CONTEMPORARY
ARCHITECTS

CONTEMPORARY ARCHITECTS

Editor
Muriel Emanuel

Architectural Consultant
Dennis Sharp

Assistant Editors
Colin Naylor
Craig Lerner

ST. MARTIN'S PRESS
NEW YORK

First published 1980 by
ST. MARTIN'S PRESS INC.
175 Fifth Avenue
New York, New York 10010

ISBN 0–312–16635–4

Library of Congress Catalog Card No. 79–67803

CONTENTS

INTRODUCTION

During the two years that I have spent preparing *Contemporary Architects,* I have come to hope that—because of our very conscious involvement with architecture in our every movement as dwellers and workers—this book will be of interest not only to the profession and its scholars, but also to the general public.

The selection of entrants has been based on the suggestions of our Advisory Board, listed on page ix. The emphasis is, of course, on living architects and on those who have recently died; as well, we have included those architects of the modern movement of the 1920's–1950's who, in the view of the Board, continue to exert an important influence on architecture. Lacunae do exist, but not for our want of trying: our editors and researchers simply were not able to establish accurate information about contemporary architecture in the U.S.S.R. and some of the countries of Eastern Europe.

We have somewhat stretched the definition of "architect." We have tried to indicate the current importance of both planning and theory by including as entrants those planners and theorists who may have few built works to show for a lifetime's career but whose thinking and imaginative visions have profoundly influenced architects throughout the world. Likewise, we have included those landscape architects who have made an outstanding contribution to our understanding of the best utilizations of open space. Also included are the most prominent structural engineers of our era—those who have increased the possibilities for architecture. The lines that separate the architect from the theorist from the planner from the engineer grow increasingly indistinct, and many entrants now work within multi-disciplinary firms. Other entrants are individuals in private practice; others are individuals who head large and diverse firms; still others are partnerships of various kinds. We hope that our choices reflect both the diversity and continuity of architecture as it enters the 1980's.

The research work was carried out mainly at the libraries of the Royal Institute of British Architects and the Architectural Association in London, the Avery Library of Columbia University in New York, and the Burnham Library of the Art Institute of Chicago. To all the librarians who answered my often seemingly unanswerable questions and searched for papers, periodicals, theses, and mislaid books—my thanks. Thanks, too, to our main translators, Fay Lunzer and Brenda Ohlman, and to those contributors who went far beyond the task of writing essays to assist, suggest and encourage throughout the project—Teresa Czaplinska-Archer, Philip Drew, Chris Fawcett, Geoffrey Jellicoe, Esther McCoy, Mitchell B. Rouda, Franz Schulze, Hiroshi Watanabe, and Arnold Whittick. The work of the dead entrants of the inter-war and post-war years has usually been well documented, but just the same there were problems: I'm grateful to all those contributors, as well as to the families and former associates of recently deceased architects, who were kind enough to look over and correct my work.

Documentation on living architects, when it is available, is less exacting, and my last acknowledgement will seem curious only to those who have never been involved in such research. I wish to thank the entrants. I am very grateful to all of them for their (often exceedingly time-consuming and painstaking) documentation of a lifetime's work, for their diligence in selecting and preparing their bibliographies, for their readiness to write statements on their work especially for this book, and for their seemingly endless patience in responding to my questions. Without the enthusiasm, cooperation and hard work of the 400 living architects included here, *Contemporary Architects* would not exist.

—**Muriel Emanuel**

ADVISERS

CONTRIBUTORS

CONTEMPORARY ARCHITECTS

Alvar Aalto
Max Abramovitz
Kurt Ackermann
Ray Affleck
Steffen Ahrends
Ahrends Burton and Koralek
Takefumi Aida
Gregory Ain
Edouard Albert
Franco Albini
Christopher Alexander
Robert E. Alexander
W. H. Alington
Osvald Almqvist
Mario Roberto Alvarez
Sydney Ancher
John Andrews
Dimitris Antonakakis
Suzana Antonakakis
Antonini Schon Zemborain and Associates
Architects Co-Partnership Inc.
Nader Ardalan
Sir Ove Arup
Yoshinobu Ashihara
Charles Herbert Aslin
Gunnar Asplund
Atelier 5
Ian Athfield
Gae Aulenti
Carlo Aymonino
Takamitsu Azuma

Sven Backström
Edmund N. Bacon
Daniel Badani
Jacob Bakema
Sir Herbert Baker
Gianluigi Banfi
Ove Bang
Edward Larrabee Barnes
Jonathan Barnett
Luis Barragán
Otto Bartning
Baudizzone-Diaz-Erbin-Lestard-Varas
Paul Baumgarten
Eugène Beaudouin
Welton Becket
Thomas Hall Beeby
Günter Behnisch
Peter Behrens
Lodovico Belgiojoso
Pietro Belluschi
Hendrik Petrus Berlage
Sergio Bernardes
Max Bill
Gunnar Birkerts
Peter Blake
Charles Blessing
Holger Blom
Piet Blom
Aulis Blomstedt
Jørgen Bo
Vladimir Bodiansky
Ricardo Bofill
Oriol Bohigas
Dominikus Böhm
Gottfried Böhm
Paul Bonatz
Pep Bonet
Victor Bourgeois
Robin Boyd
Michael Brawne
Marcel Breuer
Johannes Brinkman
Samuel Brody

Charles William Brubaker
Erik Bryggman
Gordon Bunshaft
Roberto Burle Marx
Buszko and Franta

Charles Warren Callister
Cambridge Seven Associates Inc.
Felix Candela
Georges Candilis
Douglas Cardinal
Sir Hugh Casson
Eduardo Catalano
William W. Caudill
Max Cetto
Rifat Chadirji
Chamberlin Powell and Bon
Pierre Chareau
Melvin Charney
Serge Chermayeff
Thomas D. Church
Mario J. Ciampi
Cristian Cirici
Lluis Clotet
Wells Coates
José A. Coderch
Colquhoun and Miller
Brenda Colvin
Amyas Connell
Peter Cook
Charles M. Correa
Peter Corrigan
Lúcio Costa
Keith E. Cottier
Philip Cox
Warren J. Cox
David A. Crane
Theo Crosby
Dame Sylvia Crowe
James Cubitt
Edward Cullinan

Justus Dahinden
John Dalton
Trevor Dannatt
Gustavo da Roza
J. R. Davidson
Lewis Davis
Giancarlo De Carlo
Harald Deilmann
Michel de Klerk
Alejandro De La Sota
Bernard de la Tour d'Auvergne
Enrique del Moral
Vernon DeMars
A. J. Diamond
Eladio Dieste
John Dinkeloo
Richard Döcker
Lluis Domènech
B. V. Doshi
Barry Downs
Philip Dowson
Jane B. Drew
Macy DuBois
Willem Dudok
Johannes Duiker
Werner Düttmann

Charles Eames
Norman Eaton
Garrett Eckbo
Michel Ecochard
Ezra Ehrenkrantz
Egon Eiermann

Peter D. Eisenman
Julian Elliott
Craig Ellwood
Richard England
Arthur Erickson
Ralph Erskine
Aarne Ervi
Joseph Esherick

Hassan Fathy
Hermann Fehling
Sverre Fehn
Bernard Feilden
Luigi Figini
João Filguéiras
József Finta
Kay Fisker
O'Neil Ford
Norman Foster
Revel Fox
Ulrich Franzen
Eugène Freyssinet
M. Paul Friedberg
Yona Friedman
E. Maxwell Fry
Bohuslav Fuchs
Hiromi Fujii
Buckminster Fuller
Don Hendry Fulton

Ignazio Gardella
Tony Garnier
Antoni Gaudí
Robert Geddes
Frank O. Gehry
Sir Frederick Gibberd
Robin Gibson
Irving J. Gill
Jean Ginsberg
Romaldo Giurgola
Josef Gočár
Mathias Goeritz
Bruce Goff
Daniel Gogel
Bertrand Goldberg
Ernö Goldfinger
Myron Goldsmith
Gollins, Melvin, Ward
Teodoro González de León
James Gowan
Bruce J. Graham
Michael Graves
Eileen Gray
Charles Sumner Greene
Henry Mather Greene
Herb Greene
Vittorio Gregotti
Walter Burley Griffin
Walter Gropius
Irving Grossman
Victor Gruen
Barnett Gruzen
Amancio Guedes
Joaquim Guedes
Rolf Gutbrod
Charles Gwathmey
Patrick Gwynne

N. John Habraken
Hans Hallen
Lawrence Halprin
Oskar Hansen
Norman Hanson
Hiroshi Hara
Hugh Hardy

Hugo Häring
Harwell Hamilton Harris
Wallace K. Harrison
George E. Hartman
Josef Havlíček
Zvi Hecker
John Hejduk
George F. Hellmuth
Helmut Hentrich
Ron Herron
Herman Hertzberger
Ludwig K. Hilberseimer
Tao Ho
Josef Hoffmann
Sir Charles Holden
William Graham Holford
Hans Hollein
Wilhelm Holzbauer
Clemens Holzmeister
Raymond Hood
Sutemi Horiguchi
Victor Horta
George Howe
Howell, Killick, Partridge and Amis
Richard Hughes

Kazuhiro Ishii
Arata Isozaki

Daryl Jackson
David Jackson
Arne Jacobsen
Hugh Newell Jacobsen
Helmut Jahn
Uttam C. Jain
Sir Geoffrey Jellicoe
John M. Johansen
Philip Johnson
R. N. Johnson
A. Quincy Jones
Alexis Josic
Josep María Jujol
Sumet Jumsai

Louis I. Kahn
Gerhard M. Kallmann
Dov Karmi
Ram Karmi
George Kassabaum
Tasso Katselas
George Fred Keck
György Kévés
Fazlur Khan
Frederick Kiesler
Kiyonori Kikutake
Dan Kiley
Edward A. Killingsworth
Ron Kirby
Josef Paul Kleihues
Edward F. Knowles
Knut Knutsen
Carl Koch
Pierre Koenig
Aris Konstantinidis
Arthur Korn
Arne Korsmo
Friedrich Wilhelm Kraemer
Leon Krier
Rob Krier
Lucien Kroll
Ernest J. Kump
Kisho Kurokawa

Bohdan Lachert
Morris Lapidus

Albert Laprade
Sir Denys Lasdun
John Lautner
Le Corbusier
Ricardo Legorreta
Ludwig Leo
Fritz Leonhardt
Richard Le Plastrier
William Lescaze
Rino Levi
Sigurd Lewerentz
David Lewis
William S. W. Lim
Lim Chong Keat
Horst Linde
Richard Llewelyn-Davies
Leandro V. Locsin
Marcel Lods
Adolf Loos
Bertold Lubetkin
Colin Lucas
Hans Luckhardt
Wassili Luckhardt
Anthony Lumsden
Kjell Lund
Victor A. Lundy
André Lurcat
Sir Edwin Lutyens
Hans Luz
Donlyn Lyndon
Eric Lyons
Lyons, Israel, Ellis and Gray

David Mackay
Charles Rennie Mackintosh
Col Madigan
Robert Maillart
Fumihiko Maki
Imre Makovecz
Robert Mallet-Stevens
Angelo Mangiarotti
Al Mansfeld
Manteola, Sánchez Gómez, Santos, Solsona,
   Viñoly, Architects
C. S. Mardall
Sven Markelius
Jerome Markson
Rex Martienssen
Sir Leslie Martin
Josep Martorell
Tomoya Masuda
Ernst May
Bernard Maybeck
Kunio Mayekawa
Gerald McCue
Raymond McGrath
Ian McHarg
Peter McIntyre
Noel Michael McKinnell
Richard Meier
Eric Mendelsohn
Paulo Mendes da Rocha
John Merrill
Hannes Meyer
Wilhelm O. Meyer
Giovanni Michelucci
Ludwig Mies van der Rohe
Henrique Mindlin
Ehrman B. Mitchell
José Rafael Moneo
Mozuna Monta
Arthur Cotton Moore
Charles W. Moore
Riccardo Morandi
Jorge Machado Moreira

William Morgan
Raymond Moriyama
Peter Moro
Bryce Mortlock
Werner M. Moser
Hidalgo Moya
William C. Muchow
Peter Muller
Tohgo Murano
Glenn Murcutt
Stuart Murray
Barton Myers

Wallace Neff
George Nelson
Paul Nelson
Pier Luigi Nervi
Walter A. Netsch
Richard J. Neutra
Oscar Niemeyer
Matthew Nowicki
Eliot Noyes

Gyo Obata
Dieter Oesterlen
Juan O'Gorman
Shin'ichi Okada
Masato Otaka
Sachio Otani
Frei Otto
J. J. P. Oud
Nathaniel Owings

Mario Pani
John B. Parkin
John C. Parkin
Giovanni Pasanella
Mario Payssé-Reyes
I. M. Pei
Gustav Peichl
Cesar Pelli
Luis Peña
Fabio Penteado
Timo Penttilä
William L. Pereira
Enrico Peressutti
Lawrence B. Perkins
Auguste Perret
Edoardo Persico
Marcello Piacentini
Renzo Piano
Reima Pietilä
Dimitris A. Pikionis
Hans Poelzig
Gino Pollini
James Stewart Polshek
Gio Ponti
John Portman
Paolo Portoghesi
Sir Philip Powell
James Pratt
Cedric Price
Jean Prouvé
Victor Prus
Josep Puig i Cadafalch

Ludovico Quaroni

Roland Rainer
Pedro Ramirez Vazquez
Ralph Rapson
John Rauch
Antonin Raymond
Yacov Rechter
Affonso Eduardo Reidy

Leif Reinius
Andrew Renton
Viljo Revell
Leonardo Ricci
Richard Sheppard, Robson and Partners
Bruce Rickard
Gerrit Rietveld
Roberto Architects
Sir Howard Robertson
Jaquelin Robertson
Kevin Roche
Archibald C. Rogers
Ernesto Nathan Rogers
Richard Rogers
Peter Rose
Eugene Rosenberg
Aldo Rossi
Alfred Roth
Michel Roux-Spitz
Paul Rudolph
David Russell
Aarno Ruusuvuori

Eero Saarinen
Eliel Saarinen
Francisco Saénz de Oíza
Moshe Safdie
Junzo Sakakura
Rogelio Salmona
O. R. Salvisberg
Giuseppe Samonà
Brian Sandrock
Hideo Sasaki
Louis Sauer
Henri Sauvage
Leonardo Savioli
Carlo Scarpa
Hans Scharoun
Rudolph Schindler
Frank Schlesinger
Rudolf Schwarz
Paul Schweikher
Michael Scott
Denise Scott Brown
Walter Segal
Harry Seidler
Ivan Seifert
Robin Seifert
Werner Seligmann
Josep Lluis Sert
Arieh Sharon
Kazuo Shinohara
Seiichi Shirai
John Ormsbee Simonds
Heikki Siren
Kaija Siren
Alvaro Siza
Louis Skidmore
Nils Slaatto
Ivor Smith
Whitney R. Smith
Alison Smithson
Peter Smithson
Paolo Soleri
Raphael Soriano
Josep María Sostres
Ettore Sottsass, Jr.
Albert Speer
Sir Basil Spence
Mart Stam
Douglas Stephen
Robert A. M. Stern
Stillman and Eastwick-Field
James Stirling
Edward Durell Stone

Oscar Stonorov
Hugh A. Stubbins, Jr.
Louis Sullivan
Helena Syrkus
Szymon Syrkus

Roger Taillibert
Minoru Takeyama
Kenzo Tange
Yoshiro Taniguchi
Bruno Taut
Max Taut
Ivar Tengbom
Giuseppe Terragni
Heinrich Tessenow
Clorindo Testa
The Architects Collaborative
Paul Thiry
Ron Thom
Benjamin Thompson
Stanley Tigerman
Alexandros N. Tombazis
Eduardo Torroja y Miret
R. H. B. Toy
William Turnbull, Jr.
Oscar Tusquets

O. M. Ungers
Shizutaro Urabe
Jørn Utzon
Roelof S. Uytenbogaardt

György Vadász
Pierre Vago
Gino Valle
J. H. van den Broek
Henry van de Velde
L. C. van der Vlugt
Aldo van Eyck
Jan van Wijk
Eva Vecsei
Robert Venturi
José Villagrán García
Carlos Raúl Villanueva
Alexander von Branca
Meinhard von Gerkan
C. F. A. Voysey

Konrad Wachsmann
Derek Walker
David A. Wallace
Gregori Warchavchik
John Carl Warnecke
Miles Warren
Youji Watanabe
Clifford Wearden
John Weeks
Harry Weese
Richard S. Weinstein
Hanna Wejchert
Kazimierz Wejchert
Clifford Wiens
Philip Will, Jr.
Jean Willerval
Amancio Williams
Sir Owen Williams
Sir Clough Williams-Ellis
Colin St. John Wilson
James Wines
Peter Womersley
Jackson C. S. Wong
Shadrach Woods
Ken Woolley
Frank Lloyd Wright
Lloyd Wright

William Wilson Wurster

Minoru Yamasaki
F. R. S. Yorke
Isoya Yoshida
Takamasa Yosizaka

Wojciech Zablocki
Abraham Zabludovsky
Bernard Zehrfuss
Eberhard Zeidler

A

AALTO, Alvar.
Finnish. Born Hugo Alvar Henrik Aalto in Kuortane, near Jyväskylä, 3 February 1898. Educated at the Jyväskylän Lyseo, 1908–16; Technical University of Helsinki, 1916–21, Dip. Arch. 1921. Served in the Finnish Army in 1939. Married the architect Aino Marsio in 1924 (died, 1949); children: Johanna and Hamilkar; married the architect Elissa Mäkiniemi in 1952. In private practice, in Jyväskylä, 1923–27, Turku, 1927–33, and Helsinki, 1933 until his death, 1976: in partnership with Aino Aalto, 1924–49, and with Elissa Aalto, 1952–76. Established ARTEK furniture design company, with Aino Aalto and Mairea Gullichsøn, Helsinki, 1935. Professor of Architecture, Massachusetts Institute of Technology, Cambridge, 1946–48. President of the Academy of Finland, 1963–68. Exhibitions: *Triennale,* Milan, 1933; *Alvar Aalto: Architecture and Furniture,* Museum of Modern Art, New York, 1938; *Alvar und Aino Aalto,* Kunstgewerbemuseum, Zurich, 1948; Ecole des Beaux Arts, Paris, 1950; *Möbel aus Holz und Stahl: Alvar Aalto—Mies van der Rohe,* Gewerbemuseum, Basel, 1957; Keski-Suomen Museum, Jyvaskyla, 1962; Akademie der Künste, Berlin, 1963; Kunsthaus, Zurich, 1964; *Contemporary Finnish Architecture,* Smithsonian Institution, Washington, D.C., 1965; *L'Opera di Alvar Aalto,* Palazzo Strozzi, Florence, 1965; Ateneum, Helsinki, 1967; Moderna Museet, Stockholm, 1969; *Alvar Aalto 1898–1976,* Finlandia Hall, Helsinki, and Royal Academy, London, 1978. Recipient: First Prize in the competitions for Jyväskylä Workers' Club, 1923, Paimio Tuberculosis Sanatorium, 1927, Viipuri Municipal Library, 1927, Aitta Summer Houses, 1928, Finnish Pavilion for the Paris *World's Fair,* 1936, Finnish Pavilion for the New York *World's Fair,* 1938, Forum Redivium, Helsinki, 1948, Lahti Church, 1950, Säynätsalo Town Hall, 1950, Malm Funeral Chapel, 1950, Jyväskylä Teachers University, 1950, Kuopio Regional Theatre, 1951, Rautatalo Office Building, Helsinki, 1951, Seinäjoki Church, 1952, Sports and Congress Hall, Vienna, 1953, Gothenburg, Sweden Town Hall, 1955, Kiruna, Sweden Town Hall, 1958, Aalborg, Denmark Art Museum, 1958, Essen, Germany Opera House, 1958, Seinäjoki Town Hall, 1959, and the Protestant Parish Centre, Zurich, 1967; other prizes include—Royal Gold Medal for Architecture, Royal Institute of British Architects, 1957; Sonningpriset, Denmark, 1962; Gold Medal, American Institute of Architects, 1963; Gold Cube, Svenska Arkitekters Riksförbund, Sweden, 1963; Cordon del Calli de Oro, Sociedad de Arquitetos, Mexico, 1963; Bronzeplakette, Freie Akademie der Künste, Hamburg, 1965; Medaglia d'Oro, City of Florence, 1965; Diplome des Palmes d'Or du Mérite de l'Europe, 1966; Helsingin Yliopiston Ylioppilaskunnan Puheenjohtajiston merkki purppuranauhassa, Finland, 1966; Thomas Jefferson Medal, University of Virginia, Charlottesville, 1967; Alvar Aalto Medal, Finland, 1967; Litteris et Artibus Medal, Sweden, 1969; Medaille d'Or, Académie d'Architecture, Paris, 1972; Tapiola Medal, 1975; Outstanding Architect Award, National Arts Foundation, Liechtenstein, 1975. Honorary doctorates: Princeton University,

New Jersey, 1947; Technical University of Helsinki, 1949; Norges Tekniske Højskole, Trondheim, Norway, 1960; Eidgenössische Technische Hochschule, Zurich, 1963; Columbia University, New York, 1964; Politechnico, Milan, 1964; Technische Hochschule, Vienna, 1965; University of Jyväskylä, 1969. Honorary Royal Designer for Industry, Royal Society of Arts, London; Senior Fellow, Royal College of Arts, London, 1950; Honorary Fellow, American Institute of Architects, 1958; Fellow, World Academy of Arts and Sciences, Israel, 1963. Honorary Member: Royal Institute of British Architects, 1937; Södra Sveriges Byggnadsteniska Samfund, Sweden, 1957; American Academy of Arts and Sciences, 1957; Accademia di Belle Arti, Venice, 1958; Association of Finnish Architects, 1958; Norske Arkitekterns Landsforbund, Norway, 1959; Västmanlands-Dala Nation, Uppsala, Sweden, 1965; Colegio de Arguitetos, Peru, 1965; Engineering Society of Finland, 1966; Bund Deutscher Architekten, Germany, 1966; American Academy of Arts and Letters, 1968; National Institute of Arts and Letters, U.S.A., 1968; Akademie der Bildenden Künste, Vienna, 1975; Royal Scottish Academy, 1975. Chevalier of the Légion d'Honneur, France, 1939; KømmendorsKorset av Dannebrogen, Denmark, 1957; Grand Cross of the Lion of Finland, 1965; Grande Ufficiale al Merito, Republic of Italy, 1966; Grand Croix de l'Ordre du Faucon, Iceland, 1972. *Died* (in Helsinki) *11 May 1976.*

Works:

1918 Aalto Family House remodelling, Alajärvi, Finland
      Belfry, Kauhajärvi, Finland
1921/
22 Association of Patriots Building, Seinäjoki, Finland
1922 *Industrial Exhibition,* Tampere, Finland
1922/
23 Two-family house, Jyväskylä, Finland
1923/
24 Apartment building, Jyväskylä, Finland
1923/
25 Workers' Club, Jyväskylä, Finland
1924 Church restoration, Äänekoski, Finland
      Church restoration, Anttola, Finland
1925 Church, Jämsä, Finland (competition project)
      Church remodelling, Viitasaari, Finland
1926/
29 Church, Muurame, Finland
1927 Toolo Church, Helsinki (competition project)
      Church, Viinikka, Finland (competition project)
      Belfry restoration, Pylkönmäki Church, Finland
1927/
28 Farmers' Co-operative Building and Finnish Theatre, Turku, Finland
      Apartment building, Turku, Finland
1927/
29 Association of Patriots Building, Jyväskylä, Finland

Turun Sanomat Newspaper Offices, Turku, Finland
1928 Summer houses, Aitta, Finland (competition project)
      Church restoration, Korpilahti, Finland
1929 Columbus Memorial Lighthouse, Dominican Republic (competition project)
      Church restoration, Kemijärvi, Finland
      7th Centenary Exhibition, Turku, Finland
1929/
33 Tuberculosis Sanatorium, Paimio, Finland
1930 Institute for Physical Education, Vierumäki, Finland (competition project)
      Michele Agricola Church, Helsinki (competition project)
      Stadium and Sports Centre, Helsinki (competition project)
      University Hospital, Zagreb, Yugoslavia (competition project)
1930/
31 Cellulose factory, Toppila, Oulu, Finland
1930/
35 Municipal Library, Viipuri, Finland (destroyed, 1943)
1932 Helsinki Stadium (competition project)
      Prefabricated one-family house (competition project)
      Enso-Gutzeit Week-End Cabin (competition project)
1932/
33 Villa Tammekan, Tarto, Estonia
1933 Housing for the employees and doctors of the Tuberculosis Sanatorium, Paimio, Finland
      Redevelopment plan for Norrmalm, Stockholm (competition project)
1934 Railway station, Tampere, Finland (competition project)
      Stenius Housing Development, Munkkiniemi, Helsinki
      Exhibition Hall, Helsinki (competition project)
1934/
36 Aalto House, Munkkiniemi, Finland
1936 Art Museum, Tallinn, Estonia (competition project)
1937 Finnish Pavilion, *World's Fair,* Paris
1936/
39 Cellulose factory, Sunila, Finland (1st stage of construction)
1937 Savoy Restaurant, Helsinki
      Nordic United Bank, Karhula, Finland
1937/
38 Director's house, Sunila, Finland
      Two-storey housing, Sunila, Finland
      Two-storey terrace housing, 1st and 2nd groups, Sunila, Finland
1938 Forestry Pavilion, *Agricultural Exhibition,* Lapua, Finland
      Blomberg Film Studio, Westend, Helsinki
      University of Helsinki Library extension (competition project)
      Anjala Paper Factory, Inkeroinen, Finland
1938/
39 Three-storey terrace housing, 1st and 2nd groups, Sunila, Finland

Alvar Aalto: Institute of Technology, Otaniemi, Finland, 1964

Finnish Pavilion, *World's Fair*, New York
Elementary school, Inkeroinen, Finland
Anjala Apartments Buildings, 1st group, Inkeroinen, Finland
Anjala Terrace House, 2nd group, Inkeroinen, Finland
Anjala Housing for Engineers, Inkeroinen, Finland
Villa Mäirea, Noormarkku, Finland
1938/
40 Terrace housing, Kauttua, Finland
1939/
45 Ahlström Apartment Buildings, Karhula, Finland
1940 Haka Housing Development, Helsinki (competition project)
Traffic plan and design of Erottaja Square, Helsinki (competition project)
1941 Plan for an experimental town
1941/
42 Regional plan for the Kokemaki Valley, Finland
1942/
43 Women's dormitory, Kauttua, Finland
1942/
46 Urban design project for Säynätsalo, Finland
1943 Town Centre, Oulu, Finland (competition project)
Merikoski Power Station, Oulu, Finland (competition project)
1944 Town Centre, Avesta, Sweden (competition project)
Stromberg Housing Development, Vaasa, Finland

Extension to factory, Kauttua, Finland
1944/
45 Urban design for Rovaniemi, Finland (project)
Ahlström Mechanical Workshop, Karhula, Finland
1944/
47 Strömberg Meter Factory, Vaasa, Finland
Strömberg Terrace Housing, Vaasa, Finland
1945 Engineer's house, Kauttua, Finland
Sauna, Kauttua, Finland
ARTEK Exhibition Pavilion, Hedemora, Sweden
1945/
46 Sawmill extension, Varkaus, Finland
One-family housing development, Varkaus, Finland
1946 Heimdal Housing Development, Nynäshamn, Sweden (competition project)
Master plan for Nynäshamn, Sweden (competition project)
One-family house, Pihlava, Finland
1947 Stromberg Sauna and Laundry, Vaasa, Finland
Johnson Research Institute, Avesta, Sweden
1947/
48 Baker House Dormitory, Massachusetts Institute of Technology, Cambridge
1947/
53 Regional plan for Imatra, Finland
1948 Forum Redivivum: Cultural and Administrative Centre, Helsinki (competition project)
1949 Ahlstrom Factory Warehouse, Karhula, Finland

General plan for the Institute of Technology, Otaniemi, Finland (competition project)
Woodberry Poetry Room, Lamont Library, Harvard University, Cambridge, Massachusetts
1949/
50 Tampella Housing, Tampere, Finland
1949/
54 Sports Hall, Otaniemi, Finland
1950 Church, Lahti, Finland (competition project)
Funeral chapel, Malm, Finland (competition project)
Kivelä Hospital, Helsinki (competition project)
1950/
52 Town Hall, Säynätsalo, Finland
1950/
55 Regional plan for Lappland
1951 Erottaja Pavilion, Helsinki
Regional Theatre, Kuopio, Finland (competition project)
Enso-Gutzeit Paper Factory, Kotka, Finland
One-family house, Oulu, Finland
Workers' housing, Inkeroinen, Finland
1951/
52 Typpi Oy Nitrogen Factory and housing for Typpi Oy employees, Oulu, Finland
1951/
53 Enso-Gutzeit Paper Mill, Summa, Finland
1951/
54 Paper mill, Chandraghona, Pakistan
Cellulose factory, Sunila, Finland (2nd stage of construction)

Three-storey apartment house, 3rd group, Sunila, Finland

1952 Cemetery and funeral chapel, Kongens Lyngby, Copenhagen (competition project)

Association of Finnish Engineers Building, Helsinki

Enso-Gutzeit Country Club, Kallvik, Finland

1952/
54 Housing for the personnel of the Public Pensions Institute, Munkkiniemi, Finland

1952/
56 Public Pensions Institute, Helsinki

1952/
57 Pedagogical University, Jyväskylä, Finland

1953 Sports and Congress Hall, Vogelweidplatz, Vienna (competition project)

Imatra Centre Design Project

Aalto Summer House, Muuratsalo, Finland

1953/
55 Rautatalo Office Building, Helsinki

1954 Studio R.S., Como, Italy

Housing Aero, Helsinki

1955 Urban design project for Summa, Finland

Bank building, Baghdad, Iraq (competition project)

Aalto Studio, Munkkiniemi, Finland

Theatre and concert hall, Oulu, Finland (project)

1955/
57 Apartment building, Hansaviertel, Berlin

Town Hall, Gothenburg, Sweden (competition project)

1955/
58 House of Culture, Helsinki

1956 Main Railway Station: Drottningtorget, Gothenburg, Sweden (competition project)

Director's house, Typpi Oy, Oulu, Finland

Master plan for the University of Oulu, Finland

Finnish Pavilion, *Biennale*, Venice

1956/
58 Operating Room, Tuberculosis Sanatorium, Paimio, Finland

Church, Vuoksenniska, Imatra, Finland

Villa Louis Carré, Bazoches, France

1957 Kampementsbacken Housing Development, Stockholm (competition project)

Town Hall, Marl, Germany (competition project)

1957/
61 Korkalovaara Housing Development, Rovaniemi, Finland

Sundh Centre, Avesta, Sweden

1958 Town Hall, Kiruna, Sweden (competition project)

Art Museum, Baghdad, Iraq

Post Office Administration Building, Baghdad, Iraq

Opera House, Essen, Germany (competition project)

1958/
60 Church, Seinäjoki, Finland

1958/
62 Neue Vahr High-Rise Apartments, Bremen, Germany

1959 Bjornholm Housing Development, Helsinki

Finnish War Memorial, Suomussalmi, Finland

1959/
62 Central Finnish Museum, Jyväskylä, Finland

Enso-Gutzeit Headquarters, Helsinki

Parish Centre, Wolfsburg, Germany

1959/
64 New Centre, Helsinki

1960/
61 Shopping centre, Otaniemi, Finland

Lieksankoski Power Station, Lieksa, Finland

1960/
63 Cultural Centre, Wolfsburg, Germany

Thermotechnical Laboratory, Institute of Technology, Otaniemi, Finland

1960/
64 Main Building, Institute of Technology, Otaniemi, Finland

1961/
62 Housing for nurses, Tuberculosis Sanatorium, Paimio, Finland

Office and apartment block, Rovaniemi, Finland

1961/
63 Town Hall, Seinajoki, Finland

1961/
64 Opera House, Essen, Germany (competition project)

1962 Apartment blocks, Tapiola, Finland

Enskilda Bank Building, Stockholm (competition project)

Cultural Centre, Leverkusen, Germany (competition project)

Terrace housing, Jakobstad, Finland

Stockmann Department Store expansion, Helsinki (project)

1962/
63 Heating Plant, Institute of Technology, Otaniemi, Finland

Housing development, Rovaniemi, Finland

1962/
64 Scandinavia Bank Administration Building, Helsinki

1962/
66 Student hostel, Otaniemi, Finland

1963 Urban Centre, Rovaniemi, Finland

Swimming Hall extension, Jyväskylä, Finland

Student Union Building, Jyväskylä, Finland

Town plan for Otaniemi, Finland

1963/
65 Kaufmann Conference Suite, Institute of International Education, New York

Library, Seinäjoki, Finland

Student Association House, Västmanland-Dala, Uppsala, Sweden

Heilig-Geist-Gemeinde Kindergarten, Wolfsburg, Germany

1963/
66 Parish Centre, Seinäjoki, Finland

1964 BP Administration Building, Hamburg (competition project)

Wood Technology Laboratories, Institute of Technology, Otaniemi, Finland

Tuberculosis Sanatorium extension, Paimio, Finland

1964/
65 One-family house, Rovaniemi, Finland

1964/
66 Urban design project for Stensvik, Finland

1964/
67 Ekenäs Savings Bank, Tammisaari, Finland

1965 Castrop-Rauxel Urban Centre, Germany (competition project)

1965/
68 Scandinavian House, Reykjavik, Iceland

Library, Rovaniemi, Finland

Parish Centre, Detmerode, Wolfsburg, Germany

Schönbühl High-Rise Apartments, Lucerne, Switzerland

1965/
69 Library, Institute of Technology, Otaniemi, Finland

1965/
70 Library, Mount Angel Benedictine College, Mount Angel, Oregon

1965/
72 Administration and Cultural Centre, Jyväskylä, Finland

1966 Experimental town, Gammelbacka, Porvoo, Finland (project)

Housing complex, Pavia, Italy (project)

Cultural Centre, Siena, Italy (project)

Theatre, Wolfsburg, Germany (competition project)

Prototype for the administration building and warehouse of the Società Ferrero, Turin, Italy (project)

1966/
69 Academic Bookshop, Helsinki

Town Hall, Alajärvi, Finland

1966/
76 Riola Parish Centre, Bologna, Italy

1967 Protestant Parish Centre, Zurich-Altstetten, Switzerland (competition project)

1967/
69 State Office Building, Seinäjoki, Finland

Kokkonen House, Järvenpää, Helsinki

1967/
71 Finlandia Hall, Helsinki

Institute of Physical Education, Jyväskylä University, Finland

1967/
73 City Electric Company Administration Building, Helsinki

1968/
69 Theatre, Seinäjoki, Finland (project)

1968/
71 Water Tower, Institute of Technology, Otaniemi, Finland

1969/
70 Villa Schildt, Tammisaari, Finland

Parish Centre, Alajärvi, Finland

1969/
75 Main Building extension, Institute of Technology, Otaniemi, Finland

1970 Church, Lahti, Finland

Art Museum, Shiraz, Iran

Police Headquarters, Jyväskylä, Finland

1970/
75 Theatre, 1st and 2nd stages, Rovaniemi, Finland

1971 Alvar Aalto Museum, Jyväskylä, Finland

1972 Helsinki Central Plan, 2nd stage

Art Museum, Aalborg, Denmark (with J.-J. Baruel)

1973/
75 Finlandia Congress Hall, Helsinki

Swimming Hall, Jyväskylä, Finland

1974 Midwest Institute of Scandinavian Culture, Wisconsin (project)

1975 Town Hall, Jyväskylä, Finland

1975/
76 Master plan of the university area, Reykjavik, Iceland

Publications:

By AALTO: books—*An Experimental Town*, Cambridge, Massachusetts 1940; *Post-War Reconstruction*, New York 1941; *Alvar Aalto: Synopsis*, edited by Bernhard Hoesli, Basel and Stuttgart 1970; *Alvar Aalto: Sketches*, edited by Göran Schildt, Helsinki 1972, Cambridge, Massachusetts and London 1978; articles—"Menneitten aikojen motivit" in *Arkkitehti* (Helsinki), no. 2, 1922; "André Lurcat" and "Åbo stads 700-års jubileum" in *Arkkitehti* (Helsinki), no. 6, 1929; "Bostadsbebyggelse på gammal stadsplan" in *Byggmastaren* (Stockholm), 1930; "Rationalismen och Manniskan in *Form* (Stockholm), no. 7, 1935, reprinted in *Architectural Forum* (New York), September 1935; "Utställningar" in *Byggmastaren* (Stockholm), no. 32, 1937; "Rakenteitten ja aineitten vaikutus nykaikaiseen rakennustaiteeseen" in *Arkkitehti* (Helsinki), no. 9, 1938; "The Humanizing of Architecture" in *Technology Review* (Cambridge, Massachusetts), November 1940, reprinted in *Architectural Forum* (New York), December 1940; "E. G. Asplund: In Memoriam" in *Arkkitehti* (Helsinki), nos. 11/12, 1940; "Euroopan jälleenrakentaminen tuo pinnalle aikamme rakennustaiteen keskeisimmän probleemin" in *Arkkitehti* (Helsinki), no. 5, 1941; "Bostadsutställningen en återuppbyggnadsutställning" in *Arkkitehti* (Helsinki), nos. 9/10, 1941; "Finlands Arkitektförbunds standardiseringsarbete" in *Arkkitehti* (Helsinki), nos. 5/6, 1943; "Finsk Byggstandarisering" in *Byggmastaren* (Stockholm), no. 1, 1943; "D. Dahlberg: In Memoriam" in *Arkkitehti* (Helsinki), no. 1, 1944; "Rovaniemi rediviva" in *Arkkitehti* (Helsinki), nos. 11/12, 1945; "Vad skall man göra med gardeskasernen?" in *Arkkitehti* (Helsinki), nos. 1/2, 1946; "Fin de la machine à habiter" in *Metron* (Rome), no. 7, 1946; "Un Sanatorium pour Touberculeux en Finlande" in *Architecture Francaise* (Paris), no. 62, 1946; "Architettura e Arte Concreta" in *Domus* (Milan), nos. 223/225, 1947; "Kulttuuri ja tekniikka" in *USA: Suomi-Finland* (Helsinki), no. 4, 1947; "The Decadence of Public Buildings" in *Arkkitehti* (Helsinki), nos. 9/10, 1953; "Rakennushallituksen Pääjohtajan Virka" in *Arkkitehti* (Helsinki), no. 2, 1953; "Akademisk Arkitektförening 75 år" in *Arkitekten* (Copenhagen), 1954; "Suomen Rakennustaiteen Museo" in *Arkkitehti* (Helsinki), no. 2, 1954; "Zwischen Humanismus und Materialismus" in *Der Bau* (Vienna), nos. 7/8, 1955, reprinted in *Baukunst und Werkform* (Darmstadt), no. 6, 1956; "Problemi di Architettura" in *Quaderni* (Turin), November 1956; "Annual Discourse" in *RIBA Journal* (London), May 1957; "Henry van de Velde: In Memoriam" in *Arkkitehti* (Helsinki), nos. 11/12, 1957; "Der Stadtplan von Imatra, Finnland" in *Werk* (Zurich), no. 11, 1959; "Il nuovo centro di Helsinki" in *Casabella* (Milan), August 1961; "Le Corbusier: In Memoriam" in *Progressive Architecture* (New York), October 1965; "Kaupunkisuunnittelu ja julkiset rakennukset" in *Arkkitehti* (Helsinki), nos. 3/4, 1967.

On AALTO: books—*Alvar Aalto: Architecture and Furniture,* exhibition catalog, New York 1938; *Space, Time and Architecture* by Sigfried Giedion, 2nd edition, Cambridge, Massachusetts and London 1949, and later editions (includes section on Aalto); *Alvar Aalto* by Georgio Labò, Milan 1948; *Alvar Aalto and Finnish Architecture* by E. and C. Neuenschwander, London and New York 1954; *Scandinavian Architecture* by Thomas Paulsson, London 1959; *Alvar Aalto* by Frederick Gutheim, New York and London 1960, and Milan 1963; *Alvar Aalto* by Göran Schildt and Leonardo Mosso, Jyväskylä, Finland 1962; *Alvar Aalto 1922–62,* edited by Karl Fleig, Zurich, London and New York 1963; *L'Opera di Alvar Aalto,* exhibition catalog, by Leonardo Mosso, Florence 1965; *Complexity and Contradiction in Architecture* by Robert Venturi, New York 1966; *Alvar Aalto* by Yukio Futagawa and others, Tokyo 1968, revised English edition as *Alvar Aalto* by George Baird and Yukio Futagawa, London 1970; *Alvar Aalto, vol. II: 1963–70,* edited by Karl Fleig, London 1971; *Alvar Aalto,* edited by Karl Fleig (adaptation of his previous books), London 1975; *Alvar Aalto* by Carlo Cresti, Florence 1975; *Alvar Aalto and the International Style* by P. D. Pearson, New York and London 1978; articles—"The Work of Alvar Aalto" by P. M. Shand in *Architectural Review* (London), September 1931; "Alvar Aalto: Finland's Modern Master" in *Architectural Forum* (New York), April 1938; "Due ville di Alvar Aalto" by G. Pagano in *Casabella* (Milan), no. 145, 1940; "Trends in Factory-Made Furniture" by E. Race in *Architectural Review* (London), no. 617, 1948; "Alvar Aalto" by Siegfried Giedion in *Architectural Review* (London), February 1950; "Il lungo cammino di Alvar Aalto" by Carlo Santini in *Domus* (Milan), January 1951; "The One and the Few" by Reyner Banham in *Architectural Review* (London), April 1957; "Aalto and His Influence" by Dennis Sharp in *Architecture and Building* (London), December 1957; "Alvar Aalto from Sunila to Imatra: Ideas, Projects and Buildings" by Carlo Santini and Göran Schildt in *Zodiac 3* (Milan), 1958; special issue of *Arkkitehti* (Helsinki), January/February 1958; "Finland and Architect Aalto" by John Burchard in *Architectural Record* (New York), January 1959; "Alvar Aalto baut in Deutschland" by G. Kuhne in *Bauwelt* (Berlin), no. 41, 1962; "L'Opera di Alvar Aalto" by Alessandro Mendini in *Casabella* (Milan), November 1965; "Aalto Reyisited" in *Architectural Forum* (New York), April 1966; "Alvar Aalto and the Ethos of the Second Generation" by Peter Smithson in *Arkkitehti* (Helsinki), nos. 7/8, 1967; "Aalto Ego" by Jane Holtz Kay in *Building Design* (London), August 1973; special number of

Arkkitehti (Helsinki), no. 6, 1974; 4 articles by Louis Hellman in *Building Design* (London), February and March 1975; "Alvar Aalto: The Man and His Work," special issue of *Arkkitehti* (Helsinki), nos. 7/8, 1976; "Alvar Aalto: Architecture Was His Medium" by Karl Fleig in *Werk* (Zurich), October 1976; "Alvar Aalto," special issue of *SD* (Tokyo), JanuaryFebruary 1977; "On Aalto," special issue of *Progressive Architecture* (New York), April 1977; "Reflections on the Influence of Alvar Aalto" by George Baird in *Canadian Architect* (Toronto), May 1977; "Alvar Aalto: His Life, Work and Philosophy," special issue of *L'Architecture d'Aujourd'hui* (Paris), June 1977; "An Architect of True Genius" by Malcolm Quantrill in *The Sunday Times* (London), 3 September 1978.

Bibliography: *Alvar Aalto: A Bibliography* by William C. Miller, Monticello, Illinois 1976.

"Alvar Aalto's work has meant the most to me," Robert Venturi has written, "of all the work of the Modern masters," and there are many admiring references to Aalto in Venturi's *Complexity and Contradiction in Architecture.* Visually unrelated as Aalto's and Venturi's work may seem, this acknowledged link points to the adept manipulation of "complexity and contradiction" by the Finnish master, and even to the seeds of "post-modernism" in some of Modernism's earliest monuments.

Aalto's architecture varied from International Style dogma in a number of ways: it was often rough in texture, natural in color, and lyrical rather than strictly ordered in its floor plans and even in its distribution of structural elements. In a time, now past, when the shared traits of the modern masters were being emphasized at the expense of their individuality, these variations were glossed over as the idiosyncrasies expected of an artist from such a remote land.

There is much, indeed, in Aalto's work that is perfectly fitting for the limited economic and natural resources (including limited sunlight) of Finland, and his earliest works—the Muurame Parish Church, for example, and the Farmers' Cooperative in Turku—were designed in the context of a new nation's natural self-consciousness. (Finland became an independent country only in 1917, when Aalto was 19.)

But from the completion of the Paimio sanatorium in 1933 and the Viipuri library in 1935 it was clear that Aalto was an architect of international stature. His Finnish pavilions for the Paris *World's Fair* of 1937 and the New York *World's Fair* of 1939 and the exhibition organized by John McAndrew at New York's Museum of Modern Art in 1938 established his reputation throughout the west. In the same decade, Aalto, his wife Aino, and Mairea Gullichsen formed the Artek Company for the manufacture and distribution of the beginning of a series of modest but brilliant furniture designs, the most popular of these being Aalto's three-legged stacking stool, designed in 1938 and now ubiquitous.

Aalto's first permanent American design (there were to be only three major American works, including the handsome Kaufmann Conference Suite at the Institute of International Education in New York) was the 1948 Baker House dormitory at the Massachusetts Institute of Technology. Of rough brick, with two main elevations quite different in character, and sinuously curving in plan (to give rooms views up and down, not just *at* the adjacent river), Baker House was a clear break with modern purity, unity, and planarity. (Aalto's work on Baker house was interrupted by Aino's illness and death; it is important to note that both Aino and Aalto's second wife, Elissa, were collaborating partners in his work.)

Other major buildings of Aalto's maturity include the Gullichson house, "Villa Mairea," of 1939, the modest but moving Säynätsalo Town Hall of 1952, The Public Pensions Institute, Helsinki, of 1956, the Helsinki House of Culture, 1958, the Vuoksenniska church of the same year, the Wolfsburg (Germany)

Cultural Center, finished in 1963, and a number of buildings at the Institute of Technology, Otaniemi.

Throughout the whole scope of this work—from stools, vases, and lighting fixtures to the planning of entire urban areas—it is possible to see not only those personal inclinations and poetic "complexities" that separate Aalto from the mainstream of the modern movement, but also those touches of thoughtfulness and grace that raise his work above the mainstream of the architecture of any period. For Aalto was more than a master of artistic form and of intelligent planning; he was the master as well of the details that relate a building successfully to its users. He cared for the proper shape of a handrail, for the convenience of storage elements, for the texture of a wall, and for the delights of natural light. He once advised the architecture students at M.I.T. to design their windows as if the girls they loved were sitting in them. In Aalto's work we find assuring precedents for some current trends, we find an honorable and simple humanism amongst modernism's pretensions, and we find the permanent pleasures of architecture at its highest level.

—Stanley Abercrombie

ABRAMOVITZ, Max.

American. Born in Chicago, Illinois, 23 May 1908. Educated at the University of Illinois, Champaign Urbana, 1925–29, B.S. 1929; Columbia University, New York, 1929–31, M.S. 1931; did postgraduate work at the Ecole des Beaux-Arts, Paris, 1932–34. Served as a Lieutenant-Colonel in the United States Army, in America and in the China theatre, 1942–45: Legion of Merit Award; served as a Colonel in the United States Air Force, serving at the Pentagon, Washington, D.C., 1950–52: Special Assistant to the Assistant Secretary of the United States Air Force, 1952. Married Anne Marie Causey in 1937 (divorced, 1964); children: Michael, Katherine; married Anita Zeltner Brooks in 1964. Associate Professor, Yale School of Fine Arts, Yale University, New Haven, Connecticut, 1939–42; Partner, with Wallace K. Harrison, *q.v.,* Harrison and Abramovitz, New York, 1945–76; Deputy Director of Planning, United Nations Headquarters, New York, 1947–52. Since 1976, Partner, Abramovitz-Harris-Kingsland, New York. Governor, New York Building Congress, 1957–64; Chairman of the Board, American Society of Civil Engineers, 1966–68. Director, New York Regional Plan Association; Trustee, Mt. Sinai Hospital, and Mt. Sinai Medical Center, New York. Exhibitions: University of Illinois, Champaign/Urbana campus and Chicago Circle campus, 1963; University of Michigan, Ann Arbor, 1964; Virginia Polytechnic Institute, Blacksburg, 1964; Parsons College, Fairfield, Iowa, 1964. Archive Collection: Syracuse University, Syracuse, New York. Recipient: President's Award, Columbia University, 1960; Achievement Award, University of Illinois Alumni Association, 1963. D.F.A.: University of Pittsburgh, 1961; University of Illinois, 1970; Fellow, Brandeis University, Waltham, Massachusetts, 1963. Fellow, American Institute of Architects, 1952. Address (office): 630 Fifth Avenue, New York, New York 10020, U.S.A.

Works:

1947/
53 United Nations Headquarters, first Avenue, New York (as Deputy Director of Planning; Wallace K. Harrison, Chairman of the Board of Design and Director of Planning; with advisory team of Architects, including Le Corbusier, Oscos Niemeyer, and Sven Markelius)
1951 Corning Glass Center, Corning, New York

1952 United States Embassy, Havana, Cuba
United States Embassy, Rio de Janeiro, Brazil
1955 Inter-Faith Chapels, Brandeis University, Waltham, Massachusetts
1957 Commercial Investment Trust Building, New York
1959 Corning Glass Building, New York
Loeb Student Center, New York University, New York
1960 Gateway 4 Building, Equitable Life Assurance Society, Pittsburgh
1961 Central Intelligence Agency Building, Langley, Virginia
1962 Philharmonic Hall, Lincoln Center, New York
Columbia University Law School and Plaza, New York
1963 Assembly Hall, University of Illinois, Urbana
1964 Phoenix Mutual Life Insurance Building, Hartford, Connecticut
Bell Telephone Building, *World's Fair*, New York
Institute of International Education, 809 United Nations Plaza, New York (with Wallace K. Harrison and Michael M. Harris)
1965 Erieview Plaza, Cleveland
1966 860 United Nations Plaza Building, New York
Hilles Library, Radcliffe College, Cambridge, Massachusetts
1967 Union Bank Square, Los Angeles

Temple Beth Zion, Buffalo, New York
1969 Erie County Bank and Office Building, Buffalo, New York
Cincinnati Center
Fiberglas Tower, Toledo, Ohio
Krannert Center for the Performing Arts, University of Illinois, Champaign-Urbana
1970 Westinghouse Building, Pittsburgh
Banque Rothschild Building, Paris
Brandeis University Master Plan and Academic Buildings, Waltham, Massachusetts
Currier Houses, Radcliffe College, Cambridge, Massachusetts
School of International Affairs, Columbia University, New York
Fine Arts Center, University of Iowa, Iowa City
1971 United States Steel Building, Pittsburgh
1972 First National Bank Building, Louisville, Kentucky
Music School, University of Iowa, Iowa City
Hancher Auditorium, University of Iowa, Iowa City
1976 GAN (Groupe des Assurances Nationales) Tower, La Défense, Paris
1977 GAN Building, Bordeaux, France
Nationwide Insurance Company Plaza, Columbus, Ohio
Mead Tower, Dayton, Ohio
Dayton Power and Light Building, Dayton, Ohio

Publications:

By ABRAMOVITZ: books—*Architecture and the University,* Princeton 1954; *The Architecture of Max Abramovitz,* Champaign/Urbana 1963; tapes—*Oral Memoir of Max Abramovitz,* New York 1976; articles—"An Architect's Message" in *Opera News* (New York), 29 September 1962; "The City of Tomorrow" in *Pitt* (Pittsburgh), October 1963; "Programming and the Client-User" in *Progressive Architecture* (New York), October 1965; "Designing for the Performing Arts" in *Journal of Aesthetic Education* (Urbana, Illinois), January 1969; "The Susan Morse and Frederick Wiley Hilles Library at Radcliffe College" in *Harvard University Library Bulletin* (Cambridge, Massachusetts), October 1969.

On ABRAMOVITZ: book—*The Story and Facts about the Krannert Center for the Performing Arts,* Urbana 1969; articles—"Student Religious Center Based on Synagogue" in *Architectural Record* (New York), June 1948; "Embassy Office Building" in *Progressive Architecture* (New York), October 1951; "Three Chapels" in *Architectural Record* (New York), September 1954; "New York's Biggest Building in 25 Years" in *Architectural Forum* (New York), January 1955; "An Unusual Design for Collegiate Religion" in *Architectural Record* (New York), January 1956; "A Squat Headquarters for CIT" in *Architectural Forum* (New York), January 1958; "The Big Mirror" in *Architectural Forum* (New York), May 1959; "Student Center for Big

Max Abramovitz: Assembly Hall, University of Illinois, Urbana, 1963

City University" in *Architectural Record* (New York), May 1960; "Lincoln Center, New York: Philharmonic Hall" in *Architectural Record* (New York), September 1962; "Panther Hollow Redevelopment, Pittsburgh, Pennsylvania" in *Progressive Architecture* (New York), July 1963; "Temple Beth Zion" in *Architectural Record* (New York), March 1968; "Architecture for the Arts of Music, Dance and Drama" in *Architectural Record* (New York), November 1969; "U.S. Steel Headquarters Building" in *Civil Engineering* (New York), April 1970; "Recu Chez Rothschild—La Banque Rothschild" in *Connaissance des Arts* (Paris), May 1970; "Big Steel Spike: The U.S. Steel Building" in *Architectural Forum* (New York), December 1971; "Bank in Paris —Rothschild Bank" in *Realités* (New York), October 1972.

I am trying to find in architecture a rightness that transcends the fashionable, an architecture which contains a planned order, a rhythm, with an interrelationship of spaces that is vital—wherein there is nothing that can be taken away from the building without feeling a loss and where everything contributes to the desired expression.

A building or a space should make one feel that a thought is within it, that it is more than a shelter, as a good book is more than words put together, as music is more than an arrangement of notes.

I will use the full vocabulary available to me of structure, materials, technical devices, and, when and where necessary, develop new uses for materials and structure, but always within the framework of the search for the proper design concept. I have no desire to warp the individual to technology.

Architecture can tell us more about people and the man than the other arts because it has less opportunity to be irrelevant and trivial than the other arts. Since it is in and among our buildings that we live and move, it is in our buildings that our lives are revealed.

—Max Abramovitz

Max Abramovitz is best known, perhaps, as the "other half" of the partnership of Harrison and Abramovitz. This "second billing" is understandable enough: from Rockefeller Center to the United Nations to the New York State Capital, Wallace K. Harrison has been team leader of some of the most famous architectural works of the 20th century. Yet any examination of the works list of Max Abramovitz (the former partners freely credit each other's work) reveals that Abramovitz emerges from the 30 year partnership as very much an architect in his own right.

During the great building sprees of the 1950's in the large cities of the United States there was a great deal of experimentation with new materials, and, like many others in that decade, Abramovitz was a great user of glass. The Corning Glass Building, with the first full glass skyscraper wall, contains more glass than any building built to that time. Yet, as always with Abramovitz, there is more of interest than simply statistics: The Corning Glass Building and the earlier Glass Center interestingly present the material, and the buildings exude spaciousness, airiness, light, even levity.

Abramovitz is happy when he is working with large and lofty interiors, with bare areas. And, a notable aspect of his work, he is as interested in the spaces between his buildings and their settings as he is in the structures themselves.

The Inter-Faith Chapels at Brandeis University, consisting of three buildings for the Protestant, Catholic and Jewish faiths, surround a pool; each has its own outside altar, so that joint services can take place. There is no outside "identification," but, though each building is of the same height and size and constructed of the same materials, each one has its own particular shape, the common theme appearing in the truncation of a geometric form. Glass, again, is an important feature: glass panels occupy

the full height of the "cut-off" ends facing the pool. Much thought was given to detail, and advice was taken from the three religious authorities, and, inside each building, Abramovitz's attempt to convey the relevant spiritual mood has been entirely successful.

The Philharmonic Hall at Lincoln Center received a great deal of publicity, but more interesting is the complex of buildings that form the Krannert Center for the Performing Arts at the University of Illinois, in which the truncated forms again appear. The Great Hall, seating 2100, is a complete rectangle; the Festival Theatre, seating 985, is an oval, cut across at both ends; and the Playhouse, with 678 seats, is a similar basic shape, cut off at one end only; in addition, the Center includes an Outdoor Amphitheatre for 560 spectators and a Studio Theatre, almost square, for experimental drama, with seating for 150. Again, too, the sapcing is interesting: the composition is reminiscent of a Roman Forum, a response to the obvious need for communication among the various buildings—a constant journeying from one to the other was obviously foreseen as part of the life of the Center.

Throughout his career, and throughout America, Abramovitz has built a number of important buildings. All of these works have something in common. Abramovitz believes that you cannot end up with a good result unless you start off with a good idea: from the beginning the plan and program must be based on what is wanted, not what the architect would like to impose. Ideas that are not there at the beginning will grow from discussions with the client, who must be advised about what is and what is not possible. In this way the architect involves his client in the process of design—not gratuitously, but to ensure that the building will "work" for its users, that it will be "appropriate." The fact that Abramovitz continues to be commissioned for auditoria of all kinds, for places of workshop, educational complexes, and office buildings, and by a variety of different clients, suggests that more often than not he achieves his goal.

—Muriel Emanuel

ACKERMANN, Kurt.
German. Born in Insingen, Rothenburg ob der Tauber, 2 March 1928. Educated at the Oskar von Miller-Polytechnikum and the Technische Hochschule, Munich, 1949–54. Married Eleanore Höfter in 1958; children: Katrin, Peter and Christoph. In private practice, Munich, since 1953; Principal of Professor Kurt Ackermann und Partner, Munich, since 1969 (partners: Jürgen Feit; Peter Jaeger; Richard Martin). Guest Lecturer at the Technical University, Vienna, 1971, and at the Technische Hochschule, Darmstadt, 1974. Since 1974, Professor of Design and Construction, University of Stuttgart. Member of the Executive Board, Bund Deutscher Architekten, in Bavaria, 1965–67; Member of the Governing Board, national Bund Deutscher Architekten, 1972–75; Member of the Editorial Committee, *Der Architekt,* Bonn, 1972–77. Member, Board of Patrons, *Bauen und Wohnen,* Zurich, since 1970; Member, Munich City Planning Commission, since 1973; Consultant to the Architectural Branch, German Research Organization, since 1975; Member of the Governing Council, Baden-Württemberg Building and Housing Research Society, since 1977. Recipient: Munich Culture Prize, for architecture, 1967; Bund Deutscher Architekten of Bavaria Prize, 1967, 1971 (twice), 1975; German Brick Industry Prize, 1971; Munich Honor Prize, for housing construction, 1971. Address: Profesor Kurt Ackermann und Partner, Malsenstrasse 57, 8000 Munich 19, Germany.

Works:

1956 Gartner House, Gundelfingen, Germany
1957 Holzbauer House, Gauting, Germany
     Primary school, Insingen, near Rothenburg, Germany
1958 Dr. Peters House, Berg, Germany
     Hops warehouse, Mainburg, Germany
1959 B. Höfter House, Mainburg, Germany
     E. Höfter House, Neuhausen, Germany
     Hopfenpflanzerverband Administration Building, Wolznach, Germany
     Klotz Hops Warehouse, Wolznach, Germany
1959/
  78 Märker Cement Works, Harburg-Schwaben, Germany
1960 Ackermann House, Herrsching, Germany
     Messner Housing Development, Munich
1961 Kammermeier House, Munich-Allach
1962 Dr. Fischer House, Munich
     BMW Works, Munich
1963 Graf Norman House, Icking, Germany
     Ballauf Housing Development, Munich
     FS Head Offices, Munich
1964 Federal Monopoly Building, Munich
1964/
  72 Höfter Housing Development, Munich
1964/
  78 Götz Metal Works, Deggendorf, Germany
1965 Meisel House, Feldafing, Germany
     Trade School, Mainburg, Germany
1966 Hypo Bank Administration Building, Munich
     Auto-Zentrale Korn Building, Rothenburg-ob-der-Tauber, Germany
1967 G. Moll House, Munich-Pullach
     Airport Workshops, Neubiberg, Germany
     Cramer Works, Munich
1968 Schow House, Munich
1969 Götz House, Deggendorf, Germany
1970 J. Gartner House, Gundelfingen, Germany
     Moll Housing Development, Munich
     Weissenberger Administration Building, Munich
     Schneider und Söhne Administration Building, Munich
     Weisshaupt Administration Building, Munich
     Fire Station 4, Munich
     IWIS Chain Factory, Munich
1971 Biederstein Housing Development, Munich
     Langenscheidt Publishing Company Building, Munich
     Evangelical Church, Gundelfingen, Germany
1972 Primary school, WeilheimOberbayern, Germany
     Schulz Office Building, Munich
     Evangelical Church, Füssing, Germany
     Wanderer Works, Munich
1974 Rectory and Administration Buildings, University of Regensburg, Germany
1975 Federal Administration Offices, Munich
     Wustenrot Administration Building, Munich
     Sportgastein Regional Plan, Bad Gastein, Austria
1976 EDV: Administration Building for Electronic Data-Processing, Munich
1977 Administration Building for the Corporation of the Building Trades, Munich
     OSLW: Air Force Officers' School, Fürstenfeldbruck, Germany
     Heating Plant Building, Fürstenfeldbruck, Germany

Publications:

By ACKERMANN: books—*Manifest für Architektur,* with the Architektenteam, Munich 1973; *Werkbericht Büro Prof. Kurt Ackermann + Partner,* Stuttgart 1978; articles—"Neuzeitliche Hopfenaufbereitungsanlagen" in *Hopfenrundschau* (Wolznach, Germany), February 1959; "Der Architekt und das landwirtschaftliche Bauen" in *Baumeister*

(Munich), January 1962; "Möbel kaufen in München" in *Bauwelt* (Berlin), no. 40, 1965; "Hardt-Schule in Weilheim" in *Baumeister* (Munich), February 1973; "Honorarreform—ein Trauerspiel mit Ignoranz und Unvermögen" in *Der Architekt* (Stuttgart), September 1973; "Dieses Heft sieht anders aus" in *Der Architekt* (Stuttgart), January 1974; "Zum Entwerfen von Banken" in *Architekturwettbewerbe* (Stuttgart), no. 77, 1974; "Der Architekt mit einem abermals anderen Gesicht" in *Der Architekt* (Stuttgart), January 1975; "Nachruf Karl Schwanzer" in *Der Architekt* (Stuttgart), October 1975; "Nostalgie—Laune oder Herausforderung" in *Bauen und Wohnen* (Zurich), December 1975; "Stellungnahme zur Gesamthochschulentwicklung" in *Der Architekt* (Stuttgart), December 1975; "Das Institut für Grundlagen des Entwerfens und Konstruierens" in *Baumeister* (Munich), April 1976; "Offene Umgänge an Verwaltungsbauten" in *Der Architekt* (Stuttgart), June 1976; "Planungs- und Bauablauf eines staatlichen Bauvorhabens" in *Der Architekt* (Stuttgart), February 1977; "Vorläufig nichts Neues unter der Sonne," with Paulhans Peters, in *Architekturwettbewerbe* (Stuttgart), no. 90, 1977.

On ACKERMANN: books—*Industriebau* by Walter Henn, Munich 1961, London 1965; *Stahlkonstruktionen im Hochbau* by Konrad Gatz and Franz Hart, Munich 1966; *Industriebau* by S. Nagel and S. Linke, Gutersloh 1972; *Deutsche Kunst seit 1960*, vol. 4: *Architecture* by Paolo Nestler and Peter M. Bode, Munich 1976; articles—in *Deutsche Bauzeitschrift* (Gutersloh), July 1974 and September 1974; in *Bauen und Wohnen* (Zurich), April 1975.

If we look more closely at "anti-technical criticism," there emerges the almost schizophrenic contradiction of our age, which has the highest hopes in the perfection and automation of science, industry, housing and leisure, and at the same time indulges in unrealistic daydreams of social utopias. Most publications on modern architecture deal more with ugliness than with beauty. Negative examples are legion, and no architect will deny his share of the responsibility. On the other hand, good work too is not spared. Outstanding buildings are denigrated as "solitaire" architecture, monuments to the architect, and they are often rated bad because they are new or large.

There is a distinct danger that violent rejection of aesthetic purism may issue in the opposite extreme, a revival of popular mannerism attended by arbitrary historicizing formalism. One thing, however, the negative publicity has done: it has sharpened our eye for the problems of historic monument preservation and has initiated a revision of our ideas of industrial architecture.

Nostalgia is a kind of longing. It leads to an attitude in which we merely look back; it leads to the obfuscation of problems and destroys the freedom of designer and builder. This lack of freedom can be overcome by group work on nostalgia-free social and environmental problems, by consistent and objective approaches to assignments, by the creation of alternatives as well as the technically adequate employment of materials.

The necessity of preserving historic buildings and the continuation of traditions must be taken for granted. Full of fascinated satisfaction, we have observed the rediscovery of the great values of old industrial buildings and industrially-produced constructions of the last century. These products, on a high architectural level, and often designed by engineers, were scarcely noticed by their own age and their significance was not recognized.

It is not merely the historical interest in these astonishing buildings that strikes me as important in this change of outlook. They can also support us in our work, if we carefully study and analyze these buildings, not only with regard to the influence of engineering design on architecture, but also to clarify our own standpoint and to develop our own ideas of a more imaginative technology. Many people may notice only the decorations on these old buildings.

We should not, however, be so superficial, but should derive from them a feeling for proportion, for naturalness and timelessness. Timelessness, too, is a notable feature of quality. Logical construction principles and the materials of steel and glass have not only led to bold forms but also to a new architecture. What is decisive about these buildings is their logic, precision, purity, elegance and beauty.

Transparency articulates and lightens these buildings, which were not merely prestige structures but realized correctly-understood basic functional principles. Both the aesthetic and the technical standpoints determined their expressive design.

I should now like to raise this question: What chance has such an architecture in our contemporary society? I think if clients attach the same importance to design as to function, we shall again have buildings that impose form on our environment, owing to their polyvalence, logical construction and technical perfection. This means that we want more experimentation and research, more imagination, more technology and more architecture.

—Kurt Ackermann

Kurt Ackermann was one of the young German architects who began their professional careers after the Second World War and who based their work on that of those first and second generation Modernists then still at the height of their creative powers. For Ackermann the influence was, above all, Mies van der Rohe, whose buildings in Chicago were having great influence in Germany at that time. But this turning towards Mies was due not so much to any formal reason as to a certain way of looking at architecture, a way to which Ackermann had been dedicated from the start—the development of form from the created detail and the significance of construction itself as a medium of architecture.

Ackermann was also influenced, one might say, by the simple lines of those houses that Egon Eirmann, for example, built in the 1930's—clearly defined outlines; of brick, with gable roofs; concisely proportioned; their detail moulded with infinite care. There

Kurt Ackermann: OSLW:Air Force Officers' School, Fürstenfeldbruck, Germany, 1977

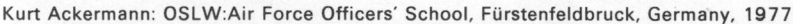

were similar buildings in Bavaria at the time—for instance, the main Post Office—that must also have played their part in influencing him.

It is from these foundations, then, that Ackermann's work has developed in the last decade. His style is characterized by the clear arrangement of the architectural totality, the attempt to make the building readable, as it were, from its external appearance, to bring construction and form into a harmonious whole. In this way Gartner House in Gundelfingen (1970) uses the existing conditions in a layout which radiates outwards, in the centre of which lies the circular dining room.

Quite different in expression is the Air Force Officer's School in Fürstenfeldbuck, completed in 1977. Here it is not so much the steel and glass architecture that is characteristic as it is, rather, the placement of the buildings around garden squares. It is the spatial concept, rather than the technical detail, that decisively and fittingly expresses the character of the site.

Instead of the usual street edge construction, the Moll Housing Development in Munich (1970) was built in a horseshoe shape around a central inner courtyard. The individual homes are in blocks that are vertically staggered and horizontally displaced: it makes for a most unusual example of town building in Germany.

At a time when there is much questioning of values, Ackermann, in his work, shows how it is possible to base one's style upon traditional methods and yet progress further, and simultaneously remain aware that design must always be a combination of both construction and creation. What emerges is not a speculative architecture but one that uses the means of our time in order to give to the people of our time a fitting environment in which to live.

—Jürgen Joedicke

AFFLECK, Ray(mond Tait).

Canadian. Born in Penticton, British Columbia, 20 November 1922. Educated at West Hill High School, Montreal, 1935–39; McGill University, Montreal, 1941–47 (Hugh McLennan Travelling Scholarship; Royal Architectural Institute of Canada Medal; Louis Robertson Prize in Design; Lieutenant-Governor's Silver Medal), B.Arch. 1947; E.T.H.: Eidgenossische Technische Hochschule, Zurich, 1948. Married Betty Ann Henley in 1950; children: Graham, Neil, Jane, Gavin, and Ewan. Architectural Assistant, McDougall Smith and Fleming, Montreal, 1948–50, and Vincent Rother, Montreal, 1950–51; Architect Principal, R. T. Affleck, Montreal, 1952–55, and Affleck Desbarats Dimakopoulos Lebensold Sise, Montreal, 1955–69. Since 1969, ArchitectPrincipal, Arcop Associates, Montreal (other principals: Fred Lebensold; Art Nichol; W. Paul Hughes; and Ramesh Khosla; associates: Imre Reichmann; Allan Thomas; Bruce Allan; Brian Hall; and Alan Woodham). Visiting Professor, McGill University, Montreal, since 1965. Exhibitions: *Architectural Work of Affleck Desbarats Dimakopoulos Lebensold Sise,* Montreal Museum of Fine Arts, 1965; *National Gallery of Canada Competition Exhibition,* National Gallery, Ottawa, 1978. Recipient: Massey Medal, 1961, 1964, 1967, 1970; Canadian Centennial Medal, 1967. Honorary doctorates: University of Calgary, 1972; Nova Scotia Technical College, Halifax, 1976. Fellow, Royal Architectural Institute of Canada, 1965; Academician, Royal Canadian Academy of Arts, 1967. Address: Arcop Associates, Post Office Box 900, Station H, 1440 St. Catherine Street West, Montreal, Quebec H3G 2L6, Canada.

Works:

1953 Klassen House, Montée des Trentes, St. Hilaire, Quebec

1954 Talbot Johnson House, Senneville Road, Senneville, Quebec
Town of Mount Royal Post Office, Graham Boulevard, Town of Mount Royal, Quebec (with Jean Michaud)
1955 Queen Elizabeth Theatre, Vancouver
1956/
65 Place Ville Marie, Montreal (with I. M. Pei)
1962 Summerlea Golf and Country Club, Pointe-aux-Cascades, Quebec
1964 Robert Tilden House, Lac Tremblant, Quebec
1964/
68 Place Bonaventure, Montreal
1965 Harry Hoy House, Lac Tremblant, Quebec
Stephen Leacock Building, McGill University, Montreal
1966 Old Arts Building renovation, Montreal
1967 Arts and Culture Centre, St. John's, Newfoundland (with Cummings and Campbell)
1969 Life Sciences Centre, Dalhousie University, Halifax, Nova Scotia (with J. Davison)
1970 John Sparling House, Georgeville, Quebec
Concourse, World Trade Center, New York (with Minoru Yamasaki)
1972/
73 Long range plan for the Toronto Harbourfront
1974/
79 Redevelopment plan for the Halifax-Dartmouth Waterfront, Halifax, Nova Scotia
Market Square, Saint John, New Brunswick
1977 Les Terrasses de la Chaudiere, Hull, Quebec
1978/
79 Core Action Program, Moncton, New Brunswick

Ray Affleck: Hotel, Place Bonaventure, Montreal, 1968

Publications:

By AFFLECK: reports—*Recent Canadian Experience in Wall Design,* for the International Council for Building Research, Oslo 1967; *Exhibitions and International Fairs as a Means of Mass Communication,* for Unesco, Paris 1968; *Implications of the Changing Society on the College of the Future,* for the Ontario Department of Education, Toronto 1968; articles — "Place Bonaventure: The Architect's View" in *Architecture Canada* (Toronto), July 1967; "The City as Process" (RIBA Discourse) in *RIBA Journal* (London), June 1968; "Urban Renewal" in the *Montreal Star,* August 1968; "Place Bonaventure: Celebration of the Mixmaster" in *Modulus 5* (Charlottesville, Virginia), 1968; "An Approach to Architectural Education at the University of Toronto" in *The Canadian Architect* (Toronto), 1969.

On AFFLECK: articles—"Stephen Leacock Building" in *The Canadian Architect* (Toronto), May 1964; "Stephen Leacock Building" in *Architectural Record* (New York), February 1966; "R. T. Affleck: A Need for More Hands" in *The Canadian Architect* (Toronto), September 1966; "Arts and Culture Centre, St. John's" in *Architecture Canada* (Toronto), January 1967; "Place Bonaventure, Montreal" in *Architectural Record* (New York), December 1967; "Place Bonaventure, Montreal" in *Architectural Design* (London), January 1968; "Place Bonaventure, Montreal" in *Progressive Architecture* (New York), July 1968; "The Unlikely Conversion of Ray Affleck" in *Saturday Night* (Toronto), May 1970.

A perennial concern in my work has been the individual's experience as he moves through a succession of spaces, an experience that is not primarily visual but involves a relationship of all the senses, especially the tactile. I have also been particularly interested in the social aspects of architecture, which, in my opinion, revolve around the sharing of space between a variety of people who are, in effect, in touch with each other through sharing the same space.

This preoccupation has been particularly significant in the design of complex mixed-use projects, such as Place Bonaventure, Montreal, or Market Square, Saint John, New Brunswick, as well as in urban design in general. This mode of perceiving architecture applies to interior space as well as exterior space and their interfaces. It applies equally well to the scale of a building or the scale of a city. Although one cannot see space, light, natural or artificial, helps to articulate space and plays a crucial role in perception and hence in the design process.

Generally speaking, I structure the design process by imagining the spaces that people will move through—not the objects they will look at. The imaging of experience is much more complex than the imaging of objects—but it is of the greatest importance to my work as an architect.

—Ray Affleck

Although in the largest city in Canada, and one that has included building spectaculars such as *Expo '67* and the 1976 Olympic Games, Montreal's architecture has had more notoriety abroad than influence at home. Similarly, its English-speaking school of architecture at McGill University has been an important source of ideas and people who have made their mark elsewhere and yet itself has failed to create a dynamic centre of its own. The exception is Ray Affleck whose professional stance and design approach have been widely influential.

Evolving out of a climate of unpleasant extremes and a city of grey stone buildings, Affleck's architecture is distinguished by its exterior heaviness and cavernous interior streets. Extending through not only his own designs but also those of adjacent buildings, this underground alternate environment concept has now spread to other urban centres. The phenomenon is an inversion of the vertical separation of vehicular and pedestrian traffic: automobiles exude their pollution into the open air while people inhabit an artificially controlled climate below the city surface. Comfortable at least for transients, if potentially as benumbing as Musak, this internal street system has other architectural advantages. Where the traditional street grid or its building equivalent, the corridor, is the pedestrian route, contemporary architects have felt impelled to get their effects by manipulating the building form, thereby producing arbitrary relationships with the urban facade, or by unnecessarily twisting the shape of rooms. By treating circulation as the experiential medium, the architect can leave the rooms left functionally intact while their juxtaposition creates the architectural space. The flowing space of early modern architecture, which necessarily opened up rooms into one another, is here confined to the link between them, producing another type of experience most nearly related to mediaeval squares or village high streets. The method has been to leave the planning elements—classrooms, stores—as standard units and to develop a multilevel, irregular spatial connection to them. While theoretically sound, the result is reminiscent of an experimental maze, especially when poorly lit and unrelated to outside reference points. Similarly the use of exposed concrete has been rationalized as an expression of its inherent integrity and as providing a neutral background for the imprint of its users' personalities, while in fact being depressingly grey and resisting any adornment.

The discrepancy between the informal, warm character of Affleck himself and that of his buildings also shows in the type of work for which he has been responsible, including the massive Place Bonaventure, which sits forebodingly in the centre of Montreal, a prototypical commercialized megastructure with its associated distortion of social values. Known for his support of such values, Affleck has nevertheless also evolved a technically sophisticated service to developers since his association with I.M. Pei and Webb and Knapp on Place Ville Marie established his initial partnership in the 1960's. That no perceived mismatch between intentions and results exists is evidenced by the similarity of solution between buildings of different purpose. Their organization and appearance relate to the climate and landscape of Quebec (and to a lesser extent elsewhere) but may be seen as symbolic of the Canadian experience—like the silos of Montreal, which once inspired the architects of the International Style. In a country searching for its own identity, this adherence to a set of rules—organizing process, ordering system, and concrete imagism—makes for a consistency of attitude that denotes an architectural personality.

—Anthony Jackson

AHRENDS, Steffen.

South African. Born in Berlin, Germany, 16 August 1907; emigrated to South Africa, 1936; naturalized, 1946. Educated at Landheim Schondorf, Bavaria, matriculated 1924; University of Berlin-Charlottenburg, 1924–25; Bauhochschule, Weimar, under Otto Bartning and Ernst Neufert, 1925–29; sat special examination, University of the Witwatersrand, Johannesburg, 1937, Dip. Arch. 1938. Married Visino in 1930 (divorced, 1944); Ruth Napier in 1946 (divorced, 1963); Jackie Popper in 1964; children: Peter, Benjamin, Sebastian and Katrina. Worked in his father's architectural studio, Berlin, 1930–31; joined Ernst May Group, Moscow, 1931–32; returned to his father's studio, Berlin, 1932–36. In private practice, Johannesburg, since 1938: in partnership with Robin Walker, 1948–53, Michael Sutton, 1952–64, and with Trevor Wellbeloved since 1965 and Adrian van Dongen since 1969. Worked in Spain on cluster-group housing, 1972–75. Address: Steffen Ahrends, Wellbeloved and van Dongen, 805–12 Saambou National Building, 130 Commissioner Street, Johannesburg, South Africa; or, Casa Uno, Bahia de Casares, Estepona, Malaga, Spain.

Works:

1938/
78 500 houses in the Transvaal, Cape Province, Natal Province and the Orange Free State of South Africa, and in Rhodesia
1950 Club House, Bryanston Country Club, Sandton, Transvaal (destroyed by fire, 1953)
 Huntingdon Shops and Flats, Sandown, Transvaal
1951 Matus Shops and Offices, Roodepoort, Transvaal
 Revolf Shops and Flats, Greenside, Johannesburg
1952 Gold and Diamond Pavilions, Van Riebeck Festival, Cape Town
1952/
60 Suzmann Showroom, Warehouse and Offices in Welkom, Orange Free State and Pretoria, Ermele and Bethal, Transvaal
1953 Transvaal Chamber of Mines Pavilion, Rand Show, Johannesburg
 Club House reconstruction, Bryanston Country Club, Sandton, Transvaal
1954 Engelhard Court House, Hurlingham, Transvaal
 Bedelia Hotel, Welkom, Orange Free State
 Daagbreek Hotel, Welkom, Orange Free State
 Transvaal Chamber of Mines Pavilion, Bloemfontein, Orange Free State, and Bulawayo, Rhodesia
 B.S.A. Pavilion, Bulawayo, Rhodesia
1955 Harmony Hotel, Virginia, Orange Free State
 30 housing units, Benoni, Transvaal
1958 Engelhard Guest House, Sabie River Bungalow, Transvaal
 Anglo-American Corporation Guest House, Welkom, Orange Free State
 Fibro Service Station, Bedfordview, Transvaal
 Balalaika Hotel, Sandown, Johannesburg
1959 Total Oil Service Station, Fairview, Johannesburg
 Callinicos Shops and Flats, Kensington, Johannesburg
1960 Barlows (Caterpillar) B.T. & M. Factory, Isando, Transvaal
1961 Total Oil Service Station, Illovo, Johannesburg
 Bayers Agrochem. Factory, Isando, Transvaal
1962 Barclays Bank, Louis Trichard, Transvaal
 Sanipass Hotel, Drakensberg, Natal
1962/
72 T and C Head Office and Warehouse, Isando, Transvaal
1962/
78 Grandstand and Club House, Johannesburg Turf Club
1963 Drum Rock Hotel, White River, Transvaal
 Commissioner-General's Residential Units, Mafeking, Cape Province
 Social Science and Speech Clinic, University of the Witwatersrand, Johannesburg
 Transvaal Provincial Administration hostels and schools in Witbank, Sanieshof, Klersdorf, Koster and Coligny, Transvaal
1963/
69 CPL (Agfa) Factory, Isando, Transvaal
1964 Barclays Bank Pavilion, *Rand Show,* Johannesburg
 Sturrock and Robson Guest House, Dullstrom, Transvaal
 Sabie Country Club House, Sabie, Transvaal
 Barlows (Caterpillar) B. T. & M. Factory, Belleville, Cape Province

Steffen Ahrends: Costa del Sol, Spain, 1975

1965 Barlows (Hyster) Factory, Isando, Transvaal
      Barlows Federated Timber Factory, Benoni,
        Transvaal
      Gallo Pavilion, *Rand Show,* Johannesburg
1966 Mbula Guest House, Sabie, Transvaal
1967 River Club House, Sandton, Transvaal
      Barlows Federated Timber Factory, Springs,
        Transvaal
1968 T and C Offices and Warehouse, Paarl, Cape
        Province
1970 SAFI Offices, Sabie, Transvaal
1971 T and C Offices and Warehouse, Milnerton,
        Cape Province
      CPL (Agfa) Factory, Milnerton, Cape Prov-
        ince
      3 houses at Sotogrande, Costa del Sol, Spain
1972/
  75 Bahia de Casares (cluster housing), Costa del
        Sol, Spain (with Aubrey David)
1974 Guest house, Piggs Peak, Swaziland

Publications:

On AHRENDS: articles—"Gold Pavilion, Van Riebeck Festival, Cape Town" and "Diamond Pavilion,
Van Riebeck Festival" in *Architect and Builder*
(Johannesburg), May 1952; "Ranch House 'V' in
Hurlingham" in *Architect and Builder* (Johannesburg), June 1952; "Chamber of Mines Pavilion,
Rand Easter Show" in *Architect and Builder* (Johannesburg), June 1953; "New Bloemfontein Chamber
of Mines Pavilion" in *Architect and Builder* (Johannesburg), June 1959; "Guesthouse Engelhard, Eastern Transvaal" in *Architect and Builder* (Johannesburg), March 1960; "Illovo Total Oil Service
Station" in *South African Architectural Record*
(Johannesburg), September 1961; "New Social Science and Speech Clinic, Witwatersrand University"
in *South African Architectural Record* (Johannesburg), August 1967; "House Vladykin, Umhlanga
Rocks, Natal" in *Artlook* (Johannesburg), February
1971; "House Skeen, Umhlanga Rocks, Natal" in
Architect and Builder (Johannesburg), September
1971; "House Gevisser, Hyde Park" in *Habitat*
(Johannesburg), 1974.

It may be that my particular interest in houses was
awakened during my last three years in Germany,
1933–36. The modern house we believed in was soon
taboo, even when treated in a moderate or disguised
way. The progressive and cultured people who
would have built modern houses were either emigrating or did not dare to express their innermost
thoughts.

I probably realized at that time that the modern
house (particularly the house of the thirties belonging to the "International Style") requires a type of
person who, although aware of the heritage of cultured tradition, is prepared consciously to break
those ties in order to live in a *contemporary* way with
a vision towards the future. It also came to me that
a house is to a certain extent merely the shell that
personifies the atmosphere of the particular mental
world a person lives in. An architect may guide up
to a certain point, but to transplant a person into a
world he has neither the inclination nor the capacity
to understand will finally create a dissonance (so
often perceptible) in the relationship between the
house and its owner, his furniture and paintings and
even his garden.

—Steffen Ahrends

Steffen Ahrends was one of the many talented men
who came to South Africa as intellectual refugees
from Nazi Germany in the 1930's. Of those who
were architects he made the greatest impact, and his
works may be found from the Cape to Rhodesia. The
large practice he achieved was the result of his training and outstanding talent combined with unfailing
enthusiasm, a compelling personality and, without
being doctrinaire, an ability to influence conservative
clients and builders to accept and appreciate new
ideas about architecture. One of his tasks, particularly in regard to domestic work, was to overcome
the always present need in the minds of white South
Africans for the reassurance of the familiar symbols
of stability and security which they identify with the
past.

A varied practice gave Ahrends the chance to explore the two different but sometimes complementary architectural impulses of his mind—the rational
and the romantic. The former directed his large,
complicated but disciplined buildings commissioned
for collective usage—a logical consequence of his
architectural education at Weimar and Moscow
under some of the advanced thinkers and exponents
who contributed to the development of the modern
international style and urban planning in the 1920's
and 30's. His informed approach and creative handling of space, light and form, an insistence on high
standards of industrial technology, and a command
of rationalized building processes make the larger
buildings not only workable but also interesting.

The romantic impulse had been nurtured by his
youthful response to the possibilities of the traditional materials used by craftsmen in the gothic, baroque and the vernacular domestic architecture he
had studied in south Germany. The quality of his
domestic work, which made him the most influential
architect in that field in Johannesburg for more than
thirty years, is generally considered to fall into this
category.

Once he had taken the measure of South African
social and geographical conditions, his designs for
houses, large and small, country hotels and clubs
evolved as being eminently suitable for the climate
and the way of life of his clients: they were planned
with free flowing spaces, conscious orientation and,
with protection from extremes of weather, for outdoor life. He employed natural finishes for floors—
flagstones, quarry tiles, brick—and rustic brick for
walls, sometimes exposed, roughly plastered and co-
lourwashed, internally and externally. He also experimented with local timbers and exposed the construction of the roofs, sometimes ceiling them with
bound canes in the old Cape Dutch fashion.

The importance that Ahrends gave to these roofs
underlined his romanticism. The functions of the
spaces they covered produced new angles, and by
following the natural changes of site levels he produced a variety of related forms which, with the
textures and colours of their coverings of thatch,
shingles or differently shaped and coloured Mediter-
ranean-like tiles, gave each house its own individuality. His houses are never boring. Moreover, whether
the site was a flat one or on the side of a mountain,
whether it was complemented with the kind of local
planting he recommended or surrounded by semi-
tropical growth or man-made forests, these beautiful
buildings rest in complete harmony with their settings.

—Doreen Greig

AHRENDS BURTON AND KORALEK.

Partnership; established, London, 1961. Partners: Peter Ahrends, Richard Burton, Paul Koralek, Paul Drake, Patrick Stubbings, and John Hermsen. Recipient: First Prize, Trinity College Library Competition, Dublin, 1960. Address: 1 Spencer Court, 7 Chalcot Road, London NW1 8LH, England.

Works:

1963   Kasmin Gallery, Bond Street, London
        Henry Moore and Ben Johnson exhibitions, New London-Marlborough Gallery, London
1964   St. Anne's Church, Soho, London (project)
        Bryan-Brown House, Thurleston, Devon
        New Inn Hall Street Development Plan, Oxford (project)
        Office building, London Road, Cheam, Surrey
1965   Chichester Theological College, Sussex
        Tate Gallery exhibition, London
1967   Library, Trinity College, Dublin
1968   Bell Tower, Canberra, Australia (competition project)
        Eastfield County Primary School, Thurmaston, Leicestershire
        South-West Area Development Plan, Basildon, Essex
        Graduate Centre Housing, Basildon, Essex (project)
1969   Centre for Management Studies, phase I, Kennington, Oxford
        Houses, Dunstan Road, Old Headington, Oxford
1971   Redcar Library, Yorkshire
1972   Maidenhead Library, Berkshire
        Roman Catholic Chaplaincy, Oxford
        St. Andrew's College, Booterstown, Dublin
        New Building, phase I, Keble College, Oxford
        Nebenzahl House, Jerusalem
1973   Ravelin House Development Plan, Portsmouth Polytechnic, Hampshire
        St. Martin's Youth Centre, Adelaide Street, London
        Plan Guinet, Valescure, Var, France (project)
        Kimbell Construction Workshop, Brixworth, Northamptonshire
        Chahar Bagh Development Study, Isfahan, Iran (project)
1974   Centre for Management Studies, phase II, Kennington, Oxford
        Habitat Warehouse and Showroom, Wallingford, Berkshire
1975   Chalvedon Housing, area I, Basildon New Town, Essex
        Whitmore Way Housing, Basildon New Town, Essex
        Post Office Headquarters Redevelopment, St. Martins-Le-Grand, London (project)
1976   New Building, phase II, Keble College, Oxford
        Chalvedon Housing, area II, Basildon New Town, Essex
1977   Chalvedon Housing, area III, Basildon New Town, Essex
        Library, Portsmouth Polytechnic, Hampshire
        Headquarters, British Airports Authority, Gatwick Airport, Surrey (project)
1978   Northlands Housing, area I, Basildon New Town, Essex
        Arts Faculty Building, Trinity College, Dublin
        Johnson and Johnson Head Office, Slough, Berkshire (project)

Publications:

On AHRENDS BURTON AND KORALEK: articles—"Architects and Their Offices" by Mary Haddock in *Building* (London), November 1966; "Trinity College Library, Dublin" by Patrick Delaney in *Architectural Design* (London), October 1967; "Retreat for Executives" in *Architectural Forum* (New York), May 1970; "Easy Reading in Redcar" by David Roessler in *Architectural Forum* (New York), November 1971; "Easy Riders" by Tim Rock in *L'Architecture d'Aujourd'hui* (Paris), December 1971/January 1972; "Profile of a Practice: Ahrends Burton and Koralek" in *The Architect* (London), December 1973; "Extrovert Library" by Lance Wright in *Architectural Review* (London), May 1974; "Five Works by Ahrends Burton and Koralek" in *L'Architecture d'Aujourd'hui* (Paris), September/October 1974; "ABK" by John Donat in *Architecture Plus* (New York), October 1974; "The Works of Ahrends Burton and Koralek" in *Architecture + Urbanism* (Tokyo), December 1974; "Designed for Flexibility" by Neil Steedman in *Building Design* (London), April 1975; "Art Object for the Post Office" by Lance Wright in *Architectural Review* (London), July 1975; "House in Jerusalem" by Ulrik Plesner in *Architectural Review* (London), August 1975; "ABK Booterstown" by Lance Wright in *Architectural Review* (London), June 1976; "Quality Through Caring: The Practice of Ahrends Burton and Koralek" by Charles Knevitt in *Building Design* (London), November 1976; "As Easy as ABK" by Stephanie Williams in *Building Design* (London), June 1977; "Basildon Blend" in *Building* (London), June 1977; "ABK Housing in Basildon" by Peter Ellis and Richard MacCormac in *The Architects' Journal* (London), September 1977; "Unbuilt England" by Peter Cook in special issue of *Architecture + Urbanism* (Tokyo), October 1977; "Oxford: New Buildings at Keble and St. John's" by John Huniadis in *Architectural Review* (London), December 1977; "Bungalows Are Back" by Stephanie Williams in *Building Design* (London), February 1978; "Social Science, User Research and the Design Process" by Peter Ellis in *The Architects' Journal* (London), February 1978; "Reading Between the Lines" in *The Architects' Journal* (London), 26 July 1978; "A Precious Testimony of Persistence: The Work of ABK" by Moriyuki Agawa in *SD: Space Design* (Tokyo), August 1978.

*

Implicit in our work is a search for quality which concerns the character and atmosphere of spaces. This has to be achieved amidst the constraints of a realistic and practical world. There are inevitable tensions between what is desirable and what is possible; between Utopian planning and society as it is; between the potential of technology and the realities of the building industry; between what one would like to spend and what one can afford. The process of design is an effort to close those gaps, using such constraints as a springboard for ideas.

Each building is a response to a new and different situation, a personal interpretation and evaluation that grows out of attitudes and standards that are the cumulative product of experience and collaboration. It is a product of shared thought and feeling and of the conviction that the quality of our surroundings cannot be dissociated from the quality of life.

—Ahrends Burton and Koralek

*

In the early 1950's, when Peter Ahrends, Richard Burton and Paul Koralek first began working together while students at the Architectural Association in London, the atmosphere around them was one of confidence, energy and enthusiasm. The agonies of the past decade had now been overcome while the potential of the new decade had been optimistically predicted by the *Festival of Britain*. Spontanaiety overcame reflection; exploration superseded academicism; imagination overpowered theory.

This atmosphere engendered in Ahrends, Burton and Koralek an approach towards design that has stayed with them throughout their practice together. To each project they seek to bring certain analytical and organisational skills but no preconceived architectural theories or forms. The first stage of their work is one of enquiry, examining and, always, questioning the brief, seeking and exploring each possible direction. The second stage is one of discovery: the design emerges, or the design is found. The design proclaims itself. For Ahrends, Burton and Koralek believe that inherent within each brief and the social circumstances in which it arises, is the form of its architectural expression. And, conversely, the finished building should become the physical symbol of the activities and the aspirations on which the design was founded. An understanding of this attitude helps to explain the apparent diversity of their work. The series of buildings that they have completed show considerable development in technique and sophistication, but, more powerfully, each one stands independently of each other as a unique solution to its initial programme.

While it is true that Ahrends, Burton and Koralek have neither embraced any specific architectural theories nor used them polemically to influence others, two particular influences of their student days should be noted. The first was Frank Lloyd Wright, in particular his concept of an organic architecture, as well as his fluid, and fluent, planning of space; interestingly, their admiration for Wright went against the conventional wisdom at the Architectural Association at that time, which favoured Le Corbusier and Mies van der Rohe. The second major shared influence was a visit to Turkey and Iran in 1956, which opened up to the three students a new architectural vocabulary of decoration and natural light.

The majority of Ahrends, Burton and Koralek's commissions have involved the design of new buildings in the context of an historical city. They have shown great respect for the traditional, well-made buildings that have constituted their neighbours, and have responded to the particular qualities of these places with considerable sympathy. But they have not forgotten, or disregarded, the time, the age in which they are building, and have consistently made use of any new technologies, new materials, new components that are available. The resulting dialogue in their buildings between the old and the new, the traditional and the modern, the hand-crafted and the machine-finished, the soft irregularity of concrete and brick and the precision of steel and glass, has almost become a hallmark of their work as well as perhaps its most influential characteristic. If this dialogue is particularly articulate, it is because of the

Ahrends Burton and Koralek: Library, Trinity College, Dublin, 1967

inventiveness and the care with which their buildings are put together, each detail referring back to, and thereby reinforcing, the primary characteristics of the design. If the dialogue is particularly compelling, it is because it is one of such significance today.

—Bob Allies

AIDA, Takefumi.

Japanese. Born in Tokyo, 5 June 1937. Educated at Waseda University School of Architecture, Tokyo, B. Arch. 1960, M.Arch. 1966, D.Eng. 1971. Married Kazuko Hama in 1966; children: Aya and Akira. Since 1970, Principal, Takefumi Aida Architect and Associates, Tokyo. Lecturer, College of Technology, Waseda University, 1972–76; Assistant Professor, Shibaura Institute of Technology, Tokyo, 1973–76. Lecturer, Iwate University, since 1972, and Nagoya Institute of Technology, since 1976; Professor, Shibaura Institute of Technology, Tokyo, since 1977. Councillor, Kanto Area, Architectural Institute of Japan, 1976–78; Juror, American Institute of Architects, Seattle Chapter, 1978. Councillor, Architectural Institute of Japan, Tokyo, since 1978. Member, ArchiteXt, with Takamitsu Azuma, Mayumi Miyawaki, Makoto Suzuki, and Minoru Takeyama, since 1971. Exhibitions: *Triennale,* Milan, 1973; *The Works of Takefumi Aida,* Tokyo, 1977; *New Wave in Japanese Architecture,* toured the United States, 1978; *Today: An Exhibition of Houses,* Tokyo, 1978. Address: Takefumi Aida Architect and Associates, 3-2 Okubo 1-chome, Shinjuku-ku, Tokyo 160, Japan.

Works:

1968 An Artist's House, Kunitachi, Tokyo
1971 Rearguard House, Fujisawa, Kanagawa, Japan
1972 Nirvana House, Fujisawa, Kanagawa, Japan
      Annihilation House, Mutsuura, Kanagawa, Japan
      Shike Showroom, Hodogaya, Kanagawa, Japan
1974 PL Institute Kindergarten, Osaka
      House Like a Die, Izu, Shizuoka, Japan
      Persona House, Suginami, Tokyo
1976 Stepped-Platform House, Kawasaki, Kanagawa, Japan
1977 Tamatsukuri Hot Springs Monument, Tamatsukuri, Shimane, Japan
      Pension-style Hotel at Shiobara, Tochigi, Japan
1979 Matsuda Building, Kawasaki, Kanagawa, Japan
      "Tomo" Dental Office, Hofu, Yamaguchi, Japan

Publications:

By AIDA: books—translation of *Architecture: Action and Plan* by Peter Cook, Tokyo 1971; *Theory of Architectural Forms,* Tokyo 1975; articles—"Approach to the Urban Residence, Symbol of the Urban Residence" in *Shinkenchiku* (Tokyo), January 1967; "Urban Design Note: City and Factory" in *Shinkenchiku* (Tokyo), October 1967; "Wall House: The Concept of Encampment" in *Toshijutaku* (Tokyo), November 1968; "Can the House Serve as a Point of Origin" in *Toshijutaku* (Tokyo), September 1969; "Image of the House" in *Kindaikenchiku* (Tokyo), September 1969; "Architecture as Rearguard" in *Kenchikubunka* (Tokyo), February 1971; "Revitalized Architecture" in *The Japan Architect* (Tokyo), July 1971; "Movement Toward the Primary" and "Plan for a Box House" in special edition of *Toshijutaku* (Tokyo), September 1971; "Robert Venturi from Our Viewpoint" in *Architecture + Urbanism* (Tokyo), October 1971; "Lightless Intellectuality" in *Shinkenchiku* (Tokyo),

Takefumi Aida: PL Institute Kindergarten, Osaka, 1974

August 1972; "Speculation in the Dark" in *The Japan Architect* (Tokyo), November 1972; "Twelve Memoranda on the House Like a Die" and "When Architecture Disappears" in *The Japan Architect* (Tokyo), July 1974; "Scenery—Even at That, Can Architecture Continue Relating Something?" in *Space Design* (Tokyo), November 1974; "Function of Individual Housing: An Architect's View" in *Kenchikuzassi* (Tokyo), December 1974; "From the Awe-Inspiring to the World of Sensuality" in *The Japan Architect* (Tokyo), February 1975; "Eliminating as a Method for Architectural Forms" in *Shotenkenchiku* (Tokyo), October 1975; "Forest Lawn Memorial Park and Mortuaries" in *Architecture + Urbanism* (Tokyo), November 1975; "Forms, Spaces of Silence, and Calm" in *Architecture + Urbanism* (Tokyo), December 1975; "About Silence" in *Shinkenchiku* (Tokyo), February 1976; "From Silence" in *Architecture + Urbanism* (Tokyo), May 1976; "My Esquisse" in *Kenchikuchishiki* (Tokyo), November 1977; "Silence: In the Culture of Sympathy" in *Architecture + Urbanism* (Tokyo), March 1978.

On AIDA: books—*Architettura Razionale* by Aldo Rossi, Milan 1973; *Japanese Contemporary Architecture 24,* Tokyo 1973; *Modern Movements in Architecture* by Charles Jencks, London 1973, Tokyo 1976; articles—"Nirvana House" in *The Japan Architect* (Tokyo), August 1972, *Domus* (Milan), January 1974, and *Casabella* (Milan), January 1974; "PL Institute Kindergarten" by Takashi Hasegawa in *Shinkenchiku* (Tokyo), January 1974; "Stepped-Platform House" by Kazuyuki Honda in *Shinkenchiku* (Tokyo), June 1976; "The ArchiteXt Group," special edition of *The Japan Architect* (Tokyo), June 1976; "Post Metabolism," special edition of *The Japan Architect* (Tokyo), October/November 1977; "Ontology of House" by Chris Fawcett in *GA Houses 4,* Tokyo 1978.

SILENCE:

Architecture of silence must be pure. Within pure forms there must be multiplicity of meaning.

Architecture of silence is dark rather than light. But within the dark space there must be as many lights as possible.

I do not like ornament that is drawn in loquacity, because it does not contain silent spaces.

Architecture of silence is especially conspicuous in noisy cities.

Architecture that is the peak of loquacity contains concealed silence.

The first significance of architectural space is in silence and loquacity.

The meaning of silent spaces must be contained in the materials, which must be handled as things that have been sublimated.

The range of view of the architect is limited; it is as if he were in the hand of the Buddha from which he can see only the smallest part of what is clear to the Buddha's eye. Therefore, I can only answer questions with silence.

The world of nature gives rise to silence. Is it possible to create architecture that does not shatter the quiet of nature?

Architecture of silence can not be created without a clear and definite framework.

Silent spaces are not seen with the eye; they are felt with the heart.

For this reason, they must be considered as metaphysical, not physical.

There is no longer any way to save architecture; only silence can help.

The architecture of silence is born of pessimism, not optimism.

The content of architecture of silence is in a calm born from motion, like the silence of space one senses when a "Noh" actor has stopped moving for an instant.

Silence should oppose noisiness. All too often noisiness makes us forget silence.

Silence and loquacity should not be treated as opposites. Silence is not the enemy of the loquacious. Silence exists—but always keeps the world of loquacity in mind.

One should sense the fragrance of silence in architectural space in the way that one can hear fish murmuring in flowing water.

Silence exists in the expectant humming of an audience at the moment that the curtain opens in a theatre. Architecture can make joint use of this kind of space of silence.

—Takefumi Aida

"It is a lot easier and more natural to put a puzzle ring back together than to take it apart" (Kobo Abe).

Takefumi Aida's "Artist's House," Kunitachi, Tokyo, 1967, features an atelier as a bit of "displaced space" perched perilously on the roof of the house proper, like a bird uncertain of its roost. The three sections of the house—the residence, the staircase, and the atelier—are separated and handled as independent entities whose arrangement on the site (we seem to see) can only be provisional: this architecture-by-parts, as if it were being rationed, is presented face on, in a literal and wry graph of house-in-the-city. It isn't comfortably honed down to a "controlling centre" with "assistant elements": each part is shown to be something in itself. It is akin to Mozuna Monta's Anti-Dwelling in Hokkaido in its box form—but there the comparison ends: Monta moves from the arbitrary to the geometrical, but what Aida has done is to remove the boxes from the natural relationship to one another and then assign them quite arbitrary relations. As Onobayashi says of "Artist's House": "The densest and most dramatic spatial sequence in the house is that leading from entrance to corridor and staircase." This is the main theme, and the other activity spaces are tucked away like closets in a sorcerer's castle. This approach reflects what Van Eyck calls "the clarity of the labyrinth."

In the Nirvana House, Annihilation House, House Like a Die, and the PL Institute Kindergarten, Aida has developed a "space of encounters"—"the very space I have been seeking is one born of a meeting between varying threads, one that produces an exalted tension as a result of that meeting." The "encounter" itself is formed by the conscious extraction and combination of straight and curved lines of hard and soft elements and by the fusion and revulsion among functional units. The "encounter" turns out to be a meeting between "consciousness and sporadic consciousness."

Aida's "speculation in the dark" concentrates on the "Ah-ness" of things *(mono-no-aware);* his designs are token hints of the "eternal in the here and now," penultimate expression of what will never fully be said. In this sense his work can't be properly called architecture but rather formulae for an architectural experience that sees all things as they are happening "by themselves" in miraculous spontaneity. *Yugen,* too, is alluded to, with all its haunting strangeness of Buddhist intimations and poetic shock. Annihilation House might well be summed up by Zeami's description of *Yugen:*

> Over foam-flecked waves in the falling
> night,
> The Wild Ducks' cries are dying, dim and
> white.

—Chris Fawcett

Gregory Ain: Tierman House, Los Angeles, 1939

AIN, Gregory.

American. Born in Pittsburgh, Pennsylvania, 28 March 1908. Studied mathematics at the University of California at Los Angeles, 1924–26, and architecture at the University of Southern California, Los Angeles, 1927–28. Married Agnes Budin in 1929; married Ruth March in 1938; children: Emily and Christopher. Worked with R. M. Schindler, Los Angeles, 1932, and Richard J. Neutra, Los Angeles, 1932–35. In private practice, Los Angeles, from 1935. Visiting Professor of Design, University of Southern California, 1947–63; Professor, and Head of the School of Architecture, Pennsylvania State University, University Park, 1963–67. Exhibitions: *Built in USA: 1932–1944,* Museum of Modern Art, New York, 1944; Museum of Modern Art, New York, 1950 (one-man show); *Sixteen Southern California Architects,* Scripps College, Claremont, California, 1950. Recipient: *House Beautiful* Award, 1937, 1938, 1940; Pittsburgh Glass Award, 1938; Guggenheim Fellowship, 1940. Fellow, American Institute of Architects. Address: 2830 Francis Avenue, Los Angeles, California 90005, U.S.A.

Works:

1936   Edwards House, 5642 Hollyoak Drive, Los Angeles
1937   Ernst House, 5670 Hollyoak Drive, Los Angeles
        Dunsmuir Flats, 1281 South Dunsmuir Avenue, Los Angeles
        Byler House, 914 Avenue 37, Mt. Washington, Los Angeles
1938   Brownfield Medical Building, Los Angeles
        Beckman House, 357 North Citrus Avenue, Los Angeles
        Kun House, 7947 Fareholm, West Hollywood, Los Angeles
1939   Daniel House, 1856 Micheltorena Street, Silver Lake, Los Angeles
        Hay House, 3132 Oakcrest Drive, Studio City, Los Angeles
        Tierman House, 2323 Micheltorena Street, Silver Lake, Los Angeles
        Vorkapich Garden House (pre-fabricated plywood house), 2100 Benedict Canyon Road, Beverly Hills, California

1941   Ain House, 7964 Willowglen Road, West Hollywood, Los Angeles
        Orans House, 2404 Micheltorena Street, Silver Lake, Los Angeles
1948   Mar Vista Housing Development (100 houses), Mar Vista, Los Angeles
        Avenel Housing Group, 2839–45 Avenel Street, Silver Lake, Los Angeles
        Hollywood Guilds and Unions Office Building, Cahuenga Boulevard, Los Angeles
        Miller House, 1634 Gilcrest, Beverly Hills, California
1949   Schairer House, 11750 Chenault Street, Los Angeles
        Wilfong House, Altadena, California
1950   House, 1350 Linda Ridge Road, Pasadena, California
        Beckman House, 15622 Meadowgate Road, Sherman Oaks, California
        Hurschler House, 1200 Hillcrest Avenue, Pasadena, California
        Museum of Modern Art House, New York
        Kun House, 7947 Fareholm, West Hollywood, Los Angeles
1951   Margolis House, 5786 Valley Oak Drive, Los Angeles
        Mesner House, 13957 Valley Vista Boulevard, Los Angeles
1952   Mesner House, 14571 Valley Vista Boulevard, Los Angeles

1954 Feldman House, 1181 Angelo Drive, Los Angeles
1955 Matthews House, San Rafael Avenue, Los Angeles
1957 153rd Street School, 1605 West 153rd Street, Los Angeles
 Asher House, 263 Loring Avenue, Los Angeles
1960 Gallas House, 5326 Sherbourne Drive, Los Angeles
1961 Elterman House, 15301 Kingswood Lane, Sherman Oaks, California
1962 Berg House, Malibu, California
1963 Lewin House, 15310 Jessen, La Canada, California

Publications:

By AIN: articles—"Small Scale Prefabrication" in *Arts and Architecture* (Los Angeles), March 1941; "In Search of Theory" in *Arts and Architecture* (Los Angeles), January 1966.

On AIN: book—*Built in USA: 1932–1944*, exhibition catalogue, New York 1944; articles—"Dunsmuir Flats" in *Architectural Record* (New York), February 1940; "Guest House" in *Architectural Record* (New York), April 1940; "Houses in Los Angeles" in *Architectural Forum* (New York), April 1940; "Los Angeles House for A. A. Ernst" in *Architectural Record* (New York), October 1940; "Tierman House" in *Arts and Architecture* (Los Angeles), April 1941; "Orans House" in *Arts and Architecture* (Los Angeles), April 1942; "Ain House" in *Arts and Architecture* (Los Angeles), May 1942; "Park Planned Homes" in *Progressive Architecture* (New York), July 1947; "100 Houses for Advance Development Company" in *Arts and Architecture* (Los Angeles), May 1948; "Basic Design for a 100-Unit Subdivision" in *Architectural Forum* (New York), April 1949; "Museum of Modern Art Exhibition House" in *Architectural Record* (New York), July 1950; "Avenel Housing Associates Project" in *Progressive Architecture* (New York), February 1951; "Two View House" in *Interiors* (New York), August 1951.

I have always felt that the architect must not regard his work as an opportunity to demonstrate his virtuosity! Instead, his work is a step to enhance the quality of living, and it can be most effective when it is produced in collaboration with many other experts as well as other colleagues in his profession.

Most contemporary work is done in a fever of ruthless money-making—that attitude must be replaced by an entirely different set of values. The architectural profession can be truly effective only if it can join hands with all the other social scientists, and work with them, and the public at large, to defeat ruthless piracy.

—Gregory Ain

Gregory Ain's impulse to study architecture came from an acquaintance as a youth with R.M. Schindler's Kings Road house, and his dissatisfaction with his Beaux Arts training determined him to work in the office of Richard Neutra. Combined in all his early work, which is his finest, are Neutra's repetitive windows and monoplanar surfaces and Schindler's broken planes and accommodation of shell to plan. In the 1939 Tierman house the modular fenestration is countered by a roof rising to a square skylight in the center of the plan and a dramatic brick chimney whose two-story height is exposed in the open stairwell to the lower level. In his Hay house of 1939 he breaks up the volumes by treating the recessed front door and patio door as dark panels which extend to the second story eaves.

Ain's interest in group housing for middle- and low-income families began in his 1937 Dunsmuir Flats, his most frequently published work. The best known view is of four staggered two-story white blocks, the ceiling levels defined by continuous ribbon windows; not seen are the private porches and patios. The panel-post construction was an early effort to reduce cost, followed in 1939 by prefabricated plywood walls for a model house.

Ain received a Guggenheim Fellowship in 1940 to continue his researches in low-cost housing, and throughout the 1940's he designed, with the participation of clients, a number of projects for attached and detached housing that were notable for site planning and innovative floor plans. Few were built because lending agencies opposed multiple ownership. One of the several schemes to be built was the 1948 Avenel housing for a musicians' union whose members worked in films. The twenty attached units were broken into two blocks for a hillside site, and private patios off the living rooms faced the view.

The 100-house Mar Vista development, begun the same year, used a staggered plan for the siting to insure greater separation; there were variations of the basic design, but the two bedroom and sleeping alcove plan was common to all. The living, kitchen, dining and bedroom alcove were essentially one space, which was opened by a glass wall to a patio.

For his more elaborate houses he borrowed freely from the flexible plan of his low-cost housing, and in most cases the alcove sleeping room became a library or guest room. Ain also adapted many contractors' practices for large or small houses to save construction time and reduce cost. Aside from Irving Gill, Gregory Ain was the first architect in California to refine and dignify the low-cost house.

—Esther McCoy

ALBERT, Edouard.
French. Born in Paris, 10 July 1910. Educated at the Lycée Voltaire, Paris, 1916–19; Collége Stanislas, Paris, 1920–28; Ecole Nationale Supérieure des Beaux-Arts, Paris, 1932–37, Dip.Arch. 1937. Served in the French Army Engineering Corps, 1931. Married Hélène Borel in 1942; children: Philippe, Anne, and Eve. Worked as an industrial designer, Paris, 1928–30; in private practice, Paris, 1938 until his death, 1968. Researcher, Alexis Carrel Foundation, Paris, 1941–44; Architect, Ministry for Prisoners and Deportees, Lorraine, 1945–46, and the Air Ministry, Paris, 1946–51; Chief Architect, Ministry of Education, Paris, 1963–68. Professor and Head of the Architecture Department, Ecole National Supérieure des Beaux-Arts, Paris, 1958–68. Member of the Jury, Grand Prix de Rome, Paris, 1960–68; Member, Editorial Board, *L'Architecture d'Aujourd'hui* Paris, 1960–68. Exhibitions: Gallery René Drouin, Paris, 1942; *Exposition des Arts Ménagers*, Paris, 1952; Musée des Arts Décoratifs, Paris, 1959, and Moscow, 1960; Musée Océanographique, Monaco, 1967; Musée des Arts Decoratifs, Paris, 1968; Mobilier Nal, Paris, 1969; Osaka, Tokyo, and Kyoto, Japan, 1969 (Retrospective). Recipient: First Prize, Town Planning Competition, Vanault-les-Dames, Marne, 1941; Grand Prix d'Architecture, Centre d'Etudes Architecturales, Paris, 1957. *Died (in Paris) 18 January 1968.*

Works:

1939 Metallurgical factory, Dreux, France
 Workmen's houses, Dreux, France
1941/
 42 Town plans, Marne et Ardennes, France
1944/
 45 7 hospital centers, Moselle and Lorraine, France
1946 Forge Factory, Dreux, France
1946/
 52 Reconstruction of Lisieux, Calvados, France
1947/
 48 "Philhome" Prefabricated Houses, for Dufay Chromex Ltd., England
1948 House, Oyonnax, Jura, France
1949/
 52 Town plans for Ajaccio, Calvi, and Corte, Corsica
1950 Long Distance Emission Center, for the Air Ministry, Etampes, France
1952 House, Champagnolles, Jura, France
 Town Hall and School, Vanault-les-Dames, Marne, France
1953 Air France Staff Restaurant, Orly Airport, France
1955 Office building (steel tubular structure), 85 Rue Jouffroy, Paris
1958 Air France Hotel interiors, Orly Airport, Paris
 Skyscraper (first in Paris), Rue Croulebarbe, Paris
1959 Air France Administration Building, Orly Airport, Paris
1960 3 churches in Vietnam
 Théâtre Populaire, Rond Point, La Defénse, Paris (project; with Jean Vilar)
1961 Montconseil Chapel, Corbeil - Essones, France
1962 Vallourec Research Center, Aulnoye, Pas de Calais, France (with Champetier de Ribes)
1962/
 68 Faculty of Literature and Human Sciences, University of Tours (project)
1963 Hotel Complex (arborescent structure), Place de la Résistance, Paris (project)
1963/
 66 Housing, Maisons - Laffitte and Melun, France
1964 Faculty of Sciences, University of Paris
1965 Circular Tower, Place d'Italie, Paris (project)
1966 Artificial Island, Monaco (project; with Commander Cousteau)
1966/
 67 Library, University of Nanterre, France (with Maroti)

Publications:

By ALBERT: book—*ABC of an Architect*, Algiers 1978; monographs—*Towards an Architecture in Space*, Dreux, France 1959; *Metallic Structures in Architecture*, Brussels 1960; *General Principles of a Contemporary Theatrical Architecture*, Paris 1963; *Aborescent Structures*, Paris 1964; *A Contemporary Process of Thinking*, Beirut 1966.

On ALBERT: articles — "Les Compagnons d'Oeuvre" by Jean Giraudoux in *Le Figaro* (Paris), 7 July 1942; "85 Rue Jouffroy, Paris" by J. de Bary in *L'Oeil* (Lausanne), April 1958; "Théâtre Populaire" in *L'Architecture d'Aujourd'hui* (Paris), February/March 1964; "Un siècle d'Architect" in *L'Architecture d'Aujourd'hui* (Paris), April/May 1964; "Artificial Island" in *L'Architecture d'Aujourd'hui* (Paris), April/May 1967; "School Buildings" in *Acier/Stahl/Steel* (Brussels), May 1967; "School Buildings" in *Technique et Architecture* (Paris), no. 3, 1968; article in *Architectural Review* (London), April 1968; "Un grand visionnaire, Albert" by Michel Ragon in *Planète* (Paris), no. 39, 1968; article by Pierre Joly in *L'Oeil* (Lausanne), February 1970; article by I. Schein in *Paris-Construit*, Paris 1970; "Faculté des Sciences" by Bernard Marrey in *Revue de l'Art* (Paris), 1975.

Edouard Albert was an architect in tune with his times. He had a sharp appreciation of its specific needs and of the possibilities it offered. But he thought that, in comparison with other scientific and artistic disciplines, architecture remained inactive. "And yet," he wrote, "if the constructed environment is not in complete harmony with its age, it will soon be largely responsible for a mounting discon-

tent among the coming generations and for the inevitable social reactions that will follow." A highly cultured man, profoundly human in the sense that nothing which touched sensibility and the arts remained foreign to him, poet and visionary, creative artist, professor of architecture, and moving spirit behind a Centre for Research into Structures, Edouard Albert was an architect convinced of the need to find new technical solutions that, together with new materials, would beget new forms.

Albert's professional life illustrated his beliefs. It is marked by works that reveal inventiveness and originality.

From 1945 he studied pre-fabrication, using lightweight materials (Dufaylite), for economic housing that could be dismantled, transformed and transported, and could be produced in aeronautical, naval or railway workshops. In 1950 he began to use hollow profiles; he initiated the use of the tubular steel framework in an office building in the rue Jouffroy in Paris in 1955, a building that can truly be called "revolutionary:

> I thought that we had finally arrived at an age of permanent inventiveness and that we could no longer settle for methods that were cumbersome, slow, subject to the vagaries of climate and demanding highly-skilled manpower. It was probable that metal in tubular form would play an important role, because columns (which tubes resemble), like welded joints or connections, are aesthetically acceptable and because the concrete infill lowers the transmission of sound and heat to the point where the Fire Services accept it for very large buildings without also requiring an exterior steel protection.

Five other qualities had determined the choice of the tube: economy of weight (13T instead of 39 in classic IPN); economy in the use of ground space, compared to that of a concrete or coated steel framework; area gain; improved long-term conservation, because the cylinder has no return angle or edge; and the usefulness of tubes for conveying certain supplies and evacuations (electricity cables, rainwater conduits, etc.)

Albert continued his research in this direction in his building in the rue Croulebarbe, Paris, a skyscraper that is the same height as the towers of Notre Dame. Posts of considerable diametral dimensions and thickness carry up to 385T, with inter-axes of 1.50m. and tubular wind braces in the form of the cross of St. Andrew. The same principle was applied to the Air France Administration Building at Orly Airport and the Vallourec Research Center in Aulnoye, where square hollow tubes were adopted for the framework.

At the same time Albert studied three-dimensional structures, convinced that this kind of tubular system would eventually predominate. He used very small diameter tubes for the Montconseil Chapel at Corbeil-Essones. Then he moved on to larger projects—a Théâtre Populaire, which should have been built with Jean Vilar at La Défense, Paris, where the roofing structure and envelope is entirely three-dimensional, with post-stressed tubes on a network of tetrahedrons and octahedrons; and an artificial island off Monaco, which should have been built in collaboration with Commander Cousteau. The island forms a kind of atoll of 220m. diameter, with an inscribed diameter of 115m. The immersed section descends for 25m., the superstructures rise to 25m., and the spiral tower, topped with a beacon, reaches 100m. The arrangement of the floatation is made up of a 6m. diameter tube connected vertically by 5 tubes of the same dimension to the crown of dodecahedrons forming the enclosure. The wind braces are secured by a series of tetrahedrons of 3.50m. diameter tubes.

Edouard Albert: Hotel Complex, Place de la Résistance, Paris, 1963 (project)

In 1963 Albert was commissioned to design a hotel complex in the Place de la Résistance in Paris opposite the Pont de l'Alma. The "given" of the architectural sector was the meeting on this site of the multiple paths along the Seine with the avenues that lead to it: the complex aimed to extend this greenery on a monumental scale by the erection of a lofty transparent structure bearing a series of suspended hotels, themselves covered in greenery. Albert's enormous "plant" emphasizes the curve of the river at the site. It is an arborescent structure containing 22 hotels on two levels, distributed in space at a height of 120m., allowing light and air to circulate among them.

> When we are able, by means of studies, to master the relationships and to solve the equation of the smallest common divisor or module of the secondary structure at the same time as that of the largest common multiple or general rhythm of the primary structure, we shall be sure of the work's unity and of its scale in relationship to man and the site. By such a procedure, one gains in strength and economy, because the easy hyperstatic relations established in the three-dimensional provide that nothing useless is preserved and that the aspect is simplified. This alleviation allows a coherent liaison of architecture with space—like the trunk and branches of a tree—and also secures the disposal of dead weight. Gothic Art was already going in this direction, and its reference to the plant world was not without deep significance. As soon as there is a breach of the compact solid, it is normal to take an option on space, which alone contains everything.

Albert created a Studio of Scientific Research into treelike structures, believing that at a time when the range of possibilities offered by science made possible the realization of everything imaginable, art should refine techniques to ensure that they were not perverted by inconsiderate usage.

Professor at the Ecole des Beaux-Arts from 1959 to his death in 1968, Albert based his teaching on a removal of barriers between the arts; he tried to initiate his pupils into a broad general culture by means of conversations with the masters of different disciplines—engineers, mathematicians, composers, painters, sculptors, men of the theatre, etc. This open-mindedness led him to create in 1960 a student architect exchange scheme between Kyoto and Paris; it continued until his death. But perhaps the best way to convey Edouard Albert is in his own words:

> The "wonderful" is beginning to disappear from our planet by our constant stripping down of the magical content of things. How can we translate our eternal hope into a style that will define us in relation to our epoch? If we want to be skilled enough to build as the spirit commands, we must not allow ourselves to be overwhelmed by sterile positivism or intellectual scepticism— for the poet is always right: the spirit of inventiveness cannot be duped by sham separations between the real and the unreal, between the concrete and the abstract.

> We have entered a new age. Its character is kinetic and universal. In the space age we should probably have a corresponding spatial architecture. Spatial architecture—like atonal music or non-representational painting—are not only expressions invented to shock man out of his conventional thinking; they also, in themselves, possess harmonious lines of strength.

—Renée Diamant-Berger

ALBINI, Franco.

Italian. Born in Robbiate, Como, 17 October 1905. Educated at the Polytechnic, Milan, Dip.Arch. 1929. Married; son: Marco. In private practice, Milan, from 1930; subsequently joined by the firm's current partners, Franca Helg, 1952, Antonio Piva, 1962, and Marco Albini, 1965. Lecturer, American-Italian Commission of Cultural Exchanges, Rome, 1954–63; Professor of Architectural Composition, Polytechnic, Milan, 1963–77. Member, Unesco Commission for the Renewal of the Museums of the United Arab Republic, 1968–69. Member of CIAM (Congrès Internationaux d'Architecture Moderne). Exhibitions: *Italian Contemporary Art, Decorative Art and Modern Architecture,* Stockholm and Helsinki, 1953; *Ten Italian Architects,* Los Angeles, 1967. Recipient: First Prize, Main Hall Competition, *Triennale,* Milan, 1954; La Rinascente Gold Compass Award, Milan, 1955, 1958, 1964; Bronze Medal, Parsons School of Design, New York, 1956; Olivetti National Medal for Architecture, Italy, 1957; IN-ARCH Award, Italy, 1963, 1965; Biscione d'Oro Award, *Ente Manifestazione Provinciale per il Turismo,* Milan, 1971; First Prize, Municipal Theatre Competition, Vicenza, Italy, 1971. Member, Italian Institute of Town Planning, and of the Scientific Institute of the C.N.R. (National Research Centre of Museography). Member, Academy of San Luca. Honorary Royal Designer for Industry, Royal Society of Arts, London; Honorary Fellow, American Institute of Architects. *Died* (in Milan) *1 November 1977.*

Works:

1936   Design of the Dwelling Exhibition, *Triennale,* Milan (with R. Camus, P. Clausetti, I. Gardella, G. Mazzoleni, G. Minoletti, G. Mucchi, G. Palanti and G. Romano)
     Design of the Antique Jewellery Exhibition, *Triennale,* Milan (with G. Romano)
     Design of Room for a Man, *Triennale,* Milan
     Fabio Filzi Workers' Housing Estate, Viale Argonne, Milan (with R. Camus and G. C. Palanti)

1938   Villa Levi alterations, Broglio, Varese, Italy
     Villa Pestarini, Piazza Tripoli, Milan
     Gabriele d'Annunzio Workers' Housing Estate, Milan (project; with R. Camus and G. C. Palanti)
     Ettore Ponti Workers' Housing Estate, Milan (project)
     Villa Toniolo, Piani d'Invrea, Riviera di Ponente, Italy
     Villa Monzino alterations, Moltrasio, Italy

1940   "Criteria for the Modern Home," *Triennale,* Milan
     Villa Neuffer alterations, Ispra, Lake Maggiore, Italy

1941   Design of the *Scipione Exhibition,* Galleria Brera, Milan

1944   Ceccon Garden, Erba, Italy
     Furniture store, Via Verri, Milan (with BBPR, Ignazio Gardella, and G. Mucchi)

1945   Villa Picolli, Torno, Lake Como, Italy (project)
     Master plan for the City of Milan (project; with others)

1946   Design of the *Home Furnishings Exhibition,* Palazzo dell Arte al Parco, Milan
     Master plan for the centre of the City of Milan (with BBPR, Piero Bottoni, Luigi Figini, Gino Pollini, and others)

1947   Villa Levi Swimming Pool and Garden, Broglio, Varese, Italy (project)

1947/
48   Development plan for Reggio Emilia, Italy (with Giancarlo De Carlo)

1948/
49   Venetian Gallery reconstruction, Galleria Brera, Milan (with L. Castiglioni)

1949/
50   Pirovano Hotel/Mountain Refuge, Cervinia, Italy

1950   Istituto Nazionale Assicurazioni Office Building, Parma, Italy
     Istituto Nazionale Assicurazioni Workers' Housing Estate, Crescenzago, Milan (with F. Marescotti)
     Mangiagalli Workers' Housing Estate, Via Jacopino da Tradate, Vialba, Milan (with Ignazio Gardella)
     Office and residential building, Piazza Repubblica, Milan (project)

1950/
51   Istituto Nazionale Assicurazioni Workers' Housing Estate, Cesate, Milan (in collaboration)

1950/
61   Palazzo Bianco conversion to a museum, Genoa

1952   Museo del Tesoro di San Lorenzo, Genoa
     Salons, *Exhibition of Arts and Customs,* Palazzo Grassi, Venice

1952/
61   Palazzo Rosso conversion to a museum, Genoa

1952/
62   Municipal Offices, Genoa

1953   Design of the *Italian Contemporary Art, Decorative Art and Modern Architecture* exhibition, Stockholm and Helsinki
     Villa alterations, Diano Marina, Italy

1954   Design of the Montecatini and Rhodatoce exhibitions, *Trade Fair,* Milan
     Main Hall, *Triennale,* Milan
     Arts School Section, *Triennale,* Milan
     Salons, *Exhibition of Arts and Customs,* Palazzo Grassi, Venice
     Design of the Italian State Exhibition, *Bienal,* Sao Paulo, Brazil
     Societa Gres Employees Residential Buildings, Colognola, Bergamo, Italy

1955   Istituto Nazionale Assicurazioni Housing Estate Creche-Kindergarten, Cesate, Milan (with G. Rigoli)
     Valletta Cambiaso Public Gardens and Sports Grounds, Genoa

1955/
56   Villa Minorini, Parco del Tigullio, Italy
     Villa Olivetti, Ivrea, Italy

1956   Palazzo dell'Arte Exhibition Galleries, Genoa (competition project; with M. Labo, Daneri, Grossi Bianchi and Zappa)
     Design of the Delacroix Exhibition, *Biennale,* Venice
     Design of the Premio La Rinascente—Compasso d'Oro Exhibition, *World's Fair,* New York
     Office and residential building, Turin (project)
     Villa Zambelli, Forli, Italy

1957   Istituto Nazionale Assicurazioni Housing Estate, Scandino, Reggio Emilia, Italy

1957/
61   Istituto Nazionale Assicurazione Office and Residential Buildings, Genoa-Piccapietra, La Rinascente Department Store, Piazza Fiume, Rome

1958   Farm building conversion, Gallarate, Varese, Italy

1959   Villa, Pesaro, Italy (project)
     Villa Strangalini, Pieve Ligure, Italy

1960   Design of the International Glass and Steel Exhibition, *Triennale,* Milan
     Design of the *History of Petroleum Exhibition,* Automobile Museum, Turin (with C. Levi)
     Design of the *History of the Tyre (Tire) Exhibition,* Automobile Museum, Turin

1960/
72   5 residential buildings, Via Argelati, Milan

1961   Organization, Productivity, Market Pavilion, *International Work Exhibition,* Turin
     Scientific Research Pavilion, *International Work Exhibition,* Turin

House, Punta Ala, Italy
1962 House, Galliate Lombardo, Italy
1962/
    63 New Egyptian Museum, Cairo, Egypt (project)
    Apartment building, Castellaro, Zoagli, Italy
    Building conversion, Via San Maurilio, Milan
    Villa Osti, Bogliasco, Italy
1962/
    65 Villa alterations, Via XX Settembre, Milan
1962/
    69 Stations for the First Line of the Underground (Subway), Milan
1963/
    67 Building, Via Moise Loria, Milan
1963/
    75 Sant'Agostino Museum, Genoa
1964 Design of the Italian Industrial Exhibition, *World's Fair,* New York
    Modissa Building, Bahnhofstrasse, Zurich (competition project)
    Forti District Landscaping Study, Genoa
1964/
    67 Building, Via Fulvio Testi, Milan
1964/
    71 Hotel, Santa Cesarea Terme, Calabria, Italy
1965 Design of the *Guardi Exhibition,* Palazzo Grassi, Venice
    Villa, Cremella, Como, Italy

Villa Contarini conversion, Valnogaredo, Padua
1965/
    67 Villa, Quinto, Genoa
1965/
    70 Apartment building, Courmayeur, Aosta, Italy
1965/
    72 Graeco-Roman Museum, Alexandria, Egypt
1966 Italsider Steel Pavilion, *Trade Fair,* Milan (with E. Gentili Tedeschi)
1966/
    70 Residential and office building, Piazza Arcole, Milan
1967 Italsider "Yesterday, Today, Tomorrow" Pavilion, *Trade Fair,* Milan (with E. Gentili Tedeschi)
    Thermal Bath Building, Salsomaggiore Terme, Italy
1967/
    69 Villa, Ponte dell'Olio, Piacenza, Italy
1967/
    70 Villa, Parma, Italy
1968 Italsider "Why Steel" Pavilion, *Trade Fair,* Milan (with E. Gentili Tedeschi)
    Alfa Romeo Technical Office Building, Arese, Italy (competition project)
    Breuil Centre, Cervinia, Italy

1968/
    69 Master plan for the Egyptian Museum and Egyptian Museum Cultural Center, Cairo
    Villa, Cremella, Como, Italy
    SNAM G.N.L. Terminal Landscaping, Lanigaglia, La Spezia, Italy (consultancy project)
1968/
    70 Brionvega Storage, Display and Office Buildings, Arzano, Padua and Florence
1968/
    71 Apartment and office building, Parma, Italy
1969 Villa, Padenghe, Lake Garda, Italy
1969/
    70 Medieval Tower conversion, Montecatini Val Cecina, Italy
1969/
    71 Villa, Rocca San Casciano, Forli, Italy
1969/
    73 Secondary school, Giussano, Milan
    SNAM Office Building III, San Donato Milanese, Milan
1969/
    74 Office and residential building, Madre di Dio, Genoa
    Civic Museum conversion, Eremitani Cloister, Padua
    Cassa di Risparmio conversion, Palazzo Pisaroni, Piacenza, Italy

Franco Albini: Thermal Bath Building, Salsomaggiore Terme, Italy, 1967

1971 Municipal Theatre, Vicenza, Italy (competition project)
1971/
72 Palladio Exhibition Plan, Basilica, Vicenza, Italy
1971/
73 Villa, Daverio, Italy
1972 Design of the *Achievements of the Pahlavi Era* exhibition, Marble Palace, Tehran
Domus Comestabilis Offices conversion, Vicenza, Italy
Office and picture gallery conversion, Sforza Castle, Milan
Villa, Daverio, Italy
1972/
75 Old Town Center Building Code Study, Brescia, Italy
1973 Design of *The School of Leonardo* exhibition, Palazzo Reale, Milan
Houses, Gavirate, Italy (project)
Villa, Daverio, Italy
1973/
74 Civic Center and Canteen, Sassuolo, Modena, Italy (project)
1974 Design of the *The School of Leonardo* exhibition, Tokyo
Design of the *50 Years of Italian Painting in the Boschi-Di Stefano Collection* exhibition, Palazzo Reale, Milan
Kindergarten, Sassuolo, Modena, Italy (with A. Pastorini)
Houses, Montichiari, Italy
Country Club, Croara, Italy (project)
1974/
75 Corso Garibaldi Study, Milan
Palazzo del Monte restoration, Piacenza, Italy
1975 Masmak restoration, Riyadh, Saudi Arabia (project)
Public Gardens and Parks Study, Saudi Arabia (with A. Porcinai)

Numerous furniture designs

Publications:

On ALBINI: books—*Storia dell'architettura moderna* by Leonardo Benevolo, 2 vols., Bari, Italy 1960; *Franco Albini* by G. C. Argan, Milan 1962; *The New Architecture of Europe* by G. E. Kidder Smith, New York and London 1961; *Dizionario Enciclopedico di Architettura e Urbanistica,* edited by Paolo Portoghesi, Rome 1969; *Orientamenti nuovi nell'Architettura Italiana* by Vittorio Gregotti, Milan 1970; *Dizionario degli Architetti,* edited by B. Oudin, Milan 1971; *Design in Italia 1945–1972* by Paolo Fossati, Milan 1972; articles—"Franco Albini and Architectural Culture in Italy" by Giuseppe Samona in *Zodiac* (Milan), no. 3, 1957; "Contemporary Italian Architects" in *Notiziario Culturale Italiano* (Paris), May 1963; "Recent Works by Albini-Helg" by F. Tentori in *Zodiac* (Milan), no. 14, 1965; "Realismo e Architettura Povera" by E. D'Alfonso in *Casabella* (Milan), no. 352, 1970.

Although Franco Albini's work covered a wide range from furniture design to town planning projects, he became best known as an outstanding exhibition and display architect whose world stature led him to be entrusted with the project for the great new museums of Egyptian art in Cairo. His influence can be seen in museums throughout the world, though it was his work in Genoa that first made him famous. There he remodelled the interiors of two Renaissance palace museums with rich art collections—the Palazzo Bianco, or White Palace; and the Palazzo Rosso, or Red Palace—displaying their art with abstract rigour yet sensitivity, so that it could be seen clearly and effectively to best advantage.

Also in Genoa he built a new museum to house the Treasury of the Cathedral of San Lorenzo, which possesses such fabulous objects as the Sacro Catino, a cup brought back from the Middle East by the Crusaders, which is supposed to have been given to Solomon by the Queen of Sheba, and from which Christ is claimed to have drunk at the Last Supper. Albini's new Museo del Tesoro di San Lorenzo is in the undercroft of the cathedral and is laid out geometrically as a series of circular rooms of various sizes, with the objects dramatically lit.

Italian designers have been best known for such things as cars or Olivetti typewriters, but Albini made a major contribution to experiments in Italian furniture design, from compact dining room furniture in graded units which pack away into a small area, to a variety of very comfortable circular armchairs such as the elegant malacca and bamboo-cane armchair Margherita, designed with his partner Franca Helg in 1950.

From his first villa in Milan in 1938 he was responsible for a great variety of works, including a number of stations for the Milan underground system. The most controversial of his buildings has been the large department store La Rinascente in Rome, the most interesting version of which was the original model, deeply influenced by the metal structures of the 19th century. As actually built, it is a savagely brutal structure with an exposed steel frame of almost windowless concrete walls built of pleated units.

Like Ignazio Gardella, with whom he worked on the development of the new Cesate district of Milan, he was one of the longest survivors of the first generation of Italian modernism or rationalism, with an exceptionally versatile career that made him a major influence in many fields of design.

—Konstantin Bazarov

ALEXANDER, Christopher.

British. Born in Vienna, Austria, of British parents, 4 October 1936. Educated at Oundle School, Northamptonshire; Cambridge University, 1956–59, B.A. in architecture, M.A. in mathematics; Harvard University, Cambridge, Massachusetts, 1960–63, Ph.D. in architecture 1963. Worked for the Village Development Planning Department of the Government of Gujarat, India, 1962; Consultant in Urban Housing, Arthur D. Little Company, San Francisco, 1963; Consultant Architect, Bay Area Rapid Transit System, San Francisco, 1963–64; Consultant on User Needs, Ministry of Public Buildings and Works, London, 1965–66. Since 1967, Director, Center for Environmental Structure, Berkeley, California. Consultant Architect to the Ministry of Information and Tourism, Spain, 1975, and Ministry of Environment, Papua New Guinea, 1976; Architect and Planner, Jewish Agency and Ministry of Housing, Israel, 1978; Consultant Architect, Infonavit, Mexico, 1978. Assistant Professor, 1963, Professor in the Humanities, 1965–66, Associate Professor of Architecture, 1966–70, and since 1970 Professor of Architecture, University of California, Berkeley. Visiting Lecturer, Royal Institute of Technology, Stockholm, 1973, and University of Mexico, Mexicali, 1975–76. Recipient: International Design Award, Kaufmann Foundation, 1965; Research Medal, American Institute of Architects, 1972. Address: Center for Environmental Structure, 2701 Shasta Road, Berkeley, California 94708, U.S.A.

Works:

1962 Master plan for the village of Bavra, Gujarat, India
Bavra Village School, Gujarat, India (project; with Janet Johnson)
1963 Urban housing program, San Francisco
1963/
64 Courtyard House, New Haven, Connecticut (project; with Serge Chermayeff)
1964 Rapid transit stations for the Bay Area Rapid Transit System, San Francisco (schematic design; with Van King and Sara Ishikawa)

1968 Multi-Service Center, Hunts Point, Bronx, New York (project; with Sara Ishikawa and Murray Silverstein)
1969 Community village of 1,500 houses, Lima, Peru (competition project; with Sanford Hirshen, Sara Ishikawa, Christie Coffin, and Shlomo Angel)
1970 "A Human City" Pavilion, *World's Fair,* Osaka, Japan (with Ronald Walkey and others)
Berkeley City Hall Complex, California (project; with Ronald Walkey and Barbara Schreiner)
1970/
73 Master plan for the University of Oregon, Eugene (with others)
1970/
78 Various experimental furniture designs
1971 Prototype houses (14), Lima, Peru
1971/
74 Community Mental Health Center, Modesto, California (with Murray Silverstein and Nacht and Lewis)
Master plan for the town of Marsta, Sweden (project; with Max Jacobson and Ingrid King)
1972 Mill Valley Housing Co-operative, California (project; with Sara Ishikawa)
1974 User-designed apartment building, St. Quentin-en-Yvelines, near Versailles (project; with Ingrid King and Walter Wendler)
Master plan for a tourist resort, Fuerteventura, Canary Islands (with Ingrid King, Halim Abdelhalim, and Lisa Heschong)
Tourist development, Malaga, Spain (project; with Halim Abdelhalim, Walter Wendler, Ingrid King, Donald Corner, and Howard Davis)
2-story building of featherweight concrete (project; with Walter Wendler, Donald Corner, and others)
Master plan for the town square of Walnut Creek, Arizona (with Ingrid King)
1975 Rockbridge Plaza (shops and apartments), Oakland, California
1975/
76 Experimental block production factory, Mexicali, Mexico
1975/
78 Various multi-colored experimental tiles and paintings
1976 Experimental houses (8), with community facilities, Mexicali, Mexico
1977 Migrant worker's house (project: for the California Department of Migrant Services)
1977/
78 Experimental designs in sprayed concrete
1978/
79 Master plan for Moshav Sof Ma'arav, Galilee, Israel
Experimental sprayed concrete house, Martinez, California

Publications:

By ALEXANDER: books—*Community and Privacy: Towards a New Architecture of Humanism,* with Serge Chermayeff, New York 1963, Tokyo and London 1966, Buenos Aires 1967, Paris and Stuttgart 1972; *Notes on the Synthesis of Form,* Cambridge, Massachusetts 1964, Milan 1967, Paris 1970; *Systems Generating Systems* (booklet), Chicago 1967; *A Pattern Language Which Generates Multi-Service Centers,* with Sara Ishikawa and Murray Silverstein, Berkeley, California 1968; *Houses Generated by Patterns,* with Sanford Hirshen, Sara Ishikawa, Christie Coffin, and Shlomo Angel, Berkeley, California 1969; *Tres Aspectos de Matematica y Desegño,* Barcelona 1969; *Mosaic of Subcultures,* Berkeley, California 1969; *A Human City,* Tokyo 1970; *La Estuctura del Medio Ambiente,* Barcelona 1971; *The Grass Roots Housing Process,* with Halim

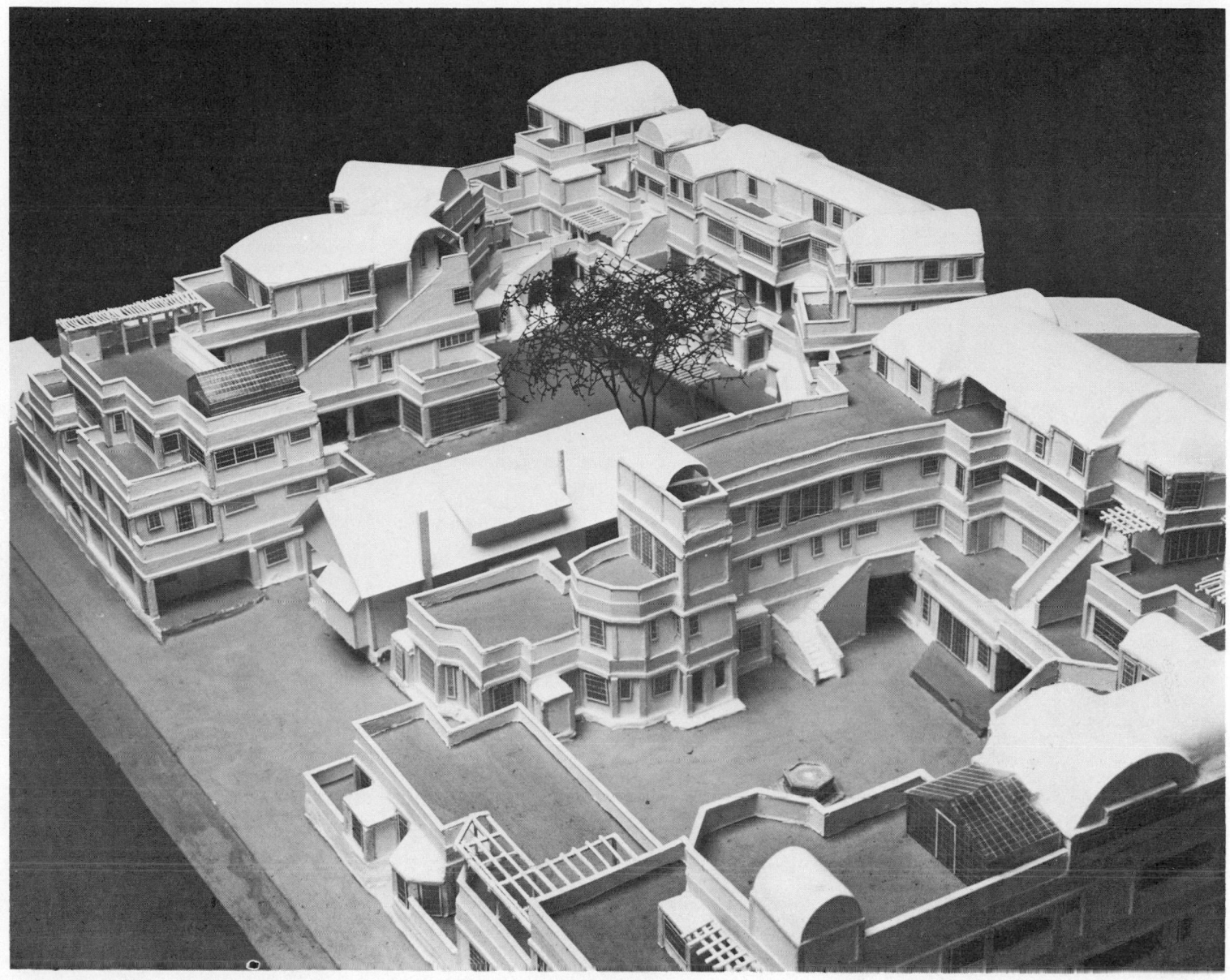

Christopher Alexander: User-designed Apartment Building, St Quentin-en-Yvelines, near Versailles, 1974 (project)

Abdelhalim and others, Berkeley, California 1975; *The New Apartment Building,* with Ingrid King and Walter Wendler, Berkeley, California 1975; *People Rebuilding Berkeley: The Self-Creating Life of Neighborhoods,* with Howard Davis and Halim Abdelhalim, Berkeley, California 1975; *The Oregon Experiment,* London 1975; *A Pattern Language,* London 1977; *The Timeless Way of Building,* London 1979; articles—"Perception and Modular Coordination" in *RIBA Journal* (London), October 1959; "The Revolution Finished Twenty Years Ago" in *The Architects Yearbook,* London 1960; "A Result in Visual Aesthetics" in *British Journal of Psychology* (London), October 1960; "The Origin of Creative Power in Children" in *British Journal of Aesthetics* (London), July 1962; "Main Structure Concept," with B. V. Doshi, in *Landscape* (Berkeley, California), Winter 196364; "On Changing the Way People See," with A. W. F. Huggins, in *Perceptual and Motor Skills* (Missoula, Montana), July 1964; "The Theory and Invention of Form" in *Architectural Record* (New York), April 1965; "A City Is Not a Tree" in *Architectural Forum* (New York), April May 1965, reprinted in *Architecture, Mouvement, Continuité* (Paris), November 1967; "The Question of Computers in Design" in *Landscape* (Berkeley, California), Spring 1965; "Relational Complexes in Architecture," with Van Maren King and others, in *Architectural Record* (New York), September 1966; "From a Set of Forces to a Form" in *The Man-Made Object,* edited by Gyorgy Kepes, New York 1966;

"The Pattern of Streets" in *Architectural Design* (London), November 1967; "Design Innovation," with others, in *Progressive Architecture* (New York), November 1967; "Subsymmetries," with Susan Carey, in *Perception and Psychophysics* (Austin, Texas), February 1968; "The Bead Game Conjecture" in *Lotus* (Venice), no. 5, 1968; "Thick Walls" in *Architectural Design* (London), July 1968; "Major Changes in Environmental Form Required by Social and Psychological Demands" in *Architectural Design* (London), March 1970; "The Environment" in *The Japan Architect* (Tokyo), no. 165, 1970; "Interview with Maria José Rague Arias" in *California Trip,* Barcelona 1971; "Houses Generated by Patterns: Summary" in *The Growth of Cities* by David Lewis, London 1971; "The Atoms of Environmental Structure," with Barry Poyner, in *Emerging Methods of Design,* Cambridge, Massachusetts 1971; "A Refutation of Design Methodology," interview with Max Jacobson, in *Architectural Design* (London), December 1971; "An Attempt to Derive the Nature of a Human Building System from First Principles" and "The Invention of a Human and Organic Building System" in *Shirtsleeve Session on Responsive Housebuilding Technologies* by Edward Allen, Cambridge, Massachusetts 1972; "The Andalusian Project," with Halim Abdelhalim, Walter Wendler, and others, in *Architectural Design* (London), January 1975; "The Architect Builder" in *AIA Journal* (Washington, D.C.), September 1977; "Value: A Reply to Protzen" in *Concrete* (Slough, Buckinghamshire), vol. 1, no. 8, 1977; etc.

On ALEXANDER: articles—"The Death of the Beaux-Arts: The Cal-Oregon Experiment in Design Education" by M. A. Milne and C. W. Rusch in *AIA Journal* (Washington, D.C.), March 1968; "Pattern Language: The Contribution of Christopher Alexander's Center for Environmental Structure to the Science of Design" by Roger Montgomery in *Architectural Forum* (New York), January February 1970; "Design Method or Beaux-Arts? Four Notes on Design Method" by Juan Pablo Bonta in *Architectural Association Quarterly* (London), Autumn 1970; "Christopher Alexander ou le Mythe de la Création Scientifique" by J. Dreyfus in *La Vie Urbaine* (Paris), no. 2, 1971; "Dossier: Récherche Habitat" in *L'Architecture d'Aujourd'hui* (Paris), July August 1974; "Christopher Alexander's Timeless Way of Building" by Kanna Hirata in *Architecture + Urbanism* (Tokyo), no. 3, 1975; "La Régression Californienne ou la Réificacion du Mythe Christopher Alexander" in *Architecture, Mouvement, Continuité* (Paris), March 1976.

Christopher Alexander is a major voice among those trying to evolve a sound theoretical basis for architecture. His influence has been through his writing and teaching rather than through completed buildings. In recent years, however, he and his collaborators have produced a number of projects that have lent visual evidence to his theoretical position.

Educated both as an architect and as a mathematician at Cambridge, Alexander later obtained his

Ph.D. in architecture from Harvard University. His doctoral work in 1962 and 1963 centered on the development of computer programs for the Hierarchical Decomposition of Sets or Systems having associated graphs (the programs were known as HI-DECS). The basic aim of this work was to develop techniques for the analysis of successful environments and for the creation of new environments. In particular, explicit analysis, it was hoped, would enable designers to capture the elusive qualities of traditional unselfconscious designs for buildings and settlements, in a way that escapes the crude rationalism of conventional architectural design.

Alexander's criticism of existing design methods, implicit in the aims of his mathematical work, found expression in two books. *Community and Privacy: Towards a New Architecture of Humanism,* written with the modernist pioneer Serge Chermayeff, explored in particular notions of privacy within the home and between home and community. Many examples were given of courtyard houses and other house forms satisfying the complex criteria of sociability and privacy in the home. *Notes on the Synthesis of Form* was one of the most important books of the decade. It presented a coherent theoretical explanation of the shortcomings of crude rationalist design, the basis for the success of many unselfconscious designs, and the necessary methods for creating better designs in the future. The impact of the book was tremendous. Architects were quite unused to serious theoretical texts outside the traditions of art history. Alexander wanted to know what made places work, not what made them look as if they worked. The theory was based on the concept of "fit" between human needs/demands and possible forms, a central theme in Alexander's thought.

Following a brief spell in an experimental group at the British Ministry of Public Buildings and Works, Alexander took up a post in 1966 at the University of California, Berkeley, where he still teaches. At Berkeley he developed the theory of "fit" in terms of what he called "patterns"—the successful resolution of a specific problem within a specific context. Patterns can be seen as "correct" solutions to sub-problems in design, and can be combined into a "pattern language" accessible to all who wish to build, not merely to professional architects. The evolution of a pattern language by Alexander and his colleagues at his design and research organization, the Center for Environmental Structure, led to a diminished confidence in mathematical methods as a basis for better design, to be replaced by empirical research to support the hypotheses of patterns.

In 1971, in an interview, Alexander shocked the large fraternity of design methodologists by condemning design methods as offering nothing useful to say on how to design buildings and as being obsessed with techniques leading nowhere. Since then the work of CES has focussed on design projects. But more important for most architects has been the publication of three books: *The Timeless Way of Building,* which sets out the philosophical basis of the Pattern Language as a medium for articulating needs and for creating buildings and environments in an adaptive rather than a wholesale manner; *A Pattern Language,* which is a compendium of 253 patterns researched at CES and ranging in scale from demographic considerations to detailed questions of ornament; and *The Oregon Experiment,* which describes a specific cooperative planning experiment for the evolution of the 15,000 student Eugene campus of the University of Oregon.

Alexander has secured an important place in the history of 20th century architecture. His critics now accuse him of a progressive slackening of rigour and the glorification of self-building, manual work and crafts at the expense of confrontation with modern technology and social institutions. But he has great resilience and originality of thought. There is much of real value in the Pattern Language concept, and it promises much for the future of the built environment in a time of increasing disillusionment with more conventional approaches.

—Andrew Rabeneck

ALEXANDER, Robert E(vans).

American. Born in Bayonne, New Jersey, 23 November 1907. Educated at Cornell University, Ithaca, New York, 1925–30, B.Arch. 1930. Married Eugenie Vigneron in 1931 (died, 1952); children: Lynne and Timothy; married Mary Starbuck in 1953; son: Robert Jr. Partner, Wilson, Merrill and Alexander, Los Angeles, 1935–41; Staff Assistant in Charge, Production Control Division, Lockheed Factory A, Burbank, California, 1942–45; in private practice, Los Angeles, 1946–49; in partnership with Richard J. Neutra, *q.v.,* Los Angeles, 1949–58. Since 1958, Principal, Robert E. Alexander and Associates, Los Angeles. Member, 1945–51, and President, 1948–50, City of Los Angeles Planning Commission; Consultant Architect, Public Housing Administration, Los Angeles, 1950, Government of Guam, 1951–52, California Institute of Technology, Pasadena, Claremont College, California, and University of Southern California, Los Angeles, 1952–61, and Federal Housing Administration, Washington, D.C., 1958–59. President, Southern California Chapter of the American Institute of Architects, 1970. Recipient: Honor Award, American Institute of Architects, 1946, 1951, 1954. Fellow, American Institute of Architects, 1956. Address: Robert E. Alexander and Associates, 825 Colorado Boulevard, Los Angeles, California 90041, U.S.A.

Works:

1935/
42 Baldwin Hills Village, Los Angeles
1942 Lakewood Village, Los Angeles
1946 Community Church, Baldwin Hills, Los Angeles (project)
1946/
50 Shops, Baldwin Hills, Los Angeles
1947/
49 Elementary School, Baldwin Hills, Los Angeles
1948 Pearce House, Los Angeles
Demonstration Elementary School, University of California at Los Angeles
1948/
55 Orange Coast College, Costa Mesa, California
1950 Urban redevelopment plan for Sacramento, California (project; with Richard Neutra)
1950/
53 Redevelopment plan for Elysian Heights, Los Angeles (project; with Richard Neutra)
1952/
54 Territorial plan, Governor's Residence, and 3 schools, Guam
1953 Community Hotel, San Pedro, California
1954 Child guidance clinic, Los Angeles (with Richard Neutra)
Business Education Building, Orange Coast College, Costa Mesa, California (with Richard Neutra)
Family housing, Mountain Home, Idaho
1955 Mellon Science Building and Francis Scott Key Auditorium, St. John's College, Annapolis, Maryland (with Richard Neutra)
1956 National Charity League Headquarters, Los Angeles
1957 Science Building, Arts and Music Auditorium, and Sports Facilities, Orange Coast College, Costa Mesa, California (with Richard Neutra)
Miramar Chapel, La Jolla, California (with Richard Neutra)
Ferro Chemical Company Office Building, Cleveland
Alamitos Intermediate School, Garden Grove, California (with Richard Neutra)
1958 Riviera Methodist Church, Redondo Beach, California (with Richard Neutra)
Fine Arts Building, University of Nevada, Reno
Palos Verdes High School, Palos Verdes, California
Fine Arts Center, California State University, San Fernando
Elementary Training School, University of California at Los Angeles (with Richard Neutra)
Visitors Center, Gettysburg, Pennsylvania
Visitors Center, Petrified Forest, Arizona
Police Facilities Building, Santa Ana, California (with Romberg and Lowry)
Family housing, Lemoore, California
1959 Museum of Natural History and Planetarium, Dayton, Ohio (with Richard Neutra)
Library, University of Nevada, Reno
1960 Megastructure, Caracas, Venezuela (project; with Richard Neutra)
1961 Great Western Savings and Loan Building, Los Angeles (with Skidmore, Owings and Merrill)
Catskill Elementary School, Los Angeles
International Student Center, University of California at Los Angeles
1962 Dining Facility, University of California at San Diego
1963 Swirlbul Library, Adelphi University, Garden City, Long Island, New York (with Richard Neutra)
United States Embassy, Karachi, Pakistan (with Richard Neutra)
Lincoln Memorial Museum, Gettsburg, Pennsylvania (with Richard Neutra)
Married Student Housing, University of Southern California, Los Angeles
1964 Hall of Records, Los Angeles (with Richard Neutra)
Richard J. Neutra Elementary School, Lemoore, California (with Richard Neutra)
1964/
71 School of Medicine, University of California at San Diego
1966 Residence Halls, Revelle College, University of California at San Diego
1968- Bunker Hill Towers, Figueroa and 1st Streets, Los Angeles
1970 Los Angeles Central Library addition (project)

Publications:

By ALEXANDER: books—*Rebuilding the City: A Study of Redevelopment Problems in Los Angeles,* with Drayton S. Bryant, Los Angeles 1951; *The Rural City* (United Nations publication), New York 1952; *Environmental Quality and Amenity in California,* with Okimoto, Sacramento, California 1966; articles—"Preview of a New Way of Life" in *Revere Magazine* (New York), no. 14, 1943; "The Suburban Campus" in *Urban Land* (Washington, D.C.), December 1966; "Southern California Transit: Too Little, Too Late, Too Bad" in *Cry California* (San Francisco), Spring 1968.

On ALEXANDER: articles — "Demonstration School" in *Architectural Forum* (New York), November 1951; "College Buildings: Space Analysis" in *Progressive Architecture* (New York), February 1952; "Planning Guam" in *Progressive Architecture* (New York), January 1953; "Guam: A Problem in Progress" in *Arts and Architecture* (Los Angeles), May 1953; "A Community Hotel" in *Arts and Architecture* (Los Angeles), September 1953; "Sacramento: A Model for Small City Redevelopment" in *Architectural Forum* (New York), June 1954; "Orange Coast College, Costa Mesa, California" in *Progressive Architecture* (New York), July 1955; "Second Group of American Embassy Buildings" in *Architectural Record* (New York), June 1956; "Genetrix: Personal Contributions to American Architecture" in *Architectural Review* (London), May 1957; "Office Building and Auditorium" in *Arts and Architecture* (Los Angeles), July 1957; "The Campus Library and the Architect" in *Architectural Record* (New York), August 1957; "An Airman's Chapel: Miramar Chapel" in *Arts and Architecture*

Robert E. Alexander: Baldwin Hills Village, Los Angeles, 1935/42

(Los Angeles), April 1958; "Libraries: Gables and Garden for Nevada Campus" in *Architectural Forum* (New York), February 1963; "Campus Planning: Building Types Study 339" in *Architectural Record* (New York), November 1964; "College Dormitories: Building Types Study No. 349" in *Architectural Record* (New York), August 1965; "Library Buildings Award Program" in *AIA Journal* (Washington, D.C.), August 1966.

My work as an architect has been soul satisfying. It has been important to the users and has satisfied their activities and feelings. The importance of the work as object is insignificant compared to the "glory of the action" of my involvement.

I have consciously managed a diverse practice in such a way that I have been personally involved in developing the concept design of almost everything with which my name is identified. Starting from a "left brain" saturation, I have tried to apply the "right brain" after the purposes of the program have been satisfied. Extensive work in "city planning" has been incorporated as a natural part of architecture, and my involvement in community and social issues as well as professional concerns has been constant.
—Robert E. Alexander

As a partner in a large firm Robert Alexander made important contributions to the planning of Lakewood Village and the well-known Baldwin Hills Village in Los Angeles. Before starting his own practice he wrote, "The form of the house is absolutely unimportant. In the field of form the community plan is the only important thing. It must have a head, a heart, a soul and a purpose. . . . Tomorrow's client is the people and it is not a beast. We must take architecture to the people." This philosophy has been evident in all of his work.

Two of his first commissions contributed to the enrichment of the area surrounding Baldwin Hills Village. A nearby shopping center established a close relationship to the circulation patterns of the Village. A community church project is notable for its free form and the close integration of architecture and landscape architecture. The landscape architect had been brought in at the very beginning of the job.

A Demonstration School built on the campus of the University of California at Los Angeles was freely disposed so that the stream running through the site was left in its natural state and became a "learning experience" for the children. In planning the individual classrooms the architect brought "the people", in this case the faculty, into the planning process to an unprecedented degree. About Alexander's technology building at Orange Coast College the editors of *Progressive Architecture* wrote, "one can hardly discuss the technology building's structure or acoustics individually; they are so interrelated that an analysis of one becomes a compendium of the other." For this job Alexander hired a well-known artist as color consultant. The consultant conferred with teaching personnel before submitting swatch-abstracts for their approval. This was typical of the way the whole job proceeded. Once again architecture was brought to the people.

Before all the buildings on the Orange Coast campus were completed, Alexander formed a partnership with Richard Neutra which lasted for a decade. Neutra's interest in form was greater than Alexander's, so that the form of the later Orange Coast buildings and the other buildings executed by the partners bears the Neutra stamp. A project for a megastructure at the intersection of two highways in Caracas was probably an Alexander concept, as after the partnership was dissolved he became interested in planning a transit system for Los Angeles, with megastructures proposed for the principal intersections in the system.

As planner in charge of the new campus for the University of California at San Diego and as architect for a group of dormitories there, Alexander succeeded in humanizing the scheme. A group of interestingly spaced low-rise dormitories was erected in place of the few high-rise buildings that had originally been proposed.

As a concerned citizen of Los Angeles, Alexander has become interested in saving the downtown urban core. He prepared a plan to save Bertram Goodhue's historic Los Angeles central library. His major commission downtown is the Bunker Hill Towers, a large apartment complex. It is one of the few recent developments in the area that respects the scale of the old city. The softened corners recall the Victorian build-

ings that once stood on Bunker Hill. Unfortunately its example has not been followed, and Bunker Hill Towers is overshadowed by fashionable monuments which lack the sense of appropriateness to site that Robert Alexander has sought to achieve in all his commissions.

—Alson Clark

ALINGTON, W(illiam) H(ildebrand).
New Zealander. Born in Lower Hutt, 18 November 1929. Educated at the University of Auckland School of Architecture, 1951–55 (Senior Scholar, 1954), B.Arch. 1956: influenced by the government architect F. G. Wilson and by Professor R. H. Toy; University of Illinois, Urbana, 1957–59 (Fulbright Scholar), M.Arch. 1959: influenced by Professor A. R. Williams. Married Margaret Hilda Broadhead in 1955; children: Elisabeth, Giles, and Catherine. Draughting Cadet, 1950–55, and Architect, 1956–65, Ministry of Works, Wellington; Architect, Robert Matthew and Johnson-Marshall, London, 1956–57; Tutor, University of Illinois, 1958; Partner, with A. L. Gabites, J. A. Beard and D. J. Edmondson, Gabites and Beard, Wellington, 1965–71, with Gabites, Beard, Edmondson, D. J. Wilson, S. W. Toomath, D. G. Irvine and G. Anderson, Gabites, Toomath, Beard, Wilson and Partners, Wellington, 1971–72, and with Gabites and Edmondson, Gabites, Alington and Edmonson, Wellington, since 1972 (office established in Christchurch, 1975). Assistant Editor, *New Zealand Institute of Architects Journal,* Wellington, 1964–69; Councillor and Vice-Chairman, New Zealand Institute of Architects, 1964–78; President, Architectural Centre Inc., 1970–72; Honorary Member of the Faculty of Architecture, Victoria University of Wellington, 1975–78; Vice-Chairman, Wellington Branch of the New Zealand Institute of Architects, 1978 Recipient: Bronze Medal, 1971, 1974, Silver Medal, 1972, Branch Awards, 1973, 1975, 1976, and National Award, 1977, New Zealand Institute of Architects. Associate, 1955, and Fellow, 1972, New Zealand Institute of Architects. Associate of the Royal Institute of British Architects, 1960. Address: Gabites Alington and Edmondson, 126 The Terrace, Post Office Box 5136, Wellington, New Zealand.

Works:

1956　Standard Water Tower, Palmerston North, New Zealand
1962　Gisborne Courthouse, New Zealand
　　　Alington House, Wellington
1965　Meteorological Office, Wellington
1966　Civic Administration Building, Upper Hutt, New Zealand
1968　Civic Hall, Upper Hutt, New Zealand
1970　Halls of Residence, Massey University, Palmerston North, New Zealand
1972　Pedestrian precinct, Upper Hutt, New Zealand
　　　Helen Lowry Hall of Residence, Wellington
　　　Wesley Haven Geriatric Hospital, Lower Hutt, New Zealand
1974　New Zealand Chancery, New Delhi, India
1976　Waipa County Council Office, Te Awamutu, New Zealand
　　　Waikanae Fire Station, New Zealand
　　　Horowhenua County Office, Levin, New Zealand
　　　Alington (Snr.) House, Wellington
1977　Waipa Lookout, Te Awamutu, New Zealand
　　　Public Library, Waikanae, New Zealand
　　　Karori Scout Hall, Wellington
1978　Public Library, Upper Hutt, New Zealand
　　　Wellington High School
　　　Wellington Planetarium

27

W. H. Alington: Civic Administration Building, Upper Hutt, New Zealand, 1966

Johnsonville Union Church, Wellington
Anglican Chinese Mission Church, Wellington

Publications:

By ALINGTON: books—drawings and appendix in
Frederick Thatcher and St. Paul's by M. H. Aling-
ton, Wellington 1965; *Old St. Paul's, Wellington: A
Pictorial Record,* with M. H. Alington, Wellington
1968; articles—"The Church and Architecture" in
Student (Wellington), June 1955; "Mies van der
Rohe" in *New Zealand Institute of Architects Jour-
nal* (Wellington), August 1963; "Francis Gordon
Wilson," entry in the *Encyclopaedia of New Zealand,*
vol. 3, Wellington 1966; "A Critique of Victoria Uni-
versity of Wellington Arts and Library Building" in
New Zealand Institute of Architects Newsletter
(Auckland), July 1967; "Some Comments on the
Christchurch Town Hall" in *Landfall* (Christchurch), September 1972; "Comment" in *New Zea-
land Institute of Architects Journal* (Wellington),
September 1974; "Architecture" in *Thirteen Facets,*
edited by I. M. Wards, Wellington 1978.

In our work we have aimed at achieving quality
buildings that occupy an unobtrusive place in the
community. The range of materials used is deliberately limited, and the occupants' requirements are
not tightly accommodated within the buildings.

The planning is usually clear and uncomplicated,
and the volumes and forms carefully proportioned to
provide calm, stable spaces within buildings that
take sympathetic cognizance of their surroundings.

In the design method followed, techniques and
spatial relationships evolve from one project to the
next. This form of development allows for careful
analysis of previous projects and the production of
work that has an immediate place in existing communities.

In most commissions the service to the clients
includes the preparation of a brief of requirements
and the design of the furnishings and gardens. Clients are constantly involved in the design process, as
are all the architectural partners, and all design policy is carefully analysed, documented, and presented
to the clients for discussions and decisions.

Because of the very limited financial resources and
the spasmodic nature of their availability in this
country, we have found that a fragmentation of the
building form is necessary if the project is to proceed
as the finances become available. This results in the
construction of smaller-scaled buildings which are
appropriate for the size of the communities they
serve. The construction period of the work is fully
monitored, and the methods of contracting allow the
architect to fully coordinate the work on the site and
to maintain strict financial control of all phases.

The methods and techniques used ensure that the
design intentions are realized. The resulting efficien-
cies have allowed more and more time to be spent in
canvassing many aspects of the clients' requirements
and in developing the designs.

—W. H. Alington

W. H. Alington deserves the title of Architect. His
work, set within the New Zealand landscape, possesses virtues of consistency, restraint, reason, order
and sensitivity. Alington's concern as an architect,
within the everyday realities and contingencies of
professional life, is the pursuit of quality—quality of
service and product. He views the role of the architect as that of a "master builder of things." This
statement of belief is not simply the pragmatic position of *l'homme engagé;* for Alington, architecture
has strong intangible characteristics.

His philosophy is built up from the idea that architecture is part of a much wider context. This realization helps him to strive for a sense of timelessness in
his work. He avoids styling his buildings in a day-to-
day sense. He believes in the classic need for a

created order in which architecture finds a meaningful place. Yet, at the same time, he wants his work
to be comprehensive enough to embrace a sense of
warmth, comfort and well-being.

Intellectually Alington is a dualist. In his work
one feels the desire for harmony and at the same time
one senses his longing to capture a feeling of naturalness. This is clearly visible in the way he sets his
buildings in the New Zealand landscape. (He is perhaps more a rural "spirit" than an urban dweller—
a New Zealand characteristic.) As far as architectural space is concerned, Alington views it as a product of all objective faculties and subjective senses.
Alington concurs with Kant in believing that the
aesthetic experience is the process of all the faculties
of concept, meshing together before the imaginative
leap is taken.

Viewed as a logical sequence of events, Alington's
architecture, from the Gisborne Courthouse, to the
Meteorological Office placed high above Wellington's dramatic harbour, to the Civic Centre set
within the valley of the Upper Hutt region, is a built
vindication of his design philosophy and of his approach to architecture. It is a dualist synthesis of
geometric resolution and his desire to embrace the
natural. On visiting one of his buildings years after
its completion, one still has the feeling of being in the
company of a man who cares for this kind of synthesis in modern architecture.

—Russell Walden

ALMQVIST, Osvald.

Swedish. Born in Trankil, near Karlstad, Värmland, 2 October 1884. Educated at Karlstad School, 1900–09; Royal Institute of Technology, Stockholm, under L. I. Wahlman and Erik Lallerstedt, 1904–08; Royal Academy of Arts, Stockholm, 1909–10; with six fellow students left the Academy and founded the Free School of Architecture, Stockholm, with Carl Westman, Ragnar Östberg, Ivar Tengbom and Carl Bergsten as teachers, 1910–11. Worked in the office of the architect Bodson, Brussels, 1908–09, in Dortmund, 1909, and in the office of Ivar Tengbom, Stockholm, 1910–11; in partnership with Gustaf Linden, Stockholm, 1911–13; in private practice, Stockholm, 1913–16; Architect and Engineer, Stora Kopparbergs Bergslag Company Domnarvet Ironworks, Dalercalia, Sweden, 1916–20; returned to private practice, Stockholm, 1920. Member, Committee on Workers' Housing, Stockholm, 1920–21; Head of the Committee on Standardization of Kitchen Equipment, Stockholm, 1922–34; Acting Head of the Parks Department, Stockholm, 1936–38; Town Planner Adviser to Södertälje, Sweden, 1940–48. Recipient: First Prize, Sundsvall Elementary School Competition, Sweden, 1924; First Prize, with Sigurd Lewerentz, Jönköping Redevelopment Competition, Sweden, 1928. *Died (in Stockholm) 6 April 1950.*

Works:

1910/
11 National Monument, Stockholm (project)
1911/
13 Apartment building, Stockholm (with Gustaf Linden)
Hotel, Nyköping, Sweden (with Gustaf Linden)
1914 Woodland Cemetery, Stockholm (Stockholm South Cemetery) (competition project)
1916/
20 Bergslagsbyn (model village for workers), at the Domnarvet Ironworks, Dalercalia, Sweden
Ironworks Manager's House, Domnarvet, Dalercalia, Sweden
1917/
21 Forshuvudforsen Hydro-Electric Power Station, Sweden (with Vattenbyggnadsbyran)
1924 Elementary school, Sundsvall, Sweden (competition project)
1925/
28 Hammarforsen Hydro-Electric Power Station, northern Sweden (with Vattenbyggnadsbyran)
Krångforsen Hydro-Electric Power Station, northern Sweden (with Vattenbyggnadsbyran)
1928 Plan for the redevelopment of 3 blocks in Jönköping, Sweden (4 competition projects; with Sigurd Lewerentz)
Katarina Secondary School, Stockholm (competition project; with Sigurd Lewerentz)
1929 Chenderoh Hydro-Electric Power Station, Malaya (with Vattenbyggnadsbyran and Rendel, Palmer and Tritton)
1930 Terraced houses, furniture, industrial products in concrete (including conical flower pot later used by Stockholm Park Department), and prefabricated cast-iron staircase, *Stockholm Exhibition*
1931 Town plan for Stockholm (with Sigurd Lewerentz)
1931/
32 Workshop training school, Domnarvet, Dalercalia, Sweden
1932 Museum, Malmo (competition project; with Sigurd Lewerentz)
1933/
36 Vocational school, Lulea, Sweden
1939/
40 Development plan for the Arsta district of Stockholm (with Albert Lilienthal)

Publications:

By ALMQVIST: books—*Byggnadsplaner för Bostadsområden, några Allmanna Synpunkter,* Stockholm 1921; *Köket och Ekonomiavdelningen,* Stockholm 1934; articles—"Forshuvudforsens Kraftverk" in *Byggmastaren* (Stockholm), no. 81, 1922; "Internationella Stadsbyggnadsutställningen ISBU" in *Byggmastaren* (Stockholm), no. 213, 1923; "Stadsplanefrågor och Bostadsområdens Planläggning" in *Byggmastaren* (Stockholm), nos. 247, 259, and 2975, 1923; "Gatubelysningsarmatur: Några Reflexioner i Anledning av Lyktstolpstävlingen" in *Byggmastaren* (Stockholm), no. 52, 1924; "Omputsning" in *Byggmastaren* (Stockholm), no. 361, 1924; "Sjätte Våningen" in *Byggmastaren* (Stockholm), no. 48, 1925; "Kökets Stadarisering: Några Synpunkter vid Pågående Utredningsarbete" in *Byggmastaren* (Stockholm), no. 105, 1927p "Nyara Kraftverksanläggningar: Synpunkter på deras Arkitektoniska Utformning" in *Byggmastaren* (Stockholm), no. 73, 1929; "Den Statsunderstödda Egnahemsverksamheten m.m." in *Byggmastaren* (Stockholm), no. 2, 1934.

On ALMQVIST: book—*Osvald Almqvist: En Arkitekt och Hans Arbete* by Björn Linn, Stockholm 1967.

As a student, Osvald Almqvist had travelled in Belgium and in Germany, but he was generally disappointed with modern architecture of the years before 1914. He seems to have derived much pleasure from what he saw of mediaeval towns, and in this respect he is similar to Camillo Sitte. In 1910 he left the Academy in Stockholm with other students to study at a private school with Östberg, Tengbom, Westman, and Bergsten as teachers. Two of his contemporary students were Gunnar Asplund and Sigurd Lewerentz, and with them Almqvist developed an architecture of national realism that was very different from the neoclassicism taught at the Academy. From the summer of 1910 Almqvist studied the timber-framed buildings of Sweden, and became steeped in the language of traditional structures and details. His early work at Nyköping with Gustaf Linden owes much to mediaeval apartment blocks and to traditional vernacular buildings.

Almqvist entered an unfinished scheme for the Stockholm Woodland Cemetery competition in 1914; it was won by Asplund and Lewerentz, but Almqvist's design clearly influenced the later realization of the project. The fact that the design was submitted in a sketchy state was an early indication of a distressing lack of decision and slowness in Almqvist that was to become more acute as the years passed. His partnership with Linden was dissolved, and he became architect to Domnarvet Ironworks for which he created Bergslagsbyn, a model village for workers that incorporated some of the lessons of Swedish vernacular housing and those of European townscapes. His Forshuvudforsen Hydro-Electric Power Station of 1917–21 is regarded as one of the most important of early Swedish industrial buildings in an idiom that owed nothing to period precedent. From this time he was to evolve his theory of sanitary aesthetics that would avoid inessentials and would express function honestly. In the years following 1922 he designed standard kitchen elements, and his ideas were consolidated in the publication of the Swedish kitchen standards in 1934 that have been the prototypes for much that is now taken for granted in domestic utilities. His most celebrated functional building is the power station at Chenderoh on the Berak River in Malaya, which he designed in collaboration with Rendel, Palmer and Tritton of London. Its success made him an international authority on the design of power stations. He prepared several designs for the *Stockholm Exhibition* of 1930, including a house, some furniture, and a cast-iron staircase that became a classic.

In later years Almqvist ran a small practice and became head of the Stockholm Parks Department in 1936, a post he relinquished two years later when it became clear that his administrative ability was unsuited to the job. His last works were in the planning of Årsta in Stockholm under Albert Lilienthal and as adviser on planning to the town of Södertälje. He succumbed to the lung disease that had plagued him since 1921 in 1950, surrounded by drawings of small projects that reflected his lifelong interest in Swedish vernacular housing.

—James Stevens Curl

ALVAREZ, Mario Roberto.

Argentinian. Born in Buenos Aires, 14 November 1913. Educated at the Colegio Nacional, Buenos Aires, 1926–32 (Gold Medal, 1932); University of Buenos Aires, Faculty of Architecture, 1932–37; (Gold Medal, and Annual Decorative Composition Prize, 1935; Gold Medal, 1937), Dip.Arch. 1937. Married Jorgelina Ortiz de Rosas in 1953; children: Juana and Mario Roberto Jr. In private practice, Buenos Aires, since 1937, as Mario Roberto Alvarez and Associates, since 1947. Architect, Ministry of Public Works, Buenos Aires, 1937–42; Municipal Architect, Avellaneda, Argentina, 1942–47; Adviser, Secretariat of Public Works of the City of Buenos Aires, 1958–62; Secretary to the World Football Cup Stadium Commission, Buenos Aires, 1972–78. Vice-President, Central Society of Architects, Buenos Aires, 1953–55; Head of the Argentine Delegation, International Union of Architects Congress, London, 1961. Exhibitions: *Bienal,* Sao Paulo, 1957; *Argentine Architects,* Buenos Aires, 1958, toured South America, the United States and Europe; *10th Exhibition of School Architecture,* Building Center, Buenos Aires, 1967; *Architects of Buenos Aires,* Centro de Arte y Comunicacion, Buenos Aires, 1977. Recipient: First Prize, Town Hall Competition, San Luis, Argentina, 1937; Ader Fellowship, Buenos Aires, 1937; First Prize, San Martin Sanatorium Competition, Buenos Aires, 1939; Gold Medal, *Fourth National Salon of Architecture,* Buenos Aires, 1942; First Prize, Club Pelota Competition, Tres Arroyos, Argentina, 1942; First Prize, Pergamino Sanatorium Competition, Buenos Aires, 1943; First Prize, Sanatorium Competition, Avellaneda, Argentina, 1948; First Prize, Orthopaedic Sanatorium Competition, Buenos Aires, 1955; First Prize, Bank of Avellaneda, Argentina Competition, 1958; First Prize, Banco Italiano Competition, Buenos Aires, 1959; First Prize, Banco Popular Competition, Buenos Aires, 1962; First Prize, Jockey Club Competition, Buenos Aires, 1963; First Prize, Somisa Headquarters Competition, Buenos Aires, 1966; First Prize, Meat and Animal Virus Technology Laboratories Competition, Buenos Aires, 1967; First Prize, Faculty of Engineering Competition, University of La Plata, Argentina, 1967; First Prize, San Martin Railway Viaduct Competition, Buenos Aires, 1967; First Prize, Banco Industrial Competition, Bahia Blanca, Argentina, 1968; First Prize, Club Aleman Competition, Buenos Aires, 1968; First Prize, International University City Competition, Belgrano, Buenos Aires, 1970; First Prize, National Technical University Competition, Buenos Aires, 1971; First Prize, Argentina/Uruguay Hydro-electric Scheme Competition, 1973; Grand National Arts Prize, Ministry of Culture, 1976. Honorary Fellow, American Institute of Architects, 1976. Address: Mario Roberto Alvarez y Asociados, Solis 370, Buenos Aires, Argentina.

Works:

1937 San Martin Sanatorium, General San Martin, Buenos Aires
Roncatti Restaurant, Julio A. Roca 537, Pergamino, Buenos Aires
1939 L.R.M. Radio Aconcagua Building, Avenida

Emilio Civit, Mendoza, Argentina

1941 Portland Cement Housing, Buenos Aires (competition projects; with M. O. Ruiz)

1944 Emergency and Urological Block, Fiorito Hospital, Avellaneda, Buenos Aires

1945 Home for the Aged, Avellaneda, Buenos Aires

1947 7-storey apartment building, Avenida Mitre y Lavalle, Avellaneda, Buenos Aires

1948 Health Center, Salta, Buenos Aires

Health Center, Santiago del Estero, Buenos Aires

Health Center, Corrientes, Buenos Aires

Health Center, Catamarca, Buenos Aires

Health Center, Tucuman, Buenos Aires

Health Center, Jujuy, Buenos Aires

M.A.D.A. Sanatorium, Avellaneda, Buenos Aires (with M. O. Ruiz)

14-storey apartment building, San Jose 1121–35, Buenos Aires (with M. O. Ruiz)

1949 Apartment building, Alsina 3263, Buenos Aires

1951 6-storey apartment building, Pozos 825, Buenos Aires

3-storey apartment buildings, Humberto 1645, Buenos Aires

1953 10-storey apartment building, Parera 65–69, Buenos Aires (with M. O. Ruiz)

Municipal Tennis Club, Olleros y. V. Alsina, Buenos Aires

Municipal Theatre, General San Martin, Buenos Aires (with M. O. Ruiz)

1953/
64 Buenos Aires City Cultural Center

1954 Puentes House, Pirovano 1149, Martinez, Buenos Aires (with M. O. Ruiz)

Podesta House, Pedro Goyena and L. Martinez, Martinez, Buenos Aires

1956 Dalbrollo House, Pergamino, Buenos Aires

1957 13-storey apartment building, Posadas 1695, Buenos Aires (with M. O. Ruiz)

1958 Mergherian House, La Lucila, Buenos Aires

Banco Popular Main Office, Florida and Cangalla, Buenos Aires

Banco Popular Branch Office, Pergamino, Buenos Aires

1959 Banco del Interior Building, Cordoba, Buenos Aires

Nuevo Banco Italiano Building, San Justo, Buenos Aires

1960 City Grain Exchange Building, Avenida Corrientes y Bouchard, Buenos Aires

Association of Banks Monument, Avenida del Libertador, Buenos Aires

Banco de Avellaneda Building, Quilmes, Buenos Aires

1961 Coca Cola Works, Luis Viale, Buenos Aires

1961/
69 Cervantes National Theatre rebuilding and additions, Avenida Cordoba, Buenos Aires

1962 Argentine National Library, Buenos Aires (competition project)

1963 Jockey Club Headquarters, Florida 559, Buenos Aires (competition project; with J. M. Borthagaray)

Cup Hipico Argentino (stadium), Avenida Figueroa Alcorta 7285, Buenos Aires

Panedile Argentina (25-storey apartment building), Avenida Libertador 3754, Buenos Aires (with Aslan and Ezcurra, and Joselevich and Ricur)

1964 San Luis Clinic, San Martin de Tours 2980, Buenos Aires

Belgrano Day School, Buenos Aires

18-storey apartment building, Virrey Loreto y Arribenos, Buenos Aires

16-storey apartment building, Paraguay y Talcahuano, Buenos Aires

1965 Pruss House, 11 de Septiembre 1382, Buenos Aires

Bank of America Headquarters, Cangallo and San Martin, Buenos Aires (with Aslan and Ezcurra)

Office building, Carlos Pellegrini 313, Buenos Aires

Ministry of Defense Laboratories, Avenida General Paz y Zufriategui, Buenos Aires (with A. Dodds and M. Cattaneo)

Santa Fe-Parana River Tunnel, Entre Rios Province, Argentina

1966 Inge Argentina Shopping Center, with offices and apartments, Acevedo 57, Buenos Aires

New Legislature Building, Buenos Aires (competition project)

Somisa Headquarters Building, Avenidas Belgrano y General Roca, Buenos Aires

Finanfor Building, Viamonte and Esmeralda, Buenos Aires

1966/
69 Covida Tower (21-storey apartment building), Villaneuva y Teodoro Garcia, Buenos Aires

1967 Railway overpass, Avenidas Juan B. Justo y Cordoba, Buenos Aires

Faculty of Engineering Building, National University, La Plata, Argentina (competition project)

1968 Colon Theatre alterations and extensions, Buenos Aires

INTA Animal Virus Laboratories, Castelar, Buenos Aires (with Ralph M. Parsons Company)

1969 Centro Corrientes (office building), Corrientes 753–63, Buenos Aires

Banco Federal Building, Buenos Aires

Ken Brown Electronics Building, Lope de Vega y Margarinos Cervantes, Buenos Aires

3-storey apartment building, Virrey Pino y Conde, Buenos Aires

El Continente (19-storey apartment building), Avenida del Liberatador y Basavilbaso, Buenos Aires (with L. Guidice)

Libertador Plaza Tower (20-storey apartment building), Avenida del Libertador 2140, Buenos Aires (with O. Zlotolow)

Playa Club Building, Miramar, Buenos Aires

15-storey apartment building, Avenida Presidente Figueroa Alcorta 3010, Buenos Aires

Hilton Hotel, Arenales y Esmeralda, Buenos Aires

1970 Office building, Rivadavia 540, Buenos Aires

12-storey apartment building, Viamonte Libertad, Buenos Aires

Club Aleman, Corrientes 319–43, Buenos Aires (with B. Davinovic and G. Iturralde)

Guemes Sanatorium, stage I, Francisco Acuna de Figueroa y Cordoba, Buenos Aires

Master plan for University City, Belgrano, Buenos Aires (competition project)

1971 Technology Buildings Complex, National Technical University, Buenos Aires (competition project; with M. Revol Luque, E. Diaz Garcia, and H. Hobbs)

Galeria Jardin Shopping Center, with offices and apartments, Florida 559, Buenos Aires

New Stock Exchange, Avenida Leandro Alem 344–66, Buenos Aires

1972 Master plan for the River Plate Athletic Club Complex, for the World Cup, Buenos Aires

Housing development, Avenida Colonel Roca, Buenos Aires (competition project)

Estadio Unico Stadium, La Plata, Argentina (competition project)

Office building, Avenida Leandro Alem 538, Buenos Aires

INTA Experimental Station Laboratories Building System (competition project)

1973 Office building, Avenida Corrientes y Reconquista, Buenos Aires (project)

Salto Grande Hydroelectric Dam, Argentine-East Uruguay Highway, Argentina (project; with Technical Commission Architects and Charles T. Main Company)

Housing development, Florencio Varela, Buenos Aires (competition project)

House for the Army Commander-in-Chief, Ruta Panamericana, Buenos Aires

Nujimovich House, La Pamba 3780, Buenos Aires

Diarben Company House, San Isidro Boating Club, Buenos Aires

1976 Office building, Sarmiento 1138, Buenos Aires

Banco Continental Building, Buenos Aires

Banco Credito Rural Argentino rebuilding, Buenos Aires

1977 Office building, Cangallo 715, Buenos Aires

Barreal Housing Development, Pampa del Indio, San Juan Province, Argentina

Pachon-Erizos Housing Development, San Juan Province, Argentina

1978/
80 Guemes Sanatorium, stage II, Francisco Acuna de Figueroa y Cordoba, Buenos Aires

Banco Rio de la Plata Headquarters, Buenos Aires

Office building, Tucuman 744, Buenos Aires

Banco Financiero Argentino, Buenos Aires

Banco Mercantil, Buenos Aires

Office building, Avenida Leandro Alem and Paraguay, Buenos Aires

Office building, Avenida Leandro Alem 456–74, Buenos Aires

Office building, Chacabuco 271, Buenos Aires

Banco Rio de la Plata, Caballito, Buenos Aires

Chacofi Office Tower, Avenida Leandro Alem 538, Buenos Aires

Master plan for the Newman Country Club, Buenos Aires

Martens Office Building, Corrientes 355, Buenos Aires

Publications:

By ALVAREZ: book—*Teatro Municipal General San Martin,* with M. Oscar Ruiz, Buenos Aires 1959; articles—"Buenos Aires y su Arquitectura" in *El Mundo* (Buenos Aires), 1960; "Buenos Aires 1990" in *Vision* (Buenos Aires), 1970; "Ciudad de Buenos Aires, su transformacion" in *Primera Plana* (Buenos Aires), 1971.

On ALVAREZ: book—*Mario Roberto Alvarez* by Marcelo A. Trabuco, Buenos Aires 1965; articles—"Building for the Club Aleman" in *Nuestra Arquitectura* (Buenos Aires), vol. 44, no. 486, 1973; special issue of *Summa* (Buenos Aires), September 1974; "Pruss Residence in Buenos Aires" in *Informes de la Construccion* (Madrid), December 1974; "Somisa Building in Buenos Aires" and Remodelling of the Theatre Colon" in *Nuestra Arquitectura* (Buenos Aires), vol. 45, no. 492, 1975.

My aims and intentions over the past 42 years could be summarized as follows: I am not committed to one particular typology; it is more a question of making the complicated simple; achieving good, efficient workmanship (I am not interested in exciting attention or in being a fashionable architect); building durably; organizing space to allow for unknown activities in the future; integrating the plastic arts to architecture; keeping an eye on the quality of space, form, proportion, and detail; anticipating growth,

Mario Roberto Alvarez: Somisa Headquarters Building, Buenos Aires, 1966

flexibility, change, and the integration of new technology to the processes of construction; using good, honest materials; and working hard, in order to make as few mistakes as possible.

—Mario Roberto Alvarez

Mario Roberto Alvarez has carried out so great a volume of work that he ranks as the most prolific architect in Argentina and perhaps in all of Latin America—yet, in more than 40 years, there has never been any diminishment in the virtues that were internationally recognized in his first constructions.

In his attitude towards architecture and in his work methods, Alvarez is a rationalist. But it is not a rationalism that involves a freezing of typologies invariably in time. His work is characterized by an adapting of form to function (therein lies the difference from Mies) and by a simplification and geometric definition of elements. Alvarez believes that permanent and universal values can be expressed through architecture. His perspective is classical, and his works contribute elements of order and clarity to the urban environment.

Alvarez's manifest intention is to "create good and enduring buildings in every aspect," an objective that he achieves both in his designs and in the choice of materials that prevent his buildings from showing the passage of years. Although the initial investment for the client may be somewhat high, because of the cost of high-quality materials and execution, the ease in upkeep more than compensates for that apparent disadvantage, and Alvarez himself contributes to keeping other costs down in his rational methods of design and in his organization of the processes of construction.

Alvarez's output can be characterized as giving simple answers to complex requirements: there is always a concern with the quality of space and form, with proportion and control of details, with centering attention on a few elements for the purpose of achieving a stylistic synthesis. At the same time, Alvarez believes that an architecture of shape-for-shape's-sake is no longer valid, that objective reality makes it imperative that qualitative and quantitative changes that take place in time, which are useful to the community, should be allowed for in the design. His projects aspire to four conditions—growth, flexibility, change, and the integration of new technology—as the only way of allowing for the unknown activities of the future.

To achieve these various goals, Alvarez and his team involve themselves in every job from the drawing stage up to final and full operation of the building, along the way controlling and directing construction, rigorously analyzing all the details of the building and its mechanical equipment. The attention given to the "technical infrastructure" is revealing of Alvarez's vision of "total building." Clarity and ease of maintenance is the basis of the correct operation of the building organism. Whether or not the architectural or mechanical elements are visible is irrelevant; they must be designed meticulously, as much for efficiency as for "formal appearance."

And it is also consistent with Alvarez's goals that he should be involved in projects not customarily part of the repertoire of architectural teams—a vehicular bridge, an underwater tunnel, a hydroelectric dam, etc. He points out that "the architect must furnish the engineer with images." Engineering works profit from the intervention of specialists in the planning of the physical environment, and they should participate in the project both in the formulation and the setting up of access elements and in the design of the structure itself so that it is formally integrated with the landscape and with other constructed elements. Including the architect in interdisciplinary teams contributes to the creation of a harmonious whole, one that is integrated into the surrounding space, within a common language, so that the structure does not stand out as foreign and unexpected but as natural and consequential within the treated and modelled space.

Alvarez is concerned with technological problems. An example is his proposal for pre-fabricated elements for a simple, functional and economical construction system made up of materials produced by domestic industry, in which the number of components is reduced to a minimum and the total system can be easily disassembled and reconstructed. Another example of this interest is his Somisa Headquarters Building, the first building in Argentina to be built wholly of steel (concrete is the usual structural material) and the first in the world to be completely welded. Another of his characteristics—the exhaustive examination of factors not explicitly assigned to the architect by the client but which may be important for the appropriate resolution of the project—is perhaps best exemplified in his suggestion (which was finally put into practice) of incorporating a corner plot into the plan for the Municipal Theatre of Buenos Aires, thus allowing for the creation of an open plaza with offices giving onto it.

The meanings that can be read into Alvarez's works are those of contemporary rationalism, in which architecture seeks no references beyond architecture itself, rejecting mannerism or decoration which, as Alvarez maintains, are simply means of evasion from objective reality. These values are obviously appealing to non-professionals—to his clients—who hold him in high regard. When, in 1976, the American Institute of Architects made Mario Roberto Alvarez an Honorary Fellow, they were recognizing the importance of a career that has enhanced and enriched architecture in Argentina.

—Jorge Glusberg

Sydney Ancher: English House, St. Ives, Sydney, 1949

ANCHER, Sydney (Edward Cambrian).

Australian. Born in Sydney, New South Wales, 25 February 1904. Educated at Sydney Technical High School, 1917–19; articled to the architect E. W. S. Wakeley, Sydney, 1924–26; studied at Sydney Technical College, 1925–29, Dip.Arch. 1929; worked in the offices of Wunderlich Ltd., Prevost Synnot and Ruwald, and Ross and Rowe, Sydney, 1926–30; awarded New South Wales Board of Architects Australian Medallion and Travelling Scholarship, 1930; travelled in England and on the Continent, 1930–36. Served in the Royal Australian Engineers, in the Middle East, 1940–41, and at Army Headquarters, Melbourne, 1942–45: Major. Married Leatha Hasemer in 1936 (died, 1970); children: John and Paul. Worked in London in the offices of Verity and Beverley, Joseph Emberton, Textaphote, and Thompson and Watford, 1930–36; returned to Australia and worked in the office of Emil Sodersten, Sydney, 1936; Partner, with Reginald Prevost, Prevost and Ancher, Sydney, 1936–39; worked in the Bank Section of the Commonwealth Department of Works, and in the office of John D. Moore, Sydney, 1939–40; Technical Officer, Commonwealth Experimental Building Station, Sydney, 1945–46; Principal, Sydney Ancher and Partners, Sydney, 1946–53; Partner, with Bryce Mortlock, q.v., and Stuart Murray, q.v., Ancher, Mortlock and Murray, Sydney, 1953–64, and, with Mortlock, Murray, and Ken Woolley, q.v., Ancher, Mortlock, Murray, and Woolley, Sydney, 1964 until he retired, 1966. Design Teacher, Sydney Technical College, 1948–49, and Newcastle Technical College, Newcastle, New South Wales, 1949–50. Exhibitions: Contemporary Art Society, Sydney, 1948–52; Royal Australian Institute of Architects, Sydney, 1948–52; *Ancher, Mortlock, Murray and Woolley, Sydney Architects, 1946–76*, Art Gallery of New South Wales, Sydney, 1976, toured Australian galleries 1977. Recipient: Sulman Award, Royal Australian Institute of Architects, New South Wales Chapter, 1945; Gold Medal, Royal Australian Institute of Architects, 1976. Fellow, Royal Australian Institute of Architects; Associate, Royal Institute of British Architects. Address: "Kingaley," Dungog, New South Wales 2420, Australia.

Works:

1946 Ancher House, 1 Maytone Avenue, Killara, Sydney
1948 Hamill House, 4 Maytone Avenue, Killara, Sydney
 Ancher House II, 2 Maytone Avenue, Killara, Sydney
 Farley House, North Curl Curl, Sydney
1949 English House, Killeaton Street, St. Ives, Sydney
1950 Riley House, Merrivale Road, Pymble, Sydney
1956 Ancher House III, 15 Bogota Avenue, Neutral Bay, Sydney
1956/
66 Shopping Centre, West Pymble, Sydney
 Shopping Centre, East Lindfield, Sydney
 Council Chambers rebuilding, Gordon, Sydney
 Public library, Gordon, Sydney
 Baby health centre, Lindfield, Sydney
 Public golf club house, Gordon, Sydney
 Three-level parking station, Gordon, Sydney
1960 Murphy House, 7 Ginahgulla Road, Bellevue Hill, Sydney
1963 Redman House, 24 Ross Street, Newport, Sydney
 Stewart House, Richmond Avenue, St. Ives, Sydney
 Housing, Northbourne Avenue, Canberra (with Stuart Murray)
1965 Students Union Building, Australian National University, Canberra

Publications:

By ANCHER: articles—"Travelling Scholar Returns" in *Architecture* (Sydney), March 1936; "Whither Architecture?" in *Architecture* (Sydney), June 1936; "Educating the Architect of Tomorrow" in *Architecture* (Sydney), May 1938; "The Evolution of Modern Architecture" in *Architecture* (Sydney), December 1939; "The Architect's Dilemma" in *RAIA News Bulletin* (Sydney), May 1976.

On ANCHER: books—*Australia's Home* by Robin Boyd, Melbourne 1952; *The Australian Ugliness* by Robin Boyd, Melbourne 1960; *Ancher, Mortlock, Murray and Woolley, Sydney Architects, 1946–76*, exhibition catalog, by David Saunders and Catherine Bourke, Sydney 1976.

*

In the years immediately following the Second World War I was able, for the first time, to shake off the tendency to think automatically of architecture along traditional lines.

A new resolve enabled me to design simple and straight-forward buildings, free from pre-conceived ideas on proportion and style. I came to believe that all work should possess a timeless quality. And I felt that if all buildings were designed in this way they would contribute to the kind of unified character you find in the grouped buildings on a Greek island.

I was also early taken with the idea of developing an Australian style. Many things favoured such an approach, including the actual character of the typical Australian, which for good or bad is certainly quite distinctive. I later realized that, as there is no positively recognizable style of any other Western country, it seemed unlikely that an Australian style would emerge.

As an aid to maintaining the desired character in all designs, I have found it essential to constantly evaluate trends. These generally are merely fashion changes—in clothes, cars and many other things which often affect our way of living. They are mostly quite transitory and as such are undesirable influences in the shaping of permanent things like buildings. Some trends do result in changes for the good, but mostly their influence is not lasting.

Altogether I find it satisfying to have evolved some direction for my work. I believe in a set line of development with leanings to simple, straight-forward, perhaps even classic, designs.

—Sydney Ancher

*

Sydney Ancher is one of the most respected architects to have practised in Sydney this century. It is remarkable that Ancher, who designed relatively few buildings, mostly houses, and certainly nothing that would be considered as a "major work," was such a pivotal figure for the local development of modern architecture. While Ancher was one of the first to introduce the "International Style" to Australia, he is a regional architect in every respect. Much of this country's better architecture has come from people who were influenced by Ancher. Of these, several worked with Ancher, worked for Ancher, or worked for someone who worked for Ancher—he is responsible for quite an extensive architectural family tree!

Australia is a conservative country and Ancher was among the few pre-war "modern" architects. Between 1930 and 1936 he worked and travelled in Europe, and returned there again in 1939. During these visits he saw much of contemporary architecture, and was particularly impressed by the pure geometry and open planning of the work of Mies van der Rohe. After four years in the Army during the War, Ancher established his own practice. His most important works are the houses of the 1946–58 period. In Australia, post-war shortages of materials and skilled labour were acute, and the quality new housing was low indeed. The average house was a stripped down version of the typical bungalow of a box under a pitched roof, with punched holes for windows, and compartmented interiors. They were

visually depressing and climatically unsound. In his own quiet way Ancher contributed to a revolution in domestic design that established the basic concepts for dwellings in Australia which persist today, despite differing expressions. Fundamental to his houses was the adaption of pre-war European examples for the Australian climate, materials, building techniques, and way of life.

With the simplicity of their crisp white forms his early houses were considered by local councils to be an affront to decency! The order of their form and the solidarity and blankness of their colour, contrast with and yet compliment the rough Australian bush sites on which (even in suburbia) they were often built. Even so, native trees, rock outcrops, and variances in terrain were always respected and integrated with the strictly man-made structures. The Australian sun casts strong shadows of posts and planting on their white exteriors.

The houses are not large, often no larger than the average post-war dwelling, but with the use of the flat roof, which allowed the freeing of interior space, and the opening up of walls with glass, they appeared generous and spacious. His plans, with central "to-be-lived-in" living rooms and minimal, yet open, secondary spaces, reflect his "hatred of secrecy and holes in the corner." With generous outlooks and the extension of the houses by patios and verandahs, the outside was closely related to the interior. The use of the continuous flat slab made for easy movement between these areas. Increased air circulation, and the protecting shade afforded by deep overhangs, pergolas, and wide covered verandahs, kept them cool in summer. On occasions, the extensive covered out-door spaces rivalled the interiors in area.

The houses received considerable publicity and their relevance was soon recognized by the architectural profession. Architects in other states became familiar with the work, and the lessons learnt had a wide effect. Ancher's planning and structural concepts were taken up and developed by others, but soon the prismatic white finishes gave way to the more rugged expression of materials "as found."

Although Ancher took no part in the designing of project housing, his firm's involvement in project housing helped introduce these buildings to the general market, and this has had a widespread effect on house design throughout the country. The further impact of this work is now evident in commercial, institutional and retail buildings as well. The result has been an architecture more compatible with its context than the majority of prior solutions.

The importance of his work for Australian architecture cannot be overstressed. With his initial, modest buildings he became one of the few leaders towards major changes in Australian design. Sydney Ancher is alone in his denial of the significance of his efforts.

—Jennifer Taylor

ANDREWS, John.

Australian. Born in Sydney, New South Wales, 29 October 1933. Educated at North Sydney Boys High School; University of Sydney (Ormonoid Prize for Design, 1956), B.Arch. 1956; Harvard University, Cambridge, Massachusetts, under Josep Lluis Sert, M.Arch. 1958. Married Rosemary Randall in 1958; children: John, Lee, Craig, and James. Worked for Edwards Madigan Torzillo, Sydney, 1957, and John B. Parkin, Don Mills, Toronto, 1958–62. Principal, John Andrews Architects, Toronto, since 1962, and John Andrews International Pty. Ltd., Sydney, since 1972. Member of Staff, 1962–69, and Chairman of the School of Architecture, 1967–69, University of Toronto. Exhibitions: *National Institute of Arts and Letters Exhibition*, New York, 1971; *Transformations in Modern Architecture*, Museum of Modern

ANDREWS

John Andrews: King George Tower, Sydney, 1976

Art, New York, 1979. Recipient: Centennial Medal,
Canada, 1967; Massey Medal, Canada, 1967; Arnold
Brunner Award, National Institute of Arts and Letters, U.S.A., 1971; Honor Award, 1973, and Bartlett
Award, 1973, American Institute of Architects; Design in Steel Citation, American Iron and Steel Institute, 1973; Award, Pre-stressed Concrete Institute,
U.S.A., 1976; Bronze Medal, Queensland Institute
of Architects, 1976. Associate, Royal Institute of
British Architects; Fellow, Royal Architectural Institute of Canada; Life Fellow, Royal Australian Institute of Architects. Address: John Andrews International Pty. Ltd., 1017 Barrenjoey Road, Palm
Beach, New South Wales 2108, Australia.

Works:

1962　Master plan for Scarborough College (Uni-
　　　versity of Toronto), Scarborough, Ontario
1963　Scarborough College (University of Toronto),
　　　phase I, Military Road, Scarborough, On-

tario
1964　Master plan for Erindale College (University
　　　of Toronto), Erindale, Ontario
1965　Bellmere Public School, Scarborough, On-
　　　tario
　　　Student Housing Complex B, University of
　　　Guelph, Ontario
　　　Apartment Tower, for the Stelco Steel Com-
　　　pany (project)
1966　Master plan of the St. George Campus of the
　　　University of Toronto
1967　Lecture Theatre, Boiler Plant, and alterations
　　　to the existing building, Prince of Wales
　　　College, Charlottetown, Prince Edward
　　　Island
　　　African Place, *Expo '67,* Montreal
　　　Activity Area F, *Expo '67,* Montreal
　　　Commonwealth Place, *Expo '67,* Montreal
　　　(project)

Weldon Library, University of Western On-
tario, London
Plan for the Metro Centre, Toronto
Student Centre, University of Toronto (pro-
ject)
Seaport Passenger Terminal, Port of Miami,
Florida
Redevelopment plan for the Civic Square,
Hamilton, Ontario (competition project)
Plan for the Yorkdale Shopping Centre,
Toronto
Student Residence, Brock University, St.
Catherines, Ontario
Library/Instructional Center, Sarah Law-
rence College, Bronxville, New York (pro-
ject)
1968　Gund Hall: Graduate School of Design, Har-
　　　vard University, Cambridge, Massachu-
　　　setts

34

Art Complex, Smith College, Northampton, Massachusetts

1969 David Mirvish Gallery, Toronto
Scarborough College (University of Toronto), stage II, Scarborough, Ontario

1970 School of Art, Kent State University, Ohio
Feasibility study for the expansion of the Behavioral Sciences Department, Tufts University, Medford, Massachusetts
Student Residence, Australian National University, Canberra

1972 Pintannie Commercial Redevelopment (multi-storey office complex), Roma Street, Brisbane (project)
Plan for the Belconnen Town Centre Retail Mall, Canberra

1973 Woden East Government Offices, Canberra (project)
Student Residence, Canberra College of Advanced Education
Chemical Engineering Building, University of Queensland, Brisbane
Design guidelines for the retention of the Great Hall of Union Station in the Metro Centre development, Toronto
Master plan for Kelvin Grove College of Advanced Education, Brisbane

1974 Development plan I for Darling Downs Institute of Advanced Education, Toowoomba, Queensland
Development plan for Ithaca Technical College, Brisbane
Regional Shopping Centre, Sydney (project)
Design study of the retail centre of Belconnen, Canberra
Study of transportation interchange and commercial/sporting development, Canberra

1975 School of Australian Environmental Studies, Griffith University, Brisbane
Low Bay Low-Income Housing Complex, Sydney
Environmental guidelines study of Palm Beach, Sydney
Urban design study of the town centre of Monarto, South Australia
Master plan for Ipswich College of Technical and Further Education, Queensland

1976 Cameron Offices, Belconnen, Canberra
King George Tower, King and George Streets, Sydney
Andrews Houses (2), Palm Beach, Sydney (project)
Educational Resource Centre, Kelvin Grove College of Advanced Education, Brisbane
Development plan II for Darling Downs Institute of Advanced Education, Toowoomba, Queensland
Belconnen Bus Terminal, Canberra

1977 Canadian National Tower, Metro Centre, Toronto
Library/Union, stage I, Royal Melbourne Institute of Technology (project)
Site location study of the Museum of Australia, Canberra
Development study of Sydney Central Station
Woden College of Technical and Further Education, stage I, Canberra
Lecture Theatre and Staff Office Buildings, Darling Downs Institute of Advanced Education, Toowoomba, Queensland (project)
Mandurah High School, Western Australia (project)

Publications:

By ANDREWS: book—*Architecture: A Performing Art*, Melbourne 1979; article—"A.A. Interview," with John Witzig, in *Architecture in Australia* (Sydney), June 1975.

On ANDREWS: books—*World Architecture 3*, edited by John Donat, London 1966; *Canadian Architecture 1960–70* by Carol Moore Ede, Toronto 1971; *Third Generation: The Changing Meaning of Architecture* by Philip Drew, London 1972; articles—"The New Campus" by Oscar Newman in *Architectural Forum* (New York), May 1966; "Beyond the Individual Building" in *Architectural Record* (New York), September 1966; "Scarborough College" by Kenneth Frampton in *Architectural Design* (London), April 1967; "Dorm City" by Kenneth B. Smith in *Architectural Forum* (New York), December 1968; "City Within a City" in *The Architect and Building News* (London), 5 June 1969; "Some Comments on the Building" by Peter Pragnell in *Architectural Forum* (New York), December 1969; "Design and Process: Four Projects by the John Andrews Office" in *Architectural Record* (New York), February 1970; "Passenger Terminal, Port of Miami" in *The Canadian Architect* (Toronto), April 1970; "Conversations with the John Andrews Architects" in *Progressive Architecture* (New York), February 1972; "Gund Hall: Harvard's Graduate School of Design under One Roof" in *Architectural Record* (New York), November 1972; "D. B. Weldon Library, University of Western Ontario, London" in *The Canadian Architect* (Toronto), November 1972; "Harvard's New Hall" by William Marlin in *Architectural Forum* (New York), December 1972; "Good Architecture—Bad Vibes" by Ada Louise Huxtable in *The Canadian ARchitect* (Toronto), January 1973; special issue of *Architecture + Urbanism* (Tokyo), May 1974; "Five Projects by John Andrews International" in *The Canadian Architect* (Toronto), July 1976; "King George Tower" in *New South Wales Builder* (Sydney), February 1977; "Civil Service City" by Jennifer Taylor in *Architectural Review* (London), March 1978.

*

1962–Scarborough College, Toronto, Ontario Canada: "The students would spend five or six months, almost the full academic year, stumbling through wind, rain, sleet and snow, from building to building, fumbling with coats and galoshes, getting wet, cold and ill. It seemed much more sensible to connect all the buildings. Our approach was to provide a ground level interior pedestrian circulation route with high use destinations plugged into it, and secondary routes above and below it."

1979–Library and Union Facilities, Royal Melbourne Institute of Technology, Melbourne, Victoria, Australia: "It is fairly evident that at the moment there is no organization, no system of movement through the campus. This was an obvious opportunity to pull the whole thing together. It puts the library at the heart of the campus, it puts the major student facilities at the heart of the campus, and it pulls all of the ground level pedestrian circulation together into the one system, maximizing the opportunity for convenience and contact. That is an old story for me, regardless of whether it is in Melbourne or Toronto. It is still the major genesis of any building."

—John Andrews

*

John Andrews' architectural intentions in Scarborough College, Ontario—the work that established him as an architect of international importance—have tended to be ignored because its "form" coincided with the avant-garde architectural language of the 1960's. Although Andrews is a fluent stylist, he is less concerned with form and style than he is with finding the right approach for each prob-

lem. His best architecture demonstrates a quality of geographical and existential appropriateness—which is "Australian" to the extent that Australia as a country is dominated by its geography. But "geography," with Andrews, refers to much more than the factors of climate and landscape; it implies the total physical environment of the building. Earl Berger has observed that John Andrews' buildings "say something simply and easily understood about where you are and what you're doing there." Andrews' concern is with the rational and commonsensical solving of problems. He agrees with the anti-aesthetic sentiments expressed by Mies van der Rohe in 1923: "We reject: all aesthetic speculation, all doctrine, and all formalism."

The Rationalism of John Andrews' architecture is expressed in the clear articulation of circulation and the emphasis on movement as a source of contact and interaction. The functional identity of the architectural elements is stressed rather than suppressed.

Though schizoid in its elevations, Scarborough College contains many of the innovations associated with Andrews, so it must be considered as a key work. His response to the harsh Canadian winter and his Scarborough site now seems both practical and beautiful. He integrated all the College functions in phase I, within a single building complex that is linked by a monumental internal street. The building forms a wall that follows the escarpment edge of a deep ravine and is breached near its centre adjacent to the meeting place. There is an important different between Scarborough College and later Andrews buildings: he usually tries to define spaces by walls and, where practicable, to avoid the use of internal columns—that is, he avoids using columns inside his buildings and tends to externalize his supporting elements. The influence of Mies' "thinking" on Andrews reveals itself in his concern for the relationship of walls and columns—when they occur.

The Student Housing Complex at the University of Guelph has a strong diagonally-aligned geometry based on Louis Kahn's dormitories at Bryn Mawr. The Housing Complex uses two distinct structural systems—loadbearing masonry walls in the courts for the small-span living quarters and long-span concrete structures for the streets, bridges and dining hills, with no attempt to establish a coherent relationship. The importance of circulation and structure of the Miami Seaport Passenger Terminal has resulted in a powerful sculptural form that is much more unified than the Guelph Student Housing.

The Cameron Offices at Belconnen, in Canberra, is structurally perverse, even Mannerist. The complex consists of seven parallel office wings linked, at their ends, by a shaded walkway system. Whereas Mies exposed roof beams above the roof in Crown Hall at I.I.T., Andrews has gone one step further and located his supporting structure in the courts adjacent to the office blocks. The staggered office floors are suspended on one edge, and supported at the other, from free-standing gallows supporting structures.

The King George Tower, on the corner of King and George Streets, Sydney, explores a fresh approach to sun control: it employs a common space frame on all three facades to support glass screens in a variety of configurations. The tower is splayed on the corner to open up the street intersection and to provide a sunken plaza.

Andrews intended that the open staggered studio terraces of the Harvard Graduate School of Design would encourage a greater degree of interaction between students. The roof over the studios is supported by exposed steel trusses and stepped to admit daylight. He conceived the GSD as a non-specific building in which learning would occur in an informal setting.

John Andrews had a significant influence on Australian architects in the early 1970's, architects whose rustic romanticism was in marked contrast to his own vigorous rationalism.

—Philip Drew

ANTONAKAKIS, Dimitris.

Greek. Born in Chania, Crete, 22 December 1933. Educated at the Experimental School, University of Athens, 1939–51; National Technical University, School of Architecture, Athens, under Michelis, Pikionis, Liapis, Marthas, Speyer and Fatouros, 1953–58, Dip.Arch. 1958. Served as a Reserve Officer in the Hellenic Air Force, 1958–61. Married the architect Suzana Kolokytha (i.e., Suzana Antonakakis, *q.v.*) in 1961; children: Aristides and Aekaterini. In partnership with Suzana Antonakakis, Athens, since 1959: Founder and Principal, with Suzana Antonakakis, Atelier 66, architects, Athens, since 1965. Assistant Instructor of Architecture, 1959–64, Instructor of Architecture, 1964–78, and since 1978 Lecturer in Architecture, National Technical University, Athens. Special Consulting Architect, Archaeological Service, Athens, 1961–62; Architect Consultant, Hellenic Committee for Nuclear Energy, 1962–63; Administrative Committee Member and Treasurer, 1962–63, and Member of the Special Committee for Information, 1971–74, Greek Architects Association; President, Association of Assistants and Instructors at the National Technical University, 1975–77; Vice-President, Central Administrative Committee, Association of Assistants and Instructors of Greek Universities, 1976–77. Exhibitions: *Modern Greek Architecture,* Patras, 1967; *Modern Greek Architecture,* Athens, 1971, 1978. Recipient: First Prize, 14th and 15th Public Schools Competition, Thessaloniki, 1961; Honor Award, *International Fair,* Thessaloniki, 1964; First Prize, Archaeological Museum Competition, Chios, Greece, 1965; First Prize, Engineers and Contractors Association Summer Homes Competition, Spetsae, Greece, 1966; First Prize, Tourist Development Competition, Paleokastritsa, Corfu, 1966; First Prize, Old Castle Development Competition, Corfu, 1967; First Prize, Children's Summer Holiday Camp Competition, St. Andreas, Athens, 1972. Address: Atelier 66, 118 Emmanuel Benaki Street, Athens 707, Greece.

Works (with Suzana Antonakakis):

1961 14th and 15th Public Schools, Thessaloniki (competition project)
1961/
62 Apartment building, Argolidos, Athens
1962/
63 Apartment building, Archelaou/Ellanikou, Athens
Apartment interiors conversion, Acchelaon, Athens
School for Handicapped Children interiors, Ag. Anarghyra, Athens
1962/
65 Private house, Phivis 15, Glyfada, Athens
1964 Reception Hall, *International Fair,* Thessaloniki (project)
1965 Private house, Chania, Kastelli, Greece (project)
School complex, Thessaloniki (project)
Hotel, Chios, Greece
1965/
66 Archaeological Museum, Chios, Greece
1965/
67 Apartment interior conversion, Alfiou 9, Athens
1965/
68 Private house additions, Hydra, Greece
Hotel, Plepi, Greece
1965/
69 Restaurant, Chania, Crete
1966 Tourist development in Paleokastritsa, Corfu (competition project)
Tourist development at Aghi Apostoli Beach, Chania, Crete (project)
Summer houses settlement, Spetsae, Greece
Museum, Komotini, Greece (project)
Old Castle Development, Corfu (competition project)
Municipal Shopping Centre, Corfu (project)
Tourist Pavilion, Amalias, Greece

Dimitris and Suzana Antonakakis: Apartment building, Emmanuel Benaki 118, Athens, 1974

1966/
67 Private consulting room, Athens
1967 Private house, N. Kifissia, Athens
Museum, Kastoria, Greece (project)
Hotel and Restaurant, Paleokastritsa, Corfu (project)
Consulting room and office furniture, Athens
1967/
68 Holiday house, Portocheli, Greece
House additions, Phaliro, Athens
1968 Tourist development at Phani Bay, Chios, Greece (project)
House additions, Kifissia, Athens
Park landscaping, Athens (project)
Hotel, Naxos, Greece (project)
Municipal Theatre, Athens (project)
1968/
69 Tourist company offices, Asklipiou 3, Athens
House extensions, Kallithea, Athens
1968/
76 Hotel, Chania, Crete
1968/
78 Tourist Complex, Plepi, Greece
1969 Mineworkers and Administrators Settlement, Distomo, Greece
Private house, Chania, Crete
Holiday house, Villia, Greece
Olive mill/lecture hall conversion, Hydra, Greece
Office building, Patission 12, Athens (project)
Storehouse/cafe conversion, Chania, Crete
Hotel furniture, Athens
1969/
70 Apartment building, Ghizi 12, Psychiko, Greece
Apartment building, Proklou 29, Athens
Holiday house, Rea, Greece
House additions, N. Psychiko, Athens
1969/
71 Hotel, Chios, Greece
Recreation development at Alcronafplia, Nafplion, Greece
1970 City Centre, Karlsruhe, Germany (project)
House, Vrilissia, Athens
Holiday house, Chania, Crete
Foreign Languages Institute, Kallithea, Athens
Wine factory, Anthoussa, Greece (project)

Akronafplia Night Club, Nafplion, Greece (project)

1970/
71 House additions, Loutraki, Greece
Hotel, Porto Ghermeno, Greece
Notary's office, Philonos 35, Piraeus, Greece

1970/
72 House additions, Kallithea, Athens
1971 House additions, Chania, Crete
Military hospital, Bengazi, Libya (project)

1971/
72 House additions, Phaliro, Athens
Hotel, Portocheli, Greece

1971/
75 House, Chania, Crete
1972 House, Politia, Athens
House, Ekali, Athens
House, Mykonos, Greece (project)
House, Hydra, Greece
Town Hall, Tavros, Athens (project)
Conservatory, Chania, Crete (project)
Loukopoulos Sculpture Exhibition layouts, Greek Hellenic Union, Athens
M. Kostakou Painting Exhibition layouts, Astor Gallery, Athens

1972/
73 Apartment building, Phaliro, Athens
House, Politia, Athens
House, P. Penteli, Athens
Apartment interior conversion, N. Kifissia, Athens

1972/
74 House, Chania, Crete
House, P. Penteli, Athens

1972/
76 Hydra Beach Village, Plepi, Greece
1973 Environmental Protection Study, Cyclades, Greece
Children's summer holiday camp, St. Andreas, Athens

1973/
74 Apartment building, Emmanuel Benaki 118, Athens
Pierrakos house, Oxylithos, Euboea, Greece
Paint factory, Koropi, Greece

1973/
75 Hydra Beach Village New Town, Plepi, Greece

1974/
75 Apartment building, Philothei, Athens
Holiday house, Alikianos, Chania, Crete
Holiday house, Spata, Athens
Apartment interior conversion, Ag. Paraskevi, Athens

1974/
77 Hotel, Heraklion, Crete
1975 Holiday house, Kouvaras, Greece (project)
House, Politia, Athens
Holiday house, Chania, Crete
House, Hydra, Greece
Shopping Centre, Athens (project)

1975/
76 Bookstore, Athens

1975/
77 House, Ano Voula, Athens
1976 House, Kifissia, Athens
House, Vrilissia, Athens
Hotel, Vouliagmeni, Athens
Kanaghini Painting Exhibition layouts, Zoumboulaki Gallery, Athens
Voghiazoglou Ceramics Exhibition layouts, French Institute, Thessaloniki, Greece
Kostakou Painting Exhibition layouts, Ora Cultural Centre, Athens

1976/
77 Apartment building, Yakinthou 18, Athens
House, Saronis, Athens
1977 Apartment building, Helioupolis, Athens
Apartment building, Ano Voula, Athens
Painting and Sculpture Exhibition layouts, Municipal Cultural Centre, Athens

1977/
78 House, Aegina, Greece

House, Oxylithos, Euboea, Greece
Office building, Navarinou, Athens
Apartments conversion, Denokratous 9, Athens

Publications:

By ANTONAKAKIS: book—*Cyclades: Identification and Recording of Important Settlements or Parts of Them,* with Suzana Antonakakis and others, 6 volumes, Athens 1974; articles—translations of Le Corbusier's "Argument," "Une Petite Maison" and "Lettre à Martienssen" in *Subjects of Modern Architecture,* Thessaloniki 1962; "Problems of Tourist Development; or, How to Avoid Destruction of Form and Equilibrium in Entire Areas: An Approach" in *Iconomikos Tachydromos* (Athens), 25 November 1971; "Notes on the Contact Limit of Public and Private Space" in *Chroniko 1973,* Athens 1973; "Open Letter to a Friend, Now That Something Can Possibly Change" in *Chroniko 1974,* Athens 1974; "Unforeseen Changes in the Dwelling Space," with Suzana Antonakakis and C. Hadjimichalis, in *Design in Greece* (Athens), no. 6, 1975; "Three Apartment Buildings," with Suzana Antonakakis, in *Design in Greece* (Athens), no. 8, 1977. "Apartment Houses in Athens: The Architect's Role," with Suzanna Antonakakis, in *Architecture in Greece* (Athens), no. 12, 1978

On D. and S. ANTONAKAKIS: book—*Architectes de la Grèce Contemporaine* by F. Loyer, Paris 1966; articles—"Greek Art and Architecture 1945–1967" by Dimitris Fatouros in *Balkan Studies,* Thessaloniki 1967; "Schulmöbel für Geistigzurückgebliebene Kinder" by Aris Konstantinidis in *Möbel Interior Design* (Stuttgart), no. 6, 1967; "L'Architecture en Grèce" by F. Loyer in *Architecture, Mouvement, Continuité* (Paris), no. 167, 1968; "A Critique of Modern Greek Architecture" by F. Loyer in *Architecture in Greece* (Athens), no. 2, 1968; "Akronafplia: The Crown of Nafplion" by D. Philippidis in *Architecture in Greece* (Athens), no. 9, 1975.

Since the early years of our studies and professional activity, we have worked under two main influences:

The first was defined by information about international modern art and architecture as it was expressed in the School of Architecture of the National Technical University of Athens through the teachings of Michelis, Ghika, and the decisive presence of J. Speyer, Professor at Illinois Institute of Technology, Chicago, a Visiting Professor at the N.T.U. from 1957–61. Speyer's original, personal manner introduced us to the methods of working and the teaching of Mies van der Rohe as well as to the international debate of that time on architecture and art.

The second influence found its origins in a more general attitude that prevailed at the time in Greece, an attitude that searched the essence of the Greek cultural heritage, rejecting superficial imitation of traditional forms. The deeper meaning of the work and teaching of Pikionis, as well as the clearness of the work of Aris Konstantinidis, exercised an important influence in this direction.

In our travels through Greece since our school days we have searched to identify relationships between open and closed, public and private space, as they could be found in built environments as expressions of socio-economic and human relations. Our major goal was to express these relationships in our own projects. We realized that the quality of built environment is directly influenced by their treatment.

We analyzed the characteristics of closed and open space and became conscious of the value of their complexity in traditional architecture. We worked on the problem of correlating private and public space as well as the problem of transition from one to the other—establishing successive degrees of higher and lesser privacy in moving from one space

to the next. We try to realize in our practical work and in a comprehensive way principles that are theoretically clear to us. This effort is made not only in large scale synthesis but also in small scale houses and apartment buildings where cost and construction limitations are great and of crucial significance.

In the course of our work we came to realize that team work enriches each team member's experience and pushes collective effort forward. Thus we organized in 1964 an architects' atelier, later named Atelier 66.

—Dimitris and Suzana Antonakakis

The work of Dimitris and Suzana Antonakakis is not only outstanding as architecture; it also offers a creative way of thinking about the organization of space that is valuable for Greek as well as international contemporary architecture. In their work the elements of space, materials, cost, geometry, and social criticism are combined in a multi-variant and consistent logical structure.

I believe that it is possible to distinguish four basic organizing principles in their work:

1) The materials and methods of construction correspond to the needs and possibilities of the Greek environment without diminishing the technological level of the construction. As physical elements, the constructions belong to the natural and man-made native environment without being "folksy."

2) Spatial organization is based on a downward gradient transition from one category of space to another, with different degrees of complexity.

3) The space produced is usually polyvalent. This is true both in the so-called main or complex spaces, like a living room or an exhibition room, as well as for the simple or secondary spaces, like a channel of communication. This is why, in the Antonakakis's architecture, a corridor is not a corridor: they create anti-institutional space.

4) Use or function in their work is always determined by, or refers to, two basic socio-spatial dimensions: the "closed-open" and the "private-public." They coordinate the functions between them. Their architectural work is usually organized around some kind of open space, and the relation of building to street becomes of great importance and is treated with special care.

As a result of the consistent use of these organizing principles, the architecture of the Antonakakis's presents these characteristics: each work has consistency and is coherent; their different works are coherent with each other (though this does not mean that they resemble one another); and their architecture is economical both in conception and realization.

No doubt these four organizing principles are not always clearly defined and clarified from the start, nor are they always apparent in every one of the Antonakakis's works. But the Antonakakis's do make a continuous effort to define and clarify the ways in which their architectural work is composed; they are scrupulous and persistent in elaborating the problems of socio-spatial organization. (This is true of any creative/intellectual work: the gradual clarification of organizing principles also characterizes the evolution of the work of creative architects.)

I would cite three examples from their work in which the four principles have been successfully integrated:

The Apartment Building in Benaki Street, Athens: The spatial organization—with an elaborated system of different levels within the block and within each flat, and the relating of indoor with outdoor spaces (street and back yard)—results in a consistent and cohesive system. This work is, typically, of average cost. It proves how small-scale elements can play a constructive role in the man-environment relationship and how it is possible to transform and use in a positive way the restructions of the conventional financial and building regulations of a typical urban milieu.

The Pierrakos House at Oxylithos: This country house involves a variation of the spatial system used in the Benaki Apartments. Here the system is developed freely in space without well-defined limits, whereas in Benaki it is "enclosed" in a restricting "trunk."

The Mineworkers Housing at Distomo: This is a project of urban scale, organized according to the same spatial concepts as Benaki or Pierrakos but within a complex of many buildings differing in size and function. The complex is well integrated into the natural landscape, with a thoughtful interplay of open and covered streets, open and closed spaces, a response to the socio-cultural activities, and a result of the physical organization, of the whole.

The spatial thinking of Dimitris and Suzana Antonakakis has proved successful not only in detached small and medium-scale buildings but also in larger urban complexes.

—Dimitris A. Fatouros

ANTONAKAKIS, Suzana (Maria).

Greek. Born Suzana-Maria Kolokytha in Athens, 25 June 1935. Educated at primary and secondary schools in Athens, 1942–53, including the French Institute, 1948–51; National Technical University, School of Architecture, Athens, under Michelis, Pikionis, Fatouros, Marthas, and Speyer, 1954–59. Married the architect Dimitris Antonakakis, q.v., in 1961; children: Aristides and Aekaterini. In partnership with Dimitris Antonakakis, Athens, since 1959: Founder and Principal, with Dimitris Antonakakis, Atelier 66, since 1965. Architect/Consultant, Archaeological and Restoration Service, Athens, 1961–63; Administrative Committee Member, Greek Architects Association, 1971–72. Exhibitions: Poster Exhibition, International Fair, Thessaloniki, 1964; Modern Greek Architecture, Patras, 1967; Modern Greek Architecture, Athens, 1971, 1978. Recipient: First Prize, 14th and 15th Public Schools Competition, Thessaloniki, 1961; Honor Award, International Fair, Thessaloniki, 1964; First Prize, Archaeological Museum Competition, Chios, Greece, 1965; First Prize, Engineers and Contractors Association Summer Homes Competition, Spetsae, 1966; First Prize, Tourist Development Competition, Paleokastritsa, Corfu, 1966; First Prize, Old Castle Development Competition, Corfu, 1967; First Prize, Children's Summer Holiday Camp Competition, St. Andreas, Athens, 1972. Address: Atelier 66, 118 Emmanuel Benaki Street, Athens 707, Greece.

Publications:

By ANTONAKAKIS: books—translation of Entretien by Le Corbusier, Athens 1971; Cyclades: Identification and Recording of Important Settlements or Parts of Them, with Dimitris Antonakakis and others, 6 volumes, Athens 1974; articles—"Unforeseen Changes in the Dwelling Space," with Dimitris Antonakakis and C. Hadjimichalis, in Design in Greece (Athens), no. 6, 1975; "Three Apartment Buildings," with Dimitris Antonakakis, in Design in Greece (Athens), no. 8, 1977; "Apartment Houses in Athens: The Architect's Role," with Dimitris Antonakakis, in Architecture in Greece (Athens), no. 12, 1978.

See ANTONAKAKIS, Dimitris

ANTONINI SCHON ZEMBORAIN.

Partnership; established, Buenos Aires, 1961, by graduates of the Universidad Nacional de Buenos Aires, Antonio Sergio Mauro Antonini (born 1936), Gerardo Saul Federico Schon (born 1936), and Eduardo Alejandro Zemborain (born 1936). Associates: Miguel Eduardo Hall (born 1943), since 1971; Juan Carlos Fervenza (born 1942), since 1973. Recipient: numerous first prizes in private and public architectural competitions in Argentina, including Ayacucho City Hall Competition, 1965; Omnibus Station Competition, Tandil, 1966; Tandil Cultural and Sports Center Competition, 1968; Chaco Provincial Bank Competition, 1970; Government Administration Center Competition, La Plata, 1971; Civic Center Competition, San Juan, 1971; La Plata World Cup Football Stadium Competition, 1972; Flores Housing and Urban Planning Competition, Rosario, 1974; University City Competition, San Luis, 1977. Address: Calle Quintana 585, Buenos Aires 1129, Argentina.

Works:

1962/
63 Sol Petrol Refineries, Francisco Solano, Buenos Aires (as consultants)

1964 Argentine Tourism Pavilion, Fifth Cotal Congress, Rio de Janeiro
National Tourist Board Pavilion, Semana de Cordoba Exhibition, Cordoba, Argentina

1964/
65 Office building, Chacabuco, Avellaneda, Buenos Aires

1964/
66 Apartment building, Repetto 473, Martinez, Buenos Aires

1965 Ayacucho Town Hall, Buenos Aires

1965/
66 Cine Majestic Building conversion, Villa Ballester, Buenos Aires
Cine Gran Liniers Building conversion, Liniers, Buenos Aires

1965/
67 Guillon Parish Church, Buenos Aires

1966 Exhibition stands, Effica 66, Buenos Aires

1966/
67 Camara Economica Mercedinia Headquarters, Mercedes, Buenos Aires (with Amaya, Devoto, Martin, Pieres and Lanusse)

1966/
69 Exhibition stands, Exposicion del Confort Humano, Buenos Aires

1967 Municipal building, 3 de Febrero, Buenos Aires (project)

1967/
70 Omnibus Terminal, Tandil, Buenos Aires
Apartment building, Gutierrez 2673, Buenos Aires (as consultant architects)

1968 Lakeside Hotel, Laguna de Monte, Buenos Aires

1968/
69 America Office Building (with cinema and car park), Avenida Callao 1057, Buenos Aires

1968/
70 Road/Rail Underpass, Avenida del Libertador, Buenos Aires (with Fernandez Long and Reggini)
Banco del Norte y Delta Argentino Computer Center, Avenida Figueroa Alcorta 7640, Buenos Aires (with Fernandez Long and Reggini)
Apartment building, Avenida del Libertador General San Martin 1080/84, Buenos Aires

1968/
71 El Chocon Housing and Community Development, Chocon Hydroelectric Works, Neuquen, Argentina (supervising architects; with Alexander Gibb and Partners and Llauro and Urgell)

1969/
70 Tandil Cultural and Sports Center Complex, Buenos Aires

Cine Ambassador Building conversion, Lavalle 777, Buenos Aires
Belgrano Athletic Club alterations and extensions, Buenos Aires (project)
Apartment building, Calle French 2377, Buenos Aires (as consultant architects)
Civic Center, La Rioja, Argentina (project)
Teatro Argentino/Channel Nine TV Studios conversion, Buenos Aires (as consultant architects)

1970 Soana Car-Wash Service Stations, Buenos Aires (project)
Plan for the Perito Moreno Highway, Buenos Aires (competition project; with Latinoconsult)
Development plan for the Ullum Tourist Resort, San Juan, Argentina (with Harz of Argentina and Edison Consult)

1970/
72 Apartment building, Blanco Encalada 5317, Buenos Aires
Campo del Pinazo Sports Fields, stages I and II, Belgrano Athletic Club, Buenos Aires

1971/
72 Naval Air Station, Ushuaia, Tierra del Fuego, Argentina (project)

1971/
73 Apartment building, Calle French and Calle Austria, Buenos Aires

1971/
74 Celulosa Argentina Building conversion, Avenida Paseo Colon y Mejico, Buenos Aires

1971/
75 El Embrujo Neighborhood Housing Development, El Talar, Tigre, Buenos Aires

1971/
79 Government Administration Center, La Plata, Buenos Aires (with Llauro and Urgell)
Chaco Provincial Bank Headquarters, Resistencia, Chaco, Argentina
Civic Center, stage I, San Juan, Argentina

1972/
73 Alcopa Complex Temporary Planning Center, Rio Limay Hydroelectric Development, Alicura, Neuquen, Argentina (project)

1972/
75 Ingenio Providencia Administration Building, Rio Seco, Tucuman, Argentina

1973/
74 Dining Hall, Futaleufu Aluminum Plant, Puerto Madryn, Argentina (project)
Cerro Chapelco Tourist Complex, Neuquen, Argentina (project; with Latinoconsult)
Plan for the Grand Aqueducts System, Argentina (competition project)
Housing development, Rio Grande, Tierra del Fuego, Argentina

1974 Housing development, Finca Lules, Tucuman, Argentina
Housing development, San Pablo, Tucuman, Argentina

1974/
75 Single-family housing, Rio Seco, Tucuman, Argentina
El Embrujo Neighborhood Housing Development extension, El Talar, Tigre, Buenos Aires
Greater Buenos Aires Electrical Services Building (project)

1974/
76 Town development plan for Minera de Tio Turbio, Santa Cruz, Argentina (with STAFF architects)
Pre-fabricated housing development, Santa Cruz, Argentina (project; with STAFF architects)
Housing and community services buildings, Minera de Rio Turbio, Santa Cruz, Argentina (with STAFF architects)
Yacimiento Carbonifero Building, Rio

Antonini Schon Zemborain: Football Stadium, Buenos Aires, 1978

Turbio, Santa Cruz, Argentina (with STAFF architects)

Barrio de Flores Neighborhood Housing Development, Rosario, Santa Fe, Argentina (with STAFF architects)

1975/
76   Hotel, Angostura, Neuquen, Argentina (project)

Civic Center, Angostura, Neuquen, Argentina (project)

Town development plan for Pocitos, San Miguel de Tucuman, Argentina

1975/
78   Mar del Plata World Cup Football Stadium and Sports Complex, Buenos Aires

1976   Plan for the center of Rosario, Santa Fe, Argentina

1976/
78   Civilian/Military Housing Development, Naval Air Station, Punta Indio, Veronica, Buenos Aires

1977   New School 4, Autopista 25 de Mayo, Buenos Aires (project; with ATEC)

Industrial plant, Comodoro Rivadavia, Chubut, Argentina (project)

Collaborators since student days, the team of Antonini/Schon/Zemborain have worked together professionally for almost 18 years, yet they are still barely more than forty years of age. Throughout this period they have developed the most varied of themes—from one-family and collective dwellings, to civic and administrative centers, multi-functional complexes, housing developments, terminals, highways, etc., to the Mar del Plata Stadium, one of the sites of the 1978 World Soccer Championship. There is a certain stylistic evolution in their work, but basically it maintains a continuity of adherence to certain principles.

Their first notable work was the Ayacucho Town Hall in 1965. As one of the team puts it, the building "created a following," and they subsequently received commissions for other similar works. At that time the team considered themselves to be influenced by the new British architecture; in particular, they valued the durability rather than the formal language of buildings. They also believed in an architecture that is not too aggressive but is adequate to its use and appropriate to its environment, and it is this attitude that continues to inform their work. And, through a continuing self-criticism, and because they

search out and respond to new tendencies in the architectural world, they keep their minds open to new solutions, an attitude that sets them apart from practitioners of spectacular but ephemeral fashions based on an a priori formalism.

But this is not to suggest that one work differs radically from another in either design or method. Each work is achieved by a very rigorous response to the program and by their as rigorously ensuring that everything—from the plan, as it were, to the carpentry—is controlled by a spatial module that acts not as a point of departure but as the coordinator of all architectural elements.

During the entire creative process, there is a set of design obligations that must be respected. These obligations are not imposed as a result of the team's adherence to some particular theory of form but as a result of their having determined the objective of each particular work, by testing alternatives against the program. When the design objective is established, they attempt synthesis with the spatial module—the method is highly analytical and highly controlled.

The adoption of a coordinating module does have several consequences. It allows for a simple building process. It creates a method of linkage of the various elements. The module is not necessarily a cube, but it *is* three-dimensional, and it can be clearly "read" in the building. It also allows for flexibility. In large-scale enterprises—The Civic Center at San Juan or the Government Administration Center at La Plata—the team has had to accept that parts of the complex may be used in ways different from their conception, that future growth must be allowed for, and that, as is frequently the case, the final purpose of the work may not be the same as the one that was initially envisaged by the program. Rigorous design criteria, and a coordinating spatial module, create not only the means but also the pattern for future change.

For the Government Administration Center at La Plata, Antonini/Schon/Zemborain created two towers facing a public square and flanking the City Hall. They chose a simple volumetric solution and avoided any need to "compete" with the environment. Set in two plots that are symmetrical in relation to the old building that they frame, the towers are both higher than the surrounding buildings and aligned to, and reflective of, each other, in their relation to the axis coordinating the whole. The City Hall rises above the axis. Because of the solution adopted, the City Hall stands out in the totality of the space, the differ-

ent characters of the towers contributing to this effect. The towers were conceived by the team as an articulated set between which, as there was a correspondence in function, there would be a correspondence in form, in coordinating module.

The center is recognizable as the work of Antonini/Schon/Zemborain. So is The Civic Center of San Juan—though here different conditions were involved. Because earth tremors are common in the area, the structures had to be strong and earthquake-resistant. More important, in this work the team tried to create a "community space" within the downtown area, a space that the city's inhabitants would identify as their own, one that would become a distinctive element in the urban fabric. Defined by the team as a work "that has a strong existence achieved by means of simple elements," The Civic Center has achieved its goals.

Antonini/Schon/Zemborain finds it difficult to point to any one work as "characteristic." They prefer to talk about a spectrum of work. Yet the Mar del Plata Stadium does very well reveal the consistent patterns in their architecture. There is the subtle yet readable presence of the coordinating module, which generates more complex forms (the horizontally extended building, the curves) appropriate to function; the attention to environment and the relation of structure to surroundings (the treatment of park areas; the fluid conditions of access and circulation); simplicity of execution, the rigorous application of pre-determined construction principles; and a flexibility achieved by clarity in design, so that the different parts of the complex can later be adapted to other uses. Moreover, a balanced image is maintained—despite a roofcovering that is a real structural accomplishment: it is not allowed to become the center of attention.

If, as they wish, one looks at their work as a whole—and if one looks at it not as a manifestation of a theory but as a series of works performing certain functions, making no reference to anything besides itself—then the best and most obvious description of the buildings of Antonini/Schon/Zemborain is that they are classical—not classical in some stylistic or formal sense but in the manifest clarity and simplicity of their solutions.

—Jorge Glusberg

ARCHITECTS' CO-PARTNERSHIP INC.

Company; established as Architects' Co-Operative Partnership, by eleven ex-students of the Architectural Association School of Architecture, London, 1939; reformed after the war, 1945, by eight of the original partners—Kenneth Capon, born 1915; Peter Cocke, born 1917; Michael Cooke-Yarborough, born 1915; Anthony Cox, born 1915; Michael Grice, born 1917; Michael Powers, born 1915; Greville Rhodes, born 1916, left the partnership 1947; Leo de Syllas, born 1917, died 1964; subsequent partners: Philip Groves, born 1928, educated at Regent Street Polytechnic School of Architecture, London—joined ACP 1955, Partner 1965; Hugh Durrant-Whyte, born 1931, educated at the University of the Witwatersrand, South Africa—joined ACP 1956, Partner 1971; John Jordan, born 1933, educated at the Birmingham School of Architecture—joined ACP 1959, Partner 1971. Name changed to Architects' Co-Partnership, 1953; office opened in Lagos, Nigeria, 1954; partnership changed to unlimited company, 1971; main office moved from central London to Hertfordshire, 1971. Recipient: Northern Region Award, 1967, London Region Award, 1968, and South East Region Award, 1971, of the Royal Institute of British Architects; Civic Trust Award, 1960, 1961, 1965, 1967, 1968, 1972; Housing Design Award, 1968. Address: Architects' Co-Partnership Inc., Northaw House, Potters Bar, Hertfordshire EN6 4PS, England.

Architects Co-Partnership: Wolfson Building, Trinity College, Cambridge, 1972

Works:

1951 Various structures for the *Festival of Britain* exhibition, South Bank, London
1952 Rubber factory and offices, Brynmawr, South Wales
1953 Richard Lee Primary School, Coventry
1954 Science laboratories, Bryanston School, Blandford, Dorset
Housing, Pitstone, Buckinghamshire
1955 Margaret Wix Primary School, St. Albans, Hertfordshire
Bedwell East Primary School, Stevenage, Hertfordshire
Roundwood Park Primary School, Harpenden, Hertfordshire
Secondary modern school, Chaddesden, Derbyshire
Secondary modern school, Hurlfield, Sheffield
1956 Shepherd's Lane Primary School, Rickmansworth, Hertfordshire
Park Lane Primary School, Waltham Cross, Hertfordshire
Infant school, Alderman's Green, Coventry
1957 Batford Infant School, Harpenden, Hertfordshire
Secondary modern school, Bingham, Nottinghamshire
1958 Secondary modern school, Thornbridge, Derbyshire
Secondary modern school, Long Sutton, Lincolnshire

Secondary modern school, Tile Cross, Warwickshire
Science laboratories, Sherborne Girls' School, Dorset
Chemical factory, Berkhamsted, Hertfordshire
President's Lodge, Corpus Christi College, Oxford
1959 Thrift Farm Secondary School, Borehamwood, Hertfordshire
Secondary modern school, Newbold, Warwickshire
1960 Risinghill Comprehensive School, Finsbury, London
Secondary modern school, Waltheof, Sheffield
Chemistry laboratories, University of Leicester
Secondary modern school, St. Austell, Cornwall
Study bedrooms, St. John's College, Oxford
1961 Secondary modern school, Wilnecote, Warwickshire
Research laboratories, Liphook, Surrey
15 primary and secondary schools, Nigeria
Bristol Hotel, Lagos, Nigeria
1962 Tye Green area housing, Harlow New Town, Hertfordshire
Radiobiological laboratories, Wantage, Berkshire
Tutors' houses, St. John's College, Oxford
1963 Harris Technical College, Preston, Lancashire (with the Department of Education and Science)

Study bedrooms, King's College, Cambridge
School for spastics, Tonbridge, Kent
1964 Physics Laboratories, University of Hull
Beaufoy Comprehensive School, Lambeth, London
Community Centre, Bethlem Hospital, Beckenham, Kent
1965 Teachers' Training College, Trinity College, Carmarthen, Wales
Biochemistry Laboratories, Imperial College, South Kensington, London
Spastics training school, Meldreth, Cambridgeshire
Spastics hostel, Broadstones, Birmingham

1967 Ophthalmic Unit, Royal Berkshire Hospital Reading
Spastics workshops, Broadstones, Birmingham
Junior Health Training Centre, Greenwich, London
Dunelm House Student Community Building, University of Durham
Science and Mathematics Laboratories, University of Hull
Laboratories, University of Keele, Staffordshire
St. Paul's Cathedral Choir School, London
Housing, Kingsley Place, Highgate, London
Music School, Lancing College, Sussex
Physics Laboratories, University of Essex, Colchester

1968 Library, University of Essex, Colchester
1969 Chemistry Laboratories, University of Essex, Colchester
Chemistry Laboratories, University College, London
Study bedrooms, Goldney House, University of Bristol
1970 Staff Hostel and Nurses' School, Maudsley Hospital, Camberwell, London
Alexander Barracks, Pirbright, Surrey
Chemistry Laboratories, Imperial College, South Kensington, London
Computer Building, University of Essex, Colchester
1971 Study bedrooms, University of Essex, Colchester
1972 Royal School of Signals, Blandford, Dorset
3 boarding schools, Tunis, Sfax and Le Kef, Tunisia
Wolfson Building (study bedrooms), Trinity College, Cambridge
1973 22 schools, Trinidad and Tobago, West Indies
1974 School of Environmental Studies, University College, London
Housing, Ethelred Street area, Lambeth, London
1975 Study bedrooms and theatre, Guy's Hospital, Southwark, London
1976 Arts Faculty Building, University of Durham
1977 Factory, offices and research laboratories, Swindon, Wiltshire
1978 Laboratories, Hatfield Polytechnic, Hertfordshire
Pavilions for the *International Fair*, Khartoum, Sudan
4 schools, Mutrah, Ruwi, Sohar, and Nizwa, Oman
Study bedrooms, Sinclair House, University of Bristol

Publications:

By ACP: articles—"Building in the Tropics" in *The Architects' Journal* (London), 16 May 1937; "Architect's Approach to Architecture" in *RIBA Journal* (London), June 1967; "Building for the Health Care Programme, Saudi Arabia" in *RIBA Journal* (London), June 1976.

On ACP: articles—"Brynmawr" by R. Furneaux Jordan in *Architectural Review* (London), March 1952; "The Team in the Office" in *Architecture and Building* (London), April 1956; "Dunelm House, Durham" by John Donat in *Architectural Review* (London), June 1966; "Schools in Trinidad" in *Building* (London), 16 November 1973.

*   *   *

The original partners of ACP were nursed in the Modern Movement in architecture in the years immediately preceding the Second World War, when the work of the architectural Establishment seemed to them bankrupt and irrelevant. They began to practise in the post-war welfare state when local authority and government architects' departments were small compared with what they have since become and when there was an acute shortage of labour and materials, severe economic stringency, and great demands for new buildings for the community.

ACP was not so much concerned with creating architectural monuments as with the provision of humane and efficient shelter for social activities, and by accident rather than by design found itself building for education, following the post-war bulge in the birth rate, through primary to secondary schools, generally using pre-fabricated systems of construction. With the subsequent expansion of the universities, its work extended into a wider field, where its largest single commitment was the master plan and most of the buildings for the new University of Essex, and also into buildings for health, medical research, and housing. Thus the majority of its commissions have been in the public sector.

It has also always been concerned with the problems of design in the developing world, and has worked in West Africa, North Africa, the West Indies, and the Middle East.

—Architects' Co-Partnership

The fact that Architects' Co-Partnership Inc. was founded early in 1939 by eleven young architects from the Architectural Association School of Architecture as Architects Co-Operative Partnership explains much of the character and consistency of the architecture they produce. The group were brought up in the early days of modern architecture in Britain, and like many of their contemporaries regarded the new approach to architecture proclaimed particularly by Le Corbusier as a crusade to which they could devote their energies and talents. Architecture through technology could be a powerful agent of the new good life in a just society.

The first major building designed by ACP in 1946 and built in 1948–52 was the new rubber factory at Brynmawr in South Wales. The site was difficult and bleak, but the architects produced a building that had a permanent effect on industrial building in Britain. By carefully analysing the factory process and interpreting this in a building of shell concrete domes and barrel vaults, approached by a communal pedestrian ramp and overlooking a man-made lake, they established an architectural standard for industry that has seldom been equalled. This building helped to make factory building an acceptable subject for architectural study and development, and it will always be regarded as one of the "classic" industrial buildings of the 20th Century.

The postwar schools programme helped to establish ACP in the field of educational buildings. They were involved in school and college design starting with the Hertfordshire "light and dry" systems, and gradually evolved their own special architectural character. As the education programme developed, so ACP's work moved into the more complex university and polytechnic buildings and later into facility planning, medical building and urban housing both in the UK and overseas.

ACP were among the first UK firms to work overseas, mainly in education and health, and their buildings show that they have not lost their ability to adapt to changing social circumstances and climatic conditions; these works underline their continued faith in the essential social value of architecture, a 1930's belief that is equally valid in the present day.

Buildings designed by ACP, on their own admission, are not intended to be architectural monuments; they are meant to fill a social need economically and practically and give aesthetic satisfaction to their users. It is not surprising that ACP prefer to remain an anonymous architectural team, and have reinforced their skills by setting up their own environmental engineering group known as Northaw Engineering Consultants (NECI).

Six of the founders are still active architects and, together with a new generation of partners, ACP has been able to demonstrate that the philosophy and attitudes that brought the original eleven together are still socially and architecturally relevant after 40 years of practice.

—Edward D. Mills

ARDALAN, Nader.

Iranian. Born in Tehran, 9 March 1939. Educated at the Carnegie Institute of Technology, Pittsburgh, 1956–61 (American Institute of Architects Scholarship), B.Arch. 1961; Harvard Graduate School of Design, Cambridge, Massachusetts, M.Arch. 1962. Married Laleh Bakhtiar (divorced, 1976); married Shahla Ganji in 1977; children: Mani, Iran, Karim, and Alireza. Designer, Skidmore, Owings and Merrill, San Francisco, 1962–64; Head, Architecture and Engineering Section, National Iranian Oil Company, Masjid-i-Sulaiman, Iran, 1964–66; Design Partner, Abdolaziz Farmanfarmaian and Associates, Tehran, 1966–72. Managing Director, Mandala Collaborative, Tehran, since 1972, and President, Mandala International, Boston, since 1977; Principal, Nader Ardalan and Associates, Boston, since 1979. Visiting Critic in Architecture, Yale University, New Haven, Connecticut, 1977, and Harvard Graduate School of Design, 1977–78. Member, Steering Committee, Aga Khan Award for Architecture, since 1977. Recipient: First Prize, Iran-America Society Culture Center Design Competition, 1975; Planning Award, *Progressive Architecture*, 1979. Address: Nader Ardalan and Associates Inc., Post Office Box 40, Boston, Massachusetts 02113, U.S.A.

Works:

1962/
64 Engineering Sciences Building, University of California, Berkeley (with Skidmore, Owings and Merrill)
1964/
66 Housing and Community Facilities, National Iranian Oil Company, Kharg Island, Aghajari, Masjid-i-Sulaiman, Iran
1965 Dr. Ali Saidi House, Tehran
1966 Dr. A. G. Ardalan House, Caspian Sea, Iran
1968 Saman Apartments, Tehran (with Abdolaziz Farmanfarmaian and Associates)
1968/
72 Asian Games Sports Center, Tehran (with Abdolaziz Farmanfarmaian and Associates)
1970/
72 Mehrabad Airport expansion, Tehran (with Abdolaziz Farmanfarmaian and Associates)
Malek House, Tehran
1971/
73 Iran Center for Management Studies, Tehran (with Abdolaziz Farmanfarmaian and Associates)
1971/
74 Behshahr Home Offices, Tehran (with Abdolaziz Farmanfarmaian and Associates)
1974 Arya Mehr University (master plan, university mosque, library, student union, and gateway), Tehran
Jondi Shahpour New Town, Ahwaz, Iran (with Skidmore, Owings and Merrill)
1974/
76 Creative Arts Center, Tehran
Pardisan Environmental Park, Tehran
Bandar Shahpour New Town, Persian Gulf, Iran (with Skidmore, Owings and Merrill)
1975 Urban design studies for the Abbassabad Development, Tehran (with Kenzo Tange and Louis Kahn)
Master plan for the Tappeh Eram New Community, Shiraz, Iran
Master plan for Bu Ali Sina University, Hamadan, Iran (with Georges Candilis)
Design of the *Sacred Space* exhibition, National Museum of Design, Smithsonian Institution, Washington, D.C. (with Karl Schlamminger)
1976/
77 Academic Buildings, Dormitories, and Administration Housing, Bu Ali Sina University, Hamadan, Iran (with Georges Candilis)
1977 Garden Apartments and Community Center, Monte Carlo
Mosque, Tehran
1977/
78 Industrial Development Bank of Iran Headquarters Building, Tehran
1978 Mercantile Bank of Iran and Holland Headquarters Building, Tehran
Tehran Center for the Celebration of Music

Development plan, and first phase housing,
Nuran Satellite Town, Isfahan, Iran
1979 University Mosque, Bu Ali Sina University,
Hamadan, Iran

Publications:

By ARDALAN: books—*The Sense of Unity: The Sufi Tradition in Persian Architecture,* with Laleh Bakhtiar, Chicago 1973; *Habitat Bill of Rights,* with Josep Lluis Sert, Moshe Safdie, Balkrishna Doshi, and Georges Candilis, Tehran 1976; *Al-Masjid al-Haram: The History and Construction of the Holy Ka'ba,* Mecca 1976.

On ARDALAN: book—*Iran: Elements of Destiny* by Roloff Beny, Toronto 1978; articles—"Contemporary Iranian Architects" by M. Eshraq in *Art and Architecture* (Tehran), June/November 1973; "Iran Today" in *Newsweek* (New York), November 1974; "Architectures Iraniennes" by Yvette Pontoizeau in *L'Architecture d'Aujourd'hui* (Paris), February 1978; "Jondi Shahpour New Community: 1979 Award for Planning" in *Progressive Architecture* (New York), February 1979.

I believe that good architecture should reflect a holistic appreciation of reality. Reality, it is held, has a hierarchy of awareness levels within which there exists both outer and inner dimensions. The outer (ecological) dimension relates to a finite world of limited energy income from the sun, of fixed energy reserves. The inner (cultural) dimension relates to humankind, who have an infinite, hidden reserve of energy —the spirit—that can often transcend the limited context of this phenomenal world. The creative imagination that has extended the art and architecture of humanity has primarily grown from this inner dimension.

It has, therefore, been my intention to develop a firm working understanding of how, traditionally, the proper and balanced relationship of both inner and outer energies has been achieved throughout history. The comparative study of outstanding traditional societies has always been undertaken with a view to discerning the underlying universal values and attitudes that are common to man, while appreciating the particular, adaptive strategies of each. The study of traditions in architecture or the normative ways of societies provide me with a sense of relaxed anticipation of the future that complements contemporary knowledge and technology.

This complementary view of existence and creativity has been applied systematically in my teaching, research, and work. At present the focus of my work centers on the re-creation of a minimum energy waste design, while my research is concerned with the aesthetics of energy in architecture.

—Nader Ardalan

Born in Iran, Nader Ardalan is now the principal of Mandala International, a group of architects and planners operating in Boston in association with the Mandala Collaborative of Tehran. Together, they have designed several buildings and planning schemes for Iran.

Ardalan's chief concern is with what he calls the "cultural dimension" of architecture. He is very disturbed that, though its architectural theories have had a broad worldwide impact, a sense of culture hardly exists in the United States. Especially in developing countries struggling to maintain identity as they rapidly adopt modern technology, the importance of the "cultural dimension" cannot be overlooked.

"We are at the threshold of the development of new architectural theories, set against the background of the ashes of the International Style," Ardalan feels. "The means lie in the domain of universal concerns that range from spiritual considerations to biosphere ecology and renewable resource usage. Most design attitudes today are parochial and re-

Nader Ardalan: Nuran Satellite Town (conceptual development model), Isfahan, Iran, 1978

source unconscious, and 90% of the world cannot afford to emulate them."

Ardalan's architecture shows that he has learned a great deal from many Third World cultures. He has absorbed lessons not only from their ancient history but also from their recent historical struggles (successes and failures) with the industrialized world. His Tehran Center for the Celebration of Music is a case in point. Through a system of pedestrian walkways, the center is linked with several other cultural facilities in the immediate area, thus creating a cultural quarter that never existed before. The concepts of walls, courtyards, outer and inner gardens, and a general progression of internalized spaces draws much from traditional Iranian design. The use of water and light (particularly dramatic is the light from the oculus above the theatre, whose shimmering opalescent surfaces add to the sense of depthless space created within the cone) make the building vibrant and inspiring.

Mandala's plan for Nuran, the City of Illumina-

tion, a new town to be built near Isfahan, is even more exciting. Within the context of a planned city, he has developed a strong sense of place, in striking contrast to so many of the new towns developed by other contemporary architects. The plan is structured with geometry, but two commercial paths designed for non-vehicular traffic meander through the town in amorphous routes. The primary axis of the town is aligned with two holy places, one to the east and one to the west, adding a spiritual justification to the plan. Parts of the plan are symbolic: the west side of the town is the imaginative or spiritual head, while the east side is the thinking or material head of Nuran. The axial spine of Nuran is a traditional "paradise garden," which enforces the spiritual axis between the two shrines, creates a cool space that is easily accessible from all points, and further connects Nuran to regional cultural traditions.

Nader Ardalan is a man dedicated to the search for origins, and it is because of that dedication that he has focussed so much attention on pure numbers, geometry, and his Islamic heritage. His designs are often highly geometrical, but his sense of geometry is finely tuned, developed from his study of Sufi traditions in ancient Persian architecture. His work should be a beacon not only for other architects practicing within the context of the developing world, but for architects in the west as well, who too often forget that without cultural connections, architecture is incapable of answering human needs.

—Mitchell B. Rouda

ARUP, Sir Ove (Nyquist).

British. Born in Newcastle upon Tyne, 16 April 1895. Educated at preparatory, primary and high schools in Germany and Denmark; studied philosophy and mathematics at the University of Copenhagen, B.A. 1916, and civil engineering at the Royal Technical College, Copenhagen, 1916–22, B.Sc. 1922. Married Ruth Sorensen in 1925; children: Anya, Jens, and Karin. Worked as a designer for Christiani and Nielson, Hamburg, 1922–23, then as Designer, 1923–25, and Chief Designer, 1925–34, for Christiani and Nielsen Ltd., London; Director and Chief Designer, J. L. Kier and Company Ltd., London, 1934–38; Director, Arup Designers Ltd. and (with his cousin) Arup and Arup Ltd., London, 1938–46; in private practice as an engineering consultant, London, 1946–49. Senior Partner, Ove Arup and Partners, London, since 1949, and Arup Associates, London, since 1963. Consultant Engineer to the Air Ministry, London, 1938–45. Visiting Lecturer, Harvard University, Cambridge, Massachusetts, 1955; Alfred Bossom Lecturer, Royal Society of Arts, London, 1970. Chairman, Society of Danish Civil Engineers in Great Britain and Ireland, 1955–59. Founder Member, Modern Architecture Research Group (MARS), London, 1933; collaborated with the Tecton Group, London, 1933. Recipient: Gold Medal, Royal Institute of British Architects, 1966; Civic Trust Award, 1968, 1971; First Prize, University of Sheffield Master Plan Competition, 1971; *Financial Times* Award, 1971, 1973; Gold Medal, Society of Structural Engineers, 1973; Structural Steel Award, 1973, 1976; Office of the Year Award, 1975; Business and Industry Award, 1976. D.Sc.: University of Durham, 1967; University of East Anglia, Norwich, 1968; Tekniske Hojskole, Lyngby, Denmark, 1974; Heriot-Watt University, Edinburgh, 1976. Fellow, Institution of Structural Engineers, 1940, and Institute of Civil Engineers, 1951. Fellow, American Concrete Institute, 1975. C.B.E. (Commander, Order of the British Empire), 1953; Knight Bachelor, 1971. Chevalier, 1965, and Commander, 1975, Order of the Dannebrog, Denmark. Address: Ove Arup and Partners, 13 Fitzroy Street, London W1P 6BQ, England.

Works (as structural engineer):

1933 Cafe and Shelter, Canvey Island, London
Highpoint I (apartment building), Highgate, London
1939 Penguin Pool, London Zoo, Regent's Park
Air raid shelters for the Finsbury Borough Council, London

With Ove Arup and Partners:

1947/
50 Waen Pond Rubber Factory, Brynmawr, South Wales
1951/
54 CIBA Ltd. Plant, Offices and Laboratories, Duxford, Cambridgeshire
1953 Irish Transport Board Bus Station Department of Social Welfare Building, Store Street, Dublin 1

1954 Hunstanton Secondary Modern School, Norfolk
1956/
80 The Barbican, City of London
1961 Smith, Kline and French Laboratories, Cambridge
Post office, Cape Coast, Ghana
1962 York Shipley Factory, Basildon, Essex
Evode Ltd. Maintenance Building, Stafford
Vaughan Building, Somerville College, Oxford

With Ove Arup and Partners or Arup Associates:

1963 Smith, Kline and French Offices and Laboratories, Welwyn Garden City, Hertfordshire
1964 Point Royal Flats, Bracknell, Berkshire
CIBA-Geigy Research Laboratories, Horsham, Sussex
Walter Jones Factory, Ashford, Kent
Leckhampton House, Corpus Christi College, Cambridge
1965 Swimming pool, Walton-on-Thames, Surrey
1965/
71 New Museums redevelopment, and new buildings for Corpus Christi and Trinity Hall, Cambridge
1965/
75 Department of Metallurgy, Department of Nuclear Physics, and new buildings for Somerville College, University College, and St. John's College, Oxford
1966 Development plan for the Old Addenbrooke's Area, Cambridge
Ove Arup and Partners Offices, South Queensferry, West Lothian, Scotland
Vic Supplies Factory, Stafford
Master plan for Loughborough University, Leicestershire
Paper mill, Jebba, Nigeria
1966/
72 Department of Arts and Commerce, Department of Mining and Metallurgy, and Department of Microbiology, University of Birmingham
1966/
74 Department of Chemical Engineering, Department of Civil Engineering, and Department of Physics and Electrical Engineering, Loughborough University, Leicestershire
1967 Wolfson Building, Somerville College, Oxford
Footbridge, Dunelm House, University of Durham
1968 The Maltings Concert Hall, Snape, Suffolk
New building for the Stock Exchange, London
Graduate and undergraduate accommodation, Trinity Hall, Cambridge
Penguin Books Offices and Warehouse, Harmondsworth, Middlesex
1969 Zunz House, 2a Drax Avenue, Wimbledon, London
Development plan for I.B.M., Havant, Hampshire
Master plan for the University of Sheffield (competition project)
Arctic City (project)
1970 Arts and Social Centre, University of Leicester
Muirhead Tower, Arts and Commerce Department, University of Birmingham
1971 Project Suroit (regional development plan), South West Mauritius
Department of Zoology, Department of Metallurgy, Department of Computer Science, and the Lion Yard City Centre Development Plan, Cambridge
Master plan for the University of Sheffield, stage II
Development plan for Aston University, Birmingham

Oxford Mail and Times Offices and Printing Works
John Player and Sons Ltd. Horizon Factory, Nottingham
Television tower, Emley Moor, Yorkshire
Sports Hall, and Teaching Block, University of Surrey, Guildford
1972 IBM Process Assembly Plant, Warehouse, Offices and Computer Center, Havant, Hampshire
Royal Yacht Squadron Pavilion, Isle of Wight
1973 Royal Opera House stage reconstruction, Covent Garden, London
Department of Music and Music School, University of East Anglia, Norwich
Concert Hall (Corn Exchange conversion), Cambridge (project)
Sydney Opera House
Cultural Centre, Abidjah, Ivory Coast (project)
1974 Married Students Community Development, University College, Oxford
British Sugar Corporation Development, Peterborough
Mosque, Hotel and Conference Center, Mecca, Saudi Arabia
Hotel and Conference Centre, Riyadh, Saudi Arabia
1975 New buildings for Ampleforth College, Yorkshire
Heavy Plate Shop, Royal Naval Dockyard, Portsmouth, Hampshire
Orchestral Rehearsal Hall, Holy Trinity Church, Southwark, London
IBM Headquarters, Johannesburg
Scottish Opera House (conversion of Theatre Royal), Glasgow
1976 Science Building, Keble Triangle, Oxford
National Exhibition Centre, Birmingham
Sir Thomas White Building, St. John's College, Oxford
Housing and Maintenance Depot, for Kensington Borough Council, London
IBM Headquarters, Portsmouth, Hampshire
Bush Lane House (office building), London
Trumans Ltd. Brewery Headquarters, Brick Lane, London
Manchester Opera House restoration (project)
Wiggins Teape Headquarters, Basingstoke, Hampshire
Computer Department, University of Sheffield
Ministry of Industry and Electricity, Riyadh, Saudi Arabia (project)
Trafalgar House Developments Office Building, Cannon Street, London
1977 Council Offices and Bus Station, Northampton
Centre Beaubourg, Paris
1978 Lloyd's Administrative Headquarters, Chatham, Kent
South West Regional Headquarters of the Electricity Generating Board, Bristol
Royal Naval Dockyard, Portsmouth, Hampshire
1978– Council of Ministers Building, Riyadh, Saudi Arabia
Britten/Pears Music School, Snape, Suffolk
1979 Buxton Opera House, Derbyshire
1980 Old Vic Theatre restoration, London (project)

Publications:

By ARUP: books—*Design, Cost, Construction and Relative Safety of Trench, Surface, Bombproof and Other Air Raid Shelters,* London 1939; *London's Shelter Problem,* London 1940; *Safe Housing in Wartime,* London 1941; articles—"Subsidence under the Tidal Pressures" in *The Structural Engi-*

neer (London), no. 12, 1929; "Planning in Reinforced Concrete," in 2 parts, in *Architectural Design* (London), nos. 9 and 10, 1935; "Reinforced Concrete" in *The Architects Yearbook,* London 1945; "Shell Construction" in *Architectural Design* (London), no. 11, 1947; "Modern Architecture: The Structural Fallacy" in *The Listener* (London), no. 1375, 1955; "Design and Construction of the Printing Works at Debden," with Sir Howard Robertson and others, in *The Structural Engineer* (London), no. 4, 1956; "A Discussion about Future Developments in Building Techniques" in *Architectural Design* (London), no. 11, 1957; "The Architect and the Engineer," with E. D. J. Matthews, in *Journal of the Institution of Civil Engineers* (London), August 1959; "Reinforced Concrete Design" in *The Financial Times* (London), 13 November 1961; "Foreword" to *Candela, The Shell Builder* by Colin Faber, New York 1963; "Discussion of Form and Structure in Engineering" in *Journal of the Institution of Civil Engineers* (London), October 1964; "Problems and Progress in the Construction of the Sydney Opera House" in *Civil Engineering and Public Works Review* (London), no. 703, 1965; "Ove Arup Talks to Peter Rawstone" in *RIBA Journal* (London), no. 4, 1965; "Art and Architecture: The Architect-Engineer Relationship" in *RIBA Journal* (London), August 1966; "The Evolution and Design of the Concourse at the Sydney Opera House" in *Journal of the Institution of Civil Engineers* (London), no. 4, 1968; "From Gorillas at the Zoo to Aussies at the Opera," interview with Martin Pawley, in *Building Design* (London), May 1970; "I Am Not a Prophet" in *Contract Journal* (London), no. 4761, 1970; "The Potential of Prestressed Concrete" in *Concrete* (Slough, Buckinghamshire), no. 6, 1970; "Sydney Opera House," with G. J. Zunz, in *Civil Engineering* (New York), no. 12, 1971; "Built Environment Professions: What's in a Name?" in *Built Environment* (London), March 1975; "I Only Used Ordinary, Plain Common Sense" in *New Civil Engineer* (London), April 1975; and numerous articles and reports in the *Arup Journal* (London).

On ARUP: books—*University Planning and Design* by Michael Brawne, London 1967; *Cambridge New Architecture* by Nicholas Taylor and Philip Booth, London 1970; *Building the New Universities* by T. Birks, Newton Abbot, Devon 1972; *Third Generation: The Changing Meaning of Architecture* by Philip Drew, London 1972; articles—"Arup's First Ten Years" in *Architecture Plus* (New York), November/December 1974; "Piece Work" by Graham Hancock in *Building Design* (London), 5 September 1975; "The Award Winners: A Profile of Arup Associates" in *Building Design* (London), 11 June 1976; "Grand Master: The Career of Sir Ove Arup and His Influence on Post-1930 Architecture" in *Building* (London), 7 October 1976; "Arup Associates" in *Architecture + Urbanism* (Tokyo), December 1977.

Ove Arup is not an architect, yet one of the best architectural practices in Britain bears his name. This is as it should be. Few people understand architecture so well, possibly because few have the driving curiosity about the universe that led this tall, vague seeming man to take a degree in philosophy before embarking upon structural engineering. In 1966 he told *The Architects' Journal:*

> Architecture has been defined as "building plus delight". . . . We know roughly what a building is. A building has to do a job and . . . has to cost as little as is compatible with doing its job well. Only in a very few cases is cost of no importance. Delight, on the other hand, has nothing to do with cost. It is not safeguarded by spending a lot of money—it may even be had for nothing, or next to nothing. It is produced somehow by the creation of spaces, sculptural relationships, light and shade, colours and tex-

Sir Ove Arup: Footbridge, Dunelm House, University of Durham, 1967

tures, and by the clarity or ingenuity with which its functional and structural problems are solved; but exactly *how* we do not know. . . . This is unfortunate because "delight" is what every architect wants to produce. . . . So naturally he spends his energies on the pursuit of delight. And perhaps neglects the building. This is unfortunate because it endangers his whole quest for delight.

I do not suppose he had it quite so clearly worked out in the 1930's when he met Lubetkin, Max Fry, Ernö Goldfinger, Wells Coates and other members of the MARS Group, but he already understood "the purpose of the whole exercise, which is not first of all to produce good plumbing, or good structure, but good architecture, total architecture, and with it delight." Ove enjoyed the enthusiasm of these pioneers, their belief in what they were doing. The social importance of architecture, he says, was rightly stressed. He shared their lively interest in the new material, reinforced concrete, and understood its limitations better than these architects for whom it was a symbol as well as a building material.

In order to work with Lubetkin on the design of

Highpoint I, Arup joined J. L. Kier and Company, the structural contractors. The box structure they evolved together was elegant to inhabit, as well as mathematically elegant, having no clumsy framing to complicate the interior. The same period was enlivened by the spiral ramps of the Penguin Pool and overshadowed by a bitter fight with Finsbury Borough Council over air raid shelters.

From the increasingly restrictive field of contracting, Arup moved into consultancy and in 1949 set up Ove Arup and Partners, Consulting Engineers. Originally 40 in London, plus 5 in Dublin to build Michael Scott's bus station, the firm now has over 1,600 in ten offices in the U.K. and 1,000 more in forty offices around the world.

Largeness is integral to the man—faintly neanderthal in outline—his thinking and activities; as it is to Philip Dowson of Arup Associates. Yet Sir Ove well knows that architectural quality bears no relation to size, that the design process is essentially the same for a chess set as for an opera house. The Barbican project, the firm's largest, is a sizeable slice of the City of London; Sydney Opera House their greatest challenge. Yet Ove has chosen to represent him here the little footbridge over the Wear between Durham

Yoshinobu Ashihara: Komazawa Olympic Gymnasium and Control Tower, Tokyo, 1964

Cathedral and Dunelm House, a late building for The Architects Co-Partnership, one of his earliest clients. He was actively involved in the design of the footbridge, where his involvement in another felicitous work, the Maltings at Snape, was indirect. But none the less real. Its designers, Arup Associates—structural, electrical and mechanical engineers, quantity surveyors and architects—are the embodiment of Ove's belief that "when engineers and quantity surveyors discuss aesthetics and architects study what cranes can do, we are on the right road."

Arup Associates, Architects and Engineers emerged as a separate entity from the consulting engineers in 1963. Ove's partners in it are the architect Philip Dowson, the engineers Ron Hobbs and Derek Sugden, who led the Maltings team. They have made a telling contribution to university residences—at Somerville, Corpus Leckhampton, Trinity Hall, and St. John's, Oxford—using the structural frame to articulate the stack of small rooms. It is, however, the firm's characteristic factory design, with the office block discreetly slung within the industrial envelope, that best demonstrates the aesthetic gains that accrue from the full integration of the building professions.

—Diana Rowntree

ASHIHARA, Yoshinobu.

Japanese. Born in Tokyo, 7 July 1918. Educated at the University of Tokyo, 1940–42, B.Arch. 1942; Graduate School of Design, Harvard University, Cambridge, Massachusetts, 1952–53, M.Arch. 1953; doctorate conferred by the University of Tokyo, 1962. Served in the Japanese Army, 1942–45. Married Hatsuko Takahashi in 1944; children: Yukiko and Taro. Draftsman, Junzo Sakakura Architect and Associates, Tokyo, 1946–47, and Marcel Breuer Architect and Associates, New York, 1953–54. Since 1955, Principal, Yoshinobu Ashihara Architect and Associates, Tokyo. Professor, Hosei University, Tokyo, 1959–64; Professor and Chairman, Musashino Fine Arts University, Tokyo, 1964–70. Since 1970, Professor at the University of Tokyo. Director, Japan Architects Association, 1959–61, and Architectural Institute of Japan, 1960–62. Recipient: Award, 1960, and Special Award, 1965, Architectural Institute of Japan; Minister of Education Award, 1968; NSID Golden Triangle Award, U.S.A., 1970. Member, Order of Commendatore, Italy, 1970. Address: Yoshinobu Ashihara Architect and Associates, Sumitomo Seimei Building, 31-15 Sakuragaoka-cho, Shibuya-ku, Tokyo 150, Japan.

Works:

1956 Chuo Koron Building, Tokyo
1959 Hotel Nikko, for Japan Air Lines, Tokyo
Nikko Youth Hostel, Nikko, Japan
1960 Yokohama Municipal Hospital
1962 Takamatsu Red Cross Hospital, Takamatsu, Japan
Ofuna Botanical Garden, Kanagawa, Japan
Okayama Prefectural Children's Hall, Okayama, Japan
1963 Kagawa Prefectural Library, Takamatsu, Japan
Master plan for the International Conference Hall, Kyoto
1964 Komazawa Olympic Gymnasium and Control Tower, Tokyo
Kawasaki Nikko, for Japan Air Lines, Kawasaki, Japan
Musashino Fine Arts University, Tokyo
1966 Ibaragi Prefectural Cultural Center, Mito, Japan
Sony Building, Tokyo
1967 Japanese Pavilion, *Expo '67*, Montreal
Kiyose Housing Community Center, Tokyo
Suginami Ward Welfare Hall, Tokyo

1969 Fuji Film Building, Tokyo
Institute for International Studies and Training, Shizuoka, Japan
Australian Pavilion, *Expo '70,* Osaka
New Zealand Pavilion, *Expo '70,* Osaka
Italian Pavilion, *Expo '70,* Osaka
1970 Iwanami Publishers' Building, Tokyo
Sekai Boeki Kaikan (restaurant), Tokyo
1971 Ibaragi Prefectural Welfare Hall, Mito, Japan
1972 Health Department Hospital, Ryukyu University, Okinawa
Shiseido Building, Tokyo
1973 Mobil Sekiyu Head Office, Tokyo
1974 KPI Town, Chiba, Japan
IBM Building, Osaka
1975 Australian Pavilion, *Ocean Expo '75,* Okinawa
Mobil Sekiyu Pegasus House, Shizuoka, Japan
1978– Dai-ichi Kangyo Bank Head Office, Tokyo
National History and Folklore Museum, Chiba, Japan

Publications:

By ASHIHARA: books—translation of *Sun and Shadow* by Marcel Breuer, Tokyo 1957; *Exterior Space in Architecture: From the Building to the City,* Tokyo 1962; *Exterior Design in Architecture,* New York 1970; *Gaibu Kukan no Sekkei,* Tokyo 1975; *Aesthetics in Townscape (Machinamino Bigaku),* Tokyo 1979.

On ASHIHARA: books—*New Japanese Architecture* by Udo Kultermann, London 1960; *New Directions in Japanese Architecture* by Robin Boyd, London and New York 1968; *Nuova architettura giapponese* by Egon Tempel, Milan 1969; *Contemporary Japanese Architecture,* edited by Paolo Riani, Florence 1969; articles—in *L'Architecture d'Aujourd'hui* (Paris), September/November 1964; in *Building Ideas* (Sydney), December 1966; in *Baumeister* (Munich), July 1967.

My efforts have been directed to the creation of architectural space, human and functional. In earlier works, I concentrated on the creation of interior space but soon I became equally interested in exterior space. In working on buildings of larger scale in recent years, I have tried to solve the problem of how to integrate interior and exterior space to make an organic unity.

In order to make space with human quality, we must try to organically combine spaces of varied sizes in a building, instead of merely filling stories of equal height with necessary functions. The use of floors of split levels is one of the answers to the problem. I have adopted this method in the Chuo Koron Building (1956) as well as in the Hotel Nikko (1958), a private house in Tokyo, clubhouse, library, and the Musashino Fine Arts University (1964).

The idea of using split levels was further extended in the Sony Building in the Ginza (1966): I made the entire interior space continuous by placing 27 floors on successive different levels. In the design of the Japanese Pavilion for the 1967 World Exhibition in Montreal, I produced continuous space by employing the same concept.

With the increase in size and number of buildings in one architectural complex, I have come to be interested in the problem of how to treat space between buildings. It is natural for an architect to study the space occupied by a building he is designing, but he should also give a meaning to the negative space not occupied by the building. My study on "exterior space in architecture" has been put to practical use in the design of the Olympic Gymnasium and the Control Tower in Komazawa Park (1964) as well as in the design of the Musashino Fine Arts University.

Architecture is the art of creating a space. We must make efforts to create space of better quality with full utilization of modern technology. My future endeavors will continue to be directed to the organic unity of interior and exterior space.

—Yoshinobu Ashihara

Yoshinobu Ashihara's most successful early work was the Sony Building in Tokyo. A cubic spiral of skip floors, it develops a space continuity that works its way throughout the built fabric, eating up the normally static and intractable elements, generating a fabulous appetite for all things spatial by the time it reaches roof level. This helter-skelter of internal connections still has time to present itself succinctly to the street—"the twenty-seven floors on successive, different levels, form a three-dimensional promenade."

From early on in his career Ashihara has pursued solutions to the questions of continuity and flow between interior and exterior spaces, but until his work on the Komazawa Gymnasium for the 1964 Tokyo Olympics he had concentrated primarily on interior spatial composition. For Komazawa, as well as for the Musashino Fine Arts University in Tokyo and the Ibaragi Prefectural Cultural Center, he was able to evolve a distinct hierarchy from exterior to interior, mediated by semi-exterior corridor spaces. But he didn't take this hierarchy at face value and apply it literally: he still possessed the wit to invest his external plazas with a certain quality of enclosure, while his interiors, fed by the quasi-external corridors, had a touch of the exterior about them.

This architecture-of-betweens, composed of discreet volumes set in "proud loneliness" and interconnected by a series of corridor-like life lines, is of course typical of Japanese retrospective space. The principle of space order involved is *Fu-seki* (placement due to circumstance), and the method of spatial composing synthesis is a cluster system *(Chidore-gake),* alterating turns *(Ore-magari),* deflected lines *(Tawani),* and recessed niches *(Kubomi).* The marrying system whereby these elements are brought together and rendered feasible for sustaining the idiosyncratic patterns of everyday social life owes much to Kurokawa's "Media-Space" or *"En-*Space." This architecture-of-the-street—or pilgrimage-space—is necessary for the activation of the scattered entities and can be known by any of these names: free space, play-space, equilibrium-zone, grey-zone, feeling of common possession, expanse for shadows, or in-between-condition.

What we have in Ashihara's work is a programme for an architecture of threshold theatre.

—Chris Fawcett

ASLIN, Charles Herbert.

British. Born in Sheffield, Yorkshire, 15 December 1893. Educated at Sheffield Central School, and the University of Sheffield. Served in the Royal Artillery, on the Western Front, 1916–19. Married Ethel Fawcett Armitage in 1920; had one daughter. Worked in the City Architect's Office, Sheffield, 1919–22; Architect, Borough Engineer's Office, Rotherham, Yorkshire, 1922–26; Deputy County Architect, Hampshire, 1926–29; Borough Architect, Derby, 1929–45; County Architect, Hertfordshire, 1945 until his retirement, 1958. President, Nottinghamshire, Derby and Lincoln Society of Architects, 1941–43; President, Royal Institute of British Architects, 1954–56. Recipient: Bronze Medal, Royal Institute of British Architects, 1957. Fellow, Royal Institute of British Architects; Associate, Institute of Civil Engineers, and Institute of Structural Engineers. Honorary Fellow, American Institute of Architects. *Died* (in Hertford) *18 April 1959.*

Works:

1929/
45 New Exeter Bridge, Police Headquarters, Bus Station, Open Market, River Gardens, Exeter House, Central Improvement Scheme, Schools, Hospitals, etc.—all Derby
1946 Cheshunt Primary School, Cheshunt, Hertfordshire
1947 Junior Mixed School, Essendon, Hertfordshire
Wilbury Junior Mixed School, Letchworth, Hertfordshire
Strathmore Avenue Infants School, Hitchin, Hertfordshire
Belswains Junior Mixed School, Hemel Hempstead, Hertfordshire
Little Green Lanes Junior School, Croxley Green, Hertfordshire
Malvern Way Infants School, Croxley Green, Hertfordshire
Warren Dell Infants School, Watford, Hertfordshire
Highwood Junior Mixed School, Bushey, Hertfordshire
1948/
49 Spencer Junior School, St. Albans, Hertfordshire
Morgan's Walk Junior Mixed School, Hertford
Monkfrith Infants School, East Barnet, Hertfordshire
Cowley Hill Junior School, Borehamwood, Hertfordshire
Leavesden Green Junior School, Watford, Hertfordshire
St. Mary's Infants School, Ware, Hertfordshire
Templewood Junior Mixed School, Welwyn Garden City, Hertfordshire
Highover Junior Mixed School, Hitchin, Hertfordshire
Batford Junior Mixed School, Harpenden, Hertfordshire
Gascoyne Cecil Junior Mixed School, Hatfield, Hertfordshire
Aboyne Lodge Infants School, St. Albans, Hertfordshire
Oxhey Wood Junior School, Oxhey, Watford, Hertfordshire
Cassiobury Junior Mixed School, Watford, Hertfordshire
Maylands Junior School, Hemel Hempstead, Hertfordshire
Maylands Infants School, Hemel Hempstead, Hertfordshire
Whitings Hill Junior Mixed School, Barnet, Hertfordshire
South Hill Junior Mixed School, Hemel Hempstead, Hertfordshire
Mandeville Junior School, St. Albans, Hertfordshire
Fairlands Junior Mixed School, Stevenage, Hertfordshire
St. Meryl Junior Mixed School, Watford, Hertfordshire
1950 Oaklands Infants School, East Barnet, Hertfordshire
St. Mary's Infants School, Baldock, Hertfordshire
Blackthorn Junior School, Welwyn Garden City, Hertfordshire
Grange Junior Mixed School, Letchworth, Hertfordshire
Brookmans Park Junior Mixed School, Hatfield, Hertfordshire
Hazelwood Infants School, Abbots Langley, Hertfordshire
Little Furze Junior School, Oxhey, Watford, Hertfordshire
Little Furse Infants School, Oxhey, Watford, Hertfordshire
Bowmans Green Junior Mixed School, London Colney, Hertfordshire

Charles Herbert Aslin: Cheshunt Primary School, Hertfordshire, 1946

Mill End Junior School, Rickmansworth, Hertfordshire

Stanstead Road Secondary Modern School, Hoddesdon, Hertfordshire

St. Julians Secondary Modern School, St. Albans, Hertfordshire

Adeyfield Secondary Modern School, Hemel Hempstead, Hertfordshire

Sandridgebury Lane Grammar School, St. Albans, Hertfordshire

Howard Secondary Modern School, Welwyn Garden City, Hertfordshire

1951 Greenfields Junior Mixed School, Oxhey, Watford, Hertfordshire

Kenilworth Drive Junior Mixed School, Borehamwood, Hertfordshire

Broom Barns Infants School, Stevenage, Hertfordshire

Cranborne Infants School, Hatfield, Hertfordshire

Brookfield Junior School, Borehamwood, Hertfordshire

Merydene Infants School, Borehamwood, Hertfordshire

Scots Hill Grammar School, Rickmansworth, Hertfordshire

1952 Lea Farm Junior School, Garston, Watford, Hertfordshire

Park Lane Junior Mixed School, Waltham Cross, Hertfordshire

Icknield Infants School, Letchworth, Hertfordshire

Havers Lane Junior Mixed School, Bishops Stortford, Hertfordshire

Livingstone Junior Mixed School, East Barnet, Hertfordshire

Hobbs Hill Junior School, Hemel Hempstead, Hertfordshire

Hobbs Hill Infants School, Hemel Hempstead, Hertfordshire

Saffron Green Junior Mixed School, Borehamwood, Hertfordshire

Site 7 Junior School, Oxhey, Watford, Hertfordshire

Barnet Lane Secondary Modern School, Barnet, Hertfordshire

Old Hale Way Secondary Modern School, Hitchin, Hertfordshire

1953/ 58 Site 7 Infants School, Oxhey, Watford, Hertfordshire

New Green Farm Junior Mixed School, St. Albans, Hertfordshire

Bennets End Junior Mixed School, Hemel Hempstead, Hertfordshire

Chaulden Junior School, Hemel Hempstead, Hertfordshire

Chaulden Infants School, Hemel Hempstead, Hertfordshire

Hillside Junior School, Abbots Langley, Hertfordshire

Bedwell East Junior School, Stevenage, Hertfordshire

Bedwell East Infants School, Stevenage, Hertfordshire

Broom Barns Junior School, Stevenage, Hertfordshire

Cowley Hill Infants School, Borehamwood, Hertfordshire

Blackthorn Infants School, Welwyn Garden City, Hertfordshire

West Shephall Secondary Modern School, Stevenage, Hertfordshire

Bennetts End Secondary Modern School, Hemel Hempstead, Hertfordshire

Bennetts End Grammar School, Hemel Hempstead, Hertfordshire

Leggatts Farm Secondary Modern School, Borehamwood, Hertfordshire

Potters Lane Grammar School, Borehamwood, Hertfordshire

Publications:

By ASLIN: article—"Specialized Developments in School Construction" in *RIBA Journal* (London), no. 1, 1950.

On ASLIN: articles—"Charles Herbert Aslin" in *RIBA Journal* (London), May 1952; "Hertfordshire Schools Development" by K. C. Twist, J. T. Redpath and K. C. Evans, in *The Architects' Journal* (London), 12 May 1955, 26 May 1955, 11 August 1955, 19 April 1956, 2 August 1956.

Charles Herbert Aslin is best known for his Hertfordshire School programme for building 175 schools in 15 years, which has become a well-known case study in the history of prefabrication. After previously working in various local government offices such as Derby, where he had been since 1929, Aslin became County Architect for Hertfordshire in 1945. This was a crucial moment, because of the destruction caused by bombing in London and the Greater London Plan's overspill policy for the creation of four new towns: the Hertfordshire architect was faced with the challenge of providing enough school places for a deluge-rate of growth. Not only was there an acute shortage of school places, but this was also unfortunately accompanied by an acute shortage of manpower, particularly craftsmen in the building industry. Since there was also a shortage of traditional building materials such as timber and bricks, there was clearly a need for some "non-traditional" system of building. Aslin faced the challenge by using prefabrication—specifically by developing a component method for prefabrication (as distinct from the alternative total unit prefabrication method) of standardized factory-made units capable of simple erection on the site by a small number of semi-skilled men. The idea that the building should mainly consist of factory-made units simply erected was the basis of the whole development, and it took advantage of the production potential of light industry that had been built up during the war.

Most of the schools were built in the constructional system that became known as the "Eight-foot three System"—a light frame with precast concrete walling and roofing units on an 8 foot 3 inch grid—of which the prototype was the Cheshunt Primary School, built in 1946. In the following years the annual plans demanded the building of an increasing number of schools. The great advantage of standardizing the component parts, rather than standardizing bay units as most manufacturers of the time had been doing, was that the component method gives much greater flexibility. As Aslin himself wrote, "If you design a whole room, all you can do with it is to stick a series on one end or the other and get something like a train; it only works on the flat. If, however, you go in for small components, you have enormous flexibility, both horizontally and vertically, and can do anything you like." At Cheshunt the 8 ft 3 inch grid was used with the concrete slabs horizontal externally, but after a short time the slabs were used vertically instead, since with 8 foot 3 inch slabs horizontally the only possible aperture in a bay was one of 8 foot 3 inch width, whereas with vertical slabs the opening could be any multiple of the width of the slabs. The 8 foot 3 inch grid was successfully applied to multi-storey buildings, and later other grid modules were also used. The flexibility was such that, with the subsequent improvement in the supply of building materials, such materials as timber could also be incorporated in the development.

The development work was of course not confined to the structure itself, but also covered the services, fittings and equipment of the schools, and Aslin also extended his ideas about prefabrication to such elements as heating and lighting. He also pioneered the use of bold, clear colours in schools.

—Konstantin Bazarov

ASPLUND, (Erik) Gunnar.

Swedish. Born in Stockholm, 22 September 1885. Educated at the Royal Institute of Technology, Stockholm, 1905–09; awarded Royal Institute of Technology Travel Scholarship, 1910: travelled in Germany; studied at a private school of architecture, Stockholm, with Bergsten, Tengbom, Westman and Östberg, 1910–11. Married in 1917. In private practice, Stockholm, 1911 until his death, 1940. Assistant Lecturer, 1912–13, Special Instructor in Ornamental Art, 1917–18, and Professor of Architecture, 1931–40, Royal Institute of Technology, Stockholm. Editor, *Arkitektur,* Stockholm, 1917–20. Recipient: First Prize, Karlshamn Secondary School Competition, 1912; First Prize, Gothenburg Law Courts Competition, 1913; First Prize, with Sigurd Lewerentz, Stockholm South Cemetery Competition, 1914; First Prize, Gustaf Adolf Square Competition, Gothenburg, 1918; First Prize, Kviberg Cemetery Competition, Gothenburg, 1926; First Prize, Kviberg Crematorium Competition, Gothenburg, 1936; First Prize, Stockholm Social Welfare Office Competition, 1938; First Prize, Stockholm City Archives Competition, 1939. *Died* (in Stockholm) *30 October 1940.*

Works:

1909 Elementary school, Hälsingborg, Sweden (competition project)
Swedish Church, Paris (competition project)
1912 Elementary school, Kalmar, Sweden (competition project)
Rosenberg Villa, Karlshamn, Sweden (project)
Timmermansorden (Order of Carpenters) Building, Stockholm (competition project; with Berven)
1912/
18 Secondary school, Karlshamn, Sweden
1913 Law Courts rebuilding and extension, Gothenburg (competition project)
Mixed school, Hedemora, Sweden (competition project)
Selander Villa, Örnsköldsvik, Sweden
Sturegarden, Nyköping, Sweden
1914 Dr. Ruth's Villa, Kuusankoski, Finland
Stockholm South Cemetery (competition project; with Sigurd Lewerentz)
1915 Entrance buildings, Hammarby Sports Ground, Stockholm
1915/
24 Carl Johan Elementary School, Gothenburg
1916 Steel Rope Factory Housing, Ekaterinoslav, Russia
Law Courts rebuilding and extension, Gothenburg (2nd project)
1917 Workers' housing, Stockholm
Götatsplatsen Square, Gothenburg (competition project)
Interiors, *Home Exhibition of the Swedish Society of Arts and Crafts,* Stockholm
1917/
18 Snellman Villa, Djursholm, near Stockholm
Tisenhult Manor restoration, near Katrineholm, Sweden
1917/
21 Lister County Court, Sölvesborg, Sweden
Workers' housing, Tidaholms bruk, Sweden
Brokind Manor extension and restoration, Ostergotland, Sweden (project)
Gustaf Adolf Square redevelopment, Gothenburg (competition project)
Cemetery, Vasteräs, Sweden (project)
1918/
20 Woodland Chapel, Stockholm South Cemetery
1919 St. Eriksplan Railway Goods Station, Stockholm (project; with Ture Tideblad)
1919/
20 Law Courts and Stock Exchange reconstruction, Gustaf Adolf Square, Gothenburg (project)
1920 Interiors, *Workshops Society Exhibition,* Stockholm
1920/
28 City Library, Stockholm
1921 Cemetery extension, Almunge, Sweden
Helgeandsholmen, Stockholm (competition project)
Prince Oscar Bernadotte's Family Vault, Stockholm North Cemetery
1922 Bridge and Road Approaches, Klevaliden, Sweden
Royal Chancellery Buildings, Stockholm (competition project; with Ture Ryberg)
1922/
23 Skandia Cinema, Stockholm
1922/
24 Offices, Stockholm South Cemetery
Pavilion, *Paris Exposition of 1925* (competition project)
1924/
25 Admiral Sten Ankarcrona's Family Vault, Stockholm North Cemetery
Assembly Hall interiors, Restaurant Gillet, Stockholm
1924/
29 Cemetery, Oxelösund, Sweden

1925 Law Courts reconstruction and extension, Gothenburg (3rd project)
Sculpture, City Library Park, Stockholm (competition project; with Ivar Johnsson)
Kviberg Cemetery, Gothenburg (competition project)
Odenhallen Market Hall, Stockholm (project)
1926/
28 Rettig Family Vault, Stockholm North Cemetery
1927/
35 Park development plan for the City Library, Stockholm
1928 Arvfursten Palace reconstruction and extension, Stockholm (project)
1928/
30 Design of the *Stockholm Exhibition*
1929/
36 Secondary school extension, Karlshamn, Sweden
1931 Swedish Society of Arts and Crafts Building renovation, Nybrogatan 7, Stockholm
1932 Stockholm Breweries Apartment Building, Norr Mälarstrand, Stockholm (competition project)
Kviberg Cemetery Chapel, Gothenburg (competition project)
Malmö Museum, Sweden (competition project)
1933 Gustaf Carlström Houseboat (project)
National Museum interiors, Stockholm (project)
1933/
35 Bredenberg Department Store, Stockholm
1933/
37 State Laboratory for Biological Research, Stockholm
1934 Bromma Airport, Stockholm (project)
B. Beckstrom Summer Residence, Stavsnas, Sweden
1934/
37 Law Courts reconstruction and extension, Gothenburg
1935 Stockholm Tower, Skansen, Stockholm (project)
1935/
37 Chapel, Oxelösund, Sweden
1935/
40 Woodland Crematorium, Stockholm South Cemetery
1936 Students Corps Building, Uppsala (project)
1936/
40 Kviberg Cemetery Crematorium, Gothenburg
Stennäs House (Asplund House), Sorunda Parish, Stockholm
Stockholm Tower and Square, Maritime Museum, Stockholm (project)
1937/
40 Skövde Crematorium, Sweden (not completed)
State Veterinary Bacteriological Laboratory, Stockholm (not completed)
1938/
39 Social Welfare Offices, Stockholm (competition project)
1939 Apartment block, Malmskillnadsgatan, Stockholm (project)
1939/
40 City Archives, Stockholm (not completed)

Publications:

By ASPLUND: articles—writings in *Arkitekture* (Stockholm), 1917–20, and *Byggmästaren* (Stockholm), 1920–40; "The City of Gothenburg" in *Byggmästaren* (Stockholm), no. 10, 1939; "The Cemetery of Stockholm" in *Byggmästaren* (Stockholm), no. 19, 1940.

On ASPLUND: books—*Swedish Architecture of the Twentieth Century* by Hakon Ahlberg, London 1925; *Verso un'Architettura Organica* by Bruno Zevi, Milan 1945; *E. Gunnar Asplund* by Bruno Zevi, Milan 1948; *Gunnar Asplund, Architect, 1885–1940*, edited by Gustav Holmdahl, Sven Ivar Lind and Kjell Odeen, Stockholm 1950; *Gunnar Asplund: A Great Modern Architect* by Eric de Maré, London 1955; articles—"Sweden's First Functionalist" by Bruno Zevi in *Architectural Record* (New York), April 1938; "The Crematorium in Stockholm" by Hakon Ahlberg in *Byggmästaren* (Stockholm), no. 19, 1940; "E. Gunnar Asplund: A Tribute" by P. Morton Shand in *Architectural Review* (London), May 1941; "L'Ultima Opera di Asplund" by Attilio Podesta in *Casabella* (Milan), September 1941; "The Work of E. G. Asplund" by Francesco Fariello in *L'Architettura* (Rome), October 1942.

Gunnar Asplund was Sweden's most important architect between the wars. He was not a great innovator like Le Corbusier, Gropius and Wright, but he was a great artist, and though by nature no doctrinaire teacher he was a leading light in a generation of pre-war designers in Sweden that included Östberg, Tengbom, Eriksson, Hedqvist, Ahren and Markelius whose work brought world-wide respect. He is recalled by those who knew him as a man of great kindliness, warmth and, in spite of his fame, surprising modesty. His early work belongs to that brilliant period of neo-classical romance called Swedish Grace—a term the functional puritans were to dub Pseudish Grace. Later he was converted to the Modern Movement of the 1930's.

Born and bred in Stockholm, he was trained at the city's Technical High School and the Academy of Art. After graduating in 1909 he entered a number of competitions, particularly for schools, in which he won two first prizes. His first major design was the extension to the Gothenburg Law Courts, for which he gained first prize in a 1913 competition. This started a controversy that lasted twenty years, and his final design, a complete departure from the original, was not executed until 1937.

At the close of 1913 Asplund set off, with funds he had earned, on a Grand Tour of Europe. On his return the following year he won, in partnership with his friend Sigurd Lewerentz, an important international competition for the lay-out of Stockholm South Cemetery with a design that sensitively exploited the Scandinavian pinewoods of the site. It was here that Asplund's greatest work, the Woodland Crematorium, was to be completed in 1940.

A number of commissions for other cemeteries, for private houses and small provincial jobs followed. He also edited *Arkitekture* for a while. During the First World War he won second prize for the Carl Johan School in Gothenburg, which was later commissioned, and he designed dwellings for the Russian Steel Rope Factory at Ekaterinoslov, some workers' emergency dwellings in Stockholm, and the charming, if stylized, Snellman Villa at Djursholm near Stockholm. After the war he won another first in a competition for the lay-out of Gustaf Adolf Square in Gothenburg, and at this time his enchanting little Woodland Chapel in the South Cemetery was built with its high-pitched roof and internal dome supported by Doric columns. A work of 1923 was the romantic and colourful fantasy of the Skandia Cinema in Stockholm, the overtones here being Pompeian pastiche. He then conceived his famous Stockholm City Library with a great central cylinder—a symmetrical, transitional design of geometrical modernity with eclectic detailing, in curious contrast with Östberg's City Hall, at last finished, after fourteen year's effort, the previous year, the swan song of Europe's Arts and Crafts Movement.

While the Library was nearing competition, the *Stockholm Exhibition* was being planned. In 1930 it burst up on an astonished public, trumpeting the new age of *Funkis*—of machine aesthetic and social realism. Le Corbusier had not shouted his staccato

Gunnar Asplund: Woodland Crematorium, Stockholm, 1940

aphorisms in vain. Here Asplund boldly but gracefully embraced the new creed. Though it had but a may-fly life, the exhibition was the herald of a revolution in Scandinavian architecture. It was not large, and it concentrated on housing and domestic artifacts, its first aim being to improve public taste in the design of everyday things made in factories.

Asplund's style had undergone a radical change, but he was too great a creative individualist to become firmly bound by the joyless rigidity of the new movement. His first important job after the Exhibition was the Bredenberg Department Store in Stockholm which is uncompromisingly "modern" in its glass walls and engineered framework, though the detailing is as meticulous and elegant as ever. This was followed between 1935 and 1937 by the austere State Laboratory for Bacteriological Research in Stockholm and the Kviberg Cemetery Crematorium in Gothenburg. A year later he built for himself and his family a small and endearing summer residence in the Stockholm archipelago that reveals his usual concern with marrying a building to its site. He then won two more competitions, but he did not live to see them accomplished: the Stockholm Welfare Offices and the Stockholm City Archives building.

Asplund's final work is an architectural landmark of our century. It has absorbed the crude but cleansing puritanism of Functionalism but goes beyond it to prove that simplicity need not be boring, monumentality be pompous, refinement be weakness or romance be sentimentality. Biblical is the word the architect himself found to describe it. This is his masterly, timeless Woodland Crematorium where buildings and landscape form a single, moving entity. It was completed the year he died in 1940. *Si monumentum requiris. . . . '*

—Eric de Maré

ATELIER 5.

Partnership; established, Berne, Switzerland, 1955. Partners: Jacques Blumer, born 1937; Anatole du Fresne, born 1939; Ralph Gentner, born 1929; Christiane Heimgartner, born 1936; Rolf Hesterberg, born 1927; Hans Hostettler, born 1925; Pierluigi Lanini, born 1938; Alfredo Pini, born 1932; Denis Roy, born 1935; Bernard Stebler, born 1935; Fritz Thormann, born 1930; administration—Christian Flückiger, born 1929. Recipient: First Prize, Lima, Peru International Housing Development Competition, United Nations, 1969; Housing Design Award, Department of the Environment, London, 1971; First Prize, Swiss National Bank Competition, Berne, 1974; Paul Bonatz Prize, Stuttgart, 1975; First Prize, Kunstmuseum Competition, Berne, 1976; Design Award, 1977, and Hugo Häring Award, 1978, Bund Deutscher Architekten. Address: Atelier 5, Architekten und Planer, Sandrainstrasse 3, CH-3007 Berne, Switzerland.

Works:

1957 Flamatt I Rowhouses, Flamatt, Switzerland
1958 House, Rothrist, Switzerland (additions in 1964)
1959 House, Motier, Switzerland (additions in 1968)
     Apartment house, Seftigenstrasse, Berne
     Muller Factory, Thun, Switzerland
1960 Flamatt II Rowhouses, Flamatt, Switzerland
     Week-end house, Zofingen, Switzerland
     Apartment house, Weissenbuhlweg, Berne
1961 Taillepied Neighborhood Development Plan, Lutry, Switzerland (project)
     Halen Housing Estate, near Berne
     Two-family house, Bolligen, Switzerland
     Gfeller Company Factory, Flamatt, Switzerland
1962 House, Villars-sur-Glane, Switzerland
     Werkhof Burren Storage Building, Flamatt, Switzerland
1963 Apartment house, Biel, Switzerland
     Apartment house, Flamatt, Switzerland
     Radio Monitoring Station, Berne
     Belmont Museum, Lausanne, Switzerland (project)
     Migros Shopping Center, Roggwil, Switzerland
1964 Local plan for Bösingen, Switzerland
     Miroir New Town, Lutry, Switzerland (project)
     La Combe Neighborhood Development Plan, Lutry, Switzerland
     House, Carona, Switzerland
     Engineering School, Biberach, Germany (competition project)
1965 Urban design for the Ruhwald District of Berlin (competition project)

Rowhouses, Park Hill Village, Croydon, Surrey, England
House, Gerlafingen, Switzerland
Apartment house, Rodtmattstrasse, Berne
Apartment house, Urtenen, Switzerland
1966 Town expansion plan for Karlstadt, Germany (competition project)
Town expansion plan, stage I, Steinhagen, Germany
District plan, stage I, for Werther, Germany
Neighborhood development plan for Bad Godesberg, Bonn, Germany (project)
Two-family house with veterinary office, Kerzers, Switzerland
Apartment building, Morillonstrasse, Berne
Open space study for a cemetery at Lutry, Switzerland
1968 Local plan for Lutry, Switzerland
Local plan for Zollikofen, Berne (competition project)
Week-end house, Sardinia, Italy
House, Boll-Sinneringen, Switzerland
Apartment building, Lyss, Switzerland
1969 Local plans for Aarberg and Tafers, Switzerland
Previ-Lima Housing Estate, Peru (competition project)
Expansion plan for Solingen, Germany (project)
National Building Code Study, Zurich
House with graphic arts studio, Oberhöchstadt, Frankfurt, Germany (additions in 1973)
1970 Regional plan for Burgdorf, Switzerland
Local plans for Bellmund, Bödeli, Interlaken and Neuenegg, Switzerland
Local plan for regional center, Lyss, Switzerland
Park Hill Village Neighborhood Development Plan, stage I, Croydon, Surrey, England
Brunnadern Apartments, Berne
Rainpark Rowhouses and Apartments, Brügg, Switzerland
Apartment building, Burgdorf, Switzerland
Highway retaining wall improvement, Flamatt, Switzerland
1971 Local plans for Flamatt, Frutigen, Ipsach, Plasselb, Port and Reichenbach, Switzerland
School Design Competition Plan, Neuenegg, Switzerland
1972 Local plan for Sutz-Lattrigen, Switzerland
City center redevelopment, Solingen, Ohligs, Germany (competition project)
Student housing, University of Stuttgart
Rowhouses, Regerstrasse, Solingen, Germany
House, Bumpliz, Germany
Meeting house, Charmey, Switzerland
Catholic church, Flamatt, Switzerland
Colora Printing Dyes Factory, Flamatt, Switzerland
1973 Economic development plan for Oberes Emmental, Switzerland (with the University of Berne Economic Study Group)
Local plans for Bühl, Kleinbösingen, Nidau, and Täuffelen, Switzerland
Neighborhood development plans for Radevormwald Dahlerau, Germany, and Burgerbeunden Nidau and Risgrund Flamatt, Switzerland
Environmental study, Biel-Löhre, Switzerland
Buhnenberg Housing Estate, Oftringen, Switzerland (project)
Schroderweg Housing Estate, Dahlerau, Germany (project)
Apartment building, Adelboden, Switzerland
Planning study, Bözingefeld, Switzerland
Local plan review, Ried Köniz, Berne
1974 Local plans for Albligen, Interlaken, Matten, Unterseen, and Sonceboz, Switzerland

Village center plans for Flamatt, Oftringen and Thörishaus, Switzerland
Neighborhood development plan for Gwanne Reichenbach, Switzerland
Thalmatt Housing Estate, Berne
Galerie Bischofberger, Zurich
Gewerbehaus Thalmatt Office Building, Thalmatt, Switzerland (project)
1975 Economic development plan for Kandertal, Switzerland
Local plans for Alterswil, Barbereche and Hochstetten, Switzerland
Village master plan for Lyss, Switzerland
Harbor neighborhood development plan, Seebucht Spiez, Switzerland
Building code regulations, State of Freiburg, Switzerland (as associates)
Apartment building, Sandrainstrasse, Berne
1976 Economic development plan for Trachselwald, Switzerland
Local plan for Tramelan, Switzerland (project)
Village center master plan for Bösingen, Switzerland
Community development plan for Bernfeld Aarberg, Switzerland
Design of the *Berne Festival*
Lorraine Housing Estate, Burgdorf, Switzerland
Orangery Stadtgärtnerei Building alterations and restoration, Berne
Kunstmuseum alterations and additions, Berne (project)
Student Center and Dining Hall, University of Stuttgart
1977 Economic development plan for Center-Jura, Switzerland (with the Neuchatel University Economic Studies Group)
Neighborhood development master plan for Scheuerfeld Tauffelen, Switzerland
Plan for a vacation community, Udrischa Ettenberg, Switzerland (project)
Staatsbank Headquarters Building, State of Freiburg, Switzerland (competition project)
1978 Commercial School alterations and renovation, Berne
1980 State Teachers College expansion, Thun, Switzerland
Savings and Loan Bank alterations and additions, Berne
1982 Amthaus Building alterations and additions, Berne
Swiss National Bank Building, Offices and Shopping Center (conversion of the Kaiser Complex), Berne

Publications:

On ATELIER 5: books—*The New Architecture in Europe* by G. Kidder Smith, London and New York 1961; *Industrial Buildings: An International Survey* by W. Henn, Munich 1962; *New Swiss Architecture* by A. Altherr, Lausanne 1964; *The New Brutalism* by Reyner Banham, Stuttgart, London and New York 1966; *New Directions in Swiss Architecture* by Bachmann and Stanislaus von Moos, New York 1969; *Entwurf und Planung Studentenheime* by Hans Schmalscheidt, Munich 1973; *Differentiated Housing Estates* by G. Schwab, Stuttgart 1974; articles—in *Werk* (Zurich), November 1958, May 1962, January 1963, March 1972, March 1975; *Architectural Design* (London), November 1959, September 1962, February 1963, April 1965, April 1970; *Casabella* (Milan), no. 258, 1961; *L'Architecture d'Aujourd'hui* (Paris), no. 103, 1962, no. 131, 1965, February/March 1968, November/December 1973; *Deutsche Bauzeitung* (Stuttgart), January 1966; *Baumeister* (Munich), September 1966, February 1970, March 1972, April 1972, December 1972, December 1973, May 1976, March 1978; *Architecture + Urbanism* (Tokyo), December 1971, October 1975, December 1977; and March 1978; *Global Architecture* (Tokyo), no. 23, 1973.

In our office an architectural design is never made by one single person, not even in the very first stage. From the beginning there are always at least two persons working together. In general the architects in charge discuss the different aspects of the problem before they begin to make the first drafts for its solution. Of course we make sketches to arrive at a mutual understanding (but these sketches are not really drafts); in doing so, we discuss various ways of tackling the problem. We look for the essential crux of the problem, the way to give the most extensive but also the most typical expression to the problem.

For example, the design of the Student Center for the University of Stuttgart took shape when we decided to tackle the problem of relating each single place or table to its surroundings. The narrow column-grid originated from this, and when we carried through this fundamental idea, the building took its shape. The fundamental principle for the building therefore originated from an extreme simplification of the whole problem and from concentrating on a central idea which a simple sketch could illustrate. This principle was the starting-point for the consequent execution of a very complex building.

As we often have long discussions before making an actual design, we almost never have to devise alternatives; they are discussed as possibilities in advance. We elaborate real alternatives only in cases where the original conditions are changed by the actual work, or where the problem or program must be determined by the work. This process is valuable in planning and town-planning, when the program becomes part of the design.

In the beginning of Atelier 5, the search for form had a greater importance than it does now; that is, our designs were more the result of formal considerations. Today, form grows as we interpret a basic idea. The design of the Student Center would probably not have been possible 15 years ago, because the problem of the unitary form of the building would have been too important to us. In those days we would have used more "traditional" methods to trying to realize the program with harmonic cubical forms. Today the form occurs when we elaborate the fundamental idea. We rarely proceed from formal conceptions because our designs are always the result of teamwork and because the same people do not always work together. Goals of essential content can be discussed, but formal conceptions are very difficult to discuss.

We see ourselves as both theorists and practitioners. Our plans always originate from theories that arise from a large number of influences from different fields—but they are not treated in a scientific manner. We work, according to our talents and experience, on a very wide basis. We always try to realize any commission by considering all the problems from as many aspects as possible, but we don't attempt to follow, or create, some theoretical treatise. All the same, we appreciate the work of the theorist who perhaps extends the profession of the architect to the point where he cannot himself build any longer because his theories can only find their realization in Utopia: the theorist can create attitudes that are important in the actual design process. The practitioner can as well be justified in developing theories about building and planning that will become a basis for carrying out actual building. In this sense it is, for us, not a solution to unify completely the profession of architect because in that way the activity that can be influenced by the architect is narrowed.

Nor do we believe that the profession of the architect should be organized like an industrial concern, that there should be a division of labor, for example between design and executive work. Our way of working attempts a continuity from planning up to supervision of the building site—not only continuity of thought but also continuity of persons. We think that the "idea" of a building cannot be preserved when it passes through different departments if it is

Atelier 5: Thalmatt Housing Estate, Berne, 1974

not accompanied by the same one or two persons from the beginning to the end. The profession of the architect should not be limited; it should be organized on a very wide basis.

—Atelier 5

Atelier 5 says: "In the beginning of Atelier 5, the search for form had a greater importance than it does now; that is, our designs were more the result of formal considerations. Today, form grows as we interpret a basic idea."

The statement is particularly informative; it calls attention to an essential aspect of the change in the ideas of the architectural avant-garde during the last twenty years. Until then "the new"—in accordance with the pioneer ideologies of the first two decades of this century—had, to a large extent, appeared as a visible interpretation of a "Manifesto for Modern Construction." In contrast, since the beginning of the 1970's a more complete relationship with the environment has begun to prevail, and greater importance is now placed on problems of historic continuity and formal integration. I don't refer to a renaissance of the ideas of the 1940's about a "native style" (though a trend in this direction, with modern trimmings, is distinctly apparent in one of the newest Swiss housing estates); I mean, rather, that contemporary avant-garde architects, and an ever-increasing circle of progressive thinkers concerned with architecture, recognize and accept as pertinent problems, in new building, the maintenance of existing constructions and a more meaningful use of human living space as a means of an improvement in the quality of life. There has been such a development in Atelier 5's conception of building, a development that is clear if one compares an early work, the

Halen Housing Estate of 1961, with the current "Kaiser" development in Berne, scheduled for completion in 1982.

Halen is one of the best-known, and, among experts, the most popular, of the new housing estates in Switzerland. There was hardly an architectural student in the 1960's who didn't attempt a "Halen Project." Similarly, there were architects who constantly produced "Halen Variations." Even now the influence of Halen in Swiss architecture remains strong. Yet Halen can in no way be taken as a model for a contemporary housing estate. It was exceptional in practically every respect—from the point of view of the planning concept ("collective estates for individualists"); in relation to the uniform class of the inhabitants (almost without exception, independent professional intellectuals); and, with regard to the particularly favorable topographical situation of the building site (a clearing surrounded on all sides by dense forest, an ideal prerequisite for a unique, architectonically planned collective total concept).

The most characteristic feature of the total concept of Halen is the estate plan itself, which is based on the traditional grid plan of the Old Town of Berne, thereby creating an extremely interesting historical building dialogue. Yet, in spite of this remarkable integration of a planning principle rooted in local tradition in a housing estate conceived for contemporary needs, Halen dominates as a deliberate manifesto for "the new architecture," the form language of Le Corbusier, the architect that Atelier 5 regarded as its true mentor.

Typically, the initial planning and erection of Halen did not allow for any subsequent extensions or additions. But it remains unique; the designers have succeeded in an outstanding way in building an es-

tate that, with one exception, the restaurant/community area, is a perfectly functioning realization of the goal of "more collectivity in planning on behalf of the greater individual freedom of all."

The Kaiser Complex was built in 1903 in a central position in the Old Town of Berne. In 1974 an architectural competition was organized for the erection of the Swiss National Bank on the same site, without modification of the existing facades. Atelier 5 won the competition.

A direct comparison of Atelier 5's Kaiser design with that of the Halen Estate makes little sense. Much more interesting are the principles which lie behind these two projects separated by twenty years.

Twenty years ago Atelier 5, with the building of Halen, brilliantly achieved the realization of a manifesto: Le Corbusier's language of form was central to their design. But Halen stood partially "on the green meadow," and did not need to take into consideration neighboring buildings. Kaiser, however, is an old building; it has been integrated for many years with the buildings of the Old Town of Berne; it is to be developed as a combined business, shopping and office centre—and such a project involves essentially different demands from those of Halen.

On the basis of the competition program Atelier 5 came to the conclusion that "the client, presented with the program for the future use of space, did not believe that it could be achieved by renovation of the old building." It says much for Atelier 5 that, in spite of this attitude, they recommended renovation and substantiated their recommendation with skilful argument, with the result that they won the competition and are now executing the project.

It is not yet completed. The coming years will show whether it will one day stand as a recommendation for the meaningful preservation of existing buildings and have as lasting an influence on the future architectural scene as Halen has had in the past on the architecture of the modern estate.

—Urs Graf

ATHFIELD, Ian (Charles).

New Zealander. Born in Christchurch, 15 July 1940. Educated at Christchurch Boys High School, 1954–58; Auckland University School of Architecture, under R. H. Toy, 1961–63, Dip.Arch. 1963. Married Nancy Clare Cookson in 1962; children: Jesse and Zachary. Architect, Stephenson and Turner, Auckland, 1963; Architect, 1963–65, and Partner, 1965–68, Structon Group Architects, Wellington. Since 1968, Principal, Athfield Architects, Wellington. Exhibitions: *5 New Zealand Architects,* Wellington, 1974; *International Union of Architects Exhibition,* Vancouver Art Gallery, 1976. Recipient: Design Award, Auckland Architectural Association, 1968, 1972, 1978; Silver Medal, 1972, and Bronze Medal, 1975, New Zealand Institute of Architects; New Zealand Tourist and Publicity Design Award, 1975; First Prize, International Housing Design Competition, Manila, Philippines, 1976. Address: Athfield Architects, P. O. Box 3364, 105 Amritsar Street, Wellington 4, New Zealand.

Works:

1968 Imrie House, Whangarei, New Zealand
P.A. 71 Housing Units, Wellington
Athfield House, Wellington
Jones House, Christchurch
Plimmers Emporium Shopping Centre, Wellington
1969 McIntyre House, Wellington
Slim House, Wellington
Porteous House, Wellington
Jackson House, Wellington
1970 Nathan House, Wellington
Arlington Apartments, Wellington (with King and Dawson)
Manson House, Wellington
Buch House, Wellington
James House, Wellington
Johnson House, Wellington
Sampsan House, Wellington
1971 Gymnasium, University of Victoria, Wellington
Elder House, Wellington
Merwood House, Wellington
Sindall House, Wellington
St. Columbans Mission House, Wellington
1972 Davis Mission House, Coromandel, New Zealand
Wakatipu Trading Post Shopping Mall, Queenstown, New Zealand
Motel units, Queenstown, New Zealand
House restoration, 12 Boulcott Street, Wellington
1973 Monopoli House, Nelson, New Zealand
Grand Hotel restoration, Palmerston North, New Zealand
Cole House, Auckland
Bailey House, Wellington
1974 Carruthers House, Wellington
Logan House, Wellington
Cates House, Auckland
McKenzie House, Wellington
Sparkes House, Wellington
King House, Wellington
Zander House, Wellington
Jamieson House, Wellington
Army Workshops, Waiouru, New Zealand
1975 Cox House, Wellington
1977 Hogg House, Wellington

Marlborough Club, Blenheim, New Zealand
Moore Wilson Ltd. Warehouse, Wellington

Publications:

On ATHFIELD: books—*Architecture an Involvement,* Wellington 1963; *The Architecture of Self-Help Communities* by Michael Seelig, New York 1978; *Joyful Architecture* by Gerald Melling, Wellington 1978; articles—"Houses for People or People for Houses" in *New Zealand Listener* (Wellington), August 1971; "Bird of Paradise" in *Designscape* (Wellington), October 1972; "Winds of Change" in *New Zealand Home Journal* (Auckland), December 1972; "A House You Can't Ignore" in *Thursday* (Auckland), September 1973; "Kiwi Concrete" in *Design* (London), December 1974; "Lots of Ups and Downs" by Nanette Cameron in *Thursday* (Auckland), December 1974; "Medieval Disney" in *Australian Post* (Sydney), February 1975; "Intuitions by Athfield" in *New Zealand Listener* (Wellington), April 1976; "Human Settlements" in *Architectural Record* (New York), May 1976; "New Zealand Architect Flouts the Rules" by Paul Goldberger in the *New York Times,* June 1976; "Prelude au Congrès de Vancouver" in *L'Architecture d'Aujourd'hui* (Paris), July 1976; "Athfield under Attack" by Boyce Richardson in *New Zealander Listener* (Wellington), July 1976; "Habitat" by Ian Hagan in *RIBA Journal* (London), August 1976; three articles in the *Christian Science Monitor* (Boston), 6, 13 and 23 August 1976; "Habitat—Self-Help Housing" in *Designscape* (Wellington), October 1976; "Urban Revival" in *New Zealand Listener* (Wellington), July 1977; "The Perfect Family Home" in *Australian Women's Day* (Sydney), August 1977; "Squatter Space" in *New Zealand Listener* (Wellington), October 1977; film —*Architect Athfield,* New Zealand National Film Unit, Wellington, 1977.

Athfield Architects is a co-operative, design-based practice of five people. The practice, which I started in 1968, has a strong influence on the current New Zealand architectural scene, albeit mainly through small-scale domestic buildings. International recognition was gained by the office in 1976 by winning the International Competition for the Urban Environment of Developing Countries, Manila, Philippines. Current interests are in community-involved building projects and knocking the bastions of architectural professionalism, the sanctity of design and town planning.

—Ian Athfield

Ian Athfield's work as an architect, brief as it has been to date, has called into question many of the

Ian Athfield: Athfield House Tower, Wellington, 1968

assumptions of the Modern Movement and is contributing to the reappraisal of architecture in New Zealand. Athfield's buildings, among the steep hills of Wellington, have from their inception commanded attention and consideration. Their apparent strident, arbitrary and flamboyant forms belie the strong sense of order and integrity in the use of materials and also the intense radical concern for society that informs Athfield's thinking.

Athfield spent his early years in Christchurch, where he was fortunate to experience a wave of enthusiasm, care and concern for buildings that was characteristic of that city in the early 1960's. Later, as a student, Athfield moved to the Auckland University School of Architecture and the tutelage of Professor R. H. Toy and Lecturer Peter Middleton. It was here in the 1960's—during the usual iconoclastic activities of students and the plethora of visual opportunities—that Athfield became attracted to the authentic use of materials in the work of Antonio Gaudi and Mies van der Rohe. He was conscious of the relationship of their work to its setting and aware of the necessity of communities to have a building heritage. He quickly set about obtaining a thorough understanding of materials and basic building techniques.

The dichotomy of allowing for complete and free-ranging change and the desire for permanence and stability of structure have produced in Athfield the flowering of a Renaissance. A fundamental part of his quest has been the need to produce a philosophical framework capable of absorbing the variety of architectural forms, while at the same time maintaining some reality in a radically changing society.

Athfield's strong social concern and his attempts to understand and design within communities have led him into some exciting and frustrating programmes both overseas and in New Zealand. Reactions to his work have been equivocal, and the conflict he has had with planning bureaucracies has caused him to fear that we could very easily destroy ourselves in the quest for learning to cope with our society and environment. In spite of many setbacks, he has remained firm in his convictions as to the value of good building to a community's life and health.

Ian Athfield's contribution to the health of architecture in New Zealand has been quite profound, and his work to date in the midst of the New Zealand landscape promises well for a significant radical architectural stake in the future.

—W. H. Alington

AULENTI, Gae(tana).

Italian. Born in Palazzolo dello Stella (Udine), 4 December 1927. Educated at the Milan Polytechnic School of Architecture, Dip.Arch. 1954; Palazzola dello Stella, Udine. In private practice in Milan since 1954. Assistant Professor of Architectural Composition, Faculty of Architecture, University of Venice, 1960–62; Adjunct Assistant Professor of the Elements of Architectural Composition, Faculty of Architecture, Milan Polytechnic, 1964. Visiting Lecturer, College of Architecture, Barcelona, and the Cultural Center, Stockholm, 1969–75. Member, Editorial Staff, *Casabella,* Milan, 1954–62. Member, Board of Directors, *Lotus,* Milan, since 1974. Member, Studies for Architecture Movement, Milan, 1955–61. Member, Association for Industrial Design, Milan, since 1960 (Vice-President, 1966). Exhibitions: *Triennale,* Milan, 1960, 1963; *Aspects of Contemporary Art,* Aquila, Italy, 1963; *Gae Aulenti,* Gimbels, New York, 1967; *Italian Design,* Hallmark Gallery, New York, 1968; *Italy: The New Domestic Landscape,* Museum of Modern Art, New York,

1972. Recipient: Grand International Prize, *Triennale,* Milan, 1960–64; First Prize, with V. Magistretti, Meda Elementary School Competition, 1967; First Prize, Directional Center Competition, Perugia, 1971. Honorary Member, Italian National Society of Interior Designers, 1967, and American Society of Interior Designers, 1976. Address (office): 4 Piazza S. Marco, 20121 Milan, Italy.

Works:

1958 House and Stable, San Siro, Milan
1960 *New Design for Italian Furniture* exhibition interiors, Milan
      Week-end house, Brianza, Italy
1962 Elementary school, Monza, Italy (competition project)
1963 Holiday house, Tonale Pass, Italy
      House in a Wood (project)
1964 Tempo delle Vacanze Pavilion, *Triennale,* Milan
1967 Olivetti Shop, Paris
      Max Mara House, Milan
      Elementary school, Meda, Italy (competition project; with V. Magistretti)
      Olivetti Shop, Buenos Aires
1970 Boutique Cadette, Milan
      Design of the *Olivetti Travelling Exhibition*
1971 Knoll Showrooms, Boston
      Garden, Granaiolo, Florence
1972 Fiat Showroom, Turin
      Collector's apartment, Milan
      Private house, Milan
1973 Fiat Showroom II, Turin
      Design of the *Christo Exhibition,* Milan
      Housing Estate, near Milan (project)
1974 Villa, San Michele, Italy
1975 Theatrical Space Project, Naples and Paris (with Luca Ronconi)
      Old House conversion, Portofino, Italy
      Fiat Exhibition Showroom, Brussels
      Fiat Exhibition Showroom, Zurich
      Week-end house, Emilian Plain, Italy
1977 Stage designs for the play *The Wild Duck,* Teatro di Genova, Genoa
      Stage designs for the play *Wozzeck,* Teatro alla Scala, Milan

Publications:

By AULENTI: articles—"Soviet Architecture" in *Casabella* (Milan), April 1962; "Marin County" in *Casabella* (Milan), April 1964.

On AULENTI: articles—"Olivetti à Paris" in *L'Oeil* (Lausanne), May 1967; "Un Ambiente di Apparenza Magica" in *Domus* (Milan), July 1967; "Per la Moda" in *Domus* (Milan), August 1968; "Il Luogo di una Collezione" in *Domus* (Milan), January 1970; "Gae Aulenti: New Force in Italian Design" in *Vogue* (New York), July 1970; "Knoll, New York" in *Architectural Forum* (New York), July-August 1970; "Medium Cool Message" by Alastair Best in *Design* (London), October 1970; "Une Architecture Intérieure pour mettre en Valeur de Précieuses Collections" in *Maison Francaise* (Paris), November 1970; "Knoll International à Boston" in *L'Oeil* (Paris), September-October 1971; "Private House, Milan" in *Japan Interior Design* (Tokyo), July 1972; "Italy: The New Domestic Landscape" in *Architectural Design* (London), August 1972; "Eine Wohnung in Mailand" in *Architektur und Wohnen* (Hamburg), February 1973; "Analisi di un Ambiente" in *Casa Vogue* (Milan), March 1973; "Vue Imprenable sur Rome" in *Connaissance des Arts* (Paris), November 1973; "Hall d'Exposition Fiat à Bruxelles" and "Hall d'Exposition Fiat à Zurich" in *L'Architecture d'Aujourd'hui* (Paris), September 1975; "A Weekend Retreat on the Emilian Plain" in *Architectural Digest* (Los Angeles), November-December 1975; "Living Around the World: Cave of Enchantment in Italy" in *Ideal Home* (London), August 1976.

Nothing is built on stone; all is built on sand, but we must build as if the sand were stone (Jorge Luis Borges).

This quote headed Gae Aulenti's text in the catalogue of the *New Domestic Landscape* exhibition held at the Museum of Modern Art, New York, in 1972, and it is as relevant to her work now—such as the Turin Showroom, Turin, 1973, and the Theatrical Space Project of 1975—as it was to the work presented at that exhibition—a "House Environment" comprising differently articulated pyramids set up at the four corners of a square plinth: this design is made up of elements so composed as always to make their original purpose evident, while at the same time remaining open to a determination of their future purposes.

Gae Aulenti views the condition of architecture as being beyond the strife of governments, war, and hunger. It is concrete space, a positive thing that has as its substance the city, in which the private and collective "join to transform nature through the exercise of reason and memory." None of man's objects, whether monument or den, can escape their relationship to the city, "the place where the human condition is manifested." The existence of an object is defined by the actual circumstance of its own relationship to the city: an object is allowed to come into being and discover its own relationship to other objects by a process not announced by its own independent voice but with that of the city too. The objects with which we deal are very numerous, ranging from the unstable and changeable to the archetype, from the precious relic to the casualty of history.

If these generalizations are true, then "the process of design can only find its proper relationship in a field of which it does not constitute the centre." Aulenti maintains that a domestic environment should not be designed in its general form, for its positive qualities can reside only in the sum of the conditions in accordance with which its spatial elements and attribution of meanings approach a synthesis, "which is possible only by using and testing all the criteria applied to designing a city." Her concern, then, is to make things appear in all their complexity and density, even if the result can represent only a limited part of the whole field.

At present, our choice is restricted to recovering the positive significance of man, who finds fulfillment through creating for himself an aesthetic atmosphere with an aesthetic intention. This choice, which looks forward hopefully to a more authentic existence for man, the rediscovery of his stable and permanent values, has been a poetic one—an arbitrary selection; it has, therefore, an emblematic value, alluding to the exorcism of a new society.

—Chris Fawcett

AYMONINO, Carlo.

Italian. Born in Rome, 18 July 1926. Educated at the University of Rome School of Architecture, Dip. Arch. 1950. Married; has several children. In private practice, Rome, since 1951; Founder/Director, with Maurizio Aymonino, Baldo de Rossi and Alessandro de Rossi, Studio AYDE, since 1960. Assistant Lecturer, University of Rome School of Architecture, 1951–63. Lecturer, 1963–67, Professor, 1968–74, and since 1974 Dean of the Graduate School of Architecture, University of Venice. Co-Editor, *Casabella,* Milan, 1959–64. Exhibition: *Triennale,* Milan, 1969. Recipient: First Prize, Pescara Covered Market Competition, 1954; First Prize, Chamber of Commerce Competition, Massa and Carrara, 1956. Address (office): Via del Boschetto 72, 00184 Rome, Italy.

Carlo Aymonino: G. Marconi School of Science, Pesaro, Italy, 1970

Plan for the center of Breuil, Italy (competition project; with others)

Plan for the city center of Bologna (with others)

Condominium, Via Anagni, Rome (with others)

Apartment and office building, Savona, Italy (with others)

1963 "Tor Carbone" (co-operative residential development), Rome (with others)

1964 Paganini Theatre reconstruction, Parma, Italy (competition project)

"Tor de' Cenci" (housing development), Rome (with others)

1966 Chamber of Deputies Building, Rome (competition project)

1967 Psychiatric Hospital, Mirano, Italy (competition project; with Constantino Dardi)

Monte Amiata Housing Development, Gallaratese, Milan (with Aldo Rossi and others)

1968 Bank of Italy Headquarters, Grosseto, Italy

1970 Centre Beaubourg, Paris (competition project)

G. Marconi School of Science, Pesaro, Italy
High school campus, Pesaro, Italy

1971/
73 Plan for the old city center of Pesaro, Italy (with others)

Plan for the city center of Reggio Emilia, Italy (competition project; with Constantino Dardi)

Plan for the city center of Perugia, Italy (with Constantino Dardi)

Master plan for the University of Florence (competition project; with others)

Elementary school, Abbiategrasso, Italy

New University of Cagliari, Italy (competition project; with others)

New University of Calabria, Italy (competition project; with others)

Piazza XX Settembre redevelopment, Fano, Italy

Cassa di Risparmio, Fano, Italy

"Roma-Est" (housing development), Rome (project; with Constantino Dardi and R. Panella)

1976 National Academy of San Luca, Rome (competition project)

1977 Prager Platz redevelopment, Berlin (competition project)

Law Courts, Ferrara, Italy (with others)

1978 Plan for the city center of Florence (competition project; with Aldo Rossi and others)

1979 Civic Center, Pesaro, Italy

"Semirurali" (housing development), Bolzano, Italy (with others)

Works:

1950 INA-Casa Housing Development, Tiburtino, Rome (with Ludovico Quaroni, M. Ridolfi and others)

1951 "La Tartaruga" (house), Via Innocenzo X, Rome (with Ludovico Quaroni)

1954 Covered market, Pescara, Italy (competition project; with others)

"Spine Bianche" (housing development), Matera, Italy (with others)

1956/
60 Chamber of Commerce Building, Massa and Carrara, Italy

Cassa di Risparmio, Rovigo, Italy (competition project; with others)

1957/
59 "Tratturo dei Preti" (INA-Casa Housing Development), Foggia, Italy (with others)

Apartment building, Via Citerni, Rome (with others)

House, Lungotevere degli Inventori, Rome (with others)

National Library, Rome (competition project; with others)

House, via Tommaso Salvini, Rome (with others)

INA-Casa Housing Development, viale Ofanto, Foggia, Italy (with others)

"Commenda Ouest" (INA-Casa Housing Development), Brindisi, Italy (with others)

Co-operative residential developments, Lecce, Italy (with others)

Piazza Guerra redevelopment, Empoli, Italy (competition project)

Law Courts, Brindisi, Italy (with others)

Co-operative residential developments, Brindisi, Italy (with others)

1960 Condominium, Via Arbia, Rome (with others)

F. Vandone Polio Center, Ospedale Spallanzani, via Portuense, Rome (with others)

Institute of Technology, Brindisi, Italy (with others)

1961 Law Courts, Lecce, Italy (competition project; with others)

Institute of Technology, Lecce, Italy (with others)

1962 Plan for the city center of Turin (competition project)

Publications:

By AYMONINO: books—*La Città Territorio,* editor, Bari, Italy 1964; *La Formazione del Concetto di Tipologia Edilizia,* Venice 1965; *L'Utopia della Realtà,* editor, Bari, Italy, 1965; *Gli Alloggi della Municipalità di Vienna 1922–32,* Rome 1965; *Origine e Sviluppo della Città Moderna,* Padua 1965; *I Centri Direzionali,* with Pierluigi Giordani, Bari 1967; *La Città di Padova,* editor, Rome 1970; *Il Significato delle Città,* Bari 1975; *Le Capitali del XIX Secolo: I Parigi e Vienna,* with others, Rome 1975; *I Catasti Storici di Padova,* editor, Rome 1976; *Lo Studio dei Fenomeni Urbani,* Rome 1977; *1977: Un Progetto per Firenze,* with others, Rome 1978; articles—"Un Dibattito sulla Tradizione in Architettura" in *Casabella* (Milan), no. 206, 1955; "Cronaca e Storia del Quartiere Tiburtino" in *Casabella* (Milan), no. 215, 1957; "Inchiesta Edilizia sulle Città Italiane: Brindisi" in *Casabella* (Milan), no. 222, 1958; "Matera: Mito e Realtà" in *Casabella* (Milan), no. 231, 1959; "Copenhagen" in *Urbanistica* (Turin), March 1960; "15 Anni di Architettura Italiana" in *Casabella* (Milan), no. 251, 1961;

"Roma: Il Sistema dei Centri Direzionali" in *Casabella* (Milan), no. 264, 1962; "La Condizione Edilizia di Roma" in *Casabella* (Milan), September 1963; "Facolta di Tendenza?" in *Casabella* (Milan), no. 287, 1964; "Berlino: Una Città Aperta" in *Casabella* (Milan), no. 288, 1964; "Dibattito sulle Tendenze Attuali dell'Architettura nel Fasciolo Dedicato a Progetti di Architetti Italiani," with others, in *Casabella* (Milan), July 1964; "Ospedale Psichiatrico di Mirano," with Constantino Dardi, and "Il P.R.G. di Bari" in *Lotus* (Venice), no. 6, 1969; "Progetto Architettonico e Formazione della Città" in *Lotus* (Venice), no. 7, 1970; "Due Insediamenti Turisitici nel Mezzogiorno" in *L'Architettura* (Rome), May 1970; "Progetti dello Studio Semerani-Tamaro 1965–1971" in *Controspazio* (Bari, Italy), July/August 1971; "Roma-Est: Proposta Architettonica," with Constantino Dardi and R. Panella, in *Controspazio* (Bari, Italy), December 1973; "The Contribution of Oswald Mathias Ungers to Architecture," with Vanna Fraticelli, in *Controspazio* (Bari, Italy), November 1975; "Architecture of Aldo Rossi" in *Architecture + Urbanism* (Tokyo), no. 67, 1976; "Materia e Materiali" in *Lotus* (Venice), June 1977; "Urban Centres: Conservation and Innovation," with Thomas Maldonado and Pierluigi Cervellanti, in *Casabella* (Milan), September 1977; "Design at Different Scales of Reference" in *Architecture + Urbanism* (Tokyo), February 1978.

On AYMONINO: books—*Il Concorso per i Nuovi Uffici della Camera dei Deputati* by Manfredo Tafuri, Rome 1968; *L'Architettura di Roma Capitale 1870–1970,* Florence 1971; *Il Dibattito Architettonico in Italia 1945–1975,* Rome 1977; *Global Architecture 45: Housing Complex at the Gallaretese Quarter, Milan* by Yukio Futagawa and Pierluigi Nicolin, Tokyo 1977; *Guida di Roma Moderna* by I. de Guttry, Rome 1978; articles—"Architetture di Giovani" by Giuseppe Samonà in *Casabella* (Milan), no. 205, 1955; "Camera di Commercio, Industria e Agricoltura di Massa e Carrara" by Giuseppe Samonà in *L'Architettura* (Rome), no. 74, 1961; "Recente Attivita dello Studio Architetti e Ingegneri" by Manfredo Tafuri in *L'Architettura* (Rome), no. 93, 1963; "Montecitorio Valle di Lacrime" by G.K. Koenig in *Casabella* (Milan), no. 321, 1967; "Le Centre de Direction de Bologna" by Marco de Michelis and Marco Venturi in *Éspace et Sociétés* (Paris), March 1971; "Un Contributo per la Fondazione di una Nuova Scienza Urbana" by M. Scolari in *Controspazio* (Bari, Italy), nos. 78, 1971; "Roofless Homes" in *Casabella* (Milan), July 1974; "La Génération de l'Incertitude" by F. Dal Co and M. Manieri-Elia in *L'Architecture d'Aujourd'hui* (Paris), no. 181, 1974; "Carlo Aymonino" in *Architecture + Urbanism* (Tokyo), February 1978.

Architectural and urban design require different scales of reference and, therefore, different techniques of representation. It is true, moreover, that these are not necessarily independent and unrelated, nor is the only possible relationship between them the strictly hierarchical one suggested by different methods of drawing and layout. Indeed, the more complete any proposed architectural solution, the greater the likelihood that it will also help to determine features at the various scales of reference involved in the project.

—Carlo Aymonino

Carlo Aymonino has been involved in the architectural/cultural debate in Italy since 1950, when he collaborated with Ludovico Quaroni on the neo-realist experiment of the Tiburtino Quarter in Rome. Aymonino has arrived at his current theoretical position through a profound critical reappraisal of his own past experiments and from an analysis of the problems of contemporary life.

Aymonino's studies of "directional centres," which he interprets as associate organisms, polyfunctional "containers" (for a variety of purposes and functions) that will yet allow for continuity in the general form of a structural complex, are based on his conception of the "physiological process of present-day society" and on the essential needs of today's cities.

The directional centre forms a link between the city centre and its surroundings, a link created by Aymonino's revival of the historic concept of typology. There is, for example, the typology of the city itself, "a place created by history." There is the typology of the individual urban component—for example, the university, "a place that produces problems." Within the urban morphology, there is also an "ideological representative" component that is fundamental to society and to democracy. It is this concept of individual types within a whole, a whole given form by a directional centre, that Aymonino tries to implement in his work as a town planner.

He speaks of needing a "rule" rather than a "regulation." He follows a process of "fundamental architectural rebuilding" that takes into account various considerations from the ideological and sociological to the technical/scientific and formal/historical.

His best known work—it might be called the Aymonino paradigm—is the Monte Amiata Housing Development in the Gallaratese district of Milan. It impresses as a complex formal fantasy that makes use of expressionist ideas and multiple quotations, which Aymonino seeks to unify in a highly-defined polysemantic design in which the memory of the past combines with a projection of the future. Tafuri speaks of the Gallaratese complex as being autobiographical, like Fellini's film *8½*. And, indeed, the complex is full of expressiveness and emotion, emphasized by its proximity to Aldo Rossi's apartment complex, which is clinically and programmatically "abstract" in accordance with Rossi's views on the importance of the rational in Italian architectural culture.

—Lara-Vinca Masini

AZUMA, Takamitsu.

Japanese. Born in Osaka, 20 September 1933. Educated at the Osaka University School of Architecture, 1952–57, B.Arch. 1957. Married Setsuko Nakaoka in 1957; daughter: Rie. Designer, Ministry of Postal Services Architecture Department, Tokyo and Osaka, 1957–60; Chief Designer, Junzo Sakakura, Architect, and Associates, Osaka, 1960–63, and Tokyo, 1963–67. Since 1967, Principal, Takamitsu Azuma Architect and Associates, Tokyo. Instructor of Architecture, Tokyo University of Art and Design, 1976–78. Member, ArchiteXt, with Takefumi Aida, Mayumi Miyawaki, Makoto Suzuki and Minoru Takeyama, since 1971. Exhibitions: *Today: An Exhibition of Houses,* Design Gallery, Tokyo, part I and II, 1978. Recipient: First Prize, Kinki Branch of the Japan Institute of Architects Competition, 1957; First Prize, Student Hall of the School of Engineering of Osaka University Competition, 1958. Address: Takamitsu Azuma Architect and Associates, 3D Aoyama Building, 3-1-1 Minami-Aoyama, Minato-ku, Tokyo, Japan.

Works:

1967 Tower House, Jingumae, Shibuya-ku, Tokyo
Kawamoto House, Aoyama-dai, Suita, Osaka
Akatsuka Lodge, Nojiriko-Daigaku-mura, Shinanomachi, Nagano, Japan
Satoya House, Higashi-Toyonaka, Osaka

1968 Yano House, Matsubara, Setagaya-ku, Tokyo
Taiyo-do Building, Nagaoka, Kyoto
Diamond Building, Higashiyodogawa-ku, Osaka

1969 Inoue House, Kanagawa-ku, Yokohama
Nakamura Clinic Building, Minami-ku, Osaka
Fukunaga-Miyata House, Honmachi, Toyonaka, Osaka
Nakahara House, Midori-dai, Kawanishi, Hyogo, Japan
Satsuki Nursery School, stage I, Ikeda, Osaka
Komoro Drivers School, Komoro, Nagano, Japan

1970 Kawabe House, Ebina, Kouza-gun, Kanagawa, Japan
Akatsuka Tower House, Kusaka-cho, Higashi-Osaka, Osaka
Oyama House, Kami-Shibutani, Ikeda, Osaka
Kano House, Shiromae, Gifu, Japan
Haijima Seaside Lodge, Iwafune, Ohara, Chiba, Japan
Mitsui Group Pavilion, *Expo '70,* Osaka (with others)

1971 Awatsuji House, Matsubara, Setagaya-ku, Tokyo
Hakusenken (Buddhist Temple), Arakawa-ku, Tokyo
Umezawa Clinic Building, Taito-ku, Tokyo
Takahashi House, Nada-ku, Kobe, Japan
Machida Lodge, Daigaku-mura, Agatsuma-gun, Gunma, Japan

1972 Ito House, Kintei, Kawasaki, Kanagawa, Japan
Machida House, Ichigaya, Shinjuku-ku, Tokyo
Airship Bowling Center, Takaishi, Osaka
Takaishi Drivers School, Takaishi, Osaka

1973 Nishimura House, Shichirigahama, Kamakura, Kanagawa, Japan
Chin House, Komaba, Shinjuku-ku, Tokyo
Ogita House, Hisagi, Zushi, Kanagawa, Japan
Komiya House, Sakurayama, Zushi, Kanagawa, Japan
Sumino House, Kurakuen, Nishinomiya, Hyogo, Japan
Satsuki Nursery School, stage II, Ikeda, Osaka
Seibu-Yatsugatake Lodge, Uminokuchi, Minami-Saku-gun, Nagano, Japan
Miyota Civic Welfare Center, Kita-Saku-gun, Nagano, Japan
Yamamichi Mountain Lodge, Karuizawa, Nagano, Japan

1974 Itaya House, Kichijyoji, Musashino, Tokyo
Ohsawa House, Narita-Higashi, Suginami-ku, Tokyo
Taira House, Yohkoh-dai, Kohnan-ku, Yokohama
Araki House, Mitaka, Tokyo
Matsumoto House, Minato-ku, Yokohama
Ohto Clinic Building, Iruma, Saitama, Japan
Yasumaru House, Hanayashiki, Takarazuka, Hyogo, Japan
Mizuno House, Koyodai, Kawanishi, Hyogo, Japan
Seijin Nursery School, Jyoyo, Kyoto
Yamazaki House, Tomizuka-cho, Hamamatsu, Shizuoka, Japan
Miyota Nursery School, Kita-Saku-gun, Nagano, Japan

1975 Yoshida House, Higashi-cho, Iwatsuki, Saitama, Japan
Shyomoto House, Hagoromo, Takaishi, Osaka
Fuji-kyuko Office and Dormitory Complex, Minato-ku, Tokyo
Green Camping Ground Center House, Fujiyoshida, Shizuoka, Japan

1976 Takahashi House, Tama-ku, Kawasaki, Kanagawa, Japan
Matsuda House, Motoazabu, Minato-ku, Tokyo
Yamamichi House, Kugenuma, Fujisawa, Kanagawa, Japan

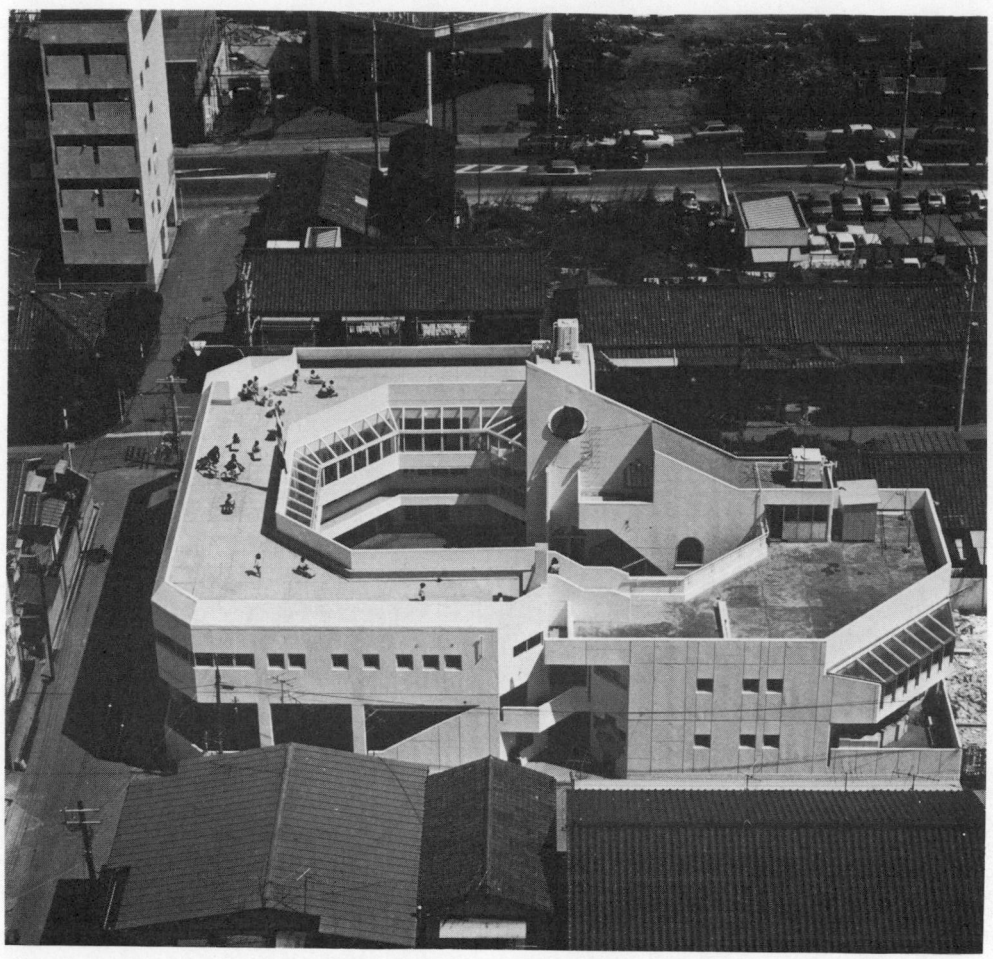

Takamitsu Azuma: Satsuki Nursery School, stage II, Ikeda, Osaka, 1973

Dantsuka Clinic and Hospital, Iruma, Saitama, Japan

Egawa House, Kohtohen, Neshinomiya, Hyogo, Japan

1977   Boh House, Nishi-Ochiai, Sinjuku-ku, Tokyo

Morita House, Sasuke, Kamakura, Kanagawa, Japan

Yamagami House, Midori-ku, Yokohama

Yonezawa Building, Nakagyo-ku, Kyoto

WAT House Complex, Yatsusaka, Iwaki, Fukushima, Japan

1978   Watanabe House, Yokohama

Kijima House, Moriyama, Komoro, Nagano, Japan

Publications:

By AZUMA: books—*Re-evaluation of the Residence,* Tokyo 1971; *Global Interiors 4: Southern Europe,* Tokyo 1972; *Planning Methodology for the Contemporary House,* Tokyo 1975; articles—"Discovery of Underground Spaces" in *Kenchiku* (Tokyo), March 1967; "Towerlike Residence: An Abstract Analysis" in *Kenchiku* (Tokyo), June 1967; "An Architect Must Have His Own Project" in *The Japan Architect* (Tokyo), June 1967; "Terminal Zones as Urban Facilities: About Their Compounding and Ecology" in *Kenchikuzasshi* (Tokyo), October 1967; "Takamitsu Azuma's Activities and Works: A Seven Day Ulysses" in *Toshijutaku* (Tokyo), July 1968; "Theory of Open Space from the Design Standpoint" in *Toshijutaku* (Tokyo), March 1969; "A Hypothesis" in *The Japan Architect* (Tokyo), November 1970; "Conception of a Creative Team System" in *Shotenkenchiku* (Tokyo), June 1971; "Living Space in the City" in *The Japan Architect* (Tokyo), July 1971; "What Urban Space Is to Me" in *Toshijutaku* (Tokyo), September 1971; "Design Memo for the Awatsuji Residence" in *The Japan Architect* (Tokyo), June 1972; "Proposal for an Image of Public Residential Spaces" in *Japan Interior Design* (Tokyo), July 1974; "What Can We Do for the Townscape" in *Shotenkenchiku* (Tokyo), June 1975; "Cognizance and Method" in *The Japan Architect* (Tokyo), June 1976; "From the Individual to the Assembled Group" in *The Japan Architect* (Tokyo), August 1978.

On AZUMA: articles—"ArchiteXt and the Problem of Symbolism" by Charles Jencks in *The Japan Architect* (Tokyo), June 1976; "Post-Metabolism: The New Wave in Japanese Architecture" by K. Ishii and H. Suzuki in *The Japan Architect* (Tokyo), OctoberNovember 1977.

*   *   *

My cognition of the way architecture ought to be and my method developed from it both depend entirely on a series of oppositional propositions: individuality and collectivity, enclosure and openness, continuity and separation, mixture and simplification, and so on. Each work includes many of these propositions, but the list given here by no means exhausts them. I often make deliberate differences between plan and section in order to generate a feeling of tension. I bring inside building elements that belong outside (urbanization of architecture) and sometimes I design the space around the building to the maximum by means of unifying it with the building (architecturalization of the city). These are the parts of many oppositional propositions that I have not explained. Many of the individual themes I employ are shared in the methods of other architects. But each architect wants to integrate his knowledge or his method and to express the resulting unity in an individualized way. Perhaps it is inconvenient to attempt to do this by organizing and preserving knowledge in the form of a series of oppositions.

Nevertheless, I want to preserve a strong feeling of tension by leaving the oppositions unresolved. Furthermore, I wish to fuse these oppositions in the work of architecture. In other words, I want my architecture to be something like a soup in which some of the vegetables remain undissolved and float about. Japanese cuisine emphasizes ways of combining the natural flavors of foods to best advantage. But one is always conscious of the tastes of the individual ingredients as one chews. I may be striving to achieve something similar in architecture. I believe that this is the only method that can result in a creative correspondence between the space created by an architect and the person who uses it. I feel that this element has been left behind in the methods of other architects. When all of the vegetables in a soup have dissolved, the only thing that remains is the blended flavor that the cook had in mind. In an architecture in which the oppositions remain unresolved, the user can select and combine the oppositions that suit his own needs and wishes at each time. Under such an arrangement, the architect prepares, and the user accepts and takes part in the creative act.

—Takamitsu Azuma

*   *   *

Takamitsu Azuma is one of those sensitive, careful, dextrous architects whose work is a pleasure to experience, but he has never been quite innovative enough to attract an international following.

After graduation from Osaka University in 1957, Azuma spent three years in relative obscurity working for the Ministry of Postal Services before he joined the offices of Junzo Sakakura. As chief designer with Sakakura from 1960 to 1967, Azuma developed his subtle, austere architectural style. After establishing his own office in 1967, Azuma, given a free hand, designed the Tower House, for himself and his family. On a very narrow sliver of land in dense downtown Tokyo, Azuma developed an ingenious vertical sequence of spaces that expresses his individuality in a neighborhood of typical Japanese tile-roofed dwellings. The smooth taut surfaces are punctured with pure openings, while the mass of the tower protrudes in bold diagonal cantilevers that extend the constricted space outward.

In 1971 Azuma helped form ArchiteXt, a group of five young, radical Japanese architects, who some thought would become the next Metabolist Group. ArchiteXt was composed of Azuma and Takefumi Aida, Mayumi Miyawaki, Makoto Suzuki, and Minoru Takeyama, and one of the purposes of the group was to attract attention to their unconventional wit and parody of modern architecture. Azuma was probably the least outrageous of the five, and yet in many ways his buildings seem some of the most lasting in their interest. The Seijin Nursery School, for example, presents a generally lean and blank facade to the street, but the uncommon cut-out entry indicates that something special lies within. Azuma has dextrously created a central space that serves as a private piazza for the children, with glimpses through geometric cut-outs into the building and out toward the street.

On yet another tight urban lot (are there any other kind in Japan?) Asuma has fashioned four superb apartments (called the WAT House) where two would have been tough. Employing the same simple white concrete surfaces of the Tower House and at the Seijin Nursery School, Azuma has again carved out a private realm off the busy street. While the WAT House is part of its neighborhood, it is also a semi-private cluster of urban dwelling units—an opposition that interests Azuma, "the relation between individuality and collectivity." The resolution of these opposing forces in architecture is what Azuma describes as "Oppositional Harmony."

In his work Azuma seeks to find a duality in which individual expression and contextualism can co-exist and in which the subjugation of the environment can occur without losing the respect for nature traditional to Japanese architecture. Thus far he has achieved his goal on a limited scale. We must look toward his future projects for a further refinement of this most intriguing concept.

—Michael Franklin Ross

B

BACKSTRÖM, Sven.

Swedish. Born in Havdhem, Gotland, 20 January 1903. Educated at the Högre Allmänna Läroverket, Visby, Sweden, graduated 1923; Royal Technical University, Stockholm, 1923–29, Dip.Arch. 1929. Married Gunvor Holmgren in 1937; children: Adam, Marie, Mårten, and Pontus. In partnership with Leif Reinius, *q.v.*, Stockholm, since 1936. Architect for the Strömsholm Royal Palace, 1951–78. Recipient: Kasper Salin Award, Svenska Arkitekters Riksförbund, 1967; Prince Eugen Medal, 1970; Olle Engkvist Medal, 1973. Member, Royal Academy for Free Arts, 1962. Knight Commander, Royal Order of Vasa, 1973. Address: Backström and Reinius, Storgatan 11, S-114 44 Stockholm, Sweden.

Works:

1938   Unmarried women's living quarters, Stockholm
1939/
40   Community house and living quarters for old people, Alvik, Sweden
1943/
45   Point houses, Danviksklippan, Stockholm
        Star Units Housing Development, Gröndal, Sweden
1946   Crematorium, Lund, Sweden
1946/
48   Nedre Norrland Law Courts, Sundsvall, Sweden
1946/
51   Terraced houses, Gröndal, Stockholm
        Nockebyhov Housing and Family Hotel, Nockeby, Stockholm
1948/
51   Björnbo Service Flats for Old People, Lidingö, Sweden
1948/
52   Rosta Housing Development, with schools, Örebro, Sweden
1948/
65   Ekliden High School, Nacka, Sweden
1953/
55   Vällingby Shopping Center, Sweden
1955/
62   Office Block 5, Sergels Torg, Stockholm
1956   Staff Quarters, Swedish Embassy, Neuilly, Paris
1956/
60   Farsta Shopping Center, Sweden
1957/
60   Crematorium additions, Lund, Sweden
1962/
64   Åhléns Department Store, Stockholm
1963   Staff Quarters, Joseph Rowntree Corporation, York, England
1964   Swedish Pavilion, *World's Fair*, New York
1964/
67   Police Headquarters, Göteborg, Sweden
1966/
69   PUNKT Department Store and Parking Garage, Västerås, Sweden
1968/
74   PK Bank Headquarters, with shops, Stockholm

1970/
73   Shops and offices, Östra Nordstaden, Göteborg, Sweden
1972/
79   AMS Education Building (offices, industrial premises, workshops, and school), Stockholm
1973/
75   Housing complex, with school, Upplands Väsby, Sweden
1974/
76   Pauves Honteux Society Old People's Home, Nockeby, Stockholm
1974/
78   Office and Shop Complex, Stockholm
1975/
79   Sveriges Arbetsgivareförening Building, Stockholm

Swedish architecture divides neatly into ten-year periods. The 1930's were the years of functionalism —of internationalism, the legacy of the Bauhaus, flat roofs, and buildings that looked as if they were built of concrete using modern industrial techniques. The 1940's by contrast, were for Sweden years of isolation due to the war in which the country was neutral, years in which the parallel development of international architecture in Europe was brutally cut off at the root. Building in Sweden was thus affected by a dearth of foreign influences and at the same time by a dearth of certain materials. The result was the rise

of an introspective, national style still (just) within the bounds of modern architecture. This was one of the high periods of Swedish architecture, and it made the country a Mecca for architects from abroad after the war. Sven Backström and Leif Reinius, more than any other architects at the time, epitomize this era.

Their work was characterized by the use of natural materials such as brick in conjunction with plenty of timber; traditional roof-forms; and an elegant, refined detailing, which in the hands of their imitators was apt to become effeminate. Their buildings of the period had a very human scale, with liberal use of breaks and bay windows to reduce the visual impact of large buildings; they had a thoroughly non-industrial look, relying on a level of craftsmanship that at the time was probably unexcelled anywhere. One of the great inventions of the partnership was the "star" housing block, a three-storey, low-pitched roofed, Y-shaped block with the three arms at an angle of 120° to each other and the staircase at the apex. These could be joined in almost unlimited numbers to form what were virtually hexagonal courts with two of the sides missing, giving pleasant proportions, human scale and economical solutions. Perhaps the most notable scheme of this kind was Gröndal in Stockholm, a scheme that also included some very early stepped housing, where each flat had a large garden terrace, and a point block where the special characteristics of various floors were lovingly exploited.

Sven Backström and Leif Reinius: Star Units Housing Development, Gröndal, Sweden, 1945

By the 1950's, the pendulum was swinging back to the International Style, but Backström and Reinius kept to the course that they had set themselves and continued to produce humane and highly individual buildings. Now that the pendulum has again swung back to humanism and away from repetitiveness, it is remarkable to note how many ideas popular in the late 1970's were pioneered by Backström and Reinius thirty or forty years ago. The small scale, the feeling of individuality, and the hand-built look so typical of many recent schemes were typical of Backström and Reinius in the 1940's. Oddly enough, this has not caused Backström and Reinius—still going strong in their seventies—to emulate the new vernacular. Their later work, perhaps because it happens to cover the more prestigious end of the market, has harder and more elegant materials than before and perhaps pays less attention to the tiny detail and the human scale. As architects, they seem intent on pursuing a logical line of development to the end, rather than doing opportunist throw-backs to what undoubtedly was a High Period.

—James Codrington Forsyth

BACON, Edmund N(orwood).

American. Born in Philadelphia, Pennsylvania, 2 May 1910. Educated at Cornell University, Ithaca, New York, 1927–32, B.Arch. 1932; Cranbrook Academy, Bloomfield Hills, Michigan, under Eliel Saarinen, 1936 (graduate fellowship in city planning). Served as a Quartermaster 2nd Class in the United States Navy, 1943–45. Married Ruth Holmes in 1938; children: Karin, Elinor, Hilda, Michael, Kira and Kevin. Architectural Designer, office of Henry Killam Murphy, Shanghai, China, 1934; worked for W. Pope Barney, Philadelphia, 1935; Supervisor of City Planning, Flint (Michigan) Institute of Research and Planning, 1937–39; Managing Director, Philadelphia Housing Association, 1940–43; Co-Designer, *Better Philadelphia Exhibition,* and Senior Land Planner, Philadelphia City Planning Commission, 1946–49; Executive Director, Philadelphia City Planning Commission, 1949–70 (Development Coordinator, 1968–70). In private practice, Philadelphia, since 1970; Vice-President, Mondev International Ltd., Montreal, since 1971. Adjunct Professor, University of Pennsylvania, Philadelphia, since 1950. Member, Task Force on the Potomac River Basin Plan, to the United States Secretary of the Interior, 1965–68; Member, Citizens' Advisory Committee on Recreation and Natural Beauty, to President Johnson, 1966–69, and on Environmental Quality, to President Nixon, 1969–70; Member, Urban Transportation Advisory Council, to the United States Secretary of Transportation. 1969–71.

Member of the Board, Franklin Institute, Philadelphia, 1969–78. Recipient: Travel/Study Grant, Ford Foundation, 1959; Medal of Achievement, Philadelphia Art Alliance, 1961; Man of the Year Award, City Business Club, Philadelphia, 1962; Brown Medal, Franklin Institute, Philadelphia, 1962; Rockefeller Foundation grant, 1963; Distinguished Service Award, American Institute of Planners, 1971; Gold Medal, Royal Institution of Chartered Surveyors, London, 1974; Honor Award, Fairmount Park Art Association, Philadelphia, 1976; Medal, American Institute of Architects, 1976; R. S. Reynolds Memorial Award for Community Architecture, 1976. Address (home/office): 2117 Locust Street, Philadelphia, Pennsylvania 19103, U.S.A.

Works:

1934 Various residences, Shanghai, China (with Henry Killam Murphy)
1937 Traffic survey of Flint, Michigan
1941 Phillips House, Torresdale, Pennsylvania (with Oscar Stonorov)
1947 Design of the *Better Philadelphia Exhibition* (with Oscar Stonorov)
1952 Penn Center, Philadelphia (original concept; with Vincent Kling)
.1957 Plan for Market East, Philadelphia (with W. von Moltke and Romaldo Giurgola)
1958 Plan for Society Hill, Philadelphia (with I. M. Pei)

Edmund N. Bacon: The Plan for Center City, Philadelphia, 1963

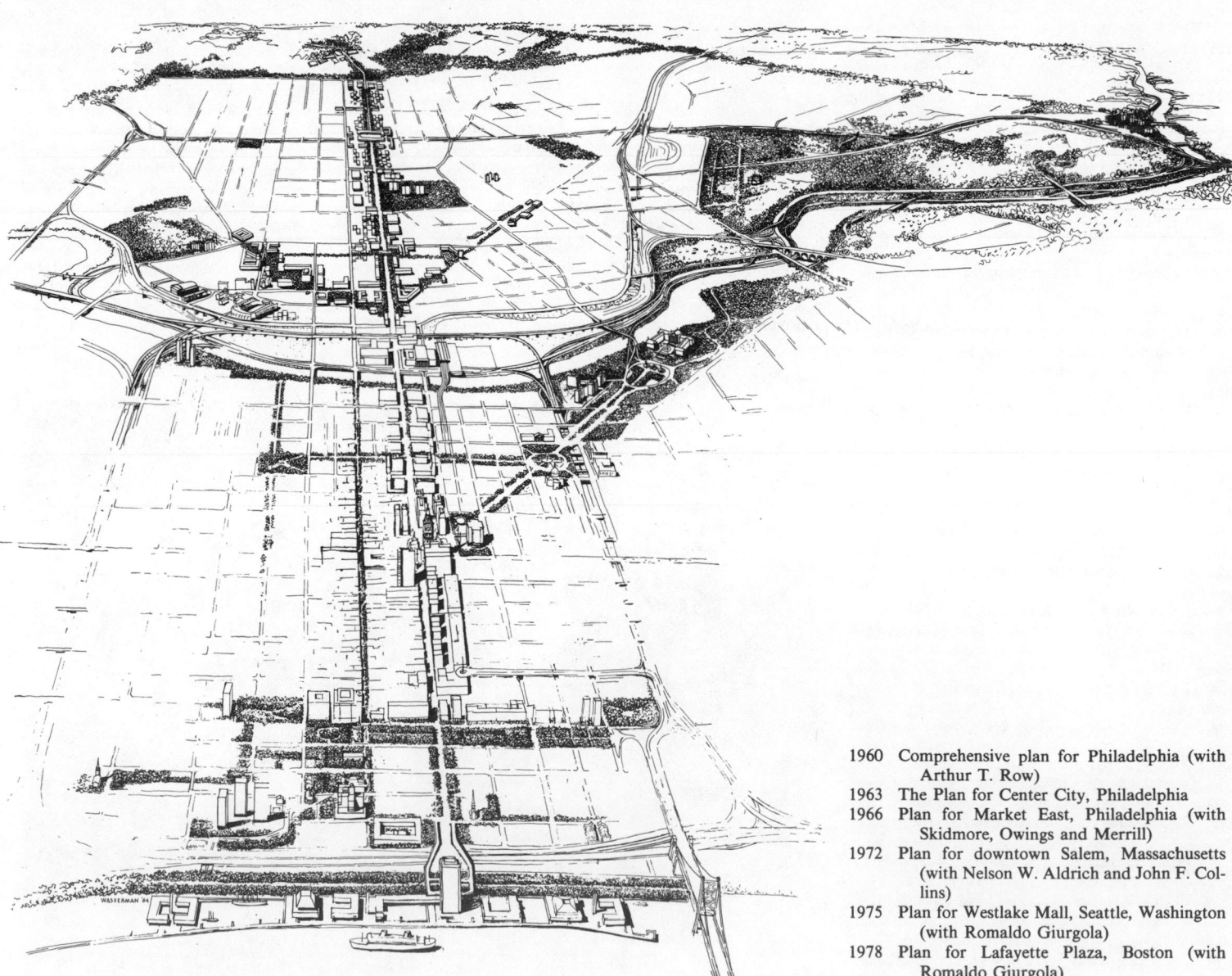

1960 Comprehensive plan for Philadelphia (with Arthur T. Row)
1963 The Plan for Center City, Philadelphia
1966 Plan for Market East, Philadelphia (with Skidmore, Owings and Merrill)
1972 Plan for downtown Salem, Massachusetts (with Nelson W. Aldrich and John F. Collins)
1975 Plan for Westlake Mall, Seattle, Washington (with Romaldo Giurgola)
1978 Plan for Lafayette Plaza, Boston (with Romaldo Giurgola)

Publications:

By BACON: book—*Design of Cities,* New York 1967, revised edition 1974, London 1976; chapters—in *Man and the Modern City,* Pittsburgh 1963; *The Conscience of the City,* edited by Martin Meyerson, New York 1970; *American Civilization,* edited by Daniel Boorstin, London 1972; *Energy Use Management,* volumes III and IV, edited by Rocco Fazzolare and George B. Smith, New York 1978; articles—"A Case Study in Urban Design" in *Journal of the American Institute of Planners* (Washington, D.C.), August 1960; "Downtown Philadelphia: A Lesson in Design for Urban Growth" in *Architectural Record* (New York), May 1961; "Architecture and Planning" in *AIA Journal* (Washington, D.C.), June 1961; "American Homes and Neighborhoods, City and Country" in *Annals of the American Academy of Political and Social Science* (Philadelphia), July 1968; "Time, Turf, Architects and Planners" in *Architectural Record* (New York), March 1976.

On BACON: books—*The Art of Government* by James Reichley, New York 1959; *Cities in a Race with Time* by Jeanne R. Lowe, New York 1967; *The Last Landscape* by William H. Whyte, New York 1968; *The Future of the City* by Peter Wolf, New York 1974; *Downtown USA* by Kenneth Halpern, New York 1978; articles—"Philadelphia Does It: The Battle for Penn Center" by James Reichley in *Harpers* (New York), February 1957; cover story in *Time* (New York), 6 November 1964; "A City's Future Takes Shape" in *Life* (New York), December 1965; "Recent Works of Edmund B. Bacon" in *Kenchiku Bunka* (Tokyo), February 1972; "Post-Renaissance Philadelphia" in *AIA Journal* (Washington, D.C.), March 1976; "Philadelphia Story" in *Progressive Architecture* (New York), April 1976; "Five Noted Thinkers Explore the Future" in *National Geographic* (Washington, D.C.), July 1976.

The building of cities is one of man's greatest achievements. The form of his city always has been and always will be a pitiless indicator of the state of his civilization. This form is determined by the multiplicity of decisions made by the people who live in it. In certain circumstances these decisions have interacted to produce a force of such clarity and form that a noble city has been born. A deeper understanding of the interactions of these decisions can give us the insight necessary to create noble cities in our own day.

I should like to dispel the idea, so widely and uncritically held, that cities are a kind of grand accident, beyond the control of the human will, and that they respond only to some immutable law. I contend that human will can be exercised effectively on our cities now, so that the form that they take will be a true expression of the highest aspirations of our civilization.

With the enormous improvement in the techniques of mathematical manipulations of electronic computers applied to the problem of projecting past trends, we are in danger of surrendering to a mathematically extrapolated future which at best can be nothing more than an extension of what existed before. Thus we are in danger of losing one of the most important concepts of mankind, that the future is what we make it.

Recent events in Philadelphia have proved incontrovertibly that, given a clear vision of a "design idea," the multiplicity of wills that constitute our contemporary democratic process can coalesce into positive, unified action on a scale large enough to change substantially the character of a city. It is my belief that a new awareness and understanding of "design idea" will enable the architectural profession over the years immediately ahead to become more relevant and effective in the building of our cities.

—Edmund N. Bacon

Edmund N. Bacon was with the Philadelphia City Planning Commission for 24 years—first as Senior Land Planner, then, from 1949 to 1970, as Executive Director.

Few city planners or urban designers ever stay put that long. A typical planner may work for several years with a commercial development company that has hired him for his grasp of federal and local renewal policies and his ability to make imaginative use of local zoning law as well as federal, state and local funding sources in the developer's behalf. For the next few years he may be on the other side of the desk, this time in a public planning agency, devising ways to attract yet control development so that it will ultimately improve the life of the city or region. At some point in the planner's career he will probably be off to Third World countries to consult with rulers who wish to rebuild their cities in the image of the West. Is it possible to be a successful and effective planner and yet stay in one job for more than a quarter of a century? It may be the only way, if Bacon's achievement is to set the standard.

A city changes slowly, conforming to patterns imprinted by transportation systems, parks, plazas, footpaths and other networks of open space, as well as landmark buildings that combine beauty with historic significance. The catalyst for change is economic; the physical form of change is shaped by zoning law. The nature of the growth of Philadelphia during Bacon's long term as Executive Director was to a significant degree established in advance by Bacon himself. What distinguishes him from almost all the planners of his own and succeeding generations is the fact that he elected to pay continuous attention to a single city over a long span of time. A street of shops reviving, a neighborhood of landmarks preserved, a subway line extended, a slum eradicated and the dwellers rehoused—all are catalysts for further change. Bacon's 24 years with the planning commission consisted of initiating such transforming ideas, getting them accepted by the public, and seeing them accomplished over decades.

Philadelphia's first planner was William Penn who laid out the city in the 18th century. The City Hall was placed at the center of two perpendicular axes. A major rectangular park marks each of the four quadrants formed by these cross axes. As the city expanded through the 19th and early 20th centuries, its urban core remained intact. In Bacon's vision Philadelphia must continue to grow organically from this nucleus. He believes that the patterns of civic space, recreation and transportation established during the city's beginnings and extended by succeeding generations of builders and planners must be understood, fostered and continued—if the city is to prosper and grow in beauty.

Nine years ago Bacon left the Philadelphia City Planning Commission to become Vice-President of Mondev International Ltd., based in Montreal. Today, the development he set in motion as Philadelphia's chief planner continues to be carried out within the framework and public consensus he established. That consensus did not always exist and, like all things political, is fragile.

Philadelphia was one of the first cities to begin to build again after the hiatus of World War II. It became a testing ground for the federal urban renewal and housing programs of the 1950's and 60's. Because Bacon was eager to take advantage of these programs, he tried most of them, finding out what worked and what didn't. Inevitably the programs favored one social class over another, and Bacon became the target of the political left, who had begun to call the nation's urban renewal projects "negro removal." The epithet "gentrification" had yet to be invented, but Bacon was criticized for his efforts to bring the middle classes back from the suburbs to the city and accused of fostering the outward dislocation of the poor. His urban design ideas were characterized as mere efforts to hide the cities ill-housed and poor behind an "antiquated City Beautiful" facade.

Although these criticisms were valid in part, they have been muted in recent years as leftist polemic found new targets. Today Philadelphia is visited regularly by busloads of planners, architects, historians, community leaders, teachers and students. They all go to learn—how to preserve landmarks, to revive neighborhoods, to build playgrounds, to renew parks, to separate pedestrian and vehicular traffic, and to house the poor and elderly. The attention paid to Philadelphia today is a tribute to Bacon, the outstanding planner of his generation.

—Mildred F. Schmertz

BADANI, Daniel.

French. Born in Vincennes, 19 June 1914. Educated at the Lycée du Puy, Haute Loire: Ecole Nationale Supérieure des Beaux-Arts, Paris. Served in the Engineers, 12th Division of the French Army, 1939–40: Lieutenant. Married Jacqueline Chaleye in 1944; daughter: Laetitia. In private practice, with Pierre Roux-Dorlut, Paris, since 1946. Inspector-General of Urban Planning, Paris, 1944–50; Consultant Architect to the Ministry of Reconstruction and Development for the Languedoc-Roussillon region of France, 1950–60, and to the Development Bureau for the La Défense complex, Paris, 1969–72. Currently, Architect-in-Chief of Civic Buildings and National Monuments; Member of the General Council of Building for France; Consultant Architect to the Ministry of Reconstruction and Development for Paris; Consultant Architect to the Ministry of Equipment for Paris; Member of the Regional Commission on Architecture for the Paris region; Consultant on Urbanism and Architecture to the Mayor of Paris; and Member of the Editorial Board, *Architecture Francaise,* Paris. Professor at the Ecole Nationale Supérieure des Beaux-Arts, Paris, 1946–55. President, Committee on Architects in Charge of Public Buildings and National Monuments, 1968–70, Syndicate of Parisian Architects, 1968–70, and National Union of French Architects, 1969–70. Exhibitions: Syndicate of Architects, Paris, 1960; Congress of Architects, London, 1960, Moscow, 1961; *Exposition Internationale des Formes Industrielles,* Paris, 1963; International Exposition, Stockholm, 1963; *Architecture Francaise de Récherches,* Paris, 1965; *Exposition Nationale des Beaux-Arts,* Paris, 1977; *Salon d'Automne,* Paris, 1977. Recipient: Silver Medal, Académie d'Architecture, Paris, 1968; Gold Medal, Société d'Encouragement à l'Art et à l'Industrie, Paris, 1972; Silver Medal, City of Paris, 1977. Member, l'Académie d'Architecture. Officer and Chevalier of the Légion d'Honneur; Chevalier des Arts et Lettres, France; Chevalier, l'Ordre de l'Etoile Noire du Benin. Address (office): 24 bis rue de Berri, 75008 Paris, France.

Works:

1946	Seafront reconstruction at Sète, France
1947	Urban plan for Abidjan, Ivory Coast
	Urban plan for Sassandra, Ivory Coast
	Urban plan for Bouake, Ivory Coast
1950/	
53	4 Courtrooms, Palace of Justice, Abidjan, Ivory Coast
1950/	
57	Central Posts and Telecommunications Building, Place Lapalud, Abidjan, Ivory Coast
	Control Building and Hangar, Abidjan Airport, Ivory Coast
1952	Quai de la Consigne reconstruction, Sète, France
1952/	
57	Cocody Mixed School, Abidjan, Ivory Coast
1953	Road Station, Bouake, Ivory Coast

1953/
54 Ministry of Public Works Offices, Abidjan, Ivory Coast
1953/
55 Abeille Company Offices and Commercial Buildings, Abidjan, Ivory Coast
    Hôtel des Relais Aériens, Niamey, Nigeria
    Bank of West Africa Building, Sassandra, Ivory Coast
1954 Urban plan for Toulouse, France
1954/
56 Palais du Grand Conseil (Palace of the National Assembly), Dakar, Senegal
1954/
57 Centre for Nuclear Studies, Marcoule, Gard, France
1955 School complexes, Herault, Vaucluse and Var, France
1955/
57 Pont Lagunaire Rail Route, Abidjan, Ivory Coast
1956/
65 Housing, Saint Maurice-Vallon des Fleurs, Nice, France
1957 Fédération Nationale du Bâtiment Headquarters, Rue Laperouse, Paris
    Canteen, Nuclear Centre, Le Bouchet, France
1957/
64 Villiers-le-Bel District Redevelopment, Paris
1958 Housing, administrative, community and commercial development, Quartier Succi, Abidjan, Ivory Coast
    Housing, Quartier N'Singa, Abidjan, Ivory Coast
    Mixed Classical and Modern College, Bagnols-sur-Ceze, France
    Master plan for housing, Cormeilles en Parisis, France
    General hospital, Bouake, Ivory Coast
    University Hospital Centre, Beirut, Lebanon
    Palais de France Pavilion, *World's Fair*, Brussels
1959 Centre for Building Research and Development, Saint Remy les Chevreuses, France
1960 School complex, Villiers-le-Bel, Paris
    Hippone-la-Royal Satellite City, Bône, Algeria (unfinished)
1960/
63 Centre for Nuclear Studies, Cadarache, Bouces du Rhone, France
    Vincennes Stadium, France (competition project)
1962 Housing and commercial development, Quartier de la Grangette, Beziers, France
    Cité Scolaire de la Dullague School and College Buildings, Beziers, France
1962/
67 Primary school, Adjame, Abidjan, Ivory Coast
1963 University, Constantine, Algeria (unfinished)
    Anna Jacquin House, Boulogne, Paris
1964 Housing, Quartier de l'Iranget, Beziers, France
    Seafront development, phase I, Saint Raphael, France
1965 Urban plan for Champigny-Chennevieres, Val de Marne, France
    Urban renewal plan for Avignon, France
    Regional urban plans for Nice, Beziers, Saint Raphael and Antibes-Vallauris, France
1966 Institut Francais de l'Afrique Noire Building, Abidjan, Ivory Coast
1966/
70 Housing, Quartier de las Planas, Nice, France
1967/
70 Secondary school, Mainvilliers, Paris
    Secondary school, Gif sur Yvette, Paris
    Secondary school, Saint-Denis, Paris
    Secondary school, Vaux-le-Penil, Paris
    Secondary school, Limours, Paris
1967/
74 Petit Defend Holiday Village, Saint Raphael, France

1968 Food warehouse, Chenneviers-sur-Marne, France
1968/
72 Tourist Centre, Maure-Vieil, Alpes Maritimes, France
    La Rague Pleasure Port, Maure-Vieil, Alpes Maritimes, France
1969 Apartment buildings and Quartier de la Balance renovations, Avignon, France
1969/
73 Agricultural Administration Offices redevelopment, Montpellier, France
1969/
74 Single people's housing, Champigny sur Marne, France
1970 Residential and community development, Valenton, Paris
    University Institute of Technology, Avenue de Versailles, Paris
    University Institute of Technology, Amiens, France
    University Institute of Technology, Clermont, near Paris
    University Institute of Technology, Lyon-la-Doua, near Paris
1971/
73 New Prefecture Building, Créteil, Val de Marne, France
    Housing and commercial development, Brunoy (Essone), Paris
1971/
74 Science Faculty Buildings, The University, Clermont-Ferrand, France
1972 Seafront development, phase II, Saint Raphael, France
1972/
75 Housing, Quartier de Saint Augustin, Nice, France
1973 Housing development, Champigny sur Marne, Paris
    Housing, Carros, Alpes Maritimes, France
1974 Hall of Archives, Créteil, Val de Marne, France
1975 Ministry of Defence Building renovations, Ilot St. Germain, Paris
    Residential tower block, Courbevoie-La Défense, Paris
1976 Housing, Créteil (Orme St. Simeon), Paris
    St. Cloud Viaduct, France
    Credit Mutuel Bank Administration Building, Lattes, Montpellier, France
1976/
77 Courts of Justice, Créteil, Val de Marne, France
    Alentours-Pont de Sevrès Road Traffic and Environmental Development, Boulogne, France
1977 Saint Bernard Gardens Development, Paris
1978 R.N.U.R. Road Station Complex, Boulogne, France

Publications:

On BADANI: articles—"Crédit Agricole Mutuel du Midi" and "Créteil Law Courts" in *Mur Vivant* (Paris), no. 47, 1978; "Créteil: A More Accessible Justice" in *Cree* (Paris), February/March 1978.

Daniel Badani met his future partner Pierre Roux-Dorlut in 1940 in Marseilles where Eugène Beaudouin had brought together various Parisian architects whose practices had been disrupted by the war. In 1946 Badani and Roux-Dorlut formed a partnership to study the rebuilding of the Languedoc, and today that partnership, based on a common architectural training and reinforced by a common regional background, is cemented by more than thirty years of work, struggle, and friendship.

A "partnership" suggests reciprocal influence, complementary enrichment, a dialogue in which the natural inclination of each partner is tempered by that of the other. However, for those who know

Badani and Roux-Dorlut well, it is possible to discern the impact of the individual personality on their joint achievements. They carry out their professional programs together, but the final embodiment in form often reveals the dominant influence of one or the other.

Daniel Badani shows a certain classicism, even a taste for the baroque, tendencies curbed by Roux-Dorlut who, five years younger and of an austere and determined character, could be accused of coldness and lack of imagination if Badani did not influence him away from these inclinations.

Their first achievements were in Africa, notably in Abidjan where they built, among other works, the courtrooms for the Palace of Justice, the Central Posts and Telecommunications Building, and various residential districts; in Dakar, where they built the Palais du Grand Conseil, which became the National Assembly of Senegal; and in Bouake, where they built the general hospital. In France they produced the principal plans and numerous buildings for the Centre for Nuclear Studies at Marcoule and at Cadarache, competition projects like the Vincennes Stadium, residential complexes both in the South and in the Paris area, and schools, industrial, public and administration buildings throughout the country.

Daniel Badani's influence shows most clearly in such works as the renovation of the Quartier de la Balance in Avignon, on the historic site of the Papal Palace, and in a special study commissed by André Malraux when Malraux was Minister of Culture, the development of a protected sector in the heart of Paris. Badani proposed that the importance of the Tuilerie Gardens be emphasized by extending them to the aracades along the rue de Rivoli, freeing the area from traffic by the creation of underground streets and parking areas. The plan is bold, intelligent, and logical.

It was also with deference to an on-site element—a large area of water—that Badani conceived the New Prefecture Building for the Val de Marne in Créteil. The most appropriate simile for the building is that it is like a ship. And Badani carefully studied the approaches, remodelled the ground, created gardens and pathways that not only provide entry but also invite one to regard the building from various aspects.

His studies for the prefectures of Chartres and Toulon also involve this concern for the complete entity, and the impact of this kind of vision is particularly strong in the elegance and power of the monumental curve of the St. Cloud Viaduct.

Yet, despite the often highly individual character of this vision, Daniel Badani does attempt, successfully, to play an active part in the main stream of architecture. He is a member of the Académie d'Architecture, and has actively served as consultant to various government ministries and to various municipalities.

—Renée Diamant-Berger

BAKEMA, Jacob (Berend).

Dutch. Born in Groningen, 8 March 1914. Educated at the Technical High School, Groningen, 1932–37; Academy of Architecture, Amsterdam, 1937–41, Dip.Arch. (cum laude) 1941; Technical University, Delft, 1939–40. During World War II, prisoner of war in France, 1941; escaped and became involved in the "underground" movement in Groningen, 1942. Married Silina Th. van Borssum Waalkes in 1939; children: Brita, Erik, and Nils. Worked in the office of Cor van Eesteren, Amsterdam, 1937, van Tijen and Maaskant, 1941, and in the Rotterdam Municipal Housing Department, 1945. Since 1948, Principal, with J. H. van den Broek, *q.v.*, (died 1978), Architectengemeenschap van den Broek en

Bakema, Rotterdam (associates: J. Boot; J. M. A. de Groot; J. E. Rijnsdorp; J. M. Stokla). Extraordinary Professor of Architecture, Technical University, Delft, since 1963; Professor in Urban Design, Staatliche Hochschule für Bildende Künste, Hamburg, since 1965. Visiting Professor, International Summer Academy, Salzburg, 1965–69, 1973–75, Columbia University, New York, 1970–71, and Cornell University, Ithaca, New York, 1972. Co-Editor, *Forum,* Hilversum, Netherlands, 1959–64; Member of the Board, *Architectura et Amicitia,* Amsterdam, 1965–67. Member of CIAM (Congrès Internationaux d'Architecture Moderne), since 1947 (Member of the Board, 1953–59), and of Team 10, since 1963. Exhibitions: *Bouwen voor een open samenleving,* Boymans Museum, Rotterdam, 1963, toured The Netherlands, Germany, Austria and Italy; *Pampus,* Stedelijk Museum, Amsterdam, 1965, toured The Netherlands, Austria and the United States; *Samen Bouwen,* Town Hall, Schoonhoven, Netherlands, 1972, toured Austria and Germany; *Progetti e Opere,* Castello Nuovo, Naples, 1974, toured Italy. Recipient: Dutch Critics Prize, International Association of Art Critics, 1972; Camillo Sitteprize, Austria, 1977; Honorary Cross, Salzburg, Austria, 1978. Member, Akademie der Künste, Berlin, since 1971; Honorary Member, American Institute of Architects, Zentral Vereinigung Architekten Oesterreichs (Austria), Bund Deutscher Architekten (Germany), Association of Scottish Architects, and Suomen Arkkitehtiliitto (Finland). Officer, Orange-Nassau Order, Netherlands, 1958; Knight, Order of Nederlandse Neeuw, 1971. Member, Order of La Couronne, Belgium, 1958. Address: Architectengemeenschap van den Broek en Bakema, Posthoornstraat 12B, 3011WE Rotterdam, Netherlands.

Works:

1947/
48 Social Centre, Rotterdam (demolished)
1947/
53 Cinema 't Venster, Rotterdam
1948/
50 2 semi-detached houses, Hornlaan, Beverwijk, Netherlands
Nederlandse Kroonkurk Mij. N.V. Factory and Office Building, Sluisjesdijk, Rotterdam
1948/
51 Termeulen-Wassen-van Vorst Shopping Bazaar, Binnenweg, Rotterdam
1948/
53 City Transport and Motor Services Building, Schiekanaal, Rotterdam
1949 Pendrecht Housing Estate, Rotterdam (project)
Artists Centre (project)
1949/
50 Layout and buildings for the *Rotterdam Ahoy* exhibition, Stadspark, Rotterdam
Zuid Shipping Union Medical Services Building, St. Jobsweg, Rotterdam
1949/
51 Van Houten and Zn. Metalworks Shop and Office Building, Bierstraat, Rotterdam
Mill and bakery extensions, Binnenhaven, Wageningen, Netherlands
Anthony Veder N.V. Shipping Bureau extensions, Westplein 11, Rotterdam
1949/
52 Van der Meer House remodelling, Prins Bernhardkade, Rotterdam
1949/
53 Lijnbaan Shopping Centre, Lijnbaan, Rotterdam
Ypenhof (van den Broek House), Kralingseweg 179, Rotterdam
Secondary school with gymnasium, Coppelstockstraat, Brielle, Netherlands
1950 Cinema, Hengelo, Netherlands (project)
Public housing, Drente, Netherlands (project)

van den Broek/Bakema Office extensions, Westerkade, Rotterdam
Van Leer Company Administration Building, Stadionplein, Amsterdam (competition project)
Auction Building, Marconistraat, Rotterdam (project)
Bataafse Petroleum Company Administration Building, The Hague (competition project)
Uttman House, Bennekom, Netherlands (project)
1950/
51 Aircraft hangar, Ypenburg, Netherlands
Terrace housing, Heeswijkstraat, Voorburg, The Hague
1950/
53 Holland-America Lines Works Building, Wilhelminakade, Rotterdam
1951 Hoving House, Drachten, Netherlands (project)
Pendrecht Housing Estate, Rotterdam (project; with Opbouw Group)
Sanders House, Vught, Netherlands (project)
1951/
52 Hispano Suiza N.V. Factory, Terheydenseweg, Breda, Netherlands
Esso Service Station, Ungerplein, Rotterdam
1951/
53 Zuid Shipping Union Station, Bananenstraat, Rotterdam
Veder N.V. Warehouse and Office Building, Ijsselhaven, Rotterdam
Public housing, Blankenburgersingel, Overschie, Rotterdam
1951/
54 Terrace shops and houses, Lange Nieuwstraat, Velsen, Netherlands
1951/
61 Metallurgy Laboratory, Technical University, Delft
1952 Veder House, Kralingseweg, Rotterdam (project)
1952/
53 Niehuis-van den Bergh Works Building, with Housing, Havenstraat, Rotterdam
1952/
54 de Klerk Furniture Shop, Nieuwe Binnenweg, Rotterdam
Public housing, Molenleystraat, Breda, Netherlands
Huf Shoe Store, Hoogstraat, Rotterdam
Horticultural School, Burgmeester H. van Sleenstraat, Brielle, Netherlands
Public housing, with shops, Burgmeester Baumannlaan, Rotterdam
Ten Cate and Company Administration Building, Spoorstraat, Almelo, Netherlands
1952/
55 Public housing, with shops and restaurant, Pleinweg, Zuidplein, Rotterdam
Boilerhouse and Laboratory of Heating Techniques, Technical University, Delft
1952/
56 Terraced and public housing, Maarten Harpertszoon Trompstraat, Brielle, Netherlands
1953 Alexanderpolder Housing Estate, Rotterdam (project; with Opbouw Group)
Van Giessen and Zn. Wharf, Office and Shops enlargement, Krimpen an der Ijssel, Netherlands
Veder N.V. Office remodelling, Westerkade, Rotterdam (project)
Hotel, Rotterdam (project)
Van Ommeren N.V. Office Building, Westerlaan, Rotterdam (project)
1953/
54 Housing, Breedveldsingel, Rotterdam
Layout and buildings for the *E 55* exhibition, Rotterdam
1953/
55 Nurses' Home, Westersingel, Rotterdam

Housing development, Geuzenveld, Amsterdam
Navy Sports Centre, Schulpweg, Rotterdam
1953/
56 Rotterdamsche Kolen Centrale Office and Warehouse Building, Waalhaven, Rotterdam
1954 Sonneveld House Redevelopment, Schiedamsevest, Rotterdam
1954/
56 Public housing, with shops, Mariniersweg, Rotterdam
1954/
57 Galeries Modernes Department Store, Hoogstraat, Rotterdam
Town Hall remodelling, Marktplein, Brielle, Netherlands (with Philippus Bolt and C. Baert de la Faille)
1954/
58 Reformed Church, Burgemeester Honnerlage Gretelaan, Schiedam, Netherlands
T.N.O. Metallurgy Laboratories, Rotterdamseweg, Delft
1955 Civic Center, St. Louis, Missouri (project)
Visser House, Papendrecht, Netherlands (project)
Zwolsman N.V. Head Office, Utrecht (project)
Sanders House, Juliaanlaan, Rotterdam
Sports Park, Madestein, The Hague (project)
Congress Hall, The Hague (project)
1955/
57 Shopping Centre, Zuiderwinkels, Nagele, Netherlands
School for the Retarded, Burgmeester H. van Sleenstraat, Brielle, Netherlands
Prefabricated public housing, Rijswijk, Netherlands
1955/
59 Terraced and public housing, Vrederust Oost, The Hague
1955/
60 Montessori School, Schimmelpenninckstraat 20, Rotterdam
1956 Hotel, Zeestraat-Javastraat, The Hague (project)
Alexanderpolder Housing Estate, Rotterdam (project; with Opbouw Group)
Single-family housing, Karpendonk, Eindhoven, Netherlands (project)
Diepen House, Wassenaar, Netherlands (project)
Youth Hostel, Oostvoorne, Netherlands (project)
Theatre, Zwartenweg, The Hague (project)
Nievelt-Goudriaan and Company Office Building, Veerkade, Rotterdam (project)
Frik House extensions, Heerenveen, Netherlands (project)
Centre Building, Emmen, Netherlands (project)
1956/
57 Public housing, Hengelolaan, The Hague
Van Giessen and Zn. Offices remodelling, Krimpen an der Ijssel, Netherlands
Wieringa House, Hobbemastraat 2, Middelharnis, Netherlands
1956/
58 Klein Driene Development, Hengelo, Netherlands
Ierland-van Zanten Shop, Lijnbaan, Rotterdam
1956/
61 World Broadcasting Building, Witte Kruislaan 55, Hilversum, Netherlands
1957 Viewing Tower, Stadtpark, Rotterdam (project)
Shopping Centre, Vlaardingen, Netherlands (project)
Maritime Centre, Scheveningen, The Hague (project)
1957/
58 't Heechterp District Development, Leeuwarden Oost, Netherlands

Jacob Bakema and J. H. van den Broek: Town Hall, Terneuzen, Netherlands, 1968

1957/
59 Nord-Kennermerland Regional Plan, North Holland
1957/
60 Apartment tower block, Hansaviertel, Berlin
Diaconessenhuis Clinic extensions, Westersingel, Rotterdam
Medical Centre, de Cordesstraat, Hook of Holland
1957/
62 Aero- and Hydrodynamics Laboratories, Technical University, Delft
Het Parool Newspaper Building, Amsterdam
1958 Netherlands Pavilion, *World's Fair,* Brussels (with Gerrit Rietveld and Joost Willem Cornelis Boks)
Lummus Nedland N.V. Office Building, Plaspoelpolder, Rijswijk, Netherlands (project)
Landbouwhuis (Agricultural Centre), Paternosterstraat, Alkmaar, Netherlands (project)
Capital Centre, Berlin (competition project)
Ter Meulen House, Oude Zeeweg, Noordwijk, Netherlands (project)
Vlaardingen Nord Building, Vlaardingen, Netherlands (project)
Margarine AG/Unilever Office Building, Valentinskamp, Hamburg (competition project)
Shopping Centre, Culemborg, Netherlands (project)
1958/
59 Van Welzenes N.V. Factory, Spijkenisse, Netherlands

1958/
60 *Floriade* horticultural exhibition layouts, Stadspark, Rotterdam
Reformed Church, Ring, Nagele, Netherlands
van Roosbroeck House, Barendrechtseweg, Barendrecht, Netherlands (demolished)
1958/
61 Dura N.V. Office Building, Raadhuisplein, Rotterdam
Analytical Chemistry Laboratories, Technical University, Delft
1958/
62 Town Hall, Marl, Germany
1958/
63 Central Post Office Building, Prinses Beatrixlaan, The Hague
1959 De Nederlanden 1845 Insurance Building, Adelheidstraat, The Hague (competition project)
Shopping Centre, Laan van Meerdervoort, The Hague (project)
1959/
61 Meerwaldt House, Baarsweg, Hoogvliet, Netherlands
Lamers and Indemans N.V. Factory extensions, Parallelweg, Hertogenbosch, Netherlands
Shopping Centre, with maisonettes, Bergen, Netherlands
Terraced houses with shops, Prins Hendrikstraat, Hook of Holland
1959/
62 Grain Testing Laboratories, Technical University, Delft

Leeuwarden Noord Housing Estate, Leeuwarden, Netherlands
Shopping Centre, with houses, Binnenhof, Amstelveen, Netherlands
1959/
63 Road Construction Laboratories, Technical University, Delft
1959/
64 School of Engineering Lecture Building, Technical University, Delft
School of Architecture Lecture Building, Technical University, Delft
1960 World Health Organization Building, Geneva (competition project)
Radio and television station, Kuwait (project)
Cultural Centre, Leverkusen, Germany (competition project)
1960/
61 Van Buchem House, Offenbachlaan 5, Hillegersberg, Rotterdam
Van Wijk House, Distelstraat 4, Hook of Holland
De Klerk House, Tsjaikofskilaan 7, Hillegersberg, Rotterdam
1960/
62 Post Office, Binnenhof 64, Amstelveen, Netherlands
Junior School and Kindergarten, Smeetslandsedijk, Rotterdam
Raiffeisenbank Building, Prins Hendrikstraat, Hook of Holland
Van Giessen and Zn. Canteen and Drawing Office, Krimpen an der Ijssel, Netherlands
Office building with shops, Tuftmarkt-Kalvermarkt, The Hague

1960/
63 High-rise apartment block, Mariahoeve, The Hague (project)
Office building, Oostingstraat, Emmen, Netherlands
Elementary School, Emmercompascum, Emmen, Netherlands

1960/
68 Town Hall, Terneuzen, Netherlands
1961 Elementary School, Erica, Emmen, Netherlands (project)
Fortgens House, Straatweg, Rotterdam (project)
Timp House extensions, Grindbank, Laren, Netherlands (project)
Steilshoop Housing Estate, Hamburg (competition project)
Frik House, Heerenveen, Netherlands (project)
Shopping Centre, Heemskerk, Netherlands (project)
High School for the Social Sciences, Linz, Austria (competition project)
Plan for Wulfen New Town, Westphalia, Germany (competition project)
Shopping Centre, Jagershoef, Eindhoven, Netherlands (project)
High-rise apartment block, Rozenburg, Netherlands (project)

1961/
62 Auditorium, Technical University, Delft
Central Post Office, Velperweg, Arnhem, Netherlands
Wierda House, Burgemeester Falkenlaan, Heerenveen, Netherlands

1961/
63 Philips N.V. Works Housing, Strijpsestraat, Eindhoven, Netherlands
Van Wilgen House, Mahlersingel, Rotterdam
1962 Development plan for the Woensel District, Eindhoven, Netherlands
Town Hall, Offenbach am Main, Germany (competition project)
Nordweststadt Centre, Frankfurt (competition project)
Centre Building, Spoorstraat, Nimwegen, Netherlands (project)
Van der Sande Wijbrand House, Straatweg, Rotterdam (project)
Lijnbaan Shopping Centre extension, Lijnbaan, Rotterdam
University of the Ruhr, Bochum, Germany (competition project)
Philips N.V. Works Housing, Geldrop, Netherlands

1962/
63 Expansion plans for Hengelo North, Netherlands
1964 Protestant Student Community Centre, Mainz, Germany (competition project)
Town Hall, Jerusalem (competition project)
Town plan for Skopje, Yugoslavia (competition project)
Sociedad Immobiliaria y del Gran Kursaal Maritimo S.A., San Sebastian, Spain (competition project)

1964/
68 Drachten Elementary School, Netherlands
1964/
69 Hermes Student Club, Rotterdam
1965 Zwijndrecht Secondary School, Netherlands
Leo van Ierland House, Rotterdam
Mobile Theatre, for the Dutch Opera Foundation (project; with Frei Otto)

1965/
70 M.B.O. Covered Shopping Centre, Leeuwarden, Netherlands

1965/
71 Drachten Elementary School for Handicapped Children, Netherlands

1965/
76 Town Hall, Ede, Netherlands

1966/
68 Corpac Office Building, Tilburg, Netherlands
1966/
69 Apartment building, Tilburg, Netherlands
1966/
73 Nurses' Dormitory, Leidschendam, Netherlands
1966/
74 I.C.Z. Hospital, Apeldoorn, Netherlands
1967 Sanders House reconstruction, Schiedam, Netherlands
1968 Medical School, Accra, Ghana
Urban district development plan for Diemen, Netherlands
Exotarium (tropical garden), The Hague
Town Hall, Amsterdam (competition project)
1968/
73 Cultural and Community Centre, Winschoten, Netherlands
1968/
76 D.S.H.B. Old People's Housing, Delft, Netherlands
1969 Shell Company Administration Building, Hamburg (competition project)
Lommerrijk Sports Centre Residential Buildings, Rotterdam
Town Hall and Apartments, Weert, Netherlands
University of Brussels (competition project)
Mummelmannsberg Comprehensive School, Hamburg (competition project)
Student Dormitories, Delft, Netherlands
1970 Netherlands Pavilion, *World's Fair*, Osaka, Japan (with Carel Weeber)
1971 University Economics Faculty Building extension, Rotterdam (project)
1971/
73 de Grave Home for the Retarded, Gorinchem, Netherlands
1971/
76 Erasmus College Secondary School, Zoetermeer, Netherlands
1973 Zeckendorf House, The Bahamas
Sunter Town Plan, Djakarta, Indonesia (project)
Kurhaus District redevelopment, Scheveningen, Netherlands (as supervising architects)
Barre Molen Windmill restoration, Zoeterwoude, Netherlands
1974 City centre plan for Eindhoven (project; with Herman Hertzberger)
World Trade Centre, Rotterdam (competition project)
Traffic plan for Kloekamp and Main Railway Station, The Hague
Kaatstraat renovation, Utrecht
1975 Renovation of the Weerdjes District, including apartment buildings, Arnhem, Netherlands

Publications:

By BAKEMA: books—*Towards an Architecture for Society,* Delft 1963; *From Doorstep to Town,* Zeist, Netherlands, 1964; *Stadtebauliche Architektur,* Salzburg 1965; *L. C. van der Vlugt,* Amsterdam 1968; *Team 10 Primer,* with others, edited by Alison Smithson, London 1968; articles—"Open Brief aan J.J.P. Oud," with J. H. van den Broek, in *De Groene Amsterdammer* (Amsterdam), 6 December 1952; "Building with Weathering Steel" in *Polytechnische Tijdschrift* (The Hague), December 1973; "BFU: Nine Evaluations," with others, in *Architecture Plus* (New York), January/February 1974; "Trees First, Then Houses" in *Bouw* (Rotterdam), May 1974; "Some Conditions Governing the Current Development of Architecture" in *Bauen und Wohnen* (Zurich), December 1975; "Bureaucracy Puts Architecture into Cold Storage" in *RIBA Journal* (London), October 1976.

On BAKEMA: books—*CIAM 1959 in Otterlo,* Stuttgart 1959; *Architektur und Stadtebau: Das Werk van den Broek und Bakema,* edited by Jürgen Joedicke, Stuttgart 1963; *Bouwen voor een open Samenleving,* exhibition catalogue, Rotterdam 1963; *van den Broek/Bakema,* edited by Camillo Gubitosi and Alberto Izzo, Rome 1976; *Architecture-Urbanism: Architecten-gemeenschap van der Broek en Bakema,* edited by Jürgen Joedicke, Stuttgart 1976; articles—"Het Bureau van den Broek en Bakema" by Willem van Tijen in *Forum* (Amsterdam), June 1957; "Costruzioni degli Architetti Jacob Bakema e Johannes van den Broek" by G. Perugini in *L'Architettura* (Rome), September 1959; "van den Broek und Bakema," special issue of *Bauen und Wohnen* (Zurich), October 1959; "Brinkman, Brinkman, van der Vlugt, van den Broek, Bakema" by B. Housden, special issue of *Architectural Association Journal* (London), December 1960.

*

Urbanistic architecture can be more than functionalism of use; it can also involve functionalism of expression. Architecture without urban dimension in our days cannot give enough information. Man is living in a field of tension between his locality—town—region and earth-moon universe. A living town-village can no longer be limited. Nowhere in the world has this proved to be possible. This is the time of total urbanization. But the process can be structured by architecture. Rhythmized and accentuated.

Perhaps, for the first time in history, art will be a condition of existence, and urbanization must find the right proportions between use and care. Architecture always was a process of proportioning. Interior is concentrated intensified exterior.

Knowing that property, power and defence can no more be continuous reasons for architecturban forms stimulates research into more universal motivation. Somehow the understanding that our existence-energy-being is a kind of network-like structure makes us try even harder for solutions for clustering, knots and transitional elements with which the built environment can be shaped.

There are knots of connection: to research what elements can be connected or knotted without losing identity—wall-like buildings, towers, transitional elements, energy lines, clustering.

Sant'Elia, Terragni, Golosov, Rietveld and Duiker (during 1925–1935) contributed to our architecturbanistic vocabulary. They expressed a new kind of simultaniety, the abandoning of hierarchy. But they could not know the problems of total urbanization of our days. The world must now deal with the worldwide administration of production and distribution.

The architectonic vocabulary has to be prepared for the expression of total urbanization. Town planning is also society planning. Clustering, wall-like buildings, transitional elements, rhythmizing and accentuation are events which can be experienced visually. They can refer to human relations and interests. Conceptions like court, square and street are signs of relationship and contrast. Urbanistic structures and forms can influence human meeting and separation. To find out what sorts of clusters are appropriate is also a question about the relationships of social forms.

The building program is named: office, house, shop, church, post office, auditorium, hospital. Every name stands for a growing idea and in every building program there is that hidden relation with all other programs and their expression by space-form conception. Every building program is part of the total built environment. The participation of every building program in the total urban structure and the expression of both participation and independence is the proper exercise of architecturbanism: it gives social, economical and political consequence.

There can grow an urban image in which both parts and the whole can be expressed. Every building program can thus be activated to develop its relationship with all others. Transitional elements are important means of expression of these events: the telephone box, a flower stand, a canopy, offices over shops can be stepping stones to higher buildings. At a distance I see something high, and at the foot of it I discover the small elements. By the speed of cars I can experience the high elements at a distance; by the speed of pedestrians I become familiar with small elements. To be information and sign is the extension of use-functionalism.

This is extended to expressive functionalism. Visual clustering, grouping and the structure of society are reciprocally defined concepts.

The space-plastic urban form is a problem of the relationship of volumes in space. The administrative urban form is, anyway, also a social-political problem. It could be more simpler for every user if urban forms and their areas of influence could be simultaneously an expression of the common interests of the user. As in history the town hall and church were meaningful, so our new forms should be the expression of the new distribution of power. (If we consider what forms, until now, have *not* been used to shape the built environment, we can better understand the expressionlessness of much modern architecture.)

There are many kinds of building programs that can stimulate and express an imaginative reality. Can we mobilize form to serve the coming total urbanization? Does our time have potential enough for such a task? Much will depend on the simultaneous employment of a lust-for-use and a lust-for-care. How does one find the architectonic expression of total urbanization?

—Jacob Bakema

Jacob Bakema was versed in technology and was tutored in hydraulic engineering as well as in architecture. As a native of Groningen he was perhaps unsympathetic to the theories of the Delft School, where he was a part-time student, for the predominantly Roman Catholic ideals of Granpré Molière found more congenial ground in which to flourish in the southern provinces of Brabant and Limburg. The craft traditions that had been a feature of Dutch architecture since Berlage purified design of excessively applied ornament had flourished during the inter-war years. Functionalist ideas, as propounded by the followers of De Stijl, were seen to be radically to the left, and a more continuous traditional manner of design was thus in favour during times of international stress. Bakema remained convinced by modernist ideas, and rejected the conservative-craft-oriented beliefs of the Delft School.

His experience in the office of Cor van Eesteren in Amsterdam, and later contact with van Tijen, brought him to know the partnership of Brinkman and van der Vlugt. He thus had a long connection with the firm that was later to consist of Brinkman and van den Broek. The partnership's buildings—such as the van Nelle factory and the Bergpolder block in Rotterdam—remained true to functionalism at a time when there was a reaction back to traditional architecture. Bakema joined van den Broek as a partner in 1948, and the older man was appointed professor at Delft, so the two partners were in a position to attack the conservative theories of the Delft School. In their attacks they were supported by the survivors of the De Stijl movement.

Bakema was solely concerned with the designs for the 't Venster Centre in Rotterdam and for the civic centre plans for St. Louis; however, it is with van den Broek that his most famous buildings have been erected. The Lijnbaan Centre in Rotterdam in 1953 was an early version of the pedestrian shopping street. The partnership also produced a number of civic centres, that at Marl being representative of a type that has become depressingly familiar all over western Europe and America. Four tower blocks linked by lower slabs, with a courtyard, the whole ensemble planned to get as far away as possible from any hint of formality, geometry, or classical memory, will be familiar to all those who have seen what has occurred in towns during the 1950's and 1960's.

Among other works by Bakema in partnership

with van den Broek are schools at Brielle and for the Montessori Lyceum at Rotterdam; the Netherlands Pavilion at the *World's Fair* in Brussels; the Rotterdam stores, Wassen van Vorst and Galeries Modernes; buildings for the Technical University at Delft; and severe modern churches at Schiedam and Nagele.

Bakema and van den Broek have been prolific and have had a great influence on developments in Britain and in Germany. The elegance of earlier works by the Brinkman and van der Vlugt partnership is missing, however, and a certain brashness perhaps prevails. The assertion by Bakema that architecture is the three-dimensional expression of human behaviour savours of a certain cliché-ridden mentality that has bedevilled architectural for so long. One suspects that any slick phrase can gain credence in a profession that has lost its values and is confused in its direction.

Bakema and van den Broek also established themselves in the field of town planning, and their proposals for the Kennemerland area of Holland set fashions in regional planning concepts during the 1950's and early 1960's. Indeed, the *opera* of Bakema and van den Broek are representative of trends in the architectural profession in the first two decades following the Second World War, examples of how traditional values were deliberately jettisoned. Little regard was paid to existing fabric, and the language of architecture, be it classical or vernacular, was ignored for an abstraction. The results of this revolution are visible in towns and cities all over Europe, especially in Britain. The insistence on brash concrete, large areas of glass, unrelated forms, crude junctions, and unrefined detail has been a familiar feature of architecture since the 1950's. Bakema's most famous work is the Lijnbaan in Rotterdam: a dispassionate examination of this large development will show that it has not worn well and that its modernity is neither elegant nor even remotely admirable.

—James Stevens Curl

BAKER, Sir Herbert.
British. Born in Cobham, Kent, 9 June 1862. Educated at the Tonbridge School, Kent, 1873–78; Royal Academy School of Architecture, London, under Norman Shaw and G. F. Bodley, 1879–81; articled to his cousin, the architect Arthur Baker, 1879–82. Married Florence Edmeades in 1904; children: Henry, Allaire, Alfred, and Ann. Senior Assistant in the offices of Ernest George and Harold Peto, London, 1882–87; associated with the Arts and Crafts movement and a group that included Herbert Read, R. Weir Schultz, C. E. Mallows, R. Blomfield, and Edwin Lutyens; in private practice, Gravesend, Kent, 1890–92; moved to the Cape of Good Hope, South Africa, began private practice in Cape Town (appointed architect to Cecil Rhodes), 1892: in partnership with Francis Masey, 1899–1902, and F. K. Kendal, 1910–12; established a practice in Johannesburg, 1902: in partnership with Ernest Wilmott Sloper, 1903–07, and Frank Fleming, 1910–21; returned to England, 1913: in private practice, London, 1913 until his death, 1946: in partnership with A. T. Scott from 1930; worked with Lutyens on New Delhi, 1913–31. A Principal Architect, Imperial War Graves Commission, 1918–28. Founder Member, South African Society of Architects, Cape Town, 1901; Vice-President, Transvaal Association of Architects, 1911; established Baker Scholarship, Transvaal, 1912. Recipient: Queen's Prize, Kensington School of Art, London, 1887; Ashpital Prize, 1889, and Royal Gold Medal for Architecture, 1927, Royal Institute of British Architects. Honorary doctorates: University of the Witwatersrand, Johannesburg, 1934; Oxford University, 1937. Fellow, Royal

Institute of British Architects, 1900. Associate of the Royal Academy, 1922, and Royal Academician, 1932. Knight Bachelor, 1926; K.C.I.E. (Knight Commander, Order of the Indian Empire), 1930. *Died* (at Owletts, Cobham, Kent) *4 February 1946.*

Works:

1881   Church of St. Padarn restoration, Llanberis, Wales (as assistant to Arthur Baker)
1882/
  87   Waterside House, Westgate-on-Sea, Kent (with Ernest George and Harold Peto)
       Redroofs (house), Streatham Common, London (with Ernest George and Harold Peto)
1886   Town House, London (competition project)
1892   The Reformatory additions, Tokai, Cape, South Africa
1892/
1902   Housing, Somerset West, Cape, South Africa
       Housing, Languedoc, South Africa
       Housing, Kimberley, Cape, South Africa
       Housing, Stellenbosch, South Africa
1894   Observatory additions, Observatory, Cape, South Africa
       St. Andrew's Church, Newlands, Cape, South Africa
1896   St. Barnabas's Church, Cape Town
       Groot Schuur (Cecil Rhodes House), Rondebosch, Cape, South Africa (destroyed by fire, 1897; rebuilt, 1898)
1897   Civic Service Club, Cape Town
       Kelvin Grove Country Club remodelling, Cape Town
       Sandhills (Herbert Baker House), Muizenburg, Cape, South Africa
1898   Union-Castle Building, Cape Town (as supervising architect)
       Wilson and Miller Building, Cape Town
       Shangani Memorial, Rhodesia
       St. Michael and All Angels Church, Observatory, Cape, South Africa
       St. Philip's Church, Cape Town
1899   The Woolsack (house), Groot Schuur Estate, Rondebosch, Cape, South Africa
1900   Welgelegen (house), Groot Schuur Estate, Rondebosch, Cape, South Africa
       Juta Building, Cape Town
       Bishop's Diocesan College Junior School, Rondebosch, Cape, South Africa
1901   Government House additions, Cape Town
       St. George's Cathedral, Cape Town (chancel only executed)
       Church of St. John the Divine, Mafeking, Cape, South Africa
1902   Rhodes Building, Cape Town
       Athol House, near Johannesburg (demolished)
       Inanda House, near Johannesburg
       De Beers Boarding House, Somerset West, Cape, South Africa
       Reef Mines Boarding House, Transvaal, South Africa
       Loch Avenue Houses, Parktown, Johannesburg
       Michaelhouse School, Balgowan, Natal, South Africa
       Stonehouse (Baker-Curtis-Balfour House), Parktown, Johannesburg
1903   St. Saviour's Church, Claremont, Cape, South Africa
       Towie, Parktown, Johannesburg (demolished)
       Enstead (Sloper House), Parktown, Johannesburg
1904   Honoured Dead Memorial, Kimberley, Cape, South Africa
       Isaac Building, Cape Town
       Bedford Court, near Johannesburg (now St. Andrew's School for Girls)
       The Big House, Westminster, Orange Free State, South Africa
       Grey College additions, Bloemfontein, Orange Free State, South Africa

New Hall, St. Peter's Home, Cape, South Africa
Roedean School, Parktown, Johannesburg
School of Music, Johannesburg
New Building, Observatory, Johannesburg
St. Michael's Home additions, Bloemfontein, Orange Free State, South Africa
Bishopskop Chapel, Parktown, Johannesburg
St. George's Church, Parktown, Johannesburg
Church of St. John the Divine, Randfontein, Transvaal, South Africa
New Government Buildings, Bloemfontein, Orange Free State, South Africa
Bishopskop, Parktown, Johannesburg
Dykeneuk, Kensington, Johannesburg
The Lodge, Northward, Parktown, Johannesburg (demolished)
Marienhof, Parktown, Johannesburg
Northward, Parktown, Johannesburg (remodelled, 1912)
Taynuilt, Waverley, Johannesburg
Abe Bailey House, Grootfontein, South Africa (project)
St. George's Grammar School, Cape Town
1905 Bank, Magersfontein, border of Cape and Orange Free State, South Africa
Bank, Malmesbury, Cape, South Africa
Findlay and Company Building, Cape Town
Guardian Building, Adderley Street, Cape Town

Marks Building, Cape Town
Rust en Vrede (Sir Abe Bailey House), Muizenberg, Cape, South Africa
Mount Nelson Hotel and Gardens, Cape Town (as supervising architect)
National Mutual Life of Australasia Building, Cape Town
Housing, Westminster, Orange Free State, South Africa
Physics Laboratory, Diocesan College, Rondebosch, Cape, South Africa
Schoolhouse, Westminster, Orange Free State, South Africa
St. Alban's Cathedral, Pretoria
St. George's Church, Cullinan, Transvaal, South Africa
St. Peter's Church, Krugersdorp, Transvaal, South Africa
Pilrig, Parktown, Johannesburg (with 1910 additions)
The Thatched House, Riviera, Johannesburg (now Shinglewood House)
1906 Bank, Kroonstadt, Orange Free State, South Africa
Housing for Witwatersrand miners, Transvaal, South Africa
Dale College, King William's Town, Cape, South Africa
Lady Chapel, Cathedral of St. Andrew and St. Michael, Bloemfontein, Orange Free State, South Africa

New Tower, Cathedral of St. Andrew and St. Michael, Bloemfontein, Orange Free State, South Africa (demolished, 1965)
Church of Christ, Arcadia, Pretoria
The White House, Sunnyside, Bryntirion, Pretoria
The Moot House, Parktown, Johannesburg
Timewell, Parktown, Johannesburg
1907 Lionel Phillips House, Haenertsburg, Transvaal, South Africa (project)
New Hall, Diocesan College, Rondebosch, Cape, South Africa
St. John's College, Johannesburg
Church of the Holy Trinity, Turffontein, Johannesburg
Church of the Innocents, Volksrust, Transvaal, South Africa
St. Luke's Church, Orchards, Johannesburg
Government House, Bryntirion, Pretoria
1908 Rhodes Memorial, Table Mountain, Cape, South Africa
Museum, Bulawayo, Rhodesia
Michaelhouse Chapel, Balgowan, Natal, South Africa
Chapel, St. Anne's Diocesan College, Hilton Road, Natal, South Africa
St. Michael's Church, Sunnyside, Pretoria
1909 Witwatersrand Native Labour Association Housing and Buildings, Johannesburg
Lower School House, St. Andrew's School, Grahamstown, Cape, South Africa

Sir Herbert Baker: Union Buildings, Pretoria, 1913

Pretoria Railway Station
St. Mary's Church additions, Richmond, Natal, South Africa
The Millin House, Parktown, Johannesburg (with J. M. Solomon; with 1920 additions)
1910 Nazareth House Chapel, Cape, South Africa
St. Boniface's Church, Germiston, Transvaal, South Africa
Blackroof, Westcliff, Johannesburg
Earnholme, Parktown, Johannesburg
The Gate House, Parktown, Johannesburg
Given-Wilson House, Yeoville, Johannesburg
Glenshiel, Westcliff, Johannesburg
Kleine Schuur, Parktown, Johannesburg
Director's House, South African Institute for Medical Research, Johannesburg
Villa Arcadia, Parktown, Johannesburg (now Jewish Orphanage)
13 Union Buildings, Pretoria
1911 Rhodes University College, Grahamstown, Cape, South Africa
Swedish Church additions, Johannesburg
St. Thomas's Church additions, Cape Town
St. Mary's and All Saints' Cathedral, Salisbury, Rhodesia
St. Peter's Pro-Cathedral, Vryheid, Zululand
St. Michael's and All Angels' Church, Boksburg, Transvaal, South Africa
Plan for Pretoria
The Angles, Parktown, Johannesburg
Duntreath, Westcliff, Johannesburg (with 1925 additions)
The Parsonage, Parktown, Johannesburg
1912 St. Mary's Church, Greyville, Durban
Bishop's House, Pietermaritzburg, Natal, South Africa
South African Institute for Medical Research, Johannesburg
Nurses' Home, Johannesburg
Chapel, St. Andrew's College, Grahamstown, Cape, South Africa
St. Peter's Church, Sabie, Transvaal, South Africa
1913 Rietbult Farm, near Balfour, Transvaal, South Africa
Union Club, Johannesburg
Belcaire (Sir Philip Sassoon House), Port Lympne, Kent
1913/
26 Secretariat and Legislative and Staff Buildings, New Delhi, India (with Edwin Lutyens)
1918/
28 112 War Cemeteries in France and Belgium (as Principal Architect)
1919/
22 Village War Memorial Crosses at Etchingham, Sussex; Ledbury, Herefordshire; Kemerton, Gloucestershire; Cobham, Kent; Wadhurst, Sussex; Potterne, Wiltshire; Meopham, Kent; Settle, Yorkshire; Sutton Valence, Kent; Ascot, Berkshire; Hatfield, Hertfordshire; Hertingfordbury, Hertfordshire; Richmond, Yorkshire; Chicheley, Buckinghamshire; Ramsgate, Kent; and other English villages.
1920 John Kipling Memorial, Etchingham, Sussex
1921 Kent County War Memorial, The Close, Canterbury
Hampshire County War Memorial, The Close, Winchester
War Memorial Lych Gate, Overbury Church, Worcestershire
Cubley Village (model housing), Penistone, Yorkshire
1922 City War Memorial, Rochester, Kent
War Memorial, The King's School, Canterbury, Kent
W. G. Grace Memorial Gates, Lord's Cricket Ground, St. John's Wood, London
1924 War Memorial Cloister, Drinking Fountain and Cross, Blackmoor Church, Hampshire

Chilham Castle restoration and additions, Kent
War Memorial Cloister, Winchester College, Hampshire
1925 Bishop Jacob Memorial Church, Ilford, Essex
1925/
28 Schools for settlers' children at Nairobi, Nakuru, Eldoret, and Kitale, Kenya
1925/
39 Bank of England reconstruction, London
1926 Meeting Hall, Royal Institute of International Affairs, Chatham House, St. James's Square, London (later remodelled by others)
South African War Memorial, Delville Wood, Longueval, Somme, France
War Memorial Building, Harrow School, Middlesex
Grandstand, Lord's Cricket Ground, St. John's Wood, London
1927 Indian War Memorial, Neuve Chapelle, France
Reserve Bank, Pretoria
War Cemetery and Memorial to the Missing, Tynecot, Passchendaele, Ypres, Belgium
Claude Johnson Memorial Garden, Rolls Royce Ltd., Derby
Howick Hall rebuilding after fire, Northumberland
Government House extensions, Mombasa, Kenya
Owletts (Herbert Baker House) alterations, Cobham, Kent
Ivo Bligh Tombstone, Cobham, Kent
1928 Government House, Nairobi, Kenya
Canon Glossop Memorial Garden, St. Albans, Hertfordshire
St. Martin's Chapel restoration, Canterbury Cathedral, Kent
1929 A. V. Lyttelton Memorial Gate, Hawarden, Cheshire
War Memorial Building additions, Harrow School, Middlesex
Indian High School, Nairobi, Kenya
Rhodes House, Oxford
1930 India House, Aldwych, London
Cloister, Merchant Taylors' Hall, Threadneedle Street, London
Mein House, Woodside, California
War Cemetery, Dud Corner, Loos, France
Ninth Church of Christ Scientist, Marsham Street, London
1931 Barclays Bank, Langham Place, London
Fairbridge Settlement Church, Pinjara, Western Australia
Kabete High School, Nairobi, Kenya (later the Prince of Wales School)
Martin's Bank, 68 Lombard Street, London
Thong Mead (A. G. Baker House), Shorne, Kent
Barclays Bank, Cape Town (with A. T. Scott)
St. Peter's Hall, Oxford (with R. Fielding Dodd)
Tudor Yeoman's House restoration, Sole Street, Kent
1932 Downing College extensions, Cambridge
War Memorial Dining Hall, Haileybury College, Hertfordshire
H.R.H. Princess Mary's Suite alterations, Harewood House, Yorkshire
Dame Millicent Fawcett Memorial Tablet, Westminster Abbey, London
Margaret McMillan Memorial Column and Lamp, Deptford, London
1933 Lord Harris Memorial Tablet, County War Memorial, Canterbury, Kent
Barham Court rebuilding after fire, Teston, Kent
Chiswick Bridge, London
Electra House facade and interior design, Victoria Embankment, London
Glyn Mills Bank, 67 Lombard Street, London
Golden Cross House alterations to facade, Strand, London

South Africa House, Trafalgar Square, London
Science Laboratories, Haileybury College, Hertfordshire
Church of St. Dunstan-in-the-East restoration, London
Church of St. Paul, Woldingham, Surrey
1934 Women's Pavilion, Bank of England Sports Ground, Roehampton, London
Lord Inchcape Memorial Chapel, Royal Merchant Seamen's Orphanage, Bear Wood, Berkshire
Scott Polar Research Institute, Cambridge
Melville (Scott House), Woldingham, Surrey
Lord Harris Memorial, Lord's Cricket Ground, St. John's Wood, London
1935 Gairdner Memorial Church, Cairo
Members' Stand, Lord's Cricket Ground, St. John's Wood, London
Moberley Library (conversion from brewery), Winchester College, Hampshire
1936 Chapel alterations, Haileybury College, Hertfordshire
Royal Empire Society Headquarters (now Royal Commonwealth Society), Northumberland Avenue, London
Boarding House, Westminster School, London
T. E. Lawrence Memorial Tablet, St. Paul's Cathedral, London
1937 London House (hostel), stage I, Mecklenburg Square, London
Church of St. John, Maadi, Egypt
1938 Atbara Church, Sudan
Somerhill House library reconstruction, Tonbridge, Kent
1939 Chapel restoration and conversion to Board Room for Rochester Bridge Trust, Kent
1940 Church House, Dean's Yard, Westminster, London
Bradbourne (house) conversion for East Malling Agricultural Research Station, near Maidstone, Kent

Publications:

By BAKER: books—*Plas Mawr, Conway, North Wales*, with Arthur Baker, London 1888; *Cecil Rhodes by His Architect*, Oxford 1934, reprinted (with Rhodes' will and chapters by W. T. Stead), Bulawayo, Rhodesia 1977; *Architecture and Personalities*, London 1944; articles—"The Origin of Cape Architecture" in *Old Colonial Houses* by Alys Fane Trotter, London 1900; "The Architectural Needs of South Africa" in *The State* (Cape Town), May 1909; "Architecture and Town Planning" in *South African Architect* (Johannesburg), August 1911.

On BAKER: books—*Three Weeks in South Africa* by F. Rothschild, London 1895; *Transvaal Problems* by Lionel Phillips, London 1905; *Historic Houses of South Africa* by Dorothea Fairbridge, Oxford 1922; *Representative British Architects* by C. H. Reilly, London 1931; *The Building Stones of the Union of South Africa* by W. Wybergh, Pretoria 1932; *The Cathedral of St. George, Cape Town* by E. Hermitage Day, Cape Town 1939; *Claremont Album* by Joyce Murray, Cape Town 1958; *St. Andrew's College, Grahamstown, 1858–1959* by R. F. Currey, London 1959; *The Unification of South Africa* by G. M. Thomson, Oxford 1960; *Cape Dutch Houses and Farms* by C. De Bosdari, Cape Town 1964; *Herbert Baker in South Africa* by Doreen E. Greig, Cape Town 1970.

As a newcomer to South Africa during a bleak period of its architectural history, Herbert Baker was given the opportunity to change the course of that architecture and to set in train ideas that were later also to benefit other countries such as Kenya, Rhodesia, and India. In the short space of twenty years he established precedents that ensured the continuation of the heritage of the traditional building forms of England, France, Italy and Greece and the extension of the Arts and Crafts movement; as well, he helped to introduce to South Africa technologies for the creation of large buildings for modern needs.

The favourable circumstances of his upbringing, the moulding of his character, and the good professional training that was then available in England made it possible for Baker to deal with the conditions he was to encounter in South Africa both before and after the South African war. His social attributes of birth, education, appearance and manner assured his acceptance among those of his own class who ran the country.

Baker's first delight in the beauty of the old Dutch gabled and whitewashed homesteads at the Cape was tempered by distress at their neglected appearance. Cape Town had lost its original urban Dutch and later Regency character, and Baker deplored the impermanent looking buildings that lined its narrow streets, just as he was to deplore those of the new towns to the North, put together with ugly, imported, industrialized components. In order to satisfy himself and his new clients, Baker had first to discover and train craftsmen to use what good indigenous materials were available and, when he was later commissioned to design churches, monuments and commercial buildings, he, his partners, and other South African architects were able to reap the benefits of his pioneering work. In the Arts and Crafts spirit he interested people in the restoration and preservation of the Cape Dutch vernacular buildings and, in the current spirit of revivalism, designed the first modern houses in that idiom.

In 1902 Baker left the Cape for the war-torn Transvaal, and there, in a difficult but dynamic environment, he met tremendous challenges. Building conditions were much the same as they had earlier been at the Cape, except that there was no building tradition, however remote, to draw on. Boer houses in the country were little more than mud or stone hovels, and in the towns everything except mud for mortar and sun dried bricks had to be imported. Labour was scarce: what had existed before had been dispersed by the war. Again he acted as an organizer of men and materials and, by 1905, his practice was country-wide and flourishing. He designed government buildings and was employed by professional men, by firms with big mining interests, and by the Anglican church.

To meet the different demands of the practice, like his contemporaries in England and other parts of the British empire, Baker drew on the building elements of other climates, countries and historical periods, combining the different forms he judged to be suitable for his designs; he compounded them into functional and often magnificent buildings: they proceeded beyond the literary quality that was discernible in his work to what he called the "human sentiment and desires" of their users.

Herbert Baker was the first architect to bring climatic conditions to bear on architectural design in South Africa. This, the nature of the dramatic sites he chose, and the use of local materials, produced a rare organic unity between the buildings and their environments—particularly in his many handsome churches and houses, which seem to be a part of the koppies from which their materials are derived, and the excellent Union Buildings in Pretoria. As works of art they hold their own with what was being built elsewhere in more favourable situations, and are the first original contribution to South African architecture since the evolution of the unique cape baroque houses of the 18th century.

—Doreen Greig

BANFI, Gianluigi.

Italian. Born in Milan, 2 April 1910. Educated at the Liceo Parini, Milan, 1921–27; Milan Polytechnic School of Architecture, 1927–32, Dip.Arch. 1932. Served in the Italian Army, 1932–34, and 1943 until the armistice, then with the Resistance: arrested by the Germans in 1944: deported to the concentration camp at Mauthausen where he died, 1945. Married Julia Bertolotti in 1939; son: Guiliano. Founder Partner, with Ludovico Belgiojoso, *q.v.*, Enrico Peressutti, *q.v.*, and Ernesto Nathan Rogers, *q.v.*, BBPR Architectural Studio, *q.v.*, Milan, 1932 until his death. Member of CIAM (Congrès Internationaux d'Architecture Moderne), from 1935; Member, Commissione per le Manifestazione d'Arte Moderne dell'Associazione trai i Cultori d'Architettura, 1935. *Died* (in Mauthausen) *10 April 1945.*

Publications:

By BANFI: articles—"Urbanistica Anno XII," with Lodovico Belgiojoso, in *Quadrante* (Milan), May 1934; "Urbanistica Corporativa," with Lodovico Belgiojoso, in *Quadrante* (Milan), August/September 1934; "La Casa Contemporanea al Regime Corporativo" in *Domus* (Milan), November 1934; "Una Casa a Milano" in *Quadrante* (Milan), January 1935; "Abitare" in *Domus* (Milan), June 1938; "La Casa e la Finestra" in *Rassegna di Architettura* (Milan), September 1939; "Città" in *Domus* (Milan), July 1941; "La Casa Ideale" in *Domus* (Milan), August 1942.

See BBPR ARCHITECTURAL STUDIO

BANG, Ove.

Norwegian. Born in Røyken, 13 September 1895. Educated at the Technical University of Norway, Trondheim, 1913–17, Dip.Arch. 1917. Worked in the office of the architect Magnus Poulsson, Oslo, 1917–19; Architect with Norsk Hydro, Rjukan, 1919–22; in private practice, Rjukan, 1922–30, then in Oslo, 1930 until his death, 1942. Recipient: Houens Fond Architectural Prize, 1935; Egers Fellowship, 1937. Member, Norwegian Architects Institute. *Died* (in Oslo) *5 May 1942.*

Works:

1922 Students Residence Hall (competition project)
       Housing prototypes for various parts of Norway (competition project)
1923 People's High School, Elverum, Norway (competition project)
1924 Frøytul Power Station, Tinn, Norway (competition project)
1925 Columbarium, Oslo (competition project)
1927 Students' Community Centre, Trondheim (competition project)
1930 Summer Houses and Cottages (competition project)
1931 Oddfellows Building, Oslo (competition project; with Øivin Grimsgaard)
       Cinema and Assembly Building, Horten, Norway (competition project; with Øivin Grimsgaard)
       Single-family house, Rjukan, Norway
       Single-family house, Sørbyhaugen, Oslo
       Single-family house, Anne Maries vei 18, Oslo
       Mountain cottage, Vågå, Norway
1932 Handelens Hus (office and assembly building), Stavanger (competition project)
1933 Single-family house, Baerumsveien 5b, Oslo
1934 Fram-huset (ship museum), Bygdøy, Oslo (competition project; with Einar F. Christiansen)
       Single-family house, Fana, Bergen
1935 Development plan for the Vestre Vika area, Oslo (project; with Johan Ellefsen)
       Apartment building, Ila, Oslo (project; with Jan Reiner)
       Norsk Rikskringkasting Broadcasting Station, Oslo (competition project; with Øivin H. Grimsgaard)
       Bibelskolen Mission Society Offices and Summer Hotel, Staffeldts gate 4, Oslo
       Single-family house, Holmenveien 87, Oslo
       Single-family house, Tuengen allé 10d, Oslo
1936 Handelsgymnasium (commercial high school), Oslo (competition project)
       Mountain cottage, Geilo, Norway
1937 Ditlev-Simonsen House, Løvenskiolds vei 32, Oslo (now the Canadian Embassy)
       Single-family house, Nypeveien 6, Oslo
       Single-family house, Holgerslystveien 10b, Oslo
       Single-family houses, Holsteinveien 7 and 9, Oslo
       Summer house, Landøen, Asker, Norway

Ove Bang: Ditlev-Simonsen House, Oslo, 1937

1938 Town Hall, Horten, Norway (competition
  project; with Øivin H. Grimsgaard)
  School, Kristiansand, Norway (competition
  project; with Øivin H. Grimsgaard)
1939 Development plan, including government
  buildings, for the Vestre Vika area of Oslo
  (project)
  Government Office Building, Oslo (competition project; with Oivin H. Grimsgaard)
  Bakkehaugen Church, Oslo (competition
  project)
  Tomb Landbruksskole (agricultural school),
  Onsøy, Norway
  Single-family house, Kongeskogen, Bygdøy,
  Oslo
  Single-family house, Sogn hageby, Oslo
1940 Oslo Court House extension, Grubbegaten 1
  Samfundshuset (Union of Workers Building,
  with community hall, cinema, shops, and
  offices), Arbeidersamfunnets plass, Oslo
1941 Reconstruction plan for Kristiansund, Nor-
  way
  Reconstruction plan for Nordnes, Bergen
  Public Library, Sarpsborg, Norway
  Metal Factory, Løren, Oslo (project)

Publications:

On BANG: book—*Arkitekt Ove Bang* by Gudolf
Blakstad and Herman Munthe-Kaas, Oslo 1943; articles—"Elastiske standardboliger" in *Byggekunst*
(Oslo), vol. 19, no. 8, 1937; "Er Vestre Vika låst
fast?" by G. Ø. Jørgen in *Byggekunst* (Oslo), vol. 21,
1939; "Ove Bang in Memoriam" by Gudolf Blakstad
in *Byggmästaren* (Stockholm), no. 17, 1942; "Before
the Moon Is Down" in *Interiors* (New York), May
1943; "Cinema in Oslo" in *The Architect's Journal*
(London), 28 March 1946; "The Samfundshuset,
Oslo" by Brian Westwood in *Architect and Building
News* (London), 26 December 1947; "Ove Bang
1895–1942" by Øivin H. Grimsgaard in *Byggekunst*
(Oslo), no. 2, 1948; "Maison du Peuple à Oslo" in
L'Architecture d'Aujourd'hui (Paris), December
1948.

Ove Bang was the outstanding representative of the
Modern Movement in Norway in the pre-war period. He had firm roots in Norwegian traditions, but
he integrated these in a series of major buildings into
a mature style inspired particularly by Le Corbusier.
  Bang was a keen open air sportsman, and his early
buildings are various mountain huts. At Vågå (1931)
he demonstrated that the traditional techniques of
"stave" (heavy vertical post and frame) and "laft"
(horizontal interlocked logs) could be used in a new
and unromantic manner, whilst at Geilo (1936) he
continued this synthesis, even achieving the technically difficult feat of integrating large plates of glass
into "laft" construction. He used a series of wooden
houses to further clarify timber construction systems
and demonstrated the ability of this system to express the ideas of the 1930's.
  Bang's two major works are the Ditlev-Simonsen
House (1937) and Samfundshuset (1940) in Oslo.
  Ditlev-Simonsen House has a strongly closed
character pierced by large panes of glass. The interior has an unusually complex spatial composition:
the three main living rooms, of differing proportions,
are in a type of split-level plan but inter-related by
a glazed central staircase. Norberg-Schulz reports
that when he showed this house to Giedion he said,
"This is as good as Corb but here it is also possible
to live!"
  Samfundshuset shows this style developed on a
major urban site. It has a complex, though typical,
set of functions: offices, shops, cinemas, etc., contained in the clearly defined body of the building. It
is one of the most successful urban statements of the
Modern Movement and still has a freshness that is
very inspiring.

—Michael Lloyd

BARNES, Edward Larrabee.

American. Born in Chicago, Illinois, 15 April 1922.
Educated at Harvard University, Cambridge, Mas-
sachusetts, under Marcel Breuer, B.S. (cum laude)
1938, M.Arch. 1942; awarded Sheldon Travelling
Fellowship, 1941–42. Served as a Lieutenant in the
United States Naval Reserve, 1942–47. Married
Mary Elizabeth Coss in 1944; son: John. In private
practice, New York, since 1949. Architectural De-
sign Critic and Lecturer, Pratt Institute, Brooklyn,
New York, 1954–59, and Yale University, New
Haven, Connecticut, 1957–64. Director, Municipal
Art Society of New York, since 1960 (Treasurer,
1961); Trustee; American Academy in Rome, since
1963 (First Vice-President, 1975; First Vice-Chair-
man, 1975–78); Member, Urban Design Council,
New York, since 1972; Trustee, Museum of Modern
Art, New York, since 1977. Exhibitions: *Architecture for the Arts*, Museum of Modern Art, New
York, 1971; *Edward Larrabee Barnes*, Scaife Gallery, Carnegie Institute, Pittsburgh, 1974. Recipient:
Distinction in the Arts Award, Yale University,
1959; Silver Medal, Architectural League of New
York, 1960; *Progressive Architecture* Award, 1963,
1974; First Honor Award, United States Federal
Housing Authority, 1963; Medal of Honor, American Institute of Architects, New York Chapter,
1971; Harleston Parker Medal, Boston Society of
Architects, 1972; Collaborative Achievement in Architecture Award, 1972, and Honor Award, 1972,
1977, American Institute of Architects; Bard
Award, City Club of New York, 1978; Louis Sullivan Award, 1979. Fellow, American Institute of
Architects, 1966. Associate, 1969, and Academician,
1974, National Academy of Design; Fellow, American Academy of Arts and Sciences, 1978. Address
(office): 410 East 62nd Street, New York, New York
10021, U.S.A.

Works:

1955 Camp Bliss, Fishkill, New York
1958/
  65 Capitol Tower Apartments, 1500 7th Street,
    Sacramento, California (with Wurster,
    Bernardi and Emmons, and DeMars and
    Reay)
1959 Woodland House, Chappaqua, New York
1962 Haystack Mountain School of Arts and
    Crafts, Deer Isle, Maine
1963 El Monte Apartments, Hato Rey, Puerto
    Rico
    Henry House, Blue Mountain Lake, New
    York
    Pan American World Airways Ticket Office,
    Vanderbilt Avenue and East 45th Street,
    New York (with Charles Forberg)
    Nieman-Marcus Shopping Center, Fort
    Worth, Texas
1965 Helen Newberry Joy Residence for Women,
    Wayne State University, Detroit
1965/
  74 Master plan and major buildings for the State
    University of New York at Potsdam
1966 W. D. Richard Elementary School, Colum-
    bus, Indiana
1968 Wye Institute Camp, Cheston-on-Wye,
    Maryland
    Rochester Institute of Technology Campus,
    New York
1968/
  78 Master plan and major buildings for the State
    University of New York at Purchase
1969 Christian Theological Seminary, Indianapolis
    Residence Halls, Bennington College, Ver-
    mont
    Snell Music Center, William Moore Dietel
    Library, and Clementine Miller Tangeman
    Apartments, Emma Willard School, Troy,
    New York
    Dormitories, St. Paul's School, Concord,
    New Hampshire
1971 New England Merchants National Bank
    Building, Boston

1973 Theatre and Outdoor Forum, Monterey Pe-
    ninsula College, Monterey, California
    Crown Center (office building complex, retail
    complex, and parking), Kansas City, Mis-
    souri
    Rockefeller Hall, Harvard Divinity School,
    Cambridge, Massachusetts
1973/
  74 South Street Seaport Development Plan, New
    York (with Jonathan Barnett and James
    Ulmer)
1974 Walker Art Center, Minneapolis
    American Savings Bank, 31–02 Steinway
    Street, Queens, New York
    Cochrane-Woods Art Center, University of
    Chicago
1975 Sarah M. Scaife Gallery, Carnegie Institute,
    Pittsburgh
1976 House on the Maine Coast, at Mount Desert
    Law School, Drake University, Des Moines,
    Iowa
1977 Farnum, Vanderbilt and Durfee Halls reno-
    vation, Yale University, New Haven, Con-
    necticut
    Chicago Botanical Garden, Glencoe, Illinois
    IBM World Trade/Americas Far East Cor-
    poration Headquarters, Mount Pleasant,
    New York
1978 Visual Arts Center, Bowdoin College, Bruns-
    wick, Maine
    Plants and Man Building, New York Botani-
    cal Garden, Bronx, New York
    Cathedral of the Immaculate Conception,
    Burlington, Vermont

Publications:

By BARNES: articles—"Defence Housing" in *Task*
(New York), no. 2, 1941; "The Design Process" in
Perspecta (New Haven, Connecticut), no. 5, 1959;
"Control of Graphics Essential to Good Shopping
Center Design" in *Architectural Record* (New
York), June 1962; "Remarks on Continuity and
Change" in *Perspecta* (New Haven, Connecticut),
no. 9/10, 1965.

On BARNES: books—*The Ideal Theatre: Eight
Concepts*, New York 1962; *Architects on Architecture*
by Paul Heyer, New York 1962; articles—"Gene-
trix: Personal Contributions to American Architecture" in *Architectural Review* (London), May 1957;
"Architecture of Ideas" in *House and Home* (New
York), March 1962; "Architect Ed Barnes: Toward
Simpler Details, Simpler Forms and Greater Unity"
in *Architectural Forum* (New York), August 1963;
"A Return to Absolute Simplicity" in *House and
Garden* (New York), April 1965; "Lines and Vol-
ume: Two Recent Projects from the Boards of Ed-
ward Larrabee Barnes" in *Progressive Architecture*
(New York), April 1969; "In Praise of the Unexcit-
ing Old Concepts Which Inspired the Work of Ed-
ward Larrabee Barnes for the College of Potsdam"
in *Architectural Record* (New York), August 1972;
"Crown Center: Urban Renewal for a Kansas City
Grey Area" in *Architectural Record* (New York),
October 1973; "Barnes Gratia Artis" in *Progressive
Architecture* (New York), March 1975; "What
Should a Museum Building Be?" by Paul Gold-
berger in *Art News* (New York), October 1975; "An
Art Center by Edward Larrabee Barnes" by Mildred
F. Schmertz in *Architectural Record* (New York),
March 1978.

In a great variety of civic, educational and ecclesias-
tic buildings, and several urban and campus plans,
Edward Larrabee Barnes has proven himself to be a
serious, adept designer with a true finesse in using
geometry to order without inhibiting space. His
buildings are exacting; they are detailed meticulously and arranged precisely. Still, there is never a
sense of the contrived: his buildings are clean and
rational without being imposing. He is, amidst ges-

tures that tend towards the monumental, acutely concerned with context, and his buildings rarely appear cold or out of place.

After working with both Gropius and Breuer, it is not surprising that Barnes displays such a love for the value of pure form. Complex programs are simplified by the employment of dominant shapes, and the final buildings are easily readable and abstract. Barnes' materials are generally homogeneous and stretch across large expanses of the external skin. This method eliminates multiple readings and aids in the clarification of the massing that characterizes his structures. In fact, very large glass walls and windows, topped by oversized spandrels, have become a trademark. His campus at Rochester Institute of Technology, the Christian Theological Seminiary in Indianapolis, and the Sarah Scaife Gallery at the Carnegie Institute in Pittsburgh, all contain this highlight.

In composing plans Barnes often uses modules. Sometimes they express themselves in unusual forms or in repetition: at the Plants and Man Building of the New York Botanical Garden, for example, hexagonal glass volumes are repeated. Often, though, his modules are merely organization devices that are barely visible when the building is complete. Precast concrete panels and large cut stone are common materials in Barnes' architecture, and both further impose modular dimension restrictions.

Some of Barnes' most recent work exhibits a lighter approach to materials, but there is still a clear reference to geometry, a formal order in the plan, and careful, precise detailing. They still incorporate abstract simplifications of massing and detail, and the results are not merely rational but also evocative, without seeming forced.

—Ching-Yu Chang

BARNETT, Jonathan.
American. Born in Boston, Massachusetts, 6 January 1937. Educated at the Noble and Greenough School, Dedham, Massachusetts, 1948–54; Yale University, New Haven, Connecticut, 1954–58, B.A. 1958; Cambridge University (Mellon Fellow), under Leslie Martin and Colin Rowe, 1958–60, B.A. 1960, M.A. 1967; Yale University, under Paul Rudolph, 1960–63, M.Arch. 1963. Designer in the office of Haines, Lundberg and Waehler, New York, 1963–64; Associate Editor, *Architectural Record,* New York, 1964–67 (Editorial Consultant since 1968); Principal Urban Designer, 1967–69, and Director of the Urban Design Group, 1969–71, New York City Planning Department. In private practice, as consultant and urban designer, New York, since 1971. Professor of Architecture, and Director of the Graduate Program in Urban Design, The City College of New York, since 1971. Member of the Board, Municipal Art Society, 1970–78. Vice-President, 1968–70, and since 1977 President, Architectural League of New York; Member of the Board, New York Landmarks Conservancy, since 1973; Member of the Executive Committee of the New York Chapter of the American Institute of Architects, since 1977. Program Director, First National Conference on Urban Design, New York, 1978. Exhibitions: *The New City: Architecture and Urban Renewal,* Museum of Modern Art, New York, 1966; *Urban Design in New York,* Architectural League of New York, 1969 (organized exhibition). Recipient: Jesse Neal Award, 1966; *Urban Design* Award, 1978. Address (office): 355 Lexington Avenue, New York, New York 10017, U.S.A.

Edward Larrabee Barnes: IBM Headquarters, Mount Pleasant, New York, 1977 (model)

Works:

1966/
67   Twin Parks Urban Renewal Plan, Bronx,
      New York (with Giovanni Pasanella, J. T.
      Robertson, Richard Weinstein and M.
      Weintraub)
1968 Standards for Planned Unit Development,
      New York (with Urban Design Group)
      Special Theatre Zoning District, New York
      (with Urban Design Group)
1969 Downtown Brooklyn Development Plan,
      New York (with Urban Design Group and
      Vincent Ponte)
      Negril Development Plan, Jamaica, West In-
      dies (with Adelates Technical Services,
      Giovanni Pasanella, J. T. Robertson and
      Richard Weinstein)
      Comprehensive Plan for New York City
1970/
71   Rapid Transit Corridors Plan, for the New
      York City boroughs of Brooklyn, Queens,
      Bronx and Manhattan (with Urban Design
      Group)
1973/
74   South Street Seaport Development Plan, New
      York (with James Ulmer and Company
      and Edward Larrabee Barnes)
1975 Various projects for Arlen Realty, in Dallas,
      Houston, Alexandria, Virginia, and New
      York City (with Arlen Planning and De-
      sign Group and J. T. Robertson)
1976/
78   Development and management plans for the
      Gateway National Recreation Area, New
      York (with the National Park Service)
1977 Louisville Alley Study, Louisville, Kentucky
      (with the Community Design Center and
      Grady Clay)
      Alaska State Capital Competition Plan, Wil-
      low, Alaska (with M. Paul Friedberg and
      Benjamin Thompson)
1977– Downtown development strategy for Pitts-
      burgh, Pennsylvania
1978 Sha Tin and Tuen Mun Town Centre Plans,
      New Territories, Hong Kong (as adviser to
      Yunken Freeman)
      Crawford-Roberts Neighborhood Plan, Pitts-
      burgh

Publications:

By BARNETT: books—*Urban Design as Public Policy,* New York 1974, Tokyo 1978; *The Architect as
Developer,* with John Portman, New York 1976; article—"A New Meaning for Modern Architecture"
in *Architectural Record* (New York), July 1966.

My work is divided among teaching, writing and
consulting, but it is all directed towards the same
purpose: trying to redirect the resources that are
being expended in any case on real-estate development, government buildings, parks, highways, and
other major changes that we make in our environment. So often, what is done wrong could just as well
be done right; as I am fond of saying: "we get what
we ask for, why can't we get what we want?"

I direct a Graduate Program that takes graduates
of schools of architecture and seeks to give them the
skills that will enable them to use their design talents
at a larger scale. We do this through a combination
of practical experience, arranged by the Program,
and intensive classroom instruction in subjects such
as law and real-estate, showing the way they relate
to design.

I wrote a description of the principles that we had
developed working for New York City, *Urban Design as Public Policy,* in the hope that I could influence other people, and other cities, to build on some

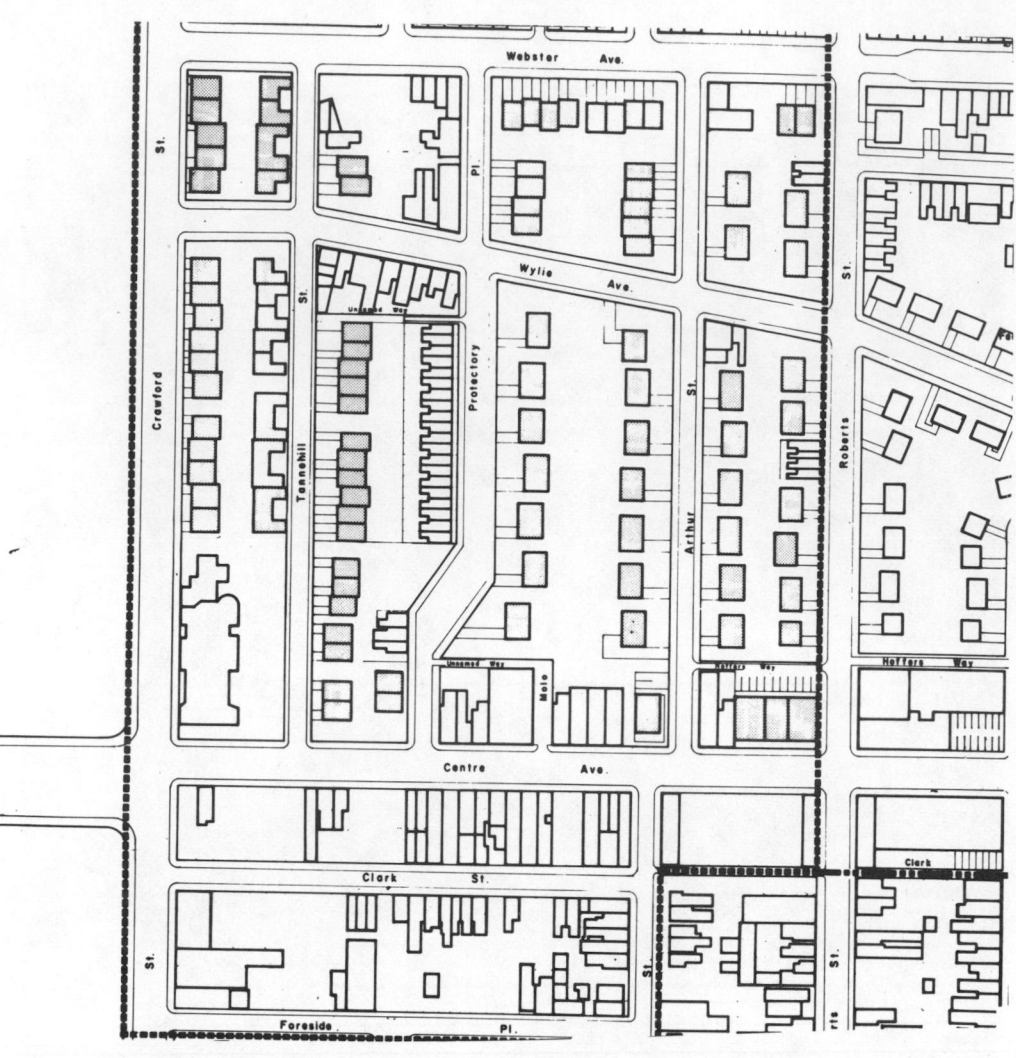

Jonathan Barnett: Crawford-Roberts Neighborhood Plan, Pittsburgh, 1978:
A—development mandated by local land-use regulations;

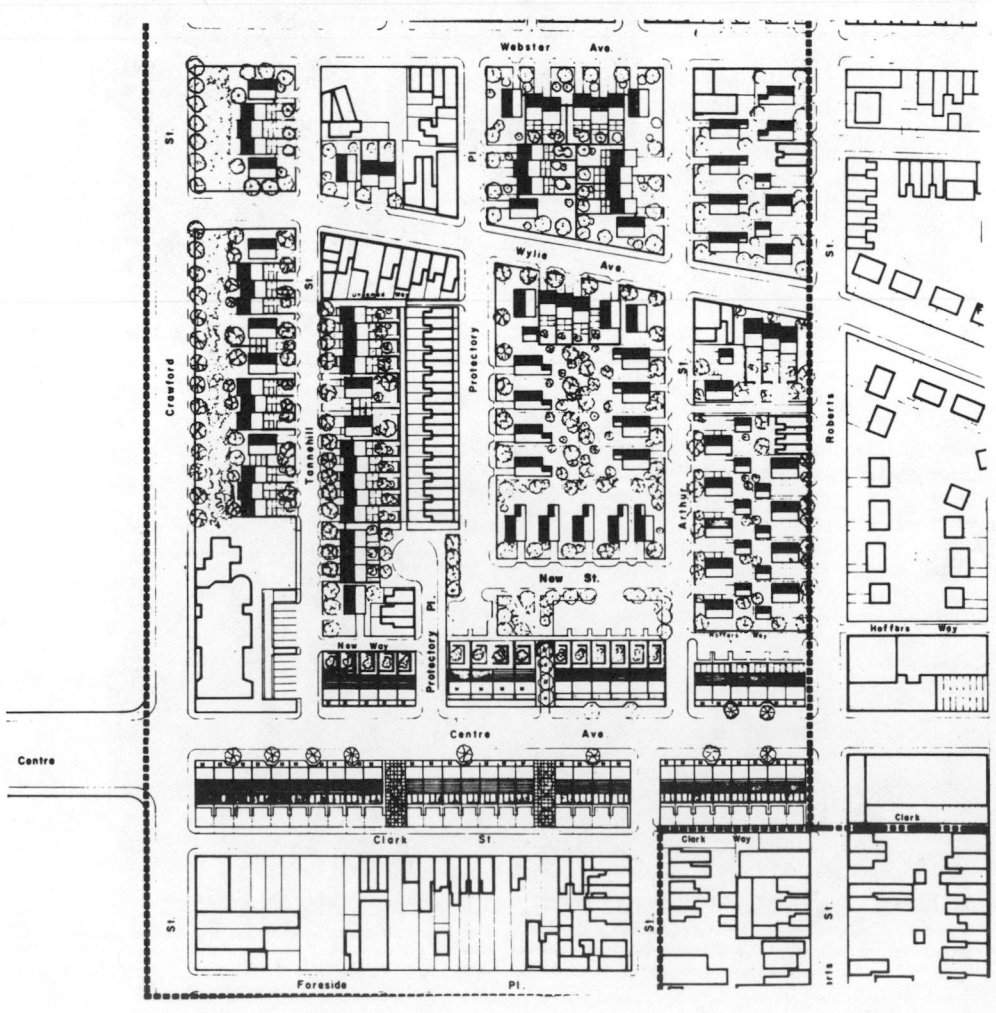

B—revised under Planned Residential
Development Scheme by Barnett as Consultant to
the Redevelopment Urban Authority of Pittsburgh

of the new ideas that I believe we started. I collaborated with John Portman on the book, *The Architect as Developer*, because Portman does, voluntarily, so many of the things that we had to give incentives for in New York City. Portman has shown that good urban design can more than pay for itself, and I was anxious to make sure that his ideas get as much recognition as possible.

My own practice is devoted to working on the context in which other architects and planners will do the more specific work—"wholesale" rather than "retail," if you will. In the Gateway National Recreation Area Plan, I believe that we have evolved a method of specifying location and relationships, without tying the hands of the architects, engineers, and landscape architects who will design the specific parts of the Park. In Pittsburgh I am working with the Redevelopment Authority and Planning Department to coordinate the massive public and private investment that is projected for the Pittsburgh downtown over the next decade.

—Jonathan Barnett

Jonathan Barnett began his career as an architect and an architectural writer, but his primary professional effort has been in the field of urban design. In many ways Barnett is the father of this discipline.

In the mid-1960's Barnett and a group of associates (who later were to become the Urban Design Group of New York City's Planning Department, with Barnett as director), rejected the existing model of unresolvable conflict between politicians, economists and developers with little sensitivity to the potential of fine design on the one hand, and architects and urban planners, who saw little relevance in the realities of politics and economics, on the other.

Barnett and his group proposed careful environmental planning, taking full advantage of architectural design possibilities, composed with strict and genuine economic sensibility. Moreover, he stressed the importance of schemes that solved problems in totality, and he placed little faith in the ability of individual architectural solutions to solve complex urban dilemmas. When John V. Lindsay created the Urban Design Group in 1967, Barnett was given the opportunity to become a truly generative force, and he explored and implemented many of his most innovative ideas in this capacity. The work that he and his group performed experimentally has become a guide for all urban design work performed since then.

Their success was attributable to several key factors in Barnett's method of approach and philosophy of execution. Besides attempting to solve problems broadly, rather than imposing only one or two changes in the hope of aggregate growth, Barnett stressed close interaction with community forces. By working with local groups and individuals, he made sure that his designs were appropriate and met with general public receptiveness. With regard to implementation, Barnett realized that no plan could be successful without great political struggle, and he often directly challenged those institutions that barred urban change. Finally, by enforcing urban design decisions through modification of the existing network of zoning laws, Barnett was able to regulate neighborhoods and actively change existing patterns without violent renewal or conflict.

His many projects for New York include revamping of the Times Square Area, the development of the Lincoln Center project, and urban renewal projects throughout the five boroughs. By implementing valid urban design via public policy, he has effectively transformed much of New York City.

Since his retirement from the Urban Design Group in 1971, Barnett has worked independently, both as a designer and an urban planning consultant. He has worked the South Street Seaport Development, a nine-block historic district in lower Manhattan, in association with Edward Larrabee Barnes. He

has developed the general management plan and environmental impact statement for the Gateway National Recreation Area, the first urban national park, located in New York City. He has also developed a series of prototype neighborhood plans with the Louisville Community Design Center, acted as consultant to the primary planners for two new town centers in Hong Kong, and produced studies for the new Alaska state capital.

Currently, Mr. Barnett is a consultant to the Urban Redevelopment Authority of Pittsburgh, where he is working on two projects. One is a development strategy for the downtown Golden Triangle Area, which includes plans for the coordination of bus and rail rapid transit, public open space, new parking facilities, downtown housing, a retail shopping strategy, and revised zoning controls. The second is a project for low income housing to be made up entirely of single family row and detached houses.

—Ching-Yu Chang

BARRAGÁN, Luis.

Mexican. Born in Guadalajara, Jalisco, in 1902. Trained as an engineer; self-taught as an architect. Travelled in Spain and France, 1924–26; practised in Guadalajara, 1927–36; lived in Paris, attending Le Corbusier's lectures, 1931–32; has worked in or near Mexico City since 1936; visited Morocco, 1951. Exhibition: *The Architecture of Luis Barragán,* Museum of Modern Art, New York, 1976. Fellow of the American Institute of Architects. Address: Calle General Francisco Ramirez 14, Mexico 18, D.F., Mexico.

Works:

1927 Robles Leon House restoration, Guadalajara
1928 Robles Leon Rental Houses, Guadalajara
Mrs. Harper de Garibi House, Guadalajara
E. Gonzalez Luna House, Guadalajara
Enrique Aguilar House, Guadalajara
1929 G. Cristo House, Guadalajara
Children's Playground, Parque de la Revolucion, Guadalajara
E. Gonzalez Luna Rental Houses, Guadalajara
1931 Barragán Family House restoration, Chapala, Jalisco
1932 House restoration, Guadalajara (with engineer Juan Palomar)
1936 House for two families, Avenida Parque Mexico, Mexico City
2 rental houses, Avenida Mazatlan, Mexico City
1937 I. Pizarro Suarez House, Las Lomas de Capultepec, Mexico City
1940 Apartment building, Calles Lerma y Guadiana, Mexico City
Rental house, Calle Guadiana, Mexico City
Apartment building, Avenida Mississippi, Mexico City
Apartment building, Plaza Melchor Ocampo, Mexico City (with José Creixell)
Apartment building with adjoining single house, Avenida Mississippi, Mexico City
Painters' studios building, Plaza Melchor Ocampo, Mexico City
3 low-cost apartment buildings, Calle de Elba, Mexico City
Eduardo Villasenor House, San Angel, Mexico City
1945 4 private gardens, Avenida Constituyentes y Calle General Francisco Ramirez, Mexico City
3 private gardens, Avenida San Jeronimo, San Angel, Mexico City

1945/
50 El Pedregal, formerly known as Parque Residencial Jardines del Pedregal de San Angel, Mexico City: master plan, 3 demonstration gardens, and entrances, including the Plaza de las Fuentes
1947 Luis Barragán House, Tacubaya, Mexico City
1948 2 houses, 10 and 12 Avenida de las Fuentes, El Pedregal, Mexico City (with Max Cetto)
1950 Eduardo Prieto Lopez House, El Pedregal, Mexico City
1953 La Plaza del Zocalo Fountain and Mall, Mexico City (project)
1955 Capuchinas Sacramentarias del Purismo Corazon de Maria Chapel, Tlalpan, Mexico City
Hotel Pierre Marquez gardens, Acapulco
Antonio Galvez House, Calle Pimentel 10, San Angel, Mexico City
Jardines del Bosque master plan, Guadalajara (project)
Capillo del Calvario Chapel, Jardines del Bosque, Guadalajara (project)
1957 Satellite City Towers, Queretaro Highway, Mexico City (with Mathias Goeritz)
1958 Las Arboledas master plan and building code, Mexico City
El Muro Rojo, Las Arboledas, Mexico City
1959 Plaza del Campanario, Las Arboledas, Mexico City
Plaza y Fuente del Bebedero, Las Arboledas, Mexico City
1964 Los Clubes master plan, public landscaping, and building code, Mexico City
Fuente de Los Clubes (Fuente de Los Amantes), Mexico City
1967 Lomas Verdes master plan and building code, Mexico City (project; with Juan Sordo Madaleno)
Open chapel for Lomas Verdes, Mexico City (project)
1968 San Cristobal stable, pools, and house for Mr and Mrs. Folke Egerstrom, Los Clubes, Mexico City (with Andres Casillas)
1969 Service entrance gate, Los Clubes, Mexico City
Cano master plan, near Tepotzotlan
1971 Guadalajara Club and Race Track (project)
1972 Monumental fountain for Lomas Verdes, Mexico City (project; with Ricardo Legorreta)
1973 Pigeon Tower, El Palomar, Guadalajara (project; with Raul Ferrera)
1976 Gilardi House, Tacubaya, Mexico City

Publications:

By BARRAGÁN: articles—"Gardens for Environment—Jardines del Pedregal" in *Journal of the American Institute of Architects* (Washington, D.C.), April 1952; "The Construction and Enjoyment of a Garden Accustoms People to Beauty, to Its Instinctive Use, Even to Its Accomplishment" in *Via 1: Ecology in Design* (Philadelphia), 1968; "Luis Barragán y El Regreso a Las Fuentes," interview with Damian Bayon in *Plural 48* (Mexico City), September 1975.

On BARRAGÁN: books—*The New Architecture in Mexico* by Esther Born, New York 1937; *18 Residencias de Arquitectos Mexicanos* by Enrique Yanez, Mexico City 1951; *Mexico's Modern Architecture* by I. E. Myers, New York 1952; *Latin American Architecture since 1945* by Henry-Russell Hitchcock, New York 1955; *Mexican Journal: The Conquerors Conquered* by Selden Rodman, New York 1958; *Moderne Architektur in Mexiko* by Max Cetto, Teufen, Switzerland 1961; *Modern Gardens and the Landscape* by Elizabeth B. Kassler, New York 1964; *Mexican Homes of Today* by Warren and Verna

Cook Shipway, New York, 1964; *Builders in the Sun: Five Mexican Architects* by Clive Bamford Smith, New York 1967; *Analisis Critico de la Arquitectura Moderna in Mexico* by Hernandez Laos, Guadalajara 1968; *Art in Architecture* by Louis G. Redstone, New York 1968; *Mexican Landscape Architecture—From the Street and from Within* by Rosina Greene Kirby, Tucson, Arizona 1972; *The Architecture of Luis Barragán,* exhibition catalogue, Museum of Modern Art, New York, by Emilio Ambasz, New York 1976; articles—"Mexican Villas: Luis Barragán, Architect" in *Architectural Record* (New York), September 1931; "Modernist Houses in Mexico Designed by Luis Barragán" in *House and Garden* (New York), October 1931; "Recent Work of a Mexican Architect—Luis Barragán" in *Architectural Record* (New York), January 1935; "The Gardens of Pedregal" by Mary Saint Albans in *Modern Mexico* (New York), April 1946; "Jardines del Pedregal, Mexico City" and "House by Luis Barragán, Architect" in *Arts and Architecture* (Los Angeles), August 1951; "Barragán's House" by Esther McCoy in *Los Angeles Times Home Magazine,* 19 October 1952; "Il Pedregal di Città del Messico" by Gio Ponti in *Domus* (Milan), March 1953; "Arbeiten von Luis Barragán, Mexico" by Horst Dohnert in *Baukunst und Werkform* (Darmstadt), November 1954; "Master Designer, Luis Barragán" in *Interiors* (New York), December 1963; "The Private World of Luis Barragán" in *Vogue* (London), April 1966; "The House of Luis Barragán" in *Harper's Bazaar* (New York), July 1968; "Dans l'Actualité le Style Mexicain, Chez un Architecte de Mexico" in *Elle* (Paris), October 1968; "I Muri di Luis Barragán" in *Domus* (Milan), November 1968; "El Palomar et son Colombier Geant" in *Vogue* (Paris), October 1974.

My house is my refuge, an emotional piece of architecture, not a cold piece of convenience.

I believe in an "emotional architecture." It is very important for human kind that architecture should move by its beauty; if there are many equally valid technical solutions to a problem, the one which offers the user a message of beauty and emotion, that one is architecture.

Any work of architecture which does not express serenity is a mistake. That is why it has been an error to replace the protection of walls with today's intemperate use of enormous glass windows.

The construction and enjoyment of a garden accustoms people to beauty, to its instinctive use, even to its pursuit.

I believe that architects should design gardens to be used, as much as the houses they build, to develop a sense of beauty and the taste and inclination toward the fine arts and other spiritual values.

—Luis Barragán

Luis Barragán is among the most perfectionist, poetic, and sublime of all contemporary architects. He is the spiritual leader of three generations of Mexican Minimalists and has become one of the revered mystics of architecture for an increasing number of designers, especially in the United States.

Working in an idiom that is at once spare and ascetic, abstract and monastic, Barragán evokes the tradition of anonymous building. He has long been interested in North African, Mediterranean, and Mexican village architecture, which he calls "architecture for the poor." Yet in the same work he can ring the overtones of the rich, almost epic tradition of all architecture. He does it by a minimalist statement that echoes, like an epitome, the continuity of uninterrupted tradition.

His work is minimal, yet sumptuous in color and texture, in visual drama and stunning juxtapositions. It is composed with the purest of planes—either wall or water—with intersecting walls of strong and stark proportions, and, above all, with a clear sense of the interaction and the union between building components and nature—between stucco and timber and

Luis Barragán: Plaza de las Fuentes, El Pedregal, Mexico City, 1950

sky, trees, and water. Much of Barragán's work, in fact, has been in urban planning and in landscape architecture—at the edges of actual shelter, where buildings merge with the landscape. His most revered project conjure up images of a roofless Barcelona pavilion, as if Mies had worked in adobe.

His early work of the 1920's consists of a number of residences in the early International Style, not unlike Le Corbusier's work at the same time. Since 1950 color has played a significant role in his work, especially in the Satellite Towers of 1957, as it had with Le Corbusier at Ronchamps (1950–53) and La Tourette (1957–60). Barragán's vibrant colors on the exteriors of his works—pink, lemon, magenta, and coral—are quintessentially Mexican. His element is the climate of Mexico—somewhat like the Mediterranean—its light, air, and open simplicity.

A confirmed religious man, Barragán's architecture is almost mystical, as is visible in his serene chapel for the Capuchinas Sacramentarias in Tlalpan and in his seemingly ineffable gardens for meditation. A horseman by bearing and interest, Barragán achieves abstract yet mythical dimensions when he designs water troughs and fountains for horses within warm-up rings and resting places. Most celebrated of these are his projects at Las Arboledas, a residential subdivision in the suburbs of Mexico City, and the San Cristobal stable, horse pool, swimming pool and house (with Andres Casillas) for Mr. and Mrs. Folke Egerstrom in Los Clubes.

There the use of falling splashing water from overhead troughs recalls for him the aquaducts of his own childhood village Mazamitla.

In his own house in Mexico City a view from the library toward the garden, over a series of interior partitions of varying heights, is like a Josef Albers painting in three dimensions—a live-in homage to the square. And the cruciform division of the window glazing is inescapable. A small white-walled patio off his architecture workshop has a rectangular black pool fed by a trickle of water coming through an old timber that projects from the wall. It is a miniature aquaduct. Sunk in the pool is an ancient terracotta amphora; a cluster of other amphoras stands alongside the pool. In this exterior room—all white and black with the terracotta of the amphoras as accent and with the blue Mexican sky for its ceiling—a rustic door to the adjacent garden is painted shocking pink—softened only by the weathering of rains and the bleaching of the inevitable Mexican sun. There is no furniture. It is an abstract composition, made kinetic and full of life by its falling water, by the changing sky, and by its colorful surprise. It is a synthesis of life and the elements, of meditation and the permanence of change.

It is a series of poetic extracts such as these—of schematic details standing as apparent symbols—that the totality of Barragán's work is known, primarily through the abstracted photographs of the architect's personally selected photographer Armando Salas Portugal. Through these images most people have come to project the apparently infinite poetic genius—the epic unreality—of Luis Barragán. And therein lies his influence, not as planner or provider of functional shelter, but as poet, as epitomizer.

Barragán has not been concerned with the larger demands of urban architecture or with the requirements of the poor for shelter—despite his admiration of anonymous building as a source of inspiration. He has remained aloof from this reality. He has built only what he himself has found interesting, primarily aesthetic problems of a romantic nature—towers, fountains, and pools. His disciples have questioned his courage and his refined goal of purity. For he has built comparatively little—less and less, it seems, as time has gone on—despite the growing reputation, respect, and demand.

Louis Kahn consulted him on the plaza design for the Salk Laboratories, but Barragán said there was no need for him because Kahn already knew the right thing to do—plant nothing, just reveal the view of the ocean. Later Kahn flew Barragán up to La Jolla to see the plaza when it was finished. Barragán approved. Unlike Kahn, who undid the day's work with new ideas each night, like Penelope taking out each day's weaving of the tapestry, Barragán, simply did not get involved in numerous commissions offered to him. His disciple Ricardo Legorreta convinced him for a while to be a partner, yet after countless revisions, Barragán would say to a client that he did not like what they had finally decided to submit—and thereby undermine and undo it all. He has been invited to design a new stable in Oklahoma, and Americans hoped to have one of his projects nearby to see, but it looks, several years later, as if the stable will not come to pass.

Still, Barragán has been a deep influence on three generations of Mexican architects, including his own generation and architects in their forties, such as Legorreta, as well as a younger generation around thirty. Yet he is determinedly modest, always emphasizing the continuity and continuum of Mexican architecture. He explains that he himself was influenced by an older generation—the sculptor and painter Jesus "Chucho" Reyes—and that his work has been influence by his longtime colleague, the sculptor Mathias Goeritz, who collaborated on the Satellite Towers and who has been a seminal influence. He also maintains that he has been influence by younger Minimalists. "We are all friends and discuss many of these things back and forth," he has pointedly stated.

What Barragán aims for is simplicity and refinement without denying the color or tradition of architecture. Although the extracted images of his architecture convey to us a kind of sculptural myth based in the realm of architecture, Barragán calls himself a landscape architect, intimating his deeper commitment to the cosmic realm of nature in its widest sense.

—C. Ray Smith

BARTNING, Otto.

German. Born in Karlsruhe, Germany, 12 April 1883. Educated at the Technische Hochschule, Charlottenburg, Berlin; Technische Hochschule, Karlsruhe; and Berlin University. In private practice, Berlin, from 1905. Director, Staatlichen Bauhochschule, Weimar, 1926–30. Chairman, Deutsche Werkbund, 1946; President, Bund Deutscher Architekten, 1950. Honorary Doctor of Theology, Albertus University, Königsberg, 1924. *Died* (in Darmstadt) *in 1959.*

Works:

1906 Evangelical Church with Vicarage and Parish Centre, Peggau, Steiermark, Austria
1907/
08 Evangelical Church, Cogealac, Black Sea, Rumania

1908 Evangelical Parish Centre, Selzthal, Steiermark, Austria
Liebscher House, Peggau, Steiermark, Austria
1909 Evangelical Chapel, Schenkenhan, Böhm. Isergebirge, Germany
1909/
10 High Lutheran Church with Vicarage, Essen
Pommer Country House, Mondsee, Pichl, Austria
Evangelical Parish Centre, Rottenmann, Steiermark, Austria
1910 Evangelical Parish Centre, Morchenstern, Böhmen, Germany
1910/
11 Woehler House, Hamburg
Westendorp House, Dusseldorf
Benfey House, Dusseldorf
Evangelical Church with Vicarage, Leibnitz, Steiermark, Austria
1911/
12 E. von Simson Country House, Dahlem, Berlin
Evangelical Church with Vicarage and Parish Centre, Neustadt, Bohmen, Germany
Evangelical Church with Vicarage, Graslitz, Böhmen, Germany
Evangelical Parish Centre, Dzieditz, Schlesien, Germany
Hartmeyer House, Vienna
Evangelical Parish Centre, Mahrenberg, Steiermark, Austria
1912 Schwerdtfeger Mansions, Nieder-Siegersdorf, Schlesien, Germany
Evangelical Parish Centre, Oberschreiberhau, Riesengebirge, Germany
1912/
13 Robert Friedlaender Country House, Dahlem, Berlin
Evangelical Church with Vicarage and Parish Centre, Krems, Donau, Austria
Hessel Country House, Grunewald, Berlin
1912/
14 Evangelical Church, Nassengrub, Böhmen, Germany
1913 A. von Simson House, Charlottenburg, Berlin
1913/
14 Von Waetjen House, Dusseldorf
G. von Simson House, Caputh, Potsdam, Germany
1914 Office building, Viktoriastrasse 25, Berlin
1914/

15 R. von Simson Country House, Dahlem, Berlin
1916 Friedlander-Fuld Office additions and alterations, Unter den Linden 9, Berlin
1918/
19 Von Bodenhausen House additions, Bendlerstrasse 6, Berlin
1919 Bendix Offices, Friedland, Germany
1919/
20 Cassirer House additions, Berlin
Krupp Company Offices, Berlin
1920 Shop building, Unter den Linden, Berlin
1921 Castle renovations, for Count Kalckreuth, Siegersdorf, Germany
1921/
22 Götz House, Sudpark, Cologne
1921/
23 Trabrennbahn Buildings, Mariendorf, Berlin
1921/
24 House, Wylerberg bei Cleve, Germany
1922 Danish Church, Berlin
Coal Works Water Tower, Zeipau, Germany
Sternkirche (Star Church) Model
1923/
24 Aschaffenburg Clothing Factory, Monchen Gladbach, Germany
Dr. Theo Meyer House, Zeipau, Germany
1924 Ceramics factory, Tempelhof, Berlin
Lieck und Heider Shop, Berlin
1924/
25 Workers' Housing, Zeipau, Schlesien, Germany
1924/
26 Merkelsdorf Warehouse, Böhmen, Germany
1925 German Red Cross Offices, Berlin
Metzger House, Potsdam, Berlin (project)
Gustav-Adolf Church, Charlottenburg, Berlin
1925/
26 Children's Home, Ruppin, Germany
German State Pavilion, *Trade Fair*, Milan
1926/
28 Housing development (48,000 units), Berlin
1927 Baptist Chapel, *Free Art Exhibition*, Berlin
1927/
28 Children's Hospital, Lichterfelde, Berlin
Elektro-Thermit Offices, Tempelhof, Berlin
1928 Geographical Foundation Headquarters renovations, Wilhelmstrasse 29, Berlin
Pressa Steel Church, Cologne
Evangelical Church, Wilhelmshof an der Havel, Austria

Otto Bartning: Pressa Steel Church, Cologne, 1928

1928/
29 State Music School, FrankfurtOder, Germany
    Theo Meyer Country House, Westend, Berlin
1929/
30 Jungfernheide Housing Development, Berlin
    Rundkirche (Round Church), Essen
1930/
31 Health Farm, Wilmersdorf, Berlin
    Stahlkirche reconstruction, Essen
    Evangelical Church, Dornbirn bei Bregenz, Austria
1931/
32 Bartning Wharf Building System
1931/
33 Gustav-Adolf Evangelical Church with Parish Buildings, Siemenstadt, Berlin
1932/
33 Haselhorst District Housing Development, Berlin
1933/
34 German Community Evangelical Church with Vicarage, Lisbon
1934 Evangelical Church, Heerlen, Netherlands
1934/
35 Astoria Hotel alterations, Berlin
    St. Mark's Evangelical Church, Baden, Karlsruhe
1935/
36 Evangelical Church of the Holy Cross, Chemnitz, now Karlmarxstadt, Germany
1936 Evangelical Church, St. Blasien, Germany
1936/
37 Kippenberg Collection, Goethe Archives, Leipzig
    Christian Science Building and Church, Wilmersdorf, Berlin
1937 Bartning House, Westend, Berlin
    German Medical Insurance Office Building, Zehlendorf, Berlin
1937/
38 Evangelical Church with Vicarage, Stetten am Heuberg, Baden, Germany
    Burkhardt House, Bodensee, Switzerland
    Evangelical Church, Gorlitz-Rauschwalde, Germany
    Tanello House, Lugano, Switzerland
    Apartment house, Schoneberg, Berlin
1938 Wichernbundes Old People's Home, Baden, Karlsruhe
1938/
39 Mayrisch House, Cannes, France
    Evangelical Church, Beirut, Lebanon
1939 Alb District Evangelical Church, Baden, Karlsruhe
1939/
40 Evangelical Church renovations, Bregenz, Austria
1940/
42 Evangelical Church with Vicarage and Parish Centre, Belgrade
1941/
42 German Protestant Church renovations, Paris
    Evangelical Church with Vicarage, Barcelona
1943/
44 German Protestant Church renovations, Brussels
1946 Experimental Clay Building Development, Neckarsteinach, Germany
    Emergency pre-fabricated churches in timber, for the German Evangelical Relief Organization (prototypes)
1950/
51 Church of the Holy Trinity reconstruction, Worms, Germany
    Women's Clinic reconstruction, Darmstadt

Publications:

By BARTNING: books—*Vom Neuen Kirchbau*, Berlin 1919; *Was ist Bauen?*, Stuttgart 1952; *Otto Bartning in kurzen Worten*, Hamburg 1954; *Erde Geliebte*, Hamburg 1955; *Kirchen: Handbuch für den Kirchenbau*, with W. Weyres, Munich 1959.

On BARTNING: book—*Der Baumeister Otto Bartning und die Wiederentdeckung des Raumes* by Hans Meyer, Heidelberg 1951.

In addition to being an architect, Otto Bartning was a doctor of theology and deeply interested in the development of the Lutheran liturgy. He was primarily a designer of churches, which in his early days were strongly gothic in feeling, although they were stripped of all ornament and mouldings. Later he experimented with many types of auditorium plan using modern construction techniques to create large clear spans and wall panels mainly of glass.

His Sternkirche of 1922 was one of these designs, with a central altar, radiating aisles, and tiered seating. Daylighting was provided from curved dormer windows carried on the vaulting ribs. The steel-framed Rundkirche in Essen was a circular pepperpot in three stages with a belfry carried on the third stage. Inside, the steel was concrete-cased. It had a gallery. The congregation sat in a semi-circle in the main body of the church, and the general effect was hard and severe.

The Pressa Church in Cologne, also known as the Stahlkirche, is his best known work, with a steel frame and steel and glass walls. The steel-clad walls are in the shape of a hyperbola on plan and rise from within a low square flat-roofed base. The church is lit through stained glass in tall narrow windows and is totally without ornament.

The fan-shaped Gustav Adolf church in Berlin Siemenstadt has a concrete-framed tower at its apex. The wall opposite the tower is of brick, almost covered by the formally arranged organ. The side walls are of glass framed in concrete.

After the Second World War Bartning built almost fifty low-cost churches using bomb rubble for their concrete walls and factory-made timber trusses for their roofs.

In his early days he designed a number of large, rather strange, frankly expressionist country houses with polygonal rooms which produced elevations with irregular eaves levels and facetted walls.

Bartning's design for a ceramics factory at Berlin-Tempelhof in 1924 is sharp and clean in outline very much in the style of Arne Jacobsen whose work it antedates by thirty years.

—Gontran Goulden

BAUDIZZONE-DIAZ-ERBIN-LESTARD-VARAS.

Partnership; established, Buenos Aires, 1966, by Miguel Andres Patricio Baudizzone, Antonio Díaz, Jorge Rufino Erbin, Jorge Horacio Lestard, and Alberto Jaime Varas. Exhibitions: *Arquitectos de Buenos Aires*, Centro de Arte y Comunicacion, Buenos Aires, 1976; *Architecten van Buenos Aires*, International Cultureel Centrum, Antwerp, 1979. Recipient: First Prize, Cultural Center Competition, Mendoza, Argentina, 1971; First Prize, City Auditorium Competition, Buenos Aires, 1972. Address: Sarmiento 552, Buenos Aires 1041, Argentina.

Works:

1965 Wilson Display Stand, *Argentine Rural Society Exhibition*, Buenos Aires
    Apartment building, Guido 1624, Buenos Aires
1966 Engineering Building, National Technological University, Avellaneda Campus, Buenos Aires
1967 Apartment building, Laprida 2044, Buenos Aires

1968 Gonzalez Porto Publishing Company Building, Avenida de Mayo 952, Buenos Aires
    Vincente Lopez Paper Factory, M. Moreno 4674, Buenos Aires
    Municipal Theatre of Balcarce City, Argentina
    Housing complex, Los Alamos Country Club, Pilar, Argentina
    Science Research Institute and Sciences Building, National University of La Plata, Argentina
1969 Travel Commission Exhibition Building, La Boca Sports City, Buenos Aires
1970 Tower apartment block, Zapiola 2191, Buenos Aires
    Apartment building, Coronel Díaz 2521, Buenos Aires
    Garay Sanatorium, Santa Fé, Argentina
1971 Bariloche Foundation Research Center, Bariloche, Rio Negro, Argentina (competition project)
    Brandsen Municipal Hospital, Buenos Aires
    Cultural Center, Mendoza, Argentina (competition project)
1972 Apartment building, Calle French 3680, Buenos Aires
    Housing development, San Clemente del Tuyu, Argentina
    Hidronor Administrative Headquarters, Neuquen, Argentina (project)
    City Auditorium, Buenos Aires (competition project)
1973 Housing development, Quilmes, Argentina (project)
    Community Medical Center, San Juan, Argentina
    Apartment building, Beruti 3180, Buenos Aires
    Pre-fabricated housing development, San Isidro, Buenos Aires (project)
1974 National University of Rio Cuarto, Argentina (as construction advisers and planners)
    Lande House, Calle Saenz Valiente 1194, Buenos Aires
    Lopez Isnardi House, Pinamar, Province of Buenos Aires
    Bernardi House, General Pacheco, Buenos Aires
    Housing development, La Verde, Chaco, Argentina
    Office building, Calle Libertad, Buenos Aires
    Sports Complex, Corrientes, Argentina (competition project)
1975 Apartment building, Calle Aguero 2008, Buenos Aires
    Apartment building, Pueyrredon 1779, Buenos Aires
    Office building, Calle Reconquista and L. N. Alem, Buenos Aires
    Apartment building, Calle Juncal 3152, Buenos Aires
    Apartment building, Calle Maipu 1230, Buenos Aires
1976 Office building, Calle Marcelo T de Alvear and L. N. Alem, Buenos Aires
    Office building, Calle Viamonte and L. N. Alem, Buenos Aires
    Tower apartment building, Calle Salguero and Cabello, Buenos Aires
    Office building, Calle Reconquista 478, Buenos Aires
    Office building, Calle Tucuman 1400, Buenos Aires (project)
1977 Celorrio House, Punta del Este, Uruguay
    Office building, Calle Suipacha 68, Buenos Aires
    Office building, 25 de Mayo and Lavalle, Buenos Aires
    Banco Hispano Building, Esmeralda 56, Buenos Aires
    Hotel San Martin de Los Andes, Neuquén, Argentina

Bus Terminal, Buenos Aires (project)
1978   Municipal Bank of Rosario Headquarters,
        Buenos Aires (project)
        2 Houses, Ingeniero Maschwitz, Province of
        Buenos Aires
1978/
   79   Housing development, Santa Fé, Argentina
        Housing Development, Catamarca, Argentina
        Housing Development, Neuquén, Argentina

Publications:

On BDELV: book—*New Directions in Latin American Architecture* by Francisco Bullrich, New York 1969; articles—in *Summa* (Buenos Aires), October 1969, November 1971, January 1975; *Hogar y Arquitectura* (Barcelona), no. 103, 1973; *Architectural Review* (London), June 1973, September 1975; *L'Architecture d'Aujourd'hui* (Paris), July 1973; *Domus* (Milan), no. 525, 1973, no. 545, 1975; *Academia Nacional de Bellas Artes: Anuario no. 4,* Buenos Aires 1976.

Despite their tacit support for systemization in what is obviously systematic in their own work, Baudizzone-Díaz-Erbin-Lestard-Varas do not wish to be classified as "systems architects."

There was a time, however, when the studio regarded itself as a "laboratory" of systematic architecture. After re-examining its past activity, it began to value an analytical vision of architecture—architecture as a search for architectural elements; architecture as the exploitation of the expressiveness of those elements. The systematic conception of architecture is that "architecture is a set of related parts." The team carried out work as from this perspective, with the elements defined as "special typologies" to be related in networks and series of networks.

Perhaps their resistance to the "systems architects" label derives from the fact that it is, as a definition, too encompassing: it might be said that all architecture, and particularly contemporary architecture, is systems based. BDELV has used elements from diverse sources in its buildings and used them according to their own criteria, adapting with which they each case to the type of building with which they

were dealing. Their dominant theory during the period 1966–75 was that there was no such thing as a single volume in which everything is situated, a conception that contradicts the ingenuous guidelines of spontaneous or naive architecture, the tradition that a building is a box that contains internal components.

The City Auditorium of 1972 is the last of their buildings to be conceived totally in a systematic way. Their reaction against systematic conception is—according to some of the partners—a reaction against the work of the Japanese architect Isozaki, specifically Isozaki's rhetoric about architecture as a manifestation of architectural language falling back on itself, "producing a metaphor on the expressed language." In other words, architecture is meta-linguistic; it talks about itself in a kind of permanent reflection, a kind of vicious circle that does not take into consideration any elements of extra-architectural reality. For example, one can imagine constructing everything on the basis of a self-repeating modular structure, like a cube reproduced an infinite number of times.

After 1972 the team very clearly moves away from these kinds of ideas by incorporating into their works and projects non-architectural factors, that is, by taking into account elements that lie beyond a particular work in itself. They make explicit their distance from modernism and the theories of Le Corbusier. Their concern has become architectural language but in the sense that the typological constitutes an important and abiding concern in the conception and design of their buildings. To a certain extent they have returned to architectural classicism in an attempt to find a way of creating architecture that is based on their own knowledge of the laws of construction; they are concerned with the elements of architecture and their relative value.

The criticism of Le Corbusier is not directed against the man himself; it is the theoretical posture of Corb and his disciples that seems wrong. As far as BDELV are now concerned, the modern movement left aside such concerns as symmetry, composition, and geometry—and it is these concerns that they now try to rescue and include in their work. Up to a certain point this interest was merely notional; now it is obvious in their work, obvious and explicit.

Their attitude with regard to architectural functionalism is now decidely hostile: its principles are rejected as chimerical and its forms as abnormal, repressing cultural values.

It is worth pointing out that, in their current efforts, they are interested in the "ideology of the box." Their purpose is not to cover up the inside with the external skin but to allow the facade to be an exhibition of the building's structural elements, so that entrails are outside and the skin inside. Rather than being conceived as a product of analysis between its parts, the building is an investigation in architectural language: there is full consciousness of working with an architectural rhetoric, with a discourse in which buildings "speak" and allude to other things, behave, in short, as "signifying" elements that express languages that are technical, aesthetic, etc.

As well, there is in their work a typological discrimination, an historical reconnaissance of architecture, an accumulation of past and present references and experiences. The team believes that there is an historical continuity in the development (and elaboration) of construction, a natural evolution of the architectural, a continuum that modernism interrupted. Today, in their effort to overcome what they see as the dead end of modernism, the team has reverted to what is, in their view, the invaluable typological and historical dialogue of architecture.

—Jorge Glusberg

BAUMGARTEN, Paul.

German. Born in Tilsit, East Prussia, 9 May 1900. Educated at the Gymnasium, Inowrazlaw, 1907–17; Gymnasium, Nordhausen, 1919; Technische Hochschule, Danzig, 1920–21; Technische Hochschule, Berlin, 1922–25, Dip. Eng. 1925. Served in the German Army, 1917–18. Married Margot Huebner in 1934. Worked as an Assistant, then Associate Architect in the office of Mebes and Emmerich, Berlin,

Baudizzone-Diaz-Erbin-Lestard-Varas: Housing Development, Santa Fe, Argentina, 1979

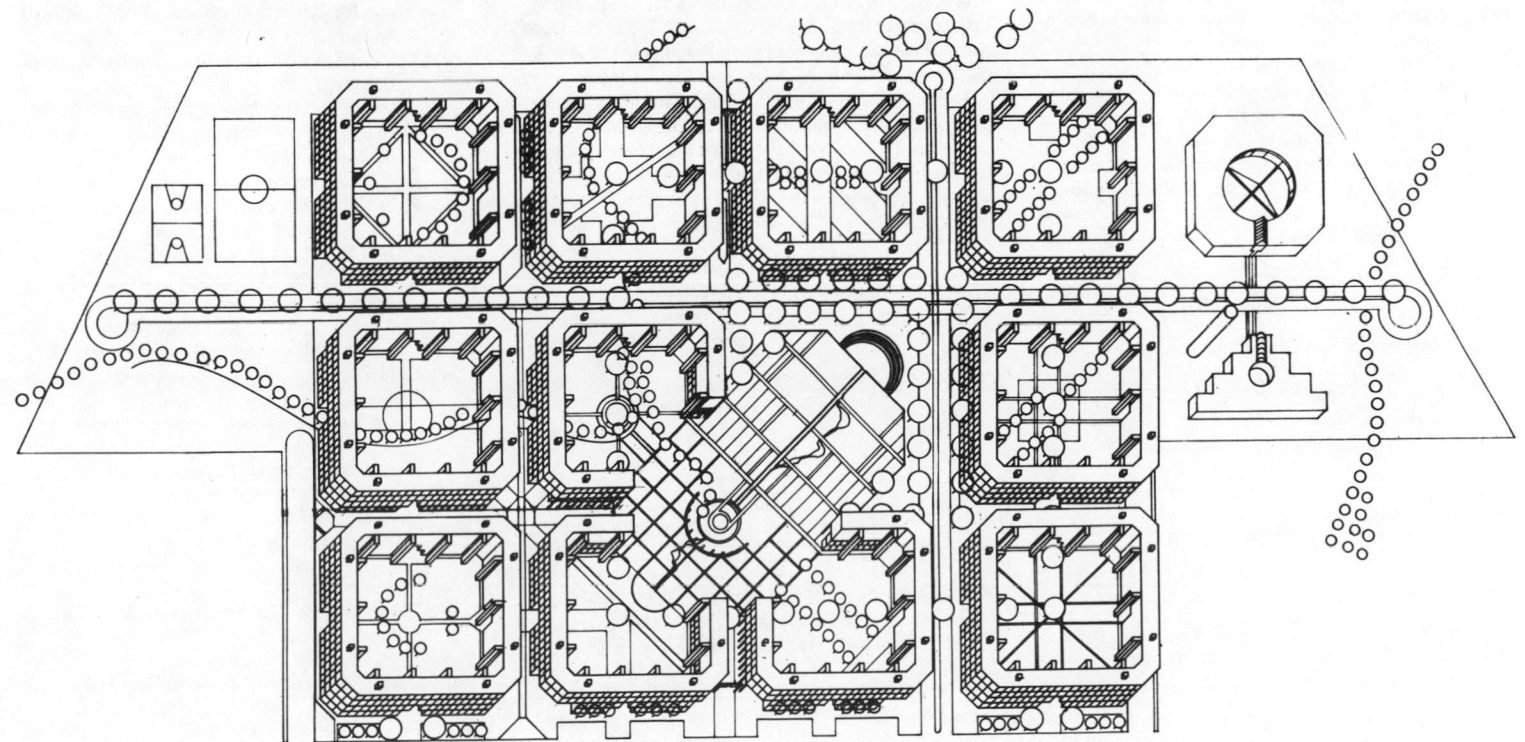

Paul Baumgarten: Federal Courts Building, Karlsruhe, 1969

1925–34; manager of a private company building department, Berlin, 1934–35; Manager of the City of Berlin Building Department, 1936; Manager of the Building Departments of Ph. Holzmann Company, Frankfurt and Berlin, 1936–46. Since 1947, in private architectural practice, Berlin. Professor of Architecture, Hochschule für Bildende Künste, Berlin, 1952–68. Recipient: Critics' Prize, Berlin, 1954; Berlin Art Prize, 1960; University of Tübingen Medal, 1968. Member, Akademie der Künste, Berlin, 1957. Address (office): Frankenallee 12, 1000 Berlin 19, Germany.

Works:

1929/
33   Housing estates, Berlin
1933 Water Sports Building, Berlin suburbs
1934 Berlin Refuse Disposal Department Office Building renovations
1935 Berlin Refuse Disposal Department loading site
1950 Rot-Weiss Club and Grounds, Berlin
1951 Hotel am Zoo reconstruction, Berlin
1953 Music Academy Concert Hall, Berlin
1955 Eternit Company Guest House, Berlin
1957 Eternit Company Industrial Buildings, Berlin
       Interbau House 25, Berlin
       Hotel am Zoo additions, Berlin
1958 Rot-Weiss Club House Building, Berlin
       Boris Blacher House, Berlin
       Ruhr Coal Company Office Building, Berlin
       Eternit Company Canteen Building, Berlin
1959 Church, Am Lietzensee, Charlottenburg, Berlin
1960 Old People's Day Centre, Wolfsburg, Germany
       Volkswagen Company residential buildings, Wolfsburg, Germany
1961 Shopping Centre, Wolfsburg, Germany
1966 Dining Halls and related buildings, University of Tübingen, Germany
1967 High rise building, Wolfsburg, Germany
       BEWAG Company Building extensions, Berlin
1969 Federal Courts Building, Karlsruhe
1970 Reichstag reconstruction, Berlin
1975 Music Academy Theatre, Berlin

Publications:

On BAUMGARTEN: article—"Reichstag Resurrection" by David Booth in *Architectural Review* (London), March 1975.

Some German industrial buildings of the middle 1930's, after the Nazi seizure of power, stand comparison with the best of Italian rationalist architec-ture. Paul Baumgarten directed the building of the Berlin Refuse Disposal Department and, avoiding any kind of monumentality, fulfilled in the best sense the demands of "new building" in relation to suitability of and respect for materials. His buildings of the period are not different in form from buildings of the 1920's: they have flat roofs, continuous window cramp irons with tubular steel profiles, unclad steel supports.

Suitability for their purpose and unobtrusive elegance are also the characteristic features of Baumgarten's post-war buildings. He frequently uses glass walls to establish a connection between the interior and the outside world—whether in a concert hall, a factory, or a church. Experience of surrounding nature becomes part of the building's purpose. For example, the individual structures of the Federal Courts open onto the Botanical Garden in Karlsruhe (the initial plan was to build the Baden State Theatre there). And Baumgarten considers as his best his unexecuted design of five circular elements permeated by nature.

In the 1960's the political differences between the two German states turned Baumgarten's reconstruction of the Reichstag in Berlin into a most exhausting task. But the result has been successful. The modern interior is in exciting contrast to the historical architecture of the building's original construction.

In the extension of the BEWAG Company Building, Baumgarten was able to alter the basic concept of his employers. They wanted to build directly onto the existing Shell-Haus. Baumgarten moved his multi-storey building away from Emil Fahrenkamp's famous building and thereby emphasized the neighbouring building, preserving it as a monument, as an independent, historically valuable structure. Baumgarten's attitude involved a restraint rarely practiced by architects in the 1960's.

—Christian Borngräber

BBPR ARCHITECTURAL STUDIO.
Partnership; established, Milan, 1932, by Gianluigi Banfi, *q.v.* (died 1945), Lodovico Belgiojoso, *q.v.*, Enrico Peressutti, *q.v.* (died 1973), and Ernesto Nathan Rogers, *q.v.* (died 1969). Exhibition: *Ten Italian Architects,* Los Angeles County Museum of Art, 1967. Recipient: First Prize, Warehouse Competition, *Ente Nazionale Risi di Lombardia e Piedmonte,* 1937. Address: via dei Chiostri 2, 20121 Milan, Italy.

Works:

1932 Hotel Quisiana and Church of Sant'Angelo, Rome (Banfi diploma project)
       Casa del Fascio Tipo per la Città (Banfi and Belgiojoso project)
1933 City plan for Pavia, Italy (project)
       Casa del Sabato per gli Sposi, *Triennale,* Milan (exhibition project; with Portaluppi, Fontana and Chiesa)
       Gairinge House interiors, Trieste
       Marietti House interiors, Palazzo Resta Pallavicini, Via Conservatorio, Milan
1934 Palazzo del Littorio, *Mostra della Rivoluzione Fascista,* Rome (competition project; with Luigi Figini, Gino Pollini, and Luigi Danusso)
       Ferrario House additions, Via Crocifisso, Milan (destroyed during World War II)
       Casa Qualunque, Via Vallazze, Milan (project)
       Exhibition Hall, *Mostra dell'Aeronautica,* Palazzo dell'Arte, Milan
       Samengo House interiors, Genoa
1935 Villa Morpurgo, Opcina, Trieste
       Home for Red Cross Nurses, Via Caradosso, Milan
       Tessiture Agosti Buildings, Legnano, Milan (project)
       Exhibition Halls, *Mostra dello Sport,* Palazzo dell'Arte, Milan (with R. Guttuso and F. Melotti)
       Pavilion, *International Exposition,* Brussels
       Exhibition Halls, *Mostra del Mare,* Trieste
       Cassa Malattie Office interiors, Trieste
       Enrico House interiors, Genoa
       Feltrinelli Studio interiors, Via Caserotti, Milan (with A. Belgiojoso)
       Feltrinelli Office/Apartment Building, Via Manin, Milan (with A. Belgiojoso)
1936 Villa Venosta conversion, Gornate Olona, Varese, Italy
       Hotel and restaurant, Opcina, Trieste (project)
       Bozzi and Crippa Society Pavilion, *Fiera Campionaria,* Milan
       Pavilion, *Triennale,* Milan (with G. Melotti and C. Cagli)
       Premoli House interiors, Corso Monforte, Milan
       Design for the "La Voce del Padrone" Radio (competition project)
1936/
37   Master plan for the Aosta Valley, Italy (with others)
1937 Palazzo della Civiltà Italiana, *International Exposition,* Rome (2 projects)
       Warehouses, *Ente Nazionale Risi di Lombardia e Piedmonte* (competition project)

Victory Monument, Piazza Fiume, Milan (competition project)

Community shopping and nursery development, Vercelli, Italy (competition project; with E. Radice Fossati)

Italian Shipping Companies' Floating Pavilion, *World's Fair*, Paris (with P. Zappa, M. Russo, and L. Fontana)

Exhibition Halls, *Leonardo da Vinci Exhibition*, Milan

Cinema Scenography Pavilion, *Mostra del Teatro Italiano*, Villa Olmo, Como

Banfi House interiors, Via Gustavo Modena, Milan

Monselise House interiors, Via M. Fanti, Milan (with P. Filippini)

1938 Master plan for the Pavilions, *Fiera Campionaria*, Milan (project; with E. Radice Fossati)

Heliotherapy Clinic, Legnano, Milan (demolished, 1956)

School, Robbio Lomellina, Pavia, Italy (project)

Romanin House interiors, Milan

1939 Tourist development plan for the Island of Elba (project)

Salsomaggiore Town Centre Plan, Parma (competition project)

Le Grazie Workers' Housing, for the Cantoni Cotton Factory, Legnano, Milan

Cucirini Milanesi Building interiors, Milan

Cozzi House interiors, Treviglio, Bergamo

Crippa Shop interiors, Montecatini Terme, Italy

Rooms for the Luini and for the Leonardo schools, *Mostra Leonardesca*, Palazzo dell'Arte, Milan

Children's Holiday and Health Centre, Legnano, Milan

Villa G., Scorcola, Trieste (project)

Gennarini-Gras House interiors, Milan

Terni Pavilion, *Fiera Campionaria*, Milan

Stipel Telephone Building interiors, Galleria Vittorio Emanuele, Milan

Crippa House interiors, Caravaggio, Bergamo

Banfi House interiors, Via Moscova, Milan

1940 Urban plan for the Belsana Paper Industry (factory/office/housing development), Valle del Lerone, Lera, Genoa (project)

Central Post Office Building, EUR Quarter, Rome

San Simpliciano Cloisters restoration (including BBPR Studio), Milan (with E. Radice Fossati)

Villa Gersony, Desenzano, Verona (not completed)

Forme nel Parco Pavilion, *Triennale*, Milan

La Lampada Bookshop, Corso Vittorio Emanuele, Milan

Belgiojoso House interiors, Via Perugia, Milan

Spiga and Corrente Galleries interiors, Via Spiga, Milan

1941 Rural Casa del Fascio (competition project)

Studio Formiggini interiors, Milan

1942 "Ideal Homes" for *Domus* magazine, Milan (projects)

Furniture store, Via Verri, Milan (with Franco Albini, Ignazio Gardella, and G. Mucchi)

1943 Centre for Facial Injuries, Milan Policlinic, Via Lamarmora, Milan (project)

Wooden House (project)

Cabrini House interiors, Milan

1944 Belsana Building, Corso Matteotti, Milan

1945 Master plan for the City of Milan (project; with others)

Residential development, Via Alcuino, Milan (with F. Ordanini Studio)

Villa Salmoiraghi, Lanzo d'Intelvi, Como (not completed)

1946 Master plan for the centre of the City of

Milan (with Franco Albini, Piero Bottoni, Luigi Figini, Gino Pollini, and others)

Monument to the Victims of German Concentration Camps, Monumental Cemetery, Milan

Banfi Gandini Tomb, Monumental Cemetery, Milan

1947 Villa Merlo, Via Duse, Vigevano, Italy

Bertoletti Alpine Resthouse, Bormio, Sondrio, Italy

Villa, Bormio, Sondrio, Italy (project)

Exhibition Halls, *Mostra della Resistenza Italiana*, Palais de Trocadero, Paris (with G. Mucchi and M. de Micheli)

Villa Riva, Saronno, Varese, Italy

Flora Bar interiors, Via Manzoni, Milan

Ravelli Apartment interiors, Milan

Oggioni House interiors, Milan

Objects and Furnishing Units Pavilion, *Triennale*, Milan

1948 Apartment/Office Building, Piazza San Erasmo, Milan (with C. Monti)

Marzoli House interiors, Milan

Melzi d'Eril House interiors, Milan

1949 Oxilia House interiors, Milan

Cinema Rosa, Via Canonica, Milan

1950 Union of Manufacturers Textile Factory, Nerviano, Italy (with A. Radaelli Studio)

Palazzo Ponti restoration, Via Bigli, Milan (with C. Monti)

Pavilion and Riva Park, Saronno Varese, Italy (with P. Porcinai and F. Ordanini Studio)

Stock Exchange and Chamber of Commerce Headquarters conversion, Via Meravigli, Milan (competition project)

Cultural Centre, Via Amedei, Milan (project)

Rollier House interiors, Via Poerio, Milan

1951 INA urban plan for Cesate, near Milan (project; with Franco Albini, G. Albricci, and Ignazio Gardella)

U.S.A. Pavilion (for the Museum of Modern Art, New York), *Triennale*, Milan

"Architecture, Measure of Man" Room, *Triennale*, Milan (Rogers only; with Vittorio Gregotti and G. Stoppino)

"Forme dell'Utile" Room, *Triennale*, Milan (Belgiojoso and Peressutti only; with F. B. Ceriani and M. Huber)

First Class Lounge on the *Neptunia* cruise ship

Grandini House interiors, Milan

Longoni House interiors, Milan

Palazzo Venier dei Leoni restoration/conversion, for the Peggy Guggenheim Museum, Grand Canal, Venice (project)

1952 Tower Apartment Buildings, Campi Elisi, Trieste (project)

Piccolo Teatro della Città di Milano conversion, Via Rovello, Milan (Rogers only; with M. Zanuso)

Camillo Olivetti Monument, Ivrea, Italy (project; with L. Fontana)

Matarazzo House, Sao Paulo, Brazil (project)

1953 INA housing developments at Albizzate, Varese, Baggio, Casorate-Sempione, Varese, Gambolo, Gazzada Schianno, Pinerolo Po, Pavia, and Sedriana, Milan, Italy

Aquila Service Station, Grumola, Port of Trieste

Ravelli Family Vault and Chapel, Bollote Cemetery, Milan

Cotonficio Valle Susa Depot and Offices, Turin

Grand Show Pavilion, *International Textile Exhibition*, Turin (with G. Lanzani Studio)

Design of the *Thonet Exhibition*, Museum of Modern Art, New York (Peressutti only)

Electric Advertisement Clock, for Soleri, Udine

1954 INA Housing Development, Bellinzago Lombardo, Milan

CUS Factory extension, Collegno, Italy

CUS Factory extension, Rivarolo, Italy

Villa Brusadelli, Capri (project)

"Labyrinth of the Children" Pavilion, *Triennale*, Milan (with S. Steinberg and and A. Calder)

Italian Pavilion, *Bienal*, Sao Paulo, Brazil (competition project)

Olivetti Showrooms, Fifth Avenue, New York

Recchia House interiors, Milan

1955 Borgo San Sergio Housing and Community Development Plan, Trieste (Rogers only; with W. A. Badalotti)

Palazzina Riva, Via Borgonuovo, Milan (not completed; with W. F. Masi and P. Portaluppi)

Apartment building conversion, Porta Vercellina, Milan (project)

Peressutti House interiors, Corso Magenta, Milan

1956 Sforza Castle conversion to a museum, stage I, Milan (with C. Baroni, R. Chiavelli, and G. Lanzani)

AGIP Office interiors, Milan

Rogers Apartment interiors, Via Bigli, Milan

Hotel, near Beirut, Lebanon (project)

1957 Rural plan for Trieste (Rogers only; with W. P. Cosulich and L. Semerani)

Sesto San Giovanni CECA Workers' Housing Development, Milan

La Loggetta CECA Workers' Housing Development, Naples

Villa Jucker, Zoagli, Genoa

Scotellaro Tomb, Tricarico Cemetery, Matera, Italy (with Carlo Levi)

ENI-AGIP Pavilion, *Fiera Campionaria*, Milan

Library interiors, *Biennale*, Venice (project)

Moriggia Housing Development, Gallarate, Varese, Italy

Civic Centre, Borgo San Sergio, Italy (with S. Bassani, S. Tintori, and L. Paiosa)

1958 Revised master plan for the centre of the City of Milan (Belgiojoso only; with L. Caccia Dominioni and P. Gazzola)

Valesca Tower Building, Milan (with A. Danusso, U. Rivolta, and F. Ordanini)

Aquila Building, Muggia, Trieste (with S. Tintori and L. Paiosa)

Olivetti Technical and Mechanical Institute, Ivrea, Italy (project; with S. Tintori)

Italian Pavilion, *World's Fair*, Brussels (with Giancarlo de Carlo, Ignazio Gardella, G. Perugini, and Lodovico Quaroni)

Canadian Pavilion, *Biennale*, Venice (with G. Bay)

Primary school, Cesate, near Milan

Conference Hall, Unesco, Paris

Ravelli Apartment interiors, Via Borgogna, Milan

Designs for Arflex Furniture, Milan

1959 Moriggia Social Centre, Varese, Italy (project)

Società Reale Mutua di Assicurazione Building, Piazza Statuto, Turin (with others)

Casa Lurani Cernuschi restoration, Via Cappuccio, Milan

Plan for the La Rinascente Shop, Via Corso, Rome (competition project)

Housing development, Via San Vittore, Milan (project)

Velarca boatsummer house conversion, Lake Como

1960 Tourist development plan for Punta Stella, Island of Elba (with P. Porcinai)

Development plan for Chiesa Rossa, Milan (competition project)

Santa Margherita Ligure Housing Development, Genoa (project; with Tekne and Bassani)

Primary school, Bellinzago Lombardo, Italy

Municipal Hall, Bellinzago Lombardo, Italy (project)

Mayer Building, Via Masolina da Panicale, Milan

Palazzina Mayer restoration, Via Bigli, Milan (with S. Steinberg and G. Lanzani)

Apartment building conversion, Tellaro, La Spezia, Italy

Randazzo Optical Shop interiors, Palermo (with B. Munari, R. Chiavelli, and G. Lanzani)

"Spazio" and "Arco" metal furniture, for Olivetti, Milan

1961 Palace of Culture, Milan (Rogers only; project; with M. Zanuso)

Town Hall, Aver El Qasar, Khartoum, Sudan (competition project)

Villa Bartolini, Castiglione della Pescaia, Italy

Patrizi Family Vault, Monumental Cemetery, Milan

Martinoli House interiors, Piazza San Erasmo, Milan

Design of lamps: "Aglia," "Enterprise," "Polinnia," "Ro," and "Talia," for the Artemide Company, Milan

1962 Villa Stabilini, Daverio, Varese, Italy

Italsider Kindergarten, Genoa (project)

Rafaello ship interiors (competition project)

Tourist development plan for Versilia, near Viareggio, Italy

1963 Sforza Castle Museum restoration, stage II, Milan (with C. Baroni, R. Chiavelli, and G. Lanzani)

Hotel Alfio, Punta Stella, Island of Elba

Tourist/residential development plan for Vecchiano, Pisa (project)

Apartment building, Via Vigna, Milan

Villa Zanetta, Lake Maggiore, Solcio di Lesa, Novara, Italy

Castello Bruni restoration, Jerago, Varese, Italy

Orfonatrofio Femminile "Stellin" restoration, Corso Magenta, Milan (project; with J. Battistoni)

Memorial Museum to the Victims of Nazi Concentration Camps, Castello de Pio, Carpi, Modena, Italy (with R. Guttuso, M. Chiavelli, and G. Lanzani)

Shell Company Entrance Hall and Exhibition Rooms, London

Einaudi Books/Galleria interiors, Manzoni, Milan

1964 Villa, Punta Stella, Island of Elba (not completed)

Gratosoglio Housing and Community Development, stage I, Milan (with others)

Electric Sub-station and Warehouse, for the Milan Underground (Subway), Sesto San Giovanni, Milan (with S. Zorzi, F. Bertolini, P. Maffioletti, and L. Paiosa)

Villa Jucker, Roncano di Bavero, Novara, Italy (with P. Porcinai and A. Radaelli)

Esso Motel, Autostrada dei Laghi, Milan (competition project)

1965 Secondigliano Housing Development, Naples (competition project)

Hispano-Olivetti Building, Ronda de la Universidad, Barcelona (with J. S. Mauri, R. Casals, and L. Paiosa)

Albertini Apartment Building, Via Zezio, Como

Belgiojoso Building, Via Maddalena, Milan

Building restoration, Via San Andrea, Milan

Church restoration, Longarone, Bulluno, Italy (competition project)

Cicogna Family Vault and Chapel, Bisuschio, Milan

1966 Master plan for the Town of Biella, Italy (project; with A. Belgiojoso)

Moriggia Nursery and Kindergarten, Italy

Touristresidential development plan for Lake Garda, Lazise, Verona (project; with A.

BBPR Architectural Studio: Chase Manhattan Bank Building, Milan, 1969

Belgiojoso and A. Radaelli)

Banca Commerciale Italiana Building, Via Ruggero Settimo, Palermo (with R. Guttuso, S. Bassani, R. Chiavelli, and G. Lanzani)

Banca Privata Finanziaria Building restoration and additions, Via Verdi, Milan

Jacini House restoration, Via dei Bossi, Milan

1967 Housing development, Via Beato Angelico, Milan

Andreatta Apartment Building, Pinzolo, Trento, Italy

Apartment/office building, Via Stampa, Milan

Villa Grandini, Luvinate, Varese, Italy

"Man in the Community" Pavilion, *Expo '67,* Montreal (Peressutti only; with F. Melotti and P. I. Tall)

Gratosoglio Housing and Community Development, stage II, Milan (with others)

IRFIS Headquarters interiors, Palermo

Revised master plan for the Town of Biella, Italy (project; with others)

Memorial, Gusen, Mauthausen, Austria

1968 Apartment/office building, Via Toino, Milan

Convent of St. Francis restoration, Rimini, Italy (project)

Hispano-Olivetti Showrooms, Piazza de Espana, Madrid (with R. Casals and A. Rodriguez)

1969 *Giornale di Sicilia* Building, Via Lincoln, Palermo

Apartment buildings, Via Pontaccio, Milan

Regional plan for the Metropolitana Veneta, Venice (as project consultants)

Reconstruction plan for the Old City of Kuwait (project; with A. Belgiojoso, G. Albertazzi, M. G. Sandri, and F. Ordanini)

Chase Manhattan Bank Building, Piazza

Meda, Milan

Romagnoli House restoration, Via Annunciata, Milan

1970 Gabriele d'Annunzio University, Chieti, Italy (with F. Ordanini and W. Passarella)

Motorways, throughout Italy (as consultants)

Tourist development plan for St. Vincent, Italy

Mazzocchi Tourist/Residential Development, Gabicce, Ancona, Italy

Apartment/office buildings, Piazza Vittorio Veneto, Biella, Italy (project)

Inverigo Housing and Community Development, Como (project)

New India Assurance Building, Cooperage Road, Bombay (with National Design Institute of Bombay and Shri J. G. Bodhe)

Mediolanum Building, Corso Vittorio Emanuele, Milan (with Ligresti and Cattozzo, R. Coluccini, and L. Paiosa)

Migliorisi Building, Corso Buenos Aires, Milan (with F. Ordanini)

Apartment/office building, Via Solferino, Milan

Tourist development plan for Ascia, Naples

Urban development plan for Canzo, Italy (project)

Hotel, Capoliveri, Island of Elba

Romagnoli Apartment interiors, Milan

1971 Apartment/office building, Via Perugia, Milan

Apartment building, Corso Lodi, Milan

Holiday houses, Gabicce, Ancona, Italy

San Simpliciano Cloisters restoration, for the Faculty of Theology, Milan

Exhibition Halls, *Trade Fair,* Dakar, Senegal (competition project)

Kindergarten, Concorezzo, Italy

1972 Central Square, Bellagio, Lake Como (project)

Ternate Quarries landscaping, Varese, Italy
Development plan for the Legnano Castle and Park, Milan
Apartment building, Viale Majno, Milan
Apartment/office building, Via Madonnina, Milan
B House, Maccagno, Italy
High school, Giussano, Italy
University of Calabria, Arcavacata, Cosenza, Italy (project)
Municipal Offices conversion, Concorezzo, Italy
St. Vincent Hotel, Sports and Cultural Centre, Aosta Valley, Italy
Circolo Hospital additions, Varese, Italy
Building conversion, Corso di Porta Nuova, Milan

1973 Plan for the Monti Berici Region of Italy (with Technital)
Pre-fabricated elements, for Fintech Italcamus
M House, Milan
University of Messina
Retirement home, Vanzago, Milan
Industrial development, near Choggia, Italy (with Lodovico Quaroni)

1974 Development plan for the communities of Lake Garda, Italy
Development plan for Dubai (competition project)
Landscape development plan for Bellagio, Lake Como (project)
M House, Bonassola, Italy
V House, Jeddah, Saudi Arabia
Schools development, Cornaredo, Milan
Technical school, Catanzaro, Italy
Technical school, Modena, Italy
Spaltenna Castle conversion, Gaiole in Chianti, Italy

1975 Memorial to the Victims of Nazi Concentration Camps, Auschwitz, Poland
Tourist development plan for Milazzo, Italy (competition project)

1976 Development plan for the central area of San Pietro all'Olmo, Milan
National Housing Authority Residential Development, Kuwait
Residential development, Masate, Milan
Residential development, Paullo, Italy
Housing developments at Riyadh, Qatif, Jeddah and Khobar, Saudi Arabia (competition project)
High school, Concorezzo, Italy
Borgo S. Sergio Parish Church, Trieste
Apartment building conversion, Via Correnti, Milan
Building conversion, Corso S. Marta, Milan
Palazzo Bagatti-Valsecchi conversion, Via S. Spirito, Milan
Development plan for the Port of Venice (as consultants; with Technital)
Road plans for Lecco, Italy (competition project)
Housing development, Nigeria

1977 Stock Exchange Building conversion, Milan

Publications:

By BBPR: books—*Stile,* Milan 1936; *Il Piano Regolatore della Valle d'Aosta,* with others, Ivrea, Italy 1943; articles—"Un Programma di Architettura," with others, in *Quadrante* (Milan), May 1933; "Relazione al Progetto del Palazzo del Littorio," with Luigi Figini, Gino Pollini, and Luigi Danusso, in *Quadrante* (Milan), August/September 1934; "Il Fatto Esposizione" in *Quadrante* (Milan), June 1935; "Urbanistica Corporativa" in *Quadrante* (Milan), September 1935; "L'Annata Architettonica" in *Almanacco Letterario Bompiani,* Milan 1936; "Il Volto delle Epoche" in *Enciclopedia Pratica Bompiani,* Milan 1936; "Riorganizzazione dell'Edilizia Rurale," with E. Radice Fossati, in *Congresso Nazionale di Urbanistica* (proceedings),

Rome 1937; "L'Architettura" in *Almanacco Letterario Bompiani,* Milan 1942; "La Città in Cura" in *Tempo* (Rome), 1942; "Il Piano A-R: La Descrizione del Piano," with others, in *Costruzioni-Casabella* (Milan), September 1946; "Sile del Museo" in *Città di Milano,* Milan 1956.

On BBPR: book—*Città, Museo e Architettura: Il Gruppo BBPR nella Cultura Architettonica Italiana 1932–1970* by Ezio Bonfanti and Marco Porta, Florence 1973 (includes bibliography); articles—"Gli Architetti BBPR" by L. Sinisgalli in *Comunità* (Milan), May/June 1950; "Continuità e Coeranza dei BBPR" by E. Paci in *Zodiac* (Milan), April 1959; "Meda Offices: Architects BBPR" in *Architectural Review* (London), January 1974; "Castle into War Memorial, Carpi, Italy" in *Architecture Plus* (New York), March/April 1974; "Project Barrier: Office Buildings, Piazza Meda, Milan" by Aileen Graham in *The Architects' Journal* (London), June 1974.

The BBPR Studio was founded in 1932, only five years after the setting up of an Italian CIAM group, an event that could be said to mark the arrival of Modern Architecture in Italy.

Despite the excitement created earlier outside Italy by Sant'Elia and the Futurists, modernist ideas had to overcome a fierce chauvinism within Italy. Italy is more accustomed to setting examples of style than to receiving them, particularly examples from the North. Banfi, Belgiojoso, Peressutti and Rogers nonetheless produced resolutely modernist thesis projects in their final year at Milan Polytechnic.

Early projects included competitions, a plan for Pavia, and a witty and spectacular weekend house for the 5th *Triennale* in Milan. Following this early burst of activity, the BBPR Studio, along with many other Italian modernists, fell under the spell of Fascist patronage. Having encountered resistance to modernism among the establishment, they hoped that Fascism would favour progressive architecture. Their eagerness to build, and their relative youth, numbed them to the true implications of Mussolini's ambitions. True, in the late 1930s BBPR did some remarkably sensitive and intelligent work, notably the Heliotherapy Clinic at Legnano of 1938. The restoration of the cloisters of San Simpliciano of 1940, which housed the firm's own offices, had a triumph of intelligent sympathy for the past, a quality to be seen again later in the magnificent conversion of the Sforza Castle to a museum (1954–56).

When Italy joined the German Axis, the progressive potential of Fascism vanished, just as Hitler had forced out German modernists as "radical" and "bolshevik." BBPR's Post Office complex of 1940 within Rome's EUR Quarter is the only building there to sustain the modernist spirit, while lesser architects "succumbed to the flattery of M. Piacentini, swallowing up and regurgitating arches, columns, pilasters, symetrical plans, static volumes, pointless scenographic perspectives" (Bruno Zevi).

The episode of EUR, the advent of war, and their own awareness of the failure of Fascism forced BBPR underground, Rogers to Lausanne, Banfi to die tragically at Mauthausen.

The war over, a renascence of Italian architecture began. Young architects who had been stifled by Fascism, able only to talk and reflect, burst on the scene and became part of the Italy the world turned to for inspiration in industrial design, naval architecture, sculpture, and fashion. Italy, as always, could provide elegance and style, both in great demand after wartime austerity. The architecture of BBPR, the more eclectic Gio Ponti, and many others, was very much part of this development.

The traditional materials of modern architecture, glass, steel and concrete were now rationed, and BBPR sought new forms based on indigenous masonry, smaller windows and careful planning. They and their colleagues such as Samona, Quaroni, Gardella, and Albini, were well equipped for such discoveries. Their knowledge of architectural history

was deep, and their love of Italy enriched by her recent horrible experiences. They began to produce a new type of modern architecture, one that did not turn its back on the past, was not frightened to copy what is good, and one that displayed great good humour—three attributes eschewed in the anglo-saxon interpretation of modernism, which is obsessed with originality, purity of form, and functional expressionism. The romanticism of the Italian movement, the concern for the symbolic rather than the expressive, was too much for the powerful British and American critics who, not seeing the wood for the trees, accused the Italians of gross eclecticism, whimsy, moral irresponsibility and worse. So vituperative was this attack that even now when the north is discovering what it calls Post-Modernism, the true genesis of that idea in the Italy of the 1950's remains unacknowledged. BBPR are among the masters of what is being learned today.

In particular, the Velasca Tower Building of 1955–58 is a seminal building. Although attacked in England for its allusive qualities (compared with mediaeval buildings), berated for its lucid and organic structure, the building is a masterful synthesis of its complex functional requirements, Milanese traditions, structural possibilities, and great art.

It is art that often seems to be lacking in Northern architecture, and one can only hope that the scorn heaped on the great Italian post-war architects, especially BBPR, is inspired by envy.

It is worth remembering that Belgiojoso, Peressutti and Rogers, along with other Italians whose best work was done in the post-war years, were mature men in the 1950's and 1960's who had seen great hopes frustrated; many of them had been fooled by Fascism; they saw their country ravaged by war; and they loved and understood their cultural heritage. The wisdom born of those experiences is felt in the maturity and great sophistication of their work. One day the rest of the world is bound to acknowledge their contribution.

—Andrew Rabeneck

BEAUDOUIN, Eugène (Elie).
French. Born in Paris, 20 July 1898. Educated at the Ecole Nationale Supérieure des Beaux-Arts, Paris; French Academy, Rome, 1929–32. Married the artist Josephine Cals in 1928; children: Francois, Sylvie, and Thierry. In partnership with Marcel Lods, *q.v.,* Paris, 1925–40. In private practice, Paris, since 1944. Chief Architect of Public Buildings and National Palaces, France, since 1933; Member, National Council of Architecture and Town Planning, since 1950. Director of Architectural Studies, University of Geneva, 1940–68. Professor of Architecture, Ecole Nationale Supérieure des Beaux-Arts, Paris, since 1946. President, International Union of Architects, 1960–64. Honorary President, French Town Planning Society, since 1965, Association of Architects' Councils of the Ministry of Equipment, since 1966, and of the Association of Chief Architects of Public Buildings and National Palaces, since 1969. Recipient: First Prize, with Marcel Lods, *World's Fair* Competition, Paris, 1937. Officer of the Grimaldi Order, Monaco, 1958; Chevalier, Order of Merit, 1960; Officer of the French Academy, 1962; Member, Fine Arts Academy, Institut de France, 1963; Commander of the Légion d'Honneur, 1971; Commander of the Order of Arts and Letters, 1972. Honorary Fellow, Royal Institute of British Architects, American Institute of Architects, and Sociedad Central de los Arquitectos Argentinos. Address (office): 38 rue de l'Yvette, Paris 16, France.

Works:

1928 Town plan for La Havane, France (with J. C. N. Forestier)

Eugène Beaudouin: Cité de la Muette, Drancy, France, 1934

1930/
  36 Plan for the Paris region (with Henri Prost)
1932 Cité des Oiseux (housing development), Bagneux, France
1933 Palais des Expositions, Paris (project; with Marcel Lods and Vladimir Bodiansky)
1934 Cité de la Muette (housing development), Drancy, France (with Marcel Lods and Vladimir Bodiansky)
1935 Open-Air School, Suresnes, France (with Marcel Lods)
1937 Aero-Club, Buc, France (with Marcel Lods and Jean Prouvé; demolished by the Germans during the Occupation, 1940–44)
     Design of the *World's Fair*, Paris (with Marcel Lods)
     French Embassy, Ottawa, Canada
1938 Dismantable Week-end House, *Exposition Habitation*, Paris (with Marcel Lods)
1939 Maison du Peuple, Clichy, Paris (with Marcel Lods, Vladimir Bodiansky, and Jean Prouvé)
1940 Town plan for Cape Town (first project)
1941/
  61 Plan for Monaco
1942/
  43 Town plan for Marseilles
1948 Town plan for Saigon
     Town plans for Montpellier and Toulon, France
     French Embassy, Accra, Ghana
1949 Industrial complex, Sarre, France
1950 Industrial centers and residential complexes in Gabon and Cameroun
1951 Cité Rotterdam (housing development), Strasbourg
     Joffre School, Montpellier, France
1954 Les Bas-Coudrais (housing development), Sceaux, France

     Housing development, including Young Workers Dormitory, Cachan, France
     University Residence Hall, Antony, France
1958 Decoration of Paris for the visit of H. M. Queen Elizabeth II
     French Embassy, Pretoria, South Africa
1958/
  74 Renovation of the Gare Montparnasse/Avenue du Maine District of Paris (with U. Cassan, L. de Marien, J. Warnery, J. Saubot, and R. Lopez)
1959 Ministries of Agriculture and Industry Building, rue Barbet de Jouy, Paris
     Residence Hall, University of Clermont-Ferrand, France
1960 Mixed School, Antony, France
     Town plan for Cape Town (2nd project)
1961 National School of Taxation, Clermont-Ferrand, France
1962 Faculty of Law, University of Clermont-Ferrand, France
     Housing development, Eaubonne, France
1962/
  74 Venissieux-les-Minguettes (satellite town), Lyons
1964 Town plan for Cape Town (3rd project)
     Plan for the reconstruction of Suresnes, France
     Housing development, Vernaison, Lyons
1964/
  69 Z.U.P. Housing Development, Venissieux-les-Minguettes, Lyons
     Z.U.P. Housing Development, La Foux, Saint Tropez, France
     Tourist housing, Saint-Cyprien, Languedox, France
1964/
  76 Administrative Center, Eaubonne, France

1965– La Croix-Laval University Complex, Lyons
1966 Housing development, Angers, France
1966/
  68 International Labor Organization Building, Geneva (with others; as Chief Architect)
1967 Post Office, Eaubonne, France
1967/
  68 Mixed School, Meuden, France
1967/
  73 Palais des Nations extension and remodelling, and new Conference Hall, United Nations, Geneva (with Pier Luigi Nervi and Alberto Camenzind)
1968 Plan for the Isfahan region of Iran
1968/
  77 National Veterinary School, Lyons
1972– Housing development, Saint-Laurent du Var, France
1973/
  74 Venissy Commercial Center, Venissieux-les-Minguettes, Lyons
1974– Montparnasse S.N.C.F. Railway Station Complex (station; housing; conference center; shops; hotels; cinemas; restaurants; and general services), Paris
1977– Apartment building, rue des Prairies, Paris
1978– Auteuil-Muette Tax Center, for the Finance Ministry, rue George Sand, Paris 16

Publications:

By BEAUDOUIN: articles—"L'Enseignement de l'Architecture" in *Werk* (Zurich), June 1943; "L'Urbanisme et l'Architecture au Cap" in *La Construction Moderne* (Paris), April 1953; "De la Composition des Plans-masse des Groupes d'Habitations" in *Forum* (Amsterdam), May 1953.

On BEAUDOUIN: articles—"Architects of Europe Today: Eugène Beaudouin" by George Nelson in *Pencil Points* (New York), February 1936; "Edificio de la Legación de Francia en Ottawa" in *Arquitectura* (Mexico City), January 1940; "Cité Rotterdam" in *Werk* (Zurich), September 1953; "Reconstruction and Housing in France," special issue of *Techniques et Architecture* (Paris), November/December 1953; "Architecture Sociale et Hospitalière" in *L'Architecture Francaise* (Paris), June 1960; "Maine/Montparnasse" in *Architecture Francaise* (Paris), July/August 1973; "Maine/Montparnasse" in *Moderner Markt* (Frankfurt), January 1974.

In the practice of architecture and urbanism, I have tried to make it my object in all my work to provide "a service" to the client, to allow him a measure of control and in this way to achieve a final result that is a collective effort.

My attitude, in all circumstances, is to work conscientiously and with complete sincerity.

—Eugène Beaudouin

Eugène Beaudouin followed in the great tradition of French architects by studying at the French Academy in Rome. However, the classical education that had had such immense international repercussions where the students of the late 18th century were concerned was not to provide Beaudouin with his inspiration. Like so many others of his generation, he became concerned with the provision of low-cost housing for the poorer members of society. He worked for the Office public d'habitation of the Department of the Seine, and later for the Société des logements économiques pour familles nombreuses. He realized that structural experiment was needed to provide low-cost housing, and that it was essential to mix such experiment with modern distributive ideas.

His Cité de la Muette at Drancy, with Marcel Lods, was a mixed development of low- and high-rise buildings in which modern prefabricated concrete components were used. There were several four-storey blocks and five sixteen-storey towers built on a steel skeleton. Roofs and non-loadbearing walls were of precast concrete, as were the outer coverings, the stairs, and the balconies, so a rigourous quality control was possible in factory conditions when the units were manufactured. The circular staircases to the towers at Drancy were expressed in vertical fins of precast concrete, and each tower was constructed with panel effects, all in concrete. These system-built towers were early prototypes of high-rise housing blocks that became usual during the 1950's and 1960's and have since attracted universal anathema. Beaudouin's system of precast concrete was also used in his school at Suresnes of 1935.

Beaudouin prepared designs for the Unesco Building in Paris after the Second World War, but by then his aggressive dogmatism and the ferociously puritan effects of his housing designs had alienated many people. His designs were not felt to be what was required by the several distinguished architects who advised on the design of the headquarters.

Other schemes by Beaudouin include the Maison du Peuple at Clichy of 1939, the Cité Rotterdam housing estate at Strasbourg, and many other developments for public buildings and housing. He is also known in the field of town and regional planning, where his peculiar blend of French logic and a ruthless devotion to systems for building have tended to produce hard and uncompromising environments.

—James Stevens Curl

BECKET, Welton (David).
American. Born in Seattle, Washington, 8 August 1902. Educated at the University of Washington, Seattle, 1923–27, B.Arch. 1927; Ecole des Beaux-Arts, Fontainebleau, France, 1928. Married; sons:

Welton Becket: Xerox Square, Rochester, New York, 1968

Bruce and Welton Jr. Worked as a designer-draftsman for a small architectural office in Los Angeles, 1929; in private practice, Seattle, 1929–33; Partner, with Walter Wurdeman and Charles Plummer, Becket, Wurdeman and Plummer, Los Angeles, 1933 until Plummer's death, 1939, then as Becket and Wurdeman, 1939 until Wurdeman's death, 1949; Becket continued the firm as Welton Becket and Associates, serving as President, 1949–68, and Chairman of the Board, 1968 until his death, 1969 (firm now continues under the direction of Welton Becket Jr.); offices established in San Francisco, 1949, New York, 1950, and Houston, 1960. Master Planner and Supervising Architect, University of California at Los Angeles, 1949–69. Recipient: First Place, Pan Pacific Auditorium Competition, Los Angeles, 1934; Honor Award, American Institute of Architects, 1936; Award, Pan American Congress of Architects, 1950. Fellow, American Institute of Architects, 1952. *Died* (in Los Angeles) *17 January 1969.*

Works:

1934 Pan Pacific Auditorium, Los Angeles (with Walter Wurdeman)
1940 Jai Alai Auditorium, Manila (with Walter Wurdeman)
1946 House of Tomorrow, Los Angeles (with Walter Wurdeman)
1947 Bullock's Department Store, Pasadena, California (with Walter Wurdeman)
1948 Prudential Square, Los Angeles (with Walter Wurdeman)
1949 General Petroleum Building, Los Angeles (with Walter Wurdeman)
1950 Bullock's Department Store, Westwood, California
1951 Stonestown Shopping Center, San Francisco, California
1955 Beverly Hilton Hotel, Beverly Hills, California
1956 Ford Motor Company General Office Building, Dearborn, Michigan
1957 Canyon Village, Yellowstone National Park, Wyoming
     Hawaiian Village, Honolulu (with Edwin L. Bauer)
1958 Beach facilities, Santa Monica, California
     Master plan for Century City, Los Angeles
1959 California Teachers Association Headquarters, Burlingame, California
     The Nile Hilton Hotel, Cairo
     Southland Center, Dallas (with Mark Lemmon)

Design of the *United States Exhibition,* Moscow
Los Angeles Memorial Sports Arena
1960 Kaiser Center, Oakland, California
     Welton Becket and Associates Building, 10000 Santa Monica Boulevard, Los Angeles
1961 Neuropsychiatric and Brain Research Institute, University of California at Los Angeles
     Veterans Administration Hospital, Palo Alto, California
1962 500 Jefferson Building, Houston
     Gateway Building West, Century City, Los Angeles
     Los Angeles International Airport (with Pereira and Luckman)
     Marion Davies Children's Clinic, University of California at Los Angeles
1963 Cullen Center, Houston
     Bullock's Department Store, Sherman Oaks, California
     Hotel Sonesta, Houston
     Humble Oil Building, Houston (with Goleman and Rolfe, and Pierce and Pierce)
     Civic Center, Orange, California
     Security Pacific Bank Building, Tishman Airport Center, Los Angeles
     U. S. Borax Building, Los Angeles
     United States Embassy, Warsaw
1964 Ford Motor Company Pavilion, *World's Fair,* New York
     General Electric Exhibit, *World's Fair,* New York
     Gateway Building East, Century City, Los Angeles
     The Meadows (apartments), San Rafael, California
     Dorothy Chandler Pavilion, Los Angeles Music Center
     Phillips Petroleum Building, Bartlesville, Oklahoma
1965 Beverly Hills/Westwood Office of the Automobile Club of Southern California, Century City, Los Angeles
     Bullock's Department Store, Lakewood, California
     North Carolina Mutual Life Building, Durham, North Carolina (with Marion A. Ham)
     Pauley Pavilion, University of California at Los Angeles
     Public Library, Pomona, California (with Everett and Tozier)
     Institute for Chronic Disease, University of California at Los Angeles
     Wells Fargo Bank, San Rafael, California
1966 Jules Stein Eye Institute, University of California at Los Angeles
     Northgate Shopping Center, San Rafael, California
     Center Plaza, Boston
     Federal Office Building, Los Angeles (with Albert C. Martin and Associates, and Paul R. Williams)
     First State Bank, Clear Lake City, Texas
1967 Fashion Island, Newport Beach, California
     Gulf Life Tower, Jacksonville, Florida (with Kemp, Bunche and Jackson)
     Hartford National Bank Building, Hartford, Connecticut (with Jeter and Cook)
     Ahmanson Theatre, Los Angeles Music Center
     Mark Taper Forum, Los Angeles Music Center
     Park Lane Apartments, Monterey, California
1968 The Manila Hilton (with C. D. Arguelles)
     City Hall, Pomona, California (with B. H. Anderson)
     Academic Building, United States Naval Postgraduate School, Monterey, California

School of Public Health, University of California at Los Angeles

Xerox Square, Rochester, New York

1969 Aetna Life and Casualty Building, San Francisco

Almaden Fashion Plaza, San Jose, California

Bullock's Department Store, La Habra, California

Canada College, Redwood City, California (with ChanRader Associates)

Equitable Life Building, Los Angeles

Hoffman Medical Research Center, University of Southern California, Los Angeles

Mutual Benefit Life Building, San Francisco

Publications:

On BECKET: book—*Total Design: The Architecture of Welton Becket and Associates* by William Dudley Hunt, Jr., New York 1972; articles—"Recent Works of Welton Becket and Associates" in *Michigan Society of Architects Bulletin* (Detroit), June 1958; "Welton Becket and Associates" in *Interiors* (New York), September 1959; "Portrait of the Artist as a Businessman" by Robert Sheehan in *Fortune* (New York), March 1967.

Discussions between architects about the influence of architects on architecture are almost always concerned, sometimes exclusively, with the subject of design. And architectural design is often taken to mean, narrowly, the form or esthetics of buildings.

Welton Becket influenced the esthetic design of buildings, but much more important was his deep influence on the complete design of buildings, including not only their forms but also their plans, functions, interiors, systems, structures and other aspects. Equally as important was the contribution of Becket to the revolutionary changes that have taken place in architectural practice.

In the early 1930's, Becket was one of the first architects to recognize that much of the architecture of the future would consist of large, complex buildings and groups of buildings. He also foresaw that such buildings, more often that not, would be designed and constructed for corporations and other organizations of great size. The owners of such buildings, the clients of architects, would be, not individuals, but groups of people, mostly businessmen, the officers and boards of directors of the organizations.

In order to serve the needs of such corporate owners, Becket set out to build an architectural practice of sufficient size and capabilities to handle properly such large and complex work. Since it would be dealing with businessmen, Becket organized the firm in a businesslike manner, along the lines of the organizations for which it would perform architectural services. In order to serve all of the needs of the clients, the firm would offer not only the usual architectural services but also what Becket came to call total design, including master planning, site planning, engineering, interior design, landscape architecture, graphic design, and other services. Thus, the firm would be able to analyze problems, perform studies and research, solve problems through design and transform the solutions into completed buildings and groups of buildings that were complete to the last detail.

Welton Becket established his practice of architecture in 1933. He practiced continuously for 36 years, devoting himself to all aspects of architecture in the broadest sense, but avoiding involvement in related but non-architectural activities such as construction, real estate or the financing of buildings. Unlike many of his contemporaries who often spent much of their time in non-practice pursuits, such as teaching or making speeches, Becket devoted himself entirely to the practice of architecture.

By the time he died, in 1969, Becket had developed one of the largest and most successful firms in the world. It was one of the first truly national, and later international, American architectural firms, with offices in a number of cities. Although he was proud of the awards his buildings earned at various times, Becket was most proud of the list of clients he developed and of the fact that many of them automatically came back to his firm, some on numerous occasions, when they had additional building projects in mind.

The firm established by Becket has continued to prosper, maintaining the same business principles and devotion to total design envisioned by its founder. Other large, multifaceted national and international firms are in practice today, but Welton Becket

pioneered the way for them.

—William Dudley Hunt, Jr.

BEEBY, Thomas Hall.

American. Born in Oak Park, Illinois, 12 October 1941. Educated at Lower Merion High School, Ardmore, Pennsylvania, 1955–58; Gresham School, Holt, Norfolk, England, 1958–59; Cornell University, Ithaca, New York, under Colin Rowe and John Hejduk, 1959–64, B.Arch. 1964; Yale University, New Haven, Connecticut, under Paul Rudolph, Vincent Scully, and Serge Chermeyeff, 1964–65, M.Arch. 1965. Married Marcia Dale Greenlease in 1960 (divorced, 1973); married Kirsten Peltzer in 1975; children: Donald, MaryAnne, and Markus. Associate, C.-F. Murphy Associates, Chicago, 1965–71; Partner, with James Hammond, Hammond Beeby and Associates, Chicago, 1971–76. Since 1976, Partner, with Hammond and B. Babka, Hammond Beeby and Babka, Chicago. Associate Professor, Department of Architecture, Illinois Institute of Technology, Chicago, since 1973. Exhibitions: *100 Years of Architecture in Chicago*, Die Neue Sammlung, Munich, and Museum of Contemporary Art, Chicago, 1976; *Chicago Architects*, Cooper Union, New York, and Time-Life Building, Chicago, 1976; *7 Chicago Architects*, Richard Gray Gallery, Chicago, 1976; *The Exquisite Corpse*, Walter Kelly Gallery, Chicago, 1977; *Designs for Urban Living*, Walker Art Center, Minneapolis, and Graham Foundation, Chicago, 1978; *Wishful Thinking*, Cooper Hewitt Museum, 1979; *Bridging Chicago*, Graham Foundation, Chicago, 1979; *Urban Fragments*, Walker Art Center, Minneapolis, 1979. Recipient: Distinguished Building Award, American Institute of Architects, Chicago Chapter, 1976 (twice), 1977, 1978. Address: Hammond Beeby and Babka, 720 North Michigan Avenue, Chicago, Illinois 60611, U.S.A.

Works:

1971 Malcolm X College, Chicago (with C. F. Murphy and Associates)

1975 One Woodfield Place (office building), Schaumburg, Illinois

1976 Beidler Conference Center, Chicago

First National Bank of Ripon, Wisconsin

1977 Champaign Public Library, Illinois

1978 Beasley House, Monroe, Wisconsin

Bank of the North Shore, Northbrook, Illinois

Doane Observatory, Adler Planetarium, Chicago

Hewitt Associates Office Building, Lincolnshire, Illinois

Highland Lakes Office Building, Lombard, Illinois

Sanders House, Barrington, Illinois

1979 Dearborn Park Townhouses, Chicago

Fultz House, Chesterton, Indiana

Tri-State Office Center, Northbrook, Illinois

North Shore Congregation Israel addition, Glencoe, Illinois

Publications:

By BEEBY: articles—"The Grammar of Ornament Ornament as Grammar" in *VIA III* (Graduate School of Fine Arts, University of Pennsylvania, Philadelphia), 1977; "Vitruvius Americanus: Mies Ornament" in *Inland Architect* (Chicago), May 1977; "Flowering Grid" in *Architectural Review* (London), October 1977; "Of Manifest Destiny and the Death of Prophets" in *AIA Journal* (Washington, D.C.), October 1978.

Thomas Hall Beeby: Hewitt Associates Office Building, Lincolnshire, Illinois, 1978

On BEEBY: books—*100 Years of Architecture in Chicago,* exhibition catalogue, by Grube, Pran and Schultz, Chicago 1976; *Chicago Architects* by Stuart Cohen, Chicago 1976; articles—"40 under 40" by Robert Stern in *Architecture + Urbanism* (Tokyo), January 1977; "Chicago 7" in *Architecture + Urbanism* (Tokyo), May 1977; special issue on Chicago of *Architectural Review* (London), October 1977; "The Diversity of Design in Chicago" by Peter Pran in *L'Architettura* (Milan), December 1977; "Ripon Pavilion" by David Morton in *Progressive Architecture* (New York), July 1978; "Chicago on the Drawing Board" by Nory Miller in *Horizons* (New York), September 1978; "Prime Square Footages" by John Dixon in *Progressive Architecture* (New York), October 1978; "Color in Architecture" by Nory Miller in *AIA Journal* (Washington, D.C.), October 1978; "Designs for Living" by Douglas Davies in *Newsweek* (New York), 6 November 1978.

*

Our approach has been to utilize the lucid systematic qualities of construction long associated with the architecture of Chicago. We employ frame construction as a pragmatic necessity and an organizing aesthetic device. Prefabricated systems and modular coordination play a major part in the visual character of our buildings. We are also interested in as free an arrangement as possible. The fluid spatial quality of early modern architecture has strongly influenced our work. We are concerned with expressive display of functional elements through arrangement of construction. This would equate with the volumetric and fenestration effects found in the 19th century balloon frame houses prevalent in Chicago. Our interests also encompass the question of meaning of forms and their derivation from the shape ideas of the past.

These methods and ideas constitute neither a revolutionary nor a radical approach; however, the full implication of these combined concepts has never been fully explored. The great break in continuity of architectural development in Chicago occurred during World War II when virtually all building stopped. At this time a schism developed which has increased with time. The choice has been between classicism pursuing pure construction and its conscious antithesis of picturesque romanticism. To ex-

plore synthesis has difficult and challenging aspects.
—Thomas Hall Beeby

*

Thomas Hall Beeby is one of the leading younger figures of the post-Miesian generation in Chicago. Typical of the designers who matured in the city during the late 1960's and 1970's, Beeby has moved from an early, rather close fidelity to the principles of Miesian structural geometry to a gradually more personal idiom marked at times by a strikingly original quality of lyric fantasy.

Beeby spent his boyhood in the suburbs of Chicago and Philadelphia, and in Norfolk, England. His professional training led to a Bachelor of Science in Architecture degree in 1964 from Cornell University, where he studied with John Hejduk and Colin Rowe, and a Master of Architecture in 1965 from Yale University, where he worked with Paul Rudolph. He accepted his first professional position with the firm of C. F. Murphy Associates, at that time one of the leading exponents of Miesian design in Chicago. Beeby quickly came under the influence of the two most talented architects on the Murphy staff, Gene Summers and Jacques Brownson. The lessons learned from that encounter are evident in the work Beeby did in the design of the Malcolm X College in Chicago.

In 1971 he joined James Hammond to form Hammond, Beeby and Associates, later (in 1977) Hammond, Beeby and Babka. Two of the more important early works which Beeby executed for the partnership are Woodfield Place (eleven-story office building) in Schaumburg, Illinois, a clear expression of the Chicago frame, and the First National Bank of Ripon, Wisconsin. Thereafter, however, a tendency away from local formula toward more experimental forms became apparent: in his library for Champaign, Illinois, the design is marked by curved walls and corrugated metal siding, as well as a free plan reminiscent of the earlier European work of Mies and Le Corbusier.

By 1979 Beeby had utilized curvilinear form to highly inventive advantage in the cylindrical volumes of the Doane Observatory in Chicago, as well as in the gleaming round white brick box which houses the Bank of the North Shore in Northbrook, Illinois. For a 1978 exhibition of the "Chicago

Seven" (a group of young local designers seeking alternatives to the traditional Chicago structuralist viewpoint), he submitted a series of drawings for a project, "The House of Vergil," which suggested he had moved, at least at the level of imagination, into a realm of luxurious visionary form altogether removed from the sternness of his early manner.

Still, among his most recent completed works, like the Hewitt Associates Office Building in Lincolnshire, Illinois, he has maintained a balance between what he himself has called "pure construction" and "picturesque romanticism."

—Franz Schulze

BEHNISCH, Günter.
German. Born in Lockwitz bei Dresden, 12 June 1922. Studied engineering at the Technische Hochschule, Stuttgart, 1947–51, Diplom-Ingenieur 1951. Oberleutnant, German Navy, 1939–45; prisoner-of-war in England, 1945–47. Married Johanna Fink in 1952; children: Sabine, Charlotte, and Stefan. Practised with Bruno Lambart, Stuttgart, 1952–56; practised on his own, Stuttgart, 1956–66; formed company, Behnisch & Partner, Stuttgart, 1966 (partners: Fritz Auer, Winfried Büxel, Manfred Sabatke, Erhard Tränkner, and Karlheinz Weber). Regional Director, Bund Deutscher Architekten, Baden-Württemberg, 1965–68. Professor, Technische Hochschule, Darmstadt, since 1975. Recipient: Paul Bonatz Prize, City of Stuttgart, 1963; Grand Architecture Prize, Bund Deutscher Architekten, 1972; Hugo Häring Prize, Bund Deutscher Architekten, Baden-Württemberg, 1972, 1974, 1977; German Architecture Prize, Bundesarchitektenkammer, 1977. Address: Behnisch & Partner, Mendelssohnstrasse 22, 7000 Stuttgart-Sillenbuch, Germany.

Works:

1957   District Council Office, Schwäbisch Gmünd, Germany (with Bruno Lambart)
1959   Hohenstaufen Grammar School, Göppingen, Germany (with Bruno Lambart)

Günter Behnisch. Olympiapark, Munich, 1072

Vogelsan School, Stuttgart (with Bruno Lambart)
1960 Technical School, Radolfzell, Germany
1961 Town Hall, Mannheim (project)
1963 State Technical College, Ulm
1965 Otto Hahn Grammar School, Furtwangen, Germany
Grammar School, Deutenberg, Schwenningen, Germany
Town redevelopment, Waiblingen, Germany (project)
1966 Droste-Hulshoff Grammar School, Freiburg
Friedrich von Keller School, Neckarweihingen, Germany
1967 Design for a university, Bremen (project)
District Hospital, Göppingen, Germany (project)
Holiday House, Schlechtbach, Germany
Sports Centre, Sindelfingen, Germany
1968 State Technical College, Aalen, Germany
Salier Grammar School, Waiblingen, Germany
Sports Hall, Schwenningen, Germany
1969 Pavilion, *Garden Exhibition,* Dortmund
Administration Building, Kronprinzenstrasse, Stuttgart
In den Berglen School, Oppelsbohm, Germany
Oskar-von-Miller School, Rothenburg, Germany
1970 Leisure Centre Park, Pfullingen, Germany (project)
Friedrich-Schiller Grammar School, Marbach, Germany
Sports Hall, Rothenburg, Germany
Purchasing Centre, Waiblingen, Germany (project)
Purchasing Centre, Ludwigsburg, Germany (project)
Korber Hohe Physical Training Hall, Waiblingen, Germany
Hymnus Choirboys Home, Stuttgart
1971 University Sports Centre, Bremen (project)
European Patent Office, Munich (project)
Nursing Home, Dahn, Germany (project)
1972 Bofingen Shopping Centre, Ulm
Rechts d. Rems School Centre, Waiblingen, Germany
Olympiapark, Munich (with Günter Grzimek)
Fritz Erler Technical School Centre, Pforzheim, Germany
School and Sports Area, Rothenburg, Germany
1973 Geriatric and Nursing Home, Reutlingen, Germany
Birkach Study and Training Centre, Stuttgart
Grammar School, Lorch, Germany
Hospital, Waldkraiburg, Germany (project)
Parliament Buildings, Bonn
1974 Josef Effner Grammar School, Dachau, Germany
Thermal Baths, Baden-Baden, Germany (project)
Olympiapark Company Administration Building, Munich
Schlossplatz Underground (Subway) Station, Stuttgart
1977 Königstrasse Pedestrian Area, Stuttgart
Neugereut Nursery School, Stuttgart

Publications:

By BEHNISCH: books—*Buildings of 19th Century Paris,* Darmstadt 1974; *Buildings of 19th Century England,* Darmstadt 1976; *Backsteinbauten,* Darmstadt 1977;

On BEHNISCH: books—*Behnisch & Partner: Buildings and Projects,* Stuttgart 1975; *Architecture in the Federal Republic* by Heinrich Klotz, Frankfurt, Berlin, and Vienna, 1977.

I am a university teacher and a "free-lance architect" in the partnership Behnisch & Partner: a free-lance architect has the opportunity and the responsibility to exercise a free and independent attitude to problems.

One consequence has been that, while we have not and would not reject such work in principle, we have not, as yet, worked for banks, combines, etc.; we have been much more involved with schools, old people's homes, kindergartens and other public-sector installations.

Practically all our commissions result from architectural competitions. In almost every case we have ourselves carried out all the architectural requirements up to the handing over of the complete project.

Our largest and most spectacular commission to date was for the Olympic Games site in Munich. The tent roof achieved notoriety because of technical, financial and labour problems, but the real achievement was in the successful integration into the structure of Munich of a site covering 3×1.5 kilometres. The park, with its sporting installations, sports grounds and recreational areas, met all the functional, technical, spatial, architectonic, organisational and financial requirements. The popular reaction is that surely it must always have been there. The Olympia Park is now the favourite recreational area of Munich, a town richly endowed in this respect.

The scale of a project is, however, not most important.

In 1977 we completed, in Stuttgart-Neugereut, a small kindergarten which, for us, is equally of great importance. It stands airy, distinctive, and carried out with affection in a new, much too densely built part of town, where the chief concern has been with the "return" on buildings. In our opinion it is an oasis, a world for children, and well worth working for.

Our next large-scale project is the Parliament Buildings in Bonn: the Upper and Lower Houses of the German Parliament together with related streets, squares and parks. An important undertaking for our company and one of interest for us. We will try to avoid representation as such, monumentality and the pursuit of the art object. We will endeavour rather to give architectonic expression to that which should distinguish a free society and which is commonly, too frequently suppressed.

—Günter Behnisch

I've asked Günter Behnisch what importance, for people, he would claim for architecture. His answer involved the demands that are made on architecture, demands that can no longer, as in former times, be considered as separate from the building itself—such as the square metre, climate, construction techniques, light, building elements, gravity, geometry, and form, as well as financing and, finally, the symbolic nature of architecture. The manner in which the architect arranges and presents his priorities determines the value that attaches to these demands. For this very reason, architecture has, of necessity, been perceived and appreciated differently by different people in different ages and in different situations.

But the value of architecture for people today also depends on how far the natural world, creation, is burdened by our constructions and how far they do or do not satisfy aesthetic needs. In any aesthetic standard Behnisch wishes to be able to perceive a concern for people, their internal natures and their external surroundings—whether the architect takes the trouble to help people or whether he hands them over to the "powerful" of our age. Behnisch does not want to create forms that are empty of content in order to generate an aesthetic goal; he wants his forms to be the consequence of a comprehensive argument with reality. Behnisch conceives of reality as power, that force in society that wants to shape people, things and nature to its own end.

His attitude begs a few questions. Who wields this power? How does this power happen? Does it have any right at all to be reflected in our architecture? And, yet, the questions are beside the point. The history of architecture demonstrates that the architect's dialogue with temporal and spiritual powers and the conversion of their demands into forms have led to the most valuable and beautiful buildings. Power is not in itself negative, only its misuse. Architecture commissioned by the powerful is in no way, by definition, inhuman; the only question is whether artistry shines through.

Behnisch also precludes "closed formal principles" from his works. As far as he is concerned there is no autonomy of form, nor are human needs established and ordained in some psychological, philosophical or religious sphere. To some extent he also denies the influence of archetypes and any inevitable continuity of tradition. For Behnisch the most important buildings are those that reveal a changing vision of the world rather than a changing set of specifications. The known and lively project that fits eloquently into the present unique situation need not immediately reveal the signature of its creator but should bear witness that, in this particular case, the "right thing" has been done. For Behnisch this "right thing," in our increasingly crowded and highly organized world, is the creation of oases, free space for the perplexed.

Behnisch is not, however, optimistic about the future development of architecture. He sees too many architects as being in one of two categories—those who simply confirm reality and thereby increase its restraints and those who avoid reality by taking refuge in Art, in the commanding heights. Behnisch feels that such architects betray their brothers and surrender them to the powerful forces of our time, in that they aesthetize architecture and place it on a pedestal; that is, they remove it from everyday life and render it incomprehensible.

Behnisch tries to be another sort of architect, and in that attempt he deserves our highest praise. He tries to achieve, and in his projects has achieved, an architecture totally related to people.

—Justus Dahinden

BEHRENS, Peter.
German. Born in Hamburg, 14 April 1868. Studied painting at the Künstschule, Karlsruhe, and in various painters' studios, Dusseldorf, 1886–89; travelled in the Netherlands: influenced by the work of the "luminist" painters, 1890. Married Lilli Kramer in 1889 (died, 1957). Moved to Munich, 1890: Co-Founder, Munich Secession group of painters, 1893; first woodcuts, 1896; Co-Founder, Union of Arts and Crafts Workshops, Munich, 1896; collaborated on the magazine *Pan,* Munich, 1898; first industrial designs for glass factory, Munich, 1898; joined the artists' group Die Sieben (The Seven), including architects J. M. Olbricht and P. Huber, painters H. Christiansen and P. Burck, and sculptors L. Habich and R. Bosselt, in Darmstadt, 1899, and began architectural work, Darmstadt, 1900; Director of the Nuremberg Master Course, 1902; Director, Künstgewerbeschule, Dusseldorf, 1903–07; in private practice, Berlin, from 1907 (pupil/assistants include Le Corbusier, Gropius and Mies van der Rohe); Director, Academy of Art, Dusseldorf, 1921–22; Director, Master School for Architecture, Akademie der Bildenden Künste, 1922–36; Head of the Department of Architecture, Prussian Academy of Arts, Berlin, 1936–40. Exhibitions: *Secession Exhibition,* Berlin and Vienna, 1893, Zurich, 1897, and Darmstadt, 1899; *Exposition of Decorative Arts,* Turin, 1902; *World's Fair,* St. Louis, Missouri, 1904; *Peter Behrens 1868–1940,* Kaiserslautern, 1966, toured Hagen, Berlin, Darmstadt and Vienna, 1967. *Died (in Berlin) 27 February 1940.*

Peter Behrens: Behrens House, Darmstadt, 1901

Works:

1900 Theatre (project)
1901 Behrens House, Darmstadt
1902 Exhibition Stand, *Exposition of Decorative Arts,* Turin
1904 Restaurant, *Building Exhibition,* Dusseldorf
 Reading Room, City Library, Dusseldorf
1905 Showrooms and Garden, *Nordwestduetsche Art Exhibition,* Oldenburg, Germany
1905/
 06 Obenauer House, Saarbrucken, Germany
1906 Delmenhorster Linoleum Pavilion, *German Arts Trade Fair,* Dresden
1907 Crematorium, Delstern, near Hagen, Germany (with the painter E. R. Weiss)
 Warehouse (project)
1908/
 10 Catholic Fellowship House, Neuss, Germany
1909 Schroeder House, Eppenhausen, near Hagen, Germany
1909/
 10 AEG (German General Electric Co.) Turbine Factory, Huttenstrasse, Berlin

1910 AEG (German General Electric Co.) High Tension Plant, Berlin
1910/
 11 AEG (German General Electric Co.) Motor Factory, Berlin
 AEG (German General Electric Co.) Workers Apartment Buildings, Henningsdorf, near Berlin
 Cuno House, Eppenhausen, near Hagen, Germany
1911/
 12 Frankfurter Gasgesellschaft Buildings, Osthafen, Germany
 German Embassy, Isaak-Platz, St. Petersburg, now Leningrad
 Goedecke House, Eppenhausen, near Hagen, Germany
 Wiegand House, Peter-Lenne-Strasse, Dahlem, Berlin (now the German Archaeological Institute)
 Continental Rubber Company, Hanover
1912/
 23 Mannesmann Tube Co. Office Building, Dusseldorf

1915/
 16 National Automobile Co. Offices, Obserschoneweide, Berlin
1916 House of Friendship, Constantinople, now Istanbul
1917 Exhibition Building, *Deutsche Werkbund Exhibition,* Berne
1919 Garden Suburb, Neusaburg, near Berlin
1920 Garden Suburb, Nowawes, near Potsdam, Berlin
 Housing Estate, Altona, near Hamburg
1920/
 24 Höchst Chemical Factory and Dyeworks, Frankfurt
1921/
 25 Hoag Steelworks, Oberhausen, Germany
1922 Stumm Administration Building, Dusseldorf (project)
1924/
 25 Monastery of St. Peter, Salzburg
1925 People's Building, Vienna
 Tomb of Reichspresident Friedrich Ebert, Heidelberg Forest Cemetery
1926 Fashion House, Frankfurt
 "New Ways" (house), Northampton, England
1926/
 27 Terrace housing, Weissenhof Estate, Stuttgart
1928 Thyssen Co. Administration Building, Dusseldorf (project)
1929/
 31 Berolina Building Complex, Alexanderplatz, Berlin
1931 Clara Ganz Villa, Cronberg, Taunus, Germany
1931/
 34 New Buildings for the State Tobacco Factory, Linz, Austria (with Alexander Popp)

Publications:

By BEHRENS: books—*Feste des Lebens und der Künst,* Jena, Germany 1900; *Behrens Schrift,* Offenbach am Main, Germany 1902; *Beziehungen der künstlerischen und technischen Probleme,* Berlin 1917; *Vom Sparsamen Bauen,* with H. de Fries, Berlin 1918; *Das Ethos und die Unlagerung der künstlerische Probleme,* Darmstadt 1920; *Terrassen am Hause,* Stuttgart 1927; articles—"Die Lebensmesse von Richard Dehmel" in *Die Rheinlande* (Mainz), April 1901; "Mein Sondergarten" in *Offizielle Ausstellungszeitung der internationalen Künst- und Gartenbauausstleung Mannheim* (Mannheim), 1 May 1907; "Die Gartenstadtbewegung" in *Berliner Tageblatt,* 5 March 1908; "Die Zukunft unserer Kultur" in *Frankfurter Zeitung,* 14 April 1909; "Uber Aesthetik in der Industrie" in *AEG-Zeitung* (Berlin), June 1909; "Künst und Technik" in *Innendekoration* (Darmstadt), July 1911; "Peter Behrens aussert sich auf eine Rundfrage uber die bauliche Entwicklung der Berliner City" in *Berliner Morgenpost,* 27 November 1912; "Zur Erziehung des baukünstlerischen Nachwuchses" in *Peter Behrens und seine Weiner akademische Meisterschule,* edited by K. M. Grimme, Vienna 1930; "Die Baukünst und das Leben" in *Baugilde* (Berlin), no. 16, 1932.

On BEHRENS: books—*Entwicklungsgeschichte der modernen Künst* by Julius Meier-Graefe, Stuttgart 1904; *Das Einzelwohnhaus der Neuzeit* by Erich Haenle and Heinrich Tscharmann, Leipzig 1906; *Moderne Baukünst* by Karl Scheffler, Berlin 1907; *Das neue Künstgewerbe in Deutschland* by Joseph August Lux, Leipzig 1908; *Die Künst Peter Behrens* by Friedrich Hoeper, Berlin 1909; *Etude sur le Mouvement d'Art décoratif en Allemagne* by Le Corbusier, La Chaux-de-Fonds, Switzerland 1912; *Peter Behrens* by Fritz Hoeber, Munich 1913; *Peter Behrens: sein Werk von 1909 bis zur Gegenwart* by Paul Joseph Cremers, Essen 1928; *Peter Behrens und seine Wiener Akademischen Meisterschule,* edited by K.

M. Grimme, Vienna 1930; *Das Gesellenhaus und eine stadtebauliche Studie von Peter Behrens in Neuss* by E. Seipe, Neuss, Germany 1961; *Bauen in Berlin 1900–1964*, Berlin 1964; *Peter Behrens* by Lida Branchesi, Rome 1965; *Peter Behrens 1868–1940*, exhibition catalogue, Kaiserslautern 1966; *Peter Behrens* by H. J. Kadataz, Leipzig 1977; articles— "L'Oeuvre de Peter Behrens" by Julius Posener in *L'Architecture d'Aujourd'hui* (Paris), March 1934; "Peter Behrens" by P. Morton Shand in *Architectural Review* (London), September 1934; special number of *Casabella* (Milan), no. 240, 1960.

Peter Behrens' work covers a wide range. In the early part of his career he worked mainly as a painter and engraver and as a designer of domestic and industrial equipment. In designing a wide variety of objects, he interpreted function in the most simple and direct manner but with an eye to effective form. The designing of the good prototype for industrial production foreshadowed the methods of the Bauhaus. It also influenced Behrens' early work as an architect at the beginning of the century. He took advantage of new methods made possible by developments in the constructional application of concrete, glass, steel and other synthetic materials and was among the first to use these with good effect. He can thus be regarded as one of the important pioneers of modern functionalism and the new architecture. At the same time, beginning as an architect in an age of eclecticism, he responded to various influences both traditional and contemporary, and was himself to some extent an eclectic—but a discriminating one. His work as an industrial architect is of a somewhat different character from his domestic work, although they are both aesthetically determined by classical feeling. The difference emerges to some extent from the type of building. Where the type has a long history, such as a house or the Monastery of St. Peter, Salzburg, then traditional influences are strong, but if the particular type has few precedents, as in much modern industrial building, then functionalism is correspondingly prominent.

Perhaps Behrens' best known building, and one of the most impressive of industrial buildings in Europe erected in the early years of the century, is the immense AEG Turbine Factory in the Huttenstrasse, Berlin. It is designed to admit the maximum of light, and the large interior space is enclosed by extensive areas of glass between tapering steel uprights, canted forward a little so that a wide cornice is formed, indicating the demarcation of the glass roof. The building has a massive grandeur resulting not only from the simple large-scale expression of function but also from the heavy masonry treatment of the corners and the cornice effect, neither of which is demanded by practical purpose; they are obviously the result of Behrens' liking for classical monumentality. In the AEG High Tension Plant, also in Berlin, motifs like classical porticos with columns and pediments are introduced in a simplified form.

A good example of Behrens' functional determinism is the office building for the Mannesmann Tube Company at Dusseldorf. Here the internal divisions are determined by the space required for the efficient operation of clerks, which in turn control the size of the standardized units in the construction of the building. The design of this building demonstrated the greater freedom of planning made possible by standardized interchangeable parts of steel, concrete and glass.

Although the planning of later industrial and office buildings was controlled by his logical interpretation of purpose, Behrens did introduce decorative motifs of a romantic or classical character. In the Hoag Steelworks at Oberhausen the whole massing gives the building a monumental character—but with the introduction of contemporary horizontal motifs in the long canopies. In the Höchst Chemical Factory and Dye Works, Behrens gives a romantic character to the large entrance hall by the flute-like treatment of brickwork in various colours and a dis-

position of forms so as to introduce dramatic effects of light and shadow.

Response to contemporary trends is clearly apparent in the tobacco factory at Linz, which he designed in 1931 in collaboration with Alexander Popp. In this factory the steel frame construction is set back a little from the long slightly convex facade, which allows for uninterrupted glass bands alternating with bands of rendered brickwork for the whole length of the building, a dramatic horizontal emphasis accentuated by wide projecting eaves. Only Mendelsohn's Schocken store at Chemnitz (now Karlmarxstadt) has a comparable dramatic character. But even in this modern factory at Linz classical motifs are introduced: the glass tower at the entrance with a band of symbolic sculpture is reminiscent in treatment of a Greek frieze.

Behrens' domestic buildings, which he began designing a little earlier than his industrial works, are the work of an eclectic. The influence of English domestic architecture is apparent in his own house at Darmstadt and in the Obenauer House at Saarbrucken, among others, in the garden suburbs he planned and built near Berlin, and in the Altona estate near Hamburg, which he built just after the First World War. These houses are traditional in character with steeply pitched roofs. Among the best is the Obenauer House: with its large plain white walls and well-disposed windows, it clearly shows Voysey's influence.

A house by Behrens that attracted much attention in architectural circles when it was built was "New Ways" in Northampton, for it was regarded, in its simplicity, orientation, large windows and flat concrete roof, as the first really modern house in England. Yet it is also eclectic in design, planned with classical symmetry and with mediaeval decorative embellishments. This characteristic blending of tradition and progressive developments occurs again in the large Ganz Villa in the Taunus Mountains, which, although modern in appearance with flat roof, plain walls and horizontal emphasis, is yet structurally traditional, with the room division of the upper floor dependent on the ground floor structure (unlike, say, Le Corbusier's houses of pole and slab construction, which make possible an independent and flexible planning of each floor). Because of its structure, the house retains a somewhat massive traditional character, and like most of Behrens' work it owes much to the classical tradition.

Behrens was an architect who combined modern functional design and the use of modern materials and methods with a degree of eclecticism, but always with an underlying classical and monumental determinism.

—Arnold Whittick

BELGIOJOSO, Lodovico (Barbiano di).
Italian. Born in Milan, 1 December 1909. Educated at the Liceo Parini, Milan, 1921–27; Milan Polytechnic School of Architecture, 1927–32, Dip.Arch. 1932. Served in the Italian Army, 1932–34, 1940; political prisoner in Germany, 1944–45. Married Carolina Cicogna Mozzoni in 1934; children: Margherita, Maria Luisa, Alberico, and Giovanni. Founder Partner, with Gianluigi Banfi, *q.v.*, Enrico Peressutti, *q.v.*, and Ernesto Nathan Rogers, *q.v.*, BBPR Architectural Studio, *q.v.*, Milan, since 1932. Member, Milan Building Commission, 1937–39; Member, Municipal Committee for the Master Plan for the City of Milan, 1946–47, and the revision, 1957–60; Member, Committee for the Lombardy Regional Plan, 1952–55; Consultant, Municipal Planning Department, Milan, 1961–65. Administrative Director, INU (Istituto Nazionale di Urbanistica), since 1948 (President, Lombardy Section, 1951–52, 1953–54); Director, Technical Committee,

PIM (Inter-Municipality Project), since 1962; Administrator, Research and Study Commission, Metropolitana Veneta, Venice, since 1967. Professor of Design, Architectural Institute, Venice, 1955–63. Since 1963, Professor of Design, Milan Polytechnic School of Architecture. Member of CIAM (Congrès Internationaux d'Architecture Moderne), from 1935; Member, Commissione per le Manifestazione d'Arte Moderna dell'Associazione tra i Cultori d'Architettura, 1935; Member, 1945, and President, 1947, MSA (Movimento di Studi per l'Architettura); Member, Maison des Artistes, Lausanne, 1949; Founder Member, Société Européenne de Culture, 1950; Member, Institut d'Esthetique Industrielle, Paris, 1951; President, Lombardy Regional College of Architects, 1959–61. Recipient: Cervo d'Oro, Italy, 1970. Member, Academy of Fine Arts, Genoa, 1949, and Venice, 1958; Member, National Academy of San Luca, Rome, 1960. Honorary Member, Royal Society of Arts, London, 1958. Address: Studio Architetti BBPR, via dei Chiostri 2, 20121 Milan, Italy.

Publications:

By BELGIOJOSO: articles—"Urbanistica Anno XII," with Gianluigi Banfi, in *Quadrante* (Milan), May 1934; "Urbanistica Corporativa," with Gianluigi Banfi, in *Quadrante* (Milan), August/September 1934; "La Casa per la Famiglia" in *Domus* (Milan), August 1942; "Per Scegliere la Casa" in *Vie d'Italia* (Rome), November 1949; "L'Evoluzione del Metodo Espositivo nelle Passate Triennali" in *Casabella* (Milan), November/December 1954; "La Ricostruzione dei Musei del Castello Sforzesco" in *Aspetti, Problemi e Realizzazioni di Milano*, Milan 1957; "Processo Estetico alle Autostrade: La Parola all'Accusa" in *Quattroruote* (Milan), October 1962; "Lettera al Direttore" in *Quattroruote* (Milan), November 1962; "Il Lavoro della Giuria: Il Concorso per il Centro Direzionale di Torino" in *Casabella* (Milan), August 1963; "Commenti alle Nuove Autostrade" in *Quattroruote* (Milan), July/August 1967; "Problemi attuali nelle Realizzazioni dell-'Edilizia Souvenzionata" in *Edilizia Popolare* (Rome), July/August 1967; "Si Progetta il Traforo dello Stelvio" in *Quattroruote* (Milan), January 1968; "Adaption of Housing to the Site" in *Revue de l'Union Internationale des Architectes* (Paris), July 1968; "Commenti alle Nuove Autostrade" in *Quattroruote* (Milan), July 1968; "Considerazioni di Ordine Urbanistico e Architettonico" in *Edilizia Popolare* (Rome), November/December 1968; "Il Salone di Torino visto da un Architetto" and "Un Buon Esempio" in *Quattroruote* (Milan), January 1969; "Commenti alle Autostrade: Quattro Recenti Construzzioni" in *Quattroruote* (Milan), January 1970; "Le Stazioni di Servizio nel Paesaggio" in *Quattroruote* (Milan), December 1970; "Un Nuovo Guasto Straddale in Toscana" in *Quattroruote* (Milan), November 1971; etc.

See BBPR ARCHITECTURAL STUDIO

BELLUSCHI, Pietro.
American. Born in Ancona, Italy, 18 August 1899; emigrated to the United States, 1923; naturalized, 1929. Educated at the University of Rome, 1919–22, D.Eng. 1922; Cornell University, Ithaca, New York, 1924. Married Helen Hemmila in 1934 (died, 1962); children: Peter and Anthony; married Marjorie Bruckner in 1965. Worked as a housing inspector in Rome, 1923; Electrical Helper, Bunker Hill and Sullivan Mining Company, Kellogg, Idaho, 1924–25; Draftsman, 1925–27, Chief Designer, 1927–42, and Associate, 1932–42, A. E. Doyle and Associates, Portland, Oregon; in private practice, Portland,

1943-50 (firm acquired by Skidmore, Owings and Merrill); Dean of the School of Architecture and Planning, Massachusetts Institute of Technology, Cambridge, 1951-65. In private practice, Boston and Portland, since 1965. Consulting Professor of Architecture, University of Oregon, Eugene, 1965; Thomas Jefferson Professor of Architecture, University of Virginia, Charlottesville, 1966. President, Oregon Chapter, American Institute of Architects, 1943-44; Member, National Fine Arts Commission, 1950-55; Trustee, American Federation of Arts, 1954; Trustee, Boston Museum of Fine Arts, 1958-65; Trustee, Lahey Clinic, Boston, 1960-65. Trustee, Portland Art Museum, since 1935 (President, 1947-48). Recipient: Committee on Education Award, 1940, First Award, 1954, 1956, Centennial Medal, 1957, Award of Merit, 1960, First Honor Award, 1963, and Gold Medal, 1972, American Institute of Architects; Design Award, *Progressive Architecture,* 1948, 1954, 1959, 1964; National Council of Churches of Christ Award, 1956; Gold Medal, AIA, Memphis Chapter, 1957; Award of Merit, Baltimore Chamber of Commerce, 1959; Distinguished Service Award, University of Oregon, 1959; Certificate of Merit, New York State Association of Architects, 1960; Citation of Excellence, AIA, Philadelphia Chapter, 1960; First Honor Award, AIA/American Library Association, 1963; "People's Architect" Award, Rice University, Houston, 1963; Gold Medal, Italian Charitable Society, 1963; Honor Award, AIA, Portland Chapter, 1965, 1971; Office of the Year Award, *Administrative Management,* 1966; Wood Structure Design Award, National Forest Products Association, 1967; Medal of Excellence, AIA, Rhode Island Chapter, 1967; PLAN Award, Junior League, Columbus, Ohio, 1969; Design Excellence Award, Oklahoma City Arts Council, 1970; Bard Award, City of New York, 1970; Architectural Award of Excellence, American Institute of Steel Construction, 1970 (three times); Design in Steel Award, American Iron and Steel Institute, 1971; Gold Medal, Dante Society of Massachusetts, 1971; Award of Excellence, American Concrete Institute, Oklahoma Chapter, 1974; Award of Excellence, AIA, Oklahoma Chapter, 1974; Award, AIA, New England Regional Chapter, 1974; Special Commendation, AIA, Western Massachusetts Chapter, 1974; Special Citation, American Association of School Administrators, 1974; Honor Award, AIA, Bay Area Chapter, 1974; Gold Medal, University of Naples, 1974. LL.D.: Reed College, Portland, Oregon,

1950; Sc.D.: Christian Brothers College, Memphis, Tennessee, 1957; D.F.A.: University of Rhode Island, Kingston, 1963; University of Massachusetts, Amherst, 1967; University of Portland, Oregon, 1977; D.Arch.: University of Michigan, Ann Arbor, 1967; L.H.D.: University of Oklahoma City, 1968. Fellow, American Institute of Architects, 1948. Fellow, American Academy of Arts and Sciences, 1952; Academician, National Academy of Design, 1953; Member, National Institute of Arts and Letters, 1955; Member, Tau Beta Phi, 1961. Fellow, Royal Academy of Fine Arts, Copenhagen, 1954; Member, Instituto Marchigiano-Accademia Scienze Lettere e Arti, Italy, 1975. Knight Commander (Commendatore), Republic of Italy, 1965. Address: Pietro Belluschi Inc., 700 N.W. Rapidan Terrace, Portland, Oregon 97210, U.S.A.

Works:

1932/
38   New wings for the Portland Art Museum, Oregon
1936   Belluschi House, Portland, Oregon
1937   Finley and Son Mortuary, Portland, Oregon
1938   Sutor House, Portland, Oregon
1941   Platt House, Portland, Oregon
        Myers House, Seattle
        Peter Kerr Beach House, Geahart, Oregon
        St. Thomas More Chapel, Portland, Oregon
        Ladd and Bush Bank Building additions, Salem, Oregon
        Wherrie Tailoring Shop Front, Portland, Oregon
1942   Boilermakers Union Building, Portland, Oregon
        McLoughlin Heights Shopping Center, Vancouver, Washington
        Bagley and Downs Shopping Center, Vancouver, Washington
1944   Belluschi Farmhouse, Aloha, Oregon
1945   Northwest Airlines Offices, Portland, Oregon
        Waddles Drive-In Restaurant, Portland, Oregon
1946   First National Bank, Salem, Oregon
        Electrical Distributing Company Building, Portland, Oregon
1947   Belluschi Office, Portland, Oregon
        Edris Morrison Photographic Studio, Portland, Oregon
1948   Oregon State Hospital, Salem
        Oregonian Newspaper Building, Portland,

Oregon
        Equitable Building, Portland, Oregon
        Menefee House, Yamhill, Oregon
1949   Moore House, Portland, Oregon
1950   Zion Lutheran Church, Portland, Oregon
1951   Central Lutheran Church, Portland, Oregon
        First Presbyterian Church, Cottage Grove, Oregon
1954   Back Bay Center, Boston (project)
1955   Louis B. Skidmore House, Winter Haven, Florida
        Lutheran Church, Walnut Creek, California (with Skidmore, Owings and Merrill)
        Central Lutheran Church, Eugene, Oregon (with Skidmore, Owings and Merrill)
1956   Temple Israel, Swampscott, Massachusetts (with Carl Koch and Associates)
1957   First Lutheran Church, Boston
1958   Library, Bennington College, Vermont (with Carl Koch and Associates)
        Life Magazine House, Palo Alto, California
1959   Church of the Redeemer, Baltimore (with Rogers and Taliaferro)
        Dining Hall and Dormitory, Rhode Island School of Design, Providence (as consultant)
        Temple Adath Israel, Philadelphia (with C. Frederick Wise)
        Portsmouth Abbey Church and Monastery, Rhode Island (with Anderson, Beckwith and Haible)
1961   Park Avenue Congregational Church, Arlington, Massachusetts (with Carl Koch and Associates)
1962   Temple B'rith Kodesh, Rochester, New York (with Waasdorp, Northrup and Kaelber)
        Pan American Building, New York (as consultant; with Walter Gropius, and Emery Roth and Sons)
1963   Goucher College Center, Towson, Maryland (with Rogers, Taliaferro and Lamb)
1964   Housing Complex, University of Rhode Island, Kingston (with Sasaki, Dawson, DeMay and Associates, and Kent, Cruise and Associates)
        Engineering Complex, University of Colorado, Boulder (as consultant; with Sasaki, Walker and Associates, and Architectural Associates)
        Trinity Church, Concord, Massachusetts (with Anderson, Beckwith and Haible)

Pietro Belluschi: Juilliard School of Music, Lincoln Center, New York, 1970

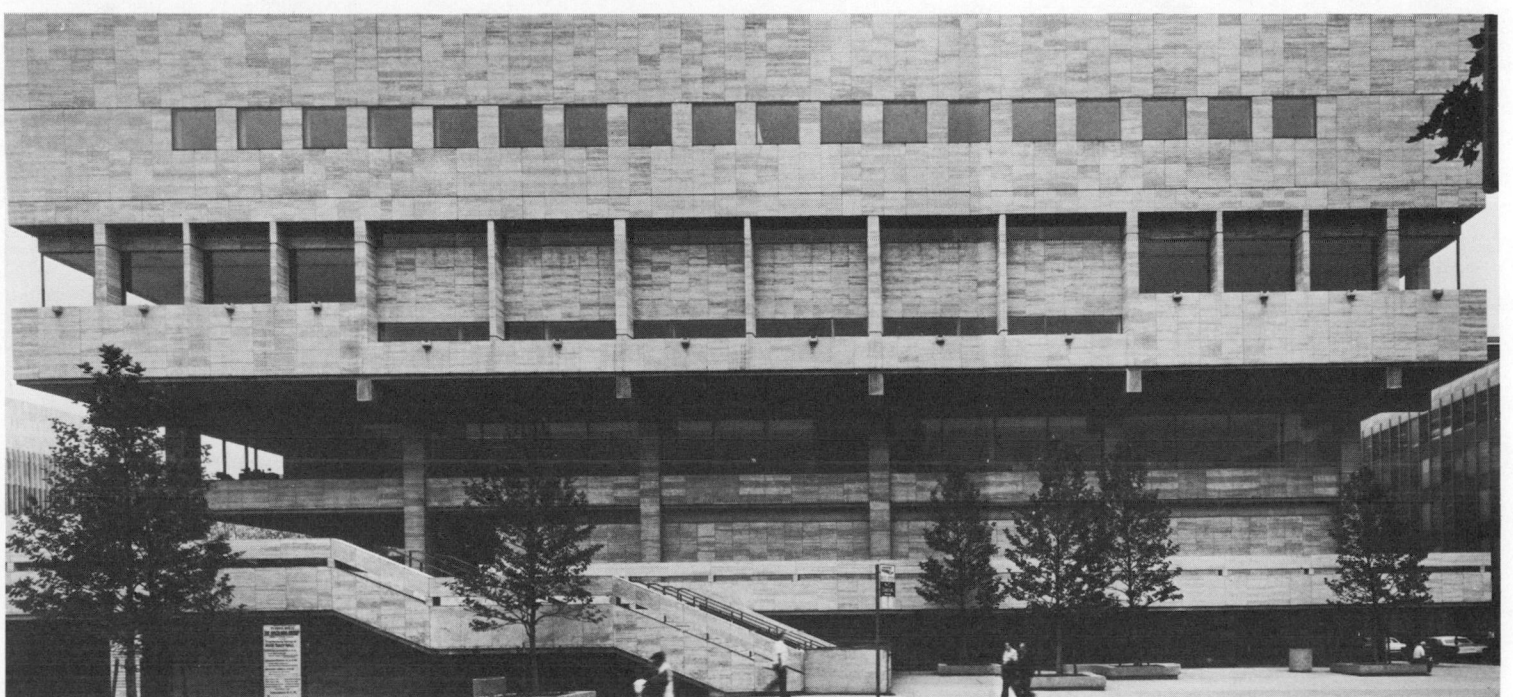

1965　Rohm and Haas Office Building, Philadelphia (as consultant; with George M. Ewing and Company)

　　　May Memorial Unitarian Church, Syracuse, New York (with Pederson, Hueber and Hares)

1966　Performing Arts Center, Ethel Walker Girls School, Simsbury, Connecticut (with Robert Brannen)

　　　Equitable Center Office Building, Portland, Oregon (with Wolff, Zimmer, Gunsul, Frasca)

　　　Science and Multipurpose Buildings, Portsmouth Abbey Boys School, Rhode Island (with Robinson, Green and Beretta)

　　　First Methodist Church, Duluth, Minnesota (with Melander and Fugelso)

　　　Sunset Mountain Park, California (as consultant; with Daniel, Mann, Johnson and Mendenahll)

1967　Unitarian Church of the Christian Union, Rockford, Illinois (with C. Edward Ware)

　　　St. Margaret of Cortona Church, Columbus, Ohio (with Brubaker and Brandt)

1968　Temple B'nai Jeshurun, Short Hills, New Jersey (with Gruzen and Partners)

　　　Bishop W. Angie Smith Chapel, Oklahoma City University

　　　St. Joseph's Church, Roseburg, Oregon (as consultant; with Wolff, Zimmer, Gunsul, Frasca)

1969　Demey Square Building, Boston (project)

　　　Technology Square Building, Cambridge, Massachusetts (project; with Emery Roth and Sons)

　　　Library Building, School of Architecture, University of Virginia, Charlottesville (with Sasaki, Dawson, DeMay and Associates, and Rawlings and Wilson)

　　　Faculty Club Dining Room, Princeton University, New Jersey (with W. C. Harrison Hill)

1970　Bank of America World Headquarters, San Francisco (as consultant; with Wurster, Bernardi and Emmons, and Skidmore, Owings and Merrill)

　　　Boston Company Building, Boston (with Emery Roth and Sons)

　　　Undergraduate Dormitory, Massachusetts Institute of Technology, Cambridge (with The Architects Collaborative)

　　　First National Bank, Seattle (as consultant; with Naramore, Bain, Brady, Joganson)

　　　Alice Tully Hall: Juilliard School of Music, Lincoln Center, New York (with Eduardo Catalano and Helge Westmann and Associated Architects)

　　　Wellesley Office Park no. 4, Massachusetts (with Jung/Brannen Associates)

1971　St. Mary's Catholic Cathedral, San Francisco (as consultant; with Pierluigi Nervi, and McSweeney, Ryan and Lee)

　　　University Lutheran Church, Philadelphia (with A. Ewing and Associates)

　　　Portland Museum Art School addition and Sculpture Court, Oregon (with Wolff, Zimmer, Gunsul, Frasca and Ritter)

1972　Kah-Nee-Ta Lodge Hotel, Warm Springs Indian Reservation, Oregon (with Wolff, Zimmer, Gunsul, Frasca and Ritter)

　　　Keystone Office Building, Boston (with Emery Roth and Sons)

　　　Baystate West Urban Complex, Springfield, Massachusetts (with Eduardo Catalano)

1973　Kerr-McGee Center, Oklahoma City

　　　IBM Center, Baltimore (with Emery Roth and Sons)

1974　Community Center, Sacramento, California (as consultant; with Sacramento Architects Collaborative)

　　　Sterling and Francine Clark Art Institute, Williamstown, Massachusetts (with The Architects Collaborative)

Tobin Elementary School, Cambridge, Massachusetts (with Sasaki, Dawson, DeMay Associates)

Wellesley Office Park no. 5, Massachusetts (with Jung/Brannen)

Publications:

By BELLUSCHI: articles—"Shopping Centers" in *Forms and Functions of Twentieth Century Architecture,* edited by Talbot Hamlin, New York 1952; "The Spirit of the New Architecture" in *Architectural Record* (New York), October 1953; "The Meaning of Regionalism in Architecture" in *Architectural Record* (New York), December 1955; "Architectural Milestones" in *AIA Journal* (Washington, D.C.), May 1973.

On BELLUSCHI: books—*The Modern House in America* by James Ford and Katherine Morrow Ford, New York 1940; *The Northwest Architecture of Pietro Belluschi,* edited by Jo Stubblebine, New York 1953; *Pietro Belluschi: Buildings and Plans,* edited by Camillo Gubitosi and Alberto Izzo, Rome 1974; articles—"An Eastern Critic Looks at Western Architecture" in *Arts and Architecture* (Los Angeles), December 1940; "Readiness for Better Architecture" in *Sunset* (Menlo Park, California), April 1943; "An Architect's Challenge" in *Architectural Forum* (New York), December 1949; "Belluschi Appraises the Gropius Challenge" in *Architectural Forum* (New York), May 1952; "Pietro Belluschi: The 1972 Gold Medallist" by Elisabeth K. Thompson in *Architectural Record* (New York), April 1972; "Lincoln Center for the Performing Arts, New York" in *Architecture + Urbanism* (Tokyo), August 1973; "Growth of a University" by Ellen Perry Berkeley in *Architecture Plus* (New York), March April 1974.

In my long professional practice, tested in the winds of change, I have held to the belief that there are certain principles of honesty, integrity and clarity that, applied in their own time and place, give meaning and permanence to architecture as a social art.

There are also trends towards the superficial and the ephemeral, perhaps as a protest against our old puritan culture.

These trends now more than ever appear to be espoused by articulate self-congratulating taste-makers engaged in the game of form-giving for its own sake.

These fickle arbiters demand new fashions every other day, soon to be bored by them, eagerly discarding them, further blurring the distinction between reality and make-believe. I don't consider these trends to constitute a "water shed," as they claim, but I am not so naive as to think that, given the subjective nature of the art, it is possible or even desirable to eliminate all attempts to escape reality.

　　　　　　　　　　　　　　　　—Pietro Belluschi

Pietro Belluschi, who was recently described by the *New York Times* as "one of America's most respected modern architects," has maintained his belief in orthodox modernism throughout a long career ranging from modest single-family houses in the Northwest to major private and public buildings on both coasts. In his early regional work Belluschi stressed the need to "derive designs from functional demand," and as the keynote speaker at the American Institute of Architects 1979 convention he reiterated this solution, attacking "today's architecture of appearances" based on "pre-conceived aesthetic theories" or cynical pandering to "mobile, rootless persons who want to be indulged with as many pleasurable sensations as possible."

Belluschi first came to national prominence in 1932 with his design for a new wing for the Portland Art Museum in a simple style, harmonious with the original building. This was followed by a second wing which added a dramatic skylit sculpture court

and typically innovative monitor lighting in the new galleries. He continued to work on the museum's development plan for forty years, culminating in a new Museum Art School with three floors of studios, a gallery, auditorium, and offices adjacent to a new pedestrian mall.

In the Portland area Belluschi designed a series of houses and churches in an elegantly simplified regional style that often suggested a distinct Japanese influence. The St. Thomas More Chapel, with its peaked roof and steeple, is reminiscent of New England churches in its simple exterior. The interior is "decorated" only by the crossed roof beams, but Belluschi reversed the traditional position of the steeple over the entrance, placing it instead over the altar, where its pleasant clerestory effect creates a subtle focal point for worship.

In another local church, the Zion Lutheran, the spire is retained for its symbolic value, with the roofline continuing over a deep sheltering porch, contributing to the sense of safety and welcome. Here the interior is marked by a rich use of contrasting textures, wood, brick, glass, copper, and the roof is supported not by cross beams but by graceful freestanding laminated wood arches.

Central Lutheran is a more complex design, using a solid round brick apse combined with an openwork wood nave and bell tower. Once again the roof is supported by laminated wood arches but with a more horizontal emphasis. The building is sensitively sited both for privacy and views and in relation to the existing trees.

The simplicity and clarity of Belluschi's early small-scale buildings are evident in his larger works as well. The 1948 Equitable Building, made of reinforced concrete clad in aluminium, is an early example of curtain wall. The starkness of its flush exterior walls boldly reflects Belluschi's admonition "to eliminate, refine and integrate." For the 1970 Boston Company Building he worked closely with engineers on an ingenious structural system of corner columns round a central core, to give that city its first column-free interior space.

Perhaps the greatest challenge of Belluschi's career was the design for the new Juilliard School of Music, Alice Tully Hall, at Lincoln Center. The monolithic travertine facade of this building masks a teaching and performing complex of great intricacy, built four storeys below street level and six above on a tight irregular site with severe height limitations. Three theatres, a library, recording and ballet studios, teaching rooms and offices all had to be insulated from each other and from the nearby subway. It was designed and built over twelve years with inflation necessitating a continual paring down of details. The resulting simplicity, particularly the exposed concrete and wood paneled interior, is a welcome change from the unconvincing glitter of other Lincoln Centre buildings and a testament to Belluschi's adherence to his own dicta.

　　　　　　　　　　　　　　　　—Lucinda Hawkins

BERLAGE, Hendrik Petrus.

Dutch. Born in Amsterdam, 21 February 1856. Studied painting at the Rijksakademie van Beeldende Kunsten, Amsterdam, 1874–75, and architecture at the Eidgenossische Technische Hochschule (E.T.H.), Zurich, under Gottfried Kinkel and Julius Jakob Stadler, 1875–78, Dip.Arch. 1878; influenced by the work of Gottfried Semper and, later, that of the Chicago architects Richardson, Sullivan and Wright. Married Marie Bienfait in 1887. Associated with Karl Koser, and lectured at E.T.H., Zurich, 1878; travelled in Germany, 1879; worked in Arnhem, 1879; travelled extensively in Italy, 1880–81; worked in the office of the engineer Th. Sanders, Amsterdam, 1881–84: in partnership with Sanders,

Hendrik Petrus Berlage: Stock Exchange, Amsterdam, 1885

1884–89; in private practice, Amsterdam and The Hague, 1889 until his death, 1934; visited the United States, and met various architects of the Chicago School, 1911. Exhibition: *H. P. Berlage, Bouwmeester, 1856–1934*, The Hague, 1975. Recipient: First Prize, Amsterdam Stock Exchange Competition, 1897; Gold Medal, Royal Institute of British Architects, 1932. Honorary doctorates: University of Groningen, 1911; Technical University, Delft, 1926; E.T.H., Zurich, 1926. *Died* (in The Hague) *12 August 1934.*

Works:

1883/
84 De Hoop Working Men's Coffee House, De Ruyterkade, Amsterdam (with Th. Sanders)

1884/
85 Stock Exchange (Bourse) additions, Amsterdam (project)

1885 Focke and Meltzer Shop and Office Building, Kalverstraat, Amsterdam (with Th. Sanders)

1886 Cathedral Front, Milan (competition project)
Villa Scheffer, Weesp, Netherlands (with Th. Sanders)
3 houses, Nieuweweg, Lochem, Netherlands

1887 Sanatorium, Baarn, Netherlands (with Th. Sanders)

1888 Terminus Building, North Holland Tram Company, Amsterdam
Painter's Studio (competition project)

1889 Mausoleum (competition project)

1890 Kerkhoven and Co. Office Building, 115 Herengracht, Amsterdam
Town Hall, Zutphen, Netherlands (project)

1891/
92 Dr. E. D. Pijzel House, 72 Van Baerlestraat, Amsterdam

1892 Community Centre, Lochem, Netherlands

1893 Frederik van Eeden House, Bussum, Netherlands
De Algemeene General Life Insurance Building, Amsterdam

1894 Dr. G. Heymans Villa, Groningen, Netherlands
Cruys Family Villa, Hilversum, Netherlands

1895 De Nederlanden van 1845 Insurance Co. Building, Muntplein, Amsterdam

1895/
96 De Nederlanden van 1845 Insurance Co. Building, Kerkplein, The Hague (with W. Wesstra)

1896 Sonnenheuvel Villa, Hilversum, Netherlands
Van Vloten Villa, Noordwijck, Netherlands

1898 Carel Henny Villa, 42–44 Oude Scheveningseweg, The Hague
Villa, Eslaan, Bussum, Netherlands

1898/
1903 Stock Exchange (Bourse), Amsterdam

1899 General Dutch Diamond Workers' Union Building, Henri-Polaklaan, Amsterdam
Jan Toorop Villa, Katwijk, Netherlands

1900 De Algemeene Building, Soerabaja, Netherlands
Parkwyck Villa, Amsterdam

1901 Amsterdamse Bank Office Building, Damrak, Amsterdam

1902 De Algemeene Building, Leipzig
Master plan for Amsterdam South
R. N. Roland Holst Villa, Laren, Netherlands
Prof. D. C. Hesseling Summer House, Noordwijk, Netherlands
D. Wiggers Villa, Beek, Netherlands

1905 De Veije Family Villa, Wassenaar, Netherlands
House, Kettingstraat, The Hague
Henri Polak Villa, Laren, Netherlands
Housing blocks (2), Linnaeusstraat, Amsterdam

1906 Walewijk Villa, Watergraafsmeer, Netherlands
Wagnertheater, Amsterdam (project)
Voorwaarts Workers' Co-operative Building, Gedempte Slaak, Rotterdam

1907 Hingst Housing, Koninginneweg, Amsterdam

1908 Master plan for The Hague
Art school, Gabriel Metsustraat, Amsterdam

1909 Concert hall, Venlo, Netherlands

1910 De Nederlanden van 1845 Insurance Co. Building, Zuidblaak, Rotterdam

1911 De Nederlanden van 1845 Insurance Co. Building, Nijmegen, Netherlands
Master plan for Purmerend, Netherlands
Workers' Housing, Zaagmolenstraat, Amsterdam

1912 Artist's studio, Amsterdam (project)

1913 L. Simons House, Prinsenvinkpark, The Hague
Berlage Family House, Violenweg, The Hague
Kröller-Müller Family Villa (project)

1914 Meddens and Son, Hofweg, The Hague
Wm. H. Müller and Co. Building ("Holland House"), Bury Street, London

1915 Revision of the master plan for Amsterdam South

1917 Museum Building (project)

1920 Master plan for Utrecht (with L. N. Holsboer)

1922 Master plan for Rotterdam-Hofplein

1925 De Nederlanden van 1845 Insurance Co. Building, Groenhovenstraat-Raamweg, The Hague (with A. D. N. van Gendt and W. N. van Vliet)
First Church of Christ Scientist Building, Zorgvliet, The Hague

Mercatorplein, Amsterdam-West

Rijksverzekeringsbank Building, Amsterdam
(project)
1926 Lenin Mausoleum, Moscow (project)
1930 De Nederlanden van 1845 Insurance Co.
Building, Utrecht
1931/
35 Gemeentemuseum, The Hague

Publications:

By BERLAGE: books—*Over Stijl in Bouw- en Meubelkunst,* Rotterdam 1904, 3rd edition 1917; *Gedanken über den Stil in der Baukunst,* Leipzig 1905; *Over de Waarschijnlijke Ontwikkeling der Architektuur,* Delft 1905; *Grundlagen und Entwicklung der Architektur,* Berlin and Rotterdam 1908; *Studies over Bouwkunst, Stil en Samenleving,* Rotterdam 1910; *Ein Drietal Lezingen in Amerika Gehouden,* Rotterdam 1912; *Amerikaansche Reisherinneringen,* Rotterdam 1913; *Bouwkunst in Holland,* Amsterdam 1913; *Schoonheid en Samenleving,* Rotterdam 1919, 1924; *L'Art et la Société,* Brussels 1921; *De Ontwikkeling der moderne bouwkunst in Holland,* Amsterdam 1925; *Mijn Indische Reis: Gedachten over cultuur en kunst,* Rotterdam 1931; *Broederschap in de Levenspraktijk,* with Roland Holst, The Hague 1933; *Het wezen der bouwkunst en haar geschiednis: Aesthetische beschouwingen,* Haarlem 1934; numerous articles in professional periodicals and newspapers.

On BERLAGE: books—*Dr. H. P. Berlage en zijn werk* by K. P. C. de Bazel and others, Rotterdam 1916; *Dr. H. P. Berlage, Bouwmeester* by Jan Gratama, Rotterdam 1925; *Dr. H. P. Berlage* by J. Havelaar, Amsterdam, 1930; *H. P. Berlage* by Pieter Singelberg, Amsterdam 1969; *H. P. Berlage: Idea and Style* by Pieter Singelberg, Utrecht 1972; *H. P. Berlage, Bouwmeester, 1856–1934,* exhibition catalogue, by Pieter Singelberg and Manfred Bock, The Hague 1975; articles—"H.P. Berlage," special issue of *Bouwkundig Weekblad Architectura* (Amsterdam), no. 51, 1934.

*

Hendrik Petrus Berlage's most celebrated building is the Bourse in Amsterdam, begun in 1898. This assured, solid structure, with its great hall and corner tower, owes much to Dutch tradition and to the late 19th century's expressionistic use of brick to form patterns and moulded shapes. The interiors of the Bourse and of Nos. 42–44 Oude Scheveningsche Wege in The Hague combine the refined craftsmanship of brick with stone dressings and a somewhat spiky decorative effect using iron and brick.

In the field of town planning, Berlage will be remembered for his work in Amsterdam after the passing of the Housing Act in 1901, which required every town of 10,000 or more inhabitants to draw up detailed and general plans that were to be subjected to revision each decade. His designs for Amsterdam South date from 1902, and were an attempt to depart from the gridiron and strongly formalistic axial approaches that had been features of contemporary town planning. He was influenced by the artistic theories of Camillo Sitte as well as by some of the ideas prevalent in Britain and America at the time, although he rejected the concept of Garden Cities.

In 1906 Berlage was introduced to the buildings of Richardson, Sullivan, and Wright, and in 1911 he visited the United States, and expressly Chicago. The works of the great Americans were the subject of various lectures Berlage later gave in Holland.

He revised his plans for Amsterdam in 1915, making the apartment blocks main elements in forming streets and reducing the importance of public buildings as visual features. The containment of urban spaces by large blocks of housing was an essentially traditional aspect of the plan, however, while greenery played a strong part in the scheme, although nature was subordinated to the general form of the built matrix.

Berlage's main achievement was to give the brick

wall something of the integrity and repose of great monuments of the past, and later he developed this to recreate a unity of streetscape by re-interpreting traditional relationships of solids to voids. He greatly influenced later generations of Dutch architects through his writings and by the example of his buildings.

His architecture owes much to the models of Early Christian and Romanesque periods as well as to the great experimenters of the 19th century, especially the Chicago School. He felt unable to join CIAM in view of his commitment to a more traditional architecture firmly rooted in his native soil of The Netherlands. This is all the more strange since his early polemical writings are ferociously anti-eclectic, and he appears to have despised the ornamentation of buildings dating from the 1850's onwards to his own time. Yet it is nonsense to think of the Amsterdam Bourse as a plain building, for the detailing is impeccable, and the craftsmanship inherent in the brick and stone walls is of a very high order. Just as the work of H.H.Richardson and Frank Lloyd Wright had disturbed European architects with a disconcerting richness of forms, so Berlage gave The Netherlands a new sense of architectural integrity that had not been experienced for generations. Berlage was the prophet, the bringer of new clean architecture from the New World, who influenced Dudok, de Klerk, and many other Dutch architects. It is almost entirely due to the teachings of this great architect that the quality of so much architecture in The Netherlands has been humane, individual, and very regional in character.

Berlage sought to give his buildings something of the quality of serenity that distinguishes so many buildings of the past. By banishing superfluity of ornament and expressing the clarity of solids against voids, he recovered something of the strength and beauty of Romanesque architecture. Polychrome interiors composed of different materials such as majolica, granite, and brick suggest the best experiments in English work of the late 19th century as well as the great traditions of European non-applied decorative effects. His uncompromising use of iron girders, cleanly laid on springing stones of granite, derives from an honourable tradition of design that knows no frontiers.

—James Stevens Curl

BERNARDES, Sergio (Vladimir).

Brazilian. Born in Rio de Janeiro, 9 April 1919. Educated at the University of Brazil, Rio de Janeiro, Dip.Arch. 1948. Married Clarice Hermos Leal in 1941; children: Christina, Sergio, and Claudio; married Maria Clara Joppert; married Christian Guarana; daughter: Bernarda; married Miriam Guanas in 1976. In private practice, Rio de Janeiro, since 1948. Professor of Architecture, University of Brazil, since 1958. Member of the Council, Brazilian Institute of Architects, 1948; Adviser to the Government of Guanabara State, Brazil, 1960–65. Exhibitions: *Bienal,* Sao Paulo, 1953, 1967. Recipient: First Prize, Housing Competition, *Bienal,* Sao Paulo, 1951; First Prize, Industrial Architecture Competition, Venice, 1955; First Prize, Brasilia Airport Competition, 1960; First Prize, Sports Center Competition, Sao Bernardo do Campo, Sao Paulo, 1967. Member, Order of the Rio Branco, Brazil, and Order of Merit Tamandre, Brazil. Address: Sergio Bernardes Associados, Avenida Niemeyer 179, Rio de Janeiro, Brazil.

Works:

1945/
48 Model shop, Rio de Janeiro
Eduardo Baouth House, Rio de Janeiro (project)

Aviation City, Galeao Airport, Rio de Janeiro (project)
1951 Jadir de Souza House, Rio de Janeiro
1952 Guilherme Brandi House, Petrópolis, Brazil
St. Dominic Church, Sao Paulo (competition project)
1953 Companhia Siderurgica Nacional Exhibition Pavilion, Sao Paulo
M. C. Macedo Soares House, Rio de Janeiro
Paulo Sampaio House, Rio de Janeiro
1954 Ivo Pitanguy House, Rio de Janeiro
1957 Brazilian Pavilion, *Bienal,* Sao Paulo
1958 Brazilian Pavilion, *World's Fair,* Brussels
1959 House, Waterloo, Belgium
Costa Brava Building, Rio de Janeiro
1960 Ortemblad House, Rio de Janeiro
Caldas Filho House, Bahia, Brazil
Marinho Office Building, Brasilia
Monumental axis extension, Supersonic Airport, Brasilia (project)
Gentil House, Ceara, Brazil
IAPB Building, Goias, Brazil
Hotel/Commercial Center, Minas Gerais, Brazil (project)
Lunardeli House, Minas Gerais, Brazil
Ensch House, Minas Gerais, Brazil
de Freitas House, Piaui, Brazil
Railway and Highway City-to-Port Link, Rio de Janeiro (project)
Sao Luiz Home for the Aged, Rio de Janeiro
Correio da Manha Newspaper Agency, Rio de Janeiro
Credito Real de Minas Gerais Bank, Rio de Janeiro
Ducal Stores Chain, Rio de Janeiro
Coca-Cola Factory, Rio de Janeiro
Borges Bank Building, Rio de Janeiro
Sao Cristovao Exhibition Pavilion, Rio de Janeiro
Araruama Club, Rio de Janeiro
Samambaia Residential Complex, Petrópolis, Brazil (project)
Engineering Development Company Building, Rio de Janeiro
Alves House, Rio de Janeiro
Figueira House, Rio de Janeiro
Guimaraes House, Rio de Janeiro
Cabral House, Rio de Janeiro
Adolfo Gentil House, Rio de Janeiro
Sergio Bernardes House, Rio de Janeiro
Caio Furtado de Mendonca House, Rio de Janeiro
Luiz Carlos Peixoto House, Rio de Janeiro
Carlos Lacerda House, Rio de Janeiro
Newton Kubrusly House, Rio de Janeiro
Carlos Albuquerque House, Rio de Janeiro
Joaquim Bento A. de Lima House, Sao Paulo
Joao Souza Dantas House, Sao Paulo
Ludovico Gavazi House, Sao Paulo
Niomar Muniz Sodre House, Rio de Janeiro
1961 City plan for Salvador, Brazil (project; with others)
Hospital Network, Brasilia (project)
Lake Hotel, Brasilia (project)
Cota 1000 Club, Brasilia
Sergio Correa Costa House, Brasilia
Coacy Oliveira House, Brasilia
Government Palace and Secretariats, Ceará, Brazil
Marshall Humberto Castelo Branco Mausoleum, Ceará, Brazil
Ouro Preto University, Minas Gerais, Brazil
Varzea de Palma Irrigation Plant and Agrarian Development, Minas Gerais, Brazil (project)
Cassio Lanari House, Minas Gerais, Brazil
Marcelo Moreira de Andrade House, Minas Gerais, Brazil
Guanabara State Plan, Brazil (project)
Dix Building, Rio de Janeiro
Bandeirantes Beach Club, Rio de Janeiro
Flower Market, Rio de Janeiro
Castelo Country Club, Rio de Janeiro

Sergio Bernardes: Naval Ministry Compound, Brasilia, 1972 (project)

Jose Olimpio Bookshop, Rio de Janeiro (project)
Jose Luiz de Magalhaes Lins House, Rio de Janeiro
Roberto Schwab House, Rio de Janeiro
Ilha Porchat Building, Sao Paulo
Commercial Center, Boqueirao, Sao Paulo
Fernao Dias Inn, Rio de Janeiro
Minas Gerais Bank Headquarters, Minas Gerais, Brazil

1962 City of Salvador Integration Plan, Brazil (project)
Reconcavo Expressway Plan, Bahia, Brazil (project)
Central Food Warehouse, Bahia, Brazil
Salvador-Itaparica Linking Bridge, Brazil
Jao Regatta Club, Goias, Brazil
Rio Palace Hotel, Rio de Janeiro (project)
Tres Solares Building, Rio de Janeiro
Jose Colagrossi House, Rio de Janeiro (project)
Francisco de Assis Figueiredo House, Rio de Janeiro
Tito Zarvos Garage, Sao Paulo
Sebastiao Almeida Ribeiro House, Sao Paulo
Tower Building, Sao Paulo (project)
Mendel Aronis House, Sao Paulo

1963 Floating University, Kuwait (project)
Virgilio Tavora House, Ceara, Brazil
Plan for Vidigal Beach, Rio de Janeiro
John Kennedy Building, Rio de Janeiro
Galeao International Hotel, Rio de Janeiro (project)
Roberto Lanari House. Rio de Janeiro

1964 Cocoa Bean Research Center (CEPEC), Bahia, Brazil
Copacabana-Niterio Tourist Bridge, Rio de Janeiro (project)
Enaldo Mendonca House, Rio de Janeiro
Plan for the city of Rio de Janeiro
Free Port, Rio de Janeiro (project)
Army Geographical Service Headquarters, Rio de Janeiro
Baronesa de Pocone Building, Rio de Janeiro
Beco Theatre, Rio de Janeiro
Rachel Demarchi House, Rio de Janeiro
Campinas University, Sao Paulo (project)
Orla Club, Sao Paulo

1965 President Strossner Port City, Paraguay (project)
Urban and Suburban Highway System, Rio de Janeiro (project)
"Play Ball" Bowling Alley, Rio de Janeiro

Sidney Latini House, Rio de Janeiro
Getulio Neves House, Rio Grande do Sul, Brazil
Thomaz Albomos House, Rio Grande do Sul, Brazil
Convergence Center, Sao Paulo (project)
Francisco Matarazzo House, Sao Paulo
Waler Building, Rio de Janeiro

1966 Francisco Souza Dantas House, Sao Paulo
Rialto Hotels, Italy (project)
Tourist development, Dubrovnik, Yugoslavia (project)
Ghana Embassy and Ambassador's Residence, Brasilia
Tambaú Hotel, Paraiba, Brazil
Highway/Railroad/Telecommunications System, Parana, Brazil (project)
Cargo Terminal, Rodotrem, Parana, Brazil
Favela Plan, Rio de Janeiro (project)
Cata-Vista Residential Complex, Sao Paulo
Jayme de Souza Dantas House, Sao Paulo
Pedro Leardi House, Sao Paulo
Joao Pessoa City Plan, Paraiba, Brazil (project)
Commerical Center, Parana, Brazil (project)

1967 Salvador Port, Brazil (project)
Flavio Guttierrez House, Minas Gerais, Brazil
Petite Art Gallery, Rio de Janeiro
G-4 Art Gallery, Rio de Janeiro
Ponta da Gavea Residential Complex, Rio de Janeiro (project)
Orcal Commercial and Residential Complex, Rio de Janeiro
Espacial Hotel, Rio de Janeiro (project)
Gerson de Freitas House, Rio de Janeiro
Sao Bernardo do Campo Satellite Town, Sao Paulo (project)

1968 Workers' Housing Development, Aratu, Brazil (project)
Tropical Hotel, Manaus, Brazil (project)
Industrial Center, Aratu, Bahia, Brazil
Study of the Alagados Poverty Areas, Bahia, Brazil
Victor Gradim House, Bahia, Brazil
Sao Luiz City Plan, Maranhao, Brazil (project)
Belem Telephone Company Building, Para, Brazil
Tropical Hotel, Reife, Pernambuco, Brazil (project)
Casa Alta Building, Rio de Janeiro
Tucuns Residential Complex, Cabo Frio, Rio de Janeiro (project)

Alvaro Salles House, Rio de Janeiro
Covered Stadium, Corinthians Club, Sao Paulo (project)
Araouara Club, Sao Paulo
Tourist plan for Campos do Jorao, Sao Paulo

1969 Jose Holanda House, Bahia, Brazil
Buriticupu and Pindare Basin Study, Maranhao, Brazil
Integrated Highway and Waterway Plan, Maranhao, Brazil
Forestry and Agrarian Development, Maranhao, Brazil (project)
Mangabeiras Farm Urban Development, Minas Gerais, Brazil
Boa Viagem Beach Club, Pernambuco, Brazil
Rio Tropical Hotel, Rio de Janeiro (project)
Swimming Pool, Yacht Club, Rio de Janeiro
Bonino Art Gallery, Rio de Janeiro
Petrobrás Research Center, Rio de Janeiro
Guanabara Pavilion, Providence Charity Fair, Rio de Janeiro

1971 Milhem Simao Racy Jr. House, Sao Paulo
Tourist development, Algarve, Portugal (project)
Brazilian Coffee Institute Headquarters, Brasilia (project)
Monument to the National Flag, Brasilia
Military Academy, Brasilia (project)
Cecilia do Rego Almeida House, Parana, Brazil
Sergio Alberto M. Carvalho House, Rio de Janeiro (project)
Roberto Boavista House, Rio de Janeiro
City Sector Plan, Albufeira, Portugal (project)

1972 Casa Forte Building, Bahia, Brazil
Super Block, Brasilia
COTELB Telphone Company Southern Peninsula Station, Brasilia
Navy Officers' Club, Brasilia (project)
Transbrasil Aircraft Hangars, Workshops, and Administration Buildings, Brasilia
Naval Ministry Compound, Brasilia (project)
Human Resources Center, Brasilia (project)
Morada do Frade Hotel, Espirito Santo, Brazil
Dorio Cardoso House, Brasilia
Schering Chemical and Pharmaceutical Industry Factory, Rio de Janeiro

1972/
80 Convention Center Complex, Brasilia
1974 Free Point, Rio de Janeiro
Helio Prates da Silverra House, Rio Grande do Sul, Brazil

1975   Paco de Pedra Residential Development, Rio de Janeiro (project)
       Alfio Russo House, Minas Gerais, Brazil
       Brazilian Computers and Systems Factory, Rio de Janeiro
       Hellan Siqueira House, Rio de Janeiro
       Moacyr del Tedesco House, Rio de Janeiro
       Jose Leme Lopes Filho House, Rio de Janeiro
       Bicudo de Castro House, Rio de Janeiro
       Rio Parque Sports Center, Rio de Janeiro (project)
1976   Caracarai Civic Center, Roraima, Brazil (project)
       Caracarai Public Market, Roraima, Brazil (project)
       Caracarai Town Hall, Roraima, Brazil (project)
       Caracarai Bus Terminus, Roraima, Brazil (project)
       Boa Vista Town Hall, Roraima, Brazil (project)
       Boa Vista Municipal Chamber House, Roraima, Brazil (project)
       Boa Vista Civic Square, Roraima, Brazil (project)
       Sea Rescue Station and Service Facilities, Rio de Janeiro
       Paqueta Tourist Hotel, Rio de Janeiro (project)
1977   Sernambetiba Residential Complex, Rio de Janeiro
       Dulce Coelho House, Rio de Janeiro
       Henrique Melman House, Rio de Janeiro
       Jose Safra House, Sao Paulo
       Sao Goncalo Urban Development, Taubate, Sao Paulo (project)
       Heavy Cargo Terminal, Rio de Janeiro (project)
       Play Center, Rio de Janeiro (project)
       Master plan for Taubate, Sao Paulo
       Municipal Technical Registry, Taubate, Sao Paulo (project)
1979   Sergio Bernardes House alterations, Rio de Janeiro

Publications:

By BERNARDES: book—*City: The Survival of Power,* Rio de Janeiro 1975;

On BERNARDES: book—*Modern Architecture in Brazil* by Henrique Mindlin, Rio de Janeiro 1956; articles—"Habitations Individuelles au Brésil" in *L'Architecture d'Aujourd'hui* (Paris), July 1948; "Twentieth Century Domestic Architecture: Brazil" in *L'Architecture d'Aujourd'hui* (Paris), October 1953; "Three Houses by Sergio Bernardes" in *Architectural Review* (London), March 1954; "Intercontinental Airport, Brasilia" in *Modulo* (Rio de Janeiro), August 1960; "Brésil—Amazonie: Hotel 'Tropical' à Manaos" in *Techniques et Architecture* (Paris), September 1969; "Flying Down to Rio" by James De Long in *House Beautiful* (New York), June 1970; "Rio—Zoo Project" by Celina Luz in *Modulo* (Rio de Janeiro), AprilMay 1978.

My aim, both in theory and in practice, is to play a part in the planning of man's environment, an environment resulting from the different ways in which man organizes himself and his space for work, living and movement.

Two concerns predominate. The first is professional and involves my contribution to the solution of specific problems, such as those of private houses, flats, clubs, estates, commercial buildings, etc.—the whole range of specific projects whose design is determined by existing circumstances, without taking the overall view into consideration.

We live in an age in which rapid communications have changed our entire life-style. Our situation must be completely reappraised if we are to consider the advance that science and technology have made on out-dated notions. Nowadays we think more in square centimetres than in square metres; and a piece of furniture that was made with the square metre in mind will have to be reconsidered both in terms of its size and its function. Transport, whether public or private, will have to be restructured. A distinction will have to be made between the right to own and the right to build, so that we can create towns that can be run economically, towns whose designers will aim at a compact and harmonious fusion of work, circulation, and living areas. Indeed, there must be a total reappraisal, from ideologies to religious views.

Spatial architecture is the art of concentration; urbanism is the art of dispersion. The two must be synchronized, yet their application is inevitably expedient, catering to popular needs and determined by the immediately prevailing circumstances.

The architect who created religious architecture, rural and civil architecture, the architecture of ports and armies, must now create an architecture of politics, of law, of administration, of economics and finance, in which the combined knowledge of these sciences produces a new spatial architecture.

My second concern is also professional. It involves my contribution to the solutions of problems of a more general nature. For these wider problems, I have been involved in the creation of L.I.C.—Laboratório de Investigações Conceptuais (Laboratory of Conceptual Research)—which is, above all, a political organization. We are a macrovision lobby. By "lobby" I mean the "explicit and legitimate articulation of the interests of any group, consisting of clear, systematic, direct pressure applied to the authorities with the aim of influencing decisions." And "macrovision" implies a global consideration of problems and a desire to solve them in the long term. It has nothing to do with award-hunting or academic results, nor does it succumb to the instant solution of problems effected within the extremely short terms of political and administrative office.

Non-conformism prevents us from accepting that, by definition, certain tasks are the exclusive preserve of universities or governments, especially when both are handicapped by outdated notions: universities create formal skills, and governments apply them. As soon as materials, machinery, techniques and formuli are shown to be inefficient, ill-conceived, costly, or counter-productive, there arises an opportunity for innovation and change. It is the responsibility of *all* of us to make the most of this opportunity; it must not be left to institutions, dubious consortia, or academics.

At the same time it is not the intention of L.I.C. simply to challenge the establishment for the sake of challenge or to add fuel to the "modernist" fire. No one should be excluded; on the contrary, I think the channels of contribution should be broadened. We must try to re-establish the practice of working together—politicians working with technicians, professionals with academics, state institutions with private institutions. There is no reason to perpetuate a wasteful confrontation. The right way is in understanding and cooperation, cooperation based on a dialogue between equals. Healthy interaction is not based on prejudice and, as members of a team, our prejudices must be forgotten. This interaction will demand the best from each contributor, and the interaction itself will be the test. It must be strong enough to relinquish preconceived notions. The languages of traditional education, of race, and of class must no longer be used; they must give way to a new language, more dangerous perhaps but a language that will be free to redefine, free enough to cater to the needs of people.

In the L.I.C. it is difficult to produce formal plans. L.I.C. formuli and proposals often outstretch the apparent dimensions of the problem. A laboratory is a "place destined for the experimental study of any type of science or for the practical application of scientific knowledge" and conceptual research ought to be concerned with questioning those views and basic ideas that are supposed to be furthering the technological advance but which are ultimately no more than its straitjacket.

—Sergio Bernardes

The work of Sergio Bernardes is an elaboration of three distinct, and successive, architectural visions.

At the beginning of his career in the late 1940's, Bernardes' architectural aims—revealed chiefly in the plans for private houses on which his reputation is based—tended towards a plasticity, which, though characteristic of Brazilian architecture of that period, is peculiar to Bernardes in its constant avoidance of gratuitious formalism. The elegant detail, the simple yet sophisticated plans, the fluid spaces, and the pleasing shapes add up to works of great precision and aesthetic appeal.

M. C. Macedo Soares House of 1953 was the start of Bernardes' concern with the expression of the construction materials themselves: this concern became increasingly important in the years that followed. This exceptional house links the rustic—stone masonry, hand-made bricks—with the industrial—large panes of glass and the light metal treliss that holds up the roof of undulating aluminum tiles. The house is a perfect metaphor, not only of the contradictory nature of the Brazilian scene but also —with its broad, linear spacing—of the country's continental vastness.

The increasing use of bare materials is notable in several buildings that could be called transitional, such as the Ivo Pitanguy House of 1954. This interest lead to a coherent rationalization of building methods, which in turn initiated the second phase of Sergio Bernardes' work: experimentation with brutalism.

A change in construction techniques is but one aspect of a transformation that affected his whole system of formulating architectural space. The structural module became the skeleton around which works were built: it exerted a classicizing and compartmentalizing influence both on internal space and also—by its "legibility"—on external form. In the architect's own house (1960), a work that symbolized the times (it was altered in 1979), this characteristic is not so evident, but in other works—the J. L. M. Lins House of 1961, the Dantas House of 1966, and the Ceará State Government Palace in 1961— the reference, whether intentional or not, to traditional Brazilian architecture is considerable.

The plastic unity that until then had predominated was now broken down into component parts. The architectural elements were no longer applied with the same dynamism, and the spatial fluidity occurred principally in the areas that link the interior with the exterior, resulting in some notable verandas and terraces. In the larger, non-residential buildings, the module imposed a standardization particularly suited to industry. This phase was also extremely important in that it offered an alternative —both logical and versatile—in an age in which the exceptional and personal nature of Oscar Niemeyer's projects for Basilia offered no possibility of imitation or adaptation in conventional architecture. The Bernardes alternative, with its accent on construction technique, developed from Rio de Janeiro, and influenced such younger architects as Arthur Licio Pontual, Marcos Vasconcellos, and Marcello Fragelli.

In 1964 Bernardes put forward a utopian plan for the city of Rio de Janeiro. To an extent, this plan has to do with Bernardes' activities in the field of design and with the two exhibition pavilions he had previously built—one in Sao Paulo for the Companhia Siderurgica Nacional in 1953, and the Brazilian Pavilion at the 1958 Brussels *World's Fair*. Both were notable for their daring suspended roofs. The first formed a bridge spanning a stream in Ibirapuera Park. It attracted attention for its lightness and for its almost "Chinoiserie" profile, defined by two inverted parabolas and inclined lateral pillars. The Brazilian Pavilion in Brussels was built around a central "impluvium" covered by an enormous floating gas balloon.

Meanwhile, Bernardes perfected and patented the most various of industrial design products: portable roofs made of wood, steel or fibre-cement; several construction materials; fittings and furniture; lighting; and even motor-launches, a bicycle, a flexible car, and the fuselage and nose of a small supersonic aircraft.

It is between these two concerns—on the one hand, a certain technological visionary approach the aims of which transcend the brutalist phase; on the other hand, a concern with design, with attention to detail—it is between these concerns that the genesis for the plan for Rio de Janeiro occurs. The plan is perhaps the only one of its kind by a Brazilian architect in an era that was noted, throughout the world, for the relative abundance of this sort of work.

Among the proposals of the plan were the creation of centers for capturing solar energy, processing plants for converting sea water into drinking water, and 500-metre telecommunication towers. The residential areas were concentrated in helical skycrapers with staggered floors allowing an open terrace for each apartment. A link between Rio and Niterói, the town on the other side of Guanbara Bay, was made by two bridges. The first, at the mouth of the bay, was a tourist bridge, supported by eight hotels in the shape of inverted pyramids. The second, the port bridge, consisted of hexagonal "islands," each side a dock 200 metres in length; inside, there were four floors of warehouses, with trafficparking on the roof. The islands linked the industrial zones of both cities.

The technical/scientific theses of this project, and the mental attitudes necessary to its conception, are reflected in all Sergio Bernardes' subsequent work. To provide for interdisciplinary research into his new concerns, Bernardes created the Laboratório de Investigações Conceptuais, L.I.C. This laboratory operates in conjunction with his office and aims "to reconsider the concepts that are at the base of all moral, ethical, political, judicial, administrative thought." The basic premises of the research are outlined in his book, *City: The Survival of Power.* In this third phase, prospective planning and theoretical considerations are the most important aspect of Bernardes' work.

Bernardes' tendency towards technology corresponds to the strengthening of a technocratic ideology in Brazilian national politics. It is significant that from the end of the 1960's Bernardes was not only invited to create various projects of a civil/official nature but also became architectural consultant to the governments of several states. In his architecture, the new phase is marked by a certain reworking of space—a tendency towards "astronautical," anti-organic shapes, often concentric, closed squares and circles as in the Tambaú Hotel of 1966, the Petrobrás Research Center of 1969, and the projects for the Military Academy and the Human Resources Center in Brasilia in 1971–72. The "nomination" of materials is no longer the principal aspect of the architecture; rather, it is characterized by the plasticity favored during the first phase but now based on other premises.

Form remains important, but it is now related to the expression of the method of construction. It is synthetic when based on the structural technology of the more daring projects, and analytical when it is a reflection of the components of buildings erected with more conventional construction techniques. The form is a marriage—within a single architectural vision—of technology and design.

The buildings that look the most simple often have complex functions and house the most sophisticated equipment. In this group could be included the most pragmatic projects such as the Tambaú Hotel, the Casa Alta Building, and the factory for the Schering Chemical and Pharmaceutical Industry. These buildings set new architectural standards—yet, paradoxically, the most audacious, even visionary projects, such as the the Tropical hotels in Manaus and Recife, and the Brazilian Coffee Institute and the Naval Ministry Compound in Brasilia, generally have functions that do not justify the singular quality of designs conceived out of a desire for technological experimentation.

Indeed, in this phase of the architect's work, concept and form are not always related. Perhaps this is why Bernardes' recent work has had so little influence on current Brazilian architectural thought. Yet Bernardes' theories are so stimulating and provocative that he is constantly being invited to give lectures and talks, more often than not to a nonarchitectural audience. He has become one of the main spokesmen of a wider architectural vision in Brazil.

—Jorge Czajkowski

BILL, Max.

Swiss. Born in Winterthur, 22 December 1908. Educated at the Kunstgewerbeschule, Zurich, 1924–27; Bauhaus School, Dessau, Germany, 1927–29. Served in the Swiss Army, 1939–45. Married Binia Spoerri in 1931; son: Johann. Has worked in Zurich as an architect, painter, sculptor, and graphic artist, since 1929, and as an industrial designer, since 1944. Lecturer on the Theory of Form, Kunstgewerbeschule, Zurich, 1944–45; Co-Founder and Rector, Hochschule für Gestaltung, Ulm, Germany, 1951–56; Professor of Environmental Design, State Institute of Fine Arts, Hamburg, 1967–74. Member of the Communal Council, City of Zurich, 1961; National Councillor, Swiss Parliament, 1967–74. Member of the Central Board, Schweizerische Werkbund, 1952–62; Member, Swiss Federal Art Commission, 1961–69; Member of the Board, Geschwisten-Scholl Foundation, Ulm, 1964; Member of the Superior Council (Création Esthetique Industrielle), French Ministry of Industrial and Scientific Development, 1971–73. Member: Abstraction-Création group, Paris, 1932–36; Allianz, Zurich, 1937; CIAM (Congrès Internationaux d'Architecture Moderne), 1938; UAM (Union des Artistes Modernes), Paris, 1949; Deutscher Werkbund, 1956. Exhibitions (paintings, sculpture, architecture, graphics): one-man—Bauhaus, Dessau, 1928; Atelier des Kunstlers, Zurich, 1929, Kunstmuseum, Basle, 1939; Galerie des Eaux Vives, Zurich, 1946; Galerie d'Art Moderne, Basle, 1949; Museu de Arte Moderna, Sao Paulo, 1950; Ulm Museum, Germany, 1956, subsequently toured Germany; Helmhaus, Zurich, 1957; Stadtisches Museum, Leverkusen, Germany, 1959; Staatsgalerie, Stuttgart, 1960; Kunstmuseum, Winterthur, Switzerland, 1960; Staempfli Gallery, New York, 1963; Galleria Cadario, Milan, 1964; Kunsthalle, Berne, 1968; Kestner Gesellschaft, Hanover, 1968; Kunstverein für die Rheinland und Westfalen, Dusseldorf, 1968; Gemeentemuseum, The Hague, 1968; Arts Club of Chicago, 1969; Centre National d'Art Contemporain, Paris, 1969; Musée de Peinture et de Sculpture, Grenoble, 1969; San Francisco Museum of Art, 1970; Musée Rath, Geneva, 1972; Marlborough-Godard Galerie, Toronto and Montreal, 1972; Marlborough Fine Art Gallery, London, 1974; Albright-Knox Art Gallery, Buffalo, New York, 1974, subsequently toured the United States; Kunsthalle, Hamburg, 1976, subsequently toured Germany; Kunstmuseum, Dusseldorf, 1977; group shows—*Abstraction-Création,* Paris, 1933; *Konkrete Kunst,* Kunsthalle, Basle, 1944; *Pevsner/Vantongerloo/Bill,* Kunsthaus, Zurich, 1949; *Bienal,* Sao Paulo, 1951; *Monument to the Unknown Political Prisoner,* Institute of Contemporary Arts, London, 1952; *Biennale,* Venice, 1958; *Konkrete Kunst: 50 Jahre Entwicklung,* Kunsthaus, Zurich, 1960; *Max Bill/Le Corbusier,* Galerie Aurora, Geneva, 1968; etc. Recipient: Grand Prize, *Triennale,* Milan, 1936; Kandinsky Prize, Paris, 1949; First Prize for Sculpture, *Bienal,* Sao Paulo, 1951; Grand Prize, *Triennale,* Milan, 1951; Gold Medal, *Triennale,* Milan, 1954; Gold Medal, Verucchio, Italy, 1966; City of Zurich Art Prize, 1968. Honorary Fellow, American Institute of Architects, 1964. Extraordinary Member, Akademie der Künste, Berlin, 1972; Honorary Member, Royal Flemish Academy of Sciences, Literature and Arts, 1973. Address: Albulastrasse 39 III, 8048 Zurich, Switzerland.

Works:

1928 Children's Garden and Shelter, Zurich (project; with Hans Fischli)
1932/
   33 Max Bill House and Studio, Höngg, Zurich
1936 Swiss Pavilion, *Triennale,* Milan
1937 Waid Country Restaurant, Zurich
1938 Swiss Pavilion, *World's Fair,* New York
1939 City Building and National Planning Display, *Swiss National Exhibition,* Zurich (with Hans Schmidt)
1942 Villiger House, Bremgarten, Aargau, Switzerland
1949 Apartment Building, Zurich (project)
   Seebach School Pavilion, Zurich (competition project)
   Die Gute Form Pavilion, *Swiss Industries Fair,* Basle
1951 Swiss Pavilion, *Triennale,* Milan
1952 Swiss Pavilion, *Biennale,* Venice
   Monument to the Unknown Political Prisoner, London (competition project)
1953/
   54
   Freudenberg Cantonal School, Zurich (competition project)
1953/
   55 Hochschule für Gestaltung, Ulm, Germany
1955 Ulm City Pavilion, *Baden-Württemberg Exhibition,* Stuttgart
1956 Georg Buchner Monument, Darmstadt (project)
1957 Swiss National Monument (project)
   Master plan for the *Olma Agricultural Fair,* St. Gallen, Switzerland (competition project)
   Design of *The Unknown Present* exhibition, Globus Department Store, Basle, St. Gallen, Chur, and Aarau, Switzerland
1957/
   58 Cinevox Cinema and Apartment Building, Neuhausen am Rhinfall, Switzerland (with Olivio Ferrari)
1959 Design of the *Swiss Design* exhibition, London
1960 Design of the *Konkrete Kunst: 50 Jahre Entwicklung* exhibition, Kunsthaus, Zurich
   Design of the *Dokumentation über Marcel Duchamp* exhibition, Kunstgewerbemuseum, Zurich
   Design Institute, Zurich (project)
1960/
   61 Imbau Administration Building, Leverkusen, Germany (with Olivio Ferrari and Rudolf Welter)
   Lichtdruck Printing Works, Dielsdorf, near Zurich (with Peter Hofmann)
   Fleckhaus (single-family house), Odenthall-Erberich, near Cologne (with Olivio Ferrari and Oswald Ungers)
1961 Fountain Courtyard, *International Hydraulic Engineering Exhibition,* Berlin
1962 Alcan Aluminium Museum, Montreal (project)
1963 Scenery for the play *Oedipus,* Municipal Theatre, Ulm, Germany
1964 "Bilden und Gestalten" Section, *Swiss National Exhibition,* Lausanne
1964/
   74 Radio Station Building (and studios), School of Applied Arts, Zurich (with Willy Roost)
1966/
   67 Lavina-Tobel Bridge, near Tamins, Switzerland (with Aschwanden and Speck)

1967 Wind Column, *Expo '67,* Montreal (now in the Musée d'Art Contemporain, Montreal)
1967/
68 Max Bill House and Studio, Zumikon, Zurich
1968/
70 Design of the *Zürcher Künstler* annual exhibitions, Zurich
1971 Denis René/Hans Mayer Art Gallery, Dusseldorf
1976 Yaacov Agam Studio, Esbly, France

Publications:

By BILL: books—*Le Corbusier: Oeuvre Complete,* volume 3, editor, Zurich 1939, London 1964; *Quinze Variations sur un Même Thème,* Paris 1938; *5 Construktionen + 5 Compositionen,* Zurich 1941; *10 Original Lithos,* Zurich 1941; *X × X,* Zurich 1942; *Leo Leuppi: 10 Compositionen,* Zurich 1943; *Konkrete Kunst,* exhibition catalogue, with others, Basle 1944; *Hans Arp: 11 Configurations,* with others, Zurich 1945; *Wiederaufbau,* Zurich 1945; *Wassily Kandinsky: 10 Farbige Reproduktionen,* Basle 1949; *Robert Maillart: Brücken und Konstruktionen,* Zurich 1949; *Moderne Schweizer Architektur 1925–45,* Basle 1950; *Wassily Kandinsky,* editor, Paris 1951; *Form: A Balance Sheet of Mid-Twentieth Century Trends in Design,* Basle 1952; *Uber das Geistige in der Kunst,* editor, Berne 1952; *Mies van der Rohe,* Milan 1955; *Essays über Kunst und Künstler,* editor,

Stuttgart 1955, Berne 1963; *Die Gute Form,* Winterthur, Switzerland 1957; *Punkt und Linie zu Flache,* editor, Berne 1959; *Enzo Mari,* with Bruno Munaro, Milan 1959; *Konkrete Kunst: 50 Jahre Entwicklung,* exhibition catalogue, with René Wehrli and Margit Staber, Zurich 1960; *7 Scarions,* Genoa 1967; *Zürcher Künstler,* exhibition catalogues, Zurich, 1968, 1969; *11 × 4,* Zurich 1970; *Jahresgabe 1972,* Berne 1972; *System mit Fünf Vierfarbigen Zentren,* St. Gallen, Switzerland 1972; *8 = (2 × 4/4) = 8,* Neuchatel, Switzerland 1974; *16 Constellations,* Paris 1974; *7 Twins,* Neuchatel, Switzerland 1977; articles—"The Beginning of a New Epoch in Architecture" in *Architectural Design* (London), no. 11, 1955; "Le Corbusier" in *Neue Zürcher Zeitung* (Zurich), no. 3867, 1965; "Das Individuelle und das Allgemeine in der Architektur" in *Diskussionsforum Schöner Wohnen,* Stuttgart 1966; "Mes Rapports avec l'Architecture Grecque" in *Monde Grec,* Fribourg 1966; "Responsibility in Design and Information" in *American Scholar* (Washington, D.C.), Spring 1966; "La Formation de l'Architecte" in *Revue de l'Union Internationale des Architectes* (Paris), no. 44, 1967; "Walter Gropius" in *Universitas* (Stuttgart), no. 11, 1969; "Ludwig Mies van der Rohe 1886–1969" in *Neue Zürcher Zeitung* (Zurich), August 1969; and numerous contributions to art journals and art exhibition catalogues throughout the world.
On BILL: books—*Max Bill,* Buenos Aires 1955;

Max Bill by Max Bense and others, Teufen, Switzerland 1958; *Max Bill* by Margit Staber, St. Gallen, Switzerland 1971; *Max Bill* by Eduard Huttinger, Zurich 1977; articles—"Variations on a Single Theme in the Fine Arts" by George Schmidt in *XX Siècle* (Paris), no. 4, 1938; "Complessita di Max Bill" by Vittorio Gregotti in *Casabella* (Milan), no. 228, 1959; "Max Bill 1963" by Max Bense in *Art International* (Lugano), no. 3, 1963; "Max Bill" by Margit Staber in *Art International* (Lugano), no. 5, 1966; "Max Bill" by Shutaro Mukai in *The Essence of Present Design Theories,* Tokyo 1966; "Max Bill's Aesthetische Zustande" by Max Bense in *Artistik und Engagement,* Cologne 1970; special issue of *Nueva Forma* (Madrid), September 1973; "Sculptor, Painter, Mathematician—Switzerland's Max Bill" by Nancy Tobin Willing in the *Courier Express Magazine* (Buffalo, New York), September 1974; "Superb Puritan" by Robert Hughes in *Time* (New York), November 1974.

Max Bill the Builder. It is necessary to make that distinction because, of our few and talented contemporaries who can claim the soubriquet "Renaissance Man," Max Bill is redolent with qualifications.

Apart from being a busy writer (his writing generally concerns himself and his exploits and his "confirmed" theories about colour and shape and content and mathematical dicta), he is also an acclaimed painter, strictly non-figurative with a Bau-

Max Bill: "Bilden und Gestalten" Section, **Swiss National Exhibition,** Lausanne, 1964

haus-trained determination to delve deep into the logistics of form and colour; he is also a sculptor able to translate mind into matter with a devastating precision that brooks no accidents, however happy; he is an ideas-man who, in the creation of stadia, layouts of large and important national and private exhibitions, and big displays, is a sure-fire success (by his own standards and those of many others), even if the demands he makes on co-workers tend to be excessive; but perhaps—is "perhaps" the right word? —above all, he is a master builder, an architect who, even though many of his projects have never been realized, has left enough of his personalized edifices around the world, along with a deep pile of blueprints, sketches, designs and plans, to ensure himself a nomination to the Empyrean where Wren rubs shoulders with Corb.

Yet a question nags: what is the true significance in world terms of Max Bill as an architect?

Bill is a loner who has stepped outside so many magic circles that he has the doubtful distinction of being even more remote—in whichever artistic role he happens to be playing—from the *Geist unserer zeitgenossische Epoche* than Frank Lloyd Wright or Tatlin. The influence of this mighty theoretician upon other contemporary architects is limited to so narrow a circle that one is prompted to wonder if it contains anyone other than Bill himself. The question can be put another way: would it have made any difference to the development of 20th century construction if Bill the architect had never existed?

Whatever the answer to that question, one has to admit that there is a wealth of personal achievement, that for fifty years Max Bill has been an outstanding artist/creator. Of some 40-odd projects, he has seen —often in co-operation with other architects—at least three-quarters of them brought to completion; and this list includes a wide variety of works from houses to exhibition layouts, from theatre-decor design to the joint undertaking, with Aschwanden and Speck, of the Lavinia-Tobel Bridge near Tamins, Switzerland.

The Lavinia-Tobel Bridge proved to be one of Bill's happiest commissions. (He would probably welcome other similar commissions.) His interest in bridge construction comes from his study of the Swiss bridge-designer Maillart about whom he wrote an informed monograph after the war, and it was through encountering the son of Ros (one of Maillart's strong adherents) that Bill came into contact with Aschwanden and Speck.

The very real success with the bridge came a few years after work on the Hochschule für Gestaltung in Ulm, started in 1953, which dragged on for two years and which Bill rated as a failure (he resigned his rectorship in 1957). Most of the buildings were allowed to fall into disuse, but the main structure won a conservation order and was converted by Ulm University into its Psychology Department; attempts have also been made to transform what remains of the accommodation area into living quarters for the university's professors and students.

Between Ulm and the Lavinia-Tobel Bridge came the "Bilden und Gestalten" Section of the *Swiss National Exhibition* at Lausanne: little of it remains today in its original Bill-conceived state except the theatre—a great and practical design in constant use.

From this brief summary it will be obvious that Bill the Architect is extremely difficult to "place." He certainly preserves the art-concrète purism of early Le Corbusier, but he is not beyond making it the formal basis from which outcrops, often aggressive outcrops, can occur. This rogue impulse—not really "rogue" or "impulse" at all because it is based on extremely sophisticated no-nonsense mathematical formulae—is early in evidence in his work, in the original version of his own home-cum-atelier in Höngg in Zurich, which was completed as long ago as 1933.

Another distinguished factor about Bill the architect is that he is supremely practical, especially in the drawing up of attractively low tenders for any contract that comes his way. Individuality, cost, work-

Gunnar Birkerts: Federal Reserve Bank, Minneapolis, 1967

duration, and scientific investigation of acceptable if heretical raw materials for building purposes all tend to answer the requirements of the most cash-conscious clients. The 1942 Villiger House in Bremgarten—prefabricated but also with wood-timbered character—was completed in 5 months!

As an architect, Max Bill has had his interesting successes; he has had just as many interesting failures. It is perhaps best to allow posterity the last word.

—Sheldon Williams

BIRKERTS, Gunnar.
American. Born in Riga, Latvia, 17 January 1925; emigrated to the United States, 1949: naturalized, 1954. Educated at the English School, Riga, 1939–44; Technische Hochschule, Stuttgart, 1945–49, Dip.Arch.Eng. 1949. Married Sylvia Zvirbulis in 1950: children: Sven, Andra, and Erik. Worked as a designer in the office of Perkins and Will, Chicago, 1950–51, and in the office of Eero Saarinen and Associates, Bloomfield Hills, Michigan, 1951–54; Chief Designer, Minoru Yamasaki and Associates, Birmingham, Michigan, 1955–59; Principal, Birkerts and Straub, Birmingham, 1959–62. Since 1962, President of Gunnar Birkerts and Associates, Birmingham. Assistant Professor, 1961, Associate Professor,

1963–69, and since 1969 Professor of Architecture University of Michigan, Ann Arbor. Exhibitions *Furniture Design Competition,* Cantu, Italy, 1954 Akron Art Institute, Ohio, 1954; *Bienal,* Sao Paulc 1962; *40 under 40,* Architectural League of New York, 1965; Katonah Museum of Art, New York, 1970; Museum of Modern Art, New York, 1971; Notre Dame University, Indiana, 1973; *Design in Michigan,* Cranbrook Academy, Bloomfield Hills, Michigan, 1977. Recipient: Young Designer of the Year Award, Akron Institute of Art, 1954; First Prize, *International Furniture Competition,* Cantu, Italy, 1955; *Progressive Architecture* Award, 1961; Award of Excellence, *Architectural Record,* 1961, 1968; First Honor Award, American Institute of Architects, 1962; Award of Merit, American Institute of Architects, Detroit Chapter, 1963, 1967; Honor Award, Church Architecture Guild of America, 1964; Award of Merit, Michigan Society of Architects, 1967; Honor Award, American Institute of Architects, 1970, 1973; Bartlett Award, 1970; National Gold Medal in Architecture, Tau Sigma Delta, 1971; American Iron and Steel Institute Awards, 1973, 1975; Honor Award, Consulting Engineers Council of the United States, 1973; Award of Honor, Michigan Society of Architects, 1974, 1977; Award of Excellence, American Institute of Steel Construction, 1974; Honor Award, and Gold Medal, American Institute of Architects, Detroit Chapter, 1975; Energy Conservation Award, Owens-Corning Fiberglas Corporation, 1977. Fellow, American Institute of Architects, Latvian Architects Association, and the Graham Foundation. Address: Gunnar Birkerts and Associates, 292 Harmon Street, Birmingham, Michigan 48009, U.S.A.

Works:

1960 Schwartz Summer House, Northville, Michigan
Haley Funeral Home, Southfield, Michigan
1961 1300 Lafayette East Apartments, Detroit
1962 Peoples Federal Savings and Loan, Royal Oak, Michigan
Lillibridge Elementary School additions, Detroit
Marathon Oil Company Office Building, Detroit
1963 University Reformed Church, Ann Arbor, Michigan
1964 Lincoln Elementary School, Columbus, Indiana
1965 Public Library, Livonia, Michigan
Tougaloo College Library, Tougaloo, Mississippi
Church of St. Bede, Southfield, Michigan
Glen Oaks Community College, Centreville, Michigan
1967 Ford Motor Company Pavilion, *Hemisfair 1968,* San Antonio, Texas
Federal Reserve Bank, Minneapolis
1968 Public Library, Duluth, Minnesota
1969 IBM Corporate Computer Center, Sterling Forest, New York
Contemporary Arts Museum, Houston
1970 Dance Instructional Facility, State University of New York at Purchase
1973 Municipal Fire Station, Corning, New York
1974 Calvary Baptist Church, Detroit
IBM Office Building, Southfield, Michigan
Law School additions, University of Michigan, Ann Arbor
1975 United States Embassy Office Building, Helsinki
1976 Museum of Glass, Corning Glass Works, Corning, New York

Publications:

By BIRKERTS: book—*Subterranean Urban Systems,* Ann Arbor, Michigan 1974.

On BIRKERTS: books—*Architecture and the College,* Urbana, Illinois 1968; *Architecture in a Revolutionary Era* by Julian Eugene Kulski, Nashville, Tennessee, and London 1971; *The Visual Dialogue* by Nathan Knobler, New York 1972; *Arts of the Environment,* edited by Gyorgy Kepes, New York and London 1972; *Architecture in the United States* by Ralph W. Hammett, New York and London 1976; *Architecture in America* by G. Kidder Smith, New York 1976; *New Architecture in the World* by Udo Kultermann, revised edition, London 1976; articles—"Gunnar Birkerts—Architect" in *Architecture and Planning* (Taiwan), November 1969; "Gunnar Birkerts" in *Kenchiku Bunka* (Tokyo), March 1970; "Eine 'Bruecke' für die Federal Reserve Bank in Minneapolis" in *Werk* (Zurich), no. 4, 1970; "Bucher-Bruecke" in *Baumeister* (Munich), December 1970; "Opere e Progetti di Gunnar Birkerts e Associati" in *L'Architettura* (Rome), May 1971; "Bridge for a Bank" in *Architectural Forum* (New York), June 1971; "To Amerikanske Biblioteksprosekter" in *Arkitekten* (Copenhagen), no. 9, 1971; "New Directions for Gunnar Birkerts" in *Architectural Record* (New York), October 1971; "This Building Is a Bridge" in *Popular Science* (New York), August 1972; "Liberating Land" in *Progressive Architecture* (New York), March 1973; "Gunnar Birkerts" in *Kentiku* (Tokyo), December 1973; "A Minneapolis La Banca" in *Domus* (Milan), January 1975; "Aktualitat, Federal Reserve Bank of Minneapolis" in *Bauen und Wohnen* (Zurich), April 1975; "Leading Architects of the World: Gunnar Birkerts" in *Nikkei Architecture* (Tokyo), 4 October 1976; "Architect Who Puts Poetry into His Buildings" in *Saudi Gazette* (Saudi Arabia), 2 March 1978.

Gunnar Birkerts has been producing significant, controversial buildings for almost twenty years. Strongly influenced by Eero Saarinen, for whom he worked as a young apprentice, having newly arrived in the United States from Latvia, his work has been shaped, as he admits, more by the times we live in than by any current ideological position. Like all contemporary architects, he acknowledges the influence of program, money and available technology and materials. He often speaks of his powers of synthesis and intuition but almost never of self expression. "To synthesize," he has written, "is to consciously search for and analyze the intrinsic structure of any design problem, while intuition is the ability to subconsciously sense the intrinsic structure of the problem. One approach deals more or less with external factors, the other with internal feelings, but both are part of the struggle to respond to human needs as they appear out of the nature of the problem. I avoid overall theories about form and try to give each building its own theoretical base."

Birkerts has always been interested in light as the means of bringing the sense of the outside to an interior space and increasing its apparent size. He borrows light from one space and transmits it to another either directly or by reflection. A second concern of his has been the simplification of form, details and construction problems. To this end he believes that he subordinates structure, never letting it become the principal element of architectural expression. Actually he does no such thing. Structure fascinates him. The Federal Reserve Bank of Minneapolis and the Tougaloo College Library in Mississippi are triumphs of structural expression.

Overriding each building's theoretical base, and the set of architectural rules that he lays down for himself, and what he takes to be the operations of his conscious and unconscious in synthesis, is a powerful talent. His work remains remarkably creative and self expressive, bursting out of its theoretical constraints. Like Saarinen, Birkerts produces strong, unforgettable building images that exist in an esthetic world that transcends their rationale.

—Mildred F. Schmertz

BLAKE, Peter.
American. Born in Berlin, Germany, 20 September 1920; emigrated to the United States, 1940: naturalized, 1944. Educated at the Bootham School, York, England, 1935–38; University of London, 1938; Regent Street Polytechnic School of Architecture, London, 1939; University of Pennsylvania School of Architecture, Philadelphia, 1940–41; Pratt Institute School of Architecture, New York, 1947–49, B.Arch. (honors) 1949. Served as an Intelligence Officer, United States 5th Armored Division, 1944–45, and as a Staff Intelligence Officer, Headquarters, United States Forces in Europe, 1945–47. Apprentice to Serge Chermayeff, London, 1938–39, and to George Howe, Oscar Stonorov and Louis I. Kahn, Philadelphia, 1940–42; Curator, Department of Architecture and Industrial Design, Museum of Modern Art, New York, 1948–50; Associate Editor, 1950–61, Managing Editor, 1961–64, and Editor-in-Chief, 1964–72, *Architectural Forum,* New York; Partner, Peter Blake and Julian Neski, Architects, New York, 1956–60, and James Baker and Peter Blake, Architects, New York, 1964–71; Contributing Editor, *New York Magazine,* 1968–76; Editor-in-Chief, *Architecture Plus,* New York, 1972–75. Since 1975, Chairman of the School of Architecture, Boston Architectural Center. Chairman, 1962, and Member of the Board of Directors, 1965–73, International Design Conference in Aspen, Colorado; Chairman, Advisory Panel to the Shah of Iran on Housing, Urban Development and New Town Planning, 1976. Member, Board of Directors, City Walls,

New York, since 1968; Member, Public Arts Council of the Municipal Arts Society, New York, since 1970. Recipient: Ford Foundation grant, 1960; Howard Myers Award for Architectural Journalism, 1960; Graham Foundation Fellowship, 1962; Architecture Critic's Medal, American Institute of Architects, 1975. Fellow, American Institute of Architects, 1970. Address: Boston Architectural Center, 320 Newbury Street, Boston, Massachusetts 02115, U.S.A.

Works:

1955/
65 Numerous houses in the New York City area
1957 Design of the *America Builds* exhibition, West Berlin
1959 Design of the *U.S. Architecture* exhibition, Moscow
1960 Hollis Unitarian Church, Queens, New York
Allen-Stevens Offices and Warehouse, Queens, New York
1961 Temple Emanu-El, Livingston, New Jersey
1963 "Ideal Theatre," for the Ford Foundation (project)
1964 Library, Darrow School, New Lebanon, New York
Plan for Tegel Airport, Berlin (competition project)
1965 Town plan for Manistee, Michigan
Institute buildings and housing, Max Planck Institute, Berlin (competition project)
1970 Mental Hygiene Center, Binghamton State Hospital, New York
1974 Roundabout Theatre Stage One, New York
1975 Neely Experimental Theatre, Vanderbilt University Drama School, Nashville, Tennessee

Publications:

By BLAKE: books—*The Master Builders: Le Corbusier, Mies van der Rohe, Frank Lloyd Wright,* New York and London 1960, revised edition New York 1976; *God's Own Junkyard: The Planned Deterioration of America's Landscape,* New York 1964; *Form Follows Fiasco: Why Modern Architecture Hasn't Worked,* Boston 1977; numerous articles in architectural journals throughout the world.

Like most young architects starting out in the United States and in Europe in the 1950's, I was tremendously influenced by the clear logic and pure beauty of Mies van der Rohe's work. I knew Mies quite well and found his theories and his performance enormously persuasive—especially since he was not only a superb artist but also a man of enormous charm and, believe it or not, of enormous humanity. Not until after he died did I really begin to question some of the hard-edged diagrams that he had built.

Since then I have been attracted increasingly to the work of certain humanists—especially Alvar Aalto—whom we used to consider rather too sentimental for a rational age. I was asked recently to identify the one building, in the Greater Boston area, built since World War II, that had really stood the test of time. Aalto's Baker House, at M.I.T., completed in the late 1940's, was the obvious answer.

Today I design and build—or try to design and build—as simply as I can, as neatly as I can, as modestly as I can, and as well as I can. And as inexpensively as I can: I am very pleased that the Rehabilitation Center, in Binghamton, New York, was constructed for about 6 per cent below the allocated budget. That produced not merely a building that I like very much indeed—but also a building that returned some money to the people who agreed to pay for such a generous gesture—in this case, the taxpayers of Binghamton. I consider myself some sort of populist, in that regard; and I don't think I would know how to design a monument—in the unlikely event that someone asked me to design and build one.

Peter Blake: Rehabilitation Center, Binghamton State Hospital, New York, 1970

I have an uneasy feeling that the modern movement, in its preachings, has been extraordinarily arrogant—telling people what was supposedly good for them, instead of *listening* to their needs and aspirations. It seems to me that the modern movement has not, until quite recently, come to terms with the idea of an egalitarian democracy—a human condition which, for better or for worse, is not compatible with super-planning à la Haussmann, Le Corbusier, Hilberseimer or, for that matter, Frank Lloyd Wright.

If the choice is between egalitarian democracy and modern architecture, I (a modern architect) today prefer the former.

—Peter Blake

Peter Blake began his architectural career through a conventional sequence of development. He went to the University of Pennsylvania School of Architecture in the 1940's at a time when the Modern Movement was supplanting the Beaux Arts tradition as the dominant theory expounded in architectural academia in the U.S. He studied the great modern masters and professed his reverence for Wright, Corbusier, and van der Rohe in his book *The Master Builders* which he wrote in 1960.

And, as if not completely convinced of those sacred cows of modernism, "form follows function," "less is more," etc, he has become a successful critic of modern architecture, challenging these time honored beliefs in his publishings and in his designs. His earlier buildings, while not numerous, seem to exhibit a strong influence of the aforementioned masters.

As a teacher and the editor of two successive yet discontinued magazines, *Architectural Forum* and *Architecture Plus,* he was constantly criticizing the built examples of current trends and their practitioners' adherence to or deviation from the precepts of the accepted philosophy. In practice, the increasing labor expenses, energy consciousness, governmental regulation in a world where time is money and money builds architecture, the phrases "shortened version," "instant house," "no frills," seem to have replaced the sacred cows. In many respects the Modern Movement has failed to provide for us in the 70's.

Well planned, "Ideal Cities," fashioned in bricks and mortar from the concepts introduced by the architects of the International Style, have developed into sterile wastelands, irresponsible to the well-being of the individual.

The culmination of Blake's criticism of modern doctrine is expressed in his 1977 book, *Form Follows Fiasco: Why Modern Architecture Hasn't Worked.* Here, he admits that the Modern Movement which he so endearingly promoted has failed. His appreciation for his mentors has not been abandoned, however, but their precepts cannot alone direct present day building.

As a critic, Blake has the intelligence, knowledge, wit and honesty to be listened to and respected. Though his essays and books speak more for his reactionary philosophy on the direction of modern architecture, as a practicing architect his works have also transformed from a pure adherence to the dogma of the masters, to an architecture more responsive to the actual constraints of the modern age. The cost of his conventionally built Mental Hygiene Center in New York (1970), for example, came in under budget because he cut out the special details, expensive materials, even prefabricated components, and fit the building construction method and its materials to those readily and inexpensively available.

The direction of architecture for the next generation will be an abandonment of this order imposed on the world, and an emergence of an order coming from within our society, based on recognition of the practical even if mundane, in essence, the actual. It will involve "shared ideals, and shared realities" with the true responsiveness to people as its generator.

—Stephen P. Hamilton

BLESSING, Charles (Alexander).
American. Born in Montrose, Colorado, 23 May 1912. Educated at the University of Colorado, Boulder, B.S.Arch. Eng. 1934; Massachusetts Institute of Technology, Cambridge, B.Arch. 1937, M.City Planning 1939. Served in the United States Army Engineers Office, 1943; Director of Urban Research, United States Navy Military Government Program, Princeton, New Jersey, 1944–45, and Monterey, California, 1945; City Planning Officer, SCAP Headquarters, Tokyo, 1945–46: Lieutenant. Married Elizabeth C. Long in 1940; children: Bayard and Curtis. Planning Engineer, New Hampshire Planning and Development Commission, 1940–41; City Planner, Chicago Plan Commission, 1942; Regional Planning Engineer, Greater Boston Development Committee, 1946–48; Director of Planning, Chicago Planning Commission, 1948–53; Director of City Planning, Detroit City Planning Commission, 1953–74. Since 1974, Director of Planning, Detroit Department of Community and Economic Development. Adjunct Associate Professor of City Planning, Wayne State University, Detroit, 1954–59. Currently, Professor of Architecture, Urban Design Studio, University of Detroit. Member, National Industrial Zoning Committee, 1949–53, 1971–73; Vice-Chairman, Detroit Commission on Neighborhood Conservation and Improved Housing, 1955–60; President, American Institute of Planners, 1958–60; Member, Michigan Cultural Commission, 1961–62; Chairman, Urban Design Committee, American Institute of Architects, 1962–63; Member, National Planning Advisory Committee, Highway Research Board, 1964–67; Member, National Advisory Council, Urban America, 1966–67; Member of the Board of Registration, 1968–75, and Chairman of the Board, 1968–75, Professional Community Planners of Michigan. Recipient: Biennial Award for Design Excellence, United States Department of Housing and Urban Development, 1970; Urban Design Award, *Progressive Architecture,* 1971; Gold Medal, American Institute of Architects, Detroit Chapter, 1972; Distinguished Engineering Alumnus Award, University of Colorado, 1972; American Institute of Architects Award, 1976. Fellow, American Institute of Architects. Address (office). 350 East Congress Street, Detroit, Michigan 48226, U.S.A.

Works:

1948/
53 Plans and planning proposals for the City of Chicago
1953/
74 Plans and planning proposals for the City of Detroit

Publications:

By BLESSING: book—*The Form of Cities in Perspective: The Graeco-Roman World 500 B.C. to A.D. 200,* exhibition catalogue, Ann Arbor, Michigan 1973; articles—"Seeing the City Whole" in *AIA Journal* (Washington, D.C.), September 1974, January 1975, and April 1976.

On BLESSING: articles—"Detroit and the Vision of Charles Blessing" by James Bailey in *Architectural Forum* (New York), June 1965; "The Other Architect" in *Architectural and Engineering News* (Philadelphia), February 1967.

Charles Blessing is an architect, yes, but he prefers to be called an urban planner. What he has done over the last quarter of a century is to combine the skills of both kinds of professional in a pioneering effort as director of city planning for Detroit.

Today, while he has retired from the position he held since 1953, he is just as busy as ever, having switched his visionary talents to a more specific place, the University of Detroit where he is a professor in the Urban Design Studio of the School of Architecture. Thus, in a sense, he has come full circle.

Meanwhile, he can look back with pride to that portion of his career spent serving a metropolis of more than 1 million people, which, surprisingly enough to some, was earning its share of recognition even though cities like Philadelphia seemed to be getting all the acclaim. Detroit, under Blessing's leadership, was the first American city to become involved in social and community organizational work, and in the 1960's was honored by the American Institute of Planners and the American Institute of Architects for its contribution to urban design. What really has mattered the most over the years, however, was that Blessing is one of the most humane persons dealing with cities in our society.

In 1976 he was cited by the AIA with a medal for his "unique and artistic documentation of many of the world's great cities." Said the jury in making the presentation: "During the course of his life as an architect and city planner, Blessing has documented the cities and places of this world as has no other person before him. His drawings . . . have become a more meaningful way of expressing and recording the drama, form and grain of the man-make environment."

Blessing understands—and visually interprets—cities in the large context of geography as well as in the intimate context of people as expressed through neighborhoods. He is broad and he is deep, going back to the ancient cities of Greece for his basic text and for a beginning to his own documentation.

When the *AIA Journal,* for its Bicentennial issue, queried professionals for a list of buildings that they felt had had the greatest influence in America, Blessing replied: "The design of the city represents the greatest challenge of the architect; the present confusion and disarray of the urban development is the real enemy of great architecture. This is not to say that no single building can qualify as an architectural masterpiece even if it lacks harmony with its surroundings, but rather to emphasize that urban visual chaos and ugliness can only be overcome by a level of thought and activity beyond the scale of a single building."

It is very likely beyond the scope of any one profession to manipulate the total form of the city, but perseverance in a search for the answers that satisfy the spirit is a must. Blessing is one of those professionals who is truly dedicated to continuing in that search, not only in Detroit but also everywhere he goes about the world in an attempt to foster a better understanding of the urban design process.

—Robert E. Koehler

Holger Blom: Play Sculpture, Humlagården, Stockholm

BLOM, Holger.

Swedish. Born in Stockholm, 2 August 1906. Educated at the Royal Institute of Technology School of Architecture, Stockholm, 1924–28; Royal Academy of Arts School of Architecture, Stockholm, 1930–32. Married Alla Feodorovna Doljenkova in 1934; son: Tarras. Worked with Lars Israel Wahlman, Stockholm, 1928–29; studied and travelled in Europe, and worked in Paris and Amsterdam, 1929–31. In private practice, Stockholm, since 1931. Worked in the Stockholm City Planning Office, 1932, and Street Office, 1933–38, and served as City Garden Director (Chief of the Parks Department), 1938–71. Address: Odengatan 15, Stockholm, Sweden.

Works:

1932/
33 Stations for Stockholm's first underground tramway
1933/
35 Slussen Traffic Cloverleaf, Stockholm (with Tage William-Olsson)
1938 "Mushroom" Concrete Rain Shelter, Sture-plan, Stockholm

1938/
71 Plans, designs, co-ordinating studies, re-organization and reconstruction of open spaces and children's play parks in Stockholm, including: Norr Mälarstrand, Fred-hälls Park, Tegnerlunden, Bellvue Park, and the Tullgården

Publications:

On BLOM: books—*Modern Gardens* by Peter Shep-heard, London 1953; *Playgrounds and Recreation Spaces* by Alfred Ledermann and Alfred Trachsel, Stuttgart and London 1959; *The Park and the Town* by George F. Chadwick, London 1966; *Planning for Play* by Lady Allen of Hurtwood, London 1968; *Landscape of Man* by Geoffrey and Susan Jellicoe, London 1975.

*

The art of building parks is part of architecture. The materials are different, certainly, but the problems are similar. Solution in plan, the forming of space, the detail. With the ground and the plants, compositions in space and color are produced that range from the most practical to the most solemn. And with these living materials all human emotions and rational requirements can be expressed.

—Holger Blom

*

While World War II was devastating most of Europe, the Swedes were exploring new concepts of landscape, especially in cities. After the war, landscape architects and laymen in the war-torn countries were astonished by the originality and inventiveness with which Holger Blom, the Director of Parks in Stockholm, brought landscape into the busiest centres of the city. The Swedish summer is short but fairly predictable; the air has never been polluted by intensive industrialization, and public vandalism is minimal. Stockholm was the first major city to prepare and execute a comprehensive landscape plan, its general shape dictated by the powerful terrain of water and rock. From the surrounding country, green fingers of landscape penetrate right to the city centre where they seem to explode into flower at Blom's magic touch.

The most popular of all of Blom's inventions (soon to be copied throughout Europe and become hack-neyed) were the portable containers on the pavements. These attractively-shaped, mass-produced concrete bowls were filled with plants in flower at a central depot, then placed wherever they could enrich an urban setting. Another of his innovations was to plant the banks of the Malärstrand, the city's principal water scenery, not as a sophisticated park but as a reflection of the city's outer landscape, with wild plants and seats set among flowers. Blom also introduced children's climbing play sculpture; he designed small areas for unusual types of play activity, such as open air stages on which children could act. His structures were all in natural materials.

It can be said that the impetus given to simplicity and grace in civic landscape by Holger Blom inspired nearly every civilized society struggling to recuperate after the war. He lifted urban park design from the traditional borough surveyor's conception of art into one that is art itself.

—Geoffrey Jellicoe

BLOM, Piet.

Dutch. Born in Amsterdam, 8 February 1934. Educated at the Architecture Academy, Amsterdam, under Aldo van Eyck, 1956–62, Dip.Arch. 1962; awarded Prix de Rome, 1962. Married Elisabeth Margaretta Maria Abels in 1958; children: Hannah, Abel, and Betje. In private practice, Monnckendam, Netherlands, since 1967. Address (office): Schoolstraat 2, Monickendam, Netherlands.

Works:

1963   Boerderij Students Building (conversion of farm building), Twente Technical University, Enschede, Netherlands
1967/
69   Bastille Students Building/Community Centre, Twente Technical University, Enschede, Netherlands
1972/
73   Kasbah Housing Development, Hengelo, Netherlands
1975   Subterranean Development under the Rozengracht, Amsterdam (project)
     Jordaan District Redevelopment Plan, Amsterdam (project)
1975/
78   Speelhuis Leisure Centre, with theatre, small halls and housing, Helmond, Netherlands
1978/
79   Apartment buildings (2), Rotterdam (project)

Publications:

By BLOM: article—"The Singular Opinions of Piet Blom" in *Bauwelt* (Berlin), 7 October 1974.

On BLOM: book—*World Architecture 3*, London 1966; articles—"Kasbah Experimental Housing in Hengelo" in *Detail* (Munich), January/February 1974; "Trial for Helmond's 'Forest of Houses'" by Ruud Brouwers in *Wonen-TA/BK* (Heerlen, Netherlands), May 1974; "Team 10 + 20: Introduction and Conclusion," special issue of *L'Architecture d'Aujourd'hui* (Paris), January/February 1975; "The Kasbah, Hengelo—A Real Experiment" by W. J. van Heuvel in *Polytechnische Tijdschrift* (The Hague), 25 June 1975; "Housing and Community Centre in Helmond" in *Bauen und Wohnen* (Zurich), January 1976; "The Dwelling Tree" by Pierluigi Nicolin in *Lotus* (Venice), no. 11, 1976; "Experimental Housing: Nine Years of Passive Conduct" by Aad Wassenaar in *Wonen-TA/BK* (Heerlen, Netherlands), March 1977; "Speelhuis Cultural Centre in Helmond" in *Polytechnische Tijdschrift* (The Hague), December 1977; "188 Homes in Helmond" in *L'Architecture d'Aujourd-'hui* (Paris), April 1978; "Boxing Clever" in *The Architects' Journal* (London), 10 May 1978; "Think of a Square and Cube It" in *Interior Design* (London), July 1978; "Het Speelhuis in Helmond" by Nathalie van den Eerenbeemt in *Bauwelt* (Berlin), 4 August 1978.

Piet Blom received his architectural education at the Architecture Academy in Amsterdam. One of his teachers was Aldo van Eyck, and van Eyck's progressive concepts exerted a decisive influence not only on Blom but also on such architects as Herman Hertzberger and Jan Verhoeven. These architects are today described as adherents of Structuralism: a reaction against decades of domination by Functionalism, it demands a humanization of architecture. The principles of Structuralism, all assimilated in Blom's work, are these:

1) Town planning should strive for a multiform urban landscape, the "casbah organisée," instead of the garden city. 2) Town planning should be based on a "sense of place" concept, rather than on the "space-time" concept of the verdant functional town. 3) There should be a deliberate creation of a "realm of the intermediate," areas where the individual and community can meet—for instance, squares, streets, and apartment building galleries that are not only functional but also life enhancing. 4) The shape, form, and identity of the town must come about according to the methods of architecture, not the scientific/analytic method of Functionalism. 5) There must be structural development, as opposed to arbitrary town growth. 6) Building mass must be articulated—as an alternative to amorphous town planning and mammoth building blocks. 7) Growth should be coherent to insure an atmosphere of order and repose. 8) The architect should prepare for future change by creating polyvalent forms and by allowing for individual interpretations, so that change is possible, so that the user may express his identity (the analogy is to the language model of linguistic Structuralism; the enemy is uniformity). 9) Time must be rendered transparent: the architect must study early and other cultures, he must offer new interpretations of these experiences for our time and place; the architect must create from the fund of knowledge in his "imaginary museum." 10) Before everything else, the architect must consider the archetypal behavior of man in a community: in this concern he is similar to Structuralist anthropologists such as Lévi-Strauss.

All of Piet Blom's works are attempts to realize his Structuralist ideals.

Boerderij, his first Students Building at the Twente Technical University: although Blom converted an existing farm building and continued to work with gable roofs, he was able to demonstrate his own formal language. The way he has handled the interior space with its empty areas and sloping views under the roof, as well as his skillful use of brick, roof tiling and timber for the exterior, is remarkable. The individually set gabled windows provide a particular emphasis. The building is architectonically very fine.

Bastille, the second Students Building at Twente: the basic plan is an extendable web of regularly ordered construction elements within which space and an organized structure are arbitrarily articulated.

Spielhuis Leisure Center, with theatre, small halls and dwellings, in Helmond: it consists of cubes that stand on their corners. Because of the "utopian" nature of the project, the client asked for three trial prototypes. They were successful, and Blom used the shapes for the theatre in the centre of the town. Here he proved that the slanting walls and window areas were no formal joke but a way to promote spatial contact. The hall, painted like a circus tent, is also worthy of mention; so is the foyer, partly roofed in glass, the colorful interior decoration, and the clear structural organization. The dwellings are single cubes arranged around the theatre. Blom achieved a very successful work—with a delighted and critically engaged client.

Within the framework of a national experimental program, Blom tried to realize Aldo van Eyck's vision of the "casbah organisée" in his Kasbah Housing Development in Hengelo: it is perhaps his most vigorous attempt to realize the ideals of Structuralism. But, as the project was not built as originally planned, and as there is no polyvalent communica-

tion structure for the collective areas under the houses, it remains architectonically interesting but its success with regard to municipal diversity is impossible to judge.

What can be said is that Piet Blom is an original artist/architect who achieves his best work when his client is able to follow and, if necessary, influence his imaginative ideas. He has a predilection for sloping roofed buildings, natural materials and colors, and he has a command over the proportions of his individual architectonic forms.

—Arnulf Lüchinger

BLOMSTEDT, Aulis.

Finnish. Born in Jyväskylä, 28 July 1906. Educated at the Institute of Technology, Helsinki, under Armas Lindgren and Lisko Nyström, 1924–30, Dip. Arch. 1930. Served in the Finnish Army in Helsinki, 1931–32, Vatnuori, 1939–40, and Vuosalmi, 1941–44: Lieutenant; awarded Cross of Liberty 4th Class. Married Heidi Sibelius in 1932; children: Juhana, Petri, Anssi and Severi. In private practice, Finland, since 1945. Professor of Architecture (Public Buildings), Institute of Technology, Helsinki, 1958–66. Exhibitions (one-man): Museum of Finnish Architecture, Helsinki, 1962; *Aulis Blomstedt: Serigraphies,* Artek Gallery, Helsinki, 1973; *Aulis Blomstedt, Architecte: Pensée et Forme,* Fondation Le Corbusier, Paris, 1977. Recipient: State Award in Architecture, Finland, 1977. Honorary Member of SAFA (Finnish Architects Association), and of OR-NAMO (Finnish Designers Association). Address (office): Otsolahdentie 8, 02100 Espoo 10, Finland.

Works:

1930/
32   Tehtaanpuisto Church, Helsinki (competition project)
1939   Apartment building, Pihlajatie 52, Helsinki
1946   University Library, Turku, Finland (competition project)
     Sauna Rysä Kallio, Kirkkonummi, Finland
1947   Walhalla Fort Restaurant, Suomenlinna, Helsinki
1948   Villa Salonen, Espoo, Finland
     "Kenno" Industrial Housing System (project)
     Imperial Palace, Addis Ababa, Ethiopia (competition project)
1950   Saimaanhovi Club Building, Imatra, Finland
     Pedagogical Institute, Jyväskylä, Finland (competition project)
1951   Apartment building, Asesepänkatu, Turku, Finland
     Villa Therman, Tolkkinen, Finland
1954   "Ketju" Terrace Houses, Tapiola, Espoo, Finland
     Apartment building, Kolmirinne, Tapiola, Espoo, Finland
1955   Artists' Terrace Houses, Tapiola, Espoo, Finland
1956/
57   Apartment building, Nallenpolku, Tapiola, Espoo, Finland
1958   Aulis Blomstedt Studio, Tapiola, Espoo, Finland
     Concert Hall, Oslo, Norway (competition project)
1959   Workers Institute Annex, Helsinki
1960   Villa Pettersson, Helsinki
     Design of the *Finnish Architecture* exhibition, Stockholm and Warsaw
1961   Apartment building, Riistapolku, Tapiola, Espoo, Finland
1962   Terrace houses, Nelikko, Tapiola, Espoo, Finland
1963   Citadelle Experimental House, Norrköping, Sweden (project)

1964 Terrace houses, Leppäkertuntie, Tapiola, Espoo, Finland
Suvikumpu Housing Area, Tapiola, Espoo, Finland (competition project)

1965 Apartment buildings, Kaskenpaja ja Allakka, Tapiola, Espoo, Finland

1967 Congregational Hall, Kulosaari, Helsinki (competition project)

1968 Villa Stig Weckström, Espoo, Finland
Villa Bjorn Weckström, Espoo, Finland
Parish Center, Maaselkä, Finland

1969 Design of the *Finland in Louisiana* exhibition, Louisiana Museum, Humlebaek, Denmark
Cubic Exhibition Unit System
Boarding School for Handicapped Children, Kuutinharju, Finland

1970 Design of the *Finnish Architecture* exhibition, Minsk, U.S.S.R.

1971 Beaubourg Centre, Paris (competition project)
Villa Auramo, Bromarv, Finland
Church Reconstruction, Kulosaari, Finland

1972 Pollution-Free House (project)

1973 Small House Unit Study (project)
Cafeteria and Custodian's Apartment, Ainola, Järvenpää, Finland

1974 Puntarpää Apartment Building, Soukka, Espoo, Finland
Design of the *25th Anniversary Exhibition,* Museum of Finnish Architecture, Helsinki

1976 Storage and industrial building for a bank, Konala, Helsinki
Church Parish House Annex, Kulosaari, Finland

1978 Reconstruction plan for Walhalla Fort Restaurant, Suomenlinna, Helsinki

Publications:

By BLOMSTEDT: articles, in *Arkkitehti* (Helsinki) —"Eliel Saarinen," no. 11/12, 1943; "Paul Nelson: The Suspended House," no. 9/10, 1945; "The Post-War Reconstruction of the World and the Architects," no. 6, 1955; "The Architect's Place Today in the Community," no. 9, 1956; "The General Foundations of House Planning," no. 3, 1957; "Public Buildings and Tradition," no. 5, 1958; "The Problem of Form in Architecture," no. 12, 1958; "Measure and Proportion," no. 9, 1962; "Urbanization and the Landscape," no. 4, 1963; "The Fourth Dimension of Architecture," no. 12, 1964; "Architectural Research," no. 6, 1967; "Man—The Measure of Architecture," no. 2, 1971; "Architect Training—

From School into Life," no. 1, 1972; "Autonomy of Architecture," no. 5, 1974; "The ABC of Architecture," no. 3, 1978.

On BLOMSTEDT: book—*Aulis Blomstedt, Architecte: Pensée et Forme,* exhibition catalogue, edited by Juhani Pallasmaa, publication of the Museum of Finnish Architecture, Helsinki 1977.

My architecture aims at simplicity and clarity. I mean that in arranging forms I resort to as few basic geometric units as possible.

My plans for private family housing always take account of the resident's wishes.

Over a period of ten years I have developed a modular system (canon 60). It was first published in the magazine *Le Carre Bleu* in 1961. We use it, my assistant and I, in all projects. I always try to look for the largest square possible in the system for use as the basic module of the plan. The plan for a bank's central storage facilities (1976) consists of four squares of 48 metres each side. I pay particular attention to aesthetic proportions.

—Aulis Blomstedt

Aulis Blomstedt is one of Finland's most devoted students of the fundamental concepts of architecture and of shape and harmony.

He has created a theoretical basis for discussion of the aesthetic foundations and social applications of module systems. In the reconstruction period of the 1940's he devised an industrially-produced cell construction system. Since the 1950's he has concentrated mainly on a system of measurements based on the dimensions of the human body and on musical harmony.

Blomstedt's aim has been primarily to discover the fundamental laws of architecture, the laws that govern the dimensions of a building. His (often aphoristic) comments stress the importance of man, nature, and individual perception, but the ultimate object of his theoretical deliberations is the building itself, its plan and its model. His scale of materials is ascetic but often warm.

Whereas Blomstedt's work in the 1940's featured "romantic" applications of wood and stone, his work in the 1950's—for example, the row and apartment houses in Tapiola, or the Workers Institute Annex in Helsinki—shows a dominant tendency towards clear and simple space, and a perception of shape that follows from a pre-determined dimensional harmony. This trend continues in Blomstedt's later work. There are sometimes bold, rhythmic patterns

—yet they are always subject to an overall harmony.

Aulis Blomstedt emphasizes the importance of graphic composition in architecture. A graphic artist himself, he has also designed jewellery in silver and gold and has produced various works of graphic art.

—Pekka Suhonen

BO, Jørgen.

Danish. Born in Copenhagen, 8 April 1919. Educated at the Royal Danish Academy of Fine Arts School of Architecture, Copenhagen, 1936–41, Dip. Arch. 1941. Married Gerda Bennike in 1941 (divorced, 1966); children: Malene, Morten, Mikkel, and Marie. In private practice, Copenhagen, since 1943. Technical Consultant, Conservation Society, Denmark, 1946–52; Member, Conservation Board, Denmark, 1952–61. Teacher, 1946–59, Assistant Professor, 1959–60, and since 1960 Professor of Building Design, Royal Danish Academy School of Architecture. Member, Censorship Committee, Charlottenborg, Denmark, 1958–71; Member of the Committee, Slotsholmen, Copenhagen, 1961–63; Member, Management Committee, San Cataldo, Italy, 1966; Member, Governing Board, Danish Institute in Rome, 1968–70. Member of the Council, Royal Danish Academy, since 1959. Recipient: Lyngy-Taarbaek Municipality Award, 1948; Gladsaxe Municipality Award, 1955, 1956; The Wood Prize, Information Council of the Timber Trade, 1958; Eckersberg Medal, Royal Danish Academy of Fine Arts, 1959; Horsholm Municipality Award, 1962; Copenhagen Municipality Award, 1965; Award from the Committee for the Embellishment of the Capital, Copenhagen, 1965. Knight of the Dannebrog, 1966. Address (office): Hovedvagtsgade 2, 1103 Copenhagen K, Denmark.

Works:

1945/
58 Terrace housing developments (Stengårdsparken, Skoleparken, Hyrdeparken, and City of Pre-fabricated Houses), near Copenhagen (with Knud Halberg)

1958 The Louisiana Museum, Humlebaek, Denmark (with Vilhelm Wohlert)
Westminster Department Store, Copenhagen

1959 Design of the *House and Garden* Exhibition, Copenhagen (with Vilhelm Wohlert)

Aulis Blomstedt: Storage and industrial building for a bank, Konala, Helsinki, 1976   Jørgen Bo: The Louisiana Museum, Humlebaek, Denmark, 1958

"Elm House," Elmvej 11, Vedbaek, Denmark (with Vilhelm Wohlert)

Jensen House, Jacosmindevej 25, Humlebaek, Denmark

Design of the *Danish Design* Exhibition, Stockholm

Vime Supermarket, Århus, Denmark

1961 Blaagaard Teachers College and Enghavegaard Elementary School, Søborg, Denmark (with Karen and Ebbe Clemmensen)

Malmmose House, Ishøj, Denmark (with Vilhelm Wohlert)

1962 Andersen House, Rungsted, Denmark (with Vilhlem Wohlert)

Design of the *Egyptian Art* Exhibition, Louisiana Museum, Humlebaek, Denmark (with Vilhelm Wohlert)

Piniehøj Terrace Houses, Rungsted, Denmark (with Vilhelm Wohlert)

1963 Overgård House, Vedbaek, Denmark (with Vilhelm Wohlert)

Gyldendal Publishing Company Office/Dispatch Hall, Copenhagen (with Vilhelm Wohlert)

1964 Kirstineparken Terrace Houses, Hørsholm, Denmark

"Parade of Northern Houses," Norköping, Sweden (with Vilhelm Wohlert)

Lindevangsgården interiors, Birkerød, Denmark

1965 The Museum of Music History conversion, Copenhagen (with Vilhelm Wohlert)

1965/
67 Works for the Birkerød Municipality, Denmark

1967 Barfred House, Viborg, Denmark

1968 Louisiana Museum extension I, Humlebaek, Denmark (with Vilhelm Wohlert)

Schiøtz House, Tibirke, Denmark

1968/
73 Danish Embassy, Brasilia (with Vilhelm Wohlert)

I.B.M. Headquarters, Lundtofte, Denmark

1969/
75 Arthur K. Watson International Education Centre, I.B.M., La Hulpe, Belgium

1973/
76 Carlsberg Foundation and Royal Danish Academy of Science and Letters restoration and interiors, Copenhagen

1971/
78 Ny Carlsberg Glyptotek, Copenhagen (as supervising architect)

1966– Thorvaldsens Museum restoration, Copenhagen (as supervising architect)

1970– Danish Institute in Rome (as supervising architect)

1970/
79 Ancient Barrows of Jelling landscaping, Denmark

1972– Museum of the Castle of Sønderborg interiors, Denmark

1975/
79 Ministry of Cultural Affairs restoration, Åbenrå 26–30, Copenhagen

1976/
79 I.B.M. Office/School Building, Lundtofte, Denmark

1976– National Museum interiors, Copenhagen

1978– City Museum, Bochum, Germany (with Vilhelm Wohlert)

Louisiana Museum extension II, Humlebaek, Denmark (with Vilhelm Wohlert)

Publications:

On BO: book—*Dansk Arkitektur* by Tobias Faber, Copenhagen 1963, 1976; articles—"The Louisiana Museum" in *Arkitektur* (Copenhagen), 3 and 4, 1959; "Various works by Jørgen Bo" in *Arkitektur* (Copenhagen), no. 5, 1963; "The Museum of Music History" in *Arkitektur* (Copenhagen), no. 1, 1968; "Blaagaard Teachers College and Enghavegaard Elementary School" in *Arkitektur* (Copenhagen), no. 2, 1969; "Extension to the Louisiana Museum" in *Arkitektur* (Copenhagen), no. 6, 1973; "Watson Education Center, IBM Headquarters-Denmark, and The Danish Embassy in Brasilia" in *Arkitektur* (Copenhagen), no. 3, 1976.

*

To a great extent it has been my fate to deal with buildings placed in surroundings of scenic beauty. Adjusting the buildings to nature has consequently been a general theme in all my works. This applies not only to the choice of materials and their mutual connection with the locality but also to the way the shape of the building is adapted to local climatic conditions and to the proportions, rhythmics, and lines of the landscape. As a result, my working method has often been, before the actual projecting has begun, to mark out the buildings on the site in such a way that it is possible to form an estimate of the connection between the interiors and the landscapes immediately outside of them, as well as of the lines of the building in relation to the ground. This thesis is best reflected in the Louisiana Museum which is, in principle, a covered walk through a varied garden where the plan of the building expresses the rise and fall of the ground, and where large windows deliberately frame picturesque landscape topics, resulting in an unbroken dialogue between nature and art. However, in the more industrialized buildings, e.g. the buildings for I.B.M., the correlation with the surrounding landscape has also been of great importance to the projects.

The Danish Embassy in Brasilia has been built on ground falling steeply down towards an artificial sea, and the fall of the ground is the main motive in the general composition. The buildings have been placed on terraces, emphasizing the fall of the ground, and they have been given their special form—the relatively narrow depth of the houses and the very large projecting roofs—from the wish to produce a building milieu pleasant to live in, in this very warm area where rainfall is infrequent but heavy. It is the main principle of the buildings that all rooms should be naturally ventilated and completely protected against the sun. This means that sunblinds, Venetian blinds, and tinted glass can be avoided and that the sliding doors can be open practically 24 hours a day, covered only by mosquito curtains. This form of building has proved to be desirable in Brasilia, a city which is otherwise characterized by completely sealed up and artificially ventilated buildings where the change between the internal and external climate is violent and inconvenient.

An essential part of my production concerns museum buildings or museum arrangements. In this connection the correlation between the works of art, the building units, and the light plays an important role. The daylight lighting of museums is critical for the experience of the art. It is a very complicated study in which, in my opinion, the point is to find the most natural ways of lighting. These may vary a great deal, depending on the type of work in question: different forms of light-intake will result in different architectural expressions. The buildings are thus characterized either by large sidelights, by lantern constructions, or, as in the museum at Bochum, Germany, by tent-shaped skylight constructions through which an optimum lighting of the rooms is obtained without letting in any actual sunlight.

—Jørgen Bo

*

As a young architect, Jørgen Bo made himself known through architectural competitions, and early in his career he collaborated with the architect Knud Halberg on the design of a number of residential developments, chiefly one- and two-storey rowhouses situated in green spaces, with fine relations between dwellings and communal areas: even today these houses hold their own among the best and most advanced residential developments of the time.

Bo soon manifested his great interest in and sensitivity to Danish scenery and the relationship of house/housing development and town/surrounding area, whether he was dealing with open landscape or existing buildings. This interest found its finest expression in the Louisiana Museum, which he designed with Vilhelm Wohlert. Here a number of lowrise museum wings are integrated in undulating park grounds, with solitary large trees on a bankside sloping down to the Sound. In the Louisiana Museum, modern open-space architecture, carried out with traditional attention to detail and fine workmanship, is combined with the simplified, textural effect of whitewashed walls around large glazed areas and accentuated roof-bearing timber girders.

Alone or in collaboration with Wilhelm Wohlert, Bo has been in charge of the restoration and conversion of older buildings of high architectural quality: he has created delightful modern settings for new activities, yet always with a deep understanding of the distinctive character of the old buildings. Special mention should be made of the conversion of a former vicarage in central Copenhagen into The Museum of Music History and of the new exhibition rooms in Gottlieb Bindesbøll's Thorvaldsen Museum of the 1880's, one of the major works of Danish architecture.

Bo has also designed a series of attractive one-family houses of distinction, and in recent years he has been awarded major commissions outside Denmark—the Danish Embassy in Brasilia and the IBM Education Centre in Brussels. These are buildings expressive of the very finest qualities of Bo's talent: a simplified and well-defined functional arrangement within an architectural framework designed in harmony with the characteristics of the site and its environment, further enriched through the choice of materials and their textural treatment.

At an early stage of his career Jørgen Bo became a member of the teaching staff of Professor Palle Suenson's department of the School of Architecture of the Royal Danish Academy of Art. In 1960 he was made Professor of Building Design. Since then, by virtue of his forceful artistic personality and his profound engagement in the creative side of the architect's work, he has attracted many students and has become an inspiring teacher to future architects.

—Tobias Faber

BODIANSKY, Vladimir.

French. Born in Kharkov, Russia, 25 March 1894; emigrated to France, 1917: naturalized, 1929. Educated at the Institute of Bridges and Causeways, Moscow, 1911–14, Dip. Ing. 1914; Ecole Nationale Supérieure de l'Aéronautique, Paris, 1919–20, Dip. Ing. 1920. Served as a Cavalry Officer, then as a Pilot-Aviator, Tsarist Army, Russia, 1915–17; Officer, French Foreign Legion, 1918–20. Married Xenia Loukomsky in 1928; children: Vladimir and Michel-Noel. Worked as an engineer for the Highways Department, Moscow, and on the Bokhara-Kabul Railway, Afghanistan, 1914–15; Chief Section Engineer, Great Lakes Railway, and Master-Planner, Town of Albertville, Lake Tanganyika, Congo, 1921–23; Engineer/Designer, Renault Car Company Research Center, Paris, 1923–24, and Caudron Aeroplane Company, Paris, 1924–25; Managing Director, Francois Villiers Aeroplanes, Paris, 1925–30; Director, Bodiansky Aeroplane Company, Paris, 1930–31; in private architectural/engineering practice, collaborating with Eugène Beaudouin and Marcel Lods, Paris, 1931–39; Managing Director, Mopin and Company, Paris, and Leeds, Yorkshire, England, 1933–39; Director, Department of Special Studies, Messier Technical Center, Pau, France, 1940–44; Member, French Town Planning and Housing Mission to the United States, 1945–46; Founder Member, 1946–49, and

Director, 1949–66, ATBAT (Atelier des Bâtisseurs), Marseilles. Professor and Studio Master (Atelier Camelot-Bodiansky), Ecole Nationale Supérieure des Beaux-Arts, Paris, 1965–66. Adviser, Monnet Plan, Paris, 1946–47; Technical Consultant, United Nations Building Committee, New York, 1947; Technical Consultant to the town of Sabende, French Guinea, 1959–61; Technical Adviser, French Polar Stations at Adelaide Island, Antarctica and Arctic Greenland, and to High Altitude Stations in the Andes, 1954–59; Technical Adviser, United Nations Missions to Cambodia, 1961–63; Co-Rapporteur, United Nations Urban Development and City Planning Committee, Geneva, 1961–66. European Vice-President, Permanent Commission on Industrialization, CIAM (Congrès Internationaux d'Architecture Moderne), 1949–66; Vice-President, Cercle d'Etudes Architecturales, Paris, 1953–55; President, Interconsult (consulting engineers group), The Hague, 1956–57; Member of the General Council, ICRPD (International Center for the Development of Overseas Territories), Paris, 1962–66. Recipient: Gold Medal, Society for the Encouragement of Arts and Industry, France, 1959. Chevalier, Légion d'Honneur. *Died* (in Paris) *10 December 1966.*

Works:

1914/
15 Bokhara-Kabul Railway constructions, Afghanistan
1920/
23 Great Lakes Railway constructions, Congo
    Plan for Albertville, Lake Tanganyika, Congo
    Furnaces, coal-mines, brickworks, plan for a river highway, etc., Congo
1924 "C.99" Reconnaissance Airplane, for the Caudron Company, Paris
1925/
30 Sea-Plane Prototypes, for the Francois Villiers Company, Paris
    Bodiansky Prototype Airplane, Paris
1933 Palais des Expositions, Paris (project; with Eugène Beaudouin and Marcel Lods)
1934 Cité de la Muette (housing development), Drancy, France (with Eugène Beaudouin and Marcel Lods)
1936 Circular Aircraft Hangar (project; with Marcel Lods)
1937 Quarry Hill Housing Estate, Leeds, Yorkshire, England (with R. A. H. Livett)
1937/
38 Suspended Highways (projects; with Azivessy and Nitzshke)
1939 Maison du Peuple, Clichy, Paris (with Eugène Beaudouin, Marcel Lods and Jean Prouvé)
1941/
42 Schmidt Telescope, and Equatorial Telescope, Pic-du-Midi Observatory, Bagneres, France
1946/
49 Unité d'Habitation (Cité Radieuse), Marseilles (with Le Corbusier)
1947/
49 France-U.S.A. Memorial Hospital, Saint-Lô, France (as technical consultant to Paul Nelson)
1951/
55 Musulman Collective Housing Development, Casablanca (with Georges Candilis and Shadrach Woods)
1952/
54 Master plan for Casablanca (with Georges Candilis and Shadrach Woods)
1954/
59 Plans for polar stations at Adelaide Island, Antarctica, and Greenland
    Igloo building for Paul-Emil Victor Polar Expedition
    High Altitude Observatory Station for Andes Expeditions (project)

1956/
61 Housing development, Bagnols-sur-Cèze, France (with Georges Candilis and Alexis Josic)
1959 Town development plan for Annassers, Algeria (with André Gomis)
1959/
61 Town plan for Sabende, French Guinea (as technical consultant)
    Urban development plans and buildings, French Guinea
    Redevelopment plan for the Dame-Blanche, Paris (with J. de Chalender)
1961/
63 South-Asia Olympic Stadium Complex, Phnom-Penh, Cambodia (with Van Moly Van, Um Samouth, Duchemin, Morin and Kandaouroff)
    Plans for various cities in Cambodia

Publications:

By BODIANSKY: book—*Chart de l'Habitat du Cercle d'Etudes Architecturales,* Paris 1957.

On BODIANSKY: book—*Dizionario Enciclopedico di Architettura e di Urbanistica,* edited by Paolo Portoghesi, Rome 1968; article— "The Work of Vladimir Bodiansky" by Marion Tournon Brahly, in *Architectural Design* (London), January 1965.

Vladimir Bodiansky was one of the most interesting, complex, exciting and extraordinary personalities among architects and builders in France from the 1930's to the 1960's. He took part in and influenced, directly or indirectly, a very large number of the most important achievements of this period.

Bodiansky was born in Kharkov in 1894; he received a higher technical education until it was interrupted by the war. As a young officer in the Tsarist Army he was forced to emigrate during the October Revolution. After an eventful journey across Siberia and China he returned to Europe and, like thousands of other White Russians, finally settled in Paris. During the 1920's he entered the Ecole Nationale Supérieure de l'Aéronautique in Paris and became an aircraft builder. Young and enthusiastic, he wanted to revolutionize everything. His aircraft were distinctive in their originality; they announced a new wave before its time. After many difficulties, he abandoned everything and went off to the Belgian Congo to work on the construction of the railway. When he returned to France he worked again in aeronautics, then in the 1930's he turned to building construction as Chief Engineer for "Mopin" prefabrication processes. He directed the construction of the very important Quarry Hill Housing Estate in Leeds, England. Meanwhile, he had become acquainted with architecture and architects, in particular the team of Beaudouin and Lods. He had finally found his true vocation.

Bodiansky collaborated, as engineer, with the team of Beaudouin/Lods on several studies and completed works, among which were the project for the Palais des Exposition (Paris) in glass and steel; a project for a circular aircraft hangar; and, in 1934, the Cité de la Muette in Drancy, an entirely prefabricated housing development—an event of some importance at that time.

During the Second World War Bodiansky met Le Corbusier, and together they assembled a team of architects and engineers, so that they might respond effectively to the problems of post-war reconstruction. Bodiansky was now convinced that the enormous demands of our time needed new skills and a new structuring of the profession of architect. He sought to combine the talents of architects, engineers and builders. This goal led to the birth of the Atelier des Bâtisseurs—ATBAT—which he founded with Le Corbusier, Wogensky, Lefèvre and the entrepreneur Py—builders like the German master builders of the Middle Ages.

As soon as the war was over Bodiansky took part in a study mission to the United States and recognized the enormous technical progress that the war had brought about in that country. Returning to France in 1946, he joined Le Corbusier to devote himself entirely to the first important achievement of ATBAT, the Cité Radieuse in Marseilles. For three years without a break the very happy collaboration continued: if it was Le Corbusier who spiritually conceived the Cité Radieuse, it was Bodiansky who was entirely responsible for its technical realization—a striking example of co-operation between architect and engineer. During this same period he accompanied Le Corbusier to New York to plan the United Nations Building: Bodiansky's participation in the team and his influence were most crucial. But at the end of the 1940's Le Corbusier withdrew from ATBAT. The collaboration of these two strong and extremely different personalities had led to an inevitable conflict.

Bodiansky continued to direct ATBAT's activities, which became more and more varied and important; it went on to produce polar habitat for Paul-Emil Victor; the France-U.S.A. Memorial Hospital at Saint-Lô, with the architect Paul Nelson; Musulman Collective Housing Development in Morocco, with the writer and Shadrach Woods; and many other noteworthy works. Among Bodiansky's personal achievements the Olympic Stadium in Pnom Penh is particularly outstanding.

Bodiansky also took part in all the activities and international conferences in the field of architecture and urbanism. In 1953 at the CIAM Congress in Aix-en-Provence he proposed a Habitat Charter that included ideas and suggestions that are still topical and valid today.

Towards the end of his life he devoted himself mainly to teaching: as Professor at the Ecole Nationale Supérieure des Beaux-Arts, he created the Bodiansky Atelier where he tried to define the necessary qualifications and skills of an architect for our time, a new kind of man who, like himself, combined the spiritual with the material, sensitivity with technical knowledge, the dream with the reality—in short, the synthesis of architect and engineer.

—Georges Candilis

BOFILL Levi, Ricardo.
Spanish. Born in Barcelona, 5 December 1939. Educated at the French Institute of Barcelona, until 1955; Escuela Tecnica Superior de Arquitectura, Barcelona, 1955–56; Architecture University of Geneva, 1957–60. Founded Taller de Arquitectura, Barcelona, 1960. Exhibitions: *Biennale,* Venice, 1976; Centre Georges Pompidou, Paris, 1978; *Setmanes Catalanes a Berlin,* Berlin, 1978; Museum of Modern Art, New York, 1979. Recipient: ADI-FAD Prize, Barcelona, 1964; Fritz Schumacher Prize, University of Hamburg, 1968; International Design Award, American Society of Interior Designers, 1978. Address: Taller de Arquitectura, Avenida de la Industria 14, Sant Just D'Esvern, Barcelona, Spain.

Works:

1960 La Elviria Urban Development, Malaga (project)
1960/
62 Rubiol Apartment Building, Calle J. S. Bach 28, Barcelona
1961 Autorremolques Industrial Building, Tarragona, Spain
1962/
63 Bargallo Apartment Building, Calle Urgel, Barcelona
    Sargazo Holiday Apartments, Castelldefels, Spain

1962/
64 Ventura Apartment Building, Calle Vilado-
mat, Barcelona
Andreu Apartment Building, Calle Maestro
P. Cabrero, Barcelona
1963 La Manzanera Resort Complex Master Plan,
Calpe, Spain (project)
1963/
65 Schenkel Apartment Building, Calle Nicaragua 99, Spain
1964/
65 Apartment house, Calle J. S. Bach 4, Barcelona
1964/
72 Barrio Gaudi Residential Complex, Reus,
Spain
1965/
66 La Manzanera Apartment Building, Calpe,
Spain
1965/
68 El Castell Apartment Building, Vallpineda,
Sitges, Spain
1966 Riomar Hotel, Delta del Ebro, Spain (project)
1966/
67 Chemical factory, Granollers, Spain
Mas-Pey Swimming Club, San Feliu de Guixols, Spain
La Manzanera (Xanadu) Apartment House,
Calpe, Spain
1967/
68 La Manzanera Housing, Calpe, Spain
1968/
69 CEEX-1 City in Space, Madrid (project)
1968/
71 La Manzanera Housing II, Calpe, Spain
1968/
73 La Muralla Roja Holiday Apartments, Calpe,
Spain
1969 El Caballo de Monte Carlo Multi-Sports Facility, Montecarlo, Concurso, Spain (project)
1969/
71 Urban, rural and residential proposal, Chile
(project)
1970/
75 Walden 7 Residential Complex, Sant Just
Desvern, Barcelona
1971/
72 Civic Centre, Evry, France (competition project)
1971/
73 La Petite Cathedrale Residential ·Complex,
Cergy-Pontoise, France (project)
1972 CEEX-1 City in Space reorganization, Madrid (project)
1972/
73 La Citadelle renovations, Fort St. Cyr,
Trappes, St. Quentin en Yvelines, France
(project)
1972/
76 Country house, Montras, Calella, Spain
1973 La Maison d'Abraxas Residential Complex,
St. Quentin en Yvelines, France (project)
Assis Home for the Aged, Sabadell, Spain
(project)
Champs Elysées/La Defénse Urban Study,
Paris (project)
Forum Blanch Civic Centre, Paris (project)
1973/
74 Hotel, St. Quentin en Yvelines, France (project)
1973/
76 La Fabrica Cement Factory remodelling
(Taller de Arquitectura offices), Sant Just
Desvern, Barcelona
1973/
78 Meritxell Religious Centre, Andorra, Spain
1974 La Maison Verte, Abidjan, Ivory Coast,
Africa (project)
1974/
75 Point "M" Civic Centre, Paris (project)
Urban master plan for Carros, Spain (project)
Urban master plan for Cala Ratjada, Palma,

Majorca, Spain (project)
1974/
76 Le Parc de la Marca Hispanica Monument,
Le Boulou-Le Perthus, France
1975 Cemetery at Montcada, Spain (competition
project)
1975/
76 Le Lac Residential Complex, Trappes, St.
Quentin en Yvelines, France
Le Couloubrier Residential Complex, St.
Maxime, France (project)
Central Plaza, St. Maxime, France (project)
Harbour at St. Maxime, France (project)
1976 La Petite Cathedrale Residential and Commercial Complex, Meaux, France (project)
Les Illetes Luxury Tourist Complex, Palma,
Majorca, Spain (project)
Prefabricated apartments, Guatemala (project)
Concurso Master Plan, Vitoria, Spain (project)
Castro-Urdiales Master Plan, Bilbao, Spain
(project)
1977 Residential complex with park and institutional buildings, Bilbao, Spain (project)
San Juan Despi District Plan, Barcelona (project)
Santa Maria de Gallecs New Town, Barcelona (project)
1978 Socialist village at Abadla, Bechar, Algeria

Publications:

By BOFILL: books—*Hacia una Formalizacion de la
Ciudad en el Espacio,* Barcelona 1970; *L'Architecture d'un Homme,* Paris 1978; films—*Circles,* with
the Taller, Barcelona 1966; *Schizo,* with the Taller,
Barcelona 1970.

On BOFILL: books—*Architecture 2000* by Charles
Jencks, London 1971; *Taller de Arquitectura* by Jose
Agustin Goytisolo, Barcelona 1977; articles—in
Forum (Hilversum, Netherlands), June 1968,
July/August 1969, November 1969, May 1971;
Baumeister (Munich), June 1968, October 1969;
Nouvel Observateur (Paris), October 1974, June/Au-
gust 1975; *Architectural Design* (London), July
1968, March 1970, August 1971; *Bauen und
Wohnen* (Zurich), June 1971; *Architektur und
Wohnform* (Stuttgart), November 1971; *Architec-
tural Review* (London), November 1973; "Espuisses
pour Les Halles" in *L'Oeil* (Lausanne), March 1975;
Progressive Architecture (New York), September
1975; *Technique et Architecture* (Paris), October
1975; "Versailles pour le peuple" in *Architecture
d'Aujourd'hui* (Paris), November/December 1975,
October 1976; *Architecture + Urbanism* (Tokyo),
December 1976; films—*Barrio Gaudi* by Hans Magnus Enzesberger, 1971; *Urbanisme et Desarroi* by J.
Darribehande and J. P. About, 1971; *Taller de Arquitectura* by Robert Cordier, 1976.

The Taller de Arquitectura is a multi-disciplinary
group involved in proposals and solutions for physical design problems within a broad spectrum of environmental issues. The atelier, which I founded in
1962, rapidly developed to include people from architectural, artistic, literary, musical, philosophical
and mathematical fields. These varied backgrounds
and experiences provide the diversity of viewpoints
which is essential to the philosophy and work of the
Taller. However, the perception and meaning of
physical form as a container of life lie at the center
of the firm's approach.

Physical form is viewed by the Taller also within
its wider political-cultural context. The failure of the
"modern movement" to evoke or include this wider
context is evident. The continued degradation of the
landscape under the principles of the "modern
movement" demonstrates that "functionalism" is a
necessary but insufficient response to the problem.
Man requires a context for social activities which
cannot be defined solely in terms of use. As Adolf

Loos wrote, "Architecture provokes spiritual reactions in man . . . the mission of architects is to make
these explicit." The use of "zoning" as a method for
analyzing social structures and built form is another
example of this failure to include the political-cultural context of the physical world. The results are
shallow environments, devoid of the rich fabric of
social interaction and meaning. It leads to an unnatural division of human activities because of its concentration on the functional relationship between a
few aspects of life. These factors, plus the lack of
personal involvement in decisions concerning one's
surroundings, lead to the well-documented loss of
aesthetic dimension and the lack of interaction with
one's physical world.

The Taller, through its research of these immediate problems, has developed various alternative solutions aimed at regaining the now-ignored quality and
value of life. A relationship between social reality
and urban and architectural forms has always existed. Thus the Taller's solutions have been created
intentionally both within the existing milieu and
with the assumption of a change in present conditions. The Taller has so defined a new position for
itself in its efforts to perceive and bring to reality new
possibilities of physical form. Obviously, creativity,
imagination and logical reasoning are the bases for
the transformation of the environment. However,
the physical designer needs new methods of synthesis to control the contradictions inherent in the work
and to reach for new forms. The designer also has the
responsibility to provide the mediating framework to
coordinate specialists working towards the improvement of the landscape. Through the achievement of
this synthesis and through the research of the Taller,
several basic concepts, or tenets, have been explored.
These have then been further defined, and given
physical form in the projects themselves.

The first of these is the generation, through a logical, abstract and recursive process, of a fabric internal to a building or complex. This is derived from the
organization of space in a traditional settlement of
the Mediterranean. Dwelling units of varying sizes
are arranged in a three-dimensional grid to form the
complementary open spaces at all levels including
streets, squares, promenades, and forums. This process is exemplified in Barrio Gaudi in Reus or La
Muralla Roja at Calpe, and especially in City in
Space, a generic study for a Mediterranean town,
and in Walden 7 in the suburbs of Barcelona, which
offers clear implications for the fabric in surrounding
areas, which is as yet unstructured.

The Taller also has been involved in research on
architectural objects as signs and symbols. The
church, the castle, and the monument have functioned historically to give orientation and identity to
an urban place. This led the Taller to a re-examination of these forms in terms of more contemporary
activities. La Petite Cathedrale in Cergy-Pontoise is
an explicit example of this. The forms and elements
of the gothic cathedral provided the inspiration for
a linear development of residential, commercial and
other uses intermingled along a covered street. Another example is La Citadelle and Abraxas in St.
Quentin en Yvelines. In this a military fortress was
re-used by converting it into an assemblage of dwellings and hotel-complex. It formed a symbolic linear
fabric and created an imposing environmental feature.

A concern of the firm has always been the common, public space. Thus the study of the generation
of architectural volumes, which can only form ultimately enclosed space, naturally led to the investigation of the negative space created by the volumes.
The goal has been the development of a new typology of urban tissue based on the ambience of the
Medieval, Renaissance, and Baroque examples of
street, square and open space. This aspect began with
the project for the structuring of the center of the
new Nanterre. The Taller also has been able to take
advantage of exceptional situations to produce examples such as Vitoria, Castro Nova, and
Echevarria, Bilbao, all in the north of Spain. This

Ricardo Bofill: La Muralla Roja Holiday Apartments, Calpe, Spain, 1973

interest in shaping open space has also led to projects in completely rural settings. The concern in these cases has been the shaping of the environment on a monumental scale to give significance to place. "El Pont de Meritxell" is a cultural, religious, and recreational center in Andorra, which forms a linear structure linking two sides of the major valley. It is part path, part bridge and part viaduct to mark the location of the patron saint of the principality. "Le Parc de la Marca Hispanica" is a symbolic pyramid on the French-Spanish border in homage to Cataluna.

Finally, the Taller has been involved in the preservation and regeneration of existing urban fabrics, and improvements to the city center. The proposal for Les Halles in Paris is basically the return to an ambience that could have existed originally when the neighborhood, Le Marais, was built. Unfortunately, the task was begun after the old pavilions were already demolished.

The offices for the firm, which were renovated from an old cement factory, are the most recent example of this line of work.

—Ricardo Bofill

The key to Ricardo Bofill's work is imagination. The strong, clear image of a central architectural idea permeates the whole design process. This process is, in itself, of almost child-like simplicity, based on the possible permutations of aggregating modular spaces that together give a built form to the image of the initial idea. Other conditioning factors—structural and constructive problems, building regulations, costs—are "subtracted" from the primary image, so that the form is eroded by these conditions rather than occurring as a result of them. Imagination and vision are given primacy of place, reviving the cultural role of architecture in society. That this revival takes physical rather than literary form makes Bofill's ideas interesting. He has managed to get his ideas built, first through family backing, then later

through agile and persuasive political maneuvering, disarming the opposition through personal charm, artistic conviction and hard teamwork.

Bofill is not an academic; he failed to complete his professional training at both the Barcelona School of Architecture and at Geneva, and this probably explains his fresh amateur approach to architecture and his surprising nonchalance about details and finishes, sadly reflected in the rather fragile durability and weathering of his buildings—like his low-cost housing, Barrio Gaudi in Reus, or his apartments in Sitges. As a result of designing from mainly models and large perspective drawings, the joints of his buildings and the joining of different materials are often crude and primitive—like the sanctuary of Meritxell in Andorra. This indifference to detail sometimes makes his buildings seem like full-size models, with abundant redundancies, cardboard images, as in the red-coloured apartments La Muralla Roja in Calpe.

Bofill's own explanations of his work should be treated with care as they are generally tactical and meant for the gallery. His work has a far more serious content: the role of architecture as a generator of urban spaces. In this role architecture must be clear and easily understood by the public, and there is no doubt that Bofill's proposals for Les Halles redevelopment in Paris contained all the elements for easy assimilation, with a formal, almost "beaux arts," layout and repetitive facades and galleries with their historical connotations.

These historical connotations are seldom absent in his work and are somewhat disconcerting. The modern movement in architecture has not, up to now, accommodated an eclectic decoration whimsically, albeit intelligently, applied, in order to obtain certain theatrical effects upon the urban stage. Bofill's vocabulary is, in this respect, extraordinarily wide, dipping into both history and geography for inspiration —Egypt for Walden 7 and neo-Gothic for his renovation of the cement factory next door. This re-use

of historical languages may be part of the modern movement's maturity, or part of "post-modern" architecture, but in Bofill's non-academic hands it appears as a provocatively polemical element.

Bofill's early buildings in the mid-1960's—the apartment houses in Barcelona, a number of private houses, a chemical factory near Granollers—fall clearly into the so-called "School of Barcelona" (neo-realist, brutalist, with strong inspiration in constructive detailing from the Modernisme architects in Barcelona at the turn of the century). The housing at Reus and the apartments at Sitges show the result of his model-making approach to design. Both projects pay for innovations by some very awkward spaces and places but these flaws are easily compensated for by the innate feeling of identity and ingenious play between public and private open areas. Walden 7, his utopian village in the sky, is an impressive tour-de-force, and makes a valid claim that architecture may yet be able to solve the problems of multi-storey dwellings.

—David Mackay

Dominikus Böhm: Caritas Institute Hospital Church of St. Elisabeth, Hohenlinde, Cologne, 1932

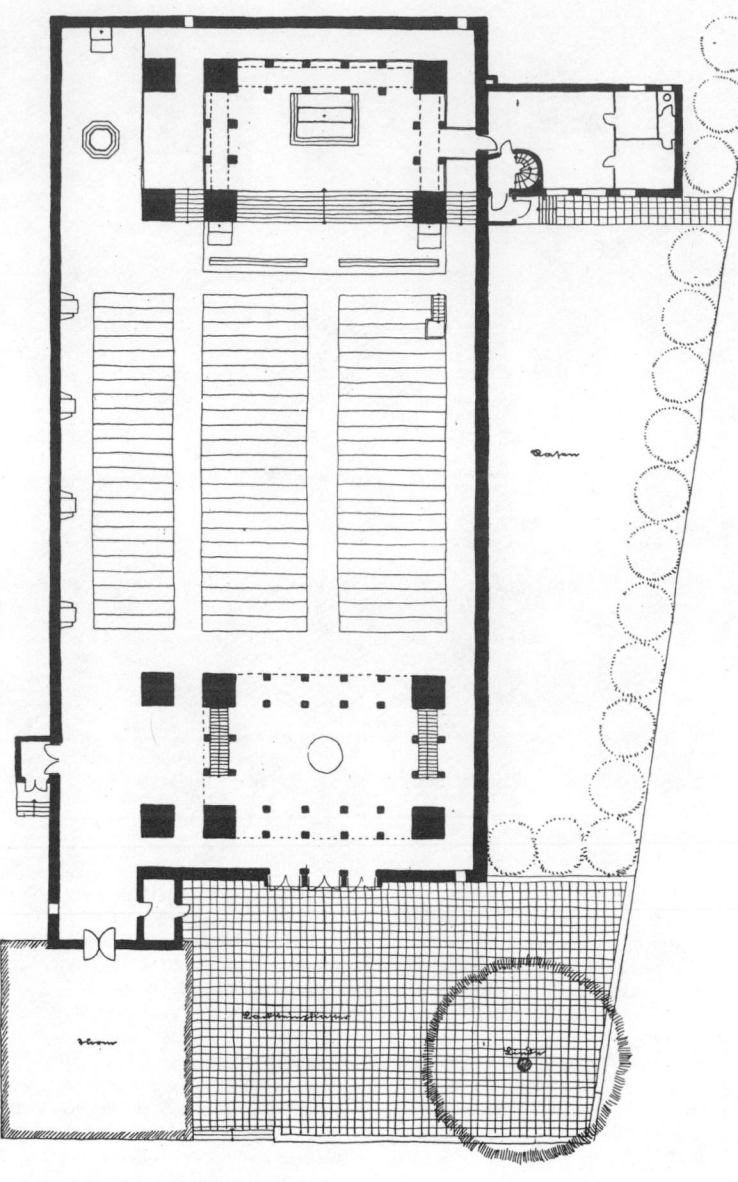

BOHIGAS Guardiola, Oriol.

Spanish. Born in Barcelona, 20 December 1925. Educated at the Escuela Tecnica Superior de Arquitectura, Barcelona, 1943–51, Dip.Arch. 1951, Dr.Arch. 1963; studied town planning at the Instituto de Estudios de la Administracion Local, Barcelona, 1961. Served in the Spanish Army, Campamento de la Granja, Segovia, 1946–47. Married Isabel Arnau in 1957; children: Gloria, Maria, Eulalia, Pere, and Josep. In partnership with Josep Martorell, *q.v.,* Barcelona, since 1951, and with Martorell and David Mackay, *q.v.,* Barcelona, since 1962. Director, Spanish Technical Office of Jespersen Prefabricated Systems, Barcelona, since 1972. Professor of Architectural Composition since 1971, and Director since 1977, Escuela Tecnica Superior de Arquitectura, Barcelona. Visiting Professor, Universidad Autonoma, Mexico City, and the College of Architecture, La Plata, Cordoba, and Rosario, Mexico, 1974, and Ball State University, Muncie, Indiana, 1976. Head of the Historial Archive, Colegio de Arquitectos de Cataluña, Barcelona, 1969; Member of the Editorial Board, *Arquitecturas Bis,* Barcelona, 1974; Editor, *Lotus,* Milan, 1975. Founder-Member, Grupo R, Barcelona, 1951. Recipient:

Biennial Prize, 1968, and Puig i Cadafalch Prize, 1970, Colegio de Arquitectos de Cataluña, Barcelona. Corresponding Member, Colegio de Arquitectos de Venezuela, 1976. Address: Martorell-Bohigas-Mackay, Camp 61, Barcelona 6, Spain.

Publications:

By BOHIGAS: books—*Un Segle de Vida Catalana,* with others, Barcelona 1960; *Tres Ensayos Polemicos sobre la Pintura de Todo,* with others, edited by Joaquín Horta, Barcelona 1961; *Llibre de l'Any 1962,* with others, Barcelona 1962; *Tres Ensayos sobre de A. Cardona Torrandell,* with others, Barcelona 1963; *Barcelona entre el Pla Cerda y el Barraquisme,* Barcelona 1963; *Llibre de l'Any 1963,* with others, Barcelona 1964; *Plan Especial de Ordenacion de la Zona Sudoeste de Montjuich,* with others, Barcelona 1967; *Architectura Modernista,* Barcelona 1968, Turin 1969; *Les Escoles Tecniques Superiors y la Estructura Profesional,* Barcelona 1968; *Contra una Arquitectura Adjetivada,* Barcelona 1969; *La Arquitectura Española de la Segunda Republica,* Barcelona 1970; *Polemica d'Arquitectura Catalana,* Barcelona 1970; *Proceso y*

Erotica del Diseño, Barcelona 1972; *Reseña y Catalogo de la Arquitectura Modernista,* Barcelona 1972; *The Anti-Rationalists,* with others, edited by Nikolaus Pevsner and J. M. Richards, London 1973; *Once Arquitectos,* Barcelona 1976; *Cataluñya: Arquitectura y Urbanisme durant la Republica,* Barcelona and Bari, Italy 1978.

See MARTORELL, BOHIGAS, MACKAY

BÖHM, Dominikus.

German. Born in Jettingen, 23 October 1880. Educated at the Technische Hochschule, Stuttgart, under Theodor Fischer. Served in the Germany Army, 1918. Married Maria Schreiber; children: Anton, Paul, and the architect Gottfried Böhm, *q.v.* In private practice, Cologne, 1903–52; in partnership with his son Gottfried, in Cologne, 1952 until his death, 1955. Professor, Kunstgewerbeschule, Offenbach, Germany, 1914–26, and Kölner Werkschule, Cologne, 1926–35, 1945–50. Recipient: First Prize, International Cathedral Competition, San Salvador, 1953. Commander, Order of St. Sylvester, Vatican, 1953. *Died* (in Cologne) *3 August 1955.*

Works:

1903 Kindergarten, Jettingen, Germany
     Herzog Guest House, Jettingen, Germany
1904 Garden Building for Karl Böhm House, Maximilianstrasse, Bad Reichenhall, Germany
1908 Design of the *Deutscher Künstlerbund Exhibition,* Darmstadt
1909 Catholic church, Ürdingen, near Krefeld, Germany (project)
     Catholic church, Memmingen, Germany (project)
1910 Gymnasium, Wettenhausen, Germany
1911 House, Kurfürstenstrasse, Bingen am Rhein, Germany
     Church, Wriezen, Brandenburg, Germany (project)
1912 Walter Villa, Offingen, Germany
1913 Zimmer House, Blumenstrasse, Offenbach am Main, Germany
     Mayer House, Taunusring, Offenbach am Main, Germany
     Tomb for Clemens Böhm, Jettingen Cemetery, Germany
1914 St. Magdalena Catholic Parish Church, Nymphenburg, Munich (2 projects)
     St. Josef's Catholic Church, Offenbach, Germany (project)
     Seashore Hospital for the South Seas (project)
     Government Building, Cameroons (project)
     House, German South-East Africa (project)
     Catholic Church of the Heavenly Glory (project)
1915 Catholic church renovation, Offenbach am Main, Germany (project)
     House renovation and Chapel, for Baroness Gumppenberg, Bad Reichenhall, Germany
1918 Catholic Garrison and Sister-Church, Parish of St. John the Baptist, Neu-Ulm, Germany (project)
     St. Elisabeth's Catholic Parish Church, Donau, Ulm, Germany (project)
     War Memorial, Pfauen Island, Lake Havelsee, Germany (project)
     Hotel, Luisenbad, Bad Reichenhall, Germany
1919 Harbour-Site Monastery and Church (project)
     St. Josef's Catholic Church, Offenbach am Main, Germany (project)

1920 Temporary Church of St. Josef, Offenbach am Main, Germany (demolished, 1947)
Catholic Chapel alterations, Heisterbacher-rott, Germany

1922 Catholic Church, Rhineland (project)
Tomb for Leonhard Thoma, Jettingen, Germany
Hotel rebuilding, Maria Laach, Germany

1923 Church of the Light of Christ (2 projects)
War Memorial Church, Göttingen, Germany (project)

1924 Munsterplatz Development, Ulm, Germany (project)
St. Josef's Catholic Church, Offenbach am Main, Germany (2nd project)

1925 Church with the Parabolic Vault (2 projects)
Monastery by the Sea (project)
St. Boniface Catholic Church, Frankfurt-Sachsenhausen am Main, Germany (project)
St. Josef's Catholic Church, Offenbach am Main, Germany (3rd project)

1926 Catholic Church of Christ the King, Bischofsheim, Mainz, Germany
St. Petrus Canisius Catholic Church, Offenbach am Main, Germany (project)
St. Martin's Catholic Church, Nuremberg, Germany (project)

1927 St. John the Baptist Catholic Parish Church and War Memorial, Neu-Ulm, Germany
Church enlargement, Grosswelzheim am Main, Germany
Catholic Church, Wiesdorf, near Leverkusen, Germany (project)
Church of the Three Kings, Bickendorf, Cologne (competition project)

1928 Catholic village church, Frielingsdorf, Germany
Catholic Church of Christ the King, Kuppersteg, Leverkusen, Germany
Mumbauer House, Bad Kreuznach, Germany
Catholic Chapel of the Immaculate Conception, *Presse Exhibition,* Cologne

1929 Catholic village church rebuilding, Freihalden, Germany
Hospital extension, Lindlar, Germany
St. Kamillusplatz Development, Hindenburg in Oberschlesien, Germany (2 projects)
Technical School, Hindenburg in Oberschlesien, Germany
Workers' Welfare Centre and Church and Monastery of St. Kamillus, Hindenburg in Oberschlesien, Germany
Kamillianer College, Berlin (project)
Cenotaph, Annaberg in Oberschlesien, Germany (project)
Catholic village church, near Pfaffenhofen, Germany (project)

1930 Kolping Works General Secretariat, Kolpingplatz, Cologne
Catholic Church, Gleiwitz in Obserschlesien, Germany (project)
Catholic village church extensions, Birken bei Wissen/Sieg, Germany
St. Elisabeth's Church Facade and Porchway, Hagen, Germany

1931 St. Kamillus Monastery, Church and Asthma Clinic, Monchen-Gladbach, Germany
Seminary, Limburg an der Lahn, Germany
St. Josef's Catholic Church, Hindenburg in Oberschlesien, Germany
Zanders Paper Factory, Bergisch-Gladbach, Germany
Catholic Church, Norderney, Germany
St. Wolfgang Catholic Parish Church, Kumpfmuhl, Regensburg, Germany (project)
Catholic Church, Geilenkirchen, Germany

1932 Caritas Institute Hospital Church of St. Elisabeth, Hohenlinde, Cologne
St. Engelbert Catholic Parish Church, Riehl, Cologne

Church, Marienberg im Westerwald, Germany
Dominikus Böhm House, Marienburg, Cologne

1933 Catholic Parish Church of the Holy Cross, Osnabruck-Schinkel, Germany
Art Gallery, Old Botanical Gardens, Munich (3 projects)
St. Francis Catholic Parish Church, Rheydt-Geneicken, Germany

1934 Country Youth House, Voiswinkel, near Bergisch-Gladbach, Germany
Spahn Building, Kaiser-Wilhelm-Ring, Cologne (project)
Savings Bank, Meppen an der Ems, Germany (project)
Dr. Scheiber Memorial, Vocklamarkt, Germany
Franciscan Church and Monastery, Garnstock, near Eupen, Belgium
Village church, Lohne in Niedersachsen, Germany (project)
Catholic village church, Hallgarten in der Rheinpfalz, Germany (project)

1935 City Hall, Augsburg, Germany (project)
Central Garage, Cologne (project)
Catholic Church, Marienburg, Cologne (2 projects)
St. Marien Catholic Church, Nordhorn-Frenswegen, Germany

1936 St. Engelbert Catholic Parish Church, Essen
Catholic Parish Church of the Heart of Jesus, Neustadt, Germany
Village church, Ringenberg, near Wesel, Germany
St. Wolfgang's Catholic Parish Church, Regensburg-Kumpfmuhl, Germany (project)
Elementary school, Borger, near Meppen, Germany
Catholic Church, Duisburg, Germany (project)

1937 St. Josef's Catholic Parish Church, Lingen-Laxten, Germany
Catholic Church of the Holy Cross, Bocholt, Westphalia, Germany
Baptismal Chapel for the Catholic Church of St. Marien, Mulheim/Ruhr, Germany
Temporary church, Marl, near Recklinghausen, Germany (project)
Catholic Church, Werne an der Lippe, Germany (project)
Catholic Church, Velbert, Rheinland, Germany (project)
"Heimat Church, Timbu, Brazil (project)
Catholic Church, Neustadt, Dresden (project)

1938 Hospital Chapel, Haselunne, Westphalia, Germany
Dr. Schilgen House, Munster, Germany
New church facade for St. Josef's Benedictine Abbey, Gerleve, Westphalia, Germany
Catholic Church, Gelsenkirchen-Buer, Germany (project)
Elementary school, Stadtchen an der Ems, Germany (project)
Elementary school, Papenburg an der Ems, Germany (project)
Catholic Church, Haltern, Westphalia, Germany (project)
Hugo Schmolz Tomb, Cologne
Catholic Church, Neuss-Reuschenberg, Germany (project)

1939 Catholic Church of the Holy Cross, Dulmen, Westphalia, Germany
Chapel extensions, Kunstrop, Westphalia, Germany (project)
Catholic Church, Hamborn, Westphalia, Germany (project)
Student House, Cologne (project)

1940 St. Wolfgang's Catholic Parish Church, Kumpfmuhl, Regensburg, Germany
Dominikus Böhm House, Jettingen in Schwaben, Germany

1941 Cinema, Weiden in der Oberpfalz, Germany (project)
Sawmill, Ottmarshausen, near Augsburg, Germany

1942 Temporary Church of the Heart of Jesus, Deuten, Germany
Community Centre and School, Jettingen in Schwaben, Germany (project)
St. Agritius Catholic Church, Trier, Germany (project)

1943 Roadside Chapel, Birken, near Wissen/Sieg, Germany (project)

1944 Catholic Church, Neuburg an der Kammel, Germany (project)

1945 New buildings for the Church of the Holy Cross, Trier, Germany (project)

1946 St. Albert's Catholic Church, Saarbrucken, Germany
St. Peter's Provost Church rebuilding, Recklinghausen, Germany (project)
St. George's Catholic Parish Church reconstruction, Vreden, Westphalia, Germany (project)
Asbach-Uralt Management Building, Rudesheim/Rhein, Germany (project)

1947 Mortuary Chapel, Burtenbach, near Jettingen, Germany (project)
Catholic Parish Church, Linz am Rhein, Germany (project)

1949 Laurenz Brothers Textile Mills extensions, Ochtrup, Westphalia, Germany
Sacristy, arcades, memorial and funeral chapels, Church at Kemnat in Schwaben, Germany
St. Karl Borromaus Catholic Church, Munster, Germany (project)
St. Matthias Catholic Church reconstruction, Bayenthal, Cologne

1950 St. Josef's Catholic Parish Church reconstruction, Duisburg, Germany
St. Wendelin Catholic Parish Church, Dirmingen an der Saar, Germany
Mortuary Chapel, Oberwaldbach in Schwaben, Germany

1951 St. Moritz Catholic Parish Church reconstruction, Augsburg, Germany
St. Martin's Catholic Parish Church extensions and new Parish House, Cochem an der Mosel, Germany
Catholic Parish Church reconstruction, Geilenkirchen-Hunshofen, near Aachen
Catholic Parish Church reconstruction, Geldern, Germany (project)
Catholic Church and Parish Plan, Bruhl, Rheinland, Germany (project)
Catholic Church, Emsdetten, Westphalia, Germany (project)
Catholic Church, The Hague, Netherlands (project)
Wallraf-Richartz-Museum, Cologne (project)

1952 St. Anthony's Catholic Parish Church reconstruction, Munster, Germany
St. Josef's Catholic Parish Church reconstruction, Kalk, Cologne

1953 St. Marien Catholic Parish Church, Ochtrup, Westphalia, Germany
Corona del Mar Cathedral, San Salvador (competition project)

1954 St. Elisabeth's Catholic Parish Church, Koblenz
Catholic Church extensions, Puttlingen an der Saar, Germany
Maria-Königin Catholic Church, Marienburg, Cologne
Catholic Church, Getulio, Brazil

1955 St. Veit's Catholic Parish Church, Mayen in der Eifel, Germany
Catholic Parish Church of the Holy Ghost, Emst, Hagen, Germany
Catholic Church, Hilgen-Burscheid, Germany

1956 St. Josef's Catholic Parish Church, Rodenkirchen, Cologne

Catholic Church extensions, Hohenberg, Cologne

St. Anna's Catholic Parish Church reconstruction, Ehrenfeld, Cologne

1957 Catholic Church of the Heart of Jesus, Oberhausen, Germany (project)

1958 St. Paul's Catholic Parish Church, Beuel/-Rhein, Germany

Publications:

On BÖHM: books—*Dominikus Böhm* by August Hoff, Berlin 1930; *Dominikus Böhm* by August Hoff and J. Habbel, Regensburg, Germany 1943; *Dominikus Böhm: Leben und Werk* by August Hoff, Herbert Muck and Raimund Thoma, Munich and Zurich 1962; *Studien zu Dominikus Böhm* by Gesine Stalling, Berne and Frankfurt 1974; articles—"Dominikus Böhm und sein Werk" by Rudolf Schwarz in *Moderne Bauformen* (Stuttgart), vol. 26, 1927; "Dominikus Böhms eigenes Wohnhaus" in *Moderne Bauformen* (Stuttgart), December 1934; "St. Joseph's Church, Hindenburg, Germany" in *Architectural Forum* (New York), August 1935; "Dominikus Böhm" in *Moderne Bauformen* (Stuttgart), August 1940; "Kirchenbau und planung von Dominikus und Gottfried Böhm" by August Hoff in *Bauen und Wohnen* (Zurich), December 1949; "Dominikus Böhm" by Rudolf Schwarz in *Baukunst und Werkform* (Nuremberg), February 1955; "Brief Biographies of German and Swiss Architects Distinguished for Church Design" in *Bauen und Wohnen* (Zurich), November 1958; "Documents of 20th Century Architecture: Priests' Seminary of the Diocese of Limburg" in *Architekt* (Stuttgart), April 1978.

Dominikus Böhm's architecture is confined to churches and ecclesiastical buildings, all of them Roman Catholic. And these may seem semi-traditional in comparison with the daringly innovative structural use of reinforced concrete by his contemporary Auguste Perret in the Church of Notre-Dame at Le Raincy, now acknowledged to be an exemplary masterpiece of 20th century architecture. But Böhm's originality lay in his emotional approach, which inspired his bold Expressionist churches of the 1920's. His War Memorial Church of 1927 at Neu-Ulm is a free fantasia on Gothic themes with little feeling of structural reality: it produces a psychological atmosphere similar to that of the strange stylized sets of German silent films of the period. His audacious Church of Christ the King at Mainz-Bischofsheim of 1926 is an early example of the use of paraboloid forms, with the concrete barrel vault of the nave intersected by lower cross-vaults over the bays of the aisles, creating a strong Expressionist-Gothic emotional effect.

Like his contemporary Rudolf Schwarz, Böhm was a pioneer of the one-room, open-plan church interior, in which a significant development was the circular plan. This is strikingly seen in what is usually considered to be the finest of Böhm's earlier churches, St. Englebert at Cologne-Riehl (1931–32). This circular church is also notable for its very ingenious roof, which is not the expected dome but eight paraboloid vaults, with small circular windows near the apex of each, so that the interior is rather dark, helping to produce a sense of religious mystery.

Others of his churches are experiments in simple rectangular forms. Böhm was in fact fulfilling that fundamental axiom of modern architecture, "form follows function," for one of the purposes of these open-plan churches was to bring the congregation into more active participation in the Mass in accordance with the Liturgical Revival. Architecturally this meant bringing priest and congregation physically closer together around the focal point of the altar. Böhm's church at Ringenberg (1936) was the first modern church in which the altar was placed so that the congregation was on three sides: he used a transeptual plan with the altar at the centre of the crossing and the congregation occupying the nave and transepts.

Böhm was not very active during the Nazi period, but after the war, when there was a great resurgence of new church building to replace those destroyed in the bombing, Böhm resumed his career. In his postwar churches he aimed at an even greater simplicity of structure, while achieving a spiritual atmosphere in other ways, such as decorative enrichment. A notable example is the Maria Königin Church in Cologne-Marienburg of 1954. The whole south wall of the church is a great curtain wall of stained glass. Its intricate pattern is a stylized leaf design in a limited palette of semi-transparent silver-grey and grey-green, harmonizing with the leaves of the trees in the park outside, with only some fragments of antique glass making accent points which blaze out in full colour: the whole wall of moving light gives a shifting veil-like effect in striking contrast to the severity of the rest of the squarish church with its slender metal supports.

Along with Rudolf Schwarz, Dominikus Böhm is generally acknowledged to be the most original of modern German ecclesiastical architects, a tradition that has been carried on by his son Gottfried. Although Dominikus Böhm was an innovatory and modern architect, his work always arose from his own deep spirituality: "Only what comes from the heart can find the way to the heart."

—Konstantin Bazarov

BÖHM, Gottfried.

German. Born in Offenbach am Main, 23 January 1920; son of the architect Dominikus Böhm, *q.v.* Educated at high school in Cologne, graduated 1938; Technische Hochschule, Munich, 1942–46, B.Eng 1946; Academy of Sculptural Art, Munich, 1947. Served in the German Army, 1938–42. Married; has 4 children. Worked as an assistant architect in his father's office, 1947–50; worked in New York, 1951; practised with his father, 1952 until his death in 1955. In private practice, Cologne, since 1955. Professor of Architecture, Institute of Technology, Aachen, since 1963. Member, Akademie der Künste, Berlin, 1968; Member, German Academy for Urban and Regional Planning, 1976. Address: Architekturbüro Böhm, Auf dem Romerberg 25, 5000 Cologne 51 (Marienburg), Germany.

Works:

1947 New membrane building structure (project)
1949 St. Columba's Church, Cologne
1955 Church in Ching Liau, Formosa
1957 Cathedral, and Chapel, Tubarao, Brazil (project)
  Herz Jesu Church, Schildgen, near Cologne
1958 St. Christopher's Church, Oldenburg, Germany
  The Queen of Grace Church, Kassel-Wilhelm-schohe, Germany
1959 Theatre, Bonn
  Corpus Christi Parish Centre, Porz-Urbach, near Cologne
  St. Joseph Parishioners' Centre, Kierspe, Germany
1960 Church, Bemkastel, Kues, Germany (project)
  Chapel, Cochem, Mosel, Germany (project)
  City Hall, Cologne (project)
  Godesburg Castle renovations, restaurant and hotel, Bad Godesburg, Bonn
1962 Thomas Morus Parishioners' Centre, Gelsenkirchen, Germany
  Church of the Pilgrimages, Neviges, Germany
  Town Hall, Bensberg, Germany
  Housing for the elderly, Garath, Dusseldorf

1963 Children's Village, Refrath, Bensberg, Germany
  Church of the Annunciation, Impekoven, Germany
  The Resurrection Church, Melaten, Cologne
1965 Cultural Centre, Bensberg, Germany (project)
  St. Ludwig Church, Saarlouis, Germany
  Children's Village, near Lake Bracciano, Italy
1966 Dr. Paul Böhm House, Munich
1967 City Hall, Amsterdam (project)
  Auditorium Centre, Aachen (project)
  City Centre Plan for Bensberg, Germany
1968 University of Dortmund, Germany (project)
  University of Bielefeld, Germany (project)
  City Hall, Wesseling Industrial District, near Cologne (project)
1969 Housing complex, Chorweiler, Cologne
  Cathedral restoration, Trier, Germany
  Kauzenburg-Ruine renovation and restaurant, Bad Kreuznach, Germany
  Diocesan Museum, Paderborn, Germany
  Music College, Cologne (project)
  Printing Factory, Cologne (project)
  State Bureau for Data Processing and Statistics, Dusseldorf
1972 Pilgrimage Church, Wigratzbad, Germany
1973 Parliament Buildings, Bonn (project)
  Housing development, Porz-Zundorf, near Cologne (project)
  City Hall and Cultural Centre, Bocholt, Germany
  St. Mathew Parishioners' Centre, Kettwig, Essen
1974 Residential quarter, Stuckenbroich, Germany (project)
1975 City Hall, Cologne (project)
  Wallraf-Richartz Museum new buildings, Cologne (project)
  Housing for the German Embassy, Moscow (project)
  Neckermann Store facade and renovation, Braunschweig am Alstadtmarkt, Germany
1976 Residential quarter on old factory site, Cologne (project)
1977 Adult Education Boarding School, Kreuzberg, Bonn (project)
  Administration Building, Marsdorf, Cologne (project)
  Viktria Insurance Building, Dusseldorf (project)

Publications:

By BÖHM: articles—in *Bauwelt* (Berlin), June 1974; in *Kunst und Kirche* (Linz), October 1975.

On BÖHM: articles—"Vacation Village for Children" in *Architecture Francaise* (Paris), January/-February 1974; "An Expressionist Presence: Gottfried Böhm" by Giuliano Chelazzi in *L'Architettura* (Rome), April 1974; "Fifteen Hundred Years Revealed in New Glory: Trier Cathedral" in *Deutsche Bauzeitung* (Stuttgart), July 1974; "Oasis in the Desert—Old People's Home in Dusseldorf-Garath" by Max Bacher in *Der Architekt* (Stuttgart), April 1976; "Observations on the Architectural Work of Gottfried Böhm" by Egon Schirmbeck and "Interview with Gottfried Böhm" by H. Klumpp and Egon Schirmbeck in *Bauen und Wohnen* (Zurich), November 1977; "Form as an Expression of Technical Function" in *Architektur und Wohnwelt* (Stuttgart), December 1977; special issue of *Architecture + Urbanism* (Tokyo), March 1978.

The actual career of Gottfried Böhm, a somewhat withdrawn architect, disinclined to sensationalism,

Gottfried Böhm: Town Hall, Bensberg, Germany, 1962

started with a bang—with the construction of the Bensberg Town Hall at the end of the 1960's. This concrete edifice is of great dramatic strength and is as unique in its way as are most of Böhm's buildings. One could say that the earlier churches, with their perfunctory dignity, had already shown that Böhm —the son of the highly illustrious master church builder, Dominikus Böhm—had freed himself entirely from any dictates of architectural fashion. All his works are thought out in an unusually sculptured way; they are intensely expressive and have a kind of rhythmically animated and joyous spaciousness. They seem to extract from their construction, and their materials, designs that are totally unexpected but in no way forced (as are those of Scharoun). Architecture, according to Böhm, "must eventually achieve its own surrender." Group of buildings, such as the Children's Village, Bensberg-Refrath, the Housing for the Elderly in Dusseldorf-Garath, or the Housing Complex at Cologne-Chorweiler, are characterized by an "organic" municipal layout that reminds one of the work of Häring. Their arrangement follows the landscape and the topography of the district, and conveys the desired social effect.

In the works of Böhm—which have avoided the International Style from the beginning—one can distinguished three more or less different phases: the first involves the recognizable traits of the 1950's; the second, to which the above-mentioned Town Hall, Children's Village, and Housing for the Elderly belong, identified itself through an inward plasticity; it is externally marked in its use of brick, concrete, and coloured wood. This phase reaches its climax in the Church of the Pilgrimages, Neviges, an enormous concrete cathedral that puts the name of Böhm on a par with that of Brunelleschi or Gaudi. In the third, the steel and glass, phase, everything that is ponderous is replaced with simplicity and transparency: here the most noteworthy examples as the State Bureau for Data Processing and Statistics, Dusseldorf, and the Diocesan Museum at Paderborn, which illustrates the exceptionally courageous, and very tensely held, symbiosis of a neighbourhood architecture that is both contemporary and historical.

—Manfred Sack

BONATZ, Paul (Michael Nikolaus).

German. Born in Solgne, Lorraine, 6 December 1877. Educated at the Humanistische Gymnasium, Hagenau, Germany, 1896; Technische Hochschule, Munich, Dip. Arch. 1900. Married Helene Frohlich in 1902; daughter: Susanne. Assistant to Theodor Fischer at the Technische Hochschule, Stuttgart, 1902–06, and Professor at the Technische Hochschule, Stuttgart, from 1907; in private practice, with F. E. Scholer, Stuttgart, 1913–27. Consultant to the Neckar Canal Authority, Germany, 1929–36; Consultant to the Inspector-General of Highways, Germany, 1935–40; Consultant Architect, City of Ankara, Turkey, 1943–46; Professor at the Technical University of Istanbul, 1946–54; returned to private practice, Stuttgart, 1954–56. Recipient: First Prize, Stuttgart Central Railway Station Competition, 1911. *Died* (in Stuttgart) *20 December 1956.*

Works:

1909 Henkell Warehouses, Biebricher, Wiesbaden
      Library, University of Tübingen
1912 School, Feuerbach, near Stuttgart
      Bonatz House, Stuttgart
1913 German Embassy, Washington, D.C. (project)
      Bridge, near Ulm, Germany

Roser House, Stuttgart
      Country house, Marienburg, Cologne
1914 Hospital, Strasbourg (with Karl Bonatz)
      Municipal Hall, Corviniusplatz, Hanover
1915 Municipal Hall, Stettin, Germany (project)
      Monument to the War Dead (2 projects)
1916 Assembly Building, Oldenburg, Germany
      Zeppelindorf Workers' Housing Development, Friedrichshafen, Germany (with F. E. Scholer)
      General Lotterer Monument, Ludwigshafen, Germany
      Turkish-German Hall of Friendship, Istanbul (competition project)
1917 Hartmannsweilerkopf Monument (project)
      Commemorative Hall (project)
1922 Office Building, Königsberg, Germany (project)
      Heymarkt Building, Cologne (project)
      Kriegerfriedhof Monument, Waldfriedhof, Stuttgart
1924 Scheibler House, Marienburg, Cologne
      Arntzen House, Marienburg, Cologne
1925 Hornschmich House, Mainleus, near Kulmbach, Germany (with F. E. Scholer)
      Am Bismarckturm Housing Development, Stuttgart
      Bonatz House, Stuttgart (destroyed, 1944)
      Trade Fair Building, Hamburg (2 projects)
1926 Buhler House, Goppinger, Germany (with F. E. Scholer)
      Dyke Project, Ladenburg bei Mannheim (project)
      Palace of the League of Nations, Geneva (competition project; with F. E. Scholer)
1927 Jeweller's Hall, Domplatz, Cologne
      Municipal Hall, Sports Hall and Museum (competition project)
      Gymnasium, Aalen, Germany
1928 Baer House, Stuttgart
      Central Railway Station, Stuttgart (with F. E. Scholer)
1929 Unterturkheim Swimming Baths, Stuttgart
      Radio Broadcasting Building, Berlin (project)
      Hotel Graf Zeppelin, Station Square, Stuttgart (with F. E. Scholer)
      House, Dortmund, Germany
      House, Bochum, Germany
1930 Cathedral Terrace/Plaza, Cologne (project)
1933 House, Gertingen, near Stuttgart
      Roser House, Stuttgart
      Vorster House, Cologne
      Strenger House, Cologne
      Muller House, Cologne
      Flag Tower, *Turnfestival,* Stuttgart
1935 Stumm Company Building, Dusseldorf (with F. E. Scholer)
      Water Tower, Kornwestheim, near Stuttgart
      Reichsnahrstandes Buildings, Goslar, Germany (project; with K. Dubbers)
1936 Locks, bridges and weirs on the Neckar Canal, Heidelberg, Rockenau, Hirschhorn and Oberesslingen, Germany
      Kunstmuseum, Basle, Switzerland (with Rudolf Christ)
      Memorial Chapel to the War Dead, Heilbronn, Germany
      Offender Rundbau Monument (project; with K. Dubbers)
1939/
42 Main Railway Station, Munich (project)
1939/
43 Naval High Command, Berlin (project)
1941 Bridges for the Autobahn: over the Waschmuhltal near Kaiserslauten; Saale near Lehesten; Donau near Leipheim (Ulm); Elbe near Hohenwarthe (Magdeburg); Elbe near Dessau; Rhine near Frankenthal (Mannheim)
      Suspension bridges at Cologne and Hamburg
1943 Stuttgart Corporation Buildings (project)
1946 Schukru-Saracogu Housing Development, Ankara, Turkey

1948 State Opera House, Ankara, Turkey

Publications:

By BONATZ: books—*Leben und Bauen,* Stuttgart 1950, 4th edition 1958; *Brücken,* with Fritz Leonhardt, Königstein, Germany 1951; articles—"Hochhauser von Paul Bonatz und F. E. Scholer teils in Gemeinschaft mit Karl Bonatz" in *Moderne Bauformen* (Stuttgart), June 1926; "The Madrid Conference" in *Revista Nacional de Arquitectura* (Madrid), November 1943.

On BONATZ: books—*Paul Bonatz und seine Schüler,* edited by G. Graubner, Stuttgart 1930; *Paul Bonatz: Arbeiten aus den Jahren 1907 bis 1937,* edited by Friedrich Tamms, Stuttgart 1937; *Neue Deutsche Baukunst* by Albert Speer, Berlin 1941; *Architecture and Politics in Germany 1918–1945* by Barbara Miller Lane, Cambridge, Massachusetts 1968; *Paul Bonatz 1877–1956* by Norbert Bongartz, Peter Dübbers and Frank Werner, Stuttgart 1977; articles—"Neue Bauten von Paul Bonatz und F. E. Scholer" by Julius Baum in *Moderne Bauformen* (Stuttgart), December 1913; "Zu neueren arbeiten von Paul Bonatz" by G.K. in *Moderne Bauformen* (Stuttgart), January 1919; "Paul Bonatz" by Julius Posener in *L'Architecture d'Aujourd'hui* (Paris), June/July 1932; "Architecture of the Nazis" in *Architectural Review* (London), October 1933; "Paul Bonatz" by Karl Bonatz in *Neue Bauwelt* (Berlin), no. 49, 1948; "A Minor Master" by Julius Posener in *Architectural Review* (London), July 1951; "Paul Bonatz 1877–1956" by Nieto and Bellmunt in *Arquitectura* (Madrid), March 1977.

Paul Bonatz, born in 1877, certainly belongs to that important and not uncontroversial group of architects known as the German Pre-Moderns. After studying architecture at the Munich Technische Hochschule, he became assistant to Theodor Fischer at the Technische Hochschule in Stuttgart: during that period he was totally influenced by Fischer who, in contrast to the movement toward an international style, was continually looking for a "regionalism" specific to place. In 1907 Bonatz succeeded Fischer as Professor at Stuttgart, and from 1913 to 1927 he maintained his own architectural practice in Stuttgart with F. E. Scholer. Important early works were the Henkell Warehouses and the Library of the University of Tübingen.

He achieved his first real breakthrough when in 1911 he won first prize in the competition for the rebuilding of Stuttgart's main railway station. With the exception of some of Peter Behren's large buildings, this construction is perhaps the most important monument of German Pre-Modernism. Bonatz succeeded not only in giving a clear function-related expression to the various technical and transport problems but also in formulating the arrangement of the masses in such a way that he largely determined the expansion of the surrounding area during the 20th century. The Stuttgart Station thus became the first "Space-Time-Architecture" in Germany. Although the building was not completed until 1928, it never really came within an International Style sphere of influence. Strongly reminiscent of Eliel Saarinen's Helsinki Railway Station in its general arrangement, the Stuttgart Station reveals an abundance of eclectic details. Nevertheless, its basic expression is matter-of-fact to a hitherto unknown degree—that is to say, it is function-oriented.

During the period from the end of World War I until about 1930 Bonatz was admittedly divided in his stylistic expression. While he turned almost exclusively to the German Biedermeier and the so-called "Heimatstil" motives for single family houses and villas, his public buildings obeyed New Building principles. But, by 1928 Bonatz was one of those architects who were strongly folk oriented and who at the time of the Weissenhof Estate in Stuttgart made a radical departure from New Building. He

Paul Bonatz: Central Railway Station, Stuttgart, 1928

was one of the signatories to the so-called "Block Manifesto," which attempted to establish "the attitudes to life of our own people." The first and only National Socialist architectural program emerged from the circle of signatories to this manifesto. In 1933 Bonatz took part in the project for the Kochenhof Estate in Stuttgart, which would later achieve sad renown as the "Anti-Weissenhof."

A further interest in his work was civil engineering. From 1929–36 Bonatz was a consultant to the Neckar Canal Authority, and as such he executed an impressive collection of locks, sluices, bridges, etc. that are among the most important engineering achievements of the time. Later, after the National Socialist seizure of power, it became increasingly difficult for so unpretentious an architect as Bonatz to build anything. In 1935, Dr. Fritz Todt, the Inspector-General of German Road Building, appointed him as his personal adviser. In this capacity, up until the Second World War, Bonatz was, at least, able to plan and executive a number of outstanding bridges.

Torn between protest at and loyalty to National Socialism, Bonatz tried to create works for the regime's leaders in Berlin. He produced gigantic and megalomaniacal projects—the Main Railway Station in Munich and the Naval High Command in Berlin—which could not be built. Like Kreis and others, he was now regarded as an elder architect, and, as such, despite his previous work for the state, of little use to the National Socialist Culture and Construction Policy.

For that reason, among others, Bonatz decided to emigrate; he went to Ankara, where the Turkish Government appointed him consultant to the City Architect. In 1946 he became Professor at the Technical University of Istanbul. In Turkey Bonatz developed a moderately antique style that, in many ways, is reminiscent of the work of Auguste Perret.

In 1954 he returned to Stuttgart where, until his death, he occupied himself chiefly with the reconstruction of his own war-damaged buildings.

Paul Bonatz's chief accomplishment—apart from his pioneer work in the German Pre-Modern style—is that over the decades at the Technische Hochschule he gathered around him a circle of architectural teachers, known as the "Stuttgart School," who were internationally acknowledged and esteemed. And he was one of the most important teachers of that time in Germany to preach the abolition of the separation between civil engineering and architecture. But he did not achieve his main ambition, which was to create a regional architecture that would be a real alternative to the New Building.

—Frank Werner

BONET Bertran, Pep.

Spanish. Born in Barcelona, 19 November 1941. Educated at the Escuela Tecnica Superior de Arquitectura, Barcelona, under Federico Correa, 1958–65, Dip.Arch. 1965. Served in the Spanish Army, in Castillejos (Tarragona) and Gerona: Lieutenant. Married Marta Monne Corbero in 1964: children: Sebas, Sara, and Elias. Formed the partnership, Studio PER, with Cristian Cirici, *q.v.,* Luis Clotet, *q.v.* and Oscar Tusquets, *q.v.* Barcelona, 1965. Professor, EINA, Barcelona, 1969–70. Professor, Escuela Tecnica Superior de Arquitectura, Barcelona, since 1976. Exhibitions: *Arquitectura del Studio PER,* Lerida, 1971; *Triennale,* Milan, 1973; *Arquitectura y Lagrimas,* Sala Vincon, Barcelona, 1975; *Centenario de la Escuela Tecnica Superior de Arquitectura de*

Barcelona, Palacio National, Barcelona, 1977; *Festival of Films about Architecture,* Centre Georges Pompidou, Paris, 1978. Address: Studio PER, Caspe 151, Barcelona 13, Spain.

Works:

1968   Design of the *Miro Otro* exhibition, Barcelona (with Cristian Cirici, Luis Clotet, and Oscar Tusquets)

1972   Llambes Offices, Barcelona (with Cristian Cirici)

1973   Profitos Factory, Polinya, Barcelona (with Cristian Cirici)

1974   C./Tokio Housing Block, Barcelona (with Cristian Cirici)

1976   Aguila House, Llavaneras, Barcelona (with Cristian Cirici)

       Bricall House, Vilasar, Barcelona (with Cristian Cirici)

       Pep Bonet House, Vilamajor, Barcelona (with Cristian Cirici)

1977   Francés House, Menorca (with Cristian Cirici)

Publications:

On BONET: articles—"Studio PER" in *Architecture + Urbanism* (Tokyo), no. 4, 1977; "Arquitectura con Ventanas" by Xavier Sust in *Arquitecturas Bis* (Barcelona), September 1977; "Per, uno per uno, tutti per tutti" by Alessandro Mendini in *Modo Milano* (Milan), November 1977.

Once in Japan I saw a Spanish juggler who impressed me a lot. He carried through his performance with just a teaspoon. He put it over his shoe, threw it up into the air, turning it over and over, and with an

Pep Bonet and Cristian Cirici: Francés House, Menorca, 1977

incredible precision made it stand vertically over his forehead. He didn't do anything else, but I found it wonderful. With such a simple performance he gave the exact measure of his great capacity to solve this or any other problem of equilibrium, and the audience applauded him, appreciating the difficulty of his work and his precise execution.

Something very different happens to architects like us. For a long time we don't know who is to be our audience, and it is with great pain that we obtain a teaspoon with which to perform. And if we pretend to do it with more spectacular contraptions, we must try to achieve equilibrium long before going on to the stage—and this is tiring.

And when we are finally able to perform, nobody understands anything or applauds us. And that is that apart from achieving equilibrium, we would like to convince the rare remaining audience that it isn't the teaspoon that they should wish to have; it's the cup of tea. Above all, we are pedants.

And meanwhile the Spanish juggler I saw in Japan is turning up all over the world, very much in demand. And we are not.

—Pep Bonet

Studio PER is four architects in two practices in one office. Apart from administrative convenience, what really binds them together is that they share the same approach to architecture in valuing positively its cultural objectives. Their architecture is essentially intellectual. They are eager to discuss, argue, and defend their work against all criticism in order to explore all the rich possibilities available to their avant-garde position. This makes their buildings, and their explanations, often contradictory—but that is the price of an open mind—adventure and doubt. But this attitude, which is almost literary rather than visual, would be of little interest if it was not backed up by secure professional ability, compositional control, and a sensitive feeling for proportions.

Pep Bonet and Cristian Cirici are one practice; they share with their partners, Lluis Clotet and Oscar Tusquets, an invigorating concern for industrial design. Between them they have a large list of products on the market. Their attention to minute detail, and the production problems involved, is reflected in the care they take in designing architectural details. Their drawings and perspectives are explicative.

Bonet and Cirici are more conservative than their partners in their architecture; they fall more clearly within the mainstream of modern architecture—as in their Profitos Factory and the C./Tokio luxury flats in Barcelona. But perhaps their most significant work is Bonet's own house in Vilamajor, where the directness of industrial architecture has inspired the conception of the house. The skeleton of two parallel naves made of block columns and pre-cast concrete beams generate two related open spaces, one partially occupied by the main body of the dwelling and the other by a studio. Details are reduced to a minimum, to the area where industrial and rural architecture meet. This voluntary simplification of architecture to the bare necessities follows Mies van der Rohe in a unsophisticated and relaxed manner.

The common freshness and professional skill of Bonet and Cirici, and that of their associates in Studio PER, together with their sensitive alertness to current architectural fashion, enable them to translate new concepts quickly into the local Catalan cultural context. It is a task that is needed if the modern movement is to take root geographically.

—David Mackay

BOURGEOIS, Victor.

Belgian. Born in Charleroi, in 1897. Educated at the Académie Royale des Beaux-Arts, Brussels, 1914–19. In private practice, Brussels, 1920 until his death, 1962. Technical Consultant, Ministry of Public Health, Brussels, 1937–40; Technical Consultant, Société des Habitations à Bon Marche, Brussels, 1938–40; Technical Counsellor to the Town Planning Administration, Province of Hainaut, Belgium, 1945–47. Professor, École Nationale Supérieure d'Architecture, Brussels; Professor, Université du Travail Paul Pastur, Charleroi. Editor or Co-Editor, *Au Volant,* Brussels, 1919; *Le Geste,* Brussels, 1920; *Sept Arts,* Brussels, 1922–28, 1948; *Bruxelles,* 1932–33. Vice-President, CIAM (Congrès Internationaux d'Architecture Moderne), 1928–40; President, Belgian Society of Modernist Town Planners and Architects, 1936–39. Exhibition: *Victor Bourgeois 1897–1962,* École Nationale Supérieure d'Architecture, Brussels, 1971. Recipient: Hainaut Architecture Prize, Belgium, 1960. Member, Free Academy of Belgium. *Died* (in Brussels) *in 1962.*

Works:

1922 Multiple housing development, rue du Cubisme, Brussels

1922/
25 Cité Moderne (300 houses and town plan), Berchem-Sainte-Agathe, Brussels

1923 Town plan for Cité de Flenu, Mons, Belgium

1924 Sept Arts-L'Equerre Display, *Exposition de Lanterne Sourd,* Palais d'Egmont, Brussels

1925 Victor Bourgeois House, 103 Avenue Seghers, Koekelberg, Brussels
Housing complex, rue Robert Scott, Uccle, Brussels

1927 Maison Belge, Weissenhof Estate, Stuttgart
1928 L'Urbaneum (Museum of Town Planning), Brussels (project)
      La Maison Blanche (Buchet House), Loth, Belgium (project)
      Jespers House and Sculpture Studio, Avenue du Prince Heritier, Woluwe, Brussels
      Apartment block, Avenue Franklin Roosevelt, Brussels
1929 Central air, rail and road transport stations, Brussels (project)
1930 House alterations and extensions, 263 Avenue Rogier, Schaerbaek, Brussels
      La Nouveau Bruxelles (city expansion plan; project)
1931 Plan for *Mont des Arts* Exhibition Terraces, Brussels (project)
      House, Wuthier-Braine, Brabant, Belgium
      Nord-Midi International Train Station, Brussels (project)
      Maison du Livre Belge Display, Brussels
1932 Cité Mondiale (new town), Tervueren, Brussels (project)
      House, Avenue Marianne, Uccle, Brussels
      Villa in a park, Anderlecht, Belgium
1933 Director's House, Avenue Prekelinden, Woluwe, Brussels
1934 Victor Bourgeois House alterations, 103 Avenue Seghers, Koekelberg, Brussels
1935 Leopold II Restaurant, and Ruwenzori Pavilion Display, *World's Fair,* Brussels
      Nouveau Frameries Development, Hainaut, Belgium
1936 La Jeannerie (villa), Rhode-Saint-Genese, Belgium
      Continental Cinema, Etterbeek, Belgium
1937 School of La Chapelle, Hornu, Belgium
1937/
49   Central Post Office, Brussels
1938 House, Avenue de l'Uruguay, Brussels (with gardens by Canccl-Clacs)
      Old people's housing, Kessel-Loo, Belgium
      Leisure and Games Complex, Hornu, Belgium
      Vacation and leisure centres plans, Congrès International de l'Habitation et de l'Urbanisme, Mexico (projects)
1938/
40   Hofstade Beach Development, Belgium (with Ministry of Public Health)
1939 Belgian Pavilion, *World's Fair,* New York
      Pavilions, *Exposition de Liège,* Belgium
1939/
40   Housing and workers' facilities buildings, for Thy-le-Chateau Iron and Steelworks, Marcinelle, Belgium
      Housing and office complex for Braine-le-Comte Factories, Belgium
1940/
41   City centre plan for Nivelles, Belgium (project; with G. Pepermans, V. Lichtert and H. Barigand)
1946 City and regional plan for Charleroi, Belgium (with Renée de Coomans)
      Housing and workers' facilities buildings, for Saint-Roch Factories and Foundries, Couvin, Belgium
1947 Gustave Boel Offices, La Louviere, Belgium
1947/
48   Baume et Marpent Offices and Shop, Haine-Saint-Pierre, Belgium
1948 Housing and workers' facilities buildings, for Belge d'Azote Company, Renory-Ougree (Liege), Belgium
1948/
49   Hainaut Women's Technical School, Saint-Ghislain, Belgium
1950 Nos Caiaux Society Housing, La Borinage, Belgium
1953 Charleroi District Social Services Offices, Courcelles, Belgium
      Sportsground, Jumet, Belgium (project)
      Old people's home, Kessel-Loo, Belgium

Victor Bourgeois: Jespers Sculpture Studio, Woluwe, Belgium, 1928

1954 New Town Hall, Ostend, Belgium
      New Saint-Camille Hospital, Namur, Belgium
      Le Foyer Montagnard (housing estate), Cité Selestat, Montigny-sur-Sambre, Belgium
1955 Medical Centre, Charleroi, Belgium
1955/
57   Francois Bovesse Cultural Centre, Namur, Belgium (with J. Ledoux, G. Lambeau, and J. Colin)
1957 Monument to the War Dead, Jemappes, Belgium (with Frans Lamberechts)
1958 Flats, Cité Moderne, Berchem-Sainte-Agathe, Brussels
      Eternit Tower and Germinal Pavilion, *World's Fair,* Brussels
1959 Grandstand, Sportsground, Kessel-Loo, Belgium
1962 Le Rayon de Soleil Hospital Centre, Montignies, Charleroi, Belgium
1966 City centre development plan for Ixelles, Belgium

Publications:

By BOURGEOIS: books—*Rationelle Bebauungsweisen,* with Cor Van Eesteren and Sigfried Giedion, Frankfurt 1931; *Charleroi: Terre d'Urbanisme,* with Renée de Cooman, Brussels 1946; *De l'Architecture au Temps d'Erasme à l'Humanisme Social de Notre Temps,* with Renée de Cooman, Brussels and Paris 1949; *L'Architecte et Son Espace,* Brussels 1955; article—"La Cité Moderne" in *L'Habitation à bon marche* (Brussels), October 1923.

On BOURGEOIS: books—*Die Wohnung für das Existenzminimum,* Frankfurt 1930; *Neuzeitlicher Verkehsbau* by H. Gescheit and K. Wittmann, Potsdam, Germany 1931; *Gli Elementi dell'Architettura Funzionale* by Alberto Sartoris, Milan 1932; *International Architecture 1924–1934,* London 1934; *Victor Bourgeois: Architecture 1922–1952* by Pierre-Louis Flouquet, Brussels 1952; *Victor Bourgeois* by Georges Linze, Brussels 1959; *Victor Bourgeois 1897–1962,* exhibition catalogue, by R. Delevoy, M. Culot and Pierre Bourgeois, Brussels 1971; articles—"Junge Kunst in Belgien" by Hannes Meyer in *Werk* (Zurich), September 1925; "La Cité Moderne" by Pierre Bourgeois in *L'Habitation à bon marche* (Brussels), October 1925; "Un Musée d'Urbanisme" in *Arlequin* (Brussels), no. 22, 1929.

Victor Bourgeois was one of the most important figures of 20th century architecture in Belgium. For most of his professional life he visualized architecture as the mirror of society, and because of his social concern, he specialized in public housing early in his career. Bourgeois claimed his primary influence was Berlage, who, with Frank Lloyd Wright, had made a deep impression on the students at the Académie Royale des Beaux-Arts in the Belgian capital, where he himself had studied.

His most celebrated work was the municipal housing scheme known as the Cité Moderne at Berchem-Ste-Agathe outside Brussels. In it, he created a variation in the appearance of terrace housing by the articulation of blocks and by the introduction of highly organized relationships between solids and voids, creating strong façades that were classics of their type. Indeed, Bourgeois attempted to give the elevations of his buildings a new language as tightly refined and controlled as that of classicism itself. Not for him was the free abstraction of shapes that were chaotically unrelated to each other. It is in these façades that the influence of the great American architect is paramount. Courtyards and squares added interest to the planning of the estates as a whole. Unquestionably, if Wright was the primary influence on the relationships between solids and voids (though he would not have approved of the hard materials), the ideas behind the layout came from Tony Garnier's Cité Industrielle and from other ideal schemes derived from French rather than from English Garden-City sources. The flat roofs, projecting flat balcony roofs, and the plain flat walls were very much in the severely formal mode of the period, and might, with some adaptation, have sprung back into the Garnier scheme.

Bourgeois also designed schools and public buildings, as well as housing estates. He was also a town planner who became influenced by English ideas and by developments in the Netherlands and in Germany. He was a member of the Congrès Internationaux d'Architecture Moderne, and, through his offices, the third congress was held in Brussels in 1930. The theme was land-use planning and rational methods of site organization. The result was the publication of a report entitled *Rationelle Bebauungsweisen* which, like so many CIAM documents, mixed prolix dogma with sound sense.

He was invited to contribute designs for the Weissenhof Housing Settlement in Stuttgart in 1927; they were distinguished in their *genre* but were perhaps overshadowed by the more famous and supremely elegant block by Ludwig Mies van der Rohe.

—James Stevens Curl

BOYD, Robin (Gerard Penleigh).
Australian. Born in Melbourne, Victoria, 3 January 1919. Educated at the Malvern Church of England Grammar School, Melbourne, 1926–36; served articles with the architect Kingsley A. Henderson, Melbourne, 1936–40, and concurrently attended evening classes at the Royal Melbourne College, 1936–39, and University of Melbourne Architectural Atelier, 1939–40, 1945–46 (Editor, *Smudges,* 1939–42); registered architect, 1946; awarded Haddon Travelling Scholarship, 1947. Served as a Warrant Officer Class II in the 3rd Field Survey Company of the Australian Imperial Forces, in New Guinea, 1941–45. Married Dorothea Patricia Madden in 1943; children: Carolyn, Penleigh, and Suzy. In private practice, Melbourne, 1946–52; Partner, with Roy Grounds and Frederick Romberg, Grounds, Romberg and Boyd, Melbourne, 1952–62; returned to private practice, Melbourne, 1962 until his death in 1971. Part-time Lecturer in Design and Architectural History, University of Melbourne, 1948–56;

Visiting Bemish Professor of Architecture, Massachusetts Institute of Technology, Cambridge, 1956–57. Member, Industrial Design Council of Australia, 1965–70; Trustee, National Gallery of Victoria, 1965–71; Member, National Capital Planning Committee, Canberra, 1968–71; Member, Melbourne Underground Rail Loop Authority, 1970–71; President, Victorian Chapter, Royal Australian Institute of Architects, 1970–71. Recipient: Gold Medal, Royal Australian Institute of Architects, 1970; Architecture Critic's Medal, American Institute of Architects, 1973. D.Litt.: University of New England, Armidale, New South Wales, 1967. Fellow, Royal Australian Institute of Architects, and Royal Society of Arts, London. Honorary Fellow, American Institute of Architects, 1960. C.B.E. (Commander, Order of the British Empire), 1971. *Died* (in Melbourne) *16 October 1971.*

Works:

1947	Boyd House, Camberwell, Victoria
1948	White House, Mentone, Victoria
1949	*House of Tomorrow* Exhibition, Melbourne
1950	Gillison House, Balwyn, Victoria
1951	Darbyshire House, Templestowe, Victoria
	Miss Elizabeth Wade House, Mount Eliza, Victoria
1953	Professor Manning Clark House, Canberra
	Finlay House, Warrandyte, Victoria
	John Boyd House, North Balwyn, Victoria
	Professor Frank Fenner House, Canberra
1954	Ctesiphon House and Shop, Jordanville, Victoria
	Bridgford House, Black Rock, Victoria
	Richardson House, Blackfriars Close, Toorak, Victoria
	Blott House, Lilydale, Victoria
1955	Troedel House, Wheeler's Hill, Victoria
	Stegbar Windowall factories in Melbourne, Sydney and Brisbane
1956	C. W. P. Wilson House, Kew, Victoria
	Kenneth Myer "Pelican" House, Mount Eliza, Victoria
	Gavin Walkley House, North Adelaide, South Australia
	Foy House, Beaumaris, Victoria
1957	Holford House, Ivanhoe, Victoria
	Haughton-James House, Kew, Victoria
	McManamny House, Beaumaris, Victoria
	Peninsula House (project)
1959	Professor Zelman Cowen House, Kew, Victoria
	Boyd House II, Walsh Street, South Yarra, Victoria
1960	Clemson House, Kew, Victoria
	Southgate Fountain, Snowden Gardens, Melbourne
	Lloyd House, Brighton, Victoria
1961	Black Dolphin Motel, Merimbula, New South Wales
1962	Phillip, Blakers and Griffin Houses, Canberra
	McNicoll House, South Yarra, Victoria
	Handfield House, Eltham, Victoria
	Richardson House, Barwon Heads, Victoria
	Domain Park Flats, South Yarra, Victoria
1963	Wright House, Warrandyte, Victoria
	Burgess House, Ivanhoe, Victoria
1965	Baker House, Bacchus Marsh, Victoria
	Kaye House, Frankston, Victoria
	Shelmerdine House, Mornington, Victoria
	Verge House, Canberra
	Simon House, Narre Warren, Victoria
	Moysey House, Echuca, Victoria
	Blackwell House, Echuca, Victoria
	Moore House, Wheeler's Hill, Victoria
	John Balman Motor Inn, Queen's Road, Melbourne
1967	Apple Tree Project Houses, Wheeler's Hill, Victoria
	McCaughey Court Student Housing, University of Melbourne
	Fletcher House, Brighton, Victoria

	Lyons House, Dolan's Bay, near Sydney
	President Motor Inn, Queen's Road, Melbourne
	Australian Pavilion interiors, *Expo '67*, Montreal
	Purves House, Kew, Victoria
	Lawrence Flats, Kew, Victoria
	Featherston-Currey House, Ivanhoe, Victoria
1968	Tower Hill Natural History Museum, Warrnambool, Victoria
	Menzies College Student Housing, La Trobe University, Melbourne
	Farfor Holiday Houses, Portsea, Victoria
	Eltringham House, Aranda, A.C.T.
1970	Australian Pavilion interiors, *Expo '70*, Osaka, Japan
1971	Hegatty House, Ringwood, Victoria
	Ian Crawford House, Canterbury, Victoria
	Churchill Memorial Trust House, Canberra

Publications:

By BOYD: books—*Victorian Modern,* Melbourne 1947; *Australia's Home: Its Origins, Builders and Occupiers,* Melbourne 1952; *The Australian Ugliness,* Melbourne 1960; *Kenzo Tange,* London and New York 1962; *The Walls Around Us: The Story of Australian Architecture,* Melbourne 1962; *The New Architecture,* Melbourne 1963; *The Puzzle of Architecture,* Melbourne, London and New York, 1965; *The Book of Melbourne and Canberra,* with Harold Freedman and Charles Troedel, Adelaide 1965; *New Directions in Japanese Architecture,* London and New York 1968, Barcelona 1969; *Living in Australia,* with Mark Strizic, Sydney 1970; *The Great, Great Australian Dream,* Sydney 1972; articles—"A New Eclecticism" in *Architectural Review* (London), September 1951; "The Functional Neurosis" in *Architectural Review* (London), February 1958; "The Engineering of Excitement" in *Architectural Review* (London), November 1958; "The Sad End of the New Brutalism" in *Architectural Review* (London), July 1967; "Anti-Architecture" in *Architectural Forum* (New York), November 1968; "A Glimpse of the Future" in *Architectural Record* (New York), March 1970; "Expo '70" in *Architectural Review* (London), August 1970.

On BOYD: articles—afterword by David Saunders to Boyd's book *Living in Australia,* Sydney 1970; "Retrospective Robin Boyd" by David Saunders in *Architecture in Australia* (Sydney), February 1972.

*

Robin Boyd began practice at a time when the Modern Movement was gaining foothold in Australia. His contribution was not to its establishment but to its maturity. He edited a student broadsheet, *Smudges,* from 1939 to 1942, in which he attacked not only the still prevalent historicist design but the crude imitations of functional forms as well. Boyd played a great part in focussing Australian interest on American modern regional movements such as the Bay Region style. He wrote the first study of modern architecture in Australia, *Victorian Modern,* in 1946, and later, from it, developed a history, *Australia's Home,* in 1952. After 1950, regionalism seesawed with internationalism in Boyd's architecture. He came to be drawn to the International Style. In particular, he became interested in the use of the cantilevered structure, crisp, simple forms, and the open plan.

In the practice of Grounds, Romberg and Boyd, he produced numerous house designs. All were marked by open planning, the extension of a functional element to a major formal theme, and the reflection of site conditions in structure. These themes found their most complete expression in his own house of 1959 and in his Featherston-Currey house of 1967. The second was a simple oblong space, where platforms replaced rooms and gardens formed part of the internal flooring. The roof lines corresponded to the slopes of their sites.

His architecture clearly took the problem-solving approach. Faced with a large roof area in his own house he simply suspended the roof on cables. Over a creek-bed site he suspended another house from two bridge arches. His work was highly conceptual, and a whole series of his designs adapted basic geometric forms for the ground plans, the crescent and semi-ellipse in particular. These interests were reflected elsewhere in contemporary designs but seldom with such purity of concepts and form. In many instances Boyd led what became popular planning solutions. He saw himself as defending the functionalism of the militant Modern Movement. His defence against its opponents was that functionalism was being discarded before it had been adequately tested. True to this principle, he constantly introduced new materials and detailing in his work.

It is not surprising that Boyd became one of the earliest critics to study new Japanese architecture where he saw architects defending functionalism in their work. He wrote the first monograph on Kenzo Tange in 1962 and followed it with the seminal *New Directions in Japanese Architecture* in 1968. He was fascinated by the promise that advanced technology held for architects and was interested in the way the Japanese and Archigram were giving leads in this area. He felt that the greatest field for the new technology was in large-scale design and entered this field for ten years before his death.

His position moved from the defence of functionalism to that of an interested observer of new trends. This stance can be seen in some of his articles for *Architectural Review.* He also expressed his views through radio and television broadcasts for the Australian Broadcasting Commission.

—Dorothea Boyd

*

Robin Boyd made a twofold contribution to Australian architecture—as a distinguished practising architect and as a critic and writer. And although he undoubtedly thought of his architecture as being more important than his writing, it was his writing about architecture, and about the life style of Australia, that has had the greatest influence. Boyd was the first Australian writer on architecture to adopt the role of social commentator. His approach led to a more critical appraisal of Australian buildings and a protracted campaign against Australian visual traditions and cultural deficiencies. The chief defect of Australian architecture, Boyd contended, was that buildings lacked a single strong idea and were instead an "assortment of little ideas which are shaken up together to make a building; typically, the 'Featuremarket' with its many loud, stale ideas mixed together."

Robin Boyd's writing and architecture were not separate and unrelated; rather, they express, in different ways, his deep involvement with people and buildings. His dual interest in architectural criticism and housing were first expressed in the student publication *Smudges* of the University of Melbourne. In 1950 he founded the Small Homes Service operated by the Victorian Institute of Architects. A few years later he designed Australia's first project house—Peninsula House—for Contemporary Homes Ltd. This concept was later to be developed in Sydney by Ken Woolley and Michael Dysart in their project homes for Lend Lease (1961) and Pettit and Sevitt. At about this time Boyd designed a stock "windowwall" system with various options for the Stegbar company. But his principal achievement is in the area of domestic architecture—he built about 100 houses in all. It was not until 1968 that a major work, Menzies College, La Trobe University, in a 1960's Brutalism idiom, was offered to Boyd. Of his houses, "Pelican," the Kenneth Myer House (1956), Robin Boyd's own house at South Yarra (1959), the Lloyd House (1960), the Lyon's House, Dolan's Bay, near Sydney (1967), a group of holiday houses, Portsea, Victoria (1968), and the Featherstone House, Ivanhoe, Victoria (1967) are some of his best works.

The intentional crudeness of the thick gumtree trunks which serve as columns in the Black Dolphin

Robin Boyd: Menzies College Student Housing, La Trobe University, Melbourne, 1968

Motel, Merimbula (1961) marks a new rustic bush phase in Australian architecture and, at the same time, reflects Boyd's growing disenchantment with the machine-made appearance of the 20th century International Style. His penchant for social comment was well suited to one of his last important projects, the design of the exhibits in the space tunnel of the Australian Pavilion at *Expo '70,* Osaka.

Boyd disapproved of style up to a point and believed that architectural form should be the product of the directness with which functional problems are solved with inventive structures. His architectural approach is essentially pragmatic; he liked to describe it as "realism." And while Boyd displayed a consistency in his buildings, he regarded each new problem as something unique and special, with the result that there is no recognizable Boyd style. One feature of his buildings, which is not much commented on, is his use of the tent. His own house at South Yarra had a simply suspended roof, and the Myer House has a parasol roof standing proud of the living components.

Robin Boyd wrote some eleven books between 1947 and 1971, of which *The Australian Ugliness* is perhaps the best known, though *The Puzzle of Architecture* is probably his most important book. His writings mark the beginning of a new self-consciousness in architecture, an important first step in establishing a coherent relationship with architectural history.

—Philip Drew

BRAWNE, Michael.

British. Born in Vienna, Austria, 5 May 1925. Educated at the University of Edinburgh, 1942–43; Architectural Association School, London, 1948–53, Dip.A.A. 1953; Massachusetts Institute of Technology, Cambridge, 1953–54 (Smith-Mundt Fellow), M.Arch. 1954. Served as a Sergeant Meteorologist in the Royal Air Force, 1944–47. Married Rhoda Dupler in 1954; children: Peter, Alison, and Nicholas. Worked for the Soullee Steel Company, San Francisco, 1954–56, Architects' Co-Partnership, London, 1956–59, British Transport Commission, 1959–61, and Denys Lasdun and Partners, London, 1961–64. Since 1964, Principal, Michael Brawne and Associates, London. Instructor in Architecture, Cambridge University, 1964–78. Professor of Architecture, University of Bath, since 1978. Visiting Lecturer: Akademie für die Bildende Künste, Berlin; Architectural Association School, London; Boston Architectural Center; University of Bristol; Gujarat University, Ahmedabad, India; University of Illinois, Chicago Circle and Urbana; University of Strathclyde, Glasgow; University College London; York Institute for Advanced Studies. Director, Architectural Association/Royal Institute of British Architects Seminar on University Planning, University of Sussex, Brighton, 1964; RIBA Representative, Illuminating Engineering Society panel on museum lighting, 1966–69; British Council Lecturer in India, 1968; Member, Advisory Panel, Centre for Advanced Studies in Environment, Architectural Association, London, 1969; Member, International Colloquium on the Technical Equipment of Central Libraries, Prague, 1974. Member of the Consultative Committee, Thames Polytechnic School of Architecture, London, since 1974. Associate, 1954, and Fellow, 1969, Royal Institute of British Architects. Address: Michael Brawne and Associates, 42 Earlham Street, London WC2H 9LA, England.

Works:

1954/
56 Wall system and door units for Soullee Steel Company, San Francisco
1956/
59 House, Enugu, Nigeria (at Architects' Co-Partnership)
Esso Oil Terminal, Apapa, Nigeria (at Architects' Co-Partnership)
1959/
61 Power Signal Box, British Railways, Manchester (at British Transport Commission)
Power Signal Box, British Railways, Edge Hill, Liverpool (at British Transport Commission)
Marshalling Yard and Amenity Buildings, British Railways, Carlisle (at British Transport Commission)
1961 House, 31 South Hill Park, London N.W.3
Trinity College Library, Dublin (competition project)
1966 Housing study for Bovis Holdings Ltd., London

1967 House, Fisher's Pond, Hampshire
1968 Bettwys Comprehensive School, Newport, Monmouthshire (competition project)
     Oxford Gallery
1969 Agricultural Research Council Maintenance Workshop, Babraham, Cambridgeshire
1969/
71   Horne Brothers Shop, 4 Oxford Street, London W.1
1970 Agricultural Research Council Animal Research Laboratories, Babraham, Cambridgeshire
     Agricultural Research Council Biochemistry Laboratory, Babraham, Cambridgeshire (with Colin St. John Wilson)
1971 Dorset County Museum extension, Dorchester
     Indoor swimming pool, Bosham, Sussex
1972 Gimpel Fils Art Gallery, London
1972/
73   Consumer Association Testing and Research Laboratory, stage I and II, Harpenden, Hertfordshire
1974 Costume Gallery, Royal Courts of Justice, London (with Colin St. John Wilson)
     Physics Building, Royal Holloway College, Egham, Surrey
1977 Arts Centre, Cambridge (project)
     Central Art Gallery conversion, Rochdale, Lancashire (with the Borough Architect)
1978 Cooper Art Gallery, Barnsley, Yorkshire
     National Gallery renovation, London (as consultant)
     National Library, Colombo, Sri Lanka (with Chief Government Architect)

Exhibition Designs: *Gauguin and the Pont-Aven Group,* Tate Gallery, London, 1966; *Naum Gabo,* Tate Gallery, London, 1966; *Jean Dubuffet,* Tate Gallery, London, 1966; *Marcel Duchamp,* Tate Gallery, London, 1966; *Rouault,* Tate Gallery, London, 1966; *David Smith,* Tate Gallery, London, 1966; *L. S. Lowry,* Tate Gallery, London, 1966; *Bomberg/Zoltan Kemeny,* Tate Gallery, London, 1966; *Great Britain/U.S.S.R.,* Victoria and Albert Museum, London, 1967; *Picasso Sculpture, Ceramics and Graphics,* Tate Gallery, London, 1967; *Cubist Art from Czechoslovakia,* Tate Gallery, London, 1967; *Derain,* Royal Academy, London, 1967; *Turkish Art,* Victoria and Albert Museum, London, 1967; *Ancient Art from Afghanistan,* Royal Academy, London, 1967; *Marzotto Prize,* Tate Gallery, London, 1967; *Alfred Wallis/Peter Lanyon,* Tate Gallery, London, 1968; *Henry Moore,* Tate Gallery, London, 1968; *Balthus,* Tate Gallery, London, 1968; *Roy Lichtenstein,* Tate Gallery, London, 1968; *Barbara Hepworth,* Tate Gallery, London, 1968; *Hungarian Art Treasures,* Victoria and Albert Museum, London, 1968; *Willem de Kooning,* Tate Gallery, London, 1969; *Magritte,* Tate Gallery, London, 1969; *Art of the Real,* Tate Gallery, London, 1969; *Pop Art,* Hayward Gallery, London, 1969; *Claes Oldenburg,* Tate Gallery, London, 1970; *Multiple Art,* Whitechapel Art Gallery, London, 1970; *Richard Hamilton,* Tate Gallery, London, 1970; *Cambridge Festival,* Corn Exchange, Cambridge, 1970; *Early Celtic Art,* Hayward Gallery, London, 1971; *Art in Revolution,* Hayward Gallery, London, 1971; *Ceramic Art of China,* Victoria and Albert Museum, London, 1971; *Victorian Church Art,* Victoria and Albert Museum, London, 1971; *Amiet and Giacometti,* Kettle's Yard Gallery, Cambridge, 1971; *Gerrit Rietveld,* Hayward Gallery, London, 1972; *French Symbolists,* Hayward Gallery, London, 1972; *The Age of Neo-Classicism,* Royal Academy, London, 1972; *The King's Arcadia: Inigo Jones and the Stuart Court,* Banqueting House, London, 1973; *Treasures from the European Community,* Victoria and Albert Museum, London, 1973; *Man and Beast: The Work of Elisabeth Frink,* Kettle's Yard Gallery, Cambridge, 1973; *The Art of Woodcarving in West Africa and New Guinea,* Kettle's Gallery, Cambridge, 1975; *The Arts of Islam,* Hayward Gallery, 1976; *John Constable Bicentenary,* British Council, London, 1977, toured overseas; multi-screen presentation at *Islam dans les Collections Nationales,* Grand Palais, Paris, 1977.

Publications:

By BRAWNE: books—*The New Museum: Architecture and Display,* Stuttgart and London 1965; *University Planning and Design: A Symposium,* editor, London 1967; *Libraries: Architecture and Equipment,* Stuttgart and London 1970; entries on architecture and town planning in *A Dictionary of Modern Thought,* edited by Alan Bullock and and Oliver Stallybrass, London 1977; articles—"Project in Steel: A House in Berkeley" in *Arts and Architecture* (Los Angeles), January 1956; "The Production of Shelter: A System of Prefabrication" in *Arts and Architecture* (Los Angeles), September 1956; "Walls off the Peg: The Curtain Wall" in *Architectural Review* (London), September 1957; "Geometry of Shade" in *Architectural Review* (London), June 1958; "Looking Up: Suspended Ceilings as an Element in Interior Design" in *Architectural Review* (London), September 1958; "Le Corbusier: A Symposium" in *Architectural Association Journal* (London), May 1959; "The Picture Wall: An Analysis of Art Gallery Design" in *Architectural Review* (London), May 1959; "Object on View: An Analysis of Museum Design" in *Architectural Review* (London), November 1959; "Polyester Fibreglass" in *Architectural Review* (London), December 1959; "Parking Terminals" in *Architectural Review* (London), August 1960; "Libraries: Communicating with Individuals" in *Architectural Review* (London), October 1961; "Airport Passenger Buildings" in *Architectural Review* (London), November 1962; "Commonwealth Institute, South Kensington: Critical Appraisal" in *Architectural Review* (London), April 1963; "Student Living: Approaches to Residential Planning" in *Architectural Review* (London), October 1963; "University Planning" in *Architectural Association Journal* (London), January 1965; "University of York: Critical Appraisal" in *Architectural Review* (London), December 1965; "The Wit of Technology: The Works of Charles Eames" in *Architectural Design* (London), September 1966; "The New Whitney: The Building: A Critical Appraisal" in *Artforum* (Los Angeles), November 1966; "Museum Design for Conservation" in *London Conference on Museum Climatology,* London 1967; "Library Planning" in *Better Library Buildings,* London 1969; "The New Universities," editor, a special issue of *Architectural Review* (London), April 1970; "Off the Shelf: A Review of the Library at Redcar" in *Architectural Review* (London), July 1971; "A Museum and Some Problems of Tradition: A Review of the North Jutland Museum of Arts" in *Architectural Review* (London), March 1973; "Briefing: Museums" in *Architectural Design* (London), October 1973; "Wolfson College, Oxford: An Appraisal" in *Architectural Review* (London), October 1974; "What Is Wrong with Eclecticism?" in *Gottfried Semper und die Mitte des 19 Jahrhunderts,* Basel and Stuttgart 1976; "Museum of London: An Appraisal" in *Architectural Review* (London), July 1977; "Art Gallery Extensions" in *The Architects' Journal* (London), 30 November 1977; "Geoffrey Bawa: An Appraisal" in *Architectural Review* (London), April 1978.

On BRAWNE: books—*New Architecture of London* by Sam Lambert, London 1963; *Maisons de Vacances en Europe* by Bernard Wolgensiger, Fribourg 1968; *Zodiac 18: Great Britain,* Milan 1968; *50 Ville de Nostro Tempo* by Roberto Aloi, Milan 1970; *Modern Houses in Town and Country* by Joyce Lowrie, London 1974; *House Conversion and Renewal* by Peter Collymore, London 1975.

*

All statements of architectural intent are difficult and risky since the correspondence between such verbal statements and the architectural end product is invariably shadowy. To say therefore that I believe it important to create an architecture of complex simplicity may not be very helpful or, in the end, accurate, even given a certain amount of explanation. Its reverse, simple complexity (to make a negative statement, which is often easier), is either the inability to resolve the enmeshed nature of all architectural problems or just an accumulation of elements for their own sake; in the end a kind of fussiness. Attempts to enrich architecture consciously but without much thought often produce just such simple complexity.

By complex simplicity I mean a kind of order which has arisen out of a set of unique circumstances, modified always of course by one's own visual likes and dislikes; an order which is intelligible to others and, hopefully, not so banal that it is boring or so weak that it has failed to deal with the important problems. This is not a matter of decoration but of the way in which all aspects are handled including those that show how a building is put together. Perhaps it has something to do with the density of visual information.

I have, as an architect, found myself involved with a limited number of building types: houses, laboratories, museums and libraries. It could be argued that the kind of attitude towards complexity which I am advocating is particularly appropriate to these buildings. I do not believe this to be the case. Firstly, the types are sufficiently disimilar in their characteristics and secondly, fifteen years of teaching have persuaded me that the attitude can be extended over a wide range of architectural tasks. The limited palette was also, of course, by no means self imposed but a matter of circumstance which has become self perpetuating. The need to test these assumptions actively on other problems is thus one of the drives which makes an involvement in practice continuously necessary and hopeful.

Architecture as both a practical and academic activity I find totally absorbing and believe it moreover to be important. Not simply because I find it enjoyable but because I am convinced that buildings, quite apart from sheltering so much of our life, can give great pleasure and security to most of us. It would be hard to think of a civilised world without architecture; not just great architecture, but any.

—Michael Brawne

Much of the flavour of Michael Brawne's architecture can be surmised from the tone and method of his writings—cool, intellectual, self-conscious, raising interesting questions about the nature of architecture, not without a mannered charm.

Very much a part of a certain Cambridge circle (though he now holds the chair at the University of Bath, leaving his frequent collaborator, Colin St. John Wilson, as professor in the fens), Brawne has had his major influence through his words, as a critic in the *Architectural Review,* and as a teacher, in the studio of the architecture department at Cambridge University. Nor, even as a designer, has his public impact been through his occasional series of finely ordered buildings. For more than ten years Brawne has produced, with great skill, a large number of major art exhibitions of a staggeringly catholic range, usually for one of the leading U.K. public galleries. With the touch of a fine accompanist, he has managed consistently to enhance both the material and its setting, whilst remaining unobtrusive himself—a point well illustrated in the Hayward Gallery's *Art in Revolution* in 1971 (the major Constructivist show, with its banners and agit-prop streaming from the presses) and in *The Age of Neo-Classicism,* an equally important but utterly contrasting event the following year in the very different setting of the Royal Academy.

Brawne's buildings—research laboratories clad in russet steel, museum and library, the occasional houses—all bear the stamp of his sense of order, immaculate yet informal. Apart from an occasional

Michael Drawne: House, Fisher's Pond, Hampshire, 1967

heaviness of frame (which is almost ungainly), there is, in his work, from the Fisher's Pond House of 1967 to the National Library of Sri Lanka of 1978, no family pattern in image or in form generator. (His recurring interest in the diagonal never becomes a trademark.)

His own house in Hampstead (1961) expresses the man. The stair had to be a certain width; the window module was less. And so, with complex simplicity, Brawne created a cranked internal wall, the return leg fully glazed into the stair well. The architecture would have been less had the glazing bar been moved, the wall angled, or the planning simply changed. He said, "The need to accommodate the difference between the width of stairs and the module of the external glazing created the opportunity for an unusual internal window. . . ." Too far, perhaps.

Brawne's civility, nevertheless, remains a precious quality.

—J.M. McKean

BREUER, Marcel (Lajko).

American. Born in Pécs, Hungary, 22 May 1902; emigrated to the United States, 1937: naturalized, 1944. Educated at the Állami Föreáiskola, Pécs, 1912–20; Bauhaus, Weimar, 1920–24, graduated 1924. Married Martha Erps in 1926; Constance Crocker Leighton in 1940; children: Thomas and Francesca. Master of the Bauhaus, in Weimar, 1924, and Dessau, 1925–28; architect and planner in Dessau, 1925–28, Berlin, 1928–31, and London, 1935–36; Associate Professor, Harvard University School of Design, Cambridge, Massachusetts, 1937–46; Principal, Marcel Breuer and Associates, Cambridge, 1937–46, and New York City, 1946 until his retirement, 1976. Member, National Council of Architectural Registration Boards, 1947. Exhibitions: *Werkbund Exhibition,* Grand Palais, Paris, 1930; *Bauausstellung,* Berlin, 1931; *Bauhaus 1919–1928,* New York, 1938; Museum of Modern Art, New York (one-man), 1949; Metropolitan Museum of Art, New York (one-man), 1972; Musée du Louvre, Paris (one-man), 1973; Bauhaus Archives, Berlin, 1974. Recipient: First Prize, International Aluminum Competition, 1930, 1933; Medal of Honor, 1965, Gold Medal, 1968, Award for Excellence, 1970, and Honor Award, 1970, 1972, 1973, American Institute of Architects; New York State Council on the Arts Award, 1967; Bard Award, City Club of New York, 1968; Thomas Jefferson Foundation Medal, University of Virginia, Charlottesville, 1968; Metropolitan Washington Board of Trade Award, 1969; Grande Medaille d'Or, French Academy of Architecture, 1976. Honorary doctorates: Pratt Institute, Brooklyn, New York, 1950; University of Budapest, 1957; University of Notre Dame, Indiana, 1968; Harvard University, 1970. Fellow, American Institute of Architects. Member, National Institute of Arts and Letters. Honorary Member, Association of Argentine Architects, 1947, and Association of Architects of Colombia, 1947. Address: 139 East 63rd Street, New York, New York 10021, U.S.A.

Works:

1924/
28 Prototype steel furniture and interchangeable cabinet units
1930 Fuld Factory, Frankfurt (project)
1932 Harnischmacher House I, Wiesbaden
1936 Doldertal Apartments, Zurich (with A. and E. Roth)
      Isokon Laminated Furniture
      Gane's Stone Exhibition Pavilion, Bristol, England
      Civic Centre of the Future, London (project; with F. R. S. Yorke)
1938 Haggerty House, Cohasset, Massachusetts (with Walter Gropius)
      Wheaton College Art Center, Norton, Massachusetts (with Walter Gropius)
1939 Breuer House I, Lincoln, Massachusetts
1940 Chamberlin Cottage, Wayland, Massachusetts (with Walter Gropius)
1942 South Boston Redevelopment (project)
      Prefabricated houses, Cambridge, Massachusetts (project)

Marcel Breuer: IBM Research Center, La Gaude, Var, France, 1961

1945 Servicemen's Memorial, Cambridge, Massachusetts (project; with L. Andersen)
Tompkins House, Hewlett Harbor, New York
Geller House, Lawrence, Long Island, New York
1947 Breuer House II, New Canaan, Connecticut
Robinson House, Williamstown, Massachusetts
1948 Breuer Cottage, Wellfleet, Massachusetts
1949 Wolfson House, Pleasant Valley, New York
Clark House, Orange, Connecticut
1950 Co-operative Dormitory, Vassar College, Poughkeepsie, New York
Stillman House I, Litchfield, Connecticut
1951 Breuer House III, New Canaan, Connecticut

1952 Art Center, Sarah Lawrence College, Bronxville, New York
Caesar Cottage, Lakeville, Connecticut
1953 Torin Corporation Building, Oakville, Ontario
1953/
70 St. John's Abbey and University, Collegeville, Minnesota (with H. Smith)
1954 Grieco House, Andover, Massachusetts
1954/
57 Institute for Advanced Study Housing, Princeton, New Jersey (with R. F. Gatje)
1956 Litchfield High School, Connecticut (with O'Connor and Killham)

1956/
61 New York University, University Heights, New York (with H. Smith and R. F. Gatje)
1957 De Bijenkorf Department Store, Rotterdam (with A. Elzas)
Laaff House, Andover, Massachusetts (with H. Beckhard)
1958 Unesco Headquarters, Paris (with Pier Luigi Nervi and Bernard Zehrfuss)
United States Embassy, The Hague
Staehelin House, Feldmeilen, Switzerland (with H. Beckhard)
Van Leer Headquarters, Amstelveen, Netherlands
El Recreo Urban Centre, Caracas (project; with E. Fuenmeyer and H. Beckhard)
Resort Development Apartments, Tanaguarena, Venezuela (project; with H. Beckhard)
1959 Convent of the Annunciation, Bismarck, North Dakota (with H. Smith)
Hunter College Library, New York (with R. F. Gatje)
Hanson House, Huntington, Long Island, New York
Ustinov House, Vevey, Switzerland (project; with R. F. Gatje)
1960 Charles Center, Baltimore, Maryland (project; with H. Smith)
1960– Flaine Ski Resort, Haute Savoie, France (with R. F. Gatje)

1961 IBM Research Center, La Gaude, Var, France (with R. F. Gatje)
Temple B'nai Jeshurun, Short Hills, New Jersey (with H. Beckhard)
1962 Torin Corporation Machine Building, Torrington, Connecticut (with R. F. Gatje)
1963/
68 United States Department of Housing and Urban Development Headquarters, Washington, D.C. (with H. Beckhard)
1963/
70 ZUP Development, Bayonne, France (with R. F. Gatje)
1964 Torin Manufacturing Plant, Nivelles, Belgium (with H. Smith)
Van der Wal House, Amsterdam (project; with H. Smith)
New England Merchant's Bank, Boston (project; with H. Beckhard)
1965 New York University Dormitory, Bronx, New York (project)
1965/
68 Laboratories Sarget, Bordeaux, France (with R. F. Gatje and Daurel)
1965/
69 University of Massachusetts Campus Center and Garage, Amherst (with H. Beckhard)
1966 Whitney Museum of American Art, New York (with H. Smith)
Stillman House II, Litchfield, Connecticut (with H. Beckhard)

Torin Corporation Administration Building, Torrington, Connecticut (with H. Beckhard)

Franklin D. Roosevelt Memorial, Washington, D.C. (project; with H. Beckhard)

1967 St. Francis de Sales Church, Muskegon, Michigan (with H. Beckhard)

Interama, Miami, Florida (project; with H. Beckhard)

Kent School Girls' Chapel, Connecticut (project; with R. F. Gatje)

Flushing Meadow Sports Park, New York (project; with Beckhard, Tange, and Halprin)

1968 175 Park Avenue Office Building, New York (project; with H. Beckhard)

Parish Church, Olgiata, Rome (project; with M. Jossa)

1968/
77 Third Power Plant and Visitors' Center, Grand Coulee Dam, Washington State (with H. Smith)

1969 New York University Technology Building II, Bronx, New York (with H. Smith)

Armstrong Rubber Company Headquarters, West Haven, Connecticut (with R. F. Gatje)

Yale University Engineering Building, New Haven, Connecticut (with H. Smith)

Convent, Baldegg, Switzerland (with Jordi and Gatje)

Soriano House, Greenwich, Connecticut (with T. Papachristou)

Office Building, Syracuse, New York (project; with H. Beckhard)

1970 Cleveland Museum of Art (with H. Smith)

1971 Cleveland Trust Headquarters (with H. Smith)

1975 Stillman House III, Litchfield, Connecticut (with T. Papachristou)

Australian Embassy, Paris (with Harry Seidler and M. Jossa)

Gagarin House II, Litchfield, Connecticut (with T. Papachristou)

1977 Hubert Humphrey Building, Washington, D.C. (with H. Beckhard)

Roxbury High School, Boston (with T. Papachristou)

IBM Complex, Boca Raton, Florida (with R F. Gatje)

Central Library, Atlanta, Georgia (with Smith, Stevens, and Wilkinson)

Federal Courthouse and Office Building, Columbia, South Carolina (with H. Beckhard, David and Floyd, and J. Hemphill)

Publications:

By BREUER: articles—"Die Möbelabteilung des staatlichen Bauhauses zu Weimar," in *Fachblatt für Holzarbeiter* (Weimar), 1925; "Metallmöbel," in *Deutscher Werkbund* (Stuttgart), 1928; "Metallmöbel und moderne Raumlichkeit," in *Das Neue Frankfurt,* January 1928; "Beitrage zur Frage des Hochhauses," in *Die Form* (Opladen), no. 5, 1930; "Das Innere de Hauses," in *Bauwelt* (Berlin), May 1931; "Aus einem Vortrag . . . gehalten im Kunstgewerbemuseum, Zürich," in *Werk* (Zurich), no. 19, 1932; "Where Do We Stand," in *Architectural Review* (London), April 1935; "Architecture and Material," in *Circle: International Survey of Constructive Art* (London), 1937; "What Is Modern Architecture," in *Museum of Modern Art Bulletin* (New York), Spring 1948.

On BREUER: books—*Staatliches Bauhaus in Weimar,* Weimar/Munich 1923; *Bauhaus 1919-1928,* exhibition catalogue. New York 1938; *Marcel Breuer and the American Tradition in Architecture* by Henry Russell Hitchcock, Cambridge, Massachusetts 1938; *Marcel Breuer: Architect,* exhibition catalogue, New York 1949; *Marcel Breuer 1921-1962* by Cranston Jones, London 1962; *Marcel Breuer: New Buildings and Projects* by Tician Papachristou, New York 1970; articles—"El Arquitecto Marcel Breuer" by Siegfried Giedion in *Arquitectura* (Madrid), no. 3, 1932; "Carattere dell'opera di Marcello Breuer" by A. Podesta in *Domus* (Milan), no. 86, 1935; "A View of Marcel Breuer" by Richard G. Stein in *Metropolitan Museum of Art Exhibition Guide* (New York), 1972.

Shall we attempt to condense the central issue facing architecture today into one sentence?

In search of a precise formulation, I wrote my first and only poem (of a sort):

Colors which you can hear with ears;
Sounds to see with eyes;
The void you touch with your elbows;
The taste of space on your tongue;
The fragrance of dimensions;
The juice of stone.

—Marcel Breuer

There can be no doubt that Marcel Breuer is the most important living architect. The extent and lasting validity of his contribution for well over half a century have no equal. And yet in contrast to other "form givers" of our time, Breuer defies classification: any attempt to label his contribution in simple terms is virtually impossible.

Breuer's unique and independently creative gifts came out early in his career, and much has been written on the subject of his origins in a provincial Hungarian town, his meteoric rise as one of the architectural "stars," the dynamic center of the Bauhaus image, his early work in Europe and England, to the period of his teaching at Harvard. My first encounter with him was when I was a student at Harvard in 1945. He gave the impression of being not that much older than his students. He exuded a warm spirit of comradeship, a yearning, searching spirit, a delight in finding satisfying solutions to design problems. We all knew his early work from books, but what made the greatest possible impression on us were the built images emanating from his Cambridge, Massachusetts office. The pilgrimages to his house at Lincoln, to the Haggerty House at Cohasset, the Chamberlain Cottage at Wayland, the Geller and Tompkins houses near New York, were absolutely shattering experiences to his students who, after all, had not seen or experienced any truly modern architecture in North America at that time, certainly none that had the air of authenticity, that generated such a sense of well-being and aesthetic joy.

Of all the teachers at Harvard at that time, it was Breuer who was the taste-setter. He combined diverse and normally irreconcilable tendencies: an almost lyrically romantic spatial aesthetic (and use of material) with disarmingly simple, uncanny "Gordian Knot" solutions to planning and structural problems. He stimulated in his students the development of designs that were at once essentially rational devices yet also deliberate, visually tantalizing compositions.

Later, when working with him in New York in 1946-48, I became intimately involved with his methodology. Every building design had as its theme a single strong idea. Plans were always basically direct in organization and resulted in beautifully related and sculptured masses. In house designs there was usually a spatially powerful living area with horizontal and often vertical interplay; sleeping areas were organized separately and were more compartmentalized. Detailing was direct and completely consequential: it was always universally applicable to the limited varieties of intersections that evolved from a design. The resulting technical systems were constantly refined and carried over from one project to another. Visual tension was generated for the world in the juxtaposition of materials as much as in elevational compositions: synthetic smooth materials to natural rough stone, natural timber against manufactured white masonry blocks. This pulling of forces also existed strongly in his Mondrianesque glass wall subdivisions and in the relationship of solids to voids. Structural devices were exploited expressively: thin steel cable tension members held up visually heavy masses; walls, stair and ramp balustrades fulfilled their function but were also sculptural forms as well as logically shaped supporting elements. Breuer always had an instinctive concern with sun control—which also aided his aesthetic aims toward deeply textured exteriors.

In the great amount of his executed work from the 1950's to the 1970's, a continuing clear direction and logical development is evident. Each Breuer project consistently grew from the visual and technical experience of those preceding it (in contrast to the wild gyrations in form language of other celebrated—but now largely forgotten—practitioners of that time). The housing designs he developed have become the essence of prototypes throughout the world. The concrete technology he developed both in prefabricated and pour-in-place forms has been emulated everywhere—but none of the imitations have that instantly warm emotional appeal or rationally satisfying quality of his work.

The consistency of Breuer's work can best be illustrated by noting that themes developed in a seminal design concept of 1936, the Civic Centre of the Future, continue to recur—in the double Y-shaped office designs of Unesco in Paris, in the IBM Research Center, La Gaude, France, in the HUD Building in Washington, and in many other buildings.

No other modern architect's work has remained as valid visually and technically for 50 years and more as has Breuer's. His earliest, as much as his latest, buildings exude that unique and characteristic warmth and give the visitor a feeling of well-being. It took half a century for the world to rediscover the magnificent qualities of his "Wassily" and "Cesca" chairs. In our shallow era of short-lived thrills of appearance, it may take as long again for the world to fully appreciate and rediscover the great genius inherent in all the wealth of his architecture.

—Harry Seidler

BRINKMAN, Johannes (Andreas).
Dutch. Born in Rotterdam, 22 March 1902. Educated at the Technische Hochschule, Delft. Worked in the office of his father, Michiel Brinkman, Rotterdam, 1921–25; in partnership with L. C. van der Vlugt, *q.v.,* Rotterdam, 1925–36; with Johannes van den Broek, *q.v.,* Rotterdam, 1937 until he retired, 1948. Exhibition: *Building for an Open City,* Boymans Museum, Rotterdam, 1963, toured The Netherlands, Germany, Austria and Italy. *Died (in Rotterdam) 6 May 1949.*

Works:

1925/
26 Theosophical Union Meeting Hall and Administration Building, Tolstraat, Amsterdam

1925/
27 Van Nelle Tobacco Company Offices, Aalmarkt, Leiden

1926 Theosophical Union Building, Ommen, Netherlands

Van Nelle Company Boilerhouse, van Nelleweg 1, Rotterdam

1926/
27 Public housing, Mathenesscrweg, Rotterdam

1926/
29 Van Nelle Tobacco Company Factory, van Nelleweg 1, Rotterdam

1928/
29 Van der Leeuw Villa, Kralingseplaslaan, Rotterdam
1929 Tennis Club, Delftshavensee Schie, Rotterdam
     Internationale Crediet en Handelsvereiniging Headquarters extensions, Wolfshoek, Rotterdam
1929/
31 Grain silos, Maashaven, Rotterdam
1930 Mees and Zoonen Bank Building, Beursplein, Rotterdam (project)
     Van der Leeuw Holiday House, Rockanje, Netherlands
     De Maas Steam Mills extensions, Maashaven, Rotterdam
1930/
31 De Bruyn Villa, Ary Prinslaan, Schiedam, Netherlands
     Mees and Zoonen Bank Building, 's-Gravendijkwal, Rotterdam
1930/
32 Van Stolk and Zn. Office Building, Abraham van Stolkweg, Rotterdam
1931 Concert Hall and Cultural Centre, Coolsingel, Rotterdam (project)
1931/
32 Graansilo N.V. Offices and Housing, Maashaven, Rotterdam
     Van Ommeren N.V. Travel Bureau rebuilding, rue Auber, Paris
     Maas Millworks Office Building, Canteen and Porter's House, Brielselaan, Rotterdam
     Prototype telephone booth, Rotterdam
1932 University buildings, Rotterdam (project)
1932/
33 Sonneveld Villa, Jongkindstraat, Rotterdam
1932/
34 Boeve Villa, Mathenesserlaan, Rotterdam
1932/
38 Van der Leeuw Holiday House, Ommen, Netherlands
1933 Van Hoey-Smith Weekend House, Rockanje, Netherlands (project)
     Golf Club, Kralingseweg, Rotterdam
1933/
34 Rotterdamse Kunstkring rebuilding, Witte de Withstraat, Rotterdam
1933/
35 Steel Skyscraper Block, Bergpolder, Rotterdam (with Willem van Tijen)
     Maas Grain and Coal Silos, Brielselaan, Rotterdam
1934 Zoological Gardens, Rotterdam (project)
     Diaconessenhuis/Schwesternheim Clinic, Westersingel, Rotterdam (project)
     Holland-America Lines Ticket Offices, rue Scribe, Paris
     Low-cost housing, Amsterdam (competition project)
1934/
35 Zuid Navigational Union Station, Vierhavenstraat, Rotterdam
1934/
36 Vaes Villa, Kortekade, Rotterdam
1935 University Extension Buildings, Westzeedijk, Rotterdam (project)
     van der Vlugt Holiday House, Noordwijk aan Zee, Netherlands
1935/
36 Feijenoord Stadium, Olympiaweg, Rotterdam
     Airport Reception Building, Ypenburg, Netherlands
     Tennis Club, Rotterdam
1936/
37 Muntz Country House, de Koog, Texel, Netherlands
1936/
38 Diaconessenhuis Clinic extensions, Westersingel, Rotterdam
1937 Hoogendijk Villa, Holyweg, Vlaardingen-Ambacht, Netherlands

Hospital, Terneuzen, Netherlands (project)
Plate Holiday House, Rockanje, Netherlands (project)
Backx Holiday House, Rockanje, Netherlands (project)
1937/
38 Holland-America Lines Departure Hall, Wilhelminakade, Rotterdam
     Ten Horst-Vogel House, Vierhouten, Netherlands
     Niehuis-van den Berg Office extensions, Pastoriestraat, Rotterdam
1937/
39 Snoek House, C.N.A. Looslaan, Hillergersberg, Rotterdam
1937/
40 Van Ommeren N.V. Office Building, Antwerp
1938 House of Art and Science, Rotterdam (project)
     Nygh House, Rotterdam (project)
1938/
39 Gestel House, Bentincklaan, Rotterdam
     Arend Central Club House, Rotterdam
     Public housing, Bentincklaan, Rotterdam
1938/
40 Low-cost housing, Tarwebuurt, Rotterdam-Sud
1939 Mass Exhibition Hall of 1941, Rotterdam (project)
     Public housing, Statensingel, Rotterdam (project)
1940/
41 Workers' housing, Rotterdam
     Temporary shops, Mathenesserlaan, Rotterdam
1941 Garden Housing Estate, Wilgenplas, Rotterdam (project)
     Blaak Development Plan, Rotterdam (competition project)
1941/
43 Tollens and Company Dye and Lacquer Factory, Overschieseweg, Overschie, Netherlands
     Public housing, Rotterdam-Sud
1941/
45 Gispen N.V. Factory and Office Building extensions, Stationsweg, Culemborg, Netherlands
1941/
48 Strijp I Terrace Housing, Strijp, Eindhoven, Netherlands
1942 Development plan for the Hofplein, Rotterdam (competition project)
     Engels N.V. Slaughterhouse, Garage and Canteen, Landsmeer, Netherlands (project)
1942/
43 Van Nelle Company Warehouse extensions, van Nelleweg, Rotterdam
1943 Reconstruction plan for Schiedamsesingel-Binnenweg, Rotterdam (project)
     Post-war public housing, Rotterdam (project; with the Woning-Architectuur Group)
     Maritime Centre, Vasteland, Rotterdam (project)
1944 Slaughterhouse and cattle-market, Rotte, Rotterdam (project)
1945 Wevers Circus, Blijdorp, Rotterdam (project)
     Parish Centre, Rotterdam-Sud (project)
1945/
49 Ardath Tobacco Company extensions, Spuiweg, Dordrecht, Netherlands
1946 Reform Church, Kralingen, Rotterdam (project)
1946/
47 Nederlandse Agrarische Industrie Factory rebuilding, Poeldijk, Netherlands
1946/
48 Aircraft Hangar reconstruction, Ypenburg, Netherlands
1946/
49 Holland-America Lines Warehouse and

Office Building, Wilhelminahaven, Rotterdam
Thomsen's Havenbedrif Harbour Building, Lekhaven, Rotterdam
1947 Aula University, Diergaardesingel, Rotterdam (project)
     Single-family housing (project)
     Terraced housing, Hook of Holland (project)
1947/
50 Strijp II Terrace Housing, Strijp, Eindhoven, Netherlands
     Holland-America Lines Harbour Building, Rijnhaven, Rotterdam
1947/
51 Lamers and Indemans N.V. Factory, Parallelweg, Hertogenbosch, Netherlands
1948 Church Community Centre, Charlois, Rotterdam (project)

Publications:

By BRINKMAN: book—*Woonmogelijkheden in het nieuwe Rotterdam,* with Willem van Tijen, Huig A. Maaskant, and J. H. van den Broek, Rotterdam 1941.

On BRINKMAN: books—*Nuova Architettura nel Mondo* by A. Pica, Milan 1938; *Geschichte der Moderne Architektur* by Jürgen Joedicke, Stuttgart 1963; *Building for an Open City,* exhibition catalogue, Rotterdam 1963; articles—"Usines de Tabac, Rotterdam" in *Cahiers d'Art* (Paris), vol. 4, 1929; "La Nuova Architettura Olandese" by Leo Lionni in *Casabella* (Milan), May 1934; "Twee Woonhuizen te Rotterdam van de Architecten Brinkman en van der Vlugt" by B. Merkelbach in *De 8 en Opbouw* (Amsterdam), no. 11/12, 1934; "Casa Populare a Rotterdam" by R. Rothschild in *Casabella* (Milan), December 1934; "Brinkman e van der Vlugt, Architetti" by Edoardo Persico and Leo Lionni in *Casabella* (Milan), March 1935; special issue of *De 8 en Opbouw* (Amsterdam), October 1936; "House van der Leeuw, Rotterdam" in *Architectural Record* (New York) October 1950; "van den Broek und Bakema: A Contribution to the History of Architecture" by Franz Fueg in *Bauen und Wohnen* (Zurich), October 1959; "Brinkman, Brinkman, van der Vlugt, van den Broek, Bakema" by B. Housden, special issue of *Architectural Association Journal* (London), December 1960; "Van Nelle Factory in Rotterdam" in *Architecture* (Paris), April 1975.

L.C. van der Vlugt enjoyed his most creative years as an architect from 1925 when he entered into partnership with Johannes Brinkman. Unquestionably the greatest work of the partnership is the Van Nelle Tobacco Factory near Rotterdam (to the design of which Mart Stam also contributed). This famous modern building, dating from 1929, is one of the most important of all 20th century industrial buildings, and one of the most elegant. It consists of a large eight-storey block with an attic, the staircases being expressed; curved wings of three storeys over basements, with attics; tall chimneys; and freely expressed ramped corridor-connections with lower industrial buildings. The cladding is one of the best examples of a fully developed curtain-wall system, while the treatment of the massing of blocks, relationships of solids to voids, and disposition of elements, is masterly.

Brinkman and van der Vlugt collaborated with Willem van Tijen on the design of the slab-shaped Bergpolder high-rise block in Rotterdam of 1933–4, one of the earliest buildings on the pilotti base made fashionable by Le Corbusier.

On the death of van der Vlugt in 1936, Brinkman entered into another fruitful partnership with J.H. van den Broek, who was to join up with Jacob B. Bakema in 1948 on Brinkman's retirement. These architects took up a philosophical stance that was derived from the theories of De Stijl, and so was seen to be functionalist and materialist by the devotees of

Johannes Brinkman and L. C. van der Vlugt: Boeve Villa, Mathenesserlaan, Rotterdam, 1934

Granpré Molière of Delft. The Professor at Delft Technical College encouraged the traditions of craftsmanship that had been a part of Berlage's work, which had followers in many countries. Brinkman and van der Vlugt were opposed to the traditionalists; they favoured a functionalism that was anathema to Granpré Molière. The office that harboured men like Mart Stam remained radically committed to industrialized non-craft techniques of design, and so remained out of favour with mainstream architectural thought in the Netherlands during the late 1930's and 40's. When van den Broek himself was appointed professor at Delft in 1948, he and Bakema attacked the traditionalists of the Delft School, and rallied support from the survivors of De Stijl.

—James Stevens Curl

BRODY, Samuel.

American. Born in Plainfield, New Jersey, 5 August 1926. Educated at Dartmouth College, Hanover, New Hampshire, B.A.; Graduate School of Design, Harvard University, Cambridge, Massachusetts, M.Arch. Married to Sally Brody; children: David, Elizabeth and Daniel. Architect, Kelly and Gruzen, New York, 1950–53. Since 1953, Partner, with Lewis Davis, *q.v.,* Davis, Brody and Associates, New York. Adjunct Professor, Cooper Union School of Architecture, New York, since 1959. Davenport Professor of Architecture, Yale University, New Haven, Connecticut, 1974. Chairman, Selection Jury for the New York City Mayor's Panel, 1969; Chairman of the Housing Committee, 1971, Chairman of the Committee on Fellows, 1971–72, Vice-President, 1971–73, and Chairman of the Committee on Ethics, 1973, American Institute of Architects, New York Chapter; Vice-President, Harvard Graduate School of Design Council, 1975. Recipient: Design Award, *Progressive Architecture,* 1954, 1955, 1958, 1961 (twice), 1962, 1966; Honor Award, American Institute of Architects, Potomac Valley, Maryland, Chapter, 1958; Design Award, Church Architectural Guild of America, 1958; Certificate of Merit, New York City Department of Commerce, 1958; Certificate of Merit, 1958, 1963, and Award, 1973, 1974, New York State Association of Architects; Award of Merit, *House and Home,* 1960; United States Department of Health, Education and Welfare Award, 1966; Honor Award, AIA, New England Regional Council, 1966; Higher Education Facilities Design Award, 1966, Honor Award, 1968, 1971 (twice), 1976, and Architectural Firm Award, 1975, national AIA; Bard Award, City Club of New York, 1969, 1973, 1975; Certificate of Merit, Municipal Arts Society, New York, 1969, 1972, 1973 (twice); Concrete Industries Award, 1969; Staten Island Chamber of Commerce Award, New York, 1970; Golden Triangle Award, National Society of Interior Designers, 1970; International Design Award, American Institute of Design, 1970; Bartlett Award, 1971, 1976; Homes for Better Living Award, 1971; Award of Honor, New York Society of Architects, 1972, 1973, 1974; Medal of Honor, AIA, New York Chapter, 1973; Mayor of New York's Citation for Distinguished Service, 1973; Brunner Award, National Institute of Arts and Letters, 1975; Louis Sullivan Award, 1977. Fellow, American Institute of Architects, 1969. Address: Davis, Brody and Associates, 130 East 59th Street, New York, New York 10022, U.S.A.

See DAVIS, Lewis

BRUBAKER, Charles William.

American. Born in South Bend, Indiana, 28 September 1926. Educated at Purdue University, West Lafayette, Indiana, 1945; University of Texas at Austin, 1947–50, B.Arch. 1950. Served in the United States Navy, 1945–46. Married Elizabeth Allen Rogers in 1955; children: William, Elizabeth and Robert. Designer, Project Manager, Partner, and Vice-President, 1950–68, President, 1968–74, and since 1974 Senior Vice-President, Perkins and Will, Chicago, with offices in New York and Washington, D.C. Member of the Board, Society for College and University Planning, 1968–70. Currently: Member of the National Urban Planning and Design Committee, Member of the City Planning Committee of the Chicago Association of Commerce and Industry, and Member of the Board of Directors of the Metropolitan Housing and Planning Council of Chicago;

President, Council of Educational Facility Planners. Fellow, American Institute of Architects, 1968. Address: Perkins and Will Architects, 309 West Jackson Boulevard, Chicago, Illinois 60606, U.S.A.

Works:

1963 National College of Agriculture, Chapingo, Mexico (with Alvarez and Carral)
Eckerd College, St. Petersburg, Florida
1964 Cairo-American College, Cairo, Egypt (with Salah Zietoun)
1965 First National Bank, Chicago (with C. F. Murphy Associates)
1966 New Trier West High School, Winnetka, Illinois (with The Architects Collaborative)
School of Technology, Southern Illinois University, Carbondale

1967 Sandhill College, Southern Pines, North Carolina (with Hayes-Howell)
1968 First National Bank Plaza, Chicago (with C. F. Murphy Associates)
Orchard Ridge College, Farmington, Michigan (with Giffels and Rossetti)
1970 Richland College, Dallas, Texas (with The Oglesby Group)
College of Alameda, near San Francisco (with Stone, Maracini and Patterson)
1972 Disney Magnet School, Chicago
1974 Whitney Young High School, Chicago
1976 Arvada Center, Arvada, Colorado (with Seracuse and Lawler)
Fort Hayes Career Center, Columbus, Ohio (with Dan Carmichael)
1978 Robert Morgan Technical-Vocational Institute, Miami

Charles William Brubaker: Richland College, Dallas, Texas, 1970

Oakton Community College, Des Plaines, Illinois

Augustana College Center, Rock Island, Illinois (with Parkhurst, Appier, Marolf)

Lake County Public Library, Merrillville, Indiana (with George Hall)

Grand Rapids Junior College, Michigan (with WBDC)

Publications:

By BRUBAKER: books—*Schools for America,* with others, Washington, D.C. 1967; *The Schoolhouse in the City,* with others, New York 1968; *Planning Flexible Learning Spaces,* New York 1977; articles —"Space for Individual Learning" in *School Executive* (Chicago), February 1959; "Planning the Community College" in *College and University Business* (Chicago), October 1967; "How to Create Territory for Learning in the Secondary School" in *Nation's Schools* (Chicago), March 1968; "Urban Design and National Policy for Urban Growth" in *AIA Journal* (Washington, D.C.), October 1969; "The Three-Generation Neighborhood" in *Interiors* (New York), November 1970; "Long Island: 2001" in *Newsday* (Long Island, New York), 24 June 1973; "The Corridor" in *Architectural Forum* (New York), February 1974; "Tomorrow's Malls" in *Chain Store Age Executive* (New York), September 1975; "Ten Decades of Chicago Architecture" in *Commerce* (Chicago), October 1977; "Chicago's New Downtown" in *Chicago Daily News,* 4 December 1977; "New Trends in Building Design" in *Dodge Construction News* (Chicago), 19 December 1977; "New Life for Chicago's Central Business District" in *Union League Men and Events* (Chicago), May 1978.

On BRUBAKER: books—*Open Space Schools* by American Association of School Administrators, Washington, D.C. 1971; *The New Downtowns* by Louis G. Redstone, New York 1976; *Human Response to Tall Buildings* by Donald J. Conway, Stroudsburg, Pennsylvania 1977.

*

Architecture for education has been, is, and will continue to be a most important component in the design of communities. The school has become the principal community center, and the college has become the principal cultural center.

Children and adults are influenced by the learning environment. Schools and colleges give each of us rich experiences that profoundly affect our lives. In the future, more people will be life-long learners, schools will be community centers, and colleges will serve a broader spectrum of people. Therefore, in the future, architecture for education will be even more important.

My work and interests are primarily in the design of educational facilities. I am particularly concerned with the creation of schools and colleges that are pleasant and humane, capable of responding to both the current and changing future needs of people.

The successful design of educational facilities depends on the ability to analyze needs and to create spaces that make learning effective. I have found this experience to be valuable in the design of other kinds of buildings which are primarily created for people.

—Charles William Brubaker

*

Though Charles William Brubaker is best known for the First National Bank Building and Plaza in Chicago, the focus of his career has been in designing buildings for educational institutions.

The sweeping, tapered form of the First National Bank Building (designed with C. F. Murphy Associates) grew out of the differing needs of the occupants. The public banking area on the ground floors required large amounts of open space, while the bank offices on higher floors needed less area. To enhance the sense of unobstructed interior space, Brubaker used twin elevator cores at two ends of the building rather than the traditional central core.

The glass and gray granite of the bank serve as back drop for the sunken plaza (also designed with C. F. Murphy Associates). In the tree-lined plaza Brubaker and Murphy play off square and rectangular shapes; at the center is a fountain composed of nine squares within a square. The spacious open areas of the plaza provide a space which Chicago's office workers and shoppers use during good weather months to enjoy either entertainment programs or the plaza's most famous feature, Marc Chagall's mural "Four Seasons."

Between 1963 and 1978 Brubaker designed buildings for fifteen educational institutions, from primary schools through colleges. In many of them he uses the conventional Bauhaus style: the buildings are clean, open, and sparse in architectural detail.

Brubaker fights the horizontality of the school buildings with vertical detail. At New Trier West High School in Winnetka, Illinois, there are echoes of Greek temple design with pseudo-pilasters instead of columns. In the Walt Disney Magnet School in Chicago Brubaker uses free-standing white columns to divide the dark curtain wall into three segments. The vertical line is enhanced by the site, which is at the top of a slight slope.

Brubaker has taken different directions in his designs for Richland College in Dallas and Alameda Community College near San Francisco. For Richland, Brubaker's design juxtaposes interlocking geometric forms. The Performance Hall is a central hexagon; from it, other buildings for Art and Music radiate at sharp angles. The effect of the angles is softened by the adjacent tree-lined lake, the open arcade supported by graceful T-shaped columns, and the clerestory windows used to light the artists' studios.

At Alameda College Brubaker has again used contrasting shapes and interlocking lines. Here he has taken the shape of the amphitheatre and in it has played with the relationship of space and solid object. By putting staircases on the outside of the buildings and thus eliminating interior corridors, Brubaker has enabled the college to cut energy costs substantially. Since rooms get natural light and cross ventilation, there is minimum cost for electricity and no need for air-conditioning.

In articles in American journals, Brubaker has proposed radical changes in access to educational institutions and in the interior design of primary and secondary schools. For example, he has suggested that community colleges be combined with shopping malls, thus creating community centers which integrate culture and commerce.

Brubaker's proposals for redesigning the interiors of secondary school would provide more flexibility in the learning process. Each student would share a space of 144 square feet with four other students plus the equipment needed for the special programs in which they might be involved. Faculty members would have individual studio areas or work as a team in the center of 20 student spaces. Students could thus work individually or in groups of varying size.

Whether in designing bank buildings, plazas, or educational institutions, Brubaker has employed the conventions of modern architecture, but he has both softened and humanized them.

—Mary Elizabeth Devine

BRYGGMAN, Erik (William).

Finnish. Born in Turku, 7 February 1891. Educated at the Turku School of Art, 1906–09; Öbo Svenska Klassiska Lyceum, Turku, 1910; Institute of Technology, Helsinki, graduated 1916. Married Agda Grönberg in 1918; daughter: Carin. Worked in the office of architect Valter Jung, Helsinki, 1916–23; in private practice, Turku, 1923–55. Exhibitions (one-man): Turku Art Museum, 1967; Museum of Finnish Architecture, Helsinki, 1968. Honorary Professor of Architecture, Finland, 1948; Honorary Member, Royal Academy of Art, Denmark, 1954, and Royal Academy of Art, Sweden, 1955; Honorary Member, Association of Finnish Architects, 1955. *Died* (in Turku) *21 December 1955.*

Works:

1913 *Otava* Magazine Prototype Villa (competition project)

1917 Town plan for Kuopio, Finland (competition project)
      Agricola Memorial, Turku, Finland (competition project; with E. Ilkka)

1918 War Memorial, Keuruu, Finland (competition project; with E. Ilkka)
      Tomb Memorial, Old Church Park, Helsinki (with E. Ilkka)

1919 Memorial of Liberty, Alimaalahti, Finland
      Petrelius Fountain, Turku, Finland (competition project; with H. Linden)
      Vaasa Theatre, Vaasa, Finland (competition project; with H. Ekelund and M. Valikangas)
      Burial Grounds and Chapel, Tammisto, Viborg, Finland (competition project)
      Sellgren's Department Store, Viborg, Finland (competition project)
      Crematorium, Helsinki (competition project)

1920 Memorial of Liberty, Oulu, Finland (with I. Saxelin)

1921 Town Hall, Iisalmi, Finland (competition project)
      Town plan for Lahti, Finland (competition project)

1922 Boman Furniture Prototypes (competition project)
      Memorial of Estonian Liberty (competition project; with E. Rautala)

1923 Hotel Hamburger Börs, Turku, Finland (project)
      Hospital for Rheumatics, Heinola, Finland (competition project)
      Church, Sveaborg, Finland (competition project)
      Medieval Cathedral Restoration, Turku, Finland (with Armas Lindgren)

1924 Suomen Sokeri Oy Employees' and Workmen's Housing, Turku, Finland
      Marketplace Stands, Turku, Finland (project)
      Residential block, Brahenkatu 9, Turku, Finland
      Savings Bank, Kemiö, Finland
      Skogsböle Farmhouse, Kemiö, Finland
      House of the Diet, Helsinki (competition project)

1925 Haartman Villa, Naantali, Finland
      Kellonsoittaja Residential Block, Turku, Finland

1926 Olympia Cinema interiors, Turku, Finland
      Power Station, Imatra, Finland (competition project)

1927 Länsi-Suomen Pankki (Western Bank of Finland) interiors, Turku, Finland
      Arts Museum Grounds Plan, Turku, Finland (with W. Aaltonen)
      Atrium Residential Block, Turku, Finland
      Lounais-Suomen Sähkö Oy (Southwestern Electricity Ltd.) Workers' Housing, Turku, Finland
      Atlas Bank interiors, Turku, Finland
      M. Solin Villa, Turku, Finland
      Lounais-Suomen Maalaisten Talo (Southwestern Farmers' House), Turku, Finland (competition project)

1928 Pharmacy interiors, Humalistonkatu 7, Turku, Finland
      Hotel Seurahuone-Societetshuset, Turku, Finland (with I. Ahonen)
      Erstan Villa, Kakskerta, Finland
      Aitta Magazine Villa Prototype (competition project)

Business block, Vaasa, Finland (competition project)
Suomi Insurance Company Office Building, Helsinki (competition project)
Kotkan Rauta Office Building, Kotka, Finland (competition project)

1929 Design of *7th Centenary of Turku Exhibition,* Turku, Finland (with Alvar Aalto)
Tuorla Manor renovation plan, Piikkiö, Finland (project)
Hotel Hospits Betel, Turku, Finland
E. Solin Villa, Hirvensalo, Finland
Sanatorium, Paimio, Finland (competition project)
South-Carelian Sanatorium, Joutseno, Finland (competition project)
Puijo Tourist Hotel and Restaurant, Kuopio, Finland (competition project)
Columbus Lighthouse, San Domingo (competition project; with H. Fürst)
Thonet-Mundus Furniture Prototype (competition project)
Church, Sortavala, Finland (competition project)

1930 Burial chapel, Parainen, Finland
Finnish Pavilion, *World's Fair,* Antwerp, Belgium
Exhibition Department, *Design Industry Exhibition,* Helsinki
Student Association Building, Ös, Norway (competition project; with H. Fürst)
Water supply plant, Turku, Finland (competition project)
Royal Summer Residence Annex, Oslo, Norway (competition project; with H. Fürst)
Central Library, Helsinki (competition project)
Stadium, Helsinki (first competition project)
Tehtaanpuisto Church, Helsinki (first competition project)

1931 Sauna for the Sports Institute, Vierumäki, Finland
T. Ylipohja Sauna, Hirvensalo, Finland
Church interiors, Luhanka, Finland
Town Hall, Kotka, Finland (competition project)
Lallukka Artists' Home, Helsinki (competition project)
St. Martin's Church, Turku, Finland (competition project)

1932 Sports Institute Residential Building, Vierumäki, Finland
Tehtaanpuisto Church, Helsinki (second competition project)
Enso-Gutzeit Holiday House (competition project)
Insulite Company Villa (competition project)
Special Construction Houses, Scandinavian Building Congress (competition project)

1933 Warén Villa, Ruissalo, Finland
Ekman Villa, Hirvensalo, Finland
Communal Hall, Korppoo, Finland (project)
J. J. Wecksell Statue Plan, Turku, Finland (project)
Railway Station, Tampere, Finland (competition project)
Temppelinaukio Church, Helsinki (competition project)
Stadium, Helsinki (second competition project)

1934 Mattsson Villa, Salo, Finland
Olympic Games Sauna, Döberitz, Germany
Exposition Hall, Helsinki (competition project)

1935 Öbo Akademi Library Book Tower, Turku, Finland
Pharmacy, Sauvo, Finland
Kaino Villa, Kakskerta, Finland

Erik Bryggman: Resurrection Chapel, Turku, Finland, 1941

Köhler Sauna, Kuusisto, Finland
1936 Sports Institute, Vierumäki, Finland
Kinopalatsi Cinema, Turku, Finland
Öbo Akademi Student Association Building, Turku, Finland
Pharmacy, Forssa, Finland (project)
Church, Varkaus, Finland (competition project)

1937 Kansallis-Osake-pankki Bank renovations, Turku, Finland (project)
Öbo Akademi Dormitories, Turku, Finland (project)
Cemetery enlargement, Turku, Finland (competition project)

1938 Kiva Cinema, Salo, Finland
Sampo Insurance Company Office Building, Turku, Finland
Café Lehtinen interiors, Turku, Finland

1939 Power plant, Harjavalta, Finland
Power plant engineers' housing, Harjavalta, Finland (project)
Oy Vilen Factory, Turku, Finland
Jaatinen Villa, Vessölandet, Finland
Salainen Manor renovation, Halikko, Finland (project)
Ministry of Social Affairs Single-Family House (competition project)

1940 Church restoration, Kakskerta, Finland
Cinema and residential building, Mariehamn, Finland (project)
War cemetery, Kotka, Finland (with E. Filén)

1941 Resurrection Chapel (Turku Cemetery Chapel), Turku, Finland
War Memorial, Parainen, Finland
Schleutker Villa, Parainen, Finland (project)
Paavola and Muuramä Single-Family Houses, Turku, Finland
Porin Puuvilla Oy (Pori Cotton Factory) Workers' Housing, Pori, Finland (project)
Provincial theatre, Kotka, Finland (project)
Molin Villa, Hirvensalo, Finland (project)
University College of Commercial Sciences, Helsinki (competition project)
Pinella Restaurant, Turku, Finland (project)

1942 Joutsen Pharmacy interiors, Turku, Finland (with Carin Bryggman)
Sharpshooters' Chapel restoration, Turku Cathedral, Finland (project)
Ginstrom Villa and Sauna, Dragsfjärd, Finland (project)
Keppo Manor conversion, Jepua, Finland (project)
Turun Asunto Oy Residential Block (competition project)

1943 Värtsilä Kone (Värtsilä Machinery) Catering Barracks, Turku, Finland
Church interiors, Naantali, Finland
Cinema, Hanko, Finland (project)
Children's Hospital, Hogsand, Finland (project)
Town centre plan for Tollered, Sweden (competition project)
Church, Sakkola, Finland (competition project)

1944 Oy W. Schauman Ab Catering Barracks, Joensuu, Finland
War Memorial, Dragsfjärd, Finland
War Memorial, Mietoinen, Finland
Kupittaa Folk Park, Turku, Finland (project)

1945 Schmandt Oy Bakery, Turku, Finland (project)
Elementary school, Mariehamn, Finland (competition project)
Savings Bank Residential Block, Turku, Finland (competition project)

1946 Vuoksenniska Oy Workers' and Foremen's Housing, Turku, Finland
Vasaramäki Congregation Hall, Turku, Finland
Grandell Villa, Parainen, Finland
Staffans Villa, Kakskerta, Finland
Uusimaa Central Hospital, Helsinki (project)

National Anthem Memorial, Kumpula, Finland (competition project)
Finnish Women's Welfare Foundation Collective House, Helsinki (competition project; with Sirkka Tarumaa)
University Library, Turku, Finland (competition project)

1947 Jaatinen Sauna, Vessölandet, Finland
Staffans Sauna, Kakskerta, Finland
Laivateollisuus Oy (Ship Industry) Residential Development, Turku, Finland
Hotel Maakunta interiors, Turku, Finland (with Carin Bryggman)
Erik Julin Statue Plan, Turku, Finland (project)
Town Hall and Hotel, Tammisaari, Finland (project)
War Memorial, Kakskerta, Finland
Congregational Hall, Järvenpää, Finland (competition project)

1948 Laivateollisuus Oy (Ship Industry) Engineers' Housing, Turku, Finland
Salon Seudun Sanomat Office Building, Salo, Finland
Blumenthal Villa, Parainen, Finland
Grandell Sauna, Parainen, Finland
National Anthem Memorial, Kumpula, Finland
Crematorium, Varberg, Sweden (competition project)

1949 Nuuttila Villa, Kuusisto, Finland
Itämeri Restaurant interiors, Turku, Finland (with Carin Bryggman)
Elementary school, Hanko, Finland (project)
Children's hospital, Turku, Finland (project)
Aleksis Kivi Statue Plan, Turku, Finland (project)
Residential block development, Läntinen Rantakatu, Turku, Finland (project)

1950 Öbo Akademi Student Association Building and Dormitory, Turku, Finland
Children's Day-Home, Oy Finlayson-Forssa Ab Residential Area, Tampere, Finland
Arvonen House restoration, Turku, Finland (project)
War Memorial, Mänttä, Finland
War Memorial, Noormarkku, Finland
Town Hall, Kajaani, Finland (competition project)

1951 Öbo Akademi Chemical Laboratory, Turku, Finland
House, Läntinen Rantakatu 21, Turku, Finland
Nuuttila Sauna, Kuusisto, Finland
District Hospital, Mänttä, Finland
War Memorial, Turku, Finland
Turku University (competition project)

1952 Water supply plant, Riihimäki, Finland
Football Stadium, Turku, Finland
Western Uusimaa Hospital, Tammisaari, Finland
University Student Association Building, Turku, Finland
War Memorial, Lassila, Finland
Residential Buildings II, Oy Finlayson-Forssa Ab Residential Area, Tampere, Finland

1953 Central Elementary School, Parainen, Finland
University Student Association Building II, Turku, Finland
Palmroth Villa I, Partola, Tampere, Finland
Finnish Savings Bank interiors, Turku, Finland (with Carin Bryggman)
War Memorial, Kemiö, Finland
Burial chapel, Nokia, Finland (project)
Burial chapel, Loviisa, Finland (project)
Congregational Office Building, Turku, Finland (competition project)
Kopenen Villa, Rymättylä, Finland

1954 Turunmaa Hospital, Turku, Finland
Swimming hall, Vierumäki, Finland (project)

Burial chapel, Lohja, Finland (completed by others)
Burial chapel, Lappeenranta, Finland (completed by others)
Turku Castle restoration, Finland (with Carin Bryggman)
1955 Elementary school, Mariehamn, Finland
Honkanummi Burial Chapel, Puistola, Finland (completed by others)
Residential Buildings III, Oy Finlayson-Forssa Ab Residential Area, Tampere, Finland
Sharpshooters' Chapel interiors, Turku Cathedral, Finland (project)
Palmroth Villa II, Partola, Tampere, Finland
University Student Association Building III, Turku, Finland
Municipal Theatre, Turku, Finland (competition project; with O. Kestilä)

Publications:

On BRYGGMAN: books—*Erik Bryggman* by Anna-Lisa Stigell, Ekenäs 1965; *Erik Bryggman,* exhibition catalogue, by Esa Piironen, Turku 1967; articles—"Finnische Landhauser" in *Monatshefte für Baukunst und Städtebau* (Berlin), vol. 30, no. 10, 1936; "Geschäftshaus Sampo in Turku" and "Sportakademie Vierumäki" in *Werk* (Zurich), vol. 27, no. 3/4, 1940; "Chapel at Öbo" in *Architectural Review* (London), vol. 103, no. 617, 1948; "Mortuary Chapel, Turku" in *Architectural Design* (London), vol. 18, no. 7, 1948; "L'Opera di Erik Bryggman nella Storia dell'Architettura Finlandese" by Leonardo Mosso in *Atti SJA* (Turin), December 1958.

When Erik Bryggman completed his architectural studies in 1916 political conditions in Finland were unsettled: the achievement of independence from Russia in the following year and the ensuing civil war hardly offered the young architect an inspiring start. In architecture, too, it was a time of change. The vigorous National Romantic period of the early part of the century had passed. It was succeeded by a return in part to a more rigid, monumental classicism and to ponderous architecture inspired by the Swedish Vasa Renaissance. As soon as contacts with other countries were resumed after the war, Italy, with Sweden and Denmark, became the focal point for young Finnish architects, and this interest is easy to understand, for architecture as taught at the Institute of Technology stressed a thorough knowledge of Italian Renaissance and Baroque architecture. On his journey to Italy in 1920 Bryggman made numerous sketches, concentrating, in addition to Renaissance architecture, on anonymous peasant architecture and the relationship of buildings to their surroundings. The influence of Italian architecture was later visible in Bryggman's works, not only in his obviously classical buildings of the 1920's, the best examples of which are the Atrium Housing Block and the Hotel Hospits Betel complex, but also, throughout his career, in his sensitive approach to building and concern for setting.

Bryggman's first work was completed in the offices of older colleagues, and, because of the post-war recession, part of it involved renovation of old buildings. He took part in the restoration of Turku's Medieval Cathedral as an assistant to his teacher Armas Lindgren, who had won his reputation early in the century as a member of the famous Gesellius-Lindgren-Saarinen team. Work with Lindgren and a thorough grounding in historical architecture apparently helped Bryggman to learn to value old cultural milieux (a concern that was not very common amongst architects from the 1930's to the 1960's). The cathedral project also brought him back to his home town of Turku, where he settled and thereafter secured most of his planning commissions.

Towards the end of the 1920's Bryggman became friends with Alvar Aalto, who moved to Turku in 1927 after his success in the competition for the

Farmers Hall in Southwestern Finland. At about this time both men became interested in Functionalism and began introducing it to Finland in late 1927. In the summer of 1928 Bryggman visited the Wiessenhof Siedlung in Stuttgart, the residential districts of Frankfurt under the direction of Ernst May, and the Bauhaus at Dessau, where he met Walter Gropius. Aalto introduced the ideas of Le Corbusier and the Dutch modernists to Turku at about the same time. The changeover to Functionalism was immediately visible in Bryggman's architecture. The Hotel Hospits Betel, which had been a straightforward classical work during the design stage, was relieved of all ornamentation during construction and emerged in the simple forms of Functionalism. The Öbo Akademi Library (1935) and the Vierumäki Sports Institute (1936) are among the purest examples of Functionalism in Bryggman's architecture. In these buildings he also retained the architectural sensitivity and lightness so characteristic of his personality.

In the late 1930's there was a widespread attempt to rid architecture of the over-simplified style of Functionalism, and Bryggman's Resurrection Chapel at Turku (1941) clearly reflects this shift to a more romantic architecture. Although the curved concrete ceiling and the colonnade of the chapel interior clearly still suggest functionalist/structuralist forms, the details, such as the ornamental door handles, the carefully placed vines, and the use of slate on the outside walls and paths, indicate a trend in a more decorative direction.

In the 1950's Bryggman received many commissions, ranging from summer villas and schools to hospitals and power plants. The influences of the 1920's are apparent in the Nuuttila Villa (1949), the water supply plant at Riihimäki (1952), and the student dormitories at Öbo Akademi (1950) and the University of Turku (1952). Yet, his buildings also became increasingly dry and matter of fact, with their dark, plastered facades and pitched roofs, features typical of contemporary Swedish architecture.

Bryggman's last works included reconstruction of Turku Castle, which had been damaged during the war. Bryggman restored the castle to its former state in part, yet he also adapted it for his own era by including modern congress and restaurant facilities. This achievement serves as a fine end to an architectural career that had begun with the renovation of another Turku monument, the Cathedral.

—Raija-Liisa Heinonen

BUNSHAFT, Gordon.

American. Born in Buffalo, New York, 9 May 1909. Educated at Lafayette High School, Buffalo, 1924–28; Massachusetts Institute of Technology, Cambridge, 1929–35, B.Arch. 1933, M.Arch. 1935; awarded M.I.T. Honorary Travelling Fellowship, 1935, and Rotch Travelling Fellowship, for study in Europe and North Africa, 1935–37. Served in the United States Army Corps of Engineers, 1942–46: Major. Married Nina Elizabeth Wayler in 1943. Chief Designer, New York office, 1937–42, 1946–49, and since 1949 Partner, Skidmore, Owings and Merrill, architects, New York, Chicago, San Francisco, etc. Visiting Critic, Massachusetts Institute of Technology, 1940–42, Harvard University, Cambridge, Massachusetts, 1954–60, and Yale University, New Haven, Connecticut, 1959–62. Member of the President's Commission on the Fine Arts, 1963–72. Trustee, Museum of Modern Art, New York, since 1975, and Carnegie-Mellon University, Pittsburgh, since 1977. Recipient: Brunner Award, National Institute of Arts and Letters, 1955; Medal of Honor, New York Chapter of the American Institute of Architects, 1961; Chancellor Norton Medal, University of Buffalo, 1969. D.F.A.: University of Buffalo, 1962. Honorary Member, Buffalo Fine Arts Academy, 1962; Honorary Professor, Universidad Nacional Federico Villareal, Lima, Peru, 1977. Academician, National Academy of Design; Fellow, American Institute of Architects, and American Academy of Arts and Sciences. Address: Skidmore, Owings and Merrill, 400 Park Avenue, New York, New York 10022, U.S.A.

Works (Partner-in-Charge of Design, Skidmore, Owings and Merrill):

1943 Hostess House, Great Lakes Naval Training Center, Illinois
1952 Lever House Corporate Headquarters, Park Avenue, New York
H. J. Heinz Company Vinegar Plant, Pittsburgh
United States Consular Housing, Bremen, Germany
1954 Manufacturers Hanover Trust Bank Branch Headquarters, Fifth Avenue, New York
United States Consulate, Dusseldorf
1955 Hilton Hotel, Istanbul
1957 Connecticut General Life Insurance Company Office Building, Bloomfield
Karl Taylor Compton Laboratories, Massachusetts Institute of Technology, Cambridge
1958 Reynolds Metals Company Building, Richmond, Virginia
1960 PepsiCo Inc., Building, New York
1961 First National City Bank, Houston
Chase Manhattan Bank, New York
Union Carbide Corporation Building, New York
1962 Albright-Knox Art Gallery addition, Buffalo, New York
1963 Emhart Corporation Building, Bloomfield, Connecticut
Beinecke Rare Book and Manuscript Library, Yale University, New Haven, Connecticut
1965 Banque Lambert Office Building and Bank, Brussels
H. J. Heinz and Company Ltd. Headquarters and Research Buildings, Hayes Park, Middlesex (with Matthews, Ryan, and Simpson)
American Republic Insurance Company Building, Des Moines, Iowa
1967 Marine Midland Building, 140 Broadway, New York
1968 No. 1 Main Place, Dallas
1970 American Can Company Suburban Corporate Headquarters, Greenwich, Connecticut
1971 Lyndon Baines Johnson Library and Sid W. Richardson Hall, University of Texas at Austin (with Brooks, Barr, Graeber, and White)
1973 W. R. Grace Building, 1114 Avenue of the Americas, New York
1974 Office Building, 9 West 57th Street, New York
Hirshhorn Museum and Sculpture Garden, Washington, D.C.
Philip Morris Cigarette Manufacturing Plant, Richmond, Virginia
1975/
85 New Jeddah International Airport, Saudi Arabia (SOM Partner-in-Charge of design of the Haj Terminal, Administration Building, RSAF, and Quarantine Building; Design Coordinator of the total project)

Publications:

On BUNSHAFT: books—*Masters of Modern Architecture* by John Peter, New York 1958; *Architecture of Today and Tomorrow* by Cranston Jones, New York 1961; *Architecture of Skidmore, Owings and Merrill 1950–1962,* introduced by Henry-Russell Hitchcock, Stuttgart 1962; *Architects on Architecture,* edited by Paul Heyer, New York 1966, London

1967; *Great Libraries* by Anthony Hobson, New York 1970; *Vacation Houses,* New York 1970; *Will They Ever Finish Bruckner Boulevard?* by Ada Louise Huxtable, New York 1970; *Architecture of Skidmore, Owings and Merrill 1963–1973,* introduced by Arthur Drexler, Stuttgart 1974; *Who's Who in Architecture from 1400 to the Present* by J. M. Richards, London and New York, 1977; article —"Gordon Bunshaft: The Establishment's Architect—Plus" by David Jacobs in *The New York Times Magazine,* 23 July 1972.

To describe properly my approach to architecture would require me to be a professional writer, which I am not. I am an architect. I express what I believe in through the buildings I have done over the past 30 years. They are the language I use—not the written word.

—Gordon Bunshaft

The names Gordon Bunshaft and Skidmore, Owings and Merrill are all but synonymous. Bunshaft has been associated with the New York office, but he has had a strong formulative influence over the work of the branches. Bunshaft's reputation and contribution rests on his pioneering influence on American corporate and industrial architecture. It is no small achievement. He was able to persuade the community of American corporations that contemporary American architecture could serve them as a signature.

The work that established this notion was the headquarters for the Lever Brothers Corporation in New York City. While not the first example of "glass box" architecture, it affirmed the role of open-space and efficient geometric enclosure as a theme for housing large office organizations.

But to say that the strictly geometric enclosure is Bunshaft's hallmark is as inaccurate as to say that his work is limited to the architectural needs of corporate America. It is more accurate to describe Bunshaft's philosophy as a disciplined contemporary classicism. He has avoided aberrant fashions; his preference is for a reasoned and always crisply-disciplined functional solution. At the same time his designs have always had a careful and steady wholeness. On occasion, they have also been innovative.

With Lever House, he set a glass box on a raised glass base. For the Manufacturers Hanover Trust Company Branch Headquarters on Fifth Avenue, New York, he revolutionized bank design: it is entirely enclosed in glass, and a vault is put on full public display at ground level. For the Beinecke Rare Book and Manuscript Library at Yale he set a translucent marble block on a series of base piers: its interior light envelopes the books in a hallow. For the Albright-Knox Art Gallery addition in Buffalo, New York, Bunshaft posed a serene glass box against a new-classical predecessor. The two complement each other in scale, delicacy, and refinement—each mirroring the difference in age and architectural attitudes. The Banque Lambert in Brussels is a box-like building of classical proportion, its facade an articulation of horizontal and vertical thrusts of force. The Connecticut General Life Insurance Company Office Building is a serene horizontal mass set in a quietly rolling landscape. In this work Bunshaft utilized a familiar theme—a clear geometric form set on a larger terrace, the building form itself punctuated by courtyards.

His urban office architecture is all but his signature, an outstanding example being the Chase Manhattan Bank in lower Manhattan. Here, again, a tower in set on a supporting base, the base's top, in this case, being a terrace.

Bunshaft—and S.O.M.—have always established a strong identity for their clients through architecture. It is at once identifiable and respectful. And it is realized with equal success in work for the corporate as well as for the institutional client. It also succeeds in work of a monumental nature, as in the Lyndon Baines Johnson Memorial Library at the University of Texas at Austin.

A particular emphasis in his work is the incorporation of embellishing sculpture. He has utilized free-standing works, such as those by Isamu Noguchi, as well as sculptural screens, such as those of Harry Bertoia. Painstakingly careful interior design and furnishing is also a characteristic of his work.

Bunshaft's development has extended into an interval of somewhat frantic if not scattered search for new principles and forms in American architecture. While not participating adventurously in that search, he has not remained static or aloof: his recent buildings have employed more daring and adventuresome forms and structures. The Hirshhorn Museum and Sculpture Garden in Washington, D.C. is a case in point. The museum, a circle in form, still remains classic in its balanced repose. The sculpture garden is a masterpiece of the placement of sculpture in space, all but unrivalled.

Gordon Bunshaft's contribution has been to be squarely at the front of his time, yet classical in his reasoned compositions.

—Paul Spreiregen

BURLE MARX, Roberto.
Brazilian. Born in Sao Paulo, 4 August 1909. Studied painting in a private studio, Berlin, and studied Brazilian flora, privately, at the Berlin Botanical Gardens, 1928–29; studied architecture at the Escola Nacional de Belas Artes, Rio de Janeiro; self-taught in landscape design. In private practice as a land-

Gordon Bunshaft: Lyndon Baines Johnson Library, University of Texas at Austin, 1971

scape architect, Rio de Janeiro, since 1934; has discovered and cultivated numerous plants that now bear his name; has also worked as a painter as well as a designer of jewellery, tapestries, stage scenery, sculptural reliefs, and fabric panels. Exhibitions (landscape design, paintings, tapestries, sculptures, fabric panels): one-man—Palace Hotel, Rio de Janeiro, 1941; Galeria Itapetininga, Sao Paulo, 1946; Museum of Art, Sao Paulo, 1952; Museum of Modern Art, Rio de Janeiro, 1956; Institute of Contemporary Arts, London, 1956; Stedelijk Museum, Amsterdam, 1957, subsequently toured Europe; *Bienal,* Sao Paulo, 1959; National Museum of Art, Buenos Aires, 1961; University of Montevideo Faculty of Architecture, 1962; Museum of Modern Art, Rio de Janeiro, 1963; Galeria Bonino, Rio de Janeiro, 1967; A Galeria, Sao Paulo, 1968; Gallery of the Banco Nacional de Minas Gerais, Sao Paulo, 1968; *Biennale,* Venice, 1970; Galeria Bancipe, Recife, Brazil, 1971; Belo Horizonte Museum of Art, Brazil, 1972; Galeria do Instituto Brasil-Estados Unidos, Rio de Janeiro, 1972; Gulbenkian Foundation, Lisbon, 1973; Musée Galerie, Paris, 1973; Galeria Bonino, Rio de Janeiro, 1974; Museum of Modern Art, Sao Paulo, 1974; Museum of Contemporary Art, Curitiba, Brazil, 1974; Teatro Castro Alves, Salvador, Brazil, 1974; Cultural Foundation, Brasilia, 1975; Hotel Ambassador, Porto Allegre, Brazil, 1976; Oficina d'Arte, Rio de Janeiro, 1976; Atelier Noth und Hauer, Berlin, 1976; Case de Olinda, Recife, Brazil, 1977; Museum of Contemporary Art, Caracas, 1977; Bolsa de Arte, Rio de Janeiro, 1978; Fine Arts Center/Contemporary Art Museum, Caracas, 1978; Atelier Internacional, Buenos Aires, 1978; Galeria AKI, Sao Paulo, 1978; Galeria Guignard, Belo Horizonte, Brazil, 1978; Fine Arts Museum, Rio de Janeiro, 1978; group—*20 Brazilian Artists,* Provincial Museum, Buenos Aires, 1945; *Modern Brazilian Painting,* Royal Academy, London, 1945; *Biennale,* Venice, 1947; *Bienal,* Sao Paulo, 1953; *Landscape Architecture,* Institute of Contemporary Art, Boston, 1955; *Brasilien Baut,* Leverkusen Museum, Germany, 1956; *International Flower Show,* Paris, 1957, Trieste, 1960; *Bienal,* Sao Paulo, 1963; *International Garden Show,* Hamburg, 1963; *Biennale,* Venice, 1978; etc. Collection: Sitio Santo Antonio da Bica, Guanabara State, Brazil. Recipient: Gold Medal, Escola Nacional de Belas Artes, Rio de Janeiro, 1941; First Prize, *Bienal,* Sao Paulo, 1953; First Prize, *International Flower Show,* Paris, 1957; Gold Medal, *International Flower Show,* Trieste, 1960; First Prize, *International Garden Show,* Hamburg, 1963; Santos Dumont Medal, Brazil, 1963; Fine Arts Medal, American Institute of Architects, 1965; Personality of the Year Award, Institute of Architects of Brazil, 1969; Museum of Image and Sound Trophy, Rio de Janeiro, 1970; Alfonso de Souza Cultural Medal, PHAN: Patrimonio Historico e Artistico da Nacao, Sao Paulo, 1975; Medal of Honor, Belo Horizonte, Brazil, 1976. Honorary Member, National Society of Interior Designers, New York, 1959, Institute of Landscape Architects, London, 1968, and British Columbia Society of Landscape Architects, 1968. Commander, Order of the Rio Branco, Brazil, 1971. Chevalier, Order of the Couronne, Belgium, 1959; Commander, Order of Merit, Chile, 1962, and Nicaragua, 1970; Member, Andres Bello Order, Venezuela, 1977. Address: Cardosso Junior 95, Laranjeiras, Rio de Janeiro, Brazil.

Works (landscape architecture):

1932 Schwarz House, Rio de Janeiro
1934 Public Gardens, Recife, Brazil
1938 Ministry of Education and Health, Rio de Janeiro
Santos Dumont Airport, Rio de Janeiro
ABI Building terraces, Rio de Janeiro
1939 IRB Building, Rio de Janeiro
Solon de Lucena Park, Joao Pessoa, Brazil
1942 Yacht Club Restaurant, Pampulha, Belo Horizonte, Brazil

Francisco Inacio Peizoto House, Cataguazes, Minas Gerais, Brazil
1943 Araxa Park, Minas Gerais, Brazil (with Henrique Lahmeyer de Mello Barreto)
1948 Odette Monteiro House, Correias, Brazil
Samambaia Farm, Petropolis, Brazil
Diego Cisneiros House, Caracas
Burton Tremaine House, Santa Barbara, California
1950 Parahyba Textile Factory, Sao Jose dos Campos, Sao Paulo State, Brazil
Olivo Gomes House, Sao Jose do Campos, Sao Paulo State, Brazil
Hotel Amazonas, Manaus, Brazil
Hotel da Bahia, Salvador, Brazil
1951 PDF Building, Rio de Janeiro
Teatro Popular de Marechal Hermes, Rio de Janeiro
Galeao Airport, Rio de Janeiro
Nossa Senhora da Conceicau da Jaqueira Church Courtyard, Recife, Brazil
Roche Laboratories, Rio de Janeiro
Cassiano Ribeiro Coutinho, Joao Pessoa, Brazil (project)
1952 Independence Square, Joao Pessoa, Brazil (project)
Cathedral Precinct, Salvador, Brazil (project)
Carlos Somlo House, Vale da Boa Esperanca, Terezopolis, Brazil (project)
1953 University of Rio de Janeiro (project)
Ibirapuera Park, Sao Paulo (project)
Pampulha Airport, Belo Horizonte, Brazil (project)
American Embassy, Rio de Janeiro (project)
1954 Promenade at Botafogo Beach, Rio de Janeiro (project)
Museum of Modern Art, Rio de Janeiro
Machado Lagoon, Rio de Janeiro
Fourth Centenary Exhibition, Sao Paulo (project)
Ernesto Waller House, Barra da Tijuca, Brazil
Edmundo Cavanellas House, Pedro do Rio, Petropolis, Brazil
1955 Labor Temple Planting Project, Los Angeles
South America Hospital, Rio de Janeiro (project)
Alberto Kronsforth House, Terezopolis, Brazil
Dr. Miranda House, Rio de Janeiro

Sergio Correia da Costa House, Rio de Janeiro
Imperial Museum, Petropolis, Brazil
1956 East and West Parks, Caracas
Canal Development, Caracas
El Castano Apartment Building, Caracas
Club Playa Azul, Caracas
Inocente Palacios House, Caracas
Diego Cisneros House, Caracas
Henrique Delfino House, Caracas
Eduardo Rahn House, Caracas
Carlos Alberto Punceles House, Caracas
Ernesto Valenilla House, Caracas
Luiz Carias House, Caracas
Hacienda Monte Sacro, Valencia, Spain
Lindoia Park, Sao Paulo State, Brazil
1957 Guararapes Airport, Recife, Brazil
Schulthess House, Havana, Cuba
1958 Olivetti Sports Ground, Buenos Aires (project)
1961 Flamengo Park, Rio de Janeiro
Monumental Axis, Brasilia (project)
Zoo/Botanical Park, Brasilia (project)
Botanical Gardens, Sao Paulo (project)
1962 Park of the Americas, Santiago, Chile (project)
1963 Unesco Building, Paris (project)
National Gardens, Vienna (project; with Karl Mang)
Brazilian Pavilion, *International Fair,* Tokyo
1965 Ministry of Foreign Affairs, Brasilia (project)
Fernandez Concha House, Lima, Peru (project)
Biological Reserve, Jacarepagua, Guanabara, Brazil
Morro da Viuva Restaurant, Rio de Janeiro (project)
Irmaos Gomes House, Ubatuba, Brazil (project)
1966 Sousa Hospital, Rio de Janeiro
Civic Center, Curitiba, Brazil
Manchete Building, Rio de Janeiro
North Park, San Isidro, Argentina (project)
Dorado Hilton Hotel, San Juan, Puerto Rico (project)
Siqueira Campos Park, Sao Paulo (project)
Ponte Alta Farm, Barra do Pirai, Rio de Janeiro State, Brazil (project)
Candido Guinle de Paula Machado House, Rio de Janeiro (project)

Roberto Burle Marx: Garden in Brazil

1967 Civic Center, Santo Andre, Brazil (project)
United States Embassy, Brasilia (project)
Santa Barbara Development, San Juan, Puerto Rico (project)
Tribunal Federal de Recursos Building, Brasilia

1968 Leoes Palace, Sao Luiz, Brazil (project)
Anhembi Park, Sao Paulo
Sao Judas Tadeu Square, Santo Andre, Brazil
Cathedral Square, Rio de Janeiro (project)
German Embassy, Brasilia (project)
Santuario de Jesus do Matosinhos, Congonhas do Camp, Minas Gerais, Brazil
Benedito Dias Macedo House, Fortaleza, Brazil
Clemente Gomes House, Sao Paulo
Gravata Condominium, Sao Paulo (project)
Brazilian Embassy, Washington, D.C.
Condominium Araucaria, Sao Paulo
National Gardens, Recife, Brazil (project)

1969 Federal University of Santa Catarina Campus, Florianopolis, Brazil (project)
National-Rio Hotel, Sao Conrado, Rio de Janeiro (project)
Bloch Building, Rio de Janeiro
Petrobras Headquarters, Rio de Janeiro
Flamengo Park Aquarium, Rio de Janeiro (project)
SESI/FIESP/DIESP Building, Sao Paulo (project)
Telepar Headquarters, Curitiba, Brazil
Santuario Dom Bosco, Brasilia (project)

1970 Botanical Garden, Federal University of Minas Gerais, Belo Horizonte, Brazil (initial project; for further development by students)
Federal University of Paraiba, Joao Pessoa, Brazil
Copacabana Promenade (with beach widening), Rio de Janeiro
Ministry of Justice, Brasilia
Esporte Clube Sirio, Sao Paulo
Hilton Hotel, Sao Paulo (project)
Londrina City Park, Parana, Brazil
Central Park, Caracas (project)

1971 Urban renovation plan for Zone 1a of Buenos Aires
Chacra Saavedra Sport and Leisure Center, Buenos Aires (project)
Estadual de Torres Park, Porto Alegre, Brazil (project)
City Park and Zoo/Botanical Gardens, Barigui, Curitiba, Brazil (project)
Sao Lourenco Park, Curitiba, Brazil (project)
Community Park, Santo Andre, Brazil (project)
Jundiai Housing Complex, Sao Paulo
Iranian Embassy, Brasilia
Hotel Belneario Laguna, Santa Catarina, Brazil (project)
DNER Residence, Brasilia
Belgian Embassy, Brasilia (project)
Urbanization plan for Patamares, Salvador, Brazil

1972 Federal University of Pernambuco, Recife, Brazil (project)
Karnak Palace, Teresina, Piaui State, Brazil (project)
Planalto Palace, Brasilia
American Embassy, Brasilia (project)
Peru Square, Buenos Aires (project)
SUDENE Headquarters, Recife, Brazil (project)
Concert Hall, Caracas (project)
Brasilia Square, Quito, Ecuador
Club Vale Verde, Campinas, Sao Paulo
Merck Factory, Rio de Janeiro
Plan for the city of Ouro Preto, Brazil (as consultant)
Ministry of Development, Brasilia
Petrobras Building and Terminal, Santa Teresa, Rio de Janeiro

1973 Teatro Jose de Alencar, Fortaleza, Brazil (project)
Cemetery, Recife, Brazil (project)
Jornal do Brasil Building, Rio de Janeiro (project)
East-West Avenue, Fortaleza, Brazil (project)
Glasner de Barros House, Recife, Brazil (project)
Municipal Prefecture, Fortaleza, Brazil (project)
Administrative Center, Salvador, Brazil (project)
Milton Campos Square, Belo Horizonte, Brazil (project)
Banco Nacional do Desenvolvimento Economico, Brasilia (project)
Sports Center, Cuiaba, Brazil (project)
Guarapirange Park, Sao Paulo (project)
Realdo Santos Guglielmi House, Criciuma, Brazil (project)
United Nations Avenue Junction, Sao Paulo (project)

1974 Governor's Palace, Alagoas, Brazil (project)
Electricity Company of Pernambuco, Recife, Brazil (project)
Comercial do Piquero Building, Tatuape, Sao Paulo (project)
Edgars Stores, South Africa (project)
Swagershoek Farm, Lydenberg District, Transvaal, South Africa (project)
Ermirio Pereira de Moraes House, Sao Paulo (project)
Juqueri Reservoir, Sao Paulo (project)
Administrative Center, Sao Paulo (project)
Jaragua Tourist Development Plan, Atibaia, Sao Paulo (project)
Olga Cunha Bueno Ferreira House, Sao Paulo (project)
Augusto Esteves de Lima Jr. House, Sao Paulo
Banco Nacional do Desenvolvimento Economico Building, Rio de Janeiro (project)
Hering Textile Factory, Santa Catarina, Brazil (project)
Rogerio Pithon Serejo Farias Recreational Park, Brasilia (project)
Maria do Carmo Nabucco de Magalhaes Lins House, Rio de Janeiro (project)

1975 Vice-President's House, Brasilia (project)
Bloch Building, Sao Paulo (project)
Hans Broos House, Sao Paulo (project)
Bicalho Goulart Park, Belo Horizonte, Brazil (project)
Da Costa and Silva Square, Piaui, Brazil (project)
Monumental Axis, Brasilia (project)
Inconfidencia Square, Belo Horizonte, Brazil
Abbey of Santa Maria, Sao Paulo (project)
Residential development, Avenida Sernambetiba, Rio de Janeiro (project)
Alberto Kronsforth House, Angra dos Reis, Brazil (project)
Rodrigo de Freitas Lagoon, Rio de Janeiro (project)
Elie Douer House, Sao Paulo (project)
Kurt Waissman House, Sao Paulo (project)
Wimbledon Park Building, Avenida das Americas, Rio de Janeiro (project)

1976 Plan for the center of Vivencia de Guarapari, Espirito Santo, Brazil
Pedro Biagi Building, Sao Paulo (project)
Riviera dei Fiore Buildings, Rio de Janeiro (project)
Enrique Delfino House, Caracas (project)
Rua Coronel Agostinho, Campo Grande, Rio de Janeiro (project)
Teatro Nacional, Brasilia (project)
River Tiete Ecological Park, Sao Paulo (project)
Gilberto Canuki Daccache House, Sao Paulo (project)
Campos do Jordao Convention Center, Sao Paulo (project)
Celso Gerbassi Ramos House, Rio de Janeiro (project)
Ipanema Farm, Sorocaba, Sao Paulo (project)
Viana Wood, Sao Paulo (project)
Joao Borges de Assis House, Aracatuba, Sao Paulo (project)
Abbey of Santa Maria, Sao Paulo
Marina, Rio de Janeiro (project)
Le Corbusier Building, Recife, Brazil (project)
Oscar Niemeyer Building, Recife, Brazil (project)
Restaurant, Conservatory and Recreational Park, Brasilia
Bangu Prison, Rio de Janeiro (project)
Fernando Conde Lorenzo House, Itacoatiara, Rio de Janeiro (project)
Renato de Toledo e Silva House, Sao Paulo (project)
Luiz Lucio Constabile Izzo House, Sao Paulo (project)
Wimbledon Park Building, Sao Paulo (project)
Juan les Pins Building, Rio de Janeiro (project)
Fernando Magalhaes Pinto House, Rio de Janeiro (project)
Emilio Maya Omena House, Maceio, Brazil (project)
Sotave Nordeste Industria e Comercio Building, Recife, Brazil (project)
Romildo de Carvalho Coutinho House, Paraiba, Brazil (project)
OMPI Headquarters, Rio de Janeiro (project)

1977 South Beach reclamation, Santa Catarina, Brazil (project)
Edgar Hargreaves House, Rio de Janeiro (project)
Sao Luiz Square, Terezopolis, Brazil (project)
Civic Center, Curitiba, Brazil
Roberto Malzoni House, Sao Paulo (project)
Linneo de Paulo Machado House, Rio de Janeiro (project)
Exhibition and Convention Center, Recife, Brazil (project)
Magaly Cannizaro-Miranda House, Caracas (project)
Artemio Furlan Filho House, Sao Paulo (project)
El Hatillo House, Caracas (project)
Pedregal Building, Caracas (project)
John Machado Urbina House, Caracas (project)
COMIND Central Administration Building, Barueri, Sao Paulo (project)

1978 Itarare Beach, Sao Vicente, Sao Paulo (project)
Glaucio Carneiro Leao House, Recife, Brazil (project)
SESC Amphitheatre, Rio de Janeiro (project)
Cerro del Vigia Development, Puerto la Cruz, Brazil (project)
International Airport, Rio de Janeiro (project)
Banco Boavista, Rio de Janeiro (project)
Walter Clark House, Rio de Janeiro (project)
Servino Y.R.S. Ortiz Building, Buenos Aires (project)

Publications:

By BURLE MARX: book—*Rino Levi*, with Nestor Goulart Reis Filho, Milan 1974; articles—"Gardens and Ecology: A Personal View" in *Plan* (Johannesburg), no. 10, 1973; "Landscape Gardening" in *Arts and Architecture* (Los Angeles), July 1954.

On BURLE MARX: book—*The Tropical Gardens of Burle Marx* by Pietro Maria Bardi and M. Gautherot, London 1964; articles—"The Gardens of Roberto Burle Marx" in *Royal Architectural Insti-*

tute of Canada Journal (Toronto), February 1952; "Burle Marx et le jardin contemporain" in L'Architecture d'Aujourd'hui (Paris), August 1952; "Roberto Burle Marx und das problem der gartengestaltung" in Werk (Zurich), August 1953; "Jardins de l'Aéroport de Rio" in L'Architecture d'Aujourd'hui (Paris), February 1954; "A Garden Style in Brazil to Meet Contemporary Needs" in Landscape Architecture (Louisville, Kentucky), July 1954; "Roberto Burle Marx: Art and the Landscape" in Architectural Record (New York), October 1954; "Musée d'Art Moderne à Rio de Janeiro" in L'Architecture d'Aujourd'hui (Paris), October 1956; "Brazilianische Garten von Roberto Burle Marx" in Baukunst und Werkform (Nuremberg), vol. 9, no. 9, 1956; "Roberto Burle Marx y sus jardines" in Arquitectura (Mexico City), June 1957; "Roberto Burle Marx: Pittore di Giardini" in Zodiac (Milan), no. 6, 1960; "Appraisal of a Master Artist" by Anthony Walmsley in Landscape Architecture (Louisville, Kentucky), July 1963; "The Versatility of Burle Marx" by Guy Playfair in Architectural Review (London), November 1964; "Roberto Burle Marx of Brazil" by Alice Graeme Korff in AIA Journal (Washington, D.C.), May 1965; "Robert Burle Marx: Parks, Gardens, Towns, Squares, Beaches" by Miguel Thomas Kerner in L'Architettura (Rome), April 1976.

The most important thing for me is the link with existing nature: a garden cannot be artificial when you are dealing with natural elements. I do admit to principles, but I hate formulas. A garden is not a painting, and a painting is not a garden, but the two have an interwoven theme. When I create a garden I speak an art language. You must have form, starting from what is there; and if it is a cleared space,

then form must be based on what is to be seen around that space. Indiscriminate planting makes a salad—it does not create a work of art. Perhaps this sounds chauvinistic, but with 5,000 trees and 50,000 plants to choose from in Brazil, why should I import plants from abroad?

—Roberto Burle Marx

The revolution of ideas created by Le Corbusier in mathematical architecture called for its complement in biological landscape. Roberto Burle Marx was the first landscape designer to evolve such an art. Painter, designer of fabrics and jewellery, stage designer, and animator of fêtes and festivals, he channelled all these qualities into the single art of landscape design. The task he undertook was the translation of abstract art into reality, using his living plant materials much as a painter uses the colour and texture of paint. Although his practice now extends all over South America and beyond, he will probably be best remembered for the pioneer gardens made among the mountains round his home town of Rio de Janeiro.

The spirit behind these gardens is his personal vision and interpretation of the Brazilian forests and their rivers. In using only indigenous plants he was influenced by William Robinson, whom he admired; but in the *manner* of using them, he is quite different. His gardens are organized as baroque gardens of movement: the sweeping and beautiful curves seem like water eddies and currents against their background of mountains. The flower beds have been described as cloud shadows passing over the landscape. To steady this movement, Burle Marx introduces geometry on plan that may originally have been inspired by that of Le Corbusier, for whose Ministry of Education and Health in Rio he made one of his most spectacular roof gardens.

Burle Marx breathes originality in all he creates, from his own home outside Rio where he grows and experiments with plants, to such inventions as a chequered lawn of two grasses kept apart by metal strips concealed below the surface. Above all, his work is stamped as the creation of an artist of many accomplishments and wide vision, an artist who first raised modern garden design to an international plane of art.

—Geoffrey Jellicoe

BUSZKO AND FRANTA.

Partnership; established, Katowice, Poland, 1950, by Henryk Buszko (born 1924) and Aleksander Franta (born 1925). Architects to the City Architectural Office (Miastoprojekt), Katowice, 1950–58. Since 1958, Senior Architects, Architectural Office of General Construction, Katowice. Exhibitions: group—Warsaw, 1951–54; Katowice, 1951–73; *Exposition International d'Urbanisme*, Paris, 1963; *International Union of Architects Exhibition*, Buenos Aires, 1969, and Madrid, 1975; *Polish Architecture Exhibition*, Moscow, 1974–75; partnership—SARP, Warsaw, 1975; Historical Museum, Koszalin, Poland, 1975; SARP, Gadansk, Poland, 1976; Architectural Museum, Wroclaw, 1976. Recipient: Town Planning and Architecture Committee Prize, 1959, 1961, 1962; Ministry of Construction Prize, 1964, 1969, 1973; SARP Medal, Katowice, 1972; Supreme Technical Organization (NOT) Prize, 1972; Ministry of Science and Technology Prize, 1973; Honorary Award, Polish Architects Association, 1975. Address: Pracownia Projektowa Budownictwa Ogolnego, ul. Marchlewskiego 19, Katowice, Poland.

Buszko and Franta: Ustron-Zawodzie Mountain Health Resort, near Bielsko, Poland, 1978

Works:

1950/
54 Trade Unions Centre, Katowice, Poland (with J. Gottfried)

1951 Malapanew Steelworks Social Centre, Ozimek, near Opole, Poland (with J. Gottfried)

Baildon Steelworks Technical College, Katowice, Poland (with J. Gottfried)

Ministry of Mining Stand, *Home Trade Fair Exhibition,* Poznan (with T. Mroszczak and B. Gorecki)

1954 Zgoda Steelworks Social Centre, Katowice, Poland (with J. Gottfried)

1955/
58 Transport Union Holiday Hotel, Olszowka-Mikuszowice, near Bielsko, Poland (with J. Gottfried)

1956 Ministry of Mining Stand, *Home Trade Fair Exhibition,* Poznan (with T. Mroszczak and B. Gorecki)

1956/
57 Torkat Winter Stadium with Ice Rink, Bankowa Street, Katowice, Poland (with J. Gottfried)

1956/
58 Regional Theatre, Rybnik, Poland (with J. Gottfried)

1957 Ministry of Mining Stand, *Home Trade Fair Exhibition,* Poznan (with T. Mroszczak and B. Gorecki)

1958 Apartments, Reymonta Street, Katowice, Poland (with J. Gottfried)

Terrace housing, Norwida Street, Tychy, Poland (with J. Gottfried)

Terrace housing, Karolinki Street, Gliwice, Poland (with J. Gottfried)

1958/
60 Mostostalu Workers' Apartment Building, Zabrze, Poland

1958/
62 Wujek Coal Mine Housing Estate, Katowice, Poland

1958/
78 "1,000 Year" Urban Housing Development, Katowice, Poland: housing blocks with service buildings; 5 schools; health centre; 4 shopping and restaurant units; Centrum Department Store; social centre; church; sports centre

1959 Buszko and Franta Architectural Office Building, Marchlewskiego Street, Katowice, Poland

1959/
60 Wedding Palace Building, Chorzow, Poland

1959/
62 Gornik Sanatorium, Szczawnica, Poland

1960 Teachers' Holiday Centre, Jaszowiec Health Resort, Ustron, Poland

Parkland Tourist Hotel, Chorzow, Poland

1960/
61 Baildon Steelworks Social Centre conversion, Katowice, Poland

1961 Miners' Seaside Holiday Centre, Leba, Poland

Apartment building, Strzelcow Bytomskich Street, Bytom, Poland

1962 Agricultural Bank Office Building, Katowice, Poland

Wedding Palace Building, Sosnowiec, Poland

1963/
65 Exhibition Stand Design, Brno, Czechoslovakia

1964 Ministry of Mining Stand, *Home Trade Fair Exhibition,* Poznan (with T. Mroszczak and B. Gorecki)

1964/
65 Polish Workers Party Office Building, Armii Czerwonej Street, Katowice, Poland

Building Industry Workers Health Centre, PCK Street, Katowice, Poland

1966/
67 Academy Teachers' Terrace Housing, Brynow, Katowice, Poland (with T. Czewczyk)

1968 Ministry of Mining Stand, *Home Trade Fair Exhibition,* Poznan (with T. Mroszczak and B. Gorecki)

1968/
78 Ustron-Zawodzie Mountain Health Resort, Ustron, near Bielsko, Poland (with T. Dzewczyk, D. Korczyk, and I. N. Lazowski): sanatorium; natural therapy centre; 18 holiday hotels; 3 shopping and restaurant sub-centres; resort medical staff housing estate; management office building

Rozdzienski Housing Settlement, Katowice, Poland (with T. Szewczyk, D. Korczyk, J. Kielski, and L. Baron): 7 housing blocks, with integral nurseries, kindergartens, and ancillary buildings; school; shopping centre with cafe and restaurant

1969 Parks Department Office Building, Chorzow, Poland

Zeto Computer Centre, Owocowa Street, Katowice, Poland (with T. Czewczyk)

1970/
72 12-storey prototype apartment block, "1,000 Year" Urban Housing Development, Katowice, Poland

1973 Gornictwa Mine Engineering Works Training Centre, Rolna Street, Katowice, Poland

1974/
77 Single-family housing, Katowice and Ustron, Poland

1977 Prototype pre-fabricated single-family housing, Stalowa Wola, Poland

The Buszko-Franta Partnership has also worked on more than two dozen competition projects, residential planning schemes, and furniture and interior designs.

Publications:

On BUSZKO/FRANTA: books—*Modern Architecture in Poland* by Bohdan Lisowski, Warsaw 1968; *Nowa Architektura Polski Diariusz lat 1966–1970* by Przemyslaw Szafer, Warsaw 1971; *Polska Architektura Wspolczesna* by Przemyslaw Szafer, Warsaw 1977; articles—"Dom Metalowca" by Z. Rzepecki in *Architektura* (Warsaw), no. 5, 1955; "Architecture of Buszko and Franta" by W. Geppert in *Architektura* (Warsaw), no. 3, 1964; "Architecture of the 1,000 Year Housing Settlement" by J. Brzozowski in *Architektura* (Warsaw), no. 10, 1964; "Bederowiec" by A. Ligocki in *Poglady* (Warsaw), no. 19, 1964; "Review of the 1,000 Year Housing Settlement in Katowice" by A. Wojda in *Architektura* (Warsaw), no. 1, 1971; "The Art of the Background" by T. Barucki in *Projekt* (Warsaw), no. 2, 1971; "Honorowa Nagroda SARP" in *Architektura* (Warsaw), no. 9/10, 1975.

Architecture is planned environmental conditioning, and the architect's task is to design space for human needs—biological, functional, and psychological. Architecture emerges and develops under conditions determined by time, place, and function. As a result, insight is needed in understanding man and his needs—an awareness of his psyche, his social background, his history and culture, and his environment. Also needed is the ability to work in different scales, from furniture and interior design to district, town and regional planning. And a wide range of technology must be mastered, from the crafts to industrial production. The building industry, with its technology and organization, is the tool to realize architecture.

We regard the process of architectural creativity as operating in a cultural sequence: it is a search for the characteristic spatial features of a particular place and a search for the individual image of settlement, town or country. Architecture conceived at a specific time is also a function of the past and deter-

mines the conditions of life in the future. Therefore, it should perhaps have a high degree of adaptability, particularly at the present time when the future is difficult to define.

We believe that the architect is a specialist, designing space for man in accordance with nature. We believe, too, that the architect, as specialist, is a social tool through which—with the help of his relatively autonomous creativity—society expresses its culture in environmental form. From this awareness results a responsibility for one's work and a sense that one is performing a service to the community; it also helps to create modesty, strength of purpose, and a desire for positive and courageous reasoning within one's professional activity.

We consider such an attitude to be a necessary condition for the practice of our profession—if we aim to achieve as high a quality of architecture as possible.

Architecture of the highest order can exist at any stage in technological development, provided that all the technical potential of that stage is used. Each building process results in new architecture—new space for human life. Each spatial pattern influences man and his psyche. Architecture of high quality influences positively; bad architecture influences negatively: it deforms, reduces sensitivity, weakens receptivity. Generally man surrenders unconsciously to its influence and does not understand the implications of its quality. It is difficult to find architecture of high quality even in highly-developed societies. We believe that every man has the right to architecture of high quality and that space shared in common should be employed for the good of the community.

The primary condition for creating such architecture is a high proficiency in making spatial decisions, for which only the architect is qualified. We believe in the future, and we believe in the human intellect and in man's abilities and his good will. Therefore we believe in the significance of our profession. We believe that future architecture will be diverse, as varied as man and his culture, and that everywhere it will be of higher quality. To achieve this goal, the work must be done by architects, the best educated ones possible, working in the right professional relationship with contractors and investors. The discovery of effective working arrangements—and appropriate means of funding—to promote a generally high standard of architecture, is the central issue in the future of architecture.

—Henryk Buszko and Aleksander Franta

Buszko and Franta regard architectural work as creating the art of the "background." The background to human life. Unlike painting and sculpture, which are arts of the object, the role of architecture is not to be striking but to organize the subtle framework within which human actions gain their meaning and significance.

Although the basic medium of architecture is building, there are a number of other relationships determining the quality of human environment that have to be considered. The most important is preservation of the balance between nature and built form, a homeostasis regarded as essential for human life, both technologically and psychologically.

The work of the Buszko and Franta practice ranges from furniture and interior design, in a variety of different types of buildings, to housing developments, holiday villages, and other large-scale town planning projects. Both Henryk Buszko and Aleksander Franta are lecturers at the Gliwice School of Architecture, and both are active members of the Polish Architects Association (Buszko was its President for several years) and the UIA (International Architects Association—in which Franta is a consultant to the General Secretary). Their work has won several architectural awards, and Buszko has been made a honorary member of both the American Institute of Architects and the Mexican Architects Association.

—Teresa Czaplinska-Archer

CALLISTER, Charles Warren.
American. Born in Rochester, New York, in 1917. Educated at the University of Texas, Austin, 1935–41, B.A. 1941. Served in the United States Army Corps of Engineers, 1941–45. In private practice, San Francisco, 1946–55; Partner, with John M. Payne and J. Martin Rosse, Callister, Payne and Rosse, Tiburon, California, 1955–69, Callister and Payne, 1969–72, and since 1972, Callister, Payne and Bischoff. Lecturer in Architecture, Stanford University, California, since 1961. Address: Callister, Payne and Bischoff, 1865 Mar West, Tiburon, California 94920, U.S.A.

Works:

1947 House, 405 Goodhill Road, Kentfield, California (with Jack Hilmer)
1949 House, 106 Diablo Drive, Kentfield, California
1952 First Church of Christ Scientist, San Raphael Avenue, Tiburon, California
House, 3456 Dwight Way, Berkeley, California
1953 House, 250 Curry Lane, Sausalito, California
1955 Portola School, 765 Portola Road, Woodside, California (with additions, 1957, 1964)
1958 House, 2637 Rose Street, Berkeley, California
1959 Bel Air School addition, 259 Karen Way, Tiburon, California
House, 176 Palo Alto Avenue, Twin Peaks, San Francisco
House, 2625 Rose Street, Berkeley, California
1960 Maybridge Cluster, Belvedere, California
O'Connell House, Elk, California
Steinhart House, Belvedere, California
1960/
65 Rossmore Leisure World (retirement community and shopping center), Walnut Creek, California
1961 Benson House, Clear Lake, California
Johnson House, Alameda, California
Deutcher House, Pleasant Hill, California
Hill House, Tiburon, California
1962 Cove Apartments, Belvedere, California
Duncan House, San Francisco
Miller House, Mill Valley, California
Haviland Hall renovation and remodelling, University of California, Berkeley
1963 Albrecht House, Los Gatos, California
1964 Callister House, Belvedere, California
Gordon House, San Francisco
Silva House, Oakland, California
1965 Granada Community School, Tiburon, California
Plan for the new town of Valencia, near Los Angeles
First Church of Christ Scientist, Mill Valley, California
Harvey's Ranch House Restaurant, State Highway 99, Valencia, California
Red Hill Intermediate School, San Anselmo, California
Grammar School additions, Ross, California
Sierra Tahoe Incline Village, Lake Tahoe, California

Plan for the center of Tiburon, California
Unitarian Church, San Mateo, California (project)
Valencia Golf Clubhouse, State Highway 99, Valencia, California
Field House and Playing Fields, University of California at Santa Cruz
1966 Barn Road Apartments, Belvedere, California
Hidden Valley School additions, San Anselmo, California
Campus Commons, Sacramento
1967 Diaz Ranch, Marin County, California (project)
Land use plan for Sycamore, Danville, California
Myers House, 455 Belvedere Avenue, Belvedere, California
Chapel, Mills College, Oakland, California
Sonoma Student Barns, Sonoma County, California (project)
1967/
72 Hiller Highlands (housing development), Hiller Drive, Berkeley, California
1968 Fair Activities Complex, and Floriculture Pavilion and Livestock Barns, *California Exposition and Fair,* Sacramento
Social Sciences and Humanities Buildings, University of California at Davis
Maloney House, Lucas Valley, California
First Unitarian Church, Franklin and Geary Streets, San Francisco
Master plan for Bania Condominium Development, Novato, California
1968/
69 Hollywood Hills Hotel, California
1969 Pacifica Condominiums, Pacifica, California (project)
1970 Ark Apartments, Belvedere, California
North Parking Facilities, California State University at San Jose
Administrative Buildings and Church School, First Unitarian Church, Franklin and Geary Streets, San Francisco
1973 The Vineyards, Saratoga, California
Toyon Farm, Los Altos, California
1974 Pier 45, San Francisco (competition project)
1975 Master plan for The Villages, San Jose, California
Pancho's Restaurant, Manhattan Beach, California (project)
1976 Davidson House, Aptos, California
1977 Foley-Corsano House, Santa Cruz, California
Jones House, Tiburon, California
Amherst fields development, Amherst, Massachusetts
1978 House, Tiburon, California

Publications:

On CALLISTER: articles—"The Bold Approach in a Magnificent New House" in *House Beautiful* (New York), February 1962; "Profiles in Design: Warren Callister" in *House and Home* (New York), July 1962; "Northern California and the Tradition of

Wood Design" in *House and Home* (New York), May 1969; "Tent Pavilion for Flower Show at State Fair" in *Architectural Record* (New York), May 1970; "Wild about Wood" by Roger Yee in *Progressive Architecture* (New York), September 1974.

Charles Warren Callister has retained a remarkable sensitivity to siting and detail while moving from small-scale designs to major community developments. He began practice in San Francisco in 1946 with designs for private houses that combined motifs from New England and Japan with the so-called Bay Area regional style. By the mid-1950's he had begun to take on bigger commissions, including schools, university buildings, and the large-scale community planning and housing projects for which he is now well known.

The influence of Frank Lloyd Wright, clearly visible in his Kentfield house of 1949, gave way to a lighter, more Japanese style. The Dwight Way house, on a steep site in the Berkeley hills, is perched on concrete piers with floor and roof beams projecting in a lively rhythm. The Oriental effect is heightened by window treatment reminiscent of shoji screens.

His Field House for the new University of California campus at Santa Cruz shows Callister's typical sensitivity to siting. Set on a gentle hill leading up to the central college clusters, the building is tucked discreetly into the slope so as not to interfere with the ocean view from the entry road or the campus above. A lower level of reinforced concrete, with narrow openings for light, supports a copper-clad hexagonal roof that blends well with the surrounding brown hills. He achieves additional visual compactness by having the roof of the locker and shower extension double as a grandstand for the playing fields below.

The Chapel at Mills College is again a circular building—but in a woodsy setting. Entry is through a low, earth-bound vestibule leading into the great round nave that acts as a compression ring for a burst of complex wood vaulting, a structural metaphor for the exultation of worship.

An unusual commission, for the Floriculture Pavilion at the *California Exposition and Fair* in the scorching Sacramento Valley, caused Callister to produce an uncharacteristically flamboyant structure. Triangular trusses of open-web steel, recalling the Snowden/Price Aviary at London Zoo, combined with sail-like tensile surfaces create an airy oasis of color and greenery over a covered walkway and meandering stream connected to a nearby lake. The canval panels can be removed completely or partially for different effects and purposes.

Callister's entry into large-scale housing and community planning necessitated fundamental changes in his work methods: he had to deal with the unpredictable tastes and lifestyles of a wide audience, to say nothing of developers' demands. Rossmore Leisure World in California, built for a projected population of 18,000, has a 2,200 acre site of which one third was left in its natural state. Garden villas and condominium apartments are grouped in clusters to lend a sense of intimacy and to blend in with the existing terrain. Facilities include a medical center,

Charles Warren Callister: House, Tiburon, California, 1978

golf courses, swimming pools, art studios, and a shopping center; all utilities are under ground.

Hiller Highlands, another California development, was built in a former rock quarry with most of the site on a 2.1 incline. Callister turned this potential disadvantage to advantage by giving each townhouse a spectacular view.

East Coast developments of the 1970's—such as Amherst Fields in Massachusetts—show increased simplification of form (with structural elements bearing full aesthetic weight) and an increased reliance on factory-made pre-fabricated parts. But the general level of design and siting indicates that Callister's sensibility has survived concessions to the mass market.

—Lucinda Hawkins

CAMBRIDGE SEVEN ASSOCIATES INC.
Partnership; established, Cambridge, Massachusetts, 1962; subsequently opened office in New York. Principals: founders—Louis J. Bakanowsky; Peter Chermayeff; Paul E. Dietrich; Terry Rankine; Ivan Chermayeff; and Thomas Geismar; since 1971—Charles Redmon. Recipient: Design Award, American Institute of Architects, 1967; Design Award, *Progressive Architecture,* 1967, 1979; United States Department of Housing and Urban Development Award, 1968; AIA/American Library Association Award, 1970. Address: 1050 Massachusetts Avenue, Cambridge, Massachusetts 02138, U.S.A.

Works:

1962 New England Aquarium, Boston
1963 Washington Park Shopping Center, Roxbury, Massachusetts
1964 United States Pavilion, *Expo '67,* Montreal
1965 Pittsfield Cooperative Bank, Massachusetts
       School study, Weston, Massachusetts
1965/
70 Arlington Station prototype modernization, Massachusetts Bay Transportation Authority, and development plan for the entire rapid transit system
1966 Knapp Shoes Office and Distribution Center, Brockton, Massachusetts
1967 Design of DC-10 airplane interiors for Douglas Aircraft
1968 Consumer Value Stores, Boston
       Allendale School, Rochester, New York
       Studies for industrialized and rationalized traditional housing
       Boston Police Station, District 11
       Visitors Center, Children's Museum, Boston
1968/
72 Harvard University Observatory, Cambridge, Massachusetts
1969 Weston Junior High School, Massachusetts
       Library, Pomfret School, Connecticut
       Arthur D. Little Inc. Office Building, Cambridge, Massachusetts
       Student Union, University of Syracuse, New York (project)
1970 1050 Massachusetts Avenue Office Building (Cambridge Seven Offices), Cambridge, Massachusetts
1971 Graphics and urban furniture for the new town of Lysander, Massachusetts
       Robinson Hall renovation, Harvard University, Cambridge, Massachusetts
       North Carolina Marine Science Center, Wilmington, North Carolina
       Chermayeff House, Concord, Massachusetts
       8th Street Station modernization, Philadelphia
1972 Graphics for Market Street East, Philadelphia
       Study for a World's Fair, for the Bicentennial Commission, Philadelphia
1973 Solar Energy Study

College 2, University of Massachusetts, Columbia Point, Boston
       Mabel Brady Garven Exhibit of American Arts, Yale University, New Haven, Connecticut
1974 Library, Smith College, Northampton, Massachusetts
       Theatre/Auditorium, New Bedford Whaling Museum, Massachusetts
       Wellesley Senior High School modernization, Massachusetts
       Graphics for the British Terminal of the English Channel Tunnel
       Solar Energy Building, Massachusetts Audubon Society, Boston (project)
1975 Music Facility, Williams College, Williamstown, Massachusetts
       Where's Boston? Pavilion, Prudential Center, Boston
       Beltway Stations, North East Rail Corridor, Boston-Washington, D.C. (prototypes)
1976 Porter Square Red Line Station extension, Massachusetts Bay Transportation Authority
       Layout for *Solar Energy Exhibit,* United States Energy Resource Development Agency, Washington, D.C.
       Wellesley Elementary Schools, Massachusetts
1977 Master plan for the IBM Corporation Complex, Essex Junction, Vermont
1978 MCI Corrections Institute, Concord, Massachusetts
       Resource Planning Associates, Cambridge, Massachusetts
       Lonestar Brewery, San Antonio Museum, Texas
       Displays for the Meldisco Shoe Company
       Boston Safe Deposit Company interiors
       Master plan for the IBM Corporation Complex, Endicott, New York
       The Talbots Inc. Office Distribution Center, Hingham, Massachusetts

Cambridge Seven Associates: New England Aquarium, Boston, 1962

Library, New Bedford Whaling Museum, Massachusetts
1979 Digital Equipment Corporation Office Building, Nashua, New Hampshire
Library addition and renovation, Trinity College, Hartford, Connecticut
1980 San Antonio, Texas Museum of Art
1981 Baltimore Aquarium

In addition to sharing the concerns of my partners in Cambridge Seven Associates in the design of a physical environment which provides a context for deeper and more meaningful human experience, I am particularly interested in the integration of all the visual arts with architecture. I feel that a more thorough incorporation of the visual arts into architecture will provide the designer with a richly-expanded environmental palette. This will be facilitated through a relational, space-field approach to architecture rather than a consideration of isolated buildings.

—Louis J. Bakanowsky

My work as an architect has been for the most part collaboration with a group of designers and others committed, without stylistic or other formal preconceptions, to finding fresh solutions to diverse problems—rationally in all cases, and dramatically where appropriate.

—Peter Chermayeff

A strong interest in all aspects of design led to my involvement in the formation of Cambridge Seven Associates. My work with my fellow principals and other designers has expanded that interest and provided the opportunity to achieve design solutions that attempt to extend beyond normal expectations and to improve the quality of our environment.

—Paul E. Dietrich

Although I have been responsible for the design of many individual buildings since the founding of Cambridge Seven Associates, I have felt that my most important contribution has been to help in the establishment, the development and the continuing ability of the group practice to produce excellence in design.

At Cambridge Seven Associates we share the design experience and help each other in the design process. We have built an organization that can, with great effectiveness, produce designs for buildings, exhibits, urban areas, multi-media events, large developments and transportation systems. We intended this at the outset, and I feel that I and all of the other principals have fashioned an effective team to achieve these goals.

—Terry Rankine

Cambridge Seven Associates Inc. was founded in 1962 by seven young men, all of whom had only recently graduated from schools of architecture or design. Six of the founders are still principals of the

firm: Louis Bakanowski, Peter Chermayeff, Paul E. Dietrich and Terry Rankine in its Cambridge office; Ivan Chermayeff and Thomas Geismar in its New York office. Charles Redmon, in Cambridge, is the seventh principal, replacing one of the founding partners.

From the beginning these talented designers decided not to limit themselves to the design of buildings. They aspired to design everything that could be designed, as did most architects before our present era of specialization. (The eclipse of the Art Nouveau, Bauhaus, and Art Deco periods marked the end of the architect's perception of himself as a universal designer, confidently engaged in as many of the arts and crafts as he had time for, including the design of furniture, fabrics, ornament and typography.)

The Cambridge Seven decided to be as many sided as today's world would allow, and became film makers, graphic designers and creators of exhibitions and interiors as well as buildings. Another American architect with a similar vision was the late Charles Eames. Like Eames, the Cambridge Seven have excelled in exhibition design, most notably at *Expo '67* in Montreal. In collaboration with Buckminster Fuller, who invented the geodesic dome in which it was housed, they devised a brilliant exhibit designed to tell the world of the scientific and cultural achievements of the United States.

Unlike Eames, however, who did more exhibitions, furniture and films than buildings, the Cambridge Seven have built or are designing aquariums, galleries, museums, display pavilions of all kinds, park visitor centers, theatres and performing arts centers. Their work includes mixed-use developments, housing, retail, office and hotel space, a police station, subway station, and school and college buildings. They are also restoring important buildings of the past and adapting them for re-use. They still, however, pursue the ideal of diversity with which they began. Their current work includes the design of a bookplate, a Harvard-Yale trophy and all the graphics for Boston's subway system.

The work they have completed since their founding 16 years ago is almost too heterogeneous to be appraised as a whole. The volume accomplished is uneven in quality, but that is inevitable. Since the firm appears not to turn down jobs that must be done quickly and cheaply, some of their work reflects this circumstance. Projects with adequate budgets and time schedules are carefully designed and meticulously constructed. The work of the Cambridge Seven that has been done under favorable circumstances is comparable with the best work of its type done anywhere.

The Cambridge Seven have developed no design style of their own. Their buildings are indistinguishable from others built throughout the United States in the late 1960's and 1970's by leading U.S. firms. But the Cambridge Seven, in the scope of their work, have sustained a vital idea—the concept of the architect as an all-encompassing artist. In today's world of ever increasing specialization, that is a major accomplishment.

—Mildred F. Schmertz

CANDELA, Felix.
American. Born in Madrid, Spain, 27 January 1910; emigrated to Mexico in 1939: naturalized, 1941; emigrated to the United States, 1971: naturalized, 1978. Educated at the Escuela Superior de Arquitectura, Madrid, 1927–35, Dip.Arch. 1935; Academia de Bellas Artes de San Fernando, Spain, 1936; study fellowship in Germany, 1936. Served as a Lieutenant in the Spanish Army Artillery, 1935, and as a Captain of Engineers in the Spanish Republican Army, 1936–39. Married Eladia Martin in 1940 (died, 1963); Dorothy Davies in 1967; children: Antonia, Jane, Manolita, Teresa, and Pilar. Worked as an architect in the Agricultural Colony, Chihuaha, Mexico, 1939–40; Partner, Candela and Bringas, Acapulco, Mexico, 1940–41; Assistant Architect, Jesus Martí and Associates, Mexico City, 1941–44; in private architectural practice, Mexico City, 1944–49; Founder-President, Cubiertas ALA S.A., design and construction company, Mexico City, 1950–69; Associate Architect, Praeger-Kavanagh-Waterbury, New York, 1969–71. In private practice, Chicago, since 1971. Consultant Architect, Project Planning Association, Toronto, since 1977, and IDEA Center, Athens, Greece, since 1978. Professor of Architecture, National University, Mexico City, 1953–70; Professor of Architecture, 1971–78, and since 1978 Professor Emeritus, University of Illinois at Chicago Circle. Charles Eliot Norton Professor of Poetry, Harvard University, Cambridge, Massachusetts, 1961–62; Jefferson Memorial Professor, University of Virginia, Charlottesville, 1966; Andrew D. White Professor-at-Large, Cornell University, Ithaca, New York, 1969–74; Honorary Professor, Escuela Tecnica Superior de Arquitectura, Madrid, 1969; William Hoffman Wood Professor of Architecture, University of Leeds, Yorkshire, 1974–77; Honorary Professor, Universidad Nacional Federico Villareal, Lima, Peru, 1977. Exhibitions: University of Southern California, Los Angeles, 1957; Harvard University, and United States tour, 1961; McNair Museum,

San Antonio, and Museum of Modern Art, Houston, Texas, 1966. Recipient: Institute of Structural Engineers Gold Medal, London, 1961; Auguste Perret Prize, International Union of Architects, 1961; Plomada de Oro, Sociedad de Arquitectos Mexicanos, 1963; Alfred E. Lindau Award, American Concrete Institute, 1965. D.F.A.: University of New Mexico, Albuquerque, 1964; D.Eng.: Universidad de Santa Maria, Caracas, Venezuela, 1968. Fellow, American Concrete Institute. Honorary Member, Sociedad Colombiana de Arquitectos, Sociedad de Arquitectos Venezolanos, American Institute of Architects, International Association for Shell Structures, Royal Institute of British Architects, Church Architectural Guild of America, Associacion Costarricense de Arquitectos, Colegio de Arquitectos del Peru, and Sociedad Bolivariana de Arquitectos. Address (office): 1514 West Jackson Boulevard, Chicago, Illinois 60607, U.S.A.

Works:

1939 Two small villages, Chihuaha Sierra, Mexico
1940 Apartment house, Acapulco, Mexico
1943 Hotel and cinema, Guamuchil, Mexico
1945 Apartment block, Mexico City
     Hotel Catedral, Mexico City
1948 Houses, Mexico City
1949 Experimental Funicular Vaults, San Bartolo, Mexico City
     Rural school, Ciudad Victoria, Tamaulipas, Mexico
1950 Fernández Factory, San Bartolo, Mexico City
     Pinedo Factory, Nativitas, Mexico City
     Boliches Marsella, Juarez, Mexico City
1951 Pisa Warehouse, San Bartolo, Mexico City
1952 Junior Club, Escandon, Mexico City
     Cosmic Ray Pavilion, Ciudad Universitaria, Mexico City
     Romero House, El Pedregal, Mexico City
     Ras Martín Flower Shop, Chapultepec, Mexico City
     Lechería Ceinsa, Tlalnepantla, Mexico
     Nash Automobile Agency, Anzures, Mexico City
     Almada House, El Pedregal, Mexico City
     Umbrella prototype, Tecamachalco, Mexico City
     Las Aduanas Warehouse, Vallejo, Mexico City
1953 Five houses for Novedades, El Pedregal, Mexico City
     Madaria Warehouse, Ciudad Victoria, Tamaulipas, Mexico
     Hidalgo School, Unidad Modelo, Mexico City
     Convent school, Guerrero, Mexico City
     Monte Alpes School, Lomas de Chapultepec, Mexico City
     Chemical Sciences Auditorium, Ciudad Universitaria, Mexico City
     Centro Gallego, Roma, Mexico City
     Ciba Laboratories, Churubusco, Mexico City
     Church of the Miraculous Virgin, Navarte, Mexico City
1954 Río Warehouse, Linda Vista, Mexico City
     Sedas Parasinas Warehouse, Xochimanca, Mexico
     La Jacaranda Cabaret, Juarez, Mexico City
1955 Lederle Laboratories, Coapa, Mexico City
     Herdez Warehouse, San Bartolo, Mexico City
     Bicardi Distillery, Matamoros, Puebla, Mexico
     Civic Center Auditorium, Ciudad Sahagun, Hidalgo, Mexico
     High Life Factory, Coyoacan, Mexico City
     Acabados Finos Factory, Puente de Vigas, Mexico
     Coyoacán Market, Mexico City
     Dock de la Tolteca, Vallejo, Mexico City
     Rastro de Pollos, Vallejo, Mexico City
     Remington Rand Factory, Vallejo, Mexico City

Celestino Warehouse, Vallejo, Mexico City
Cabero Warehouse, Vallejo, Mexico City
Jamaica Wholesale Market, Mexico City
Banco Núñez, Havana, Cuba
Presidential Palace, Havana, Cuba (project)
Low-cost housing, Monterrey, Nuevo Leon, Mexico
Cross Roads Restaurant, Great Southwest District, Texas
Insignia of the Great Southwest District, Texas
Stock Exchange Hall, Mexico City (with Enrique de la Mora)
El Altillo Chapel, Santo Angel, Mexico City (with Enrique de la Mora)
Rivetex Treadmill, Cuernavaca, Mexico
La Fama Factory, Tlalpan, Mexico City
Aceros de México Factory, Monterrey, Mexico
Cafés de México Factory, Santa Clara, Mexico
Toyoda Factory Canteen, Ciudad Sahagun, Hidalgo, Mexico
Belron Factory, Ixtapalapa, Mexico
Swimming pool, Lomas de Chapultepec, Mexico City
Church of Santa Teresa del Niño Jesús, Monterrey, Mexico
Champagnac Church, Las Charcas, Guatemala
Television transmitting tower, Mexico City
El Léon Confectionery, Vallejo, Mexico City
Borges House, Havana, Cuba
Mexican Travel Association, Juarez, Mexico
Lederle Laboratories Boiler House, Coapa, Mexico City
Oratory, Havana, Cuba
Beach Club, Playa Azul, Venezuela
Synagogue, Guatemala City
Lederle Laboratories Entrance Pavilion, Coapa, Mexico City (with Alejandro Prieto)
1956 Band shell, Santa Fé, Mexico City (with Mario Pani)
     Church of San Antonio de las Huertas, Tacuba, Mexico City (with Enrique de la Mora)
1957 Sign Post, Tequesquitengo, Mexico
     Plaza de los Abanicos, Lomas de Cuernavaca, Mexico
     Bazaar, Lomas de Cuernavaca, Mexico
     La Jacaranda Night Club, Acapulco, Mexico (with J. Sordo Madaleno)
     Texas Instruments Factory, Dallas (with O'Neil Ford and Associates)
     Entrance Monument, Cuernavaca, Mexico (with Guillermo Rossell)
1958 Centro Electrónico, Ciudad Universitaria, Mexico City
     Restaurant, Xochimilco, Mexico City (with J. Alvarez Ordonez)
     Auditorium and restaurant, Casino de la Selva, Cuernavaca, Mexico
1959 Open chapel, Lomas de Cuernavaca, Mexico (with Guillermo Rossell)
     Church of San José Obrero, Monterrey, Mexico (with Enrique de la Mora)
1960 Chapel of San Vicente de Paul, Coyoacan, Mexico City (with Enrique de la Mora)
     Bicardi Bottling Plant, Carretera Mexico, Queretaro, Tlalnepantla, Mexico
     Sales office, Guadalajara, Jalisco, Mexico
1963 John Lewis Warehouse, Stevenage, Hertfordshire, England (with Yorke, Rosenberg and Mardall)
1964 Aztec Stadium, Mexico City (project)
1968 Mexican Olympic Sports Palace, Mexico City (with E. Castaneda and A. Peyri).
1969 Brown University Sports Complex, Providence, Rhode Island (project; with Praeger-Kavanagh-Waterbury)
     City for Sports, Kuwait (competition project)
1975 Bernabeu Stadium, Madrid (project)

1977 King Abdulaziz University, Jeddah, Saudi
    Arabia (consultant; with Project Planning
    Associates)

Publications:

By CANDELA: book—foreword to *Frei Otto:
Spannweiten* by Conrad Roland, Berlin, Frankfurt
and Vienna, 1965; articles—"Cubierta Prismática de
Hormigón en la Ciudad de México" in *Revista Na-
cional de Arquitectura* (Mexico City), March 1950;
"Simple Concrete Shell Structures" in *American
Concrete Institute Journal* (Detroit), December
1951; "Structural Digressions on Style" in *Espacio*
(Mexico City), May 1953; "The Shell as Space En-
closer" in *Arts and Architecture* (Los Angeles), Janu-
ary 1955; "A New Way to Span Space" in *Architectural Forum* (New York), November 1955;
"Construction en Voiles Minces, au Méxique" in
Techniques et Architecture (Paris), January 1956;
"Shell Concrete Construction in Mexico" in *Municipal Journal* (London), March 1956; "Lezione di
Modestia di Felix Candela" in *L'Architettura*
(Rome), August 1957; "Hyperbolic Paraboloids" in
Conferencia (Chicago), 11 December 1957; "Understanding the Hyberbolic Paraboloids" in *Architectural Record* (New York), July 1958; "Felix Candela" in *Arquitectura* (Madrid), October 1959;
"Planta Embotelladora Bacardí en México" in *Nuestra Arquitectura* (Buenos Aires), March 1961; "Design and Construction in Mexico: Shell Construction" in *Industrial Building* (New York), September
1961; "Une Suele Conscience pour l'Oeuvre à Créer"
in *Architecture d'Aujourd'hui* (Paris), December
1961/January 1962; "Comprender il Paraboloide
Iperbolico" in *Casabella* (Milan), October 1965;
"Architettura e Strutturalismo" in *Casabella*
(Milan), no. 306, 1966; "Shell Structure Development" in *Canadian Architect* (Toronto), January
1967; "The Heritage of Maillart" in *Archithese* (Niedertaufen), no. 6, 1973; etc.

On CANDELA: books—*Candela: The Shell Builder*
by Colin Faber, New York and London 1963; *Builders in the Sun: Five Mexican Architects* by Clive B.
Smith, New York 1967; articles—"Una Casa de En-
sueno" in *Novedades* (Mexico City), 1 June 1951;
"The New University City of Mexico" by Esther
McCoy in *Arts and Architecture* (Los Angeles), September 1953; "Shell Concrete Today" in *Architectural Forum* (New York), August 1954; "The Work
of Felix Candela" in *Progressive Architecture* (New
York), July 1955; "Folded-Slab Church" in *Architectural Review* (London), January 1956; "Incon-
tro con Felix Candela" by Manfredi Nicoletti in
L'Architettura (Rome), February 1957; "Felix Candela" in *Concrete Quarterly* (London), April/June
1957; "Fyller, Candela, Headline AIA Convention"
in *Architectural Record* (New York), December
1957; "Felix Candela: Architect of Shells" in *Time*
(New York), 8 September 1958; "Engineering of Excitement" by Robin Boyd in *Architectural Review*
(London), November 1958; "Wizard of the Shells"
in *Architectural Forum* (New York), November
1959; "Enrique de la Mora y Palomar—Felix Candela—Deux Eglises au Mexique" in *Architecture
d'Aujourd'hui* (Paris), September/November 1960;
"Felix Candela" by Betty Campbell in *The Guilds'
Engineer* (London), no. 13, 1962; "Felix Candela at
the A.A." in *Architectural Association Journal* (London), vo. 80, no. 883, 1964; "Casing the Olympics"
in *AIA Journal* (Washington, D.C.), December
1967; "Mexico and the Olympics—The Daring Design" in *Saturday Review* (New York), 22 June 1968;
"Candela: Recent Works" in *Zodiac* (Milan), October 1973.

Felix Candela: Church of the Miraculous Virgin, Navarte, Mexico City, 1953

Like Prouvé in France and Nervi in Italy, Felix Candela is both builder and designer, and he shares with
them the advantages and disadvantages of this situation. The advantages are a close relationship between
design and construction and an interest in the formal
possibilities of building very cheaply. The chief

disadvantage is that the work is often carried out for
indifferent architects, so that Candela has himself
confessed to preferring many of his buildings half
finished—"before the architecture is added."

Candela has made himself effective by narrowing
the range of what he has to offer and by being uninterested in problems—like multi-storey buildings—
that do not readily lend themselves to his chosen
form of construction. Candela's achievement has
been in the field of thin shell vaulting in concrete
reinforced with mild steel, and for this a Spanish
upbringing and a Mexican practice could not be bet-
tered. In the Madrid of the 1930's, the young Candela witnessed the construction of the vaults of the
Zarzuela race track and the Fronton Recoletos, two
of the first masterpieces of thin concrete shell design,
and he could learn from their designer Eduardo Torroja that a great engineer is a poet, one who uses
imagination and intuition as much as he uses calculation. However, war-torn Europe could not offer
Candela the chance to build, and the USA, that
magnet for European emigrés, could not offer the
low labour costs required to make shell vaulting an
economical way to roof buildings. Mexico, with its
post-war building boom combined with cheap labour, gave Candela his opportunity.

Candela built his first shell structure in the summer of 1949. It was a development of the war-time
British Cresiphon system where the vault is rippled
to give greater rigidity to a thin shell. As a contrac-

tor, Candela was concerned to simplify the formwork into which the concrete was poured, and to this
end he evolved shells whose geometry was such that
the forms could be entirely constructed of straight
timbers. The roof of the Fernandez factory uses con-
oids to this end, but the really dramatic breakthrough came with the use of hyperbolic paraboloids, a form that became almost a Candela
trademark, and the economy of construction was
such that he was able to win many contracts on cost
alone.

In the early 1950's the vast campus of Mexico
University was built. The scientists wanted a small
building for research into cosmic rays, and they
needed a concrete structure no more than 15mm
thick to admit the rays to the interior. This was
Candela's opportunity, and he seized it with both
hands. The Cosmic Ray Pavilion is a delightful
structure, with its undulating shell vaulted building
standing on slender arches. From being an unknown
contractor Candela was catapulted to the forefront
of the design world, and his practice grew in size and
importance.

The period following the completion of the Cosmic Ray Pavilion was the most productive of Candela's career. Concrete columns supporting an umbrella consisting of four hyperbolic parabloids
became his norm for factory and warehouse building, sometimes used in a straightforward way as in
the warehouses at Linda Vista in Mexico and Steven-

age, England, and sometimes distorted to enable light to enter between the shells, as at the Coyoacan High Life Factory. Warping of the hyperbolic paraboloid form was taken further in the Church of the Miraculous Virgin, where concrete, 37mm thick, twists and bends to give a Gaudi-like spookiness without ever losing its structural logic. Other churches followed—the exteriors were often kitsch in the extreme, but the logic of the structure usually created an interior of real quality. The roofs were beautiful, but the walls spoilt the magic, and in the early 1960's Candela found himself in the same dilemma as Buckminster Fuller. Both had evolved structural systems that were sane, logical and beautiful, but in each case the clarity of the structure was marred when incorporated into a real building. However, both Fuller and Candela were so widely admired that they were commissioned to design and build structures that remained structures—beautiful sculptures without the enclosures that destroyed their charm. Candela built a whole series of shells that are really playful demonstrations of what shells can do; the entrance to the Lederle laboratory complex, the Bandshell at Santa Fé and especially the bird at Lake Tequesquitengo can be regarded as pure sculpture, with form the only aim.

Shells as sculpture were fun, but Candela is essentially a builder. After the tours-de-force he was content to turn his mind back to buildings, and a second constructive period begins with the three 30 metre square groined vaults that he built for Bacardi Rum in Mexico City. This last building stands next to an office building by Mies van der Rohe, two very different buildings but both by designers who believed that form comes from structure, in one case concrete, in the other steel.

—John Winter

CANDILIS, Georges.

French. Born in Bakou, Azerbaydzhan, Russia, 11 April 1913; emigrated to France, 1945: naturalized, 1946. Educated at the Athens Polytechnic, Dip. Arch. 1936. Served as a First Lieutenant in the Greek Army, 1940–42: awarded Order of St. George. Married Christiane Richard in 1959; children: Alexis, Alexandrine, and Panaghyote. Worked in the office of Le Corbusier, Paris, 1945–48, and Marseilles, 1948–50; in partnership with Shadrach Woods, q.v., and Vladimir Bodianky, q.v., in AT-BAT-Afrique, Casablanca, 1951–54; in partnership with Woods and Alexis Josic, q.v., as Candilis-Josic-Woods, Paris, 1955–63. In private practice, Paris, since 1963. Assistant Professor of Architecture, Athens Polytechnic, 1936–40; Professor, Greek National School for Building Techniques, Athens, 1940–45. Since 1959, Professor of Architecture, Ecole Nationale Supérieure des Beaux-Arts, Paris. Member, CIAM (Congrès Internationaux d'Architecture Moderne), and of Team 10. Recipient: First Prize, Marseilles Housing Competition, 1959; First Prize, Toulouse-le-Mirail New Town Competition, 1960; Grand Prize for Urban Development, New Town of Bagnols-sur-Cèze, 1961; First Prize, Free University of Berlin Competition, 1963. Honorary Fellow, American Institute of Architects. Chevalier, Légion d'Honneur. Address (office): 18 rue Dauphine, 75006 Paris, France.

Works:

1946/
52 Unité d'Habitation (Cité Radieuse), 280 Boulevard Michelut, Marseilles (with Le Corbusier and others)
1949 Chalets, Megeve, St. Gervais, France
1951/
55 Musulman Collective Housing Development, Casablanca (with Vladimir Bodiansky and Shadrach Woods)

1952/
54 Master plan for the City of Casablanca (with Vladimir Bodiansky and Shadrach Woods)
1953/
56 Apartment buildings, Algiers
1954 Housing for Tropical Countries (competition project)
Tobacco Factory, Lebanon (competition project)
1954/
55 Opération Million: 3,600 housing units, France, particularly the Paris suburbs (with Shadrach Woods and Alexis Josic)
1955 Elementary and secondary schools, French Guiana
1956 Low-cost housing, Nicaragua (project)
1956/
59 Housing complex for oil company employees, Abadan, Iran (project)
1956/
61 Plan and housing for the new town of Bagnols-sur-Cèze, France (with Shadrach Woods and Alexis Josic)
1957 Low-cost housing, Panama (project; with Jean Prouvé)
1958 Plan for tourist development in New Caledonia
Hotel, San Juan, Puerto Rico (project)
1959 Caribbean Hotel (project)
Housing (4,000 units), Marseilles (with Shadrach Woods and Alexis Josic)
1959/
62 Tropical housing, Martinique (with local firms)
1960 Urban pre-fabricated houses, Algeria (competition project; with Shadrach Woods and Alexis Josic)
Master plan for the new town of Toulouse-le-Mirail, France (with Shadrach Woods and Alexis Josic)
1961 French Secondary School, Geneva
New town of 30,000 inhabitants, Caen, France (competition project; with Shadrach Woods and Alexis Josic)
New town of 10,000 inhabitants, Hamburg (competition project; with Shadrach Woods and Alexis Josic)
1962 University for 2,000 students, Bochum, Germany (competition project; with Shadrach Woods and Alexis Josic)
Hotel Complex and Leisure Center, Phalere Bay, Greece (project)
Plan for tourist development, Spetsai, Greece
Plan for hotel accommodation, New Caledonia
1962/
63 Schools, Fort-de-France, Martinique (with local firms)
1962/
65 Apartment buildings, Paris
1963 Plan for the center of Frankfurt (with Shadrach Woods and Alexis Josic)
Master plan of Fort Lamy, Chad, Africa (with Shadrach Woods and Alexis Josic)
Master plan for the Free University of Berlin (with Shadrach Woods and Alexis Josic)
Leisure Center and Harbour, Beirut (project; with El Khoury)
Hotel, Tahiti (project)
Hotel, Guadeloupe (project)
Cultural and Sports Center, Bagnols-sur-Cèze, France
Gypsy Settlement, Avignon
1963/
65 Apartment buildings and maisonettes, Aix-en-Provence, France
1964 Apartment buildings, Marseilles and Nimes, France
1964/
65 Ski Resort, Vallée de Belleville, France (with Shadrach Woods and Jean Prouvé)

Apartment buildings, Lyons (with others)
Cité Artisanale (Workshop Center for Artisans), Sèvres, France (with Shadrach Woods and Alexis Josic)
1964/
67 Tourist Development, Languedoc-Roussillon, France (project; with others)
1965/
75 Leisure Center of Barcarès-Leucate, Languedoc-Roussillon, France
1966 Tourist Development, Tahiti
Steilshoop Regional Center, Hamburg (with Shadrach Woods)
Hotel, Cesarea, Israel
1966/
67 Water Treatment Plant, Toulouse-le-Mirail, France (with Alexis Josic)
1966/
68 Faculty of Literature, Restaurant, Administration Building, and Sports Facilities, University of Toulouse-le-Mirail, France (with Alexis Josic)
Tourist Development, Corsica (project)
1966/
69 3 apartment buildings, Paris
1967 Experimental housing, stage I, Fort Lamy, Chad, Africa (project)
Plan for the city of Athens
University of Zurich (competition project)
1967/
77 New town of Toulouse-le-Mirail, France
Free University of Berlin
1968 Covered Market, Toulouse
Technical Office Building, Toulouse
Garage, Toulouse
Master plan for Plovdiv, Bulgaria (competition project)
Leisure housing development, Cap Martin, France
1968/
72 Low-cost apartments, Paris
1969 University of Madrid (competition project)
Master plan for the Old City of Kuwait (competition project)
Marina-type housing, with harbor facilities, St. Raphael and Deauville, France (project)
1969/
70 Housing (10,000 low-cost units), Lima, Peru (competition project; with Alexis Josic)
1970 Hilton Hotel, Lahore, Pakistan (with Alexis Josic)
Leisure housing development, Cannes (with others)
1970/
79 Luxury apartment buildings, Le Havre, France
1971 Tourism facilities for the Peninsula of Lavrotto, Monaco (competition project; with Alexis Josic)
1972 Plans for the residential areas of the Old City of Kuwait
1972/
74 Residential complexes, Jeddah, Al Khobar, and Dammam, Saudi Arabia (with R. H. Sanbar)
1973 University of Lattakia, Syria (competition project)
1973/
75 Master plan and design of Bu Ali Sina University, Hamadan, Iran (with the Mandala Collaborative)
Luxury residential complex, Kuwait (with the Kuwaiti Engineering Office)
1973/
76 Master plans for the cities of Dammam, Al Khobar, Qatif, Al Ahsa, and Al Jubayl, Saudi Arabia (projects; with the Metra Consulting Group)
1974 NIRT Employees Apartment Buildings, Tehran (project)
1974/
78 Housing development, Dohar, Qatar

Plans for residential areas in Jeddah, Al Khobar, Medina, and Mecca, Saudi Arabia
1975 Qatar Embassy renovation, Paris
1976/
77 Academic Buildings, Dormitories, and Administration Housing, Bu Ali Sina University, Hamadan, Iran (with the Mandala Collaborative)
1976/
78 Plan for naming and numbering city streets and buildings, Dammam, Saudi Arabia (with Denco)
1976/
79 Eastern Province Corniche, Saudi Arabia (project; with Denco)
1977/
78 Bus Terminal, Depot, Garage, and transport system plan, Dammam, Saudi Arabia (with Denco)
1977- Umm Said Residential Area, phase I, Qatar (with R. H. Sanbar)

Publications:

By CANDILIS: books—*Planning and Design for Leisure*, Stuttgart 1972; *Habitat Bill of Rights*, with Nader Ardalan, Balkrishna Doshi, Moshe Safdie, and Josep Lluis Sert, Tehran 1976; *Bâtir la Vie*, Paris 1978; articles—"Problème d'une Ville: Barcelone" in *L'Architecture d'Aujourd'hui* (Paris), March 1960; "New Town in France: Bagnols-sur-Cèze" in *Architectural Association Journal* (London), April 1960; "Le Corbusier et Notre Epoque," "1918–1930: Le Moment Héroique de l'Architecture Moderne en U.R.S.S." and "De Stijl, Hollande, 1920–1930, et le Bauhaus, Allemagne, 1922–1933" in *L'Architecture d'Aujourd'hui* (Paris), April/May 1964; "Problèmes d'Urbanisme" in *L'Architecture d'Aujourd'hui* (Paris), December 1964/February 1965; "Le Corbusier" in *L'Architecture d'Aujourd'hui* (Paris), June/July 1965; "La Formation de l'Architecte" in *Architecture: Formes et Fonctions* (Lausanne), vol. 12, 1965–66; "Le Mythe de l'Habitat Individuel" in *L'Architecture d'Aujourd'hui* (Paris), February/March 1968; "A la Récherche d'un sens nouveau au mot l'Architecte" in *Architecture: Formes et Fonctions* (Lausanne), vol. 15, 1969; "Ideas" in *Architecture: Formes et Fonctions* (Lausanne), vol. 16, 1971.

On CANDILIS: books—*Candilis, Josic, Woods* by Jürgen Joedicke, Stuttgart 1968; *Toulouse-le-Mirail: Birth of a New Town*, Stuttgart 1975; articles—"Habitat Collectif: Morocain Etude ATBAT-Afrique" in *L'Architecture d'Aujourd'hui* (Paris), February/March 1953; "New Apartment Houses in Rabat and Casablanca" in *L'Architecture d'Aujourd'hui* (Paris), December 1954; "L'Architecte Georges Candilis" in *L'Architettura* (Rome), July 1958; "Low-Cost Housing in Blanc Mesnil" in *Architectural Design* (London), May 1959; "Bagnols-sur-Cèze" in *Architectural Design* (London), May 1960; "Candilis, Josic, Woods" in *Cimaise* (Paris), January/February 1961; "Récherches: Candilis-Josic-Woods" in *L'Architecture d'Aujourd'hui* (Paris), June/July 1964; "Riviera Wall: Vast Candilis Scheme" in *Architectural Review* (London), November 1964; "Atelier Candilis, Josic, Woods" in *Architectural Design* (London), January 1965; "Freie Universität Berlin" in *Deutsche Architektur* (East Berlin), July 1967; "Toulouse-le-Mirail" by Peter Smithson in *Architectural Design* (London), October 1971.

More than ever before our society needs architects. But we have to define which society and which architects.

Man's habitat, the habitat of all men, expresses the focal spirit of our society. These men, omnipotent by their number, make up the Society of the Greatest Number. The Greatest Number, an idea without limit, has its own way of thinking. Numbers disappear and are replaced by facts: white, black, yellow; cold, temperature, hot; poor, rich. We must not confuse Number with the Greater Number. A Number has limits; the Greatest Number has none. The spirit of the Greatest Number sets conditions for everyone —whereas yesterday's problem was that of only a few.

Enormous technical progress, social struggles, and the century's wars have upset completely the order of values: limits, frontiers, distances lose their importance and indeed all significance. Growth is universal; the same needs, rights, and duties occur at the same time in China, Africa, Russia and America. Today man occupies more and more of the earth's surface. In order to live, the man of tomorrow will need more and more square kilometers, more and more kilowatt hours. Villages will turn into towns; towns will become regions. Under the pressure of the Greatest Number, sooner or later, architecture, urbanism, technique, and the technology of construction will change completely.

In our time architects and town planners have unconsciously become experts in the "organization of disorder" and in confusion. Town planning programs conform to a so-called efficacy. In reality they advocate an appalling and artificial vision of our future—tentacular motorways, fathomless underground parking areas, super-hyper markets, vertiginous skyscrapers and other towers of Babel where everything is provided for except the presence of a child. Now, today, only the poet can shout out this truth: No child, no town! How can we establish the relationship of town, vehicle, and child? Who can really achieve this? Who can be made responsible?

Everything changes, everything grows, everything becomes more complicated. Man alone is out of date. So man alone will inevitably be replaced by a team. But, in order for that to happen, we have to train men who can work as a team and who will speak the same language while contributing their complementary disciplines. The presence of the architect—or, rather, the architectural point of view—must be assured at all levels within the team, which will bring together engineers, sociologists, economists, biologists, lawyers, politicians, artists, and—poets.

First, teams of programmers will effectively interpret the country's politico-economic program and create an executive program. Then, teams of normalizers will be entrusted with making things "normal," that is, with establishing the normalization of needs first and of objects thereafter. In this way we will achieve real standards for serial production and the creation of urban industry, and we will achieve quality and prices that will allow us to avoid penury, excess, and wastage. The programmers and normalizers will clear the way for the executors—architects, town planners, engineers, entrepreneurs and industrialists who will carry out the functional, useful and necessary work, truly expressive of our age.

Whether we like it or not, we live in a consumer society. There is nothing wrong with that as long as the consumption is controlled. Consumption implies change, elimination and renewal. It leads and encourages us to think of a house as an impermanent object. And, indeed, it is absurd to think that because a building now exists, it must necessarily continue to exist. The "machine for living" should not have to survive the family for which it was conceived. Kafka, visiting an abandoned and derelict house, described, in a novel, the family that had lived there: "No family, no house!" It is the family that creates the house.

The crinolines and wigs of the marchionesses determined Louis XV's architecture. Our grandmothers' and our great grandmothers' corsets influenced 19th century bourgeois architecture. The couturier Paul Poiret, in dispensing with "bonework," liberated women and inspired the modern movement in architecture. Today, more than ever before, men and women, young and old, wear jeans. Jeans are not only clothing; they are also the expression of an attitude that sooner or later must provoke an upheaval and give rise to a truer, younger, and more candid architecture. Jeans architecture? Why not?

But to be truer, younger and more candid, the act of building must also and above all be an act of love. As, in the creation by Paul Valéry of the words of the architect Eupalinos: "This little temple that I have built for Hermes a few steps from here—if you knew what it means to me! The passer-by sees only an elegant chapel. It is nothing—just four columns, a very simple style. I have put into it the memory of a bright day in my life. Oh gentle transformation. This delicate temple, though no one knows it, is the mathematical image of a girl from Corinth whom I dearly loved. . . ."

—Georges Candilis

Among those who worked for a long time for Le Corbusier, it was perhaps Georges Candilis who first learned how to free himself from the influence of the master in order to assert his own personality. His temperament—the opposite of that of his patron— prompted him to the break. Born in the capital of Azerbaydzhan of a Greek family, he studied in Athens and immediately after the war, on arriving in Paris, joined the studio of Le Corbusier in the rue de Sèvres. Responsible for representing Corbu during the construction of l'Unité d'Habitation in Marseilles, Candilis then directed the Moroccan offshoot of ATBAT created by Le Corbusier, whose only real contribution to the enterprise was that he succeeded in encouraging, in a rather autonomous manner, his young protegé. Returning to France, Candilis set up on his own account, and thanks to a very happy choice of associates—Josic the Yugoslav and Woods the American—he created in the rue Dauphine a studio whose style was soon recognized, and a research center whose achievements were soon known, throughout the world.

Candilis has always remained a Mediterranean. He is interested in man before he is interested in form; he is guided by his heart rather than by his head; his intelligence is supple, his approach infused with warmth. He possesses to the highest degree what we call the "human touch." He has all the necessary qualities to be an excellent actor—he "goes over well," as one says in the jargon of that profession. That is what makes him so popular, particularly with the young.

Though nothing that comes out of the studio in the rue Dauphine is unimportant, and though the average level of its production is distinctly superior to that of most of the architectural practices in France, the interest and merit of the projects and achieved works is variable. There are some that I consider frankly poor, such as the project for the creation of a very dense property development on the site of a navy yard in Le Havre. Among the non-successes, I would also cite the Free University of Berlin, a Mediterranean conception that is lost on the banks of the Spree—but it seduced a competition jury and inspired, more or less happily, many student architects. The buildings give the impression of an immense, abandoned military camp.

Yet the accomplishments are great too. The hotel built for Rothschild at Cesarea in Israel is a small jewel. The sector of the Languedoc-Roussillon coast development entrusted to Candilis is, without question, the most successful. And at the summit of his achievement is the Mirail district of Toulouse. The project was remarkable. If, since the completion of the first phase, Candilis has had to make concessions, the result is still indisputably one of the best urban complexes built in France since the beginning of this century, a complete justification of an architectural vision.

—Pierre Vago

Georges Candilis: New town of Toulouse-le-Mirail, France, 1977

CARDINAL, Douglas (Joseph).
Canadian. Born in Red Deer, Alberta, 7 March 1934. Educated at the University of British Columbia, Vancouver, 1953–54; University of Texas, Austin, 1956–63, B.Arch. 1963. Married Marilyn Gale Zamar in 1973; children: Lisa, Nancy, Guy, and Bret. Design Architect, Bissell and Holman, Red Deer, 1963–67. Principal, Douglas J. Cardinal Architect, Reed Deer, 1964–67, and Edmonton, 1967–76, and Douglas J. Cardinal Architect Ltd., Edmonton, since 1976. Exhibitions: Burnaby Art Gallery, British Columbia, 1978; *Transformations in Modern Architecture,* Museum of Modern Art, New York, 1979. Recipient: Honor Award, Alberta Association of Architects, 1968; Award of Excellence, *The Canadian Architect,* 1972; Achievement of Excellence Award in Architecture, Province of Alberta, 1974. Address: Douglas J. Cardinal Architect Ltd., Number 1601—8830 85th Street, Edmonton, Alberta T6C 3C3, Canada.

Works:

1967　Guloien House, Sylvan Lake, Alberta
1968　St. Mary's Church, Red Deer, Alberta
1970　Master plan for the Alberta Indian Education Centre, Edmonton
1971　Stettler Municipal Hospital, Alberta
1972　Hay River High School, North West Territories
　　　Provost Provincial Building, Alberta
　　　St. Michael's School, Bow Island, Alberta
1975　Kehewen School, Alberta
1976　Ile à La Crosse School, Alberta
　　　Bonnyville Rehabilitation Centre, Alberta
　　　Grande Prairie Regional College, Alberta

1977　La Ronge Elementary School, Saskatchewan
　　　Alberta Government Services Centre, Ponoka
1978　Slake Lake Senior Citizens Residence, Alberta
　　　Slake Lake Drop-In Centre, Alberta
1978-　Community Development Studies
1979　Grotski House, Edmonton

Publications:

On CARDINAL: book—*Of the Spirit* by G. Melnyk, Edmonton 1977; articles—"Alberta Indian Education Centre" by R. Gretton in *The Canadian Architect* (Toronto), September 1970; "The Work of Douglas Cardinal" by Abraham Rogatnick and A. Balkind in *Artscanada* (Toronto), October 1976.

In my profession and in my daily living I have always maintained that the endeavours of all Canadians should be towards a betterment of the human condition. Therefore, in my role as a planner and architect, as the co-ordinator of technologists, I see tremendous opportunity to petition the needs of the individual and to reinstate our humaness as the most important element in all our efforts.

Learn from your body. Solve the problem organically. You have a brain, a stomach, a mouth, a heart, a pair of lungs. You think, eat, talk, feel, breathe. Build around what you are and want to be.

I have found that placing the needs of the human being before the systems created by modern man ensures that man is indeed served by these systems rather than becoming a slave to them.

—Douglas Cardinal

Douglas Cardinal's aim has been to give architectural expression to a synthesis of the indigenous culture of the Indians of North America with that of the dominating Euro-American culture. Although his ancestry is largely Indian, he has had to take deliberate steps in his adulthood to learn and absorb Indian lore and philosophy, an effort that, coming after his study of architecture, inexorably influenced his philosophy of architecture as profoundly as it influenced his philosophy of life.

It is mainly the culture of the Plains Indians of Central Canada and the North-Central United States that Cardinal has studied and, to a considerable extent, practices. Since the Plains Indians are not noted for a strong building tradition, the impression of their culture on the work of an architect would be assumed to be slight. However, in Cardinal's case, the lack of dominating structural techniques or architectural stylistic details as base ingredients for an eclectic porridge has been both unmissed and irrelevant. It is the Indian attitude toward life, toward nature, toward man, and toward collective and private functions that Cardinal is most interested in utilizing, expressing and practicing. Formal influences do indeed enter, however, since Cardinal believes that the Indian way is based on certain spatial conceptions that pervade Indian thought, which, when taken into account, result in superior architectural solutions, as well as superior solutions to the problems of life itself.

Thus the emphasis on the circle and on curvilinearity, which, in Cardinal's view, tend to facilitate the most natural physical as well as symbolic functions of man. The circle symbolizes, but also facilitates, the double function of face to face group contact, as well as the communication, radiation and dissemination of ideas from a central point; of the double-need of the individual to face toward the company of society and also to face away into the loneliness of the wider world.

Cardinal's emphasis on curvilinearity is inspired on the one hand by a positive response to the notion of man and his works as constituting an integral part of nature, a nature that seems to favour curvilinear forms flowing easily and felicitously in and out and from and to every direction at once. On the other hand, there is also a kind of negative defiance in Cardinal's use of curves which, in his mind, contradicts the rectilinearity, the rigid sequential thinking, the strait-lacedness of the culture that he feels the Europeans brought to and imposed upon the western hemisphere with an arrogant and erroneous conviction of its superiority over the indigenous ones.

In his efforts to educate and to impress the non-Indian world with what he feels are quite practical and non-romantic expressions of his philosophy, Cardinal makes a special point of using the most sophisticated methods of design and construction in order to execute the unusual shapes of his buildings. This was probably best illustrated in the construction of the suspended reinforced concrete roof of St. Mary's Church in Red Deer, Alberta, for which computerized calculations furnished the structural solution.

According to Cardinal, the influence of the Indian approach has deeply affected every aspect of his architectural practice; and he prides himself on having successfully handled client-architect relations in new and satisfactory ways, placing great emphasis on patiently fostering group decision-making on the part of the client and on an open-minded, honest response to these decisions on the part of the architect.

—Abraham Rogatnick

CASSON, Sir Hugh (Maxwell).

British. Born in London, 23 May 1910. Educated at Eastbourne College, Sussex; St. John's College, Cambridge, 1929–32; British School, Athens (Craven Scholar), 1932–33; Bartlett School of Architecture, University College, University of London, 1933–35. Served as a Camouflage Office in the Air Ministry, London, 1939–45. Married Margaret Macdonald Troup in 1938; children: Carola, Nicola, and Dinah. In private practice, London, 1933–39; Technical Officer, Ministry of Town and Country Planning, London, 1944–46; resumed private practice, 1946; Director of Architecture, Festival of Britain, London, 1948–51. Since 1953, Senior Partner, Casson, Conder and Partners, London. Professor of Environmental Design, Royal College of Art, London, 1953–75. Architectural Editor, *Arts and Technics,* London, 1947–50; Editor, *Architectural Review,* London, 1948–65. Member, Royal Fine Arts Commission, since 1960, Royal Mint Advisory Committee, since 1972, Post Office Design Advisory Committee, since 1975, Greater London Council Historic Buildings Board, since 1975, and British Rail Development Panel, since 1977; Member of the Council and Executive of the National Trust, since 1965; President, Greater London Arts Association, since 1974; President, Royal Academy of Arts, London, since 1975; Trustee, British Museum of Natural History, and National Portrait Gallery, both London, since 1976. Honorary doctorate: Royal College of Art, 1975; University of Southampton, 1977; LL.D.: University of Birmingham, 1977. Fellow, Royal Institute of British Architects, and the Society of Industrial Artists. Royal Designer for Industry, 1951 (Master of the Faculty, 1969–71); Royal Academician, 1960. Honorary Member, Royal Danish Academy, 1954; Honorary Associate, American Institute of Architects, 1968. Knighted, 1952; K.C.V.O. (Knight Commander, Royal Victorian Order), 1978. Address: 35 Victoria Road, London W8 5RH, England.

Works:

1951   Design of the *South Bank Exhibition,* London

1952/
55   Sidgwick Avenue Development, Cambridge
1954   Master plan for the University of Birmingham

1963/
64   Elephant House, London Zoo
1963/
70   National Westminster Bank Headquarters, Manchester
1971/
78   W. H. Smith Headquarters, London
1973/
76   Education Centre, London Zoo
1973/
77   Civic Centre Assembly Rooms, Derby

Other design work including ships, trains, and theatre and opera sets at Glyndebourne in Sussex and Covent Garden, London.

Publications:

By CASSON: books—*New Sights of London,* London 1938; *Bombed Churches,* London 1946; *Homes by the Million,* London 1946; *Houses: Permanence and Prefabrication,* with Anthony Chitty, London 1947; *An Introduction to Victorian Architecture,* London 1948; *Red Lacquer Days,* London 1956; *Fol-*

Douglas Cardinal: St. Mary's Church, Red Deer, Alberta, 1968

lies, editor, London 1963; *Monuments,* editor, London 1963; *Craftsmanship and Life* (lecture), Birmingham 1966; *Inscape: The Design of Interiors,* editor, London 1968; illustrations in *The Pillow-Book Puzzle* by Ivan Morris, London 1969; *Nancy Says,* with Joyce Grenfell, London 1972; *Spirit of the Age,* with others, London 1975; *Sketch Book: A Personal Choice of London Buildings,* London 1975; articles—"On Architectural Journalism" in *Concerning Architecture,* edited by John Summerson, London 1968; "At the Zoo" in *The Architects' Journal* (London), July 1975; "The Importance of Design Education" in *Building Design* (London), May 1976; "Royal Academy Summer Exhibition" in *RIBA Journal* (London), July 1976; "Looking Back at a National Tonic: The Festival of Britain 1951" in *Country Life* (London), November 1976.

On CASSON: articles—"Looking Back" by Peter Murray in *Building Design* (London), January 1975; "Casson Perspectives" in *Building* (London), November 1976; "Sir Hugh Casson" by Joan Bakewell in *Illustrated London News,* August 1977.

Since the foundation of the partnership our work has been mostly in the field of education (particularly universities) and in, "one-off" projects—theatres, civil halls, and prestige buildings often in conservation areas where special care is needed. Most of our largest projects have been won in competition, and we have also received many design awards and commendations.

My personal interests have developed also in the fields of conservation, interior design (including ships and trains) and theatre design.

—Sir Hugh Casson

Sir Hugh Casson is a complete and well-rounded person with as many facets as the working head of a golf-ball typewriter. He is, above all, an artist combining the skills of architect, environmentalist, conservationist, interior designer, industrial designer, water colourist, author, illustrator, teacher, public speaker, star performer on the media, supporter of good causes, inveterate writer to *The Times*—and many other things besides.

Casson is the senior partner of a well-known firm of architects and as such has been concerned over the years with a steady output of buildings of many kinds. It is not easy to pick out those with which he has been most closely concerned but it is comparatively easy to see where he has added a touch, often a magic touch, to a scheme. The work of the firm, which is never less than distinguished, is usually given a good send-off with one of his inimitable perspective sketches, which have the remarkable quality of accurately suggesting what the finished building will look like, presented with a masterful economy of line and colour. His photographically accurate memory enables him to produce in a trice a drawing of a building in its true setting. It is the same with his architecture, and in this particular skill he resembles Erich Mendelsohn whose miniature sketches from the trenches of World War I so closely resemble his later completed buildings.

Casson seems to design by intuition. The whole building is contained in the first sketch, but there may be many sketches: designing may stop only with the last coat of paint. A Casson building must fit its environment; it may be placed there firmly but it will never be obtrusive and above all it will be friendly to its neighbours. Sometimes it may suffer from an over-keen awareness of both sides of a problem and thereby fall between two stools, but very gently and

without hurt. Excessive interest in high technology and structure are not to be found in the Casson armoury, but choice of materials, colour, and every aspect of interior design are among his sharpest weapons.

Casson first showed his flair and lightness of touch in his layout of the South Bank Exhibition in London in 1951. His flow of good ideas has continued unabated and is still supporting him admirably in his highly influential position as President of the Royal Academy of Arts.

—Gontran Goulden

CATALANO, Eduardo.

American. Born in Buenos Aires, Argentina, 1 December 1917; emigrated to the United States, 1951: naturalized, 1963. Educated at the University of Buenos Aires; University of Pennsylvania, Philadelphia, 1944, M.Arch. 1944; Harvard University, Cambridge, Massachusetts, 1944–45 (Institute of International Education/United States Department of State Scholarship), M.Arch. 1945. Children: Alejandrina and Adrian. Since 1958, Principal, Eduardo

Sir Hugh Casson: Elephant House, London Zoo, 1964

Catalano, Architects and Engineers, Cambridge, Massachusetts. Visiting Professor of Architecture, Architectural Association School, London, 1950–51; Professor of Architecture, University of North Carolina, Raleigh, 1951–56, and Massachusetts Institute of Technology, Cambridge, 1956–77. Exhibition: *Eduardo Catalano,* toured European cities, 1978. Recipient: First Prize, Carrier Company National Competition, 1953; First Prize, Ferro-Enamel National Competition, 1954; First Prize, Health Center Competition, Philadelphia, 1954; Award, American Institute of Architects, North Carolina Chapter, 1956; Award, *Progressive Architecture,* 1969. Address: Eduardo Catalano, Architects and Engineers, 300 Franklin Street, Cambridge, Massachusetts 02139, U.S.A.

Works:

1954 Raleigh House, Raleigh, North Carolina
1961 Master plan for the campus of the University of Buenos Aires (with H. Caminos and E. Sacriste)
  Burton-Connor Dining Room, Massachusetts Institute of Technology, Cambridge (with W. Brown)
1962 Science Building, University of Buenos Aires (with H. Caminos)
1963 Student Center, Massachusetts Institute of Technology, Cambridge
1965 Architecture Building, University of Buenos Aires (with H. Caminos)
  Married Student Housing and Polaroid Building, Massachusetts Institute of Technology, Cambridge
1968 Juilliard School of Music, Lincoln Center for the Performing Arts, New York (with Pietro Belluschi and Helge Westermann)
  Central Plaza, Cambridge, Massachusetts
1969 Civic Center, Springfield, Massachusetts
  Bay State West Urban Complex, Springfield, Massachusetts
  Charlestown Library, Boston
1970 Governmental Center, Greensboro, North Carolina
1971 Washington Mall, Boston
1973 Hall of Justice, Springfield, Massachusetts
1974 United States Embassy, Buenos Aires
1975 Civic Center, Portland, Maine
1976 Cambridge High School, Massachusetts
  La Guardia High School, New York

Publications:

By CATALANO: books—*Teoria de las Sombras y Tratados de Perspectiva,* with Oscar Crivelli and Rene Nery, Buenos Aires 1940; *Structures of Warped Surfaces,* Raleigh, North Carolina 1958, as *Estructuras de superficies Alabeadas,* Buenos Aires 1962; articles—"Un Concurso de Arquitectura en U.S.A." and "Auditorium Ciudad de Buenos Aires" in *Nuestra Arquitectura* (Buenos Aires), July 1946; "From the Crystal Palace to the 1951 Exhibition" in *Nuestra Arquitectura* (Buenos Aires), July 1951; "Three Stadiums" in *Nuestra Arquitectura* (Buenos Aires), December 1952; "Two Warped Surfaces" in *Student Publication of the School of Design* (University of North Carolina, Raleigh), no. 1, 1955; "A Talk to Students" in *Northwest Architect* (Minneapolis), July/August 1966; "Por una arquitectura de sistemas" in *La Prensa* (Buenos Aires), 23 March 1969; "A Case for Systems" in *Progressive Architecture* (New York), November 1969; "A New Scale for Architecture Through Systems" in *Systems Building News* (Chicago), July 1970.

On CATALANO: books—*A Decade of New Architecture* by Sigfried Giedion, Zurich 1951; *Eduardo Catalano* by Gazaneo Scarone, Buenos Aires 1956; *Aluminum in Modern Architecture* by John Peter, New York 1956; *Architecture, You and Me* by Sigfried Giedion, Cambridge, Massachusetts, 1958;

Structures in Art and in Science by Gyorgy Kepes, New York 1965; *Architects on Architecture,* edited by Paul Heyer, New York 1966, London 1967; articles—"The State of Contemporary Architecture" by Sigfried Giedion in *Architectural* Record (New York), February 1954; "Raleigh House" in *Progressive Architecture* (New York), September 1955; "A New Way to Span Space" in *Architectural Forum* (New York), November 1955; "Structure of Hyperbolic Paraboloids" in *Architectural Review* (London), November 1958; "Structures of Warped Surfaces" in *Arts and Architecture* (Los Angeles), December 1963; "MIT Student Center: Eduardo Catalano Starts with Systems and Creates Architecture" in *Architectural Record* (New York), March 1966; "Sobre una obra de Eduardo Catalano" by Fernando Alvarado in *La Prensa* (Buenos Aires), 18 September 1966; "Prefabricated Housing System—Ledgewood" in *Progressive Architecture* (New York), January 1970; "La arquitectura actual segun Eduardo Catalano" by Fernando Alvarado in *La Prensa* (Buenos Aires), 9 August 1970; "Baystate West Shopping Mall" in *Architectural Record* (New York), April 1974; "Greensboro Governmental Center" in *Architectural Record* (New York), June 1974; "Como nacio la arquitectura moderna" by Peter Blake in *La Nacion* (Buenos Aires), 5 November 1975; North Carolina Governmental Center" in *L'Industria Italiana del Cemento* (Rome), December 1978.

*

Like politics, architecture has changed only its face through the use of new visual slogans. Buildings of the last decades, considered outstanding examples of architecture, are merely archaeological resurrections disguised by short-lived visual slogans.

We have made no attempt to find the common denominators of human behavior and needs to formulate the few building constants from which a systematized design and construction process evolves to achieve flexible and long-lasting buildings.

The emphasis on an architecture to satisfy individuals and temporary needs has wrongly led to the construction of frozen structures without flexibility for growth and change.

We cannot aspire to work as individuals, producing individual solutions to satisfy individual whims and needs through custom-made construction, and at the same time pretend to be part of a generation that is searching for an architectural alternative of social and technological dimensions.

The scale of our collective unsatisfied needs is too great to satisfy them through small "museum pieces" and isolated individual efforts, infested with personal mannerisms and romantic techniques. The art gallery of yesterday has been replaced today by the entire city.

The origin of a system is life and its capability to adapt itself to changing human physical environments. They are not sterile patterns but topological networks in constant transformation.

In 1851 Joseph Paxton proved that systems could become the means to structure a poetic thought. After Paxton, there has not been continuity in research and development.

—Eduardo Catalano

*

The Argentine Catalano believes that contemporary architects must abandon individualistic design and turn to the paths opened by science and technology and industrialization to develop a systems architecture responsive to the ever expanding population, increasing governmental control of urban construction, and introduction of new materials.

Architecture is presently moving but not advancing when compared to the achievements of science and technology. And because the population, legislation, economics, energy consumption, etc. have expanded all known proportions, so too must architecture abandon the isolated individual building as we see it today, and respond with new systematized urban complexes of a new porportion and scale.

Catalano suggests that the future of architecture rests in the hands of the students of this new approach who can combine the advances of industry and science with the designing of space. But, so far, architecture schools have not taken their share of the responsibility to develop this alliance. They should participate more in the research and development of new construction materials and processes. And teachers should encourage the study of total systems of urban design, rather than dabble with little single solutions to individual buildings that are responsive only to a limited user population.

His own designs exhibit an underlying and visible expression of pure form, often pure geometry in their structural systems. His buildings make bold statements. Several of his houses employ the simplest of structure, for example, the hyperbolic paraboloid. All of the inside spaces and functions are subservient to the powerful geometric shape. The Student Center at MIT, with its simple horizontality of large cantilevers, resists gravity and declares its structural integrity in an expression of unilateral boldness.

Both a city and a house have a pattern of behavior that comes from spatial and structural systems that overlap and interplay to create shelter as a main theme. The architect designs and builds systems and subsystems. Like a city with its layers of circulation paths from limited access highways to the neighborhood alleys, the form changes as the shapes and scales change, but all exist in a cohesive network exclusive of construction inconsistencies or random moods. Architecture is the three-dimensional event that constitutes growth and change according to a pattern of behavior and construction.

In his teachings and in his designs, Catalano expresses architecture as a system responsive to technological and behavioral order generated from a purity of geometry and structure. A building is an offering to this order of nature, following the norms of organization, responding to a value far above the constraints imposed by individual sites or individual clients or individual programs.

—Stephen P. Hamilton

CAUDILL, William W(ayne).
American. Born in Hobart, Oklahoma, 25 May 1914. Educated at Oklahoma State University, Stillwater, 1933–37, B.Arch. 1937; Massachusetts Institute of Technology, Cambridge, 1937–39, M.Arch. 1939. Served in the United States Navy during World War II. Married Edith Rosellel Woodman in 1940; children: Susan and William Jr.; married Aleen Plumer Harrison in 1974. Since 1946, Principal of Caudill Rowlett Scott, Houston, Texas: Chairman of the Board, CRS Inc., since 1950. Professor of Design, 1939–42, 1946–49, and Research Architect, Texas Engineering Experiment Station, 1946–49, Texas A and M University, College Station; Director of the School of Architecture, 1961–69, and William Ward Watkin Professor of Architecture, 1969–71, Rice University, Houston. Chairman of the National School Committee, 1956–59, and Member of the Research Committee, 1963–66, American Institute of Architects; Director, Association of College Schools of Architecture, 1965–66; Member of the Advisory Committee for New Educational Media, United States Department of Health, Education and Welfare, 1966–68; Member of the Advisory Panel on Architectural Services, United States General Services Administration, 1966–69; Director, Council of Educational Facility Planners, 1968–69; Member of the Advisory Panel for Building Research, United States Academy of Sciences, 1969–71; Architectural Consultant to the United States Department of State on Foreign Buildings, 1974–77. Member, United States Energy Research and Development Ad Hoc Advisory Committee, since 1977. Recipient: College of Engineering Hall of Fame

Eduardo Catalano: Governmental Center, Greensboro, North Carolina, 1970

Award, 1964, and University Hall of Fame Award, 1973, Oklahoma State University; Planner of the Year Award, Council of Educational Facilities Planners, 1970; Dean's Council Award, University of California at Los Angeles, 1976; Gold Medal, Tau Sigma Delta Fraternity, 1978. LL.D.: Eastern Michigan University, Ypsilanti, 1947. Fellow, American Institute of Architects, 1961. Founding Member, Academy of Texas, 1969. Address: CRS Inc., 1111 West Loop South, Houston, Texas 77027, U.S.A.

Works:

1969	CRS Office Building, Houston
1970	First Hutchins-Sealy National Bank, 2200 Market Street, Galveston, Texas
	Four College Science Center, Claremont, California
	Rehabilitation Building, Manhattan Psychiatric Center, Wards Island, New York
1973	Desert Samaritan Hospital, Phoenix, Arizona
	Fodrea Community School, Columbus, Indiana
1974	State and Mapleton Banking Center, 301 Washington, Columbus, Indiana
	Hyatt Regency Hotel, Houston
	Salanter-Akiba Riverdale Academy, 655 West 254th Street, Bronx, New York
	Houston National Bank
1975	Thomas E. Leavey Student Activity Center, University of California at Santa Clara
1975-	University of Petroleum and Minerals, Dhahran, Saudi Arabia
1976	County Office Building, 1555 Berger Drive, Santa Clara, California
1976-	Mass Seating and Natatorium, Gainesville, Florida
1977	Tulane University Hospital and Teaching Center, 1430 Tulane Avenue, New Orleans
	Rochester General Hospital, Rochester, New York
	Public School/Intermediate School 229, Bronx, New York
1978	Bahrain Monetary Building, Manama
	University for Girls, Riyadh, Saudi Arabia
1979	IBM Office Building, Riverway, Houston

Albert Thomas Convention Center, Houston
Federal Youth Center, Bastrop, Texas

Publications:

By CAUDILL: books—*Space for Teaching,* College Station, Texas 1942; *Your Schools: An Approach to Long Range Planning,* College Station, Texas 1950; *Toward Better School Design,* Chicago 1953; *In Education the Most Important Number Is One,* Houston 1964; *Memos from Russia,* Boston 1969; *Architecture by Team,* New York 1971; *A Bucket of Oil: The Humanistic Approach to Building Design for Energy Conservation,* with Frank Lawyer and Thomas A. Bullock, Boston 1975; *Problem Seeking: An Architectural Programming Primer,* with William M. Pena and John Focke, Boston 1977; *From Infancy to Infinity,* with Charles Schorre and Jeffrey Conroy, Houston 1977; *Architecture and You: How to Experience and Enjoy Buildings,* with Paul Kennon and William M. Pena, New York 1978; numerous articles and technical reports.

On CAUDILL: articles—"An Image for Technology" by Sharon Lee Ryder in *Progressive Architecture* (New York), May 1974; "Houston's Hyatt Regency: Coherent Expression of Multi-Use Space" in *Architectural Record* (New York), May 1974; "I'm an Architecture: Fodrea Elementary School" by Sharon Lee Ryder in *Progressive Architecture* (New York), May 1974; "How to Work with the Health Client" by James Falick in *Progressive Architecture* (New York), July 1974; "Rust City" by Jonathan King in *Architectural Design* (London), June 1975; "Productive Elegance for Industry" by Charles Hoyt in *Architectural Record* (New York), July 1975; "Bank Transparency: A Visual Come-on: The Houston National Bank" in *Interiors* (New York), August 1975; "Tilt to the River: S.A.R. Academy, New York" by Jack W. Smith in *Progressive Architecture* (New York), December 1975; "Joint Ventures and Associations" by C. A. Carlson and Wallie E. Scott Jr. in *AIA Journal* (Washington, D.C.), June 1976; "Evaluations" by Jonathan King in *AIA Journal* (Washington, D.C.), August 1976; "Money-changers in the Temple of Architecture" by Roger Yee in

Interiors (New York), November 1976; "Construction Management, in a Miami Test" in *Architectural Record* (New York), January 1977; "The Corporate Architect" by James Murphy in *Progressive Architecture* (New York), May 1977.

I am a professor/architect involved in theory and practice since 1947, committed to the team concept of practice. The practice is international. CRS Inc. has grown from two members in 1947 to over 1,000 employees. This figure includes affiliate companies. Probably I am best known for innovations in educational architecture and management procedures, although the firm of CRS has received literally hundreds of awards.

—William W. Caudill

William Caudill is the founder of Caudill-Rowlett-Scott of Houston, Texas. Now known as CRS Inc., the company has been in existence for more than thirty years: during that time it has grown enormously, has been a pioneer in the development of management techniques, and has been a leader in technological advance in architecture; but, perhaps most important, CRS has become a highly influential model for other American architectural firms in its concept of architecture by team.

Caudill, now Chairman of the Board, is a firm believer in the team—a team comprised not only of architects but of the client as well. His vision has proved highly successful. A team of architects, other specialists, and client(s), often on site, quickly devise design objectives, work together during the process of design refinement, execution and completion of a project, then, post-occupancy, come together to discuss success or failure. A simple questionnaire is given to the client; it includes such questions as: Are the materials withstanding wear? Has the building merged well with its environment? What do you consider to be the building's assets and its problems? In Caudill's own words:

> We believe that many people should be involved in the design process, particularly if they are the users of the building. . . . The key to this approach is communication. But communication must have a broad meaning. It is being direct and frank with people. And when you can successfully do that, you have a good chance to produce a direct and frank architecture. The quality of ruggedness found in this approach is also reflected in our buildings—no namby-pamby architecture. From the beginning of Caudill-Rowlett-Scott, we have not been able to separate our *process* from our *architecture.*

Such directness (and prompting of frank criticism) has produced considerable respect and prestige from clients, from potential clients, and from within the architectural profession.

Caudill also maintains that a designer sitting in his Houston office is not going to be able to assess the environmental requirements in, say, the Bronx or the Colorado Mountains with just a couple of hurried site visits. Far better to send a team to the spot. A good example of this attitude in practice is the CRS work on Saudi Arabia's University of Petroleum and Minerals. To accomplish this huge project, CRS sent their top people and a carefully chosen crew of builders and engineers to the site, established stringent quality control, worked closely with the local client, and are producing a showplace for Saudi Arabia. Caudill again:

> Our "formula" for a building is this: take a client, teach him to speak architecture and make him a part of your team. Add technologists as well as designers to the team. Condition the reflexes of each of the members to absorb and accept ideas. Then go directly to the site and mix them up in

William W. Caudill: CRS Office Building, Houston, 1969

a group. We feel that if, after programming is completed, we have not educated our clients and raised their aspirations for a better physical environment, then we have not done our professional job.

This is not to suggest, however, that CRS produces design-by-vote. All group action is led by a strong designer of outstanding abilities in leadership, quality control and creativity, and, indeed, many well-known designers, not least Caudill himself, have emerged from within the company. It would probably be fair to say that CRS strives for diversity through team effort, a diversity to match the requirements of the varying environments of different American states and different foreign countries—yet assures design excellence by always remembering that creativity is still the province of the individual. As usual, Caudill puts it better:

> There must be strong leadership, plus plenty of imagination, as well as competence and skill, to pull off one of these things. And even more important, there must be the freedom of choice for using analyzed elements which seem capable of giving architecture a strong art form. Again, it is people involvement, but with strong architectural leadership. . . .

> Architecture is more than a reflective art of civilization. It is a regenerative force—the force that is created through group dynamics. We believe that architecture must reflect the excitement of life found in our democratic society, which respects the individual. We believe in the individual over the team, and that architecture is for everybody, not just the privileged few.

—Colin Naylor

CETTO, Max.

Mexican. Born in Coblenz, Germany, 20 February 1903; emigrated to the United States, 1938, then to Mexico, 1939: naturalized, 1947. Educated at the Technical Universities of Darmstadt and Munich, 1921–23; Technical University of Berlin, under Hans Poelzig, 1923–26, Dip.Ing. 1926. Married Gertrude Catherine Kramis in 1940; children: Veronica, Ana Maria, and Bettina. Designer, City Planning and Building Office, Frankfurt, 1926–31; Supervisor of industrial construction in various parts of Germany, 1932–38; worked with Richard Neutra, in San Francisco, 1938; worked as a designer for various architects in Mexico City, 1939–45. Since 1945, in private practice, Mexico City. Professor, School of Architecture, Universidad Nacional Autonoma, Mexico City, 1965–79. Founder Member, CIAM (Congrès Internationaux d'Architecture Moderne), 1928. Address: Calle del Agua 130, Mexico 20, D.F., Mexico.

Works:

1926/
30 . Various works, including park pavilions, university dental clinic, teachers seminary, old people's asylum, electrical generating/transforming plants, etc., for the Frankfurt Building Office
1927 League of Nations Building, Geneva (competition project; with Wolfgang Bangert)
1939 Hotel, San José Purrua, Mexico (with Jorge Rubio)
1945 Wolfgang Paalen Studio, San Angel, Mexico City
1946 Señor House, Gen. Cano, Tacubaya, Mexico City
1947 Quintana Week-end House, Lago de Tequesquitengo, Morelos, Mexico
1948 Hill House, Guerrero 10, San Angel, Mexico City (with John McAndrew)
1949 Tamayo House, Leibnitz 248, Col. Anzures, Mexico City
    Max Cetto House, Agua 130, Pedregal, Mexico City
1950 Pedregal Show House, Fuentes 130, Mexico City (with Luis Barragan)
1951 Berdecio House, Fuentes 140, Mexico City (with Luis Barragan)

1952 Friedeberg House, Agua 330, Mexico City
1953 Boehm House, Agua 737, Mexico City
1954 Kirk House, Creston 232, Mexico City
1955 Deutsch Week-end House, Tepozotlan, Morelos, Mexico
    Reforma Office Building, Reforma 134, Mexico City
1956 Deutsch House, San Jeronimo, Mexico City
1957 Krupenski House, Pirules 106, Mexico City
1959 Vetter House, Picacho 239, Mexico City
1960 Ehni House, Fuente de Diana 45, Tecamachalco, Mexico
1961 Cold Rolled Company Workshop, Calz. del Moral 186, Ixtapalapa, Mexico
1962 Novick House, Avenida 3, 43, Las Aguilas, Mexico City
1963 Kirchhoff House, Juarez 18, Tlacopac., Mexico City
1964 Crevenna House, Av. San Jeronimo 136, Mexico City
1965 Ezquerro House, Cerro del Tesoro, Coyoacan, Mexico City
1966 Sevilla House, Santiago 258, San Jeronimo, Mexico City
    Moore House, Genung Road, Ithaca, New York
1967/
68 Morelos Tanning Company, Cuautla, Morelos, Mexico
1968/
71 Office Building, Obrero Mundial 629, Mexico City
1970/
79 German Club of Mexico, Aldama 153, Tepepan, Mexico
1974 Strötgen House, San Diego de los Padres 51, Club de Golf Hacienda, Mexico
1975 Cold Rolled Company Office Building, Calz. del Moral 186, Ixtapalapa, Mexico
1977 Frenk Week-end House, Jiutepec, Morelos, Mexico
1979 Brody House, Cerro del Agua 43, Mexico City

Publications:

By CETTO: books—*Moderne Architektur in Mexico,* Stuttgart 1960, as *Modern Architecture in Mexico,* New York 1961; *Knaurs Lexikon der Modernen*

Architektur, with others, Munich 1963; *Candela und seine Schalen,* translation into German of *Candela, The Shell Builder* by Colin Faber, Munich 1965; articles—"External Influences and the Importance of Tradition" in *America Latina en su Arquitectura,* Unesco, Mexico City 1975; "Architecture Mexicaine" in *Techniques et Architecture* (Paris), June/-July 1978.

On CETTO: books—*18 Homes of Mexican Architects* by E. Yanex, Mexico City 1951; *Mexico's Modern Architecture* by I. E. Myers, Mexico City 1952; *Encyclopédie de L'Architecture Nouvelle* by Alberto Sartoris, Milan 1954; *Latin American Architecture since 1945* by Henry-Russell Hitchcock, New York 1955.

A generation ago the term Ecology was only used by biologists and was widely unknown to the general public, including architects. For me it always meant, and goes on meaning, the most important auxiliary science in planning the human "habitat." That does not mean that other, humanistic or technological, aspects should be neglected. The following is a quotation from an article that I wrote 28 years ago (in *Arts and Architecture,* Los Angeles, 1951) that is still valid today, despite the fact that in the meantime building procedures have been more and more mechanized in Mexico:

Because of the lack of qualified personnel with sufficient intermediate technical knowledge, houses cannot be built by simply providing a complete set of drawings and specifications. . . . If the architect cares to see the building finished according to his concepts, he has to supervise the work every day, playing the part of a general contractor himself. Knowing that even the most careful preparation on the drawing board would not free him from spending at least half his time to put them through on the job, he very often prefers to rely on sketches and oral directions.

This method is not as bad as one would imagine. What is lost in efficient preparation is gained in directness of approach, new suggestions coming out of the work in progress, and a flexibility that allows one to make improvements on a moment's notice.

Under such circumstances it seems considerably wiser to renounce certain ideals of mechanical perfection, which we adored in the first years of functional architecture, and accept the blessings of a rather rustic, handmade and more human touch, which is probably the most adequate expression of the natural and spiritual resources of this country.

Obviously the romantic working habits of an archi-

tect, as described above, will not last any longer than the underdevelopment of any given population of which he is a part.

—Max Cetto

In 1939, when Max Cetto came to Mexico, fundamental changes were occurring in the politics of the country, changes that were having repercussions in the field of architecture. Private capital was regaining the power it had lost during the period of revolution and was once again becoming a powerful patron. During the 1930's Mexican architecture had been characterized by an open struggle between, on the one hand, a young generation fighting to establish functionalism in a purely technical sense as the means of resolving social need and, on the other, the traditionalists, with their concept of beauty and culture, defending the styles and fashions of the past. After 1940 the political climate favored functionalism, a potentially lucrative international idiom that would achieve maximum gain at minimum cost. This was the sad fact that Cetto, having fled from European fascism, and hoping to live in a socialist country, had to accept on his arrival in Mexico.

His career had begun—after his studies under the great master, Hans Poelzig—in the Frankfurt City Planning and Building Office. There, he was responsible for several impressive municipal works, but it was his competition entry for the League of Nations Building in Geneva that brought him to public notice and earned him a place in CIAM at the early age

Max Cetto: Max Cetto House, Pedregal, Mexico City, 1949

of 24. The fascist escalation in Germany halted what promised to be a brilliant career, and finally, in 1938, Cetto abandoned Germany and went to the United States, where he worked for a year with Richard Neutra. A year later he established himself in Mexico.

Cetto's first important Mexican project, built in collaboration with Jorge Rubio, was the Hotel at San José Purrua. With this building Cetto established the basis of an integral functionalism of a kind different from that which had formerly been practised in the country. As the site—around an area of natural springs—was rugged and uneven, Cetto actually sketched his plan on the earth with chalk. He wanted to make the best use of the topographical variations and to incorporate views of the countryside as well as its rocks and trees: he studied the various surrounding elements in order to utilize them to best advantage or, alternatively, to avoid them. His method showed that his was an architecture that arose out of nature and was inextricably bound up with it. Three years later, after visiting the hotel, Walter Gropius wrote to him: "The work at San José appeals to me very much indeed. One needs imagination to implant a building among the rocks. The concept of different levels is carried out in a masterly fashion. The details may be a little rough, but the line of the whole, its 'elan,' stands out above everything."

By 1949 Cetto had become famous in Mexico, and was known affectionately as "Le Hombre del Pedregal." He had built and now lived in the first house in Pedregal, an area of Mexico City devastated during two millenia by volcanic eruption and again threatened by a large and new split in the earth. The rough ground, formed of volcanic lava, with its strange vegetation and colouring, was a challenge to the imagination of the architect, and the complete and successful way in which he overcame the problems, humanizing a hitherto purely technical functionalism in order to solve the psychological problems involved, became a great example to contemporary architects. It might even be claimed, without exaggeration, that without this work Mexican residential architecture would have taken a different road. The use of natural materials—lava stone, mosaic, wood—created the feeling of a construction sown among the natural folds of the earth, integrating the internal and external vistas. The house was a revelation, the basis of a new kind of construction.

The other dwellings that Cetto built in the same volcanic zone of El Pedregal—either alone or in collaboration—are equally successful and beautiful variations of this architectural theme. He applied the same principles when building the Morelos Tanning Factory in the torrid Valle de Cuautla, where he dispensed with the hitherto indispensable international-style window and inserted open tile shutters to create currents of air. He employed a similar solution for the Quintana Week-end House in the tropical region of Tequesquitengo, by taking advantage of the cool freshness provided by a nearby lake.

Max Cetto has also been interested in the history of architecture, in criticism, and in practical teaching. Part of his role as craftsman has been to devise a method of teaching the result of which can be of service to rural and outlying communities. He has shown his students the uselessness of working in an office in a kind of conceptual vacuum. Creation, according to Cetto, is the product of contact, study, and the appraisal of the reality of a situation in all its aspects. Only an exact but loving comprehension of reality can transform it in the service a man—a truth that Cetto has never stopped preaching: to students, whom he has taken to deprived villages in order to study economic, social and building problems at first hand; to architects, the "visionaries of the future," to whom he has spoken out, cautioning them against faith in technology as a solution to social problems; and, as it were, to architecture itself, in the example of his own work. The problem that preoccupies him is that of alienation and conflict—between nature and man, the individual and society, pure materialism and pure aesthetics. The struggle

and commitment of his life has been to bring about the harmony of man with the world in which he lives.

—Ida Rodriguez

CHADIRJI, Rifat.

Iraqi. Born in Baghdad, in December 1926. Studied at the Hammersmith School of Arts and Crafts, London, under Arthur Korn, 1946–52, Dip.Arch. 1952. Married Balkis Sharara in 1954. Since 1952, Founder, Senior Partner, and Director, Iraq Consult, Baghdad. Building Department Section Head, Waqaf Organization, Baghdad, 1954–57; Director-General of Housing, Ministry of Planning, Baghdad, 1958–65; Head of the Planning Committee, Ministry of Housing, Baghdad, 1959–63; returned to full-time private practice with Iraq Consult, 1965. Member of the Mayor's Council, Baghdad, 1958–61; Member of the Iraqi Government Tourist Board, 1970–75. Exhibitions: Beirut, 1966; Madrid, 1966; Sudan, 1967; Ghana, 1967; Tunisia, 1967; Kuwait, 1967; Ankara, 1968; Baghdad, 1972; Damascus, 1973; Kuwait, 1975; Tunisia, 1975; *Modern Arab Architecture,* London, 1978. Recipient: First Prize, Mortgage Bank Building Competition, Baghdad, 1956; First Prize, Al-Pasha Al-Sajheer Building Competition, Baghdad, 1961; First Prize, Tobacco Monopoly Administration and Stores Building, Baghdad, 1965; Honors Prize, Ministry of Municipalities Competition, Baghdad, 1965; Bronze Medal, International Interior Architecture and Design Competition, Madrid, 1966; First Prize, Commercial Bank of Iraq Competition, 1967; Co-First Prize, Kuwait Parliament Complex Competition, 1971; First Prize, Council of Ministers Building, Baghdad, 1975; First Prize, National Theatre Competition, Abu Dhabi, 1977. Address: Iraq Consult, Hasib Saleh Building, Nidhal Street, Post Office Box 2291, Alwiyah, Baghdad, Iraq.

Works:

1957 Munir Abbass Building, Iraq
1959 Unknown Soldier Monument, Baghdad
1960 National Insurance Company Building, Baghdad
1961 Tobacco Monopoly Offices, Baghdad
1962 Al Azzawi House, Baghdad
1964 Rifidain Bank, Sinak, Baghdad
       Veterinary hospital, Baghdad
1965 Waqaf Office Building, North Gate, Baghdad
       Tobacco Monopoly Headquarters Building, Baghdad
       M. Othman Villa, Baghdad
       Yasoob Rafiq Villa, Baghdad
1966 Tobacco Monopoly Offices II, Baghdad
       Iraqi Federation of Industries Building, Baghdad
       National Insurance Offices, Mosul, Iraq
       Commercial Bank, Mansoor, Iraq
1967 Al Hamad Villa, Kuwait
       Veterinary college, Baghdad
1968 Iraqi Scientific Academy, Baghdad
       Hawalli Residential Complex, Kuwait (with Pan Arab Consultants)
1969 Monument for the workers' housing scheme, Baghdad
       Kufa Cement Factory, Iraq (with N. Fetto and P. Nacy)
       Central Communication Building, Baghdad (with Henry Svoboda)
       Waqaf Building, Alwiyah, Iraq
       Orphanage, Dohuk, Iraq
       Orphange, Arbil, Iraq
       Medical Auxiliary Training Institute, Baghdad
       Andulus Cinema, Manama, Bahrain

       Housing complex, Salimiya, Kuwait
1970 Office building, Bahrain
       Sheikh Khalifa Building, Bahrain
1971 Arbil Citadel Conservation Study, Iraq (with Colin Buchanan Partners)
       Gali Ali Beg Sector Development Study, Iraq
1972 Qatar Cinema Complex, Doha Qatar
       Kurdish Scientific Academy Building, Baghdad
       H. H. Hmood Villa, Baghdad
1973 Gate of Arbil Fortress Conservation, Iraq
       General Federation of Trade Unions Assembly Hall, Baghdad
1975 Reinsurance Company Building, Baghdad
1976 Cabinet of Ministers Building, United Arab Emirates
1977 National Theatre, Abu Dhabi, United Arab Emirates
       Al Ain Public Library, United Arab Emirates

Publications:

On CHADIRJI: articles—"Modern Arab Architecture" by W. Mason in *Building Design* (London), 21 April 1978; *Arts Review* (London), 12 May 1978; *Al-Watan Al-Arabi* (London), 20–26 May 1978; *Al Dastor* (London), 22–28 May 1978; "Modern Arab Architecture" by Konstantin Bazarov in *Art and Artists* (London), June 1978.

Starting in 1952, I have been concerned to find an appropriate path for a modern Arab architecture. The point of departure in this search was intensive discussion between architects, painters, sculptors and thinkers in Baghdad in the 1950's. The question was whether contemporary art and architecture should continue to be a by-product of European ideas or whether it could be influenced by local environment, tradition and materials.

I set out to learn from traditional architecture and to achieve a synthesis between traditional forms and the inevitable advent of modern technology. My aim was to create an architecture which at once acknowledges the place in which it is built, yet which sacrifices nothing to modern technical capability. At the same time I was concerned to understand analytically the reasoning behind traditional devices of environmental control such as courtyards, screen walls, natural ventilation and reflected light.

Until 1965 my work on understanding traditional elements of Iraqi architecture led to an idiosyncratic regional modern architecture. The roots of inspiration were clearly apparent in the buildings, and yet they continued to subscribe to the European functionalist concept of form being determined by structural considerations.

Only later, in the early 1970's, again through close study of traditional buildings, did I reach the view that this connection between form and structure is not inevitable. This realization has led to increased freedom of composition and an increase in the plastic possibilities of building form.

Within the context of Arab architecture generally, I can say that my earlier search for understanding of traditional elements has had some influence on the younger generation of architects who have seen the buildings themselves or published projects.

My present concern is to develop further the abstraction of national and regional traditional forms —their aesthetic values—independent of the structural concept of the building. This endeavour is essential, I believe, if we are to escape the possibility that by the end of the century the whole world will be covered by a uniformly mediocre travesty of some European ideas which are now half a century old.

—Rifat Chadirji

Cities in various parts of the world used to be radically different in character, not merely because they arose out of distinctive artistic traditions but also because they were constructed out of quite different local materials. But the growing internationalism in the arts and the triumph of functionalistic modernism in architecture has meant that many once beautiful cities have had their own unique cultural identity swamped in a sea of indifferent international-style architecture. The Iraqi architect Rifat Chadirji, since returning to his native Baghdad after studying in England, has faced this crucial dilemma of our time by gradually rediscovering the cultural and social traditions of his own country—but always in the context of the need to keep abreast of the realities of modern technology and rapid technological change. His work shows a development from the early European influence of Le Corbusier and Mies van der Rohe to his gradual re-discovery of the qualities of Iraqi traditional architecture and so to an individual style that aims to reconcile the need to use modern building technology with the cultural traditions of Iraq.

In the earliest phase of his work from 1952–1962, when he was mainly designing private houses, he was still heavily under European influence, but he was already concerned with the central issue of whether contemporary art in Iraq should continue to be a by-product of European art and how far it should respond to local environment and tradition. He was exploring those traditional approaches to environmental control, insulation and ventilation, and cool courtyards that have been highly developed in the extreme climates of the Middle East. So that, for instance, in his Wahab residence of 1953 he exploited the possibilities of filtered light through screens and environmental control through the use of air corridors. He was also experimenting with Islamic decorative patterns and with traditional Arab architectural features such as doors, windows, balconies and screens, to determine whether they could become elements of composition in a new modern architecture.

Chadirji's understanding of Arab tradition was greatly enhanced when from 1954–57 he was head of the Building Department of Waqaf, the government body responsible for the maintenance of mosques, khans and old houses throughout Iraq. During the 1960's he used this experience of traditional architecture to develop his own style in public buildings such as the National Insurance Company offices at Mosul, with its almost baroque use of traditional forms to make the building a sculptural entity. At this time he was still holding to the basic functionalist doctrine of expressing the building's structure in its form. But by the 1970's he had realized, through studying the Yemeni capital city of San'aa, Iraqi village architecture, and the ancient buildings of Baghdad itself, that this doctrine of form expressing the underlying structure did not necessarily apply in traditional Arab architecture, where the sculptural treatment of volumes and surfaces is a more important factor in determining form. He has thus, since 1975, been freeing himself from functionalist dogma, a freedom that brings with it the need for a rich vocabulary of symbolic forms with which to develop a "post-modern" architecture.

Chadirji's work has been a major influence on other young Arab architects from Iraq and the Gulf States, because it does explore alternatives to the standardized international-style architecture that has proliferated in the Middle East, moving towards renewed diversity and variety. And in its acknowledgement of the importance of searching beyond the bald and often brutal statements of functionalism, his work is an interesting contribution to the debate about the path recent contemporary architecture has been taking.

—Konstantin Bazarov

Rifat Chadirji: Iraqi Federation of Industries Building, Baghdad, 1966

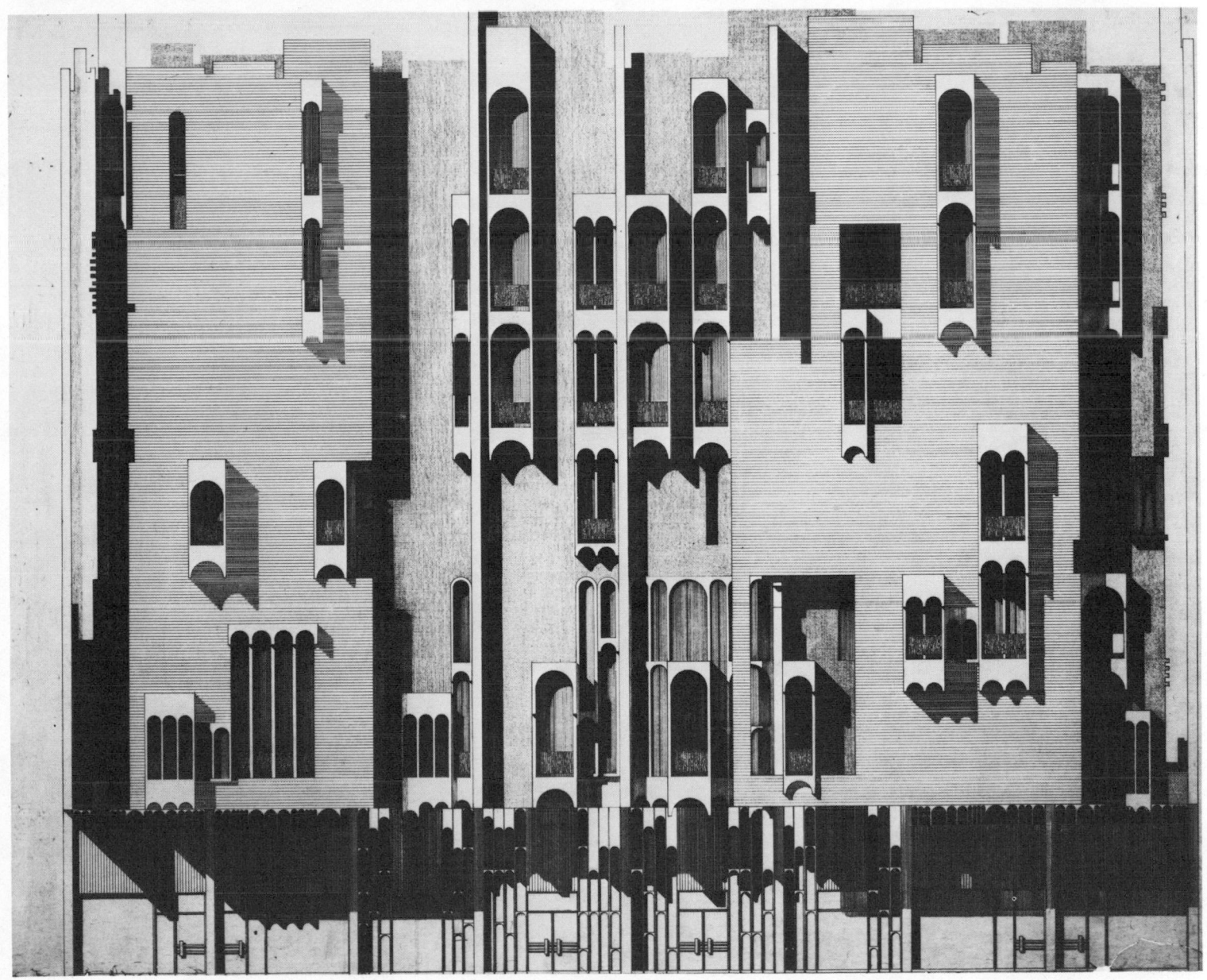

CHAMBERLIN POWELL AND BON.

Partnership; established, London, 1952, by Peter Chamberlin (born 1919; died 1978), Geoffrey Powell (born 1920), and Christoph Bon (born 1921); additional partner, Frank Woods. Associate company: Chamberlin, Powell and Bon (Barbican), London, established 1960; additional partner, Charles Greenberg. Recipient: Bronze Medal, Royal Institute of British Architects, 1956, 1957; Ministry of Housing and Local Government Medal, 1965; Civic Trust Commendation, 1973; RIBA Architecture Award, 1973, 1974. Address: 1 Lamont Road Passage, Kings Road, London SW10 OHW, England.

Works:

1955	Cooper Taber Factory, Witham, Essex
1956	Bousefield Primary School, South Kensington, London
1957	Rossdale House, 30a Hendon Avenue, London N.3
	Golden Lane Estate, Finsbury, London
1960	Two Saints Primary School, London
1962	Goswell Road Extension, London
1963	Shipley Salt Grammar School, Shipley, Yorkshire
	Henry Price Buildings, University of Leeds
1965	Vanbrugh Park Housing, Greenwich, London
	New Hall Residential College, Cambridge
1966	Physical Education Centre, University of Birmingham
	Physical Education Centre, stage II, University of Leeds
	New Hall College, phase II, Cambridge
1966/	
80	The Barbican, City of London
1967	Squash Courts, New Hall College, Phase IIa, Cambridge
	Mathematics Building and Senior Common Room, University of Leeds
	Charles Morris Hall of Residence, University of Leeds
	Cheltenham Grammar School, Gloucestershire
1968	Television Centre, University of Leeds
1969	Biology Multipurpose Building, University of Leeds
	Biophysics Building, University of Leeds
	Physics Building, University of Leeds
	St. George's Fields Garden, University of Leeds
	Students Union Extension, University of Leeds
1970	Lecture Theatre Block, University of Leeds
	J. Sainsbury Shop, Folkestone, Kent
	Moravian Corner, Chelsea, London
1971	Welfare Insurance Company Building, The Leas, Folkestone, Kent
	Computer Laboratory Extension, University of Leeds
	Medical Multipurpose Building, University of Leeds
1972	Library Building, University of Leeds
	Chancellor's Court, University of Leeds
	Flats and maisonettes, 9–15 The Leas, Folkestone, Kent
1973	Offices, 69 Sandgate Road, Folkestone, Kent
1974	General Electric Technical Marketing Centre, Warrington, Lancashire
	Physics Education Centre and School of Physiotherapy, University of Leeds
	Arts Block, University of Leeds
	Flats and maisonettes, 5–6 The Leas, Folkestone, Kent
	Houses and maisonettes, 35–37 Earls Avenue, Folkestone, Kent
1975	Undergraduate Library, University of Leeds
	Block 19, University of Leeds

Also designed modular furniture for the University of Leeds complex, 1964–75.

Publications:

On CHAMBERLIN POWELL AND BON: articles —"Barbican: Metropolitan Neighbourhood" in *Bauen und Wohnen* (Zurich), April 1974; "Barbican: London's Domestic Fortress" by Will Howie in *New Civil Engineer* (London), August 1975; "New Towns: English Encampments" by Barbara Goldstein in *Progressive Architecture* (New York), July 1977; "The Right Note: Guildhall School of Music and Drama" by Joseph Boys in *Building Design* (London), November 1977.

*

The practice started in 1952, and from the first one of our principal interests has been the creation of places—not just buildings. With a romantic enthusiasm for the cities of Italy and the colleges of Oxford and Cambridge, we have been concerned to bring together buildings and related elements to make places with strong identities of their own. If the greater part of our work has been on large projects, this has been partly accidental; our approach is to avoid specialisation as we welcome and enjoy fresh opportunities of any size and type. In a difficult period culturally and economically we believe that architecture is still far more than a technology and that some buildings have a magic that others conspicuously lack.

—Chamberlin Powell and Bon

*

Urban architecture is a continuous source of disenchantment between the end user, urban man, and the creator of his environment, the architect. In winning the Barbican Development Plan competition in the early 1950's, the partners of a practice that on the strength of their success became known as Chamberlin Powell and Bon, made sure of their own positive contribution to the dialogue.

Peter Chamberlin was quoted as saying of their work "that architects have to somehow pin down the aspects of living" and that "the fundamental element an architect deals with is space."

But it is in the very development of wholesale areas of living, sleeping and working space by deliberate design, rather than by the softer mellowing of time and change on established city settlements, that so many architects fail to appreciate the importance people place on their need to identify with their environment. High-rise urban dwellings seen from a distance at sunset may well appear aesthetically satisfying and maximize the use of space, but they fail dramatically for the old age pensioner on the sixth floor attempting to use a vandalized lift. Successful identification in urban housing must include the territory outside the immediate unit of shelter.

The Barbican is now a reality, and the innovation and excitement of the original proposal can be seen in perspective with other and later developments on a similar scale. The development will continue to be a classic example of how a particular generation dealt with the problem of urban renewal. The strength and sense of identity of the project will continue to be in its honest approach to the almost insoluble problem of creating wholesale areas of urban environment that provide areas of living space for people, rather than mere units of shelter.

—T. Q. Battle

CHAREAU, Pierre.

French. Born in Bordeaux, 3 August 1883. Studied painting, music and architecture at the Ecole des Beaux-Arts, Paris, 1900–08. Served in the French Army, 1914–18. Married. Worked as an apprentice at Waring and Gillow Furnishings, Paris, 1908–13; in private practice as an architect and designer, Paris, 1918–40; worked with Bernard Bijovoet, 1925–35; emigrated to the United States and settled in East Hampton, Long Island, New York, 1940; practiced in New York, 1940 until his death, 1950. Founder Member, with Mallet-Stevens, Barbe, Herbst, Jourdain and Perriand, Union des Artistes Modernes, Paris, 1929. Exhibitions: *Salon d'Automne,* Paris, 1919; *Salon des Arts Décoratifs,* Paris, 1925. *Died* (in New York) *in 1950.*

Works:

1918/	
19	Dalsace Apartment interiors, rue Saint-Germain, Paris
1925	Embassy Office interiors, *Salon des Arts Décoratifs,* Paris
1927	Golf Club, Beauvallon, France (with Bernard Bijovoet)
1928	Hotel interiors, Tours, France
1928/	
31	Dalsace House (Maison de Verre), rue St. Guillaume, Paris (with Bijovoet and Dalbet)
1931/	
32	Compagnie du Téléphone Offices, Paris
1937	Djemel Anik Country House, near Paris
	Office interiors, Ministry of Foreign Affairs, Paris
	Union des Artistes Modernes Pavilion, *International Exposition,* Paris (with others)
1939	Soldat Colonial Foyer, Grand Palais, Paris
1940/	
50	Exhibition layouts for the French Cultural Center, New York
	Library interiors, French Cultural Center, New York
	Robert Motherwell House, near New York
	"La Colline" (Monteux-Laughlin House) alterations, New York
	Chareau House, East Hampton, Long Island, New York

Publications:

By CHAREAU: book—*Meubles,* Paris 1929; article —"La Création Artistique et l'Imitation Commerciale" in *L'Architecture d'Aujourd'hui* (Paris), September 1935.

On CHAREAU: books—*Art d'Aujourd'hui,* Paris 1928; *Pierre Chareau* by René Herbst, Paris 1954; *Global Architecture 46: Maison Dalsace* by Yukio Futagawa and Fernando Montes, Tokyo 1977; articles—"Maison de Verre" in *Werk* (Zurich), February 1965; "Maison de Verre" by Kenneth Frampton in *Arena* (London), April 1966; "La Casa di Verro di Pierre Chareau" by Richard Rogers in *Domus* (Milan), October 1966; "Modern Antiques: 20th Century Landmarks" by Cervin Robinson in *Architectural Forum* (New York), June 1967; "Maison de Verre" by Kenneth Frampton in *Perspecta* (New Haven, Connecticut), vol. 12, 1969; "The 1929 Paris House of Glass" in *House and Garden* (London), October 1973; "Le Corbusier, Mallet-Stevens, Chareau and Some Others" by Michel Lugnier in *Architecture Francaise* (Paris), October 1975.

*

"The creative man is dangerous; the craftsman is annoying and rigid." This comment, written by Pierre Chareau in 1935, helps to define his own personality and reveals the cause of the particular treatment he receives in French architectural criticism.

In effect, Chareau built only one house, the Maison de Verre (the Glass House) for Dr. Dalsace, in collaboration with the Dutch architect Bijovoet and the artisan Dalbet. He came relatively late to architecture, having passed through a hard apprenticeship, and he had not previously had many opportunities to express himself. With the Maison de Verre he was revealed as a great architect, but, at the same time, he became an embarrassment to the architectural milieu of the 1930's because of his ideas and his consummate mastery of his craft.

Chamberlin Powell and Bon: Chancellor's Court, University of Leeds, 1972 .

Like many others of his generation, Chareau had a difficult start in life. His career was interrupted in 1914 by the war; later, the economic crisis of 1929 prevented him forever from finding his own place as an architect. From then on his field of activity was almost entirely restricted to interior decoration and furniture design. The label "decorator" attached itself and remained with him. In 1940 he emigrated to the United States, where he worked with the French Embassy, concerned more with cultural programs than with architecture. He arranged exhibitions and interiors and—unusually—built two small houses.

Chareau passed for an eccentric, but in fact his reserved and timid character hid an honest man, intransigent and totally incapable of coming to terms with error. His own curiosity was the basis of his education and of his knowledge of materials. He mastered them as if by magic. With a good team of workmen he was capable of turning iron into gold: indeed, this was the result he achieved with the Maison de Verre. For Chareau all materials were worthy of attention, as if each were rare and precious. Each detail of his construction became an object in itself which he linked with the environment, creating a space proper to itself.

As he worked primarily in the late 1920's and 1930's, Chareau remains linked with Art Deco, yet his interiors and furniture do not reveal the formalist or decadent approach characteristic of this period. We may eventually discover that the origin of his method of working and his conception of objects is to be found in the masters of Art Nouveau; this would also explain his almost instinctive ease with architecture. For Chareau, the arrangement of an interior or an exhibition, the creation of a piece of furniture or of architectonic space, comes from the same approach. All of his works are the result of a mastery, invention and precision that very often produce poetry.

A man of his time, Chareau admitted no compromises. Even among the group of artists with whom he was linked and worked, the Union des Artistes Modernes, Chareau remained fundamentally isolated, respected by his contemporaries but as often feared. The impression made by his Maison de Verre remained an isolated event in the French cultural debate of the 1930's: it was a period in which architects confused style with architecture. Apart from his most intimate friends—Jourdain, Paul Nelson, Herbst—the only man to have realized the value of his contribution to modern architecture was Le Corbusier, who is said to have often visited the site in the rue Guillaume.

Even the most recent criticism portrays Pierre Chareau as an "enigmatic" personality. Apart from the rediscovery of his now famous house, a rediscovery linked with a revival of interest in the years 1920–30, he has still not been given his rightful place in the history of architecture. This neglect may have something to do with the lack of a *History of Modern French Architecture,* and the "Chareau case" can, in effect, be studied only as a example of the constraints upon French architectural culture in those years.

—Luciana Miotto-Muret

Pierre Chareau: Maison de Verre, Paris, 1931

CHARNEY, Melvin.

Canadian. Born in Montreal, Quebec, 28 August 1935. Educated at the McGill University School of Architecture, Montreal, 1952–58 (C.P.I. Design Scholarship; A. F. Dunlop Travelling Scholarship), B.Arch. 1958; Yale University School of Architecture, New Haven, Connecticut, under Louis I. Kahn, 1958–59 (W. S. McCay Fellowship), M.Arch. 1959. Married Ann Korsower in 1960; daughter: Dara. Worked for John M. Johansen, New York, 1959–61, Guillaume Gillet, Paris, 1961–62, and Victor Prus, Montreal, 1962–63. Since 1964, Principal of Melvin Charney, Architect, Montreal. Assistant, then Associate Professor, 1964–72, Director of the Graduate Program, 1966–70, and since 1972 Professor of Architecture, University of Montreal School of Architecture. Visiting Critic in Design, Graduate Program, University of Toronto Department of Architecture, 1968–70. Member, Architects Committee, American Academy of Arts and Sciences, 1968–69; Director, Canadian Government Task Force on the Production and Adequacy of Low-Income Housing, 1970–71. Exhibitions: *Montréal . . . plus ou moins,* Museum of Fine Arts, Montreal, 1972; *Canada Trajectoires—'73,* Musée d'Art Moderne de la ville de Paris, 1973; *Triennale,* Milan, 1973; *Quebec '75,* National Museums of Canada, 1975; Graduate School of Design, Harvard University, Cambridge, Massachusetts (one-man show), 1977; Art Gallery of Ontario, Toronto (one-man show), 1978; Musée d'art contemporaine, Montreal (one-man show), 1979. Member, Royal Architectural Institute of Canada, 1963–74; Member of the Ordre des architectes du Québec, 1974. Address (office): 3620 Marlowe Avenue, Montreal, Quebec H4A 3L7, Canada.

Works:

1964 Ecole Notre-Dame des Laurentides, Lac Beauport, Quebec
1967 Canadian Pavilion, *Expo '70,* Osaka, Japan (project; with J. Baracs and H. Parnass)
1969 Canadian Air Force Museum, Trenton, Ontario (project)
1972 Conception and design of the exhibition *Montréal . . . plus ou moins,* Montreal
1976 "Corridart" (five-mile long Museum-in-the-Street), *21st Olympiade,* Montreal
   "Les Maisons de la rue Sherbrooke," Montreal (exhibition project)
1978 "Streetwork," Art Gallery of Ontario, Toronto (exhibition project)

Publications:

By CHARNEY: books—*Pour une définition de l'architecture au Québec,* Montreal 1971; *The Adequacy and Production of Low Income Housing in Canada,* Ottawa 1972; articles—"A Journal of Istanbul: Notes on Islamic Architecture" in *Journal of the Royal Architectural Institute of Canada* (Toronto), June 1962; "Troglai: Rock Cut Architecture" in *Landscape* (Santa Fe, New Mexico), no. 3, 1963, reprinted in *La Vie des Arts* (Montreal), no. 34, 1964, and (in part) in *Caves of God* by Spiro Kostof, Cambridge, Massachusetts 1972; "The Trulli of Southern Italy" in *Landscape* (Santa Fe, New Mexico), no. 1, 1965, reprinted in *La Vie des Arts* (Montreal), no. 38, 1965; "Environmental Chemistry: Design Application of Plastics Technology" in *Journal of the Royal Architectural Institute of Canada* (Toronto), May 1966; "Environmental Conjecture: In the Jungle of the Grand Prediction" in *Landscape* (Santa Fe, New Mexico), no. 3, 1967, reprinted in *Planning for Diversity and Choice,* edited by Stanford Anderson, Cambridge, Massachusetts 1969; "An Environment for Education" in *Canadian Architect* (Toronto), March 1967; "Grain Elevators Revisited" in *Architectural Design* (London), July 1967; "Naissance d'une Architecture" in *Cimaise* (Paris), July 1967; "Beyond Flexibility: A Study of Educational Environments" in *Architecture Canada* (Toronto), March 1968; "Concrete: A Material, a System, an Environment" in *Architecture Canada* (Toronto), June 1968; "A Self-Erecting Exhibit System" in *Architecture Canada* (Toronto), March 1969; "Experimental Strategies: Notes for Environmental Design" in *Perspecta 12* (New Haven, Connecticut), March 1969, reprinted in *Deutsche Bauzeitung* (Stuttgart), August 1969, and in *Formalism, Realism, Contextualism,* edited by Hajime Yatsuka, Tokyo 1979; "Memo Series: On the Liberation of Architecture" in *Artforum* (New York), May 1971; "Learning from the Wire Services" in *Architectural Design* (London), April 1974; "Understanding Montreal" in *Exploring Montreal,* edited by Pierre Beaupré and Annabel Slaight, Toronto 1974; "Dead-End Choices: Housing in Canada" in *Architectural Design* (London), April 1975; "Other Monuments: Four Works 1970–76" in *Vanguard* (Vancouver Art Gallery), March 1977; "Art as Urban Activism" in *Architectural Design* (London), July/August 1977; "Modern Movements in French Canadian Architecture" in *Process: Architecture* (Tokyo/Pittsburgh), March 1978; "Monuments Now: On Contemporary Architecture and the Avant-Garde" in *Avant-Garde:*

A History of Innovation and Invention in Architecture, Eindhoven, Netherlands 1978.

On CHARNEY: book—*Megastructures: Urban Futures of the Recent Past* by Reyner Banham, New York 1976; articles—"Progretto canadese per Osaka '70" in *L'Architettura* (Rome), December 1967; "The Real Housing Report" by Sara Berger in *Canadian Dimension* (Toronto) 1972; "Corridart: Instant Archeology in Montreal" by Dale McConathy in *Artscanada* (Toronto), July/August 1976; "Les Maisons de la rue Sherbrooke" in *Process: Architecture* (Tokyo/Pittsburgh), March 1978; "Melvin Charney" by Chantal Pontbriand in *Parachute* (Montreal), December 1978.

*

The kind of architecture I do is involved in two areas of activity outside the sphere of traditional office practice. The first is the creation of autonomous (i.e., client-free) projects which delve into experimentation with built form, with social symbolism in architecture, and with processes of building. This work has evolved from projects based on the use of off-the-shelf hardware, to the reproduction of images transmitted by the wire services, to the insertion of full-scale constructions as commentaries on existing urban contexts. Much of this work is published and exhibited. The second and complementary aspect of this work is the research, teaching and writing on critical themes in contemporary architecture, particularly on the relationship between built form and social processes.

—Melvin Charney

*

The general territory of contemporary Canadian architecture may be seen to be limited by two extreme forms of professional practice. On the one extreme, one finds a mode of commercial practice that raises programmatic expediency to a very high order; the practitioners now find themselves in demand from a commercial clientele not only in Canada but also around the world. On the other extreme, one finds a poetic—sometimes even mystical—mode of practice whose adherents are elevated to the rank of acclaimed national gurus by the media of this country. Needless to say, most architectural activity in Canada proceeds within the vast territory that lies between these two extremes, but the majority of practitioners who occupy that middle ground continue to find themselves less successful than their more commercially oriented fellow-practitioners and less well recognized than the celebrated poets of the media. What is perhaps less evident to the world at large is that the sad tendency of Canadian architecture to polarize in this fashion has prevented much architecture of world rank from being created in Canada in recent years.

   No one has challenged the resultant poverty of architectural praxis in this country with more acumen than has the Montreal architect, artist and theorist, Melvin Charney. In 1970 Charney challenged the assumptions of the architectural establishment in his submission to the competition for an Air Force Memorial for Trenton, Ontario. Refusing to meet the programme requirement for a "Memorial Hall of History," Charney proposed instead to organize a decentralized cross-Canada network of existing buildings and objects, many of which have played a crucial role in the training of personnel and in the development of machinery for flight. Since 1970, Charney has moved further and further away from any address to the norms of conventional architectural practice, turning instead to a new role in which his chief forums for intervention have been the art gallery and the street. In 1973, for example, he organized the exhibition *Montréal . . . plus ou moins* at the Montreal Museum of Fine Arts, incorporating within the walls of the museum for the first time a vast array of heterogeneous—often almost dada—fragments of "everyday life" in Montreal. In 1978 Charney showed "Six Other Monuments" at the Art Gallery of Ontario. The two most significant of these

Melvin Charney: "Les Maisons de la rue Sherbrooke," Montreal, 1976

were "Le Trésor de Trois Rivières" and "Street-work." The first is a modest, but highly charged house facade Charney had admired; which had been subsequently demolished; and which Charney reconstituted in an extensive series of modes—photographs, drawings and models. The second, created especially for the Toronto show, consisted of a "wall" created by Charney, which in an arrested process of erection/dismantling figuratively penetrated the gallery from outside to inside.

By far the most important of Charney's recent interventions occurred in the street. This was Corridart, the collective work he organized along five miles of Sherbrooke Street in Montreal during the 1976 Olympics. Corridart constituted a striking transformation of this major street into an instant history of itself, and into a series of appropriations of its contemporary reality. Large metal scaffoldings displayed historical episodes of the street's history, giant hands pointed to elements of major but unappreciated significance along its length. Some dozen other artists contributed a range of icons of Sherbrooke Street's contemporary reality to its overall sequence of street events. Perhaps as a reward for Charney's all-too-acute perception of the reality of architectural praxis in Canada, Corridart was destroyed in its entirety by orders of the Mayor of the City of Montreal.

Some of Charney's admirers have been concerned, in the wake of the 1978 show, by what appears to be a discernible new tendency in his activities, a tendency that might be characterized as a retreat to the gallery and, within the gallery, as a retreat from forms to texts. But it has to be said that this perceived "retreat" must be viewed reciprocally with the territory of feasible architectural praxis in Canada today. To the extent that Charney's recent "retreat" is a real one, it mirrors the difficulties encountered by any practitioner making any primary commitment to architecture as cultural praxis in this country.

—George Baird

CHERMAYEFF, Serge (Ivan)

American. Born in Grosny Azerbaijan, Caucasus, Russia, 8 October 1900; emigrated to England, 1910: naturalized, 1928; emigrated to the United States, 1939: naturalized, 1946. Educated privately in Moscow; at Peterborough Lodge Preparatory School, Hampstead, London, 1910–13; Royal Drawing Society School, London, 1910–13; Harrow School, 1914–17 (scholarship; Yates Thompson Prizes); studied art and architecture at various schools in Germany, Austria, France, and the Netherlands, 1922–25. Married Barbara Maitland in 1928; sons: the graphic artist Ivan Chermayeff and the architect Peter Chermayeff (see CAMBRIDGE SEVEN ASSOCIATES). Worked as a journalist for the Amalgamated Press, London, 1918–23; Chief Designer for the decorators E. Williams Ltd., London, 1924–27; Director of the Modern Art Department, Waring and Gillow, London, 1928–29; in private architectural practice, London, 1930–32; in partnership with Eric Mendelsohn, q.v., London, 1933–36; in private practice, London, 1937–39, San Francisco, 1940–41, and in New York, 1942–46; Professor of Architecture and Chairman of the Department of Design, Brooklyn College, New York, 1942–46; President and Director of the Institute of Design, Chicago, 1946–51; Lecturer, Massachusetts Institute of Technology, Cambridge, 1951–52; Professor of Architecture, Harvard Graduate School of Design, Cambridge, Massachusetts, 1953–62; Professor of Architecture, 1962–71, and since 1971 Emeritus Professor, Yale University School of Architecture, New Haven, Connecticut; Gropius Lecturer, Harvard University, 1974. Consultant on Planning, Architecture and Industrial Design, Museum of Modern Art, New York, 1942–47; Member, Editorial Board, American Federation of Art, 1942–47; Consultant, Chicago Plan Commission, 1946–48. Founder, 1942, and Member of the Executive Council, 1942–47, American Society of Planners and Architects. Exhibitions: First London Exhibition of Art, 1929; White City Exhibition, London, 1936; Whiteley's Housing Exhibition, London, 1936; Tomorrow's Small House, Museum of Modern Art, New York, 1945; Chicago Planning Exhibition, 1949. Recipient: Gold Medal, Royal Canadian Institute of Architects, 1974. D.F.A.: MacMurray College, Jacksonville, Illinois, 1946; Washington University, St. Louis, 1964. Fellow, Royal Institute of British Architects, Royal Society of Arts, London, and the American Institute of Architects. Address: Box NN, Wellfleet, Massachusetts 02667, U.S.A.

Works:

1929 Ambrose Wilson Ltd. office interiors, Vauxhall Bridge Road, London
1930 Chermayeff House interiors, London
Chermayeff Office interiors, 173 Oxford Street, London
Cambridge Theatre interiors, Seven Dials, London (with Wimperis, Simpson and Guthrie)
1931 Venesta Plywood Company Exhibition Stand, Building Trades Exhibition, Olympia, London (competition project)
1932 British Broadcasting Corporation interiors, Broadcasting House, London
English Country House (project)
A. G. Gibbons Grinling Flat interiors, London
1933 "Kernal" House Prototypes and Exercise Court, British Industrial Art Exhibition, Dorland Hall, London
1934 House in reinforced concrete, Rugby, Warwickshire
Living Room, Contemporary Industrial Design in the Home Exhibition, Dorland Hall, London
British Broadcasting Corporation interiors, Broadcasting House, Birmingham
Corset showrooms, Regent Street, London
1935 Working men's flats (competition project; with Helsby-Hamann-Samuely, and Cyril Sweet and J. Stinton-James)
House, Chalfont St. Giles, Buckinghamshire (with Eric Mendelsohn)
Flat interiors, 42 Upper Brook Street, London
Hotel, Southsea, Hampshire (project; with Eric Mendelsohn)
de la Warr Pavilion, Bexhill-on-Sea, Sussex (with Eric Mendelsohn)
1936 House, Frinton Park, Essex (with Eric Mendelsohn)
White City Housing Development, London (project; with Eric Mendelsohn)
House, 64 Old Church Street, Chelsea, London (with Eric Mendelsohn)
Music Room, Piano Exhibition, Dorland Hall, London
1937 Gilbey House Office Building, James Street and Oval Road, Camden Town, London
Flat interiors, Connaught Place, London
1938 Chermayeff House, Bentley, near Halland, Sussex
Imperial Chemical Industries Research Laboratories, Blackley, Manchester
Imperial Chemical Industries Offices and Works Canteen, Huddersfield, Yorkshire (project)
Ciro Jewelry Shop, 48 Old Bond Street, London
1939 Government Evacuation Camps in England (with others)
1941 Walter Horn House, Richmond, California
Park-Type Apartments, New York (exhibition project; with Black and Sorensen, and Fletcher and Hebbeln)
Revere Copper and Brass Company Nursery School (project)
1945 Neighborhood Development and Community Buildings, Tomorrow's Small House Exhibition, Museum of Modern Art, New York (with others)
1946 House, Piedmont, California
Duplex flat interiors, New York
Studio, New York (with Konrad Wachsmann)
1947 House, Redwood, California
1948 Ciro of Bond Street Store, San Francisco (with Raphael Soriano)
1950 British Railways Inc. Offices, Rockefeller Center, New York (with Ketchum, Gina and Sharp)
1952 Chermayeff Studio, Wellfleet, Massachusetts
Cottage interior renovations, Chermayeff Compound, Wellfleet, Massachusetts
1953 Sigerson Cottage, Wellfleet, Massachusetts
Herbert Payson Jr. House, Portland, Maine
1954 Wilkinson Cottage, Wellfleet, Massachusetts
Cape Codder Newspaper Plant, Orleans, Massachusetts
1956 Weekend House, Flato, Massachusetts (with Heyward Cutting)
Edwin O'Connor House, Wellfleet, Massachusetts
1957 Harvard Prototype Houses, Cambridge, Massachusetts (project)
1962 Chermayeff House, 28 Lincoln Street, New Haven, Connecticut
1963/
64 Courtyard House, New Haven, Connecticut (project; with Christopher Alexander)
1972 Chermayeff Studio II, Wellfleet, Massachusetts

Numerous exhibition and furniture designs, 1928–49.

Publications:

By CHERMAYEFF: books—Plan for A.R.P.: A Practical Policy (pamphlet), London 1939; Community and Privacy, with Christopher Alexander, New York 1963, Tokyo and London 1966, Buenos Aires 1967, Paris and Stuttgart 1972; The Shape of Community, with Alexander Tzonis, New York 1970, London 1971.

On CHERMAYEFF: books—20th Century Houses by Raymond McGrath, London 1934; New Research Laboratories, Manchester (ICI pamphlet), London 1938; Projects and Theories of Serge Chermayeff by Richard Plunz, Cambridge, Massachusetts 1972; articles—"Bexhill Entertainment Hall Competition" in The Builder (London), 9 February 1934; "Working Details: BBC Studios, Birmingham" in The Architects' Journal (London), 23 February 1934; "House at Rugby Designed by Serge Chermayeff" in The Architects' Journal (London), 19 April 1934; "House at Chalfont St. Giles" in Architectural Review (London), November 1935; "The de la Warr Pavilion, Bexhill" in The Builder (London), 20 December 1935; "Leisure at the Seaside" in Architectural Review (London), July 1936; "Two Houses in Church Street, Chelsea" in The Architects' Journal (London), 24 December 1936; "Gilbey House, Camden Town" in Architectural Review (London), July 1937; "Research Laboratories, Manchester" in RIBA Journal (London), 7 March 1938; "Offices and Factories" in Architectural Design and Construction (London), June 1938; "House near Halland, Sussex" in The Architects' Journal (London), 16 February 1939; "Trends in Shop Construction" in Architectural Design (London), May 1939; "Profile: Serge Chermayeff" in Der Aufbau (Vienna), September 1957; "Time and Chermayeff" in Architectural Review (London), June 1960; "Perspective: In

Serge Chermayeff: Chermayeff House, Bentley, near Halland, Sussex, 1938

Hampstead in the 30's" in *Building Design* (London), 17 January 1975; "Technology in the 1930's" by Alvin Howard in *Building Design* (London), 8 October 1976.

During my lifetime, entirely and precisely of this century, I have witnessed a series of events in my chosen field announcing profound change: I have seen Eclectic Architecture respectfully buried. I have observed, with some pleasure, that the mythical beast "International Style" did not rise from the ashes of World War II. I have seen with deep chagrin the anarchic, fashionable western shapes confront the dull paraphernalia of western commerce in cities, and even in remote islands, all over the world. Embassies, universities, hospitals, housing, offices and factories—Western Buildings without rhyme or reason, interlopers in cultures, places, economies and climates unable to accommodate them.

I hope that our "Shape-Makers" will, like old soldiers or the Cheshire Cat, fade away along with their "creations." I hope to see these replaced by "Problem-Solvers." I hope to see an "International Space Agency" established for here below. I continue to believe that artistic independence is not a myth. I am therefore confident that the beauty of nature and art will join the elegance of science in a new amalgam. And I feel that once this is achieved, this new excellence will be recognized.

—Serge Chermayeff

Serge Chermayeff, born in Russia in 1900, emigrated

to England at the age of 10 and received his formal education in architecture in that country. Notable among his first achievements in the profession were the projects designed in collaboration with Eric Mendelsohn between 1933 and 1936. Chermayeff's work in England was at the forefront of modern architecture in the 1920's and 1930's and gave the country some of its first International Style buildings. In 1939 Chermayeff and his family moved to America where his interests expanded more deeply into the field of education. In addition to an active professional practice, Chermayeff has taught and/or served as director at Brooklyn College, the Institute of Design in Chicago, Harvard University, M.I.T., and Yale University—a total of twenty-nine years of active involvement with architectural education in this country.

Chermayeff is also known for his writings. In 1963 he wrote *Community and Privacy* with Christopher Alexander. As a response to their concerns over basic social problems in architecture, the book proposed criteria for urban housing generated from a necessary balance of public and private spaces. Chermayeff's concern involves a broad range of levels from an urban to a domestic scale, all based on the assumption that a more meaningful architecture can be created through utilizing the contrast inherent in the public/private dichotomy, a balance between individual privacy and the possibilities for communal interaction.

The same theme is again addressed in *The Shape of Community,* written with Alexander Tzonis in 1970. The focus of this book is the problem of urban

design, and the authors provide a theoretical model for contemporary and future urban planning. Again, the basic premise concerns the social and formal need for public gathering places to be provided in conjunction with elements of privacy. The movement between spaces in an urban environment is given great emphasis as the basis for communication. In any concept of "community," communication by definition becomes one of the dominating features of urban life. Chermayeff considers an understanding of, and the design potential in, these communication networks to be a prime issue in architecture and planning on an urban scale.

His philosophy, however, is applicable to small-scale projects as well. In 1962 Chermayeff built his own house in New Haven as a prototypical example of his ideas about residential living. The house is arranged as a series of one-storey pavilions and courtyards. This pattern of open and closed spaces is an attempt to provide a physical separation between private and communal functions in the house. As a prototype, the house provides an economical solution to domestic programs.

Chermayeff's own studio and guest house on Cape Cod (1952) is another example of his interest in simple, contextual architectural forms. The design was developed on a modular geometry, for ease of construction. The materials and architectural elements are borrowed from the vernacular of traditional New England architecture. The sense of order created by this type of construction is very similar to that of the repetitive structure and bay system so integral to the International Style and to the work of Mies van der

Rohe in particular.

It could be said that Chermayeff's work and attitudes are a direct result of his belief in functional planning and of his sense of social responsibility.

—S. Fiske Crowell, Jr.

CHURCH, Thomas D(olliver).

American. Born in Boston, Massachusetts, 27 April 1902. Educated at Berkeley High School, California, 1914–18; University of California, Berkeley, 1918–23, B.A. Landscape Arch. 1923; Harvard Graduate School of Landscape Architecture, Cambridge, Massachusetts, 1924–26, M.S. 1926; awarded Sheldon Travel Scholarship, 1926–27. Married Elizabeth Roberts in 1930; daughters: Judith and Belinda. Assistant Professor of Landscape Architecture, Ohio State University, Columbus, 1927–29, and University of California, Berkeley, 1929–30; Landscape Architect for Pasatiempo Estates, Santa Cruz, California, 1930–32; Principal of Thomas D. Church and Associates, San Francisco, 1933 until his death, 1978. Consultant Landscape Architect, Stanford University, Palo Alto, 1957–77, and to the University of California at Berkeley and Santa Cruz, 1959–77. Recipient: Fine Arts Medal, American Institute of Architects, 1951; Oakleigh Thorne Medal, Garden Club of America, 1969; Honor Award, 1971, and Gold Medal, 1976, American Society of Landscape Architects; Citation for Outstanding Contributions, American Horticultural Society, 1974. Honorary Fellow, American Institute of Interior Designers, 1970; Fellow, American Academy of Arts and Sciences, 1978. *Died* (in San Francisco) *30 August 1978.*

Works:

Approximately 2,000 private gardens throughout the United States, 1930–77, and landscape design for:

1935 War Memorial Opera House Garden Court, San Francisco
1941/
50 Park Merced, San Francisco
1945 General Motors Research Center, Detroit
1946 El Panama Hotel, Panama City
Des Moines Art Center, Iowa
1958 Stanford Medical Center, Palo Alto, California
Stuart Pharmaceutical Company, Pasadena, California
1961 Master plan for the University of California, Berkeley
1963 *Sunset Magazine* Gardens, Menlo Park, California
Master plan for the University of California at Santa Cruz
Strybing Arboretum Home Demonstration Gardens, Golden Gate Park, San Francisco
Master plan for Harvey Mudd College, Claremont, California
1964 Caterpillar Tractor Company, Peoria, Illinois
1965 Master plan for Stanford University, Palo Alto, California
1969 Master plan for Scripps College, Claremont, California

Publications:

By CHURCH: books—*Gardens Are for People,* New York 1955; *Your Private World: A Study of Intimate Gardens,* San Francisco 1969; articles—in *Arts and Architecture* (Los Angeles), May 1932, May 1933, April 1934, June 1935; in *House Beautiful* (New York), July 1944, January 1948, April 1948, July 1948, October 1948, January 1949, October 1952, April 1955, September 1955, May 1957; in the *New York Times,* 9 January 1966; in *Horticulture* (Boston), October 1967; numerous articles in *Bonanza,* Sunday magazine of the *San Francisco Chronicle* from the late 1950's to the early 1960's.

On CHURCH: articles—in *Sunset* (Menlo Park, California), April 1935, February 1937, June 1941, May 1942, June 1946; in *Pencil Points* (New York), May 1941, January 1944, June 1944; in *House Beautiful* (New York), March 1948, May 1961, February

Thomas D. Church: Mr. and Mrs. C. Wagner Garden, Tacoma, Washington, 1967

1964, November 1967, September 1969; in *Better Homes in Gardens* (Des Moines, Iowa), April 1948; in *Architectural Forum* (New York), April 1951; in *Landscape Design and Construction* (Elm Grove, Wisconsin), March 1964; "Thomas Church and the Evolution of the California Garden" by Michael Laurie in *Landscape Design* (London), February 1973; "Thomas D. Church: His Role in American Landscape Architecture" by P. A. Messenger in *Landscape Architecture* (Louisville, Kentucky), March 1977.

Gardens are for people. In every case they should please and serve the people who live in them.

The only limit to your garden is at the boundaries of your imagination.

Your entrance should say "Welcome" and the steps should be an invitation.

Landscaping is not a complex and difficult art to be practised only by high priests. It is logical, down-to-earth, and aimed at making your plot of ground produce exactly what you want and need from it.

The site may be a garden in the true sense of providing trees and flowers, fruits and vegetables; it should be a place where man can recapture his affinity with the soil, if only on Saturday afternoons. It must be a green oasis where memories of his bumper to bumper ride from work will be erased.

The direction in which to move will be determined by the desires of the people who expect to find happiness in their gardens. Happiness will come by adding as much beauty and by eliminating as many irritations as possible within the limits of the problem. The limits of the problem will be the restrictions and opportunities of the site and the ability of the owner and designer to overcome or make use of them.

No definite style of gardening from the past will answer all the needs of today's small garden. Many old gardens do help us, however, to understand the underlying principles of building gardens for maximum enjoyment. There were the smart town gardens of Pompeii, the courtyards of Spain, the walled flower gardens of Queen Elizabeth and Henry VIII. They all contribute to our knowledge of scale and livability as applied to the areas surrounding the house. This is a new era in garden-making because, while many things have entered our life to make the problem complex, our ideas and requirements tend toward simplicity of solution.

To weigh, advise, interpret, integrate, and come up with some answers beyond the ability and imagination of the layman, is the role of the landscape architect.

—Thomas D. Church

Thomas D. Church began his professional career in San Francisco in the 1930's after conventional Beaux Arts training at the University of California at Berkeley and the Harvard Graduate School of Design. The timing coincided with a rapidly changing social context in California and a revolution in art and architecture on an international scale. By the 1950's Church had become one of the leading landscape architects in the United States working on large commercial and institutional projects with eminent architects of the modern movement including Eero Saarinen and Edward Durell Stone. But the bulk of his practice was at the domestic scale, and it was on garden design that his reputation was based.

His sensitivity to historical precedent, the environment of California, the changing life style and values of his clients, together with a mind receptive to new concepts in Art and Architecture, brought to his early work unique forms and new spatial qualities. His best gardens seem to be natural products of time and place and reflect the changes in taste and attitude already growing and requiring to be given form. These gardens not only fall into the realm of fine art but also represent an important milestone in the evolution of the modern garden and landscape architecture.

Locally, Church associated with young modern architects of the Bay Area (William Wurster, Gardener Daily, Ernest Born and others) and together,

for adventurous clients, they produced integrated houses and gardens based on the new aesthetic and designed for California living. The ratio of house to garden was frequently high, and the automobile further contributed to a reduction of useable garden space for the average home owner.

Church's designs to accommodate the increasing use of small gardens by families and the need to reduce maintenance included hard surfaces and ground cover planting, screens to separate areas and provide privacy, techniques and illusions to increase apparent size, and shapes suited to topography, function and upkeep. The combination of this relatively new design problem, the small garden, with the new approach to form resulted in a major breakthrough for Landscape Architecture. While satisfying all practical criteria, the central axis was abandoned in favor of a multiplicity of viewpoints. Simple planes and flowing lines, texture and color, space and form, were manipulated in a manner reminiscent of the cubist painters. Not only did the gardens which Church designed in the late 1930's look different, they also represented a new and improved way of dealing with landscape design at any scale. Each design derived form and uniqueness from careful appraisal and analysis of the site, from the architecture of the house and from the client's personality and preferences.

Historical precedent was not rejected by Church. In fact, his work drew strength from an appreciation of good design of whatever age and an understanding of the present as it evolves out of the past. Church had an exceptional ability to translate a client's requirements into a logical and intelligent plan, which at the same time derived specific quality from the surrounding environment. His deep understanding of the California landscape, its tradition and history, and of the life style and values of his clients, makes his work, albeit for a small section of society, a logical part in its evolution.

Thomas Church had an enormous influence on modern landscape architecture as it evolved in the post-war years in the United States, and his office nurtured many young landscape architects who are now leaders in the profession.

—Michael Laurie

CIAMPI, Mario J(oseph).
American. Born in San Francisco, California, 27 April 1907. Educated at the Night College of the San Francisco Architectural Club, 1927–29; Harvard University Graduate School of Design, Cambridge, Massachusetts, 1930–32; Beaux-Arts Institute of Design, Paris, summers 1932–33. Married Loretta Keane in 1939 (died, 1972). Draftsman, office of Alexander Cantin and Dodge A. Riedy, San Francisco, 1927–29; Associate Architect, office of Dodge A. Riedy, San Francisco, 1932–38. Since 1945, Principal, Mario J. Ciampi and Associates, San Francisco. Design Critic, San Francisco Architectural Club, 1935–40. Urban Design Consultant, San Francisco Market Street Development Plan, since 1963, and San Francisco Yerba Buena Project, since 1971. Recipient: Collaborative Medal of Honor, Architectural League of New York, 1960; Albert John Evers Environmental Award, 1972; Supervisors Award, County and City of San Francisco, 1973; San Francisco Art Festival Award, 1974. Fellow, American Institute of Architects. Address: Mario J. Ciampi and Associates, 617 Front Street, San Francisco, California 94111, U.S.A.

Works:

1950 War Memorial Community Center, 6655 Mission Street, Daly City, California

1953 Vista Grande Elementary School, Wyandotte Avenue and Thiers Street, Daly City, California

1954 Olympia Primary School, 200 Northgate Avenue, Daly City, California

1955 Westlake Elementary School, Daly City, California

1956 Garden Village Elementary School, 208 Garden Lane, Daly City, California

House, 760 Chiltern Road, Hillsborough, California (with Germano Milano)

1957 Pauline Margaret Brown Elementary School, 305 Eastmoor Avenue, Daly City, California

Olympia Primary School addition, 200 Northgate Avenue, Daly City, California

1958 Westmoor High School, 131 Westmoor Avenue, Daly City, California

1959 Vista Mar Elementary School, 725 Southgate Avenue, Daly City, California

1960 Fernando Riviera Elementary School, 101 Lake Merced Boulevard, Daly City, California

1962 Master plan for downtown San Francisco

1963 Embarcadero Plaza, phase I, San Francisco (with Lawrence Halprin and John S. Bolles)

1964 Oceana High School, Pacifica, California

Jefferson High School District Master Plan, for Pacifica, Brisbane, and Daly City, California

St. Peter's Roman Catholic Church, 700 Oddstad Way, Pacifica, California

1965 Development plan for St. Mary's College, Moraga, California

1966 Study of the Panhandle and Golden Gate Freeway, San Francisco (as urban consultant)

1967 Newman Center and Chapel, University of California, Berkeley

1967/
74 Site selection study, for the State College of San Mateo/Santa Clara Counties, California

1968 Market Street Development Plan, San Francisco (with John Carl Warnecke and Associates)

Humanities Complex, San Francisco State College

1970 University Art Museum, University of California, Berkeley

1971 Menlo Circus Club, Atherton, California (project)

Ferry Park, San Francisco (phase II of the Embarcadero Plaza)

1971/
74 Market Street reconstruction, San Francisco (with Lawrence Halprin and John Carl Warnecke)

1972 Tennis Center, Olympic Club, San Francisco (project)

1973 Powell Plaza, Powell, Eddy and Market Streets, San Francisco (with Lawrence Halprin and John Carl Warnecke)

Office Building Complex, West San Mateo, California (project)

1974 Seton Provincial House, Los Altos Hills, California

Development plan for Pier 45, Fisherman's Wharf, San Francisco

Master plan for Parking Center, Embarcadero Park, San Francisco

1975 Performing Arts Theatre, San Francisco (project)

Publications:

On CIAMPI: articles—"University Arts Center" in *Arts and Architecture* (Los Angeles), October 1965;

"UC Shows Art Center Plans" by Alexander Fried in *San Francisco Examiner,* 5 January 1966; "Three New Museums" by Peter Selz and Spiro Kostof in *Art in America* (New York), January/February 1968; "The Great Museum Debate" by C. Ray Smith in *Progressive Architecture* (New York), December 1969; "An Art Museum Designed for the Campus" in *Architectural Record* (New York), July 1972.

By the early 1950's California's post-war expansion was in full flood: the state's population was increasing by 5,000 people a week, mostly accommodated in the new suburbs of the San Francisco Bay Area and the Los Angeles Basin. Bay Area Region architecture had achieved recognition as an identifiable style, continuing the material and craft traditions of half a century earlier but reinterpreting forms and spaces for the culture of the 1950's. Brilliantly successful in responding to and forming the lifestyle of the Bay Area's cultured upper middle class, the style —and its creators—struggled to find as comfortable an expression for its institutions, its schools, universities, and city halls. Where these works could be interpreted at the residential scale, there were some successes, but, as state expansion continued, the size of building programs destroyed the fiction that such works could be designed as if they were houses.

During this period Mario Ciampi executed a series of public buildings that put the San Francisco suburbs of Daly City and Pacifica on the architectural tour map. As architect for the local school district, Ciampi designed—and, more remarkable, had built —a series of schools that replaced the current idiom of wood frame and pink stucco with one of bright hard materials, steel and ceramic tile, and forms such as concrete folded plates that, at the time, were more familiar in Europe and Brazil than in San Francisco.

These buildings showed promise of a sophistication and world reference that were missing in a Bay Area architecture already become cozy and self-satisfied with small-scale triumphs. Westmoor High School in Daly City was a cheerful version of a 2,000 student loft-plan high school, a huge one-story warehouse penetrated by courts, its gymnasium a rippling shell roof, its walls enlivened by bright paint and ceramic color. Oceana High School in Pacifica opposed a square space framed gymnasium by a huge crescent of concrete and glass classrooms. St. Peter's Roman Catholic Church, also in Pacifica, brought a whiff of Brasilia to this raw and foggy oceanside suburb.

This flurry of activity and hope lasted about 15 years. Ciampi's attempt to insert color and excitement into the local school environment failed, stifled by the grim humorlessness of the educational establishment, and he was replaced by an anonymous hack. Ciampi went on to execute one other work of great interest, the Art Museum of the University of California in Berkeley. This monolithic concrete building, with its linked fan-shaped galleries stepping up to form a single exhibition space of great vitality, unfortunately shows the weakness of an exterior that is allowed to happen as a result of the interior.

In fact, Ciampi's work must be evaluated as placed uncomfortably in a middle range: too sophisticated for his clients, yet too casual and glib in its acceptance of fashionable forms and materials to have the staying power of the work of the more meticulous craftsmen of his generation. But his work cheered us up a lot in its time, and, as the Bay Area style never did find a way to do public buildings, Ciampi's defects weigh light against his accomplishments.

—Christopher Arnold

CIRICI Alomar, Cristian.

Spanish. Born in Barcelona, 26 September 1941. Educated at the Escuela Tecnica Superior de Arquitectura, Barcelona, under Federico Correa, 1958–65, Dip.Arch. 1965. Served in the Spanish Army, in Castillejos, Tarragona, 1961, 1962, 1965: Lieutenant. Married Ana Bricall Orellana in 1967; children: Carla, Marc, and Iu. Formed the partnership, Studio PER, with Pep Bonet, *q.v.,* Luis Clotet, *q.v.,* and Oscar Tusquets, *q.v.,* Barcelona, 1965. Professor, EINA, Barcelona, 1969–70. Since 1976, Professor at the Escuela Tecnica Superior de Arquitectura, Barcelona. Member of the Board of Governors, Collegi Oficial d'Arquitectes de Cataluña, Barcelona, since 1976. Exhibitions: *Arquitectura del Studio PER,* Lérida, 1971; *Triennale,* Milan, 1973; *Arquitectura y Lágrimas,* Sala Vincon, Barcelona, 1975; *Centenario de la Escuela Tecnica Superior de Arquitectura de Barcelona,* Palacio Nacional, Barcelona, 1977; *Festival of Films about Architecture,* Centre Georges Pompidou, Paris, 1978. Address: Studio PER, Caspe 151, Barcelona 13, Spain.

Works:

1968   *Miró Otro* exhibition plan, Barcelona (with Pep Bonet, Luis Clotet, and Oscar Tusquets)

1972   Llambes Offices, Barcelona (with Pep Bonet)

1973   Profitos Factory, Polinya, Barcelona (with Pep Bonet)

       Housing, Queralbs, Gerona, Spain (with Santi Loperena)

1974   C./Tokio Housing Block, Barcelona (with Pep Bonet)

1976   Aguila House, Llavaneras, Barcelona (with Pep Bonet)

       Bricall House, Vilasar, Barcelona (with Pep Bonet)

       Pep Bonet House, Vilamajor, Barcelona (with Pep Bonet)

1977   Francés House, Menorca (with Pep Bonet)

Publications:

By CIRICI: articles—"El Plan que Sale del Armario" in *Destino* (Barcelona), 2 December 1967; "Popularidad del Diseño?" in *Destino* (Barcelona), 23 February 1968; "En el Proceso de Consumo" in *Destino* (Barcelona), 22 March 1968; "La Arquitectura de Vanguardia" in *Destino* (Barcelona), 20 April 1968; "Una Banca Catalana" in *Destino* (Barcelona), 18 May 1968; "Vivir en Barcelona" in *Destino* (Barcelona), 7 June 1968; "Premios FAD 1967" in *Destino* (Barcelona), 13 July 1968; "El Boom del Turismo de Verano" in *Destino* (Barcelona), 10 August 1968; "En Torno a la Parcelacion de un Area de Spot" in *Destino* (Barcelona), 7 March 1969; "En la Muerte de Ernesto Rogers" in *Destino* (Barcelona), 15 September 1969; "Revestimientos" in *Nuevo Ambiente* (Barcelona), no. 17, 1969; "El Esqui, Juego de Sociedad de los años 70" in *Cuadernos de Arquitectura* (Barcelona), no. 95, 1973; "Una Historia de Oficinas" in *Nuevo Ambiente* (Barcelona), no. 24, 1974.

On CIRICI: articles—"Studio PER" in *Architecture + Urbanism* (Tokyo), no. 4, 1977; "Arquitecturas con Ventanas" by Xavier Sust in *Arquitectura Bis* (Barcelona), September 1977; "Per, uno per uno, tutti per tutti" by Alessandro Mendini in *Modo Milano* (Milan), November 1977.

I remember that in 1965, when we were students of architecture in Barcelona, we used to get together in order to speak about our future as professionals. We specially debated the sociological, political and moral circumstances under which we would accept future commissions.

During the following ten years, in the practice of my profession, I never got the opportunity of that debate, and in order to keep myself in training, expecting the *great opportunity,* I accepted almost any commission, which taught me various things. It may be a long time before my expectations are realized, and now, just in case, I have gone back to school to explain to others younger than I the most exciting and subtle things I learned in my training.

Some may reach the great opportunity and others may go back to school as professors.

—Cristian Cirici

See BONET, Pep

CLOTET Ballus, Lluis.

Spanish. Born in Barcelona, 31 July 1941. Educated at the Escuela Pías, Barcelona, 1951–57; Escuela Tecnica Superior de Arquitectura, Barcelona, 1958–65: studied with Federico Correa Ruiz. Married Nuria Bohigas in 1966. Formed the partnership, Studio PER, with Cristian Cirici, *q.v.,* Pep Bonet, *q.v.,* and Oscar Tusquets, *q.v.,* Barcelona, 1965. Exhibitions: *Arquitectura del Studio PER,* Lérida, 1971; *Triennale,* Milan, 1973; *Arquitectura y Lágrimas,* Sala Vincon, Barcelona, 1975; *Centenario de la Escuela Tecnica Superior de Arquitectura de Barcelona,* Palacio Nacional, Barcelona, 1977; *Festival of Films about Architecture,* Centre Georges Pompidou, Paris, 1978. Recipient: Premio F.A.D., 1965, 1972. Address: Studio PER, Caspe 151, Barcelona 13, Spain.

Works:

1963   Colegio Mayor San Raimundo de Peñafort, Barcelona (with Oscar Tusquets)

1965   Editorial Lumen Offices, Barcelona (with Oscar Tusquets)

       Emilio Blay House Interiors, Barcelona (with Oscar Tusquets)

       Apartment Block I, Cadaqués, Gerona, Spain (with Oscar Tusquets and Xavier Carulla)

       Sonor Hi-Fi shop and studio, Barcelona (with Oscar Tusquets and Xavier Carulla)

1968   Gremio Vidrieros Building, Barcelona (with Oscar Tusquets and Xavier Carulla)

       Maspons-Ubiña Studio, Barcelona (with Oscar Tusquets and Xavier Carulla)

       Fonda Sala Restaurant, Olost de Llusanes, Barcelona (with Oscar Tusquets and Xavier Carulla)

       Ibars Offices, Barcelona (with Oscar Tusquets and Xavier Carulla)

       Casa Fullá apartment building, Barcelona (with Oscar Tusquets and Santiago Loperena)

       Single-family housing, La Atmella del Vallés, Barcelona (with Oscar Tusquets and Xavier Carulla)

       Solitari Apartments, Cadaqués, Gerona, Spain (with Oscar Tusquets and Xavier Carulla)

       El Colomer Apartment Complex, Cadaqués, Gerona, Spain (with Oscar Tusquets, Santiago Loperena, and Anna Bohigas)

       Casa Penina (house), Cardedeu, Barcelona (with Oscar Tusquets, Santiago Loperena, and Anna Bohigas)

       Ancla Roja Apartments, Salou, Tarragona, Spain (with Oscar Tusquets and Anna Bohigas)

       Miró Otro exhibition plan, Barcelona (with Oscar Tusquets, Pep Bonet, and Cristian Cirici)

1970   Gil Sala residential additions, Barcelona (with Oscar Tusquets, Santiago Loperena, and Anna Bohigas)

1971 Casa Regás (house), Llofriu, Gerona, Spain (with Oscar Tusquets, Santiago Loperena, and Anna Bohigas)

Puig and Cadafalch Housing Block, Mataró, Barcelona (with Oscar Tusquets, Santiago Loperena, and Anna Bohigas)

Unión Lloyd Travel Agency Building, Barcelona (with Oscar Tusquets, Santiago Loperena, and Anna Bohigas)

1972 Aerojet Travel Offices, Barcelona (with Oscar Tusquets, Santiago Loperena, and Anna Bohigas)

Belvedere Georgina (house), Llofriu, Gerona, Spain (with Oscar Tusquets, Santiago Loperena, and Anna Bohigas)

1973 Mozart-Fortuny Apartments, Sant Cugat del Valles, Barcelona (with Oscar Tusquets, Santiago Loperena, and Anna Bohigas)

Aerojet Travel Offices, Palma, Majorca (with Oscar Tusquets and Santiago Loperena)

Alpes Building, Hospitalet, Barcelona (with Oscar Tusquets, Santiago Loperena, and Anna Bohigas)

1974 Tusquets Family Apartment alterations, Barcelona (with Oscar Tusquets, Santiago Loperena, and Anna Bohigas)

Casa Vittoria (house), Pantelleria, Italy (with Oscar Tusquets)

Stephanie Apartment, Barcelona (with Oscar Tusquets, Santiago Loperena, and Anna Bohigas)

Sahatuje Studio, Barcelona (with Oscar Tusquets, Santiago Loperena, and Anna Bohigas)

1975 Jacob Levy Apartment, Barcelona (with Oscar Tusquets, Santiago Loperena, and Anna Bohigas)

Editorial Lumen Offices, Barcelona (with Santiago Loperena)

Feria Textiles Exhibition Stand, Valencia (with Oscar Tusquets)

1976 Housing group, Sardanola, Barcelona (with Oscar Tusquets, Santiago Loperena, and Anna Bohigas)

Gloria Rognoni House, Sant Cugat del Valles, Barcelona (with Santiago Loperena)

1977 Ramirez House, Alella, Barcelona (with Santiago Loperena)

Publications:

By CLOTET: books—*Arquitectura Modernista*, with Oscar Tusquets, Barcelona 1968; *Arquitectura Gótica Catalana*, with Oscar Tusquets, Barcelona 1968; *Arquitectura y Lágrimas*, with Oscar Tusquets, Barcelona 1975; *Vivir en el Campo*, Barcelona 1976; articles, with Oscar Tusquets—"Acondicionamento sala estar y comedor" in *Cuadernos Arquitectura* (Barcelona), no. 4, 1965; "Viviendas en Hospitalet de Llobregat" in *Hogar y Arquitectura* (Madrid), Octobrr 1968; "Casa Regás" in *Cuadernos Arquitectura* (Barcelona), July/August 1972; "El chalet masia" in *Mobelart* (Barcelona), October 1972; "Belvedere Georgina casita unifamiliar" in *Cuadernos Arquitectura* (Barcelona), September-/October 1973; "Mi Terraza, Studio PER en el Industrial Design de la Triennales de Milan" in *Hogares Modernos* (Barcelona), November 1973; "Biblioscala de un piso en Barcelona" in *Nuevo Ambiente* (Barcelona), March/April 1974; "Manzana Puig i Cadafalch" in *Cuadernos de Arquitectura Anuario* (Barcelona), no. 109, 1975; "Viviendas en Sant Cugat" in *Cuadernos de Arquitectura Anuario* (Barcelona), no. 110, 1975.

On CLOTET: books—*Casa Vittoria, Pantelleria* by the Habitat editors, Barcelona 1976; *El Studio PER o los confines de la Arquitectura actual* by J. Muntañola, Barcelona 1976; *Arquitecturas Catalanas* by Helio Piñón, Barcelona 1977; articles—"Los Premios FAD" by Oriol Bohigas in *Serra d'Or* (Barcelona), January 1967; "Canaletas Neighbourhood"

by David Mackay in *World Architecture*, London 1968; "Uma lonja em Barcelona" in *Arquitectura* (Lisbon), July 1968; "Chalet en una ciudad jard." in *Nuevo Ambiente* (Barcelona), no. 15, 1969; "Exposición Miró Otro" in *Summa* (Buenos Aires), 20 November 1969; "Vivre dehors: Autour de patios-terrasses" in *Maison Francaise* (Paris), June 1971; "Obras de Clotet-Tusquets," special issue of *Hogar y Arquitectura* (Madrid), July 1971; "Los Premios de interiorismo FAD 1971" in *Hogares Modernos* (Barcelona), January 1972; "Allestimento a Barcelona" in *Domus* (Milan), October 1972; "Nuevas Tendencias de la Arquitectura española" in *Arquitectura* (Madrid), May 1972; "Belvedere Georgina" in *Nuevo Ambiente* (Barcelona), September 1973; "Casa Regas Llofriu" in *Nuevo Ambiente* (Barcelona), November 1973; "Casa Georgina" in *Toshi Yutaku* (Tokyo), November 1973; "Introducir una vivienda funcional en un Belvedere Palladiano" in *Domus* (Milan), no. 522, 1973; "Opiniones sobre el Belvedere" by Correa, Sust, and Flores in *Jano Arquitectura* (Barcelona), December 1973; "Agencia Viajes Aerojet" in *Nuevo Ambiente* (Barcelona), March 1974; "Gil Sala Building" in *Toshi Yutaku* (Tokyo), no. 8, 1975; "Casa Vittoria en la isla de Pantelleria" in *Arquitecturas Bis* (Barcelona), May/-June 1976; "Anarchist's Guide" by Chris Fawcett in *Architectural Association Quarterly* (London), vol. 7, no. 3, 1976; "C'e un designer sul trapezio" by Bruno Zevi in *Espresso* (Milan), 23 July 1977; "Studio PER," special issue of *Architecture + Urbanism* (Tokyo), April 1977; "Per, uno per uno, tutti per tutti" by Alessandro Mendini in *Modo Milano* (Milan), November 1977.

*

It was the first woman's bottom I saw in my life. I was five and looked at her while she was dressing herself. My cousin and I slept in the same bed.

She still lives in that village, and now I am putting her house in order.

Arturo, the best centre-halfback the team has ever had, is the bricklayer. The plumber is the only guy I ever fight with.

There are no estimates, no permissions, no discussions; everything is as plain and simple as it should be. And the pies and sausages they give me for my work are delicious.

—Lluis Clotet

Studio PER is four architects in two practices in one office. Apart from administrative convenience, what really binds them together is that they share the same approach to architecture in valuing positively its cultural objectives. Their architecture is essentially intellectual. They are eager to discuss, argue, and defend their work against all criticism in order to explore all the rich possibilities available to their avant-garde position. This makes their buildings, and their explanations, often contradictory—but that is the price of an open mind—adventure and doubt. But this attitude, which is almost literary rather than visual, would be of little interest if it were not backed up by secure professional ability, compositional control, and a sensitive feeling for proportions.

Lluis Clotet and Oscar Tusquets are one practice. From the beginning they were immersed in the neo-realist, historically-based, so-called Barcelona School of Architecture that achieved a coherent local style during the 1960's and 70's. It was based on program analysis, environmental integration, economic use of materials, and constructional detailing as a basis for decoration. Their apartment building Casa Fullá in Barcelona and the private house Casa Penina are the most representative of this period.

The small week-end house, "Belvedere Georgina," in Llofriu, is so ironic in poking fun at the modern movement and so dexterous in its use of historical vocabulary that at first it seems to be just a brilliant example of pop art in architecture. The house is conceived as a garden pavilion in the form of a temple in homage to the motor-car, which makes the week-end house possible. The car is parked under a classical pergola, and one enters the house down through the pit. Part of the pavilion is cut away to form a sheltered court, and the missing section is painted on the walls. The window shutters are designed and placed according to the proportions and rules of classical composition, allowing the real windows to be placed haphazardly behind, according to the dictates of the interior function. Though the image of the house is an irrelevant exercise in pop history, it has given the the authors the freedom to extend the frontiers of architectural composition in its own right to give a cultured solution to the building so that it reads well in the landscape and allows the exterior and interior design to overlap independently.

It is through this "second reading" of their architecture that one finds the common denominator that runs through their buildings—be it the outside rooms defined by concrete columns in the Vittoria

Lluis Clotet and Oscar Tusquets: Belvedere Georgina (house), Llofriu, Gerona, Spain, 1972

house on the Island of Pantelleria or the split-level row housing in Sant Cugat.

The common freshness and professional skill of Clotet and Tusquets, and that of their associates in Studio PER, together with their sensitive alertness to current architectural fashion, enable them to translate new concepts quickly into the local Catalan cultural context. It is a task that is needed if the modern movement is to take root geographically.

—David Mackay

COATES, Wells (Wintemute).

Canadian. Born in Tokyo, Japan, of Canadian parents, 17 December 1895. Educated privately in Tokyo; at the University of British Columbia, Vancouver, 1914–16, 1919–21, B.S. in engineering 1921; University of London, 1922–24, Ph.D. in engineering 1924. Lieutenant in the Canadian Infantry, in France and Belgium, 1915–17; served as a pilot in the Royal Naval Air Service and the Royal Air Force, in Italy, 1917–18; Technical Staff Officer, with rank of Wing Commander, Royal Air Force, 1939–45. Married Marion Grove in 1927 (separated, 1935); daughter: Laura. Worked as a journalist for the *Daily Express* in London and Paris, 1923–26; worked in the office of Adams and Thompson, with Maxwell Fry, London, 1924; Engineer/Architect, Chrysede Textiles Company, London and Cornwall, 1927–28; in private practice as designer and architect, London, 1929–39, 1945–49; in partnership with Jacqueline Tyrwhitt, London, 1949–52; Architect and Planner for Iroquois New Town, Ontario, Canada, 1952–54; Visiting Professor, Harvard University, Cambridge, Massachusetts, 1955–56; returned to private practice in London, 1956 until his death, 1958. Design Consultant, Cresta Silks Shops, London, 1929–33; Consultant, De Havilland Aircraft Company, 1946, and EMI Electrical Industries, London, 1952. Member, Executive Council, Twentieth Century Group, London, 1930–31; Founder Member, Modern Architectural Research Group (MARS), London, from 1933; Member, Unit One, London, 1933–35. Exhibitions: *Hampstead in the Thirties*, London 1974; *PEL*, London 1977; *The Wireless Show!*, London 1977. Fellow, Royal Institute of British Architects; Member, Royal Architectural Institute of Canada. Associate, Royal Society of Arts, 1944; Royal Designer for Industry, 1944; Master of the Faculty of Design for Industry, 1951–53. O.B.E. (Officer, Order of the British Empire), 1944. *Died* (in London) *17 June 1958.*

Works:

1928 Chrysede Silks Shop, Cambridge
1929 Cresta Silks Factory interiors, Welwyn Garden City, Hertfordshire
Cresta Silks Shop, Brompton Road, London
Cresta Silks Shop, Bournemouth
1930 Cresta Silks Shop, Brighton
Cresta Silks Shop, Bromley, Kent
2 linked houses, Lawn Road, Hampstead, London (project)
1931 Cresta Silks Shop II, Brompton Road, London
British Broadcasting Corporation Studios, Broadcasting House, London
House conversion, 1 Kensington Palace Gardens, London
Flat conversion, 34 Gordon Square, Bloomsbury, London
Venesta Plywood Display, *Empire Trade Exhibition*, Manchester
Venesta Plywood Display, *Empire Trade Exhibition*, Buenos Aires
Venesta Plywood Display, *Brewers' Exhibition*, London

Venesta Plywood Display, *Commercial Motor Exhibition*, Olympia, London
Isotype House (project)
1932 British Broadcasting Corporation Studios, Newcastle
Airport (project)
Cresta Silks Shop, Baker Street, London
Cresta Silks Shop, Bond Street, London
Office conversion, Elizabeth Street, London
Venesta Plywood Display, *Empire Trade Exhibition*, Olympia, London
1933 Lawn Road Flats, Hampstead, London
Minimum Flat, *British Industrial Art Exhibition*, Dorland Hall, London
House conversion, 78 Addiscombe Road, Croydon, Surrey (with David Pleydell-Bouverie)
Layout for *Artists of Today* exhibition, Zwemmer Gallery, Litchfield Street, London (with David Pleydell-Bouverie)
Second Feathers Club, Norland Gardens, London (with David Pleydell-Bouverie)
Venesta Plywood Display, *Building Trades Exhibition*, Olympia, London
Permanent stage set for the 1933–34 season, Old Vic Theatre, Waterloo, London
1934 Sunspan House, *Ideal Home Exhibition*, Olympia, London (with David Pleydell-Bouverie)
MARS Group Display, *Building Exhibition*, Olympia, London (with David Pleydell-Bouverie)
Embassy Court Flats, Brighton
1935 Sunspan Single-Storey House, Welwyn Garden City, Hertfordshire
Studio flat, 18 Yeoman's Row, Knightsbridge, London
School camp, Ogmore, Glamorgan, Wales (with Elizabeth Denby)
Flats, Sleepy Hollow, Hove, Sussex (project)
Venesta Plywood Display, *Building Trades Exhibition*, Olympia, London
1935/
38 Sunspan House, Angmering, Sussex
Sunspan House, Portsdown Hill, Hampshire
Sunspan House, Wentworth Close, Ditton Hill, Kent
3 Sunspan Houses, Surbiton, Surrey
2 Sunspan Houses, Avondale Avenue, Esher, Surrey
2 Sunspan Houses, Southwood Gardens, Esher, Surrey
3 Sunspan Houses, Woodlands Avenue, New Malden, Surrey
1936 Ekco Factory, Southend-on-Sea, Essex
Hampden Nursery School, Holland Park, London
Flat conversion, 2 Devonshire Street, London
Hairdressing salon, Canterbury, Kent (with Edric Neel)
Flats, Durdham Park, Bristol (project)
1937 Flats, 10 Palace Gate, Kensington, London
House, Benfleet, Essex
SCS Slum Clearance, Bethnal Green, London (project)
News Chronicle School (competition project; with Denys Lasdun)
1938 The Homewood (house), Esher, Surrey (with Patrick Gwynne)
Layouts for the *MARS Group Exhibition*, New Burlington Galleries, London
1944 Share Farm alterations and additions, Horsmonden, Kent (project)
1945 AIROH Aluminium House (project)
1946 St. Lawrence Cliffs Hotel conversion and additions, Isle of Thanet, Kent (project)
1947 BOAC Aircraft interiors
A. W. Hawksley Display, and Thomas French and Sons Display, *Building Trades Exhibition*, Olympia, London
1949 James Clark and Eaton Display, *Building Trades Exhibition*, Olympia, London
1950 British Broadcasting Corporation Television

Studio, *Festival of Britain*, London (project)
Telekinema, *Festival of Britain*, South Bank, London (with Peter Bender)
Television Pavilion, *Festival of Britain*, South Bank, London (with Peter Bender and Denys Hinton)
1951 James Clark and Eaton Display, *Building Trades Exhibition*, Olympia, London
1953 Master plan for Iroquois New Town, Ontario
1954 Toronto Island Development Plan (project; with J. B. Parkin)
1955 Flats, The Drive, Hove, Sussex (project; with Michael Lyell)
Prince's Gardens Development, Kensington, London (project; with Michael Lyell)
1956 House, Thames Ditton, Surrey (with Michael Lyell)
Hope Brothers Shop, Regent Street, London (with Michael Lyell)
House, West Wittering, Sussex (with Michael Lyell)
Flats, Ottawa, Ontario (project)
1957 Flats, Vancouver (project)
Project 58, Vancouver (project; with Arthur Erickson, Geoffery Massey, Peter Oberlander and E. J. Watkins)
Mass Rapid Transit System (project)

Designs: numerous items of furniture and fitments for incorporation into his building projects, as well as commissioned projects for radio and television sets and boats, 1928–55.

Publications:

By COATES: articles—"Critics: A Reader's Way to Reconcile Their Unfriendliness" in *The Architects' Journal* (London), 11 February 1931; "Inspiration from Japan" and "Material for Architecture" in *The Architects' Journal* (London), 4 November 1931; "Furniture Today—Furniture Tomorrow" in *Architectural Review* (London), July 1932; "Response to Tradition" in *Architectural Review* (London), November 1932; "Modern Shops and Modern Materials" in *Building* (London), December 1932; "Wells Coates: Interview," with J. Craven, in *Advertisers' Weekly* (London), March 1933; "Design in Modern Life: Modern Dwellings for Modern Needs," with Geoffrey Boumphrey, in *The Listener* (London), 24 May 1933; "Planning in Section" in *Architectural Review* (London), August 1937; "The Conditions for an Architecture of Today" in *Architectural Association Journal* (London), April 1938; "Planning the Festival of Britain Telekinema" in *British Kinematography* (London), April 1951; "The Cine-Theatre Today and Tomorrow" in *Atti e Rassegna Tecnica della Società degli Ingegnieri e degli Architetti* (Turin), December 1952; "The Film Theatre of the Future" in *Ideal Kinema* (London), 26 May 1953; "Graduation Banquet Address" in *Royal Architectural Institute of Canada Journal* (Toronto), June 1959.

On COATES: books—*Unit One: The Modern Movement in English Architecture, Painting and Sculpture*, edited by Herbert Read, London 1934; *Interior Decorating* by Duncan Miller, London 1937; *The Modern Flat* by F. R. S. Yorke and Frederick Gibberd, London 1950; *The Politics of Architecture: A History of Modern Architecture in Britain* by Anthony Jackson, London 1970; *Hampstead in the Thirties*, exhibition catalogue, edited by Michael Collins, London 1974; *PEL*, exhibition catalogue, edited by Dennis Sharp, Tim Benton and Barbie Campbell Cole, London 1977; *The Wireless Show!*, exhibition catalogue, edited by Carol Hogben, London 1977; *Wells Coates* by Sherban Cantacuzino, London 1978; articles—"The Year's Work" by C. H. Reilly in *The Architects' Journal* (London), 10 January 1935; "The Year's Work at Home" by C. H.

Reilly in *The Architects' Journal* (London), 16 January 1936; "The Designers: Wells Coates" by Geoffrey Boumphrey in *Architectural Review* (London), January 1936; "The Year's Work" by C. H. Reilly in *The Architects' Journal* (London), 18 January 1940; "Broadcasting Comes of Age: The Radio Cabinet 1919–1949" by Nikolaus Pevsner in *Architectural Review* (London), May 1940; "Isokon Flats" by Reyner Banham in *Architectural Review* (London), July 1955; "English Architecture from the Thirties" by E. Maxwell Fry in *The Architect's Yearbook 8,* London 1957; "Wells Coates 1895–1958" by J. M. Richards in *Architectural Review* (London), December 1958.

Wells Coates was one of the small group of cosmopolitans who were the spearhead of the modern movement during the 1930's in England. Born in Japan in 1895 of Canadian parents who were missionaries, he was educated in Canada and at the University of London, from which he obtained a doctorate in engineering in 1924. By the time he focussed fully on architecture in the late 1920's he had had a versatile career as war-time pilot, research student, journalist and exhibition display designer. Between 1929 and 1932 he established himself at the forefront of English modern tendencies with a series of designs for Cresta shops and with the planning of the BBC Special Effects studios.

Coates' formation as an architect corresponded with the "heroic phase" of the European Modern Movement. His innate sense of abstract form had already received stimulus from the controlled proportions and clean forms of Japanese architecture, and he was naturally attracted to abstract art of the 1920's and to the stripped shapes of the International Style. Moreover, Coates' engineering sensibility was in sympathy with Le Corbusier's machine aesthetic, and he was also attracted to the quality of dynamic expression in the work of Eric Mendelsohn.

These disparate influences and attitudes were synthesised in Coates' first major work, Lawn Road Flats in Hampstead (1933), designed for Jack Pritchard. Here the rationally arranged apartments have been packed into a tight oblong form from which the access balconies have been cantilevered and to which a block containing vertical circulation and garages has been attached. The result is a disciplined communal statement and a demonstration of the potentials of reinforced concrete: it is entirely fitting that the flats should have been the temporary home of such cosmopolitan emigrés as Walter Gropius, who fled Nazi oppression by coming to England. Lawn Road embodied a manifesto for a new way of life in the English context.

Coates was involved with the political and propaganda activities surrounding the formation of English modern architecture during this period and took part in such avant-garde manifestations as the Twentieth Century Group, Unit One and The Modern Architectural Research Group (MARS), the English wing of the Congrès Internationaux de l'Architecture Moderne (CIAM). His personality was well suited to liaison with foreign architects, as he delighted in demonstrating his broad range of knowledge of foreign cultures and cut an elegant figure in his reticent but immaculate clothes and his Ronald Colman moustache. It was entirely consistent with Coates' persona that he should have driven a flamboyant Lancia Lambda sports car and that his flat in Kensington should have contained a radio set of his own design with a transparent front. But beneath this self consciousness and theatricality there was a passionate character of great integrity: Coates' architectural activities were rooted in aesthetic and moral principles and in the quest for a new social ethos.

Coates' other major work of the 1930's, the flats at Palace Gate, Kensington, resulted from an attempt at synthesising this social vision with new forms and techniques. The architect here combined the plan arrangements of Le Corbusier's Pavillon

Wells Coates: Lawn Road Flats, Hampstead, London, 1933

Suisse with an ingenious, space-saving 3/2 section derived from Russian Collectivist dwellings of the late 1920's. Whatever the sources, the result is uniquely Coates' own and, along with Lubetkin and Tecton's High Point Flats at Highgate, must rank as one of the clearest statements of the highrise urbanistic principle before the Second World War in England.

Coates applied his mind to a broad range of architectural problems: the creation of house prototypes (the "Sunspan" house of 1934), the study of urban problems (studies for Bethnal Green slum clearance, 1937), even the design of catamarans and radio sets (his EKCO wireless cabinet of 1934 is a classic of the period). But in the broad context his output must be seen as of secondary importance alongside the original thinkers who created the modern movement. Moreover Coates' extremely individualistic temperament was better suited to the atmosphere of the battlegrounds for modern architecture of the 1930's than to the more complacent post-war years, and his later development did not lead to the fulfilment of the early promise. His last

years, up until his death in 1958, were spent mostly in Canada working on urban schemes and teaching.

Coates was a complex man who impressed most who met him with the quality of his high ideals and with a certain sadness. The historian Sigfried Giedion perhaps spoke the truth when he suggested that Coates was "never completely at home in architecture or in life."

—William J. R. Curtis

CODERCH y de Sentmenat, José A(ntonio). Spanish. Born in Barcelona, 25 November 1913. Educated at the Escuela Tecnica Superior de Arquitectura, Barcelona, under José Maria Jujol y Gibert, José Rafols, and Professor Florensa, 1929–36, 1939–40, Dr.Arch. 1940; influenced by the work of the Madrid architect Secundino Zuazu and by popular Mediterranean architecture. Served as a Lieutenant in the Spanish Civil War, 1936–39: Cruz de Guerra al mérito en Campana; Cruz Roja al mérito militar. Married Ana Maria Giménez Ramos in 1943; children: José Antonio, Ana Maria, Gustavo, and Elvira. Worked in the offices of the Director-General of Architecture, Madrid, 1940–42, offices of the City Architect, Sitges, Spain, 1942–45, Obra Sindical del Hogar, Barcelona, 1944–52, and at the Naval Institute, Barcelona, 1949–52. In private architectural practice, Barcelona, since 1947 (partner since 1947: J. Sanz Luengo; partners since 1967: G. Coderch Giménez; J. A. Coderch Giménez). Professor, Escuela Tecnica Superior de Arquitectura, Barcelona, 1965–68. Member of Team 10, 1961. Exhibitions: National Architecture Congress, Barcelona, 1949; *Triennale,* Milan, 1951; *National Fine Art Exhibition,* Madrid, 1960; Centre Pompidou, Paris, 1978. Recipient: Gold Medal and Grand Prize, *Triennale,* Milan, 1951; Gold Medal, *National Fine Art Exhibition,* Madrid, 1960; Gold Delta, ADI-FAD, Barcelona, 1962, 1964; Obelisk Prize, *Domus,* 1963; National Design Prize, Argentina, 1964; Professional Merit Medal, FAD, Barcelona, 1977. Academician of the Real Academia Catalana de Bellas Artes de San Jorge, Barcelona, 1977. Address: Estudio de Arquitectura Coderch de Sentmenat, Plaza Calvó 4, Barcelona 22, Spain.

Works:

1945 Las Forcas Urban Plan, Sitges, Spain (project)
1946 Ferrer Vidal House, Cala d'Or, Majorca
1947 Garriga Nogues House, Sitges, Spain
1949 Union Building, Madrid (project)
1951 Ugalde House, Caldetas, Spain
House, Barceloneta, Barcelona
Pescadores Housing Block, Barceloneta, Barcelona (project)
1952 Capilla chimney design
1955 Experimental housing (project)
Coderch House, Caldetas, Spain (project)
Polo chimney design
1956 Transatlantic Bank Building, Barcelona (project)
Catasus House, Sitges, Spain
Senillosa House, Cadaques, Gerona, Spain
1957 Lamp design
Ballve House, Camprodon, Spain
Olano House, Comillas, Santander, Spain (project)
1958 Residential block, Comp. Bach, Barcelona
Coderch and Milá House, Cadaques, Spain
1959 Torre Valentina Urban Plan, Costa Brava, Spain (project)
1960 Hoechst Office Building, Barcelona (project)
Casa Tàpies House and Studio, Barcelona
1961 Paricio House, San Feliu de Codines, Spain
Club Nautico Building, San Feliu de Guixols, Spain (project)
Uriach House, Atmetlla del Vallés, Spain
1962 Rozes House, Rosas, Spain
Hotel de Mar, Palma, Majorca
1964 Casa Pairal (Coderch House), Espolla, Spain
1965 Luque House, Sant Cugat del Valles, Spain
Gili House, Sitges, Spain
Trade Office Building, Barcelona
1966 Girasol Residential Block, Madrid
Entrecanales House, Madrid
Encarnación House, Barcelona
Chapel of Santa María, Queralt, Spain
Monitor (Augusta-Amigo) Housing Block, Barcelona
1967 Rovira House, Canet de Mar, Spain
Savings Bank, Sabadell, Spain (competition project)
Banco Urquijo Residential Block, Barcelona
1968 Cocheras Housing Block, Sarria, Barcelona
1969 Zobel de Ayala House, Sotogrande, Cadiz, Spain (project)
1970 Raventós House, Matadepera, Spain
1971 Guell House, Barcelona
Gran Kursaal House, San Sebastian (competition project)

1972 French Institute Building, Barcelona
1973 SEAT Technical Centre, Martorell, Spain
1976 Housing block, Madrid (competition project)
Lacua House, Vittoria, Spain (competition project)

Publications:

By CODERCH: articles—"No son genios lo que necesitamos ahora" in *Arquitectura* (Madrid), February 1962; "Un proyecto de viviendas" in *Arquitectura* (Madrid), June 1972; "Conjunto de viviendas, Barcelona" in *Informes de la Construccion* (Madrid), September 1975.

On CODERCH: articles—"Proyecto de viviendas maritimas en Sitges" in *Arte y Hogar* (Madrid), December 1945; "Due ville à Sitges" in *Domus* (Milan), November 1949; "La nueva arquitectura rural" by Alberto Sartoris in *Revista Nacional de Arquitectura* (Madrid), December 1949; "Deux Villas a Sitges" in *L'Architecture d'Aujourd'hui* (Paris), July 1950; "Giro d'orizzonte alla T9" by Marco Valsecchi in *Edilizia Moderna* (Milan), December 1951; "Casa a Maiorca" in *Domus* (Milan), November 1952; "Per i pescatori di Tarragona" in *Domus* (Milan), September 1952; "Villa en Caldetas" in *Revista Nacional de Arquitectura* (Madrid), December 1953; "Casa a Barcelona" in *Domus* (Milan), May 1955; "Jose Coderch y Manuel Valls" by Juan Teixidor in *Zodiac 5* (Milan), October 1957; "L'Architecture de Coderch et Valls Verges" by Alberto Sartoris in *Architecture: Formes et Fonctions* (Lausanne), no. 4, 1957; "Real Club de Golf del Prat, Barcelona" in *Cuadernos de Arquitectura* (Barcelona), no. 31, 1958; "Hotel and Apartments at Torre Valentina" in *Architectural Design* (London), May 1960; "Casa a Camprodón" in *Domus* (Milan), December 1960; "Hotel und Aparthenthauser en Torre Valentina, Costa Brava" in *D.B.Z.* (Gutersloh), February 1961; "Casa per vacanze in Spagna" in *Edilizia Moderna* (Milan), December 1961; "Maison Coderch" in *L'Oeil* (Lausanne), April 1962; "Luxury Flats, Barcelona" in *Architect and Building News* (London), July 1962; "Village de Vacances sur la Costa Brava" in *Réalités* (Paris), April 1963; "Conversacion con José A. Coderch" by Rafael Marquina in *Clima* (Madrid), 1964; "José Antonio Coderch, Manuel Valls" in *Arquitectura* (Madrid), December 1965; "Zwei Wohnhauser in Spanien" in *Baumeister* (Munich), May 1966; "New Ideas Revive an Ancient House" in *House Beautiful* (London), August 1966; "Une parfaite maison de vacances" in *Maison Francaise* (Paris), April 1968; "Tutta Bianca sul Mare" in *Ville-Giardini* (Milan), January 1970; "Dernier grand maitre solitaire de l'architecture espagnole" in *L'Architecture d'Aujourd'hui* (Paris), January/February 1975; "J.A. Coderch," special issue of *Architecture + Urbanism* (Tokyo), February 1976; "Institut francais à Barcelona" in *L'Architecture d'Aujourd'hui* (Paris), October 1977.

An old and famous American architect said to another who was very much younger and was asking for his advice: "Open wide your eyes and look; it is much easier than you think." He also said to him: "Behind every building that you see there is a man that you don't see." A man, he said. He did not mention whether he was an architect or not.

No, I do not think that it is miracles or geniuses that we need at this time. I believe genius is an occurrence that is an Act of God, not a goal or an end. Nor do we need High Priests or dubious Prophets of Architecture or great doctrinaires. There is something of a living tradition that is still within our reach, and there are also many ancient moral doctrines concerning our trade or profession (and I use these terms in their best traditional sense) of architect. We need to take advantage of what little there is left of the constructive tradition and, above all, the moral tradition in this epoch when the most beautiful of our words have practically lost their real and true meaning.

The thousands and thousands of architects in the world should think less about Architecture (with a capital A), about money or about cities of the year 2000, and more about their trade as architects. Let them work tied by a leg so that they cannot stray too far from the earth in which they have their roots or from men they know best; let them always clutch a firm foundation based on dedication, good will and honour.

I am convinced that any present-day architect moderately endowed and developed or formed who is able to understand this, is easily capable of producing truly living work. This is, for me, the most important, more important than any consideration or end that only *apparently* takes precedence.

I believe that it is from works, possibly of the greatest diversity, carried out with a sound knowledge of the fundamentals and also great conscientiousness, without worrying about the final result (which, fortunately anyway, escapes us and is not an end but a consequence) that an authentic, live new tradition will be born.

To bring this about, I believe that we must first rid ourselves of many ideas which appear clear but are false, of many hollow words, and work, each and every one of us, with that good will that is translated into one's work and teaching rather than with a mere concentration on doctrinairism. I think that the best teaching is that which teaches our trade, teaches us to work with great faith, or, in short, that which teaches us to be architects, knowing, at the same time, as we must, that we can all makes mistakes. It is also the example of working, continuously watching in order not to confuse human frailty, the right to be mistaken (a cloak which if wrongly used can cover a multitude of sins), with inconstancy of will, immorality or the cold calculation of the climber or "getter-on."

I imagine society as a sort of pyramid, with, at the peak, the best and least numerous and at the wide base, the masses. There is an intermediate zone where may be found people of all sorts who are aware of some superior values and have decided to act accordingly. These people are aristocrats and on them everything depends. They enrich society upwards towards the peak with words and deeds, and downwards towards the base by example, as the masses are enriched only through respect and mimicry. Today this aristocracy hardly exists, swallowed by materialism, the philosophy of success, State technocracy and bureaucracy, incompatible with liberty and creative initiative, with what is holy.

My parents used to tell me that a gentleman, an aristocrat, is the person who finds himself unable to do certain things which even the law, the Church and the majority approve or permit. Each one of us, if we are aware, must try to form a new aristocracy. This is an urgent problem. We must begin soon, and then go on without losing heart. The main thing is to begin to work, and then, and only then, can we talk about it.

We must pit ourselves against money, against the vanity of success, against excess of property or earnings, against inconstancy or haste, and against the lack of spiritual life and conscience; we must put instead dedication, craftsmanship, good will, time, the bread we need for every day and, above all, love, which is acceptance and giving, not possession and domination—all these must be taken hold of and clung to, for these are the true values.

Seeing and knowing more or less profoundly the works or forms (the exterior signs of spiritual richness) of the great masters is considered to be culture or architectural formation. The same means of classification are applied to our craft or profession as are used (exterior signs of economic richness) in our materialistic society. And then we complain or lament because there are no great architects now, that the majority of architects are bad, that the new urbanization is anti-human almost without exception through the world, that our towns and villages are destroyed, and houses and towns are built like film

José A. Coderch: Trade Office Building, Barcelona, 1965

sets along the length of our beautiful Mediterranean coasts.

The value, merit and acclaim bestowed upon the great masters, who are not within our reach, contrast vividly with the silence, indifference or even ignorance concerning their moral values or their attitude to their work, which is, let it be clearly said, something we can aspire to. Is it not curious that people write and talk of their weakness and frailty as an attractive oddity or a tit-bit for gossip or just as being mistaken, and at the same time conceal as a forbidden subject or as an anecdote their attitude to life or to their work? Is it not also strange that we have here, very near to us, Gaudi (I myself have known people who worked with him), and so much is said

about his work and so little about his moral position and his dedication?

Almost the same thing happens with the great masters of our time; their works are admired, or rather the shapes of their works, and nothing else. There is no attempt to go deeper and discover what there is within, the most valuable, which is, after all, exactly that which is within our reach. Of course it is clear that this would mean accepting our own limitations, which is not possible when one wishes to be a Le Corbusier or make a great deal of money.

The real spiritual culture of our profession has always belonged to a few. The circumstances that enable nearly anyone to have the possibility of access to this culture is the heritage of nearly all, and is one

that is not generally taken. Neither, unfortunately, do we accept cultural behavior which should be obligatory and in the consciousness of us all.

In ancient times architects had a certain solid support. Many things existed that were accepted by the majority as good or, at any rate, inevitable, and the organization of society, as much in its social problems as in its economic, religious and political ideas, was stable or evolved slowly. On the other hand, there was greater faith, more dedication, less false pride and a living tradition on which to lean. With all their defects, the upper classes had a clear idea of their duty and seldom did they err in their choice of the best architect or artist, so spiritual culture was naturally propagated. The little cities grew like plants in different ways, but slowly, and gathering together the common life of the people. Seldom was there sloth, improvisation or irresponsibility. Works of all sorts were created which had a human value seldom found today. Sometimes, but not often, there were growth problems to overcome, but without that feeling, inevitable today, that the evolution of the cities is extremely rapid and, except in the short term, difficult to plan for.

Nowadays, the ruling classes have lost their sense of mission, and all, including the aristocracy of the blood, of money, of intelligence, of politics and the Church or Churches, with only a few and personal exceptions, serve to contribute decisively to the chaos of present-day architecture by their uselessness, their money-grabbing souls, their cowardice, their love of power and lack of any sort of consideration for their responsibilities.

On the other hand, the circumstances on which we have to base our work vary continually. There are religious, moral, social and economic problems; those of education, the family and energy sources, which can all play a part in changing, unsuspectingly, the face and structure of our society. Brutal changes whose meanings are lost to us are also possible, but their existence can impede honest long-range planning.

As I've said before, a live tradition is not clear to us, a tradition that to the majority of us is essential. That which has so far been done (a great deal in certain cases, of course) is not sufficient to light the necessary path the great majority of architects must follow. Lacking this live tradition, our solution is at best looked for in formalism, in the application of fashionable methodology or in routine and the topic of some of the great and old masters of modern architecture, forgetting their mistakes and leaving out their spirit, their circumstances and, above all, carefully hiding with magnificent words our great irresponsibility (which is often only lack of thought), our ambition and our inconstancy.

It is ingenious to think, as is thought, that the ideal and the practice of our profession may be condensed into slogans such as the sun, light, air, greenness, the social, the political and so many others. A formalistic base, dogmatic, above all if it is only partial, is in itself bad, save in exceptional and catastrophic circumstances. From all this I deduce that among the different paths that each thinking architect will choose to follow, there must be some common factor, something which must be in all of us, without forgetting history and its ancient wisdom.

Goethe, as an old man, said: "The true subject of world history and humanity, the only and most profound subject to which all the rest are subordinate, is the conflict between faith and incredulity. All the periods of history marked by faith, regardless of the form in which it appears, are brilliant, lift the soul and bear fruit in the present and in the future. On the other hand, all periods when incredulity, in whatever guise, has gained its sad victory, even when it happens to shine for a time with false brilliance, disappear from view for posterity, because there is nobody willing to take the trouble to know what has not borne fruit."

A sentence of Einstein's hung in our office for many years: "The most beautiful thing to be felt by man is the mysterious side of life. There is the cradle of Art and real Science."

Note: The text is practically the same as a letter I wrote to my good friend the architect Bakema, secretary of the Team 10, concerning my joining this team of architects in 1961, so that they should know my beliefs before admitting me. In this version I have made slight changes in order to make the text clearer.

—José A. Coderch

José A. Coderch's work has been a consistent stabilizing force in post-Civil War Catalan architecture. His extraordinarily sensitive designs spring from a profound love for the art and science of his profession and the reality of human nature. The cultural content of his work, though never absent, takes second place to the human problems involved. His buildings are always disarmingly pure, often reducing complex problems to incredible simplicity. There is always great care taken with the proportions of his buildings and their elements, not only with form but also with materials, allowing large expanses of blind walls to induce a constant note of tranquillity. This urge to simplicity is applied to every detail and joint in the building. His work is not just rooted in the observation of popular Mediterranean architecture but also in the great static spaces of the Catalan civic and religious medieval architectural tradition. It is this quality that makes his work transcend the purely local arena and makes it relevant to the wider sphere of the modern movement in architecture.

Although he is a recluse, Coderch's isolation is only apparent. His work responds not to the whims of fashion but to the strong cultural currents of a turbulent 20th century architecture. It is this that has made him a constantly young architect whose work, whatever year it was built, remains a fresh reminder that the craft of architecture still exists.

Because of the Civil War Coderch qualified late as an architect. He was 27 years old in 1940, and after a brief encounter with official work in Madrid, close to the mentality of dictatorship, he moved back to the Mediterranean as municipal architect to the seaside resort of Sitges. Here he made his first attempt at popular architecture—Las Forcas, a housing estate that was never built. It consisted of a series of aggregated volumes for each function, extended over the sites, forming outside courts that were designed as extensions of the living space. The style was clearly Ibizan, the same popular architecture from the island that had inspired the rationalist architects in the 1930's. Although official architecture, when not concerned with the imperial image of Escorial, was bent on the revival of rural architecture as the true "blood and earth" response to nationalism, Coderch's Mediterranean model was more cubic than stylistic. As an abstraction from this model, and as a rupture from the cultural vacuum of the dictatorship, Coderch took refuge in surrealism in his Ugalde House in Caldetas: orthogonal planning is destroyed; cubes explode into bent and curved forms to gather in the external views and immediate countryside. Although he was never to repeat this exercise—his feeling for reality was too strong—this flight beyond realism to destroy rigidly-contained spaces is present in all of his buildings. It is immediately apparent in the plan of his Pescadores Housing Block in Barceloneta, where the splayed walls increase the richness of the space by making it flow slightly beyond immediate comprehension, thus releasing the restrictive feeling of a tiny flat. These flats are contained within a double facade, which acts as a climatic filter, that is almost diagramatically simple, alternating splayed tiles and louvered vertical strips slightly cantilevered over the street from the first floor upwards. This concern to contain a complex plan within a simple envelope is another of Coderch's recurring themes.

For many years his work lay mostly in the design of private houses for which he evolved an almost standard single-storey, L-shaped plan with rows of parallel walls set back to contain balcony windows between them. This system of fenestration is another personal feature of Coderch's work. We find it in the Hotel de Mar in Majorca and in the Cocheras Flats in Sarria, Barcelona (though in the Cocheras he combines this composition with corner windows).

Two non-residential buildings of note—The Trade Office Building, Barcelona, obviously inspired by Mies van der Rohe's glass skyscraper project of 1921, and the French Institute, Barcelona—demonstrate Coderch's ability to sheathe his buildings with simple skins.

However, his design of urban spaces rests more on complexity rejecting the usual approach of an ordered street front. The jagged plan and broken facade of the Cocheras Flats, and his project for housing in Vittoria, may be ingenious in removing the obligatory enclosed light and ventiliation wells for deep plans, but the monotony of constant movement is a wearing experience, even when mitigated by an elegance in design details and careful paving and gardening around the base of the buildings. Is this perhaps Coderch's substitution of an urban city for a rural one?

What is certain is that the example of Coderch remains a living force not only in Catalan architecture but also in the modern movement as a whole.

—David Mackay

COLQUHOUN AND MILLER.

Partnership; established, London, 1961, by Alan Colquhoun and John Miller; additional partner, since 1975, R. J. Brearley. Exhibition: University of Architecture, Palermo, Italy, 1974. Recipient: South West Region Award, Royal Institute of British Architects, 1975. Address: 23 Neal Street, London WC2H 9PU, England.

Works:

1965 Forest Gate High School, West Ham, London

1969 Weinreb and Douwma Print Shop and Offices, 22 Bloomsbury Street, London
Hotel du Cap, Antibes, France (project)
Library, Eaton Square, London S.W.1 (project)
Derby Civic Centre (project)

1970 Chemistry Building, Royal Holloway College, Englefield Green, Surrey

1972 Canon Lee School, Clifton, North Yorkshire

1973 Holiday chalets, Aviemore, Scotland (project)

1974 Pillwood House, Feock, Cornwall
Melrose Avenue Activity Centre, Bletchley, Buckinghamshire

1975 Private house, Feock, Cornwall (project)
Colnaghi Gallery conversion, Bond Street, London W.1 (project)
U.K. Canning Plant for Coca Cola Export Corporation (project)

1977 Two Mile Ash (housing), Milton Keynes, Buckinghamshire (project)
2 community centres, Welbourne and Tenterden Road, Haringey, London
Milbank Housing, London (project)

1978 West Green Road Old People's Home, Haringey, London
Exhibition layout for *Dada and Surrealism Reviewed,* Hayward Gallery, London
Housing, Gaisford Street, Camden Town, London
Infill housing, Fenny Stratford, Buckinghamshire
Single person flats, Hornsey Lane, London N.6

1979 Whitechapel Art Gallery renovation and extension, London (project)
Royal Holloway College Theatre Workshop, Englefield Green, Surrey (project)
150 rental houses, Central Milton Keynes, Buckinghamshire (project)

Publications:

On COLQUHOUN/MILLER: book—*British Buildings 1960–1964* by Douglas Stephen, Kenneth Frampton and Michael Carapetian, London 1965; articles—in *Zodiac* (Milan), no. 18, 1965; *Casabella* (Milan), May 1976; *Architecture + Urbanism* (Tokyo), January 1978.

Colquhoun and Miller: Chemistry Building, Royal Holloway College, Englefield Green, Surrey, 1970

The architectural problem presents itself as the need to satisfy the demands of distribution, environment, site, construction, etc.

But the designer would be unable to decide on a distributive scheme unless he already had a certain ideal configuration in his mind. This is the constant against which possible solutions are measured.

The design process would seem to be more dialectical then deductive. It is similar to what in the context of painting Gombrich calls "making and matching."

Since one no longer designs according to a set of rules, as was the case with the Beaux-Arts, the guiding principles are eclectic. They are extracted from one's experience of existing architecture. The "programme" itself is formless. It does not suggest an architectural solution until it has been subjected to classification and has become generic rather than particular. The value of typology is that it shows the result of this classification. There are a limited number of possible architectural forms.

What Levi-Strauss says of structuralism applies to architecture; "A resolutely intellectual approach, a bias in favour of systematic arrangements, a mistrust of mechanistic and empirical solutions."

Our work, like that of many other architects, discloses the existence of a conflict between functionalism and older typologies.

The old avant-garde functionalism, which was associated with a unique vision of society, is no longer possible.

The symbolism of the plan as "a machine at rest" is constantly challenged by more static forms of order. (The dialectic was already present in the 1920's and 30's in the work of Le Corbusier.) But it is not possible simply to turn one's back on functionalism and try to outflank history by treating historical forms as belonging to a kind of specious present.

Functionalism intervenes between us and the past, and modifies anything we take from it.

—Colquhoun and Miller

Shying away from the architecture-of-leftovers which "participation" and the supposed de-mystification of the environment proposed by Krool, Alexander and others has inevitably led to, and similarly not impressed by the architecture-of-decomposition that litters the city, and certainly uninterested in architecture as a conflux of not too clear images based on very slender conceptions of democracy, Colquhoun and Miller hone in on a more classicizing skeleton of possibility: their work is a stereometric distribution of almost glacial tectonics, within which invitations, vistas, fissures and stops are framed and architecturalized.

Their aim, as Colquhoun puts it, is the fabrication of a universe, a non-dispersed, centralized Renaissance whole, with sufficient autonomy to be able to take on the kind of semantic role expected of a building by its context—but with sufficient gaps at its perimeter to meet the social expectations as well. This image is best exemplified in their Forest Gate High School, which features a porous threshold connecting with a more consolidated focus by means of "annular rings of innerness." The red brick finish typifies their earlier primitivism with regard to materials (earth-affirming echoes of Louis Kahn) and was employed in the struggle against dispersion.

Colquhoun and Miller are not afraid of the "institution"; neither are they afraid of giving it expression through their work. The Chemistry Building of Royal Holloway College is a good example of their cool, unflinching, institutional-typology: each of their projects involves a similar act of assembling elements most typical of the programme in hand. The civic face of the building, fronting a communications spine, has all the symmetrical sense of purpose and frontality of Isozaki's museum at Gumma; but from behind it turns into a more dynamic projectile that could for all the world be the Katsura Palace refurbished by Craig Ellwood—it bolts down the sloping section at a superb A-B-A rhythm, and would break away completely, making for the surrounding parkland, if it weren't for the facade tethering it to its location.

The Chemistry Building impresses us with its turns and ways: we feel intuitively that the architects responsible must have entered into a pact with the sublime; one feels sure that "what they know is worth knowing." This contrasts with the vicarious dignity of so many buildings that are merely the product of the bickerings and jealousies of the ethics of commerce. Colquhoun and Miller prefer to construct an architecture that waits for the time when it will come into its own, rather than accept an architecture that assumes any guise the marketplace might demand—Palladian one moment, Venturian the next, its thousand masks as unpredictable as the thousand eyes of a primitive deity, with vague historical epochs coming forward in turn, as though auditioning. In place of this kind of transient Rent-a-Style plurality, which at worst can be a blundering disruption of the events and sequences that existence insists on, Colquhoun and Miller prefer a more unwavering and penetrating solution.

—Chris Fawcett

COLVIN, Brenda.

British. Born in Simla, India, 8 June 1897. Educated in Paris; studied at the Swanley Horticultural College, c.1920; privately with Madeline Agar. Worked as site assistant for Madeline Agar on War Memorial Garden, Wimbledon, 1921–22. In private practice, as landscape architect, England, 1922–69. Since 1969, Senior Partner, with Hal Moggridge, Colvin and Moggridge, landscape consultants, Filkins, Gloucestershire. Landscape Consultant to the East Kilbride Development Corporation, 1950. Lecturer, Department of Architecture, Regent Street Polytechnic, London, 1937, and Architectural Association School, London, 1937. Founder-Member, 1929, Honorary Secretary, 1941–48, Vice-President, 1949–50, President, 1951–53, and since 1968 Trustee, Institute of Landscape Architects, London. Founder Member, International Federation of Landscape Architects. Exhibition: Gardens Section, *Royal Horticultural Society Show,* London, 1928. C.B.E. (Commander, Order of the British Empire), 1973. Address: Colvin and Moggridge, Filkins, near Lechlade, Gloucestershire GL7 3JQ, England.

Works (landscape architecture):

1935 West Stowell House, near Marlborough, Wiltshire
1937 Chateau Zywiec, Poland

1948   Sutton Courtenay Manor Gardens, Oxford-
        shire
        Garden for the Port of London Authority,
        Tower Hill, London
1953   Compton Beauchamp Estate, Oxfordshire
1956   Salisbury Crematorium, Wiltshire
1958   Shotton Steelworks, Cheshire
1959   Queen Elizabeth Gardens, Wiltshire
        Drakelow Power Station, Burton-on-Trent,
        Staffordshire (grounds layout)
1961   Eggborough Power Station, Yorkshire
        Halls of Residence, Queen's University of
        Belfast
1962   Rugeley Power Station, Staffordshire
        (grounds layout; with Rendel, Palmer and
        Tritton)
        Trimpley Reservoir, Worcestershire (with
        Binne and Partners)
1962   Ash Disposal Scheme, Gale Common, Egg-
        borough, Yorkshire
1971   Lower Farm, Coombe, Berkshire

Numerous private and public gardens and parks

Publications:

By COLVIN: books—*Trees for Town and Country*, with Jacqueline Tyrwhitt, London 1947, 3rd edition 1972; *Land and Landscape*, London 1947, 1970; articles—"Planting Design" in *Landscape Design* (London), March 1951; "Presidential Address" in *Landscape Design* (London), November 1951; "Garden Architecture" in *Country Life* (London), September 1952; "Planting as a Medium of Design" in *Landscape Design* (London), August 1961; "Landscape Maintenance of Large Industrial Sites" in *Landscape Design* (London), November 1968; "Of Time and Trees: What the Eye Will See, the Imagination Foresees" in *Landscape Design* (London), February 1974; "Power Station, Didcot, Berkshire" and "Potash Mine, Boulby, Yorkshire" in *Architectural Review* (London), August 1974; "Beginnings" in *Landscape Design* (London) February 1979.

On COLVIN: articles—"Gale Common, Eggborough, Yorkshire" in *Landscape Design* (London), November 1968; "Ideas into Landscape" by David Streatfield in *Landscape Architecture* (Louisville, Kentucky), January 1972.

I have had some part in the development of the profession of landscape architecture and am a founder member of the Institute of Landscape Architects and of the International Federation of Landscape Architects. I think the profession has an important role in the future. Its value will gain increasing recognition if it continues to be non-political and if it emphasizes that in landscape design it is essentially a problem of long-term issues rather than immediate short-term policy. Landscape design differs from architectural design in fundamental aspects of both time and space.

Most landscape design projects take far longer to mature than those of architecture, and they are far more vulnerable to short-term destruction or inadvertent neglect. The time required for the successful establishment of major landscapes is related to, and must influence, the initial design from the outset of operations. Long-term management in harmony with the intention of the design is essential if the intention is to reach maturity; flexibility and the possibility of change must be built into the design.

Spacially, landscape covers larger areas than architecture. Agriculture, forestry, reservoirs and other land uses form an important element of many major landscape projects. In many cases architectural features may be absent or of secondary importance, although where they are, in themselves, of importance, man-made artifacts form the focus of attention.

The basis of landscape design is biological rather than geometrical: the laws of nature remain dominant over human fashion and convention.

—Brenda Colvin

One of the pioneers of modern landscape design, Brenda Colvin has throughout her life been dedicated to her profession and has become highly respected both for her work and her writings. Perhaps, above all, her place in history is assured for her unstinted efforts to help create an independent landscape profession in a country previously dominated by gifted laymen. A founder member of the Institute of Landscape Architects, later President and now Trustee, she has encouraged younger members in every way open to an established practitioner. Before schools of landscape design were created, Miss Colvin's office was one of the few that were in a position to take in students. Later, when students were leaving school and seeking practical experience, her office was foremost in taking on the idealistic but immature assistant. There are many practitioners today who remember their office experience with her with affection and gratitude.

Like others of her generation, Brenda Colvin had no formal education in landscape architecture, for there was none to have. She emerged from horticulture, virtually teaching herself the elements of design. Prior to World War II the employment of landscape designers, slight as it was, was confined almost entirely to private gardens. With an immense experience of such works behind her, Miss Colvin played an invaluable part when the clientele changed from private to public. Her experience, technical skill, good judgment and increasing wisdom made her advice acceptable to committees who chiefly relied on the reputation of the professional involved. Although her work for the War Office at Aldershot was probably her largest contract, the most spectacular

Brenda Colvin: Trimpley Reservoir, Worcestershire. 1962

was the proposal for disposing of fly-ash from the Central Electricity Generating Board's power station at Gale Common, Eggborough, Yorkshire. Here she proposed a new undulating agricultural countryside made out of waste, presenting her scheme in the manner of Humphry Repton's Red Books, with photo-montage of "before" and "after."

Although Brenda Colvin early published an invaluable technical guide to forest trees, gave many lectures and contributed countless articles to the landscape press, her literary claim to fame rests on one work, *Land and Landscape*, Known and read throughout the English speaking world, respected in Europe and translated into Japanese, it has become a standard work on good landscape practice.

Still in practice in a charming house in the Cotswold village of Filkins, with a younger partner, Hal Moggridge, Miss Colvin recently circulated privately a beautifully printed *credo* of a philosophy that ranges from the small plant to the mysteries of the universe.

—Geoffrey Jellicoe

Amyas Connell: "New Farm," Grayswood, Surrey, 1933

CONNELL, Amyas (Douglas).

New Zealander. Born in Eltham, New Zealand, 23 June 1901; emigrated to England, 1924. Educated at the Stratford High School, New Zealand, 1912–16, and studied painting with his father; articled to the architect Stanley Fearn, Wellington, 1919–24; studied at the Bartlett School of Architecture, University of London, 1924–26, Dip.Arch. 1926; British School, Rome, 1926–29 (Rome Scholarship). Served in the British Army as a Garrison Engineer, Royal Engineers, Aldershot, Hampshire, 1939–43, and as Architect to the Ministry of Works, London, 1943–45. Married Maud Hargroves in 1930; Margret Stroud in 1957; children: James, Graham, Diane, and Katharine. In private practice, London, 1929–31; in partnership with Basil R. Ward, London, 1932–33; Partner, with Ward and Colin Lucas, *q.v.*, Connell, Ward and Lucas, London, 1933–39; in private practice, Tanganyika and Kenya, 1947–77. Founder Director, TRIAD Architects and Engineers, Nairobi, Kenya, 1967; Consultant to TRIAD Architects and Planners, London, since 1975. Founder Member, MARS (Modern Architecture Research) Group, London, 1931. Served as President, Kenya Institute of Architects, Nairobi. Exhibitions: *Contemporary Industrial Design in the Home*, Dorland Hall, London, 1934; Exhibition of Drawings of Blocks of Working Class Flats in Reinforced Concrete, Imperial Institute, London, 1935; *Contemporary Industrial Design*, London, 1935; Museum of Modern Art, New York, 1939. Recipient: Bronze Medal, Royal Institute of British Architects, 1960. Fellow, Royal Institute of British Architects, 1964. Address: TRIAD Architects and Planners, 9 Tufton Street, London S.W.1, England.

Works:

1928 "High and Over" (Professor Bernard Ashmole House), Amersham, Buckinghamshire
1929 "Noah's House," Bourne End, Buckinghamshire (destroyed)
Trent Park garden design
Lyme Park garden design
1932/
33 "New Farm" (Sir Arthur Lowes Dickenson House), Grayswood, Surrey (with Basil Ward)
1933 "The Hop Field" (house), St. Marys Platt, Wrotham, Kent (with Basil Ward and Colin Lucas)
1934 "The Saltings" (Dr. R. D. Lawrence House), Sinah Lane, Hayling Island, Hampshire (restored, 1977)

3 houses, Wiclands Avenue, Saltdean, Sussex (destroyed)
4 houses, High and Over Estate, Amersham, Buckinghamshire (with Basil Ward and Colin Lucas)
1935 Kent House Flats, Ferdinand Street, Chalk Farm, London (with Basil Ward and Colin Lucas)
2 pairs of semi-detached houses, Parkwood Estate, Ruislip, Middlesex (with Basil Ward and Colin Lucas)
"The Firs" (house), Brighton Road, Redhill, Surrey (with Basil Ward and Colin Lucas)
Hertford County Buildings (competition project; with Basil Ward and Colin Lucas)
1936 Individual Health Centre (project)
"Dragons" (house), Woodmancote, Sussex (with Basil Ward and Colin Lucas)
"Concrete House" (Ronald Gunn House), The Ridgeway, Westbury-on-Trym, Bristol (with Basil Ward and Colin Lucas)
Civic Buildings, Newport, Monmouthshire (competition project; with Basil Ward and Colin Lucas)
1937 House, Wentworth, Virginia Water, Surrey (with Basil Ward and Colin Lucas)
Geoffrey Walford House, 66 Frognal, Hampstead, London (with Basil Ward and Colin Lucas)
House, Worcester Park, Surrey (with Basil Ward and Colin Lucas)
Sound City Film Studios, Shepperton, Middlesex (with Basil Ward and Colin Lucas)
1937/
38 Tarburn House, 6 Temple Gardens, Moor Park, Hertfordshire (with Basil Ward and Colin Lucas)
1938 "Potcraft" (Dr. Thomas House), Sutton, Surrey (with Basil Ward and Colin Lucas)
1938/
39 Major Proudman House, 26 Bessborough Gardens, Roehampton, London (with Basil Ward and Colin Lucas)
1939 Lords Court (apartment building and shops), 32 St. John's Wood Road, London (partially built with Basil Ward and Colin Lucas)
Edith Edwards Preventorium, Papworth Village Settlement, Cambridgeshire (project)

1941 Cathedral, Auckland (competition project)
1948 Executive Houses, Tanga, Tanganyika
Cinema, Tanga, Tanganyika
Dalgety Office Building, with shops, Tanga, Tanganyika
Tzambourakis Office Building, Tanga, Tanganyika
1949 Village development (with mosque, hospital, market, and church), Kangi, Tanganyika
1955 Kenya Legislative Council Building, Nairobi (with H. Thornley Dyer)
1959 Aga Khan Platinum Jubilee Hospital, Nairobi
Out-Patients Clinic, King George VI Hospital, Nairobi
1960 Crown Law Offices, Nairobi
1963 Parliament Buildings, Nairobi

Publications:

By CONNELL: articles—"For and Against Modern Architecture," with Sir Reginald Blomfield, in *The Listener* (London), 28 November 1934; "Heroes of the Modern Movement: Amyas Connell Talks about the Problems of Modern Architects in the 30's," interview with Walter Menzies, in *Building Design* (London), 27 February 1976; "Basil Ward 1902–1976" in *RIBA Journal* (London), October 1976.

On CONNELL: articles—"Auckland Cathedral" in *The Architects' Journal* (London), 27 February 1941; "Parliament Buildings for the Government of Kenya at Nairobi" in *The Architects' Journal* (London), 13 January 1955; "Connell, Ward and Lucas 1927–1939," special issue of *Architectural Association Journal* (London), November 1956; "Connell, Ward and Lucas" by Peter Smithson in *Architectural Association Journal* (London), December 1956; "Aga Khan Platinum Jubilee Hospital, Nairobi" in *Architect and Building News* (London), 18 February 1959; "Side View of 66 Frognal" and "Block of Flats, Ferdinand Street, Designed in 1936 by Connell, Ward and Lucas" in *Design* (London), December 1974; "Connell, Ward and Lucas" in *RIBA Journal* (London), March 1976; "Architect's Approach to Architecture: Connell, Ward and Lucas" in *The Architects' Journal* (London), 10 March 1976; "Mending the Modern Movement: Restoration of

The Saltings, Hayling Island" in *The Architects'*
Journal (London), 30 March 1977.

From inception to completion, each building for
which I, as the architect, have been responsible
been the best that I could do. I have looked on each
project as a projection of my past experience, and, on
completion, it becomes the prime subject for exercising my critical faculty.

I have travelled widely and have learned that the
understanding of the timeless quality of a great work
of art begins with the analytical study of social history related to the aesthetic expression of its creator,
and grows with the realization that those moments
of delight and joy felt when one is in the presence of
a great work of art are indelibly implanted in one's
memory. Consciously or unconsciously they become
part of one's aesthetic expression.

So, a target is set for achievement, and the core of
my critical faculty was established.

—Amyas Connell

English architecture had its heroic period in the
1930's, and the most memorable buildings of that
period were private houses. The finest of the private
houses were designed by the firm of Connell, Ward
and Lucas. The star of Connell, Ward and Lucas was
Amyas Connell.

New Zealand, the Bartlett School of Architecture,
and the British School in Rome does not sound like
the background for a major innovatory architect.
Nor does the ex-director of the British School in
Rome sound like the sort of client who would commission an architect who had not built anything to
design his house. Yet that is what happened. "High
and Over" at Amersham, built in 1928 for Professor
Bernard Ashmole, is the most inventive English
house of the 1920's. It stands on a bluff, commanding
a view over a beautiful valley. The plan, a three-
pointed star, has a sense of classical ordering that
might be expected with both architect and client
fresh from the British School in Rome. But the concrete is frankly a reinforced concrete frame, with a
formal language taken from a villa that André Lurcat had just completed overlooking the Parc Montsouris in Paris. The result was both inventive and
spectacular, and the widespread publicity was
enough to make modern architecture a "cause."

In "New Farm" at Grayswood, Surrey, Connell
finally abandoned the classical approach to planning.
the house is expressed as a series of cubes fanning out
from the circulation area. He turned to Le Corbusier's Maison Domino for the structural parti,
with the columns placed internally and continuous
strip windows used to demonstrate that the walls
contained no structure. In his "Concrete House" at
Bristol, Connell reversed the idea and pulled the
columns outside the skin, as in Le Corbusier's Villa
at Carthage.

Connell formed a partnership with Basil Ward in
1932 and Colin Lucas joined them in 1933 to form
Connell, Ward and Lucas, a team that continued
throughout the 1930's to build houses of increasing
clarity and formal confidence, culminating in the
magnificent Tarburn House at Moor Park and Walford House in Frognal, Hampstead. Increasing clarity and formal confidence yes, because the partners
obviously worked well together, but the work is
maybe duller than Connell's early houses--as if
group discussion had killed off the more outlandish
formal inventiveness of the Grayswood and Amersham houses.

Connell, Ward and Lucas gave credit to the individual partner responsible for each of their houses,
and it cannot be said that those attributed to Connell
are amongst the firm's best works; however, they
were a team, and Connell remained the spokesman
for the practice.

After the war Connell developed a practice in East
Africa, and he built on a far larger scale than his
pre-war English houses. The work, however, did not
again reach such high standards of quality.

—John Winter

COOK, Peter (Frederic Chester).
British. Born in Southend, Essex, 22 October 1936.
Educated at Stoneygate School, Leicester, Ipswich
School, Suffolk, and Bournemouth School, Hampshire, until 1953; Bournemouth College of Art De-
partment of Architecture, under Ronald Sims, 1953–
58; Architectural Association School, London,
under James Gowan, John Killick and Peter Smith-
son, 1958–60, Dip.A.A. 1960. Married the painter
Hazel Fennell in 1960. Architectural Assistant,
Jackson and Greenen, Bournemouth, 1956–58, and
James Cubitt and Partners, London, 1960–62; Founder Member, with Ron Herron, Dennis Crompton,
Warren Chalk, Mike Webb and David Greene, Archigram Group, London, 1960, and Co-Editor of
Archigram magazine, 1961–70; Assistant Architect,
Taylor Woodrow Design Group, London, under
Theo Crosby, 1962–64; Partner, with Ron Herron
and Dennis Crompton, Archigram Architects, Lon-
don, 1969–75; Director, Institute of Contemporary
Arts, London, 1973–74. Director, Art Net, London,
since 1974 (Editor of *Net* magazine, 1974–78); Part-
ner, with Christine Hawley, Cook-Hawley Ar-
chitects, London, since 1978. Assistant 5th Year
Master, 1964–66, 5th Year Master, 1966–70, Head
of the Diploma School, 1970–72, and since 1973
Unit Master, Architectural Association School,
London. Visiting Critic, University of California at
Los Angeles, 1968–69; Visiting Fellow, Institute of
Architecture and Urban Studies, New York, 1975;
Visiting Critic, Rhode Island School of Design,
Providence, 1976; Visiting Professor, School of Ar-
chitecture, University of Strasbourg, 1978. Exhibi-
tions: *Living City,* Institute of Contemporary Arts,
London, 1963; *New Designers,* Woollands, London,
1965; *Summer Show,* Royal Academy, London,
1965, 1976, 1977; *Biennale,* Paris, 1967; *Triennale,*
Milan, 1968; *Expo '70,* Osaka, Japan, 1970; *Monte
Carlo Casinos,* Victoria and Albert Museum, London, 1972–73, toured Europe; *Archigram,* Institute
of Contemporary Arts, London, 1973; *New Work:
Peter Cook,* London, 1976; *40 London Architects,*
Art Net Gallery, London, 1977, toured Europe; *Ron
Herron and Peter Cook,* London, and New York,
1978. Recipient: First Prize, Gas Council Old People's Housing Competition, London, 1962; First
Prize, Monte Carlo Entertainment Centre Competition, 1970; Graham Foundation Award, Chicago,
1970; Japan Foundation Award, Tokyo, 1977. Associate of the Royal Institute of British Architects,
1968; Fellow, Royal Society of Arts, London, 1974.
Address: Cook-Hawley Architects, 12 Ladbroke
Square, London W.11, England.

Works:

1956 Furniture for Kinson Congregational
       Church, Bournemouth
1956/
58   Detailing for various buildings, Bournemouth
1960/
62   Detailing for various buildings, London
1962 Euston Station Detail Plans, London (pro-
       ject)
       Berkshire County Offices, Reading (project;
       with David Greene)
1963 Design of the *Living City* exhibition, Institute
       of Contemporary Arts, London (with oth-
       ers)
       Shopping Centre, Nottingham (project; with
       David Greene)
1964 Fulham Housing Study, London
       Plug-in City (project)
1965 Plug-in University (project)
1965/
66   Plug and Clip Room, Woollands, London
1966 Plug and Clip Housing (project)
1967 Control and Choice House, *Biennale,* Paris
       (exhibition project; with Dennis Cromp-
       ton and Ron Herron)
       Plug-in City (project model)
1968/
69   Electric Car for Plug-in Projects (project;
       with Hornsey College of Art students,
       London)
1969 Monte Carlo Entertainments Centre (project;
       with C. Fournier)
1969/
70   Archigram Capsule, *Expo '70,* Osaka, Japan
       (with Archigram Group)
       Instant City (project; with Ron Herron and
       Dennis Crompton)

Peter Cook: "Arcadia." 1977

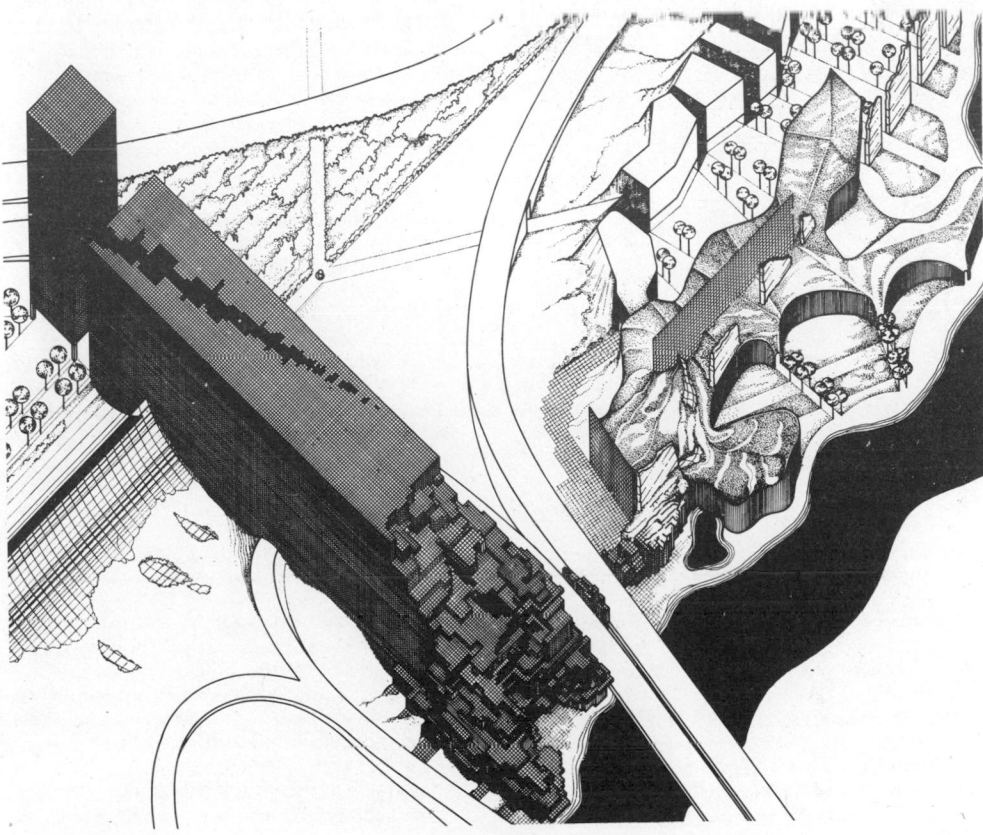

1970 Bournemouth "Steps" (project; with Archigram Group)
1971 Cheek-by-Jowl (project)
"Addhox" Urban Housing (project)
Foulness Airport City alternatives, Essex (project)
1971/
73 Development plans for the Monte Carlo Entertainments Centre
1972 "Urban Mark" (project)
Hedgerow Village (project)
Monte Carlo Casino (competition project; with B. Tschumi and D. Jowsey)
1973 "Lump" (project)
1974 "Prepared Landscape" (project)
Riverside Housing (competition project; with D. Jowsey)
1975 "Sponge" (project)
Roosevelt Island Housing, New York (project; with others)
1976 Shinkenchiku House (House on the Via Appia) (competition project; with Christine Hawley)
1976/
77 Trondheim Library, Norway (competition project; with Christine Hawley)
1977/
78 "Arcadia" Housing and Town Plan (project)
1978 "Mesh" Projects (with Christine Hawley)
Antique Exchange, London (project; with Christine Hawley)

Publications:

By COOK: books—*Fulham Study* (report), London 1964; *Architecture: Action and Plan,* London and New York 1967; *Experimental Architecture,* London and New York 1970; *Archigram,* London and New York 1974; *Melting Architecture,* exhibition catalogue, London 1976; *The Arcadian City* (pamphlet), London 1978; articles—"Living City" in *Living Arts* (London), 1963; "Plug-in City" in *The Sunday Times* (London), October 1964; "Instant City" in *Architectural Design* (London), November 1970; article in *The Japan Architect* (Tokyo), December 1976/January 1977; "Unbuilt England," editor and contributor, special issue of *Architecture + Urbanism* (Tokyo), September 1977; article in *The Japan Architect* (Tokyo), December 1977/January 1978.

On COOK: articles—"Archigram" by Claude Parent in *L'Architecture d'Aujourd'hui* (Paris), 1965; "Monte Carlo" by Reyner Banham in *The Architects' Journal* (London), 1970; "The Work of Archigram" in *Russian Architect* (Leningrad), 1972; "A Green-Obsessed Architect" by Arata Isozaki in *Space Design* (Tokyo), 1977; "Arcadias" by F. Bernard in *L'Architecture d'Aujourd'hui* (Paris), 1977; article by Deyan Sudjic in *The Architects' Journal* (London), 12 July 1978.

I was a founder member of the "Archigram Group." I am the author of many projects that have been published all over the world. I am also a teacher, and I lecture all over the world. My projects are much discussed by *other architects.* But I consider myself a designer rather than a theoretician.

My work in the mid 1960's was inspired by the possibilities of technology: by the possibility that architecture could break out of its narrow-mindedness if it acquired elements (a vocabulary of form) from outside itself.

Towards the end of the 1960's I began to break down the notions of "definite subject:" a moving and robot-like architecture that conceptually dismembered "the city," "the university," "the house," etc. As well as physically dismembering it, Plug-in City was a "throw-away" city—with expendable parts. The Control-and-Choice House was a home like a robot—made up of apparatus that could flex and respond to the individual members of the family.

Towards the early 1970's the notion of "metamorphosis"—implicit in the earlier work—could be explored more as a romantic and simbiotic study, so that the "urban mark" could take a prognosis of urban form: from the earlier, more rigid, more "architectural" state to the final state whereby the landscape had taken over. (The straight-forward functional demands of the Monte Carlo Building were meanwhile developing one's physical design abilities.)

During the 1970's the idea of incorporating natural, and quasi-natural, elements has re-asserted one's basic desire to break architecture out of its narrow limits, particularly those of its formal vocabulary, so the "Lump" and "Sponge" projects suggest an architecture where high technology and nature are mixed together, the overall form being often "melted" together, rather than formally composed.

In the most recent work, the combination of "sleek" or highly-tailored architectural elements with free-form and vegetal architecture has composed itself around a "back-front" format (as in the Roosevelt Island Housing and some of the "Arcadia" housing). Or in a smooth exterior containing a disintegrative or "Gothic" internal architecture (as in the Trondheim Library). This is allied to a developing interest in the idea of a matrix (or grid) as the point of departure: overlaid and "eaten into" so that the final building is a dismembering or "melting" of the matrix. The Shinkenchiku House of 1976, designed with my partner, Christine Hawley (who has even more extreme abilities with "melting" aesthetic), is the prototype project for most of the recent output.

—Peter Cook

Speaking of England, in an article in the Japanese magazine *A + U,* Peter Cook says "in the country at large, architecture is discussed in pragmatic terms. Style is mistrusted, unless it is in the traditional style of the area. Innovation occurs more frequently in plan or in section, the dimensions that cannot be understood by a layman." It is an interesting observation, and it is probably true. In matters of building, art is best kept as a secret activity that does not obtrude on the simple and dominant processes of reasoning and selection.

In the late 1950's Peter Cook came to the Architectural Association from Bournemouth to complete his studies, and, happily, an aspect of that south-coast background remains uppermost in his thoughts. Holidays, when the whole family relaxes and behaves less formally and predictably; the pier and its fun and amusements; childish foods, ice-cream, candy floss, and lemonade. Several of his early projects—or I should say Archigram's, because much of his work has been done with that group—harness this mood and its licence too. Fairs, circuses, arriving by air and bombarding the sleepy inhabitants with noise and excitement. Like that of the clowns in a Continental movie who embarrass staid folk with their antics and advances, this is a most theatrical view of what life might be. It is also a very abrasive artistic gesture—small wonder that this vision of play and pleasure has been met with reserve and even the antagonism of main-stream architects. In another context, Peter Cook gives one a clue to his stance when he says, "Pragmatism can only be fought (and fortified) by bouts of loony optimism. Dreams and fancies undermine the Puritan instincts and rekindle the Romantic." Perhaps it would not be unfair to remind him of "invention can be piled upon invention until the resultant beast resembles a monster."

Speaking of English design he says, directly and not without justification, that it "comes from the strongest area of English art, the compositions and observations of rural painters such as Constable, the suggestiveness of the watercolour tradition, and from the gardeners of the 18th century who combine an instinct for the picturesque with the reality of diminutive undulation that is the raw material of the English countryside. All of this is soft, Romantic, episodic." It is clear that he does not rate trivial and small-scale incident too highly. Elsewhere he says of English conversation that it is "discussive rather than polemical; mood is a substitute for form."

From this particular selection of quotations it would seem that Peter Cook's work is addressed critically to two streams of traditional architectural thought, the formal and the picturesque, and (at the risk of oversimplification) the former is represented as dull and the latter petty. Necessarily, he engages these established cultures with grand Utopian gestures, and, much in the spirit of the 19th century French visionaries, his canvases are large and their ramifications panoramic. His is a formidable commitment, but he brings into this field of the imagination a skill and attack that are a match for it.

—James Gowan

CORREA, Charles M(ark).

Indian. Born in Hyderabad, 1 September 1930. Educated at St. Xavier's College, Bombay, 1946–48; University of Michigan, Ann Arbor, under Buckminster Fuller and Walter Sanders, 1949–53, B.Arch. 1953; Massachusetts Institute of Technology, Cambridge, under Buckminster Fuller and Lawrence Anderson, 1953–55, M.Arch. 1955. Married Monika Sequeira Kamat in 1961; children: Nondita and Nakul. Worked in the office of architect Minoru Yamasaki, Detroit, 1953; Partner, firm of G. M. Bhuta and Associates, Bombay, 1956–58. In private practice, Bombay, since 1958. Chief Architect, City and Industrial Development Corporation, Government of Mamarastra, 1971–74. Albert Bemis Professor, M.I.T., 1962; Visiting Critic, Harvard University, Cambridge, Massachusetts, 1963, 1974; lectured at Indian Institute of Technology, Kharagpur and the University of Roorkee, 1964, University of Baroda, 1966, 1969, University of Ahmedabad, 1967, Industrial Design Centre, Institute of Technology, Bombay, 1970, University of Delhi, 1971, University of Queensland, Brisbane, 1973, and Cambridge University, 1973; Bannister Fletcher Professor, University College London, 1974; lectured at the Architectural Association, London, 1974, Yale University, New Haven, Connecticut, 1974, University of Pennsylvania, Philadelphia, 1974, and University of Bombay, 1976. Member of the Council, Indian Institute of Architects, since 1972; Member of the Western Board, Reserve Bank of India, since 1973; Consultant Architect, Government of Karnataka, Bangalore, since 1974; Member, Bangalore Development Authority, since 1976; Member, Steering Committee, Aga Khan Architecture Awards, Paris, since 1977. Exhibition: *Contemporary Architecture in India,* Boston and United States tour, 1975. Recipient: First Prize, Gujarat Low-Cost Housing Competition, 1962; Padma Shri Award, Government of India, 1972; *Time* magazine New Leadership nomination, 1974. Fellow of the Indian Institute of Architects, 1964. Address: Office of C. M. Correa, 9 Mathew Road, Bombay 400 004, India.

Works:

1958 Handloom Pavilion, *Industrial Fair,* Delhi
1959 Vallabh Vidyanagar University new campus buildings, Gujerat, India
Merchant Houses, Bhavnagar, India
Lalbhai House, Ahmedabad, India
Sen House, Calcutta
1960 Gun House Office Building, Ahmedabad, India
Plutonium plant, Bombay
Cricket Stadium and Sports Complex, Ahmedabad, India
1961 Suhrid-Geigy Laboratory and Workshop, Bombay

Lever Pavilion, *All-India Fair,* Delhi
Workshop and bus terminals for Ahmedabad Municipal Transport Service
Low-cost housing, Ahmedabad, India
1962 Futehally House, Bandra, Bombay
Asansol Polytechnic College, India
Ramkrishna House, Ahmedabad, India
1963 Mahatma Gandhi Memorial Museum, Ahmedabad, India
Sonmarg Apartments, Bombay
1964 Catering Institute, Bombay
Chemicoat Factory, Baroda, India
1965 Kasturba Memorial, Poona, India
Dutta House, Delhi
1966 Rajendranagar Office Centre for the Delhi Development Authority
Electronics Corporation of India Office Building, Hyderabad, India
Mascarenhas House, Bangalore, India
1967 Ushanagar Housing Estate, Bombay
Menezes House, Poona, India
Fereira House, Bombay
1968 Cablenagar Township, Kota, India
1969 Gandhi Darshan Museum, Delhi
Union Carbide Factory, Hyderabad, India
Parikh House, Ahmedabad, India
Heredia House, Bombay
Patwardhan Houses, Poona, India
1970 Previ low-income housing for the United Nations and Government of Peru, Lima
Jeevan Bima Nagar Township, Bombay
Kovalam Beach Development, Trivandrum, India
Union Carbide Factory, Bombay (with Dasturco)
Mazumdar House, Delhi
1971 Jeevam Bima Nagar Township, Bangalore, India
1971/
74 Plan for New Bombay
1972 Group housing, Ahmedabad, India
Kanchanjunga Apartments, Bombay
1974 Salvacao Church, Bombay
1975 Tara Group Housing, Delhi (with Mahendra Raj and J. Sawhney)
1976 Kala Art Centre, Goa, India

1977 Crafts Museum, Delhi
Bharat Bhavan Museum, Bhopal, India
1978 New India Centre, Bangalore, India
Visvesvaraya Centre, Bangalore, India

Publications:

By CORREA: articles—"Fatehpur Sikri" in *Architectural Forum* (New York), November 1963; "Corbusier in Chandigarh" in *Architectural Review* (London), June 1964; "Our Cities" in *Seminar* (Delhi), March 1965; "Planning for "Bombay" in *Marg* (Bombay), June 1965; "Architecture and Climate" in *Architectural Design* (London), March 1970; "On Urban Planning" in *Science Today* (Bombay), May 1971; "India Today: Programmes and Priorities" in *Architectural Review* (London), December 1971; "Self-Help City: The Internal Organisation" in *United Nations Bulletin* (Stockholm), August 1973; "Mass Transport" in *Seminar* (Delhi), November 1973; "La Citta che si fa da se" in *Lotus* (Milan), September 1974; "Urban Pollution" in *Times of India Annual,* Bombay 1974; "Space as a Resource" in *Ekistics* (Athens), January 1976; "India: The Urban Scene" in *The Guardian* (London), November 1977; "Functional and Spatial Planning in Low-Cost Housing" in *International Journal for Housing Science* (Oxford), December 1977; "Housing for All" and "Towards the New Landscape" in *Urbanisation: 2001,* Paris 1977.

On CORREA: books—*New Buildings in the Commonwealth,* edited by J. M. Richards, London 1961; *World Architecture 3,* edited by John Donat, London 1965; *Architecture in Dry, Hot Climates* by Balwant Saini, Melbourne 1973; articles—in *Architectural Review* (London), July 1960, December 1971; *Architectural Design* (London), April 1960; *Architectural Forum* (New York), September 1962; *Marg* (Bombay), December 1963; *L'Architecture d'Aujourd'hui* (Paris), September 1969; *Daily Telegraph Magazine* (London), 28 September 1973; *Architecture Plus* (New York), March/April 1974; *Design and Environment* (New York), Spring 1976; *Arts et Techniques* (Paris), December 1976.

To build in India is to respond to climate. We simply can't afford to squander the kind of money—and energy—required to put up a glass tower in a tropical climate (or in most other climates, for that matter). And this, of course, is an advantage, for it means that the architecture itself must create the "controls" which the user needs. Such a response necessitates much more than just sun angles and louvres; it needs must involve the section, the plan, the shape, and the heart of the building.

Because of this, a country like India is really a pleasure for an architect to work in. It is one of the few occasions left when the two (contradictory) compulsions that precipitated modern architecture can be synthesised: namely, on the one hand the credo that function, however broadly defined, is the progenitor of form; on the other, the equally compulsive fascination that architects have always felt for new and exotic form. Thus, too often, an office building in New York is made interesting, as Mies pointed out, only at the expense of being good. But here in India one is dealing with a unique set of social and economic conditions, climate, living habits, materials, and so forth. In other words, the kind of occasion which—without contortion, without exaggeration—must sooner or later surely precipitate new forms, new patterns, new techniques—in short: a new landscape.

—Charles M. Correa

Like most of his contemporaries, Charles Correa is one of the post World War II generation of Indian architects who acquired their professional training in the West and who returned to their homeland to revive the profession of architecture which lay dormant during the 150 years of colonial rule. After years of absence abroad, these architects have shown little sensitivity to local conditions, and many, to this day, continue to inappropriately transplant European forms of building in what is essentially a tropical Indian setting. Charles Correa is an exception. His record to date clearly indicates that he realized the folly of this approach and set about systematically familiarizing himself with the local environment and developing solutions that show sensitivity to and awareness of the local culture.

Charles M. Correa: Mahatma Gandhi Memorial Museum, Ahmedabad, India, 1963

To achieve this, he did not look to ancient monuments of the past; rather, he sought inspiration from the humble peasant buildings of the land. Some of Correa's best work, such as the Ghandi Memorial Museum in Ahmedabad, is low cost, utterly simple in concept, and utilizes materials and techniques widely employed in the villages of Goa on the west coast of India where his roots lie. He has used white washed stucco walls and red clay tiled roofs, which remind one of the thousands of villages scattered throughout the Southern Indian landscape that blend happily with their environment.

Correa's early work mostly involved architecture in a limited sense, the design of individual buildings, ranging from housing to buildings for tourism, education, commerce, and industry. These projects still continue to form an important part of his work. In fact, his output has expanded both in range and complexity ever since he established his multi-disciplinary professional practice.

During the past decade Correa has also increasingly concerned himself with the plight of homeless people who are the victims of urbanization in the Third World countries. His theories and solutions to these urgent problems are pragmatic and are based on his own work as planner of New Bombay, a settlement of 2 million people across the harbour from the existing city. These solutions have attracted worldwide attention because they get to the source of the problem and have relevance to similar situations faced by governments in many developing regions of Africa, Asia and Latin America.

Correa suggests that in order to build reasonable living environments for the maximum number of people, governments should not concentrate on building houses but should leave this to the resources of the people themselves. In proposing this solution Correa is, of course, fully aware that self-help housing has been most successful in rural areas where people have access to building materials and sufficient spare time on their hands to construct their own shelter. It is much more difficult to accomplish this task in urban areas, and here lies the challenge for planners and architects to use their expertise and innovative abilities to generate low-cost building activity.

This is a refreshing view, particularly since it emanates from a representative of a profession that has always been preoccupied with building forms. He believes the main effort of housing authorities should be directed to the provision of infrastructure of basic services, that the problem is not one of low-cost housing but of proper land use planning. Correa's major contribution in this area lies in developing planning proposals that can lend themselves to high densities in order to reduce development costs of land, yet ensure adequate community facilities.

Charles Correa has already proved himself as a thinker and pace-setter in pointing the way in which architects may possibly contribute to solve the enormous problems of urban environmental crises, particularly in the Third World.

—B. S. Saini

CORRIGAN, Peter.

Australian. Born in Daylesford, Victoria, 6 May 1941. Educated at the University of Melbourne, 1959–65, B.Arch. 1966; Yale University, New Haven, Connecticut, 1967–69, M.Environmental Design 1969. Design Draftsman, Godfrey and Spowers Pty. Ltd., Melbourne, 1964, and Best Overend Pty. Ltd., Melbourne, 1965–66; Draftsman, Mockridge, Stahle and Mitchell, Melbourne, 1966; Draftsman/Theatrical Engineer, George Izenour and Associates, New Haven, 1967; Senior Urban Planner, New Haven Redevelopment Agency, 1967–68; worked in the Design Department of Roche Dinkerloo and Associates, Hamden, Connecticut, 1969; De-

sign Architect for Paul Rudolph, New York, 1971; worked in the Design Group, Gruen Associates, New York, 1973–74; Design Architect, Johnson and Burgee, New York, 1974. Since 1975, Partner, with Maggie Edmond, Edmond and Corrigan, Architects and Planners, Melbourne. Tutor, Yale University, 1968–69; Guest Critic, City University of New York, 1971–73; Guest Lecturer in Stage Design, University of Melbourne, 1976. Lecturer in Design Theory and Design Studio, Royal Melbourne Institute of Technology, since 1973. Member, Australian Performing Group, Melbourne, since 1974. Member, Education Services Board, Royal Australian Institute of Architects, Victoria Chapter, since 1976. Address: Edmond and Corrigan, 40 Little Latrobe Street, Melbourne, Victoria 3000, Australia.

Works:

1965 Mercovich House, Burwood, Victoria
     McCarthy House, Lillydale, Victoria
1966 Schmidt House, Eltham, Victoria
     Hosking House, Donvale, Victoria
1974 Resurrection Parish Centre, Keysborough, Victoria
     St. Colman's Church, Mortlake, Victoria
1975 Resurrection Church, Keysborough, Victoria
     Resurrection School, stage I, Keysborough, Victoria
     Amenities Block, Nagambie, Victoria
     City Square, Melbourne (competition project)
     Freedom Club Kindergarten, Keysborough, Victoria
1976 St. Joseph's Chapel, Surrey Hills, Victoria
     Resurrection School, stage II, Keysborough, Victoria
1977 Wonthaggi Arts Activity Centre, Wonthaggi, Victoria
     Housing for the elderly, Keysborough, Victoria
     Sister Nance's Studio, Keysborough, Victoria
     Union Theatre renovations, University of Melbourne
1978 Westcott House, Burwood, Victoria
     Last Laugh Restaurant, Collingwood, Victoria
     Barber House, Carlton, Victoria
     Industrial park and high-rise development, for McIvor Village, Footscray, Victoria
1979 Performing Arts Centre, Sale, Victoria
     National Archives, Canberra (competition project)

Theatre: sets and costumes for 14 student productions, University of Melbourne, 1963–66; sets and costumes for *Don Giovanni*, Sydney Opera House, 1974; stage designs since 1974—7 Australian Performing Group productions, Pram Factory, Carlton, Victoria; 1 Melbourne Theatre Company production, St. Martin's Theatre, Melbourne; 6 Last Laugh Theatre Restaurant productions, Collingwood, Victoria; 2 Adelaide Arts Centre productions; 2 Grant Street Theatre productions, Melbourne; 1 Victorian Opera Company touring production (children's opera); 1 Australian Performing Group touring production, Bergamo, Italy; 2 Night Shift Company busking productions, Melbourne; 9 Hoopla Theatre Company productions, Playbox Theatre, Melbourne, and Nimrod Theatre, Sydney.

Publications:

By CORRIGAN: articles—"Featurism and Our Spire" in *Farrago* (Melbourne), 5 May 1961; "Smudges" in *Melbourne University Architecture School Broadsheet*, November 1961; "Stage Space" in *Theatre* (Melbourne), July 1962; "Church Architecture" (lecture), published by the Newman Society, Melbourne University 1964; "2 Houses at Burwood and Croydon" in *Cross-Section* (Melbourne), February 1967; "Life in the Plug-In Age" in the

Herald (Melbourne), 3 April 1967; "Reflections on a New North American Architecture—The Venturi's" in *Architecture in Australia* (Sydney), February 1972; "Inside the Third Reich" in *Architecture in Australia* (Sydney), December 1972; "On Non-Architecture" in *Architecture in Australia* (Sydney), December 1973; "Education, Hobart" in *Architecture in Australia* (Sydney), February 1974; "Workbook of an Unsuccessful Architect" in *Architecture in Australia* (Sydney), June 1974; "Architecture's Changing Role" in *The Age* (Melbourne), 14 October 1974; "Bronze Medal and Brute Steel" in *Meanjin Quarterly* (Melbourne), no. 1, 1976; "Molnar House, Glen Waverley" in *Architect* (Melbourne), September 1976; "Passion in the Suburbs" in *Architecture in Australia* (Sydney), February/March 1977; "Church News" in *Architect* (Melbourne), May 1977; "Carlton Designs" in *Theatre Australia* (Newcastle, New South Wales), August 1977.

On CORRIGAN: articles—"Civic Square Competition" in *Architecture in Australia* (Sydney), September 1976; "Exorcism of the Modernist Spirit" by Norman Day in *The Age* (Melbourne), 23 May 1978; "The Australian Eleven" by Philip Drew in *Architecture + Urbanism* (Tokyo), August 1978; "Suburban Manifesto" by Cathy Peake in *The National Times* (Sydney), 10 February 1979.

This office's search for form is conducted as a search for both content and value for money. It is intended as a fruitful interplay between the traditions of architecture and the social philosophies of our time. Mind you, there is now an emerging Australian urban culture, and it would be a serious blue to miss the tram.

—Peter Corrigan

Peter Corrigan studied architecture at the University of Melbourne, then completed a post-graduate degree in Environmental Design at Yale and worked for five years in the United States. As a student, and since graduation, Corrigan has been active as a designer of sets and costumes for numerous theatrical productions, most of which have had to be carried out with little money. This experience of "poor theatre" in Off-Broadway companies and Melbourne (1974–) has exerted a strong influence on his ideas concerning architecture. Much as in the theatre, Corrigan improvises his architecture; he uses cheap ordinary materials in a decorative, entertaining manner.

In the direct intervention of the architect in the building process, in the decorative use of brickwork, and in the exploitation of local building motifs, Peter Corrigan's architecture closely resembles that of the Amsterdam Expressionist Michel de Klerk. The inspiration for the decorative ideas in Corrigan's buildings is the common and ugly buildings of the new suburbs—he prefers to describe his architecture as "poor architecture." The form and structure of these buildings, as opposed to the imagery, is far from unsophisticated, having benefited from Corrigan's studies with Venturi.

Corrigan's development over a period of four years, in creating a unique style based on local suburban motifs, is an impressive achievement. It has not been easy, and some of Corrigan's buildings, such as the Parish Centre, Keysborough, and St. Joseph's Chapel, Surrey Hills, testify to the struggle, while others, notably the Resurrection School, Keysborough, are far more successful in relating all the individual themes in a coherent whole.

Corrigan's architecture is rich and complex, so it is not easy to come to a concise assessment of its full import. His buildings ignore the taboo against decoration and introduce a rich decoration of patterned brickwork. They are open and inclusive, rather than closed and exclusive. And instead of seeking to correct and improve on Australian visual traditions as Robin Boyd wanted to, Peter Corrigan exploits these traditions in much the same fashion as, in another genre, Barry Humphries does, by employing them

Peter Corrigan: Resurrection Church, Keysborough, Victoria, 1974

within a strong artistic framework. Corrigan's architecture will not satisfy those who demand an architecture of equilibrium, poise and harmony. His architecture, after all, is true to life.

—Philip Drew

COSTA, Lúcio.

Brazilian. Born in Toulon, France, of Brazilian parents, 27 February 1902. Educated at the Royal Grammar School, Newcastle, England, 1911–13; Collège National de Montreux, Switzerland, 1914–16; National School of Fine Arts, Rio de Janeiro, 1917–22, Dip.Arch. 1924. Served in the Brazilian Army, 1920. Married Julieta Guimaraes in 1928 (died, 1954); children: Maria Elisa and Helena. In private practice, Rio de Janeiro, since 1924 (collaborated with Gregori Warchavchik, 1931–33). Director, National School of Fine Arts, Rio de Janeiro, 1930–31. Since 1937, Consultant Architect, IPHAN: Instituto do Patrimonio Historico e Artistico Nacional, Rio de Janeiro. D.F.A.: Harvard University, Cambridge, Massachusetts, 1960. Honorary Member, Royal Institute of British Architects, American Institute of Architects, and the Académie d'Architecture, France. Commandeur, Légion d'Honneur, France. Address: Avenida Delfim Moreira 1212, Leblon, Rio de Janeiro, Brazil.

Works:

1932 Alfredo Schwartz House, Rio de Janeiro (with Gregori Warchavchik)
San Miguel Church restoration, Rio Grande Do Sul, Brazil
1937/
43 Ministry of Education and Health, Rio de Janeiro (with Le Corbusier, Oscar Niemeyer, Affonso Eduardo Reidy, Jorge Machado Moreira; now the Palace of Culture)
1939 Brazilian Pavilion, *World's Fair,* New York (with Oscar Niemeyer)
1942 Hungria Machado House, Rio de Janeiro
1943 Saavedra House, Correias, Brazil
1944 Park Hotel, Friburgo, Brazil
1948/
54 Guinle Park Apartments, Rio de Janeiro
1957- Master plan for Brasilia
1969 Master plan for Baixada de Jacarepagua, Rio de Janeiro

Publications:

By COSTA: books—*Arquitectura Carioca,* Rio de Janeiro 1952; *The Architect and Contemporary Society,* Venice 1952; *About My Work in Brazil,* Rio de Janeiro 1958; *Scientific and Technological Humanism,* Cambridge, Massachusetts 1961; articles—"A Necessary Documentation" in *Revista do Servico do Patrimonio Historico Artistico* (Rio de Janeiro), no. 1, 1938; "Portuguese-Brazilian Furniture" in *Revista do Servico do Patrimonio Historico Artistico* (Rio de Janeiro), no. 3, 1940; "Jesuit Architecture in Brazil" in *Revista do Servico do Patrimonio Historico* (Rio de Janeiro), no. 5, 1941; "L'Urbaniste Défend sa Capitale" in *Architecture: Formes et Fonctions* (Lausanne), no. 14, 1968; "Manifestation Normale de Vie" in *Architecture: Formes et Fonctions* (Lausanne), no. 15, 1969.

On COSTA: books—*Modern Architecture in Brazil* by Henrique Mindlin, Rio de Janeiro and Amsterdam, 1956; *Lúcio Costa* by J. O. Gazenco and M. M. Scarone, Buenos Aires 1959; *Doorway to Brasilia* by A. Magalhaes and E. Feldman, Philadelphia 1959; article—"Individualidades na historia da atual arquitectura no Brasil" by G. Ferraz in *Habitat* (Sao Paulo), October 1956.

Scientific and technological development is not opposite to nature but the secret side of nature itself—with its virtual potentialities disclosed through man's intellect, that is, through nature again in its state of lucidity and consciousness. Man is, therefore, nature's *lucid* link between two abysses, the microcosm and the macrocosm, both *natural* phenomena whose "elaborated" products are the counterpart of "raw" natural phenomenon.

So we have, on one side, nature at the *reach of our senses, of our hands,* and on the other, nature at the reach of our *intellect and technology.*

Man's intellect and consciousness are the *quintessence of nature as a whole.* Everything is, for that reason, tightened together—immanently or transcendentally—and scientific and technological de-

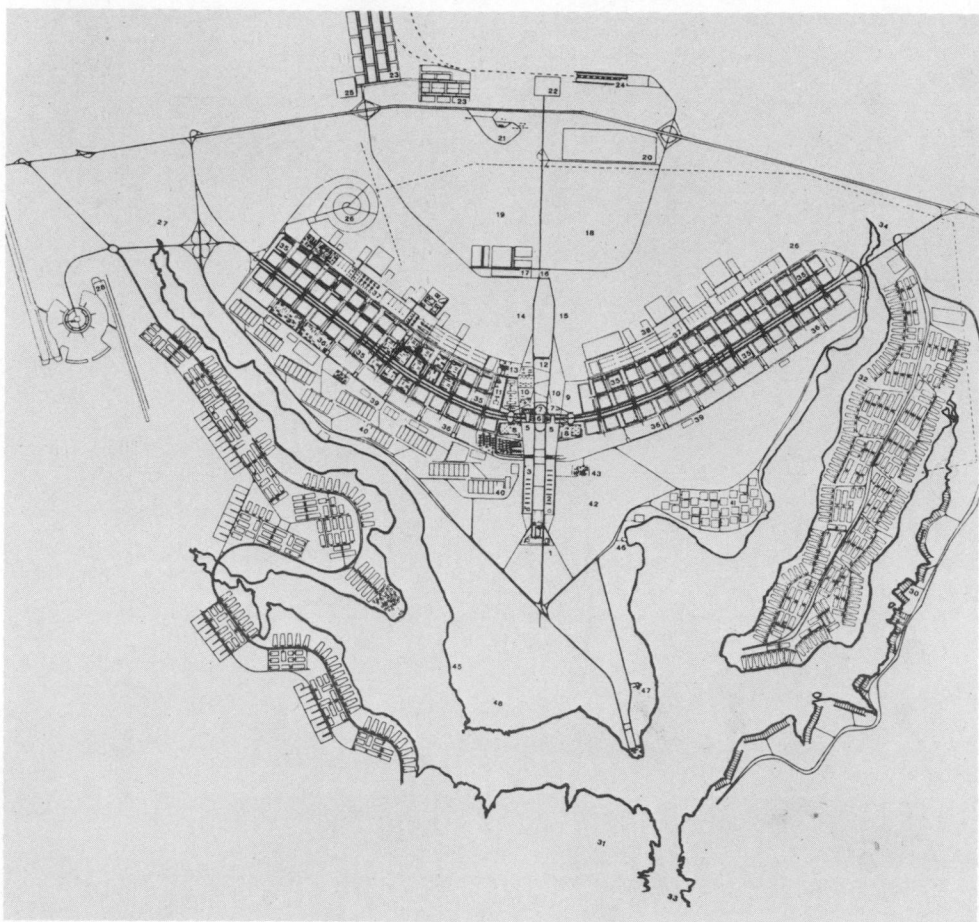

Lúcio Costa: Master Plan for Brasilia, 1957–

velopment, when free to pursue its own penchant in view of a normal conclusion, cannot be against man, because man is a key part in this process into which life's drama is inserted.

Of course continuous interventions of all sorts of interests—economic, commercial, political, ideological—act to deviate scientific and technological development from its normal course. But one cannot maintain indefinitely such deviations; one will be forced back as if attracted by an "imponderable" gravitational force and will gradually tend to lose such centrifugal impulses and to adapt to a sort of resultant consensus in obedience to intrinsic scientific and technological command.

If one tries to stop midway, confused by so many contradictions produced by the deviations from rational and technological normalcy, the result is *chaos.* That is precisely where world affairs, and the world itself, now stand.

But one should not despair, because it is exactly when perplexity attains its climax that new perspectives suddenly open through the intricate and apparently illogical pattern of events, and everything seems again clear and easy.

—Lúcio Costa

Lúcio Costa established himself as a leader of the avant-garde in Brazil after the revolution in 1930. He worked in partnership with Gregori Warchavchik who had brought new Cubist ideas from Europe to developing Brazil. Costa himself was appointed Director of the School of Fine Arts in Rio de Janeiro (which embraced architectural studies), and so was able to influence subsequent generations of architects in the ideals of the modern movement.

One of the most significant of his buildings was the Ministry of Education and Health in Rio de Janeiro, 1937–43, for which Le Corbusier acted as consultant. This huge slab building was erected to the designs of a team led by Costa which included Niemeyer. The *brise-soleil* and the *pilotis,* trademarks of Le Corbusier, were ideal for the Brazilian

climate, and the architecture was enthusiastically hailed by Brazilians. Costa's next building was the Brazilian Pavilion for the New York *World's Fair* of 1939, again designed in collaboration with Oscar Niemeyer.

Costa has always been devoted to the study and conservation of historic buildings in Brazil; as well, he has been a perceptive discoverer of architectural and innovatory talent. His early championing of Niemeyer ensured the rise of that architect to the singular position he later held for many years.

Following the Second World War, Costa designed the Guinle Park Apartments in Rio de Janeiro. His most famous work, however, is his design for the new capital of Brasilia. The master plan has a shape rather like a crossbow that recalls the geometrical simplicity of Renaissance and classical town plans. Significantly, Costa's extremely pellucid plan serves as a framework for the great number of buildings erected to designs by Oscar Niemeyer.

—James Stevens Curl

COTTIER, Keith E(ric).

Australian. Born in Sydney, New South Wales, 27 May 1938. Educated at the Sydney Technical College, 1954–60 (Board of Architects Travelling Scholarship, 1960). Married Elizabeth Wickham Barrett in 1962; children: Sarah, Benjamin, and Hugo. Travelled in Europe for two years, and worked with Ian Fraser and Associates, London, for two years, 1960–64; returned to Australia to work with John Allen and Russell C. Jack, 1964. Since 1965, Partner, Allen, Jack and Cottier, architects, Paddington, Sydney. Recipient: Blacket Award, 1967, 1970, and New South Wales Merit Award, 1971, 1976, Royal Australian Institute of Architects; ACI-St. Regis Travelling Scholarship, 1972. Fellow of the Royal Australian Institute of Architects, 1975. Address: Allen, Jack and Cottier, 6a Liverpool Street, Paddington, New South Wales 2021, Australia.

Works (with Allen, Jack and Cottier):

1965 House, 99 Riverview Road, Clareville, Sydney
1967 Clubbe Hall, Frensham School, Mittagong, New South Wales
1969 Bryant House school dormitory, Frensham School, Mittagong, New South Wales
1970 Library, Frensham School, Mittagong, New South Wales
   Rothbury Winery, stage I, Pokolbin, New South Wales
1971 Kuringai College of Advanced Education, Lindfield, New South Wales (with the New South Wales Department of Public Works)
1972 Rothbury Winery, stage II, Pokolbin, New South Wales
1974 Swimming Pool Complex, Mount Druitt, New South Wales
1975 Seymour Centre for the Performing Arts, University of Sydney

Publications:

On COTTIER: books—*Architecture in Australia* by J. M. Freeland, Melbourne 1968; *Towards an Australian Architecture* by Harry Sowden, Sydney 1968.

Much of my work has been concerned with relatively low cost buildings, often using quite traditional materials and construction techniques. The architecture is seen as a direct response to the demands of both the existing environment or "place" and the functional needs of the users. The resultant character of the built forms may therefore differ considerably from one project to another, "appropriateness" to the particular problem being the guiding principle. Whilst the functional needs are becoming increasingly complex and technical, underlying all my work is an attempt to maintain human scale, and to produce a relaxed, easily-understood organization of spaces.

—Keith E. Cottier

Keith Cottier's work could be classified as within the style of what has come to be known as the Sydney School, an idiom of brick and timber construction, appropriate as being within the capacity of available expertise of the traditional Australian builder (applied as it was to mainly domestic work) but using a new approach towards traditional materials. Cottier's approach to design is, in his own words, pragmatic. His initial concentration is on planning, the relationship of building to environment, the sequence of internal spaces, and, finally, the influence of the subsequent forms on the three-dimensional qualities of the design.

One of his earlier works is a house in the beach suburb of Clareville. It is set on a steep site, amongst trees, overlooking the water. It is of timber construction, with the frame pulled out from the wall surface, creating what is almost a cage of timber members to relate to the surrounding trees.

His work at Frensham School, Mittagong, includes the multi-purpose Clubbe Hall, Bryant House dormitory, and a Library. The Hall, in addition to its school function, provides a well-used and much-needed venue in a country town for visiting musical and dramatic groups. Cottier's realization of the importance of spaces external to a building is shown in his design of the Library: by careful siting of the Library, he turned existing spaces into protected external courtyards that have proved to be a major social congregation point for the school.

In 1970 he completed stage I of the Rothbury

Keith E. Cottier: Rothbury Winery, Pokolbin, New South Wales, 1972

Winery (stage II was completed in 1972), which he feels to be his most satisfying project. It provides accommodation not only for wine making and storage but in addition for a large banqueting hall used for promotion. This was an ambitious building programme for a new winery, and in part the programme was responsible for creating "image." The clients were a group of wine makers and connoisseurs whose tastes are somewhat romantic: that attitude influenced the establishment of atmosphere. The building's form, enclosing as it does the paraphernalia of wine making, needed to be a blend of factory and traditional Australian country style. Cottier was influenced by the classic Australian woolshed, with its strong timber detailing and simple forms, and the site provided few constraints.

The Seymour Centre for the Performing Arts at the University of Sydney best exemplifies Cottier's concentration on external spaces between buildings, the need to have good working spaces internally, and the growth of forms from these work points. The site is surrounded by a multiplicity of buildings and interspersed by services that constrained the physical limits of planning. Three theatres provide venues for drama, chamber music and experimental theatre. The complex thus provides for a wide variety of users, a necessity that influenced him in his selection of materials, both simple and sophisticated. There was no client in the form of a resident company, and Cottier was required to make many of the decisions that normally would have been made by such a client. His over-riding determination was to provide workable, flexible theatres.

Cottier regards the psychological analysis of the client's needs, immediate and future, as a paramount influence. He sees every job as an individual problem in which there is always a need to recognize, isolate and solve the problem at the core of the situation. When it has been grasped, all other decisions—in planning, massing and detailing—will fall within the pattern prescribed. Each building needs to work but on many different levels, and the greatest test is whether it stands the test of time.

—Diane Kell

COX, Philip (Sutton).

Australian. Born in Sydney, New South Wales, 10 September 1939. Educated at the Church of England Grammar School, Sydney, 1949–55; University of Sydney, 1956–62, 1969–71 (Royal Australian Institute of Architects Silver Medal, 1962), B.Arch. (honours) 1962, and Diploma in Town and Country Planning 1971. Married Louise Gowing in 1973; daughter: Charlotte. Worked with Bruce Rickard, Sydney, 1962–63, and Ian McKay, Sydney, 1963–66. Since 1967, Principal, Philip Cox and Partners, Sydney (practice divided into three separate parts, 1974: Philip Cox and Partners, architectural services; Cox, Tanner, architectural conservation and publishing; Cox and Corkill, environmental planning). Tutor, University of Sydney, 1963–70, and University of New South Wales, Sydney, 1971–73. Chairman, Historic Buildings Committee, Royal Australian Institute of Architects, 1971–76; Member, Historic Buildings Committee, National Trust, New South Wales, 1971–78. Exhibition: *Sydney Young Contemporaries,* Blaxland Galleries, Sydney, 1966. Recipient: Silver Medal, 1963, and Merit Award, 1973, 1976 (twice), 1977 (twice), and Urban and Community Design Award, 1977, Royal Australian Institute of Architects; Sir John Sulman Medal, with Ian McKay, 1964, 1966; Wilkinson Award, 1970; ACI-St. Regis Travelling Scholarship and Institute of Valuers Prize, University of Sydney, 1971; Gray and Mulroney Award, with Louise Gowing, 1975. Address: Philip Cox and Partners, 2 McManus Street, McMahon's Point, New South Wales 2060, Australia.

Works:

1964 St. Andrews Presbyterian Preparatory College, Leppington, New South Wales (with Ian McKay)
1966 C. B. Alexander Presbyterian Agricultural College, stage I, Paterson, New South Wales (with Ian McKay)
Yarrawarra Boys Home, Kurri Kurri, New South Wales (with Ian McKay)
1968 Ferguson House, Palm Beach, New South Wales
1969 Hawkins House, Cheltenham, New South Wales
1971 Hotel, Minto, New South Wales
1971/
 81 Norfolk Island restoration, Kingston, Norfolk Island
1972 Hotel, Leppington, New South Wales
1974 Union Building, stages II and III, Macquarie University, Sydney
1975 Non-Collegiate Student Housing, Macquarie University, Sydney
Special Education Centre, Macquarie University, Sydney
Denham Court restoration, Ingleburn, New South Wales
Admiralty House restoration, Kirribilli, New South Wales
Housing development, McMahon's Point, Sydney (with Louise Gowing)
Doctor's house, Kellyville, New South Wales

1976 C. B. Alexander Presbyterian Agricultural College, stage II, Paterson, New South Wales

Burrundulla Homestead restoration, Mudgee, New South Wales

Report on official residences' grounds, Sydney and Canberra, A.C.T.

1977 Dalwood House restaurant conversion, Branxton, Hunter Valley, New South Wales

National Sports Stadium, Bruce, Canberra, A.C.T.

Kambah Health Centre, Canberra, A.C.T.

Conservation study: Braidwood, New South Wales

1978 Reid Medium Density Housing, Canberra, A.C.T.

Akuna Bay Marina, Coal and Candle Creek, New South Wales

Family Court and Australian Capital Territory Juvenile Court, Canberra, A.C.T.

Woolloomooloo Housing Development, Woolloomooloo, New South Wales

1980 Hawkesbury Agricultural College, Richmond, New South Wales

Mudgee Shire Council Chambers, Mudgee, New South Wales

Villawood Housing Commission Development, Villawood, New South Wales

Publications:

By COX: books—*Rude Timber Buildings in Australia,* with J. M. Freeland and Wesley Stacey, London 1969; *Building Norfolk Island,* with Wesley Stacey, Melbourne 1970; *The Australian Homestead,* with Wesley Stacey, Melbourne 1972; *Historic Towns of Australia,* with Wesley Stacey, Melbourne 1973; *Restoring Old Australian Houses and Buildings,* with Howard Tanner, Melbourne 1975; *Colonial Architecture of Australia,* with Clive Lucas and Wesley Stacey, Melbourne 1978; *South Coast of New South Wales,* Melbourne 1978; articles—"Housing over the Past Ten Years" in *Architecture in Australia* (Sydney), October 1973; "Belltrees, Scone, N.S.W." in *Architecture in Australia* (Sydney), 1976.

On COX: books—*Towards an Australian Architecture* by Harry Sowden, Sydney 1968; *Architecture in Australia* by J. M. Freeland, Melbourne 1968; *Australian Housing in the Seventies* by Howard Tanner, Sydney 1976; articles—"'Tocal': C. B. Alexander Presbyterian Agricultural College in *Architecture in Australia* (Sydney), September 1966; "Special Education Centre, Macquarie University" and "Doctor's House, Kellyville" in *Architecture Australia* (Sydney), October/November 1976; "Special Education Centre, Macquarie University, Ryde, N.S.W." in *Builder NSW* (Sydney), March 1977; "Architecture as Spatial Enclosures" by Neville Couten in *Architecture Australia* (Sydney), April/May 1977; "House, Castle Hill, N.S.W." and "National Athletics Stadium, Bruce, A.C.T." in *Architecture Australia* (Sydney), January 1978; "National Athletics Stadium" in *Architecture + Urbanism* (Tokyo), September 1978.

*

The work undertaken has been directed towards an Australian architecture which satisfies the peculiar geographical situation of this country. It is aimed at solving problems within a human-scale framework with direct structural expression. The architecture produced generally is limited in material vocabulary. In the early years of practice, brick, glass, timber and tile were used exclusively. This has now developed to concrete, steel and glass in recent larger structures. However, the same desire to express the structure in its purest sense, where the observer can sense the forces of the structure and its function, has still persisted. A great love for the landscape has generated buildings integrally. Houses take the landscape form, horizontally or inclined, depending on slope; stadiums are moulded out of the ground and are very much part of a wider landscape. Most importantly, the architecture is influenced by the vernacular tradition of Australian architecture, particularly in smaller-scale buildings—traditional roof forms, verandahs and horizontality. These are adapted and revised in such a way as to produce new shapes which relate to 20th century problems. Housing has recently been the main subject of study, particularly low cost housing, where social problems coupled with economic restrictions have produced a wide range of solutions.

—Philip Cox

Philip Cox was born into a family whose pioneer ancestors had created an architectural legacy in their homesteads and construction feats. This background, and a natural skill at drawing, doubtless influenced his choice of profession. During his formative years an initial interest in architectural history was broadened by employment with Bruce Rickard and travels in New Guinea. Rickard had studied landscape architecture with McHarg in Pennsylvania and had experienced Frank Lloyd Wright's architecture first-hand, and was endeavouring to integrate these influences with a human-scaled archi-

Philip Cox: National Sports Stadium, Bruce, Canberra, A.C.T., 1977

tecture appropriate to the Sydney region. New Guinea revealed the rich variety of vernacular architecture and provided an abiding interest in abstract and primitive forms of art.

At 23 Philip Cox was presented with his first major design commission by the Presbyterian Church. A bequest of one C. B. Alexander, grazier of "Tocal," Paterson, New South Wales, sought to establish a private agricultural college whose architecture would reflect the traditions and materials embodied in "Tocal" homestead. The scope of the project was beyond the capabilities of a recent graduate, and so Cox began an association with Ian McKay, an older architect with a range of practical experience and a similar design direction. For a "test run" the Presbyterian Church commissioned the new practice to undertake St. Andrews Preparatory College, centred around an old verandahed farmhouse at Leppington to the south west of Sydney. New pitch-roofed and verandahed buildings formed courtyard spaces and extended the vernacular tradition of the homestead group. During this time the scheme for Tocal developed—a great range of buildings set on a hilltop in countryside of extraordinary beauty. The spired chapel was the central pivot, with planes of roof defining the other functions. Timber, brick and tile, of local origin, combined in massive walls, trusses and roofscapes to make an impressive organic composition.

The association with McKay produced as well a range of sensitively detailed brick and timber houses, forming a significant "slice" of the "Sydney School" of domestic architecture of the 1960's—informal houses of rustic materials nestled in bushland settings.

Philip Cox set up practice on his own in 1967 and commenced an involvement in architectural education and publishing; his interest in architectural history provided the basis for several books. One outgrowth of these books was an involvement in the area of architectural restoration—for example, the military buildings at Kingston, Norfolk Island. During this period his commissions were generally domestic, and Cox experimented with massed form in the landscape, notably roofs, chimney stacks and angled glazing, with internal spaces about fireplaces and solid blocks extending out onto terraces and into the landscape. Two houses—Ferguson at Palm Beach, N.S.W., and Hawkins at Cheltenham, N.S.W.—best show this trend.

In hotels at Leppington and Minto, N.S.W., and a doctor's residence at Kellyville, N.S.W., he further explored these themes, linking them to the Australian vernacular tradition examined in his books on historic homesteads and towns.

In 1975, in his Special Education Centre for Macquarie University, there was evidence that Cox was revising his philosophy towards built form: the spine brick walls follow a series of horizontal steps, and the general roof and fenestration lines are horizontal. Garden walls and pergolas extend these lines out into the landscape. And recently his work has changed direction from the exploration and development of vernacular prototypes to a much more controlled and individual expression of form and space. The change is shown in several large-scale commissions from the National Capital Development Commission:

The Reid Housing Scheme introduces medium-density, low-rise housing into central Canberra, thus reversing its Los Angeles sprawl pattern. In character this scheme is derivative of the Special Education Centre, though on a minimal budget. The horizontal, stepped brickwork theme has been further pursued in the Family Law Courts Building, here combined with an unusual translucent ribbed roofing system, to provide a gentle quality of light to all major interiors. Each courtroom overlooks a leafy courtyard, and the building is linked to the Griffin ceremonial axis—city to university—by a carefully modelled pedestrian precinct. The largest work undertaken to date in Canberra is the National Sports Stadium, completed for the Pacific Conference Games in 1977.

Built to a six million dollar budget, the site has been carefully remodelled to provide graded surrounds to the arenas and to emphasize the natural forest landscape towards Black Mountain. The cable-suspended roof structure provides a distinctive focus for the site.

These recent works hold out enormous promise for future projects. It would appear that Philip Cox has a new-found affinity in architecture quite different from that of his work in the 1960's. The historic overtone has vanished.

—Howard Tanner

COX, Warren J(acob).

American. Born in New York City, 28 August 1935. Educated at the Hill School, Pottstown, Pennsylvania, graduated 1953; Yale University, New Haven, Connecticut, 1953–57 (History of Art Prize), B.A. (magna cum laude) 1957, and Yale University School of Architecture, 1957–61 (Editor of *Perspecta: The Yale Architectural Journal*, 1961; American Institute of Architects Prize, 1961), M.Arch. 1961. Married Susan Elizabeth Shifley in 1966 (divorced, 1974); married Claire A. Christie-Miller in 1975. Worked in the BBPR Studio, Milan, summers 1954, 1958; Technology Editor, *Architectural Forum*, New York, 1961–62; Designer and Draftsman, Keyes, Lethbridge and Condon, architects, Washington, D.C., 1962–65. Since 1965, Partner, with George E. Hartman, *q.v.*, Hartman-Cox Architects, Washington, D.C. Lecturer on Architecture, Washington Gallery of Modern Art, 1965; Visiting Design Critic, 1966, and Lecturer on Architecture, 1972, Yale University; Visiting Design Critic, Catholic University of America, Washington, D.C., 1966–67; Visiting Professor of Architecture, University of Virginia, Charlottesville, 1976. Chairman of the Jury, Louis Sullivan Award, 1975, and AIA/*House and Home* Awards Program, 1978. Exhibitions: *The Work of Hartman-Cox*, University of Virginia, Charlottesville, 1973; *Recent Work of Hartman-Cox*, University of Maryland, College Park, 1974; *Award Winning Architecture by Yale Graduates*, Yale University School of Architecture, 1976. Collections: Museum of Modern Art Archives, New York. Recipient: Award, American Institute of Architects, Potomac Valley Chapter, 1968, 1970, 1972, 1974, 1976; Honor Award, 1970, 1971, and Homes for Better Living Award, 1976, national AIA; Louis Sullivan Prize, 1972; Honor Award, AIA/Concrete Reinforcing Steel Institute, 1977. Fellow, American Institute of Architects, 1977. Address: Hartman-Cox Architects, 1071 Thomas Jefferson Street N.W., Washington, D.C. 20007, U.S.A.

Works (with George E. Hartman):

1964 Office for Cox, Langford and Brown, New Hampshire Avenue, Washington, D.C.
1965 Symington House additions, stage I, Washington, D.C.
1966 Tager House additions, Bethesda, Maryland
Office for James Symington, 19th Street, Washington, D.C.
Ballroom addition, Saudi Arabia Embassy, Washington, D.C.
1967 Long-range development plan for Mount Vernon College, Washington, D.C.
1968 Walinsky House, McLean, Virginia
Phillips-Brewer House, Connecticut Avenue, Chevy Chase, Maryland
Symington House additions, stage II, Washington, D.C.
Fairfax Village Recreational Center, National Park Service, Washington, D.C.
1969 St. Alban's Tennis Club, Mount St. Alban's, Washington, D.C.

Chapel and Gate House, Mount Vernon College, Washington, D.C.
Leventhal House additions, Washington, D.C.
1970 Dormitory, Mount Vernon College, Washington, D.C.
Stable for the National Park Service, Rock Creek Park, Washington, D.C.
Offices for the Washington Chapter of the American Institute of Architects, Washington, D.C.
1971 Euram Building, Dupont Circle, Washington, D.C.
Carmichael House, Annapolis, Maryland
Watts House additions, Washington, D.C.
Tennis stadium, Washington, D.C.
1972 Kenney House additions, Washington, D.C.
Student Lounge, St. Alban's School, Washington, D.C.
New Chancery, French Embassy, Washington, D.C. (project)
1973 Saltonstall Farm, Rappahannock County, Virginia
Carousel Shelter Study for the Smithsonian Institution, Washington, D.C.
Visitors Center, Washington Monument, Washington, D.C.
1974 Walker House, St. Mary's County, Maryland
Preservation plan for the urban core of New Hanover County, Wilmington, North Carolina
1976 Conant House, Potomac, Maryland
The National Bookstore, National Visitors Center, Washington, D.C.
Swimming pool, Brown House, Washington, D.C.
Resort hotel complex, Williamsburg, Virginia (project)
Recreation Centers, Department of the Army, Washington, D.C. (project)
Study of public places for the National Archives, Washington, D.C.
1977 Dodge Center, Wisconsin Avenue, Washington, D.C.
National Permanent Building, Pennsylvania Avenue, Washington, D.C.
Office building for the Arnold and Porter law firm, Washington, D.C. (project)
Long-range development plan for the National Humanities Center, Raleigh, North Carolina
1978 Stable, Saltonstall Farm, Rappahannock County, Virginia
Law Enforcement Center, Wilmington, North Carolina (with V. J. Ballard, McKim and Sawyer)
Headquarters Building, Maryland National Capitol Park and Planning Commission, Silver Spring, Maryland
National Humanities Center, Raleigh, North Carolina
Folger Shakespeare Library additions and remodelling, Capitol Street, Washington, D.C.
Medical Office Building, Warrenton, Virginia

Interiors: Symington House, Washington, D.C., 1968; Leventhal House, Washington, D.C., 1969; Chapel, Mount Vernon College, Washington, D.C., 1969; offices, Washington Chapter, American Institute of Architects, 1970; Gate House, Mount Vernon College, Washington, D.C., 1970; Dormitory, Mount Vernon College, 1971; offices, Euram Corporation, Washington, D.C., 1971; offices, Cox, Langford and Brown, Washington, D.C., 1972; residence rooms, Cosmos Club, Washington, D.C., 1973; Robert House, Washington, D.C., 1973; offices, Koteen and Burt, Washington, D.C., 1976; offices, Financial General Bankshares Inc., Washington, D.C., 1976; Research Center, National Humanities Center, Raleigh, North Carolina, 1977.

Warren J. Cox and George E. Hartman: Folger Shakespeare Library, Washington, D.C., 1978

Publications:

By COX: book—*AIA Guide to the Architecture of Washington, D.C.*, editor with others, Washington, D.C. 1965, 1974; article—in *Architectural Forum* (New York), May 1965.

On HARTMAN/COX: book—*Houses Architects Live In* by Barbara Plumb, New York 1977; articles—"Brewer Residence" in *House and Garden* (New York), April 1969; "Chapel for Mount Vernon College" in *Architectural Forum* (New York), March 1971; "Hartman-Cox Wins First Sullivan Award" in *AIA Journal* (Washington, D.C.), October 1972; "The Euram Building" in *Architectural Forum* (New York), October 1972; "Dormitory and Plan for Mount Vernon College" in *Progressive Architecture* (New York), June 1972; "Brewer House/Leventhal Remodelling" in *Architecture + Urbanism* (Tokyo), November 1973; "Mount Vernon College

Dormitory" in *Architecture Plus* (New York), December 1973; "Cox Residence" in *House and Garden* (New York), June 1974; "Conant Residence" in the *New York Times*, 6 June 1976; "Evaluation: Euram Building" in *AIA Journal* (Washington, D.C.), September 1976; "Forty under Forty" in *Architecture + Urbanism* (Tokyo), January 1977; "In Washington—A Serious Design" by Paul Goldberger in the *New York Times*, 9 February 1977; "Conant Residence" in *Architectural Record* (New York), May 1977; "National Permanent Building" in *Progressive Architecture* (New York), December 1977; film—*Architects/Architecture*, International Masonry Institute, 1977.

*

One hopes that the work of Hartman-Cox is marked by a lack of recognizable office style and by a variety of response.

Most of our work has been in the quite unique environment of Washington, D.C. and its surrounds, usually on difficult, prominent and very particular sites. This has been coupled with an unusually wide variety of commissions, ranging from libraries to houses, jails to stables. We have attempted to honor these situations and programs rather than ignore or oppose them.

In principal, therefore, the buildings vary in design (or "style") the one from the other, based on the premises (1) that each combination of site, program and client is unique and deserves treatment specific to its particular demands, and (2) that the use of the same aesthetic or design vocabulary on quite different and unrelated projects is not only likely to be counter to that end but is irresponsible.

This should not be confused with the hopefully discredited fifties' approach of a new, spectacular "concept" for each job, usually, if not invariably, unrelated to or dominating its environment.

On the contrary, we assume that the old is as valid as the "new" and, for example, that the level of assertiveness of a building or its scale should be a rational choice based on its context, not predicated on an abstract design prejudice.

I suppose we are proposing a mixture of eclecticism and contextualism for want of better terms.

We aspire to a level of design professionalism where one is able to work in a wide variety of styles or aesthetics (as was the case in past eras) as required. This seems particularly relevant now that "modern" architecture has become a style and it is obvious that, thankfully, we are not going to rebuild the world according to the precepts of the "modern movement."

—Warren J. Cox

George E. Hartman and Warren J. Cox, working in the quasi-isolation of the small Washington, D.C. architectural community and without a conscious polemic, were among the early defectors from the Modern Movement in the United States. "We were just never convinced that Modern was the answer," they say and trace this attitude to their schooling—both took degrees in art history before attending professional schools (Hartman at Princeton and Cox at Yale)—and to their early practice, which in conservative Washington consisted of dozens of remodelings, giving them an appreciation for older architecture. Further, Hartman's professional education at Princeton was under Jean Labatut, one of the America's last remaining believers in Ecole des

Beaux-Arts training, and, for a short time, Louis Kahn.

The design of Hartman-Cox is purposefully eclectic and widely varied from one project to another. Primary is an effort to relate each building to its particular site, for instance the horseshoe plan of their Euram Building as a way of fronting on a traffic circle. The stepped pyramid is their frequent response to siting on a hill. For their dormitory at Mt. Vernon College, they not only used a variation of this form to deal with the sloped landscape but also distinguished between its various facades, turning a quiet brick face to the neo-Georgian campus and a dramatic chiaroscuro elevation away from it.

The whole point of their design repertory has been to avoid the minimalism of their elders. "Modern architecture," Cox says, "gives you five shapes and tells you they will solve all problems. But you can't get there from here. You need more pieces." For years, one of the pieces was the angle, a formal tool exploited not only by them but also by an entire generation to such an extent that it has become a cliché of the 1960's. Today, the firm is more likely to turn to an historical or contemporary quotation to enrich a building's vocabulary and modulate its scale. Their National Permanent Building superimposes huge concrete columns, a reference to a French Second Empire landmark nearby, on a grid of black pipes, inspired by Piano and Rogers' high-tech Place Beaubourg. The glass bays are derived admittedly from Adler and Sullivan's Guaranty Building.

In keeping with their attitudes toward site and

scale, Hartman and Cox prefer molded spaces to free-flowing ones, which they call "ill-defined." Their Conant House, with its octagonal library, or Folger Library, with its barrel vaulted spine, simultaneously disregard the Modern concepts of planes in space and interior form reading through on the exterior.

Yet Hartman-Cox does not consider itself—nor is it considered by the propagators of the term—postmodern. The firm enjoys an impressive local reputation and a growing national one, but has eschewed identification with any architectural group or theoretical position.

—Nory Miller

CRANE, David A(lford).
American. Born in Mutoto, Belgian Congo, now Zaire, of American parents, 25 January 1927. Educated at lower schools in the Belgian Congo, 1932–40; Tuscaloosa Senior High School, Alabama, 1941–43; Davidson College, North Carolina, 1943–44, 1946–47; Georgia Institute of Technology, Atlanta, 1947–50, B.S. and B.Arch. 1950; Harvard Graduate

David A. Crane: Radisson New Town, near Syracuse, New York, 1974 (model)

School of Design, Cambridge, Massachusetts, under Walter Gropius and G. Holmes Perkins, 1950–52 (Lehman Fellow; Rumrill Scholar), M.City Planning 1952. Served in the United States Navy, in the Pacific, 1944–46: Quartermaster 2nd Class; and as a Reserve Officer in the United States Corps of Engineers, 1950–57: First Lieutenant. Married Bonnie Beth Loyd in 1954; children: Melinda, Matthew and Lauren. Assistant Director, Tampa, Florida Housing Authority, 1951; Designer, IBEC Housing Corporation, New York, 1952–53; Draftsman, Marcel Breuer Associates, New York, 1953–54, and Wiener and Sert Associates, New York, 1954; Planner, Mayer and Whittlesey Associates, New York, 1954–55; Designer, Carl Koch Associates, Cambridge, Massachusetts, and Research Associate, Massachusetts Institute of Technology School of Architecture and Planning, Cambridge, 1955–57; Assistant Professor of Architecture and Planning, Graduate School of Fine Arts, University of Pennsylvania, Philadelphia, 1957–61; Director of Design and Planning Administrator, Boston Redevelopment Authority, 1961–65; Professor of Architecture and Chairman of the Urban Design Program, Graduate School of Fine Arts, University of Pennsylvania, 1965–72. Since 1966, Founding Partner, David A. Crane and Partners, and Chairman of the Board, DACP Inc., Philadelphia, Boston, and Cairo, Egypt. Dean and Distinguished Professor of Architecture, Rice University School of Architecture, Houston, 1972–77, and Founder, Chairman of the Board, and Chief Executive Officer, Rice Center for Community Design and Research, Houston, 1973–77; Program Director, Sadat City Development Group, Cairo, Egypt, 1978–79. Member, National Architectural Accrediting Board, 1968–71; Special Consultant to the United States Department of Housing and Urban Development for the Urban Development Action Grants, 1977. Exhibitions: *Fort Lincoln New Town,* Corcoran Gallery, Washington, D.C., 1969; *New York State Urban Development Corporation Projects,* Whitney Museum, New York, 1972. Recipient: Young Engineer of the Year Award, Tau Beta Pi Engineering Society, 1950; Italian Government Travelling Fellowship, 1955; Award, *Progressive Architecture,* 1969, 1970; Award, American Institute of Architects, Philadelphia Chapter, 1969, 1970; Award, Texas Society of Architects, with W. T. Cannady, 1974. Address: David A. Crane and Partners, 1316 Arch Street, Philadelphia, Pennsylvania 19107, U.S.A.

Works:

1952/
53 Low-cost housing systems designs for Cuba, Puerto Rico, Venezuela, etc. (with IBEC Housing Corporation)

1953/
54 Houses and schools projects (with Marcel Breuer Associates)

1954 Urban design projects for Latin American countries (with Wiener and Sert Associates)

1954/
55 Master plan for Krobo New Town, Ghana (with Mayer and Whittlesey Associates)

1955/
57 Housing designs and hotel projects in various American cities (with Carl Koch Associates: F. Day)
"Image of the City," Los Angeles, Boston, and Jersey City (M.I.T. research project; with Kevin Lynch)

1958/
61 Urban renewal design plans and site designs, Philadelphia, Washington, D.C., and Pennsylvania and Delaware towns (with various collaborators)

1961/
65 General plan for Boston and the Boston Regional Core

General neighborhood renewal area plans (10), Boston
Urban renewal project design plans for: Government Center; Water-Front-Faneuil Hall; Washington Park; South End; Charlestown; South Cove; Central Business District; Back Bay—all Boston
Project briefs and design review management for Boston redevelopment projects: City Hall and other Government Center buildings; Washington Park housing, commercial, and public facilities; Water-front Aquarium; etc.

1966 "Planning and Design in New York" (policy study for the Mayor of New York; with Edward J. Longue)

1966/
67 Master plan for the Main Street Campus of the State University of New York at Buffalo
Area renewal plan for Bedford-Stuyvesant, Brooklyn, New York (with E. J. Logue, I. M. Pei Associates, and Raymond and May Associates)

1967 Multi-Use Center, for Food Fair Inc. and Horn and Hardart Inc., Philadelphia

1967/
68 Master plan for the in town new town of Spring Creek-East New York, New York City (with S. W. Killinger)
Education Park prototypes, for the Corde Corporation
North Philadelphia School Facilities Systems Design
Buffalo-Amherst Corridor Development Plan and Transport Systems Concept Design, Buffalo, New York (with S. W. Killinger)

1968/
69 Master plan for Ft. Lincoln New Town, Washington, D.C. (with Keyes, Lethbridge and Condon)
"Applications of New Technology in Developing New Communities," Washington, D.C. (development study for the U.S. Department of Housing and Urban Development; with Keyes, Lethbridge and Condon)

1968/
70 Plan for the 1976 *Philadelphia Bicentennial Exposition* (with S. W. Killinger and others)

1969/
70 "Quality in Environment" (policy study of public design processes in Albuquerque, New Mexico)
Campus master plan for the Université Libre de Congo, Kisangani (with J. Lane and others)
South Central Corridor Transport Design and Impact Study, Philadelphia (with A. M. Voorhees and Associates, and J. Lane)

1969/
73 Master plan, demonstration building systems coordination, and architectural designs for Total Energy Plant, School, and Commercial Structure, U.S. Department of Housing and Urban Development "Operation Breakthrough" Project, Jersey City, New Jersey

1969/
74 Master plan for Radisson New Town, formerly Lysander New Town, near Syracuse, New York (with J. N. Kise, R. Glaser, P. Franks, J. Straw and others)

1970/
72 Building systems development and architectural designs, Université Libre de Congo, Kisangani: Proto Classroom Building; Proto Dormitory; Proto Lecture Hall; Library; Chapel/Socio-Cultural Center; Dining Commons; Central Kitchen (with J. Lane and others)
Industrialized housing systems, for various

clients, various U.S. locations
New town feasibility studies for Tennessee Valley Authority, Illinois Housing Development Authority, etc.

1972/
73 Village center and subdivision design, Flower Mound New Town, Texas (with J. V. Thomas)
Crane House, Houston (with W. T. Connaly)

1973/
75 Bedford-Pine in town new town, and other renewal projects for Atlanta, Georgia (with S. W. Killinger, P. Franks and others)

1974 City master plan revision and Glenloch Village design plan, Peachtree City, Georgia (with J. V. Thomas and others)

1974/
77 Project designs and strategy services for developers in Houston, Dallas and El Paso, Texas, and Atlanta, Georgia

1975/
77 Oklahoma City Plan for Growth Management and Community Development (with RERC, Haines, Luudberg and Waehler, and Marshall Kaplan, Gans and Kahn)

1976/
79 Master plan for Sadat City, Egypt (with J. N. Kise and S. W. Killinger, Parons Brinckerhoff, Marcel Breuer Associates, and Sabbour Associates)

1977 Design plan for the Capitol Gateway Community, Washington, D.C. (with Gibbs and Hill, and P. Franks)

1978/
79 Nasr City Center, Cairo (with S. Heikin, Marcel Breuer Associates, and Sabbour Associates)

Publications:

By CRANE: books—*Philadelphia Tomorrow* (AIA Guidebook), Philadelphia 1961; *Planning and Design in New York: A Study of Problems and Processes of the Physical Environment Developing New Communities,* with Keyes, Lethbridge and Condon, New York 1966, Washington, D.C. 1968; articles—"The Vital City: The Gift of America Unchallenged" in the *Daily Pennsylvania* (Philadelphia), March 1959; "The Dynamic City" in *Architectural Design* (London), April 1960; "Chandigarh Reconsidered" in *AIA Journal* (Washington, D.C.), May 1960; "The City Symbolic" in *Journal of the American Institute of Planners* (Washington, D.C.), Fall 1960; "Alternative to Futility: Design in the Boston Redevelopment Authority" in *The Architect and the City* (seminar proceedings), Cranbrook, Michigan 1962, reprinted in *AIA Journal* (Washington, D.C.), November 1962; "Education for City Form Makers, Not Cosmeticians" in *Education for Urban Design,* St. Louis 1962; "The Public Art of City Building" in *Annals of the American Academy of Political and Social Science* (Philadelphia), March 1964; "Design and Urban Renewal in Boston" in *The Role of Government in the Form and Animation of the Urban Core* (conference report), Cambridge, Massachusetts 1964; "Architecture and the Urban Revolution" in *Connection* (Cambridge, Massachusetts), Winter 1966; "Achieving Quality in Environment," with George Rolfe, in *Proceedings of the Institute of Planning, Zoning and Eminent Domain,* New York 1971; "Responsiveness in the Design of Transportation and Environment" in *Transportation* (Boston Architectural Center Proceedings), 1971; "In Search of 'New' New Towns" in *New Towns in America,* edited by James Bailey, New York 1973; "Back to the City: Atlanta Points Toward New Housing Options" in *Real Estate Atlanta* (Georgia), no. 1, 1976; "Energy and Urban Living" in *Energy and the Quality of Life* (proceedings of a conference in Houston), 1976.

On CRANE: articles—"Design Awards" in *Progressive Architecture* (New York), January 1969, January 1970; "Awards" in *Texas Society of Architects Journal* (Austin), Spring 1975; "Houston Architects" in *Inland Architect* (Chicago), July 1977.

The nature of my work—both its material and immaterial results—has been a product of a continuing dialectic among competing ideals of design achievement, professional ethic, urban realism, and social reform. I am an architect needing to plan, a planner needing to develop, a developer needing social justification. When I am in the university, I am looking for the intersection of abstract theory and strategic action. When I am in the field, I have an unquenchable desire to learn. There is no surcease from this dialectic for those like myself who love cities and want them again to be good places to live.

Urban form and urban process are the mirrors of each other, and that is another dialectic in which I have always dealt. My earlier theoretical urban design works, with students, reflected the practical observation that our cities cannot be the work of a single genius but are formed by the modern realities of the "Dynamic City": the "City on Wheels," the "City of a Thousand Designers," and the "City of Growth and Change." But, with our "Capital Design" schemes, we sometimes overreached these realities of the "Dynamic City" and came close to resurrecting Baron Haussmann, who was a grand designer of an undemocratic and non-dynamic age.

In the vast redevelopment programs for Boston during the early sixties I found a more practical illustration of how process and form are mirrored. Even more revealing was the experience of being a front-line participant in urban renewal efforts during the social agonies of American cities from 1966 through 1971. Neighborhood rehabilitation schemes, intown new towns, urban schools prototypes, transportation systems design, and downtown revitalization programs were carried out in an environment of maximum citizen participation. Clearly, this period confirmed the power of the "City of a Thousand Designers." It was a thrilling and humbling period to work in the American city.

When the American northeast became more somnolent I was persuaded to go to Houston, as the Rice University Dean of Architecture. With the creation of Rice Center for Community Design and Research, as well as other community benefit projects, I brought the reality of the city into the classroom and the talents of the university into humanizing the city. Only time will tell whether that great American boomtown senses a difference!

Always an internationalist because of my origins in the Belgian Congo, I am very pleased now to be working for the execution of Sadat City, the "flagship" of Egypt's hopes to redirect its rapid population and urban growth into the desert and away from the valuable agricultural lands and overcrowded cities of the Nile Valley. Creating a desert city is a complex task, ranging from the gut issues of water supply, recycling of wastes, or self-help housing, on one hand, to the design of sophisticated buildings, infrastructure, investment systems, and human institutions on the other hand. Again the development of Sadat City illustrates the urban dialectic (i.e., between the material and the immaterial) which is what makes it all worthwhile!

—David A. Crane

David Crane is one of the architects who has pioneered in the development of effective urban design techniques, and the firm he founded is one of the leading practitioners of urban design and planning. Crane is also well-known as an educator, particularly for his contributions to urban design education.

A major professional opportunity opened up for Crane in 1961, when Edward J. Logue, the administrator of the Boston Redevelopment Authority, made Crane, in effect, the director of planning for the City of Boston. Under the centralized system of administration created by Logue in Boston, the planning administrator had less autonomy than is customary in such positions, but in exchange became part of an exceptionally effective implementation process. While he was with the Boston Redevelopment Authority, Crane was responsible for a number of specific development plans, but his major work was the production of the General Plan for Boston and the Boston Regional Core. This plan was unusual for a number of reasons: it was one of the few detailed, comprehensive plans to be adopted in a major American city; it went beyond the official boundaries of the City to consider Boston's role in the metropolitan region; it was not solely a physical plan (although the emphasis was certainly on physical planning); and—most unusual of all—large parts of it have actually been carried out. In this plan Crane developed the concept that he calls "The Capital Web," using government capital expenditure strategically to achieve larger objectives.

In 1965 Crane returned to the University of Pennsylvania as a professor and chairman of the Graduate Program in Civic Design. With several younger associates he opened the office now called David A. Crane and Partners. This office is best known for its work with large-scale urban design plans, including the new communities of Lysander (now called Radisson), near Syracuse, New York, and Fort Lincoln in Washington, D.C. These plans have distinctive urban design elements, notably the use of a grid pattern with a strong diagonal emphasis, that mark them as the work of the Crane office and show a kinship to the distinctive approach to architecture developed at the School of the Fine Arts at the University of Pennsylvania in the years when Louis I. Kahn was its leading figure.

From 1972 through 1977 Crane was the Dean of the School of Architecture at Rice University in Houston, Texas, a move that necessarily cut down his involvement with David A. Crane & Partners in Philadelphia. Crane's most significant achievement at Rice was the creation of a research center, supported in part by the Houston business community, that investigates large-scale planning and community design issues. In Houston, noted for its laissez-faire attitude towards planning, the creation of such a center was a major achievement.

At the present time, Crane has returned to a full-time association with his firm and is devoting most of his energies to Sadat City, a major new community in Egypt, which is to be the keystone of Egyptian national planning policies.

—Jonathan Barnett

CROSBY, Theo.

British. Born in Mafeking, South Africa, 3 April 1925; settled in England, 1947. Educated at the University of the Witwatersrand, Johannesburg, 1940–47, B.Arch. 1947. Served in the South African Army, 1944–45. Married Anne Buchanan in 1960; children: Dido, Emily, and Matthew. Worked in the office of Maxwell Fry and Jane Drew, London, 1947–52; Technical Editor, *Architectural Design*, London, 1953–62; Founder Partner, with Alan Fletcher and Colin Forbes, Crosby/Fletcher/Forbes, London, 1965–72. Since 1972, Partner, with Fletcher, Forbes, Mervin Kurlansky, Ken Grange, John McConnell, David Hillman and Ron Herron, Pentagram Design Partnership, London. Exhibition: Sculpture, ICA Gallery, London, 1960. Recipient: Grand Prize, *Triennale*, Milan, 1963; 2 Architectural Heritage Year Awards, 1973. Associate, Royal Institute of British Architects, 1944; Fellow, Society of Industrial Design, 1963. Address: Pentagram Design, 61 North Wharf Road, London W.2, England.

Works:

1961 Design of the *International Union of Architects Exhibition*, South Bank, London
1962/
64 Euston Station reconstruction, London (as supervising architect for Taylor Woodrow)
1963 Design of the British Section, *Triennale*, Milan
1964 "Twilight Areas" Study, Fulham, London (for Taylor Woodrow)
1967 Industry Section of the British Pavilion, *Expo '67*, Montreal
1968 "The Lookout" (observation lounge), *Queen Elizabeth II*
1969 Design of the Cape Universal Buildings Products display, *International Building Exhibition*, Olympia, London
Rowe Rudd office interiors, 63 Moorgate, London
1971/
73 Ulster Terrace reconstruction, Regent's Park, London (with Edward Armitage)
Chalcot House renovation and conversion, Westbury, Wiltshire
1972 Boase Massimi Pollit Advertising Agency conversion and interiors, Paddington, London
1972/
73 Cherry Garden Pier development, Bermondsey, London (project; with others)
1973 Design of *The Environment Game* exhibition, Hayward Gallery, London
1975 Malaysia House conversion and interiors, London
Geers Gross Advertising Agency interiors, London
1976 Design of the *British Genius* exhibition, Battersea Park, London
1978 Unilever House refurbishment, London
1979 Boase Massimi Pollit Advertising Agency further conversion and interiors, Paddington, London

Publications:

By CROSBY: books—*This Is Tomorrow*, exhibition catalogue, London 1956; *Le Corbusier*, exhibition catalogue, London 1959; *An Anthology of House*, with Monica Pidgeon, London 1960; *The Architecture of Technology*, editor, London 1961; *Architecture: City Sense*, London and New York 1965; *The Necessary Monument*, London 1970; *A Sign Systems Manual*, with Alan Fletcher and Colin Forbes, London 1970; *Pentagram: The Work of Five Designers*, with Pentagram Partners, London 1972; *How to Play the Environment Game*, London 1973; *Living by Design*, with Pentagram Partners, edited by Peter Gorb, London and New York 1978; articles—editor, with John Bodley, of 5 issues of *Uppercase* (London), 1958–61; editor of 3 issues of *Living Arts* (London), 1962; "The Modern Movement" in *RIBA Journal* (London), February 1974; "Arup Museum" in *Architectural Review* (London), February 1974; "Another World!," with Idris Watts, in *Building Design* (London), 5 July 1974; "Docklands Feedback" in *Architectural Design* (London), April 1975; "Johannesburg Revisited" in *RIBA Journal* (London), February 1976; "Architect's Approach to Architecture" in *The Architects' Journal* (London), 11 February 1976; "Port Sunlight: The First and Only Good Housing Estate in England" in *RIBA Journal* (London), July 1978.

On CROSBY: articles—"Exhibition Design" in *Architectural Review* (London), January 1974; "Six Design Offices in Europe" by Gilles de Bure and Gerard Negreaunu in *Cree* (Paris), May 1974; "Nash Conversion with Imagination" in *House and Garden* (London), October 1975; "Living by Design" in *RIBA Journal* (London), February 1976; "Pentagram: Style and Content" in *Building* (Lon-

Theo Crosby: Ulster Terrace, Regent's Park, London, 1973

Dame Sylvia Crowe: Roof garden, Scottish Widows Fund and Life Assurance Society Building, Edinburgh, 1976

don), 13 February 1976; "A Return to Ornament?" in *Architectural Review* (London), October 1976; "Technology in the 1930's" by A. Howard in *Building Design* (London), 8 October 1976; "Advertising Agency" in *RIBA Journal* (London), November 1976; "Corridor Street Life Detail" in *Design* (London), January 1977; "Tentative Genius" in *Building Design* (London), 3 June 1977.

Pentagram is a partnership which explores a great variety of problems. Its strength is in its self-limiting organization, which places total responsibility on the partner. Each partner has a small, young team. There is no pyramidal structure but an association of determined equals.

With regard to my own work, I am concerned with the extension of the barren and commercially worn language of modern architecture, not in the direction of an ever more streamlined technology but through the involvement of other disciplines.

Designers and artists can add a dimension to architecture, a way of mediating between architect and the public. Nothing new in this. It was the normal mode in building until the 1950's, before our puritan masters changed the rules.

For a new, and responsive, architecture, and a decent environment, we need more intelligent input at every level.

Thus I am concerned with public art, monuments and monumentality, with decoration, with the sensuous use of material.

It has also become clear that my training has quite unfitted me for this task, though it is very enjoyable, if painful, trying to rediscover skills that were common to every 19th century draftsman.

—Theo Crosby

When Theo Crosby arrived in England from South Africa in 1947, he was just in time to experience the mixture of optimistic euphoria about the possibilities of modern architecture in post-war Britain and the reality of economic depression, a mixture exemplified by the *Britain Can Make It* exhibition at the Victoria and Albert Museum in 1946 and by the Festival of Britain five years later. Crosby's first job was with the Fry/Drew partnership where he could have been expected to absorb the traditional and received truths about modernism as they were defined before 1939. He went on to the influential journal, *Architectural Design*, and, later, to found Pentagram.

Crosby is the only qualified architect in the Pentagram group which makes it a speciality to offer a wide range of design services in diverse fields, services defined by the group as those that are "not quite architecture," including signs, posters, exhibitions and shopping centres. The Lewisham Shopping Centre (architects: Bernard Eagle Partnership) is one recent example of Pentagram's work in shaping the whole environment: the possibilities of the shopping arcade included integrating graphics into the fabric of the building. The Arts Council Shop in Sackville Street, London W.1, is another popular example of Pentagram's environmental design. The group has also been very influential in the fashionable areas of design, including the Art Nouveau revival (which began with Pentagram's logo for the Biba Department Store) and extending to corporate identity programmes for large companies such as BP, Reuters and St. Ivel.

In 1976 Crosby, together with his partners Fletcher and Forbes, addressed the Royal Institute of British Architects in the popular "Architect's Approach to Architecture" series of lectures. The lecture gave the only architect in a prominent design partnership an opportunity to define and clarify his views. Crosby offered a view of architecture that stressed the importance of visual complexity and compound symbolism. He complained of architectural imaginations being dessicated by imposed economies and, reversing Mies' awesome *diktat* (rather as Robert Venturi had already done), maintained the "less is not more, it is actually less."

Pentagram's most famous building is the complex remodelling of a part of Nash's Ulster Terrace in Regent's Park, where the architectural effect depends on elaborate brick-work and fine detailing. Crosby is opposed to the monopoly that architects have over the appearance of our environment, and maintains, as one might expect from an architect who spends most of his time with professional designers, that "good building is rich with the work of many men."

—Stephen Bayley

CROWE, Dame Sylvia.
British. Born in Banbury, Oxfordshire, 15 September 1901. Educated at the Berkhamsted Girls' School, Hertfordshire, 1908–12; Swanley Horticultural College, Kent, 1920–22; pupil of the landscape architect Edward White, London, 1926. Served as a Volunteer Ambulance Driver with the Polish Army in France, 1940; with Motor Transport Companies in the Auxiliary Territorial Service, in the U.K., 1940–45: Sergeant. Garden Designer for Cutbush Nurseries, Barnet, Hertfordshire, 1939. In private practice as a landscape architect, London, since 1945. Consultant to Harlow and Basildon New Town, 1948–58, Central Electricity Generating Board, 1948–68, Essex County Council, 1957, Forestry Commission, 1964–76, and since 1969 to the Southern and South West Water Authorities. Founder Honorary Secretary, 1948–58, and Vice-President, 1958–70, International Federation of Landscape Architects; President, Institute of Landscape Architects, London, 1957–61. Recipient: Woman of the Year Award, *The Architects' Journal*, 1960. D.Litt.: University of Newcastle, 1976; Heriot-Watt University, Edinburgh, 1976; LL.D.: University of Sussex, Brighton, 1978. Honorary Fellow, Royal Institute of British Architects, 1969, and Royal Town Planning Institute, 1970. Corresponding Member,

American Society of Landscape Architects; Honorary Fellow, Australian Institute of Landscape Architects. C.B.E. (Commander, Order of the British Empire), 1967; D.B.E. (Dame Commander, Order of the British Empire), 1973. Address (office): 182 Gloucester Place, London NW1 6DS, England.

Works (landscape architecture):

1927/
39 Numerous private gardens
1946 Public gardens, Mable Thorpe, Lincolnshire (destroyed by floods, 1953)
1948/
68 Harlow and Basildon New Towns, Essex (as consultant)
Nuclear power stations, Trawsfynydd and Wylfa, Wales
Power line routing in Southern England (as consultant)
Coastal reclamation and restoration of the public gardens, Mable Thorpe, Lincolnshire
Coastal reclamation, Sutton-on-Sea, Lincolnshire
1950 St. Mary's Churchyard, Banbury, Oxfordshire
Quadrangles, University College, Oxford
Rose Garden, Magdalen College, Oxford
Neville Hall Hospital, Abergavenny, Wales
Housing for the United States Air Force in Britain
Friern Barnet Hospital, London
1957 Nuclear power station, Bradwell, Essex (as consultant)
Landscape master plan for Washington New Town, County Durham
Landscape master plan for Warrington New Town, Lancashire
Knaresborough Churchyard, Yorkshire
County Hall and Colleges, Bedford
Teachers' Training College, Norham Gardens, Oxford
Cement and Concrete Association Research Station, Wexham Springs, Buckinghamshire (roof garden moved to Edinburgh, 1978)
1966 Master plan for the Commonwealth Gardens, Canberra, A.C.T., Australia
1976 Scottish Widows Fund and Life Assurance Society Office Building, Edinburgh
Bewl Bridge Reservoir (as consultant)
Bough Beech Reservoir (as consultant)
Empingham Pumping Station, Rutland Water (as consultant)
Wimbleball Reservoir (as consultant)
Imperial College, South Kensington, London (as consultant)
Cumberland Basin and Ashton Park Parkway, Bristol

Publications:

By CROWE: books—*Tomorrow's Landscape,* London 1956; *Garden Design,* London 1958; *The Landscape of Power,* London 1958; *The Landscape of Roads,* London 1960; *Space for Living,* editor, Amsterdam 1961; *Shaping Tomorrow's Landscape,* with Zvi Miller, Amsterdam 1964; *Forestry in the Landscape,* London 1966; *The Gardens of Mughul India,* with others, London 1972; articles—"Garden Design" in *Country Life* (London), 1958; "Roads in the Landscape" in *Landscape Design* (London), November 1967; "Landscape of Unity and Surprise: The Wye Valley" in *Country Life* (London), May 1977; "International Scene" in *Landscape Design* (London) February 1979.

On CROWE: articles—"Power and the Landscape" and "Making the Landscape Plan" in *Landscape Design* (London), November 1960; "Upland Catchment Management" in *Landscape Design* (London),

February 1969; "Empingham Pumped Storage Project" in *Architecture East Midlands* (Lincoln), November/December 1976; "Pumping Stations in the Landscape" in *Concrete Quarterly* (London), April/June 1977; "New Head Office for the Scottish Widows Fund Life Assurance Society" by David Colley in *Arup Journal* (London), December 1977; "Scottish Widows Fund and Life Assurance Society Office Building, Edinburgh" in *Landscape Design* (London), May 1978; "In Person: Lady in the Landscape" by Sally Festing in *New Scientist* (London), January 1979.

*

The object of my work and writing is to reconcile the needs and aspirations of men with the welfare of the natural order and to create beauty out of the fusion of the human spirit and the workings of nature. I try to enter into the spirit of each landscape and to express its individual character.

—Sylvia Crowe

*

Sylvia Crowe was first recognised as a sensitive designer for her exhibition garden at the *Chelsea Flower Show* shortly before the war. Her more important career, however, was to lie outside domestic gardens. While still an officer in the ATS during the war, and while stationed in Kent, she made a landscape plan for the Isle of Sheppey during her spare time. The combination of horticultural knowledge and planning instinct at that time made her unique, and post-war architects and town planners employed her to fill a vacuum in their knowledge. Particularly valuable were her pioneer landscape survey reports on the new towns and, later, her detailed designs, under Sir Frederick Gibberd, for Harlow New Town. Her practice in the 1950's developed with ever-widening scope. One recalls with pleasure her little fountain garden at the Cement and Concrete Association Research Station at Wexham Springs, her original treatment of the centre of a roundabout at Basildon, or a more recent roof garden in Edinburgh, designed to merge with the surrounding landscape. But her greatest ambition, as she herself has said, was fulfilled when she was appointed landscape consultant to the Forestry Commission—an assignment that called for all her wide vision, ecological knowledge and aesthetic sense.

Apart from her own practice, Sylvia Crowe (like her colleague Brenda Colvin, with whom for a long time she shared a London office) has been dedicated to the interests of landscape as a whole. Her various books were written at a time when the information was sorely needed. She has been a continuous and highly respected supporter of the professional body, now the Landscape Institute. As founder Honorary Secretary of the International Federation of Landscape Architects she worked unsparingly for its development. Behind a singularly charming manner lies an ordered and acute mind that can penetrate unhesitatingly to the root of a problem. Factors on all sides are weighed, seen to be weighed, and presented to committee or lecture audience with eloquence and clarity.

—Geoffrey Jellicoe

CUBITT, James (William Archibald).
British. Born in Melbourne, Victoria, Australia, 1 May 1914. Educated at the Harrow School, Middlesex, 1928–32; Brasenose College, Oxford, 1932–35, B.A. (honours) 1935; part-time student at Ruskin School of Art, Oxford; studied at the Architectural Association School, London, 1935–40, A.A. Diploma (honours) 1940. Served with the Royal Engineers, in West Africa, India, and Burma, 1940–46: Major; commanded the 5th West African Field Company; M.B.E. (Member, Order of the British Empire), 1945. Married Ann Tooth in 1939 (di-

vorced, 1947); Constance Anne Sitwell in 1950 (divorced, 1972); Eleni Alkmene Kiortsis in 1973; children: Jennifer, Benjamin, and Francis. Studio Master, Department of Architecture, Kingston School of Art, Surrey, 1946–48. Senior Partner, James Cubitt and Partners, London, since 1949 (as James Cubitt Fello Atkinson and Partners since 1967—partners: Cubitt, Atkinson, John Baker, and Alan Craig), with branches in Ghana, 1951–55, Burma, 1954–58, Malaysia, 1955–70, Nigeria since 1956, and Libya since 1965. Architectural Correspondent, *Westminster Review,* London, 1957–61. Member of the Council, 1959–66, President, 1965–66, and since 1969 Trustee of the Development Fund, Architectural Association, London. Exhibitions: Royal Academy of Art, London, 1959; Eastern Region House of Assembly, Enugu, Nigeria, 1959. Also a sculptor, since 1957; one-man shows at the John Whibley Gallery, London, 1962, and Burgos Gallery, New York, 1966. Associate, 1940, and Fellow, 1955, Royal Institute of British Architects. Address: James Cubitt Fello Atkinson and Partners, 25 Gloucester Place, London W1H 4BT, England.

Works:

1949/
51 minor works, including airline offices, London (with Stefan Buzas and R. M. Maitland)
1950/
57 Office group, Accra, Ghana (with Cubitt, Scott and Partners)
1951/
54 Teacher training college, Berekum, Ghana (with Cubitt, Scott and Partners)
Teacher training college, Secondi, Ghana (with Cubitt, Scott and Partners)
Teacher training college, Jasikan, Ghana (with Cubitt, Scott and Partners)
Secondary School, Jasikan, Ghana (with Cubitt, Scott and Partners)
College of Technology, Kumasi, Ghana (with R. M. Maitland)
1952/
54 Technical Institute, Accra, Ghana (with Cubitt, Scott and Partners)
Technical Institute, Kumasi, Ghana (with Cubitt, Scott and Partners)
1954/
57 Ryburn Secondary School, Sowerby Bridge, Yorkshire (with Gerry Richards and Don Lee)
Carleton Primary School, Pontefract, Yorkshire (with Stefan Buzas)
1954/
58 Pharmaceutical factory, Rangoon, Burma (with R. M. Maitland)
1957/
59 First development, University of Nigeria, Nsukka (not completed; with John Baker and Keith Banks)
1958 Nsukka New Town, Nigeria (project; with Keith Banks and Otto Koenigsberger)
1958/
61 Paramount Hotel, Freetown, Sierra Leone (with Henry Smith and Keith Banks)
1958/
62 Elder Dempster Shipping Offices, Freetown, Sierra Leone (with Keith Banks)
Elder Dempster Shipping Offices, Lagos, Nigeria (with Keith Banks)
1959 Churchill College, Cambridge (project; with Keith Banks)
1960/
62 2 schools for delicate and handicapped children, Putney, London (with Dennis Marshall)
1961 St. Anthony's College, Oxford (project; with Keith Banks)
1961/
65 Flats and houses, Harlow New Town, Essex (with Dennis Marshall)

James Cubitt: University of Garyounis, Benghazi, Libya, 1978

1962/
67 Old people's home, Islington, London (with Peter Gray)

Old people's home, Stoke Newington, London (with Peter Gray)

Faculty of Medicine and Teaching Hospital, Kuala Lumpur, Malaysia (with J. L. Middleton and Alan Craig)

1964/
66 Secondary modern school, Highbury, London (with Peter Gray)

1966/
74 Academic and Administrative Buildings, University of Garyounis, Benghazi, Libya, master plan phase I (with Alan Craig, Keith Banks, and Ward Koss)

1971 Redevelopment of the University of Nigeria Campus, Nsukka (with Keith Banks)

1974/
78 University of Garyounis, Benghazi, Libya, phases II and III (with Craig and Grant)

1977 University of Garyounis, Benghazi, Libya, phase IV

Publications:

By CUBITT: articles—in the bi-monthly *Westminster Review* (London), 1958–60; "University of Malaya Medical Centre, Kuala Lumpur" in *Hospital Management Planning and Equipment* (Sevenoaks, Kent), November 1964; "The Need for Self Awareness" in *Arena* (London), January 1966.

On CUBITT: articles—"70 Piccadilly" in *Art News and Review* (London), October 1950; "The Work of James Cubitt and Partners" in *Architect and Building News* (London), April 1957; "B.P.I. Burma" in *International Monthly Journal for Prefabrication and New Building Techniques* (London), May 1957; "James Cubitt and Partners: Work in Ghana" in *Architectural Forum* (New York), July 1957; "University of Nigeria" in *Architectural Review* (London), February 1959; "Sowerby Bridge School" in *Architectural Design* (London), July 1959; "Special School" in *Interbuild* (London), April 1961; "I.D.C. Group, Accra" in *West African Builder and Architect* (Lagos), 1961; "University of Garyounis, Benghazi" in *The Times* (London), 6 March 1968; "Medical Centre, Kuala Lumpur" in *Architectural Review* (London), July 1968; "University of Garyounis" in the *Architectural Association Quarterly* (London), vols. 3–4, 1974; "University of Garyounis, Benghazi" in *L'Archittetura* (Rome), April 1975; "Garyounis University" in *The Observer* (London), 13 June 1976.

My architectural qualification is dated 1940. From then until 1950 my contribution to architecture was a bamboo officers' mess in the jungle south of Chittagong. The war took ten vital years in exchange for an intimate knowledge of the tropics and, in 1951, the commission for a large education programme in Ghana, part of which was carried out. In 1957 I started sculpture "to improve my architecture and for itself if successful," returning to early passions rendered impossible in the lost years. Sculpture played a part in forming my own leanings, beliefs and wishes in architecture, bits and pieces of which began to emerge in the late fifties. The context was seldom right for me until abundant opportunity came in 1966 with the start of design for the University of Garyounis at Benghazi, leading to the completion, so far, of three phases.

A new and mature period starts about 1967/68 when I felt liberated in architecture, in sculpture, and in my personal life. By then I had many years' knowledge of different peoples, customs and cultures outside Europe. Certainly I have never looked on architecture abroad as an export product, like a car or a radio, more or less suitable to greatly differing physical and cultural conditions. On the contrary, architecture is significant only in its response to specific needs. It is the response which creates the formal values: the architect's concern with the interaction of people, place, climate, and function brings everything together as "architecture," a highly-formal art having its own discipline of volume, scale and materials, as other arts have theirs.

—James Cubitt

When I met James Cubitt in the mid 1950's and watched him at work giving shape, coherence and sense to the groups of buildings destined for the University of Nigeria, I was reminded of a remark made by my teacher Hans Poelzig in 1930 in an address to architecture students in Berlin. Poelzig warned his audience not to rely too much on the certainty that "form would follow from function." "Buildings," he asserted, "tend to outlive their functions. You work your fingers to the bone to meet your client's brief, you invoke science and technology or even sociology to make your building perfectly functional and give your client good value for his money—only to find, 30 years later, that few people remember the reasons for your virtuous thrift and the special circumstances that governed your efforts at the time of designing. All that future generations will see will be the forms you have created, and it is by these that you will be judged." These were bold words at a time when Hannes Mayer at the Bauhaus could declare "ornament is crime" and progressives, especially students, considered "form" a dirty word. A quarter of a century later, the pendulum had only just begun to swing back, and James Cubitt's unashamed concern with the art of architecture was still viewed with suspicion by a generation of professionals who preferred to consider themselves as scientists, artisans, technologists, economists—anything rather than artists.

James Cubitt would have been a man after Poelzig's heart. Not that he is a formalist; on the contrary, his great University of Garyounis at Benghazi, on which he has worked since 1966, is the result of more than 15 years of intensive study of university building and university design. This preoccupation with the physical background of academic life began when he became architect for the University of Science and Technology in Kumasi and several teachers training colleges in Ghana in the 1950's. In 1957 he was commissioned by Dr. Nnamdi Azikiwe, Premier of the Eastern Region of Nigeria, to plan the University of Nigeria at Nsukka. University work in West Africa was followed by the Churchill College competition in Cambridge in 1958/59, a design for St. Anthony's College, Oxford, in 1961, the Medical Centre (Faculty of Medicine and University Teaching Hospital) at Kuala Lumpur, 1963/67, the start in 1966 of design at Benghazi and the return in 1971 to the University of Nigeria at Nsukka. Work on the last two continues.

What is essential in the context of Poelzig's remarks is that James Cubitt's involvement with university life and university buildings coincided with an intensive preoccupation with drawing and sculpture. This was no accident. James Cubitt was fully conscious of the importance of his work as a sculptor for his own architectural development. He made this clear in his presidential address to the Architectural Association in October 1965: "Compared with painting and sculpture, very few buildings have survived for more than a few centuries. Yet these, which have obviously far outlived their creators' purposes, can still be judged—are *always* judged—by their formal/spiritual qualities. To know much beyond their general purpose and historical context is irrelevant to this judgement: our response is much too direct. Of course, this process is happening today too. In fact, today change is so rapid in some fields—hospitals, factories—that the functional edge is blurred

even before the contractor moves out and the client in." In keeping with this philosophy, James Cubitt's buildings are not only the results of long and painstaking involvement with his clients' life and needs, but they are also deliberate and positive statements in the language of colour and shape.

Architects in Northern Europe, particularly in England, are trained to fit their buildings into a friendly, man-made landscape which is often of great beauty. The people who live or work in these buildings want to look out onto this landscape and enjoy the reassuring effect of familiar meadows, hedgerows and trees. Well-designed buildings in England are outward looking and liked best if they are so well in harmony with their surroundings that they appear a natural part of the countryside. The situation is different in the Libyan desert. The desert climate is not friendly, but severe. Desert scenery can be dramatic and exciting, but it is seldom restful; it can be terrifying in its stark contrasts. Human beings who are exposed to it for long periods feel the need for refuge and protection among the man-made surroundings of towns and buildings. It is no accident that the best architects have used geometrical forms in arid climates, thereby emphasizing the contrast between an orderly built environment and a hostile outer world. Good desert buildings have few outside windows and look inward to small but carefully-controlled and tended courtyards or gardens. Some of the famous historical buildings of the arid world meet this psychological need perfectly. The palaces of Shush and Persepolis, the desert cities of north Africa, and the great mosques of Isfahan or Kairuan are well-known examples.

The University of Garyounis at Benghazi shows that James Cubitt and his partners have learned to speak the language of desert architecture and, I believe, have produced something that future generations will value as a powerful statement in this language. The strength of the architecture of the University at Benghazi will help it to satisfy another function that was often overlooked by the pioneers

of the modern movement of the 1920's and 30's; that is, the essential role of public buildings in providing a city or country with an image or point of identification. Libya, one of the youngest among the new countries, needs emotional rallying points and images, features that visitors and natives alike remember as characteristic to their country or city. Even if this were not specifically mentioned in his brief, James Cubitt was clearly meant to create at Benghazi a memorable image for a newly awakened nation that was proud of putting a large part of its resources into a peaceful endeavour—the creation of a large central university. I believe he has achieved this and found an architectural language that will be understood even after the oil wells have run dry and life on the north coast of Africa has assumed a character that cannot be predicted or visualized today.

One can imagine future visitors admiring the boldness of placing this monumental group of buildings in a barren, windswept and treeless plain by the sea. One can imagine their excitement at meeting strong colours and shapes in the glaring sunlight and their surprise and pleasure on entering the courtyards and spaces between university buildings with their sense of protection, calm and even gentleness.

—Otto Koenigsberger

CULLINAN, Edward.

British. Born in London, 17 July 1931. Educated at Ampleforth College, Yorkshire, 1944–49; Cambridge University (Anderson and Webb Scholarship), 1951–54, B.A. (first-class honours) 1954; Architectural Association School, London, under Arthur Korn, John Killick, Denys Lasdun, and Peter Smithson, 1954–56; University of California, Berkeley (George VI Memorial Fellowship), 1956–

Edward Cullinan: Olivetti Offices and Workshops, Dundee, Scotland, 1971

57. Served in the British Army, 1949–51. Married Rosalind Yates in 1961; children: Emma, Kate, and Tom. In private architectural practice, London, since 1957. Second-Year Master, Cambridge University, 1968–73; Visiting Critic, University of Toronto, 1973–78, and University of Cincinnati, 1977–78; Tutor, Polytechnic of the South Bank, London, 1977–78. Exhibitions: British Olivetti Ltd., London, 1970; Architectural Association, London, 1973; *British Architecture Exhibition*, Tehran, 1977. Recipient: Industrial Architecture Award, *Financial Times*, 1973; Heritage Year Award, Civic Trust, 1975. Address: Edward Cullinan Architects, 57d Jamestown Road, London N.W.1, England.

Works:

1958 Bell Tout Lighthouse, Birling Gap, Eastbourne, Sussex
1960 Horder House, Ashford Chase, Petersfield, Hampshire
     Marvin House, Panoramic Boulevard, Stinson Beach, California
1964 Knox House I, New Maltings, Nayland, Suffolk
1965 Cullinan House, Camden Mews, London
     Kawecki House, Bartholomew Villas, London
     Church (project)
1966 Garrett House, Greenholm Road, London
     Garage and filling station, Nayland, Suffolk
     Surgery, Church Road, Ashford, Kent
1967 Warehouse and printshop, Stepfield, Witham, Essex (with Julyan Wickham)
     Morrison House (project)
     Houses at Wilmslow, Cheshire (project)
1968 House and barns, Little London Farm, Oakley, Aylesbury, Buckinghamshire (with Julyan Wickham)
1969 Conference and study centre, Minster Lovell Mill, Oxfordshire (with Julyan Wickham and Julian Bicknell)
     Knox House II, New Maltings, Nayland, Suffolk (with Julyan Wickham)
1971 Olivetti Offices and Workshops, Dundee, Scotland, Belfast, Derby and Carlisle (with Julyan Wickham, Julian Bicknell, Michael Chassay, and Giles Oliver)
1972 Residential Wing, Olivetti Training Centre, Haslemere, Surrey (with Julyan Wickham, Julian Bicknell, Michael Chassay, and Anthony Peake)
     Apartment conversion, Powis Terrace, London (with Michael Chassay)
     Olivetti Training Centre, stage II, Haslemere, Surrey (project)
     Olivetti Branch Offices, Edinburgh (project)
     North End Road Development, London (project)
     Houses and apartments, Montpelier Estate, London (project)
     Olivetti office conversions, Cardiff, Coventry, Thornton Heath (Surrey), Hove (Sussex), and Bootle (Merseyside).
     Trojan Factory, Stonebroom Industrial Estate, Chesterfield, Derbyshire (with Michael Chassay)
     House conversion, Gilston Road, London (with Philip Tabor)
1974 Village Hall, Mildenhall, Wiltshire (with Mark Beedle)
1975 House conversion, Cambridge Gardens, London (with Brendan Woods and Michael Chassay)
     Maisonettes, Selhurst Road, South Norwood, London (with Anthony Peake)
     The Orchard Development, Nassington Road, Hampstead, London (project)
1976 Studio, Powis Terrace, London (with Michael Chassay)
     Old people's apartments, Roy Road, Northwood, Middlesex (with Philip Tabor)
1977 Housing estate, Highgrove, Ruislip, Middle-

sex (with Michael Chassay, Mark Beedle, Anthony Peake, Brendan Woods, and Philip Tabor)
1978 Housing estate and house conversions, Chester Road and Green Lane, Northwood, Middlesex (with Anthony Peake, Philip Tabor, and Michael Chassay)
1979 Flats and maisonettes, Westmoreland Road, Bromley, Kent (with Brendan Woods and Sunand Prasad)

Publications:

By CULLINAN: articles—"British Architecture" in *Architectural Design* (London), September/October 1977; "Materials in Use—The Roofs of Highgrove" in *RIBA Journal* (London), November 1977; "Cullinan and Hillingdon," with Thurston Williams, in *RIBA Journal* (London), February 1978.

On CULLINAN: books—*World Architecture One*, edited by John Donat, London 1964; *British Architecture: Arts and Leisure*, edited by Sherban Cantacuzino, London 1977; *Architectural Association Annual Review*, London 1977; articles—"A Studio Near Petersfield" in *House and Garden* (London), May 1963; "Non Profit Architektur" in *Baumeister* (Munich), April 1969; "AR Preview—Olivetti Edinburgh" by Peter Collymore in *Architectural Review* (London), January 1973; "Architect's Work" in *Architectural Association Quarterly* (London), Spring 1973; "Olivetti's New Branches in England" in *Architectural Design* (London), April 1973; "Houses for Tomorrow—Hunters Hill, Wilmslow" in *The Architects' Journal* (London), May 1973; "Four Olivetti Offices" by Mark Girouard in *The Architects' Journal* (London), June 1973; "Olivetti's New Branches" in *Architecture + Urbanism* (Tokyo), February 1974; "Two for Olivetti" by Reyner Banham in *Architectural Review* (London), April 1974; "Pick of the Projects" in *Architectural Design* (London), May 1974; "Study Centre, Minster Lovell, Oxfordshire" by Sherban Cantacuzino and Anthony Ambrose in *Architectural Review* (London), July 1976; "Interior Architecture—Artist's Flat" by Gordon Bowyer in *RIBA Journal* (London), November 1976; "Olivetti Aujourd'hui" in *L'Architecture d'Aujourd'hui* (Paris), December 1976; "Building Study—Highgrove Housing" by David Wild in *The Architects' Journal* (London), July 1977; "British Architecture—Edward Cullinan Architects 1959–1977" by David Wild in *Architectural Design* (London), September/October 1977; "Radical Alternatives—Cullinan's Co-op" by Tom Woolley in *The Architects' Journal* (London), October 1977.

*

I started at the beginning; I encouraged my friends to build houses, studios and conversions, however small: we sometimes built them ourselves.

Minster Lovell, a place for conferences in the Cotswold National Park, followed: I designed it with Julian Bicknell and Julyan Wickham as a series of new buildings that connected old ones and made useful an existing graceful garden.

We were joined by Michael Chassay and Giles Oliver to make new branch offices for Olivetti. We made each one as if it were a home for its fifty occupants, gathered round a partial courtyard, designed to expand to complete it.

With Mark Beedle, we designed a group of a hundred low-lying, relaxed, wide frontage houses at Highgrove in the North West London suburbs—laid out as a series of paths, hedges, houses, trees and bushes; formally like an Elizabethan garden, they deliberately embrace and progress a suburban ideal.

At Chester Green with Anthony Peake, the same ideals were carried forward to embrace both new houses and modifications to existing ones; intermeshed and supporting one another.

Our latest schemes of houses move from the country and suburb into the city, and with Brendan Woods, Sunand Prasad and Philip Tabor, we have

enjoyed devising houses that support the city fabric, that understand the street, the close and the square as rooms with the sky for a ceiling, whose walls are the public fronts of the buildings through which doorways lead to a more personal world beyond.

We propose a future that joyfully accepts the materials and methods of our time to support and enhance the rural, suburban or urban context we find, to make an art of Architecture in the service of our shared humanity.

—Edward Cullinan

*

The clarity of the thinking that underlies each of Edward Cullinan's designs is immediately apparent in the building's sections and its plans: each drawing reads almost like a diagram of an idea. Invariably, it is the section that most eloquently expresses this idea, a key section that acts as a sort of three-dimensional template from which the more complex forms of the building may then develop, not one by which they are restrained. Cullinan is forced to rationalize and order the relationships within the building in order to achieve this key section, but he does so for two reasons, firstly because it will facilitate a modular, repetitive system of construction, and secondly because it will plant the seed from which a variety of spatial inter-relationships may then begin to grow.

This fascination on the one hand for the use of new constructional systems and, on the other, for the intricate manipulation of space, points to Cullinan's firm roots in the architectural philosophies of the Modern Movement. But, to Cullinan, as important as the philosophies themselves was the force of the social responsibility and concern that accompanied them, a view reflected in his personal commitment to the design of low-cost housing, to maximizing the physical return to be gained from very limited financial resources. (It is interesting to note that Cullinan's own office is run as a cooperative.) Where Cullinan has moved beyond the Modern Movement is in his particular response to the need for simplicity and economy. His interest has been in simplicity of technique rather than simplicity of form. He has adopted straight-forward and additive, rather than refined and reductive, methods of construction, partly because of his own experience of self-building, but also because he believes that it is through the manifestation of its construction that a building gains its particular meaning. Cullinan retains a conventional masonry structure at the base of his buildings, but the solidity and permanence of this part of the construction then gives way to a lighter, more flexible structure towards the roof. Paradoxically, it is the base of the building which is formally most fluid and relaxed while the lightweight structure above is very rigidly defined and ordered; ultimate flexibility necessitates preliminary restraint.

These primary elements, base, wall, roof, then receive an accretion of secondary elements, decks, entrances, porches, planting boxes, rainwater butts, balustrades, modulating and ornamenting the facade. Each building has one, or sometimes two, facades, consistent, linear and open-ended. The facade commands the external space before it in the rather formal relationship of building to landscape, house to garden. These traditional relationships Cullinan respects, as he does the conventional values of the prospective tenants of his houses. But while endeavouring to embody these traditional relationships and conventional values, Cullinan is equally committed to experimentation, invention, to the search for new ways of building. His own work is continually evolving, lessons are always being learnt. But the ideas and the principles originally expressed in the design of his first, small, private house are those that he still carries with him today.

—Bob Allies

D

DAHINDEN, Justus.

Swiss. Born in Zurich, 18 May 1925. Educated at the Federal Institute of Technology, Zurich, 1945–49, Dip.Arch. 1949, D.Sc.Tech. 1956. Sergeant in the Swiss Army since 1958. Married Marta Arquint in 1950; children: Zeno, Ivo, and Delia. In private practice, Zurich, since 1955. Member of the Town Planning Commission of Zurich since 1971. Professor of Architecture, and Director of the Institute for Environmental Design, Technical University, Vienna, since 1973. Member, International Congress of Religion, Architecture, and the Visual Arts, New York/Montreal, 1967, Brussels, 1970, and Jerusalem, 1973. Member of the Groupe International d'Architecture Prospective, Paris, since 1968, and of the International Society of Food Service Consultants, U.S.A., since 1969. Exhibitions: Paris, 1967; Salzburg, 1968; Munich, 1968; Moscow, 1969; London, 1969; St. Louis, 1969; New York City, 1973; Lyons, 1973; Zurich, 1974; Poland, 1975; Lausanne, 1976; Moscow, 1978. Recipient: three awards for excellence in design, Guild for Religious Architecture, 1969; two awards for achievement in interior design, *Institutions Magazine,* 1969; Grand Prix International d'Urbanisme et d'Architecture, 1970. Honorary Fellow, American Institute of Architects, 1973; Honorary President, International Society of Christian Artists, 1976. Address (office): Heuelstrasse 21, 8032 Zurich, Switzerland.

Works:

1960 Dreikonig Movenpick Restaurants, Zurich
1962 St. Paulus Catholic Church, Dielsdorf, Switzerland
    Bosco della Bella Holiday Village, Fornasette, Switzerland
    Primary School, Weggis, Switzerland
1963 St. Franziskus Catholic Church, Huttwilen, Switzerland
1964 St. Bartholomaus Catholic Church, Rielasingen, Germany
    Silberkugel Restaurant Chain, Zurich
    Ventilator AG Administrative Building, Stafa, Switzerland
1965 St. Stefan Catholic Church, Arlen, Germany
    Maria Kronung Swiss Academy and Parish Centre, Witikon, Zurich
    Herz-Jesu Catholic Church, Buchs, Switzerland
    Rundfunkrestaurant, Munich
    Claridenhof Movenpick Restaurant, Zurich
    Hotel Continental, Lausanne
1966 Craftsmen School and Church, Taitung, Formosa
1967 Dominican Monastery, Kinshasa, Zaire
    Hostellerie Rigi Hotel Centre, Rigi-Kaltbad, Switzerland
1968 Swiss Fair Restaurants and Shopping Centre, London
1969 Doldertal Trigon Village, Zurich
1970 St. Antonius Catholic Church and Parish Centre, Wildegg, Switzerland
    Ferrolegeringar Pyramidal Administrative Building, Zurich

1971 St. Antonius Catholic Church and Parish Centre, Kleindottingen, Switzerland
1972 Martyrs' Shrine, Church, Convent, School, and Social Centre, Mityana, Uganda
    Tantris Restaurant, Munich
    Hotel Aarauerhof, Aarau, Switzerland
    Ratia Shopping Centre, Davos, Switzerland
1973 Hotel Alpha Palmiers, Lausanne
    Trigon Village, Cala en Bosc, Menorca, Spain
    Justus Dahinden House, Kienastenwiesweg 41, Zurich
1974 Bruder Klaus Catholic Church and Community Centre, Spiez, Switzerland
    Schwabylon Leisure City, Munich
1975 Catholic Cathedral and Martyrs' National Shrine, Namugongo, Uganda
1976 San Giuseppe Catholic Church and Community Centre, Monza, Italy
1977 Zur Gottlichen Vorsehung Catholic Church and Community Centre, Königsbrunn, near Augsburg, Germany
    St. Michael Catholic Church and Community Centre, Vettelschoss, Germany
    Heilig Geist Catholic Church and Parish Centre, Weingarten, Germany
    Trottenhof Historic Residential Building, Weggis, Switzerland
    Villa on Lake Geneva, Villette, Switzerland
    Family houses, Rotzenbuhlstrasse, Oberwil, Switzerland
    Residential area for elderly people, Königsbrunn, Germany
1978 St. Josef Catholic Church and Community Centre, Dotzheim, Wiesbaden
1979 St. Jakobus Catholic Church and Civic Centre, Limburg-Lindenholzhausen, Germany
    St. Elisabeth Catholic Church and Community Centre, Wiesbaden
    Catholic Church and Community Centre, Ingelheim-West, Germany
    Waidburg Restaurant, Zurich
    Hotel Zentrum Gaggenau, Gaggenau, Germany
    Twannberg Holiday Village, near Biel, Switzerland
    Technical University Library, Vienna
    Pearl-of-Cairo Floating Hotel, Egypt
    Ivoirexpo African International Exhibition, Abidjan, Ivory Coast

Research: Floating structures, such as "Athens Seatel" at the Saronic Gulf, and "Floating Theatre on the Lake of Zurich;" Urban structural system TRIGON for housing, schools, offices, restaurants, hotels, and motels; Town planning system AKROPOLIS; housing systems—BUBBLE system for low cost housing; TUBBY system for housing; CUBO system for low cost housing.

Publications:

By DAHINDEN: books—*Standortbestimmung der Gegenwartsarchitektur (Theoretical Research on Modern Architecture),* Zurich 1956; *New Trends in*

Church Architecture, New York 1968; *Urban Structures for the Future,* London 1971; *Urbanisme,* Brussels 1972; *Thinking—Feeling—Acting,* Stuttgart 1973; *Leisure Cities,* Stuttgart 1974; articles—in numerous periodicals throughout the world.

On DAHINDEN: books—*The Church of the Future,* New York 1970; *Buildings for Hospitality,* Zurich 1968; articles—"Contemporary Catholic Church Building" in *Building and Home* (Zurich), 1963; "New Trends in International Hotel Building" in *Building and Home* (Zurich), 1964; "Holiday Hotels for the Future" in *Building and Home* (Zurich), 1965; "La Città di Domani" in *Chiesa e Quartiere* (Milan), 1967; "Architecture?" in *Arch* (Stuttgart), no. 3, 1968; "Prospective Environmental Design" in *Baumeister* (Munich), no. 4, 1968; "Leisure Society and Leisure City" in *Transparent* (Vienna), no. 7/8, 1971; "The Visual Environment" in *Kunst und Kirche* (Linz), 1971; "Animation by Holiday Architecture" in *Building and Home* (Zurich), 1976; "Acculturation in Architecture" in *Schweizerische Bauzeitung* (Zurich), 1978; "Architectural Education" in *DBZ Deutsche Bauzeitung* (Gutersloh), no. 4, 1978.

My work is my life and my love. In principle it is an occupation of leisure and never a constraint. The need for relaxation that I feel at the end of a busy day disappears as soon as I relax. To do nothing produces in me a biologically negative reaction.

I have never wished for a profession other than that of architect. In my childhood, a solid basis was laid for my life to come. As a child I learnt a great deal. My parents were tolerant and affectionate; they offered me above all the maximum of security. When I was at primary school I liked to draw and I took photographs with a simple camera. My father told me then, "It is not the camera that counts, it is the eye." I taught myself when very young to observe the world around me. This exercise had positive effects: I look for, and I find, the imagé of the urban environment.

My family comes from Central Switzerland and something intangible links me to the heart of my tiny homeland, the mountains and the lakes among them: a fondness for the rocks, for trees and water which I cannot explain to myself. If someone said that I no longer belonged to Central Switzerland, I would feel dispossessed.

I received a strict Catholic education and religion is for me a staff and a concern. My attitude toward the church has, it is true, been modified; before, I respected it profoundly as an institution; it offered me visionary prospects, imaginary bonds but also triumphant flights of imagination; today, the church for me has lost most of its radiance, the glory has faded. We know that the church must seek new ways and new forms. The critical attitude toward the church has not, however, lessened the emotional engagement that I feel in church architecture: its uncertainties fascinate me.

Most of our contracts are carried out abroad. My professorship is abroad. Nevertheless, I live very

Justus Dahinden: Martyrs' Shrine, Mityana, Uganda, 1972

willingly in little Switzerland. It is a country propitious to human structures, to friendship and close contacts, but from the point of view of work, I must go abroad. I should be starved mentally if I had to renounce all communication with the international scene.

Like everyone else it is difficult for me to define my character. One of my basic traits is spontaneity. I am the kind of person who makes rapid decisions and I like improvising according to circumstances: spontaneous solutions. The profession of architect is constantly changing. Too much thinking about mechanisation and the pressure of mass production in architecture are injurious, increasing output for more profit; this seems to me less essential than the individual and artistic aspect. In the context of industrialized architecture, spontaneous and emotional decisions can lead to frictions. However, where I can express myself freely on individual planning, I mistrust all preconceived strategy. I consider abstract systems as nonsense, for they never cease to outrun themselves. In reality, I am against systems, but systematic in my way of life. Is this a paradox?

In all aspects of life we need more individuality. I have always been an individualist and I shall remain one. In dissociating myself from society, I can view it from a wider angle and can, to a certain extent, have an outside judgment of it. If I integrated myself too closely to society I would lose, I fear, the faculty of judging events around me. It is thus that a permanent conflict reigns between my wish to enter into contact with the world around me and my tendency to remain aloof. My father told me one day that his antagonists became dearer to him than his friends and that it was basically just because with an antago-

nist one always knows where one stands. This guiding principle, more philosophically approached, has remained with me and has in fact always helped me. I seek contact with people throughout the world, actually more in connection with common interests by erecting a common project than in hasty friendship. I have few real friends, but those I have are true ones.

People say that I am basically an egoist. I interpret thus the words of *The Bible*, "love thy neighbour as thyself": so as you love yourself you love also your neighbour. However, at the same time, I demand much of myself and I force myself to remain self-critical, which is not always easy. Finally, the requirements I have for myself, I expect them also from my collaborators.

I believe that one of the essential motives of the architectural profession, which is dear to me, is the need to be prepared, to accept problems as they come and to draw from failure a new imaginative spirit. When no sparks fly, it is that the fire has died down. I want to remain mobile and I try to retain my receptivity and always to take a decision in virtue of the situation. This mobility, this adaptability—two factors which are indeed very important in my profession—have led me to a strong, but not a blind, positivism. I have faith in the future with the conviction that the problems with which mankind will be faced will find their solution not only on the practical level but also even as real qualities of life.

Pessimism and depression are never profitable. Of course, there are deceptions; one loses a competition or a contract that one would willingly have accepted, but then the following day something happens which one had not envisaged and which appears much

more fascinating. An idea once developed is realized sooner or later, in one form or another. I have always had this experience, which has led me to a "strategic" optimism. To grieve at setbacks is to destroy activity and vitality. A conscious optimism, which at the same time involves knowledge of one's limitations, always finds a way out.

Because I have faith in the future, I believe deeply in the need for utopian developments. It has a great fascination for me. It is at the basis of utopian visions which will change our future environment. Utopian research has always been the driving force of coming to better conditions of living and even to the sector of urbanism. It has led to new sciences, to new materials and to new methods of manufacture. It offers to every architect the possibility of realizing his dreams. On the other hand, I want to keep traditions. I fight against the danger that man, an "earthbound" being with many attachments of long-standing tradition and proven and established values, will be lost if uprooted. I do not believe in general alternations of social structures; on the contrary, I think there will be attempts towards a new symbiosis in group living, such as family life.

My faith in the future is linked to the faculty for illusion, to the ability to devise valuable imaginings and to take them occasionally as guides of conduct. However, valuable imaginings often are far away and the major human problems are near and imperiously urgent. To my mind, one focal point is to be found in a general way in the spiritual field. An important aspect is the relationship of man with religion. The secular urban society of the future—will it need a new religion?—and to what extent, when, where, and how? What kind of spiritual life do men want and what degree of mental intensity do they wish to realize? What are the forms of architecture corresponding to this mental intensity? What kind of believing will there be in the future society? To my mind a society without religion at all cannot eixst. I can imagine a regenerating effect of religion on future society: in the sense of hope, of a theology of hope!

Here, I think, are some other fundamental questions; they also will have to be answered. Shall we have one day a society that is totally disintegrated in social, cultural and religious life? Or, on the contrary, will there be reintegrated societies where groups will be unceasingly in creative contact with others?

Our era overvalues functionalism. Functional thought is nevertheless only one of the facets of every creation, the other being the irrational, that is to say all that goes beyond the practical purpose and transcends logic. I think that a society which does not possess this balance between rationalism and irrationalism is likely to finish badly. The image of the environment, which for us only partly depends on the logistic function, is very important for the requirements of our soul. We need a humanized image of our built surroundings for identification and creation of homelike feelings.

Every architect has some dream project; for me it would be to build a leisure city for a leisure society. For me leisure means to be more creative in a gambling manner under democratic conditions. I am enthusiastic about the new dimensions of such a philosophy: leisure cannot be separated from labour, but labour can be as an individual working without constraints and orders!

Social relationship theories in architecture, the philosophical reflections and psychology of form, of colour and of light on the one hand, as well as the execution of the buildings, the atmosphere of the sites where are given birth and grow the structures on the other hand, create in me an interior balance which is infinitely precious to me. It is thus that during my studies, to compensate for all the rational knowledge, I wrote a book entirely concerned with the origin of contemporary architecture. I continue to write and to publish with pleasure, but not to publicize myself. For me it is a question of the mission to be fulfilled, of the idea and of the interior conflict. The theory must correct practice, and practice shall involve the theory. If one of my buildings incites controversy, if feelings are aroused by use or sight of it, then I am glad of the discussion. It is witness of people's involvement. It is the awareness that interests me, in other words a reaction of people when I try to motivate men's behaviour by my architecture—however modest my intervention may be. When no reaction occurs, then I am disappointed.

It is in a situation of conflict that I am placed in relation to the arts. I prefer what is plastic—that is, sculpture. What we need is space to live in; and space is sculpture. It is an essential part of my architectural compositions to create space to take in people; it is the generator of existence and as such it has to be integrated in all my architectural visions. To painting I have less relation because painting is reduced to two dimensions only. As to music, I draw on different sources, according to my humour, my mood, the moment, and the place. I am strongly drawn to the romantics—Liszt, Dvorak, Richard Strauss—but rock and beat can also give me pleasure. In an abstract space, even Stockhausen can move me. For me music is always linked to space.

If I had to live in an historic building, it could only be of Roman style. The candour and the strength of Roman architecture, simple facts without ostentation, are convincing to me. It offers an environment which is at the same time a powerful expression and yet restrained and quiet. There I could develop my personality without being fixed at the beginning—as in a baroque building, for example. I have need of space which leaves many possibilities and yet remains powerfully present. My new residence is "Roman."

Karl Schwanzer, at the University of Vienna, told me one day that I had within me three abilities—to think, to feel, and to act. This statement made me very happy, for if it is the truth, then I have obtained what I always wanted.

—Justus Dahinden

Switzerland has made a notable contribution to European architectural culture since the war, and the Zurich Polytechnic, with its great traditions linked with the Mosers, Haefeli, Hubacher, and Roth, has been the standard-bearer of new architectural trends. Justus Dahinden, a native of Zurich, has been one of its most illustrious graduates.

Dahinden decided very early in life to be an architect. His study of the work of Frank Lloyd Wright expanded his vision as well as created a sound professional ethic; his contact with Gaudi's extraordinary structures galvanized his lively imagination and enabled him to achieve an ideal balance between radical design and sound method. In an effort to continually excel himself, he began, in his works, to work to the limits of his intuition, beyond the goals he had earlier set himself. The Church also played a part in his development, because he is himself a Christian and because the Church provided his first commissions. His analyses of religious complexes became the basis of his first theories on urban complexes.

Dahinden has also been influenced by the avant-garde projects of the Archigram group and by the theories of the Metabolist Group in Japan. He has developed a vocabulary for devising and testing his works: *biotectonics,* covering the totality of life in its evolutionary processes; *geometrics,* the ordered and disciplined expression of original forms; *psychologics,* the inter-related processes that affect the environment; and *cosmics,* the superior force able to overwhelm human constructs. The unit of measurement of his modular constructional system is the *trigon,* a triangular prism made stable by angular columns. Among his achievements in the trigon mode are the village in Cala en Bosc, Menorca, and the village at Doldertal in Zurich.

In Dahinden's work on "urbanotopia," he seeks an alternative to the dehumanization of the megalopolis, a new orientation in the use of leisure as an integral part of individual life and behaviour and as a pattern of socio-economic structure. Schwabylon Leisure City, Munich, was one effort in that direction, but the "precociousness" of the contents proved fatal to the functioning of the complex and condemned it to early demolition. The floating town centres, based on the same principle, and planned for the Aegean and on the Nile, reached a successful execution in a new lagoon city on the Ivory Coast. What Dahinden has achieved is a projection of the integrated urbanistic system of the "fantascientific" design of Radio City.

The wealth of his imagination can also be seen in smaller, individual works, such as his houses. The Villa on Lake Geneva is a successful demonstration of the articulation of surroundings centred on a vacation or holiday: the villa is the centre of activities and communications and its space is extended down to the lake by terracing. The roof is made to conform, also descending through inclined planes down to the quay.

On a larger scale, Dahinden's religious centres are designed according to the same principle—an open flexible church integrated with the social and urban texture. His work on these complexes clearly demonstrates that normally "immobile structures" can be rendered in dynamic, flexible forms, forms that closely relate to, and participate in, their surroundings. One of his most significant achievements of this kind is to be found a Mityana, a centre of pilgrimage in Uganda, where Dahinden masterfully integrates indigenous tribal forms with secular surroundings as the key to his architectural solution.

—Giuliano Chelazzi

DALTON, John.

Australian. Born in Leeds, Yorkshire, England, 30 December 1927; emigrated to Australia, 1950: naturalized, 1960. Educated at the Adel School, Leeds, 1939; Leeds Technical College, 1940–45; Queensland University, Brisbane, under R. P. Cummings, 1952–58, Dip.Arch. 1958. Served in the Royal Air Force, 1946–48. Married Sheila Harvey in 1952; Suzanne Elizabeth Crozier in 1970; children: Penelope and Amanda. Since 1958, Principal of John Dalton Architect and Associates, Brisbane. Part-time Lecturer in Design, Faculty of Architecture, 1963–71, and since 1969 Member of the Faculty Board of Architecture, Queensland University. Executive Member of the Council for the Queensland Art Gallery Society, Brisbane, 1960–74; Chairman of the Publications Committee, 1962–71, and Member of the Council of the Queensland Chapter, 1966–70, Royal Australian Institute of Architects; Executive Member of the Contemporary Art Society of Australia, 1965–74. Exhibitions: Australian Pavilion, *Lausanne Fair,* Switzerland, 1959; Qantas Australian Architecture Exhibition, London, 1962; Australian Pavilion, *Expo '67,* Montreal, 1967; Australian Pavilion, *Expo '70,* Osaka, Japan, 1970. Recipient: First Prize, Queensland Plywood Competition, 1956; *Arts and Architecture* (Brisbane) Award, 1960, 1961, 1962; First Prize, Brick Manufacturers of Queensland Competition, 1962; Bronze Medallion, Queensland Chapter of the Australian Institute of Architects, 1964, 1967, 1972, 1975; Timber Development Association Award, South Australia, 1971; Merit Award, Royal Australian Institute of Architects, 1977. Fellow of the Royal Australian Institute of Architects, and of the Royal Institute of British Architects. Address: John Dalton Architect and Associates, 333 Queen Street, Brisbane, Queensland 4000, Australia.

Works:

1956　Spinks House, Quentin Street, Indooroopilly, Brisbane
　　　Head House, Fleming Road, Chapel Hill, Brisbane

1957　Young House, Frost Street, Mount Gravatt, Brisbane

1960　Battersby Flats, Quinton Street, Kangaroo Point, Brisbane
　　　Dalton House, Fig Tree Pocket, Brisbane
　　　Farbach House, Moordale Street, Indooroopilly, Brisbane
　　　Henricks House, Homestead, Roma, Queensland
　　　Masters House, Sophia Street, Kenmore, Brisbane
　　　Tennett Town Houses, Terrace Street, Toowong, Brisbane
　　　Professor Whitehead House, Kirkdale Street, Chapel Hill, Brisbane

1961　Mayo House, Kroshanne Street, Aspley, Brisbane

1962　Brick Manufacturers House, Ipswich Road, Brisbane
　　　Clayton House, Retreat Road, Aspley, Brisbane
　　　Collier House, Equinox Street, Kenmore, Brisbane
　　　Leverington House, Kenmore Road, Kenmore, Brisbane

1963　Arts Theatre, Petrie Terrace, Brisbane
　　　Burke House, Waterworks Road, Ashgrove, Brisbane
　　　Hinstedt Town Houses, East Brisbane
　　　Magee House, Woodfield Road, Kenmore, Brisbane
　　　Morrocco Homstead, St. George, West Queensland
　　　Pickworth Town Houses, Waterloo Road, East Brisbane
　　　Stirling House, Moggill Road, Moggill, Brisbane

Wipple Homestead, St. George, West Queensland

1964 Deignan House, Hoya Street, Holland Park, Brisbane

Stoneham House, Kenmore Road, Kenmore, Brisbane

Watson House, Deerhurst Road, Brookfield, Brisbane

Wareham House, Kenmore Road, Kenmore, Brisbane

Wilson House, Mount Coot-tha Road, Brisbane

1965 Belligoi House, Munro Street, Indooroopilly, Brisbane

Davidson House, Ardell Street, Kenmore, Brisbane

Quilpie Memorial Pool, Western Queensland

Dr. Whitfield House, Cadiz Street, Indooroopilly, Brisbane

1966 Barrett House, Kingussie Street, Kenmore, Brisbane

Buckley House, Fontayne Street, Aspley, Brisbane

Graham House, Gower Street, Indooroopilly, Brisbane

1967 Kaeshagen House, Musgrave Street, Kenmore, Brisbane

1968 Barclay House, Indus Street, Whites Hill, Brisbane

Bucknell House, Sutton Street, Chelmer, Brisbane

Clark House, Prospect Street, Sherwood, Brisbane

Dr. Douglas House, Hill Crescent, Gladstone, Queensland

Crozier House, Woodfield Road, Brookfield, Brisbane

Gamin House, Skyline Drive, Burleigh Heads, Queensland

Hodges House, Clontarf Beach, Redcliffe, Queensland

Hollingsworth House, Helse Street, Bardon, Brisbane

Krebs House, Ventura Street, Mermaid Beach, Queensland

Leitch House, Sunset Road, Kenmore, Brisbane

McDonald House, Banbury Street, Carina, Brisbane

Professor Neale House, Roseberry Street, Chelmer, Brisbane

Rabaa House, Kimba Street, Indooroopilly, Brisbane

Swan House, Lois Street, Kenmore, Brisbane

1969 Bolton Holiday Units, Attunga Heights Road, Noosa Heads, Queensland

Bowers House, Castile Street, Indooroopilly, Brisbane

C.H.I. House, Mimosa Downs, Mount Gravatt, Brisbane

Ebzery House, Tallaro Street, Jindalee, Brisbane

Hughes House, Brookfield Road, Kenmore, Brisbane

Jamieson House, Kenmore Road, Kenmore, Brisbane

King House, Castile Street, Indooroopilly, Brisbane

McGregor House, Musgrave Street, Kenmore, Brisbane

Nell House, Queenscroft Street, Chelmer, Brisbane

Smith House, Brookfield Road, Brookfield, Brisbane

1970 Cameron House, Bycroft Street and Heron Road, Pullenvale, Brisbane

Griffin House, Long Road, Mount Tamborine, Queensland

Handicrafts of Asia Shop, Lennons Plaza, Brisbane

Meek House, Haven Road, Brisbane

Robinso House, Luckins Street, Aspley, Brisbane

1971 Read House, Lavereigh Street, Indooroopilly, Brisbane

Roberts House, Orme Road, Buderim, Queensland

1972 Myers House, Wonalee Street, Kenmore, Brisbane

Salter House, Fig Tree Pocket Road, Fig Tree Pocket, Brisbane

Strugnell House, Grandview Road, Brookfield, Brisbane

Vice-Chancellor's Residence, University of Queensland, Brisbane

1973 Musgrave House, Roseberry Street, Chelmer, Brisbane

Rosenblum House, Kneele Street, Holland Park, Brisbane

1974 Arts, Crafts and Music Centre, Darling Downs Institute of Technology, Toowoomba, Queensland

1975 Anderson House, Kruger Road, Carbrook, Queensland

Covacevich House, Cairns, North Queensland

Dunlop House, Jesmond Street, Indooroopilly, Brisbane

Louis House, Alton Estate, The Gap, Brisbane

Peden Farm, Waroolba A.I.S. Stud, Moggill, Brisbane

University House, Griffith University, Nathan, Brisbane

1976 MacFarlane House, Repton Street, Pullenvale, Brisbane

Bardon Professional Development Centre, Bardon, Brisbane

1977 Hall of Residence, College of Technical Education, Kelvin Grove, Brisbane

Publications:

On DALTON: books—*Best Australian Homes* by Neil Clerehen, Melbourne 1961; *Towards an Australian Architecture* by Harry Sowden, Sydney 1968; *Architecture in Australia* by J. M. Freeland, Sydney 1968; *Architecture in Tropical Australia* by Balwant Singh Saini, London 1970; *Living and Partly Living: Housing in Australia* by Ian McKay and others, Melbourne 1971; *The Visual Arts* by M. Symonds, Brisbane 1972; *Understanding Art* by B. Churcher, Adelaide 1973; *Australian Housing in the 70's* by Howard Tanner, Sydney 1976; articles—"We Should Build to Suit the Climate" in *Courier Mail* (Brisbane), 21 July 1965; "Architect of Sun and Shadow" by Babette Hayes in *Belle* (Sydney), July/August 1977.

Design for climate is the simple solution for all our architectural endeavour in Queensland. It is the mainspring for all the magical qualities that add up to a vital architecture. The broad verandahs and the cool, serene arcades found in our early architecture are qualities that we recognize and unconsciously delight in. The delicate tracery of shadow on a simple light-washed wall reveal the ever-changing character of buildings in the sun. We instinctively love these patterns of climate, as they are part of our experience, and we have every right to expect them in contemporary design. Our delight is to build in the sun and gather our poetic inspiration from the sunlight, shade, and shadow that is our heritage.

—John Dalton

John Dalton belongs to a small band of English architects who migrated to Australia after the Second World War. Most of them chose to live and work in the comparatively temperate cities of Melbourne, Adelaide and Sydney, but Dalton decided to settle in the sub-tropical environment of Brisbane, where he extended his earlier training in building and finally qualified as an architect. Dalton's early practice was confined to domestic building, mainly single houses, and it was in this kind of work that he built his reputation as a highly sensitive and skilful designer. During the 1970's, however, his work has considerably expanded, and it now includes a number of larger projects—educational, professional and student residential buildings.

Dalton built houses at a time when many of the existing large old colonial timber houses with high ceilings and generous rooms and verandahs were

John Dalton: Peden Farm House, Moggill, Brisbane, 1975

being pulled down and were being replaced by more compact brick and brick veneer houses popular in the more temperate zones of south and east Australia. His buildings offered a refreshing contrast. He adapted quickly to his new humid, sub-tropical surroundings and realized that the main problem in building design lay in control of the sun, provision of cross ventilation, and reduction of glare. The roots of Dalton's earlier buildings, however, did not lie in the traditional Queensland vernacular, though he did make occasional gestures to the local domestic building tradition by adding wooden lattice work between verandah posts, louvres and horizontal lattice blinds. His earlier solutions were more in tune with the prevalent domestic architecture of Richard Neutra, William Wurster, and others who were busy on the west coast of the U.S.A.

Over the years Dalton has absorbed some of the casual semi-outdoor lifestyle of Queenslanders, and his recent houses reflect this influence. The rooms are planned to suit the specific needs of the owners, and the verandahs and terraces are generous and cantilevered well beyond the houses to reach out to nature. They have resulted in a highly personalized style that has been born out of his use of white coloured masonry walls, natural timbers and sloping roofs admirably suited to steep sites typically found in some of the outer areas of Brisbane.

John Dalton is thorough, meticulous in detail, and is extremely sensitive to the needs of his client. He has already established himself as an important designer and, judging by his recent work, should continue to make significant contributions to architecture in tropical Australia.

—B. S. Saini

DANNATT, (James) Trevor.

British. Born in London, 15 January 1920. Educated at Colfe's School, London; Regent Polytechnic, London, Dip.Arch. 1942. Married Joan Howell Davies in 1953; children: Clare and Adrian. Studio Assistant, School of Architecture, Regent Polytechnic, 1942–43; Assistant Architect, office of Jane B. Drew, London, 1943–44; office of E. Maxwell Fry and Jane B. Drew, London, 1944–48, and London County Council Architects' Department, Royal Festival Hall Group, 1948–52. In private practice, London, since 1952: formed Trevor Dannatt and Partners, 1972 (with Colin Dollimore and Ronald Paxton; currently, with Colin Dollimore). Instructor, Central School of Arts and Crafts, London, 1952–54; Chair of Architecture, University of Manchester, 1975; Visiting Professor, Washington University School of Architecture, St. Louis, 1976. Editor, 1945–46, and Joint Editor, with Jane B. Drew, 1946–62, *The Architects Yearbook*, London. Secretary, MARS Group, London, 1948–54. Exhibitions: *British Architecture*, Arts Council, London, 1955; *Architecture Today*, with Alan Irvine, Arts Council, London, 1961. Recipient: First Prize, Conference Centre and Hotel Competition, Riyadh, Saudi Arabia, 1968. Associate, 1943, and Fellow, 1961, Royal Institute of British Architects; Associate of the Royal Academy, 1977. Address: Trevor Dannatt and Partners, 115 Crawford Street, London W.1, England.

Works:

1957 Congregational Church, Blackheath, London
1958 Dobbs House, Hampstead, London
      Laslett House, Cambridge
1960 Plante House, Hampstead, London
      College Hall Student Residence, University of Leicester (with Sir Leslie Martin)
1962 Vaughan College and Museum, Leicester
1964 Interiors and reconstruction, 40 Berkeley Square, London

Needler Hall, University of Hull
      Fellows Social Building, Trinity Hall, Cambridge
1965 Library and Council Chamber, University of Leicester
      Gymnasium and Science Building, Rosa Bassett School, London S.W.17
1966 Assembly Hall, Bootham School, York
      House, Colinsburgh, Fife, Scotland
      Housing, Poplar High Street, London E.14
1969 Classroom Building, Eltham Hill School, London S.E.9
      Old people's home, Cedars Road, London S.W.4
1971 Children's Reception Home, Davey Street, London S.E.15
      Old people's home, Sumner Road, London S.E.15 (with John Shaw)
1972 Meeting halls, Acorn Estate, and Sceaux Gardens, Southwark, London
      Friends' Meeting House, Blackheath, London
1974 Conference Centre, Riyadh, Saudi Arabia
      Intercontinental Hotel, Riyadh, Saudi Arabia (with Colin Dollimore and Ronald Paxton)
      Mosque and villas, Riyadh, Saudi Arabia (with Colin Dollimore and Ronald Paxton)
      Housing, Charminster Road, Mottingham, London S.E.9 (with Colin Dollimore)
      Building society offices, Greenwich, London (with Colin Dollimore)
1975 Housing, Union Road, Lambeth, London (with Colin Dollimore)
      Welfare home, Union Road, Lambeth, London (with Colin Dollimore)
1976 Playground, Greenwich Park, London (with Colin Dollimore)
      Meeting hall, Warwick Estate, London W.2 (with Colin Dollimore)
1977 Housing, Langton Way, London S.E.3 (with John Shaw)
      Playground, Lilestone Estate, London W.2 (with Colin Dollimore)
      Sheltered Housing Extension, Whittington College, Felbridge, Surrey (with Colin Dollimore)

Designs: interior for Richard Church, Curtisden Green, Kent, 1950; tea bar, *Festival of Britain*, South Bank, London, 1951; Spry Cooking Centre, London, 1954; reception area, Lund Humphries, publishers, Bradford, 1955, and London, 1958.

Development Studies: Hatcliffe Charity, 1965; London University Precinct, with Sir Leslie Martin, 1965; Trinity Hall, Cambridge, 1966; Trinity College, Cambridge, 1967; Bootham School, York, 1969; Parcorm Estate, Beirut, 1972; Society of Friends Euston Road Building, London, 1973.

Publications:

By DANNATT: books—*Architects Yearbook*, editor, nos. 1–2, joint editor, with Jane B. Drew, nos. 3–10, London 1946–62; *Modern Architecture in Britain*, London 1959; article—"The Architect's Approach to Architecture" in *RIBA Journal* (London), March 1969.

On DANNATT: book—*Trevor Dannatt: Buildings and Interiors 1951–72*, introduced by Theo Crosby, London 1972; articles—in *Architectural Design* (London), May 1963, and *Architectural Review* (London), March 1967, April 1973, and April 1975.

It is not the size of what we build but the quality of thought and the task evaluation that matters. There is a time to be noble and a time to be modest—which doesn't mean relaxing thought but possibly intensifying it to decide what can be discarded and what is appropriate.

Where does design start? At the conscious level, no doubt, the functional/practical—but at the same time maybe with a vision, the idea of a space or form, or perhaps with a magic image of a conjunction of materials and light. The clarification of the problems, the accommodation/site equation determine the generating line. Sometimes an idea does spring out of the side of a problem, unsought, and development in one way is explored and then stopped or redirected for this or that severely practical reason, or because of one's inner censor. The process is one of continuous fusion, sometimes clear, sometimes mysterious.

We extend from the practical field of circulation and function, structure, services and economy, to consideration of well-being—psychological as well as physical needs. In certain areas we cannot just refer to intuitions but need to support them with more informed knowledge; thus it is "Not only thought, not only intuitions, but a terrible amount of disciplined labour"—at the level of the task (the function/folk equation) and then at the level of a building design (the means/milieu equation) and its realization.

We *may* start with a "concept" along with the analysis and consideration of parts, the latter a necessary study, albeit crude, a design process that sorts out basic accommodation and makes an arrangement serving convenience, economy—securing appropriate advantages to each part while considering structure and services. Such a *synthetic* result is a reassuring stand-by but one which should be taken apart immediately for recreation as an *organic* entity. For that deeper structuring which, however we may start, is the essential basis of architecture, the organizational/spatial pattern which should pervade a building in all dimensions, transmuting the utilitarian into significant order to produce "the architectural totality, the building task realized within a characteristic formal organization," and through this we are concerned with *ambience*, something to which we respond beyond convenience, a milieu which connects us to the poetry of living, heightening our awareness of today as part of yesterday and the day before yesterday. This is the *organic* architecture for which to strive.

—Trevor Dannatt

Trevor Dannatt is an eminent example of a dedicated professional whose maturity came about in the immediate post-war years. His work bears the stamp of deep consideration for the user combined with a strongly disciplined aesthetic sensibility. No seeker for huge commissions and someone who would not wish to approach the "executive" role as the ruler over a large commercial practice, Dannatt keeps his finger on the design process throughout, with the result that the whole range of his considerable achievement is utterly consistent.

There is a modesty and tolerance in his approach that is exemplified in his own words: "I am amazed at the certainty with which others speak about matters that to my mind can be seen in at least two ways." For this reason, perhaps, Trevor Dannatt, although producing work of the greatest significance, cannot be regarded as an "influence" in the sense that he has turned the direction of architectural design by his own example, a task that in any case demands a single-minded obstinacy. Such a tremendous steering of a whole generation of the profession, however, has two sides to be considered: it may powerfully influence design towards a new aesthetic, but it equally engenders a following of enthusiasts many of whom misinterpret and vulgarize it, often with a self-destructive result.

Even his largest work—an hotel, conference centre and mosque, won in an international competition—is unlikely to influence work in this country, for it is in Riyadh, Saudi Arabia, where nevertheless it might well influence the "emergent" architects of the Middle East.

Trevor Dannatt: Assembly Hall, Bootham School, York, 1966

The most important aspect of Dannatt's widely diverse practice is that the results stand as examples to be digested by any student and to those in the profession who can bring themselves to study the work of their contemporaries, for in Dannatt's work can always be detected the absolute dedication of the man both in his control of form and in the smallest detail of design, with the proper and logical use of materials, the reaching back as well as forward to uphold the essential continuity of architectural development. He has expressed his antipathy to "the idea of architecture as business, and the fallacy of size, the thought that we might solve our problems by making them bigger. . . . I believe we should aspire to relieve the anthill of society and technology rather than be the apostles of the brave new world."

Architecture is fortunate in having amongst its practitioners such a pure professional whose example, both practical and aesthetic, has been expressed in such permanent ways and whose strength of character shows nothing of the arrogance that is so often the accompaniment of great gifts.

—H. A. N. Brockman

da ROZA, Gustavo.

Canadian. Born in Hong Kong, of Portuguese nationality, 24 February 1933; emigrated to Canada, 1960: naturalized, 1966. Educated at the School of Architecture, University of Hong Kong, under R. Gordon Brown, 1950–55, B.Arch. (first class honours) 1955. Married Gloria Go in 1961; children: Guia, Gabriella, Gina, Gustavo III, and Gil. Assistant Architect to R. Gordon Brown, Hong Kong, 1955–56; Designer, The Architects Collaborative, Cambridge, Massachusetts, summer 1959, and office of E. Lloyd Flood, San Francisco, 1959–61. Since 1961, Principal, da Roza Architects, Winnipeg. Instructor in Architecture, University of Hong Kong, 1956–58, and University of California, Berkeley, 1958–60. Assistant Professor, 1960–65, Associate Professor, 1965–71, and since 1971 Professor in Architecture, University of Manitoba, Winnipeg. Chairman, Canadian Housing Design Council, 1975–77. Honorary Consul of Portugal in Winnipeg since 1970. Exhibitions: Royal Academy, London, 1956, 1958; *Indianapolis Home Show,* Indiana, 1959, 1960. Recipient: First Prize, with others, Winter Olympic Games Project Competition, Banff, Alberta, 1963; First Prize, Canadian Lumbermen's Association National House Design Competition, 1965; First Prize, Winnipeg Art Gallery Competition, 1967; House Design Award, Canadian Housing Design Council, 1967; Special Arts Award, 1967, and Senior Arts Award, 1975, Canada Council. Fellow, Royal Architectural Institute of Canada, 1973; Academician, Royal Canadian Academy of Arts, 1973. Address: da Roza Architects, 515 Shaftesbury Boulevard, Winnipeg, Manitoba R3P OM3, Canada.

Works:

1955 F. Remedios House, 10 Kent Road, Kowloon, Hong Kong
1957 Wan Yan College Chapel, Waterloo Road, Kowloon, Hong Kong (design only)
1958 P. Remedios House, Clear Water Bay Road, New Territories, Hong Kong
       Chiap Hua Clock Factory, Matauwei Road, Kowloon, Hong Kong
1962 da Roza House, 23 Waterford Bay, Fort Garry, Manitoba

1963 Speers House, 3304 Assiniboine Avenue, Assiniboia, Manitoba
       Scalena House, 3276 Assiniboine Avenue, Assiniboia, Manitoba
1964 Hutcheson House, River Road, Selkirk, Manitoba (with A. J. Donahue)
       Kalef House, 403 Doreham Boulevard, Tuxedo, Manitoba
       Sokolov House, 413 Shaftesbury Boulevard, Tuxedo, Manitoba
       Bergman House renovations, 209 Yale Avenue, Winnipeg
1965 Pitcairn House, 516 Laidlaw Boulevard, Tuxedo, Manitoba
       4 houses, Cuthbertson Avenue, Tuxedo, Manitoba
1966 Lockhead House, 634 Kilkenny Drive, Fort Garry, Manitoba
       C. Smith House, 3354 Assiniboine Avenue, Assiniboia, Manitoba
       "Man and His Home" Pavilion, *Expo '67,* Montreal
1967 da Roza House II, 515 Shaftesbury Boulevard, Tuxedo, Manitoba
       Ferguson House renovations, 78 Thatcher Drive, Fort Garry, Manitoba
       Fingold House renovations, 236 Victoria Crescent, St. Vital, Manitoba
1968 Nitikman House, 519 Shaftesbury Boulevard, Tuxedo, Manitoba
       Walder House, 513 Shaftesbury Boulevard, Tuxedo, Manitoba
       Frame House, 3348 Assiniboine Avenue, Assiniboia, Manitoba
1969 Burstein House, 455 Park Boulevard East, Tuxedo, Manitoba
       Yip House, 14 Paradise Bay, Charleswood, Manitoba
       Bihler House, 507 Shaftesbury Boulevard, Tuxedo, Manitoba

Gustavo da Roza: Winnipeg Art Gallery, 1971

Publications:

On da ROZA: book—*Winnipeg* by Mitchell and Benham, Winnipeg 1974; articles—in *The Architect and Building News* (London), 10 May 1956; *Star Weekly* (Toronto), 3 September 1966; *Canadian Builder* (Toronto), April 1967; *Chatelaine* (Toronto), May 1967; *Artscanada* (Toronto), April 1968, and February/March 1971; "Branch Bank, Winnipeg" in *Canadian Architect* (Toronto), June 1971; "Winnipeg Art Gallery" in *Canadian Architect* (Toronto), July 1972; Canadian issue of *Progressive Architecture* (New York), September 1972; *Kenchiku Bunka* (Tokyo), January 1973; *Asian Architect and Builder* (Hong Kong), April 1973; "A Perspective of Modern Canadian Architecture" in *Process: Architecture* (Tokyo/Pittsburgh), no. 5, 1978.

Architecture is the art of resolving our needs for physical shelter harmoniously with the environment, while responding to visual aspirations, thus contributing to our cultural heritage.

Architecture is more than sound building. It must meet ALL design determinants: functional requirements, environmental conditions, technical and economic limitations, and visual aspirations.

Architecture is a continuous and dynamic challenge to contribute positively to society in spite of difficulties of contradictions, of time, of place, and of personalities. It is a pragmatic art requiring dedicated application of knowledge and principles, thus adding to the fountain of ideas, experience and experiments, and contributions made by the profession through history to date.

—Gustavo da Roza

Mechanical Consultants Western Ltd. office interiors, Winnipeg
1970 Standing House, 14 King's Drive, Fort Garry, Manitoba
R. Smith House, Southboine Avenue, Charleswood, Manitoba
Schwartz House additions, Thatcher Drive, Fort Garry, Manitoba
Decorations for the Royal Visit, Manitoba Centennial Celebrations, Winnipeg
Decoration of the National Arts Centre, Manitoba Centennial, Ottawa
1971 Winnipeg Art Gallery, Memorial Boulevard, Winnipeg (with Number Ten Architectural Group)
Vincent Week-end House, Victoria Beach, Manitoba
WAG System Furniture, for Krug Furniture, Kitchener, Ontario
1972 Ringers Drug Store renovations, 1151 Pembina Highway, Fort Garry, Manitoba
Wong House, 2 Paradise Bay, Charleswood, Manitoba
Owens Art Gallery, Mt. Allison, Sackville, New Brunswick (with Brown, Brisley and Brown)
1973 Bank of Montreal Branch, Mountain and McGregor, Winnipeg
Wittman House additions, 516 Laidlàw Boulevard, Tuxedo, Manitoba
Berkowitz House additions, 23 Carmarthen Boulevard, Tuxedo, Manitoba
YIP Orthodontic Clinic, 1887 Portage Avenue, St. James, Manitoba
Feasibility study: Little Grindstone Develop-

ment Proposal, Manitoba
1974 Summer Cabins for Provincial Parks, Hecla Island, Manitoba
Art Bank, for the Canada Council, Ottawa
Thomas Art Gallery, River and Osborne, Winnipeg
Venture Manitoba Tours Convention Centre interiors, Winnipeg
Feasibility study for the redevelopment of Chinatown in Winnipeg
Functional program for the Consulate General Residence of Japan, Winnipeg
1975 Apartments (45 units), 727 Nassau Street South, Winnipeg
Ferguson Week-end House, Clytie Bay, Ontario
1976 Asper House renovations, 1063 Wellington Crescent, Winnipeg
Stephens House additions, 1536 McCreary Road, Charleswood, Manitoba
Len Steingarten office interiors, Winnipeg
Functional program for the Vancouver Art Gallery
1977 Gull Harbour Resort Hotel, Hecla Island, Manitoba (also furniture for the hotel)
Tadman Hornstein Kalef and Company office interiors, Winnipeg
Nassau Square Townhouses (95 units), Winnipeg
Ringer Week-end House, Falcon Lake, Manitoba
1978 Payne House, Lot 1, Headingley, Manitoba
Sellers House, Lot 218, Riverbend Farms, St. Francois Xavier, Manitoba
1978- Church of the Immaculate Conception, 181

Gustavo da Roza is an exotic plant in an alien environment in which he not only flourishes unexpectedly but also provides unique fruits to enrich his new land.

Fundamental to da Roza's architectural style is the belief that the natural environment must be accepted and not fought. Working primarily on the great prairie of Canada, he must cope with powerful forces: the extreme flatness of the land and the limited color in the plant life it supports; the dominant horizontality that is reinforced by the great sky and its abundant sunshine; above all, the snow and ice of the long winters, which da Roza loves for the constantly changing sun-washed tints and frigid purity. In response, da Roza's buildings invariably hug the ground and present solid faces to the winds; openings are few and judiciously placed for visual and functional reasons. His palette is restricted to whites, browns, and grays, though he orchestrates these to enhance space and defeat monotony; when strong color appears, such as a red door, it is as a definite statement of function and never as ornament.

Da Roza's most celebrated building is the Winnipeg Art Gallery, a triangular mass on an urban site that dictated the ground plan. The gallery is virtually windowless and the form is simple; its austere silhouette is low; it is faced with an off-white local limestone that resembles frozen oatmeal. Yet, the modulations to the austerity are telling: a simple cut-out from the roof line reveals the walled outdoor roof sculpture gallery and allows the eye to pierce deeply into an important sheltered function otherwise hidden; a wedge protruding from the main mass announces the entrance, and a grid of clear glass lamps intensifies the event of arrival without disturbing the monochromatic whole. Inside, the gentle gradations of warm grays, whites and browns provide a muted background for art and comfortable spaces for viewing. It is a building that responds perfectly to the environment according to its designer's beliefs, and the response is intensely cerebral without the inhumanity of mere single-minded restraint.

But da Roza is not primarily a designer of monuments. For one thing, his practice is intentionally limited; he is primarily an architectural teacher. One of his great interests is housing, and he has expressed his ideas through the design of numerous houses. On the whole, these tend to be small, introverted, and practical, with interest provided by the same subtle techniques of light and form manipulation used in the art gallery. His designs provide a rich yet simple backdrop for family living and do not intrude.

Da Roza has built a solid reputation on this solid approach to his art. The oriental delicacy of his sensitivity and the clarity of his intellectual approach to design have produced works of peaceful dignity not usual for a designer so comparatively young. In this era of bravura exhibitionism and mass-produced extrusions, his sweet reasonableness is welcome.

—Kent Hurley

DAVIDSON, J(ulius) R(alph).

American. Born in Berlin, Germany, 7 February 1889; emigrated to the United States, 1924: naturalized, 1938. Educated at gymnasium in Berlin, and at preparatory college in Posen, now Poznan, Poland. Married Greta Wollstein in 1914; son: Ralph Thomas. Worked as a delineator for the architect Moritz Hirschler, Berlin, 1908–09; detailer and designer for the architect Frank Stuart Murray, London, 1910–12; designer for architects Paul and Alfred Dumas, Paris, 1913–14; in private practice as an architect, Berlin, 1919–23; detailer and designer for the architect David Farquhar, Los Angeles, 1924–25; set designer for Cecil B. DeMille, Los Angeles, 1925; architect in the office of Hite and Bilike, Los Angeles, 1926; in private practice, Los Angeles, 1927 until he retired to Ojai, California, 1972. Recipient: *Progressive Architecture* Award, 1946; Special Award, California Council of the American Institute of Architects, 1977. *Died* (in Ojai, California) *2 May 1977.*

Works:

1922   3 shops for Stiller Shoes, Berlin
1923   Hupfeld Piano Showroom and Auditorium, Berlin
1927/
    29   Office building with shops and restaurant, Wilshire Boulevard, Los Angeles
1932/
    35   Knickerbocker Hotel alterations, Chicago
        Shoreland Hotel alterations, Chicago
        Pearson Hotel alterations, Chicago
1937   Maitland House, 230 Strada Corta, Bel' Air, Los Angeles
        Stothart House, 2501 La Mesa Drive, Santa Monica, California (now Phillips House)
1940   Gretna Green Apartment Building, 12201 Dunoon Lane, Los Angeles
        Sabsay House, 2351 Silver Ridge, Silver Lake, Los Angeles
1941   Medical building, 6222 Wilshire Boulevard, Los Angeles
        Thomas Mann House, 1550 San Remo Drive, Pacific Palisades, California
        Vigeveno House, Ojai, California
1945   Cron House, 540 South Barrington Avenue, Los Angeles

1946   Kingsley Houses, 1620 and 1630 Amalfi Drive, Pacific Palisades, California
        Davidson House, 560 South Barrington Avenue, Los Angeles
        Crosby-Furniss House, 473 Denslow Avenue, Los Angeles (with addition, 1954)
1948   McFadden House, 1052 Toluca Lake Avenue, North Hollywood, California
        Case Study House, 4756 Lasheart Drive, La Canada, California
1949   Osherenko House, 1005 North Alpine Drive, Beverly Hills, California
        Schapiro House, Waverly and Maxwell Streets, Los Angeles
1951   Dann House, 1369 Londonderry Place, Los Angeles
1957   Dr. Egeberg House, 6918 Oporto Drive, Los Angeles
        Dr. Fenichel House, Tigertail Road, Los Angeles
        Dr. Munk House, 290 Westgate Avenue, Los Angeles
        Dr. Rabinowitz House, 2262 Stradella Road, Los Angeles
1958   Dr. Jokl House, 563 North Bundy Drive, Los Angeles
1966   Westgate Apartment Building, Westgate and Darlington, Brentwood, Los Angeles

Publications:

On DAVIDSON: books—*Tomorrow's House* by George Nelson and Henry Wright, New York 1945; *Houses* by Thomas Creighton, New York 1947; *The American House Today* by Thomas Creighton, New York 1951; *Contemporary Houses* by Thomas Creighton, New York 1961; *Modern California Houses* by Esther McCoy, New York 1962; *The Architecture of the Well-Tempered Environment* by Reyner Banham, Chicago 1969; *Los Angeles* by Reyner Banham, New York 1971; articles—"30 Distinguished Houses and Plans" in *House and Garden* (New York), November 1939; "Villa a Santa Monica" in *Casabella* (Milan), December 1940; "Small House on a Hill" in *Arts and Architecture* (Los Angeles), October 1941; "Interiors by J. R. Davidson" in *Arts and Architecture* (Los Angeles), June 1944; "40 Houses," special issue of *Architectural Forum* (New York), May 1948; "Sixteen Southern Californian Architects Exhibit Contemporary Trends" in *Arts and Architecture* (Los Angeles), April 1950; "Arts and Architecture Case Study Houses" by Esther McCoy in *Perspecta* (New Haven, Connecticut), no. 15, 1975; "J. R. Davidson" by Esther McCoy in *L.A. Architect* (Los Angeles), May 1977; "J. R. Davidson, 1889–1977" by Esther McCoy in *Progressive Architecture* (New York), September 1977.

*

J. R. Davidson was essentially a designer of interiors, and these were so carefully studied in terms of plan, circulation, storage spaces and human use that eventually the exterior form was little more than a loose envelope around a complex plan. His early work was mainly in the design of shops. His Stiller bootery shops and Hupfeld piano showroom and auditorium in Berlin were notable for the elegant use of metals, glass, flush surfaces, ingenious storage spaces, experiments in indirect lighting, and the discreet introduction of *fauve* colors. His first work in Los Angeles, a group which included a two-story office building, a restaurant and shops brought into harmony a collage of materials and colors; his remodellings of three Chicago hotels included what were to become prototypes of the post-Prohibition intimate cocktail lounge.

In 1937 he turned to the design of houses, and from then on his commissions were mainly residential. He adapted for his houses many of the practices for shops, especially indirect lighting and the glass screen wall—in the Stothart house they are used to separate entrance hall from living room, and bedroom from dressing room. In his experiments in floor planning he minimized halls or pressed them into a dual use (Cron house); in his "gallery" plan, used in most of his later houses, he broadened and lengthened the entrance hall to connect with the bedroom and service wings, and placed a glass screen above built-in cabinets between the gallery and living room. His skill in the design of storage units came from his three years in London as a detailer and designer of interiors of ocean liners and yachts for Frank Stuart Murray, while his sensitivity to colors and fabrics was heightened during the early Art Deco period in Paris.

J. R. Davidson: Stothart House, Santa Monica, California, 1937

His early houses and flats (Gretna Green Apartments) fell into the International Style, but he never strictly obeyed its tenets. By the end of the 1940's many of his roofs were sloped and no module was respected; walls were often of plywood, and a combined ceiling/roof surface of wood planking replaced plastered surfaces.

Davidson's most complex plans came in the late style; most successful among them were ones for psychiatrists whose offices were attached to the house (Dr. Jokl house, Dr. Fenichel house).

—Esther McCoy

DAVIS, Lewis.

American. Born in New York City, 31 July 1927. Educated at the University of Pennsylvania, Philadelphia, B.Arch.; Columbia University, New York. Served in the United States Air Force, 1942–45. Married to Anne Davis; children: Steven, Michael, Peter, and Ariel. Architect, Kelly and Gruzen, New York, 1948–51, Mayer and Whittlesey, New York, 1951–52, and Samuel Juster, New York, 1952. Since 1953, Partner, with Samuel Brody, q.v., Davis, Brody and Associates, New York. Adjunct Professor, Cooper Union School of Architecture, New York, since 1958. Davenport Professor of Architecture, Yale University School of Architecture, New Haven, Connecticut, 1974. Member, Mayor's Advisory Committee on Housing in New York, 1965; Member of the Executive Committee, 1965–69, Vice-President, 1969, and Chairman of the Housing Committee, 1972, American Institute of Architects, New York Chapter; Member, National Commission on Urban Problems, 1967–69; Chairman, Progressive Architecture Design Awards Jury, 1968; Member, Task Force Advisory Council, United States Department of Housing and Urban Development, 1973. Recipient: Design Award, Progressive Architecture, 1954, 1955, 1958, 1961 (twice), 1962, 1966; Honor Award, American Institute of Architects, Potomac Valley, Maryland Chapter, 1958; Design Award, Church Architectural Guild of America, 1958; Certificate of Merit, New York City Department of Commerce, 1958; Certificate of Merit, 1958, 1963, and Award, 1973, 1974, New York State Association of Architects; Award of Merit, House and Home, 1960; United States Department of Health, Education and Welfare Award, 1966; Honor Award, AIA, New England Regional Council, 1966; Higher Education Facilities Design Award, 1966; Honor Award, 1968, 1971 (twice), 1976, and Architectural Firm Award, 1975, national AIA; Bard Award, City Club of New York, 1969, 1973, 1975; Certificate of Merit, Municipal Arts Society, New York, 1969, 1972, 1973 (twice); Concrete Industries Award, 1969; Staten Island Chamber of Commerce Award, New York, 1970; Golden Triangle Award, National Society of Interior Designers, 1970; International Design Award, American Institute of Design, 1970; Bartlett Award, 1971, 1976; Homes for Better Living Award, 1971; Award of Honor, New York Society of Architects, 1972, 1973, 1974; Medal of Honor, AIA, New York Chapter, 1973; Mayor of New York's Citation for Distinguished Service, 1973; Brunner Award, National Institute of Arts and Letters, 1975; Louis Sullivan Award, 1977. Fellow, American Institute of Architects. Address: Davis, Brody and Associates, 130 East 59th Street, New York, New York 10022, U.S.A.

Works (with Samuel Brody):

1963 Waterside (apartments), New York
Riverbend (apartments), New York
East Midtown Housing, New York
Science Building, State University of New York at New Paltz
Estée Lauder Cosmetics Plant, Melville, New York (with Richard Dattner)

Library, Cooper Union, New York
Social Science Building, Long Island University, Brooklyn, New York (with Horowitz/Chan)
1965 Bronx Park South Housing, Bronx, New York
1966 Brody House, Brooklyn, New York
Westport Office Building, Connecticut
River Park Towers, New York
Science Building, State University of New York at Binghamton
Lambert Houses (apartments), Bronx, New York
1967 United States Pavilion, Expo '70, Osaka, Japan
Sachs Furniture Stores, New York
Boston Road Apartments, Bronx, New York
1968 100 William Street Office Building, New York (with Emery Roth and Sons)
Dormitories and Dining Halls, State University of New York at Buffalo
Group Residence, Children's Aid Society, Staten Island, New York
Library, Long Island University, Brooklyn, New York (with Horowitz/Chan)
1969 Interiors for the State University of New York at Binghamton
Central Refrigeration Plant, State University of New York at Buffalo
1971 Cathedral Parkway Housing, New York
1972 Robert Crown Athletic and Recreation Center, Hampshire College, Amherst, Massachusetts
Coney Island Housing, Brooklyn, New York
Waterside Health Club and Pool, New York
1973 St. Lawrence State Hospital, Ogdensburg, New York
1974 Quadrangle renovation, University of Pennsylvania, Philadelphia
Brooklyn College of Pharmacy, Brooklyn, New York (with Horowitz/Chan)
1975 Athletic facilities for Massachusetts Institute of Technology, Cambridge
Estée Lauder Cosmetics Plant, Switzerland (with Richard Dattner)
Federal Correctional Institution, Otisville, New York (with Large/Moger)
Office Building rehabilitation, for American Airlines, Hartford, Connecticut (with Associated Architects)
Allan Harvey House, Vermont
1976 Biochemistry Building, Princeton University, New Jersey
Town Hall, Huntington, Long Island, New York
1977 Corning Glass Works Building, Corning, New York
Yale/New Haven Medical Center, New Haven, Connecticut (with Russo and Sonder)
Atlantic-Richfield Research Building, Newtown Square, Pennsylvania (with Llewelyn-Davies Associates)
Intercontinental Hotel, Isfahan, Iran (with DAZ)
1978 Arco Chemical Corporation Research and Development Center, New Town Square, Pennsylvania (with Jaquelin Robertson)

Publications:

On DAVIS/BRODY: books—Religious Buildings for Today by John Knox Shear, New York 1957; Schoolhouse by Walter McQuade, New York 1958; Architecture of Monuments by Thomas Creighton, New York 1962; Architectural Design Preview U.S.A. by John Dixon, New York 1962; New Directions in American Architecture by Robert A.M. Stern, New York 1969; Will They Ever Finish Bruckner Boulevard? by Ada Louise Huxtable, New York 1970; Principles of Pneumatic Architecture by Roger Dent, London 1971; Industrial Buildings and Factories by

Oswald Grube, London 1971; articles—"10 Projects" in Kenchikubunka (Tokyo), August 1970; "Work of Davis, Brody and Associates" in L'Architecture d'Aujourd'hui (Paris), August 1971; "The Work of Davis, Brody and Associates" in Architecture + Urbanism (Tokyo), December 1972; "Davis, Brody and Associates" in AIA Journal (Washington, D.C.), May 1975.

* * *

In more than 25 years of partnership Lewis Davis and Sam Brody have consistently produced architecture of outstanding quality. Their buildings are handsome and carefully detailed, but, far more important, they are unpretentious examples of a rational, humanistic approach to architecture that displays uncommon integrity and conscientiousness.

Their work has been remarkably varied; they have completed major commercial, industrial, educational, and residential projects. Without doubt, though, their most significant contribution has been in the field of public housing, which they have almost single handedly revolutionized. Rejecting the pattern of Pruitt-Igoe, which continued to be a model for low-income residential development in America well into the 1960's, Davis and Brody have created projects that are highly economical, offer up-to-date facilities, and yet, unlike earlier projects, still preserve human identity and existing urban patterns.

The key to their success has been sophisticated architectural maneuvers, accomplished not at the expense of contextual and human concerns but in support of them. Unusual massing gives many of the buildings a sculptural quality: inhabitants sense individuality in them, and they have therefore become sources of inspiration—a change from the dreary mediocrity to which residents are usually condemned. Any extra expense incurred by formal manipulation, though, has been more than recovered by Davis and Brody's efficient planning and careful choice and application of materials.

Most of the projects employ standard masonry construction because it is inexpensive, allows great planning flexibility, and is resistant to the "urban vandal's ultimate weapon—the spray paint gun." At Lambert Houses, an urban renewal project for New York City's decayed South Bronx, a special brick was developed by Davis and Brody that was larger (requiring fewer courses of brick), extruded with horizontal cavities (for lighter weight), and finished with a handle (for easier laying). Estimates suggest that the man hours saved as a result of this innovation cut more than half a million dollars off the total project budget.

In other projects Davis and Brody have been given opportunities to design with less restrictive budgets, but one still never senses any sort of wastefulness, and their concern for creating dynamic spaces for people has remained unfaltering. In an office building in New York's commercial district, for example, the architects have presented the public with an 80' high passage from one street to another. The huge galleria is lined with shops and suggests a visual connection with an existing plaza across the street, thus extending the site, conceptually, in that direction. They developed a new Science Building Complex for the State University of New York Center at Binghamton only after completing a remarkably elaborate user requirement study, further demonstrating their genuine concern with user satisfaction over formal architectural statement.

Nevertheless, their work is visually excellent, and Davis and Brody cannot be accused of aesthetic insensitivity. They are masters who have skillfully used their ability to mold space for the benefit of those people who most frequently are abused by architects. Not only have they created institutions that maintain human scale and propriety, but they have also offered decent, pleasant, and gaily exciting housing to the people of the city of New York. The residents of that city ought to be deeply grateful, and we, as architects, ought to take great heed of the lessons Davis and Brody have, through their work, offered us.

—Mitchell B. Rouda

Giancarlo De Carlo: Faculty of Education, Free University, Urbino, 1976

DE CARLO, Giancarlo.
Italian. Born in Genoa, 12 December 1919. Educated at the Polytechnic, Milan, Dip.Ing. 1942; Institute of Architecture, Venice, 1945–49, Dip.Arch. 1949. In private practice, Milan, since 1950. Professor of Urban Design, Institute of Architecture, Venice, since 1955. Member, Team 10. Recipient: INA-Casa National Prize, 1949; National Prize, Urban Development Competition, Aldisio, Italy, 1953; First Prize, Housing Development Competition, Matera, Italy, 1954; First Prize, Urban Development Competition, Donoratico, Italy, 1957; First Prize, with others, Master Plan for the City Centre of Padua Competition, 1960; Edoardo Caracciolo Prize, 1963; Sir Patrick Abercrombie Prize, International Union of Architects, 1967; First Prize, General Hospital Competition, Milan, 1967; First Prize, Community Education Centre Competition, Perugia, 1976. Honorary Member, American Academy of Arts and Sciences, and American Institute of Architects. Member, National Academy of San Luca, Rome. Address (office): via Mascheroni 18, 20145 Milan, Italy.

Works:

1946 Small houses for ex-servicemen, Quarter T.8, Milan (competition project; with others)
1947 Youth Hostel, Quarter T.8, Milan (competition project; with others)
Standardization and Industrialization Display, *Triennale,* Milan
1948 Master plan for Reggio Emilia, Italy (with Franco Albini)
Public housing development, Sicily (competition project; with others)

1949 Workers' housing development, Varese, Italy
1950 Master plan for Tortona, Italy (competition project)
Spontaneous Architecture Display, *Triennale,* Milan
INA-Casa Housing Development, Sesto S. Giovanni, Italy
1951 Flight of steps, Viale delle Palme, Nervi, Italy (project)
INA-Casa Apartment Buildings, Arona, Baveno, and Stresa, Italy
1952/
60 Free University reconstruction, Urbino
1953 Cesate Residential Centre, Varese, Italy (competition project)
1954 Structural frame for the *Santa Lucia* cargo boat, constructed at Pietra Ligure, Italy
Residential development, Matera, Italy
Urbanism Exhibition, *Triennale,* Milan
1955 Student Housing, Free University, Urbino
Congress House, Stresa, Italy (competition project)
Cassa del Mezzogiorno Housing Developments (3), Matera, Italy (projects)
2 urban plans for the Canton Vesco Quarter, Ivrea, Italy
1956/
57 Apartment building, Matera, Italy
Pineta Costiera di Donoratico Urban Development, Livorno (competition project)
INA-Casa Apartment Building, Villanuova sul Clisi, Italy
1957 Farmhouse, Colbordolo, Urbino (project)
Elementary school, Pievebovigliani, Italy
1957/
59 Cedas e Santi Co-operative Apartment Building, Urbino
School, Fiastra, Italy
1958 Zigiaina House, Cervignano del Fiuli, Italy
Urban plan for the Feltre Quarter of Milan (with others)
1958/
64 Master plan for the City of Urbino
1959 School, Campione d'Italia, Italy (competition project)
Italian/Swiss Education Centre Children's Home, Rimini, Italy
Children's Mountain Resort (project)
1960/
68 School of Humanities restoration, Milan
Plan for the centre of Padua (competition project; with others)
1961 Apartment and shop building, Feltre Quarter, Milan (project)
Marcello Ceccarelli House, Bologna
Residential Zone, Marbella, Spain (competition project)
Master plan for Volterra, Italy (competition project; with others)
1961/
63 SIP Children's Colony, Riccione, Italy (with Armando Barp)
1961/
64 Marine Colony, Classe, Ravenna (project)
1961/
66 High school, Feltre Quarter, Milan
Azienda Trasporti Holiday Home, Bordighera, Italy
1962 SIP Recreational Centre, Viverone Lake, Italy
Lavagine Quarter, Urbino (enquiry/reclamation project)
Master plan for the Commune of Ameglia, Italy (with Paolo Ceccarelli)
1962/
65 Residential Development for 25,000 Inhabitants, Assago, South Milan (project)
1962/
66 Faculty buildings, Free University, Urbino
1963 Apartment buildings, Assago, South Milan
Palazzo degli Anziani restoration and reconstruction, for the Faculty of Economics and Commerce, Free University of Urbino

at Ancona
Children's Library, School of Humanities, Milan
1964 University of Dublin (competition project; with Armando Barp)
Houses for journalists, Anzano del Parco, Milan (project)
Master plan for the Commune of Sarzana, Italy (with others)
1965 Italian/Swiss Education Centre, Rimini, Italy
1965/
66 School for the Disabled, Bologna (project)
Open-Air School and Heliotherapy Centre, Bologna
1965/
68 Giovanni Santi Co-operative Apartment Building, Urbino
1966 Plan for the Piansevero zone of Urbino (with others)
Re-organization of the Free University buildings within the master plan of the City of Urbino (with others)
Cultural Centre, Riyadh, Saudi Arabia (competition project)
1966/
68 XVII Century Convent restoration and reconstruction, for the Faculty of Law, Free University, Urbino
1967 Faculty of Economics and Commerce, University College, Ancona, Italy (project)
Livio Sichirollo House, Cavallino, Urbino
General Hospital, Mirano, Italy (competition project)
Town Hall, Amsterdam (competition project; with Armando Barp and George Solms)
Plan for the Petriccio zone of Urbino
1967/
69 La Pineta Residential Complex, Urbino
1968 Plan for the Cesane area, Urbino (with others)
Plan for the reconstruction of the centre of Plovdiv, Bulgaria (competition project; with F. Spirito and P. de Brerleville)
Development plan for the coastline between Antignano and Quercianella, Livorno (with others)
Commercial Centre reconstruction, Urbino (project)
1968/
76 XV Century Convent restoration and reconstruction, for the Faculty of Education, Free University, Urbino
1969 International Pavilion, *Expo '70,* Osaka
Matteotti Quarter reconstruction, Terni, Italy (project)
"Casa dei Ragazzi," Urbino (project)
Oil company headquarters, Garbagnate, Milan (project)
1969/
72 Underground Carpark, Commercial Centre, Urbino
1970 Plan to re-site the "Orto dell'Abbondanza," Urbino (project)
Underground Terminal, Colle delle Vigne, Urbino (project)
1970/
72 Plan for the centre of Rimini, Italy
1970/
77 Restoration of the ramp of Francesco di Giorgio and re-opening of a passage under the Theatre Sanzio, Urbino
1970/
79 Theatre Sanzio reconstruction, Urbino
1971/
74 Matteotti New Village, phase I, Terni, Italy
1972/
75 Development plan for the University of Pavia, Italy
1972/
80 Institute of Art, Urbino
1974/
76 CNR Laboratories, and Faculty of Engineer-

ing, University of Pavia, Italy
1976 Institute of Genetics, University of Pavia, Italy
Community Education Centre, Perugia (competition project; with others)
1976/
79 Development plan for the San Miniato area and the Lizza area, Siena (with others)
1977 United Nations Environment Program Headquarters, Nairobi (with others)
1977/
80 Buia Elementary School, Friuli, Italy
Osoppo Elementary and Middle School, Italy
1979 Novafeltria Theatre, Marche, Italy (project)
Plan for the reconstruction of the Vigne e dell'Orto degli Scalzi area, Urbino

Publications:

By DE CARLO: books—*Le Corbusier,* Milan 1945; *William Morris,* Milan 1947; *Questioni di Architettura e Urbanistica,* Urbino 1965; *Proposal for a University Structure,* Venice 1965; *Urbino: La Storia di Una Città e il Piano della sua Evoluzione Urbanistica,* Padua 1966, Cambridge, Massachusetts 1970; *Pianificazione e Disegno delle Università,* Venice 1968; *La Piramide Rovesciata,* Bari, Italy 1968; *An Architecture of Participation,* Melbourne 1972, Milan 1973; articles—"L'Insegnamento di F. L. Wright" in *Domus* (Milan), no. 207, 1946; "William Morris: Pioniere dell'Arte Sociale" in *Domus* (Milan), no. 211, 1947; "Formalismo, Continuità dell'Accademismo" in *Casabella* (Milan), no. 199, 1954; "Discussione sulla Valutazione Storica dell'Architettura e sulla Misura Umana" in *Casabella* (Milan), no. 210, 1956; "Una Precisazione" in *Casabella* (Milan), no. 214, 1957; "Il Contributo degli Architetti Italiani alla Cultura Internazionale" in *L'Architettura* (Rome), no. 33, 1958; "Furniture, Exhibition and Industrial Design in Contemporary Italian Architecture" in *The Architects Yearbook,* London 1958; "The Situation of Contemporary Architecture: CIAM 1959" in *Dokumente der Modernen Architektur,* Stuttgart 1959; "I Piani Paesistici e il Codice dell'Urbanistica" in *Urbanistica* (Turin), no. 33, 1961; "Programmi di Sviluppo Economico e Pianificazione Urbanistica: Proposte Operative" in *Casabella* (Milan), no. 270, 1962, reprinted in *Urbanistica* (Turin), no. 38, 1963; "Why/How to Build School Buildings" in *Harvard Educational Review* (Cambridge, Massachusetts), no. 4, 1969; "Il Pubblico dell'Architettura" in *Parametro* (Bologna), no. 5, 1971; "Architecture Between Self and System" in *Parametro* (Bologna), March 1975; "Rimini: A Plan for Today and Tomorrow" in *Parametro* (Bologna), September/October 1975; "Giancarlo De Carlo, Architect," interview with P. Korose-Serfaty, in *Neuf* (Brussels), September/October 1975; "Team X at Royaumont, 1962" in *Architectural Design* (London), November 1975; "Further Notes on Participation" in *Parametro* (Bologna), January/February 1977; "Reflections on the Present State of Architecture" in *Architectural Association Quarterly* (London), no. 2, 1978.

On DE CARLO: book—*Giancarlo De Carlo* by C. Colombo, Milan 1964; articles—"University College in Urbino" by Aldo van Eyck in *Zodiac* (Milan), no. 16, 1960; "De Carlo" in *Architectural Review* (London), October 1970; "Counterpoint in Concrete" in *Architectural Forum* (New York), May 1972; "Works by Giancarlo De Carlo" in *Architecture + Urbanism* (Tokyo), July 1974; "Giancarlo De Carlo: La Réconciliation de l'Architecture et de la Politique" in *L'Architecture d'Aujourd'hui* (Paris), January/February 1975; "Monastery, Urbino; Convent, Urbino; Orto dell'Abbondanza, Urbino" in *New Uses for Old Buildings,* edited by Sherban Cantacuzino, London 1975; "Matteotti Housing Development" by Naomi Miller in *Progressive Architecture* (New York), December 1976; "The Work of Giancarlo De Carlo" in *Architect and Builder* (Cape Town), November 1977; "Urbino: A Story Which

Continues" by Pier Carlo Santini in *Ottagono* (Milan), September 1978; "Urbino Outlook" by Judy Loach in *Architectural Review* (London), April 1979.

Against a background of constant political change and cultural turmoil, Giancarlo De Carlo has remained committed to his fundamental belief in the inevitability of Socialism. It is with this attitude firmly in mind that his contribution to the evolution of the new architecture of Italy must be considered. In every sense he is an architect of social commitment; he believes that what he builds is but a facet of the total human, social, and, often unpredictable, economic situation.

The history of post-war Italian architecture is riddled with movement and counter-movement, and that history, coupled with the traditional enmity between North and South, between Milan and Rome, has made it extremely difficult for an Italian architect to arrive at any coherent formal plan. Like other Italians, De Carlo has had to learn to live with the splendours of the past; he has had to make a very deliberate attempt to blend the best of traditional methods and accomplishments with what he realizes are the vital necessities of the present. He is constantly looking for new ways and, more important, new forms with which to answer today's problems. He is a realist; he knows what he is up against.

An intellectual in the true Italian sense, De Carlo has proposed changes not only in the building process but also, at the very earliest stages, in committee procedures. Constantly frustrated by the ever changing pattern of local authority politics and by uninformed public opinion, he has become one of the most articulate polemicists in the whole of Western Europe. He realizes the need to maintain contact with the general public in order to enlist sympathy and interest: he wants to build for the individual so as to give him a sense of value in his everyday existence. Those who are to live and work in his buildings are given every possible say in the initial design, and his concept of architecture is truly democratic.

De Carlo is internationally respected for his work on the Free University in Urbino, one of the most traditional of all Italian cities, where he has built what amounts to a "cartoon" of a hill-top town: it is at once physically unlike anything that has been built before, yet in essence it is highly familiar. His ability to keep the balance between past and present is remarkable.

A regular member of Team 10 in recent years, De Carlo has also become one of the dominant personalities of the 1970's, with a particular appeal for the younger generation. He is an inspiring teacher. His avowed distrust of an "expressionist" answer to a possible anti-formalist method makes him one of the men of the moment, and his contribution to the new architecture of the future is awaited with interest by all those concerned with the steady evolution of the Modern Movement.

—John Furse

DEILMANN, Harald.

German. Born in Gladbeck, Westphalia, 30 August 1920. Educated at the J. C. Schlaun Gymnasium, Munster, graduated 1938; Technische Hochschule, Stuttgart, under Richard Döcker, Gunter Wilhelm, Hans Volkart, and Rolf Gutbrod, 1946–48, Dip.Ing. Arch. 1948. Served in the German Army, 1938–46. Married Elsbeth Schole in 1949; children: Thomas, Andreas, and Cordula. Lecturer, Technische Hochschule, Stuttgart, 1949–51; Partner, with H. Bartmann, Bartmann and Deilmann, Munster, 1951–53; Partner, with Max von Hausen, Ortwin Rave, and Werner Ruhnau, Architektenteam, Munster, 1953–

55. In private practice, Munster, since 1955; offices established in Dortmund, 1969, and Dusseldorf, 1973. Professor, Technische Hochschule, Stuttgart, 1963–69, and Director of the Institute for Building Studies, University of Stuttgart, 1964–69. Since 1969, Professor at the University of Dortmund. Exhibitions: *Christliche Kunst*, Schloss Corvey, Germany, 1972; *Kirchenbau in der Diskussion*, Stadtmuseum, Munich, 1973. Recipient: Northrhine/Westphalia Prize, 1962; Federal Distinguished Service Medal, 1977. Member, Akademie der Künste, Berlin, 1967; Member, Akademie für Städtebau und Landesplanung, 1970. Address (office): Prinzipalmarkt 13, 4400 Munster, West Germany.

Works:

1954/
56 Municipal Theatre, Munster (with Max von Hausen, Ortwin Rave, and Werner Ruhnau)
1955 Wustener Strasse Treatment Clinic, Bad Salzuflen, Germany
    Fraling Weaving Mill, Bahnhofstrasse 41–43, Nordwalde, Germany
1956 Tuberculosis Sanatorium, Engelskirchen, Germany
    Heerde College, Munster
1957 Vocational Training School, Bockum-Hovel/Ludinghausen, Germany (competition project)
    Vocational Training School, Bielefeld, Germany (competition project)
    High School, Marl, Germany (competition project)
    Town Hall, Dillingen/Saar, Germany (competition project)
    Central Regional Bank, Dusseldorf (competition project)
    Guildhall, Nordwalde, Germany
1958 School Hospital, Sendenhorst, Germany (competition project)
    Religious Seminary, Essen (competition project)
    Nordwest-Lotto Office Building and Administration Centre, Munster
1959 Concert Hall, Saarbrucken (competition project)
    Boys' Vocational School, Munster (competition project)
    Eye Clinic, Essen (competition project)
    Vicarage, Kindergarten and Library, Stromberg, Germany
1960 District Administration Centre, Munster (competition project)
    Hospital, Lintfort, Germany (competition project)
    Public Health Department and Administrative Savings Bank School, Munster (competition project)
    Heuting-Esch Community Centre, Bocholt, Germany (competition project)
    Natural Sciences Faculty, University of Munster (competition project)
    Student Hostel, Essen (competition project)
    Sanatorium, Bad Driburg, Germany
    Agricultural Centre, Munster (project)
1961 C. and F. Fraling Needlework Establishment, Saerbeck, Germany
    Engineering School, Cologne (competition project)
    Secondary school, Dorsten, Germany
    Metalwork school, Gelsenkirchen, Germany
    Martin Luther Primary School, Bielefeld, Germany
1962 District Council Centre, Ludgeriplatz, Munster
    DRK Centre, Munster (competition project)
    Theatre Square, Gelsenkirchen, Germany (competition project)
    City Hospital and Staff Housing, Siegburg, Germany

Pötterhoek Primary School, Munster (competition project)
    Deutsche Bank, Alter Fischmarkt/Vossgasse, Munster
    Special school, Gescher, Germany
    Concert Hall, Bochum, Germany (project)
    High School, Oelde, Germany (competition project)
    Primary and secondary schools, Versmold, Germany
    Student Centre, Stuttgart (competition project)
1963 Agricultural Insurance Association, Munster (competition project)
    Clinics, University of Munster (competition project)
    Sanatorium, Bad Lippspringe, Germany (competition project)
    Electricity Works, Hamburg (competition project)
1964 Council Building, Leverkusen, Germany (3 projects)
    State Library, Berlin (competition project)
    Market/Church Square restoration, Lubbeck (project)
    Primary School, Hürth, Germany (competition project)
    Modern School, Senden, Germany (competition project)
    Professional School, Altena-Lüdenscheid, Germany (competition project)
    City and District Hospital, Herford, Germany (competition project)
    Hospital, Waldbröl, Germany (competition project)
    SOS Children's Village, Materborn, Germany
1965 Modern school, Lemgo, Germany
    Church of St. Michael, Gievenbeck, Munster
    Plan for the restoration of Moers, Germany (project)
    Tourist Hotel, Bamberg, Germany (competition project)
    Primary School, Selm, Germany (project)
    Max-Planck Institute for Child Nutrition, Dortmund (competition project)
    Rehabilitation Centre, Dortmund (competition project)
    Cathedral Square, Munster (competition project)
    Herz-Jesu Church, Bad Homburg, Frankfurt
    Montessori School Centre, Cologne (competition project)
    Church of St. Joseph, Mülheim-Ruhr, Germany (competition project)
    Parish Church, Coesfeld-Goxel, Germany (competition project)
    Hospital, Itzehoe, Germany (competition project)
    Plan for the restoration of Beckum, Germany (project)
    J. F. Kennedy School, Zehlendorf, Berlin
    Space utilization plan for Warendorf, Germany (project)
    German Legation, Vatican City (competition project)
    Agricultural Building, Stuttgart (project)
    High School, Brandenburg Quarter, Reinickendorf, Berlin (competition project)
1966 Institute for the Promotion of Housing Construction, Dusseldorf (competition project)
    Hospital, Freudenstadt, Germany (competition project)
    Urban District Administration Building, Cologne (competition project)
    Tegel Airport, Berlin (competition project)
    Robert Bosch Hospital, Stuttgart (competition project)
    Hürth District Administration Building, Cologne (competition project)
    Town Library and Adult Education Centre, Gelsenkirchen, Germany
    District Administration Centre, Halle, Ger-

Harald Deilmann: Westdeutsche Landesbank, Munster, 1967

many (competition project)

Max Planck Institute, Göttingen, Germany (competition project)

Town restoration plan for Emmerich, Germany (project)

Regional Savings Bank, Aegidiiplatz, Munster (project)

District Administration Centre, Warendorf, Germany (project)

Plan for restoration and slum clearance of Ibbenbüren, Germany (project)

Secondary School with Sports Centre, Emsdetten, Germany (competition project)

Vocational Training School, Coesfeld, Germany (competition project)

Town restoration plan for Warendorf, Germany (project)

School Centre, Ochtrup, Germany (competition project)

Cathedral Academy, Schwerte, Germany

Max Planck Institute for Biochemistry, Martinsried, Munich (competition project)

Max Planck Institute, Berlin (competition project)

St. Anna Cathedral Church Centre, Mecklenbeck, Munster

1967 Hospital, Göppingen, Germany (competition project)

District Hospital, Donaueschingen, Germany (competition project)

Technical College Centre, Aachen (competition project)

District Administration Centre, Schwelm, Germany (competition project)

St. Joseph Church Centre, Oelde, Germany

(competition project)

Swimming Centre, Lake Zurich (competition project)

Matriculation Institute, Paderborn, Germany (competition project)

Children's Home, Gutersloh, Germany (competition project)

Accountancy Department, Administrative Centre, Hibernia, Herne, Germany

Day Centre Gymnasium, Osterburken, Germany (competition project)

Vocational School, Gutersloh, Germany (competition project)

Gymnasium, Marl, Germany (competition project)

Administration and Exhibition Building, Hochdahl, Germany (competition project)

Town Hall, Munster (competition project)

Hotel by the Zoo, Munster (project)

Westdeutsche Landesbank, Munster

Administration and Bank Building, Heilbronn Street, Stuttgart

District Administration Centre, Büren, Germany (competition project)

Slum clearance plan for Lemgo, Altstadt, Germany (project)

1968 Regional Vocational School, Wiedenbrück, Germany (competition project)

High School, Barmen, Wuppertal, Germany (competition project)

Bergisch-Gladbach School, Paffrath, Germany (competition project)

Haus Hall School for the Mentally Handicapped, Gescher, Germany

Commerzbank, Munster

Laurentianum High School, Warendorf, Germany

Social Welfare Building, Dortmund

Regional Vocational School, Wiedenbrück, Germany (competition project)

University of Dortmund (competition project)

University of Bremen (competition project)

Allianz Administration Building, Stuttgart

University of Bielefeld, Germany (competition project)

Haus Hall Clinical Centre, Gescher, Germany (project)

Gymnasium and Swimming Hall, Secondary School, Lemgo, Germany

High School Hall and Sports Centre, Ochtrup, Germany (competition project)

West German District Bank, Dortmund

Teaching Workshops, for the Apostolic Governing Body, Sibolga, Germany (project)

1969 Administration/Research Centre, Siemens-Perlach, Munich (competition project)

All-Weather Zoo, Munster

Capuchin Monastery Mission Headquarters, Munster

Town Savings Bank, Erkelenz, Germany (competition project)

High School, Rheda, Germany (competition project)

Zimmerman Villa, Kinderhaus, Munster (project)

Aula Theatre, Menden, Germany (competition project)

Plan for Perlach Urban Building Development, Munich (competition project)

Town Savings Bank, Dusseldorf (competition project)
Town Hall, Gronau, Germany
Guildhall, Gronau, Germany (competition project)
Guildhall and Adult Education Centre, Porz, Germany (project)
Rhineland Savings Banks Administration Centre and Central Clearing House, Dusseldorf
St. Barbara Hospital, Gladbeck, Germany (project)
Provincial Insurance Building, Munster (competition project)
German Radio Building, Cologne (competition project)
School Centre, Oerlinghausen, Germany (competition project)
1970 Diocesan Museum, Paderborn, Germany (competition project)
Cultural Centre, Herne, Germany (competition project)
Guildhall, Iserlohn, Germany (competition project)
Hospital Nurses' Home, Gladbeck, Germany
Ostermann and Schweiwe Plastics Factory, Munster
Hospital, Osnabrück, Germany (competition project)
School and Sports Centre, Kreuztal, Germany (competition project)
Factory, Buer, Gelsenkirchen, Germany (competition project)
Old Peoples' Home, Amrum, Norddorf, Germany (project)
German Savings Bank Training Centre, Bad Godesberg, Germany (competition project)
Postal Headquarters, Bremen (competition project)
Caroline Hospital, Neheim/Husten, Germany (competition project)
School Centre, Soest, Germany (competition project)
1971 Guildhall, Wanne Eickel, Germany (project)
Guildhall and Adult Education Centre, Wesel, Germany (competition project)
Clemens Sels Museum, Neuss, Germany
Service Centre, Langenberg, Germany (competition project)
Rhine Province State Insurance Organization Building, Dusseldorf
Bus Station, Ibbenbüren, Germany
House restoration, Turmhof Porz, Cologne (project)
Town Hall and Park, Schwelm, Germany (project)
Town Savings Bank, Schwelm, Germany
District Leisure Park, Karkortsee/Hengstaysee, Hagen, Germany (project)
Finance Bureau, Aachen (project)
Finance Bureau, Dusseldorf (project)
1972 Town Hall, Paderborn, Germany (competition project)
Administration Centre, Government Quarter, Dusseldorf (competition project)
Postal Headquarters, Dortmund (competition project)
Market Place rebuilding, Staelen, Germany
1973 "Flexible Living" Housing Development, Barop, Dortmund
Town Savings Bank, Bad Honnef, Germany (competition project)
German Legation, Rome (competition project)
Sports School of the Armed Forces, Warendorf, Germany (competition project)
Guildhall, Menden, Germany (competition project)
Old Peoples' Centre, Porz-Urbach, Cologne
Central Law Courts, Munster
School Centre, Altena, Germany (competition project)

Town Savings Bank, Oberhausen, Germany (competition project)
Colonia Insurance Building, Hamburg (competition project)
Hospital, Ibbenbüren, Germany (competition project)
1974 Cultural Centre, Lingen, Germany (competition project)
Guildhall, Minden, Germany
Business Centre, Neumarkt, Cologne (competition project)
Dresdner Bank, Kampstrasse, Dortmund
Casino, New Health Farm, Aachen
Leisure Pool, Wulfen, Germany (competition project)
Hospital, Reinickendorf, Berlin (competition project)
Clinic, Bohlmke, Dortmund
Kudamm Karree Casino, Berlin (project)
Karstadt Department Store, Munster (project)
German Student Foundation Headquarters, Wurzburg, Germany (competition project)
North Rhine-Westphalia Provincial Diet, Dusseldorf (competition project)
Old Peoples' Home, Boelerheide, Hagen, Germany (competition project)
1975 Banking Hall, Westdeutsche Landesbank, London
Plan for an integrated city centre extension, Dülmen, Germany (competition project)
Open-Air Baths, Elmsdetten, Germany (competition project)
District Council Centre, Osnabrück, Germany (competition project)
District Council Centre, Recklinghausen, Germany (competition project)
Guildhall, Montabaur, Germany (project)
1976 Financial Training Centre, Munster (competition project)
Health Guest House, Staatsbad, Salzüflen, Germany (competition project)
Warendorf District Vocational School Centre, Beckum, Germany (competition project)
Old Peoples' Centre, Emmerich, Germany (competition project)
Krupp Headquarters remodelling and conversion, Essen
Mannesmann Headquarters, Ratingen-Lintorf, Germany
Banking Hall, Westdeutsche Landesbank, New York
Westdeutsche Landesbank Branch, Luxembourg
Westdeutsche Landesbank Branch, Frankfurt
Westdeutsche Landesbank Headquarters, Dusseldorf
Communications Centre, Dortmund-North (competition project)
Pilgrims' Centre, Kapellenplatz, Kevelaer, Germany (project)
Musselmann Estate, Hygstetten/Donau, Germany
1977 Gelsenwasser AG Laboratory Buildings, Gelsenkirchen, Germany
Federal Academy, Brühl, Germany (competition project)
Youth and Sports Centre, Gronau, Germany (competition project)
Communications Centre, Gladbeck, Germany (competition project)
Nigerian Legation, Bad Godesberg, Bonn (project)
Covered and Open-Air Baths, Lüdenscheid, Germany (competition project)
Ministry of Food, Agriculture and Environment, Stuttgart (competition project)
Casino, Bottcherstrasse, Bremen (project)
Restroom, United Nations Building, New York (project)

1978 Flight Simulator, for Lufthansa, Frankfurt
National Library, Tehran (competition project)
Television Tower, Dusseldorf (project)
Restaurant and Bistro, in the Casino, Aachen
Guildhall and Adult Education Centre, Porz, Cologne
Hotel Malek-Shar, Iran (project)
Casino, Bad Oeynhausen, Germany (project)
Mosque, Malek-Shar, Iran (project)
Multi-Purpose Hall, Malek-Shar, Iran (project)
Garniran New Town, for the Tehran Housing Development Corporation, Iran (competition project)
Rehabilitation and Leisure Centre, Wilgertswiesen, Germany (project)

Publications:

By DEILMANN: books—*30 Junge Deutsche,* with others, exhibition catalogue, Leverkusen, Germany 1961; *Zehn Jahre Grosser Kunstpreis des Landes Nordrhein/Westfalen,* with others, exhibition catalogue, Dusseldorf 1962; *Einfamilienhaus für morgen,* with Einar Ridderström, Stuttgart and Berne 1967; *Umstrukturierung historischer Stadtgebiete,* with K. F. Gehse and B. Jensen, Dortmund and Stuttgart 1970; *Schulbauten: Planungsgrundlagen für allgemeinbildende Schulen,* Gutersloh, Germany 1971; *Lerne Wohnen,* with others, exhibition catalogue, Dusseldorf 1971; *Menschlich Bauen,* with others, exhibition catalogue, Dusseldorf 1972; *Bauten des Gesundheitswesen: Planungsgrundlagen für allgemeine Krankenhäuser,* Gutersloh, Germany, 1972; *System der Gebäudeerschliessung und ihre Auswirkung auf die Baukosten und den Nutzwert der Wohnungen,* with Herbert Pfeiffer, Dortmund 1972; *Bebauungssysteme I: Wohnungsbau,* Dortmund 1972; *Stadt in Test,* with others, exhibition catalogue, Dusseldorf 1973; *Wohnungsbau/The Dwelling/L'Habitat,* with Jörg C. Kirschenmann and Herbert Pfeiffer, Stuttgart 1973; *Wohnsysteme Anwendungsbeispiele,* Dortmund 1973; *Bebauungssysteme II,* volume 1, *Anlagen für Bildung und Kultur,* with K. H. Merkel, volume 2, *Anlagen für Gesundheit, Soziales und Sport,* with K. H. Merkel, and volume 3, *Anlagen für Handel, Gewerbe und Verwaltung,* with H. Brettschneider and K. H. Merkel, Dortmund 1974, *Umstrukturierung historischer Stadtbegiete: Kriterien, Methoden, Beispiele,* with others, Dortmund 1974; *Bau- und Wohnforschung,* Bonn 1974; *Die Eignung des Grossraumbüros für die kommunale Verwaltung,* Bonn 1975; articles—"Post War Architects," with others, in *Zodiac* (Milan), February 1956; "Für Architektur," with others," in *Bauwelt* (Berlin), January 1974; "Thus They Project" in *Proceedings of the World Congress of the International Union of Architects,* Madrid 1975.

On DEILMANN: articles—"Porträt Harald Deilmann" by Udo Kultermann in *Deutsche Bauzeitung* (Stuttgart), April 1961; "Dem Menschen und dem Material gerecht" by Hannelore Schubert in *Die Welt* (Hamburg), 3 May 1965; "Harald Deilmann: Werkbericht 1955–1965" by Jürgen Joedicke in *Deutsche Bauzeitung* (Stuttgart), August 1965; "Werkbericht Harald Deilmann" in *Die Ziegelindustrie* (Wiesbaden), no. 24, 1967; "Harald Deilmann" in *Japan Interior Design* (Tokyo), February 1975.

Architecture is mainly a question of overcoming certain practical problems. Solutions must be found for the many different projects arising out of human needs, and these solutions must take into account physical as well as psychological facts. This, in a nutshell, is the formula that these days seems so difficult for us to achieve. But the deplorable deterioration of the 3-dimensional imagination is due not only to an unsympathetic and materialistically oriented world but also to a hostility towards architects and to the lack of an educated clientele.

For when it comes to artistic production of any kind, including architecture, the question is not one of individual taste but of absolute values that can be established by anyone with the requisite understanding. There are certain forces underlying every perception, for which every epoch has its own collective sensibility. The architect, looking for original solutions to present-day problems, must be familiar with current forces in order to integrate them in the dialogue, as it were, to be expressed.

A change of form, resulting from a change in awareness—a coming to terms with the spiritual and social currents of the day—must not be seen as short-lived modernism. Intrinsic expression of contemporary conditions can only originate from a fundamental reference to the spiritual issues that have developed. My ambition in my work is to satisfy both those factors that are unique to time and place and those that relate to a universal validity and are archetypal and timeless. This creative symbiosis of present and unique elements with those that are universal and timeless is the only identifiable common characteristic of the works for which I have taken responsibility. I concern myself with the greatest variety of forms and modes of expression possible for each individual assignment, rather than adhere to any consistent and uniform style or set of rules.

It was Walter Gropius who said that "specialists are people who always repeat the same mistakes." I do not feel that his warning applies to me: I constantly make new mistakes, but I hope thereby to make my own contribution to the development of architecture.

My work method is this. If architectural planning is seen as the solving of problems for new and unique assignments, then it follows that one must look for solutions that derive from an ever-changing technology. The reason that stereotyped plans and buildings fail so disastrously is that there has been a neglect of the dimension of time—in the sense of historical development. With the fast-moving advances of our day, any restriction to previous plans creates anachronism. Because building systems are various and flexible does not mean that no further thought is necessary: one must plan ahead, taking decisions that will not become obsolete too quickly.

As far as my design methodology is concerned, I can best describe it by describing the day to day running of my practice, which deals with all kinds of commissions connected with the human environment.

In the first place we sift the basic information regarding the task to be carried out—such factors as its special requirements; programming of work; surface ground conditions; intended function of the building; and local building regulations. All are thoroughly analyzed and studied. Of the greatest importance, however, is the search for an Idea: the essence of the task and its unique formula must be formed into a comprehensive unity that takes account of all the given circumstances. In this first phase the integration of functional requirements with architectural image must be so fused that one can no longer conceive of the one without the other. There is no hard and fast rule about the method of this conceptual form-finding stage, and it will vary according to the situation and the frame of reference. One cannot repeat past experience exactly, and yet the knowledge gained in previous situations will play a role in solving the new problems. The design conception may occur spontaneously, through the working of the imagination in relation to the job content, or through an inspiration provoked by the setting, tradition, or visual suggestion.

It is this Idea that is the foundation of design and sets off the work process, the process of harmonizing the various technical and creative details. The final outcome must be a compatible interpretation of planning in 3-dimensional or even 4-dimensional spatial reality, so as to enrich the human environment.

The various necessary work processes—plans, building regulation procedures, and actual realization of the project with all its technical details—are all processes that also vary from task to task; there is very little point, therefore, in trying to systematize. In an experienced practice, all these duties are discharged as a matter of routine, naturally, with the help of modern planning aids and computerized cost- and time-planning.

The creative process itself cannot be rationalized, but with increased experience it can be better guided and directed. In order to synthesize the details of production, one must make both quantitative and qualitative analyses, within the terms of reference of the limited possibilities of the particular task. It is more difficult to analyze the process of designing than to analyze the design itself, and this problem may explain the many unfruitful attempts to make attractive and appealing so much that was previously better lost to sight.

—Harald Deilmann

Harald Deilmann was only in his thirties when, in collaboration, he built the Municipal Theatre at Munster. Prior to this first work, he had been a Lecturer at the Technische Hochschule in Stuttgart where many of the post-war architects of the Federal Republic had connections. Deilmann started practice firmly in the modern camp, and he seems to have eschewed constantly any thought or any sense of formality in his designs. Even the Munster theatre is almost self-consciously informal, as though its authors were deliberately going out of their way to make the building as un-grand as possible. This informality is accentuated by the setting back of the structure diagonally on the site, thus creating a restless and uneasy sense of gaiety. The curved upper works around the foyer area combine with the fly-tower to give the building a centre of gravity. Paradoxically, Deilmann and his colleagues integrated a neoclassical ruin into the scheme, which remains a brilliant essay in refined understatement. The tendency to an informal approach is peculiar to the post-1945 German architects who were concerned to reject the neoclassical planning of so much work produced during the era of the Third Reich.

Deilmann's subsequent work includes hospitals, cultural buildings, and many office blocks. The Nordwest-Lotto building at Munster is perhaps his best-known office structure, but all of his work reveals the same careful, intellectual approach, an approach that has led him into academic life as well as professional practice. In general, Deilmann's oeuvre inspires a quiet admiration for its intellectual rigour and for the refinement of his detailing. He did much to re-establish the pre-eminence of German architecture in its European context in the difficult years after the war.

—James Stevens Curl

de KLERK, Michel.

Dutch. Born in Amsterdam in 1884. Studied at the Industrial School, Amsterdam; mainly self-taught as an architect. Worked in the studio of the architect P. J. H. Cuijpers, Amsterdam, 1898–1910; travelled in Scandinavia, 1910–11; collaborated with P. Kramer, Amsterdam, 1911–16; in private practice, Amsterdam, 1916 until his death, 1923. Exhibition: *Nederlandse Architectuur*, Amsterdam, 1975. *Died* (in Amsterdam) *in 1923*.

Works:

1906   Railway Station (competition project)
1907   Sports Club House (competition project)
       Town House (competition project)
       Cafe-Restaurant (competition project)
1908   Workers' Association Housing Block (competition project)
       Workers' Terrace Housing (competition project)
1909   Semi-Detached Houses (project)
       Resort Hotel by the Sea (competition project)
1910   Reincarnation Church and Cemetery (competition project)
1911   House, Uithoorn, Netherlands (project)
1911/
12   Hillehuis Housing Block, Johannes Vermeerplein and Gabriel Metsustraat, Amsterdam
1911/
16   Scheepvaarthuis Shipping Offices, Amsterdam (project; with van der Mey and Kramer)
1912   Water Tower and Service Building (competition project)
1913/
14   Veerhoff-Kothe Country House, Hilversum, Netherlands
1913/
18   Eigen Haard Housing Estate, Spaarndammerplantsoen and Zaanstraat, Amsterdam
1914   Billeke Country House, Hilversum, Netherlands
1915   Semi-detached housing, Amsterdam (project)
       Housing Complex for a Provincial City (project)
       Voorbereidende School, Amsterdam (project)
       Van Leering Bank Building, Amsterdam (project)
1917   Rijksacademie voor Beeldende Kunsten, Amsterdam (competition project)
1920   Gezellenhuis Single Men's Lodging House, Maastricht, Netherlands (project)
       Friedman's Emigrants' House, Amsterdam (project)
1921   Church Tower restoration, Ijsselstein, Netherlands (project)
1922   de Dageraad Housing Estate, Takstraat and Henriette Ronnerplein, Amsterdam
       Bloemenlust Flower Market, Oosteinde, Aalsmeer, Netherlands
1923   Plan Zuid Housing Estate, Amstellaan, Amsterdam
       de Hoop Sailing Club House, Weesperzijde, Amsterdam (demolished, 1942)
       Flower Market, Amsterdam (project)
       Barendsen House, Aalsmeer, Netherlands
       Country house, Wassenaer, Netherlands

Publications:

On de KLERK: books—*Architettura Moderna in Olanda* by Giovanni Fanelli, Florence 1968; *Nederlandse Architectuur 1910–1930: Amsterdamse School*, exhibition catalogue, by A. Venema, E. Bergvelt, W. de Wit and others, Amsterdam 1975; articles—"Onze Tijd en het werk van M. de Klerk" by K. P. C. de Bazel in *Wendingen* (Amsterdam), no. 2, 1919; "Modern Dutch Architecture" by Howard Robertson in *Architectural Review* (London), August 1922; "Over het Teekenwerk van M. de Klerk" by J. P. Mieras in *Wendingen* (Amsterdam), no. 2, 1924; "On uitgevoerde ontwerpen" by J. F. Staal in *Wendingen* (Amsterdam), no. 4–5, 1924; "De Bouwwerken van Michel de Klerk" by P. Kramer in *Wendingen* (Amsterdam), no. 9–10, 1924; "La Escuela de Amsterdam y su tiempo" by Mariano Bayon in *Arquitectura* (Madrid), June 1966; "Michel de Klerk's Design for Amsterdam Spaarndammerbuur 1914–1920" by Suzanne S. Frank in *Nederlands Kunsthistorisch Jaarboek 22*, Amsterdam 1971; "Michel de Klerk and the Street Parade of the Amsterdam School" by Nic H. M. Tummers in *Tijdschrift voor Architectuur en Beeldende Kunsten* (Heerlen), October 1973.

Michel de Klerk was one of a great generation of Amsterdam architects who followed Berlage. He was closely involved with the influential architectural journal *Wendingen,* and was one of the leading lights of the Amsterdam School with Kramer and van der Mey. The Amsterdam School broke away from the ideas propounded by Berlage, and evolved shapes for buildings that were essentially plastic, in contrast to the sharply rectangular forms favoured by the De Stijl movement based in Rotterdam. The Amsterdam School was a parallel body to contempo-rary German Expressionism. To de Klerk and his colleagues, individual expression of design was para-mount; highly personal detail was favoured, often with little regard to logic in construction or use of appropriate materials. The work of the Amsterdam School, and especially that of de Klerk, attracted international attention from about 1912 until shortly after de Klerk's death in 1923.

Michel de Klerk was eminently successful in ap-plying interesting modelling to the façades of low-cost housing, especially in his work in Amsterdam South, which was being developed to designs by Berlage. The most interesting of de Klerk's designs are the Eigen Haard flats (1913/18) with their for-mal, symmetrical arrangements of windows, can-tilevered curved balconies of brick, and central spire-let. His de Dageraad Housing Estate in Amsterdam of 1922 incorporates numbers of four-storey linked pairs, with tall chimneys between, a form that was developed in London from 1820–1850 and was greatly admired on the Continent. Certainly, the reg-ularity of the façades of de Klerk's buildings recalls the traditional approach to townscape that had been successful in creating great urban environments. The apartment blocks of the Amstellaan of 1923 really belong to the mainstream of 19th century town de-sign. The street frontages were designed as units, and the scale is very much traditional. Five-storey ranges of flats faced in fine brickwork recall the tall blocks of Paris or the streets of Victorian London, yet the detail and architectural handling of the fronts are quite new. Cantilevered balconies with brick fronts, semicircular bows cantilevered from various points of the façade, and a light, clean, agreeably propor-tioned mass of building stripped of all allusions to classical or other ornament, speak of a great achieve-ment in the liberation of architectural design. Com-pared with the grim tenements of Liverpool, Lon-don, or Glasgow, these splendid buildings are perhaps de Klerk's greatest contribution to the knowledge of how to build cheap mass-housing that is at once humane, architecturally pleasing, and a gracious ornament to the townscape.

Some commentators have described the work of de Klerk, and that of the Amsterdam School, as retarding the "progress" of modern architecture. To such writers, Expressionist architecture, and espe-cially the humane face of Dutch Expressionism, with its interesting façades and unboring silhouettes, is a "fantastic aberration." De Klerk and his colleagues, not to mention Dudok and others who do not fit conveniently in any tidy compartment, are a great nuisance, spoiling the theory of the evolution of a rational "functionalist" architecture that was mor-ally pure. Such simplistic and bogus notions are, of course, quite absurd in any consideration of architec-tural history. De Klerk realized that it is a *function* of architecture to delight the beholder and to enliven the streetscape and that something more than an ugly moralistic and pure box was necessary to house the masses. Indeed, de Klerk must not be seen as either an aberration or as a seminal figure. He was a gifted architect working within an honourable tra-dition of providing decently designed housing within an urban matrix that not only housed people satis-factorily but also ornamented the townscape and added delight to the passer-by. Amsterdam consists largely of houses that are individually fine and to-gether form a homogeneous city. De Klerk worked within that tradition, and it is a measure of his great-ness that he reinterpreted tradition in his own time to produce buildings that have worn gracefully and still give delight.
—James Stevens Curl

Michel de Klerk: Eigen Haard Housing, Amsterdam, 1918

Alejandro De La Sota: Commercial and residential development, Zamora, Spain, 1959

DE LA SOTA Martinez, Alejandro.
Spanish. Born in Pontevedra, 20 October 1913. Edu-cated at the Escuela de Madrid, Dip.Arch. 1941. Designer, Instituto Nacional de Colonización, Ma-drid, 1942–49. In private practice, Madrid, since 1950. Professor of Design, Escuela de Madrid, 1956–63, 1965–66, 1969–71. Recipient: First Prize, Trea-sury Office Competition, Tarragona, 1954; First Prize, Housing Competition, La Coruna, Spain, 1956; First Prize, Civilian Government Building Competition, Tarragona, 1957; National Prize for Architecture, 1974. Address (office): Breton de los Herreros 66 (3), Madrid, Spain.

Works:

1942/
49 Rural housing development, Gimenells, Spain
Rural housing development, Valuengo, Spain
Rural housing development, La Bazana, Spain
Rural housing development, Jerez de los Caballeros, Spain
1948/
52 Rural housing development, Esquivel, Spain
1954 Local Treasury Office, Tarragona
Chalet, calle Doctor Arce, Madrid
1956 Housing development, La Coruna, Spain
1956/
59 Commercial and residential development, Zamora, Spain
1957 Civilian Government Building, Tarragona
1958 TABSA Workshops Building, Barajas Highway, near Madrid
1959 Workers' Children's Center, Miraflores de la Sierra, Madrid (with J. A. Corrales and R. Vasquez Molezun)
1959/
65 Clesa Dairy Works, Madrid
1960 Residential development, Salamanca, Spain
1965 Gymnasium, Maravillas College, Madrid
1966 Sports Club, Pontevedra, Spain
1970 Cesar Carlos High School, Madrid
Faculty of Law Building, University of Granada, Spain
1974 Lecture Hall Pavilion, University of Seville

Publications:

On DE LA SOTA: articles—"Vivienda Agrupada—Pueblo de Gimenells" in *Revista Nacional de Arquitectura* (Madrid), November 1948; "El Nuevo Pueblo des Esquivel" in *Revista Nacional de Arquitectura* (Madrid), January 1953; "Seven Masters of Madrid and 7 + 7 Young Architects" by Alberto Campo Baeza in *Architecture + Urbanism* (Tokyo), March 1978.

In the isolationist climate of the first post-war years in Spain, Alejandro de la Sota began his career as a designer in the Instituto Nacional de Colonización in Madrid. During those years—1942-49—he worked on a series of new rural developments, works in which he allowed patterns similar to those of the modern tradition to act as the foundation for a style that accepts the inheritance of vernacular elements and uses them as plastic means. During the 1950's, after the isolated experience of the Instituto, de la Sota quickly accepted the ideal of modernism and thereafter remained faithful to it, making function and technique the criteria of architecture. But the plastic/aesthetic considerations that informed his first designs did not disappear; they continued to impregnate his work; and some of his most successful buildings have been those in which his impulses took over, making use of technical means to create a plastic medium, an architectural language. At the same time his evolution as an architect has involved an increasingly restricted language, a purism that suggests both Mies and the rationalism typical of Italy in the 1930's.

In the early 1950's, de la Sota joined the modernists with some works that share the informal plasticity of the International Style of that period. Examples are the Local Treasury Office in Tarragona, the housing development at La Coruna, and the "chalet" in c. Doctor Arce, Madrid. But, by 1957, in his Civilian Government Building in Tarragona, he had begun to suggest the nature of his future career, the works of his maturity. The loyalty is still to modernism, but to a less informal modernism; there is now an interest in something more plain, unadorned, purist. The striving is for a sparkling quality, for the kind of rationalist style fathered by Terragni—a quest for formal radiance, simple and perfected, which alone can be the expression of functional and

spatial rationality. Thereafter, de la Sota's work is pervaded with that neo-Platonism implicit in so many works of the modern movement, especially those that took technology as guiding star and linguistic medium.

de la Sota's buildings, then, are more or less inclined to convert the functional and the technical into an architectural language. Besides the Civilian Government Building, such buildings include the commercial and residential development at Zamora, the residential development at Salamanca, the Gymnasium at Maravillas College, Madrid, the Cesar Carlos High School, Madrid, and the Faculty of Law at the University of Granada. More decidedly inclined towards the technical, and prone therefore to the ambiguity associated with much of the avant garde architecture of Europe in the 1960's, are the Clesa Dairy Works in Madrid and the Sports Club at Pontevedra.

Like Mies, de la Sota feels that architecture, in spite of appearances, is not determined by technology but adopts connotations of order, smoothness, simplicity, purity—the synonyms of technology for some of the modernists. The demands of the technical elements may be great, but the architect, consciously or unconsciously, turns technology into language.

Whatever the validity of these premises, Alejandro de la Sota has created works of such high standards as to make him one of the giants of contemporary Spanish architecture.

—Anton Capitel

de la TOUR d'AUVERGNE, Bernard.

French. Born in Maisons-Lafitte, 9 September 1923. Educated at the Ecole Nationale Superieure des Beaux-Arts, Paris; Ecole Spécial d'Architecture, Paris, graduated 1948. Served as a volunteer in the Royal Air Force, in North Africa, 1940-44. Worked in the offices of Palmer Krissel, Los Angeles, Philip Johnson, New York, and Eugène Beaudouin, Paris, 1948-55. In private practice, Paris, 1955 until his death, 1976. Professor, Ecoles d'Art Américaines, Fontainebleau, 1960-61; Professor and Studio Master, Ecole Spécial d'Architecture, Paris, 1961-68; Professor, California Polytechnic University, San Luis Obispo, 1968-71; Director, Ecoles d'Art Américaines, Fontainebleau, 1972-75. Recipient: Bronze Medal, Society for the Encouragement of Arts and Industry. Member, Order of Architects, France, 1951. *Died* (in Paris) *8 October 1976.*

Works:

1952 House, Cuernavaca, Mexico
1955 Museum, Aleppo, Syria (competition project; with J. Lauffroy)
1957 City Centre, West Berlin (competition project; with M. Tournon Branly, P. Devinoy, J. Faugeron Associates, and M. Schlote)
Mausoleum, Quay Azam Jinnah, Karachi, Pakistan (competition project; with M. Andrault, P. Parat and M. Calka)

Bernard de la Tour d'Auvergne: Centre Européen d'Educátion Permanente, Fontainebleau, France, 1969

Palace of Justice, Lille, France (competition project; with M. Calka)

1958 Automobile Museum and Congress Hall, Le Mans, France (project; with M. Andrault and P. Parat)

1959 S.C.I.C. Housing Development, Gonesse, France (competition project; with M. Andrault and P. Parat)

1960 Tourist Centre, Saut-du-Doubs, France (project; with M. Tournon Branly)

Club Martini, Champs Elysees, Paris (with M. Tournon Branly, M. Pechere and M. Calka)

1961 Civic and Cultural Centre, Cape Town, South Africa (project; with E. Beaudouin, A. Fournier, and A. Laprade)

ZUP Housing Development, Caen-Herouville, France (competition project)

1962 Housing development, Limeil-Brevannes, France (project; with J. Viallefond)

Mehringplatz Redevelopment, West Berlin (project; with M. Tournon Branly)

1963 Housing development, Chilly-Mazarin, France (project)

1964 National School of Taxes, with Residences, Clermont-Ferrand, France (with E. Beaudouin)

1965 Housing, Limeil, France (project; with P. Lacroix)

1966 Institut Européen d'Administration des Affaires, Fontainebleau, France (with R. Cidrac)

1967 Pavilions, Parc de Chambly, France (project; with P. Lacroix)

Town Hall, Amsterdam (competition project)

Air and Space Museum, Paris (competition project)

1968 Fiat Planning Centre, Trappes, France (project)

Winter sports centre, Vallée de Chasse, France (project)

Housing and leisure complex, Vallée de Risle, France (project)

1969 Centre Européen d'Education Permanente, Fontainebleau, France

1970 Tourist centre, Caicos Island, Bahamas (project)

S.C.I.C. Cultural Centre, Maffliers, France (project)

ARCS 2000 Winter Sports Centre, Mont Pourri, France (project; with B. G. Huidobro)

1971 Small tourist complex, Megeve, France (project; with P. Lacroix)

1972 French Embassy, Peking (project)

Institute of Management, Front de Seine, Paris (project; with E. Duhart and M. Le Caisne)

L'Oréal Headquarters and Laboratories, Clichy, France (project; with A. Bailly)

S.C.I.C. Planning Centre, Menucourt, France (project)

1973 National School of Treasury Services, Marne-la-Vallée, France (with C. Costantini)

Tourist complex, Port-de-l'Orb, Languedoc-Roussillon, France (project; with C. Costantini and M. Regembal)

Pavilions, La-Queue-les-Yvelines, France (project; with M. Regembal)

ELF Conference Rooms and Museum of Gabon, Libreville (competition project)

Saint-Germain Market redevelopment, Paris (competition project; with C. Costantini, G. Hoym de Marien, and M. Regembal)

Plateau de Vanves renovation, Vanves, France (competition project; with C. Costantini and M. Regembal)

1974 Four Seasons Hotel, Les Halles, Paris (project; with the Webb Zerafka Menkes Housden Partnership)

Redevelopment plan for Les Halles, Paris (project)

Educational complexes for Tehran, Shiraz and Isfahan, Iran (projects; with C. Costantini and M. Regembal)

Tax Centre (competition project; with C. Costantini and M. Regembal)

Damascus Public Library, Syria (competition project; with D. Harding)

Museum of Prehistory of the Ile de France, Nemours (competition project)

1975 Village of the West (tourist complex), Leucate-Barcares, France (project)

Redevelopment plan for Les Halles, Paris (2nd project; with others)

Hotel complex, Moulin de Paillas, Les Combes, France (project)

Publications:

On de la TOUR d'AUVERGNE: book—*Bernard de la Tour d'Auvergne,* Paris 1975.

*

During his 25 years of activity Bernard de la Tour d'Auvergne was motivated by a desire to protect the sensitivity of other people, to respond to the human need for equilibrium and harmony, and to accomplish the modest but essential task of creating an architectural object that could be experienced with discreet exaltation, then looked upon with joy. Because of these goals, one finds in his work a coherence both in the process of creation and in the direction of his research.

This coherence has principally to do with the relationship of contents to container and with the articulation of volumes, each responding to its own function but intimately linked with each other according to a subtle hierarchy implying a progression towards the fundamental element, the heart of the composition. The variety of these volumes is expressed not only by their forms and their siting but also by the choice and use of materials employed. Contrasts, counterpoint, and rhythm are created that visually express the "elements" of the architecture in an undisguised, open manner.

For example, one can cite two particularly characteristic studies: the Centre Européen d'Education Permanente at Fontainebleau and the National School of Treasury Services at Marne-la-Vallée.

At the Centre Européen d'Education Permanente a large transparent volume on a orthogonal plane has as its centre a vast cylinder containing four amphitheatres, and alongside the two facades there are eight towers comprising sixteen chambers, little "oratories" for group work. For the cylinder and the towers, de la Tour d'Auvergne designed massive walls in a warm tinted brick, to contrast with the light polished steel skeleton and curtain facade of the overall structure.

The National School of Treasury Services is defined as a curved, linear building sliding between cylindrical masses of the amphitheatres. All the activities of the school converge on the areas essential to study and reflection, and the contrast is emphasized in a differentiation of construction principles: unclad brick for the interior and exterior of the amphitheatres, bronze-coloured steel skeleton and tinted glass for the linear building.

These principles of contrast and relation are, in fact, to be found in all of his work, whether in the Club Martini in Paris or in some of his projects for the many competitions in which he took part—the Palace of Justice in Lille, the Amsterdam City Hall, the Museum of the Prehistory of the Ile de France, or the study he was asked to complete of a Social Centre for l'Oréal.

His principal work could have been the architectural complex he conceived for the development of the Les Halles area of Paris; it included a 5-acre garden designed to set off that marvellous jewel, the Church of St. Eustache, and, in counterpoint to the Bourse du Commerce, volumes of resolutely contemporary architecture sited around a vast "crater" and bringing together very varied activities. When one considers the present disastrous treatment of this "crater," one can only regret that de la Tour d'Auvergne's project was not accepted, for he brought

light and animation to the densest sectors of the project.

de la Tour d'Auvergne was an aesthete, a cultured man who had travelled a great deal; he loved travel, and in his youth he had been strongly influenced by Egypt and by Greece, countries to which he liked to return. He was very interested in the United States of America, and he had very close contacts with young American architects. He devoted himself to his task as Professor and then Director of the Ecoles d'Art Américaines, in Fontainebleau, where he was joined and then succeeded by Marion Tournon Branly.

Finally, one must not forget his origins. He belonged to one of the great families of France. His uncle was Emilio Terry, a gifted creator with a powerful imagination, who encouraged him, while very young, to reflect upon architecture and to develop his knowledge and sensitivity: perhaps as a reaction to this early influence, he later devoted himself to a search for austerity and rigour.

Apparently retiring but in reality remote and vulnerable, de la Tour d'Auvergne gave all of his strength to his work.

—Renée Diamant-Berger

del MORAL, Enrique.

Mexican. Born in Irapuato, Gto., 20 January 1905. Educated at the Instituto Franco Ingles, Mexico City, 1913–22; Universidad Nacional Autonoma, Mexico City, at the National School of Architecture, under José Villagrán García and Carlos Obregón Santacilia, 1923–27, Dip.Arch. 1928, and at the School of Philosophy and Letters, under José Gaos, 1943–46. Married Elisa Madrid in 1940. Worked in the studio of Carlos Obregón Santacilia, Mexico City, 1928–35. In private practice, Mexico City, since 1935. Member, Federal School Construction Administration Committee, Guanajuato, 1944–46; Member, Medical Center Construction Committee, Mexico City, 1945–46; Architectural Coordinator and Director, Ciudad Universitaria, Mexico City, 1947–54; Executive Member, National Commission of Hospitals, 1954–58. Professor of Architectural Drawing, 1934, Adjunct Professor of Architectural Composition, 1934–36, Professor of Architectural Composition, 1938–50, Member of the Technical Council, 1940–44, and Director, 1944–49, National School of Architecture, Universidad Nacional Autonoma, Mexico City; Adviser to the School of Architecture, Universidad Iberoamericana, Mexico City, 1958–62. Secretary, 1967, 1973, and Treasurer, 1972, 1973, Academy of Arts, Mexico; President, Seminar on Mexican Culture, 1968, 1969; President, Sociedad de Arquitectos de Mexico, 1972–73, 1974, 1975. Recipient: Monterrey Prize, 1972; National Architecture Prize, 1978. Member, Sociedad de Arquitectos de Mexico, Colegio de Arquitectos de Mexico, and Association of Mexican Art Critics; Founder Member, Mexican Academy of Arts. Honorary Member, Sociedad Bolivariana de Arquitectos, Caracas, Venezuela. Address (office): Calle General Francisco Ramirez 5, Mexico 18, D.F., Mexico.

Works:

1936 10 workers' houses, Irapuato, Mexico (with M. Gutierrez Camarena)

1937 R. E. Calles House, Pirineos 519, Mexico City (with M. Gutierrez Camarena)

1938 4 rental houses, for R. E. Calles, Monte Altai 215, Mexico City (with M. Gutierrez Camarena)

Palomino House reconstruction, Tabasco y Valladolid, Mexico (with M. Gutierrez Camarena)

Banco Capitalizador de Ahorros Building conversion, Calle de las Cruces, Mexico City (with M. Gutierrez Camarena)
1939 Juan Gallardo Moreno House, Paseo de la Reforma 1115, Mexico City (with M. Gutierrez Camarena)
J. Gama Apartment Building, Abraham Gonzalez 123, Mexico City (with M. Gutierrez Camarena)
Andre Guieu House, Cuernavaca, Mexico
Saenz House, Paseo de la Reforma 414, Mexico City
1940 Palomino Apartment Building, Calle del Panuco, Mexico City
General P. E. Calles Apartment Building, Plaza Melchor, Ocampo 64, Mexico City
1940/
41 J. Gama Apartment Building, Zacatecas y Cordova, Mexico
3 rental houses, for Gallardo Moreno, Cuernavaca, Mexico
1941 4 rental houses, Sierra Nevada 315, Mexico City
1941/
42 Apartment/Office Building, for J. Gama, Independencia 67, Mexico City
1942 7 rental houses, Monte Altai 215, Mexico City
R. E. Calles Apartment Building, Plaza Melchor, Ocampo 56, Mexico City
L. Avalos House, Payo de Rivera 240, Mexico City
1942/
43 C. Palomino Apartment Building, Tigris, Mexico
Palomino House alterations, Tabasco y Valladolid, Mexico
1943 Carlos Tejeda House, Aida y Cedros, Mexico City
V. Gama House, Tlacopac, San Angel, Mexico
1943/
46 General Hospital, San Luis Potosi, Mexico
1944 Alteration of 2 houses for J. Gama, General Farias 41, Mexico City
José Iturbi House, Acapulco
Fregoso House, Avenida Pirineos, Mexico City
Zumpano Apartment Building, Sinaloa 75, Mexico City
1944/
46 15 schools, Jefe de Zona, Guanajuato, Mexico
1945 R. E. Calles House, Cajema, Mexico
Flavio Borquez House, Cajeme, Mexico
1945/
46 J. and V. Gama Apartment Hotel, Farias 39, Mexico City
Nursery School, Colonia Buenos Aires, Mexico City
1946 José Iturbi House, San Angel, Mexico City
1947/
54 Master plan for Ciudad Universitaria (University City), Mexico City (with Mario Pani)
1948/
49 del Moral House, Francisco Ramirez 5, Mexico City
1950 Coghlan House, Puebla, Mexico
Office building, Avenida 5 de Mayo, Mexico City (with José Villagrán García)
Alterations to 4 shops, Avenida 5 de Mayo and Condesa, Mexico City (with José Villagrán García)
Hydraulic Resources Secretariat Building, Paseo de la Reforma-Artes, Mexico City (with Mario Pani)
Sports Fields, Ciudad Universitaria (University City), Mexico City (with Mario Pani)
Men's Bathing and Changing Rooms, Ciudad Universitaria (University City), Mexico City (with Mario Pani)
5 houses, Costera M. Aleman 36–44, Acapulco, Mexico (with Mario Pani)

Apartment building, Hamburgo 5, Mexico City (with Mario Pani)
1951 Sierra de Fernandez House, Tennyson 117, Mexico City (with Mario Pani)
Flores Zavala House, Calle de Andre Dumas, Mexico City (with Mario Pani)
Raya Manrique Rental Bungalows, Acapulco (with Mario Pani)
1951/
52 Miguel Arias House, Acapulco (with Mario Pani)
Hotel Pozo del Rey, Acapulco (with Mario Pani)
Hotel Posada de los 7 Mares, Acapulco (with Mario Pani)
Hotel Villas Monte Mar, Pinzona 126, Acapulco (with Mario Pani)
Mexico Golf Club Building, Tlalpan, Mexico City (with Mario Pani)
1951/
53 Reaseguros Alianza Building, Insurgentes and Hamburgo Streets, Mexico City
Arturo Pani House, Mexico City (with Mario Pani)
1952 Club de Pesca, Puente Hotel, Acapulco (with Mario Pani)
Airport Building, Laguna Tres Palos, Acapulco (with Mario Pani)
A. L. de Rabell House, Acapulco (with Mario Pani)
1952/
53 Gallardo Moreno House, Mexico City
Gallardo Moreno Rental House, Caucaso, Mexico
1953 Bullfight Ring, Acapulco (with Mario Pani)
Luis R. Montes House, Acapulco (with Mario Pani)
1954/
55 Bernardo Quintana House, Pedregal San Angel, Mexico City
R. de la Roziere House, Colonel Flores Magon, Mexico City
Kaye House, Pedregal San Angel, Mexico City
1955/
58 Federal Medical Center Emergency Hospital, Central Laundry Building, and Laboratory Building, Mexico City
1956 Children's Hospital, Villahermosa, Tabasco, Mexico
1956/
57 La Merced Market Hall, Mexico City
1958 Chemical Industry Building, Atenas y Versalles, Mexico City
1958/
60 Hirsch House, Lipodromo Edo, Mexico City
1959/
60 Attorney-General's Office Building, Mexico City
1960/
61 Secondary school, Postal, Mexico City
1961/
62 Federal Penal Court Building, Mexico City
1962 House renovation, Jonacatepec, Mexico
1962/
63 Federal Treasury Building, Mexico City
Sears Roebuck Department Store, Mexico City
1964 Federal Employees Social and Security Institute Nurses' School and Medical Investigation Center, Mexico City
Federal Employees Social and Security Institute Hospital and Clinic, Monterrey, Mexico
1964/
65 Federal Employees Social and Security Institute Hospital and Clinic, Tampico, Mexico
1966/
67 Gildred Foundation Geriatric Hospital, Lindavista, Mexico City
1966/
68 Mexican Social Security Institute Hospital and Clinic, Ciudad Obregon, Sonora, Mexico

Mexico
1967 Mexican Social Security Institute Hospital and Clinic, Cuautla, Mexico
1967/
68 Subway stations, Tlalpan, Mexico City
1968 Mexican Social Security Institute Medical Center, Olympic Village, Mexico City
1969 Federico Sanchez Fogarty Picture Gallery and Studio, Nepantla, Morelos, Mexico
1969/
74 Mexican Social Security Institute Complex (Gynaecological Clinic, Branch Office Building, Laundry Building, and Hospital and Clinic), Monterrey, Mexico
1972 Mexican Social Security Institute Hospital and Clinic, Nogales, Sonora, Mexico
1973/
74 Mexican Social Security Institute Psychiatric Hospital, Mexico City
1975/
77 Bernardo Quintana Apartment Building, Acapulco

Publications:

By del MORAL: book—*Enrique del Moral: Collected Essays,* Mexico City 1979.

On del MORAL: books—*Mexico's Modern Architecture* by I. E. Myers, New York 1952; *Modern Architecture in Mexico* by Max Cetto, Stuttgart and London 1961.

It is indispensable, if we are to talk about Style, to consider the two forces involved: first, the one that both confirms and defines it by determining the "general" tone of the epoch which is established by just a few countries; and second, the one that represents the "particular features" of other nations within the same period of time.

Considering the above in terms of architecture, there are in Mexico two positions that co-exist: they are neither opposed one to the other nor contradictory, and they can be defined more or less clearly. One of them, "internationalism," is the position wherein forms are born as a product of the dominant ideas in world architecture; this position involves pretending, although it is not completely possible, not to consider local features or ways of being. The formal expressions that derive from this posture are characterized by their lack of regional identity, their internationalism: that is where the name comes from.

The other posture, the "regionalist" one, is also a response to dominant architectural ideologies, but as well it takes into account particular regional conditions of all kinds, integrally and with all the complexities involved; it is concerned, too, with cultural, psychological, physical and economic factors, as well as others of an atavistic nature. That is, attention is paid to differences; the architect struggles towards the goal that his creations be not "transplanted," that they show clearly they belong to Mexico, being within our scope and circumstances.

Undoubtedly, communications nowadays create a link with other countries which facilitates and makes available to us not only the ideas but also the products, systems and methods of building of other countries. But it is also true that this modern world, which we did not invent, which has been "manufactured" and "supplied" to us by nations whose ideas are sometimes contrary to our ways of thinking, is—at least in part—difficult for us to understand and to swallow.

Those things that may distinguish us will be more outstanding in solutions to programs in which man appears as a differentiated being—for instance, in residences, either individual or collective. I think too that, on some occasions, it might happen that the expression of our particularity could reflect a lack of resplendent modernity due to the fact that Mexico is

Enrique del Moral: La Merced Market Hall, Mexico City, 1957

not a characteristic or outstanding country in terms of modernism.

—Enrique del Moral

During the late 1920's and through the 1930's, Enrique del Moral, along with Villagrán García and O'Gorman, played a leading role in a movement among Mexican architects to construct severely functional buildings—mostly pure white boxes that looked as if ornament were to be regarded as some symptom of mental poverty. Concurrently with this "anti-ornament" feeling there was a belief that the new architecture had a social propagandist role to play, and that somehow the work of the most talented Mexicans was not fulfilling that role. On the international scene, "integration of the arts" was fashionable currency, and many architects collaborated with painters like Orozco, Siqueiros and Rivera, whose murals filled the interior (and sometimes exterior) surfaces of their buildings with distinct accents of social protest. The movement, either through lack of energy and real direction or the political climate, petered out in the early 1950's. The lessons gained from these experiences were not lost on del Moral, however, and traces of the search for a truly "national" Mexican architecture remain in his work today.

Consequently, we find in one of del Moral's best-known works, the La Merced Market Hall complex in Mexico City, a rigorous practicality. Large prestressed concrete shells span the open-plan layouts of the 20 acres of main halls; the produce from the extensive agricultural regions around Mexico City flows freely through the bays where up to 140 trucks can be unloaded at at a time; clean concrete walls and a high roof contribute to the cool airiness of the building in the height of summer. And, as in many public buildings throughout Mexico, the market is also a social centre, containing an auditorium, 300 public baths, and 8 day nurseries that can cope with approximately 1500 children. Despite the complexity such a description suggests, the formal simplicity and social awareness del Moral brought to La Merced's design and construction meant it was built in a record time of 8 months.

An earlier work, the rural school at Casacuran, eschews the use of high technology in its construction but, nonetheless, is of a sophisticated standard in it amenities. Here, del Moral displays his concern for the social needs of the area, creating simple, open classrooms, each with its own kitchen, bathroom and sleeping quarters, often necessary in rural areas. Local materials are employed throughout, both as a practical and environmental consideration: peeled logs are used as columns supporting the shady patio roof overhang, native tiles cover the surface of the roof itself, local brick and stone for the walls—all blending with the existing village buildings. The school, for 200 students, set a high standard even by today's criteria for rural amenities on a severely limited budget.

Nor does del Moral, for all his strict adherence to functional concerns, lose sight of the "aesthetics" of the environment for which he is building. In an apartment house in Mexico City, designed in 1952 in collaboration with Mario Pani, the somewhat stark character of the neighborhood is relieved by his skilful handling of everyday materials. The ground floor is shaded by a perforated screen of hollow cement brick, concrete has a hammered texture and is painted in earth colours, a discreet glass mosaic on the facade delineates each level of the building, and the basically simple structure is "off-set" from the street by a long, low trough planted with native Mexican cacti and succulents.

Again, in a 1951 house in Polanco, Mexico City, del Moral makes successful use of difficult terrain. The confined site is bounded by a retaining wall in warm buff-coloured stone, and the upper floors of the house, with their plain deep terracotta walls and white trim, actually project beyond the retaining wall, whilst its spacious upper terrace looks inward over the private garden. Its pleasing combination of carefully chosen colours, volumes and proportions prevent the somewhat "daring" structure from overwhelming the observer.

—Colin Naylor

DeMARS, Vernon (Armand).
American. Born in San Francisco, California, 26 February 1908. Educated at the University of California, Berkeley, 1925–31, B. Arch. 1931. Served in the United States Navy, 1944–45, as Lieutenant Junior Grade and Navigator on the U.S.S. Yakona, later as Lieutenant and Naval Aide to the Governor of Puerto Rico. Married Betty Bates in 1940. Member, Monument Valley-Rainbow Bridge Expedition, Arizona, 1934; Architectural Draftsman, United States Resettlement Administration, 1936; District Architect, for the Western States, United States Farm Security Administration, 1937–43; Founder, with Burton Cairns, Joseph McCarthy, Garrett Eckbo, T. J. Kent Jr. and Francis Violich, of TELESIS (city and regional planning organization), San Francisco, 1939; Chief of the Housing Standards Section, Technical Division, National Housing Agency, Washington, D.C., 1943–44; Visiting Professor in Architecture, Massachusetts Institute of Technology, Cambridge, 1947–49; Partner, with Donald Reay, DeMars and Reay, Berkeley, California, 1950–65. Since 1965, Principal, with John Wells, DeMars and Wells, Berkeley. Lecturer in Architecture, 1951–52, Professor of Architecture, 1953–75, and Chairman of the Department of Architecture, 1959–62, University of California, Berkeley. Exhibitions: *TELESIS,* San Francisco Museum of Art, 1940; *Built in U.S.A. 1932–1944,* Museum of Modern Art, New York, 1944; *Homes for Tomorrow,* Museum of Modern Art, New York, 1944; *10 Buildings in America's Future,* American Institute of Architects, Washington, D.C., 1957, toured the U.S.S.R., 1958. Recipient: Parker Medal, with others, Boston, 1951; Regional Award of Merit, 1957, and Merit Award, 1963, American Institute of Architects; First Prize, Student Center Competition, University of California, Berkeley, 1957; First Prize, Capitol Towers Competition, Sacramento, California, 1958; Design Award, 1958, and First Design Award, 1959, 1960, *Progressive Architecture;* Special Award, *Sunset Magazine,* 1959; First Prize, Golden Gateway Competition, San Francisco, 1959; First Prize, The Plaza Redevelopment Competition, Richmond, California, 1959; First Prize, Marin City Urban Renewal Competition, California, 1960; Award of Merit, AIA/*House and Home/Life,* 1960; First Honor Award, with others, Urban Renewal Administration, 1964; First Honor Award, Community Facilities Administration, 1964; California Governor's Design Award, 1966 (twice); Award of Merit, 1967, and First Honor Award, 1978, AIA, Northern California Chapter; United States Department of Housing and Urban Development Award, 1968; American Society of Landscape Architects Award, 1971; San Francisco Planning and Urban Renewal Award, 1972; Association of American Universities Award, 1974; "The Berkeley Citation," University of California, 1975. Fellow, American Institute of Architects, 1964. Address: 240 The Uplands, Berkeley, California 94705, U.S.A.

Works:

1937/
43   40 Farm Workers' Communities in the Western United States, including the Farm Workers' Center at Yuba City, California, Cooperative Farm and Workers' Housing at Chandler, Arizona, and the Woodville Farm Workers' Center near Porterville, California

1949   Bannockburn Cooperative Houses, Washington, D.C. (with Rhees Burket and Joseph Neufeld)

1950   Eastgate Apartments (for the Massachusetts Institute of Technology faculty), 100 Memorial Drive, Cambridge, Massachusetts (with Brown, Kennedy, Rapson and Koch)

1951   DeMars House, 240 The Uplands, Berkeley, California

1954   Easter Hill Village (public housing development), Richmond, California (with Donald Hardison)

1955   Cathedral Precinct, Cologne (competition project)

1956   Residence Halls, University of California, Berkeley (competition project)

1957   Sydney Opera House (competition project)

1958/
65   Marin City Redevelopment, near San Francisco

       Capitol Towers (four-block apartment development), Sacramento, California (with Wurster, Bernardi and Emmons, and Edward Larrabee Barnes)

1959/
66   The Golden Gateway (high-density redevelopment project), San Francisco (with Wurster, Bernardi and Emmons)

Vernon DeMars: Student Center, University of California, Berkeley, 1969

1960/
69 Student Center: Sproul Plaza, Student Union, Dining Commons, Eshleman Hall (office building for student activities), and Zellerbach Hall (Auditorium, Concert Hall, and Playhouse), University of California, Berkeley (with Donald Hardison, Donald Reay, and John Wells)

1960/
73 Master plan for the Walnut Creek Civic Center, California

1961 Ocean Park (urban renewal: high-rise and terrace apartments), Santa Monica, California (competition project)

1962 Master plan for Mililani New Town, Oahu, Hawaii (with Livingston and Blayney, and Lawrence Halprin)
   Columbia Plaza, Washington, D.C. (with Keyes, Lethbridge and Condon)
   Lawrence Hall of Science, University of California, Berkeley (competition project)

1963 Master plan for the redevelopment of the Historic Old Sacramento Waterfront, California (with Candeub, Fleissig and Associates)

1965 Wurster Hall: College of Environmental Design, University of California, Berkeley (with Joseph Esherick and Donald Olsen)
   Wells Fargo Bank, El Cerrito, California
   Master plan for Hamilton New Town, near San Jose, California (with Livingston and Blayney, and Lawrence Halprin)

1966 Housing designs for Mililani New Town, Oahu, Hawaii

1968 701 Projects (urban design guide), Oakland, California (with Jack T. Sidener)
   Urban design plan for the Historic Old Sacramento Waterfront, California (with Robert D. Hill)
   Library and Classroom Buildings, California College of Arts and Crafts, Oakland (with Donald Reay)

1969/
75 San Francisco Performing Arts Center (preliminary planning and design)

1970 Library, Mount Angel Abbey, Oregon (with Alvar Aalto)

1971 Grattan Elementary School, San Francisco
   Cutting and Fairmont Stations, in El Cerrito, California, for the San Francisco Bay Area Rapid Transit District

1973 Wheeler Hall Auditorium reconstruction, University of California, Berkeley

1974 Aster Park (moderate-income housing), Sunnyvale, California

1975 Student Union, California State University, Sacramento

Publications:

By DeMARS: articles—"Look Homeward, Housing" in *Architectural Record* (New York), April 1946; "Design Awards Seminar" in *Progressive Architecture* (New York), December 1958; "Urban Design and the Great Exhibitions" in *Daily Pacific Builder* (for the AIA Convention), San Diego 1967.

On DeMARS: books—*The New Architecture* by Alfred Roth, Zurich 1940; *The People's Architects,* edited by Harry Ransom, Chicago and London 1964; *Architects on Architecture,* edited by Paul Heyer, New York 1966, London 1967; articles—"Farm Security Administration" in *Architectural Forum* (New York), January 1941; "Farm Security Architecture" by Talbot Hamlin in *Pencil Points* (New York), November 1941; "War Housing Dormitories, Vallejo, California" in *Arts and Architecture* (Los Angeles), June 1943; "Eastgate Apartments" in *Architectural Record* (New York), February 1949; "Boston Builds Balconies" in *Magazine of Building* (New York), May 1951; "Easter Hill Village" in *House and Home* (New York), July 1955; "Redevelopment of Marin City, California" in *Progressive Architecture* (New York), January 1960; "Golden Gateway Redevelopment" in *Arts and Architecture* (Los Angeles), November 1960; "Planned Chaos on the Piazza" by Allan Temko in *Architectural Forum* (New York), October 1961; "Neues Wohngebiet in Santa Monica, Kalifornien" in *Baumeister* (Munich), June 1962; "La Wurster Hall della Università di California a Berkeley" in *L'Industrie Italiano del Cimento* (Rome), November 1970; "Center of Action" by Robert Montgomery in *Architectural Forum* (New York), reprinted in *Cities Fit to Live In,* edited by Walter McQuade, New York 1971.

I have always approached my architecture as a *setting* for life's events and people's activities. As in theatre, "the play's the thing"—not the setting. This should not lower the architect's aspirations to provide as rewarding a total experience as possible—in usefulness, stability and esthetic satisfaction—the Vetruvian components. But it does raise a danger signal against unheeding, often arrogant pursuit of novelty or of Art for Art's Sake alone.

I have never held that mere honest problem-solving would yield an automatic, soul-uplifting result, but I did expect that the basic tenets of "Modern" architecture, thoughtfully and sensitively pursued, would produce a more satisfactory total environment than now seems to be the case.

The strong, simple forms of the New Architecture in the hands of the pioneering masters had an exciting initial impact when set amid the typical complex tapestry of older street and city scapes. Now, complete street scenes of "Modern" buildings, whether in New York, Rotterdam or Berlin, are often uninteresting, bland and monotonous. The man-in-the-street has long held this to be so. The architect is beginning to agree with him.

The collective architecture of the city needs a richer complexity than the limited vocabulary of "Modern" architecture now seems to produce. The vernacular urban architecture of the 19th century, even in the hands of lesser talents than the masters of the time, added needed texture to the urban scene. A conscious search for its equivalent should be a prime concern for our time.

I have been fortunate in having had the experience of so many problems for which there were few, if any, satisfactory precedents. For the Migratory Farm Workers Communities of the West there were only pitiful, unsatisfactory examples to draw upon for guidance. This experience in the provision of modest dwellings for low-income families led to both my interest and opportunities in a wider range of housing problems in more normal communities. Easter Hill Village attempted to bring individuality and personal identification to each dwelling of a low-income housing development. The Golden Gateway pioneered a high-density, inner city housing solution which fully accommodates the automobile in storage as well as movement. The Berkeley Student Center provided the rare opportunity to plan and to execute, over a period of years, a contemporary version of the medieval town square and its important buildings.
—Vernon DeMars

Working mainly as a designer of "contained streetscapes," Vernon DeMars denegrates the sterility of uniformity and Miesian formalism. As one of America's strongest advocates of the need for variety in modern design, he stresses in his work the "accidental" or semi-planned urban situation. His spaces, instilled with a sense of the familiar and a variety of forms, elevations, and materials, handsomely succeed in evoking an easily related to, human-scale environment.

From his experience as the Farm Security Association's district architect for the western states from 1937–1943, DeMars recognized the tendency of uniformity to produce a lack of vitality. During this period he suggested the creation of mixed neighborhoods in government projects, to include high-rise apartments, townhouses, duplexes and single-family dwellings. He has successfully carried out this concept in several of his designs including the Marin City redevelopment project, the Golden Gateway project, and the Santa Monica Ocean Park project. The last is indicative of his approach. Confronted with the need to provide as much outdoor recreation space as possible, DeMars designed seven high-rise, tower apartments that rise from multi-level parking garages. The sloping exteriors of the garages are given over to townhouse-like, terraced apartments with flora covered patios. This arrangement provided for a fifty-fifty ratio between high-and low-rise dwellings, which gave this community a desirable population diversity as well as providing large open recreational spaces.

The Student Center at the University of California, Berkeley, well demonstrates DeMars' "planned chaos" ideology. Perhaps his most successful and certainly his most controversial undertaking, the Student Center consists of four buildings placed on each side of a sunken central square with a plaza serving as a transition area for the remainder of the campus. The four buildings, the student union, the dining commons, the two thousand seat Zellerbach auditorium, and the eight-story office tower, Eshleman Hall, are individual entities with distinct styles, scales and characters. No one structure can be considered an architectural masterpiece, but taken as a whole they compliment one another and contribute enormously to the patina of the square. Such a diversity exudes visual excitement and allows a vibrant tension to exist between the structures that in turn enhances the dynamics of the central courtyard.

The buildings, which are in scale with their surroundings, do not obtrude on the spatial freedom of the square, the main attraction of the Student Center. The square's openness, coupled with the eclectic employment of such familiar elements as the fountain on the plaza, Maybeck-inspired trellises in the dining commons and as a cornice on the student union, kiosks which serve as bulletin boards, trees and street furniture, provides a casual, rather European, and extremely viable human space. With a mixture of modern and familiar forms, open and private spaces, multi-level pedestrian pathways and a diversity of materials, the Student Center provides a pleasingly provocative campus streetscape.

By recognizing a community's need for diversity in building types, and by an intermixing of the traditional and modern, DeMars has taken a large step towards combating the critical assertions leveled against the sterility of much of modern architecture. He has developed a workable synthesis that incorporates traditional haphazard urban planning and design with modern architecture's preoccupation with rationality and order.

—Don J. Hibbard

DIAMOND, A(bel) J(oseph).
Canadian. Born in Piet Retief, South Africa, 8 November 1932; emigrated to Canada, 1964: naturalized, 1965. Educated at the University of Cape Town, South Africa, 1951–56 (Thornton White Prize, 1952), B.Arch. (honours) 1956; Oxford University, England, 1956–58, M.A. 1958; University of Pennsylvania, Philadelphia, 1961–62 (Marley Scholarship, 1961; Italian State Bursary, 1961; Graham Foundation Scholarship, 1962), M.Arch. 1962. Married Gillian Mary Huggins in 1959; children: Andrew and Alison. Assistant Professor, University of Pennsylvania, 1962–64; Associate Professor, University of Toronto, 1964–69; Professor, York University, Toronto, 1969–73. In private practice, as A. J. Diamond Architect, Toronto, 1965–69; Partner, with Barton Myers, *q.v.*, Diamond and Myers, Toronto, 1969–74. Since 1975, Principal of A. J. Diamond Associates, architects and planners,

A. J. Diamond: Beverley Place, Toronto, 1977

Toronto (associates: Wilfrid Worland; Kevin Garland; Leslie M. Klein); branch office in Ottawa. Member, Registration Board, Ontario Association of Architects, 1974–78; Chairman of the Visiting Committee, Ontario Schools of Architecture, 1977–78. Exhibition: *This City Now,* Art Gallery of Ontario, Toronto, 1969. Recipient: Canada Council Grant, 1967. Member, Royal Architectural Institute of Canada; Associate, Royal Institute of British Architects. Address: A. J. Diamond and Associates, 322 King Street West, Toronto, Ontario M5V 1J4, Canada.

Works:

1967   Eedee Chair for the Canadian Federal Government (project)
1969   York Square (restaurant/shops complex), Yorkville, Toronto (with Barton Myers)
          Housing/Union Building, University of Alberta, Edmonton (with Barton Myers)
          Alcan Executive Headquarters interiors, Toronto (with Barton Myers)
          Long range development plan for the University of Alberta, Edmonton (with Barton Myers)
          Vidal Sassoon Salon interiors, Toronto (with Barton Myers)
1970   Roy Foss Motors Building, Toronto
          Ontario Medical Association Headquarters, Toronto (with Barton Myers)
1971   Dofasco/Ibis Steel Manufacturers Housing, Hamilton, Ontario
          Warehouse to office conversion, 322 King Street West, Toronto
1973   Union Facilities, University of Maryland, Baltimore (project; with Barton Myers)
1974   Pickering Airport Impact Study, Toronto
          Rideau Street Mall, Ottawa, Ontario

Union Station Feasibility Study, Toronto
1975   Innis College, University of Toronto
1976   Student housing, Queen's University, Kingston, Ontario (partly complete)
          Citadel Theatre, Edmonton, Alberta (with Barton Myers and R. L. Wilkin)
          Dundas/Sherbourne Housing, Toronto (with Barton Myers)
1977   Beverley Place: Hydro Low-Rise, High-Density Housing Block, Toronto
          Gerrard Library, Toronto
          Le Breton Flats, Ottawa (project)
          Downtown revitalization plans for St. Mary's, Barrie, Perth, Dundas, and Prescott, Ontario
1978   Rail relocation plan for Sudbury, Ontario
          Victoria Park Infill Housing, London, Ontario
          St. Michael's Lands Multiple Housing, Forest Hill, Toronto

Publications:

By DIAMOND: articles—"Eye Witness—Cranbrook" in *AIA Journal* (Washington, D.C.), December 1962; "Critique of the UBC Student Centre" in *Royal Architectural Institute of Canada Journal* (Toronto), October 1964; "Expo" in *AIA Journal* (Washington, D.C.), February 1967; "Shopping Centres—New Urban Nucleii" in *Toronto Daily Star,* 3 February 1968; "There Are Solutions to the Housing Crisis" in *Toronto Daily Star,* 2 March 1968; "Residential Density and Housing Form" in *Journal of Architectural Education* (Washington, D.C.), February 1976; "Big City Trends Eroding the Quality of Life in Small Centres" in the *Globe and Mail* (Toronto), 29 July 1976; "Taking Risks out of Design" in the *Globe and Mail* (Toronto), 28 December 1977; "On Sleeping with an Elephant" in

Process: Architecture (Tokyo/Pittsburgh), March 1978.

On DIAMOND: articles—"The Diamond Residence" in *Canadian Homes* (Toronto), August 1968; "Mobile Homes" in *Canadian Homes* (Toronto), April 1969; "York Square" in *Canadian Architect* (Toronto), June 1969; "Long Range Development Plan, University of Alberta" in *Canadian Architect* (Toronto), July/August 1969; "Long Range Plan—Alberta" in *Architecture Canada* (Toronto), July/August 1969; "York Square" in *Progressive Architecture* (New York), September 1969; "York Square" in *Byggenkunst* (Oslo), September 1969; "York Square" in *Canadian Architect* (Toronto), April 1970; "York Square and Student Union House, Alberta" in *Architecture Canada* (Toronto), April 1970; "York Square" in *Abitare* (Milan), October 1970; "Alcan Interiors" in *Canadian Architect* (Toronto), March 1971; "Ontario Medical Association" in *Canadian Architect* (Toronto), June 1971; "Vidal Sassoon Salon" in *Architectural Record* (New York), August 1971; "Ontario Medical Association" in *Architectural Record* (New York), September 1971; "York Square" in *Architecture + Urbanism* (Tokyo), November 1971; "Alcan Interiors" in *Architectural Record* (New York), March 1972; "Work of Diamond and Myers" in *Architecture + Urbanism* (Tokyo), May 1972; "Dofasco Steel Housing" in *Chatelaine* (Toronto), May 1972; "The Campus as a Lesson in Urban Form—Students' Union Housing" in *Progressive Architecture* (New York), September 1972; "York Square in Toronto" in *Baumeister* (Munich), October 1972; "Old Is New in Office Space" in *Executive* (Toronto), November 1972; "The Low Rise Alternative Urban Recycling" in *Time* (New York), 16 April 1973; "To Save a Fabric" in *Progressive Architecture* (New York), May 1973; "Student Street" in *Progressive Architecture* (New York), February 1974; "La Cantinetta Restaurant" in *Interiors* (New York), June 1974; "Students' Union Housing, University of Alberta" in *Architecture + Urbanism* (Tokyo), December 1974; "Diamond and Myers: The Form of Reform" in *City Magazine* (Toronto), August 1975; "999 Queen Street West" in *City Magazine* (Toronto), Summer 1976; "The Democratization of Canadian Architecture" in *Library of Canadian Architecture,* Halifax, Nova Scotia 1978; "A Hybrid Rival to High-Rise Has Character" in the *Globe and Mail* (Toronto), 15 March 1978; "Hydro Block" in *Toronto Star,* 18 March 1978.

*   *   *

There are several characteristics to my work.

The first is the range of scales of projects, from urban planning (for example, the towns of Sudbury, Barrie, Dundas and Perth and Ottawa, Ontario) to building interiors (executive offices and residential projects).

The second is the conviction that existing conditions must be seen as a resource, to be utilized in new development. Examples of this aspect of my work are infill housing, re-using of existing buildings for new purposes, and using alternatives to high rise in existing neighbourhoods so that the surrounding community is not traumatized or overshadowed by new development.

The third characteristic is a concern for the social content and impact of architecture—that architecture (unlike other arts) is not merely a set of formal physical considerations: the *user's* needs and satisfactions are paramount.

Finally, I am concerned with scale and historical precedent.

—A. J. Diamond

Doubtless what sticks in the public mind as most exemplary of A. J. Diamond's work was his demonstration, by turning an architectural model on its end, that high-density low-rise was no more than high-rise on a human scale. At Beverley Place, the Hydro Site project in Toronto, he went on to put into

Eladio Dieste: Brick Shell Bus Station, Salto, Uruguay, 1972

action just this principle, thereby saving some fine old houses and providing a liveable high-density project that interestingly combines new and old.

Diamond brings to his architecture his career as a designer and his care for intimate spaces. In 1969 he first demonstrated this (with Barton Myers) in the creation of York Square, a complex of shops and restaurants around a tree-shaded square behind a set of old houses. That the tree was preserved and is central to the attractiveness of the square was a pleasant feature uncharacteristic of much other "development" in Toronto at that time. More recently, at Innis College, he has similarly preserved old houses in conjunction with a new building. In spite of economies in the project and the use of an unattractive brick, the complex as a whole works better than many more expensive and attractive academic buildings. The use of exposed ductwork in this complex and in Diamond's conversion of 322 King Street West, a bow to trendy functionalism, is less successful. In the latter offices, however, there is a skilful use of exposed brick and lightwells that gives what was an unprepossessing building a surprising grace. This is especially obvious in "La Cantinetta," the restaurant on the ground floor of the building, where the Diamond-Myers Partnership succeeded in combining intimacy with an airy lightness.

Diamond's participation (with Barton Myers) in the long-range development plan for the University of Alberta as well as his own more recent Le Breton Flats in Ottawa, show his capacity for large-scale planning. And this is borne out too in his numerous ambitious plans for the renovation of a number of small urban centres in Ontario. Indeed, when his career as a whole comes to be assessed, it seems likely that his concern for "urban recycling" by conversion and adaptation will be seen as his major achievement.

—D.D.C. Chambers

DIESTE, Eladio.

Uruguayan. Born in Artigas, 1 December 1917. Educated at the Faculty of Engineering of the Universidad de la Republica, Montevideo, Dip.Ing. 1943. Married Elizabeth Friedheim Utke in 1944; children: Juan, Esteban, Eduardo, Antonio, Marta, Teresa, Bernardo, Pedro, Tomás, Inés, and Isabel. Engineer, Ministry of Public Works, Montevideo, 1943–45; Engineer, Represa Rincon del Bonete, Montevideo, 1945–46; Chief Engineer, Head Architectural Technical Office, Ministry of Public Works, Montevideo, 1946–48; Chief Engineer, Viermond S.A., Montevideo, 1948–55. Since 1955, Founder and Chief Engineer, with Eugenio R. Montañez, Dieste and Montañez, Montevideo. Consultant Engineer for the Salto Grande and Palmar Dams, Uruguay, since 1973. Professor of Engineering, Universidad de la República, Montevideo, 1943–73. Visiting Professor and Lecturer, University of Buenos Aires, since 1959. Member, Academia Nacional de Ingenieria del Uruguay, 1966. Address (office): Carlos Roxlo 1606, Montevideo, Uruguay.

Works:

1957 Ceramic Shell Garage, for the Insurance Bank, Avenida Rondeau, Montevideo (with Eugenio R. Montañez)

1958 TEM S.A. Industrial Plant, Cno. Carrasco 5975, Montevideo (with Eugenio R. Montañez)

Church, Atlántida Station, Canelones, Uruguay

1968 CALNU Industrial Plant, Bella Union, Artigas, Uruguay (with Eugenio R. Montañez)

1969 St. Peter's Church, Durazno, Uruguay (with A. Casto and A. Romero)

1971 Caputto Orange Packing Plant, Salto, Uruguay (with Eugenio R. Montañez)

Central Market, Porto Alegre, Brazil (with C. M. Fayet and C. Araujo)

1972 Brick Shell Bus Station, Salto, Uruguay

Market Building, Maceió, Brazil

1975 Agro-Industrial Complex, Vergara, Treinta y Tres, Uruguay

1977 Massaro S.A. Industrial Plant, Joanico, Canelones, Uruguay

Agro-Industrial Complex, Young, Rio Negro, Uruguay

1978 Port of Montevideo Industrial Building

Refrescos del Norte S.A. (Coca-Cola Export) Industrial Plant, Salto, Uruguay (with E. Dieste)

Industrial building for construction company, Avenida Italia 3656, Montevideo

Publications:

By DIESTE: monographs—*Problems of the Foundations of Turbo-Alternators,* Montevideo 1969; *Buckling of Double Curvature Shells,* Montevideo 1970; *The Action of Wind over Long-Span Industrial Buildings,* Montevideo 1972; *Reinforced Ceramic Hollow Towers,* Montevideo 1972; articles—"Atlántida Church" in *Informes de la Construccion* (Madrid), no. 127, 1961; "Reinforced Ceramic Structures" in *Ingenieria* (Montevideo), nos. 657/660, 1963; "Double Curvature Shells of Reinforced Ceramic" in *Proceedings of the World Conference on Shell Structures,* Washington, D.C. 1964; "About Reinforced Brick Constructions," "Technique and Underdevelopment" and "St. Peter's Church" in *Summa* (Buenos Aires), no. 70, 1973; "About Reinforced Brick Construction" in *Summa* (Buenos Aires), no. 85, 1975.

On DIESTE: books—*Eladio Dieste* by Juan P. Bonta, Buenos Aires 1963; *New Directions in Latin American Architecture* by Francisco Bullrich, New York 1969; articles—"Eglise Paroissiale d'Atlántida" in *L'Architecture d'Aujourd'hui* (Paris), June 1961; "Atlántida Parish Church" in *Architectural Review* (London), September 1961; "Brick Shell Construction" in *Progressive Architecture* (New York), April 1962; "Architecture in Uruguay" in *Summa* (Buenos Aires), no. 27, 1970.

I have been trained as a civil engineer. I graduated in 1943, and my initial work was in the areas of pilings, foundations, bridges, construction machinery, and the design of big structures. In 1948 I made my first reinforced ceramic shells.

My purpose has been to create rational and economical structures, and I have, gradually, refined the shapes that I have created. Both aims—technical rationality and aesthetic worth—are, in fact, different aspects of the same attitude. I am pleased that architects are now very interested in our work.

I believe that the techniques that we have developed provide the beginnings of a new kind of construction, one that really works. Despite current opinions about reinforced ceramics (based on the fact that both the material cost and the labor cost are low), I do not believe that the technique need be restricted to under-developed countries.

—Eladio Dieste

For thousands of years man used such materials as brick, stone or wood for construction and created buildings based on processes of trial and error: history has taught us that the architecture of the past was the result of the very experience of building. But in the last two centuries this situation has changed: new structural materials—iron, concrete—have created new technologies, and the science of engineering has been so refined as to allow us to project construction and to forecast its behavior. Roman or Gothic architecture were the results of techniques learned in the actual process of construction, without pre-planning. In our century very few architects work in that way; in a highly-technical age, we can hardly conceive of an architecture that does not involve elaborate prior controls. The advantages of the new materials and technologies are obvious: architecture has been rationalized, industrialized, internationalized. But there are disadvantages too: in the process architects have been drawn away from a direct experience and intimate contact with construction, and this withdrawal has, in turn, brought about an impoverishment of forms, a lessening in creativity.

Eladio Dieste is an exception to these generalizations. He attempts to rescue the experience of artisan labor; he believes in the value of actual involvement in the building process and in the environment in which buildings are created. Dieste does not subscribe to the tenets of international, rational, industrialized architecture: he believes that most of such architecture is inhuman. His country, Uruguay, is not in a period of industrialization, so Dieste has been able to pursue his goals of rescuing the traditional values of intimate contact with material and of "living with" construction as a creative process. He uses the same material used by the workmen of Mesopotamia thousands of years ago—brick, the fundamental element in his work.

A quarter of a century ago, Dieste, in association with Eugenio Montañez, began to construct vaults made of brick (though, then, he strengthened his structures with an iron frame able to withstand traction stresses), and from that time, with the vaults, he has created a constructive language, which, given his formal sensibility, has been inevitably transformed into an architectural language. The vaults have been fundamentally of two kinds—the self-supporting, made solely of ordinary bricks, and the gaussian, made both of ordinary bricks and of special bricks: their distinctive geometric feature is their double curvature.

Eladio Dieste's accomplishment, then, has been in the rescue of artisanship and in the bringing of the language of brick to its maximum expression. The works he has created possess a series of qualities that emerge directly from the materials used and from an experimentation in form during the actual process of construction. The expression profits to a great extent from site conditions, economy, and speed of execution and from his attention to natural lighting.

All of Eladio Dieste's work reveals a concern to understand building as a totality, a totality that is essentially on a human scale.

—Jorge Glusberg

DINKELOO, John (Gerard).
American. Born in Holland, Michigan, 28 February 1918. Educated at Holland High School, 1924–30; Hope College, Holland, 1936–39; University of Michigan School of Architecture, Ann Arbor, 1939–42, B.Arch. in architectural engineering 1942. Served in the United States Navy, in the South and Central Pacific, 1943–46: Lieutenant. Married Thelma Ann Van Dyke in 1943; children: Carter, Janje, Dirk, Tessa, Christiaan, Hanni, and Kaaren. Designer, 1942–43, and Chief of Production, 1946–50, Skidmore, Owings and Merrill, Chicago; Head of Production, Eero Saarinen and Associates, Bloomfield Hills, Michigan, 1950–56; Partner, Eero Saarinen and Associates, Bloomfield Hills and Birmingham, Michigan, 1956–61, and Hamden, Connecticut, 1961–66. Since 1966, Founder Partner, with Kevin Roche, *q.v.*, Kevin Roche John Dinkeloo and Associates, Hamden, Connecticut. Trustee, Hope College. Exhibitions: Museum of Modern Art, New York, 1968, 1971. Recipient: Medal of Honor, New York Chapter of the American Institute of Architects, 1968; California Governor's Award for Excellence in Design, 1968. Address: Kevin Roche John Dinkeloo and Associates, 20 Davis Street, Hamden, Connecticut 06517, U.S.A.

See ROCHE, Kevin

DÖCKER, Richard.
German. Born in Weilheim an der Teck, Württemberg, 13 June 1894. Educated at the Staatliche Beratungsstelle für Baugewerbe, Stuttgart, 1912–14, 1916–18, Dip.Arch. 1918. Served in the German Army, 1914–16: wounded in action. Married Claire deLatue in 1926; Erna Clara Tsuneko Grosse in 1943; had two daughters. Worked as an architect in the Town Planning Office, Stuttgart, 1920–22; Assistant to Paul Bonatz, Technische Hochschule, Stuttgart, 1922–25; in private practice, Stuttgart, 1922 until his death, 1968. Architect-in-Charge, Building Works, *Die Wohnung* exhibition, Weissenhof Estate, Stuttgart, 1927; Director of Reconstruction, Saarbrucken, 1941–43, and Stuttgart, 1946–50. Professor of Urban Planning and Design, Technische Hochschule, Stuttgart, 1947–68. Member, German Werkbund, and Der Ring architects group, Germany. Exhibitions: *Die Wohnung,* Stuttgart, 1927. *Died (in Stuttgart) 9 November 1968.*

Works:

1923 Friedenschule, Trossingen, Germany
1926 Hospital, Waiblingen, Germany
1926/
28   Hospital, Maulbronn, Germany
     Goppingen Housing Development, near Stuttgart
     Hechingen Housing Development, near Stuttgart

1927 Lichthaus Building, Stuttgart
     Houses 21 and 22, Weissenhof Estate, Stuttgart (destroyed in World War II)
1941 Redevelopment/rebuilding plan for Saarbrucken
1946 Redevelopment/rebuilding plan for Stuttgart
1948/
51   Rebuilding plan for the Technische Hochschule, Stuttgart
1953 Library, University of Saarbrucken
1954/
57   Master plan for University City, Hyderabad, Pakistan
1955/
68   Great Katharine Hospital restoration and additions, Stuttgart

Publications:

By DÖCKER: book—*Terrassentyp,* Stuttgart 1929.

On DÖCKER: articles—"Sanatorium à Waiblingen" in *Architecture Vivante* (Paris), vol. 7, no. 2, 1928; "Richard Döcker" in *Bauwelt* (Berlin), 9 July 1931; "Richard Döcker" in *Baumeister* (Munich), no. 29, 1931.

Richard Döcker began his career in the Stuttgart Town Planning Office; later, after qualifying as a master builder, he was appointed assistant to Professor Paul Bonatz at his former college, the Technische Hochschule in Stuttgart. As a young architect Döcker became involved in the German "New Building" movement of the 1920's, then in its initial phase. He was a member of the German Werkbund and also of the architects' union Der Ring, with which avant garde architects of the time—like Häring, Scharoun, Gropius, May, Mendelsohn, Mies van der Rohe and the Taut brothers—had associated themselves.

When the Werkbund was planning its exhibition *Die Wohnung* in Stuttgart in 1927, it was Döcker who was the spokesman for a group of young architects and artists who were eager to make sure that the orientation of the exhibition would be towards the "New Building" philosophy. The plan that was finally accepted for the Weissenhof housing development was designed by van der Rohe, but Döcker himself was in charge of the building works, and it was he who designed and built numbers 21 and 22 of the houses (which were later destroyed in the war).

As a result of this assignment, and, even more, the Waiblingen Hospital, designed on the terrace principle, Döcker became internationally famous. He developed his ideas on this kind of building in his book *Terrassentyp,* published in 1929. Yet after 1933 he found it progressively more difficult to achieve his new kind of building. Like Hugo Häring, with whom he felt an affinity, he stayed on in Germany, but increasingly he had to restrict his architectural activities. It was for this reason that in 1939 he began to study biology.

Then, in 1941, he was drafted to direct the rebuilding of Saarbrucken. In 1946 he was chosen to direct the rebuilding operations in Stuttgart, and a year later he was appointed to the Chair of Urban Planning at the Stuttgart Technische Hochschule. As director of the Department of Architecture, he was able to put the aims of the "New Building" movement in practice: in effect he founded a second school in Stuttgart, and his influence as a teacher of urban planning was decisive for a whole new generation of young architects.

Among his buildings of the post-war period, one must mention, above all, the University Library at Saarbrucken as well as the first general rebuilding plan for the Stuttgart Technische Hochschule. From 1954–57 he led the planning of University City in Hyderabad, Pakistan. His last works include the restoration of, and additions to, the Great Katharine Hospital in Stuttgart.
—Jürgen Joedicke

DOMÈNECH i MONTANER, Lluis.

Spanish. Born in Barcelona, 21 December 1850. Educated at the Escuela de Arquitectura, Madrid, 1870–73, graduated 1873. Married Maria Roura Carnesoltes in 1875; children: Maria, Ana, Pedro, Delores, Luis, Felix, Enrique and Ricardo. Practised with the architect Vilaseca, Barcelona, 1873–78; in private practice, Barcelona, 1878 until his death, 1923. Temporary Professor, 1875–77, Professor of the Knowledge of Materials and the Application of Physical and Natural Sciences, 1877–1900, and Director, 1900–23, Escuela de Arquitectura. Barcelona. Director, with J. Puig i Cadafalch, Montaner i Simon publishing company, Barcelona, 1886–97; Deputy of the Cortes (Parliament), Barcelona, 1901, 1903. President, Jocs Florals (poetry contest), Barcelona, 1881, 1895, Lliga de Catalunya, Barcelona, 1887–1904, Unió Catalanista, Barcelona, 1892, and Ateneo Barcelona, 1898–1900, 1904–06, 1911–14. Recipient: First Prize, Clavé Monument Competition, with Vilaseca, Barcelona, 1874; First Prize, Provincial Institute of Public Instruction Building Competition, with Vilaseca, Barcelona, 1874; Municipal Prize, Barcelona, 1904, 1905, 1908, 1912. Member, Centre Nacional Catalana, Barcelona, 1899, Royal Academy of Fine Arts of San Fernando, 1903, and Royal Academy of Literature, Barcelona, 1921. *Died* (in Barcelona) *27 December 1923.*

Works:

1873/
74   Monument to Clavé, Barcelona (competition project; with Vilaseca)
      Provincial Institute of Public Instruction Building, Barcelona (competition project; with Vilaseca)
1874/
88   House, Ronda Universidad 4, Barcelona
      House, Calle Trafalgar 54, Barcelona
      House, Calle Méndez Núñez 15, Barcelona
1881/
85   Editorial Montaner i Simon Building, Calle Aragon 255, Barcelona
1887 Casino of Canet de Mar, Barcelona
1888 Café-Restaurant (Castillo de los Tres Dragones), *Universal Exhibition,* Parquede Cuidadela, Barcelona
      International Hotel, for the *Universal Exhibition,* Paseo de Colon, Barcelona (demolished)
      Town Hall conversion to Royal Lodgings, *Universal Exhibition,* Barcelona
      Monument to the First Marques de Comillas, Santander, Spain
      Comillas Seminary, Santander, Spain
      Casa Roura, Canet de Mar, Barcelona
1889 Plan for the Vía Transversal, Barcelona
1893 Palau Montaner, Calle de Mallorca 273, Barcelona
1897/
1919 Pedro Mata Institute, Reus, Barcelona
1899 Casa Thomas, Calle Mallorca 291, Barcelona
1900 Casa Rull, Reus, Barcelona
1901 Casa Navàs, Reus, Barcelona
1902 Casa Lamadrid, Calle Gerona 113, Barcelona
      Fonda España, Calle San Pablo 9, Barcelona
1902/
12   Hospital of St. Paul, phase I, Avenida San Antonio Maria Clavet 167, Barcelona (later completed by Pedro Domènech)
      Grand Hotel, Palma, Majorca (now the National Institute of Social Security)
1905 Casa Lleó Morera, Paseo de Gracia 35, Barcelona
1905/
08   Palace of Catalan Music, Barcelona
1907/
09   Castle of Santa Florentina restoration, Canet de Mar, Barcelona
1908/
11   Casa Fuster, Paseo de Gracia 128, Barcelona

1911/
12   Casa Gasull, Reus, Barcelona
1913/
16   Casa Solà restoration, Olot, Gerona, Spain

Publications:

By DOMÈNECH: books—*Historia General de Arte,* with others, 8 volumes, Barcelona 1876–97; *Arquitectura Moderna de Barcelona,* with F. Roget y Pedrosa and F. Casanovas y Gorchs, Barcelona 1897; *Primer Congrés Universitari Català,* Barcelona 1903; *Estudis Politichs,* Barcelona 1905; *Abastecimiento de aguas para saneamiento y alumbrado eléctrico de Barcelona,* Barcelona 1914; *Historia i Arquitectura del Monestir de Poblet,* Barcelona 1925; *La Iniquitat de Casp i la fi del Comtat d'Urgell,* Barcelona 1930; *Centcelles,* Barcelona 1931; *Ensenyes Nacionals de Catalunya,* with Felix Domènech, Barcelona 1936; articles—"En busca de una arquitectura nacional" in *La Renaixensa* (Barcelona), January 1878; "La Reforma de Barcelona resolta pel sentit comú" in *La Renaixensa* (Barcelona), 3 January 1892; "De com se pot fer lo Museo de la Historia a Barcelona" in *La Renaixensa* (Barcelona), 26 February 1892; "L'Emili Vilanova" in *Illustracio Catalana* (Barcelona), 12 August 1906; "Les primeres imatges conegudes de Jaume I" in *Illustracio Catalana* (Barcelona), 14 June 1908; "L'art en l'Institut d'Estudis Catalans" in *El Poble Català* (Barcelona), 7 May 1909; "En defensa de l'Escola d'Arquitectura" in *El Poble Català* (Barcelona), 8 May 1909; "L'apartament de l'Ildefons Suñol" in *Ateneu Barcelonés* (Barcelona), vol. I, 1917.

On DOMÈNECH: books—*Don Lluis Domènech i Montaner* by J. Puig i Cadafalch, Barcelona 1902; *Gaudi e il Movimento Catalano* by Oriol Bohigas, Turin 1968; *Domènech i Montaner: Arquitecto del Modernismo* by Maria Lluisa Borràs, Barcelona 1971; articles—"Lluis Domènech i Montaner" by Guitart Trulls in *Arquitectura* (Madrid), January 1924; "Lluis Domènech i Montaner" by Serra i Pages in *Boletin de la Real Academia de Buenas Letras de Barcelona,* 1926; "Lo Decorativo en la Obra de Domènech i Montaner" by J. F. Rafols in *Cuadernos de Arquitectura* (Barcelona), February 1956; "Lluis Domènech i Montaner a traves de un edificio cincuentenario" by José Maria Sostres Maluquer in *Revista Nacional de Arquitectura* (Madrid), October 1958; "Lluis Domènech i Montaner," special issue of *Cuadernos de Arquitectura* (Barcelona), April/June 1963; "Lluis Domenech i Montaner 1850–1923" by Oriol Bohigas in *Architectural Review* (London), December 1967; "Lluis Domènech i Montaner 1850–1923" by Michele Costanzo in *L'Architettura* (Rome), June/July 1973; "Domènech i Montaner: Works in Reus" by José Maria Buqueras Bach in *Jano Arquitectura* (Barcelona), March 1975.

Though less well known than his contemporary Antoni Gaudi, Lluis Domènech i Montaner nevertheless made outstanding contributions to the Catalan Modernisme Movement and to the ideals of the Renaixenca as an architect, teacher and politician.

After graduating from the Escuela de Arquitectura in Madrid, Domènech practised successfully with Vilaseca, winning several competitions. The most important of these was the Provincial Institute of Public Instruction, which broke with historicism and demonstrated an understanding of the new technology that was shaping European building elsewhere, particularly in Germany, Austria and Switzerland. Puig i Cadafalch, writing in 1902, commented on the importance of this building and its technological message. Unfortunately the Institute was not built, but it contrasted sharply with Domènech's earlier eclectic neo-classical work such as the house at Ronda Universidad 4 in Barcelona's Ensanche. It was, for Domènech, a complete architectural re-appraisal.

Lluis Domènech i Montaner: Palace of Catalan Music, Barcelona, 1908

Appointed to a professorship at Barcelona's Escuela de Arquitectura, he made conspicuous contributions and reforms, which led to his being appointed to a personal chair in 1877. He defined his architectural philosophy and experiments in "En busca de una arquitectura nacional," and broke his partnership with Vilaseca, in 1878.

Domènech's first important building on his own was Editorial Montaner i Simon. Commissioned by relatives, the building is logically planned and well organized throughout in terms of circulation, light, ventilation and in the use of structural steel. Great attention is devoted to detail as seen in the use of brick, refined carpentry and superb ironwork—in which Catalan craftsmen excelled.

The Barcelona exhibition of 1888 gave Domenech additional opportunities to extend his feelings for rationalism into yet higher planes. He contributed two buildings of importance, The Café-Restaurant (or Castillo de los tres dragones) and the International Hotel, which was demolished at the end of the exhibition. The Café-Restaurant is undoubtedly one of the great European buildings of its time, especially in its spatial planning, use of materials and constructional techniques. Often compared with Berlage's Amsterdam Exchange, completed some ten years later, and cited as having De Stijl as the basis of its style, the Café-Restaurant is an indication of Domènech's visionary zeal. The International Hotel—which, from the fragmentary evidence available, seems to have resembled the Provincial Institute of Public Instruction—was one of the most important constructional achievements of the era. Five storeys high with a facade 160 metres wide, it was erected in 63 days. This phenomenal achievement was attributed to Domènech's extraordinary capacity for organization and the utilization of industrialized methods of building and prefabrication techniques.

The years 1885–1908 were the climax of Domènech's career as an architect. He implemented important architectural commissions and held important political and academic appointments. His most important building was undoubtedly the Palace of Catalan Music, now considered to be his masterpiece and also that of the Modernisme Movement. True to Domènechian precedent, the building is superbly planned in response to an extremely difficult and irregular urban site. Space and light are handled with great imagination and skill, as seen in the vestibule, stairs and concert room, which are incredibly beautiful. Among the features of this building are free planning assisted by the use of structural steel and a continuous curtain wall protected by balconies and applied decorative columns that function as *brise soleil*. The overall impression of this exuberantly decorated building is ethereal. Its functional message inspired a whole series of buildings and led to the purism and rationalism of the 1920's and 30's.

Between 1902 and 1912 Domènech completed the first phase of the Hospital of St. Paul in Barcelona (it was completed by his son Pedro). Conceived as a series of pavilions linked by subterranean passages, it is unique in the annals of hospital planning. Because it was flexible it permitted change in hospital procedures and medical practise, as well as providing good environmental conditions for patients; it also facilitated the phasing of the enormous project. It created, moreover, a human scale and atmosphere in contrast to the monumental and awesome concepts for hospital buildings then prevelant. In detail the building reflects Domènech's passion for the revitalization of the crafts and techniques of his country, not only for aesthetic but also for ethical reasons. The result is a bold, moving, inspired decorative theme which is certainly therapeutic.

Domènech's domestic works—for example, Casa Lleó Morera in Barcelona and the Casas Rull and Navàs in Reus—are pleasing with a gay sensitivity that belies his intensely rational approach; they demonstrate a human touch.

In order to carry out such a large practice, along with government and academic appointments, Domènech was assisted by a team of talented architects, sculptors, painters and artists. The office was efficiently organized, but the spirit was apparently akin to that of the Bauhaus.

Critics have compared Domènech unfavourably with Gaudi, portraying him as some sort of disciple of Gaudian philosophy. The Noucentistes, too, pledged to bring order to the apparent madness of Modernisme, denounced his work as being excessively decorative, superficial, and lacking at a conceptual level. But, in retrospect, it is clear that Domènech represents an alternative route to Gaudi and Expressionism. Beneath the exuberant decoration that the age demanded there is evidence of vision and genius. In moving towards Rationalism, Domènech made an immeasurable and brilliant contribution not only within Modernisme but also within the Modern Movement. He deserves greater universal recognition.

—Harold Booton

DOSHI, B(alkrishna) V(ithaldas).

Indian. Born in Poona, 26 August 1927. Educated at Fergusson College, Poona, 1946; J. J. School of Art, Bombay, 1946–50. Married Kamala B. Doshi in 1955; children: Tejal, Radhika, and Manisha. Senior designer with Le Corbusier, in Paris, for major buildings in Chandigarh and Ahmedabad, 1951–57, and represented Le Corbusier and supervised his works in Ahmedabad, 1954–57; in private practice, as Vastu-Shilpa, Ahmedabad, 1956–77. Since 1977, Senior Partner, with Joseph Allan Stein and Jai Rattan Bhalla, Stein Doshi and Bhalla, Ahmedabad and New Delhi. Since 1978, Founder Director, Vastu-Shilpa Foundation for Studies and Research in Environmental Design. Founder, 1962, Honorary Director of the School of Architecture, 1962–72, and since 1972 Honorary Director of the School of Planning, and Dean, Centre for Environmental Planning and Technology (CEPT), Ahmedabad. Visiting Professor, Washington University, St. Louis, 1958, 1960, 1964, 1967, University of Pennsylvania, Philadelphia, 1964, 1967, 1968, 1974, and University of Illinois, Urbana, and Rice University, Houston, 1977. Member, Building International, London, 1972–76; Vice-President, Council of Architecture, Government of India, 1973–74; Member, Advisory Council, International Institute of Architecture, 1978. Member, Advisory Board, *Architecture + Urbanism*, Tokyo, since 1971; Member, Scientific and Technical Advisory Council, Kent State University, Ohio, since 1975. Member of Team 10 since 1967. Recipient: Graham Foundation Fellowship, 1958; Padma Shree, Government of India, 1976. Fellow, Indian Institute of Architects, 1971. Associate Member, Royal Institute of British Architects, 1954; Honorary Fellow, American Institute of Architects, 1971. Address: Stein Doshi and Bhalla, Dhun House, Bhadra, Ahmedabad 380 001, Gujarat State, India.

Works:

1958   City Hall, Toronto (competition project)
1958/
77   Atual Products Ltd. Plant, Bulsar, India
    Anil Starch Products Factory, Ahmedabad
    Silver Cotton Mills, Ahmedabad
    Anup Engineering Ltd. Factory, Ahmedabad
    Jupiter Mills, Ahmedabad
    Shri Ambica Mills, Ahmedabad
    Navabharat Mills, Ahmedabad
    Sarabhai Merck Ltd. Factory, Baroda, India
    Electrical Manufacturing Company Factory, Calcutta
1961   Doshi House, Ahmedabad
1962   Master plan for Gandhidham Township, Kandla, Kutch, India (with Kanvinde and Rai)
    Institute of Indology, Ahmedabad
1962– Indian Institute of Management, Ahmedabad (with Louis I. Kahn, 1962–74)
1963   Science Buildings and Housing, Gujarat University, Ahmedabad
1965   Shreyas Foundation Comprehensive School, Ahmedabad
1966– Centre for Environmental Planning and Technology (CEPT), Ahmedabad
1967   Tagore Memorial Theatre and Cultural Centre, Paladi, Ahmedabad
1968   Housing, for the Gujarat State Fertilizers Company, Baroda, India

B. V. Doshi: Housing, for the Electronics Corporation of India, Hyderabad, 1972

Housing, for the Adinath Cooperative Housing Society, Poona, India

1970 Master plan for the Srinagar Lake areas of India (with Joseph Allen Stein)

1972 Housing, for the Electronics Corporation of India, Hyderabad

National Assembly Complex, Kuwait (competition project)

Master plan for the Gulmarg-Tangmarg area of India (with Joseph Allen Stein)

1973 Housing, for the Indian Farmers Fertilisers Cooperative Ltd., Kalol, North Gujarat, India

Housing, for the Bhabha Atomic Research Centre/Department of Atomic Energy Heavy Water Project, Kota, Rajasthan, India

1973- Ahmedabad Municipal Corporation Office Building and Council Chamber, Victoria Gardens, Ahmedabad

1974 International Crops Research Institute for the Semi-Arid Tropics, Hyderabad

Indian Petrochemicals Corporation Research and Development Laboratories, near Baroda, India

1974/
77 Housing, for the Life Insurance Corporation of India, Hyderabad

1975 Central Bank of India Bank/Office Building, Lal Darwaja, Ahmedabad

Housing and Staff Quarters, Physical Research Laboratory, Ahmedabad Education Society, Gujarat University, Ahmedabad

1976 Premabhai Hall for Gujarat Vidyasabha (multi-purpose theatre/hall and commercial centre), Ahmedabad

India Tourism Development Corporation Hotel, Aurangabad, India

Plan for the redevelopment of the Bhadra area, Ahmedabad

Computer Centre and Library, Administrative Staff College of India, Hyderabad

1977 Indian Institute of Management, Bangalore (with Kanvinde and Rai)

Publications:

By DOSHI: articles—"Self-Sufficiency and Generative Centres" in *Ekistics* (Athens), March 1970; "Human Stake in Environmental Improvement" in *Ekistics* (Athens), November 1970; "The Impetus to Build," interview with William Marlin, in the *Christian Science Monitor* (Boston), 16 June 1977.

On DOSHI: article—"Designing Shady New Buildings for India" by William Marlin in the *Christian Science Monitor* (Boston), 16 June 1977.

Educational background affects interpretation of the environment. It affects an individual's performance and decision-making processes. When one is trained abroad, as I was, and then has to practice in his own country, which has a long tradition and varied needs, he is bound to be confronted with new situations and challenges.

I learned from Le Corbusier to observe and react to climate, to tradition, to function, to structure, to economy and to the landscape. To an extent, I also understand how to build buildings and create spaces and forms. However, I have, in the last two decades, gradually discovered that the buildings that I have designed seem somewhat foreign and out of milieu; they do not appear to have their roots in the soil. With the experience of my work over the years and my own observation, I am trying to understand a little about my people, their traditions and social customs and their philosophy of life.

The best way to know a culture is to study its existing settlements, their way of life, their crafts and their arts. They offer insight into many problems. One observes the heat and cold, the sunshine and moonlight, the starry heavens above, the directions of the wind, and the religious and social ceremonies, the feasts and festivals and pilgrimages to sacred places—things that mould the life of the people and relate them to their environment.

One understands the subtle significance of the porches, verandahs, staircases, open spaces, balconies, terraces, carvings, etc., which constitute the form and the character of their indigenous architecture. Seen in depth they show the relation of classes and communities, their mutual actions and reactions—in short, the whole web of life. One understands, too, the connections with the general economy and the use of energy.

When studying existing buildings from huts to mansions, from a workman's house to a market place, one sees the technical insight of the past in keeping buildings cool, achieving cross ventilation, providing direct and indirect natural light, and providing protection from the sun, the rain or the dust. Economy, of course, played an important role and affected the major aspects of design, such as choice of materials, methods of construction and the ultimate expression itself. In some of these buildings one even comes across indigenous and ingenious methods of insulation through landscaping and positive use of local conditions matched with the life style of the day. One often finds the simplest and most direct ways of building a total eco-system giving architecture its due place of reverence.

There have been examples of water architecture in stepped wells and reservoirs or tanks, of sun architecture in terraces and Jallis porches, and of earth architecture in mud houses and forts. All of these examples highlight the economical use of materials, ingenuity of local skills, and an understanding of the sanctity of the world around us. To this I often feel that we can perhaps add new ideas based on new technology, new spatial understanding, perhaps a new function and a new aesthetic. For example, we could add an efficient internal lighting system to make the building more suitable for frequent use in different seasons and at different times. We could provide varieties of space for specific or general functions or even make the building an extension of the outside space. We could try to reorganize functional and service elements within and outside the house to make it more efficient, save energy and create a new orientation. These are the innovations, the new expressions—but there are still many more issues that remain unresolved.

It is necessary to consider the family ties and local associations of older buildings, associations that we cannot afford to give up. We should draw the inference that buildings that survive in time have more than material utility. They indicate meaning in a building, as opposed to the present-day functional structure that has no meaning except in its craving for modernity. Such structures do not appeal for long. It is not strange that these buildings do not "feel" as good as local buildings. They look incongruous or alien or without roots.

Often new buildings do not come up to the expectations of their occupants: the structures, forms and spaces are unfamiliar; the occupants do not acclimatize. Buildings go through innumerable changes, and we ask ourselves, What is appropriate? What kind of buildings should we build? At this juncture one feels the limitations of one's education and has to learn anew.

Building in India must provide for growth, fluctuating economic conditions and a changing social situation. This demand becomes obvious and compulsory when society is growing rapidly. Changes occur in the time between the start of a project and its completion, because of economic constraints, non-availability of materials, or a change in the social environment, and these changes sometimes result in a partially-built construction or a building double the size originally planned. I have observed that the concept of growth and the provision for change and modification in the design lead to better efficiency and economy. The need to up- or downgrade the functions of a building leads us to provide for vertical or horizontal expansion, fulfilling both immediate and future demands. Such a concept is not widely in practice today but it is of great importance. Strangely enough, many of the buildings in the historic cities of India are built according to such a concept, cities like Jaisalmer, Udaipur, Ahmedabad, and Jaipur.

Generally, local customs and nuances and cultural peculiarities are lost sight of and therefore do not operate in the design. For example, it is essential to understand the pattern, scale and type of streets so as to accommodate variable functions during different seasons and plan outdoor space for different economic activities in different social groups. Yet, very often, the most economical way of providing these services is disturbing to the local community. This fact suggests that when an irrelevant intention based on a particular consideration becomes the main theme of design, it leads to communal disparities and incongruities. I now realize that such an approach to design rarely helps; on the contrary, it very often obstructs the overall efficiency of a society or an organization. I believe that all design should be based on community considerations.

Unless the socio-cultural tradition is understood, one finds it difficult to locate or design streets or places or extensions to buildings or the buildings themselves. The forms of the built environment cannot become a fabric and they cannot be used. It is necessary to speak about a cultural environment rather than about a building or a technology or an economy. A house in Ahmedabad or Jaisalmer or Udaipur has behind it centuries of tradition. This tradition has given the house its form, and many factors tie the generations together. For example, very often at least three generations stay in one house, and it is difficult to perceive this factor immediately in the original design. However, seen through the activities and functions and personal activities of three generations, one perceives a hidden message and becomes aware of a continuity of culture, security and identity provided within a particular framework.

I believe that institutions are the primary elements of an environment. When one is to design either a building or a settlement, he must, first of all, study the interaction between the individual and the community and then provide the community spaces and the institutions of the community.

—B. V. Doshi

B. V. Doshi is a devout Hindu and a vegetarian. He is also eminently cosmopolitan, teaching, leading seminars and lecturing in many of the leading American architectural schools, collaborating on major projects with internationally known architects, and participating in international conferences. He is the founder and dean of the Centre for Environmental Design and Technology in Ahmedabad and honorary director of its School of Planning.

Since he began private practice as an architect and planner under the name of Vastu Shilpa, he has executed approximately 684.7 million rupees worth of work. A breakdown of this figure indicates the nature and scope of his practice. He has created the master plans and designed vast institutional and co-operative housing projects within urban areas for which 150.8 million rupees have been spent; educational and other institutional buildings for 200.5 million rupees; public buildings for 78.4 million rupees; master plans and designs for industrial complexes for 20 million rupees; and entire townships for these complexes, for 67 million rupees; and, finally, town and regional planning projects for 169 million rupees.

Works of such magnitude in the hands of large American or European firms are too often executed in a mechanical, dull manner with little attention paid to the human needs of their users, their culture or their traditions of building. Notice is seldom taken of the problems posed by man's inter-relation to the natural environment. Doshi's work, by contrast, has from the beginning been shaped by his humanity, understanding of the Indian culture and love of nature. For example, in preparing the master plan for the development of tourism in the unspoiled lake area of the Valley of Kashmir for the Government of India Department of Tourism, he made every effort to preserve the area's quietness and serenity—the heritage of the people of Kashmir. Although his assignment had been solely to design facilities that would attract tourists into the Valley, he studied the problem much more deeply.

He examined the relationships between the nearby city of Srinagar and its surrounding lands, the social patterns between the local population and the tourists and between the proposed development patterns and the ecological balance of the region. He urged that the urban penetration that had begun be stopped and future construction controlled. He warned that the noise pollution, the visual pollution and the sanitary pollution that results from today's unenlightened planning practices, architectural forms and urban growth be kept away from the lakes. "It is of prime importance," he wrote in his report to his client, "to recognize and accept that a beautiful land is a privilege for all and a common trust for the future. It must be accepted and enforced that permission to build does not confer the right to damage or despoil the beauty of the surroundings to the loss of everyone."

Doshi's design esthetic has been influenced by Le Corbusier for whom he worked in Paris on major buildings in Chandigarh and Ahmedabad. Later he supervised Le Corbusier's works in Ahmedabad. Doshi was also associated with Louis I. Kahn from 1962 until the latter's death in 1972, and he is at present carrying to completion Kahn's Indian Institute of Management in Ahmedabad.

The Indian government invited Le Corbusier and Kahn to Chandigarh and Ahmedabad to create masterpieces. It hires Doshi to help solve housing problems, plan for industrial expansion and deal with the practical needs of a developing country from the scale of a single kindergarten to the scale of a new city. Although the late styles of Le Corbusier and Kahn can be discerned in Doshi's work, the latter's projects are more profoundly shaped by the everyday aspects of building in India than by the precepts of his famous predecessors. Doshi is very conscious of the vernacular styles of whatever locality in which he is working; he is interested in using local materials and craft methods wherever possible and in making labor-intensive buildings so as to employ the huge reservoir of workers available.

Doshi's accomplishments cannot be assessed apart from the governmental policies that have helped create them. Because of these policies, however, he has had the opportunity to design and construct projects that have considerable impact on their surroundings. Fortunately, his mind is engaged with an aesthetic beyond style—an art with moral and ethical roots—springing from his care for the earth, its people and how they live.

—Mildred F. Schmertz

DOWNS, Barry (Vance).

Canadian. Born in Vancouver, British Columbia, 19 June 1930. Educated at Lord Byng High School, Vancouver, 1941–47; University of Washington, Seattle, 1949–54, B.Arch. 1954. Married Mary Hunter in 1955; children: William and Elizabeth. Architect/Draftsman/Designer, Thompson Berwick Pratt and Partners, Vancouver, 1954–63; Part-

ner, with Fred Hollingsworth, Hollingsworth and Downs, West Vancouver, 1963–67; in private practice, Vancouver, 1967–69. Since 1969, Partner, with Richard B. Archambault, Downs/Archambault Architects, Vancouver. Visiting Lecturer, University of British Columbia, Vancouver, 1960–63. Member, Vancouver Civic Design Panel, 1967–68; Member, Housing Design Council of Canada, 1969–73; Member, Heritage Advisory Committee, Vancouver, 1974–76. Member, City of Vancouver Historical Advisory Board, since 1971. Recipient: First Prize, Canada Art Gallery Competition, 1957; Massey Medal, Canada, 1964; First Award, Canadian Wood Design Awards, 1965; Canadian Housing Design Award, 1967, 1969, 1974, 1976; Award of Excellence, *Canadian Architect,* 1969, 1971, 1974; Canadian Education Showplace Award, 1973. Member, Architectural Institute of British Columbia; Fellow, Royal Architectural Institute of Canada. Member, Royal Canadian Academy of Art. Address: Downs /Archambault, 1272 Richards Street, Vancouver, British Columbia V6B 3G2, Canada

Works:

1960   Winnipeg City Hall (competition project)
1961   Ladner Public Library, Ladner, British Columbia (with Richard Archambault)
1964   Rayer House, West Vancouver
1966   Cocking House, West Vancouver
1967   Smith House, West Vancouver
1968   Canadian Pavilion, *Expo '70,* Osaka, Japan (competition project)
       Toy Ski Cabin, Whistler, British Columbia
       Bowker House, West Vancouver
1969   Prettie House, Bowen Island, British Columbia
       Strathcona Girls' School, Shawnigan Lake, British Columbia (with Ian Davidson)
1970   Guerin House, Point Roberts, Washington
       Lamont House, Langley, British Columbia
1971   Sedgewick Building, University of Victoria, British Columbia
       Botanical Gardens, University of British Columbia, Vancouver
1972   McNairn House, Salt Spring Island, British Columbia
       Caine House, West Vancouver
1973   Lions Paraplegic Lodge, Vancouver
       FP.18 (public housing development), Vancouver
1973/
75   North Vancouver Civic Centre
       Britannia Community Services Centre, Vancouver
1974   Murphy House, Hernando Island, British Columbia
       Master plan for Champlain Heights, Vancouver
       Single women's apartments, Vancouver
       MacInnes Place (courtyard housing), Burnaby, British Columbia
1974/
77   Lester Pearson College of the Pacific, Pedder Bay, Vancouver Island (with Ron Thom)
1975   Burke Mountain Environmental Planning Study, Coquitlam, British Columbia (with others)
1976   Multi-Purpose Complex, Simon Fraser University, Burnaby, British Columbia
1977   RCMP Building, Prince Rupert, British Columbia
       R. C. Macdonald Elementary School, Coquitlam, British Columbia
       False Creek Housing, Vancouver
1978   Chinese Cultural Centre, Vancouver (competition project)
       Public Library, New Westminster, British Columbia
       Carnegie Building Community Centre, Vancouver
1979   Patio Houses, Champlain Heights, Vancouver

       Gymnasium/Arts Building, York House School, Vancouver
       Arts Club Theatre, Granville Island, Vancouver
       Alder Bay Co-op Housing, Vancouver (with Davidson/Johnson)

Publications:

By DOWNS: articles—"Vancouver" in *Canadian Architect* (Toronto), October 1963; "A Plea for What Counts" in *Western Homes and Living* (Vancouver), January/February 1970; "Focus on British Columbia" in *Architecture Canada* (Toronto), 22 May 1972; "The Royal Engineers in British Columbia" in *Canadian Collector* (Toronto), May/June 1976; "Dawson City: A Tour of a Heritage Town" in *Western Living* (Vancouver), September 1976; "A Richness of Form, Space and Books" in *Canadian Architect* (Toronto) January 1978.

On DOWNS: book—*Canadian Architecture 1960–70,* Toronto 1970; articles—"This Is a Factory Built House?" in *Plywood World* (Vancouver), January–April 1968; "Projects: Barry Downs" in *Canadian Architect* (Toronto), August 1968; "Faculty Club" in the *Canadian Architect Yearbook,* Toronto 1971; "A House Built Open to Nature" in *House and Garden* (New York), July 1973; "Community Effort to Make Allies of Education and Leisure" in *Architectural Record* (New York), May 1975; "Vancouver's Land Shortage Gets Citizens into the Design Process" in *Landscape Architecture* (Louisville, Kentucky), March 1976; "Britannia Community Services Centre, Vancouver" and "North Vancouver City Centre" in *Canadian Architect* (Toronto), June 1977; "Strandhaus am Pazifik" in *Baumeister* (Munich), January 1978.

Architecture cannot divorce itself from social and humanistic needs. In our practice it has been possible to include these major considerations in a planning process where user and client play a major part in shaping the building or master plan. We often act as a catalyst in this process and supply background material, talk out psychic, social and physical needs, help establish design criteria and provide a full range of design alternatives. In so doing, our work remains consistently flexible, although always concerned with human scale, the use of natural materials, and appropriateness of building to site (and/or street), and embodies all the design elements so essential in the North-West, including the harnessing of natural light and the insuring of a strong sense of shelter.

Through design, architectural styles are explored as the program and client demands, yet an underlying language prevails. A building's aesthetic results, which is at once familiar, sometimes unique, often romantic or borrowed from history. All this is fused to its urban or natural setting, which in the end acts as the primary force at work.

—Barry Downs

Now that the functional concerns of modern architecture have been broadened to include the psycho-social needs of its users, some architects have realized that cultural values differ between groups and yet are equally valid. Under our educational system the architect's taste is usually shaped away from that of the people for whom he designs, and a number of approaches have been evolved to somehow bridge this gap: for example, limiting the architect's role to the provision of basic frameworks on which users may imprint their personalities; do-it-yourself kits; feeding sociological norms into the computer. Barry Downs has favoured another approach, that of bringing the users into the design process instead of restricting client participation to owners and administrators.

Downs' method has been to determine the key elements of design, such as entrances or lighting effects, then with the users to work out appropriate

Barry Downs: North Vancouver Civic Centre, 1975

environmental responses, thereby establishing a range of patterns to be later organized into a building solution. Citizen participation in this sense is a feedback mechanism that reacts to the architect's design proposals; the user does not initiate those proposals. The resultant architecture, while looking as if it has responded to its users' concerns, is therefore likely to be really a modified projection of the architect's own beliefs concerning the sort of architecture that is socially relevant. For instance, while some widely popular buildings take advantage of their bigness to create dramatic effects, the buildings of Barry Downs are small in scale even when they are large in size, a reflection of his own design philosophy. Similarly, the domestic range of materials with which he works is of the West Coast residential idiom rather than of the internationalism of industrial technology.

Small is beautiful, a homely style, citizen participation: that this is what the majority believes or wants is difficult to prove. The West Coast style is different in character from the sort of homes and furnishings that are generally sold on the open market. Conversely the West Coast style was admired by certain architects and their middle class clients long before it was associated with other virtues. In this context the work of Barry Downs does not reach the highest qualitative level. On the other hand, unlike most of his contemporaries, he has successfully extended his philosophy into the public realm, seemingly reducing the architectural schism between small-scale and large-scale environments. The virtue of his work is that it accommodates a humane way of life without pretentiousness, and in its time and place this achievement is sufficiently rare to warrant notice and respect.

—Anthony Jackson

DOWSON, Philip (Manning).
British. Born in Johannesburg, South Africa, 16 August 1924. Educated at Gresham's School, England, 1937–42; studied mathematics at University College, Oxford, 1942–43, and fine arts at Clare College, Cambridge, 1947–50, M.A. 1950; studied at the Architectural Association School, London, 1950–53, Dip.A.A. 1953; influenced by Arthur Korn, Ernesto Rogers, and Eduardo Catalano. Served in the Royal Navy, in the North Atlantic, Mediterranean and Far East, 1943–47; Lieutenant in the Royal Naval Volunteer Reserve. Married Sarah Crewdson in 1950; children: Anna, Charles, and Katherine. Worked as an architect with Ove Arup and Partners, London, 1953–63; Architectural Founder Partner, Arup Associates, London, since 1963 (group practice: with Sir Ove Arup, Ronald Hobbs and Derek Sugden, engineers); Senior Partner, Ove Arup Partnership, London, since 1969. Member of the Crafts Advisory Committee, London, 1971–75. External Examiner for Cambridge University since 1965; Member, Royal Fine Art Commission, since 1970; Governor, St. Martin's School of Art, London, since 1975. Exhibitions: Lyons, France, 1966; Royal Academy, London, 1974, 1976, 1977, 1978; British Council, London, 1977, 1978; Design Council, London, 1977; *Jubilee Exhibition,* Architectural Association, London, 1977. C.B.E. (Commander, Order of the British Empire), 1969. Address: Arup Associates, 7 Soho Square, London W1V 6QB, England.

Works:

1954/
64 Ciba (ARL) Ltd. plants, offices and laboratories, Duxford, Cambridgeshire
1958/
62 Vaughan Building, Somerville College, Oxford
1959/
64 Point Royal Flats, Bracknell, Berkshire
1960/
71 Department of Nuclear Physics, Oxford
1961/
64 Leckhampton House, Corpus Christi College, Cambridge
1962/
64 Long Wall House, Long Melford, Suffolk
1964/
66 Department of Metallurgy and Mining, University of Birmingham
1964/
70 Department of Arts and Social Sciences, University of Leicester
1964/
71 New Museums Building, Departments of Zoology, Metallurgy, and Computer Science, Cambridge
1965/
66 Old Addenbrooke's Area Development Plan, Cambridge
1965/
67 The Maltings Concert Hall, Snape, Suffolk
1965/
69 House, 2a Drax Avenue, Wimbledon, London S.W.20
1965/
71 *Oxford Mail and Times* Headquarters and Printing Works, Oxford
1966/
68 Graduate and Undergraduate Accommodation, Trinity Hall, Cambridge
Penguin Books Offices and Warehouse, Harmondsworth, Middlesex
1966/
72 IBM Process Assembly Plant, Warehouse, Offices and Computer Centre, Havant, Hampshire
1967/
74 Married Students Community Development, University College, Oxford
1968/
71 Horizon Factory, John Player and Sons Ltd., Nottingham
1969/
71 Development plan, stage II, University of Sheffield, Yorkshire
1969/
75 IBM Headquarters, Johannesburg, South Africa
1970/
73 Department of Music and Music School, University of East Anglia, Norwich

Philip Dowson: Leckhampton House, Corpus Christi College, Cambridge, 1964

1970/
76 Sir Thomas White Building, St. John's College, Oxford
1971/
78 Dock and support buildings, Portsmouth Dockyard, Hampshire
1972/
76 Trumans Ltd. Brewery Headquarters, Brick Lane, London
1973/
76 Wiggins Teape Headquarters, Basingstoke, Hampshire
1973/
78 Lloyd's Administrative Headquarters, Chatham, Kent
   Central Electricity Generating Board South-West Regional Headquarters, Bristol

Publications:

By DOWSON: articles—"The Architect's Approach to Architecture" in *RIBA Journal* (London), March 1966; "Building for Science" in *Architectural Design* (London), April 1967; "A Room of One's Own" in *Architectural Design* (London), April 1968; "Architecture and Professional Integration" in *Public Works Congress Report,* London 1972; "Integration—Disintegration?" in *JLO Conference Report,* York 1973; "Complex Yet Humane Architecture" in *The Times* (London), 7 May 1975; "Offices" in *Arup Journal* (London), December 1977; "Some Personal Thoughts During European Architectural Heritage Year, 1976" in *Architecture + Urbanism* (Tokyo), December 1977.

Architecture requires us constantly to re-interpret and revalue technology in human and social terms.

The conviction that close-knit, interdisciplinary design teams are necessary to confront the scale and complexity of modern buildings if an architecture is to survive which embodies humane ideas, led directly to the creation of Arup Associates.

However, whilst method and analysis can never substitute for an architecture which helps to enrich and not diminish our lives and surroundings, nevertheless, in considering means and ends, the "ends" have become so complex that it has become necessary to design new ways of designing buildings, if an architecture is to be derived from all the sources that can nourish it.

We are faced with a daunting problem of creating an environment for mass need that will not itself be despoiled by the very measures designed to meet the need.

The teachings of Gropius and the example of the Bauhaus have perhaps been the main influence.

—Philip Dowson

It is exceptional for a distinguished architect to be a member of a firm of structural engineers, but Philip Dowson almost uniquely spans the gap that exists today between science and the arts. Ove Arup and Partners have acquired an international reputation not only for their own pure structural form but also for their interpretation of an architect's idea, such as the Sydney Opera House, imaginatively if vaguely designed by the Danish architect Utzon. With the head of the firm so sensitive to architecture himself, it is not surprising that he should have encouraged architecture as one of the multi-disciplines within his organization.

Since architects usually employ engineers rather than the other way round, the architectural profession felt some concern over what was described as a "package deal." It is to the credit of Philip Dowson

that he has risen above any criticism that he is making the arts subservient. On the contrary, in all the work that he has designed under the firm's name (with full acknowledgement to himself personally), he seems never to have been anything other than an artist working freely and without restraint in a medium that he thoroughly understands and can control.

Dowson's work is clearly inspired and enriched by the closeness to his varied colleagues and by the constant interchange of ideas that is only possible in a multi-purpose and friendly office. This reversal of the normal relationship between architect and engineer has probably called for a special approach. Usually, an architect expands outwards, as it were, from the creative artist within himself, and his early ideas of form may later be modified by the engineer; in the process his building may lose some of its original humanity. The evidence suggests that Dowson begins from the functional and structural angle and afterwards gives it warmth and humanity as only an artist can. Certainly all his work has an element of classicism in its pure geometry and in the charm that it holds for the layman so easily overwhelmed by bigness, hostility of material and inelegance.

—Geoffrey Jellicoe

Jane B. Drew: Torbay Hospital and Nurses' Residence, Devon, 1973

DREW, Jane B(everley).

British. Born in Thornton Heath, Surrey, 24 March 1911. Educated at Croydon High School, Surrey; Architectural Association School, London. Dip. A.A. Married the architect James Thomas Alliston in 1937; the architect E(dwin) Maxwell Fry, *q.v.*, in 1942; children: Jennifer and Sarah. Assistant to architect Joseph Hill, London, 1938–39; Partner, with James Alliston, Alliston and Drew, London, 1939; Principal, Office of Jane B. Drew, London, 1940–45: Consultant to the British Commercial Gas Corporation, 1941–43, and Assistant Town Planning Adviser to the Resident Minister for the West African Colonies, 1944–46. Founder Partner, with E. Maxwell Fry, of Fry, Drew and Partners, London (including Fry, Drew, Drake, and Lasdun, 1951–58), 1946–73, and Fry, Drew, Knight and Cramer (with Frank S. Knight and Norman Creamer), London, since 1973. Senior Architect to the Punjab Government, India, 1952–54. Beamis Professor, Massachusetts Institute of Technology, Cambridge, 1961; Visiting Professor of Architecture, Harvard University, Cambridge, Massachusetts, 1970; Bicentennial Professor, University of Utah, Salt Lake City, 1976. Joint Editor, with Trevor Dannatt, *Architects Yearbook*, London, 1946–62. President, Architectural Association, London, 1969. Member of the Council, Royal Institute of British Architects. Exhibitions: *Kitchen Planning*, Dorland Hall, London, 1941; *Britain Can Make It*, Olympia, London, 1942; *Rebuilding Britain*, National Gallery, London, 1943; *South Bank Exhibition*, Festival of Britain, London, 1951. LL.D.: University of Ibadan, Nigeria, 1966; Open University, Milton Keynes, Buckinghamshire, 1973. Fellow, Royal Institute of British Architects, Institute of Arbitrators, and the Society of Industrial Artists. Associate, Indian Institute of Architects; Honorary Fellow, American Institute of Architects, 1978.

Address: Fry, Drew, Knight and Creamer, 63 Gloucester Place, London W1H 4DJ, England.

Works:

1940 Walton Yacht Works, London
1946 Prempeh College, Kumasi, Ghana
Adisadel College, Ghana (with E. Maxwell Fry)
Amedzofe Teacher Training College, Togoland (with E. Maxwell Fry)
1947 Wesley Girls School, Cape Coast, Ghana
1949/
51 Hospital buildings, Kuwait Oil Company
1950 Passfields (flats), Lewisham, London (with E. Maxwell Fry)
1951 Waterloo Bridge Entrance and Harbour Bar, *South Bank Exhibition*, Festival of Britain, London (with E. Maxwell Fry)
1953 Flats, Whitefoot Lane, Lewisham, London (with E. Maxwell Fry)
1953/
59 Ibadan University College, Nigeria (with E. Maxwell Fry)
1954/
56 New Capital City, Chandigarh, India (with E. Maxwell Fry, Le Corbusier, and Pierre Jeanneret)
1957/
59 Housing, health and amenity buildings, Iran Oil Company, Tehran
1959 Gach Saran New Town, Iran
Co-operative Bank Offices and Shop, Lagos, Nigeria
Co-operative Bank Assembly Hall and Maisonettes, Ibadan, Nigeria
Gulf House, Gulf Oil Company, London
1960 Lionel de Wint Art Centre, Ceylon

1964 Apowa Training Centre, Ghana
Institute of Contemporary Arts, London
Housing, Hatfield, Hertfordshire
Housing, Mark Hall Neighbourhood, Harlow, Essex
Housing, Welwyn, Hertfordshire
1965 Kaduna Olympic Stadium and Swimming Pool, Nigeria
Hotel, Colombo, Ceylon
1968 School for the Deaf, Herne Hill, London
1969/
77 Open University, Milton Keynes, Buckinghamshire
1970 Carlton House Terrace and Art Gallery, London
1973 Torbay Hospital and Nurses' Residence, Devon
1976 Gestetner Building, Stirling, Scotland
1977 Institute of Education, Mauritius

Publications:

By DREW: books—*Kitchen Planning*, London 1945; *Architects Yearbook*, editor, 14 numbers, 1946–62; books, with E. Maxwell Fry—*Architecture for Children*, London 1944, re-issued as *Architecture and the Environment*, London 1976; *Village Housing in the Tropics*, in collaboration with Harry L. Ford, London 1947; *Tropical Architecture in the Humid Zone*, London 1956; *Tropical Architecture in the Dry and Humid Zones*, London 1964; article—"Some Work by Women Architects" in *Architectural Design* (London), August 1975.

On DREW: article—"Nigeria Today" by Noel Moffett in *RIBA Journal* (London), June 1977.

My work has ranged from specialist studies on kitchen planning when I was a consultant to the British Commercial Gas Corporation during the War, to large-scale town planning work first in West Africa and later in India and Iran. A major part of my work is in West Africa and India, but there is some in Ceylon, France, Mauritius, Kuwait and some in England.

I have been a friend of artists and very interested in contemporary artists' work. My friendships have included Ben Nicholson, Henry Moore, Barbara Hepworth, Eduardo Paolozzi, Lynn Chadwick, Graham Sutherland, Victor Pasmore, Le Corbusier and Gropius, Burle Marx and, above all, my husband Maxwell Fry. These friendships have much influenced me, including the work of Denys Lasdun who was our partner, and the work of the CIAM Group and the MARS Group.

The support of staff and partners has been invaluable to me; more and more do I agree with Professor Lethaby who said that a good building is many men thick.

I have liked to be concerned with buildings where the purpose of the building itself is a challenge—such as the first university in West Africa, Ibadan University, or the School for Deaf Children at Herne Hill, or the Open University, or, perhaps most of all, the Institute of Contemporary Arts. When working on hospitals I have tried to make them friendly, not frightening, whilst remaining efficient. I love good colour and find it lacking in most contemporary work. Luckily our overseas practice has given us good opportunity to use colour—which is less important than material and form but which can compliment both. I think scale is the most difficult problem in architecture and regret that teaching about it is negligible now. Le Corbusier, Lutyens and Louis Kahn all considered it an essential ingredient in good architecture.

—Jane B. Drew

That the designing of buildings starts with human needs and climatic conditions and the most efficient methods to satisfy them is perhaps obvious, but the methods and the success vary. Much of Jane Drew's architectural work has been in tropical countries, chiefly Ghana, Nigeria, India and Ceylon, and the study of climatic conditions (very different from those in Northern Europe) and their effects on buildings have been a paramount consideration. By residing in these countries and studying how modern building technology could best answer these needs, she has created some outstanding work—what might be called a functional adaptation of the modern idiom to tropical building. Some of her best earlier work has been in Chandigarh (1954–56) with Le Corbusier, Pierre Jeanneret, and Maxwell Fry, where each was responsible for various buildings. Jane Drew's consisted of government and private housing, shops and shopping areas, health centres, schools and colleges. In speaking of her work in Chandigarh she said that a house there is essentially a shade and shelter from the sun. She realized that it is also necessary to consider established customs and taboos, to respect them and to combine them with modern efficient structural methods. She concluded, however, that tradition was not important except where it followed the climate and habits of living—determining factors for the architect.

The government housing with its minimum accommodation and economy hardly gave scope for notable design, with long low blocks and plain walls, yet she was able to introduce attractive features in the passage-ways between houses with lintel and post entrances. More scope was provided by the larger private housing, where an early experience in kitchen design prompted some very practical designs. In the exteriors of these houses she appears as a designer on geometric principles probably much influenced by Le Corbusier whom she greatly admires. The pale walls and nicely calculated relations of volumes with sun-protecting canopies and deep shadowed recesses are often impressive. In the designs of long rows of shops with flats above, in the schools and colleges, hospitals and health centres, the sun is a determinant in the character of the geometric design. Canopies, recesses, and egg-crate walls often result in a fascinating decorative appearance.

Among her best work in England is some housing in the Mark Hall neighbourhood of Harlow consisting mainly of long terraced units and four-storey blocks of flats. The general effect in terrace housing depends much on the excellence or otherwise of the repeated unit; and here it is well proportioned with a mono-pitched roof. The contrasting squarish blocks of flats provide a varied note, resulting in a very satisfactory ensemble in a spacious setting.

Among Jane Drew's most notable later work are the buildings for the Open University at Milton Keynes. The necessity of harmonizing with the existing late Georgian Walton Hall, which is a centre of the complex, may have been an inhibiting influence, resulting in very restrained architecture, but it has been tastefully designed with windows between broad vertical slabs. Starting from scratch is always an advantage in this kind of grouping.

Actuated in much of her work by geometric precision, she sometimes achieved in her designs the kind of aesthetic satisfaction that one derives from a typical painting of Ben Nicholson. She is an imaginative architect, rich in ideas that often had interesting fruition. For example, she suggested to Le Corbusier that he should set up in the heart of the Capitol of Chandigarh the symbols of his philosophy governing his conception of city design. From this suggestion arose the idea of the great esplanade where the signs of the modulor, the harmonic spiral and the open hand are displayed on a generous scale.

—Arnold Whittick

DuBOIS, Macy.

Canadian. Born in Baltimore, Maryland, 20 December 1929; emigrated to Canada, 1929. Educated at the Baltimore Polytechnic Institute, 1943–47; Tufts University, Medford, Massachusetts, 1947–51, B.S. Eng. (cum laude) 1951; Harvard Graduate School of Design, Cambridge, Massachusetts, under Sigfried Giedeon, 1954–58, M.Arch. 1958. Served in the United States Navy, as a Lieutenant Junior Grade, in the Mediterranean area, 1951–52, and in the Pacific area and Korea, 1952–54: Korean Service Medal; United Nations Battle Star. Married Sarah Buchanan in 1957; children: Mark and Lindsay; married Helga Plumb in 1975. Architectural Designer, John B. Parkin and Associates, Toronto, 1958–59; Architectural Designer, Rounthwaite and Fairfield, Toronto, 1959–60; Associate in charge of Design, Robert Fairfield Associates, Toronto, 1960–62; Partner in charge of Design, Fairfield + DuBois, Toronto, 1962–75. Since 1975, Principal, DuBois + Associates, Toronto. Exhibitions: group shows— *Plan for Toronto,* Art Gallery of Ontario, Toronto, 1963; *Bienal,* Sao Paulo, Brazil, 1965; one-man shows—University of Toronto, 1970, 1978; University of Waterloo, Ontario, 1970, 1978; Carleton University, Ottawa, 1978; Harvard University, 1978; Toronto Dominion Centre, 1978; Ontario College of Art, Toronto, 1979. Fellow, Royal Architectural Institute of Canada; Academician, Royal Canadian Academy of the Arts. Address: DuBois + Associates, 76 Richmond Street East, Toronto, Ontario M5C 1P1, Canada.

Macy DuBois: Joseph Shepard Building (Government of Canada Office Building), North York, Ontario, 1973

Works:

1958   City Hall, Toronto (competition project; with John Andrews, William Morgan, and Byron Ireland)

1960   Oxford University Press, Don Mills, Ontario

        Canadian Ambassador's Residence, Ankara, Turkey

1961   Smyth Road Housing, Ottawa (competition project)

        Central Technical School Art Centre, Toronto

        Residences, New College, University of Toronto

1964   45 Charles Street East Office Building, Toronto

        Dow Corning Silicones Ltd. Office Building, North York, Ontario

        Ontario Government Pavilion, *Expo '67,* Montreal

1965   Master plan and various buildings, Lakehead University, Thunder Bay, Ontario

        The ECE Group Office Building, Don Mills, Ontario

        Ithaca Festival Theatre, Ithaca, New York (project)

        York Regional School of Nursing, North York, Ontario (project)

1966   Hamilton Civic Theatre, Ontario (project)

        Tecumseh Senior Public School, Scarborough, Ontario

1968   Albert Campbell District Library, Scarborough, Ontario

        Fischbach and Moore Office Building, Etobicoke, Ontario

        City Hall, Amsterdam (competition project)

1969   Greenwood Vocational School, Toronto

        Consumer's Gas Company Office Building, Toronto

        Casa Loma Campus of the George Brown College of Applied Arts and Technology, Toronto

        Rogers Public School, Newmarket, Ontario

1970   Residences, and Academic and Student Building, Otonabee College, Trent University, Peterborough, Ontario

1971   Sarnia Opera House, Ontario (project)

        Garrison Motor Inn, Fort Erie, Ontario

1972   Ontario Police College, Aylmer

Foxboro Senior Elementary School, Belleville, Ontario (project)
1973 Houses of Parliament, London, England (competition project)
Joseph Shepard Building (Government of Canada Office Building), North York, Ontario
Baha'i National Offices, North York, Ontario
1974 Bloor Park Squash Club interiors, Toronto
1975 Grand River Cable TV Company Offices and Studio, Kitchener, Ontario
Master plan and several buildings, Lakefield College School, Ontario
1978 The Oaklands (housing development), Toronto
Ambulance Services Headquarters for Metropolitan Toronto, North York, Ontario
Bell Canada Alness Street Bar X Building, North York, Ontario
The Longboat Junior Public School, Scarborough, Ontario

Publications:

By DuBOIS: book—*Exploring Toronto*, with others, Toronto 1972, 1973, 1974; articles—"The Impact of Size: Reflections of a Seasoned Traveler" in *Canadian Architect* (Toronto), May 1967; "Toronto-Dominion Centre: A Critique" in *Canadian Architect* (Toronto), November 1967; "Winnipeg Art Gallery Competition" in *Canadian Architect* (Toronto), February 1968; "Critique: Towards a New Prose Architecture" in *Canadian Architect* (Toronto), November 1968; "New College II: Straight Line and Curve" in *Canadian Architect* (Toronto), May 1970; "The Sixties: A Decade of Innovation?," with others, in *Canadian Architect* (Toronto), July 1971; "A Protestant Work of Architecture" in *Canadian Architect* (Toronto), January 1973; "Two Schools" in *Canadian Architect* (Toronto), April 1973; "Book Review: 'The Prairie School: Frank Lloyd Wright and His Midwest Contemporaries' by H. Allen Brooks" in *Architecture Plus* (New York), September 1973; "Architectural Concepts: George Brown College of Applied Arts and Technology, Toronto" in *Canadian Architect* (Toronto), March 1974; "Erickson" in *Canadian Architect* (Toronto), November 1974; "Commentary: Otonabee College, Trent University, Peterborough, Ontario" in *Canadian Architect* (Toronto), July 1975.

On DuBOIS: article—"Portfolio: Fairfield and DuBois" in *Canadian Architect* (Toronto), May 1965.

True architecture responds to people using buildings in a particular place and time. We attempt to produce architecture which satisfies specific requirements but which also expands the known. We try to respond to people's needs, the local climate, the demands of site, our surroundings and what is affordable. This results in a design process which creates an architecture with something of a regional character.

It is our responsibility to assure that our work is socially responsive. We are concerned about the building's neighbourhood and the larger social structure in which it must operate. It is our feeling that a social concept must precede an architectural one.

Our built forms derive much of their uniqueness from the site. Existing plant material, sun orientation, views from and to the building, land contours and accessibilities are plan shapers.

Climate is harsh. Our Canadian winters are cold and our summers are hot. The temperature range and precipitation are severe tests against which current design fashions usually fall. The testing keeps us honest.

Architectural manners, response to our environment and building context are part of good design. We care that the total community benefits from our work.

We try to learn from our colleagues with as clear an eye as we can muster. We greatly admire the inventive and committed work of every era without ever feeling the need to duplicate it. To that extent the work of the past is our starting point and inspiration.

Finally, we feel the quality of our work is not conditional on the cost. Sometimes we have found that tough budgets have encouraged our inventiveness and can give our buildings an additional character. We try to use unpretentious materials in ways which increase their impact.

Above all else, we work hard to create buildings which will serve and invigorate the people who use them.

—Macy DuBois

While some of the images of modern architecture could be seen in earlier Canadian buildings, the underlying principles of the style were not at first consistently applied except in the work of John B. Parkin Associates. Quickly passing from a Gropius idiom to that of Mies, the office endeavoured to maintain its lead into the 1960's by hiring talented new designers, one of whom was Macy DuBois.

At this time, although very little good modern architecture existed in Canada, in the U.S.A. there had already been a reaction to the first phase of actual building based on the example of the European pre-war leaders who now resided there. This reaction showed itself in a greater freedom of form, a wider choice of materials, and a more decorative treatment of facades. The even more basic difference in approach taken by Eero Saarinen, who returned to the use of metaphorical form, also underlay the Finnish architect Viljo Revell's winning competition design for the Toronto City Hall, which inaugurated the effective spread of modern architecture in that city.

The work of DuBois, which matured during this later period, has been based on the accepted credo of the early modern movement, which stressed rational planning, structural order, and a straightforward attitude to design; that is, a belief in honesty of expression that came down from Gothic Revival theory and a functionalist concern for measurable space rather than its psychological qualities.

At the same time DuBois has enlarged his architectural vocabulary both from other sources and his own. Different building problems have suggested different precedents. He has exploited the current interest in large multi-storey interior spaces as well as the breaking up of large exterior masses into smaller cubic units so as to produce a more human scale and interest. Similarly, with the recent broadening of functional expressionism, he has exposed mechanical services. Elsewhere the influence of Aalto is apparent in an undulating facade or ceiling and also in the sensitive handling of brick and other masonry. This attention to detail distinguishes the work of DuBois, and his intelligent resolution of constructional situations gives it an overall consistency of design. His own contribution to the enrichment of a working vocabulary includes distinctive elements such as the architectural use of standard commercial siding and a collaboration with artists that adds a symbolic dimension to his work, which, as part of what may be categorized as the extended modern style, has integrity and a pervasive seriousness.

—Anthony Jackson

DUDOK, Willem (Marinus).

Dutch. Born in Amsterdam, 6 July 1884. Educated at the Cadet School, Alkmaan, Netherlands, 1899–1902; Royal Military Academy, Breda, Netherlands, 1902–05. Served as a telegraphist and engineer in the Dutch Army, in Utrecht and Parmerend, 1905–13, and in the Engineering Corps, 1914–15: Lieutenant. In private practice, Leiden, 1913–14, and Hilversum, Netherlands, from 1915. Acting Municipal Engineer, Leiden, 1913–14; Director of Municipal Works, Hilversum, 1915–27; Municipal Architect, Hilversum, from 1927. Recipient: Gold Medal, Royal Institute of British Architects, 1935; Gold Medal, Municipality of Hilversum, 1949; Gold Medal, Municipality of The Hague, 1949; Gold Medal, American Institute of Architects, 1955. Honorary Member: Koninklijke Maatschappij der Bouwmeesters, Antwerp; Academic Corps, Koninklijke voor Schone Kunsten, Antwerp; Zentralvereinigung der Architekten Osterreichs, Austria; Bund Deutscher Architekten; Vereinigung Bildender Künstler Wiener Secession, Vienna; Société Centrale des Architectes, Paris; Académie d'Architecture, Paris; Sindicato Nacional dos Arquitectos, Lisbon; Architectural Association, London; American Institute of Architects. Officer, Orange of the Oranje Nassau, Netherlands; Knight of the Order of the Nederlandse Leeuw. Officer, Order of the Crown of Belgium. *Died* (in Hilversum, Netherlands) 6 April 1974.

Works:

1916 Secondary school, Leiden
1917 *Leidse Dagblad* Offices, Leiden
1918 Residential development, 1st Municipal Quarter, Hilversum
1920 Rembrandt School, Hilversum
"Huize Sevensteijn," Zorgvliet Park, The Hague
1921 Residential development, Naarden, Netherlands
Municipal Baths, Hilversum
Dr. H. Bavinck School, Hilversum
Residential development, 4th Municipal Quarter, Hilversum
1922 Oranje Primary School, 5th Municipal Quarter, Hilversum
1923 Slaughterhouse, Hilversum
1925 Jan van der Heyden School, Hilversum
Minckelers School, Hilversum
Manager's office and dressing rooms, Sports Ground, Hilversum
1926 Juliana School, Hilversum
Fabritius School, Hilversum
Columbarium, at the Crematorium, Westerhaven, Netherlands
Dudok House, Hilversum
1927 Van Heutsz Monument, Gambir, Indonesia
1928 Netherlands House, Cité Universitaire, Paris
Ruysdael School, Hilversum
Nassau School, Hilversum
1928/
30 Town Hall, Hilversum
1929 Vondel School, Hilversum
De Bijenkorf Department Store, Rotterdam (destroyed in World War II)
Noorder Cemetery, Hilversum
1930 Multatuli School, Hilversum
Johannes Calvijn School, Hilversum
Valerius School, Hilversum
Marnix School, Hilversum
1931 Snellius School, Hilversum
1932 Town Hall, The Hague (project)
1933 Monument on the Zuyderzee Dike, Netherlands
1934/
35 H.A.V. Bank, Schiedam, Netherlands
1936 Aquatic Sports Pavilion, Hilversum
Garden Theatre and Lighthouse Cinema, Calcutta, India
1937 Harbour Master's Office, Hilversum
1938 De Burgh Garden City, Eindhoven, Netherlands

Town Hall, Amsterdam (project)
1939 Bridge over the River Vecht, near Vreeland, Netherlands
Erasmushuis Office and Apartment Building, Rotterdam
Office building, Dam Square, Amsterdam (project)
De Nederlanden van 1845 Office Building, Arnhem
1940 Reception and office building, Crematorium, Westerveld, Netherlands
1941 Municipal Theatre, Utrecht
1943 Plan for the redevelopment of the town centre of Alkmaan, Netherlands
1945 Plan for the reconstruction of The Hague
1947 Residential development, 19th Municipal Quarter, Hilversum
Protestant church, Schiedam, Netherlands (project)
Cultural Centre, Soest, Netherlands (project)
1948 Royal Dutch Steelworks Offices, Velsen, Netherlands
1951 House, Oegstgeest, Netherlands
1952 De Nederlanden van 1845 Office and Apartment Building, Rotterdam
Old people's flats, Amsterdam (project)
1953 Race course grandstand, Sports Ground, Hilversum
Park Flats, Bussum, Netherlands
Bungalow, Jacobus Pennweg, Hilversum
Residential development, Jacobus van Campenlaan, Hilversum
Esso Service Stations, Netherlands

Publications:

By DUDOK: lectures—in *Willem M. Dudok* by G. Stuiveling, F. Bakker-Schut and others, Amsterdam 1954.

On DUDOK: books—*W. M. Dudok* by G. Friedhoff, Amsterdam 1930; *Willem M. Dudok* by G. Stuiveling, F. Bakker-Schut and others, Amsterdam 1954; articles—"La Nuova Architettura Olandese" by Leo Lionni in *Casabella* (Milan), May 1934; "Baukunst des Auslandes: Holland" in *Deutsche Bauzeitung* (Stuttgart), April 1937; "Willem Marinus Dudok" by Jan de Meyer in *Bouwkundig Weekblad* (The Hague), 23 November 1940; "Dudok and the Repercussions of His European Influence" by R. F. Joran in *Architectural Review* (London), April 1954; "Forty Years of Hilversum" in *Town and Country Planning* (London), November 1955; "Willem Marinus Dudok: In Memoriam" by Gert Jonker in *Bouw* (Rotterdam), 20 April 1974; "Willem Dudok 1884–1974" by Richard Padovan in *Architectural Review* (London), June 1974.

*

Willem Dudok was remarkable in a number of ways. As city architect of a provincial Dutch town, Hilversum, and after training to be an army engineer, he produced and fully developed a personal style in little more than ten years. Although he designed some distinguished buildings here and there outside Hilversum, the great bulk of his work was done within the city boundary. His style was attractive and much imitated outside Holland, though never really successfully. Popular though it was, it left no permanent mark in the development of modern architecture, and he had no successors.

The main features of Dudok's work were the dramatic massing of asymmetrical blocks of plain, high-quality brickwork, often with deeply-raked horizontal joints; ranges of continuous low, deep-set horizontal windows set under projecting concrete hoods; deep-set semi-circular-headed entrance doors, and skilfully managed corner treatments between blocks, often incorporating large windows and towers. His details were always very carefully worked out, and the general effect of his buildings was handsomely comfortable. All these features can be found in the Vondel School, Hilversum.

Dudok's most important building was the Hilversum Town Hall, where the pale yellow brick masses are dominated by a tower in a setting of formal pools and gardens. The carefully chosen materials look as fresh today as they did when they were first used. Internally the building holds the attention by the skilful use of differing ceiling heights.

Besides a number of schools, Dudok's other important buildings in Hilversum include the abattoir and the public baths. Outside Hilversum his most important building was the Bijenkorf Department Store in Rotterdam, destroyed in the Second World War. Large areas of glass were contrasted with mass brickwork without ornament but with strongly-marked horizontal projecting balconies and a well-managed corner tower.

—Gontran Goulden

DUIKER, Johannes.
Dutch. Born in The Hague, 1 March 1890. Educated at the Delft Technical College, under Professor Evers, 1911–13, Dip.Arch.Eng. 1913. Worked with Bernard Bijvoet in Professor Evers' office in Delft, 1913–16; in partnership with Bijvoet, Amsterdam, 1916 until his death, 1935. Member of the De Stijl group. Editor, *De 8 en Opbouw* magazine, Amsterdam, 1932–35. *Died* (in Amsterdam) *23 February 1935.*

Willem Dudok: Town Hall, Hilversum, 1930

Works:

1913 Village Church, Rotterdam (competition project)
1915 Resort Hotel, Rotterdam (competition project)
     Workers' Housing, Meerweg, Buiksloot, Netherlands (project)
1917/
  19 Karenhuizen Old People's Housing, Alkmaar, Netherlands
1918 2 houses, Eikstraat, The Hague
     Housing and shops, Thomsonplein 10–15, The Hague
1919 Rijksacademie voor Beeldende Kunsten, Amsterdam (competition project)
1920 House, Jacob Catslaan 12, The Hague
     Housing development, Johan van Oldebarneveldlaan and Doornstraat, The Hague
     Housing block, Doornstraat, The Hague
     Housing development, Scheveningselaan, Kijkduin, The Hague
1922 *Tribune* Tower, Chicago (competition project)
     Third Technical Training School, Scheveningen, Netherlands (project)
1924 Country house, Stommerkade 64, Aalsmeer, Netherlands
1924/
  25 Copper Rods Fund Soap Factory, Diemerbrug, Netherlands
1925 Chemist's shop, Haltestraat 8, Zandvoort, Netherlands
1926/
  28 Zonnestraal Sanatorium Complex, Hilversum, Netherlands (with Bernard Bijvoet)
1927 Palace of the League of Nations, Geneva (competition project)
1927/
  30 Nivana Flats, Benoordenhoutseweg and Willem Witsenplein, The Hague (with Wiebenga)
1928 Zonnestraal Open-Air School, Hilversum, Netherlands (project)
     Single-family housing (project; with Wieberg)
1929 Strand Hotel, Salesel an der Elbe, Germany (competition project)
1929/
  30 Open-air public school, Cliostraat, Amsterdam
1930 Third Technical Training School, Scheveningen, Netherlands
     Basic housing units, *International New Building Congress,* Brussels
1930/
  34 Bioscope Theatre, Klein-Gartman-Plantsoen, Amsterdam (project)
     Jamin Shop (project)
1932 Zonnestraal Servants' Quarters, Hilversum, Netherlands (with Bernard Bijvoet)
1934 Handelsblad-Cineac Cinema, Regulierbreestraat, Amsterdam
     Meel-and Brodd Factory Complex, Vijzelgracht/Lijnbaansgracht, Amsterdam (project)
     Enci-Cernij Exhibition Stand, Utrecht
     Winter's Department Store, Weteringschaus/Vijzelstraat, Amsterdam
1934/
  36 Grand Hotel Gooiland, Hilversum, Netherlands (completed by Bernard Bijvoet)
1935 A.V.R.O. Radio Station, Hilversum, Netherlands (completed by Merkelbach and Karsten)

Publications:

By DUIKER: book—*Hoogbouw,* Rotterdam 1930; articles—in *De 8 en Opbouw* (Amsterdam), 1932–35.

On DUIKER: articles—"Jan Duiker" by Leo Lionni in *Casabella* (Milan), April 1935; "Grand Hotel Gooiland te Hilversum" in *Bouwkundig*

Johannes Duiker: Zonnestraal Sanatorium Complex, Hilversum, 1928

Weekblad (The Hague), 26 December 1936; "La Stazione Radio A.V.R.O. di Hilversum" in *Casabella* (Milan), January 1939; "Hotel at Hilversum" in *Architectural Review* (London), October 1947; "Duiker and the Zonnestraal," special issue of *Forum* (Amsterdam), January 1962; "Bauten von Johannes Duiker" in *Bauwelt* (Berlin), 12 February 1968; "Bijvoet and Duiker" by Robert Vickrey in *Perspecta* (New Haven, Connecticut), no. 13/14, 1971; "Duiker 1" and "Duiker 2," special issues of *Forum* (Amsterdam), November 1971 and January 1972.

Johannes Duiker studied at Delft Technical College and was a member of the De Stijl group. He was also connected with the radical journal *De 8 en Opbouw.* One of his earliest and most influential buildings was the Zonnestraal Sanatorium at Hilversum of 1926–8, designed in collaboration with Bijvoet. The long horizontal sweeps of concrete, strips of fenestration, and long thin roof edges were very much *à la mode* for the period, but were softened and set off by the circular stair motifs that recalled de Klerk's housing schemes in Amsterdam, especially the use of semicircular bowed balconies to model façades.

The Sanatorium was followed by the Open-Air School at Cliostraat in Amsterdam of 1928–30. This had an L-shaped plan with fully glazed walls and the

corner of the L open to the air. The arrangement gave the building a somewhat toothless appearance, accentuated by the restless canting of the slabs. The philosophy of knocking the corner elements out instead of accentuating them with a strong architectural feature (as had been the usual treatment during the 19th century) was carried one stage further in the designs for the Handelsblad-Cineac Cinema in Amsterdam of 1934. The upper walls, of plain surfaces pierced only by large areas of glass, are supported on the thinnest of corner posts. The stark concrete and glass box, with a deliberately weakened ground-floor storey, contained an oval-shaped cinema auditorium. Almost as tall as the structure itself was the spidery metal superstructure that supported the illuminated signs. This astonishing building owed something to Le Gorbusier's houses but also a great deal to the Constructivists.

Duiker's early death in 1935 precluded further experiment, yet his small *oeuvre* is extremely interesting, if eccentric. It is doubtful if his arrogance in ignoring existing townscape when filling corners with voids would be acceptable today. But as a catalyst and as an experimenter Duiker takes his place among the most significant of Dutch architects of this century.

—James Stevens Curl

DÜTTMANN, Werner.

German. Born in Berlin, 6 March 1921. Educated at high school in Berlin, 1939–42, and at the Technical University of Berlin, 1947–48, Dip.Arch. 1948; Town and Country Planning Institute, King's College, University of Durham, England, 1950–51. Served in the German Army, 1942–46. Architect with the Planning Board, Kreuzberg, Berlin, 1949; architect in the design office of the Public Buildings Administration, Berlin, 1951–56; free-lance architect, Berlin, 1956–60; City Architect and City Planner of Berlin, 1960–66. Honorary Professor since 1963, and Ordinary Professor, 1966–70, Technical University of Berlin. President, Akademie der Künste, Berlin, since 1971. Recipient: Bildende Kunst Prize, Association of German Critics, 1959/60; Berliner Kunstpreis, 1964. Honorary Fellow, American Institute of Architects, 1971. Address: Westendallee 97F, 1000 Berlin 19, West Germany.

Works:

1953   Old People's Home, Wedding, Berlin
1954   Youth Center, Zehlendorf, Berlin
1956   Congress Hall, Tiergarten, Berlin (as associate architect to Hugh Stubbins)
1957   District Library and Metro Entrance, Tiergarten, Berlin
1960   Academy of Arts (Akademie der Künste), Tiergarten, Berlin
1961   Edinburg House (hotel), Charlottenburg, Berlin
1964   Salzenbrodt House, Wachstrasse, Tegel, Berlin
1965   Dr. Dienst House, Bismarckallee, Grunewald, Berlin
1966   Dr. Menne House, Zingerleweg, Kladow, Berlin
        Plan for Märkisches Viertel Satellite Town, Wittenau, Berlin (with Georg Heinrichs and Hans Christian Müller)
1967   St. Agnes Church and Community Center, Kreuzberg, Berlin
        An der Urania Office Building, Schöneberg, Berlin
        Mensa Technical University, Charlottenburg, Berlin
        Brücke-Museum, Dahlem, Berlin

1970   Apartment buildings, Märkisches Viertel, Wittenau, Berlin
1971   Apartment buildings, Heerstrasse, Spandau, Berlin
1972   Kudamm-Eck Shopping Center, Charlottenburg, Berlin
1973   Office building extension, Ernst-Reuter-Platz, Charlottenburg, Berlin
1974   Apartment buildings, Mehringplatz, Kreuzberg, Berlin
        Rodenkirchen-Sürth Housing Estate, Cologne
1975   Urban renewal apartment housing, Ritterstrasse, Friedrichstrasse and Putkamer Strasse, Kreuzberg, Berlin
        St. Martin's Church, Kindergarten, Old People's Home and Community Center, Märkisches Viertel, Wittenau, Berlin
        Kleiner Wannsee Housing Estate, Wannsee, Berlin
        Hotel Schweizer Hof extension, Schöneberg, Berlin
        Low-density housing, Heiligensee, Berlin
1976   Schiepe House, Griegstrasse, Dahlem, Berlin
1977   Lentzealle Housing Estate, Dahlem, Berlin
        Youth Hostel, Schöneberg, Berlin
        Dohnenstieg Housing Estate, Dahlem, Berlin (project)
        Art Museum extension, Bremen (project)
        Apartment building, Markgrafenstrasse, Kreuzberg, Berlin (project)
        Apartment building, Klausener Platz, Charlottenburg, Berlin (project)

Publications:

By DÜTTMANN: article—"Berlin Freie Universität: Nine Evaluations," with others, in *Architecture Plus* (New York), January/February 1974.

On DÜTTMANN: articles—"Europe 5: Housing in Berlin" in *The Architect* (London), May 1974; "The Brücke Museum in Berlin" by Leopold Reidemeister in *Du* (Zurich), March 1975.

I hope that my architecture will be recognizable and understandable and livable in without any comment.

I think that if interpretation becomes necessary, architecture may have failed.
—Werner Düttmann

Werner Düttman was City Architect of Berlin during the 1960's, and it was his judgment and his work that created the image of the city during this period of its reconstruction and redevelopment. He invented concepts as contradictory as the "Märkisches Viertel" and the movement "Rettet den Stuck" (Save the Stucco—of the 19th century facades). And it was he who persuaded Mies van der Rohe to come back to Berlin to realize his last work, The Nationalgalerie.

Düttman is now President of the Academy of Arts, and his efforts remain the same, gathering to Berlin creative people from all over the world to maintain the city's liveliness, cultural activity and meaning. He remains a "Zeitgenosse," someone who combines sensible judgment, creative strength and a feeling for reality. The work of Werner Düttmann is concentrated on Berlin, and the new Berlin would have been very different without him.

Comprehensive and strong in judgment, he creates architecture that is lively, amorous and warm. It is "architecture for people," and he does not relie on any individual formal language to express his goal. In some ways his buildings are a reflection of the different styles and dreams that architecture has lived through during the past thirty years. His works look simple, almost incidental, from the outside, but they are welcoming within. The proportioning of space, the hidden order of wide and narrow, of dark and light, of intimate and generous, make his buildings livable, easy to use and accommodating.

His Academy of Arts, completed in 1960, is still the centre of cultural life in Berlin, and on Sunday mornings, when the exhibitions open, it buzzes with activity; it is a place that people like to go.

During this period of search for meaning in architecture—when solutions range from a new formal expressionism to re-evaluation of the forms of the past—one is almost relieved to find so simple a quality in architecture as that which one discovers in the work of Werner Düttman. It makes you feel good.
—Martina Schneider

Werner Düttmann: Brücke-Museum, Dahlem, Berlin, 1967

E

EAMES, Charles.

American. Born in St. Louis, Missouri, 17 June 1907. Educated at the Washington University School of Architecture, St. Louis, 1924–26. Married Ray Kaiser in 1941; daughter by previous marriage: Lucia. Worked for the architectural firm of Trueblood and Graf, St. Louis, 1925–27; in private practice, St. Louis, 1930–34; travelled and worked in Mexico, 1934; returned to private practice, St. Louis, 1935–36; Fellow, 1936, and Head of the Department of Experimental Design, Cranbrook Academy, Bloomfield Hills, Michigan, 1937–40; worked in the Art Department of Metro-Goldwyn-Mayer, Los Angeles, while experimenting in molding plywood, 1941; began development laboratory, with John Entenza, Gregory Ain, Margaret Harris, and Griswald Raetze, Los Angeles, 1942–45; in partnership with wife Ray Eames, Los Angeles, subsequently Venice, California, 1944 until his death, 1978: formed Molded Plywood Division of Evans Products Company, Los Angeles, 1944; Consulting Designer, Herman Miller Inc., Los Angeles, 1946. Lecturer, California Institute of Technology, Pasadena, 1953–56. Charles Eliot Norton Professor of Poetry, Harvard University, Cambridge, Massachusetts, 1970. Member, National Council on the Arts, 1970–78. Exhibitions: Museum of Modern Art, New York, 1946; *Triennale*, Milan, 1954, 1957; Museum of Modern Art, New York, 1973; Walker Art Center, Minneapolis, 1974; Sainsbury Centre, East Anglia University, Norwich, England, 1978. Recipient: First

Charles Eames: Eames House, Pacific Palisades, California, 1949

Prize, with Eero Saarinen, Organic Design Chair Competition, Museum of Modern Art, New York, 1940; National Award, Industrial Designers Institute, 1951; Gold Medal, *Triennale*, Milan, 1954; Grand Prize, *Triennale*, Milan, 1957; Gold Medal, 1957, Industrial Arts Medal, 1972, and, with Ray Eames, Distinguished Service Citation, 1974, American Institute of Architects; Kauffmann International Design Award, with Ray Eames, 1960; Honor Award, with Eero Saarinen, American Institute of Architects, New York Chapter, 1964; Honor Award, American Institute of Architects, Los Angeles Chapter, 1967; Design Medal, Society of Industrial Artists and Designers of Great Britain, 1967; Elsie de Wolfe Award, with Ray Eames, American Society of Interior Designers, 1975; Royal Gold Medal, Royal Institute of British Architects, 1979. D.F.A.: Kansas City Art Institute, 1955; California College of Arts and Crafts, Oakland, 1962; Pratt Institute, Brooklyn, New York, 1964; D.Art: Washington University, St. Louis, 1970. Fellow, Royal College of Art, London, 1960. Member, American Academy of Arts and Sciences. *Died* (in St. Louis) *21 August 1978.*

Works:

1940   Molded Plywood Chair (competition project; with Eero Saarinen)
1942   Molded Plywood Leg Spring, for the United States Navy
1944   Child's Chair, for the Evans Products Company, Los Angeles
1946   Molded Plywood Chair
      Molded Plywood Folding Screen
1947   Folding Dining Table
1948   ETR (Eames Table Rod) Table
1949   Fiberglass Chair
      Eames House, 203 Chautauqua, Pacific Palisades, California
      John Entenza House, 205 Chautauqua, Pacific Palisades, California
      Herman Miller Showroom, 8806 Beverly, Los Angeles
1950   Eames Storage Units
      Good Design Show, Museum of Modern Art, New York
1951   LTR (Low Table Rod) Table
      Wire Chair
      "The Toy," for Tigrett Enterprises, Chicago
1952   "House of Cards," for Tigrett Enterprises, Chicago
      "The Little Toy," for Tigrett Enterprises, Chicago
1953   Upholstered Fiberglass Chair
      "Giant House of Cards," for Tigrett Enterprises, Chicago
1954   Sofa Compact
1955   Stacking Fiberglass Chair
1956   Lounge Chair and Ottoman
1957   "Solar Toy," for Alcoa Aluminum, Pittsburgh
1958   Aluminum Group
1959   *American National Exhibition*, Moscow (with George Nelson)

1960   La Fonda Chair
      Time/Life Chair
1961   Eames Contract Storage
      Mathematica exhibition, for IBM, California Museum of Science and Industry, Los Angeles
1962   Tandem Sling Seating
      Stock Certificate, for the Herman Miller Company, Los Angeles
      House of Science, *Century 21*, Seattle
1964   IBM Exhibit, *World's Fair*, New York
1965   *Nehru: His Life and His India* exhibition, Ahmedabad, India, toured New York, London, Washington, D.C., and Los Angeles (with Alexander Girard)
1968   "Billy Wilder" Chaise
      Photography and the City exhibition, Smithsonian Institution, Washington, D.C.
1969   Soft Pad Chair
1971   Loose Cushion Chair
      A Computer Perspective exhibition, IBM Exhibition Center, New York
1972   Executive Oval Table
      Wallace Eckert: Celestial Mechanic exhibition, IBM Exhibition Center, New York
      Fibonacci: Growth and Form exhibition, IBM Exhibition Center, New York
      Nicholas Copernicus: An Exhibition in Celebration of His 500th Anniversary, IBM Exhibition Center, New York
1973   *Movable Feasts and Changing Calendars* exhibition, IBM Exhibition Center, New York
      The Shoulders of Giants exhibition, IBM Exhibition Center, New York
      Isaac Newton exhibition, IBM Exhibition Center, New York
1975/
76   *The World of Franklin and Jefferson* exhibition, for the American Revolution Bicentennial Administration, toured the Grand Palais, Paris; National Museum, Warsaw; British Museum, London; Metropolitan Museum of Art, New York; Art Institute of Chicago; and the Los Angeles County Museum of Art

Films: with Ray Eames—*Traveling Boy*, 1950; *Parade; or, Here They Come Down the Street*, 1952; *Blacktop*, 1952; *Bread*, 1953; *Calligraphy*, 1953; *Communications Primer*, 1953; *Sofa Compact*, 1954; *Two Baroque Churches in Germany*, 1955; *House*, 1955; *Textiles and Ornamental Arts of India*, 1955; *Eames Lounge Chair*, 1956; *The Spirit of St. Louis* (aerial sequences only), 1956; *Day of the Dead*, 1957; *Tocatta for Toy Trains*, 1957; *Information Machine*, 1957; *Expanding Airport*, 1958; *Herman Miller at the Brussels Fair*, 1958; *DeGaulle Sketch*, 1959; *Glimpses of the U.S.A.*, 1959; *Jazz Chair*, 1960; *Introduction to Feedback*, 1960; *Fabulous Fifties* (sequences in CBS-TV Special), 1960; *IBM Mathematics Peep Show*, 1961; *Kaleidoscope*, 1961; *Kaleidoscope Shop*, 1961; *ECS*, 1962; *House of Science*, 1962; *Before the Fair*, 1962; *The Good Years* (sequences in CBS-TV Special), 1962; *Think*, 1964; *Think* (revised version), 1965; *IBM at the Fair*,

1965; *Westinghouse ABC,* 1965; *The Smithsonian Institution,* 1965; *The Smithsonian Newsreel,* 1965; *Horizontes,* 1966; *Boeing: The Leading Edge,* 1966; *IBM Museum,* 1967; *A Computer Glossary,* 1967; *National Aquarium Presentation,* 1967; *Schuetz Machine,* 1967; *Lick Observatory,* 1968; *Babbage,* 1968; *Powers of Ten,* 1968; *Photography and the City,* 1969; *Tops,* 1969; *The U.N. Information Center,* 1970; *Man's View of Himself,* 1970; *Memory,* 1970; *The Perry Expedition,* 1970.

Publications:

By EAMES: books—*A Computer Perspective,* Cambridge, Massachusetts 1973; *The World of Franklin and Jefferson,* exhibition catalogue, Los Angeles 1976; articles—"Design Today" in *Arts and Architecture* (Los Angeles), September 1941; "Organic Design" in *Arts and Architecture* (Los Angeles), December 1941; "General Motors Revisited" in *Architectural Forum* (New York), June 1971.

On EAMES: book—*Charles Eames,* exhibition catalogue, by Arthur Drexler, New York 1973; articles—"Charles Eames" by Eliot Noyes in *Arts and Architecture* (Los Angeles), September 1946; "Three Chairs/Three Records of the Design Process" in *Interiors* (New York), April 1958; "Some Thoughts about Eames" by Jane McCullough in *Zodiac* (Milan), no. 8, 1961; "Mathematica" by J. R. Miller in *Industrial Design* (New York), May 1961; "Design in America: The Last 25 Years" by George Nelson in *Interiors* (New York), November 1965; "Eames Celebration," special issue of *Architectural Design* (London), September 1966; "Poetry of Ideas: The Films of Charles Eames" by Paul Schrader in *Film Quarterly* (Berkeley, California), Spring 1970; "Eames Perspective" by Esther McCoy in the *New York Times Magazine,* 15 April 1973; "At the Modern Museum: The Thoughts of Chairman Eames" by Paul Goldberger in *Art News* (New York), Summer 1973; "An Affection for Objects" by Esther McCoy in *Progressive Architecture* (New York), August 1973; "Charles Eames Isn't Resting on His Chair" by Walter McQuade in *Fortune* (New York), February 1975; "Charles Eames" by John Winter in *Architectural Review* (London), October 1978; "The Keen and Loving Eye of Charles Eames" by Paul Goldberger in *Art News* (New York), October 1978.

Charles Eames occupied a unique position in the design world from 1940 when he and Eero Saarinen won the competition for the design of a chair sponsored by the Museum of Modern Art in New York. But it is not just for his designs that he is important. Charles Eames, and his wife and partner Ray Eames, achieved something much more rare: they caused a shift in the way that we look at everything. Bright and cheerful objects that are commonplace in one culture or another, be they tin trains or carved Indian animals, were placed to form a montage of images that spread from Eames' own living room to those of designers around the world. No money was needed, just a good eye.

Part of the secret of Eames' success was that the items that he picked for display were never from the world of high-art. Normal commercially-made objects, often not highly regarded in their place of origin, were combined with natural objects to make a kaleidoscopic collection of bric-a-brac that is cheerful, fascinating, pleases the senses, and makes no moral or political point. Perhaps only Los Angeles, with its free-wheeling cultural ambience and its questioning of European values, could have nurtured and sustained such a frankly hedonist approach to design. The rest of the world is still too serious about art.

Charles Eames designed exhibitions and showrooms, made films, invented toys, and spread his skills over the whole field of design, but the artifacts that have made the greatest impact on architects are his chairs and the house that he built for himself in Pacific Palisades, California. The house was sponsored by the architectural magazine *Arts and Architecture* as one of its series of "Case Study Houses," surely one of architectural journalism's most adventurous and rewarding notions (it also brought Raphael Soriano and Pierre Koenig to fame). Eames House is on a beautiful site: a steep bank with eucalyptus trees along one side. When the steel framing members were already fabricated, Eames completely changed the design, from a bridge house spanning between two supports to a ground-hugging house tucked into the bank, a demonstration of his calm flexibility of approach—most architects are very uptight about making changes once the project has reached a certain point. The steel frame, cleverly detailed to emphasize its lightness, has a skin that is typically Eames—windows and panels just as found in the catalogue. Like his toys and bric-a-brac, the house is designed on the select-and-arrange technique, not on the I-must-design-it-all-myself approach.

Equalling the house in importance are the series of chairs he designed over a period of thirty years. As Charles Eames grew older, so his chairs became less stark, more comfortable and more expensive, as if he were always designing for his own age group. In retrospect, it is the youthful inventiveness of the early chairs that appeals, those shells of formed plywood or fibreglass on light metal supports that may well strike the antique collector of the future as the noblest product of the 1940's.

The story of modern design has been a very sombre one, deadly serious about its responsibilities and totally lacking in any sense of fun. Charles Eames added a touch of whimsy, of lightness and delicacy. He could get away with it because he combined these characteristics with superlative technical know-how and a sharp discerning eye for colour and for form.

—John Winter

EATON, Norman.

South African. Born in Pretoria, in October 1902. Educated at the Diocesan College, Cape Town, 1915–21; University of the Witwatersrand, Johannesburg, under G. E. Pearse, Dip.Arch. 1928; articled to Gordon Leith, Johannesburg and Pretoria, 1927–28; studied at the British School of Architecture, Rome (Herbert Baker Scholarship), 1930–32. In private practice, Pretoria, 1933 until his death, 1966: in partnership with T. J. Louw, as Norman Eaton and Louw, from the mid-1950's. Recipient: Gold Medal, Suid-Afrikaanse Akademie vir Wetenskap en Kuns, 1960; Posthumous Gold Medal of Honour, Institute of South African Architects, 1968. Honorary Member, Suid-Afrikaanse Akademie vir Wetenskap en Kuns. *Died* (in Pretoria) *in November 1966.*

Works (all South Africa):

1933/
34   Boyes House, Pretoria
1935   Nicolson House, Pretoria
1937/
38   Van Wouw House, Pretoria
       De Loor House, Pretoria
1940   Land Bank Building, Potchefstroom, Transvaal
       Children's Art Centre, Pretoria
1940/
41   Van der Merwe House, near Pretoria
1941/
43   Land Bank Building, Pietermaritzburg, Natal
1943/
44   Land Bank Building, Kroonstad, Orange Free State
1944/
48   Ministry of Transport Building, Pretoria (project; with R. Cole-Bowen and A. L. Meiring)
1946/
53   Netherlands Bank Building, Pretoria (with A. L. Meiring)
1949/
50   Anderssen House, near Pretoria
1949/
51   Greenwood House, near Pretoria
1954/
56   Holsboer House, Pretoria
1955/
60   Wachthuis Building, Pretoria
1961/
62   Moolman House, Pretoria
1961/
65   Netherlands Bank Building, Durban
1964   Van den Berg House, Pretoria

Publications:

By EATON: articles—"Pretoria of the Future" in *Journal of the Society of Old Pretoria,* August 1958; "The Architect Today" in *South African Architectural Record* (Johannesburg), June 1964; "Aims and Procedures in the Preservation and Restoration of Historic Buildings" in *Preservation and Restoration of Historic Buildings in South Africa,* edited by R. F. M. Immelmann and G. D. Quinn, Cape Town 1968.

On EATON: book—*Norman Eaton: Architect* by Clinton Harrop-Allin, Cape Town and Johannesburg 1975.

Norman Eaton's training and early experience prepared him for the rôle of an architect whose work was to be based upon historical themes and precedents. He nevertheless emerged, during the 1940's and 1950's, as one of South Africa's foremost modern architects, merging in his work the traditional and the contemporary. Although his plans were as modern as anything produced by his contemporaries who followed the precepts of the International Style, Eaton's work showed from the outset a regional emphasis.

His success in establishing a special relevance and harmony of building and environment springs from a more profound faculty than the mere ability to reproduce traditional detailing or the satisfaction of regional demands of climate, techniques and materials. His evocation of locality does not rest upon an exploitation of the picturesque, and the emotions it evokes are far removed from mere sentimentality. In his striving for a harmony between building and place, or in the suggestion through detailing of an African touch, there is also a realization that this could only be done with success if it could be brought into the context of his own time and society and the basic problems of function and structure with which he was involved. The evocation of the regional and the indigenous thus occurs at a level which precludes any suggestion of a vernacular character. With Eaton, the creative process was intuitively subjected to a refinement determined by his deep feeling for the landscape, climate, materials and crafts of Africa. The result is a capturing of a regional ethos: the intangibles of mood, atmosphere and tradition and, in the last analysis, a sense of belonging.

He concentrated largely upon traditional and indigenous materials, exploiting their inherent qualities, extending their possibilities, and showing that modern architecture can attain a richness and warmth without compromising its principles. In the handling of stone, wood, terra-cotta and above all the simple brick, no other South African architect can be compared to Norman Eaton for inventiveness and creative originality.

Finally, through his study of architectural history, including South Africa's own Cape Dutch heritage, Eaton became convinced that the achievements of the past held vital lessons of continuing applicability. This study and this conviction enabled him to rise

Norman Eaton: Wachthuis Building, Pretoria, 1960

above the constricting precepts of styles and movements. His work is significant in the development of a modern architecture in South Africa because of, not in spite of, the fact that he was steeped in tradition and man's architectural accomplishments over the ages. His best work is that of an artist who did not stand in awe of conventions, either of his own day or of the past. He understood the meaning of tradition. He grasped its spirit. His work is part of it, and, within the considerable powers at his command, an extension of it.

—Clinton Harrop-Allin

ECKBO, Garrett.
American. Born in Cooperstown, New York, 28 November 1910; raised in California. Educated at Marin Junior College, now College of Marin, California, 1930–31; University of California, Berkeley, under H. L. Vaughan, 1932–35, B.S. in Landscape Design 1935; Harvard University Graduate School of Design, Cambridge, Massachusetts, under Walter Chambers, 1936–38, M.L.A. 1938. Married Arline Williams in 1937; daughters: Marilyn and Alison. Worked at Armstrong Nurseries, Ontario, California, 1935–36; worked for Kastner and Berla, architects, Washington, D.C., United States Housing Authority, Washington, and the designer Norman Bel Geddes, New York, 1938; Landscape Architect, Farm Security Administration, San Francisco, 1939–42; Partner, Eckbo and Williams, San Francisco, 1942–45, Eckbo, Royston and Williams, San Francisco, 1945, Los Angeles, 1946–58, Eckbo, Dean and Williams, Los Angeles, 1958–64, and

Eckbo, Dean, Austin and Williams, San Francisco, 1964–68; Principal, Eckbo, Dean, Austin and Williams Inc., San Francisco, Los Angeles, Honolulu and Minneapolis, 1968–73. Principal, Garrett Eckbo and Associates, San Francisco, since 1973, and Eckbo-Kay Associates, San Francisco, since 1979. Lecturer, then Associate Professor, University of Southern California, Los Angeles, 1948–56. Professor, College of Environmental Design, 1965–78, Chairman of the Department of Landscape Architecture, 1965–69, and since 1978 Professor Emeritus, University of California, Berkeley. Visiting Lecturer, University of Osaka, 1969, and the University of New South Wales, Sydney, and University of Queensland, Brisbane, 1974. Recipient: Award of Merit, Homes for Better Living, American Institute of Architects/*House and Home/Sunset Magazine,* 1956; Award of Merit, AIA/*Sunset Magazine,* 1961–62; First Honor Award, 1962, Honor Award, 1966, 1978, Merit Award, 1970 (twice), 1972, 1976, Bradford Williams Award, 1963, Medal of Honor, 1975, and Special Honor Award, 1978, American Society of Landscape Architects; California Governor's Design Award, 1966; Merit Award, United States Department of Housing and Urban Development, 1968; Achievement Award, California Landscape Contractors Association, 1968; Certificate of Merit, American Association of Nurserymen, 1971; Grand Award, Council of Engineering Consultants, 1972; Certificate of Achievement, Department of Landscape Architecture, Harvard University, 1976. Fellow, American Society of Landscape Architects; Member, American Institute of Planners, and International Federation of Landscape Architects; Associate, National Academy of Design. Honorary Fellow, American Institute of Interior Designers;

Honorary Member, American Institute of Landscape Architects. Address: Eckbo-Kay Associates, 1045 Sansome Street, Suite 302, San Francisco, California 94111, U.S.A.

Works:

1939   General Motors Building, *World's Fair,* New York (project)
       Federal Building, *International Exposition,* San Francisco (project)
1939/
42   Site planning and landscape development for 50 rural housing/camp developments in the Western United States, for the Farm Security Administration, San Francisco
1940   Plan for a cooperative housing development at Ladera, California
       Weltner House garden, Woodside, California
1942/
45   Plans for 50 war and public housing developments in Northern California
1947   Park Planned Homes landscaping, Altadena, California
1948   Mar Vista Homes landscaping, West Los Angeles
1950   Olivet Memorial Park (cemetery), Colma, California (project)
       Plan for cooperative housing development at Reseda, California (project)
       Rich's Department Store landscaping, Knoxville, Tennessee
       Mankowski Homes landscaping, Azusa, California
       Central Quadrangle, Long Beach City College, California

Campus development plan for Orange Coast College, Costa Mesa, California
1952 Campus development plan for Occidental College, Los Angeles
1953 S. A. Camp Company landscaping, Shafter, California
1954 Aeronautical District Lodge 727 landscaping, Burbank, California
1955 Plan for parks and recreation spaces for Lakewood, California
Lucky Lager Brewery landscaping, Azusa, California
Neighborhood plan for Wonderland Park, Los Angeles
Sunset Capri Apartments landscaping, Los Angeles
City Hall Plaza and Gardens, Civic Center, Whittier, California
1955/
60 Designs for power generating plant landscapes at Point Arena, Oxnard and Huntington Beach, California, and Agua Fria, Arizona
1955/
65 Campus development plan for Ambassador College, Pasadena, California
School ground development plans for 6 high schools, 7 intermediate schools, and 53 elementary schools, throughout southern California
Gardens for Frank House, Holmby Hills, California; Johnson-McFie Houses, Los Angeles; Duke House, Benedict Canyon, Los Angeles; Cooper House, Holmby Hills, California; Sudarsky House, Bakersfield, California; Gelman House, Bakersfield, California; Cameron House, Beverly Hills, California; Frick House, Arvin, California; Karlen House, Thunderbird Ranch, Palm Springs, California; Keatinge House, San Marino, California; Mayer House, Bel Air, California; LeRoy House, Bel Air, California; Koolish House, Bel Air, California; May House, Beverly Hills, California; Mandel House, Beverly Hills, California; Prinzmetal House, Holmby Hills, California; Goetz House, Holmby Hills, California; Goldstone House, Beverly Hills, California; Hartman House, Beverly Hills, California; Fisk House, Atherton, California; Bagley House, San Francisco.
1956 El Caballero Country Club landscaping, Tarzana, California
Longwood Redevelopment landscaping, Cleveland
Douglas Aircraft Company landscaping, Long Beach, California
Churchill Apartments landscaping, West Los Angeles
Design plans for Live Oak Cemetery, Monrovia, California
Plan for cooperative housing development at Kenter Canyon, West Los Angeles
Collins Radio Inc. landscaping, Newport Beach, California
Campus development plan for Loyola University, Los Angeles
Neighborhood Church landscaping, Pasadena, California
1956/
58 Mayfair, Jose San Martin, Jose del Valle, and Simon Bolivar Parks, Lakewood, California
1957 Plan for parks and recreation spaces for Casper, Wyoming
Farnsworth and Chambers Office Building landscaping, Houston
Parkway systems, Lakewood, California
Bellehurst Country Club landscaping, Buena Park/Fullerton, California
Civic Center, Buena Park, California
Bel-Air Lanai Apartments landscaping, Los Angeles

1958 Great Lakes Carbon Corporation Land Reclamation Plan, Palos Verdes, California
Bellehurst Community Development landscaping, Buena Park/Fullerton, California
Neighborhood plan for Nichols Canyon, Los Angeles
Twenty-eighth Church of Christ Scientist landscaping, Westwood, California
Eagle Rock Park, Los Angeles
Civic Center landscaping, El Monte, California
La Canada Country Club landscaping, La Canada, California
Design study for the Hipodromo Nacional, Caracas, Venezuela
Alcoa Forecast Garden, Los Angeles
Design plans for Crestlawn Memorial Park (cemetery), Norco, California
Los Angeles All-City Outdoor Art Festival
Communities Facilities Planners Offices landscaping, South Pasadena, California
Dow Chemical Company Administrative Center landscaping, Freeport, Texas
1958/
65 Campus development plan for Ambassador College, Bricket Wood, England
1959 Central park, lake and waterfall, California City
Wilderness Park, Arcadia, California
1960 Harper Humanities Garden, University of Denver
Fifth Church of Christ Scientist landscaping, Hollywood, California
Special playground, City of Hope, Duarte, California
Waterside Promenade, Newport Beach, California
1960/
62 Campus development plan for St. John's College, Santa Fe, New Mexico
1961 Mt. Sinai Hospital Playground, Los Angeles
Long Beach Community Hospital landscaping, Long Beach, California
1962 Design study for the Golden Pagoda Hotel, Hilo, Hawaii
House of the Book landscaping, Brandeis Camp Institute, Brandeis, California
1962/
67 Campus development plan for Monterey Peninsula College, Monterey, California
1962/
78 Open spaces master plan for the University of New Mexico, Albuquerque
1963 Downtown pedestrian mall, Fresno, California
Housing for the elderly landscaping, Las Vegas, California
Temple Mt. Sinai landscaping, El Paso, Texas
Urban design study for El Centro, California
El Paso International Airport landscaping, Texas
1963/
65 Campus development plan for California State College, San Bernardino
1964 Union Bank Square, Los Angeles
1965 Urban-Metropolitan Area Open Space Study, Southern Section, State of California
Mission Bay Park, San Diego, California
1966 Old Monterey Plaza, Monterey, California
Plan for City/County Civic Center, Santa Ana, California
Campus development plan for Leeward Oahu Community College, Honolulu
1968 Plan for the Sausalito Waterfront, California
Science-Engineering Mall, University of California at Davis
Land-use plan for Redwood Shores, Redwood City, California
Master plan for Lodi Park, New Delhi, India
Downtown pedestrian mall, Sacramento, California
Ford Foundation Headquarters landscaping, New Delhi, India
1969 Plans for service facilities relocation, Yosem-

ite National Park, California
Critique of environmental and urban design proposals for the State Foundation for Culture and the Arts, Hawaii
1970 Master plan for the river channel, Mississippi River at St. Paul, Minnesota
Right-of-way and station design studies, San Francisco Municipal Railway
Urban design study for Hayward, California
The Villages (housing), San Jose, California
Design plan for Community Center Park, Castro Valley, California
McKeon House garden, Hillsborough, California
Design plan for a downtown pedestrian mall, Sunnyvale, California
Tucson Community Center, Arizona
Quaill Hill landscaping, Terra Linda, Marin County, California
1971 Expressway location and design, Minneapolis
P.G. & E. Building landscaping, San Francisco
Bechtel Corporation Office Building landscaping, San Francisco
1972 Master plan for the Berkeley Waterfront, California
Yosemite Village Mall, Yosemite Valley, California (design only)
Design plan for Horse Ranch Park, Cupertino, California
Freeway location and design, Dubuque, Iowa
1973 Freeway location and design, Duluth, Minnesota
Plan for the Civic Center, Mountain View, California
Denver Botanic Garden
Housing rehabilitation study for the Navajo Nation, Arizona-New Mexico
Park/parkway system review and rehabilitation plan, Minneapolis
1974 Public Safety Building landscaping, Mill Valley, California
North County Coach Terminal landscaping, San Jose, California
Plan for parks, recreation areas and open spaces, Ojai, California
Jeffrey House garden, San Rafael, California (with Kenneth Kay)
Comparative study of Sydney/San Francisco Bays
American Falls International Board, Niagara Falls, New York/Ontario
1974/
75 Plans for Penasquitos Canyon Regional Park, San Diego, California
1974/
76 Plan for urban squares, malls and plazas, University of California, Berkeley
1974/
78 Bayhill Office Building landscaping, San Bruno, California (with Kenneth Kay)
1975 Plan and program for the public use of Shelby Farms, Memphis, Tennessee
1976 Central Park, University of New Mexico, Albuquerque
Land-use, circulation, and vegetation management plan for Strawberry Canyon, University of California, Berkeley
Plan for the Esplanade/Great Highway Corridor, San Francisco
Study for the California State Parks and Recreation Commission
Cypress Lawn Cemetery, Colma, California (as consultant)
New master plan for the Botanic Garden, Memphis, Tennessee
Tri-Cultural Fountain, College of Santa Fe, New Mexico
Plans for the Living History Center, Novato/Black Point, California
1976/
78 Kaiser Medical Clinics landscaping, Santa Clara, California
1977 Plan for radio communication facilities, Mt.

Garrett Eckbo: Student Union Square, University of New Mexico, Albuquerque, 1977

Diablo, California

Plan for solar access for residential communities (with Living Systems)

Church of the Winding Way landscaping, Sacramento, California (project)

Black's Beach Access Trail, San Diego, California (project)

1978 Capital improvement development plan for Garin Regional Park, Hayward, California

Galvez Mall, Stanford University, California

Sand Bay Village Condominiums landscaping, Discovery Bay/Byron, California

Buena Vista Park, San Francisco (as consultant)

California Shakespearean Festival, Visalia/Three Rivers, California (as consultant)

Oakmead Office Building landscaping, Sunnyvale, California

Plans for Puerto Azul Resort Community, Ternate, Cavite, Philippines

Hellinger House garden, Pacific Palisades, California

1978– Master plan for Baylands, Palo Alto, California (with Kenneth Kay)

Publications:

By ECKBO: books—*Landscape for Living,* New York 1950; *Urban Landscape Design,* New York 1964, Tokyo 1970; *The Art of Home Landscaping,* New York 1965, revised edition as *Home Landscape,* New York 1977; *The Landscape We See,* New York 1969, Tokyo 1972; *Environment and Design,* Tokyo 1971; *Public Landscape,* Berkeley, California 1977; articles—"Small Gardens in the City" in *Pencil Points* (New York), September 1937; "Sculpture and Landscape Design" in *Magazine of Art* (New York), April 1938; "Landscape Design in: The Urban Environment; The Rural Environment; The Primeval," three articles with James Rose and Daniel Urban

Kiley, in *Architectural Record* (New York), May and August 1939 and February 1940; "Outdoors and In" in *Magazine of Art* (New York), October 1941; "Site Planning" in *Architectural Forum* (New York), May 1942; "Landscape Gardening," two articles in *Architectural Forum* (New York), February and March 1946; "Land Planning Knits House and Site Together" in *Sunset Magazine* (Menlo Park, California), May 1946; "Landscape Architecture: A Professional Adventure" in *Architect and Engineer* (San Francisco), September 1946; "Planning and Design Today" in *Parks and Recreation* (Washington, D.C.), March 1948; "Urban Landscape" in *Journal of the Town Planning Institute* (London), February 1950; "Landscape Design in the Pacific Southwest Today" in *Architectural Record* (New York), January 1953; "Living with Gardens" in *California Garden* (Berkeley), Spring 1956; "Converging Forces on Design" in *Journal of Architectural Education* (Washington, D.C.), Autumn 1956; "The Urban Landscape in *Synthesis* (Cambridge, Massachusetts), April 1957; "A Splendid View of Mission Bay in *San Diego Magazine,* February 1960; "Longwood: Antidote for Pomposity" in *Landscape Architecture* (Louisville, Kentucky), Spring 1960; "Landscape Design Potentials for Education" in *American School and University Yearbook,* New York 1960–61; "Is It Possible to Design a City?" in *Landscaping* (Washington, D.C.), February 1961; "Urban Design: A Definition" in *AIA Journal* (Washington, D.C.), September 1963; "Design and Criticism" in *AIA Journal* (Washington, D.C.), September 1964; "Architecture and the Landscape" in *Arts and Architecture* (Los Angeles), October 1964; "Landscape and Garden in Japan" in *Garten und Landschaft* (Stuttgart), October 1964; "Creative Design of the Landscape" in *Landscape Architecture* (Louisville, Kentucky), January 1965; "Planning the Gross Society" in *Landscape Architecture* (Louisville, Kentucky), July 1965; "Landscape Continuity" in *Image* (Austin, Texas), 1965; "The Personalized Landscape" in *AIA Journal* (Washington, D.C.), May

1965; "Campus Landscape" in *American School and University* (New York), April 1966; "The Mission of the Department of Landscape Architecture" in *Journal of Environmental Design* (Berkeley, California), May 1966; "Design and Landscape Character" in *Landscape and Human Life,* edited by Cru Tandy Diambatan, Amsterdam 1966; "The Decision-Making Totem Pole" in *AIA Journal* (Washington, D.C.), July 1966; "The Quality of Urbanization" in *Centennial Review* (East Lansing, Michigan), vol. X, no. 3, 1966; "Defining the Cultural Environment" in *Landscape* (Santa Fe, New Mexico), Autumn 1966; "Parklands in the Urban Desert" in *Cry California* (Sacramento), Winter 1966; "People in Landscape Space" in *Mountain States Architecture* (Denver), September/October 1966, reprinted in *New Mexico Architecture* (Albuquerque), November/December 1966; "Commentary on Qualification of Professional School Graduates" in *Grounds Maintenance Magazine* (Kansas City), May 1968; "Garden or Jungle?" in *American Institute of Landscape Architects Journal* (Los Angeles), June 1969; "The Landscape of Tourism" in *Landscape* (Santa Fe, New Mexico), Spring/Summer 1969; "Too Much Analysis or Designer's Fantasy?: An Eckbo-Porterfield Interchange" in *Landscape Architecture* (Louisville, Kentucky), April 1970; "K Street Mall, Sacramento" in *Design and Environment* (New York), June 1970; "Green Land in Japan" in *Landscape Architecture* (Louisville, Kentucky), April 1971; "Ecology and Design" in *Journal of Soil and Water Conservation* (Washington, D.C.), July/August 1971; "Shopping in Gardens" in *Yearbook of the United States Department of Agriculture,* Washington, D.C. 1972; "Open Space and Land Use" in *Land Use and Landscape Planning,* edited by Derek Lovejoy, London 1973; "Sculpture in the Garden—Wood" in *House and Garden Garden Guide,* New York 1973; "Garden and Landscape Design" in *Encyclopedia Britannica,* Chicago 1974.

On ECKBO: articles—"Landscape Design in the

U.S.A." in *Architectural Review* (London), January 1949; "The Landscape We See" by D. Streatfield in *Landscape Architecture* (Louisville, Kentucky), January 1972; "Northstar" by Henrik Bull in *Architectural Record* (New York), January 1974; "Nine Landscaping Projects in America" in *Building Ideas* (Sydney), November 1974.

I am a planner and designer of outdoor environments, particularly where qualitative experience is important. That is, or should be, everywhere that people will see rather than only where the well-to-do and discriminating live.

Outdoor environments begin just outside all of the doors and windows of every building and extend to the next visual or movement block—or other structure, land, or water form or vegetation mass. Outdoor environments therefore begin in everyone's back or front yard and extend around the world. At individual and/or urban scale, buildings dominate outdoors; at regional or larger scale, outdoors dominates buildings, even cities. Small towns and suburbs fall between.

Outdoors is where people and society meet nature or the existing landscape as a composite of structural and natural elements. Construction (architecture, engineering) is the representative technology of society in the landscape. Agriculture and horticulture are the intermediate technologies which remodel nature without losing its vitality.

Planning sets policy for land use, change and developed character in general terms. Design establishes specific forms for change and development when they are to occur. Outdoor design begins with situations as they exist and with programs for change as they are presented. It functions as intermediary between people and nature or, more specifically and qualitatively, between architecture and ecology.

The most traditional product of outdoor design is the agricultural landscape, followed by gardens, parks, malls, plazas and planned/designed communities and urban sectors in which there is a symbiotic relationship between indoor and outdoor development. Qualitative standards for form and space, scale and proportion, rhythm and balance, with unstable or incomplete equilibrium as the ultimate goal, are as demanding and compelling as in any of the other fine/social arts. Ultimate success will come from a balance of social, ecological and qualitative design standards.

—Garrett Eckbo

Garrett Eckbo has been in the forefront of those trying to articulate the need for a contemporary expression of American ideals in the urban landscape. He has severely criticized the undemocratic, exploitative, and mechanical aspects of the rapid urbanization that has taken place in the United States during and since World War II. In response he has formulated a design philosophy for gardens, parks, and the urban landscape based on equality, sharing, and humanism. This philosophy stresses rural-centered values of maximum interpenetration of natural with made elements in urban and suburban settings. The stress is on keeping urbanized individuals and communities in touch with their non-urban roots through maximum use of accessible social areas based on aesthetic and variable landscaping. He thus stands opposed both to the helter-skelter suburbanization (private development for maximum profit) and to high density urban cores with their stress on totally human-made forms. He stands for the essentially romantic main stream of American aesthetics: preservation and cultivation of values and technologies tying the industrial and post-industrial environment to its agrarian past.

In terms of his professional practice, Garrett Eckbo is perhaps the individual most responsible for the "Quality California Look" in American landscape design. Although he viewed his solutions as prototypic to any urban or suburban environment, the distinct regional climate of California overcame even the most technologically sophisticated attempts

at a homogeneous American aesthetic of landscape design. His work out-of-state tends to look either out-of-place or out-of-phase with the bulk of his work which is located in California.

His 1941 Garden in Oakland (Figures 15–20 in *Landscape for Living*) serves as an illustration of this look for a private garden. It presents an idealized California landscape, totally removed from the visual and auditory urban fabric and stressing leisure living on outside patios surrounded by trees and screens. Communication with neighbors would involve the telephone, a car trip, or a detour around the front gate. The illusion of country-in-the city is as near-perfect as can be accomplished on a small lot.

José del Valle Park (Lakewood, California) demonstrates these same principles on the scale of a neighborhood park. A strong separation is achieved from the displeasing visual forms of the city by surrounding the park with screens, berms, and trees. The internal environment intersperses small paved areas and leisure activity centers with nodes of plantings. The philosophy of interpenetration works out in practice to be a quasi-rural retreat in what is perceived as an urban wasteland.

The grounds of the Polytechnic High School, Long Beach, operate on the level of a building cluster. Here the plantings are more formal and less intraverted than on the garden or park scale design. The rural clumps of trees and meadows in the center of an educational complex again reach for a nature-culture interpenetration.

In theory and practice Eckbo has made a great contribution to the improvement of the American landscape. From today's perspective, the main weaknesses of his approach, both in theory and practice, seem to be an excessive fragmentation of experience from the realities of contemporary life and a mannered aesthetism not directly related to the ecology of the region, area, or the particular site. The main strengths are a genuine concern for the welfare of users rather than clients alone and an ability to relax the severity of the contemporary urban landscape.

—Joseph B. Juhasz

ECOCHARD, Michel.

French. Born in Paris, 11 March 1905. Town Planner in Syria, 1932–45; Director of Town Planning and Architecture, Morocco, 1946–53. In private practice, Paris, since 1953. Member of the High Council for Civic Buildings, Paris, since 1962; Chief Architect of Civic Buildings and National Palaces, France, since 1962. Recipient: First Prize, Kuwait National Museum Competition, 1960; Grand Prix d'Architecture, Cercle d'Etudes Architecturales, Paris, 1964; Gold Medal, Société d'Encouragement à l'Art et à l'Industrie, Paris, 1967. Address (office): 55 Boulevard du Montparnasse, Paris 6, France.

Works:

1931 Antioch Museum, Turkey
1936 Damascus Museum
French Institute, Damascus
Master plan for Damascus
1943 Master plan for Beirut
1946/
53 Master plans for Casablanca, Fez, Rabat and Meknes, Morocco
1955 French Protestant School for Girls, Beirut (with Le Coeur)
Kindergarten, Beirut
1955/
58 University of Karachi (with Riboulet and Thurnauer)
1958 Mohenjodaro Museum, Pakistan
City plan for Sabende, Guinea
1959 Marist Brothers School, Saida, Lebanon (with Amine Bezri)

Master plan for Conakry, Guinea
Master plans for Jounieh and Byblos, Lebanon
1959/
60 Secondary school, Beirut (with Faez Ahdab)
1960 Kuwait National Museum (competition project)
Antonine Fathers Boys' College and Seminary, Baabda, Lebanon (with Gabriel Tabet)
1961 Sisters of Charity Hospital, Beirut (with Henri Edde and ATBAT)
Sisters of Charity School, Church and Convent, Tripoli
Governmental city plan for Beirut
Plan for a summer resort, Coti-Chiavari, Corsica
1962/
78 University of the Ivory Coast, Abidjan
Master plan for Satellite City, near Marseilles
Master plan for the city and suburbs of Beirut
Plan for an express highways network, Lebanon
1963 College of Further Education, Brazzaville, Congo
University of the Federation of the Cameroons, Yaounde
Social Security Training Center, Lyons (project)
Master plan for Dakar, Senegal
City Center Plan, Beirut
Satellite City, Beirut
1964 Primary School, Martigues, France
Master plan for Damascus
1967 House of Culture, Nanterre, France
Master plan for Tabriz, Iran
1969 University Center for the Health Sciences, Yaounde, Cameroons
Center for African Studies, British Foundation, and Open Amphitheatre, Yaounde, Cameroons
French Embassy, Yaounde, Cameroons
General plan for Corsica
1971 City Center Plan, Mashhad, Iran
1972 Museum, Bahrain (project)
University of Yaounde Polytechnic School, Cameroons
1973 University of Yaounde Amphitheatre, Cameroons
Master plan for a new capital city, Sultanate of Oman
1977 Farabi Arts University, Karadj, near Tehran (with Lombard and Vakili)
Kuwait National Museum
1978 Study of the city center of Tehran

Publications:

On ECOCHARD: articles—"Transformation of the Centre of Mashhad" and "Damascus Centre Renewal" in *L'Architecture d'Aujourd'hui* (Paris), September/October 1973; "The Mohenjo-Daro Museum" by Mohammed Ishtiaq Khan in *Museum* (Paris), no. 2/3, 1977; "Casablanca" by Jean-Claude Delorme and others in *Architecture, Mouvement, Continuité* (Paris), June 1977.

The major part of Michel Ecochard's career as a town planner and architect has been spent abroad—from 1932 to 1945 in Syria, then in Morocco where he was in charge of the Department of Town Planning and Architecture. A man of rare integrity, he necessarily found himself in conflict with speculators and opportunists. The probity of his character and the firmness of his convictions made him an inconvenience to an administration subject to many kinds of pressures and predisposed to compromise.

As a government servant he was "transferred" to France and condemned to an inactivity that weighed heavily on him. A mission to Pakistan got him out of the way. There he drew up very fine plans for a university that were rejected thanks to a change of

Michel Ecochard: City Center Plan, Mashhad, Iran, 1971

generals at the head of the government. He had to begin again. The project as finally executed has indisputable qualities, but unfortunately it does not stand comparison with the initial project.

Looking over Ecochard's list of works, one is impressed by the number of plans, proposals and town planning studies that resulted in little or nothing! It is a story of difficult struggles that were rarely crowned with success—that is to say, with execution. Ecochard's work—and he was a town planner in the fullest sense of the words—poses serious questions. His works in the architectural sphere are less characteristic of Ecochard the man; however, they reveal a certain strength in idea, a sobriety in form, and honesty in conception tempered by a profound sense of humanity.

Ecochard continued his struggles in the Near East and in Black Africa, always enthusiastic, always ready to fight for idealistic and progressive solutions for towns and their populations. Many futile struggles, many disappointments and a great deal of travelling have worn him down. It is a great pity that our society has not known how to make better use of a man of such professional and moral worth.

—Pierre Vago

EHRENKRANTZ, Ezra (David).
American. Born in Newark, New Jersey, 20 February 1933. Educated at the Massachusetts Institute of Technology, Cambridge, 1950–54, B.Arch. 1954; Building Research Station, England (Fulbright Fellow), 1954–55; University of Liverpool, 1955–56 (Ford Fellow), M.Arch. 1956. Served as a Lieutenant in the United States Navy. Since 1966, President and Chairman of the Board, Building Systems Development Inc., San Francisco. Associate Professor of Architecture, University of California, Berkeley, 1967–70. Member: Presidential Task Force on Cit-

ies, 1966; National Committee on Urban Problems, 1966–68; Technological Advancement Board, and the Construction Affairs Committee, United States Chamber of Commerce, 1968–69; National Committee on Architectural Education, 1968–70, and the National Committee on Research in Architecture, 1969, American Institute of Architects. Recipient: Innovation in Building Award, *American Builder*, 1965; Service to the Building Industry Award, 1966; Construction Man of the Year Award, *Engineering News Record*, 1968. Address: Building Systems Development Inc., 120 Broadway, San Francisco, California 94111, U.S.A.

Works:

1964   School Constructions Systems Development (SCSD) Pilot Unit, 770 Pampas Lane, Stanford, California (now the Stanford Employees Credit Union)

1966   DeLaveaga Elementary School, Santa Cruz, California

1969   Silvercreek High School, San Jose, California

1974   Canaday Hall, Harvard University, Cambridge, Massachusetts

1976   Interdisciplinary Resource Center, Pratt Institute, Brooklyn, New York (with Daniel Tully)

1978   Aaron Davis Hall, City College of the City University of New York, Convent Avenue and West 135th Street, New York (with Abraham Geller)

Publications:

By EHRENKRANTZ: book—*The Modular Number Pattern: Flexibility Through Standardization,* London 1956; articles—"Flexibility Through Standardization" in *Progressive Architecture* (New York), July 1957; "How to Make Things Fit Together" in *Architectural Forum* (New York), August 1960; "The Remarkable Dr. Doxiadis" in *Architectural Forum* (New York), May 1961; "Modular Materials and Design Flexibility" in *Arts and Architecture*

(Los Angeles), April 1967; "The System to Systems" in *AIA Journal* (Washington, D.C.), May 1970; "Systems Building" in *Ekistics* (Athens), February 1971; "BSD Building Systems Development" in *Architectural Design* (London), November 1971.

On EHRENKRANTZ: articles—"Architecture by the Carload" in *Architectural Forum* (New York), April 1965; "SCSD Project, U.S.A.: School Construction Systems Development" in *Architectural Design* (London), July 1965; "School Construction Systems Development Program" in *Arts and Architecture* (Los Angeles), April 1967; "R and D Takes a Sea Change" by Michael Hacker in *The Architects' Journal* (London), November 1967; "Pratt's Athletic Facility Opens" in *Progressive Architecture* (New York), January 1976.

Ezra Ehrenkrantz first attracted national attention with his plan to use standardized components to assemble low-cost school buildings with flexible interiors that retained architectural integrity. The pilot unit for the School Construction Systems Development (SCSD), built at Stanford, California in 1964, was hailed as a "jewel-like pavilion," and it was quickly followed by DeLaveaga Elementary School at Santa Cruz and Silvercreek High School at San Jose. The choice of non-systematized outer walls meant that the schools were quite different in external appearance, and users could modify the interiors to suit their changing needs.

Building Systems Development Inc., Ehrenkrantz's firm, pursued this approach, designing self-perpetuating building systems such as those for University of California residences and for academic buildings there and at the University of Indiana.

Ehrenkrantz went on to design such notable works as Aaron Davis Hall at the City College of New York and the Interdisciplinary Center at the Pratt Institute, Brooklyn. Davis Hall is an intricate building that expresses the complexity of its task, to house three separate theatres and serve an open-air amphitheatre. The Interdisciplinary Resource Center is dominated by an enormous hyperbolic paraboloid roof that results from the upward curve of two diagonally opposite corners of the square and the downward curve of the other two corners. The huge clear span of the upper level houses the gymnasium, with athletic offices and dance studios on the mezzanine and other offices and laboratories under ground. The need for expensive air-conditioning was circumvented by an ingenious system of wells and pumps, using water from an underground stream (aquifer) with a constant temperature of 54 degrees to cool the structure.

—Lucinda Hawkins

EIERMANN, Egon.
German. Born in Neuendorf, near Berlin, 29 September 1904. Educated at the Technische Hochschule, Charlottenburg, Berlin, under Hans Poelzig, 1923–27. Married Brigitte Feyerabendt in 1954; children: Andreas (from previous marriage) and Julie Anna. Worked in the architectural office of the Rudolf Karstadt Company, Hamburg, 1927–28, and for BEWAG, Berlin, 1928–30; in private practice, Berlin, 1930–45, and Karlsruhe, 1947 until his death, 1970. Dean of the Faculty of Architecture, University of Karlsruhe, 1947–70. Chairman, Olympic Buildings Jury, Munich, 1968. Recipient: Good Design Award, Museum of Modern Art, New York, 1953; Architecture Prize, Cercle d'Etudes Architecturales, Paris, 1959; Berlin Art Prize, 1962; Best Building Award, *Architectural Forum*, 1963; Hessen Landspreis, Wiesbaden, 1965; Architectural Award of Excellence, American Institute of Steel Construction, 1965; Architecture Prize, Board of Trade,

Washington, D.C., 1965; Institutional Landscaping Award, Washington, D.C., 1967; Nordrhein/Westfalen State Prize, 1965; Cross of Merit, German Federal Republic, 1968; Grand Prize, Bund Deutscher Architekten, 1968. D.Eng.: Technical University, Berlin, 1965. Honorary Member, Zentralvereinigung der Architekten Österreichs, Vienna, 1960; Honorary Corresponding Member, Royal Institute of British Architects, London, 1963. Member, Akademie der Künste, Berlin, 1955; Member, German Order of Merit for Science and Art, 1970. Member, Order of Leopold, Belgium, 1958. *Died* (in Baden-Baden, Germany) *19 July 1970.*

Works:

1929/
30 Berlin Electricity Company Transformer Station
1930 Central Justice Building, Berlin (competition project: preliminary sketches; with Fritz Jaenecke)
1930/
31 Price-controlled, modern, self-contained private house (competition project; with Fritz Jaenecke)
1931/
32 "The Growing House," Berlin (with Fritz Jaenecke)
1931/
33 Hesse House, Berlin (with Fritz Jaenecke)
1934/
35 Bolle House, Berlin
1934/
37 Grieneisen Undertakers Quarters, Berlin
1935 Friedrich Theatre, Dessau, Germany (competition project; with Fritz Jaenecke and Gunther Andretzke)
1935/
36 Dienstbach House, Berlin
Mathies House, Babelsberg, near Berlin

Egon Eiermann: Olivetti Headquarters, Frankfurt, 1972

1936/
37 Steingroever House, Berlin
Display and Cinema for the *Gebt mit 4 Jahre Zeit* exhibition, Berlin
1936/
39 Foerstner and Company's Totalwerke alterations and extensions, Apolda, Germany
1937/
39 Dega-AG-Auergesellschaft Production and Administration Buildings, Berlin
1938/
42 Vollberg House, Berlin (with Rudolf Büchner)
1939/
41 Märkische Metallbau GmbH Factory Administration Building, Canteen, Boiler House and Porter's Lodge, Oranienburg, Germany
1942/
43 Plan for town of 20,000 inhabitants with an aircraft repair works, Udetfeld, Germany (project)
1946/
48 Community estate, Hettingen, Germany
Community estate, Buchen, Germany
1947 Airline Terminal and Hotel, Frankfurt (competition project; with Robert Hilgers)
1947/
48 Textile/Leather Goods Factory, Hassmersheim, Germany (project; with Robert Hilgers)
1948/
51 Südd.-Rundfunk Broadcast and Administration Building, Stuttgart (competition project)
1948/
52 Ciba AG Administration and Factory Buildings, Wehr, Germany (with Robert Hilgers)
1949/
51 Handkerchief Weaving Mill and Boiler

House, Blumberg, Germany (with Robert Hilgers)
1950/
53 Vereinigten Seidenweberei AG Administration Building, Krefeld, Germany (with Robert Hilgers)
1951 Merkur Store, Heilbronn, Germany (with Robert Hilgers)
Textile Engineering School, Krefeld, Germany (competition project)
1951/
52 University of Saarbrucken extension (competition project; with Robert Hilgers)
1951/
60 Merkur Store, Stuttgart (with Robert Hilgers)
1951/
65 Experimental Generating Station, Technische Hochschule, Karlsruhe (with Robert Hilgers)
1952 Chemical/Pharmaceutical Institute reconstruction, University of Munich (competition project; with Robert Hilgers)
Merkur Store, Reutlingen, Germany (with Robert Hilgers)
1952/
53 Small Hall reconstruction, Wurttemberg State Theatre, Stuttgart (competition project)
1952/
56 Matthäus Church, Pforzheim, Germany (with Robert Hilgers)
1953 German House, Cité Universitaire, Paris (competition project)
St. Nikolai Church redevelopment, Hamburg (competition project)
1953/
54 Evangelical Church with Community Centre, Baden-Baden, Germany (competition project)
1953/
55 Burda-Moden Depot, Offenburg, Germany (with Robert Hilgers)
1954 German Section, *Triennale,* Milan
Main Fruit and Vegetable Market, Hamburg (competition project)
Lecture Hall extension, University of Freiburg (competition project)
1955/
57 Volkshilfe-Lebensversicherungs AG Office Building, Cologne (with Robert Hilgers)
1956 Theatre, Recklinghausen, Germany (competition project)
1956/
60 Essener Steinkohlenbergwerke AG Administration Building, Essen (with Robert Hilgers)
1956/
62 Mannheimer Lebensversicherungsgesellschaft AG Headquarters, Mannheim (project)
1957 "Object 13," *International Building Exhibition,* Berlin (with Robert Hilgers)
1957/
63 Kaiser-Wilhelm Memorial Church, Berlin
1958 German Pavilion, *World's Fair,* Brussels (with Sep Ruf)
1958/
60 Horten Store, Heidelberg (with Robert Hilgers)
Hardenberg House, Baden-Baden, Germany (with Georg Pollich)
1958/
61 Steel Works Administration Building, Offenburg, Germany (with Robert Hilgers)
Josef Neckermann KG Dispatch Building, Frankfurt (with Robert Hilgers)
1958/
64 Chancery, German Embassy, Washington, D.C. (with Eberhard Brandl)
1959 Red Sand Artificial Island Lighthouse, Outer Weser, Bremerhaven, Germany (competition project)

1959/
60 Baden State Theatre, Karlsruhe (competition project)

1959/
62 Egon Eiermann House, Baden-Baden, Germany

1960 Johannis Church and Community Center, Mulheim/Ruhr, Germany (competition project)

1961/
63 Dea-Scholven GmbH Refinery, Karlsruhe (with Robert Hilgers)

1962 Town Hall, Essen (competition project)

1962/
67 Hotél Prinz Carl extension, Buchen, Germany

1963/
64 Housing, South Backenberg Sector, Wulfen New Town, Germany (competition project)

1964 Office building, Frankfurt (project; with Theo Ambos)

1964/
65 Prefabricated atrium houses, Offenbach, Germany

1964/
66 Fichtel & Sachs AG Administration Building, Schweinfurt, Germany (project)

1965/
66 Town Centre, Castrop-Rauxel, Germany (competition project)
   IBM Administration Building, Böblingen, Germany (project: planning study)

1965/
69 Members Building, Bundestag, Bonn (design and artistic direction; with Georg Pollich)

1966 Biochemical Centre, Max Planck Institute, Martinsried, near Munich (competition project)

1966/
68 Hochtief AG Office Building, stage I, Frankfurt

1967/
72 IBM-Germany Headquarters, Vaihingen, Stuttgart

1968/
72 Olivetti-Germany Administration and Development/Training Centre, Frankfurt

1972/
74 Hochtief AG Office Building, stage II, Frankfurt

Publications:

By EIERMANN: book—*Planungsstudie Verwaltungsgebaude: am Beispiel für die IBM-Deutschland,* with Heinz Kuhlmann, Stuttgart 1967; articles—"Das Theater in Dessau und die Baukunst von heute" in *Monatschefte für Baukunst und Städtebau* (Berlin), no. 19, 1935; "Hans Poelzig unserem Lehrer" in *Bauwelt* (Berlin), no. 27, 1936; "Einige Bermerkungen über Technik und Bauform" in *Baukunst und Werkform* (Frankfurt), no. 1, 1947; "Der arbeitende Mensch und die Technik" in *Baukunst und Werkform* (Frankfurt), no. 4, 1951; "Der Neubau des Versandhauses der Josef Neckermann KG" in *Baukunst und Werkform* (Nuremberg), no. 14, 1961; "Wohnhaus der Familie des Grafen Hardenberg in Baden-Baden" in *Baukunst und Werkform* (Nuremberg), no. 15, 1962; "Taufschale und Orgel der neuen Kaiser-Wilhelm-Gedächtniskirche in Berlin" and "Raffinerie Dea-Scholven GmbH, Karlsruhe" in *Architektur und Wohnform* (Stuttgart), no. 73, 1965; "Neubau der Kanzlei der Deutschen Botschaft in Washington, D.C." in *Architektur und Wohnform* (Stuttgart), no. 74, 1966.

On EIERMANN: book—*Landhäuser* by H. J. Zechlin, Tubingen 1951; articles—"Wohnhaus H. in Lankwitz" in *Bauwelt* (Berlin), no. 24, 1933; "Ein Fabrikbau im Norden Berlins" in *Bauwelt* (Berlin), no. 29, 1938; "Erweiterung und Umbau der "Total"-Werke Foerstner & Co." in *Moderne Bauformen* (Stuttgart), no. 38, 1939; 'Ein Wohnhaus im Grunewald" in *Moderne Bauformen* (Stuttgart), no. XLI, 1942; "Vom Sauerteig des Künstlerischen: Zu den Arbeiten von Professor Egon Eiermann" by Alfons Leitl in *Baukunst und Werkform* (Heidelberg), April 1951; "Kaufhaus Merkur in Heilbronn der Kaufhaus Merkur AG in Nürnberg" in *Bauen und Wohnen* (Zurich), no. 7, 1952; "St. Nicolai Kirche in Hamburg" in *Architekturwettbewerbe* (Stuttgart), October 1956; "Ein verlorener Beitrag zur Bauaustellung: Hansaviertel-Projekte von Egon Eiermann, Karlsruhe" in *Baukunst und Werkform* (Heidelberg), no. 10, 1957; "Deux Projets Récents" in *L'Architecture d'Aujourd'hui* (Paris), September/October 1960; "Verwaltungsgebäude eines Stahlbauwerkes in Offenburg" in *Bauwelt* (Berlin), September 1961; "Steel Company Offices, Offenburg" in *Architectural Design* (London), June 1963; "Haus und Nebenhaus in Baden-Baden" in *Architektur und Wohnform* (Stuttgart), no. 71, 1963; "West German Chancery: Bauhaus Precision Overlooking the Potomac" in *Interiors* (New York), May 1965; "Deutsche Botschaft in Washington" in *Bauen und Wohnen* (Zurich), January 1966; "One, Two, Three" in *Architectural Forum* (New York), March 1966; "Egon Eiermann 1904–1970" by H. Werner Rosenthal in *RIBA Journal* (London), January 1971; "Das Abgeordneten-Hochhaus in Bonn" in *Deutsche Bauzeitschrift* (Stuttgart), September 1972; "Hauptverwaltung IBM Deutschland GmbH, Stuttgart-Vaihingen" in *Bauen und Wohnen* (Zurich), March 1973; "Egon Eiermann" in *Architecture Plus* (New York), September 1973; "Headquarters of Olivetti Germany" and "Headquarters of IBM Germany" in *Architecture + Urbanism* (Tokyo), June 1974.

One of the vices of post-war architectural criticism has been that of returning too often and too readily to categories that were already showing signs of wear in the 1930's. Such an attitude risks doing less than justice to those personalities in architecture who have developed mainly since the war. A good example is Egon Eiermann; his widely publicized support of rationalism has caused him to be placed in that critical "category" occupied by Mies van der Rohe, Gropius, the Bauhaus. And, to a certain extent, it was because of that identification that Eiermann received some of his most important commissions: Olivetti, a firm always careful and particular in its choice of architects and designers, chose him to design their Administration Center in Frankfurt; the American Government, for the German Embassy in Washington, also chose this "awkward" architect, veteran of outstanding work on the German Pavilion at the 1958 Brussels *World's Fair* and the Kaiser Wilhelm Memorial Church in Berlin, two works that attracted both enthusiasm and criticism.

Yet, looking at these four works and trying to compare them, we can deduce everything but a common denominator—i.e., the rationalist constant. And when we go on to look at his other work, we recognize Eiermann's creative breadth and variety.

With the 30-story building for members of the Bundestag in Bonn, Eiermann copes admirably with the problems of the skyscraper: he achieves a lightness by arranging the glazed surfaces horizontally and an elegance by emphasizing the fixed sun-screens in wavy fibre, varying them in height from sector to sector. The marked "gap" half way up also lightens the upper bulk of the building, and the cooling towers are a screened prism. Two of these features figure prominently in Eiermann's work—the fixed sun-screen; the technical facilities in a compact form placed at the margin of the architectural complex.

The Washington scheme quite rightly reminds one of Frank Lloyd Wright's organic creed, not so much in its actual architectural effect (though some of the structural elements do recall well-known features of Wright's work), as in Eiermann's architectural attitude. For Mies, the technical treatment came to determine design to such an extent that many of his works simply repeat themselves, often losing contact with environmental conditions that might well have suggested a different treatment. In his Washington design, Eiermann offers an alternative that seems to have disappeared since Wright's time: he rejects showy, expensive materials in favor of a more "human" choice—brick walls both inside and outside, tiled floors, lighting by ordinary electric light bulbs. The building earned him high praise throughout America.

This more "human" quality is always found in Eiermann's work, and the master's last works should perhaps be looked at from this perspective. Of course, a certain rigidity of approach is evident, but most of all there is a plastic power and an elegance unique in Germany, achieved by a brilliant architectural self-control together with an exceptional attention to detail that extends down to the smallest particular. In the Essener Steinkohlenbergwerke Administration Building in Essen, or the more recent IBM Building at Stuttgart, every structural point is given a fascination of its own by the ease and lightness with which the problem involved has been solved. No one travelling on the Autobahn in the area of Vaihingen can miss the IBM Building: it creates a profound impression, as does the Olivetti Building, which can be seen along the Autobahn from Frankfurt to Kassel, with its graceful shape of sixteen stories, nine of them visible, tapering at the base to form an inverted pyramid, the windows in the shade brightened by the fixed sun-screens.

—Giuliano Chelazzi

EISENMAN, Peter D.

American. Born in Newark, New Jersey, 12 August 1932. Educated at Cornell University, Ithaca, New York, 1951–55 (Charles G. Sands Memorial Medal for Senior Thesis, 1955), B.Arch. 1955; Columbia University, New York, 1959–60 (William Kinne Fellowship, 1960–61), M.S.Arch. 1960; Cambridge University, England, 1960–63, M.A. in theory of design 1962, Ph.D. in theory of design 1963. Married to Elizabeth Henderson; children: Nicholas and Julia. Worked for Percival Goodman, New York, 1957–58, and The Architects Collaborative, Cambridge, Massachusetts, 1959; Assistant Lecturer, 1960–63, Assistant First Year Master, 1960–61, and First Year Master, 1962–63, Cambridge University; Assistant Professor, 1963–67, and Third Year Master, 1965–66, Princeton University, New Jersey. Since 1967, Director of the Institute for Architecture and Urban Studies, New York. Editor, *Oppositions* magazine, New York, since 1973. Lecturer, 1967–75, and since 1975 Adjunct Professor, The Cooper Union, New York. Architect-in-Residence, American Academy in Rome, 1976; Kea Professor, University of Maryland, College Park, 1978. Co-Founder of CASE (Conference of Architects for the Study of the Environment), 1964; Vice-President, Architectural League of New York, 1970. Exhibitions: *40 under 40,* Architectural League of New York, 1966; *The New City: Architecture and Urban Renewal,* Museum of Modern Art, New York, 1967; *Architecture of Museums,* Museum of Modern Art, New York, 1968; *Another Chance for Housing,* Museum of Modern Art, New York, 1973; *Architettura Razionale,* Triennale, Milan, 1973; *Contemporanea,* Rome, 1973–74; *Five Architects,* Princeton University and the University of Texas at Austin, 1974; *Five Architects,* Castel Nuovo, Naples, 1975; *The New York Five,* Art Net, London, 1975; *Biennale,* Venice, 1976; *Two Hundred Years of American Architectural Drawing,* Cooper-Hewitt Museum, New York, 1977, and toured the United States; *Abraham, Eisenman, Hedjuk, Rossi,* New York, 1977; *House X,* Princeton

Peter D. Eisenman: House VI: Frank House, Cornwall, Connecticut, 1972

University, 1977; *Numerals,* Yale University, New Haven, Connecticut, 1978; *Assenza-Presenza,* Bologna, 1978. Recipient: Graham Foundation Fellowship, 1966; Guggenheim Fellowship, 1976. Address: The Institute for Architecture and Urban Studies, 8 West 40th Street, New York, New York 10018, U.S.A.

Works:

1960 Liverpool Cathedral (competition project)
1961 Boston City Hall (competition project; with Anthony Eardley)
1963 Boston Architectural Center (competition project; with Michael Graves)
1964 American Institute of Architects Headquarters, Washington, D.C. (competition project; with Michael Graves)
1964/
65 Jersey Corridor Study (New York/ Philadelphia urban corridor) (project; with Michael Graves and Anthony Eardley)
1965 University of California Arts Center, Berkeley (competition project; with Michael Graves)
1966 The Manhattan Waterfront, New York (project; with Michael Graves)
1967/
68 House I: Barenholtz House, Princeton, New Jersey
1968 Town houses, Princeton, New Jersey (project)
1969/
70 House II: Falk House, Hardwick, Vermont
House III: Miller House, Lakeville, Connecticut
1971 House IV, Falls Village, Connecticut (project)
1972 House VI: Frank House, Cornwall, Connecticut
1973 Low-rise, high-density housing, Fox Hills, Staten Island, New York (project)
1975 Roosevelt Island Housing, New York (competition project)
House X: Aronoff House, Bloomfield Hills, Michigan (project)

1978 House 11a: Forster House, Palo Alto, California (project)

Publications:

By EISENMAN: books—*Giuseppe Terragni,* Cambridge, Massachusetts 1978; *House of Cards,* New York 1978; articles—"Towards an Understanding of Form in Architecture" in *Architectural Design* (London), October 1963; "The Big Little Magazine: Perspecta 12 and the Future of the Architectural Past" in *Architectural Forum* (New York), October 1969, reprinted in *Casabella* (Milan), January 1970; "Notes on Conceptual Architecture I" in *Design Quarterly* (Minneapolis), no. 78/79, 1970, reprinted in *Casabella* (Milan), December 1971; "Ordinariness and Light" in *Architectural Forum* (New York), May 1971; "Meier's Smith House: Letter to the Editor" in *Architectural Design* (London), August 1971; "The City as Artifact," editor, special issue of *Casabella* (Milan), December 1971; "From Object to Relationship II: Giuseppe Terragni" in *Perspecta* (New Haven, Connecticut), no. 13/14, 1972; "From Golden Lane to Robin Hood Gardens; or, If You Follow the Yellow Brick Road You May Not Get to Golders Green" in *Architectural Design* (London), September 1972, reprinted in *Oppositions* (New York), September 1973; "Notes on Conceptual Architecture II" in *Arquitectura: Historia y Teoria de los Signos,* Barcelona 1973; "Notes on Conceptual Architecture II A" in *Environmental Design Research* (Stroudsburg, Pennsylvania), vol. II, 1973; "Cardboard Architecture" in *Casabella* (Milan), February 1973; "From Adolf Loos to Bertold Brecht" in *Progressive Architecture* (New York), May 1974; "Real and English: Destruction of the Box I" in *Oppositions* (New York), October 1974; "Post Functionalism" in *Oppositions* (New York), Fall 1976; "Behind the Mirror: On the Writings of Philip Johnson" in *Oppositions* (New York), Fall 1977.

On EISENMAN: books—*The New City: Architecture and Urban Renewal,* exhibition catalogue, New York 1967; *New Urban Settlements: Analytical Phase,* New York 1971; *Five Architects* by Kenneth Frampton and Colin Rowe, New York 1972; *An-*

other Chance for Housing, exhibition catalogue, New York 1973; article—"On Reading Architecture" by Mario Gandelsonas in *Progressive Architecture* (New York), March 1972.

The critical establishment within architecture has told us that we have entered the era of "post-modernism." The tone with which this news is delivered is invariably one of relief, similar to that which accompanies the advice that one is no longer an adolescent. Two indices of this supposed change are the quite different manifestations of the "Architettura Razionale" exhibition at the Milan Triennale of 1973 and the "Ecole Des Beaux Arts" exhibition at The Museum of Modern Art in 1975. The former, going on the assumption that modern architecture was an outmoded functionalism, declared that architecture can be generated only through a return to itself as an autonomous or pure discipline. The latter, seeing modern architecture as an obsessional formalism, made itself into an implicit statement that the future lies paradoxically in the past, within the peculiar response to function that characterized the 19th century's eclectic command of historical styles.

What is interesting is not the mutually exclusive character of these two diagnoses and hence of their solutions, but rather the fact that *both* of these views enclose the very project of architecture within the *same* definition: the terms continue to be function (or program) and form (or type). In so doing, an attitude toward architecture is maintained that differs in no significant way from that of the 500-year-old tradition of humanism.

The various theories of architecture that properly can be called "humanist" are characterized by a dialectical opposition: an oscillation between a concern for internal accommodation—the program and the way it is materialized—and a concern for articulation of ideal themes in form—for example, as manifested in the configurational significance of the plan. These concerns were understood as two poles of a single, continuous experience. Within pre-industrial, humanist practice, a balance between them could be maintained because both type and function were invested with idealist views of man's relationship to his object world. In a comparison first suggested by Colin Rowe, of a French Parisian *hôtel* and an English country house, both buildings from the early 19th century, one sees this opposition manifested in the interplay between a concern for expression of an ideal type and a concern for programmatic statement, although the concerns in each case are differently weighted. The French *hôtel* displays rooms of an elaborate sequence and a spatial variety born of internal necessity, masked by a rigorous, well-proportioned external façade. The English country house has a formal internal arrangement of rooms that gives way to a picturesque external massing of elements. The former bows to program on the interior and type on the façade; the latter reverses these considerations.

With the rise of industrialization, this balance seems to have been fundamentally disrupted. In that it had of necessity to come to terms with problems of a more complex functional nature, particularly with respect to the accommodation of a mass client, architecture became increasingly a social or programmatic art. And as the functions became more complex, the ability to manifest the pure type-form eroded. One has only to compare William Kent's competition entry for the Houses of Parliament, where the form of a Palladian Villa does not sustain the intricate program, with Chalres Barry's solution where the type-form defers to program and where one sees an early example of what was to become known as the *promenade architecturale.* Thus, in the 19th century, and continuing on into the 20th, as the program grew in complexity, the type-form became diminished as a realizable concern, and the balance thought to be fundamental to all theory was weakened. (Perhaps only Le Corbusier in recent history has successfully combined an ideal grid with the architectural promenade as an embodiment of the original interaction.)

This shift in balance has produced a situation whereby, for the past fifty years, architects have understood design as the product of some oversimplified form-follows-function formula. This situation even persisted during the years immediately following World War II, when one might have expected it would be radically altered. And as late as the end of the 1960's, it was still thought that the polemics and theories of the early Modern Movement could sustain architecture. The major thesis of this attitude was articulated in what could be called the English Revisionist Functionalism of Reyner Banham, Cedric Price, and Archigram. This neo-functionalist attitude, with its idealization of technology, was invested with the same ethical positivism and aesthetic neutrality of the prewar polemic. However, the continued substitution of moral criteria for those of a more formal nature produced a situation that now can be seen to have created a functionalist predicament, precisely because the primary theoretical justification given to formal arrangements was a *moral* imperative that is no longer operative within contemporary experience. This sense of displaced positivism characterizes certain current perceptions of the failure of humanism within a broader cultural context.

There is also another, more complex, aspect to this predicament. Not only can functionalism indeed be recognized as a species of positivism, but also, like positivism, it now can be seen to issue from within the terms of an idealist view of reality. For functionalism, no matter what its pretense, continued the idealist ambition of creating architecture as a kind of ethically constituted form-giving. But because it clothed this idealist ambition in the radically stripped forms of technological production, it has seemed to represent a break with the pre-industrial past. But, in fact, functionalism is really no more than a late phase of humanism, rather than an alternative to it. And in this sense, it cannot continue to be taken as a direct manifestation of that which has been called "the modernist sensibility."

Both the Triennale and the Beaux Arts exhibitions suggest, however, that the problem is thought to be somewhere else—not so much with functionalism *per se* as with the nature of this so-called modernist sensibility. Hence, the implied revival of neo-classicism and Beaux Arts academicism as replacements for a continuing, if poorly understood, modernism. It is true that sometime in the 19th century, there was indeed a crucial shift within Western consciousness, one that can be characterized as a shift from humanism to modernism. But, for the most part, architecture, in its dogged adherence to the principles of function, did not participate in or understand the fundamental aspects of that change. It is the potential difference in the nature of modernist and humanist theory that seems to have gone unnoticed by those people who today speak of eclecticism, postmodernism, or neo-functionalism. And they have failed to notice it precisely because they conceive of modernism as merely a stylistic manifestation of functionalism, and functionalism itself as a basic theoretical proposition in architecture. In fact, the idea of modernism has driven a wedge into these attitudes. It has revealed that the dialectic form and function is culturally based.

In brief, the modernist sensibility has to do with a changed mental attitude toward the artifacts of the physical world. This change has not only been manifested aesthetically, but also socially, philosophically, and technologically—in sum, it has been manifested in a new cultural attitude. This shift away from the dominant attitudes of humanism, which were pervasive in Western societies for some four hundred years, took place at various times in the 19th century in such disparate disciplines as mathematics, music, painting, literature, film, and photography. It is displayed in the non-objective abstract painting of Malevich and Mondrian; in the non-narrative, atemporal writing of Joyce and Apollinaire;

the atonal and polytonal compositions of Schönberg and Webern; in the non-narrative films of Richter and Eggeling.

Abstraction, atonality, and atemporality, however, are merely stylistic manifestations of modernism, not its essential nature. Although this is not the place to elaborate a theory of modernism, or indeed to represent those aspects of such a theory which have already found their way into the literature of the other humanist disciplines, it can simply be said that the symptoms to which one has just pointed suggest a displacement of man away from the center of his world. He is no longer viewed as an *originating agent*. Objects are seen as ideas independent of man. In this context, man is a discursive function among complex and already-formed systems of language, which he witnesses but does not constitute. As Levi-Strauss has said, "Language, an unreflecting totalization, is human reason which has its reason and of which man knows nothing." It is this condition of displacement which gives rise to design in which authorship can no longer either account for a linear development that has a "beginning" and an "end"— hence the rise of the atemporal—or account for the invention of form—hence the abstract as a mediation between pre-existent sign systems.

Modernism, as a sensibility based on the fundamental displacement of man, represents what Michel Foucault would specify as a new *épistème*. Deriving from a non-humanistic attitude toward the relationship of an individual to his physical environment, it breaks with the historical past, both with the ways of viewing man as subject and, as we have said, with the ethical positivism of form and function. Thus, it cannot be related to functionalism. It is probably for this reason that modernism has not up to now been elaborated in architecture.

But there is clearly a present need for a theoretical investigation of the basic implications of modernism (as opposed to modern style) in architecture. In his editorial "Neo-Functionalism," in *Oppositions* 5, Mario Gandelsonas acknowledges such a need. However, he says merely that the "complex contradictions" inherent in functionalism—such as neo-realism and neo-rationalism—make a form of neo-functionalism necessary to any new theoretical dialectic. This proposition continues to refuse to recognize that the form/function opposition is not necessarily inherent to any architectural theory and so fails to recognize the crucial difference between modernism and humanism. In contrast, what is being called post-functionalism begins as an attitude that recognizes modernism as a new and distinct sensibility. It can best be understood in architecture in terms of a theoretical base that is concerned with what might be called a modernist *dialectic*, as opposed to the old humanist (i.e., functionalist) opposition of form and function.

This new theoretical base changes the humanist balance of form/function to a dialectical relationship within the evolution of form itself. The dialectic can best be described as the potential co-existence within any form of two non-corroborating and non-sequential tendencies. One tendency is to presume architectural form to be a recognizable transformation from some pre-existent geometric or platonic solid. In this case, form is usually understood through a series of registrations designed to recall a more simple geometric condition. This tendency is certainly a relic of humanist theory. However, to this is added a second tendency that sees architectural form in an atemporal, decompositional mode, as something simplified from some pre-existent set of non-specific spatial entities. Here, form is understood as a series of fragments—signs without meaning dependent upon, and without reference to, a more basic condition. The former tendency, when taken by itself, is a reductivist attitude and assumes some primary unity as both an ethical and an aesthetic basis for all creation. The latter, by itself, assumes a basic condition of fragmentation and multiplicity from which the resultant form is a state of simplification. Both tendencies, however, when taken together, constitute

the essence of this new, modern dialectic. They begin to define the inherent nature of the object in and of itself and its capacity to be represented. They begin to suggest that the theoretical assumptions of functionalism are in fact cultural rather than universal.

Post-functionalism, thus, is a term of absence. In its negation of functionalism it suggests certain positive theoretical alternatives—existing fragments of thought that, when examined, might serve as a framework for the development of a larger theoretical structure—but it does not, in and of itself, propose to supply a label for such a new consciousness in architecture as I believe is potentially upon us.

—Peter D. Eisenman

Peter Eisenman has been more active as an educator than as a builder of architecture, and it is as an educator, author, critic, and publisher that he has been most influential. As the founder of New York City's Institute for Architecture and Urban Studies in 1967, he has provided a forum for discussion among the profession and with students and laymen that has made that organization the most public and polemic voice of architecture in New York, perhaps on the East coast. To the lecture platform, exhibition walls, and published pages of the Institute have come virtually every distinguished practitioner, thinker, author, and critic in today's architecture world. Eisenman's aim is to "bridge the gap between architecture and contemporary culture." His espousal of aestheticians' latinate complexity of language hardly facilitates his progress, however.

As architect of some dozen house designs, Eisenman also is a polemicist. He feels that "mechanization, prefabrication, repetition, and standardization have made our existence merely routine, and that the role of art is to alienate and dislocate man from his environment so that he is jolted into seeing what it is again." In his house designs, therefore, Eisenman abrasively jars and jabs, tricks and stuns the occupants into seeing architecture—their environment— in a new way. Stairs have no railings; columns do not touch the ground but hang obviously suspended; the functional requirements of kitchens and baths are denied; air conditioning is needed on the north side. He wants us to break through the habits of seeing and hearing and to experience new insights into reality.

In his House VI for Suzanne and Richard Frank, a stair is too low for one to descend without ducking; a door is too narrow for one to enter without turning sideways; a column comes down between the chairs on one side of the dining table. Eisenman wants to force people to see their new dinner partner—architecture. For him physical hardship or readjustment is the elected eye-opener. For him architecture is a kind of shock therapy.

He aims to make us see architecture "through creating a climate that accepts architecture as necessary," and to understand that "the actual tactile sensation of space as an independent object is necessary." That may not be the most winning way to lure back to architecture a public that has been alienated by abstraction for 50 years, but it is a way to make architecture unavoidable.

At a larger scale, Eisenman's architecture is concerned with a further abstraction of Miesian structural play clothed in Corbusian forms. He is concerned with a basic grid to which he makes reductive and additive variations. He has professed an interest in constructing architecture as if it were a language composed of columns, beams, and walls—like words, sentences, and paragraphs. In his houses the structural grid is left exposed as much as possible, and the overlapping of columns and beams is often treated as the joint of a Chinese puzzle. Where elements are not articulated by separation or reveals, they are often distinguished by color. It is an architecture that is highly photogenic, cubistic and volumetric, interlocking and ambiguous, perhaps mythic in its expression of the protean elements of construction. It is also purely intellectual, coldly alienating, maddeningly non-functional, and as maddeningly impossible to ignore. By espousing neither *utile dulci* nor firmness, commodity, and delight, Peter Eisenman strikes out as a polemical iconoclast of forceful influence.

—C. Ray Smith

ELLIOTT, Julian (Arnold).

South African. Born in Cathcart, 27 August 1928. Educated at the University of Cape Town, 1948–53, B.Arch. 1953. Married Helene Joubert in 1953; children: Paul and Mary. Assistant Architect, with Fry, Drew and Partners, London, 1951, and with Frederick Gibberd and Partners, London, 1953–54; Partner, with Philippe Charbonnier, Charbonnier and Elliott, Lubumbashi, Congo, 1955–58; in private practice, Ndola, Zambia, 1959–68. In private practice, Newlands, Cape Town, since 1969. Visiting Lecturer, University of Cape Town, 1967, and University of Natal, 1968, 1969. Director of the University of Cape Town Planning Unit since 1969. Recipient: Bronze Medal, for religious, community, and domestic buildings, Zambian Institute of Architects, 1967; Ernest Oppenheimer Study Grant, 1969; University of Cape Town travel grant, 1977. Associate of the Royal Institute of British Architects, 1955. Address: 5 Pembroke Lane, Newlands 7700, South Africa.

Works:

1956   Bocskay Flats, Lubumbashi, Congo (with Philippe Charbonnier)
1958   Border Motors Building, Kitwe, Zambia (with Philippe Charbonnier)
1959   Attala House, Ndola, Zambia (with Gluckman, de Beer, and Peters)
1960   Border Motors Building, Kabwe, Zambia (with Neil Grobbelaar)
1961   Bracaire Shop, Ndola, Zambia (with Neil Grobbelaar)
        Groenewald House, Ndola, Zambia (with Neil Grobbelaar)
1962   Llewelyn High School, Ndola, Zambia (with Neil Grobbelaar)
1963   Chifubu Community Hall, Ndola, Zambia
        Ndola Library, Zambia (project)
1964   Kasama Cathedral, Zambia
1964/
68   University of Zambia, Lusaka (with Anthony Chitty, Douglas Yetton, and Munnik, Visser and Black)
1965   Pilcher House, Ndola, Zambia
        Ndola Museum, Zambia (project)
1966   Allen House, Ndola, Zambia
1971   Schuurmans House, Cape Town, South Africa
1972   Huyghe House, Cape Town, South Africa
1974   Elliott House, Cape Town, South Africa
1975   Middle Campus, University of Cape Town (with Neil Grobbelaar)
1977   Catholic Church, Cape Town
1978   Sciences Building, University of the Witwatersrand, Johannesburg (with Neil Grobbelaar, and Montgomerie, Oldfield and Kirby)

Publications:

By ELLIOTT: articles—"Zambian Architecture" in *Edilizia Moderna* (Milan), 89–90, 1967; "University Planning" in *Architectural Review* (London), April 1970.

On ELLIOTT: books—*New Architecture of Africa* by Udo Kultermann, London 1963; *Pianificazione e Disegnio della Universita* by Giancarlo De Carlo, Venice 1968; *New Directions in African Architecture*

Julian Elliott: University of Zambia, Lusaka, 1968

by Udo Kultermann, London 1969; *The Phenomenon of Architecture in Cultures of Change* by David Oakley, Oxford 1970; articles—"Commonwealth Architecture" in *Architectural Review* (London), June 1961; "University of Zambia" in *Architectural Review* (London), January 1967; "Kasama Cathedral" in *Architect and Builder* (Salisbury, Rhodesia), February 1968; article in *Bauen und Wohnen* (Zurich), November 1969; "Kasama Cathedral" in *Architectural Review* (London), July 1971.

*

The projects and completed works to date have all been undertaken on the African sub-continent and are the direct result of four architectural understandings:

Firstly, that architecture is a lived environment; that form/container, space/contained, and observer/experience are locked together into a single reality.

Secondly, that there are timeless ways of building which have evolved organically over time and that

the relevance of these patterns, structures, and processes is always travelling with us into contemporary time.

The third factor follows directly from this, in that the African timeless way has had a particular influence. One aspect of this is the African idea of space, whereby buildings are placed within external open space (lapas), and it is these external "courtyards" with their sense of protection, order, and repose that are the dominant architectural element. This idea is best experienced in the Zimbabwe ruins in Rhodesia/Zimbabwe and the Ndabele villages in the Transvaal, South Africa. It has particular relevance in the domestic architecture of Africa.

Finally, most of the work has been concerned with developing generic building types: families of houses, libraries, churches, and, most importantly, a family of university building types. It is the range of university building types which has provided the most interesting research in appropriate assembly of space and structure in order to make buildings which accommodate a diverse range of activities, some highly specialized, and which can readily respond to change in use and user over time.

—Julian Elliott

Julian Elliott's best-known project has been the coordination and development of the design for the University of Zambia, which, when it was produced, was in the forefront of thinking about new universities. The careful control of open space, the creation of linking elements between buildings, an ingenious lineal plan which allowed for growth, and the meticulous approach to the programming of the project are its most impressive characteristics. There is a sure attitude to form in all of Elliott's work—for example, his use in the Kasama Cathedral and in several houses of brick barrel vaults together with crisp detailing of voids and openings gives the buildings a sharp and characteristic form. There is also in his work an appealing empathy with older traditions in South Africa.

The number of Elliott's works is not vast, but their quality has had a considerable influence upon his colleagues. Although the works are for the most part "one-off," they seek to be generic solutions. His most recent projects—for example, The University of Cape Town Middle Campus—reveal a concern for the organization of buildings within a suitable geometry. Further, Elliott is concerned to find an appropriate density of site usage that allows for simple pedestrian movement and access and for a humane relationship in scale between open space and building.

Elliott is an incisive thinker on architectural problems and an excellent architectural critic. Although one at first gains the impression of strong links with the early era of the modern movement, there is in his work a much more personally-developed vocabulary of ideas: these are best seen in Kasama Cathedral, the Pilcher House and his own house in Cape Town.

Working for much of his career in Central Africa in an area with little urban building tradition either in cultural values or technology, Elliott has been able to develop both, as well as managing to build buildings appropriate to climate and social setting. These are rare qualities.

—Hans Hallen

ELLWOOD, Craig.
American. Born in Clarendon, Texas, 22 April 1922. Studied structural engineering at night classes at the University of California at Los Angeles Extension Division, 1949–54. Served in the United States Air Force, 1942–46. Married Gloria McInery in 1949 (divorced, 1976); children: Jeffrey, Erin, and Adam; married Anita Gail Eubank in 1978. Worked for a construction company, Los Angeles, 1946–48; Principal, Craig Ellwood Associates, Los Angeles, 1948–76. Since 1976 has devoted himself to painting and sculpture, and lives part of the time in Italy. Visiting Lecturer, Yale University, New Haven, Connecticut, 1959, 1960, Cornell University, Ithaca, New York, 1960, and Syracuse University, New York, 1961. Exhibitions: architecture—*International Exhibition of Architecture*, Sao Paulo, 1953, 1957; *Craig Ellwood*, Sioux Falls Art Museum, South Dakota, 1955; *Three Young Architects*, Long Beach Art Museum, California, 1956; *The Architecture of Steel*, The Architectural League of New York, 1962; *The Twentieth Century House*, Museum of Modern Art, New York, 1962; painting—Anhalt-Barnes Gallery, Los Angeles, 1979; Art Center College of Design, Pasadena, California, 1979. Recipient: First Prize, Collective Dwelling Category, *International Exhibition of Architecture*, Sao Paulo, 1953; Governor's Design Award, California, 1966; American Institute

of Architects Award, 1967; Los Angeles Beautiful Award, 1972, 1975; National Endowment for the Arts grant, 1973; Pasadena Beautiful Award, 1976; Design Award, *Progressive Architecture*, 1976; Graham Foundation grant, 1978. Honorary doctorate: University of Mexico, 1966. Address: 7488 Mulholland Drive, Los Angeles, California 90046, U.S.A.; and, Casanovalta, Pergine/Valdarno, 52020 Arezzo, Italy.

Works:

1948 Lappin House, Cheviot Hills, California
1949 Epstein House, 401 North Cliffwood, Brentwood, Los Angeles
    Broughton House, 909 North Beverly Glen Boulevard, Bel Air, Los Angeles
1949/
50 Hale House, 9618 Yoakum Drive, Beverly Hills, California
    Zimmerman House, 400 North Carmlina Avenue, Brentwood, Los Angeles
1950 Brown House, 902 North Roxbury Drive, Beverly Hills, California
    Anderson House, 656 Hightree Road, Pacific Palisades, California
    Unity Church, Santa Monica, California (project)
1951 Elton House, Pacific Palisades, California
    Case Study House 16, Los Angeles (for *Arts and Architecture*)
1952 Courtyard Apartments, 1570 Labaig Avenue, Hollywood, California
1953 Pierson House, Malibu Beach Road, Malibu, California
1954 Case Study House 17, Los Angeles (for *Arts and Architecture*)
1955 Smith House, Crestwood Drive, West Los Angeles
    Case Study House 18, Los Angeles (for *Arts and Architecture*)
1955/
56 South Bay Bank, Manhattan Beach, California
1957 Hunt House, 24514 Malibu Beach Road, Malibu, California
1957/
58 Westchester Post Office, California
1958 Carson-Roberts Building, 8233 Beverly, West Hollywood, California (now rental office building)
1960 Daphne House, 20 Madrone Place, Hillsborough, California
1960/
61 Acme-Arcadia Building, Los Angeles (project)
1961 Pierson House, 32320 Pacific Coast Highway, Malibu, California (destroyed by fire)
    Rosen House, 910 Oakmont Drive, Brentwood, Los Angeles
1962 Office Building, Los Angeles (project)
    Carson-Roberts Square, Los Angeles (project)
1962/
63 Litton Systems Factories (2), New York (project)
    Chamorro House, Los Angeles (project)
1964 Moore House, 4791 Bonvue, East Hollywood, California
    Kubly House, 215 La Vereda, Pasadena, California
    Courtyard House (project)
1965/
66 Craig Ellwood Associates Office Building remodelling, 1107 South Robertson Boulevard, Los Angeles
1966 Scientific Data Systems Building, 555 South Aviation Boulevard, El Segundo, California (now Xerox Building)
1967 Scientific Data Systems Buildings 2 and 3, El Segundo, California
    Weekend house, San Luis Obispo, California

Craig Ellwood Associates Building Annex remodelling, 1111 South Robertson Boulevard, Los Angeles
1967/
68 Goldman House, Beverly Hills, California
1968 Scientific Data Systems PCM Building, Pomona, California
    Bridge House (project)
    Kawahara House, Rolling Hills Estates, California
    Design of "Knockdown" Computer Exhibit, for Scientific Data Systems Company
    Airport Business Center, Irvine, California
1968/
69 Palevsky House, 1021 Cielo Drive, Palm Springs, California
1969 Master plan for the Rand Corporation, Santa Monica, California
    Security Pacific Place, Wilshire and Bedford, Beverly Hills, California
1970/
75 Art Center College of Design, Pasadena, California
1972 Performing Arts Building, Immaculate Heart College, Los Angeles (project)
1972/
73 Joy Manufacturing Company, 4565 Colorado, Glendale, California
    Security Pacific National Bank, 1811 North Western, East Hollywood, California
1973 Xerox Computer and Data Processing Center, Culver City, California (project)
1974 GF Furniture Showroom, Pacific Design Center, Los Angeles (subsequently altered)
1978 15th century farmhouse restoration, Tuscany, Italy

Publications:

By ELLWOOD: book—*Architects on Architecture*, edited by Paul Heyer, New York 1966, London 1967; articles—"Form, Function and Architecture" in *L'Architecture d'aujourd'hui* (Paris), April 1955; "On Prefabrication and the Product House" in *Arts and Architecture* (Los Angeles), February 1956; "Nonsensualism" in *Bauen und Wohnen* (Zurich), April 1962; interviews with Thomas Vreeland in *L.A. Architect*, December 1975 and March 1978; "The Search for Post-modern Architecture" in *Crit* (Washington, D.C.), Fall 1978.

On ELLWOOD: books—*Quality Budget Houses* by Katherine Morrow Ford and Thomas H. Creighton, New York 1954; *Aluminum in Modern Architecture* by John Peter, 2 volumes, New York 1956; *Craig Ellwood: Architecture* by Esther McCoy, New York 1968; articles—"Designers of Change: Craig Ellwood" by Olga Gueft in *Interiors* (New York), November 1970; special issue of *Bauen und Wohnen* (Zurich), December 1971.

The essence of architecture is the interrelation and interaction of mass, space, plane and line. The purpose of architecture is to enrich the joy and drama of living. The spirit of architecture is its truthfulness to itself: its clarity and logic with respect to its materials and structure.

Building comes of age when it expresses its epoch. The constant change in technology demands a continuously maturing expression of itself. When technology reaches its fulfillment in perfect equilibrium with function, there is a transcendence into architecture.

The consciousness of truth is not static but ever progressively unfolding. We must strive for intrinsic solution, not extrinsic effect. The moment form becomes arbitrary, it becomes novelty or style—it becomes something other than architecture. Materials and methods will certainly change, but the basic laws of nature make finally everything timeless.

Architecture, by its own nature, must certainly be

Craig Ellwood: Art Center College of Design, Pasadena, California, 1975

more than an expression of an idea. Art in architecture is not arbitrary stylism or ethereal symbolism but rather the extent to which a building can transcend from the measurable into the immeasurable. The extent to which a building can evoke profound emotion. The extent to which a building can spiritually uplift and inspire man while simultaneously reflecting the logic of the technique which alone can convey its validity to exist.

—Craig Ellwood

In an age when architects are expected to spend years at university learning their craft, what can one make of the builder's cost estimator who leaves his employer and sets up practice as a designer and, within a few years, is acclaimed as one of the most sensitive and sophisticated architects in the world? The earlier Los Angeles architects, Neutra and Soriano, had come to the machine very much as to an aesthetic idea. Craig Ellwood learnt about building in steel and plastic sheet before he owned up to any aesthetic theories, and this gave him a fluency and ease with steel construction that his contemporaries from architectural schools could never acquire.

Hale House, one of his first independent commissions, is very much a builder's house in steel, although the use of "flash-gap" detailing shows a thoughtful, craftsmanly mind at work in the relationship of material to material. His third Case Study House for the magazine *Arts and Architecture* moves some way to exploiting the elegance of steel with its thin (2½e square) columns, but the 8 ft. spans do not exploit the spanning potential of steel with the confidence of contemporary houses in Chicago.

In 1953 came the first real breakthrough: a group of four dwellings, "Courtyard Apartments" in Hollywood, won the world's top architecture award. Of beautiful and simple elegance, the structure introduces what was to become one of Craig Ellwood's favourite structural devices—the exposed warren truss, using small members to span big distances. In the Courtyard Apartments, the trusses just span the width of an apartment under the first floor windows, but they are a portent of what was to become a dominant motif in his work.

In the early 1960's the world of architectural fashion swung against the hard pristine style of Mies van der Rohe. The decorative and crumbly manner was all the rage. Yet it was at this moment that the full

impact of the work of Mies hit Ellwood, and his Daphne House and his Rosen House take the Miesian parti to unequalled heights of elegance and luxury. In the Rosen House, in particular, architecture reaches near to perfection.

But Ellwood was, in many ways, a Los Angeles man and thus closer to the light-steel cage of Charles Eames than to the structured formalism of Mies van der Rohe. Ellwood loved his exposed trusses, and in the Scientific Data Systems plant at El Segundo he got his chance to build on a big scale—a spreading factory with glorious trusses clearly expressed externally: the columns, and hence the beam ends, are pulled well outside the skin. The El Segundo factory was designed and built very quickly—Ellwood had the advantage of having a lifetime's work on one idea behind the design.

In a more fanciful mood, Ellwood proposed storey high trusses enclosing the living area of a house: the entire building becomes a beam spanning its length, glazed on the long sides so that the diagonals of the warren truss can be seen from within. The first of these designs, the Chamorro House, was never realized, but, due largely to Jerry Horn's seductively beautiful perspectives, the idea caught on, and students at the California State Polytechnic College built a slightly smaller version spanning a modest ravine.

Trusses are fascinating for small houses, but the idea really demands size. In the Arts Centre College of Design in Pasadena, Ellwood got his chance. Here a linear building, gently Miesian in form, lays on the landscape and suddenly leaps across a valley with four parallel warren trusses, starkly exposed inside and out—a permanent exemplar to the students within of the importance of structure in the design of buildings.

—John Winter

ENGLAND, Richard.
Maltese. Born in Sliema, 3 October 1937. Educated at St. Edward's College, Malta, 1947–53; Royal University of Malta, 1954–61, B.Arch. (Architecture and Civil Engineering) 1961; Polytechnic, Milan (studied interior design), 1960–61. Married Myriam

Borg Manduca in 1962; children: Sandra and Marc. Student Architect, Studio Ponti, Fornaroli and Rosselli, Milan, 1960–62. Formed the company, England + England, Malta, 1961; Partner/Director and Head of the Design Section of Architectural Plus Engineering Services Limited (A Plus E), Malta, since 1976. Visiting Lecturer, Architectural Association, London, the University of Liverpool and the University of Manchester, 1974, Sheffield Polytechnic, 1975, and Yale University, New Haven, Connecticut, the University of Pennsylvania, Philadelphia, and the University of Florida, Gainesville, 1977. Exhibitions: *Art from Malta,* Richard Demarco Gallery, Edinburgh, 1970; *Malta Now,* St. George's Park, Malta, 1970; Grand Hotel Ambasciatori, Turin, 1971; *Henraux Collection,* Palazzo dei Diamanti, Ferrara, Italy, 1972; *Mostra Internazionale del Marmo,* Carrara, Italy, 1972; *Form Is My Language,* Phoenicia Hotel, Floriana, Malta, 1973; Richard Demarco Gallery, Edinburgh, 1974; University of Manchester School of Architecture, 1974; *Sculpture and Maquettes,* Architectural Association, London, 1974; University of Liverpool School of Architecture, 1974; *Terra I,* Wroclau, Poland, 1975; *Threads of Stone,* Commonwealth Art Gallery, London, 1975; Bund Deutscher Architekten exhibition, Oldenburg, Germany, 1976; University of Florida School of Architecture, 1977. Recipient: First Prize, Yorkton International Film Festival, Canada, 1973. Fellow of the Institute of Professional Designers, London, 1977. Addresses: Richard England, Oleander Street, The Gardens, St. Julian's, Malta; England + England, 26 Merchants Street, Valletta, Malta; A Plus E, 3B Il-Piazzetta, Tower Road, Sliema, Malta.

Works:

1964 Paradise Bay Hotel, Marfa, Malta
       Ramla Bay Hotel, Marfa, Malta
       Mid Med Bank, formerly Barclays Bank, Sliema, Malta
       Bank of Valletta, formerly Tagliaferro Bank, St. John Square, Valletta, Malta
1965 Dolphin Court Apartments, Ta'Xbiex, Malta
1966 Joinwell Furniture Showrooms, Sliema, Malta
       Mid Med Bank, formerly Barclays Bank, Spinola, Malta
1967 Dolmen Hotel, St. Paul's Bay, Malta
       Hyperion Hotel, St. Paul's Bay, Malta

Mariners Court Apartments, St. Paul's Bay, Malta

Haro Fashion Boutique, Valletta, Malta

Villa "La Maltija," Naxxar, Malta

1968 Villa "Brockland," St. Julian's, Malta

Cavalieri Hotel, St. Julian's, Malta

Malta Hilton Hotel, Spinola, Malta (with Thomas E. Stanley and Associates)

Leroy Hotel, Sliema, Malta

1969 Cavalli Marini Apartments, St. Paul's Bay, Malta

St. George's Park Apartments, Spinola, Malta

Salina Bay Hotel, Salina, Malta

Trilithon Court Apartments, St. Paul's Bay, Malta

1970 Tower Palace Hotel, Sliema, Malta

Dinmore Court Apartments, Sliema, Malta

Bahar-ic-Caghaq Studio Apartments, Salina, Malta

Joinwell Furniture Factory, Qormi, Malta

Edwin England Sant Fournier Office Block, Spinola, Malta

1971 Edrichton Court Apartments, St. Paul's Bay, Malta

Central Bank of Malta, Valletta, Malta

Ta' Monita Apartments, Marsascala, Malta

Malta Development Corporation office interiors, Floriana, Malta

Printex Limited Factory, Qormi, Malta

Mid Med Bank, formerly Barclays Bank, Floriana, Malta

Mid Med Bank, formerly Barclays Bank, St. Paul's Bay, Malta

1972 Villa complex, St. Julian's, Malta

Mid Med Bank, formerly Barclays Bank, Msida, Malta

Bank of Valletta (Tagliaferro Centre), Sliema, Malta

Aragon Court Apartments, Marsascala, Malta

Villa "Gascan," Naxxar, Malta

Twin villas, St. Julian's, Malta

Villa "The Blessings," Ta'Xbiex, Malta

1973 American Embassy Offices, Floriana, Malta

Mid Med Bank, formerly Barclays Bank Computer Centre, Qormi, Malta

Philips Pavilion, *Malta Trade Fair*, Naxxar

1974 Church of St. Joseph, Manikata, Malta

Chapel, Addolorata Cemetery, Malta

Mid Med Bank, formerly Barclays Bank, Rabat, Gozo

Mid Med Bank, formerly Barclays Bank, Valletta, Malta

1975 Villa "It-Tina 1-Helwa," Naxxar, Malta

Il-Piazzetta Offices and Apartments, Sliema, Malta

1976 Stones Boutique, Sliema, Malta

Villa "La Saracena," Marsascala, Malta

House of Representatives, Valletta, Malta (with Uhlin and Malm)

1977 Dragonara Court Apartments, Spinola, Malta

American Ambassador's Residence, Lija, Malta

1978 Mid Med Bank, formerly Barclays Bank, extension, Spinola, Malta

Mid Med Bank, formerly Barclays Bank, Mosta, Malta

Museum Chapel, Naxxar, Malta

Penthouse, Sliema, Malta

Malta Exhibition Stand, Commonwealth Institute, London

H.R.H. Prince Mohamed Ibn Fahd Guest House, Jeddah, Saudi Arabia

Conference Centre, Sports City, Riyadh, Saudi Arabia (with Suter and Suter)

Villa Abdul Aziz al Malik Al Sheikh, Riyadh, Saudi Arabia

Publications:

By ENGLAND: books—*Walls of Malta* (photo-prose poem), Malta 1973; *White Is White* (Poems and epigrams), Malta 1973; *Contemporary Art in Malta,* editor, Malta 1974; *Carrier-Citadel Metamorphosis,* Malta 1974; articles—"L'Architettura di Malta" in *L'Ingegnere* (Rome), March 1968; "Cinque Progetti a Malta" in *L'Ingegnere* (Rome), January 1969; "Contemporary Architecture in Malta" in *Architectural Review* (London), June 1969; "The Architecture of the Maltese Islands" in *Architectural Association Quarterly* (London), April 1970; "Notes on the Maltese Vernacular" in *Richard England, Architect in Malta* by Emile Henvaux, Brussels 1970; "Internal Pressures" in *Architectural Conservation in Europe,* London 1975; "Foreword" to *Megalithic Monuments of Malta* by G. Formosa, Vancouver 1975; "Mdina" in *European Heritage* (London), October 1975; also numerous articles in the *Sunday Times of Malta* and Maltese daily newspapers; other—graphic offset litho sets in limited editions, Malta, 1972–76.

On ENGLAND: books—*Richard England, Architect in Malta* by Emile Henvaux, Brussels 1970; *Contemporary Art in Malta,* Malta 1974; articles—"Modern Vernacular in Malta" in *Architectural Review* (London), August 1965; "Travaux de l'architecte Richard England" in *La Maison* (Brussels), February 1966; "The Maltese Fashion" in *Progressive Architecture* (New York), June 1966; "Richard England el gran arquitecto actual de la isla de Malta" in *Obras* (Madrid), October 1966; "Richard England nel avant-guardia d'arquitectura de Malta"

Richard England: Ramla Bay Hotel, Marfa, Malta, 1964

in *Obras* (Madrid), February 1967; "La Maltija" in *L'Architettura* (Rome), March 1967; "Récherches et Travaux de l'architecte Richard England" by Emile Henvaux in *La Maison* (Brussels), July 1967; "Malta—Rebirth or Death of an Island" by Eric Ambrose in *Ideal Home* (London), May 1968; "England in Malta" in *Concrete Quarterly* (London), October 1968; "The England Look Is So Maltese" by Robert Langton in *Evening News* (London), 23 September 1969; "Explosie op Malta" by R. Blijstra in *Plan* (The Hague), no. 6, 1970; "Malta: Richard England's Visionary View" by Richard Demarco in *Malta News*, 14 October 1973; "The Architect as Artist" by P. Serracino Inglott in *Times of Malta,* 7 December 1973; "Richard England's Exhibition" by A. C. Sewter in *Royal Society of Arts Journal* (London), February 1974; "Richard England, Architect, Sculptor and Poet of Malta" by Mitzi Cunliffe in *Sunday Times of Malta,* 22 December 1974; "A Bit of England" by Charles Knevitt in *Building Design* (London), 19 March 1976.

Voices of a Site
The Site constitutes the land within its
boundaries
And yet it extends beyond.

The Site is the hill, the valley, the rocks,
The very earth itself.

The Site is the climate, the sun, the rain,
the wind,
The lights and shadows which fall on it.

The Site is the sum of the very materials
    which constitute it:
Materialistic and etheric.

The Site is the tradition: the background,
    the past, the present
The whole totality of that particular place:
    visible and invisible.

The Site is place
The Site is totality
The Site is environment.

An environment which sends out vibra-
    tions
Vibrations of esoteric waves
Impregnating and pulsating through the
    enveloping surrounding air
The very air which belongs to and limits
    that environment.
For that environment has its own personal-
    ity
Not only material but also spiritual
Not only visual but also aural.

It is here that the role of the architect
An an intruder to this harmony is para-
    mount.

He must first of all look
Then he must listen
But most of all he must understand

He must discover the tuning in and switch-
    ing off distance of the Site.
In other words he must understand what is
    included in
And what is excluded from the environ-
    ment.
Its aural and visual, spiritual and material-
    istic boundaries and limitations.

It is a moment of pause and reflection
It is a moment of silence and contempla-
    tion
A moment of almost mystical expectation
Before man and site, man and environment
    reciprocate
And establish the right wave lengths and
    vibrations

It is an almost frightening moment of
    soundless silence,
Of loneliness and nothingness

Then suddenly contact is established:

The voices are heard . . .
The voice of the land
The voice of the hill
The voice of the rocks
The voice of the earth, sky, sun and winds,
The voice of totality.
The totality of that site
The totality of that environment.

These are the voices which in a moment of
mystic rare faery-like contact will reveal
the traces and images of the solution required. Voices which will tell the architect
(if he is a sensitive one) whether the environment is weak and this in turn requires
him to be strong and dominant; or they will
tell him perhaps that the environment is
strong, and that he, in turn, should be doc-
ile and servient.

The architect must now listen . . . listen
. . . listen . . . listen. . . .

Only after this spiritual contact has been
established can the mechanical materialistic wheels of the rest of the architectural
creative process continue, then and only
then is one able to produce a truly inspired
architecture: an architecture of *evolution,*
an architecture of *place,* an architecture of
environment.

                 —Richard England

The work of Richard England in Malta shows up one
of the paradoxes of modern architecture since the
Second World War. The most easily recognized distinguishing feature of most design derived from the
European Modern Movement is its anonymity and
internationalism, despite the fact that figures like Le
Corbusier, Mies van der Rohe, Alvar Aalto and
many others were individual artists whose work was
instantly recognizable. But they did not create architecture that was rooted in a particular place and its
qualities. Their idioms and ideas were exported all
over the world and copied without discrimination,
and the assumption has been that this is an unavoidable and inevitable result of industrialization, ease of
travel and communication. But when a body of work
as large and consistent as that of Richard England
seems to contradict this tendency, one has to question the inevitability of the process.

In a way the circumstances in Malta contributed:
an island with a very restricted range of available
materials; a local traditional vernacular that had developed undisturbed by industrial or cultural revolutions for centuries; an economy that suddenly
boomed as a result of tourist development in the
Mediterranean, creating a demand for new building
that was catastrophic. But in these circumstances,
where so many other architects failed to produce
anything worthwhile, Richard England succeeded in
making a subtle synthesis of local traditional forms
and materials, the possibilities inherent in newer
materials like reinforced concrete, and the new visual expectations of his generation.

Beginning as soon as he went into his father's
established architectural practice in Malta, he has
been extraordinarily prolific in his architectural output, as well as finding time for making sculpture,
drawings, and photographs, and for writing poetry,
criticism and essays on the Maltese townscape and
landscape. He is sensitive to the qualities of a site to
a degree and in a way that was preached (but not
always practised) by Frank Lloyd Wright. The geometry and massing of his buildings and sculpture
are organic in the true sense of the word. Some, like
the Manikata Church, seem to have grown out of the
landscape—to have been formed with it. On a sun-
drenched land without much natural vegetation,
dominated by the angular forms of natural limestone
formations, organic expression in buildings, as
shown by the vernacular, will be angular, cubic, geometric, full of contrast of light and shadow and emphatic in massing. Richard England's work also
shows a deeply felt response to the history of Malta,
going right back to the mysteriously impressive
megalithic remains there. It never copies but comments in a completely contemporary way, sometimes
with subtle irony.

But the paradox is that such a deep-rooted architecture cannot be exported, and as his work becomes
quite deservedly internationally well-known, its
genesis may be obscured and give rise to imitations
in inappropriate places. The hope is that Richard
England himself, exercising his skill, sensitivity and
analysis in new environments, will demonstrate that
connection that should exist between a place and its
architecture.

                 —Cedric Green

ERICKSON, Arthur (Charles).

Canadian. Born in Vancouver, British Columbia, 14
June 1924. Educated at the University of British
Columbia, Vancouver, 1942–45; McGill University,
Montreal, 1946–50 (Lieutenant-Governor's Bronze
Medal), B.Arch. (honours) 1950; awarded McLen-
nan Travelling Scholarship, for architectural re-
search in the Middle East and Europe, 1950–53.
Served in the Canadian Army, 1943–45: Captain,
Canadian Intelligence Corps in India, Ceylon and
Malaya, 1945. In private practice, Vancouver, 1953–
62; Partner, with Geoffrey Massey, Erickson/Mas-
sey Architects, Vancouver, 1963–72. Since 1972,
Principal, Arthur Erickson Architects, Vancouver
and Toronto; since 1977, President, Arthur Erickson
Associates, Vancouver, Toronto, Kuwait, and Jeddah, Saudi Arabia. Assistant Professor, University of
Oregon, Eugene, 1955–56; Instructor, 1956–57, Assistant Professor, 1958–60, and Associate Professor,
1961–64, University of British Columbia. Broadcaster, Canadian Broadcasting Corporation, 1956–
62. Exhibitions: *The Architecture of Arthur Erickson,*
Vancouver Art Gallery, 1966; *Art in Architecture—
Arthur Erickson,* University of Calgary, 1976; *Arthur Erickson: Recent Work,* University of Toronto,
1977; *Transformations in Modern Architecture,* Museum of Modern Art, New York, 1979. Recipient:
Massey Medal, 1955, 1958, 1967 (3 times), 1970 (3
times); Canada Council Fellowship, 1961; Pan-
Pacific Citation, American Institute of Architects,
Hawaii Chapter, 1963; First Prize, Simon Fraser
University Competition, Burnaby, British Co-
lumbia, 1963; *Tokyo International Trade Fair*
Award, 1965; Vancouver Citation Award, Architec-
tural Institute of British Columbia, 1965; Prestressed
Concrete Institute Award, 1966, 1967, 1972; Molson
Prize, Canada Council, 1967; Centennial Design
Award, National Housing Design Council, 1967;
Design Award, Architectural Institute of British Co-
lumbia, Vancouver Chapter, 1967 (twice), 1968
(twice); Award of Merit, *Canadian Architect,* 1968;
House Award, *Architectural Record,* 1969; Ar-
chitectural Institute of Japan Award, 1970; Triangle
Award, National Society of Interior Designers,
1970; First Prize, Elementary School Competition,
Southeast Sector of Vancouver, 1970; Award of Ex-
cellence, *Canadian Architect Yearbook,* 1970, 1977;
Royal Bank of Canada Award, 1971; First Line
Award, 1971, and Residential Design Award, 1975,
Canadian Housing Design Council; Man of the Year
Award, Greater Vancouver Visitors and Convention
Bureau, 1972; Gold Medal, Tau Sigma Delta, 1973;
Auguste Perret Award, International Union of Ar-
chitects, 1974; President's Award of Excellence,
American Society of Landscape Architects, 1979.
D.Eng.: Nova Scotia Technical College, Halifax,
1971; LL.D.: Simon Fraser University, 1973; McGill
University, 1975; University of Manitoba, Winnipeg,
1978. Fellow, Royal Architectural Institute of Can-
ada, 1953; Academician, Royal Canadian Academy
of Arts, 1953. Honorary Fellow, American Institute
of Architects, 1978. Officer, Order of Canada, 1973.
Address: Arthur Erickson Architects, 2412 Laurel
Street, Vancouver, British Columbia V5Z 3T2, Canada.

Works:

1958 Filberg House, Comox, British Columbia
1962 Graham House, West Vancouver
1963 Simon Fraser University, Burnaby, British
      Columbia
1964 Lloyd House, Vancouver
      Danto House, Vancouver
      Bayles House, Vancouver
      Smith House, West Vancouver
1965 Pavilion for the *International Trade Fair,*
      Tokyo
1966 Development study of the downtown core of
      Vancouver
      Townhouses, Point Grey Road, Vancouver
1967 Craig House, Kelowna, British Columbia
      Catton House, West Vancouver
      Theme Building, *Expo '67,* Montreal
      Campus development plan for the University
      of Victoria, British Columbia
      Transportation study of Vancouver
1968 Faculty Club, University of British Co-
      lumbia, Vancouver
      Snauq Harbour, Vancouver
      Marathon Realty M-3 Development, Mont-
      real (with David Boulva Cleve)
1969 Married Student Housing, Simon Fraser Uni-

Arthur Erickson: Blocks 51-61-71 Project (government offices and courthouse complex), Vancouver, 1979

versity, Burnaby, British Columbia
MacMillan Bloedel Office Tower Block, Vancouver
Cité des Terrasses (housing development), Montreal (with David Boulva Cleve)
Campus development plan for the University of Lethbridge, Alberta
Development study for the Bank of Canada, Ottawa
West Seattle Freeway

1970 Sikh Temple, Vancouver
Canadian Pavilion, *Expo '70*, Osaka, Japan
Biological Sciences Building, University of Victoria, British Columbia
1971 Nelson Towers (housing), Vancouver
Centre Beaubourg, Paris (competition project)
University of Lethbridge, Alberta
Bank of Canada, Ottawa (with Marani, Rounthwaite, and Dick)

Village Lake Louise, Alberta
1971/
77 Museum of Anthropology, University of British Columbia, Vancouver
1972 Queen's University Centre, Vancouver
Home Lumber Company, Saanich, British Columbia
Study of downtown Vancouver
1973 Shannon Mews (housing), Vancouver
Oppenheimer Lodge, Vancouver

Christ Church Cathedral, Vancouver
Elementary school, Vancouver
Canadian Pacific Hotel, Vancouver
Intermediate Transit Demonstration Project,
for the Government of Ontario
Inner Harbour, Victoria, British Columbia
False Creek East End Lake, Vancouver
Area plan for Langley, British Columbia
Traffic study for the University of British Columbia at Fort Camp

1973/
79 Blocks 51–61–71 Project (government offices and courthouse complex), Vancouver
1974 Arthur Erickson House, Vancouver
Hilborn House, Cambridge, Ontario
Eppich House, West Vancouver
1975 Ghajere Ski Condominiums, Tehran
Kanata Recreation Plan, Ottawa
Development plan for East End Lake, Vancouver
Expansion study for British Columbia Hydro and Power Authority Head Office, Vancouver
Midtown Terrace, Toronto
1976 Sawaber Housing Development, Kuwait
Habitat Pavilion, Vancouver
British Columbia Medical Centre, Vancouver
Downtown West (commercial development) and City Park, Toronto (with Mathers and Haldenby)
Hornby-Smithe Development, Vancouver
Office building, Abbotsford, Ontario
Centro Simon Bolivar, Caracas, Venezuela
1976/
80 New Massey Hall, Toronto
1977 Islamic Centre, Richmond, Ontario
National Art Gallery of Canada, Ottawa
Eglinton West Subway Station, Toronto
Yorkdale Rapid Transit Station, Toronto
1978 Performing Arts Centre, Calgary, Alberta
Hotel/Convention Center, Victoria, British Columbia
Federal Office Building, Vancouver
Ministry of Foreign Affairs Interim Headquarters, Jeddah, Saudi Arabia
1979 Wright House, Seattle, Washington
Town Centre, Fintas, Kuwait
1980 Bank of Canada Building, Ottawa

Publications:

By ERICKSON: book—*The Architecture of Arthur Erickson* (text by Erickson), Montreal 1975; articles—"The Weight of Heaven" in *Canadian Architect* (Toronto), March 1964; "The Roots" and "A Tendency Towards Formalism" in *Canadian Architect* (Toronto), December 1966; "The Language of Erickson" in *Lotus* (Venice), no. 5, 1968; "The University: The New Visual Environment" in *Canadian Architect* (Toronto), January 1968; "Architecture, Urban Development, and Industrialization" in *Canadian Architect* (Toronto), January 1975; "The Context for Urbanization and Industrialization" in *Towards a Quality of Life: The Role of Industrialization in the Architecture and Urban Planning of Developing Countries,* Tehran 1976; "Ideation as a Source of Creativity" in *A Political Art,* edited by W. H. New, Vancouver 1978.

On ERICKSON: book—*The Architecture of Arthur Erickson,* Montreal 1975; articles—"The Design of a House" in *Canadian Art* (Toronto), November 1960; article in the *New York Times Sunday Magazine,* 20 November 1961; article in *Architectural Design* (London), March 1962; article in *Design* (Bombay), January 1965; article in *Time* (New York), 25 August 1967; "Canadian Architect Arthur Erickson Gets Major Award for His Expo '70 Pavilion" in *Design* (Bombay), October 1971; article in *Progressive Architecture* (New York), September 1972; article in *Architecture Plus* (New York), February 1973; "Erickson" by Macy DuBois in *Canadian Architect*

(Toronto), November 1974; "Design for Transit" in *Canadian Architect* (Toronto), May 1976; "Architecture as Cultural Expression" in *Arts Canada* (Toronto), October/November 1976; "Meet the Architect: Arthur Erickson" in *Global Architecture: Houses,* Tokyo 1977; "The Architect as Artist" in *The Illustrated London News,* January 1978.

*

I like to think of building design not as the product of an architect's imagination but as the inevitable result of the two conditions of its being: its purpose and its context. These, in my view, become like two opposite forces, one pushing out the form through the programmatic pressures from within and the other molding it through the environmental pressures from without.

I probably don't differ from other contemporaries in this stance, except perhaps that these become equal sources of inspiration. The context or site, in the broadest sense of site, pervades the design so irrevocably that the building form is meaningless without it. The program goes beyond the definition of building requirements to the redefinition of purpose in the context of the society and the culture at that particular time and place. This is the real source of innovation—not the forms themselves, nor the structure or materials—and from it a building injects into its culture a fresh response to its traditions. All my building forms can be traced to these sources.

Of course the matter of personal taste must play a role. My preference is for the horizontal line and for simple forms and materials that are uncomplicated, if not austere. Surfaces are unadorned to the extent of rejecting ornament of any kind—even board formwork. I abhor subterfuge or disguise, crave frankness, especially in exposing and featuring structure, though structure never determines the form but rather is the result of it. Things should be themselves above all, which is sometimes difficult in this age of the artificial. Life is rich, always changing, always challenging, and we architects have the task of transmitting it into wood, concrete, glass and steel, of transforming human aspirations into habitable and meaningful space.

—Arthur Erickson

*

"... the greatest architect in Canada, and maybe the greatest on this continent", according to Philip Johnson (quoted by Edith Iglauer in *The New Yorker,* 4 June 1979), Arthur Erickson gained international recognition for his (and Geoffrey Massey's) conceptual plan and covered mall for Simon Fraser University in 1963. This striking conception extended a linear university plan across the two high points of a low mountain. The saddle between the peaks accommodates a vehicular underpass and terminal for entry to the pedestrian campus above. Individual buildings were awarded to the competition finalists; Erickson chose to build the huge covered mall which created a central weather protected gathering place adjacent to the point of arrival, stretching between the university library and theatre. The mall roof itself is a composite wood, steel and glass space frame, spanning 40 metres by 90 metres long, designed by the structural specialist, Jeffrey Lindsay.

Simon Fraser suggests a key to Erickson's particular interests and abilities; his essential contribution was more the orchestration of space and movement than a matter of detailed physical design. The same fascination with movement, with place, route and destination appears in other major structures such as the Museum of Anthropology and the Provincial Government Offices and Courthouse in Vancouver.

Instead of a consistent and single minded fascination with particular forms, materials, or patterns of organization, Erickson seems to pursue particular effects, appropriate to the place and program. Architecture is seen as performance, with physical structure, users, and landscape or urban context all as actors. Though the forms of his buildings are often striking, his materials and colours tend to neutral tones, lending unity to the overall shapes and creat-

ing a background for people and planting. Conflicts arise, however, between the large scale gesture, as at the two universities—Simon Fraser, spanning its mountain tops; Lethbridge, damming a coulee—and the internal environments, in these examples overextended, attenuated.

A variety of techniques and memorable images characterize Erickson's other buildings: the visually dominating horizontal timber beams in the Smith House, the deeply recessed in-situ concrete openings of the massive moated MacMillan Bloedel Office Tower, the glittering facetted mirror glass canopy over the New Massey (Concert) Hall for Toronto. Each building suggests a different hand, but the concern for the dramatic—in form, use and setting—is constant.

Erickson's architecture suggests a contemporary eclecticism based on the immense variety of forms and structures available to the designer. Earlier 20th century architects were preoccupied with a rigorous consistency in the use of preferred materials, in choice and expression of structure, and in the relation between building form and program of use. While each of Erickson's projects is internally consistent, in form, colour, materials and detail, these show little continuity from one project to the next. The architect is no longer the rigorous theorist, or moralist, whose work follows his manifesto. Instead, he is a virtuoso, immensely talented, knowledgeable and sensitive, able to dispose the manifold effects at his command as appropriate to each occasion.

—Michael McMordie

ERSKINE, Ralph.

British. Born in London, 24 February 1914; moved to Sweden, 1939. Educated at the Friends School, Saffron Walden, Essex, 1920–32; Regent Street Polytechnic, London, 1932–37, Dip.Arch. 1937; Royal Academy of Arts, Stockholm, 1944–45. Married Ruth Monica Francis in 1939; children: Jane, Karin, and Patrick. In private practice, Drottningholm, Sweden, since 1946: now in partnership with Aage Rosenvold; acquired Thames barge *Verona,* sailed it to Drottningholm, and converted it to offices, 1956–63; established branch office on the Byker Estate, Newcastle, England, 1968. Guest Professor, E.T.H.: Eidgenössischen Technische Hochschule, Zurich, 1964–65, and McGill University, Montreal, 1967–68. Member, Team 10, since 1959. Exhibitions: *Architecture in Cold Climates,* Cornell University, Ithaca, New York, 1959; *The Climate,* Tokyo, 1960; *Ralph Erskine/Ilhan Koman,* Schindler Gallery, Berne, 1962; *Ralph Erskine,* travelling exhibition, Sweden and Canada, 1963. Recipient: Kasper Salin Prize, Sweden, 1972; Ytong Prize, with Höjer and Ljungqvist, Sweden, 1974. Dr.Tech.: University of Lund, Sweden, 1975. Associate, Royal Institute of British Architects, 1937; Member, Royal Town Planning Institute, 1938; Member, S.A.R.: Swedish Arkitekts' Riksforbund, 1965. Honorary Fellow, American Institute of Architects, 1966; Foreign Member, Swedish Royal Academy of Arts, 1972. C.B.E. (Commander, Order of the British Empire), 1978. Address: Ralph Erskines Arkitektkontor, S-170 11 Drottningholm, Sweden.

Works:

1941/
42 Erskine House, Lissma, near Stockholm
von Platen House, Djupdalen, near Stockholm
1942/
43 Skiing Hotel/Centre, Lida Friluftsgard, Stockholm (with Birch-Lindgren)
1945/
55 Housing development for workers, Gyttorp, Sweden

Ralph Erskine: Byker Housing Estate, Newcastle, 1969

Publications:

By ERSKINE: articles—"Town Planning in the Swedish Subarctic" in *Habitat* (Ottawa), November/December 1960; "The Challenge of the High Latitudes" and "Community Design for Production, for Publication, or for People" in *Royal Architectural Institute of Canada Journal* (Toronto), 1964; "Construire dans le Nord" in *L'Architecture d'Aujourd'hui* (Paris), no. 134, 1967; "Architecture and Town Planning in the North" in *Polar Record* (Cambridge), no. 89, 1968; "Climate" in *Werk* (Zurich), no. 4, 1969; "8 Riposte a 8 Domande" in *L'Architettura* (Rome), November 1974; "Ralph Erskine Talks to AJ" in *The Architects' Journal* (London), 3 March 1976; "Working on Projects Abroad" and "Byker," with J. Sjostrom, in *Arkitektur* (Stockholm), October 1976; "On the Situation of the Architect," in special Erskine issue of *Bauen und Wohnen* (Zurich), January 1977; "Byker: New Building Best Solution" in *Arkitektur* (Stockholm), February 1977; "Nya Bruket: Daynurseyr in Sandviken" in *Arkitektur* (Stockholm), August 1977.

On ERSKINE: articles—"Individual Houses in Sweden" in *Récherche et Architecture* (Paris), no. 19, 1974; special Erskine issue of *L'Architettura* (Rome), November 1974; "Byker by Erskine" by Colin Amery in *Architectural Review* (London), December 1974; "Byker: Architect Ralph Erskine" by Diana Rowntree in *Architectural Design* (London), June 1975; "Housing—Still More New Ideas?" by John McKean in *The Architects' Journal* (London), 2 July 1975; "The Village Lives!" by G. Darley in *Building Design* (London), 14 November 1975; "Ralph Erskine" by M. Corominas and I. Castineira in *Jano Arquitectura* (Barcelona), March 1976; "Byker in Newcastle" by J. Gomez Morata in *Arquitectura* (Madrid), March/April 1976; "Romantic Pragmatism and Lyric Continuity" in *L'Architecture d'Aujourd'hui* (Paris), October 1976; special Erskine issue of *Bauen und Wohnen* (Zurich), January 1977; "Ralph Erskine, The Human Architect" by M. Egelius in *Architectural Design* (London), November/December 1977; "Children's Day Centre in Sandviken" in *Baumeister* (Munich), January 1978; "In Newcastle—Byker" in *Abitare* (Milan), December 1978.

After studying architecture at the Regent Street Polytechnic in London, Erskine moved to Sweden just before the war started in 1939. Sweden represented the idea of the new welfare state, with a new architecture to go with it, and was the Mecca for many architects at that time.

The "culture shock" of moving to Sweden and, perhaps, the physical shock of the northern climate, formed Erskine's architectural philosophy, based on a functional response to climate and related to social and political requirements. Erskine felt that "modern" architecture paid only lip-service to these fundamental ideals of the movement, and had got sidetracked by aesthetic and formal considerations. Face to face with the problems of building in Sweden, Erskine, in his arctic studies, attracted interest from countries with similar problems such as Canada and Russia. He evolved building types to take advantage of what sun there was, to keep out the arctic winds, and to control the snow drifts.

The northern perimeter of his sketch for an arctic town became a continuous wall-building, turning its back on the cold winds and opening out to the south. This wall-building has appeared in many of his projects since then, principally at Svappavaara in the Swedish north, Byker in the English north at Newcastle, in the Canadian township for Eskimoes and white Canadians at Resolute Bay, and to a lesser extent in other schemes. Apart from their functional appropriateness, these wall-buildings have given Erskine an opportunity to exercise his romantic inclinations—to have gateways through the wall and to decorate it on its northern face, where there are few windows, with brick murals as at Byker or bright coloured stained boarding as at Resolute Bay.

Too much emphasis should not be placed on the wall-buildings, however. Erskine has built tower blocks at Kiruna and Växjö, courtyard housing, factories, and single houses, and he has designed many town planning projects. The town plans have a casual, intimate and informal atmosphere on the ground, but, when examined, often reveal a strong backbone of geometrical regularity, planned groups with informal spaces between them.

One of Erskine's strongest held ideals is that of participation with the people who will use or live in his buildings. This goes beyond dealing with the client; it has been extended to making direct contact with the potential inhabitants of his housing schemes. Erskine feels that the professions have distanced themselves from the people they purport to serve and have erected barriers through using special professional language when plain language would be more sensible. Thus at the Byker housing scheme at Newcastle, Erskine set up his English office in a disused building in the middle of the housing area where tenants go to raise points about their accommodation and future tenants can see their housing being designed, after previous open discussion meetings. The Byker office has become something of a communal centre as well as being Erskine's office.

Byker is only one example of this principle at work. Erskine tries to make this special contact in all his work.

Erskine has designed some 80 projects, most of which have been built in collaboration with his partner Aage Rosenvold. Principal among these many varied buildings are the village at Storviks-Hammarby 1947; houses at Lisö (a dome house), Lidingö, Södertälje and Drottningholm; factories at Hammarby and Fors; housing schemes at Kiruna and Svappavaara (in sub-arctic Sweden), Tibro, Sandviken, and Newcastle-upon-Tyne, Newmarket and Milton Keynes in England; a school at Gyttorp; a post-graduate college at Cambridge; a housing township in North Canada at Resolute Bay; a ski hotel at Borgafjäll as well as an enclosed shopping centre at Lulež, both in North Sweden. These buildings show an early eclecticism and the development of a personal style, taking ideas from traditional building in Britain and Sweden but very much related also to the mainstream modern movement, a relationship sustained through Erskine's meetings with CIAM and Team 10.

—Peter Collymore

ERVI, Aarne (Adrian).
Finnish. Born Aarne Adrian Elers in Forssa, 19 May 1910; adopted the surname Ervi, 1935. Educated at the Helsingin Suomalainen Yhteiskoulu, Helsinki, 1930; Technical University of Helsinki, 1930–35, Dip.Arch. 1935. Married Naemi Inkeri Hanninen in 1935 (divorced, 1957); Rauni Maria Erika Luoma in 1957; children: Heikki, Heidi and Matti. Assistant Architect, City Building Office, Helsinki, 1934; worked in the office of Alvar Aalto, Helsinki, 1935, and Toivo Paatela, Helsinki, 1937; in private practice, Helsinki, 1938 until his death, 1977. Worked in the Standardization Department, Finnish Rebuilding Office, Helsinki, 1942–44; Director, Standardization Institute, Association of Finnish Architects (SAFA), 1942–45; Director, City Planning Office, Helsinki, 1965–68. Special Instructor, Central School of Arts and Crafts, Helsinki, 1937–38; Instructor, Technical University of Helsinki, 1943–46. Assistant Editor, *Arkkitehti,* Helsinki, 1937–43. Exhibition: *Finnish Building,* Helsinki, 1953. Recipient: First Prize, University of Helsinki Library Extension Competition, 1937; First Prize, University of Helsinki Building Institute Competition, 1949; First Prize, Tapiola Garden City Town Centre Competition, 1954. D.Tech.: Technische Hochschule, Stutt-

Aarne Ervi: Library, Turku University, Finland, 1952

gart, 1966; Honorary Professor, Finland, 1967. Honorary Fellow, American Institute of Architects, 1966. *Died* (in Helsinki) *26 September 1977.*

Works:

1931 Student Union Building alterations, Technical University, Helsinki (competition project; with Erkki Taimi)
1936 Temppeliaukio Church, Helsinki (competition project; with Toivo Paatela)
Plan for the centre of Tampere, Finland
1937 Heinolan Liike Oy Office Building, Heinola, Finland
Library extension, University of Helsinki
1938 Apartment building, Lauttasaarentie 9, Helsinki
Design of the *International Air Exhibition,* Helsinki
Cap factory, Kurikka, Finland
Karjala Insurance Company, Viipuri, Finland (competition project)
1939 Private house, Harjavalta, Finland
Kupittaa Park, Turku, Finland (competition project)
Small house design, for the Finnish Ministry of Agriculture
Church, Härmälä, Finland (competition project)
1940 Berger House, Inkoo, Finland
1941 Institute of Economics, Helsinki
1942/
 46 Oulujoki Oy Power Plants, and their housing areas, at Pyhäkoski, Jylhämä, Nuojua, and Pälli, Finland
1944 Rikkihappo Oy Housing Development, Harjavatta, Finland
1945 Secondary school, Kurikka, Finland
Secondary school, Kauniainen, Finland
1945/
 49 Regional master plan for Oulu, Finland (with Otto Meurman)
1947 Finland House (store and restaurant), New York
1947/
 53 Voimatalo Commercial and Office Building, Helsinki (with Tapani Nironen)
1949 Parish Centre, Lohja, Finland
City development plan for Helsinki (competition project)
1950 Ervi House, Kuusisaari, Helsinki
KOP Casino, Otaniemi, Espoo, Finland
1950/
 57 Helsinki University Institute, Porthania, Helsinki
1952 Secondary school, Lohja, Finland
Secondary school, Somero, Finland
1952/
 56 Library, Main Building, and Institute of Natural Sciences, Turku University, Finland
1952/
 64 Town centre, houses, apartments, and row housing, Tapiola Garden City, Espoo, Finland
1954 Himberg House, Helsinki
1955 Office building, Ruoholahdenkatu 8, Helsinki
1956 Hotel Management School, Helsinki
Keri Oy Stocking Manufacturing Company, Tornio, Finland
Secondary school, Urjala, Finland
1957 Furniture prototypes for the Merivaara Company, Finland
1958 Mannerheimintie Secondary School, Helsinki
1959 Secondary school, Voikka, Finland
Secondary school, Salo, Finland
Office building, Eerikinkatu 27, Helsinki
1960 Town Hall extension, Tampere, Finland
Cafe Töölönranta, Helsinki
1961 Atelier Ervi (extension to Ervi House), Kuusisaari, Helsinki
Apartment building, Mylltie 3, Helsinki
Rikkihappo Oy Chemical Factory, Kokkola, Finland

Oulujoki Oy Power Plant, Seitenoikea, Finland
Merivaara Factory, Kerava, Finland
Secondary school, Messukylä, Finland
Kauppa-Häme Commercial Building, Tampere, Finland
1962 Swimming Hall, Tapiola Garden City, Espoo, Finland
Apartment building, Vantaanpuisto, Vantaa, Finland
1963 Town Hall extension, Kemi, Finland
Terrace houses, Itaranta, Tapiola, Finland (with Heikki Koskeloand and Markus Tavio)
Rikkihappo Oy Chemical Factory, Uusikaupunki, Finland
1964 Swimming Hall, Kemi, Finland
M/S Finnhansa interiors, Helsinki
1965 *M/S Finnpartner* interiors, Helsinki
Heikintori Department Store, Tapiola Garden City, Espoo, Finland
1966 Municipal Office Building, Tampere, Finland
1967 Institute of Natural Sciences Building II, Turku University, Finland
1968 Töölö Library, Helsinki
1969 Kaleva Insurance Company Offices, Espoo, Finland
1970 Imatran Voima Oy Thermal Power Plant extension, Finland
1971 Housing development, Stuttgart (competition project)
Plan for Hanko Island, Uusikaupunki, Finland
1973 Swimming Hall, Salo, Finland
1974 Tapiola Garden Hotel, Espoo, Finland

Publications:

On ERVI: books—*Finnish Building,* exhibition catalogue, Helsinki 1953; *Esempi di Pianificiazione edilizia in Finlandia* by H. J. Becker and W. Schlote, Milan 1960; *New Finnish Architecture* by Egon Tempel, London 1968; *Aarne Ervi arkkitehtuuria* by Pentti Solla, Helsinki 1970 (includes bibliography); articles—"Nouveau Bâtiments de l'Université de Turku" in *L'Architecture d'Aujourd'hui* (Paris), vol. 31, no. 93, 1960/61; "Centre de Tapiola, Cité Satellite d'Helsinki" in *L'Architecture d'Aujourd'hui* (Paris), vol. 33, no. 101, 1962; "Terassenhaus, Tapiola" in *Architektur und Wohnform* (Stuttgart), vol. 75, no. 4, 1967; "Aarne Ervi: Ein Ritter der Alten Schule" by Pentti Solla in *Deutsche Bauzeitung* (Stuttgart), vol. 102, no. 9, 1968.

*   *   *

Among the small countries (in terms of population), Finland has made one of the richest contributions to the evolution of modern architecture and town planning, and Aarne Ervi, with Aalto and a few others, can be regarded as one of the authors of this achievement. He has designed power-stations and industrial and university buildings, but his crowning achievement has been as planner and architect at Tapiola.

Among his earlier works the University Library at Turku is distinctive. It is a long, squarish, fourstorey building with the two lower floors housing the book-stacks and the two upper floors the reading rooms, with vertical services to provide rapid supply of books. It is a reinforced concrete structure, and the broad simple massing, with ample fenestration of the upper floors, makes a very effective exterior.

Tapiola Garden City is one of the most beautiful small new towns in Europe. Ervi won the competition for its over-all plan and also for the design of its town centre. The site is a forest by the sea, seven miles west of Helsinki. It is flat in the centre surrounded by low hills, while in the forest there are large granite protuberances. Ervi took full advantage of these natural features in planning the town. He placed the centre in flattish land, and built three neighbourhoods to the east, north and west. These neighbourhoods, separated from the centre by forest belts, are mixed developments of tower and slab

blocks of flats with family houses, and all are grouped round gardens and childreńs' playgrounds. Particularly successful is the Western neighbourhood. It is approached from the town centre by a short paved footpath through the forest. The path rises on a rocky hill, and at the summit are tall white tower blocks among the dark pines, as if the granite protrusions were continued upwards. A little beyond, slab blocks enclose extensive gardens and childrens' playgrounds. Many of the granite boulders are used as garden features and as bases for sculpture.

Ervi was responsible for the design of the centre and of many of its buildings. In the middle of the area there was an old gravel pit, and it was converted to a 2½ acre square pool surrounded by buildings and gardens. Adjacent is the shopping centre, which is a complete pedestrian precinct approached by a broad flight of steps and enclosed on three sides by arcaded shops with a garden with trees in the centre. To the right of the approach is a tall 13 storey block; it gives a note of contrast to the general horizontality. A restaurant at the top provides views of the lovely surrounding country. This centre has a Greeklike quiescence that conveys a happy sense of peace.

Tapiola is necessarily a product of team work, but Ervi was the main planner and architect of its centre, and he necessarily set the style for much of the architecture of this lovely town. In the integration of architecture with scenery and natural features, Tapiola and the work of Ervi are unsurpassed.

—Arnold Whittick

ESHERICK, Joseph.
American. Born in Philadelphia, Pennsylvania, 28 December 1914. Educated at the University of Pennsylvania, Philadelphia, 1933 37, B.Arch. 1937. Served in the United States Navy, 1943–46. Married Rebecca Wood in 1939, children: Lisa, Joseph and Peter; married Ann Rowe in 1953; children: Maria and Julia. In private architectural practice, San Francisco, 1946–53; President, Joseph Esherick and Associates, San Francisco, 1953–72. Since 1972, President, Esherick Homsey Dodge and Davis, architects and planners, San Francisco (partners: George Homsey; Peter Dodge; Charles Davis). Instructor, 1952–56, Associate Professor, 1956–58, since 1958 Professor of Architecture, and since 1977 Chairman of the Department of Architecture, University of California, Berkeley. Secretary, Northern California Chapter, American Institute of Architects, 1959–60; Member, San Francisco Art Commission, 1959–69; Member, Architectural Advisory Committee, San Francisco Housing Authority, 1965; Jury Chairman, Nebraska Honor Awards, American Institute of Architects, 1975; Architectural Consultant to the United States Department of State on Foreign Buildings Operations, 1975–78; Member, Architectural Review Panel, United States Federal Reserve System, 1976–79. Recipient: American Institute of Architects Award, 1953, 1965, 1966, 1970, 1973; Graham Foundation Fellowship, 1962; Bay Area Honor Award, 1967; Homes for Better Living Award, 1966. Honorary Fellow, Adlai E. Stevenson College, University of California at Santa Cruz, 1968. Fellow, American Institute of Architects, 1965; Associate, National Academy of Design, 1976. Address: Esherick Homsey Dodge and Davis, 2789 25th Street, San Francisco, California 94110, U.S.A.

Works:

1940 Esherick House, Ross, California
1946 Holt House, Stockton, California
Guide Dogs for the Blind School, Marin County, California
Grill House, Oakland, California

Campbell House, Sacramento, California
Cahill House, San Francisco
Lewis House, Belvedere, California
1947 Smith House, Orinda, California
1948 Walker Summer House, Lake Tahoe, California
Revere Quality House Institute House, San Bruno, California
Metcalf Summer House, Lake Tahoe, California
McCoy House, Kentwoodlands, California
Kelham Summer House, Lake Tahoe, California
Huish House, Contra Costa County, California
Harrington House, San Joaquin County, California
Frohlick House, San Rafael, California
Bradley Summer House, Lake Tahoe, California
1949 Wiper House I, Sausalito, California
Smith House, Piedmont, California
Norton House, San Rafael, California
MacChesney House, San Rafael, California
Campbell House, Palo Alto, California
Brown House, Stockton, California
Albert Field Recreation Center, San Rafael, California
1950 Squaw Valley Ski Lodge and Facilities, Sun Valley, Idaho
Women's Athletic Club alterations, San Francisco
Rose House, Sausalito, California
Perry House, Sausalito, California
Wiper House II, Sausalito, California
Kimball House, Kentwoodlands, California
Gassman House, Palo Alto, California
American Home Company Houses, Sacramento, California
Alden House, Woodside, California
1951 Summers House, Hillsborough, California
Smith House, Orinda, California
San Rafael Fire Department alterations, California
Jurs House, Contra Costa County, California
Hellyer House, San Francisco
Goldman House, San Francisco
Gibson House, Sacramento, California
Dern House, San Mateo, California
1952 Starr House, Mission San Jose, California
Smith House, Happy Valley, California
W. N. Breeze Commercial Building, San Bruno, California
Borregard House, Oakland, California
Beardslee House, Stockton, California
1953 Pike House, San Mateo, California
Medical office building, San Francisco
Lezin House, Woodside, California
Eastman House, Woodside, California
Daly House, Eureka, California
Bewley House, San Joaquin, California
1954 Tobin House, Hillsborough, California
Pan American Airways Sales Office, Oakland, California
Bergin House, Kentwoodlands, California
Belvedere Land Co. Houses, Belvedere, California
1955 Wiley House, Belvedere, California
Weigel House, Bolinas, California
Teigland House, Orinda, California
Pan American Airways Sales Office, San Francisco
Pacific Overseas Showroom, San Francisco
Kelham House, San Francisco
Franck House, Woodside, California
Ecker House, Greenbrae, California
Buck Summer House, Lake Tahoe, California
Burman House, Kentfield, California
Atwater House, Sausalito, California
Ackerman House, Berkeley, California
1956 Svend Wohlert Showroom, San Francisco
Pelican Building, University of California, Berkeley

Gallo House, Livingston, California
Fisher-Harlow Co. Houses, Atherton, California
Bridge House, Belvedere, California
1957 Wieser House, Kentfield, California
Walker House, San Francisco
Hubbard House, Dover, Massachusetts
Holt Guest House, Stockton, California
Fisher House, Berkeley, California
Cappeller House, Woodland, California
Best House, Woodland, California
Baum House, San Francisco
1958 Lyon House, Berkeley, California
Kibbey House, Sacramento, California
Grant House, Hillsborough, California
1959 Martin House, Ross, California
1960 Y.M.C.A., Berkeley, California
Mantegani House, Belvedere, California
1961 Thompson House, Modesto, California
McIntyre House, Hillsborough, California
Heller House, Atherton, California
Hartzell House, Sonoma, California
Hamilton House, Atherton, California
Child Study Center, Berkeley, California
Cary House, Mill Valley, California
1962 Pan American Airways Ticket Office, San Francisco
McLeod House, Belvedere, California
Lowe House, San Francisco
Lehman House, San Francisco
Larsen House, San Francisco
Dennis House, Woodside, California
1963 Wheary House, San Francisco
Steffanides House, Piedmont, California
Roth House, Hawaii
Kesten House, Inverness, California
Joseph Esherick and Associates Office Building alterations, San Francisco
4 townhouses, Culebra Terrace, San Francisco
Burr House, Sunol, California
Botsford Office, San Francisco
Bermak House, Oakland, California
Bacci House, San Anselmo, California
1964 Management Science Laboratory, University of California, Berkeley
1965 7 demonstration houses, general store/restaurant and entry marker, The Sea Ranch, California
Kylling House, Live Oak, California
Wurster Hall: College of Environmental Design, University of California, Berkeley (with Vernon DeMars and Donald Olsen)
1966 Romano House, Kentwoodlands, California
Carlson House, The Sea Ranch, California
Oestreicher House, Sausalito, California
Longyear House, Sacramento, California
Hewlett House, Berkeley, California
Church of Christ the Saviour, San Francisco
1967 Very Very Terry Jerry Dress Shop, The Cannery, San Francisco
Splendiferous Dress Shop, The Cannery, San Francisco
Palo Alto Unitarian Church additions, Palo Alto, California
1968 Cahill House, Woodside, California
The Cannery, San Francisco
Mini-Mod I and II, The Sea Ranch, California
1973 Rounds House, The Sea Ranch, California
Botsford House, Los Altos Hills, California
Roscoe House, Walnut Creek, California
Coblentz House, Pajaro Dunes, California
Family Development Center, San Francisco
1975 Willoughby Vacation House, Sugar Bowl, California
1977 New Exhibits, San Francisco Zoological Gardens
Gallo House, Modesto, California

Publications:

By ESHERICK: books—*Hollein Peichl Architektur: Work in Progress,* exhibition catalogue, Vienna 1963; contributor to *Color in Architecture* by Tom Porter, New York 1976; *The Architect: Chapters in the History of the Profession,* with others, edited by Spiro Kostof, New York 1977; articles—"Graduate Programs, I: The University of California," with others, in *AIA Journal* (Washington, D.C.), September 1963; "Management Teamwork Ensures Better Design" in *Pacific Factory* (San Francisco), May 1965; "Some Notes on Wood Frame" in *Architecture Canada* (Toronto), December 1965; "Réalités et significations de l'architecture" in *Aujourd'hui: Art et Architecture* (Paris), January 1967; "A Laboratory to Facilitate Computer-Controlled Behavioral Experiments," with others, in *Administrative Science Quarterly* (New York), June 1969; "A Planned Campus: The University of California Santa Cruz Experiment" in *Architecture Canada* (Toronto), June/July 1969; "Highlands of American Architecture 1776–1976," with others, in *AIA Journal* (Washington, D.C.), July 1976.

On ESHERICK: books—*Architects on Architecture* by Paul Heyer, New York 1966, London 1967; *Global Interiors I,* edited by Yukio Futagawa, Tokyo 1971; *Observations on American Architecture* by Ivan Chermayeff, New York 1972; *Adhocism* by Charles Jencks and Nathan Silver, New York 1973; *The Place of Houses* by Charles Moore and others, New York 1974; *Dimensions* by Charles Moore, New York 1976; *Bay Area Houses,* edited by Sally Woodbridge, New York 1976; *Supermannerism: New Attitudes in Post Modern Architecture* by C. Ray Smith, New York 1977; articles—"Joseph Esherick: Theory and Practice" in *Western Architect and Engineer* (Portland, Oregon), December 1961; "Form Is What Things Are" in *Progressive Architecture* (New York), May 1964; "World Architects: Joseph Esherick" in *The Japan Architect* (Tokyo), March 1965; "A Building for People" in *California Monthly* (Berkeley), November 1965; "Aujourd'hui USA" in *Aujourd'hui: Art et Architecture* (Paris), January 1967; "The Use of Human Use" by Nathan Silver in *The Nation* (New York), 15 May 1967; "What the Architect Tried to Do" in *Architectural Forum* (New York), June 1968; "Focus: Grass Roots in American Architecture II" in *Toshi-Jutaku* (Tokyo), November 1968; "World Famous Architects: Joseph Esherick" in *Nikkei Architecture* (Tokyo), 21 March 1977; "A View of Contemporary World Architects" in *Architecture + Urbanism* (Tokyo), December 1977; "Evaluation: A Class Recycling after 11 Years" by James Burns in *AIA Journal* (Washington, D.C.), July 1978.

In architecture today a multitude of small voices is being raised to tell us that we are not on the right track, that we must go this way or that way. For the most part they are subjective and trivial, because they are concerned only with esthetics. They are part of a new cult of beauty for beauty's sake, at all costs and no matter how arrived at.

Beauty is a consequential thing, a byproduct of solving problems correctly. It is unreal as the goal. Preoccupation with esthetics leads to arbitrary design, to buildings which take a certain form because the designer "likes the way it looks." No successful architecture can be formulated on a generalized system of esthetics; it must be based on a way of life. We must decide what is alive and vital in our culture and approach each problem with this in mind. By approaching things subjectively and in a materialistic way we will never learn what things are. We need to know what things are, and what they are for. We need to discover realities and meanings.

Architecture is a process, a way of bringing together spoken and unspoken needs in relation to reality. I think we have been confusing the process with the end product. We have been thinking of the building instead of man living in space and using space. We have been concerning ourselves with expressions instead of realities.

Consider the often stated relationship between functionalism and the industrial process. The prewar buildings of the Bauhaus group and the postwar functionalist buildings in this country—Lever House, the Seagrams Building, Crown Zellerbach in San Francisco—are claimed to be expressions of the industrial approach, but in fact they represent merely a handcraft approach, the only change being that machines are used to do what otherwise would have been done by hand: a machine esthetic has been constructed, and while this has transient importance in indicating future possibilities, it is still an esthetic system and therefore a limiting thing.

The industrial process, for example, has nothing built into it that suggests a modular system. There are modular systems in certain related activities such as cataloging, distribution, shipping, and warehousing, but the industrial process itself can be as fluid as we want it to be. I would suggest a radically different concept of its application to architecture. Conceive the implications of an enormous, completely automatic factory that never produces the same thing twice. Today this is possible. If we will look beyond esthetics, we will find that tools are avilable to deal with particularity that did not previously exist.

I would suggest that a few sentences in the internal revenue code have far more effect today on the general physical form of our communities than all the architects in the country. The reason may be that we have lost sight of the total impact of our work. We have run out of steam on the big problems like urban ghettos, which can be created either by abandonment or by construction.

A scientific and systematic approach to the process of architecture has one radical difference from the majority of classical systems: it does not depend on broad general laws, but on the particular nature of each individual problem, so that everything can be considered for what it is and nothing need be relegated to arbitrary categories. With this it should be possible to move on to a plastic, free approach where our primary media are space, light and time—where the building itself disappears and we sense only space, light and time.

—Joseph Esherick

In an attempt to break with "dogmatic" tradition, including the formalism of the Bauhaus, Joseph Esherick has reverted to a utilitarian approach to design. Rejecting formal aesthetics and concepts of beauty, he pragmatically believes a building should not be judged by any arbitrary standards but only as good or bad in relation to its specific purpose. He rules out the associative functions of architecture as insignificant; he attempts to discover unique solutions to the problems of form and function.

Although sounding very mechanistic, Esherick retains a semblance of humanism and recognizes the need for ambiguity in architecture. The Cannery project in San Francisco, which gutted and transformed a Del Monte cannery into a shopping mall, well demonstrates Esherick's desire to create a rationalized irrationality. Its three-story interior and roof plaza feature a stimulating and delightful pedestrian space of many turns, zig-zags and corners, which offers the hint of a maze. While it is possible to go through the mall in a clear and obvious way, the option of "getting lost" also presents itself to the consumer. Ten means of vertical circulation, of which the most dramatic is a free-standing, glass-encased elevator, further contributes to the spatial experience.

Even the extremely brutalistic Wurster Hall, the environmental design building at the University of California, Berkeley, attempts to retain a sense of ambiguity. The utterly utilitarian building was described by *Architectural Forum* as a "wonderland of perhaps premeditated but evidently uncensored mechanical happenings." The plumbing, ventilation and electrical conduits remain exposed and the walls are either of dense, smooth concrete or resawn redwood plywood panels which serve as bulletin boards. Little effort seems to have been expended to meld the various shapes and forms, including a ten-story tower, into a coherent entity. The exterior window sill heights vary to accommodate the lighting needs of the rooms without reference to massing or alignment with adjoining windows. As such, the building stands as a testament to Esherick's belief that architecture should not attempt a series of compromises to resolve conflict but rather should preserve oppositions and tensions.

The majority of Esherick's residential designs tend to be simple and rather stark, vertically elongated, two-story boxes. Several are distinguished by pergola-like sun shading devices that project out above each window. This innovation supplants the function of the traditional roof with overhanging eaves. One of the more exciting dwellings designed by Esherick is the McIntyre House, which features a central living space covered by a skylight. The concrete beams that support the glass roof also serve as gutters in rainy weather. This solarium-like room opens on a terraced garden court with rectilinear pools and waterways. The house itself, which is extremely compartmental to provide privacy for the various family members, displays very sleek lines which evoke a Spanish mission spirit and unite the varying roofline elevations.

The work of Joseph Esherick displays an enormous diversity, as well it should if he has indeed forsaken the dictates of any universal laws of taste. By approaching all projects with a mental set devoid of preconceived appearances, he provides the design process with tremendous latitude. Whether Esherick's capacity to continually create original solutions can resist becoming in itself a dogmatic equation remains to be seen.

—Don J. Hibbard

Joseph Esherick: The Cannery, San Francisco, 1968

FATHY, Hassan.

Egyptian. Born in Egypt in 1899. In private practice, Cairo. Professor of Fine Arts and Head of the Architectural School, University of Cairo. Fellow, Adlai Stevenson Institute of International Affairs, Chicago. Recipient: National Prize for Arts and Letters, Cairo, 1969. Honorary Fellow, American Institute of Architects. Address: 4 Darb el Labbana, Citadel, Cairo, Egypt.

Works:

1937 Royal Society of Agriculture Building, Bathim, Egypt
1938 Prototype House, near Cairo
1945/
  48 New Town of Gourna, Egypt
1954 Village of Mit-el-Nasara rebuilding, Egypt
1966 Prototype Houses, El Dareeya, Saudi Arabia
1974 V.I.P. Mansion, Jedda, Saudi Arabia (project)
  Middle-Class House, Jedda, Saudi Arabia (project)

Publications:

By FATHY: books—*Gourna: A Tale of Two Villages,* Cairo 1969, as *Architecture for the Poor,* Chicago and London 1973; *The Arab House in the Urban Setting: Past, Present and Future,* London 1972; articles—"Beyond the Human Scale," interview with Yorick Blumenfeld, in *Architectural Association Quarterly* (London), no. 3/4, 1974; "Self-Help/Mud Building, Egypt" in *Architectural Design* (London), October 1976; "Gourna—Peasant Houses" in *L'Architecture d'Aujourd'hui* (Paris), February 1978.

On FATHY: articles—"Le Nouveau Village de Gourna" in *Architecture Francaise* (Paris), no. 73/74, 1947; "Model Houses for El Dareeya, Saudi Arabia" in *Ekistics* (Athens), March 1966; "Gourna: A Lesson in Basic Architecture" by J. M. Richards in *Architectural Review* (London), February 1970; "An Architect Whose Clients Are Peasants" in the *Christian Science Monitor* (Boston), 5 September 1974; "Designers of Human Settlements" in *Design and Environment* (New York), Spring 1976; "Hassan Fathy" in *L'Architecture d'Aujourd'hui* (Paris), February 1978.

Hassan Fathy is an Egyptian architect who has devoted himself to the task of housing the poor in developing nations. His work in a particular village in Egypt deserves the closest study by anyone involved in rural improvement.

The essense of his work and his approach in directing architectural planning to the needs of the poor are seen in the rural village of New Gourna, Egypt. It is located near Thebes and Luxor, on the eastern side of the Nile River near the famous Colossus of Memnon. The objective of New Gourna was to create an indigenous environment at a minimal

cost, and in so doing to improve the economy and the standard of living in a rural area. Fathy planned a complete village in all its parts, using the familiar forms of Egyptian village design. He also planned the construction method of these buildings: it, too, corresponded to local tradition. The main materials were to be mud brick formed on site—in exactly the same way that brick had been made since ancient times. The forms of the structures also derived from ancient experience: thick dense walls to absorb heat in daytime and to release it at night, and courtyards affording utility, openess, and privacy to both houses and communal buildings. Fathy also planned for the revival of ancient crafts.

In short, he devised a system for bringing together ancient design methods by using modern organizational skills. In so doing he integrated a knowledge of the socio-economic composition of rural Egyptian society, of ancient architectural and town design techniques, of climate, of public health considerations, and of ancient craft skills. Fathy saw New Gourna not as an end in itself but as an experiment whose lessons could inform a national rural redevelopment program.

New Gourna was built, but numerous problems, including a sluggish if not resistant bureaucracy, prevented full success. But, as built, in three construction seasons, from 1945 to 1948, it was a strikingly beautiful architectural and urban ensemble.

—Paul Spreiregen

FEHLING, Hermann.

German. Born in Hyeres, France, of German parents, in 1909; raised in Lubeck and Hamburg. Educated at the Baugewerkschule, Hamburg. Served in the German Army. In private practice, Berlin, 1946–53. In partnership with Daniel Gogel, *q.v.,* Berlin, since 1953. Recipient: Berlin Arts Prize, 1965. Honorary Professor, Technical University of Berlin, 1966. Member, Akademie der Künste, Berlin, 1961. Address (office): Margartenstrasse 4, 1000 Berlin 33, West Germany.

Works:

1951 Student Union, Free University of Berlin (with Peter Pfankuch)

With Daniel Gogel:

1956 Berlin Philharmonie (competition project)
1957 German Glass Industries Pavilion, and Hansaviertel Pavilion, *Interbau Exhibition,* Berlin
  Student Village, Nikolassee, Berlin
1960 R. Platte House, Dahlem, Berlin
1961 Paul-Gerhard Church, Schöneberg, Berlin
  St.-Norbert Church, Schöneberg, Berlin

1963 Haas und Sohn Administration Building, Sinn, Germany
  Hela Gerber House, Dahlem, Berlin
1964 Dr. Prawitz House, Gelnhausen, Germany
1965 Meeting Hall and Kindergarten, Paul-Gerhard Church, Schöneberg, Berlin
1967 Schatz House, Baden-Baden, Germany
1972 Hallesches Ufer Apartment Building, Berlin
  Cemetery chapel, Tegel, Berlin
1974 Institute for Hygiene and Medical Microbiology, Lichterfelde, Berlin
  Max Planck Institute for Educational Research, Dahlem, Berlin
1977 Student Union extension, Free University of Berlin
1978 Max Planck Astrophysics Institute, Garching, Munich

Publications:

On FEHLING/GOGEL: articles—"Fehling et Gogel: Projets Récentes" in *L'Architecture d'Aujourd'hui* (Paris), October 1967; "Max Planck Institute for Educational Research" in *Bauwelt* (Berlin), 14 October 1974; "Institute for Hygiene and Medical Microbiology" in *Bauwelt* (Berlin), 14 March 1975; "A Work of Art for Science" by Gerhard Ullmann in *Bouw* ('s Gravenhage), 5 June 1976; "The Max Planck Institute" by Hans Moldenschardt in *Der Architekt* (Stuttgart), June 1977; "Institute for Astrophysics in Garching, near Munich" in *Baumeister* (Munich), February 1978; "Contemporary Architects: Hermann Fehling and Daniel Gogel" in *Architecture + Urbanism* (Tokyo), August 1978.

The list of the buildings of Hermann Fehling and Daniel Gogel is not long. For, in their joint practice, each work is personally designed and drawn down to the smallest detail with a devotion and patience worthy of a medieval craftsman. Each work has a distinct personality; there is no trace of "international" match-making.

The apparently free forms of their architecture show slight traces of the potent graphics of Le Corbusier's white architecture, of the Luckhardt brothers, of the playful visions of Bruno Taut, and the "organic functionalism" of Hugo Häring. Superficially, therefore, Fehling and Gogel could be placed in a line of descent from Scharoun—I say "superficially" because their work is unmistakably their own and free from any fashionable or inherited attitudes.

Fehling and Gogel develop their designs principally from the ground plan. Because a building for them is a body that (like that of man) is not square as a matter of course, and because they feel that a building should have a face, an expression of its destiny, they arrive at impressive, plastic, extremely rhythmic spatial compositions. The buildings achieve their logic by means of a distinct, well composed, functional structure.

In two of their most expressive buildings—the Max Planck Institute for Educational Research and the Institute of Hygiene, both in Berlin—the distinct

Hermann Fehling and Daniel Gogel: Max Planck Institute for Educational Research, Dahlem, Berlin, 1974

order achieves harmony by the musicality of the free but not arbitrary spatial forms. It could be said that Fehling and Gogel's informing principle in these two buildings was this: "A building must be a pleasure to its users. When they are at work there, they should feel at home."

—Manfred Sack

FEHN, Sverre.

Norwegian. Born in Kongsberg, 14 August 1924. Educated at the Tønsberg Gymnasium; Oslo School of Architecture, Dip. Arch. 1948. Married Ingrid Løvberg Pettersen in 1952; son: Guy. In private practice, Oslo. Professor, Oslo School of Architecture, since 1970. Exhibitions: CIAM (Congrès Internationaux d'Architecture Moderne), Aix-en-Provence, France, 1953; *Bienal,* Sao Paulo, 1957; Vasa University, Finland, 1964; Galerie des Beaux-Arts, Paris, 1965; Museum of Modern Art, New York, 1968. Recipient: First Prize, Norwegian Pavilion Competition, for the *World's Fair,* Brussels, 1956; First Prize, Nordic Pavilion Competition, for the *Biennale,* Venice, 1958; Anton Christian Hougens

Award, Federation of Norwegian Architects, 1961, 1975; First Prize, Church of Cap Nord Competition, 1965; First Prize, Tønsberg Housing Competition, 1967; Wood Prize, Norwegian Concrete Association/Council for Tree Information, 1973; Concrete Prize, Federation of Norwegian Architects/Norwegian Concrete Association, 1976. Member, Order of Leopold, Belgium. Address (office): Nordraaks gt. 23, Oslo 2, Norway.

Works:

1953 Handicraft Museum, Lillehammer, Norway (with Geir Grung)
1955 Økern Home for Elderly People, Oslo (with Geir Grung)
1958 Norwegian Pavilion, *World's Fair,* Brussels
1962 Nordic Pavilion, *Biennale,* Venice
1964 Villa Schreiner, Langmyrgrenda 79, Oslo
      Villa Norrkøping, Sweden
1966 Villa Arne Sejersted Bodtker, Setra vei 18, Oslo
1967 Villa Carl Sejersted Bodtker, Setra vei 16, Oslo
1970 Bøler Community Center, Oslo
      Bøler Library, Oslo
1973 Archeological Museum, Hamar, Norway
1974 School for Deaf Children, Skadalsveien 33, Oslo

Publications:

By FEHN: articles—in *Byggekunst* (Oslo), March 1950, October 1951, May 1952, June 1952, April 1956, April 1958, April 1962, June 1962, May 1964, July 1968, August 1968, February 1971, April 1973, March 1975, and June 1978; *Arkitekten* (Helsinki), September 1954, August 1956, July 1966, and August 1966; *Byggmerstaren* (Stockholm), August 1958; *Architectural Design* (London), August 1958 and October 1963; *Domus* (Milan), no. 345, 1958, no. 424, 1965, no. 409, 1963, no. 461, 1968, and no. 481, 1969; *L'Architecture d'Aujourd'hui* (Paris), no. 27, 1960, no. 38, 1962, and no. 49, 1964; *Werk* (Zurich), July 1961; *Forum* (Amsterdam), November 1962; *Bauen und Wohnen* (Zurich), December 1964; *Deutsche Bauzeitung* (Stuttgart), January 1965.

On FEHN: books—*Esposizioni Esempi* by Roberto Aloi, Milan 1960; *The New Architecture of Europe* by G. E. Kidder-Smith, New York and London 1961; *Musei Architectura Technica* by Roberto Aloi, Milan 1962; *Intentions in Architecture* by C. Norberg Schulz, London 1963; *World Architecture I* and *II,* edited by John Donat, London 1964, 1965; *Decorative Art and Modern Interiors,* London 1979.

*

By walking through the wood, you made a path. The rhythm of your foot-prints are marks for the column's base. The path, indicating your adventures, is architecture written on earth. In this image we are all architects.

The materialized construction is the language of architecture, born by poetic thought. When constructions meet the earth, dimensions are born and the room is created.

No constructions have ever been more beautiful and great than those made around death—poems of life after death.

—Sverre Fehn

*

Sverre Fehn was one of the post-war generation of architects who emerged from the Oslo School with Norberg-Schulz, Grung, Mjelva, and Vesterlid. The influence of this generation on the post-war architecture in Norway was of the greatest importance. This group created a new architecture that was clearly based on the Modern Movement, but was expressed in a regional form both in the choice and use of materials and in the formal language. This renewal was essential to overcome the nationalistic tendencies of the immediate pre- and post-war periods which had resulted in an enfeebled aesthetic. The

Sverre Fehn: Nordic Pavilion, *Biennale,* Venice, 1962

group was closely involved with CIAM, *Carré Bleu,* and Team 10. While Norberg-Schulz is the outstanding theoretician, Fehn is without doubt the most gifted practitioner in the group.

The Handicraft Museum at Lillehammer of 1953 was a major event in Norwegian architecture. It established the new language. It was characterised by great clarity in form, organisation, and the use of materials. Twenty-five years later it is still an outstanding museum building.

Fehn has never been a dogmatist; his buildings have always had a human and poetic quality beyond and transforming the clear Modern Movement statement. This quality is perhaps most clearly revealed in his Nordic Pavilion at the Venice *Biennale* of 1962: the building, of the greatest simplicity, has also poetic qualities of light and subtleties of form.

Fehn has also explored the ideas of Japanese architecture in some deceptively simple timber houses. In the planning of these houses, he demonstrates a great sensitivity to the needs of the client, resulting in a refreshing freedom from the conventional plan. His recent work at Hamar (an archaeological museum) and in Oslo (a school for deaf children) continues to exhibit his bold and firm grasp of form and materials at the same time as he continues to explore new architectural language.

—Michael Lloyd

FEILDEN, Bernard (Melchior).

British. Born in London, 11 September 1919. Educated at Bedford School, 1927–37; worked in the office of O. P. Milne, architect, London, 1937–38; studied at the Bartlett School of Architecture, London (exhibitioner), 1938, and the Architectural Association School, London, 1946–49, Dip.A.A. (honours) 1949; awarded Bratt Colbram Travelling Scholarship, 1949. Served in the Royal Engineers, in India, the Middle East, and Italy, 1940–46: Captain. Married Ruth Bainbridge in 1949; children: Henry, Harriet, Mary, and Francis. Assistant in the office of J. Douglas Matthews, London, 1949–50, and E. Boardman and Son, Norwich, 1950–54; in private practice, Norwich, 1954–56; Partner, with David Mawson, Feilden and Mawson, Norwich, 1956–77. Architect, Norwich Cathedral, 1963–77; Surveyor to the Fabric, York Minster, 1965–77; Surveyor to St. Paul's Cathedral, London, 1969–77; Consultant Architect to the University of East Anglia, Norwich, 1969–77. Hoffman Wood Professor of Architecture, University of Leeds, 1973–74. Since 1977, Director of the International Centre for Conservation, Rome. Member of the Council, Royal Institute of British Architects, 1972–77; President, Ecclesiastical Architects and Surveyors Association, 1975–77, and Guild of Surveyors, 1976–77. Member of the Ancient Monuments Board of England since 1964. Recipient: Civic Trust Award, 1960, 1968; Architectural Heritage Year Award, and Royal Institute of Chartered Surveyors Conservation Award, 1975. Honorary doctor of the University of York, 1973. Associate, 1949, and Fellow, 1968, Royal Institute of British Architects; Fellow of the Society of Antiquaries, 1969, and of the Royal Society of Arts,

1973. O.B.E. (Officer, Order of the British Empire), 1969; C.B.E. (Commander, Order of the British Empire), 1976. Address: International Centre for Conservation, Via di San Michele 13, 00153 Rome, Italy.

Works:

1954 Trinity Presbyterian Church, Norwich
1955 North Transept Roof, Norwich Cathedral (conservation)
1956 Feilden and Mawson Offices, The Close, Norwich
1957 May and Baker Chemical Warehouses, Norwich
      F. W. Harmer Warehouse, Norwich
      Civic Trust Scheme, Magdalen Street, Norwich (project)
1958 May and Baker Warehouse, Dagenham, Essex
1959 Ambulatory Roof, Norwich Cathedral (conservation)
1960 South Transept Roof, Norwich Cathedral (conservation)
      Ethelberg Gateway, Norwich (conservation)
1961 Alysham Scheme, Norfolk (project)
1962 Heslington Hall and Kings Manor, University of York (conservation)
1963 Spire, Norwich Cathedral (conservation)
      The Village, University of East Anglia, Norwich (with David Luckhurst)
1964 Wessex Hotel, Winchester, Hampshire (with consultant Lord Esher)
      Raynham Hall, Norfolk (conservation)
1967 Tower and Bells, Wymonham Abbey, Norfolk (conservation)

Bernard Feilden: University of East Anglia, Norwich, 1970

1968 Tower, Norwich Cathedral (conservation)
St. Paul's School, Barnes, London (with Ray Thompson and Graham Keith)
Bauchim Chapel Screen, Norwich Cathedral
Bauchim Chapel Ceiling, Norwich Cathedral (conservation)
Bishop's Throne, Norwich Cathedral
Bell Hotel, Thetford, Norfolk (conservation and extension; with Mary Reader)

1969 Feilden and Mawson Offices, Riverside Road, Norwich (with Malcolm Rose)

1970 Nave Roof, Norwich Cathedral (conservation)
Teaching Hall, University of East Anglia, Norwich (with David Luckhurst)
Dining Halls, University of East Anglia (with Geoffrey Mitchell)
Chapel, University of East Anglia (with Simon Crosse)
Registry and Senate, University of East Anglia (with David Luckhurst)
The Square, University of East Anglia (with Geoffrey Mitchell)
The Broad, University of East Anglia (with Rosamunde Reich)
University of East Anglia Master Plan and Landscaping (with Maldwyn Morgan)
Science Block, Greshams School, Holt, Norfolk (with Graham Keith)
Barclays Bank, Swaffham, Norfolk (with Charles Carus)

1972 Watney Mann Brewery, Norwich (with Graham Keith)
Dining Halls, Greshams School, Holt, Norfolk (with Graham Keith)

1973 York Minster (conservation)
Nave Aisles, Norwich Cathedral

1975 Welcoming Area, Norwich Cathedral

1976 Chesterfield Town Centre Conservation Plan, Derbyshire (project)

1977 West Tower, St. Paul's Cathedral, London (restoration)
Doors, organ rebuilding, lighting, and choir cleaning, St. Paul's Cathedral, London (restoration)
West Front and Upper Close, Norwich Cathedral (landscaping)
Hyde Park Estate, London (as consultant)
St. Giles Cathedral, Edinburgh (as consultant)
Kitchens, Buckingham Palace, London (with Graham Keith)

Publications:

By FEILDEN: books—*The Wonder of York Minster,* York 1976; *Conservation of Historic Buildings,* London 1978; articles—"Training for Restoration" in *Architectural Review* (London), November 1970; "Saving York Minster" in *International Nickel* (London), 1970; "The Restoration of York Minster" in *Chartered Surveyor* (London), August 1974; "Vibration from Motor Traffic" in *European Heritage* (London), no. 2, 1974; "Training for Conservation: A European View," with Derek Linstrum, in *Architectural Review* (London), January 1975; "Craftsmen for Conservation" in *Quantity Surveyor* (London), January 1975; "The Storehouse of Tradition" in *Architectural Association Quarterly* (London), January/March 1975; "The Care of Cathedrals and

Churches" in *Royal Society of Arts Journal* (London), March 1975; "Feasibility Study for Setting Up Training Schools for Craftsmen in Venice" in *Council of Europe Pro Venetia Report,* Strasbourg 1977; "An Introduction to Conservation," report for Unesco, Paris 1978.

On FEILDEN: articles—"The Road to Rome: Bernard Feilden Takes Over as Director of the International Centre for the Preservation and Restoration of Cultural Property" by Vic Tapner in *Building Design* (London), July 1977; "The Conservation Brotherhood" by Vic Tapner in *Building Design* (London), October 1977.

*

I have believed in architecture but learned that it can be both good and bad. Architecture enables man to become human and should, therefore, be humane and not totalitarian. Architects should define what they mean by the word "Architecture." Through architecture man is enabled to fulfill his needs for living, working, leisure, social, cultural and spiritual activities. Architecture includes, by extension, town or city, the whole built environment. I have learned much from my work with amenity societies.

Architecture must be structurally stable, weatherproof, able to moderate the external climate to give internal comfort, be economical in scarce materials and metals, be durable and have low maintenance costs. Design should be for long life, flexibility, and low energy consumption. All this may seem simple common sense, but, with the exception of stability, modern technology in the last twenty-five years has not been outstandingly successful in solving the above problems, nor have designers understood buildings as unified spatial environmental systems. Historic buildings are a laboratory of experience.

I believe that to produce human architecture the architect must have a deep rooted empathy with the users of his buildings, a fellow feeling for their fears and hopes, and a responsible attitude to possible dangers. The practice of architecture is not for self-expression and nothing is less original than trying to be original. Design must have unity if the architect is to be an effective artist and the skilled men who carry out their work must have an appreciation of the artist's aims as well as job satisfaction in its execution—hence my deep interest in the state of the building craftsman and my writings on the subject, and my gratitude to them.

Conservation of historic buildings and a modern practice go hand in hand, as the latter proposes new techniques and the former teaches humility and old lessons if the building is understood as a spatial environmental system. In this work the architect must accept responsibility and not be afraid of decisions—some of which must be made quickly if men's lives are at stake, as I found in my work on the Spire at Norwich or in ordering the evacuation of San Michele twelve hours before a part fell. In conservation the architect is like a conductor—with the building as the musical score, and the building team as the orchestra.

To produce humane architecture that looks better ten years after it has been built has been the policy of my partnership who have nobly supported me in my major works of conservation, at Norwich, York, and St. Paul's.

—Bernard Feilden

Before his departure to head the International Centre for Conservation in Rome, Bernard Feilden's English architectural practice was devoted to both new building and conservation, reflecting his own interests and capabilities. Much more than that in most other countries, British architecture in the 1960's and '70s particularly centred on problems of combining new with old and making the best of the old (in the long run this attitude may produce one of the most interesting national architectures of the time). Feilden has been a leader in this movement.

Infill buildings in Norwich and on the Hyde Park Estate, London, are among the subtle works he directed. At the end of a terrace of historic houses, a new Feilden building might be a bold facsimile done with integrity, or a complementary contemporary one: he has ample self-confidence to rely on his personal judgement above rulebook principles to determine which course to follow, not unlike the bold eclectics of years ago. In conservation matters he recognizes that taste and discretion must combine with historical knowledge. That attitude makes a difference from the hack conservationism sometimes practised by official planners and design controllers; Feilden has had his battles with these experts but has usually won.

An able scholar and charismatic teacher, Feilden nevertheless deserves consideration mainly on the basis of his practice. His reliance upon judgement augmented with advanced scientific capability is like that of an updated Viollet-le-Duc. As appreciation of the useful life of historical architecture continues to grow, our pains to preserve the existing stock of buildings will have to increase, and we are probably only at the beginning of an endless interest in architectural conservation: any idea about continuity in the man-made world that excludes conservation is inconceivable. The kind of skill and insight Feilden has demonstrated is fundamental to architecture's immediate future. He must be reckoned a crucial exemplar in a national and now international sphere.

—Nathan Silver

FIGINI, Luigi.

Italian. Born in Milan, 27 January 1903. Educated at the Liceo Classico, Milan; School of Architecture, Milan Polytechnic, 1921–26, Dip.Arch. 1926. Served in the Italian Army, 1928. Married Teresa Bottinelli in 1935. Founder Member, with Guido Frette, Sebastiano Larco, Adalberto Libera, Gino Pollini, q.v., Carlo Enrico Rava and Giuseppe Terragni, q.v., Gruppo 7, Milan, 1927–29. Since 1929, in partnership with Gino Pollini, Milan. Member, MIAR (Movimento Italiano per l'Architettura Razionale), 1930–32, and Quadrante, Milan, 1933–35. Member of CIAM (Congrès Internationaux d'Architecture Moderne). Exhibitions: Rationalist Architecture Exhibition, Biennale, Monza, Italy, 1927; Triennale, Monza, 1930; Modern Architecture Exhibition, Museum of Modern Art, New York, 1931; Union des Artistes Modernes, Paris, 1932; IV CIAM, Athens, 1933; CIAM Pavilion, Triennale, Milan, 1933; Italian Aeronautical Exhibition, Milan, 1934; Triennale, Milan, 1936; VII CIAM, Bergamo, 1949; Italian Architecture, London, and toured the United Kingdom, 1952; The Modern Movement in Italy: Architecture and Design, Museum of Modern Art, New York, and toured the United States, 1953; Triennale, Milan, 1954; Mostra Documentaria dell' Architettura Sacra Italiana del Dopoguerra, Bologna, 1955; Triennale, Milan, 1960; Milano 70–70, Museo Poldi Pezzoli, Milan, 1971; Domus: 45 Anni de Architettura, Louvre, Paris, 1973; Il Razionalismo e l'Architettura Italiana durante il fascismo, Venice, 1976. Member, Accademia di San Luca, and the Accademia Tiberina. Address: Architetti Figini/Pollini, Via Manin 3, 20121 Milan, Italy.

Works:

1927 Garage (project; with Gruppo 7)
Casa del Dopolavoro (project; with Gruppo 7)
1930 Electric House, Triennale, Monza, Italy (with Gruppo 7)
1931 De Angeli-Frua Offices, Milan (with Gino Pollini and Luciano Baldessari)
Bar Craja, Milan (with Gino Pollini and Luciano Baldessari)
1933 Artist's House and Studio, Triennale, Milan (with Gino Pollini)
1934 Sala dei Precursori, Italian Aeronautical Exhibition, Milan (with Gino Pollini)
Figini House, Villaggio dei Giornalisti, Milan
Palazzo del Littorio, Mostra della Rivoluzione Fascista, Rome (competition project; with Gino Pollini, BBPR, and Luigi Danusso)
1934/
57 Olivetti Factory, Nursery School, Workers' Housing and Social Services Centre, Ivrea, Italy (with Gino Pollini)
1935 Plan for the New Town of Ivrea, Italy (with Gino Pollini)
1936 Living Room and Roof Garden, Triennale, Milan (with Gino Pollini)
Brera Academy, Milan (with Gino Pollini, Pietro Lingeri, and Giuseppe Terragni)
Master plan for the Val d'Aosta (with Gino Pollini, BBPR, Piero Bottoni and others)
1939 Sala del Volo, Milan (exhibition project; with Gino Pollini)
1942 Villa Manusardi, Cartabbia, Italy (with Gino Pollini)
1946 Master plan for the centre of Milan (with Gino Pollini, BBPR, Piero Bottoni, Franco Albini, and others)
1948 Apartment and Office Building, Via Broletto, Milan (with Gino Pollini)
1951 INA-CASA Housing Estate, Via Harar, Milan (with Gino Pollini and Gio Ponti)
1952 Plan for the Borgo Porto Conte, Sardinia (with Gino Pollini)
1954 Church of the Madonna of the Poor, Milan (with Gino Pollini)
1957 Apartment building, Via Circo, Milan (with Gino Pollini)
Hoepli Building, Milan (with Gino Pollini)
1963 Pozzi Ceramic Factory Industrial Complex, Sparanise, near Caserta, Italy (with Gino Pollini)
Church for the CEP Housing Scheme, near Bergamo (project; with Gino Pollini)
Hotel Largo Augusta, Milan (with Gino Pollini and C. Blasi)
1974 Villa Guida, Guanzate, Italy (with Gino Pollini)
1976 IACP Housing Development, S. Giuliano Milanese, Italy (with Gino Pollini and G. Marini)
1977 Church of Mater Ecclesiae, Rome (project; with Gino Pollini and G. Marini)

Publications:

By FIGINI: books—Il Piano Regolatore della Valle d'Aosta, with Gino Pollini, BBPR, Piero Bottoni and others, Ivrea, Italy 1943; L'Elemento Verde e l'Abitazione, Milan 1950; articles—"Architettura," with Gruppo 7, in Rassegna Italiana (Milan), December 1926; "Gli Stranieri," with Gruppo 7, in Rassegna Italiana (Milan), February 1927; "Impreparazione, Incomprensione, Pregiudizi," with Gruppo 7, in Rassegna Italiana (Milan), March 1927; "Una Nuova Epoca Arcaica," with Gruppo 7, in Rassegna Italiana (Milan), May 1927; "Un programma di Architettura," with Gino Pollini and others in Quadrante (Milan), May 1933; "Realazione al Progetto del Palazzo del Littorio," with Gino Pollini, BBPR, and Luigi Danusso, in Quadrante (Milan), August/September 1934. "Appunti per una Casa" in Quadrante (Milan), no. 33, 1936; "Diario Illustrato di Ibiza, Isla Blanca" in Domus (Milan), November 1951; "Origines de l'Architecture Moderne en Italie," with Gino Pollini, in L'Architecture d'Aujourd'hui (Paris), June 1952; "Comunicazione al Congresso Nazionale di Architettura Sacra" in Dieci Anni di Architettura Sacra in Italia, Bologna 1956; etc.

On FIGINI: books—Figini e Pollini by Eugenio Gentili, Milan 1959; Figini e Pollini by Cesare Blasi, Milan 1963 (includes bibliography).

Luigi Figini and Gino Pollini, exact contemporaries, both trained at the Polytechnic in Milan. With their junior by one year, Giuseppe Terragni, and four others, they founded the Gruppo 7, with which Italian "modern" or "rational" architecture begins in 1927, and showed a project in the first exhibition of Rationalist architecture at the Monza Biennale of that year. Their first important commission was the Electric House for the Monza Triennale of 1930, followed, in 1931, by their first industrial building, the De Angeli Frua Offices in Milan (with Luciano Baldessari). For the V Triennale in Milan in 1933 they designed an Artist's House and Studio: the studio looked on Marino Marini's first large horsemen. Like most Italian architects, in 1934 they entered the competition for the Palazzo Littorio in Rome (with Luigi Danusso and BBPR). They went on to design the new Brera Academy, with Pietro Lingeri and Giuseppe Terragni. Although by 1935 they were doing much domestic and exhibition work, as well as furniture, their most important next step was their collaboration with Adriano Olivetti for whom they designed the new Olivetti factory in Ivrea (first stage, 1934–35; second stage, 1939–41; third stage, with Annibale Fiocchi, 1947–49; fourth stage, 1956–57). They also built the nursery school there (1939–41), workers' housing (1940), projected (unbuilt) cafeteria (1940), and built the social services centre (1954–57).

Olivetti also promoted the regional development plan for the Valle d'Aosta, which Figini and Pollini ambitiously prepared with Piero Bottoni and BBPR in 1936. Its publication during the war was seen as a harbinger of post-war ideas. This was not the case,

Luigi Figini and Gino Pollini: Church of the Madonna of the Poor, Milan, 1954

and Olivetti's campaign for regional development in Italy has had little effect.

After the wartime hiatus their first important building was the flat/office block in the Via Broletto, Milan, a return to the pre-war elegance of their geometrical refinements. But perhaps their most influential single building is the small Church of the Madonna of the Poor in an industrial suburb of Milan: it transforms the geometries developed in industrial and office building to the needs of a suburban parish, in a new translation of the early Christian basilica. Another church, for the CEP Housing Scheme near Bergamo, adopts this approach less successfully to a much larger scale.

The general loss of direction Italian architecture suffered in the 1950's is reflected by their INA-CASA Housing Estate in Milan (with Gio Ponti) and in some other less happy housing blocks. The large ceramic factory for Pozzi at Sparanise near Caserta (Naples) has, however, much of the earlier assurance and inventiveness. In the last ten years most of Figini and Pollini's work has been in housing and office building in Milan.

—Joseph Rykwert

FILGUÉIRAS Lima, João.

Brazilian. Born in Rio de Janeiro, 10 January 1932. Educated at the Colegio Santa Catarina, Rio de Janeiro, 1939–43; Colegio Militar, Rio de Janeiro, 1943–49; Escola Militar, Aqulhas Negras, 1949; National Faculty of Architecture, University of Rio de Janeiro, 1950–55, Dip.Arch. 1955. Married Alda Rabello Cunha in 1960; children: Luciana, Adriana, and Sonia. Worked as a clerk in the Naval Ministry, Rio de Janeiro, 1949–50; Technical Designer, Arquitec Ltda., Rio de Janeiro, 1950–52; Technical Designer, 1952–55, and Architect, 1955–58, 1961–62, IAPB (Institute of Retirement and Pensions of Bankers), Rio de Janeiro; Managing Architect, Constructions Ltda., Brasilia, 1958–60; Executive Secretary, with Oscar Niemeyer, Planning Centre, University of Brasilia, 1962–65; worked in collaboration with Oscar Niemeyer, Brasilia, 1962–70; Head Architect, Department of Architecture, Projectum Ltda., Brasilia, 1970–71. Since 1971, in private practice, Brasilia. Coordinator of the Post-Graduate Course, Faculty of Architecture, University of Brasilia, 1962–65. Architectural Consultant, Hospital Foundation, Brasilia, 1969–72. Exhibitions: *Architecture Bienal*, Brasilia, 1969; *Bienal*, Sao Paulo, 1974. Address: SCRN Q-714, Block G-1 17/19, W-3-N Brasilia, Brazil.

Works:

1958 Temporary residence for IAPS employees, Brasilia
1960 Cesar Prates House, SHI, S-QL-1, Brasilia
1962 Staff Residence, University of Brasilia
      General Services Building, University of Brasilia
      Colina Housing Complex, University of Brasilia
1963 Faculty of Sciences, University of Brasilia (with Oscar Niemeyer)
1965 Volkswagen Factory, Brasilia
      Dishrave Headquarters, Brasilia
1966 Waldir Fonseca House, SHI, S-QL-1/8, Brasilia
1967 Public Libraries, Brasilia (with Oscar Niemeyer)
      Cultural Centre, Brasilia (with Oscar Niemeyer)
1968 Taguatinga Hospital, Brasilia
      National Congress Annex I, Brasilia (with Oscar Niemeyer)
1969 Aloysio Campos da Paz House, ML-1, Brasilia
1970 Ministry of Defence, Brasilia (with Oscar Niemeyer)
1971 Residence of the Minister of Planning, Brasilia
      Rabello Construction Building, Brasilia
1972 Tennis Academy, Brasilia
      Museum, Brasilia (with Oscar Niemeyer)
      National Congress Annex II, Brasilia (with Oscar Niemeyer)
      Assembly Hall, House of Deputies, Brasilia (with Oscar Niemeyer)
      João Machado House, Est. Tres Rios-Jacarepagua, Rio de Janeiro
1973 Rogério Ulissea House, SHI, S-QL-3, Brasilia
      Portobras Building, Brasilia
      Engine Rebuilding Plant, Brasilia
      DASP Training Centre, Brasilia
      Mercedes-Benz Factory, Brasilia
      Ford-Planalto Factory, Brasilia
1974 Church of Ascensão do Senhor, Salvador, Brazil
      Commercial Federation of Brasilia Headquarters, Brasilia

João Filguéiras Lima: Taguatinga Hospital, Brasilia, 1968

Comargo Correa Complex, Brasilia
Disbrave Building, Brasilia
Salvador Administration Centre Secretariat, Salvador, Brazil
Exhibition Centre, Salvador, Brazil
1975   José da Silva Netto House, S-1, Brasilia
Codipe Building, Public Utility Sector, Brasilia
Nivaldo Borges House, Mansion Sector, Brasilia
1976-   Hospital for Locomotor Diseases, Brasilia
1977   DAHER Surgical Clinic, Brasilia
Filguéiras Studio, SCRN 714, BGL 17/19, Brasilia
1979-   Research Centre for the Cerrado Regions, Brasilia
Mario Kertesz House, Pituba Beach, Salvador, Brazil
Eduardo Kertesz House, Mansion Sector Lake, Brasilia
Secretariat of Finance, for the Government of Bahia, Salvador, Brazil

Publications:

By FILGUÉIRAS: articles—"Block of Flats for the Teachers of the University of Brasilia" and "General Services Building of the University of Brasilia" in *Modulo* (Rio de Janeiro), no. 28, 1963; "Disbrave: Volkswagen Workshop" in *L'Oeil* (Lausanne), no. 184, 1970; "Church for the Administration Centre of Salvador, Exhibition Centre of Salvador, and Secretariat of the Administration Centre of Salvador" in *Architecture Review* (Rio de Janeiro), no. 7, 1974; "Church for the Centre of Salvador, Exhibition Centre of Salvador, and Centre of Administration of Salvador" in *Modulo* (Rio de Janeiro), no. 40, 1975; "Residence of José da Silva Netto" in *Modulo* (Rio

de Janeiro), no. 43, 1976; "Hospital of Taguatinga" in *Modulo* (Rio de Janeiro), no. 44, 1976; "Hospital Planning" in *Modulo* (Rio de Janeiro), no. 45, 1977; "Research Centre for the Cerrado Regions" in *Modulo* (Rio de Janeiro), no. 48, 1977; "Headquarters of Portobras" in *Modulo* (Rio de Janeiro), no. 52, 1978.

On FILGUÉIRAS: articles—"Les Progrès de Brasilia" by Francois Loyer in *L'Oeil* (Lausanne), no. 184, 1970; "A Arquitetura Brasileira ate hoje" by Italo Campofiorito in *Modulo* (Rio de Janeiro), no. 42, 1976.

*

One of the essential factors which enables me to exercise the liberty of creation and to guarantee a result that is architecturally valid is the comprehension of the process of construction from the initial phase of conception.

This does not simply mean that I must go into the chosen techniques in depth and that I must also search for sources of material and labour beyond those available.

What is demanded, above all, is a realization of the fact that the construction starts from a constant critical awareness of the social and technological context and the will to confront the distorted, unjust and predatory structures that man has instituted.

—João Filguéiras Lima

*

João Filguéiras Lima's work is of two co-existing kinds, differentiated from each other by the nature of the building methods employed. The first, of traditional construction, is marked by a strong expression of structural concrete and results in massive-looking architectural objects with compact and unitary volumes. Examples are the Exhibition Centre in Sal-

vador, the Portobras Building in Brasilia, and the houses for the Minister of Planning and José da Silva Netto, both in Brasilia. A certain reference to Oscar Niemeyer's latest work can be detected, the architect having collaborated with Niemeyer for quite a long time at the beginning of his career. However, unlike the master, it is not when employing free-flowing forms but when relying on the disciplinary support of the constructive units, which characterizes his second manner, that Filguéiras Lima is most successful. This second manner is important for its use and improvement of pre-fabrication methods. Pre-fabrication is not a common practice in Brazil, but Filguéiras Lima has obtained outstanding results with the formal and spatial qualities of his buildings.

At an early stage he worked on a concrete pre-fabrication system reminiscent of wooden construction—as in the General Services Building and, much more sophisticated, in the charming Colina Housing Complex at the University of Brasilia. Precise technology is vigorously displayed inside the flats as well as on the facades, and the very long spans, which give the buildings their lightness, are "conquered" by pre-stressed concrete beams attached to the pillars by steel pins.

More recently, Filguéiras Lima has been using a system of structural concrete boxes that form the load-bearing facades that support the floor-slabs. Despite the restrictions of such a repetitive vocabulary, the resulting mass, which expresses the demands of the different functions, has quite a variegated profile and suggests a discreet organic tendency. Two very important examples are the Taguatinga Hospital, near Brasilia, and the Salvador Administration Centre.

Because it stretches flatly over a large area, Taguatinga Hospital emphasizes the gentle slope of the site on which it is built and reaches out to the vast horizon in a way that is so typical of Brasilia. The building is composed of two blocks, tied together by towers for vertical circulation. The wards are in a long and echeloned building of structural concrete boxes. The ambulatory areas, surgical centre and other services are located in a low lying construction, lighted and ventilated by a "shed" roof of concrete "Y" beams. Both blocks can be extended at will without interfering with existing activities and without disrupting the appearance of the whole. Such "open-ended" aesthetics, clearly readable in the complex articulation of the mass, plus the subtle relationship of the building to the surrounding countryside, and the high quality of the technical solutions, make Taguatinga Hospital one of the most important recent projects on the Brazilian architectural scene.

The Salvador Administration Centre is placed on very uneven ground: it can only be reached "from the top." Respecting the existing topography, Filguéiras Lima designed seven long and narrow buildings that are mounted on "bridges" that follow the winding contour of the hill side. This system of construction on "bridges" is the same as that used for the ward block at Taguatinga: vertical circulation, auditoria, cafeterias and other special functions are enclosed in individual volumes attached to the office-block spines.

João Filguéiras Lima's most recent work, the Hospital for Locomotor Diseases in Brasilia, is distinguished by the use of Virendeel trusses, with octagonal openings that support and enclose the floors, which are in turn supported by eight powerful pylons containing the stairs and lifts. The functional solution is carefully thought out—Filguéiras Lima is a specialist in hospital building—and the wards, which open on two sides onto double-height "loggias" (reminiscent in disposition and elevation of Le Corbusier's first project for a house in Carthage), provide the patients with generous amounts of light, sun, and greenery.

—Jorge Czajkowski

FINTA, József.

Hungarian. Born in Kolozsvar, Cluj, Rumania, in 1935. Educated at the Budapest Technical University, graduated 1958; Master School of the Association of Hungarian Architects, Budapest, 1958–60. Since 1958, Member of the Staff of the Housing Planning Company, Budapest: currently, Head Architect. Recipient: First Prize, Salgótarján City Centre Plan Competition, 1963; First Prize, Danube-bank Competition, Budapest, 1966; Hungarian State Prize, 1970. Lives in Budapest.

Works:

1963- Master plan for Salgótarján, Hungary
1966 Shopping Centre, Salgótarján, Hungary
       Plan for reconstruction of hotels on the Danube-bank, Budapest
1969 Hotel Duna Intercontinental, Budapest
1971 Hotel Volga, Budapest
1972 Housing, Salgótarján, Hungary
1974 Hotel Bratislava, Pozsony, Czechoslovakia
1979 Hotel Voronyezs, Brno, Czechoslovakia

Publications:

By FINTA: books—*Blocks of Buildings,* Budapest 1970; *Hungarian Architecture,* with Jenö Szendröi, Budapest 1972; *Neue Architektur in Ungarn,* Budapest and Munich 1978; *Plans—Troubles—Thoughts,* Budapest 1978.

Along with Gyorgy Keves and Gyorgy Vadasz, József Finta is one of the middle generation of Hungarian architects who started working after the so-called period of socialist realism in Hungarian architecture in the 1950's had ended.

József Finta: Hotel Duna Intercontinental, Budapest, 1969

The first ten years of Finta's planning activity can be characterized as having involved a certain attraction towards some interesting, even unique, commissions, as well as towards the problems of city and settlement planning. He has taken part in several local competitions for the construction of housing estates and the reconstruction of city centers. He was awarded first prize in the competition for the rehabilitation of the downtown part of the Danube-bank on the Pest side of Budapest: this success helped him to obtain the commission for the Hotel Duna Intercontinental, completed in 1969. Finta's plan proposed the building up of the Pest riverside sector of the inner city by reconstructing the hotels, famous throughout Europe, that had once stood there but had been destroyed during the Second World War. As a result of winning another competition, he has also been working since 1963 on the reconstruction of the center of Salgótarján, an industrial and mining town in North Hungary. With two of his colleagues, he was awarded the State Prize in 1970 for this work. From their work within an unsettled and miserable mass of old mining colonies, we see a new vision of the city that could influence Hungarian planning: suitable utilization of natural potentialities; artistic ordering of buildings and squares; a humanistic sense of scale.

Although Fintz is still working on the plans for Salgótarján, he has, since 1966, that is since the commission of the Hotel Duna Intercontinental, been primarily involved with hotel planning. In 1970 he completed the plans for the Budapest Hotel Volga, a building with 700 rooms, constructed with concrete panels. This task turned his attention in a new direction and to a new set of problems; namely, the analysis of the contradictory relations between prefabricated construction based on standardized production and a construction based on compliance with special, functional and formal demands. The Hotel Volga, the Hotel Bratislava and, most recently, the Hotel Voronyezs have all been built from prefabricated ferro-concrete panels. With their chiselled exteriors and exciting interior constructions, these buildings effectively contradict the belief that buildings constructed of such materials can only be monotonous and boring.

—Anonymous

FISKER, Kay.

Danish. Born in Frederiksberg, 14 January 1893. Educated at Gustav Vermehren's School of Art, Copenhagen, 1909; and School of Architecture of the Academy of Fine Arts, Copenhagen, 1909–20, Dip.Arch. 1920; studied English housing legislation, London, 1919; travelled and studied in Italy, France, India, China and Japan, 1920–22. Editor, *Arkitekten* magazine, Copenhagen, 1919; Assistant to Edvard Thomsen, Academy of Fine Arts, Copenhagen, 1919–20; in private practice, Copenhagen, 1920–30; in partnership with C. F. Møller, Copenhagen, 1930–43; returned to private practice, 1944 until his death, 1965. Visiting Lecturer, Technical School, Helsinki, 1928; Professor of Architecture, Academy of Fine Arts, Copenhagen, from 1936, and Dean of the Architectural School, from 1941; Visiting Professor, Harvard Graduate School of Design, and Massachusetts Institute of Technology, Cambridge, 1952; Visiting Lecturer, Tulane University, New Orleans, and Georgia Institute of Technology, Atlanta, 1952; Visiting Lecturer, Royal Technical School, Stockholm, 1954; Visiting Professor, Massachusetts Institute of Technology, 1957. Chairman, Academic Architects Society, Copenhagen, 1937–42; Chairman of the School Committee, Academy of Fine Arts, Copenhagen, 1940; Member of the Council, State Building Research Institute, Copenhagen, 1946; Member of the Council, Society for Architectural History, Copenhagen, 1947; Member of the Council, Danish Architects National Association, 1952; Vice-President, Academic Council, Copenhagen, 1959. Exhibitions: Charlottenborg, Denmark, 1934 (one-man); Charlottenborg and Aarhus, Denmark, 1954 (one-man); *Interbau Exhibition*, Berlin, 1956. Recipient: City Council Prize, Copenhagen, 1923, 1927, 1928, 1929, 1934, 1941, 1942, 1953, 1960; Eckersberg Medal, Academy of Fine Arts, Copenhagen, 1928; First Prize, Aarhus University Competition, 1932; City Council Prize, Lyngby-Taarbaek, Denmark, 1946; C. F. Hansen Medal, Copenhagen, 1947. Member, Royal Academy for the Liberal Arts, Stockholm, 1936; Honorary Corresponding Member, Royal Institute of British Architects, 1946; Member, Royal Society of Arts, London, 1948; Extraordinary Member, Heinrich Tessenow Gesellschaft, Berlin, 1948; Honorary Member, Architectural League of New York, 1952; Honorary Fellow, American Institute of Architects, 1955; Extraordinary Member, Society of Architectural Historians, Philadelphia, 1960; Extraordinary Member, Akademie der Künste, Berlin, 1960. *Died* (in Copenhagen) *21 June 1965.*

Works:

1915 Railway stations, Almindingen-Gudhjem Railway, Denmark (with Aage Rafn)
1918 F. W. Friis House, Rønnebarallé, Snekkersten, Denmark
    Exhibition layouts for the Society for Art and Design, Liljevalchs Konsthall, Stockholm
    Kristiana Tivoli Circus Building, Oslo (project; with Carl Petersen)
1918/
21 Co-operative Building Society Housing, Borups Allé and Stefansgade, Copenhagen
1919 Race-course, Amager, Denmark (project)
1920 Holiday hotel, Solrød Strand, Denmark (project)
1920/
22 Hornbaekhus Co-operative Society Housing, Borups Allé, Aagade and Hornbaekgade, Copenhagen
1921 Handelsbanken Building, Rønne, Denmark
    Jantzens Hotel extension, Gudhjem, Denmark (project)
1922 2 single-family houses, Lundeskovvej, Hellerup, Denmark
1924 Jagtgaarden Housing, Jagtvejen, Copenhagen (with Christian Holst)
1924/
26 Amagerbo Housing, Englandsvej and Østerdalsgade, Copenhagen (with S. C. Larsen)

1925 Danish Exhibition Stands, *World's Fair*, Paris
1925/
27 Glaenøgaard Housing, Vognmandsmarken, Copenhagen
1926/
27 Brigadegaarden Housing, Brigadevej, Copenhagen (with S. C. Larsen)
1927 Gullofshus Housing, Artillerivej and Gullofsgade, Copenhagen
1928 Richard von Hauen House, Hellebak, Denmark
1929/
32 Østergaarden Housing, Vognmandsmarken, Copenhagen
1930 Housing, Herman Triers Plads, Copenhagen
    Single-family house, Egehøj 4, Ordrup, Denmark
    Single-family house, Exnersvej 44, Ordrup, Denmark
    Single-family house, Schimmelmannsvej 47, Klampenborg, Denmark
    Jarner Summer House, Jonstrup Hegn, Hellerup, Denmark
    Single-family house, Damstien 27, Vanløse, Denmark
    Single-family house, Frølichsveg 17, Ordrup, Denmark
    Housing, Vodroffsvej 2–4, Copenhagen
1930/
32 Housing, Aaboulevarden and Rosenørns Allé, Copenhagen
1931 Nürnberggaarden Housing, Nürnberggade, Copenhagen
    Single-family house, Bispebjerg Parkallé 29, Copenhagen
    Tagensgaard Housing, Tagensvej, Copenhagen
1932 District Hospital, Aarhus, Denmark
    Radium Centre, Aarhus, Denmark
1932/
45 Aarhus University, Denmark (with Pøul Stegmann until 1937; with C. F. Møller until 1945)
1933 Housing, Grøndals Parkvej and Gudenaavej, Copenhagen
    Fisker Summer House, Udsholt Strand, Denmark
    Single-family house conversion, Kildeskovvej 50, Hellerup, Denmark
    Single-family house, Fyrrehøj 11, Gentofte, Denmark
    Single-family house, Skolevangen, Aarhus, Denmark
    Single-family house, Gardevej, Aarhus, Denmark

Housing, Marselis Boulevard, Aarhus, Denmark
Commemorative Park Buildings, Aarhus, Denmark
Corn-Silo, Vejle Harbour, Aarhus, Denmark
1934 Housing, Godthaabsvej and Grøndals Parkvej, Copenhagen
    Otto Summer House, Ramløse Strand, Frederiksvaerk, Denmark
    Radium Centre, Strandboulevarden, Copenhagen
    Sandberg Summer House, Løkken, Aarhus, Denmark
    Natural History Museum, Aarhus University, Denmark
    Summer House, Vejlby Fed, Aarhus, Denmark
    Housing, Skovvej, Aarhus, Denmark
    A/S Jernkontoret Office Building, Aarhus, Denmark
    Housing, Aalborggade, Aarhus, Denmark
1935 State School, Vordingborg, Denmark (project)
    Golf Clubhouse, Skaade Bakker, Aarhus, Denmark
    Summer House, Abeltoft Vig, Mols, Denmark
    Kolding Amts og Bys Sygehus Hospital conversion and extensions, Copenhagen (with Ernst Petersen)
    Jutland Trade and Agricultural Bank, Riisskov, Aarhus, Denmark
    Finsen Institute conversion and extensions, Strandboulevarden, Copenhagen
    Single-family house, Skovgaardsvej 11, Charlottenlund, Denmark
    Vestersøhus I Housing, Vester Søgade, Copenhagen
1936 *M/S Hammershus* ship interiors
    Hotel, Rønne, Denmark (project)
    Vintersbølle Children's Sanatorium, Vordingborg, Denmark
    Albani Hotel, Odense, Denmark (project; with Viggo Jacobsen)
    M/S Kronprins Olav ship interiors
    Ship interiors for the East Asiatic Company (projects)
1937 Hegnshusene Terraced Housing, Brønshøjvej, Copenhagen (with Erik Jensen)
    M/S Frem ship interiors
1938 *M/S Hans Broge* ship interiors
    M/S C. F. Tietgen ship interiors
    Vestersøhus II Housing, Vester Søgade, Copenhagen
1939 Hotel Richmond, Copenhagen (project)
    M/S Rotna ship interiors

Kay Fisker: Aarhus University, Denmark, 1932–45

Housing, Griffenfeldsgade 37–39, Copenhagen (with Eske Kristensen)
Vestersøhus III Office Building, Vester Søgade, Copenhagen (project)
Hillerødsholm Housing, Hillerød, Denmark
Town Hall conversion, Mariager, Denmark
M/S Kronprins Frederik ship interiors

1939/
44 Stefansgaarden Housing, Stefansgade, Copenhagen (with Eske Kristensen)
1941 Movable pre-fabricated houses
State Youth Camp, Avdebo, Denmark
Monastery Work-Supervisors' Housing, Vitskol, Denmark
State Youth Camp Work-Supervisors' Housing, Asserbo, Denmark
Shipbuilding Works extensions and conversions, Helsingør, Denmark

1941/
56 Ny Søndergaard Apartment Blocks and Terraced Housing, Vangedevej, Copenhagen (with Eske Kristensen)
1942 Housing, Dronningens Tvaergade and Adelgade, Copenhagen (with Eske Kristensen)
Doctor's House, Helsinge, Denmark
1943 Vintersbølle Children's Sanatorium extensions I and II, Vordingborg, Denmark
Egeparken Terraced Housing, Bredevej and Lindevangen, Lyngby, Denmark
Book designs for Nyt Nordisk Forlag, Copenhagen
Fogedgaarden Old People's Housing, Copenhagen
Sandmose Camp, Denmark (project)
Housing, Lystoftevej, Lyngby, Denmark (with Viggo Møller-Jensen)
Broparken Housing, Lyngvyvej and Brogaardsvej, Gentofte, Denmark
1944 Housing, Aaboulevarden and Blaagaardsgade, Copenhagen (project)
Brøndbyøster Town Plan, Denmark (with M. Askjar Ravn)
Svanholm Estate Farmworkers' Housing, Hornsherred, Denmark
Beringparken Housing, Køgevej, Copenhagen
1945 Hotel, Køge, Denmark (project)
Lundehøjgaard Soldiers' Home, Høvelte Camp, Denmark
Voldparken Housing and School, Husum, Denmark
1946 Villa Højstrup conversion and extension, Strandvejen 257, Copenhagen (project)
1947 Single-family house conversion, Nyelandsvej 115, Copenhagen
M/S Kronprinsesse Ingrid ship interiors
M/S Kronprins Frederik ship interior conversion
1948 Plan for the pedestal and installation of King Christian X Statue, Bispetvorvet, Aarhus, Denmark
1949 Catholic Grammar School, Strandvejen, Copenhagen (project)
Lundehøjgaard Soldiers' Home II, Høvelte Camp, Denmark
1950 *M/S Kongedybet* ship interiors
1951 Nygaardsparken Housing and Shopping Centre, Brøndbyøster, Denmark
Praestekaershave Housing, Frederikssundsvej and Praestekaersvej, Copenhagen
Scho Factory conversion and extensions, Copenhagen
1954 Housing, Dronningens Tvaergade, Copenhagen (with Eske Kristensen)
M/S C. F. Tietgen ship interiors
M/S Hans Broge ship interiors
Brondbyoster School, Brondbyerne, Denmark
1955 National Council for Unmarried Mothers Administration Building and Home, Strandboulevarden, Copenhagen
Housing, Dronningens Tvaergade and Borgergade, Copenhagen (with Eske Kristensen)

1956/
57 Interbau Housing, Hansaviertel, Berlin
Mogens Schubart House, Solbakken 17, Virum, Denmark
1957 Soldiers' Home, Troldevej, Fredericia, Denmark
1958 Hans Buus House, Skovmindevej 1, Holte, Denmark
Egmontgaarden College for Single Mothers, Faaborggade, Copenhagen (with Robert Duelund Mortensen)
1959 Nygaard School, Roskildevej, Brøndbyøster, Denmark (with Robert Duelund Mortensen)
Nygaardsparken Children's Home, Brøndbyøster, Denmark (with Robert Duelund Mortensen)
Commercial and Residential Building, Østervold, Randers, Denmark (with Robert Duelund Mortensen)
1960 Beringgaarden Housing Development and Shopping Centre, Køgevej, Copenhagen (with Robert Duelund Mortensen)
Multi-storey development, Backa, Göteborg, Denmark (with Robert Duelund Mortensen)

Publications:

By FISKER: books—*Modern Danish Architecture,* with F. R. Yerbury, London 1927; *Kobenhavnske Boligtyper,* with others, Copenhagen 1936; *Danish Architectural Drawings of All Periods,* with others, Copenhagen 1947; *Den Funktionelle Tradition,* Copenhagen 1950; *Danske Arkitekturstromninger 1850–1950,* Copenhagen 1951; *Danish Architectural Drawings,* with C. Elling, Copenhagen 1961; articles—numerous in *Arkitekten* (Copenhagen), 1917–60; "The Danish House" in *Berlingske Tidende* (Copenhagen), vol. 27, no. 1, 1942; "Better Dwellings" in *Berlingske Tidende* (Copenhagen), vol. 31, no. 3, 1942; "Gunnar Asplund and Scandinavian Architecture" in *Svenska Dagbladet* (Stockholm), vol. 10, no. 9, 1942; "The History of Domestic Architecture in Denmark" in *Architectural Review* (London), November 1948; "The Development of Architecture in Denmark" in *L'Architecture d'Aujourd'hui* (Paris), June 1949; "The Moral of Functionalism" in *Magazine of Art* (New York), February 1950.

On FISKER: books—*The New Architecture* by Gregor Paulsson, Copenhagen 1920; *Nordic Calendar,* Copenhagen 1934; *Denmark's Building Culture* by Harald Langberg, Copenhagen 1955; *Arkitekten Kay Fisker* by Hans Erling Langkilde, Copenhagen 1960; articles—numerous in *Arkitekten* (Copenhagen) from 1915; "U.S.A. Exhibition" in *AIA Journal* (Washington, D.C.), June 1958; "Bay Region—stilens ophavsmaend" in *Arkitekten* (Copenhagen), January 1962; "Kay Fisker—70 Years," special issue of *Arkitekten* (Copenhagen), February 1963; "Den Klintske Skole," special issue of *Arkitekten* (Copenhagen), April 1963.

Kay Fisker was a traditionalist who resolutely refused to be drawn into the Modern Movement and even, in his early days, set up a group in opposition to it. Afterwards he took the lead in establishing the high standards of modern Danish housing which became the admiration of the world. Having worked in the offices of Asplund and Lewerentz, he had an approach that was essentially human, and he was a keen follower of Voysey, Baillie-Scott, and the English planners.

In partnership with Pøul Stegmann and C. F. Møller, Fisker won the competition for Aarhus University. The partnership broke up, and Møller completed the project alone. Fisker, however, was responsible for the large Institute of Chemistry, Physics and Anatomy. Here the architects demonstrated their opposition to the "new efficiency" of functionalism by designing a building that was a frank develop-

ment of mediaeval brick tradition. Strong material unity combines with simplicity and clarity. The university site is in undulating parkland, and the whole conception is devoid of pomposity or even formality. Unity of composition is maintained by siting all primary building groups to run north-south and secondary groups east-west. Added cohesion is provided by maintaining the same steep angle of the tiled roofs which are designed without eaves. Many of the details of these buildings became part of the grammar of late modern Danish architecture.

Kay Fisker was largely responsible for the introduction of projecting but partly recessed balconies, coupled with informal fenestration, in Danish housing. These features are illustrated in the main facade of the Vestersøhus Flats in Copenhagen, built with C. F. Møller in 1935–39. The Vestersøhus, completed in two stages, has 264 flats; a third stage was abandoned because of the war.

Another large development, Voldparken, at Husum, near Copenhagen, includes a notable school with classrooms giving on to courtyards. The Voldparken flats include six seven-storey blocks, but the majority of the blocks are three-storey with lower buildings for shops, garages, and a recreation centre. The tiled roofs with projecting eaves are rather heavy. The layout of the blocks shows the beginning of the fashion of dividing very large residential districts into smaller groups of blocks, which, with varying design in the blocks themselves, helps to avoid monotony. There are, in all, 1075 flats.

Kay Fisker also designed a number of distinguished ship interiors. Outstanding among them was that of the DFDS Company's *Kronprinsesse Ingrid* (1947) for the Harwich-Esbjerg service.

—Gontran Goulden

FORD, O'Neil.

American. Born in Pink Hill, Texas, 3 December 1905. Educated at North Texas State University, Denton, 1924–26. Served in the United States Army Air Force, 1942–45. Married Wanda Graham in 1940; children: Wanda, Michael, John, and Linda. Draftsman, David R. Williams, Dallas; 1926–32; in private practice, Dallas, 1932–34; Chief Architect, Rural Rehabilitation Association, in East Texas and Georgia, 1934–36; Partner, with A. B. Swank, Ford and Swank, Dallas, 1936–39, and with Jerry Rogers, Ford and Rogers, San Antonio, Texas, 1939–53; Principal, O'Neil Ford and Associates, San Antonio, 1953–65. Since 1965, Partner, with Boone Powell and Chris Carson, Ford, Powell and Carson, San Antonio. Consultant to the United States Corps of Engineers, since 1967. Visiting Professor, Harvard University, Cambridge, Massachusetts, 1953; Ward-Lucas Lecturer, Carleton College, Northfield, Minnesota, 1971; Visiting Professor, University of Texas at Austin, 1974. Member, National Council on the Arts, 1968–74. Recipient: Thomas Jefferson Award, University of Virginia, Charlottesville, 1967; Pitts Award, Texas Society of Architects, 1978. D.F.A.: Trinity University, San Antonio, 1968; Skidmore College, Saratoga Springs, New York, 1978; D.H.L.: Southern Methodist University, Dallas, 1970; University of Dallas, 1976. Fellow, American Institute of Architects, 1960. Honorary Fellow, Sociedad Arquitectos Mexicano, 1975. Address: Ford, Powell and Carson, 528 King William Street, San Antonio, Texas 78204, U.S.A.

Works:

1949- Trinity University, San Antonio (with Bartlett Cocke and Associates)
1956/
59 Library, Science Building, Planetarium, and Gymnasium, St. Mark's School, Dallas

O'Neil Ford: Laurie Auditorium, Trinity University, San Antonio, 1949

1956- Pan American School, Kingsville, Texas
1959 Texas Instruments Laboratory and Plant, Houston (with Colley and Tamminga)
1960 Texas Instruments Factory, Bedford, England (with Richard Colley)
1960/
65 Science Building, Dining Hall, and Library, Greenhill School, Dallas
1962- New campus of Skidmore College, Saratoga Springs, New York
1963 Carter House, Tulsa, Oklahoma
Commercial development plan for San Antonio (with Allison B. Peery)
Science and Mathematics Quadrangle, St. Mark's School, Dallas (with Sam Zisman)
1964/
76 Selwyn School, Denton, Texas
1965 Design of *Hemisfair*, San Antonio
1965/
72 New Graduate Center, Lecture Hall, College Tower, Gymnasium, and College Center, University of Dallas (with Duane Landry Associates)
1966 Printing plant, St. Gallen, Switzerland
1966/
69 St. Mary's Hall (school), San Antonio (with Bartlett Cocke Associates)
1967 Steves House, San Antonio
1967/
68 Tower of the Americas, San Antonio
1967- Holland Hall (school), Tulsa, Oklahoma (with H. B. Bernard)

1968 Texas Instruments Building, Dallas (with Richard Colley)
1970 Hotel, Lima, Peru
1970/
74 Plan for a resort community at Lake Texoma, Texas
1974/
78 Master plan, Humanities Building, Art Building, Science Building, Library and Field House, University of Texas at San Antonio (with Bartlett Cocke Associates)
1977- Information center and office buildings, Riyadh, Saudi Arabia
Oakwell Farms (housing, offices, shops), San Antonio
Plaza Nacional Hotel, San Antonio
Hyatt Regency Hotel, San Antonio
1978 Texas House, Mission Trace, San Antonio
1978- Chamber Music Hall, Vienna, Virginia
Bexar County Office Building, San Antonio
Glen Lakes Center (hotel, office buildings, shops), Dallas
San Fernando Cathedral restoration, San Antonio
Wulff House restoration, San Antonio
Moody Building restoration and additions, Galveston, Texas
Blum Building restoration, Galveston, Texas
Whiteside House restoration, Galveston, Texas
St. Paul's Square (neighborhood commercial buildings) restoration, San Antonio

Hicks House restoration and additions, Bandera, Texas
Alamo National Bank rehabilitation, San Antonio
Stockman's Restaurant rehabilitation and additions, San Antonio

Publications:

On FORD: articles—"Laurie Auditorium, Trinity University: Art for Art's Sake" in *Texas Architect* (Austin), September/October 1973; " 'Landmark' Ford: Nation's Leading Architect" by Wolf Von Eckardt in the *Washington Post,* 24 April 1976; article in *Building Design* (London), 5 November 1976; "Interview: O'Neil Ford" by Larry Paul Fuller in *Texas Architect* (Austin), May/June 1978; "Doing What Comes Naturally" by Michael Ennis in *Texas Monthly* (Austin), June 1978; "Built Especially for Texas" by Philip Morris in *Southern Living* (Birmingham, Alabama), November 1978.

Fame, international acclaim, and an influential architecture are concerns that occupy the least of O'Neil Ford's time. Yet he has had a good deal of public exposure for *Hemisfair* in 1965 and for his work at Trinity University, both in San Antonio, Texas. Various articles have recently sung his praises as one of the nation's best unknown architects. And, until recently, his schedule has been filled with lectures to various organizations across the country. Why, then, isn't he better known?

The answer can be found in his architecture. It could be called vernacular, and America does not aspire to vernacular architecture. Though the problems of energy shortages are changing this situation, most architects are still seekers after the avant-garde. Ford doesn't even join the competition. Nor is he interested. As well, his work doesn't cry out for attention, which is what it would have to do to be heard above the noise in America today. It is, instead, quiet, low-key, and comfortable. Most often his interiors are detailed by craftsman—up until his recent death, by Ford's brother Lynn. Ford's willingness to consider as many ideas and opinions as possible reflects his effort to achieve a total design, not unlike that of Eliel Saarinen. And—as, for example, in one of his most recent works, at Skidmore College in New York—the user's needs and the environmental requirements are successfully resolved in a humane, non-pretentious design.

Bricks, glass (in moderate amounts), wood, and stone are Ford's principal building materials. Rooted in the requirements of a region of America known for its torrid summers and miserable cold winters, his designs have one attribute above all others—good common sense. Few people can claim such simplicity of approach, and few can claim to have adhered to such a credo and succeeded. It is simplicity that returned San Fernando Cathedral, in San Antonio, to its original elegance.

Ford has also made important contributions in planning and preservation. Preservation, which was an unheard of endeavor just a few years back, is one of Ford's priorities. His exemplary work in Texas has helped to make preservation/restoration a viable alternative to the destructiveness of "urban renewal."

Ford has been around for nearly 40 years, and he continues to practice "common sense architecture." (He will preach it too, but be prepared for his brash Texas charm. You won't know what hit you.) Many people have missed and will continue to overlook his accomplishments by labelling his work as "regional" or "vernacular" or merely "Texana." And the American public, and many of its architects, are quick, too quick, to criticize when the architect doesn't shine, shout and/or intellectualize. Ford is too modest and too busy to bother defending himself. It is up to the public to educate itself.

There is no need to be hesitant about making firm predictions about his reputation in the future. Ford will be known and admired in ever growing circles, both within the United States and without.

—Logan Cravens

FOSTER, Norman (Robert).

British. Born in Manchester, 1 June 1935. Educated at the University of Manchester School of Architecture and Department of Town and Country Planning, 1956–61 (Builders' Association Scholarship; Royal Institute of British Architects Silver Medal; Heywood Medal; Manchester Society of Architects Bronze Medal), Diploma in Architecture and Certificate of Town Planning 1961; Yale University School of Architecture, New Haven, Connecticut, 1961–62 (Henry Fellowship), M.Arch. 1962. Served in the Royal Air Force, 1953–55. Married Wendy Cheeseman in 1964; children: Ti and Cal. Partner, with Wendy Foster and Richard Rogers, Team 4, London, 1963–67. Since 1967, Partner, Foster Associates, London (associates: Loren Butt; Chubby S. Chaabra; Spencer de Grey; Roy Fleetwood; Birkin Haward; James Meller; Frank Peacock; Graham Phillips; Mark Robertson). Exhibitions: Heinz Gallery, Royal Institute of British Architects, London, 1979; *Transformations in Modern Architecture,* Museum of Modern Art, New York, 1979. Recipient: Project Award, *Architectural Design,* 1964, 1965, 1966, 1969; Industrial Architecture Award, *Finan-cial Times,* 1967, 1974; Royal Institute of British Architects Award, 1969, 1972, 1977, 1978; Structural Steel Award, 1972, 1978; Business and Industry Award, 1976; International Prize for Architecture, 1976; Reynolds Memorial Award, American Institute of Architects, 1976, 1979. Fellow of the Society of Industrial Architects; Associate of the Royal Institute of British Architects. Address: Foster Associates, 12–16 Fitzroy Street, London W1P 5AJ, England.

Works:

1965   Mews Houses, Camden, London
1966   Creek Vean House, Feock, Cornwall
         Skybreak House, Radlett, Hertfordshire
         Reliance Controls Factory, Swindon, Wiltshire
1971   Fred Olsen Passenger Terminal and Operations Centre, Millwall, London
         Computer Technology, Hemel Hempstead, Hertfordshire
         Foster Associates Studio, Fitzroy Street, London
         I.B.M. Advance Head Office, near Portsmouth, Hampshire
1973   Modern Art Glass Warehouse, Thamesmead, Kent
         Spastics Society Special Care Unit, Hackney, London
         Orange Hand Shops, London, Nottingham, Brighton and Reading
1974   Fred Olsen Showroom, Regent Street, London
1975   Bean Hill Rental Housing, Milton Keynes, Buckinghamshire
         Palmerston Special School, Bellvale, Liverpool
         Willis Faber Country Head Office, Ipswich, Suffolk
1977   SAPA Aluminum Extrusion Plant, Tibshelf, Derbyshire
1978   I.B.M. Technical Park, Greenford, Middlesex
         Sainsbury Centre for the Visual Arts, University of East Anglia, Norwich
1979   I.B.M. Technical Park, phase II, Greenford, Middlesex
         Norman and Wendy Foster House, Cannon Place, Hampstead, London
         Joseph Shop, Sloane Street, London
1986   Hammersmith Centre, London

Publications:

By FOSTER: articles—"How to Design Low-Cost Flexible Quick-Build Buildings" in *Building Design* (London), October 1973; "Alvar Aalto 1898–1976" in *RIBA Journal* (London), July 1976; "Foster Associates: Buildings and Projects" in *Architectural Design* (London), September/October 1977.

On FOSTER: books—*Principles of Pneumatic Architecture* by Roger N. Dent, London 1971; *New British Architecture* by Robert Maxwell, London 1972; *Design and Planning of Retail Systems* by David Gosling and Barry Maitland, London 1976; articles—"Foster Associates' Recent Work" in *Architectural Design* (London), May 1970; "Architect's Approach to Architecture" in *RIBA Journal* (London), June 1970; "Foster Associates: Assembly Without Composition" in *Casabella* (Milan), March 1973; "Orange Hand: The Shops for Boys" in *Architecture + Urbanism* (Tokyo), September 1973; "Teamwork" in *L'Architecture d'Aujourd'hui* (Paris), November/December 1973; "Perspective" in *Building Design* (London), March 1974; "Fred Olsen Operations—Amenity Building" in *Byggekunst* (Oslo), April 1974; "Orange Hand Shops" in *Baumeister* (Munich), August 1974; "Orange Hand: The Image of a Children's Clothing Shop" in *Domus* (Milan), August 1974; "Foster Associates—IBM UK, Cosham" by Roberto Collova in *Parametro* (Bologna), February 1975; "Foster Associates" in *Architecture + Urbanism* (Tokyo), September 1975; "High-tech to Appropriate: A View of Foster Associates' Approach to Appropriate Technology" in *Architectural Design* (London), March 1976; "Engineering Design and Foster Associates" in *Northern Architect* (Sunderland, England), April 1976; "Low-Profile School" in *Architectural Review* (London), November 1976; "Palmerston Special School in London" in *Bauen und Wohnen* (Zurich), May 1977; "Unbuilt England" by Peter Cook in *Architecture + Urbanism* (Tokyo), October 1977; "Preview 78: Distribution Centre, Greenford, Middlesex" in *Architectural Review* (London), January 1978; "Stretching Glass" and "Roundabout" by Stephanie Williams in *Building Design* (London), February 1978; "Fostering the Arts" in *The Architects' Journal* (London), April 1978; "Art Shed" by Martin Spring in *Building* (London), April 1978; "East Anglia Arts Centre" in *Architectural Review* (London), December 1978.

Design can be many things to many people. To us, as an office, it is a means of integrating and resolving conflicts, to avoid an either/or situation, to recognise needs which might be spiritual as well as material, and to recognise that beautiful things can and should be reconciled with moving through the maze of cost, time and quality control. We really do not see why "art" and "business" have to be put into separate pigeon holes. If you break down the conflict between private and public, the individual and the community, and the conflict between short and long term requirements—this raises the whole issue of multi-use and flexible building, flexibility for choice, change and growth, and the problems of flexibility as well as the bonuses. In the end, it means resolving and integrating many conflicting requirements.

High technology is not an end in itself, but rather a means to social goals and wider possibilities. High technology buildings are hand-crafted with the same care as bricks and mortar, or timber. Hand-crafted care is the factor which makes a building loved by its users and by those who look at it. Materials have changed; quality control no longer comes from site based crafts.

—Norman Foster

By the mid-1960s the architectural scene in England was sliding into chaos. Many leading architects were disillusioned, and it became normal for the architectural magazines to attack the modern movement without knowing what to put in its place. Into this vacuum came many theorists for a post-modern architecture, but they, too, had neither images to convince nor ideas to hold the imagination. Throughout this period of turmoil the work of Norman Foster has steadily and consistently developed. Far more advanced in concepts than the apologists for "post-modernism" could imagine, it yet remained rooted in one wing of the modern movement.

Stripped of the formal ideas put forward by various of its practitioners, the architecture of the modern movement basically involved two ideas. The first was that the architecture of our time was to be founded on a serious, objective study of the needs of the client; the second was that the new buildings would not only be built by machines but also that they would celebrate their origins by being light, shiny and orderly. It is an amusing historical irony that the modern movement in England first achieved these ideals in Foster's work just at the moment when the magazines and the writers had given up hope. The result is that the *Architectural Review,* for example, writes of Foster's work with incomprehension and bewilderment.

Norman Foster first achieved fame when he was a partner of Team 4 and they completed a low industrial building at Swindon for Reliance Controls. This little building relied for much of its quality on an

Norman Foster: Sainsbury Centre for the Visual Arts, University of East Anglia, Norwich, 1978

elegant structure, beautifully expressed externally with cantilever beams all round, indicating the possibility of extension. Such a strong horizontally proportioned structure made up of rolled sections clearly owed much to the work of Skidmore, Owings and Merrill, and in fact one of the partners in Team 4, Richard Rogers, had worked in their office. With the break up of Team 4 and the departure of Rogers, structure ceased to play such a strong formal role in Foster's buildings.

In Foster's work of the 1970's, the structure is retained as an ordering device, but it is played down externally and interest is concentrated on a minimal skin that pushes glazing technology to the limit. Earlier glassy buildings had retained top rails, had kept a demonstration of floors and structures; Foster dispensed with all this, and his first mature work, the Olsen building at Millwall, is surely more minimal than any building had ever been before—and with its calm proportions, its reflections, and its top melting into the sky, it is a beautiful building to see. "This line of development can obviously go no further," said the critics. Norman Foster spent the next eight years taking it further, and saved English architecture from dying of boredom.

Millwall was followed by a series of industrial buildings. Here the architectural requirement was low key, and the Foster approach worked well. His housing at Milton Keynes suffered somewhat from tenants used to tougher buildings: it serves to show that there is far to go before this kind of minimum hi-tech building is appropriate for low-cost housing.

The completion of the Willis Faber office building at Ipswich and the Sainsbury Centre for the Visual Arts in Norwich showed Foster to be an architect of world stature. The Ipswich building, externally re-

flecting the surrounding buildings and following the old street pattern, is internally planned around an escalator bank that must be one of the few great spaces in a modern office building. The Norwich building is of great constructional originality, with its curtain walling being carried over the roof and its clear glazed ends. This building shows both the glories and the limitations of the open, flexible plan (restaurant, offices, senior common room and art gallery share one great room), for the scale and the calm atmosphere is magnificent, but the noise of one vacuum cleaner can disturb the entire building.

—John Winter

FOX, Revel (Albert Ellis).

South African. Born in Durban, 20 September 1924. Educated at the University of Cape Town School of Architecture, 1942–44, 1946–48, B.Arch. 1948; University of Cape Town Department of Urban and Regional Planning, 1966–69, M.Urban and Regional Planning (with distinction) 1969. Served in the Union Defence Force, in the Special Service Battalion, 6th Armoured Division, in Italy, 1944–46. Married Suzanne Hermine Krige in 1948; children: Grethe-Maria, Revel, and Justin. Assistant and Associate, Ayers, Wilson and Parker, Bulawayo and Gwelo, Rhodesia, 1948–51; Assistant in the studio of Ivar and Anders Tengbom, Stockholm, 1951–52; in private practice in Worcester, Cape Province, South Africa, 1953–56; Partner, Revel Fox and George

Krige, Worcester and Cape Town, 1957–62; in private practice, Cape Town, 1962–66. Since 1966, Principal of Revel Fox and Partners, Cape Town (partners: William Ritchie, Bruce Milne, and Feo Sachs). Regional Editor, *South African Architectural Record,* Cape Town, 1959–60. Studio Master, School of Architecture, University of Cape Town, 1959–63; Visiting Lecturer/Critic, University of the Witwatersrand, Johannesburg, 1962, University of Pretoria, 1963, Yale University School of Art and Architecture, New Haven, Connecticut, 1964, and the University of Natal, 1965, 1966, 1967. Member of the Central Council, 1966–70, Chairman of the Board of Education, 1970, Member of the National Board, 1971–75, and Member of the Executive Committee of the National Board, 1974, Institute of South African Architects; Chairman of the Educational Advisory Committee, 1971–75, and Chairman of the Visiting Board, 1972–75, South African Council for Architects; Chairman, National Architectural Education Conference, Cape Town, 1972; President, Cape Provincial Institute of Architects, 1974–75, and Representative of the Institute on the Environmental Advisory Board of the Cape Town City Council, 1975–76. Chairman of the Architectural Heritage Committee of the Cape Provincial Institute of Architects, since 1975. Exhibitions: *Architecture as We See It,* University of Cape Town, 1969; *The Work of Revel Fox,* Institute of South African Architects, Cape Town, 1977. Recipient: Ernest Oppenheimer Memorial Trust Fund Grant, 1963;

Revel Fox: BP Centre, Cape Town, 1973

Carnegie Travel Grant, 1964; Cape Provincial Institute of Architects Medal, 1968, 1969, 1973; South African Institute of Architects Travel Grant, 1970, and Gold Medal, 1977. Associate of the Royal Institute of British Architects, 1951; Member of the Institute of South African Architects, 1953, and of the South African Council for Architects, 1971. Address: Revel Fox and Partners, 117 Waterkant, Cape Town 8001, South Africa.

Works:

1954 Courtyard House, Worcester, Cape Province
1955 Fox and Ross houses, Worcester, Cape Province
Droomer House, Worcester, Cape Province
1956 Hill House, Worcester, Cape Province
1959 Giannellos House, Camps Bay, Cape Province
High school and school hall buildings, De Doorns, Cape Province
Meerlust Homestead restoration, Faure, Cape Province
1960 Deanery, Cathedral Church of St. George, Cape Town
1961 "Rust en Vreugd" Town House restoration, Cape Town
Esselen Park High School, Worcester, Cape Province
La Cock House, Higgovale, Cape Town
1962 Le Roux House, Llandudno, Cape Province
Robinson House, Higgovale, Cape Town
Theunissen House, Klipvlei, Philadelphia, Cape Province
Ballet School, stage I, University of Cape Town
1963 Odes House, Clifton, Cape Province
Vlok House, Bishopscourt, Cape Province
1964 Municipal Market, Worcester, Cape Province
Municipal Workshop, Worcester, Cape Province
Faure House, Rondebosch, Cape Province
Ballet School, stage II, University of Cape Town
1967 Faure House, Bloubergstrand, Cape Province
Fischer House, Milnerton, Cape Province
Shell and British Petroleum Properties Development Report (project)
Housing development, Claremont, Cape Province (project)
Housing development, Pinelands, Cape Province (project)
1968 Montebello Apartments, Newlands, Cape Province
Van Lennep House, Monterey, Wynberg, Cape Province
Zaaiman House, Hout Bay, Cape Province
Moses Beach Development Study (project; with E. W. N. Mallows and Julian Beinart)
Port Elizabeth Civic Centre Development Plan (project; with E. W. N. Mallows and Julian Beinart)
Scott House, Constantia, Cape Province
1969 Post Office Development Report (project; with E. W. N. Mallows and Julian Beinart)
Faculty of Education, University of Cape Town
Eoan Group Cultural Centre and Joseph Stone Auditorium, Athlone, Cape Province
Shell Company experimental open office layouts, Port Elizabeth
1970 Worcester Library, Cape Province (project)
School for Botanical Studies, Kirstenbosch, Cape Province (with Lindsay Falck)
Revel Fox and Partners Offices and Studios conversion, Cape Town
1971 Krige House restoration and museum conversion, Worcester, Cape Province (with Henry Villet)
1972 Early Learning Centre, Athlone, Cape Province
Rhenish Parsonage restoration, Stellenbosch, Cape Province (with Henry Villet)

1973 BP Centre, Cape Town
Crematorium extension, Maitland, Cape Province
Tafelberg Petrol Service Station, Cape Town
Entokozweni Early Learning Centre, Moletsane, Soweto
Kanetvlei Homestead renovation, Sandhills, Cape Province
Devon Valley Development, Stellenbosch, Cape Province (with A. and A. de Souza Santos)
Ballet School, stage III, University of Cape Town
1974 Demonstration houses, Marina da Gama, Muizenberg, Cape Province
Nieuwenhuizen House, Somerset West, Cape Province
Geustyn House, Camps Bay, Cape Province (project)
1975 Hunyani Early Learning Centre, Salisbury, Rhodesia
Port Zimbali Resort Town, Natal (project; with Wilhelm O. Meyer and Partners)
Urban and dwelling unit plan for a sector of Mitchell's Plain, near Cape Town (project; with Lowe, Simpson and Associates, Louis Karol and Peter Land)
1976 Maria van Riebeeck Domestic Science High School, Riebeek West, Cape Province
Cullinan Holdings Administration Building, Olifansfontein, Transvaal
Hertford Estate Farm Village Community (project)
Lion's Kloof cluster housing development (project)
1977 Geustyn House, Stellenbosch, Cape Province
Gamsberg Zinc Township Development, Cape Province (project)
1978 Leeusig Telephone Exchange, Cape Town
Mitchell's Plain Urban and Dwelling Unit Plan, near Cape Town (with Lowe, Simpson and Associates, and Louis Karol)
Shelter Housing Schemes:
Expandable Starter Units, Valhalla Park, Cape Province
Family house conversions, Lange, Cape Province
Emergency Relief Housing, Kensington, Cape Province (project)
Federal Theological Seminary, Edendale, Natal
Franschhoek School Hostel, Cape Province
St. George's Cathedral extensions, Cape Town
Cape of Good Hope Provincial Administration Offices, Long Street, Cape Town

Publications:

By FOX: book—*The Preservation and Restoration of Historic Buildings in South Africa,* with others, Cape Town 1968; articles—"Investigation into the Use of Plastics in Architecture" in *South African Architectural Record* (Johannesburg), August 1962; "The Squares of Cape Town" in *South African Architectural Record* (Johannesburg), February 1963; "Cape Town: The Old and the New in a Changing Environment" in *Cape Times,* 24 September 1965, reprinted in *South African Architectural Record* (Johannesburg), February 1966; "Serendipity as Education" in *Architectural Education Symposium,* Johannesburg 1969; "The Education of the Disadvantaged Pre-School Coloured Child at the Cape of Good Hope" and "Proposals for an Experimental Pre-School Centre at Athlone," with others, in *Plan* (Johannesburg), December 1969; "Conservation in Cities" in *Plan* (Johannesburg), December 1972; "Strategies to Solve Urban Dilemmas" in *Society for the Protection of the Environment Newsletter* (Stellenbosch), vol. 3, no. 1, 1973; "Traffic and People" in *Cape Times,* 29 March 1973; "Those Who Care Must Organize" in *Cape Times,* 12 March 1974; "Conservation in the

City, the Historical Process, Conservation of Urban Artifacts: The Methods and the Results" in *Metropolitan Dialogue,* Cape Town 1974; "Urban Design as an Aid to Conservation" in *Plan* (Durban), December 1974; "Housing Objectives in Southern Africa" in *Housing People,* edited by Michael Lazenby, Johannesburg 1977; "The Role of the Quantity Surveyor as Seen by an Architect" and "Architects Speak" in *Institute of South African Architects and Association of South African Quantity Surveyors' Golden Jubilee Congress Report,* Johannesburg 1977; "The Residential Component: Conservation and Rehabilitation of the Existing Housing Stock" in *Urban Revitalisation: New Life for Our Cities,* Johannesburg 1978.

On FOX: articles—"The Small House in Modern South African Architecture" by Alan Lipman in *Lantern* (Pretoria), December 1962; "The House" by Michael Munnik and Dirk Visser in *South African Architectural Record* (Johannesburg), June 1965; "The Work of Revel Fox" by Danie Theron in *Credo* (Pretoria), April 1967; "Architecture as We See It" in *Architect and Builder* (Cape Town), vol. 19, no. 11, 1969; "Visitors' Guide to Cape Town" by Paul Righini in *Credo* (Pretoria), April 1973; "Letter from Cape Town" by James D. Morgan in *Architecture Plus* (New York), March/April 1974; "The Institute Gold Medal Award" in *Institute of South African Architects Newsletter* (Johannesburg), no. 1, 1976; "Institute's Gold Medal Awards" in *Architect and Builder* (Cape Town), May 1977; "Architects Gold Medal Award" in *Planning and Building Developments* (Braamfontein), May 1977.

*   *   *

After training at the University of Cape Town under L. Thornton White, and working 1951–52 with Ivar and Anders Tengbom in Sweden, Revel Fox quickly established a reputation as an avant-garde architect of outstanding sensitivity and skill in detailing, in the small country town of Worcester in the Cape Province. His courtyard house for the Wilson family, 1954, and the Fox and Ross houses, 1955, exerted great influence on a generation of young architects, who often travelled great distances to study them.

Although primarily interested in the development of a new and personal domestic architecture, Fox was too responsive to the continuity of tradition not to be influenced by the past. His houses shared with those of the 18th century a concern with the articulating of light-coloured surfaces and the use of openings to make precise punctuations related to internal and external volumes. The appreciation shown in his work for the essential qualities of Dutch colonial architecture was soon sensed by the more perceptive among the public, with the result that he was chosen as architect for the most important restoration projects of the 1950's and early 1960's, Meerlust and Rust en Vreugd. This field has continued to involve him deeply throughout his career.

After moving the centre of his activities to Cape Town, Fox exerted a much more direct influence on students through his association with the University, and this association also resulted in several of the most important of his buildings, the new Ballet School, 1962, and the Eoan Group Cultural Centre and Joseph Stone Auditorium, 1969.

Meanwhile, his concern with domestic architecture had taken him into the field of multiple housing, in which he first came to the attention of the general public with his award-winning "Montebello" Apartments in Newlands and subsequently with demonstration housing at Marina da Gama, Muizenberg. Increasing social involvment, together with a more favourable investment situation, enabled him to apply his high standards of design to low-cost housing in the Mitchell's Plain development of 5000 dwellings and in projects for Shelter focusing on the provision of emergency and minimum shelter, using self-help expansion and up-grading.

The growth of his reputation and practise resulted in his being given the commission for a number of large commercial buildings, each one of which exhibits his tireless concern with the search for original solutions and the polished detailing of every element; the most notable is the BP Centre. These commissions were paralleled by an increasing involvement in large-scale planning projects, such as those for parts of Port Elizabeth and the development of a new mining township in the North West Cape.

Fox has earned a reputation for commitment to design integrity even at the sacrifice of remunerative commissions. Public acknowledgement of his achievement led to a number of awards for specific buildings, culminating in the Gold Medal of the South African Institute of Architects in 1977.

—Ronald Lewcock

FRANZEN, Ulrich.

American. Born in Dusseldorf, Germany, 15 January 1921; emigrated to the United States, 1936: naturalized, 1943. Educated at Williams College, Williamstown, Massachusetts, 1938–42, B.A. 1942; Harvard Graduate School of Design, Cambridge, Massachusetts, 1944–48, M.A. 1948. Served in the United States Army, 1942–44: Bronze Star; Croix de Guerre. Married to Josephine Burgess; children: Peter, David, and April. Worked for I. M. Pei and Partners, New York, 1950–55. Since 1955, Principal, Ulrich Franzen and Associates, New York. President, Architectural League of New York, 1966. Exhibitions: *Boston Arts Festival,* 1961; *Transformations in Modern Architecture,* Museum of Modern Art, New York, 1979. Recipient: Excellence in Design Award, *Architectural Record,* 1956, 1957, 1959, 1960, 1963, 1964, 1965, 1966, 1967, 1968; Arnold Brunner Prize, National Institute of Arts and Letters, 1962; Award of Merit, 1962, 1964, Homes for Better Living Award, 1966, and Honor Award, 1971, 1972, American Institute of Architects; Award Citation, 1964, and Medal of Honor, 1972, AIA, New York Chapter; Louis Sullivan Award, AIA/Bricklayers International Union, 1970; Thomas Jefferson Award, University of Virginia, Charlottesville, D.H.L.: Williams College, 1972; Postgraduate Center for Mental Health, New York, 1978. Fellow, American Institute of Architects. Address: Ulrich Franzen and Associates, 555 Madison Avenue, New York, New York 10022, U.S.A.

Works:

1950 Cook House, Palo Alto, California (project)
1955 Bejan House, Katonah, New York (project)
1956 Franzen House, Rye, New York
1958 Weissman House, Rye, New York
      Barkin Levin Factory, New York
1959 Beattie House, Great Neck, Long Island, New York
      Scheinman House, York, Pennsylvania (project)
1961 Miller House, Brewster, New York
      Franklin Delano Roosevelt Tidal Basin Project, Washington, D.C. (competition project)
      Philip Morris Research Center I, Richmond, Virginia
      Bernstein House, Great Neck, Long Island, New York
1962 Elliot House, Pound Ridge, New York
      Hubbard House addition, Greenwich, Connecticut
      Tenafly Cluster Housing, New Jersey
      Philip Morris Power Plant, Richmond, Virginia
      Helen Whiting Dress Factory, Pleasantville, New York
1963 Dana House, New Canaan, Connecticut
      Philip Morris Operations Center, Richmond, Virginia
      Fleschner House, Westport, Connecticut

Ulrich Franzen: Agronomy Building, Cornell University, Ithaca, New York, 1968

      Castle House, New London, Connecticut
      Towers House, Essex, Connecticut
1963/
  64 MVR Hall, Cornell University, Ithaca, New York
1964 Buttenwieser House, Mamaroneck, New York
      Growth Chamber Laboratories, Cornell University, Ithaca, New York
1965 United States Consulate, Montreal (project)
      Bloedel Guest House, Williamstown, Massachusetts
1966 Jefferson Memorial, Birmingham, Alabama (competition project)
      Motel, Westhampton Beach, Long Island, New York (project)
      Weathersfield Motor Inn, Westport, Connecticut (project)
1966/
  69 Residence Hall, University of New Hampshire, Durham
1967 Elk Grove Presbyterian Church, Elk Grove, Illinois (project)

1968 Bronx State School, New York (project)
      House, Pound Ridge, New York (project)
      Alley Theatre, Houston
      Agronomy Building, Cornell University, Ithaca, New York
      Forest Hills Public Housing, New York (project)
1969 Dormitory and Classroom Building, Watchtower Bible and Tract Society, Brooklyn Heights, New York
      Astor Place Building, Cooper Union, New York (project)
      Harpers Ferry Center, Harpers Ferry, Virginia
      Torrington Housing, Torrington, Connecticut
1970 Urban Development Corporation Housing, Binghamton, New York (project)
      First Unitarian Church, Richmond, Virginia
      Kennedy Plaza Apartments, Utica, New York
      Paraphernalia (boutiques), Lexington Avenue, New York

Dining Hall, University of New Hampshire, Durham

1971 Philip Morris Research Center II, Richmond, Virginia

The Evolving City (service megastructure), New York (project)

1972/
77 English and Modern Languages Building, New York State University, Amherst

1973 First City National Bank, Binghamton, New York

Mono Rail Station at Interstate Highway, New York (project)

Urban design plan for Ossining, New York (project)

Library, Wesleyan University, Middletown, Connecticut

1973/
75 William Street Student Housing, Wesleyan University, Middletown, Connecticut

1974 Plymouth Street College, University of New Hampshire, Plymouth

Research Tower, College of Veterinary Medicine, Cornell University, Ithaca, New York

1975 Undergraduate Library, University of Virginia, Charlottesville

Residential Community in Southern California (project)

Hunter College, New York

1977 Harlem School of the Arts, 645 St. Nicholas Avenue, New York

1978 E. Krauss House, Old Westbury, Long Island, New York

Visitors Center, Miller Brewing Company, Eden, North Carolina

Miller Brewing Company Headquarters, Milwaukee

Franzen House, Bridgehampton, New York

800 Fifth Avenue (housing), New York

1978/
80 Music Building, State University of New York, Amherst

Champion International Headquarters, Stamford, Connecticut

1979 A. Krauss House, Old Westbury, Long Island, New York

Boyce Thompson Institute, Cornell University, Ithaca, New York

Student Center, University of Michigan at Flint

1979/
81 Philip Morris Headquarters Building, New York

Publications:

By FRANZEN: book—*The Evolving City*, with Paul Rudolph, New York 1974.

On FRANZEN: books—*The New House for Family Living* (Treasury of Contemporary Living), New York 1956; *Architecture U.S.A.*, London 1959; *Observations on American Architecture* by Ivan Chermayeff, New York 1972; *The Current Situation in Architecture* by Paul Heyer, New York 1978; articles—"Five New Projects by Ulrich Franzen" in *Architectural Record* (New York), February 1969; "Four Current Projects by Ulrich Franzen" in *Architectural Record* (New York), July 1971; "Ulrich Franzen" in *Architecture + Urbanism* (Tokyo), June 1973; "Multi-Cat's Veterinary Lab" by Peter Blake in *Architecture Plus* (New York), May 1974; "Studenthauser Universität von New Hampshire" in *Baumeister* (Munich), August 1974; "Ulrich Franzen," special issue of *Architecture + Urbanism* (Tokyo), May 1975; "Changing Design Solutions for a Changing Era" in *Architectural Record* (New York), September 1975; "A View of Contemporary World Architects," special issue of *Shinkenchiku* (Tokyo), October 1975; "Philip Morris Plans Tower at 42nd Street" in the *New York Times*, 4 December

1978; "Ulrich Franzen" in *Process Architecture* (Tokyo/Pittsburgh), May 1979.

In the last few years the idea of modern architecture as the puritanical uniform of political as well as social reform has finally expired. The current architectural situation offers no mainstream but many contending positions of validity. Thus, there is neither the crutch of socio-political salvation nor a correct aesthetic system to lean on. The most important aspect, therefore, of the serious architect's approach today and in the future is a philosophical frame of reference, a sensitive understanding of the relationship of idea systems and a particular cultural situation. While we are, now, decrying the anti-historical and anti-intellectual stance of the so-called "modern movement," we fail to recognize that the reformist zeal of the modern movement was nurtured within the cultural ideas of Marxism, Futurism, and even Fascism. The formal solutions of that era were emblems of a "brave new world," and their alienation from any context was, in fact, perceived as witness of ideological correctness and, therefore, architectural importance. Now that the folly of "brave new world" attitudes is recognized by broad numbers of not only architects but also, more importantly, society, a cultural situation is arising as a pre-condition for an architecture which is generous, where "modern" architecture was didactic. What flows from this are design notions not based on holistic systems but on combinations of idea systems, often unresolved within a single scheme, but related nonetheless as symbols of our delight in the often perverse but always intriguing multiplicity of ideas that sustain man.

Perhaps this explains why there is in my work, today, a preoccupation to fuse into a single concept both abstract ordering devices as well as easily recognized fragments of reality. In the same vein, but of a different tune, are those buildings I have recently designed which combine within a single broad solution more than one organizing idea, as well as several architectural vocabularies corresponding to the different organizing geometries. Just as our conceptual thinking today must stem from a full knowledge of architectural history and become a commentary to it, in the same spirit our form language will become more eclectic. The effort is then to make buildings that are assemblages or "combines" of parts and ideas, evoking a multi-faceted present and past. I see architecture, today, as creating bridges for valid formal elements of the past and present, including aspects of modernism, to move into fresh compositional systems.

—Ulrich Franzen

The work of Ulrich Franzen has been constant in its variety of experimentation. This variety stems perhaps from Franzen's knowledgability about the work of his peers, but also perhaps equally from his sensitivity to the social context within which he and they work. In either case, the significance of Franzen's work strongly rests on his responsiveness to the social context.

He has said, "Architecture is the servant of its time, and significant designs are experiments of an era. The buildings that are designed become footprints of our own socio-cultural history, reflections of the ideas and concerns of an era, and not those of an individual." Indeed, Franzen's work reflects much of what modern architecture has been attempting in its search for directions.

Franzen's influences were varied, and he was certainly affected by the time and place in which he studied, under Marcel Breuer and Walter Gropius at Harvard's Graduate School of Design in the 1940's. In many ways their effect was negative, however, and Franzen's own inclinations in his earliest independent work were towards the only other available model (one that would have been somewhat less acceptable to the GSD faculty at that time), Mies van der Rohe. This may have been partly due to a mildly

rebellious streak in a young architect, but it must have been due as well to a strong natural affinity.

Particularly, Franzen adopted Mies' characteristic hardness, and his designs were also dominated by materials that are physically tough, permanent, and precise. As this Miesian respect for permanent materials (without Mies' penchant for luxurious materials) has pervaded Franzen's work, so also was his earliest work pervaded by Miesian plan compositions. One characteristic of this type that Franzen has used repeatedly are free planes: walls which almost intercept each other but slip past, never quite touching, and extending into the landscape. Franzen's use of symmetry can also be traced, however indirectly, to Miesian themes. Although most of Mies' smaller buildings were dramatically asymmetrical, he experimented with symmetry at a larger scale, and Johnson's variation on Mies' work, at a residential scale, provided a link that extended to Franzen.

Angularity, and the frequent use of modules, also characterized Franzen's earliest work, and many of his more recent designs continue to exhibit these traits as well. Additionally, a preoccupation with the qualities of collage, or juxtaposition of parts, has been periodically evident in his architecture.

Despite the formal nature of many of these properties, Franzen has linked them together through a careful and consistent analysis and response to zeitgeist and social conditions. Franzen has always attempted to integrate "form and reality," and his formal designs are responsive not merely to physical reality but also to the realities of attitude, fashion and spirit. To whatever extent a cohesive zeitgeist exists, Franzen senses it. In this sense of form yielding to "cultural context," his Paraphernalia shops of 1970 are a perfect case in point. Responding to the multi-media audiovisual craze of that time, none of the merchandise was directly displayed; images of the stock were flashed continuously on screens around the walls.

More recently, his designs have reflected current trends towards social responsiveness as well as conscientious planning of movement within space. Context, established as a primary concern in Franzen's work of the late 1960's, remains important in all of his later designs. Even Franzen's recent formal preoccupation with juxtaposition, and the dynamism created by many parts that are combined but not quite unified, often stems from a study of context. His display of natural conflict between polar forces is often one that arises in response to site conditions.

The sense of diversity within his buildings that arises from his combination of strictly ordered spaces with parts that fragment that order is further responsive to social climate, because it appropriately reflects the pluralism of American culture today. Art that invites us to recognize and take pleasure in surprising combinations may prepare us to enjoy the contradictions of a society that can be both violent and sentimental, both conventional and permissive, and both idealistic and intensely pragmatic.

—Stanley Abercrombie

FREYSSINET, Eugène.
French. Born in Objat, Corneze, France, in 1879. Educated at the Ecole Polytechnique, Paris, and the Ecole Nationale des Ponts et Chaussées, Paris; apprentice to the engineer Rabut. Served as an engineer in the French Army, 1904–07, 1914–18. Worked as a road engineer for local authorities in Central France, 1907–13; Director, Société des Enterprises Limousin, Paris, 1918–28; in private practice as an engineer/architect, Paris, 1929 until his death, 1962. President, International Federation of Pre-stressed Concrete. D.Sc.: University of Leeds, Yorkshire, 1953. *Died* (in Saint-Martin-Vesubie, France) *8 June 1962.*

Eugène Freyssinet: Airship Hangars, Orly Airport, Paris, 1924

Works:

1907 Bridge, Boutiron, France
      Bridge, Le Veurdre, France (destroyed, 1944)
1913 Arched Concrete Bridge with 607-foot Span
      (project)
1916/
   24 2 Airship Hangers, Orly Airport, Paris (de-
      stroyed, 1944)
1922 St. Pierre-du-Vauvray Bridge, France (de-
      stroyed, 1944)
1926/
   29 Plougstel Bridge, Elorn River Estuary, Brit-
      tany, France (partly destroyed, 1944; re-
      built)
1932 Tranenberg Bridge, Stockholm
1937/
   39 Harbour structures, Brest, France
1946/
   47 Runways, Orly Airport, Paris
1946/
   52 Ocean Terminal, Le Havre, France
1949 5 pre-fabricated, pre-stressed concrete
      bridges, River Marne, France
1958 Basilica of St. Pius, Lourdes, France (with
      Pierre Vago)

Publications:

By FREYSSINET: book—*Les Grandes Constructions,* Paris 1930; articles—"Les Hangars d'Orly" in
Le Genie Civil (Paris), September 1923; "Les Ponts
en Beton Armée de tres Grande Portée" in *Architecture Vivante* (Paris), Spring/Summer 1931.

On FREYSSINET: books—*Baukunst der Neuester*
Zeit by G. A. Platz, Berlin 1927, 1930; *Concrete: The*
Vision of a New Architecture by P. Collins, New
York and London 1959; *Eugene Freyssinet* by José
A. Fernandez Ordonez, Barcelona 1978; articles—
"Les Hangars à Dirigeables de l'Aéroport d'Orly par
E. Freyssinet" by Jean Badovici in *Architecture Vi-*
vante (Paris), no. 2, 1924; "Eugene Freyssinet" by
Jean Badovici in *Architecture Vivante* (Paris),
Spring/Summer 1931; "The Freyssinet Process of
Pre-Stressing Concrete" by Archibald Kirkwood
Dodds in *Architect and Building News* (London), 26
June 1942; "Basilica of St. Pius" in *Architectural*
Design (London), June 1959; "Freyssinet: A Revolu-
tion in the Art of Construction" by José A. Fer-
nandez Ordonez in *2C Construccion de la Ciudad*
(Barcelona), June 1978.

It is to Eugène Freyssinet that we owe some of the
most beautiful architectural works in reinforced concrete. The most beautiful—the hangars for airships
at Orly Airport, Paris—were unfortunately destroyed during the Second World War. The "father
of pre-stressed concrete" had many achievements to
his credit. He did not consider himself as an architect, but architecture interested him. He hoped for
collaboration with architects, but few such opportunities arose.

I had the good fortune to live through one of these
valuable experiments at the time of the conception of
the subterranean Basilica at Lourdes. It was an exemplary experiment in real collaboration, in a patient search for a common language. It resulted in
the free expression of a rigorously logical purity put
at the disposition of a spatial will but accepting all
the constraints imposed by technique and economy.

—Pierre Vago

FRIEDBERG, M(arvin) Paul.

American. Born in Brooklyn, New York, 11 October
1931. Educated at Cornell University, Ithaca, New
York, 1950–54, B.S. in horticulture 1954; Art Students League, New York, 1959; New School for Social Research, New York, 1962. Served as a Lieutenant in the United States Army, 1954–56. Married
Ester Louise Hidary in 1962; children: Mark and
Jeffrey. Landscape Architect, with Arthur Hoffman,
Hartford, Connecticut, 1954, and with Joseph Gan-
gemi, New York, 1956–58. Since 1958, Principal, M.
Paul Friedberg and Partners (landscape architecture
and urban design), New York. Founder Director,
Urban Landscape Program, City College, City Uni-
versity of New York, since 1971. Member, Board of
Directors, Municipal Arts Society, New York,
1968–71; Vice-President, Architectural League of
New York, 1969–70; Member, Art Commission of
the City of New York, 1971–72; Chairman/-
Designer, *Not Too Late* exhibition, Guild Hall, New
York, 1972; Vice-President, American Society of
Landscape Architects, 1973. Member of the Board,
1975–78, Chairman of the 1976 Conference, "Exploring Change," and since 1978 Member of the
Advisory Board, International Design Conference at
Aspen, Colorado; Trustee, American Academy in
Rome, since 1978. Recipient: Commercial Landscape Design Award, 1962, *World's Fair* Award,
1964, Merit Award, 1970, 1971, 1974, and Certificate of Merit, 1977, American Association of Nurserymen; Client Award, 1964, Certificate of Merit,
1970, and Excellence in Design Award, 1973, New
York State Association of Architects; Commendation, New York Park Association, 1965 (twice); Albert S. Bard Award, City Club of New York, 1965,
1967; Honor Award, 1965 (three times), 1968, 1970,

Merit Award, 1965 (twice), 1967 (three times), 1968, 1969, 1971 (three times), 1974 (three times), 1975, and Special Award, 1978, American Society of Landscape Architects; Honor Award and Merit Award, United States Department of Housing and Urban Development, 1966; New York Council of the Arts Award, 1967; Merit Award, 1967, and Bronze Plaque, 1967, 1974, New York Municipal Arts Society; Honor Award, 1967, and Award Citation, 1969, American Institute of Architects; Special Citation, American Association of School Administrators, 1970; Residential Design Award, National Landscape Association, 1971; Mayor's Medal, New York City Diamond Jubilee, 1973; Excellence in Environmental Design Award, *Industrial Design,* 1973; Award of Merit, Concrete Industry Board of New York, 1974; Design in Steel Citation, American Steel Institute, 1975; Award, *Progressive Architecture,* 1977; Certificate of Excellence, Urban Awards Program, 1978. Address: M. Paul Friedberg and Partners, 4 West 62nd Street, New York, New York 10023, U.S.A.

Works (landscape and urban design):

1965 Bay Ridge Air Rights, New York
Carver Houses, New York
Chatham Towers, New York
Commodore John Rogers School Number 27, Baltimore
Israel Senior Citizens Housing, New York
Ittelson Center, New York
Jacob Riis Houses and Jacob Riis Plaza, New York
Leesburg Prison, New Jersey

1966 Bridgeport Courthouse Plaza, Connecticut
Dag Hammarskjold Plaza, New York
Lancaster Public Square, Pennsylvania
Letchworth Village, Haverstraw, New York

1967 Bedford-Stuyvesant Superblock, New York
Playground, Buchanan School, Washington, D.C.
Buttenweiser House, Mamaroneck, New York
Capper Plaza Urban Renewal, New York
Madison Public Library, New Jersey
New York Institute of Technology, Westbury
Ottumwa Central Business District, Iowa
Temple B'nai Jeshurun, Short Hills, New Jersey
Wilton State School, Wilton, New York
Woodlawn Park, Buffalo, New York

1968 Essex Community College, Newark, New Jersey
Fall River Housing, Massachusetts
Gottesman Plaza, New York
Master plan for the Harlem River State Park, Bronx, New York
Humboldt School, Boston
Kent General Hospital, Easton, Pennsylvania
Nassau County Civic and Social Services Center, Mineola, Long Island, New York
Site evaluation: New York University at Sterling Forest
Paerdegat Housing, New York
Parks improvement plan for Poughkeepsie, New York
Peachtree Center, Atlanta
Public School 166, New York
Queens College, New York
Temple B'nai Abraham, South Orange, New Jersey
Vest Pocket Parks, New York
Wilson College, Chicago
Worcester Center Development, Massachusetts
Central Park Police Stable, New York

1969 Beef Island Environmental Study, British Virgin Islands
Canadian Jewish Congress, Montreal
Chelsea Park, New York
Creedmore State Hospital, Queens, New York

IBM, Burlington, Vermont
Jeanette Plaza, New York
Kaufman Campgrounds, Sullivan County, New York
Mid-Westchester YM-YWHA, Scarsdale, New York
Roberto Clemente State Park, Bronx, New York
Schaefer Brewery, Scranton, Pennsylvania
Seton Park, Riverdale, New York
State University of New York, at Brockport, Buffalo, Delhi, New Paltz, and Stony Brook
Stevens Institute, Hoboken, New Jersey
Wall Street Park, Staten Island, New York
Washington Street Urban Renewal, New York
Model Cities Open Space Study: Waterbury, Connecticut

1970 Cadman Plaza Urban Renewal, New York
Consolidated Edison Indian Point Project, Westchester County, New York
Open Space Study: East Hampton, New York
East Orange Housing, New Jersey
Easton Hospital, Pennsylvania
Ellicot Neighborhood Facility, Buffalo, New York
Lindsay Bushwick Housing, New York
Lindsay Park, New York
Marcus Garvey Park Village, New York
Nassau Community College, Long Island, New York
Newark Vest Pocket Parks, New Jersey
New Jersey Housing Authority, Morristown
New York City Housing Authority Developments: Allen Stanton, Amherst Houses, Amsterdam Houses, Coney Island Site 13, East Houston, First Avenue and 110th Street, Mermaid Avenue, Penn Wortmann, and Warren Street
Operation Breakthrough, Wilmington, Delaware
Townland Housing Systems, Operation Breakthrough, Newark, New Jersey
Model Cities Training Program, New York
Twenty-four Forty Boston Road, Bronx, New York
29th Street Park, New York
University Towers, New York
Urban Development Corporation Mobile Home Project, Brooklyn, New York
Urban Nature Study, New York
Watertown East New Town, Massachusetts
West Side Urban Renewal (5 sites), New York

1971 A.T.&T. Long Lines Headquarters, Bedminster, New Jersey
Clinton Towers, New York
Kings County State School, New York
Kingsborough Community College, Queens, New York
Dr. Martin Luther King Boulevard, Miami
Nielsen Building, Chicago
Rochester Recreational Parks, Rochester, New York
Rome State School, Rome, New York
Smithbridge Towers, New York
South East Loop Housing, Rochester, New York
South Hall Housing, Albany, New York
Village Mall, Queens, New York

1972 Harlem River Houses, New York
Metropark/Tri-State Regional Planning Commission, New York
Middletown Urban Development Corporation, Middletown, New York
Oakley Oval, Jersey City, New Jersey
Pearl Ridge Shopping Center, Honolulu
Recreational facilities, Pittsburgh
River Plaza, New York
Stevenson Commons, New York
Summer Street Plaza, Boston
Synthetic Land: Ford Foundation, New York

1973 Bergdorf-Goodman Store, White Plains, New York
College Point, Queens, New York
Cook County Hospital, Chicago
East Boston Housing
First of Denver Plaza
Fitzgerald Park, Beckley, West Virginia
Site development impact study: Leonia Golf Course, New Jersey
Minneapolis Orchestra Hall
Urban beautification: Yonkers, New York
Village Green, Staten Island, New York
Washington Market Urban Renewal, New York

1974 Cité Concordia, Montreal
Fordham Medical and Mental Hospital, Bronx, New York
Model Cities Open Space Plan for Harlem, New York
Hancock/Saratoga Housing, New York
Hofstra University, Hempstead, New York
Kemper Williams Park, Patterson, Louisiana
Loring Park Development, Minneapolis
Melrose Housing, Bronx, New York
Menorah Park Home for the Aged, Beechwood, Ohio
Police Plaza, New York
Rainbow Center Mall/Winter Garden, Niagara Falls, New York
Social Security Administration, Metro West, Baltimore
Staten Island Theme Park, New York
State Street Mall and Capitol Concourse, Madison, Wisconsin

1975 African Square Park, Miami
Arya Sheraton Hotel, Tehran
Farahzad Housing, Tehran
Home Furnishing Center, Aurora, Illinois
Department of Housing and Urban Development Beautification Demonstration: Ten Demountable Parks, New York
Jamaica "El" Study, New York
Plan for Main Street, Poughkepsie, New York
Moscow World Trade Center
State Street South Operations Center, Quincy, Massachusetts

1976 Jersey City State College, New Jersey
John F. Kennedy Plaza and Civic Center, Lowell, Massachusetts
Junior High School 320, New York
Kissena Park and Park Corridor, Queens, New York
Lafayette Boynton Housing, New York
Monroe Center, Grand Rapids, Michigan

1977 Bowling Green Park restoration, New York
Alaska State Capital Competition Plan, Willow, Alaska (with Jonathan Barnett and Benjamin Thompson)

1978 Baychester Housing, New York
Campau Square, Grand Rapids, Michigan
Peavey Plaza, Minneapolis

1979 Fort Lincoln New-Town In-Town, Washington, D.C.
Garden Court Apartments, New York
Gateway National Recreation Area, New York
Poughkeepsie Central Business District Redevelopment, Poughkeepsie, New York

Publications:

By FRIEDBERG: books—graphics and captions in *Planning for Parks and Recreation in Urban Areas* by Elinor Guggenheimer, New York 1968; *Playgrounds for City Children,* Washington, D.C. 1969; *Creative Play Areas,* Portland, Oregon 1970; *Play and Interplay,* New York 1970; *Handcrafted Playgrounds,* New York 1975; articles—"In Search of Eden" in *Interiors* (New York), July 1963; "Patios for Parlous Suburbia" in *Landscape Architecture* (Louisville, Kentucky), January 1964; "Programming Play" in *Schoolhouse in the City*, edited by Alvin Toffler, New York 1968; "Manhattan Protest" in *Landscape Architecture* (Louisville, Kentucky), October 1968; "Systems for Play" in *Small Urban Spaces*, edited by Whitney North Seymour Jr., New York 1969; "Sharing the Spaces, Sharing the Yields" in *AIA Journal* (Washington, D.C.), March 1969; "Dealing with Public Agencies" in *Journal of the Industrial Designers Society of America* (Washington, D.C.), June 1969; "Roofscapes" in *Architectural and Engineering News* (Philadelphia), September 1969; "A Further Proposal" in *The New York Society of Architects Annual Report*, 1970; "Projects for Urban Spaces" in *Design Quarterly* (Minneapolis), Spring 1970; "What Is an Adventure Playground" in *New York Planning Review*, Fall 1970; "Is This Our Utopia?" in *The Social Impact of Urban Design*, Chicago 1971; "Park Power" in *Parks and Recreation* (Arlington, Virginia), July 1971; "Clustering Is for Sharing" in the *New York Times*, 12 March 1972; "Plazas" in *Site* (New York), August 1973; "Where Have All the People Gone?" in *The Designer* (New York), September 1973; "Community Renewal: A Position Paper" in *Proceedings of the ASLA National Growth Task Force*, Washington, D.C. 1974; "Performance as Energy (in Public Spaces)" in *Site* (New York), Fall 1974; "How to Develop New Open Space Inside Our Cities" in *Inland Architect* (Chicago), January 1975.

On FRIEDBERG: books—*Design on the Land* by Norman T. Newton, Cambridge, Massachusetts 1971; *New York* by Dore Ashton, New York 1972; *Alive in the City* by August Heckscher, New York 1974; articles—"Parks Are Not for Planners" by J. C. Ely in *Progressive Architecture* (New York), March 1966; "Riis Houses Replanned Open Space, New York City; Capper Plaza and Buchanan School Playground, Washington, D.C." in *Architectural Record* (New York), December 1966; "Parc de Loisirs de l'Ensemble Jacob Riis" in *L'Architecture d'Aujourd'hui* (Paris), April 1967; "His Work" in *Architectural and Engineering News* (Philadelphia), September 1967; "Designing the Spaces in Between" in *Architectural Record* (New York), March 1968; "Playgrounds in Temporary Vacant Lots, New York" and "Play Space Any Space" in *Architectural Forum* (New York), November 1968; "Bedford-Stuyvesant Superblock" in *L'Architecture d'Aujourd'hui* (Paris), February 1971; "Designing the Urban Landscape: New Projects by M. Paul Friedberg" by Mildred F. Schmertz in *Architectural Record* (New York), March 1972; "M. Paul Friedberg: Designer of Spaces for City People" by Ursula Cliff in *Design and Environment* (New York), Winter 1973/74; "M. Paul Friedberg" in *Kenchiku Bunka* (Tokyo), March 1974; "Towering Urban Garden Under Glass" in *Life* (New York), December 1978.

The actual process of design is a mystery to me. I have no notion of where ideas come from. As most people in creative fields, I work by a trial and error process. I try an idea, and if I like it, I pursue it; if I don't, I discard it or hold it in abeyance.

Design for me is an intuitive process by which I attempt to solve the problem of transferring a verbal, intellectually conceived idea into three dimensional form. It's my wish to be sensitive to the client and his needs, so that I might satisfy him in a manner that is not only understandable and functional but also will provide him with new insights and an expanded view of the world. I don't believe it is necessary to put myself in the place of a client in order to provide him with a fulfilling environmental experience.

Design is the interplay of form or aesthetics with function. The dynamic poles from both sides of this polarized arrangement create the tension that gives drama to the process of designing. I seek solutions which are open ended, if not in form, then in interpretation. In this way the design can be both dynamic and offer opportunities for participation in a fixed environment.

One of the joys of working with plants is that, like all living things, they are always in a state of change —growing and responding to climatic changes of light, wind and other environmental forces. I seek to simulate this state of flux and motion in my designs. I provide environments that are stage settings in which all of us become actors and spectators. Spontaneity, interaction and involvement are the script and scenario; the drama is provided by our encounters and the ways in which we see each other. Both the stage and the seats are fluid, depending upon the activity taking place. I design to provide a choice, a

M. Paul Friedberg: Peavey Plaza, Minneapolis, 1978

chance for participation and interpretation in a wide variety of experiences—without this, my designs have no meaning. That is why I enjoy design problems ranging from playgrounds, which challenge and allow children to display the unplumbed depths of their imagination, to plazas which serve as outdoor rooms, to parks which are spaces for encounters with the natural environment.

Because we change, environments change; therefore, there is no one solution which allows my work to provide constant challenge and interest. There is always room for new ideas, new experiments and adventures. For me, design is a hands-on exercise in which we talk to one another. Through the vocabulary of form, we provide the opportunity for understanding and participation in our environment.

—M. Paul Friedberg

The large volume of work produced over the past twenty years by M. Paul Friedberg and his staff of 35 landscape architects, architects, engineers, planners, urban designers, and graphic and product designers is broad in scope. It includes open space and recreational analysis and programming; comprehensive master planning; development of site and landscape designs; civil engineering; environmental surveying and analysis; research and technology; as well as services patterned for community participation.

Early in his career Friedberg developed a formula for his landscape design to which he remains faithful. It is highly successful with owners and is essentially what each client who hires him hopes he will produce. Friedberg takes the area with which he is working, whatever its size, and breaks it down into spaces of a more human scale by means of steps, platforms, occasional clusters of regularly spaced trees, other trees or flagpoles in rows, play sculpture, playing grounds for particular sports, cantilevered terraces, trellises of heavy lumber, wading pools, fountains, waterfalls, amphitheatres, yacht basins, bollards, kiosks, benches, tables, lighting fixtures and specially designed trash cans. Almost all surfaces are hard and consist of bricks, concrete slabs or granite setts. His larger spaces do not encourage biking, jogging or cross-country skiing because they have few paths which are not interrupted by flights of steps or sudden changes of pattern. His urban landscapes have no sylvan glens, little juxtaposition of soft greenery against asphalt streets and brick facades, no relief from the tough unyielding textures of the city —only more of the same. Friedberg's work bears no resemblance to the urban parks and squares built in the United States in the 19th century, which are still leafy, green, filled with birds and squirrels, and restful.

It is true that today these lovely places are wearing out through over-use, neglect, and lack of money for maintenance. But for grafitti and the fragility of trees (always used sparingly by Friedberg not only because of their initial cost but also because of the expense of pruning and care), his landscapes are virtually indestructable. He doesn't use grass because it wears out, nor earth because it is complicated to drain and gets muddy. Shady glens invite mugging and worse. Friedberg's urban landscapes may be the best we in the United States can do today, and this may be why they are to be found everywhere at every scale from small mid-block playgrounds to cheer a city slum to grand cadenced plazas to enhance the importance of proud new civic monuments.

—Mildred F. Schmertz

FRIEDMAN, Yona.

French. Born in Budapest, Hungary, 5 June 1923; emigrated to France, 1945: naturalized, 1966. Educated at the Technical University, Budapest, 1943; The Technion, Haifa, Israel, Dip.Arch. 1948. Married Denise Charven in 1960; children: Anat and Marianne. Worked as a free-lance architect, 1949–

Yona Friedman: Spatial Town, 1959

57; has worked on theoretical projects and concepts since 1956; settled in Paris, 1958; Founder-Member, GEAM (Groupe d'Etude d'Architecture Mobile), Paris, 1958; published the manifesto *Architecture Mobile,* 1958. Visiting Lecturer, Massachusetts Institute of Technology, Cambridge, University of California at Los Angeles, Harvard University, Cambridge, Massachusetts, University of Michigan, Ann Arbor, Rutgers University, New Brunswick, New Jersey, and Princeton University, New Jersey, 1958–74. Exhibition: French Exhibition, Moscow, 1960; *Une Utopie Réalisée,* Musée d'art Moderne de la ville de Paris, 1975, toured South America. Recipient: Grand Prize, *Venice Film Festival,* 1962; Grand Prix de Récherches et Formes de Demain, Paris, 1967; Architecture Prize, Academy of Arts and Sciences, Berlin, 1972. Honorary Member, Royal Academy of Fine Arts, Amsterdam; Honorary Fellow, Academy of The Hague, 1976. Address: 42 Boulevard Pasteur, 75015 Paris, France.

Works (projects/concepts):

1953/
  58 Cylindrical Shelters
1957/
  58 Span-over Blocks
1958 Cabins for the Sahara
     Stacked Concrete Boxes
1958/
  59 Spatial Town (including Tunis Spatial, Paris Spatial, etc.)
1959 The Venice of Monaco
     African Proposals
1963 Bridge-Town over the English Channel
1964 American Projects
     Headquarters of the SNCF (French National Railways) and Neighbourhood Centre over the marshalling yards of the Gare St. Lazare, Paris
1969 Venice
     The Flatwriter
1971 Alternative plan for the Place Beaubourg, Paris
1972 The Manuals
1974 Architecture by Yourself
1976 CDC Headquarters, Ivry, France

Publications:

By FRIEDMAN: books—*L'Architecture Mobile,* Paris and Tournai, Belgium, 1970; *Pour Une Archi-*

tecture Scientifique, Paris 1971, Cambridge, Massachusetts 1975; *Les Mécanismes Urbains,* Brussels 1968; *La Planification Urbaine,* Brussels 1968; *Société-Environnement,* Brussels 1972; *Meine Fiebel,* Dusseldorf 1974; *Comment vivre entre les autres,* Paris 1974; *It's Your Town—Know How to Protect It,* Strasbourg 1975; *Utopies Réalisables,* Paris, 1975; *Une Utopie Réalisée* (catalogue: Musee d'Art Moderne de la ville de Paris), Paris 1975; *Les Pictogrammes de la Genèse,* Paris 1975; *Comment habiter la terre,* Paris 1976; *L'Architecture de Survie,* Tournai, Belgium 1978; *Où Commence la Ville?,* Paris 1978; articles—more than 500 articles in periodicals throughout the world.

On FRIEDMAN: article—"Yona Friedman: An Appreciation" by Anthony Hill in *RIBA Journal* (London), March 1976.

From 1956 on I have believed that architectural objects should be determined and designed not by the architect but by their future users—the inhabitants. Obviously this does not exclude, for the architect, a technician's role. My research, my publications, my books, all had this basic statement as their starting point.

It is evident that, as a consequence, I had to endure unfriendly reactions from various professional bodies. My first book, *Mobile Architecture,* appeared in print twelve years after its first photocopied publication.

I was trying to develop the possibility of implementation of my thesis; I had many difficulties. In the first years (1957–62) I developed the principle of "infrastructure," a skeleton in which the effectively used space-defining elements (walls, floors, partitions, etc.) could be "mobile" and thus be manipulated directly by the inhabitant. The next step (1962–65) was to demonstrate the enormous combinatory range resulting by such manipulation, and only after 1966 did I start to present these ideas (and some simple methods to help the inhabitant to become master of his own design) to a public of architects rather than to laymen (who are professional inhabitants). I worked for a long time to refine these methods for laymen (using cartoons for explanations—as in the "manuals" distributed in many countries by U.N. agencies, endeavouring to improve conditions in shantytowns).

The first occasion to implement "Mobile Architecture" (in the sense explained before) was at the project C.D.C. in Ivry, near Paris, where 300 people working in a firm conceived for themselves their own future premises, after having had an introductory course based on the "manual." The project was finished in 1976, but the building could not be realized because of C.D.C.'s being absorbed by another company. Actually, other similar implementations are in progress.

Most of my projects prior to 1974 were conceived of as demonstrations of the feasibility of my theses, and many of them influenced architects in many countries, if not to follow the idea, at least to become inspired by the forms and organization of space visualized in my projects.

—Yona Friedman

Yona Friedman is considered more a theoretician than a practicing architect, but he holds an accepted place in 20th century architecture and his projects and concepts are valued by the profession.

Mobility is his theme, and Friedman himself could be described as mobile. He left his native Hungary for France as a young man of 22, and, after completing his architectural studies in Israel during the War of Independence, he returned to Paris. He has since made numerous journeys to the United States and Canada, Brazil, Great Britain, and Germany, where he has presented papers at conferences and lectured at universities and architectural schools.

It was at CIAM in Dubrovnik in 1956 that he realized that his ideas on the mobility of architecture were still largely unexplored. He began his search for young architects throughout Europe with ideas similar to his own, and formed his Group d'Etude d'Architecture Mobile (GEAM) in 1958. By "mobility" Friedman suggests that the functional planning of a building must involve the ultimate user/owner: he must make the planning decisions; he must also be able to alter them again and again as situations change over a period of time. The purpose of GEAM was to research the possibilities of implementing changes for any possible use without having to demolish a building or any part of it. His concept of a non-determined infrastructure and the technique of "spanning over" a clear ground level allow the self-planner to design or re-design his space as he needs to use it.

Friedman's ideas were very slow to gather interest, but in the 1960's his first projects were published in Japan with the encouragement and help of Kenzo Tange. Interest in his work appeared across a wide spectrum of the profession, from the young student, Moshe Safdie, who used the subject for his master's thesis, to the wise and experienced Buckminster Fuller.

Despite his success and the interest now shown in his concepts, Friedman has remained a theoretician, not a builder, yet he derives enormous satisfaction from seeing his ideas implemented in the work of other architects and planners. He is also interested in putting into simple language, understood by the layman, the necessary instructions for the self-planner. This goal involves more than simple "do-it-yourself" planning instructions. Friedman's theories—to involve the occupant/worker/user in his surroundings, to allow him to plan them, to allow him the possibility of change to suit his routine and to facilitate his day to day work—require continual reassessment and refinement. He spends his time re-researching and re-formulating his original ideas and working out what he sees as faults in his own proposals.

His book, *Towards a Scientific Architecture,* has been compared to Le Corbusier's *Towards a New Architecture;* and it is considered by some to contain deeper and more innovative architectural thought.

—Muriel Emanuel

FRY, E(dwin) Maxwell.

British. Born in Wallasey, Cheshire, 2 August 1899. Educated at the Liverpool Institute, 1910–17; School of Architecture, University of Liverpool, under Charles Reilly, 1920–23. Served in the King's Regiment, 1918–20: Lieutenant; served with the Royal Engineers in the Department of Fortifications and Works, War Office, London, 1939–42: Staff Captain/Major; Deputy Commandant, Royal Engineers, Gold Coast, West Africa, 1942–44. Married Ethel Speakman in 1927 (divorced, 1942); the architect Jane B. Drew, q.v., in 1942; daughter: Ann. Assistant to the architects Adams and Thompson, London, 1925–27; Chief Assistant, Architects Department, Southern Railway, London, 1927–30; Partner, with Thomas Adams and Longstreth Thompson, Adams, Thompson and Fry, London, 1930–34; Partner, with Walter Gropius, Gropius and Fry, London, 1934–36, and continued alone until 1939; Town Planning Adviser to the Resident Minister, West Africa, 1944–46; Founder Partner, with Jane B. Drew, Fry, Drew and Partners, London (including Fry, Drew, Drake, and Lasdun, 1951–58), 1946–73, and Fry, Drew, Knight and Creamer (with Frank S. Knight and Norman Creamer), London, since 1973: now retired. Senior Architect for the New Capital, Chandigarh, Punjab, India, 1951–54. Vice-President, Royal Institute of British Architects, 1961–62. Exhibition: Drian Gallery, 1974 (paintings and drawings). Recipient: Royal Gold Medal for Architecture, Royal Institute of British Architects, 1964. LL.D.: University of Ibadan, Nigeria, 1966. Fellow of the Royal Institute of British Architects, and of the Royal Town Planning Institute; Associate of the Royal Academy, 1966, and Royal Academician, 1972. Honorary Fellow, American Institute of Architects, 1973. C.B.E. (Commander, Order of the British Empire), 1953. Address: The Lake House, The Old Hollow, Rowfant, Sussex, England.

Works:

1933 Showroom for Westminster Electricity Supply Corporation, Victoria Street, London (demolished)
1934 "Little Winch" (house), Chipperfield, Hertfordshire
1935 The Sun House, Frognal Way, Hampstead, London
R. E. Sassoon House, St. Mary's Road, Peckham, London
Apartments, St. Leonard's Hill, Windsor, Berkshire (project; with Walter Gropius)
1936 Kensal House, Ladbroke Grove, London
House, 66 Old Church Street, Chelsea, London (with Walter Gropius)
Impington Village College, Cambridgeshire (with Walter Gropius)
The Wood House, Skipbourne, near Sevenoaks, Kent (with Walter Gropius)
Papworth Sanatorium School, Cambridgeshire (project; with Walter Gropius)
Histon School, Cambridgeshire (with Walter Gropius)
London Film Productions Worshops, Denham, Hertfordshire (with Walter Gropius)
Donaldson House, Sussex (with Walter Gropius)
1937 "Miramonte" (house), Coombe, near Kingston, Surrey
1938 Electricity showrooms, Regent Street, London
Flats, Ladbroke Grove, London
1940 Homerton College Nursery School, Cambridge
Cecil House (girls hostel), Gower Street, London
1946 Aburi School and College, Ghana
Adisadel College, Ghana (with Jane Drew)
Accra Community College, Ghana
Amedzofe Teacher Training College, Togoland (with Jane Drew)
1948 Broadcasting House, Nigerian Broadcasting Company, Kaduna

1949 The Tea Centre, London
1950 Passfields (flats), Lewisham, London (with Jane Drew)
Cooperative Bank of Western Nigeria, Ibadan
Ashanti Secondary School for Boys, Kumasi, Ghana
Royal Exchange Assurance Company Ltd., Ibadan, Nigeria
1951 Waterloo Bridge Entrance and Harbour Bar, *South Bank Exhibition,* Festival of Britain, London (with Jane Drew)
1953 Flats, Whitefoot Lane, Lewisham, London (with Jane Drew)
Flats, Bromley Road, Lewisham, London
1954 Oriental Insurance Company Office Block, Calcutta
1956 New Capital City, Chandigarh, India (with Jane Drew, Le Corbusier, and Pierre Jeanneret)
1958 Teacher Training Centre, Wudil, Nigeria
Women's Teachers Training College, Kano, Nigeria
1959 University College, Ibadan, Nigeria (with Jane Drew)
1960 Holy Cross School, Lagos, Nigeria
St. Matthias School, Lagos, Nigeria
St. Patrick's School, Lagos, Nigeria
College of Engineering, and Veterinary Science Building, University of Liverpool
Dow Agro Chemicals Ltd. Plant and Offices, King's Lynn, Norfolk
1961 British Petroleum Company Offices, Lagos, Nigeria
Housing, Lagos, Nigeria
Offices for Longmans Green, publishers, Lagos, Nigeria
1963 Wates Ltd. Head Office, Norbury, London
Plan for the University of Sheffield, Yorkshire
1964 Isle of Thorns College, Chelwood Gate, Sussex
1965 Chelwood House, Gloucester Square, London
1966 Legislative Assembly, Port Louis, Mauritius
1967 Kingston House, Hull
Macintosh Square Development, Gibraltar
1969 Mid-Glamorgan Crematorium
1972 Redevelopment of Hatfield Old Town, Hertfordshire
Garage, Old Hatfield, Hertfordshire
Shop Block A, Hatfield, Hertfordshire
1973 A1 Trunk Road Development Study
1974 Flats, Porchester Terrace, London
1975 Breakspear Crematorium, Northwood, London
1977 Institute of Education, Le Reduit, Mauritius

Publications:

By FRY: books—*The Need for Planning Town and Countryside* (pamphlet), with John Gloag, London 1933; *English Town Hall Architecture,* London 1934; *Fine Building,* London 1944; *The Bauhaus and the Modern Movement,* London 1968; *Art in a Machine Age,* London 1969; *Maxwell Fry: Autobiographical Sketches,* London 1975; books with Jane B. Drew—*Architecture for Children,* London 1944, revised edition as *Architecture and the Environment,* London 1976; *Village Housing in the Tropics,* in collaboration with Harry L. Ford, London 1947; *Tropical Architecture in the Humid Zone,* London 1956; *Tropical Architecture in the Dry and Humid Zones,* London 1964; articles—in *The Architects' Journal, RIBA Journal, Building, Contemporary Review,* etc.

On FRY: book—*Fry, Drew, Knight, Creamer: Architecture,* introduction by H.A.N. Brockman, London 1978; articles—"Max Fry Remembers" by Maurice Cooper in *Building Design* (London), 24 January 1975; "The Origins of Impington" by Jack Pritchard and Alan Moody in *Northern Architect* (Sunderland), April 1975; "Modern Architecture in England" by Miguel Corominas in *Arquitectura* (Ma-

E. Maxwell Fry: The Sun House, Frognal Way, Hampstead, London, 1935

drid), May 1975; "Max Fry" by A. E. J. Morris and Cornelius Murphy in *Building* (London), 31 October 1975; "Nigeria Today" by Noel Moffett in *RIBA Journal* (London), June 1977.

I entered architecture sufficiently versed in medieval architecture to win a history essay prize soon after joining the Liverpool School of Architecture. By the time I set my real course in architecture I had immersed myself in its classical interpretation of which I could value its detailed modulations as I could its larger modellings.

It was my appreciation of its excellence *in itself* that justified me in finding no place for it in a technocratic world and renouncing it. It was the prompting of my moral as of my reasoning nature that decided me in favour of a clean sweep of historical and associational references and that brought me at once to the centre of the Modern Architectural Movement, but without the widespread but foolish revolutionary gesture of condemning all that came before me.

In the hey-day of the Movement I found all the warmth and humanity I needed, for it freely encompassed what we have now, unwisely, I think, separated into the pseudo-science of sociology, into the amorphous pursuit of an environment, into a vain and vapid historicism, and into town-planning divorced from its roots in architecture.

The basic principles of the Movement enabled me to analyse the human and climatic conditions of the humid West African tropics and to harmonise them in a manner that remained valid over a respectable period of time in any but the centres of high technology, money and nationalism.

A devastating war bringing in its wake vast increases in mechanical reproduction and instrumentation, together with an intensification of both commercialism and bureaucracy, prevented modern architecture from a gradual diversification in various materials at the expense of reinforced concrete as the sole means of expression, though not of support. I have never used it in its "brut" state on account of its manifest inability to weather in any but the dryest climates.

For all my working life I have been an independent individual for whom work has been the greatest pleasure. I believe that art is a celebration of life and is so recognised by those who value life. In my old age I paint, which is the next best thing.

—E. Maxwell Fry

E. Maxwell Fry can be rightly regarded as the father of the Modern Movement in architecture in Britain. Born in Liverpool, he trained at the University School of Architecture under Professor Charles Reilly and joined the London town planning practice of Adams and Thompson in the mid 1930's. One of the first examples in London of Fry's work was the showroom for the then Westminster Electricity Supply Corporation in Victoria Street. The building has since been destroyed in the redevelopment of Victoria Street, but it was one of the outstanding examples of shop design in Europe. By the use of a large non-reflecting window set back from the pavement, Fry united interior and exterior of the showroom. The interior fittings and furniture were all designed with great care and set a standard for shop design that has seldom been equalled.

In the 1930's much of Maxwell Fry's work was concerned with individual houses, many of which were built only after prolonged battles with planning authorities and local objectors. Fortunately, several still survive and today, more than 40 years later, it is difficult to understand the heated debate caused by "Little Winch" at Chipperfield, Hertfordshire, a flat roofed, brick house with a weather-boarded studio, and the Sun House, Frognal Way, Hampstead, a concrete house on a south facing steeply sloping site with splendid views over London.

The problem of low rental housing was one to which Fry devoted much attention and research at a time when local authority housing was universally conceived in "mock Georgian" style. The block of flats built in Peckham and known as R. E. Sassoon House was unique. Admittedly, the size of the scheme was modest by today's standards—twenty flats on five floors with balcony access and no lift—but each flat had a large balcony and generously sized rooms, fitted kitchen and a separate bathroom. This latter feature was a novelty in "working class" dwellings where the norm was a bath under a tabletop in the kitchen. By careful standardization of details and repetition throughout, Fry built the flats of in-situ concrete at an average cost of £362 per flat (including professional fees), just over 50 pence per square foot; they were let at economic rents of little more than 50 pence per week. Kensal House, a second low-cost housing project, was built on the site of an abandoned gas-holder in Ladbroke Grove. The scheme, which was sponsored by the Gas Light and Coke Company to demonstrate the use of coal gas,

consisted of 68 flats and included a social club, tenants' recreation room, shops, and a nursery school and playground. Like Sassoon House, Kensal House was limited to 5 floors without lifts, but staircase access was provided to each pair of flats instead of the common gallery approach. The flats were spacious and well planned, and each had both sitting and drying balconies; once again the structure was in-situ reinforced concrete, and Fry paid great attention to detail and to standardization. Rents at Kensal House also averaged 50p per week. Few modern housing projects can compare favourably with these schemes both in overall conception and detailed design: after 40 years Kensal House is still a model of its kind. Maxwell Fry's early housing work set the standard, influenced by the Gropius's housing work of the early '30s, by which all subsequent housing must be judged.

Fry himself admits that his pre-war work was influenced by Mies van der Rohe, and both The Sun House and Miramonte show that influence clearly in the horizontal window pattern, the white walls and the projecting balcony roofs, all reminiscent of Mies' Tugendhat House of 1930. Walter Gropius joined Fry in London from 1934 to 1936, having left Germany as a refugee from the Nazi regime; but during his residence in Britain little advantage was taken of the presence of such a distinguished educationalist and designer. A number of interesting projects were produced with Fry, but they were often rejected because they were too modern. The most important building actually erected by the Fry-Gropius partnership was the Impington Village College. This building, small by present-day school standards, was a landmark in school design in its integration of building and site; the simple internal spatial arrangements and human scale resulted in a complex that caused a contemporary critic to describe it as "one of the finest sets of school buildings in the country."

During the war years Maxwell Fry spent part of his period of war service in West Africa and later advised on village planning in Nigeria. This led to the establishment of a practice with Jane Drew which was responsible for large scale planning and building work in that country. It was typical of the Fry approach to architecture that a great deal of basic research was carried out on tropical architecture, and the book by Fry and Drew on the subject soon became the standard textbook for architects involved in building in the tropics. Much of the work of the practice was concerned with school and university building. In the immediate post-war years Maxwell Fry was one of the first British architects to become involved in overseas work, and his distinctive style of building, using local materials combined with careful detailing intended to reduce the impact of the climatic extremes, resulted in a series of buildings, such as the University of Ibadan, which demonstrate Fry's role as a pioneer.

In 1951 Le Corbusier invited Maxwell Fry to join the team at Chandigarh, the new capital of the Punjab in India. Fry, with Jane Drew, took on the task of translating Le Corbusier's design for a new city in the arid plains of North India into a reality. They were particularly concerned with the housing zones of the project, and it is in these areas that Chandigarh is most successful, in spite of the rigid road grid established by Le Corbusier's master plan. The architectural achievements of the new capital were largely due to the influence of Maxwell Fry and his concern not only for good buildings but also for the people who would use them.

Throughout his professional career Maxwell Fry has always been a pioneer. Attention to detail, the understanding of basic needs, and his insistence on the importance of a building in its environment has earned him a place in the history of 20th century architecture.

—Edward D. Mills

FUCHS, Bohuslav.

Czechoslovakian. Born in Všechovice, Bystřice Pod Hostýnem, 24 March 1895. Educated at the Academy of Arts, Prague, under Jan Kotěra, 1916–19. Married. Worked in the architectural office of Jan Kotěra, Prague, 1919–21. In private practice, Brno, from 1923. Architect to the City Building Department, Brno, 1923–29. Lecturer, School of Art, Gottwaldov, Czechoslovakia, in the 1930's; Lecturer, 1945–47, and Professor of Architecture, 1947–58, Technical University of Brno. Member, CIAM (Congrès Internationaux d'Architecture Moderne). Honorary Corresponding Member, Royal Institute of British Architects, 1937. *Died* (in Brno) *25 September 1972.*

Works:

1920 Master plan for Malá Strana, Prague (competition project)
Master plan for Letná, Prague (competition project; with J. Štěpánek and A. Moudry)
Master plan for the city of Prostějov, Czechoslovakia (competition porject; with J. Štěpánek)
1923 Administration Building, Bystřice Pod Hostýnem, Czechoslovakia
1924 Meat Exchange, Brno
1925 Ceremonial Hall, Central Cemetery, Brno
Cafe Zeman, Brno
1927 Hotel Avion, Brno
Bohuslav Fuchs House, Brno
1928 Nový Dům Housing Estate, Brno
International Trade Fair and Exhibition Hall, Prague (with O. Tyl)
Exhibition Pavilion, *Exposition of Contemporary Culture,* Brno
1929 Moravian Bank, Brno (with Wiesner)
Workers' Colony, Lyskov u Frýdku-Kistek, Czechoslovakia
Masaryk Student Hotels, Brno
1930 Public baths, Zábrdovice, Brno
Vesna Women's Trade School and Hostel, Brno (with J. Polášek)
1935/
36 Zelena Zaba Open-Air Swimming Pool, Cafe and Restaurant, Trenčianské Teplice, Slovakia, Czechoslovakia
1935/
39 Numerous town and country houses in Czechoslovakia
1938 Railway Station Post Office, Brno
1948 Bus Terminal Building, Brno (partially constructed)
1962/
64 Master plan for the National Theatre area, Prague

Publications:

On FUCHS: articles—"Die Neue Frauenschule in Brunn" and "Das Brunner Studenthaus" in *Wasmuth's Monatshefte für Baukunst* (Berlin), vol. 15, 1931; "Das Haus der Mahrischen Bank in Brunn" in *Wasmuth's Monatshefte für Baukunst* (Berlin), vol. 16, 1932; "Das Stadtische Bad in Brunn" by Wilhelm Bisom in *Wasmuth's Monatshefte für Baukunst* (Berlin), vol. 17, 1933; "A Swimming Pool in Czechoslovakia" in *Architect and Building News* (London), 23 September 1938; "Piscine Thermale en Plein Air à Trencianske Teplice, Tchechoslovaquie" in *L'Architecture d'Aujourd'hui* (Paris), October 1938; "Bathing Pool, Czechoslovakia" in *The Architects' Journal* (London), 16 March 1939; "Piscina en Checoslovaquia" in *Arquitectura* (Madrid), July 1943; "Bohuslav Fuchs, 1895–1972" in *Bauwelt* (Berlin), 13 November 1972; "Obituary: Bohuslav Fuchs" in *RIBA Journal* (London), January 1973; "Bohuslav Fuchs" by Frank Arneil Walker in *The Architects' Journal* (London), 7 November 1973.

Bohuslav Fuchs was 23 years of age in 1918 when the Czechoslovak Republic came into being. He was then a student at the Academy of Arts in Prague under Professor Jan Kotěra in whose celebrated School of Architecture a number of leading Czechoslovak architects were trained, among them Gočár, Chochol and Janák. Fuchs inevitably caught the enthusiasm and optimism that swept through the new independent Republic, an ideal social and cultural climate for the development of a highly-gifted architect who had already had a thorough technical training before becoming Kotěra's pupil.

As early as 1920 Fuchs, while working as an assistant in Kotěra's studio, was among the prize winners in two town planning competitions for the Malá Strana district of Prague and the new City of Prostějov.

During the formative years of the early 1920's, which were of great importance in the evolution of modern architecture, there was a struggle to break from the already sterile but still prevailing formalism of the past and to find a new visual and functional expression of the rapidly changing social and political conditions. Fuchs' first buildings of this period—the Administrative offices in Bystřice and the Meat Exchange in Brno—vividly illustrate this struggle. They are a mixture of Dutch influence (Dudok), Behrens' monumentality and the starkness of Adolf Loos, but Fuchs' planning already shows the clarity and functional logic which would mark his later work.

His 1925 buildings in Brno—the Ceremonial Hall for the City Cemetery and the Cafe Zeman—marked the next step towards a definitive breakthrough, which came two years later with the Hotel Avion and the housing estate Nový Dům. Mies van der Rohe, in a lecture at the Technical University in Brno in 1930, said that the Hotel Avion was one of the most important buildings in the modern international movement. It stands on a very narrow and deep site in a small street in the centre of the city and is a little masterpiece of spatial and functional design. The progression of interlocking spaces, both in plan and section, is perfectly handled and visually exciting. The Vitrolite-clad elevation has a crispness and precision that could only have been achieved by the new industrial technology. Fuchs repeated it on his Moravian Bank in Brno, and the cladding was subsequently widely used by other architects.

The International Trade Fair and Exhibition Hall, bold in conception, with a daring reinforced concrete structure, gave Fuchs an opportunity to take his understanding of space a step further. On a visit to Prague in 1938 Le Corbusier commented: "It is instructive for me to see architecture on this scale in actual reality. I, who have so far built only a few relatively small buildings, understand now how I must design big buildings."

In the foothills of the Carpathian Mountains in a beautiful thickly wooded valley, Fuchs built the Zelená Žaba (Green Frog) Open Air Swimming Pool, Café and Restaurant. This light and airy building, its long curving balconies and terraces following the contours of the hills, belongs in its setting as if it had grown up with the trees. It was his last major work before the Second World War.

After the War Fuchs devoted most of his time to town planning and teaching at the Technical University of Brno. Town planning—then a purely statistical and technical problem, the exclusive domain of the civil engineer—was for Fuchs an integral part of architecture. To clear logic, strict discipline in functional planning, thorough understanding of structure and an appreciation of existing social conditions, he added a feeling for form and composition that gave his work an added dimension.

Fuchs' contribution to the shaping of modern architecture in the 1920's and '30's in Czechoslovakia and in Europe as a whole was very considerable, but he was, perhaps, less well known abroad than some of his contemporaries. This may to some extent have been due to the fact that he lived and worked not in the capital Prague but in Brno, Moravia, the second city of Czechoslovakia.

—Eugene Rosenberg

FUJII, Hiromi.

Japanese. Born in Tokyo, 23 August 1935. Studied at the Waseda University School of Architecture, Tokyo, 1958; studied and worked in Professor Take's studio at Waseda University, 1958–64. Married Hiroko Todoroki in 1968; child: Yuri. Worked for Angelo Mangiarotti, Milan, 1964–66, with Peter Smithson, London, 1966, and for Yorke, Rosenberg, Mardall, London, 1967. Since 1968, Principal, Hiromi Fujii Architect and Associates, Tokyo. Lecturer, 1968, and Associate Professor, 1973, Shibaura Institute of Technology, Tokyo; Visiting Critic, Waseda University School of Architecture, 1978. Exhibitions: *Matwya Exhibition,* Tokyo, 1978; *New Wave of Japanese Architecture,* toured the United States, 1978. Address (office): Room 402, 37–4 Toyama-cho, Shinjuku-ku, Tokyo, Japan.

Works:

1971 Suzuki House, Tokyo
Suzuki Apartment, Tokyo
Project C (house)
Project E (house)
Project S (house)
Project L (house)
Project for Mr. Y (house)
Project for Mr. A (house)
1972 Snack 7 (restaurant), Tokyo
1973 Miyajima House, Tokyo
1975 Todoroki House, Chiba, Japan
Project: Similar, Connotation (house)
Project: Continuity (house)
Project: Similar, Symmetry (house)
Project: Congruity, Symmetry (house)
Project: Similar, Connotation, Junction (house)
1976 M Office Building, Saitama, Japan

Publications:

By FUJII: articles—"Architectural Senses of Anonymity" in *Toshijutaku* (Tokyo), January 1969; "On Negativity" in *Space Design* (Tokyo), February 1969; "A Note on the Negativity of Materialism" in *Architecture + Urbanism* (Tokyo), February, April and July 1971; "Architecture of Negativeness" in *Toshijutaku* (Tokyo), October 1971; "Now What Are We Asking of Architecture" in *Space Design* (Tokyo), March 1972; "Articulation" in *Toshijutaku* (Tokyo), June 1972; "Indication of the Visual Point of Absence" in *Space Design* (Tokyo), August 1972; "The Meaning of Negativeness" in *The Japan Architect* (Tokyo), July 1973; "Sympathy for the 'Solid' " in *Architecture + Urbanism* (Tokyo), December 1973; "Reflection and Transparency" in *Architecture + Urbanism* (Tokyo), June 1974; "Aspects of Intimacy to Objects" in *Toshijutaku* (Tokyo), June 1974; "On Deep Structure" in *Kenchikubunka* (Tokyo), April 1975; "The Castle of Cards" in *The Japan Architect* (Tokyo), July 1975; "Expression for Itself" in *Kenchikubunka* (Tokyo), November 1975; "Zero Degree of Recognition" in *The Japan Architect* (Tokyo), June 1976; "Liberation from Existence" in *The Japan Architect* (Tokyo), February 1977.

On FUJII: book—*New Wave of Japanese Architecture,* exhibition catalogue, by Kenneth Frampton, New York 1978; articles—"Hiromi Fujii" by Veda Makoto in *Mizue* (Tokyo), July 1975; "The Game of Intellectual Matter" by Kazuyuki Honda in *The Japan Architect* (Tokyo), August 1975; "Intension to Architectural Language" by Masahiko Mineo in *Shotenkenchiku* (Tokyo), August 1975; "The Work of Hiromi Fujii" by David Stewart in *Architecture + Urbanism* (Tokyo), September 1975; "An Anarchist's Guide to Modern Architecture" by Chris Fawcett in *Architectural Association Quarterly* (London), no. 3, 1975.

It happened several years ago. I used to pass in front of an old building near my office that was being

Hiromi Fujii: Todoroki House, Chiba, Japan, 1975

walls, ceiling, floor and a straight edge stretching to the infinity of the grey square box. It was as if I was under an hallucination, absorbed by the infinity of the tunnel. I felt a certain response: I thought of the scene as beautiful. Surrounded by these objects, I was more comfortable in the complete silence than in the noises of the town, deeply impressed more by the existence of the grey color than by the bright colors of the outside world. Is it possible to explain exactly about this tunnel? Of course, it is correct to say that it is an underground communication road from one place to another—but that is not the point: an explanation of function does not explain my experience in the tunnel. The only explanation of the experience of the tunnel is that it involved blank, square geometrical patterns and grey color; the reason of my partiality for the tunnel is that it refused every usual significance. It is an ultimate shape without any banal explanation, without any meaning in our everyday life. This ultimate shape is the very form of the blank geometrical patterns and the grey color which I have been repeating, over and over again. This form can also be said to be a negative object. When I stand in front of this negativeness I am aware of the uselessness of expression, of the terms which I have learned in order to explain. There, negative form and color is so neutral that we have to create its meaning as we like. It may also be said that this negative object is absolute existence, which is impartial, neither objective nor subjective, neither rational nor irrational.

I have been explaining my experiences of these encounters with the object at great length—but I have been trying to show that my new theory is on the same lines as that of something as material as a manhole cover and something as abstract as the color grey. It is difficult to generalize or to formulate a logical theory here and now. At the moment, on one hand, I am trying to put the theory of the manhole cover and the color grey into a logical pattern, but, on the other hand, I am searching for a pattern more practical and more radical to replace it.

—Hiromi Fujii

The information immediately available to us before one of Hiromi Fujii's houses is both slender and rich. He feels no need to inform. He wants to express nothing, consequently his buildings are without the burden of language. He presents us with an objective denial of any representation. By expressing nothing he is acting in accordance with his perception of what he calls the encompassing "emptiness." This expression of nothing is the paradoxical basis of his work, for one of his buildings is quite clearly a threat to the emptiness. His designs, therefore, have a way of simultaneously portraying and effectively diminishing the emptiness, and through this dialectical process we come to envisage the limits within which architecture can be found. Imagining and understanding aren't so very different.

Fujii is appraising architecture on a time scale far removed from our usual reckoning. The past that he faces could be said to be our future, and this is how the menacing aspect enters in. It's the fellowship of the marvellous and the ominous: his designs don't fit current facts but are more predictive, probing into what others shun. Can we say we learn enough from one of his designs to guide us through our surroundings? What can we recognize there apart from architecture itself? Faces have two eyes, and only one needs to be seen for a face to be identified. If a head, one can guarantee a body and a pair of legs. In much the same way we can make great sense of a house by just glimpsing its pitched roof, and through a chain of associated images readily picture it. This isn't the case with a house by Fujii, and identification of its function is impeded by its form, scale and materials, so that its setting in a residential context only serves to exaggerate the ambiguity, i.e. the richness of conflicting associations. Are we being urged to help salvage architecture from the 20th century? Or is it beyond assistance, does it need something more?

To see one of Fujii's buildings is to see the whole

pulled down. On that particular day, as it was already late in the evening, I could see no one working on the building. Several stories of the old building had been demolished, leaving only a few concrete pillars and the first and second floors.

The buildings nearby were already lit up; neon lights were beginning to brighten; people were hurrying for their homes. The thick, clouded sky echoed commotion and the noises of the town. Yet, in spite of the clamour of the town, I felt a different atmosphere, as if of a completely different time and space, over the block of the demolished building. Inside and outside of the building there were lumps of stone, concrete and iron scattered about: there was no space to put a foot.

At the one corner retaining some of its original shape, the thick concrete wall's section produced irregular geometrical patterns. They dispersed so much that they looked almost beautiful. Surrounded by these bare "objects," which seemed lurid and frightful, I was more impressed with the grave importance of existence than with magnificent town buildings. "Is our meaningless and useless existence untrue—or are you who grasp it only in that way mistaken?" This encounter with objects was one of the few experiences that appealed to my inner life.

A ruin is, fundamentally speaking, a place which is bare or useless. The real shape or phase of objects can be visible here, whereas in our daily life it is

difficult to face up to the reality of a structure because of its effective value, its necessity, or the terms we artifically believe. But ruins no longer flatter us, they are no longer subordinate to men. They recover their real expression, and this existence itself appeals exactly to our inner life. From the ordinary point of view, this bare object, after effacing its effectiveness or its ordinary affectation, can be described as simply meaningless or "negative." On the other hand, from a spiritual point of view, it can be described as "positive." But I dare to name it a "negative object" because of its daily occurrence, and also name the process effacing its usual meaning as "negativeness."

Putting aside the question of whether this negative object can be recognized as architecture, I convey my new encounter between the mind and the object in a concept of "negativeness." Moreover, it is not only this bare object in the ruins that can be called a "negative object;" we are also able to find unexpected objects when we enlarge the encounter between man and objects.

Even now, I am struck from time to time by the old encounter with the space abruptly seen at the corner of the town where there are splendid buildings and colorful displays in shop windows.

A previous encounter with space was in a tunnel, an encounter I still remember as of blank geometric patterns stretching straightforwardly. Nothing in particular appealed to me there. I saw nothing but grey color fading away between the boundaries of the of architecture on trial, and in this way he can be considered the watching institution of Japanese architecture, tackling many problems not only overlooked by architects, but also more generally ignored. He goes directly to the authentic processes of architecture, while ignoring what seems to be the actual components. He does not begin with a site and derive from it some particular values; instead, at the outset, he has an a priori formulation, which he doesn't so much apply to the site as apply to the whole world. Everything must be compatible with the real world, and his buildings are no exception, despite the rigorous standard he pursues in his own way. Seeing Fujii's work is one way of seeing more than I have ever seen before.

—Chris Fawcett

FULLER, (Richard) Buckminster.

American. Born in Milton, Massachusetts, 12 July 1895. Educated at Milton Academy, 1904–13; Harvard University, Cambridge, Massachusetts, 1913–15; United States Naval Academy, Annapolis, Maryland, 1917. Served in the United States Navy, 1917–19: Lieutenant. Married Anne Hewlett in 1917; children: Alexandra and Allegra. Assistant Export Manager, Armour and Company, New York, 1919–21; National Accounts Sales Manager, Kelly-Springfield Truck Company, 1922; President, Stockade Building System, Chicago, 1922–27; Founder and President, 4D Company, Chicago, 1927–32; Editor and Publisher, *Shelter* magazine, Philadelphia, 1930–32; Founder, Director, and Chief Engineer, Dymaxion Corporation, Bridgeport, Connecticut, 1932–36; Assistant to the Director of Research and Development, Phelps Dodge Corporation, New York, 1936–38; Technical Consultant on the staff of *Fortune* magazine, New York, 1938–40; Vice-President and Chief Engineer, Dymaxion Company Inc., Delaware, 1940–50; Chief Mechanical Engineer, United States Board of Economic Warfare, Washington, D.C., 1942–44, and Special Assistant to the Deputy Director of the United States Foreign Economic Administration, Washington, 1944; Chairman and Chief Engineer, Dymaxion Dwelling Machine Corporation, Wichita, Kansas, 1944–46; Chairman, Fuller Research Foundation, Wichita, 1946–54; President, Synergetics Inc., Raleigh, North Carolina, 1954–59. Since 1949, President of Geodesics Inc., Forest Hills, New York; since 1957, President of Plydomes Inc., Des Moines, Iowa; since 1959, Chairman, Tetrahelix Corporation, Hamilton, Ohio. Research Professor, 1959–68, University Professor, 1968–75, Distinguished University Professor, 1972–75, and University Professor Emeritus since 1975, Southern Illinois University, Carbondale. Charles Eliot Norton Professor of Poetry, Harvard University, 1962–63; Harvey Cushing Orator, American Association of Neuro-Surgeons, 1967; Nehru Lecturer, New Delhi, 1969; Hoyt Fellow, Yale University, New Haven, Connecticut, 1969; Fellow, St. Peter's College, Oxford, 1970; World Fellow in Residence, consortium of the University of Pennsylvania, Haverford College, Swarthmore College, Bryn Mawr College, and the University City Science Center, Philadelphia, and Consultant to the Design Science Institute, Philadelphia, 1972–75; Tutor in Design Science, International Community College, Los Angeles, 1975. Editor-at-Large, *World Magazine,* New York, 1972–75. President, Triton Foundation, Cambridge, Massachusetts, 1967; International President, MENSA, Paris, 1975, and World Society for Ekistics, Athens, 1975. Exhibitions: Dymaxion House, Harvard University, 1929, and American Institute of Architects, Washington, D.C., 1930; Dymaxion Automobile, *World's Fair,* Chicago, 1933; Dymaxion Bathroom, Museum of Modern Art, New York, 1937; Dymaxion Deploy-

Buckminster Fuller: United States Pavilion, *Expo '67,* Montreal, 1967

ment Unit, Museum of Modern Art, New York, 1940; Dymaxion World Map, Museum of Modern Art, New York, 1943; outdoor garden exhibit, Museum of Modern Art, New York, 1959; United States Embassy, London (one-man), 1962; Spoleto Festival, Italy (one-man), 1967; Dymaxion Car No. 2, Museum of Modern Art, New York, 1968; Museum of Science and Industry, Chicago (retrospective), 1973, subsequently toured the United States; Tetrascroll, Museum of Modern Art, New York, and Museum of Art, Philadelphia, 1977; *50 Years of Buckminster Fuller,* Ronald Feldman Gallery, New York, 1977. Recipient: Award of Merit, American Institute of Architects, New York Chapter, 1952; Grand Prize, *Triennale,* Milan, 1954, 1957; Award of Merit, United States Marine Corps, 1955; Gold Medal, Scarab: National Architectural Society, 1958; Gold Medal, AIA, Philadelphia Chapter, 1960; Frank P. Brown Medal, Franklin Institute, Philadelphia, 1962; Allied Professions Gold Medal, 1963, Architectural Design Award, 1968, and Gold Medal, 1970, national AIA; Plomado de Oro Award, Society of Mexican Architects, 1963; Delta Phi Delta Gold Key, 1964; Creative Achievement Award, Brandeis University, Waltham, Massachusetts, 1965; First Award of Excellence, Industrial Designers Society of America, 1966; Order of Lincoln Medal, Lincoln Academy, Illinois, 1967; Gold Medal for Architecture, National Institute of Arts and Letters, 1968; Royal Gold Medal for Architecture, Royal Institute of British Architects, 1968; Citation of Merit, United States Department of Housing and Urban Development, 1969; Citation of Excellence, National Institute of Steel Construction, 1969; Humanist of the Year Award, American Association of Humanists, 1969; McGraw-Hill Master Designer in Product Engineering Award, 1969; Alpha Rho Chi Master Architect Life Award, 1970; President's Award, University of Detroit, 1971; Sal-

magundi Medal, Salmagundi Club, 1971; Annual Award of Merit, Philadelphia Art Alliance, 1973; Honorary Citizenship Award, City of Philadelphia, 1973; Planetary Citizens Award, United Nations, 1975. Doctor of Design: North Carolina State University, Raleigh, 1954; Doctor of Arts: University of Michigan, Ann Arbor, 1955; Southern Illinois University, 1959; D.Sc.: Washington University, St. Louis, 1957; University of Colorado, Boulder, 1964; Bates College, Lewiston, Maine, 1969; University of Maine, Orono, 1972; Pratt Institute, Brooklyn, New York, 1974; McGill University, Montreal, 1974; D.H.L.: Rollins College, Winter Park, Florida, 1960; Monmouth College, West Long Branch, New Jersey, 1965; California State Colleges, 1966; Long Island University, Greenvale, New York, 1966; Dartmouth College, Hanover, New Hampshire, 1968; University of Rhode Island, Kingston, 1968; New England College, Henniker, New Hampshire, 1968; Brandeis University, Waltham, Massachusetts, 1970; Columbia College, Chicago, 1970; St. Joseph's College, Philadelphia, 1974; University of Pennsylvania, Philadelphia, 1974; Hobart and William Smith Colleges, Geneva, New York, 1975; D.L.: Clemson University, South Carolina, 1964; Park College, Parkville, Missouri, 1970; Grinnell College, Iowa, 1972; Emerson College, Boston, 1972; Nasson College, Springvale, Maine, 1973; D.F.A.: University of New Mexico, Albuquerque, 1964; California State College of Arts and Crafts, Oakland, 1966; Ripon College, Wisconsin, 1968; Boston College, 1969; Minneapolis School of Art, 1970; Rensselaer Polytechnic Institute, Troy, New York, 1973; D.Eng.: Clarkson College of Technology, Potsdam, New York, 1967; University of Notre Dame, Indiana, 1974; D.Arch. Eng.: University of Wisconsin, Madison, 1969; Doctor of Science and Humane Letters: Wilberforce University, Ohio, 1970; Doctor of Fine and Applied Arts: Southeastern Massachusetts University, North

Dartmouth, 1971; D.Lit.: Beaver College, Glenside, Pennsylvania, 1973. Member, National Academy of Design; Fellow, American Institute of Architects, and of the Building Research Institute of the National Academy of Sciences; Life Fellow, American Association for the Advancement of Science. Member, National Institute of Arts and Letters; Fellow, American Academy of Arts and Sciences. R. Buckminster Fuller Chair of Architecture established at the University of Detroit, 1970. Member, Mexican Institute of Architects; Honorary Member, Society of Venezuelan Architects, Israel Institute of Engineers and Architects, Zentralvereiningung der Architekten Österreichs, and Royal Society of Siamese Architects; Benjamin Franklin Fellow, Royal Society of Arts; Honorary Fellow, Royal Institute of British Architects. Address (office): 3500 Market Street, Philadelphia, Pennsylvania 19104, U.S.A.

Works:

Geodesic domes (there are now more than 100,000 domes in more than half the countries of the world), including:

1954 United States Air Force Early Warning System Domes, in the Arctic
1958 Union Tank Car Company quarter sphere, Baton Rouge, Louisiana, and Wood River, Illinois
1959 United States Pavilion, Sokolniki Park, Moscow
      Palais de Sports, Paris
1960 "Climatron" Botanical Garden, St. Louis
1963 Cinerama Theatre, Hollywood, California
1964 Yomiuri "Star" Golf Club Field House, Tokyo
1966 County Administration Headquarters, Placer County, California
1967 United States Pavilion, *Expo '67*, Montreal
1969 Airplane Museum, Skipoel Airport, Amsterdam
1972 United States Research Station, Antarctica
1973 Weather Radome, Mt. Fuji, Japan

Patents: Stockade (building structure), 1927; Stockade (pneumatic forming process), 1927; 4D House, 1928; Dymaxion Car, 1937; Dymaxion Bath, 1940; Dymaxion Deployment Unit, 1944; Dymaxion Airocean World, 1946; Fuller House, 1946; Geodesic Dome, 1954; Paperboard Frame, 1959; Plydome, 1959; Catenary, 1959; Octetruss, 1961; Tensegrity, 1962; Submarisle, 1963; Aspension, 1964; Monohex, 1965; Laminar Dome, 1965; Octa Spinner, 1965; Star Tensegrity, 1967; Rowing Device, 1970; Tensegrity Dome with Spaced Lesser Circles, 1973; Geodesic Hexa Pent, with Shoji Sadao, 1974; Floating Breakwater, 1975; Non-symmetrical Tension-integrity Structures, 1975.

Publications:

By FULLER: books—*4D Timelock,* Chicago 1928; *Nine Chains to the Moon,* New York 1963; *The Dymaxion World of Buckminster Fuller,* with Robert W. Marks, New York 1960; *Untitled Epic Poem on the History of Industrialization,* New York 1962; *Education Automation,* New York 1963; *Ideas and Integrities,* Englewood Cliffs, New Jersey 1963; *No More Secondhand God,* New York 1963; *World Design Decade Documents,* with others, 1965–75; *Operating Manual for Spaceship Earth,* New York 1968; *What I Have Learned,* with others, New York 1968; *Utopia or Oblivion,* New York 1969; *The Buckminster Fuller Reader,* edited by James Meller, London 1970; *I Seem To Be a Verb,* with Jerome Agel and Quentin Fiore, New York 1970; *Intuition,* New York 1971; *Buckminster Fuller to Children of Earth,* New York 1972; *Earth Inc.,* New York 1973; *Synergetics: Explorations in the Geometry of Thinking,* with E. J. Applewhite, New York 1975; *It Came to Pass, Not to Stay,* New York 1977; articles—"The

Case for a Domed City" in the *St. Louis Post Dispatch,* 26 September 1965; "City of the Future" in *Playboy* (Chicago), January 1968; "The Earthian's Critical Moment" in the *New York Times,* 11 December 1970; "Ethics" in the *Saturday Review* (New York), 6 November 1973; "Energy Through Wind Power" in the *New York Times,* 17 January 1974; "Time Present" in *Harper's Magazine* (New York), March 1975; and numerous others.

On FULLER: books—*R. Buckminster Fuller* by John McHale, New York 1962; *Wizard of the Dome —R. Buckminster Fuller, Designer for the Future* by Sidney Rosen, Boston 1969; *Bucky: A Guided Tour of Buckminster Fuller* by Hugh Kenner, New York 1973; *Mind's Eye of Buckminster Fuller* by Donald W. Robertson, New York 1974; *Buckminster Fuller at Home in the Universe* by Alden Hatch, New York 1974; articles—"The Dymaxion American" in *Time* (New York), 10 January 1964; "Profile" by Calvin Tomkins in *The New Yorker,* 8 January 1966; "Meet Bucky Fuller, Ambassador from Tomorrow" in the *Reader's Digest* (New York), November 1969; "A Buckminster Fuller Survival Kit" in *Queen* (London), May 1970; "Relax—Bucky Fuller Says It's Going To Be All Right" by Hal Aigner in *Rolling Stone* (San Francisco), 10 June 1971; "The World of Buckminster Fuller" in *Architectural Forum* (New York), January/February 1972; "Whole Earth Man" by Tony Lang in the *Cincinnati Enquirer,* 11 November 1973; "Bucky Fuller and the Final Exam" by Hugh Kenner in the *New York Times Magazine,* 6 July 1975.

*

Although "Bucky" Fuller was long ago recognized and embraced by the architectural community, and while he identifies himself as an architect, he is much more. He is also an author, inventor, cartographer, mathematician, engineer, futurist, philosopher, poet, teacher and resource expert. He is as much of a universal man as our century can produce. His work embraces the principal issues of the 20th century, and his thinking points to the future with a sense of constructive reason.

Born in Milton, Massachusetts, in 1895, he attended Harvard for two years, leaving to hold a variety of jobs in industry, interrupted by two years of service in the United States Navy. His experience in industry, in several capacities, established an insight into technical processes and the relation between materials and manufacturing. Similarly, his experience in the navy afforded him a sense of the wholeness and inter-relatedness of complex but integral systems. In future lectures he was, often, to comment on the self sufficiency of modern warships and of the knowledge required on the part of a ship's captain of the resources of the ports to which he had access. He was to enlarge on this theme, later, in reference to the conduct of nations and, indeed, "spaceship earth."

The death of one of his two children while still an infant imbued a seriousness of purpose in Fuller. A sense of moral purpose in the sharing of the world's resource bounty, including knowledge and technique, has been at the root of his work ever since.

His efforts to design for a more judicious apportionment began with housing and automobiles. He sought to apply new industrial techniques to housing in particular, but he also experimented with automobile transportation. The broad researches he made in the 1920's and 30's included examinations of world resources for *Fortune* magazine in the late 30's. During the war he worked on problems of economic welfare and foreign economies.

After the war Fuller developed the Dymaxion House, a circular structure supported on a central mast. He also developed insights into the mathematics of highly-efficient structures. His particular emphasis was to make the most appropriate use of each material. He also probed the nature of efficiency in structural form. These investigations lead to the work that all but characterizes Fuller—the Geodesic

Dome. It was a configuration of structural members forming a dome, the intersection points being equiposed spherical great circles.

Fuller espoused a philosophy of resource-sharing made possible by the application of a technology of efficiency. This moral attitude, as well as his frequent criticism of inefficient techniques and the obsolete institutions that both stem from them and support them, made him a favorite of schools of architecture. Many are the students, world-wide, who have had the benefit of hours with him.

His dome concept is applicable to small-scale domestic as well as large-scale industrial usage. It has been used in hundreds, if not thousands, of applications, short, however, of covering an entire city. The essential purpose of his domes is to achieve a maximum of structural rigidity and strength with a minimum of materials. Thus, a maximum of space and useful surface area is enclosed by a minimum of materials.

Among his other innovations are the concept of a geodesic world map. Using "geodesic" geometry he has developed a map in which the continents and ocean masses can be portrayed flat or in three dimensions without great distortion. A further application was to construct a huge electronic version of this map. Computerized, it could be used to play world resources relationship games. Fuller called them "World Games." A further structural innovation was his concept of discontinuous compression. With this compression, forces were translated into series of short tension increments. In application this created lighter compression members.

A remark that Fuller once made about thinking and doing characterizes his life. He said: "You can't re-order the world by talking to it."

—Paul Spreiregen

FULTON, Don Hendry.
Australian. Born in Melbourne, Victoria, 30 January 1925. Educated at the Royal Melbourne Institute of Technology, 1942, 1946–47 (Illuminating Engineering Society Award for Lighting Design in Architecture, 1946, 1947), Dip.Arch. 1947; University of Melbourne, under Sir Roy Grounds, 1948–50 (Picton Hopkins Award), B.Arch. 1950; University of California, Berkeley, under William Wurster, Catherine Bauer, Vernon DeMars, Joseph Esherick, Charles Eames, and John Carl Warnecke, 1953–54 (Fulbright grant; Skidmore, Owings and Merrill Fellow in Architecture), M.Arch. 1954. Served as a Cartographer in the Royal Australian Air Force, 1943–45. Married in 1954; children: Simon, Joel, and Mathew. Architect, office of Brian Lewis and Roy Grounds, Melbourne, 1950, Mussen, Mackay, Potter and Grounds, Melbourne, 1951–53, and Mussen, Mackay and Potter, Melbourne, 1955; Principal Partner, E. E. Milston and Don Fulton, Melbourne, 1956. Since 1956, Principal, Don Hendry Fulton Pty. Ltd., Melbourne. Councillor, Historic Buildings Council, Victoria, 1974–78. Councillor, Royal Australian Institute of Architects, Victoria Chapter, since 1972. Exhibition: Abstract Graphics, *International Art Fair,* Dusseldorf, 1973. Recipient: Bronze Medal, Royal Australian Institute of Architects, Victorian Chapter, 1966; Bronze Award, Illuminating Engineers Association of Australia, 1976. Fellow, Royal Australian Institute of Architects, 1967. Address: Don H. Fulton Pty. Ltd., 439 King Street, Melbourne, Victoria 3000, Australia.

Works:

1955 Mary Kathleen Township (new uranium mining township for Conzinc Riotinto), Central Queensland (with E. E. Milston)
1960 Weipa Township (new bauxite mining township for Comalco), Northern Queensland

1962 Studio 9, General Television Corporation, Richmond, Victoria

1963 Ministry of Education and Fine Arts, for the Royal Cambodian Government and the Australian Government, Phnom Phen, Cambodia (project)

1966 Administrative Centre, BP Refinery, Westernport, Victoria

1970 St. Kilda Marina, Victoria

1972 Australian and New Zealand Banking Group Regional Bank, Darwin, Northern Territory

1976 Municipal Offices, Flinders Civic Centre, Rosebud, Victoria

1978 Robertson Township, Narracan, Victoria

Publications:

By FULTON: articles—"Philosophy and Design Approach to Weipa Township in Tropical Australia" in *Australian Mining Journal* (Sydney), May 1967; "This Is Munich" in the Saturday Review Magazine of *The Age* (Melbourne), 26 August 1972; "Ein australischer Architekt sieht Ulm" in *Ulmer Forum* (Ulm, Germany), Winter 1972/73.

An early confrontation with the images of Ankor: I think this propelled the dream/need to become an architect.

And I'm sure that the vital elements of ancient Asian architecture—rhythmically structured, strongly shaped, sheltering—have had an important influence on founding a particular aesthetic mechanism.

We all begin with the urge to push forward the conceptual frontiers, to considerably influence the shape of buildings in one's own time—fortunately for all, a few of the talented and tough manage to do so and make the marks of history.

But from the threshold of the school to that of one's own practice—indeed, that now seems a great leap by the unknowing into the unknown—the dreamer perforce becomes legally and financially accountable—called "responsible."

Who was it said "I don't want to be interesting, I want to be good"—Mies, I think.

Well, to me, architecture necessarily is all about *buildings that are both good and interesting.*

It's about the good and interesting shapes and forms of buildings and the spaces within and between them.

And, of course, it's also about the proper functioning of systems and equipment in buildings and how properly buildings use energy, modify the climate, and fit their sites.

If, in the course of time and well beyond its first purpose, a building is somehow still good and interesting, then perhaps it's touched that quality of art called style that sets certain man-made things apart, whether buildings, sculpture, music, tools, or toys.

But isn't our involvement in architecture essentially about the whole built fabric working well and looking good in our time?

I think this "overview" attitude leads to architecture of the overall, to town-planning.

Indeed, fortunately, it has led us to the planning of small new self-contained townships associated with Australia's developing mining industries and major civil works, in remote areas of the country.

From the development "go"-point to that of people moving in, in layout, systems and building, they are usually towns "in a hurry." The challenge is to help make them good and interesting to work and live in.

—Don Hendry Fulton

Against stiff competition from large and expensive city buildings, a small economical, out-of-the-way administration block at an oil refinery won the top architectural award for any building in the state of Victoria in the years 1963–66. This modest building is typical of architect Don Hendry Fulton's work: austere, rational and elegant. At first sight it appears to owe much to the temple form of U.S. embassies built during the 1950's (notably by the Architects' Collaborative in Athens, and John Carl Warnecke in Hawaii). But this building is not a simple exercise in the International style. It results from a careful study of functional requirements, climatic conditions, and

socio-cultural influences. These determinants of form are the raw material from which the architect must seek the underlying order and derive the appropriate style.

For Fulton, who was strongly influenced by American architecture during his studies for Master of Architecture at the University of California in Berkeley, style is of major importance: for he sees architecture as an art, and style as the mediator between art and mere building. In the refinery administration block the style is uncompromisingly classic: a tetrastyle peripteral temple form with wide overhanging eaves is poised delicately around a symmetrical but direct response to a complex brief. To one side is a small gatehouse, the roof of which is visually accommodated by a slight inflection of the ground floor walls of the main building. The two-storey high columns are slender square-section shafts, necked and splayed to give visual strength to the base. They are topped with a steel capital that passes through a slot in the eaves soffit, so that the roof appears to float. The same separation and articulation of parts, and the careful attention to detail, are apparent throughout the building.

Besides a number of buildings with a high technical component such as radio and television studios, the major part of Fulton's practice has been the planning layout and building design of a number of "company" towns for large civil engineering projects in remote areas all round Australia, from Robertson in Victoria in the south, to Weipa in Queensland in the north. In each case his design approach is as direct as possible. The elements of vernacular buildings are the basic forms from which the architectural style and planning geometry are derived. The resulting buildings are simple, elegant and formal; above all, they are experienced as familiar places.

—David Watson

Don Hendry Fulton: Administrative Centre, BP Refinery, Westernport, Victoria, 1966

GARDELLA, Ignazio.

Italian. Born in Milan in 1905. Studied engineering at the Polytechnic, Milan; studied architecture at the Istituto Universitario di Architettura, Venice. In private practice, Milan: in partnership with Anna Castelli Ferrieri since 1950. Professor of Architecture, Istituto Universitario di Architettura, Venice. Member, Executive Committee, *Triennale,* Milan, 1959. Exhibition: *Ten Italian Architects,* Los Angeles, 1967. Recipient: Olivetti National Prize, 1955. Address (office): Corso di Porta Romana 87/B, 20122 Milan, Italy.

Works:

1932 Venzahi Apartment alterations, Piazza Italia 3, Milan
      Caruso Dairy and Stables, Retorato, Arquata Scrivia, Italy
1933 Calvi Cottage, San Vito, Italy
1934 Bell Tower, Piazza del Duomo, Milan (project)
      Theatre restoration, Busto Arsizio, Italy
      Hospital Isolation Unit, Busto Arsizio, Italy (1st project)
1935/
  36 Villa Borletti extensions and alterations, Milan
1936 Chapel-Altar, Varinella, Arquata Scrivia, Italy (project)
1936/
  37 Hospital Isolation Unit, Busto Arsizio, Italy (2nd project)
1936/
  38 Anti-Tuberculosis Dispensary, Alessandria, Italy (with L. Martini)
      "Milano Verde:" City Plan for Milan (project; with others)
1937 Gardella Apartment interiors, Milan
1937/
  39 Provincial Laboratory for Hygiene, Alessandria, Italy
1938 Cattle Market Building, Alessandria, Italy (competition project)
      Hotel for the E.42 Development, Rome (project; with others)
      Palazzo della Civiltà Italiana Building, E.42 Development, Rome (project; with others)
1939 Palace of Water and Light, E.42 Development, Rome (project; with others)
1940/
  41 Pirovano Shrine, Municipal Cemetery, Missaglia, Italy
1942 CNASA Employees Apartment Building, Marina Carrara, Italy (not completed)
1942/
  47 La Fergan Housing Block, via Severino Boezio, Milan (not completed)
1946 Apartment building, Castana, Italy
      Borsalino Company Exhibit, *Trade Fair,* Milan
1947 Redevelopment plan for the Angeli Quarter, Genoa (project; with others)
      Redevelopment plan for the Balzaretti and Modigliani Glassworkers' Quarter, Livorno (project; with Alberto Menghi)
1947/
  48 Apartment House by the Park, Piazza Castello, Milan
1948 Redevelopment plan for Turin (competition project)
1950 Regina Isabella Spa Building, Lacco Ameno, Isle of Ischia (with Elena Balsari Berrone)
1951 Condominium Apartments, Milan (with Anna Castelli Ferrieri and Alberto Menghi)
      Italian Chairs Exhibition, *Triennale,* Milan
1951/
  53 Borsalino Employees' Block of Flats, Corso Teresio Borsalino, Alessandria, Italy
1952 Villa Baletti, Lesa, Lake Maggiore, Italy
      Terrace apartment houses, INA-CASA Quarter, Cesate, Milan
1953 Gallery of Modern Art, Giardini della Villa Reale, Milan
1953/
  59 Olivetti Recreation Centre Complex, Ivrea, near Turin
1955 Columbus House and Museum, Genoa
1956 Fabric-Cutting Building, Borsalino Factory, Alessandria, Italy
      New Exhibition Rooms, Uffizi Gallery, Florence
1957 New Building, Cesar Arrigo Children's Hospital, Alessandria, Italy
      Brick Church, Cesate, Milan
      Alle Zattere Apartment Building, Grand Canal, Venice
      Edizioni Paoline Bookstore, Piazza del Duomo, Milan
      Thermo-Electric Plant, Ravenna
1958 Grassi Collection Rooms, Villa Belgioioso, Milan
      Hotel Punta San Martino, near Genoa (with Marco Zanuso)
1959 C.P.E. Pilot Residential Development, Vicenza, Italy (with Anna Castelli Ferrieri, Plinio Marconi, Valeriano Pastor, and Guido Pravato)
1960 Alitalia DC-8 Aircraft interiors
1960/
  61 Piazza with Shops and Housing, Arenzano Pineta, Capo San Martino, Italy
1960/
  62 Villa, Arenzano, Capo San Martino, Italy (with Anna Castelli Ferrieri)
1961 Agricultural Pavilion, *Fiera Campionaria,* Milan
1961/
  62 Olivetti Showrooms and Offices, Königsallee, Dusseldorf
1962/
  63 Einaudi Bookstore, via Veneto, Rome (with Luigi Parisi)
1963 Elementary school, Alessandria, Italy
1964 San Enrico Church, Metanopoli, near Milan
1966/
  68 IBM Offices, Vimercate, near Milan
      Kartell Factory and Offices, Binasco, Italy
      Porto di Punta Ala Residential Development, Grosseto, Italy (with Alberto Mazzoni, Diego Guicciardi, and Vito Sonzongni)

1968 Parish Church, Forlanini Quarter, Milan
1970 Theatre, Vicenza, Italy (competition project)
      House, via Marina, Milan
1970/
  72 Alfa Romeo Technical Offices, Arese, Milan
1970- Plan for the restoration of the centre of Genoa (with Daniele Vitale and others)
1974 Shahrestenak Winter Tourist Resort, near Tehran (project)

Numerous designs for furniture and light fittings, especially for the Azucena Company of Milan, 1947–51.

Publications:

On GARDELLA: book—*Ignazio Gardella* by Giulio Carlo Argan, Milan 1959; articles—"Concorso per il mercato bestiame di Alessandria" in *Casabella* (Milan), April 1939; "Espressione di Gardella, espression di Rouault" in *Domus* (Milan), June 1954; "Ignazio Gardella" by Giulio Carlo Argan in *Architects Yearbook,* London 1956; "Casa di Abitazione in Condominio" and "Galleria d'Arte Moderna" in *Forum* (Amsterdam), October 1957; "Umanesimo di Gardella" by Giuseppe Mazzariol in *Zodiac* (Milan), no. 2, 1958; "Progetto per il quartiere pilota C.P.E. a Vicenza" in *Casabella* (Milan), August 1959; "Appunti sulla progettazione di Gardella" and "La Mensa Olivetti a Ivrea" in *Casabella* (Milan), January 1960; "Nel centro residenziale di Arenzano Pineta, sul Capo San Martino: La Piazza" in *Domus* (Milan), August 1960; "Negozio Olivetti a Dusseldorf" in *L'Architettura* (Rome), December 1961; "A Roma, una libreria in via Veneto" in *Domus* (Milan), June 1962; "Un teatro di Gardella" in *Domus* (Milan), November 1969; "Ignazio Gardella" by Aldo Rossi in *Architecture + Urbanism* (Tokyo), December 1976.

Although Ignazio Gardella's career has coincided with the often tortuous development of modern architecture in Italy, which has been accompanied by lively controversy and fierce commitment, Gardella himself has never been committed to any social or aesthetic ideology. Indeed, his famous Zattere Apartment House, on the Grand Canal in Venice, has been something of an embarrassment to modernist extremists: nobody can deny that it is not supremely functional, yet so far from having the ugly brutality too often associated with functionalism, this witty variation on modern and vernacular themes fits in perfectly with its environment.

Gardella has in fact always shown great sensitivity to the demands of the environment. Many of his works have indeed been whole environments rather than single buildings. For instance, the Hotel Punta San Martino of 1958, which he designed with Marco Zanuso, is splendidly set on the cliffs of the gulf of Genoa as part of a whole Gardella plan for Arenzano, to develop this stretch of coastline without allowing it to be ruined by speculators (as, in fact, to some extent it unfortunately has been).

Many of his most important works have been at Alessandria, an important market town and communications centre between Milan and Genoa. His first work there was the splendid Anti-Tuberculosis Dispensary, an outstanding early example of modern Italian architecture. It already suggests the lines along which Gardella was to develop; it shows his respect for the traditional environment in its use of techniques and materials drawn directly from the local tradition. For though this is a reinforced concrete building, and its windows and plane surfaces are all clearly modern, its facing of grillwork in the local coloured bricks not only gives it a lively surface but also helps it blend harmoniously with the local architecture. His many other works in Alessandria include the Provincial Laboratory for Hygiene, the Children's Hospital, and the block of flats built for the Borsalino workers, which has been called "bourgeois neoclassicism" yet is a highly original building with such unusual features as its deeply overhanging eaves.

Gardella has also created some interesting furnishings. He began his career with interior decoration and rebuilding schemes, such as the renovation of the theatre at Busto Arsizio in 1934. But his most distinctive contribution to architecture has been his remarkable ability to use the formal vocabulary of Italian rationalism or modernism while at the same time reinterpreting regional and traditional elements in a modern key—as in his block of flats at Castana. Similarly his work in the Cesate district of Milan involves a subtle geometric layout very much in the contemporary spirit, yet it also includes a brick-built church with historic overtones. As used by Gardella, such traditional elements can never be accused of being merely fancy-dress architecture, for they embody his characteristically thoughtful and critical attitude to the landscape and environment.

—Konstantin Bazarov

GARNIER, Tony.

French. Born in Lyons, 13 August 1869; son of the architect Charles Garnier. Educated at the Ecole National des Beaux-Arts, Lyons, under Eldin and Louvier, 1886–89; Ecole des Beaux-Arts, Paris, under Paul Blondel and Scellier de Gisors, 1889–99; also studied in the studio of J. Guadet, Paris; Prix de Rome Scholar, 1899–1904. In private practice in Lyons, 1904 until his death, 1948: City Architect, 1905–19. Professor at the Ecole Régionale d'Architecture, 1912. Exhibitions: Prix de Rome, Ecole des Beaux Arts, Paris, 1901, 1904; Congress of French Architects, Lyons, 1914; *Exposition des Arts Décoratifs*, Paris, 1925; one-man shows—Musée des Arts Décoratifs, Paris, 1925; Musée des Beaux-Arts, Lyons, 1953; Libreria Salto, Milan, 1961. Collections: Musée des Beaux-Arts, Lyons; Musée St. Pierre, Lyons. Recipient: Medal of the French Order of Architects, 1909. Honorary Member, Royal Institute of British Architects. *Died* (in La Bédoule, France) *19 January 1948*.

Works:

1900/
04 Cité Industrielle (project)
1903/
04 Reconstruction of the city of Tusculum (project)
1905 Fondation Rothschild Building, Paris (competition project)
Municipal Dairy, Parc de la Tête d'Or, Lyons
1905/
19 Expansion and redevelopment plan for Lyons
1906 Development plan for the La Bourse District, Marseilles (competition project)
1907 Cattle Market Abattoir rebuilding, Reims

1908/
13 La Mouche Cattle Market and Abattoirs, Lyons
1909 Garnier House I, St. Rambert, Lyons
1910 Villa Gros, Mont d'Or, Saint-Cyr, near Lyons
1911 Garner House II, St. Rambert, Lyons
Housing on Mont d'Or, Saint Didier, near Lyons
1911/
25 Edouard Herriot Hospital Complex, Grange Blanche, Lyons
1913 Municipal Sports Centre, Lyons (project)
1913/
14 Master plan for the *Exposition Internationale Urbaine,* Lyons
1913/
18 Olympic Sports Stadium, Lyons
1918 Monuments to the 1914–1918 War Dead, Lyons (4 projects)
1918/
24 Monument to the Dead of Paris and Monplaisir (project)
League of Nations Building, Geneva (competition project)
1919 Monument to Edouard Aynard, Place de la Bourse, Lyons
Moncey Central Telephone Exchange, Lyons (project)
1920/
35 Etats-Unis District Housing Development, Lyons
1924 Monument to the War Dead, Parc de la Tête d'Or, Lyons (with the sculptor Larrive)
1925 Lyons-St. Etienne Pavilion, *Exposition des Arts Décoratifs,* Paris
1927 Moncey Central Telephone Exchange, Lyons
1929 Christopher Columbus Monument, Santo Domingo, West Indies (competition project)
1930/
31 Villa by Lake Geneva, Switzerland (project)
Monument to Pierre Mouillard (project)
Monument to the aviator Ferber (project)
1930/
33 Textiles School, Croix-Rousse, Lyons
1931/
34 Town Hall, Boulogne-Billancourt, Paris (with Debat-Ponsan)
1935/
39 Theatre, Saint-Etienne, France (competition project)
Hospital, Reims (competition project)
Parilly Park, Lyons (competition project)

Tony Garnier: La Mouche Abattoirs, Lyons, 1909

Publications:

By GARNIER: books—*La Désaffection de l'Hotel-Dieu,* with E. Herriot, Lyons 1910; *Une Cité Industrielle: Etude pour la Construction des Villes,* Paris 1917, 1932; *Les Grand Travaux de la Ville de Lyon,* Paris 1920; *Rapport Général sur l'Etat des Bâtiments Departementaux,* Lyons 1937; article—preface to *Quelques Problèmes d'Urbanisme* by M. Kharachnick, Paris 1927.

On GARNIER: books—*L'Oeuvre de Tony Garnier* by Jean Badovici and A. Morancé, Paris 1938; *Tony Garnier* by G. Veronesi, Milan 1948; *Tony Garnier et les Débuts de l'Urbanisme Fonctionnel en France* by Christophe Pawlowski, Paris 1967; articles—"L'Oeuvre de Tony Garnier" by Jean Badovici in *Architecture Vivante* (Paris), Autumn/Winter 1924; "A Propos de l'Exposition de Tony Garnier au Musée des Arts Décoratifs à Paris" by P. Bourdeix in *Construction Moderne* (Paris), 5 April 1925; "La Cité Industrielle de Tony Garnier" by P. Bourdeix in *Construction Moderne* (Paris), 10 January 1926; "Tony Garnier, Précurseur de l'Architecture d'Aujourd'hui" by P. Bourdeix in *L'Architecture d'Aujourd'hui* (Paris), March 1931; "Chez l'Architecte Tony Garnier" by A. Goissaud in *Construction Moderne* (Paris), 6 November 1932; "La Cité Industrielle de Tony Garnier" by Julius Posener in *L'Architecture d'Aujourd'hui* (Paris), July 1935; "Tony Garnier: Le Premier Architecte qui a Concu la Cité Industrielle" by Bernard Champigneulle in *Le Figaro Littéraire* (Paris), 28 February 1948; "Tony Garnier au Musée des Beaux-Arts de Lyon" by J. J. Lerrant in *Bulletin des Musées Lyonnais,* no. 2, 1953; "La Mostra dei Disegni di Tony Garnier" in *L'Architettura* (Rome), December 1961; "Utopian Aspects of Tony Garnier's Cité Industrielle" by D. Wiebenson in *Journal of the Society of Architectural Historians* (Philadelphia), no. 1, 1962.

Tony Garnier is well known for having been, at the very beginning of our century, an innovator in two fields: he was one of the first in France to see the necessity for a mass solution in architectonic and urbanistic terms to deal with the need for large numbers of dwellings, and he logically translated this choice into a rationalist architecture and urbanism at a time when eclecticism dominated.

These social and rational notions and the two being linked were due, on the one hand, to his birth in a working class area of Lyons, a town which in his youth experienced a rapid transformation in urban and industrial development and, on the other hand, to the ferment of the progressive culture that he encountered in the different schools he attended.

As a young student Garnier belonged to the Society of Friends of Emile Zola. The author of *Travail* exercised a considerable influence on the whole of his work: Garnier occupied himself a great deal with social habitat. He spent four years at the Ecole National des Beaux-Arts in Lyons and then received a scholarship for Paris. He arrived there in 1889, at the time of the *Universal Exposition,* and he visited the Eiffel Tower with great interest. As a student in J. Guadet's studio he benefitted from both a classical and a rational education. A centre of positivist culture, this studio was the most progressive in the teaching of architecture. After winning a Prix de Rome in 1899, he devoted his time, during his stay at the Villa Medici, to the study of a modern town, taking his inspiration also from classical Greek culture.

In the first sketches of 1907 for a "Cité Industrielle," Tony Garnier stresses that "modern architecture should draw inspiration from the beauty of antiquity without making it the sole basis of education, for social needs require other studies." He defended this idea throughout his life. Rejected by the Institute's members, his project shows regulatory, land, economic, and social preoccupations that would be of interest much later on and that would place their author as an "Urbanist" ante litteram. "Searching for solutions that will give the greatest satisfaction to the material and moral needs of the individual," he said, "I was led to create regulations concerning roads, sanitation, etc. . . . and to presuppose certain developments in the social order." From 1904, the date of the presentation of this project, to 1939, the time of his last achievements, Garnier occupied himself methodically with giving substance to his theories, with achieving, element by element, the different components of his industrial city.

The opportunity to execute the major works for the city of Lyons for which he is now famous was due to his meeting with Edouard Herriot, the radical mayor elected in 1904. The creation of the Lyons works was based on the extraordinary collaboration of these two personalities of the same generation with the same political and cultural convictions.

In the La Mouche Abbatoirs, a masterpiece of functional organization, he employed a technology very close to that of the Galerie des Machines. According to his theories, technological evolution was a component of social democratic progress. In the project for the Municipal Sports Centre of 1913, classical inspiration is very evident—not in the "monumental" sense but in the handling of polyfunctional areas, a characteristic of the stadia of Greek towns (only the Stadium was built, as the work was interrupted by the First World War). In the Herriot Hospital at Grange Blanche and in the Etats-Unis District, Garnier used models left over from the "Cité Industrielle" project and used a modern material—reinforced concrete. His use of roof terraces created "strong horizontals and verticals necessary to give to the constructions a calm and equilibrium in harmony with the lines of nature." The brutality of the modern materials is balanced by the development of urban furniture which is useful and which gives a lively aspect to the districts.

Tony Garnier was not only the precursor of contemporary urbanism; he was also a very important point of reference for French architects of the 1920's and 1930's.

—Luciana Miotto-Muret

GAUDÍ, Antoni.

Spanish. Born Antoni Gaudí i Cornet in Riudoms, Catalonia, 25 June 1852. Educated at the Escuela Superior de Arquitectura, Barcelona, 1874–78, Dip. Arch. 1878. Worked with the architects Juan Martorell and Emilio Sala, Barcelona, 1874–75, with Francisco de Paula del Villar y Lozano, Barcelona, 1875–77, and with the engineer José Serramalera, Barcelona, 1876; Draughtsman, Padrós i Borràs industrial machinery firm, Barcelona, 1876, and with the architectural firm of José Fontseré, Barcelona, 1877–82. In private practice, Barcelona, 1882 until his death, 1926. Exhibitions: Société Nationale des Beaux-Arts, Paris, 1910 (one-man); Madrid, 1911; Gerona, 1915; Olot, 1915; Reus, 1916; Sagrada Familia Church Crypt, Barcelona, 1917 (one-man); Valls, 1917; *Liturgical Art Exposition,* Barcelona, 1925; Sala Pares, Barcelona, 1927 (one-man); *2nd Exposition of Liturgical Art,* Barcelona, 1928; *Triennale,* Milan, 1951; Salon del Tinell, Barcelona, 1956 (one-man); Museum of Modern Art, New York, 1957 (one-man); Milan, 1957 (one-man); *Bienal,* Sao Paulo, Brazil, 1959; Baden-Baden, Germany, 1961 (one-man); *Fifty Years of Gaudí,* Building Centre, London, 1979. Collections: Amigos de Gaudí, 3–5 Conde de Asalto, Barcelona (founded, 1952); Municipal Museum, Reus. Recipient: First Prize, Street Lighting Competition, Barcelona, 1878; Ayuntamiento Prize, Barcelona, 1900. *Died* (in Barcelona) *10 June 1926.*

Works:

1869/
70 Monastery restoration, Poblet, Barcelona (project)
1875/
77 Chapel of the Virgin, Monastery of Montserrat (with Francisco de Paula del Villar y Lozano)
1877/
82 Parque de la Ciudadela Monuments, Barcelona (with José Fontseré)
1878 Writing desk
Furniture for Commilas Chapel, near Santander, Spain
Church Monstrance (project)
Comella Showcase, *Paris Exposition*
1878/
79 Street lighting, Plaza Real, Barcelona
1878/
80 Casa Vicens, 24–26 calle de las Carolinas, Barcelona (altered by J. B. de Serra Martinez, 1925–26)
1878/
82 Mataronese Co-operative Machinery Shed and Kiosk, Mataro, near Barcelona
Mataronese Co-operative Workers' Housing, Mataro, near Barcelona (project)
1879 Farmacia Gibert, Barcelona (demolished)
Plan for Allegorical Cavalcade, Vallfogona de Riucorp, near Lerida, Spain
1880 Street lights for the Paseo Nacional, Barceloneta Waterfront, Barcelona
Muralla de Mar Waterfront electric lighting, Barcelona (project; with José Serramalera)
1880/
81 Casino, San Sebastian (competition project)
1880/
82 Altar and furniture for the Colegio de Jesus-Maria Chapel, calle Mendez-Nunez, Tarragona, Spain (lost)
1882 Church, Villaricos, Almeria, Spain (project)
Eusebio Güell Hunting Pavilion, Garraf, near Barcelona (project)
"El Capricho" (Maximo Diaz de Quijano Summer House), Comillas, near Santander, Spain
1883 Chapel, Alella, near Barcelona (project)
1884/
1926 Church of the Sagrada Familia, Barcelona (remains unfinished)
1885 Altar, José M. Bocabella Oratory, 31 calle Ausias March, Barcelona (dismantled, 1936)
1885/
89 Palau Güell (mansion), 3–5 calle Conde de Asalto, Barcelona
1887 Salon de Ciento alterations, Barcelona (project)
Finca Güell (estate), Las Corts de Sarriá, Barcelona
1887/
93 Episcopal Palace for Bishop Juan Bautista Grau, Astorga, Spain (work abandoned, 1893; additions by Luis de Guereta, 1905–07)
1888 Compañia Trasatlántica Pavilion, *Exposición Universal,* Barcelona
1889/
94 Colegio de Santa Teresa de Jesus, 41 calle Ganduxer, Barcelona
1891/
94 Casa de los Botines (commercial/residential building), Plaza de San Marcelo, Leon, Spain (altered, 1954–55)
1892/
93 Spanish Franciscan Mission, Tangier (project)
1895 Güell Family Tomb, Montserrat, Spain (project)
1898/
1904 Casa Calvet, Calle Caspe 48, Barcelona
1898/
1915 Colonia Güell Chapel, Santa Coloma de Cervello, near Barcelona
1900 Misericordia Sanctuary alterations, Reus, Spain (project)
1900/
02 "Bellesguard" (Figueras Villa), Bonanova, Barcelona
1900/
14 Park Güell Garden Suburb, Montaña Pelada, Barcelona
1901/
02 Miralles Estate Wall and Gate, Paseo de Manuel Girona, Barcelona
Castelldosrius House alterations, Barcelona (demolished)
1904 Luis Graner House, 40 calle nueva de Santa Eulalia, Barcelona (project)
Cinema Sala Merce, Barcelona (demolished)
Mystery of the Rosary Statuary Groups, Montserrat, Spain (project)
1904/
14 Cathedral of Palma de Mallorca interior alterations (unfinished)
1905 Pulpits for the Blares Parochial Church, near Gerona, Spain
1905/
07 Casa Batlló ("Casa de los Huesos") remodelling, 43 Paseo de Gracia, Barcelona
1905/
10 Casa Milà ("La Pedrera") Apartment Building, 92 Paseo de Gracia, Barcelona (interior alterations by F. J. Barba Corsini, 1954)
1908 Barrio Gotico restoration, Barcelona (project)
1908/
10 Chapel, Colegio de Santa Teresa de Jesus, Barcelona (project)
1909 School buildings, Sagrada Familia Church, Barcelona
1922 Shrine, Church of the Virgin, Rancagua, Chile (project)
1923 Chapel and schools, Colonia Calvet, Torello, near Vich, Spain (projects)

Antoni Gaudí: Palau Güell, Barcelona, 1889

Publications:

On GAUDÍ: books—*Antoni Gaudí: La seva vida, les seves obres, la seva mort*, Barcelona 1926; *La Visió Artística i Religiosa d'En Gaudí* by Francesc Pujols, Barcelona 1927; *Gaudí: el gran arquitecto espanol* by J. F. Ráfols and F. Folguera, Barcelona 1928, 1929; *El Arte de Gaudí* by J. E. Cirlot, Barcelona 1950, 1954; *Gaudi 1852–1926* by J. F. Ráfols, Barcelona 1952; *Antoni Gaudí: l'Home i l'Obra* by Joan Bergós, Barcelona 1954; *Guadinismo* by César Martinell, Barcelona 1954; *Antonio Gaudí* by César Martinell, Milan 1955; *Gaudi*, exhibition catalog, by Henry-Russell Hitchcock, New York 1957; *Gaudi* by Le Corbusier, Gomis and Prats-Valles, Barcelona 1958; *Antoni Gaudí* by James Johnson Sweeney and J. L. Sert, London and New York 1960; *Antoni Gaudí* by George R. Collins, New York and London 1960; *Defensa de Gaudí* by J. M. Guix Sugranes, Reus, Spain 1960; *Antoni Gaudí* by R. Pane, Milan 1964; *Nueva Vision de Gaudí* by E. Casanelles, Barcelona 1965; *Park Güell* by C. Giedion-Welcker, Barcelona and New York 1966; *Gaudí* by J. E. Cirlot, Barcelona 1966; *Casa Batlló, Barcelona, Spain 1905–07*, edited by Yukio Futagawa and M. L. Borras, Tokyo 1972; *Gaudí en Astorga* by M. J. Alonso Gavela, Leon, Spain 1972; *Antoni Gaudí: Inspiration in Architektur und Handwerk* by J. Wiedermann, Munich 1974; *Gaudí: His Life, His Theories, His Work* by C. Martinell, Barcelona 1975; *Gaudí* by D. Mower, London 1977; articles—"Gaudí" by Evelyn Waugh in *Architectural Review* (London), June 1930; "Antonio Gaudí" by N. Tesch in *Byggmastaren* (Stockholm), no. 10, 1948; "Un Genio Catalano: Antonio Gaudí" by Bruno Zevi in *Metron* (Rome), September/October 1950; "Antoni Gaudí" by James Johnson Sweeney in *Magazine of Art* (New York), May 1953; "Bildhafte Kachel-Kompositen von Antonio Gaudí" by C. Giedion-Welcker in *Werk* (Zurich), April 1955; "Gaudianism in Catalonia" by A. Kerrigan in *Arts* (New York), December 1957; "The Work of Antoni Gaudí i Cornet" by Henry-Russell Hitchcock in *Architectural Association Journal* (London), November 1958; "Willkür und Bindung im Werk con Antonio Gaudí" by Jürgen Joedicke in *Bauen und Wohnen* (Zurich), no. 5, 1960; "Antonio Gaudí" by J. J. Khadem in *Art et Architecture* (Paris), March/August 1975; "Gaudí: Master of Arts and Crafts" by H. Spiegel in *Architectural Record* (New York), August 1978; etc.

Bibliography: *A Bibliography of Antoni Gaudí and the Catalan Movement* by G. R. Collins and M. E. Farinas, Charlottesville, Virginia 1973.

*

Antoni Gaudí's place in the history of the modern movement in architecture is based upon both the intrinsic value of his works and the major part he played in the period of Catalan Modernisme, 1880–1914.

150 years after Filip V removed Catalonia from the political map, the Romantic movement kindled the embers of the Catalan cultural inheritance. This rebirth (Renaixença) aroused interest not only in Catalan language and literature but also in Catalan archaeology, the monuments of the Romanesque and medieval periods. It led, too, to political claims for autonomy that immersed the whole population in a unified struggle for national identity. The Romanticism of the 19th century gave coherence to these historical claims, but the practical and commercial instinct of the Catalans, combined with the rapid industrialization of production, developed this romanticizing of a medieval past into a search for the expression of a progressive society. These circumstances produced the style known as Modernisme and distinguish it from other Art Nouveau movements—with the possible exception of the work of the architect Charles Rennie Mackintosh who undeniably combined, like the Catalans, a national expression within an international movement.

The main characteristics of the architecture of Modernisme are its concern for total design (mother architecture gathering to its bosom, in unity, all the other arts); fluidity of space, especially in the use of the double facade and continuity of line; definition of aggregated elements; constructive elements as the bases of ornamentation; the use of ornamentation independent of the architectural structure but often symbolic of structure; the strong influence of historicism, a strong current of accepted eclecticism throughout the movement; and, finally, a generous allowance for bourgeois comforts, creating, in turn, a domestic charm.

Antoni Gaudí's effervescent imagination led him to interpret Modernisme in a Baroque manner. His Baroque Modernisme became a sort of collective Orphism for Catalans in search of a lost 18th century denied them by Castile. Perhaps this may explain the apparent contradiction between the normal sobriety of Catalan architecture and the public acceptance of Gaudí's exorbitance noted by Nikolaus Pevsner. Gaudí filled a cultural gap.

His early works show a disciplined control over the composition of the architecture, which combines the eclectic vocabulary of the transition from the Romanticism of the Renaixença to the personalization of Modernisme. The Casa Vicens, his earliest major work, has a hesitant symmetrical plan that hides an agile aggregation of domestic rooms. This inherent difficulty has been superbly camouflaged in the design of the facades: a symmetrically pitched roof in the form of a "W" over a continuous gallery, combined with a gradual change in intensity of materials, from stone rubble with brick ribbons, to tiles, to corbelled turrets over the awkward corners, gives unity and apparent coherence to the house. The metalwork has its source in Viollet-le-Duc whose illustrated works were familiar to Gaudí. The famous metal fence, with its palm-leaf design, was installed at a later date. The Casa Vicens reveals what was to be Gaudí's basic approach to architecture: a strong architectural idea or concept to which the plan is fitted, and a careful elaboration of a decorative theme developed as the building proceeded, concealing the inconsistencies of the project. Architects at that time rarely drew plans, but in his early works Gaudi did so—suggesting that the inconsistency was a deliberate choice, a way to regulate the plan to the discipline of the main architectural idea.

In the Palau Güell the central hall is really based on the idea of a covered court. The other rooms are placed around this court in a deliberately casual way, as if they had been added to the best ability of the architect. Both the street and interior facades reveal a great deal of care in the drawing stage: the former responds to the restrictions of a narrow street with its double facade, to protect the intimacy of the inside and enrich the spatial transition of light. The parabolic arch of the entrance and the rich texture of its wrought-iron gate demonstrates Gaudí's creative ability in experimenting with form. The rather severe Scottish baronial facade of the interior is a relaxed expression of the internal functions, held together by the rather forced symmetry of the tribune. The chimneys and ventilation shafts, which are curiously out of scale with the rest of the building, display the first full range of Gaudí's primitive and exciting fantasies in form, material, and colour.

Other important early works are the Colegio de Santa Teresa, the Casa Calvet, "Bellesguard," and the gatehouse and stables at Las Corts de Sarriá. All of these buildings show us a Gaudí doing ordinary work extraordinarily well. Bellesguard is a formal exercise in the unity of material, with a stone facing on walls, roof, even the drain pipes—but the study under the roof, with its dextrous thin brick arches and cantilevers, abuses structural economy not only for decoration but also for spatial effects that are masterly. No doubt there are simpler ways of building, but Gaudí seems to have created problems in order to demonstrate how he could solve them. The result is of extraordinary interest, for it demonstrates the role of redundant design in architecture—a role that was destroyed by the later "rational approach"

in architecture.

A sudden increase in commissions around 1900, and no doubt more confidence, led Gaudí to evolve his design methods through sketches and models, which were a more appropriate means of composing his architecture around a strong idea; they would act as a catalyst for elements encountered in the creative process. The oval plan of the crypt of the Chapel in Colonia Güell, which gathers the people around the altar; the imitation of nature and architecture in Park Güell; the flowing form of the Casa Batlló, based on the theme of St. George and the Dragon; "La Pedrera," with its free plan of luxury apartments made possible by the use of a steel frame and a stone-hung curtain wall; the structural form of the school buildings of the Sagrada Familia Church; and, finally, the tapered cylinders of the towers of Sagrada Familia itself—all these works add up to Gaudí's Baroque corpus, his contribution to Modernisme.

Gaudí's role in these buildings was obviously that of the persistent and determined creator holding to and developing a single architectural purpose through the instrument of his team—from the precise sobriety of Berenguer and Rubio to the "rococo" graphics of Jujol. Apart from these immediate assistants, Gaudí also gathered around him able craftsmen and artists who, completely identified with the Modernisme movement, were able to add their own contributions to the overall vision of Gaudí. His genius thrived within, and inspired, this kind of teamwork.

The Baroque style within which Gaudí chose to work allowed him to break away from the classical disciplines of architecture. If it were not for the strength of his imposed ideas, unifying each composition, the results would have been chaotic. The common elements that we find in these Baroque buildings are the attention to human circumstances and the constructional basis of many of his details, which he infused with an enormous sense of humor. His wit helps us to enjoy his buildings; no doubt it also sustained him, and his creativity, during the long process of work on each project and construction of each building.

The enigma of Gaudí is that although he was a very able architect, he failed to consolidate a viable architectural discipline that could be reinterpreted by followers. His abundant imagination, private wit, and public arrogance were corrupted by a superficial and reactionary religion that grew up around him through his work on the Sagrada Familia. He misread the brief, and it destroyed him. He subjected his architecture to a religion of symbols, and from 1914 onwards, with the Catalan cultural elite rejecting the "barbarism" of Modernisme in favor of the classic rules of Mediterranean culture, and the death of his client Güell and his chief assistant Berenguer, Gaudi became a cultural recluse. A revered mystic. It is from this later period that a group of well meaning collaborators have drawn their experiences of Gaudí, and their accounts have led to a profusion of publications that tell the story of Gaudi the "outsider." But it is as an "insider" in the Modernisme movement that Gaudí's contribution to the modern movement really lies.

—David Mackay

GEDDES, Robert.
American. Born in Philadelphia, Pennsylvania, 7 December 1923. Educated at Yale University, New Haven, Connecticut, 1941–42, 1945; Harvard Graduate School of Design, Cambridge, Massachusetts, 1946–50, M.Arch. 1950. Served in the United States Army, 1942–45. Married Evelyn Basse in 1947; children: David and Ann. Professor of Architecture and Civic Design, University of Pennsylvania, Philadelphia, 1951–65. Since 1954, Principal, Geddes Brecher Qualls Cunningham, architects, Princeton,

New Jersey, and Philadelphia. Kenan Professor of Architecture, and Dean of the School of Architecture and Urban Planning, Princeton University, since 1965. Member, Board of Directors, Johns-Manville Corporation, since 1970, and Butler Manufacturing Company, since 1971. Fellow, American Institute of Architects, 1967. Address: Geddes Brecher Qualls Cunningham, 12 Nassau Street, Princeton, New Jersey 08540, U.S.A.

Works:

1954 Fotteral Square, Philadelphia
      Geddes House, Radnor, Pennsylvania
1955 Lawncrest Center, Philadelphia
1956 Wister Playground, Philadelphia
      Beachcomber Swim Club, Gwynedd, Pennsylvania
      Alter House, Brockton, Massachusetts
      Bentman House, Lancaster, Pennsylvania
      Schaeffer House, Rydal, Pennsylvania
1957 Roosevelt Playground, Philadelphia
      Bulk Zoning Controls Study, Philadelphia
      Eastwick New House, Philadelphia (project)
1957/
  65 Tarkin Playground, stages I and II, Philadelphia
1958 Dolphin Swim Club, Lower Bucks County, Pennsylvania
      Urban renewal plan for the North Marshall Street Shopping Mall, Philadelphia
      Pender Laboratory, Moore School of Electrical Engineering, University of Pennsylvania, Philadelphia
1959 Development proposal for Eastwick Urban Renewal Area, Philadelphia
1960 F. J. Cooper Jewelry Shop, Philadelphia

      Plan for undergraduate men's housing, University of Pennsylvania, Philadelphia
1962 Police Headquarters, Philadelphia
      Huntington Laboratories, Lansdale, Pennsylvania
1963 Northeast Regional Library, Philadelphia
      Temple Beth Sholom, Manchester, Connecticut
      Master plan for Penn's Landing, Philadelphia
1963/
  64 Land plan for the Southern Sector of Reston, Virginia
1964 Master plan for the University City Science Center, Philadelphia
      Development plan for the Community College of Philadelphia
1965 Pine Street Row Houses, Philadelphia
      Development plan for cluster housing and recreational facilities, Reston, Virginia
      Master plan for the Peddie School, Hightstown, New Jersey
      Master plan for the Center City YM-YWHA, Philadelphia
1966 Community College of Philadelphia Department Store remodelling
      Unitarian Church of Delaware County, Springfield, Pennsylvania
      Geddes House, Princeton, New Jersey
      Master plan for the town center of Rockville, Maryland
      Bernards Street Housing, West Chester, Pennsylvania
1966/
  68 Theatre and Fine Arts Complex, Beaver College, Glenside, Pennsylvania
1967 Residence and Dining Halls, University of Delaware, Newark
      Graduate Research Center, Moore School of

      Electrical Engineering, University of Pennsylvania, Philadelphia
      Proposal for Kukui Redevelopment Area, Honolulu
1968 Middle-income housing, Princeton, New Jersey (project)
      Holmcrest Houses, Philadelphia
      Master plan for the central campus of Southern Illinois University, Carbondale
1968/
  72 Study/Dining Hall and Academic Buildings, Institute for Advanced Study, Princeton, New Jersey
1969 Development plan for Beaver College, Glenside, Pennsylvania
1970 Classroom/Office Building, Rutgers: The State University, Newark, New Jersey
      Research Laboratories, Academy of Natural Sciences, Philadelphia (project)
      Library, Southern Illinois University, Carbondale (project)
1971 Science/Academic Building, Beaver College, Glenside, Pennsylvania
      Pickett Middle School, Philadelphia
      Fine Arts Building, Goucher College, Towson, Maryland (project)
      Master plan for the Haile Selassie I University, Addis Ababa, Ethiopia
      Plan for the Vienna South New Community, Austria (competition project)
1971/
  76 Stockton State College, Pomona, New Jersey
1972 Downing renewal plan for Corning, New York
      Stauffer Dormitory and Dining Hall, University of Pennsylvania, Philadelphia
      IBM Branch Office Building, Bethlehem, Pennsylvania

Robert Geddes: Humanities and Social Sciences Center, Southern Illinois University, Carbondale, 1975

Master plan for a new town at Ken-Caryl
Ranch, Colorado
Design of public works for the town center of
Rockville, Maryland
Urban design study of the center of Trenton,
New Jersey
1973 Coatesville Public Housing, Coatesville,
Pennsylvania
Plan for a proposed new community in Read-
ington Township, New Jersey
Study of the Spring Garden Street Campus,
Community College of Philadelphia
Building systems research for the Johns-Man-
ville Corporation, Denver
Urban design study of the Henderson Street
Urban Renewal Area, Jersey City, New
Jersey
1974 Psychology Building, Rutgers: The State Uni-
versity, New Brunswick, New Jersey
United States Mint renovation, Philadelphia
1975 Humanities and Social Sciences Center,
Southern Illinois University, Carbondale
Trenton Commons Garage, Trenton, New
Jersey
1976 Dock Street Theatres and Shops, Philadel-
phia
1977 Master plan for Howell Farm, Mercer
County, New Jersey
1978 Master Plan, New Gallery, Chapel and reno-
vations, Trinity Church, Princeton, New
Jersey
United States Navy Recreation Facility,
Sandy Hook Bay, New Jersey
Master plan for the Columbian Mutual Life
Insurance Company, Binghamton, New
York
School of Medicine, Medical Education
Building, and Hamilton Walk Develop-
ment, University of Pennsylvania, Phila-
delphia
1979 Housing for the elderly, West Orange, New
Jersey
Housing for the elderly, Trenton, New Jersey
Columbian Mutual Life Insurance Company
Office Building, Binghamton, New York
1979/
85 Liberty State Park, Jersey City, New Jersey
1980 Master plan of the Downtown Government
Center, Miami

Publications:

By GEDDES: articles—"Theory in Practice: The
Dual Values of Teacher and Practitioner" in *Architectural Forum* (New York), September and October 1972; "The Nature of the Built Environment"
in *Progressive Architecture* (New York), June 1974;
"The Responsibilities (and Joy) of Architecture,"
interview with Diane Hempel, in *University Magazine: A Princeton Quarterly*, Summer 1974; annual
review of architecture and civil engineering in *Encyclopaedia Britannica Yearbook*, Chicago 1976, 1977,
1978; "Possibilities in Architecture" in *Architectural
Record* (New York), November 1977.

On GEDDES: articles—"Interiors as an Integral
Part of Practice" by Andrea Dean in *AIA Journal*
(Washington, D.C.), July 1975; "Kind of Uptown—
Concert Hall in Jefferson Civic Center" by David
Morton in *Progressive Architecture* (New York), No-
vember 1975; "The Home Towns Come Back" in
Architectural Record (New York), December 1976;
"Faner Hall at Southern Illinois University" by John
Morris Dixon in *Progressive Architecture* (New
York), December 1976; "It's Back to School for the
Systems Approach: Stockton State College" by Wil-
liam Marlin in *Architectural Record* (New York),
May 1977; "Humanities and Social Sciences Build-
ing, Southern Illinois University" by Mary E.
Osman in *AIA Journal* (Washington, D.C.), May
1977.

*

Architecture arises out of our need to shelter the
human animal in a spatial environment and to enclose the social animal in a group space. In this sense
architecture serves our institutions and expresses the
values of our culture.

Architecture is a public art, not a private expression of a single person. The production of architecture involves historical and cultural factors, social
and behavioral factors, economic and political factors.

Architecture is the expression of institutions, their
purposes, activities, and qualities. While the architecture of an institution should provide for future
change and growth, it must also be responsive to the
immediate satisfactions of the users and community.

Architect should be both coherent and complex in
form. It should be colorful and stimulating to the
senses, yet modest and economical in use of resources. It is an "enabling" mechanism, which
makes possible, but does not determine, the achievement of individual and social goals. In the construction of its spaces, its walkways and rooms, its landscapes, architecture participates in creating a
framework for living.

—Robert Geddes

Robert Geddes is an architect who would disagree
with Oscar Wilde that "Art never expresses anything
but itself." Geddes believes that the art of architecture expresses the nature of institutions—the family,
church, school, state—and that it communicates
emotion and ideals. He is convinced that architecture can improve society and influence character,
and that the aesthetics of architecture cannot be separated from moral and ethical purpose. For him,
both are "two parts of a unity; to emphasize either
at the expense of the other is improper. The social
responsibility of the architect is to be aesthetic. His
total responsibility is to bring the two together.
When he does, there is great joy in architecture."

Geddes the philosopher translates these articles of
faith into his everyday practice of architecture by
accepting commissions which he deems to be of the
most social importance to a community and its individuals—housing, educational buildings, and
urban design projects. He believes housing to be one
of the most important social and aesthetic responsibilities of our time. It is his credo that school buildings by the nature of their forms instruct the young,
in and out of the classroom. As an urban designer he
contends with all the forces that continually transform the city in his effort to create new physical
patterns that will enable people to lead better lives.

Geddes' buildings as sculptural forms are influenced by the works of Le Corbusier in the master's
pre-Brutalist, 1920's period. Geddes develops complex, interlocking volumes by means of alternatingly
curving or flat thin planes which, in combination
with transparent glass, dramatically advance and re-
cede. In most of his projects he articulates rather
than conceals structure. His completed works are
precise and elegant solutions of technical as well as
social problems.

Geddes believes that buildings should be constructed to last, and, if they do, that their functions
will change through time, as those of today's valuable old structures usually have. He therefore designs flexible, adaptable structures because, as he has
said, "the fit between form and function should not
always be close." He hopes that each of his buildings
will have second and third lives after their first use
is past. Such meticulously conceived and executed
works deserve the future he hopes for them.

—Mildred F. Schmertz

GEHRY, Frank O.

American. Born in Toronto, Ontario, Canada, 28
February 1929. Educated at the University of Southern California, Los Angeles, 1949–51, 1954, B.Arch.
1954; Harvard Graduate School of Design, Cambridge, Massachusetts, 1956–57. Served in the Special Services Division of the United States Army,
1955–56. Architectural Designer, Victor Gruen Associates, Los Angeles, 1953–54; Planner and Designer, Robert and Company, architects, Atlanta,
1955–56; Architectural Designer and Planner,
Hideo Sasaki Associates, Boston, 1957; Architectural Designer, Pereira and Luckman, Los Angeles,
1957–58; worked in planning, design and project direction for Victor Gruen Associates, Los Angeles,
1958–61; Project Designer and Planner, André Remondet, Paris, 1961. Since 1962, Principal, Frank O.
Gehry and Associates Inc., Los Angeles. Assistant
Professor, University of Southern California, 1972–
73; Visiting Critic, University of California at Los
Angeles, 1977, 1979. Member, Los Angeles 12. Exhibitions: *International Design: New Attitudes, New
Forms*, Contemporary Arts Museum, Houston,
1972; *45 Years of Architectural Design*, Musée des
Arts Décoratifs, Paris, 1973; *Innovations: Contemporary Home Environs*, La Jolla Museum of Contemporary Art, California, 1974; *Drawings of American
Architects*, Cooper-Hewitt Museum, New York,
1977. Recipient: Special Award, American Institute
of Architects/*Sunset Magazine*, 1975; Honor
Award, 1975 (twice), 1976, 1978, and Merit Award,
1975, 1977, AIA, Southern California Chapter;
Honor Award, national AIA, 1977; Award of Excellence, American Institute of Steel Construction,
1977. Fellow, American Institute of Architects. Address: Frank O. Gehry and Associates Inc., 1524
Cloverfield Boulevard, Santa Monica, California
90404, U.S.A.

Works:

1963 Kay Jewellers Office Building, Los Angeles
1964 Faith Plating Company, Los Angeles
1965 Danziger Studio/House, 7001 Melrose Avenue, West Hollywood, California
Design of the *Art Treasures from Japan* exhi-
bition, Los Angeles County Museum of
Art
1967 Merriweather Post Pavilion of Music, Co-
lumbia, Maryland
Feasibility study of the central business dis-
trict of Hermosa Beach, California
O'Niel Hay Barn, San Juan Capistrano, Cali-
fornia
1968 Joseph Magnin Store, South Coast Plaza,
Costa Mesa, California
Joseph Magnin Store, Almaden Fashion
Plaza, San Jose, California
Bixby Garden Townhouses, Garden Grove,
California (with Walsh and O'Malley)
Design of the *Billy Al Bengston* exhibition,
Los Angeles County Museum of Art
1970 University Park Apartments, Irvine Ranch,
California
Vernon-Central Redevelopment Plan, Los
Angeles
Temporary acoustical shell for the Holly-
wood Bowl, Los Angeles
1972 Ron Davis Studio/House, 29715 West Cuth-
bert Road, Malibu, California
Easy Edges Cardboard Furniture
1973 Cochiti Indian Reservation Commercial Cen-
ter, Cochiti, New Mexico
1974 Westinghouse Office Building, Los Angeles
Larkspur Center, Larkspur, California
Janss House, West Los Angeles
Rouse Company Headquarters, Columbia,
Maryland
1975 Concord Pavilion, Performing Arts Center,
Concord, California
1976 Gemini G.E.L. Lithography Shop and Gallery remodelling, 8365 West Melrose, Hollywood, California

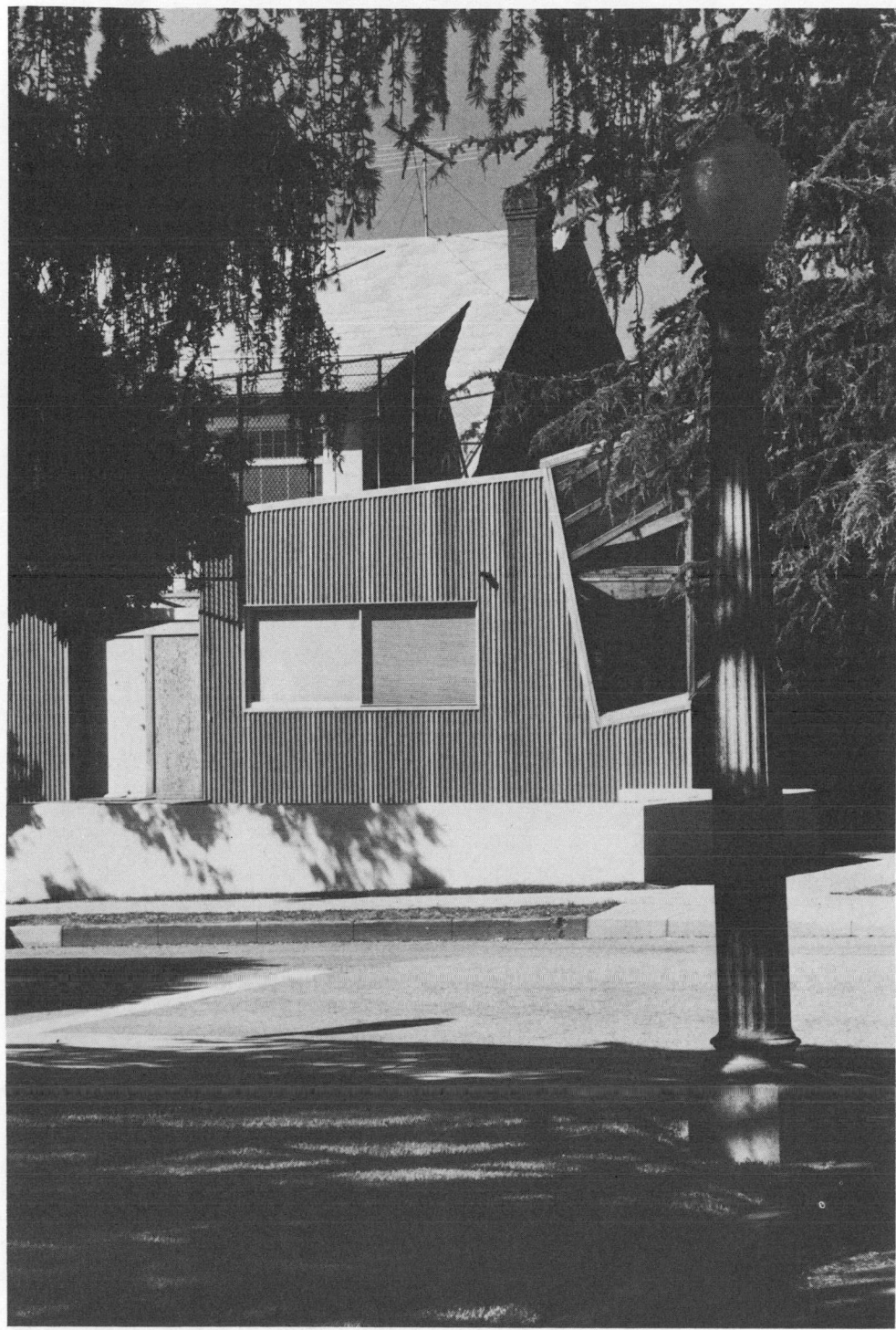

Frank O. Gehry: Gehry House, Santa Monica, California, 1979

Norton Simon House, Malibu, California
Santa Monica Pier renovation, Santa Monica, California
Harper House Condominiums, Village of Cross Keys, Baltimore
Hollywood Bowl Shell, phase I, Los Angeles
1977 Ron Davis Studio/House interior additions, 29715 West Cuthbert Road, Malibu, California
Rudge and Guenzel "The Atrium," Lincoln, Nebraska
Berger, Berger, Kahn and Shafton Law Offices, Los Angeles
Cheviot Hills House remodelling, Los Angeles
Design of the *King Tut Exhibition*, Los Angeles County Museum of Art
Design of the *Heeramaeneck Exhibition*, Los Angeles County Museum of Art
1978 Mid-Atlantic Toyota Distributorship (ware-

house and offices), Glen Burnie, Maryland
1979 Cabrillo Marine Museum, San Pedro, California
Santa Monica Place (mall and parking structures), Santa Monica, California
DeMenil Townhouse, New York
Frank O. Gehry House, Santa Monica, California
Spiller House, Venice, California
Los Angeles Children's Museum

Publications:

On GEHRY: book—*Innovations: Contemporary Home Environs,* exhibition catalogue, La Jolla, California 1973; articles—"The Quiet Townhouse" in *House and Home* (New York), December 1968; "Alfresco Spectacular" by Arthur C. Risser in *AIA Journal* (Washington, D.C.), August 1969; "Innovations: Easy Edges Does It" in *Architectural Forum*

(New York), April 1972; "Ready-to-Go-Zest: Cardboard Furniture" in *House and Garden* (New York), August 1972; "Report from the Malibu Hills" by Esther McCoy in *Progressive Architecture* (New York), December 1974; "Studied Slapdash" by Paul Goldberger in the *New York Times Magazine,* 18 January 1976; "Frank Gehry: The Search for 'No Rules' Architecture" by Janet Nairn in *Architectural Record* (New York), June 1976; "And Then There Were Twelve: The Los Angeles 12" in *Architectural Record* (New York), August 1976; "Law Offices, Los Angeles" and "Offices and Warehouse, near Baltimore" in *Architectural Review* (London), May 1979.

I am interested in finishing work, but I am interested in the work's not appearing finished, with every hair in place, every piece of furniture in its spot ready for photographs. I prefer the sketch quality, the tentativeness, the messiness if you will, the appearance of "in progress" rather than the presumption of total resolution and finality. The paintings of Cézanne, Monet, DeKooning, Rauschenberg, to name a few, compared to the hard edge painters, Albers, Kelly, etc.—perhaps that comparison makes my point more explicit.

I have been searching for a personal vocabulary. This search has been far ranging, from childlike exploration of my fantasies—a fascination with incoherent and seemingly illogical systems—to a questioning of orderliness and functionality.

If you try to understand my work on the basis of fugal order, structural integrity and formalized definitions of beauty, you are apt to be totally confused.

A client's programs are interesting to me but are not the driving force in creating his building. I approach each building as a sculptural object, a spatial container, a space with light and air, a response to context and appropriateness of feeling and spirit. To this container, this sculpture, the user brings his baggage, his program, and interacts with it to accommodate his needs. If he can't do that, I've failed.

The manipulation of the inside of the container is for me an independent, sculptural problem and no less interesting than the design of the container itself. This manipulation tests the adaptability of the space for a program that by now can have changed several times. In my work the perception of the object is primary. The imagery is real and not abstract, using distortion and juxtaposition of cheap materials to create surrealistic compositions.

All in the pursuit of firmness, commodity, and delight.

—Frank O. Gehry

Frank O. Gehry practices in an avant-garden manner. His design concepts have to do with creating architecture as pure art and sculpture. He has concentrated on flexibility and economy as expressed in angular forms and an unusual use of materials.

One of his goals is that of minimal construction: he strongly defines the outer walls, forcing the user to totally define the interior space. He is also acutely aware of building economics—what he refers to in his own work as "cheapscape architecture"—and his structures are clad in materials that have been stereotypically relegated to other building types. In particular, he has explored the use of corrugated metal panels, chain link fence, and exposed structural trusswork, to give the effect of industrial structures, in both commercial and residential work.

Gehry's artistic panache is obvious in such works as the warehouse and offices for Toyota in Maryland. The metal supports and bridges form patterns against the corrugated background of the roof and the colorful partitions, which vary in height and width. The horizontal is interrupted at times by diagonals, forming triangles. There are panels of metal caging, and the divisions meet and cross at different levels, sometimes right through the middle of a paneless window or a doorless entrance. The shapes created for such purposes are irregular, and the whole effect is that of a Mondrian painting.

The exposed service transmitters are another example of Gehry's creation of abstract sculptural effects, and add further interest to the structures of this original designer.

—Janet Nairn

GIBBERD, Sir Frederick.

British. Born in Coventry, 7 January 1908. Educated at the King Henry VIII School, Coventry, 1913–25; studied architecture in the office of Crouch, Butter and Savage, Birmingham, and at the Birmingham School of Architecture, 1925–29. Married Dorothy Phillips in 1938 (died, 1970); children: Geoffrey, Kate, and Sophie; married Patricia Fox Edwards in 1972. In private practice, London, since 1930: formed partnership, Frederick Gibberd and Partners, London, 1966. Principal, Architectural Association School, London, 1942–44; Architect-Planner, Harlow New Town, Essex, 1946–72. Member, Royal Fine Art Commission, 1950–70; Member of the Council, Royal Institute of British Architects, 1951–70; President, Building Centre, London, 1959–76. Exhibitions: MARS Group, London, 1936; Museum of Modern Art, New York, 1936; Playhouse Gallery, Harlow, 1978. Recipient: Festival of Britain Award, 1951 (three times); Civic Trust Award, nine times; Bronze Medal, Royal Institute of British Architects, 1955; European Architectural Heritage Award, 1975 (twice); Housing Medal, three times; Gold Medal, Royal Town Planning Institute, 1978. Honorary Professor of Architecture, National Engineering University, Peru, 1965; LL.D.: University of Liverpool, 1969. Fellow, Royal Institute of British Architects, 1939, Society of Industrial Artists, 1943, Royal Town Planning Institute, 1948, and the Institute of Landscape Architects, 1956. Associate of the Royal Academy, 1961, and Royal Academician, 1969. C.B.E. (Commander, Order of the British Empire), 1954; Knighted, 1967. Address: Marsh Lane, Harlow, Essex CM17 ONA, England.

Works:

1933 Pullman Court, Streatham, London
1935 Park Court, Crystal Palace, London
1936 Ellington Court, Southgate, London
1937 Macclesfield Nurses Home, Cheshire
1943 Howard Pre-Fabricated House (project)
     British Iron and Steel Federation Pre-Fabricated House
1945 Somerford Estate, Hackney, London
1946 Cladwell and Marston Estates, Nuneaton, Warwickshire
     Nuneaton Town Centre, Warwickshire
     Master plan for Harlow, Essex
1947 Steel rolling mill, Scunthorpe, Lincolnshire
     Civic Centre, Harlow, Essex
1948 Dempster Court, Town Centre, Nuneaton, Warwickshire
     Beecholme Housing Estate, Prout Road, Hackney, London
     Cofton Common School, Worcestershire
1949 Lansbury Market, London
     Stow Shopping Centre, Harlow, Essex
     The Lawns, Harlow, Essex
1950/
69   Terminal Buildings, London Airport
1951 Hull College of Technology, Yorkshire
     College of Further Education, Kidderminster, Worcestershire
     Westcliffe Secondary School, Scunthorpe, Lincolnshire
     Foley College of Technology, Stourbridge, Worcestershire
     Guinness Trust Flats, Cadogan Street, Chelsea, London
1952 Orchard Croft Housing Estate, Harlow, Essex
     Oakside Housing, Rutland Road, Hackney, London
     Market Square, Harlow, Essex
     National Dock Labour Board Office, Albert Embankment, London
1953 Ulster Hospital, Belfast
1955 Hancock House Office Block, Vincent Square, London
     Shell Research Centre, Thornton, Cheshire
     College of Technology, Huddersfield, Yorkshire

Hill County Secondary School, Upton-on-Severn, Somerset
High School, Henley-in-Arden, Warwickshire
Hinkley Point Nuclear Power Station, Somerset
1956 The Beckers Estate, Rectory Road, Hackney, London
     Sion Hill Secondary School, Kidderminster, Worcestershire
     ICI Offices, Runcorn, Cheshire
     Kingsgate Estate, Tottenham Road, Hackney, London
     Bath Technical College, Somerset
     Civic Centre, St. Albans, Hertfordshire
1957 Kennedy Square, Leamington Spa, Warwickshire
     Redditch Secondary School, Worcestershire
1958 Shell Agricultural Research Centre, Sittingbourne, Kent
     St. Neots Bridge, Huntingdon
     Derwent Reservoir, Durham and Northumberland
1959 Alconbury Bridges, A1 Trunk Road, Huntingdon
     Fulwell Cross Library and Swimming Pool, Ilford, Essex
     Roseberry Square Neighbourhood Centre, Redcar, Yorkshire
     The Lakes Estate, Redcar, Yorkshire
     Llyn Celyn Reservoir, Merioneth, Wales
     Nuneaton Library, Warwickshire
     Corn Exchange Development, Stratford-upon-Avon
     Civic Centre, Doncaster, Yorkshire
1960 Roman Catholic Cathedral, Liverpool
     Colonnade Shopping Precinct, Birmingham
     Hopwood Hall Chapel, Middleton, Lancashire
     Old Harlow Redevelopment, Essex
1961 Barclays Bank, Bletchley, Buckinghamshire
1962 Douai Abbey, Berkshire
     South East Highgate Housing, Kendal, Westmorland
     Lowfellside Housing, Kendal, Westmorland
     Northumberland Court, Leamington Spa, Warwickshire

Sir Frederick Gibberd: Harlow New Town, Essex, 1946–72

Sydenham Farm Neighbourhood and Housing, Leamington Spa, Warwickshire
Catholic Chaplaincy, University of Liverpool
Leamington Spa Courthouse, Warwickshire
Hull Youth Centre, Yorkshire

1964 St. George's Chapel, London Airport
Didcot Power Station, Berkshire

1965 The Royal Spa Centre, Leamington Spa, Warwickshire
Newbold Comyn Park, Leamington Spa, Warwickshire
Crown Offices, Leamington Spa, Warwickshire
Longman House, Harlow, Essex

1966 Arundel Great Court, The Strand, London
Grays South Redevelopment, Grays, Essex
The Howard Hotel, Temple Place, London

1967 Cleveland Potash Mine, Yorkshire

1968 Inter-Continental Hotel, Hyde Park Corner, London
York House, The Parade, Leamington Spa, Warwickshire
Godfrey Holmes Offices, Lincoln
Memorial University of Newfoundland, St. John's
Town Centre, Haverhill, Suffolk
Bell Court Shopping Centre, Stratford-upon-Avon

1969 The Harpur Centre Shopping Centre, Bedford
Coutts Bank, The Strand, London
London Central Mosque, Regent's Park, London
Kielder Reservoir, Northumberland
Thomas Cooper Memorial Chapel, Lincoln

1970 Dinorwic Pump Storage Power Station, Snowdonia, Wales

1971 Lion Walk Shopping Centre, Colchester, Essex
Castle Centre Shopping Centre, Banbury, Oxfordshire

1973 Environmental Centre, Llanberis, Caernarvon, Wales
The Harvey Shopping Centre, Harlow, Essex

Publications:

By GIBBERD: books—*The Modern Flat*, with F. R. S. Yorke, London 1937; *The Architecture of England*, London 1938, 5th edition 1965; *Harlow New Town*, Harlow, Essex 1947, 1952; *Report of the Oxford University Drama Commission: Supplementary Architectural Report*, Oxford 1948; *Town Design*, London 1953, 4th enlarged edition 1962; *Design in Town and Village*, with others, London 1953; *Architecture in the New Towns*, London 1963; *Metropolitan Cathedral of Christ the King*, London 1968; *Sculpture in Harlow*, Harlow, Essex 1973; *Harlow Expansion 1974*, Harlow, Essex 1974; *A Tonic for the Nation—Lansbury*, London 1976; articles—"Wall Textures" in *Architectural Review* (London), July 1940; "The Schools and Practice" in *Architectural Review* (London), November 1943; "Landscaping a New Town" in *Architectural Review* (London), March 1948; "Three Dimensional Aspects of Housing Layout" in *RIBA Journal* (London), August 1948; "Detail in Civic Design" in *Town Planning Institute Journal* (London), March 1951; "Expression in Modern Architecture" in *RIBA Journal* (London), January 1952; "High Flats in Medium Sized Towns" in *RIBA Journal* (London), February 1955; "Mark Hall Neighbourhood" in *Architectural Review* (London), May 1955; "Ten Years After" in *The Sunday Times* (London), 19 May 1957; "Designing a New Town" in *Far and Wide* (London), Winter 1957/58; "The Landscape of Reservoirs" in *Journal of the Institute of Water Engineers* (London), March 1961; "New Towns in Britain" in *AIA Journal* (Washington, D.C.), March 1961; "Reflections on Architecture, 1965" in *The Builder* (London), December 1964; "The Landscaping of Reservoirs" in *Architectural Review* (London), July 1966; "Environmental Aspects of Boulby Mine" in *Minerals and the Environment* (London), June 1974; "A New Lake for Northumbria" in *Country Life* (London), December 1974; "Sculpture in the Landscape: The Private Garden" in *Journal of the Institute of Landscape Architects* (London), February 1978.

On GIBBERD: articles—"A 50 ft. Living Room" in *House and Garden* (London), June 1966; "Hotel, Hyde Park Corner" by Lance Wright in *Architectural Review* (London), December 1975; "London Central Mosque" in *RIBA Journal* (London), June 1976; "The Making of Harlow" by Stephanie Williams in *Building Design* (London), 27 August 1976; "Arundel Great Court, Strand" by Sutherland Lyall in *The Architects' Journal* (London), 3 November 1976; "Harpur Centre, Bedford" by James Madge in *The Architects' Journal* (London), 24 November 1976; "The Gibberd Touch" by Tony Aldous in *The Architects' Journal* (London), 11 January 1978.

My interest is in design. I have spent most of my life at the drawing board and have never been interested in a professional career as such. I do not produce imaginative sketch designs and leave them to others to work out. To me design is a long and laborious process, and I am involved until it is finally settled. I have avoided specialising because the more varied the design problems, the more interesting life is.

Unlike most architects, I practise Landscape Architecture and Town Planning. My imagination is probably at its best when I am able to combine these three arts into a complete environment.

I came to town planning from architecture because, apart from the design problems being more complex, it enabled me to determine the environment for my buildings and to relate buildings to each other and to the landscape to make urban spaces. The English landscape has had a strong influence on my work. Harlow is based on the land form, and large-scale industrial projects like Didcot Power Station and the Cleveland Potash Mine were fundamentally landscape problems.

I am told that I have a reputation for being sensitive to the character of English towns and villages. I received European Architectural Heritage Awards for the village of Old Harlow and Lowfellside housing in Kendal and design awards for Lansbury Market and schemes at Stratford-upon-Avon, Bedford and elsewhere.

I have a capacity for realising my designs (I swallow my pride and do not resign) with the consequence that I remained with Harlow until its completion, and at places like Leamington Spa and Nuneaton I carried out a whole series of designs over long periods.

My concern for the environment has been a strong influence on my architecture: Liverpool Cathedral has a tower to give, with the Catholic Cathedral, two crowns to the urban composition; the Inter-Continental Hotel is designed to terminate the long frontage of Piccadilly, leaving Apsley House as a pavilion in the park; and Arundel Great Court in the Strand has given London a new landscaped court.

—Frederick Gibberd

Although, as the list of his works demonstrates, Sir Frederick Gibberd has designed a wide variety of buildings, it is possible to discern definite and persistent characteristics that pervade most of his work. In his concepts, whether in individual structures, groups of buildings or town planning schemes, he has been socially progressive in answering human needs, he has been anxious to conserve and introduce amenities, and in doing this he has kept abreast of technical developments so as more efficiently to satisfy needs. Aesthetically, simplicity and restraint, with a few exceptions, have generally prevailed in his designs.

In these three main aspects of his work the last, because it is the most apparent, claims first attention. Throughout most of his work Gibberd has been a designer in rectangles, with a studied adjustment of their relations, of the parts to each other and of the parts to the whole, so that the appearance of most of his buildings might be described as a rectangular massing of the parts, with variety secured by various textures of wall and patterning of fenestration, with projections and recessions giving light and shade. Occasionally there is a horizontal emphasis, but it is rarely sufficient to disturb a general sense of repose. These qualities are seen in Pullman Court, Streatham, one of his earliest buildings, where the large rectangular blocks arranged round a court have well spaced windows and balconies which give variety. A simpler treatment is seen in the three-storey blocks at Park Court, Crystal Palace, where the flatness of square windows on plain walls is saved perhaps from dullness by the integration with an attractive landscape setting. In his tall square blocks of flats at Harlow, the good effect depends on the slightly curved facades, on the vertical recessions, the well-proportioned window spacing, and the landscape setting. The rectangular motif controls much of Gibberd's planning of many town centres, of which that for Harlow is a conspicuous example, where Gibberd started from scratch. This centre, looked at on plan, is a rectangular pattern and the buildings—the shops, offices and those surrounding the market square—have this same characteristic with occasional horizontal emphasis. It is seen too in the water gardens, south of the centre, with long straight pools and rectangular flower beds, while the theme is continued horizontally and vertically in the adjacent tower hall. The consciousness of this square formal massing is strong because of the simplicity and the restrained articulations. At its best it achieves a Greek-like serenity, and dignity; when it is less successful, as in some of the extremely simple terrace housing and blocks of flats, it is dull, monotonous and cold, where regularly spaced, squarish windows on smooth plain pale walls wait for shrubs and trees to grow nearby to make them acceptable.

One of Gibberd's best works in the idiom is the Civic Hall, St. Albans, the principal building in the Civic Centre that he planned. It is very broadly and effectively treated. A broad canopy projects above the ground floor, which has extensive glazed areas, while on the first floor the extensive fenestration at the corners of the block relate very well to the plain walls. The building is in a sunken area from the main approach ways, and thus the broad massing can be well seen.

Gibberd is probably best known for Harlow New Town, Heathrow Airport terminal buildings and the Liverpool Roman Catholic Cathedral. The best of the airport buildings is the last, which represents an advance in functional design with its two main levels for arriving and departing passengers and two level road access. It is the most dramatic in appearance of the group—a long rectangular building with the horizontal bands of wall and fenestration giving a more dynamic emphasis than is usual in his work.

Gibberd's designing for human needs is seen both in his work as a town planner and in his housing. The visit of a resident to a town centre may include a dozen calls to shops, bank, post office, library, etc. located there; it is a great advantage if these are concentrated to minimize movement from one to the other. In Harlow town centre Gibberd has achieved this concentration and has grouped his buildings round squares and pedestrian ways. Gibberd must also be accounted one of the pioneers of pedestrianization, and good examples are seen in his many designs for town centres. That at Nuneaton, designed at the end of the Second World War, is a good example, and here Gibberd made use of the natural feature of the river Anker that runs through the centre to introduce the amenities of a park and tree planting while retaining some of the old features, like flour mills, achieving a happy blending of old and new, something that he also achieved at St. Albans and in the old town or rather village of Harlow, where the narrow High Street was bypassed and converted into a pedestrian way, with some new modern buildings in excellent harmony in scale and massing.

Robin Gibson: Mayne Hall, University of Queensland, Brisbane, 1973

In designing for human needs, Gibberd has always been ready to use and develop modern materials and methods of construction. During the Second World War he designed the Howard House, which structurally had a light steel frame with panels of suitable weatherproof and insulating materials and a kitchen made in the factory and transported complete to the site. With other designs of the period, it was a useful contribution to prefabrication. A valuable factor in the design of the house was a service unit consisting of kitchen, utility room on the ground floor, and bathroom on the first, kept separate from the living and sleeping sections and ingeniously arranged to come together in terrace housing. A further example is the structural innovation in his design for the Liverpool Cathedral, which is rather a departure from Gibberd's other work. With its circular plan and central altar (following the modern liturgical movement), it is of tent-like form similar to the old bell tent of the British Army, surmounted by a tower and culminating in a crown of thorns. The construction is of reinforced and pre-stressed concrete with a careful calculation of compression and tension, making possible an economy of bulk and material. But the conical roof coming low on the cylindrical wall hardly gives the spatial feeling that is desirable in a church of this size. It is not typical of Gibberd's best work, which resides more in the attractive and often ingenious variations of rectangular massing.

—Arnold Whittick

GIBSON, Robin.

Australian. Born Robert Findlay Gibson in Brisbane, Queensland, 15 May 1930. Educated at the University of Queensland, Brisbane, 1948–54, Dip. Arch. 1954. Married Moorea Roach in 1957 (died, 1977); children: Kristina and Nicholas. Student Architect, City Architect's Department, Brisbane, 1948, office of Frank Cullen, Brisbane, 1949, Hayes and Scott, Brisbane, 1950, and Theo Thynne, Brisbane, 1951–54; Architect, James Cubitt and Part-

ners, London, 1955, and Sir Hugh Casson and Neville Conder, London, 1955. Since 1957, Principal of Robin Gibson and Partners, Brisbane. Exhibitions: Queensland Art Gallery, Brisbane, 1974; Australian Pavilion, Spokane, 1976. Recipient: First Prize, Queensland Art Gallery Competition, 1973; Bronze Medal for Meritorious Architecture, Royal Australian Institute of Architects, Queensland Chapter, 1973, 1976. Address: Robin Gibson and Partners, 233 Elizabeth Street, Brisbane, Queensland 4000, Australia.

Works:

1961 Miss Shirley's Shop, Brisbane
1963 Perrins House, Ascot, Brisbane
      Wallace Bishop Store, Fortitude Valley, Brisbane
1964 Shirley Shoes and Players, Surfers Paradise, Queensland
      British Overseas Airways Corporation, Brisbane
1965 Qantas House, Brisbane
1966 Mocatta House, Yeronga, Brisbane
1968 Kenmore Presbyterian Church, Brisbane
      Robinson's Sports Store, Queen Street, Brisbane
      Wallace Bishops' Store, Toombul Shopping Town, Brisbane
1969 Commonwealth Industrial Gases Office Building and Stores, Brisbane
      Commonwealth Industrial Gases Research Centre, Sydney
1970 I.A.C. House, Brisbane
1972 Office building, 40 Queen Street, Brisbane
1973 Mayne Hall, University of Queensland, Brisbane
      Central Library, University of Queensland, Brisbane
      Mathers Shoes Warehouse, Brisbane
1974 Administration and Psychology Building, Mount Gravatt Teachers College, Brisbane
1975 Library and Humanities Complex, Griffith University, Brisbane
      Mathers Shoes Retail Premises, Townsville, Queensland

1975/
  78 Queensland Cultural Center, Brisbane: Art Gallery; Performing Arts Complex; Museum; and State Library
1976 Library/Arts and Crafts and Music Students Union, Mount Gravatt Teachers College, Brisbane
1977 State Control Centre, Queensland Electricity Generating Board, Brisbane

Publications:

On GIBSON: books—*Towards an Australian Architecture* by Harry Sowden, Sydney 1968; *University Library Buildings in South East Asia,* University of Singapore Library, 1976.

Architecture is the truthfulness of creating spaces effective for their use and enjoyable to the user in the answering of those usages.

"In the beginning" are magical works, and the opportunity to create and bring into being a tangible reality is the joy of architecture.

The processes to achieve it are a complex matrix based on a continuing assessment of applied techniques overlaid with modern technological advances.

Problems to be solved are analysed and abstracted to the minimal elemental bases so that the end result is the essence of the problem.

From this base architecture is created with an emotional and subjective but, above all else, an imaginative input.

An architecture which is on-going with previous experiences and examples is the basis for development.

Architecture that relies on the purity of material use, the clarity of structural solutions, and the objectivity of planning solutions as the language creates a poetry which is known and seen as a personal architecture.

The built result is seen as a place which is in context with its use, brings joy and happiness to the user, and contributes to the improvement of the total environment.

—Robin Gibson

Robin Gibson practices architecture in the State of Queensland in Australia, which is the only known part of the world where five generations of Europeans have lived and worked in what is largely a hot, humid, tropical climate. These families successfully adapted themselves to an environment different from that of their historical experience. They also developed a distinctive vernacular building tradition that extensively used light, durable, low-cost materials, such as timber and tin. This tradition is unique to Queensland, and it has also substantially helped to establish what is considered by many as a transitory environment.

In sheer contrast to this tradition, Gibson's buildings are solid, carefully detailed, and permanent enough to give the impression that they are likely to stay there for some time. In a region where fortunes are quickly made and lost, Gibson's buildings continue to provide a sense of stability and order.

Robin Gibson's projects are associated with cultural, civic and educational institutions. His design approach has its links with the Bauhaus which reached Australia via the U.S.A., particularly the Californian west coast, where the climate is not unlike that of Queensland. His style is tightly controlled in the Miesian tradition, with judicious use of concrete—mainly precast—and glass and steel. The details are meticulous and highly refined. However, unlike Mies van der Rohe's architecture, Gibson's buildings are open-ended and can be extended to satisfy the changing requirements.

Since most of Gibson's buildings are air-conditioned, climate, as a basis of design, plays only a minor role. He uses large glass areas and extensive terraces that lend themselves to enjoyment of the outdoors.

Irving J. Gill: Dodge House, Los Angeles, 1916

Gibson has designed a large cultural centre complex in Brisbane on the banks of the river, which includes buildings for the performing arts, a museum, an art gallery, restaurant, auditorium and the State Library. It is one of the most ambitious projects ever undertaken by the Government of Queensland. The design incorporates the best elements of Gibson's approach and indicates a high level of sensitivity for its unique location. When completed it will firmly establish its designer as one of the most significant contributors to the architectural heritage of the State.

—B. S. Saini

GILL, Irving J(ohn).
American. Born in Syracuse, New York, in 1870. Educated in Syracuse public schools. Married Marion Breashears in 1929. Worked as a draftsman for Adler and Sullivan, Chicago, 1890–93; in private practice, San Diego, 1895–1916: in partnership with W. S. Hebbard, 1898–1906, and with his nephew, Louis J. Gill, 1914–16; also maintained an office in Los Angeles. Exhibition: *Irving Gill 1870–1936,* Los Angeles County Museum of Art, 1958. *Died* (in Carlsbad, California) *7 October 1936.*

Works:

1895 Normal school, San Diego
1898 George McKenzie House, Front and Kalmia Streets, San Diego
     Bernard McKenzie House, Coronado, California
     Stephens House, 1156 Ocean Boulevard, Coronado, California
1902 Ellen Mason House, Newport, Rhode Island
1904 Christian Science Church, 3rd and Ash Streets, San Diego
     George Marston House, Upas and 7th Streets, San Diego
     Wagenheim House, 148 Juniper Street, San Diego
     Barker House, 108 Robinson Street, San Diego
     Pickwick Theatre, San Diego
     Gill House, 3109 Albatross Street, San Diego
     Kline House, Lakeside, California
1905 Tutt House, 519 Ocean Boulevard, Coronado, California
     Douglas House, 202 Maple Street, San Diego
     Fox House, 3100 Brant Street, San Diego
     John Olmstead House, Chepiwanoxet, Rhode Island
     House, Apponaug, Rhode Island
     McCagg House, Bar Harbor, Maine
     Lee House I, 3578 7th Street, San Diego

     Lee House II, 3353 Albatross Street, San Diego
1906 Burnham House, 3565 7th Street, San Diego
     Cossitt House, 3526 7th Street, San Diego
     Lee House III, 3574 7th Street, San Diego
     Teats House I, 3560 7th Street, San Diego
     First Methodist Church, 9th and C Streets, San Diego
     Porterfield House, San Diego
     House, 280 Olive Street, San Diego
1907 Bailey House, 1962 Princess Street, La Jolla, California
     Laughlin House, 666 West 28th Street, Los Angeles
     Allen House, Sweetwater Valley, California
     Melville Klauber House, 3060 6th Street, San Diego
     Mitchell House, 2720 4th Street, San Diego
1908 St. James Chapel, La Jolla, California
     Alice Klauber Studio, 3060 6th Street, San Diego
     Waterman House, 2104 Front Street, San Diego
     Cottage, 212 Hawthorn Street, San Diego
     Cottage, 220 Hawthorn Street, San Diego
     Goff House, 3580 5th Street, San Diego
     House, 3353 2nd Street, San Diego
     Bishop's Day School, 3072 1st Street, San Diego
     Wilson Acton Hotel, La Jolla, California

Gill Row Houses (2), Robinson Mews, San Diego

Gill Rental House, 3776 Front Street, San Diego

Webster House, 7th and Beech Streets, San Diego

Wheaton House, 6th and Redwood Streets, San Diego

Darst Apartments, 2266 5th Street, San Diego

Dart House, 502 Kalmia Street, San Diego

Hugo Klauber House, 2626 6th Street, San Diego

Scripps Institute of Oceanography, La Jolla, California

Holly Sefton Memorial Hospital for Children, San Diego

Christensen Apartments, 22nd Street between J and K, San Diego

1909 Plaza Foundation, San Diego

Bentham Hall, Bishop's School, La Jolla, California

Christian Science Church, 2nd and Laurel Streets, San Diego

1910 Lewis Courts (housing development), Mt. Trail and Alegria Street, Sierra Madre, California

Scripps Hall, Bishop's School, La Jolla, California

National City High School alterations, National City, California

San Diego Country Club, 1740 Upas Street

Gorham House, 6th and Palm Streets, San Diego

Fulford House, 7th Street, San Diego

1911 Multimore House, 1301 South Chelton Way, South Pasadena, California

Timken House, 335 Walnut Street, San Diego

House, 3404 Front Street, San Diego

1912 Thompson House, 1156 Isabella Avenue, Coronada, California

Teats House II, 3415 Albatross Street, San Diego

Lee House IV, 3367 Albatross Street, San Diego

House, 2728 6th Street, San Diego

Belcher House, 1st and Kalmia Street, San Diego

Echo Park Court, Los Angeles

Banning House, 503 South Commonwealth Avenue, Los Angeles

1913 Supervisor's Residence, Community House, La Jolla, California

Women's Club, Prospect Street, La Jolla, California

Kautz House, Girard Street, La Jolla, California

Torrance Boulevard Bridge, Torrance, California

Pacific Electric Station, Torrance, California

Workmen's cottages (12), 1800–1900 Gramercy, Torrance, California

Office building, Torrance, California

1914 Community House, La Jolla, California

House, 7233 Hillside Avenue, Los Angeles

Cottages, 1003 4th Street, Santa Monica, California

1916 Mason House, 2434 Langdale Avenue, Eagle Rock, California

Dodge House, 950 Kings Road, Los Angeles

Ellen Scripps House, La Jolla, California

Gilman Hall, Bishop's School, La Jolla, California

Cottage Court, Los Angeles

1917 Morgan House, Arden and Melrose, Los Angeles

1919 Wilde Apartments, 500 D Street, Coronada, California

Horatio West Court, 126 Hollister Street, Santa Monica, California

1922 Teats House III, 3407 Albatross Street, San Diego

Jean Ginsberg: Les Speluges Complex, Monte Carlo, 1977

1929 City Hall, Oceanside, California

Fire and Police Station, Oceanside, California

Auditorium, Recreation Hall and Swimming Pool, Oceanside, California (project)

Nevada Street School, Oceanside, California

Christian Science Church, Avenue C and 8th Street, Coronado, California

1931 Kindergarten, Division and Center Streets, Oceanside, California

1933 Rancho Barona Resettlement Development for Indians, California

1935 Beauty shop, 311 South Elena Avenue, Redondo Beach, California

Publications:

By GILL: article—"New Ideas about Concrete Floors" in *Sunset Magazine* (Menlo Park, California), December 1915.

On GILL: books—*Irving Gill 1870–1936,* exhibition catalogue, Los Angeles 1958; *Five California Architects* by Esther McCoy, New York 1960; *The Roots of Contemporary Architecture,* edited by Louis Mumford, New York 1972; *A Guide to Architecture in Los Angeles and Southern California* by David Gebhard and Robert Winter, Santa Barbara, California 1977; articles—"The Garden Apartments of California" by E. M. Roorbach in *Architectural Record* (New York), December 1913; "Roots of California Contemporary Architecture" by Esther McCoy in *Arts and Architecture* (Los Angeles), October 1956; "Irving Gill" by Esther McCoy in *L'Architettura* (Rome), December 1959, January 1960, February 1960, and March 1960; "More Is Less" in *Arts and Architecture* (Los Angeles), October 1963; "Irving Gill's Dodge House 1916–1965" in *Arts and Architecture* (Los Angeles), September 1965; "Green Between the Gray" in *AIA Journal* (Washington, D.C.), November 1967; "Irving Gill, Architect" by Esther McCoy in *Historic Preservation* (Washington, D.C.), April/June 1972.

Irving J. Gill was born in Syracuse, New York, in 1870, the son of a building contractor. He attended public schools in that city but never went to college. Following a short stay in a Syracuse architectural office, he made his way west to Chicago, aged 20, to join the firm of Adler & Sullivan. Sullivan looked with favor on him, partly because he was pleasantly uncorrupted by the formal training for which Sullivan had so little use, also because he possessed a poetic nature and romantic outlook not unlike that of the master himself. Certainly Sullivan's yearning for an "American architecture," as well as his suspicion of the classical past, were influences that remained with Gill during his whole career.

Gill stayed in Chicago for only two years, then for reasons of health he moved to San Diego. He was much taken by the look of the native vernacular he found there—by the adobe, the redwood houses and the missions with, as he wrote, "their long low lines, graceful arcades, tile roofs, bell towers, arched doorways and walled gardens." These formal elements would eventually appear, personally modified, in Gill's finest later work. In his early California years, however, he practiced a variety of eclectic manners, ranging from Beaux-Arts to Shingle Style to Prairie Style. In 1906, when he ended a partnership with W.S. Hebbard which had been formed eight years earlier, Gill began to realize his mature potential. In the wall construction of the Klauber House (San Diego, 1907) and the Laughlin House (Los Angeles, 1907), he made bold use of concrete and hollow tile, a technique that became one of the hallmarks of his career. He used it innovatively, pioneering a tilt-wall construction system that provided for cheaper costs in concrete building. Gill rapidly developed into one of the 20th century's most expressive artists in the medium. It served him well in his modifications of the mission style into a clean, sheer, stripped-down modern that bore a resemblance to the work done at roughly the same time—1900–1910—by the Viennese Adolf Loos. Gill very likely arrived at his solutions independent of Loos; in fact his Acton Hotel in La Jolla (1908) antedates Loos' famous Steiner House by two years.

The climax of Gill's career as a designer of houses came in his handsome, elegantly appointed Dodge House in Los Angeles (1916), in which cubist volume took on an identity with the white stucco box of the mission manner.

Gill was also a tireless designer of small-scale, low-cost housing projects, some of which, like Lewis Courts, Sierra Madre (1910), have seldom if ever been surpassed for their commodity and grace. His commission to design a plan for the city of Torrance,

California (1913), however, fell through, and in fact with the ascendancy of the virtuoso Beaux-Artsman Bertram Goodhue, who sparked a revival of florid Spanish neo-Baroque in southern California, Gill's career after World War I went into a decline from which it never fully recovered.

—Franz Schulze

GINSBERG, Jean.

French. Born in Czestochowa, Poland, 20 April 1905; emigrated to France, 1924: naturalized, 1939. Educated at the Technical College, Warsaw, B.A. 1922; Berlin University, 1923; Ecole Spéciale d'Architecture, Paris, 1924–29, Dip.Arch. 1929. Married May d'Ornhjelm in 1954; children: Corinne and Christiane. Principal, Jean Ginsberg & Associés, Paris, since 1932. Permanent Member, Housing Committee of the International Union of Architects. Recipient: First Prize, Academy of Architecture, Paris, 1962; First Prize, Beauty of Paris Competition, 1967; First Prize, National Housing Program Consultation, Paris, 1967; First Prize, Ministry of Equipment Housing Competition, Paris, 1969, 1973; First Prize, Center of the New Town of Evry, France Competition, 1972. Member: Academy of Architecture, Paris; French Society of Town Planning; Cercle d'Etudes Architecturales; Industrial Aesthetic Institute; and Franco-British Union of Architects. Chevalier of the Légion d'Honneur, and of the National Order of Merit; Chevalier de Saint Charles, Monaco. Address: Jean Ginsberg & Associés, 25 rue Michel Salles, 92210 Saint Cloud (Paris), France.

Works:

1927 Apartment building, 25 Avenue de Versailles, Paris (with Bertold Lubetkin)

1930/
72 Group of 2,000 flats, Meaux, France
Group of flats, Meudon, France
Group of 275 flats, Massy, France
Group of 220 flats, Montrouge, France
Group of 360 flats, Courbevoie, France
Group of 300 flats, Gif-sur-Yvette, near Paris
Group of 320 flats, Poissy, France
Building, Boulogne sur Seine, Paris
Group of 1200 flats, Argenteuil, France
Group of 2080 flats, Le Mureaux, France
Building, Saint Cloud, Paris
Embassy of Finland, Paris
O.E.C.D. (Organization for Economic Cooperation and Development) Offices, Paris
Administrative Offices, Orly Airport, Paris
General Secretary's Office, Civil Aviation Board, Paris
Government Administration Buildings, Monaco
Holiday centre at Biarritz and at Lacanau, France
Holiday centre at Ibiza, Spain
1972 Centre of the new town of Evry, France (competition project)
1975 Gif-sur-Yvette Commercial Centre, near Paris
City Centre of the new town of Vitrolles, near Marseilles
1975/
77 Technical University, Libreville, Gabon (with others)
Les Speluges Complex, Monte Carlo: Palais Heracles; Mille Fiori Tower; Las Palmeras Building; Monte Carlo Star Building; Loew's Hotel and Casino; and International Convention Centre and Auditorium

Publications:

On GINSBERG: articles—"A Different Kind of Building Complex: Les Speluges at Monte Carlo" by

Abel Blanc in *La Construction Moderne* (Paris), September/December 1974; "Residential Complex, Marly-le-Roi" in *Bauen und Wohnen* (Zurich), September 1975; "Les Speluges Complex in Monte Carlo" in *Récherche et Architecture* (Paris), no. 28, 1976; "Luxury Hotel with Convention Hall and Flats on the Mediterranean" in *Bauen und Wohnen* (Zurich), May 1976; "Technical High School at Libreville for 3,000 Pupils" in *Mur Vivant* (Paris), no. 48, 1978.

Jean Ginsberg's practice, in association successively with Lubetkin, Heep and others, shows a continuity in architectural ideas, a search for imaginative solutions, an attention to detail, and a quality in the completed work that clearly bear the stamp of this excellent architect's personality.

His first-class organizing ability and business competence do not detract from this excellence. Fate has made of him an architect chiefly concerned with property developments for various clients whose main concern is profitability. He has given them satisfaction without sacrifice of architectural quality. Nor does he bow to fashion: Ginsberg remains faithful to "line" and develops it wherever possible.

We do not choose our clients, and to a certain extent they fashion us. It is to Jean Ginsberg's great credit that he has always known how to please his clients and yet produce good architecture—as every architect knows, not always an easy task.

—Pierre Vago

GIURGOLA, Romaldo.

American. Born in Rome, Italy, 2 September 1920; emigrated to the United States, 1954: naturalized, 1959. Educated at the School of Architecture of the University of Rome, 1945–49, B.Arch. (honors) 1949; Columbia University, New York, 1949–51, M.Arch. 1951. Married Adelaide F. Bercivenga in 1952; daughter: Paola. Since 1958, Partner, with Ehrman B. Mitchell, *q.v.*, Mitchell/Giurgola Architects, Philadelphia; office established in New York, 1966. Assistant Professor of Architecture, Cornell University, Ithaca, New York, 1952–54; Professor of Architecture, University of Pennsylvania, Philadelphia, 1954–66. Chairman of the Department of Architecture, 1966–71, and since 1971 Ware Professor of Architecture, Columbia University, New York. Architect-in-Residence, American

Romaldo Giurgola and Ehrman B. Mitchell: Liberty Bell Pavilion (foreground) and Penn Mutual Tower, Philadelphia, 1975

Academy in Rome, Autumn 1977. Member of the Advisory Council, Princeton School of Architecture, New Jersey, 1975–77; Member, Architectural Review Board, Charles Center/Inner Harbor, Baltimore, 1975–77. Exhibitions: University of Pennsylvania Museum, Philadelphia, 1965; Pennsylvania Academy of Fine Arts, Philadelphia, 1975; Columbia University, New York, 1977; *200 Years of American Architectural Drawing,* American Federation of Arts travelling exhibition, 1977–78; *Drawing Toward a More Modern Architecture,* The Drawing Center, New York, 1977, and Otis Art Institute Gallery, Los Angeles, 1978; *Roma Interrotta,* Rome, 1978. Recipient: First Award, 1961, Gold Medal, 1964, Honor Award, 1974, 1975, 1977, Architectural Firm Award, 1976, and Award of Merit, 1978, American Institute of Architects; Gold Medal, AIA, Philadelphia Chapter, 1961, 1964, 1972, 1974, 1977; Silver Medal, 1965, 1974, 1975, 1977, Distinguished Building Award, 1971, 1975, 1977, and First Honor Award, 1977, Pennsylvania Society of Architects; Gold Medal, Artists Guild of Philadelphia, 1966; Arnold Brunner Award, National Institute of Arts and Letters, 1966; First Prize, Wainwright State Office Complex Competition, St. Louis, 1974; Medal of Honor, AIA, New York City Chapter, 1975; Bard Award, City Club of New York, 1978; Design Award, *Urban Design,* 1978. Fellow, American Institute of Architects, 1975; Institute Member, American Academy and Institute of Arts and Letters, 1977. Commendatore, Republic of Italy, 1972. Address: Mitchell/Giurgola Architects, 170 West 97th Street, New York, New York 10025, U.S.A.

Works (with Ehrman B. Mitchell):

1958 Crockett House, Corning, New York
    Mitchell House, Lafayette Hill, Pennsylvania
    Far East Asia Development (project; with Wright and Mitarachi)
1959 Stine House, Bryan, Ohio
    Public Health Center 9, 13 East Cheltan Avenue, Philadelphia
1960 Evansville Petroleum Club interiors, 420 Main Street, Evansville, Indiana
    Wright Brothers Memorial Visitors Center, Kill Devil Hills, North Carolina
1961 Mednick House, Philadelphia
    Lumberyard Town House Development, Philadelphia (project)
    Franklin Delano Roosevelt Memorial, Washington, D.C. (competition project)
    Huebner Hall: American College of Life Underwriters National Headquarters, Bryn Mawr, Pennsylvania
1962 Philadelphia Life Insurance Company Office Building addition, Philadelphia
    Boston City Hall (competition project)
    Campus Plan, and Dormitory, Academy of the New Church, Bryn Athyn, Pennsylvania
    Market Street East Development, Philadelphia
1963 White House, Chestnut Hill, Pennsylvania
    Patzau House, Philadelphia (project)
    Andale Company Office Building, Lansdale, Pennsylvania
    Frankford Arsenal Metrology Laboratories, Philadelphia
    Administration Building, Academy of the New Church, Bryn Athyn, Pennsylvania
    Maintenance Building, Academy of the New Church, Bryn Athyn, Pennsylvania (project)
    Parking Garage I, University of Pennsylvania, Philadelphia
    Classroom and Laboratory renovation, University of Pennsylvania, Philadelphia (project)
1964 Bethlehem Steel Company Office Building, Philadelphia (project)
1965 International House, Philadelphia (competition project)

Headquarters Building, Acadia National Park, Bar Harbor, Maine (project)
    Newman Center, University of Kentucky, Lexington (project)
    Swarthmore Presbyterian Church and School, Swarthmore, Pennsylvania (project)
    American Institute of Architects National Headquarters, Washington, D.C. (competition project)
    Myrick Pavilion, The American College, Bryn Mawr, Pennsylvania
1966 Five Cents Savings Bank, Boston
    Campus plan for The American College, Bryn Mawr, Pennsylvania
1967 Hotel and Office Building, Wilmington, Delaware (project)
    William Jeanes Memorial Library, Whitemarsh, Pennsylvania (project)
    Parking Garage, State University of New York at Oneonta (project)
    Plan for the central business district of Wilkes Barre, Pennsylvania
1968 Zebooker House, Philadelphia
    Roberts House, Philadelphia
    Rockefeller Center Theatre, New York (project)
    United States Embassy, Bogota, Colombia (project)
    Interim facilities for the United Nations International School, New York
1969 United Nations International School, New York (project)
1970 Dayton House, Wayzata, Minnesota
    Parking Garage II, University of Pennsylvania, Philadelphia
    Women's Physical Education Facility, Swarthmore College, Swarthmore, Pennsylvania (project)
    Master plan for the 30th Street Site, Philadelphia (with David A. Crane)
    Campus plan for Swarthmore College, Swarthmore, Pennsylvania
1971 United Fund Headquarters, Philadelphia
    South End Branch Public Library, Boston
    Subway Concourse Entrance, Market and 8th Street, Philadelphia
    University Museum Academic Wing, University of Pennsylvania, Philadelphia
    Apartment Building, Welfare Island, New York (project)
1972 Peacock Hill Redevelopment, Williamsburg, Virginia (project)
    Bok Tower, Mountain Lake Sanctuary, Lake Wales, Florida
    Mission Park Residential Houses, Williams College, Williamstown, Massachusetts
    Adult Learning Research Laboratory, MDRT Foundation Hall, The American College, Bryn Mawr, Pennsylvania
    Master plan for the Eastwick Site, Philadelphia (with others)
    Convention Center, Philadelphia (project)
    Twin Parks East Apartment Building, Bronx, New York (project)
1973 Administrative Office interiors, N and G Buildings, Westminghouse Electric Corporation, Lester, Pennsylvania
    Worship Assembly Building, Benedictine Society of St. Bede, Peru, Illinois
    Lang Music Building, Swarthmore College, Swarthmore, Pennsylvania
    Columbus High School, Columbus, Indiana
    Undergraduate Housing, Yale University, New Haven, Connecticut
1974 Central Service Building, Westinghouse Electric Corporation, Lester, Pennsylvania
    Student Union, State University College of New York at Plattsburgh
    Casa Thomas Jefferson (United States Information Agency/Thomas Jefferson Cultural Center), Brasilia
    Master plan for the Springhouse Research

Center, Rohm and Haas Corporation, Springhouse, Pennsylvania
1975 William Penn High School, Philadelphia
    Condon Hall: School of Law, University of Washington, Seattle
    Indian Point Energy Education Center, Buchanan, New York
    Penn Mutual Tower, Philadelphia
    Liberty Bell Pavilion, Philadelphia
    Two INA Plaza (office building), Philadelphia
    Feasibility study for the Philadelphia College of Art
    Master plan for the Volvo Manufacturing Plant, Chesapeake, Virginia
    University City Science Center office interiors, Philadelphia
1976 Philadelphia College of Art renovation and alterations
    Volvo of America Office and Assembly Building, and Power House, Chesapeake, Virginia
    Girard Bank main office renovation, Philadelphia
    Living History Center, *Philadelphia '76*
    Tredyffrin Public Library, Tredyffrin Township, Strafford, Pennsylvania
    St. Joseph's Village for Senior Citizens, Brookhaven, New York (competition project)
1977 Benjamin F. Feinberg Library, State University College of New York at Plattsburgh
    Sherman Fairchild Center for the Life Sciences, Columbia University, New York
    Master plan for Harbor Plaza (office/parking/hotel complex), Stamford, Connecticut
    Master plan for the future development of the United States Capitol, Washington, D.C. (design consultant; with Wallace, McHarg, Roberts and Todd)
1978 Harbor Plaza, Stamford, Connecticut
    Hardie A. Beloff Nursing Home, West Goshen, Pennsylvania (project)
    Development plan for the East Campus, Massachusetts Institute of Technology, Cambridge (with Gruzen and Partners)
    Bershad House kitchen addition, Philadelphia
    DeCordova Museum renovation and addition, Lincoln, Massachusetts
1979 Beni Stabili Apartment/Retail Complex, Houston (competition project)
    South Central Bell Telephone Company Regional Headquarters, Nashville, Tennessee (competition project; with Gassner, Nathan and Partners)
    Newman House, Bedford, New York
    Harristown Key Block, phase I, Harrisburg, Pennsylvania (with Lawrie and Green)
    Physical Activities Building, Swarthmore College, Swarthmore, Pennsylvania
    Administrative Resources Center, Lukens Steel Company, Coatesville, Pennsylvania
    General Services Building, The American College, Bryn Mawr, Pennsylvania
    Ten Stamford Forum (office building/parking garage), Stamford, Connecticut
    Master plan for the Art Museum, Princeton University, New Jersey
    Central Chilled Water Plant, Massachusetts Institute of Technology, Cambridge (project; with Gruzen and Partners)
    Blank, Rome, Comisky and McCauley office interiors, Philadelphia
1980 Geology Library renovation and addition, Princeton University, New Jersey
    Wainwright State Office Complex, St. Louis (with Hastings and Chivetta)
    Graduate Studies Center, The American College, Bryn Mawr, Pennsylvania
    Maintenance Facility, Independence Park, Philadelphia

1981 Lafayette Place (hotel/retail/parking complex), Boston
    College of Health Sciences Technology and Management Building, and Health Services Building, Massachusetts Institute of Technology, Cambridge (with Gruzen and Partners)
    Technical High School, Maniago, Italy
    Elementary School, Aviano, Italy
    Student Housing, San Pietro al Natisone, Italy
    Concert Theatre renovation and reconstruction, C. W. Post Center, Long Island University, Greenvale, New York
1982 Central Research Library, University of North Carolina at Chapel Hill (with Leslie N. Boney)
    Los Palos Grandes (office building/retail complex), Caracas, Venezuela (with W. James Alcock)
    Cell Biology Research Center renovation, New York University
    Library renovation, Union Theological Seminary, New York
    Student Center, Bryn Mawr College, Bryn Mawr, Pennsylvania
1983 Westlake Park (museum/retail/parking complex), Seattle
    Pennsylvania Avenue Development (hotel/office/retail/parking complex), Washington, D.C. (with Frank Schlesinger)

Publications:

By GIURGOLA: book—*Louis I. Kahn*, with Jaimini Mehta, Zurich and Boulder, Colorado 1975; articles—"Eric Mendelsohn 1887–1953" in *Interiors* (New York), December 1953; "Architecture in Change" in *Journal of Architectural Education* (Washington, D.C.), November/December 1962; "Reflections on Buildings and the City: The Realism of the Partial Vision" in *Perspecta* (New Haven, Connecticut), no. 9/10, 1965; "Aldo Giurgola" in *Arts and Architecture* (Los Angeles), April 1965; "On Louis Kahn" in *Zodiac* (Milan), no. 17, 1967; "Five on Five," with others, in *Architectural Forum* (New York), May 1973; "Louis I. Kahn 1901–1974" in *Progressive Architecture* (New York), May 1974; article in *Space Design* (Tokyo), December 1975; article in *Christian Science Monitor* (Boston), 21 April 1977; "Roma Interrota" in *Architectural Design* (London), no. 3/4, 1979; "Forces Shaping Current Design" in *AIA Journal* (Washington, D.C.), May 1979.

On MITCHELL/GIURGOLA: articles—"Conscious Contrasts" in *Progressive Architecture* (New York), May 1965; "Should Anyone Care about the 'New York Five' or about Their Critics, the 'Five on Five'" by Paul Goldberger in *Architectural Record* (New York), February 1974; "Mitchell/Giurgola" in *Architecture + Urbanism* (Tokyo), December 1975; "On Trying to Understand the Significance of Mitchell/Giurgola" by William Marlin in *Architectural Record* (New York), April 1976; "Profile of Mitchell/Giurgola" by Andrea O. Dean in *AIA Journal* (Washington, D.C.), April 1976; "Structures with a Social Value" by William Marlin in *Christian Science Monitor* (Boston), 21 April 1977; "Mitchell/Giurgola," special issue of *Process: Architecture* (Tokyo/Pittsburgh), July 1977; interview with Kenneth Frampton in *Controspazio* (Bari, Italy), July/August 1977.

Arts were begot by chance and observation, nursed by use and experience, and improved and perfected by reason and study—Alberti

Our buildings are reflections of aspects of life, expressing continuity, history, and the desire of a future. They are manifestations of projects for life that

people everywhere pursue. In them all is design, from the texture of a wall to the caliber of a space. They aspire to be architecture.

—Romaldo Giurgola

The work of Romaldo Giurgola and Ehrman B. Mitchell continually exhibits strong consistency in design—but with a flavor all its own. At a time clouded with rhetoric and doctrine, Mitchell/Giurgola Architects have produced singular buildings, relying on new perceptions of design criteria. They have worked to develop new directions, expressions, and alternatives, in order to give FORM to a PLACE. This approach has emerged from Romaldo Giurgola's concern with reality—reality, in all its aspects, is what makes Mitchell/Giurgola distinct from other firms.

Their buildings do not participate in the profession's preoccupation with intra-architectural arguments; instead, they emerge from a clear synthesis of external constraints. Much thought is applied to the nature of functional relationships and visual implications, but, most importantly, architecture is always seen in context. The product is not an individual monument; it is part of both a social and an architectural environment.

Theory is important, nevertheless, and Giurgola is an academician trained in Europe and reared in the tradition of the Beaux-Arts. He maintains an acute interest in tradition and history, and he sees architecture as a continuous progression. It is because of this temporally conscious view that he shies away from fashion or what he calls "perennial eclecticism," preferring an expression of more meaningful connections with change and the "dynamics of life." His buildings establish a sense of propriety free from style or time.

Giurgola's notions of order are reflective of his deep debt to his teacher Louis Kahn, but the ideas have been modified and adapted to suit Giurgola's environmentalist approach. He loves Kahn's work, not for shape but for the sudden discoveries or "realizations," as Kahn used to say. He refers to Kahn's architecture as deriving from "the architecture of the past and tangentially the Beaux-Arts connection." He respects Kahn's approach to place and sympathizes with the value of conceptual operations in design.

Modern technology makes of our society fast-track representatives of a particular event. "Forget the past and create the new present," we say. But while many people enjoy instant happenings, Mitchell/Giurgola continues to fight for the importance of the process. Process not only represents a contemporary idea of architecture but also reflects the past in combination with the dynamics of the present.

This methodological concern, coupled with Giurgola's conviction that architecture's major task is in giving FORM to a PLACE, reflects a desire to go far beyond functional satisfaction. His architecture becomes the realization of his own personal sense of place, accomplished skilfully and rationally.

—Ching-Yu Chang

GOČÁR, Josef.

Czech. Born in Semin, Bohemia, 13 March 1880. Educated at primary and secondary schools in Pardubice, Czechoslovakia, and secondary school in Prague; Technical School for Building, Prague, 1899–1902; Arts School, Prague, 1903–08. Served in the Austrian Army, 1917–24. Married; son: the architect Jiří Gočár. In private practice, Prague, 1908–45. Professor of Architecture, 1924, and Dean, 1924–28, Academy of Fine Arts, Prague. Founder, with the architect Pavel Janak, Prague Art Workshops, 1912; President, Mánes Association of Artists, 1912; President, Czechoslovak Association of

Architects. Exhibitions: *Austro-Hungarian Exhibition,* Earl's Court, London, 1906; *Contemporary Artists,* Berlin, 1912; *Grosse Berliner Kunstausstellung,* Berlin, 1913; *Werkbund Exhibition,* Cologne, 1914; *Manes Association,* Berne, 1919; *Czechoslovak Exhibition,* Lyons, 1920; *World's Fair,* Brussels, 1920; *Künstlerbund Hagen,* Vienna, 1923; *Arts Décoratifs et industriels modernes,* Paris, 1925; *International Town Planning Exhibition,* Vienna and Leipzig, 1926; *Czechoslovak Art Exhibition,* Warsaw, 1927; *Oeuvres Tchecolovaque,* Barcelona, Bucharest and Strasbourg, 1929; *Deutsche Bauausstellung,* Berlin, 1931; *Oeuvres Tchecoslovaque,* Stockholm 1931; *International Exhibition of Architecture,* Brussels, 1935; *Arts et Techniques,* Trocadéro, Paris, 1937; *Mánes Retrospective Exhibition,* Prague, 1947. Recipient: Grand Prix, *Exposition des Arts Décoratifs,* Paris, 1947. Member, Czechoslovak Academy of Sciences and Arts. Corresponding Member, Royal Institute of British Architects; Member, Légion d'Honneur, France, 1926. *Died* (in Prague) *10 August 1954.*

Works:

1904/
05 Houses, Magdaleny Dobromily Street, Hradec Králove, Czechoslovakia
1907/
09 Binka Villa, Krucemurk, Czechoslovakia
1909/
10 Winternitz Brothers Mills and Silos, Pardubice, Czechoslovakia
    Wenke Department Store and interiors, Jaromir, Czechoslovakia
1910 Water Tower, Bohdaneč, Czechoslovakia
    Town Hall, Staroměstské Nàměsti, Prague (competition project)
    Jaroušek Villa, Brno, Czechoslovakia
    Sanatorium, Prague (project)
1910/
14 Austrian Regiments of Uhlans Barracks, Bohdaneč, Czechoslovakia
1911 Experimental houses for workers, Kolín, Czechoslovakia
    Kustov Villa, Kolín, Czechoslovakia
    Apartment building, Černé Matky Boží Street, Prague
1911/
12 2 villas, Tycho de Brahe Street, Prague
    Spa buildings, Bohdaneč, Czechoslovakia
1912/
13 Bauer Villa, Librodice, Czechoslovakia
1914 Pension Vesely, Bohdaneč, Czechoslovakia
1919 Winternitz Silos extension, Pardubice, Czechoslovakia
    Experimental housing, Prague and Strašnice, Czechoslovakia
1920/
21 Offices and warehouses, Prague and Kbely, Czechoslovakia
1921 Bank of the Czechoslovak Legions, Prague (with sculptors Stursa and Gutfreund)
1921/
23 Bank of Brno, Jindřiská, Prague
1923 State Gymnasium, Hradec Králove, Czechoslovakia
1923/
24 Koželuž School, Hradec Králove, Czechoslovakia
    Anglobank, Pardubice, Czechoslovakia
    Anglobank, Ostrava, Czechoslovakia
    Hus Square reconstruction, Hradec Králove, Czechoslovakia
1923/
25 Anglobank, Hybernská, Prague
1924/
25 Czechoslovak Pavilion, *Exposition des Arts Décoratifs,* Paris
1924/
26 Farmers Union Headquarters, Vinohrady, Prague
1925 Primary and secondary schools, Hradec Králove, Czechoslovakia

Josef Gočár: Bank of the Czechoslovak Legions, Prague, 1921

1925/	1927/
26 Strnad Villa, Prague	32 Czechoslovak Railways Headquarters, Hradec Králove
1925/	
27 Schools, Hradec Králove, Czechoslovakia	1928 Final town plan for Hradec Králove, Czechoslovakia
1926/	1928/
27 President Masaryk Monument, and Masaryk Square reconstruction, Hradec Králove, Czechoslovakia	29 St. Wenceslas Church, Prague
Elbe Valley Town Planning, Hradec Králove, Czechoslovakia	1928/
	30 Main Post Office, Užhorod, Czechoslovakia
Infant school, Hradec Králove, Czechoslovakia	1930 Bata Offices, Karlsbad, Czechoslovakia
1926/	1931/
28 Embankment and Museum District reconstruction, Hradec Králove, Czechoslovakia	32 Tyrs Bridge, Hradec Králove, Czechoslovakia
	1931/
1927/	36 County Finance Office, Hradec Králove, Czechoslovakia
28 County Offices and Grand Hotel, Pardubice, Czechoslovakia	1932/
	33 Kytlica Villa, na Babě, Prague
	1933 Loma Villa, na Babě, Prague

1933/
35 Med Villa, Humpolec, Czechoslovakia
1934/
35 Offices and flats, Ulrich Square, Hradec Králove, Czechoslovakia
1935/
36 Böhm Apartment Block, Prague
1937 President Masaryk Monument, Humpolec, Czechoslovakia (with sculptor V. Makovsky)
1939 Post Office Square reconstruction, Humpolec, Czechoslovakia

Publications:

On GOČÁR: books—*Tschechische Bestrebungen um ein modernes Interieur* by V. V. Stech, Prague 1914; *Contemporary Czech Art* by A. Matejček and Zd. Wirth, Prague 1921; *Contemporary Slovakia* by Zd. Wirth, Prague 1925; *Contemporary Architecture* by J. Krejcar, Prague 1928; *Josef Gočár* by Zd. Wirth, Vienna and London 1930; *Josef Gočár, Hradec Králove,* introduction by Zd. Wirth, Prague 1930; *Modern Architecture in Czechoslovakia* by Karel Teige, Prague 1930; *The Churches of Prague* by O. Štefan, Prague 1936; *Prague: The City of Churches* by M. Chalupníček, Prague 1937; *The History of Our Art* by J. Pavel, Prague 1939; *New Czech Architecture* by J. E. Koula, Prague 1940; *Prague in Photographs* by K. Plicka, Prague 1940; *L'Architecture Contemporaine en Tchecoslovaquie* by K. Teige, Prague 1947; *Prague* by Vojtech Volavka, Prague 1948; *Prague Step by Step* by Emanuel Poche, Prague 1948; *Josef Gočár* by Marie Benešová, Prague 1958.

Josef Gočár was born into a Czech minority in a country of many minorities during one of the more liberal periods of the 19th century in Central Europe. At the turn of the 20th century he was twenty years old, and his professional life spanned the political, social and artistic turmoil of the first half of the century.

He became a pupil of Jan Kotera and later his assistant. Kotera, "the father of Czech modern architecture," had in turn been a pupil of Otto Wagner, an active member of the Secession in Vienna. When the influence of Art Nouveau began to fade, the more radical artists and architects in Prague turned to Cubism, perhaps the most important visual philosophy of the 20th century. They fought against the Secession, the monumentality of Wagner, and for a new rationalism. Gočár played a leading role in the movement and in 1912 became the first President of the new breakaway Association of Artists in Prague. Throughout his life he was actively connected with the arts, and many leading painters and sculptors were his friends and collaborators.

The Wenke Department Store was an early attempt by Gočár to free himself from the School of Vienna. The ground and first floors of this small three-storey building were fully glazed (one of the first examples of curtain walling), without any visible structural elements. The third floor, with its heavy coffered cornice and series of non-structural decorative columns, is, however, still late Secession. His design for a Sanatorium in Prague, with five interconnected three storey pavilions, was severe, the walls punctuated only by windows and balconies without cornices or applied decoration.

In 1910 Gočár submitted a competition design for the Town Hall in the Staroměstské Nàmèsti in Prague—a huge stepped-back pyramid which, had it been built, would have wrecked the beautiful 15th/16th century square. It created a furore and led to Gočár's complete break with the spirit of Wagner and Vienna. A spa building in Bohdaneč, designed in the following year, was based on Cubist principles with strong prismatic elements, creating—to use Gočár's own words—"a dramatic sense of movement."

When the Czech Republic was created in 1918 there was a nationalist upsurge which was reflected in architecture in the use of folklorist decoration and vivid colours. Gočár's exhibition pavilion for the Artists Club (Mánes) and his Legion Bank in Prague in 1921 are covered with ornamentation echoing peasant embroidery. This, however, was a shortlived period, and by 1924 his work showed a connection with Dutch architecture and progressive involvement with the Modern Movement. From this time on, his architecture was consistent and had a personal unity. The Headquarters for the Czechoslovak Railways in Hradec Králove and the beautiful St. Wenceslas Church in Prague are among the best modern buildings in Europe.

In the early 1920s Gočár was commissioned by an enlightened mayor to prepare a town plan for the rebuilding and extension of the old town of Hradec Králove. He was responsible not only for the planning but also for the design of many of the important new buildings. This collaboration between a farsighted client and an architect-planner of determination resulted in the building of a modern city in which, despite opposition, everything of architectural and historic value was retained.

In 1924 Gočár was appointed Professor of Architecture at the Academy of Arts in Prague and shortly after became Dean. The art students numbered more than one hundred, but Gočár's department was small with never more than fourteen to sixteen students who were required to have had previous technical training. He was against formal teaching; he never gave lectures, concentrating on studio work. The free, enthusiastic and hardworking atmosphere in the studio was the result of an exceptionally good master-pupil relationship.

Gočár was a prolific architect; some 250 works are documented as are 190 projects that were never realized. He was neither an innovator nor a theoretician but reacted intuitively, sensitively and in a very personal way to the tendencies of his time.

—Eugene Rosenberg

GOERITZ, Mathias.

German. Born in Danzig, Germany, 4 April 1915; moved to Mexico, 1949. Educated at the Kaiserin-Augusta-Gymnasium, Charlottenburg, Berlin, 1924–34; Friedrich-Wilhelms-Universität, Berlin, 1934–40, Ph.D. 1940; Kunstgewerbeschule, Charlottenburg, Berlin, 1937–39. Married Marianne Gast in 1942 (died, 1958); Ida Rodriguez Prampolini in 1960; son: Daniel. Professor, Centro de Estudios Marroquies, Tetuan, Spanish Morocco, 1940–44; worked as a painter in Granada, Spain, 1945–47, and Madrid, 1947–49; Professor of Visual Education and Design, Escuela de Arquitectura, Universidad de Guadalajara, Jalisco, Mexico, 1949–54. Since 1953, painter, sculptor and architect in Mexico City, and Founder/Professor, Department of Basic Design, Universidad Nacional Autónoma de Mexico, Mexico City. Founder/Director, Escuela de Artes Plasticas y Escuela de Diseño Industrial, Universidad Iboamericana, Mexico City, 1957–60; Artist-in-Residence, Aspen Institute for Humanistic Studies, Aspen, Colorado, 1970–72. Editor, Art Section, *Arquitectura Mexico,* Mexico City, since 1958. Founder, La Escuela de Altamira movement, Santillana del Mar, Santander, Spain, 1948, and Los Hartos movement, with José Luis Cuevas, Pedro Friedeberg, Jesus Reyes Ferreira, and others, Mexico City, 1961. Member of GIAP (Groupe International d'Architecture Prospective), since 1965. Exhibitions: one-man shows—Sala Clan, Madrid, 1946; Salon Alerta, Santander, Spain, 1948; Galeria Palma, Madrid, 1949; Galeria Camaraux, Guadalajara, 1950; Galeria Clardecor, Mexico City, 1950; Galeria Jardin, Barcelona, 1952; Galeria de Arte Mexicano, Mexico City, 1952; Galeria Proteo, Mexico City, 1955; Carstairs Gallery, New York, 1956; Galeria de

Arte Mexicano, Mexico City (retrospective), 1959; Carstairs Gallery, New York, 1960; Galerie Iris Clert, Paris, 1960; Galeria de Antonio Souza, Mexico City, 1960; Galeria de Arte Mexicano, Mexico City, 1961; Carstairs Gallery, New York, 1962; group shows—*New Media-New Forms,* Martha Jackson Gallery, New York, 1960; *Aspects de la sculpture américaine,* Galerie Claude Bernard, Paris, 1960; *New Europeans,* Contemporary Arts Museum, Houston, 1960; *Art of Assemblage,* Museum of Modern Art, New York, 1961; ceased exhibiting, 1962. Collections: Museum of Modern Art, New York; Museo de Arte Moderno, Mexico City; The Israel Museum, Jerusalem; etc. Member, Akademie der Künste, Berlin, 1973; Honorary Fellow, Royal Academy of The Hague, 1976. Address: Apartado 20–390, Mexico 20, D.F., Mexico.

Works:

1952/
53   EL ECO Experimental Museum, Calle Sullivan 43, Mexico City (now altered)

1957   Open Chapel, Guadalajara (with Luis Barragán; unfinished)
     Towers, Satellite City, near Mexico City (with Luis Barragán and Mario Pani)

1959/
61   Studio, Avenida Hidalgo Temixco, Morelos, Mexico

1964   Automex Towers, near Toluca, Mexico (with Ricardo Legorreta)

1966   House, Calle Dr. Manuel Mazari 112, Cuernavaca, Morelos, Mexico

1975   The Jerusalem Labyrinth: Community Center Alejandro and Lilly Saltiel, Jerusalem (with Arthur Spector and Micha Amisar)

1977/
78   Belfry of the Instituto Technologico, Monterrey, Mexico (with Team Gocadiguse)

Publications:

By GOERITZ: books—*Manifesto of the School of Altamira,* Santander, Spain 1948; *Manifesto: Estoy Harto,* Mexico City 1960; *Manifesto: Estamos Hartos,* Mexico City 1961; articles—"Manifesto: Arquitectura Emocional" in *Cuadernos de Arquitectura* (Guadalajara), no. 1, 1954; "Statement" in the catalog for his one-man show, Carstairs Gallery, New York 1962.

On GOERITZ: books—*Encyclopédie de l'Architecture Nouvelle* by Alberto Sartoris, Milan 1954; *Encyclopaedia of Modern Architecture* by Max Cetto, London 1963; *Art in Latin American Architecture* by Paul F. Damaz, New York 1963; *Arquitectura Contemporanea Mexicana* by Israel Katzman, Mexico City 1964; *Bouwmeesters van morgen* by J. J. Beljon, Amsterdam 1964; *El Arte Contemporaneo* by Ida Rodriguez Prampolini, Mexico City 1964; *Les Cités de l'Avenir* by Michel Ragon, Paris 1966; *Builders in the Sun* by Clive B. Smith, New York 1967; *The Aesthetics of Contemporary Architecture* by Michel Ragon, Neuchatel 1968; *A History of Latin American Art and Architecture* by Leopoldo Castedo, New York 1969; *Histoire Mondiale de l'Architecture et de l'Urbanisme Modernes* by Michel Ragon, Paris 1972; articles—"El Eco: Ein Experimental-Museum in Mexiko" in *Baukunst und Werkform* (Frankfurt), no. 4, 1954; "Architektur in Mexiko" by Helmuth Borcherdt in *Baumeister* (Munich), November 1959; "Mathias Goeritz" by Michel Ragon in *Cimaise* (Paris), no. 106, 1972.

Art in general, and naturally also architecture, reflects man's spiritual state. But the impression exists that modern architects, too individualistic and intellectual—perhaps because they have lost their close ties with the community—emphasize the rational side of architecture. As a result, the 20th century man feels crushed by the exaggerated "functionalism." logic and usefulness of modern architecture.

He looks for a solution, but neither exterior aesthetics defined as "formalism," nor organic regionalism, have adequately faced the problem of the common man of our times—creative or receptive—who aspires to something more than a pretty, pleasant and comfortable house. He asks—or will one day ask—that architecture with its modern means and materials give him a spiritual lift or—said in a simpler way—move him, as did in its time the architecture of the Pyramid, the Greek temple, the Romanesque or Gothic cathedral, or even that of the Baroque palace. When architecture causes an emotive response in man, he will again consider it an art.

—Mathias Goeritz

Functionalism claims to have invented an environment in which architecture would adopt as its aesthetic principle the new technology of mechanics and engineering. Thus, for more than three decades—between 1920 and 1950—and even today, the landscape of many of the cities of Europe, the United States, and Latin America has been invaded by monotonous units of construction whose square outlines and glass walls give the impression of space planned with a utilitarian aim in mind. Mathias Goeritz, painter, sculptor, and architect, who was born in Germany but settled in Mexico, questions both the plastic and the spiritual values of Functionalism. His attitude is obviously not an isolated one. The horrors of the Second World War implanted in the Western mentality a mistrust of reason and caused a revaluation of subjectivity and emotion as valid means and forms of knowledge and understanding of the world.

In 1952, the time of the triumph of Functionalism, Goeritz chose to construct the El Eco Experimental Museum, a work accompanied by a manifesto in which he developed his idea of an emotional architecture: he used the building as an example of a kind of architecture whose principal function is to arouse emotion. The modern architect, according to Goeritz, is out of touch with man and society, and as a result he has created constructions that are merely "decorative, pleasant and adequate." As far as Goeritz is concerned, however, as artist-philosopher the architect, with his new methods and materials, must be able to create works that invoke a spiritual response: "Only when architecture inspires real emotions can it again be regarded as an art."

The aim of the experimental museum was not merely to make good use of space; the architectural features—walls of between 7 and 11 metres in length; corridors; open and enclosed spaces—were arranged in such a way as to involve man and awaken in him the emotion that at one time he was able to feel when confronted by the Greek temple, the Pyramids, or a Gothic cathedral—before the onset of a modern architecture of indifference.

The importance of El Eco is in its integrated plasticity—the way in which paintings and sculptures are not superimposed but grow naturally with the walls of the building. It has become a living example of "collective artistic production," combining experience in music, literature, the theatre, and the cinema.

In the years that followed Goeritz created monumental sculpture. The gigantic Towers of Satellite City are symbols of the town, as medieval cathedrals once were. In this way sculpture and architecture unite. Sculpture fulfils the symbolic functions of architecture, and in return architecture makes sculpture inhabitable—as for example in the house that Goeritz built at Cuernavaca in 1966.

Goeritz has been concerned to articulate a philosophy of need for an aesthetic based on a new morality that leaves out the self complacency of much of contemporary art. The inability of society and its artists to produce structures and images of significance is more and more apparent. Art has become tepid—on the one hand because everyone is competing to produce the most brilliant gesture, on the other because of an increasing assimilation with the mentality of technology. Goeritz replies with spec-

Mathias Goeritz: EL ECO Experimental Museum, Mexico City, 1953

tacular forms, pure and monumental, which throw down a challenge to the ugliness of towns, the products of growing industrialization, and the gratuitous gestures of so many contemporary experimentalists.

—Rita Eder

GOFF, Bruce.

American. Born in Alton, Kansas, 8 June 1904. Educated at Lincoln Public School, Tulsa, Oklahoma, 1914–22; apprenticed to the firm of Rush, Endacott and Rush, Tulsa, 1916. Served in a United States Navy Construction Batallion, in the Aleutian Islands and California, 1942–45. Married Evelyn Hall in 1926 (divorced, 1926). Worked for Rush, Endacott and Rush, Tulsa, 1916–30; Partner, Endacott and Goff, Tulsa, 1930–33; worked for the industrial products design firm of Alfonso Iannelli, Chicago, 1934; in private practice in the Chicago suburb of Park Ridge, 1935; Teacher of Art Composition, Chicago Academy of Fine Arts, 1935; Director of Design, Libbey-Owens-Ford Glass Company, Toledo, 1935–36; in private practice, Chicago, 1936–42, and Berkeley, California, 1945–46; Professor, 1947–55, and Chairman and Head of the School of Architecture, 1948–55, University of Oklahoma, Norman; in

private practice, Bartlesville, Oklahoma, 1956–64, Kansas City, Missouri, 1964–69, and Tyler, Texas, since 1970. Exhibitions: The Architectural League, New York, 1970; Yellowstone Art Center, Billings, Montana, 1978. Address: 1302 Roseland, Tyler, Texas 75701, U.S.A.

Works:

1918 Indiana Limestone Residence (project)
      Stucco House and Reflecting Pool (project)
      Frame House with Four-Way Fireplace (project)
1920 A Modern House of the Midwest Type (project)
      Mausoleum for Grant McCullough, Tulsa, Oklahoma (project)
      Way House, Tulsa, Oklahoma
      Consolidated Cut Stone Company Offices, Tulsa, Oklahoma
      McClure House, Tulsa, Oklahoma
      Graves Summer House, Los Angeles
      Marquee for the Lorton Building, Tulsa, Oklahoma
1921 Hansen House, Tulsa, Oklahoma
      Police Station, Tulsa, Oklahoma (competition project)
1922 Directors' Dining Room, First National Bank, Tulsa, Oklahoma
      Concrete and Glass Hill House, Tulsa, Oklahoma (project)
      Stucco and Shingle Tile House, Tulsa, Oklahoma

Concrete Auditorium, Tulsa, Oklahoma (project)
1923 Tulsa Building, Tulsa, Oklahoma
      Atlas Office Building, Tulsa, Oklahoma (project)
      Hodgson House, Tulsa, Oklahoma (project)
1924 Robinson Studio, Tulsa, Oklahoma
1925 Medical Arts Building, Tulsa, Oklahoma (project)
1926 Boston Avenue Methodist/Episcopal Church, Tulsa, Oklahoma
      Cole Commercial Building, Tulsa, Oklahoma
1927 Page Warehouse, Tulsa, Oklahoma
1928 Genett Furniture Store, Tulsa, Oklahoma (project)
      Guaranty Laundry, Tulsa, Oklahoma
      Riverside Music Studio, Tulsa, Oklahoma
1929 Indian Memorial, Tulsa, Oklahoma
      Gas Company Building, Tulsa, Oklahoma (project)
      Tulsan Athletic Club, Tulsa, Oklahoma (project)
      Memorial Hospital, Tulsa, Oklahoma (project)
      Children's Pre-School, Tulsa, Oklahoma (project)
      City Market, Tulsa, Oklahoma (project)
      Glass House, Tulsa, Oklahoma (project)
      Tulsa Convention Hall interior remodelling, Tulsa, Oklahoma
1930 Merchants Exhibit Building, Fair Grounds, Tulsa, Oklahoma

Phi Beta Delta Fraternity House, University of Oklahoma, Norman (project)

East Methodist Church, Tulsa, Oklahoma (project)

Catholic Cathedral, Oklahoma City (project)

Baptismal font, side alters, mosaics, bishop's throne and priest's bench in Christ the King Church, Tulsa, Oklahoma

Lathan House, Tulsa, Oklahoma

Higgins House additions, Tulsa, Oklahoma

Skelly Building additions, Tulsa, Oklahoma

1931 Pittsburgh Equitable Meter Company Warehouse, Sand Springs, Oklahoma

Parental Home, Tulsa, Oklahoma (project)

Railway Passenger Station, Sand Springs, Oklahoma (project)

Chicago War Memorial (competition project; with Alfonso Iannelli)

1935 Cole House, Park Ridge, Illinois

Badlands Hotel, South Dakota (project; with Alfonso Iannelli)

Turzak House, Edison Park, Chicago

1936 Rant House, Northfield, Illinois

Elin House, Northfield, Illinois

1937 Colmorgen House, Glenview, Illinois

Showroom for Libbey-Owens-Ford Glass Company, Toledo, Ohio

Advertising designs for Libbey-Owens-Ford Glass Company, Toledo, Ohio

1938 Theobald House, Chicago (project)

Langdon House, Chicago (project)

Burt House, LaGrange, Illinois (project)

1939 Unseth House I, Park Ridge, Illinois (project)

1940 Unseth House II, Park Ridge, Illinois

Triaero Vacation House, Fern Creek, Kentucky

1942/
43 United States Navy Seabee Base Complex, Camp Parks, California

1944 Chapel, United States Navy Seabee Aleutian Base Facilities, Adak, Attu

Durfee House, Birmingham, Albama (project)

Wold House, Altadena, California (project)

Ennis House, Coronado, California (project)

1945 Leidig House, Hayward, California (project)

1946 San Jule House, Sausalito, California (project)

Patri Studio, Sausalito, California (project)

Warren House, Orinda, California (project)

1947 Giganto House, San Francisco (project)

Butley Packing Company Executive Offices, Oakland, California

Riley House, Oakland, California (project)

Kozak House, Marin City, California (project)

Hudson House, Oakland, California (project)

Gillis House, Bend, Oregon (project)

Church of Jesus Christ of Latter Day Saints, Cody, Wyoming (project)

Ledbetter House, Norman, Oklahoma

Family Circle House, Midwest City, Oklahoma (project)

Ledbetter Summer Lodge, Texoma Lake, Oklahoma (project)

1948 Garden City Apartments, Norman, Oklahoma (project)

Cox House, Boise City, Oklahoma

Bachman House alterations and additions, Chicago

Kinkaid Apartment, Oklahoma City (project)

1949 Ford House, Aurora, Illinois

Newton House, Bradenton, Florida (project)

Crystal Chapel and Student Religious Center, University of Oklahoma, Norman (project)

1950 Blakely House, Dallas (project)

Goodman House, Norman, Oklahoma (project)

Key House, Norman, Oklahoma

R. Goff House, Norman, Oklahoma (project)

Reece House, Norman, Oklahoma (project)

Bruce Goff: Bavinger House, Norman, Oklahoma, 1950

Whitaker House, Norman, Oklahoma (project)

Angelina House, Norman, Oklahoma (project)

Bavinger House, Norman, Oklahoma

Magyness House, Norman, Oklahoma (not completed)

Plan for the Wetzler Subdivision, Norman, Oklahoma

Concrete Block House, Norman, Oklahoma (project)

Wilson House, Perdido Bay, Pensacola, Florida

1951 Stulman House, Baltimore (project)

Blakely House, Dallas (2nd project)

1952 Garvey House, Urbana, Illinois (project)

Hopewell Baptist Church, near Edmond, Oklahoma

1953 Murdoch House, Midwest City, Oklahoma (project)

Perez House, Caracas, Venezuela (2 projects)

Corsaw House, Norman, Oklahoma

1954 Cunningham House, Lawton, Oklahoma (project)

Garvey House, Urbana, Illinois (2nd project)

Allen House, Tulsa, Oklahoma (project)

1955 Frank House, Sapullpa, Oklahoma

Barnes House, Canyon, California (project)

Pi Lambda Phi Fraternity House, University

of Oklahoma, Norman

Trinity Baptist Church, Duncan, Oklahoma (project)

1956 Bass House, Tulsa, Oklahoma (project)

Circle Tower (project)

McCullough House, Wichita Falls, Texas

Comer House, Dewey, Oklahoma

Circle Center Development, Bartlesville, Oklahoma (project)

Tele-Movies Theatre, Bartlesville, Oklahoma (project)

Space Study Institute (project)

Price House, Bartlesville, Oklahoma

1957 Dord Fitz Studio-School, Amarillo, Texas (project)

Dewlen Aparature, Amarillo, Texas (project)

Grain Bin House (project)

Motsenbocker House, Bartlesville, Oklahoma (2 projects)

Van Dall House, Bartlesville, Oklahoma (project)

Price Studio, Bartlesville, Oklahoma

1958 Pollock House, Oklahoma City

Darling House, El Dorado, Kansas (project)

Snyder House, El Dorado, Kansas (project)

Kennedy House, Bartlesville, Oklahoma (project)

White House, Bartlesville, Oklahoma

Adams House, Vinita, Oklahoma (project)

Stull House, Dewey, Oklahoma (project)
Gutman House, Gulfport, Mississippi
Allen House, Bartlesville, Oklahoma (project)
Durst House, Houston
Deutsch House, Jacksonville, Florida (project)
J. and S. Foundry, Dewey, Oklahoma (project)
Jones House, Bartlesville, Oklahoma (2 projects)
Rudd House, Portola Valley, California (project)
Collins House, Bartlesville, Oklahoma (2 projects)
1959   Freeman House, Joplin, Missouri (3 projects)
Swambt House, Michigan City, Indiana (project)
Venus Soft Drinks Bar, Wichita, Kansas (project)
Tolff House, Lake Koshkonong, Wisconsin (project)
Gelbman House, Jacksonville, Florida (2 projects)
Kennedy House, Bartlesville, Oklahoma (2nd project)
Daphne House, Hillsborough, California (project)
Allen House, Bartlesville, Oklahoma (2nd project)
Rudd Store remodelling, San Francisco
Akright House alterations and additions, Bartlesville, Oklahoma
Education Building, Redeemer Lutheran Church, Bartlesville, Oklahoma
Plan for the development of Redeemer Lutheran Church, Bartlesville, Oklahoma
McBryde House, Kansas City, Missouri (project)
1960   Daphne House, Hillsborough, California (2nd project)
Beal House, Wichita, Kansas (project)
Darling House, El Dorado, Kansas (2nd project)
Gryder House, Ocean Springs, Mississippi
Floral Hills Memorial Park, Las Vegas, Nevada (project)
Cowboy Hall of Fame (competition project)
1961   Viva Hotel and Casino, Las Vegas, Nevada (project)
Rodin House, Libertyville, Illinois (project)
Blackbear Motor Lodge, Jackson Hole, Wyoming (project)
Giacomo Motor Lodge, McAlester, Oklahoma (project)
Blackwell Clinic, Dallas (project)
Fitchette House, Bartlesville, Oklahoma
Grady House, Casa Grande, Arizona (project)
Unitarian Fellowship Hall, Bartlesville, Oklahoma (project)
Plan for the Baxter Subdivision, Quincy, Illinois
Rudd House, Portola Valley, California (project)
1962   Quail Valley Country Club, Rogers, Arkansas (project)
H. and B. Goff House, Tulsa, Oklahoma (2 projects)
Barby House, Beaver, Oklahoma (2 projects)
Rudd House, Portola Valley, California (2nd project)
Entrance for the Woodland Hills Subdivision, Roland, Oklahoma (project)
Miller House, Kennedy Mountain, Harrison, Arkansas (project)
Phi Sigma Epsilon Fraternity House, Tahlequah, Oklahoma (project)
Slater House, Roland, Oklahoma (project)
1963   Giacomo Motor Lodge, McAlester, Oklahoma (2nd project)
Loosen Lodge, Okarche, Oklahoma (project)
Butler Mortuary, Tulsa, Oklahoma (project)

Stewart House, Tulsa, Oklahoma (2 projects)
Playtower and Moebius Strip Crawler, Sooner Park, Bartlesville, Oklahoma
Seventh Day Adventist Church, Bartlesville, Oklahoma (project)
Apartment building, Tyler, Texas (project)
Fitzgerald Realty Office, Tyler, Texas
1964   Van Doll House, Bartlesville, Oklahoma (project)
Bird Rehabilitation Center, Kansas City, Kansas (project)
Dace House, Beaver, Oklahoma
Briar Associates Doctors Building, Kansas City, Missouri
Housing, for Briar Associates, Kansas City, Missouri (project)
Vacation cabins, for Briar Associates, Kansas City, Missouri
Haven House Nursing Home, Las Vegas, Nevada (project)
1965   Combs Farmhouse, Gower, Missouri
Van Doll House, Bartlesville, Oklahoma (2nd project)
Hyde House, Kansas City, Kansas
Riddle House, Kansas City, Kansas (project)
Hollander House additions and alterations, Missouri City, Kansas (project)
Phi Kapp Tau Fraternity House, Kansas State University, Lawrence (project)
Price House, Lake Tahoe, California (project)
Duncan House, Cobden, Illinois
Jacquart House, Sublette, Kansas
Ski Lodge, Crested Butte, Colorado
1966   Searing House, Kansas City, Kansas (3 projects)
Yockey House, Tonganoxie, Kansas (project)
Nichol House, Kansas City, Missouri (4 projects)
Youngstrom House, Lake Quivira, Missouri (project)
Heft House, Racine, Wisconsin (project)
Plunkett House, Tyler, Texas (project)
Plunkett Apartment Building, Tyler, Texas (project)
Price House additions and alterations, Bartlesville, Oklahoma
1967   Mercedes-Benz Sales and Shops Building, Atlanta
Youngstrom House, Lake Quivira, Kansas (2nd project)
Abraham House, Kansas City, Kansas (project)
Heft House, Racine, Wisconsin (2nd project)
1968   Mitchell House, Dodge City, Missouri
Britton House, Warrensburg, Kansas (project)
Nichol House, Warrensburg, Kansas (project)
Youngstrom House, Lake Quivira, Kansas (3rd project)
Heft House, Racine, Wisconsin (3rd project)
Searing House additions, Kansas City, Kansas
Ford House additions, Aurora, Illinois
1970   Plunkett House, Lake Village, Tyler, Texas
Glen Harder House, near Mountain Lake, Minnesota
1970/
75   Various speculative houses for Lake Village, Tyler, Texas
1971   Jacob Harder House, Mountain Lake, Minnesota
1974   Price House additions, Bartlesville, Oklahoma
Barby House, Tucson, Arizona

Publications:

By GOFF: portfolio—*Bruce Goff, Architect,* Chicago 1978; articles—"A Declaration for Independence" in *Western Architect* (Los Angeles), January 1930; "Notes on Architecture" in *Bauwelt* (Berlin), January 1958; "Absolute Architecture" in *L'Architecture d'Aujourd'hui* (Paris), June/July 1962; "Architecture as Art" in *Progressive Architecture* (New York), December 1962; "Frank Lloyd Wright: Le Roi des Etoiles" in *L'Architecture d'Aujourd'hui* (Paris), April/May 1964; "Originality and Architecture" in *Bruce Goff in Architecture* by Takenobu Mohri, Tokyo 1970.

On GOFF: books—*Utopian Architecture* by Ulrich Conrads, New York 1963; *An Architectural Biography of Bruce Goff* by John A. Zaluski (student paper: Columbia University, New York), 1965; *Bruce Goff: A Portfolio of the Work of Bruce Goff,* compiled by William Murphy and Lois Muller, New York 1970; *Bruce Goff in Architecture* by Takenobu Mohri, Tokyo 1970; *Bruce Goff: Bavinger House and Price House* by Yukio Futagawa, Tokyo 1975; *The Architecture of Bruce Goff: Buildings and Projects 1916–1974* by David DeLong, London and New York 1977; *The Architecture of Bruce Goff* by Jeffrey Cook, London and New York 1978; articles—"Bruce Goff: Architecture Without Style" by G. S. Thomas in *Baukunst und Werkform* (Nuremberg), July 1953; "Bruce Goff" in *Wisconsin Architect* (Madison), January 1956; "Bruce Goff" by Ben Allan Park in *Architectural Design* (London), May 1957; "Bruce Goff" by Ian McCallum in *Architectural Review* (London), May 1957; "Bruce Goff's Architecture" by H. Waichter in *AIA Journal* (Washington, D.C.), December 1959; "The Master Builder" by Ian Nairn in *Punch* (London), 1 June 1960; "Pavilions on the Prairie" by John Canady in *Horizon* (New York), November 1961; "Portrait" in *Architectural Forum* (New York), July 1962; "Goff Rides Again" in *Architectural Review* (London), March 1963; "The Serious American" by Alan Pryce-Jones in *Harpers* (New York), September 1963; "Principles of Design: A Seminar with Bruce Goff" by Linda Troxel and Julian Ominski in *Kansas Engineer* (Lawrence), March 1964; special issue of *Kentiku* (Tokyo), March 1969; "A View of Contemporary World Architecture" in *The Japan Architect* (Tokyo), July 1970; special issue of *Architectural Design* (London), October 1978.

*   *   *

For well over half of the 20th century Bruce Goff has generated a world architectural presence based almost exclusively on isolated idiosyncratic and inaccessible one-family houses scattered through rural and suburban American locations of the Great Plains and their neighboring states. Without urban or rural theories and without apparent connection with current tastes and trends, Goff's work simultaneously epitomizes the vagaries of the century and some of its most creative variants.

Bruce Alonzo Goff was born on the 37th birthday of Frank Lloyd Wright in the heartland of the U.S.A. Apprenticed at the age of 12, he had major buildings to his credit before he left high school. At 22 he designed the Boston Avenue Methodist Episcopal Church, Tulsa, Oklahoma, whose international publication brought attention to Goff before he was 25. An early imitator and life-long friend of Frank Lloyd Wright, Goff quickly established his own much more pluralistic approach in which each building program was regarded as unique and particular.

Goff's designs for the Seabees during World War II examined the free use of "as found" and "ad hoc" materials. His most exploratory designs followed during his teaching years. His professional office years (1956–1969) produced work that was increasingly regular and polished both technically and aesthetically. Goff's mature work has extended his skill with materials, space, and structure.

Although his polychromatic originality seems unfettered by academic discipline, Goff is among the most informed architects of his time—his personal library, both in 20th century architecture and in post-classical musical recordings, is probably unparalleled. His homespun, broadly-based leadership of the school at the University of Oklahoma (1948–1955) established it as one of the most stimulating and distinctive architectural curricula. Since then, a series of apprentices have always assisted in his small office.

Goff's creative method of free association and subconscious techniques has pushed certain architectural explorations well beyond most expectations. Anthracite walls, goose feather ceilings, and carpeted roofs are among his protagonist architectural inventions that have challenged his inclusion in many contemporary surveys. He freely uses the word "beauty" and persists in designing sometimes lavishly ornamental buildings. But structural clarity and material integrity are also characteristic of his richly tactile spatial compositions.

In spite of the regularity and even symmetry of his plans, there is no institution, style, movement, or association that represents Goff. The individuality of his designs and the profusion of potential sources defy attempts at classification.

Goff has explored virtually every geometry and most construction materials and structural techniques: handmade and mass produced components; Woolworth ashtrays and suspension cables; sequins and plastic rain; disposable pie plates and boiler tubing; stencils and glass culletts abound to frustrate all attempts at categorizing his "place."

From abroad, Goff's apparent exuberance is assumed to be characteristically American; at home, he has been regarded as an irrelevent eccentric. Indeed, the settings and ultimate quietude of many of his houses, together with the richness of his craft, suggest that Goff is left over from the 19th century of some other place. But TV antenae and all kinds of cars are especially compatible with Goff houses. Goff can be associated with the "organic" not only in his esteem for that triumvirate, Richardson, Sullivan, and Wright, but also in his intimate considerations of function and site, client and climate. Goff's sensitive client response has produced a succession of "client" styles unparalleled in architecture. The "transcendental" label identifies Goff's sense of the natural world and man's perception of its harmonies —a subliminal Emerson influence on many native-born Americans. But "visionary" and "fantastic" are adjectives that hardly apply to an architect who has built almost one-third of everything he has ever designed. "Expressionistic" themes often seem evident but with a colorful wit and whimsey never allowed the obsessive monochromatic German and Dutch Expressionism of the 1920's. Goff's architectural expressions are generated abstractly, without the narrative or subjective allusions often applied by critics.

Goff's dramatic approaches are also personal and unpredictable; he imitates neither himself nor others. Perhaps Goff's most published work is the owner-built Bavinger house with its spiral plan and floating saucers suspended from a central mast. The succession of house designs and additions for Joe Price, built from 1956 to 1978, is the most complex, rich, and elegant summary of his later work. The unbuilt Dewlin Aparture was both apartment and departure in its playful, animistic, and amorphous imagery. But the teepee cluster of the Nicol House, the farmhouse working elegance of the Harder House, the crystalline Gutman House, and the interlocking spheroids of the Ford House, are among many that represent great maturity in Goff's distinctive and uniquely imaginative buildings. Goff's work is living and entertaining proof that the artistic potentials of the 20th century are continuously realizable.

—Jeffrey Cook

GOGEL, Daniel.

German. Born in Berlin in 1927. Educated at the Hochschule für Bildende Künste, Berlin, under Max Taut. Worked with Ludwig Leo and Hans Müller, as part of a study/architectural co-operative, Berlin. In partnership with Hermann Fehling, *q.v.,* Berlin, since 1953. Guest Lecturer, Technical University of Berlin, 1975–76. Address (office): Margartenstrasse 4, 1000 Berlin 33, West Germany.

See FEHLING, Hermann

GOLDBERG, Bertrand.

American. Born in Chicago, Illinois, 17 July 1913. Educated at Harvard College, Cambridge, Massachusetts, 1930–32; Bauhaus, Berlin, 1932–33 (worked in the office of Mies van der Rohe, Berlin, 1932); Armour Institute of Technology, now Illinois Institute of Technology, Chicago, 1933–34. Married Nancy S. Florsheim in 1946; children: Nan, Lisa and Geoffrey. Principal of Bertrand Goldberg Associates, architects and engineers, Chicago, since 1937; branch office established in Boston, 1964; also Director of the subsidiary companies (all Chicago) of Computer Service Inc., since 1969, Environmental Engineering Corporation, since 1974, and Copy Corporation, since 1975. Exhibitions: *Sculpture in Architecture,* Paris, 1967; Museum of Modern Art, New York, 1968; *Bauhaus Travelling Exhibition,* 1970; Glessner Foundation, Chicago (one-man), 1972; *Bauhaus Archives Exhibition,* Germany, 1974. Recipient: *Architectural Forum* Award, 1945, 1951; Apartment Project Award, *Progressive Architecture,* 1954; First and Second Awards, Fine Hardwoods Association, 1956; Apartment Project Award, American Institute of Architects/Chicago Chamber of Commerce, 1959; Chicagoan of the Year Award, in architecture, Chicago Junior Association of Commerce and Industry, 1965; Silver Medal, Architectural League of New York, 1965; Distinguished Building Award, American Institute of Architects, Chicago Chapter, 1967; Award for Concrete Shell Structures, *Engineering News Record,* 1975; Design Excellence Award, Society of American Registered Architects, 1978. Fellow, American Institute of Architects, 1966. Address: Bertrand Goldberg Associates, Marina City, Chicago, Illinois 60610, U.S.A.

Works:

1937/
44   Prefabricated houses and industrial units for the United States Government
       Town of Suitland, Maryland (prefabricated housing)
1938   Prefabricated housing, Lafayette, Indiana
1939   Prefabricated housing, Indian Head, Maryland
1945/
48   Stanfab prefabricated unit bathroom
1948   Master plan for Calumet New Town, Calumet City, Illinois
1949   Unicel Plastic Freight Car for the Pressed Steel Car Company
1950   Unishelter Prefabricated Unit Houses for the Pressed Steel Car Company
1955   Michael Todd Theatre, Chicago
       Michael Todd Theatre, Paris
1957   Drexel Town and Garden Apartments, Chicago
1959   Marina City, Chicago
       The Happy Medium Theatre, Chicago
       Astor Tower Hotel, Chicago
1960   Joseph Brennemann School, Chicago

1962   Civic Auditorium, West Palm Beach, Florida
       Elgin State Hospital, Elgin, Illinois
1963   Raymond Hilliard Center, Chicago
1965   Squantum Point, Squantum, Massachusetts
       Outpatient Clinic, Menninger Foundation, Topeka, Kansas
1966   Burns-Jackson Center, Dayton, Ohio
1967   Biology Building, State University of New York at Stony Brook
       Stanford University Medical Center and Stanford University Master Plan, Palo Alto, California
1968   La Trinidad Medical University and Health Center Campus, Caracas, Venezuela
       Health Services Center, State University of New York at Stony Brook (with Abam Engineers and Seifert, Forbes and Berry)
1968– River City, Chicago
1969   St. Joseph Hospital, Tacoma, Washington
       Sidney Farber Cancer Center, Boston
1970   Prentice Women's Hospital and Maternity Center, and Institute of Psychiatry, Northwestern Memorial Hospital, Chicago
1972   St. Mary's Hospital, Milwaukee
1974   University of Illinois Replacement Hospital, Chicago (with A. Epstein and Sons, and Schmidt, Garden and Erickson)
       Basic Science Research Building, State University of New York at Stony Brook
1976   Affiliated Hospitals Center, Boston
       Good Samaritan Hospital, Phoenix, Arizona (with Associated Samaritan Architects)

Publications:

On GOLDBERG: books—*Architects on Architecture,* edited by Paul Heyer, New York 1966, London 1967; *Conversations with Architects* by John Cook and Heinrich Klotz, New York 1973; *The New Architecture of Bertrand Goldberg* by Linda Legner, Chicago 1974; articles—"Marina City Architect Is Still Throwing Curves" by Rita Tatum in *Building Design and Construction* (Chicago), March 1974; "Towers' Cores Implanted Idea for Cantilevered, High-Rise Shell" in *Engineering News Record* (New York), July 1974; "Bertrand Goldberg" in *Architecture + Urbanism* (Tokyo), July 1975; "The Goldberg Variations" by Gregg W. Downey in *Modern Healthcare* (New York), March 1976; "The Goldberg Effect" in *Architectural Record* (New York), July 1976; "L'Ospedale St. Joseph a Tacoma" by Federico Zabo in *L'Industria Italiana del Cemento* (Milan), November 1977.

Both contemporary architecture and modern physics have their roots in similar Victorian concepts of duality. As the 19th century closed, that sibling relationship between neutron and proton was matched by the incest of form and function.

Continuing investigation by scientists in this century has shown the neutron-proton to have developed a family of quarks, pis and mesons, while the architects have only discovered that life with form and function was a void.

Why were form and function so sterile? Why didn't we do as well as the physicists? The world of the physicist was what they had started off with in the Victorian days—it has never changed and they are finding what is there. The world of the architect is a changing world wherein form and function no longer can play their role as a lovely couple.

Form is no longer *the form,* the perfect ur-form in a simple Miesian world of columns and beams produced by the universal machine administered by a Faustian Speer. Form is whatever we can think. We have reached that moment of freedom for the first time in the history of man where we almost can economically produce whatever we can imagine. Form no longer is a box made by columns and beams, but spaces made by tubes, shells and even by

air. Material is not brick, steel and glass, but poly, moly and ium.

Function is no longer the knee-jerk function of the Victorian mass man controlled by a latter-day Hitler. Function is rather that aspiration, that spirit-given action that identifies each individual emerging from and merging with neighborhood and society. These new social changes demand new forms to shelter them. The box is not the universal package for functions of living in contemporary society.

Will the architect study himself? Will the architect make new promises to a new humanism? For the first time in the history of the world, we now can build whatever we think. What shall we build for people?

—Bertrand Goldberg

Bertrand Goldberg's early work was a direct outgrowth of his training at the Bauhaus and his years with Mies van der Rohe's office in Germany. Throughout his career, Goldberg has continued to show this influence, regarding the task of architecture to be one of finding new structural solutions and improving social and psychological conditions through building design. But, with time, Goldberg has broken with Mies. He rebelled against what he calls "the engineer's module applied to society," "the anonymous development of space as yardgoods." He considers rectilinear shapes antithetical to much human activity and espouses instead nuclear forms. Activity revolves around focal points, he says, so circular buildings serve activity better and help to create a sense of community in anonymous situations like hospitals and large apartment buildings. In addition, he claims that circular buildings provide more efficient wind resistance, more direct mechanical distribution and, frequently, more usable interior square footage. "Industrialization has developed beyond straight line objects," says Goldberg, lamenting that, "architects continue to use concrete as if it were wooden logs." His towers represent a line of experimentation in concrete shell structure.

Most famous of these towers, however, is still the first one, Marina City, famous also as the first American government-sponsored downtown housing and among the first multi-use projects in the United States, public or private. Marina City, which has long been nicknamed "The Corncobs" because of the shape of its two towers, provides apartments, parking, movie theaters, a marina, shops, restaurants and office space. It was with Marina City that Goldberg developed his theory of kinetic space. Nonparallel walls, he believes, give the illusion of expanded room size because the space is set in motion—a further rationale.

Goldberg is often heralded as proof of a continuing Chicago School of Architecture, a label he denies. Ignoring here the question of whether such a continuing school can be postulated, it is probably sufficient, and more to the point, to see Goldberg as a true student of the principles, if not the forms, of the German Bauhaus. Though widely published and well-known, he has operated virtually in a vacuum and his utopian ideas have not, as yet at least, developed what could be called a following.

—Nory Miller

GOLDFINGER, Ernö.
British. Born in Budapest, Hungary, 11 September 1902; emigrated to England, 1934; naturalized, 1945. Educated at the Gymnasium, Budapest, 1912–19; Le Rosay School, Gstaad, Switzerland, 1919–20; Ecole National et Supérieure des Beaux-Arts, Paris, 1923,

Bertrand Goldberg: Marina City, Chicago, 1959

DPLG 1931; Co-Founder of the breakaway Beaux-Arts "Atelier Auguste Perret," 1924; Ecole d'Urbanisme, La Sorbonne, Paris, 1927–28. Married Ursula Ruth Blackwell in 1933; children: Peter, Elisabeth, and Michael. In private practice, Paris, 1924–34, and London, 1934 until he retired, 1979. Correspondent for Great Britain, *L'Architecture d'Aujourd'hui,* Paris, 1934–74. Honorary Member, Association of Building Technicians, 1937; Member, Foreign Relations Committee, Royal Institute of British Architects, 1937–45; Member of the Council, Architects Registration Council of the U.K., 1941–50; Honorary Organizing Secretary, International Union of Architects, 1946; Member of the Council, Architectural Association, London, 1960–63, 1965–68; Council of Industrial Design, 1961–65, and the Royal Academy, 1974. Member of CIAM (Congrès Internationaux d'Architecture Moderne), 1928–59; Honorary Secretary, French Section, Athens Congress, 1933; also, Member of the MARS Group (U.K. Section of CIAM), 1935–60. Exhibitions: *CIAM Exhibition,* Athens, 1934; *Housing Exhibition,* Grand Palais, Paris, 1934, and Olympia, London, 1935; *MARS Group Exhibition,* Burlington Gallery, London, 1938; *CIAM Exhibition,* Aix-en-Provence, 1952; *This Is Tomorrow,* Whitechapel Art Gallery, London, 1955; *UIA Sports Buildings Commission Exhibition,* Moscow, 1968. Fellow, Royal Institute of British Architects, 1966; Fellow, Royal Society of Arts, 1968; Associate of the Royal Academy, 1971, and Royal Academician, 1975. Honorary Member, Association of Hungarian Architects, 1963. Address: 2 Willow Road, London NW3 1TH, England.

Works:

1926 Library (Aghion), in (the Auguste Perret building) Aghion House, Alexandria, Egypt
Helena Rubinstein Beauty Salon, 24 Grafton Street, London W.1
1927 Central European Express, rue Godot de Mauroy, Paris 9
1928 La Portique (picture gallery), Boulevard Raspail, Paris 6
Cheftel Apartment furniture and interiors, 6 rue d'Astorg, Paris 8
Grossman Apartment furniture and interiors, 6 rue d'Astorg, Paris 8
Alpina Exhibition Stand, *Foire de Paris*
Alpina Exhibition Stand, *British Industries Fair,* Olympia, London
1929 Luteaux Monument, Jardin d'Acclimatation, Algiers
Hotel, Philippeville, Algeria (project)
Housing, Philippeville, Algeria (project)
Nursery School, Vitry-Seine, near Paris (with Pierre Forestier)
1930 Hollender Apartment interiors, Paris 7
Susanne Blum Offices and Apartment, 53 rue de Varenne, Paris 7
Dick Wyndham Studio interiors, rue Froidevaux, Paris 14
1931 Ernö Goldfinger Studio and Apartments interiors, 3 rue de la Cité Universitaire, Paris 14
Entas Steel Stacking Chairs, Paris
Aero Club (project)
1932 Heliometer (scientific instrument for measuring insolation)
1933 15-Storey Apartment Building (exhibition project)
P. and M. Abbatt Toy Showroom, Endsleigh Street, London W.C.1
Lahousse House and Studio, near Le Touquet, France
1934 Abbatt Apartment, Tavistock Square, London W.C.1
1935 S. Weiss Shop, Golders Green, London N.W.11
"Easiwork" Toys and Furniture, for P. and

M. Abbatt Company, London
1936 P. and M. Abbatt Toy Shop, Wimpole Street, London W.1
1937 House, Broxted, Essex (with Gerald Flower)
Children's Section, British Pavilion, *World's Fair,* Paris
Terrace houses (3), including Goldfinger House, 1–2–3 Willow Road, London N.W.3
1938 ICI Exhibition Stand, *British Industries Fair,* Olympia, London
Children's Section, *MARS Group Exhibition,* Burlington Gallery, London W.1
Benroy Apartment, Hendon, London N.W.4
Wordsworth House, 13 Westhill, London N.5
1939/
45 Educational exhibitions for the British Army, Royal Navy, and Royal Air Force
1940 Air Raid Shelter, Bedales School, Petersfield, Hampshire
Blastproof Housing (competition project)
1945 Planetarium for Hyde Park, London (project)
1947 Newspaper Office and Printing Press, 75 Farringdon Road, London E.C.1
1949 Fletcher Hardware Company Warehouse and Offices, Pershore Street, Birmingham
Fletcher House, Henley-in-Arden, Warwickshire
1950 Brandlehow Road Primary School, Wandsworth, London S.W.15
Westville Road Primary School, Hammersmith, London W.6
Dairy farm, Ibstone, Buckinghamshire
House with two apartments, 74 Avenue des Chênes, Uccles, Brussels
1951 S. Weiss Shop, Shaftesbury Avenue, London W.1 (with Lilian Ladlow)
Kiosks, *Festival of Britain,* South Bank, London
1952 Houses (4), Broadstairs, Kent
1954 Block of flats, 10 Regent's Park Road, London N.W.1
1955 Carr and Company Offices, Shirley, West Midlands
1956 Albemarle Street Office Building, 45–46 Albemarle Street, London N.W.1
Taylor Woods Showrooms, 45–46 Albemarle Street, London N.W.1
Design of the *This Is Tomorrow* exhibition, Whitechapel Art Gallery, London (with Victor Pasmore and Helen Phillips)
1957 Wallis House, Amersham, Buckinghamshire
1957/
60 Hille Factory, 134 St. Albans Road, Watford, Hertfordshire
1958 Abbotts Langley Housing, Hertfordshire
French Government Tourist Office, 66 Haymarket, London S.W.1 (with Charlotte Perriand; now Belgium Tourist Office)
1959 Elephant and Castle Development, London S.E.1 (competition project)
1960 Hille House (offices and showroom), 134 St. Albans Road, Watford, Hertfordshire
1962 Player House, Coombe Hill Road, Coombe Hill, Surrey
Westminster Bank, Elephant and Castle, London S.E.1
1962/
66 Alexander Fleming House (Ministry of Health), in 2 phases, Elephant and Castle, London S.E.1
1963 French Government Tourist Office, 177 Piccadilly, London S.W.1 (with Charlotte Perriand)
1965 Motz House, 16 Bedford Street, Oxford
1966 Odeon Cinema, Old Kent Road, Elephant and Castle, London S.E.1
1966/
78 Rowlett Street Housing, in 3 phases, St. Leonard's Road, London E.1
1967 Martins Bank, Wigmore Street, London W.1 (now Barclays Bank)

French Government Tourist Office and SNCF (French Railways) Office, 127 Avenue des Champs Elysées, Paris (with Pierre Forestier)

1968 Teesdale (Perry House), Westwood Road, Windlesham, Surrey

Haggerston Comprehensive School, Queensbridge Road, London E.1

1968/
69 Edenham Street Housing, in 2 phases, Cheltenham Estate, Golborne Road, London W.10

Publications:

By GOLDFINGER: books—*County of London Plan Explained*, with E. J. Carter, London 1945; *British Furniture Today*, London 1951; articles—"Der Neue Baustil" in *Pester Lloyd* (Budapest), 8 August 1925; "Der Baumeiter Unserer Lieben Frau" in *Pester Lloyd* (Budapest), 30 December 1925; articles in *L'Organisation Ménagère* (Paris), 1928–29; "Heliometer" in *L'Architecture d'Aujourd'hui* (Paris), March 1934; "MARS Group Exhibition" in *L'Architecture d'Aujourd'hui* (Paris), July 1938; "Art of Enclosing Space" in *Architectural Review* (London), November and December 1941 and January 1942; "Town and Country Planning Conference" in *The Architects' Journal* (London), April 1942; "Standardisation" in *Architect and Building News* (London), 15 January 1943; "Organisation of Science" in *The Architects' Journal* (London), 11 March 1943; editor, *MARS News* (London), July 1944, February 1945, July 1945; "Building Research in Great Britain" in *Das Werk* (Zurich), April 1947; "Problèmes du Logement en Grande Bretagne" in *L'Architecture d'Aujourd'hui* (Paris), September 1950; special issue on Great Britain of *L'Architecture d'Aujourd'hui* (Paris), February 1952; "Perret" in *Architectural Review* (London), May 1954; "Aesthetic Control" and "France Rebuilds" in *Architectural Design* (London), July 1954; "André Sive" in *The Times* (London), 25 September 1958; "Londres et sa Région" in *L'Architecture d'Aujourd'hui* (Paris), February/March 1960; "Corbusier at Pessac" in *RIBA Journal* (London), September 1969; "Auguste Perret: The Last of the Master Builders" in *Building Design* (London), 7 March 1975.

On GOLDFINGER: books—*Junge Franzosische Architektur* by Roger Ginsburger, Geneva and Ghent 1930; *Shops* by Brian and Norman Westwood, London 1937; *Modern Houses in England* by F. R. S. Yorke, London 1944; *Houses for the People*, London 1946; *Architects' Homes* by Robert Winkler, Zurich, 1955; *Public Interiors* by Misha Black, London 1960; *Exterior Space in Architecture* by Yoshinobu Ashihara, Tokyo 1962; *Office Building* by Leonard Manessah, London 1962; *Glass* by Raymond McGrath, London 1967; *Ernö Goldfinger* by Mate Major, Budapest 1970; articles—"Ernö Goldfinger," special issue of *Architectural Design* (London), January 1963; "Elephant and Castle" by Kenneth Frampton in *Architectural Design* (London), October 1967.

ARCHITECTURE: THE ART OF ENCLOSING SPACE

A particle is snatched from space, rhythmically modulated by membranes dividing it from surrounding chaos: that is Architecture.

There is other enclosed space, not modulated, not rhythmic, but that is not Architecture.

The "sensation of space" is to Architecture what looking at a picture is to painting, moving around and touching to sculpture, or listening to music. But "sensation of space" is a sub-conscious phenomenon; to undergo its effect it is not necessary to be aware of it.

To undergo the effects of Architecture you have to

Ernö Goldfinger: Alexander Fleming House, London, 1966

be in it; you need not contemplate it or be conscious of it. If you shut your eyes, the painting disappears. If you stop your ears, the music no longer exists. But as long as you are inside "the rhythmically enclosed space" of Architecture, you undergo its effects.

You cannot see Architecture; you can only be in it, as in music (what you see are the real or imaginary membranes which divide space).

You can move through Architecture, and when doing so the spatial sensation becomes four-dimensional.

It is the Architect who, when he identifies with the anticipated user, creates a "thing" which has never existed before. While creating this "thing" he undergoes an emotion (call it an artistic or creative inspiration, if you will), which then is transmitted to the subconsciousness of the "user."

Whenever "space" is enclosed, "spatial sensation" will automatically result for the person within this "space"; it is therefore axiomatic that the creator of

Architecture must be an artist, and Town Planning and Building is not merely the work of the Sociologue, the Drain-layer, the Statistician, the Health Inspector, or the Politician.

Politics, Statistics, Social Relations, Economics, Transport, Hygiene—are all part of it, but it is the artist who comprehends and identifies with the SOCIAL REQUIREMENTS of his time and is able to integrate them with the TECHNICAL POTENTIALITIES to create the shape of the SPACES OF THE FUTURE—ARCHITECTURE.

—Ernö Goldfinger

The 1930's was the great period for Modern English domestic architecture. At the beginning of the decade, a few local architects were taking tentative steps in the new direction, but it was the arrival of the European emigres, including Ernö Goldfinger, that gave real quality and a sense of confidence to the nascent movement. As years went by, some of the distinguished emigrants departed, mainly to the USA, and some retired; by the 1970's Ernö Goldfinger was one of the very few who remained.

As a man, Goldfinger's total commitment to architecture, his unshakeable integrity of outlook, and his indifference to passing fashions earned him the respect of younger architects; however, he was not an easy person to work with, and he had no long term collaborators, so that his work, at times, ploughed a lonely furrow. This isolation of ideas can be seen in the mid-1970's when he seemed the only man left who believed in hi-rise flats.

As an architect, there are two high points in his English career. The first was undoubtedly in the late 1930's. The completion of his Willow Road houses just before the Second World War sums up the English modern movement at that time: the white cube period was over and bricks were again acceptable but with the underlying concrete structure made plain on the highly-modelled facades. After the extremes of a few years previously, a quiet sanity now reigns supreme, and Goldfinger sums this up at Willow Road with a design that is thoughtful and gives evidence of common sense at every turn. Moreover, there is a concern for urbanistic problems: for Goldfinger, as a European, was very impressed with the English 18th and early 19th century town building tradition of Bath and Bloomsbury, and he designed his houses as a prototype urban terrace, publishing elevations to show how the design might be extended. These proposed extensions to his Willow Road houses had a profound influence ten years later when, in coarsened form, they formed the basis of such designs in Gibberd's work at Harlow New Town.

The second high point occurred some twenty years after the first. Goldfinger's Albemarle Street Office Building is one of the very few successful examples of urban infill in London, a demonstration that a calm, modern building of quality can fit well into a distinguished traditional street. The Carr and Company Office Building at Shirley, near Birmingham, showed similar quality in a free-standing structure, unfortunately marred in this case by poor surroundings and lack of landscaping. A few years later, on a suburban site at Coombe Hill, the Player House shows Goldfinger at his best—a clear clean building for an upper middle class life-style.

—John Winter

GOLDSMITH, Myron.

American. Born in Chicago, Illinois, 15 September 1918. Educated at the Armour Institute of Technology, Chicago, 1935–39, B.S. in Architecture 1939; Illinois Institute of Technology, Chicago, under Mies van der Rohe, 1939–40, 1947–53, M.S. in Architecture 1953; University of Rome (Fulbright Fellow), under Pier Luigi Nervi, 1953–55. Served as a Staff Sergeant in the United States Army Corps of Engineers, Fort Belvoir, Virginia, 1944–46. Married Robin W. Squier in 1962; children: Marc and Chandra. Worked as a structural engineer in various offices, 1939–44; Architect and Structural Engineer, Office of Ludwig Mies van der Rohe, Chicago, 1946–53. Joined Skidmore, Owings and Merrill, 1955: Chief Structural Engineer, Skidmore, Owings and Merrill, San Francisco, 1955–58; Associate Partner and Senior Designer, 1958–67, and since 1967 General Partner, Skidmore, Owings and Merrill, Chicago. Professor of Architecture, Illinois Institute of Technology Graduate School of Architecture, since 1961. Chairman, Friends of Mies van der Rohe Archive, Museum of Modern Art, New York, 1972. Exhibitions: *Twentieth Century Engineering*, Museum of Modern Art, New York, 1964; *100 Years of Architecture in Chicago*, Museum of Contemporary Art, Chicago, 1976. Recipient: Honor Award, 1963, 1970, 1977, Citation of Merit, 1966, and Distinguished Building Award, 1969 (twice), 1970, 1971, American Institute of Architects, Chicago Chapter, and Chicago Association of Commerce and Industry; Architectural Award of Excellence, American Institute of Steel Construction, 1963, 1964, 1971; Award of Merit, American Society of Civil Engineers, 1967; Honor Award, AIA, Northern California Chapter, 1967; James F. Lincoln Arc Welding Foundation Award, 1970; 4th Biennial Award for Design Excellence, United States Department of Housing and Urban Development, 1970; Citation of Excellence for Design of Low-Rise Construction, American Iron and Steel Institute, 1973; Honor Award, National AIA, 1975; Excellence in Masonry Award, Metropolitan Chicago Masonry Council, 1976; Architectural Merit Award, Association of School Business Officials, 1976 (twice); Award of Merit, Chicago Lighting Institute, 1976. Fellow of the American Institute of Architects, 1972. Address: Skidmore, Owings and Merrill, 30 West Monroe Street, Chicago, Illinois 60603, U.S.A.

Works:

1959 Norton Office Building, Seattle, Washington
1960 United Air Lines Hangars and Flight Kitchen Complex, San Francisco
1962 United Air Lines Headquarters Building and Stewardess Training School, Chicago
      Solar Telescope, Kitt Peak, Arizona
1964 Home News Enterprises Building, Franklin, Indiana
1965 Brunswick Office Building, Chicago
      De Witt-Chestnut Apartments, Chicago
1966 Life Science Building, Illinois Institute of Technology, Chicago
1967 Gymnasium, Illinois Institute of Technology, Chicago
      Ultra High Energy Cosmic Ray Physics Facility feasibility study, Mount Evans, Colorado (project)
      Inland Steel Research Laboratory, East Chicago, Indiana
      Engineering Building No. 1, Illinois Institute of Technology, Chicago
      Spectrum Arena, Philadelphia
1968 Oakland-Alameda County Coliseum, Oakland, California
1969 Central business district plan for Columbus, Indiana (project)
1970 Central business district plan for Elkhart, Indiana (project)
1971 *The Republic* Newspaper Plant, Columbus, Indiana
1972 Stellar Telescope, Kitt Peak, Arizona
      Management Building, Illinois Institute of Technology, Chicago
      Rapid Transit Stations for the Kennedy Expressway and Dan Ryan Expressway, Chicago
      Crosstown Expressway, Chicago (project)
1973 Diamond Shamrock Building, Cleveland
      Arthur Andersen Center, St. Charles, Illinois
1974 St. Joseph Valley Bank Headquarters, Downtown Drive-In Branch, and Concord Mall Branch, Elkhart, Indiana
      The Royal Gazette Newspaper Plant, Hamilton, Bermuda
1975 Illinois Tool Works Deltar Plant, Chicago
      Percy L. Julian High School, Chicago
      George Henry Corliss High School, Chicago
      Equibank Building, 2 Oliver Plaza, Pittsburgh
1976 Europoint II and III Office Buildings and Parking Garage, Rotterdam
1978 Tropic World of Primates, Chicago Zoological Park, Brookfield, Illinois
      Fort Dearborn Station Post Office, Chicago
      Europoint IV Office Building, Rotterdam
1979 National City Bank Building, Cleveland
1980 Jefferson Park Rail/Rapid Transit Station Parking Structure, Chicago
      Ruck-a-Chucky Bridge, Auburn, California (as consultant)
      International Museum of Photography, George Eastman House, Rochester, New York
1989 New Jeddah International Airport, Jeddah, Saudi Arabia

Publications:

On GOLDSMITH: articles—"Dimensione e Struttura" in *Architettura* (Rome), July/August 1955; "Three Projects by Myron Goldsmith and James D. Ferris" in *Arts and Architecture* (Los Angeles), August 1958; "Pre-stressed Concrete: The Big Stretch" in *Architectural Forum* (New York), March 1959; "Punctured Pre-stressed Beams Frame West Coast Skyscraper" in *Architectural Forum* (New York), March 1960; "Jet Age Hangars" in *Architectural Forum* (New York), March 1961; "A Dream of Splendor for Oakland" by Allan Temko in *San Francisco Chronicle*, 30 April 1962; "Goldsmith: Chicago's New Structural Poet" by Allan Temko in *Architectural Forum* (New York), May 1962; "Structer Studien aus der Meisterklasse von Professor Myron Goldsmith am Illinois Institute of Technologie" in *Bauwelt* (Berlin), October 1962; "United Air Lines Offices, Des Plaines, Illinois" in *Architectural Design* (London), April 1964; "A Diagonally-Braced Tall Office Building" by Mikio Sasaki in *Column* (Tokyo), June 1965; "Annual Discourse" in *RIBA Journal* (London), June 1966; "Brunswick Building" in *Kenchiku Bunka* (Tokyo), November 1966; "Daily Journal" in *Vitrum* (Milan), July/August 1967; "Solar Telescope, Kitt Peak" in *Bauen und Wohnen* (Zurich), December 1969; "Urban University" by Dorman D. Anderson in *Column* (Tokyo), January 1970; "Large, Clear Span Structures" by Peter Pran in *Byggekunst* (Oslo), January 1971; "Follow Mies" in *Architectural Review* (London), July 1973; "Chicago Architektur" by Peter Pran in *Byggekunst* (Oslo), September/October 1974; "Mantled Printing Plant" in *Bauen und Wohnen* (Zurich), December 1974; "Prairie Showplace" by Paul Goldberger in the *New York Times*, 4 April 1976; "Structure, Scale and Architecture" in *Casabella* (Milan), October 1976; "Engineering Marvels Spanning the Ages" by Paul Weingarten in the *Chicago Tribune*, 1 December 1977; "E una ragnatela? No, e un ponte" in *L'Espresso* (Milan), March 1978.

The spreading organisation of Skidmore, Owings and Merrill has acted as an umbrella for many architects of talent, amongst whom are a few of world stature—Gordon Bunshaft, Walter Netsch, Charles Bassett, Myron Goldsmith. These men are essentially members of a team, and Myron Goldsmith has collaborated closely with many others, notably James Ferris in the early days and Bruce J. Graham more recently; but, though much credit must be shared with his colleagues, a number of buildings can be discussed as being, in large part, his own creation.

The key to Myron Goldsmith's approach is to be found in Mies van der Rohe and Pier Luigi Nervi, each of whom regarded Goldsmith as his protégé. Mies the architect and Nervi the engineer both believed that structure is the basis of architecture, and Goldsmith, who is both an architect and an engineer, combines the concept of structural purity of Mies with Nervi's concern for shaping the structure to enjoy and to explain the forces within. During his years of apprenticeship with Mies and with Nervi, Goldsmith produced a series of designs which have proved to be the basis of his subsequent work with Skidmore, Owings and Merrill. From his studies under Mies emerged the design for a high-rise building with its skeleton boldly expressed and with beams chamfering into columns to resist sheer forces; from these days also date studies of towers

Myron Goldsmith: Solar Telescope, Kitt Peak, Arizona, 1962

with horizontal forces taken by boldly expressed diagonals. From his period in Rome with Nervi there are designs for sports arenas and a bridge with every member profiled in sinuous curves to correspond to and to demonstrate the stresses within.

Myron Goldsmith's hangars for San Francisco airport, his first job within S.O.M., owe much to Nervi's recently completed Palace of Labour at Turin. For the main hangar there are steel roof beams on concrete columns, all tapering and profiled to explain the stresses in a very large structure. For a smaller wash hangar, tapered steel plate portals create an exceptionally economical structure which is quite delicious as an object; it's so unforced as to seem calm, natural, almost sweet, and it is clear that Goldsmith had been building up skills for many years that made his first built work a modest masterpiece.

In the years around 1960 the concepts of the formative years one by one achieved reality in various S.O.M. buildings, but the going was never easy and there were false starts and abandoned schemes along the way. The multi-storey frame chamfering to respond to the nature of the forces within was first proposed by Goldsmith when a student of Mies, and later within S.O.M. for a hotel in Chicago: the latter project was abandoned, but the idea realized, not very elegantly, in the firm's Hartford Building in Chicago. The diagonally braced tower, which similarly dates from Goldsmith's days with Mies, was first proposed within S.O.M. by Goldsmith for the Norton Building in Seattle: the idea stayed and was incorporated by other S.O.M. designers in San Francisco's Alcoa Building and Chicago's John Hancock Center. The sports arenas Goldsmith had designed

for Nervi were the basis for his subsequent designs within S.O.M., first for Portland, Oregon, where his design was discarded, and then for Oakland, where the concept was realized by others.

The arrival of Goldsmith into the Chicago office in 1958 had an effect far beyond those schemes for which he was personally responsible. His input of ideas based on the poetry of a rational, structural architecture was just what part of that office was looking for, and he became a kind of guru from whom ideas circulated, often to be executed by others with varying degrees of skill and understanding. In terms of architectural quality, the smaller buildings which Goldsmith could control himself show the true measure of the man. He has become known as a prime theorist of the Chicago school of thought, which is fascinated by the nature of truly giant structures, but the more modestly scaled buildings show his skill as a sensitive architect for more normal requirements. His newspaper office building for *The Republic* in Columbus, Indiana, has a lightness and a delicacy that is new to the Mies tradition. It has no special features; it is its sense of calm, effortless quality that makes it architecturally significant, whilst historically it is important as a link building from Mies to those English architects like Norman Foster who are seeking to lighten the Chicago inheritance.
—John Winter

GOLLINS, MELVIN, WARD.

Partnership; established, London, 1947, by Frank Gollins, James Melvin and Edmund Ward; branch office established, Berkhamsted, Hertfordshire, 1965. Current partners: W. Robert Headley; Brian Mayes; Robert Smith; Anthony Gregson; Julian Ryder Richardson; Neil Southam; with Frank Gollins, James Melvin and Edmund Ward consultants to the practice. Recipient: Concrete Society Award, London, 1970; Civic Trust Award, London, 1970; Special Structural Steel Design Award, London, 1970, 1974; Concrete Industry Board Award, New York, 1971; Bronze Medal, New York Borough of Queens, 1971; *Financial Times* Industrial Architecture Award, London, 1975. Address: GMW Partnership, 18 Manchester Square, London W1M 6AY; and Castle Mill, Berkhamsted, Hertfordshire, England.

Works:

1947   Trades Union Congress Memorial Building, London (competition project)
1948   Leigham Court Road Residential Development, Streatham, London (competition project)
1950   Infant and junior school, Oxhey, Hertfordshire
1951   Infant and junior school, Little Furze, Hertfordshire
1952   Secondary modern school, St. Julians, St. Albans, Hertfordshire
1953   Master plan for the central redevelopment of the University of Sheffield, Yorkshire
1956   Secondary school, Southborough, Kent

1957 Office buildings, 93–97, 118–126 New Cavendish Street, London

1959 Library and Arts Tower, University of Sheffield, Yorkshire

Fracture Clinic and Rehabilitation Centre, St. Mary's Hospital, Praed Street, London W.2

Grammar and modern school, Stokesley, Yorkshire

Home for Aged Seamen, Belvedere, Erith, Kent

1960 Classrooms and Assembly Hall, Radley College, Berkshire

Castrol House (office building), 174–204 Marylebone Road, London

E.M.I. House (including GMW Offices), Manchester Square, London W.1

1961 Technical College, Scarborough, Yorkshire

Department of Pharmacy extension, Oxford University

Civic Centre, Lincoln (competition project)

1962 University House, University of Sheffield, Yorkshire

Spencer Steel Works, Newport, Monmouthshire (with Sir Percy Thomas and Son)

1964 Regional Hospital Administration Offices, Headington, Oxford

District General Hospital, stage I, Kettering, Northamptonshire

Secondary school, Ecclesfield, Yorkshire

Residential development, Hermitage Lane, Hampstead, London N.W.2

Pavilion, West Hendon Playing Fields, London

1965 College of Education, Loughborough, Leicestershire

Women's Royal Army Corps College, Camberley, Surrey

Outpatients' and Maternity Departments, Sevenoaks Hospital, Kent

Arts, Economics and Social Studies Buildings, University of Sheffield, Yorkshire

1966 District General Hospital, Hillingdon, Middlesex

Equitable Life Assurance Society Headquarters Offices, Coleman Street, London E.C.

Grammar school, Lutterworth, Leicestershire

Residential development, St. George-in-the-East, Stepney, London

1967 Boadicea House Computer Building, London Airport, Heathrow

Rawlins Grammar School, Quorn, Leicestershire

Holophane Ltd. Factory and Offices, Bletchley, Buckinghamshire

1968 Royal Military College of Science, Shrivenham, Wiltshire

South Wales Electricity Board Headquarters Offices, St. Mellons, Monmouthshire

P and O Tower Offices, Leadenhall Street, London

Administrative Offices, Epcner Steel Works, Newport, Monmouthshire (project)

British Airways Flight Catering Centre, London Airport, Heathrow (project)

Chemistry Building, University of Sheffield, Yorkshire

Samuel Fox and Company Canteen and Dining Rooms, Stockbridge, Derbyshire

1969 Commercial Union Tower Offices, Leadenhall Street, London

House, Campden Hill, London W.8

British Airways Freight Terminal, London Airport, Heathrow

1970 The Polytechnic, Sheffield, Yorkshire

Post Office Savings Department, Durham (with P. O. Directorate of Works)

HMS Caledonia Naval Barracks, stage I, Rosyth, Scotland

Royal Air Force Residential Accommodation, West Drayton, Middlesex

Royal Military Academy, Sandhurst, Camberley, Surrey

Upper School, Desford, Leicestershire

British Airways/Air Canada International Airport Terminal, J. F. Kennedy Airport, New York

Air Canada Services Building, London Airport, Heathrow

Hoverlloyd Hoverport, Weymouth, Dorset (project)

Master plan for the District General Hospital, Barnet, Hertfordshire

1971 HMS Caledonia Naval Barracks, stage II, Rosyth, Scotland

Upper School, Syston, Leicestershire

Biological Sciences Building, University of Sheffield, Yorkshire

Library extension, Cambridge University, Grange Road, Cambridge

Teaching hospital, Goldhawk Road, Hammersmith, London (project)

1972 Teacher training college, Portsmouth, Hampshire

District General Hospital, Harold Wood, Essex

1973 Manufacturers Life Insurance Company Headquarters Offices, Stevenage, Hertfordshire

Woking Centre Swimming Pool, Surrey

District General Hospital, stage II, Kettering, Northamptonshire

1974 Junior mixed and infant school, Chipperfield, Hertfordshire

Department of Drama Building, Portsmouth College of Education, Hampshire

Lennox Estate, stage I, Wandsworth, London

1975 Equitable Life House, Walton Street, Aylesbury, Buckinghamshire

Kingfisher House Office Building, Aylesbury, Buckinghamshire

Centre Halls, Woking, Surrey

New Covent Garden Market, Nine Elms, London S.W.8

Central Fish Market, Djeddah, Saudi Arabia (competition project)

Town Hall, Medina, Saudi Arabia (competition project)

District General Hospital, stage III, Kettering, Northamptonshire

Michelin Tyre Company Headquarters Offices, Fulham Road, London S.W.3

Feasibility study for the Munich 2 Airport

Holiday resort and hotel, Cesme Peninsula, Turkey (with Transport and Tourism Technicians Ltd.)

Westminster City School, Nine Elms, London S.W.8 (project)

Royal Opera House additions, Covent Garden, London W.C.2

1978 Mombasa Airport Development, Kenya

American Express International Banking Corporation Headquarters Offices, Brighton, Sussex (with Peter Wood and Partners)

Banque Belge, London

Zurich House, Portsmouth, Hampshire

Crown House, Woking, Surrey

Publications:

By GMW PARTNERSHIP: book—*Architecture of the Gollins Melvin Ward Partnership,* with an introduction by Tony Aldous, London 1974.

On GMW PARTNERSHIP: articles—"Imaginative Approach to New Market Development" in *Asian Building and Construction* (Hong Kong), November 1973; "Perspective: In the Swim" in *Building Design* (London), November 1973; "Two Office Buildings in the City of London" in *Bauen und Wohnen* (Zurich), January 1974; "Spring Start on £5M. Portsmouth Offices" in *Building* (London), January 1974; "Insurers Cut Their Ground Risks" in *Contract Journal* (London), March 1974; "Wok-

ing Pool" in *Surveyor* (London), May 1974; "Contract Awarded for Zurich Insurance Headquarters at Portsmouth" in *Building* (London), November 1974; "Business as Usual, or Almost, at the New Covent Garden Market" in *The Architect* (London), December 1974; "Flower Power Relies on Steel" in *Design* (London), January 1975; "New Covent Garden Market, Nine Elms, London" in *Bauwelt* (Berlin), January 1975; "Architect's Approach to Architecture" in *The Architects' Journal* (London), February 1975; "Good Gollins" by Maurice Cooper in *Building Design* (London), February 1975; "A 30-year-old Practice Looking at Architecture" by David Crawford in *Building* (London), February 1975; "Woking Centre Pool" in *The Architects' Journal* (London), May 1975; "Woking's New Swimming Pool" in *Concrete Quarterly* (London), October/December 1975; "VIP Treatment for BSC's Computer House" in *Building* (London), December 1975; "Design Confidence in Assurance Offices" in *Interior Design* (London), September 1976; "A Tale of Two City Banks" in *Building Design* (London), March 1978.

In 1947 when the Gollins Melvin Ward Partnership was formed and when the partnership's work was confined to the re-habilitation of bomb destroyed dwellings for the London boroughs, the partners realized that only by combining all of their resources and skills and eschewing the cult of personality could design and technical abilities be developed sufficiently to face the demands and challenges of the 1950's and 1960's. These skills stood the partnership in good stead, for as the new generation grew up, the demands in the field of education, first for primary and secondary schools then technical colleges and universities as well as colleges for teachers' training and further education, increased immensely. Simultaneously with this ever increasing programme went the need for the construction and extension of buildings for the National Health Service, admission units, clinics, general and specialized hospitals and post-graduate teaching facilities.

Parallel with this local authority government and corporation work, the partners developed also the commercial side of the partnership, starting with comparatively restricted office schemes in London. The scope of this division gradually increased to include high-raise developments in the city of London, many for the headquarters the leading insurance and banking firms.

The partnership now has, in addition to six partners, nine associates and an average total staff of 150. The practice has experience in most aspects of building—educational, medical, commercial, residential—and has developed specialist groups with detailed knowledge of user requirements and an awareness of the complexities of present day and future construction and environmental technology. The principle determining the character of the organization is that each of the specialist groups be headed by a partner or partners supported by an associate and project architect who provide the basic link with the client during the life of the project. The policy remains that a partner or partners are always readily available for discussion with the client on all matters of policy and administration, and are actively involved in the progress of each project through its various phases. Computer techniques are used for accounting, job costing, budgeting, forward planning and pre-contract and contract programmes, architectural design, architectural drafting and services coordination. The differing age groups of the partners has allowed the structure of the practice to be so developed that there is a continuing process of growth, ensuring in particular that clients with long-term development schemes can rely on a sequence of service.

There are separate sections including interior design, working in close liaison with the architectural teams, specializing in the selection of furnishings, fittings and materials together with the preparation of detailed schemes in all types of interiors. There is

also a separate section concerned with landscape design in all its aspects, both in the UK and abroad. Considerable experience has also been gained abroad on research and development studies, particularly in relation to the design of airports, shopping centres, offices, hotels, holiday resorts and hospitals. With overseas projects the policy is normally to collaborate with local architects by setting up a joint overseas office. Currently operating on this basis are offices in Hong Kong, Riyadh, Belgium, Kenya and Greece.

—Anthony Gregson

GONZÁLEZ de LEÓN, Teodoro.

Mexican. Born in Mexico City, 29 May 1926. Educated at the Universidad Nacional Autonoma, National School of Architecture, Mexico City, 1942–47, Dip.Arch. 1947. Married Ulalume Ibanez in 1948; children: Berenice, Diego, and Sofia. Worked in the architectural studio of Le Corbusier, Paris, 1948–49. In private practice, Mexico City, since 1949: in partnership with Abraham Zabludovsky, q.v., since 1968. Director of Rural Housing, National Housing Institute, 1956–58; Technical Director, Council of Economic and Social Planning, Mexico City, 1958; Adviser, Operating and Banking Discount Fund for Housing, Mexico City, 1966–70, and Public Works Department, Mexico City, 1970–76. Adviser to the Ministry of Public Education, Mexico City, since 1978. Exhibitions: *XX Centuries of Mexican Architecture,* El Colegio de México, Mexico City, 1965, and toured Mexico; Colegio Nacional de Arquitectos, Mexico City, 1969; *Arquitectura Contemporánea Mexicana,* Galeria Misrachi, Mexico City, 1969; *The Photography of Architecture and Design,* Los Angeles, 1977; *Mexican Architecture,* Mexico City, 1978; *Transformations in Modern Architecture,* Museum of Modern Art, New York, 1979. Recipient: First Prize, with Abraham Zabludovsky, El Colegio de México Competition, Mexico City, 1974. Address: Zabludovsky/González de León, Avenida Mexico 9, Mexico 11, D.F., Mexico.

Works:

1953   Catan House, Reforma 2135, Mexico City (with Armando Franco)
1957   Orozco Housing Estate, Guadalajara, Jalisco, Mexico
1957/
  58   Rural towns research project, Mexico (with Luis Lesur)
1958   Plan for Barra de Navidad, Jalisco, Mexico
1962   Sahagun Housing Estate, Hidalgo, Mexico
1962/
  64   Urban research project, Mexico (with Luis Lesur)
1964   IMSS Housing Estate, Toluca, Mexico
1965   Bodega Dina Building, Sahagun, Hidalgo, Mexico
1966   Sears Roebuck Building, Guadalajara, Mexico
       School of Law, University of Tamaulipas, Tampico, Mexico
1969   Gonzáles de León House, Galeana 107, Mexico City
1972   Office building, Leibnitz 20, Mexico City
1973   Weekend house, Cocoyoc, Morelos, Mexico
1978   Ex-Hacienda de Enmedio (1150 units), Mexico City

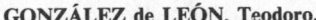

Gollins, Melvin, Ward: Library and Arts Tower, University of Sheffield, 1959

Teodoro González de León and Abraham Zabludovsky: El Colegio de México, Mexico City, 1975

The following works are with Abraham Zabludovsky:

1963/
  77   8 planning surveys for various Mexican cities
1968   José Luis Cuevas House, Galeana 109, Mexico City
1969/
  70   Office building, Nuevo León and Campeche Street, Mexico City
       Office building, Campos Eliseos 169, Mexico City
       Office building, Presidente Masarik 191, Mexico City
1969/
  71   Mixcoac Towers, Mixcoac-Lomas de Plateros, Mexico City
1970/
  73   Vallejo-La Patera (1418 apartments), Avenida Vallejo/Torres/de los Cien Metros/Margarita M. de Juárez, Mexico City (with Armando Franco)
1971   Apartment buildings (2), Avenida de las Fuentes and Fuente de la Templanza, Tecamachalco, Mexico City
1972   Apartment buildings (2), Victoria 34, Echegaray, Mexico
       Sports and Civic Center (public square; movie theatre; library; club; gymnasium; swimming pool; etc.), Sor Juan Inés de la Cruz 45, Tlalnepantla, Mexico
1972/
  73   Cuauhtémoc District Municipal Building, Mexico City (with Luis Antonio Zapiain and Jaime Ortiz Monasterio)
       Apartment buildings (2), Fuente de las Pirámides 20 and 22, Tecamachalco, Mexico City (with Rosemberg)
1973   Conasupo Branch Stores, throughout Mexico
       INFONAVIT Building (administrative offices for workers' housing development), Mexico City
1973/
  75   Mexican Embassy, Brasilia (with J. Francisco Serrano)
1974/
  75   El Colegio de México (library; seminar rooms; computer center; offices; auditorium; cafeteria; parking), Mexico City
1975   25-story apartment building, Tecamachalco, Mexico City
       Rufino Tamaya Museum, Oaxaca, Mexico (project)

Publications:

By GONZÁLEZ de LEÓN: books—*Barra de Navidad: Survey of an Area,* Mexico City 1958; *Housing in Mexico,* Mexico City 1960; *Research on Housing in Eleven Mexican Cities,* 3 volumes, Mexico City 1966; *Catalogue of Cartograms,* compiler, Mexico City 1969; articles—"Problems of Sunlight and Control of Temperature in the Work of Le Corbusier" in *Espacios* (Mexico City), 1949; "Le Corbusier" in *Dialogos* (Mexico City), January 1966.

See ZABLUDOVSKY, Abraham

GOWAN, James.

British. Born in Glasgow, Scotland, 18 October 1923. Educated at the Glasgow School of Art, Department of Architecture, 1940–42; Kingston School of Art, Surrey, with tutors Philip Powell, James Cubitt, and Peter Chamberlin, 1946–48. Served as a radar instructor in the Royal Air Force, 1942–46. Married Margaret Aileen Barry in 1946; children: Lindy and Joanna. Worked as an occasional assistant to architect Brian O'Rorke, London, 1946–50; architect with Powell and Moya, London, 1950–51, with the New Town Corporation, Stevenage, Hertfordshire, 1952–53, and with Lyons, Israel and Ellis, London, 1954–56; Partner, firm of James Stirling and James Gowan, London, 1956–63. In private practice, London, since 1964. Tutor at the Architectural Association School, London, 1958–60, 1970–72; Visiting Professor, Princeton University, New Jersey, 1965; Banister Fletcher Professor, University College, London, 1975. Member of the Council of the Architectural Association, 1963–64. Exhibition: *Triennale,* Milan, 1973. Recipient: Reynolds Memorial Award, Leicester, 1965. Associate of the Royal

James Gowan: Housing, Trafalgar Road, Greenwich, London, 1968

Institute of British Architects, 1950. Address: 2 Linden Gardens, London W.2, England.

Works:

1957 Expandable House (project; with James Stirling)
1958 Private house, Baring Road, Cowes, Isle of Wight (with James Stirling)
Low-rise flats, Ham Common, Richmond, London (with James Stirling)
1960 Private house, Grenville Place, London (with James Stirling)
Churchill College, Cambridge (project; with James Stirling)
1961 Low-rise houses and flats, Preston, Lancashire (with James Stirling)
Selwyn College, Cambridge (project; with James Stirling)
1963 Dining Hall, Brunswick Park Primary School, London (with James Stirling)
Engineering Department, University of Leicester (with James Stirling)
1964 Old people's dwellings, Blackheath, London (with James Stirling)
Children's home, Frogmore, Wandsworth, London (with James Stirling)
Private house, West Heath Road, Hampstead, London (with Frank Newby)
1965 Furniture warehouse, Birkbeck Mews, London (project; with Stephen Revess)
1967 Private house, St. Davids, Wales
City Hall, Amsterdam (project; with Brian Richards)
Low-rise housing, Creek Road, Greenwich, London (with Stephen Revess)
1968 Swimming pool, West Heath Road, Hampstead, London (with Frank Newby)
Neighbourhood housing, Runcorn, Cheshire (project)
Old people's dwellings, Byfleet, Surrey (project)
Low-rise housing, Trafalgar Road, Greenwich, London (with Stephen Revess)

Laminated timber furniture (with C. S. Schreiber)
1969 Luxury flat, Fountain House, Mayfair, London
1970 Unit warehouses, Pages Walk, London S.E.1 (with Stephen Revess)
1971 Unit warehouses, Crimscott Street, London S.E.1 (with Stephen Revess)
1972 Rural housing, Bembridge, Isle of Wight (with Stephen Revess)
Nelson House restoration, Rotherhithe Street, London (with Jampel and Partners)
Redevelopment, Oban, Argyll, Scotland (project)
1973 Warehouse and offices, Evelyn Street, London S.E.8
1974 Unit warehouses, Blackhorse Road, London S.E.8 (with Jampel and Partners)
Family health clinic, Polygon Road, London N.W.1 (project)
Rural housing, East Hanningfield, Essex

Publications:

By GOWAN: books—*Projects: Architectural Association 1946–71,* London 1972; *A Continuing Experiment: Learning and Teaching at the Architectural Association,* London 1975; articles—"Le Corbusier Exhibition in London" in *Architect and Building News* (London), February 1959; "Architectural Association: Review of the Annual Exhibition" in *Architectural Association Journal* (London), June 1959; "Curriculum: A Structure for Teaching Architecture" in *Architectural Review* (London), December 1959; "Notes on American Architecture" in *Prospecta* (New Haven, Connecticut), no. 7, 1963; "British Ministry of Works Exhibition" in *The Architects' Journal* (London), January 1964; "Le Corbusier" in *RIBA Journal* (London), October 1965; "Architectural Education and Its Technical Aspects" in *The Architects' Journal* (London), November 1970; "AA Architects" in *Architectural Association Quarterly* (London), Spring 1973; "Five Architects: Review of the New York Five" in *The Architects' Journal*

(London), May 1975; "Millbank Exhibition: Sketches and Comments" in *Architectural Design* (London), Autumn 1977.

On GOWAN: books—*New English Architecture* by Robert Maxwell, Stuttgart 1972; *Multiple Family Housing* by David Mackay, London 1977; articles—in *Casabella* (Milan), October 1972; in *Arquitecturas Bis* (Barcelona), July 1974; film—*Two Architects: James Stirling and James Gowan,* British Aluminium 1965.

Some years back I wrote a programme for the Architectural Association Diploma School: the domestic refurbishment of the room I worked in . . . large, bay-windowed, scruffy. Unusually so, there was a big response; the projects filled several rooms and were restless with ideas and complications. One project was different and, I thought then, a little facile, but the image has stayed with me. It is an ink-line drawing of the room, empty, and as it was when new: clean, with the ornamental plasterwork perfect and precise. There was a second drawing which was a repeat of the first, except for an open suitcase in the middle of the floor. This was crammed and neatly compartmented with everything one needed: a heater, bedding, books . . . all trimmed down to essentials.

The drawings and their implications have needled me occasionally since. Though I regard myself as observant in architectural matters, I had never seen my room as a fresh fine space . . . only as a room in transition, genteelly fighting off seediness. Secondly, the drawings arrested or questioned my thoughts on architecture . . . the grand spread of design and action that was unlikely ever to be realized. And the possibility that architecture of the future would have more to do with a shrinking compass of events, the room, significantly, and perhaps its enrichment with cultural symbols and gestures not attainable by any other means. There are signs enough that the promise for many may be no better than a slice of old building stock, and our nearest visual experience of what this might be is through photographs and films of the immediate post-revolutionary Russia . . . stark rooms and stripped shared establishments. In such a condition, the architect's role, if it continued to exist at all, could shrink to advising on the most simple requirements—where best to hang one's finery, where best to place a precious nail in the wall.

—James Gowan

James Gowan is remembered by many architects as the co-designer with James Stirling of what was perhaps the most startlingly original work of architecture to be built in Britain since the war—the Engineering Department at the University of Leicester, completed in 1963. This was a milestone in British architecture for a number of reasons: it exemplified a new and expressive use of materials—particularly patent glazing which had previously had only industrial uses; a new and bold formal articulation that was much imitated in subsequent years; and, perhaps most significantly, a departure from the influence of Le Corbusier which had until then dominated British architecture.

The Leicester building was the last major work which Stirling and Gowan worked on together, and it represents the summit of their mutual achievement: neither architect has since produced its equal. Since the partnership split up Stirling has enjoyed great public acclaim, producing a series of brilliantly inventive though often controversial works which unfortunately seem to lack the intellectual rigour of those produced by the partnership. Gowan, meanwhile, has worked mainly on small projects, remaining renowned within the profession but without much public recognition. Some call him an "architect's architect," meaning that his work is better appreciated by fellow professionals than by laymen, but he might more justly be called a client's architect, for he leaves in his wake a train of satisfied clients, many of whom have returned to him with further commissions. He is careful on every occasion to produce a design appropriate to its purpose and surroundings, so that his work is varied in style, somewhat unpredictable, and often baffling to critics. It reflects well his personal modesty, his reluctance to attach himself to any one movement or design philosophy, and his considerable historical knowledge. In recent years he has been involved in some extremely low-cost projects, such as East End warehousing at £3 per square foot, and has proved his ability to make a silk purse out of a sow's ear, never relaxing his strict attention to detail no matter how humble the task. His reputation for efficiency and thoroughness in the execution of his works is legendary.

Gowan also taught for some years at the Architectural Association, where he is respected for his penetrating judgement and loved for his infectious and sometimes rather reckless wit.

—Peter Blundell Jones

GRAHAM, Bruce J(ohn).

American. Born in LaCumbre, Bogota, Colombia, of American parents, 1 December 1925. Educated at the University of Dayton, Ohio, 1942–43; Case School of Applied Sciences, Cleveland, Ohio, 1943–44, 1946; University of Pennsylvania, Philadelphia, 1946–48, B.Arch. 1948. Served in the United States Navy, 1943–45. Married Jane Johnson in 1960; children: George, Lisa and Mara. Worked in the offices of Holabird, Roche and Burgee, now Holabird and Root, Chicago, 1949–51. Chief of Design, 1951–60, and since 1960 Partner, Skidmore, Owings and Merrill, Chicago. Exhibition: *Architecture of Chicago*, Museum of Contemporary Art, Chicago, 1976. Fellow, American Institute of Architects, 1966. Address: Skidmore, Owings and Merrill, 30 West Monroe Street, Chicago, Illinois 60603, U.S.A.

Works:

1957 United States Navy Service School, Great Lakes, Illinois
1958 Inland Steel Company Headquarters, Chicago
Standard Oil Company Technical Service Buildings, Whiting, Indiana
1960 Parke Davis and Company Offices and Research Laboratories, Ann Arbor, Michigan
1961 Upjohn Company Corporate Headquarters, Kalamazoo, Michigan
1962 Central Motor Bank, Jefferson City, Missouri
1964 Business Men's Assurance Company of America Corporate Headquarters, Chicago
1965 Brunswick Office Building, Chicago
Civic Center, Chicago
Equitable Life Assurance Society of the United States Office Building, Chicago
1968 Boots Pure Drug Company Ltd. Corporate Headquarters, Nottingham, England
1969 One Marine Midland Plaza Bank and Office Building, Rochester, New York
1970 John Hancock Center, Chicago
International Bank for Reconstruction and Development, Washington, D.C.
Eastman Kodak Company Marketing Education Center, Henrietta, New York
1971 One Shell Plaza Office Building, Houston
Bond Court Office Building, Cleveland
Office Building, 1010 Common Street, New Orleans
Hartford Fire Insurance Company Building, Chicago
Trans World Airlines Office Building, Kansas City, Missouri
1972 Two Shell Plaza Office Building, Houston
One Shell Square Office Building, New Orleans
Gateway III Office Building, Chicago
Office building, O'Hare Plaza, Chicago
Central area study, Milwaukee, Wisconsin
1973 National Life and Accident Insurance Company Headquarters, Nashville, Tennessee

MGIC Plaza Office Building, Madison, Wisconsin
Chicago 21 Plan
Woodfield 76 Office and Commercial Development, Schaumburg, Illinois
1974 First Wisconsin Center Bank and Office Building, Milwaukee, Wisconsin
First Wisconsin Plaza Bank and Office Building, Madison, Wisconsin
Fourth Financial Center Bank and Office Building, Wichita, Kansas
Sears Tower, Chicago
W. D. and H. O. Wills Corporate Headquarters and Tobacco Processing Facility, Bristol, England
1975 Baxter Travenol Laboratories Inc. Corporate Headquarters, Deerfield, Illinois
Harris Trust and Savings Bank, Chicago
Marathon Realty Development Office and Commercial Complex, Montreal (project)
1976 Ohio National Bank Building, Columbus
Charles Stark Draper Laboratory, Cambridge, Massachusetts
Central Bank of Iran, Tehran (project)
1977 Office building, 60 State Street, Boston
Apparel Mart and Holiday Inn Hotel, Wolf Point, Chicago
Master plan for the Chicago Dock and Canal Trust
Master plan for Dearborn Park New Town, Chicago
Group Alfa Corporate Headquarters, Monterrey, Mexico (project)
Khaneh Center Multi-Use Complex, Tehran
1978 New World Center Multi-Use Complex, Hong Kong
Hyatt International Hotel, Surabaya, Indonesia
1979 Banco de Occidente Building, Guatemala City
Central Trust Center Bank and Office Building, Cincinnati, Ohio
1980 Arab International Bank Multi-Use Complex, Cairo, Egypt
Hyatt International Hotel, Cairo, Egypt
1981 Hyatt International Hotel and Cultural Center, Kuwait City

Bruce J. Graham: John Hancock Center, Chicago, 1970

In Architecture, as in many other arts, it should be unnecessary to explain the work's existence within the certain time and special relationship. To discover and understand this position is the role of the Architect. To function within that framework, to understand the transitory quality, and to place the work within this context and then be sure of its validity is the satisfaction of an Architect. Recognition is not to be expected for this labor as it is not the product of life, but of a whole sequence of lives. We judge not a building; but, rather, let an architectural vocabulary illuminate an Age. We are, at this particular time, in an Age of discovery of a new Civilization. We have the technical tools as well as the crude consciousness of a new Age.

I feel very much that this time is a beginning; and, as such, our buildings must be clear, free of fashion, and simple statements of the truth.

—Bruce J. Graham

Bruce J. Graham is one of the leading American designers of high-rise buildings in the third quarter of the century. After graduating from the University of Pennsylvania, he moved to Chicago, where he has lived and worked ever since. Following a tour of duty with the firm of Holabird, Root and Burgee, he accepted a position in the Chicago office of Skidmore, Owings and Merrill, and nine years later, in 1960, he became a general partner. By that time he had already begun to specialize in the design of large commercial structures. He played a leading role in the design of the Inland Steel Building, one of the most important works in the recent history of Chicago architecture. Inland was the first major building to be erected in the Loop after World War II, as well as the first to incorporate clearly the principles and the lean, directly structural look of Miesian building. For about 15 years following Inland, Chicago commercial architecture, like that of most of the United States, was in debt to the Miesian manner, and Graham—though he never studied with Mies—became one of the ablest and most enthusiastic practitioners of the genre.

In 1965 three of the best known skyscrapers of the "Second Chicago School" were completed: the Brunswick Building, the Civic Center, and the Equitable Building. Graham played a significant role in the planning of all three. His reputation took on international luster in the later 1960's and early 1970's when, together with the brilliant Bangladesh-born engineer Fazlur Khan, he designed a number of towering skyscrapers utilizing the revolutionary tubular frame principle: the John Hancock Center, Chicago; the First Wisconsin Center, Milwaukee; One Shell Plaza, Houston; and the Sears Tower, Chicago. The last of these, composed of nine bundled tubes, the tallest of which rises 1,454 feet from the ground, is the world's loftiest building.

In the later 1970's Graham and SOM have continued to build on the large urban scale, in locales as far flung as Hong Kong (the New World Center, a multi-use complex) and Cairo (the Arab International Bank, another multi-use facility). As the popularity of the classical Miesian look has waned in the 1970's, Graham, in his recent work, has often grown consciously more lyrical and complex, as in the imaginatively prismatic First Wisconsin Plaza in Madison.

—Franz Schulze

GRAVES, Michael.
American. Born in Indianapolis, Indiana, 9 July 1934. Educated at the University of Cincinnati, Ohio, 1954–58, B.Arch. 1958; Harvard University, Cambridge, Massachusetts, 1958–59, M.Arch. 1959; American Academy, Rome, 1960–62 (Prix de Rome; Brunner Fellowship). Divorced; children: Sarah and

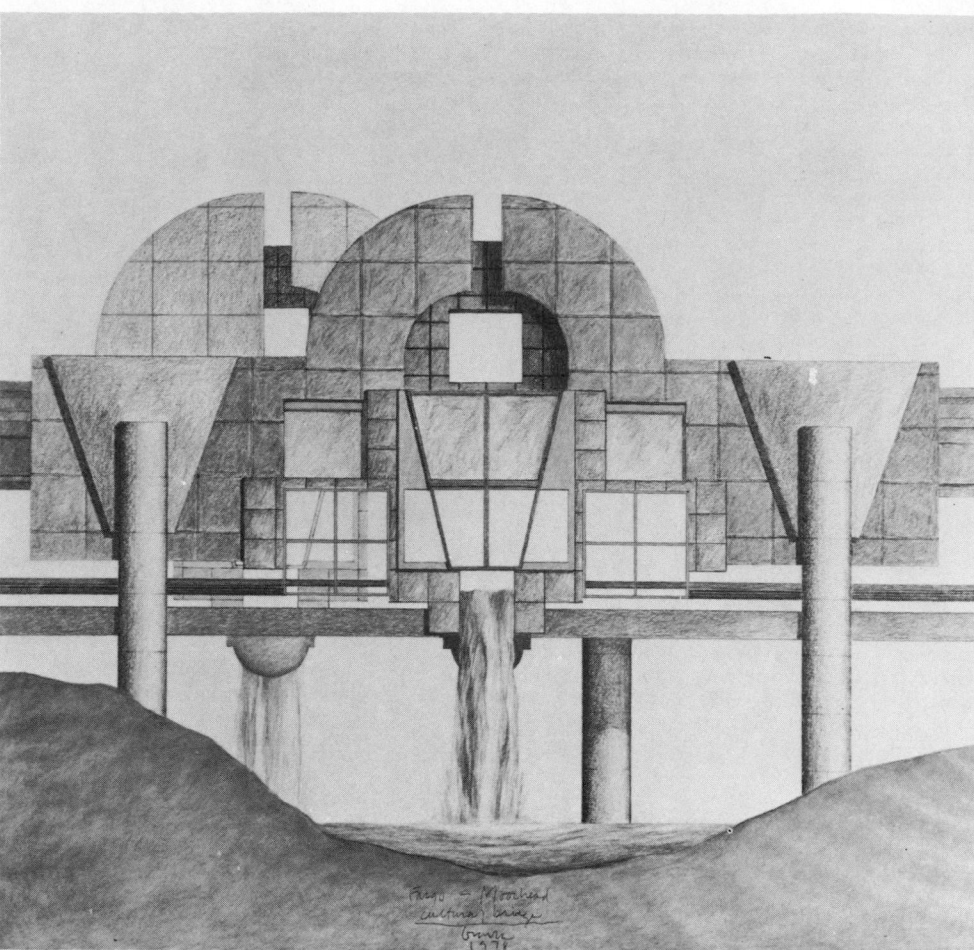

Michael Graves: Fargo-Moorhead Cultural Center Bridge, between Fargo, North Dakota and Moorhead, Minnesota, 1977

Adam; step-children: Anne and Elizabeth. Since 1964, Principal, Michael Graves, Architect, Princeton, New Jersey. Lecturer, 1962–63, Assistant Professor, 1963–67, Associate Professor, 1967–72, and since 1972 Professor of Architecture, Princeton University. Visiting Fellow, Institute for Architecture and Urban Studies, New York, 1971–72; Visiting Professor, University of Texas at Austin, 1973, 1974, University of Houston, Texas, 1974, 1978, New School for Social Research, New York, 1975, and the University of California at Los Angeles, 1977. Exhibitions: *40 Under 40*, Architectural League, New York, 1966; *The New City: Architecture and Urban Renewal*, Museum of Modern Art, New York, 1967; *Union County Nature and Science Museum*, Princeton University, 1967; *Architecture of Museums*, Museum of Modern Art, New York, 1968; *Birch Burdette Long Memorial Drawing Exhibition*, Architectural League, New York, 1973; *Triennale*, Milan, 1973; *Due Architetti*, USIS Gallery, Milan, 1974; *Five Architects*, Princeton University, and University of Texas at Austin, 1974; *Architectural Drawing*, Institute for Architecture and Urban Studies, New York, 1974, and Carnegie Mellon University, Pittsburgh, 1974; *Architectural Studies and Projects*, Museum of Modern Art, New York, 1975; *The New York Five*, Art Net, London, 1975; *Five Architects*, Castel Nuovo, Naples, 1975; *1975 AIA Honor Awards*, Kimbell Art Museum, Fort Worth, Texas, 1976; *Michael Graves: Projects, 1967–1976*, Columbia University, New York, 1976, toured the United States; *Two Hundred Years of American Architectural Drawing*, Cooper-Hewitt Museum, New York, 1977, toured the United States; *Drawing Toward a More Modern Architecture*, Drawing Center, New York, and Otis Art Institute, Los Angeles, 1977; *Beyond the Modern Movement*, Harvard University, Cambridge, Massachusetts, 1977; *Artists' Postcards*, Drawing Center, New York, 1977, toured the United States; *Grafica 80—*

Architettura, Milan, 1977; *Architecture: Service, Craft, Art*, Rosa Esman Gallery, New York, 1978, toured the United States; *Collage*, Goddard-Riverside Community Center, New York, 1978; *Roma Interotta*, Rome, 1978, toured internationally; Max Protetch Gallery, New York (group show), 1978; *Ornament in the Twentieth Century*, Cooper-Hewitt Museum, New York, 1978; *Trends in Contemporary Architecture*, The New Gallery of Contemporary Art, Cleveland, 1978. Recipient: Design Award, *Progressive Architecture*, 1970, 1976, 1977, 1978 (twice), 1979; National Honor Award, American Institute of Architects, 1975. Fellow, Society for the Arts, Religion and Culture. Address: Michael Graves, Architect, 34 Witherspoon Street, Princeton, New Jersey 08540, U.S.A.

Works:

1963 Boston Architectural Center (competition project; with Peter Eisenman)
1964 American Institute of Architects Headquarters, Washington, D.C. (competition project; with Peter Eisenman)
1964/
65 Jersey Corridor Study (New York/ Philadelphia urban corridor) (project; with Peter Eisenman and Anthony Eardley)
1965 University of California Arts Center, Berkeley (competition project; with Peter Eisenman)
1966/
68 Urban design plan for Oyster Bay, Long Island, New York (project)
1967 Hanselmann House, Fort Wayne, Indiana
Urban County Nature and Science Museum, Mountainside, New Jersey
Upper West Side of Manhattan Urban Design Plan (exhibition project; with Peter Eisenman)

1967/
68 Low-income and elderly people's housing, Coatsville, Pennsylvania (with Geddes, Brecher, Qualls and Cunningham)
1967/
71 Rehabilitation housing for N.E.S.T., Trenton, New Jersey
1968 Middle-income housing, Newark, New Jersey (project)
Master plan for the Newark Museum, New Jersey (project)
1969 Benacerraf House, Princeton, New Jersey
Rockefeller House, Pocantico Hills, New York (project)
1970 Drezner House, Princeton, New Jersey (project)
1971 Ear, Nose and Throat Associates Medical Office, Fort Wayne, Indiana
1971/
73 Alexander House, Princeton, New Jersey
1972 Gunwyn Ventures Investment Office, Princeton, New Jersey
Keeley Guest House, Princeton, New Jersey (project)
Snyderman House, Fort Wayne, Indiana
1973 Mezzo House, Princeton, New Jersey (project)
Sklute House, Bucks County, Pennsylvania (project)
Mural, *Triennale,* Milan
1974 3 murals, Transammonia Inc. Offices, New York
Mural, School of Architecture, University of Texas at Austin
Claghorn House, Princeton, New Jersey
Wageman House, Princeton, New Jersey (project)
1975 Housing for the elderly, Trenton, New Jersey (competition project)
Newark Museum Carriage House renovation, Newark, New Jersey (project)
Newark Museum Art School renovation, Newark, New Jersey
1976 Crooks House, Fort Wayne, Indiana
Schulman House, Princeton, New Jersey
1977 Chem-Fleur Inc. Factory addition and renovation, Newark, New Jersey (project)
Warehouse/house conversion, Princeton, New Jersey
Plocek House, Warren Township, New Jersey
Abrahams Dance Studio, Princeton, New Jersey
Fargo-Moorhead Cultural Center Bridge between Fargo, North Dakota and Moorhead, Minnesota
1978 Railroad station conversion and office building, Millburn, New Jersey
Mural, John Witherspoon School, Princeton, New Jersey
Porta Maggiore, *Roma Interotta,* Rome (exhibition project)
Kalko House, Green Brook, New Jersey
Newark Museum Children's Museum, Newark, New Jersey
House, Aspen, Colorado (project)
Furniture Demonstration Center, E. F. Hauserman Corporation, New York
Furniture Showroom and Offices, E. F. Hauserman Corporation, Cleveland

Publications:

By GRAVES: articles—"The Swedish Connection" in *Journal of Architectural Education* (Washington, D.C.), Fall 1975; "Elusive Outcome, Mental Mise-en-scene" in *Progressive Architecture* (New York), May 1977; "The Necessity of Drawing: Tangible Speculation" in *Architectural Design* (London), June 1977; "Snyderman House," with M. Perkins, in *GA Houses 2,* Tokyo, 1977; "Porta Maggiore" in *Roma Interotta,* exhibition catalogue, Rome 1978, "Three

Architects, Three Approaches to Color Use" in *AIA Journal* (Washington, D.C.), October 1978; "Thought Models" in *Publication of the School of Design* (North Carolina State University, Raleigh), 1978; "Referential Drawings" in *Journal of Architectural Education* (Washington, D.C.), Fall 1978.

On GRAVES: books—*Five Architects: Eisenman, Graves, Gwathmey, Hejduk, Meier* by Kenneth Frampton and Colin Rowe, New York 1972; *Architettura Razionale* by E. Bonfanti, R. Bonicalzi, A. Rossi, M. Scolari and D. Vitale, Milan 1973; *Five Architects NY,* Rome 1976; *The Language of Post-Modern Architecture* by Charles Jencks, London 1977; *200 Years of American Architectural Drawing* by David Gebhard and Deborah Nevins, New York 1977; *New Directions in American Architecture* by Robert A. M. Stern, New York 1977; articles—"Private Residence, Pocantino Hills, New York" in *Progressive Architecture* (New York), January 1970; "On Reading Architecture: Eisenman and Graves: An Analysis" by Mario Gandelsonas in *Progressive Architecture* (New York), March 1972; "Michael Graves: Doctor's House" in *Architecture + Urbanism* (Tokyo), November 1972; "Towards a Pluralist Architecture" by Peter Carl in *Progressive Architecture* (New York), February 1973; "Five on Five" by Robert A. M. Stern, Jaquelin Robertson, Charles Moore, Allan Greenberg and Romaldo Giurgola in *Architectural Forum* (New York), May 1973; "Architecture's '5' Make Their Ideas Felt" by Paul Goldberger in *The New York Times,* 26 November 1973; "Should Anyone Care about the New York Five . . . ?" by Paul Goldberger in *Architectural Record* (New York), February 1974; "Rockefeller House and Keeley Guest House" and "About Michael Graves" by Takeo Hatac in *Architecture + Urbanism* (Tokyo), March 1974; "Five Architects" by Kenneth Frampton in *Lotus 9* (Venice), February 1975; "The Architect as Intellectual Artist" by John McKean in *Building Design* (London), 10 October 1975; "Les Cendres de Jefferson" by Manfredo Tafuri, and "Michael Graves: Maison Snyderman" in *L'Architecture d'Aujourd'hui* (Paris), August-/September 1976; "Living in a Work of Art" by Suzanne Stephens in *Progressive Architecture* (New York), March 1978.

There appear to be two major positions in current architectural thought. Although they are not mutually exclusive, these two attitudes can be seen in opposition to each other.

The first can be characterized as constituting a part of symbolic and mythic representations of the culture. One assumes that there is a correspondence between cultural values and physical artifacts, and that these physical artifacts provide representations both of symbolic objects and of ritual participation. This position, by its nature, relies on the literal, often familiar characteristics of form which are thought of as representational.

The second position is primarily abstract in nature, having been derived from an early twentieth century, self-conscious rejection of historical precedent in favor of an interest in machine technology and its symbolism. The building is seen as a technical artifact whose abstract geometric devices are generally unadorned and read as minimal. The loss of those figurative elements thought to be derived from classical analogies of man and nature leads to a sense of alienation or a lack of association with the architecture.

If we are to increase the participation in and identification with architecture by the culture at large, we must begin to re-establish the former, somewhat classical, mode of thinking which is capable of representing in physical form the symbolic and mythic aspirations of that culture.

—Michael Graves

By the time he had been in practice for 15 years—in the late 1970's—the Princeton, New Jersey-based

Michael Graves was one of the most inspirational and influential American architects for the younger generation that was exploring the poetry—allusion and metaphor—and the meanings—semiology—in architecture. His work is in the realm of built architecture, though still small in number—a dozen houses, five of them built, half a dozen museums and galleries, and a half-dozen additions and alterations. It is also in the form of murals, paintings, and drawings, which are among the most persuasive and appealing by today's architects. In addition Graves is an educator—teaching at Princeton University and lecturing across the country with great popularity. He is one of the most cerebral theorists and exciting aestheticians of architecture today.

The principal feature of his work is a cubist simultaneity of images, meanings, and inspirations or derivations. He is concerned with multiple layers of space, structure, and symbolism. In his early work the forms and images were those of the Cubists themselves, especially Juan Gris, and of the early Le Corbusier—fragments, overlay and superimposition, multiple perspective, and the juxtaposition of the grid against such unexpected shapes as the violin curve. In more recent work the inspirations or derivations have been ever more far reaching into forgotten or rejected history—to Ingres and Poussin, to Ledoux and Boullée, to early 19th century English landscape painting, and constantly to classical Greece and Rome. Always these forms and images are overlaid to produce a new language of almost polyphonic simultaneity.

Questions about contextual continuity—the relationship of his architecture to its physical site and its cultural background—are the primary concerns of Graves and place him in the forefront of those architects dealing with historicism or historical allusion. His is architectural storytelling. Questions about the relationship of architecture to the site bring him to statements about the relationship of his work to nature. He relates foreground, middle-ground, and background or ground, horizon, and sky to base, wall, and roof; or he relates foot, body, and head to base, wall, and cornice. It is anthropomorphic rather than machine symbolism. It rejects abstraction in favor of the representational, the humanistic, the communicative.

Most accessible of Graves's architectural metaphors of nature is his use of color—a much wider and fuller use of color and patterned color than most of his contemporaries—to create "metaphorical landscapes." The landscape of Graves's mind believes that it is part of our cultural heritage to make a simile, if not to equate, blue with sky and water, green with plants and leaves, yellow with sunlight, and red with wall. He believes we have an inherent tradition—long felt, if for a while forgotten by the Modern movement—that red, since the time of the Etruscans, has meant wall. So he locates his colors high or low in his architecture as they are located in nature. This makes or tells special meanings: blue on the ceiling means sky; on the floor it might symbolize pool; yellow on a pipe signifies a streak of sunlight; green on a floor can connote grass, on a wall can mean a bush or a hedge, or on an overhead duct can say, "leaves of trees."

But that is not enough for Graves. He compounds his work with multiple images and multiple meanings for each. Blue on the floor, in the Claghorn kitchen, means the reflection of the sky through the window—and the shadow of a muntin should tell us so. And there, too, brown on the exterior base relates not only to the ground but also to the stone base of the original house; dark green not only connotes leaves but also reiterates the shutters on the existing house. Forms of architecture can serve the same double purpose. The *tabula rasa* and the mountain are mythic images for him that convey both their own meanings and their prototypical messages as structure, space, and extension—especially in the House in Aspen project.

With ever more delicate and sophisticated colorings and poetic allusions therefrom, and with ever more abstruse and interrelated historical inspirations or derivations, Michael Graves's work is among the most lively mosaics of overlaid grids and diaper patterns, of classicism and neo-classicism, of high art and late pop, of delicacy and boldness, of functional circulation and historical memory, and it reflects one of the most complete aesthetic mythologies at work in architecture today.

—C. Ray Smith

GRAY, Eileen.

Irish. Born at Brownswood, Enniscorthy, County Wexford, Ireland, 9 August 1879. Educated at the Slade School of Art, London, 1898–1902, and Académie Colarossi and Académie Julien, Paris, 1902–05; studied furniture-making and lacquerwork with Sugawara in Paris, 1907–14. Served as an ambulance driver in the French Army, 1914–15. Proprietor of a lacquerwork/furniture studio and workshop, with Sugawara, in London, 1915–17, and Paris, 1977–22; Proprietor of the Galerie Jean Désert, Paris, 1922–30; first architectural projects, with Jean Badovici, Roquebrune, France, 1926; worked in Castellar, France, 1939–45, and Paris, 1945 until her death, 1976. Exhibitions: *Exposition des Artistes Décorateurs,* 1913, 1912; *World's Fair,* Paris, 1937; Heinz Gallery, Royal Institute of British Architects, London, 1973; *1925,* Musée des Arts Décoratifs, Paris, 1976; *Eileen Gray: Designer 1879–1976,* Victoria and Albert Museum, London, and Museum of Modern Art, New York, 1979. Royal Designer for Industry, Royal Society of Arts, London, 1972; Fellow, Royal Institute of Irish Architects, Dublin, 1973. *Died* (in Paris) *28 November 1976.*

Works:

1919/
22 Suzanne Talbot (Madame Mathieu-Lévy) Apartment interiors, Rue de Lota, Paris
1923 Monte Carlo Boudoir (exhibition project)
1925/
28 Eileen Gray Apartment interiors, 21 Rue Bonaparte, Paris
1926 House for an Engineer (project)
1927/
29 E-1027 (Eileen Gray House), Roquebrune, Cap Martin, France (with Jean Badovici)
1930 Jean Badovici Studio/Apartment interiors, rue Châteaubriand, Champs Elysées, Paris
1932/
34 Tempe à Pailla (Eileen Gray House), Castellar, near Menton, France (now Graham Sutherland House)
1933 House for Two Sculptors (project)
1937 Tube House (project)
Centre des Vacances (project; exhibited at the *World's Fair,* at Le Corbusier's Pavillon des Temps Nouveaux, 1937)
1939 Eileen Gray Apartment interiors, St. Tropez, France (destroyed, 1944)
1946/
49 Cultural and Social Centre (project)

Publications:

By GRAY: article—"La Maison Minimum," with Jean Badovici, in *L'Architecture d'Aujourd'hui* (Paris), no. 1, 1930.

On GRAY: books—*Gli Elementi dell'Architettura Funzionale* by Alberto Sartoris, Milan 1932; *Des Canons, des Munitions? Merci! Des Logis . . .* by Le Corbusier, Paris 1938; *Eileen Gray: Designer 1879–1976,* exhibition catalogue, by Stewart Johnson, London 1979; articles—"Les Lacques de Miss Ei-

Eileen Gray: Dressingcupboard, E-1027: Eileen Gray House, Roquebrune, Cap Martin, France, 1928

leen Gray" by E. de Clermont-Tonnerre in *Feuillets d'Art* (Paris), February/March 1922; article by Jan Wils and Jean Badovici in *Wendingen* (Amsterdam), no. 6, 1924; "Maison en Bord de Mer" by Jean Badovici in *Architecture Vivante* (Paris), 1929; "Projet Centre Culturel" in *L'Architecture d'Aujourd'hui* (Paris), no. 82, 1949; "Un Imaggio di Eileen Gray" by Joseph Rykwert in *Domus* (Milan), December 1968; "Eileen Gray: The Houses and an Interior" by Joseph Rykwert in *Perspecta* (New Haven, Connecticut), no. 13, 1971; "Eileen Gray: Pioneer of Design" by Joseph Rykwert in *Architectural Review* (London), August 1972; "The Complete Designer" in *Design* (London), January 1973; "Eileen Gray" in *RIBA Journal* (London), February 1973; "Eileen Gray" in *The Sunday Times Magazine* (London), 22 June 1975; "Eileen Gray Lives" by Richard Carr in *Building Design* (London), 30 June 1978.

Overshadowed as she was by the giants of her era, Eileen Gray is a comparatively little known exponent of the modern movement. Unlike many of her contemporaries, she intensely disliked self publicity, and that attitude contributed to her neglect by clients and critics alike. Her total output is two houses,

some interiors and unexecuted projects—her work nevertheless displays a full and original understanding of the language of that style.

It is difficult to categorize Ms. Gray's work, falling as it does between the over-ornamentation of Art Deco and the purely functional of the machine aesthetic. Some critics have associated her with the De Stijl group, and parallels can be found, but she rejected the group's intellectual austerity, reasoning that "Man is not purely Spirit." She was essentially an individualist, believing that her creations, whilst reflecting her artistic outlook, should first and foremost be practical.

The one European whose philosophy attracted Gray was her friend Le Corbusier. They were in many ways kindred spirits. Neither had been subjected to a recognized architectural training, and they were able to view the world with unblinkered eyes. Both had a clear vision of the way ahead for modern design in the "New World" that was emerging. Yet—whilst agreeing in principal with ideas expressed in his contributions to *L'ésprit Nouveau* in 1920–26—she nevertheless revolted against the over mechanisation of things to the exclusion of emotion.

Apart from Rietveld's Schroder house, Utrecht, completed in 1924, and Adolph Loos' house for Tristan Tzara in 1926, there were few precedents for such completeness of design as displayed in Gray's first building begun in 1927 at Roquebrune in collaboration with the Rumanian architect Badovici. The spaces are furnished with floor coverings, light fittings, murals, furniture of absolute appropriateness, all designed and made to specification in her Paris workshop. She pioneered the use of a variety of the "new" materials—cork, aluminium, tubular steel, suede, leather, perforated metal sheeting, always sensitive to the nature of the material. A fusion of formal invention with craftsman's skills, which received a fully articulated expression only in the work of the early Bauhaus masters, is very evident in her creations.

Her houses and interiors are a celebration of Corbusier's *machine à hâbiter* ideal in its true sense but with an entirely humanistic approach. "In the limited confines of domestic space,' she said, "everything must be made to adjust—to be adaptable." Thus she initiated folding windows, sliding screens and blinds, false ceilings concealing storage space, staircases hidden in cupboards or under seating, adjustable skylights, extending wardrobes, all things functioning with the maximum of ease, every detail adjusting to form part of a larger and potentially variable spatial composition, the exterior spaces becoming an extension of the interior.

In retrospect, Eileen Gray's work can be seen to be a product of its time, but it was her feeling that artists should "be of their era"—should live in their own epoch and express it with honesty. "The beautiful work of art is more real than the artist" must surely be her epitaph.

—Elizabeth Murphy

GREENE, Charles Sumner.

American. Born in Brighton, Ohio, 12 October 1868; brother of the architect Henry Mather Greene, *q.v.* Educated at the Manual Training High School of Washington University, St. Louis, 1886–88; Massachusetts Institute of Technology School of Architecture, Cambridge, 1888–91. Married Alice Gordon White in 1901; had five children. Worked for Winslow and Weatherall and other Boston architects, 1891–94; Partner, with Henry Mather Greene, Greene and Greene, Pasadena, California, 1894–1903, Los Angeles, 1903–06, and Pasadena, 1906–22; practised independently, in Carmel, California, from 1922. Recipient: Certificate of Merit, 1948, and Citation, 1952, American Institute of Architects. *Died* (in Carmel, California) *11 June 1957.*

Works (with Henry Mather Greene; all California unless noted):

1894   John Breiner House, Pasadena
Mrs. Martha Fynn House, Pasadena
Conrad A. Covelle House, Pasadena
Pasadena Security Investment Company House, Pasadena
Pasadena Security Investment Company House II, Pasadena

1895   Robert Eason House, Pasadena
Willis M. Eason House, Pasadena
Dr. Thomas J. Rigg House, Pasadena
Charles Eldred House, Pasadena
Pasadena Presbyterian Church additions
Edward S. Crump House, Pasadena

1896   Robert S. Allen House, Pasadena
Minney-Kendall Building, Pasadena
Rollin H. Miller House, Pasadena
Edward B. Hosmer House, Pasadena
Mrs. C. Gartzman House, Pasadena

1897   Theodore P. Gordon House, Pasadena
Dr. Fenyes House, Pasadena (project)
J.J. Neumeister House, Pasadena
Dr. George S. Hull House, Pasadena
Dr. George S. Hull Office, Pasadena
Elizabeth A. McLean House, Pasadena
Howard Longley House, South Pasadena

1898   Dr. W.H. Roberts Office, Pasadena
Winthrop B. Fay House, Pasadena
Wilson School addition, Pasadena (project)

William B. Tomkins House, Pasadena
James Swan House, Pasadena

1899   J.M. Smith House, Pasadena
Charles W. Hollister House, Pasadena
Pasadena Library addition, Pasadena (project)
Dr. William T. Bolton House, Pasadena
George H. Coffin House, Pasadena

1900   Pasadena Ice Company Building, Pasadena
John C. Bentz Building, Pasadena
Mrs. Mary R. Milnor House, Pasadena
Katherine M. Duncan House, Pasadena

1901   Mrs. Metilde Phillips House, Pasadena
Mrs. Benjamin C. Brown House, Pasadena
Lorenz P. Hansen House "A", Pasadena
Lorenz P. Hansen House "B", Pasadena
James F. Ker House, Pasadena
Dr. John M. Radebaugh House additions, Pasadena
Miss H. Sybil Swett Private School, Pasadena
Charles S. Greene House, Pasadena

1902   George H. Barker House, Pasadena
Mrs. Rose J. Rasey Rooming House, Pasadena
All Saints Episcopal Church Rectory, Pasadena
James A. Culberton House, Pasadena
W.B.T. House, near Pasadena (project)
George G. Guyer House additions and alterations, Altadena

1903   F. J. Martin Studio Apartments, Pasadena

Emma M. Black House, Pasadena
Martha, Violet and Jane White House, Pasadena
Philip L. Autin House, Pasadena
Katherine M. Duncan House additions, Pasadena
Samuel P. Sanborn House and Stable, Pasadena
Arturo Bandini House, Pasadena
Dr. Frances F. Rowland House and Office, Pasadena
Mrs. Mary R. Darling House, Claremont
Dr. Edith J. Claypole House, Pasadena

1904   Mrs. Jennie A. Reeve House, Long Beach
Henry M. Greene House, Pasadena
Charles W. Hollister House, Hollywood
Edgar W. Camp House, Sierra Madre
Mrs. James A. Garfield House, South Pasadena
R. Henry/C. Green House, Vancouver, British Columbia
Adelaide M. Tichenor House, Long Beach
Thomas Palmer House additions, Los Angeles
Rev. Alexander M. Merwin House, Pasadena
Kate A. White House, South Pasadena
Dr. William T. Bolton House alterations, Pasadena

1905   Mrs. William A. Bowen House, Altadena
S. Hazard Halsted House, Pasadena

Greene and Greene: David B. Gamble House, Pasadena, California, 1908

South Pasadena Realty and Improvement Company Entrance Gates, Fence, and Bridge, South Pasadena
Dr. Arthur A. Libby House, Pasadena
Charles J. Willet House, Pasadena
Lucy E. Wheeler House, Los Angeles
Mrs. T. Stewart White House, Santa Barbara (project)
Iwan Serrurier House, Pasadena
A. C. Brandt House, Altadena
Tod Ford House alterations, Pasadena
Henry M. Robinson House, Pasadena
Mrs. L. G. and Marion Porter House, Los Angeles
1906 Mrs. Josephine Van Rossem House additions and alterations, Pasadena
James A. Culbertson House additions and alterations, Pasadena
Tod Ford House additions, Pasadena
Pasadena Ice Company Offices, Pasadena
Pomona Valley Ice Company Offices, Pomona
Mrs. Jennie A. Reeve House, Sierra Madre
Caroline S. DeForest House, Pasadena
Louis K. Hyde House, Plainfield, New Jersey (project)
John B. Phillips House, Pasadena
Robert Pitcairn Jr. House, Pasadena
Dr. William T. Bolton House, Pasadena
Katherine M. Duncan House alterations and additions, Pasadena
John C. Bentz House, Pasadena
John A. Cole House, Pasadena
F. W. Hawks House, Pasadena
Charles S. Greene House alterations and additions, Pasadena
1907 Fred Stahlhuth House, Pasadena
James A. Culbertson House alterations and additions, Pasadena
Mary L. Ranney House, Pasadena
Pasadena Hospital Association Nurses' Home, Pasadena (project)
S. Hazard Halsted House additions, Pasadena
Charles W. Leffingwell Bunk House, Whittier
Robert R. Blacker House, Pasadena
Freeman A. Ford House, Pasadena
Lon F. Chapin House alterations and additions, Pasadena
William W. Spinks House, Pasadena
Rev. Alexander M. Merwin House additions, Pasadena
John Wadsworth House additions, Pasadena
Theodore Irwin House additions, Pasadena
Tod Ford House additions, Pasadena
Shelter for Viewlovers, Pasadena
1908 David B. Gamble House, Pasadena
Robert R. Blacker House additions, Pasadena
S. Hazard Halsted House alterations, Pasadena
Charles K. Silent House, Glendora (project)
William J. Lawless House, Sierra Madre
James W. Neill House additions, Pasadena
Theodore Irwin House alterations, Pasadena
Armenian Pilgrims Church, Fresno (project)
1909 John B. Phillips House additions, Pasadena
Charles M. Pratt House, Nordhoff
William R. Thorsen House, Berkeley
William W. Spinks Garage, Pasadena
Dr. S. S. Crow House, Pasadena
Earle C. Anthony House, Los Angeles
1910 John G. Neumeister House, Redondo (project)
John Lambert House, Pasadena (project)
John C. Bentz House alterations and additions, Pasadena
James A. Culbertson House additions, Pasadena
Ernest W. Smith House, Pasadena
James W. Neill House alterations, Pasadena
Howard Longley House alterations and additions, South Pasadena
Samuel L. Merrill House, Pasadena
Keith Spaulding Bunk House, Fillmore

John C. Bentz Garage, Pasadena
A. C. Drake House, Pasadena (project)
Henry M. Robinson House additions, Pasadena
1911 Alexander M. Drake House, Pasadena (project)
Mortimer Fleishhacker House, Woodside
S. Hazard Halsted House additions, Pasadena
William W. Spinks House alterations, Pasadena
Crow-Crocker Garage additions, Pasadena
Nathan Bentz House, Santa Barbara
Earle C. Anthony Automobile Showroom interiors, Los Angeles
Henry M. Greene House additions, Pasadena
Cordelia A. Culbertson House, Pasadena
Longfellow School, Pasadena
S. C. Graham House, Los Angeles (project)
Charles P. Wilcox House, Pasadena
Mrs. Charles G. Brown House, Pasadena
Pasadena Ice Company Building alterations, Pasadena
Joseph K. Huston House, Pasadena
1912 Mrs. Parker A. Earle Apartment House, Pasadena
Charles M. Pratt House alterations, Nordhoff
Annie Blacker House, Pasadena
Edward S. Crocker House, Pasadena
Dr. Frances F. Rowland House moving and alterations, Pasadena
Charles S. Greene House alterations and additions, Pasadena
Frank L. Palmer House, North Pomona (project)
S. Hazard Halsted House alterations and additions, Pasadena
Michael Kew House, San Diego
George A. Gibbs House additions, Pasadena
Vista del Arroyo Hotel east annex and bungalow alterations, Pasadena
Dr. Robert P. McReynolds House alterations, Los Angeles
F. W. Hawks House alterations, Pasadena
J. S. Silverberg House alterations, San Mateo
1913 Henry A. Ware House, Pasadena
Earle C. Anthony House alterations and additions, Los Angeles
Dr. Edward H. Angle House, Pasadena (project)
William M. Ladd House, Nordhoff
Mrs. J. Herbert Ballentine House alterations and additions, Altadena
Sidney D. Gamble House, Escondido (project)
James W. Neill House alterations, Pasadena
1914 James A. Culbertson House additions, Pasadena
Vista del Arroyo Building, Pasadena (project)
Dr. Rosa Engelmann House, Pasadena
Cordelia A. Culbertson House additions, Pasadena
Charles S. Greene Garage, Pasadena
Theodore Irwin House additions, Pasadena
Henry A. Ware House additions, Pasadena
Dr. William T. Bolton House additions, Pasadena
1915 John T. Greene House, Sacramento
Dr. Robert P. McReynolds House additions, Los Angeles
Mortimer Fleischhacker House additions, San Francisco
William E. Hamlin House, Pasadena
F. W. Hawks House alterations, Pasadena
Charles M. Pratt House alterations, Nordhoff
Dr. Nathan H. Williams House, Altadena
S. Hazard Halsted House alterations and additions, Pasadena
Dr. Rosa Engelmann House additions, Pasadena
Dr. Arthur A. Libby House additions, Pasadena
Herbert Fleishhacker House alterations, Atherton

Pasadena Ice Company Offices alterations and additions, Pasadena
Pasadena Ice Company Ice Storage Building additions, Pasadena
William E. Hamlin Garage, Pasadena
Dr. Frances F. Rowland House alterations, Pasadena
1916 H. T. Proctor House, Cocoa Nut Beach, Florida (project)
J. Herbert Hall Apartment House alterations and additions, Pasadena
Dr. Robert P. McReynolds House alterations, Los Angeles
Westmoreland Place Portals and Gates, Pasadena
Mortimer Fleishhacker House additions, Woodside
S. Hazard Halsted House additions and garage, Pasadena
1917 Charles H. Stoddard House, Burlingame (project)
Dr. Martha J. Kuznik House, Hollywood (project)
John H. Poole House, Pasadena
Earle C. Anthony House alterations and additions, Los Angeles
Cordelia A. Culbertson House alterations, Pasadena
Henry M. Robinson House alterations and additions, Pasadena
1919 John H. Poole House, Pasadena (project)
Hubert F. Krantz Development for Prospect Park, Palm Beach County, Florida (project)
Hubert F. Krantz House, Pasadena (project)

Works (by Charles Sumner Greene only; all California):

1902 W.B.T. House, near Pasadena (project)
1918 Daniel L. James House, Carmel Highlands
1920 Charles S. Greene House, Carmel
1921 Thomas C. Greene House, Carmel
Carmel Country Club Clubhouse (project)
1922 Carmel War Memorial
Rudolf Schevill House alterations and addition of Music Studio, Berkeley
1923 Robert Tolmie House and Music Studio, Piedmont
Mortimer Fleischhacker House additions, Woodside
Charles S. Greene Studio, Carmel
1925 Jessie H. Payne House, Carmel (project)
1926 Mrs. Willis Walker Stable, Pebble Beach
Mrs. Jennie Crocker Whitman House, Pebble Beach (project)
1927 Mortimer Fleischhacker House water garden, Woodside
Violet Campbell House additions, Carmel
1928 Martin Flavin House entry walls and gates, Carmel Highlands
Robert R. Blacker House fountain, Pasadena
Mortimer Fleishhacker Dairy House, Woodside
1929 Ralph C. Lee House garden pergola, Hillsborough (project)
John L. Howard House and Studio, Monterey
Mrs. Frank J. Kelley House alterations and additions, San Jose
Martin Flavin House alterations, Carmel Highlands
Mortimer Fleischhacker House gothic room addition, San Francisco (project)
Violet Campbell House alterations, Carmel
1931 Mrs. Frank J. Kelley House additions, San Jose
Mortimer Fleischhacker House fountain, Woodside
1932 Martin Flavin House alterations, Carmel Highlands
1934 Rinehart House (project)
Martin Flavin House alterations, Carmel Highlands

Mortimer Fleishhacker House alterations and additions, Woodside (project)
1937 Park Abbott House and Offices, Oakland (project)
1938 Adelaide Howard House (project)
1939 Martin Flavin House alterations, Carmel Highlands
1940 Daniel L. James House library addition, Carmel Highlands

See GREENE, Henry Mather

GREENE, Henry Mather.
American. Born in Brighton, Ohio, 23 January 1870; brother of the architect Charles Sumner Greene, *q. v.* Educated at the Manual Training High School of Washington University, St. Louis, Missouri, 1886–88; Massachusetts Institute of Technology School of Architecture, Cambridge, 1888–91. Married Emeline Augusta Dart in 1899; had four children. Worked for Stickney and Austin, then for Shepley, Rutan and Coolidge, Boston, 1891–94; Partner, with Charles Sumner Greene, Greene and Greene, Pasadena, 1894–1903, Los Angeles, 1903–06, and Pasadena, 1906–22; practised independently, in Pasadena, from 1922. Recipient: Certificate of Merit, 1948, and Citation, 1952, American Institute of Architects. *Died* (in Altadena, California) *2 October 1954.*

Works (with Charles Sumner Greene; all California unless noted):

1894 John Breiner House, Pasadena
Mrs. Martha Fynn House, Pasadena
Conrad A. Covelle House, Pasadena
Pasadena Security Investment Company House, Pasadena
Pasadena Security Investment Company House II, Pasadena
1895 Robert Eason House, Pasadena
Willis M. Eason House, Pasadena
Dr. Thomas J. Rigg House, Pasadena
Charles Eldred House, Pasadena
Pasadena Presbyterian Church additions, Pasadena
Edward S. Crump House, Pasadena
1896 Robert S. Allen House, Pasadena
Minney-Kendall Building, Pasadena
Rollin H. Miller House, Pasadena
Edward B. Hosmer House, Pasadena
Mrs. C. Gartzman House, Pasadena
1897 Theodore P. Gordon House, Pasadena
Dr. Fenyes House, Pasadena (project)
J.J. Neumeister House, Pasadena
Dr. George S. Hull House, Pasadena
Dr. George S. Hull Office, Pasadena
Elizabeth A. McLean House, Pasadena
Howard Longley House, South Pasadena
1898 Dr. W.H. Roberts Office, Pasadena
Winthrop B. Fay House, Pasadena
Wilson School addition, Pasadena (project)
William B. Tomkins House, Pasadena
James Swan House, Pasadena
1899 J.M. Smith House, Pasadena
Charles W. Hollister House, Pasadena
Pasadena Library addition, Pasadena (project)
Dr. William T. Bolton House, Pasadena
George H. Coffin House, Pasadena
1900 Pasadena Ice Company Building, Pasadena
John C. Bentz Building, Pasadena
Mrs. Mary R. Milnor House, Pasadena
Katherine M. Duncan House, Pasadena
1901 Mrs. Metilde Phillips House, Pasadena
Mrs. Benjamin C. Brown House, Pasadena
Lorenz P. Hansen House "A", Pasadena
Lorenz P. Hansen House "B", Pasadena
James F. Ker House, Pasadena

Dr. John M. Radebaugh House additions, Pasadena
Miss H. Sybil Swett Private School, Pasadena
Charles S. Greene House, Pasadena
1902 George H. Barker House, Pasadena
Mrs. Rose J. Rasey Rooming House, Pasadena
All Saints Episcopal Church Rectory, Pasadena
James A. Culberton House, Pasadena
George G. Guyer House additions and alterations, Altadena
1903 F. J. Martin Studio Apartments, Pasadena
Emma M. Black House, Pasadena
Martha, Violet and Jane White House, Pasadena
Philip L. Autin House, Pasadena
Katherine M. Duncan House additions, Pasadena
Samuel P. Sanborn House and Stable, Pasadena
Arturo Bandini House, Pasadena
Dr. Frances F. Rowland House and Office, Pasadena
Mrs. Mary R. Darling House, Claremont
Dr. Edith J. Claypole House, Pasadena
1904 Mrs. Jennie A. Reeve House, Long Beach
Henry M. Greene House, Pasadena
Charles W. Hollister House, Hollywood
Edgar W. Camp House, Sierra Madre
Mrs. James A. Garfield House, South Pasadena
R. Henry/C. Green House, Vancouver, British Columbia
Adelaide M. Tichenor House, Long Beach
Thomas Palmer House additions, Los Angeles
Rev. Alexander M. Merwin House, Pasadena
Kate A. White House, South Pasadena
Dr. William T. Bolton House alterations, Pasadena
1905 Mrs. William A. Bowen House, Altadena
S. Hazard Halsted House, Pasadena
South Pasadena Realty and Improvement Company Entrance Gates, Fence, and Bridge, South Pasadena
Dr. Arthur A. Libby House, Pasadena
Charles J. Willet House, Pasadena
Lucy E. Wheeler House, Los Angeles
Mrs. T. Stewart White House, Santa Barbara (project)
Iwan Serrurier House, Pasadena
A. C. Brandt House, Altadena
Tod Ford House alterations, Pasadena
Henry M. Robinson House, Pasadena
Mrs. L. G. and Marion Porter House, Los Angeles
1906 Mrs. Josephine Van Rossem House additions and alterations, Pasadena
James A. Culbertson House additions and alterations, Pasadena
Tod Ford House additions, Pasadena
Pasadena Ice Company Offices, Pasadena
Pomona Valley Ice Company Offices, Pomona
Mrs. Jennie A. Reeve House, Sierra Madre
Caroline S. DeForest House, Pasadena
Louis K. Hyde House, Plainfield, New Jersey (project)
John B. Phillips House, Pasadena
Robert Pitcairn Jr. House, Pasadena
Dr. William T. Bolton House, Pasadena
Katherine M. Duncan House alterations and additions, Pasadena
John C. Bentz House, Pasadena
John A. Cole House, Pasadena
F. W. Hawks House, Pasadena
Charles S. Greene House alterations and additions, Pasadena
1907 Fred Stahlhuth House, Pasadena
James A. Culbertson House alterations and additions, Pasadena
Mary L. Ranney House, Pasadena

Pasadena Hospital Association Nurses' Home, Pasadena (project)
S. Hazard Halsted House additions, Pasadena
Charles W. Leffingwell Bunk House, Whittier
Robert R. Blacker House, Pasadena
Freeman A. Ford House, Pasadena
Lon F. Chapin House alterations and additions, Pasadena
William W. Spinks House, Pasadena
Rev. Alexander M. Merwin House additions, Pasadena
John Wadsworth House additions, Pasadena
Theodore Irwin House additions, Pasadena
Tod Ford House additions, Pasadena
Shelter for Viewlovers, Pasadena
1908 David B. Gamble House, Pasadena
Robert R. Blacker House additions, Pasadena
S. Hazard Halsted House alterations, Pasadena
Charles K. Silent House, Glendora (project)
William J. Lawless House, Sierra Madre
James W. Neill House additions, Pasadena
Theodore Irwin House alterations, Pasadena
Armenian Pilgrims Church, Fresno (project)
1909 John B. Phillips House additions, Pasadena
Charles M. Pratt House, Nordhoff
William R. Thorsen House, Berkeley
William W. Spinks Garage, Pasadena
Dr. S. S. Crow House, Pasadena
Earle C. Anthony House, Los Angeles
1910 John G. Neumeister House, Redondo (project)
John Lambert House, Pasadena (project)
John C. Bentz House alterations and additions, Pasadena
James A. Culbertson House additions, Pasadena
Ernest W. Smith House, Pasadena
James W. Neill House alterations, Pasadena
Howard Longley House alterations and additions, South Pasadena
Samuel L. Merrill House, Pasadena
Keith Spaulding Bunk House, Fillmore
John C. Bentz Garage, Pasadena
A. C. Drake House, Pasadena (project)
Henry M. Robinson House additions, Pasadena
1911 Alexander M. Drake House, Pasadena (project)
Mortimer Fleishhacker House, Woodside
S. Hazard Halsted House additions, Pasadena
William W. Spinks House alterations, Pasadena
Crow-Crocker Garage additions, Pasadena
Nathan Bentz House, Santa Barbara
Earle C. Anthony Automobile Showroom interiors, Los Angeles
Henry M. Greene House additions, Pasadena
Cordelia A. Culbertson House, Pasadena
Longfellow School, Pasadena
S. C. Graham House, Los Angeles (project)
Charles P. Wilcox House, Pasadena
Mrs. Charles G. Brown House, Pasadena
Pasadena Ice Company Building alterations, Pasadena
Joseph K. Huston House, Pasadena
1912 Mrs. Parker A. Earle Apartment House, Pasadena
Charles M. Pratt House alterations, Nordhoff
Annie Blacker House, Pasadena
Edward S. Crocker House, Pasadena
Dr. Frances F. Rowland House moving and alterations, Pasadena
Charles S. Greene House alterations and additions, Pasadena
Frank L. Palmer House, North Pomona (project)
S. Hazard Halsted House alterations and additions, Pasadena
Michael Kew House, San Diego
George A. Gibbs House additions, Pasadena
Vista del Arroyo Hotel east annex and bungalow alterations, Pasadena

Dr. Robert P. McReynolds House altera-
tions, Los Angeles
F. W. Hawks House alterations, Pasadena
J. S. Silverberg House alterations, San Mateo
1913 Henry A. Ware House, Pasadena
Earle C. Anthony House alterations and ad-
ditions, Los Angeles
Dr. Edward H. Angle House, Pasadena (pro-
ject)
William M. Ladd House, Nordhoff
Mrs. J. Herbert Ballentine House alterations
and additions, Altadena
Sidney D. Gamble House, Escondido (pro-
ject)
James W. Neill House alterations, Pasadena
1914 James A. Culbertson House additions,
Pasadena
Vista del Arroyo Building, Pasadena (project)
Dr. Rosa Engelmann House, Pasadena
Cordelia A. Culbertson House additions,
Pasadena
Charles S. Greene Garage, Pasadena
Theodore Irwin House additions, Pasadena
Henry A. Ware House additions, Pasadena
Dr. William T. Bolton House additions,
Pasadena
1915 John T. Greene House, Sacramento
Dr. Robert P. McReynolds House additions,
Los Angeles
Mortimer Fleischhacker House additions,
San Francisco
William E. Hamlin House, Pasadena
F. W. Hawks House alterations, Pasadena
Charles M. Pratt House alterations, Nordhoff
Dr. Nathan H. Williams House, Altadena
S. Hazard Halsted House alterations and ad-
ditions, Pasadena
Dr. Rosa Engelmann House additions,
Pasadena
Dr. Arthur A. Libby House additions,
Pasadena
Herbert Fleischhacker House alterations,
Atherton
Pasadena Ice Company Offices alterations
and additions, Pasadena
Pasadena Ice Company Ice Storage Building
additions, Pasadena
William E. Hamlin Garage, Pasadena
Dr. Frances F. Rowland House alterations,
Pasadena
1916 H.T. Proctor House, Cocoa Nut Beach,
Florida (project)
J. Herbert Hall Apartment House alterations
and additions, Pasadena
Dr. Robert P. McReynolds House altera-
tions, Los Angeles
Westmoreland Place Portals and Gates,
Pasadena
Mortimer Fleischhacker House additions,
Woodside
S. Hazard Halsted House additions and ga-
rage, Pasadena
1917 Charles H. Stoddard House, Burlingame
(project)
Dr. Martha J. Kuznik House, Hollywood
(project)
John H. Poole House, Pasadena
Earl C. Anthony House alterations and addi-
tions, Los Angeles
Cordelia A. Culbertson House alterations,
Pasadena
Henry M. Robinson House alterations and
additions, Pasadena
1919 John H. Poole House, Pasadena (project)
Hubert F. Krantz Development for Prospect
Park, Palm Beach Country, Florida (pro-
ject)
Hubert F. Krantz House, Pasadena (project)

Works (by Henry Mather Greene only; all California
unless noted)

1901 All Saints Episcopal Church alterations,
Pasadena

1917 Jennie A. Reeve House moving and altera-
tions, Long Beach
Charles S. Witbeck House, Santa Monica
Howard F. Mundorff House, Fresno
Dr. William T. Bolton House alterations,
Pasadena
1918 John Whitworth House additions, Altadena
1922 S. Hazard Halsted House alterations,
Pasadena
1923 Earle C. Anthony House moving, Beverly
Hills
Pasadena Drapery Workshop
1924 Thomas Gould Jr. House, Ventura
Mrs. J.H. Jones House garden plan, Pasadena
Mrs. Datus C. Smith House alterations and
garden, Pasadena
Mrs. Kate A. Kelley House, Los Angeles
Mrs. D.G. Wilson House alterations, Los An-
geles
Rev. Charles Hibbard House alterations,
Pasadena
Mrs. Paran F. Rice House additions, Mon-
rovia
1925 J.H. Huntoon Duplex, Visalia (project)
Earle C. Anthony House garden develop-
ment, Beverly Hills
Dr. Robert P. McReynolds House altera-
tions, Los Angeles
Haigag H. Khazoyan Store alterations,
Pasadena
A. C. Blumenthal Garage, Los Angeles
Walter D. Valentine Garage additions, Al-
tadena
Samuel Z. Mardian Store and Apartment
Building, Pasadena
William Thum House, Pasadena
Lloyd E. Morrison House, South Pasadena
"The Dugout," California Institute of Tech-
nology, Pasadena
Ernest E. Wennerberg Store alterations,
Pasadena
Miss Hatcher House, Pasadena (project)
Arthur Savage Duplex, Pasadena
Mary R. Darling House additions and garage,
Claremont
Mary R. Darling House garage, Claremont
James W. Neill House alterations, Pasadena
James Swan House alterations and moving,
Pasadena
1926 Mrs. C. P. Daly House, Ventura (project)
Pacific Southwest Trust and Savings Bank al-
terations, Pasadena
Dr. William T. Bolton House alterations,
Pasadena
Dr. Robert P. McReynolds House altera-
tions, Los Angeles
Mrs. James E. Saunders House, Pasadena
1927 Crow-Crocker House alterations and addi-
tions, Pasadena (project)
Jennie A. Reeve House alterations, additions
and second moving, Long Beach
1928 Lucy E. Wheeler House alterations, Los An-
geles
1929 Mrs. Edward Strasburg House, Covina
Walter L. Richardson House, Porterville
Whitworth Corporation Building alterations,
Pasadena
1930 Frank M. Brininstool House alterations,
Pasadena
Mrs. Carrie Whitworth House alterations,
Altadena
Mrs. Fred W. Horne House alterations,
Pasadena
1931 Emma M. Black House alterations, Pasadena
Cordelia A. Culbertson House potting house
addition, Pasadena
1932 George W. Gain House alterations, Pasadena
B. O. Kendall House alterations, Pasadena
1933 George F. Kernaghan House alterations,
Pasadena (project)
Carl Mencerberg Shop, Pasadena (project)
William H. Rapp House alterations,
Pasadena (project)

James Howard House alterations, Pasadena
1934 William M. Beeson Shop Building, Pasadena
(engineering consultant)
1935 Howard K. Brick House, Philadelphia (project)
L. C. Johnson Garage, Altadena
George H. Barker House alterations,
Pasadena
William H. Sloane House alterations and additions to garage, South Pasadena
1936 J. M. Ritson House alterations, Pasadena
1938 Cordelia A. Culbertson House alterations,
Pasadena
1941 Mrs. Louise Thum House alterations and additions, Glendora
1943 Mrs. James E. Saunders House alterations,
Pasadena
1944 William S. Greene House, Pittsburg (project)

Publications:

On the GREENES: books—*Five California Architects* by Esther McCoy, New York 1960; *Greene
and Greene: Architects in the Residential Style* by
William Current, Fort Worth, Texas 1974; *A Greene
and Greene Guide* by Janann Strand, Pasadena, California 1974; *A Guide to the Works of Greene and
Greene* by Randell L. Makinson, Salt Lake City
1974; *Greene and Greene Collection in the Avery Li-
brary: Inventory and Index* by John K. McAskill,
New York 1976; *Greene and Greene* by Randell L.
Makinson, volume I: *Architecture as a Fine Art,* vol-
ume II: *Furniture and Related Designs,* Salt Lake
City, 1977, 1979. articles—"Greene and Greene" by
Jean Murray Bangs in *Architectural Forum* (New
York), October 1948; "A obra dos irmaos Greene"
by Jean Murray Bangs in *Arquitectura Portuguesa*
(Lisbon), April/June 1949; "Greene and Greene of
Pasadena" by L. Morgan Yost in *AIA Journal*
(Washington, D.C.), September 1950; "Prophets
Without Honor" by Jean Murray Bangs in *AIA Jour-
nal* (Washington, D.C.), July 1952; "Notes on
Greene and Greene" by Esther McCoy in *Arts and
Architecture* (Los Angeles), July 1953; "California:
The Emergence of a Tradition" in *Architectural Re-
cord* (New York), May 1956; "Roots of California
Contemporary Architecture" by Esther McCoy in
Arts and Architecture (Los Angeles), October 1956;
"Recognizing Our Own Architectural Traditions"
in *House Beautiful* (New York), January 1957; "A
Parting Salute to the Fathers of the California Style"
in *House and Home* (New York), August 1957;
"Some Sources of Greene and Greene" by Clay Lan-
caster in *AIA Journal* (Washington, D.C.), August
1960; "The Gamble House by Greene and Greene"
in the *Prairie School Review* (Chicago), no. 4, 1968;
"Architecture West" in *Progressive Architecture*
(New York), November 1972; "Greene and Greene"
by Randell L. Makinson in *Approach* (Tokyo),
Spring 1975; "The Brothers Greene" by Harwell
Hamilton Harris in *Architectural Record* (New
York), November 1975; "Recent Books on Greene
and Greene" by Esther McCoy in *Progressive Archi-
tecture* (New York), January 1976; "Greene and
Greene" by Philip Jodidio in *Connaissance des Arts*
(Paris), December 1977; "Greene and Greene" in
American Preservation (Little Rock, Arkansas),
April/May 1978.

For nearly a decade the young architects Greene and
Greene explored and experimented with a variety of
styles in their search for an architectural expression
that, in their minds, would represent the natural
living patterns and regional characteristics of California. They had been trained in the principles of
William Morris, enchanted by the California missions, intrigued by the valley landscapes, fascinated
by Oriental art and architecture and by the publication of Swiss chalets and Italian gardens and villas.
In 1902 their dramatic shift from traditional styles
and their embrace of the concepts of the Arts and
Crafts Movement was clearly revealed in the James

Culbertson house. Although the exterior was reminiscent of the half-timbered construction of English country houses, their use of local cobblestones and clinker brick, the influence of Japanese timber construction in the interiors, and the selection of Gustav Stickley furnishings suggested a more relaxed life style. The brothers themselves regarded their 1903 bungalow for Arturo Bandini as the turning point in their work. The significance of this design, however, lay in its "U"-shaped courtyard plan, incorporating the garden into the total living pattern and introducing floor plan concepts into the Greenes' work that were less formal and a synthesis of relationships between indoor and outdoor space.

The elements of true care and craftsmanship appeared in various of their designs during 1902 and 1903, but it was the 1904 house for Jennie A. Reeve that brought together, for the first time, the full range of the Greenes' architectural vocabulary and established their California Bungalow style. Here in this two-story shingle-clad bungalow were the articulated timber structure, multiple gabled overhanging roofs, projecting support beams now carefully shaped on the ends, open sleeping porches, vertical slit windows, horizontal bands of casement windows, combinations of cobblestones and brick masonry, leaded stained glass and lantern designs, the coordination of landscape, walks, fencing and gates, and the full development of furniture and interior accessories. Here, as in other unpretentious designs, they demonstrated that modest dwellings could be endowed with grace, dignity and character.

In the Adelaide Tichenor house, also of 1904, their growing interest in the Orient was reflected throughout the structure, interiors and gardens. At this time their own furniture designs began to depart from the four-square directness of Stickley's work. The lines of their designs were more relaxed, and, as their experience and convictions grew, they gracefully combined integrity, craftsmanship and human personality into their works.

As larger commissions came into the office the Greenes, through careful handling, easily adapted the bungalow philosophies for more sophisticated designs by stretching its flexibility of concept and their personal sensitivities to the fullest. Structure and site became one. In order to relate the larger structures to the landscape, they emphasized and expressed the horizontal line in cantilevered roof lines, broad bands of casement windows, and sleeping porches. Outdoor terraces with wide stairways provided positive transitions to the grounds. The Greenes firmly maintained that a wooden structure should express the integrity and identity of each separate part, each treated as a design element. It was their handling of this concept that produced a symphony of wooden joinery. Wood panelling and trim were fastened with brass screws covered at times with square pegs of ebony, mahogany and oak. Woodwork was brought together in different planes. Materials other than wood—brick, tile, boulders, metal and glass—retained their own identity and function, yet each contributed to the richness of the total composition. No detail was overlooked. Every peg, wedge, downspout, air vent, and fixture was designed into the whole.

At the height of their career, in the elaborate residences designed between 1907 and 1910, the Greenes' meticulous attention to detail, their insistence upon the highest quality of craftsmanship and materials, and the latitude given by clients for the design of nearly all of the interior furnishings developed in the brothers so exalted a set of standards for their work that soon very few people were able to afford their creations. At this same time public tastes were changing, poor emulation of their work obscured the progressive spirit and integrity of the originals, and thus fewer and fewer commissions came into their offices. Concurrently the brothers' individual interests again surfaced. Charles in particular wanted time to pursue his painting, photography, writing and philosophical studies. The brothers' mutual respect allowed each of them to follow an

independent path while they continued to work together. In the years that followed, their independent commissions and the clearly identifiable individual input into joint work attest to their unique and varying personal genius.

Today, their reputation as the leading architects of the Arts and Crafts Movement in America presently rests on the incredible craftsmanship and progressive designs for their ultimate bungalows for the Blacker, Ford, Gamble, Pratt, Thorsen and Culbertson families. Time will, however, focus considerable importance upon the swift evolution and refinements of their works between 1902 and 1906 as well as their independent designs after 1910, where their personal responses to changing attitudes reveals the brothers' sensitivity to each new day, client and site.

—Randell L. Makinson

GREENE, Herb(ert).

American. Born in Oneonta, New York, 13 September 1929. Educated at Syracuse University, New York, 1947; University of Oklahoma, Norman, under Bruce Goff, 1948–52 (First Prize, Indiana Limestone Competition, 1951), B.Arch. 1952. Married Mary Morrison in 1955; children: Tom and Lauren; married Nanine Hilliard in 1977. Worked in the office of John Lautner, Hollywood, California, 1952, Bruce Goff, Norman, Oklahoma, 1950–53, and Wirtz, Calhoun, Tungate and Jackson, Houston, Texas, 1954; Associate Architect with Joseph Krakower, Houston, 1955–57. In private practice, Houston and Norman, 1957–64, and in Lexington, Kentucky, since 1964. Associate Professor, University of Oklahoma, 1957–63. Since 1963, Professor of Architecture, University of Kentucky, Lexington. Exhibitions: *Modern Architecture U.S.A.*, Museum of Modern Art, New York, 1965; *American Churches*, United States Information Agency tour of Europe, 1966; *Environmental Architecture*, Kansas City Art Institute, Missouri, 1967; Florence Duhl Gallery, New York (one-man show of architectural drawings), 1977; *An American Architecture*, Milwaukee Art Center, 1977. Also a painter; exhibitions—Oklahoma City Art Museum, 1962; *Illinois Biennial*, 1965; Fine Arts Gallery, University of Arkansas,

Fayetteville (one-man), 1966; Kovler Gallery, Chicago (one-man), 1966; Phoenix Gallery, New York (one-man), 1970, 1971; University of Kentucky Fine Arts Gallery (one-man), 1974; Living Arts and Science Center, Lexington (one-man), 1975; Lousville Arts Association (one-man), 1976. Recipient: National Endowments for the Arts Grant, 1977. Address: 75 Hampton Court, Lexington, Kentucky 40508, U.S.A.

Works:

1955 Lurie House, Houston (with Joseph Krakower)
Rainey House, Houston (with Joseph Krakower)
Gulf Coast Finance Company Offices, Houston (with Joseph Krakower)
1956 Long Point Clinic, Houston (with Joseph Krakower)
Folloder House, Houston (with Joseph Krakower)
Houston Typewriter Exchange Building (with Joseph Krakower)
Salsman House, Houston (with Joseph Krakower)
Mendel House, Houston (with Joseph Krakower)
1957 Lyne House, Houston
1958 Southwestern Bell Telephone Company Office Building, Houston
Baylor Medical College Research Building, Houston (project)
1960 Mr. and Mrs. John Joyce House, Snyder, Oklahoma
Roosevelt Granite Company Offices, Snyder, Oklahoma
Burton's IGA Supermarket, Holdenville, Oklahoma
Northwestern Electric Cooperative Office and Warehouse alterations, Woodward, Oklahoma
1961 Herb and Mary Greene House ("Prairie House"), Norman, Oklahoma
Downtown urban remodelling plan for Norman, Oklahoma
Lyons House and Museum, Holdenville, Oklahoma
1962 Metropolitan Pedestrian Overpass System (project)
Theatre-in-the-Round (project)

Herb Greene: Greene House ("Prairie House"), Norman, Oklahoma, 1961

1964 Housing for the Elderly, Paris, Kentucky (with Jim Clark)
  Low-Cost Mountain Housing Research Project, Eastern Kentucky
  Dr. and Mrs. Earl Cunningham House, Quail Creed Road, Oklahoma City (with Robert Alan Bowlby)
  Unitarian Church, Higbee Mill Road, Lexington, Kentucky
1966 Painting and photography research project, Lexington, Kentucky
  Dr. and Mrs. Richard French House, Paynes Mill Road, Versailles, Kentucky
1967 Multi-Use Space for Urban Areas (project; with C. A. Coleman, Jr.)
  Mr. and Mrs. Harry Furchess House, Murray, Kentucky
1969 Mr. and Mrs. Philip Lovaas House, Grimes Mill Road, Lexington, Kentucky
1970 Parking Structure II, University of Kentucky, Lexington (design consultant; with C. A. Coleman, Jr.)
  University of Kentucky Academic Facilities Building, Ashland Community College, Ashland, Kentucky (design consultant; with C. A. Coleman, Jr.)
  Community Park Shelter, Lexington, Kentucky (with C. A. Coleman, Jr.)
1971 Dr. and Mrs. Will Ward House, 5801 Orion Road, Glenview, Kentucky
  Polyurethane foam experimental project, Lexington, Kentucky
1972 Courtyard Housing (project)
1974 Medical Center, Harrodsburg Road, Lexington, Kentucky
  Dr. and Mrs. Richard O'Neill House, Evans Mill Road, Lexington, Kentucky
1978 Urban studies and armatures (projects)
  Dr. and Mrs. Clinton Cook House, Glenview, Kentucky

Publications:

By GREENE: book—*Mind and Image: An Essay on Art and Architecture,* Lexington 1976; articles—in *The Kentucky Architect* (Louisville), October 1966, June 1968, July 1968.

On GREENE: books—*Photography of Architecture* by Julius Shulman, Los Angeles 1964; *Residential Architecture in America* by Helmut Borchardt, Munich 1965; *Architecture at Rice, 15,* Houston 1965; *Architects on Architecture,* edited by Paul Heyer, New York 1966, London 1967; *Photographic History of Modern Architecture* by Dennis Sharp, New York 1972; *Modern Movements in Architecture* by Charles Jencks, New York 1973; *Ad Hocism* by Charles Jencks and Nathan Silver, New York 1973; articles —"Greene Residence" in *Architectural Design* (London), May 1957; "Greene Residence" in *Progressive Architecture* (New York), May 1962; "Greene Residence" in *L'Architecture d'Aujourd'hui* (Paris), June 1962; "Greene Residence" in *Life* (New York), November 1962; "Joyce Residence" in *Progressive Architecture* (New York), November 1962; "Greene Residence" in *Look* (New York), September 1963; "Cunningham Residence" in *Progressive Architecture* (New York), May 1965; "The Unitarian Church of Lexington" in *Progressive Architecture* (New York), March 1966; "A Modern Farmhouse for the Kentucky Blue Grass" in *The Kentucky Architect* (Louisville), June 1966; "The Paintings of Herb Greene" in *Arts and Architecture* (Los Angeles), November 1967; "Four House Projects" in *Progressive Architecture* (New York), August 1968.

I conceive the architectural image as an assemblage to which significant harmonized experience of the user and the audience can be attached. Ideas of shelter, sanctuary, social gathering, valued historic ar-

chitecture, characteristics of particular sites and climate are primary sources for images, as are feelings and associations from bodily life and memory.

The Prairie House (illustrated) communicates protection by enveloping forms. The soft textures, rhythms and warm color of the shingles and boards seem human. At the same time they relate the house to the American shingle style and the exposed prairie site which is left in a natural condition. Ideas such as looking out at the world and bodily sentience are also consciously included. The image contains references ranging from primordial creature to futurist object and represents my interest in creating metaphors of age and the passage of time.

I am at present developing new forms of urban architecture in which similar aims are expressed in long-lasting frameworks or armatures that can be added to by many participants over generations. Human beings, with our unique ability to remember and anticipate, need to develop an architecture whose primary esthetic impact gives direction to an imaginative mingling of past, present and future. This architecture, as a built continuum, should be a receptacle for many individualized acts of expression which are symbolic of a democratic society and the diversity and indeterminacy of the world. Orchestrated in an armature whose forms are grounded in long-sanctioned relationships to region and historic form, individualized acts become a mosaic for reverie and a record of social and esthetic comment.

—Herb Greene

Herb Greene is the major prophet of American vernacular high-art architecture practicing today. His Prairie House of 1961 quickly established him as the primary artistic spokesman for the organicism developed by Bruce Goff from elements of the Frank Lloyd Wright heritage. The continuity with Wright and Goff is evident in the use of native materials, ikonic organic forms, comfortable sheltering proportions, and in the integration into the solid earth of the site and the human culture of the region. While the continuity of form is evident, the new departure is both striking and daring. Prairie House, much more than an organic form of bird-pyramid that settled down on the Oklahoma prairie, is a personal talisman or sheltering power-object and transformation place of the Greene family.

Wright's struggles for a contemporary organicism were always in the context of the prototypic rather than the personal solution to the shelter problems if not of the whole world, then at least of America. Goff's fantasy places were indeed unique creations, but they also remained on an impersonal plane of purely formal aestheticism. It is the infusion of the personal statement into the fixed medicine-bag of the abode that transforms this ikonic tradition into Greene's talismanic Prairie House. In creating a personal statement, a modern vernacular becomes possible, and the "professionalism" of the architect comes under severe strain.

It is to the tension between the personalism of the truly organic power object and the universalism of our conception of art that I referred when I said "vernacular high-art architecture." On the face of it, this is a contradiction in terms, a contradiction that has at least in part been responsible for the divergence in Greene's more recent work. The highly personalistic and subjective has become increasingly concentrated into collages, which, hung on a wall, are sharable talismanic objects. The residences and projects have evolved into much more "general" solutions that leave room for personalization by users and inhabitants.

This divergence in Greene's work may be both unfortunate and inevitable. Yet, one is struck by the enormous influence that Greene's early work has had on self-built housing in the late 1960's and since, particularly in California and in mountainous regions in the United States. Similarly, attempts to "give away" architecture as a profession, as in the populist projects of Christopher Alexander and his

group, have radically redefined the role of the architect as professional in an evolution toward a new vernacular folk art in the built environment. Prairie House can be seen as the starting point of both of these trends—a starting point from which Greene has himself retreated perhaps due to a high regard for museum art or the exigencies of professional career, or both.

Alternatively, Greene may have correctly perceived that the exterior shells that house private lives gain their power in and through use rather than through the direct formal reflection of the dreams they shelter. Instead of giving a place, form, and habitation to a dream then, the architectural artist may only make it possible to create a safe place for dreaming.

—Joseph B. Juhasz

GREGOTTI, Vittorio.

Italian. Born in Novara, Italy, 10 August 1927. Educated at the Milan Polytechnic, School of Architecture, 1948–52, Dip.Arch. 1952. Married Marina Mazza in 1975. Partner, with Lodovico Meneghetti and Giotto Stoppino, Architetti Associati, Milan, 1952–67; in private practice, Milan, 1968–74. Since 1974, Partner, with Pierluigi Cerri and Hiromichi Matsui, Gregotti Associati, Milan. Architectural Consultant, La Rinascente Stores Group, Milan, 1968–71; Director, Visual Arts Section, *Biennale,* Venice, 1974–76. Professor of Architectural Composition, Milan Polytechnic, since 1964, and School of Architecture, Venice, since 1978. Associate Editor, with Ernesto N. Rogers, *Casabella,* Milan, 1952–60; Editor, *Edilizia Moderna* monographs, Milan, 1962–64; Architectural Editor, *Il Verri,* Milan, 1963–65. Co-Editor, *Lotus,* Venice, since 1974. Exhibitions: *Triennale,* Milan, since 1951. Recipient: Grand Prize, *Triennale,* Milan, 1963; Compasso d'Oro, Milan, 1968; First Prize, IACP Housing Development Competition, Palermo, 1970; First Prize, University of Florence Competition, 1971; First Prize, University of Calabria Competition, 1973. Address: Gregotti Associati, via Bandello 20, 20123 Milan, Italy.

Works:

1953 Exhibition Pavilion, *Market Fair,* Novara, Italy
1956 Worker's house, Novara, Italy
1958/
 59 3 apartment buildings, Novara, Italy
  Istituto di Credito Headquarters, Novara, Italy
1961/
 62 Co-operative housing development, Novara, Italy
  Cottage on a Slope, near Varese, Italy (project)
  3 single-family houses, Lake Maggiore, near Stresa, Italy (project)
1962 2 houses, Portofino, Italy (project)
1962/
 67 Co-operative housing development, via Palmanova, Milan
  Master plan for the city of Novara, Italy
1964 Entrance Pavilion, *Triennale,* Milan (with Peppo Brivio)
1964/
 68 Co-operative housing development, via Desiderio Settignano, Milan
1967 Gregotti Apartment conversion, via Regaldi 2, Milan
1968 Bossi Cotton Mill, Novara, Italy
  Istituto di Credito Headquarters, Bra, Italy
1969 La Rinascente Supermarket, Milan
  La Rinascente Supermarket II, Milan

La Rinascente Department Store, via Carlo Alberto, Turin (project)

La Rinascente Department Store, via Ruggero Settimo, Palermo (project)

1970/
72 Science Department, University of Palermo
1970- IACP Zen Housing Development, Cardillo District, Palermo
1971/
78 Community Centre, Gibellina, Sicily
1971- New buildings, University of Florence
1972/
74 Gabel's Offices and Warehouse, Como
1972/
75 New University of Calabria, Cosenza, Italy
1974/
75 Ricordi Music Store, Milan

Publications:

By GREGOTTI: books—*Territorio dell'Architettura,* Milan 1966; *New Directions in Italian Architecture,* London 1968, New York 1969; articles—"Marco Zanuso, un Architetto della Seconda Generazione" in *Casabella* (Milan), no. 216, 1957; "Complessita di Max Bill" in *Casabella* (Milan), no. 228, 1959; "Classicita a Razionalismo di Auguste Perret" in *Casabella* (Milan), no. 229, 1959; "Peter Behrens 1868–1940" in *Casabella* (Milan), no. 240, 1960; "L'Architettura dell'Expressionismo" in *Casabella* (Milan), no. 254, 1961; "Facolta del Costruire" in *Casabella* (Milan), May 1964; "La Ricerca Storica in Architettura" in *Edilizia Moderna* (Milan), no. 86, 1965; "L'Art Nouveau" in *L'Arte Moderna* (Milan), no. 91, 1967; "L'Architettura Tedesca dal 1900 al 1930" in *L'Arte Moderna* (Milan), no. 94, 1967; "Les Nouvelles Tendances de l'Architecture Italienne" in *L'Architecture d'Aujourd'hui* (Paris), September 1968; "Italian Design 1945–1971" in *Italy: The New Domestic Landscape,* exhibition catalogue, New York 1972; "ANIACAP/IN/ARCH Competition for Low-Cost Housing" in *Domus* (Milan), October 1973; "Auguste Perret 1874–1974," with Jean Prouvé, in *Domus* (Milan), May 1974; "Per una Storia del Design Italiano" in *Ottagono* (Milan), nos. 32, 33, 34, 36, 1974. "For Which Modern Movement?" in *Parametro* (Bologna), June 1977; "Palermo: The Necessity of Architecture," with Pierluigi Nicolin, in *Casabella* (Milan), September 1977; "Bellinzona: Architecture for the Ancient City" in *Casabella* (Milan), November 1977; "Il Filo Rosso del Razionalismo Italiano" in *Casabella* (Milan), no. 440–441, 1978.

On GREGOTTI: articles—"Padiglioni in un Parco alla Terza Fiera-Mercato di Novara" in *Domus* (Milan), December 1953; "Case d'Affito a Novara 1958–59" in *Casabella* (Milan), July 1960; "Due Case di Portofino 1962" in *Casabella* (Milan), no. 276, 1963; "Architettura Italiana 1963," special issue of *Edilizia Moderna* (Milan), no. 82/83, 1964; "Contemporary Italian Architects" in *L'Architecture d'Aujourd'hui* (Paris), no. 48, 1965; "Apartment in Milan" in *House and Garden* (London), March 1968; "Le Cento Città d'Italia: Milano" in *Controspazio* (Bari, Italy), September/October 1969; "L'Architettura Interrota: Tre Progetti di Vittorio Gregotti" in *Controspazio* (Bari, Italy), March 1971; "Civile Abitazione: Complessita di Linguaggio per il Recupero dell'Unita Architettonica alla Periferia di Milano" in *Casabella* (Milan), April 1972; "Vittorio Gregotti" in *Architecture + Urbanism* (Tokyo), July 1977.

Vittorio Gregotti's career spans a wide artistic spectrum. He is well known as an architect and planner; he has also been involved in furniture and industrial design; and he is a prolific writer and an impresario. During the period of his co-editorship with Ernesto N. Rogers of *Casabella,* he became the main apologist of the Art Nouveau revival (Stile Liberta), but his essays have a forthright quality that puts them

above the more morbid and extreme exercises in the style.

Gregotti's commitment to historicism was very sophisticated, and he soon passed beyond the limitations that the revival imposed—as may be seen in his section of the *XIII Triennale* in Milan, a radical departure in exhibition design. In his most important book to date, *Territorio dell'Architettura,* he sets out his theoretical position, which owes something to phenomenology and something to the structuralists. It also discusses the planner's almost geographical concern with environment, which has been one of Gregotti's overriding interests, evident in his early plan of Novara and in his more recent planning work, explicitly in the winning schemes for the universities of Florence and Calabria. His architecture, meanwhile, was becoming increasingly stereometric. The Architetti Associati office was dissolved in the late 1960's, and thereafter Gregotti became an independent practitioner, working with a number of different associates. The most considerable of his later works is the Zen Housing Development in Palermo.

His exhibition work and his writings have made Gregotti one of the best-known architects of his generation in Italy. Although the volume of his built work to date is not vast, all that he has done has had a great influence. His development has been accompanied by polemics that have elucidated the rationale of every step he has taken, in a way that cannot be paralleled by any other European architect.

—Joseph Rykwert

GRIFFIN, Walter Burley.

American. Born in Maywood, Illinois, 24 November 1876. Educated at Oak Park High School, Illinois, graduated 1895; University of Illinois, Urbana, 1895–99, B.A. 1899. Married the architect Marion Lucy Mahoney in 1911, who subsequently worked as his draftsman. Worked in Chicago on commission and in the offices of various architects, including Dwight Perkins, Robert Spencer and Webster Tomlinson, 1899–1901; worked for Frank Lloyd Wright, Chicago, 1901–05; in private practice, Chicago, 1905–14, in association with Barry Byrne, 1913–14; Director of Design and Construction for the New Federal Capital of Australia, Canberra, 1913–20; in private practice, Australia, 1915–35: designed and patented the Knitlock system of construction, 1917; involved in the development and promotion of Castlecrag residential suburb, Sydney, 1921–35; accepted commission to design library for the University of Lucknow, and left Australia for India, 1935: lived in Lucknow, 1935 until his death, 1937. Exhibitions: *Clay Products Exposition,* Chicago, 1913. Collections (drawings): Avery Library, Columbia University, New York; New York Historical Society Archives; Burnham Library, Art Institute of Chicago; Department of Art, Northwestern University, Evanston, Illinois. Recipient: First Prize, New Capital of Australia Competition, Canberra, 1912. *Died (in Lucknow, India) 11 February 1937.*

Works:

1898 Elmhurst Electric Light and Power Cottage, Illinois (elevations)
1900 C. A. Stone Barn, Elmhurst, Illinois
Wilder Barn, Elmhurst, Illinois
Compton Garage and Barn, Glencoe, Illinois
Landscaping for Eastern Illinois State Normal School, Charleston
1901 Elmhurst Golf Club, Illinois
1901/
02 Emery House, Elmhurst, Illinois
1906 Iverson House, Chicago
Landscaping for Northern Illinois State Normal School, DeKalb

Jenkins/Lewis/Dickinson House, Hollister, California (project)
1907 Temple of Music, Riverside, Illinois (project)
Hall Cottage, Glencoe, Illinois (project)
1908 Orth Twin Houses, Kenilworth, Illinois
F. W. Itte House, Chicago
P. Itte House, Chicago
Bovee House, Evanston, Illinois
Gauler Twin Houses, Edgewater, Chicago
Moulton House, Chicago
1909 Sloan House, Elmhurst, Illinois
Ralph Griffin House, Edwardsville, Illinois
Niles Club, Michigan
Gunn House, Chicago
Garrity House, Chicago
Fox Store and Apartment, Chicago
Amberg House landscaping, Grand Rapids, Michigan
Bolte House landscaping, Hubbard Woods, Illinois
1910 Dr. Stecher House, Maywood, Illinois
Carter House, Evanston, Illinois
Blount House, Chicago
Olmsted House, Chicago
Mueller House landscaping, Decatur, Illinois
Cooley House, Monroe, Louisiana
Dickinson House Street Scheme (project)
Marshall House, Kenilworth, Illinois (project)
1911 Ricker House, Grinnell, Iowa
Bovee Cottage, Ludington, Michigan
Irving House landscaping, Decatur, Illinois
Van Nostrand House, Chicago
Tolles House, Chicago
Bayless House, Evanston, Illinois (project)
Purnell House, Attica, Indiana (project)
Shirley House, Chicago (project)
Ravines Private Community landscaping (project)
Community Center, and E. J. Staten Store, Idalia, Florida (project)
1912 Comstock House I and II and landscaping, Evanston, Illinois
Melson House, Mason City, Iowa
Rule House, Mason City, Iowa
Page House, Mason City, Iowa
Mess House, Winnetka, Illinois
Community plan for Rock Crest/Rock Glen, Mason City, Iowa
Blunt House, Chicago
Salmon House, Chicago
Jenkinson House, Chicago
Ridge Quadrangles, Chicago (project)
Plan for the Trier Center Neighborhood, Winnetka, Illinois
Walter Burley Griffin House, Trier Center, Winnetka, Illinois (project)
First House, Trier Center, Winnetka, Illinois (project)
House of Interlocking Squares, Trier Center, Winnetka, Illinois (project)
Harvey Community Plan, West Chicago
Holahan House, Mason City, Iowa (project)
Emory Hills Community Plan, Wheaton, Illinois
Dudley Walker House, Wheaton, Illinois (project)
Community plan for the Rogers Park district, Chicago
Wilder Community Plan, Elmhurst, Illinois
Temple House, Chicago (project)
City Club of Chicago (competition project; with Edgar H. Lawrence)
1913 Blythe House, Mason City, Iowa
Schneider House, Mason City, Iowa
Stinson Memorial Library, Anna, Illinois
Furneaux House, Chicago
Clarke House, Chicago
P. F. Volland Offices, Monroe Building, Chicago
Hugh Gilmore House, Mason City, Iowa (with Barry Byrne; completed to Byrne design)

Walter Burley Griffin: Incinerator, Willoughby, New South Wales, 1934

Model Brick Cottage, *Clay Products Exposition,* Chicago
Monroe Club, Monroe, Louisiana (project)
Melson House, Mason City, Iowa (project; with Barry Byrne)
Franke House, Fort Wayne, Indiana (project; with Barry Byrne)
Koehne House, Palm Beach, Florida (project)
Cohn Two-Flat Building, Chicago (project)
1913/
20 Federal Capital City of Australia, Canberra
1914 Clark Memorial Fountain, Grinnell, Iowa
Temple Houses (2), Winnetka, Illinois
Hornbaker House, Chicago
Collins House, Melbourne (with A. S. Eggleston)
Rasmussen House, Moore Park, Sydney (with Clamp)
Palais de Danse, St. Kilda, Victoria
Holy Trinity Church, Dulwich Hill, Sydney (with Clamp; completed to a Clamp design)
Street environment, Lower Esplanade, St. Kilda, Victoria

Plan for the University of Sydney
Workmen's Cottages, Canberra (project)
Melbourne Post Office remodelling (as consultant)
Morse House, Ithaca, New York (project)
City plan for Leeton, New South Wales
City plan for Griffith, New South Wales
1915 Cafe Australia, Melbourne
Australia House, Sydney (with Clamp)
Henry George League Club Rooms and Shops, Melbourne
Plan for the University of New Mexico at Albuquerque
Chemistry Building, University of New Mexico at Albuquerque (project; with Barry Byrne)
Liberty Hall, Melbourne (project)
Plan for the University of Western Australia, Perth
Graham House, Toorak, Victoria (project)
Fairy Harbour Estate, Manly, Sydney (project)
1915/
17 Newman College, University of Melbourne (with August Fritsch)

1916 City plan for Tuggeranong, A.C.T.
1916/
17 General Post Office alterations and additions, Sydney (project)
1916/
23 Community plan for Mount Eagle (Eaglemont), Heidelberg, Victoria
1917 Quartermaster's Store, Duntroon, A.C.T.
Administration Building, Duntroon, A.C.T.
Community plan for City View Estates, East Keilor, Victoria
Canteen, Duntroon, A.C.T. (project)
Australia Picture Palace (Paris) Theatre, Sydney (with Clamp)
1918 Arcadia Restaurant, Upper Esplanade, St. Kilda, Victoria
Lippincott House, Eaglemont, Victoria
1919 Kindergarten, Methodist Church, Kew, Victoria (with Roy Lippincott)
Barrachi House landscaping, Ivanhoe, Victoria
Soldiers' Club, Toowoomba, Queensland (project)
City plan for Port Stephens, New South Wales
Jervis Bay City Home extension, New South Wales (project)
1920 Home of Five Rooms, Melbourne (project)
Young Australia League, Perth (project)
Major General Sir William T. Bridges Tomb, Canberra, A.C.T.
1920/
35 Community plan for Castlecrag, New South Wales
1921 Walter Burley Griffin House ("Pholiota"), Eaglemont, Victoria
Skipper House, Eaglemont, Victoria
Johnson House, Parapet, Castlecrag, New South Wales
Moon House, Parapet, Castlecrag, New South Wales
1922 Chinese National Society Rooms, Melbourne
Twin Cottages, Olivers Hill, Frankston, Victoria
Real Estate Office, Carrum, Victoria
O'Malley House, Sortie Point, Castlecrag, New South Wales
Cheong House, Parapet, Castlecrag, New South Wales
Ferguson Twin Dwellings, Parapet, Castlecrag, New South Wales
Towler House, Castlecrag, New South Wales (project)
Barwon Heads Golf Club, Geelong, Victoria (project)
1923 Salter House, Toorak, Victoria
Community plan for Croydon Hills Estate, Victoria
Railway Yards Reclamation, Jolimont, Melbourne (project; with Nicholls)
Ascot Theatre, Ascot Vale, Victoria (project)
White Sales Building, Melbourne (project)
1924 Capitol Theatre, Melbourne (with Peck and Kemper)
Clendon Lodge, Toorak, Victoria
Leonard House, Melbourne
Vaughan Griffin House, Heidelberg, Victoria
Jefferies House, Surrey Hills, Victoria
Paling House, Toorak, Victoria
Felsted House, Edinburgh, Castlecrag, New South Wales
Shops, Edinburgh, Castlecrag, New South Wales
Community plan for Ranelagh Estates, Mornington Parish, Victoria
Kanewsky Mercantile Building, Latrobe Parade, Victoria (project)
1925 Guy House, Parapet, Castlecrag, New South Wales
Palais Pictures, St. Kilda, Victoria
Chapel, Scotch College, Melbourne (competition project)
Alexandra Gardens Kiosk, Melbourne (competition project)

Wearne and Finlay Semi-Detached Housing, Castlecrag, New South Wales (project)

1926 Creswick House, Barbette, Castlecrag, New South Wales

Manager's Quarters, Castlecrag, New South Wales

Shops, High Street/Glenferrie Road, Malvern, Victoria

Community plan for Middlecove, New South Wales

Wirth House, Castlecrag, New South Wales (project)

Mower House, Castlecrag, New South Wales (project)

1927 Barrachi House, Fairfield, Victoria

Romance Theatre, Melbourne (project)

The Cloisters, Toorak, Victoria (project)

Cromer Sanatorium, Castlecrag, New South Wales (project)

1928 Langi Flats, Lansell, Toorak, Victoria

Rivett House, Sortie Point, Castlecrag, New South Wales

Cabarisha Private Hospital, Sortie Point, Castlecrag, New South Wales

Community plan for Milleara Estates, East Keilor, Victoria

Duncan House, Castlecrag, New South Wales (project)

1929 Lucas House remodelling and landscaping, Frankston, Victoria

Wilson House, Barbette, Castlecrag, New South Wales

Fyshwick House, Citadel, Castlecrag, New South Wales

Incinerator, Kuring-gai, New South Wales

Incinerator, Moonee Ponds, Victoria

Wills House, Woodend, Victoria

Incinerator, Unley, South Australia (project)

Keith Drygoods Building, Melbourne (project)

Lee House, Castlecrag, New South Wales (project)

Holman House, Castlecrag, New South Wales (project)

Garett House, Castlecrag, New South Wales (project)

Symington House, Castlecrag, New South Wales (project)

Richards House, Castlecrag, New South Wales (project)

1930 Williams House remodelling, Toorak, Victoria

Incinerator, Granville, New South Wales (project)

1931 Nurses' Quarters, Castlecrag, New South Wales

Incinerator, Waratah, New South Wales

Castlecove Golf Club Pro Shop, Castlecrag, New South Wales

Community plan for Castlecove, New South Wales

1932 Cameron House, Killara, New South Wales

Incinerator, Randwick, New South Wales

Incinerator, Moore Park, Sydney (project)

Incinerator, Chatswood, New South Wales (project)

1933 James House, Avalon, New South Wales

Duncan House, Barbette, Castlecrag, New South Wales

Incinerator, The Globe, Sydney

"A Residence," Haven Estate, Castlecrag, New South Wales (project)

1934 Incinerator, Brunswick, Victoria

David Pratten House, Pymble, New South Wales

Incinerator, Willoughby, New South Wales

Incinerator, Pyrmont, New South Wales

Winter House, Telopea, New South Wales

Eric Pratten House, Pymble, New South Wales

Incinerator, Hindmarsh, South Australia

Incinerator, Ipswich, Queensland

Incinerator, Covecrag, New South Wales (project)

Campus plan for the University of Lucknow, India

1935/
36 Library, University of Lucknow, India (project)

1936 Incinerator, Leichhardt, New South Wales

Van der Lay Duplex, Clifton Gardens, Sydney

Incinerator, Thebarton, South Australia

Watson House, Pymble, New South Wales

Incinerator, Lane Cove, New South Wales (project)

Narian Singh House, Benares, India

Mather House, Lucknow, India (partially realized)

Community plan for Agra, India

House for the Treasurer of Benares University, India (project)

Mosque for the Raja of Jahangirabad, India (project)

Medical College and Hospital, Aligarth, India (project)

Jaani Bank, Agra, India (project)

Woollen Mills, Kanpur, India (project)

Offices and stores, Lucknow, India (project)

Gupta House, Lucknow, India (project)

Bahtia Subdivision, Lucknow, India (project)

Bhargava House, Lucknow, India (project)

House for the Raja of Tagore, Calcutta (project)

Student Union, University of Lucknow, India (project)

Capitol Theatre, Lucknow, India (project)

Library and Museum for the Raja of Mahmudabad (project)

Town Hall, Ahmedabad, India (project)

Club House, Lucknow, India (project)

Prince of Nepal House, Bholanpur, India (project)

Paper mill, Lucknow, India (project)

Mohsin House, Lucknow, India (project)

1937 Shant i Devi House, Lucknow, India

Raza House, Lucknow, India

Zenana Palace, for the Raja of Jahangirabad, India (project)

Sahni House, Lucknow, India (project)

1939 Pioneer Press Building, Lucknow, India

Publications:

On GRIFFIN: books—*The Chicago School and Walter Burley Griffin 1893–1914* by Mark L. Peisch, New York 1959; *The Chicago School of Architecture: Early Followers of Sullivan and Wright* by Mark L. Peisch, New York 1964; *Walter Burley Griffin* by James Birrell, Brisbane 1964; *Walter Burley Griffin: Selected Designs*, Chicago 1970; *The Prairie School: Frank Lloyd Wright and His Midwest Contemporaries* by H. Allen Brooks, Toronto 1972; *Walter Burley Griffin: Comprehensive Subdivision Planning in the Midwest* by Albert J. Drap Jr. and Thomas A. Heinz, Urbana, Illinois 1972; *Prairie School Town Planning 1900–1915: Wright, Griffin, Drummond* by Courtney Graham Dommell, New York 1974; *The Architecture of Walter Burley Griffin* by Donald Leslie Johnson, Melbourne 1977; articles—"Canberra: A Garden Without a City" by Benjamin Higgins in *Royal Architectural Institute of Canada Journal* (Toronto), September 1951; "The Early Works of the Prairie Architects" in *Society of Architectural Historians Journal* (Philadelphia), March 1960; "Griffin in Melbourne" by Robin Boyd in *Architectural Review* (London), February 1965; "The Prairie School" by H. Allen Brooks in *Edilizia Moderna* (Milan), no. 86, 1965; "Rock Crest/Rock Glen: Prairie Planning in Iowa" by Robert E. McCoy in *Prairie School Review* (Chicago), no. 3, 1968; article by Nory Miller in *Inland Architect* (Chicago), May 1972; "Castlecrag: A Physical and Social Planning Experiment" by Donald Leslie Johnson in *Prairie School Review* (Chicago), no. 3, 1972; "Walter Burley Griffin in India" by Donald Leslie Johnson in *Architecture Australia* (Sydney), April/May 1977.

Both in his life and architecture, Walter Burley Griffin was profoundly committed to spiritual and intellectual principles, the influence of Theosophy and, later, to Rudolf Steiner's movement Anthroposophy. These metaphysical involvements deeply affected his work as an architect, landscape designer, and land planner. In Australia, a country whose architecture is notable for its lack of principles or doctrine, Griffin's devotion to principle was incomprehensible.

Griffin's outstanding contribution lies in the relationship of buildings to other buildings, in forming building clusters; and of buildings to landscape, in binding all the elements of the neighbourhood or city in a semi-mystical union with nature. The built environments that Griffin designed in the mid-western United States, Australia and India matter more than his individual buildings (not that these are unimportant), for in the final assessment, Griffin's outstanding achievement is as an environmental designer. Besides his plan for the capital of Australia, Canberra, Griffin designed a number of neighbourhoods: Rock Glen, Mason City, Iowa, and the Trier Center Neighbourhood, Winnetka, Illinois, in America; and Eaglemont, Victoria, and Castlecrag, Sydney, including plans for the cities of Griffith and Leeton, in Australia. In his concern for ecology and preservation of the natural environment Griffin was far ahead of his time and anticipated many of the principles in such matters that only came to the fore in the 1960's. Griffin's town planning ideas were influenced by the work of Frederick Law Olmstead, Ebenezer Howard's Garden City movement, the sociological approach of Patrick Geddes, and the revival of classical planning principles following the *World's Columbian Exposition* in Chicago in 1893. The plan for Canberra reapplied the lessons of Le Enfant's plan for Washington, and more particularly Cass Gilbert's plan of 1900, and the plan for New Delhi. Griffin retained the axiality of main boulevards focussing on points or nodes that generate a concentric geometry of streets. The axes are related to the principal landscape elements such as surrounding mountains or rivers.

The question of the relative influence of Griffin on Wright and vice versa is difficult to assess, and this is further complicated by the fact that Marion Mahony, whom Griffin married in 1911, had spent fourteen years in Wright's studio (1895–1909) and was responsible for many of Wright's beautiful renderings. With his concept for the Emery House in Elmhurst, Illinois (1901–02), Griffin may have encouraged Wright to experiment with a more informal geometry in his own prairie houses. But, though Griffin is unquestionably an important member of the Chicago School of Architecture, he does not rank with Wright in either inventiveness or the mastery of spatial form. Griffin's houses are much more classical than Wright's, and he employs such Palladian motifs as linked pavilions, symmetry, and rusticated basements.

Griffin's Australian houses are smaller, meaner and less sophisticated spatially than his earlier American domestic work. His outstanding works are his fine American houses, particularly the Emery, Sloan (1909) and Bovee (1908) in Chicago, and the Ricker (1911), Melson (1912), and Blythe (1913) in Mason City. Of his Australian work, Newman College, University of Melbourne (1917), the superb Capitol Theatre, Melbourne (1924), Griffin's own house (1921) and the T.R. Wilson houses (1922) at Castlecrag, the "knitlock" building system (Creswick House, Castlecrag, 1926), and his incinerator buildings, particularly the Pyrmont and Willoughby incinerators (1934), are amongst the most distinguished.

From 1935 until his death in February 1937, Griffin worked in Lucknow, India, on a bizzare series of projects. The Pioneer Press Building and Shant i Devi House have the same horizontal forms with squarish proportions, a general squat appearance and rusticated surface treatment associated with his earlier buildings, but here Griffin imposed a blend of decorative motifs derived from the transitional architecture of the Nawab period.

—Philip Drew

GROPIUS, Walter (Adolf).
American. Born in Berlin, Germany, 18 May 1883; emigrated to England, 1934; emigrated to the United States, 1937. Educated at the Humanistisches Gymnasium, Berlin, 1903; Technische Hochschule, Munich, 1903–04; Technische Hochschule, Charlottenburg, Berlin, 1905–07. Served as an Officer in the German Army, 1904–05, 1914–18: Iron Cross (first and second class); Bavarian Military Medal; Royal Austrian Decoration. Married Alma Schindler Mahler (widow of the composer) in 1916 (divorced); daughter: Alma; married Ise Frank in 1923; daughter: Beate. Worked in the office of the architects Solf and Wichards, Berlin, 1904; travelled in Europe, 1906–07; Chief Assistant in the office of architect Peter Behrens, Berlin, 1907–10; in private practice, Berlin, 1910–14; Director, Grand Ducal Academy of Arts, Weimar, and Grand Ducal Saxon School of Applied Arts, Weimar, 1915–19: merged the two schools under the name Das Staatliche Bauhaus, 1919: Director of the Bauhaus, at Weimar, 1919–25, and at Dessau, 1925–28 (associates: Herbert Bayer; Marcel Breuer; Josef Albers; Laszlo Moholy-Nagy; Wassily Kandinsky; Paul Klee; Lyonel Feininger; Johannes Itten; Gerhard Marcks; Adolf Meyer; Ludwig Mies van der Rohe; Georg Muche; Oskar Schlemmer); in private practice, Berlin, 1928–33; in partnership with E. Maxwell Fry, London, 1934–36, and with Marcel Breuer, Cambridge, Massachusetts, 1937–41; Founder/Partner, with seven associates, TAC: The Architects' Collaborative, Cambridge, 1945–69. Professor of Architecture, 1937–52, Chairman of the Department of Architecture, 1938–52, and Professor Emeritus, 1952–69, Graduate School of Design, Harvard University, Cambridge. Founder Member and President, 1928, and Vice-President, 1929–57, CIAM (Congrès Internationaux d'Architecture Moderne); Vice-President, Institute of Sociology, London, 1937. Exhibitions: *World's Fair,* Ghent, Belgium, 1913; *Deutsche Werkbund,* Cologne, 1914; *Deutsche Werkbund,* Stuttgart, 1927; *Wohnen im Grünen,* Berlin, 1928; *Deutsche Werkbund,* Paris, 1930; *Bund Deutscher Architekten Exhibition,* Berlin, 1931; *The Extendable House,* Berlin, 1932; *German People—German Work,* Berlin, 1934; *Non-Ferrous Metals Exhibition,* Berlin, 1934; *The Bauhaus 1919–1928,* Museum of Modern Art, New York, 1938; *World's Fair,* New York, 1939; *Bauhaus,* London, 1969. Recipient: Gold Medal, *World's Fair,* Ghent, 1913; First Prize, Dammerstock District Development Competition, Karlsruhe, 1928; First Prize, Spandau-Haselhorst Experimental District Competition, Berlin, 1929; Gold Medal of Honor, The Architectural League of New York, 1951; Grand Prix d'Architecture, Sao Paulo, 1953; Royal Gold Medal, Royal Institute of British Architects, London, 1956; Hanseatic Goethe Prize, University of Hamburg, 1956; Ernst Reuter Medal, City of Berlin, 1957; Gold Medal, American Institute of Architects, 1959; Grand State Professor of Architecture Award, Germany, 1960; Prince Albert Gold Medal, Royal Society of Arts, London, 1961; Goethe Prize, Frankfurt, 1961; Kaufmann International Design Award, 1961; Cornelius Gurlitt Medal, Germany Academy for City and Regional Planning, 1962. Dr. Ing.: Technische Hochschule, Hannover, 1929; M.A.: Harvard University, 1942; D.Sc.: Western Reserve University, Cleveland, 1951; University of Sydney, 1954; D.Arts: Harvard University, 1953; D.Arch.: North Carolina State College, Raleigh, 1953; Dr.: University of Brazil, 1955; D.F.A.: Pratt Institute, New York, 1961; D.H.L.: Columbia University, New York, 1961; Williams College, Williamstown, Massachusetts, 1963; Dr.Phil.: Free University, Berlin, 1963. Fellow, American Institute of Architects, 1954; Member, National Institute of Arts and Letters; Associate, National Academy of Design, 1967. Honorary Member, Royal Institute of British Architects, London, 1937; Honorary Member, Royal Society of Arts, London, 1946; Fellow of the Society of Industrial Artists and Designers, London, 1950; Honorary Senator, Hochschule für Bildende Künste, Berlin, 1962; Honorary Royal Academician, London, 1967. Grand Cross of Merit with Star, Germany, 1958. *Died* (in Boston) *5 July 1969.*

Works:

1909 Farm-workers' houses, Janikow, near Dramburg, Germany
1911 Fagus Shoe Factory, Alfeld-an-der-Leine, Germany (with Adolf Meyer)
1913 Design of railway car for a factory at Königsberg, Germany
    Interior design for the *World's Fair,* Ghent, Belgium
    Single-family houses, Wittemberg, Frankfurt-on-Oder, Germany (with Adolf Meyer)
    Plan for the Fitz District, Frankfurt-on-Oder, Germany (with Adolf Meyer)
    Hospital, Alfeld, Germany (project; with Adolf Meyer)
    Regional Councillor's Office, Rummelsberg, Germany (project)
    Savings Bank, Dramburg, Germany (project; with Adolf Meyer)
    Shops and regional plan for Posen, Germany, now Poznan, Poland (project)
    House, Semmering, Vienna
    Car factory employees' housing, Bernburg, Germany
    Shops, Märkisch Friedland, Germany
    Kleffel Cotton Factory, Dramburg, Germany (with Adolf Meyer)
    Mendel House furniture and interiors, Berlin
    Langerfeld House furniture and interiors, Königsberg, Germany
    Dr. Herzfeld House furniture and interiors, Hanover, Germany
    Rural houses on the von Brockhausen estate, Pomerania, Germany, now Poland
1914 Industrial complex (administration building, garage compound, and medium-sized factory), *Deutsche Werkbund* Exhibition, Cologne (with Adolf Meyer)
    Steel furniture for the warship *Von Hindenburg, Deutsche Werkbund Exhibition,* Cologne (with Adolf Meyer)
    Farm-workers' houses and shops, Dramburg, Germany
1921 Sommerfeld House, Dahlem, Berlin
    Workers' houses for the Hess Stocking Factory, Erfurt, Germany (competition project; with Adolf Meyer)
    Chicago Tribune Tower (competition project; with Adolf Meyer)
1922 War Memorial, Weimar, Germany
    Bauhaus Building, Weimar, Germany
1923 Villa Hausmann, Pyrmont, Germany (project; with Adolf Meyer)
    State Theatre renovation, Jena, Germany (with Adolf Meyer)
1924 Auerbach House, Jena, Germany (with Adolf Meyer)
    Academy of Philosophy, Erlangen, Germany (project; with Adolf Meyer)
    Fröbel Institute, Bad Liebenstein, Germany (with Adolf Meyer)
    Hanover Paper Mill, Alfeld, Germany (with Adolf Meyer)
    von Klitzing Beach House (project; with Adolf Meyer)
    Engelhard Workshops (project; with Adolf Meyer)
    Banqueting Hall, Frankfurt (competition project; with Adolf Meyer)
    Reis and Mendel Tombs, Berlin
1925 Kappe Shops, Alfeld, Germany (with Adolf Meyer)
    Fagus Shoe Factory Annex, Alfeld-an-der-Leine, Germany (with Adolf Meyer)
    Benscheidt House, Alfeld-an-der-Leine, Germany (project)
    Benscheidt Jr. House reconstruction, Alfeld-an-der-Leine, Germany

    Old people's home, Alfeld-an-der-Leine, Germany (project)
    Teachers' Association Headquarters, Dresden (project)
    Sanatorium, Thuringia, Germany (project)
    Teachers' houses at the Bauhaus, Dessau, Germany
1926 The Bauhaus, Dessau, Germany
    Müller Factory, Kirchbraach, Germany
    Terrace houses, groups I and II, Törten, Dessau, Germany
1927 Terrace houses, group III, Törten, Dessau, Germany
    2 prefabricated houses, *Deutsche Werkbund Exhibition,* Stuttgart
    Co-operative store, Dresden (project)
    Dairy, Törten, Dessau, Germany (project)
    Apartment building, Marburg, Germany (project)
    Hecke House, Hamburg (project)
    Small houses for the firm of Molling and Company (project)
    House for the Austellung Press, Cologne (project)
    "Totaltheater" (project; with Erwin Piscator)
    Zuckerkandl House, Jena, Germany
    Wooden week-end houses (project)
    Town hall, museum and sports grounds, Halle, Germany (competition project)
    Biesenhorst District development, Berlin (project)
1928 Municipal Labor Office, Dessau, Germany
    Dammerstock District development, Karlsruhe (competition project; in collaboration)
    Lewin House, Zehlenderf, Berlin
    Harnischmacher House, Wiesbaden (project)
    Country district development, Wolfen, Dessau, Germany (project)
    Co-operative District, Merseburg, Germany (project)
    Co-operative Store, Törten, Dessau, Germany
    Terrace houses, group IV, Törten, Dessau, Germany
    Prefabricated houses for the Mirsch Copper and Brass Factory, Finow, Germany
1929 Spandau-Haselhorst Experimental District, Berlin (competition project)
    Prefabricated furniture for the Feder Shops, Berlin
    Houses, Sommerfeld, Berlin (project)
    Professional School, Kopenick, Berlin (project)
    Engineering School, Hagen, Germany (competition project)
    Old people's home, Kassel (project)
    Gagfah District, Lindenbaum, Frankfurt
1930 Bodywork for Adler cars
    Siemensstadt District, Berlin (supervising architect; with Bartning, Forbat, Häring, and Scharoun)
    Cheap flats and houses for the Reichsforschungsgesellschaft (project)
    Deutsche Werkbund Exhibition, Paris (with Herbert Bayer, Marcel Breuer, and Laszlo Moholy-Nagy)
    House with a steel structure (project)
    Law Courts, Berlin (project)
    Theatre, Charkov, Russia (competition project)
    Houses of recreation and education at the Tiergarten, Berlin (project; with R. Hillebrecht)
    School of Physical education, Schwarzerden, Germany (project)
1931 Meeting room and gymnasium, *Bund Deutscher Architekten Exhibition,* Berlin

Walter Gropius: Apartment block, Hansa District, Berlin, 1959

Erich Mendelsohn Sanatorium (project)

Bienert Tomb, Dresden

Soviet Headquarters, Moscow (competition project)

Electrical machinery for the Voss Factory, Hanover

Houses and flats, Wansee, Berlin (project)

Apartment buildings, Nagel, Nuremberg (project)

Kass House interiors, Zehlendorf, Berlin

Apartment buildings, Paris (project)

1932 Adler Workshops reconstruction, Frankfurt (project)

Club Building, Buenos Aires (project)

Standardized houses, Buenos Aires (project)

1933 Stoves for the Frank Factory

Prefabricated houses, A. Rosa Works, Barcelona (project)

Reichsbank, Berlin (project; with J. Schmidt)

Bahner House, Berlin

Maurer House, Dahlem, Berlin

1935 Apartments, St. Leonard's Hill, Windsor, Berkshire, England (with E. Maxwell Fry)

1936 London Film Productions Workshops, Denham, Buckinghamshire, England (with E. Maxwell Fry)

House, 66 Old Church Street, Chelsea, London (with E. Maxwell Fry)

Donaldson House, Sussex, England (with E. Maxwell Fry)

Impington Village School, Cambridgeshire, England (with E. Maxwell Fry)

Papworth Sanatorium School, Cambridgeshire, England (project; with E. Maxwell Fry)

School, Histon, Cambridgeshire, England (with E. Maxwell Fry)

Christ's College, Cambridge, England (project)

1937 Kindergarten, Cambridge, Massachusetts (project)

Art Center, Wheaton College, Norton, Massachusetts (competition project; with Marcel Breuer)

1938 Gropius House, Lincoln, Massachusetts (with Marcel Breuer)

Breuer House, Lincoln, Massachusetts (with Marcel Breuer)

Professor J. Ford House, Lincoln, Massachusetts (with Marcel Breuer)

Hagerty House, Cohasset, Massachusetts (with Marcel Breuer)

1939 Chamberlain House, Sudbury, Massachusetts (with Marcel Breuer)

Frank House, Pittsburgh (with Marcel Breuer)

State of Pennsylvania Pavilion, *World's Fair*, New York (with Marcel Breuer)

G. House, Lincoln, Massachusetts (with Marcel Breuer)

Black Mountain College, Lake Eden, North Carolina (project; with Marcel Breuer)

1940 Leisure center at Key West, Florida (project; with Konrad Wachsmann)

1941 Dr. Abele House, Framingham, Massachusetts (with Marcel Breuer)

1942 Storrow Land Division, Lincoln, Massachusetts (with Marcel Breuer)

Convalescent home, Key West, Florida (project; with Konrad Wachsmann)

1943 Aluminum City, New Kensington, near Pittsburgh (with Marcel Breuer)

1943/
45 Packaged House System for the General Panel Corporation (project; with Konrad Wachsmann)

1944 Jeweller's Shop, New York

Factory, Greensboro, North Carolina

Factory, Cali, Colombia

1945 Catholic church, Torreon, Mexico (with J. Gonzales Rejna)

1946 Town planning consultancy, Black Mountain College, North Carolina (with Marcel Breuer)

Ryan House, Cambridge, Massachusetts

Poppleton House, Dayton, Ohio

Lexington Nursery School, Lexington, Massachusetts (project)

Skiing hut, Franconia, New Hampshire (project)

Library, Willimantic, Connecticut (project)

Kaplan House, Newton, Massachusetts

Usiskin House, Long Island, New York (project)

1947 Brockelman House, Worcester, Massachusetts

Neil House, Andover, Massachusetts

Wolfers House, Maine

Peter House, Cape Code, Massachusetts

Catheron House, Foxboro, Massachusetts

Heywood House reconstruction, Maine

Town plan for Michael Reese Hospital, Chicago

1948 Hua Tung University, Shanghai, China (project)

Peter Thacher Junior High School, Attleboro, Massachusetts

Lawrence House, Lexington, Massachusetts

McMahon House, Lexington, Massachusetts

House, Providence, Rhode Island

England House, Pittsfield, Massachusetts

Howlett House, Belmont, Massachusetts

Elementary school, Sherborn, Massachusetts (project)

1949 Pillsbury House, Rumford, Rhode Island

Field House, Cape Cod, Massachusetts

Graduate Center, Harvard University, Cambridge, Massachusetts (with Brown, Lawford and Forbes)

1950 Park buildings, Lexington, Massachusetts

Apthop House, Concord, Massachusetts

Hechinger House, Washington, D.C.

England House, Washington, D.C.

Napoli House, Concord, Massachusetts

Theatre, New Rochelle, New York (project)

Medical center, Mt. Kisco, New York (project)

Barnes House reconstruction, Belmont, Massachusetts (project)

1951 Business school, Attleboro, Massachusetts

Burncoat Secondary and Senior Schools, Worcester, Massachusetts (with A. Johnson)

Pillsbury House, Milton, Massachusetts

Vischer House furniture, Indiana

Vannah House, Foxboro, Massachusetts

Stichweh House, Hanover, Massachusetts

Elementary and secondary schools, Amesbury, Massachusetts (project)

Donelly Bureau reconstruction, Boston (project)

Bradley House (project)

Housing and Home Finance Agency Headquarters, San Jose, Costa Rica (project)

1952 Wasco Flashing Corporation, Cambridge, Massachusetts (project)

Five Fields Housing Complex, Lexington, Massachusetts

Houses, Lake Barcroft, Falls Church, Virginia

American University Office Building, Washington, D.C. (project)

Mulcahey Elementary School, Taunton, Massachusetts

Pilgrim Park Elementary School, Warwick, Rhode Island

Elementary school, Providence, Rhode Island

Senior school, Concord, New Hampshire

American Association for the Advancement of Science Office Building, Washington, D.C.

Shops, for the Hechinger Company, Falls Church and Alexandria, Virginia

Designs/models for school and college furniture for the Thonet Factory

Cole House, Cambridge, Massachusetts

Baruch House, Newton, Massachusetts

Lang House, Newton, Massachusetts

Elementary school, Cambridge, Massachusetts

Elementary school, North Adams, Massachusetts

Caulfield House reconstruction, Washington, D.C.

1953 McCormick and Company Office Building, Chicago

Wherry District Housing, for the United States Navy, Quonset, Rhode Island

Back Bay Center, Boston (with Pietro Belluschi, Carl Koch, Hugh Stubbins and Walter Bogner)

National Education Association Building (project)

1954 Flagg Street Elementary School, Worcester, Massachusetts (with A. Roy)

Shopping center, Saugus, Massachusetts (with Ketchum, Gind and Sharp)

Overholt Thoracic Clinic, Boston

1955 Elementary school, Waltham, Massachusetts

Secondary school, Attleboro, Massachusetts

1956 Elementary school, West Bridgewater, Massachusetts

Housing at Otis Air Force Base, Falmouth, Massachusetts

United States Embassy, Athens

1957 Oheb Shalom Temple, Baltimore

Littleton Junior-Senior High School, Littleton, Massachusetts

Pioneer Valley Regional High School, Northfield, Massachusetts

1958 William F. Pollard Junior High School, Needham, Massachusetts

Elementary school, Stoughton, Massachusetts

2 dormitories for Phillips Academy, Andover, Massachusetts

Reyim Synagogue, Newton, Massachusetts

Murchison House, Provincetown, Massachusetts

Pan American Building, New York (consultant architect, with Pietro Belluschi, on plan of Emery Roth and Sons)

1959 Elementary school, Acton, Massachusetts

Britz-Buckow-Rudow Settlement, West Berlin (project)

Apartment block, Hansa District, Berlin

Academic Quadrangle, Brandeis University, Waltham, Massachusetts

1960 L. G. Hanscom Field Elementary School, Lincoln, Massachusetts

Elementary School additions, Kingston, Massachusetts

Northeast Elementary School, Waltham, Massachusetts

Gould Hospital, Presque Isle, Maine

Hemoglobin Laboratory Alterations, Children's Hospital Medical Center, Boston

1961/
69 Wayland High School, Wayland, Massachusetts

1964 Britz-Buckow-Rudow Center, West Berlin (project)

1965 Rosenthal China Factory, Selb, Germany

Master plan for a university at Mosul, Iraq

1967 Experimental buildings for a primary and secondary school at Britz-Buckow-Rudow, West Berlin

Huntington Art Gallery addition, San Marino, California

Tower East Office and Commercial Building, Shaker Heights, Ohio

Thomas Glassworks, Hamburg

Town plan for Selb, Germany

1968 Kennedy Federal Building, Civic Center, Boston

Publications:

By GROPIUS: books—*Programm des Staatlichen*

Bauhauses, Weimar 1919; *Idee und Aufbau des Staatlichen Bauhauses,* Weimar and Munich 1923; *Internationale Architektur,* Weimar and Munich 1925, 1927; *Neue Arbeiten in Bauhauswerkstätten,* editor, Munich 1925; *Bauhausbauten* Dessau, Munich 1928; *The New Architecture and the Bauhaus,* London 1935, New York 1936; *Bauhaus 1919–1928,* with Herbert Bayer and Ise Gropius, New York 1938, Stuttgart 1955; *Rebuilding Our Communities,* Chicago 1945; *Architecture and Design in the Age of Science,* New York 1952; *The Scope of Total Architecture,* New York and London 1955, Buenos Aires 1956, Tokyo 1958, Milan 1959; *Architektur: Wege zu optischen Kultur,* Frankfurt and Hamburg 1956; *Arquitectura y Planeamiento,* Buenos Aires 1958; *Katsura: Tradition and Creation in Japanese Architecture,* with Tange and Ishimoto, New Haven, Connecticut 1960; *Apollo in the Democracy: The Cultural Obligation of the Architect,* New York 1968; articles—"Die Entwicklung moderner Industriebaukunst" in *Jahrbuch des Deutschen Werkbundes,* Berlin 1913; "Das flache Dach: Internationale Umfrage über die technische Durchfuhrbarkeit horizontal abgedeckter Dächer und Balkone" in *Bauwelt* (Berlin), 25 February, 4 March, 8 and 22 April 1926; "Offset-, Buch-, und Werbekunst" in *Bauhaus* (Leipzig), no. 7, 1926; "Geistige und technische Voraussetzung der neuen Baukunst" in *Umschau* (Frankfurt), no. 31, 1927; "Der Architekt als Organisator der moderner Bauwirtschaft und seine Forderungen an die Industrie," with F. Block, in *Wohnbau* (Potsdam), no. 1, 1928; "Das Ergebnis des Reichsforsehungs—Wettbewerbes" in *Bauwelt* (Berlin), February 1929; "Grossiedlungen" in *Zentralblatt der Bauverwaltung* (Berlin), 26 March 1930; "Flach-, Mittel-, oder Hochbau?" in *Neues Frankfurt,* February 1931; "Arquitectura Functional" in *Arquitectura* (Madrid), no. 2, 1931; "The Small House of Today" in *Architectural Forum* (New York), March 1931; "Wohnhochhauser im Grunen: Ein Grosstadtische Wohnform der Zukunft" in *Zentralblatt der Bauverwaltung* (Berlin), no. 49/50, 1931; "The Formal and Technical Problems of Modern Architecture and Planning" in *RIBA Journal* (London), May 1934; "Theaterbau" in *Atti della Reale Accademia d'Italia* (Rome), October 1934; "The Role of Reinforced Concrete in the Development of Modern Constructions" in *The Concrete Way* (Chicago), September/October 1934; "Grandes Polaciones" in *Nuestra Arquitectura* (Buenos Aires), September 1934; "Education Toward Creative Design" in *American Architect* (New York), May 1937; "Architecture at Harvard University" in *Architectural Record* (New York), May 1937; "Essentials for Creative Design" in *The Octagon* (Philadelphia), July 1937; "Background of the New Architecture" in *Civil Engineering* (New York), December 1937; "Towards a Living Architecture" in *American Architect* (New York), January/February 1938; "General Panel System" in *Pencil Points* (New York), April 1943; "A Program for City Reconstruction" in *Architectural Forum* (New York), July 1943; "Field Experience and the Making of an Architect" in *AIA Journal* (Washington, D.C.), November 1945; "A Frank Letter and Its Answer" in *AIA Journal* (Washington, D.C.), April 1947; "Design Topics" in *Magazine of Art* (New York), December 1947; "What Is Happening to Modern Architecture" in *Museum of Modern Art Bulletin* (New York), Spring 1948; "Organic Neighborhood Planning: Housing and Town and Country Planning" in *UN Bulletin* (New York), April 1949; "Plan pour un enseignement de l'Architecture" and "Le théatre total" in *L'Architecture d'Aujourd'hui* (Paris) February 1950; "Architecture fonctionnelle" in *L'Architecture Francaise* (Paris), no. 11, 1950; "The Position of Architecture in the Century of Science" in *The Architect and Building News* (London), 19 July 1951; "Not Gothic but Modern for Our Colleges" in *AIA Journal* (Washington, D.C.), April 1952; "Gropius on Gropius: Letter to the Editor" in *Architectural Forum* (New York), August 1952; "Faith in Planning" in *American Society of Planning Officials Journal* (Chicago), October 1952; "Eight Steps Toward a Solid Architecture" in *Architectural Forum* (New York), February 1954; "Is There a Science of Design" in *Journal of the Royal Australian Institute of Architects* (Sydney), July/September 1954; "The Necessity of the Artist in a Democratic Society" in *Arts and Architecture* (Los Angeles), December 1955; "Architecture in Japan" in *Perspecta* (New Haven, Connecticut), no. 3, 1955; "Kompass für architekten" in *Werk* (Zurich), June 1955; "Discorso di Gropius alla inaugurazione della scuola di Ulm" in *Domus* (Milan), February 1956; "The Curse of Conformity" in *Saturday Evening Post* (Philadelphia), 6 June 1958; "Einheit in der vielfalt: ein paradox der kultur" in *Bauen und Wohnen* (Zurich), December 1959; "Una testimonianza diretta" in *Casabella* (Milan), June 1960; "True Architectural Goals Yet to Be Realized" in *Architectural Record* (New York), June 1961; "The Architect in Society" in *Architectural Association Journal* (London), January 1962; "Creative Education: Key to Good Architecture and Design" in *Architectural Record* (New York), November 1963; "Traditional and Continuity in Architecture" in *Architectural Record* (New York), May, June, July 1964; "L'Architetto e la societa" in *Casabella* (Milan), October 1965; "Ludwig Mies van der Rohe" in *Bauen und Wohnen* (Zurich), May 1966; "Programm zur Grundüng einer Allgemeinen Hausbaugesellschaft auf künstlerisch einheitlicher Grundlage MbH" in *Baumeister* (Munich), April 1969; etc.

On GROPIUS: books—*Walter Gropius* by Siegfried Giedion, Paris 1931; *Walter Gropius e la Bauhaus* by Giulio Carlo Argan, Milan 1951; *Walter Gropius* by Chikatada Kurata, Tokyo 1953; *Walter Gropius: Work and Teamwork* by Siegfried Giedion, Stuttgart, Paris, London and New York 1954; *Walter Gropius* by Masakazu Koyama, Tokyo 1954; *Walter Gropius: The Man and His Work* by Siegfried Giedion, Milan 1954; *Bauhaus: Weimar, Berlin* by Mityiko and Iwao Yamawaki, Tokyo 1954; *Walter Gropius* by the Centro Estudiantes de Arquitectura, Montevideo 1955; *Gropius in Japan* by the editors of the International House of Japan, Tokyo 1956; Gropius section by Ernesto Rogers of *Universal Encyclopaedia of Art,* Rome 1958; *The Synthetic Vision of Walter Gropius* by Gilbert Herbert, Johannesburg 1959; *Walter Gropius* by James Marston Fitch, New York 1960; *Walter Gropius und das Faguswerk* by H. Weber, Munich 1961; Gropius section by Elio Piroddi in *Encyclopaedic Dictionary of Architecture and Town Planning,* Rome 1969; *Four Great Makers of Modern Architecture,* Columbia University, New York 1970; *Gropius* by Alberto Busignani, Florence 1972, London 1973; *Masters of Modern Architecture* by Edwin and Joy Hoag, Indianapolis 1977; articles—"Das neue Bauhaus in Weimar" by Dr. Fritz Hoeber in *Der Architek* (Vienna), no. 22, 1919; "The Work of Walter Gropius" by Herman George Scheffauer in *Architectural Review* (London), August 1924; "Exposition du 'Werkbund' à Stuttgart" in *Cahiers d'Art* (Paris), no. 7/8, 1927; "The 'Total-theatre' Proposed by Walter Gropius" in *Architectural Record* (New York), April 1930; "Der deutsche Werkbund in Paris" in *Bauwelt* (Berlin), June 1930; "Bauhaus School" in *Architectural Record* (New York), October 1930; "Walter Gropius" by J. M. Richards in *Architectural Review* (London), August 1935; "Professor Gropius Designs in Glass" in *The Architects' Journal* (London), 4 October 1945; "Le Préfabrication aux Etas Unis" in *L'Architecture d'Aujourd'hui* (Paris), January 1946; "Walter Gropius et son école," special issue of *L'Architecture d'Aujourd'hui* (Paris), February 1950; "Gropius in Retrospect" in *Architectural Record* (New York), February 1952; "Gropius Symposium" in *Arts and Architecture* (Los Angeles), May 1952; "Gropius, 1952" by William Holford in *Architectural Review* (London), July 1952; "Labatut on Gropius" by Jean Labatut in *Architectural Forum* (New York), August 1952; "Walter Gropius" by E. Maxwell Fry in *Architectural Review* (London), March 1955; "Presentation of the Royal Gold Medal to Dr. Walter Gropius" by Charles Aslin in *RIBA Journal* (London), May 1956; "Gropius and Van de Velde" by Nicholas Pevsner in *Architectural Review* (London), March 1963; "Architectural Details: Walter Gropius" in *Architectural Record* (New York), February 1964; "Gropius, Wright, and the Intentional Fallacy" by Charles Jencks in *Arena: Architectural Association Journal* (London), June 1966; "All Purpose Old Master of Design" by Peter Blake in *Life* (New York), 7 June 1968; "Gropius Throws His Hat in the Ring" in *AIA Journal* (Washington, D.C.), July 1968; "Gropius: Young at His Passing" by Wolf Von Eckardt in the *Washington Post,* 31 July 1969; "Bauhaus Birthday" by Stanley Abercrombie in the *Wall Street Journal* (New York), 16 October 1969; "Meeting Gropius Again" by Walter Segal in *The Architects' Journal* (London), 13 February 1974; "The True Relevance of Walter Gropius" by Stan Scott in *RIBA Journal* (London), March 1974; "Analyzing the Gropius House as Energy-Conscious Design" by Neil Summers in *AIA Journal* (Washington, D.C.), February 1977.

Walter Gropius deserves to be considered as one of the chief architectural innovators of this century. He was essentially progressive, making full use of new materials and methods of construction made possible by modern technology, and, with Le Corbusier, he contributed much towards the transformation of building from an empirical craft to a science in which precise mathematical calculations are possible. He made the Das Staatliche Bauhaus, of which he was director from 1919 to 1928, the most vital and influential school of industrial design in Europe. He was an important theorist and teacher, and he advocated and contributed much to the acceptance of standardization, prefabrication and team work.

His qualities as a progressive designer are first significantly apparent in the Fagus Shoe Factory at Alfeld-an-der-Leine, built in 1911 in collaboration with Adolf Meyer. The structure is a steel frame that supports the floors, while the external walls are glass screens that continue, without interruption of corner supports, round the building. This admits the maximum of light and minimizes the distinction between outer and inner space. It was a design that had far-reaching influence. A building with a similar motif was the administration building at the *Deutsche Werkbund Exhibition* at Cologne in 1914. Here continuous fenestration is carried from the circular glass corners on the first floor along the sides and for the entire length of the rear of the building. These circular glass structures enclose spiral staircases, another motif widely adopted in much modern building, especially in departmental stores.

One of the best and most complete examples of the glass screen wall occurs in the workshop that forms part of the Bauhaus building erected at Dessau in 1926. This workshop is of four storeys with a post and slab construction; supports are set well back to allow a large uninterrupted glass screen of the three upper floors to continue without the interruption of any structural supporting member round three walls. This was the most complete utilization of the glass screen to date, and it was a long time before anything comparable was used.

The main purpose of these buildings by Gropius was to admit the maximum of light, for even today there is no satisfactory substitute for daylight either from an amenity or functional standpoint. This preoccupation with light influenced much of Gropius' domestic architecture. One of the best early examples is the Siemensstadt Development near Berlin of 1929–30, for which Gropius was, as supervising architect, responsible for the general layout. The estate consists mainly of long four- and five-storey apartment blocks designed by Gropius, Scharoun, and Forbat. In siting these parallel slab blocks Gropius aimed, within the required densities, to make them of such a height as to provide as much sunlight as possible, at the same time providing for maximum space for lawns and gardens between the blocks. The calculations on which the layout are based are given in his book *The New Architecture and the Bauhaus,* and this exercise in site planning had much influence at the time.

Siting of domestic buildings for maximum sunlight was always a prime consideration with Gropius. Another notable example is the Aluminium City housing estate near Pittsburgh, designed in collaboration with Marcel Breuer in 1943. A road winds through a hilly wooded site; the blocks of terrace houses are orientated to get maximum sunlight, and thus there is an irregular relation to the road: some face it, some abut it end-wise, and others are away from it, reached by branching service ways. At the time this unusual yet functional siting excited controversy.

Gropius was a functionalist and most of his buildings in Germany, England and America are constructions that aim to be logical interpretations of purpose. This is seen conspicuously in the Impington Village School, designed in collaboration with Maxwell Fry in 1936, and the Harvard Graduate Center of 1949.

All of these works demonstrate that Gropius was very much an experimenter. He was also an experimenter in his projects. Conspicuous among these is his project in 1927 for a total-theatre. In this design three forms are combined: the circus with the central area, the Greek semi-circular shape, and the proscenium stage. The theatre is so arranged that tiers of seats can be revolved in sections so that change from one form to another can be effected quickly.

As a progressive architect Gropius was quick to see the advantages of economy and speed in building and was a strenuous advocate of standardization, prefabrication and dry assembly, making possible mass production and large factory-made units. This advocacy of industrialized building carried with it a belief in team work.

Aesthetically Gropius was a classicist, as his most beautiful buildings prove, such works as the houses built with the Bauhaus in 1925–6, the Harvard Graduate Centre of 1949, the apartment block in the Hansa District of Berlin, 1957–9, and the American Embassy building at Athens 1956. Although in most of these buildings there is a slight horizontal emphasis, it is balanced by verticals that, together with rectangular windows moving towards squares and large areas of plain walls always well proportioned, create a feeling of classic repose and serenity. Almost all his buildings have flat roofs condusive to this feeling of repose. But it was not only aesthetically that he liked the flat roof; he also realized its functional advantage in freedom of planning.

Gropius has sometimes been criticized on aesthetic grounds and for his advocacy of team work. For architecture is an art, the creation of individual artistic feeling, and therefore cannot be the work of equals in a team. It is possible that there is some contradiction here between advocacy and practice: it is difficult to imagine that Gropius was not the determining influence in any design that bore his name.

—Arnold Whittick

GROSSMAN, Irving.

Canadian. Born in Toronto, Ontario, 7 December 1926. Educated at the University of Toronto, 1945–50 (Ontario Association of Architects Scholarship, 1947; Hobbs Glass Prize, 1948; Toronto Brick Prize, 1949; Architectural Guild Medal, 1950; Pilkington Glass Fellowship, 1950), B.Arch. 1950. Married Helena Derwinger in 1971; sons: Adam and Jonas. Assistant in the offices of R. M. Schindler, California, 1947, Fry, Drew and Partners, London,

Irving Grossman: Edgeley (residential community), Toronto, 1973

1950–51, and in the Housing Department of the London County Council, 1952–53. Since 1954, in private practice, Toronto. Teacher at the School of Architecture, University of Toronto, 1954–62. Exhibitions: School of Architecture, University of Toronto, 1974; Canadian Exhibition, Hungary, 1979. Recipient: Regional Design Award, 1957, and National Design Award, 1962, 1971, Canadian Housing Design Council; Canada Council Research Award, 1959; Massey Medal, 1967; Design Award, Ontario Association of Architects, 1967; Canadian Centennial Medal, 1967; Design Award of Excellence, *Canadian Architect's Yearbook,* 1970, 1972; Ontario Masons Relations Award, 1970, 1973; Design Award, Scarborough, Ontario Planning Board, 1972; Annual Design Award, *Canadian Architect,* 1978. Fellow, Royal Architectural Institue of Canada, 1970; Fellow, Royal Canadian Academy, 1973. Address (office): 7 Sultan Street, Toronto, Ontario M5R 1L6, Canada.

Works:

1955	Winesanker House, 24 Croydon, Toronto
	Houzer House, Maple Lane, Ottawa
1955/	
59	Shaarei Tefellah Synagogue, 3 phases, Toronto
1956	Adath Israel Synagogue, phase I, Toronto
	MacPherson House, Bayview Village, Downsview, Ontario
	Betel House, 55 York Downs Drive, Downsview, Ontario
	Berman House, Hog's Hollow, Toronto
	Fogel House, Sandringham Avenue, Toronto
1957	Korn House, Toronto
1958	Ison House, Denmark Crescent, Downsview, Ontario
	Klamer House, Wilket Road, Bayview, Ontario
1958/	
60	Beth David Synagogue, Toronto
1959/	
65	Flemingdon Park (residential community), Toronto
1960	Morris Winchevsky School, Toronto
	Central Library Theatre interiors, Toronto
1961	Isaacs Gallery interiors, Toronto
1961/	
64	Temple Emanu-El Synagogue, Toronto
1963	Puppet Theatre, Toronto Island
	Yorkdale Fountain, Toronto (with Graham Coughtry)
	Somerset Apartments, Toronto
	Kiosks, on the Centre Islands, Toronto
1964	Administration and News Building for *Expo '67,* Montreal
	Tea House, Toronto Islands

Beth David Synagogue expansion, Toronto
1964/
  73 Edgeley (residential community), Toronto
1965 Cedarbrae Library, Scarborough, Ontario
1966 Condominium Town Houses, Edgeley, Toronto
     Shoreham Drive Public School, Edgeley, Toronto
1968 Edgeley in the Village Apartments, Toronto
1969 Student Residence, Elrond College, Kingston, Ontario
1970 YWCA Women's Residence, Toronto
     Highlands (residential community), phase I, Ottawa
1976 St. Lawrence (residential community), phase I, Toronto

Publications:

By GROSSMAN: articles—"Mathematics in Architecture" in *Royal Architectural Institute of Canada Journal* (Toronto), February 1956; "Human Patterns" in *Canadian Architect* (Toronto), April 1956; "Seminar on Colour in Architecture" in *Canadian Architect* (Toronto), August 1960; "The Forgotten Image" in *Canadian Architect* (Toronto), September 1960; "In Search of the Lost Street" in *Canadian Arts* (Ottawa), November 1960; "Le Corbusier" in *Architects of Modern Thought* (radio talks), Toronto 1962; "The Monstrous Menace," with H. Blumenfeld, in *Ontario Housing* (Toronto), June 1964; "City Hall" in *RAIC Journal* (Toronto), September 1965; "Building the City" in *Ontario '66*, Toronto 1966; "Flemingdon Park (Revisited)" in *Canadian Architect* (Toronto), April 1967; "Edgeley" in *Canadian Architect* (Toronto), August 1971.

On GROSSMAN: articles—"Betel Residence" in *Arts and Architecture* (Los Angeles), May 1959; "Beth David Synagogue" in *The Face of Toronto,* Toronto 1961; "Flemingdon Park" by M. Hancock in *Plan Canada* (Toronto), May 1961; "Flemingdon Park" in *House and Home* (New York), April 1962; "Flemingdon Park" by G. Ritter in *Architectural Design* (London), May 1962; "Flemingdon Park as an Example of Design for the Car" by William Goulding in *Canadian Art* (Ottawa), February 1962; "Flemingdon Park" in *Architectural Forum* (New York), August 1962; "Flemingdon Park" by Mayer in *American Journal of Housing* (Washington, D.C.), April 1963; "Expo Building" in *Progressive Architecture* (New York), June 1964; "Expo Building" in *Architectural Review* (London), August 1967; "Edgeley" in *Ontario Housing* (Toronto), February 1968.

Much of my thinking over the years of my practice has revolved around the forms and uses of residential groupings. While I have produced a number of "one-off" buildings that contained kernels of innovative ideas about form and space, I believe that my deepest interest has been in the larger scale issues of urban form.

It occurred to me many years ago that in this field of activity, the general direction, "formally" speaking, was backward—that is, while the architectural magazines publish each week a good project here and there in the world, thousands of acres of "junk" are built at the same time, which we tend to ignore.

In my housing work, I have tried to evolve a vocabulary that allowed a system to grow, producing ultimately "un-architected" house-forms. Working for builder clients has of course meant profits, and that concern has added discipline and tightness to one's thinking.

—Irving Grossman

Irving Grossman's contribution to architecture is primarily in the area of housing and community design. His sensitivity to the human scale and to ground-related housing, coupled with his recognition of the wastefulness associated with urban sprawl, has led to a continuous search for viable housing alternatives. As a result, he was one of the early proponents of medium-density housing when the choice for Canadians was (and to a great extent still is) limited to two extremes, namely the low-density, low-rise family detached house in the suburb or the high-density, high-rise apartment block in the city.

Grossman's first accomplishment was the design of the initial stages of Flemingdon Park, a mixed housing development hailed in the early 1960's as a breakthrough. Designed for middle-income groups at a density of 18 to 25 dwelling units per acre, this development received international recognition for its "linear-attached" concept, which introduced the practise of vertical traffic separation to modest housing developments. It suggested a solution to the incompatible needs of pedestrian and vehicular traffic in a low-rise residential environment. The solution involved a slightly raised pedestrian deck giving access to the dwellings, while a slightly depressed garage concealed the car and stored it in close proximity to the owner's house. The Flemingdon concept has since been emulated by many Canadian architects and has no doubt contributed to the acceptance of the once ill-famed row house, now known as the "town house."

Edgeley, a suburban medium-density housing development, was envisaged as an integrated community of free-market and subsidized housing linked to each other by a community center. Grossman was commissioned in the late 1960's to design the master plan and the public housing component as well as the public school for this development. The housing of Edgeley is a continuation of the "linear-attached" housing concept used at Flemingdon Park but with horizontal rather than vertical traffic separation. A thirty-foot wide pedestrian street links all the houses and, in spite of the budgetary constraints implicit in subsidized housing, a charming and picturesque environment resulted through good design. The traditional row house monotony was avoided by juxtaposing various dwelling unit types next to each other and by individualizing the design of each unit through color, texture and building materials. In fact, the public housing sector of Edgeley is, in my opinion, as attractive as its freemarket housing counterpart, if not more so.

In the early 1970's Grossman was commissioned to design a large condominium community in Ottawa, "The Highlands." Once again, he developed a linear concept, with a pedestrian spine separating two rows of multiple housing units—one row of six-storey apartments punctuated by point blocks paralleled by a four-storey stacked town house row. These linear buildings were superimposed upon a garage substructure and, when all stages are completed, will encircle a large central park and recreational area with some community facilities. Although this development exceeds 60 dwelling units per acre in density, it still retains cross ventilation and two-sided exposure for most units.

Most recently, Irving Grossman has designed a high-density sector of the St. Lawrence re-development area of downtown Toronto. Featuring mixed land-use and a medium-profile housing development for both low-and middle-income families, this development when completed may become a trend-setter for urban housing in Canada. Grossman's sector involves housing accommodation for 210 households in a six-storey linear building incorporating two elementary schools and several commercial and community facilities at sidewalk level.

Of course, Irving Grossman has also designed several private homes as well as non-residential buildings of some renown. A synagogue in North York, highly sculptural, and a community library in Scarborough, consisting of a cluster of skylit pyramids, are just two examples of well-designed community buildings. The three-storey administrative office building he designed for *Expo '67* has since become the headquarters of the Harbour Authorities and is still a landmark at the harbour front of Montreal.

—Norbert Schoenauer

GRUEN, Victor (David).

American. Born Viktor Grünbaum in Vienna, Austria, 18 July 1903; emigrated to the United States in 1938; naturalized, 1943. Educated at the Architectural School, Vienna, 1918–23, and the Academy of Arts, Vienna, under Peter Behrens, 1924–25; influenced by the work and writings of Le Corbusier. Married Lizzie Kardos in 1930 (divorced, 1941); Elsie Krummeck in 1941 (divorced, 1951); Lazette van Hauten in 1952 (died, 1962); Kemija Salihefendic in 1963; children: Michael and Margaret. Worked as a technician for Melcher and Steiner, Vienna, 1923–32; organizer, author, and actor in "Politische Kabarett," Vienna, 1926–34; in private architectural practice, Vienna, 1932–38; Designer, IVEL Corporation, New York, 1938, and in the office of Norman Bel Geddes, New York, 1938; organizer and producer, Viennese Theatre Group, New York, 1938–40; with Elsie Krummeck, formed design partnership, Grünbaum and Krummeck, New York and Los Angeles, 1940–48; in private architectural practice, as Victor Gruen, Los Angeles, 1948–51; Founder and Chief Architect, Victor Gruen Associates, Los Angeles, New York, Washington, and Tehran, 1951–68, and Victor Gruen International, Vienna, Paris, and Los Angeles, 1963–72. Since 1968, President of the Victor Gruen Center for Environmental Planning, Los Angeles; since 1969, Chief Architect of Victor Gruen AG, Switzerland, Vienna, and Paris; since 1973, President of the Zentrum für Umweltplanung, Vienna. Exhibitions, 1955–68: National Gallery, Washington, D.C.; *World's Fair,* Brussels; United States Information Service, Washington, D.C.; Architectural League of New York; 8th Pan-American Congress of Architects, Mexico City; American Institute of Architects Exhibition in Moscow; Berlin International Building Exhibition; American Embassy, Paris; Brooklyn Museum, New York. Recipient: Honor Award, American Institute of Architects, Southern California Chapter, 1949, 1951; Avenue of the Americas Association Award, New York, 1953; Gold Medal, AIA, Detroit Chapter, 1955; Gold Medal, AIA, Memphis Chapter, 1958; Special Medallion, "Architect of the People," Rice University, Houston, Texas, 1963; Community Architecture Citation, New York State Association of Architects, 1965; *Who's Who in America* Award, 1966; Significant Artistic Achievement Award, City of Vienna, 1972; etc. Honorary doctorate: Pepperdine University, Los Angeles, 1976. Fellow, American Institute of Architects, 1948. Address: Zentrum für Umweltplanung, Traungasse 7, A-1030 Vienna, Austria.

Works:

(Only the most important buildings and projects, as selected by Mr. Gruen, are listed. More than 1,000 works have been executed under Mr. Gruen's direction—including offices, hospitals, hotels, department stores, city plans, and interior design projects.)

1939 Lederer Shop, Fifth Avenue, New York
1939/
  51 12 stores for Barton's Bonbonnerie, New York
1940 Altmann and Kuehne Candy Store, Fifth Avenue, New York
1954 Northland Center, Detroit
     Master plan for 5,000 acres, Palos Verdes, California
     Dayton Department Store, Rochester, Minnesota
1955 Revitalization plan for Fort Worth, Texas (project)
1956 Southdale Shopping Center, Minneapolis
1957/
  65 Various office buildings for the Tishman Company
1958 Wilshire Terrace Apartment House, Los Angeles
     Revitalization plan for the city core of Kalamazoo, Michigan

2500 apartments, Charles River Park, Boston

1958/
64 Commercial, recreational and civic center project at Redondo Beach, California

1958/
65 Southdale Medical Building, Minneapolis

1959 World's Fair Plan, Washington, D.C. (project)

City, County and Federal Civic Center, Syracuse, New York

1960 Museum of Arts and Sciences, Evansville, Indiana

Cherry Hill Center, Camden, New Jersey

Winrock Center, Little Rock, Arkansas

27 acre commercial, residential and institutional complex at Newark, New Jersey

Master plan for Welfare Island Model Town, New York

1960/
66 9 department stores for the May Company in California

1962 Midtown Plaza, Rochester, New York

Randhurst Shopping Center, Mt. Prospect, Chicago

Doheny Towers Apartment Building, Los Angeles

Marina del Rey, Los Angeles

Redevelopment study of 27 acres, The Rocks, in downtown Sydney

12 block redevelopment project in the central area of Urbana, Illinois

1963 Square block central area multi-functional

development in Salt Lake City, Utah

Wilshire Comstock Apartment Building, Los Angeles

1963/
66 California Mart, Los Angeles

1964 Leo Baeck Temple, Los Angeles

1965 New satellite town in Valencia, California (in development)

1966 Sea World (marine exhibit), San Diego, California

Business sector revitalization plan, Boston (in process)

Fox Plaza, San Francisco

1968 City core revitalization plan, Fresno, California

City master plan for Teheran (project)

1969 Harbor and city core revitalization plan for Antwerp (project)

1971 University City plan, Louvain-la-Neuve, Belgium (in process)

City core revitalization plan, Vienna (in process)

1972- City core plans for 7 satellite cities in the Paris region

Publications:

By GRUEN: books—*How to Live with Your Architect,* New York 1949; *Shopping Towns USA,* with Larry Smith, New York 1960; *Stadsfornyelse i Forenta Staterna,* Stockholm 1963; *Heart of Our Cities,* New York 1964; *The Ideal City,* with others,

New York 1964; *The People's Architect,* with others, Chicago 1964; *New Cities USA,* Washington, D.C. 1966; *Who Designs America?,* with others, New York 1966; *The Downfall and Rebirth of City Cores on Both Sides of the Atlantic,* Los Angeles 1972; *Centers for the Urban Environment,* New York 1973; *Das Überleben der Städte,* Vienna 1973; *Die Alte Schuhschachtel,* Vienna 1973; *Die Lebenswerte Stadt,* Munich 1975; *Ist Fortschritt ein Verbrechen?,* Vienna 1975; numerous articles in architectural magazines throughout the world.

On GRUEN: books—*Architecture, You and Me* by Siegfried Giedion, Cambridge, Massachusetts 1948; *Urban Pattern: City Planning and Design* by Arthur B. Gallion, New York 1950; *Shopping Centers* by Geoffrey Baker, New York 1951; *Forms and Functions of 20th Century Architecture* by Talbot Hamlin, New York 1952; *Mixed Blessing: The Motor in Britain* by Colin Buchanan, London 1958; *Shops and Stores* by Morris Ketchum, New York 1958; *Cities in the Motor Age* by Wilfred Owen, New York 1959; *An Introduction to Modern Architecture* by J. M. Richards, London 1960; *Architecture and the Esthetics of Plenty* by James Marston Fitch, New York 1961; *Death and Life of Great American Cities* by Jane Jacobs, New York 1961; *Man-Made America* by Christopher Tunnard, New Haven, 1963; *Urban Landscape Design* by Garrett Eckbo, New York 1964; *1976: Agenda for Tomorrow* by Stewart Udall, New York 1968; *Art in Architecture* by Louis G. Redstone, New York 1968; *Les Villes Nouvelles aux*

Victor Gruen: Midtown Plaza, Rochester, New York, 1962

USA by Nardin, Paris 1968; *Die Ohnmacht des Bürgers* by Theodor Leuenberger and Rudolf Schilling, Frankfurt 1977.

I regard architecture as an integrating professional art, which combines all activities which contribute to the shaping of the man-made and man-influenced environment. To these belong, of course, architecture, planning, and engineering, but also ecology and last, but not least, philosophy. I see the architect as a generalist, who knows much about something, namely architecture in the narrower sense, but also something about everything. This striving for the acquisition of multi-disciplinary knowledge and interest has shown itself early, but has become stronger with age. I am, in fact, still a student, and I try to widen my horizon by a steady dialogue with scientists of all disciplines.

As far as the term "architecture" is concerned, I base it on the teachings of Pollio Vitruvius, which—though they are nearly 2,000 years old—seem to me still applicable. He states in his work about architecture, in the volumes devoted to the "true art of building," the following: "Architecture is based on three conditions—firmness, commodity and delight." What I have tried to achieve in my building is the provision of firmness in a manner in which the structure does not interfere or impose upon the conditions of commodity and delight. I have always understood the term "commodity" in a very wide sense. Buildings have not just to be useful but commodious in the physical, psychological, and spiritual sense. Delight is to me one of the most important conditions and to create it one of my greatest aims.

With these aims before me, it should not be surprising that I have tried to move in my career from the single structure to the creation of environmental compositions and finally to the rehabilitation of existing cities and the planning of new urban units.

Recognizing the importance of all environmental aspects to every individual person and every individual structure, I have turned my interests increasingly to the task of becoming an environmental planner.

—Victor Gruen

Victor Gruen, like Neutra and Schindler before him, emigrated from Vienna to Los Angeles, but unlike them he is not noted for the design of innovative or beautiful buildings. Gruen has said that he sees little value in buildings themselves and that energies should be devoted to improving the environment; but in such pronouncements he is not thinking in baroque terms of architecture on a city scale, for to him formal values are of less importance than providing a comfortable and convenient place for the American life-style.

From his earliest days of practice, both in Vienna and in the U.S.A., Gruen had been concerned with the design of shops, and it is in the design of retailing establishments that he became well known in the decade following World War Two. With the knowledge of traffic and concern for traffic-free zones learnt from shopping centres, he felt emboldened to tackle urban problems and gained a reputation as the planner who would put the automobile in its place.

Gruen's concern that people should have the convenience of cars without letting their lives be destroyed by them is a continuing and constructive thread in his work. He believes that the car is right for individual mobility but wrong for mass transport: we ought to be able to make social life and shopping journeys by car, but office workers in the big cities should use public transport for the journeys to and from work. By the late 1960's, this was conventional thinking in planning circles; in post-war Los Angeles it was heresy. It is perhaps somewhat cruel that Victor Gruen has had great success with his shopping centres which encourage the use of cars, yet his planning advice to numerous cities to require greater use of public transport has more often than not fallen on deaf ears.

Soon after the war Gruen designed a department store outside Los Angeles with its image derived from ramps giving access to rooftop parking. This store, besides revealing Gruen's fascination with vehicular movement, was his only memorable piece of architecture until younger partners, like Cesar Pelli, designed for the firm a couple of decades later.

In 1954 Victor Gruen Associates completed the Northland Center, outside Detroit, the first large scale shopping centre designed to serve the motorists of an entire region. As architecture the Northland Center is pleasant if bland; as a circulation system, a series of systems, it demonstrates a clear grasp of the problem. Servicing of the stores is by underground truck route, freeing the ground around the building for the base acreage of shoppers' cars, which are on turn served by a highway net of mammoth proportions which surrounds the site. The actual shopping area of the Northland Center stands in the centre of the sea of cars and is completely traffic free: shoppers can walk and children can play as if the internal combustion engine had never been invented.

When the Northland Center had been completed, the next logical step in pampering the shopper still further was to enclose completely the shopping complex by roofing over the "pedestrian malls." This was accomplished in subsequent shopping centres, such as the Southdale Shopping Center in Minneapolis. The inside space now becomes multi-storey with different shopping levels, and the space itself filled with pools, hanging lamps and a whole paraphernalia of commercial kitsch.

Despite the success of the suburban shopping centres, Victor Gruen was genuinely concerned with the decay of American cities, a decay hastened, perhaps, by the very success of the shopping centres. He was given opportunities to construct shopping centres in the old city cores—his Midtown Plaza in Rochester, New York, for example, covers a quarter of the downtown area.

Buildings like Midtown Plaza did indeed help to revitalize the downtown area, but Gruen had always known that shopping alone could not solve the problem. When he was asked to make proposals for Fort Worth, Texas, he seized the chance to show his ideas for the centre of cities. The Fort Worth plan was never realized, but it remains Gruen's most important work, and there can be few city planners anywhere in the world that have not been influenced by it. In Britain, for example, Colin Buchanan's famous report *Traffic in Towns* follows many of the strategies proposed for Fort Worth.

The Fort Worth plan consists, in essence, of ringing the downtown area with a highway and parking garages, and within this area all is pedestrianized except for a gentle public transport system. The concept was clear, and one would have thought appealing, but in the 1950's Texans were not yet in the mood to be told that they could not take their cars wherever they wanted.

The fame of the Fort Worth plan brought Victor Gruen Associates work for various smaller cities and Gruen himself wrote his book *Heart of Our Cities*. He was fascinated by metropolitan scale and on his own initiative prepared a plan for Manhattan that proposed cross-town freeways to divide the island into segments.

In retrospect, it is the Northland Center and Fort Worth that are memorable. Both were optimistic about the possibilities of the good life for Americans. The Northland Center took the squalor of roadtown, made sense of it and gave it an image. The Fort Worth plan took a step on the road to making cars compatible with a great city.

—John Winter

GRUZEN, Barnett (Sumner).

American. Born in Dankera, Latvia, 25 July 1903; emigrated to the United States, 1905: naturalized, 1925. Educated at the Massachusetts Institute of Technology, Cambridge, 1921–28, B.Arch. 1926, M.Arch. 1928; Ecole des Beaux-Arts, Paris, 1930–32 (Rotch Traveling Fellowship). Married Ethel Brof in 1930; children: Jordan and Maxson. Worked in the offices of Ritchie, Parsons and Taylor, Guy Lowell, and Perry Shaw and Hepburn, Boston, 1928–30, and Stone and Webster, and Emery Roth, New York, 1930–32; in private practice, Jersey City, New Jersey, 1932–37; Partner, with Hugh Kelly, in Kelly and Gruzen, Jersey City, 1937–41; Chief Executive, Kelly and Gruzen, Jersey City, 1941–46, and New York, 1946 until Kelly's death, 1967; name changed to Gruzen and Partners, 1967; served as Consultant to the Partnership, 1971 until his death, 1974; direction of the firm assumed by son Jordan, 1971. President, American Society for Technion: Israel Institute of Technology, 1936–64; Chairman, Architectural Division, United Jewish Appeal and Federation of Jewish Philanthropies, New York, 1951. Recipient: Diamond Jubilee Citation, New York City, 1973; Medal of Honor, American Institute of Architects, 1974. Fellow, American Institute of Architects, 1957. *Died* (in New York) *27 September 1974.*

Works:

1955 Milton Steinberg House, Park Avenue Synagogue, East 87th Street, New York
Forchheimer Medical Science Building, Albert Einstein College of Medicine, Bronx, New York
1956 Junior High School 22, and adjoining Hamilton Fish Park Branch of the New York Public Library, Houston Street, New York
1958 Robbins Auditorium, Friedman Lounge, and Gottesman Library, Albert Einstein College of Medicine, Bronx, New York
1961 United States Mission to the United Nations, U.N. Plaza, New York
1962 Chatham Green Apartments, Park Row, New York
1963 Litho City, New York (project)
University Terrace Apartments, Brooklyn, New York
1964 Spanish Pavilion, *World's Fair*, New York
Congregation Knesseth Israel Synagogue, Empire Avenue, Queens, New York
1965 Chatham Towers Apartments, Park Row, New York
1966 Loeb Pavilion, Montefiore Hospital and Medical Center, Bronx, New York
1967 Lindsay Park Houses, Montrose Avenue, Brooklyn, New York
1968 Goldfine Pavilion, Hebrew Home for the Aged, Bronx, New York
1969 Bache and Company Headquarters, 100 Gold Street, New York
1970 Southbridge Towers Apartments, Gold, Frankfort, Water and Fulton Streets, New York
Annie Lichtenhein Pavilion, Montefiore Hospital and Medical Center, Bronx, New York
Kissena II Apartments, 45th Avenue, Flushing, New York
1971 Bronx State Hospital Rehabilitation Center, Waters Place, Bronx, New York
Japan House, East 47th Street, New York (with Junzo Yoshimura)
New Amsterdam Apartments, Amsterdam Avenue at West 95th Street, New York
Reuther Houses (apartments), Seagirt Avenue, Queens, New York
1972 Beekman Downtown Hospital Staff Residence, New York
1974 Police Headquarters Building and Pedestrian Plaza, Park Row, Pearl, Henry and New Streets, New York

United States Courthouse annex and modernization, New York

Beth Israel Medical Center, Newark, New Jersey

1975 Beekman Downtown Hospital Ambulatory Care Facility, New York

Murray Bergtraum High School, Pearl Street, New York

Publications:

On GRUZEN: articles—"The 1968 AIA Honor Awards" in *AIA Journal* (Washington, D.C.), June 1968; "Age-Old Problem" in *Industrial Design* (New York), July/August, 1969; "Bauen für Kranke Menschen" in *Baumeister* (Munich), September 1970; "Barnett Sumner Gruzen" in *AIA Journal* (Washington, D.C.), November 1974; "Barney Gruzen, FAIA, Dies at 71" in *Architectural Record* (New York), November 1974.

*

During Barnett Gruzen's partnership with Hugh A. Kelly he built numerous public housing schemes, hospitals and community centers, and this experience stood him in good stead for his later work. Towards the end of the partnership, Gruzen was responsible for gaining no less than ten separate commissions for developments in downtown Manhattan, and it is for these substantial contributions to that area that he is now best known.

After Kelly's death in 1967, Gruzen reorganized the office into Gruzen and Partners, taking on five new associates, including his son Jordan. The strength of the company during the next five years, before he retired to become a consultant to the firm, lies in Gruzen's political acumen, diplomacy, and almost bulldozing determination. When it came to a complicated civic development involving the sort of long-term wrangles with publicly funded agencies that big-city projects often entail, Gruzen had the patience and stamina to follow through.

A good example is one of the later downtown Manhattan works (which was finally completed by Jordan Gruzen), the new Police Headquarters Building. Originally commissioned in 1960 and opened in 1974, this project spanned the reign of two mayors, six police commissioners, and nine public works commissioners. During the inevitable and vexing delays, Gruzen and Partners were the only continuing presence.

The project required the shifting of several approach ramps to the Brooklyn Bridge, which in turn required the co-operation of a spate of city agencies and a helping hand from the Office of Lower Manhattan Development. In spite of fierce opposition from promoters of alternative and temporarily expedient projects, Gruzen helped the city to gain a sound and coherent piece of civic planning in an area where that virtue had been absent for too long.

The building itself, clad in brick, with its echoing grid of regularized deep set windows, towers over its basement car park and open lobby, but it is the use of the irregularly shaped site that is most impressive. A 75 foot wide pedestrian plaza—designed with the landscapists Friedberg and Associates, with whom Gruzen had often collaborated—has been planted with rows of honey locust trees, fitted with benches, with a large steel sculpture placed in the center, creating such a grand and spacious outdoor lounging area that it is difficult for the visitor to realize that he is actually on a bridge with a busy traffic artery —Park Row—cutting beneath it. The Police Department is now physically and symbolically linked both to the residential neighborhood to the South and to the courthouses along Center Street.

New York has sometimes seemed a city intent on bleeding itself to death in fragmented and ad hoc planning decisions. It is to Barnett Gruzen's credit that he never gave up when others did, and that he persevered against what many would regard as for-midable odds to create such an intelligently planned addition to the city center.

—Colin Naylor

GUEDES, Amancio (d'Alpoim Miranda) ("Pancho" Guedes).

Portuguese. Born in Lisbon, 13 May 1925. Educated at the São Tome School, 1930: Gulf of Guinea Primary School, Lisbon, 1931; Manjacaze Primary School, Mozambique, 1932–33; Lourenco Marques High School, Mozambique, 1934–38; Maritz Brothers College, Johannesburg, South Africa, 1939–44; University of the Witwatersrand, Johannesburg, under Donald Pilcher, 1945–50, B.Arch. 1950. Married Dorothy Ann Phillips in 1947; children: Pedro Paulo, Veronica, Godofredo and Katarina. In private practice, Lourenco Marques, Mozambique, 1949–75. Since 1975, Professor and Head of the Department of Architecture, University of the Witwatersrand. Exhibitions: *Bienal,* Sao Paulo, 1961; *Biennale,* Venice, 1975; Institute for Architecture and Urbanism, New York, 1976. Address: 17 Ninth Avenue, Melville, Johannesburg, South Africa.

Works:

1950 Sacadura Botte House, Lourenco Marques
1951/
52 Leite Martins House, Lourenco Marques
Dragão Apartments, Lourenco Marques
1951/
53 Prometheus Apartments, Lourenco Marques
Mendes d'Almeida House, Machava, Mozambique
1952/
53 Hotel and shops, Palmeira, Mozambique
Semi-Detached Houses for Matos Ribeira, Lourenco Marques
1952/
54 Saipal Bakery, Lourenco Marques
1953 Santos Marques e Silva Building, Lourenco Marques
1953/
54 Otto Barbosa Garage and Offices, Lourenco Marques
Co-Op Rowhouses, Lourenco Marques
8 houses, Avenida Belgarde da Silva, Lourenco Marques
1953/
59 Abreu, Santos e Rocha Building, Lourenco Marques
1954 Nucleo de Arte Art Club, Lourenco Marques
Zambi Restaurant, Lourenco Marques
Exhibition pavilions, Lourenco Marques
1954/
55 Pylon Cement Factory, Matola, Mozambique
Abreu Family Rowhouses, Lourenco Marques
1954/
56 Mann George Shipping Company Building, Lourenco Marques
12 houses, Avenida Miguel Bombarda, Lourenco Marques
Dr. Simoes Ferreira Apartment Block, Lourenco Marques
1954/
57 Tonelli Condominium, Lourenco Marques
1954/
59 Polana Bar, Polana Hotel, Lourenco Marques
1955 Hotel, San Martinho do Bilene, Mozambique
1955/
56 House, Avenida Caldas Xavier, Lourenco Marques
1955/
57 Barclays Bank Building, Lourenco Marques
1956/
57 Engenheiro Gomes Rowhouses, Lourenco Marques
1956/
58 House of the Three Giraffes, Lourenco Marques
Smiling Lion Apartments, Lourenco Marques
1957/
62 Isauro Lopes Building, Lourenco Marques

1958/
60 Saturio Pires House, Lourenco Marques
1958/
61 The Pyramidal Kindergarten, Lourenco Marques
1958/
63 Spence e Lemos Building, Lourenco Marques
1959/
72 Boror Building, Lourenco Marques
1960/
61 Service Station, Komatipoort, South Africa
1960/
63 Motel, Komatipoort, South Africa
1961/
62 Yes House, Lourenco Marques
1962/
64 Sagrada Familia Church, Machava, Mozambique
1963 Mayers House, Piet Retief, South Africa
Associacão dos Naturais Building, Lourenco Marques
1963/
65 Church of St. James the Great, Nyamandhlovo, Rhodesia
Casa Salm, Lourenco Marques
1963/
72 Waterford School, Mbabane, Swaziland
1964/
65 Dr. Jose da Costa Building, Lourenco Marques
Primary school, Antioka, Magude, Mozambique
1964/
66 Church of Santa Ana da Munhuana, Lourenco Marques
Casa Almiro do Vale, Lourenco Marques
1965 Enfermagem School, Lourenco Marques
1965/
66 Agricultural Adviser's House, Mavuvulane, Mozambique
1965/
67 Police Widows and Orphans Savings Bank Building, Lourenco Marques
Dr. Lopes da Silva House, Lourenco Marques
1966/
68 San Jose de Lhanguene Convent, Lourenco Marques
Hospital extension, Chicumbane, Gaza, Mozambique
1966/
69 Octavio Lobo Building, Lourenco Marques
1966/
73 Khovolar Hostel, Lourenco Marques
1967 College of Nossa Senhora da Conceicão, Inhambane, Mozambique
1967/
68 Desirello House, Illovo, Johannesburg
1968 Canha St. Andrews House, Johannesburg
1968/
69 The Clandestine Nursery School, Canico, Lourenco Marques
Congregational Church, Choupal, Mozambique
1968/
71 The Red House, Lourenco Marques
1969/
71 The House of the Broken Pediment, Lourenco Marques
1970/
72 Standard Totta Bank Director's House, Lourenco Marques
1970/
74 Parque Condominium, Lourenco Marques
Nurses' Hostel, Chicumbane, Gaza, Mozambique
Church of San Cipriano do Chamanculo, Lourenco Marques
1971 Church of the Twelve Apostles, Gala Massala, Maputo, Mozambique (with Pedro Guedes)
1971/
73 Boesch House, Lourenco Marques

Waterford School Girls Hostel, Mbabane, Swaziland (with Pedro Guedes)

1972/
74 Post Office School, Inhambane, Mozambique
1972/
75 Hostel and Farm School, Estevel, Boane, Mozambique
1973 Governor's Palace, Vila Pery, Mozambique
1973/
75 Totta Standard Building, Porto Alexandre, Angola
Hotel, Alto Mahe, Lourenco Marques
1974/
75 Regentes Agricolas School, Vila Pery, Mozambique

Publications:

By GUEDES: book—*Fragments from an Ironic Autobiography,* Johannesburg 1977; articles—"Les Mapogga" in *Aujourd'hui* (Paris), June 1962; "Amancio Guedes: Y aura-t-il une architecture" in *L'Architecture d'Aujourd'hui* (Paris), June/July 1962; "Things Are Not What They Seem To Be" in *Proceedings of the First National Congress of African Culture,* Salisbury 1962; "Four Sights and the Whosing of Sakes" in *For Us,* Johannesburg 1963; "The American Egyptian Style" in *World Architecture 1,* edited by John Donat, London 1964; "The Practice of Architecture" in *South African Architectural Record* (Johannesburg), June 1964; "Architects as Magicians, Conjurors, Dealers in Magic Goods, Promises, Potions, Spells—Myself as Witchdoctor" in *World Architecture 2,* edited by John Donat, London 1965; "Buildings Grow Out of Each Other; or, How My Own Sagrada Familia Came To Be" in *World Architecture 4,* London 1967; "The Intuitive Process and Some Other Ideas" in *Architectural Education Symposium,* Johannesburg 1967; "The Language of Sculpture" in *Faculty of Arts Colloquium,* Johannesburg 1975; "Bush Schools" in *RIBA Journal* (London), no. 10, 1976.

On GUEDES: articles—"Amancio Guedes, Architect of Lourenco Marques" by Julian Beinart in *Architectural Review* (London), April 1961; "Pancho Amancio d'Alpoim Miranda Guedes: Arquitecto escultor—escultor arquitecto" by Salette Tavares in *Coloquio* (Lisbon), April 1977; "On Amancio d'Alpoim Guedes" by Alison Smith and "Down There on a Visit" by Alan Berman in *Architecture + Urbanism* (Tokyo), no. 6, 1978.

For twenty-five years I invented and made enough buildings to make up a city. An imaginary but quite probable city, chaotic and layered with memories, a city of many separate and tiny cases of obsessive regularity.

I am also a painter and sculptor. I cannot tell painting and sculpture apart from architecture. Many of the ideas of my architecture have originated in drawings which are common to the three. Some of the other ideas are paraphrases or distorted quotations from other architects' works and ideas. I believe that buildings grow out of each other, that each artist invents his own precursors, that there is an incessant dialogue with many pasts. Sometimes I have ridden a track of ideas for a number of years with other ideas interspersed. Often the ideas have crashed and turned into other ideas. I have worked in many styles simultaneously. I have dismissed any sort of chronology long ago. I have, instead, classified my architectural inventions into twenty-five families and filed them into a catalogue of twenty-five architectures. In that catalogue there is a family of learning machines, some slices of street face, some slabs, some temporary towers, buildings in parts of rings, wedges and circles, a whole neo-colonial revival, some transformations and resurrections, a set of parts of villages, remembering other villages far away in my mother country, many disparate churches, a collection of Euclidian palaces, a few grass houses, a chain of service stations, thirty or forty little blue banks on the east side and ten little black and white ones on the west side, buildings in my arched and somewhat roman manner, the Wrightian works and the earlier Wright houses, a whole industrial zone of factories and warehouses, the clubs and associations, the passages, steps, places and squares of the city, the bargains in a bush style, the bubblies, a number of tents and sails, a couple of box houses, all the works in the American-Egyptian style, the buildings with walls twisting and turning and stilo guedes.

I have always worked at home with the help of a few draughtsmen who, in most cases, I have trained myself. I have always done all the design work myself (and by all I mean all, from the invention to the detail which is as much a part of the invention) except for the few times when I have collaborated with my son, Pedro.

Most of my works now lie dead or wounded, casualties and victims of four revolutions. I now live in exile. I carry the ideas of all these twenty-five architectures within me. They have become the drawings and photographs I have with me. I have become a teacher. My task is now to explore the borders of architecture, to expand its territories, to illuminate the new lands and sign-post them for my students and for myself.

—Amancio Guedes

Amancio Guedes: Smiling Lion Apartments, Lourenco Marques, 1956–58

Pancho Guedes is an amalgam. Born in Portugal, schooled in South Africa and having practised in Mozambique, he is both Dadaist and Renaissance Man.

His writing, sparkling and irreverent, illustrates this creative tension, which has resulted in some of the most exhilarating buildings in Southern Africa. The stance is theatrical, but it is founded on a deep-rooted love, and enthusiasm, for Architecture. His personal brand of Dada is that of an artist who is secure in the knowledge of his own formal ingenuity, one who can savour the excitement of hurling himself off a precipice, knowing he will land on his feet. As the joker in the pack, Guedes can afford to make faces at his architectural contemporaries, whilst acknowledging and developing their ideas in his own work.

His buildings are not merely refreshing: their abundance runs into hundreds. The full number is not yet established, even by Guedes himself, as some of his designs for the remoter parts of Mozambique may have been built without his knowledge, but it probably surpasses even that of Frank Lloyd Wright. In pursuit of this achievement, he would work all week, except for Sunday evenings, conducting his site visits at a blistering pace, never hesitating to personally demolish a wall if it was built incorrectly, or get to work with a brush and a pot of paint if the building had been painted the wrong colour. The activity of creation, and its expression, is one of the underlying themes throughout all his Styles and Families.

His earliest style, Stilo Guedes, is certainly the most outrageous—giant spikes of concrete stick out on either side of strident murals inspired by Ndebele art; crosswalls hang in space, deliberately designed to engender anxiety in the beholder. Later work becomes more orthogonal: the American Egyptian Style features the pyramidal roofs of Louis Kahn's Trenton Center; the Euclidean Palaces (some of which show a marked tendency towards disintegration) are based on a strict geometry; whilst his "arched and somewhat Roman manner" includes the Red House, which succeeds in being both toy-like and monumental at the same time, with an internal organization which refers both to Corb's double volumes and to Michelangelo's "staircase room" at the Laurentian Library. But it would be futile to attempt to summarize the whole range of his work here.

What is most important is his approach. From the few buildings which have been at all publicized in the more orthodox architectural centres of the world, it is easy to perceive his erudition in the field of architectural ideas. Indeed, his work might even be cast in the role of the collective unconscious of contemporary architecture, as in his buildings its chief preoccupations are expounded and discussed. Certain patterns predominate at different times—Gaudí, Corb, Kahn, Wright, Palladio—even Venturi. But far from being a slavish imitator, Guedes develops his own and others' ideas into architecture of the most satisfying humanity, forming an object lesson in how to use the mechanism of influence creatively—and this could prove to be his greatest contribution.

—Timothy Ostler

GUEDES, Joaquim.
Brazilian. Born in Sao Paulo, 18 June 1932. Educated at the University of Sao Paulo, Faculty of Architecture and Urbanism, 1949–54, Dip.Arch. 1954, D.Arch. 1972. Married Liliana Marsicano in 1953; children: Joaquim José, Maria Clara, Alberto, Francisco, and Tereza Matilde. In private practice, Sao Paulo, since 1955. Professor of Building Materials, 1958–69, and since 1969 Professor of Town Plan-

ning, University of Sao Paulo. Associate Professor, Institute of Architecture and Urbanism, Strasbourg, France, 1970–73. Director, Sao Paulo Division, 1959–62, and Member of the Council, 1959–69, Brazilian Institute of Architects; Member, International Union of Architects/Unesco Commission on Habitat, Paris, 1963–69. Exhibitions: *Salão Paulista de Arte Moderna,* Sao Paulo, 1959, 1961, 1969; *Bienal,* Sao Paulo, 1965; *Premiação Anual,* Brazilian Institute of Architects, Sao Paulo, 1969; *Joaquim Guedes,* Buenos Aires, 1978. Recipient: Governor's State Prize, Sao Paulo, 1959, 1969; Prize, *Bienal,* Sao Paulo, 1965; Rino Levi Prize, Brazilian Institute of Architects, 1969. Address: Joaquim Guedes e Associados, Avenida Paulista 1776, 21st Floor, Sao Paulo 01310, Brazil.

Works:

1957 J. A. Guedes House, Rua Georgia, Sao Paulo
1958 Cunha Lima House, Rua Silvio Portugal, Sao Paulo
1959 Itapira Forum, Sao Paulo
  Ataliba Nogueira Primary School, Itapira, Sao Paulo
1961 Costa Neto House, Rua Itapanhau, Sao Paulo
  São Domingos High School, Sao Paulo (project)
1962 Toledo House, Rua Samuel Neves, Piracicaba, Sao Paulo
  Areia Branca Primary School, Taubaté, Sao Paulo (project)
1963 Mathematics Institute, University of Sao Paulo (project)
1965 Breyton House, Rua Souza Ramos, Sao Paulo
  Landi House, Rua Guilherme Milward, Sao Paulo
1966 Pereira House, Rua Carangola, Sao Paulo
  Agricultural School, Lorena, Sao Paulo
  Campinas Electronics School, Sao Paulo (project)
  Faculty of Philosophy, Lorena, Sao Paulo (project)
  Carvalhosa House, Rua Polonia, Sao Paulo
  Reinach House, Braganca Paulista, Sao Paulo
1967 São José High School, Sororcaba, Sao Paulo (project)
  Preparatory institute, Jandira, Sao Paulo
1968 Apartment building, Al. Ministro Rocha Azevedo, Sao Paulo (project)
  Vila Galvão State High School, Guarulhos, Sao Paulo
  Central Library of Bahia, Salvador, Brazil (project)
1969 Urban plan for Sao Paulo
  Preliminary plan for Campinas, Sao Paulo
  United Nations Conference Center, Vienna (project; with E. S. Mello)
1970 Monteil House, Itanhaem, Sao Paulo
  Master plan for Mogí Guaçú, Sao Paulo
1971 School of Architecture, Strasbourg, France (project; with P. Chemetov and R. Chomel)
1972 Urban plan for Porto Velho, Rondonia, Brazil
  Civic and Cultural Center, Mogí Guaçú, Sao Paulo (project)
1973 Urban plan for the Carajás Iron Mines new town project, Pará, Brazil
  Urban plan for Marabá, Pará, Brazil
1974 J. Guedes House, Rua Prof. Luciano Gualberto, Sao Paulo
  Urban plan for Piracicaba, Sao Paulo
  Residential complex, Campinas, Sao Paulo
  Marsicano Factory, Salto, Sao Paulo
  Plan for the island of Tamandua, Sao Paulo
  São Bernardo Satellite Town, Sao Paulo (project)
  Dourado House, Rua Albert Einstein, Sao Paulo
1975 Convention Center, Foz do Iguaçú, Paraná, Brazil (project)
  Beer House, Rua Jacupiranga, Sao Paulo

  Romero House, Campinas, Sao Paulo
  Monteil House, Avaré, Sao Paulo
1976 Hotel, Rua Ministro Nelson Hungria, Sao Paulo
  Urban plan for Taquaral, Piracicaba, Sao Paulo
  Monteiro Lobato Public Library, São Bernardo, Sao Paulo (project)
  Urban plan for Caraiba, Bahia, Brazil
1977 Campinas Maternity Hospital, Sao Paulo (project)
1978 Urban plan for Paiva, Recife, Brazil
  Anna Mariani House, Ibiuna, Sao Paulo
1979 Urban plan for Barcarena, Belém, Brazil

Publications:

By GUEDES: book—*Arquitectura Brasileira após Brasilia/Depoimentos,* Rio de Janeiro 1978; articles —"José Anthero Guedes House" in *Bem Estar* (Sao Paulo), no. 4, 1957; "Architecture in the VIII Bienal" in *Acrópole* (Sao Paulo), October 1965; "O Exercício da Profissão em Função da Arquitetura e o meio Ambiente," "A Integração do Arquiteto no Planejamento" and "Arquitetura e Planejamento Urbano," with J. Wilheim, in *Acrópole* (Sao Paulo), November 1966; "Concurso para Bilioteca Central de Salvador" in *Acrópole* (Sao Paulo), November 1968; "The Private Home in Brazilian Tradition and the Problem of the New Generation" in *Global Interiors 2,* Tokyo 1972; "Obras y Proyetos del Estudio Joaquim Guedes y Associados" in *Revista Summa* (Buenos Aires), June 1979; "Caraiba New Town and Other Works" in *Spazio e Società* (Milan), no. 7, July 1979.

On GUEDES: books—*New Directions in Latin American Architecture* by Francisco Bullrich, New York 1969, London 1970; *Profile of New Brazilian Art* by P. M. Bardi, Sao Paulo 1969; *Panoramica de la Arquitectura Latinoamericana* by P. Gasparini and D. Bayon, Barcelona 1975; articles—"Cunha Lima House" in *Kokusai Kentiku* (Tokyo), July 1967; special issue of *Acrópole* (Sao Paulo), February 1968; "Nouvelle Ecole d'Architecture à Strasbourg" in *L'Architecture d'Aujourd'hui* (Paris), September 1971.

*

All projects are important, even the smallest and most incoherent. They are laboratories allowing one to think about and to work with man, his complex and marvellous needs, with materials, matter and technologies, with light, economics, ethics, politics. "A house is a small town" (V. Eyck).

For many years I thought that construction was the important thing. Architecture was a construction to house a system of activities/spaces organized for man. This way of seeing guided and even differentiated my work. As a result, it was characterized by a certain severity in the analysis of factors and was, in consequence, severe in its end solutions; it was an architecture opposed to ornament, to decoration, and to traditional national or foreign forms, a point of departure for many projects.

I did not know and even denied the importance of beauty.

As time has passed I have become aware that, even with an aversion to any kind of forcibly pre-conceived aesthetic, my great desire has always been to create beauty, to produce increasingly beautiful architecture, marked, nevertheless, by a sense of human, social and anthropocentric destiny. But who, in all conscience, can imagine himself to be in possession of such reserves of beauty as to offer it so prodigally to others? Beyond all the rhetoric—what criteria must be satisfied to produce beauty? What is beauty? How to learn it? How to teach it? How to create it?

Looking into myself, looking for points of reference that have guided me in this quest for beauty, I can identify: an analysis of the relationship between

habitat and landscape, the perfect siting of a work, its integration into the town from a functional, atmospheric, cultural and yet formal point of view; a compromise with man, whose needs and sensibilities are the prime reasons for the project—and this compromise involves more than simply and conveniently supposing his participation; it involves guaranteeing his participation, his freedom, in relation to the work; and, finally, a rigorous, coherent and accurate construction, one that realizes and is expressive of these relationships and compromises.

—Joaquim Guedes

*

Joaquim Guedes is one of a few modern Brazilian architects who have chosen the path of experimentation, and his completed buildings, though hardly numerous, are clearly representative of his proposals and research. At first sight his works present a deceptively large number of different forms; on closer inspection, they are manifestations of a systematic and coherent work process, a solving of the problems posed by all the factors that go to make up a work of architecture. These factors may be intrinsic and specific, such as the technology, the building program, or the economics; or they may be part of a larger context, factors around which the building will emerge. And a crucial concern for Guedes is that each project is started from scratch—creation in its purest form, abandoning existing notions and earlier premises in favor of a complete return to the drawing board and a fresh start.

This philosophy and method accounts for the predominant organic quality in Guedes' architecture; at the same time, his work is characterized by a clear logic that often results in a sensitive rationalism. The dynamic relationship between these two tendencies, co-existing within a single project, creates a special tension.

Guedes' architectural output can be divided into three groups.

The first group is characterized by importance of the structural system, the element that organizes space. External surfaces and other architectural elements are clearly subservient to the structure, which determines the volume—as in the Cunha Lima House of 1958, the Campinas Electronics School of 1966, and the Guedes House of 1973.

The second group involves works of much greater complexity of form, and here it is that Guedes gives his virtuoso performances. Here, structure loses its importance and becomes subservient to a stronger organic tendency. The mass is divided into smaller volumes, often with irregular shapes: prismatic surfaces of frameless panes of glass, which break up the dividing line between interior and exterior; overhangs and *brises-soleil* that give rhythm to the facades. The resulting combination is powerfully dynamic, its cohesion assured by its very logic. Buildings in this group include the Pereira House, Dourado House, the Itapira Forum, and the unbuilt plans for the São José High School, the Central Library of Bahir, and the Mogí Guaçú Cultural and Civic Center.

Of his third group it can be said that Guedes reverts to the vision of simplicity that existed in Brazilian architecture in the works of Lúcio Costa and a few others, a vision that was abandoned by the end of the 1940's in the wake of the great "Brazilian Style." Without favoring any particular trend (though he was, perhaps, influenced most directly by the works of Alvar Aalto), Guedes rediscovers the human subtleties of this early vision and, in doing so, returns to an option far better suited to the realities of everyday life in Brazil. The Landi House—notable for its subtle use of space, its mass, and its architectural elements, and built by extremely economical means—is a perfect example. Others are the group of architectural projects for the town of Caraiba.

Yet another, fourth group could be made up by linking certain buildings whose structure plays a less important part than in those of the first group and whose appearance is more compact and less elaborate externally than those of the third. Examples are

Joaquim Guedes: Guedes House, Sao Paulo, 1974

the Toledo House, Beer House, and the project for the United Nations Center in Vienna. But this excessive categorization is valid only as a means of explanation: in Guedes' work as a whole, the most diverse, even contradictory, solutions are merely ways of dealing with certain facets of the total situation within which the architect is working.

Town planning has also been an important part of Guedes' career from the beginning. Among the more recent of these plans, Caraiba stands out by virtue of its staying within basic limitations and restricting itself to a simplicity of function and construction that has resulted in the elimination of all superfluity and the consequent minimalization of production costs. It has a modest dignity rare in this kind of work.

The new town of Caraiba—currently under construction in the interior of Bahia—is a "company town" for the 15,000 employed by a mining company. Its conception was based on socio/anthropological research, a facet of town planning that is usually neglected. The plan is based, too, on traditional urban models in the region and on the study of vehicular and pedestrian circulation patterns. The plan relies on the archetypal solution of the grid pattern but develops it in a way that optimizes urban integration. Social stratification and limitation is avoided by a distribution of dwellings of varying size within the urban area and by creating open spaces within the city for the accommodation of external or neighboring populations that will no doubt be attracted to this economic center. The structure allows for a natural, ordered growth. The existing houses can be altered by their occupiers, and the buildings are endowed with a certain spontaneity.

Guedes' architectural projects for Caraiba are simple and in perfect accord with local conditions. They have an irregular plan, resulting from the informal distribution of functions that are, in turn, organized and supplied by means of interlinked circulation axes. The basic module is elaborated and disappears behind the volumes, which play an important part in plastic terms, without losing their entirely functional role and without compromising the rationale and the economy of construction. Guedes deals with the region's severe climatic conditions (semi-desert) by various means—in the urban planning (streets running east-west, buildings oriented north-south), in the architecture (buildings with patios, covered walkways, etc.), and in the building techniques (thick walls of bricks specially made from local clay).

Caraiba illustrates clearly all the professional views of Joaquim Guedes. It is also one of the most interesting experiments in town planning ever attempted in Brazil.

—Jorge Czajkowski

GUTBROD, (Konrad) Rolf (Dietrich).

German. Born in Stuttgart, 13 September 1910. Educated at the Freie Waldorfschule, Stuttgart; Technical Universities of Berlin and Stuttgart, 1929–35, Dip.Ing. 1935; worked with Professor Günter Wilhelm, in Stuttgart, 1935–36. Has three children: Christiane, Verena and Ghita. Served on the Government Building Council, 1940–45. In private practice, Stuttgart, since 1946; established offices in Berlin, 1961, and Riyadh, Saudi Arabia, 1977. Professor, Technical University of Stuttgart, since 1953 (Chair of Interior Decoration and Design since 1961). Guest Professor, Technical University of Istanbul, 1957–59; Walker Ames Professor, University of Washington, Seattle, 1963. Recipient: First Prize, IBM Administration Building Competition, Berlin, 1959; First Prize, Cologne University Centre Competition, 1960; First Prize, Württembergische Bank Competition, Stuttgart, 1963; First Prize, Student Hostel Competition, Stuttgart, 1963; First Prize, Max-Planck-Institut and Dahlem Row Houses Competition, Berlin, 1965; First Prize, Museums of European Art Competition, Berlin, 1966; First Prize, with Frei Otto, Hotel and Conference Centre Competition, Mecca, Saudi Arabia, 1966; Auguste Perret Prize, International Union of Architects, 1968; First Prize, SDR Radio Station Building Competition, Stuttgart, 1968; Paul Bonatz Prize, Stuttgart, 1970, 1972; First Prize, Sparkassen-Versicherung Ag Building Competition, Stuttgart, 1970; Grand Cross of Merit, German Government, 1972; Hugo Häring Award, 1972. Member, Akademie der Künste, Berlin, 1963; Member, Ordre pour le Mérité, 1971. Address: Büro Gutbrod, Ebereschenallee

27, 1000 Berlin 19; or Schoderstrasse 10, 7000 Stuttgart 1, West Germany.

Works:

1954 Chamber of Commerce, Stuttgart (with Rolf Gutbier)
1956 Concert Hall, Berliner Platz, Stuttgart (with Adolf Abel and B. Spring)
1957 SDR Broadcasting Studios, Villa Berg, Stuttgart (with Helmut Weber and Hertha-Maria Witzemann)
1962 IBM Administration Building, Ernst-Reuter-Platz, West Berlin
1965 German Embassy, Metternichgasse, Vienna
SDR Television Studios, Villa Berg, Stuttgart (with Helmut Weber and Hertha-Maria Witzemann)
1966 Advertising Center, Berlin (with Hermann Kiess)
Teachers' College, Freie Waldorfschule, Uhlandshöhe, Stuttgart (with Wolfgang Henning)
Volkswagen Building, Stuttgart
1967 German Pavilion, *Expo '67*, Montreal (with Frei Otto)
Library, University of Cologne
1968 Auditorium Building, University of Cologne
Württembergische Bank, Stuttgart (with Hermann Kiess)
1969 Britz-Buchow-Rudow Housing, Gropiusstadt, Berlin
Student Hostel, Schwerzstrasse, Birkach, Stuttgart (with Hermann Kiess)
1970 Opernplatz Housing, Berlin

1971 Max-Planck-Institut, Dahlem, Berlin
Development plan for the Kurfürstendamm Quarter of Berlin
1972 Row houses, Dahlem, Berlin
1973 Classroom Building, for the Freie Waldorfschule, Uhlandshöhe, Stuttgart (with Wolfgang Henning)
Master plan for the Museums of European Art (Museum of Arts and Crafts; Picture Gallery; Sculpture Gallery; Print Gallery; Art Library), Tiergarten, Berlin
Cultural Center, Abidjan, Ivory Coast (project; with Frei Otto and Ove Arup and Partners)
1974 Hotel and Conference Center, Mecca, Saudi Arabia (with Frei Otto and Ove Arup and Partners)
Spa and Recreation Center, Baden-Baden (competition project; with Frei Otto)
ZDF Television Center, Lerchenberg, Mainx (competition projects; with Hermann Kiess)
Pilgrims' Accommodation, Muna, Saudi Arabia (competition project)
1976 SDR Radio Station Building, Neckerstrasse, Stuttgart
Sparkassen-Versicherung Ag (insurance company) Building, Löwentorstrasse, Stuttgart
Ministry of Industry and Electricity, Riyadh, Saudi Arabia (project; with Frei Otto and Ove Arup and Partners)
Mannesmann Administration Building, Stuttgart (competition projects; with Wolfgang Henning)

Publications:

On GUTBROD: books—*Konzerthaus Stuttgarter Liederhalle* by Dr. Pollert, Stuttgart 1956; *Bibliotheksbauten in der BRD*, Frankfurt 1968; *Funkhaus Stuttgart*, Stuttgart 1976; *Frei Otto* by Philip Drew, Stuttgart 1976.

If an architect like Felix Candela, the great inventor of new structures, who was invited to report on his ideas about the "influence of technology on architectural creativity," reveals himself as a non-technologist—being disappointed with the tendencies of today's technology—and if Candela demands an entirely different attitude from us architects, and if he thinks it necessary to stop the "inhuman and bureaucratic production of buildings," and if he invites us to "rediscover the pleasure of creation"—and if, too, Arthur Erickson, speaking about the "influence of ideology on architectural creativity" comes to the conclusion that our ideology today is valid for only a very small part of the world and has to be reflected and revised in view of world-wide needs, and that all ideology can be valued only in the context in which it has to serve—then it is quite obvious that the high aim of creativity (creativity as understood and hoped for as the salvation of our profession) cannot be achieved simply by combining technology and ideology.

There is a world-wide concern about the changes that have taken place in our surroundings during the last 20 years. Everyone seems shocked about the escalation of needs and about the way in which changes for the worse always happen most quickly.

At the University of Stuttgart, for a few years, our

Rolf Gutbrod: Hotel and Conference Center, Mecca, Saudi Arabia, 1974

young students were enthuasiastic about the scientific approach; they had slogans like "death to the artist-architect;" they were negative about design; they voted against learning to be draftsmen. Now, the great majority seems to realize that this belief in research only and the adoration of the quantifiable is a danger to our built surroundings.

The reports of the Club of Rome have made it clear to everyone where this road leads—and even the stupid now understand that once everyone has a bathroom, a washing-machine and a dish-washer, there will not be enough hot water; and if everyone in the world has a color television set or two, and a car or two, there can not be enough energy to run them.

So a change *must* come, and surely this is not a problem that requires more analysis, more futurology, more perfection, or—worst of all—more production.

We architects will never have the possibilities and means for research as do those groups working for governments or for, say, armaments and mass-production industries, and if we look at what these experts, with all this support, have produced in response to relatively simple problems (as, for instance, the price and availability of crude oil), we cannot hope to come up with better answers for the problems connected with accommodating the fast growing world population, building in harmony with existing topography and culture, and using more technology without further destroying and polluting our surroundings. So, I think, we have to admit that only a fundamental change in our attitude will give us a chance to meet the challenge.

We must convince ourselves and our clients and the public that the problems cannot be solved with more technology but that we are confronted with a spiritual problem and that we must learn to have confidence in ingenuity, in ideation, in creativity. And it is *our* job to achieve this change.

The more complex our problems became the more we looked for help—we formed teams, we collaborated with sociologists, ecologists, doctors, psychologists, experts of all kinds; we resigned ourselves to being the leader of the team. But in the public mind, we, the architects and engineers, are responsible for the destruction of existing values, for the dreariness of the newly built environment, for the production of new slums. And—maybe—this serves us right.

As architects *we* should have known that, though our work is becoming more and more specialized, and though the problems to be solved are becoming more and more complex, and though, naturally, our work today is involved with and is characterized by technology, our profession must remain an art, must allow for spiritual values, must leave room for intuition, must reflect philosophy.

These most valuable notions, inherent in our profession, are not so easily quantifiable as the other elements that influence the construction of buildings and surroundings. But why are we not looking for new methods of integration? We must not allow ourselves to be outmaneuvered. No, I don't want to go back to the old image of the artist-architect as someone wearing a special hat and a funny tie. And, of course, what we need is the well-informed and educated architect who has an excellent knowledge of today's technology or, at least, knows where to find and how to use it. But the more architecture is rationalized, "progressive" and profit-oriented, the more the creative element must balance this development.

The important ideas, the creative guidelines, and the solutions for tomorrow cannot be expected to come from the computer.

—Rolf Gutbrod

In 1974 an interesting architectural manifesto was published, a manifesto in open opposition to the renunciatory and classicist tendencies of contemporary architecture. Among was signatories was Rolf Gutbrod who was then, with Frei Otto, putting the finishing touches to the Hotel and Conference Center in Mecca, a work that in itself marks a fundamental stage in the progress of architectural planning in Arab countries.

Gutbrod's career has been a preparation for the manifesto. His Volkswagen Building of 1966, together with Scharoun's towers and the elegant houses of Chen Cuen Lee, was one of the most significant buildings completed in Stuttgart in the 1960's. That the irregular ground plan of the Volkswagen Building is derived from Scharoun is easily recognizable in the facades set at different angles. A little later Gutbrod completed the Student Hostel in Birkach: in a way similar to the Volkswagen Building, it burst out from the sides of an acute-angled triangle, with the single rooms along the sides directed toward the central nucleus of the service complex.

These designs would lead one to describe Gutbrod as an organic architect, to associate him with Scharoun and German expressionism—but that is perhaps rather too common an exaggeration. His conceptions are in a field and in an epoch that have already emerged from the classical currents of expressionism. Born in Stuttgart, and educated at the Freie Waldorfschule, Gutbrod was raised in a basically humanistic-naturalistic tradition. His work on the Freie Waldorfschule, on the Uhlandshöhe, Stuttgart, completed in 1973, is evidence of Gutbrod's humanistic interests and sensitivity; it is obviously a task in which he cared particularly deeply. And Gutbrod is a Muslim convert: he has shifted the axis of his activities more and more to the Middle East.

Collaboration with Frei Otto has also constituted an important chapter in his life: it has given Gutbrod the opportunity to dedicate himself to a search for associative forms and to work with tensile roofs. This technological instrument has enabled him to broaden his units of measurement and to adapt tensile forms to the requirements of the Arab peoples, who perform their religious devotions mainly in the open air. The German Pavilion at *Expo '67* in Montreal was another stage in his coming to a global view of the concept of community, a concept that he had been developing ever since he won international recognition for his Concert Hall in Stuttgart in 1956.

Gutbrod's recent work, the Museums of European Art Complex in Berlin, of which the Museum of Arts and Crafts is already being built, is also certain to attract international attention. The site is, in fact, the completion of the quadrangle formed by Scharoun's Philharmonie and Library and Mies van der Rohe's National Gallery. To design a complex to stand next to these buildings must have been, for Gutbrod, a delicate task. Yet he at once rejects any seductive monumental gesture: he has designed a continuous articulated block surrounding closed and open courts, forming an organic urban texture that contributes to the richness of the architectural landscape, a landscape characterized by blocks that are, in contrast, closed and compact. Once again Gutbrod has given priority to the social obligation of architecture—the most significant aspect of his work.

—Giuliano Chelazzi

GWATHMEY, Charles.

American. Born in Charlotte, North Carolina, 19 June 1938. Educated at the Music and Art High School, New York, 1952–56; University of Pennsylvania School of Architecture, Philadelphia, under Louis I. Kahn, Robert Venturi, and Thomas Vreeland, 1956–59; Yale University School of Architecture, New Haven, Connecticut, under Paul Rudolph, James Stirling, and Shadrach Woods, 1959–62, M.Arch. 1962; awarded William Wirt Winchester Travelling Fellowship, 1962; Fulbright Fellow in France, 1962–63. Married Bette Ann Damson in 1974. Professor of Architectural Design, Pratt Institute, Brooklyn, New York, 1964–66, Yale University, 1966, Princeton University, New Jersey, 1966–69, Harvard University, Cambridge, Massachusetts, 1970–72, Cooper Union, New York, 1971–72, University of California at Los Angeles, 1973–74, Princeton University, 1975–76, and Columbia University, New York, 1976–77. Partner, Gwathmey-Henderson, New York, 1966–70, and Gwathmey-Henderson-Siegel, New York, 1970–71. Since 1971, Partner, with Robert Siegel, Gwathmey Siegel Architects, New York. Trustee, Institute of Architecture and Urban Studies, New York, since 1978. Recipient: National Honor Award, American Institute of Architects, 1968, 1976 (twice); House Award, *Architectural Record,* 1968, 1969, 1970, 1973, 1975; Residential Design Award, AIA, New York Chapter, 1968, 1969, 1971, 1973, 1974, 1975; Arnold Brunner Prize, National Institute of Arts and Letters, 1970; Design Award, *Progressive Architecture,* 1973; Design Award, New York State Association of Architects, 1973, 1974; Interior Award, *Architectural Record,* 1974; Leadership in America Citation, *Time* magazine, 1974; Honor Award, New York Society of Architects, 1974; Bartlett Award, 1976; Honor Award, AIA, Connecticut Chapter, 1976; VFM Award, *Institutions* magazine, 1977; Lumen Council Award, 1977; Bard Award, City Club of New York, 1977; United States Plywood Award, 1977. Member, National Institute of Arts and Letters, 1976. Address: Gwathmey Siegel Architects, 154 West 57th Street, New York, New York 10019, U.S.A.

Works:

1967 Gwathmey Residence and Studio, Amagansett, New York
1968 Straus Residence, Purchase, New York (with Henderson)
Sadacca Residence, East Hampton, New York (with Henderson)
1969 Goldberg Residence, Manchester, Connecticut (with Henderson)
Cooper Residence, Orleans, Massachusetts (with Henderson)
1971 Steel Residence, Bridgehampton, New York (with Robert Siegel)
Grey Residence, Bridgehampton, New York (with Robert Siegel)
1972 Cogan Residence, East Hampton, New York (with Robert Siegel)
Whig Hall Student Center, Princeton University, New Jersey (with Robert Siegel)
1973 Service Group and Boiler Plant, State University College of New York at Purchase (with Henderson)
Dormitory, Dining and Student Union Facility, State University College of New York at Purchase (with Henderson and Robert Siegel)

With Robert Siegel:

1973 Brooklyn Friends School
New York Friends School
Elia Bash Residence, Tewksburg, New Jersey
Cohn Residence, Amagansett, New York
Friday Residence, Greenwich, Connecticut
Geffen Residence, Malibu, California (project)
Sagner Residence, West Orange, New Jersey (project)
1975 Charof Residence, Montauk, New York
1976 Urban Development Corporation Perinton Housing, Rochester, New York
Buettner Residence, Sloatsburg, New York
Student Apartment Housing, State University College of New York at Purchase
Damson Oil Office Building, Houston, Texas
1977 Evans Shure Office Buildings (5), Piscataway, New Jersey

International Energy Building, Houston, Texas

Kislevitz Residence, West Hampton, New York

1978 Colorforms Inc. Warehouse and Offices, Norwood, New Jersey

Thomas and Betts Office Building, Elizabeth, New Jersey

Northpoint Office Building, Houston, Texas

Knoll International Offices and Showrooms, Boston

Amax Corporation, Houston, Texas

Island Walk Cooperative, Fairfax County Department of Housing and Community Development, Reston, Virginia

Haupt Residence, Amagansett, New York

Weitz Residence, Quoque, New York

Benenson Residence, Rye, New York

Crowley Residence, Greenwich, Connecticut

Taft Residence, Cincinnati, Ohio

1980 East Campus Student Housing, Columbia University, New York

Playboy Hotel and Casino, Aruba, Netherlands Antilles

Northgate Housing, Roosevelt Island, New York

Columbus Housing, Columbus, Indiana

Interiors: with Henderson—Herlinger Bristol Ltd., New York, 1966; with Siegel—Dunaway Apartment, New York, 1970; Pearl's Restaurant, New York, 1974; Blum Hellman Gallery, New York, 1974; Transammonia Corporation, New York, 1974; Vidal Sassoon Salons in La Costa, California, New York, Chicago, Atlanta, and Beverly Hills, California, 1974–77; Breslow Apartment, New York, 1975; General Motors Acceptance Corporation, Brooklyn, New York, 1975; U.S. Steakhouse Restaurant, New York, 1976; Shezan Restaurant, New York, 1976; Poster Originals Ltd., New York, 1976; Unger Apartment, New York, 1976; Bower and Gardner Law Offices, New York, 1976; Damson Oil Corporation, Houston, Texas, 1976; Lisner/Richelieu Corporation Showroom, New York, 1977; Barber Oil Corporation, New York, 1977; Vidal Sassoon International, Los Angeles, 1977; Vidal Sassoon Inc., New York, 1977; Swirl Inc., New York, 1977; Garey Shirtmakers Inc., New York, 1977; Swid Apartment, New York, 1978; Geffen Apartment, New York, 1978; General Mills Corporation Headquarters, New York, 1978; F.D.M. Productions, New York, 1978; Lincoln Center for the Performing Arts, New York, 1978; Evans Shure Corporation, New York, 1978.

Publications:

On GWATHMEY: books—*The New York Times Book of Interior Design and Decoration,* edited by George O'Brien, New York 1965; *Vacation Houses: An International Survey* by Karl Kaspar, New York 1967; *Young Designs in Living* by Barbara Plumb, New York 1969; *Observations on American Architecture* by Ivan Chermayeff, New York 1972; *Five Architects* by Kenneth Frampton and Colin Rowe, New York 1972; *Great Houses* by Walter F. Wagner, New York 1976; *Charles Gwathmey and Robert Siegel: Residential Architecture,* edited by Kay and Paul Breslow, Tokyo 1976.

Our approach to design is based upon three propositions that inter-relate: 1) There is no aesthetic preconception of form. Every program generates new and different sets of information and constraints. Form is generated by site, orientation, climate, program and technological references. 2) The essential

Charles Gwathmey: Kislevitz Residence, West Hampton, New York, 1977

organizational components in any design are circulation, light, and volumetric clarity. 3) All buildings are similar in abstraction, thus the design process for specific programs is similar. This position was clearly stated by Michael Graves as an introduction to our book:

There appear to be two major positions in current architectural thought. These two attitudes can be seen as opposing orientations although they are mutually exclusive. However in attempting to characterize them as intrinsic modes of thought they are nonetheless generally seen as polar.

The first can be characterized as constituting a part of the symbolic and mythic representations of the culture. This position holds that there is an architectural thought process in the transferral of cultural values to physical artifacts and a corresponding interpretation of symbolic themes which requires one's perception to make the connection between cultural value and architectural symbol. This architectural position must by its nature rely on somewhat literal characteristics of form which could be thought of as representational.

The second architectural position is primarily abstract in nature, based on the assumption that there is a correspondence between Euclidian geometry and human action; there is a parallel drawn between the cardinal axes of geometry and human movement patterns. This architecture which relies heavily on the counter distinctions of passage and rest is able to capitalize on the natural tension established by these two phenomena. An additional interest of this position is that provided by the possibilities of geometrical overlay or transparencies which contribute toward a spatial interlock developed through plan and section. The abstract geometric devices used to articulate these spatial correspondences are generally unadorned and read as minimal in order to clarify the original assumption of man's action related to geometry.

Without the work of Gwathmey Siegel we would not be able to give precise definition to the latter mode of thinking, as they are significant authors of the genuine ideas embodied in an architecture of abstraction and continue to develop the strengths of that position by the sheer artistry of their compositions.

The transcendence of accommodation is the difference between the art of architecture and building.

—Charles Gwathmey

In the search for an American architecture, Charles Gwathmey has found an appropriately distinctive Northeastern expression. His work imports the sophisticated vocabulary of the International Style as developed by Le Corbusier and builds it—and builds on it—in a distinctly American way. From Le Corbusier, Gwathmey has adopted a family of forms—the cube, the cylinder, the partial cylinder—and a set of details—round columns, ribbon windows, ship railings, and glass block. All these elements are expressed with a decidedly Yankee twang—with spontaneity, exaggeration, and clear-eyed pragmatism.

The neo-Corbusian forms are overlaid, intersected, and telescoped in a neo-cubist time-space simultaneity that suggests the brashness and bustling vitality of American activity. The cube is slashed open, gouged out, interspersed with rotated elements—fragments of cylinders, steep shed roofs, diagonal stripes of stairways in a continuum of inside-outside space. Asymmetrical geometries are caught in collision. Overall, however, there is no confusion or ambiguity in the richness and complexity of detail but a disciplined clarity of parts.

Gwathmey also invests his forms with the exaggeration of American superscale, which is sometimes described as never big enough, sometimes as too big. Perhaps this is due to the forms' being sliced off and not ended, suggesting an infinite open-endedness. Perhaps it is due to the emphasis on verticality, both inside and outside, which may be influenced by Paul Rudolph.

Then the forms are sheathed with wood siding, which suggests the rustic New England vernacular and the Shingle Style, the latter surely an influence of Vincent Scully. And the cube is set squarely on the ground, like the sober New England saltbox house—not elevated in a structural pirouette, what Frank Lloyd Wright called "boxes on stilts." Gwathmey's work also shows a craft of construction that sets him apart from other "Cardboard Corbu" architects, perhaps due to the influence of Louis Kahn—another poet of materials—who combined the handcraft of 19th century brickwork with the Modern movement's passion for industrial buildings. Similarly, Gwathmey combines the Corbusian forms and the American vernacular of wood construction, in sleek, smooth, and unarticulated surfaces (despite their wood textures) that suggest the tight skinned minimalism of Edward Larrabee Barnes.

The most significant achievement of this architect's work, however, is in its volumetric invention and spatial variety. Inside, the exterior geometry seems to be only the framing of continuous spatial juxtaposition, high against low, long against short, flat against curved, and enclosed against the calculated vista. This is a spatial vision that owes greatly, but not entirely, to the process of axonometric presentation. It is experiential, luminescent, and related to both site and time-space—even the variety of flooring materials from country to city bears this out. In the volumetric variety is housed functional appropriateness—good planning that recognizes physical activity patterns as well as orientation for access and view.

This synthesis of European and American influences is strong and robust, sophisticated yet simple, angular and curved, crisp yet cosy, static yet lively, monumental yet in rotated action, seductive and sentimental in its nostalgia for the early 1920's.

Theoretically Gwathmey's work raises a significant opposition to proponents of representational architecture. Although Gwathmey himself generally abjures aesthetic pronouncements, his work posits a demonstrably attractive kind of abstraction. That abstract geometry, which is itself without reference to other cultural or historical associations—except for the vernacular wood siding—is strong and resolute, iconographic and perhaps mythic. In this abstraction lies the elegance and the sophisticated achievement of his architecture.

—C. Ray Smith

GWYNNE, Patrick.

British. Born in Porchester, Hampshire, 24 March 1913. Educated at preparatory school, 1923–27; Harrow School, Middlesex, 1927–30; articled pupil, 1930–32. Served as a Squadron Leader in the Royal Air Force, in Britain, Canada and Europe, 1940–45. Worked as an assistant, then as Associate Architect, in the office of Wells Coates, London, 1935–37. In private practice, Esher, Surrey, since 1946. Recipient: First Prize, Furniture Competition, London, 1935; Civil Trust Award, 1968. Address: Office of Patrick Gwynne, The Homewood, Esher, Surrey, England.

Works:

1938 The Homewood, Esher, Surrey (with Wells Coates)

1949 EMG Gramophone Showroom, Newman Street, London

1951 Restaurant building, Battersea Park, London

1952 Supreme Radio Shop, Edmonton, London

Patrick Gwynne: The Homewood, Esher, Surrey, 1938

1953	Freeman-Hardy-Willis Shop, Catford, London
1954	Clifford Curzon Music Studio, Highgate, London
	Ox-on-Roof Restaurant, Chelsea, London
1955	House reconstruction, Blackheath, London
1958	House, Spaniard's End, Hampstead, London
	Chesnut Lodge House conversion, Cobham, Surrey
	Jack Hawkins House, Bournemouth, Hampshire
1959	House, Henley-on-Thames, Oxfordshire
1960	Group of 4 houses, Kingston, Surrey
1961	House, 4 Beechworth Close, Hampstead, London
1962	Gerald Bentall House, Witley Park, Godalming, Surrey
1963	House, 3 Beechworth Close, Hampstead, London
1964	Serpentine Restaurant, Hyde Park, London
1965	Dell Restaurant, Hyde Park, London
	House, Virginia Water, Surrey
1966	Quantity surveyor's offices, Hobart Place, London
1967	Theatre Royal remodelling, York
1968	Flats, St. Paul's Bay, Malta
1969	House, Blackheath, London
1970	Doctors' group practice surgery, Henley-on-Thames, Oxfordshire
	House, Angmering-on-Sea, Sussex
1971	Pergola Restaurant, Hyde Park, London
	Lawrence Harvey House, Hampstead, London
	House, Esher, Surrey
1974	M62 Motorway Service Area, Burtonwood, Lancashire
1975	Restaurant building, Dubai, United Arab Emirates

Publications:

On GWYNNE: articles—"Awards: 7 U.K. Entries for Cembureau—Theatre Royal Extension, York" in *Building* (London), 14 February 1975; "Three Theatres—Restored, Extended and Modernized" in *Lighting and Environmental Design* (London), September/October 1975.

Mine is a small practice and the works so far have been mainly divided between private houses of a fairly luxurious standard designed for individual clients and larger works mostly connected with the catering trade. I have been sought out by clients who wanted an unusual solution in the modern manner and where attention to detail was considered important.

Particularly in regard to the houses I was strongly influenced by my client's views and character, and each design would have been completely otherwise, I believe, if the clients had been different people—or if they had gone to another architect. Nevertheless, people seem to recognize my work as being from my hand in spite of the strong influence of client and site in each case.

The larger works—such as the Hyde Park restaurants and the York Theatre—were intended to be showy buildings albeit with the need to fit into the famous park scenery and into the historic centre of York. It has pleased me that these buildings seem to be popular with the ordinary people who see them and use them.

I have also striven through my work to produce buildings which would be reasonably easy to maintain without undue expense and would remain looking in good condition over the years.

—Patrick Gwynne

A happy-go-lucky building with a hop-scotch plan gambolling like a young deer by the waterside: such is Patrick Gwynne's Serpentine Restaurant in Hyde Park, London. Its busy indentations, facetted glazing, sketchy run-through sections would like to have us believe that the Festival of Britain has never quite ended. Its balustrades serve perfectly as footing for the pigeons. The mini-ramps and decks suggest so many things for the children. Its fairy-tale, grotto-like crystalline resolution can be traced, via Taut's Alpine architecture, back into folklore and legends of another, more paradisic world where people live in jewel-like houses—or else the dwellings are made from eagles' feathers, human eyes, fused sand, or a myriad of materials inconceivable to those condemned to mere mortal life on earth. Gwynne's extension to the Theatre Royal at York has this same fabulous touch, as though it had been revealed to him in a reverie.

This fanciful architecture delights with its innocent language, its rhyming, its exquisite miniaturist flourishes: this is the kind of architecture we can see in Miro's earlier canvases, in Chagall, Rousseau . . . its unflinching love of architecture is akin to the frontal emphasis found in children's art and in that of the naive and primitive artist. The Serpentine Restaurant is given strong outline, and one can imagine the process whereby it was designed and realised as being not altogether different from the way a child would sit down and draw it. Fountains of transparent quartz, alabaster windows, rainbow-tinted pools, a seesaw of black glass—such is the Tolkien-like associational journey one embarks on from the contemplation of the Serpentine Restaurant. The stream of consciousness blur of images opens up a world so much closed by this century.

—Chris Fawcett

H

HABRAKEN, N(icolaas) John.
Dutch. Born in Bandung, Indonesia, 29 October
1928. Educated at the Department of Architecture,
Technical University, Delft, Netherlands, 1948–55,
Bouwkundig Ingenieur 1955. Served in the Royal
Dutch Air Force, 1955–57. Married Emmie Marlene
Van Hall in 1959; children: Julie and Gysbert. Instructor, Department of Architecture, Technical
University, Delft, 1958–60; freelance architect in the
Netherlands, 1960–62; Job Captain, architectural
office of Lucas and Niemeyer, Voorburg, Netherlands, 1962–65; Director, Stichting Architecten Research (SAR), Voorburg, 1965–67, and Eindhoven,
Netherlands, 1967–75. Chairman of the Department
of Architecture, 1967–70, and Professor of Architecture and Urban Design, 1967–75, Technical University, Eindhoven. Since 1975, Professor and Head of
the Department of Architecture, Massachusetts Institute of Technology, Cambridge. Address: Department of Architecture, Massachusetts Institute of
Technology, 77 Massachusetts Avenue, Cambridge,
Massachusetts 02139, U.S.A.

Works:

1959 Private house, 63 Wildernislaan, Apeldoorn,
      Netherlands
1962 Arntz House, Millingen, Netherlands
1965/
  75 Design method for open-ended systems and
      their evolution; and method for design of
      "urban tissues"
1968 Amsterdam Town Hall (competition project)

Various studies and designs for support systems

Publications:

By HABRAKEN: books—*Supports: An Alternative
to Mass Housing,* Amsterdam 1962, London and
New York 1972; *Three R's for Housing,* Amsterdam
1970; *Variations: The Systematic Design of Supports,*
with J. T. Boekholt, A. P. Thyssen and P. M. J.
Dinjens, Alphen, Netherlands 1974, Cambridge,
Massachusetts 1976; articles—"The Tissue of the
Town" in *Forum* (Amsterdam), no. 1, 1964; "Quality and Quantity: The Industrialization of Housing"
in *Forum* (Amsterdam), no. 2, 1964; "Supports, Responsibilities and Possibilities" in *Architectural Association Quarterly* (London), Winter 1968/69; "The
Pursuit of an Idea" in *Plan* (Amsterdam), no. 3,
1970; "L'Habitat, l'Home et l'Industrie" in *L'Architecture d'Aujourd'hui* (Paris), February/March
1970; "You Can't Design the Ordinary" in *Architectural Design* (London), April 1971; "Support Structure and Detachable Unit, on the Basis of Industrialization and Participation" in *Toshi-Jukaku* (Tokyo),
September 1972; "Das Ende des Wohnbahn-
projektes" in *Archithese* (Zurich), no. 1, 1972; "Playing Games" in *Architectural Design* (London), no. 4,
1972; "Involving People in the Housing Process" in
RIBA Journal (London), November 1972; "SAR
Design Method for Housing: Seven Years of Development in the Real World" in *DMG-DRS Journal*

for Design Research and Methods (San Luis Obispo,
California), July/September 1973; "Création Architectural et Industrie: Intervention au Colloque
d'Yerres" in *Techniques et Architecture* (Paris),
March 1975; "Fragments" in *Techniques et Architecture* (Paris), October/November 1976; "The Limits
of Professionalism" in *Architectural Association
Quarterly* (London), no. 1, 1978; "The Leaves and
the Flowers" in *Via* (Philadelphia), December 1978.

On HABRAKEN: books—*SAR 65* report, Voorburg, Netherlands 1965; *SAR 73* report, Eindhoven,
Netherlands 1973; *N. J. Habraken e il Gruppo SAR:
Materiali di Sicerca sulla Progettazione della Residenza* by Marcello Mamoli and others, Venice 1973;
*Deciding on Density: An Investigation into High Den-
sity Allotment with a View to the Waldeck Area,* The
Hague 1977; articles—"The Perfect Barracks and
the Support Revolution" by Martin Pawley in *Interbuild Arena* (London), October 1967; "Mass Housing: The Desperate Effort of Pre-Industrial Thought
to Achieve the Equivalent of Mass Production" by
Martin Pawley in *Architectural Design* (London),
January 1970; "SAR" by Makato Uyeda in *Toshi-
Jutaku* (Tokyo), September 1972; "Nikolaas Habraken: du regne de la quantité à l'ordre de la qua-
lité?" by B. B. Taylor in *L'Architecture d'Aujour-
d'hui* (Paris), July/August 1974; "Involving People
in the Housing Process: The Story of Habraken's
Supports and Detachables" by Eric Dluhosch in *Industrialization Forum* (Montreal), no. 1, 1976.

*

Looking back at years of research, writing, teaching
and consulting, it seems that those efforts reveal
some consistency. What runs through it as a continuous thread could perhaps be best described as an
attempt to introduce the concepts of time and
change in architectural thinking.

As architects we still operate in a social role bestowed on us in the Renaissance. We dream of
monuments and try—by building—to stop time; try
to erect a symbol that transcends everyday life.

Simultaneously, we embrace today the whole built
environment as worthy of our attention or service.
But the built environment is a living thing. Change
within durable patterns is its primary characteristic.
Although one can design for it, it cannot be designed
but wants to be cultivated.

Thus, we find ourselves in conflict with our chosen
subject matter. Neither our theories, nor our methods, nor our education give us the understanding or
the tools needed to operate in the broader realm of
the everyday world. Some of us have to sit and think;
the dilemma is as fascinating as its solution is crucial.
—N. John Habraken

*

In the early 1960's international architecture was in
a transitional phase in the sense that fundamental
theories from the 1920's and 30's were being rejected
and new, partly utopian proposals were emerging.
Criticism was mainly directed against the fundamental concepts for planning a functional town. The
essays of Jane Jacobs who, inter alia, supported municipal diversity, are well known in this respect.

Aldo van Eyck held similar views when, in 1960, he
suggested replacing the traditional "Space-Time"
concept of Giedion with a "Sense of Place" concept:
"Whatever space and time mean, place and occasion
mean more." Similarly, we can point to the utopian
town planning proposals of the Japanese Metabolists
and to the English Archigram projects.

N. John Habraken's utopian town planning proposals, with their emphasis on co-determination by
the inhabitant, also come from this period. His ideas
appeared in his book *Supports: An Alternative to
Mass Housing,* which was enthusiastically received.
In the book Habraken criticized the uniform character of new housing and its surroundings, where individual endeavors are unwelcome and personal initiative undesirable. He starts his argument from the
idea that one can only identify with one's surroundings if one has contributed something to those surroundings, something for which one is responsible.
The inhabitants should also be able to take possession of their surroundings. According to Habraken,
possession (which is different from property) is connected with action. Something will belong to us, become part of our lives, only by our own efforts. Because man wants to take possession of his
surroundings, he touches them, puts his personal
stamp on them.

Habraken distinguishes between two kinds of architecture: the architecture of specific buildings
(public buildings, private houses, etc.) and the architecture of the ordinary environment (mass housing,
etc.). He himself is concerned with the latter, and he
points out that architects still believe that they can
solve the problems of mass housing with the same
approach as for specific buildings. He considers that,
in comparison with specific buildings, an ordinary
environment is built up differently and has different
but equally valuable qualities.

Habraken proposes the building of prefabricated
housing structures (terrains artificiels/artificial sites)
which can be individually filled in—like Le Corbusier's project "Fort l'Empereur," designed for Algiers in 1933. He puts forward the idea that dwellings could be assembled like built-in kitchens. The
housing structures would belong to the community
and would be built to last, while it would have to be
expected that the built-in dwelling would be built,
altered and demolished.

On the image of the new town, he comments:
"There is one architecture that makes uniform and
another that gives form to diversity. With the latter
the principle is structure with built-in elements. In
this way a form can be designed for a facade of such
strength that anything can happen inside without
giving a totally chaotic impression on the outside.
This will provide an experience of lively diversity."

Fascinated by these ideas, architects from ten
well-known practices in Holland decided, in 1964, to
form a working party to make a reality of the "support" town. The working party was called SAR (Architects Research Foundation) and was led by Habraken. In the course of time various mass and support systems appeared which were partly adopted by
foreign architects. But, as the SAR made hardly any

pronouncements about the form of the structure or about basic town planning concepts, their influence on house building remained on the whole rather insignificant.

Yet Habraken's original and imaginatively written vision of a town-planning utopia still has an influence and, as he himself expressed it in 1961, it continues to represent "a formidable challenge to the greatest talents in design for living."

—Arnulf Lüchinger

HALLEN, Hans (Heyerdahl).
South African. Born in Durban, 31 August 1930. Educated at Durban High School, 1944–48; University of Natal, Durban, under Barrier Bierman and Ronald Lewcock, 1949–53 (Kimberley Scholarship; Government Scholarship), Dip.Arch. 1953. Married June Wendy Meiring in 1955; children: Martin, Andre and Michele. Worked in the offices of Frolich and Kass, Durban, 1948–50, and A. B. Adkin, Durban, 1950–53; Architect, London County Council, 1956; associated with O. Pretorius, Durban, 1959. In private practice, Durban, since 1959: Partner with A. J. Diamond, 1959–62, with M. Dibb, 1963–69, with J. D. Theron, since 1969, and with M. J. Speed, since 1970. Part-time and Full-time Lecturer, University of Natal, 1966–78. Member of the Natal Provincial Committee, 1964–77, Member of the National Board, 1968–77, and President-in-Chief, 1974–75, Institute of South African Architects; Member of the Council for Architects, 1970–78, and Chairman of the Fees Committee of the Council for Architects, 1976–78; Member of the Council, International Union of Architects, 1975–81; Delegate of the Institute of South African Architects to the United Nations "Habitat" Conference, Vancouver, 1976. Consultant to the Urban Foundation, Johannesburg, since 1977. Exhibitions: *The City Is a Walking Place,* Durban, 1964; *Riebeeck Festival,* Cape Town, 1970. Recipient: First Prize, Voortrekker Monument Competition, Winburg, 1964; First Prize, La Lucia Civic Centre Competition, 1971; Institute of South African Architects Award, 1977. Address: 741 Musgrave Road, Durban 4001, South Africa.

Works:

1959 Eckhoffs Corner, Durban
1960 Hallen House, Nicolai Crescent, Durban
Norwegian Lutheran Mission Church, Kwa Mashu Umlazi Glebe, South Africa
1961 Bassudey House, Crescent Street, Durban
Sparks House, Westville, South Africa
Masojada House, Essenwood Road, Durban
1962 Stellenberg Flats, Essenwood Road, Durban
Illing House, Kloof, South Africa
Hattingh House, Kloof, South Africa
Sculptural reliefs and panels, Marine Terminal Restaurants, Durban (with Warunkiewicz)
Lutheran Seminary, Zululand, South Africa (project)
1963 Drosdy Flats, Silverton Road, Durban
Musgrave Mews Flats, Musgrave Road, Durban
Reed House, Durban
Maisonettes Zakrzewski, 602 Essenwood Road, Durban
1964 Fouche House, Durban
Riebeeck Flats, Durban
Bellevue Flats, Durban
St. Luke's Church, Chatsworth, South Africa
Powell House, Westville, South Africa
Voortrekker Monument, Winburg, South Africa (competition project)
Ulundi Court, Durban

Hans Hallen: Huletts Head Office, La Lucia, South Africa, 1976

1964/
66 Residences, University of Natal, Durban
1965 Seedat House, Westville, South Africa
Lakhi House, Reservoir Hills, South Africa
Ceza Mission Hospital, Ceza, South Africa
1966 Barker House, Gillets, South Africa
Dublin Library (competition project; with Danie Theron)
Hall House, Durban
1967 Thabane Li Mele Arts and Crafts School, Lesotho
St. Olav's Church, St. Thomas Road, Durban
Lunn House, Durban
Umlazi Polyclinic, Durban (project)
St. John's Convent, Durban
Reservoir Hills Mosque, Reservoir Hills, South Africa
Norwegian Seamen's Mission, Durban
1968 Habib Factory, Durban
Nkonjeni Mission, South Africa
Shaw House, Lamont Road, Durban
Ceza Mission, South Africa
1969 Fine Fare Supermarket, Pietermaritzburg, South Africa
Smit House, Westville, South Africa
Habib Duplexes, Durban
Entabeni Hospital redevelopment, Durban (with M. Dibb)
Little Top Beach Pavilion, Durban
Alleson House, Durban
Mosque, Chatsworth, South Africa
Castle Wine and Brandy Factory, Cape Town (with L. Louw and Partners)
Sacca Ltd. Factory, Durban
Reform Church, Durban
1970 Rustomjee House, Reservoir Hills, South Africa
Sacca Ltd. Factory, Kimberley, South Africa
Golden Hours Centre for Retarded Children,

Sherwood, South Africa
Taikyo Restaurant, Durban
Jacobson House, La Lucia, South Africa
Beckerling House, Zinkwazi, South Africa
Tollman Towers by the Sea, Umhlanga Rocks, South Africa (project)
1971 Civic Centre, La Lucia, South Africa (competition project)
Beach Offices, Durban
1972 Villa Road Flats, Durban
1972/
77 South African Railways Service Buildings, Durban
1974 Kara House, Westville, South Africa
1974/
76 Huletts Head Office, La Lucia, South Africa
1974/
78 Hospital redevelopment, Wentworth, South Africa
1975 St. John's School, Pietermaritzburg, South Africa
St. John's Church Hall and Nursery School, Pinetown, South Africa
Plan for the redevelopment of Tel Aviv (competition project; with Danie Theron)
1976 Catholic Church, Bluff, South Africa
Technical School, Clairwood, South Africa
1977 Anglican Church, Amanzimtoti, South Africa
Redevelopment proposals for Durban North Beach
1978 Business and Community Centre, Kwa Mashu, South Africa
Sacca Ltd. Factory, Cape Town
Restaurant, President Hotel, Bloemfontein, South Africa
Mangosuthu College of Technology, Umlazi, South Africa (with Julian Elliott)
Schmidt House, Kloof, South Africa

Publications:

By HALLEN: books—introduction to *Housing People*, Johannesburg 1977; *Needs and Resources Survey: Durban,* Durban 1977; articles—"Quality of Place" in *ISAA Record* (Johannesburg), July 1965; editor of special issue on Natal in *ISAA Record* (Johannesburg), July 1965; "Voortrekker Monument" in *ISAA Record* (Johannesburg), August 1965; "Greek Islands—Cycladic Architecture" in *ISAA Record* (Johannesburg), March 1966; editor of the Congress issue of *ISAA Record* (Johannesburg), October 1966; "University and Profession" in *Plan* (Johannesburg), July 1970; "Beggar, Borrowers and Fat Colonials" in *New Check* (Johannesburg), October 1970; "Hindu Temples" and "Indian Temples and Mosques" in *Plan* (Johannesburg), June 1973; "Towards the City University" in *Concept Five* (Durban), June 1974; "Architecture and the World Around Us" in *South African Builder* (Johannesburg), November 1974; "Urban Heritage in *Plan* (Johannesburg), 1975; "The Quality of Life and Urban Development" in *Optima* (Johannesburg), April 1976.

On HALLEN: articles—"Bassudey, Hallen, Masojada—3 Houses" by B. E. Bierman in *ISAA Record* (Johannesburg), July 1963; "Huletts Building" in *Planning and Building Development* (Johannesburg), April 1971; "Houses of the Sixties" by Danie Theron in *Lantern* (Pretoria), September 1972; "Huletts Head Office" in *Architecture South Africa* (Cape Town), July 1978.

*

The small houses in my first period of practice were white and cube-like experiments in geometry —the houses such as Masojada, Hattingh, Hallen, Seedat attempted to escape from the prevalent three-bedroomed layout used in Durban and sought in plan and section new and more valid solutions to orientation and ventilation in a sub-tropical climate with a very direct relationship of the interior and exterior with associated rich planting. Most of this and subsequent work has been done for sloping sites.

The early churches and mosques used a formal geometric shape, cladding around a plan form that uses the new liturgical attitudes of closeness to the focus of workship which emphasise a sense of community. Churches such as St. Olav's, St. John's Convent and various mission churches as well as the Reservoir Hill's Mosque are expressive of this phase.

Some of the earliest experiments with low-rise, high-density housing in this area were done in the early sixties using crosswall construction both in brick and concrete with apartments opening onto private and semi-private courts. The early examples were in white-washed brick, and such buildings as Stellenberg, Drosdy and Musgrave Mews were typical.

The larger buildings of the mid-sixties such as the University of Natal Student Residences, competition entries for Dublin and for Tel Aviv (both of these with Danie Theron) focused upon the organisation of pedestrian movement through buildings. These buildings show a concern for the use of changes of level with open and expressed staircases and ramp systems.

Much of the later work, from 1970 on, has been concerned with large span roof structures where any number of variations of the problems of sheet roofing of various types have been resolved to give new forms, and the series of buildings that include the railway buildings, Huletts Head Office, Wentworth Hospital buildings and other industrial buildings are typical. They have deeply shaded areas and large simple volumes. Colourful facades and a degree of overt symbolism has been used in later years.

My work and that of my colleagues (in latter years Danie Theron and Mike Speed) has emphasised close links with site—often with full landscaped and conceived environs, emphasis upon the gentle treatment of changes of level, the creation of buildings that also react to and encourage socially desirable use of buildings both in terms of the movement areas and in the scale of the spaces, nearly always enclosed in clearly expressed structural form.

I feel the closest affinity with the work of Aalto; I enjoy the scale of his work and the lightness of touch and ingenuity of his detailing.

—Hans Hallen

*

There are many ways in which an architect can be of service to the public and to his profession. Hans Hallen has explored probably every one and excelled in all. Urging international architectural circles to greater tolerance, his own government and local authorities to greater flexibility, and educationists and fellow practitioners to higher standards, he has had to draw on reserves of talent, energy and character at the expense of his own practice. Nevertheless, his design work constitutes a remarkable record of achievement of the same restless probing, catholic nature. A sound apprenticeship in the eclectic design procedures prevailing before the advent of dogmatic modern architecture in the university schools provided a base from which he could operate with confident independence.

His first contact with architecture beyond local confines came on a visit to the Cape of Good Hope where he was captivated by the humanity and simplicity of the historical style and the rich pictorial quality of its peasant materials—an experience he expanded by visits to the Mediterranean homeland of the Cape style. These cultural forays found expression on his return to Durban in a wide range of building types developing the potential of white modulated surfaces in the local tropical context.

By way of reaction to this "soft" period, there followed an intense investigation of in situ concrete structure and finish of uncompromising angularity but with spatial qualities related to his more humanistic early works. By degrees he passed on to a somewhat doctrinaire exploitation of the local red brick together with glass and metal in prismatic association. It was an obsession with him to master every material and structural technique, and in the process he contributed a series of new formal solutions to conventional design problems, derived from precast concrete, epoxy resins, and the newly available range of non-ferrous metals.

After some fifteen years in practice, versatility fully demonstrated, Hallen is now creating designs that reflect increasingly the style of our age, each new project not only engendering its appropriate formal language (form follows function) but also determining the use of specific materials handled in a particular way: technological eclecticism.

—B. E. Biermann

HALPRIN, Lawrence.

American. Born in New York City, 1 July 1916. Educated at Cornell University, Ithaca, New York, 1935–39, B.S. 1939; University of Wisconsin, Madison, under Professor Aust, 1939–41, M.S. 1941; Harvard University, Cambridge, Massachusetts, under Walter Gropius, Marcel Breuer and Christopher Tunnard, 1941–42, B.Land.Arch. 1942. Served as a Lieutenant Junior Grade in the United States Navy, 1942–45. Married Anna Schuman in 1940; children: Daria and Rana. Senior Associate Architect with Thomas D. Church and Associates, San Francisco, 1945–49; Principal, Lawrence Halprin and Associates, San Francisco, 1949–76. Since 1976, Partner, with Sue Yung Li Ikeda, RoundHouse, San Francisco. Design Consultant, California Division of Highways, 1963–65; Landscape Architect and Urban Consultant, San Francisco Bay Area Rapid Transit District, 1963–66. Visiting Lecturer, University of British Columbia, Vancouver, 1954, University of North Carolina, Raleigh, 1955, and University of Pennsylvania, Philadelphia, 1956; Lecturer, University of California, Berkeley, 1960–65, 1978; Director, Halprin Summer Workshop, San Francisco, 1966, 1968. Exhibitions: San Francisco Museum of Art, 1952, 1960, 1976; Bolles Gallery, San Francisco (paintings), 1965; Berkeley Museum, California, 1971; Columbia University, New York, 1972; Kennedy Gallery, New York (drawings), 1978. Recipient: Honor Award, 1953, 1957, 1968 (twice), Merit Award, 1953 (three times), 1956, 1957, 1959, 1966, 1972, and First Honor Award, 1961, American Institute of Architects; Design Award, 1954, 1958, 1959, 1963 (three times), 1964, 1966, and First Design Award, 1959, 1960, *Progressive Architecture;* Special Award for Land Planning, *House and Home,* 1956; Collaborative Medal of Honor, Architectural League of New York, 1960; Honor Award, AIA, Southwest Washington Chapter, 1962; Honor Award, AIA, Chicago Chapter, 1963; Honor Award, Federal Housing Authority, 1963; California Governor's Design Award, 1966 (three times); Industrial Design Award of Excellence, The Smithsonian Institution, Washington, D.C., 1968 (twice); Certificate of Merit, Municipal Art Society of New York, 1969; Merit Award for Environmental Design Excellence, American Institute of Planners, 1970; Fourth Biennial Award, 1970 (three times), and Fifth Biennial Award, 1972, and Design Award, 1974 (three times), United States Department of Housing and Urban Development; Commercial Landscaping Award, 1972, and Municipal Landscaping Award, 1973, 1974, American Association of Nurserymen; Annual Art Directors Award for Report Design, Art Directors Club of Metropolitan Washington, 1973; Award of Excellence, *Design and Environment,* 1975, 1976 (twice); First Place Award, Association of Landscape Contractors of America, 1976; Merit Award, American Society of Landscape Architects, 1977. Fellow, American Society of Landscape Architects; Honorary Fellow, American Institute of Interior Designers; Member, American Academy of Arts and Sciences. Address: Round-House, 1500 Sansome Street, San Francisco, California 94111, U.S.A.

Works (Landscape Architecture):

1949 Schuman House, Bay Area, San Francisco
 Bissinger House, Bay Area, San Francisco
1950 Esherick House, Bay Area, San Francisco
1951 Woerner House, Bay Area, San Francisco
1952 Master plan for the University of California at Davis
1953 Halprin House, Kentwoodlands, California
1954 Baer House, Berkeley, California
1955 Greenwood Common, Berkeley, California
 Halprin House and Dance Deck, Kentfield, California
 Washington Water Power Company Corporate Headquarters, Spokane, Washington
 Old Orchard Shopping Center, Skokie, Illinois
1956 Grant House, Berkeley, California
1957 Stanford Medical Plaza, Palo Alto, California
 Sproul Plaza and Student Union, University of California, Berkeley
 Married Student Housing, University of California, San Francisco
 Public housing, Marin County, California
 Master plan for the Seattle Center, *World's Fair,* Seattle
1958 McIntyre House, Bay Area, San Francisco
1959 Navajo Nation Master Development Program, Window Rock, Arizona
 Crocker Industrial Park, Brisbane, California
1960 Capitol Towers Housing, Sacramento, California

Lawrence Halprin: Lovejoy Plaza, Portland, Oregon, 1961

1961   Lovejoy Plaza, Portland, Oregon
        Pettigrove Park, Portland, Oregon
1962   Nicollet Mall, Minneapolis
1963   Stevenson, Cowell, and Crown Colleges, University of California at Santa Cruz
        Woodlake Housing, San Mateo, California
        Ghirardelli Square, San Francisco
        Urban Freeways Study, State of California
        St. Francis Square Housing, San Francisco
1965   California State Capital Plan, San Francisco (project)
        Customs House Plaza, Monterey, California
        Hadassah Medical Center Master Plan, Ein Karem, Israel
1966   BART (Bay Area Rapid Transit) Design Criteria and Open Space Amelioration, San Francisco
        Ida Crown Museum Garden, Jerusalem
        Halprin House, Sea Ranch, California
1967   New York New York Open Space Study
        Oakcreek Apartments, Palo Alto, California

        Flushing Meadow Sports Park, New York
1968   Environment Workshop Studies, San Francisco
        Trojan Nuclear Power Plant, Portland, Oregon
        Jewish Home for the Aged, San Francisco
        Anacostia River Master Plan, Washington, D.C.
        Virgin Islands Master Plan
        Oakbrook Shopping Center, Illinois
        Community Plan, Everett, Washington
        Auditorium Forecourt Plaza, Portland, Oregon
        Sea Ranch, Mendocino County, California
        Foothills Ecological Study, Palo Alto, California
        California State Fairgrounds, Sacramento
        Trinity River Plan, Fort Worth, Texas
1968–   Market Street, San Francisco
1969   Bank of America World Headquarters, San Francisco

1970   State Capital Plan, Olympia, Washington
        Embarcadero Plaza, San Francisco
        Willemstad Downtown Plan, Curacao
        Welfare Island, New York
        Urban Design Study, Caracas, Venezuela
1971   Cold Springs New Town, Baltimore, Maryland
        Israel National Park, Mount Carmel, Jerusalem
1972   Fox Valley East New Town, near Aurora, Illinois
        Willamette Valley: Choices for the Future, Willamette Valley, Oregon
1973   Workshop and Village Plan, Yountville, California
        Main Street Mall, Charlottesville, Virginia
        Concept for Cleveland and Master Plan
1974   Settlers Landing, Cleveland
        Manhattan Square Park, Rochester, New York
        Babi Yar Memorial, Denver, Colorado

1974– Franklin Delano Roosevelt Memorial, Washington, D.C.
Battery City Park, New York
1975 Skyline Park, Denver
1976 Freeway Park, Seattle
Transit Mall, Portland, Oregon
1976– Second Avenue Mall, New York
1978 Levi Strauss Headquarters, San Francisco

Publications:

By HALPRIN: books—*Cities,* New York 1963, revised edition, Cambridge, Massachusetts and London 1972; *Freeways,* New York 1966; *New York New York,* New York 1968; *The Freeway in the City,* with others, Washington, D.C. 1968; *RSVP Cycles: Creative Processes in the Human Environment,* New York 1970; *Notebooks of Lawrence Halprin 1959–1971,* Cambridge, Massachusetts 1972; *Taking Part: A Workshop Approach to Collective Creativity,* with Jim Burns, Cambridge, Massachusetts 1974; articles—"The Choreography of Gardens" in *Dance* (New York), July 1953; "Dance Deck in the Woods" in *Impulse* (San Francisco), 1956; "The Edge of the Garden" in *Landscape Architecture* (Louisville, Kentucky), Winter 1956/57; "Landscape Between Walls" in *Architectural Forum* (New York), November 1959; "Houses and Landscapes" in *Progressive Architecture* (New York), May 1960; "Israel: The Man-Made Landscape" in *Landscape* (Berkeley, California), Winter 1960; "The Landscape of Israel" in *Landscape Architecture* (Louisville, Kentucky), April 1961; "The Community and the Landscape" in *AIA Journal* (Washington, D.C.), September 1961; "The Gardens of the High Sierra" in *Landscape* (Berkeley, California), Winter 1961; "The City Tree" in *Architectural Forum* (New York), October 1961; "Portrait of a Garden" in *Progressive Architecture* (New York), December 1961; "The Shape of Erosion" in *Landscape Architecture* (Louisville, Kentucky), January 1962; "Transportation and the City" in *Architectural Forum* (New York), April 1963; "San Francisco, Panhandle Freeway" in *San Francisco Examiner,* May 1964; "Motation" in *Progressive Architecture* (New York), July 1965; "This Is a City" in *Western Building Design* (Los Angeles) 1973; films—*Le Pink Grapefruit,* 1976; *How Sweet It Is!,* with Anna Halprin, 1976.

On HALPRIN: book—*The Third Generation Architect and Concept* by Ted Itoh, Tokyo 1974; articles—"Riding a Revolution: A Radical Experiment in Reorganization" by Nilo Lindgren in *Innovation* (New York), February 1971; "Lawrence Halprin: Humanizing the City Environment" by Elin Schoen in *The American Way* (New York), November 1972; "The Halprin Revolutions Revisited" by Nilo Lindgren in *Landscape Architecture* (Louisville, Kentucky), April 1974; "FDR and the Cherry Blossoms: A New Design for a Roosevelt Memorial" in *Horizon* (New York), May 1977; "Lawrence Halprin," special issue of *Process: Architecture* (Tokyo/Pittsburgh), February 1978.

I have always felt that design is a total involvement and that it is not purely visual. The process for me has been always inextricably intertwined with the results. This is a hard concept to explain, in a sense, except perhaps through a diagram.

You can view process as a way to arrive at a solution, in which case it is a means towards an end

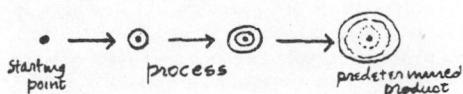

or you can perceive it as important and valid in itself —full of twisting and turning, unknown explorations, reactive to many different inputs and influ-

ences along the way and lacking a clear image of what the end product is or should be. What emerges then is, in fact, *part* of the process. This diagram looks more like this:

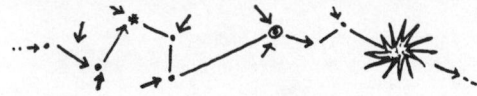

It is really more like life itself—unforeseen, adventurous, exploratory: with only two fixed points—a beginning and an end but even those linked up with larger changes.

It is in this way—a holistic way—that I have designed.

For me too the progression of problems which I have been solving has been important. I started with issues of personal relationships: gardens and houses —evocative of private family needs, tract houses and gardens after the war. After that I attempted to link these together: group housing, suburban villages, shopping centers. Gradually these issues have aggregated into larger ones—how people, in regions, can live together in town and villages without raping the land and destroying the very environment they live in. This led to concerns about transportation, both freeways for cars and mass transportation (BART), with particular concern for how these mammoth constructions could do more than just function as carriers, but go further and become forms of sculpture (as well as sociology) in the landscape.

Eventually—perhaps inevitably—I came into the city whose decaying cores, streets and ghettos were losing ground yearly. I felt that somehow *cities* could be reconstituted and that many of the lessons we had learned in the new communities could be brought to bear in our older cities—amenities, liveliness, open spaces, pedestrian networks, re-cycled old buildings —and that if we conceived of cities as places of enjoyment and creativity they could flower once again.

During this time of working—particularly during the latter part when projects became larger and more and more complex, reaching into whole regions and very large urban complexes—many dedicated and talented young people spent time in my office and contributed profoundly to the projects you see listed here. Lawrence Halprin & Associates was, itself, an example of collective creativity—of the process itself. It exemplified in its best moments the idea that a group can work synergistically and develop more than the sum of its individual components—an organism in itself. We were full of high energy, of boundless enthusiasm, high spirits and an eager search for new ways of doing things!

In the past few years, in addition to designing actual projects, I have turned to new explorations, trying to dig deeper into the sources of collective creativity. Though my new group, RoundHouse, with my partner, Sue Yung Li Ikeda, I am concentrating on the issue of people's inter-actions with their environment both as individuals *and* in groups —both aspects are important. We have been searching for archetypal relationships in workshops which take place primarily out in the field. These TAKING PART workshops allow people the opportunity to discover and articulate their own needs and desires for themselves and for their communities. Working with the RSVP cycles they discover ways of communicating with each other and arriving at creative decisions based on multiple input. Then they can implement what they want with the full support and enthusiasm of the entire group.

We hope to reveal two things—what is the fundamental human environment symbiosis . . . and how people can go about providing it for themselves. It is a hope to design *with* its inhabitants a human ecosystem biologically and emotionally satisfying.
—Lawrence Halprin

In the annals of landscape architectural history, few individuals have had such an impact on the human

environment as Lawrence Halprin. He has responded to current social needs, created imaginative sculptural places for all segments of society and provided leadership in the related design professions with new design processes.

Following an apprenticeship with Thomas Church, where he helped develop the contemporary California garden concept, Halprin opened his own office in 1949. Continued concern with the private personal space saw him linking them together in suburban villages, shopping centers and educational facilities. Scattered centers of habitation called for freeways and public transportation, which, in turn, led to problems at the urban core. Perhaps Halprin's career will be best known for his innovative and imaginative response to urban renewal, downtown malls and recycling of old buildings. Regional planning and very large urban design projects complete the scale cycle.

Design process is as important to Halprin as the end result, and every human activity is as important as the notes in a musician's score. The activities are orchestrated and analyzed to develop diagrams and designs that are translated into organic built spaces.

A greater awareness and concern by the public for their total environment and an infusion of young, enthusiastic, free-thinking designers into his office resulted in Halprin's developing a design methodology involving client and user. Workshops were organized in communities where representatives of different interest groups would come together under the leadership of a professional designer/facilitator. Their dreams, desires, aspirations and needs were discussed in a creative, collective effort and synthesized by the professional into a final design statement.

To Halprin, the whole of life is design process. Everything we need to know as creative environmental designers can be observed in nature, from the cascading waters of the Sierras to the freedom seen in the flight of a bird. The organic, free flowing, romantic people spaces created by Halprin express these lessons from nature as well as being a response to mid-20th century environmental needs.
—Roger Usbaldeston

HANSEN, Oskar.
Polish. Born in Helsinki, Finland, of Norwegian parents, 12 April 1922; emigrated to Poland, 1922: naturalized, 1926. Educated at the Technical College, Vilnius, Lithuania, 1942, Dip.Ing. 1942; Institute of Technology, Warsaw, under Romuald Gutt, 1946–51; Fernand Léger Studio, Paris (studied painting), 1948–49; CIAM International Summer School of Architecture, London, 1949. Served in the Polish Partisan Army, 1944. Married the architect Zofia Garlinska in 1950; children: Igor and Alvar. Assistant Architect, Workers Housing Association, Warsaw, 1948; worked in the studio of Pierre Jeanneret, Paris, 1948–49, and of Jerzy Soltan, Warsaw, 1950–56. Senior Architect, 1958–60, and since 1960 Chief Architect, Housing Co-operative, Warsaw. Assistant, 1950–51, Adjunct Professor and Chairman of the Studio of Basic Design, 1952–55, Assistant Professor and Chairman of the Visual Structures Studio of the Sculpture Department, 1956–64, and since 1964 Professor and Chairman of the Unit of Sculpture in Architecture, Academy of Fine Arts, Warsaw. Exhibitions: *Oskar Hansen: Architecture, Sculpture, Painting,* Jewish Theatre, Warsaw, 1957; *Oskar Hansen: In Search of Methods of Teaching Art,* Mickiewicz Museum, Warsaw, 1966; with Zofia Hansen—Rotterdam, 1962; Helsinki, 1962; Delft, 1963; Oslo, 1964; Warsaw, 1967; Zielona Gora, Poland, 1967; Warsaw, 1971. Recipient: CIAM Housing Prize, London, 1949; Polish 10th Anniversary Medal, 1955; Architecture Prize, Warsaw, 1957; Art

Oskar Hansen: Monument, Auschwitz-Birkenau, Poland, 1959

Prize, Warsaw Journalists Committee, 1958; Silver Medal, *Triennale*, Milan, 1959; Polonia Restituta Cross, 1959; Silver Badge, Housing Co-operatives Union, Poland, 1964; Silver Medal, *Exempla '74*, Munich, 1974. Address (office): ul. Sędziowska 3/4, 02-081 Warsaw, Poland.

Works:

1948 Dębiec Housing Estate, near Poznan
1948/
    49 Aluminium Villas, Villeneuve St. Georges, France (with Pierre Jeanneret)
1949 Housing Estate, London (project)
1951/
    52 Interior designs, Warsaw and Służewiec, Poland (with Jerzy Sołtan)
1953 Polish Pavilion, *Trade Fair*, Stockholm (with Stanislaw and Wojciech Zamecznik)
1955 Plan for the *Folk Art Exhibition*, Warsaw (with Jerzy Sołtan)
    Hansen Apartment interiors, Warsaw (with Zofia Hansen)
1956 Polish Pavilion, *Trade Fair*, Izmir, Turkey (with Lech Tomaszewski)
1957 Plan for the *National Exhibition of Interior Design*, Warsaw (with Zofia Hansen and J. Meisner)
1958 Polish Pavilion, *World's Fair*, Brussels (with others)
    Rakowiec Housing Estate, Warsaw (with Zofia Hansen, Z. Malicki, M. Szymanowski, and Z. Gurtzman)
    Cultural Centre, Montevideo (project; with Zofia Hansen and Lech Tomaszewski)
    Zacheta Building extension, Warsaw (with Lech Tomaszewski and Stanisław Zamecznik)
1959 Monument, Auschwitz-Birkenau, Poland (project; with Zofia Hansen, Jerzy Jarnuszkiewicz, Julian Pałka, and Lechostaw Rosiński)
    Polish Pavilion, *Bienal*, Sao Paulo (with Zofia Hansen and Lech Tomaszewski)
1960 Polish Radio Experimental Music Centre, Warsaw (with J. Piatkowski)
    Polish Pavilion, *Triennale*, Milan
1960/
    61 Master plan for the Słowacki Housing Estate, Lublin, Poland (with Zofia Hansen and J. Dowgiałło)

1961 City Monument, Westerplatte, Poland (with J. Kucz)
1962 Open Form Theatre, Lublin, Poland (with Zofia Hansen and M. Konieczny)
    Energetyk-Torwar Housing Estate, Warsaw (with Zofia Hansen and B. Ufnalewski)
1963 Przyczołek Grochowski Estate, for the Young Men's Housing Co-operative, Warsaw (with Zofia Hansen, J. Dowgiałło, and M. Konieczny)
    Teacher Training College, Lublin, Poland (with Zofia Hansen, J. Wolski, and M. Konieczny)
1964 Skoczylas Monument, Warsaw (with E. Cieślar)
1965 Słowacki Housing Estate, Lublin, Poland (with Zofia Hansen and Jerzy Dowgiałło)
1966 Shopping Centre, Słowacki Housing Estate, Lublin, Poland (with Zofia Hansen)
    Linear Continuous System Housing Estate (project; with Zofia Hansen, M. Konieczny, T. Kujawa, G. Marczak, and H. Rzenca)
    Museum of Modern Art, Skopje, Yugoslavia (with B. Cybulska, Lars Fasting, and Svein Hatløy)
1967 Linear Continuous System Settlement Definition Study (with Zofia Hansen)
1968 Hansen Country House, Szumin, Poland (with Zofia Hansen)
    Linear Continuous System Housing Development, Ursynów-Lasy Kabackie, near Warsaw (with others)
1969 Low-cost housing, Lima, Peru (competition project; with Svein Hatløy, J. Dowgiałło, and J. Kozierski)
1971 Development plan for the Warta River, Poznan
1972 Polish Regional Development Forecast Plan (Linear Continuous System study; with Svein Hatløy)
    Linear Continuous System Housing Development, near Poznan (project; with Svein Hatløy)
    Studio Theatre modernization, Warsaw
1973 Monument, Lodz, Poland (project; with J. Kucz)
    Polish Embassy, Washington, D.C. (with P. Damięcki)
    St. George Church/Cultural Centre conversion, Gdansk, Poland (with Zofia Hansen)

1974 Linear Continuous System Housing Development, near Przemyśl, Poland (project; with Zofia Hansen, P. Damięcki, and Svein Hatløy)
    Polish Pavilion, *Exempla '74*, Munich
1975 Environmental study of the city centre of Lubin, Poland (with E. Bartman, H. Górka, T. Banovitz and P. Piwowarczyk)
1976 Linear Continuous System Housing Development, Legnica, Lubin, and Głogów, Poland (project; with E. Bartman, and M. Czernicki)
1977 Polish Pavilion, *Biennale*, Venice
1977/
    78 Work-environment study for the Automats Factory, Chocianów, Poland (with E. Bartman, H. Górka, E. Kun, and H. Szmalenberg)

Publications:

By HANSEN: articles—"Biotechnique" in *Projekt* (Warsaw), no. 5, 1957; "Open Form" in *Przeglad Kulturalny* (Warsaw), no. 355, 1958; "Open Form—The Art of the Great Number," with Zofia Hansen, in *CIAM 1959 Otterlo*, edited by Oscar Newman, Stuttgart 1959; "Auf der Suche nach der Offenen Form" in *Bauwelt* (Berlin), no. 37, 1963; "Evolution où Revolution," with Zofia Hansen, in *L'Architecture d'Aujourd'hui* (Paris), no. 119, 1965; "Komposisjonsundervisningen ved akademiet i Warszawa" in *Arkitektnytt* (Oslo), no. 14, 1965; "Linear Continuous System" in *Diekorativnoje Isskustwo* (Moscow), no. 9, 1967; "Towards the Architecture for 30 Million Caesars" in *Kenchiku Bunka* (Tokyo), no. 1, 1967; "Dipoli ist Architektur" in *Bauwelt* (Berlin), no. 28, 1968; "Proposition pour un Urbanisme Lineaire" in *Le Carre Bleu* (Paris), no. 2, 1969; "Lima, Peru," with Svein Hatløy, in *Bafnytt* (Bergen), no. 2, 1972; "Pilotsprojektet i Lima" in *Byggekunst* (Oslo), no. 5, 1977.

On HANSEN: books—*Oskar Hansen: Architecture, Sculpture, Painting*, exhibition catalogue, by Jerzy Sołtan, Warsaw 1957; *Oskar Hansen: In Search of Methods of Teaching Art*, exhibition catalogue, Warsaw 1966; *L'Architecture Polonaise Contemporaine* by B. Lisowski, Warsaw 1968; *Nowa architektura Polska* by P. Szafer, Warsaw 1972; *Przygody Architektury XX wieku* by P. Trzeciak, Warsaw 1974; *Biennale di Venezia: Polonia*, exhibition catalogue, Venice 1976; articles—"Oskar Hansen Exhibition" in *Projekt* (Warsaw), no. 3, 1957; "De Technische en Riumtelijke Experimenten von Oskar Hansen" in *Het Bouwwerk* (The Hague), no. 1, 1961; "Oskar Hansen and His Open Form" by S. Stopczyk in *Projekt* (Warsaw), no. 1, 1962; "The Searches of Oskar Hansen" by A. Oseka in *Poland* (Warsaw), no. 4, 1962; "In Defence of Professor Hansen's Ideas" in *Poland* (Warsaw), no. 2, 1967; "Oskar Hansen" by A. Moffet in *Architectural Design* (London), no. 2, 1968; "About Lima, Peru Housing" in *Architectural Design* (London), no. 6/7, 1970; "Hansen—en aporte al diseño de rivienelas colectivas" in *Summa* (Buenos Aires), no. 67, 1973; "Slowacki—Newcastle" by Svein Hatløy in *Bafnytt* (Bergen), no. 6, 1977.

The growing discord between man and his physical surroundings and the disharmony between man and man result first of all from the objective organization of space, which I have called the "Closed Form," being the semantically-spatial derivative of a consumer life-style. In order to create a balance between man and his natural and technical environments, and harmony between men, one ought to realize the spatial conditions for a different qualitative style of life. The consumer model should be exchanged for a cognitive model—encouraging the growth of the level of life rather than the standard of living, which is merely based on growth in the quantity of goods produced in relation to the number of inhabitants. Achieving a cognitive model requires us to grasp the problems in a complex and integrated way. In the 1950's these premises promoted the idea of ordering space based on the "Open Form" concept.

The idea of architecture and art based on "Open Form" results from the principles of situational relations. The aim of an architect or an artist should not be to create finished works of art but to provide a background for the user's expression and, in this process, to search for an expressional synthesis. Life-processes and man himself should develop these forms.

The term "Open Form" derives from the fact that works of art created by its conventions are based on the user's intervention; therefore, they are forms that will adopt to the evolutionary process. It may seem that the freedom given to users by "Open Form" is synonymous with spatial anarchy. But this is not so. The content of "Open Form" revealed, for example, in housing—a process for evolving the user's consciousness, expressed by an active transformation of space—is expressed through the interpretation of a background of events taking place in accordance with the readability of individual constituent elements. The user is liberated from the rigour with which space has been previously arranged. This type of environment makes it possible to broadly compare the various concepts for organizing living space, and it creates possibilities for development and progress through choice and natural selection.

Regional planning in the context of "Open Form" implies that the objective elements—permanent and scientifically defined—would be applied in such a way that the subjective elements—the development processes—would become organic events and constitute the basic wealth and character of the surrounding built forms.

In considering the postulates of "Open Form" in the context of both the function and form (or colour), and the architect's or artist's new approach to design, one realizes that there is a need to create new didactic programmes. These programmes should derive from the reality of development processes, not from the reality of static situations. Technical knowledge should be conveyed in the context of a humanist education.

In organizing space in accordance with "Open Form," painting and sculpture lose their consumer character and become integral components of the whole. Their new function, I believe, is to make the events occurring in space more legible, to clarify their spontaneous character, and to articulate the compositional open-ness of their surroundings. The interpenetration of spontaneous elements with conscious artistic creativity should lead us to an authentic environmental art.

—Oskar Hansen

The inspiration of Oskar Hansen's work is a search for a future relationship between Man and his surroundings that corresponds to an egalitarian social system and that solves the problems of mass population. Hansen contrasts the old objective approach to architecture with an architecture created by a series of events—man and nature in a developing process. An absence of events would mean the absence of Hansen's architecture, the architecture of Open Form; that is, in his opinion, his activity only initiates one of the elements of architecture—the organisation of a framework for coming events. Closely related to Hansen are Svein Hatløy, Herman Hertzberger, Lucien Kroll and Ralph Erskine, who are also searching for a crystallization of the Open Form concept, working in the much more difficult conditions of a civilization dominated by the myth of consumption and commodity.

Oskar Hansen, with his wife Zofia, search for a concept of social space, the creation of certain frameworks in which individual activities—irrespective of personal intentions—will by necessity be in agreement with the spirit of the community, creating a

type of community life in which each member, while attending to his own minor everyday needs, will contribute to the creation of the whole. This view is connected with his belief in the necessity for a profound re-evaluation in architecture, the acquisition of new vision and imagination.

The ideas of "Open Form" and the "Art of Great Numbers," defined by Hansen in 1958 and presented at the 11th Congress of CIAM in Otterlo (1959), are attempts to specify the contemporary philosophy of architectural thought, based on an awareness of the role played by social factors in the creation of our environment. The concept of "Closed Form" formerly used by CIAM (which Hansen felt neglected the psychic needs of the individual, did not allow flexibility in lifestyle, and did not solve the problems of mass living) he contrasts with that of Open Form, which accepts the individual in the community as a whole, helping him to identify himself in the building of his own environment. It is a synthesis of impersonal social elements and the subjective elements of the individual.

Using as an analogy the development of Christian ideology, Hansen remarks that, in the development of a new social outlook on life and the new forms that result, we also have to pass through a period of "Christian basilicas built of pagan columns." Step by step we have to break with the present forms of our human environment (and change people's spatial and social imagination), which are the result of the needs of former times—such as the atrophy and disintegration of human settlements on a village scale, the concentric patterns of cities, specialized education based on static values—reflected in the dogmas of Closed Form. The goal of Open Form is to free man from the present consumptional, objective model of life and to direct his interests towards the development of social conciousness, towards authentic creative interests, and finally towards the needs of his own "nest."

The Open Form concept formed the basis for Hansen's "Linear Continuous System" (LCS), which attempts to answer the problems of settlement patterns that lag behind growth processes and the organization of mass living when it is in a state of continuous motion.

The Linear Continuous System is a proposal for creating man's environment within a socialist framework, based on the growth of organic structure: a flexible, proportionally correlated interdependance of urban zones running parallel to each other, clearly relating the service zones to those serviced. It is the kind of urban profile whose interpretation depends on the number of inhabitants, their social structure, their technical resources, etc. Thus it is a model with an open and highly flexible character, a set of organically linked functional systems, each of which goes through biotechnical evolution both qualitative and quantitative in nature.

LCS proposes coordinated action on the scale of a whole country; it is an attempt to bring together the combined resources of state-owned land, funding and industry—an attempt to get a "percentage" for the individual from the national economy.

LCS defines three linear planning zones on both sides of an axis of major communication routes and rivers. Immediately adjacent is the housing and light industry and an appropriate service infrastructure; beyond this is a zone of open land containing existing historical settlements, woods and farmland; the outermost zone contains heavy industry appropriate to the available natural resources. LCS creates a approach to planning different from that of the concentric pattern, and some structural units characteristic of concentric patterns disappear or change their meaning, such as the market place, shopping centre, or residential neighbourhood. Instead, new structural units arise, such as housing lines, service lines, lines of communication and lines of work. The linear concentration of this approach causes a rise in the individual's standard of living, enables closer contact with a less spoilt natural environment, and creates a more balanced relationship between work and recre-

ation. The high standard of living, the variety of local countryside, the scale of the social milieu, this great linear concentration of people, equipped with efficient, rationally used communication—these are the advantages of LCS, the attractiveness of which, in Hansen's opinion, will draw people to it, and at the same time will rescue the towns from further pathological expansion.

In LCS an individual has a clear image of relationships, both objective—of a scientifically motivated public area; and subjective—of his own private area. The primary axis consists of a bearing structure together with infrastructure and services—this is a public area. The private houses on the structure—this is a private area. During the developing process the relationship between public and private areas in LCS form harmonious dependencies that come together at various times, unlike the zonal relationships in a concentric town.

In Hansen's view of human surroundings, there are no inert, indifferent forms. Each spatial activity expresses a certain idea, a philosophy related to man's affairs. Open Form is an activity for the sake of mankind, for those who are creative and conscious, understanding, and prepared to be individuals in the framework of community life.

Two somewhat compromised attempts to put Hansen's LCS idea into practice are the Słowacki Housing Estate in Lublin and Warsaw's Przyczołek Grochowski. They are, in Hansen's view, still only objects, individual items, still using the old language but at the same time being experimental vehicles for the Open Form concept.

Hansen agrees that he is a little doctrinaire, with clearly stated views on the essence of his creativity. He consistently accepts only those design commissions in whose solution he can sense the potential for making the next step forward, for bringing Open Form to fruition. He is often accused of turning the problem of people into the problem of the idea, of preaching the pragmatism of utopia, and of an uncompromising attitude in making judgements. But Hansen believes that the realization of the LCS model will be the expression of an integrated social consciousness, and he is conscious that the LCS model will not be fully realized in his lifetime. This is an idea for many generations to come, an idea that he is trying to implant in his students and the younger generation of architects.

Oskar Hansen believes that, now, one must be an "enfant terrible," must design so-called utopias and must try to arouse and shape social consciousness, so that tomorrow LCS may become a reality.

—Teresa Czaplinska-Archer

HANSON, Norman (Leonard).
South African. Born in Johannesburg, 19 June 1909; resident in England since 1963. Educated at the King Edward VII School, Johannesburg, 1921–24; University of the Witwatersrand School of Architecture, Johannesburg, under G. E. Pearse and A. Stanley Furner, 1925–31, B.Arch. 1932. Married Matle Joyce Frank in 1961; children: Caroline and Roger (Hanson); Natalie and Vivienne (née Frank). Partner, with S. N. Tomkin and N. I. Finkelstein, in Hanson, Tomkin and Finkelstein, later Hanson and Tomkin, Johannesburg, 1932–70; Partner, with Tomkin and latterly C. E. Harris, in S. N. Tomkin, Hanson and Harris, Durban, 1946–78. Development Consultant, New Town of Ashkelon, Israel, 1949–61. Visiting Professor, University of New South Wales, Sydney, 1962. Professor and Director, School of Architecture, 1963–71, and since 1971 Professor Emeritus, University of Manchester. President, Transvaal Provincial Institute of Architects, 1943, and Institute of South African Architects, 1947; Executive Member of the National Housing and Planning Commission, Founder-Member of the Building

Norman Hanson: Architecture and Planning Building, University of Manchester, 1970

Research Advisory Committee of the National Building Research Institute, Founder-Member of the Management Committee of the National Development Fund for the Building Industry, Member of the Board of the Faculty of Architecture of the University of the Witwatersrand, and Member and Chairman of the Board of Education of the Institute of South African Architects, all South Africa, 1946–63. Recipient: Award of Merit, 1948, and Gold Medal, 1959, Institute of South African Architects. M.A.: University of Manchester, 1966. Norman Hanson Bursary and Fellowships established by the Institute of South African Architects, Council for Scientific and Industrial Research, Association of South African Quantity Surveyors, and Building Industry Federation of South Africa, 1963. Associate, Royal Institute of British Architects, 1935. Address: 5 Straffan Lodge, Belsize Grove, London NW3 4XE, England.

Principal Works:

1932 Saffer House, Johannesburg (project)
1933 Harris House, Johannesburg
1934 Brookstone House, Johannesburg
     Hotpoint House (showrooms, offices and flats), Johannesburg
1935 Yeoville Flats, Johannesburg (project)
1936 Suzman House, Johannesburg
     Reading Court, Johannesburg
1937 Denstone Court, Johannesburg
1938 Hanson House, Johannesburg
1940 20th Century Cinema, Johannesburg (with Cowin and Ellis)
1948 Medical Centre, Johannesburg
1956 Zionist Centre, Johannesburg (with Cooper and Hellmann)
     Government Offices, Esplanade, Durban (with S. N. Tomkin)
1958 Broadway Building, Foreshore, Cape Town (with Kantorowich and Skacel)

1961/
66 Medical School and Library, University of the Witwatersrand, Johannesburg (with P. Aneck-Hahn and H. M. J. Prins)
1962 Geology and Mining Engineering Building, University of the Witwatersrand, Johannesburg (with H. M. J. Prins)
1963 Electrical Engineering Building, University of Natal, Durban (with S. N. Tomkin)
1963/
77 Science Complex, University of Natal, Durban (with S. N. Tomkin)
1970 Architecture and Planning Building, University of Manchester, England (with Roy Kantorowich, M. Schonegevel and G. Skacel)

Publications:

By HANSON: book—*Zerohour,* editor with Rex Martienssen and Gordon McIntosh, Johannesburg 1933; articles—"Metaphysics of Space" in *South African Architectural Record* (Johannesburg), September 1932; "Architecture and the New Aesthetic" in *South African Architectural Record* (Johannesburg), November 1936; "An Architect's House" in *South African Architectural Record* (Johannesburg), October 1939; "The Twentieth Century Cinema" in *South African Architectural Record* (Johannesburg), August 1940; "Rex Martienssen: In Memoriam" and "The Student and Philosopher of Architecture" in *South African Architectural Record* (Johannesburg), November 1942; "Community Planning" in *South African Architectural Record* (Johannesburg), October 1943; "South Africa—Architecture from 1700 to 1930," special issue of *Architectural Review* (London), October 1944; "The Architect's Dilemma" in *Manchester Literary and Philosophical Society Proceedings 1964–65,* Manchester 1965; "Professional Education" in *Research for Better Building* (Proceedings of the Third South African Building Congress), Durban 1974.

On HANSON: books—*Twentieth Century Houses* by Raymond McGrath, London 1934; *Martienssen and the International Style* by Gilbert Herbert, Cape Town and Rotterdam 1975; articles—"An Experiment in Technique" in *South African Architectural Record* (Johannesburg), January 1935; "Formal Problems in Cinema Design" by Monte Bryer in *South African Architectural Record* (Johannesburg), November 1941; "Contemporary Building" by J. Fassler in *Architectural Review* (London), October 1944; "Contemporary Architecture in South Africa" by J. Fassler in *Architectural Design* (London), June 1956; "Le Corbusier and the South African Movement" by Gilbert Herbert in *Architectural Association Quarterly* (London), January/March 1972.

My work as a practising architect over a period of 46 years has had two distinct phases, the first dominant in the years preceding the war, that is, from 1932 to 1939, and the second, part development and part reorientation, dating from 1946 to the present time.

In the first phase, as a young architect, I participated actively in the evolution of the modern movement in South Africa, itself an offshoot of the architectural revolution in Europe, epitomised in the work, theoretical and practical, of the pioneers, Gropius, Mies van der Rohe and, above all, Le Corbusier. With Le Corbusier a strong link was forged, essentially through the contact made with him by Rex Martienssen, then teaching at the University of the Witwatersrand. The small band of young architects, recently graduated from that University, absorbed and put into practice the principles enunciated by the master, and were labelled by him "The Transvaal Group." In spite of some initial public and professional opposition, a considerable body of work was carried out by the group, mainly in the domestic field, but culminating, in my case, in the building of a large project, the 20th Century Cinema in Johannesburg. The history of that period has been written by Gilbert Herbert in his monumental *Martienssen and the International Style.*

After the hiatus of the war years (during which Martienssen died while in military training), the problem of re-starting practice brought new challenges. An introspective review and re-appraisal of past attitudes indicated for me the need to recast my architectural approach. Though valuing the achievements in many respects of the proponents of the modern movement, I nevertheless saw a profound weakness in the technical base of the pre-war work (as well as social shortcomings). As I now believed that sound constructional techniques were the foundation of all good architecture, I re-shaped my approach from first principles and found much common ground with architects and constructors such as Perret and Nervi. Under prevailing immediate post-war conditions, building resources were scarce, the most readily available materials being brick and concrete. I concentrated on these age-old materials and have stayed with them ever since. Developing techniques in factory production and site assembly have transformed the use of concrete, and modern science, applied to building, has improved, and is improving, building standards. For myself, I believe that the mainspring of the creative process may be found in structure, though architecture itself arises from an amalgam of social, functional and constructional factors brought to the level of an art form.

—Norman Hanson

Norman Hanson played a considerable role in the development of modern architecture in South Africa, as a close associate of Rex Martienssen, a leading member of the Transvaal Group, and as the designer of some of the finest examples of modern buildings of the day outside of Europe.

After his overwhelming confrontation (together with Martienssen) with the new architecture at Stuttgart in 1930—the Weissenhofsiedlung and Mendelsohn's Schocken Store—Hanson unequivocally accepted the International Style. He was moved by the austere power of its forms and stimulated by the philosophy that informed them. His early papers in the *South African Architectural Record* ("Metaphysics of Space" and "Architecture and the New Aesthetic") indicate the formidable mind of a very capable theoretician; but his principal contribution was to be in the field of architectural practice. In 1932, in Johannesburg, he established the firm of Hanson-Tomkin-Finkelstein, which was the pioneer firm of architects undertaking work only in the contemporary manner: this integrity of purpose ensured an outflow of high quality but, naturally, inhibited the quantity of work produced. The influence of Mies van der Rohe is evident in much of the early work, sometimes explicitly in the plan forms adopted, as in the virtuoso Saffer House project, or the simpler Brookstone House swimming pool—which formed the basis for a polemical article by Martienssen in the *Record* ("An Experiment in Technique"). The less superficial and more enduring effect of the Miesian influence, however, lay in Hanson's respect for the precision of Mies's designs and his emphasis on the primacy of technology as a form-giving force.

In a series of notable houses in the 1930s, Hanson allied this creative use of technology with a growing mastery of the language of the International Style, notably the idioms of Le Corbusier. From the very first realized example, Harris House—the first South African work to receive international recognition, being published in Raymond McGrath's *Twentieth Century Houses*—there is a consistent use of white wall surfaces and large glazed areas; the frequent juxtaposition of a dominant prismatic architecture with sensuously curved, sculptural forms; spacious exercises in the free flow of the plan; and an overall character of power and strength. To an even greater degree, these characteristics may be seen in his larger buildings: Hotpoint House, a tall building on a narrow centre-city site, with a beautifully modelled fa-

cade; the Yeoville flats project, which combines a free-flowing plan with a vigorously plastic external form; and Reading Court, a relatively small building which somehow is almost monumental in scale. In Reading Court, and more explicitly in Denstone Court, Hanson emphasized the communal aspects of the building—the open spaces, recreation areas, etc. —for the idea of the flat, the communal residential building, had for Hanson, as it had for Gropius, a social basis, an ideological as well as an architectural motivation.

In his last works prior to the war—his own house and the outstanding 20th Century Cinema building —the sensuous, almost baroque elements are still present but in combination with strong forms of geometric precision, taking the architecture beyond the formal limits set by the International Style and presaging the romantic modernism then being evolved, unknown to Hanson, in Brazil.

The outbreak of the war, and the caesura it enforced on building, enabled Hanson to pause and to re-examine the premises upon which he had built his architectural philosophy. He came to question the social validity of Le Corbusier's proposals, the lack of realism which the new aesthetic had imposed upon building technology, the invalidity of the International Style in respect to the South African climate —in effect, the very ethical bases of the architecture he had espoused. He retreated—in such postwar buildings as the Medical Centre and the Zionist Federation building in Johannesburg—into a conservative mode, sacrificing the exuberance of his earlier buildings to the interests of rational planning and meticulous detailing of constructional elements. The strong controlling hand of Hanson was always evident, but the forms became subdued, austere almost, neo-classical in spirit in their strict modularity. With difficulty, it seemed, a new architecture gradually emerged, of which the Architectural School buildings at Manchester University (where he had taken up the chair of architecture) is a late flowering.

—Gilbert Herbert

HARA, Hiroshi.

Japanese. Born in Kanagawa Prefecture in 1936. Educated at Nagano Prefectural High School, graduated 1955; Tokyo University, under Kenzo Tange and Professor Uchida, 1955-59, Dip.Arch. 1959, D.Arch. 1964. In private practice, Tokyo: Founder/Director, Research Studio for Architecture and Space (RAS). Associate Professor, Institute of Industrial Science, Tokyo University, since 1969. Exhibition: *From Space to Environment,* Tokyo, 1966. Address (office): Sakuragaoka High Home no. 701, 13-10 Sakuragaoka, Shibuya-ku, Tokyo, Japan.

Works:

1965 Hotel Yamagishi (project)
1966 Primary School (project)
     Wooden House, Tokyo (project)
1967 Itoh House, Tokyo
1968 Keisho Kindergarten, Machida City, near Tokyo
     Induction House (project)
1969 Mountain Lodge, Tanazawa, Japan
1970 Hakone International Culture Center, Japan (competition project)
1972 Toba Maritime Museum, Tokyo
     Awazu House, Kawasaki, Kanaga Prefecture, Japan
     Izu Fishing Lodge, Japan
1974 Hiroshi Hara House, Machida City, near Tokyo
     School, Kasumageseki, Japan
1975 Villa Kudo, Tokyo
1978 Niramu House, Tokyo

Publications:

By HARA: book—*Global Architecture 4: Kevin Roche, John Dinkeloo and Associates—The Ford Foundation Building, New York 1967; The Oakland Museum, California 1969,* with Yukio Futagawa, Tokyo 1971; articles—"E. N. Rogers, the Critic," with Ken-ichi Karasaki, in *Kokusai Kentiku* (Tokyo), June 1960; "Architecture and Individuality" in *The Japan Architect* (Tokyo), June 1966; "Notes Concerning Spatial Concepts" in *Space Design* (Tokyo), no. 96, 1972; "Okaya Municipal Minato Primary School" in *The Japan Architect* (Tokyo), January 1974.

On HARA: articles—"Japanische enfamiliehuse" by Helle Klint in *Arkitekten* (Copenhagen), no. 10, 1968; "A New Generation of Architects" in *The Japan Architect* (Tokyo), June 1968; "Awazu Residence" and "Toba Ocean Museum" in *Kenchiku Bunka* (Tokyo), September 1972; "Houses" in *The Japan Architect* (Tokyo), November 1972; "House for a Graphic Artist: Awazu Residence, Kawasaki" in *Architecture Francaise* (Paris), October 1975; "Villa Kudo" in *Kenchiku Bunka* (Tokyo), January 1977; "Hiroshi Hara: An Introduction" by Chris Fawcett in *Architectural Association Quarterly* (London), no. 4, 1978.

"The basic nature of architecture is in its holes. The geometric relations between 'open' and 'closed' determine what the piece stands for."

I first saw Hiroshi Hara's own house in the rain, against a copper sky, in Machida City, some kilometres south-west of Tokyo. The self-effacing exterior ran away from the hill, its timber cladding vanished in the site overrun with vegetation—"even in a city, architecture is a device for evoking the natural strengths of location." While the outside was intent on doing a disappearing act, the inside made its presence felt the instant one entered—the levels cascade down, Mediterranean hill-village style, with servant spaces on either side of the processional descent. The extraordinary topography of dwelling is emphasized by the quality of light, fluttering through roof-lights, intermediary translucent perspex membrances, and apertures of various kinds. One had the feeling of standing in the centre of some mysterious mass that had over a period of time been punctured, pierced, tunneled and, through a process of attrition, worn down into a porous, honey-combed space where cavities and hollows overlapped in a warren of hideaways. The Ninja Yashiki is a pertinent metaphor here, the place of a refuge of the Ninja, a 17th century Japanese mercenary: fold-away stairs, secret passageways, one-way views, hidden floors, the very apotheosis of our idea of the flexibility of the Japanese house.

Hara's school at Kasumageseki, the Keisho Kindergarten at Machida City, the Awazu, Itoh and his own house—all are characterized by a hollowing out, a concavity, excavation, cave, recess, niche. Internally, his buildings tend to string the concavities together on a linear basis—"to equipmentalize the building so that its spaces participate in the control of the activities of the occupants."

More recently, since the completion of his Toba Maritime Museum, Hara has had fewer opportunities to build, and he has had the opportunity, therefore, to visit and study world village types: his investigation has been of the relation between the "morphology of dwelling groups" and domain theory. The interaction of village domain and individual house domain he explains by the ordering concept of "threshold," which supports the interior order of the group and regulates the intercourse between one group and others. In other words, he is finding in the remote, vernacular villages, elements of articulation parallel to those that he himself has employed in his own urban projects. The "architecture of holes" was already there in the "morphological complexity of dwelling groups." The eternal return.

—Chris Fawcett

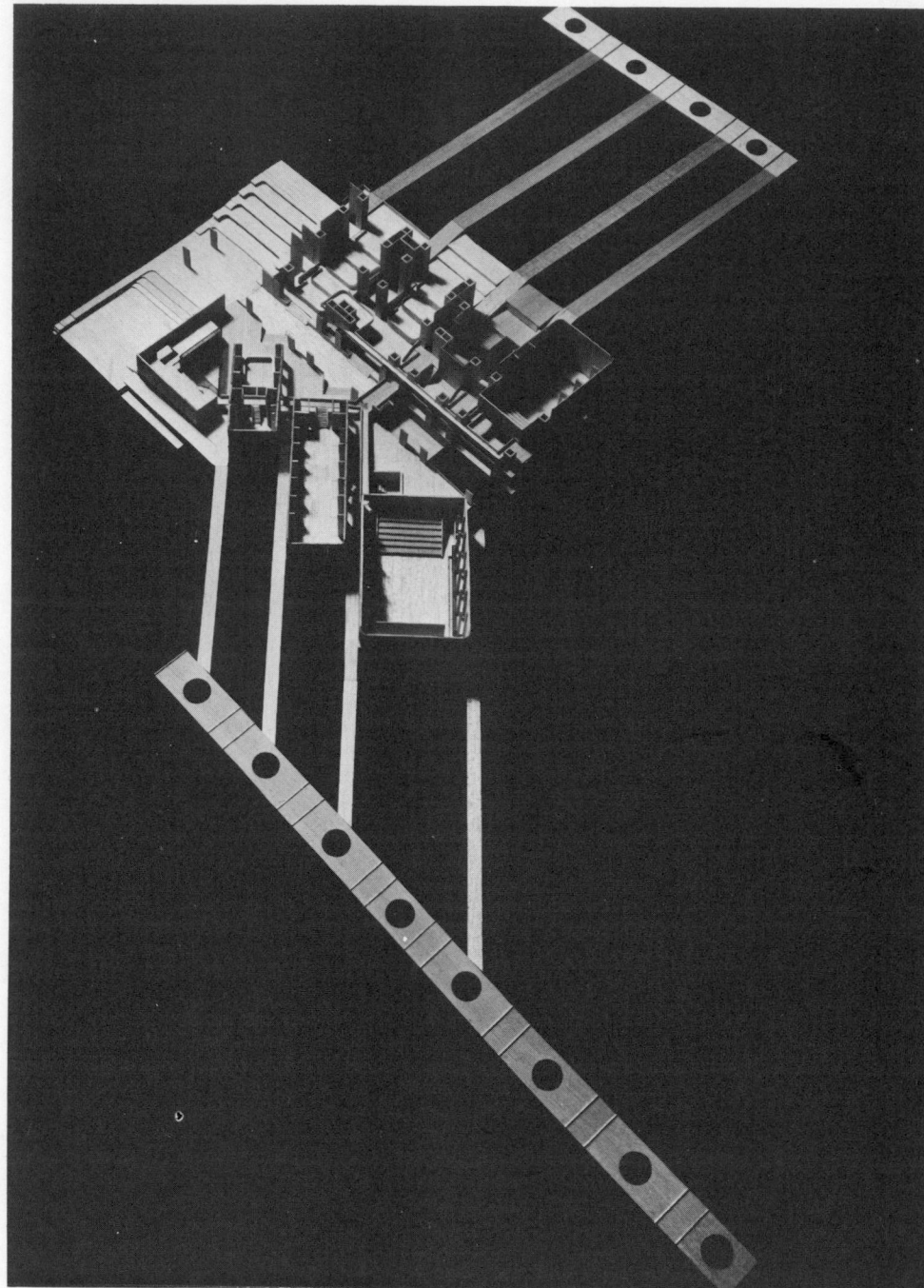

Hiroshi Hara: Hakone International Culture Center, Japan, 1970 (competition project)

HARDY, Hugh (Gelston).

American. Born in Majorca, Spain, of American parents, 26 July 1932. Educated at Princeton University, New Jersey (D'Amato Prizeman), B.Arch. 1954, M.F.A. 1956. Served in the Engineering Corps of the United States Navy, 1956–58. Architectural Assistant to the scenic designer Jo Mielziner, New York, 1958–62; Principal, Hugh Hardy and Associates, New York, 1962–67. Since 1967, Partner, with Malcolm Holzman and Norman Pfeiffer, Hardy Holzman Pfeiffer Associates, New York. Vice-President for Architecture, The Architectural League of New York; Vice-President and Member of the Executive Committee, The Municipal Art Society of New York (also, Chairman, Committee to Save Grand Central Terminal, and Member of the Advisory Board to its Public Arts Council); Member, Advisory Committee to the National Design Network. Davenport Professor, with partners, Yale University, New Haven, Connecticut, 1976. Recipient: Design Award Citation, *Progressive Architecture*, 1967; Architectural Award Citation, American Institute of Steel Construction, 1969; Beautifying America Award, *Holiday Magazine*, 1969; Certificate of Merit, 1970, and Citation of Merit, 1978, Municipal Art Society of New York; Bard First Honor Award, 1970, and Bard Award of Merit, 1977, City Club of New York; First Honor Award, American Institute of Architects/*House and Home/American Home*, 1973; Excellence of Design Award, *Industrial Design*, 1974; Brunner Prize, National Institute of Arts and Letters, 1974; Lumen Citation, Illuminating Engineering Society, 1975; Award for Excellence in Environmental Design, *Design and Environment*, 1975; Honor Award, American Institute of Architects/New York State Association of Architects, 1976 (twice); Bartlett Award, 1977, Honor Award, 1977, and Honor Award for Extended Use, 1978, 1979, American Institute of Architects; Award of Honor, New York Society of Architects, 1977; Medal of Honor, American Institute of Architects, New York Chapter, 1978. Fellow, American Institute of Architects. Address: Hardy Holzman Pfeiffer Associates, 257 Park Avenue South, New York, New York 10010, U.S.A.

Works:

1963/
65 Playhouse in the Park adaptive re-use, Cincinnati, Ohio
1966 Simon's Rock Art Center adaptive re-use, Great Barrington, Massachusetts
Ingersoll House, Sharon, Connecticut (with T. Merrill Prentice, Jr.)
Dobell House, Ottawa, Ontario, Canada
1967 Performing Arts Center, University of Toledo, Ohio (project)
Hadley House, Martha's Vineyard, Massachusetts
1968 New Auditorium, for Playhouse in the Park, Cincinnati, Ohio
Avery Johnson House adaptive re-use, Boston
MUSE (museum) adaptive re-use, Brooklyn, New York
New Lafayette Theatre adaptive re-use, New York
1969 Exeter Assembly Hall adaptive re-use, New Hampshire
Taylor Theatre adaptive re-use, Lockport, New York
Knowlton House adaptive re-use, Sneden's Landing, New York
Newark Community Center of Arts adaptive re-use, New Jersey
1970 Cloisters Condominium, Cincinnati, Ohio
Exeter Theatre, New Hampshire
Community Services Center, Shaw University, Raleigh, North Carolina
1971 Dance Theatre of Harlem School adaptive re-use, New York
1972 Cultural Ethnic Center adaptive re-use, New York
Salisbury School, Maryland
Mt. Healthy School, Columbus, Indiana
Schaefer House (project)
Emelin Theatre, Mamaroneck, New York
Weber Ski House, Straton Mountain, Vermont
Spaeth House, Easthampton, Long Island, New York
1973 American Film Institute Theatre, Washington, D.C.
American Film Institute Headquarters, Washington, D.C.
Occupational Health Center, Columbus, Indiana
1974 Artpark, Lewiston, New York
Orchestra Hall, Minneapolis (with Hammel Green and Abrahamson)
Olmsted Theatre, Adelphi University, Garden City, New York
von Bernuth House, Dobbs Ferry, New York
Pratt House adaptive re-use, Bridgewater, Connecticut
1975 Firemen's Training Center, New York
Agnes deMille Theatre adaptive re-use, Winston-Salem, North Carolina
1976 Baskerville Hall and Wingate Gymnasium adaptive re-use, City College of New York
Terry Dintenfass Gallery adaptive re-use, New York
Cooper-Hewitt Museum adaptive re-use, New York
1977 Brooklyn Children's Museum, New York
Eliot Feld Ballet Studio and Headquarters adaptive re-use, New York
St. Louis Art Museum restoration for extended use
1978 The Eye Institute, Pennsylvania College of Optometry, Philadelphia
Boettcher Concert Hall, Denver Center for the Performing Arts
1979 Langworthy House, New York

Publications:

By HARDY: report—*Re-Using Railroad Stations,*

Hugh Hardy: Boettcher Concert Hall, Denver Center for the Performing Arts, 1978

with Malcolm Holzman and Norman Pfeiffer, Washington D.C. 1974; articles—"Flexible Theatres of Performance" in *Theatre Design and Technology* (New York), Spring 1968; "Designing Random Focus" in *The Drama Review* (New York), Spring 1968; "The Overpermanent Architecture" in *Theatre I* (annual), New York 1969; "An Architecture of Awareness for the Performing Arts" in *Architectural Record* (New York), March 1969; "An Interview with Hugh Hardy" in *Historic Preservation* (Washington, D.C.), July/September 1972; "Architecture as Environment" in *Design Quarterly* (Minneapolis), Spring 1975; "Music, Architecture and Choice" in *Symphony News* (Vienna, Virginia), August 1975; "Machines, Man and Architecture" in *Architectural Record* (New York), October 1975; "Acts of Conscious Choice" in *Canadian Architect* (Toronto), March 1976; "An Evocative Approach to Adaptive Re-Use," interview, in *AIA Journal* (Washington, D.C.), June 1976; "Between Science and Scenery" in *Architectural Record* (New York), Summer 1977.

On HARDY: articles—"Supermannerism" by C. Ray Smith in *Progressive Architecture* (New York), October and November 1967; "Design for Learning" in *Architectural Record* (New York), April 1971; "Hardy Holzman Pfeiffer on America" by Stuart E. Cohen in *Progressive Architecture* (New York), February 1975; "Hardy Holzman Pfeiffer Associates" in *Architecture + Urbanism* (Tokyo), March 1976;

'Hardy Holzman Pfeiffer Associates Projects in Re-Use" in *AIA Journal* (Washington, D.C.), June 1976; "Re-using Railroad Stations" in *Domus* (Milan), September 1976; "Hardy Holzman Pfeiffer Associates" in the *New York Times,* 20 February 1977; "Hugh Hardy: Approaches to Color" in *AIA Journal* (New York), October 1978.

The process of collaboration is redundant, sometimes noisy, given to compromise, but essential if architecture is to make structures that are responsive to people. Although there is no reason to believe that the urge to build monuments is past, architecture now has more pressing things to do than look backward and beautiful. It must deal with the present, giving us buildings that are responsive to change, expressive of our pluralistic society, and cognizant of economic and technological realities.

The design of a building passes from abstract to specifics and requires conscious choice. The advantage of collaboration is that these choices are externalized through a process of continuing pin-up reviews, some informative, some competitive. Competitive pin-ups are used to elicit design ideas that are publicly synthesized into the design intent of each project. Informative pin-ups are conducted by the project architect and provide the design group with an opportunity to assess how well the project is proceeding in relation to its design intent.

Good ideas can come from anywhere. Collaboration solicits them without prejudice from all partici-

pants, whereas the idea of an individual creative genius radiating superior instinct over a network of technical drones is at once too monarchistic and too machine-like an image for a people-oriented architecture.

With this summer of 1979 our collaboration has survived a 15-year span of exploration. The results have produced buildings in a variety of shapes, uses and locations. This activity has given rise to the series of ideas outlined below:

1) *Old and new are of equal importance.* There is no present without the past, and putting new life in old structures is as valid as the creation of new buildings. The present includes the past. The future is more of the present, not utopia.

2) *A variety of spaces gives flexibility of use* for far less than movable walls, ceilings, or floors. (It is easier to make people move than architecture.)

3) Architectural elements need not be unified to provide order. It is possible to have an *order of disparate parts.*

4) Buildings need *not* appear the same from all sides. They can and often *should* appear different from different sides.

5) Buildings are *never* complete. They cannot be permanent when the society that surrounds them is in flux. In fact they grow or decline in appearance and importance—without physically changing—and should not be thought of as fixed in time.

6) Buildings *should,* therefore, be incomplete.

7) Open planning can best be achieved through the

inclusion of fixed enclosed elements, a process called Residual Space Planning.

8) Activities need *not* match space enclosures. Some activities are best housed *both* in and between places.

9) Standard parts can be combined to make a non-standard enclosure.

10) Architecture must now be built to imagine the future—not to memorialize the past.

11) Architecture is a language through which society both expresses and confronts itself. It is made for people, not architects.

12) Metal and plastic technology offer new ways to enclose space.

13) Architects have a responsibility to consider their clients' intent in relation to overall social well-being, especially in a time of potential environmental disaster.

14) Architecture is composed of five kinds of consciousness: social purpose; technology; geometry; time; and money.

—Hugh Hardy

Of all the flamboyant, young, revolutionary architects of the 1960's Hugh Hardy and his partners Malcolm Holzman and Norman Pfeiffer have survived the maturing process most successfully and have progressed from houses and other small commissions to generally approved major civic monuments. It has been an unlikely transformation, but not entirely surprising. For additive growth and transformation, or recycling, have been fundamental interests and explorations of the three partners from the beginning in the early 1960's.

Even before the firm of Hardy Holzman Pfeiffer Associates (HHPA) was formed, Hugh Hardy had defined his interest in the concept of the "additive assemblage" in the Ingersoll house (designed with T. Merrill Prentice Jr.). And from the first works of the three partners this collage idea was apparent: it was a collage of many parts, with "inclusion"—the early equivalent of today's "pluralism"—as the catchword. HHPA has always posited that architects should include more of the world than the limited range of natural and elegant materials that their predecessors had accepted for the International Style. HHPA expand that architectural vocabulary to include low art as well as high, the old as well as the new, applied decoration as well as integral, tinsel as well as bronze.

Therein lies their growth pattern to maturity and their lifeline to large-scale projects. It is not the witty or scandalizing use of unexpected materials, with which pranksterism they began, that gives them significance, but rather their larger view that sees more of the world, that looks to see the whole environment as it is. With that overview they came to portray a picture of contemporary America that is both true and harsh, witty and painful, sophisticated and common, sleek and kitsch. For America, like life, is all of those things—accommodating, aspiring, acquisitive, additive, and more. This is an overview that is real, and therefore more accessible to the lay public, because it accepts and includes more known objects.

Still, the first thing noticeable about each of the buildings by HHPA is that as a totality each is a work of non-architecture. That is, their buildings are either literally underground, bermed structures, and therefore ostensibly invisible, like the Brooklyn Children's Museum (1977), or they are virtually formless, non-geometrical, and free-form faceted envelopes like the Toledo Performing Arts Project (1966–67) that seem to reject any appearance of unified exterior composition. This derived in the beginning from a rejection of architecture as their predecessors made it and from a rejection of monumentality as an inaccurate expression of the tradition, context, and fact of American building. Yet this contextual awareness seems at times antithetical to the individual building in relation to its specific physical context. A kind of Palladian siting is evident in some HHPA buildings that are not actually underground. Instead, their self-effacing exterior envelopes are

tents for the occupants and for the components of which they are built—for the found objects of our culture, the known fragments with which HHPA composes, like signs on a building. Essentially this is a pop direction that involves two routes. The most prominent route throughout the nearly 20 year development of the firm's work is the industrial image, with its catalogue of prefabricated industrialized components. These the firm uses freely for their functional and economic values as well as leaving them exposed for their aesthetic contributions—structural elements such as steel decking and preassembled stairways; mechanical elements such as ducts and anemostats; and lighting systems with their wiring conduits. Superficially this could be seen as a development into a full-scale aesthetic of Charles Eames's house at Venice, California of 1947–49. Certainly it is a rococo cadenza of the industrial revolution and of man's fascination with the machine. And as certainly it is a romantic revival in representational terms of the classical period of Modern architecture, which used the machine and industry as its pre-eminent abstraction.

The second route in the search for pop components by HHPA is vernacular building and the roadway culture. Vernacular via Shingle Style is the main source. Objects from the roadway, including the airport runway, are standard building components for these architects—signs, neon, lights of all kinds, and whatever can be used decoratively out of the roadway context. As a sub category of this pop direction, kitsch and camp objects are also in the expanded HHPA vocabulary—stuffed animal heads, "hideous" theatre and hotel carpeting, and a riot of "ordinary" colors. From what began, seemingly, as pranks and games, inconsequential manipulations and inversions, HHPA have developed a serious and significant architecture.

Also the partners have always been open to the old as well as the new, to historical artifacts as building components—such as the train kiosk from the Queensborough Bridge that is used as the entry to the Brooklyn Children's Museum—as well as to the preservation of complete old buildings and the adaptation of them to new uses. They were forerunners in the recycling movement, and that activity as well as the early interest of Hugh Hardy in theatre design has led HHPA into the restoration and recycling of cultural facilities—theatres and museums of large scale, such as Cincinnati's Playhouse in the Park (1965), the Cooper-Hewitt Museum (1976), and the St. Louis Museum (1977). New symphony halls are also a part of their practice—Orchestra Hall in Minneapolis (1974) and Boettcher Concert Hall in Denver (1978).

All of this new vocabulary is assembled or collaged into collisions of form (Hadley House, 1967) or superimpositions of one plan idea on another, as in the parallel banks of stairs rising up both legs of an A-shaped plan (von Bernuth house 1974) or rising up across a crescent shaped plan (Schaefer house project 1972). Other collages are shifted grids, sometimes carried to their ultimate completion even if outside the building envelope (Mt. Healthy School, 1972). These superimpositions—an essentially additive process like the firm's early collisions with supergraphics—reflect the use of the diagonal to "break out of the box" of International Style architecture to produce something more free, informal, and humanistic.

The questions that the work of HHPA raises, then, are twofold: What is an architecture that is so generally self-effacing on the exterior and primarily concerned with the interior? And how can collage or assemblage be considered a higher achievement than architectural decorating? Furthermore, can any one architecture be representative of all America? Is a synthesis of America with all its regions and diversities ever really possible? And, finally, by including so wide a range of human experience as possible vocabulary for architecture, HHPA includes the possibility of the bad as well as the good. How can that do other than leave critics nonplussed for several years?

In their new American statement, HHPA seems to omit one large segment—the formally elegant, the classical, refined, and serene, the world of international diplomacy and protocol, of high society and tact. Only Orchestra Hall in Minneapolis appears to accommodate traditional elegance in a consistent way, and consistency seems almost mutually exclusive from the HHPA collage technique. Instead the HHPA view of our environment is of a more popularized America—a youthful, democratic, domestic, and middle class common man. This is a sure reality of much of America, perhaps even the majority. But it seems to accept the myth of the classless society, of the one-class democracy, and that is less than total realism. Still, in their ever youthful outlook, HHPA have given us an architecture of fun and vitality, of joy and chaos, of additive collage and recycled treasures that is among the realest architecture of our time. Theirs is certainly one valid and illuminating view of American architecture.

—C. Ray Smith

HÄRING, Hugo.

German. Born in Biberach, Württemberg, 22 May 1882. Educated at the Technische Hochschule, Stuttgart, under Theodor Fischer, 1899–1902; Technische Hochschule, Dresden, under Gurlitt, Schumacher and Wallot, 1901–02; studied privately in Stuttgart, 1903. Served in the German Army, 1914–15, 1917–18; Architect for the rebuilding of East Prussia, 1915–16. In private practice, Ulm, 1903–04, Hamburg, 1904–14, Berlin, 1918–43, and Biberach, 1943 until his death, 1958. Director, Reimann School (Kunst und Werk School), Berlin, 1935–43. Member of the Novembergruppe, Berlin, from 1918; Founder Member, Zehner Ring, Berlin, 1924 until it expanded to form Der Ring, 1926: served as Secretary of Der Ring, 1926–33; Founder Member, CIAM (Congrès Internationaux d'Architecture Moderne), 1929, and served as the Vice-Chairman of the German Section. Exhibitions: *Berlin Architectural Exhibition,* 1924; *Werkbund Exhibition,* Vienna, 1932. Honorary doctorate: Technische Hochschule, Stuttgart, 1950. *Died* (in Göttingen, Germany) *17 May 1958.*

Works:

1907 Main Railway Station, Leipzig (competition project)
1912 Royal Opera House, Berlin (competition project; with Gustav Blohm)
1916/
  18 Manor House, Gr'Plauen, East Prussia, Germany
1916/
  19 Hans Romer House, Neu Ulm, Germany
1917 Reimann Shop and Living Quarters, Allenburg, East Prussia, Germany
1921 Reception Building, Main Railway Station, Leipzig (project)
1922 Gaffre Guinle Hospital, Rio de Janeiro
    Skyscraper, Friedrichstrasse, Berlin (competition project)
1923 Garkau Complex, near Lubeck
    Germania Club rebuilding, Rio de Janeiro
    Revenue Office rebuilding, Schöneberg, Berlin
1924 Auction Rooms, Lubeck
    Prince Albert Garden alterations, Berlin
1925 Tobacco Goods Factory, Neustadt, Holstein, Germany
1925/
  26 Berlin Sezession Building (competition project)
1926 Terrace housing, Zehlendorf, Berlin
1927 Max Voythaler Building, Lankwitz, Berlin

Hugo Häring: Garkau Complex, near Lubeck, 1923

Tiergarten rebuilding, Berlin (competition project)

Reichstag rebuilding, Berlin (competition project)

1928 Art Exhibition Hall, Tattersalle, Berlin

Adler Week-end House, Wannsee Country Club, Berlin

Apartment buildings, Stockholmstrasse and Christianistrasse, Wedding, Berlin

1928/
29 Frentzel House, Elbing, East Prussia, Germany

1929 Plan for Zagreb, Yugoslavia (competition project)

Bin-Copernick Vocational School, Germany (competition project)

Siemensstadt (North) Housing Development, Charlottenburg, Berlin

1930 Behrendt House, Berlin

Karlshorst Housing Development, Treskowallee, Berlin

Roderstrasse Housing Development, Lichtenberg, Berlin

1930/
31 Beck/Segmehl House, Biberach, Germany

1932 Eichkamp Housing Development, Berlin

Hugo Haring House, Berlin

1933 Design of the *Werkbund Exhibition*, Stuttgart

Kochenhof Housing Development, Stuttgart (project)

Trade Union Housing Development, Vienna (project)

1937/
41 von Prittwitz Building, Tutzing, Germany

1938 Open-air school, Torbole sul Garda, Italy

1942 Kunst and Werk School, Berlin

1947/
48 Housing development, Birkendorf, Germany

1949/
50 Outer harbour, Friedrichshafen, Germany

1949/
52 Outer harbour, Biberach, Germany

Werner Schmitz House, Biberach, Germany

1950 Outer harbour, Aulendorf, Germany

Gert Schmitz House, Biberach, Germany

1951/
54 Outer harbour, Krefeld, Germany

Publications:

By HÄRING: book—*Hugo Häring: Schriften, Ent-*

würfe, Bauten by H. Lauterbach and Jürgen Joedicke, Stuttgart 1965; (includes writings); monographs—*Vom Neuen Bauen,* Berlin 1952; *Vom Geheimnis der Gestalt,* Berlin 1954; articles—"Probleme des Bauens" in *Der Neubau* (Berlin), September 1924, February 1925; "Wege zur Form" in *Die Form* (Berlin), October 1925; "Geometrie und Organik" in *Baukunst und Werkform* (Nuremberg), no. 9, 1951; "Beispeil einer Wohnung" in *Deutsche Architektur* (East Berlin), July 1967.

On HÄRING: book—*Hugo Häring: Schriften, Entwürfe, Bauten* by H. Lauterbach and Jürgen Joedicke, Stuttgart 1965 (includes bibliography); articles—"Häring at Garkau" by Jürgen Joedicke in *Architectural Review* (London), May 1960; "Hugo Häring: Zur Theorie des Organheften Bauen" by Jürgen Joedicke in *Bauen und Wohnen* (Zurich), November 1960; "Hugo Häring" by Jürgen Joedicke in *Arts and Architecture* (Los Angeles), February/March 1966.

Hugo Häring is an important representative of the "New Building" in Germany. Although he adopted the posture of an outsider, he was one of the few German avant-garde architects who brought a quite unmistakable personal touch to the International Style.

After studying architecture with Theodor Fischer in Stuttgart and Fritz Schumacher in Dresden, Häring set up in private practice in Ulm and then in Hamburg. One of his most important works from this period is undoubtedly his design for the Main Railway Station in Leipzig: Häring broke away from the traditional ground plan and worked his way to flowing, function-related solutions that precipitated a plastic transformation of structure.

During the years following his military service in World War I, after he had settled in Berlin, Häring produced a series of buildings and projects that brought him world renown. In the Prince Albert Garden in Berlin, the Neustadt Tobacco Goods Factory, the Garkau Complex, and his design for the Berlin Sezession Building, Häring used curves to mark out space, and, while maintaining traditional spatial sub-divisions, defined its flowing continuity. Unlike Erich Mendelsohn, for whom architecture was the expression of stasis in movement, Häring tried to show outwardly the function-related movements taking place inside the building.

During this period Häring's credentials in the

modernist movement were impeccable. He joined the Novembergruppe in 1918; he exhibited at the *Berlin Architectural Exhibition* of 1924, and that same year (with Hilberseimer, Mendelsohn, Mies van der Rohe and Bruno Taut, among others) he helped to found the Zehner-Ring, the aim of which was to counteract all anti-modern interpretations of architecture. In 1926 Zehner Ring expanded to form the famous Ring, and Häring was named as its first secretary: in this capacity he took part, in 1929, in the founding of CIAM, which he served as Vice-Chairman of the German Section.

But, from about 1926, Häring's interest began to change; he no longer projected or carried out in his buildings the curved demarcations of space. He began to see form not as "premeditated" fixed masses but, rather, as the result of individual design processes. In the following years his main interest became "basic existence" houses and housing development. He built a terraced housing estate in Zehlendorf, multi-family apartment buildings in Wedding, and the Siemensstadt Housing Development in Charlottenburg—all in Berlin. At the same time, he became interested in the problems of creating rational high-rise buildings and in the requirements of the growing family within a single-family house. With these works, and others, of the late 1920's and early 1930's, and with these interests, Häring had come some way from a simple concern with form. Also, in contrast to the then current purist interpretations of white, abstract structure, Häring worked with warm, natural materials—for example, he used bricks for visible masonry, slates for exterior wall cladding. He was also the first avant-garde architect to employ the concrete shell as an architectonic element.

Häring's last designs, prior to the National Socialist period, were the 1933 projects for the Trade Union Housing Development in Vienna and the Kochenhof Housing Development in Stuttgart. After the Nazi seizure of power, he was labelled a "degenerate architect," and from then until the end of the war he was able to build very little. In 1935 he became Director of the Reimann School, a private design school in Berlin, and in 1943 he returned to his birthplace, Biberach, where he practiced until his death. Even after 1945, Häring, who had used the enforced idleness of the previous years to clarify and define his architectural theories, was commissioned to build very little.

More than twenty years after his death Hugo Häring is honored, much too one-sidedly, as a protagonist of a formalist, organic architecture. In reality, he was a man to whom form alone signified little. Häring felt a great obligation to the social demands of his profession. His criterion was, first and foremost, the human being with his material needs, his wishes, his movements. Form, as an exterior covering, took second place. Häring's merit lies less in his alleged function as spokesman for organic building than in his search, during the flowering of the International Style, for consciously more human, warmer variants of architecture.

—Frank Werner

HARRIS, Harwell Hamilton.
American. Born in Redlands, California, 2 July 1903. Educated at San Bernardino High School, California, 1917–21; Pomona College, California, 1921–23; Otis Art Institute, Los Angeles, 1923–26; Frank Wiggins Trade School, Los Angeles, 1928–29. Married the historian Jean Murray Bangs in 1937. Worked as a sculptor, Los Angeles, 1926–28; collaborated with Richard J. Neutra, Los Angeles, 1928–32; in private practice, Los Angeles, 1933–51, Austin, Texas, 1955–56, Fort Worth, Texas, 1956–58, and Dallas, 1958–62. In private practice, Ra-

345

Harwell Hamiliton Harris: Havens House, Berkeley, California, 1941

leigh, North Carolina, since 1962. Lecturer, Chouinard Art Institute, Los Angeles, 1938–39, 1945–46, University of Southern California, Los Angeles, 1940, 1941, 1945, 1946, Art Center School, Los Angeles, 1941–45, and Columbia University, New York, 1943–44; Professor and Director, School of Architecture, University of Texas at Austin, 1951–55; Adjunct Professor, Columbia University, 1960–62; Professor of Architecture, School of Design, North Carolina State University, Raleigh, 1962–73. Member of CIAM (Congrès Internationaux d'Architecture Moderne), from 1929: Secretary, American Chapter, 1930–32, and Secretary, Relief and Postwar Planning Chapter, 1944–45. Exhibitions: Museum of Modern Art, New York, 1939, 1942, 1943, 1945, 1953; San Francisco Museum of Art, 1940, 1942; American Federation of Arts, New York, 1947; *Triennale,* Milan, 1957; National Gallery, Washington, D.C., 1957, toured Europe, Asia, and the United States; *International Fair,* Moscow, 1959; *Olympiad,* Munich, 1972; *200 Years of American Architectural Drawing,* Cooper-Hewitt Museum, New York, 1977, toured Chicago, Fort Worth, and Jacksonville, Florida, 1978. Recipient: First Prize, Class 1-A, Pittsburgh Glass Institute Competition, 1937, 1938; Honor Award, American Institute of Architects, Southern California Chapter, 1938; Honor Award and Merit Award, Texas Society of Architects, 1961. Fellow, American Institute of Architects, 1965. Address: 122 Cox Avenue, Raleigh, North Carolina 27605, U.S.A.

Works:

1934 Lowe House, 596 East Punahou, Altadena, California
1935 Fellowship Park House (Harwell Hamilton Harris House), 2311 Fellowship Park Way, Los Angeles
Laing House, 1642 Pleasant Way, Pasadena, California
1936 De Steiguer House, Glen Sumner Road, Pasadena, California
1937 Entenza House, 475 North Mesa Road, Santa Monica, California
Kershner House, Brilliant Way, Los Angeles
1938 Bauer House, 2538 East Glenoaks, Glendale, California
Blair House, 3762 Fredonia Drive, Los Angeles
Clark House, Valley View and 17th, Carmel, California
Granstedt House, Woodrow Wilson Drive, Hollywood, California
1939 Hawk House, 2421 Silver Ridge, Los Angeles
Harris House, 410 North Avenue 64, Pasadena, California
Pumphrey House, 615 Kingman Avenue, Santa Monica, California
Power House, 5160 La Cañada Boulevard, La Cañada, California
1940 Comstock House, Del Mar, California
Grandview Gardens Restaurant, Los Angeles

McHenry House, 624 South Holmby Avenue, West Los Angeles
Sox House, Ridgeview Drive, Menlo Park, California
1941 Havens House, 255 Panoramic Way, Berkeley, California
Naylor House, 40 Arden Road, Berkeley, California
Snyder House, 10879 Whipple Street, North Hollywood, California
Treanor House, 343 Greenacres Drive, Visalia, California
1942 Birtcher House, Sea View Drive, Los Angeles
Lek House, 1600 Mecca Drive, La Jolla, California
Meier House, 2240 Lakeshore, Los Angeles
1945 Fellowship Park Studio, Los Angeles
1946 Calvin House, Sitka, Alaska
Sobieski House, 1420 San Marino Boulevard, San Marino, California
Treanor Equipment Company, Delano, California
1947 Ingersol Demonstration House, Kalamazoo, Michigan
1948 Cruze Studio-House, 2340 West 3rd Street, Los Angeles
Johnson House, 10280 Chrysanthemum, West Los Angeles
Wylie House, 1964 Rancho Drive, Ojai, California
1949 Loeb House, Redding, Connecticut

Mulvihill House, 580 North Hermosa, Sierra Madre, California

1950 Chadwick School, Rolling Hills, Palos Verdes, California

English House, 1260 Lago Vista Drive, Beverly Hills, California

Havens Apartments, Milvia and Blake, Berkeley, California

Ray House, Burma Road, Fallbrook, California

1951 Elliott House, 10443 Woodbridge, North Hollywood, California

Hardy House, Portuguese Bend Club, Palos Verdes, California

1952 Cranfill House, 1901 Cliff Drive, Austin, Texas (with Eugene George)

Harwell Hamilton Harris House, Fallbrook, California

Lang House, 700 Alta Street, San Antonio, Texas

1953 Duhring House, Greenwood Common, Berkeley, California (with Hervey Parke Clark)

House Beautiful Pace-Setter House, Dallas

National Orange Show Exhibition Building, San Bernardino, California (with Jerome Armstrong)

1954 Barrow House, 4101 Edgemont, Austin, Texas

1956 Antrim House, 6160 North Van Ness, Fresno, California

Johnson House, 1200 Broad, Fort Worth, Texas

Motel-on-the-Mountain, Suffern, New York

St. Mary's Episcopal Church, Big Spring, Texas

Townsend House, 230 Simpson, Paris, Texas

1957 Kirkpatrick House, 457 Harbor Road, Southport, Connecticut

1958 Cranfill Apartments, 1911 Cliff Drive, Austin, Texas

Eisenberg House, 9624 Rockbrook, Dallas

Security Bank and Trust Company remodelling (Louis Sullivan building), Owatonna, Minnesota (with A. Moorman and Company)

1959 Greenwood Mausoleum, Fort Worth, Texas

Treanor House, 2617 Oldham Road, Abilene, Texas

Talbot House, 1508 Dayton Road, Big Spring, Texas

Woodall House, 808 West 14th Street, Big Spring, Texas

1960 Trade Mart Court, Dallas

Havens Memorial Plaza, Berkeley, California

1961 Wright House, 3504 Lexington, Dallas

1963 First Unitarian Church, Dallas (with Beran and Shelmire)

Paschal House, 1527 Pinecrest, Durham, North Carolina

1964 Lindahl House, 305 Clayton Road, Chapel Hill, North Carolina

Security Motor Bank, Owatonna, Minnesota (with Hickey and Little)

1965 North Country School Cottages, Lake Placid, New York

Pugh House, Kerr Lake, Virginia

Sweetzer House, Laurel Park, Hendersonville, North Carolina

1966 Van Alstyne House, 1702 Woodburn, Durham, North Carolina

1967 Sugioka House, 1 Bayberry Drive, Chapel Hill, North Carolina

1968/
77 Harwell Hamilton Harris Studio and House, 122 Cox Avenue, Raleigh, North Carolina

1969 Bryant House, Lake Dam Road, Raleigh, North Carolina

St. Giles Presbyterian Church, Raleigh, North Carolina

1970 Bennett House, Jones Ferry Road, Chapel Hill, North Carolina

1978 Cullowhee Presbyterian Church, North Carolina

Publications:

By HARRIS: articles—"Ein Amerikanischer Flughafen" in *Die Form* (Berlin), April 1930; "In Designing the Small House" in *California Arts and Architecture* (Los Angeles), January 1935; "Wood" in *California Arts and Architecture* (Los Angeles), May 1939; "What the Architect Can Contribute to the Knowledge of Tropical Housing" in *Proceedings of the Mid-Southwestern Conference on Tropical Housing and Building,* Austin, Texas 1952; "Architecture as an Art" in *AIA Journal* (Washington, D.C.), November 1952; "Rythmic Integration of Panel Elements" in *Perspecta-2* (New Haven, Connecticut), 1953; "Observations on Mexico's University City" in *AIA Journal* (Washington, D.C.), January 1953; "How a House Can Enrich Life Within" in *House Beautiful* (New York), May 1953; "Regionalism and Nationalism" in *Texas Quarterly* (Austin), no. 1, 1958; "The Architecture" in *Dallas Theater Center* (brochure), Dallas 1959; "Harwell Hamilton Harris: A Collection of His Writings and Buildings" in *Student Publication* (School of Design, North Carolina State University, Raleigh), no. 5, 1965; "Design Dimensions" in *North Carolina Architect* (Raleigh), September 1966; "A Museum Building Is Special" in *North Carolina Architect* (Raleigh), May/June 1967; "Why Nature?" in *North Carolina Architect* (Raleigh), June/July 1968; "The Brothers Greene" in *Architectural Record* (New York), November 1975; "Richard Neutra and the Gold Medal" in *North Carolina Architect* (Raleigh), May/June 1977; "Regionalism" in *North Carolina Architect* (Raleigh), January/February 1978; "An Other View" in *Crit* (Washington, D.C.), Fall 1978.

On HARRIS: books—*Architecture, Ambition and Americans* by Wayne Andrews, New York 1955; *Masters of Modern Architecture* by John Peter, New York 1958; *American Art: An Historical Survey* by Samuel M. Green, New York 1966; articles—"Houses by Harwell Hamilton Harris" in *Architectural Forum* (New York), March 1940; "Interior Decoration, 1940" by Talbot Hamlin in *Pencil Points* (New York), July 1940; "Architect Harwell Hamilton Harris" in *Kentiku Sekai* (Tokyo), April 1941; "Hillside House for Weston Havens" in *Architectural Forum* (New York), September 1943; "Harwell Hamilton Harris, Arquitecto" in *Revista de Arquitectura* (Buenos Aires), August 1944; "Meet Harwell Harris" in *House Beautiful* (New York), July 1945; "Three California Houses and a Tradition Revitalized" by Douglas Haskell in *Magazine of Building* (New York), October 1951; "Simple Ideas from a Complex House" by Douglas Haskell in *House and Home* (New York), January 1953; "Bostadsbygge in Californien" by Gosta Edberg in *Byggmartaren* (Stockholm), November 1958.

The soil in which these houses are rooted is the same soil that led to the flowering of California architecture almost fifty years ago. It is a combination of abundance, free minds, love of nature, and unspoiled countryside. Simple as such a combination seems, it has happened but seldom in the world's history. The eventual reward for its cultivation is a spontaneous architecture in tune with democratic aspirations.

This statement was written in 1948 to accompany pictures of my work exhibited in Australia. Of course, other influences have shaped me and so shape my work. Among them are: 1) an early love of sculpture, especially Asiatic sculpture; 2) the discovery of Louis Sullivan—his writing before I had seen even a picture of a Sullivan building; 3) the discovery of a Frank Lloyd Wright building before I had even heard Mr. Wright's name: it had everything to do in deciding me to be an architect; and 4) a meeting with R. M. Schindler and Richard Neutra —the men and their buildings: they introduced me to the present and to the particulars of creation.

Though there were other influences, none were as powerful as these in determining my direction. They were made more powerful by the time. It was the time of awakening, and what I had just seen was the birth of the modern spirit, a spirit that had been germinating throughout the whole of the 19th century and, with the conclusion of World War I, was bursting out everywhere. I had watched painting, sculpture, music, literature and psychology budding. Next it would be architecture, for I had just seen expressiveness in a building. Whether or not these influences appear in my buildings, they nevertheless determined me to be an architect.

—Harwell Hamilton Harris

Harwell Hamilton Harris's sensitivity to site and materials, and his special sympathy with wood, produced a group of buildings, mainly houses, that carried on the tradition of the Greenes of Pasadena and Maybeck of Berkeley. He did not celebrate wood as the Greenes did, using it instead in an orderly and refined way, and he had little of the wilfulness of Maybeck, but he developed a style uniquely his own —one particularly at home in Southern California, his birthplace. Traces of the vernacular practices of California gave a vigor to his work, and from Neutra came a familiarity with modular practices, which, when applied to wood, carried directly to the source, the Japanese house.

His reputation was established three years after he opened his office, with a small pavilion which had removable walls. The simple platform, capped by a hipped roof with broad eaves, floated above a slope. The house (1935) was for himself and wife, a historian who was the first to rediscover and write about Greene and Greene and Maybeck.

In his houses of the 1930's and 1940's he rarely repeated himself, although his skill in bringing different roof forms into a quiet composition was evident. In his floor planning, to which he was indebted to Wright, there were several variations of the cruciform plan. His many hipped roofs were expressed on the interior; indeed there was a tension between exterior and interior that sprang from his early training as a sculptor; he projected himself into interior forms, and without slighting the exterior gave a sinuosity to interior spaces.

In the Lowe house (1934) there are two minor hipped roofs projecting from a major one; a blunt wedge-shaped clerestory rises above rooms ranged in a line to face the canyon view in the Granstedt house (1938); the cruciform plan of the Wylie house (1948) has a major gable rising above a minor trellised gable covering an entrance walk, and a clerestory opposes the two—a measure of Harris's gifts is his ability to order and simplify exterior forms that expand the life within. He could do beautiful little exercises in wood —the scissor truss built up of small framing members, Johnson house (1948)—but seldom took his mind off the exterior-interior relationship to practice the art.

The most dramatic use of the gable was in the Havens house, Berkeley (1941), in which inverted gables appear to tie the two-story house into a steeply sloping site facing into the strong winds off the bay. He pushed the house out over the slope to carve out a wind-free garden between house and street.

Work in stucco in California was larger scaled and the roofs were flat; the Entenza house (1937) was essentially one space, which was extended through a large glazed opening to a deck; the large, cubistic English house (1950) with its emphasis on wall predicted his buildings after 1951, when he went to Texas to head the school of architecture at Austin.

His work in Texas was more compact and had fewer openings; the First Unitarian Church, Dallas (1963), had glass at the perimeter of the roof that bathed the walls in light. Buildings were turned inward to courts as protection against sun and wind; the courts soon evolved from rectangular to more complex shapes—ones to which another leaf or link-up could be added, but which were balanced at all stages. The Greenwood Mausoleum, Fort Worth (1959), has a cruciform court.

Many of his later works have been in North Carolina where he moved in 1962. Here he continued the exploration of negative spaces begun in his courts; in St. Giles Presbyterian Church, Raleigh (1969), the functions of the church were separated into detached buildings, all designed as a family of forms in a family of spaces.

—Esther McCoy

HARRISON, Wallace K(irkman).

American. Born in Worcester, Massachusetts, 28 September 1895. Studied in the atelier of Harvey Corbett, New York, 1916–17, and Gustave Umbdenstock, Paris, 1919–20; awarded Rotch Travelling Fellowship, 1922: studied at the Ecole Nationale Supérieure des Beaux-Arts, Paris, 1923–24. Served in the United States Navy as a Lieutenant on a submarine chaser, in Greece, 1917–19; Director of the Cultural Relations Division, 1941–44, Deputy Coordinator, 1944–45, and Director, 1945–46, Office of Inter-American Affairs, Washington, D.C. Married Ellen Hunt Milton in 1926; daughter: Sarah. Worked as a Draftsman for Norcross Brothers, Worcester, Massachusetts, 1911–13; worked for Frost and Chamberlain, Worcester, 1913–16, McKim, Mead and White, New York, 1916–17, 1919, and Bertram Goodhue, New York, 1920–21, 1924; in partnership with Robert Rogers, New York, 1924–25; Associate Architect, New York City Board of Education, 1925–27; Partner, with Harvey Corbett and Frank J. Helmle, in Helmle, Corbett and Harrison, New York, 1927–29, and, with Corbett and William H. MacMurray, in Corbett, Harrison and MacMurray, 1929–34; in private practice, New York, 1934–35; Partner, with André Fouilhoux, Harrison and Fouilhoux, New York, 1935–41, and, with Fouilhoux and Max Abramovitz, q.v., Harrison, Fouilhoux and Abramovitz, 1941–45, and, after Fouilhoux's death, Harrison and Abramovitz, 1945–76. In private practice, New York, since 1976. Since 1929, Member of the Rockefeller Center Architectural Team, New York. Taught at Columbia University, New York (3 years), and at Yale University, New Haven, Connecticut (3 years). Recipient: Gold Medal, American Institute of Architects, 1957. L.H.D.: Dartmouth College, Hanover, New Hampshire, 1950; LL.D.: Harvard University, Cambridge, Massachusetts, 1958; Clark University, Worcester, Massachusetts, 1960; University of Michigan, Ann Arbor, 1968. Address (office): One Rockefeller Plaza, New York, New York 10020, U.S.A.

Works:

1931/
40   Rockefeller Center, New York (as member of a team of architects including Harvey Corbett and Raymond Hood)
1936   Rockefeller Apartments, 17 West 54th Street, New York (with André Fouilhoux)
1937   Avila Hotel, Caracas, Venezuela
1939   The Trylon and Perisphere (theme pavilion), *World's Fair,* New York
1941   African Plains, Bronx Zoo, New York (with André Fouilhoux)
1947/
53   United Nations Headquarters, First Avenue, New York (as Chairman of the Board of Design and Director of Planning; Max Abramovitz, Deputy Director of Planning; with advisory team of architects, including Le Corbusier, Oscar Niemeyer, and Sven Markelius)
1952   Alcoa Building, Pittsburgh
1953   Carnegie Endowment International Center, 345 East 46th Street, New York
1955   Socony-Mobil Building, 150 East 42nd Street, New York
      New York Aquarium, West 8th Street and Boardwalk, Brooklyn, New York
1956   First Presbyterian Church, Stamford, Connecticut
1957   Caspary Auditorium, Rockefeller University, New York
1958   President's House, Rockefeller University, New York
      Daily News Building addition, 220 East 42nd Street, New York
1962/
68   Lincoln Center for the Performing Arts, New York (as Architect of the Metropolitan Opera House; other architects—Max Abramovitz, Philharmonic Hall; Philip Johnson, New York State Theatre; Pietro Belluschi, Juilliard School of Music; Eero Saarinen, Vivian Beaumont Theatre; Gordon Bunshaft, Library)
1962/
78   New York State Capital, Albany, New York (now known as Nelson A. Rockefeller Plaza; as Overall Architect, and, with Max Abramovitz, responsible for all of the complex except for the Automotive, Justice and Legislative buildings)
1964   Institute of International Education, 809 United Nations Plaza, New York (with Max Abramovitz and Michael M. Harris)
      Hall of Science, *World's Fair,* New York
1965   Nurses Residence, Cornell-New York Hospital School of Nursing, 1320 York Avenue, New York

Wallace K. Harrison: First Presbyterian Church, Stamford, Connecticut, 1956

Central Terminal and Control Tower, La-Guardia Airport, Queens, New York (later altered by others)

1972 *Daily News* Gravure Plant, 2nd Street at Newtown Creek, Queens, New York

1977– Battery Park City, New York

1978 Metropolitan Opera House office alterations, Lincoln Center, New York

Pershing Memorial design alterations, Washington, D.C.

Publications:

By HARRISON: book—*School Buildings of Today and Tomorrow,* with C. E. Dobbins, New York 1931; articles—"Drafting Room Practice" in *Architectural Forum* (New York), January 1932; "Orientations of Contemporary Architecture," with others, in *Plush* (New York), December 1938–May 1939; "Skyscrapers" in *Forms and Functions of 20th Century Architecture,* edited by Talbot Hamlin, New York 1953.

On HARRISON: articles—"Profile" by Herbert Warren Wind in *The New Yorker,* in 3 parts, 20 November, 27 November, and 4 December 1954; "New York's Biggest Building in 25 Years" in *Architectural Forum* (New York), January 1955; "Architecture for the Arts of Music, Dance and Drama" in *Architectural Record* (New York), November 1969.

*

I am preparing a short biographical sketch for the Oral History Department of Columbia University, but, unfortunately, it is not yet ready. Also, prior to his death, Nelson Rockefeller was working on a book about the projects we had worked on together: no decision has yet been made about publication.

I have often tried to write about architecture over the years, including the war years 1917–19 and the six years I spent in Washington during World War II with the Office of Inter-American Affairs—but I never had time to write, and, as my friend Nervi once said, "it is hard."

I have worked for more than 50 years on one group of buildings—Rockefeller Center. At the start it became absolutely clear to me that the only sound approach to architecture is to think in terms of the people who will be using the building—that the function of architecture is to take care of human beings in a pleasant way. The question is, How do I utilize the best principles of design and the advances of modern technology to create the most agreeable atmosphere for the user. When all is said and done, an architect is a designer with a client.

—Wallace K. Harrison

*

Until the latter part of the 19th century few American architects had any formal training in their chosen profession. And many of those that did have such training obtained it at the École des Beaux Arts in Paris. Most learned their profession by working in the offices or ateliers of practicing architects and by supplementing that experience with independent study. By the early 20th century, when Wallace K. Harrison was a young man, university training for architecture had become general, usually in American professional schools, though many young architects still attended the Beaux Arts; a decreasing number learned their profession by working in architectural offices.

After very little formal training as a child and young man, Harrison attended the Beaux Arts for just one year. But before and after that year he worked in the offices of McKim, Mead and White, Bertram Goodhue, one of the noted architects of the time, and Helmle and Corbett, with whom he later joined in partnership. Thus almost all of his training was received by actually working in architectural offices, a feat that had been common in the past but one that had become quite rare by the 1920's.

No one probably could have predicted that Harrison, with so little in the way of formal training,

would eventually become one of the most successful architects of his time, make a great reputation, particularly for the design of office and other commercial buildings, and become the leader of several teams of architects who designed great complexes. No one could probably have predicted that he would become possibly the most urbane of American architects of his time and would practice as a principal for more than fifty years.

Although Harrison has always said that he prefers his work on single buildings, much of his reputation is derived from his involvement with large complexes. The first was Rockefeller Center, New York City, completed in 1940. Harrison, his partner Harvey Wiley Corbett, and Raymond Hood are acknowledged as the primary designers of this great urban complex. Later, Harrison headed the teams that designed the United Nations Headquarters and the Lincoln Center for the Performing Arts, both in New York City.

For the United Nations, Harrison directed the work of an international team of 15 architects that included LeCorbusier of France, Oscar Niemeyer of Brazil and Sven Markelius of Sweden. Buildings at Lincoln Center were designed by Philip Johnson, Pietro Belluschi, Eero Saarinen and Skidmore, Owings and Merrill. Harrison himself designed the Metropolitan Opera House, and his longtime partner, Max Abramovitz, designed Philharmonic Hall.

During his long career, Harrison, mostly in partnership with Abramovitz, has designed a very large number of buildings of many types, including apartments, churches, museums, auditoriums, college buildings and research buildings. But it is in the tall urban office building type that he most plainly made his mark on architecture. These buildings are not usually distinguished for innovation or pioneering but for straightforward, functional designs and plans that perform properly and efficiently for their owners and users. For his work, Wallace K. Harrison was awarded, in 1957, the highest honor of his fellow architects, the gold medal of the American Institute of Architects.

—William Dudley Hunt, Jr.

George E. Hartman and Warren J. Cox: National Humanities Center, Raleigh, North Carolina, 1978

HARTMAN, George E(itel).

American. Born in Fort Hancock, New Jersey, 7 May 1936. Educated at Princeton University, New Jersey, 1953–60, B.A. 1957, M.F.A. 1960. Served in the Field Artillery of the United States Army, at Fort Sill, Oklahoma, 1960: 2nd Lieutenant. Married Ann Burdick in 1965; children: Sarah and Joshua. Architect to Princeton University's archaeological excavation in Italy, 1960; Project Manager, Keyes, Lethbridge and Condon, architects, Washington, D.C., 1960–64; in private practice, as George E. Hartman Jr., Architect, Washington, D.C., 1964–65. Since 1965, Partner, with Warren J. Cox, *q.v.,* Hartman-Cox Architects, Washington, D.C. Design Critic, Catholic University of America, Washington, D.C., 1964–69, Design Critic, 1972–73, and Kea Distinguished Professor of Architecture, 1973–74, University of Maryland, College Park; Visiting Professor, North Carolina State University, Raleigh, 1977. Director, 1969–71, Treasurer, 1972, Secretary, 1973, and President, 1975, Washington Metropolitan Chapter of the American Institute of Architects; Chairman, AIA National Capital Committee, 1974–76. Member of the National Council of Architectural Registration Boards, since 1965; Member of the AIA Committee on Design, since 1972 (Chairman, 1977); Contributor Editor, *Journal of Architectural Research,* Washington, D.C., since 1975. Exhibitions: *Contemporary Chairs,* Washington Gallery of Modern Art, 1964; *The Work of Hartman-Cox,* University of Virginia, Charlottesville, 1973; *Recent Work of Hartman-Cox,* University of Maryland, College Park, 1974; *Princeton Architectural Drawings,* Institute of Architecture and Urban Studies, New York, 1977. Collections: Museum of Modern Art Archives, New York. Recipient: AIA Potomac Valley Chapter Award, 1968, 1970, 1972, 1974, 1976; National Honor Award, AIA, 1970, 1971; Louis Sullivan Prize, 1972; Homes for Better Living Award, AIA, 1976; AIA/Concrete Reinforcing Steel Institute Honor Award, 1977. Fellow of the American Institute of Architects, 1975, and of the American Academy in Rome, 1977. Address: Hartman-Cox Architects, 1071 Thomas Jefferson Street N.W., Washington, D.C. 20007, U.S.A.

Architecture is, as a commissioned art, intended to serve a specific purpose on a given site. The architect's inter-action with the decision to modify an existing order creates most of architecture's unique possibilities as well as many of its problems. The balance between expression, function and context is a tension which at best can neither be resolved nor denied. Architecture emerges as a formal realization of these issues.

—George E. Hartman

See COX, Warren J.

HAVLÍČEK, Josef.

Czechoslovakian. Born in Prague, 5 May 1899. Educated at the Technical High School, Prague, 1916–23, Dip. 1923; Academy of Fine Arts, Prague, 1923–26, Dip. 1926. In partnership with Karel Honzík, Prague, 1928–36; in private practice, Prague, 1936 until his death, 1961. Exhibition: *Exhibition of Contemporary Culture*, Brno, Czechoslovakia, 1928. Recipient: First Prize, State Pensions Institute Headquarters Competition, Prague, 1929. *Died* (in Prague) 30 December 1961.

Works:

1924/
25 Apartment block, Smíchov, Prague
1926/
28 House, Smíchov, Prague (with Karel Honzík)
    Dílo Apartment Block, Štěpánská, Prague (with Karel Honzík)
1927 Habich Flats, Offices and Stores Complex, Štěpánská, Prague (with J. Polivka)
    Department store, Danube, Prague (project)
1929/
33 State Pensions Institute Headquarters, Žižkov, Prague (with Karel Honzík)
1931 Koldom Collective Apartment Block, Prague (project; with Karel Honzík)
1936 Sanatorium, Poděbrady, Czechoslovakia
1937 Apartment block, Letná, Prague
1938 Apartment block, Letohradská, Prague
1939 Czechoslovak Red Cross Headquarters, Prague (project)
1940 Žižkov Redevelopment, Prague (project; with E. Hruška)
1942 Regional dairy, Tábor, Czechoslovakia (project)
1943 Car park, Gottwaldov, Czechoslovakia (project)
    Crematorium, Kolín, Czechoslovakia (project)
1944 Crematorium, Prostějov, Czechoslovakia (project)
1945/
50 Town expansion plan for Hradec Králove, Czechoslovakia (project; with F. Bartoš)
1946 Town plan for Záluží u Mostu, Czechoslovakia (project; with F. Pacholík and J. Pokorny)
    Ministry for Post and Telegraph Headquarters, Prague (competition project; with S. Semrád)
1947 Crematorium, Slané, Czechoslovakia (project)
    Crematorium, Havlíčkuv Brod., Czechoslovakia (project)
    University City, Albertov, Prague (project)
    United Nations Housing Scheme, New York (project)
1948/
50 Town plan for Jindřichúv Hradec, Czechoslovakia (project; with K. Filsák)
1950 Regional dairy and milk processing plant, Strakovice, Czechoslovakia
    Health and hospital centre, Most, Czechoslovakia (project; with V. Dohnal)
1952 Gottwald Square Redevelopment, Bratislava, Czechoslovakia (project; with K. Filsák)
1952/
58 Vitězného Února Redevelopment, Kladno, Czechoslovakia (with K. Neuman, V. Hílsky, N. Konerža and E. Kovařík)
1954 Nusle Viaduct and Pankrác Development, Prague (project; with J. Černohorský and Z. Vávra)
    Department store, Bíla Labut, Prague (project)
1956 Czechoslovak Embassy Complex, Peking, China (project)
1957/
60 ROH Area Redevelopment, Žižkov, Prague (project; with K. Honzík and J. Sedláček)
    Town Hall, Toronto (competition project)
1958 Housing Types Report, Prague (project; with K. Neumann and L. Honeiser)
    Industralized housing, Prague (competition project; with K. Neumann)
1958/
60 Regional hospital, Jindřichúv Hradec, Czechoslovakia (project)
1959 Veletržní Tř. Redevelopment Study, Prague (project; with K. Neumann)
1960 Holešovice-Bubny Redevelopment, Prague (project; with K. Neumann, J. Cila and L. Honeiser)

Publications:

By HAVLÍČEK: articles—"Economy and Architecture," with Karel Honzík, in *Kvart* (Prague), 1935; "High Rise Buildings in Boxframe Construction," with K. Neumann, in *Architekt* (Prague), no. 23, 1958.

On HAVLÍČEK: books—*Maisons d'Habitation*, edited by Morancé, Paris 1926; *Modern Architecture in Czechoslovakia* by J. Krejcar, Prague 1928; *Contemporary International Architecture* by K. Teige, Prague 1929; *The Studio Year Book*, London 1933; *The Modern House* by F. R. S. Yorke, London 1934; *The Modern Flat* by F. R. S. Yorke and Frederick Gibberd, London 1935; *The New Architecture* by Alfred Roth, Zurich 1940; *An Introduction to Modern Architecture* by J. M. Richards, London 1940; *Gli elementi dell'Architettura funzionale* by Alberto Sartoris, Milan 1941; *A Book about Czech Architecture* by J. E. Koula, Prague 1943; *Skyscrapers* by V. Kolář, Prague 1946; *The New Dictionary of Czechoslovak Artists* by Toman, Prague 1947; *Architecture for Everybody* by Karel Honzík, Prague 1956; *The Road to Socialist Architecture* by Karel Honzík, Prague 1960; *Contemporary World Architecture*, Tokyo 1961; *Josef Havlíček: Projects and Buildings*, Prague 1964; articles—"Josef Havlíček—Oeuvres" in *Cahiers d'Art* (Paris), 1926; "Modern Architecture in Czechoslovakia" by J. Setnička in *Vedag* (Prague), 1931; "Storia dell'architettura funzionale" by G. Pagano in *Casabella* (Milan), April 1942; "The Question of Monumentality" in *Architekt SIA* (Prague), no. 8, 1944; "The Work of Josef Havlíček" in *Perspective* (Winnipeg), 1948; "The Work of Josef Havlíček" in *Architektura CSR* (Prague), no. 4, 1959.

Josef Havlíček rejected the national romantic revival that prevailed after the establishment of the Czechoslovak Republic in 1918 and played an active role in the running battle by younger architects and artists against the imitation of past styles. Cubism held a strong attraction for him in the early 1920's, but the transition from Viennese Hoffmann-type Cubism to the new Functionalism was a natural and inevitable process. His deep convictions made him a fighter for what he believed to be of paramount importance. He saw in Functionalism the promise of a solution to the pressing social needs of the time, leading to a new visual expression.

In 1925 at the age of 24 he designed blocks of flats for a Trade Union in Prague. The buildings had flat roofs—then one of the hallmarks of modern archi-

tecture—but the Trade Union "boss" had steep pitched roofs added. Characteristically, whenever Havlíček published photographs of the buildings the roofs were left out.

The Habich building in Prague (1927) is a classic example of functional architecture. Behind the street elevation of this comparatively small building are shops, offices and flats. Above the ground floor, with its large plate glass shop windows, are three floors of offices with uninterrupted horizontal windows from party wall to party wall, topped by three set-back strongly modelled floors with balconies. The different uses are clearly expressed; one can read them. It is a resolved elevation where the individual elements do not compete.

A limited competition for the Headquarters of the State Pensions Institute in Prague was won by Havlíček and his partner Karel Honzík in 1929. The scheme was ferociously attacked from all quarters, and it took a man of Havlíček's determination and staying power to get the project through, but the opposition continued unabated throughout the construction period. Morton Shand called the building "the white cathedral of Prague." It is undoubtedly the best example of "White Architecture" and remains an outstanding contribution to contemporary architecture in Central Europe.

During the late 1930s, before the Nazi occupation of Czechoslovakia, very few of Havlíček's projects were realized. He designed a sanatorium in Poděbrady and two blocks of flats in Prague. After the War only two projects were built—a Milk Processing Plant in Strakovice and a development for 8,000 inhabitants in Kladno (1952–58) in which Havlíček was involved as a member of an Architects' Collective.

Soon after the War he was sent by the Czechoslovak Government to New York as a member of the Committee of Architects for the United Nations Building. This was his first visit to the United States and he was strongly influenced by the scale and technology of what he saw. During the last fifteen years of his life the skyscraper in a variety of strongly modelled pyramidal forms dominated his work.

Havlíček was one of a number of gifted architects who came out of the school of Professor Gočár at the Academy of Fine Arts in Prague where, despite the slogans of Functionalism, Rationalism and Constructivism, the emphasis was on the Art of Architecture.

—Eugene Rosenberg

HECKER, Zvi.

Israeli. Born in Cracow, Poland, 31 May 1931 (lived in Syberia, Russia, 1939–41, and Samarkand, Russia, 1941–45); emigrated to Israel, 1950. Educated at elementary schools in Cracow and Samarkand, 1937–45; Sobieski Liceum, Cracow, 1945–49; Cracow Polytechnic School of Architecture, 1949–50; Technion: Israel Institute of Technology, Haifa, under Alfred Neumann, 1950–54, B.Arch. 1954; Avni Academy of Art, Tel Aviv, 1954–56. Served in the Corps of Engineers of the Israel Defence Forces, 1955–57. Married Deborah Houchman in 1957; children: Ronnie and Ella. Worked in the office of Arieh Sharon and Benjamin Idelson, Tel Aviv, 1957–58; in partnership with Eldar Sharon, Tel Aviv, 1959–65, and with Alfred Neumann, Tel Aviv, 1960–68; Visiting Professor, 1968–69, and Adjunct Professor of Architecture, 1969–72, Laval University, Quebec, Canada; also, Visiting Lecturer and Critic in Architecture, McGill University, Montreal, and University of Pennsylvania, Philadelphia, 1969–72. In private practice, Tel Aviv, since 1972. Distinguished Foreign Visiting Lecturer, School of Architecture and Environmental Design, University of Texas at Arlington, 1977. Exhibitions: *Today's Form*, Bezalel Museum, Jerusalem, 1963; *Proportion in Architecture*, Carpenter Center, Harvard University, Cam-

Zvi Hecker: Synagogue, Military Academy Campus, Negev Desert, Israel, 1969

bridge, Massachusetts, 1966; *Bienal,* Sao Paulo, 1969; *Introduction to Design,* Israel Museum, Jerusalem, 1973; *Zvi Hecker: Polyhedral Structures,* Julie M. Gallery, Tel Aviv, 1975; *Zvi Hecker: Polyhedric Architecture,* Israel Museum, Jerusalem, 1976; *Alternativ Arkitektur,* Louisiana Museum, Humlebaek, Denmark, 1977. Address (office): 22 David Yellin Street, Tel Aviv 62964, Israel.

Works:

1959/
63   City Hall, Bat-Yam, Israel (with Alfred Neumann and Eldar Sharon)

1960/
61   Club Mediterranee Holiday Village, Arhziv, Northern Israel (with Alfred Neumann and Eldar Sharon)

1961   Arab Village, Ein Raffa, near Jerusalem (with Alfred Neumann and Eldar Sharon)

1961/
63   Dubiner Apartment House, Ramat-Gan, Israel (with Alfred Neumann and Eldar Sharon)

1963/
67   Military Academy, Negev Desert, Israel

1964   City Hall, Natania, Israel (project; with Alfred Neumann)

1964/
67   Danciger Hall: Mechanical Engineering Laboratory, Technion: Israel Institute of Technology, Haifa (with Alfred Neumann)

1965   City Centre Plan, Ashdod, Israel (competition project; with Alfred Neumann)

1966/
69   Synagogue, Military Academy Campus, Negev Desert, Israel

1967   City Hall, Amsterdam (competition project)

1969   Dissentshik House, Tel Aviv (project)

1969/
70   Youth Vacation Camp, Beit-Zayit, Jerusalem

1970   Plan for the City Centre of Montreal

1972   Synagogue, Ben-Gurion Airport, Tel Aviv (project)

1972/
78   Ramot Housing, Jerusalem

1974/
76   Marine Restaurant, Coral Beach, Eilat, Israel

1975   Monument, Negev Desert, Israel (project)

1976/
78   Band Shell, Hatikva Park, Tel Aviv

1977   Synagogue, Ramot, Jerusalem (project)

Publications:

By HECKER: books—*Polyhedric Furniture,* exhibition catalogue, Jerusalem 1973; *Polyhedric Structures,* exhibition catalogue, Tel Aviv 1975; articles— "Gate for Peace" in *B'machane* (Tel Aviv), July 1967; "A New City Centre for Montreal" in *Architectural Association Quarterly* (London), Winter 1972; "Polyhedric Architecture" in *Architectural As-* *sociation Quarterly* (London), Summer 1972; "Polyhedra" in *Mussag* (Tel Aviv), no. 12, 1976; "The Geometry of My Polyhedral Sculptures" in *Leonardo* (Oxford), Summer 1977; "Beauty Is the Essence of Architecture" in *Ha'aretz Literary Supplement* (Tel Aviv), 10 September 1977.

On HECKER: book—*Zvi Hecker: Polyhedric Architecture,* exhibition catalogue, by Itzhak Gaon, Jerusalem 1976; articles—"Bat-Yam City Hall" by David Yaarin in *Ha'aretz* (Tel Aviv), 13 September 1963; "A House with a Personality" by Rachel Ramati in *Yediot-Acharonot* (Tel Aviv), 18 March 1966; "Het Stadhuis can Bat-Yam, Israel" by F. E. Rontgen in *Polytechnische Tijdschrift* (The Hague), 17 August 1966; "How to Be an Unsuccessful Architect" by Amos Kenan in *Yediot Achronot* (Tel Aviv), 21 October 1966; "Honeycomb House on a Hill" by David Rubinger in *Life* (New York), 19 February 1968; "Israeli Architecture Spreads Its Influence in Other Areas" by Satish Dhar in *The Lively Arts* (Montreal), 27 April 1968; "Geometric Prefabbing" by C. Ray Smith in *Progressive Architecture* (New York), March 1969; "Tinker Toy City Hall in Israel Is 'Spaced Packed' " by Ada Louise Huxtable in the *New York Times,* 5 June 1969; "An Architect Who Breaks Things" by Evelyn Dumas in *Montreal Star,* 10 October 1970; "Revaloriser Montreal" by Claudette Chauveau in *Culture Vivante* (Quebec), June 1971; "The Responsibility of the Architect" by Lesley Hazleton in *Ariel* (Jerusalem), no. 36, 1974; "Das Polyedrische Bausystem des Zvi Hecker" by Wulf

351

Brackrock in *Architektur und Wohnen* (Hamburg), October 1975; "Hecker's Housing" by Meir Ronen in *Jerusalem Post Magazine*, 23 July 1976; "The Pentagonal Neighborhood of Zvi Hecker" by Menachem Michelson in *Yediot-Acharonot* (Tel Aviv), 3 March 1978; "Geometri på et bjerg ved Jerusalem" by Henrik Sten Møller in *Politiken* (Copenhagen), 9 May 1978; "New Angle on Architecture" by Abraham Rabinovich in *Jerusalem Post*, 13 October 1978.

Relieved of the long-standing slogans of modern architecture, we are now in a position to raise questions that have been gradually shaping themselves for the last few decades. We can recognize now that architecture is not merely a self-evident phenomenon and cannot be justified by cause and effect alone. Great architecture never comes into being by absolute necessity. On the contrary, it originates its own demand. Though it records the spirit of the culture to which it belongs, it also casts a lasting image and shapes a symbolic meaning for future generations.

Our growing perception of the complexity of man's environment excludes also the narrow view of architecture as a mere sum of programmatic requirements, even if such requirements can be arranged in orderly functionalistic patterns. Architectural form cannot be derived from function alone but must unfold harmoniously within the confines of an artist's consciousness. He confers meaning on the basic geometric form, which only then becomes architecture.

To express our sense of reality in a more powerful conception of architecture, we must explore and enrich the language of our message: the vocabulary of form and its grammar, the geometry upon which it rests. The deeper our insight and the more profound our mastery of the treasury of form, the greater our freedom of imagination and the greater our chances to avoid stereotyped platitudes, allowing for architectural statements of poetic intensity.

As I see it, the spatial configurations of the ubiquitous cube-form, still predominant in architecture because of inertia, seem particularly exhausted and limited when compared with the vast richness of all the possibilities of polyhedral form, as yet untapped by architecture. Polyhedric Architecture, by assimilating the new-found bounty of polyhedral forms, unfolds, through new possibilities of industrial building techniques, a richness and diversity hitherto unprecedented in architecture.

However, the geometry of polyhedra by itself, inexhaustible and intriguing as it certainly is, must not be confused with the intensity of expression of architectural forms displaying such geometry. Geometry *per se* serves architecture only as an imaginary scaffolding, securing its construction, to be finally removed, its traces only suggested by the created architectural form.

I consider the geometrical principles underlying Polyhedric Architecture to be as much reflections of our ever broadening insights into the structure of matter in space as they are images invoked by the great mathematical and ornamental tradition of the Mediterranean cultural heritage to which I belong.

—Zvi Hecker

Zvi Hecker's contribution to the modern architectural movement is best seen in the contrast between his forms and those of nearly all the other modernists. Firmly rooted in the utilitarian notion "form follows function," classical modernists demand from their architecture economy of materials and construction, pragmatic partis, and flexible, accommodating plans. The forms accordingly should be the logical extension of these demands and should evolve from an unbiased design process generated solely from reason. Hecker's fundamental contribution derives its significance from the architectonic means he uses to satisfy these conditions, means quite different from those of the classical modernists, which are based exclusively on the right angle geometry.

As a metaphor for his buildings Hecker uses the crystalline geometry of nature. From his studies in crystallography he has extracted a myriad of sources for giving organization and form to his architecture. The appropriateness of this model comes from the parallel needs inherent in both the natural and built worlds. Nature's various physical forces present a need for organizing her constituent elements in a fashion extremely efficient in its use of matter, energy, and space. The system which satisfies this need is a spatial close-packing one. Also involved with the spatial ordering of constituent parts, architects are confronted with the need to build with fewer materials, in shorter time, using less space. By carrying the analogy one step further, Hecker employs these extremely flexible close-packing systems in order to develop an architecture responsive to the needs of his time.

Hecker uses the metaphor of crystalline geometry both in his individual building projects and in his plans for the restructuring of major cities. As a source for his synagogue in the Negev Desert he employed the crystalline structure of a boron and metal compound. The resulting structure is a three-dimensional complex of cube-octahedrons, a strikingly unique building. For his Montreal City Center project he used a combination of truncated octahedrons superimposed on a plan grid of regular and semi-regular hexagons as a means of reconciling a growing population and a dwindling of available space. The resulting complex is in many ways similar to the snowflake-patterned utopian city plans of the Renaissance.

Fundamentally, Hecker works with conventional architectural ideas. His planning notions, his handling of a building's programmatic requirements, and his use of the repetitive element as an aesthetic device are all quite common to the modern architect. Hecker's basic building blocks, however, are unique. His three-dimensional polyhedric components and their corresponding two-dimensional planning grids lead him to unusual forms. These forms may indeed be thought of as mere idiosyncratic, esoteric, sculptural exercises—or they may be seen as brilliantly utilitarian responses to the mandates of the modern movement.

—Robert B. Nevel

HEJDUK, John.
American. Born in New York City, 19 July 1929. Educated at the Cooper Union School of Art and Architecture, 1947–50; University of Cincinnati, Ohio, 1950–52, B.Arch. 1952; Harvard Graduate School of Design, Cambridge, Massachusetts, 1952–53 (HGSD Scholarship), M.Arch. 1953; University of Rome School of Architecture, 1954 (Fulbright Scholarship). Married Gloria Fiorentino in 1951; children: Renata and Rafael. Worked in various architectural offices, New York, 1947–52, and in the office of I. M. Pei and Partners, New York, 1956–58; Chief Designer, A. M. Kinney Associates, New York, 1960. In private practice, New York, since 1965. Instructor in Architectural Design, University of Texas, Austin, 1954–56; Assistant Professor of Architecture, Cornell University, Ithaca, New York, 1958–60; Critic in Architectural Design, Yale Graduate School of Design, New Haven, Connecticut, 1961–64. Professor of Architecture, and Dean, School of Architecture, Cooper Union, New York, since 1964. Exhibitions: *Architectural Projects*, Graham Foundation, Chicago, 1966; *The Diamond in Painting and Architecture*, Architectural League of New York, 1967; *Projects/John Hejduk, Architect*, Le Corbusier Foundation, Paris, 1972; *Architectural Projects*, Eidgenössische Technische Hochschule, Zurich, 1973; Architectural Projects, *Triennale*, Milan, 1973; Architectural Projects, Lausanne and

Stuttgart, 1974; *Five Architects*, Princeton University, New Jersey, 1974; *Cemetery of the Ashes of Thought*, at the *Biennale*, Venice, also toured Naples and Rome, 1975; *The New York Five*, Art Net, London, 1975; *Five Architects, New York*, Naples, Genoa, Zurich, Lausanne, Paris, Brussels and Helsinki, 1976; Architectural Projects, Nova Scotia School of Architecture, Halifax, 1976; *Cooper Union Foundation Building Renovation*, University of Houston, Texas, 1976; *Hejduk, Rossi, Abraham and Eisenman*, Cooper Union, New York, 1977; Architectural Projects, Drawing Center, New York, 1977; *American Drawing*, Cooper Hewitt Museum, New York, 1977; Architectural Projects, Oslo Society of Architects, 1978; Architectural Projects, Architectural Association, London, 1978; *The Thirteen Watchtowers of Cannareggio*, Venice, 1978–79; *Sculpture and Painting*, Dortmund, Germany, 1979; *Mind, Child and Architecture*, Newark Museum, New Jersey, 1979. Recipient: Graham Foundation grant, 1967; Architectural League of New York grant, 1967; National Endowment for the Arts Award, 1972; Duke Foundation Award, 1973; Municipal Arts Society Award, New York, 1975; New York State Council on the Arts Award, 1975; Graham Foundation/National Endowment for the Arts grant, 1976. Address: 5721 Huxley Avenue, Riverdale, New York 10471, U.S.A.

Works:

1955 Skinner Duplex Apartments, Austin, Texas (project)
1959 Friedlander House, Waverly, New York (project)
1960 Demlin House, Locust Valley, Long Island, New York
1967 Design for Exhibition, Architectural League of New York
1968 Bernstein House, Mamaroneck, New York (project)
1969 Hommel Apartment, New York
1971 Design of the *Education of an Architect* exhibition, Museum of Modern Art, New York
1972 Design of the *Projects/John Hejduk* exhibition, Le Corbusier Foundation, Paris
1973 Bye House, Ridgefield, Connecticut (project)
1975 Foundation Building restoration, Cooper Union, New York

Publications:

By HEJDUK: books—*Three Projects: John Hejduk*, New York 1968; *Projects/John Hejduk*, exhibition catalogue, Paris 1972; *Fabrications*, New York 1974; articles—"Lockhart, Texas" in *Architectural Record* (New York), March 1957; "Out of Time and Into Space" in *L'Architecture d'Aujourd'hui* (Paris), September 1965.

On HEJDUK: books—*Five Architects: Eisenman, Graves, Gwathmey, Hejduk, Meier* by Kenneth Frampton and Colin Rowe, New York 1972; *John Hejduk, Architect*, Zurich 1973; *Five Architects, New York* by Manfredo Tafuri, Rome 1976; articles—in *Architecture + Urbanism* (Tokyo), March and April 1974, May 1975; "Five on Five" in *Architectural Forum* (New York), May 1973; "Architecture's Big Five Elevate Form" by Paul Goldberger in the *New York Times*, 26 November 1973; articles in *Progressive Architecture* (New York), June and July 1974, July 1975; "European Graffiti" by Manfredo Tafuri in *Oppositions 5* (New York), Summer 1976.

My projects are the result of a twenty-year effort and search into generating principles of form and space. There is an attempt to understand certain essences in regard to an architectural commitment with the hope of expanding a vocabulary. The discovery of the workings and dictates of an organic development

John Hejduk: Foundation Building, Cooper Union, New York, 1975 (model)

of specific ideas becomes a necessary function of the search. It was from undertaking these projects that I hoped to establish a point of view, a belief; the belief that through self-imposed discipline, through intense contained study, through an aesthetic, a liberation of the mind and hand would be possible, leading to certain visions and transformations of form regarding space.

The realization that profound works in the arts are the embodiment of specific plastic points of view, that the hand and mind are one, working on first principles, and of filling these principles with meaning through juxtaposition of basic relationships such as point, line, plane, and volume opened up the possibility of argumentation. The mind played a most significant part in the support of the creative act. The first gropings were arbitrary; but once the arbitrary beginning was committed, once the initial intuitions were experienced, it was necessary that the organism go through its normal evolution—and whether the evolution of form continued or stopped depended on the use of the intellect, not as an academic tool but as a passionate living element.

The problems of point-line-plane-volume, the facts of square-circle-triangle, the mysteries of central-peripheral-frontal-oblique-concavity-convexity, of right angle, perpendicular, perspective, the comprehension of sphere-cylinder-pyramid, the questions of structure-construction-organization, the questions of scale, position, the interest in post-lintel, wall-slab, vertical-horizontal, the arguments of two dimensional-three dimensional space, the extent of a limited field, of an unlimited field, the meaning of plan, of section, of spatial expansion-spatial contraction-spatial compression-spatial tension, the direction of regulating lines, of grids, the meaning of implied extension, the relationships of figure to ground, of number to proportion, of measurement to scale, of symmetry to asymmetry, of diamond to diagonal,

the hidden forces, the ideas on configuration, the static with the dynamic—all these begin to take on the form of a vocabulary.

The projects were begun not knowing the above, but knowing that basic orders needed to be searched for, becoming known as the work progressed, as the work was analyzed, as the work was criticized, as the work was formed. In order to have a-priori principles meaningful, and to give up and put forth organic revelations, there had to be a given form. The arguments and points of view are within the work, within the drawings; it is hoped that the conflicts of form will lead to a clarity which can be useful and perhaps transferable.

—John Hejduk

In approaching John Hejduk's work and his attitude to it, one is reminded of a musical evening at which a composer plays a new piano composition. When he finishes, he is asked to explain the work. The composer replies by playing the piece again. Hejduk's work over the last twenty or more years, with few exceptions, has comprised drawings and models exploring the harmonic possibilities of architecture. He has been content to allow these explorations to be ends in themselves. They are a sufficient reality. He has accepted the role of the poet whose sensual explorations clarify and expand the perceptual possibilities to which others give concrete life. In this cause he has resolutely pursued a narrowly defined set of themes and variations. At first, it was cubes, grids, frames, and the nine square problem, and when his graphics hinted at architecture, it was brutalist. Then came the diamond series, square grids in diagonal containers, an open pleasure in Mondrian, and an occasional curving wall. This determined evolution moves into the present with flat planes entertaining curved masses in various combinations

and colors: salted with memories of "Les Heures Claires" and the other Gris.

The objects are all very pretty and free from any socially redeeming virtue. As is much that is pleasurable in architecture. Perhaps love of beauty is essential to all that we praise in architecture; other ingredients, the technical, the rational, the political, merely highlight the pleasure but in no way alter its essential basis. Hejduk allows himself complete freedom, complete detachment, from context, materials, structure, climate. Such freedom makes high demand upon the intellect to provide sufficient constraints to convince. It is in his limitations that the work is flawed. Contained within the exuberant confections sits the untransformed equipment of living —toilet bowls, fireplaces, dull kitchens, commonplace furniture arrangements—that share no part in their exotic surroundings. In responding to the surface pleasure of the drawings and models, there is a willingness to suspend disbelief, yet such pedestrian reality detracts from pleasure. There is no irony here, just inconsistency.

Hejduk's drawings pose a curious problem. They are in two forms, freehand drawings, often in series, which explore and annotate a theme, and the mechanically precise descriptions of discrete projects. The exploratory drawings, frequently done with marker pens, have none of the precision implied in the mechanical drawings. They are heavy-handed and insensitive, and the accompanying verbiage— code, ode—detracts. But they have a robust presence which, as with the rest of his work, is not enhanced by inquiring too deeply. Either the intentions are too obscure or what you see is all you get. Although this may not be the way to increase respect for the objects, it no way diminishes their pleasure. Delightful and satisfying architecture can also be insubstantial and trivial. Hence the composer's reply should be Hejduk's reply to the critic, "My work speaks for itself, and it tells of elemental pleasures and architectural harmonies and composition." But why the toilet bowl?

Hejduk's one major completed building is the extensive renovation of Cooper Union in New York City. Here the merely pleasurable interests are set aside to produce a convincing rearticulation of this vast Victorian Hulk. His solution is clear and simple, and in its strength it possesses the stuff of sheer architecture.

—Alan Balfour

HELLMUTH, George F(rancis).

American. Born in St. Louis, Missouri, 5 October 1907. Educated at Washington University, St. Louis, B.Arch. 1928, M.Arch. 1930; Ecole des Beaux-Arts, Fontainebleau, France, 1930–31 (Steedman Travelling Fellow), Dip.Arch. 1931. Served in the Reserve Corps of the United States Army, 1930–33. Married Mildred Lee Hennings in 1941; children: George, Nicholas, Mary, Theodore, and Daniel. In general practice with his father, George W. Hellmuth, St. Louis, 1935–40; Assistant to the President, Smith, Hinchman and Grylls, Detroit, 1940–49; Partner, with Minoru Yamasaki and Joseph Leinweber, Hellmuth, Yamasaki and Leinweber, St. Louis, 1949–55. Since 1955, Principal, with Gyo Obata, *q.v.,* and George Kassabaum, *q.v.,* Hellmuth, Obata and Kassabaum, St. Louis: Chairman of the Board of Hellmuth, Obata and Kassabaum Inc., 1955–78, and of HOK-International Inc., St. Louis, since 1978. Chairman, St. Louis Landmarks and Urban Design Commission, 1950–70. Recipient: Outstanding Alumni Citation, Washington University, St. Louis, 1966; Citation, *Engineering News-Record,* 1977. Fellow, American Institute of Architects. Address: Hellmuth, Obata and Kassabaum Inc., Architects, 100 North Broadway, St. Louis, Missouri 63102, U.S.A.

I came from a family of architects, having a father and uncle who practiced the profession in St. Louis and throughout the Midwest. At the beginning of my professional experience, I realized that the greatest professional satisfaction could be derived from the very highest level of accomplishment.

My natural skills—although I have a bachelor's and master's degree in architecture—were in working with people and in understanding the organization of an architectural/engineering practice. In a sense, I have worked with men, rather than with my hands, and the result of this effort has culminated in the vast accomplishments of our organization, Hellmuth, Obata and Kassabaum.

I am convinced that any individual who depends only on himself puts a definite ceiling on his potential accomplishments. However, if he is willing to work with the best men he can find and has enough skill to identify these best men, there can be absolutely no limit to his professional accomplishments.

—George F. Hellmuth

See HELLMUTH, OBATA AND KASSABAUM

HELLMUTH, OBATA AND KASSABAUM.

Partnership; established, St. Louis, 1955, by George F. Hellmuth, *q.v.,* Gyo Obata, *q.v.,* and George Kassabaum, *q.v.* Recipient: First Honor Award, American Institute of Architects, 1956. Address: 100 North Broadway, St. Louis, Missouri, 63102, U.S.A.

Works:

1955 United States Military Personnel Records Building, St. Louis County
1956 Bristol Primary School, Webster Groves, Missouri
1957 Belleville Memorial Hospital, Belleville, Illinois
1958 Parkway High School, St. Louis County
      KSD-TV Transmitter Building, St. Louis County
      St. Louis Five Alarm Headquarters, St. Louis
      St. Sylvester's Church, Eminence, Missouri
1959 Good Samaritan Home for the Aged, St. Louis
      Warson Woods Elementary School, St. Louis County
      St. Thomas Aquinas High School, San Fernando Hills, Missouri
      Riverview Gardens High School, Bellefontaine Neighbors, Missouri
1960 Kirksville High School, Missouri
      Steger Junior High School, Webster Groves, Missouri
      Plaza Square Apartments, St. Louis
1961 Blue Cross Building, St. Louis
      St. Louis County Juvenile Treatment Center
      Villa Duchesne Student Activity Building, St. Louis County

Hellmuth, Obata and Kassabaum: Smithsonian Institution National Air and Space Museum, Washington, D.C., 1976

1962 Wohl Mental Health Institute, St. Louis
Temple Israel, Ladue, Missouri
Maryland Heights School, St. Louis County
St. Louis Priory School, St. Louis County
United States Naval Reserve Training Center, St. Louis
1963 Berkeley Junior High School, Missouri
McDonnell Planetarium, St. Louis
United States Federal Office Building, Washington, D.C.
1964 IBM Research Center Advanced Systems Development Labs, Los Gatos, California
United States Federal Penitentiary, Marion, Illinois
Psychoanalytic Foundation, St. Louis
Lindell Terrace Apartments, St. Louis
Municipal Ice Rink, Webster Groves, Missouri
1964/
68 Dormitories, 5 Dining Halls, School of Fine Art, Mathematics Building, and Social Science Building, University of Missouri, Columbia
1965 American Zinc Building, St. Louis
Student Union, MacMurray College, Jacksonville, Illinois
Conservation Commission Building, Jefferson City, Missouri
Chapel, Mississippi State College for Women, Columbus
Federal Office Building, East St. Louis, Illinois
1966 Dormitory, Science Building, and Library, Hannibal-LaGrange College, Hannibal, Missouri
Wydown Junior High School, Clayton, Missouri
Dormitories, Washington University, St. Louis
Chronic Illness Hospital, St. Louis
Dormitory, Cafeteria, Married Student Housing, Student Union, and Field House, University of Missouri at Rolla
1967 Library, St. Benedict's College, Atchison, Kansas
Apartment Community of Our Lady of the Snows, Belleville, Illinois
Wind Tunnels, Parks Air College, Cahokia, Illinois
United States Embassy, San Salvador, El Salvador
Federal Bureau of Reclamation Building, Denver
Office Building, George Washington University, Washington, D.C.
Office Building, Avenue of the Stars, Los Angeles
Prototype for Canadian Maximum Security Prisons
Dormitories and Fine Arts Building, Maryville College, St. Louis County
Priory Chapel, St. Louis County
1968 Library, Ohio Northern University, Ada
New York Telephone Company Equipment Building, Pearl River, New York
The Galleria, Houston
Neiman-Marcus Store, Houston
Prototypes (5) for Canadian Medium Security Prisons
Laboratory and Classroom Building, and Mathematics and Languages Building, University of Missouri at St. Louis
1969 Science Building, Women's Physical Education Building, and General Arts Building, Southeast Missouri State College, Cape Girardeau
Library, University of the West Indies, St. Augustine, Trinidad
New York Telephone Company Equipment Building, Elmsford, New York
Technicon Instrument Corporation, Tarrytown, New York
Ralston Purina Corporate Headquarters, St. Louis

Post Oak Tower, Houston
Salem Memorial Hospital, Missouri
Catholic Seminary Foundation, Indianapolis
1970 Convention Center, Winston-Salem, North Carolina
Y.M.C.A., St. Louis
St. Christopher Church and School, Florissant, Missouri
1971 Emerson Electric Company Building, St. Louis
Equitable Building, St. Louis
New York City Correctional Institution for Women
Hawaii Adult Correctional Training Facility, Pauwela Point
Valancia Community College, Orlando, Florida
Dormitories, Cornell University, Ithaca, New York
Dormitories, Berea College, Kentucky
MAC Building, Scott Air Force Base, Belleville, Illinois
Houston Oaks Hotel, Houston
1972 Married Student Housing, University of Alaska, Fairbanks
E. R. Squibb World Headquarters, Laurenceville, New Jersey
Kimberly Clark Research and Engineering Center, Menasha, Wisconsin
Sumitoma Bank Building, Pleasant Hill, California
Metropolitan Correctional Facility, San Francisco
1972/
76 Belleville Area College, Illinois
1973 Dallas/Fort Worth Airport, Dallas
Dupont Company United States Headquarters, Teaneck, New Jersey
Western Union Telegraph Company, Upper Saddle River, New Jersey
IBM Office Building, Columbus, Ohio
Science Building, West Texas State University, Canyon
Bartlett-Begich Junior/Senior High School, Anchorage, Alaska
Penrose Library, University of Denver
Library/Learning Center, University of Wisconsin at Kenosha
Library, University of Alaska, Anchorage
Missouri Botanical Garden, St. Louis
Bent Oak Apartments, Lake St. Louis
Franciscan Sisters Convent, Ferguson, Missouri
Married Student Housing, University of Michigan, Ann Arbor
St. Louis Symphony Pavilion
1974 Singapore International Airport
Quito and Guayaquil Airports, Ecuador
First National Building, Dallas
Sheraton Park Hotel, Washington, D.C.
Executive Plaza Office Building, Kansas City, Missouri
CAV Building, New York
Blue Cross Office Building, Indianapolis
Lord and Taylor Store, Houston
South Central Correctional Institution, Eagle River, Alaska
Lake County Junior College, Grayslake, Illinois
Christ Prince of Peace Church, Manchester, Missouri
Community School renovation, Ladue, Missouri
Kodiak High School, Kodiak Island Borough, Alaska
Maryland Gardens Apartments, St. Louis
Central Laundry Facility, Kansas City, Kansas
1975 Kaskaskia Junior College, Centralia, Illinois
Southeastern Illinois Junior College, phase I, Harrisburg
Instituto Central, Tegucigalpa, Honduras
Library, Northern Illinois University, De-Kalb

United States Marine Barracks, Washington, D.C.
Murphy-Blair Housing, St. Louis
Western States Bank Card Association Building, San Francisco
Illinois Security Hospital, Chester
St. Edward Community Medical Center, Fort Smith, Arkansas
Incarnate Word Hospital, St. Louis
Health Science Facility, and Pharmacy and Biology Buildings, State University of New York at Buffalo
Xerox Research Center, Palo Alto, California
Greenwich Savings Bank, New York
St. Clair County Courthouse, Belleville, Illinois
1975– West Texas Air Terminal, Lubbock
Riyadh International Airport, Saudi Arabia
1976 Boatmen's Tower, St. Louis
Stix, Baer and Fuller Offices, Chesterfield, Missouri
Smithsonian Institution National Air and Space Museum, Washington, D.C.
1977 Mallinckrodt Corporate Center, St. Louis
International River Center, New Orleans
Hilton Hotel International, New Orleans
District of Columbia Courthouse, Washington, D.C.
Medical Center, University of Wisconsin, Madison
1978 Galleria II, Houston
Library, Vassar College, Poughkeepsie, New York
Science Complex, Butler University, Indianapolis
1978– University of Riyadh, Saudi Arabia

Publications:

On HOH: articles—"Aéroport de Dallas-Fort Worth" in *L'Architecture d'Aujourd'hui* (Paris), March/April 1974; "Bibliotek, University of Wisconsin" in *Baumeister* (Munich), no. 5, 1974; "The Arabian Building Boom Is Making Construction History" by Walter McQuade in *Fortune* (New York), September 1976; "HOK" in *Space Design* (Tokyo), September 1976; "Saudi Jobs: How HOK +4 Won a Big One" in *Engineering News-Record* (New York), 11 November 1976; "U.S. Builders Prepare for Superprojects" in *Business Week* (New York), 26 September 1977; "Glass, Concrete Triangles, Roof, Saudi Airport Terminals" in *Engineering News-Record* (New York), 17 November 1977; "Museo Nacional Aeroespacial" in *Informes de la Construccion* (Madrid), November 1977; "Modules Bloom in the Saudi Desert for $3-Billion University Job" in *Engineering News-Record* (New York), 9 March 1978; "Universidad de Ciencias de Butler" in *Informes de la Construccion* (Madrid), March 1978; "Ristrutturazione di Complessi Ospedalieri in USA" by Denise Lupi Schmid in *Prefabbricare Edilizia in Evoluzione* (Milan), March/April 1978; "Hellmuth, Obata and Kassabaum et amerikansk arkitektfirma" in *Arkitekten* (Copenhagen), April 1978; "Bibliothek, Vassar College" in *Baumeister* (Munich), November 1978; "Erweiterung einer Bibliothek in Poughkeepsie" in *Deutsche Bauzeitung* (Stuttgart), December 1978.

After George Hellmuth completed his architectural education, he did what most young architects do. He went to work for other architects. He spent 10 years in various offices but was never completely content as a designer. The longer he practised, the more aware he became of his abilities to communicate with and motivate people. He also began to develop an idea for the organization of his own firm. Since every architectural commission involves three essential steps—securing the job, creating the design, and executing the building—it seemed only logical to Hellmuth that an architectural office should also be structured along those lines: in essence, one principal would oversee administrative and marketing activities, another would be responsible for design, and a third would supervise production and construction services.

Hellmuth put his idea to the test in 1949 by forming the firm of Hellmuth, Yamasaki and Leinweber. Although this office was dissolved six years later, he had proved to himself and others that a troika approach in architecture was definitely effective. In 1955, with Gyo Obata and George Kassabaum, he founded the now famous partnership on the same efficient principle. Once again Hellmuth took over administration, promotion and client relations. Obata headed design. Kassabaum directed production.

Hellmuth, Obata and Kassabaum has not only remained viable; it has also become one of the most prolific architectural offices in the United States. Designs are diverse and solutions are fresh and practical —yet the quality is always consistently high. Because commissions are varied rather than specialized, the firm has worked on a wide range of projects at various scales—education, health care, criminal justice, transportation, housing, urban planning, adaptive re-use, and industrial, commercial and institutional development.

Gyo Obata has been the design force in the firm. Although his work is clearly organized and based on sound functionalist principles, Obata's projects do not bear an identifiable signature. Rather, each commission is approached individually, so that the results represent an expression appropriate to the problems involved. His designs are exceptionally diverse and almost always interesting. They tend to reflect the natural features of the site, as well as those of the surrounding area. He takes great care to consider the movement of people, vehicles and supplies within and around his buildings: that care is one reason why his projects are so successful. And, in most cases, his designs include special interior spaces that seem to have been created purely for drama and enjoyment.

Obata has designed across the broadest spectrum of building types, and he is an experienced urban planner. His projects for HOK have included commissions as large as the complex and innovative Dallas/Fort Worth Airport and as small as the humane but practical Married Student Housing for the University of Alaska. Other major commissions have included the National Air and Space Museum in Washington, D.C., and The Galleria in Houston, which includes two office towers, a hotel, a private club, parking, and America's first enclosed retail mall.

As the partner in charge of project management, George Kassabaum oversees the general administration of all HOK's commissions once they leave the design phase and enter the construction process. He is responsible for such critical production services as estimating, scheduling, and the preparation of bid and construction documents. Under his direction, HOK has earned a remarkable reputation for completing projects on time and within budget limitations, and, as a result of Kassabaum's inventiveness, the firm is now known as one willing to experiment with new production approaches.

Unlike many professionals who view architecture as a purely creative pursuit, Kassabaum is committed to the concept that architecture is a specialized service that requires precise administrative expertise during the construction process. He has devoted most of his career to this effort, and has been recognized throughout the United States for his refined system of cost analysis and control.

—Linda Legner

HENTRICH, Helmut.

German. Born in Krefeld, 17 June 1905. Educated at the University of Freiburg, 1924; Technical University of Vienna, 1924–25; Technical University of Berlin, 1925–28, Dip.Arch. 1928; Dr. Ing., Technical University of Vienna, 1929. Assistant to the architect Ernö Goldfinger, Paris, 1930, and to Norman Bel Geddes, New York, 1932–33; in private practice, Dusseldorf, 1933–35; Partner, with Hans Heuser, Dr. Helmut Hentrich-Hans Heuser, Dusseldorf, 1935–53. Since 1953, Partner, with the architectural engineer Hubert Petschnigg, Hentrich and Petschnigg, Dusseldorf (Hentrich-Petschnigg and Partner, 1969; HPP: Hentrich-Petschnigg and Partner KG, since 1972); formed Hentrich-Petschnigg and Partner Planning Company, Dusseldorf, 1971, and IPLA Planning and Consulting AG (an association of Hentrich-Petschnigg and Partner Planning Company and Suter and Suter, architects and engineers, Basel), 1973. Recipient: National Prize and Schinkel Medal, 1929; Honorary Professor, National Government of Nordrhein-Westfalen, 1970; Jan Wellem Ring Award, Dusseldorf, 1970; State Medal, Dusseldorf, 1975; IBI Medal, Liechtenstein, 1975; Verdienst Cross of the Bundesrepublik Deutschland, 1976. Member, Academy of Town and Country Planning, Dusseldorf, 1936. Associate of the Royal Institute of British Architects, 1974. Address: HPP: Hentrich-Petschnigg and Partner KG, Neusser Strasse 111, 4000 Dusseldorf, West Germany.

Works:

1952 Drahthaus, Dusseldorf
1953 Bürohaus Pempelfort, Dusseldorf
1955 Jagerhof Castle, Dusseldorf
1957 BASF Skyscraper, Ludwigshafen, Germany
1960 Thyssen Building, Dusseldorf
    School, Karl-Muller-Strasse, Dusseldorf
1962 Kaiserhof Office Building, Hamburg
    Casino Bayer AG, Uerdingen-Krefeld, Germany
    British American Tobacco Building, Hamburg
    High-rise apartments, Dorotheenstrasse, Hamburg
1963 Applied Technology Department of the BASF Company, Ludwigshafen, Germany
    Bayer Skyscraper, Leverkusen, Germany
    Knoll Research Centre, Ludwigshafen, Germany
    Horten Department Store, Neuss, Germany
1964 Europa Centre, Berlin
    Klockner-Humb. Main Administration Building, Deutz, Cologne
    Unilever House, Hamburg
1965 Family housing estate, Elbchaussee, Hamburg
    Garath Church, Dusseldorf
    Research Building C6 for BASF, Ludwigshafen, Germany
1966 Finnlandhaus, Hamburg
    A and M Administration Building, Aachen
    BASF Laboratory, Ludwigshafen, Germany
1967 German Africa Lines Building, Hamburg
1968 Hoechst Calculating Centre, Frankfurt
    Carp-Haus, Dusseldorf
    Wayss and Freytag Administration Building, Dusseldorf
1969 Finance Management Building, Munster, Germany
1970 Procter and Gamble Main Administration Building, Schwalbach, Germany
    WDR Administration Building, Cologne
    Engineering School, Dusseldorf
    Standard Bank Centre, Johannesburg, South Africa
    Horten Department Store, Krefeld, Germany
    Rank Xerox Main Administration Building, Dusseldorf
    Ruhr University, Bochum, Germany
1971 Post Office Headquarters, Hanover

1972 Hillbrow Centre, Johannesburg, South Africa
    Sternhaus, Dusseldorf
    Thyssen Trade Fair Building, Hanover
1973 Town Hall, Hovel, Germany
    Municipal Savings Bank, Dusseldorf
    ERCO Factory, Ludenscheid, Germany
    Post Office, Hanover
1974 VEBA House, Dusseldorf
    TUV Main Administration Building, Cologne
    A and M Main Administration Building, Frankfurt
    Diamond sorting building, Kimberley, South Africa
    RWI House, Dusseldorf
    Town Hall, Wesel, Germany
    Old Leipzig Administration Building, Oberursel, Germany
    Kapuziner Housing Estate, Cologne
1976 Preussenlektra Administration Building, Hanover
    South German Iron and Steel Administration Building, Mainz
1977 Klockner Administration and Calculating Centre, Bremen
    Rhein Braun Main Administration Building, Cologne
    West District Telephone Exchange, Cologne
1978 Klockner House, Duisburg, Germany
    Concert Hall, Dusseldorf

Publications:

By HENTRICH: books—*Buildings 1953–1969*, with Hentrich-Petschnigg and Partners, Dusseldorf, 1969; *Standard Bank, Johannesburg*, Johannesburg 1970; *Buildings 1970–71*, with Hentrich-Petschnigg and Partners, Dusseldorf 1971; *Denkmalpflege 1947–1972*, with Hentrich-Petschnigg and Partners, Dusseldorf 1972; *Buildings 1972–75*, with Hentrich-Petschnigg and Partners, Dusseldorf 1975.

On HENTRICH: books—*The BASF Skyscraper*, by BASF editors, Stuttgart 1959; *The Thyssenhaus* by Martin Mittag, Essen 1962; *The BASF Laboratory Building* by Martin Mittag, Essen 1963; *The Bayer Skyscraper* by Martin Mittag, Essen 1963; *Klockner-Humboldt-Deutz* by Paulhans Peters, Munich 1965; *Unilever-Haus, Hamburg*, by Paulhans Peters, Munich 1966; *Finnlandhaus, Hamburg* by Fritz Rafeiner, Munich 1968; *The Hoechst Calculating Centre* by Bruno Krekler, Munich 1970; *The Procter and Gamble Administration Centre* by Bruno Krekler, Munich 1970; *Administration Buildings* by Bruno Krekler, Munich 1973; *Research Laboratories* by Bruno Krekler, Munich 1975; *The New Administration Buildings of Old Leipzig in Oberursel* by the Old Leipzig Administration Editors, Oberursel 1975.

My guiding principle is from Georges Bernanos: "I do not know whether life loves me but by the Grace of God I love this life through which fools rush without giving themselves time to look, this life full of amazing mysteries held in readiness for mankind."

—Helmut Hentrich

Helmut Hentrich, with his partner Hubert Petschnigg, now known as HPP: Hentrich-Petschnigg und Partner, became well known mainly for their office and administration buildings in a style that even today characterizes post-war German architecture. The International Style of Mies van der Rohe or Skidmore, Owings and Merrill did not, in the march of the Americanization of Western Europe, halt at the borders of the Federal Republic. Uniform sky-

Helmut Hentrich: Thyssen Building, Dusseldorf, 1960

scrapers arose that, unlimited and immoderate, standardized and monotonous, the casual passer-by could, in his thoughts, freely re-compose.

The best-known example of HPP architecture is the Thyssen Building in Dusseldorf, and the best-known photograph of this edifice is one taken from the nearby Park Lake: it shows two of the three sections in a highly-distorted side view. It mirrors the attempt at elegance of a young Federal Republic aspiring at the same time to economic power. Seen from the front, the building, in spite of the different heights of the two visible sections, looks like a monolithic box: the typical German steel skeleton building totally lacks American luxury in the use of building materials (as in Mies's Seagram's Building in New York); in Germany there is additional "frugality" for those who admire the coolness and severity of curtain walling.

HPP's Europa Centre is presented as the first covered shopping centre in Berlin. But violent gusts of wind in the shopping arcades below made structural alterations necessary in the 1970's. HPP also developed the first standard facade components for the department store concern Horten AG. They determine today the appearance of all branches in the Federal Republic, whether in a large city or a small town, whatever the characteristics of nearby old or modern architecture. "Identification" of a particular town or city by the forms of its facades or building masses is made increasingly difficult.

HPP have adjusted the facades of their skyscrapers to the fashionable tendencies of the age—from the smooth curtain walling of the 1950's, via the window hatches set into exposed concrete of the 1960's, to the bevelled corners of the 1970's. HPP won the competition for the Ruhr University in Bochum. After a more than ten year construction period the building complex was handed over for use to the students, a practically structureless example of gigantomachy. The two monotonous rows of the layout, the lack of differentiation in the buildings, the negation of the individuality of the interior courts, and the brutal exposed concrete were all found continually more oppressive by the users. On the other hand, HPP did find inspiration in technical and economic necessity in the Standard Bank Centre in Johannesburg, an office building in three sections, each of nine storeys, which are hung one over the other on a central core. No problem in that: in Johannesburg buildings may be high so that the built-over surface at pedestrian level is limited.

In the post-war period HPP produced small format designs for churches and single-family houses, and they have been involved in the restoration and careful rebuilding of historic buildings. They have won more than fifty national and international competitions.

—Christian Borngräber

HERRON, Ron(ald James).

British. Born in London, 12 August 1930. Educated at various elementary and secondary schools in London, 1934–44; Brixton School of Building, London, 1944–47, and the Brixton School of Building Department of Architecture, evening course, 1950–54; Regent Street Polytechnic, London, evening course, 1954–56. Served in the Royal Air Force, in Germany, 1949–50. Married Patricia Ginn in 1952; children: Andrew and Simon. Architect with the Greater London Council, 1954–61; Founder Member, with Peter Cook, Dennis Crompton, Warren Chalk, Mike Webb and David Greene, Archigram Group, London, 1960, and Co-Editor of *Archigram* magazine, 1960–70; Deputy Architect, Taylor Woodrow Construction Ltd., London, 1961–65; Associate, Halpern and Partners, London, 1965–67; Consultant Architect to Colin St. John Wilson, Cambridge,

1967; in private practice, London, 1968; 2nd Year Master, North East London Polytechnic School of Architecture, 1968; Visiting Professor in Urban Design, University of California at Los Angeles, 1968–69; Director of Urban Design, William Pereira and Partners, Los Angeles, 1969–70; Partner, with Cook and Crompton, Archigram Architects, London, 1970–75; Artist-in-Residence, University of Wisconsin, Madison, 1972; in private practice, as Ron Herron, Architect, London, 1975–77; Visiting Professor, University of Southern California, Los Angeles, 1976–77. Since 1977, Partner, Pentagram Design, London. Tutor at the Architectural Association School of Architecture, London, 1965–68, and since 1970. Exhibitions: *Biennale de Paris,* 1967; *Triennale,* Milan, 1968; *Archigram,* Institute of Contemporary Arts, London, 1973; *House for a Superstar,* Art Net Gallery, London, 1975; *40 London Architects,* Art Net Gallery, London, 1977, subsequently toured Europe; *Ron Herron: Insertion Projects,* Art Net Gallery, London, 1977. Recipient: Graham Foundation Fellowship, with Cook and Crompton, 1968; First Prize, with Archigram Group, Monte Carlo Entertainment Centre Competition, 1970. Associate of the Royal Institute of British Architects; Fellow of the Royal Society of Arts. Address: Pentagram Design, 61 North Wharf Road, London W2 1LA, England.

Works:

1954/
58 Starcross Secondary School, London
    Prospect County Secondary School, St. Pancras, London
    Student Hostel, Northampton College of Advanced Technology
1963 City Interchange (project; with Warren Chalk)
1964 Study of Twilight Areas: Fulham (with Theo Crosby)
    "Walking City" (project)
1965 Clarksons Shipping Ltd. Headquarters Building, London (project; with Theo Crosby)
    Maternity Wing, Royal Berkshire Hospital, Reading
    Gasket House (project; with Warren Chalk)
1966 Free-time Node (project; with Barry Snowden)
    Inflatable Dwellings (project; with Barry Snowden)
    "Air-Hab" (project; with Barry Snowden)
    Shopping Centre, Tredegar, Wales
    Shopping Centre, Aberdare, Wales (project)
1967 "House 199-90" (project; with Archigram Group)
    "Control and Choice" (project; with Peter Cook and Dennis Crompton)
    Amsterdam Town Hall (project; with Alex Pike and Barry Snowden)
1968 "Tuned Suburb" (project)
    "Oasis" (project)
    "Instant City" (project; with Peter Cook and Dennis Crompton)
    Housing development at Pacific Palisades, California (project; with Warren Chalk)
1969 Master plan for a new town for the Ford Motor Company at Dearborn, Michigan (project)
    "Manzak" (project)
    Air terminal at Los Angeles International Airport for Pan American Airlines (project)
1970 Hotel and offices for the Embarcadero Site, San Francisco (project)
    Teaching facility for the University of Missouri (project)
    "Holographic Scene Setter" (project)
    Entertainment facility for Monte Carlo (project)
1971 Conference facility and shopping complex at Bournemouth, Hampshire (project)
1972 Casino at Monte Carlo (project; with Archigram Architects)

"Promotional Event Kit" (project; with Barry Snowden)
Development plan for Margate, Kent (project)
1973 Swimming pool and kitchen block for Rod Stewart, Windsor, Berkshire (with Archigram Architects)
    "Tuning London" (project; with Diana Jowsey)
    Northampton Civic Centre (project; with Archie McNab)
    Glasgow river front (project; with Archie McNab)
    Offices for the British Oxygen Company, Dublin (project; with Archigram Architects)
1974 Furniture for Cassina, Milan (project; with Archigram Architects)
    "Suburban Sets" (project; with Andrew Herron)
    Student Centre, Trondheim, Norway (project; with C. Price, P. Kartvedt, T. Dugdale, and Archigram Architects)
1975 Play centre at Calverton End, Milton Keynes (with Archigram Architects)
    "Sets Fit for the Queen" (project)
    Theatre extension, Trondheim, Norway (project; with Per Kartvedt)
1976 Government offices, Mineritenplatz, Vienna (project; with Theo Crosby)
    Development of the central area of Heathrow Airport, London (project)
1977 Trondheim Library, Norway (project; with Per Kartvedt)
    St. Christopher's Place Development, London (with Pentagram)

Designs: British Industry section, *British Design* exhibition, with Archigram, Paris, 1971; *Malaysia Exhibit,* Commonwealth Institute, with Archigram, London, 1973; *Islamic Art and Architecture Exhibition,* Architectural Association, with Dennis Crompton, London, 1976; *Frei Otto Exhibition,* Architectural Association, London, 1976; *Trailer Exhibition,* with Pentagram, Milton Keynes, 1978.

Publications:

By HERRON: book—*Archigram,* editor with Peter Cook, London 1973; articles—various projects and writings in *Archigram* (London), nos. 1–9, 1960–70; "Living City" in *Living Arts* (London), no. 2, 1963; "Japan's Arata Isozaki" in *Lotus* (Venice), no. 6, 1969; "Archigram" in *Design Quarterly* (Minneapolis), no. 74/75, 1969; "Instant City in Progress," with Peter Cook, in *Architectural Design* (London), November 1970; "Trondheim Theatre" in *RIBA Journal* (London), November 1976; "Set Pieces" in *Space Design* (Tokyo), September 1977; "Sets" in *Architecture + Urbanism* (Tokyo), October 1977; "Palace of the League of Nations: An Architectural Competition in Its Social and Historical Context" in *Pentagram Papers* (London), no. 5, December 1977.

On HERRON: books—*British Architecture* by Royston Landau, London 1968; *Experimental Architecture* by Peter Cook, London 1970; *Architecture 2000* by Charles Jencks, London 1971; *The Third Generation* by Philip Drew, London 1972; *Modern Movements in Architecture* by Charles Jencks, London 1973; *Architectura Radicale* by P. Navone, Milan 1974; *Storia dell'Architettura Contemporanea* by Renato de Fusco, Rome 1974; *Korunk Epiteszete* by Vamossy Ferenc, Budapest 1975; *Mega Structures* by Reyner Banham, London 1976; articles—"Suburban Sets" by Peter Cook in *Casabella* (Milan), no. 398, 1975; "Sets Fit for the Queen" by Arata Isozaki in *The Japan Architect* (Tokyo), February 1976; "Ron Herron" by Sutherland Lyle in *Building Design* (London), 6 May 1977; "Magician of Virtual Images" by Arata Isozaki in *Space Design* (Tokyo), September 1977; "Palace of the League of

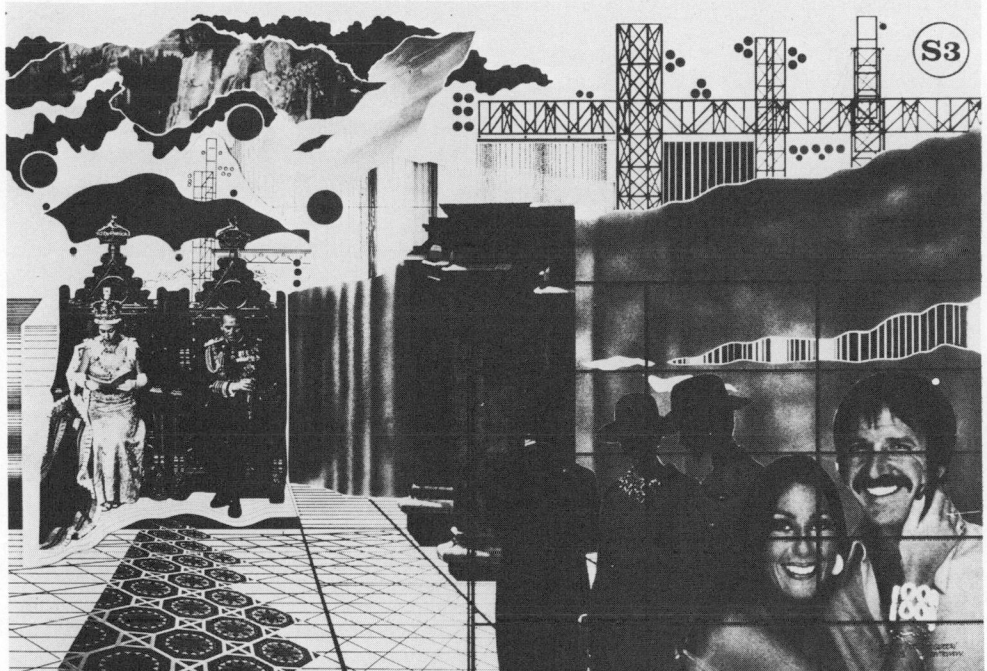

Ron Herron: "Sets Fit for the Queen", 1975

Nations" by David Pierce in *Building Design* (London), 16 December 1977.

Architecture is concerned with: people / what might be / invention / history / art / intuition / order / adaptability / society / change / consistency / structure / needs / beauty / movement / connectivity / response / flexibility / experience / wit / inconsistency / pleasure / ordinariness / complexity / compatibility / environment / context / changing the rules / systems / simplicity / the weather / the city / space / planning / colour / texture / light / view / statics / comfort / the banal / imagination   and so on

Architecture is: the fusing of building and art to make something "special."

My own work concerns itself with all these things and attempts to make architecture by fusing building and art. I hope, one day, to do this successfully.

—Ron Herron

Ron Herron is best known as a leading member of Archigram, an organization that has played a prominent role in British architecture during the past two decades. Archigram started as a magazine founded by Peter Cook in 1960. It was brash, exuberant, and very much part of the "Swinging Sixties." From Pop culture it bothered its graphics, its vulgarity and its love of the ephemeral; from the American Space Programme and science fiction its technological imagery. From contemporary architectural thinking came an interest in mobility and prefabrication and a new acceptance of mass-media: "Today we read ads," the Smithsons had written.

Archigram was also part of the new youth culture, a reassertion of identity after the privations of postwar austerity. Like the music of The Beatles and Rolling Stones it was meant to shock older generations, and it succeeded. But of course cultural movements thrive on controversy, and *Archigram* was hungrily read in architectural schools throughout the country. "This is the space age," it asserted. "What are we doing still building with bricks and mortar? Look what we could do with the technology that is already at hand." Seductive images flowed thick and fast, often just about within the bounds of technical possibility but never worked out in detail. Instant City, Walking City, Tuned Suburb, came and went. It was wonderful propaganda, and it paved the way to new applications of technology and to a new kind of non-building, since realized by Piano and Rogers with their Pompidou Centre in

Paris and by Cedric Price in his Inter-Action Centre in London.

When the effects of the images had worn off, though, what was left? Archigram was always justly criticised for having no real substance behind its graphics. Would it ever build anything? Ron Herron and Warren Chalk had built when working for the Greater London Council in the early 1960's, and were in fact responsible for the conception of the South Bank Arts Complex, though it was not built as the ambiguous half-hived mound building covered in vegetation that they had originally envisaged but as an unrelenting bunker-like mass of grey concrete. Other Archigram members had built nothing of significance. Their chance to put theory into practice came in 1970 when they were invited to join a limited competition for an entertainments complex in Monte Carlo: they won first prize. This was to be the Archigram *tour de force*, with plenty of high technology in its multi-purpose interior, and no exterior at all—instead, the beloved mound covered with trees and a park. The project was developed over the next three years, but, like so many competition projects, it was eventually dropped, in this case because a developer offered the client a more tempting deal on an adjacent site.

By the mid-1970's Archigram had lost its urgency: its message had either been absorbed or rejected. High technology did not fit in with ecology and conservation or with a new call for craftsmanship. Archigram had had its heyday, and its members moved apart, though remaining close friends. Ron Herron moved to Pentagram, where he is now a partner. He builds, albeit at a modest scale, and continues to produce visionary drawings in the evenings. He teaches at the Architectural Association, where one of the essential messages of Archigram still needs to be heard by each generation of students: "When you are looking for a solution to what you are told is an architectural problem—remember, it may not be a building."

—Peter Blundell Jones

HERTZBERGER, Herman.
Dutch. Born in Amsterdam, 6 July 1932. Educated at the Technical University, Delft, graduated 1958. Married Hans van Seters in 1959; children: Akelei, Veronica, and Titus. In private practice, Amsterdam, since 1958. Town Planning Consultant, Deventer, 1969. Instructor, Academy of Architecture, Amsterdam, 1965–70. Since 1970, Professor at the University of Delft. Visiting Professor, Massachusetts Institute of Technology, Cambridge, 1966–67, 1970, Columbia University, New York, 1968, and the University of Toronto, 1969, 1970, 1971, 1974. Editor, with Aldo van Eyck, Jacob Bakema and others, *Forum,* Amsterdam, 1959–63. Exhibitions: *Biennale des Jeunes,* Paris, 1967; Stedelijk Museum, Amsterdam, 1968; Historical Museum, Amsterdam, 1971; *Biennale,* Venice, 1976. Recipient: Amsterdam Architectural Award, 1968; Eternitaward, 1974; Fritz Schumacher Award, 1974. Address: Architektenburo Herman Hertzberger, Vossiusstraat 3, 1071 AB Amsterdam, The Netherlands.

Works:

1959/
66 Students residence, Weesperstraat, Amsterdam
1964 Lin Mij factory extension, Molenwerf, Sloterdijk, Amsterdam
Church in Driebergen, The Netherlands (project)
1966 Montessori School, Jacoba van Beierenlaan, Delft
Town Hall in Valkenswaard, The Netherlands (project)
1967 House conversion, Laren, The Netherlands
Town Hall, Amsterdam (project)
1968 Monogoon housing (project)
1970 Kindergarten and Primary School extension, Jacoba van Beierenlaan, Delft
Neighbourhood Nieuwmarkt, Amsterdam (project)
1971 Eight experimental houses (Diagoon), Gebbenlaan, Delft
1972 Renewal plan for the old city of Groningen (project)
Centraal Beheer Office Building, Prins Willem-Alexanderlaan, Apeldoorn (with Lucas and Niemeijer)
1974 De Schalm Community Centre, Dreef, Deventer
De Drie Hoven Old People's Home, Louis Chrispijnstraat 50, Slotervaart, Amsterdam
City centre plan for Eindhoven (project; with Van den Broek and Bakema)
1978 Vredenburg Music Centre, Utrecht

Publications:

By HERTZBERGER: articles—"Some Notes on Two Works by Schindler" in *Domus* (Milan), September 1967; "Montessori Primary School in Delft" in *Harvard Educational Review: Architecture and Education* (Cambridge, Massachusetts), vol. 39, no. 4, 1969; "Looking for the Beach under the Pavement" in *RIBA Journal* (London), 1971; "Homework for More Hospitable Form," special number of *Forum* (Amsterdam), no. 3, 1973.

On HERTZBERGER: articles—"Buildings Designed as Street" by Raymond Lifchez in *Architectural Record* (New York), July 1968; "Young Dutch Architects" by Mette van Regteren Altena in *Arkitekten* (Copenhagen), no. 20, 1972; "Strukturalismus-Architektur als Symbol der Demokratisierung" by Arnulf Lüchinger in *Bauen und Wohnen* (Zurich), May 1974; "Strukturalismus: Eine neue Stromung in der Architektur" by Arnulf Lüchinger in *Bauen und Wohnen* (Zurich), no. 1, 1976; "Herman Hertzberger: Musical Architecture" in *The Architects' Journal* (London), April 1976; "Little Things Mean a Lot: The Philosophy of Herman

Hertzberger" by Walter Menzies in *Building Design* (London), April 1976; "Variaciones de Hertzberger sobre temas del team 10" by Oriol Bohigas in *Arquitectura* (Madrid), no. 11, 1976; "Herman Hertzberger, Dutch Architect" by Arnulf Lüchinger in *Architecture + Urbanism* (Tokyo), March 1977.

Designing in such a way that several interpretations are possible should mean not only that the things we make can play several roles, but also that the users themselves are thereby encouraged to play more roles. Not only do we interpret the form, the form simultaneously interprets us, shows us something of who we are.

Thus user and form begin mutually to interpret each other; their identities are strengthened by each other; each becomes more itself. It is like the actor who interprets his role and is himself interpreted by it at the same time; not only does he manifest something of the play; the play also manifests something of him: actor and play affirm each other.

The more roles the actor plays, the more facets of his identity are expressed; his identity becomes more complete, or is magnified, in the same way as the play, too, through differing interpretations, releases more of its being.

Just as the identity of the actor extends as he plays more roles, so our identity will grow as we are drawn into a greater diversity of roles, that is, relationships to others.

Thus we have to make things such that it becomes in reality possible for everyone to show as many facets of himself, to be himself in as many ways, as possible.

As the possibilities for interpretation are increased, so the more facets of himself the individual can express are increased, and a greater number of people can simultaneously be drawn into related behavior.

Our purpose, then, should be to make as many possibilities for interpretation as possible, in the sense of giving each place its maximum "capacity."

Of essential importance here is that the differences should in fact be qualitative; otherwise, they will all only offer the same thing: it will thus be only a question of pseudo-interpretation, and a new stereotype pattern will be born.

Only with a diversity of interpretations that is qualitative will there be a question of choice on which the establishment of a maximally variegated social pattern can be based.

Everything we make must be the catalyst to stimulate the individual to play the roles through which his identity will be enlarged. The aim of architecture is then: to reach the situation where everyone's identity is optimal, and because user and thing manifest each other, affirm each other, make each other more itself, the problem is to find the right conditioning for each thing.

It is a question of the right dimensions, placing, beat, interval, the right articulation, that things and people offer each other.

Form makes itself, and that is less a question of invention that of listening well to what person and thing want to be.

Form, directed towards a given purpose, functions as an apparatus, where both form and programme are reciprocally evocative; the apparatus evolves into an instrument.

A properly functioning apparatus does the work for which it is programmed, and that is what we expect of it, not less, but also not more. By pressing the right knobs we get the expected result—the same for everybody, constantly the same.

An instrument essentially contains as many possibilities as can be drawn out of it; an instrument must be played. Within the range of the instrument, it is up to the player to draw what he can from it, within the limits of his own ability.

Thus instrument and player reveal their ability to complement and fulfil each other. Form as instrument offers the scope for each person to do what he

has most at heart, and above all to do it in his own way.

It is because of this that a form must house both private and communal activities, intentions and associations and, moreover, must be able to suggest different ways in which it can be adjusted constantly to suit the needs of each person. Therefore the building itself must contain the incentive that provokes each person into making the choices that he feels are most suited to his circumstances at that particular time.

This extraordinary quality of hospitality is the scope a form must provide for people, for their values and dignity, in order to create the conditions that enable everyone to be who he wants to be—whoever that may be.

Just as people must put themselves in the place of a form in order to be able to appropriate it, so must form put itself in the place of people to be appropriated.

Thus we could look upon this quality of hospitality of a form as the spatial equivalent of entering into a part.

The architect's task is above all to apply more than cut-to-fit, ready-made solutions and as much as possible to free in the users themselves whatever they think they need, by evoking images in them which can lead to their own personally valid solutions.

What we offer cannot be neutral; it must be the raw material, as it were, containing the "intentions" out of which everyone can make his choice in a particular situation, extracting from it precisely the intention which "resonates" with his intentions—intentions which give the prospect of his doing, or being, whatever will strengthen his ego-ideal.

Each user interprets what's offered in such a way that he gets information out of it which is relevant to him and which he can use with relevance.

—Herman Hertzberger

Herman Hertzberger is part of an architectural movement that is essentially different from Machine-Aesthetic, International Style, Brutalism, Mannerism, Rationalism, or Classicism: his architecture has a basis that is broader than the purely aesthetic and formal. He is a descendant of the architectural tradition that had its beginnings at the end of the 1920's in the CIAM movement, a movement that itself diverged into another path at the end of the 1950's. Kenzo Tange speaks of two principal tendencies: Functionalism, from 1920 to 1960, and Structuralism, from 1960 to the present. With the change in direction, there was as well a change in name—from Congrès Internationaux d'Architecture Moderne to Groupe de Récherches des Interrelations Sociales et Plastiques. In the first period (1920–60), importance was attached to the development of a contemporary architectural expression that would replace the stylistic chaos of the 19th century. In the second period (1960 to date), there has been an essentially different approach: formalist "isms" now hardly count; the "interrelations sociales et plastiques" are thought to be more valuable. Herman Hertzberger is today the most influential representative of Structuralism in relation to these "interrelations sociales et plastiques," and he has carried out exemplary work both in theory and in practice.

Both Functionalism and Structuralism have political ideologies. The socially committed CIAM Functionalists felt themselves deeply allied with socialist ideology and tried to introduce the scientific materialism of Marxist thought into their architecture. In some ways, Structuralists have a similar attitude. Hertzberger writes: "The architect, as we know, has never been very human: throughout history he has always served the happy few, never the great number. Since buildings cost money, he has always been on the side of money—the wrong side." But the Structuralists totally reject any belief in architecture as a science. With due respect for Marx, they proceed from the fact that he made no competent statements about architecture and art because he had insufficient insight into that sphere of human activ-

ity. While Marx can be considered the guru of the CIAM Functionalists, it is Claude Lévi-Strauss, with his structuralism in anthropology, who is spiritual father to the Structuralists. And, while various CIAM Functionalists tried to realize their ideas in Communist Russia, Structuralist architects have followed the example of Lévi-Strauss and carried out studies in distant lands among primitive peoples, their intention being to learn about archetypal man in his community and to integrate that experience into contemporary architecture.

Team 10, the most active group within CIAM during the 1950's, made a significant contribution to the formation of the theory of Structuralism. Aldo van Eyck, one of the most prominent of the team, exerted great influence, with his theories and in his works, on younger architects like Hertzberger and Piet Blom. Influenced as well by John Habraken's book *Supports: An Alternative to Mass Housing,* Hertzberger went on to develop his own major theme—co-determination in architecture. With his nuanced treatises on polyvalent form, identity, structure, infill, etc., he produced theories that compensated for the one-sided conception of form of Functionalism.

Hertzberger has always shown a lively interest in the international development of architecture, with the consequent advantage that, in building, he has never copied himself. The influence is perceptible not only of the great masters like Le Corbusier, Kahn and Tange, but also, among others, of Duiker, Chareau, Bofill, and the architects of other cultures. Hertzberger creates ideas (to borrow from Malraux) from the "Musée Imaginaire." He has a special affection for the Dutch architect Duiker. One of the least understood and therefore most underestimated Dutch architects of the 1920's, Duiker had anticipated an important principal of later Structuralism, the legitimate possibility of extension. Further, Duiker's poetic Concrete Constructivism offers many more possibilities for the realization of co-determination (structure and infill) than the modern architecture of the pure cube. Duiker was a musician as well as an architect. So is Hertzberger.

But, finally, it has only been of secondary importance to Hertzberger to function as a theorist. His prime intention has always been to translate into reality the social theories that he and others have developed. As a builder, he has proved to be an unsurpassed master. Four examples from the 1970's will suffice:

Diagoon Houses, Delft, 1971—8 terraced, single-family houses. A test case for co-determination in house building—in the inside, the facade, and the environment. Hertzberger regards the houses as "half-works" (though certainly not neutral works), to be completed by the occupants.

Centraal Beheer Office Building in Apeldoorn, 1972—for an insurance company with 1,000 employees. A statement from Hertzberger, from 1965, is relevant: "A building must be essentially anti-monumental in the sense that monumentality is connected with power. A building must be essentially monumental in the sense that monumentality is connected with democracy." The basis of the design is a work island for each group of 16 employees, and the building is comprised of cubic building components that are connected by a gridiron plan. It is a classic example of co-determination at the place of work, whereby the identity of each employee can be expressed.

De Drie Hoven Old People's Home, Amsterdam, 1974—a variable structure with vertical communications units. Hertzberger pays special attention to the "spaces between"—that is, he creates contact-promoting access areas between the dwellings (seating areas, stable-type doors, interior windows, etc.). There is a smooth transition from the public to the

Herman Hertzberger: Centraal Beheer Office Building, Apeldoorn, 1972

private realm. The building is a demonstration of the goal of "sense of place," and the central image is that of the village square.

Vredenburg Music Centre, Utrecht, 1978—a structure with construction units. Within an amorphous whole that relates to its surroundings, Hertzberger has crystallized ordered, symmetric forms—the main hall block, the other halls and foyers—and the play of free and ordered forms is very exciting. There is also a symmetrically formed main facade: this symbolic exterior form is no longer typically Structuralist but is, rather, related to Expressionism. If one compares Centraal Beheer Office Building, the De Drie Hoven Old People's Home, and the Music Centre, a development of the total form from basic structure to symbolic form is apparent. Ideologically, the Music Centre (with passages, shops, restaurants, information desk, etc.) involves the opposite of the well-known separation of functions in Functionalism. It is more appropriate to talk about "osmotic" architecture with "semi-permeable" openings. There are fluent transitions—Foyer/Hall and Foyer/Public Passages—in which the view from the public to the private realm strengthens the "osmotic" effect. This effect is perceptible even in the perforated parapet details, the edges of the glass projecting roofs, and even in the lamps, which Hertzberger designed himself, as the architects of the 1920's designed their furniture. He considers lighting an important component of space arrangement.

Hertzberger is an excellent theoretician, of the intellectual level of van Eyck, yet his greatest strength lies in his translation of new social ideas into reality. He has artistic talent, a wealth of ideas, and a tremendous creative capacity. He works roughly on a level comparable to that of Duiker, van der Vlugt and van Eyck—which is to say, he must be numbered among the most important of avant-garde architects.

—Arnulf Lüchinger

HILBERSEIMER, Ludwig K(arl).

American. Born in Karlsruhe, Germany, 14 September 1885; emigrated to the United States, 1938: naturalized, 1944. Educated at the Technische Hochschule, Karlsruhe, 1906–11. Architect and planner in various European cities, mainly Berlin, 1918–38; in private practice as a town planner, Chicago, 1938 until his death, 1967. Founder and Director of the City Planning Department at the Bauhaus, Dessau, Germany, 1929–32; Professor and Director of the Department of City and Regional Planning, 1938–57, and Professor Emeritus, 1957–67, Illinois Institute of Technology, Chicago. European Architectural Correspondent, *Chicago Tribune,* 1925; Member, Advisory Board, Burnham Library, Art Institute of Chicago, 1938–60; organized the Town Planning Exhibition at the Art Institute, 1944. Member, Noverbergruppe, Berlin, 1919, Der Sturm artists' group, Berlin, 1925, Der Ring, Berlin, 1927, and CIAM (Congrès Internationaux d'Architecture Moderne), from 1928; served as a Director of the Deutsche Werkbund from 1931. LL.D.: Western Reserve University, Cleveland, 1962; D.Eng.: Technical University of Berlin, 1963. Fellow, American Institute of Architects. Member, Akademie der Künste, Berlin. *Died (in Chicago) 6 May 1967.*

Works:

1911   Opera House, Berlin (project)
1919/
24   "Minimal Standards" City Planning Studies, Berlin (projects)
1924   Skyscraper City, Berlin (project)
1924/
27   Housing studies, Berlin (projects)

1927   Werkbund Exhibition House, Weissenhof Estate, Stuttgart
1930   Furnished houses (2), *Die Wohnung Exhibition,* Berlin
         Housing, Adlershof Estate, Berlin
1931   Town Hall, Nuremberg (project)
1932   Housing, Zehlendorf Estate, Berlin
1935   "Minimal Standards" Housing Studies, Berlin (projects)
1936   Housing, Rupendorn Estate, Berlin
         Housing, Fichteberg Estate, Berlin
1937/
38   City redevelopment plan for Chicago
1939/
45   City plan for Montreal
1947   City plan for Maui, Hawaii
1950   Revised city redevelopment plan for Chicago
1955   Lafayette Park Development Plan, Detroit
1957   City plan for Seattle
1959   Lafayette Park Development, stage I, Detroit
1961   Revised city redevelopment plan for Chicago

Publications:

By HILBERSEIMER: books—*Grossstadtbauten,* Hanover 1925; *Grossstadt Architektur,* Stuttgart 1927; *Beton als Gestalter,* with Julius Vischer, Stuttgart 1928; *Internationale Neue Baukunst,* Stuttgart 1928; *Hallenbauten,* Leipzig 1931; *The New City: Principles of Planning,* Chicago 1944; *The New Regional Pattern,* Chicago 1949; *The Nature of Cities,* Chicago 1955; *Mies van der Rohe,* Chicago 1956; *Entfaltung einer Planungsidee,* Berlin 1963; *Contemporary Architecture: Its Roots and Trends,* Chicago 1964; *Berliner Architektur der 20 Jahre,* Mainz and Berlin 1967; articles—"Reichstagerweiterung und Platz der Republik" in *Die Form* (Berlin), 1 July 1930; "Neue Literatur über Städtebau" in *Die Form* (Berlin), 15 October 1930; "Vorschlag zur city Bebauung" in *Die Form* (Berlin), 15 December 1930; "Die Wohnung unserer Zeit" in *Die Form* (Berlin), 15 July 1931; "Die Bewohner des Hauses Tugendhat aussern sich . . ." in *Die Form* (Berlin), 15 November 1931; Reflections on a Greek Journey" in *Inland Architect* (Chicago), February 1967.

On HILBERSEIMER: book—*Bauen seit 1900 in Berlin* by Rolf Rave and Hans-Joachim Knöfel, Berlin 1968; articles—"Entwurf für die Stadthalle Nurnberg" in *Die Form* (Berlin), 15 October 1931; "Haus Dr. B. in Berlin-Zehlendorf" in *Die Form* (Berlin), 15 November 1932; *"The New City:* Social Planning Is a Social Task" by Jan Reiner in *Architect and Engineer* (New York), June 1945; "Plan d'urbanisme de Chicago" in *Architecture: Formes et Fonctions* (Lausanne), 1957; "Profile: Ludwig Hilberseimer" in *Der Aufbau* (Vienna), March 1959; "Seidlung Lafayette Park, Detroit" in *Bauen und Wohnen* (Zurich), November 1960; "Modern Proposals for the Physical Decentralization of Community" by Henry Winthrop in *Land Economics* (Madison, Wisconsin), February 1967; "Elementos de la nueva ciudad: La obra de Ludwig Hilberseimer" by Reginald F. Malcolmson in *Hogar y Arquitectura* (Madrid), May/June 1968; "The Development of the Weissenhof Estate in Stuttgart" by Bodo Rasch in *Deutsche Bauzeitung* (Stuttgart), November 1977.

*   *   *

Ludwig Hilberseimer was one of the leaders of that singular generation of central European designers born in the 1880's (Gropius, Mies van der Rohe, and Mendelsohn were others) who revolutionized building in Germany during the 1920's, then emigrated to the United States during the following two decades and contributed equally to the reconstitution of architecture in this country.

After taking his training at the Technische Hochschule in Karlsruhe, Hilberseimer settled in Berlin, where he practiced for nearly two decades and where his abiding architectural philosophy was shaped. That outlook was uncompromisingly modernist:

Hilberseimer became devoted to the direct structural expression of technological elements in building; he has been called one of the founders of the International Style. As early as 1911 he saw and was impressed by the work of Frank Lloyd Wright, and he later formed a lifelong friendship with Ludwig Mies van der Rohe. He was an early member (in 1919) of the Novembergruppe in Germany and a contributor to the magazine *G,* both radical instruments of the modern movement in art and architecture. He was the first architect to show in the Der Sturm exhibitions in Berlin, and in 1927 he became a member of yet another organization of major German vanguard architects, Der Ring.

By this time Hilberseimer had earned a reputation not only as a designer but also as a writer and city planner. His book *Grossstadtbauten* appeared in 1925, and two years later he contributed the design of a house to the Weissenhof Estate project in Stuttgart. In 1929 he became the Founder/Director of the City Planning Department of the Dessau Bauhaus.

Hilberseimer spent most of the 1930's, bleak years for the modern arts in Germany, in his homeland. He was elected to the directorate of the Deutsche Werkbund in 1931, the same year his book *Hallenbauten* was published. He meanwhile designed housing in Berlin, in Adlershof, Zehlendorf, Rupenhorn and Fichteberg.

Hilberseimer's career took an important turn in 1938, when he accepted the post of Director of the Department of City and Regional Planning of the School of Architecture of the Illinois Institute of Technology (then the Armour Institute) in Chicago. There he and his countryman Walter Peterhans joined the School's newly appointed director Mies van der Rohe in a full-scale reorganization of the architecture curriculum. The modern structuralist principles that the three men had espoused in their European years were communicated to several generations of younger designers who in turn did much to engender the skin-and-bones look of American commercial architecture during the 1950's.

—Franz Schulze

HO, Tao.

British. Born in Shanghai, China, 17 July 1936; emigrated to Hong Kong, 1949: British subject, 1976. Educated at Pui Ching Middle High School, Kowloon, Hong Kong, 1950–56; Williams College, Williamstown, Massachusetts, 1956–60 (Bowdwin Scholarship; Hutchinson Prize, 1960), B.A. 1960; Harvard University Graduate School of Design, Cambridge, Massachusetts, under Josep Lluis Sert and Siegfried Giedion, 1960–64 (Arthur Lehman Fellowship), M.Arch. 1964. Married Chi-Ping Lu in 1960 (divorced, 1978); children: Suenn, Shu, and Dien; married Irene Lo in 1978. Research Assistant, Albright-Knox Art Gallery, Buffalo, New York, Summer 1959; Architectural Assistant, Harvard University Planning Office, 1961, Boston Redevelopment Authority, 1962, and The Architects Collaborative (TAC), Cambridge, 1963–64; architect with various firms in Hong Kong, 1964–68. Since 1968, Principal of TAOHO Design, architects and designers, Hong Kong. Core Member, with Fumihiko Maki and Koichi Nagashima of Tokyo, William S. M. Lim of Singapore, and Sumet Jumsai of Bangkok, APAC (Asian Planning and Architectural Consultants Ltd.), since 1975. Visiting Lecturer, Fine Arts Department, Chinese University of Hong Kong, 1965–67; Visiting Critic, Harvard University Graduate School of Design, 1975. Part-time Lecturer, Architecture Department, University of Hong Kong, since 1977. Chairman, Visual Arts Committee, Hong Kong Arts Centre, 1972–77 (organized 25 art exhibitions at the Centre; President, Harvard Club of Hong Kong, 1975–77; Member, EROPH (Eastern

Tao Ho: Hong Kong Arts Centre, 1977

Regional Organization for Planning and Housing), 1975–76. Exhibitions (paintings): Museum of Art, Springfield, Massachusetts, 1959; Hong Kong Museum of Art, 1959; Boston Art Festival, 1960; Hong Kong Museum of Art, 1969. Collections (graphics): Art Museum, Lawrence, Massachusetts. Recipient: Design Award, Trade Development Council of Hong Kong, 1969; Silver Medal, Hong Kong Institute of Architects, 1978; Silver Award, Hong Kong Designers Association, 1978. Fellow of Robert Black College, University of Hong Kong; D.H.L.: Williams College, Williamstown, Massachusetts, 1979. Member, Hong Kong Institute of Architects, 1971, World Society of Ekistics, 1973, and American Institute of Graphic Arts, 1973. Address: TAOHO Design, 4 Sunning Road, 9th Floor, Causeway Bay, Hong Kong.

Works:

1968   Olivetti Pavilion, *C.M.A. Exhibition,* Hunghom, Hong Kong
1969   Hong Kong Government Pavilion, *C.M.A. Exhibition,* Hunghom, Hong Kong

1971   Rediffusion Pavilion, *C.M.A. Exhibition,* Wanchai, Hong Kong
1973   Feasibility study of village planning policy for New Territories, Hong Kong (as consultant architect to Wilbur Smith and Associates)
1975   Elementary Section, Hong Kong International School, Repulse Bay, Hong Kong (with Wong and Ouyang Associates)
1976   Project Office, Mass Transit Railway Corporation, Admiralty, Queensway, Hong Kong
1977   Hua Hsia Building, Gloucester Road, Hong Kong
       Hong Kong Arts Centre
1979   K. S. Lo Residential Development, Shouson Hill, Hong Kong (with K. C. Lye)
       H. K. Lee House, Black's Link, Hong Kong Master Plan, Special Studies Building, and Gymnasium, St. Stephen's College, Stanley, Hong Kong

Interiors: Foreign Correspondents' Club, Sutherland House, Hong Kong, 1968; Johnson, Stokes and Master, Hong King and Shanghai Bank Building, Hong Kong, 1969; Merrill Lynch, Pierce, Fenner and Smith, St. George's Building, Hong Kong, 1969; United States Information Service Libraries, Hong Kong, Bangkok, and Taipei, 1969; Hong Kong

branches of the Far East Bank Ltd., 1969–72; The Shell Company of Hong Kong, Hong Kong and Shanghai Bank Building, Kowloon, 1969–73; Munichre Service Ltd., Connaught Centre, Hong Kong, 1972; Vickers da Costa and Company, Connaught Centre, Hong Kong, 1972; Union Insurance Society of Canton Ltd., Swire House, Hong Kong, 1972; Coca-Cola Export Corporation, Connaught Centre, Hong Kong, 1973; Marubeni Corporation, Connaught Centre, Hong Kong, 1973; Sing Tao Newspaper Ltd., News Building, Hong Kong, 1973; Hong Kong Stock Exchange, Edinburgh House and Hutchinson House, 1973–76; Charles Fulton (Hong Kong) Ltd., Sincere Insurance Building, Tai Seng Building, Hong Kong, 1973–78; Duty Free Shoppers Ltd., Hyatt Regency Hotel, J. Hotung House, Kai Tak Airport, Kowloon, 1973–78; Lufthansa head office and ticket offices, Pedder Building, Prince's Building, Peninsula Hotel, 1974; Italian Consulate, Hutchison House, Hong Kong, 1975; Nan Fung Textiles Ltd., Central Building, Hong Kong, 1975; Hong Kong Institute of Architects, Cheong Sun Building, Hong Kong, 1975; International Maritime Carriers, Connaught Centre, Hong Kong, 1975; Barberlines (Hong Kong) Ltd., Melbourne Plaza, Hong Kong, 1975–77; Slaughter and May, Connaught Centre, Hong Kong, 1976; Zim Israel Navigation Company Ltd., Alexandra House, Hong Kong, 1976; Austin Centre public space and lobbies, Austin Avenue, Kowloon, 1976; SGV-Sun Hung Kai Ltd., Alexandra House, Hong Kong, 1976; Rigoletto Ristorante Italiano, East Town Building, Hong Kong, 1976; China Engineering Ltd., Ching Lung Tau Facility, Texaco Road, Tsuen Wan, New Territories, Hong Kong, 1976; Longines Hong Kong Ltd., Ocean Centre, Kowloon, 1977; Hambro Pacific, Connaught Centre, Hong Kong, 1977; Li Residence, Mt. Cameron Road, Hong Kong, 1977–78; Sumitomo Bank, Hong Kong, 1978; Exxon Chemical East Pacific Ltd., Connaught Centre, Hong Kong, 1978; Grindlay's Bank Ltd., China Building, Hong Kong; IBM World Trade Corporation, Bank of Canton Building, Hong Kong, 1978; Hong Kong Tourist Association, Connaught Centre, Hong Kong, 1978.

Publications:

By HO: articles/monographs—"Chinese Paintings and Paul Cezanne: A Comparison" in *Williams Review* (Williamstown, Massachusetts), May 1960; "Chinese Architecture and Town Planning, B.C. 1500–A.D. 1911" in *Landscape Architecture* (Louisville, Kentucky), July 1963; "Hong Kong Waterfront Development" in *Ekistics* (Athens), June 1964; "Some Thoughts on the Theory and Technique of Art" in *Art Review of New Asia College* (Hong Kong), September 1966; "A Chinese Architectural Spirit" in *Ekistics* (Athens), November 1965; *Graphic Art in Germany Today: A Brief Development of Art from 1907–1973,* TAOHO Design Publication, Hong Kong 1973; "Design Criteria for Human High-Density Housing" in *Ekistics* (Athens), June 1975; "Hong Kong: A City Prospers Without a Plan" in *City Planning Review* (Tokyo), August 1976; "The Hong Kong Arts Centre—A Piece of Functional Sculpture" in *Hong Kong Exporter and Far Eastern Importer* (Hong Kong), Winter 1977/78; *Music in Architecture,* TAOHO Design Publication, Hong Kong 1978; *German Expressionism,* TAOHO Design Publication, Hong Kong 1978; *The Colour of Monet, The Sound of Debussy, and The Spiritual Realm of Huang Pin-Hung,* TAOHO Design Publication, Hong Kong 1978; introductions for Hong Kong Arts Centre exhibition catalogues, 1972–77.

On HO: books—*Delos Symposium 1974,* Athens 1974; *The Architecture of Self-Help Communities* by Michael Seelig, New York 1978; *Unesco School Furniture* by Bo Fritzell, Paris 1978; articles—"Tao Ho Sees Great Things Ahead for Arts Centre" by Sheila

Wyndham in *South China Morning Post* (Hong Kong), 28 September 1971; "Hong Kong Arts Centre" in *Architecture and Planning* (Taipei, Taiwan), December 1972; "An Interview with Mr. Tao Ho" by Ioh Lee in *Grove Magazine* (Hong Kong), 1 January 1973; "11th Delos Symposium 1974" in *Ekistics* (Athens), December 1974; "Stimulating Environment for Learning" by Peter Leung in *Building Materials and Equipment in Hong Kong* (Hong Kong), October 1975; "Hong Kong Arts Centre: Simple, Compact and Functional" by Peter Leung in *Building Journal* (Hong Kong), May 1976; "Arts Centre—Intricate, Economical, Imaginative Design" in *Asian Architect and Builder* (Hong Kong), November 1976; "A Place of Their Own" in *Asiaweek* (Hong Kong), 28 October 1977; "Asian Planning and Architectural Consultants" in *Nikkei Architecture* (Tokyo), 14 November 1977; "Hong Kong's Oasis" by Lesley Nelson in *Peninsula Group Magazine* (Hong Kong), April 1978; "Hong Kong Arts Centre" by Michael Outhwaite in *Tabs* (London), Spring 1978.

*

The history of civilization is the cycle of man's continuous effort to shape and to reshape his environment. During this process the architect has played a very important role.

It is, perhaps, historically inevitable that architecture will become more and more complicated because of the increasingly complex nature of our society. We have also reached a point in history where, for the first time, almost any conceivable structure can be built in a technological sense. Whether this is a blessing to mankind remains to be judged. The test of the architect in this respect seems to me to be one of his attitude towards the future of humanity.

In order to humanize our future world, which we should do if we do not wish to be ruled by mechanization, an architect must possess both social and spatial imagination. The former is the amorphous ideal of improving our life pattern while the latter is the formal representation of that ideal in terms of better spatial organization for our activities.

An architect, therefore, must be able to penetrate the superficial, the chaotic and the transitory social phenomena in order to formulate a new dynamic and inspiring social order for tomorrow. At the same time, an architect must have the innovative design ability to create functionally and economically whilst aesthetically and poetically expressing his social ideals by means of well articulated and integrated forms in space.

Good architecture is like a piece of beautifully composed music crystallized in space that elevates our spirits beyond the limitation of time.

The Hong Kong Arts Centre is an example of my belief. In addition to being the architect, I was one of the initiators nine years ago who promoted and fought for the idea of providing a people's cultural oasis in the highly commercially oriented city of Hong Kong. It is a very small building on a tiny 30 m. × 30 m. site. But it symbolizes a vision. I hope this vision will help to shape the future.

—Tao Ho

*

Tao Ho is probably the only architect in Hong Kong who is fearlessly committed to the art of making spaces in a city so thoroughly committed to commercial imperatives. His background is an interesting one; he is a cosmopolitan Chinese well versed in art and literature of the East and the West. His early work at Harvard exhibited a degree of formalism that was probably generated by his knowledge of disciplines surrounding Chinese architecture—a frame of mind not dissimilar to Beaux Arts attitudes. But his exposure to Le Corbusier and Sert over the years also provided certain relevant contradictions that have allowed him as an architect to recognize the worth of formalism with all its constraints and positive attributes. Like Sert, he has acquired the ability to externally

and internally decompose formalism to an extent that permits his architecture the possibility of indeterminacy within a whole.

Tao Ho is, perhaps, the only one among a small band of young architects in Hong Kong who has remained a constant source of irritation to the establishment, whose preference is for Honky-Tonk Han (Bloodsworth) on the one hand and the Puerile-Virile Pop on the other. It can be said that it is ultimately the Baroqueness of Tao Ho's work that makes him controversial, much discussed and never a source of boredom. His architecture always delights or frightens, depending on the viewer's frame of mind. He is a cheeky architect and a perfect gentleman—am I describing an English public school boy up to some mischief at the vicar's party in a country churchyard?

—K.C. Lye

HOFFMANN, Josef (Franz Maria).

Austrian. Born in Pirnitz, Moravia, now Brtnice, Czechoslovakia, 15 December 1870. Studied architecture at the Academy of Art, Vienna, under Carl von Hasenauer and Otto Wagner, 1892–95; awarded the Rome Prize, 1895. Married Anna Hladik in 1903, and Karla Schmatz in 1925; son: Wolfgang. Worked with Joseph Olbrich in the studio of Otto Wagner, Vienna, 1896–97. In private practice, Vienna, 1898 until his death, 1956. Professor, Vienna School (now Academy) of Applied Arts, 1899–1936. Founder Member, Sezession Group, Vienna, 1897; Founder, with Kolo Moser and Fritz Wärndorfer, Wiener Werkstätte, 1903; Director, with Gustav Klimt, Kunstschau (secession from the Sezession), Vienna, 1908–09; Co-Founder Director, Austrian Werkbund, Vienna, 1910; Director, Künstlerwerkstätte, Vienna, 1943–56. Exhibitions: *Josef Hoffmann: 60th Birthday Retrospective*, Vienna, 1930; *Triennale*, Milan, 1933 (retrospective); *Josef Hoffmann*, Vienna, 1950; *Josef Hoffmann*, Galerie Würthle, Vienna, 1960, 1970; *Josef Hoffmann: Drawings*, Austrian Institute, New York, 1975; *Josef Hoffmann 1870–1956: Architect and Designer*, Fischer Fine Art Gallery, London, 1977; *Frühes Industriedesign: Wien 1900–1908*, Galerie Nächst St. Stephan, Vienna, 1977. Recipient: Honor Award, City of Vienna, 1950. Honorary doctorates: Technische Hochschule, Dresden, Berlin, and Vienna. Honorary Member, Akademie der Künste, Vienna and Berlin. Commander, Légion d'Honneur, France, 1926. *Died* (in Vienna) *8 May 1956.*

Works:

1898 Ver Sacrum Salon, *Sezession Exhibition*, Gartenbaugesellschaft Palace, Vienna
      Secretariat, Sezession Building, Vienna (building by Joseph Olbrich)
      Pollak House interiors, Atzgersdorf, Lower Austria
1899 Wooden Exhibition Pavilion, in the courtyard of the Austrian Museum for Art and Industry, Vienna
      Kurzweil Studio interior, Vienna
      Apollo Candle Shop, Vienna
      Brix Office interiors, Vienna
      P. Wittgenstein Hunting Lodge, Bergerhöhe, Lower Austria
1899/
1902 Exhibition designs for the Sezession, Vienna
1900 Mahogany dining-room, *World's Fair*, Paris
1900/
  01 Wittgenstein Foresters' Office and Housing, Hohenberg, Lower Austria
1901/
  03 Kolo Moser House, Hohe Warte, Vienna

      Karl Moll House, Hohe Warte, Vienna
      Henneberg House, Hohe Warte, Vienna
      Spitzer House, Hohe Warte, Vienna
1902 Klinger Salon, *XIV Sezession Exhibition*, Vienna
      Sezession Room, *Art Exhibition*, Dusseldorf
      Poldihütte Steelworkers' Hostel, Kladno, Bohemia, now Czechoslovakia
      Hochstätter House interiors, Vienna
      Mauthner Apartment interiors, Vienna
      Wärndorfer House interiors, Vienna
      Biach Apartment interiors, Vienna
      Koller House interiors, Vienna
1903 Church, Hohenberg, Lower Austria
      Knips House, Seeboden, Kärnten, Austria
      Wiener Werkstätte Headquarters interiors, Neustiftgasse, Vienna
      Design of the *Wiener Werkstätte Exhibition*, Vienna (with Kolo Moser)
1904 Design of the *Wiener Werkstätte Exhibition*, Hirschwald Applied Arts House, Berlin
1904/
  06 Sanatorium, Purkersdorf, Lower Austria
1905/
  06 Beer-Hofmann House, Vienna
1905/
  11 Stoclet House, Brussels
1906 Kohn Tomb, Vienna
1906/
  07 Wittgenstein Hunting Lodge, Hochreith, near Hohenberg, Lower Austria
1907 Hochstätter House, Hohe Warte, Vienna
      Hamburger Apartment interiors, Vienna
      Fledermaus Theatre/Cabaret, Vienna
      Johann Strauss Tomb, Vienna (project)
      Music Pavilion on the River Danube, Vienna (project)
      Wiener Werkstätte Shop, Graben, Vienna
      Building Complex for the 1908 *Austrian Applied Arts Jubilee*, Vienna (project)
1908 Pavilion for the Emperor's Jubilee (project)
      Temporary building for the *Kunstschau*, Vienna
1909 Sales Room, State Printing House, Vienna
      Pickler House alterations and interiors, Budapest
      Knips Apartment interiors, Vienna
      H. Böhler Apartment interiors, Vienna
      H. Böhler House remodelling and interiors, Baden, Lower Austria
      C. Böhler House, Kapfenberg, Austria
      Moll House II, Vienna
1910 Böhler Company Theatre, Kapfenberg, Austria (project)
      Legler House, Döbling, Vienna
1910/
  11 Ast House, Hohe Warte, Vienna
1911 Austrian Pavilion, *International Art Exhibition*, Rome
      Hanak Salon, *Dresden Art Exhibition*
      Stoclet Tomb, Brussels
      Marlow Apartment interiors, Vienna
      Steckelberg Apartment interiors, Vienna
1912 Graben Coffee House, Vienna
      Austrian Pavilion, *Art Exhibition*, Venice (project)
      Ast Tomb, Vienna
      Zuckerkandl Apartment interiors, Vienna
      Josef Hoffmann House renovations and interiors, Pirnitz, Moravia, now Brtnice, Czechoslovakia
      Böhler Tomb, Kapfenberg, Austria
      Cellar Bar, Hotel Pitter, Salzburg
      Koller House renovations, Oberwaltersdorf, Lower Austria
      Koller House interiors, Vienna
1912/
  14 Poldihütte Steelworks Office remodelling, Vienna
      Bernatzik House, Hohe Warte, Vienna
      Wellesz House, Kaasgraben, Vienna
      Botstieber House, Kaasgraben, Vienna
      Vetter House, Kaasgraben, Vienna

Yella Herzka House, Kaasgraben, Vienna
Küper House, Kaasgraben, Vienna
Drucker House, Kaasgraben, Vienna
Hodler Apartment interiors, Geneva
Gallia Apartment interiors, Vienna
Förster Tomb, Vienna

1913/
14 Günther Wagner Company Building, Vienna
(project)
Design of the *Bugra Graphic Arts Exhibition*,
Leipzig
Primavesi Bank renovations, Olmütz,
Moravia, now Olomouc, Czechoslovakia
Austrian Pavilion, *Werkbund Exhibition*,
Cologne

1913/
15 Skywa (Panzer) House, Heitzing, Vienna
Primavesi House, Winkelsdorf, Moravia, now
Kouty, Czechoslovakia
1915 H. Böhler House interiors, Munich
Gödl-Olajossy Apartment interiors, Linz,
Austria
1916 Knips Apartment interiors, Vienna
Zuckerkandl Apartment interiors, Vienna
P. Wittgenstein Apartment interiors, Vienna

1916/
17 Salesroom, Fashion Department, Wiener
Werkstätte, Vienna
1917 Böhler Studio, Vienna
Display cases for porcelain, for P. Wittgenstein Jr., Vienna
Exhibitions for Copenhagen and Stockholm
(projects)
Palace of World Peace, Stockholm (project)

1917/
18 E. Böhler Apartment interiors, Vienna
Town Hall reconstruction, Ortelsburg, now
Czczytno, Poland (project)

1917/
19 Poldihütte Steelworks Buildings corrections,
Komotau and Kladno, Bohemia, now
Czechoslovakia
1918 Primavesi Apartment interiors, Vienna
Berstel Apartment interiors, Wiener Neu-
stadt, Vienna
Steiner Tomb, Vienna
Displays, *Trade Fair*, Leipzig
Pazzani Palace, Vienna
1919 Hamburger Tomb, Freudenthal, now Brun-
tal, Czechoslovakia
Knips House, Vienna (project)

1919/
20 Knips Tomb, Vienna
1920 Convalescent Home remodelling, Gross-
Ullersdorf, Moravia, now Velke Losiny,
Czechoslovakia
Gamekeeper's Cottage for Dr. Pazzani, Ad-
mont, Austria (project)
Hostel and Bank, Novi-Sad, Serbia, Yugoslavia (project)
Cafe/Restaurant, Laxenburg, Austria (project)

1920/
22 Pazzani House alterations, Pichl, Steiermark,
Austria
Berl House, Freudenthal, now Bruntal, Czech-
oslovakia
F. Grohmann House, Würbenthal, now
Vrbno pod Praded, Czechoslovakia
Bernatzik Apartment interiors, in the Ast
House, Hohe Warte, Vienna
Gallia Apartment interiors, Vienna
1921 Hotel, Zagreb (project)
1922 K. Grohmann House interiors, Pochmühl,
Silesia, now Czechoslovakia
G. Nebehay Building Entrance Doors and
Shop, Vienna

1922/
23 Dunckel House, Budapest
Baru Apartment interiors, Vienna
1923 Grohmann Company Offices, Würbenthal,
now Vrbno pod Praded, Czechoslovakia
Josef Hoffmann Apartment interiors, Vienna

Josef Hoffmann: Stoclet House, Brussels, 1911

Baron Bachofen-Echt House, Vienna (pro-
ject)
Heller House, Vienna (project)
Grohmann Company Workers' Housing,
Würbenthal, now Vrbno pod Praded, Cze-
choslovakia

1923/
24 Ast House, Velden on the Wörthersee,
Austria

1924/
25 Knips House, Döbling, Vienna
1925 Public housing, Felix Mottl Strasse, Vienna
Public housing, Stromstrasse, Vienna
Austrian Pavilion, *Exposition des Arts
Décoratifs*, Paris
1928 Design of the *Viennese Applied Arts Jubilee
Exhibition*
Sarmej Office Building, Cluj, Rumania
Altmann and Kühne Pastry Shop, Vienna
Record shop, Vienna
Sanatorium, Salzburg (project)
Pre-fabricated house in steel, Vienna
1929 Design of the *Austrian Werkbund Exhibition*,
Vienna

1929/
30 Grand Palace of Art, Karlplatz, Vienna (project)

1930 Lengyel House interiors, Bratislava, Czecho-
slovakia
Central Room and Coffee Terrace, *Werkbund
Exhibition*, Vienna
Austrian Section, *International Exhibition*,
Stockholm
Graben Cafe/Restaurant remodelling, Vienna
Railway carriage interiors for Austrian Railways
Otto Wagner Monument, Vienna
1932 Four low-cost terraced houses, Werkbund
Estate, Vienna
Public housing, Laxenburgerstrasse, Vienna
1934 Austrian Pavilion, *Biennale*, Venice
1935 Austrian Pavilion, *World's Fair*, Brussels
(project)
1936 Austrian Pavilion, *World's Fair*, Paris (project)
1937 Boudoir for a Great Actress, *World's Fair*,
Paris
1938 Hanak Museum, Augarten, Vienna (project)

1939/
44 German Officers' Club, Vienna
1940 Reinforced concrete monumental bridges
across the Danube Canal, Vienna (projects)

365

1945 Low-cost terraced housing (project)
 Low-cost housing in circular layout (project)
1950 Public housing, Blechturmgasse, Vienna
1952 Public housing, Silbergasse, Vienna (with Josef Kalbac)
1954 Public housing, Heiligenstätterstrasse, Vienna (with Josef Kalbac)

Publications:

On HOFFMANN: books—*Josef Hoffmann* by Leopold Kleiner, Berlin, Leipzig and Vienna 1927; *Josef Hoffmann* by Armand Weiser, Geneva 1930; *Josef Hoffmann zum 60. Geburtstag,* edited by the Austrian Werkbund, Vienna 1930; *Josef Hoffmann* by L. W. Rochowanski, Vienna 1950; *Josef Hoffmann* by Giulia Veronesi, Milan 1956; *Josef Hoffmann 1870–1956: Architect and Designer,* exhibition catalogue, by Eduard F. Sekler and Robert Judson Clark, London 1977; *Frühes Industriedesign: Wien 1900–1908,* exhibition catalogue, by O. Oberhuber and J. Hummel, Vienna 1977; articles—"Josef Hoffmann 1870–1920" by Max Eisler in *Wendingen* (Amsterdam), nos. 8/9, 1920; "The Work of Josef Hoffmann" by Peter Behrens in *Architecture* (London), no. 2, 1923; "Josef Hoffmann und seine Schule" in *Moderne Bauformen* (Stuttgart), no. 26, 1927; "Josef Hoffmann, maestro dimenticato" by Vittoria Girardi in *L'Architettura* (Rome), October 1956; "Josef Hoffmann und die Wiener Werkstätte" by Günther Feuerstein in *Der Aufbau* (Vienna), April/May 1964; "Josef Hoffmann 1938–1945" by Othmar Birkner in *Werk* (Zurich), October 1967; special issue of *Alte und Moderne Kunst* (Vienna), November/December 1970; "Gli schizzi del viaggio in Italia di Josef Hoffmann" by Eduard F. Sekler in *Artisti Austriaci a Roma,* exhibition catalogue, Rome 1972; "Little Square Hoffmann" by Peter Vergo in *Architectural Review* (London), December 1977.

For many readers it will be a surprise to discover that half a century ago a critic could write "No recent architect has influenced Europe more comprehensively than Hoffmann" (*Architectural Forum,* November 1928). In the meantime many of his buildings have been drastically altered or pulled down, and little has been written about the historic significance of his contribution as a prodigious inventor of forms. There are personal, doctrinal and typological reasons for this neglect.

As a person, Josef Hoffmann was full of inhibitions and distrustful of the intellectual approach to the arts. He disliked discussions about architecture and did not formulate a body of theory to go with his works; in this respect he differed from his teacher Otto Wagner or his more articulate and aggressive contemporary and competitor Adolf Loos. As far as types of buildings are concerned, he built none that were in the public eye or the focus of public discussion except for some short-lived exhibition pavilions such as those at Rome (1911), Cologne (1914), and Paris (1925). Instead, he designed primarily houses and their furnishings for artistically inclined clients who valued privacy more than publicity. His largest commission was the sumptuous and much admired Stoclet House in Brussels. As far as architectural doctrine is concerned, Hoffmann's oeuvre did not fit easily into any of the great movements of the period, from Bauhaus to CIAM; the Secession movement to which he belonged at the outset of his career remained a local development and moreover soon had run its course.

Much of Hoffmann's creative energy over almost thirty years went into running the "Wiener Werkstätte," the workshops for artistic craftsmanship he had helped to found in 1903. But to some critics his unfaltering belief in artistic craftsmanship seemed anachronistic in an age of rapid industrialisation. Moreover, he mostly worked for a vanishing stratum of Austrian society: the rich, liberal, often Jewish, haute bourgeoisie. Thus his temporary eclipse becomes understandable.

Hoffmann's architectural activity can be divided into at least five periods. After a brief initial infatuation with curvilinear Art Nouveau, which found expression in such works as the Bergerhöhe interiors and the Apollo candle shop, he evolved a mode of expression more truly his own and created a more restrained architecture based on rectilinearity, a predilection for the square and a preference for the colors of white and black against which a few accents of ornament and chromatic color were set off to greatest advantage. The Purkersdorf Sanatorium best illustrates this phase. In tune with developments in the rest of Central Europe, Hoffmann then turned to a reformulation of classicist and folkloristic themes and at the same time relied on increasingly rich schemes of decoration by means of a very personal kind of ornament, as in the Ast, Primavesi (at Winkelsdorf), Berl and Knips Houses.

Then the impact of the Modern Movement in its "classic phase" was duly felt in a number of designs from the late 1920's and early 1930's, some of them, such as the Altmann and Kühne shop, joint designs with his chief assistant and head of office, Oswald Härdtl. Finally, during Hoffmann's old age, there is a last phase with a few designs done during the Nazi regime and with a few post-war housing schemes done in partnership with others. During the later periods Hoffmann built comparatively little, but he never ceased to pour out highly decorative designs for textiles, wall papers, ceramics, table ware and furniture, even when there was no actual commission.

Hoffmann's best creations are characterized by an unfailing sense of form and color and often by a delightful playfulness and ease of presence, which, however, turns out to be perfectly compatible with great restraint and at times puristic severity and with a directness of formal and functional solution that may impart a deceptive air of simplicity. As an architectural draftsman Hoffmann was a master, especially when it came to making small, dramatically foreshortened perspective sketches that convincingly summed up a building's three-dimensional characteristics.

From 1899 till 1936 Hoffmann was professor at the Vienna School (now Academy) of Applied Arts, and there as well as in his private office he made it a point to encourage and promote young talents—among them Charles Edouard Jeanneret to whom he offered a position. "Les oeuvres de Hoffmann étaient pour moi l'expression la plus lumineuse de l'évolution architecturale," Le Corbusier remembered in 1928. Fifty years later many others are beginning to rediscover Hoffmann. Forms of his architecture seem to reverberate in recent Italian designs, patterns from the "Wiener Werkstätte" turn up in modern fashion design, Hoffmann furniture fetches high prices in the art market, and some pieces are back in production as facsimiles. Considering the abundance of Hoffmann's formal invention and the sensuous appeal of his colors, textures and forms, it was almost inevitable that he would be rediscovered by the leading architects of of today with their renewed interest in the pursuit of pure form.

—Eduard F. Sekler

HOLDEN, Sir Charles (Henry).

British. Born in Lancashire, 12 May 1875. Educated at the Manchester Institute of Technology, 1893–96; articled to E. W. Leeson, 1896–97, and C. R. Ashbee, London, 1898. Married to Margaret Macdonald. Entered the office of the architect H. Percy Adams, London, 1899: Partner, 1907; firm known as Adams, Holden and (J.L.) Pearson from 1913. Member, War Graves Commission, 1918–22; Member, Royal Fine Art Commission, 1933–47; Vice-President, Royal Institute of British Architects, 1935–37.

Recipient: Soane Medal, 1896; Godwin Bursary, 1913; Bronze Medal, 1929, and Gold Medal, 1936, Royal Institute of British Architects. D.Litt.: University of Manchester, 1936; University of London, 1946. Associate, 1906, and Fellow, 1921, of the Royal Institute of British Architects; Royal Designer for Industry, 1943. *Died 1 May 1960.*

Works:

1903 Belgrave Hospital for Children, Clapham Road, Kennington, London
1904 Library Block, Law Society Building, Chancery Lane, London
 Norwich House, 127–129 High Holborn, London
1906 King Edward VII Sanatorium, Midhurst, Sussex
 Central Library, Bristol
 British Medical Association, 429 Strand, London (now Rhodesia House)
1910 Evelyn House, 62 Oxford Street, London
1911 Royal Infirmary, Marlborough Hill, Bristol
1914 Queen Mary's Hostel, Duchess of Bedford Walk, Notting Hill, London
 Sutton Valence School and Chapel, Kent
1920 War Memorials, for the War Graves Commission, in Northern France
1922/
39 London Underground Stations: 1922, Oval, Westminster, Bond Street, St. Paul's, Mansion House; 1925, Clapham South; 1928, Balham, Piccadilly Circus, Leicester Square, Tooting Bec, Tooting Broadway, Colliers Wood, South Wimbledon, Morden, Ealing Common, Hounslow West; 1932, Sudbury Town, Sudbury Hill, Alperton, Manor House, Turnpike Lane, Bounds Green, Wood Green, Arnos Grove, Southgate; 1934, Oakwood (formerly Enfield West), Cockfosters, Chiswick Park, Acton Town, Northfields, Boston Manor, Osterley, Rayners Lane, Hammersmith; 1939, East Finchley
1929 London Passenger Transport Board Headquarters, 55 Broadway, London S.W.1
1931 Empire Marketing Board Stand, *British Industries Fair,* London (with C. H. James)
1936/
40 London University Complex, phase I, including Senate House (1936), Tower for Bookstacks (1937), and Institute of Education and Historical Research (1938)
1946 Plan for the South Bank, London (project)
 Plan for the City of London (project; with William Holford)
1948/
55 London University Complex, phase II

Publications:

By HOLDEN: papers—*The Conditions Influencing Contemporary Architecture* (London Passenger Transport Board publication), London 1930; *The City of London: A Record of Destruction and Survival,* with William Holford, London 1947.

On HOLDEN: books—*Edwardian Architecture* by A. Service, London 1977; *Charles Holden: Underground Architect* by Gerald Adler (unpublished M.A. thesis), University of Sheffield 1978; articles—"Patient Progress: The Life Work of Frank Pick" by Nikolaus Pevsner in *Architectural Review* (London), September 1942; "Singing the Body Electric with Charles Holden" by B. Hanson in *Architectural Review* (London), December 1975; "Charles Holden" by G. Middleton in *Architectural Association Quarterly* (London), vol. 8, no. 2, 1976.

Of much significance for the prevailing character of Sir Charles Holden's architectural designs is that he

Sir Charles Holden: London Passenger Transport Board Headquarters, 1929

ward to form the spine of the various university buildings branching east and west, with the squarish massive blocks of Senate House at the southern end. The great square tower to house the books stacks of the library rises above the spine just north of Senate House. Heavy load bearing walls of stone and brick (of which there is long experience) were employed, as the building is designed to last for hundreds of years. The result is a heavy, massive, monumental building with, in the context of the design, a seemingly unavoidable monotony of windows.

The interior is more effective, for something of the dignity and repose associated with the architecture of ancient Greece has been recaptured, particularly in the ceremonial hall of Senate House. The Greek atmosphere pervades the entrance hall with its coffered ceiling and bronze bowls along the walls, with sconces for indirect lighting at night. The feeling that ancient Greece was the cradle of culture no doubt prompted these visual reminiscences. The question arises whether a heavy monumental building of this kind can so easily be adapted to changes in educational methods as could a more flexible structure. In the work of Charles Holden the massive, static and monumental, often excellent in design, is perpetuated into our era, an era with an accent on change.

—Arnold Whittick

HOLFORD, William Graham (Lord Holford).
British. Born in Johannesburg, South Africa, 22 March 1907. Educated at The Diocesan College, Johannesburg (also student apprentice in the architectural office of Cowin, Powers and Ellis, Johannesburg) 1920–24; Liverpool School of Architecture, under Charles Reilly and Patrick Abercrombie, 1925–30, B.Arch. (first class honours) 1930; worked in the office of Voorhees, Gmelin and Walker, New York, 1929 (American Society of Arts and Sciences Scholar); attended British School in Rome, 1930–33 (Royal Institute of British Architects Rome Scholar). Married Marjorie Brooks in 1933. In private practice, as architect and town planner, Liverpool, 1933–46, and London, 1946 until his death, 1975. Architect to the North Eastern Trading Estates, England, 1935; Chief Architect for Wartime Hostels, U.K. Ministry of Supply, 1941; Member, Reconstruction Secretariat, U.K. Ministry of Works, 1942; Chief Technical Officer, U.K. Ministry of Town and Country Planning, 1943; Planning Consultant, City of London, 1946–48, University of Liverpool, 1946–55, County of Cambridge, 1948–53, City of Pretoria, South Africa, 1948–49, Corby New Town Development Corporation, Northamptonshire, 1950–54, and the Government of Australia, 1951–57; Architect and Consultant, University College of the Southwest, later University of Exeter, 1954–58; Consultant Architect, Piccadilly Redevelopment, London, 1960, and University of Nottingham, 1960. Lecturer in Architecture, 1933–36, and Lever Professor of Civic Design, 1936–46, University of Liverpool; Professor of Town Planning, 1947–70, and Professor Emeritus, 1970–75, University College, University of London; Romanes Lecturer, Oxford University, 1969. Member of the Council, 1938–39, Vice-President, 1951–52, and President, 1960–62, Royal Institute of British Architects; Member, Royal Fine Art Commission, 1943–69; Chairman, Advisory Committee on Buildings of Architectural and Historic Interest, 1952–75; President, Royal Town Planning Institute, 1953–54; Trustee, British Museum, 1969–75; Treasurer, Royal Academy of Arts, 1970–75; Director, Leverhulme Trust, 1972–75. Recipient: Florence Bursary, Royal Institute of British Architects, 1935; Gold Medal, Royal Town Planning Institute, 1961; Gold Medal, RIBA, 1963. D.C.L.: University of Durham,

began practice at about the time that the revival of historical styles was coming to an end and serious architects were looking for an architecture that was expressive of contemporary life. One of the somewhat negative manifestations of this trend was a strong movement towards simplicity and a getting rid of the debris of historical ornament before starting afresh. The greater prominence of structural engineering in the media of steel and concrete facilitated this evolution.

In his early years as a student and then as an assistant to H. Percy Adams, Holden was, in some buildings, associated with mediaeval effects of roofs and windows, but these were soon abandoned when he became a responsible partner in the firm: he essayed designs with rectangular massing and a general simplicity sometimes faulted by contemporary critics as being unusually severe. A significant early example is the Royal Infirmary in Bristol. Here the squarish treatment, broad and massive, seemed at the time severe and simple, yet it carried a stylistic reminiscence in the Ionic columns of the upper portions. If the ornament of bases and capitals disappeared in his later buildings, the Greek-like forms of a lintel architecture with the serenity of balanced verticals and horizontals remained and was a dominating character in all of his work. An even better

early example is the fine British Medical Association Building in The Strand, London, where the feeling for stone in the exterior design is strong.

Although well known for his simple and effective London Underground stations, Holden is most likely to be chiefly remembered for the important and impressive London Passenger Transport Board Headquarters and for the London University Complex in Bloomsbury. In both these works a classic dignity and even monumental grandeur are apparent, yet Holden always endeavoured to reconcile these attributes with functional building. In the design of the Passenger Transport Board Headquarters, which had to be combined with St. James Station, the convenience of passengers was carefully studied, together with the convenient disposition of offices. The result was a cross-shaped plan which, in his own words, made possible "good light, no interference with neighbour light, short corridors, and a compact centre containing all services, complete with lifts and staircase communicating directly with all four wings." Above the seven storeys the four arms build up a satisfying sequence of diminishing masses to the central tower. A few accents of sculpture relieve the general simple treatment.

In the London University Complex the central axis of the British Museum was continued north-

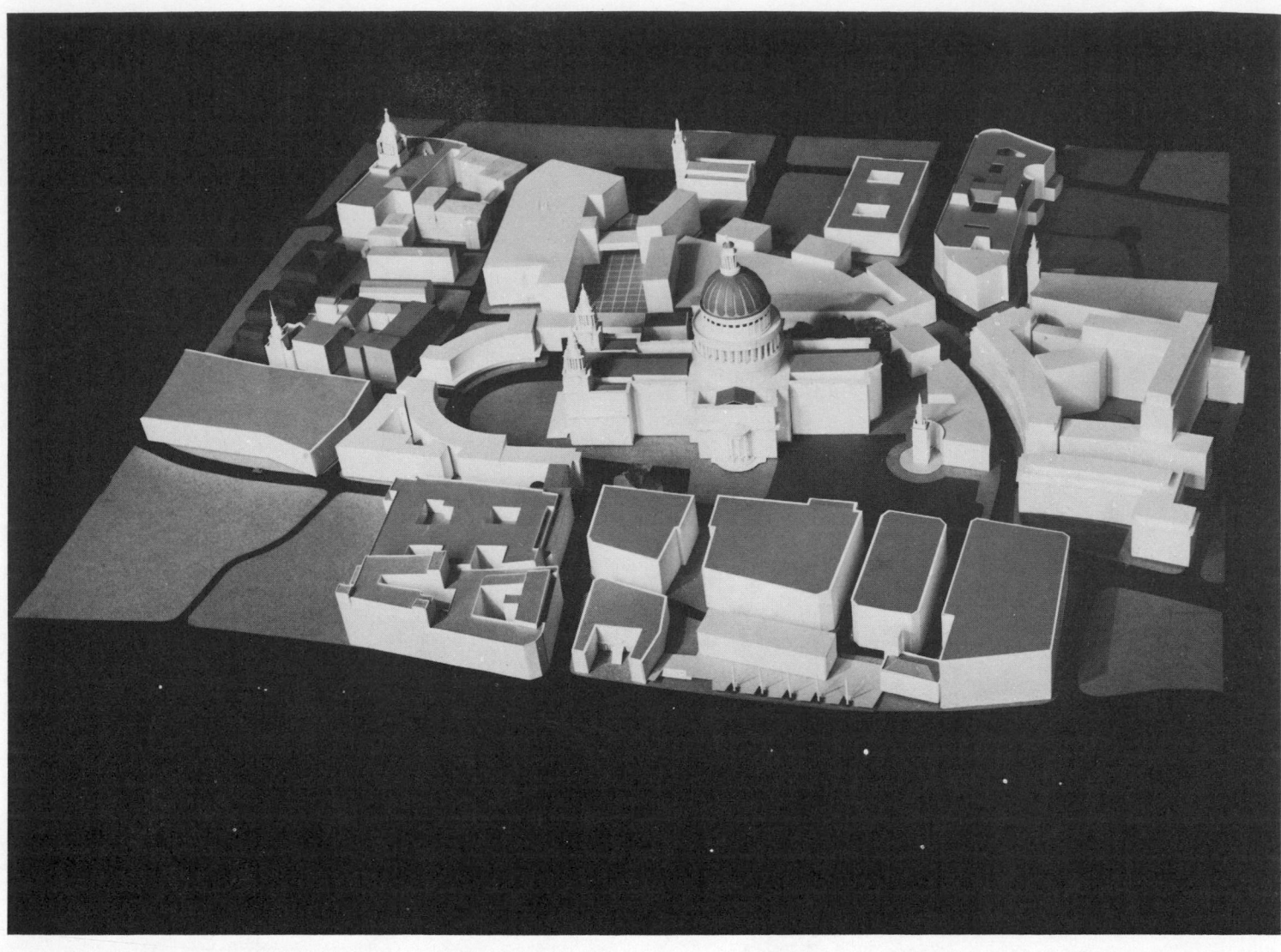

William Graham Holford: City of London Development, 1947 (model)

1960; LL.D.: University of Liverpool, 1961; D.Litt.: Oxford University, 1964; University of Exeter, 1968; Honorary Fellow, University College London, 1973. Associate, 1932, and Fellow, 1948, Royal Institute of British Architects; Fellow, Institute of Landscape Architects, and Royal Town Planning Institute; Associate of the Royal Academy, 1961, and Royal Academician, 1968. Knight Bachelor, 1953; Life Peer, 1965. *Died* (in London) *17 October 1975.*

Works:

1939   Royal Ordnance Factory, Kirby, Lancashire
1941   Wartime hostels for the U.K. Ministry of Supply
1941/
  45   Team Valley Industrial Estate, near Newcastle upon Tyne
1946/
  47   Development plans for the City of London
1949   Development plan for the University of Liverpool
    City plan for Pretoria, South Africa
    Liverpool Playhouse Theatre interiors
    War Memorial, Eton College, Buckinghamshire
1950   Regional plan for Cambridgeshire
    Courtyard, Kings College, Cambridge
    Bodley's Building Extension, Kings College, Cambridge
1950/
  60   House conversions, Eton College, Buckinghamshire
1951   Plan for Corby New Town, Northamptonshire

1952   Town centre plan for Corby New Town, Northamptonshire
1953   Nuclear Physics Complex, University of Liverpool
1954   Revised development plan for the University of Liverpool
    Market Square and Housing, Corby New Town, Northamptonshire
1955/
  56   Foundation Buildings restoration, Eton College, Buckinghamshire
1955/
  75   Development plan for the University of Exeter, Devon
1956   Study of St. Paul's Cathedral Precinct, London
1957   Development plan for Canberra, Australia
1958   Science Schools, Eton College, Buckinghamshire
    Queen's Building, Refectory and Union Building, University of Exeter, Devon
    King's Avenue Bridge, Commonwealth Avenue Bridge, and Central Parkway, Canberra, Australia (with W. H. Maunsell and Partners)
    Plan for the University of Kent, Canterbury
1960/
  70   Administration and Senate Chamber Buildings, University of Exeter
    Jeremiah Ambler Factory, Peterlee, Durham
    Woolworth Building, Cornmarket, Oxford
    Farrer House, Eton College, Buckinghamshire
    High-rise flats and maisonettes, Kensal New Town, London

    Villiers House, Eton College, Buckinghamshire
    Barclays Bank, Maidstone, Kent
    Wholesale Market, Sheffield
    Housing, Gidea Park, Icklesham, Sussex
    Courtyards, King's College, Cambridge
    Viaduct and Queenhill Bridge, Gloucestershire
    Narrows Bridge, Perth, Western Australia (with W. H. Maunsell and Partners)
1961   Redevelopment plan for Piccadilly Circus, London
    Government Offices, Bridge Street, Westminster, London (project)
    Science Buildings, Oxford University (project)
    Chapel Ceiling, Eton College, Buckinghamshire
1962   Library, Tonbridge School, Kent
    Memorial Cloister, Overbury, Gloucestershire
1964/
  67   Conversion of four houses in Carlton House Terrace, London, for the Royal Society
1969/
  75   Buildings for Lloyds Register of Shipping, City of London
1970   Royal Liverpool Hospital

Publications:

By HOLFORD: books—*The Future of Merseyside,* with W. A. Eden, Liverpool 1937; *The City of London: A Record of Destruction and Survival,* with C. H. Holden, London 1947; *Cambridge Planning*

Proposals, Cambridge 1950; *Design in Town and Village,* with Frederick Gibberd and Thomas Sharp, London 1953; *The Future of Canberra,* Canberra 1958; *Land Use in an Urban Environment,* with others, Liverpool 1961; *Our Heritage of Landscape and Building,* Bristol 1975.

On HOLFORD: articles—"Sir William Holford" in *The Architects' Journal* (London), 17 January 1957; "Man at the Hub of the Circus" by Robert Harling in *The Sunday Times* (London), 8 October 1961; "Sir William Holford Answers Six Questions" in *Official Architecture and Planning* (London), January 1962; "Profile '67: Lord Holford: To Hell with Talking" by Ivor Herbert in the *Evening News* (London), 19 January 1967; "Anatomy of an Architect" by Leslie Jerman in *The Scotsman* (Edinburgh), 19 January 1968; "Obituary" by John Summerson and others in *Building Design* (London), 24 October 1975; "Obituary" by Bernard Collins in *The Planner* (London), December 1975; "Obituary" by Lord Esher in *RIBA Journal* (London), January 1976.

William Holford was born in South Africa and trained as an architect under the noted Professor Charles Reilly at the School of Architecture, Liverpool. He was a brilliant student: he obtained a first class honours degree and won the Rome Scholarship in Architecture in 1930. In 1933 he commenced his long teaching career, first at Liverpool as Lever Professor and later, in 1947, as Professor of Town Planning at University College London.

During the war years Holford was instrumental, with Lord Silkin, in laying down the framework of British town planning legislation and administration, which has since been followed by many other countries throughout the world. His wartime architectural work included the vast Team Valley Industrial Estate near Newcastle upon Tyne: it was the first major large-scale industrial scheme and became the model for many subsequent industrial estates.

Holford was closely associated with Abercrombie's County and Greater London Plans; he also prepared plans for the City of London, Cambridge, and Corby New Town, as well as special reports on St. Paul's precinct and Piccadilly Circus. His planning work extended to Australia (where he replanned the capital, Canberra), South Africa, Brazil, and other parts of the world. He was particularly interested in university planning, and his development plan for the University of Liverpool in 1949 was the first of its kind in Britain and became the prototype for university campus design throughout the world. As an architect he was able to put his plans into practice at the University of Exeter and at the new University of Kent in Canterbury.

He was an early exponent of modular design, and his 14-storey block of flats at Kensal, London, was the first large-scale modular building.

William Holford's skill as an adviser and administrator in all matters concerning art, architecture and town planning was always in great demand, and his involvement in professional affairs took much of his time and energy. He held the Presidency of both the Royal Institute of British Architects and the Royal Town Planning Institute, and received the Gold Medals of both institutions. The many honours and awards, both in Britain and overseas, which marked his career in architecture and town planning, culminated in the award of a life peerage in 1965.

It has been said that William Holford "came as near as the modern world permits to being one of the artist-craftsmen of the Renaissance who tried to master all branches of knowledge." He was a brilliant speaker, a convincing writer, a gifted administrator, and a skilful draughtsman (he originally intended to be a professional artist); he was even a good amateur actor. With his death in 1975 at the age of 68 the world of architecture and town planning lost a practical pioneer who had, by his personal tact, charm and brilliance, established standards and guidelines that have left a mark on the cities of the world and have helped to make that world a more pleasant place in which to live and work. Holford was, in every sense, a great man.

—Edward D. Mills

HOLLEIN, Hans.

Austrian. Born in Vienna in 1934. Educated at the Academy of Graphic Arts, Vienna, graduated 1956; Illinois Institute of Technology, Chicago, 1958–59; University of California, Berkeley, 1959–60, M.Arch. 1960. Worked in various architectural offices in Australia, South America, Sweden, and Germany, 1960–64. In private practice, Vienna, since 1964. Professor, Academy of Art, Dusseldorf, since 1970. Editor, *Bau,* Vienna, since 1965. Exhibitions: *Hans Hollein/Walter Pichler, Architektur,* Galerie Nächst St. Stephan, Vienna, 1963; *Triennale,* Milan, 1968; *Hans Hollein: Work and Behavior, Life and Death, Everyday Situations,* at the *Biennale,* Venice, 1972. Address (office): Argentinierstrasse 36, 1040 Vienna 4, Austria.

Works:

1963/
64 University Theatre, St. Louis (project)
1965 Retti Candle Shop, Kohlmarkt, Vienna
1966 Savings Bank, Florisdorf, Vienna (project)
Design of the *Selection 66* exhibition, Osterreichisches Museum für Angewandte Kunst, Vienna
1967 Christa Metek Boutique, Vienna
1968 Austrian Pavilion, *Triennale,* Milan
1969/
72 Carl F. Von Siemens Foundation Headquarters, Nymphenburg, Germany
1970 Richard Feigen Gallery, New York
Olivetti Building, Amsterdam
1972 Guest Rooms, Siemens Headquarters, Wittelsbacher Platz, Munich
1974 Schullin Jewellery Shop, Vienna
Villa Strozzi Museum conversion, Florence (project)
Development plan for the Municipal Square District, Vienna
Museum of Modern Art, Monchengladbach, Germany (project)
Principal Room, Sigmund Freud Museum, Vienna (project)
1976 Church in the Mountains, Turracher Höhe, Austria
Design of the *Man Transforms* exhibition, Cooper-Hewitt Museum, New York
1978 Austrian Tourist Office, Vienna

Publications:

By HOLLEIN: book—*Global Architecture 47: Otto Wagner,* with Yukio Futagawa, Tokyo 1978; articles—"Hans Hollein: A Biographic Interview," with Federico Correa in *Arquitecturas Bis* (Barcelona), November 1975; "Everything Is Architecture" in *Bauen und Wohnen* (Zurich), April 1976; "Position and Move" in *Space Design* (Tokyo), April 1976; "Church in the Mountains at Turracher Höhe" in *Kunst und Kirche* (Linz, Austria), February 1977.

On HOLLEIN: books—*Hans Hollein/Walter Pichler, Architektur,* exhibition catalogue, by Joseph Esherick, Vienna 1963; *Hans Hollein: Work and Behavior, Life and Death, Everyday Situations,* exhibition catalogue, Venice 1972; articles—"Hans Hollein and Walter Pichler—Forms and Designs" by Joseph Esherick in *Arts and Architecture* (Los Angeles), August 1963; "Keyhole Shop" in *Architectural Forum* (New York), June 1966; "Mobili nel Museo" in *Domus* (Milan), March 1967; "Architectural Fabergé" in *Progressive Architecture* (New York), February 1970; "Richard Feigen and Company: Hans Hollein's Design for a New York Gallery" in *Architectural Design* (London), March 1970; "A View of Contemporary World Architecture: Hans Hollein" in *The Japan Architect* (Tokyo), July 1970; "Vienna Orchestra" by Franco Raggi in *Casabella* (Milan), August/September 1974; "Municipal Museum, Abteiberg, Monchengladbach" and "Two Projects for the Conversion and Extension of the Villa Strozzi, Florence" in *Baumeister* (Munich), May 1975; "Man Transforms: The Opening Exhibition of the Cooper-Hewitt Museum, New York" in *Space Design* (Tokyo), December 1976; "Austrian Tourist Office in Vienna" in *Baumeister* (Munich), February 1979.

Hans Hollein is one of the few Vienna-born architects who have successfully derived a dialectical creative advantage from a combination of detachment from, and an intimate knowledge of, the city's culture. Although experience of American plurality of style and the almost uncontrolled treatment of architectonic phenomena were certainly of importance to Hollein's development, his work would be inconceivable without reference to the aesthetic precision and the semantic spectrum of Viennese historicism and the Secession.

At the beginning of the 1960's, Hollein, together with Walter Pichler, began actively criticizing Functionalism, not only verbally but also with sketches and projects that brought about a broader and more comprehensive understanding of architectonic and extra-architectonic phenomena. The theoretically untenable, almost tautological, extension of the architectural idea—"everything is architecture"—nevertheless proved to be a useful vehicle with which to get away from the trap of Functionalism and to discover a crucial theme for his subsequent works. The success of the small Retti Candle Shop consisted not only in its aesthetic complexity but also, and more precisely, in its new interpretation of a functional problem. It is an apparent paradox of his methods that Hollein's works arrive at a sort of Super-Functionalism, modified by a complex view of the building problem and an aesthetic demonstration of its contents.

From a Viennese standpoint, it is difficult to be fair to Hollein. There is, in Vienna, too much experience, and too developed a sensibility, of substitutes for reality. Since the Baroque era, possibly because of the Hapsburg's firm suppression of literature, the ambivalence of music or architecture has been favored for the staging of semblances of reality, extending even to the reflection of individual or collective psychic states. The funeral cortèges and festive processions of the Hapsburgs were forerunners of the "staging of the downfall" of the aristocratic-bourgeois world, prior to the First World War, accomplished primarily within the Secession. Vienna has its tradition of aesthetizing and equalizing realities—a kind of domestic repression. Assembly, collage, and the alteration of old meanings through new relationships are cultivated in media other than just language.

Hans Hollein seems not only to personify this tradition but, as well, to exaggerately express it. Otto Wagner, Sigmund Freud, Adolf Loos and Ludwig Wittgenstein have not altered the situation—they are merely new figures in the game of ambiguity. This background seems visible again in Hans Hollein's works, and he also possesses the technical skill with which to depict it.

—Friedrich Achleitner

HOLZBAUER, Wilhelm.

Austrian. Born in Salzburg, 3 September 1930. Educated at the Technical College, Salzburg, 1946–50; Academy of Fine Arts, Vienna, under Clemens Holzmeister, 1950–53 (Golden Füger Medal, 1952; Austrian State Student Prize, 1953), Dip.Arch. 1953; Massachusetts Institute of Technology, Cambridge, 1956–57. Married Ursula Mattes in 1966; children: Svilena, Boris, and Philipp. In partnership with F. Kurrent and J. Spalt, Vienna, 1952–56; Partner, Arbeitsgruppe 4, Vienna, 1959–64. In private practice, Vienna, since 1964; office established in Amsterdam, 1970. Visiting Critic/Professor, University of Manitoba, Winnipeg, 1958, Yale University, New Haven, Connecticut, 1959, 1965, University of Illinois at Chicago Circle, 1967, 1968, and Technische Hochschule, Graz, Austria, 1974–76. Professor of Architecture, Academy of Applied Arts, Vienna, since 1976. Exhibitions: Salzburg, 1968; Graz, Austria, 1968; New Haven, Connecticut, 1968; Vienna, 1976; Stuttgart, 1977; Moscow, 1977. Recipient: Theodor-Körner Prize, Austria, 1954; Austrian State Prize, 1960; City of Kapfenberg Prize, 1967; First Prize, Amsterdam Town Hall Competition, 1967; City of Vienna Prize for Architecture, 1971. Address: Wilhelm Holzbauer, Architect, Franziskanerplatz 3, 1010 Vienna, Austria; or, Staalkade 4, Amsterdam C, The Netherlands.

Works:

1953/
56 Parish Church, Parsch, Salzburg (with F. Kurrent and J. Spalt)
1960/
64 St. Joseph Seminary, Aigen, Salzburg (with F. Kurrent and J. Spalt)
1965 Residenz Publishing House, Salzburg
1966/
72 St. Vitalis Parish Center, Salzburg
1966/
76 St. Virgil Educational and Cultural Center, Salzburg
1967 Bettelheim House, Vienna
1970/
82 27 stations of the Vienna Underground System (with Marschalek, Ladstätter and Gantar)
1971 Urban renewal plan for Salzburg
1973 Austrian Cultural Institute, Budapest (project)
1975 Stifter House, Ottensheim, Austria
1976/
79 Living Tomorrow Municipal Housing, Vienna
1976/
80 Provincial Government Building, Bregenz, Austria (with Rapf, Mätzler and Schweitzer)

1977 Residenz Publishing House New Quarters, Salzburg
1978 Conference Center, Abu Dhabi (project)
1978/
82 De Bijenkorf Department Store, Utrecht
1978/
84 City Hall, Amsterdam
1979 Dichand House, Vienna

Publications:

On HOLZBAUER: books—*Neue Architektur in Österreich 1945–1970*, Vienna 1971; *Österreichische Architektur 1960–1970*, Vienna 1972; *Wilhelm Holzbauer: Porträt eines Architekten* by Heinrich Hübl, Vienna 1977; *Sechs Architekten vom Schillerplatz*, Vienna 1977; articles—"Design for the New Amsterdam Town Hall" by Sokratis Dimitriou in *Bauforum* (Vienna), January/February 1974; "New City Hall for Amsterdam" in *Parametro* (Bologna), July 1974; "Wilhelm Holzbauer" by Naisu Akashi in *Architecture + Urbanism* (Tokyo), October 1976; "St. Virgil Centre for Continuing Education in Salzburg-Aigen," "The Church of St. Vitalis in Salzburg" and "St. Joseph's College in Salzburg-Aigen" in *Art d'Eglise* (Ottignies), January/March 1977; "Religious Centre in Salzburg" in *Kunst und Kirche* (Linz), February 1977; "Study and Meditation Centre in Salzburg" in *Domus* (Milan), May 1977; "St.

Wilhelm Holzbauer: Sir Virgil Educational and Cultural Center, Salzburg, 1976

Virgil Institute, Salzburg" in *Bauen und Wohnen* (Zurich), April 1978.

Wilhelm Holzbauer is one of those Holzmeister students who have stayed close to their master in their attitude towards architecture. This has nothing to do with architectural vocabulary, as it were, but above all concerns the art of developing a construction out of all of the given circumstances, seeing architecture both as historic phenomenon and as autonomous medium.

Looking at it superficially, Holtzbauer's conception of architecture is nonpolitical and not particularly given to reform. His works show no easily labelled tendencies. Their underlying theories are hidden, and theory is replaced by a stance which gives priority to the traditional values of architecture. Holzbauer does not bow to any system; there are no obvious fundamental premises that can easily be identified. It is more that the philosophy somehow develops itself in the course of the realization of the task in hand and within its unique historical setting. Quality is understood on the one hand as the repeated reflection of the complexity of the assignment and on the other as the interpretation of its optimum possibility.

Holtzbauer is more likely than not to be uncritical of his commissions. He is interested less in the "what" than in the "how." He wants to change neither his client nor society in general; rather, he tries to interpret their thoughts and wishes. In this he finds himself entirely in the Viennese tradition of "therapeutic Nihilism" and "Aestheticism" (in the manner of William M. Johnston). That is to say, he has more of an interest in the factual, the great variety of reflections and relationships, than in alteration or in therapy. With this attitude one might easily underrate the realism of the architectural medium or its possibilities and effects. Holtzbauer sees architecture as having the power to influence life, making it better or more beautiful; but he is sceptical about the greater power that some claim for it, to change society.

This realism of Holzbauer's, which is not necessarily solely sceptical, is above all noticeable in the balance of his materials. His structures often show a good comprensible and functional concept of space. Materials are used fundamentally where they can make a definite contribution, not merely for their own sake, as their statement can be made only in a structurally coherent relationship. His inclination is therefore towards synthesis, beginning with an acceptance of the commitment to the client's specification. This, however, does not mean that the architectural and spatial resources relate only to themselves and one another. They develop, one might say, a dialectic of reactions, a mannered relativity of form, that makes the building come alive quite independently of its actual function. So perhaps one could say that his Cultural Center in Salzburg stands over and above its original conception as a dialogue with the Salzburg mannerist-baroque tradition and setting, without having recourse to collage or quotation. Holzbauer avoids the literary or psychological; his manner remains within the frame of pure architecture. For him, architecture is itself a medium of fascination.

—Friedrich Achleitner

HOLZMEISTER, Clemens.

Austrian. Born in Fulpmes, Tyrol, 27 March 1886. Educated at the Technische Hochschule, Vienna, under Ferstel, Simony and Kong, 1913. In private practice, Vienna, 1914–38, 1954–57. Assistant Teacher, 1914–19, and Professor of Architecture, 1919, Technische Hochschule, Vienna; Professor,

Clemens Holzmeister: Festival Theatre, Salzburg, 1960

Staatsgewerbeschule, Innsbruck, 1919–24; Professor and Head of the Architectural Master Class, 1924–38, and Rector, 1933–37, Academy of Fine Arts, Vienna; Professor of Architecture, Kunstakademie, Dusseldorf, 1928–32; lived in Turkey, 1938–54: Professor of Architecture, Technical School, Istanbul, 1940–49; Professor, 1954–57, and Rector, 1955–57, Academy of Fine Arts, Vienna; teacher of his own master class, Salzburg, since 1957. Lives in Salzburg.

Works:

1922/
23   City Crematorium, Simmeringer Hauptstrasse 234, Vienna
1923   Parish Church, Batschuns, Vorarlberg, Austria
1924   Heroes' Church of Mary, Vorkloster, near Bregenz, Austria
1924/
25   Public housing development, Linzerstrasse 128, Vienna
1926/
28   Women's School, Linz, Austria
1930   Parish Church of Judas Thaddeus, Vienna School, Grinzingerstrasse 6, Vienna
1931   Government and bank buildings, Istanbul
1931/
32   Presidential Palace, Ankara, Turkey
1933   Parish Church of Saint Albert, Berlin
1933/
34   Seipel-Dollfuss Church, Vienna
1953/
60   Festival Theatre additions and development, Salzburg
1960   Evangelical Church, Kitzbuhl, Austria
1965   German Embassy, Metternichgasse, Vienna (with Rolf Gutbrod)

Publications:

By HOLZMEISTER: books—*Entwürfe und Zeichnungen,* Vienna 1927; *Bauten, Entwürfe und Zeichnungen,* Salzburg and Leipzig 1937; *Kirchenbau ewig neu, Baugedanken und Beispiele,* Innsbruck and Vienna 1951.

On HOLZMEISTER: books—*Clemens Holzmeister* by A. Weiser, Berlin, Leipzig and Vienna 1927; *Clemens Holzmeister: Das Architektonische Werk* by J. Gregor, Vienna 1953; *Das Neue Salzburger Festspielhaus,* Salzburg 1960; articles—"Clemens Holzmeister" in *Casabella* (Milan), July 1934; "Alcuni Ultimi Lavori di Clemens Holzmeister" by Luigi Lenzi in *L'Architettura* (Rome), August 1934; "Clemens Holzmeister als Raumgestalter" in *Innendekoration* (Darmstadt), March 1936; "L'Eglise Commemorative de Vienne" in *La Construction Moderne* (Paris), 9 May 1937; "Clemens Holzmeisters Bauten in der Turkei" by Hans Henniger in *Deutsche Bauzeitung* (Stuttgart), June 1938; "Clemens Holzmeister" in *Der Aufbau* (Vienna), March 1957; "Autriche: Nouveau Theatre du Festival de Salzbourg" in *Techniques et Architecture* (Paris), September 1957; "Das Neue und das Alte Festspielhaus" in *Der Aufbau* (Vienna), November/December 1961; "Clemens Holzmeister" by Friedrich Achleitner in *Bau* (Zurich), no. 1/2, 1966.

It was certainly no accident that Clemens Holzmeister, teacher of three generations of Austrian architects at the Vienna Academy of Fine Arts, should have continued a master class tradition that included the work of Friedrich von Schmidt, Viktor Luntz and Friedrich Ohmann, rather than the tradition of Theophil Hansen, Karl von Hasenauer and Otto Wagner (the tradition of the "gothic" and later the romanticized-baroque, the classicism of Hansen leading to the functionalism of Wagner). Holzmeister regards himself as part of the former tradition: it presents itself less as a formal school than as a principle of designing in which, as it were, the thematic, or graphically developed, or that which emanates from one point and proceeds to relate to a definite situation—that is to say, the anti-rational, emotional and sensual—plays an important part.

Holzmeister's theoretical world remains intact; the old established hierarchies still stand; cult, monument, and signs have all retained their content and significance. His baroque theory of life, with its "triad of the fine arts," and his feeling for stage management—not only of his architecture but also of his way of life—have left room in his work for elements that do not necessarily represent his main interest. Thus, for example, the typological elements in his structures are not there as part of an intellectual exercise, but simply because newly worked out formulae required the adaptation, re-interpretation and transformation of traditional space design. His very striking graphical work sets up a strong colloquy with the existing building substance, and his work is, in fact, a constant dialogue with the medium of space. If these terms suggest the theatre, that is appropriate: "theatre" is the key to his temperament.

But, though Holzmeister's training was of the old school of Viennese historical emphasis, and though he has, throughout his life, designed and theorized from a background of historical awareness, it would nevertheless be untrue to say that he is historically oriented in the sense of being an architect who works strictly within historical forms. In the euphoria of Expressionism, and the realism that followed, Holzmeister learned to transform historic forms, to distance them from their traditions, and so to give them a breath of new life.

Holzmeister has now been designing and building for more than 70 years, yet even his most recent structures indicate that stagnation has not set in. Rather, there has been a new freedom in his use of materials. His work is enjoying a new recognition after a long period of disparagement during the time of Viennese "Positivism." Of course, his architecture does involve a playing back of only one side of the Austrian "soul"—but it is one that is too easily described as "barock-kulinarisch," not taking into account its contemplative, basically Liebnitzian, world view. Holzmeister's spiritual and cultural background is Alpine Catholicism, with its existentialist dialectic between reality and make-believe, between realism and mysticism. It is not surprising that the Tyrolean Holzmeister finally made himself at home not in Vienna but in Salzburg.

—Friedrich Achleitner

HOOD, Raymond (Mathewson).

Born in Pawtucket, Rhode Island, 2 March 1881. Educated at Pawtucket public schools; Brown University, Providence, Rhode Island, 1898–1899; Massachusetts Institute of Technology, Cambridge, 1899–1901; Atelier Calarossi, Paris, 1905–06; Ecole des Beaux-Arts, Paris, 1908–10, Dip.Arch. 1910. Married Elsie E. Schmidt in 1920; children: Raymond Jr., Trientje and Richard. Draftsman for Cram, Goodhue and Ferguson, Boston, 1903–04; 1906; worked for Palmer, Hornbostel and Jones, Pittsburgh, 1906–08; Assistant to Henry Hornbostel, Pittsburgh, 1911–14; in partnership with Rayne Adams, New York, 1914–24; Partner, with Frederick A. Godley and J. André Fouilhoux, in Hood, Godley and Fouilhoux, New York, 1924–31; Partner, Hood and Fouilhoux, New York, 1931 until his death, 1934. President, Architectural League of New York, 1929–31. Trustee, Beaux Arts Institute of Design, New York. Exhibition: *Modern Architecture International Exhibition,* Museum of Modern Art, New York, 1932. Recipient: First Prize, *Chicago Tribune* Tower Competition, with John Mead Howells, 1922; Medal of Honor, Architectural League of New York, 1926; Gold Medal, American Institute of Architects, Chicago Chapter, 1927. M.A.: Brown University, 1931. Fellow, American Institute of Architects. Chevalier de la Couronne, Belgium. *Died* (in Stamford, Connecticut) 15 August 1934.

Works:

1920 John Green House alterations, New York
1924 Mori's Restaurant remodelling, Bleecker Street, New York
  St. Vincent de Paul Asylum, Tarrytown, New York (with J. André Fouilhoux)
  American Radiator Building, New York
1925 *Chicago Tribune* Tower (with John Mead Howells)
  Raymond Hood House, Stamford, Connecticut

1926 Bethany Union Church, Chicago
1927 McCormick Mausoleum, Rockford, Illinois
  Morris House, Greenwich, Connecticut
  National Broadcasting Company Studios, New York
1928 Apartment building, 3 East 84th Street, New York (with John Mead Howells)
  National Radiator Building, London (with J. Gordon Jeeves)
1929 Masonic Temple and Scottish Rite Cathedral, Scranton, Pennsylvania (with Godley, Fouilhoux and H. V. K. Henderson)
  Daily News Building, New York (with John Mead Howells)
1930 Beaux Arts Apartments, New York (with Godley and Fouilhoux; plan by the firm of Kenneth Murchison)
  DuPont Building additions, Washington, D.C. (with Godley and Fouilhoux)
  Patterson House and Garage, Ossining, New York (with John Mead Howells)
  McGraw Hill Building, New York (with Fouilhoux)
1931 Rex Cole Showrooms, Bay Ridge and Flushing, Long Island, New York (with Godley and Fouilhoux)
1931/
34 Rockefeller Center, New York (as consultant architect; with Fouilhoux; Reinhardt and Hofmeister; and Corbett, Harrison and McMurray; died before completion)
1932 Country Tower, New York suburbs (project)
1933 Electricity Building, *Century of Progress* exhibition, Chicago

Publications:

By HOOD: articles—"The Chicago Tribune Competition" in *Architectural Record* (New York), February 1923; "The American Radiator Building" in *American Architect* (New York), 19 November 1924; "The National Broadcasting Studios, New York" in *Architectural Record* (New York), July 1928; "Business Executive's Office" in *Pencil Points* (New York), March 1929; "The Spirit of Modern Art" in *Architectural Forum* (New York), November 1929; "Beauty in Architecture" in *Architectural Forum* (New York), November 1930; "The News Building" in *Architectural Forum* (New York), November 1930; "Three Visions of New York" in *Creative Art* (New York), August 1931; "Hanging Gardens of New York" in the *New York Times Magazine,* 23 August 1931; "The Design of the Rockefeller Center" in *Architectural Forum* (New York), January–June 1932; "The Apartment House Loggia" in *Architectural Forum* (New York), January 1934.

On HOOD: books—*Contemporary American Architects: Raymond Hood,* New York and London 1931; *Raymond Hood: The Unheralded Architect* by John B. Schwartzman, Charlottesville, Virginia 1962; *Raymond Hood, Architect* by Walter H. Kilham, New York 1973; articles—"American Radiator Building, New York City" by Harvey Wiley Corbett in *Architectural Record* (New York), May 1924; "Draftsmanship and Architecture as Exemplified by the Works of Raymond M. Hood" by Francis S. Swales in *Pencil Points* (New York), May 1928; "New York Daily News" in *Architectural Record* (New York), December 1930; "McGraw Hill Building" in *Architectural Record* (New York), April 1931; "Theatre Designs for Rockefeller Center" in *Architectural Record* (New York), June 1932; "Raymond Mathewson Hood" by Henry-Russell Hitchcock in *Modern Architecture International,* exhibition catalogue, New York 1932; "The Super Block as a Core: Unity and Harmony at Rockefeller Center" by Douglas Haskell in *Architectural Forum* (New York), January/February 1966; "The Way of an Architect with a Client" by Walter A. Kilham in *AIA Journal* (Washington, D.C.), September 1972.

*

If the term "meteoric" can be applied with precision to the career of an architect, or anyone else, it certainly must accurately apply to that of Raymond Hood.

For many years he spent his professional life in almost complete obscurity, at first working for other architects and later designing small, unimportant buildings that brought him little income and no recognition. Then, when he was 41 years old, he emerged suddenly, in a blinding light, as does a meteor when it is first sighted on a dark night. With John Mead Howells, he won, in 1922, one of the most highly publicized international competitions in history, that for the *Chicago Tribune* Tower. From the darkness of obscurity, Hood emerged as a recognized celebrity. No matter that the Tribune Tower design was the epitome of Beaux Arts Gothic eclecticism. No matter that the second place design, by Eliel Saarinen, was considered superior to the winner by many people and that the designs of Walter Gropius and others were highly praised. Hood had designed the winner. After so many years of poverty and frustration, he had begun his meteoric rise, a rise that would be extinguished in midflight by his premature death 12 years after the competition, when he was only 53 years of age.

During his 12 years of successful practice Hood accomplished a great deal. He became an internationally famous architect with a growing practice. He designed a number of buildings of note, among them commercial buildings of various kinds and even houses, but his major accomplishments were made in the design of office buildings, particularly the high-rise types that became known as skyscrapers.

Most importantly, Hood began an evolution from eclectic toward modern architecture. His first tall building in New York City, the American Radiator Building, completed in 1924 one year before the completion of the Tribune Tower, was in eclectic Gothic style but with simpler, more subdued forms than the Chicago building. Later, the buildings of Rockefeller Center, for which Hood, Harvey Wiley Corbett and Wallace K. Harrison were the principal designers, certainly were eclectic in many ways. However, the brilliance of the site plan and the relationships between buildings and open spaces, as well as the overall design of the buildings themselves, dominate the eclectic details, subduing and subordinating them to the overall scheme.

Near the end of his career Hood designed two other New York City buildings that had considerable influence on the tall office towers that came after them. These were the *Daily News* Building, completed in 1929, and the old McGraw-Hill Building, completed a year later. In the designs for these buildings Hood came very close to deserting the eclectic idiom completely in favor of the modern. In the *Daily News* Building he avoided almost all ornament on the exterior, choosing instead very simple, vertical bands of limestone, alternating with bands of windows, that rose from the ground floor to the top. In the McGraw-Hill Building he went the other way, with an exterior of unadorned, horizontal terra cotta bands, alternating with windows.

During the depression years Hood was able to obtain almost no architectural commissions, and after a year of illness he died. Many believe that he had not really approached the height of his powers and that if he had lived longer he would have carried his designs for modern tall buildings to a much higher zenith.

—William Dudley Hunt, Jr.

Raymond Hood: *Daily News* Building, New York, 1929

HORIGUCHI, Sutemi.

Japanese. Born in Mushiroda Village, Gifu Prefecture, 6 January 1895. Educated at the University of Tokyo, under Chyuta Ito, 1916–20, B.Arch. 1920, Dr.Arch. 1944. Married Suzuko Suzumura in 1922; children: Masako, Keiko, Ohi, and Yoshiko. In private practice, Tokyo, since 1920. Professor, Teikoku University of Art, 1932–38; Lecturer, Tokyo Women's Normal High School, 1938–46; Lecturer, University of Tokyo, 1946–55; Professor, 1949–65, Head of the Engineering Department, 1952–70, and Lecturer, 1965–70, Meiji University, Tokyo. Founder Member, the Secession Group, Tokyo, 1920; Founder Member, Japan Construction Culture League, 1936 (issued the magazine *Contemporary Architecture*); Director and Trustee, Japan Garden Society, and Japan Ceramics Society, since 1938; Organizer, Symposium on the Culture of the Tea Ceremony, Tokyo, 1943. Exhibitions: *Japan New Tea Ceremony Exhibition,* Matsuzakaya Department Store, Ueno, Tokyo, 1951; Kindai Art Gallery, Kyobashi, Tokyo, 1955. Recipient: Kitamura Tokoku Award, 1941; Award, 1950, 1951, and Grand Prix, 1969, Architectural Institute of Japan; Mainichi Publications Award, 1953; Art Academy Award, 1957; Medal of Honor, 1963, and Third Class Order of the Sacred Treasure, 1966, Japanese Government; First Chubu Architectural Award, 1969. Address (office): 4-6-5 Sanno, Ota-ku, Tokyo 143, Japan.

Works:

1922 4 Pavilions, *Tokyo Exhibition*
Makita House, Koishikawa, Japan
1926 Shien-So ("Purple Smoke" Cottage), Warabi, Saitama Prefecture, Japan (destroyed by fire)
1927 Soshokyo House, Koishikawa, Tokyo
1928 Makita Building, Nihonbashi, Tokyo
1930 Kikkawa House, Meguro, Tokyo
1931 Tokugawa House, Koishikawa, Tokyo
1932 Fukuoka Meteorological Observatory, Fukuoka, Japan
1934 Okada House, Omori, Tokyo
1935 Arao House, Tokyo
Mito Weather Station, Ibaragi Prefecture, Japan
1936 Nakanishi House, Tokyo
Toride Racecourse, Ibaraghi Prefecture, Japan
1937 Villa Chokin-Ryo, Yamanaka Lakeside, Yamanashi Prefecture, Japan
1938 Yamakawa House, Nishinomiyashi, Hyogo Prefecture, Japan
Kobe Marine Observatory
Oshima Weather Station, Oshima Island, Tokyo
1940 Wakasa House, Shibuya, Tokyo
1950 The Emperor's Room, Hotel Hasshokan, Nagoya, Japan
1951 Bijikyo Tearoom (and 4 other tearooms), *Japan New Tea Ceremony Exhibition,* Matsuzakaya Department Store, Ueno, Tokyo
Hiyoshigaoka High School, Kyoto
1953 Bath Room, Hotel Hasshokan, Nagoya, Japan
"Nakamise," Hotel Hasshokan, Nagoya, Japan (destroyed by fire, 1965; rebuilt, 1967)
1954 Okayama Branch of the Fuso Sogo Bank
Japan Pavilion, *Bienal,* Sao Paulo
1955 Lecture Hall, Meiji University, Tokyo
Number 8 Building, Meiji University, Tokyo
Mannyo Park, with Exhibition Pavilion and Tea Ceremony Pavilion, Yugawara, Kanagawa Prefecture, Japan
Koraku Hotel, Misasa Hot Springs, Tottori Prefecture, Japan
Uemura Restaurant, Tokyo
1956 "A Small House in Omori," 4-6-5 Sanno, Ota-ku, Tokyo
Izumi Gymnasium, Meiji University, Tokyo

1957 Lecture Hall and Gymnasium, Futaba Gakuen (girls' junior and senior high school), Shizuoka, Japan
Iwanami House, Bunkyo-ku, Tokyo
1958 Sakura Room and Kiku Room, Hotel Hasshokan, Nagoya, Japan
Otokiki Golf Clubhouse, Hotel Hasshokan, Nagoya, Japan
Number 6 Building and Number 7 Building, Meiji University, Tokyo
1959 Library, Meiji University, Tokyo
1960 Izumi Lecture Hall, Meiji University, Tokyo
Student Union, Meiji University, Tokyo
1961 Tokoname Ceramic Art Research Center, Aichi Prefecture, Japan
1962 St. Maur Abbey, Shizuoka, Japan
1964 Shirakawa House, Setagaya, Tokyo
Number 4 Building, Faculty of Engineering, Meiji University, Kawasaki, Kanagawa Prefecture, Japan
Number 1 Building, Faculty of Engineering, Meiji University, Kawasaki, Kanagawa Prefecture, Japan
1965 Number 2 Building and Number 3 Building, Faculty of Engineering, Meiji University, Kawasaki, Kanagawa Prefecture, Japan
Kankyo Tea Room, Minato-ku, Tokyo
1968 Ohara Sanso (mountain villa), 238 Uenomachi, Ohara, Sakyo-ku, Kyoto
1971/
72 Uraku-En (Jo An Tea Room and surrounding garden), Inuyama, Aichi Prefecture, Japan

Publications:

By HORIGUCHI: books—*Complete Study of the Tea Ceremony,* editor, 15 volumes, Tokyo 1935–37; *The Katsura Imperial Villa,* Tokyo 1952 (included in *The Complete Works*); *Collected Cubic Plans of the Japanese Tea Room,* supervising editor, 12 volumes, Tokyo 1963–67; *The Complete Works of Sutemi Horiguchi,* in 7 volumes: volume I, *The Tradition of Japanese Gardens and Space Construction,* Tokyo 1965; volume II, *Tea Rooms by Rikyu,* Tokyo 1968; volume III, *The Study of Tea Rooms,* Tokyo 1969; volume IV, *Tea by Rikyu,* Tokyo 1970; volume V, *Works of Sutemi Horiguchi: Space Construction of Houses and Gardens,* Tokyo 1974; volume VI, *Collected Papers on Architecture,* Tokyo 1978; volume VII, *Study of the Shoin-Zukuri and the Sukiya-Zukuri,* Tokyo 1978; *Kusaniwa,* Tokyo 1968 (included in *The Complete Works*); *Ise Jingu,* Tokyo 1973; articles—"The Growth of the Japanese Garden" in *Bunkazai* (Tokyo), November 1963; "Gardens in the Asuka and the Nara Era" in *Bunkazai* (Tokyo), August 1965; "The Origin of the Japanese Concept of Beauty," discussion with Kiyonori Kikutake, in *Approach* (Tokyo), Autumn 1972; "Tea Rooms," editor, in *Japanese Art* (Tokyo), 15 April 1973.

On HORIGUCHI: books—*History of Modern Architectural Design* by Ryuichi Hamaguchi, Tokyo 1962; *Sutemi Horiguchi* (in Contemporary Japanese Architects series), edited by Isamu Kurita, Tokyo 1971; *Eight Japanese Architects: Witnesses of Modern European Architecture,* edited by Hiroshi Sasaki, Tokyo 1977; articles—"A University Is Circulation" in *Architectural Review* (London), June 1959; "On the Gardens of Sutemi Horiguchi and Masayuki Nagare" by Hiroshi Ohe and Yuichiro Kojiro in *Space Design* (Tokyo), March 1973.

*

Japan was opened to the West when eclecticism was still supreme. Thus the adaptation of the Western building art meant learning the styles. The man who through his roles as teacher and architect exerted the greatest influence on the first generation of modern Japanese architects, Josiah Conder, came from England in 1877. Within a year of his arrival, he had three buildings of his design under construction, one Romanesque, another Indian-Islamic, and the third Venetian Gothic. The greatest achievement of this initial period of modernization was perhaps the Akasaka Palace (architect: Tokuma Katayama), modelled after Versailles and the Louvre. Ironically Japan caught up with the West just when eclecticism was being overthrown. One of the first to take a stand for the Modern Movement in Japan was Sutemi Horiguchi, who with fellow students formed the Secession Group in 1920. Having thrown off the older styles, the members of the group experimented with a number of newer styles, notably Expressionism, then current in Europe.

At the same time, however, Horiguchi became increasingly attracted to Japanese traditional architecture. As a scholar he made important contributions to the study of the tea-ceremony and tea-ceremony rooms. In his domestic architecture, Horiguchi was very conscious of these two opposite tendencies toward modernism and tradition, even as he deprecated the duality that remained unresolved in some of his own designs. He wrote of the Okada House, with its mixture of styles, that "although inevitable, it is by no means an architecture that ought to be." He labelled it "a house of a transitional period."

Sutemi Horiguchi: Izumi Lecture Hall, Meiji University, Tokyo, 1960

In his first house, the Shien-so of 1926, the ground floor Western style rooms and the upper floor Japanese style room are in a sense pulled together by the bold thatched roof, reminiscent of contemporary Dutch architecture. This pastoral design might be said to express his youthful optimism for the eventual reconciliation of the two modes.

Horiguchi was from the start concerned with bringing the house and the garden into active relationship. Here a geometricized stretch of space—a terrace and a pond—is created between the house proper and an auxiliary building.

In the Okada House of 1934 the two modes are more frankly expressed. The house is divided into a front Japanese style section and a back Western style section. Though the two parts may be integrated in plan by the central courtyard, the *sukiya* style Japanese section and the International Style Western section abut in elevation in an awkward, unresolved manner. (In the Meiji Period it was not uncommon for a member of the oligarchy to build two houses for himself, one in front in the Western style in which to receive guests and an adjacent one in the Japanese style in which to actually live. In Horiguchi's scheme the order has been reversed.) The garden too is divided into two distinct parts, their only mediation a narrow channel of water. It is as if Horiguchi had decided to admit that the two modes could not be so easily reconciled.

The Wakasa House of 1940 is outwardly completely Western: a white International Style structure. Yet this may be his most trenchant comment on the state of modern Japanese society. The heart of the house is the 2-storey living room located half a floor above the garden. Looking out from the living room, one sees the long, narrow pool which divides the garden in two and which seemingly continues under the house. The apparently serene dwelling is in reality standing precariously atop a fault in the earth, just as Japanese society, superficially successful in adapting to the West, was being threatened by contradictory tendencies.

This state of inner conflict could not be long sustained. Horiguchi's pre-war houses, full of tension, gave way eventually to highly refined *sukiya* style architecture (as in Hasshokan) of impeccable details—of air conditioning intakes and outlets neatly hidden behind beautifully designed "traditional" grills—from which all impure and disharmonious elements have been excised. Horiguchi's scholarly background perhaps accounts for the "correctness" that marks his work in contrast to the oeuvre of Isoya Yoshida and Togo Murano, two other major practitioners of the *sukiya* style.

The path of initial Westernization and eventual return to native traditions is one taken by many Japanese of Horiguchi's generation. It is, however, his pre-war work, which attempted to give form to the essential cultural conflict in himself and in Japanese society, that is most interesting today to the post-modernist who finds value in the expression of contradiction and ambivalence.

—Hiroshi Watanabe

HORTA, Victor.

Belgian. Born in Ghent, 6 January 1861. Studied music theory at the Conservatoire, Ghent, 1873; drawing, textiles and architecture at the Academy of Ghent, 1874–77; and architecture at the Académie des Beaux-Arts, Brussels, 1881. Worked in the office of the architect Jean Dubuysson, Paris, 1878–80; Assistant Architect, office of Alphonse Balat, Brussels, 1884–85; in private practice, Brussels, 1886–1915; lived in London, 1915, and in the United States, 1916–18; resumed practice in Brussels, 1918 until his death, 1947. Head of the Architecture Department, 1892–97, Professor Extraordinary, 1897–1911, and Professor of Architecture and Drawing, 1912–15, Université Libre, Brussels; Professor from 1912, and Director, 1927–31, Académie des Beaux-Arts, Brussels; Professor of Architecture, 1919, Institut Supérieur des Beaux-Arts, Antwerp. Member, Royal Commission on Sites, Brussels, 1921; President, Beaux-Arts Section, Académie Royale, Brussels, 1925; President of the Jury, League of Nations Building Competition, Geneva, 1925–27. Exhibitions: Atelier Devreese, Brussels, 1887, 1888; *Exposition Internationale*, Brussels, 1897; *Exposition de la Libre Esthetique*, Brussels, 1897; *Exposition des Arts Décoratifs*, Turin, 1902, Monza, 1906; *Pionniers du XXe Siècle: Guimard, Horta, Van de Velde*, Paris, 1971; *Victor Horta*, Musée Horta and Town Hall, Brussels, 1973. Collections: Musée Horta, 25 rue Americaine, St.-Gilles, Brussels. Recipient: Prix Godecharle, Brussels, 1884; Grand Prix, Triennial of Architecture, Académie des Beaux-Arts, Brussels, 1887; Architecture Prize, Académie des Beaux-Arts, Brussels, 1888; First Prize, Vanduyse Monument Competition, Termonde, 1892. Honorary Professor, Université Libre, Brussels, 1912; Honorary Correspondent, 1913, and Associate, 1919, Académie Royale, Brussels; Honorary Professor, Institut Supérieur des Beaux-Arts, Antwerp, 1932; created Baron, 1932. Corresponding Member, Institut de France, 1936. *Died* (in Brussels) *11 September 1947.*

Works:

1884   Parliament Buildings (competition project)
       Prison Buildings, Verviers, Belgium (competition project)
       Funerary Monument, Ghent (with the sculptor Devreese)
       Casino (competition project)
1885   3 houses, 35, 36 and 37 rue des Douze Chambres, Brussels (with the sculptor Leroy and the painter De Witte)
1887   Palfyn Monument, Courtrai, Belgium (with the sculptor Vincotte)
       Museum of Natural History, Brussels (competition project)
1888   Augustus and Livia Temple restoration, Vienne, France (project)
       Baudouin Lighthouse (competition project)
       Seghers Belemont Family Vault, Courtrai, Belgium (with the sculptor Devreese)
       Provincial Government Building (project)
1889   Lambeaux Building, Parc du Cinquantenaire, Brussels (to contain Jef Lambeaux' bas-relief, The Human Passions; altered, 1905)
       L. Gallair Monument, Tournai, Belgium (with the sculptor Charlier)
1890   Mattyn House, 50 rue de Bordeaux, Brussels
       Reception and Exhibition Hall, La Madeleine Market, Schaerbeek, Brussels (project)
1891   Table-top model of the city of Brussels (with the sculptor Van der Stappen)
1892   Vanduyse Monument, Termonde, Belgium (competition project; with the sculptor Devreese)
1893   Autrique House, 242 chaussée de Haecht, Brussels
       Hôtel Tassel (Tassel House), 6 rue Paul-Emile Janson, Brussels
1894   Frison House, 27 rue Lebeau, Brussels
       Godefroid Devreese Studio, Ghent
       Hôtel Winssinger (Winssinger House), 66 rue Hôtel des Monnaies, Brussels
       Constantin Meunier Monument to Work (project)
       Solvay Monument, Couillet, Charleroi, Belgium (with the sculptor Thomas Vincotte)
       Solvay Funerary Monument, Ixelles Cemetery, Belgium
       Artan Funerary Monument, Oosterduinkerke, Belgium (with the sculptor Van der Stappen)
       Solvay Chateau alterations and furnishings, La Hulpe, Belgium (destroyed)
1895   Jardin d'Enfants, 40 rue St.-Ghislain, Brussels
       Boch House interiors, 73 avenue de la Toison d'Or, Brussels (destroyed)
1895/
1900   Hôtel Solvay (Solvay House), 224 avenue Louise, Brussels
1896   Brossel House, rue des Champs Elysées, Brussels (destroyed)
       Van Beneden Monument, Ghent (with the sculptor Van der Stappen)
       Deprez-van de Velde House alterations, 3 avenue Palmerston and 14 rue Boduognat, Brussels
       Remy Factories, Louvain, Belgium (project)
1896/
99   Maison du Peuple, place Emile Vandervelde, Brussels
1897   Val St.-Lambert Pavilion, *Exposition Internationale*, Brussels
       Ompdraille Monument, avenue Louise, Brussels (with the sculptor Van der Stappen)
       Baron Wangen Chateau, Chambley, Meurthe-et-Moselle, Belgium (destroyed during the First World War)
       Timberman Villa, 563 chaussée d'Alsemberg, Uccle, Belgium (destroyed)
       Vandersypen House, Cologne
1897/
1900   Hotel Van Eetvelde (Van Eetvelde House), 4 avenue Palmerston, Brussels
1898   Furnemont Villas "Rouge" and "Rose," Wenduyne, Belgium (destroyed)
       Pavilion of the Independent State of the Congo, for the 1900 *Paris Exposition* (project)
       Horta House/Studio, 23–25 rue Américaine, Brussels (now the Musée Horta)
1899   "Les Espinglettes" (Frison Country House), 70 avenue Circulaire, Uccle, Belgium
       Carmouche Villa, La Panne, Belgium
       St. Anne Maternity Pavilion (project)
       Carpentier Villa, route de Tournai, Renaix, Belgium
       Remy Monument, Louvain, Belgium (with the sculptor Braecke)
       Hôtel Aubecq (Aubecq House), 520 Avenue Louise, Brussels (destroyed, 1950)
1900   Villa Lotte alterations, Wenduyne, Belgium
       Furnemont Country House, Uccle, Belgium
       Cousin House alterations, 24 chaussée de Charleroi, Brussels (dismantled, 1969, and reconstructed in the Musée des Beaux-Arts)
       Dapsen House alterations, 417 avenue Louise, Brussels
1901   A l'Innovation Department Store, rue Neuve, Brussels (destroyed by fire, 1967)
       Dopchie Building ("La Bruyere") alterations, Renaix, Belgium
       Hôtel Dubois (Dubois House), 80 avenue Brugmann, Brussels
       Solvay Laboratories, rue des Champs Elysées, Brussels (destroyed)
       Hotel Roger alterations, 459 avenue Louise, Brussels
       Braeck House/Sculpture Studio, 31 rue de l'Abdication, Brussels
       Delgouffre House alterations, 4 rue Hôtel des Monnaies, Brussels (destroyed)
       Dubois House, Forest, Belgium
1902   Moury Restaurant, rue de l'Ecuyer, Brussels (destroyed)
       Belgian Pavilion, *Exposition des Arts Décoratifs*, Turin
       Brahms Monument, Vienna
       Bara Monument, Tournai, Belgium (with the sculptor G. Charlier)
1903   Max Hallet House, 344 avenue Louise, Brussels
       Grand Bazar Anspach Department Store, Brussels (partly destroyed)

Grand Bazar Department Store, Frankfurt (with the sculptor Van der Stappen; destroyed)

Sander Pierron House, 157 rue de l'Aqueduc, Brussels

Waucquez Department Store, 20 rue des Sables, Brussels

Solvay Pavilion, *Liege Exposition*

Gymnastics Hall, Maredsous Abbey, Belgium (project)

Hôtel Winssinger alterations, 66 rue Hôtel des Monnaies, Brussels

A l'Innovation Department Store, chaussée d'Ixelles, Brussels

Vinck House alterations, 85 rue Washington, Brussels

1903/
28 Musée des Beaux-Arts, Tournai, Belgium (work interrupted by First World War)

1904 Féron Country House, La Petite Espinette, Uccle, Belgium

Les Peupliers Gymnastics Hall, Vilvorde, Belgium

1905 Villa Dubois, Sosoye, Belgium

Lambeaux Building alterations, Parc du Cinquantenaire, Brussels

1906 Exhibition stand, *Exposition des Arts Décoratifs*, Monza, Italy

Hiclet Building, rue Neuve, Brussels (destroyed)

Wolfers Building, 11–13 rue d'Arenberg, Brussels

Wolfers Country House alterations, La Hulpe, Belgium

Horta Country House ("La Bastide") alterations, La Hulpe, Belgium

A l'Innovation Department Store, Meir, Antwerp (destroyed)

Wiener House, Brussels (destroyed, 1966)

Cavalier Luttant Monument, Brussels

1906/
26 Brugmann Hospital, Jette, Brussels

1910 Hôtel Verstraete (formerly Hôtel Roger) alterations, 459 avenue Louise, Brussels

Terwagne House, Antwerp

1911 Horta House alterations, 23–25 rue Américaine, Brussels (now Musée Horta)

Absalon Department Store alterations, 47–49 rue St. Christophe, Brussels

1913/
52 "Halte Centrale" Main Railway Station, Brussels (completed by Brunfaut)

1919 Redevelopment plan for the Place de Héros, Brussels (project)

Grand Hotel alterations, Boulevard Anspach, Brussels (destroyed)

Monument, Place de Heros, St.-Gilles, Brussels (project)

1920 Horta House alterations, 136 avenue Louise, Brussels

1920/
28 Palais des Beaux-Arts, Brussels

1922 Lazard Building alterations, 12 Avenue Brugmann, Brussels

1923 Institut Medico-Chirurgical du Cinquantenaire extensions, 152 rue de Linthout, Brussels

School of Arts and Crafts, Brussels (project)

1925 Belgian Pavilion, *Exposition des Arts Décoratifs*, Paris

1927 Municipal Development Plan (siting of the Shell Building), Brussels (project)

1929 Boys' and Girls' Schools, rue des Sols, Brussels (projects)

1929/
36 Musées Royaux des Beaux-Arts extensions, Brussels (project)

1930 Wolfers Building extensions, 11–13 rue d'Arenberg, Brussels

1934 Feasibility study: Albert I Library, Brussels

1937 King Albert Monument, Boulevard Piercot, Liège (project)

Victor Horta: Hôtel Solvay, Brussels, 1900

1943 Braecke Funerary Monument, Nossegem, Belgium (with the sculptor De Jonckeere; original design by Braecke)

Publications:

By HORTA: books—*Considérations sur l'Art Moderne*, Brussels 1925; *L'Enseignement Architectural et l'Architecture Moderne*, Brussels 1926.

On HORTA: books—*Victor Horta* by Robert Delevoy, Brussels 1958; *Victor Horta* by R. Puttemans and others, Brussels, 1964; *Victor Horta* by Franco Borsi and Paolo Portoghesi, Rome 1969, Tokyo 1976, Brussels 1977; *Pionniers du XXe Siècle: Guimard, Horta, Van de Velde*, exhibition catalogue, by Robert Delevoy and others, Paris 1971; *Victor Horta*, exhibition catalogue, by Suzanne Henrion-Giele, Brussels 1973; articles—"Horta: Works and Style of Victor Horta Before 1900" by S. T. Marsden in *Architectural Review* (London), December 1955; special issue of *L'Architettura* (Rome), nos. 23–29, 1958; special issue of *Rythme* (Brussels), April 1964;

"Quelques Hôtels Particuliers Construits par Victor Horta" by Suzanne Henrion-Giele in *La Maison d'Hier et d'Aujourd'hui* (Brussels), December 1972.

It is universally agreed that what distinguishes modern architecture from what precedes it is its disdain for the revival of historical styles or their eclectic mixing. It is generally agreed that Victor Horta's Hôtel Tassel (Tassel House, Brussels) of 1893 marks the beginning of modern architecture according to that definition. Yet, the surface characteristics of the decorative, ornamental, organic forms of Art Nouveau architecture as established by Horta hardly look like our stereotype of modern architecture with its surface simplicity, redundancy, and high polish.

The contrast between Horta's architecture and the predominant themes of the dominant architecture after the First World War is easy enough to establish. Horta provided monuments to the wealth, power, and sense of beauty of the bourgeois family, the private patron. After the First World War, as the power of these families and patrons waned, the dominant architecture produced monuments to the wealth, power, and sense of beauty of the modern corporation or the corporate state. The decorative, the ornamental, the organic of the Art Nouveau were appropriate to the aesthetism and introversion of a last-generation Buddenbrooks or a bourgeois manqué just as they look decadent from the point of view of the emerging corporation and corporate state and its bureaucratic preoccupation with paper efficiency, control, and simplicity.

The similarities between modern architecture as initially conceived of by Horta and the International Style that followed it that are more difficult to detect and articulate. Here, a first approach is to focus on the insides of Horta's grand series of private residences and compare them to the exteriors of paradigmatic contemporary buildings. This is in line with the intraversion of Horta's work and with the extroversion of the International Style. On the one hand we have Horta's staircase of the Tassel House with its structural/ornamental ironwork interlaced with stone, painted-on tracery, stupendous wooden millwork, and colorful mosaic. On the other hand we have the exterior steel framework that is brought slightly out of the plane of the building, which is so characteristic of the Modern Movement as exemplified in the mature work of Mies or of SOM office buildings. In his staircase Horta, for the first time, reveals the sinews of a building in naked iron: an internal treasure of the industrial age. For the Modern Movement iron or steel no longer relate to the internal connectedness of things but rather to external, redundant structure. But still, both make manifest and visible what previous architectures hid or knew nothing about: industrial strength. It is the Art Nouveau pioneers who, in revealing the internal workings of their buildings, laid the groundwork for what gets admired as "honesty," "directness," or "technical solutions" by the Modern Movement.

But what of the outsides of Horta's buildings? Perhaps the most prototypic of his residences that achieves a mature integration of inside and outside is his Hôtel Dubois (Dubois House, Brussels) of 1901. If the interior cast ironwork here, as in the Tassel House, is a visible sinews, and thus the rooms and corridors form the interior chambers of the smooth muscle organs, then surely here we have an instance of a façade no more nor less than skin. (Once again, a foretaste of the "curtain wall" beloved of the Modern Movement.)

This body metaphor carries forward a line of development that begins at least as far back as the Renaissance in European architecture. After all, it was the Renaissance spirit that first allowed us to look at the naturalistic forms of life through buildings as well as other ways. The physicality of the Renaissance became amazingly delicate as it transformed itself into Mannerism. The body was now in movement, oscillation, in a delicate tension between the hidden and the manifest, the spiritual and the physical. For Horta, in the Dubois House at any rate, that delicate interpenetration between spirit and matter is taken up 300 years later at the critical points of the skin (façade): at the orifices, the doors, windows, and street-level openings. The focus becomes *interpenetration* of the insides and outsides.

But, if for the mature Horta what unites insides with outsides is the orifice, then the naturalism so evident in his Art Nouveau forms, the aesthetism so blatant in his flagrant custom-made asymmetries, is but a screen for a deeper concern. Horta's naturalism is not sincerely concerned with the imitation of the forms of nature for their own sake, any more than it is concerned with the classicist's externalization of solid geometry. Rather, Horta centers on the *rules* underlying the generation of natural forms, the *relations* between insides and outsides. The focus on the interpenetration amounts to a concern for rules and relations of translating the outside to the inside and vice versa. Modern architecture, as conceived by Horta, then, centers not on the imitation of other forms (whether from nature, previous cultures, or modern science) but rather on the abstract principles of generation of form, of relations rather than enti-

ties. At this point it is easy to see Horta as the *direct predecessor* of people whose work would at the surface appear extremely different if not opposed: Le Corbusier, Mies (or indeed Philip Johnson), Buckminster Fuller and Paolo Soleri. Each of these men, in his own way, overtly or covertly, centers in on the relational principles of form generation rather than on the forms themselves.

Modern architecture is special and new because it not only does not imitate previous styles but also does not imitate anything at all; rather, it seeks for the rules for generating things, the relations between things. It has indeed transcended, then, surface opposition between Classical, Romantic, or Mannerist tendencies. In transcending the historical styles it has, however, focused itself on abstraction: on an abstract concern with the fundamental rule structures and relations that underlie any form. In this way, whether modern architecture is "naturalistic" as in Horta's Art Nouveau or "spiritualistic" as in the best of Mies, it is never humanistic, for it is always a step removed from direct experience.

It is commonplace to fault Horta for turning to "classicism" at the end of his career. It is easy to see a structure such as the Brugmann Hospital or Musée des Beaux-Arts at Tournai as both retrograde and out of step with mainstream architecture. Yet, perhaps in these unfashionable forms some future critic might yet detect the birth of an authentic non-narcissist, post-Modern architecture based on a humanism of direct experience.

—Joseph B. Juhasz

HOWE, George.

American. Born in Worcester, Massachusetts, 17 June 1886. Educated at schools in Switzerland and New England, 1896–1904: Groton School, Connecticut, 1900–04; Harvard University, Cambridge, Massachusetts, 1904–07, graduated 1907; Ecole des Beaux-Arts, Paris, 1908–12, graduated 1912. Served as a Lieutenant in the Corps of Interpreters, United States Army, as Assistant Military Attaché at Berne, Switzerland, 1917–19. Married Maritje Patterson in 1907; children: Anne and Helen. Practiced in Philadelphia: worked for the firm of Furness, Evans and Company, 1914–16; Partner, with Walter Mellor and Arthur I. Meigs, in Mellor, Meigs and Howe, 1916–28; in private practice, 1928–29; Partner, with William Lescaze, *q.v.*, Howe and Lescaze, 1929–34; in private practice, 1935–40; in partnership with Louis I. Kahn, *q.v.*, 1941, and with Kahn and Oscar Stonorov, *q.v.*, 1942–43; Supervising Architect, 1942–44, and Deputy Commissioner for Design and Construction, 1944–45, Public Buildings Administration, Federal Works Agency; in private practice, 1945–48; in partnership with Robert Montgomery Brown, 1949 until his death, 1955. Chairman of the Department of Architecture, Yale University, New Haven, Connecticut, 1950–54. Exhibition: *Modern Architecture International Exhibition,* Museum of Modern Art, New York, 1932. Recipient: Gold Medal, American Institute of Architects, 1922, 1939. Fellow, American Institute of Architects. *Died* (in Cambridge, Massachusetts) *16 April 1955.*

Works:

1913   George Howe House I renovation, Chestnut Hill, Philadelphia
1914   Kermit Roosevelt House additions and renovation, Oyster Bay, Long Island, New York
1914/
16   High Hollow (George Howe House II), 101 West Hampton, Chestnut Hill, Philadelphia (garage added, 1923; swimming pool, 1928; now the Paley Conference Center of the University of Pennsylvania)

1921   4-house development, Germantown Avenue, Chestnut Hill, Philadelphia (with Walter Mellor and Arthur I. Meigs)
      Leeds Farm Buildings, Clonmell, Pennsylvania (with Walter Mellor and Arthur I. Meigs)
      Howe-Fraley House, 10 West Chestnut Hill Avenue, Chestnut Hill, Philadelphia
1921/
23   Stikeman House, West Hampton, Chestnut Hill, Philadelphia
1921/
24   Newbold Estate, Laverock, Pennsylvania (with Arthur I. Meigs; swimming pool added, 1928)
1922   Illoway House, Bell's Mill Road, Chestnut Hill, Philadelphia
1924   Willowbrook Farms (Page House), Paoli, Pennsylvania (with Walter Mellor and Arthur I. Meigs)
      Philadelphia Saving Fund Society Main Office renovation, 7th and Walnut Streets, Philadelphia (with Walter Mellor and Arthur I. Meigs)
      Philadelphia Saving Fund Society Branch Office, 11th Street and Lehigh Avenue, Philadelphia
      Philadelphia Saving Fund Society Branch Office, Broad and McKean Streets, Philadelphia
      McManus House, Germantown, Philadelphia (with extensions, 1930)
1924/
28   United States Coast Guard Memorial, Arlington National Cemetery, Virginia (with the sculptor Gaston Lachaise)
1925   Siebecker House, Bethlehem, Pennsylvania
      Open-air auditorium, Fairmount Park, Philadelphia (project; with Walter Mellor and Arthur I. Meigs)
1926   Philadelphia Saving Fund Society Branch Office, 52nd and Ludlow Streets, Philadelphia
      Philadelphia Saving Fund Society Branch Office, Broad and Ruscomb Streets, Philadelphia
1927   Baker House, Harrisburg, Pennsylvania (with Walter Mellor and Arthur I. Meigs)
      Oxmoor (Bullitt House), Fort Washington, Pennsylvania
      Holden House, Haverford, Pennsylvania
      McLean House, Whitemarsh Valley, Pennsylvania (with Arthur I. Meigs)
      Magill House, Germantown, Philadelphia (with Arthur I. Meigs and Walter Mellor)
      Philadelphia Saving Fund Society Temporary Banking Offices, 8 South 12th Street, Philadelphia
1928   George Howe House III renovation, Bell's Mill Road, Chestnut Hill, Philadelphia
      Sinkler House, Sugartown and Goshen Roads, Westchester, Pennsylvania
      Tyler House renovation, Elkins Park, Pennsylvania
      Airport, Camden, New Jersey (project)
      Christopher Columbus Memorial Lighthouse, Dominican Republic (competition project)
      War Memorial, Somme American Cemetery, Bony, Aisne, France
      Wasserman House I, Whitemarsh, Pennsylvania (project)
1929   Howe and Lescaze Offices, Philadelphia (with William Lescaze)
      Ingersoll Museum, Pennlyn, Montgomery County, Pennsylvania (project; with William Lescaze)
      Monument in Honor of the 27th and 30th Divisions, Kemmels, near Vierstataelt, Ypres, Belgium (with the sculptor Sidney Waugh)
      Philadelphia Saving Fund Society Main Building renovation, 7th and Walnut Streets, Philadelphia

William Stix Wasserman Offices, Philadelphia (with William Lescaze)

Wasserman House II, Whitemarsh, Pennsylvania (project; with William Lescaze)

1930/
31 Museum of Modern Art, New York (project: preliminary designs; with William Lescaze)

1931 Hessian Hills School, Mt. Airy Road, Croton-on-Hudson, New York (with William Lescaze; later remodelled; now part of a synagogue complex)

Philadelphia Saving Fund Society Building, 12th and Market Streets, Philadelphia (with William Lescaze)

Stikeman Cottage, Sennerville, near Montreal

Emigrant Savings Bank and Office Building, East 42nd Street, New York (project; with William Lescaze)

1931/
32 Frederick V. Field House, New Hartford, Connecticut (with William Lescaze)

Philadelphia Saving Fund Society Garage, 12th and Filbert Streets, Philadelphia (with William Lescaze)

Housing development, Chrystie-Forsyth Streets, New York (project; with William Lescaze)

1932 50 small houses (project; with William Lescaze)

1932/
34 Square Shadows (Wasserman House III), Butler Pike, Whitemarsh, Pennsylvania

1934/
35 Welsh House, Laverock, Pennsylvania

1935 Speiser House, 2005 Delancey Place, Philadelphia

1936/
37 Levy House, Germantown, Philadelphia

1936/
41 *Evening Bulletin* Office renovation, Juniper and Filbert Streets, Philadelphia (with Louis McAllister)

1937 Hale House renovation, Dover, Massachusetts

1937/
39 Fortune Rock (Thomas House), Northeast Harbor Road, Ellsworth, Soames Sound, Mount Desert Island, Maine

1938 Arts Center, Wheaton College, Norton, Massachusetts (competition project)

1939 America at Home Exhibit, *World's Fair,* New York

Children's World Exhibit, *World's Fair,* New York (with Oscar Stonorov, Herbert Spiegel, and Cornelius Bogert)

House Prototype, for *Life* magazine, Amityville, Long Island, New York (with Robert Montgomery Brown)

1940/
42 Pine Ford Acres (defense housing), Middletown, near Harrisburg, Pennsylvania (with Louis I. Kahn)

1941 Newhall House, Scarsdale, New York (project)

1941/
43 Carver Court Housing, Coatesville, Pennsylvania (with Louis I. Kahn and Oscar Stonorov)

1942 Information Center, Office of War Information, Washington, D.C. (temporary structure; now demolished)

Pennypack Housing, Philadelphia (project; with Louis I. Kahn and Oscar Stonorov)

West Potomac Women's Residence Halls, Public Buildings Administration, Washington, D.C. (as supervising architect; temporary structures; now demolished)

1943 Lincoln Road Housing, Coatesville, Pennsylvania (project; with Louis I. Kahn and Oscar Stonorov)

Lily Ponds Housing, Washington, D.C. (project; with Louis I. Kahn and Oscar Stonorov)

1947 United States Consulate, Naples (project)

1952 WCAU Television Studio, City Line Avenue, Philadelphia (with Robert Montgomery Brown)

1954/
55 *Evening* and *Sunday Bulletin* Building, 30th and Market Streets, Philadelphia (with Robert Montgomery Brown)

1955 Wholesale Food Distribution Center (project; with Robert Montgomery Brown)

Publications:

By HOWE: articles—"Functional Aesthetics and the Social Ideal" in *Pencil Points* (New York), April 1932; article in *Architectural Forum* (New York), April 1940; "Two Architects' Credos: Traditional Versus Modern," with W. A. Delano, in *Magazine of Art* (New York), April 1940; "New York World's Fair" in *Architectural Forum* (New York), July 1940; "The Meaning of Art Today" in *Magazine of Art* (New York), May 1942; "Monuments, Memorials, and Modern Design—An Exchange of Letters" in *Magazine of Art* (New York), October 1944; "Relation of the Architect to Government" in *Michigan Society of Architects Bulletin* (Detroit), 31 July and 7 August 1945; "Master Plans for Master Politicians" in *Magazine of Art* (New York), February 1946, reprinted in *Metron* (Rome), no. 25, 1948; "Statement by George Howe at Princeton University's Bicentennial Celebration" in *Michigan Society of Architects Bulletin* (Detroit), 24 June 1947; "A Lesson from the Jefferson Memorial Competition" in *AIA Journal* (Washington, D.C.), March 1951; "Old Cities and New Frontiers" in *AIA Journal* (Washington, D.C.), January 1952; "Training for the Practice of Architecture" in *Perspecta* (New Haven, Connecticut), no. 2, 1953.

On HOWE: books—*George Howe, Architect, 1886–1955* by Helen Howe West, Philadelphia 1973; *George Howe* by Robert A.M. Stern, New Haven, Connecticut 1975; articles—"Howe and Lescaze" by Henry Russell Hitchcock in *Modern Architecture International,* exhibition catalog, New York 1932; "Low-cost houses" in *Architectural Forum* (New York), November 1942; "George Howe" by Bruno Zevi in *Metron* (Rome), no. 25, 1948; "George Howe: An Aristocratic Architect" by Bruno Zevi in *AIA Journal* (Washington, D.C.), October 1955; "Philadelphia Saving Fund Society Building: Its Development and Its Significance in Modern Architecture" by William Jordy and "Philadelphia Saving Fund Society Building: Beaux Arts Theory and Rational Expressionism" by Robert A.M. Stern in *Journal of the Society of Architectural Historians* (Philadelphia), May 1962; "Philadelphia Saving Fund Society Building" by Henry Wright in *Architectural Forum* (New York), May 1964; "PSFS: A Source for Its Design" by H. Allen Brooks in *Journal of the Society of Architectural Historians* (Philadelphia), December 1968; "Yale 1950–65" by Robert A.M. Stern in *Oppositions* (New York), October 1974.

*

Although he is known principally for his contributions to the distinguished International Style skyscraper, the Philadelphia Saving Fund Society Building, George Howe encompassed a wide variety of architectural achievements in his career.

Born in 1886 into the wealth and position of Philadelphia society, Howe was, both by education and temperament, suited to be the prototypical "gentleman architect." His early career was restricted largely to residential work in Philadelphia's fashionable suburbs, and as a partner in the firm of Mellor, Meigs and Howe he contributed to the design of country houses and estates in historical styles. Both picturesque and dignified, the best of these houses include Howe's own "High Hollow" and the more extensive Newbold Estate. Although they are conventional in plan and overall conception, these houses exhibit a concern for the clear expression of materials and their construction, complementing the building's charm with directness.

By the late 1920's Howe grew dissatisfied with his successful career: he quit both his firm and many of the architectural precepts that guided it. What he earnestly sought was a modern architecture, the architecture developing in Europe and beginning to make its presence felt in America through various publications. As the decade came to a close, Howe received the commission to design the Philadelphia Saving Fund Society Building (PSFS)—a large bank building conceived, ironically, during the worst years of the financial depression.

In 1929 Howe formed a partnership with the Swiss architect William Lescaze, with whom he was to do the most significant work of his career. Responsibility for the actual design of PSFS has been a topic of considerable dispute. Original contracts show that Howe was responsible primarily for business and administrative matters, while Lescaze took charge of architectural issues. Lescaze was later to claim full credit for PSFS, although early schemes by Howe, dating from before the partnership with Lescaze, indicate that crucial elements of massing and structure were conceived by Howe. Consisting of a commercial ground floor, a spectacular double story second floor banking room, and a twenty-eight story office tower, PSFS was perhaps the first skyscraper in America to be designed according to the structural and aesthetic tenets of the International Style. Historian William Jordy has pointed out the importance of its "composite image created of a diverse mechanomorphology . . ." and of its machine image as both "container" and "component." In its compositional asymmetry, the curved sweeping lines of the base, the extraordinary uninterrupted expanse of glass, the boldness of its huge juxtaposed forms, and in its sumptuous use of materials—all accomplished under the imperative of "functional architecture"—the PSFS was, and in many ways still is, the standard against which subsequent skyscraper design must be measured.

The seeming adventurousness of the PSFS was significantly never subsumed by Howe's quest for an authentically functional architecture. Fascinated by the modern quest for anti-gravitational effects in building, Howe was also concerned (as he himself later wrote) with the "true sculptural quality of an organic design" arising from "the moulding of interior space and the shaping of the skeleton to contain it. The functional architect delights in the huge torso of a building swaying on tendoned ankles."

Later projects from the office of Howe and Lescaze all contain their special felicities. The Chrystie-Forsyth Housing Development in New York was a concerted attempt at a large-scale scheme designed to alleviate the acute housing shortage during the early years of the Depression. Sharing certain structural principles with the Chrystie-Forsyth scheme was a group of proposals for the new Museum of Modern Art in New York, in which a skeletal frame held structurally independent gallery boxes. Also, during the early 1930's, Howe and Lescaze designed several private houses (though remarkably few were actually built). The most famous was Wasserman House, "Square Shadows," a large, boxy house, which, for all its notoriety, now seems rather clumsy on the outside and too full of stagey effects on the inside.

In 1935, after several disputes, Howe and Lescaze terminated their partnership, and Howe's career thereafter is an odd jumble of some pedestrian projects, one splendid house, "Fortune Rock," which is notable for its extravagant cantilevered decks and vernacular approach to building, and his own gradual transformation into teacher and elder statesman of American architecture. In 1940 Howe hired Louis Kahn, then a novice architect; they were joined by Oscar Stonorov, and the three men worked together on several housing schemes, including the interesting

George Howe: Philadelphia Saving Fund Society Building, Philadelphia, 1931

Carver Court at Coatesville, Pennsylvania. After the war Howe returned to private practice, and in 1949 he was invited to teach at Yale, where from 1950 to 1954 he was the popular and irrepressible chairman of the architecture department.

Noted for his sardonic wit and sartorial flair, George Howe abandoned an easy and lucrative career as a fashionable patrician architect to, instead, attempt to define the shape and direction of modern American architecture. A talented designer in his own right, he had the intelligence and largesse to recognize the talent of others. Most importantly, in the PSFS he contributed to the design of a building that, now divorced from the ideological struggles of fifty years ago, still retains its spirit of vigor, inventiveness and sheer excellence.

—Richard Lavenstein

HOWELL, KILLICK, PARTRIDGE AND AMIS.

Partnership; established, London, 1959, by former London County Council architects William G. Howell (born 1922; died 1974), John A. Killick (born 1924; retired 1969; died 1972), and John A. Partridge (born 1924); joined by Stanley F. Amis (born 1924) in 1961. Current partners: Partridge, Amis, Stephen Osgood (born 1937) since 1973, and R. J. Murphy (born 1932) since 1976; associates: A. H. Miller; L. Goodchild; P. J. Lawlor. Recipient: Civic Trust Award, 1965, 1968, 1969, 1970, 1978; Architecture Award, Royal Institute of British Architects, 1966, 1970 (twice), 1971, 1975, 1978; House Design Award, Ministry of Housing and Local Government, 1968; Camden Society of Architects Award, 1969; Concrete Society Award, 1970, 1971; Popular Architecture Award, RIBA, Plymouth Branch, 1978. Address: 20 Old Pye Street, Westminster, London SW1P 2DG, England.

Works:

1951/
    60 Roehampton Lane Housing, London (with London County Council Architect's Department)
1954/
    55 Terrace houses, Hampstead, London
1958/
    60 Timber framed house, Bromley, Kent
1960/
    64 Faculty of Commerce and Social Science, University of Birmingham
1960/
    65 Wolfson Residential Building, St. Anne's College, Oxford
1961/
    63 Metal Box Company Offices and Computer Centre, Worcester
1961/
    66 Acland Burghley School, London
1962/
    63 Planning study of Mill Lane, Cambridge
1962/
    66 Furniture Industry Research Association Headquarters, Stevenage, Hertfordshire
       Graduate Flats at Summertown House, Oxford University
1963/
    67 University Centre, Cambridge
1963/
    69 Weston Rise Housing, Islington, London
1964/
    65 Ramsay Rae House extension, Little Wakestone, Sussex
1964/
    66 Old Merchant Taylors' Society Squash Courts, London
       Gatehouse Building, St. Anne's College, Oxford
1964/
    68 Old people's housing, Stonegrove, Harrow, Middlesex
1964/
    69 Residential Building, Sidney Sussex College, Cambridge
1964/
    70 Hall and Residential Building, Darwin College, Cambridge
1965 Lenham School, Kent
       Planning study of Heythrop College, Oxfordshire
1965/
    69 Rayne Residential Building, St. Anne's College, Oxford
1965/
    70 Combination Room, Hall and Kitchens, Downing College, Cambridge
1966/
    69 House of Studies for Philosophers, House of Studies for Theologians, Astro Physics Out-Station, and House of Studies for Nuns of the Holy Child, Heythrop College, Oxfordshire (projects)

Howell, Killick, Partridge and Amis: College of Estate Management, University of Reading, 1973

Alton Road Housing, Roehampton, London
1966/
71 New Hall and Common Rooms, St. Antony's College, Oxford
1967/
70 Houses for visiting mathematicians, University of Warwick
1968/
71 Young Vic Theatre, Waterloo, London
1968/
73 College of Estate Management Faculty Building, University of Reading
Hall of Residence, University of Reading
1969/
71 Children's Playground, Roehampton, London
1970/
71 Development studies for teaching, music, sports, and study bedrooms, for the Merchant Taylors' School, London
1970/
72 Convent Building conversion, St. Antony's College, Oxford
1970/
74 Arts Centre, Christ's Hospital School, Horsham, Sussex
The Grove Old People's Housing, Haringey, London
1971 Children's Reception Home, Kent (project)
1971- Fleet Maintenance Base and Submarine Refit Complex, H. M. Dockyard, Devonport
Redevelopment Area Housing, Russell Road, Haringey, London
1971/
72 Harris and Sutherland Engineering Office conversion, Whitfield Street, London

1972 Arts Based Building, University of Reading (project)
Cement and Concrete Association Office Building, Wexham Springs, Buckinghamshire (project)
1972- Magistrates Courthouse, Chatham, Kent
Faculty of Art and Design, phase II, Middlesex Polytechnic, Enfield, London
1972/
73 Teaching Block, Music School and Swimming Pool, Merchant Taylors' School, Northwood, Middlesex (project)
1972/
74 Squash Courts, Merchant Taylors' School, Northwood, Middlesex
1972/
75 New Auditorium, Open Air Theatre, Regent's Park, London
1973/
75 Farmhouse and outbuildings conversion, Saltash, Cornwall
1973/
76 Development studies of Great Scotland Yard and Whitehall, London
1973/
78 Redevelopment Area Housing, Somerville Road, Lewisham, London
1974 New housing and rehabilitation, Trewsbury Road, Lewisham, Road (project)
Development study of Ilford High Road, Essex
1974/
76 Regency Cottage restoration, Cudham, Kent
Old People's Housing, Haringey, London
1976- Box Office, Scenery Workshop, Dressing and Administration Rooms, Open Air Thea-

tre, Regent's Park, London
New Kitchens and Boiler House, Farnborough Hospital, Kent
1977- Community Building and Theatre, The Albany, Deptford, London
Offices and shops conversion and restoration, 45–51 Whitehall, London
1978- Feasibility study for Ranby Prison, Nottinghamshire
Modernization study for the Royal Naval College, Dartmouth, Devon
Hall of Justice, Port of Spain, Trinidad

Publications:

On HKPA: articles—"Two Oxford Colleges" in *Aujourd'hui: Art et Architecture* (Paris), July 1965; "Universitätsgebaude in England," special issue of *Werk* (Zurich), January 1966; "University Centre, Cambridge" and "Young Vic Theatre, London" in *Architecture + Urbanism* (Tokyo), May 1973; "HKPA Vertebrae" by C. Amery in *Architectural Review* (London), November 1973; "Wells Hall Residential Building, University of Reading" in *Architectural Review* (London), July 1975; "Christ's Hospital Arts Centre" in *RIBA Journal* (London), July/August 1975; "Theatre in the Park" in *Building Design* (London), 25 June 1977; "Young Vic Theatre in London" in *Baumeister* (Munich), February 1978; "Urban Housing Variations" by J. M. McKean in *Building Design* (London), 21 July 1978; "Precast Concrete Walling for a Naval Base" by Stephen Osgood in *Concrete* (London), August 1978; "New Housing: New Cross Area" by Peter Collymore in *Architectural Review* (London), October 1978.

We have no "house style," though no doubt the authorship of our buildings can usually be guessed by those who know our work. However, this is not due to our having any particular formal obsessions or predilection for certain materials or structural methods. We aim to choose materials, structures and geometrical systems appropriate to the locations, the budget and the function of the building. We have designed brick buildings, stone, timber, concrete and steel buildings, and buildings which combine these materials.

We have developed certain themes which can be traced through a series of jobs. From our work at Roehampton, the first large scale use of pre-cast concrete cladding in this country, we have gone on, particularly in our Oxford College work, to try to achieve richness and quality from this often misused material. This we have done partly by using three-dimensional forms of pre-cast units, which derive from the splayed window units we have developed to introduce light into rooms in a well modulated way and partly from our research into ways of detailing, surfacing and assembling pre-cast concrete so that it weathers well and ages gracefully.

Another theme has been the evolution of less box-like geometry than that which characterizes much of modern building. This rather crude angularity no doubt partly results from most building materials being rectilinear (sheets, blocks or linear elements like timber or steel beams). However, we have developed, in a series of buildings, ways of using these materials that, while respecting their inherent geometry and avoiding expensive cutting or bending, build up from them more complex geometrical forms which may well be more suitable to the internal functions or characteristics of the environment in which the building is to go. (Our octagonal dining hall at Darwin College, Cambridge is an example.) We have also developed an approach to interiors, using "as found" materials, natural timber, bricks and blocks (painted or natural), which we feel avoid the bleakness often associated with modern interiors and give a humanity and warmth often hard to achieve, especially in institutional buildings.

In all our work we attempt to pay particular attention to neighbouring buildings and existing landscape. We prefer to blend rather than stick out like a sore thumb, and tend to choose materials, colours, textures and scale of elements that will fit naturally, especially when faced with an existing environment of quality.

—Howell, Killick, Partridge and Amis

Bill Howell, who was born in 1922, became Professor of Architecture at Cambridge, and died in a car crash in 1974, was the best known partner of Howell, Killick, Partridge and Amis. In his obituary *The Times* offered an explanation of the significance of HKPA, saying that Howell "belonged to the generation that made British architecture, in the years after the war, respected all over the world." Almost as a model of the whole post-war profession in Britain, HKPA have been concerned with the public sector: they have specialized in housing and schools and have attempted to find an architectural expression of the social responsibilities that have characterized the age.

Howell, Killick, Partridge and Amis was set up in 1959 by architects who had been employed by the London County Council in the immediate post-war years. In a period of economic depression, the offices of Britain's largest local authority provided an opportunity for architectural experimentation that made it one of the centres of the contemporary architectural enlightenment. One of the major schemes produced by the LCC in these years, and one in which Howell and the others were prominent, was the award-winning Roehampton Housing Estate in south-west London. Often reproduced as a symbol of the best in British housing, Roehampton was the superficial vernacular expression in England of the ideas that Le Corbusier had made the everyday stuff of architectural education.

Howell left the LCC in 1956, and in eighteen years of improving and declining economic conditions he managed to make himself and his firm leading, articulate spokesmen of the conservative best in current British architecture. The architecture of the whole group was heavily influenced by the example of the Smithsons, and each HKPA building concentrates heavily on what older architectural jargon calls "circulation" and what Reyner Banham has called "connectivity." Asked just before his death to cite the partnership's most important buildings, Howell listed St. Anne's and St. Antony's Colleges, Oxford; Darwin, Downing, and Sidney Sussex Colleges, Cambridge; the University Centre, Cambridge; Young Vic Theatre, London; and the Arts Centre at Christ's Hospital School, Horsham. Of the Roehampton episode he concisely referred only to "GLC Housing," a suggestion that with maturity the naive expectations and empty rhetoric of the immediate post-war period were best forgotten.

—Stephen Bayley

HUGHES, (Henry) Richard.

British. Born in London, 4 July 1926; emigrated with his parents to East Africa in 1937. Educated at Hilton College, Natal, South Africa, 1940–44; Architectural Association School, London, under R. F. Jordan, Arthur Korn, Felix Samuely, and Ernesto Rogers, 1947–50, 1951–53, A.A. Diploma 1953; attended short course in city and regional planning at Massachusetts Institute of Technology, Cambridge, Summer 1954. Corporal in the Kenya Regiment, attached to the Royal Engineers, 1944–46. Married Anne Hill in 1951; children: Bridget, Penelope, and Mervyn. Assistant Architect to Henry J. Ludorf, Hartford, Connecticut, 1953–55, and to Blackburn and Norburn, Nairobi, Kenya, 1955–57; in private practice, as H. Richard Hughes, Nairobi, 1957–76; Partner, with Brian Arthur Smith, Richard Hughes/Smith Partnership, Nairobi, 1976–78; resumed private practice, Nairobi, 1978. Member of the Council, East African Institute of Architects, 1956–57; Chairman, Kenya Branch, Capricorn Africa Society, 1958–61; Governor, Hospital Hill School, Nairobi, 1962–75; Vice-President, Kenya Arts Society, 1965–73; Chairman, East African Institute of Architects Board of Architectural Education, 1972–74; Governor, Kenya Polytechnic, 1972–75; Chairman, Kenya Museum Society, 1974–75; Consultant to the United Nations Environment Programme on Human Settlements Technology, 1976; Chairman, Environment Liaison Centre, Nairobi, 1976–78; Chairman, Lamu Society, 1977–78. Exhibitions: Overseas League and Imperial Institute, London, 1953; East African Institute of Architects, Nairobi, 1963; Commonwealth Arts Festival, Cardiff, 1965; German Africa Society, Bonn and Berlin, 1966. Associate, 1954, and Fellow, 1969, Royal Institute of British Architects. Address: Post Office Box 14390, Nairobi, Kenya.

Works:

1957/
74 Alliance Girls' High School Chapel and Redevelopment, Kikuyu, Kenya
1957/
75 Private houses in Nairobi, Mombasa, Gilgil, and Nanyuki, Kenya, and in The Seychelles
1958 Council chamber and offices, Kenya Federation of Labour, Nairobi
1958/
76 Hospital Hill Primary School Assembly Hall and Classrooms, Nairobi

1960/
62 University of Nairobi Institute of Adult Studies, Kikuyu, Kenya
1960/
70 Churches in Embu, Meru, Kilifi, Maralal, Mombasa, Maguga, Masasi, Nairobi, and Nambale, and in Zululand, South Africa
1962 Television Studios, Nairobi
Egerton Agricultural College redevelopment, Njoro, Kenya
Kaimosi Teachers' Training College redevelopment, Kenya
1963 Trinity College for the Anglican Church, Nairobi
1964 Makerere University Chapel extensions, Kampala, Uganda
Town Hall, Bukoba, Tanzania
1964/
67 Radio studios, control rooms and offices, Nairobi
1965 Broadcasting House, Mauritius
1965/
73 Limuru Girls' School extensions, near Nairobi
1965/
76 East African Posts and Telecommunications staff housing, Nairobi
1967 Coast Hotel, Watamu Beach, Kenya
Transmitter Building, Ngong, Kenya
1967/
73 Student residences, University of Nairobi
1968 Houses, Moi Estate, Nairobi
Development House (office building), Nairobi
Lutheran Cathedral, Bukoba, Tanzania
Industrial and Commercial Development Corporation industrial estate, Nairobi (with Sir Alexander Gibb and Partners)
Kenya Institute of Mass Communication, Nairobi
All-Africa Conference of Churches Radio and TV Training Centre, Nairobi
1968/
72 Tea factory and extension, Mauritius
1969 Makerere University Art Gallery, Kampala, Uganda
VOK Outside Broadcasting and Transport Unit, Nairobi
1970/
78 East African External Telecommunications Company Headquarters Buildings, Nairobi and Kampala, Uganda
1971 Coast Transmitting Station, Mombasa, Kenya
1972 New Stanley Hotel alterations, Nairobi
Block Hotels Office Building extensions, Nairobi
1973 University of Nairobi Senior Staff Houses, Kabete, Kenya
Flats and maisonettes, Nairobi
Katoke Teachers' College redevelopment, Tanzania
Two secondary schools, Bukoba, Tanzania
Norfolk Hotel extensions, Nairobi
1974 Civil servants housing, Old Racecourse, Nairobi
Murang'a College of Technology, Kenya
Town Hall, Embu, Kenya
1975 Hillcrest Secondary School, Nairobi
1976 Residential estate, near Nairobi
Christian Students Leadership Centre, Nairobi
University of Nairobi Library, Chiromo Campus, Nairobi
1977 Mombasa Airport, Kenya (production drawings and supervision as joint production architects; design by Gollins, Melvin and Ward Partnership)
National Bank of Kenya Headquarters, Nairobi
1978 S. M. Githunguri Office Development, Nairobi
Development House II, Nairobi

Richard Hughes: National Bank of Kenya Headquarters, Nairobi, 1977

Insurance Company of East Africa Office Building, Nairobi

Publications:

By HUGHES: articles—"East Africa" in *New Buildings in the Commonwealth,* edited by J. M. Richards, London 1951; "Proposals for an Inter-Racial Settlement in Kenya" in *East Africa and Rhodesia* (London), August 1953; "Town Plan to Facilitate Racial Integration" in *New Commonwealth* (London), September 1953; "Continuing Boom in New Construction" in *Manchester Guardian,* 25 April 1956; "Five Church Buildings in Kenya" in *Church Buildings Today* (London), January 1962; "Protestant Churches of Kenya" in *East African Annual,* Nairobi 1964/65; "Development of a Private Practice in Kenya" in *The Architects' Journal* (London), October 1969; "Religious Architecture and Planning" in *Kenya Churches Handbook,* edited by D. B. Barrett, Nairobi 1973; "Lamu: A Lesson in Townscape," with U. Ghaidan, in *Architectural Review* (London), November 1973; "Instruments of Creativity" in *Thus They Project,* International Union of Architects, Madrid 1975; "Lamu: A Study in Conservation" in *Azania* (Nairobi), no. XI, 1976; "Planning Policies and Proposed Byelaws for Lamu" in *Lamu: A Study in Conservation,* Nairobi 1976.

On HUGHES: books—*East African Institute of Architects Year Book,* Nairobi 1961; *New Architecture in Africa* by Udo Kultermann, London 1963; *East African Institute of Architects Jubilee Handbook,* Nairobi 1963; *Modern Churches of the World* by R. Maguire and K. Murray, London 1965; *University Hostel Research Project* by D. M. Ferguson, London 1968; *New Directions in African Architecture* by Udo Kultermann, London 1969; *The History of the Alliance High School* by J. S. Smith, Nairobi 1973; *Then and Now: The Norfolk Hotel* by Jan Hemsing, Nairobi 1975; articles—editorial comment in *East Africa and Rhodesia* (London), August 1953; "A Nairobi House" in *Trade and Industry* (Nairobi), July 1958; illustrations in *Architectural Review* (London), July 1960; "New Churches" in *Church Buildings Today* (London), January 1962; illustrations in *The Architects' Journal* (London), October 1969; "New Churches in Kenya" in *Church Buildings Today* (London), October 1969; illustrations in *Architectural Review* (London), February 1970, July 1973; illustrations in *Plan East Africa* (Nairobi), February 1975; "National Bank Building" in *Build Kenya* (Nairobi), August 1977; "Murang'a College of Technology" in *Build Kenya* (Nairobi), January 1978; "Richard Hughes: A Man for All Reasons" in *Build Kenya* (Nairobi), June 1978.

My design objectives are easily stated but hard to achieve: to meet all the client's requirements, including those he has not thought of or formulated; to reflect the constraints and nature of the site and the environment; to be concerned about all those who will use and be influenced by the building; to have regard for the economic level of the area, regardless of the actual budget; and to create a series of spaces that are coherent and defined. The subconscious synthesis of all these and myriad other inputs to produce a three-dimensional concept requires time to evolve (usually just the period available up to the last minute) and, even more important, time for the rigorous testing of the solution against the requirements, both those that are absolute and those that are negotiable depending on one's judgement of priorities.

Although the external appearance of a building and the materials used are important, they are less so than the clarity of the enclosed spaces, for it is space that distinguishes architecture from the other visual arts, plus the need to meet functional requirements.

The relationship to the local environment, social, economic and physical, is vital, particularly in new countries like Kenya, if the building is not to seem alien and out of context. Many long-absorbed and unrecorded scraps of information have to be part of the synthesis at the design stage, which is why the developing world suffers from jobs designed overseas by architects who think it sufficient to study the site plan and climatic data and then impose their preconceptions.

It is my belief that the environment, in the broader context, must be a major concern and responsibility of any architect: not only human settlements or "Habitat," but the whole spectrum of energy, water, waste, appropriate technologies and the fundamental problems of development within environmental constraints.

Seen from the Third World, many of the technologies that are imposed or transferred through sale of equipment and expertise by the industrialized countries on the less developed are inappropriate in scale and in the relation between capital and labour. They often seem wasteful of resources in their country of origin too.

—Richard Hughes

Nairobi resembles the capital cities of many developing nations in, being young and growing fast. From having been a small administrative and commercial town on the Uganda railway, it has become the principal focus for development, commerce and communications in Kenya and eastern Africa. Most of Richard Hughes' work has been in East Africa, much of it in Nairobi itself, and his professional practice has spanned the major period of growth in this region and in the city.

The recent expansion of opportunities for architects in Kenya is mirrored in the fact that though many of Hughes' earlier buildings were on a relatively domestic scale, some of his more recent works are very large complexes in the city centre. What is unusual about his work is the consistency of approach in more than twenty years of practice and the exposition of principle that is as evident in a tiny youth hostel chapel as in a vast communication centre. In spite of the changing scale of his buildings over the years, Hughes has continued to express and develop an imaginative but essentially functionalist aesthetic. The most immediately striking features of his buildings are a bold, sometimes almost brutally deliberate, articulation and interplay of volumes and spaces, an equally deliberate parsimony in the number of materials or finishes that go into the fabric, and an unusual sensitivity to the relationship between the needs and activities of people, the numbers likely to use a space and the modelling and scale of the rooms, halls and passages they occupy. Detailing in his buildings is invariably simple and unobtrusive but immaculate.

All too often fancied needs for pretentious facades, irrelevant gimmicks or "prestige" have been indulged or pandered to by architects working in developing countries. When I interviewed Hughes for an article in 1961 he remarked "good buildings result from imaginative and honest solutions to the many problems of site, climate, clients, brief and budget. . . . I believe that grossly expensive buildings, even if the money happens to be available, are out of place in a country without enough school buildings, housing or hospitals. The budget dictates standards of finish and workmanship and the architect must design and detail accordingly."

It is significant that Hughes has never departed from these principles nor have his major clients (government agencies, education authorities, the communications industry and banks) imposed irrelevant demands. Hughes special talent for buildings of a social nature has led to numerous commissions from Protestant organizations for cathedrals, churches, chapels, community centres, clinics and educational complexes.

Hughes has never clad a building in marble or used imported materials in preference to suitable local ones. Wherever budgets have allowed his doing so, he has involved reputable local artists in murals, sculpture, stained glass and ceramics so that, in addition to his own creative role, he has done more to actively foster the fine arts in East Africa than any other architect.

The arrival of the United Nations Environmental Programme in Nairobi in 1973 stimulated Hughes' sustained concern for architectural principles and channelled his energies and vision into the wider field of human habitat (the subject of a book he is currently writing with a colleague).

Hughes believes that architects should not only use technologies that are appropriate to "place" and site, but they must also accept responsibility and be concerned for every aspect of human settlements, particularly the environmental constraints on water supplies, waste disposal, energy sources and the less tangible social problems of rapid development.

In his buildings, in words and in print, Hughes continues to call for greater awareness of our environment and action to save us from the spreading cancer of urban and rural squalor.

—Jonathan Kingdon

ISHII, Kazuhiro.

Japanese. Born in Tokyo, 1 February 1944. Educated at the University of Tokyo, under Arata Isozaki, B.A. 1968, M.A. 1970; Yale University, New Haven, Connecticut, under Charles Moore, James Stirling, and Louis I. Kahn, M.Ed. 1974. Worked for Isozaki, in Tokyo, 1969. In private practice, Tokyo, since 1970: Principal, Kazuhiro Ishii Architect and Associates. Lecturer, Waseda University, Tokyo, 1978; Visiting Professor, University of California at Los Angeles, 1978. Address: Kazuhiro Ishii Architect and Associates, Takegami Building 201, 2 chome 3–30 Jingumae, Shibuya-ku, Tokyo 150, Japan.

Works:

1970 "Genshu" Tea House, Oizumigakuen, Tokyo
       Naoshima Elementary School, Naoshima, Kagawa, Japan
1971 Cyclotron House, Tokorozawa, Saitama, Japan
1972 Ishii Residence, Kokubunji, Tokyo
1974 Naoshima Kindergarten, Naoshima, Kagawa, Japan
1975 "54 Windows" (Soya Clinic and Residence), Hiratsuka, Kanagawa, Japan
1976 "Strawberry" Cafe, Kanda, Tokyo
       Naoshima Gymnasium, Naoshima, Kagawa, Japan
1977 Takahashi Residence, Kichijoji, Tokyo
1978 Honda Residence, Aoyama, Tokyo
       Ishii Garden House, Kokubunji, Tokyo
1979 Naoshima Junior High School, Naoshima, Kagawa, Japan
       "54 Roofs" (Takebe Nursery School), Takebe, Okayama, Japan

Publications:

By ISHII: book—*Yale, Architecture, Commuting,* Tokyo 1977; translations of books—*James Stirling* by John Jacobs, Tokyo 1975; *MLTW Houses* by Donlyn Lyndon, Tokyo 1975; *Dimensions* by Charles Moore and Gerald Allen, Tokyo 1978; *Learning from Las Vegas* by Denise Scott Brown, Robert Venturi and Steven Izenour, Tokyo 1978; *Place of Houses* by Charles Moore, Gerald Allen and Donlyn Lyndon, Tokyo 1978; articles—"Analysis of Kohou-an, Daitokuji-Temple" in *Kenchikubunka* (Tokyo), April 1971; "Independence or Isolation" in *Toshijutaku* (Tokyo), May 1972; "Total Institution," editor, in *Toshijutaku* (Tokyo), October 1972; "Los Angeles," editor, in *Architecture + Urbanism* (Tokyo), November 1972; "Documents on Motomachi, Hiroshima" in *Shinkenchiku* (Tokyo), May 1973; "Notes on Open School" in *Space Design* (Tokyo), June 1973; "The Column Culture and the Wall Culture in Japanese Architecture" in *Shinkenchiku* (Tokyo), June 1975; "Notes on Arata Isozaki" in *Space Design* (Tokyo), April 1976; "Post Metabolism" in *The Japan Architect* (Tokyo), October/November 1977; "Sukiya Concept" in *GA Houses 3,* Tokyo 1978; "Kisho Kurokawa" in *Shinkenchiku*

(Tokyo), March 1978; "Deliberate Regression from Modern Architecture: Eleven Points, The Contribution of Charles Moore" in *Architecture + Urbanism* (Tokyo), May 1978; "Kenji Kawaii and Osamu Ishiyama" in *Shinkenchiku* (Tokyo), May 1978; "Togo Murano" in *Shinkenchiku* (Tokyo), June 1978; "Fumihiko Maki" in *Shinkenchiku* (Tokyo), September 1978; "Junzo Yoshimura" in *Shinkenchiku* (Tokyo), November 1978.

On ISHII: article—"Reality and Mask" by Koji Taki in *Japan Interior* (Tokyo), November 1977.

Unlike most architectural students who see their projects die in the oblivion of their portfolios, Kazuhiro Ishii has managed to make reality some of the products of his student days. Furthermore, in the years of his short but extraordinary career, Ishii has continued to create projects that retain the spark of student freshness; his works are intolerant of conventional professional compromises, yet they are highly disciplined at all levels of their architecture—conceptual, spatial, structural and functional. So far there has been no project of Ishii's that can not be regarded as a unique case study. All of his works, covering a wide range of building types (educational facilities, residential buildings, ceremonial structures), have been studied intensely; he has produced a series of prototypes that other architects will find it difficult to surpass.

Ishii's design method is heavily dependent on history. Although not an historian, he is highly conversant in world and Japanese history of architecture. Observation and hard analysis of historical examples

have been his tutors in design, and his exercises in design history have often stimulated his imagination in the creative process. The tea ceremony room, the "54 windows" project, and the curved colonnade of the Naoshima Gymnasium are all results of Ishii's interpretations of historical examples. His scholasticism is empirical: combined with his socio-worldly concerns and creative drive, it produces projects that are consistent with the theories and circumstances of their making.

An intentional inclusion of conventional symbols and schemata, as well as an appropriate display of occasional subtle "humor," distinguish Ishii's architecture from mainstream architecture. His humor is reminiscent of Gaudi's (the Gaudi of the non-vertical colonnade of the Park Güell in Barcelona). Ishii has totally omitted two columns in the curved colonnade of his Naoshima Gymnasium. The Visible Bar reinforcement suggests the two columns that ought to have been there but are not there; it suggests, too, that our current high technology can permit us to play such non-conventional games.

The house in Hiratsuka, known as "54 Windows" or "Tokyo Boogie Woogie," is Ishii's answer to current building practices in today's conventional environment. It demonstrates his concern and offers his answer to contemporary Japanese regionalism, which, in his own words, is characterized by "excess and display." This house—Ishii's masterpiece, in my opinion—offers a diagrammatic intellectual answer to metropolitan alienation. The easily built, thus economic, rigid-frame structure permits the display of abundant information on the elevations by means of clipped window cubicles (54 or 171), each conveying to the outside the varying "meanings" of the inside.

Kazuhiro Ishii: "54 Windows" (Soya Clinic and Residence), Hiratsuka, Kanagawa, Japan, 1975

"54 Windows" is a symphony of "messages," subordinate to the severe discipline of a low-budget structural system and an efficient functional layout.

Ishii's school buildings (kindergarten, elementary school, gymnasium, etc.) on the Island of Naoshima, all designed in his late twenties and constructed by his early thirties, have already opened new horizons for the architecture of Japanese educational facilities.

Ishii is, in my opinion, the happiest product of Oriental and Western influences. His education at Yale under the guidance and inspiration of Charles Moore, along with his strong concern for meaningful contemporary Japanese regionalism, have produced a most sensitive architecture, unique in Japan and the world.

Tange, Kurokawa and Isozaki tried to show the world that Japan could do equally well, and perhaps even better, what everybody else was doing architecturally. Tange tried it through structural expressionism and metabolism, Kurokawa through a multiplicity of expressions, and Isozaki through a Japanese version of often ultra-incomprehensible interpretations of New York "metaphysics." Kazuhiro Ishii has gone beyond all that. He belongs to a post-metabolist, much younger, generation, a down-to-earth but highly dedicated generation in which a claim to immortality can be made even through involvement with trivia.

This young talented architect, also a dedicated scholar and tireless writer, is a model not only in his joyful, pleasing, consistent and human architecture but also in the way in which he practices architecture as a vocation—an example for architects and ar-

chitectural students in our complex and demanding era. I believe that in the years to come, when fashions and the works of various fashionable architects have been faded by time, Ishii will most probably shine at the top of the Japanese architectural pyramid.

—Anthony C. Antoniades

ISOZAKI, Arata.

Japanese. Born in Oita City, 23 July 1931. Educated at the University of Tokyo, Faculty of Architecture, Dip.Arch. 1954. Married the sculptor Aiko Miyawaki in 1972. Worked with Kenzo Tange's Team and Urtec, Tokyo, 1954–63. Since 1963, Director of the Arata Isozaki Atelier, Tokyo. Visiting Professor, University of California at Los Angeles, 1969, University of Hawaii, Honolulu, 1974, Rhode Island School of Design, Providence, 1976, and Columbia University, New York, 1976, 1979. Exhibitions: *Space and Color,* Tokyo, 1966; *From Space Towards Environment,* Tokyo, 1966; *Triennale,* Milan, 1968; *Operation Vesuvius,* Naples, 1972; *Terra-1: International Exhibition of Architecture,* Warsaw, 1975; *Arata Isozaki: Retrospective,* London, 1976; *Dortmunder Architecturausstellung,* Dortmund, Germany, 1976; *ManTransForms,* Cooper-Hewitt Museum, New York, 1976–77; *Architecture of Quotation and Metaphor* (one-man show), Tokyo, Chicago, and Lodz, 1977; *Assenza/Presenza,* Bologna, 1977; *Bienal,* Sao Paulo, 1977; *Numerals: Mathematical Concepts in Contemporary Art,* Leo Castelli Gallery, New York, 1977; *A New Wave of Japanese Architecture,* toured the United States, 1978–79; *MA-Space/-Time in Japan,* Cooper-Hewitt Museum, New York, 1979. Recipient: Annual Prize, 1967, 1975, and Special *Expo '70* Prize, 1970, Japan Architectural Association; Annual Prize, *Architectural Year Book,* Japan, 1968; Artist Newcomer Prize, Ministry of Culture, Japan, 1969. Member, Accademia Tiberina, Italy, 1978. Address: Arata Isozaki Atelier, Kyo Building 2F, 15 Tenjin-cho, Shinjuku-ku, Tokyo, Japan.

Works:

1959/
60 Oita Medical Hall, Oita City, Japan
1960 Joint Core System for large-scale urban development (project)
    Tokyo Plan 1960 (with the Kenzo Tange Team)
1960/
62 Future Dwelling (project)
    Process Planning (project)
    Ruin Future City (project)
    Clusters in the Air (project)
1962/
66 Oita Prefectural Library, Oita City, Japan
1963 Upper Structure, for the Central District of Tokyo (project)
1963/
64 Iwata Girls' High School, Oita City, Japan
1964 Nakayama House, Oita City, Japan

Arata Isozaki: Gunma Prefectural Museum of Fine Arts, Takasaki City, Japan, 1974

1965 Set designs for the film *The Other Man's Face*
1965/
66 Plan for the reconstruction of Skopje, Yugoslavia (with the Kenzo Tange Team)
1966 Monument for a Poet, Kuju Mountain, Oita, Japan
1966/
67 Oita Branch of the Fukuoka Mutual Bank, Oita City, Japan
1966/
70 *Expo '70*, Osaka: site planning; cybernetic environment for the Festival Plaza; layout of urban trunk facilities; and mechanics of the Festival Plaza
1968/
69 Daimyo Branch of the Fukuoka Mutual Bank, Fukuoka City, Japan
1968/
71 Fukuoka Mutual Bank Head Office, Fukuoka City, Japan
1970/
71 Tokyo Branch of the Fukuoka Mutual Bank (with Kijo Rokkaku)
Computer Aided City (project)
1970/
72 Annex, Oita Medical Hall, Oita City, Japan
1971 Nagazumi and Ropponmatsu Branch of the Fukuoka Mutual Bank, Fukuoka City, Japan
1971/
74 Gunma Prefectural Museum of Fine Arts, Takasaki City, Japan
1972/
74 Kitakyushu City Museum of Art, Kitakyushu City, Japan
1972/
75 Kitakyushu Central Library, Kitakyushu City, Japan
1973 Saga Branch of the Fukuoka Mutual Bank, Saga City, Japan
1973/
74 Fujimi Country Club, Oita City, Japan
1974 Katsuyama Country Clubhouse (project)
I and T House, Karuisawa, Japan (project)
Cultural Center, Oita City, Japan (project)
1974/
75 Shuko-sha Office Building, Fukuoka City, Japan
1975 Yano House, Takaishi, Tama-ku, Kawasaki City, Japan
Kawarayu Spa Removal (project)
1975/
77 West Japan General Exhibition Center, Kitakyushu City, Japan
Kamioka Town Hall, Gifu Prefecture, Japan
1976 Kaijima House, Honcho, Kichijoji, Musashino City, Tokyo
Hayashi House, Kozasa, Nishi-ku, Fukuoka City, Japan
Information/Cultural Center (project)
Layout of the Japanese Section, *Biennale,* Venice
1977/
79 Audio-Visual Center, Oita City, Japan
1978 Sueoka Clinic, Kogazuru, Oita City, Japan
Karashima House, Chiyo-machi, Oita City, Japan
1978- Hakubi Kyoto Kimono School, Tokyo
Town Center, Tsukuba Academic New Town, Tsuchiura City, Japan
1978/
79 Design of the "MA-Espace-Temps au Japon" exhibition at the *Festival d'Automne,* Paris
1979 Aoki House, Tokyo

Publications:

By ISOZAKI: books—*Kukan-e* (collected writings, 1960–69), Tokyo 1971; *Kenchiku-no-kaitai* (monograph on contemporary architecture), Tokyo 1975; *Kenchiku Oyobi Kenchikugai-teki Shiko* (dialogue with other architects and people from various fields), Tokyo 1976; *Kenchiku-no-1930-nendai* (architecture of the 1930's: dialogue with other architects), Tokyo 1978; *Shuho-ga* (collected writings, 1969–78), Tokyo 1979; *Kenchiku-no-Shuji* (notes on a counter architecture), Tokyo 1979; articles in English—"About My Method" in *The Japan Architect* (Tokyo), August 1972; "The Metaphor for the Cube" in *The Japan Architect* (Tokyo), March 1976; "A Metaphor Relating with Water" in *The Japan Architect* (Tokyo), March 1978; "Formalism" in *The Japan Architect* (Tokyo), January 1979.

On ISOZAKI: books—*New Directions in Japanese Architecture* by Robin Boyd, London and New York 1968; *Third Generation: The Changing Meaning of Architecture,* London 1972; *Modern Movements in Architecture* by Charles Jencks, London 1973; *Decorative Art and Modern Interiors,* London 1977; *Beyond Metabolism: The New Japanese Architecture* by Michael Franklin Ross, New York 1978; articles—"Architecture for the Mini-skirt Age" by Yoshiaki Tono in *The Japan Architect* (Tokyo), May 1968; "Recent Works by Arata Isozaki" in *The Japan Architect* (Tokyo), August 1972; "Die Maniera des Arata Isozaki" by Jürgen Joedicke in *Bauen und Wohnen* (Zurich), March 1975; "Arata Isozaki," special editions of *The Japan Architect* (Tokyo), March and April 1976; "Position and Move" by Hans Hollein in *Space Design* (Tokyo), April 1976; "The Unreal Architecture of Arata Isozaki" by Jennifer Taylor in *Progressive Architecture* (New York), September 1976; special issue of *Architectural Design* (London), January 1977; "Arata Isozaki" by Jennifer Taylor in *Architecture Australia* (Sydney), September 1977.

The last 20 years of my architectural career manifest two fairly distinct tendencies which coincide with two periods, the 1960's and the 1970's. The transition between these two periods stems from my situation as architect in the stream of social, economic and cultural events of Japan in these years.

In my work of the 1960's I attempted to represent the rapid expansion of the Japanese city and the extensive development of technology and economy in Japan by my architectural method. At this same time, in the early 1960's, the Metabolist Movement was begun by a group of young Japanese architects. This architectural movement aimed to express directly the specific development of technical method itself, which could correspond to the changing situation of the city and architecture. Although I was not a member of the Metabolist Group, I remained sympathetic but always critical, while trying to find my own method. I sympathized with the Metabolists primarily on the technical and expressive levels. My Joint Core System of 1960, a project working with architectural concepts on an urban scale, and Oita Prefectural Library (1960), the concrete realization of the earlier project, represent this tendency. Later this tendency was further developed in the Master Plan for *Expo '70* in the idea of the Festival Plaza and, moreover, in the design of mechanical equipment and in the direction of performance at the Festival Plaza in 1970.

My criticism of the Metabolist Movement was directed against what I considered to be their somewhat facile and naive interpretation of modern architecture—the tendency to reduce architecture to simply an answer to utilitarian needs. My objection, in purely conceptual terms, argued that architecture must possess its own independent form and that this would ultimately secure for architecture an original cultural meaning. This attitude would be kept in my work in the 1970's. My Nakayama House of 1964, based on purely geometric form, is important when seen from this point of view.

In the 1970's the number and functions of my buildings increased, from private houses to public buildings (The Kitakyushu Central Library, 1975; Gunma Prefectural Museum of Fine Arts, 1974), from the structural development at the West Japan General Exhibition Center of 1977 to the organization of a new-style exhibition, *MA-Space/Time in Japan* (1978–79), introducing the unique and deeply-rooted Japanese concept of MA to the West. Through these various works, I have consistently intended to locate architecture in the context of culture, by clarifying conceptualization and method. Such a pursuit may represent a unique point of view, missing not only in Japanese architecture but also in modern architecture in general. Therefore, in my work, I have always regarded architecture as a play of pure forms, simultaneously containing economic, functional, technical and various other solutions.

In order to synthesize in architecture these posited but undefined dimensions, I have adopted an architectural method, a "Maniere (=Maniera)" as a means of critically passing beyond the Modern Movement.

More explicitly, in attempting to establish "architecture," my work includes quotations from the whole of our cultural legacy up to the present, bringing forth, hopefully, unique metaphors. This architectural attitude will continue to preoccupy me in the future.

—Arata Isozaki

Arata Isozaki is one of the most prolific and creative personalities in international contemporary architecture. In terms of boldness of design and creative power, he can be compared only with James Stirling, Richard Meier and Aldo Rossi. Like them, he must be acknowledged to be one of the masters of the 1970's. Isozaki's early architectural work in his home town of Oita in the south of Japan, his work with the Kenzo Tange Team in Tokyo, his proposals for Clusters in the Air of 1962, and especially his work since 1970 show innovative exploration into the complexity of architectural space and its meaning.

Most characteristic of Isozaki's buildings is their ambiguous nature, an ambiguity that includes a sense of irony and wit. The complexity of meaningful spatial articulations in his work is often hidden by an academic perfection of execution. Yet the basic goal remains the revelation of the autonomous and complicated meaning of spaces. In Isozaki's own terms: "Architecture is a machine for the production of meaning." And he continues: "I attempt to use the simplest possible techniques to embody my methods because I feel that without the intermediary of what I call the traces of human hands, the method itself will be more effective and the range greater. Of course the method involves the use of the hands, and the traces of their activities only begin to vanish as the result of the virtually automatic process originating with the use of the ruler."

In order to achieve his goals, Isozaki makes the images and quotations of earlier architectural solutions integral parts of the design process; he aims at what could be called "architectural multimedia." Isozaki's term "maniera" designates the re-use or variation of pre-conceived themes from different periods and places at the same time and in the same work. This method results in a pluralization of elements and a multi-level approach that, in itself, causes a multiplicity of meaning and eclecticism of radical dimensions. The conceptual presence of all historical phases from the past—Greek temples, Shinto shrines, Buddhist temples, Palladio's villas, the buildings of Kenzo Tange, Superstudio design, and technological images in general—makes Isozaki's work one of international, universal synthesis. As with other contemporary pioneers of an autonomous architecture, Isozaki defends his medium against its exploitation as a language of social comment, cultural or personal expressionism, and political propaganda.

Arata Isozaki's major buildings include the Saga Branch of the Fukuoka Mutual Bank; Gunma Prefectural Museum of Fine Arts, Takasaki; Fujimi Country Club in Oita; Kamioka Town Hall; Kitakyushu Central Library; and the Yano House in Kawasaki.

—Udo Kultermann

J

JACKSON, Daryl.

Australian. Born in Clunes, Victoria, 7 February 1937. Educated at Wesley College, Melbourne, 1950–53; Royal Melbourne Institute of Technology, 1954–56, Dip.Arch. 1956; University of Melbourne, 1957–58, B.Arch. 1958. Married Kay Jackson in 1960; children: Timothy, Sara, Olivia and Melissa. Assistant, Edwards, Madigan and Torzillo, 1959, Don Hendry Fulton, Melbourne, 1960, Chamberlin, Powell and Bon, London, 1961–63, Paul Rudolph, New Haven, Connecticut, 1963–64, and Skidmore, Owings and Merrill, San Francisco, 1964. Since 1965, Partner, Daryl Jackson/Evan Walker Architects Pty. Ltd., Melbourne. Address: Daryl Jackson/Evan Walker Architects Pty. Ltd., 6 Brunswick Place, Fitzroy, Victoria 3065, Australia.

Works:

1967/
69   Special Studies Building and Gymnasium/ Music School, Lauriston Girls' School, Malvern, Victoria

1969   E.S. and A. Bank, Hawthorn, Victoria
    Harold Holt Memorial Swimming Centre, Melbourne (with Kevin Borland)

1971   Residential Wing, St. Hilda's College, University of Melbourne
    Science/Humanities Wing, Presbyterian Ladies' College, Burwood, Victoria
    Sports Complex and Kindergarten, Eltham, Victoria

1972   Redevelopment of Wesley College, Prahran, Victoria (with McGlashan and Everist)
    Library/Resource Centre, St. Leonard's College, Brighton, Victoria
    The Hermitage Church of England Girls' Grammar School Education Complex, Highton, Geelong, Victoria

1973   Princes Hill High School Education Complex, Carlton, Victoria
    Resource Centre, Methodist Ladies' College, Kew, Victoria

1973/
75   Student Union and Student Housing, Ballarat College of Advanced Education, Victoria

1974   New Courts and Clubrooms, Royal Melbourne Tennis Club, Sherwood Street, Richmond, Victoria
    Y.W.C.A., Suva, Fiji
    Tenaden School, Belgrave, Victoria
    Senior Centre, Kingswood College, Box Hill, Victoria
    Library/Resource Centre, Mount Scopus Memorial College, Burwood, Victoria
    Australia and New Zealand Bank Building, Kyabram, Victoria
    Queen's College renovations, University of Melbourne, Parkville, Victoria

1974/
79   St. Paul's School, Woodleigh, Baxter, Victoria

1975   New Music School, Presbyterian Ladies' College, Burwood, Victoria
    Australia and New Zealand Bank Building,

Glen Waverley, Victoria
    Art Gallery and Old Physics Building renovation, University of Melbourne
    Resource Centre, St. Patrick's CBC College, Ballarat, Victoria
    Staff Quarters, Government House, Canberra

1976   Junior Library and Art/Craft Building, St. Leonard's College, Brighton, Victoria
    Hall/Synagogue, Mount Scopus Memorial College, Burwood, Victoria
    Yooralla Special Day School, Glenroy, Victoria
    City Edge (high-density housing development), Eastern Road, South Melbourne
    School of Music, Canberra
    Tullamarine Sports Pavilion, Keilor, Victoria
    New Teaching and Library Facilities, St. Alipius Parish School, Ballarat, Victoria
    State Bank of Victoria Building, Richmond, Victoria

1977   Student Housing, University of Melbourne, Cardigan Street, Carlton, Victoria
    New Biology Laboratory, St. Patrick's CBC College, Ballarat, Victoria
    Residential Staff College, State Bank of Victoria, Richmond
    Indoor Swimming Complex, Collingwood, Victoria
    Squash Courts, Dickson Square Centre, Canberra
    Association for Modern Education School, Weston Creek, Canberra

1978   Pre-School Building, Yooralla Special Day School, Glenroy, Victoria
    Boarders' Wing, St. Patrick's CBC College, Ballarat, Victoria
    Camberwell City Council Branch Library, Balwyn, Victoria
    Student Union extensions, Ballarat College of Advanced Education, Victoria
    Staff Housing, Royal Melbourne Hospital, North Melbourne
    Activities Centre, Blackburn South High School, Melbourne
    Synday Primary School, Wesley College, Melbourne (with McGlashan and Everist)
    Collingwood Branch Library, Victoria
    Emu Ridge High Density Housing, Belconnen, Canberra
    Moorabbin Indoor Swimming Pool, Victoria
    Moorabbin Link Shopping Centre, Victoria
    Union and Administration Building, Deakin University, Geelong, Victoria

1979   National Circuit Offices, Canberra
    Ashburton Branch Library, Melbourne
    Lecture Theatre, Deakin University, Geelong, Victoria

Publications:

By JACKSON: articles—"Getting Away from It All" in *Design Australia* (Melbourne), February/ March 1973; "Daryl Jackson on Robin Boyd" in *Architecture in Australia* (Sydney), April 1973; "A Show of Hands" in *Architect* (Melbourne), Novem-

ber 1976; "Every Hand Counts" in *Architect* (Melbourne), January 1977; "Where Is Your Hand" in *Architect* (Melbourne), March 1977; "Handing It Up" in *Architect* (Melbourne), May 1977; "Hands Up (Gloves Off)" in *Architect* (Melbourne), July 1977; "Put Your Hands Together" in *Architect* (Melbourne), November 1977; "Lost Chance at the Last Laugh?" in *Architect* (Melbourne), August 1978.

On JACKSON: book—*Modern Houses, Melbourne* by Norman Day, Melbourne 1976; articles— "Princes Hill High School," "M.L.C. Resource Center," and "Y.W.C.A., Suva" in *Constructional Review* (Sydney), June/September 1974; "YWCA Community Resource Centre, Suva, Fiji" in *Architecture in Australia* (Sydney), December 1974; "Two Recent Projects by Jackson/Walker" in *Architect* (Melbourne), July 1976; "Scuola in Australia" in *Domus* (Milan), November 1976; "Royal Tennis Club" and "Mt. Scopus College" in *Constructional Review* (Sydney), August 1977; "The Golden Rules of Brutalism" by Norman Day in *The Age* (Melbourne), 30 August 1977; "A Bush Haven for Bank Men" by Norman Day in *The Age* (Melbourne), 13 September 1977; "Pool Plan Still in the Swim" by Norman Day in *The Age* (Melbourne), 25 October 1977; "Three Approaches to Preserving the Past" by Norman Day in *The Age* (Melbourne), 28 November 1977; "Sins to Avoid in Design for the Faith" by Norman Day in *The Age* (Melbourne), 3 January 1978; "Daryl Jackson Designs an End or a Beginning" by Brian Talbot in *Architect* (Melbourne), April 1978; "Terraces for the Seventies" by Norman Day in *The Age* (Melbourne), 25 April 1978; "Calling the Tune in the Schoolyard" by Norman Day in *The Age* (Melbourne), 25 July 1978; "Music School, Canberra" and "St. Paul's School, Woodleigh, Baxter" in *Architectural Review* (London), September 1978.

*

In a democratic society architecture is, we believe, an essentially social art with a level of accountability/expectation extending well beyond those notions of aesthetic morality which are so closely identified with the development of the "modern movement."

The act of design, while it remains an intrinsic function of architecture, does so as part of an inclusive life-process which in itself is a key function of the society for whom things are built.

There are three critical areas: 1) the context or problem solving; 2) ideas and idea making; and 3) architectural form, object and symbol . . . (out of ideas and into context), about which it could be assumed architects will be moral.

None of these aspects can be ignored; they are fundamentally related or associated; and architecture, if it is to be of value—moral value—can only become so by addressing "the whole" or universal proposition, not merely one of its parts.

Idea-making on behalf of society remains a necessary function of architecture, with architectural form seen in the first instance as a *fertile proposition* against which ideas (of use, shape and materials utili-

Daryl Jackson: School of Music, Canberra, 1976

sation) can be tested and a hierarchical structuring · established.

Our preference is to develop forms which are not visually constrained and which therefore enable us to hold the proposition "open to verification" for as long as possible.

The substance of our approach to architectural composition and architectural morality can be summarized as follows: 1) *The Social Stance Adopted*—associative understanding, not dissociative method; front end decision making; 2) *Assembly of Parts*—space realms as a cue to enabling and facilitating human encounter; exposing the circulation; 3) *Place and Identity*—context determinants as a basic for physical expression; 4) *Expressionism and Symbolism*—geometric abstraction; formal complexity; adaptability and changeability; industrial vernacular.

We are convinced that architecture is concerned with creative fit, and in the ultimate sense this is the measure of the art.

—Daryl Jackson

Find a nice safe niche, my boy, develop a fashionable style of building, attract all the right sort of clients and then relax—you will enjoy a comfortable practice. Such a philosophy would be poisonous to Daryl Jackson, who has no apparently consistent architectural style and no special group of clients (except perhaps educational ones), and he seldom sits back because he enjoys too much the business of life.

If you like the comfort of labels, you could say that

Daryl Jackson's work ranges somewhere between vernacular sophistication and a subtle brand of brutalism. A better description would be that he brings an open mind to each project. With a wide range of projects and a mind not closed, he produces results that are seldom predictable. When a client wanted to collect the rays of the sun to heat his bath water, Jackson gave him a bank of solar absorbers and stood them proudly on the roof. If a government authority needs a public swimming pool, he makes it a happy and colourful place, one that opens to the gardens in good weather and withdraws into an exciting shell when the fogs come. In Fiji he has built with concrete because it is an economic and thermally successful material; in the country he uses local materials and techniques; in the city he uses materials that will survive the fetid air and grit.

Jackson has developed some sort of a following with school and college buildings and more recently with housing groups, but even then the products are as varied as the problems. The working spaces of his buildings are clear expressions of their functions, but because he works from the inside out he often ends up with unobvious boundaries to the spaces. This is all very confusing to the receiver of his messages. Usually the real mechanics of his designs, and their logical systems, become clear only after trying them out.

The process of design is seldom concealed in a Jackson building. Conflicts and contradictions faced in that process end up as conflicts and contradictions in the building fabric. He can juggle nuts and bolts

with one hand and sinuous curves with the other, when many of his fellows would probably have put one set of problems down to polish the act of the other. He would seem to be a disquieting influence in the quiet school of Melbourne architects, yet he can also give a flat street a serene little house or an extensive group of apartments, buildings that sit calmly denying that anything else could ever have been there.

There is a strong connection between the visual variety of his buildings and his quest for a valid role for the architect in society. From Jackson's searches will come one day a better understanding of the essential catholicity of an environmental scientist. In the interim, a whole lot of clients are getting the sort of architecture that is too rarely found, architecture that feels good.

—Roger Pegrum

JACKSON, David.
Australian. Born in Gloucester, England, 12 November 1931; emigrated to Australia, 1958: naturalized, 1976. Educated at the Architectural Association School, London, 1950–55 (5th Year Prize), Dip.A.A. 1955; Yale University School of City Planning, New Haven, Connecticut (King Georve VI

David Jackson: Rosemont Gardens Housing, Edgecliff, New South Wales, 1972

Memorial Fellowship), 1955–56. Married Barbara Hansen in 1962; children: Ann, Sophie, Rachel and Theo. Architectural Adviser, City Planning Commission, New Haven, Connecticut, 1955–56; Architectural Assistant, Norman and Dawbarn, Kingston, Jamaica, 1956–58; Architectural Assistant, subsequently Associate then Partner, McConnel, Smith and Johnson, Sydney, 1958–71. Since 1971, Director, with J. D. Chesterman, A. L. Teece and F. D. Willis, of Jackson Teece Chesterman Willis Pty. Ltd., Sydney. Chairman, New South Wales Board of Architectural Education, 1972–78; President, Royal Australian Institute of Architects, New South Wales, 1978. Fellow, Royal Australian Institute of Architects, 1967, and Royal Institute of British Architects, 1970. Address: Jackson Teece Chesterman Willis Pty. Ltd., 40 King Street, Sydney, New South Wales 2000, Australia.

Works:

1971 Development Finance Corporation Head Office renovations, Sydney
Guardian Royal Exchange Assurance Office Building, Chatswood, New South Wales
Young and Green Pty. Ltd. Car Sales Offices, Newcastle, New South Wales
Guardian Royal Exchange Assurance Open Office Plan, Kindersley House, Sydney
1972 Rosemont Gardens Housing, Edgecliff, New South Wales
Retirement Village Plan, Eastern Suburbs Hospital, Waverley, New South Wales
Public Transport Interchange remodelling and pedestrian tunnel, Railway Square, Sydney (with Rankine and Hill)

6 houses, Armidale, New South Wales
Receiving Home Experimental Documentation Study, Lidcombe, New South Wales (with the New South Wales Government Architect)
20 town houses, William Street, Double Bay, New South Wales
Flookies Boutique interiors, Sydney
Apartment tower block, Darling Point, New South Wales
Angus and Robertson Bookshop interiors, Elizabeth Street, Melbourne, and Ballarat, Victoria (with Jackson and Walker)
35 town houses, Bellevue Hill, New South Wales
1973 Chandlers Ltd. Electrical Retail Shop interiors and warehouse, Cairns, Townsville and Rockhampton, Queensland
School of Behavioral Science, Macquarie University, Ryde, New South Wales (with the University Architect)
Medical Centre, Dee Why, New South Wales
Field staff management and organization study for the University of New England, New South Wales
Socio-economic study for the preservation of a suburb, Glebe, Forest Lodge, New South Wales
1974 Holiday resort plan, Burra Burra, New South Wales
Mass housing plan, East Balmain, New South Wales
Teachers College New Campus Plan, Carillon Avenue, Sydney
Harris House, Simmons Street, Balmain, New South Wales

1975 Ore loader repairs, Darwin, Northern Territory
Freeway routes analysis, Sydney
College of Art Site Planning Study, Ryde, New South Wales
Library extension, Macquarie University, Ryde, New South Wales
Blackbutt Estate Plan, Shell Harbour, New South Wales
College/Community Activity Centre, Wanniassa, A.C.T.
Social and Educational Facilities Integration Study, Lanyon, A.C.T.
Warehouse conversion to Science Centre, Clarence Street, Sydney (with Ruth Inall)
1976 New Sydney Stock Exchange, Bond Street
Wabo Dam Town Planning Study, Papua New Guinea
Factory buildings conversion to shops and marina, Birkenhead Point, Drummoyne, New South Wales
Teachers College renovations and landscaping, Carillon Avenue, Sydney
1977 Police College and Services Centre, Weston, A.C.T.
Beach management study, Maroubra, New South Wales
Medibank Head Office, Woden, A.C.T.
Botany Bay Visual Study, Botany Bay, New South Wales
R. Young House, Cherry Road, Warners Bay, Newcastle, New South Wales
Medical Centre Plan, Ryde, New South Wales
1978 Kindersley House renovations, Sydney (with L. J. Hooker)

Ski Resorts Development Plan, Kosciusko National Park, New South Wales

My work is my firm's work. Each project is dealt with by a team of people with the range of skills we see as appropriate to the tasks. We like the client to be active in the team because we think it is the best way to identify accurately his problems and needs, and by participating progressively in the decision making, he develops an informed appreciation of the final product as well as an understanding of the community impact it may have.

We base our judgements on common sense, economy, good looks, performance on time and professional and community responsibility. We try to encourage people in the teams to contribute as individuals rather than shadows of the firm.

The contemporary architectural practice needs a wider range of skills than was provided in the past to satisfy the increasingly complex needs of society. Our list of projects reflects the variety of skills we bring together in our team approach. In support of our building design abilities, we provide urban planning and economic analysis, expertise in building technology and in management. It is critical to our work to recognise our own limitations and bring to a team the necessary external skills we do not possess. Some of the projects listed are not quite architecture, like the temporary repair of the Darwin ore loader after Cyclone Tracy, but they exploit the skills we bring to the central task of architecture.

Our buildings do not have a consistent architectural style because our management method responds to the differences in time, location, technology and client's needs in each project. The photograph of Rosemont Gardens is included because we like the picture rather than to suggest that it is typical of the appearance of our buildings. It is a high density housing development designed to satisfy the client's investment, to preserve mature trees and to have minimum impact in an area of two storey traditional houses.

—David Jackson

David Jackson emphasizes the importance of team work. He considers that the buildings in whose design he has participated are the work of his firm rather than of himself as an individual. He also disclaims the need for consistency of style in his architecture because each building is designed to respond to the client's requirements and the limitation set by its surroundings. David Jackson's work is therefore marked by a quiet competence rather than by flamboyant touches.

This attitude is demonstrated by his Pedestrian Subway at Railway Square, used daily by many thousands of people. Placed in a part of the city where buildings have been declining for several decades, it provides not merely efficient pedestrian circulation and a pleasant shopping area, but also a small oasis of trees at a busy traffic intersection. The Birkenhead Point project is another example of a re-development of a declining neighbourhood. An old industrial area is being turned into a major shopping centre and a site for the Sydney Maritime Museum.

David Jackson's designs are notable for their wide range, and their consistently successful solution of the client's problems. They include several office buildings, among them the complex new headquarters of the Sydney Stock Exchange; several residential buildings, of which the fifty-unit Rosemont complex in Edgecliffe is particularly noteworthy; a number of educational buildings; some renovations, including the highly successful interior of the new Angus and Robertson Bookshop in Melbourne; and several town-planning projects.

—Henry Cowan

JACOBSEN, Arne.

Danish. Born in Copenhagen, 11 February 1902. Educated at the School of Architecture of the Academy of Arts, Copenhagen, Dip.Arch. 1928. Married; had two sons. Worked in the office of the city architect Paul Holsoe, Copenhagen, 1927–30; in private practice, Copenhagen, 1930 until his death, 1971; also designed textiles and furniture from 1943. Professor of Architecture, Academy of Arts, Copenhagen, 1956–71. Exhibitions (one-man): Royal Institute of British Architects, London, 1959; McLellan Galleries, Glasgow, 1968; Ministry of Cultural Affairs, Copenhagen, 1971. Recipient: First Prize, Bellevue Seaside Development Competition, 1932; Eckersberg Gold Medal, Academy of Arts, Copenhagen, 1936; First Prize, Aarhus Town Hall Competition, 1937; First Prize, Søllerød Town Hall Competition, 1939; Grand Prize, *Bienal,* Sao Paulo, Brazil, 1953. D.Litt.: Oxford University, 1966; LL.D.: Strathclyde University, Glasgow, 1968. Honorary Corresponding Member, Royal Institute of British Architects; Honorary Fellow, American Institute of Architects. *Died* (in Copenhagen) *24 March 1971.*

Works:

1926/
27 C.V.E. House, Knutsvej 9, Copenhagen
House, Knutsvej 11, Copenhagen
1928/
29 Jacobsen House, Gotfred Rodesvej 2, Copenhagen
House, Baunegardsvej 22, Copenhagen
1929 House of the Future, *Danish Building Exhibition,* Copenhagen (exhibition project; with Flemming Lassen)
1930 Rothenborg House, Klampenborgvej 37, Copenhagen
Friis House, Tranegardsvej 25, Copenhagen
Mattsson's Riding School, Bellevuevej 12, Klampenborg, near Copenhagen
1930/
31 House, Ole Olsens Alle 28, Copenhagen
House, Baunegardsvej 81, Copenhagen
House, Hegelsvej 8, Copenhagen
1932 Bellevue Seaside Development, Denmark
Bellevue Tower and Restaurant, Denmark (project)
1933 Brobjerg House, Hegelsvej 18, Copenhagen
Grumstrup House, Vemmetofte Alle 10, Copenhagen
Povl Munck House, Hegelsvej 17, Copenhagen
Bellavista Housing Estate, Klampenborg, near Copenhagen
1934 Steinthal House, Hegelsvej 9, Copenhagen
Erik Dugdale House, Kratvaenget 9, Copenhagen
Erhardt House, Hegelsvej 3, Copenhagen
Seaside Bathing Complex, Dragor, Denmark (demolished)
1934/
35 Novo Therapeutic Laboratories, Fuglebakkevej, Copenhagen
1935 Juncker's Tennis Hall, Malthegardsvej, Gentofte, Denmark
1936 Landmandsbanken, Norrebrogade 160, Copenhagen
1936/
42 Gentofte Stadium, Jaegersborg, Gentofte, Denmark
1937 Christensen House, Skovvangen 17, Copenhagen
Bellevue Theatre and Gammel Bellevue Restaurant, Copenhagen
Hellerup Idraetsklub Tennis Hall, Hartmannsvej 37, Gentofte, Copenhagen
Jacobsen Country House, Gudmindrup Lyng, Denmark
1937/
38 Stelling House, Gammel Torv 6, Copenhagen

1937/
42 Town Hall, Aarhus, Denmark (with Erik Møller)
1938 Pedersen House, Kongehojen 3, Copenhagen
1939 Housing Estate, Jaegersborg Alle, Annettevej, Copenhagen
1939/
42 Town Hall, Søllerød, near Copenhagen (with Flemming Lassen)
1940 Ibstrupparken I Housing Estate, Horsholmvej, Jaegersborg, Gentofte, Denmark
1943 Smoke House, Oddenhavn, Denmark
Terraced housing, Ellebaekvej, Copenhagen
1944/
45 Ebbe Munck Country House, Arild, Sweden
1946 Ibstrupparken II Housing Estate, Smakkegardsvej, Jaegersborg, Gentofte, Denmark
1947 Young People's Housing, Gentofte, Denmark
1948 Paulsen and Company Building interiors, Frederiksgade 19, Copenhagen
1949 Creche and Kindergarten, Bornevenneme, Copenhagen (project)
Yacht Harbour, Vejle, Denmark (project)
1950 Søholm Terraced Housing, Strandvejen, Klampenborg, near Copenhagen
1951 Islevvaenge Terraced Housing, Rødovre, Denmark
C. A. Møller House, Vedbaek, Denmark
Harby Central School and Teachers' Housing, Funen, Denmark
1952 Allehusene Housing Estate, Jaegersborg Alle, Gentofte, Denmark
Massey-Harris Showroom and Spares Depot, Roskilde Landevej 183, Copenhagen
1952/
56 Munkegaard School, Vangedevej, Gentofte, Denmark
1953/
58 Town Hall, Glostrup, Denmark
1954 Upton Hansen House, Kalundborg, Denmark
Henning Simony House, Geelsvej 10, Copenhagen
1955 Town Hall, Rødovre, Denmark
Jespersen and Son Office Building, Copenhagen
1956 Ruthwen Jurgensen House, Vedbaek, Denmark
Koktelt Summer Cottage, Tisvilde, Denmark
1957 Landskrona Sports Hall (project)
Circular House, Odden, Denmark
Atrium Houses, Hansaviertel, Berlin
Terraced housing, Ornegardsvej, Jaegersborg, Gentofte, Denmark
Carl Christensen Factory, Aalborg, Denmark
Town Hall, Marl, Germany (project)
Atrium Houses, Carlsminde, Søllerød, near Copenhagen (project)
1958 Town Hall extensions, Cologne (project)
1958/
59 Nov Industri A/S Factory, Gladsaxe, Denmark (project)
1958/
60 SAS Royal Hotel and Air Terminal, Vesterbrogade, Copenhagen
1959 Erik Siesby House ("Sorgenfri"), Prinsessestien, Lyngby, Denmark
School, Rodovre, Denmark (project)
Orderinges Headquarters Building, The Hague (project)
1960 Edwin Jensen House, Mosehojvej, Ordrup, Denmark
Housing block, Rødovre, Denmark
St. Catherine's College, Oxford
World Health Organization Headquarters, Geneva (project)
Bellevue Bay Housing Estate, Klampenborg, near Copenhagen
1961 Gertie Wandel House, Ordrup, Denmark
Library, Rodovre, Denmark (project)
Novo Industri A/S Factory, Hillerogade, Copenhagen

Arne Jacobsen: Town Hall, Rødove, Denmark, 1955

National Bank and Bill Printing Plant, Copenhagen (project)
Tom's Chocolate Factory, Ballerup, Copenhagen
1962 Electricity Company Headquarters, Hamburg, Germany (with Otto Weitling)
Parliament Building, Islamabad, Pakistan (project)
Landskrona Sports Hall II (project)
Town Hall, Essen, Germany (competition project)
1966/
77 Town Centre, Castrop-Rauxel, Germany (with Otto Weitling)
1969/
70 Novo Factory, Mainz, Germany
Novo Factory, Chartres, France
1970 HEW Offices, Hamburg
Hotel, Newcastle, England (project)

1970/
73 Modular Cubic House Type (with Otto Weitling)
1970/
74 Town Hall, Mainz, Germany (with Otto Weitling)
1970/
75 Holiday Resort Development, Fehmarn Island, Germany (with Otto Weitling)
1970/
77 Danish Embassy, Sloane Street, London (with Dissing/Weitling)
1971 National Bank of Kuwait (project)
Danish National Bank, Copenhagen

Publications:

On JACOBSEN: books—*Arkitekten Arne Jacobsen* by J. Pedersen, Copenhagen 1954; *Arne Jacobsen:* *Architecture, Applied Art,* exhibition catalogue, by Poul Erik Shriver, London 1959; *Arne Jacobsen* by T. Faber, London 1964; *Arne Jacobsen at the McLellan Galleries, Glasgow,* exhibition catalogue, Glasgow 1968; *Arne Jacobsen* by Jorgen Kastholm, Copenhagen 1968; *Arne Jacobsen: A Danish Architect* by Poul Erik Shriver, Copenhagen 1972; articles—"Evoluzione di Jacobsen nella Moderne Architettura Danese" by E. Gentili in *Casabella* (Milan), September/October 1956; "Recent Buildings by Arne Jacobsen" in *Zodiac* (Milan), no. 5, 1959; "L'Oeuvre d'Arne Jacobsen" by Poul Erik Shriver in *L'Architecture d'Aujourd'hui* (Paris), December 1960/January 1961.

Arne Jacobsen was the leading exponent of the International School in Denmark in the middle of the 20th century. Combining the comfortable humanity of Gunnar Asplund, a close friend of his early professional days, and the absolute and uncompromising precision of Mies van der Rohe, Jacobsen reached in his work a zenith of perfection in the Rødovre Town Hall of 1955. Devoid of all showmanship and gimmickry, he had a sureness of touch that was also reflected in the domestic industrial design in which he also excelled. Nevertheless, his work was more highly revered abroad than in his own country.

Jacobsen was first noticed at a Danish building exhibition in 1929, the year before Asplund's famous exhibition in Stockholm. There, with Flemming Lassen, he built a revolutionary circular show house that broke entirely with tradition. At that time Danish architecture was still narrowly neo-classical. Much of his early work consisted of private houses that combined the best of traditional techniques and materials with a growing sense of functionalism and fitness for purpose. His ability to find simple and logical solutions to problems made him a successful competitor in many architectural competitions. His first real chance came in 1932 when he won the competition for a seaside development at Bellevue, north of Copenhagen. The open planning and carefree atmosphere which his skill in architecture and landscaping gave to this scheme made a deep impression on the thousands of holiday makers who used it and enormously helped its general acceptance. Jacobsen returned to add other buildings to this development on several more occasions: it became a record of the development of his domestic architecture.

One of his first commercial buildings was Stelling House in old Copenhagen on a site surrounded by plain neo-classical domestic apartment houses. Jacobsen's was the first modern building to be built in the area and produced violent protests because of its "inconsiderate" treatment of the old civic environment. Today it is accepted as a fine example of the considerate adjustment of a modern design to surroundings of an earlier and different style. The building is a parallel to Gunnar Asplund's skilful additions to the law courts at Gothenburg, which were much admired by Jacobsen.

Immediately before the Second World War Jacobsen won two important town hall competitions—the first, in partnership with Erik Møller, at Aarhus in Jutland; the second, with Flemming Lassen, at Søllerød, north of Copenhagen. Both designs owe much to the influence of Asplund.

In 1943 Jacobsen took refuge from the Germans in Sweden. There, in collaboration with his wife Jonna, a textile printer, he produced some distinguished designs for floral furnishings fabrics based on his watercolour studies of Danish flora. These designs were much imitated.

He returned to Denmark immediately after the war, and once again a competition win took him back to the site near Bella Vista. It was a small development known as Søholm. Terraced and linked in echelon, these houses aroused tremendous interest internationally. Admirably sited among old trees and beautifully planted, Søholm is a masterpiece of small scale domestic architecture. It is not surprising that Jacobsen chose to live there himself, continuing to do so even after he became rich and famous. "We have never lived grandly or in style," he said in an interview published in 1971, the year of his death, "and one reason for that is that, although at times I may have made money, I have always had the feeling that you can't go on doing it, and so why should you have the upset of having a high standard of living reduced to a more sensible one?" You can feel this kind of sensible reasoning in his work.

His next important work was the Munkegaard School at Gentofte, north of Copenhagen. In a single-storied building of formal and rigid layout the class rooms are arranged around individual internal courtyards, each differently planted and laid out. Good lighting and a pleasant outlook make the rooms excellent for work; each has the feeling of an individual summer house.

Although a master in the use of traditional materials and techniques, Jacobsen was interested in industrialized buildings and the introduction of new materials and techniques. In Rødovre Town Hall the reinforced concrete skeleton has centrally placed vertical members, the lightweight curtain walling being suspended from the floor slabs. Many of the components are factory made. Externally the building is as severe as ruled paper, but internally, where Jacobsen designed all the furniture and fittings, it is as light and delicate as a cobweb. The rod-suspended staircase and the council chamber are specially notable. Jacobsen's other major exercise in industrialized building was the SAS Royal Hotel in Copenhagen. One of that city's only tall buildings, eighteen stories high, it is very much less bulky than it might be because of the skilful way in which Jacobsen used the glass of his curtain walling to reflect the passing cloud patterns. The heavier design of the lower stories housing the air-terminal forms a solid base for the much lighter looking tower. Jacobsen designed everything in this building down to the ashtrays, and the result is unique and very satisfactory. Much of the furniture was made available to the general market and has become famous in its own right, like that of Alvar Aalto.

Jacobsen's industrial building followed the same distinguished pattern of simplicity, good proportion and fitness for purpose. To these qualities he added the discipline of standardized, factory-made building components. A factory at Aalborg for Carl Christensen, in 1957, and Tom's Chocolate Factory, 1961, are both outstanding by the highest standards.

Arne Jacobsen built a lot abroad in the last ten years of his life, his most important commissions being St. Catherine's College, Oxford, where he managed to combine something of the traditional college quadrangle with his own classical quality and simplicity of design. Speaking of the buildings, Alan Bullock, the master, said: "The longer I live in them, the more I find they delight and satisfy me."

—Gontran Goulden

JACOBSEN, Hugh Newell.

American. Born in Grand Rapids, Michigan, 11 March 1929. Educated at the University of Maryland, College Park, B.A. 1951; Architectural Association School, London, Dip.A.A. 1954; Yale University, New Haven, Connecticut, B.Arch. 1955. Served in the United States Air Force, at the Headquarters of the Tactical Air Command, 1955–57: Lieutenant. Married Robin Kearney in 1952; children: John Matthew and Simon. Architect/Draftsman in the office of Philip Johnson, New Canaan, Connecticut, 1955, and Keyes, Lethbridge and Condon, Washington, D.C., 1957–58. Since 1958, in private practice, Washington, D.C. Visiting Professor for the Arts and Humanities, University of Cairo, Egypt, 1970; John Fitzgerald Kennedy Memorial Fellow, New Zealand, 1971. Trustee, Washington Gallery of Modern Art, 1965–69; Trustee, Washington Theatre Club, 1965–72. Member of the Board of Governors, 1968–73, and since 1973 Trustee, Corcoran Gallery of Art, Washington. Recipient: Honor Award, American Institute of Architects, 1965, 1968, 1969 (twice), 1972, 1973, 1974, 1978; Awards for House Design, *Architectural Record*, 1973, 1975, 1976, 1977, 1978. D.H.L.: Gettysburg College, Pennsylvania, 1974. Fellow, American Institute of Architects, 1971. Address (office): 1427 27th Street N.W., Washington, D.C. 20007, U.S.A.

Works:

1960 Robert E. Lee House, Q Street N.W., Washington, D.C.
1961 Alan Naftalin House, Riva, Maryland
1962 Robert Shorb House, Montgomery County, Maryland
1963 Benjamin Thoron House, Martha's Vineyard, Massachusetts
William Shaw House, New York
1964 Woods/Vest Guest House, 28th Street N.W., Washington, D.C.
Calvin Cafritz House, Cambridge Place N.W., Washington, D.C.
Bolton Square Townhouses, Baltimore
1965 Ronald Gainer House, McLean, Virginia
1966 Stephen Millett House, Poppasquash Road, Bristol, Rhode Island
Robert Newmyer House, Washington, D.C.
1968 Stephen Trentman House, 27th Street N.W., Washington, D.C.
1969 Gerald Smernoff House, Montgomery County, Maryland
Hugh Jacobsen House, P Street N.W., Washington, D.C.
1970 Stuart Land House, North Shores, Rehoboth Beach, Delaware
Clyde's Bar, Georgetown, Washington, D.C.
King of the Road Motor Inn, Nashville, Tennessee
Tidesfall Lake Townhouses, Columbia, Maryland
Dr. Proctor Harvey House, McLean, Virginia
Edward Echeverria House remodelling, Olive Street N.W., Washington, D.C.
Arthur Hartman House additions and swimming pool, McKinley Street N.W., Washington, D.C.
Cord Meyer House remodelling, 33rd Street N.W., Washington, D.C.
Mrs. V. V. King Vacation House, Springs, Long Island, New York
1971 Alexander Blumenthal House, Easton, Maryland
Washington Theatre Club (church conversion), Washington, D.C.
Miller and Smith Detached Houses, Fairfax County, Virginia
C. Woods Vest House, St. Croix, Virgin Islands
1972 Renwick Gallery, Smithsonian Institution, Washington, D.C.
Ralph Schwaikert House, Salisbury, Connecticut
Robert Porter House, Newark Street N.W., Washington, D.C.
Guggenheim Products Inc. Office remodelling, South Street N.W., Washington, D.C.
Alfred Moses Houses, Georgetown Pike, McLean, Virginia
James Kemper House, 57th Street, Kansas City, Missouri
1973 Berton Korman House, Philadelphia
Burton Reiner House, Chevy Chase, Maryland
Mr. and Mrs. Peter Peterson Apartment remodelling, 10 Gracie Square, New York
Sam Korman Apartment remodelling, Philadelphia
1975 Hugh Jacobsen House, 28th Street N.W., Washington, D.C.
Half Moon Bay Hotel and Golf Club additions, Antigua, West Indies
1976 Michael Straight House remodelling, Montgomery County, Maryland
10 houses, Robert Butts, Virginia (project)
Mr. and Mrs. Robert Burling House additions, 29th Street N.W., Washington, D.C.
Mr. and Mrs. Edwin Stetson House swimming pool addition, Montgomery County, Maryland
Arts and Industries Building restoration, Smithsonian Institution, Washington, D.C.
1977 Bricklayers and Allied Craftsmen Office design, 15th Street N.W., Washington, D.C.

Hugh Newell Jacobsen: Alexander Blumenthal House, Easton, Maryland, 1971

Calvin Cafritz House, R Street N.W., Washington, D.C.

1978   Master plan and feasibility study for Gallaudet College, Washington, D.C.
        Library, Deree-Pierce Colleges, Athens, Greece
        Gymnasium, Anatolia College, Thessaloniki, Greece
        Library, American University in Cairo
        Library, Harvard University, Dumbarton Oaks, Washington, D.C. (project)

Publications:

By JACOBSEN: book—*A Guide to the Architecture of Washington, D.C.,* editor, New York 1965.

On JACOBSEN: books—*A Place to Live* by Wolf Von Eckardt, New York 1967; *Interior Spaces Designed by Architects* by Barclay Gordon, New York 1974; *Great Houses* by Walter Wagner, New York 1976; *Kicked a Building Lately?* by Ada Louise Huxtable, New York 1976; *Houses Architects Live In* by Barbara Plumb, London and New York 1977; articles—"Naftalin and Newmyer Residences" in *L'Architecture d'Aujourd'hui* (Paris), January 1967; "Naftalin, Newmyer and Millett Residences" in *Tochi-Jutaku* (Tokyo), January 1967; "Bolton Commons" in *Detail* (Munich), no. 5, 1968; "Vest Residence, St. Croix" in *Casa Vogue* (Milan), July/August 1972; "Tidesfall, Columbia, Maryland" in *Architecture + Urbanism* (Tokyo), October 1973; "Hugh Jacobsen" in *Architecture + Urbanism* (Tokyo), November 1973; "Five Current Projects from the Office of Hugh Jacobsen" in *Architectural Record* (New York), May 1974; "Eichholz Residence" in *Casa Vogue* (Milan), October 1974; "Pennsylvania Avenue" in *Baumeister* (Munich), December 1974; "Hartman House" in *House and Garden* (London), July/August 1977.

All an architect does is make spaces. It is the quiet and thoughtful arrangement of these spaces that makes houses, neighborhoods, streets and environments. Good architecture never shouts. It is like a well-mannered lady that is polite to its neighbors. The order and progression of the street is more important than the individual building. In looking back over my work for the past twenty years it seems I have been obsessed with the quality of light. I am still learning.

—Hugh Newell Jacobsen

Hugh Newell Jacobsen has spent a career upholding the tradition of the gentleman architect. He has upheld it in the face of utopian architects, corporate architects, radical architects and avante-garde architects. He is none of these. Jacobsen is concerned primarily with the sensory aspects of design. He talks about buildings in terms of how they will be experienced. How they look from far away and how they look close up. How the light comes through the windows in the morning and how it moves through the building during the day. How space is gathered up in one place and how linked. Formally, there are certain tendencies—pavilion arrangements, pyramid and prism shapes, flat arches, plans with elements slipped back and forth to break up masses. But there are not consistent stylistic mannerisms nor rigorous intellectual underpinning. Jacobsen's houses—he has done other buildings but many houses—are designs that have their moments. They show taste and judgment and erudition. And they are carefully attuned to their practical requirements. In one sense, Jacobsen is more a client's than an architect's architect.

He has emerged as well as one of the few American architects capable of truly sensitive restorations. His Renwick Gallery and Smithsonian Arts and Industries Building stand as examples of how to integrate contemporary service technologies delicately

within the shadows. Jacobsen has as well tackled the difficult problem of building new construction in the midst of harmonious older buildings. His taste in architecture is catholic—"there are no bad periods, only bad buildings"—and he has drawn freely on historic motifs for both "loaded" sites and in isolation.

—Nory Miller

JAHN, Helmut.

German. Born in Nuremberg, 4 January 1940; moved to the United States, 1966. Educated at the Technische Hochschule, Munich, 1960–65, Dip.Ing./Arch. 1965; Illinois Institute of Technology, Chicago, under Myron Goldsmith and Fazlur Khan, 1966–67. Married Deborah Ann Lampe in 1970; son: Evan. Worked with P. C. von Seidlein, Munich, 1965–66. Joined C. F. Murphy Associates, Chicago, 1967: Assistant to Gene Summers, 1967–73; Partner, Director in charge of Planning and Design, and Executive Vice-President, since 1973. Member, "Chicago 7," since 1977. Exhibitions: *Exquisite Corpse,* Walter Kelly Gallery, Chicago, 1978; *Townhouses,* Walker Art Center, Minneapolis, 1978. Recipient: Bartelt Award, 1975; National Honor Award, American Institute of Architects, 1975, 1978, 1979; Award, AIA, Chicago Chapter, 1975, 1976, 1977, 1978; Design Citation, *Progressive Architecture,* 1976, 1977; First Prize, *Minnesota II* Competition, St. Paul, 1977; Honor Award, AIA, Illinois Council, 1977; First Honor Award, AIA/American Library Association, 1978. D.F.A.: St. Mary's College, Notre Dame, Indiana, 1979. Address: C. F. Murphy Associates, 224 South Michigan Avenue, Chicago, Illinois 60604, U.S.A.

Works:

1970   McCormick Place (convention center), Chicago
1972   Grant Park Bandshell, Chicago (project)
1974   Kemper Arena, Kansas City, Missouri
1975   Auraria Library (learning center), Denver
1976   Fourth District Courts Building, Maywood, Illinois
        John Marshall Courts Building, Richmond, Virginia (with Wright/Jones/Wilkerson)
        Kansas City Convention Center, Missouri (with Seligson Associates, and Horner, Blessing, Howard, Needles, Tammen, and Bergendoff)
        Conference City, Abu Dhabi (project)
        One Exchange Place, Chicago (project)
        Minnesota II, St. Paul (competition project)
1977   Michigan City Library, Indiana
        Athletic Facility, St. Mary's College, Notre Dame, Indiana
        Monroe Garage (parking facility), Chicago
1978   Springfield Garage (parking facility), Springfield, Illinois
        Glenbrook Professional Building, Northbrook, Illinois
        La Lumiere Gymnasium, La Porte, Indiana
        Rust-Oleum Corporate Headquarters, Vernon Hills, Illinois
        Pahlavi National Library, Tehran (competition project)
        St. Paul Convention Center, Minnesota (project)
        Plan for the redevelopment of the North Loop, Chicago (project)
1978– W. W. Grainger Inc. Corporate Headquarters, Skokie, Illinois
        De La Garza Career Center, East Chicago, Indiana
        Springfield Garage/Hotel Complex, Springfield, Illinois

Xerox Center, Chicago
Area 2 Police Headquarters, Chicago
Post Office, Oak Brook, Illinois
Agricultural Engineering Building, University of Illinois, Champaign
Support Facility, Argonne National Laboratory, Illinois
Commonwealth Edison Company District Headquarters, Downers Grove, Illinois
First Bank Center, South Bend, Indiana
Wacker-Madison Office Building, Chicago
Board of Trade extension, Chicago
O'Hare Rapid Transit Station, Chicago
Federal Life Insurance Headquarters, Lincolnshire, Illinois
State of Illinois Building, Chicago

Publications:

On JAHN: book—*After Mies* by Werner Blaser, New York 1977; articles—"Analysis of Planned and Completed Projects by C. F. Murphy Associates" in *Bauen und Wohnen* (Zurich), September 1974; "Kemper Arena" in *Domus* (Milan), April 1976; "Grand Structures" in *Techniques et Architecture* (Paris), May 1976; "Abu Dhabi Conference City" in *Progressive Architecture* (New York), January 1977; "CFMA Portfolio" in *L'Architettura* (Rome), December 1977; "Design Directions: Looking for What Is Missing" in *AIA Journal* (Washington, D.C.), May 1978; "The Chicago Seven" in *Architecture + Urbanism* (Tokyo), June 1978; "Contemporary Architects: Helmut Jahn" in *Architecture + Urbanism* (Tokyo), July 1978; "Chicago on the Drawing Boards" in *Horizon* (New York), September 1978; "Minnesota II" in *Progressive Architecture* (New York), January 1979; "St. Mary's Athletic Facility" in *L'Industria delle Costruzioni* (Rome), February 1979; "Kansas City Convention Center" in *Domus* (Milan), February 1979; "Missing Mies" by William Marlin in *Architectural Record* (New York), July 1979.

Our approach to design is both rational and intuitive; it attempts to give each building its own philosophical and intellectual base and establishes an opportunity to exploit its particular elements to achieve a visual and communicative statement. The rational part deals with the realities of a problem, consciously analyzing the many discrete but related planning and technical aspects of a design problem and synthesizing them along functionalist construction principles. The intuitive aspect deals with the theoretical, intellectual aspects, a subconscious ability to sense the intrinsic structure of a problem and establish priorities for the elements of design which deal with space, form, light, color, and materials, and the way architecture communicates through symbol and meaning of architectural language.

There is a strong relationship between the problem and the way that architecture articulates it. It may come with the conditions of the site, the program, the circulation and general organization of the plan, with the structure, with the enclosure, with the technical systems, or with the effect of light, reflections and transparency, the creation of space or form, and the expression of symbol or meaning through communicative associations. Such attitudes free our skills to practice architecture beyond a mere problem solving, functionalist methodology, resulting in a pluralism, which is multi-directional, less restrictive and less dogmatic, characterized by a loss of conviction as to exclusivist principles and more communicative and user-oriented. It may contain much of the past or present. It doesn't always contain something new, but it is based on idea content.

—Helmut Jahn

Helmut Jahn: Kemper Arena, Kansas City, Missouri, 1974

Helmut Jahn's architectural career at C. F. Murphy Associates in Chicago has been a parallel of the recent history of international movement in architecture known as Rationalist Functionalism. The shadow of Mies van der Rohe was long and apparently all-pervasive.

Jahn began as a strict believer in functionalism; design was a matter of problem-solving according to firmly rational and theoretically "correct" principles and, as such, was a purely "objective" process. Critics have characterized this attitude to design as "exclusivist" or "reductive," and questioned the value of a conceptual grid that yielded so many icy, if elegant, edges. Today, it is clear that many architects *were* boxed in—more by their acceptance of the austerity and apparent "ease" of the style than by any real understanding of Mies' concept of functionalism. (Far from being a dogma which hemmed architecture in, the concept made room for adventure. Moreover, it has actually made that adventure inevitable.) In the ten years since the master's death, Jahn has been changing the strictly "Miesian" character of the output at C. F. Murphy Associates.

The difference now, as Jahn perceives it, is that the post-Modernist sees architecture more as a social art, and he uses many codes to signal the building's relationship to context, history, or the popular vernacular of its own, or some other, time, creating an architecture that—aided by the latest developments in technology—is engineered rather than designed. He stresses the intuitive nature of creative rationalism, which in the design process becomes a conscious assignment of priority to the expressive power of space, form, light, colour and material within a framework of cultural and human references. Such an attitude frees the architect to develop an approach that is multi-directional, less restrictive, and less dogmatic.

In appearance, Jahn's recent designs don't seem to make any radical departure from those of the Mies period. For instance, his current First Bank Center complex in South Bend, Indiana, looks to be a mere geometrical permutation of the box; the Energy Conservation Offices for the Argonne National Laboratories is also rigidly "geometric"—regular ridges of building across a circular format; the Rust-Oleum Headquarters at Vernon Hills, Illinois, is a bright, white floating box, split lengthwise by a skylit circulation spine. All make extensive use of glass sheathing to achieve that quality of lightness so characteristic of late Mies. Observers of the "strange" doings at C. F. Murphy Associates focus on details like a pediment or organically curved edge to explain their notions of what is different about Jahn's approach. And, indeed, there is the odd neo-Georgian facade (Agricultural Engineering Building at the University of Illinois), or Art Deco outline (Board of Trade Building extension, Chicago).

But the difference doesn't lie in "geometric" instead of "organic" form, or decorative elements or the lack of them, or pedimented platform or clean cantilever. It isn't really in the outward appearance of his buildings that Jahn is radically different; what is important is the way the buildings *work*.

The First Bank Center design isn't merely of two angled building blocks with a dramatic glasshouse section slicing downwards between them; the whole complex becomes a metaphor for city life itself. The central glass section functions as a public plazza with retail shopping areas leading to a hotel block and the bank offices themselves, the big space relating symbolically to the pattern of the surrounding streets.

Similarly, the interior spaces of the University of Illinois Agriculture Building, devised on a linear plan as demanded by the site, has a long, wide spine running its entire length, with tall single-storey workshops on one side and smaller laboratories on three levels on the other. Effectively, the spine becomes a sunny "street," illuminated from outside during the day by virtue of glass-block panel walls and skylights.

The Rust-Oleum central circulation spine also splits the complex lengthwise, its lofty single-storey

avenue sheathed in glass with ramped pathways encouraging movement through the various levels of the building, whilst the openness of its plan links the green landscape outside to the interior flow of space.

This attention to performance rather than just appearance is combined in Jahn's work with context, with metaphor and symbol, and visual and physical richness—a true synthesis of many viable pathways to post-Modernist architecture.

—Colin Naylor

JAIN, Uttam C(hand).

Indian. Born in Malwara, 15 January 1934. Educated at Sardar High School, Jodhpur, 1948–51; Jaswant College, Jodhpur, 1951–53; Indian Institute of Technology, Kharagpur, 1953–58 (Merit Scholarship) B.Arch. (first class honours) 1958; National University of Tucuman, Argentina, 1958–59 (Advanced Study Scholarship). Married Rasila Shah in 1953; children: Chirag, Leela, Neena, Seema, and Maya. Travelled abroad, 1959–60. In private practice, as Uttam C. Jain, Architects and Planners, Bombay, since 1961. Visiting Lecturer, University of Roorkee, 1962–63, Academy of Architecture, Bombay, 1965–66, 1972–73, 1975–76, and the J. J. College of Architecture, University of Bombay, 1973–77. Member of the Public Affairs Board, 1972–73, and Member of the Council, 1973–77, Indian Institute of Architects, and Editor of the Institute's Journal, 1975–77. Recipient: First Prize, Contemporary Indian Architecture Essay Competition, Commonwealth Association of Architects, London, 1969. Fellow, Indian Institute of Architects, and Institute of Valuers, New Delhi. Address: Uttam C. Jain, Architects and Planners, 408 Regent Chambers, 208 Nariman Point, Bombay 400 021, India.

Works (all India):

1960 Rural school at Kuha, Ahmedabad
Girls school, Bhavnagar
1961 High school at Bhayli, Baroda
Warden's Residence, Boys Hostel, Malwara
1962 Bright Tubes Corporation Plant for lightweight steel components, Bombay
1965 Nayan Co-op Society Residential Flats, Bombay
Urvashi Co-op Society Flats, Bombay (with Romesh Pathare)
Sanjog Co-op Society Flats, Bombay (with Romesh Pathare)
Guest house for Raisil India, Juhu Lane, Bombay
1966 Themis Pharmaceuticals Ltd. Vitamin B-12 Producing Plant, Vapi
Modern Water Proof Paper Manufacturing Company Plant, Thana
1968 Chamosyn Ltd. Plant, Vapi
Pre-cast, pre-stressed housing project, Surat
Amichand Bungalow, Surat
Kirtibhai Bungalow, Surat
Main Gate, University of Jodhpur
1969 Pump Houses, University of Jodhpur
Zoology Experimental Field Station, University of Jodhpur
1970 Printing Plant, University of Jodhpur
1971 Junior Staff Housing, University of Jodhpur
1972 Lecture Theatre Complex, University of Jodhpur
Amphitheatre, University of Jodhpur
1973 Department of Botany, University of Jodhpur
Department of Zoology, University of Jodhpur
Boys' Hostels, University of Udaipur
1974 Residences for the deputy and assistant registrars, University of Jodhpur
Oil and Gas Plant, University of Jodhpur

Memorial to the Chief Minister, Miramar, Panaji, Goa
Flour mill plant, Thana
1975 Faculty Residences (4 variations), University of Jodhpur
Vice-Chancellor's Residence, University of Jodhpur
Boys' Hostel, University of Udaipur, Jobner
Faculty of Parasitology, Bikaner Veterinary College
Students' Cafeteria, Bikaner Veterinary College
Ambika Electrolytic Capacitators Ltd. Factory, Jodhpur
1976 Student dormitory, University of Jodhpur
Faculty of Surgery and Radiology, Bikaner Veterinary College
Home Science College, University of Udaipur
Faculty of Agronomy and Soil Sciences, University of Udaipur
Block of flats for Mrs. Sarlabahen Vyas, Bombay
1977 Week-end cottage, Lonawla
Resort hotel, Colva, Margoa, Goa
1978 Tradewinds Resort Hotel, Bogmalo Beach, Goa
Central Library, University of Jodhpur
Gymnasium, University of Jodhpur

Publications:

By JAIN: articles—"Turning Point in Architecture" in *Indian Builder* (New Delhi), September 1965; "Obituary of a Poetic Genius" in *Architects Trade Journal* (Bombay), May 1974; "Anonymous Architecture and Naive Art in Western India" in *Architecture + Urbanism* (Tokyo), June 1975.

On JAIN: books—*New Architecture in the World* by Udo Kultermann, London 1966; *Building Environment* by B. S. Saini, Sydney 1973; articles—"Indian Prints" in *Architectural Forum* (New York), October 1971; "Jain's Clusters" in *Architectural Review* (London), December 1973; "Jain at Jodhpur" in *Architectural Review* (London), February 1976; "Uttam C. Jain" in *Architecture + Urbanism* (Tokyo), October 1977; "The Third World: Continuity of the Modern Style among Native Architects" in *Bauen und Wohnen* (Zurich), October 1977; "A View of Contemporary World Architects" in *The Japan Architect* (Tokyo), December 1977.

The word "modern" in India acquires a different connotation than in the advanced communities in the West. Modern India is unable to modify her texture because of a lack of a rapid rolling culture and remains untouched by super industrialism as well. 70 per cent of her population dwells in a rural setting, primarily under thatched shelters.

Social landscape having a rural tinge and high technology remaining a distant drum beat, India is at the intermediate level of technology. Manpower is a factor to reckon with at all levels of national planning.

As an architect I am presently involved in creating physical environments for two universities in western India—the University of Jodhpur and the University of Udaipur.

Jodhpur and Udaipur have their origins in mediaeval India. Their architectural heritage is so intense that its streaking into the new town's fabric is natural. The present practice of producing buildings in these towns retains its flavour for indigenous building materials locally available. Experience through observations here focussed on two principles. Firstly, creation of many architectural objects over centuries enabled craftsmen to master the art of controlling rigours of extreme climate and rugged terrain. Secondly, the intensive use of local stone through structural permutations and combinations improved economics of building at regional level. Universities funded by the public exchequer could ill

Uttam C. Jain: Lecture Theatre Complex, University of Jodhpur, 1972

afford consumption of factory products, when local materials, coupled with high craftsmanship, could be the logical answer. Besides, this adaptation (not imitation) permitted a sense of historical linkage in these towns.

Again, in seeking answers to climatic problems, the accepted process seemed simpler—smaller openings, over-scaled walls, bare exteriors, stone-textured faces, weighty roofs and the emphasized narrow lanes with still shorter distances, became parameters for my works.

At grassroots level I observed and assimilated what was authentic. I also became aware of confining my architectural indulgence at different levels of micro-detailing.

This way I strived to enhance the physical ambient without playing a discordant note on the cultural wave-lengths of the towns. My concern was that preservation and progress should go hand in hand.
—Uttam C. Jain

The work of the Indian architect Uttam C. Jain is directed toward harmony with the traditional values of India and the specific requirements of the contemporary situation in that country. His buildings for the universities at Jodhpur and Udaipur parallel the steps taken in other countries that question the doctrines of the Modern Movement.

Jain advocates a learning experience from the works of Le Corbusier and Louis I. Kahn in India as well as from the architecture of cultural identity of old Indian cities such as Rajasthan. Both lines of tradition have to be integrated into a new Indian architecture. Jain's historical studies into Indian cities and buildings thus blend with the recent trends in international developments which aim at a more concrete and realistic understanding of the local situation. Jain says: "Architecture is a social activity and must not leave any aspect of human life untouched."

Materials of traditional and local character dominate Jain's buildings in Jodphur, Udaipur, Goa and Bombay. Landscape and climate, the Indian tradi-

tion, and modern technology merge into a new vocabulary with which Jain attempts to create a new level of architecture in India, to "manifest the creative mind of the simple people in rural India as an organic part of human existence."
—Udo Kultermann

JELLICOE, Sir Geoffrey (Alan).

British. Born in London, 8 October 1900. Educated at Cheltenham College, Gloucestershire, 1915–18; Architectural Association School, London, under Howard Robertson, 1919–23 (Bernard Webb Scholarship; Neale Bursary), Dip.A.A. 1923. Married Ursula Pares in 1936. Partner, with J. C. Shepherd, Shepherd and Jellicoe, London, 1925–31; Principal, G. A. Jellicoe, London, 1931–38; Senior Partner, with Russell Page and Richard Wilson, Jellicoe, Page and Wilson, London, 1938–39; Principal, G. A. Jellicoe, London, 1939–58; Senior Partner, with Alan Ballantyne and Francis Coleridge, Jellicoe, Ballantyne and Coleridge, 1958–64; Senior Partner, Jellicoe and Coleridge, London, 1964–73. Since 1973, Consultant to Jellicoe, Coleridge and Wynn, Pershore, Worcestershire. Studio Master, 1929–34, and Principal, 1939–42, Architectural Association School, London. Founder Member, 1929, and President, 1939–49, Institute of Landscape Architects; Founder President, 1948–54, and Honorary Life President since 1954, International Federation of Landscape Architects; Member, Royal Fine Arts Commission, 1954–68; Trustee, Tate Gallery, London, 1967–74. Associate, Royal Institute of British Architects. Honorary Corresponding Member, American Society of Landscape Architects, and Venezuelan Society of Landscape Architects. C.B.E. (Commander, Order of the British Empire), 1963;

Knighted, 1979. Address: 19 Grove Terrace, London NW5 1PH, England.

Works:

1929   Gordon Russell Ltd. Workshops, Broadway, Worcestershire
1933   Advisory plan for Broadway, Worcestershire
1934   Development plan for Goldsmiths' Company Estates, Acton, London
1934/
36   Caveman Restaurant, Cheddar Gorge, Somerset (with Russell Page)
1935/
36   House, Stanmore, Middlesex (with Russell Page)
1935/
39   Ditchley Park gardens, Oxfordshire
1936/
37   Gordon Russell Showrooms, Wigmore Street, London
      Gordon Russell Factory, Park Royal, London
1936/
39   Royal Lodge gardens, Windsor, Berkshire
      Kelmarsh Hall gardens, Northamptonshire
      The Holme gardens, Regent's Park, London
      Pusey House gardens, Faringdon, Oxfordshire
      Hever Castle gardens, Kent
      Mottisfont Abbey gardens, Hampshire
      Overbury House gardens, Gloucestershire
      Cottesbrook gardens, Northamptonshire
      St. Paul's gardens, Walden Bury, Hertfordshire
1938/
40   Calverton Colliery Buildings, Bestwood, Nottinghamshire (with Richard Wilson)
      Calverton Village and Landscaping, Bestwood, Nottinghamshire
1939/
43   Housing for the U.K. Ministry of Supply, in

Sir Geoffrey Jellicoe: Kennedy Memorial, Runnymede, Berkshire, 1965

Theale, Berkshire; Hereford; Newport, Monmouthshire; Cardiff; Worcester; and Poole, Dorset

1942 Landscape plan for Earle's Cement Works, Hope Valley, Derbyshire

1943 *Motorways for Britain* exhibition, British Road Federation, London

1944 Landscape plan for Pitstone Cement Works, Buckinghamshire

1945 Landscape plan for Imperial Chemical Industries, Wilton, Yorkshire

Town and country plan for Wolverton, Buckinghamshire

Outline plan for Guildford, Surrey

1945/
53 Mulgrave Castle garden, Whitby, Yorkshire

1946 Outline plan for Wellington, Shropshire

Foreshore development plan for Mablethorpe and Sutton-on-Sea, Lincolnshire

1947 Sandringham House garden, Norfolk

New town plan for Hemel Hempstead, Hertfordshire

1947/
50 Livingstone Airport, Zambia (with Ronald Rutherford)

Broken Hill Hospital, Zambia (with Ronald Rutherford)

Schools in the Copper Belt, Zambia (with Ronald Rutherford)

1949/
52 Gardens and housing, Church Hill Memorial Landscape, Walsall, West Midlands

1950 Town plan for Lusaka, Zambia

1951 Lansbury Neighborhood Housing, Poplar, London

Ashmore, Benson and Pease Engineering Works and Offices, Stockton-on-Tees, Cleveland

Palladian House, Heron's Beach, Barbados

Cement works, Shoreham-by-Sea, Sussex

1951/
52 Ridgeway Hotel, Lusaka, Zambia (with Denis Lennon)

1952/
53 Bennett's End Housing, Hemel Hempstead, Hertfordshire

1954 Landscaping for Cadbury Brothers Factory, Moreton, Cheshire

Housing at Levylsdene, Merrow, Surrey (with F. S. Coleridge)

Pilkington Brothers "Glass Age" Project, Soho, London

1955 Landscape development plan for the University of Nottingham

Landscape plan for St. Margaret's Bay, Kent

Landscape design for the Volta River Project, Ghana

1955/
56 Sylvania-Thorn Colour Television Laboratories, Enfield, Middlesex (with Alan Ballantyne)

1956 Landscape design for the Barry foreshore, South Wales

Housing, Basildon New Town, Essex (with F. S. Coleridge)

1956/
57 Harvey's Department Store, Guildford, Surrey (with F. S. Coleridge)

Harvey's Department Store Roof Garden, Guildford, Surrey

1957 Civic and Market Hall, Totnes, Devon

1957/
58 Pilkington Brothers Sports Pavilion and Recreation Ground, Ruskin Drive, St. Helen's, Lancashire

1957/
59 Water Gardens, Hemel Hempstead, Hertfordshire

1957/
62 Civic Centre and Great Square, Plymouth, Devon (with Alan Ballantyne)

1959 Gardens, Cement and Concrete Association Research Centre, Wexham Springs, Slough, Berkshire

Motopia: Pilkington Brothers "Glass Age" Project

Artificial hills for Guinness, Park Royal, London

Redevelopment plan for Digbeth Street, Walsall, West Midlands

1960 Artificial hills for Rutherford High Energy Laboratory, Harwell, Berkshire

Landscape plan for the Nuclear Power Station, Oldbury-on-Severn, Gloucestershire (with John Ingleby)

1960/
63 Landscape for the Queen Elizabeth II Hospital, Welwyn, Hertfordshire

1961 Crystal 61: Pilkington "Glass Age" Project (with Hal Moggridge)

Cornwall County Hall, Truro (as consultant; with F. K. Hicklin)

Comprehensive plan for the centre of Gloucester (with Hal Moggridge)

1961/
64 Civic Centre, Chertsey, Surrey (with F. S. Coleridge)
1962 Garden at Cliveden, Buckinghamshire
1963 Proposals for Christchurch Meadow inner relief road, Oxford
Crystal Span: Pilkington "Glass Age" Project (with Hal Moggridge)
1964 Report on the M4 Motorway, Berkshire
1964/
65 Kennedy Memorial, Runnymede, Berkshire
1965 Outline scheme for the redevelopment of the Tollcross area, Edinburgh (with C. Davidson)
Westcliff Estate Flats, Scunthorpe, Humberside (with F. S. Coleridge)
Landscape charter for the Isles of Scilly
Garden, Horsted Place, Uckfield, Sussex
1966 Report on the Oaklands Development, Nassau, Bahamas
Report on a Height of Buildings Policy for cathedral and other historic English cities
1966/
67 Crematorium, Grantham, Lincolnshire (with F. S. Coleridge)
1967 Landscape plan for Sark, Channel Islands
Landscape plan for Armagh Cathedral, Northern Ireland
1968 Sea City: Pilkington "Glass Age" Project (with Hal Moggridge)
Control Building and Office Block for the Central Electricity Generating Board at Durley Park, Keynsham, Avon (with F. S. Coleridge)
1968/
71 Landscape plan, with swimming baths, for Pittville, Cheltenham, Gloucestershire (with F. S. Coleridge)
1970/
78 Garden at Shute House, Donhead St. Mary, Dorset
1971 Report on urban road through Cardiff
1971/
72 Pools at the Royal Horticultural Society Gardens, Wisley, Surrey
1971/
74 Country park at Fish Hill, Broadway, Herefordshire and Worcestershire
1971/
75 Landscape plan for the river area, Stratford upon Avon
Gardens, Hilton Hotel, Stratford upon Avon
1972 Landscape for bypass, Warwick
Landscape advisory plan for the Chequers Estate, Buckinghamshire
Landscape plan for Chevening, Kent
1972/
75 Landscape for Delta Metal Works, West Bromwich, Staffordshire
Landscape for New Palace Yard, Westminster, London (not completed)
1972/
77 Landscape for Fitzroy Square, London W.1
1973 Landscaping of roads in central area, Leicester
Terrace and general landscape at Stratfield Saye, Berkshire
1974 Landscape development plan for oil platform construction works, Kishorn, Wester Ross, Scotland
Processional way, Exeter Cathedral, Devon
Garden at Everton Park, Sandy, Bedfordshire
1975 Garden at Northington, Hampshire
1976 Garden and landscape at Dewlish House, Dorset
1977/
78 Landscape development plan at Buckenham Broad, Norfolk

Publications:

By JELLICOE: books—*Italian Gardens of the Ren-* *aissance*, with J. C. Shepherd, London 1925; *Gardens and Design*, with J. C. Shepherd, London 1927; *Baroque Gardens of Austria*, London 1932; *Garden Decoration and Ornament*, London 1936; *Gardens of Europe*, London and Glasgow 1937; *Conurbation: Report for the West Midland Group on Post-War Reconstruction and Planning*, London 1948; *Motorways: Their Landscaping, Design and Appearance*, London 1958; *Studies in Landscape Design*, 3 volumes, 1960–70; *Motopia*, London 1961; *Modern Private Gardens*, with Susan Jellicoe, London, Toronto and Paris 1968; *L'Architettura del Paesaggio*, Milan 1969; *Water: The Use of Water in Landscape Architecture*, with Susan Jellicoe, London and New York 1971; *The Landscape of Man*, with Susan Jellicoe, London and New York 1975; articles—in *Architectural Review* (London); *Country Life* (London); *Landscape Design* (London); etc.

Post-student research into the classical Italian garden (with fellow student J. C. Shepherd—published in 1925 as *Italian Gardens of the Renaissance* and still the standard work) convinced me unhesitatingly that architecture was part of the environment and therefore incomplete when considered in isolation. This timeless idea has always remained the basis of the thought, design and execution of my work.

—Geoffrey Jellicoe

Geoffrey Jellicoe is widely known for his influence on the profession of landscape architecture, which has been profound and worldwide. His practice as an architect led him to see the importance of the setting —the relationship of buildings to their context. He studied gardens and garden design, and his books on these subjects have inspired a whole generation of designers and will remain as outstanding classics of this period.

The Institute of Landscape Architects had begun rather unsteadily in 1929, just before he joined it, and would probably have collapsed but for the support he brought it from the architectural world and for his continuing support through the years of World War II, when he provided secretarial and office accommodation in his Gower Street office. Other distinguished architects and town planners who shared his views on the relationship of buildings to landscape followed his example and brought further recognition to the art of landscape design which, though it had been described as a "new art" in the 18th century, had languished in a sort of doldrums (at least in Britain) since the days of Kent, Repton and Brown.

Soon after the war, heavy correspondence from other countries on the subject of landscape design proved that there was a revival of interest and showed that the time had come to launch an International Federation of Landscape Architects. Earlier meetings held in Paris and elsewhere in Europe had not foreseen this brave possibility, but Jellicoe saw the matter in its broadest light as a common interest capable, if suitably focussed, of healing wartime antagonisms and containing perhaps some seeds of peaceful international co-operation in the future. He used the resources of his office to organize an international conference to be held in Cambridge; he was elected first President and then Life President of Honour of IFLA and has been constantly in touch with its development: since then it has greatly outgrown—at least in numbers—the Institute of Landscape Architects, its parent body.

During that time several important books by Jellicoe appeared, all concerned with garden or landscape matters. In particular his 3 volumes of *Studies in Landscape Design* and his important work *The Landscape of Man* (written jointly with his wife Susan) have expanded the basis of his wide philosophic thinking on the subject, and these books have exerted untold influence on public appreciation of the growing art wherever it has been practiced. His keen realization of the links between the arts of painting and sculpture and that of landscape design is a main characteristic of his approach. He has also fully understood the limitations imposed on landscape design by the laws of nature—the inevitable ecological necessities and the land sciences that must govern landscape design far more stringently than they do the visual arts.

He was among the first landscape architects to be consulted by a major industry on the setting of its works. His report and plans for Earle's Cement Works in Derbyshire set an example and precedent for the treatment of open-cast mining and quarrying to prevent disfigurement of the landscape and showed how multiple land use, properly balanced, could create fine new landscapes. This recognition of the function of landscape design has since become generally adopted by industry and planners. On a smaller scale Jellicoe showed a different aspect of his design in the little park at Hemel Hempstead, making delightful gardens in an area of disused urban space.

His work and his writings constantly emphasise the role of each individual site. The spirit of place, "genius loci," is a main inspiration of every serious landscape project, but whereas many buildings have been designed on the drawing board with little reference to the individuality of the site, Jellicoe has underlined the designer's need to draw inspiration from the existing conditions of every site—an approach tending to counteract the risk of monotony which seems to be a bane of the architecture and town planning of this age throughout the world.

A summary of his views and his influence on contemporary thought may be found in his own words from *The Landscape of Man*:

The world is moving into a phase when landscape design may well be recognized as the most comprehensive of the arts. Man creates around him an environment that is a projection into nature of his abstract ideas. It is only in the present century that the collective landscape has emerged as a social necessity. We are promoting a landscape art on a scale never conceived of in history.

—Brenda Colvin

JOHANSEN, John M(acLane).
American. Born in New York City, 29 June 1916. Educated at Harvard University, Cambridge, Massachusetts, 1935–39, B.S. (cum laude) 1939; Harvard Graduate School of Design, Cambridge, 1939–42, M.Arch. 1942. Married Mary Lee Longcope in 1946 (divorced, 1954); Mary Ellen Goode in 1959 (divorced, 1967); daughters: Deborah and Christen. Worked as a draftsman for Marcel Breuer, Cambridge, 1942; Researcher, National Housing Agency, Washington, D.C., 1943–45; Designer, Skidmore, Owings and Merrill, New York, 1945–48; in private practice, New Canaan, Connecticut, 1948–70. Since 1970, Partner, with Ashok M. Bhavnani, Johansen and Bhavnani, New York. Professor of Architecture, Yale University School of Architecture, New Haven, Connecticut, 1955–58, and Columbia University, New York 1964–66; lectured in Italy, 1974; Architect-in-Residence, American Academy in Rome, 1975. Professor of Architecture at the Pratt Institute, New York, since 1976. Exhibitions: *Built in U.S.A.: Post-War Architecture*, Museum of Modern Art, New York, 1952; *International Exhibition of Architecture*, Berlin, 1962; *Selected Works of American Architects*, Moscow, 1965; *Architecture U.S.A.*, United States Pavilion, *World's Fair*, Osaka, 1970; *Exhibition U.S.A.*, Katowice, Wroclaw, Posnan and Warsaw, Poland, 1970; *Architecture in America*, United States Information Agency tour, 1976. Recipient: Record House Award, *Architectural Record*, 1956, 1958, 1977, 1978; Award of Merit, 1963, and Honor Award, 1972, American Institute of Architects; Honor Award, AIA, Connecticut Chapter,

John M. Johansen: Oklahoma Theatre Center, Oklahoma City, 1970

1964; Honor Award, Indiana Association of Architects, 1965; Honor Award, Connecticut Association of Architects, 1965, 1966; First Award, Florida Society of Architects, 1966; Award of Merit, United States Department of Health, Education and Welfare/AIA, 1966; First Honor Award, Baltimore Chamber of Commerce/AIA Baltimore Chapter, 1967; First Honor Award, AIA, Mid-Atlantic Region, 1968; Brunner Award, National Institute of Arts and Letters, 1968; Award of Merit: Library Buildings, AIA, 1970; Honor Award, American Concrete Association, Florida Chapter, 1971; Medal of Honor, AIA, New York Chapter, 1976; Bard Award, City Club of New York, 1977. D.F.A.: Maryland Institute, Baltimore, 1965; Clark University, Worcester, Massachusetts, 1970. Fellow, American Institute of Architects, 1969. Address: Johansen and Bhavnani, 401 East 37th Street, New York, New York 10016, U.S.A.

Works:

1948 Coggeshal House, Schenectady, New York
1949 Langenwalter House, Schenectady, New York
     Bengst House, Schenectady, New York
1950 Johansen House I, New Canaan, Connecticut
1951 Barlow House, New Canaan, Connecticut
1952 Dunham House, New Canaan, Connecticut
     Lake Dwellers House (project)
1953 Henvelle House, Litchfield, Connecticut
     Campbell House, New Canaan, Connecticut
     Goode House, New Canaan, Connecticut
1954 Dickenson House, New Canaan, Connecticut
1955 Sprayform Houses I and II (projects)
     McNiff House, Stockbridge, Massachusetts

Stillman House, Newburgh, New York
1956 Goodyear House, Darien, Connecticut
     Sprayform United States Pavilion, Zagreb, Yugoslavia
1957 Warner House, New Canaan, Connecticut
     Sprayform Church, Norwich, Connecticut (project)
     Sprayform Restaurant, Mount Kisco, New York (project)
1958 Roe House, Greenwich, Connecticut
1959 Durst House, Mount Kisco, New York
1960 Franklin Delano Roosevelt Memorial, Washington, D.C. (competition project; with John McVitty)
1961 Museum of Art, Science and Industry, Bridgeport, Connecticut
1962 Church, Norwich, Connecticut
1963 Schwarzenbach House I, Norwalk, Connecticut
     Simon House, Bedford, New York (project)
     Clowes Hall, Indianapolis, Indiana
1964 United States Embassy, Dublin
1965 Florence Virtue Housing (120 units), New Haven, Connecticut
     Helen Grant Elementary School, Dixwell Renewal Area, New Haven, Connecticut
     Theatre, Vassar College, Poughkeepsie, New York (project)
     Cultural Center, Wallingford, Connecticut (project)
1966 Taylor House, Westport, Connecticut
     Public Library, Orlando, Florida
     Leapfrog City, New York (project)
     Master plan of the new campus for the State University of New York at Old Westbury, Long Island (with Alexander Kouzmanoff

and Victor Christ-Janer)
1967 Morris Mechanic Theatre, Baltimore, Maryland
     Leapfrog Housing, New York (project)
1968 Ritts House, Greenwich, Connecticut
     Goddard Library, Clark University, Worcester, Massachusetts
     Junior High School, Litchfield, Connecticut
1969 Dixwell Avenue Congregational Church, New Haven, Connecticut
     KQED TV Studio, San Francisco (project; with George Rockwise)
     Twin Parks Housing, Bronx, New York (project)
     Car Body Office Building, Baltimore, Maryland (project; with Ashok Bhavnani)
     L. Francis Smith School, Columbus, Indiana
1970 Oklahoma Theatre Center, Oklahoma City
     Western Connecticut State College, Danbury (project; with Ashok Bhavnani)
     Guest House, Fishers Island, Connecticut (project)
     Foster and Company Corporate Headquarters and Plant, Hanover Park, New Jersey
1971 High school, New York (project; with Ashok Bhavnani)
1972 State University of New York at Old Westbury, Long Island
1974 Johansen House II, Stanfordville, New York
1975 Library and TV Resource Center, Staten Island Community College, New York (project; with Ashok Bhavnani)
1976 Roosevelt Island Neighborhood, New York (with Ashok Bhavnani)
     Ellsworth House, Salisbury, Connecticut
1977 Pope House, Salisbury, Connecticut

1978 Schwarzenbach House II, Vieques, Puerto Rico
       Kinetic House (project)
1979 Barna House, Bedford, New York

Publications:

By JOHANSEN: book—*The New Urban Aesthetic,* New York 1972; articles—"Johansen Declares Himself" in *Architectural Forum* (New York), January 1966; "An Architecture for the Electronic Age" in *American Scholar* (Washington, D.C.), 1966, reprinted in *McLuhan, Hot and Cool,* New York 1967; "New Town" in *Architectural Forum* (New York), September 1967; "The Mummers Theatre, A Fragment, Not a Building" in *Architectural Forum* (New York), May 1968; introduction to *Islamic Architecture,* Milan 1971; article in *On Philosophies of Construction,* compiled by Abby Suckle, New York 1979.

On JOHANSEN: book—*Built in U.S.A.: Postwar Architecture* by Stephen Mahony, New York 1952; articles—"A Platform Raised Above a Field: House in New Canaan, Connecticut" in *Architectural Forum* (New York), July 1951; "Textbook House, New Canaan, Connecticut" in *House and Home* (New York), May 1952; "Genetrix: Personal Contributions to American Architecture" in *Architectural Review* (London), May 1957; "Jeunes Architects aux Etats Unis" in *L'Architecture d'Aujourd'hui* (Paris), September 1957; "The New House of 1958" in *Architectural Record* (New York), May 1958; "Embassy with a New Twist" in *The Architects' Journal* (London), August 1958; "Sculpting with Sprayed Concrete" in *Architectural Forum* (New York), October 1959; "Design for the Architect's Own House, New Canaan, Connecticut, and U.S. Embassy Office Building, Dublin" in *Art in America* (New York), vol. 49, no. 1, 1961; "Architecture of Ideas: The Romantic House" in *House and Home* (New York), March 1962; "Labyrinthian Environs: Residence, Westport, Connecticut" in *Progressive Architecture* (New York), May 1962; "Architectural Changes Forecast New Adventures in Living: House at Westport, Connecticut" in *House and Garden* (New York), October 1962; "Theatre Block, Charles Center, Baltimore, Maryland" and "U.S. Embassy Office, Dublin" in *Architectural Design* (London), November 1964; "Theatres and Auditoriums" in *Architectural Record* (New York), December 1964; "College Buildings" in *Architectural Record* (New York), June 1965; "Anti-Architecture" by Robin Boyd in *Architectural Forum* (New York), November 1968; "A View of Contemporary World Architecture," special issue of *The Japan Architect* (Tokyo), July 1970; "The Mummers Theatre" by Peter Blake in *Architectural Forum* (New York), March 1971; "Towards a New Slang" by Robert Hughes in *Time* (New York), 31 May 1971; "Rigged House" in *Architecture Plus* (New York), December 1974; "A Model City Within a City" in *U. S. News and World Report* (Washington, D.C.), December 1977/January 1978; "Mechanic Theatre" in *AIA Journal* (Washington, D.C.), February 1978; "Private House" in *Architectural Record* (New York), May 1978.

After a rather nonsequential search in my early career, I have more recently come to see buildings and building complexes in terms of their parts—i.e., individuation. For some time I have considered the most essential elements in architecture to be enclosures, generalized or specific, to accommodate function. These functions were seen to be "static" and contained, as opposed to elements which served as access to static elements in the kinetic function of moving people and mechanical services. The third category of elements were structural, which held it all up in some sort of mutually agreeable disposition. In concept and procedure I saw it to be as simple as 1) "place it," i.e., the enclosures; 2) "support it," i.e., hold it together structurally; and 3) "connect it," i.e.,

provide access. However the sequence might be in reverse: Starting with a structural frame to which are attached enclosures later to be connected. Or, starting with a circulation system, add structure and then enclosures.

Still another "dimension," as it were, is kinetics. We are now able to satisfy that basic fascination with movement, not by illusion, as in the baroque period, but with the technology we now command, producing buildings which, in part, do indeed move. As the history of architecture bears out, most innovations are drawn from either humble or crude and vulgar utilitarian origins. The barrel vault and arch were known to the Egyptians and Greeks who used them only for underground sewage, whereas the Romans and those for centuries later got, as we might say, a "lot of mileage" out of them. Hidden steel tension structures used to hold Renaissance domes from collapsing, and have now come to be commonly exposed. Kinetic devices first appeared in industrial buildings in the form of attached hoists, overhead conveyors, power scaffolding, pneumatic tube intercom, trackage, self-erecting cranes, etc. Now when an improved service is performed, sooner or later an architect will make it somehow publically acceptable on an aesthetic level. Increasingly there appear kinetic devices, vividly expressed, in airports, supermarkets and flashy hotels. Kinetics is here; to perform greater service, and to delight in.

Except for the most usual moving elements such as elevations, I have not yet designed a kinetic building. Yet following the sequence of my works, and with my continuing interest in an architecture of parts, it is with kinetics that I now come face to face. And as the house, as building type, is always a good proving ground, I sketched, in 1960, a house of parts, assembling and disassembling themselves on railroad trackage. A central element containing the entrance, living room, kitchen, bath, power source, etc., had other parts, i.e. master bedroom, guest room, studio and a "folly" or "mood room," grouped around it. For the practicabilities of domestic life, or for reason of pure whim, this house could change its functional grouping. From an aesthetic point of view, this house is never a static composition, but enters that field of experience now limited to kinetic sculpture.

I believe kinetics is more and more a part of our lives. The fusion of transportation and the building, people-moving devices, theatre technology, museum and exposition display, and opening and closing of solar heated buildings—all these current developments confirm the functional justification of moveable parts, while the public's delight in the exposed machinery of the Roosevelt Island cable car system, or the exposed elevator cabs of the Portman hotels, or the scenic railroad entering the hotel lobby in Orlando's Disney World, and now the "Super-Mannerists'" growing involvement with changeable facades and changeable "room liners" confirms the aesthetic acceptance of kinetics as well.

My philosophy of construction, then, would develop around "the part." The part appears first in analysis of the program, then in synthesis, in the typing of parts, then the grouping of parts, assembly, interchange, reshuffling, and finally in movement. This seems to be the basis of my "ordering devices" or "organizing ideas." The vivid expression, articulation, detailed connections and couplings are the "poetic touches" I give in the design process, thereby making of problem solving and building technology possibly something more. And if I add to this my other concerns—our sense of life, our basic psychological motivations, newly awakened perception of the impact of our electronic age, and our historic derivations—I hope I may come up with something which can be called architecture.

—John M. Johansen

John Johansen's is a punchy, loose-limbed architecture, full of solidified desire: his designs don't get bogged down in the quagmire of impulsive forms; they embody a surprisingly wide strain of social factors, though without for a single moment ever denying that, when all is said and done, they nonetheless owe something to form too. But in his case the forms are strong and roughly woven shapes going out to greet function. His Mechanic Theatre in Baltimore, the result more of thrust than intention, comprises brute concrete embracing the functional parameters in a dizzy architectural rewriting of Léger's Ballet Mechanique. His "Leapfrog City" project takes off in multi-determinate axes, like trails of smoke from a team of aerobatic aircraft.

His starting point is, how to make a human but unpredictable project? It must be the product of an enormous argument between everyone concerned, resulting in an agglutinative whole, alive with associations and suggestions. It is the way his buildings have obviously been argued through into their final form that prevents them from succumbing to that no-go area between architecture and sculpture: the reference-point established by means of the argument guarantees that only a few responsibilities and obligations at the most are lost in the formation process. Under such conditions, real, hard-headed "content" is very much on the cards.

The danger facing the designer today is that his parameters are all moving along similiar lines and that one criteria has come to be as good as another. Johansen instead insists on a provocative hierarchy of conditions as the only way of trying to get to the end of a sentence: this pugnacious vocabulary is what saves him from the spatial fixations and mechanical obsessions of the megastructure: he manages to come up with a language half given, half shared . . . fighting against the ghost seriality of the ultimate cliches.

His buildings, through their consideration of the social and anthropological, and through their lucid expression of the urban, seem to magnify one's whole being: the charitable gesture that characterizes his buildings is an index of the way they give themselves not just to ourselves but to the whole of the world—this might seem ludicrous only because of our current notions of selfishness. He recognizes that architecture can be a candidate for another dimension. Having admitted the power architecture commands over the elements, he has sworn not to abuse his own powers as architect. Architecture is something we ought to chase after, although we seldom do—we are led from it by personal foibles, mad impulses, eccentric codes of conduct: Johansen tries to reverse this, inviting us back directly to architecture. In order to do this, his buildings must boast many points of fusion with one's mind, which they do. He is afraid that the architect today could best be compared to an old woman who considers she is a lover of flowers when she presses them in a book instead of planting them.

—Chris Fawcett

JOHNSON, Philip (Cortelyou).
American. Born in Cleveland, Ohio, 8 July 1906. Educated at Harvard University, Cambridge, Massachusetts, 1923-30, A.B. (cum laude) 1930; Harvard Graduate School of Design, 1940-43, B.Arch. 1943. Director, Department of Architecture, Museum of Modern Art, New York, 1930-36; practised architecture in Cambridge, Massachusetts, 1942-46; again served as Director, Department of Architecture, Museum of Modern Art, 1946-54; returned to private practice in New York, 1954-64; Partner, with Richard Foster, Philip Johnson and Richard Foster, New York, 1964-67. Since 1967, Partner, with John Burgee, Johnson/Burgee Architects, New York. Trustee of the Museum of Modern Art since 1958. Recipient: Silver Medal of Honor, Architectural League of New York, 1950; First Prize, *Bienal,* Sao Paulo, 1954; Grand Festival Award, Boston

Philip Johnson: Pennzoil Place, Houston, 1976

Arts Festival, 1955; Merit Award, 1956, First Honor Award, 1956, 1961 (twice), Twenty-Five Year Award, 1975, and Gold Medal, 1978, American Institute of Architects; Award of Excellence, *Architectural Record,* 1957, 1962; Gold Medal of Honor, with Mies van der Rohe, Architectural League of New York, 1960; Best New Institutional Building, Fifth Avenue Association, New York 1962; Design Award, *Progressive Architecture,* 1964; First Honor Award, City Club of New York, 1966; Louis Sullivan Award, Bricklayers, Masons, and Plasterers International Union of America, 1975; R. S. Reynolds Memorial Award, 1978; Thomas Jefferson Medal, University of Virginia, Charlottesville, 1978; Bronze Medallion, City of New York, 1978; Pritzker Architecture Prize, Hyatt Foundation, 1979. D.F.A.: Pratt Institute, Brooklyn, New York, 1962. Fellow, American Institute of Architects, and American Academy of Arts and Letters. Address: Johnson/Burgee Architects, 375 Park Avenue, New York, New York 10022, U.S.A.

Works:

1942 Philip Johnson House, Cambridge, Massachusetts
1944 Townsend Farms Barn, New London, Ohio

1947 Farney House, Sagaponack, Long Island, New York
1949 Philip Johnson House, New Canaan, Connecticut
1950 Annex, Museum of Modern Art, New York
 John D. Rockefeller III Guest House, New York
1951 Hodgson House, New Canaan, Connecticut (with Landes Gores)
 Oneto House, Irvington, New York (with Landes Gores)
1952 Davis House, Wayzata, Minnesota
 Schlumberger Administration Building, Ridgefield, Connecticut
1953 Alice Ball House, New Canaan, Connecticut
 Rockefeller Sculpture Garden, Museum of Modern Art, New York (with James Fanning)
 Wiley House, New Canaan, Connecticut
1956 Boissonnas House, New Canaan, Connecticut
 Kneses Tifereth Israel Synagogue, Port Chester, New York
 Leonhardt House, Lloyd's Neck, Long Island, New York
1957 Auditorium and Classroom Buildings, University of St. Thomas, Houston (with Howard Barnstone and Partners)

1958 Seagram Building, 375 Park Avenue, New York (with Mies van der Rohe and Kahn and Jacobs)
1959 Asia House, New York
1960 Museum Building, Munson-Williams-Proctor Institute, Utica, New York
 Nuclear reactor, Rehovot, Israel
 Roofless Church, New Harmony, Indiana
 Dormitories, Sarah Lawrence College, Bronxville, New York
1961 Amon Carter Museum of Modern Art, Fort Worth, Texas
 Computing Center, Brown University, Providence, Rhode Island
1962 Pavilion, Philip Johnson House, New Canaan, Connecticut
1963 Museum for Pre-Columbian Art, Dumbarton Oaks, Washington, D.C.
 Sheldon Memorial Art Gallery, University of Nebraska, Lincoln
1964 Boissonnas House, Cap Benat, France
 Kline Geology Laboratory, Yale University, New Haven, Connecticut (with Richard Foster)
 East and Garden Wings, Museum of Modern Art, New York
 New York State Theatre, Lincoln Center, New York (with Richard Foster)
 New York State Pavilion, *World's Fair,* New York (with Richard Foster)
1965 Epidemiology and Public Health Building, Yale University, New Haven, Connecticut (with the Office of Douglas Orr)
 Geier House, Indian Hills, Ohio
 Painting Gallery, Philip Johnson House, New Canaan, Connecticut
 Kline Science Center, Yale University, New Haven, Connecticut (with Richard Foster)
 Henry L. Moses Institute, Montefiore Hospital, Bronx, New York
 Hendrix College Library, Conway, Arkansas (with Wittenberg, Delony, and Davidson)
1968 Bielefeld Art Gallery, West Germany (with Cäsar Pinnau)
 WRVA Radio Station, Richmond, Virginia (with Rudina and Freeman)
 Kreeger House, Washington, D.C. (with Richard Foster)
1970 Sculpture Gallery, Philip Johnson House, New Canaan, Connecticut
 John F. Kennedy Memorial, Dallas
1971 List Art Building, Brown University, Providence, Rhode Island
1972 Art Museum of South Texas, Corpus Christi (with John Burgee, and Barnstone and Aubry)
 Burden Hall, Harvard University, Cambridge, Massachusetts (with John Burgee)
 Neuberger Museum, State University of New York at Purchase (with John Burgee)
1973 Elmer Holmes Bobst Library, New York University, New York (with Richard Foster)
 Hagop Kevorkian Center for Near East Studies, New York University, New York (with Richard Foster)
 I.D.S. Center, Minneapolis (with John Burgee, and Edward F. Baker Associates)
 Boston Public Library addition (with John Burgee, and Architects Design Group)
1974 Convention Center, Niagara Falls, New York (with John Burgee)
1975 Water Garden, Fort Worth, Texas (with John Burgee)
 Morningside House, Bronx, New York (with John Burgee)
1976 Pennzoil Place, Houston (with John Burgee, and Wilson, Morris, Crain and Anderson)
 Post Oak Central 1, Houston (with John Burgee, and Wilson, Morris, Crain and Anderson)
 Avery Fisher Hall interiors, Lincoln Center, New York (with John Burgee)

1977 Muhlenberg College Fine Arts Center, Allentown, Pennsylvania (with John Burgee, and Coston, Wallace and Watson)
General American Life Insurance Company, St. Louis (with John Burgee)
Thanks-Giving Square, Dallas (with John Burgee)

Publications:

By JOHNSON: books—*Modern Architects*, with others, New York 1932; *The International Style*, with Henry-Russell Hitchcock, New York 1932, 1966; *Machine Art*, New York 1934; *Mies van der Rohe*, New York 1947, 1953; *Selected Writings*, Tokyo 1975; *Philip Johnson: Writings*, edited by Robert A.M. Stern, New York 1978.

On JOHNSON: books—*Philip Johnson* by John Jacobus, Jr., New York 1962; *Philip Johnson: Architecture 1949–1965* by Henry-Russell Hitchcock, New York and London 1966; *Philip Johnson* by Charles Noble, Tokyo 1968, London 1972; *Johnson House, New Canaan, Connecticut*, edited by Yukio Futagawa, text by Bryan Robertson, Tokyo 1972; *Conversations with Architects*, edited by John W. Cook and Heinrich Klotz, New York and London 1973; article—"The New Age of Philip Johnson" by Paul Goldberger in the *New York Times Magazine*, 14 May 1978.

Bibliography: "Writings by and about Philip C. Johnson," compiled by William B. O'Neal, in the *American Association of Architectural Bibliographers Papers*, vol. I, 1965, vol. II, 1966.

Philip Johnson occupies a unique position in the architectural world. A man of unequalled taste and sensibility, but one with no consistent idea of the kind of buildings that he should be building, he has left a trail of admiration and confusion. Most of the admiration is centred on the period of his work in the decade after the war when, briefly, he settled on a Miesian direction: if it were not for the buildings of this period, he would certainly not be regarded as a major architect.

It is significant that Philip Johnson came to designing buildings comparatively late in life, after a period as client, critic, author, and museum director. It was in pursuing these activities that he found his real training, and it was in these capacities that he became an important figure in the American East Coast architectural scene of the 1930's. He organized the first visits of both Mies van der Rohe and Le Corbusier to America. An affluent young man, he commissioned Mies to design his New York apartment for him in 1930, then found Mies his next American client; subsequently he wrote a book on Mies (based on the catalogue he had written for the New York Museum of Modern Art exhibition he had organized), which still remains the best of many books on its subject. Most important, in the years before and after the war he was the Director of the Department of Architecture at the Museum of Modern Art, a post he used forcefully to promote the causes in which he believed.

Johnson was a key propagandist for the Modern Movement in architecture, and the subsequent history of modern architecture in the U.S.A. is in many respects influenced by its having been brought to the country by Johnson, with his particular set of values. In Europe, the modern movement in architecture was closely related to social problems: it involved a belief that the good life must be for everyone, and working class housing was considered a major building type. Philip Johnson, the hedonist, filtered out these notions of social responsibility and sold America the new architecture as a new style. From Le Corbusier he gave them Poissy, but not the Ilot Insalubre, with the result that the movement had a very different history in America from, say, England,

where architecture and welfare were seen as closely related.

Johnson's apprenticeship was long and thorough, and when, at the age of 43, he built his first significant building, the result was a knock-out. The Glass House (Johnson House) at New Canaan states his position well: it is a historian's modern building. At a time when history was anathema to architects, Johnson published his house and illustrated some of the many sources of his design, not only Mies van der Rohe but also Schinkel, Choisy, Ledoux and Ben Nicholson. The modern movement had lost the innocence of its notion of a clean sweep of history. Yet, however clever the polemic that surrounded the completion of the Glass House, it would have remained an intellectual game had it not been for the manifest quality of the building itself. This was not the work of a mere critic but of a designer of the first rank. The building can be enjoyed for its historical allusions or for the quality of its materials. It can be appreciated for the clarity of its structure or for the elegance of its siting. Most of all, it must be admired as one of architecture's magic spaces, with the play of reflections and transparency of glass: thanks to the genius of Richard Kelly, the lighting consultant, the space at night is a veritable wonderland, as glass walls disappear and grass and trees are illuminated.

Johnson never again matched the memorability of the Glass House, but in the years following its completion he designed and built a series of middle-class family houses, often on modest budgets, that take much of the formalism and the quality of the Glass House and make it work in load-bearing brickwork for a plan with separate bedrooms. The Hodgson House and the Oneto House are particularly successful in this respect and must rate as amongst the most habitable family houses yet designed—one of the many curious twists to be found in Johnson's work is that he castigates architects who over-emphasise the functional basis for architecture, yet his own buildings often function superlatively well, while those of supposedly functionalist architects prove impracticable.

But by the mid-1950's, Johnson was becoming bored with the limitations imposed by the Miesian world. Mies had worried about the disorder apparent in cities, but Johnson welcomed chaos as preferable to order. "It's chaos and I love it," he said of the architectural situation in New York. First he turned to Louis Kahn, and Johnson's Boissonnas house of 1956 had brick piers and a rambling plan in the manner of Kahn's Adler and de Vore houses. The Boissonnas house was a lovely building, but Johnson did not feel that he had gone far enough. He wanted to overthrow not just Mies but the whole modern movement. The sheer architectural quality of his houses, and his prestige as Mies's assistant on the Seagram Building, meant that Johnson was an architect who had to be taken seriously, but from 1960 onwards he devoted his energies and his talents to twisting the tail of the modern movement.

In his design for Asia House, New York, Johnson published "alternative elevations": one involved sensuous curves, devoid of structural meaning, and these he employed in the Sheldon Memorial Art Gallery at the University of Nebraska. Later buildings, such as the theatre at Lincoln Center, often had the overblown banality of Mussolini's buildings, while others, such as the Moses Institute for Montefiore Hospital, New York, are just plain dull. A dull building is something Johnson himself would not wish for, and his recent project for an office building on a Chippendale cabinet parti can be seen as an effort to maintain interest almost at any price.

Whatever we may make of his flamboyant later buildings, consistent qualities remain. A certain exquisiteness, an instinctive understanding for quality in artificial lighting, and a sure sense of the way a building is walked through—the processional route that has fascinated him for thirty years, ever since he placed his glass house at the end of an elaborate route from the highway.

—John Winter

JOHNSON, R(ichard) N(orman).
Also known as Peter Johnson. Australian. Born in Armadale, Victoria, 15 December 1923. Educated at Sydney Boys' High School, 1936–40; University of Sydney, 1946–50, B.Arch. (honours) 1951. Served as a Flight Lieutenant in the Royal Australian Air Force, in Australia, Canada, the United Kingdom and France, 1942–45. Married Jane Margaret Adria Meade-Waldo in 1944; children: Christopher, Timothy, and Simon. Partner, McConnel Smith & Johnson, architects and planners, Sydney, 1955–71, and since 1971 Director, McConnel Smith & Johnson Pty. Ltd., Sydney; since 1974, Director, MSJ Keys Young Planners Pty. Ltd., Sydney. Director, YRM +MSJ Pty. Ltd. (Architects), Sydney, 1971–78. Professor of Architecture since 1967, and Dean of the Faculty of Architecture since 1968, University of Sydney. Foundation Chairman, The Architectural Society, Sydney, 1960–65; President, New South Wales Chapter, Royal Australian Institute of Architects, 1968–70; Member of the Senate, University of Sydney, 1968–72; Member of the Commonwealth Board of Architectural Education, 1971–77, Chairman, 1973–77, and Member of the Executive, 1976–77, Commonwealth Association of Architects; Member of the Council, New South Wales Branch, National Trust of Australia, 1972–77. Member, Board of Architects of New South Wales, since 1966; Member of the Council, New South Wales Institute of Technology, since 1967; Member of the Advisory Council, Sydney Building Information Centre, since 1970; Federal Councillor, Royal Australian Institute of Architects, since 1977. Recipient: Wilkinson Award, 1964; City of Sydney Award for Architectural Merit, 1971; Merit Award, Royal Australian Institute of Architects, New South Wales Chapter, 1977. Address: McConnel Smith & Johnson Pty. Ltd., Post Office Box 210, Darlinghurst, New South Wales 2010, Australia.

Works:

1960 Western Assurance Company Offices, Sydney
1963 R. N. Johnson House, Sydney
1965 Sydney Water Board Building
1966 School of Architecture, University of New South Wales, Sydney
1969 Law School, University of Sydney
1977 Federal/State Law Courts, Sydney
1978/
79   Benjamin Government Offices, Belconnen, Canberra

Publications:

By JOHNSON: articles—various articles, including "Annual Review of Architecture in Australia," in *Sydney Morning Herald*, 1963–70; "Suggestions for a Course in Architecture," with others, in *Architecture in Australia* (Sydney), June 1963; "Architect's Own House" in *Architecture in Australia* (Sydney), December 1963; "Internal Use of Plastics in Buildings" in *Architectural Science Review* (Sydney), March 1964; "The Board's Head Office Building" in *Sydney Water Board Journal*, July 1964; "No, Architects Do Not Have Their Heads in the Sand" in *Australian Financial Review* (Sydney), August 1969; "Five Buildings Tight or Loose: Contrasting Approaches to Design" in *Art and Australia* (Sydney), September 1969; "Joseph Fowell" in *Architecture in Australia* (Sydney), August 1970; "Does Town Planning Retard Development" in *Builder NSW* (Sydney), November 1972; "Emeritus Professor Leslie Wilkinson" in *Architecture in Australia* (Sydney), December 1973; "Leslie Wilkinson and His Architecture" in *Art and Australia* (Sydney), July/September 1974; "Sydney Opera House Since Utzon" in *Current Affairs Bulletin* (University of Sydney), August 1974; "Community Attitudes: New Respectability for an Ancient Custom" in *The Building Economist* (Sydney), December 1976; "Commonwealth State Law Courts, Sydney" in *Architecture Australia* (Melbourne), May 1978; "(Professional Responsibil-

R. N. Johnson: Federal/State Law Courts, Sydney, 1977

ment of an Australian architecture which will have a character responding to the nature of the people and the country, growing out of, expressing, and contributing to Australian traditions.

—R. N. Johnson

The characteristic feature of R. N. (Peter) Johnson's buildings is the rationality of their design. The needs of the people who are going to use the buildings, not merely the needs of the client organization, are carefully studied, and the design revolves around the satisfaction of those needs. This is apparent in his three best-known buildings, the new head office of the Sydney Water Board, the high-rise building housing the Federal/State Law Courts in Sydney, and the Benjamin Government Offices in Belconnen, Canberra.

For the Water Board Building the study of the needs of the occupants was relatively simple, as they consisted of the staff of the Board. For the Law Courts it was necessary to ascertain not merely the views of judges, administrators, and lawyers, but also of the members of the public who would use the courts as jurors and as litigants. This was done by interviews and questionnaires, with advice from psychologists, a process that took almost two years. Models were used extensively to explain the layout to various user groups. The result is an environment that is exceptionally humane without sacrificing the dignity appropriate to a court of law. Several of the courts are octagonal; this shape provoked discussion in the conservative legal profession, but it has proved to be successful. The law courts require three circulation systems that must be kept separate: one for the judges, one for the prisoners, and one for the public.

The Benjamin Offices were designed for government departments as yet unspecified, so flexibility was needed. Peter Johnson avoided the anonymity often associated with a "flexible" layout by using a hexagonal plan, which fitted the site, gave fine views over the lake on one side, and provided favourable orientation to the sun. The hexagons created some interesting interior spaces that counteracted the blandness of the office atmosphere. Each block has a distinctive colour to give identity to the building and to aid the visitor to find his way. The colours, initially conceived as an aid to circulation, are well chosen and constitute an important visual element.

Peter Johnson has attached particular importance to the space between the inside and the outside of his buildings, occupied by a verandah or balcony in traditional Australian architecture. He devoted a great deal of attention to sun control and energy conservation long before they became fashionable. In his office buildings "the space between the inside and outside" becomes a neutral zone occupied by sunshades and sun screens, which are accurately designed in accordance with solar altitude and azimuth. The visual character of the buildings owes a great deal to this aspect of his design.

Although Peter Johnson has a good understanding of structure, he never uses it purely for show. In the Water Board Building exceptionally long spans produce large spaces uninterrupted by supports, but generally his structures are the simplest and most economical that will serve the purpose. His buildings therefore lack the demonstrative elements evident in the work of some other Australian architects. Johnson admits that it is sometimes necessary to rearrange the interior spaces to satisfy the aesthetic needs of the facade, but essentially the buildings are designed to serve a purpose, and to satisfy human needs.

—Henry Cowan

ity) Is There a Solution?" in *The Building Economist* (Sydney), June 1978.

On JOHNSON: books—*Towards an Australian Architecture* by Harry Sowden, Sydney 1968; *Australian Art and Artists in the Making* by Craig McGregor, Melbourne 1969; articles—"World" in *Architectural Review* (London), February 1964; "Commonwealth State Law Courts, Sydney" in *Architecture Australia* (Melbourne), January 1978; "Commonwealth State Law Courts Building, Sydney" in *Architectural Review* (London), September 1978.

*

Society has made increasingly insistent demands on architects that their buildings should meet social and economic needs while still contributing to the quality of the built environment as art.

McConnel Smith & Johnson accept that, in architecture, serving society comes before the pursuit of personal artistic goals. For us architecture is a social art in which we aim to meet the shelter needs of the people who use the spaces we design in a way which evokes a positive response. We believe that architects must consider all the information available about the needs of those for whom they design and, whenever possible, share with them the experience of developing the design.

Architecture takes place in context—an organisational context, a physical context and a cultural context. We believe that the inspiration for architectural form should be drawn from the functional need for which the building exists, from the physical location, whether natural or man-made, and from the historical tradition of the community.

For us architecture is a social art in another sense —today it is rarely the product of one man. We believe in working together as a team so that not only those in the architects office but also the specialist consultants and the builder and his artisans should have a sense of involvement and be able to contribute actively to the nature and the quality of the final work. As a consequence we have always thought of our buildings as products of the firm as a whole and not as the products of particular individuals.

Architects now working in Australia do not have the long local traditions which surround architects working in other, older, countries. They are however aware of the influences brought to Australia by migrants during its relatively short history, and, in this century, of the pervasive influence of the ideas of the modern movement.

An Australian tradition will grow as the Australian culture itself becomes more mature and more self-assured. Its beginnings can be seen in a response in architecture to the strong sun and clear light and the need for shade. The country itself has a sense of space; it is big and varied and still uncluttered.

We hope that we will contribute to the develop-

JONES, A. Quincy.
American. Born in Kansas City, Missouri, 29 April 1913. Educated at the University of Washington, Seattle, 1931–36, B.Arch. 1936. Served in the United

States Navy, 1945. Married Ruth E. Schneider in 1937 (divorced, 1942); married Anne B. Austin in 1943 (divorced, 1961): children: Michael, Hillary, and Timothy; married Elaine Kollins Sewell in 1962. In private practice, Los Angeles, from 1937: in partnership with Frederick E. Emmons, 1950–69. Professor of Architecture, University of Southern California, Los Angeles, 1951–67. President, 1960, Member of the Housing Committee, 1963–64, 1969–79, and Member of the International Relations Committee, 1969–79, American Institute of Architects, Southern California Chapter. Recipient: First Honor Award, 1950, and Award of Merit, 1952, 1955, 1957, American Institute of Architects. Fellow, American Institute of Architects. *Died* (in Los Angeles) *3 August 1979.*

Works (all California):

1938   Jones House and Studio, 8661 Nash, West Hollywood, Los Angeles
1948   Nordlinger House, 11492 Thurston Circle, Bel Air, Los Angeles
1949   Fuller House, 3068 Chevy Chase, Glendale
       Griffith Park Girls' Camp, Griffith Park Boulevard, Hollywood (with Smith and Contini)
1950   Mutual Housing Association Development, Los Angeles (with Smith and Contini)
       Hvistendahl House, San Diego
1951   Campbell Hall School, 4717 Laurel Canyon, North Hollywood
1952   House, Bienveneda and Marquette Streets, Pacific Palisades
1953   Greenmeadows Subdivision, Palo Alto (with Anshen and Allen, and Claude Oakland)
       St. Matthew's Episcopal Church, Pacific Palisades
1954   Emmons House, 661 Brooktree, Pacific Palisades
1955   Jones House, 1223 Tigertail Road, Los Angeles (destroyed by fire)
       Research Village, Barrington, Illinois
1959   Biological Sciences Building, University of California at Santa Barbara
1960   Faculty Center, University of Southern California, Los Angeles
1963   Shorecliff Tower Apartments, 535 Ocean Avenue, Santa Monica
1964   Joseph Eichler Housing Development, Granada Hills
       University Research Library, unit I, University of California at Los Angeles
       Laguna/O'Farrell Apartments, 66 Cleary Court, San Francisco
       Joseph Eichler Housing Development, Thousand Oaks, California
1965   The Barn, 10300 Santa Monica, Westwood
       Library (unit I), Crawford Hall, Steinhaus Hall, and the Humanities-Social Sciences Building, University of California at Irvine (with William L Pereira, and Blurock and Ellerbrock)
1966   Carillon Tower, University of California at Riverside (competition project)
1967   Chemistry Building, University of California at Riverside
1969   Medical Unit, I and II, University of California at Riverside
       Library, unit II, University of California at Irvine
1971   University Research Library, unit II, University of California at Los Angeles
1972   Educational Resources Center, State University of California at Dominguez Hills
1975   Mandeville Center for the Arts, University of California at San Diego, La Jolla.
       Warner Brothers Records Office Building, Burbank
1976   Annenberg School of Communications, unit I, University of Southern California, Los Angeles
1979   Annenberg School of Communications, unit II, University of Southern California, Los Angeles

A. Quincy Jones: Annenberg School of Communications, University of Southern California, Los Angeles, 1976

Publications:

On JONES: articles—"Pushbutton Paradise in California" in *House and Garden* (New York), April 1953; "Escape for City Children" in *Progressive Architecture* (New York), March 1954; "Research Village" in *Arts and Architecture* (Los Angeles), April 1955; "Four Offices of Distinction" in *Architectural Forum* (New York), November 1956; "Genetrix: Personal Contributions to American Architecture" in *Architectural Review* (London), May 1957; article in *Arts and Architecture* (Los Angeles), May 1966; "Modular Project for More Flexible Hospitals" in *Progressive Architecture* (New York), September 1971; "School of Communications, University of Southern California" in *Progressive Architecture* (New York), May 1977.

*   *   *

Much of A. Quincy Jones's work from the 1960's to the present has been in the design of buildings for university campuses and of office buildings, but he first gained recognition in residential work in the postwar era when the need for housing was acute. His houses set standards of excellence that affected all house design of the period, especially the tract house, to which he was one of the few to give architectural consideration. A characteristic of these small houses was the simplified structural system which allowed for spatial diversity, in contrast to the usual static box.

Typical of his early planning was Mutual Housing, a development of 100 houses, in which the houses were adjusted to a hilly terrain with little disturbance of the contours. He was not opposed to changing the natural terrain, however, when it served environmental purposes, as in his unique proposal in 1962 to contour a flat building tract for 260 houses in order to create sight and sound barriers between houses.

Certain characteristics of Jones's large-scale work grew out of his solutions for residences, particularly in siting and in the development of flexible structural systems, although in his larger buildings his experiments were aimed at the integration of mechanical systems; previous to his researches each system was treated as a separate element, and their haphazard installation reduced their efficiency and retrievable space. The aesthetic of the Jones buildings emerges very often from structural or mechanical simplification: the 1959 Biological Sciences Building on the Santa Barbara campus, and the 1967 Chemistry Building on the Riverside campus of the University of California are visually dominated by a heavy continuous cap which houses an integrated mechanical system, and it is expressed on the interiors by a prefabricated coffered ceiling of concrete which carries conduits in the channels.

Jones never hesitates to mix a heavy with a delicate scale, often with great success, as in the University Research Library at UCLA (Unit I, 1964, Unit II, 1971), in this case the delicate almost Gothic scale deriving from the structural expression of narrow study carrels.

A planning practice initiated with the University Research Library that effectively minimized the height and simplified circulation was to depress the ground story somewhat below grade and place the entrance at the second level. The ground level workrooms and offices are naturally lighted by windows facing a terrace which ends in a landscaped gentle upslope to grade level. The main entrance is reached by a series of stairs which are interrupted by plazas at two levels, the plazas serving as meeting places for students, with one extended to a protected patio furnished with tables. This scheme was adapted for the 1972 Educational Resources Center for the State University of California at Dominguez Hills, Units I and II (1976, 1979) of the Annenberg School of Communications at University of Southern California, the Mandeville Center for the Arts at the University of California at San Diego, and for a woodsheathed office building for Warner Brothers Records. The latter, planned around interior patios, is in the spirit of many of Jones's large houses, although even in his university buildings there are definite traces of the residential scale—a friendly scale which, combined with the exercises in simplification, created warm and principled buildings.

—Esther McCoy

JOSIC, Alexis.

French. Born in Stari Becej, Yugoslavia, 24 May 1921; emigrated to France, 1953: naturalized, 1964. Studied painting at the National Fine Art School, Belgrade, 1940–46, graduated 1946, and at the Josic Fine Art School, Belgrade (founded by his father Mladen Josic), 1940–46; studied architecture at the Grate Technical School, Belgrade, 1940–48, Dip. Arch. 1948. Served in the Yugoslav Army, 1951–52. Married Douchanka Ivanovic in 1961; children: Jovan and Marko. Architect, Ministry of Construction, Belgrade, 1945–47; Professor of Painting, Josic Fine Art School, Belgrade, 1946–47; Scenographist, National Movie Industry, Belgrade, 1948–50; Architect, ATBAT (Atelier des Bâtisseurs), Paris, 1953–54; Partner, with Georges Candilis, q.v., and Shadrach Woods, q.v., Atelier Candilis-Josic-Woods, Paris, 1955–63. In private practice, Sèvres, France, since 1963. Professor of Architecture, Fine Arts School of Paris (Atelier Candilis-Josic), 1961–64, and Faculty of Architecture of the Unité Pédagogique 5, Paris, 1971–74. Recipient: First Prize, Marseilles Housing Competition, 1959; French Government Prize in Town Planning, 1959; First Prize, Toulouse-le-Mirail New Town Competition, 1960; First Prize, Free University of Berlin Competition, 1963; First Prize, Hilton Hotel Competition, Dakar, Senegal, 1972; First Prize, Lille-Est New Town Competition, 1972; Gold Medal for Architecture, Society for the Encouragement of Arts and Industry, France, 1974. Member, l'Ordre des Architectes Français, 1963. Address: Alexis Josic—Architecte, 5 rue Carle Vernet, 92310 Sèvres, France.

Works:

1953/
54 Housing for the North Pole (project; with ATBAT)
Operation Emmaus (low-cost housing), France (competition project; with ATBAT)

1954/
55 Opération Million: 3,600 housing units, France, particularly the Paris suburbs (with Georges Candilis and Shadrach Woods)

1956/
61 Plan and housing for the new town of Bagnols-sur-Cèze, France (with Georges Candilis and Shadrach Woods)

1959 Housing (4,000 units), Marseilles (with Georges Candilis and Shadrach Woods)

1960 Urban pre-fabricated houses, Algeria (competition project; with Georges Candilis and Shadrach Woods)
Master plan for the new town of Toulouse-le-Mirail, France (with Georges Candilis and Shadrach Woods)

1961 New town of 30,000 inhabitants, Caen, France (competition project; with Georges Candilis and Shadrach Woods)
New town of 10,000 inhabitants, Hamburg (competition project; with Georges Candilis and Shadrach Woods)

1962 University for 2,000 students, Bochum, Germany (competition project; with Georges Candilis and Shadrach Woods)

1963 Plan for the centre of Frankfurt (project; with Georges Candilis and Shadrach Woods)
Master plan of Fort Lamy, Chad, Africa (with Georges Candilis and Shadrach Woods)
Master plan for the Free University of Berlin (with Georges Candilis and Shadrach Woods)

1964/
65 Cité Artisanale (Workshop Centre for Artisans), Sèvres, France (with Georges Candilis and Shadrach Woods)

1965/
66 Housing (2,000 units), Morangis, France (project)

1965/
67 Regional plan for the development of tourism, Aveyron, France

1965/
72 Master plan for the centre of Sèvres, France

1966/
67 Water Treatment Plant, Toulouse-le-Mirail, France (with Georges Candilis)

1966/
68 Faculty of Literature, Restaurant, Administration Building, and Sports Facilities, University of Toulouse-le-Mirail, France (with Georges Candilis)

1967 Rural plan for Brittany (competition project)
Housing for a holiday resort, Collioure, France (project)

1968 Thermo-Electric Building, Toulouse-le-Mirail, France
Plan for Chamarande, France

1969/
70 Commercial Centre and Housing, Sèvres, France
Plan for a neighborhood of Limoges, France
Housing (10,000 low-cost units), Lima, Peru (competition project; with Georges Candilis)

1970 Hilton Hotel, Lahore, Pakistan (with Georges Candilis)

1971 Tourism facilities for the peninsula of Lavrotto, Monaco (competition project; with Georges Candilis)

1972 Water Treatment Plant, Neuilly-sur-Marne, France
Hilton Hotel, Dakar, Senegal (competition project)

1972/
78 New town of Lille-Est, France (with François Calsat)

1973 Plan for the redevelopment of Vanves, near Paris

1974 Administrative Centre, Besançon, France (competition project)

Department of Sciences, University of Isfahan, Iran (competition project; with Fereydoun Davarpanah)

1974/
78 Les Passage District, Evry New Town, France: master plan; dwellings; university department of technology; commercial art and workshop centre; international youth hotel

1977/
78 Fine Art School, Mashad, Iran (with Fereydoun Davarpanah)

Publications:

On JOSIC: books—*CIAM 59 in Otterlo* by Oscar Newman, Stuttgart 1961; *Architecture and the Phenomenon of Transition* by Siegfried Giedion, Cambridge, Massachusetts 1967; *Candilis, Josic, Woods* by Jürgen Joedicke, Stuttgart 1968; *Toulouse-le-Mirail: Birth of a New Town,* Stuttgart 1975; articles—"Candilis, Josic, Woods" in *Cimaise* (Paris), January/February 1961; "Atelier Candilis, Josic, Woods" in *Architectural Design* (London), January 1965; "The Work of the Architect Josic" in *Arhitektura-Urbanizam* (Belgrade), no. 58, 1969.

The continuously increasing, explosive and uncontrollable population growth, together with the reduction in space available for the life of the individual, provoke a deep and universal anxiety, and a search for additional space becomes mankind's obsession. The lack of vital space obliges mankind to use all of its resources to recover lost space; distribute and reorganize the space still available; and create new physical environments where the man of tomorrow can live.

The organization of life for the "mass" is the fundamental problem facing contemporary civilization. The vast increase in our numbers leads to a violent break with tradition and hastens the world towards an unavoidable transformation and change in scale. The scale of man? The scale of many men. The "mass." That is the point of reference for our world today.

The policy of "land usage" provides one of the fundamental answers to the problem of co-existence with the "mass," and town planning provides the most adequate methods of organization for the sites of collective life, the towns.

We have carried out our studies in this sphere by research into the idea of a town as an environment; we have been guided by methods of perception of architectural space. In consequence, the research has been related to the elaboration of urban systems. The prime objective of the research was to establish a system that created a vast structure that would favour the relationship of man with his environment, a reception site for the sum of man's activities, and a suitable environment for social activity. The pre-established system (mental approach) must be perceived physically (in reality) as a sum of spaces built with continuity. It is brought into being by a spatial structure that includes and organizes the "full" and the "empty" space.

In the structure that is advocated, the act of building is twofold: it creates simultaneously a "full" and "empty" space; it makes them interdependent and complementary. It creates a totality of modulated and differentiated spaces, assigned to programmed functions, thus eliminating insignificant and superfluous residual space from the urban structure.

Man inhabits the empty space that is defined, articulated and organized by the constructed area (the house, the street, the square). The house is an inhabited, contained space, defined by the "constructed area" (walls) but it is itself also the limit of an empty space on a superior scale (the street, the square). Man inhabits the total system: he lives in his dwelling, his street, his district, his town, his world. The structure must provide the idea of a spatial hierarchy that will arouse the feeling of belonging to the largest unit employed by man—the town.

This goal calls for the voluntary abandonment of

Alexis Josic: New Town of Lille-Est, France, 1978

a contained and definitive architecture, an architecture of objects that separate human activities, for an open and continuous architectural web that unites human activities and favours the perception of the town as an entity. The modulated geometric grid is an integral part of the structure and serves only as a language for the architecture that results. Such an architecture does not impose its specific character by architectural form. It is an open architecture whose form is never definitive but always developing, an architecture in waiting, of which one dimension is time.

—Alexis Josic

Alexis Josic's architectural personality is fully expressed in his Cité Artisanale (Workshop Centre for Artisans) in Sèvres, conceived and built in 1965, where he has now set up his practice: five interlocking levels of open-plan spaces overlooking a wood, with a team of young architects, his architect wife at his side, large-scale plans on the walls, on the drawing tables paper cut-outs for studying planning modules, proportions, volumetric relationships, colours, rhythms. . . .

His architecture is based essentially on the three-dimensional modular system. That is the tool, the methodology, and the process by which he is able to organize his space into constructed and open areas, the filled-in and the unoccupied, allowing him to define and integrate different themes without "left-over" areas. The constructed masses, together with the streets and squares, form an entity that ensures a relationship between dwelling and town, domestic space and public space, and environment, and provides for continuity and the possibility of growth. It was with this research into modular space in mind that he devised Cité Artisanale. The continual process of growth and evolution in time is clearly visible in the built form of the upper stories added when and where necessary without destroying the unity of the original conception—a form awaiting change, the

antithesis of an object architecture that is in essence definitive.

Josic arrived at this language, this modular system, which he uses in very diverse programs, not as a matter of improvisation but as the result of long experience and deliberation. From his earliest youth he was aware of space, of the significance of volume, and of "ambiance." His father, Mladen Josic, was a well-known Yugoslav painter who founded an art school that rapidly became a centre of creative encounter and exchange of ideas. He created an exciting atmosphere, and he instilled in his son the value of "approach" and "method." Josic grew up and studied while immersed in this stimulating atmosphere. Through painting, he mastered volume; from his researches, he constructed a working method; through a constant feedback from intuition to verification, he arrived, beyond a simple response to function, at "something indefinable that touches the heart—architecture" (Le Corbusier).

Josic arrived in Paris in 1953. He settled quickly into ATBAT (Atelier des Bâtisseurs), then into partnership with Georges Candilis and Shadrach Woods. This association was decisive for each of them. The project "Opération Million" placed the team in the forefront of research into economical habitat, and in two years they built more than 3,600 dwellings in France. Then there were ten years of strenuous work, of prize winning in national and international competitions, of executed works, and, above all, of research that would give birth to an ideology. They proposed an "organization of space" instead of the "juxtaposition" of buildings and "spirit of composition." They developed the idea of "spatial continuity," where the object disappears to the benefit of the whole, creating a bond between all things, and the polyvalent urban system is the basis of architectural language.

Each work was a step in the process of the doctrine—from Bagnols-sur-Cèze to the new town at Toulouse-le-Mirail, from Bochum University to the Free University of Berlin.

In 1963 Josic established his own studio, and since then he has independently created a number of works, worked again with Candilis (Faculty of Literature at the University of Toulouse-le-Mirail), and, on a completely different scale, produced a theoretical study for the Aveyron, an important development in the search for a grid plan for the development of regional tourism. In 1972 he won the important national competition for the new town of Lille-Est. It gave him the opportunity to develop and to apply his theories on "filled" and "empty" spaces to achieve spatial continuity, to create a sense of belonging to a structure greater than that of the simple dwelling. It was also an open door to constructive research toward a flexible system that would lead to a personalized architecture. This period was marked by a very fruitful collaboration with François Calsat, who died, unfortunately, in 1976.

Since then there has been a succession of projects: master plan for a district of Vanves (2,000 dwellings along the Paris Ring Road) and the execution of 300 dwellings; the Les Passages district in Evry New Town; continuation of Lille-Est; the competition for the University of Isfahan; and the Fine Art School at Mashad in Iran. At present he is completing a study of a workers' town of 30,000 inhabitants, in the desert, near a steelworks, not far from Isfahan. In principle it is a linear town comprising two superimposed urban structures: one fulfills the need for a traditional habitat, a closely-woven structure freely interlaced with small streets and little squares; the other responds to another tradition of habitat that is typically Iranian, terraced buildings around areas of water, creating a landscape, conferring on the town its own silhouette. In this project Josic was able to give free rein to his abilities, form a synthesis of his experience, and realize his most profound aspirations as an architect, a man, and a creator.

Today, Alexis Josic, in full possession of his powers and certain of his convictions, is an international architect of whom we can still expect a great deal.

—Renée Diamant-Berger

JUJOL (i GIBERT), Josep María.

Spanish. Born in Tarragona, 16 September 1879. Educated at primary school in Tarragona, 1885–88; De Gracia Elementary School, Barcelona, 1888–91; Provincial Institute of Higher Education, Barcelona, 1891–96; School of Architecture and Engineering, University of Barcelona, 1897–1906, Dip.Arch. 1906. Married Teresa Gilbert Mosella in 1927; son: Josep María, Jr. Worked in the studio of the architect Gallissà, in Barcelona, 1901–03, and in the studio of Font i Gumá, Barcelona, 1903–06; collaborated with Antoni Gaudí, Barcelona, 1906–10: first furniture designs, 1908; in private practice, Barcelona, 1907 until his death, 1949. Auxiliary Municipal Architect, Sant Joan Despí, Barcelona, from 1926. Exhibitions: *Furniture Exhibition,* Barcelona, 1923; *World's Fair,* Barcelona, 1929. Recipient: Architecture Prize, Fiesta de la Virtud y el Trabajo, Barcelona, 1905. *Died* (in Barcelona) *5 May 1949.*

Works:

1902 Merced Festival street decorations, Calle Fernando, Barcelona (with Gallissá)
Gallissá House architectural graphics and staircase, Barcelona
Cloister decorations, Barcelona (project)
Doorway, Ensanche, Barcelona (project)

1903 House, Calle Valencia 339, Barcelona (with Gallissá)
Altar, Church of the Holy Trinity, Santa María del Mar, Spain (with Font i Gumá)
Watchman's cabin, gates and fences, Municipal Park, Barcelona (projects)

1904 Ateneo Redevelopment Plan, Barcelona (with Font i Gumá)
Palace with Museum (project)
Country Palace (project)
Historical Archives Building, Barcelona (project)

1905 Mosaics for the Basilica of Our Father, Jerusalem (with Font i Gumá)
Amusement Park, Barcelona (project)
Church of St. Eulalia, Barcelona (project)
Tower (project)
Street decorations, Calle Cos del Bou, Tarragona (project)

1906 Monument of the 1905 African War (project)
Health Spa (project)
Casa Batlló remodelling ("Casa de los Huesos"), 43 Paseo de Gracia, Barcelona (assisted Antoni Gaudí)
Gallissa House entrance architectural graphics, Barcelona

1907 Casa Milá ("La Pedrera") Apartment Building, 92 Paseo de Gracia, Barcelona (assisted Antoni Gaudí)
Apartment building, Poble Sec, Barcelona
Alcover Church and Square temporary decorations, Tarragona
Theatre of Patronato del Obrero, Tarragona

1909 Torre San Salvador (house), Paseo de Nuestra Senora del Coll, Barcelona
Farinera Teixidor Building, Gerona, Spain (project)

1910 Casa Escofet Mosaics, Barcelona (project)
Gibert-Romeu Tombstone, Barcelona
Cathedral of Palma, Majorca interior alterations (assisted Antoni Gaudí)

1911 Casa de Familia, Calle del Carmen, Barcelona (destroyed)
Manach Store, Calle Fernando 57, Barcelona (destroyed)
Manach Workshop alterations, Calle de Barbara 9, Barcelona (destroyed)

1912 Designs for the roof of the Cathedral, Tarragona (projects)

1913 Cases dels Periodistes, Barcelona (project)
Urban development plan for Les Corts, Barcelona (project)
Apartment building alterations, Calle Sant Oleguer, Barcelona (project)
Lift/Elevator in the Casa Iglesias, calle Mallorca 284, Barcelona
Slaughterhouse, Sant Feliu del Llobregat, Spain (project)
Torre de la Creu (house), Calle Canalias 12, Sant Joan Despí, Barcelona

1913/
15 Baptistry and presbytery in Constantí, Tarragona

1914 Casa Ximenis, Paseo de Saavedra 17, Tarragona
Casa Befarull, Els Pallaresos, Tarragona
Apartment building, Poble Sec, Barcelona
Chapel, La Secuita Cemetery, Tarragona (project)
Gate for the main square, Montferri, Tarragona (project)

1915 Agua Radial Mines Building, 98 Paseo Nuestra Senora del Coll, Barcelona
Apartment building alterations, Calle Masens, Barcelona
Casa Negre extensions and alterations, Torrent del Negre 37, Sant Joan Despí, Barcelona

1916 Tower, Calle de las Torres, Barcelona
Manach Workhouses, Riera de Sant Miguel 39, Barcelona
Coro de Flora Tower, Calle Falanga, Sant Joan Despí, Barcelona
Apartment building, Calle del Oro, Gracia, Barcelona

1917 Queralt Tower, Calle Pineda 1, Barcelona
Casa Xatruc extensions, La Canonja, Tarragona
Church Bell-Tower, Creixell de Mar, Tarragona
La Budallera Country House alterations, Tarragona
Estate Buildings, Calle Alcolea, Barcelona
Planells Family Tombstone, Barcelona
Parish church baptistry, Alforja, Tarragona (project)

1917/
20 Schools, Els Pallaresos, Tarragona

1918 House, Calle Verge del Pilar 24, Barcelona
Casa Iglesias, Tarragona (project)
Del Carmen Chapel, Tarragona
San Salvador Family Tombstone, Barcelona
Vda. Casanovas Factory alterations, Barcelona
Convent of the Carmelitas de Badalona, Barcelona (project)
House extensions, Plaza de la Concordia, Barcelona

1918/
23 Vistabella Church, Tarragona

1920 Casa Malaquer alterations, Sant Joan Despí, Barcelona
Town Hall, Els Pallaresos, Tarragona
Casa Andreu, Plaza de la Iglesia, Els Pallaresos, Tarragona
City Theatre, Barcelona (project)
Gozos de San Silverio (project)

1921 Sisters Oblatas de Bellesguard Building alterations, Barcelona
Senoras Tangenelli Tower, Vallcarca, Barcelona

1922 House, Calle de la Independencia, Barcelona
Samontá (Negre Estate) Development Plan, Sant Joan Despí, Barcelona (project)
Apartment building, Calle del Bruc, Barcelona
Tower, Calle Sicilia, Barcelona (project)
House, Calle Sant Benet, Barcelona
Hospital Espanol, Mexico (competition project)
Public Library (competition project)
Tower, Calle Verdaguer 9, Sant Joan Despí, Barcelona

1924 Casa Planells, Avenida Diagonal 332, Barcelona
Apartment building, Calle San Salvador, Barcelona
Apartment building, Calle de Sant Benet 20, Barcelona
Jujol House, Paseo de Canalías, Sant Joan Despí, Barcelona (project)
Tombstones, Municipal Cemetery, Tarragona

1925 Camprubi Family Vault (project)
Ermita del Roser interior decoration, Vallmoll, Tarragona
Marble Tombstones, Municipal Cemetery, Tarragona (with Arana)

1926 Casa Manach Store electric sign, Barcelona
Ermita de Lloret alterations, Renau, Tarragona
Llobregat Cinema, Sant Joan Despí, Barcelona
Sant Francesc Chapel, Rambla Sant Carles, Tarragona
Reconstruction and development plan for the Roman Amphitheatre, Tarragona (project)
Shrine, Montserrat, Montferri, Tarragona
Casa Rovita architectural graphics and alterations, Calle Mossen Cinto Verdaguer 41, Sant Joan Despí, Barcelona
Lloret Shrine Fountain, Bràfim, Tarragona (later altered)
Ermita del Roser floors, Vallmoll, Tarragona
Casa Joaquím oratory, Sant Joan Despí, Barcelona
Apartment building extensions, calle Libertat, Barcelona
Blessed Sacrament Chapel, Parish Church, Sant Joan Despí, Barcelona (destroyed)
Escuela del Trabajo Arches, Barcelona
Casa Solé window-grille, Els Pallaresos, Tarragona

1927 Esperanza Xaux House extensions, Calle Verdaguer, Sant Joan Despí, Barcelona

1927/
29 Palacio del Vestido, *World's Fair,* Plaza de Espana, Barcelona (with Calzada; later altered)

1928 Town Hall alterations, Montferrí, Tarragona (project)
Samontá (Negre Estate) Development Plan II, Sant Joan Despí, Barcelona (project)
Church of Sant Joan Despí garden development, Barcelona
Torre Dot extensions and alterations, Sant Joan Despí, Barcelona (destroyed)
Torre Campubrí, between Sant Joan Despí and Cornellà de Llobregat, Barcelona

1928/
29 Fountain, *World's Fair,* Plaza de Espana, Barcelona

1929 Land development plan for Sant Joan Despí, Barcelona (project)

1930 Commemorative gravestones, Tarragona (with Arana)

1931 Rectory renovations, Bisbal del Penedès, Tarragona

1932 Torre Jujol (house), Calle Mossèn Cinto Verdaguer 45, Sant Joan Despí, Barcelona

1933 Baptistry windows and chapel renovations, Parish Church, Sant Joan Despí, Barcelona (destroyed)
Fomento Sindicato Agrícola Theatre, Sant Joan Despí, Barcelona (later altered)
Pacual-Carrera House oratory, Barcelona (destroyed)
Casa Pujol facade, Vallmoll, Tarragona (project)

1934/
35 Presbytery windows, floors and furnishings, Parish Church, Rodà de Barà, Tarragona

1935 Mas Carreras renovations, Rodà de Barà, Tarragona
New Rectory, Sant Joan Despí, Barcelona (project)

1939 New Parish Church, Sant Joan Despí, Barcelona (project)
Lloret Shrine Presbytery, Bràfim, Tarragona (project)

Monument to the Fallen, Fosos de Santa Elena, Castillo de Montjuic, Barcelona (project)

Apartment building renovations, Calle del Arco del Teatro, Barcelona

House extensions, Sant Joan Despí, Barcelona

Parish Church renovation, Rodà de Barà, Tarragona (project)

Parish Church renovation, Campins, Barcelona (partially destroyed)

Carmelitas de la Caridad Convent School alterations, Tarragona

House extensions, Calle Augusto 7, Sant Feliú de Llobregat, Barcelona

Parish Church of Santa Mónica, Barcelona (project)

1940 Monument to the Holy Assumption (project)

Classroom and work archives alterations, School of Architecture, Barcelona

Presbytery and altar, Guimerà, Lerida, Spain

"Gremí de Pagesos" Church alterations, Placa Sant Llorenc, Tarragona

Presbytery floors and altar, El Vendrell, Tarragona

1941 Holy Week Float (project)

Monument to the Fallen, Placa del Marcat, San Joan Despí, Barcelona

1941/
45 Bonastre Church restoration, Tarragona

1942 Rose Window and Santa Vedrina Memorial Stone, Baptistry of the Basilica del Pino, Barcelona

Casa Solé alterations, Els Pallaresos, Tarragona

Bonastre Baptistry, Tarragona

Blessed Sacrament Altar, El Vendrell, Tarragona

1943 Carmelitas de la Caridad Convent extensions, Calle Agusta 7, Tarragona

"Old Custodia" Guard-House reconstruction, Belltall, Tarragona

Carmelitas de la Caridad Convent, Gerona, Spain (project)

Parish Church interiors, Sant Joan Despí, Barcelona

Casa de l'Abadessa alterations, Tarragona

Pulpit and confessionals, Blessed Sacrament Chapel, El Vendrell, Tarragona

Presbytery, Bonastre Church, Tarragona

1943/
48 Colonia Güell Church altar, Barcelona

1943/
49 Torre Codina alterations, del Canyet, Badalona, Barcelona

1944 Emilia Fortuny House alterations, Els Pallaresos, Tarragona

Chapel of Mas Carreras alterations and renovation, Roda de Bara, Tarragona

Samontá (Negre Estate) Development Plan III, Sant Joan Despí, Barcelona (project)

Shrine, Bonastre Church, Tarragona

San José Altar, El Vendrell, Tarragona

1945 Parish Church of Pobla de Claramunt alterations, Barcelona

1945/
47 Side altars, Church of Els Pallaresos, Tarragona

1945/
49 Parish Church of Capellades alterations, Barcelona

1946 Sanctuary, Church of the Hospital at Capellades, Barcelona

1947 Parish Church of San Antonio windows, Vilanova i la Geltrú, Barcelona

"Casa de Amparo" presbytery and main altar, Vilanova i la Geltrú, Barcelona

Pared Delgada Hermitage, Le Selva del Camp, Tarragona, Spain (project)

Parish Church facade and main altar, La Selva del Camp, Tarragona

Utilitarian Bungalows (projects)

Chapel of the Sacrament, La Bisbal del Penedès, Tarragona (project)

Dominicas de la Annunciata Convent extensions, Calle Doctor Dou, Barcelona

1948 Parish Church of Santa Colomba de Gramenet alterations, Barcelona

Blessed Heart Altar, Parish Church of Sant Antoni, Vilanova i la Geltrú, Barcelona (unfinished)

1949 Carmelitas de la Caridad Convent extensions, Vinalesa, Valencia

Bank Agency Building, Sant Joan Despí, Barcelona (destroyed)

Samontá (Negre Estate) Development Plan, Sant Joan Despí, Barcelona (final project)

Publications:

By JUJOL: articles—in *Catalunya Nova* (Barcelona), 2 February 1908; "Necrologia de Concepcion Mallafre" in *La Veu de Catalunya* (Barcelona), 5 July 1922; "L'Esglesia Primera de Vistabella" in *Lo Missatger del Sagrat Cor de Jesus* (Barcelona), March 1923; "Necrologia de Angel Bru" in *Tarragona,* 29 April 1924; "El Nuevo Pendon" in *La Cruz* (Tarragona), 18 November 1925; "Fiestas Centenarias C. de la C." in *Tarragona,* 30 May 1926; "Necrologia de Casimir Llobet" in *La Veu de Catalunya* (Barcelona), 24 January 1929; "El Palacio del Vestido" in *El Iman* (Barcelona), December 1929.

On JUJOL: books—*El Arte Modernista Catalan* by A. Cirici Pellicer, Barcelona 1951; *Arte Religioso Actual en Cataluña* by J. Ferrando Roig, Barcelona 1952; *Barcelona, entre el Pla Cerda i el Barraquisme* by Oriol Bohigas, Barcelona 1963; *Arquitectura Modernista* by Oriol Bohigas, Barcelona 1968; *La Arquitectura de Josep María Jujol* by Josep María Jujol Jr., J. F. Ràfols and C. Flores, Barcelona 1974.

The force that pushed Josep María Jujol to the limits of architectural creativity has left us with an astounding lesson in design. His works are characterized by their ability to solve the problems created by the interaction of his two methods of artistic creation —a juxtaposition of different geometrical systems and an independent pictorial composition applied to the resulting form. He was no doubt a precursor of Dada and Surrealism, working from both the cultural freedom of the Catalan Modernisme movement and the discipline of the Noucentist cultural reaction.

The juxtaposition of different geometrical systems can be clearly observed in his Casa Planells, with the curvilinear facade added on to the regular plan, and in his Torre de la Creu, where the merging of five cylinders is regulated by the clean cut of the party wall and the other orthogonal divisions. The unity of the cylindric composition destroys the semi-detached function, which in turn is set against the curvilinear space inside. This tense double-game is one of the great creative characteristics of Jujol's work that sets it apart from, and to some extent above, the work of Antoni Gaudí.

Jujol's most satisfying work is his country parish church in Vistabella. It is essentially a building within a building. The spire, in the centre, consists of a pyramid formed by four columns, which in turn support the vaults that rise over the main space. Wrapped around this space is an aisle, the roof of which spirals up, supporting steps that can take the visitor from the ground to the belfry without his having to enter the church. The plan, which is square, is composed axially along the diagonal, with the entrance at one point and the altar at the other. This tendency to introduce the diagonal in his compositions is found not only in the planning of major elements but also in the design of details, like the fences that surround several of his small houses, from Torre San Salvador to the Torre Jujol in Sant Joan Despí.

Jujol's other characteristic method is one of architectural graphics, a technique *(esgrafiats* in Catalan) of coloured "stucco," a favourite decorative element used by most Modernist architects on facades. The highly original "calligraphic" style of Jujol is unmistakable, be it a severe, classic rectangular composition or one of baroque lyricism. This graphic ornamentation follows its own internal design structure independent of the architecture that supports it. Independent, but not separate, as Jujol drew lines of colour casually linking a window to a door or a ceiling. Venturi's suggestion that architecture also consists of decorated sheds is a particularly happy phrase to describe this essential part of Jujol's work. Jujol's metalwork is also essentially graphic, with hatched bars contrasting with thin plate strips—best seen in the balcony railings of the Casa Milà, designed in collaboration with Gaudi. Once one has observed Jujol on his own, it is easy to identify his work when collaborating with Gaudí—for example, the "sea-weed" balconies and plaster ceilings of the Casa Milà or the alterations to the Cathedral in Palma.

Jujol took form and pattern and destroyed their normal limits so that they emerged together to produce an architecture that is still extraordinarily stimulating and relevant to the 20th century.

—David Mackay

JUMSAI, Sumet.
Thai. Born in Bangkok, 30 March 1939. Educated at Cambridge University (Brancusi Travelling Fund Award, 1963; Breezewood Foundation Scholarship, 1965; JDR III Scholarship, 1965), B.A. 1961, M.A. 1963, Dip. Arch. 1963, and Ph.D. in architectural studies 1967. Married Suthini Jumsai in 1970; children: Siriprapha and Prisdha. Architect, and Assistant to the Chief of the Division of Comprehensive Planning, Thailand Department of Town and Country Planning, Bangkok, 1965–69; Principal, DEC Consultants, Bangkok, 1970–72, and Sumet Likit Tri and Associates, Bangkok, 1972–75. Since 1975, Managing Director, Sumet Jumsai Associates Co. Ltd., Bangkok. Executive Director, APAC (Asian Planning and Architectural Consultants), Hong Kong, since 1969. Guest Lecturer and Visiting Critic, Faculty of Architecture, Silpakorn University, Bangkok, since 1967, and Chulalongkorn University, Bangkok, since 1970. Member, Government Committee for the Conservation and Registration of Historic Monuments, Bangkok, 1972–75; Chairman, Arts Committee of the Siam Society, Bangkok, 1975. Member, National Board of Environment, Bangkok, since 1976. Exhibition: Museum of Modern Art, New York, 1979. Member, Association of Siamese Architects under Royal Patronage; Member, World Society of Ekistics. Address: Sumet Jumsai Associates, 106/1 Sukhumvit 53, Bangkok 11, Thailand.

Works:

1969 Office for the Private Properties of H. M. The King, Bangkok

1970 Nava Nakorn Satellite Town, Pathumthani District, near Bangkok (with Likit Hongladarom and David A. Bailey)

British Council Building, Bangkok

1971 Dr. Pierra Foundation Children's Canteen, Bangkok

Residence for the President of Siam Motors, Sukhumvit 55, Bangkok

1972 Siam Country Club, Pattaya, Thailand

Daikin Showroom/Offices, Bangkok

School for the Blind, Bangkok

1973 Guest House, Siam Country Club, Pattaya,

Thailand (with Vunchai Nitisophon)
Siam Motors Showroom, Ubol, Thailand
Siam Motors Showroom, Nakorn Pathom, Thailand
Apartments and architect's office, Bangkok
1974 Refrigerator plant, Bangna-Trad Highway, Thailand
1975 Car air-conditioner factory, Bangna-Trad Highway, Thailand
Ambassador Cinema, Bangkok
Private museum/library, Bangkok
1976 Bank of Asia Branch Office, Bang Pakong, Thailand
Bank of Asia Branch Office, Cholburi, Thailand
Bank of Asia Warin Branch Office, Ubol, Thailand (with Somboon Skoolisariyaporn)
1977 Science Museum, Bangkok (with Tri Devakul and Mrs. Kwanchai Laksanakorn)
Siam Motors Industrial Estate, Bagna-Trad Highway, Thailand
Nissan Car Assembly Plant, Bangna-Trad Highway, Thailand (with Sawan Imarom)
Nissan Car Assembly Plant Canteen, Bangna-Trad Highway, Thailand (with Sawan Imarom)
Yamaha Motorcycle Factory, Bangna-Trad Highway, Thailand
Low-cost housing, Nava Nakorn Satellite Town, Pathumthani District, near Bangkok
Engineer's studio house, 1/46 Patanawate 10, Sukhumvit 71, Bangkok
1978 Indoor Stadium, Siam Motors Industrial Estate, Bangna-Trad Highway, Thailand (with Jarin Kamklai)
Car inspection plant, Bangna-Trad Highway, Thailand
Industrial showroom/office, Bangna-Trad Highway, Thailand
Bus assembly factory, Bangna-Trad Highway, Thailand
Bottle factory, Rangsit, Bangkok
Bank of Asia Branch Office, Chiangmai, Thailand (with Pong Wibhvanuwong)
Bank of Asia Branch Office, Phuket, Thailand (with Somboon Skoolisariyaporn)

Bank of Asia Head Office, Bangkok (project)
Advance factories, Nava Nakorn Satellite Town, Pathumthani District, near Bangkok (with Praphont Thanakul)
Siam Motors Head Office, Bangkok (with Kwanchai Laksanakorn)

Publications:

By JUMSAI: books—*Architectural Forms of Northern Siam and Old Siamese Fortifications,* Bangkok 1970; editor and translator of *Six Hundred Years of Work by Thai Artists and Architects* by Joti Kalyanamitra, Bangkok 1977; articles—"Some Comparative Aspects of Angkor Thom and Ayutya" in *Journal of the Association of Siamese Architects* (Bangkok), no. 2, 1965; "Bangkok Plan: Technological Changes versus Historical and Geographical Factors" in *Bangkok World,* 9 February 1965; "Some Recollections and a Tribute to Le Corbusier, 1887–1965" in *Bangkok World,* 31 August 1965; "Ayutya, Venice of South Asia" in *Unesco Courier* (Paris), October 1966; "City Plan Thwarted" in *The Times* (London), 3 September 1970; "Sexual Connotations in Urban Symbolism" in *Nation* (Bangkok), 6 and 13 August 1972; "The Proposed Town and Country Planning Act: Towards Urban Dynamics or Standstill?" in *Nation* (Bangkok), 17 November 1974; "Polycentric Plan: Answer to the City's Problem" in *Nation* (Bangkok), 29 July 1975; "Mountain and Water: How Cities Strove for Harmony by Being Macrocosmically Planned" in *Ekistics* (Athens), September 1975; "Urbanization on Low Technology: A Strategy for Majority Survival into an Exponential World" in *City Planning Review* (Tokyo), July/August 1976; "Strategy to Combat World Urbanization" in *Bangkok Post,* August 1976; "Cartography and Beyond" in *Nation* (Bangkok), 26 March 1978; "The World of Buckminster Fuller" in *Nation* (Bangkok), 19 March 1978.

On JUMSAI: book—*Architecture of the Seventies* by Udo Kultermann, London 1979; articles—"Thai Design for the English" in *Progressive Architecture* (New York), October 1970; "But the Ladies Hate It" by Charles Correa in *Architecture Plus* (New York), November 1973; "Siam Country Club" in

Asian Architect and Builder (Hong Kong), February 1974; "Bangkok's British Beatnik Building" in *South China Morning Post* (Hong Kong), 3 May 1974; "Apartments and Architect's Office/Private Library" in *Architecture + Urbanism* (Tokyo), October 1976; "A Bangkok Colori: 18 Apartments + 1 Atelier" in *Domus* (Milan), March 1977; "Per le Scienze in Thailandia" in *Domus* (Milan), July 1977; "Wissenschaftliches Museum" in *Bauen und Wohnen* (Zurich), October 1977; "Science Museum" in *Architecture + Urbanism* (Tokyo), November 1977; "APAC" in *Nikkei Architecture* (Tokyo), November 1977; "Letter from Bangkok" by Harry Rolnick in *Far Eastern Economic Review* (Hong Kong), 10 February 1978.

We find from the dawn of history that people in the northern hemisphere were forced by the cold climate to lay food and other essentials in store and hence to plan, contemplate and calculate interests, resulting subsequently in a whole host of other intellectual activities in which they are highly capable, and resulting also in their world hegemony. This hegemony includes architecture and architectural education as we know it.

In the land-water (but mainly water) configurations of the equatorial Pacific and Southeast Asia, the at least 2½ million year old humanity found an oasis for survival through two intervening glacial periods and has, therefore, formulated the oldest continuous culture. This culture, which is instinctive and spontaneous, as against intellectual, is a link to the longest human experience and possibly a key to humanity's next test in survivability.

Although I am from this original survival oasis, I was brought up in the northern (western) hemisphere and was conditioned for a long time by its intellectualism which I now know has blunted a great deal of the instinctive approach ingrained in the people of the equatorial Pacific.

I am convinced that if this exponential world is to survive into the future, alternative design and technology will have to replace those created by the present intellectual impasse—and where would such alternatives be found if not in the area where humanity has for 2½ million years accumulated the codes for survival, codes that generated a wealth of instinct and spontaneity in design?

I am now gradually unlearning what I have learned in architecture, and if my work reflects this unlearning approach, then perhaps I shall be contributing something useful to the future of humanity.
—Sumet Jumsai

Sumet Jumsai's own remarks accurately reflect his architecture and need no further elaboration. He studied under Martin at Cambridge, and to a considerable extent, especially early in his carrer, a Corbusier/Martin duality can be recognized in his works. Thai sensitivity in the size and delicacy of materials that he chooses to envelope his buildings also creates vernacular spaces that can be thoroughly appreciated, even if they are somewhat Western-looking.

One of his later works is much too *Domus*-esque—a Lamborghini may look fine on an Italian autostrada but it is totally surrealistic and even frightening in the context of the boats on the Klongs of Bangkok.

Jumsai is perhaps the most intellectual architect in Southeast Asia, but while this intellectualism is acceptable at the Architectural Association or in Cambridge, it does not sit easily with the Southeast Asian businessmen and politicians who have just "made it" or, for that matter, with the masses aspiring toward only the understandable.

Sumet Jumsai is intelligent enough to have observed this difficulty, and I suppose he must live with and through these contradictions if he is to find an Architecture of Thailand. If a new Thai architecture does develop, he will be at the forefront.
—K. C. Lye

Sumet Jumsai: Science Museum, Bangkok, 1977

KAHN, Louis I(sadore).

American. Born on the Island of Saarama, Estonia, now U.S.S.R., 20 February 1901; emigrated to the United States, to Philadelphia, 1905: naturalized, 1915. Educated at the Central High School and Pennsylvania Academy of Fine Arts, Philadelphia, 1912–20; Graphic Sketch Club, Fleisher Memorial Art School, and the Public Industrial Art School, Philadelphia, 1916–20 (Pennsylvania Academy of Fine Arts Prize, 1920); University of Pennsylvania, Philadelphia, 1920–24, B.Arch. 1924. Married Esther Virginia Israeli in 1930; daughter: Sue Ann. Draftsman with the architects Hofman and Henan, Philadelphia, 1921, and with Hewitt and Ash, Philadelphia, 1922; Teaching Assistant, University of Pennsylvania, 1923–24; Senior Draftsman, 1924–27, and Chief of Design for the *Sesqui-Centennial Exhibition*, 1925–26, City Architect's Department, Philadelphia; studied and travelled in Europe, 1928–29; Designer, office of Paul Cret, Philadelphia, 1929–30, and Zantziger, Borie and Medary, Philadelphia, 1930–32; Organizer and Director, Architectural Research Group, Philadelphia, 1932–33; Squad Head in charge of Housing Studies, City Planning Commission, for the W.P.A. (Works Progress Administration), Philadelphia, 1933–35; Assistant Principal Architect, office of Alfred Kastner and Partner, Philadelphia, 1935–37; in private practice, Philadelphia, 1937 until his death, 1974: in association with George Howe, *q.v.*, 1941–42, with Howe and Oscar Stonorov, *q.v.*, 1942–43, and with Stonorov, 1943–48. Consultant Architect, Philadelphia Housing Authority, 1937, and United States Housing Authority, 1939; Consultant Architect to the Philadelphia City Planning Commission, 1946–52, 1961–62; Consultant Architect, Philadelphia Redevelopment Authority, 1951–54. Chief Critic in Architectural Design and Professor of Architecture, Yale University, New Haven, Connecticut, 1948–57; Resident Architect, American Academy, Rome, 1950–51; Albert Farwell Bemis Professor, School of Architecture and Planning, Massachusetts Institute of Technology, Cambridge, 1956; Professor of Architecture, 1957–66, Paul Cret Professor, 1966–71, and Emeritus Professor, 1971–74, University of Pennsylvania. Member, Team 10. Exhibitions: Pennsylvania Academy of Fine Arts, Philadelphia (drawings and paintings), 1930, 1933; *Architecture in Government Housing*, Museum of Modern Art, New York, 1936; *Houses and Housing*, Museum of Modern Art, New York, 1939; *Better Philadelphia Exhibition*, Philadelphia, 1947; *The Works of Louis I. Kahn*, La Jolla Museum of Art, California, 1965; *Louis I. Kahn*, Museum of Modern Art, New York, 1966; *Louis I. Kahn*, ETH: Swiss Federal Institute of Technology, Zurich, 1969, and toured Europe; *Louis I. Kahn: Drawings*, Pennsylvania Academy of Fine Arts, Philadelphia, and toured the United States, 1978. Recipient: Arnold Brunner Prize, National Institute of Arts and Letters, 1960; Graham Foundation Fellowship, 1961; Philadelphia Art Alliance Medal, 1962; Frank P. Brown Medal, Franklin Institute, Philadelphia, 1964; Medal of Honor, Danish Architects Association, 1965; Annual Award, Philadelphia Sketch Club, 1966; International Silver Medal, University of Connecticut, Storrs, 1969; Centennial Gold Medal, American Institute of Architects, Philadelphia Chapter, 1969; Gold Medal of Honor, AIA, New York Chapter, 1970; Gold Medal, national AIA, 1971; Philadelphia Book Award, 1971; Creative Arts Medal, Brandeis University, Waltham, Massachusetts, 1972; Royal Gold Medal, Royal Institute of British Architects, 1972; Gold Medal, National Institute of Arts and Letters, 1973. H.H.D.: University of North Carolina, Raleigh, 1964; D.Arch.: Polytechnic, Milan, 1964; D.F.A.: Yale University, 1965; Maryland Institute College of Art, Baltimore, 1968; Bard College, Annandale-on-Hudson, New York, 1970; University of Pennsylvania, 1971; LL.D.: LaSalle College, Philadelphia, 1967; D.L.: Tulane University, New Orleans, 1972; D.H.L.: Columbia University, New York, 1974. Fellow, American Institute of Architects, 1953. Member, National Institute of Arts and Letters, 1964, American Academy of Arts and Sciences, 1968, and American Academy of Arts and Letters, 1973. Honorary Member, Royal Swedish Academy of Fine Arts, 1966, and College of Architects of Peru, 1967; Fellow, Royal Society of Arts, London, 1970. *Died (in New York City) 17 March 1974.*

Works:

1920/
24   Entrance, United States Veterans Hospital, Philadelphia (competition project)
       Shopping Center, United States Army Post, Philadelphia (competition project)

1924/
26   Buildings for the *Sesqui-Centennial Exhibition*, Philadelphia

1926/
27   Municipal Building, Philadelphia (project)
       City planning studies for Philadelphia

1929/
30   Buildings for the 1933 Chicago *World's Fair* (project)

1929/
32   Folger Library, Washington, D.C. (with Paul Cret)

1930/
32   Department of Justice Building, Washington, D.C. (project)

1933   Slum block reclamation, Philadelphia (project)

1933/
35   Housing studies for the Philadelphia Planning Commission

1935/
39   Ahavath Israel Synagogue, Philadelphia
       Homesteads Development, Hightstown, New Jersey (project)

1939   Rational City (exhibition project)

1940   Jesse Oser House, 688 Stetson Road, Melrose Park, Pennsylvania

1941/
42   Pine Ford Housing, Middletown, Pennsylvania (with George Howe)

1941/
43   Carver Court Housing, Coatesville, Pennsylvania (with George Howe and Oscar Stonorov)

1942   Pennypack Housing, Philadelphia (project; with George Howe and Oscar Stonorov)
       Stanton Road Housing, Washington, D.C. (project; with George Howe)

1943   Lincoln Road Housing, Coatesville, Pennsylvania (project; with George Howe and Oscar Stonorov)
       Lily Ponds Housing, Washington, D.C. (project; with George Howe and Oscar Stonorov)
       Willow Run Housing, Detroit (project; with Oscar Stonorov)
       194X Hotel, Philadelphia (competition project; with Oscar Stonorov)

1944   Pennypack Buildings, Philadelphia (project; with Oscar Stonorov)

1944/
45   Health Clinic extension and alterations, 22nd and Locust Streets, Philadelphia (with Oscar Stonorov)

1944/
46   Psychiatric Hospital, Monument Avenue, Philadelphia (project; with Oscar Stonorov)

1945/
49   Philip Roche House, Harts Lane, Whitemarsh Township, Pennsylvania

1946/
54   Mill Creek Redevelopment, Philadelphia (project; with Kenneth Day, Louis McAllister and Anne Tyng)

1947   Offices and Cafeteria, Container Corporation of America, Philadelphia (project; with Oscar Stonorov)

1947/
48   Plan for the Midtown City Center, Philadelphia (exhibition project)

1947/
49   Winslow Tompkins House, Apalogan Road and School House Lane, Germantown, Philadelphia (project)

1948   Jefferson Memorial, St. Louis (competition project)
       Radbill Oil Company Office interiors, 1724 Chestnut Street, Philadelphia (project)

1948/
49   Morton Weiss House, Norristown, Pennsylvania

1949   Coward Glass Front Shoe Store, Philadelphia (with Oscar Stonorov)
       Samuel Genel House, Lancaster Avenue and Indian Creek Drive, Lower Merion Township, Pennsylvania

1949/
50   Pincus Therapy Building, Psychiatric Hospital, Ford and Monument Roads, Philadelphia (with Isadore Rosenfield)

1950   St. Luke's Hospital alterations, Philadelphia (project)
       Jacob Sherman House, 414 Sycamore Avenue, Lower Merion Township, Pennsylvania

1950/
53 Radbill Psychiatric Hospital, Philadelphia (with Isadore Rosenfield)
Temple and Poplar Public Housing, Philadelphia (project; with Kennedy Day, Louis McAllister and Anne Tyng)
1951/
53 Yale Art Gallery, New Haven, Connecticut (with Douglas Orr)
1952/
53 Midtown-Penn Center, Philadelphia (project)
1952/
57 City Tower Municipal Building, Philadelphia (project; with Anne Tyng)
1952/
62 Mill Creek Public Housing, 46th Street and Fairmount Avenue, Philadelphia (with Kenneth Day, Louis McAllister and Anne Tyng)
1953 Ralph Roberts House, School House Lane, Germantown, Philadelphia
1954 Adath Jeshurun Synagogue, Elkins Park, Pennsylvania (project)
Weber de Vore House, Montgomery Avenue, Springfield Township, Pennsylvania (project)
Francis Adler House, Davidson Road, Germantown, Philadelphia (project)
1954/
56 Medical Service Building, AFL-CIO, Philadelphia (demolished, 1973)
1954/
59 Bath House, and Master Plan, Jewish Community Center, Lower Ferry Road, Trenton, New Jersey
1955/
57 Martin Research Institute, Fort Meade, Maryland (project)
1956 Library, Washington University, St. Louis (competition project)
1956/
57 Midtown City Center Forum, Philadelphia (project)
Enrico Fermi Memorial, Chicago (competition project)
1957/
59 Irving Shaw House additions and alterations, 2129 Cypress Street, Philadelphia
1957/
61 Fred Clever House, Hunt Tract, Delaware Township, Pennsylvania
1957/
64 Richards Medical Research Building, University of Pennsylvania, Philadelphia
1958 Lawrence Morris House, Mount Kisco, New York (project)
1958/
61 *Tribune Review* Building, Greensburg, Pennsylvania
1959 Robert Fleisher House, Woodland Glen, Elkins Park, Pennsylvania (project)
Morton Goldenberg House, Rydal, Pennsylvania (project)
1959/
61 Esherick House, Chestnut Hill, Pennsylvania
Bernard Shapiro House, Hidden River Road, Penn Valley, Narberth, Pennsylvania
United States Consulate, Luanda, Angola (project)
1959/
62 Mill Creek Community Center, 46th and Aspen Streets, Philadelphia
1959/
65 Laboratory Buildings for the Salk Institute, La Jolla, California
1959/
67 Unitarian Church and School Building, Rochester, New York
1960 Norman Fisher House, Mill Road, Hatboro, Philadelphia
Municipal Building, Mill Creek and Bath Road, Levittown, Bristol, Pennsylvania (project)

1960/
61 Franklin D. Roosevelt Memorial, Washington, D.C. (competition project)
1960/
65 Erdman Hall Dormitories, Bryn Mawr College, Pennsylvania
1961 Thames Barge, London, for the American Wind Symphony Orchestra, Pittsburgh
Carborundum Co. Warehouse and Sales Office, Niagara Falls, New York (project)
General Motors Exhibition Building, for the 1964 *World's Fair,* New York (project)
Plymouth Swim Club Building, Pennsylvania (project)
Chemistry Building, University of Virginia, Charlottesville (project)
Shapero Hall of Pharmacy, Wayne State University, Detroit (project)
1961/
62 Mid-town/Market Street East Development, Philadelphia (project)
1961/
64 Levy Memorial Playground, Riverside Park, New York (project; with Isamu Noguchi)
1961/
70 Mikveh Israel Synagogue, Philadelphia (project)
1962/
74 Sher-E-Banglanagar: New Capital of Bangladesh, Dacca: Citadel of Assembly; National Assembly; Prayer Hall; Hostels; Ayub Hospital
Institute of Management, Ahmedabad, India (with B. V. Doshi and A. D. Raje)
1963 President's Estate, Islamabad, Pakistan (project)
1963/
64 Master plan for the Gandhinagar Capital City, Gujarat, India
1964/
67 Philadelphia College of Art (project)
Interama/Pan American Center, Miami (project)
1964/
72 Jewish Martyrs' Memorial, Battery Park, New York (project)
1965/
68 Dominican Sisters Convent, Media, Pennsylvania (project)
1965/
74 Theatre of the Performing Arts, Fine Arts Center, Fort Wayne, Indiana
1966 St. Andrew's Priory, Valyermo, California (project)
Stern House, Washington, D.C. (project)
1966/
70 Olivetti-Underwood Factory, Harrisburg, Pennsylvania
1966/
72 Kimbell Art Museum, Will Rogers Road West, Fort Worth, Texas (with Preston M. Gerne and Associates)
Temple Beth-El Synagogue, Chappaqua, New York
1966/
73 Kansas Office Building, Kansas City (project)
1967/
68 Broadway Church of Christ Church and Office Building, New York (project)
1967/
72 Library and Dining Hall, Phillips Exeter Academy, New Hampshire
1968 Delaware Valley Family Living Mental Therapy Building, New Britain, Pennsylvania (project)
1968/
73 Hill Central Area Redevelopment, Columbus and Washington Avenues, New Haven, Connecticut (project)
1968/
74 Hurva Synagogue, Jerusalem (project)
Congress Hall, Venice (project)

Wolfson Center, University of Tel Aviv, Israel (project)
1969/
74 Center for British Art and Studies, Yale University, New Haven, Connecticut
1970 Dual Movie Theatre, Sansom Street, Philadelphia (project)
1970/
74 Family Planning Center, Khatmandu, Nepal
1971/
73 Inner Harbor, Baltimore (project)
1971/
74 Design for the 1976 *Bi-centennial Exposition,* Philadelphia
1972/
74 Independence Mall Area Development, for the 1976 *Bi-centennial Exposition,* Philadelphia (project)
Hotel, Government Hill Development, Jerusalem (project)
1973/
74 Theological Library, University of California, Berkeley (project)
Roosevelt Memorial, Roosevelt Island, New York (project)
Pocono Arts Center, Luzerne County, Pennsylvania (project)
1974 Abbasabad Development, Government Complex, Tehran (project; with Kenzo Tange)
Korman House, Whitemarsh Township, Pennsylvania

Publications:

By KAHN: books—*Why City Planning Is Your Responsibility,* with Oscar Stonorov, New York 1942; *You and Your Neighborhood,* with Oscar Stonorov, New York 1944; *The Notebooks and Drawings of Louis I. Kahn,* edited by Richard Saul Wurman and Eugene Feldman, Philadelphia 1962, 2nd edition Cambridge, Massachusetts 1973; *Louis I. Kahn: Talks with Students,* Houston, Texas 1969; *Light Is the Theme: Louis I. Kahn and the Kemball Art Museum* (commentary by Kahn), compiled by Nell E. Johnson, Fort Worth, Texas 1975; articles—"Monumentality" in *New Architecture and City Planning,* edited by Paul Zucker, New York 1944; "Toward a Plan for Midtown Philadelphia" in *Perspecta* (New Haven, Connecticut), no. 2, 1953; "Architecture Is the Thoughtful Making of Spaces" in *Perspecta* (New Haven, Connecticut), no. 4, 1957; "Form and Design" in *Architectural Design* (London), April 1961; "A Statement" in *Arts and Architecture* (Los Angeles), May 1964; "Remarks" in *Perspecta* (New Haven, Connecticut), no. 9/10, 1965; "Structure and Form" in *Royal Architectural Institute of Canada Journal* (Toronto), November 1965; "Louis Kahn: Statements and Architecture" in Zodiac (Milan), vol. 17, 1967; "Architecture: Silence and Light" in *On the Future of Art* by Arnold Toynbee and others, New York 1970; "Not for the Faint-Hearted" in *AIA Journal* (Washington, D.C.), June 1971; "The Room, The Street, and Human Agreement" in *AIA Journal* (Washington, D.C.), September 1971; "Louis I. Kahn: Royal Gold Medallist" in *RIBA Journal* (London), August 1972; "The Invisible City: An Architect Speaks His Mind: Louis Kahn Talks . . ." in *House and Garden* (New York), October 1972; "Room, Window and Sun" in *Canadian Architect* (Toronto), June 1973; "L'Accord de l'homme et l'architecture: une conférence de Louis Kahn" in *La Construction Moderne* (Paris), July/August 1973; "Clearing: Interview with Louis Kahn" in *Via* (Philadelphia), vol. 2; 1973; "Harmony Between Man and Architecture" in *Design* (Bombay), March 1974.

On KAHN: books—*Louis I. Kahn* by Vincent Scully Jr., New York 1962 (includes bibliography); *Man Made Philadelphia* by Richard Saul Wurman, Philadelphia 1972; *Modern Movements in Architecture* by Charles Jencks, London 1973; *Louis I. Kahn*

Louis I. Kahn has become a legend of modern architecture. The architecture he produced, and the philosophy he professed, have had an absolutely monumental impact on the development and redirectioning of progressive design. Apart from his importance as leader of the most dramatic shift in architectural thought since the dawn of modern architecture in the 1920's, the sheer talent that Kahn possessed compelled him to create several of the most sensitive, beautiful and thrilling buildings erected in this century.

Kahn's major work spans barely fifteen years, but it documents a change in architectural perception that, although only recently identified, has certainly become the most salient trend of the 1970's. When Kahn's work first gained recognition at the end of the 1950's, the western world was still mesmerized by the advancements of rapid industrialization, and the new construction techniques and materials technology offered. Kahn identified this as blind idolatry, and rejected the uniformity of design response that had made most modern architecture at that time nameless, faceless, and crude. Instead, he espoused individuality, sensitivity, and freedom to respond in unique ways to the particular constraints of each building's program. He never rebelled against the new technology, materials, and aesthetics that had come to characterize contemporary building, but he insisted on reworking the process of design to allow the inclusion of both greater personal artistic statement and occupant concern. What is more, he developed and preached certain formal organizational maneuvers, claimed to be demanded by the integrity of the created pieces themselves, that suggested an architectural order more strict than any imposed since the classicism of antiquity.

While teaching at the University of Pennsylvania in Philadelphia, Kahn had a chance to fully develop his concepts, which he labeled with a unique vocabulary of names that have since become catchwords of architectural rhetoric. "Servant and served space," for example, described formal zoning differentiation between the primary spaces of a building and the portions of a structure reserved for mechanical equipment and ancillary use. "Silence and light" was a more spiritual analogy of the same concept of duality expressed in the physical distinction of servant and served spaces. Kahn's concern with expressing the contrasts of duality are repeatedly evident; his juxtaposition of the "light" of expression against the "silence" of the pre-inspirational void, his interest in the physical modulation of light against darkness, and his insistence on clear distinction between zones of use and zones of service all reflect a similar focus on exposing and identifying opposing forces. These concepts, together with his affinity for geometrical systems of organization in plan (perhaps a vestige of his Beaux-Arts training), account for the most marked features of Lou Kahn's architecture.

Kahn's design process was labeled with a different set of jargon. He used the word "Form" to describe the pure, ideal existence of an architectural program. "Order" was used to refer to architectural maneuvers, including geometry, linearity, symmetry, asymmetry, etc., that could create physical, architectural entities. "Design" was the attempt to approach perfect Form through the imposition of Order.

"Searching for what a material wants to be" was another favorite expression of Kahn's. It implies the importance of using materials in ways that most effectively capitalize on their physical attributes. A "society of rooms" was also an important phrase. It was used to connote a plan that contains dramatic, active architectural response between one area and another, so that there is a level of interactive resonance in the communication of the spaces.

Although Kahn's words often seem cryptic (and he consistently expressed dissatisfaction with his own ability to express himself verbally, even while others lauded him as a poet), his buildings shine through as gems of bursting creativity and instantaneous accomplishment. Each clearly displays the excitement of truly inspirational production, and never

Louis I. Kahn: Richards Medical Research Building, University of Pennsylvania, Philadelphia, 1964

by Romaldo Giurgola and Jaimini Mehta, Zurich and Boulder, Colorado 1975; *Eighteen Years with Architect Louis I. Kahn* by August Komendant, Englewood, New Jersey 1975; *Louis I. Kahn: The Complete Works 1935-1974* by Heinz Ronner, Sharad Jhaveri and Alessandro Vesella, Basle, Stuttgart, and Boulder, Colorado 1977 (includes bibliography); *Between Silence and Light: Spirit in the Architecture of Louis I. Kahn* by John Lobel, 1979 articles—"The Philadelphia Cure" in *Architectural Forum* (New York), April 1952; "Les Reseaux à Trois Dimensions" by Robert Le Ricolais in *L'Architecture d'Aujourd'hui* (Paris), September 1954; "The New Brutalism" by Reyner Banham in *Architectural Review* (London), December 1955; "Architect Louis I. Kahn and His Strong-Boned Structures" by Walter McQuade in *Architectural Forum* (New York), October 1957; "Louis Kahn" by E. and R. Katan in *L'Architecture d'Aujourd'hui* (Paris), no. 105, 1962/63; "Louis Kahn" in *Zodiac* (Milan), October 1967; "Louis I. Kahn," special issue of *L'Architecture d'Aujourd'hui* (Paris), February/March 1969; "Louis I. Kahn," special issue of *Architectural Forum* (New York), July/August 1972; "Louis I. Kahn," special issue of *Architecture å Urbanism* (Tokyo), January 1973; "Review of Recent Work: Louis Kahn" by Alison Smithson in *Architectural Design* (London), August 1973; "Within the Folds of Construction" by William Marlin in *Architectural Forum* (New York), October 1973; "Homage to Louis Kahn," special issue of *Werk* (Zurich), July 1974; "Yale Center for British Art" by Vincent Scully Jr. in *Architectural Record* (New York), June 1977; "Kahn at Yale" by William Jordy in *Architectural Review* (London), July 1977.

is their any evidence of labored attempts to fulfill academic prescriptions. Often his buildings do appear to be full of conflict and doubt, but the tension arises far more from conflict of artistic and expressive intent than from any stifling effort to follow formula.

Kahn's work was inconsistent, sporadic, and frantic, and only a few of his buildings were completely successful. Even those obscured by many unresolved problems, however, still display massive creative effort and the stroke of a hand more artistically impulsive than analytical.

In the Richards Medical Research Laboratories built on the University of Pennsylvania's campus in 1964, for example, Kahn appears to express servant and served space with a clarity not achieved in his later projects. The viewer does not sense this to be the primary issue, though. Instead, one is absorbed with the romantic display of stairtowers and ventilation ducts as futuristic monuments of ascension and simplicity, reminiscent of Sant'Elia's drawings from before the First World War.

The Salk Laboratory, in La Jolla, California, is clearly a continuation of the same exploration for Form, since the programs for the two projects are very much the same. Here, servant and served space is distinguished vertically, and an intermediate storey houses both the structure (huge Veerendell Trusses) and the mechanical facilities. The artistic thrust here is also not on the resolution of servant-/served organization, however, but on the creation of a spiritual environment for meditation, conducive to the spontaneous emergence of ideas. The starkness of the interior court, livened only by a thin stream of water analogous to Life Force, makes the site awesome and rich despite the minimalism of the environment.

Several projects in the late sixties, most notably the library of the Phillips Exeter Academy (a prestigious New England preparatory school), evidenced growing interest in material richness and volumetric complexity. In three outstanding projects in South Asia, the Institute of Management in Ahmedabad, India, and the Ayub Hospital and National Capital of Bangladesh, both in Dacca, Kahn used simpler materials (brick and concrete spandrels) but with equally perfect placement and execution. His masterful use of arches and structural brick remains unequalled, and the powerful forms created by using the material the way it wants to be ("A brick wants to be an arch," he used to say) are compelling, stark, and monumental.

Kahn's work often failed, economically, because of his unwillingness to compromise his artistic and social goals. Many of his buildings were more costly and more time-consuming than originally planned, and he himself suffered great financial difficulties because he revised plans long after he had expended all of the money he received from commissions.

Kahn's efforts seem so terribly significant, not because of the successes or failures of his particular projects, nor the validity or invalidity of his architectural proposals, but because of his sincere effort to reassign the role of architecture as supplying spiritual values and inspiration to those that use it. This is what made Kahn such a powerful figure. The fact that his talent matched his fine intentions, and his pure sense of beauty was remarkably sharp, elevated his work still higher, far above the class of noble effort, to the level of those few divinely inspired geniuses who occasionally rise above the mundanity of most architectural production.

—Mitchell B. Rouda

KALLMANN, Gerhard M(ichael).

American. Born in Berlin, Germany, 13 February 1915; lived in England, 1936–49; emigrated to the United States, 1949: naturalized, 1962. Educated at the Architectural Association School, London, 1936–41, Dip.A.A. 1941. Assistant Editor, *Architectural Review,* London, 1945–49; Assistant Professor, Institute of Design, Chicago, 1949–51; Lecturer, Cooper Union, New York, 1951–55; Associate Professor, Columbia University, New York, 1958–62. Since 1962, Professor of Architecture, Harvard Graduate School of Design, Cambridge, Massachusetts, and Partner, with Noel Michael McKinnell, *q.v.,* and Henry Wood, Kallmann, McKinnell and Wood, Architects, Inc., Boston. Bemis Professor, Massachusetts Institute of Technology, Cambridge, 1963–64; Bishop Professor, Yale University, New Haven, Connecticut, 1976. Exhibitions: Museum of Fine Arts, Boston, 1962; Metropolitan Museum of Art, New York, 1970; De Cordova Museum, Lincoln, Massachusetts, 1974. Recipient: Honor Award, American Institute of Architects, 1969; Precast Concrete Institute Award, 1969; Bartlett Award, 1969; Harleston Parker Medal, 1970, 1975; Award of Merit, Concrete Industry Board, 1974; Bard Award, City Club of New York, 1977. Address: Kallmann, McKinnell and Wood, Architects, Inc., 127 Tremont Street, Boston, Massachusetts 02108, U.S.A.

Works (with Noel Michael McKinnell):

1968 City Hall, Boston
1970 City Hall Plaza, Boston
       Government Center Garage, Boston
       Phillips Exeter Academy Athletics Facilities, New Hampshire
1972 Boston Five Cents Savings Bank
       Master plan for Harvard University athletic facilities, Cambridge, Massachusetts
1973 West Bank Student Union, University of Minnesota, Minneapolis
1975 Government Center open spaces, Boston
       Roosevelt Island Motorgate, New York
1976 Dudley Street Library, Boston
1977 Woodhull Medical and Mental Health Center, Brooklyn, New York
       Cardinal Cushing Park, Boston

Publications:

By KALLMANN: articles—editor of a special issue on the reconstruction of London of *Architectural Review* (London), June 1945; "Structural Trends in Contemporary City Planning" in *Architectural Review* (London), 1946; "Design," with Ian McCallum, in *Physical Planning,* London 1947; "The Way of Technology," special issue of *Architectural Review* (London), December 1950; "Reflections on Design Education" in *Transformation* (New York), March 1952; "Theatres" in *Interiors* (New York), September 1956; "New Tower in Milan" in *Architectural Forum* (New York), February 1958; "Lessons of the Bauhaus for the Second Machine Age" in *Four Great Makers of Modern Architecture,* New York 1963; "Action Architecture of a New Generation" in *Architectural Forum* (New York), October 1969; "Movement Systems as Generators of Built Form," with Noel Michael McKinnell, in *Architectural Record* (New York), November 1975.

On KALLMANN/McKINNELL: book—*A Competition to Select an Architect for the New City Hall in the Government Center of the City of Boston,* Boston 1961; articles—"Boston City Hall Design Finalists Announced" in *Architectural Record* (New York), March 1962; "End of the Glass Box?" in *Time* (New York), 25 May 1962; "La Tourette Comes to Boston: Boston City Hall" in *The Architects' Journal* (London), July 1962; "Toughness Before Gentility Wins in Boston" by Walter McQuade in *Architectural Forum* (New York), August 1962; "Boston City Hall" in *Arkitekten* (Copenhagen), no. 26, 1963; "Boston City Hall" in *Casabella* (Milan), January 1963; "Ein Projekt für die Boston City Hall" by J. G. Mertz in *Werk* (Zurich), February 1963; "Projet pour l'Hotel de Ville de Boston, Etats Unis" in *L'Architecture d'Aujourd'hui* (Paris), February 1963; "A Great Plaza for Boston's Government Center" in *Architectural Record* (New York), March 1964; "Office Buildings Sprout in New Hybrids" in *Fortune* (New York), April 1965; "The Boston Government Center: A Study in Urban Design" by Paul Spreiregen in *Arts and Architecture* (Los Angeles), October 1965; "Boston's Emerging Architectural Monument" in *Architectural Forum* (New York), November 1966; "Bold Bastion" in *Time* (New York), 29 December 1967; "Facade: Boston City Hall" in *The Architects' Journal* (London), January 1969; "Boston's City Hall: It Binds the Past to Its Future" by Sibyl Moholy-Nagy in *Architectural Forum* (New York), January/February 1969; "You Can Fight City Hall" by David L. Shirey in *Newsweek* (New York), 1 July 1969; "An Airy Fortress" in *Time* (New York), 21 February 1969; "Boston: Where Old and New Meet Graciously" by Alexander Roll in *Cue* (New York), 11 April 1970; "A Prep School Athletics Building—Controlled, Concentrated, Balanced and Alive with Distilled Energy" by Mildred F. Schmertz in *Architectural Record* (New York), June 1971.

The architecture of Gerhard M. Kallmann and Noel Michael McKinnell is rooted in two aesthetic movements of the 1950's: the "New Brutalist" and the "Compositional Rigorist" canons of design. The style which came to be called New Brutalism first appeared in the late work of Le Corbusier. Louis I. Kahn led the Compositional Rigorists. Brutalist work can be dramatic, eccentric, aggressive and antirational; Rigorist work has an inner coherence and logic shaped by structural and mechanical systems but also ordered by patterns of movement and the concept of space as either serving or served.

These contradictory approaches overlap in Kallmann and McKinnell's work, most notably in their masterpiece, the Boston City Hall. The power of this building to celebrate the idea of government, to dramatize the concept of citizen participation, to heighten the sense of meaning in the activities of ordinary life stems from the Brutalist canon. Like all Brutalist architecture the building is without small elegances and refinements. Kallmann, in a speech given in 1959, pointed out that he and other architects of like mind were "contemptuous of agreeable and acceptable aesthetic effect. [The new trends] are expressive only of the process of their genesis; they communicate fundamentally only the manner of their own making, and they do not declare themselves in terms other than those of architectural actuality.... It appears [that thus is ending] a phase of overmuch gratification of the desire to please, and that an architecture more stern and less sensorially directed is in the making."

As a Compositional Rigorist building, Boston City Hall is ordered by a geometry that controls its paths of movement, sequences of space, and its structural and mechanical parts. It is the movement system which is the foundation of this order. The visitor moves across a great square, up broad steps and into and through magnificent public space and then beyond toward Boston's historic Faneuil Market district. This movement system links the Boston City Hall to the venerable network of the old city with a degree of style and authority which is seldom seen.

Movement systems are of particular interest to Kallmann and McKinnell who describe them as "generators of built form." Another important work, the athletics facility at the Phillips Exeter Academy in New Hampshire, like the Boston City Hall, consists of spaces supported by an armature of circulation. If Boston City Hall celebrates government and public participation, the Exeter gym dramatizes sport. Swimming, skating, basketball, squash and gymnastics are totally visible to visitors

Gerhard M. Kallmann and Noel Michael McKinnell: City Hall, Boston, 1968

and athletes as they move through the building's circulation system. For Exeter, as for the Boston City Hall, these paths are the ordering device of the design.

A well-planned movement system makes a building a legible, comprehensible assemblage of functions. As the permanent elements in a building's organization, these routes become the arteries and veins along which other permanent building elements are set. Columns and piers are placed along the movement system instead of within the spaces served by the system. Such great circulation networks become the best place for social interaction within a building. To make them memorable, Kallmann and McKinnell attenuate their heights and introduce light by means of skylights, thus using sky time and weather to connect the user with the world outside. These networks are open ended and can link up later additions to a building or tie into existing or proposed networks beyond the site.

Kallmann and McKinnell use the structural system as well as the movement system to communicate visual information about a building, paying attention to joinery and expressing the multiplication of parts. Thus four principal themes characterize their architecture—dramatization, compositional rigor, the primacy of movement, and the expression of structure. These are the keys which open the mind to an understanding of their distinguished work.

—Mildred F. Schmertz

KARMI, Dov.

Israeli. Born in Odessa, Russia, in 1905; emigrated to Palestine, 1921: Israeli citizen, 1948. Educated at the Harali High School, Haifa, graduated 1923; Bezalel School of Painting and Sculpture, Jerusalem, 1923–26, graduated 1926; University of Ghent, Belgium, 1926–30, Dip.Arch.Ing. 1930. Married; children: Ram (i.e., the architect Ram Karmi, *q.v.*) and Ada. Partner, Karmi and Barak, Jerusalem, 1931–36; in private practice, Tel Aviv, 1936–50; Principal, Dov Karmi Collaborative, Tel Aviv, 1950–56; Partner, with his son Rami and Z. Melzer, Karmi-Melzer-Karmi, Tel Aviv, 1956 until his death, 1972. Visiting Teacher of Architecture, Technion: Israel Institute of Technology, Haifa. President, Association of Israeli Architects, 1952–56. Recipient: National Prize for Architecture, Israel. *Died* (in Tel Aviv) *in May 1962.*

Works:

1930/
39 Feller House, Jerusalem
Hairdressing salon interiors, Jerusalem
Zlotopolsky Apartment Building, Tel Aviv
Simkin Apartment Building, Tel Aviv
Idelson Apartment Building, Tel Aviv
Hershkovitch Apartment Building, Tel Aviv
Armenian Monastery School, Jaffa

1940/
49 Bezzerano House, Tel Benjamin, Israel
Frumchenko Apartment Building, Tel Aviv
Mazur Apartment Building, Tel Aviv
Goldman Apartment Building, Tel Aviv
Arnon Apartment Building, Tel Aviv
Allenby Passage (commercial building), Tel Aviv
Biderman Apartment Buildings, Tel Aviv
Fellman Apartment Buildings, Tel Aviv

1950/
56 Histadrut Headquarters, Tel Aviv
Town center of Ashkelon, Israel
Institute of Building Materials, Technion, Haifa
Yaron Cinema, Tel Aviv
Bar Shiva, Lautman, Frumchenko and Katz Apartment Buildings, Tel Aviv

1956/
62 Administration Building, and Weiss Auditorium, Hebrew University of Jerusalem
Mann Auditorium, Jerusalem (with Jacob Rechter)
Parliament House, Sierra Leone
Zim Navigation Company Building, Tel Aviv
ORT Vocational School, Tel Aviv
El Al Office Building, Tel Aviv
Commercial/Residential Center, Beer Sheva, Israel

Publications:

On KARMI: articles—"Bureau de la Fédération du Travail, Tel Aviv" in *L'Architecture d'Aujourd'hui* (Paris), December 1956/January 1957; "Histadrut" and "University Campus" in *Werk* (Zurich), April 1958; "Dov Karmi 1905–1962" in *L'Architecture d'Aujourd'hui* (Paris), February/March 1963; "Palazzo per Uffici del'El Al" in *L'Architettura* (Rome), March 1965.

Dov Karmi, born in Russia but educated in Israel, must be regarded as one of the founding fathers of the modern movement in architecture in Israel. After graduating from the Bezalel Academy of Art in Jerusalem, he went overseas to continue his professional studies, receiving his diploma in architecture and engineering from the University of Ghent in 1930. On his return to Eretz Israel he set up an office in Jerusalem (in association with the architect Barak), and a few years later moved to Tel Aviv, where the bulk of his early work is located.

Two very different examples of his work of the 1930's indicate his approach as an architect and give evidence of his great ability. The school of the Armenian Monastery in Jaffa is a stone building of cut ashlar blocks, with triple round-headed windows and a bold arched entrance on the ground floor, and a row of well-proportioned french windows set deep and opening on to elegant shallow balconies above. A block of flats in Tel Aviv, of the same period, is a simple white cubic structure, with windows and recessed balconies banded together to form shadow-filled horizontal slits. In architectural style the Armenian school is timeless, almost vernacular (albeit an architect-designed and most subtle vernacular); on the other hand, the apartment building is uncompromisingly modern, as Gropius or Mendelsohn might have built it. But despite the apparent differences, the two buildings are remarkably similar in architectural approach: both emphasize the cubic form, the clipped roof-line, the dominance of simple unadorned wall surfaces, the boldness of deep-set fenestration, and the overriding importance of sunlight and shadow.

Throughout the productive years that followed, many of these qualities still obtained in Karmi's work. In the large commercial and institutional projects of the 1950–56 period (the Karmi Collaborative), and the subsequent partnership with Z. Melzer and son Rami Karmi, the architecture of necessity became more complex. The famed Mann Auditorium of Tel Aviv (in association with Rechter) has a magnificent interior, and together with the associated buildings of the cultural centre forms a monumental group of tremendous civic presence. In the commercial and office buildings the expression of structure becomes more dominant, and the modular nature of the facade is indicative both of the constructive imperatives of pre-cast concrete and the planning imperatives of repetitive cellular space divisions. One sees fine examples of this approach in the Histadrut Building in Tel Aviv, in the Administration Building of the Hebrew University in Jerusalem, and in the Zim Navigation Company headquarters in Tel Aviv.

All these examples of the 1950's show the strength, discipline and restraint of a master architect thoroughly in control, in buildings that may not aspire to the highest levels of architectural poetry but are never prosaic. The last in this series of excellent buildings, the El Al Building in Tel Aviv, is something of a departure, and perhaps indicates the growing influence of the young Ram Karmi in the design office: the vigour of the curved facade, the bravura sculptural effect of the exposed spiral staircase, and the greater textural richness of the facade all point to new directions, to be explored by Ram Karmi in the 1960's, following the death of his father.

The design talents of the son are his own, and highly individual. The standard of excellence to which he aspires was set for him, as it was for a whole generation of Israeli architects, by pioneers such as Dov Karmi.

—Gilbert Herbert

KARMI, Ram.

Israeli. Born in Jerusalem in 1931; son of the Israeli architect Dov Karmi, *q.v.* Educated at the Tichon Hadash High School, Tel Aviv, graduated 1947; Technion: Israel Institute of Technology, Haifa, 1949–50; Architectural Association School, London, 1950–55, Dip.A.A. 1955. Partner, with his father and Z. Melzer, Karmi-Melzer-Karmi, Tel Aviv, 1956 until his father's death, 1962; Principal, with his sister Ada, Karmi Associates, Tel Aviv, from 1962. Currently, Director of the Design Department, Israel Ministry of Housing, Tel Aviv. Adjunct Teaching Fellow in Architecture, subsequently Holder of the Special Chair in Architecture, Technion, Haifa, since 1968. Visiting Lecturer and Critic, Columbia University, New York, 1969, Princeton University, New Jersey, 1969, Massachusetts Institute of Technology, Cambridge, 1972, and the University of Houston, 1972. Associate, Royal Institute of British Architects, 1973. Address: Karmi Associates, Ben Zion Boulevard 5, Tel Aviv, Israel.

Works:

1956/
62 Administration Building, and Weiss Auditorium, Hebrew University of Jerusalem
Mann Auditorium, Tel Aviv (with Jacob Rechter)
Parliament House, Sierra Leone
Zim Navigation Company Building, Tel Aviv
El Al Office Building, Tel Aviv
Commercial/Residential Center, Beer Sheva, Israel

1965/
77 Hadar-Dafna Office Complex, Tel Aviv
Lady Davis Amal School, Tel Aviv
Argaman Factory, Yavneh, Israel
Student dormitories, Ben Gurion University of the Negev, Beer Sheva, Israel
Central Bus Station, Tel Aviv
Second Avenue Subway, New York (project)

Humanities Building, Hebrew University of Jerusalem
Consolidated Edison Master Plan for Kip's Bay, New York (project)
Plan for Long Island City, Queens, New York (project)
1979 Giloh Housing, near Jerusalem

Publications:

On KARMI: articles—"Palazzo per Uffici del'El Al" in *L'Architettura* (Rome), March 1965; "Architektur: Kunst und Planung in Israel" in *Werk* (Zurich), January 1973; "Student Residences, Negev University" in *Architecture Plus* (New York), June 1973; "An Israeli School Shaped for Community" in *Architecture Plus* (New York), December 1973; "Les Murailles de Jericho" in *L'Architecture d'Aujourd'hui* (Paris), July/August 1974.

After qualifying at the Architectural Association School of Architecture, Ram Karmi worked in association with his father, the well-known Israeli architect Dov Karmi, in the firm of Karmi, Melzer and Karmi. During the 1950's this firm was responsible for several fine buildings in Israel, including the Administration Building at the Hebrew University of Jerusalem, the Zim Building in Tel Aviv, and the striking El Al Building, perhaps Tel Aviv's most handsome structure of that period. All these buildings are in reinforced concrete, which is handled—both in precast and in situ form—with skill and sensitivity: the resultant architecture is both spirited and ordered, the strict modularity imposing an insistent discipline.

In later years, when head of his own architectural office, Ram Karmi remained faithful to the medium of reinforced concrete but used it with much greater virtuosity and freedom. The series of buildings which then came from his office are monuments to a creative talent that delights in strong complexes of sculptured but geometric form, with intricate silhouettes and boldly modelled surfaces, sparkling in the bright Israeli sunshine. The commercial centre at Beersheva, the Hadar-Dafna Office Complex in Tel Aviv, both of the 1960's, and the Lady Davis Amal School, all indicate a mastery of form, and interplay of mass and space, that first catch, and then maintain, the interest. Internal public spaces—the roof-lit atrium in the Negev centre, the lobby and sweeping staircase of Hadar-Dafna, the amphitheatral courtyard of the Amal School—are often breathtaking, always memorable. One may sometimes question the programmatic aspects of Karmi's design, or the aptness of the architectural character for the function served—the school is, in my view, too aggressive and abrasive an environment in which to nurture the young learning mind—but its formal strength is undeniable.

More recently, as in the student dormitories for the Ben Gurion University of the Negev, of the 1970's, or the housing clusters at Giloh, near Jerusalem, now building, one senses a growing interest in the round form and the perforated wall surface as an element that, through its bold penetrations and the use of strong primary colour, develops a layering of space, an envelope subtly unfolding to reveal the inner planes of the building's form. The influence of Le Corbusier, present ever since the 1950's, is here brought into fusion with that of Louis Kahn—and especially the later work of Kahn at Dacca. There are some affinities, too, between the formal approach of Karmi, and that of John Andrews, especially Andrews' Scarborough College.

Despite the monumentality of these powerful buildings, Karmi's philosophy of housing tends towards the humane and the romantic. He seeks, through the paradigm of Mediterranean vernacular, the intimate scale of the small dwelling cluster, whose image and whose sense of place derives from the judicious design of pathway, staircase, entrance. In the pursuance of this vision, he has recently—in an unprecedented move for a creatively successful

architect—given up private practice to become director of the Design Department of the Israel Ministry of Housing.

—Gilbert Herbert

KASSABAUM, George (Edward).

American. Born in Atchison, Kansas, 5 December 1920. Educated at Taft Junior High School, Oklahoma City, 1932–35; Classen Senior High School, Oklahoma City, 1935–38; Washington University, St. Louis, 1938–42, 1946–47, B.Arch. 1947. Served in the United States Air Force, 1945–46: Sergeant. Married Marjory Verser in 1949; children: Douglas, Anne and Karen. Worked at the Boeing Aircraft Company, Wichita, Kansas, 1942–45; Instructor, Washington University, 1947–51; Architect, with Hellmuth, Yamasaki and Leinweber, St. Louis, 1951–55. Since 1955, Principal, with George Hellmuth, *q.v.*, and Gyo Obata, *q.v.*, Hellmuth, Obata and Kassabaum, St. Louis. Director, Tower Grove Bank, St. Louis, since 1973. President, 1968–69, and Chancellor of the College of Fellows, 1977–78, American Institute of Architects. Director, Metropolitan St. Louis Y.M.C.A., since 1970, and Downtown St. Louis Inc., since 1974; Trustee, Washington University, since 1975. Recipient: Alumni Citation, Washington University, 1972; Missouri Architect of the Year Award, 1978. Fellow, American Institute of Architects, 1967. Honorary Fellow, Royal Architectural Institute of Canada, and La Sociedad de Arquitectos Mexicanos; Honorary Member, Sociedad Colombiana de Arquitectos. Address: Hellmuth, Obata and Kassabaum Inc., Architects, 100 North Broadway, St. Louis, Missouri 63102, U.S.A.

See HELLMUTH, OBATA AND KASSABAUM

KATSELAS, Tasso.

American. Born in Pittsburgh, Pennsylvania, 15 July 1927. Educated at the Carnegie Institute of Technology, now Carnegie Mellon University, Pittsburgh, 1946–50, 1952–54, B.Arch. 1950, M.Arch. 1954. Served in the United States Navy, 1945–46. Married Jane Banning in 1951; children: Dana and Lisa. In private practice, Pittsburgh, since 1956. Exhibitions: *Gold Medal Exhibition,* New York, 1960; *New Form in Concrete,* New York, 1961. Recipient: Architectural Design Award, *Progressive Architecture,* 1961; Architectural Award, Dow Corporation, 1964; Award of Design Excellence, 1964, 1970, House Award, 1974, and Apartments of the Year Award, 1974, *Architectural Record;* Architectural Award, *College and University,* 1970. Address (office): 4951 Centre Avenue, Pittsburgh, Pennsylvania 15213, U.S.A.

Works:

1955 Katselas House, Churchill Sector, Pittsburgh
1958 Evanson House, Pittsburgh
1959 Medical building, Pittsburgh
Neville House Apartments, Pittsburgh
1960 O'Hara Parking Plaza, Pittsburgh
Berman House, Pittsburgh
Rich House, Pittsburgh
1961 410 Craig Street Medical Building, Pittsburgh
Berger House, Pittsburgh
1962 Katselas House II, Fox Chapel Sector, Pittsburgh
1963 City and Moon Township Campus, Robert

Morris College, Pittsburgh
Highland House, Pittsburgh
1964 Forbes Pavilion Nursing Home, Pittsburgh
1965 Pennley Park North Apartments, Pittsburgh
Cree House, Corapolis, Pennsylvania
1966 Schenley House Apartments, Pittsburgh
Cavender House, Pittsburgh
Penthouse Apartments, Pittsburgh
1967 American Institutes for Research, Pittsburgh
The Edge Restaurant/Motel, Pittsburgh
Pennley Park South Apartments, Pittsburgh
St. Vincent Monastery, Latrobe, Pennsylvania
Zion Evangelical Lutheran Church, Bridgeville, Pennsylvania
Roberts House, Pittsburgh
1968 Greek Orthodox Church, Poughkeepsie, New York
1969 Berkeley School, White Plains, New Jersey
Centre Towne Mall, Johnstown, Pennsylvania
Johnstown Savings Bank, Johnstown, Pennsylvania
Masterwork Paint Company, Pittsburgh
Pressley Street Highrise Apartments, Pittsburgh
St. Vincent Science Building, Latrobe, Pennsylvania
Rogal House, Pittsburgh
1970 McKeesport Highrise Apartments, McKeesport, Pennsylvania

McKeesport Garden Apartments, McKeesport, Pennsylvania
Penn Circle Tower Apartments, Pittsburgh
1971 East Mall Apartments, Pittsburgh
St. Nicholas Serbian Orthodox Church, Monroeville, Pennsylvania
Winthrop Square I and II, New London, Connecticut
1972 East Hills Highrise Apartments, Pittsburgh
East Hills Housing, phase I and II, Pittsburgh
East Hills Elementary School, Pittsburgh
Rovida House, Pittsburgh
Dining Hall, Indiana University, Pennsylvania
Oakmont North (housing complex), Norfolk, Virginia
1973 Allegheny Commons Housing, Pittsburgh
Community College of Allegheny County, Pittsburgh
Schneirov House, Pittsburgh
1974 Allegheny Airlines Components Overhaul Building, Pittsburgh
American Institutes for Research, Washington, D.C.
Mahoning East Civic Center, Punxsutawney, Pennsylvania
Kamin House, Pittsburgh
1975 City Towers Highrise Apartments, Harrisburg, Pennsylvania
Greater Pittsburgh International Airport
1975/

77 Wimmerton (Mini-City), Latrobe, Pennsylvania
1976 Highpoint Towers Apartments, Erie, Pennsylvania
Mid-City Towers Apartments, Erie, Pennsylvania
Midtown Plaza, McKeesport, Pennsylvania
777 Court Street Apartments, Reading, Pennsylvania
St. Vincent Mental Health Facility, Erie, Pennsylvania
Hirsch House, Pittsburgh
1977 Bidwell United Presbyterian Church, Pittsburgh
Budget Rent-a-Car, Pittsburgh
YIKC Monroeville Camp, Monroeville, Pennsylvania
1978 St. Vincent Community Center, Latrobe, Pennsylvania
The Pennsylvania Apartments, Erie, Pennsylvania
Neuberg House, Pittsburgh
Katselas House III, Pittsburgh

Publications:

By KATSELAS: book—writings/speeches in *Tasso Katselas, Architect Planner,* Pittsburgh 1969; articles —"The Architects: A Chance for Greatness" in *Fortune* (New York), January 1966; letter in *Architectural Record* (New York), September 1966.

Tasso Katselas: Community College of Allegheny County, Pittsburgh, 1973

On KATSELAS: book—*Tasso Katselas, Architect Planner,* Pittsburgh 1969; articles—"Campus in Motion: Tasso Katselas' New Campus for the Robert Morris Junior College" in *Progressive Architecture* (New York), February 1966; "Community and Privacy for Benedictines at Latrobe" in *Architectural Record* (New York), November 1967; "A New Benedictine Monastery in Pennsylvania" in *Art d'Eglise* (Brussels), January/March 1968; "Pittsburgh's Poet in Concrete" by M. Carlin in *Pittsburgh Press Roto,* 9 September 1969; "Architectural Analogy: New Science Center, St. Vincent Archabbey and College" in *Architectural Record* (New York), May 1970; "Greater Pittsburgh Airport Remodels and Expands with Interim Facilities" in *Architectural Record* (New York), October 1972; "Pittsburgh Architect Tasso Katselas: The Architect and His City" in *Space Design* (Tokyo), June 1975.

The question is, Are we able to produce buildings that will not succumb to obsolesence but which can mature and evolve in man's heart and mind.

Life in architecture is a call to share in the world's making. It is a chance to intervene, to contribute, to enhance what exists by the sheer power of one's presence and activity. I believe that human life must know ecstasy; I am young enough to hope for a world where this is possible. Where the ugly will no longer be tolerated. Ugliness sins against the fundamental order; ugliness betrays a technical blunder and denies, for me, the fact that intense beauty is liberation. I am old enough to know that the words economy and profit in architecture are not ugly words but necessary ones that may limit the vocabulary of the architect, the engineer, the technician, but not the poet. I am optimistic enough to see our era as one teeming with lyric possibilities. I sense a kind of song, a yearning for an exuberant symphony. And we, the architects, must make the music. Some of us are in full chorus; some are on the side quietly humming or tapping their feet; some are undecided, afraid to leave a well-worn groove; some, alas, have not heard a single note, but it is not too late, it is never too late to make our spaces sing.

My hope is that somehow we can combine practical wisdom and philosophy with our art. The architect's job must be re-defined as taking care of the living. Men are difficult, troublesome creatures, but nevertheless valuable. The creative care of man is an artful and beautiful task. The arts and skills of the architect, the creation and inspiration of which he is capable, must be brought fully into life as consequential beauty. We can no longer pretend that the living moment is unreal and only the future actual.

The architect must be involved totally in the character of the activity where use limits yet provokes, develops and chooses content. This is where our magic lies—the ability to choose content. Choice is significantly the act of recognition—composition—design. Architecture is the fact and effect of such activity. Where form and content occur simultaneously.

Design is an activity whose content is anticipated in space. Design is determined space—through it, architecture has the power to structure environment. Architecture is declaring: it anticipates without boundaries or necessary conclusions of activity. Intent to create, to build, is necessary, yet it is finally what an architect makes that is significant. If his perception is intense, the result might become architecture born from the processes of life to support intrinsic movement that will continually verify its authenticity. Like the muscles in our body, our work should improve with use, and as artists we must never forget that the most important muscle is the heart.

—Tasso Katselas

Like most architects, Tasso Katselas sometimes invents, sometimes adapts. But for him design is primarily a challenge to his geometrical and spatial skills. And yet his architecture is also a form of self expression and pure creativity emerging from his psyche. These two contradictory aspects of design challenge Katselas's powers of synthesis, and the achievement of such a synthesis has become the principal preoccupation of his life as an artist. The success of each of his his works can be measured in part by the degree to which he has solved this basic problem that he has set himself.

As in every art, and as with all architecture that aspires to art, Katselas' buildings are rooted in the architecture of others. He is strongly influenced by Frank Lloyd Wright and by the Le Corbusier of the Jaoul houses. Both these progenitors themselves struggled to achieve the very synthesis that Katselas seeks. Sharing their ambition, he has learned from them, but it is their attitude toward design, rather than their specific geometrical and structural solutions, that informs his work.

Katselas began his practice in the late 1950's and has never had a partner. He has always worked with a small team of never more than eight people, and he exercises complete control over design. His small force has developed designs for almost every building type, including housing, office buildings, schools, churches, shopping centers, college buildings, medical facilities, industrial buildings, airport structures and recreational facilities. The greatest amount of work has been in housing, but his finest design is to be found in his campus work. Such a varied practice, which includes so many buildings the purpose of which is mainly commercial, does not permit Katselas to treat each project as an opportunity for the heroic endeavor that interests him most. He is at his best, however, when he is so engaged, as proved by his finest achievements—the monastery and college for St. Vincent in Latrobe, and the Community College of Allegheny County.

—Mildred F. Schmertz

KECK, George Fred.

American. Born in Watertown, Wisconsin, 17 May 1895. Educated at the University of Wisconsin, Madison, 1914–15; University of Illinois, Urbana, 1915–20, B.S. 1920. Served in the United States Coastal Artillery, 1917–18: 2nd Lieutenant. Married Lucile Liebermann in 1921. Worked as a designer in various architectural offices in Chicago, 1920–26. In private architectural practice, Chicago, since 1926: in partnership with his brother William Keck, as Keck and Keck, Chicago, since 1946. Instructor in Design, University of Illinois, Urbana, 1923–24; Head of the Department of Architecture, Institute of Design, Chicago, 1938–44. Exhibitions: *Keck on Architecture,* Taylor Museum of the Colorado Springs Fine Arts Center, 1947, toured American universities; *Thirties and Forties Modern in Chicago,* Chicago School of Architecture Foundation, 1975; *Chicago Architects,* Cooper Union, New York, 1976, and toured the United States; *100 Years of Architecture in Chicago: Continuity of Structure and Form,* Museum of Contemporary Art, Chicago, 1976, and toured the United States. Also a painter in watercolors: exhibitions—Kathryn Kuh Gallery, Chicago; Baldwin-Kingery Gallery, Chicago; Colorado Springs Fine Arts Center; Feingarten Gallery, Chicago; Feingarten Gallery, San Francisco; Lawrence University, Appleton, Wisconsin; Syracuse University, New York; University of Minnesota, Minneapolis; University of Kansas; Elgin Academy, Illinois; Circle Gallery, New Orleans; Art Institute of Chicago; Main Street Gallery, Chicago. Recipient: Honor Award, 1953, 1958, 1959, 1964, 1967, and Citation of Merit, 1957, 1958, 1961, 1964, American Institute of Architects, Chicago Chapter; Award of Merit, national AIA, 1955; Annual Award, Fine Hardwoods Association, 1956; Award of Merit, AIA/*Life/House and Home,* 1958; Award, *Architectural Record,* 1958, 1962, 1963, 1967; Award, Chicago Beautiful Committee, 1972. Address: Keck and Keck, 612 North Michigan Avenue, Chicago, Illinois 60611, U.S.A.

Works:

1927 Newton B. Lauren House, Flossmoor, Illinois

1929 "Miralago" (nightclub), Wilmette, Illinois

1933/
34 House of Tomorrow, *Century of Progress Exposition,* Chicago (now Miller House, Beverly Shores, Indiana)

1934 Crystal House, *Century of Progress Exposition,* Chicago (demolished)

1935/
36 Herbert Bruning House, 2716 Blackhawk Road, Wilmette, Illinois

1936/
37 Edward Morehouse House, Ely Place, Madison, Wisconsin
    Bertram J. Cahn House, 270 South Western Avenue, Lake Forest, Illinois

1936/
38 William H. Fricker House, Case Street, Whitewater, Wisconsin

1937 Keck-Gottschalk-Keck Co-op Apartment Building, 5551 University Avenue, Chicago

1939 William Kellett House, Winnefox Point, Menasha, Wisconsin
    Dr. J. R. Buchbinder House, Fish Creek, Wisconsin

1940 Dr. Maurice Rice House, Stevens Point, Wisconsin

1941 Hugh D. Duncan House, 1612 Sylvan Street, Flossmoor, Illinois (now Cohen House)
    John Bennett House, Cuba Road, Barrington, Illinois
    Pete Keck House, 5713 North Lake Road, Oconomowoc, Wisconsin
    Richard E. Pulliam House, 825 East Morningside Drive, Sunset Hills Estate, Lake Forest, Illinois (now Mathews House)
    Dr. Emile Quenneville House, Grandy, Quebec, Canada

1942 Green's Ready-Built Prefabricated Homes, Rockford, Illinois and Lake Geneva, Wisconsin

1946 Thaddeus Stevens Shopping Center, Altgeld Gardens, South Ellis Avenue, Chicago
    Charles Huckins House, 541 West Grant Street, Hinsdale, Illinois

1946/
47 Joseph D. Krueger House, 23 Lake View Terrace, Highland Park, Illinois

1947/
49 Dr. Anne Benjamin House, Dune Acres, Indiana

1948 Howard A. DeMyer House, Indiana Avenue, LaPorte, Indiana
    Abel E. Fagen House, 1581 Old Mill Road, Lake Forest, Illinois

1949 Ezra Levin House, Elmwood and University Avenue, Champaign, Illinois
    Pioneer Co-operative Housing, 5400 South Dorchester Avenue, Chicago
    Avery Craven House, Dune Acres, Indiana

1949/
52 Harold Friedman House, Lincoln Street, Glencoe, Illinois

1950 Prairie Avenue Courts (public housing), Chicago
    Manuel Fink House, 573 Longwood Avenue, Glencoe, Illinois (now Knight House)
    Hyde Park Neighborhood Center, 5480 Kenwood Avenue, Chicago

1951 Dr. Jacques Olivier House, Sherbrooke, Quebec, Canada
    Marshall Goldman House, 430 South Evanslawn Avenue, Aurora, Illinois (now Snell House)

Herman Grossman House, 815 Tostenabe Lane, North Muskegon, Michigan
Sigmund Kunstadter House, 1436 Waverly Road, Highland Park, Illinois
Art Gordon House, 240 Country Club Road, Chicago Heights, Illinois (now Berg House)
1951/
52 Don McNeill House, Dundee, Illinois
1952 Robert Feldman House, Miami Road, Benton Harbor, Michigan
1952/
53 Edwin C. Tukey House, 222 Otis Road, Barrington, Illinois
1953 Edward McCormick Blair House, Lake Bluff, Illinois
1954 Walter Gray House, 7 Graymoor Lane, Olympia Fields, Illinois
1955 Harold E. Levin House, Olympia Fields, Illinois
Robert D. Misch House, 151 Maple Avenue, Highland Park, Illinois
1955/
56 Walter Placko House, Dune Acres, Indiana
1955/
59 Ben Marcus House, Bear Lake, North Muskegon, Michigan
1957 Donald Buser House, Riverdale, Iowa

1957/
58 John S. Patton House, Deep Creek, Maryland
Dr. and Mrs. Robert Hohf House, 303 Sheridan Road, Kenilworth, Illinois
1958 Mortimer M. Bortin House, Mequon, Ozaukee County, Wisconsin
1959 Frank E. Payne House, Box 398, Springtown, Bucks County, Pennsylvania
Dr. Edward Isaacson House, 2747 Ridge Road, Highland Park, Illinois
Dr. Robert Bloom House, North Muskegon, Michigan
1959/
61 Chicago Child Care Society Building, 5467 University Avenue, Chicago
1960 Eugene F. LaBorde House, 103 Idlewild Street, Kaukauna, Wisconsin
Thomas Florsheim House, 730 Redwood Lane, Glencoe, Illinois
Gerald Lindquist House, 19239 North Shore Drive, Grand Haven, Michigan
1960/
61 Joe Weix Jr. House, Beggs Isle, Oconomowoc, Wisconsin
1961 T. M. Koenig House, 2887 Blackthorne Road, Riverwoods, Deerfield, Illinois
1961/
62 Norman Weinrib House, Highland Park, Illinois

1962 Jack Teplinsky House, Highland Park, Illinois
1962/
63 Julian Levi House, Door County, Wisconsin
1964 Roy Golze House, Bloomfield Township, Michigan
James Schramm House, Burlington, Iowa
1964/
65 Peerless Confectionery Co. Warehouse additions, 1250 W. Schubert Avenue, Chicago
Norman Karlin House, 5812 South Blackstone Avenue, Chicago
Edwin Rothschild House, Ellison Bay, Door County, Wisconsin
1965/
66 Lewis Weinberg House, Fisher Lane, Winnetka, Illinois
Ben Marcus House II, 3985 Scenic Drive, Whitehall, Michigan
1967 George Wiss House, 28WO21 Marion, Winfield, Illinois
1967/
72 Harper Square (co-operative housing complex), 4800 Lake Park Avenue, Chicago
1970 Dr. Kyung Ahn House, 1901 Mirmar Road, Munster, Indiana
1972 Cyrus C. DeCoster House, 17 Martha Lane, Evanston, Illinois
Dr. Edward A. Wolpert House, Troy Village, Route 1, Sauk County, Spring Green, Wisconsin
1973 Dr. Robert A. Wolf House, 1447 Oak Park Drive, Munster, Indiana
1975 Dr. Andrew J. Griffin House, Lake Front Drive, Beverly Shores, Indiana

Publications:

By KECK: book—*Keck on Architecture,* exhibition catalog, Colorado Springs 1947; article—"The House of Tomorrow May Be on Wheels," interview with William C. Wertz, in the *Washington Post,* 29 May 1977.

On KECK: articles—"Keck and Keck, Architects," special issue of *Inland Architect* (Chicago), June 1965; "Child Care Society of Chicago" in *Vitrum* (Milan), July/August 1967; "Architect Specializes in Design of Homes" in the *Chicago Tribune,* 7 April 1968; "The Crystal House of 1934" by Thomas M. Slade in *Journal of the Society of Architectural Historians* (Philadelphia), December 1970; "Chicago Child Care Society and Harper Square Housing Project" in *Architectural Review* (London), November 1973; "Let the Sun Keep You Warm" in *Chicago Sun-Times,* 17 February 1974; "A New Look at Chicago Architecture" by Paul Goldberger in the *New York Times,* 4 March 1976; "Chicago Architects: The New Show in New York" by Nory Miller in the *Chicago Daily News,* 6/7 March 1976; "Rediscovering Chicago Architecture" by Ada Louise Huxtable in the *New York Times,* 14 March 1976; "Report from Chicago—Architecture City: Two Views" by Franz Schulze in *Art in America* (New York), March 1976; "The Makers of the Chicago School—Keck and Keck" by Don Klimovich in *Chicago Magazine,* April 1976; "New York Looks at Chicago Architecture" by Carol Diehl in *New Art Examiner* (Chicago), May 1976; "Battle of the Buildings" by Douglas Davis in *Newsweek* (New York), 21 June 1976; "City of Towers Exposed—Two Architecture Shows" by Jane Allen and Derek Guthrie in *New Art Examiner* (Chicago), June 1976; "A Window on Chicago Architects" by John Dreyfus in *Los Angeles Times,* 26 April 1977; "House of Tomorrow, Herbert Bruning House and B. J. Cahn House" in *Architecture + Urbanism* (Tokyo), September 1977.

As its most important function, architecture gives an expression in form to the needs and requirements of

George Fred Keck: Keck-Gottschalk-Keck Co-op Apartment Building, Chicago, 1937

the day and age in which it is created. Aesthetic expression in the form of any structure develops directly from the need. Such a form arrives instinctively and grows from the requirements of the plan. Its appearance derives from the nature of the materials available at any given time, and, when there is a choice, the selection should be dictated by that material which best fits the particular need.

How that is achieved is the function of the living, contemporary architect who must work with the materials at hand and available, with understanding workmen who can turn architectural ideas and plans into reality. In the last analysis, contemporary architecture is a democratic art expressing the needs, requirements and desires of many people in its accomplishment.

—George Fred Keck

George Fred Keck was one of the pioneer architects of the modern movement in Chicago. He has only lately received his fair share of honor, having long stood in the shadow of Mies van der Rohe, popularly and somewhat inaccurately presumed to be the bringer of modernism to Chicago.

After graduating from the University of Illinois in 1920, Keck worked for several Chicago architectural firms, then opened his own office in 1926. One of his earliest independent works was the Newton B. Lauren House in Flossmoor, Illinois, a curious though fetching mixture of Beaux-Arts and modern manners, which suggested Keck's will toward simplicity of form held in check by the more conservative tastes of his client. In 1929 he completed the strikingly avant-garde "Miralago," a night club in Wilmette, Illinois, whose sleek white exterior prefigured the International Style in America. Its interior contained some of the most elegant Art Deco ever designed by a Chicago architect.

Keck's contributions to the 1933–34 *Century of Progress Exposition* in Chicago were even more forward-looking. His House of Tomorrow, a dodecagonal vitreous box in two levels, the upper set back from the lower, was uncompromising in its abstraction. It included a hangar for a small airplane, a feature evidently suggestive of early 1930's visions of future American transportation habits. Still more startling in its departure from tradition was the Crystal House, a ruthlessly stripped down structure in which all-glass walls were hung behind a steel exoskeleton.

In 1938 Keck was named head of the architecture department of the Institute of Design, a progressive art school which Laszlo Moholy-Nagy had opened in Chicago a year earlier as a revival of the Bauhaus. Keck retained that position until 1944, then devoted his time more fully to his practice, since 1946 in partnership with his brother William. In those years Keck produced several of his most accomplished works, mostly residences. Notable among these are the Herbert Bruning House in Wilmette and the Bertram J. Cahn House in Lake Forest, Illinois.

In the years since World War II, Keck has gradually slipped from sight, as the Miesian influence spread, as the big commercial firms took command of Chicago building in the 1950's and 60's, and finally as post-modernist taste came to dominate the late 1970's. It is nonetheless this last development that has reawakened interest in Keck's groundbreaking early efforts.

—Franz Schulze

KÉVÉS, György.

Hungarian. Born in Budapest in 1935. Educated at the Technical University, Budapest, graduated 1959. In private practice, Budapest, since 1961. Lecturer, Faculty of Architecture, Technical University, Budapest, since 1964. Chief Architect, Circle of Young Architects Postgraduate School, Budapest, since 1974. Recipient: Ybl Prize, 1973. Lives in Budapest.

Works:

1964 Ministry of Metallurgy and Machine Industry, Budapest
1965 Block of flats, Meredek Street, Budapest
1967 Block of flats, Hernánd Street, Budapest
       Cultural House, Esztergom, Hungary
1969 Block of flats, Alsó Törökvész Street, Budapest
1970 School, Budapest
       Block of flats, Zólyomi Street, Budapest
1971 Vocational Secondary School of the Catering Trade, Budapest

Block of flats, Nárcisz Street, Budapest
1972 Block of flats, Pajsz Street, Budapest
       Block of flats, Bimbó Street, Budapest
       Block of flats, Fodor Street, Budapest
       Nursery for children of employees of the Hungarian Radio and Television Authority, Budapest
1973 Vocational School of the Printing and Textile Industry, Budapest
       Block of flats, Hegytető Street, Budapest
1974 Youth House, Budapest
1975 Block of flats, Dobsina Street, Budapest

In the 1930's the pioneers of modern Hungarian architecture planned numerous family houses in the Buda mountains of the capital. After the Second World War—because of new social conditions—the need in the area was for flats rather than single family houses, but talented architects avoided planning and constructing these flats: they felt this kind of work was "beneath their dignity." Consequently, standards became extremely low. At the beginning of the 1960's György Kéves planned a whole series of terraced houses on the mountains of Buda, harmoniously appropriate to the character of the city and surrounding scenery. Approximately 30 blocks of flats have now been built according to his plans. By this example he has succeeded in raising this kind of architectural planning to a high standard and making it, as well, a sought-after commission.

Since the beginning of the 1970's there has been a new architectural demand in Hungary—for steel-structure construction to satisfy increased need for public housing. In 1970, with his planning team, Kéves constructed a steel-framed, light-structured architectural system called I + F, with which he has now realized several important public buildings, especially educational institutions. These buildings are outstanding examples of current Hungarian architecture with their clear structural systems and rational accomplishment of ground plans.

—Anonymous

KHAN, Fazlur (Rahman).

American. Born in Dacca, India, now Bangladesh, 3 April 1929; emigrated to the United States, 1952: naturalized, 1967. Educated at the University of Dacca, 1946–50, B.Eng. 1950; University of Illinois, Urbana, 1952–55 (Fulbright Scholar), M.Sc. in structural engineering 1952, M.Sc. in theoretical and applied mechanics 1955, and Ph.D. in structural engineering 1955. Married Liselotte Lurba in 1959; daughter: Yasmin. Lecturer, University of Dacca, 1950–52. Joined Skidmore, Owings and Merrill, Chicago, 1955: General Partner since 1970. Adjunct Professor of Architecture, Illinois Institute of Technology, Chicago, since 1966. Exhibition: *Architecture of Chicago,* Museum of Contemporary Art, Chicago, 1976. Recipient: Construction Men of the Year Award, 1966, 1969, 1971, and Man of the Year Award, 1972, *Engineering News-Record;* Chicagoan of the Year in Architecture and Engineering, 1970; Wason Medal, American Concrete Institute, 1970; Special Citation, American Institute of Steel Construction, 1971; Chicago Civil Engineer of the Year, American Society of Civil Engineers, 1972; Alumni Honor Award, University of Illinois, 1972. D.Sc.: Northwestern University, Evanston, Illinois, 1973. Member, National Academy of Engineers, 1973. Address: Skidmore, Owings and Merrill, 30 West Monroe, Chicago, Illinois 60603, U.S.A.

György Kévés: Block of flats, Zólyomi Street, Budapest, 1970

Fazlur Khan: Sears Tower, Chicago, 1974

Works:

1962 United Airlines Administration and Training Center, Elk Grove Village, Illinois
United States Air Force Academy, Colorado Springs
1964 DeWitt Chestnut Apartment Building, Chicago
1965 University of Illinois at Chicago Circle
Brunswick Building, Chicago
1968 500 North Michigan Avenue Building, Chicago
1969 Marine Midland Bank Building, Rochester, New York
1970 John Hancock Center, Chicago
1971 One Shell Plaza Building, Houston
Latter and Meltzer Building, New Orleans
1972 Two Shell Plaza Building, Houston
One Shell Square, New Orleans
1974 First Wisconsin Center Bank and Office Building, Milwaukee
Imperial Tobacco Company, Bristol, England
Sears Tower, Chicago
1975 Baxter Travenol Laboratories Corporate Headquarters, Deerfield, Illinois
1976– Jeddah International Airport, Saudi Arabia
1977 National Life Building, Nashville, Tennessee
1977– King Abdul Aziz University, Makkah, Saudi Arabia

Publications:

By KHAN: monographs—*A Study of Tests on Prestressed Concrete Beams,* Urbana, Illinois 1974; *Analytical Studies of Relations Among Various Design Criteria for Prestressed Concrete Beams,* with N. Khachaturian and C. P. Siess, Urbana, Illinois 1955; articles—"Gantries Set Prestressed Bridge Beams," with A. J. Brown, in *Engineering News-Record* (New York), January 1958; "Load Test of 120 Foot Precast, Prestressed Bridge Girder," with A. J. Brown, in *American Concrete Institute Journal* (Detroit), July 1958; "Proposed Revision of Building Code Requirements for Reinforced Concrete" in *American Concrete Institute Journal* (Detroit), November 1962; "Proposed Recommended Practice for Concrete Formwork" in *American Concrete Institute Journal* (Detroit), March 1963; "Interaction of Shear Walls and Frames," with J. A. Sbarounis, in *Journal of the American Society of Civil Engineers* (New York), June 1964; "Effects of Column Exposure in Tall Structures: Temperature Variations and Their Effects," with Mark Fintel, in *American Concrete Institute Journal* (Detroit), December 1965; "Effect of Column Exposure in Tall Structures," with Mark Fintel, in *American Concrete Institute Journal* (Detroit), August 1966; "The Bearing Wall" in *Architectural and Engineering News* (Philadelphia), September 1966; "Computer Design of the 100-Story John Hancock Center," with S. H. Iyengar and J. P. Colaco, in *Journal of the American Society of Civil Engineers* (New York), December 1966; "Voies Nouvelles dans la Conception des Ossatures Metalliques de Bâtiments" in *Journal Construction Metallique* (Paris), December 1966; "The Nature of High-Rise Buildings" in *Indian Builder* (Bombay), June 1967, reprinted in *Inland Architect* (Chicago), July 1967; "The John Hancock Center" in *Civil Engineering* (New York), October 1967; "Effects of Column Exposure in Tall Structures," with Mark Fintel, in *American Concrete Institute Journal* (Detroit), February 1968; "Office Tower Design Cuts Framing Costs" in *Engineering News-Record* (New York), 15 February 1968; "Shock-Absorbing Soft Story Concept for Multi-Story Earthquake Structures" in *American Concrete Institute Journal* (Detroit), March 1968; "Analysis and Design of the 100-Story John Hancock Center in Chicago," with S. H. Iyengar and J. P. Colaco, in *Acier Stahl Steel* (Brussels), June 1968; "The Bearing Wall Comes of Age" in *Architectural and Engineering News* (Philadelphia), October 1968; "The Chicago School Grows Up" in *Architectural and Engineering News* (Philadelphia), April 1969; "Temperature Effects on Tall Steel Framed Buildings," with Anthony F. Nassetta, in *Engineering Journal* (New York), October 1970; "Response of Buildings to Lateral Forces," with others, in *American Concrete Institute Journal* (Detroit), February 1971; "Buildings" in the *McGraw-Hill Yearbook of Science and Technology,* New York 1972; "The Future of High Rise in America" in *Progressive Architecture* (New York), October 1972; "The Changing Scale of the Cities" in *Consulting Engineer* (New York), April 1974; "Megastructure" in *Actual Specifying Engineer* (Dayton, Ohio), September 1974; "Tabular Structures for Tall Buildings" in *Handbook of Concrete Engineering,* edited by Mark Fintel, New York 1974.

On KHAN: articles—"Hancock Center Represents Breakthru for Construction" by Alvin Nagelberg in the *Chicago Tribune,* 5 May 1968; "Building Design Reduces Steel with Concrete-Tube Wind Bracing" in *Engineering News-Record* (New York), June 1971.

The 110-story Sears Tower is the world's tallest building at 1450 feet. It uses the bundled tube concept. This concept makes it possible to build super tall buildings without any cost premium for height.

—Fazlur Khan

Fazlur Rahman Khan, one of America's leading structural engineers, was born in 1929 in Dacca. Following completion of the engineering curriculum at the University of Dacca in 1950, he lectured at that institution for two years before emigrating in 1952 to the United States. Most of his subsequent professional training was at the University of Illinois in Urbana, where he was awarded a Ph.D. in structural engineering in 1955. His first professional connection, with the Chicago office of Skidmore, Owings and Merrill, was formed in 1955, and he has remained with the firm ever since; he became a general partner in 1970. In 1966 he was appointed Adjunct Professor of Architecture at the Illinois Institute of Technology.

Khan's academic appointment suggests something of the eminence he enjoys in architecture as well as in engineering. In Chicago—where a strong structural tradition can be traced back to the metal-frame skyscrapers of the 1880's and 1890's—architecture and engineering have been historically allied, and the relationship was never more pronounced than during the 1950's and 1960's, when Mies van der Rohe was the leading spirit in building art in the city. During the 1960's Khan and his I.I.T. and S.O.M. colleague Myron Goldsmith, a former student of Mies, advanced several new theories about the construction of very tall buildings.

Among the most important results of these studies was the tubular frame, a construction system that facilitates the building of tall, wind-resistant structures, with a minimum of interior bracing and exterior cladding. Khan and Bruce Graham, another general partner at S.O.M.'s Chicago office, have worked as a team to produce a remarkable group of such buildings in Chicago, including the DeWitt Chestnut Apartments, the John Hancock Center, a 100-story multi-use complex, and Sears Tower, at 1454 feet the world's tallest building. Khan and Graham also played major roles in the design of the Central Facilities Building of the Baxter Travenol Laboratories Corporate Headquarters in Deerfield, Illinois. This structure features a 288-foot-long cable suspension roof, which at the time of its completion was the longest such structure in the world.

During the late 1970's Khan has devoted most of his energies, administrative as well as architectural, to several vast and as yet unfinished building complexes in Saudi Arabia. Most notable are the King Abdul Aziz University in Makkah and the Jeddah International Airport.

—Franz Schulze

KIESLER, Frederick (John).
American. Born in Vienna, Austria, 22 September 1890; emigrated to the United States, 1926: naturalized, 1936. Educated at the Akademie der Bildenden Künste, Vienna, 1911–12; Technische Hochschule, Vienna, 1912–14. Served in the Austrian Army, 1914–17. Married Steffie Fritsch in 1919. Worked with Adolf Loos on the first slum clearance and rehousing project in Vienna, 1920; began designing theatre sets/decor, Vienna, in the early 1920's; joined the de Stijl group, with Van Doesburg, J. P. Oud and Mondrian, Leyden, Netherlands, 1923; first endless form/continuous space projects, Vienna, 1923; Artistic Director and Architect, *International Exhibition of New Theatre Technique,* Konzerthaus, Vienna (devised suspension method of exhibition), 1924; Architect/Director, Austrian Section, *Exposition international des arts décoratifs et industriels modernes,* Grand Palais, Paris, 1925; in partnership with Harvey Wiley Corbett, New York, 1926–28; Consulting Architect, National Public Housing Conference, 1931–32; Director of Scenic Design, Juilliard School of Music, New York, 1934–47; Director, Laboratory for Design Correlation, School of Architecture, Columbia University, New York, 1936–42; began association with the Surrealists, 1939: directed installation of the *Exposition International du Surréalisme,* Paris, 1947; in partnership with Armand Bartos, as Kiesler and Bartos, New York, 1957 until his death, 1965. Member, Advisory Board for Advancement of Science and Art, Cooper Union, New York. Exhibitions: *International Theatre Exposition,* Steinway Building, New York, 1926; *Cubism and Abstract Art,* Museum of Modern Art, New York, 1936; *Ten Years of American Opera Design 1931–1941,* New York Public Library, 1941; *Bloodflames 1947,* Hugo Gallery, New York, 1947; *Exposition International du Surréalisme,* Galerie Maeght, Paris, 1947; *The Muralist and the Modern Architect,* Kootz Gallery, New York, 1950; *De Stijl,* Stedelijk Museum, Amsterdam, 1951; *Fifteen Americans,* Museum of Modern Art, New York, 1952; *Two Houses: New Ways to Build,* Museum of Modern Art, New York, 1952; *De Stijl 1917–1928,* Museum of Modern Art, New York, 1952–53; *Galaxies by Kiesler,* Sidney Janis Gallery, New York, 1954; *Beck, Cage, Kiesler, Rexroth,* Great Jones Gallery, New York, 1960; *Visionary Architecture,* Museum of Modern Art, New York, 1960; *Shell Sculptures and Galaxies by Kiesler,* Leo Castelli Gallery, New York, 1961; *The Ideal Theatre: Eight Concepts,* Museum of Contemporary Crafts, New York, 1962; *Frederick Kiesler: Environmental Sculpture,* Guggenheim Museum, New York, 1964; *Frederick Kiesler,* Galerie Nächst St. Stephan, Vienna, 1975; André Emmerich Galleries, New York, 1978–79. Recipient: First Prize, Community Center/Playhouse Competition, Woodstock, New York, 1928; Best Store Design Award, City of Buffalo, 1936; Honor Award, American Institute of Architects (posthumous), 1966. *Died (in New York) 27 December 1965.*

Works:

1920 Slum clearance and rehousing project, Vienna (with Adolf Loos)
1923 Endless House (project; and subsequent revisions)
Production design of *R.U.R.,* Theater am Kurfürstendamm, Berlin
"Space Stage" for production of *The Emperor Jones,* Berlin
1924 Endless Theatre (project)
1925 Austrian Pavilion, *Exposition international des arts décoratifs et industriels modernes,* Grand Palais, Paris
Optophon: A "Neoplastic" Building (project)
1927/
28 Museum for the Société Anonyme (project)
1929 Eighth Street Playhouse, New York
1930 Film Guild Cinema, New York
1933 The Universal Theatre, Woodstock, New York

1934 Space House (project)
1934/
47 Sets for productions of the Juilliard School and the Metropolitan Opera, New York
1936 Store, Buffalo, New York
1937/
39 Exhibition Hall, School of Architecture, Columbia University, New York
1942 Art of This Century Gallery for Peggy Guggenheim, New York
1945/
65 Environmental Sculptures
1946 Stage design for *No Exit,* New York
1949 Stage design for *Angélique,* New York
1955 Festival Theatre, Ellenville, New York
1956 John Jacob Astor House extension, West Palm Beach, Florida (project)
1957 World House Gallery, New York (with Armand Bartos)
Javitts House, Greenwich, Connecticut (project; with Armand Bartos)
Robbins House, West Palm Beach, Florida (project; with Armand Bartos)
1958 Venetian Theatre ("Caramoor"), Katonah, New York
1959 Hospital section of the Albert Einstein Medical Center, New York (project; with Armand Bartos)
Ullman Research Center, Albert Einstein

Medical Center, New York (with Armand Bartos)
Kamer Gallery, New York (with Armand Bartos)
Shrine of the Book, Hebrew University of Jerusalem (with Armand Bartos)
1960 Endless House (expanded model; exhibition project)
1961 Universal (Ideal) Theatre, New York (project; for the Ford Foundation)
1963 Grotto for the New Being, New Harmony, Indiana (project)

Publications:

By KIESLER: books—*International Exhibition of New Theatre Technique,* exhibition catalogue, Vienna 1924; *Contemporary Art Applied to the Store and Its Display,* London 1930; *Ten Years of American Opera Design 1931–1941,* exhibition catalogue, New York 1941; *Inside the Endless House,* New York 1966; articles—"Erneuerung des Theaters" in *De Stijl* (Leyden), no. 75/76, 1926; "Eintritt 75 cents" in *G: Zeitschrift für elementare Gestaltung* (Berlin), April 1926; "L'Architecture élementarisée" in *De Stijl* (Leyden) no. 79/84, 1927; "Notes d'Amérique" in *Cahiers d'Art* (Paris), March 1931; "Homage to Theo van Doesburg" in *De Stijl* (Leyden), January 1932; "Notes on Architecture: The Space

House: Annotations at Random" in *Hound and Horn* (Camden, New Jersey), January/March 1934; "Notes on Improving Theatre Design" in *Theatre Arts Monthly* (New York), September 1934; "Murals Without Walls: Relating to Gorky's Newark Project" in *Art Front* (New York), December 1936; "The Architect in Search of . . . Design Correlation" in *Architectural Record* (New York), February 1937; "Design Correlation" in *Architectural Record* (New York), April, May, June, July and August 1937; "On Correalism and Biotechnique: A Definition and Test of a New Approach to Building Design" in *Architectural Record* (New York), September 1939; "Design Correlation as an Approach to Architectural Planning" in *VVV* (New York), March 1943; "Les Larves d'Imagerie d'Henri Robert Marcel Duchamp" in *View* (New York), March 1945; "Art and Architecture: Notes" and "Trends in Exhibitions" in *Partisan Review* (New York), Winter 1946; "Pseudo-functionalism in Modern Architecture" in *Partisan Review* (New York), July 1949; "Endless House and Its Psychological Lighting" in *Interiors* (New York), 4 November 1950; "A Symposium on How to Combine Architecture, Painting and Sculpture" in *Interiors* (New York), May 1951; "Design in Continuity" in *Architectural Forum* (New York), October 1957; "The Art of Architecture for Art" in *Art News* (New York), October 1957; "Is Today's Artist with or Against the Past?" in *Art News* (New York), September 1958; "Art Is the Teaching of Resistance" in *College Art Journal* (New York), Spring 1959; "Frank Lloyd Wright" in *It Is* (New York), Autumn 1959; "Hazard and the Endless House" in *Art News* (New York), November 1960; "Kiesler's Pursuit of an Idea" (interview) in *Progressive Architecture* (New York), July 1961; "Breaking the Strait Jacket" in *Show* (New York), March 1964; "Kiesler by Kiesler" in *Architectural Forum* (New York), September 1965; "The Future: Notes on Architecture as Sculpture" in *Art in America* (New York), May/June 1966.

On KIESLER: books—*Frederick Kiesler: Environmental Sculpture,* exhibition catalogue, New York 1964; *Frederick Kiesler,* exhibition catalogue, Vienna 1975; articles—"New Theatre Architecture in Europe" by K. Lönberg-Holm in *Architectural Record* (New York), May 1930; "Space House by Frederick Kiesler" in *Architectural Record* (New York), January 1934; "New Display Techniques for Art of This Century, Designed by Frederick Kiesler" in *Architectural Forum* (New York), February 1943; "Design's Bad Boy" in *Architectural Forum* (New York), February 1947; "The Endless House: Frederick Kiesler, Architect" in *Architectural Forum* (New York), November 1950; "Frederick Kiesler's Theaterprojekte" in *Bauen und Wohnen* (Zurich), November 1951; "Greatest Non-Building Architect of Our Time Expounds His Ideas" by Ada Louise Huxtable in the *New York Times,* 27 March 1960; "The Ideal Theatre: Eight Concepts" in *Progressive Architecture* (New York), December 1961; "Kiesler: Exhibition of His Work in Vienna" by Joseph Rykwert in *Domus* (Milan), May 1975.

Frederick Kiesler was a visionary architect, sculptor, and theater designer whose fundamental genius was in the time-space continuum. Yet he was always one step away from whatever vantage point he took to look at that continuum. From the time-space of the Cubists to the De Stijl group, to the Surrealists to the Space Age of outer space, he was always ahead of each period or art group with which he identified himself. He was always able to add just one more dimension, to flip the coin one more time, to do the opposite, the contrary, the different, the revealingly but not always appealingly new. His interests and energy were seemingly endless, like the continuum to which he related virtually all of his work.

In 1923 his stage setting for Karel Chapek's

Frederick Kiesler: World House Gallery, New York, 1957

R.U.R. in Berlin included, for the first time, a motion picture as a backdrop to live actors. His setting for the subsequent production in Berlin of O'Neill's *The Emperor Jones* demonstrated the time-space idea by means of revolving flats and drops and a stage flowing continually with light, color, and kinetic scenery that reinforced the increasing drum-heartbeats of the play. Kiesler called it "multiple mobility," "constant change," and "continuous tension."

In 1925, for the *Exhibition international dès arts décoratifs* in Paris, Kiesler designed and built an exhibition of intersecting and overlapping columns, beams, and panels that was an epitome of the goals of De Stijl and of the articulated architecture that was to be called The International Style. But Kiesler went one step father; his City in Space exhibition was entirely suspended—a floating, orbiting, time-space satellite that anticipated the grade-level open parkland of Le Corbusier's Voisin Plan and that was not to be fully realized until the Space Age began in the late 1950's.

And in 1924 when he first designed his "Endless" as a theater, he included a continuous intertwining ramp and elevators for both actors and audience that prefigured both Walter Gropius's multi-form Total Theater project and Frank Lloyd Wright's spiral Guggenheim Museum design.

But at a time when Modern design was preoccupied with the grid and the rectangle, with the flat plane and with structural clarity, Kiesler was offering curved corners, continuous wall-and-ceiling planes with no beginning and no end—a three-dimensional, live-in, act-in, Moebius strip. "The time was not ripe," he mused later; yet he had continued to work out these early themes for the rest of his long life.

Then when the Kootz Gallery in 1950 and the Museum of Modern Art in 1952 exhibited his later Endless House model—a smooth egg shape on a rough pedestal surrounded by fern fronds—Eero Saarinen was designing his hockey rink for Yale and his TWA Terminal at JFK Airport. It was clear that the times had changed. Still, Kiesler got to build little. He had continued to design time-space stage settings of astonishing invention for the Juilliard School of Music for 15 years; he had joined the Surrealists and built in a surrealist vein at Peggy Guggenheim's Art of This Century Gallery in 1942; he had designed and built walk-in or "environmental sculpture" from the mid 40's to the mid 60's. And he redesigned his Endless Theater concept for the Ford Foundation's exploration of the Ideal Theater in 1962, having a great egg-shaped theater model cast in gleaming polished aluminum with a movable multi-form stage. It was a lifeline of continuity.

His verve and enthusiasm, his joie de vivre and seemingly endless invention were an influence on all who came in contact with him or his work. He was a perfectionist of the most demanding character that was sometimes exasperating: toward the end of his life he could not let go his personal control; he could not let anything out of his own hands but continually had to rework it to make it better and better in his view—but never finished. So he built little permanent architecture. His World House Gallery of 1957 may have been the best demonstration of his Endless interior concept. Only his Shrine of the Book in 1959 —the sanctuary for the Dead Sea Scrolls in Jerusalem, with Armand Bartos—approaches the full realization of his pursuit of an expression of the continuum of architecture, art, and life.

—C. Ray Smith

KIKUTAKE, Kiyonori.

Japanese. Born in Kurume City, 1 April 1928. Educated at Waseda University, Tokyo, under Kenji Imai, Takeo Sato, Tachu Naito, Motoo Take and Saburo Soshiroda, 1946–50 (Graduate Design Prize, 1950), B.Arch. 1950. Married Norie Sasaki in 1953; children: Yuki, Kasumi and Mitsunori. Since 1953, Principal of Kiyonori Kikutake and Associates, Tokyo. Director of the Urban Industry Company, Tokyo, since 1965. Lecturer at Waseda University, Tokyo, since 1959. Director, Architectural Institute of Japan, 1972–74. Director, Japan Architects Association, since 1974, Association of Tokyo Architectural Design Supervision, since 1974, and Japan Society of Future Research, since 1974; Executive Director, Tokyo Y.M.C.A. Institute of Design, since 1978. Exhibitions: *Japanese Ancient Art Jomon Exhibition,* Tokyo, 1960; *View of Today from Primitive Arts,* Tokyo, 1960; *New Module of Living,* Tokyo, 1961; *Metabolism Exhibition,* Tokyo, 1962; *Kiyonori Kikutake,* Honolulu, 1964; *Modern Japanese Architecture,* Florence, 1964; *Future Garden City Planning of Tama Exhibition,* Tokyo, 1965; *Today's Exhibition,* Tokyo, 1977; *Visual Architecture,* New York, 1978. Recipient: First Prize, Shimonoseki City Hall Competition, 1951; First Prize, Low-Cost Housing Competition, Ministry of Construction, Japan, 1952; Award of Excellence, Japanese Ministry of Construction, 1963; Arts Award, Japanese Ministry of Education, 1964; Pan Pacific Architecture Citation, American Institute of Architects, Hawaii Chapter, 1964; Architectural Institute of Japan Award, 1964, and Special Award, 1970; Building Constructors Society Award, 1965; Low-Cost Housing Competition Prize, Lima, Peru, 1969; Gold Medal, 1972, and Silver Medal, 1973, Sign Design Association, Tokyo; Tokyo Metropolitan Governor's Special Award, 1972; Cultural Merit Award, Kurume City, 1975; Auguste Perret Award, International Union of Architects, 1978. Honorary Fellow, American Institute of Architects, 1971. Address: 1-11-15 Otsuka, Bunkyo-ku, Tokyo 112, Japan.

Works:

1956 Tonogaya Apartment House, Yokohama
1958 Sky House (Kikutake House), Tokyo
Tower Shaped City (project)
1959 Shimane Prefectural Museum, Matsue, Japan
Marine City (project)
1960 Factory and employees' apartment house, Tokyo
Metabolism Floating City (project)
1961 Indoor gymnasium, Hitosubashi Junior High School, Tokyo
1963 Izumo Shrine Administration Building, Izumo, Japan
Floating City (project)
City Hall, Tatebayashi, Japan
International Conference Hall, Kyoto (competition project)
1964 Tokoen Hotel, Yonago, Japan
Dining Hall, Olympic Village, Tokyo
1965 Iwate Education Hall, Morioka, Japan
Tokyo Channel Development (project)
1966 Civic Center, Miyakonojo, Japan
Pacific Hotel, Chigasaki, Japan
1967 Sado Grand Hotel, Ryozu, Japan
1968 Iwate Prefectural Library, Morioka, Japan
Shimane Prefectural Library, Matsue, Japan
Civic Center, Hagi, Japan
1969 Civic Center, Kurume, Japan
United Nations Low-Cost Housing, Lima, Peru (competition project)
1970 Tower for *Expo '70,* Osaka
Martial Arts Hall, Matsue, Japan
1971 Suruga Bank Computer Center, Numazu, Japan
Floating City, Hawaii (project)
Toto Pavilion, Ginza, Tokyo
Mass Housing (project)
1972 Tokoen Hotel extension, Yonago, Japan

Ube Kosan Factory, Matsuyama, Japan
Kyoto Community Bank Branch Offices, Kyoto
Gymnasium, City University, Shimonoseki, Japan
1973 Tokyo Bay Floating Project (project)
1974 Porsche Showroom, Tokyo
City Hall, Hagi, Japan
Pasadena Heights Housing, Mishima, Japan
1975 Aquapolis, *International Ocean Exposition,* Okinawa
Nikkei Aluminium Factory, Funabashi, Japan
City Center Redevelopment, Yamaga, Japan
1976 Biwako Shopping Center, Otsu, Japan
Floating Hotel (project)
KIC Floating Platform (project)
1977 Floating Cassette System (project)

Publications:

By KIKUTAKE: books—*Architecture Textbook no. 1: Drawing,* Tokyo 1955; *Architecture Textbook no. 6: Planning and Design,* Tokyo 1957; *Metabolism,* Tokyo 1960; *Metabolic Architecture,* Tokyo 1968; *Wooden Culture, The Japanese Language* (high school textbook), Tokyo 1969; *Human Architecture,* Tokyo 1970; *A Human City,* Tokyo 1970; *Essence of Architecture,* Tokyo 1973; *Kiyonori Kikutake: Works and Methods 1956–1970,* Tokyo 1973; *Floating City,* Tokyo 1973; *Ideology of Design,* Tokyo 1974; *Environment of Design,* Tokyo 1974; *Creation of Design,* Tokyo 1974; *Field of Design,* Tokyo 1974; *Method of Design,* Tokyo 1974; *Future of Design,* Tokyo 1974; *Community and Man,* Tokyo 1975; *Community and Civilization,* Tokyo 1975.

On KIKUTAKE: books—*This Is Japan* by Noboru Kawazoe, Tokyo 1962; *World Architecture 4,* London 1967; *New Directions in Japanese Architecture* by Robin Boyd, London and New York 1968, Barcelona 1969; articles—"The Kikutake House" in *The Japan Architect* (Tokyo), January/February 1959; "1963 Pan Pacific Citation Awarded to Japan's Kikutake" in *Architectural Record* (New York), March 1964; "The Approach of Kiyonori Kikutake" by Günter Nitschke in *Architectural Design* (London), October 1964; "Hotel Tokoen, Yonago, Japan" in *Baumeister* (Munich), February 1966; "Suruga Bank Lakeside Lodge" in *L'Architecture d'Aujourd'hui* (Paris), April 1966; "The Morioka Grand Hotel" in *The Japan Architect* (Tokyo), July 1966; "The Miyakonojo City Hall" in *The Japan Architect* (Tokyo), October 1966; "A Profile of Kiyonori Kikutake" by Hiroki Onobayashi in *The Japan Architect* (Tokyo), March 1967; "Kritische Anmerkungen" by Manfred Speidel in *Bauen und Wohnen* (Zurich), July 1967; "Wettbewerbsentwürfe für die International Kongresshalle, Kyoto" by Manfred Speidel in *Bauen und Wohnen* (Zurich), July 1967; "Children's Land School in a Grove" in *The Japan Architect* (Tokyo), November 1967; "The Iwate Prefectural Library" in *The Japan Architect* (Tokyo), November 1968; "Shimane Prefectural Library" by Shigeru Furukawa in *Approach* (Osaka), March 1969; "Expo Tower" in *The Japan Architect* (Tokyo), May/June 1970; "New Developments in Japanese Architecture" by Mildred F. Schmertz in *Architectural* Record (New York), September 1970; "Pragmatischer Metabolists: Kurume City Hall" in *Baumeister* (Munich), December 1970.

My design method involves three steps. These are: 1) ka (image); 2) kata (prototype); and 3) katachi (form). Above all, I consider the problems of metabolism within the prototype stage. That is to say, I pursue a "replacement system" through the fields of city planning, architecture, equipment, tools and details. The reason is that I tend to believe that it creates a more favorable environmental system for man. These ideas have been realized in projects such

Kiyonori Kikutake: Aquapolis, *International Ocean Exposition,* Okinawa, 1975

In the Izumo Shrine Office Building and the Tokoen Hotel, for example, he tried to reconcile historical and modern forms, reflecting the "Tradition Debate" that was most active in the 1950's (and that produced, among other buildings, Tange's Kagawa Prefectural Government Office). Izumo, with its slanted screen-like walls, is meant to recall the way rice is left to dry out in the fields, and Tokoen employs traditional wood structural details (in concrete) and a shell roof for the restaurant on top, which gives the hotel a "traditional" silhouette.

Though the two buildings are different in spirit, they both reveal the architect's preoccupation with structure. Like Tange, Kikutake deliberately sets himself challenging structural problems to be solved for each project: at Izumo there is a 40 meter span cleared by prestressed beams, and in Tokoen the fifth and sixth floor hotel rooms are suspended from above.

But he is unlike Tange in one respect: where Tange integrates the design into a tightly-knit whole, Kikutake is often content to let the parts remain individuated—hence the little parabolic explosion in the otherwise monolithic Izumo building or the exuberant articulation of functions in Tokoen.

Perhaps the work that best reveals Kikutake's structural and traditionalist concerns is the one that was never built, his entry for the Kyoto International Conference Hall competition. Cruciform in plan, it had a central core of elevators to the conference halls at the top level. The building expanded in volume as it went up, and its precast, prestressed beams were staggered to create a structural expression recalling Buddhist temple construction. The jury, though strongly attracted to the project, finally rejected it on the grounds that the placement of the halls on top made the circulation too difficult. (The Conference Hall was built eventually on the basis of Sachio Otani's design.)

Though Metabolism has come to be identified with a futuristic image, Kikutake rarely resorts to the more obvious devices such as capsules in his actual buildings. The Pacific Hotel, with its bathroom units cantilevered out, is one exception and can stand comparison with Kurokawa's later yet more awkward Nakagin Building. Rather, Kikutake's work is most striking precisely when he has applied Metabolist ideas to conventional programs.

He has developed over the years proposals for floating cities as a means of expansion for land-starved societies. The Aquapolis, a pavilion built for the Exposition in Okinawa, is a partial realization of these ideas. This is the most futuristic of his buildings, yet it may also be one of his least successful. The architect has lost control in this almost purely engineering enterprise, and the interior with its curiously banal hotel-lobby atmosphere is disappointing.

Like Tange's Osaka Exposition Theme Pavilion, the Aquapolis marked the end of an era of rapid economic growth and uncritical worship of technology in Japan. Kikutake's recent work indicates a new direction, but his past accomplishments already assure him a place among the most imaginative architects of his generation.

—Hiroshi Watanabe

as a marine city and a mouvenette and in other movable systems and flexible and changeable systems that I have proposed.

Furthermore, I believe that it is necessary to create a favorable environment for man by expanding the alternatives of his life activities. I'm trying to introduce a multi-channel system. This means that I advocate a finiteness, fluidity and co-existence of architecture as opposed to the historical concepts of architecture such as eternality, completion and unity. Especially, when it comes to modern architectural problems, I define the period after 1950 as the equipmental/technological age, brought about by highly-developed equipmental technology such as artificial lighting, elevators, air conditioning, communication, computers, electronics, etc. I believe that the situation calls for the creation of a new type of architecture, one that is entirely different from the structural/technological architecture of the past.

Such ideas of mine towards architecture as well lie behind traditional Japanese architecture and they exist in Japanese culture. My ideas are derived from them. My ideas are characterized by the three-step methodology, in which Image and Form are brought freely into the open by placing Kata (Prototype) as the axis: I consider this the distinctive feature.
—Kiyonori Kikutake

When Metabolism was launched in 1960 at the time of the World Design Conference, Kiyonori Kikutake was already known for his Sky House. Supported on tall wall columns, it is essentially a single room marked off by storage units, with the services located on the periphery to facilitate later change of models. Additional rooms for children were to be suspended underneath the floor slab. Thus he anticipated the Metabolist philosophy of change and growth, despite the deceptively orthodox vocabulary of the design.

Throughout the 1960's Kikutake was a member of the Metabolism Group, which emphasized the cyclical, organic character of cities, and he himself contributed utopian proposals for cities built out on water. Yet despite this association, Kikutake never tied himself to any single style or doctrine, and his output during the decade is characterized by great variety.

KILEY, Dan(iel Urban).
American. Born in Boston, Massachusetts, 2 September 1912. Educated at the Graduate School of Design, Harvard University, Cambridge, Massachusetts, 1936–38. Served in the United States Corps of Engineers, 1942–45: Chief of Design Presentation Branch, Office of Strategic Services; awarded Office of the United States Chief of Council Legion of Merit for design and construction of the Nuremberg Courtroom Internal Trials, 1945. Married Anne Lothrop Sturges in 1942; children: Kathleen, Kor,

Christopher, Antonia, Gracie, Timothy, Aaron and Caleb. Draftsman, Warren H. Manning, Cambridge, 1932–38; Apprentice Associate Draftsman, Landscape Design and Regional Planning, National Park Service, Concord, New Hampshire, 1939; Associate Town Planning Architect, United States Housing Authority, Washington, D.C., 1939–40; President, Office of Dan Kiley, Washington, D.C., and Middleburg, Virginia, 1940–41, and Franconia, New Hampshire, 1940–51; President, Dan Kiley and Partners, Charlotte, Vermont, 1951–74; President, Kiley/Tyndall/Walker, Charlotte, 1974–79. Since 1979, President, Dan Kiley/Peter Ker Walker, Landscape Architect/Planning Architect, Charlotte. Member: Board of Design, University of Minnesota, Minneapolis, 1960; President Kennedy's Advisory Council for Pennsylvania Avenue, 1962–65; Board of Design, University Circle, Cleveland, 1965–68; Boston Redevelopment Authority Board of Design, 1966–67; Architectural Registration Board, Vermont, 1967; Board of Design, Redevelopment Land Agency, Washington, D.C., 1967–69; Cambridge, Massachusetts Redevelopment Authority, 1968; Vermont Governor's Committee of Manufacturing/Housing, 1969–70, and Technical Review Committee for State Planning, 1973; Vermont Council for the Arts, 1974. Member, Minnesota Capitol Area Architectural and Planning Commission, since 1968. Graham Foundation Lecturer, Chicago, 1975; Landscape-Architect-in-Residence, American Academy in Rome, 1975–76. Exhibition: Architectural League of New York, 1958 (one-man); American Federation of Arts Travelling Exhibition, 1958–61; Museum of Modern Art, New York, 1960; National Academy of Design, New York, 1968; Iowa State University, Ames, 1968. Recipient: First Prize, with Eero Saarinen, Jefferson Memorial National Competition, St. Louis, 1948; First Prize, with Ron Gourlay, Student Union Competition, University of New Hampshire, Durham, 1951; Residential Design Award, American Society of Landscape Architects, 1962; Allied Professions Medal, 1971, and Collaborative Achievement in Architecture Award, 1972, American Institute of Architects; Residential Design Award, National Landscape Association, 1973. Associate Member, National Academy of Design. Address: Kiley/Walker, East Farm, Charlotte, Vermont 05445, U.S.A.

Works (landscape design and planning):

1940   Collier House, Leesburg Pike, Washington, D.C.
1942   Willow Run Housing, Michigan
        Lily Ponds Housing, Washington, D.C.
        Penny Pack Woods (housing), Philadelphia
        Coatesville Housing, Pennsylvania
1945   Nuremberg Internal Trials, Germany (as architect)
1947/
48   Jefferson Memorial, St. Louis (competition project)
1951   New Town Aluminium Ltd., Kitimat, British Columbia, Canada
        Student Union, University of New Hampshire, Durham (competition project)
        Mill Creek Housing, Philadelphia
        Baker House, Greenwich, Connecticut
        Federal Reserve Bank, Detroit
1953   Miller House, Columbus, Indiana
1955   Concordia Junior College, Fort Wayne, Indiana
1956   IBM Building, Rochester, Minnesota
        Union Carbide and Carbine Company, Eastview, New York
        United States Air Force Academy, Colorado Springs
        Reynolds Metals Building, Richmond, Virginia
1957   Chicago Filtration Plant
1958   Law Library, University of Chicago
        Dulles International Airport, Chantilly, Virginia
1959   Third Block, Independence Mall, Philadelphia
1960   North Court, Lincoln Center, New York
1962   Stanley McCormick Court, Art Institute of Chicago
        Oakland Museum, California
        Design of Pennsylvania Avenue, Washington, D.C.
        Burr Memorial, Hartford, Connecticut

1963   Stiles and Morse Colleges, Yale University, New Haven, Connecticut
1964   Irwin Union Bank and Trust Company, Columbus, Indiana
        IBM Building, Milwaukee
        Rochester Institute of Technology, New York
1965   Study of the Washington Mall and Tidal Basin, Washington, D.C.
        Fredonia College, New York
        Kenwood-Hyde Park Housing, Chicago
1966   New Haven Parks, Connecticut
        Snowbird Ski Resort, Alta, Utah
        Tenth Street Overlook, Washington, D.C.
        Tufts University, Medford, Massachusetts
        University of Lagos, Nigeria
1967   Ottauquechee River Basin, Vermont
        Calgary Place, Alberta
1968   Cummins Engine Company, Columbus, Indiana
1969   Chicago Inland Regional Parks
        Squibb Corporate Headquarters, Lawrenceville, New Jersey
1970   Rockfeller University, New York
        Mall and Plazas for Dalle Centrale, La Defénse, Paris
        Miami River Corridor, Dayton, Ohio
1971   National Gallery of Art, Washington, D.C.
        Blackwell Park, Roosevelt Island, New York
1972   Baltimore Inner Harbor
1973   Fort Lawton Park, Seattle
        McLean Hospital, Belmont, Massachusetts
        McLean Hospital, Boston
1974   South Court, Smithsonian Institution, Washington, D.C.
        Minnesota State Capitol, St. Paul
        Riverfront development, Springfield, Massachusetts
1975   Washington Cathedral
        Woodruff Plaza, Atlanta, Georgia
        Detroit Art Institute
1977   Gallaudet College, Washington, D.C.
        Conservatory surround, New York Botanical Gardens
1978   Urban renewal development plan for Winooski, Vermont

Dan Kiley: Oakland Museum, California, 1962

Flood control study of Trout Brook, West Hartford, Connecticut

Overlake (condominium), Burlington, Vermont

John F. Kennedy Library, Boston

East Shore Park, New Haven, Connecticut

Cummins Engine Company, Brussels

Chace Mill Hydro-Electric Dam, Burlington, Vermont

Amalgamated Transit Union, Bethesda, Maryland

Publications:

By KILEY: articles—"Landscape Design in Urban, Rural and Primeval Environments," with Garrett Eckbo and James C. Rose, in *Architectural Record* (New York), May 1939; "Site Planning: The Modern Way to Expand Your Living" in *Better Homes and Gardens* (Des Moines, Iowa), 1951; "Three Landscape Architects Look Ahead" in the *New York Times,* 5 January 1959; "Nature: The Source of All Design" in *Landscape Architecture* (Louisville, Kentucky), January 1963; "Man Is Nature: Thoughtful Planning" in *Echo Vermont* (Thetford Center), January 1963.

On KILEY: articles—"Dan Kiley" by Clemens Kalischer in *Vermont Life* (Montpelier), Summer 1967; "Renowned Landscape Architect Here to Give View on Moving Monument" in *Lancaster News Era* (Pennsylvania), 23 June 1970; "Landscaping the Urban Jungle" by Henry Mitchell in the *Washington Post,* 10 October 1971.

I first saw Landscape Design, in the 1930's, as a parallel to modern art and architecture, a development concerned with function expressed in terms of a continuous spatial structural order. The use of trees and other plant materials in large scale geometry extend and connect out with the cosmos in a spatial system, comparable to Le Notre but expressed in modern terms. Most of my work is typified by allees and groves of trees set close together to define space and set up relationships with buildings and other elements in a continuing large scale system. First examples of this are the Jefferson National Expansion Memorial, St. Louis, 1947/48, the Irwin Miller Residence, Columbus, Indiana, 1953, and the Third Block, Independence Mall, Philadelphia, 1956.

—Dan Kiley

Dan Kiley is a pioneer of modern landscape architecture. His education at Harvard Graduate School of Design in the late thirties exposed him to the transitional period in that school's curriculum, from the Beaux-Arts tradition to architectural modernism. Walter Gropius had not yet arrived at Harvard, but the seeds of the modern style were already planted and Kiley and his contemporaries were searching for expression in landscape design to compliment the new architectural modernism.

At first, Kiley was interested in the development of form as a pure art rather than in the development of solutions to problems from a functional viewpoint. In his early work, his preoccupation with design form led him to ignore the functional aspects, to exploit the ground and design idea, and to use too little restraint.

The great designers, Kiley believes, analyze all the conditions and specific aspects of a problem, and go through all the analyses and processes of design. Then, almost automatically, a larger view presents itself. Although seemingly disconnected, this emergence of understanding develops the solution by itself, and transcends conditions and requirements.

Form does not come by searching for it. It comes as a byproduct of solving problems with functional solutions. Form should be forgotten in the process of design and it becomes a reality by way of the solution. Beauty, excitement and possibility come from addressing the simple need, as tools of a primitive

culture, whose forms we celebrate in museums, are but objects created to solve a simple need.

Kiley believes each problem requires a new set of investigations, endeavors and values. Design values which are carried from place to place, from problem to problem, are dangerous if they are preconceived. Often a grave task of the designer is to dispel the client's preconceived impressions based on solutions he has seen elsewhere but which do not apply to his problem. The conditions and requirements of each problem are very different, and the designer must approach each problem in a new light. The designer should work to enlighten people of the variety of the possibilities of solutions open to them. He should be looking at the overall idea first and not be thinking of making little designs in space out of reference to any other part.

Many of Kiley's works are not landscape designs surrounding buildings, but works where buildings surround his landscapes. His collaborations with architects are numerous, and his landscape projects, integrally related to buildings, show a genius of design harmony of landscape and building.

The education of the designer should include the knowledge of his materials, his tools, plant materials, structure, drainage, details, etc. The broader the background, the more potent the designer. But Kiley believes his greatest inspiration has come from the great, broad philosophers, who have waded through the specific and individual ideas and solutions, and have emerged to a world of overviews and general insight. The strength of a design depends on the sensitivity in working out the functional aspects, to become released from them, and to become connected to the Universe in the broadest, poetical sense.

—Stephen P. Hamilton

KILLINGSWORTH, Edward A(bel).

American. Born in Taft, California, 4 November 1917. Educated at the University of Southern California, College of Architecture, Los Angeles, 1935–40 (Newcomb Prize, 1940), B.Arch. 1940. Served in the United States Army Engineers, in Europe, 1941–45 (Bronze Star, 1944): Captain. Married Laura Catherine Baird in 1943; children: Gregor and Kim. Associate, office of Kenneth S. Wing, Long Beach, California, 1945–53; Partner, with Jules Brady and Waugh Smith, Killingsworth, Brady, Smith and Associates, Long Beach, 1953–67. Since 1967, President, Killingsworth, Brady and Associates, Long Beach; since 1970, Vice-President, Killingsworth, Brady and (Fred) Sutter, Honolulu. Professor of Architectural Design, University of Southern California, 1963–68. Chairman, American Institute of Architects Fellowship Jury, 1976. Recipient: First Prize, *Bienal,* Sao Paulo, 1961; California Governor's Award, 1966. Fellow, American Institute of Architects, 1962. Address: Killingsworth, Brady and Associates, 3833 Long Beach Boulevard, Long Beach, California 90807, U.S.A.

Works:

1957 Clock-Waestman-Clock Attorneys Offices, Long Beach, California

1958 Hertz Auto Rentals Offices, Pasadena, California

Opdahl House, Long Beach, California

1959 Cambridge Office Building, Long Beach, California

1961 Community Bank, Huntington Park, California

Shell Chemical Laboratory, Torrance, California

Reef, Oakland, California

Hancock House, Long Beach, California

Case Study Triad, for *Arts and Architecture* magazine, La Jolla, California

Alondra Junior High School, Paramount, California

1961– Master plan for the California State University at Long Beach

1962 Montecito Park Apartments, Glendale, California

DeBell Country Club and Facilities, Burbank, California

Case Study House No. 25, for *Arts and Architecture* magazine, Naples, California

1963 Duffield Lincoln-Mercury Showroom, Long Beach, California

Peninsula Shopping Center, Palos Verdes, California

Buffums Peninsula (store), Palos Verdes, California

1964 Kahala Hilton Hotel, Honolulu

1965 Buffums Lakewood (store), Lakewood, California

Coyote Point Restaurant, San Mateo, California

1966 Religious Center, University of Southern California, Los Angeles

Virginia Country Club additions and alterations, Long Beach, California

Atlantic Research Corporation, Costa Mesa, California

Van Luit and Company Offices, Glendale, California

Hof's Hut Restaurant, Long Beach, California (with Eldredge Combs)

1967 Student Union, University of California at Riverside

Dining Facilities, Pitzer College, Claremont, California

1968 Buffums (store), La Habra, California

Kahala Beach Condominiums, Honolulu

Marina Pacifica Condominiums, Long Beach, California

Riviera Methodist Church, Redondo Beach, California

1969 Buffums Fashion Valley (store), San Diego, California

Plaza Inn, Rancho California

Castaway Restaurant, Burbank, California

Marina, Berkeley, California

Lutheran Church, Newport Harbor, California

1970 Brady House, Long Beach, California

Killingsworth House, Long Beach, California

Roberts House, Laguna Beach, California

1971 Plaza and Access Ways for the *Queen Mary,* Long Beach, California

1972 Married Student Housing, University of California at Santa Barbara

College Union, California State University at Long Beach

Terminal Island Federal Correctional Institution, California

Seaport Village, Long Beach, California

Janss House, Sun Valley, Idaho

1973 Hollywood Park Hotel, Inglewood, California

Halekulani Hotel, Honolulu

Al Khobar Hilton Hotel, Saudi Arabia

Al Jubail Hilton Hotel, Saudi Arabia

Sun Valley Inn, Sun Valley, Idaho

College of Architecture and Fine Arts, University of Southern California, Los Angeles (with Sam Hurst)

Buffums Laguna (store), Laguna Hills, California

Navy Cafeteria, Naval Shipyard, Long Beach, California

Women's Housing, Terminal Island Federal Correctional Institution, California

Harbor Square Condominiums, Honolulu

Dominguez Water Corporation, Long Beach, California

1974 Oceangate Building, Long Beach, California
Buffums Westminster (store), Westminster, California
Buffums Santa Anita Fashion Park, Arcadia, California
Mercedes-Benz Sales and Service Building, Hollywood, California
Honolulu Medical Group Building
Center for Continuing Education, Long Beach Memorial Hospital, California
Elkhorn Condominiums, Sun Valley, Idaho
1975 Ascuaga's Nugget Gambling Casino remodelling, Reno, Nevada
1976 Jakarta Hilton Hotel, Indonesia (with Raglan Squire)
Headquarters Building, California State University at Long Beach (with Deasy and Bolling)
1977 Marina Pacifica Shopping Center and Village, Long Beach, California
1978 Korea Hilton Hotel, Seoul
Kapalua Bay Hotel, Maui, Hawaii
Boca Raton Hotel and Cabanas, Boca Raton, Florida
Pacific Terrace Convention Center, Long Beach, California (with Architects Associates)
City Hall and Main Library, Long Beach, California (with Allied Architects)
Los Angeles County Sheriff's Administration Building and Crime Laboratory, Los Angeles
Kapalua Bay Shopping Center, Maui, Hawaii

Publications:

On KILLINGSWORTH: books—*Photographing Architecture and Interiors* by Julius Shulman, New York 1960; *Contemporary Houses Evaluated By Their Owners* by Thomas H. Creighton and Katherine M. Ford, New York 1961; *Mid-Century Architecture in America,* edited by Wolf Von Eckardt, Baltimore 1961; *Modern California Houses* by Esther McCoy, New York 1962; *Beautiful Homes and Gardens in California* by Herbert Weisskamp, New York 1964; *Architects on Architecture,* edited by Paul Heyer, New York 1966, London 1967; *International Private Houses* by Werner Weidert, Stuttgart 1967; *Art in Architecture* by Louis G. Redstone, New York 1968; *Hotels. An International Survey* by Herbert Weisskamp, New York 1968; *The Illustrated Guide to the Houses of America* by Richard M. Ballinger and Herman York, New York 1971; *They Chose to Be Different: Unusual California Homes* by Chuck Crandall, San Francisco 1972; *Los Angeles: The Architecture of Four Ecologies* by Reyner Banham, London 1973; *Houses Architects Design for Themselves* by Walter F. Wagner Jr. and Karin Schlegel, New York 1974; *Santa Barbara Architecture* by Herb Andree and Noel Young, Santa Barbara, California 1975; *Case Study Houses 1945–1962* by Esther McCoy, Los Angeles 1977; *A Guide to Architecture in Los Angeles and Southern California* by David Gebhard and Robert Winter, Santa Barbara, California and Salt Lake City, Utah 1977; *The Photography of Architecture and Design* by Julius Shulman, London 1977.

It is difficult to say what really punched the button, turning me to architecture. I'm not sure that I know. I suspect that I am a classicist at heart, and what I liked most about architecture is to be found in its rich past. I love balance, a clear and compelling axis, careful proportion, respect for tradition. What does this love of classical characteristics have to do with my own work? Well, I suspect that, somehow, in my

Edward A. Killingsworth: Case Study House No. 25, Naples, California, 1962

way, I have been trying to recapture what was done so well in the past, although in an idiom consistent with the materials and needs of our own time. This is especially true of our "Case Study" work for that powerful editor, John Entenza, when he was running *Arts and Architecture.* I was searching for an elusive something in residential design which gave me a feeling deep down, absolutely true to myself, of serenity, simplicity and, perhaps because of these, significance.

It was with those "Case Study Houses" that I started my search for good spaces. High ceilings, rooms flowing into one another without walls, tall doors—in fact, if I have a "trademark," it must be those tall doors. But this is important only in that a tall door points up the importance of space. It is so good to be in a space where the spirit can soar, and, with all of this, it must soar with the sense of balance and proportion set up by the spaces we create. What better goals in life can there be? To create a condition in which you can really *see* the spirit soar?

My original goal was not toward architecture but toward painting and sculpture; once, I would rather paint than eat. Although this love has since been transfused into building, it does say a lot about my roots as an architect.

Probably this love is the main reason I have such a respect for indigenous architecture, no matter where it may be. And this is also probably why I have gradually developed an approach to design which I call "the architect as collector." Every work is a collection of, and a sorting out of, a variety of influences and circumstances that swirl about the process of design. It is an especially vital perception when building in other lands, as we are doing in Bali and Jakarta, where the elements of indigenous culture are so worthy of respect and can be used as sources of design. As a "collector," I develop, through design, the basic parameters and planning concepts and, into this framework, we bring the local experts and artisans and craftsmen to "do their own thing" which, as in Bali or Jakarta, has been a great tradition for hundreds of years. This is much more than a plasticized pasting on of old images and symbols, which is why so many "authentic" buildings, set into *really* authentic locales, come off as travesties of the very traditions the architecture is trying to emulate. At our Bali Hilton, for example, we are working with the craftsmen to create a great piece of Balinese architecture that will *incidentally* be a hotel. Here sculptors will work for five to ten years, as part of the hotel staff, embellishing themes that have been used over and over through time.

My major quarrel with "modern architecture" is that so many building designers seem to be searching for what they think is new rather than for what is good. Most modern buildings make bad neighbors—to me an unforgivable sin. For many years now there has been a theoretical permissiveness about this, as though originality at any cost is all right. This is why, after the similarity and sterility of the machine-like structures of the early modernist period, you see so many strange, forced, contrived forms passing for "innovation" and "expressiveness." This has to do with another major quarrel of mine—that too many architects would rather "do their own thing" than respect the character and scale of the locale or district or street in which they are building. Why can't more of us architects be good neighbors?

Then there is one more quarrel. This has to do with the architect's relationship with his client. Architecture as an outgrowth of ego is an imposition on the needs to be served, the people to be accommodated, the community which will have to live with the building, and certainly it is an imposition on the man paying the bills. Not that an architect should bow down and pander to the mediocre, just to get a job. But I feel that an architect can, by identifying himself with the problems and values of his client, help that client to become part of the creative process and, in doing so, instill a sense of quality that might not have been there before. The highest praise that I can have is when the client

identifies so much with his *building* that he forgets I ever existed.

—Edward A. Killingsworth

Edward A. Killingsworth's approach to architecture is consistent with a quiet but rich variety. His simple wood post and beam construction is carefully detailed to overcome the problem of shrinking and twisting. The entrances to his buildings are frequently through a garden overlooked from the interior spaces surrounding it. Fountains and reflection pools are often employed to utilize the spatial feeling of the intimately scaled proportions. The landscaping becomes an integral part of the whole, with soft textures and irregular outlines contrasting with the refined dimensions of the precise structures.

His award-winning Opdahl House, built in Long Beach in 1958 on a small 30' × 80' lot, was oriented to the courtyard and reflection pool for a sense of spaciousness. Stepping stones across the pool lead to a two-story-high living room with glass from floor to ceiling. The success of this residence influenced his commercial design. His own office is approached over a shallow pool with round pebble-concrete stepping stones stopping at a blank crimson-colored wall before turning left to a tall entrance door flanked by fixed glass. The parking lot, in front, is beautifully landscaped with trees and vines. Elements of his residential design appear in his Duffield Lincoln-Mercury Agency, also in Long Beach—high ceilings with plate glass walls framed in white timber post and beam construction.

In the early 1960's the magazine *Arts and Architecture* commissioned him to design several case study houses, among them a triad in La Jolla. Here he was allowed to be innovative, expressing all of his fresh, new ideas—17' high entrance doors leading into a two story atrium surrounded by plate glass. The interplay of light and shadow from the trellises he designed for these houses influenced his future work.

The publication of his architectural genius attracted the attention of Hilton Hotels who were looking for an architect for their hotel in Hawaii, one who could reflect the quiet and casual elegance of the islands in a romantic setting. Killingsworth's design for the Kahala Hilton Hotel, near Waikiki, met all their requirements. His aim was an unobtrusive environment in the natural setting of a lagoon, embellished with waterfalls. The main ten-story structure, in the shape of two rectangles raised above the ground, is approached through a grand 30' high lobby. The trellises of precast, pre-stressed concrete, covered with flowering vines, support the lanai balconies of the guestroom wings. From each window there are framed views of the gardens, which have been laid out according to traditional principles of the Italian Renaissance. Double rows of palms line the entrance driveway. While the structure of the hotel is a work of art, the guests are influenced to remember only the gracious rooms, the lush gardens, and the elegant informality.

Because of the wide publicity given to the Kahala Hilton, the firm of Killingsworth, Brady and Associates was also commissioned to design hotels in Saudi Arabia, Indonesia, Bali, Korea, Tahiti, Noumea New Caledonia, Fiji, and Florida. Their luxurious Kapalua Bay Hotel and shopping center in Maui, Hawaii is thought by many people to surpass even the beauty of the Kahala Hilton.

Killingsworth has also been active in his home city of Long Beach, where he designed the Civic Center, which includes a City Hall tower of concrete spires, separated by smooth planes of glass, reaching toward the sky, the city library, an underground parking structure, and public parks graced with weeping willow trees. Close to the Civic Center is his Pacific Terrace Convention Center. The main form is a large glass structure, topped by a massive concrete cornice, set on a multi-level concrete structure. The 50' high lobby, with its cantilevered grand staircase, takes full advantage of the spectacular view of the Pacific Ocean surrounding it. The interior is simple, devoid of ornament, so as not to distract from the natural setting.

Although Killingsworth sums up his architectural philosophy by saying, "I'm not looking for new principles in architecture, only good principles," he has created a style of his own that is not just "good," but unique in its graceful, delicate simplicity.

—Peggy Cochrane

KIRBY, Ron(ald Hubert).

British. Born in Lusaka, Northern Rhodesia, now Zambia, 3 January 1936. Educated at Lusaka Convent, 1940–44; Muir College, Uitenhage, South Africa, 1945–52; University of Cape Town, South Africa, 1953–59 (Muir College Bursary; Northern Rhodesia Government Bursary), B.Arch. 1959. Married Rosemary Longridge in 1964; daughter: Jane. Joined the architectural firm of Montgomerie and Oldfield, Salisbury, Rhodesia, 1960: Partner, with H. G. (Nick) Montgomerie and Peter Oldfield, Montgomerie, Oldfield, Kirby, Salisbury, and Lusaka, Zambia, since 1962; Partner, in association with Denis Clarke-Hall, Montgomerie, Oldfield, Kirby, London, 1964–68; established branch offices of Montgomerie, Oldfield, Kirby, in Blantyre, Malawi, 1966, in London (in association with APT International), 1975, and in Cape Town (in association with Elliott, Grobbelaar), 1977. Founder, Zambia Institute of Architects Board of Education, 1968–71; President, Zambia Institute of Architects, 1970–72; Chairman, Commonwealth Association of Architects Africa Region Meeting, 1971; Chairman, Zambian Southern Planning Authority, 1972–77; Registrar, Architects and Quantity Surveyors Registration Board of Zambia, 1972–78; Zambia Representative, Commonwealth Association of Architects Board of Education, 1977. Chairman, Council for the Construction Industry, Zambia, since 1973. Recipient: Bronze Medal, Royal Institute of British Architects, 1962; Industrial Architecture Award and Commercial Architecture Award, 1964, Commercial Architecture Award and Civic Architecture Award, 1968, Institutional Architecture Award, 1971, Institutional Architecture Award, 1973 (twice), and Domestic Architecture Award, 1978, Zambia Institute of Architects; First Prize, Central Medical Stores Complex Competition, Lusaka, 1973; First Prize, New Central Ministerial Headquarters Competition, Lusaka, 1975; First Prize, Ndola Civic Centre Competition, Zambia, 1975; First Prize, United Arab Emirates National Assembly Complex Competition, Abu Dhabi, 1976; First Prize, New Life Sciences Complex Competition, University of the Witwatersrand, Johannesburg, 1977. Address: Montgomerie, Oldfield, Kirby, Goodman House, Cairo Road, Box 721, Lusaka, Zambia.

Works:

1963 Queen Victoria Memorial Library, Salisbury (with Peter Oldfield and Andrew Stein)

1964 Refined Oil Products Factory and Offices, Lusaka (with Nick Montgomerie)
John Sisk Headquarters, Lusaka (with Nick Montgomerie)

1965 Development plan for the Evelyn Home College of Further Education, Lusaka (with Nick Montgomerie)

1966 Zambia National Assembly Complex, Lusaka (with Nick Montgomerie and Bob Anderson)

1968 African Farming Equipment Showrooms and Offices, Lusaka (with Nick Montgomerie and Bob Anderson)
National Housing Board Headquarters, Lusaka (with Nick Montgomerie and Bernard Gouveia)

International Air Terminal Buildings, Ndola, Zambia (project; with Nick Montgomerie)

1969 Lochinvar Game Camp, Zambia (project; with Nick Montgomerie)

1971 Lukashya Trades Training Institute, Kasama, Zambia (with Nick Montgomerie and Bob Anderson)
Mansa Trades Training Institute, Mansa, Zambia (with Paul Andrew and Richard Martin)
Development planning study of the Central Government Office Area, Lusaka (with Nick Montgomerie and Paul Andrew)
Prototypical office block for the Central Government Office Area, Lusaka (project; with Nick Montgomerie and Bob Anderson)
Bank of Zambia Town House Complex, Lusaka (with Peter McGurn and Craig Wilson)
Department of Lands and Surveys Headquarters, Lusaka (project)

1972 Development and planning study of Naperi Farm, Blantyre, Malawi (with Mike Denn and Craig Wilson)
Professorial Department, Lusaka Teaching Hospital (with Nick Montgomerie)

1973 Town planning and architectural design for a new Mine Town, Kansanshi, Zambia (with Bob Anderson)
U.S.S.R. Embassy, Lusaka (with Derek Simpson and Nick Montgomerie)

1974 Teaching Block, Evelyn Home College of Further Education, Lusaka (with Bob Anderson)
British High Commission Residence, Lusaka (project; with APT Partnership and David Wager)
Development feasibility studies for Mining Administrative Headquarters, Kankola and Chingola, Zambia (with Bob Anderson)
Development and redevelopment studies for the Lusaka Hotel (with Francis Ndilila)
Mines Trust Schools, Kankola, Chingola, and Kitwe, Zambia (with Ken Barnes)

1975 Government Ministerial Complex, Lusaka (competition project; with Lewis Construction, Nick Montgomerie, Bob Anderson, Walter Dobkins, and Mick Pilcher)
International School Media Centre, Lusaka (with Bob Anderson)
Ndola Civic Centre, Ndola, Zambia (with Nick Montgomerie and Bob Anderson)

1976 Cathedral Centre, Pietermaritzburg, South Africa (competition project; with Peter Oldfield and Peter Boer)
Federal Headquarters, University of Zambia, Lusaka (project)
Intercity Bus Terminus, Lusaka (with Peter Jackson)
National Assembly Members Motel, Lusaka (with Tony Logan)

1977 National Assembly Speakers Lodge, Lusaka (with Ken Barnes)
Radford House, Leopard's Hill Road, Lusaka (with Tony Logan)
United Arab Emirates National Assembly Complex, Abu Dhabi (competition project; with APT Partnership and David Wager)
Work Bank Student Hostels, Evelyn Home College of Further Education, Lusaka (with Nick Montgomerie and Peter Jackson)
Ravenna Town House, Lusaka (prototype; with Roy MacLachlan)
National Medical Stores Complex, Lusaka (with Lewis Construction and Nick Montgomerie)
Clinic, University of Zambia, Lusaka (with Roy MacLachlan)

1978 Life Sciences Complex, University of the Witwatersrand, Johannesburg (with Julian Elliott and Niel Grobbelaar)
Lonrho Headquarters, Lusaka

Publications:

By KIRBY: articles—"A Review of Educational and Related Problems in Small Developing Countries" in *Insitu* (Lusaka), April 1969; "The Role of

Ron Kirby: Ravenna Town House, Lusaka, 1977

the Architect in Development Planning in Africa" in *Insitu* (Lusaka), May 1971; "The Challenge of the Next Two Years" in *Times of Zambia Building Supplement* (Lusaka), October 1971; "Education of the Architect to Meet His Role in Africa" in *Insitu* (Lusaka), no. 18, 1972; "Civil Service Housing in Zambia" in *Insitu* (Lusaka), July 1977; "Science and Technology in the Construction Industry" in *Insitu* (Lusaka), July 1978.

On KIRBY. book—*Economic Housing in Africa* by R. Jährling (United Nations Economic Commission for Africa Publication), Addis Ababa 1976; articles —by Jim Morrison and Ian Whittaker in *Insitu* (Lusaka), July 1969; in *Z Magazine* (Lusaka), April 1973; in *Insitu* (Lusaka), no. 23, 1974; in *Insitu* (Lusaka), no. 24, 1975; in *Insitu* (Lusaka), April 1977; by Alex Brown in *Insitu* (Lusaka), July 1977; by Alex Brown in *Insitu* (Lusaka), December 1977.

*

One of a new generation of native Central African architects, I joined the firm of Montgomerie and Oldfield in 1960. The strong iconography of the firm's international style, their liberal social and political attitudes, together with their concern for developing team skills, form the background to the body of work completed post-independence in Zambia and, more recently, internationally. The work is to be seen as a reflection of both personal and collaborative design energies, not least those of the original but also the new partners and the many colleagues with whom I have worked. If there has been any sustained philosophy it has been that of eschewing exclusivity while attempting to structure inclusivity.

Independence saw the start of a massive demographic shift in Zambia and, amongst many requirements, the urgent need for urban employment opportunities in the construction sector. This was paralleled by a sharp outflow of politically alienated middle management construction skills, which, coupled to a history of job reservationism, led to the need for new design techniques to deal with rapidly declining levels of craft and technological skills in an industry which had become remote from its traditions and saw no need to explore or return to them in the face of the national and international "brave new world" euphoria of the sixties.

Projects at this stage reflected the need to change from imported carpenter to locally developed masonry technology. Particular emphasis was placed on rationalized labour intensive construction systems designed to utilize simple component assemblages and to optimize scarce on-site management skills. Rationalized methodological design systems led to the development of an egalitarian design philosophy, much encouraged by the international development agencies, but much railed against by the image-conscious new political forces.

New energies are now being brought to bear in our work at the interface of imagery, traditional product/process design and community/systems design. Our later works reflect these new inputs and attempt to respond to evolving inclusive understandings of architecture and the unfolding expressive socio-political economic iconography of our times.

Future Zambian design needs are seen as innovative, inclusive and dynamic, with African imagery playing a key role.

—Ron Kirby

*

The architectural work of Ron Kirby is built firmly on the foundation laid by his partners, Nick Montgomerie and Peter Oldfield. Oldfield, a post-war graduate of the Liverpool School, and Montgomerie, from the London office of Denis Clarke-Hall, started practice in Salisbury after winning the Peterhouse School competition in the early 1950's—the first of many competition successes that the firm was to enjoy in the future. A characteristic of the firm's work has been the analytical clarity of problem definition, together with direct and efficient problem so-lution in the modern idiom. To this Ron Kirby, who was born in Zambia, has added regional concerns and understandings that include the central as well as the southern and western parts of the African continent. He has also added architectural skills and enthusiasms, as well as administrative involvement, of remarkable dimensions.

Kirby's Zambian work is prolific and consistent. The range of commissions includes important state and civic buildings, a large range of educational buildings, commercial and industrial developments, as well as individual and group housing.

The early work is characterized by a simple palette of materials, mainly unplastered brick with wall dominated edges incorporating adaptive shading devices and flat roofs (African Farming Equipment Offices). At the same time a recurrent built form model has been the low-rise, fat-bodied building with large top lighted and ventilated internal spaces (National Housing Board Headquarters; Department of Land and Surveys Headquarters [project]; and the Evelyn Hone College of Further Education). The latest work reflects a similar built form model but a different and more appropriate architectural image, a large roof-dominated structure with free standing polychrome walls—as in the Clinic for the University of Zambia.

Any review of the work of Ron Kirby must note his impressive involvement in the affairs of architecture, particularly education, at a local professional, national and international level.

—Julian Elliott

KLEIHUES, Josef Paul.

German. Born in Rheine, Westphalia, 11 June 1933. Educated at the Gymnasium Dionysianum, Rheine, graduated 1955; Technical University, Stuttgart, 1955-57, and Berlin, 1957-59, Dip.Ing. 1959; Ecole Nationale Supérieur des Beaux-Arts, Paris, 1959–60. Married Sigrid Müller in 1961; children: Jan, Hein, Jo, and Anna. In private practice, as architect and town planner, Berlin, since 1962 (in partnership with H. H. Moldenschardt, 1962–67). Professor of Design and Architectural Theory, University of Dortmund, since 1973. Initiator and Director, "Life and Work on the Ruhr" Industrial Environmental Study Project, 1975–78. Initiator and Director, Dortmund Architecture Days, since 1975, and Dortmund Architecture Exhibitions, since 1976; Editor and Publisher, *Dortmunder Architekturhefte,* since 1975. Exhibitions: *Tendenzen,* toured Germany and Switzerland, 1976; *Wohnen im Revier,* toured Germany and France, 1978; *Museen,* Dortmund, 1979. Recipient: Young Generation Art Prize, Berlin, 1967; Building in Brick Prize, 1968; Sandstone Building Prize, 1971; Concrete Building Prize, 1975. Address (office): Holsterbrink 1, 4408 Dülmen-Rorup; or Schlickweg 4, 1000 Berlin 38, West Germany.

Works:

1960/
66   Kopfklinik Westend Mental Hospital, Berlin (with Peter Poelzig)

1963/
66   Housing, Fussgängerstrasse, Gropiusstadt, Berlin (with H. H. Moldenschardt)

1965   German Embassy, Vatican City (competition project)
     Housing, Titusweg, Berlin (project; with H. H. Moldenschardt)

1966   Housing, Ruhwald, Berlin (project; with H. H. Moldenschardt)

1966/
67   Old People's Club, Reinickendorf, Berlin (with H. H. Moldenschardt)

1967/
68   Housing II, Ruhwald, Berlin (project; with H. H. Moldenschardt, O. M. Ungers, and others)
     Hospital, Göppingen, Germany (competition project)
     Plan for housing and development of the town center of Perlach, Munich (competition project; with H. Goepfert)

1967/
71   "Open Hand" Housing, Gropiusstadt, Berlin (with H. H. Moldenschardt)

1968   Congress Center, Berlin (project)

1968/
69   University of Bielefeld, Germany (competition project; with H. Goepfert)

1968/
74   Kleihues Studio, Schlachtensee, Berlin

1969/
70   Hospital, Ingolstadt, Germany (competition project)

1969/
73   Main Workshops, phase I, Municipal Refuse Collection Depot, Berlin (with W. Stepp)
     Lewis-Ham Towers Housing Development, Charlottenburg, Berlin (project; with Leon Krier)

1972   Lamp in Oxidized Aluminum
     Sprengel Museum, Hanover (competition project)
     House for Georg Baselitz with fractured basis (project)
     House for Friedrich Meckseper (project)

1972/
75   Housing Block (600 units) by the Water, Charlottenburg Sluice, Berlin (project; with M. Kausch, Leon Krier, and B. Tonon)

1972/
76   Block 270 Housing Development, Vineta Plaza, Wedding, Berlin (with M. Schonlau)

1973/
81   Neukölln Hospital, Berlin (with J. König)

1974/
75   School, Borken, Germany (competition project; with U. Falke)

1975   Reconstruction plan for Dinslaken, Germany (with U. Falke and R. Hauser)
     Berliner Ring Redevelopment, Berlin (competition project; with W. Stepp)
     Dusseldorf Museum (competition project; with U. Falke and R. Hauser)
     Town Center, Dulmen, Germany (project; with U. Falke and R. Hauser)

1975/
78   Dahlhauser Heide Workers' Housing Development, Bochum, Germany (with R. Hauser)

1975/
79   Main Workshops, phase II, Municipal Refuse Collection Depot, Berlin (with W. Stepp)

1975/
80   Town Center Housing and Commercial Development, Wulfen New Town, Germany (with U. Falke)

1976   Financial Administration Building and School, Munster (competition project; with G. Schumann)
     Exhibition Pavilion, *Documenta,* Kassel (project)
     St. Martin Oratory, Kevelaer, Germany (project; with U. Falke and R. Hauser)

1976/
81   Museum, Blankenheim, Germany (with R. Hauser)

1977   Park Lenné Inner-City Housing (project; with M. Baum, U. Falke, and R. Hauser)

1978   Dr. Sluka House, Munster (with M. Baum)
     Ephraim Palais (Jewish Museum), Berlin (with M. Baum, U. Falke, and R. Hauser)

1978/
82   German Steel Museum, Solingen (with M. Baum)

Josef Paul Kleihues: Main Workshops, Municipal Refuse Collection Depot, Berlin, 1979

1979/
82 Gerleve Monastery extensions, Coesfeld, Germany (with Eggers and U. Falke)

Publications:

By KLEIHUES: books—*Berlinatlas zu Stadtbild und Stadtraum,* Berlin 1974; *Park Lenné: Eine innerstädtische Wohnform,* Berlin 1977; article— "Siedlung Dahlhauser Heide," with Spiegel and Boennighausen, in *Dortmunder Architekturhefte,* no. 12, 1978.

On KLEIHUES: book—*Wohnungsbau/The Dwelling/L'Habitat* by Harald Deilmann, Jörg C. Kirschenmann and Herbert Pfeiffer, Stuttgart 1973; articles—"Junge Berliner Architekten" in *Deutsche Bauzeitung* (Stuttgart), no. 8, 1968; "Milieu, Surrogat einer besseren Welt" in *Der Architekt* (Stuttgart), no. 9, 1975; "Architekturzeichnungen heute" in *Bauwelt* (Berlin), no. 19, 1975; "Landesgalerie Düsseldorf" in *Domus* (Milan), no. 4, 1976; "J. P. Kleihues," special issue of *2C Construccion de la Ciudad* (Barcelona), June/September 1977; "Gestörte Form" by Feuerstein in *Transparent* (Vienna), no. 11/12, 1977; "Hauptwerkstatt der Berliner Stadtreinigung" in *Bauwelt* (Berlin), no. 40, 1977; "Work by J. P. Kleihues" in *Space Design* (Tokyo), no. 10, 1977; "Block 270, Geschichte der Blockbebauung" in *Baumeister* (Munich), no. 12, 1977; "J. P. Kleihues: Recent Work" in *Lotus International* (Venice), no. 15, 1977; "Apologie für die Architektur als Kunst . . ." in *Bauwelt* (Berlin), no. 1, 1978; "5 Arbeitersiedlungen im Revier" in *Bauwelt* (Berlin), no. 14, 1978; "Park Lenné and Block 270" in *Lotus International* (Venice), no. 19, 1978; "Architektur in Deutschland" by H. Bofinger and H. Klotz in *Das Kunstwerk* (Baden Baden), no. 4/6, 1979.

Expecting nothing,
Mostly humourless,
At times angry as well,
Architecture will be talked into nothingness
The Word will, with indifferent agreement, be spoken against architecture.
Architecture is rare:
Architecture as encouragement in an increasingly organized world in which client and architect absolve themselves from responsibility and involvement.
Architecture as opposition
To political technicity and an instrumental way of thinking that reduce to routine planning and construction.
Architecture as example
Against pre-formed belief in experience and function that negates any poetry.
Architecture as poetry
Against the blind arrangement of expedient arrogance.
Architecture looking back
Timid and enchanted.
Architecture as instructive
In classical landscapes, Nepalese mountain villages, and in Las Vegas.
Architecture as renovative
In dialectic with Alberti, Palladio, Schinkel, and all the saints.
Architecture as a potential category of the new
In recognition of ever-similar among ever-changing new hells.
Architecture in search of broader autonomy

Loving planning ahead, collecting attributes,
Set up against the moral terror of pure reason and empiric realities,
Avoiding the market.
Architecture as yearning
Boundlessly.

—Josef Paul Kleihues

"I would describe myself as a rationalist, though not in the Italian sense. . . . I have nothing of the Latin in me." So says Josef Paul Kleihues, who also calls himself a "poetic rationalist" in order to explain his position. This attitude would account for the way in which he incorporates a playful element, based on the given spatial arrangements of a building, into his otherwise strictly "purist" geometrical forms, which relate to functional purpose with an extraordinarily confident feeling for space.

The roots of Kleihues's characteristically semiotic architecture clearly stretch back as far as the classicism of Schinkel, and the strong feeling for design, combined with a clear humanitarian awareness, as well as a kind of intellectual sense of humor, has led throughout his career to exceptional works of construction. These include the classically-oriented Workshops of the Berlin Municipal Refuse Collection Depot—a large hall with three nave-like areas in which the collection vehicles are renovated and repaired; the "Wohnblock 270," a typical Berlin red-brick town development housing block in Vineta-Platz; the center of Wulfen New Town, consisting of shops and houses; the Neukölln Hospital, Berlin; and several other designs that, "à la Ledoux," are not more than "thoughts on paper," daydreams.

430

Kleihues has also gained a reputation as a pedagogue, particularly because of "Dortmund Architecture Days," which he founded in 1975. This international symposium on architectural theory is held each year and produces a regular flow of relevant literature.

—Manfred Sack

KNOWLES, Edward F(rank).

American. Born in New York City, 12 August 1929. Educated at Brooklyn Technical High School, 1943–47; Pratt Institute, Brooklyn, New York, 1947–51, B.Arch. 1951. Married Barbara Lee Dupree in 1952; children: Christopher, Sarah, Mary, and Emily. Worked as an assistant to Abraham Geller, New York, 1953–55, to Philip Johnson and Mies van der Rohe, New York, 1955–56, and to Edward Larrabee Barnes, New York, 1957–58; Instructor, Pratt Institute, 1959–60. In private practice, New York, since 1961. Partner, with Gerhard Kallmann and Noel McKinnell, Kallmann, McKinnell and Knowles, Boston, 1963–67; Partner, with John MacFadyen, MacFadyen and Knowles, New York, 1967–68. Professor of Architecture, Cooper Union, New York, 1960–64, and Columbia University, New York, 1965–66. Chairman, LeBrun Scholarship Committee, American Institute of Architects, 1966–67. Recipient: First Prize, New Boston City Hall Competition, with Kallmann and McKinnell, 1962. Address (office): 130 West 56th Street, New York, New York 10019, U.S.A.

Works:

1957 Fairchild Experimental Laboratory, Yonkers, New York
1959 Wiggins Beach House, Ocean Ridge, Fire Island, New York
1960 Knowles Beach House, Davis Park, Fire Island, New York
Edward Molyneux Townhouse, East 52nd Street, New York
1961 IBM Offices, New York
1962 Fleischmann Shopping Center, Naples, Florida
Holy Trinity Episcopal Church, Hicksville, New York (with Seth Hiller)
1964 Pine Manor Junior College, Brookline, Massachusetts (with Kump Associates)
1967 Richmond Foundation Housing, New York
New Boston City Hall (with Kallmann and McKinnell)
Sachs Department Store, Brooklyn, New York
Study of American art museums for the National Endowment for the Arts, Washington, D.C.
Bernbaum Townhouse, East 52nd Street, New York
Brooklyn Academy of Music Opera House restoration, Brooklyn, New York
1968 Casey's Restaurant, New York
Forbes House, Briarcliff Manor, New York
1969 Art resources study for the City of San Francisco (with John H. MacFadyen)
Davis Beach House, Bayberry Dunes, Fire Island, New York
U.S.O. Club, Portsmouth, Virginia
City Center of Music and Drama, New York
Coudert House, Lyme, Connecticut
Stifel House, Short Hills, New Jersey
1970 The LePerc Space (theatre), Brooklyn Academy of Music, New York

The Chelsea Theatre, New York
Newhouse Pavilion, Manhattan School of Music, New York (with John H. MacFadyen)
1971 Forstmann House, Montauk, Long Island, New York
Filene Center for the Performing Arts, Wolf Trap Farm Park, Vienna, Virginia (with John H. MacFadyen)
1973 Richard Lippold Greenhouse, Locust Valley, Long Island, New York
Music Hall Study, Troy, New York
1974 Birdsall Horse Farm, Southampton, Long Island, New York
ANTA Theatre Study, New York
Seattle Opera House
1975 Lowell Nesbitt Studio, New York
Hubay House, Fishkill, New York
Blust House, Beacon, New York
Kislak House, Pound Ridge, New York
1976 Exotic Gardens Greenhouse Complex, Long Island, New York
Janics House, New York
The Drawing Center, New York
1977 Friedman-Kien Estate, Garrison, New York
Bory House, Douglas Manor, New York
Geoffrey Holder House, New York

Publications:

On KNOWLES: articles—"The New Boston City Hall" by Mildred F. Schmertz in *Architectural Record* (New York), February 1969; "Boston's City Hall" by Sibyl Moholy Nagy in *Architectural Forum* (New York), February 1969; "Boston's City Hall" by Ada Louise Huxtable in the *New York Times*, 8 February 1969; "A Happy Union, A Grand Simplicity" by Wolf Von Eckardt in the *Washington Post*, 23 January 1971; "New Arts Site Near Capitol" by Harold C. Schonberg in the *New York Times*, 1 July 1971; "Washington Joins Showbiz" by Robert J. Landry in *Variety* (New York), 18 August 1971; "Wolf Trap's New Crop" by Phillis Funke in the *Wall Street Journal* (New York), 3 September 1971; "New Boston Center" by Ada Louise Huxtable in the *New York Times*, 11 September 1972; "Mating of Traditional and Modern" by Norma Skurka in the *New York Times*, 1 October 1972; "High, Dry and Handsome" by Richard W. Langer in *New York Magazine*, 10 March 1975; "A 'Bare Bones' Pavilion" in *Architectural Record* (New York), November 1975; "Sculptor of Space" in *MD* (New York), October 1976; "Background for an Artist" by Peter Carlsen in *Architectural Digest* (Los Angeles), April 1977; "Just One Room Can Do It All" in *House and Garden* (New York), Spring 1978.

My designs are generated inductively as the result of the interplay of the requirements of the project. Significant architecture must express the emotional factors of the problem in addition to the obvious requirements of program, site, budget, and structure, or it ceases to be an art form. The rejection of any of the phenomena that are experienced at any point in history is short sighted. Historical references, popular idioms, avant garde statements, sculptural and painterly concepts all have a potential role in the design of buildings.

Any academic approach to architecture is arbitrary and limiting. We are in an era that is a tornado of ideas. Our architecture should be no less.

—Edward F. Knowles

In 1962 Edward F. Knowles of New York, with Gerhard Kallmann and Noel McKinnell of Boston, won the national competition for the new Boston City Hall. The jury decided that the three young architects had solved the problem of designing an open, accessible structure through which the life of the city could pass—the result of the "rich expressive form" and sensitively scaled interior space. Since its opening, the reinforced concrete City Hall has been acclaimed as "magnificently monumental" without being austere or forbidding. The building doesn't merely *stand* on its sloping, trapezoid site; it is rooted to it, as if growing from the brick-faced gradient, two of its lower floors being partially buried in the mound, the outer staircases echoing the angled incline of the hill. Almost classically detailed, the concrete pillars and cross-members recall archaic Greek temples, but the building clearly forges a link between past and future. Inside, broad concourses are interconnected by escalator ramps and stairs for the 5,000 people who do business there every day. The main offices are built around an open, upper courtyard, through which light shafts illuminate the

Edward F. Knowles: Filene Center for the Performing Arts, Wolf Trap Farm Park, Vienna, Virginia, 1971

spacious inner public courts below—and all of these public areas, open night and day, allow the citizens to walk through and be part of City Hall without once having to open a door.

Since the City Hall competition in 1962, Knowles has also become known for his houses and, particularly, for his work on buildings for the arts. He is noted, too, for his skill in conversions and for his sensitivity in handling materials, especially wood.

Knowles' Fire Island beach houses are notable for their maximum utilization of space and their handling of wood and glass. Even more impressive is his conversion of an abandoned New York police stables building into a studio-home for the painter Lowell Nesbitt: it demonstrates both Knowles' genius for moulding space into elegant, functional forms and his ability to harmoniously combine conservation and innovation. A skylight greenhouse roof floods the old building with sunlight, so that details like the well-crafted old timber beams are highlighted by being presented in their new context. Another very impressive conversion is in upstate New York, where Knowles created a series of dwelling units for a physician from eight old farm buildings and an ice house. The farm's greenhouse was revived to its original splendor, and a cottage was raised on jacks and rebuilt from the bottom to form two apartments. Whenever possible, Knowles retained the original timbers, beamed ceilings and fine old masonry.

Apart from Boston City Hall, the Knowles' commission that has received the most publicity is the Filene Center Auditorium at Wolf Trap Farm Park in Virginia. It deserves its fame. Sheathed in red cedar for minimal environmental impact and maximum acoustical efficiency, the structure is set in a natural, grassy amphitheatre, so that both those inside the building and those out on its front lawn all sit on the natural slope of the ground with a clear view of the performers.

All of his designs for the musical arts are noteworthy. His work at Brooklyn Academy of Music reveals great care in the refurbished mosaic floors, lobby chandeliers, and re-designed interior spaces. For the Newhouse Pavilion of the Manhattan School of Music he created additional lounge and dining spaces, and shafts of natural light were introduced to a dark old locker room that he converted to a center of student activity.

In contrast to many contemporary architects, whose works are cold and impersonal steel and glass boxes, Knowles has built, converted and restored for people, for their human needs and activities. He follows the dictates of the environment and produces structures that are appropriate to their surroundings yet clearly state their purpose through the use of well-conceived forms and textures.

—Colin Naylor

KNUTSEN, Knut.

Norwegian. Born in Oslo, 4 December 1903. Educated at the State School of Arts and Crafts, Oslo, 1920–25. Married Hjørdis Christiansen in 1930; son: the architect Bengt Espen Knutsen. In private practice, Oslo, from 1933. Design Teacher, State School of Arts and Crafts, 1937–47; Instructor, 1956–66, and Professor, 1966–69, Oslo School of Architecture. Chairman, Oslo Architects' Association, 1952. Exhibitions: *Knut Knutsen/Arne Korsmo,* Henie-Onstad Kunstsenter, Høvikodden, Norway, 1972. Recipient: Henrichsens Fellowship, 1930; Egers Fellowship, 1948; First Prize, Norwegian Embassy for Stockholm Competition, 1952; Treprisen (Wood Architecture Award), 1961; Houens Fond Prize, 1961; Sundts Prize, 1962. *Died* (in Portør, Norway) *9 July 1969.*

Works:

1930 Salicath House, Lillevannsveien 61, Oslo
1936 Nølke House, Holmenkollen, Oslo
1937 Norwegian Pavilion, *World's Fair,* Paris (with Arne Korsmo and Ole Lind Schistad)
Office building, Munchsgate 5b, Oslo
Office building, Møllergaten, Oslo
Summer cottage, Ildjernet, Nesodden, Norway
Tåsen Home for the Elderly, Oslo
1938 Folk High School, Sørmarka, Norway
Design of the *Vi Kan* exhibition, Oslo (with Arne Korsmo)
Norwegian Pavilion, *World's Fair,* New York (project)
1939 Knutsen House, Lillevannsveien 8, Holmenhollen, Oslo
1941 Staff House (project)
Pfeiffer Summer House, Kragerø, Norway
1942 Bjørum Summer House, Jomfruland, Norway
Hauen House (project)
1944 Natvig House, Østhorn, Oslo
1946 Church, Snarøya, Norway (project)
Bergman House (project)
Borgan House (project)
Strand Hotel, Gjøvik, Norway
Fossen House, Blommenholm, Baerum, Norway
1948 Knutsen Summer House, Portør, Norway
1949 Housing development, Borstad, Norway (with Rolf Prag)
Forest cottage, Bjørum, Norway
Viking Hotel, Oslo
Town Hall, Vågå, Norway
Villa Rynning, Larvik, Norway
1952 Norwegian Embassy, Stockholm

Sjøfartsmuseet (maritime museum), Bygdøy, Oslo (project)
1953 Sundt House, Holmenkollen, Oslo
1955 Venstres Hus (office building), Møllergaten 16, Oslo
1956 Strand Cinema, Gjøvik, Norway
1958 Wathne House, Sarbuvollveien 11b, Høvik, Norway
Town Hall, Askim, Norway (project)
Lie House, Pans vei 6, Ulvøya, Oslo (with Bengt Knutsen)
Lionaes House, Pans vei 8, Ulvøya, Oslo (with Bengt Knutsen)
1959 Romsdal Vocational School (project)
Folkets Hus (Labor Movement Headquarters), Youngsgate 11, Oslo
Home for the Elderly, Erling Skjalgssonsgate 25, Oslo
Eckhoff House, Lyder Sagens gate 6, Oslo (with Bengt Knutsen)
1960 Bergendal Summer House, Tjøme, Norway
Brumunddal Church (project; with Bengt Knutsen)
1961 Thorkildsen Summer House, Portør, Norway
1962 Landasen Church, Bergen (project)
1963 Henie-Onstad Art Center, Høvikodden, Norway (project; with Bengt Knutsen)
Sollid House, Dalsveien 21, Oslo
Aasgaard House, Smestad, Oslo
1964 Town Hall, Mo I Rana, Norway (project; with Bengt Knutsen)
1965 Sundt House II, Bygdøy, Oslo
Holmen Church, Asker, Norway
Minister's House, for the Holmen Church, Asker, Norway
Grieghallen (Grieg Concert Hall), Bergen (project; with Bengt Knutsen)
1966 Cranner Summer House, Tjøme, Norway
1967 Rydning House, Besserud, Oslo
1968 Täby Church, Sweden (project)
Kontorhus (office building), Oslo (project)
Sørkedalen Residential Development, Oslo (project)

Publications:

By KNUTSEN: articles—"Samtidens billigste massemøbler" in *Byggekunst* (Oslo), no. 1, 1934; "Norges paviljong på Verdensutstillingen i Paris" in *Byggekunst* (Oslo), no. 1, 1938; "Om arkitektkurset" in *Byggekunst* (Oslo), no. 9, 1949; "Arkitektur eller pynt" in *Byggekunst* (Oslo), no. 10, 1951; "Forslag til undervisningsplan for avdeling Bygg og Statens arkitektkurs ved SHKS" in *Byggekunst* (Oslo), no. 3, 1958; "Mennesket i sentrum" in *Byggekunst* (Oslo), no. 4, 1961; "En mesterarkitekt i Norden" in *Byggekunst* (Oslo), no. 3, 1963.

Knut Knutsen: Knutsen Summer House, Portør, Norway, 1948

On KNUTSEN: book—*Knut Knutsen/Arne Korsmo,* exhibition catalogue, by Per Cappelen and Christian Norberg-Schulz, Høvikodden, Norway 1972; articles—"Norvège" in *L'Architecture d'Aujourd'hui* (Paris), May/June 1954; "House in Oslo" in *Architectural Design* (London), October 1961; "Knut Knutsen 1903–1969" by Per Cappelen in *Arkitektnytt* (Oslo), no. 12, 1969; "Arne Korsmo/ Knut Knutsen: Arkitekturutstilling, Henie-Onstad Kunstsenter" in *Byggekunst* (Oslo), no. 6, 1972.

Knut Knutsen believed that buildings have always been used to publicize their individual owners. He thought that "things" should be made unimportant. Mankind was what mattered. He felt, too, that "nature is the most valuable and greatest source of inspiration. We are never bored with nature but we are with buildings. We must preserve nature, and we can best do this by seeking harmony with it and making our buildings subservient to it." In an article he called his own house "the unimportant house," and his winning entry in the competition for the Stockholm Embassy was titled "The Considerate."

Knutsen was an opponent of the Modern Movement as it was understood in the immediate pre- and post-war periods; he also rejected the concept of style and all style-based architecture. His belief that buildings could express freedom, poetry and harmony with nature suggests the ideas of Frank Lloyd Wright, but Knutsen shows no signs of having been stylistically influenced by Wright. Ideally, Knutsen felt, a building should be invisible, and he very nearly achieved his goal in his own summer house at Portør. This spontaneous design looks like an accidental pile of planks, hidden amongst the rocks.

His buildings demonstrate his evolving ability to embody his concepts. His pre-war Folk High School at Sørmarka is a rather conventional building and, to a high degree, so is his Tåsen Home for the Elderly. But after these works his formal language becomes less constrained. His own house on Holmenhollen is an assemblage of small units staggered one to another. He added elements to two-storey houses to make the basic shape less clear. Windows seem to be placed where they will, without order in shape and size. But in the Stockholm Embassy these ideas are combined with a definite architectural order: it is probably his major work. The ground floor has a very free plan, creating lively spatial relationships both between the rooms and between the interior and exterior, but the facade is contained in a clear structural framework. The upper floor uses larger and simpler forms to unite the whole, and walls and terraces tie the building to its site. The Viking Hotel in Oslo and the Strand Hotel in Gjøvik are works from the same period. The Viking Hotel has an irregular plan that relates well to its site; the Strand has a simple form enriched by the varied use of forms and materials in the facade panels within the structural frame. The later Folkets Hus is a more conventional office building, but Knutsen's later houses continue to involve the theme of distintegration into elements and the use of rustic materials.

Knutsen's influence on the post-war generation that he taught was considerable. His work gave them positive and constructive ideas without resort to nationalistic or romantic precedents, and his ideas have continued to be an influence on several outstanding Norwegian architects who are now themselves teachers.

—Michael Lloyd

KOCH, (Albert) Carl.

American. Born in Milwaukee, Wisconsin, 11 May 1912. Educated at Harvard College, Cambridge, Massachusetts, 1930–34, B.A. (cum laude) 1934;

Harvard University, Cambridge, Massachusetts, 1934–37, M.Arch. 1937; awarded Bacon Traveling Fellowship, 1938–39. Senior Architect, National Housing Agency, 1942–44; served as a Lieutenant in the United States Navy, 1944–46. Married Persis White in 1934 (divorced, 1949); children: Cyrus, Otto, Molly and Carl Jr.; married Jean Emery in 1951; children: David, Samuel and Elizabeth. Worked with Sven Markelius, Sweden, 1937, and with Walter Gropius and Marcel Breuer, Cambridge, Massachusetts, 1938; President, Carl Koch and Associates, Cambridge and Boston, Massachusetts, 1939–78. Since 1978, in private practice, as Carl Koch, Architect, Boston. Exhibition: De Cordova Museum, Lincoln, Massachusetts, 1965. Recipient: Honor Award, 1949, and Industrial Arts Medal, 1969, American Institute of Architects; Bronze Medal, AIA, Philadelphia, 1951; Gold Medal, The Architectural League of New York, 1953; *Parents Magazine* Award, 1954; Award of Merit, AIA/American Library Association, 1956; Boston Arts Festival Award, 1963; Frank P. Brown Medal, Franklin Institute, 1967; Quarter Century Citation, Builders Research Advisory Board, 1977. Fellow, American Institute of Architects. Address (office): 54 Lewis Wharf, Boston, Massachusetts 02110, U.S.A.

Works:

1940/
46   Snake Hill Cooperative Housing Community, Belmont, Massachusetts

1948   Design of Lustron Panelized System Houses

1949/
51   Conantum (community development), Concord, Massachusetts

1952/
63   Techbuilt Houses and Furniture (prototypes)

1953   Back Bay Center, Boston (with Pietro Belluschi, The Architects Collaborative, Hugh Stubbins and Walter Bogner)

1954/
57   Master plans for Pease Air Force Base, Portsmouth, New Hampshire; Dow Air Force Base, Bangor, Maine; Westover Air Force Base, Springfield, Massachusetts; Hanscom Air Force Base, Bedford, Massachusetts; and Kindley Air Force Base, Bermuda

1954/
58   Urban renewal planning studies for Webb and Knapp: Laurel Richmond Community and Kenyon Barr Community, Cincinnati; Airport Project, Camden, New Jersey; River Park, Hartford, Connecticut; Seneca Square, Buffalo, New York; Thompson Townsite, Manitoba.

1956/
59   Acorn Pre-fabricated Houses

1957/
59   Residential construction research project for National Steel

1958   Fiberglas bathroom for Owens-Corning

1959   Design of air conditioning for residential construction for the Carrier Corporation

1959/
60   Basic panels for the Ferro House (research house)

1960   East Hills, Pittsburgh (with The Architects Collaborative and Sert, Jackson)

1960/
61   Adaptation and development of new products for housing for Armco Steel
    Lane Apartments, Antioch College, Yellow Springs, Ohio

1961/
62   College Dormitory Research Project for the Alcoa Corporation

1962   Downtown renewal plan for Louisville, Kentucky (with Doxiades)

1963   Research project for moderate income housing, Boston

1964   Relocatable House, for the United States Air Force
    Urban planning study for a new satellite community, for the Union Carbide Corporation
    Academy Homes I, Boston

1964/
71   Techcrete Modular Building System

1965   USAHOME Pre-Fabricated Buildings, for the United States Department of Defense

1966/
67   Scotia Square, Halifax, Nova Scotia

1966/
72   Lewis Wharf, Boston

1967   Military housing research and development program, for the United States Department of Defense
    Academy Homes II, Boston
    Westminster Court, Boston

1968   Cambridge School, Weston, Massachusetts

1969   Stowe House Motor Lodge, Brunswick, Maine

1969/
72   Elmwood Park, Detroit

1970   Housing for the elderly, Lewiston, Maine

1970/
71   Tarlton, Piermont, New Hampshire

1970/
72   Arverne, New York

1971   Housing for the elderly, Brunswick, Maine

1971/
72   Madison Park North, Baltimore

1974   Elmwood Park, stage II, Detroit

1975   Lewis Wharf, stage II, Boston
    Arverne, stage II, New York

1976   Madison Park North, stage II, Baltimore

1978   Housing for the elderly, Waterville, Maine

Publications:

By KOCH: book—*At Home with Tomorrow,* with Andy Lewis, New York 1958.

On KOCH: articles—"Rehab Creates an Inner-City PUD" by Michael J. Robinson in *House and Home* (New York), February 1974; "Wharf into Village" in *Architecture Plus* (New York), March/April 1974.

Carl Koch and Associates are working toward an architecture consistent with both the changing tools and materials of today's exploding technology and also those human aspirations which remain unchanged.

This, we think, involves continually fresh thinking without straining for novelty. We believe that cities, buildings and their smallest parts achieve beauty only if they function well. Good architecture must express primary concern for the people it serves— the individual and the community.

We have long believed that response to the critical problems of speed, economy and quality-control must include design of new building systems using 20th century industrial techniques, without sacrificing the flexibility vital to individual expression and modes of living. Close collaboration with business, industry and government is essential in this process.

We believe in conserving the best elements of the past in our cities and in trying to reflect in new construction a sympathy with this heritage. Our principal commitment is toward improving the quality of life through design . . . to achieve vitality and enrichment of the total living environment.

—Carl Koch

Carl Koch was a pioneer of industrial housing. After spending the beginning of his architectural career designing handsome, single houses for handsome budgets, he realized that since eighty-five percent of all houses built come from little or no architectural design, the traditional architect is misdirecting his efforts. Koch saw the need to simplify and modularize multiple housing, by using the advantages of industrialization to create sensible and comfortable housing for the increasingly mobile and concentrated fast-growing population.

Koch, trained at Harvard in the late thirties when the Beaux-Arts tradition was being pushed out by modernism, was struggling for direction. At this time of architectural confusion, he felt his contemporaries also lacked direction, and he packed himself off to Europe to see for himself what modernism and the International Style were all about. He went to work with Sven Markelius in Sweden, where he gained a great and long lasting reverence for the simple, clean, uncluttered houses of Scandinavia.

The new architecture for Koch lay in the successful combining of the advances of factory production of building component parts with the aesthetics of spatial and material arrangement. Working closely with the modular parts industry, he developed the "Techbuilt" house, an industrialized structure which was cheaper than the one-off singly designed house, yet more individualized than the mobile home. It included a set of prefabricated stressed skin plywood panels arranged and connected in a simple rectilinear plan. Each set of standardized parts could be arranged with some variety and uniqueness to fit an individual client's needs.

The architect, Koch feels, must design the architectural means, not the architectural answers. He must relinquish the heavy-handedness which often leads to over design. The architectural elements of buildings must be left to stand on their own. The architect is, in a sense, the moderator of a dialogue between the functional components of construction and the spatial needs of the client. Koch admits he

initially thought that the remedy to the housing problem was in the building of more and more systems housing, but later realized that in his overwhelming concern for the construction process, he slighted the resident's humanistic needs. The success of Koch's later efforts were due to his ability to make industrialized commercial housing personally livable.

Koch's houses have a spatial and structural simplicity based on the logical and straightforward process of construction, allowing for individuality of expression in the variety of component arrangement.

—Stephen P. Hamilton

KOENIG, Pierre.

American. Born in San Francisco, California, 17 October 1925. Educated at the University of Utah, School of Engineering, Salt Lake City, 1943; Pasadena City College, California, 1946–48; University of Southern California, Los Angeles, 1948–52, B.Arch. 1952. Served in the United States Army, in Europe, 1943–46: Corporal. Married Merry Sue Thompson in 1953 (divorced, 1959); Gaile Elodie Carson in 1960 (divorced, 1975); children: Randall and Jean. Draftsman in the office of Raphael Soriano, Hollywood, California, and Kistner, Wright and Wright, Los Angeles, 1952. In private practice, Los Angeles, since 1952 (worked as a Draftsman for Jones

and Emmons, Los Angeles, 1956). Instructor, Architectural Design Studio, 1961–69, Associate Professor, Institute of Building Technology, 1970–71, and since 1970 Associate Professor of Architecture, University of Southern California, Los Angeles (Director, Chemehuevi Planning Program, 1971–76). Visiting Critic and Lecturer, Yale University, New Haven, Connecticut, 1963; Visiting Lecturer, Pratt Institute, New York, 1963, Arizona State University, Tempe, 1964, and University of California at San Luis Obispo, 1965; Participant, Cranbrook Seminar, Illinois, 1965; Guest Lecturer, Architectural Panel, Los Angeles, 1966. Exhibitions: *Bienal,* Sao Paulo, Brazil, 1957; Architectural League of New York, 1957; American Federation of Arts Traveling Exhibition, 1958–59; *Bethlehem Steel Traveling Architectural Exhibit,* 1963; *Environment U.S.A.,* Los Angeles, 1964; *Architecture in Southern California,* Los Angeles County Museum, 1965. Recipient: Award, *Bienal,* Sao Paulo, 1957; Award, American Institute of Architects/*House and Home,* 1957, 1960, 1962, 1963; Award, Architectural League of New York, 1957; Honor Award, 1959, and Award, 1961/62, AIA/*Sunset Magazine;* Award, Architectural Institute of Southern California, 1963; Best Exhibition Building Award, Portland, Oregon, 1964; Los Angeles Grand Prix Award, 1967. Fellow, American Institute of Architects, 1971. Address (office): 12221 Dorothy Street, Los Angeles, California 90049, U.S.A.

Works:

1950 Koenig Exposed Steel House, Glendale, California

Carl Koch: Lewis Wharf, Boston, 1972

1953 Lamel Exposed Steel House, Glendale, California

1954 Squaire Exposed Steel House, LaCanada, California

1955 Scott Exposed Steel House, Tujunga, California

1957 Burwash Exposed Steel House, Sunland, California

1958 Case Study House 21, for *Arts and Architecture* magazine, Hollywood, California
Radio Station KYOR, Blythe, California
Western Saw Works, Los Angeles

1960 Case Study House 22, for *Arts and Architecture* magazine, Hollywood, California

1961 Seidel Beach House, Malibu, California
Pre-fabricated Steel Tract, Quebec, Canada

1962 Seidel Exposed Steel House, West Los Angeles
Johnson Exposed Steel House, Carmel, California

1963 Oberman Exposed Steel House, Palos Verdes, California
Mosque, Los Angeles
Willheim Wood House, West Los Angeles
Exhibition Pavilion, *Bethlehem Steel Traveling Architectural Exhibit*
Beagles Steel House, Pacific Palisades, California

1966 Factory, El Segundo, California

1968 Iwata House, Monterey Park, California

1971 Television station, Cypress, Florida

1971/
77 Chemehuevi Indian Reservation, Lake Havasu, California

1972 West Exposed Steel House, Vallejo, California

1978 Burton House, Malibu, California

Publications:

By KOENIG: books—*The Chemehuevi Project*, with P. Rodemier and K. H. Grey, Los Angeles 1971; *The Chemehuevi Future*, Los Angeles 1973; *This Is Our Land*, Los Angeles 1974; *Remaking the Homeland*, Los Angeles 1975; *The Chemehuevi Today*, Los Angeles 1976; *Graphic Communication*, Los Angeles 1977.

On KOENIG: books—*Einfamilienhauser in den U.S.A.*, Munich 1963; *Modern California Houses* by Esther McCoy, New York 1962, 1978; *Hauser und Garten in Kalifornien*, Stuttgart 1965; *Los Angeles* by Reyner Banham, London 1971; *Drawings by American Architects* by Alfred Kemper, New York 1973. articles—"Steel and Concrete Hillside House" in *Arts and Architecture* (Los Angeles), January 1959; "Case Study House 21" in *Arts and Architecture* (Los Angeles), February 1959; "Pierre Koenig" by Esther McCoy in *Zodiac* (Milan), no. 5, 1959; "Wasser, Stahl und Glas" in *Bauen und Wohnen* (Zurich), December 1960.

I became interested in modern technology and mass production as applied to housing early in my career. In 1950, while still a student at the University of Southern California, I designed and built my first exposed steel and glass house as an extra-curricular project. The house had exposed steel columns, wide flange beams and a steel roof deck, with the underside of the decking working as the ceiling. Sliding glass doors, industrial windows and metal siding completed the shell. Rather than style, my search was for a new aesthetic based on simplicity and economy.

From this start I went on to design many houses with these systems, refining and extending ideas as new materials and processes became available. Although the houses were custom designed for private clients, each of them was a prototype for mass production.

Notable among the many steel and glass buildings over the years are the Case Study Houses 21 and 22,

Pierre Koenig: Case Study House 21, Hollywood, California, 1958

sponsored by *Arts and Architecture* magazine. John Entenza, editor of *Arts and Architecture*, called Case Study House 21 (see the photo) "some of the cleanest and most immaculate thinking in the development of the small contemporary house."

I have expanded my basic ideas into large-scale projects: factories, commercial buildings such as radio and tv stations, and medical facilities, all of which require unique solutions.

My designs include mass-produced housing for two extreme climatic conditions, one for the near-arctic (Pre-fabricated Steel Tract, Quebec) and one for the desert (Chemehuevi Indian Reservation). The first project dealt with temperatures of -40°F and the other with +120°F. Both projects represented climatic extremes, yet each problem was solved with similar advanced technological means, using pre-fabricated combination steel and wood panels and steel frames. For the arctic houses the frames were separate and on the inside of the envelope. For the desert houses the separate frames were outside the envelope.

Believing that conservation and ecological balance starts at the land planning level, I spent six years planning the 28,000 acre Chemehuevi Indian Reservation, with the help of a Department of Housing and Urban Development grant for the design of the residential and commercial installations.

While carrying on a professional practice, I am currently involved in researching the effects of natural forces on architectural forms, at the University of Southern California. My emphasis is on technology and adaptive architecture, and my research has included an investigation of the relationship between sun and form as well as experimental work with a wind tunnel which I designed and built with the help of my students.

—Pierre Koenig

The lucidity of the steel frame, utilizing industrial methods of technology, is the basis of Pierre Koenig's architectural style. Koenig is a perfectionist who believes that truth in architecture lies in the natural expression of materials, devoid of ornamentation, fakery or fad. His approach is straight-forward simplicity based on economy—not just of cost,

but economy of means and of methods of energy conservation. For example, he shuns air conditioning in favor of cross-ventilation; even his buildings in the desert are air-cooled by means of evaporative coolers rather than by refrigeration. In spite of opposition by loan companies, building departments, and contractors, Koenig has remained dedicated to his own unique style.

When the magazine *Arts and Architecture* was seeking inventive architects for their case study houses, they chose Koenig to design two of them. His first case study house utilized the monoplaner wall together with glass curtain walls and exposed steel beams, with ceilings of steel decking. By orienting the glass walls toward the north and south, he achieved a minimum of heat gain. The house was cooled, in summer, by pumping the water from the reflection pool onto the roof. The striking color scheme of black structural elements contrasting with smooth white planes was achieved by spray painting with a machine.

The site for his second case study house was on the edge of a canyon with a sweeping view of the city lights below. The factor of the design was a 10' cantilever to extend the living space and allow for a swimming pool on the same level. Large, flat concrete slab bridges connect the house with the garden.

Both case study houses emerged as pure pavilions with flat roofs and wide overhangs. Industrial materials were handled with unusual spareness to obtain noble perspective. The crispness of the steel frame was accompanied by an inventiveness of plan and detail, combined with a sensitivity of proportion. In both schemes water became an integral part of the floor plan.

These houses, and others he designed for private clients, became prototypes for Koenig's large-scale projects—the 28,000 acres Chemehuevi Indian Reservation on Lake Havasu in California and a housing project near the Arctic Circle in Canada.

Koenig believes that many floor plans can be evolved from the structural plan, and that the simple multiplication of standard structural parts can produce even more variations. This is one reason why he chooses steel, rather than wood—for economy of mass production.

—Peggy Cochrane

435

KONSTANTINIDIS, Aris.

Greek. Born in Athens, 4 March 1913. Educated at the Varvakion Model School, Athens, 1926–30; Technical University Architectural School, Munich, 1931–36, Dip.Ing.Arch. 1936. Served in the Greek Army, 1937–38, 1940–41, 1945–47. Married Natalia Melas in 1951; children: Dimitri and Alexandra. In private practice, Athens, since 1938. Architect, Town Planning Department, Athens, 1938–40, and Ministry of Public Works, Athens, 1942–53; Director of the Design Department, Organization of Labour Housing, Athens, 1955–57, and Greek National Tourist Organization, Athens, 1957–67. Since 1975, Special Adviser for Architecture and Environment, Greek National Tourist Organization. Guest Professor in Architectural Design, Polytechnic School (ETH), Zurich, 1967–70. Exhibitions: *Greek Anonymous Architecture* (photographs and drawings by Aris Konstantinidis), Athens, 1967; *The Work of Aris Konstantinidis: Buildings 1938–1966*, University of Stuttgart, 1967, Polytechnic, Zurich, 1967, Architectural Association, London, 1968, Bauzentrum, Vienna, 1968, School of Architecture, Aarhaus, Denmark, 1969, and the Art Academy of Copenhagen, 1969; *Aris Konstantinidis: Drawings*, Desmos Gallery, Athens, 1975. Also, a photographer; exhibitions—Athens, 1951; *Greece by Eleven Greek Photographers*, Art Institute of Chicago, 1957; *Two Greek Photographers*, with Harissiadis, Underground Gallery, New York, 1967; *Aris Konstantinidis: Photographs*, Desmos Gallery, Athens, 1976. Honorary doctorate: University of Thessaloniki, 1978. Address: Aris Konstantinidis, Architect, 24 Rigillis Street, Athens 138, Greece.

Works:

1938   Country residence, Eleusis, near Athens
1939   Garden exhibition, Kifissia, near Athens
1940   Cine-News Cinema, Athens
1951   House, Vasil. Sofias Street 4, Athens
        Week-end house, Sikia, near Corinth
1952   Exhibition pavilion, Thessalonica
1955   Housing development, Athens
1956   Housing development, Pyrgos, Greece
        Housing development, Thessalonica
        Housing development, Serres, Greece
        Housing development, Piraeus
1957   Housing development, Iraklion, Crete
1958   Theatre Dressing Rooms Building, Epidauros, Greece
        Hotel Triton, Andros, Greece

1959   Motel Xenia, Igoumenitsa, Greece
        Motel Xenia, Larissa, Greece
        Exhibition pavilion, Thessalonica
1960   Hotel Xenia, Mykonos, Greece
        Hotel pavilions, Epidauros, Greece
        Motel Xenia, Kalambaka, Greece
1961   House, Kleitomachou Street, Athens
        House, Pholothei, near Athens
        House, Vouliagmeni, near Athens
1962   Week-end house, Anavyssos, near Athens
        Hotel pavilions, Epidauros, Greece
        Motel Xenia, Paliouri/Calkidiki, Greece
1963   House, Spetses, Greece
        Motel Xenia, Olympia, Greece
        Motel Xenia, Iraklion, Crete
1964   Hotel Xenia, Poros, Greece
1965   Museum, Ioannina, Greece
1966   House, Spetses, Greece
1967   Museum, Momotini, Greece
1971   4-flat building, Philiothei, near Athens
1974   House, Penteli, near Athens
1975   House and studio, Agina, Greece
        Week-end house, Agina, Greece

Publications:

By KONSTANTINIDIS: books—*Two Villages of Mykonos*, Athens 1947; *Old Athenian Houses*, Athens 1951; *Chapels of Mykonos*, Athens 1953; *Elements for Self-Knowledge: Towards a True Architecture*, Athens 1975; articles—"Die Zukunft des Architektenberufs" in *Detail* (Munich), no. 5, 1961; "Jedes Alte Bauwerk hat Bezug zu unseren eigenen Problemen" in *Detail* (Munich), no. 1, 1964; "Architecture" in *Architectural Design* (London), May 1964; "Heutige Architektur und Anonymes Bauen" in *Baumeister* (Munich), no. 4, 1965; "Summer House, Anavysso" in *World Architecture 2*, London 1965; "Architecture of the Xenia Hotels" in *World Architecture 3*, London 1966.

On KONSTANTINIDIS: books—*The New Architecture of Europe* by G. E. Kidder Smith, New York 1961; *One-Family Houses* by Pfau and Zietzschmann, Zurich 1964; *World Architecture*, vols. 1–3, edited by John Donat, London 1964–66; *Histoire Mondiale de l'Architecture*, vol. 2, by Michel Ragon, Paris 1972; *Geometry and Spatial Organization: A Syntax of Architecture* by Dimitris A. Fatouros, Athens 1979; articles—"The Work of Konstantinidis" in *Architectural Design* (London), May 1964; "Aris Konstantinidis" in *Arquitectura* (Madrid), October 1965; "Aris Konstantinidis" by Josef Krawina in *Domov* (Prague), no. 1, 1966; "Aris

Konstantinidis" by S. Dimitrou in *Bauforum* (Vienna), no. 5/6, 1968; "Aris Konstantinidis" by Szilagyi Istvan in *Hungarian Architecture* (Budapest), no. 3, 1975.

True architecture rises above the ephemeral and the transient and evokes in man the deepest psychological feelings and emotions, according to the conditions existing in every period and to the intellectual climate in each country.

There is always a constructional problem that must be solved in harmony with sociological aims, artistic standards, and the economy. Above all, the problem of architecture is a problem of intellectual perception. Architecture reflects not only the technique of the time but also, and most important, the spirit of the time, the social life, the manners and customs and the deepest personal emotions of man. Inasmuch as each building might be contemporary to its time from the point of view of technique (economy, hygiene, construction, etc.), it is as much a monument from the point of view of its artistic merit.

The purpose to which the architect dedicates himself is to create throughout the medium of his work the framework of a comfortable and pleasant life for the good of all—in other words, the architect works for one good and standard way of life, one that will be common to everyone. In this effort to achieve the universal panacea, the architect envisages the perfection of form. This will be based on the perfection of construction. Perfect construction means the research into a "typical construction," because "type" (the ancient Doric temple is a typical form; it is the perfection of a typical form, a *type* of a construction and of a form) is the result of the good and the perfect. With this type of construction and form we serve the common needs for a good and productive social life.

Good architecture starts always with efficient construction. Without construction there is no architecture. Construction embodies material and its use according to its properties, that is to say stone imposes a different method of construction from iron or concrete. I believe that we can create contemporary architecture with all materials—with any material as long as we use it correctly according to its properties. In areas where we can find nothing but stone, we should build with that local stone. We will create contemporary architecture just as we would have done with any other material, because the important things will be the spirit of construction and the flexibility of our outlook and not a constructional whim foreign to the site.

Aris Konstantinidis: Week-end house, Anavyssos, near Athens, 1962

I also believe that true architectural work cannot exist without a finite location just as it cannot be created without the people who live in each environment (country, area, etc.)

The finite location, the climate, the topography and the materials available in each area determine the constructional method, the functional disposition, and finally the form. Architecture cannot exist without landscape, climate, soil, and manners and customs. This is the reason why we sometimes see old buildings looking contemporary, and for the same reason we build today contemporary buildings which could have been built in the past. Since man, from time immemorial to this day, has always lived, moved about, and breathed in the same way, perhaps nothing in our way of life has basically changed.

If something today has changed, it is the techniques of new material and the new constructional possibilities which enable us to build in a different way from our ancestors. What we build is not entirely original or new, for if our ancestors could have had our materials and techniques, they would have created the architecture of our time! However, today, we do have something different from them. It is the way in which we come into contact with our natural surroundings, with nature and landscape. Today we love landscape and nature in a different way, for when we endeavour to live more healthily, when playing sports, we are confronted with nature and landscape not as an image but as a living space. We live with nature, in nature, as we live indoors. So, the new element in contemporary architecture (and this is entirely new) is that we aim to link the interior and exterior as *one* harmonious unit. Interior and exterior space (the natural surroundings, the landscape) become an organic entity with various aesthetics results. This is always in relation to the climate of the country, the nature of the country and the landscape. Thus building and landscape combine to create harmony. Architects today organize the landscape as an architectural space—we work differently today because as architects we organize the natural landscape, integrating the exterior and interior into one space.

There are cases when the form of the landscape imposes the use of a material which varies according to area. The first object of care in good and true architecture is to relate the construction harmoniously with the landscape. The form of the building (in texture, colour and quality) originates from the material as much as from its method of treatment. There comes a moment when the landscape will indicate the material and the method of construction when, in spite of having both concrete and iron, we shall build only in stone. Otherwise we will be out of character with the landscape and out of step with its organic qualities.

I can build with the most modern materials (iron, concrete, and with the *artificial* materials of contemporary building construction) a building which will be related harmoniously with the character of the landscape. I shall do this frequently in order to challenge my architectural inventiveness, and this I must do in order to be able to prove that true architecture can be created in any place with any material. But I cannot ignore a sentimental factor, which we must reveal in our construction; otherwise, we will be stagnant and inhuman . . . we must choose our material not only according to the standards of economy and pure science but also with the spirit of emotional freedom and artistic imagination. Architecture finally stands beyond pure purpose, higher than the achievements of logic and cold calculation.

If the architect is primarily a builder, he becomes finally an inspired organizer of life who designs spaces and creates forms with meaning, liveliness and character. In the end, when his work exists as a living organism, the individual who lives in it must be able to appreciate it and to let it become a part of himself.

—Aris Konstandinidis

Aris Konstandinidis has created a wise, austere and consistent kind of architecture, one that is particularly instructive for his contemporaries. His work, at any point in time or space, is a strict application of his socio-spatial philosophy, that architecture is a "container of life." This attitude is firmly based on the Greek spatial tradition, which means, for Konstandinidis, that architecture should be organized with a network of communications, should involve well-defined orientations, simple construction materials and methods and orthogonal geometric elements, and should be in harmony with, or be in dialectic contrast but not contradiction to, the geometry and light of the landscape.

More particularly, these basic principles can be detected in his work: 1) a strict organization based on a rectangular grid; 2) simple methods of construction and simple materials used in their natural state; 3) a persistent effort to relate the architectural work to the natural environment and to the psychological and physical scale of man; 4) space distribution, mainly through absolute and not intermediate limits: "contour" and variants in size—as well as, in particular cases, a series of columns in front of semi-covered spaces—act as transitional elements; and 5) a consistent application of these principles—yet though he strictly follows his organizational and construction principles, even to the most minute details, he does not simply repeat himself: by using different materials and because of different environmental conditions, he creates architecture of the same theme but with many variations.

The Xenia Hotel on Mykonos and the tourist hotel complex at Epidaurus are two examples of his method: Konstandinidis uses a simple and clear code of conceptualization and distribution of his space and succeeds in creating solutions of a multivariant quality, appropriate for particular (and different) conditions and needs, yet with a common spatial and geometric organization.

It is also interesting that his work has developed in the same ways as he has developed his relations with his employees and with the authorities. He has insisted in formulating a life style through architecture, and he has defended his propositions against any intervention.

—Dimitris A. Fatouros

KORN, Arthur.

British. Born in Breslau, Germany, 4 June 1891; emigrated to England, 1937. Educated at gymnasium in Berlin; Imperial College of Arts and Crafts, Berlin, graduated 1911. Served in the 5th Grenadier Guards of the German Army, 1914–18: Iron Cross. Married Regina Israel in 1919; children: Eva and Susanna. Worked as an assistant in various architectural offices in Berlin, 1911–14; planner in the Town Planning Department of Greater Berlin, 1914; worked with Erich Mendelsohn, Berlin, 1919; in partnership with Sigfried Weitzmann, Berlin, 1922–30; in private practice, Berlin, 1930–35; worked in Yugoslavia, 1935–37; practised in London, working with F. R. S. Yorke and E. Maxwell Fry, 1938–41; Teacher, Oxford School of Architecture, 1941–45, and Architectural Association School, London, 1945–65; retired to Austria. Secretary of the November Group, Berlin, 1924; Member, Berlin Ring, 1926; German Delegate, with Walter Gropius, CIAM, London, 1934; Chairman, MARS Town Planning Committee, London, 1938. Fellow, Royal Institute of British Architects. Member, Akademie der Künste, Berlin. *Died* (in Vienna) *14 November 1978.*

Works:

1922 Goldstein Villa, Grünewald, Berlin (with Sigfried Weitzmann)

Arthur Korn: Ullstein Shops, Berlin, 1930

1922/
30 Kopp and Joseph Shops, Berlin (with Sigfried Weitzmann)
Ullstein Building, Berlin (with Sigfried Weitzmann)
1928 Factory, Friedrichshagen, Germany (with Sigfried Weitzmann)
Fromm Rubber Factory, Cöpenick, Berlin (with Sigfried Weitzmann)
Business Centre, Haifa, Israel (competition project; with Sigfried Weitzmann)
1929 Intourist Shop, Unter den Linden, Berlin (with Sigfried Weitzmann)
1930 Master plan for Berlin: "The Town as Hotel and Factory" (with the Collective for Socialist Building)
1940 8 flats, Lettsom Street, Camberwell, London (with F. R. S. Yorke)
1942 Town plan for Nish, Yugoslavia (competition project)
Study of London (as Chairman of the MARS Town Planning Committee)

Publications:

By KORN: books—*Glas im Bau und als Gebrauchsgegenstand,* Berlin 1929, as *Glass in Modern Architecture,* London and New York 1967; *History Builds the Town,* London 1953; articles—"Analytische und utopische Architektur" in *Das Kunstblatt* (Berlin), December 1923; "Factory at Copernick—Berlin, 1928" in *The Architects' Journal* (London), September 1934; "1891 to the Present Day" in *Architectural Association Journal* (London), December 1957; "55 Years in the Modern Movement" in *Architectural Association Journal* (London), April 1966.

On KORN: books—*Internationale Architektur* by Walter Gropius, Munich 1925, 1927; *Berlin Architektur der Nachkriegszeit* by E. M. Hajos and L. Zahn, Berlin 1928; articles—"Hinweis auf Arthur Korn" in *Das Kunstblatt* (Berlin), December 1923; "Arthur Korn," special number of *Architectural Association Journal* (London), December 1957; "The Ring and Arthur Korn" in *Architectural Association Journal* (London), February 1958.

While I first worked as a town planner I discovered an interest in the nature and organization of the community. Ever since then I have asked myself three questions: What is a town? What way is a modern town different from an ancient town? How can we express the uniqueness of modern life, with its industry and transport problems in an adequate art form?

In the beginning of the town planning movement, it was the Russian and German revolutions that released a stream of new thoughts; Le Corbusier with his design, "La Ville Contemporaine," and the Constructivists with their new conceptions based on the visual attraction of industrial forms.

In 1928 after preliminary studies on the specific crystal character of individual towns—their morphology—and Law of Evolution, I took up the meaning of the town with greater vigour. Of the many aspects involved two seemed to stick out: living and working. These two activities have to be linked by transport and supplied with amenities. In this way the plan for Berlin was evolved conceiving two parallel areas, one for living and one for working, and in between a spine with a cultural centre, shopping facilities and a power grid.

In 1938, as a result of this spade work on Berlin, I wrote to the MARS executive outlining a way to study London. The idea was taken up and during the war we published our results. Having investigated the growth and changing structure of London, dependent upon her unique position in the world, we studied the four main components, housing, work, transport and amenities.

Housing proved to be the most formidable problem. Gradually a fundamentally new solution emerged which, until now, has not received the recognition it deserved. There is a progression, a hierarchy from the individual and the family to the larger unit which is London and further to the country as a whole.

There is still much hard work to be done in town planning. We must explore the possibility of the town, its physical implications and its artistic and symbolic form, and the way these things will change as our lives change under the impact of technical and industrial innovations. The questions are still in the air and demand an answer.

In the end there is still only ONE task—to establish our work—from the whole region, to the town in all its manifestations down to the individual cell; and not to fake the issues, either by analysis or any other device, but just to establish our world with all our passion, courage and integrity.

—Arthur Korn

The career of Arthur Korn can be divided into three phases. The first phase covers his period as a practicing architect in Berlin during the time of the Weimar Republic; the second is a period of thinking about cities and proposing planning theories and remedies for the ills that beset great cities; and the final phase is of the years after the Second World War, when Korn was as an influential teacher in London.

After the First World War, Germany was in chaos, physically and intellectually. It was the vital moment when a new architecture was being born. Walter Gropius, Mies van der Rohe, Bruno Taut and others were evolving a new architecture in an atmosphere where tradition was equated with defeat and the demand was to forget the old world and build a new. Arthur Korn shared an office with the young Richard Neutra, and all his life he remained unswervingly loyal to the Berlin architecture of the 1920's.

There may have been plenty of ideas in the Berlin of the 1920's, but there were not many commissions for architects, and in 1929 Arthur Korn published a book, *Glas im Bau*, which showed the work of his friends and the fascination that glass held for them, both for its connotations as an industrially produced material and for its "it's there and it's not there" quality that could be used to play spatial games on a modest budget. Several designs by Korn and his partner, Sigfried Weitzmann, show this fascination with glass, notably the Kopp and Joseph shop where the entire shop front is of obscure and clear glass.

In 1930, and again in collaboration with Weitzmann, Korn produced his one masterpiece, the Fromm Rubber Factory at Copernick. Largely de-

stroyed during the war, pathetically little of the building now exists in this East Berlin suburb. At a time when most modern buildings were of smooth white stucco, the Fromm factory was a celebration of steel, clearly expressed and painted bright red. Korn did not develop the idea, but Mies van der Rohe took its image as his starting point for the buildings at I.I.T.

With the coming of the Nazis, Korn came to England and lived modestly in a small, South London terraced house filled with the memorabilia of the heroic days in Berlin. He became chairman of the group that produced the MARS plan for London, and, although he built one small apartment building in South London, his real interest in that time was city planning: the MARS plan and his book *History Builds the Town* sum up his views. As a Hegelian and as a Marxist, Korn took an extreme view of planning, which he regarded as the means of redeeming the world. A later generation, including many of his own students, was to react sharply against his belief in a totally planned environment.

For twenty years after the Second World War, Arthur Korn taught at the Architectural Association School in London. His willingness to consider and respond to any proposal, however outrageous, made him a well-loved teacher and a lasting influence on the very many students whose vision of architecture and of planning he had extended.

—John Winter

KORSMO, Arne.

Norwegian. Born in Oslo, 14 August 1900. Educated at the Technical University, Trondheim, 1920–26, Dip.Arch. 1926; toured Europe on a Henrichsens Fellowship, 1928–29. Married Öse Thiis in 1928; Grete Prytz in 1945; Hanne Refsdal in 1965; children: Nora, Anne, and Marie. Worked in the architectural office of Bryn and Ellefsen, Oslo, 1927, and Arneberg and Poulsson, Oslo, 1928; in private practice with Sverre Aasland, Oslo, from 1929; Local Government Architect, Kristiansund, Norway, 1940–41; war fugitive in Sweden, 1941–45; resumed private practice, Oslo, 1945. Teacher, and subsequently Head of the Department of Interior Design, State School of Arts and Crafts, Oslo, 1936–41, 1945–56; Professor of Architecture, Technical University of Trondheim, 1956–68. Founder of the Norwegian section of CIAM (Congrès Internationaux d'Architecture Moderne), 1950. Exhibitions: *Triennale*, Milan, 1954, 1957; *Knut Knutsen/Arne Korsmo*, Henie-Onstad Kunstsenter, Høvikodden, Norway, 1972. Recipient: Sundts Prize, 1933; Grand Prize, *Triennale*, Milan, 1954. *Died* (in Cuzco, Peru) *29 August 1968*.

Works:

1929   10 single-family houses and area development plan, Frøen, Oslo (with Sverre Aasland)
Bagatelle Restaurant, Bygdøy Allé, Oslo (with Sverre Aasland)
Shops, Bygdøy Allé 3 and 7, Oslo (with Sverre Aasland)
1930   Louis Benjamin Shop, Oslo
Dammann House, Havna Allé 8, Oslo (with Sverre Aasland)
Apartment building, Pavelsgate 6, Oslo (with Sverre Aasland)
1931   3 single-family houses, Apalveien, Oslo (with Sverre Aasland)
1933   Eriksen House, Kristiansand, Norway (with Sverre Aasland)
1935   Hansen House, Tuengen Allé 6b, Oslo
Terrace houses, Apalveien, Oslo (with Sverre Aasland)

Riise House, Hamar, Norway (with Sverre Aasland)
1935/
36   Heyerdahl House, Slemdalsveien, Oslo
Benjamin House, Slemdalsveien, Oslo
1936   Grain Silo, Kristiansand, Norway (with Sverre Aasland)
Design of the *Trade Fair*, Halden, Norway
1937   Norwegian Pavilion, *World's Fair*, Paris (with Knut Knutsen and Ole Lind Schistad)
Stenersen House, Tuengen Allé 10c, Oslo
Design of the *Polar Exhibition*, Bergen (project)
1938   Design of the *Vi Kan* exhibition, Oslo (with Knut Knutsen)
1947   Von der Fehr Summer House, Larkollen, Norway
Central Railway Station, Oslo (project; with Jørn Utzon)
1948   School of Commerce, Göteborg, Sweden (project; with Jørn Utzon)
Mountain School (project)
Development plan for the Vestre Vika area, Oslo (project; with Jørn Utzon)
1950   Korsmo Apartment, Bygdøy, Oslo
1951   Alfredheim Pikehjem Home for Girls, Tåsen, Oslo
Atrium Houses (project; with Christian Norberg-Schulz)
1952   Prototype apartments (project)
Development plan for the Skøyen-Oppsal area, Oslo (project; with Jørn Utzon)
Aquarium, Bergen (project; with Christian Norberg-Schulz)
1952/
53   Development plan for the central city, Oslo (project; with Christian Norberg-Schulz)
1952/
55   Terrace houses (3), including Korsmo House, Planetveien, Oslo (with Christian Norberg-Schulz)
1953   Crematorium (project; with Gunnar Gundersen)
Institute of Architecture and Design, Oslo (project)
Tostrupgården Office Building, Oslo (project)
1955   Prytz House (project)
1957   Environmental Center, Technical University of Trondheim (project)
1958   Displays, *Unesco Exhibition*, Paris
1960   Single-family house, Halden, Norway (with Terje Moe)
1962   Britannia Hotel, Trondheim (with Terje Moe)

Designs: furniture, glassware, cutlery, jewellery, and airline cabin equipment, 1950–64.

Publications:

By KORSMO: articles—"Om butikker" in *Byggekunst* (Oslo), no. 5, 1931; "Romeksperimenter: Innredning av egen leilighet på Bygdøy" in *Byggekunst* (Oslo), no. 3, 1952; "Brukskunsts høstutstilling og hus 'Grete' " in *Byggekunst* (Oslo), no. 8, 1952; "Treavdelingen ved Statens håndverks—og kunst—industriskole" in *Byggekunst* (Oslo), no. 12, 1952; "Konferanse hos Aalto" in *Byggekunst* (Oslo), no. 1, 1954; "Drøm og virkelighet" in *Byggekunst* (Oslo), no. 2, 1954; "Japan og Vestens arkitektur" in *Byggekunst* (Oslo), no. 3, 1956; "Arme Student—hvor blir det av ditt arkite sinn?" in *Byggekunst* (Oslo), no. 3, 1958.

On KORSMO: book—*Knut Knutsen/Arne Korsmo*, exhibition catalogue, by Per Cappelen and Christian Norberg-Schulz, Høvikodden, Norway 1972; articles—"Arne Korsmo og den Norske Funktionalisme" by Nils-Ole Lund in *Byggekunst* (Oslo), no. 1, 1966; "Arne Korsmo/Knut Knutsen: Arkitekturutstilling, Henie-Onstad Kunstsenter" in *Byggekunst* (Oslo), no. 6, 1972.

Arne Korsmo was a vital influence on the post-war development of architecture in Norway—by example but especially as a source of ideas and as a teacher. He was the first Norwegian to build from the outset in the style of the Modern Movement, having been inspired by a visit in 1927 to the Stuttgart "Siedlung."

Korsmo's ideas are fully developed in the Dammann House of 1930, even though the influence of Mendelsohn and Dudok is detectable. The lounge, which was designed to contain a painting collection, is 15.5 × 4.7 × 3.8 metres, closed to the south but with gable walls fully glazed. One experiences the great panoramic view in a small semi-circular room of glass attached to the south wall. These rooms thus give a complex set of perceptions between closed and open spaces, changes of scale, and a highly-controlled relationship between the interior and exterior. The main facade uses ramps and a loggia to tie the house to its site and to express a typical vertical versus horizontal theme.

In 1938 Korsmo was responsible for the *Vi-Kan* exhibition where, despite great differences in architectural language, he collaborated with Knut Knutsen. His work in this exhibition underlines his great sensitivity to the form, colour and significance of the designed object. This not only enabled him to mount extremely effective exhibitions; it was also the foundation of his industrial design work, for which he was awarded the Grand Prix in the 1954 Milan *Triennale*.

The same sensitivity made him a master of interior design: his apartment on Bygdøy in 1951 is an outstanding example. In 1951 he also built Tåsen girls' home where, with a freer planning technique, he continues the ideas of the 1930's. At this same time he founded and led the Norwegian CIAM group, and through it, and his teaching as Head of the Department of Interior Design at the Oslo State School of Arts and Crafts, he had a powerful influence on the post-war work of younger architects. This group was responsible for examining most of the critical questions facing architecture in Norway in the 1950's and early 1960's.

In 1955, Korsmo, together with Norberg-Schulz, built a small group of houses that are significant not only for integrating industrial design ideas into building and for the extremely flexible planning made possible by these techniques but also for illuminating new paths that architecture might take.

—Michael Lloyd

KRAEMER, Friedrich Wilhelm.
German. Born in Halberstadt, 10 May 1907. Educated at the Technische Hochschule, Braunschweig, Germany, and Vienna, 1925–29, Dip.Arch. Ing. 1929, Dr.Ing. 1945. Married Inge Roedenbeck in 1947; children: Annette, Kaspar, Matthias, and Sabine. In private practice, Braunschweig, since 1935; in partnership as Kraemer, Sieverts und Partner, Braunschweig, since 1962, and Cologne, since 1974. Assistant Lecturer, 1929–35, and Professor (chair in architectural theory and design), 1947–74, Technische Hochschule, Braunschweig. Exhibition: *Friedrich Wilhelm Kraemer: Aus 50 Jahren eines Architekten,* Artothek, Haus Saaleck, Cologne, 1979. Recipient: Peter Joseph-Krahe Prize, 1952; Laves Medal, 1952; Bund Deutscher Architekten Prize, for Northrhine/Westphalia, 1965, Hesse, 1966, Bremen, 1974, Cologne, 1975, and Lower Saxony, 1976. Address: Kraemer, Sieverts und Partner, Am Romerturm 3, 5000 Cologne 1, West Germany.

Works:

1948 NWDR Radio Station, Hanover
Royal Palace, Addis Ababa, Ethiopia (competition project)

1949 Ministry of Trade Building, Bonn (competition project)
1950 High School, Wolfsburg, Germany
"Constructa" Housing, Hanover
1951 Waterways and Navigation Headquarters, Bremen
School Centre, Misburg, Germany (competition project)
Unterharz Mining and Foundry Works, Goslar, Germany
1952 Intermediate School, Peine, Germany
Golf Club, Braunschweig, Germany (competition project)
1953 Seaside House, Cuxhaven, Germany (competition project)
Trade School, Heidelberg
1954 Evening School Building, Dortmund
1955 City Savings Bank, Osnabruck, Germany (competition project)
State Bank, Salzgitter-Lebenstedt, Germany
1957 Landeszentralbank, Dusseldorf
1958 BASF Building, Tor 7, Ludwigshafen, Germany
City Savings Bank, Dusseldorf
1959 Community Building, Aluminium Rolling Mills, Singen, Germany
1960 Centennial Hall, Dyeworks, Hoechst, Germany
Student Union, University of Kiel
1961 State Chancery, Hanover (competition project)
1963 HEW Building, Hamburg (competition project)
1964 Town Hall, Essen (competition project)
British Petroleum Headquarters, Hamburg
Constanze Company Headquarters, Hamburg (competition project)
Insurance Buildings Complex, Hanover (competition project)
Savings Bank, Einbeck, Germany
1965 Tiergarten Museum, Berlin (competition project)
School Center, Wolfsburg, Germany (competition project)
1966 Simonbank Building, Dusseldorf
DKV Insurance Headquarters, Cologne
Volkswagen Foundation Building, Hanover (competition project)
Sports Forum, University of Kiel (competition project)

1968 Vogel Building, Hamburg (competition project)
Grammar School, Burgdorf, Germany (competition project)
1969 Veba-Chemie Headquarters, Dortmund (competition project)
Town Hall, Bonn (competition project)
Bayer Sales Department Building, Leverkusen, Germany (competition project)
1970 Siemens Building, Perlach, Munich (competition project)
Shell Company Headquarters, Hamburg (competition project)
Landeszentralbank, Hamburg (competition project)
1971 Colonia-National Headquarters, Cologne (competition project)
1972 German Embassy, Helsinki (competition project)
1973 Bavarian Insurance Company Headquarters, Munich
Landeszentralbank, Ludwigshafen, Germany (competition project)
1974 Social Democratic Party Headquarters, Bonn (competition project)
School Center, Gifhorn-Ost, Germany
1975 DEVK State Railways Insurance Bank Building, Cologne (competition project)
Neckermann Company Building, Braunschweig, Germany (competition project)
North German and Hamburg-Bremer Insurance Company Building, Hamburg (competition project)
Town Hall, Wuppertal, Germany (competition project)
WDR West German Radio Station, Cologne
1976 Deutsche Bank, Dusseldorf
GEW Headquarters, Cologne
Thyssen Gas Company Building, Duisburg, Germany
United Insurance Group Building, Munich (competition project)
1977 Ministry of Public Works and Housing, Riyadh, Saudi Arabia

Publications:

By KRAEMER: books—*BASF Rechenzentrum,* Stuttgart 1965; *Kraemer, Sieverts, Huth: Grossraum-*

Arne Korsmo: Dammann House, Oslo, 1930

Friedrich Wilhelm Kraemer: DKV Insurance Headquarters, Cologne, 1966

büros, Stuttgart 1968; *Kraemer und Meyer: Büro-hausgrundrisse,* Stuttgart 1974; *Kraemer, Sieverts und Partner: Grossraumbüros,* Stuttgart 1975.

On KRAEMER: articles—by Meinhard von Gerkan in *Braunschweiger Zeitung,* 3 April 1977; by Von Werner Strodthoff in *Kölner Stadt-Anzeiger,* 3 July 1979.

The course of Friedrich Wilhelm Kraemer's career was interrupted by the Second World War, after which, in 1946, he was appointed to the chair in architectural theory and design at the Technische Hochschule in Braunschweig. Like Hans Scharoun in Berlin, Egon Eiermann in Karlsruhe, and Richard Döcker in Stuttgart, Kraemer was one of those architects of the early days who took up their teaching again as soon as the war was over and went on to impress their particular stamp on a whole new generation of architects.

Kraemer's main achievement in the 1950's—and one of the monuments of the German architectural scene—was the Unterharz Mining and Foundry Works in Goslar. It is a building that impresses for the clarity of its structural order. Compared with the usual frame buildings of the time, buildings by Kra-

emer, as a result of a variation in the dimensions of the supporting struts, actually succeed in presenting the technology of their construction. It was this architectural method that informed a large number of the buildings that he designed at this time, including private houses, industrial installations, and schools.

In 1962 Kraemer's practice changed, and all his subsequent works emanated from a new partnership, Kraemer, Sieverts und Partner. At the end of the 1960's he built the DKV Insurance Headquarters in Cologne, which signalled a change in the functional concept of office block construction as a series of cellular subdivisions. Instead of the conventional rectangular arrangement, Kraemer and his partners created a multi-dimensional block in relief, based on the fitting together of a chain of mutually displaced triangles, resulting in a succession of areas that were unconnected but inter-related with one another. This functional shaping and three-dimensional organization of the office areas re-emerges on the exterior of the building, to create an architectural composition of powerful effect.

Kraemer has also made a name for himself as an architectural theorist. The subject of his thesis was the planning and building of the classical theatre, and he has written extensively on the construction of office blocks.

—Jürgen Joedicke

KRIER, Leon.

Luxembourger. Born in Luxembourg, 7 April 1946; brother of Rob Krier, *q.v.;* moved to England, 1968. Attended the University of Stuttgart for six months, 1967–68. Assistant to James Stirling, London, 1968–70, 1973–74; Project Partner, with J. P. Kleihues, Berlin, 1971–72. In private practice, London, since 1974. Lecturer, Architectural Association School, London, 1973–76, Royal College of Art, London, 1977, and Princeton University, New Jersey, 1977. Exhibitions: *Triennale,* Milan, 1973; *Rational Architecture* (organiser), London, 1975; *Mercati Trajani,* Rome, 1978; *Une Nouvelle Architecture,* Centre Pompidou, Paris, 1978. Recipient: Berlin Prize for Architecture, 1975. Address (office): 16 Belsize Park, London N.W.3, England.

Works:

1967 Lake resort, Heilbronn, Germany (project)
1968 University of Bielefeld, Germany
1969 Siemens A. G. Computer Centre, Munich (project; with James Stirling)
1969/
  73 Lewis-Ham Towers, Charlottenburg, Berlin (project; with Josef Paul Kleihues)
1970 Lycée Classique, Echternach, Luxembourg (project)
  Civic Centre, Derby (project; with James Stirling)
1972/
  75 Housing Block (600 units) by the Water, Charlottenburg Sluice, Berlin (project; with Josef Paul Kleihues, M. Kausch, and B. Tonon)
1974 Meyer House, Bagnano, Tuscany (project)
1976 La Villette Quarter, Paris (project)
1977 Social Centre, Piazza Navona, Rome (project)
  Social Centre, Piazza San Pietro, Rome (project)
  Social Centre, Via Corso, Rome (project)
  Motorway Intersection Park, Piraeus, Greece (project)
  City Centre, West Berlin (project)
  Blundell Corner, Hull, Yorkshire (project; with Rita Wolff)
1978 School for 500 children, St. Quentin en Yvelines, France
  Herrlichkeit Island, Bremen, Germany
  Capital of Europe, Luxembourg (project)

Publications:

By KRIER: books—*Buildings and Projects of James Stirling 1950–1974,* editor, Stuttgart 1974; *The Reconstruction of the European City,* Brussels 1978; *The City Within the City,* editor, Rome 1979; articles—"Progetti di Leon Krier 1968–72" in *Controspazio* (Bari, Italy), no. 10, 1972; "Projects on the City" in *Lotus* (Venice), no. 11, 1976; "The City Within the City" in *Architectural Design* (London), March 1977; "Cities Within the City" in *Architecture + Urbanism* (Tokyo), November 1977; "The Blind Spot" in *Architectural Design* (London), April 1978; "The Lesson of the Urban Block" in *Lotus* (Venice), no. 18, 1978.

On KRIER: articles—"Projects in a Bottle" by G. K. Koenig in *Casabella* (Milan), November 1972; "Les Frères Krier" by Antoine Grumbach in *L'Architecture d'Aujourd'hui* (Paris), July 1975; "Culot —Krier" by Robert Maxwell in *Architectural Design* (London), March 1977.

My projects are a series of polemical statements. They are not experiments; they are reflections on the specific structure of the European city (the streets, the squares, the communities)—a meditation on the true and constant elements of architecture and building and their necessary and precise relationships within the urban and social fabric. For architecture to be an art, building must be a craft. A reconstruction of these cannot be a matter of industry nor can it be a matter of science; it is a cultural and a political project.

A new generation is now discovering the urban cultures of pre-industrial Europe as documents of intelligence, memory and pleasure. This investigation is being led on different levels—political, cultural, economic—all over Europe; it leads to a clear conclusion. The necessity is for a global plan which opposes the global destruction of European culture through industrialization.

—Leon Krier

In line with the ideas of Aldo Rossi, Carlo Aymonino, Oswald Mathias Ungers, James Stirling, and his brother Rob Krier, the architectural concept of Leon Krier involves a basic re-evaluation of the total urban fabric as a medium for change and morphological growth.

A most important part of his concept is the distinct concentration of urban activities in "quartiers" (not separated into artificial zones as advocated by Le Corbusier and still seen as relevant by the majority of modern planners and architects). Krier says: "Dezoning is the first step in an anti-monopolistic and democratic planning policy." He is, in this sense, against the continuation of ideas which, from his point of view, interrupted tradition by means of building codes and anti-human ideas. He is against the architect's being the uncritical servant of the building industry; he wants the architect to be responsible for society and the total human environment. Krier advocates the rediscovery of building typologies and an urban experience based on and directed toward the value system of the individual with emphasis on the "public realm." A place is defined by him as "where the individual identifies himself as a being with full cultural and political responsibility." His concern is urban form and the integration of its social meaning.

In several of his projects (for example, La Villette Quarter, Paris) Leon Krier shows a close affinity to the works of painters and sculptors whose imaginative qualities he tries to integrate into his own urbanistic and architectural work. Subconscious elements often enter his work with direct reference to buildings and images from the past (Boullée, Ledoux, Loos, Le Corbusier). Krier says: "Architecture must be refounded in the intelligence of history. This it must take as its concern, the understanding, adaption and evolution of building types which express human needs and experience."

Through his basic education by his brother Rob Krier and the practical experience in the architectural offices of Josef Paul Kleihues and James Stirling, Leon Krier absorbed a great amount of experience which enabled him to look at architecture with a fresh approach. This has been further enhanced by a brilliant drawing technique of imaginative and realistic elements which has been widely influential.

—Udo Kultermann

KRIER, Rob(ert).

Austrian. Born in Grevenmacher, Luxembourg, 10 June 1938; emigrated to Austria: naturalized, 1975; brother of Leon Krier, *q.v.* Educated at the Lycée Classique, Echternach, Luxembourg, 1951–59; Technical University, Munich, 1959–64, Dip.Ing. Arch. 1964. Married Gudrun Schnitzer in 1964; children: Caren and Nadine. Worked in the office of O. M. Ungers, Cologne, 1965–66; and Frei Otto, Berlin and Stuttgart, 1967–70; engaged in work on the book *Stadtraum,* 1970–75; taught in Stuttgart and Lausanne, 1973–75. In private architectural and urban studies practice, Vienna, since 1976. Professor at the Technical University of Vienna, since 1975. Exhibitions: University of Stuttgart, 1970; *Triennale,* Milan, 1973; Kunstverein, Stuttgart, 1975; Institute of Architecture and Urban Studies, New York, 1977; Architectural Bookstore, San Francisco, 1977; Museum of Modern Art, Bologne, 1978, and toured Germany. Address (office): Elisabethstrasse 13/18, 1010 Vienna, Austria.

Works:

1968 Siemer House, Warmbronn, Germany
1974 Dickes House, Bridel, Luxembourg
1978 Social housing, Ritterstrasse, Berlin

Publications:

By KRIER: books—*Stadtraum in Theorie und Praxis,* Stuttgart and Barcelona 1975, London, Brussels and Tokyo 1979; *Notizen am Rande: Sketch-Book,* Berlin 1975.

On KRIER: articles—"The Work of Rob Krier" in *Nueva Forma* (Madrid), April 1973; "House Siemer" in *Bauen und Wohnen* (Zurich), October 1974; "Royal Mint Housing" in *Casabella* (Milan), no. 396, 1974; "The Work of Rob Krier" in *Nueva*

Leon Krier: Lycée Classique, Echternach, Luxembourg, 1970

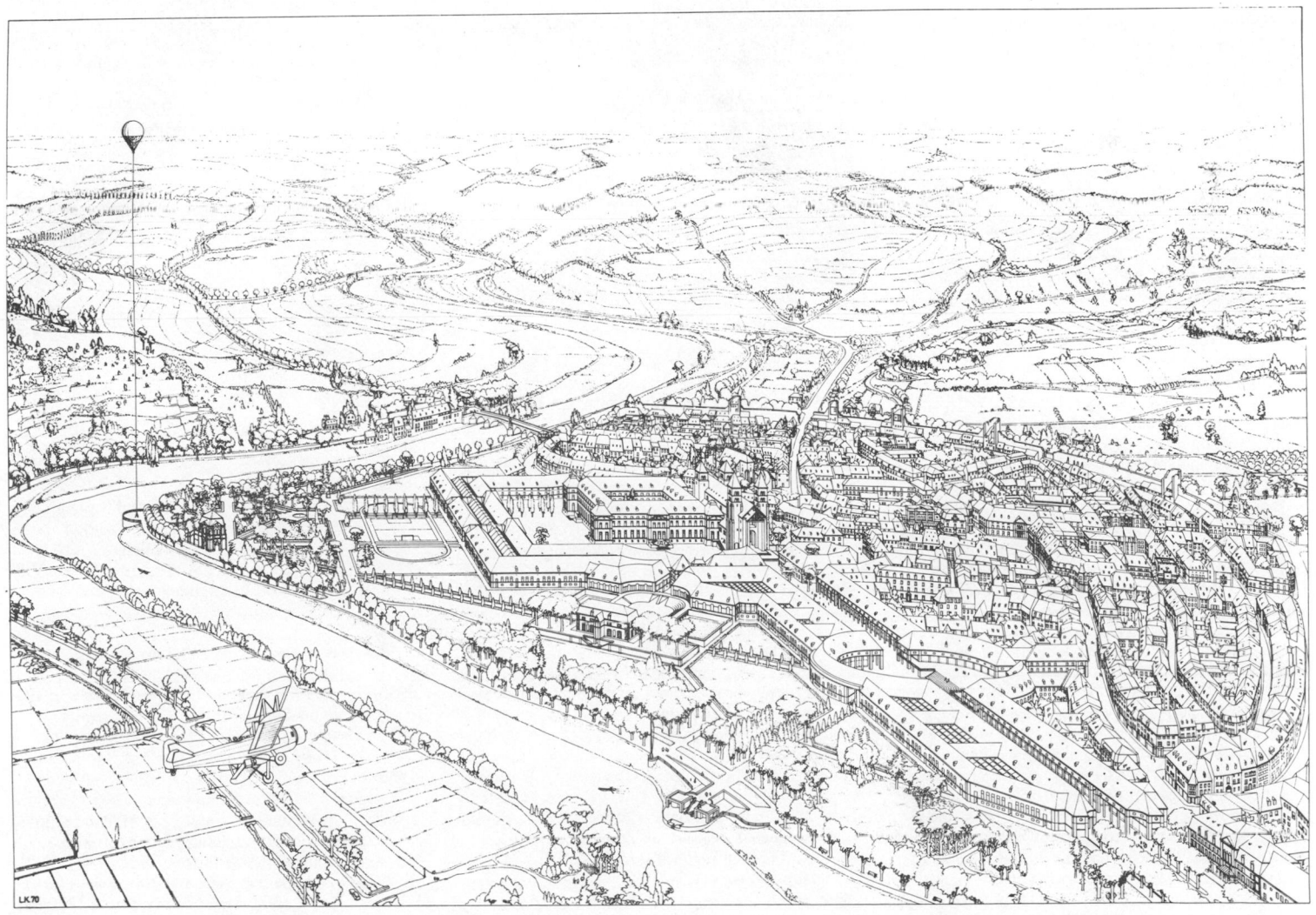

Forma (Madrid), February 1975; "Haus Dickes" in *Bauen und Wohnen* (Zurich), February 1975; "Les Freres Krier" by Antoine Grumbach in *L'Architecture d'Aujourd'hui* (Paris), July 1975; "The Work of Rob Krier" in *Architecture + Urbanism* (Tokyo), June 1977.

If you ask a 40 year old architect what he plans to do with the rest of his professional life, you will soon notice that he stands there like a child counting flowers petals: "I love you, I love you not, I love you" and so on.

As an architect I would like to achieve three things:

1) Learn to master the building of a house. I know that that doesn't happen at the first attempt. I would like to build a number of types of houses which are not drawn up according to one-sided criteria but which should, over several generations, be able to gain acceptance as prototype dwellings. That might sound like a touching architect's dream, but I mean, rather, to exclude from the building all fashionable trimmings, to limit myself to a few elements without becoming mean-minded.

2) Put together a few buildings in a town building complex in such a way that they form a street sector or a square which can serve as an area for public life. I should like very much to plan so sensibly and generously that the buildings would last well.

3) Finally, I would like to build a house open to the public, preferably one room devoted to worshipful purposes and which by virtue of its sublime function can raise a claim to the monumental. I should like to prepare myself at length and patiently for this most difficult of all architect's problems.

—Rob Krier

In the current re-evaluation of urban reality, the work proposals and research analyses of Rob Krier are of fundamental importance. Krier's main goal is the re-establishment of articulated space in cities; architecture and urbanism are to be united in creating a realistic basis for contemporary solutions. In his book, *Stadtraum in Theorie und Praxis,* he tries to establish a systematic typology of urban space systems and the basis for further research and alternative creative endeavors.

Krier's theoretical and practical work is a counter-attack against the domination of technological means, not against the means themselves. Zoning laws and the division of functions in cities, as proposed by Le Corbusier and many other orthodox modern planners, are seen as basic evils which prevent active and harmonious urban life and exclude the human element. For Krier typologies should dominate city space, not constructions for specific functions that are subject to change. For transportation he postulates a strict separation of car traffic and streets for people: the latter is seen as the relevant element in urban space.

Krier's main concerns are the use of spaces by humans, new perspectives in the creation of squares, and streets and their humanistic function in the larger fabric of cities. He sees the work of Camillo Sitte from the late 19th century in a new perspective, especially in regard to the ideas about urban spaces, in comparison with the much more successful ideas of the Garden City as advocated by Ebenezer Howard. For Krier it is the complexity of urban space, with its multiple and changing functions, not the limited restriction of space to one function only, that creates life and harmony in cities.

Rob Krier's arguments do not remain theoretical; they are manifested in several concrete proposals for cities like Stuttgart, Vienna and Berlin. His building activity as an architect is restricted to two houses, the Siemer House in Warmbronn and the Dickes House in Luxembourg, and social housing in the Ritterstrasse, Berlin.

—Udo Kultermann

Rob Krier: Siemer House, Warmbronn, Germany, 1968

KROLL, Lucien.

Belgian. Born in Brussels, 17 March 1927. Educated at the Ecole Nationale Supérieure de la Cambre, Brussels, Dip.Arch. 1951; studied city planning at the Institut Supérieur de la Cambre and at the Institut Supérieur International d'Urbanisme, Brussels, 1951. In partnership with architect Charles Vandenhove, Brussels, 1951–57. In private practice, Brussels, since 1957: established Atelier Kroll, with Vincent Klaus, Daniel de Cooman, Simone Kroll, Edouard Lambin, Didier Mersch, Genevieve Poelaert, and Gilbert Wampach, Brussels. Professor of Architecture, Ecole Saint-Luc de St.-Gilles, Brussels, since 1970. Founder Member, Institut d'Esthetique Industrielle, Brussels, 1956. Exhibitions: *Architecture Vivante,* Colegio de Arquitectos de Cataluña y Baleares, Barcelona, 1965; *Triennale,* Milan, 1965; Avionpuits and Louvain, Belgium, 1966; University of Louvain, 1966. Has also organized numerous art and architecture exhibitions in Belgium since the 1950's. Member, Order of Belgian Architects. Address (office): 20 Avenue Louis Berlaimont, Auderghem, 1160 Brussels, Belgium.

Works:

1952/
53 Chapel of Pont-de-Bonne, Modave Highway, Huy, Modave, Belgium (with Charles Vandenhove and G. Watelet)

1953 Parish Hall, La Roche, Tangissart, near Villers-la-Ville, Belgium (with Charles Vandenhove)

1954/
55 House, Avenue des Vallons, Waterloo, Belgium (with Charles Vandenhove)

1955 House, 28 Vijverstraat, Kiewit, Hasselt, Belgium (with Charles Vandenhove)

1956 Design of the *Exposition Esthetique Industrielle,* Liége (with Charles Vandenhove)

1956/
57 Tourist Restaurant, Eupen Dam, Belgium (with R. Bassin and Charles Vandenhove)

1957 Industrial Development Plans (projects; with Charles Vandenhove)
 Workshops and Permanent Campsite for the Boy Scouts, Abbey of Maredsous, Belgium

1957/	
58	Toussaint House, Uccle, Belgium
1958	House, 6 Avenue des Etangs, Sept Fontaines, Braine l'Alleud, Belgium
1958/	
59	House, route de Dinant, Sorinnes, Belgium
1958/	
62	Design of the travelling exhibition *Le Signe d'Or Industriel,* Bruges, Ghent, Antwerp, and Brussels
1959	House, 18 rue G. Dellince, Auderghem, Brussels
1960	Monin House, rue de Namur, Dinant, Belgium
1960/	
61	Lahaut House, rue Joseph Waregne, Salzinnes, Belgium
1960/	
62	Church of Ste.-Marie-le-Haut-Clocher restoration, Chevigny, Libramont, Belgium (with G. Watelet)
1960/	
63	't Holleken Church, 6 Boesdalstraat, Linkebeek, Belgium
1961/	
62	House, rue Soldat La Rivière, Jodoigne, Belgium
	Italian Social Center, rue Beaujean, Seraing, Belgium (with A. Constant)
	Chapel, between Rendeux and Marche, Waharday, Belgium
1961/	
63	Abbey of Gihindamuyaga, near Butare, Ruanda
	House, Nihersant, near Poilvache, Evrehaines, Belgium
1961/	
64	Medical Building, rue Graffe, Namur, Belgium
1961/	
65	Housing complex, 20 Avenue Louis Berlaimont, Auderghem, Brussels
1962	Electronic Instruments for MBLE, Belgium (projects)
	Belgian Pavilion, *International Fair,* Helsinki
1962/	
63	Oury House, Old Quarter of Liége
1962/	
65	Martens House, 180 rue Victor Hugo, Waterloo, Belgium
1963/	
65	Dom Lambert Bauduin Ecumenical Center, Abbey of Chevetogne, Belgium
1963/	
68	AITA School, rue de la Montagne, Namur, Belgium
1964	Dominican Chapel, 5 rue Leys, Brussels
	Design of the *Lyons Fair*
	Design of the *Roger de la Pasture Exhibition,* Cathedral of Tournai, Belgium
1964/	
65	Pirotte House, 8 Dreve des Equipages, Watermael-Boitsfort, Belgium
	Von Scholz House, 47 Avenue des Faisans, Kraainem, Belgium
	Villa, Route de Modave, Pont-de-Bonne, Belgium
1965	"Louisville" Development, Porte Louise, Brussels (project)
	Design of the *Belgian Architecture* exhibition, Colegio de Arquitectos, Barcelona
	Design of the *4,000 Years of Craftsmanship in Palestine* exhibition, Brussels
1965/	
66	Godet House, 213A rue Haute, Heer-Agimont, Belgium
	La Maison Familiale Primary School, 150 Chaussée Bara, Braine-l'Alleud, Belgium
	Design of the *Cadeaux de Firmes* exhibition, Design Center, Brussels
1966/	
67	University Hospital, Butare, Ruanda

1966/	
68	Technical School, Fontaine-l'Evêque, Belgium (with E. Lambin)
1966/	
70	Government Ministerial Building, Kigali, Ruanda
1967/	
68	Jam Production Works, Gihindamuyaga, Butare, Ruanda
1967/	
69	Toussaint House, 13 Avenue G. Mercator, Wemmel, Belgium
	Le Cheval Brun House (farmhouse conversion), Route de Huy, Tihange, Belgium
	Agricultural Co-operative Administration Center, Nyabisindu, Ruanda
	Crahay House, 11 Avenue de l'Aiglon, Waterloo, Belgium
1967/	
70	Filles de Marie Primary School, rue de Bouvy, La Luvière, Belgium
1968/	
69	"Organ" Shop, 13 rue de la Station, Jemeppe-sur-Meuse, Belgium
	Vandermensbrugghe House, 58 Bruyningstraat, Kortrijk, Belgium
	Church, Biesmeree, Namur, Belgium
1968/	
70	House, 1 Avenue de Beau Feuillage, Kraainem, Belgium
	Dresse House, 47 Warandeberg, Wezembeek, Belgium
1969	Town plan for Barvaux-sur-Ourthe, Belgium
	Parking Garage, rue Hotel des Monnaies, Saint-Gilles, Belgium (project)
	Benedictine Monastery, Gihindamuyaga, Ruanda
1969/	
70	Witte Brug House, Oostduinkerke, Belgium (with J. L. Franchimont)
1970	Iproma School, Namur, Belgium
	Presidential Palace, Kigali, Ruanda
1970/	
75	Master plan for the new capital city of Kimihurura, Ruanda
1970/	
77	Paramedical Faculty Buildings Complex, Catholic University of Louvain, Woluwe, Belgium (partially built)
1974/	
75	Convent for the Dominican Sisters, Ottignies, Belgium
1975	Dominican House, Froidment, Belgium
1978	Sperling House, near Brussels
1978/	
79	Housing development, Cergy-Pontois New Town, near Paris

Publications:

By KROLL: articles—"Le Stand d'Esthétique Industrielle" in *Bouwen en Wonen* (Antwerp), no. 6, 1956; "La Vocation de l'Industrial Designer" in *La Relève* (Brussels), no. 3, 1965; "Réponse Architecturale à une Attitude Non Directive" in *Neuf* (Brussels), no. 8, 1967; "Industrial Design en Grande Bretagne" and "Archigram" in *La Maison* (Brussels), no. 4, 1968; "Reply to Christopher Alexander" in *Architectural Design* (London), no. 7, 1968; "L'Institute de l'Environnement" in *La Maison* (Brussels), no. 3, 1970; "Why I Could Build Woluwe" in *Wonen TA/BK* (Heerlen, Netherlands), June 1977.

On KROLL: book—*La Construction en Belgique 1945–1970* by Geert Bekaert and Francis Strauven, Brussels 1971; articles—"Quelques Réalisations Religieuse de Lucien Kroll" in *Art d'Eglise* (Ottignies, Belgium), July/September 1970; "Portrait de Lucien Kroll" by Christian Hunziker in *L'Architecture d'Aujourd'hui* (Paris), January/February 1976; "Lucien Kroll" in *Art d'Eglise* (Ottignies, Belgium), January/March 1976; "The Anarchitecture of Lucien Kroll" by Francis Strauven in *Architectural Association Quarterly* (London), no. 2, 1976; "Lucien Kroll: Architecture et Participation" by Nicolas Godebski in *Crée* (Paris), December 1976; "The Ideas of Lucien Kroll" in *Architecture* (Paris), April 1977; "Anarchy and Architecture" by Gerald R. Blomeyer in *Bauwelt* (Berlin), 9 December 1977; "Kroll's Krunch" in *The Architects' Journal* (London), 7 June 1978; "Kroll Rocks the Boat" by Joe Holyoak in *Building Design* (London), 30 June 1978; "Lucien Kroll: The Holiday Is Over, Now Order Rules Again" in *Architekt* (Stuttgart), January 1979; "The Ecological Architecture of Lucien Kroll" by Stephanie Williams in *Architectural Review* (London), February 1979.

From the outset of his independent career Lucien Kroll refused to engage in the semantic competition to which many Belgian architects abandon themselves and instead aspired to a mild neo-vernacular described by one critic as "the denial of architecture." His early work seemed to show no sign of "progressiveness;" rather, it involved a modest and constrained use of basic means and materials employed in a natural and apparently haphazard fashion. None of his walls was built entirely of the same material: concrete blocks were mixed with brick of different sizes and colours, rough stone ran into slate—frequently at the discretion of the bricklayer or eventual occupant. Kroll has always favoured materials that live with the weather, that harbour lush growths of moss, lichen and ivy, so that his buildings look as if they have been there forever, absorbed into the landscape. It is Kroll's way of building organically, of trying to create buildings that do not impose themselves on their occupants, buildings that relate to people.

This interest in people informs his 1961/65 housing complex (including his own house and office) in Auderghem, near Brussels: he created a kind of communal dwelling as an experiment in open form, with highly adaptable living/working/playing areas for friends, acquaintances and strangers—all under one roof. The experiment led him to a deeper involvement with "group participation." Kroll even applied group dynamics to the organization of his own office, aiming at a more personal involvement of his assistants in the design process. To achieve his goals, he found that he had to reduce his authority-as-expert as much as possible in order to involve his clients in a kind of neo-anarchist therapy, refusing institutionalized solutions, moving toward self-consciousness and self-determination.

Probably as a result of these experiences, Kroll's descriptions of the conventional products of the Modern Movement are laced with the adjectives of oppression: the administrators who commission designers are fond of "paramilitary models;" the Pruitt-Igoe housing development in St. Louis (and developments like it) are the products of a generation of "somewhat militaristic architects;" the dark glazed windows of contemporary office blocks present a "fascist facade;" programmes call for completely regular, separate rooms "like ruled metric paper;" and facades of reflecting glass are "like the sunglasses of American policemen."

With views so much at variance with those of the Establishment, it is not surprising that, despite all his care for those who will use his buildings, Kroll is not widely popular in Belgium. His reputation may have had something to do with his not having been invited by the academic authorities to participate in the design of Louvain-La Neuve, the new university town near Ottignies. It was at the request of the students that in 1969 Kroll was commissioned to design the medical complex at Woluwe. The authorities probably granted the request thinking that "group dynamics" meant only another of that kind of harmless verbal participation by which conflict is often reduced. Kroll, however, was as good as his reputation: he involved the students in design decisions that normally belong to the architect—including a de-emphasis of the elitism of Henri Montois' original campus master plan. The new complex was designed in such an open, flexible way that internal walls can be built or taken down to give more or less space, sun can come in at the right places, areas can be communally shared or made into self-contained units, all parts have access to outside balconies or terraces, and living quarters can easily be converted into ordinary dwellings and are great fun to be in. Incorporated into the complex is a primary school that was soon occupied by a nearby school that had to be evacuated for underground works: in fact, it seems as if the whole complex could function as a district centre for the adjacent town suburb of Kapellveld.

At first sight the Woluwe complex looks a complete jumble, like the fragments of an old city, the facades a totally disordered collection of brick, glass, grills, balconies, grey tiles, staircases—the sort of "organic disorder" that Kroll had in mind from the beginning. With its intentional promiscuity of quotes (Aalto, Mies, Le Corbusier, Stirling, SITE), the buildings have been characterized as a collage of "war surplus materials. discarded on the battlefield after the defeat of the avant garde." The authorities disliked it so much that in 1977 they dismissed Kroll as architect, and threatened to tear down the buildings. They have already destroyed the planting that was beginning to climb up the walls (Kroll had commissioned Louis Leroy, a Dutch "anarchist" gardener, to make an ecological garden, intertwining itself with the built structures). Ultimately, Woluwe remains a utopian dream to the extent that the complete participation process has had to remain imaginary—though, whereas classical utopia was always the exclusive work of one enlightened man, this utopia did grow from the involvement of many people.

But that Kroll can indeed bring about a successful ecological marriage between the old and the new, between landscape and "organic" architecture, is illustrated by his Dominican House at Froidment. One occupant, despite some reservations about the materials and details of the building, said, "When we moved in, we felt at home immediately. He did exactly what we wanted—in his completely original way."

—Colin Naylor

KUMP, Ernest J(oseph).
American. Born in Bakersfield, California, 29 December 1911. Educated at the University of California, Berkeley, 1928–32, B.A. 1932; Harvard University, Cambridge, Massachusetts, 1932–33, M.Arch. 1933. Married Josephine Clark Miller in 1934; children: Peter Clark and Mondi. Principal, Ernest J. Kump Associates, Bakersfield, Fresno, and San Francisco, California, 1934–45, and Palo Alto, California, 1945–75. Founder, Tekkto Systems Research, New York, 1964–66, Palo Alto, California, 1968–76, and London, since 1977. Visiting Lecturer, Harvard University, 1945, University of Michigan, Ann Arbor, 1945, University of Texas at Austin, 1946, and University of Melbourne, 1948; Adjunct Professor and Chairman of Advanced Research, 1961, and Professor of Architecture and Chairman of Advanced Research and Educational Planning, 1962, Columbia University, New York. National Chairman for School Buildings, American Institute of Architects, 1948–49. Exhibitions: Museum of Modern Art, New York, 1943; *World's Fair*, Brussels, 1958; *World's Fair*, Seattle, 1962; Museum of

Lucien Kroll: Paramedical Faculty Buildings Complex, Catholic University of Louvain, Woluwe, Belgium, 1970–77

Ernest J. Kump: Foothill College, Los Altos Hills, California, 1962

Modern Art, New York, 1965. Recipient: United States Navy Meritorious Civilian Service Emblem, 1944; *Progressive Architecture* Award, 1947, 1948, 1949, 1957, 1958, 1960, Award of Merit, 1954, Honor Award, 1955, and Architectural Firm Award, 1970, American Institute of Architects. Fellow, American Institute of Architects, 1956. Fellow, Royal Society of Arts, London, 1950. Address: Tekkto Systems Research Ltd., 6–7 Grosvenor Place, London S.W.1, England.

Works:

1932/
36   Memorial Auditorium, Fresno and O Streets, Fresno, California (with others)
1933   United States Post Office, Madera, California
1933/
35   Tulare County Welfare Building, 210 North Court, Visalia, California
1936   Reedley Junior College, California
School Administration Building, Fresno, California (with others)
1937/
39   Fowler Elementary School, California
1937/
41   School complex, Shafter, California
1938   Development plan for the Greeley Elementary School District, Bakersfield, California
Sill Property Company Office and Store, Bakersfield, California
El Tejon Hotel, Bakersfield, California
Tollhouse High School, California
Dinuba Joint Union College, California
1938/
39   School complex, Patterson, California
1938/
41   School complex, Wasco, California
1939   Gymnasium, Raymond, California
Tollhouse High School classroom addition, California
Elementary school, Ducor, California
Sierra Vista Elementary School, Mineral King and Dollner Streets, Visalia, California
1939/
40   School complex, Taft, California
1939/
49   Carmel High School, California

1940   United States Army Engine Repair and Storage Building, McClellan Field, Sacramento, California
Edison Technical High School, Fresno, California
Sierra Union High School, 4330 East Garland, Fresno, California
School Administration Building, Tranquillity, California
City Hall, Fresno, California
Commercial building, Chester and 18th Streets, Bakersfield, California
Acalanes High School, Lafayette, California
Exeter Union High School, 820 San Juan, Exeter, California
1941   Defense Housing School and Community Center, Vallejo, California
Carmel Woods School, Carmel, California
Housing, San Diego
United States Army Sierra Ordnance Depot, Lassen County, California
Kern Mutual Telephone Company Building, Maricopa, California
1942   Chabot Acres (housing development), Vallejo, California
Runways, hangars and living quarters for the United States Navy at Oakland Municipal Airport, California
Chabot Terrace School and Community Center, Vallejo, California
1943   Alameda Unified School and Community Center, California
Dover Street School, San Pablo, California
1944   Development plan for the Antioch/Live Oak Unified School District, California
Elementary school, Albany, California
White Oaks School, San Carlos, California (with additions, 1948, 1953)
United States Army Base Engineers Maintenance Building, Suisun, California
United States Army Test and Storage Building, McClellan Field, Sacramento, California
1944/
45   School complex, St. Helena, California
1945   Development plan for the Tracy Union High School District, California
Development plan for the Orinda Union Elementary School District, California
Healey and Popovich Store and Warehouse, Fresno, California

United States Navy Ordnance and Optical Shop Building, San Francisco Naval Shipyard
California Packing Corporation Plant and Warehouse, San Francisco
"Pre-Bilt" Model House, San Anselmo, California
1945/
50   Hoover Elementary School, Redwood City, California
Lincoln Elementary School, Redwood City, California
John Gill School, Redwood City, California
Beresford Park School, San Mateo, California
Borel School, San Mateo, California
College Park School, San Mateo, California
George W. Hall School, San Mateo, California
Laurel Elementary School, San Mateo, California
Lawrence School, San Mateo, California
Shoreview School, San Mateo, California
Sunnybrae School, San Mateo, California
1946   School complex, Santa Clara, California
John Marsh Elementary School, Antioch, California
Tracy High School, California
High school, Antioch, California
Merced Passenger Terminals, Modesto, California
Los Lomitos Elementary School, Atherton, California
San Jose High School, California
Broadway Elementary School, San Jose, California
Asilomar Buildings, Pacific Grove, California
YMCA Conference and Guest Buildings, Asiolmar, California
1946/
50   Barstow Union High School, California
Las Lomas High School, Walnut Creek, California
1947   Locker Building, San Mateo, California
Line Street Elementary School, Hollister, California
Aquatic Center, Richland, California
Plan for the long-range building program of San Bernardino City Elementary School District, California
Plan for the long-range building program of the Alameda Unified School District, California
1948   Field House, Tamalpais High School, Larkspur, California
Moorpark School, Campbell, California
San Tomas School, Campbell, California
Eliot School, Gilroy, California
Civic Center, Phoenix, Arizona (project)
1949   Laureola School, San Carlos, California
Richland School, Hanford, Washington (project)
Michele and Pfeffer Shop, San Francisco
1950   Encinal High School, Alameda, California
1950/
53   Franklin Elementary School, Berkeley, California
Jefferson Elementary School, Berkeley, California
1950/
56   North School Complex, Hillsborough, California
1951   Bessie Carmichael School, San Francisco
Richland School, Shafter, California
Christ Episcopal Church additions, Los Altos, California
1951/
57   Rickey's Studio Inn, Palo Alto, California
1952   San Jose High School, California (with addition, 1961)
University Village Houses, Redwood City, California
1953   Columbus Park Elementary School, San Francisco

1955	Portable classrooms, Alameda, California
	District plan for the Crestmoor Site, San Bruno, California
	Plan for the long-range building program of the San Bruno Park School District, California
	Vernon J. Pick Laboratory, Saratoga, California
1955/ 56	Rollingwood School, San Bruno, California
	New classrooms for the Edgemont School, San Bruno, California
	New classrooms for the Parkside School, San Bruno, California
	Herbert Hoover Junior High School, San Francisco
1956	Parking study for Palo Alto, California
1957	Halfway House Recreation Center, Hillsborough, California
	Woodside High School, Atherton, California
1958	United States Navy and Air Force Housing at Zaragoza and Madrid, Spain
	Kump Office Building, Lytton Square, Palo Alto, California
	Franklin School additions, Berkeley, California
	Jefferson School additions, Berkeley, California
1959	Crestmoor Elementary School, San Bruno, California
	Northbrae Elementary School additions, San Bruno, California
	Eldorado Country Club, Palm Desert, California
	United States Embassy and Staff Residence, Seoul, Korea
1959/ 65	William H. Crocker Jr. High School, Hillsborough, California
1960	Civic Center, Los Altos, California
	United States Coast Guard Indoor Training Pool, Alameda, California
	Youth Center, Los Altos, California
	Pioneer Senior High School, San Jose, California
	Water Treatment Plant, Santa Cruz, California
	John Muir School, San Bruno, California
1961	Master plan for the American University, Beirut
	Carl Sandburg School, San Bruno, California
	Stowell Manor Shopping Center, Santa Maria, California
	Chester F. Awalt High School, Mountain View, California
1962	Carmel Valley Junior High School, Carmel, California
	All Saints Church, Watsonville, California
	San Lorenzo Plaza Redevelopment, Santa Cruz, California
	Conference and Commercial Building, Palo Alto, California
	Foothill College, Los Altos Hills, California (with others)
	Garden Hotel, Oxnard, California
1962/ 64	Santa Clara County Superior Court Building, San Jose, California
1964	California Water Service Company, Civic Center, San Jose, California
1965	Cabrillo College, Aptos, California (with others)
	Henry M. Gunn High School, Palo Alto, California
	Lucie Stearn Hall, Mills College, Oakland, California
	Central Service Building, University of California at Santa Cruz
1966	Civic Center, Concord, California
	Isabella Cowell Health Center, Mills College, Oakland, California
1967	Crown College, University of California at Santa Cruz

1968	DeAnza College, Cupertino, California (with others)
1971	Union Bank, 400 University, Palo Alto, California
	Walter H. Haas Pavilion, Mills College, Oakland, California
1972	Student Union, San Jose State College, California
1973	San Joaquin Delta College, Stockton, California
1978	Bendigo College of Advanced Education, Victoria, Australia (as consultant architect)

Publications:

By KUMP: book—*A New Architecture for Man,* Palo Alto, California 1957; article—"Architecture for the College Campus" in *AIA Journal* (Washington, D.C.), March 1963.

On KUMP: articles—"Pioneer School" in *Architectural Forum* (New York), October 1949; "Design" in *Architectural Forum* (New York), October 1953; "Finger-Plan School Refined" in *Architectural Forum* (New York), October 1955; "Design Notes" in *Architectural Forum* (New York), September 1956; "Quality of School Design" in *Architectural Record* (New York), April 1957; "The Space Module School" in *Architectural Forum* (New York), December 1957; "Colleges for the Community" in *Architectural Forum* (New York), November 1959; "Architect Ernest Kump" by Georgia Hesse in the *San Francisco Examiner,* 8 April 1962; "An Environmental Grid" in *Architectural Forum* (New York), August 1962; "Education: New Two-Year Colleges" in *Time* (New York), 5 March 1965; "Bendigo College of Advanced Education" by Nick Walter in *Architecture in Australia* (Sydney), September 1978.

*

Architecture, to be relevant in today's world, requires a whole new philosophy—an architecture without buildings!

This means essentially that architecture must be intrinsically a total dynamic and living environmental system, in harmony with nature.

It must immediately cease to continue to be merely an art or method for the design and construction of inert static structures known as buildings. As the result of the relentless growth of this false concept of architecture, our environment in its present state bears witness to the unconscionable degree of pollution and soulless decadence in which today's society finds itself immersed.

Building Architecture is dead. This is born out by the fact that one idea that is emphasized and is also a recurring theme in the world of science is that reality in the universe can only be understood as being intrinsically dynamic in terms of flow and movement, change and transformation, and that the whole of nature is engaged in endless motion and activity resulting in a constant state of ever-becoming form. So must architecture be!

Without this vision a hostile, soulless, environmental wasteland will be the ultimate destiny of humanity—and in it "the people will perish."

—Ernest J. Kump

*

Foothill College, in the suburbs of San Francisco, is Ernest J. Kump's masterpiece. It solved a problem in California architecture, that of finding a form for larger institutional suburban buildings that would match the comfortable casualness of the redwood and glass suburban house.

Foothill College provided an immediately successful solution. It did it by a planning method that broke down a huge campus into a large number of smaller—but still clearly institutional rather than residential size—buildings. This method had been used before, but Kump introduced a crucial formal innovation in roof form that is reminiscent of the

traditional shapes of rural California redwood farm structures. The combined hip and flat roof was attractive in itself, and the flat top allowed Kump to cover a large space with a wide eave pitched roof that did not need to go so high as to cause a problem of both cost and appearance. And the flat roof served as a perfect concealment area within which the elaborate mechanical system now required by a large public building could be placed.

The romantic imagery of Foothill came as a surprise, for prior to its design Kump had been known and respected for his thoughtful rationalist approach to school design. Kump had investigated and expounded the merits of modular design and construction; in his school work he evolved a refined and economical system of construction using available materials and practices, which he then developed into a space module—a wide span supermodule within which a variety of plans could be accommodated (it formed the basis of the planning of Foothill). Kump also worked on, and promoted, technological inventions such as an integrated ceiling system, and he experimented with and used advanced methods of communication and coordination in the construction document process long before such ideas became a matter of more general professional concern.

Foothill College had instant popular appear, and the Kump office was flooded with commissions for large-scale projects. None succeeded in equalling the strength and conviction of the original, though nearby DeAnza College comes close. Unfortunately, clients saw and loved only the romantic softness of the Foothill image: later projects of the firm seemed to lose the firm rationality upon which Foothill was based and which gave it the timeless quality of great architecture.

All of Kump's work has an old-fashioned respect for materials and a delight in using them as a small scale design element. Although the success of Foothill almost forced the office into an endless repetition of wood gamesmanship, Kump has, over the years, worked intelligently and sensitively in steel and concrete. His office was also old-fashioned in its management style. California offices are populated not only by Kump's ex-employees but also by his ex-partners. He was known to arrive in the morning and fire, sack or dismiss his entire staff. He kept a castle on the Rhine, no small feat for a California-based tycoon. But he created an environment in which first class design work was done for education, an institutional field notable, in architecture, for its mediocrity and compromise.

—Christopher Arnold

KUROKAWA, Kisho.

Japanese. Born in Aichi Prefecture, 8 April 1934. Educated at Kyoto University, Department of Architecture, B.Arch. 1957; Tokyo University, Department of Architecture, under Kenzo Tange, M.Arch. 1959, D.Arch. 1964. Married Sumie Tsuchiya in 1959; children: Kako and Mikio. Founder, Kisho Kurokawa and Associates, Tokyo, 1962–68. Since 1968, President, Kisho Kurokawa, Architect, and Associates, Tokyo. Principal, Institute for Social Engineering Inc., Tokyo, since 1969; President, Urban Design Consultants Inc., Tokyo, since 1969; Adviser to the Japanese National Railways, since 1970; Analyst for the Japan Broadcasting Corporation, since 1974. Member, Metabolist Group, from 1960. Exhibitions: World Design Conference, Tokyo, 1960; *Metabolism,* Tokyo, 1962; *Team Ten,* Urbino, Italy,

Kisho Kurokawa: Sony Tower, Osaka, 1976

1964; *Contemporary Japanese Architecture,* Florence, 1968; *Capsule Architecture,* Rome, 1973. Recipient: Takamura Kotaro Design Prize, 1965; First Prize, International Competition for Pilot Low-Cost Housing in Peru, 1969; First Prize, International TANU Headquarters Competition, Tanzania, 1972; Silver Prize and Gold Prize, Japan Sign Design Association, 1977; Building Contractors Society Prize, 1977; Mainichi Art Award, 1978. Address: Kisho Kurokawa, Architect, and Associates, Aoyama Building 11F, 1–2–3 Kita-Aoyama, Minato-ku, Tokyo, Japan.

Works:

1962   Mass-Production Apartments (project)
       Nishijin Labor Center, Kyoto
1963   Shiga Residence, Tokyo
1964   Head Office and Main Factory, Takeda Riken
       Company, Yamagata Prefecture, Japan
       Nitto Food Company Factory, Yamaguchi
       Prefecture, Japan
1965   Yoshimatsu Residence, Tokyo
       Rest Station, National Children's Land,
       Kanagawa Prefecture, Japan
       Hans Christian Andersen Memorial Museum, Kanagawa Prefecture, Japan
1966   Irako Vacation Village, Aichi Prefecture,
       Japan
1967   Irako Vacation Village extension, Aichi Prefecture, Japan
       City Hall, Sagae, Japan
       Resort center, Yamagata Prefecture, Japan
1968   Goshikidai Vacation Village Lodge,
       Yamagata Prefecture, Japan
       Space Capsule Discotheque, Tokyo
1969   Takeda Riken Factory, Gyoda, Japan
       Service area, Tokyo-Nagoya Highway, Kanagawa Prefecture, Japan
       Otome Toge Drive-In Restaurant, Hakone,
       Japan
1970   Odakyu Restaurant in Ashinoko, Hakone,
       Japan
       Capsule House at the Celestial Theme Pavilion, *Expo '70,* Osaka
       Toshiba IHI Pavilion, *Expo '70,* Osaka
       Takara Group Pavilion, *Expo '70,* Osaka
1971   Omori Keisi Department Store, Omori,
       Japan
       City Hall, Sakura, Japan
       Agricultural Experimental Station, Yamanashi Prefecture, Japan
       Long Beach Bowl, Oiso, Japan
1972   Leisure Capsule LC-30X
       Employees' Dormitory, Prince Hotel, Sapporo, Japan
       Capsule House K, Karuizawa, Japan
       Prince Hotel, Sapporo, Japan
       Nakagin Capsule Tower Building, Tokyo
1973   Sanpo Construction Company Head Office,
       Tokyo
       Prince Hotel, Shimoda, Japan
       Prince Hotel, Karuizawa, Japan
       Club House, Guam
1974   Koito Office Building, Tokyo
       Hotel White Town, Gunma Prefecture, Japan
       Azabu no. 1 Town House, Tokyo
       Big Box Seibu recreation center, Tokyo
1975   Conference City, Abu Dhabi, United Arab
       Emirates
       City Hall, Waki Cho, Japan
       Daido Mutual Life Insurance Building, Sapporo, Japan
       Hotel New Otani, Tottori, Japan
       Fukuoka Bank Head Office, Fukuoka, Japan
1976   Wildlife Protection Center, Yamanashi Prefecture, Japan
       Astronomical Observation Building and
       Guest Houses, Tadeshina Society Club,
       Tadeshina, Japan
       Aoyama Bell Commons (multi-use plaza),
                          Tokyo
                          Hotel New Otani, Saga, Japan

       Sony Tower, Osaka
1977   Wataya Villa Annex, Saga Prefecture, Japan
       Cottage on Mt. Kitadake, Yamanashi Prefecture, Japan
       Wacoal Building, Tokyo
       Sakuradai Branch Office, Tokai Bank, Tokyo
       Peace Memorial, Gamagori, Japan
       Japanese Red Cross Society Head Office,
       Tokyo
       Ishikawa Cultural Center, Kanazawa, Japan
       National Ethnology Museum, Osaka

Publications:

By KUROKAWA: books—*Metabolism '60,* with others, Tokyo 1960; *Prefabricated Houses,* with Noboru Kawazoe, Tokyo 1964; *Urban Design,* Tokyo 1965; *Action Architecture,* Tokyo 1967; *Homo Movense,* Tokyo 1969; translation into Japanese of *The Death and Life of Great American Cities* by Jane Jacobs, Tokyo 1969; *Kisho Kurokawa: Architectural Creation,* Tokyo 1969; *Works of Kisho Kurokawa,* Tokyo 1970; *The Creation of Contemporary Architecture,* Tokyo 1971; *Lectures in Urban Sociology: Modern Society,* co-author, Tokyo 1972; *The Future of Informative Archipelago—Japan,* Tokyo 1972; *The Concept of Metabolism,* Tokyo 1972; *Dialogue for Futurology,* Tokyo 1972; *Introduction to Urbanology,* Tokyo 1973; *The World of Kisho Kurokawa,* Tokyo 1975; *Metabolism in Architecture,* London and New York 1977; *Concept of Cities,* Tokyo 1977; *Concept of Space,* Tokyo 1977; *Culture of Gray,* Tokyo 1977; articles—"The Japanese Housing Problem: A Personal View" in *The Planner* (London), February 1975; "En-Space" in *Bauen und Wohnen* (Zurich), December 1975; "Sony Tower" in *The Japan Architect* (Tokyo), November 1976; "Head Office of the Japan Red Cross Society," with Yasuhiko Nagata, in *The Japan Architect* (Tokyo), September 1977; "Rikyu Gray" in *The Japan Architect* (Tokyo), January 1978; "National Museum of Ethnology" in *The Japan Architect* (Tokyo), April 1978.

On KUROKAWA: book—*Beyond Metabolism: The New Japanese Architecture* by Michael Franklin Ross, New York 1978; articles—"Kurokawa" by Robert Williams in *Building Design* (London), 2 November 1973; "Kurokawa" by Yasuo Uesaka in *Architecture Plus* (New York), January/February 1974; "Team 10 at Royaumont" by Alison Smithson in *Architectural Design* (London), November 1975; "The Enigma of Kurokawa" by Charles Jencks in *Architectural Review* (London), March 1976; "Kurokawa and Metabolism" by Agnoldomenico Pica in *Domus* (Milan), December 1977; "Kisho Kurokawa" by Claude Lévi-Strauss in special issue of *Space Design* (Tokyo), April 1978; "Kumamoto City Museum" in *Building Design* (London), 19 May 1978.

*   *   *

I have been engaging in many creative activities based upon the theory of "Metabolism" which I developed as an architectural movement in the 1960's. This theory of metabolism is best explained in my book *Metabolism in Architecture.* The following summarizes the major points that I stressed in my book:
1) I consider architecture as part of a space opened to society, rather than as a work of art.
2) I have put into my architecture the elements of growth and change.
3) Architecture should not be a world to be thought of as an end in itself. It should be considered as a theatre stage setting where the leading actors are the people, and to dramatically direct the dialogue between these people and space is the technique of designing.
4) Since architecture is closely connected to the culture of each country, its international quality should be gained by discovering a theory to univer-

salize this cultural characteristic.
5) By abolishing the philosophy of dualism which sees the individual in contrast to society, the part to the whole, art against technology, I intend to postulate a new philosophy—the philosophy of co-existence. This philosophy considers these elements in unification with the whole of what's going on.
—Kisho Kurokawa

Kisho Kurokawa is truly one of the boy-wonders of modern Japanese architecture. Born in Nagoya in 1934, at twenty-six he was the youngest and most precocious member of the original Metabolist Group. In their futurist manifesto, *Metabolism 1960,* the metabolists called for a new method of urban structuring using large interlocking megastructures. From his experience in Kenzo Tange's office, working on the Plan for Tokyo 1960, Kurokawa evolved his own Helix City concept. This extraordinary beginning has been followed by an unending series of innovative and intriguing projects.

Kurokawa's interest in new technology has had various repercussions. He visited the Soviet Union in the early sixties and wrote a book on Soviet prefab systems. He captured the imagination of the international architectural community with his high-tech pavilions at *Expo '70,* including the Capsule House at the Celestial Theme Pavilion and the Takara Beautillion. Both projects implied an architecture of tomorrow that would be composed of plug-in modules and clip-on capsules suspended from a structural space-frame.

The hopes inherent in the metabolist dream were not simple, and converting them to reality was equally difficult, but Kurokawa persevered and achieved the Nakagin Capsule Building in 1972. The implications of the capsules suspended from the central towers were awe inspiring. Perhaps the future had finally arrived. Kurokawa continued to pursue the capsule concept whenever it seemed to be appropriate as in the LC-30X Leisure Capsule, the Sony Tower in Osaka completed in 1976, and in his own country retreat at Karuizawa. In the final analysis the capsule concept was limited and had only a finite number of intelligent applications.

As an alternative to the purity of the Metabolist manifesto, Kurokawa has been developing a concept which is parallel to and complements his high-tech imagery. This is the traditional Japanese concept of "en" or in-between space. Every Japanese home has a *genkan* or foyer as a transition zone, and some more elaborate buildings have the *engawa* or veranda which is an extension of the interior space while also serving as an introduction to the outdoor space. Kurokawa has attempted to incorporate this concept in his modern architecture. It is most apparent in the Head Office of the Fukuoka Bank, the National Ethnology Museum, and the Waki-Cho City Hall. The Fukuoka Bank is clearly indebted to the Ford Foundation Building by Kevin Roche and John Dinkeloo, and Kurokawa admits that he was influenced by the design but that he has extended the concept and adapted it to the Japanese condition. The *en*-space is part interior and part exterior and forms one layer of a series of transition zones in the sequence of spaces.

Kurokawa is himself a multi-dimensional architect who has written nearly twenty books, designed half a dozen new towns and built almost fifty major buildings. He agrees that "some may be puzzled at my work, which sometimes expresses technology and sometimes reflects the tradition of Japanese architecture." However, this combination of the past, the present and the future is the key to understanding Kurokawa's work. He further explains that "my creative practice probes the point of contact between modern architecture and Japanese culture; and it is my pleasure to contribute, if it be but a little, to the world of architecture by presenting a different quality." For this we can all be thankful, for Kurokawa has brought us a variety of work that is stimulating and often beautiful.
—Michael Franklin Ross

LACHERT, Bohdan.

Polish. Born in Moscow, of Polish parents, 13 June 1900. Educated at the Technical University, Warsaw, under Professor Swierczynski, 1920–26, Dip. Arch. 1926. Served in the Polish Cavalry, 1918–20: prisoner of war, 1920–21; served in the Polish Resistance, 1939–45. Married Irene Nowakowska in 1922; children: Krzysztof, Rudolf, and Krystyna; married Maria Ceglinska in 1945. In partnership with Jozef Szanajca, Warsaw, 1926–39; Lecturer, Underground Polytechnic, Warsaw, 1940–44; Chairman of the Planning Department, Polish Rebuilding Bureau, Warsaw, 1944; Chairman of the Architectural Department, Capital Rebuilding Bureau, Warsaw, 1945–48; Chairman and Chief Designer, Muranow District Architectural Office, Warsaw, 1948–52. Since 1952, Chairman of the Architectural Programming Team, Home Office, Warsaw. Assistant Professor, 1926–28, Senior Assistant Professor, 1928–29, Adjunct Professor of Civil Engineering, 1929–37, Assistant Professor of Architecture, 1945–48, Associate Professor, 1948–66, Dean of the Faculty of Architecture, 1950–54, Professor, 1966–70, and since 1970 Professor Emeritus, Technical University, Warsaw. Founder Member, 1926, Chairman of the Warsaw Section, 1937–38, 1948–50, and National Chairman, 1944–45, Polish Architects Association (SARP), Warsaw; Founder Member, Praesens avant-garde group, Warsaw, 1926–39; First Secretary, Polish Workers Party at the Technical University, Warsaw, 1947–48, 1955–61; Member, Scientific Publications Committee, 1950–53, and Central Qualifying Committee, 1953–57, Ministry of Higher Education, Warsaw. Exhibitions: *First Exhibition of Modern Architecture,* Warsaw, 1926; *Architectural Exhibition,* Budapest, 1930; *Constructivism in Poland 1923–1936,* Muzeum Sztuki, Lodz 1973, toured Essen and Otterlo, 1973; *Tendenzen der Zwanziger Jahre,* Berlin, 1977. Collection: Museum of Architecture, Wroclaw. Recipient: Gold ,Medal, with Jozef Szanajca, and Grand Prix, *Exposition Internationale,* Paris, 1937; Golden Cross of Merit, Warsaw, 1946, 1947; State Art Award, Warsaw, 1950; Polish Tenth Anniversary Medal, 1955. Commander, Cross of the Order of Polonia Restituta, Warsaw, 1967. Officier, Légion d'Honneur, Paris, 1946. Address (office): ul. Katowicka 9, 03–932 Warsaw, Poland.

Works:

1924 Mansion House, Ciechanki, Poland
Hydro-Biological Research Station, Lake Wigry, Poland (with Jozef Szanajca)
1927 League of Nations Building, Geneva (competition project; with Jozef Szanajca and S. Hempel)
1928/
31 3 houses, 9–13 Katowicka Street, Warsaw (with Jozef Szanajca)
House, Czeska Street, Warsaw (with Jozef Szanajca)
1929 Officers' Housing Estate, Cracow (competition project; with Jozef Szanajca and W. Winkler)

Tabita Mansion House, Skolimov, Poland (with Jozef Szanajca)
Centrocement Pavilion, *Home Trade Fair,* Poznan (with Jozef Szanajca)
Sanatorium, Ustronie, Poland (competition project; with Jozef Szanajca)
1930 School of Political Science, Warsaw (competition project; with Jozef Szanajca)
1931 Krakowskie Przedmiescie Bank, Lublin, Poland (with Jozef Szanajca)
1932 Hospital, Lagiewniki, Poland (competition project; with Jozef Szanajca)
1932/
35 Rakowiec Housing Estate, Warsaw (with the Praesens Group)
1933 Ministry of Works Building, Warsaw (competition project; with Jozef Szanajca and W. Winkler)
Ministry of Social Security Building, Warsaw (competition project; with Jozef Szanajca)
1934 Private house, Wolozyn, Poland (with Jozef Szanajca)
Saski Place, Warsaw (competition project; with Jozef Szanajca, and S. and B. Brukalski)
Church, Warsaw (competition project; with Jozef Szanajca)
1935 Post Office Building, Stanislawow, Poland (with Jozef Szanajca)
Aircraft Hangar (competition project; with Jozef Szanajca and S. Hempel)
Tuberculosis Sanatorium (competition project; with Jozef Szanajca)
1936 Mokotowski Stadium, Warsaw (competition project; with Jozef Szanajca, and S. and B. Brukalski)
Store, Warsaw (competition project; with Jozef Szanajca)
1937 Polish Pavilion, *World's Fair,* Paris (with Jozef Szanajca)
Polish Radio Building, Warsaw (competition project; with Jozef Szanajca)
Post Office Building, Warsaw (competition project; with Jozef Szanajca)
1938 Pilsudski Bridge, Warsaw (competition project; with Jozef Szanajca, F. Szelagowski, and Z. Wasiutynski)
Post Office Building, Stalowa Wola, Poland (competition project; with Jozef Szanajca)
1939 Polish Pavilion, *World's Fair,* New York (competition project; with Jozef Szanajca)
Hospital, Warsaw (competition project; with Jozef Szanajca)
School of Trade, Wilnok, Poland (competition project; with Jozef Szanajca and W. Winkler)
1945 *Polish Word* Newspaper Building, Warsaw (competition project)
1946 Victory Monument, Warsaw (competition project; with J. Knothe)
1947 Office building, Marszalkowska Street 124, Warsaw
Post Office and Telecommunications Building, Targowa Street, Warsaw

PKO Bank Building, Warsaw (competition project)
1948 Polish Workers Party Central Committee Building, Warsaw (competition project)
National Bank Building, Warsaw (competition project)
1948/
52 Muranow District Development, Warsaw (with the Architectural Office Team)
1949 Soviet Army Cemetery, al. Zwirki i Wigury, Warsaw (with Architectural Office Team)
Ministry of Finance Building, Warsaw (competition project)
Ministry of Security Social Home, Warsaw (competition project)
1950 Triumphal Arch, Lublin, Poland (competition project; with J. Jarnuszkiewicz)
1952 Marszalkowska Street Development, Warsaw (competition project)
1959 Heroes' Monument, Warsaw (competition project; with J. Jarnuszkiewicz)
1963 Old People's Home, Warsaw (competition project; with W. Benedek and J. Lucki)
1968 Apartment building, Kazimierz Dolny, Poland
Town Hall, Amsterdam (competition project; with J. Cianciara and H. Dabrowski)
1968/
70 Low-rise housing development, Pulawy, Poland (with the Architectural Office Team)
1969 Museum of Modern Art, Lodz (competition project)
1976 Railway and Bus Station, Lublin, Poland (competition project; with J. Lubanski and A. Pawlik)
1978 National Library, Tehran (competition project; with W. Szober and J. Lubanski)

Publications:

By LACHERT: articles—"The PKO Building in Warsaw" in *Architektura* (Warsaw), no. 2, 1948; "Experimental Building Methods" and "The Streets of Saka Kepa" in *Architektura* (Warsaw), no. 4, 1948; "Muranow Housing District" in *Architektura* (Warsaw), no. 5, 1948; "Two Currents in Contemporary Polish Architecture" in *The Fight for Building Materials,* Warsaw 1949; "Warsaw Bridges" in *Polish Review* (Warsaw), no. 9, 1949; "Muranow" in *Miasto* (Warsaw), no. 9, 1952; "Reflections and Remarks" in *Przeglad Kulturalny* (Warsaw), no. 4, 1955; "Low-Rise Housing District: An Architect's Thoughts" in *Architektura* (Warsaw), no. 4, 1963; "Friends Who Have Gone" in *Architektura* (Warsaw), no. 10, 1964; "Mieczyslaw Szczuka as an Architect" in *Mieczyslaw Szczuka,* edited by Anatol Stern and Mieczyslaw Berman, Warsaw 1965; "Institutes of Architectural Design" in *Warsaw School of Architecture 1915–1965,* Warsaw 1967; "Style or School" in *Architektura* (Warsaw), no. 7, 1969.

On LACHERT: books—*Gli Elementi dell'Architettura Funzionale* by Alberto Sartoris, Milan 1932, 1940; *Introduzione all'Architettura Moderna* by Al-

Bohdan Lachert: 3 houses, Katowicka Street, Warsaw, 1931

berto Sartoris, Milan 1944; *Warsaw: The Destruction and Rebuilding of the Town* by A. Ciborowski, Warsaw 1964; *Polish Avant-Garde Architecture 1918–1939* by I. Wislocka, Warsaw 1968; *Constructivism in Poland 1923–1936,* exhibition catalogue, Lodz 1973; *William Morris und die Socialen Ursprünge der Modernen Architektur* by E. Goldzamt, Dresden 1976; *Towards the Theory of the Social Housing Unit* by Helena Syrkus, Warsaw 1976; *Atlas of Warsaw Architecture* by J. Chroscicki and A. Rottermund, Warsaw 1977; *Tendenzen der Zwanziger Jahre,* exhibition catalogue, Berlin, 1977.

The designer's vision of an urban development may be considered only in the form of a model which reflects the order of people's existence and the pattern of their movement in the area to be developed.

The designer's vision of an architectural work, evolving as it is designed, is not recognizable a priori.

The vague character of both visions—as I see them—means that, although I took part from the very beginning in the rebuilding of Warsaw after the destruction of the Second World War, I have never had a firm image of the future capital.

The progressive increase in density of urban built form makes one aware of the futility of anticipating its future image.

The creator of an architectural work ought to possess not the intuition for recreating an original vision but an awareness of the need to subordinate himself to an autogenous end product, a design method for generating the shape of an unknown object: the shape that it progressively arrives at will be the result of the accumulation of random and non-random partial decisions taken by the creator.

The later the vision of a work is crystallized in its shape, the more likely it is to become unique and the less it will reflect solutions for analogous subjects that already exist.

The development process of an architectural design has a certain kind of analogy with the development process of a living organism, and only in this way can one see the reason for calling architecture "organic"—formed organically in a creative process but not having the features of an organism.

—Bohdan Lachert

The work of Bohdan Lachert cannot be discussed without paying a tribute to his inseparable prewar partner, Jozef Szanajca, killed by the Nazis in September 1939. Over 17 years of fruitful cooperation,

Lachert and Szanajca produced numerous projects, many of which were constructed; of their competition projects, 51 received awards.

While still at the Warsaw School of Architecture in the 1920's, Lachert's and Szanajca's student works attracted the attention of Szymon Syrkus, and as a result they were both invited to join the newly-formed avant garde group Praesens. Their competition project for the League of Nations Building in Geneva also attracted special attention among the Polish entries. One of the most remarkable of their early projects is the unrealized design for the School of Political Science in Warsaw, characterized by outstanding visual values and extremely modern construction. These young architects were constantly looking for new solutions and experimenting with new building methods and materials. Their house in Katowicka Street in the Saska Kepa district of Warsaw provided a real testing ground for their new ideas. The use of transverse structural walls allowed a horizontal arrangement of windows along the whole facade. The internal division into 3 dwelling units, with differently treated levels, was reflected in the garden elevation. Lachert and Szanajca's houses for the Warsaw Housing Cooperative and their projects for two tuberculosis sanatoria are also among their best designs.

Since the war Lachert has developed his own philosophy for teaching architects, his own "school of thinking." He has been interested in the mystery of creativity. As the physicist Robert Oppenheimer said, "Scientists and artists perpetually live on the edge of mystery, being always surrounded by it."

Lachert is interested in the ontological problems as well as the methodology of architecture, and he regards architectural creativity as worthy of separate study and deeper attention—from four aspects: the juxtaposition of preferences and opinions; the intentional object and visionary image; compromise and the hierarchy of problems; and, lastly, the eidetic determinants of design work. With this rigorous analysis of creativity Lachert undermines the "stability" of architectural opinions, depreciates the authority of the visionary image, and demonstrates his disapproval of compromise solutions. He considers the intellectual qualities of the designer to be of most significance in creative architectural work, for it is the intellect that generates and stores the abstract visions related to the intentional object, the visions motivated by the design subject.

—Teresa Czaplinska-Archer

LAPIDUS, Morris.
American. Born in Odessa, Russia, 25 November 1902; emigrated to the United States, 1903: naturalized, 1914. Educated at New York University, 1921–23; Columbia University School of Architecture, New York, 1923–27, B.Arch. 1927. Married Beatrice Perlman in 1929; sons: Richard and Alan. Junior Draftsman, Warren and Whetmore, New York, 1926–27; Draftsman, Block and Hess, New York, 1927–29; Chief Draftsman, Arthur Weiser, New York, 1929–30; Architect, Ross Frankel, New York, 1930–43. Since 1943, Principal, Morris Lapidus Associates, New York and Miami Beach. Exhibitions: *40 Years of Art and Architecture,* Lowe Gallery, Miami University, 1967; *An Architecture of Joy,* American Federation of Arts, New York, 1970. Recipient: Outstanding Citizen Award, Miami Beach, 1960; Justin P. Alman Award, Wallcovering Wholesalers Association, 1963; Citation for Excellence in Community Architecture, American Institute of Architects, 1965; Outstanding Specifications Award, Gypsum Drywall Contractors, 1968; Variety Children's Hospital Award, 1972; Distinguished Service in the Arts Award, Brandeis University, Waltham, Massachusetts, 1974. Address: Morris Lapidus Associates, 1301 Dade Boulevard, Miami Beach, Florida 33139, U.S.A.

Works:

1943   Martin's Department Store, Brooklyn, New York

1944   A. S. Beck Shoe Corporation, New York

1945   Namm's Department Store, Brooklyn, New York
      Crawford Clothes Shops, various U.S. cities
      Bond's Clothing Stores, various U.S. cities

1946   Ludwig Baumann Furniture Store, Jamaica, New York, and various U.S. cities

1948   Columbia Mills Showroom, Syracuse, New York

1950   Fresh Meadow Country Club, Long Island, New York

1951   Jewish Center, Long Island, New York
      Ainsley Building, Miami
      Biltmore Terrace Hotel, Miami Beach

1952   Laurel in the Pines Hotel, Monticello, New York
      Fontainebleau Hotel, Miami Beach
      Flagler Hotel, Miami Beach
      Hicksville Shopping Center, Long Island, New York
      Trump Village Housing, Brooklyn, New York

1953   Ocean Haven Shopping Center, Brooklyn, New York
      Shopping center, Jackson Heights, New York
      Harrison Country Club, Harrison, New York
      Sand and Surf Hotel, West End, New Jersey
      DiLido Hotel, Miami Beach
      Algiers Hotel, Miami Beach
      Shopping center, Pritchard, Alabama
      Shopping center, Clearwater, Florida
      Shopping center, Bradenton, Florida
      Airport hotel, New York
      Tamarack Lodge, Greenfield Park, New York

1954   Rainbow-Whitestone Beechurst Shopping Center, Whitestone, New York
      Westchester Highway Hotel, Westchester, New York
      St. Augustine Store Center, Florida
      Nautilus Hotel, Atlantic Beach, New Jersey
      Surf Club Hotel, Atlantic Beach, New Jersey
      Eden Roc Hotel, Miami Beach
      Broadway Maintenance Office Building, Long Island City, New York

1955   Bee Hive Department Store, Patchogue, New York
      New Rochelle Country Club, New York
      Kutsher's Country Club, Monticello, New York
      Aruba Hotel, Netherlands Antilles

1956 American Fore Office, Brooklyn, New York
Arawak Hotel, Jamaica
Charlotte Harbor, Punta Gorda, Florida
Federation of State, County, and Municipal Employees Building, New York

1957 The Saxony (apartments), Jamaica, New York
The Highlander (apartments), Jamaica, New York
Shelbourne Hotel, Miami Beach
Voyager Motel, Miami Beach
North Plaza Shopping Center, St. Petersburg, Florida
Biscayne Terrace Hotel, Miami
Mayfair Apartments alterations, Akron, Ohio
Fort Lauderdale Hotel, Broward, Florida
Sea Isle Hotel, Miami Beach
Executive House (apartment hotel), Chicago
Blauvelt Country Club, Nyack, New York
Lincoln Road Mall, Miami Beach
Continental Restaurant, Monmouth, New Jersey
Bay Harbor Isle Apartment Building, Bay Harbor Isle, Florida
Deauville Hotel, Miami Beach
Sunny Isles Shopping Center, Sunny Isles, Florida

1958 Daytona Beach Hotel, Florida
Mayfair Hotel, Palm Beach, Florida
Concord Hotel, Kiamesha Lake, New York
Lucerne Hotel, Miami Beach
Leisure Lake Hotel, Leisure Lake, Florida
Colonial Plaza Hotel, Orlando, Florida
Massena Hotel, Massena, New York
Chicopee Motel, Chicopee, Massachusetts
Brookhaven Laboratory, Long Island, New York
State Office Building, Fall River, Massachusetts
Harrison Hot Springs Hotel, Vancouver

1959 Lobby of the Blair Towers, Washington, D.C.
Lido Beach Hotel, Lido Beach, New York
Golden Triangle Hotel, Norfolk, Virginia
Clason Houses, New York
New Madison Avenue Office Building, New York
Three Chopt Apartments, Norfolk, Virginia
Syracuse Motel, Syracuse, New York
Stadium Lanes Bowling, New York
The Narrows Shore Road Apartments, Brooklyn, New York
Bank of Miami Beach
Condado West Hotel, San Juan, Puerto Rico
Sheraton Motor Inn, New York
Shaare Zion Temple interiors, Brooklyn, New York
Kansas City Motel, Missouri
Ambassador Hotel, Los Angeles
Newark Motel, New Jersey
Motel/Boatel, New Port Richey, Florida
Shelburne Apartment Hotel, Hartford, Connecticut
International Inn, Tampa, Florida
Fresh Meadows Country Club, Lake Success, New York
New Street Building (office building), Newark, New Jersey
Summit Hotel, New York
Australian House, New York
Murphy Houses, Bronx, New York

1960 Ponce de Leon Hotel, San Juan, Puerto Rico
Duck Key Yacht Club and Lanai, Florida
Golden Triangle International Hotel, Norfolk, Virginia
Kipnis Causeway Motel, Tampa, Florida
Indianapolis Motel
International Inn, Washington, D.C.
Loew's Motor Inn, New York
Loew's Midtown Inn, New York
Hebrew Academy, Miami Beach
Sheraton Hotel, New York
Terrace Towers Apartments, Belle Isle, Florida

Meridian Office Building, Miami Beach
Sterling Gardens Lodge, Tuxedo, New York

1961 Crescent Park (housing development), East Orange, New Jersey
Skyline Motel, Washington, D.C.
Temple Beth Tfiloh, Baltimore
Arlington Office Building, Virginia
Cadman Plaza (housing development), Brooklyn, New York
Richmond Motel, Virginia
White Plains Motel, New York

1962 Kings Bay Yacht Club, Miami
South Harrison Apartments, East Orange, New Jersey
Variety Children's Hospital, Miami
1800 G Street (office building), Washington, D.C.
Fairfield Towers, Brooklyn, New York
Concordia Gardens (apartments), San Juan, Puerto Rico
San Patricio Apartments, San Juan, Puerto Rico
Bay Towers (office building), Miami
Horizon House (apartments), San Juan, Puerto Rico
Professional Staff Apartments, Baltimore

1963 Miramar Towers, San Juan, Puerto Rico
Lobby of Clyde Hall, Brooklyn, New York
Lobby of Ocean Terrace, Brooklyn, New York
Skylake Gardens (apartments), Miami
Grossinger's Hotel, Grossinger, New York
Trump Village Shopping Center, Brooklyn, New York

1965 El San Juan, San Juan, Puerto Rico
Metairie Avenue Apartments, New Orleans
Seacoast Towers East (apartments), Miami Beach
El Conquistador (hotel), San Juan, Puerto Rico
North Meeting Room, Seacoast Towers, Miami Beach

Morris Lapidus: Fontainebleau Hotel, Miami Beach, 1952

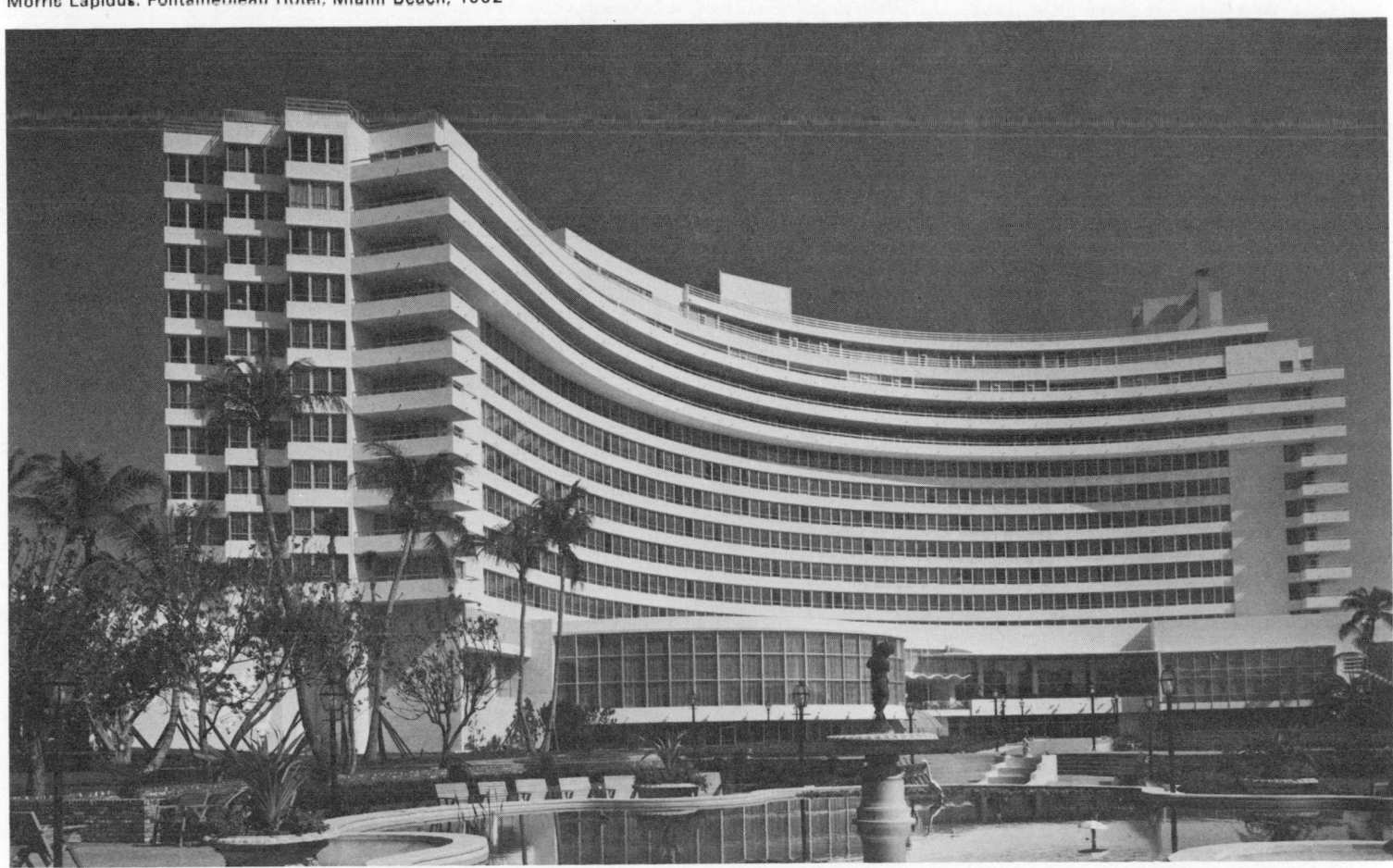

Park Towers (apartments), New Orleans

Fairview Country Club, Greenwich, Connecticut

1966 Paradise Island Hotel, Bahamas

Hilton Hotel, Macon, Georgia

Jr. Chamber International Building, Miami Beach

Skylake Shopping Center, Miami

Municipal Swimming Pool, Brooklyn, New York

Fire Station, Miami Beach

Quality Courts Inc., Memphis, Tennessee

1967 Medical Office Building, Bay Harbor Islands, Florida

Americana of New York, New York

Belle Isle Apartments, Miami Beach

Portman Square Hotel, London

Oceanside Plaza (apartments), Miami Beach

Kensington Apartments, Jade Beach, Florida

Americana Hotel, San Juan, Puerto Rico

Mahoe Bay Hotel, St. Maarten's Isle, West Indies

Penn Wortman Apartments, Brooklyn, New York

1968 Parker Towers (apartments), Hallandale, Florida

Parker Plaza (apartments), Hallandale, Florida

Americana Hotel, Bal Harbour, Miami Beach

Regency Tower Apartments, Miami Beach

Crystal House, Miami Beach

Royal Coast Apartments, Pompano Beach, Florida

Arlen Beach Apartments, Miami Beach

Greater Miami Jewish Federation Office Building, Miami

Lauderdale Seasons Apartments, Fort Lauderdale, Florida

Great Neck Office Building, Great Neck, New York

1969 17 Battery Place (office building), New York

Surfside Royale Apartments, Surfside, Florida

1970 Second National Bank, North Miami

Jacksonville Skycenter (hotel/motel), Jacksonville, Florida

1971 555 Griffin Square (office building), Dallas

Trelawny Beach Hotel, New Falmouth, Jamaica

Rivergate Office Building, Miami

Villa Dorada Complex, Miami

Holiday Springs Complex (housing), Margate, Florida

Bonavista Hi-Rise, Miami

Maurice Gusman Concert Hall, Coral Gables, Florida

Blackstone Office Building, Jacksonville, Florida

Bonavida Hi-Rise, Miami

1122 Connecticut Avenue (office building), Washington, D.C.

1972 Arlen House East (apartments), Miami Beach

Coronado Condominiums, Miami

Office Building, New York Avenue at 13th Street, Washington, D.C.

Citizens Federal Savings and Loan Building, Miami

Oceans Two (apartments), Daytona Beach, Florida

Oceans Three, Five, Seven (apartments), Daytona Beach, Florida

1973 Bal Harbour 101 (apartments), Bal Harbour, Florida

Copa City Office Building, Miami Beach

Theatre of the Performing Arts, Miami Beach

Flamenco (apartments), Miami

South Shore Community Center, Miami Beach

1975 *TSS Carnivala* cruise ship, Dodge Island, Florida

TSS Mardi Gras cruise ship, Dodge Island, Florida

Carnival Cruise Lines Terminal Building, Dodge Island, Florida

1976 Ogun State Hotel, Abeokuta, Nigeria

Community College, Key West, Florida (with Carr Smith)

1977 Nueva Casa (apartments), Miami

1978 Grandview at Emerald Hills (apartments), Hollywood, Florida

Lausanne (apartments), Naples, Florida

Publications:

By LAPIDUS: books—*Architecture: A Profession and a Business,* New York 1967; *Time Saver Standards: Hotel Design,* New York 1973; *An Architecture of Joy,* Miami 1979; articles—"Planning Today for the Store of Tomorrow" in *Chain Store Age* (New York), 1944; "Good Architecture Is Good Business" in *Institutions Magazine* (Chicago), 1960; "A Quest for Emotion in Architecture" in *AIA Journal* (Washington, D.C.), 1961; "Living Space in Architecture" in *AIA Journal* (Washington, D.C.), 1962.

On LAPIDUS: books—*Design for Modern Merchandising* by Caleb Horbostel, New York 1945; *The Specialty Shop* by Jose Fernandez, New York 1950; *Hotels and Motor Hotels* by Henry End, New York 1963; *Hotel Planning and Management* by E. A. Braben, New York 1965; *Hotel Restaurant and Business* by Donald E. Lundberg, Chicago 1970. *Conversations with Architects,* edited by John W. Cook and Heinrich Klotz, New York 1973.

During most of my architectural practice I have been known as a Controversial Architect. The controversy began when I made a decision that I was not going to follow the precepts set down by Walter Gropius and Mies van der Rohe of the German Bauhaus. I felt that what this school and these architects were advocating was a cold clinical architecture that lacked an appeal which I felt architecture should always have. I followed my own theories, namely that architecture must first of all solve the problems presented by each project and, more important, that each project should have popular appeal. My work has been pragmatic and eclectic. In 1967, Dr. A. L. Freundlic, the present Dean of Art at Syracuse University, said that "Lapidus is an architect by training, but a mob psychologist through experience. He balances architectural forms and textures as units of design with what will attract public attention and what is, therefore, a sound financial return for the investor. He combines showmanship and shape with dramatic texture and lighting to achieve an effect which seems desirable to the average American. Where a Gropius might seek for elegance through a sparsity of materials and linear elements, Lapidus strives for a joyful feeling of overabundance sometimes referred to as an overspilling of the cornucopia of goodies."

Especially in hotels and to a lesser degree in other types of buildings, I employed all of the elements that Dr. Freundlic speaks of. When my first major hotel, the Fontainebleau in Miami Beach, was completed, it became instantly famous, but it also gave rise to some very acrimonious criticism by some architects and some critics; they felt that I had gone too far. Now, in 1979, I find that I am in rather constant demand as a lecturer, because the younger generations of architects, who have embarked on what is called "post-modernism" in architecture, see things in my work which they seem to relate to.

My basic theory is based on the fact that in earliest pre-historic time primitive man sought to adorn his cave with phenomenally beautiful wall paintings and to adorn himself with shells, feathers and flowers. The basic human instinct (the love of adornment) is a part of our genes and has manifested itself throughout history up to the present time. It was only during the period from 1930 until about 1975 that we tried to forget those basic human instincts. Now we are coming back to them. Our architecture of today—or "post-modernism"—reflects a desire to adorn our buildings and so plan and shape them that once again we are satisfying man's inborn instinct—which the Bauhaus halted but which has become only a passing phase in the history of architecture.

—Morris Lapidus

"My convictions are that good architecture and good profit are both possible, if we maintain a happy balance between convictions and compromise." This sentence, from Morris Lapidus' major written work *Architecture: A Profession and a Business* serves as an excellent summary of his design philosophy. Lapidus' work seems to be a consistent compromise between strivings for what he believes to be design excellence on the one hand ("aesthetics") and what are the requirements for attracting large and profitable commissions on the other ("business").

The working out of these compromises in physical form results in sacral embodiments of the complex and contradictory elements that characterized the high point of American optimism about the possibility of combining Power, Profit, and Fun. The Trinity of Power, Profit and Fun has perhaps never been more eloquently worshipped than in Lapidus' justly famous hotels such as the Fontainebleau (Miami Beach), and the New York or Bal Harbour Americana.

Curving the slab of the Fontainebleau was one of those master strokes that looks simple and logical in retrospect but was imaginative and daring in its time. Here, contemporary design dogma would have demanded the power and honesty of a straight building; Good Business might have called for Rumple, Bieder, or some other Meyer—the compromise put fun and profit into the power and honesty of post World War II aesthetics. The interiors of the Fontainebleau in fact betray the same compromise, although this may be difficult to see for those who are simply struck by the opulence and vulgarity of its greedy profit seeking.

The New York Americana transported Miami Beach to Sixth Avenue just as the Fontainebleau had previously transported Sixth Avenue to Miami. That is, Lapidus' approach paved the way for the penetration of the urban form into the resort, and vice versa, an approach which has finally come to fruition in Portman's work in this decade. This interpenetration of megastructure with beach, and resort ambiance with Manhattan, is a kind of ultimate celebration of human ability to dominate and supplant nature, exact a profit from its contemplation, and have fun doing it.

Both the Fontainebleau and the New York Americana share a strong emphasis on the horizontal linearity of the multiple storeys. It is almost as if the high-rise profitable verticality were once again being compromised with the humanistic values of equality, visual access, and physical groundedness. The lower property values at Bal Harbour gave Lapidus the opportunity to accent the horizontal integration to an extreme. The high-rise human warehouse is tucked behind the beach-level plaza/piazza and meeting rooms almost as an afterthought to the profit motive. The move from here to the 1970's Portman indoor piazza becomes simple and logical.

The architecture of compromise is perhaps a more valid reflection on contemporary existence than the various purisms experimented with by less frankly commercial designers. In this respect, the work of Lapidus, master compromiser, has a validity and timelessness that architects with seemingly higher aspirations might well envy.

—Joseph B. Juhasz

LAPRADE, Albert.

French. Born in Buzançais, Indre, 29 November 1883. Educated at the Lycée de Chateauroux, Indre, 1894–1900; Ecole des Beaux-Arts, Paris, 1903–1910. Served in the French Army, 1900–03, 1914–15; wounded at Ypres. Married Marie-Louise Gaillot in 1914; children: Jacqueline, Claude and Arlette. Worked in Morocco, under Maréchal Lyautey and for the architect Prost, 1915–20; in private practice, Paris, 1920 until his death, 1978. Inspector, then Inspector-General, Ecole des Beaux-Arts, Paris, 1932–45. Member of the Institut de France from 1959: President, 1965. Recipient: Silver Medal, City of Paris. Member, Syndicate of the Arts Press and Men of Letters, Paris. Honorary Corresponding Member, Royal Institute of British Architects; Member, Royal Academy of Belgium. Commander of the Légion d'Honneur, 1945. *Died* (in Paris) *9 May 1978.*

Works:

1915/
20 City plan for Casablanca, Morocco
Residence General, Rabat, Morocco
1920 Private houses and gardens, Paris and Paris region
1925 Design of the *Garden Exhibition,* Paris
1928 Marbeuf Garage: Citroen Showroom, rue Marbeuf, Champs Elysées, Paris
E.D.F. Building, 76 rue de Rennes, Paris
1931 *Exposition Coloniale,* Musée des Arts Africains, Paris (with Janniot)
1934 *Echo du Nord* Newspaper Offices, Lille
1935/
37 French Embassy, Ankara, Turkey
1939/
49 E.D.F. Hydro-Electric Dam, Genissiat-sur-le-Rhone, France
Maison de Cuba, Maison de la France d'Outre Mer, and Maison du Maroc, Cité Universitaire, Paris
Kleber-Colombes Factory, Paris
Central Thermique, Oran, Algeria
1943 Redevelopment plan for Valenciennes, France
Redevelopment plan for Lille
Redevelopment plan for Gournay-en-Bray, France
1944/
58 Old City Quarter Development, Le Mans, France
1950/
62 Schneider Company Buildings, Le Creusot, France (as consultant)
1954 Administrative Centre, Lille
"Ilot XVI" Development, Paris
Old City Development, Alençon, France
E.D.F. Factories at Seyssel sur le Rhone, La Bathie sur le Rhone, and Villarodin sur le Rhone, France
1961/
62 Renault Offices, Champs Elysées, Paris (with Claude Barré)
Hilton Hotel, Orly Airport, near Paris (with Claude Barré)
1962 Maréchal Lyautey Tomb, Les Invalides, Paris
1965 Cité Administrative, Paris

Publications:

By LAPRADE: books—*Carnets de Croquis: Le Nord de la France, L'Est, Le Midi, Le Centre, L'Ouest, Paris, Espagne-Portugal-Maroc, L'Italie et l'Asie Mineure,* 8 volumes, Paris 1940–70; *Francois d'Orbay, Architecte de Louis XIV,* Paris 1965; *Conte la Démolition de Paris,* edited by Berger-Leurault, Paris/Nancy 1967.

On LAPRADE: book—*La Maison et le Jardin Arabe au Maroc,* Paris 1926.

Albert Laprade: E.D.F. Building, Paris, 1928

Albert Laprade. A strange character! I met him when I was a very young student architect writing some articles of "architectural criticism" for my school magazine. I had been carried away by the Citroen Showroom, in Paris, so without further ado, I presented myself at the home of the architect who (with his young associate Bazin) had signed the work. He received me very amicably, in his old fashioned and very "average French bourgeois" apartment in the rue des Eaux in Passy. He did not understand my enthusiasm. He disclaimed authorship of the too audacious window of 400 square metres. In fact it was the work of the engineer Perrin and the "client" who had prescribed it. As for the architects, they had masked the elegant metal framework with "casings" which gave the impression of heavy pillars. With all the impudence of my 20 years my criticism was severe. But at that moment a friendship was borne that lasted a lifetime.

Of retiring and modest appearance, Laprade was an able man of great sensitivity. His words and his writings always displayed much delicacy, culture and common sense. Unfortunately his achievements regularly contradicted his writings. Let us ignore the works of his youth conceived in Morocco in the shadow of Prost and under the rather disdainful authority of Lyautey. But then later on: the building for the principal newspaper of the north, in Lille, is a lamentable pastiche. The enormous Administrative Centre not far away from it is worse than mediocre: entrusted with "protecting" the site of the Seine, Laprade bears the heavy responsibility for a building that in fact disfigures the site. Less questionable are those buildings in good classical form such as the Museum of the Colonies and the lost opportunity that is the hydroelectric complex at Genissiat on the Rhone. Let us forget the work and keep the memory of a delightful man who loved beauty and appreciated the true qualities of all past architectural creation from the most monumental to the most humble, and whose wisdom united with a genuine intellectual and an artistic subtlety that did not know how to express itself other than in words.

—Pierre Vago

LASDUN, Sir Denys.
British. Born in London, 8 September 1914. Educated at the Rugby School, 1928–31; Architectural Association School, London, 1931–34. Served as a Major in the Royal Engineers, British 2nd Army, 1939–45: M.B.E. (Member, Order of the British Empire). Married Susan Virginia Bendit in 1954; children: Louisa, James and William. Worked in association with Wells Coates, founder of the MARS Group, London, 1935–37; joined Tecton, London (partners: Lubetkin, Skinner and Drake), 1937–38; Partner in Tecton, 1946 until the firm was dissolved, 1948; taught at the Architectural Association School, London, 1948–49; in partnership with Lindsey Drake, London, 1949–59. Since 1960, Principal, Denys Lasdun and Partners; renamed Denys Lasdun Redhouse and Softley, 1978. Lectured at Massachusetts Institute of Technology, Harvard University, Illinois Institute of Technology, and the University of Chicago, 1954; Visiting Critic, University of Manchester, 1961; Hoffman Wood Professor of Architecture, University of Leeds, 1962–63; British Council Lecturer in Spain and Portugal, 1964. Member of the Jerusalem Town Planning Committee, 1970. Member of the Advisory Council of the Victoria and Albert Museum, London, since 1973; Member of the Council of the Architectural Association, since 1974; Trustee of the British Museum, London, since 1975; Member of the Slade Committee since 1976. Exhibitions: *Twentieth Century Form,* Whitechapel Art Gallery, London, 1953; *Ten Years of British Architecture 1945–1955,* Arts Council Gallery, London, 1956; *Architecture Today,* British Council Gallery, London, 1961; *National Theatre Exhibition,* Royal Institute of British Architects, London, 1968; *Bienal,* Sao Paulo, Brazil, 1969; *Singapore Planning and Urban Research Group Exhibition,* Singapore, 1971; *The Architecture of Denys Lasdun and Partners,* Heinz Gallery, RIBA, London, 1976; *Art and Leisure,* British Council, Iran, 1977–78; *RIBA Drawings Exhibition,* Luxembourg and Germany, 1978. Recipient: Student Award for design of Students Hostel, London, 1935; First Prize, Cement and Concrete Association Competition, 1950; London Architecture Bronze Medal, RIBA, 1960, 1964; Ambassador Award, for contribution to the London skyline, 1965; Civic Trust Award, Class I, 1967, and Group A, 1969; Special Award, *Bienal,* Sao Paulo, 1969; Royal Gold Medal for Architecture, RIBA, 1977; Concrete Society Award, 1977; London Region Award, RIBA, 1978. Honorary Associate, Manchester College of Art and Design, 1966; D.Litt.: University of East Anglia, Norwich, 1974; University of Sheffield, 1978. Fellow, Royal Institute of British Architects, 1945. Honorary Fellow, American Institute of Architects, 1966; Honorary Fellow, Royal College of Physicians, London, 1975. C.B.E. (Commander, Order of the British Empire), 1965; Knighted, 1976. Address: Denys Lasdun, Redhouse and Softley, 50 Queen Anne Street, London W1M ODR, England.

Works:

1937/
38　House, 32 Newton Road, Paddington, London
1948　Hallfield Housing Scheme, Paddington, London (with Tecton)
1950　Whiteleigh Footbridge, Plymouth, Devon (with Harris and Johns, engineers)
1951　Hallfield Primary School, Paddington, London
1952　Usk Street Cluster Block Housing, Bethnal Green, London
1955　Claredale Street Cluster Block Housing, Bethnel Green, London
1958　Flats, 26 St. James's Place, London
　　　Peter Robinson Store and Offices, Strand, London (now London headquarters of the New South Wales Government)
1959　Fitzwilliam College, Cambridge

1960　Royal College of Physicians, Regent's Park, London
　　　Wartski shopfront, Regent Street, London
　　　Metropolitan Cathedral of Christ the King, Liverpool (competition project)
1961　Complex of Science Laboratories, New Museum Site, Cambridge (project)
1962　Stamford Hall, University of Leicester
　　　New buildings for St. John's College, Cambridge (competition project)
　　　Royal Institution of Chartered Surveyors, Parliament Square, London (project)
1962/
68　University of East Anglia, Norwich
1963　Charles Wilson Social Centre, University of Leicester
　　　Sports Centre, University of Liverpool
1965　National Theatre and Opera House, Shell Site, London (project)
　　　Comprehensive redevelopment for the University of London: School of Oriental and African Studies; Institute of Education; and Institute of Advanced Legal Studies
1966　Residential building, Christ's College, Cambridge
1967/
76　National Theatre, Waterloo Bridge Site, London
1971　Burrell Collection, Glasgow (competition project)
　　　Feasibility study: Broad Sanctuary, Parliament Square, London
1972　Cannock Community Hospital, Staffordshire (project)
1973　European Investment Bank (EEC Headquarters building), Luxembourg
1975　Sotheby and Company Headquarters Building, New Bond Street, London (project)
　　　Plant Protection Division Headquarters Building, Imperial Chemical Industries, Fernhurst, Surrey
1977　Feasibility study: Courtauld Institute, University of London precinct
1978　Feasibility study: IBM United Kingdom Ltd. Headquarters Building, South Bank (adjacent to the National Theatre) London

Publications:

By LASDUN: articles—"Housing in London" in The *Architects' Yearbook,* London 1951; "Impressions of American Architecture" in *Architectural Association Journal* (London), June 1954; "Le Corbusier's Maison Jaoul" in *Architectural Design* (London), March 1956; "LCC Housing Scheme: Picton Street, Camberwell" in *Architectural Association Journal* (London), June 1956; "Thoughts in Progress," monthly discussions with J.H.V. Davies, in *Architectural Design* (London), December 1956 to December 1958; "MARS Group 1953–57" in *Architects' Year Book* (London), no. 8, 1957; "Means not Ends" in *RIBA Journal* (London), June 1961; "Process of Continual Cooperation" in *The Financial Times* (London), 2 August 1961; "7 Keys to Good Architecture" in *20th Century* (London), Winter 1962/63; "An Architect's Approach to Architecture" in *RIBA Journal* (London), April 1965; "Le Corbusier" (obituary) in *L'Architecture d'Aujourd'hui* (Paris), September/November 1965; "A Sense of Place and Time" (radio broadcast) in *The Listener* (London), 17 February 1966; "The National Theatre" (radio broadcast, with J. M. Richards) in *The Listener* (London), 22 February 1968; interview in the series "The Arts Today" in *The Observer Magazine* (London), 16 September 1973; introduction to *A Language and a Theme: The Architecture of Denys Lasdun and Partners* by William J. R. Curtis, London 1976; edited version of talk between Lasdun and Peter Hall originally televised on "Aquarius" in *The Complete Guide to Britain's National Theatre,* London 1977; statements in special issue on National Theatre of *Architectural Re-*

view (London), January 1977; "Random Thoughts on Creativity" in *RIBA Journal* (London), May 1977; transcript of RIBA Royal Gold Medal address in *RIBA Journal* (London), September 1977; "Architectural Aspects of the National Theatre" in *Royal Society of Arts Journal* (London), November 1977.

On LASDUN: books—*The New Architecture of Europe* by G. E. Kidder Smith, New York and London 1961; *Architecture in Britain Today* by Michael Webb, London 1969; *The Politics of Architecture* by Anthony Jackson, London 1970; *Neue Englische Architektur* by by Robert Maxwell, Stuttgart 1972; *A Visual History of Twentieth Century Architecture* by Dennis Sharp, London 1972; *Age of the Masters: A Personal View of Modern Architecture* by Reyner Banham, London 1975; *A Language and a Theme: The Work of Denys Lasdun and Partners* by William J. R. Curtis, London 1976; *Who Who's in Architecture,* edited by J. M. Richards, London 1977; articles—introduction by John Summerson to *Ten Years of British Architecture, 1945–1955,* exhibition catalogue, London 1956; "The Anti-Pioneers" by Nikolaus Pevsner in *The Listener* (London), 5 January 1957; "Denys Lasdun: England" by Robert Furneaux Jordan in *The Canadian Architect* (Toronto), September 1962; "Evolution of a Style" in *Architectural Review* (London), May 1969; "National Monument" by Reyner Banham in *New Society* (London), 18 March 1976; "Building a Landscape for Figures" by Brian Connell in *The Times* (London), 24 March 1975; "University of East Anglia" by William J. R. Curtis in *Archithese* (Zurich), no. 14, 1975; "Denys Lasdun: A New National Role" by Dennis Sharp and Colin Davies in *Building* (London), 17 September 1976; review by William J. R. Curtis in *Architectural Review* (London), January 1977; article by William J. R. Curtis in *The Complete Guide to Britain's National Theatre,* London 1977.

*

Architecture, by its form and language and concern for human scale, can maintain its responsibility to bring the highest insights of which art is capable into the lives of everyone. Architecture is a social art and only makes sense as the promoter and extender of human relations. Architectural creation demands a fresh understanding of physical order and the nature of man and particularly of man in society—the clarification, in fact, of order and diversity. Perhaps this clarification is the key to an architectural language which is in tune with what ordinary people want.

—Denys Lasdun

*

The architecture of Denys Lasdun provides a rare example of a set of forms based on principle. Each of his buildings represents the gradual clarification of ideas expressed in a vocabulary of standard elements which are limited in number but flexible in scope. At the core is the idea of architecture as "urban landscape:" Lasdun's buildings are composed of vertical towers and horizontal terraces and extend into the urban or natural surroundings; the overall effect of these walkways and promenades, which cascade as horizontal planes and stepped levels inside and outside, is of an artificial landscape of "hills" and "valleys." Indeed the architect calls the terraces "strata," a word that suggests geological sources of inspiration. The system is seen most clearly in such works of the 1960's and 1970's as the University of East Anglia or the National Theatre. Lasdun explains the principle of the "strata:"

　　Most activities take place on "platforms"—floors, paths, terraces, bridges etc. (see Le Corbusier's pronouncement of 1915: "The actual ground of the town is a sort of raised floor, the streets and pavements as it were bridges. Beneath this floor and directly accessible are places for the main services"). A building can be looked at in the same way, as a matter of platforms

Sir Denys Lasdun: National Theatre, London, 1976

and connections and interlocking spaces. Sensitive gradations of levels and heights can be made to respond to site and function, creating an endless variety of rhythms and scales, satisfactory in themselves and adaptable to any existing urban situation, including the architecture of the past.

The vocabulary of strata and towers can be seen evolving gradually in Lasdun's work and is in some respects an extension of the vocabulary and concerns of the architect's predecessors in the history of the modern movement. Lasdun was born in 1914 and entered the mainstream of modern architecture before the Second World War when the formative impulses and visions were still fresh and were just beginning to influence the English situation. He worked with both Berthold Lubetkin and Wells Coates before designing a house in Paddington of 1938 which shows clearly the impact of Le Corbusier's Maison Cook of 1926. Certain foundations were thus defined early: an interest in the horizontal cantilever in reinforced concrete as a generator of vocabulary; a concern for the unity of townplanning and architecture; an ethical conviction that the architect might enhance the quality of life with forms matched to modern functions; and an instinctive feeling for abstract form, initially nurtured on the white geometrics of the International Style, later inspired by works in the classical tradition, particularly the English Baroque.

Lasdun's personal synthesis began to emerge after the Second World War in works like the Hallfield Primary School and the Bethnal Green cluster blocks. In each case the program was broken down into distinct formal elements united by articulated spines of circulation. At Bethnal Green a critique of the standard modern block was implied. The raised bridges and levels linking the stacked maisonettes represent an attempt at turning the local street type on its end. In the late 1950's, in such works as the St. James' flats and the Royal College of Physicians, the vocabulary of elegantly proportioned horizontals and overhanging soffits becomes clearer. The college with its neo-classical white shell enclosing the areas of ceromonial, and its sprawling mauve brick hump containing a sunken auditorium, is a rare case of truly honorific modern building. Without resorting to pastiche, the college incorporates within itself a modern re-statement of the urban sequences of Nash's surrounding terraces. To pass into the airy hallway with its receding levels of white balconies linked by steps is to experience features that were to become central to the Lasdun vocabulary.

This is clearly seen in the university schemes designed in the 1960's: The University of East Anglia; Christ's College, Cambridge; and The University of London. At the University of East Anglia the site was some fields tilting down to the River Yare, and the social problem was to lay down the core of an educational experiment involving the rejection of the collegiate ideal. Accordingly a basic division was adapted between a flexible "teaching wall" containing a spine of the various teaching disciplines ("schools"), and the residences which were to be sited with maximum use of the astounding views over the landscape. Translated into architectural terms these priorities led to a linear plan form disposed around a central landscape space and to the creation of an upper social plane of raised pedestrian streets linking all parts of the university with minimum recourse to lifts. The architect organized the residences into steps, thus breaking down their scale and introducing a strong horizontal, unifying theme. The result is, indeed, an artificial landscape grafted to the previous contours.

In the case of the schemes for the National Theatre and Opera House and the final National Theatre the urban landscape idea and its central element, the strata, came fully into their own and revealed their relevance to a public building.

Over and above the immensely complex tasks of designing the auditoria and interiors of the theatre, there was obviously the need to exploit to the full the scenographic possibilities of the riverside site, and to give a suitable image to the institution of a public monument. A plan arrangement was found which registered the hierarchy between the main auditoria and their flytowers and which disposed the public zones of the building alongside the river and linked them to Waterloo Bridge and the riverside walkways. The strata pass through the building and have internal and external volumes cut out of them to provide here an open-air theatre, here a foyer, here an interior auditorium. When the theatre is in use and people pass over the levels, inside and outside, the building resembles a teeming hill. The strata open out the contents of the building to the public and link the theatre visually with the river and the surrounding vistas of London.

Since the National Theatre was designed Lasdun's ideas and vocabulary have naturally continued to evolve. But the National Theatre is the clearest and most conspicuous demonstration of the urban landscape ideal to date.

—William J. R. Curtis

LAUTNER

LAUTNER, John.

American. Born in Marquette, Michigan, 16 July
1911. Educated at high schools in Marquette and
New York City; Northern Michigan University,
Marquette, A.B. in English 1933; worked under
Frank Lloyd Wright at Taliesin (Wisconsin and Ari-
zona), 1933–39. Married Mary Lautner in 1934;
Elizabeth Lautner in 1950; children: Karol, Michael,
Mary, and Judith. Associate in the office of Douglas
Honnold, Los Angeles, 1944–46. In private practice,
Los Angeles, since 1946. Exhibitions: *The Three
Worlds of Los Angeles,* toured Europe, 1974; *A View
of California Architecture 1960–76,* San Francisco,
1977. Fellow, American Institute of Architects,
1970. Address (office): 7046 Hollywood Boulevard,
Los Angeles, California 90028, U.S.A.

Works:

1939 Lautner House, 2007 Micheltorena, Los An-
geles
1940 Bell House, 7714 Woodrow Wilson, Los An-
geles
1946 Mauer House, 932 Rome, Los Angeles
R. and H. Motors Showroom, 600 Colorado,
Los Angeles (now Rayco)
1947 Desert Hot Springs Motel, Desert Hot
Springs, Colorado
Gantvoort House, Flintridge, California
Henry's Restaurant, Glendale, California
Polin House, Los Angeles
Carling House, Pacific View and Hockey
Trail, Los Angeles
1948 Schaeffer House, Glendale, California (now
Wallace House)
Sheats ("L'Horizon") Apartments, 10901-19
Strathmore, Beverly Hills, California

1949 Dahlstrom House, South Pasadena, California
United Productions of America Studios, Burbank, California
1950 Foster House, 4235 Las Cruces, Sherman
Oaks, California
Harvey House, Los Angeles
Shusett House, Beverly Hills, California
1953 Bergren House, Los Angeles
1954 Beachwood Market remodelling, Los Angeles
1955 Baldwin House, Los Angeles
1956 Harpel House, Hollywood, California
Speer Contractors' Office Building, Los Angeles (now World Supply Company)
1957 Henry's Restaurant, Pomona, California
Pearlman Mountain Cabin, Idyllwild, California
Zahn House, Hollywood, California
1958 Hatherell House, Sun Valley, Idaho
1959 Ernest Lautner House, Florida
1960 Concannon House, Los Angeles (now Chester House)
Malin House ("Chemosphere"), 776 Torrey-
son Drive, Los Angeles (now Kuhn
House)
Midtown School, Los Angeles
Alto Capistrano Apartments and Shopping
Center, San Juan Capistrano, California
(project)
1961 Wolff House, Hollywood, California
1962 Garcia House, Mulholland Drive, Los Angeles
1963 Sheats House, Beverly Hills, California (now
Goldstein House)
"Silvertop" (house), 2138 Micheltorena, Los
Angeles
1966 Alto Capistrano Headquarters, San Juan
Capistrano, California

Harpel House, Alaska
1968 Elrod House, 2175 Southridge Drive, Palm
Springs, California
Stevens House, Malibu, California
Zimmerman House, Studio City, California
1969 Walstrom House, Beverly Glen, Los Angeles
1971 Familian House, 1011 Cove Way, Beverly
Hills, California
1973 Jordan House, Laguna Beach, California
Nature Center, Griffith Park, Los Angeles
(project)
1976 Bob Hope House, Southridge Drive, Palm
Springs, California (partially destroyed by
fire)
Trancas Beach House, Malibu, California
Segal House, Malibu, California
Crippled Children's Society Rehabilitation
Center, Rancho del Valle, California
1977 Arango House, Acapulco, Mexico
1978 Rawlins House, Newport Beach, California

Publications:

On LAUTNER: books—*Petites Maisons en Amerique du Nord,* Paris 1957; *Einfamilienhouser in den
U.S.A.,* Munich 1962; *Beautiful Homes and Gardens
in California* by Herbert Weisskamp, New York
1964; *Drawings by American Architects* by A. M.
Kemper, New York 1974; *A View of California Architecture 1960–76,* exhibition catalogue, by David
Gebhard and Susan King, San Francisco 1977; articles—"West Coast Architecture V: John Lautner"
by Esther McCoy in *Arts and Architecture* (Los Angeles), August 1965; "Modern Palace in the Desert"
in *Architectural Digest* (Los Angeles), Spring 1970;
"Five Distinctive Houses" in *Architectural Record*
(New York), November 1970; "You've Got to Fight
for Good Design" in *Los Angeles Times Home Mag-*

John Lautner: Arango House, Acapulco, Mexico, 1977

azine, 14 February 1971; "The Architect's Perspective" in *Architectural Digest* (Los Angeles), September/October 1971; article in *Architecture + Urbanism* (Tokyo), no. 40, 1974.

Architecture, in its truest sense, may not be academically defined. If it is, it becomes a dead, non-growing entity of style or cliché. I see it as a continuous search for total basic human needs in shelter; emotional, psychological, etc., as well as mere physical; then it becomes a valid enduring Art. In the business of building, when people become commodities or merchandise, we have facilities to house or shelter, but not Architecture.

—John Lautner

John Lautner's dramatic domestic designs are notable even in Southern California, which is famous for its architectural extravagances. Esther McCoy has called him "a lyrical technologist with a style spanning Frank Lloyd Wright and the year 2,000." He boldly experiments with new industrial processes in what he terms his "continual search to answer total basic human needs—emotional as well as physical—in shelter."

The 1948 apartment building "L'Horizon," like much of Lautner's work, shows the influence of his six year fellowship at Taliesin. Visually intriguing and functionally ingenious, his design gives each of the nine units its own deck and outdoor garden. The Pearlman Cabin of 1957 is a successful attempt to integrate a modern building into a wooded site without resorting to "rusticness." The sharply angled glass walls of the house are supported by a circle of peeled log pillars, as if the building simply grew out of the surrounding trees. The result is refreshingly direct but not overly intrusive.

Perhaps Lautner's best known building is Malin House ("Chemosphere") of 1960. This flying saucer shape perched on a single concrete column may look like futuristic indulgence, but, as Reyner Banham has pointed out, it is also a very sensible solution for a small steep site. The one column foundation minimized destruction of the existing terrain and obviated the usual bull-dozing and retaining walls of hillside building. The clear span interior of the hexagonal house leaves 1,300 square feet of uninterrupted living space and offers amazing views of the valley below.

Wolff House is again characteristically bold, made of dressed boulders, concrete and jutting glass, with the carport projecting like a great lip. "Silvertop," with a cantilevered driveway *and* swimming pool, is a cascade of projecting forms: it was several years in the building because of difficulties in obtaining permits for its unorthodox structure.

Another Lautner design with space ship overtones is the Elrod House in Palm Springs. Here, however, the circular form is not on a stalk but fit snugly into the rocky hillside. The immense concrete spokes of the roof provide shade and also frame wedge-shaped windows with views of the distant mountains. The indoor-outdoor effect is increased by rocky intrusions on the interior and by the placement of the pool.

One of Lautner's largest private commissions, a house for the comedian Bob Hope, was sadly nipped in the bud. The swooping concrete roof, reminiscent of Saarinen's TWA Terminal, spanned 25,000 square feet of pools, garden and living space arranged around a private central court. Begun in 1972, the house burnt down to its steel skeleton in 1976 and may only be rebuilt in a modified form.

South of the border, the Arango House in Acapulco is Lautner at his most elegant and imaginative. Again a colossal concrete roof covers the whole complex, extending over a vast living terrace bordered by a cantilevered moat, which seems to merge with the bay beyond, giving the house a sense of hovering between sky and sea. A lower level has nine bedrooms with quiet terraces sheltered by the overhanging moat; steps lead down to the main swimming pool. The use of space is daring and inventive—but never at the expense of the human needs central to Lautner's view of architecture.

—Lucinda Hawkins

LE CORBUSIER.

French. Born Charles-Edouard Jeanneret in La Chaux-de-Fonds, Switzerland, 6 October 1887; adopted pseudonym Le Corbusier, 1920; emigrated to France, 1917: naturalized, 1930. Studied engraving at the School of Applied Arts, La Chaux-de-Fonds, under l'Eplattenier, 1900–05. Married Yvonne Gallis in 1930 (died, 1957). Worked in the office of the architect Josef Hoffmann, Vienna, 1907, Auguste Perret, Paris, and, with Walter Gropius and Mies van der Rohe, in the office of Peter Behrens, Berlin, 1910; Founder Director, L'Atelier d'Art Réunis, La Chaux-de-Fonds, 1909–14, and Instructor, l'Eplattenier's Nouvelle Section de l'Ecole d'Art, La Chaux de Fonds, 1911–14; also worked as a painter and lithographer from 1912. In private practice as an architect, Paris, 1917 until his death, 1965: in partnership with his cousin Pierre Jeanneret, 1922–40; collaborated with the architect Charlotte Perriand, 1927–29; practised as ATBAT (Atelier des Bâtisseurs), from 1942; developed Modulor System, with Hanning and Elisa Maillard, 1943–48. Chief Planner, La Rochelle-Pallice, France, 1945; Architectural Adviser, Capital City, Chandigarh, India, 1951–59. Founder Editor, with Amédée Ozenfant and Paul Dermée, *L'Esprit Nouveau,* Paris, 1919–25. Founder Member, CIAM (Congrès Internationaux d'Architecture Moderne), 1928; Founder, ASCORAL (Assemblée de Constructeurs pour une Renovation Architecturale), Paris, 1942. Lectured extensively at universities in Europe and the United States, 1921–56. Exhibitions: group—*Exposition Internationale d'Art Décoratif,* Turin, 1902; *Salon d'Automne,* Paris, 1912; *Après Le Cubisme,* Galerie Thomas, Paris, 1918; *Salon d'Automne,* Paris, 1922; *Salon des Indépendants,* Paris, 1922; *L'Effort Moderne,* Galerie Leonce Rosenberg, Paris, 1923; *Exposition des Arts Décoratifs,* Paris, 1925; *Salon d'Automne,* Paris, 1929; *L'Art Primitif,* Studio Louis Carré, Paris, 1935; *World's Fair,* Paris, 1937; *Ideal Home Exhibition,* London, 1939; *France d'Outremer,* Paris, 1940; *Vienna Exhibition,* 1947; *Exposition de Nature Morte,* Musée de Saint-Etienne, France, 1955; *La Machine à s'asseoir: Le Corbusier, Charlotte Perriand, Pierre Jeanneret,* Rome, 1976. one-man—Galerie Drouet, Paris, 1921; John Becker Gallery, New York, 1933; Galerie Louis Carré, Paris, 1938; Kunsthaus, Zurich, 1938; Galerie Boesiger, Zurich, 1941; Radio City, New York, 1945; Stedelijk Museum, Amsterdam, 1947; Institute of Contemporary Art, Boston, 1948; Paul Rosenberg Gallery, New York, 1950; Museum of Modern Art, New York, 1951; Galerie Denise René, Paris, 1952; Musée National d'Art Moderne, Paris, 1953, toured the Institute of Contemporary Arts, London, and the Samleven Gallery, Stockholm; Kunsthalle, Berne, 1954; Villa del Olma, Como, Italy, 1954; Pierre Matisse Gallery, New York, 1956; Musée d'Art, Lyons, 1956; Kunsthaus, Zurich, 1957; Neue Galerie, Linz, Austria, 1957; Moderna Museet, Stockholm, 1958; Walker Art Gallery, Liverpool, 1958; Musée National d'Art Moderne, Paris, 1961–62; Weber Galerie, Zurich, 1962; Palazzo Strozzi, Florence, 1963; Musée National d'Art Moderne, Paris, 1964; Weber Galerie, Zurich, 1968; Nielson Gallery, Boston, 1976; Galerie Kornfeld, Zurich, 1976. Collections: Fondation Le Corbusier, 8–10 Square du Docteur Blanche, Paris 16; Centre Le Corbusier, Hoschgasse 8, Zurich. Recipient: Medal, *Exposition International d'Art Décoratif,* Turin, 1902; First Prize, with Pierre Jeanneret, League of Nations Competition, Geneva, 1927; Gold Medal, Royal Institute of British Architects, 1959. Honorary doctorates: University of Zurich, 1933; E.T.H: Eidgenössische Technische Hochschule, Zurich, 1955; Cambridge University, 1959. Chevalier, 1937, Commandeur, 1952, and Grand Officier, 1963, of the Lègion d'Honneur. *Died* (at Cap Martin, France) *27 August 1965.*

Works:

1906 Fallet House, 1 chemin de Pouillerel, La Chaux-de-Fonds, Switzerland

1908 Stotzer House, 6 chemin de Pouillerel, La Chaux-de-Fonds, Switzerland

Jacquemet House, 8 chemin de Pouillerel, La Chaux-de-Fonds, Switzerland (supervised by Chapallaz)

1910 School of Arts and Crafts, La Chaux-de-Fonds, Switzerland (project)

1912 Favre-Jacot House, rue de la Montagne, Le Locle, near La Chaux-de-Fonds, Switzerland

Jeanneret House, 12 chemin de Pouillerel, La Chaux-de-Fonds, Switzerland

1914 Domino House (project)

Norman Houses, Deauville, France (project)

Felix Klipstein House, Loubach, Switzerland (project)

Bank, Neuenburg, Switzerland (project)

1915 Butin Bridge, near Geneva (competition project)

Buildings on "pilotis" (project)

House, Lons-le-Saunier, France (project)

1916 Scala Cinema, 32 rue de la Serre, La Chaux-de-Fonds, Switzerland (demolished)

Schwob House, 167 rue du Doubs, La Chaux-de-Fonds, Switzerland

Fritz Zbinden House, Erlach, Switzerland (project)

Administrative Building, Le Locle, near La Chaux-de-Fonds, Switzerland (project)

Watch Factory, La Chaux-de-Fonds, Switzerland (project)

1916/
21 Paul Poiret Seaside Villa (various projects)

1917 Water Tower, Les Landes, France

Abbatoir, Challay, France (project)

Abbatoir, Garchizy, France (project)

Workers' housing estate, near Dieppe, France (project)

Dam, Ile Jourdain, France (project)

1918 Factory, Saintes, France (project)

1919 Pre-cast concrete houses, Troyes, France (project)

In-situ concrete housing (project)

Monol Housing (project)

Hotel, Rabat, Morocco (project)

Distillery, near Lyons (project)

1920 Citrohan House (1st project)

Painter's studio (project)

1921 Citrohan Seaside House (project)

Garage, Lille (project)

1922 Besnos House, La Chataigneraie, 49 Avenue du Chesnay, Vaucresson, Paris (now altered)

Ozenfant House, 53 Avenue de Reille, Paris (now altered)

Contemporary City for 3 Million People, *Salon d'Automne,* Paris (exhibition project)

Group of villas and apartments (project)

Citrohan House (2nd project)

Artist's house (project)

Worker's house (project)

La Roche-Jeanneret Houses, Auteuil, France (1st project)

1923/
25 Villa La Roche-Jeanneret, 8–10 Square du Docteur Blanche, Paris 16 (now Fondation Le Corbusier)

Jeanneret House, 21 Route Lavaux, Corseaux-Vevey, Switzerland

1924 Lipchitz/Miestschaninoff House, 9 Allée des Pins, Boulogne, Paris
Tonkin House, Bordeaux
10 houses, Lege, near Bordeaux (now altered)
Week-end house, Rambouillet, France (project)
Pre-fabricated workers' housing (project)

1925 Pavillon de l'Esprit Nouveau, *Exposition des Arts Décoratifs,* Paris
Cité Universitaire (project)
Meyer House, Paris (project)
Voisin Plan for Paris (project)
Housing, Cité Audincourt, France (project)

1925/
26 Cité Fruges Development, Pessac, near Bordeaux (now altered)

1925/
27 2 houses, Weissenhof Estate, Stuttgart

1926 Ternisien House, 5 Allée des Pins, Boulogne, Paris
Cook House, 6 rue Denfert-Rochereau, Boulogne, Paris
Salvation Army Dormitory (Palais du Peuple), 29 rue des Cordelieres, Paris
Guiette House, Antwerp (now altered)
Raspail Garage, Paris (project)
Cardinet Stadium, Paris (project)
Fruges Factory (project)

1927 "Les Terraces," 17 rue du Professeur Victor Pauchet, Garches, Paris (now altered)
Plainex House, 24 bis Boulevard Massena, Paris
League of Nations Headquarters, Geneva (competition project)

1928 Villa Baizau, Carthage, Tunisia (now in grounds of presidential palace)
Church House, Ville-Avray, Paris (demolished)

Le Corbusier: Notre-Dame-du-Haut Chapel, Ronchamp, France, 1955

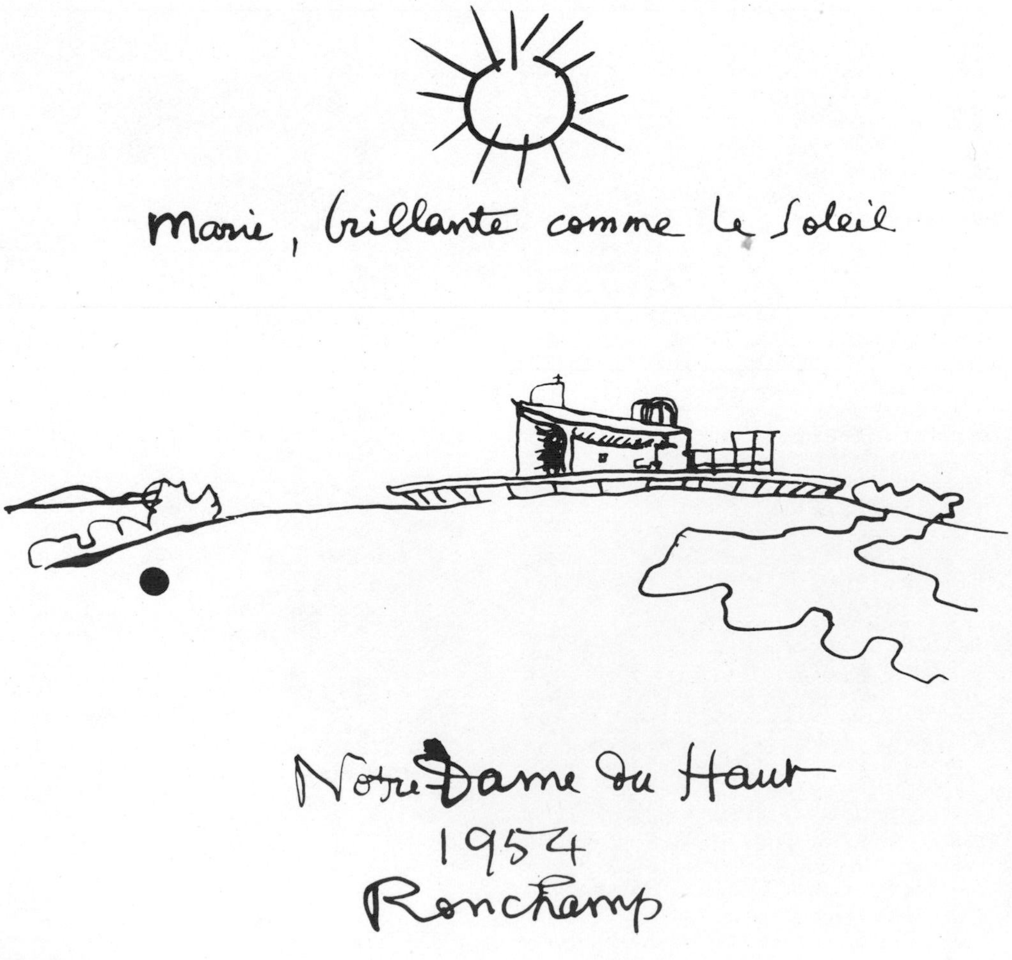

Wanner Apartment Block, Geneva (project)

1929 Salvation Army Floating Dormitory, Pont d'Austerlitz, Paris
Planning study of Montevideo
Planning study of Sao Paulo
Planning study of Rio de Janeiro
Planning study of Buenos Aires
Plan for Porte Maillot, Paris
"Mundaneum" (world museum), Geneva (project)
Loucher Housing (project)
Draeger Printing Works, Paris (project)
Canneels House, Brussels (project)

1929/
31 "Les Heures Claires" (or "Villa Savoye"), 82 chemin de Villiers, Poissy, France

1929/
33 Centrosoyus Building, Kirova Ulitsa, Moscow (now altered)
Salvation Army Hostel (Cité de Refuge), 12 rue Cantagrel, Paris (now altered)

1930 City plan for Algiers (1st project)
Ville Radieuse (project)
Errazuris House, Chile (project)

1930/
31 Charles de Beistegui Penthouse Apartment, rue de Balzac, Paris
Madrot House, Le Pradet, near Toulon

1930/
32 Swiss Students' Hostel, Cité Universitaire, Paris (now altered)
"Clarte," 2 rue Saint-Laurent, Geneva

1931 Palace of the Soviets, Moscow (competition project)
Museum of Contemporary Art, Paris (project)

1932 Apartment block, Zurichhorn, Zurich (project)

1933 Apartment block, 24 rue Nungesser-et-Coli, Paris
MACIA Plan, Barcelona
Plan for the Right Bank, Geneva
City plan for Stockholm
Plan for the Scheldt Left Bank, Antwerp (with H. Hoste and P. Otlet)
City plan for Algiers (2nd project)
Durand Housing, Oued-Ouchaia, Algeria (project)
Apartment block, Algiers (project)
Rentenanstalt Building, Zurich (project)

1934 City plan for Nemours (Jamad-el-Ghazuar), Algeria (with N. Bezard)
Workers' housing, Zurich (project)
Apartment block, Esplanade des Invalides, Paris (project)
City plan for Algiers (3rd project)

1935 Villa le Settout, La Tremblade, Les Mathes, near Marennes
Week-end House, 85 Boulevard de la République, La Celle-Saint-Cloud, Paris
Young man's apartment, *International Exhibition,* Brussels (exhibition project)
Study of New York
Bata Shoe Factory, Hellocourt, Lorraine, France (project)
Bata Shoe Factory, Zlin, Czechoslovakia (project)
Apartment block, rue Fabert, Paris (project)
Bastion Kellerman, Paris (project)
Apartment block, Nemours (Jamad-el-Ghazuar), Algeria (project)
Swimming pool with wave machine, Badjarah, Algeria (project)
College president's house, near Chicago (project)
Museum, Paris (project)
"Cartesian" Tower (project)

1936 University, Rio de Janeiro (project; with Lúcio Costa and Oscar Niemeyer)
"Ilot Insalubre no. 6" Plan, Paris (project)
"Paris 37" Plan (project)
National Sports Centre, Bois de Vincennes, Paris (project)
Studies for Bata Shops (projects)

1937 Pavillon des Temps Nouveaux, *World's Fair,* Paris
Monument to Vaillant-Courturier, Villejuif, France (project)
Jaoul Week-end House (project)

1937/
43 Ministry of Education and Health, Rio de Janeiro (with Lúcio Costa, Oscar Niemeyer, Affonso Eduardo Reidy, and Jorge Machado Moreira; now the Palace of Culture)

1938 Tower and master plan for the Quartier de la Marine, Algiers (project)
Plan for Pont Saint-Cloud, Boulogne, Paris (project)
City plan for Buenos Aires (project)
Co-operative Village (project)

1939 Exhibition Pavilion (project)
Museum of Endless Growth, Philippeville, Algeria (project)
Pavilion, *Ideal Home Exhibition,* London (project)
Research Laboratory, Roscoff, France (project)
Clarke Arundell House (project)
Plan for the Main Square, Boulogne, Paris (project)
Sports Centre, Var Valley, France (project)
City plan for Algiers (4th project)

1940 Layout for the *France Outremer* exhibition, Grand Palais, Paris
Murondins Housing (project)
Refugee School (project; with Jean Prouvé)
Pre-fabricated housing (project)
Foreman's house (project)
Engineer's house (project)

1941 Plans for the Cure Valley, Vezelay, Asquins,

Marie, brillante comme le Soleil

Notre-Dame du Haut
1954
Ronchamp

Saint-Père, France (projects)

1942 Peyrissac House, near Cherchel, Algeria (project)

Plan for the Linear Industrial City (project)

Plan 7, Algiers (project)

1945 Unité d'Habitation, Marseilles (1st project)

City plan for La Rochelle-Pallice, France (project)

City plan for Saint-Gaudens, France (project)

1946 Duval Factory, 1 Avenue de Robache, Saint-Die, France

Airport (project)

1946/
51 City plan for Saint-Die, France (projects)

1946/
52 Unité d'Habitation, 280 Boulevard Michelet, Marseilles

1947 Redevelopment plan for the Vieux Port, Marseilles

Redevelopment plan for Veyres, Marseilles

2 Unités d'Habitation, Antony, France (project)

CIAM Grid (project)

"Sept Voies" (7 V's) Planning Studies

City planning study of Bogota, Colombia

1947/
53 United Nations Headquarters, First Avenue, New York (as one of team of international architects—Wallace K. Harrison, Chairman)

1948 Plan for La Sainte Baume, France (with E. Trouin)

City plan for Izmir, Turkey

"Roq" and "Rob" Housing, Cap Martin, France (projects)

1949 Currutchet House, La Plata, Argentina

1950 Holiday huts, Cap Martin, France

Fueter House, Lake Constance, Switzerland (project)

Studies for the Museum of Endless Growth

City plan of Bogota, Colombia (with J. L. Sert and P. L. Wiener)

Exhibition Pavilion, *Synthese des Arts Majeurs*, Porte Maillot, Paris (project)

Delgado Memorial Chapel (project)

1950/
55 Notre-Dame-du-Haut Chapel, Ronchamp, France

1951 Master plan for the capital city at Chandigarh, India

2 Unités d'Habitation and Tower, Strasbourg (project)

City plan for Marseilles South

1951/
59 High Court, Chandigarh, India

1952 Open Hand Monument, Chandigarh, India (project)

Workers' houses, Chandigarh, India (project)

1952/
54 Jaoul Houses, 81 rue de Longchamp, Neuilly-sur-Seine, Paris

1952/
55 Unité d'Habitation, Reze-les-Nantes, France

1953 Governor's Palace, Chandigarh, India (project)

1953/
59 Couvent de la Sainte-Marie-de-la-Tourette, Eveux-sur-l'Arbresle, near Lyons

1954/
56 Millowners' Association Building, Ahmedabad, India

1955 Bhakra Dam, Himalaya Mountains, India

1955/
56 Sarabhai House, Ahmedabad, India

1956 Shodhan House, Ahmedabad, India

Museum, Ahmedabad, India

Pre-fabricated houses, Lagny, France (project; with Jean Prouvé)

Hospital, Flers, France (project)

Sports Centre, Baghdad (project; with G. Presente)

1957 Unité d'Habitation, Tiergarten, Charlottenburg, Berlin

Unité d'Habitation, Meaux, France

Unité d'Habitation, Briey-en-Foret, France

Unité de Camping, Cap Martin, France

5 Unités d'Habitation, Meaux, France (project)

1957/
59 Brazilian Students' Hostel, Cité Universitaire, Paris (with Lúcio Costa)

National Museum of Western Art, Tokyo (with Kunio Mayekawa, Takamasa Yosizaka, and Junzo Sakakura)

1958 Philips Pavilion, *World's Fair*, Brussels

Secretariat Building, Chandigarh, India

City plan for Berlin (competition project)

1959 Pre-fabricated housing, France (project; with Renault Engineers)

1960 Museum of Knowledge, Chandigarh, India (project)

City plan for Firminy-Vert, France

1961 Conference Centre and Hotel, Quai Anatole France, Paris (project)

1961/
64 Carpenter Center for the Visual Arts, Harvard University, Cambridge, Massachusetts (supervised by J. L. Sert)

Legislative Assembly Building, Chandigarh, India

1962 Ahrenberg Exhibition Pavilion, Stockholm (project)

1962/
65 Church of St.-Pierre, Firminy-Vert, France (project)

1963 International Art Centre, Erlenbach, near Frankfurt (project)

Church, Bologna (project)

Olivetti Computer Centre, Rho-Milan (project)

1964 Club House, Chandigarh, India

Congress Hall, Strasbourg (project)

French Embassy, Brasilia (project)

1964/
65 Hospital, Venice (project)

1964/
66 Centre Le Corbusier, Hoschgasse 8, Zurich

1964/
68 Museum and Art Gallery, Chandigarh, India

1965 Youth Centre, Firminy-Vert, France

Stadium, Firminy-Vert, France

Museum of the Twentieth Century, Nanterre, Paris (project)

1965/
68 Unité d'Habitation, Firminy-Vert, France

Publications:

By LE CORBUSIER: books—*Feuille d'Avis de La Chaux-de-Fonds*, La Chaux-de-Fonds 1911; *Etude sur le Mouvement d'Art Décoratif en Allemagne*, Paris 1912; *Après Le Cubisme*, exhibition catalogue, with Amédée Ozenfant, Paris 1918; *Architecture d'Epoque Machiniste*, with Amédée Ozenfant, Paris 1918; *Vers une Architecture*, Paris 1923, revised edition Paris 1924, Stuttgart 1926, London 1927, 2nd revised edition Paris 1928; *Urbanisme*, Paris, 1925, as *The City of Tomorrow and Its Planning*, London 1929; *L'Art Décoratif d'Aujourd'hui*, Paris 1925, 1959; *La Peinture Moderne*, with Amédée Ozenfant, Paris 1925; *Almanach d'Architecture Moderne*, Paris 1927; *Une Maison—un Palais*, Paris 1928; *Précisions sur un Etat Présent de l'Architecture et de l'Urbanisme*, Paris 1930; *Croisade; ou, Le Crépuscule des Académies*, Paris 1932; *La Ville Radieuse*, Paris and London 1935; *Aircraft*, Paris, London and New York 1935; *Quand les Cathédrales Etaient Blanches*, Paris 1937, as *When the Cathedrals Were White*, New York 1947; *Des Canons, Des Munitions?—Merci! Des Logis . . . S.V.P.!*, Paris 1938; *Le Lyrisme des temps nouveaux et l'urbanisme*, Paris 1939; *Destin de Paris*, Paris 1941; *Sur les Quatres Routes*, Paris 1941, as *The Four Routes*, London 1947; *Les Constructions Murondins*, Paris 1941; *La Maison des Hommes*, with Francois de Pierrefeu, Paris 1942, as *The Home of Man*, London 1948; *Entretien avec les Etudiants des Ecoles d'Architecture*, Paris 1943, as *Le Corbusier Talks with Students from the Schools of Architecture*, New York 1961; *La Charte d'Athènes*, Paris 1943, 1957; *Les Trois Etablissements Humains*, Paris, 1944; *Propos d'Urbanisme*, Paris 1946, as *Concerning Town Planning*, London 1947; *La Grille CIAM d'Urbanisme*, Paris 1948; *Le Modulor 1948*, Paris 1950, London 1954; *Poèsie sur Alger*, Paris 1950; *L'Unité d'Habitation de Marseille*, Paris 1950, as *The Marseilles Block*, London 1950; *Une Petite Maison, 1923*, Paris 1954; *Le Modulor 2*, Paris 1955, London 1958; *Le Poème de l'Angle Droit*, Paris 1955; *Architecte du Bonheur*, Paris 1955; *La Chapelle Notre-Dame-du-Haut à Ronchamp*, Paris 1956, as *The Chapel at Ronchamp*, London 1957; *Les Plans de Le Corbusier de Paris 1922–1956*, Paris 1958; *Le Poème Electronique*, with others, Brussels 1958; *L'Atelier de la Récherche Patiente*, Paris 1960; *Petites Confidences*, Paris 1960; *My Work*, London and Stuttgart 1960; *Gaudí*, Barcelona 1967; *Les Maternelles*, Paris and New York 1968.

On LE CORBUSIER: books—*Zwei Wohnhauser von Le Corbusier* by Alfred Roth, Stuttgart 1927; *Le Corbusier: Complete Works*, 7 volumes, edited by W. Boesiger, Zurich, subsequently London and New York, 1929–65; *Le Corbusier and Contemporary Architecture* by Siegfried Giedion, Paris 1930; *La Machino-Latrie de Le Corbusier* by Angel Guido, Rosario, Argentina 1930; *Le Corbusier et Pierre Jeanneret* by Francois de Pierrefeu, Paris 1932; *Revision der Kunstgeschichte: Prolegomena zu einer Kunstgeschichte aus dem Ceiste de Gegenwart, mit einer Anhang "Semper und Le Corbusier"* by Joseph Ganther, Vienna 1932; *L'Abitarie nell'Architettura di Le Corbusier* by Alberto Gatti, Rome 1933, 1953; *Von Ledoux bis Le Corbusier: Ursprung und Entwicklung der Autonomen Architektur* by Emil Kaugmann, Vienna and Leipzig 1933; *Le Corbusier; ou, l'Architecture au Service de l'Homme* by Maximilien Gauthier, Paris 1944; *Le Corbusier* by Giancarlo De Carlo, Milan 1945; *Que Répose Le Corbusier* by Jacques Clair, Paris 1946; *Le Corbusier, Architect, Painter* by Stamo Papadaki, New York 1948; *A Critical Review of Le Corbusier/Leitura Critica de Le Corbusier* by Pietro Maria Bardi, Sao Paulo 1950; *Le Corbusier* by Jean Alazard, Florence 1951, New York 1960; *Le Corbusier: Idealistisch Architect* by W. S. van de Erve, Utrecht 1951; *Two Standpoints Towards Modern Architecture: Wright and Le Corbusier* by Carl Berger Troedsson, Göteborg 1951; *Eight European Artists* by Fel H. Man, London, Melbourne and Toronto 1953; *Le Corbusier: Dessins* by Maurce Jardot, Paris 1955; *Ronchamp: Le Corbusiers erster Kirchenbau* by Anton Henz, Recklinghausen 1956; *Le Corbusier* by Anton Henz, Berlin 1957; *Chapelle Notre-Dame-du-Haut à Ronchamp* by Jean Petit, Paris 1957; *Architecture of Truth* by Francois Cali, London 1958; *Besuch in Ronchamp* by Karl Anton Rohna, Nuremberg 1958; *Le Corbusier* by Henri Perruchot, Paris 1958; *Le Corbusier's Wohneinbeit "Typ Berlin"* by Frithjof Miller-Beppen, Berlin 1958; *The Philips Pavilion at the 1958 Brussels World's Fair*, London 1959; *The Master Builders* by Peter Blake, New York 1960; *Le Corbusier* by Francoise Choay, New York and London 1960; *La Couvent Sainte Marie de la Tourette, Construit par Le Corbusier*, edited by M. Francois Mathey, Paris 1960; *De La Fenetre au Pan de Verre dans l'Oeuvre de Le Corbusier* by Jean Alazard, Paris 1961; *Un Couvent de Le Corbusier* by Jean Petit, Paris 1961; *La Tourette: Le Corbusiers erster Klosterbau* by Anton Henz and B. Moosbrugger, Starnberg 1963, Paris, Fribourg and New York 1966; *Le Corbusier: Architecture and Form* by Peter Blake, Baltimore 1964; *Le Corbusier: Presentations Choix de Textes, Bibliography, Portraits, Facsimiles*, edited by Sophie Daria, Paris 1964; *Le Corbusier* by Henrik Sommerschild, Oslo 1965; *Le Corbusier en la Historia* by Leonides Guadarrama, Mexico City 1966; *Le Corbusier* by Vittorio Franchetti Pardo, Florence 1966, Paris 1968, New York and London

1971; *Chandigarh* by Norman Evenson, Berkeley, California 1966; *Le Corbusier Parle* by Jean Petit, Paris 1967; *Le Corbusier: Oeuvre Graphique,* edited by Heidi Weber, Zurich 1967; *Documentation of the Centre Le Corbusier* by Heidi Weber, Jean Prouvé and Albert Jeanneret, Zurich 1967; *Four Compositions of Le Corbusier* by John Petit West, New York 1967; *Pavillion de Vendome: Le Corbusier,* Marseilles 1967; *Le Corbusier* by Willy Boesiger and Hans Girsberger, Zurich 1967; *Le Corbusier: Elemente einer Synthese* by Stanislaus von Moos, Frauenfeld 1968; *Les Erreurs de Le Corbusier et leurs Consequences* by J. Riboud, Paris 1968; *Qui Etait Le Corbusier?* by Maurice Besset, Geneva and Cleveland 1968; *Diskussion über Chandigarh: Antworten zu Fragen Europaischer Architekten* by M. Sharma, Zurich 1968; *Le Corbusier: Chandigarh, Neue Hauptstadtes Punjab Indien,* Nuremberg 1969; *Pessac de Le Corbusier* by Philippe Boudon, Paris 1969; *Le Corbusier: The Machine and the Grand Design* by Norman Evenson, New York and London 1969; *Fondation Le Corbusier,* Paris 1970; *Le Corbusier Lui-Même* by Jean Petit, Geneva 1970, New York 1971; *Ausstellungsgebaude von Le Corbusier in Zurich,* Dusseldorf 1970; *Le Corbusier* by Jean Petit, Lausanne 1970; *Le Corbusier: Artist and Writer* by Marcel Joray, New York 1970; *Le Corbusier* by Martin Pawley, New York 1971; *Le Corbusier and the Articulation of Architectural Elements* by G. H. Baker, Newcastle 1971; *Global Architecture 7: Chapelle Notre-Dame-du-Haut, Ronchamp* by Yukio Futagawa and Takamasa Yosizaka, Tokyo 1971; *Global Architecture 11: Couvent Sainte Marie de la Tourette* by Yukio Futagawa and Arata Isozaki, Tokyo 1971; *Le Corbusier: L'Architecte et Son Mythe* by Stanislaus von Moos, Paris 1971; *Le Livre de Ronchamp: Le Corbusier* by Jean Petit, Paris 1971; *Le Corbusier* by Robert Furneaux Jordan, New York and London 1972; *Le Corbusier* by Willy Boesiger, Zurich and New York 1972; *Global Architecture 18: Unité d'Habitation, Marseilles; Unité d'Habitation, Berlin* by Yukio Futagawa and Takamasa Yosizaka, Tokyo 1972; *Global Architecture 13: Villa Savoye, Poissy* by Yukio Futagawa and Richard Meier, Tokyo 1972; *Begegnung mit Pionieren* by Alfred Roth, Basle 1973; *Le Corbusier and the Tragic View of Architecture* by Charles Jencks, London and Cambridge, Massachusetts 1973; *Global Architecture 30: Chandigarh* by Yukio Futagawa and Takamasa Yoshizaka, Tokyo 1974; *Global Architecture 32: Sarabhai House, Shodhan House* by Yukio Futagawa and B. V. Doshi, Tokyo 1974; *Le Corbusier* by Stephen Gardiner, London and New York 1974; *Urbanistica e Mobilita* by P. G. Gerosa, Zurich 1974; *Le Corbusier in Perspective* by Peter Serenyi, New York 1975; *Le Corbusier e "L'Esprit Nouveau"* by R. Gabetti and C. Olmo, Turin 1975; *Le Corbusier: Evolution of His Architecture* by W. Curtis, London 1975; *Global Architecture 37: Millowners Building; Carpenter Center* by Yukio Futagawa and Kenneth Frampton, Tokyo 1975; *Le Corbusier in Selbstzeugnissen und Bilddokumenten* by N. Huse, Hamburg 1976; *The Education of Le Corbusier* by P. V. Turner, New York and London 1977; *Masters of Modern Architecture: Frank Lloyd Wright, Le Corbusier, Mies van der Rohe, and Walter Gropius* by Edwin and Joy Hoag, Indianapolis 1977; *The Early Drawings of Charles-Edouard Jeanneret* by M. P. M. Sekler, New York and London 1977; *The Open Hand* by Russell Walden, London and Cambridge, Massachusetts 1977; *Le Corbusier* by E. Nagy, Budapest 1977.

Le Corbusier (Charles Edouard Jeanneret), architect, painter, author, journalist and lecturer, urbanist, wood sculptor, and designer of furniture, enamels and tapestry, was during his lifetime the doyen, idealistic conscience and chief propagandist of modern architecture. He inspired fanatical devotion and exercised a magnetic and often barely rational hold over his followers throughout the world. Ferociously egocentric and difficult to work with, he possessed tremendous vitality, high artistic perception, the deepest feelings, remarkable receptiveness, a sense of drama, and a love of nature—and throughout his life he was an outsider in Parisian society.

Intellectually Le Corbusier was a dualist. He was fundamentally a divided human being, torn between precision and sensibility. His brilliant intuitive approach to design originated in nature, in the rich and diverse landscape of the Swiss Jura. Because of his Calvinist upbringing and individualistic temperament, he never grew into a benevolent man of peace, propriety or gentility. Indeed, he became the very reverse. Egotistical, proud and avid for recognition, he drove himself ruthlessly forward in a lifetime of struggle, of intellectual and professional combat.

Le Corbusier experienced the world in a profoundly emotional way and in so doing exposed the Dionysian-Appollonian polarities of his vision. As an artist-architect his themes were: the tension between the individual—especially the creative artist—and society; the notion of the artist as genius, seer and visionary prophet; the value of spontaneous feeling and expression of emotion, the original as against the traditional in art, values, morality and social conventions. These themes undeniably suggest the romantic. Yet the High Romantic in Le Corbusier vied with another facet of his personality—that side of him that preferred Cartesian clarity of thought. This more classical aspect of his personality explains his preoccupation with harmony and his interest in the world of the abstract. In fact functions of this binomial—space, precision, order, form, machine aesthetic, scale, *béton brut*, mathematics, proportion and the modulor—are concepts that appear over and over again in his thinking.

As a product of a late 19th-century art education and despite his experiences with Perret and Behrens, the young Jeanneret pitched himself into life's battles in the style of his bedside hero Don Quixote. He never rejected the machine as William Morris had done. In fact, as a young man in Paris he tried unsuccessfully to become an industrialist. Eventually he emerged under his new name Le Corbusier, not as a technical director of industrialized building systems but as a purist painter and architect of the white, cubic architecture of the 1920's. His most poetic examples were the Villa La Roche-Jeanneret, 1923–25; Le Pavillon de L'Esprit Nouveau, 1925 (rebuilt in Bologna, 1977); Les Terraces at Garches, 1927; and Les Heures Claires at Poissy, 1929–31. In effect Le Corbusier's answer to the industrialization of housing was Purism. The fact that all his Purist houses demanded a high degree of craft skills to build them meant that the final result was purely symbolic of first-machine-age architecture.

Architectural practice for Le Corbusier in the 1920's was complicated. He had no technical background. He was no builder. He was not even a good technician. Yet he did have technical ideas and he wanted desperately to be thought of as a man of the 20th century. One has the feeling about Le Corbusier that, as a man of action, he would have been much happier had he been practising in the age of Palladio.

An even more striking example of Le Corbusier's idealistic predicament is provided by his encounter with the City of Paris. It was the testing ground of all his urbanism. Le Corbusier hoped that if he could bring order to the disorder of Paris, the event would trigger an urban revolution: within this new framework the architecture of the new age could arise. Le Corbusier's intuitive capacity to anticipate the urban consequences of the car and the motorway showed remarkable foresight and imagination. At the same time, his answer to meet the future needs of the inner city demonstrated that he was not a pure intellectual with a classical mentality, who used logic as the organizing principle *par excellence*. His visions were the mystical product of a man who desired the harmonious solution of Nature as the model for 20th-century man. Le Corbusier's desire for harmony was the fundamental goal behind all his work.

Nowhere is Le Corbusier's archilles heel more painfully exposed than in his plans for Paris. On the basis of a Cartesian-geometrical system he developed his notorious vision of high-density office towers, motorways and underpasses, so familiar now to Western man. For all his visionary capacity he never fully appreciated the effect of excesses in transportation and centralization on *people*. As an experimental model Le Corbusier took the historic right bank of Paris and autocratically applied his heavenly vision to the Marais quarter. Between 1922 and 1946 Le Corbusier put forward five separate schemes for Paris, and each time he abundantly demonstrated his political naivety. As an urbanist he always considered that he had observed people's needs, and he thought that he had solved the problem of the ugliness of the suburbs. But it is now quite clear that Le Corbusier never understood other people. He conceived his plans messianically and then wondered why he "got kicked in the arse for his pains."

There were other inherent weaknesses in his method of working as an architect. From early in his career his artistic abilities as an architect greatly exceeded his administrative skills. Moreover, under the puritanical influence of Ozenfant, Le Corbusier's creation was strictly limited within the Purist ideology of *objet-types*. Moreover, he had difficulties with land tenure, technical servicing and the clinical workability of his Purist houses.

By 1925 Le Corbusier had begun to feel his way beyond the Purist impersonal condition of his painting, and he finally abandoned it in his architecture in 1929. From that time he tried to adjust his thinking in urbanism, which widened along with his humanity, though perhaps never enough. He embraced the human condition more confidently and richly. He got married. Through his wife Yvonne Gallis he made his final and irrevocable conversion to the light of Provence and to the psychological spontaneity of the French Mediterranean temperament. These influences are to be found in his paintings from the 1930's onwards. The liberating effect of the Mediterranean upon his work aesthetically, psychologically and spiritually cannot be overemphasized. Le Corbusier turned his back on Purism, although he retained the Apollonian desire for visual clarity and harmonic measurement through his modulor. Above all it was in the Dionysian sphere of feeling and intuition that Le Corbusier's personal development began to leap forward energetically, and his paintings glory in a rich vocabulary and intensity of curvilinear form and colour that leave one in no doubt about the influence of women in his life.

By the mid-1950's Le Corbusier was as complete an artist as he would ever be. His paintings were full of a rich multiplicity of meanings. Even in maturity his artistic psyche was still the principal source of his unwavering strength and rebelliousness. Like a monk he painted every morning in his apartment above the Rue Nungesser-et-Coli, and from the late 1920's onwards this discipline of plastic research was the basis of his aesthetic leadership. There in his studio his ideas germinated, were imaginatively sorted and reviewed, ready for admission to his mature architecture.

As far as materials were concerned, all his life Le Corbusier had wanted to build a steel building with exactitude, but in the economic climate of post-war France he was restricted to working in reinforced concrete and using cheap Algerian labour. But what a success he made of this stringency. In spite of the often sloppy workmanship his office permitted, Le Corbusier did for concrete what Michelangelo had done for marble. His *béton brut* potency marked all his mature work from the Unité d'Habitation, Marseilles, 1946–52; Notre-Dame-du-Haut de Ronchamp, 1950–55; Couvent de La Sainte-Marie-de-la Tourette, Eveux-sur-l'Arbresle, 1953–59; The High Court at Chandigarh, 1951–59; to the Carpenter Centre for the Visual Arts, Harvard University, 1961–64.

Amongst all the heroic poetry of his mature work, the Chapel at Ronchamp is his enigmatic masterpiece, "the pearl of my career." This commission came at a fortunate time in Le Corbusier's creative life when he had reached artistic and intellectual maturity. His ideas had been fully developed, and he now unashamedly and passionately responded to nature and her inherent rhythms. The idea of pilgrimage, of worship before the spectacle of nature, was extremely appealing to Le Corbusier's developed notion of the spiritual. Such a programme stimulated and excited his imagination. The Chapel is situated on a high point above the village of Ronchamp in the Haute-Saône, where the surrounding configurations of earth and sky reveal a rare richness—basic and profound. For this reason alone, the Chapel of Ronchamp became one of his most revealing commissions. Unhesitantly, he called forth a powerful response before the drama of nature. For Le Corbusier, Ronchamp is the meeting-place of the sense-world and the spiritual. In his nature mysticism he unrelentingly projected the principle of a free, spontaneous and creative life as the essence of reality, and gave instinctual expression to the whole world of nature, that aspect of creation neglected by Christianity.

Although this isolated programme of pilgrimage practically made Le Corbusier a household name, his spontaneous success on the hill of Bourlémont concealed a variety of problems for modern architecture. In the first place, many thought Le Corbusier had betrayed the rational principles upon which modern architecture was based. Several church architects mistakenly aped Le Corbusier's imagery without realizing the individuality of the Ronchamp programme or the uniqueness of its site. Many more misguided architects thought Ronchamp was the signal enabling their liberation to do anything they wanted. Le Corbusier unwittingly prolonged the life of an ideal, that of the Renaissance architect as a messianic prophet. As far as Le Corbusier himself was concerned, these problems of misrepresentation of his vision did not interest him. Ronchamp for him was a spontaneous moment of ecstasy where, in one day, he defined an idea which captured a higher level of reality than the previous chapel. He said of the experience:

This pilgrim chapel is no baroque
    pennon
May Ronchamp bear witness,
Five years of work isolated on the hill.
I have never in my life explained a
    work,
The work may be liked or disliked,
    understood or not,
What difference does that make to me.

At Ronchamp Le Corbusier was as near to expressing his inner voice as he ever came to doing. In this commission he successfully brought together the ideals and realities of the situation, and for that reason Ronchamp was and still is a masterpiece.

To historians, however, the problem becomes one of interpreting the architect's *oeuvre*. To understand Le Corbusier one must discover him creatively. There is no shortcut to an understanding of his work. There is, for example, the question of whether Le Corbusier's architecture changed fundamentally during the course of his career. Although his work of the 1950's is more richly expressive and laden with a multiplicity of meanings than his Purist architecture of the 1920's, the differences between the two periods is one of degree, not of kind. During both periods his work owed allegiance and inspiration to nature and to a form of measurement which varied from *les tracés régulateurs* of the 1920's to the modulor—a proportioning harmonic grid—that underlaid all his mature work from the 1950's onwards. In Le Corbusier's Purist period his work was under the discipline and exactitude of *objet-types,* yet there was still a strong abstracted link with nature, although that link is sometimes difficult to see. Le Corbusier's mature work has a more obvious and richer affinity with nature, which becomes all the more apparent when one has personally experienced the influence of the Mediterranean. The answer to the question of

whether or not Le Corbusier's vision as an architect changed categorically is, therefore, no, but it must be admitted that until he built Ronchamp, his nature mysticism was not fully visible to the world.

Le Corbusier was a brilliant artist. Yet, as a designer, his artistic autocracy often led him, particularly in urbanism, towards sterility and worse. This contagious condition was part of the thinking of all the pioneers of modern design from William Morris to Gropius. And, indeed, Le Corbusier's personality mirrors all the major problems that have beset the 20th century: authoritarianism, fascism, opportunism and artistic autocracy. Politically, Le Corbusier's dilemma was that he was a nature mystic operating autocratically in the century of mass democracy. Plagued by this disease, whichever way he turned, he suffered defeats. He was rejected at Vichy by an authoritarian body, but his plans were also rejected by the people of Paris. Le Corbusier's problem was that he acted like a God when he was not one, and therefore the gap between his idealism and the political realities was one that could never be closed. However, when commissions came to which Le Corbusier could respond idealistically as a nature mystic, he did create architecture that was original not only within the period in which he worked but also within his own *oeuvre*. He never stood still artistically, and he never created the same building twice.

As an artist-architect Le Corbusier could be both devastatingly brilliant and overwhelmingly a tragic figure, depending upon the circumstances. Where the architect's mysticism was alien to the sociopolitical programme, there was stalemate. But where the architect's vision coincided with the requirements of the client's situation, he achieved a masterpiece—as at Ronchamp. Le Corbusier shared both the brilliance and the central weakness of his spiritual mentor, Jean-Jacques Rousseau: both men radically disturbed the periods within which they worked; both were nature mystics, both were politically impotent, and both died alone. Nevertheless, whatever influence others had on him, Le Corbusier followed his own path, he was master of his own fate, faithful only to himself, lonely as the sun but one who glowed with much the same intensity.

—Russell Walden

LEGORRETA Vilchis, Ricardo.

Mexican. Born in Mexico City, 7 May 1931. Educated at the Universidad Nacional Autonoma de Mexico, Mexico City, 1948–52, Dip.Arch. 1953. Married Maria Luisa Hernandez in 1956; children: Lucia, Lourdes, Elisa, Luis, Ricardo, and Victor. Worked as a Draftsman, 1948–52, and Project Manager, 1953–55, for José Villagrán García, Mexico City; in partnership with José Villagrán García, 1955–60; in private practice, Mexico City, 1961–63. Since 1963, Principal, Legorreta Arquitectos, Mexico City (partners: Noe Castro and Carlos Vargas); since 1977, President, Legorreta Arquitectos Diseños, furniture and accessory design, Mexico City. Design Professor, 1959–62, and Chief of the Experimental Architecture Group, 1962–64, Universidad Nacional Autonoma de Mexico. Member of the International Council, Museum of Modern Art, New York, since 1970. Exhibitions: *Borrowings and Lendings,* University of Wisconsin at Milwaukee, 1977; *Mexican Architecture of Today,* Mexico City, 1978; *Master Builders: The Architecture of Mexico,* University of California at Los Angeles, 1979. Distinguished Honorary Fellow, Mexican Society of Architects, 1978. Honorary Fellow, American Institute of Architects, 1979. Address: Ricardo Legorreta Arquitectos, Palacio de Versalles 285-A, Col. Lomas Reforma, Mexico 10, D.F., Mexico.

Works:

1963 Fabricas Automex Chrysler Office Building and Warehouse, Mexico City
1963/
  64 Smith, Kline and French Laboratories, Mexico City
1963/
  69 Fabricas Automex Chrysler Office Building and Engine Plant, Mexico City
1966 Nissan Mexicana Office and Manufacturing Building, Cuernavaca, Mexico
1966/
  68 Celanese Mexicana Office and Laboratory Buildings, Mexico City (with Roberto Jean)
1967 Cedros School, Mexico City
1968 Camino Real Hotel, Mexico City
      Plunket House, Mexico City
1970 Pedro de Gante School, Tulancingo, Hidalgo, Mexico
1972 Camino Real Hotel, Cabo San Lucas, Baja California, Mexico
      Office building, Insurgentes and Algeciras, Mexico City
      Palacio de Iturbide restoration, for the Financiera Banamex, Mexico City
      Monumental fountain for Lomas Verdes, Mexico City (project; with Luis Barragán)
1973 Houses, Valle de Bravo, Mexico City
1974/
  75 IBM Office Building, Mexico City
1975 IBM Factory, Mexico City
      Kodak Mexicana "Mexicolor" Laboratories, Mexico City
      Camino Real Hotel, Can Cún, Quintana Roo, Mexico
1976 Urban design and architectural coordination of "El Rosario," for Infonavit, Mexico City
      Gomez House, Mexico City
1976/
  77 Seguros America Banamex Office Building, Mexico City
1977 Pedro de Gante School expansion, Tulancingo, Hidalgo, Mexico
      IBM Technical Center, Mexico City
1978 La Estadia Housing Development and Equestrian Club, Mexico City
1979 Camino Real Hotel, Ixtapa, Guerrero, Mexico
      Las Brisas Hotel renovation, Acapulco
      Camino Real Hotel renovation, Mexico
      Camino Real Hotel expansion, Can Cún, Quintana Roo, Mexico
      Lomas Sporting Club, Mexico City
      DESC Office Building, Mexico City
      IBM Factory expansion, Guadalajara

Publications:

On LEGORRETA: articles—"Forma y Funcion: Legorreta Arquitectos" in *Arquitectura* (Mexico City), March 1966; "Ricardo Legorreta" in *Arquitectura* (Mexico City), April/July 1968; "Camino Real" by Victor R. Zevallos in *Architectural Forum* (New York), November 1968; "Hotel Camino Real, Mexico City" in *Architecture: Formes et Fonctions* (Lausanne), 1969; "Everyman's Mexican Home" in *Progressive Architecture* (New York), June 1969; "Hotel Camino Real in Mexico City" in *Deutsche Bauzeitung* (Stuttgart), February 1970; "La Arquitectura Mexicana en la Industria," special issue of *Arquitectura* (Mexico City), no. 104, 1971; "The Mexican Minimalism of Ricardo Legorreta" by C. Ray Smith in *Architectural Record* (New York), October 1976; "Ricardo Legorreta" in *Teccnodomica* (Athens), March 1977; "Ferienwohnungen in Mexico" in *Baumeister* (Munich), May 1977; "Ricardo Legorreta: Mexico's Mexican Architect" by Anthony C. Antoniades in *Architecture + Urbanism* (Tokyo), no. 4, 1978.

Ricardo Legorreta: Camino Real Hotel, Can Cún, Quintana Roo, Mexico, 1975

Post-war architecture in Mexico was an assembly of foreign imitations. Versions of International Style thrived. If it were not for the murals by some of Mexico's most famous artists that were incorporated on the elevations, many of the buildings could be taken to belong anywhere on earth but in Mexico. This was an architecture of the "column culture," the Corbusier pilotis, and a concern for proportional appeal in the elevations. The "wall culture" of native architecture had been totally forgotten by contemporary Mexican architects.

Ricardo Legorreta brought back the "wall culture;" he brought Mexico's contemporary architecture back to Mexico. His work, along with that of Luis Barragán (who, however, did some works in International Style at the beginning of his career), has evolved out of the study and understanding of the values of traditional architecture in Mexico. Its language recognizes the "wall" rather than the "column," the supremacy of solids over voids, the importance of three-dimensional continuity, the use of color to enclose wall space, and the preference for privacy that is to be encountered in Mexican cloisters and haciendas. Legorreta does responsive regional architecture but does not indulge in the imitations and set design techniques of that "Mexican-looking" architecture so abundant in Mexico as well as in Southern California.

The architect of a diverse number of building types, Legorreta is mainly known as the creator of the superb series of Camino Real hotels. The Camino Real in Baja California, a semi-underground complex facing the Pacific, is totally integrated with its landscape. It is energy-efficient and is distinguished by the superb quality of its interiors as well as by the ingenious treatment of its exterior grounds.

The Camino Real in Can Cún, in the Yucatan Peninsula, is as an ocean liner floating in vast oceans. Its linear form, its strong cross-section, and the ingeniously planned sequence of its functions, make it a "vessel of life," one of the most relaxing environments on our planet.

The dream of the city dweller can become reality: Legorreta's hotels are opened to a cross-section of the population. The Camino Real in Mexico City, perhaps the most "homey" hotel on earth, is an outstanding example of a mixture of moderation and grandeur, and rich and poor are both to be found in the various bars and restaurants of this machine of integration. The hotel is the Mexico City address of the extravagant American conventioneer; it is also the place where the Mexican worker takes his date. Legorreta's hotels are palaces for everyone, not just monuments to the vanity of the rich. Something of his attitude is suggested in his acknowledgement that he has been influenced by Hassan Fathy's book *Architecture for the Poor.* The Camino Real in Mexico City is also distinguished by a most appealing use of color and by the incorporation of other visual arts, painting and sculpture, as integral parts of the architecture. A huge stabile by Calder and some works by Mathias Goeritz complete the hotel environment, one that eventually becomes a total experience.

The introverted plan of the Camino Real in Mexico City, as well as the strong grey wall that defines the property of the IBM Factory in the same city, very clearly express Legorreta's concern for privacy and the hacienda prototype. His other factories and some of his residential projects are also case studies in response to landscape, interior simplicity, and three-dimensional continuity of interior space.

Ricardo Legorreta achieves what he does through extremely hard work. By constructing very large scale models during the design stage, he exploits completely the space possibilities of his project.

Legorreta's architecture has been consistently good, and it has evolved because, despite the capital-making nature of his major commissions (hotels, IBM factories, etc.), he has never regarded architecture as from the perspective of a businessman. He has always remained a dedicated artist. Along with perhaps two other Latins, Ricardo Bofill in Barcelona and Luis Barragán in Mexico City, Legorreta occupies the top place in Spanish-decendant architecture in the world. He is certainly Mexico's Mexican architect.

—Anthony C. Antoniades

LEO, Ludwig.

German. Born in Rostock, 2 September 1924. Educated at the Hochschule für Bildende Künste, Berlin, 1948–54, Dip.Arch. 1954. Married Sheila Leo in 1955; children: Miriam and Morag. Worked in the office of Hans and Wassili Luckhardt, Berlin, 1953–55. In private practice, Berlin, since 1956. Professor, Hochschule für Bildende Künste, Berlin, since 1975. Recipient: Baukunst Prize, Berlin Senat, 1969. Address (office): Fasanenstrasse 72, Charlottenburg, Berlin, West Germany.

Works:

1958   Kindergarten, Loschmidstrasse, Berlin
1959   Eichkamp Students Residence, Berlin (with Müller and Heinrichs)
1962/
63   Sports Hall, Charlottenburg, Berlin
1965   Town Centre, Gropiusstadt, Berlin (competition project)
1966   Town Hall extensions, Zehlendorf, Berlin (competition project)
       French Lycée, Berlin (competition project)
       Sewage Plant, Marienfelde Building, Berlin (project)
       Multi-purpose floating station, on the River Havel, Berlin (project)
1967/
70   Märkisches Viertel Development, Berlin
1969/
72   DLRG (Deutsche Lebens Rettungs Gesellschaft) Multi-Purpose Station, Am Pichelsee, Spandau, Berlin
       Circulation Tank, Institute for Waterways and Shipbuilding, Tiergarten, Berlin
       School Building, Bielefeld, Germany (prototype)
       Lighting plan for the Kurfürstendamm, Berlin
       Rudolf Virchow Hospital extensions, Berlin (project)
       Autobahn redevelopment, Rehberge, Berlin (project)

Publications:

On LEO: articles—"Serious Sport" in *Architectural Review* (London), July 1966; "Progetti di Ludwig Leo a Berlino" by A. Carlini in *Controspazio* (Bari, Italy), November/December 1972.

It is a difficult task to write about the architect Ludwig Leo. Difficult because there are no authoritative or interpretative studies that explain his work and because his buildings and projects do not correspond to any of the current and well-known architectural tendencies. In effect, there is no available frame of reference. We can, however, rely on the evidence of the work itself. Specialized knowledge and historical memory are unnecessary, for there is no formal quotation, no aesthetic reference to a previous style, model, or even to his own evolution. Leo is radically unconcerned with history in his work: each building is a new, striking, and above all individual formal solution to a particular problem. If one looks more closely, even the means toward the expression of function seem novel, and here we discover the real significance of Leo's buildings: they modify the otherwise over-riding demands of pure function. The aesthetic and social aims of the artistic programs of the historical avant garde of functionalism—the Bauhaus—floundered because of the priority given to function. Since then, function has established itself as an absolute—and it is this problem that Leo addresses in his work. The fact that so far he has been able to realize very little is evidence that he continues the struggle of historical functionalism without wishing to be involved in its later compromises. Beyond the trappings of convention, prejudice and stereotype, his search has been for the essence of the building task, the true function required by the client. Paradoxically, it is usually this contemporary search for social universality by means of a particular building task that deters clients.

A building such as the DLRG Station was completed after a long process of engineering, involving research into construction, materials, spatial arrangement, and self-expression, but it fails to conform to urban and formal context by its radical reference to its own particular function. Yet, whatever their effect, DLRG Station and Leo's other buildings are not elitist—just the opposite. The precision and intelligence of their functionalism and their visible "usefulness" suggest another kind of society, not one of hierarchy and oppression but one of equality and freedom, a dynamically permeable society in which things also are liberated so that they may really work in co-operation with people.

Both in his theorizing and in his works, Leo has furthered an enlightened thinking about the machine age. He has worked not only against the decline into vulgar functionalism but also against the fashions of rationalism and populism that altogether ignore function and are preoccupied with the aesthetic shell. Of course, Leo's desperate struggle is naive in a deeply human sense, and of necessity he has worked in isolation, away from the prevailing architectural milieu of commercial success. But his failure is important, because it stimulates, it leads forward. Most of the work of his successful colleagues, during a time of architectural crisis, achieves only the opposite.

—Günther Uhlig

LEONHARDT, Fritz.

German. Born in Stuttgart, 11 July 1909. Educated at the University of Stuttgart, 1927–31, Dip.Ing. 1931, D.Eng. 1938; Purdue University, West Lafayette, Indiana, 1932–33. Married Liselotte Klein in 1936; children: Sabine, Monika, Heidemarie, Hans-Jorg, and Christine. Bridge Engineer of the Autobahn in Stuttgart, Berlin and Cologne, 1934–38. In private practice, as consulting engineer, Stuttgart, since 1938: in partnership with Wolfhart Andrä, as Leonhardt und Andrä, since 1953. Professor and Director of the Institute for Concrete Structures, 1958–74, and Rector (President), 1967–69, University of Stuttgart. Member, Deutsche Akademie für Städtebau und Landesplanung, since 1952; Vice-President, Comité Européen du Béton, since 1971. Recipient: Honor Award, Verein Deutscher Ingenieure, 1953; Paul Bonatz Prize, Stuttgart, 1959; Fritz Schumacher Prize, 1961; Gold Medal, Austrian Engineers and Architects Association, 1965; Werner-von-Siemens-Ring, 1965; Emil Mörsche Medal, 1967; Gustave Magnel Gold Medal, Belgium, 1968; First Prize, Straits of Messina Bridge Competition, 1969; Grashof Medal, Verein Deutscher Ingenieure, 1973; Freyssinet Medal, Federation Internationale de la Précontrainte, 1974; Distinguished Service Award, Oregon State University, Corvallis, 1974; Gold Medal, Institution of Structural Engineers, London, 1975; Distinguished Service Medal, Baden-Württemberg, 1976; Gold Medal, Associazione Italiana Cemento Armato e Precompresso, 1977; Honor Award, Washington Roadside Council, U.S.A., 1978. Dr.Ing.: Technical University, Braunschweig, Germany, 1972; Dr.Tech.: Technical University of Denmark, Lyngby, 1974. Honorary Member of the Chamber of Architects of Baden-Württemberg, 1974. Honorary Member of the American Concrete Institute, 1972; First Honorary Member, Comité Euro-International du Béton, 1977. Address: Leonhardt und Andrä, Lenzhalde 16, Postfach 742, D-7000 Stuttgart 1, West Germany.

Works:

1935   Sulzbach Viaduct, Denkendorf, for the Stuttgart-Ulm Autobahn
1938/
41   Cologne-Rodenkirchen Suspension Bridge, across the River Rhine
1947/
48   Cologne-Deutz Bridge, across the River Rhine
1949   Bridge across the River Elz, on the Freiburg-Offenburg Highway, near Emmendingen, Germany
1950/
51   Heilbronn-Böckingen Bridge, across the River Neckar, Germany
1952/
53   Untermarchtal Bridge, across the Danube Valley, Germany
1952/
56   North Bridge, across the River Rhine, Dusseldorf
1954   Ziegelhausen Bridge, across the River Neckar, near Heidelberg

Ludwig Leo: Circulation Tank, Institute for Waterways and Shipbuilding, Berlin, 1972

1955/
56 Television Tower, Stuttgart
   Indoor Swimming Arena, Wuppertal, Germany

1955/
59 5 bridges, crossing the Delta of the Rio Jacui, near Porto Alegre, Brazil
   Bridge across the Rio Guaiba, near Porto Alegre, Brazil

1957 Bridge across the River Rhone, St. Moritz, Switzerland

1957/
62 Bayer Building, Leverkusen, Germany
   Mannesmann Building, Dusseldorf

1959 Suspension bridge, across the River Tejo, Lisbon (project)

1960/
61 BASF Building, Ludwigshafen, Germany

1960/
62 Elevated highway, Jan-Wellem-Platz, Dusseldorf (with T. Tamms)

1961 Mono-cable suspension bridge, across the River Rhine, Emmerich, Germany (project)
   Bridge, Port Elizabeth, South Africa

1961/
63 Unilever Building, Hamburg

1962 Agnashini Bridge, India
   Lapinlahti Bridge, Helsinki (project)
   Alvsborgsbridge, near Göteborg, Sweden (project)

1963 Bridge across the River Ager, near Attersee, Austria

1964 Bridge across the Rio Caroni, near San Felix, Venezuela

1965/
68 Heinrich Hertz Telecommunications Tower, Hamburg

1967 German Pavilion, Expo '67, Montreal (with Frei Otto)

1968 Bridge across the River Inn, Kufstein, Austria

1968/
69 Knie Bridge, across the River Rhine, Dusseldorf
   Sechslingspforte Indoor Swimming Arena, Hamburg

1969 Bridge over the Straits of Messina, Italy (competition project)
   Ravi Bridge, near Lahore, Pakistan

1971 Andarax Bridge, Spain

1972 Roofing for the Sports Arenas, Olympic Games, Munich
   Guadalimar Bridge, Spain

1972/
77 2 bridges across the River Parana, near Buenos Aires

1973 Viaduct No. 302, Peripheral Highway, Istanbul
   Val Restel Bridge, near Trento, Italy

1975 Viaduct, across the Neckar Valley, near Weitingen, Germany

1975/
76 Dusseldorf-Oberkassel Bridge, across the River Rhine

1978 Columbia River Bridge, connecting Pasco and Kennewick, Washington, U.S.A.
   Bridge across the Gronach Valley, Heilbronn-Nuremberg Autobahn
   Geislingen Bridge, across the Kocher Valley, Heilbronn-Nuremberg Autobahn
   Allgemeine Rentenanstalt Administration Building, Stuttgart
   University of the Federal Army, Hamburg
   Bridge II across the Rio Caroni, near San Felix, Venezuela
   Telecommunications Tower, Frankfurt

Development of several pre-stressing methods for pre-stressed concrete, since 1949; development of the Incremental Launching System, since 1959.

Publications:

By LEONHARDT: books—*Die Gestaltung der Brücken,* with K. Schaechterle, Berlin 1938; *Brücken,* with Paul Bonatz, Königstein, Germany 1951; *Spannbeton für die Praxis,* Berlin 1955, 3rd edition 1973, English translation as *Prestressed Concrete Design and Construction,* Berlin 1964; *Brücken aus Stahlbeton und Spannbeton* by Emil Mörsch, editor with H. Bay and K. Deiniger, Stuttgart 1958; *Vorlesungen über Massivbau:* volume I, *Grundlagen zur Bemessung im Stahlbetonbau,* with E. Mönnig, Berlin 1973; volume II, *Sonderfälle der Bemessung im Stahlbetonbau,* with E. Mönnig, Berlin 1975; volume III, *Grundlagen zum Bewehren im Stahlbetonbau,* with E. Mönnig, Berlin 1974; volume IV, *Nachweis der Gebrauchsfähigkeit,* Berlin 1976, 1978; and volume VI, *Grundlagen des Massivbrückenbaues,* Berlin 1979; *Ingenieurbau-Bauingenieure gestalten die Umwelt,* Darmstadt 1974.

For all the many bridges, towers, halls, and industrial structures that I have designed, I have always struggled for beauty. In my experience beauty can only be obtained by observing rules that can be traced to the oldest monuments. Such rules are good proportions between all elements, order by restriction to only a few directions of lines, edges etc. in space, simplicity and clearness of structural systems, no unnecessary additives, harmonious colours, and scale appropriate to surroundings and to the human senses.

Sometimes slenderness, lightness, and keenness of structures can help to enhance good appearance.

The aesthetic qualities of all that we build are more important for the future of mankind than most of us realize; they have influence on the health of our soul and, therefore, on social peace and human welfare.

—Fritz Leonhardt

Fritz Leonhardt: Cologne-Deutz Bridge, across the River Rhine, 1948

Fritz Leonhardt is one of the most influential engineers in Germany, and his research and development work have had a considerable effect on the building of bridges and other engineering works throughout the world.

Leonhardt's development of lightweight tracks made of cellular steel plates led to the building of steel girder bridges and later to the first steel beams for steel bridges. In order to construct large viaducts —such as the Sulzbach Viaduct at Denkendorf and the Neckar Viaduct at Weitingen—he introduced the use of slender steel supports, and so created transparent and filigree-like valley crossings that could be easily integrated into the landscape according to scale. In 1934, at the start of his career in bridge building, it was customary to use statically-determined single-span beams. It took great strength of conviction and perseverance to replace the multispan girders with a largely continuous construction that had no expansion joints. It was in the 1950's that Leonhardt's bridge over the Hochstrasse in Dusseldorf spanned 38 support openings without a joint; today these jointless constructions are generally accepted in Germany as well as in many parts of the world.

Leonhardt's research on aerodynamically-stable suspension bridges began in 1950. He replaced the gigantic trussed reinforcing girders of the earlier American suspension bridges with slender, aerodynamically-formed carriageway slabs, and achieved wind stability without any bracing struts. These developments were based on experiments carried out in the wind tunnel at the National Physical Laboratory at Teddington, near London. The first pioneering projects for this kind of suspension bridge —such as the Tejo Bridge at Lisbon and the Rhine Bridge at Emmerich—came too early for their time; they were too *avant garde* to be adopted. It was left to other engineers, inspired by Leonhardt, to take up his ideas in the suspension bridges across the Severn, the Bosphorus, and the Humber. The knowledge and experience gained thereby led to the development of improved cross sections for slanting cable bridges, and Leonhardt's trials for the Parana bridges resulted in an aerodynamic stability for slanting multicable bridges through systematic shock absorption. For the bridge over the Straits of Messina, he suggested and executed a slanting cable bridge of 1500 metre span width.

In his conversation and his lectures, Fritz Leonhardt often reminds one of his architect father, whom he talks of as his first teacher and the one who first showed him how to observe. Later guiding spirits were the engineers Freyssinet and Maillart and the architect Paul Bonatz. Architects and engineers alike have influenced his achievements, and it is not surprising that he feels strongly about the need for cooperation between them. He has always passed on to his engineering students a necessary understanding of the work of the architect. It has been his concern to make these two professionally autonomous groups work as one team. This is not to say that he trained engineers who dabbled in architecture or that he wanted architects to act as if they were engineers. He advocates an arrangement in which the engineer is a specialist with a particular responsibility and the architect is the general practitioner with an overview of the project.

Leonhardt has practiced this concept in his daily work. He was the engineer in charge of the German Pavilion at *Expo '67* in Montreal and of the Olympic tent constructions in Munich. His designs for television/communications towers have influenced the building of such towers throughout the world: the best example of his work is the impressive and original television tower in Stuttgart, the first concrete tower with a revolving restaurant—an entirely convincing structure, due to its genuine and uncluttered form. In high-rise blocks, Leonhardt, at an early stage, used the idea of incorporating lifts and staircases in cores and of regarding them—also from the statistical point of view—as stressed towers with boxed sections restrained in the foundations: exam-

ples are the BASF Building in Ludwigshafen and the Mannesmann Building in Dusseldorf. This idea inspired engineers and architects in the United States to design the external walls of skyscrapers as hollow boxed sections, as in the World Trade Center in New York and the Hancock Center in Chicago.

Fritz Leonhardt is one of the great engineers of his time, continuing the line of such renowned figures as Freyssinet, Maillart, and Pier Luigi Nervi, Franz Dischinger, Felix Candela, and Ulrich Finsterwalder. Broadly educated, Leonhardt has been concerned to approach problems from all aspects—in professional practice, in his teaching, in his writings, in his sense of vocation, and in the breadth of his general knowledge as well as professional expertise.

He once said that he feels committed to "well being and beauty," and that, "just as no teacher, lawyer, or sociologist should do so, so too no engineer should any longer be allowed to go out into his profession without at least having come to certain basic convictions about the worth and existence of beauty and its relation to man."

—Kurt Ackermann

LE PLASTRIER, Richard.
Australian. Born in Melbourne, Victoria, 7 November 1939. Educated at the University of Sydney School of Architecture, under Lloyd Rees, 1958–63 (Board of Architects Fellowship and Prize), B.Arch. 1963; Kyoto University Foreign Students' Group, under Tomoya Masuda, 1966–67. Architect with Clark, Gazzard and Yeomans, Sydney, 1963–64, Jørn Utzon, Sydney, 1964–66, Kenzo Tange and Urtec, Tokyo, 1967–68, and Lobb and Partners, London, 1969–70. Since 1971, in private practice, Sydney. Part-time Architect/Tutor, University of Sydney, 1971–78. Address: "Sitting Pretty," Lovett Bay, via Church Point, New South Wales 2105, Australia.

Works:

1961 Changing shed and toilets, Castlecrag Boatshed, Sydney
1963 Halford House, 26 Corniche Road, Church Point, New South Wales

Richard Le Plastrier: Walker House, Bilgola Beach, near Sydney, 1978

1969/
70 Motorway Service Areas, Hartshead Moor, Killington, and Membury, England (competition projects; with Brian Leather)
1972/
78 Buddhist Meditation Retreat, Cliff Drive, Katoomba, New South Wales
1973/
74 Spencer House, Lovett Bay, near Sydney
1973/
78 Walker House, 4 The Serpentine, Bilgola Beach, near Sydney
1974 High Court of Australia (competition project; with Lawrence Nield)
1974/
75 Paludan House, Gilwinga Drive, Bayview Heights, near Sydney
1976/
78 Craigie House, Wyong Creek Road, Yarramolong Valley, near Wyong, New South Wales (with David Jacobson)
1978/
79 Hebden House, Lovett Bay, near Sydney (project)
Housing, Bathurst, New South Wales (competition project; with Stephen Wells)
Sussman House, Cammeray, near Sydney
Le Plastrier House alterations, Lovett Bay, New South Wales (with Shelley Ludyk)

After graduating from the University of Sydney, Richard Le Plastrier worked with Don Gazzard and then in Jørn Utzon's Sydney office. From 1966 to 1970 he travelled extensively in South East Asia, the Middle East and Europe. He studied with Professor Masuda at Kyoto University, and worked in Kenzo Tange's office on the Kuwait Stadium project.

Le Plastrier's architectural language exploits the confrontation of opposites as a means of generating an architectural dialectic and synthesis. Thus his buildings involve a series of contradictions: they are at once romantic and rational, rich in landscape values and highly engineered, primitive and advanced, soft and hard, and warm and cold. This pervasive complementarism explains the subtlety, richness, and hidden strength of his formal architectural language.

He has also made extensive use of corrugated iron formed into elegant barrel-vault or combined segmental and planar profiles for the roofs of his houses.

Each house by Le Plastrier is important even when, as in the Paludan House in Bayview Heights, his intentions have not been realized fully, because he invests much time and thought to their design and construction. The Walker House at Bilgola Beach is one of the most significant post-war Australian buildings. It consists of two corrugated copper barrel-vaulted pavilions connected at the rear by a rammed earth wall and linear circulation/service space, facing onto a magnificent tropical garden.

—Philip Drew

LESCAZE, William.

American. Born in Geneva, Switzerland, 27 March 1896; emigrated to the United States, 1923. Educated at the College de Geneve; E.T.H: Eldgenössische Technische Hochschule, Zurich, under Karl Moser, M.A. 1919. Married Mary Hughes; son: Lee Adrian. Worked in the war devastated areas of France, and in the office of Henri Sauvage, Paris, 1919–20; worked for Hubbell and Benes, Cleveland, Ohio, 1925; in private practice, New York, 1925–29; Partner, with George Howe, q.v., Howe and Lescaze, Philadelphia, 1929–34; Principal, William Lescaze and Associates, New York, 1934 until his death,

William Lescaze: Headmaster's House, Dartington Hall, Totnes, Devon, England, 1931

1969. Member, New York State Building Code Commission, 1949–59. Fellow, American Institute of Architects. *Died* (in New York) *9 February 1969.*

Works:

1928 The Future American Country House (project)
Penthouse Studio, *Macy's International Exhibition of Art in Industry,* New York
President's Room, Amos Parrish and Company, New York
1929 Dreyfus Apartment, New York
Howe and Lescaze Office, Philadelphia (with George Howe)
Ingersoll Museum, Pennlyn, Montgomery County, Pennsylvania (project; with George Howe)
Oak Lane Country Day School, Second Street and Oak Lane Road, Philadelphia (demolished)
William Stix Wasserman Office, Philadelphia (with George Howe)
Wasserman House II, Whitemarsh, Pennsylvania (project; with George Howe)
Mrs. Leopold Stowkowski Apartment, New York
1930 Ben Herzberg Apartment, New York
C. Phillips Apartment, New York
Porter House, Ojai, California
1930/
31 Museum of Modern Art, New York (project: preliminary designs; with George Howe)
1931 Hattie Carnegie Shop, New York
Headmaster's House (Curry House), Dartington Hall, Totnes, Devon, England
Hessian Hills School, Mt. Airy Road, Croton-on-Hudson, New York (with George Howe; later remodelled; now part of a synagogue complex)
Philadelphia Saving Fund Society Office Building, 12th and Market Streets, Philadelphia (with George Howe)
Trans-Lux Theatre, New York
Emigrant Savings Bank and Office Building, East 42nd Street, New York (project; with George Howe)
Peck House, Paoli, Pennsylvania (project)
Wertheim House, Cos Cob, Connecticut (project)
Charles Harding Apartment, New York

1931/
32 Frederick V. Field House, New Hartford, Connecticut (with George Howe)
Philadelphia Saving Fund Society Garage, 12th and Filbert Streets, Philadelphia (with George Howe)
Housing development, Chrystie-Forsyth Streets, New York (project; with George Howe)
1932 Belmont-Lincoln Hotel, Park Avenue and 42nd Street, New York (project)
50 small houses (project; with George Howe)
Storefront, Dorothy Gray, New York (project)
Amos Parrish and Company Office Building, New York (project)
Wilbour Library, Brooklyn Museum, New York
1933 Auditorium, Connecticut College, New London, Connecticut (project)
1934 Lescaze House, 211 East 48th Street, New York
1935 Brooklyn Children's Museum, New York (project)
1936 High school, Ansonia, Connecticut
Brooklyn Children's Museum, New York (revised project)
1937 Administration Building, Kimble Glass Company, Vineland, New Jersey
Williamsburg Houses, Brooklyn, New York (with others)
1938 Cherry Lawn School, Connecticut
CBS Radio Building, Hollywood, California (with E. T. Heitschmid)
1939 Aeronautics Pavilion, *World's Fair,* New York
Swiss Pavilion, *World's Fair,* New York
1941 Longfellow Building, Washington, D.C.
House, 124 East 70th Street, New York
1946 Elliott House, New York
1949 Calderone Theatre, Hempstead, Long Island, New York
1950 Medical Center, Crosset, Arkansas
Harbor Homes Development, Port Washington, Long Island, New York
Spinney Hill Homes Development, Manhasset, Long Island, New York
1951 India Exchange Ltd. Offices, Calcutta
1954 Dune Deck Hotel, Westhampton Beach, Long Island, New York
1955 Houses, Salamanca, New York (project)

Offices, 711 Third Avenue, New York
1956 Laurel Homes Development, Roslyn, Long Island, New York
1958 Offices, 30 West Broadway, New York
1959 Chancellery, Swiss Embassy, Washington, D.C.
1960 Civil and Municipal Courthouse, Centre Street and White Street, New York (with Matthew Del Gaudio)
Manhattanville Residences, New York
The Churchill Apartments, Los Angeles
1961 School of Art and Design, New York
1962 "Christian Peace" Building and Chapel, United Nations, New York
Offices, 300 East 42nd Street, New York
1964 First National City Bank Pavilion, *World's Fair,* New York
Offices, 777 Third Avenue, New York
1969 One New York Plaza, Water, Whitehall, South and Broad Streets, New York

Publications:

By LESCAZE: book—*On Being an Architect,* New York 1942; articles—"The Classic of Tomorrow" in *American Architect* (New York), December 1935; "A Community Theatre" in *Architecture for the New Theatre,* New York 1935; "America's Outgrowing Imitation of Greek Architecture" in *Architectural Record* (New York), August 1937; "The Meaning of Modern Architecture" in *North American Review* (Cedar Falls, Iowa), Autumn 1937; "Why Modern Architecture" in *Royal Architectural Institute of Canada Journal* (Toronto), 1937; "Marginal Notes on Architecture" in *Virginia Quarterly Review* (Charlottesville), Spring 1939; article in *Pencil Points* (New York), July 1940; "These Documents Called Buildings" in *The Intent of the Artist,* Princeton, New Jersey 1941; "New York State Building Code Commission: Aims and Accomplishments" in *Architectural Record* (New York), June 1951; "The Correlation of the Arts" in *AIA Journal* (Washington, D.C.), November 1952.

On LESCAZE: articles—"The Future American Country House" in *Architectural Record* (New York), November 1928; "City House of William Lescaze, New York" in *Architectural Forum* (New York), December 1934; "The Proposed Children's Museum, Brooklyn" in *American Architect* (New York), December 1935; "CBS Broadcasting Studios, Hollywood, California" in *Architectural Forum* (New York), June 1938; "Longfellow Building, Washington, D.C." in *Architectural Forum* (New York), June 1941; "Steel House, Factory-Built in Seven Pieces" in *Architectural Forum* (New York), December 1949; "Multi-Family Housing" in *Architectural Record* (New York), June 1954; "Proposed City and Municipal Courts" in *Architectural Record* (New York), December 1955; "Genetrix: Personal Contributions to American Architecture" in *Architectural Review* (London), May 1957; "Philadelphia Saving Fund Society Building: Its Development and Significance in Modern Architecture" by William Jordy and "Philadelphia Saving Fund Society Building: Beaux Arts Theory and Rational Expressionism" by Robert A. M. Stern in *Journal of the Society of Architectural Historians* (Philadelphia), May 1962; "Philadelphia Saving Fund Society Building" by Henry Wright in *Architectural Forum* (New York), May 1964.

William Lescaze, born in Geneva, Switzerland in 1896, spent most of his life in the United States, where he is remembered as one of the first Europeans to carry the gospel of the modern movement across the Atlantic. Following general schooling at the College de Geneve, he took his architectural training at the Technische Hochschule in Zurich, where he worked under Karl Moser, an early advocate of modernism and one of the central forces in Lescaze's life.

In 1919 and 1920 Lescaze worked in areas of France devastated by World War I, and did a tour of duty in the Paris office of another pioneer modernist, Henri Sauvage. Early on he developed a yearning to design monumental architecture, a passion which contributed to his decision to emigrate to America in 1923. Employment proved difficult to find in New York, however, and he moved to Cleveland for what turned out to be no more than a six-month stint with Hubbell and Benes, a firm of conservative tastes. He returned to New York late in 1925.

At that time America as a whole had little sympathy for, and less knowledge of, avant-garde European architecture. Lescaze found himself producing work, mostly commercial and residential interiors, in the eclectic manners of the day. Following a number of projects done more or less after the Art Deco style, Lescaze designed a strikingly modern and experimental penthouse studio for R.H. Macy Company's International Exhibition of Art in Industry in 1928. The following year he met the Philadelphia architect George Howe, with whom he was destined to do his most important work. Howe was then moving closer and closer to modernism himself, and he wanted to form a partnership with someone who knew and stood for the principles of the International Style. Lescaze seemed to be that man. The firm of Howe and Lescaze was begun in May of 1929.

The most significant fruit of this relationship was the majestic Philadelphia Savings Fund Society Building of 1931, which Howe had sketched out before he met Lescaze but to which Lescaze contributed several important refinements. Howe's plan had been at first symmetrical, influenced by Beaux-Arts tradition; Lescaze changed this to an informal organization more in keeping with modernist ideas. The result has been called the first American skyscraper in the International Style.

Howe and Lescaze broke up their partnership in 1934, after which Lescaze worked mostly on his own. In his later years he vacillated between a form of streamlined moderne (e.g., the CBS Radio Building in Hollywood, California, designed with E.T. Heitschmid, 1937–38) and a manner nearer that of the International Style (e.g., the Longfellow Building, Washington, D.C., 1941). He continued practicing after World War II but ceased to be a figure of prominence, and little notice was taken of his death in 1969.

—Franz Schulze

LEVI, Rino.

Brazilian. Born in Sao Paulo, 31 December 1901. Educated at primary and secondary schools in Sao Paulo; Academy of Fine Arts, Milan, 1921–22; School of Architecture, Rome, 1923–26, Dip.Arch. 1926. Married Yvonne Theodora Arié in 1933; daughter: Barbara. In private practice in Sao Paulo from 1927: in partnership with Roberto Cerqueira Cesar from 1941 and with L. R. Carvalho Franco from 1952 (firm constituted as Rino Levi Arquitetos Associados Ltda., 1965, and continues under the direction of Cerqueira Cesar and Carvalho Franco). Consultant, Interamerican Centre for Housing, Bogota, Colombia, 1957. Professor of Architecture and Urbanism, University of Sao Paulo, 1954–59; Visiting Professor of Architecture and Urbanism, University of Caracas, Venezuela, 1959. President, Brazilian Institute of Architects, Sao Paulo, 1954–59. Member of CIAM (Congrès Internationaux d'Architecture Moderne), from 1945. Exhibitions: *Bienal Hispano America,* Madrid 1951; Pan American Congress of Architecture, Mexico City, 1952, Washington, D.C., 1965. Recipient: First Prize, Santo André Civic Centre Competition, 1956; First Prize, Albert Einstein Hospital Competition, Sao Paulo, 1957. Honorary Member, Sociedad Colombiana de Arquitectos, 1957, Sociedad Central de Arquitectos, Argentina, 1958, and Sociedad de Arquitectos, Mexico, 1960; Honorary Fellow, American Institute of Architects, 1965. *Died* (in Sao Paulo) *29 September 1965.*

Works:

1932 Columbus Apartment Building, Sao Paulo
1935 Do Chá Viaduct, Sao Paulo
1936 Cine UFA Movie Theatre, Sao Paulo
1938 Porchat Building, Sao Paulo
1939 I.A.P.I. Office Building, Sao Paulo
1941 Hotel Excelsior and Ipiranga Cinema Building, Sao Paulo
Saedes Sapientiae Girls' School, Sao Paulo
1943 Cultura Artística Theatre, Sao Paulo
Trussardi Building, Sao Paulo
Stig Building, Sao Paulo
Companhia Jardim Coffee Processing Plant, Sao Paulo
1944 Rino Levi House, Sao Paulo
Prudencia Apartment Building, Sao Paulo
1945 Maternity Hospital, University of Sao Paulo (project; with R. Cesar)
1947 Banco Paulista do Comercio Building, Sao Paulo
Central Institute for Cancer Diseases, Sao Paulo
1948 Sao Paulo Chapter Headquarters of the Brazilian Institute of Architects
1950 Gomes House, Sao Jose dos Campos, Sao Paulo
Cruzada Pro-Infancia Children's Hospital, Sao Paulo
1951 Milton Guper House, Sao Paulo
1952 Industrial workers' housing, Sao José dos Campos, Sao Paulo
1953 Paulo Hess House, Sao Paulo
1956 Copana Parking Garage, Rio de Janeiro (with Luis Roberto Carvalho Franco)
America Parking Garage, Sao Paulo
Electrocloro Engineers' Housing, Rio Grande, Brazil
Paulista Biological Laboratory, Sao Paulo
Concordia Office Building, Sao Paulo
1957 Master plan for Brasilia (competition project)
1958 Castor Delgado Perez House, Sao Paulo
Albert Einstein Hospital, Sao Paulo
1959 R. Monteiro Office Building, Sao Paulo
1961 Plavinil-Elcror Building, Sao Paulo
1962 Social Centre, University of Sao Paulo
Banco Itau America Building, Sao Paulo
1963 Parahyba Milk Plant, Sao José dos Campos, Sao Paulo
1964 Gravatá Apartment Building, Sao Paulo
1965 Tecelagem Parahyba Hangar, Sao José dos Campos, Sao Paulo
Araucaria Apartment Building, Sao Paulo
Civic Centre, Santo André, Brazil

Publications:

By LEVI: articles—"The Parking Problem in Sao Paulo" in *Acropole* (Sao Paulo), no. 207, 1950; "The Via 4th Congress" in *Acropole* (Sao Paulo), no. 203, 1955; "Research in Hospital Planning" in *Acropole* (Sao Paulo), no. 204, 1955; "Architects and Professional Regulations" in *Bem Estar* (Sao Paulo), no. 4, 1959; "The Role of Acoustics in Architecture" in *Engenharia Municipal* (Sao Paulo), no. 22, 1961.

On LEVI: books—*The Architectural Record Book of Commercial Buildings,* New York 1953; *Selezione Mondiale di Edilizia Ospedalieri* by Augusto Moral, Turin 1954; *Latin American Architecture since 1945* by Henry-Russell Hitchcock, New York 1955; *Garten und Haus* by Julius Hoffmann, Stuttgart 1956; *Modern Architecture in Brazil* by Henrique Mindlin, Rio de Janeiro and London 1956; *L'Architettura Moderna in Brazile* by Sergio Bracco, Milan 1967; *Diccionario da Arquitectura Brasileira* by E. Corona and C. Lemos, Sao Paulo 1972; *L'Ar-*

Reno Levi: Civic Centre, Santo André, Brazil, 1965

chitecture Moderne au Brésil by Yves Bruand, Lille 1973; *Rino Levi,* Milan 1974; *Diccionario de la Arquitectura* by Gerd Hatje, Barcelona 1975; *Profile of the New Brazilian Art* by Pietro Maria Bardi, Rio de Janeiro 1975; article—"Una Nuova Dignitad al Habitat" by Bruno Alfieri in *Zodiac* (Milan), no. 6, 1960.

Throughout his career Rino Levi was particularly concerned to maintain a correct professional attitude within the reality of the milieu in which he worked. His work always maintained its excellence despite the enormous pressures exerted by real estate speculation in Sao Paulo, the city where most of it was built. His constant concern with ecology influenced a generation of younger architects and his work helped to focus the search for integration of inside and outside spaces.

In his first works in the late 1930's—the Columbus Apartment Building, the UFA Movie Theatre, and the Porchat Building—the mass is worked in a manner close to expressionism, opposing full and empty, light and dark, indentations and juttings. (They are all buildings of some excellence, compared to the usual work of that period.) Then, progressively, the mass is simplified, losing this sculpture-like quality, and the surfaces flatten out, as in the Trussardi and Stig buildings of 1943. In the Banco Paulista do Comercio Building of 1947, the pure geometry of the glass tower is subtly broken by the curving of one facade, by the jutting-out of the floor slabs, and by the set-back and the glass-brick wall on the ground floor.

This language is further developed in the Head-

quarters for the Sao Paulo Chapter of the Brazilian Institute of Architects, in the Concordia Building, and in the Banco Itau Building: it forms one of the distinct currents in Levi's work and is characterized by an apparently meaningless contradiction in the articulation of some architectural elements—a "contradiction" that is the means by which he signals the different functions and the constructive hierarchy of the building.

In the Brazilian Institute of Architects Headquarters the curtain wall is fractioned in the same way as in the Banco do Comercio Building, and the prism is further interrupted by the insertion of the twisted volume of the restaurant on the 2nd and 3rd floors. In the Concordia Building the interplay of the "brise-soleil," the hollowed-out elements, and the glazed areas adds an unexpected depth and ambiguity to the facades, enlivening the box-like volume of the building. Banco Itau, a late work—in a phase that was discreetly brutalistic in other, more typical, cases—is an excellent example of the slab-and-tower typology in the tradition of the Lever Building of Skidmore, Owings and Merrill. Its connection with the syntax is in a contradictory fragility that seems to deny the solidity of the volumes. The blocks seem to hover, the facades barely touching one another, and the kinetic quality of the aluminum "brise-soleil" underlines a certain immateriality of the whole.

Another and parallel current in Rino Levi's work, no less involved in the expression of functions but heavier in aspect, encompasses such distinct works as the Companhia Jardim Coffee Processing Plant, all of his hospitals, the Paulista Biological Laboratory, and the Civic Center of Santo André.

The hospitals are all planned on the same principle of sheltering different activities in separate blocks. The complex relationship of the various units sometimes fails to produce a successful whole, but the technical and functional solutions proposed are always paradigmatic. The Santo André Civic Center is the last and the largest of Rino Levi's works. It comprises three different buildings—the City Hall, the Council Chamber, and the Cultural Center. The architectural language is very simple, plastically defined by the clear and sober design of the exposed concrete structure, and particularized in each instance by the functional distinctions of each building. The horizontal "brise-soleil" reinforce the grid of the structure and create planes of light and shadow that lend depth to the facades.

From the 1940's onwards Rino Levi's work also shows a growing concern for the specific conditions of the environment in which he built. This concern can take the simple form of providing adequate sun protection for an over-exposed facade or it can involve the whole project in a much more profound way. In the Rino Levi, Milton Guper, Paulo Hess, and Delgado Perez houses, the theme of inside/outside integration is developed in such a way as to create some of the most important propositions so far devised in urban domestic architecture for subtropical climates. The gardens, in a determining relationship with the house, either isolate the house from the street by merging it with the public space or they extend it by extending the rooms—shadowed, intimate, protected by walls and pergolas, directly connected to the inside through large openings that allow for a pleasant interflow of space.

In the Sedes Sapientiae Girls School, in addition

to the light-modulating devices, there is a careful balance between open and built areas. The undulating marquee surrounding and crossing the garden becomes an intermediary zone and connects the blocks of classrooms, bedrooms, and the auditorium. There is a similar distribution at the Parahyba Milk Plant.

Rino Levi's office is still one of the most important in Brazil, and since his death in 1965 his partners, Roberto Cerqueira Cesar, Luis Roberto Carvalho Franco, and, since 1972, Paulo Julio Valentino Bruna, have continued to turn out large scale projects such as the Industries Federation Building, the Siemens Headquarters, and the Gessy-Lever Cosmetics Plant.

—Jorge Czajkowski

LEWERENTZ, Sigurd.

Swedish. Born at the Sandö Glass Works, Bjärtrå, near Sundsvall, Sweden, 29 July 1885. Educated at the School of Building, Chalmers Technical College, Gothenburg, 1905–08; Academy of Arts, Stockholm, 1910: with six fellow students left the Academy and founded the Free School of Architecture, Stockholm, with Carl Westman, Ragnar Östberg, Ivar Tengbom and Carl Bergsten as teachers, 1910–11 Married Edit Engblad in 1911; children: Per, Ewa and Carl. Worked in the office of Bruno Möhring, Berlin, 1907–08, Theodor Fischer, Munich, 1909, and Richard Riemerschmid, Munich, 1910; in partnership with Torsten Stubelius, Stockholm, 1911–17; in private practice, Stockholm, 1917–43, Eskilstuna, Sweden, 1943–58, Skanör, Sweden, 1958–70, and in Lund, Sweden, 1970 until his death, 1975. Founder Director (with Claës Kreüger, 1928–35), Idesta Metal Window Company, Stockholm, 1928–40, and Eskilstuna, Sweden, 1940–75. Exhibitions: Architecture School, Aarhus, Denmark, 1969; Swedish Museum of Architecture, Stockholm, 1969. Recipient: First Prize, with Gunnar Asplund, Stockholm South (Woodland) Cemetery Competition, 1914; First Prize, with Osvald Almqvist, Jönköping Redevelopment Competition, Sweden 1928. Died (in Lund) 29 December 1975.

Works:

1911 Building plan for the Marma Works, Söderhamn, Sweden (project)
1913 Holiday houses, Kummelnäs, near Stockholm
Chinese Garden Pavilion, Drottningholm, Stockholm
1913/
14 Assembly Rooms, Färe Glassworks, Sibbhult, Sweden (with Torsten Stubelius)
1914 Development plan for Brantevik, Sweden
Chapel, Forsbacka, Sweden (with Torsten Stubelius)
Crematorium, Hälsingborg, Sweden (project; with Torsten Stubelius)
Ahxner House, Djursholms-Ösby, Sweden
Ramen House, Hälsingborg, Sweden
Plan for the Stockholm South (Woodland) Cemetery, Stockholm (with Gunnar Asplund)
1914/
15 Workers housing, Forsbacka, Sweden
1917 Shop, Marma, Sweden (project)
Plan for Götaplasten Square, Gothenburg (competition project)
1917/
18 Eneborg Housing Estate, Hälsingborg, Sweden (with Torsten Stubelius)
1920/
25 Burial Chapel, Valdemarsvik, Sweden
1920/
58 Eastern Cemetery, Malmo

1926 Chapel of the Resurrection, Woodland Cemetery, Stockholm
1928 Plan for the redevelopment of 3 blocks in Jönköping, Sweden (4 competition projects; with Osvald Almqvist)
Katarina Secondary School, Stockholm (competition project; with Osvald Almqvist)
1929 Tombstone, Utterö Island, Stockholm Archipelago
1929/
58 Industrial development, Skoghall, Sweden
1930 House, apartment, small pavilions, furniture, 3 coaches for General Motors, and official exhibition sign and posters, Stockholm Exhibition
1931 Filips Tea-Rooms, Regeringsgatan, Stockholm
Town plan for Stockholm (with Osvald Almqvist)
National Insurance Building, Adolf Fredriks Kyrkogata, Stockholm
Burial Chapel, Enhöping, Sweden
1932 Museum, Malmo (competition project; with Osvald Almqvist)
Marabou Shop-front, Gothenburg
1932/
44 Municipal Theatre, Malmo (with D. Hellden and E. Lallerstedt)
1933 Villas, Djursholm, Sweden (project)
Johanneberg Church, Gothenburg (competition project)
1935 Burial Chapel and Crematorium, Djursholm, Sweden (project)
1936 Edstrand House, Falsterbo, Sweden
Karolinska Institutet, Stockholm (competition project)
1938/
45 Chapel, Eastern Cemetery, Malmo
1939 New National Insurance Buildings, Gärdet, Stockholm (project)
1943 Crematorium, Eastern Cemetery, Malmo
Lewerentz Apartment, Eskilstuna, Sweden
1946/
62 Cathedral restoration, Uppsala (competition projects; developed with Peter Celsing)
1956/
60 St. Mark's Church, Skarpnäck, Stockholm
1958 Lewerentz House/Office conversion, Skanör, Sweden
1966 St. Petri Church, Klippan, Sweden
1969 Service Building, Eastern Cemetery, Malmo (with Bernt Nyberg)
1970/
71 House of Parliament, Stockholm (competition project; with Bernt Nyberg)

Publications:

On LEWERENTZ: book—Sweden Builds by G. E. Kidder Smith, New York and Stockholm 1950, London 1957; articles—"Sigurd Lewerentz" by H. Ahlberg and "Kapel og Krematorium i Malmö" by A. Jacobsen in Byggmästaren (Stockholm), no. 19, 1945; "Takvåning for arkitekt SAR Sigurd Lewerentz i Eskilstuna" in Byggmästaren (Stockholm), no. 1, 1948; "Markuskirken i Björkhagen" by Kay Fisker in Arkitektur (Copenhagen), February 1963; "Björkhagen Church, near Stockholm" in Architectural Design (London), March 1963; special issue of Arkitektur (Stockholm), September 1963; "Kyrka i Klippan" by S. I. Lind in Arkitektur (Stockholm), May 1968; "St. Petri Kirke i Klippan" in Arkitektur (Copenhagen), October 1968; "Sigurd Lewerentz in Memoriam" in Arkitekten (Copenhagen), 10 February 1976; "Sigurd Lewerentz's Last House" by Bernt Nyberg in Arkitektur (Stockholm), May 1976; "Sigurd Lewerentz 1885–1975" by J. Codrington in Architectural Review (London), April 1976.

*

Sigurd Lewerentz, with Almqvist, Asplund and Wernstedt, studied under the distinguished ar-

chitects Westman, Östberg, Tengbom and Bergsten at a private school of architecture established in Stockholm in 1910 as a reaction against the policies and teachings prevalent in the Academy of Arts at that time. Lewerentz and his colleagues belonged to a movement known as "national realism," which attempted to return to a national identity in architecture. This movement was opposed to the development of neo-classicism so fashionable in respectable academic circles in most European countries before 1914.

With Gunnar Asplund, Lewerentz entered a design for the new Woodland Cemetery competition and won first prize. Prior to this success, Lewerentz had co-operated with Stubelius in a project for a new crematorium in Hälsingborg, and indeed many of his later most elegant designs were for buildings with a certain formal or ritualistic function—although his holiday houses in the Stockholm Archipelago (1913) are both traditional and timeless.

Like many architects of his generation, Lewerentz was influenced not only by his immediate mentors but also by the writings and examples of professionals as diverse as the great German, Tessenow, and contemporary Englishmen who followed in the wake of the Arts and Crafts movement.

Lewerentz entered a number of competitions with his friend Almqvist; in 1928 they won first, second and third prizes in a competition for the development of three blocks in Jönköping. He was responsible for a number of residential buildings and housing estates, but his major architectural successes are his design, with Asplund, for the Stockholm Cemetery; his solo work for the crematorium at Malmo of 1943; and his beautiful brick church at Skarpnäck of 1960. Some interesting projects, produced in collaboration with Almqvist, include Katarina Secondary School in Stockholm, the Malmo Museum, and a town plan for Stockholm.

Sigurd Lewerentz is one of the most important Swedish architects of the 20th century. With his contemporaries Gunnar Asplund and Osvald Almqvist, he helped to change the course of Scandinavian design. Perhaps the drastic move away from the picturesque, delicious eclecticism of his teacher, Ragnar Östberg, was necessary to purify architectural thought, but the final result is somewhat dessicated. It is also a function of architecture to delight, and Lewerentz undoubtedly achieved delight in his design, with Asplund, for the Woodland Cemetery. The landscape around Asplund's famous crematorium is chiefly the work of Lewerentz, and it is of a very high order. His crematorium in Malmo is also set in a cemetery, one that he had designed as early as 1920. Paradoxically, just as Lewerentz had been in the vanguard of a move away from a tradition of classicism, so he was a leader in the revolt against international functionalism. The private house that he designed in 1936 at Falsterbo heralded the beginning of a swing in his development that was to end with his simple brick church at Skarpnäck. Eternal architectural values rather than an hysterical belief in progress prevailed as Lewerentz returned to an architecture that respected nature and his native soil.

—James Stevens Curl

LEWIS, David.

American. Born in Southampton, England, of South African parents, 24 January 1922; emigrated to the United States, 1963. Educated at the University of Cape Town, South Africa, 1939–41; Leeds College of Art, Yorkshire, England (Lovis Aaron Fellow, 1961–63), Dip. Arch. 1961, Dip.Arch. (with distinc-

David Lewis: Gananda Neighborhood Center, Gananda, New York, 1974

tion in thesis) 1963. Petty Officer, South African Navy, 1941–44. Partner, Design Collaborative, London, 1956–61; Senior Architect, City of Leeds, 1961–63; Andrew Mellon Professor of Architecture and Urban Design, Carnegie-Mellon University, Pittsburgh, 1963–68. Since 1965, Founder-Partner, Urban Design Associates, Pittsburgh (partners: Raymond L. Gindroz; James P. Goldman). Visiting Critic in Urban Design, Faculty of Architecture, Yale University, New Haven, Connecticut, 1968–70; William Henry Bishop Visiting Professor of Architectural Design, Yale University, 1975, 1977; Visiting Professor of Urban Design, Ohio State University, Columbus, 1977–78. Member, Board of Directors, Pittsburgh Council for the Arts, and Director, Gallery for Contemporary Arts, Pittsburgh, 1968–70; Vice-Chairman, 1977, and Chairman, 1978, National Urban Design and Planning Committee, American Institute of Architects; Member, Arts Commission of Pittsburgh, 1978. Trustee, Pittsburgh History and Landmarks Foundation, since 1967. Exhibitions: British Exhibit, International Union of Architects, London, 1958; *This Is Tomorrow,* Whitechapel Gallery, London, 1962; *Confluences,* Pittsburgh, and Cincinnati and Columbus, Ohio, 1976. Recipient: William C. Bellamy Award, National Association of Housing and Redevelopment Officials, 1975, 1977; Biennial Honor Award, United States Department of Housing and Urban Development, 1976; Honor Award, *Urban Design Magazine,* 1977. Associate of the Royal Institute of British Architects; Fellow, Royal Society of Arts, England, 1971. Address: Urban Design Associates, 249 North Craig Street, Pittsburgh, Pennsylvania 15213, U.S.A.

Works:

1968/
72 Human Resources Center, Pontiac, Michigan
1971/
73 Master plan for the Methodist Hospital, Brooklyn, New York
1971/
77 Queensgate II Town Center, Cincinnati, Ohio
1973/
74 Gananda Neighborhood Center, Gananda, New York
1974 Master plan for Station Square, Pittsburgh (re-use of P. and L.E. Station and Yards)
      Master plan for the new Indiana University/-Purdue University at Indianapolis (with Woollen Associates)
1976/
78 Master plan and student housing for the University of Pittsburgh at Johnstown, Pennsylvania

1976– New Court Plaza (offices, apartments, commercial and garage), Pittsburgh
1977 Highland Elementary School, DuBois, Pennsylvania
      Sports Center, University of Pittsburgh at Johnstown, Pennsylvania
1977– Shadyside Estates (condominiums and apartments), Pittsburgh
1978 Phoenix-Hills Shopping Center, Pittsburgh
      Luthersburg Elementary School, Pennsylvania
      Forward/Shady Apartments for the Elderly, Pittsburgh
      Glen Hazel Housing, Pittsburgh
      Frank B. Fuhrer Office Building, O'Hara Township, Pittsburgh
      Ethnic Village, Settler's Cabin Park, Pittsburgh
      Oakland Planning Study, Pittsburgh
      Restoration of Historic York, for the National Register of Historic Places, York, Pennsylvania (with UNIPLAN)

Publications:

By LEWIS: books—*End and Beginning,* Johannesburg 1945; *The Naked Eye,* Cape Town 1946; *Piet Mondrian,* London 1956; *Constantin Brancusi,* London 1957, London and New York 1975; *New Hous-*

ing in Great Britain, with Hansmartin Bruckmann, London 1961; *The Pedestrian in the City,* editor, London 1966, New York 1967; contributor to *The People Versus the System,* edited by Sol Tax, New York 1968; contributor to *Education and Urban Renaissance,* edited by R. F. Campbell, L. A. Marx and R. L. Nystrand, New York 1968; *Urban Structure,* editor, London and New York 1969; contributor to *Values and the Future,* edited by Kurt Baier and Nicholas Rescher, New York 1969; *The Growth of Cities,* editor, London 1971; *The Olden Triangle,* with Raymond Gindroz, Pittsburgh 1977; articles—numerous in various professional and academic journals; also, editor, with Jules Gregory, "Community Design: By the People," special issue of *Process: Architecture* (Tokyo), March 1977.

The work for which my firm, Urban Design Associates, is best known involves users directly in planning and design.

We have over the years developed techniques for including citizens in the programs and decisions affecting their physical environments. We have included children and teachers in the design of schools, townsfolk in the design of parks and open-space systems and in the design of neighborhoods and town centers, and we have included the elderly in design processes dealing with their issues and problems too.

Many of these techniques are not only widely recognized as innovative but they have had a potent impact on design and on community pride in the product.

Among the projects that have received most recognition are the Human Resources Center, Pontiac, Michigan, and the Queensgate II Town Center in Cincinnati, Ohio. The Pontiac project was the first in the U.S.A. in which users developed the program, participated in the design, and became an integral part of the administration of the building which came out of the process. The Queensgate II project was the first town center in the U.S. to be developed in this way too.

These projects (and several others) are a dramatic break from the usual processes of modern architecture and client-architect relationships. They reconfirm the ancient traditions of urban places as the artifacts of citizens. In our processes, the user and architect gradually "speak with one voice." The built form emerges as *appropriate* not only in its utilitarian aspects, but socially, culturally, and politically also.

—David Lewis

In 1965 David Lewis founded Urban Design Associates in Pittsburgh, which has since become one of the leading urban design firms, especially well-known for its identification with community participation in the design and planning process.

Lewis came to the United States in 1963 when he was appointed Andrew Mellon Professor of Architecture and Urban Design at Carnegie-Mellon University in Pittsburgh. A native of South Africa, Lewis had spent his earlier professional career as an architect, educator and author in Great Britain. Soon after Lewis's arrival, Pittsburgh was to begin a period of reaction against the "Pittsburgh Renaissance," which had made astonishingly successful improvements in pollution abatement and in the development of the downtown and other commercial centers. Controlled, however, by a small group of business and political leaders, the "Renaissance" was perceived as making the over-all business climate of the City more successful at the expense of individual small property holders and neighborhoods.

Perhaps made sensitive to such issues by the social welfare policies prevailing in British planning (although planning of the time in Great Britain was at least as much *de haut en bas* as it was in Pittsburgh), Lewis became active on behalf of the people of the Hill District, an area of run-down small houses inhabited mainly by Blacks that lay just to the east of the central business district. As a consultant he also worked with the Pittsburgh Board of Education on a new building policy to promote school desegregation, and began work on a whole series of proposals for small communities and city neighborhoods, where ordinary people, living in the area, were encouraged to comment and make suggestions during the development of designs and plans.

The best-known example of this work by Lewis's firm is the Queensgate II Town Center in Cincinnati, for which Urban Design Associates were both the planners and the architects. This development fulfills a number of purposes, including providing a safe and pleasant transition between parking spaces and the building housing the Cincinnati Symphony Orchestra, creating a sense of urban place and identity, and bridging two inner-city neighborhoods.

Lewis's architectural and urban design philosophy can perhaps best be summarized by his own statement: "Five hundred years ago Alberti encouraged the architect to be an artist, an intellectual and a noble. Today we encourage him to be a citizen."

—Jonathan Barnett

LIM, William S(iew) W(ai).

Singaporean. Born in Hong Kong, 19 July 1932. Educated at the Architectural Association School, London, under John Killick, Bill Howell, Peter Smithson, Ove Arup and Robert Furneaux, Dip. A.A. 1955; Harvard University Department of City and Regional Planning, Cambridge, Massachusetts, under Jaqueline Tyrwhitt, 1956–57 (Fulbright Fellow). Married Lena U. Wen in 1962; children: Lim Chiwen and Lim Weiwen. Worked for the London County Council, 1955–56, and James Ferries and Partners, Singapore, 1957–60; Partner, Malayan Architects Co-Partnership (MAC), Singapore, 1961–67, and Design Partnership, Singapore, 1967–75. Managing Director, APAC (Asian Planning and Architectural Consultants Ltd.), Hong Kong, since 1970 (core members: Tao Ho, Hong Kong; Fumihiko Maki and Koichi Nagashima, Tokyo; Sumet Jumsai, Bangkok; Charles Correa, Bombay); Chairman, DP Consultant Service Pte. Ltd., Singapore, since 1971; Principal Partner, ABC Akitek, Malaysia, since 1974; Chairman and Principal Partner, DP Architects, Singapore, since 1975; also, Chairman, Select Books Ltd., Singapore, since 1977; Director, Solectra Ltd., Singapore, since 1977, and Gallery Asia, Singapore, since 1978. Chairman, Singapore Planning and Urban Research Group, 1966–68; External Lecturer, School of Architecture and Faculty of Law, University of Singapore, 1967–71; Member of the Transport Advisory Board and Chairman of the Working Committee, Ministry of Communications, Singapore, 1968–71; Member, International Advisory Committee, Pacific Asrama, 1974–75. Address: DP Architects, 5881 Golden Mile Shopping Centre, Beach Road, Singapore 7.

Works:

1962/
64   Singapore Conference Hall
1966/
67   2 houses, 11 and 11a Mount Rosie Road, Singapore
1967/
69   4 houses, 3 Chancery Hill Road, Singapore
Telephone Board Exchange and Engineering Centre, Singapore
1968/
69   House, 114 Windsor Park Road, Singapore
1969   Conference Centre, Vienna (competition project)
1969/
72   People's Park Shopping Complex, Singapore
1970/
71   House, 9 Frankel Street, Singapore
House, 464 Holland Road, Singapore
1970/
72   Golden Mile Shopping Complex, Singapore
Tanglin Shopping Centre, phase I, Singapore
1971   Jurong Town Hall, Singapore (competition project)
1971/
73   Katong Shopping Centre, Singapore
Ampang Park Shopping Centre, Kuala Lumpur, Malaysia
1972/
73   Plastics factory, Jurong, Singapore
Asia Radio Showroom, Singapore
1972/
76   Housing development, Bartley Road, Singapore
1973/
74   Shops and housing development, East Coast Road/Siglap Road, Singapore
1975   Dagat-Dagatan Low-Cost Housing, Manila, Philippines (competition project)
Dumai Complex, Kuala Lumpur, Malaysia
Ridgewood Condominium, Singapore
1975/
76   House renovation, 5 Victoria Park Close, Singapore
1976   Bandar Park Shopping/Entertainment Centre, Kuala Lumpur, Malaysia
St. Andrew's Junior College, Singapore
1976/
77   Yeo Hiap Seng Factory, Singapore
1977/
78   Yeo Hiap Seng Factory, Johor, Malaysia
Shops and housing development, Jln. Larkin, Johor, Malaysia
1978   Shops, hotel and entertainment centre, Malacca, Malaysia
Shopping centre, Temple Street, Singapore
Low-cost housing development, Kota Tinggi, Johor, Malaysia
Low-cost housing development, Plentong, Johor, Malaysia
Jalan Campbell Shopping Complex, Kuala Lumpur, Malaysia
Jalan Imbi Complex, Kuala Lumpur, Malaysia
Merlin Hotel, Johor Bahru, Malaysia
Prefabricated housing for the Middle East (project)
Sim Lim Tower, Singapore
Tanglin Shopping Centre, phase II, Singapore
2 houses, Coronation Road West, Singapore
Abu Dhabi Tower, Dubai (competition project)
Low Keng Huat Offices, Kuala Lumpur, Malaysia

Publications:

By LIM: book—*Equity and Urban Environment in the Third World,* Singapore 1975; articles—"Urban Transport and Mobility of People: Singapore as a Case Study" in *Singapore: A Decade of Independence,* edited by Charles Ng and T. P. B. Menon, Singapore 1975; "Options for Public Housing in Singapore: Some Policy Implications" in *New Directions* (Singapore), December 1975; "Driving Away Cars" in *The Times* (London), 19 July 1976; "Low Resource Urban Centres, with Special Reference to Asian Countries" in *City Planning Review* (Tokyo), 15 August 1976; foreword to *Questioning Development in Southeast Asia,* edited by Nancy Chng, Singapore 1977; "Money Well Spent" in *Singapore Trade and Industry Yearbook,* Singapore 1977; "Going Public—A Gone Case?" in *New Directions* (Singapore), June 1977; "An Overview of Some Policy Guidelines to Low-Income Urban Housing in Third World Countries" in *International Journal for Housing Science* (New York), no. 1, 1978; "If Buildings Could Speak . . ." in *Business Times* (Singapore), 25 August 1978; "When a City Is Not a

Home" in *Business Times* (Singapore), 25 September 1978.

On LIM: book—*Architecture in the Seventies* by Udo Kultermann, London 1979; articles—"William Lim" by Colin Gibson in *Nikkei Architecture* (Tokyo), no. 3, 1976; "The Ginger Man" by Ilsa Sharp in *Singapore Business,* February 1977; "William Lim" in *Nikkei Architecture* (Tokyo), no. 14, 1977.

Values, attitudes and visual images are changing at an accelerating rate. The speed of these changes is now unprecedented. A talented architect who practices mainly what he learnt during his formal education 15–20 years ago may be financially successful, but he is professionally irrelevant. The master-architect is dead!

In the last decade we have experimented with group working methods based on a complex blending of group-dynamic theories from the West with traditional practices in Asia. We work with and learn from talented young architects, who are fully integrated into the design-team. The group-dynamic process is practiced in the design team to intensify idea-interactions and to generate creativity. This continuous learning process is essential and must include new ideas drawn from other related disciplines. I can honestly state that the design of all of our major buildings was produced through joint, integrated efforts and cannot therefore be claimed by any single member of the team.

Our experience has shown that the team must be relatively small—4 to 8 persons at most. Team members should be of different ages and with different professional talents. The talent and personality of a single individual must not dominate the team. Common ground—especially relating to architectural theories—must be developed. Personal relationships, trust and respect must be established. These are essential conditions for effective idea-interactions; so, too, are frank and often heated discussions during design working sessions.

Team members must have common objectives and social values and concern for the improvement of the urban environment for the benefit of the majority. Writings and lectures can be used to articulate complex social and environmental issues. Professional excellence must take absolute precedence over monetary rewards. Recognition by the Establishment can be counter-productive, as it often restrains and discourages new design experimentation. The continuous development and evolution in our design approach has often made it impossible for our firm to continue applying certain design idioms, which we have used successfully 5–10 years previously, without being dishonest with ourselves. In the context of the restrictive creative architectural environment of Singapore, we often stand alone professionally, though still unbending and undefeated.

—William S. W. Lim

William Lim combines a busy group practice with jetting about attending conferences and producing a constant stream of papers ranging from "The Impending Urban Crisis" to "The Case Against Tall Buildings" to "If Concrete Could Speak." He holds frequent forums in his penthouse flat overlooking Singapore Harbour. He has been labelled an "Econut" by the local press, perhaps mainly because of his association with the Singapore Planning and Urban Research Group (SPUR), which has criticized official proposals affecting the environment.

William Lim also leads a young coterie of local, Southeast Asian and international associates in an atelier that has produced a string of interesting buildings; their speciality has been shopping centres in Singapore like the People's Park, Golden Mile, and Tanglin. "We firmly believe in group work," he says, "and we do not believe in a master designer." All professional personnel in the firm are encouraged to initiate and criticize ideas, and the resultant solutions are the combined effort of all participants. Out

William S. W. Lim: Golden Mile Shopping Complex, Singapore, 1972.

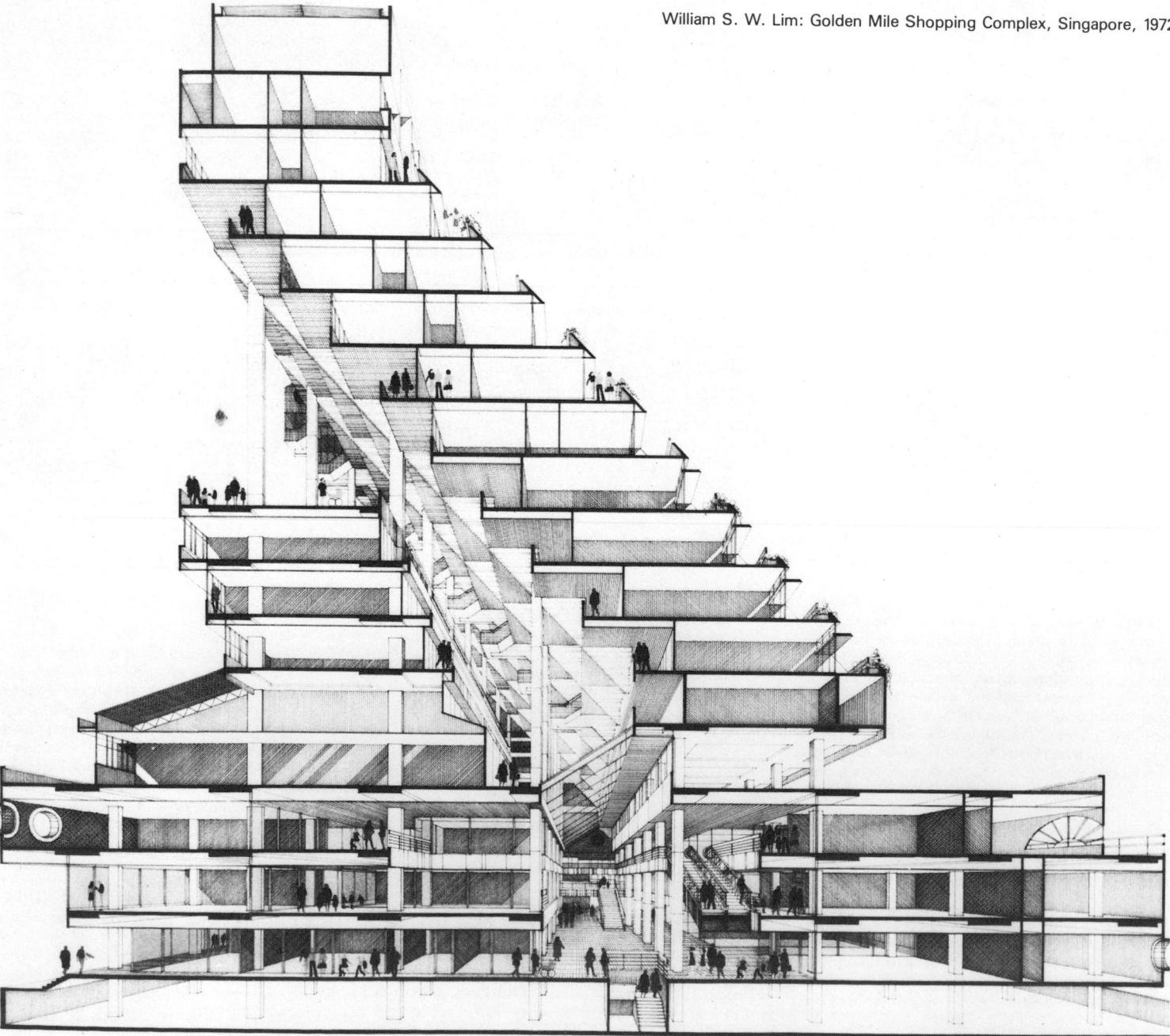

of this "think tank" approach has surprisingly arisen a recognizable group style, focusing on imaginative use of space, natural materials such as raw concrete, mill timber and plain asbestos cement, bold building forms, and simple details.

Lim, of course, has been the coordinator, catalyst and indeed the spur of his group, which feels committed to make a positive contribution to society and the architectural environment—and to comment on public issues like housing, transportation and the environment. The atmosphere he creates provides the bubbling ferment from which his "think tanks" emerge with their design solutions. The whole group is limited 30 members, 10 of whom are professional, 20 technical. Each project is led by a member of the group supported by a consultant member and by others responsible for the technical side of the project. Complete freedom and criticism are required—and apparently it works, while it lasts.

Lim is continually probing the social environment and seeking new architectural alternatives, particularly for the urban environment in the Third World. His buildings are fresh and innovative, with particular attention paid to the division of space, accessibility, movement and circulation. The architectural images he contrives to achieve and has achieved in his group appear to be unified and consistent.

—E. J. Seow

LIM Chong Keat.

Malaysian. Born in Penang, 22 December 1930. Educated at the University of Manchester, England, 1951–56 (Hayward Medallist, Royal Manchester Society, 1955), B.Arch. (first-class honours) 1956; Massachusetts Institute of Technology, Cambridge, 1955–57 (Commonwealth Fellow), M.Arch. 1957. Lecturer at the School of Architecture and Building, Singapore Polytechnic, 1959–61; Founder-Partner, Malayan Architects Co-Partnership, Singapore, 1961–67. Since 1967, Founder-Partner, Architects Team 3, Singapore, Kuala Lumpur, and Penang (with Dato Baharuddin Abu Kassim; Kok Siew Hoong; Raymond Kuah Leong Heng; Lim Chin See; Terry Tay Hui Tiong; and Teoh Ong Tuck). Member, Housing and Development Board, Singapore, 1960–69; Governor, Singapore Polytechnic, 1965–67; President, Singapore Institute of Architects, 1966–69; Chairman, Streets Naming Committee, Singapore, 1968–78; Member, United Nations Review Panel for State and City Planning, Singapore, 1969–71; Chairman, Architects Regional Council of Asia (ARCASIA), 1969–74; Member, National Museum Advisory Committee, Singapore, 1974–76. Member, 1972–77, and since 1977 Chairman, Commonwealth Board of Architectural Education. Recipient: First Prize, Singapore Conference Hall Competition, 1961; First Prize, Seremban State Mosque Competition, 1962; Federation of Malaya Society of Architects Award, 1964; Bintang Bakti Masharakat Public Service Star, Singapore Government, 1966; First Prize, Jurong Town Hall Competition, 1971. Member, Singapore Institute of Architects, and Royal Institute of British Architects. Address: Architects Team 3, 211 Upper Bukit Timah Road, Singapore 21.

Works:

1961 Conference Hall and Trade Union House, Singapore
1962/
67 Seremban State Mosque, Negri Sembilan, Malaysia
1964 Dr. A. F. H. Aeria House, Cantonment Avenue, Penang
1967 Malaysia-Singapore Airlines Building, Singapore

Lim Chong Keat: United Overseas Bank Headquarters Building, Singapore, 1974

1969 Bank Negara Malaysia Building, Penang
1969/
75 Development Bank of Singapore Building
1970 Petaling Jaya Town Hall, Selangor, Malaysia
1971/
73 Jurong Town Hall, Singapore
Starpoint Condominium, Pasir Panjang Road, Singapore
1971/
74 United Overseas Bank Headquarters Building, Singapore
1973 Loh House, Stubbs Road, Hong Kong
1974 Penang Urban Centre/Kompleks Tun Abdul Razak, phase I, Penang

Publications:

By LIM: articles—"Regeneration of the City: The Planning Crossroads in Singapore" in *Singapore Institute of Architects Journal*, July/August 1969; "Communication and Organization Problems Within Professional Institutes" in *Far East Builder* (Hong Kong), January 1970; "The Role of the Professions in Society" in *Singapore Institute of Architects Journal*, September/October 1971; "Peasant

Painters from Bali" in *Asian and Pacific Quarterly* (Seoul), Autumn 1976.

On LIM: articles—"MSA Building" in *Singapore Institute of Architects Journal*, March/April 1969; "MSA Building Sets a Pattern" in *Far East Builder* (Hong Kong), May 1969; "Jurong Town Hall Architectural Design Competition" in *Singapore Institute of Architects Journal*, March/April 1970; "Life at the Top—Lim Chong Keat: 'Architects Should Work Together' " by Anthony Ramasamy in *Singapore Trade and Industry*, October 1971; "The Science Centre Design Competition" in *Singapore Institute of Architects Journal*, November/December 1971; "The Man Behind the Face of Singapore" in *Singapore Trade and Industry*, February 1972; "The Public Utilities Board Building" in *Singapore Institute of Architects Journal*, May/June 1972; "Urban Centre Will Bring City Changes into Focus" in *Malaysian Business* (Kuala Lumpur), April 1974; "Penang Urban Centre" in *Asian Architect and Builder* (Hong Kong), May 1974; "UOB Building" in *Building Materials and Equipment* (Singapore), September 1974; "DBS Building" in *Building Materials and Equipment* (Singapore), May 1975;

"Huge Multi-Million Dollar Penang Urban Centre" in *Asian Building and Construction* (Hong Kong), September 1975; "Kompleks Tun Abdul Razak: A Mixed Use Project in Penang" in *Building Materials and Equipment* (Singapore), December 1976.

The architect in the developing world has to face a comprehensive range of problems embracing the whole urbanisation process in his country and its cultural evolution in relation to total world change. His work must be conscientious and be free from mimicry, alien concepts or pseudo-folksiness. He has to extend himself in four dimensions: including a time-frame interrelating the past, the present and the future. His general architectural education will not have equipped him for all this, and he has to search and develop extensively and comprehensively so as to be meaningful in his professional work.

—Lim Chong Keat

Lim Chong Keat now heads a large practice in Singapore and Malaysia, and his impact on the local architectural scene during the last two decades has been significant.

He began his career as a teacher and had a profound influence on students in the School of Architecture of the Singapore Polytechnic, now part of the University of Singapore. Whilst still a lecturer at the school he won the competition for the design of the Singapore Conference Hall and Trade Union House. The same year, 1961, he formed Malayan Architects Co-Partnership, with William Lim and others; in 1967 he formed Architects Team 3, which continues to develop to the present day with commissions such as the Development Bank, Jurong Town Hall, United Overseas Bank, and other buildings in Singapore and Malaysia.

The Singapore Conference Hall is still perhaps his best major work; it reveals the purity of his architectural approach and individual style, with its imaginative and creative use of space and materials, its disciplined articulation, and the aptness and fluency that he displays not only in his buildings but also in his speeches and writings. His buildings are machine-finished, the concepts well-defined, the details functional and intellectually derived and sometimes playful.

Lim Chong Kong initiates, directs, corrects, attacks, checks, selects, justifies and defends his works like the grand master he is. His interests are wide; he keeps in touch with other architects as well as with architectural education; he continuously searches for models and antecedents for a meaningful architecture; and he is a prolific producer of significant buildings.

—E. J. Seow

LINDE, Horst.

German. Born in Heidelberg in 1912. Educated at primary and secondary schools in Baden-Baden; studied architecture at the Technische Hochschule, Karlsruhe, 1931–36, Dip.Ing. 1936. Served in the German Army, 1939–46; prisoner-of-war. Government Architect, Berlin, 1939; Town Planner, Lahr, Baden, Germany, 1939; worked as an architect for the reconstruction in France, 1941; Director, Office of Reconstruction, University of Freiburg, 1947–49; Director, State Building Administration, South Baden, Germany, 1949–57; Director, State Building Administration, Baden-Württemberg Region of Germany, and Section Head, Finance Ministry, Stuttgart, 1957–72. In private practice, Freiburg, since 1972. Professor, 1961–74, and since 1977 Professor Emeritus, Technische Hochschule, Stuttgart (Director, Institute for University Building, 1969–74). Recipient: Paul Bonatz Prize, Stuttgart, 1961, 1963; Fritz Schumacher Prize, University of Hano-

ver, 1963; Architecture Prize, University of Oulu, Finland, 1967. Honorary doctorate: University of Freiburg, 1957. Member, Akademie der Bildenden Künste, Stuttgart, 1962, and Akademie der Künste, Berlin, 1970; Member, Academy of Town and Country Planning, Berlin, 1970. Honorary Member, Royal Institute of British Architects, Institute of Finnish Architects, and Finnish Academy of Technical Sciences, 1974. Address (office): Schlierbergstrasse 33, 7800 Freiburg, West Germany.

Works:

1928 Timber Houses, Berlin (competition project)
1931 Memorial Tower, Triberg, Black Forest, Germany
1934 Spa Hotel, Bad Dürrheim, Germany (competition project; with Bottling)
1935 Private house, Baden-Baden, Germany
1947 Forest Cafe, Badenweiler, Germany (with Haas)
1947/
57 Master plan for the reconstruction/-redevelopment of the University of Freiburg (with others)
1948 Zoning plan for Badenweiler, Germany (with Haas)
      Vocational School, Gaggenau, Germany
      Plan for the town center of Karlsruhe (competition project; with Diehm)
      Plan for the town center of Frankfurt (competition project)
1949 Commercial and Vocational Trades School, Sackingen, Germany (with W. Müller)
1950 Ludwig Evangelical Church, Freiburg (with Diehm, Hampe and Heine)
      Chapel, at the Catholic Hospital, Freiburg (with Kaufmann, Hesselbacher, and Rolli)
1951 Private houses, Wehr, Freiburg
1952 CIBA Ink Factory, Wehr, Baden, Germany (with Geier and Heinrich)
1953 Spa Hotel, Bad Dürrheim, Germany (with Heid)
      Private houses, Wehr, Baden, Germany
      Markgrafen Baths extension, Badenweiler, Germany (with Geier)
      Weinbrenner City Church reconstruction, Karlsruhe (with Pfeiffer)
      Local Government Administration Building, Freiburg (with Wolf and Heim)
1956 Church of St. John the Evangelist, Bad Dürrheim, Germany (with Heinrich)
      Engineers' School and Clock Museum, Furtwangen, Germany
1957 Plan for the town center of Stuttgart (with Frey and Fecker)
1958 Spa Hotel, Bad Krotzingen, Germany (with Heinrich and Geier)
1961 Design of the *Federal Garden Show*, Stuttgart
1962 Master plan for the University of the Ruhr, Bochum, Germany (competition project; with Conradi and Klose)
      Hotel and Service Station, Freiburg (with Dorr)
1965 St. Michael's Chapel, Ebersteinburg, Germany (with Reichenecker and Schwab)
1967 Design of the *Federal Garden Show*, Karlsruhe
1968 Evangelical Church, Marbach, Black Forest, Germany (with Dorr)
      Deutsche Bank, Schwäbisch Gmünd, Germany (with Markelin)
1969 Max Planck Institute, Freiburg (competition project; with Weber)
1970 Deutsche Bank Headquarters, Frankfurt (with Dionisius)
1973 Development plan for the spa and town of Baden-Baden, Germany (with the Baden-Baden Town Development Study Group)
      Casino extension, Baden-Baden, Germany (with Pfluger, Witzemann, Stadelmaier and Partners)

      Town Hall extension, Bad Dürrheim, Germany (with Weber)
1975 Salt Works conversion to Guest House, Bad Dürrheim, Germany (with Weber and Wrangel)
1976 Grand Auditorium and Spa Hotel, Baden-Baden, Germany (with Witzemann, Stadelmaier and Partners)
1977 Master plan for Guilan University, Iran (with Heinle, Wischer and Partners, and Zwirn, Weber, Heinrich and Aminde)

Publications:

By LINDE: books—*Die Eignung Detmolds als Universitätsstandorf,* with W. Rath and others, Stuttgart 1965; *Bremen University,* with others, Berne 1967; *Standortbestimmung einer Universität,* with others, Munster 1967; *Hochschulplanung: Beiträge zur Struktur und Bauplanung,* editor, 4 volumes, Dusseldorf 1969–71; *Tendenzen und Ziele der Hochschulplanung in der Bundesrepublik Deutschland,* Aargau, Germany 1971; *Die Ausbildung des Architekten im Wandel der Zeit,* Stuttgart 1972; *Für Architektur: Ein Manifest,* with others, Stuttgart 1973; *Stadt- und Kurortentwicklung Baden-Baden,* with others, Baden-Württemberg, Germany 1974.

On LINDE: book—*Horst Linde: Architekt und Hochschullehrer,* edited by the Institut für Hochschulbau, Stuttgart 1977.

Horst Linde studied at the Technische Hochschule, Karlsruhe, where he was influenced by Oscar Ernst Schweizer, an important exponent of the New Building. As with all architects of his age group, Linde had his early professional career interrupted by the war. After his military service, he became, in 1947, Director of the Reconstruction Office at the University of Freiburg, then, in 1949, Director of the State Building Administration for South Baden. It was there and especially after his appointment in 1957 as Director of the State Building Administration for the whole of Baden-Württemberg that he discovered a broad and fruitful field of activity that suited both his personality as an architect and his political philosophy. From then on, Linde directed, influenced and stimulated building activity in an important *land* of the Federal Republic.

Characteristic of his work as Director of Building Administration for both South Baden and Baden-Württemberg is a thorough analysis of problems, the formulation of comprehensive development objectives, and the achievement of those objectives by means of intelligent and clear-sighted policies.

In Freiburg, immediately after the war, Linde directed the reconstruction of the university and completed new buildings that obviously bear his signature as architect. As early as 1950 he built the Chapel at the Catholic Hospital, Freiburg, one of the most important buildings of this period in Germany. In Stuttgart, in the 1960's, he had a significant influence on developments in university building. In 1961 he was appointed a professor-in-ordinary at the Technische Hochschule, Stuttgart, then in 1963 he founded the central archive for university building and in 1969 the special research facility for university building: he directed both establishments until 1974, creating institutions that could carry out the research and basic work necessary for progress in this field. The results of his work were felt far beyond Germany's borders.

Apart from his obligations—and contributions—as administrator, teacher and researcher, Horst Linde has also been active as an architect. Among his most impressive works are the plan for the town center of Stuttgart, the Church of St. John the Evangelist in Bad Dürrheim, and the Evangelical Church in Marbach.

—Jürgen Joedicke

LLEWELYN-DAVIES, Richard
(Lord Llewelyn-Davies).

British. Born in London, 24 December 1912. Educated privately; at Trinity College, Cambridge, 1931–33, M.A. in engineering 1933; Summer School, Ecole des Beaux-Arts, Paris, 1930–33, Diploma 1933; Architectural Association School, London, 1933–37, Dip.A.A. (honours) 1937. Married Patricia Parry, now Baroness Llewelyn-Davies of Hastoe, in 1943; children: Melissa, Harriet and Rebecca. Engineering Draughtsman, Sir Alexander Gibb and Partners, London, 1939–42; Architect, London Midland and Scottish Railway Company, London, 1942–48; Director, Investigation into Function and Design of Hospitals, Nuffield Foundation, London, 1948–60. In partnership with John Weeks, *q.v.*, London, since 1960: currently, Senior Partner of the successor firm, Llewelyn-Davies Weeks Forestier-Walker and Bor. Professor of Architecture, 1960–69, Professor of Urban Planning, 1969–75, Head of the School of Environmental Studies, 1971–75, and since 1976 Emeritus Professor of Urban Planning, University College London. Gropius Lecturer, Harvard University, Cambridge, Massachusetts, 1975. Member, Royal Fine Art Commission, 1961–72; President, World Society for Ekistics, 1965. Chairman, Centre for Environmental Studies, London, since 1967. Recipient: Bronze Medal, Royal Institute of British Architects, 1957; West Suffolk Award to Architects, 1957. Fellow, Royal Institute of British Architects, 1956, and Royal Town Planning Institute, 1966. Honorary Fellow, American Institute of Architects, 1970, and Sri Lanka Institute of Architects, 1973. Created Baron (Life Peer), 1963. Address: Llewelyn-Davies Weeks, Brook House, 2–16 Torrington Place, London WC1E 7HN, England.

Works (all with John Weeks):

1952 Nuffield House, Musgrave Park Hospital, Belfast

1954 Diagnostic Centre, Corby, Northamptonshire

1955 House, Mayford, Surrey

1957 Mignot Memorial Hospital, Alderney, Channel Islands
Rushbrooke Village Housing, Bury St. Edmunds, Suffolk

1958 *The Times* Newspaper Office Building, London (with Ellis, Clarke and Galleraugh)

1960 Students Residence and Dining Room, Imperial College of Tropical Agriculture, Trinidad, West Indies (with Colin Laird Associates)
Meeting halls and laboratories, Zoological Society, London
Nuffield Institute of Comparative Medicine, London

1961 The Stock Exchange redevelopment, London (with Fitzroy Robinson)
Sun Alliance Insurance Building, London (with Fitzroy Robinson)
Northwick Park Hospital and Clinical Research Centre, Harrow, Middlesex

1963 Tate Gallery extension, London
Town Centre Development, phase I, and Sports Centre, Basingstoke, Hampshire (with Ian Fraser Associates)

1966 Barmston Village Housing Project, Washington New Town, County Durham

1968 Experimental Pathology Research Building, St. Mary's Hospital, Paddington, London
Stantonbury Housing Scheme, Milton Keynes, Buckinghamshire

1970 Youth Treatment Centre; Birmingham
University Children's Hospital, Leuven, Belgium (with Felix Tanghe and Delarue)
Medical Centre, Flinders University, Adelaide, South Australia (with the South Australia Department of Public Works)

Richard Llewelyn-Davies: Sun Alliance Insurance Building, London, 1961

1971 York District Hospital
Sciences Laboratories, National Hospital for Nervous Diseases, London
Salmaniya Medical Centre, Bahrain

1972 Metal Box Company Headquarters Building, Reading, Berkshire
Singapore General Hospital, Outram Road, Singapore (with INDECO)
General Hospital, Doha, State of Qatar

1973 Normanby College Education Centre, King's College Hospital, London

1974 Health Sciences Centre, University of Khon Kaen, Thailand (with Kingston Reynolds Thom and Allardice)

1975 Cancer Research Foundation, Sutton, Surrey
Rayne Institute Research Laboratories, University College Hospital, London

1975/
78 Shahestan Pahlam, Tehran (with Jaquelin Robertson)

1976 Voluntary Research Trust Research Laboratory Building, King's College Hospital, London

Publications:

By LLEWELYN-DAVIES: books—*Studies in the Functions and Design of Hospitals,* with others, London 1955; *Building Elements* (textbook), with D. J. Petty, London 1956; *Psychiatric Services and Architecture,* with A. A. Baker and P. Sivadon, Geneva 1959; *Design of Research Laboratories,* with others, London 1961; *Children in Hospital,* with others, London 1963; *Hospital Planning and Administration,* with H. M. C. Macaulay, Geneva 1966; *New Cities—a British Example: Milton Keynes,* Washington, D.C. 1969; foreword to *British Hospitals: Home and Overseas,* 9th edition, London 1973; *The Tuscan Artist: Thought and Action in Design,* Cambridge, Massachusetts 1975; articles—"The Hertfordshire Achievement," with John Weeks, in *Architectural Review* (London), June 1952; "Facilities and Equipment for Health Services—Needed Research" in *Millbank Memorial Fund Quarterly* (New York), no. 3, 1966; "Similarities and Differences in Hospital Design International Trends" in *American Journal of Public Health* (Washington, D.C.), October 1966;

"Town Design" in *Town Planning Review* (Liverpool), October 1966; "Problems and Principles of Synthesis in Planning" in *Ekistics* (Athens), December 1966; "Research for Planning" in *Journal of the Town Planning Institute* (London), June 1967; "Planning to Meet Demand" in *Hospital Administration* (Sydney), October 1967; "New Cities—The British Experience" in *Indiana Architect* (Indianapolis), May 1968; "The Architect in 1988," with Lord Esher, in *RIBA Journal* (London), October 1968; "Educating the Professionals of the Built Environment" in *Architectural Record* (New York), February 1969; "Future of Environmental Studies" in *Architectural Design* (London), March 1969; "The Problems of Design" in *Journal of the Royal Institute of Chartered Surveyors* (London), April 1969; "Modern British Hospital Building" in *Hospital Management* (Sevenoaks, Kent), May 1969; "Villes Nouvelles: L'Expérience Britannique" in *Revue Politique et Parlementaire* (Paris), June 1969; "Science and the City," with Peter Cowan, in *Science Journal* (London), October 1969; "Milton Keynes: Goals of the Plan" in *RIBA Journal* (London), July 1970; "How Others See the U.S." in *Daedalus* (Cambridge, Massachusetts), Fall 1972; "The Role of the Social Sciences in Architecture and Planning" in *Anthropology and Society* (Washington, D.C.), 1975; "The Architect as a Planner" in *RIBA Journal* (London), July 1976.

On LLEWELYN-DAVIES: books—*Changing Ideals in Modern Architecture* by Peter Collins, London 1965; *The New Brutalism* by Reyner Banham, London 1966; articles—"To Plan or Not to Plan: Some Interim Thoughts on Milton Keynes" by Hugh Roper in *Journal of the Town Planning Institute* (London), May 1969; "The Plan Is a Beginning: Some Further Thoughts on Milton Keynes" by Hugh Roper in *Journal of the Town Planning Institute* (London), April 1970; "Milton Keynes: L'Etablissement d'un planning en prévision de la société urbain des temps futurs" by Jan Tanghe in *Environment* (Brussels), October 1970; "The Shah's New Town" by Miles Chapman in *Harpers & Queen* (London), April 1977.

*

My work as an architect has been based on belief in the power of human reason. I believe that creative design must be based on real depth of understanding. I believe that an architect has to understand the purpose of his building in a very broad sense, which includes understanding a lot about the society and culture within which he works. I also believe that his technical understanding of the means of building needs to be very complete. I believe that only when he has mastered a design problem in all its rational aspects can he be comfortable with his design. This does not mean that I find that design itself is a deductive process based on a series of steps, one following another. I think that ideas about design come suddenly and unexpectedly in a creative flash, but I think that the result will be shallow and inadequate unless the creative moment comes against a background of deep and wide understanding. I do not think there is a great deal of difference in the creative activity of a designer and that of a scientist. I think both use inspiration on a basis of reason.

—Richard Llewelyn-Davies

Sometimes, but not often, an architect comes along whose interests are so wide-ranging, activities so diversified and accomplishments so varied that he is difficult, if not impossible, to categorize. Richard Llewelyn-Davies is that kind of architect.

For much of his early career Lord Llewelyn-Davies was deeply involved in architectural and planning work for various institutions and trusts. As architect for the Nuffield Foundation, he directed and participated in many important research and other studies of hospitals and their functions, design and planning. The research and studies developed and promoted important new concepts for hospitals

and other health care facilities. From these experiences came an interest in research and teaching. He has been Professor of Architecture and Professor of Urban Planning at University College London. His other interests led him to establish, in 1960, his practice of architecture and planning in London and later to expand the practice internationally.

The Llewelyn-Davies practice has developed in a manner unlike that of any other firm that comes to mind. In the first place, it is truly international. In the second, it encompasses work of a scale, completeness and complexity unknown to most architects. The firm performs architectural services in the usual manner not only for hospitals, a building type in which it is pre-eminent; it is as well noted for housing and shopping centers and for urban design and planning services for new towns, cities and other urban areas.

Unlike almost any other firm in the world, that of Llewelyn-Davies performs a great variety of other services. These includes research, studies, analyses and consultation of many kinds—social, economic, institutional, strategic, as well as environmental and physical; and the firm continues to perform services for a large number of private and governmental clients in the fields of hospital and health care planning and facilities.

The firm that Llewelyn-Davies has developed produces excellent architecture and planning, along with large-scale programs and plans that are socially, economically and physically sound, yet creative and pioneering.

—William Dudley Hunt, Jr.

*

LOCSIN, Leandro V.

Filipino. Born in Silay City, 15 August 1928. Educated at De La Salle College High School, graduated 1947; University of Santo Tomas, 1949–53, B.Arch. 1953. Married Maria Cecilia Yulo in 1960; children: Leandro Jr. and Luis. In private practice, Makati, Manila, since 1955: Founder Director, L. V. Locsin and Associates, 1955–78; President, L. V. Locsin and Company Inc., since 1967; President and Manager, L. V. Locsin and Partners, since 1978. Executive Vice-President, Laguna Estates Development Corporation, since 1974; Chairman, LVL-CYL Foundation Inc., since 1974; President, YCLA Sugar Development Corporation, since 1975; President, YNTALCO Investment Corporation, since 1975—all Makati. Vice-President, 1963, and President, 1964–66, Philippine Institute of Architects; Trustee, De La Salle University, 1973–79. Exhibitions: *Leandro V. Locsin*, University of Hawaii, Honolulu, 1960; *Expo '70*, Osaka, 1970; Fulbright Scholars Exhibition, Cultural Center of the Philippines, Manila, 1978. Recipient: Outstanding Young Man Award, Philippines Junior Chamber of Commerce, 1959; Pan Pacific Architectural Award, American Institute of Architects, Hawaii Chapter, 1960; Rizal Centennial Award for Architecture, Philippines, 1962; Gold Medal, University of Santo Tomas, 1968; Philippine Republic Cultural Heritage Award, 1970; Philippine Arts and Architecture Award, 1971; Araw ng Maynila Cultural Award, Manila, 1972; Gold Medal, Philippine Institute of Architects, 1978; Professional Award, United Architects of the Philippines, 1978; Architect of the Year Award, Philippines, 1978. Fellow, United Architects of the Philippines, 1978. Address: Leondro V. Locsin and Partners, 448 E. de los Santos Avenue, Makati, Manila, Philippines.

Works (Philippines unless noted):

1955 Chapel of the Holy Sacrifice, University of the Philippines, Quezon City
1957 Monterrey Apartments, Ayala Avenue, Makati
1958 Ayala Building I, Ayala Avenue, Makati

(now Elizalde Building)
    Marcelo Fernando House, Panay Road, Quezon City
    Fernando Zobel House additions and gardens, Forbes Park, Makati
    G. Yvanovich House, Hidalgo Street, Makati
    José Aldeguer House, Diliman, Quezon City
    Howard Cavender House, Urdaneta Village, Makati
    Robert Ho House, Forbes Park, Makati
1959 Filipinas Life Assurance Company Building, Ayala Avenue, Makati
    Fernando Garcia House, Cubao, Quezon City
    Jaime Zobel de Ayala House, Forbes Park, Makati
    Michael Joseph House, San Lorenzo Village, Makati
    Jaime Lacson House, Makati
1960 Ozamis City Cathedral
    John T. Quimzon House, La Vista, Quezon City
    Angel Heredia House, La Vista, Quezon City
    José Tuason Jr. House, La Vista, Quezon City
    Sergio Montinola House, Forbes Park, Makati
    Residence for the National Life Insurance Company, Urdaneta Village, Makati
    Manuel Escaler House, Wack-Wack, Mandaluyong
    Arturo Rotor House, Urdaneta Village, Makati
1961 Davao Insular Hotel, Davao City
    Commercial Credit Corporation Building, Buendia Avenue, Makati
    Pacita Soriano House, Forbes Park, Makati
    Nicanor Yniguez House, Shaw Boulevard, Mandaluyong
1962 Integrated Realty Building, Buendia Avenue, Makati
    Joaquin de Sequerra House, Urdaneta Village, Makati
    Robert Sy House, Forbes Park, Makati
    José Yulo Sr. House, Forbes Park, Makati
    Ramon Pertierra House, Forbes Park, Makati
    Manuel del Rosario House, Forbes Park, Makati
    René Unson House, Bel-Air Village, Makati
1963 Phil-Am Life Company Building, Cagayan de Oro City
    Enrique Carlos House, Forbes Park, Makati
    Alberto Quiroz del Rio House, Forbes Park, Makati
    Leandro V. Locsin House, Forbes Park, Makati
    Jesus de Veyra House, Greenhills, Mansaluyong
    Johnny de Leon House, Forbes Park, Makati
1964 Emerson CoSeteng House, Marikina
    Domingo Locsin House, Urdaneta Village, Makati
    Henry Moran House, Greenhills, Mandaluyong
    Francisco Tansengco House, Makati
    José San Buenaventura House, Forbes Park, Makati
    Ramon Cojuangco House, Forbes Park, Makati
    Salvador de Leon House, Paranaque
1965 Manila Memorial Park Chapel, Paranque
    Sarmiento Office Building, Ayala Avenue, Makati
    American International Underwriters Building, Ayala Avenue, Makati
    Dona Corazon L. Montelibano Memorial Chapel, De La Salle College, Bacolod City
    Mauro Prieto House, Forbes Park, Makati
    Ramon Yulo House, Forbes Park, Makati
1966 Sikatuna Office Building, Ayala Avenue, Makati
    Tuason Building, Ayala Avenue, Makati
    Locsin Office Building, de los Santos Avenue, Makati

Leandro V. Locsin: Theatre of the Performing Arts, Cultural Center of the Philippines, Manila, 1969

5 executive houses, and pavilion, Central Azucarera, Tarlac
1967 Hyatt Regency Hotel, Roxas Boulevard, Pasay City
Ricardo Cu Unjeng House, Forbes Park, Makati
Enrique Zobel House renovations and additions, Forbes Park, Makati
Antonio Floirendo House, Forbes Park, Makati
Manolo Lopez House, Wack-Wack, Mandaluyong
1968 Josefa Apartment Building, M. Adriatico, Malate, Manila
Church of St. Andrew, Bel-Air Village, Makati
Miguel Yulo House, Forbes Park, Makati
Florencio Reyes House, Dasmarinas Village, Makati
1969 Filipinas Life Assurance Company Building, Iloilo City
Manila Intercontinental Hotel, Ayala Avenue, Makati
First National City Bank Building renovations, Juan Luna, Manila
Philippine Bank of Commerce, Ayala Avenue, Makati
Theatre of the Performing Arts, Cultural Center of the Philippines, Manila
College of Agriculture Dormitories, University of the Philippines, Los Banos, Laguna
Magnolia Dairy Products Plant, Aurora Boulevard, Quezon City
Amalgamated Office Building, Makati
Filipinas Life Assurance Company Building, Mandaue, Cebu

Holy Cross Memorial Park Chapel, Novaliches, Manila
Leland Villadolid House, Dasmarinas Village, Makati
Vicente Paterno House, Paterno Avenue, San Juan, Manila
Clemente Gatmaitan Jr. House, Dasmarinas Village, Makati
1970 Chapel of St. Alphonsus Liguori, Magallanes Village, Makati
Union Carbide Office Building, Mandaue, Cebu
Continuing Education Center of the College of Agriculture, and Student Union Building, University of the Philippines, Los Banos, Laguna
Filipinas Life Assurance Company Building, Naga City
David Consunji House, Pasay Road, Makati
Alejandro Roces House, Forbes Park, Makati
Cesar Zalamea House, Dasmarinas Village, Makati
1971 Filipinas Life Assurance Company Building, Cagayan de Oro Coty, Mindanao
Filipinas Life Executive Center, Mandaue, Cebu
Church of the Immaculate Heart of Mary Teachers' Village, Diliman, Quezon City
Auditorium, College of Agriculture, University of the Philippines, Los Banos, Laguna
Hall of Congress renovations, Philippine National Legislative Assembly, Manila
Romago Office Building, Mandaluyong, Manila
Filipinas Life Assurance Company Building, Batangas City

Filipinas Life Assurance Company Building, Dagupan City
Stock Exchange, Ayala Avenue, Makati
Luis Maria Guerrero House, Dasmarinas Village, Makati
1972 Cadiz Church
Filipinas Life Assurance Company Building Annex, Ayala Avenue, Makati
Session Hall renovations, Congress of the Republic of the Philippines, Taft Avenue, Manila
Filipinas Life Assurance Company Building, Davao City, Mindanao
Asian Reinsurance Pool Building, Legaspi Village, Makati
Terminal Buildings renovation, Manila International Airport
Philippine Commercial and Industrial Bank Building, Greenhills, Mandaluyong
Gregorio Locsin House, Greenhills, Mandaluyong
José Cruz House, Pasig, Manila
Ang Maharlika State Guest House restoration, San Miguel, Manila
Leondro V. Locsin Beach House, Puerto Galera, Oriental Mindoro
1973 Kodak Office Building renovations, Pasong Tamo, Makati
Edon Yap House, Greenhills, Mandaluyong
Anton Roxas House, Forbes Park, Makati
Stephen Zuelling House, Forbes Park, Makati
1974 SEARCA Dormitory, College of Agriculture, University of the Philippines, Los Banos, Laguna
Ayala Museum, Makati Avenue, Makati

Design Center, and Folk Arts Theatre, Cultural Center of the Philippines, Roxas Boulevard, Manila

Population Center, Makati

Conrado Ocampo House, Dasmarinas Village, Makati

Ileana Maramag House, Dasmarinas Village, Makati

Rest house for President Marcos, Olot, Leyte

1975 First National City Bank Building, Paseo de Roxas, Makati

Nutritional Center of the Philippines, Makati

Ralph Panganiban House, Dasmarinas Village, Makati

1976 Filipinas Life Assurance Company Building, Tacloban City, Leyte

Asian Center for Social Welfare Training and Research, Makati

Marbella Condominium, Roxas Boulevard, Manila

National Arts Center, Mount Makiling, Los Banos, Laguna

Fast Food Center, International Convention Center, and Plaza Hotel, Cultural Center of the Philippines, Roxas Boulevard, Manila

Australian Embassy Residence, Forbes Park, Makati

1978 EEI Office Building, Pasig, Manila

Canlubang Golf and Country Club, Laguna

Generoso Villanueva House, Tamarind Road, Forbes Park, Makati

1979 Canlubang Sports Complex, Laguna

Philippine Long-Distance Telephone Company Building, Makati

Johnny Widjaya House, Djakarta, Indonesia

1979– New Terminal Buildings, Manila International Airport

Terminal, Manila Domestic Airport

Various buildings for Canlubang City, Laguna

Publications:

By LOCSIN: book—*Oriental Ceramics Discovered in the Philippines,* with Cecilia Y. Locsin, Rutland, Vermont 1967; article—"Architecture in the Philippines" in *Pamana Magazine* (Manila), 1970.

On LOCSIN: books—*The Art of the Philippines* by Rodrigo Perez, Manila 1958; *Philippine Contemporary Art* by Manuel Duldalao, Manila 1972; *The Struggle for Philippine Art* by P. Kalaw Ledesma, Manila 1974; *The Philippine Art Scene* by Manuel Duldalao, Manila 1977; *The Architecture of Leandro V. Locsin* by Nicholas Polites, New York and Tokyo 1977; *Philippines* by Richard Chesnoff, New York 1978; *The Manila Hotel* by Beth Day, Manila 1979.

*

Equally weighed with considerations of space is the element of time: the past, present and future as seen through the architect's soul, from which emanate his aesthetic perceptions and the strength to transform into architectural conceptualization that which he knows is truth. The process, intuitive or deliberate, represents a synthesis of the designer's personality—the sum total of his experience and his criteria—in dynamic interaction with his understanding of and identification with national traditions, linking generations, periods, epochs, and those traditions which are living, developing and ever-changing with the demands of the present.

Architecture is not to be experienced in isolation. The architect is ever with his audience: the users, the onlookers, the people. It is, however, left to the architect from his vantage point in the time-continuum to synthesize the arts, beliefs, technology, life-styles and aspirations of his people; and, by translating these into structures of concrete, stone, wood or steel, adding one more statement to his country's architectural record by which he, his society and his times will ultimately be measured.

—Leandro V. Locsin

Many western artists have a particularly unfortunate habit of acute ethnocentrism, and rarely if ever look at work produced beyond the Pacific Ocean or the Ural Mountains. For this reason the sensitive and innovative work of Leandro V. Locsin of the Philippines has gone largely unnoticed. That is too bad, because there are many lessons we could learn from Locsin, and much delight we could reap merely from becoming acquainted with his unusual architecture.

Locsin has risen to an extremely difficult challenge, for his work attempts to discover, not in superficial terms, what aspects of his rich tradition retain meaning in a now rapidly changing environment. Although we in the west also face this dilemma of reconciliation between old styles and patterns and contemporary technology, it is an amplified conflict in the Philippines, where many traditional values stand in direct opposition to the current social atmosphere that has been largely imported from the west. Locsin has compounded the struggle still further, by attempting to validate his expression of his heritage through sophisticated abstraction. Had Locsin been a less talented architect than he is, the results could have been chaotic, and in many ways, much of the work of his Asian colleagues has been just that. Locsin's brilliant sense of mass, space, and structure, coupled with a simple and consistent style of personal expression have, though, produced many extremely fine buildings that seem to stand up to these challenges with extraordinary ease.

Locsin's architecture begins with sincere introspection, both of himself and his nation. He is very attuned to Filipino living patterns, and has avidly studied vernacular Filipino building. He frequently incorporates common vernacular spatial qualities into his designs.

His nation's tropical climate, for example, has always exerted considerable influence on architecture produced there, and Locsin responds to the weather in much the same ways as his ancestors. Large open spaces and few ceiling to floor partitions, frequent use of lattices and other partial partitions, and the expression of the roof as the dominant shape, are all qualities of Locsin's work that have been adopted from the vernacular. An exuberant sense of ornament, detail, and architectural intent, contrasted against great simplicity is another characteristic that marks Locsin's buildings, and has been drawn from his own culture.

Locsin is very careful in his adaptations, though. "We must avoid the temptation towards gimicky, carnival architecture," he warns. "The brass tacks are that we *are* using western technology. But we must think of this as an enrichment of our own vocabulary, not an exclusion of it."

Locsin's buildings are fine constructions that are rational, climatically sound, and deftly scaled. They are composed of unusual and carefully selected materials. He uses concrete freely, because of low labor costs, but several of his buildings use earth berms integrally; others use a concrete he devised with a shell aggregate, and his houses are composed of fine wood panels, wood lattice work, masonry, stone, tile, and (as perfectly tangible as all other materials) open air. They are handsome sculptural pieces and demonstrate superb exploration of the expressive potentialities of shade and shadow.

Locsin has been remarkably prolific, and has demonstrated his vitality and truly vibrant creative impulse by completing several very large projects on impossibly tight schedules. Without doubt his biggest project, and to Locsin his greatest honor, has been his virtually single handed execution of the new Cultural Center of the Philippines. The production of four large buildings, two theatres, an exhibition hall, and a convention center, as well as a large, on-site hotel, afforded Locsin the unique opportunity to create variations on principle themes. The result (although the landscaping is not fully completed to date) is an exciting, harmonic arrangement of similar shapes, colors, and mass. Locsin exhibits his affection for massive roof shapes, for example, in repeat-

edly huge, plain cantilevers extending over shaded areas.

The Theatre for the Performing Arts shines as the most outstanding example of Locsin's material restraint informed by spirited, energetic, compositional sense. Today it is becoming a symbol of, and a monument to, that Filipino spirit so deeply entrenched in Locsin's perceptions. Like all of Locsin's work, it documents a struggle, and a triumph, of a national spirit over the modern world.

—Mitchell B. Rouda

LODS, Marcel (Gabriel).

French. Born in Paris, 16 August 1891. Educated at the Ecole Nationale des Arts Décoratifs, Paris; Ecole Nationale Supérieure des Beaux-Arts, Paris, Dip. Arch. 1923. Served in the French Army, 1914–18: Lieutenant; volunteer in 1940. Married Germaine Lucy Empereur Bissonet in 1919; children: Gilbert, Francis and Denise; married Jacqueline Albert Lambert; children: Martine and Bernard; married Denise Marcelle Martineau. Worked with L. H. Brileau, Paris, 1922–23; in partnership with Eugène Beaudouin, *q.v.,* 1925–40. In private practice, Paris, since 1945. Studio Master, with André Hermant and Trazzini, Ecole des Beaux-Arts, Paris, 1948–64. Architect-in-Charge of Public Buildings and National Monuments; Architect-in-Charge of the Reconstruction of Sector II of Rouen; City Architect and Urbanist, Sotteville les Rouen, Drancy and Mayence, France; City Architect to the Government of Guinea. Member of the French Section of CIAM (Congrès International des Architectes Modernes). Recipient: Reynolds Prize, 1970. Officer of the Légion d'Honneur, of the Order of Merit, and of the Order of Arts and Letters. Address (office): 90 Avenue Niel, 75017 Paris, France.

Works:

1933 Palais des Expositions, Paris (with Eugène Beaudouin and Vladimir Bodiansky)

1934 Cité de la Muette, Drancy, France (with Eugène Beaudouin and Vladimir Bodiansky)

1935 Open-Air School, Suresnes, France (with Eugène Beaudouin)

1936 Circular Aircraft Hangar (project; with Vladimir Bodiansky)

1937 Aero-Club, Buc, France (with Eugène Beaudouin and Jean Prouvé; demolished by the Germans during the Occupation, 1940–44)

Design of the *World's Fair,* Paris (with Eugène Beaudouin)

1938 Dismantable Week-end House, *Exposition Habitation,* Paris (with Eugène Beaudouin)

1939 Maison du Peuple, Clichy, France (with Eugène Beaudouin, Vladimir Bodiansky, and Jean Prouvé)

1945 Retreat House, housing, and 2 school complexes, Sotteville les Rouen, France (with Alexandre, Bloquel and Yvelin)

1955 Church of Joan of Arc, Belfort, France

Church of the Cross, Sochaux, France

1955/
65 Housing, Drancy, France

1956 Air Base, Strasbourg (with Arsene Henry)

Air Base, Metz

Housing, Argenteuil, France

1958 Les Grandes Terres Housing Estate, Marly le Roi, France (with Honegger)

1960 5 currency exchange kiosks in Paris depots

Technical college, Paris

Supermarket, Sotteville les Rouen, France (with Alexandre and Malizard)

GEAI: La Grand Mare (apartments), Rouen (with Depondt and Beauclair)

Marcel Lods: Open-Air School, Suresnes, France, 1935

1962/
63 School, Ivry-sur-Seine, France
College of Chemistry, Mulhouse (with Fischbach and Steinmetz)
University Restaurant, Mulhouse (with Fischbach and Steinmetz)
Banque Populaire Offices, Mulhouse (with Meyer)
1964/
65 Z.U.P. Housing, Meaux, France (with Depondt and Beauclair)
Faculty of Sciences Building, University of Reims (with Durand de Guillarbois)
Halls of Residence, University of Reims (with Durand de Guillarbois)
1967 Maison des Sciences de l'Homme, Paris (with Depondt and Beauclair)
French National Printing Works, Douai

Publications:

By LODS: book—*Le Metier d'Architecte,* with Hervé Le Boterf, Paris 1976.

On LODS: articles—"Architecture Between the Wars: A Conversation with Marcel Lods" in *Architecture Mouvement Continuité* (Paris), March 1974; "Marcel Lods" by Manfred Schiedhelm in *Architectural Design* (London), October 1974; "Imprimerie Nationale Francaise: New Printing Works at Douai" by Themis Constantinidis in *Acier Stahl Steel* (Brussels), January 1975; "Imprimerie Nationale à Douai" in *Usines d'Aujourd'hui* (Paris), no. 127, 1975; "National Printing Works, Douai" in *Informes de la Construccion* (Madrid), June 1976; "Grandeur and Misery of a Rationalist Masterpiece" by Francois Laisney and Ginette Baty-Tornikian in *L'Architecture d'Aujourd'hui* (Paris), October/November 1976.

The team of Eugène Beaudouin and Marcel Lods was remarkable for the complementary qualities of the two partners. Together they built the first prefabricated housing schemes, the best known of which is Cité de la Muette, in Drancy, in the suburbs of Paris, sadly renowned for its use as a transit centre for Jewish deportees during the German occupation, and the excellent open-air school in Suresnes. With

the collaboration of Jean Prouvé, they built the Maison du Peuple in Clichy, too quickly forgotten in spite of its indisputable interest and merit.

Unfortunately, events led to the separation of the partners. Lods continued in his independent practice with his strong commitment to industralized architecture. He pleaded for pre-fabrication with characteristic vigour and with the inner conviction that the future of architecture depended on the capacity of architects to infiltrate the industrialization process and so guide its future development. He has had the opportunity to illustrate his ideas in many important works, some of them undeniably successful.

But, since the war, Marcel Lods, the enthusiastic and spirited warrior, has really devoted his inexhaustible energy to another cause—to what has become a crusade: trying to persuade the political authorities, the public, and, above all, other architects of the absolute priority that should be given to land and town planning. He has campaigned tirelessly—in his writings, in public conferences, in radio broadcasts—never allowing himself to become discouraged by the feeble echo that his pleadings and warnings evoke.

A real force of nature, who visited his sites on a powerful motorcycle and who liked to pilot his own aircraft, Lods, with his astonishing youthfulness of spirit, is and will remain one of the most attractive figures of 20th century French architecture.

—Pierre Vago

LOOS, Adolf.

Austrian. Born in Brünn, now Brno, Czechoslovakia, 10 December 1870. Educated at the Royal and Imperial Grammar School, Melk, Lower Austria, 1884–85; Royal and Imperial State Technical College, Reichenberg, Bohemia, 1887–88; College of Technology, Dresden, 1890–93. Served in the Austrian Army, 1889–90, 1916–18. Married Lina Loos in 1902. Worked for the building firm Czpka and Neusser, Brünn, 1887; lived in the United States, working as a mason, floor-layer and dish-washer, 1893–96: influenced by the Chicago architects, particularly Louis Sullivan; Assistant to Carl Mayreder, Vienna, 1896–97; in private practice, Vienna, 1897–1922: Journalist for the *Neue Freie Presse,* Vienna, 1897–1900; Founder Director, Free School of Architecture, Vienna; lived in Paris, 1922–28: Lecturer at the Sorbonne, 1926; returned to practice in Vienna, 1928 until his death, 1933. Visiting Lecturer, University of Stuttgart and University of Graz, 1926–27. Exhibitions: *Salon d'Automne,* Paris, 1923; Wurthle Gallery, Vienna, 1961; *Fruhes Industriedesign, Wien 1900–1908,* Galerie Nächst St. Stephan, Vienna, 1977. Collection: Loos Apartment Reconstruction, City Historical Museum, Vienna. *Died* (in Vienna) *23 August 1933.*

Works:

1898 4,000-seat Theatre, Vienna (project)
Goldman and Salatsch Shop, Vienna (destroyed)
1899 Emperor's Jubilee Memorial Church, Vienna (project)
Museum Cafe, Vienna (now altered)
Eugen Stossler Apartment, Vienna
Hugo Haberfeld Apartment, Vienna
Fireplace design
Vienna Ladies' Club interiors
1900 Otto Stoessl Apartment, Vienna
Gustav Turnowsky Apartment, Vienna
Alfred Sobotka Apartment, Vienna
1901 Leopold Langer Apartment, Vienna
1902 Aufricht Apartment, Vienna
1903 Loos Apartment, Vienna
Reifler Apartment, Vienna

Adolf Loos: Goldman Building, Vienna, 1910

Müller House, Prague
House, Paris (project; with Kurt Unger)
1931 Semi-detached house, *Werkbund Exhibition*, Vienna
Dentist's Consulting Rooms, for Dr. Teichner, Pilsen, Czechoslovakia
Willy Kraus Apartment, Pilsen, Czechoslovakia
Esplanade Nursing Home interior reconstruction, Karlovy Vary, Czechoslovakia (with Kurt Unger)
Small Timber House, for Mitzi Schnabel, Vienna
Babi Workers' Estate, near Nachod, Northern Bohemia
Heinrich Jordan Apartment, Brno, Czechoslovakia (project)
Fleischner Villa, Haifa, Palestine (project; with Kurt Unger)
Hotel, Juan-les-Pins, France (project)
Dining Room, *International Exhibition of Interiors,* Cologne
Drinking glasses, made by J. and L. Lobmeyr, Vienna

Publications:

By LOOS: books—*Wohnungswanderungen,* Vienna 1907; *Richtlinien für ein Kunstamt,* Vienna 1919; *Ins Leere Gesprochen,* Paris 1921, Innsbruck 1932; *Trotzdem: 1900–1930,* Innsbruck 1931; *Die Schriften von Adolf Loos,* 2 volumes, Innsbruck 1931, 1932; *Sämtliche Schriften,* edited by Franz Glück, 2 volumes, Vienna and Munich 1962.

On LOOS: books—*Adolf Loos* by A. Marilaun, Vienna 1922; *Adolf Loos zum 60 Geburtstag* by Berg, Taut, Oud, Schoenburg and others, Vienna 1930; *Adolf Loos* by Franz Glück, Paris 1931; *Adolf Loos: Das Werk des Architekten* by Heinrich Kulka, Vienna 1931; *Adolf Loos* by B. Markalaus, Vienna 1931; *Adolf Loos* by Ludwig Münz, Milan 1956; *Der Architekt Adolf Loos* by Ludwig Münz and Gustav Künstler, Vienna and Munich 1965, as *Adolf Loos: Pioneer of Modern Architecture,* London 1966; *Funktionalismus heute* by Th. W. Adorno, Frankfurt 1967; *Adolf Loos der Mensch* by Elsie Altmann Loos, Vienna and Munich 1968; *Oikos da Loos a Wittgenstein* by F. Amendolagine and M. Cacciari, Rome 1975; *Das Looshaus* by Czech and Mistelbaur, Vienna 1976; *Die Verdrängung des Ornaments: Zum Verhältnis von Architektur und Lebenspraxis* by Michael Müller, Frankfurt 1977; articles—"Loos" by P. Morton Shand in *Architectural Review* (London), October 1934; "Ornament a Crime: The Decisive Contribution of Adolf Loos" by Reyner Banham in *Architectural Review* (London), February 1957; special edition of *Casabella* (Milan), November 1959; special edition of *L'Architettura* (Rome), May 1965; "Der 'Traditionalist' Adolf Loos" by Gustav Künstler in *Oesterreichische Zeitschrift für Kunst und Denkmalpflege* (Vienna), no. 2, 1968; "Il Centenario di Hoffmann e di Loos" by A. Pica in *Domus* (Milan), November 1970; "Adolf Loos: House for Tristan Tzara" by J.-P. Fortin and M. Pietu in *Architecture Mouvement Continuité* (Paris), March 1976; "Adolf Loos: Language and Difference" by B. Gravagnuolo in *Controspazio* (Bari, Italy), September 1977; "The Loos Idea" by H. Czech in *Architecture + Urbanism* (Tokyo), May 1978.

Adolf Loos is one of those architects who became better known for what he wrote than for what he built. He contributed to this vision of himself: he intended his entire work to be a criticism of the conditions and prejudices of his time, and he intended that it should provoke controversy.

His most significant works—certainly his most successful works—appeared during a short space of years shortly before the First World War. His essay "Ornament und Verbrechen" (Decoration and Crime) appeared in 1908 and the not less important

"Architektur" in 1910; in the same year he created Steiner House and the—one has to admit—"controversial" Goldman Building on the Michaelerplatz in Vienna. The Viennese could not accept such undecorated architecture, and they tried to impose an historicized facade. Loos resisted, but he was not an established architect like Otto Wagner; he was not in a position to impose his own will. The argument raged, and Loos was eventually so upset that he had to receive medical treatment. He prevailed, however, thanks to his clients, who had convictions similar to his own. This episode was not unique. Throughout his life Loos felt keenly that he was not understood. He published his collected essays as *Trotzdem* (In Spite Of) and as *Ins Leere Gesprochen* (Spoken to the Void).

Yet Loos was no illusionist; on the contrary, he wanted an intelligently established building method supported by reason. He believed that everything that could not be justified on rational grounds was superfluous and should be eliminated. He meant, primarily, decoration. In articles and essays composed between 1897 and 1900 he had begun the struggle against form that achieved its quality not from its usefulness but from its richly-ornamented decoration. At the same time Henry van de Velde, in his search for a new architecture suited to the era of industrialization, believed that it was necessary to have a new kind of decoration that would unite artistic and industrial interests, individual needs and the universal aims of capital. In contrast, Loos maintained in 1898—and the development of architecture supports his view—that the goal to which mankind aspired was a beauty of form independent of decoration. Twenty years later he wrote:

> In place of the fanciful forms of past centuries, and in place of the flourishing ornaments of past times, clean, pure construction, straight lines, and right-angled edges had to appear: the craftsman works in this manner, with nothing but the object in view, his materials and tools in front of him. When I abuse the use of the object with ornament, I shorten its life because, subject to fashion, it must die sooner.

It was for economy and effectiveness that Loos wanted his pure forms. But he never seriously considered how this "effectiveness" could actually be brought about—whether it corresponded to what he considered to be rational human needs or whether it passed over those needs. Decoration—goes one of his well-known claims—is wasted manpower, squandered capital. He wanted to have inscribed on his tomb, "Adolf Loos, who freed mankind from superfluous work."

Loos saw himself as an innovator, and he had in mind the far-reaching goal of building a new culture, but he saw his goal hindered by decoration. In his attempt to make culture dependent upon the subjugation of decoration to the effectiveness of capital, he differed from other thinkers of the time—Hermann Muthesius, for example—who also believed in an environment free of decoration. What makes Loos' challenge so interesting is that he did not restrict his attack to the imitative style of the 19th century; he judged contemporary decoration—and rightly—to be mass-produced and mass-consumed trash. And Loos went further than other thinkers: his attack and his concept of form are based on the notion that cultural evolution is synonymous with, and proportional to, the total removal of decoration. In other words, Loos was not simply thinking of economy or beauty of form; it was on ethical grounds that he renounced decoration. The cultural goal is to be achieved not only by the removal of mechanical decoration but also by our emancipation *from* decoration.

What Loos was aiming at was the acceptance of a purified, objective form by means of renunciation—a significant repression of any decoration that conflicts with objectivity. And it has remained unclear

to this day what Loos actually wanted to put in place of decoration—for he speaks of his purified forms as having not only an aesthetic but also a sensual-mimetic and psychic effect.

In fact, Loos did make use of the psychoanalytical findings of his time, especially the cultural and "driving-force" theories of Sigmund Freud. Particularly in "Ornament and Verbrechen," Loos tried to produce a coherent substantiation of his discrimination against decoration by pointing to economic and historical reasons for its development, but he also described the suppression of decoration as necessary to the regulation and thereby control of vast uncontrolled passions or driving-forces. Culture—and here he appropriated psychoanalysis—is built on a renunciation of these passions. And that which brings man to the absence of ornamentation is spiritual power. Loos is relentless:

> But the man of our time who, because of his inner tensions, daubs the walls with erotic symbols is a criminal or a degenerate. It is evident that these tensions most violently overwhelm men in institutional establishments. One can measure the culture of a country by the degree of scrawling on lavatory walls. With children it is a natural occurrence that their first artistic expression is the scrawling of erotic symbols on walls. But what is natural in Papua and for children is a sign of degeneration in modern man. I have made the following discovery and presented it to the world: the evolution of culture is synonymous with the removal of decoration from the useful object.

This and other of his statements are to be taken very seriously. For they refer to the treatment of wishes and sensual needs in capitalist society. Loos recognized, realistically, the dominance of a profit-making interest, and he had far fewer illusions about this domination than did certain of the Bauhaus theorists who came after him. Everything that conflicted with the logic of this profit-making interest was to be repressed, for it was either superfluous or sick.

Whatever one thinks of such notions, the great merit of Loos with regard to an "engaged architecture" cannot be sufficiently praised. He had to fight very hard against the "bourgeois poison" of the 19th century to give social critical form to the new objectives for which other architects, those who came after him, especially those of the 1920's, also had to fight. For them Loos was a model and a seer. In 1941, Hans Schmidt, a determined believer in building toward a socialist future, spoke of Loos as a "very important contributor without whose work architecture would perhaps have remained in general only an interesting game, a speciality of the artist, as abstract painting and the plastic arts."

Schmidt was doubtless right. Yet the question begged by the image of the game remains unanswered. Loos rigorously ignored such questions. He was a realist. Perhaps it is for that reason that people have not wished to understand him.

—Michael Müller

LUBETKIN, Berthold.

Russian. Born in Tiflis, Georgia, Russia in 1901; emigrated to England, 1930. Studied at the Moscow Technical School, 1920–22; Atelier Auguste Perret and other architectural schools, Paris, 1925–27. In private practice, Paris, 1927–30, and London, 1930–32; Partner, with Anthony Chitty, Lindsey Drake, Michael Dugdale, Val Harding, Godfrey Samuel and Francis Skinner, TECTON Group, London, 1932–52, and Lubetkin, Bailey and Skinner, London, 1952–55; has farmed in Gloucestershire since 1955. Founder Member, MARS (Modern Architecture Research) Group, 1933.

Works:

1927 Apartment building, 25 Avenue de Versailles, Paris (with Jean Ginsberg)
1932 Gorilla House, London Zoo, Regent's Park
1933 Penguin Pool, London Zoo, Regent's Park
1934/
35 Giraffe and Elephant houses, Whipsnade Zoo, Bedfordshire
1935 High Point I Flats, Highgate, London
1937 Dudley Zoo Buildings, Worcestershire
2 bungalows, Whipsnade, Bedfordshire
1937/
38 High Point II Flats, Highgate, London
1938 Finsbury Health Centre, London
1942 Lenin Memorial Monument, Holford Square, Holborn, London
1951 Spa Green Housing Development, Finsbury, London
Priory Green Housing Development, Finsbury, London
1955 Plan for Peterlee New Town, Durham (project)

Publications:

By LUBETKIN: books—*Opening of Finsbury Health Centre,* London 1938; *Planned A.R.P.,* London 1939; *Report to Finsbury Borough Council on Structural Protection for People Against Aerial Bombardment,* London 1939; *Spa Green Estate,* London 1952; articles—"The Builders," in special Russian issue of *Architectural Review* (London), May 1932; "Modern Architecture in England" in *American Architect* (New York), February 1937; "Soviet Architecture: Notes on Developments from 1917–1932" in *Architectural Association Journal* (London), May 1956; "Soviet Architectufe: Notes on Developments from 1932–1955" in *Architectural Association Journal* (London), September/October 1956; "Milton Keynes" in *L'Architecture d'Aujourd'hui* (Paris), no. 192, 1977.

On LUBETKIN: articles—"Flats on Spa Green Estate, Finsbury" in *The Architects' Journal* (London), 26 April 1951; "Groupe d'Immeubles Spa Green à Finsbury, Londres" in *Techniques et Architecture* (Paris), April 1953; "Lubetkin" by Robert Furneaux Jordan in *Architectural Review* (London), July 1955; "Historic Pioneers: Architects and Clients" by Sam Lambert in *The Architects' Journal* (London), 11 March 1970; "Berthold Lubetkin on 'Socialist' Architecture in the Diaspora" by William J. R. Curtis in *Archithese* (Niedertaufen, Switzerland), no. 12, 1974; "High Point Flats, Camden" in *Design* (London), December 1974; "Perspective: Hampstead in the 30's" in *Building Design* (London), 17 January 1975.

In 1930, Berthold Lubetkin, a Russian-born architect, arrived in London from Paris. Although he was only twenty-nine years old his architectural outlook was already well formed. Lubetkin had been influenced by the political and cultural upheavals of the Russian Revolution of 1917 and by the architectural transformations which occurred in Paris in the late 1920's, especially the work of Le Corbusier. He had studied at the atelier Perret in Paris, had learned the basics of reinforced concrete construction and had imbibed something of the classical principles underlying the work of the master.

The young architect who arrived in England in 1930 was well prepared for the building tasks of a modern society and might well have preferred to have practised in Russia except that official dogma there soon turned against modern architecture. Instead, Lubetkin set up a practice in London with six Architectural Association graduates, and the group became known as TECTON. Before his arrival Lubetkin had demonstrated the range of his talents in an apartment building on the Avenue de Versailles in Paris, but in England his earliest works were for

Berthold Lubetkin: High Point, Highgate, London, 1938

animals rather than men. The first of these was an ingenious "machine à habiter" for two Congolese gorillas in London Zoo. This was built in the form of an environmentally adaptable cylinder that simulated some of the climatic conditions of the jungle while protecting the beasts from germs and providing a circulation route for public viewing. The other main building, for the same client, was the better known Penguin Pool of 1933. With its taut, interlacing ramps and its abstract sculptural quality, it shows clearly the influence of Russian Constructivists like Gabo and Pevsner.

High Point I flats in Highgate of 1935 also indicate Lubetkin's debt to the architecture of the revolutionary avant-garde in Russia, particularly the communal buildings of the OSA group. Thus despite its upper-middle class inhabitants, the building has the quality of a polemic for a new social order and contains communal zones on top, on the roof terrace, and below, in a hallway that is a sort of emblematic forum. As well as the imagery of socialist architecture, High Point I incorporates a formal vocabulary and system of concrete construction derived from Le Corbusier. Indeed Le Corbusier visited the building and praised it highly, announcing it as "The Vertical Garden City" of the future. Clearly he recognized in it a personal re-interpretation of his own urban doctrines and utopian fantasies in favor of the employment of modern technique to create a high density communal existence in an idyllic natural setting.

High Point II, which Lubetkin designed a few years later, represents an extension of the International Style vocabulary of High Point I so that more materials and a more complex facade design can be realized. The later building has a strong neoclassical quality and contains blatant historical references in some of its details—for example, the classical caryatids supporting the cantilevered entrance slab. The materials and the expensive 2/1 section of High Point II are luxurious, and it seems in retrospect as if the polemical quality of the earlier building has been replaced by superficial stylistic formulae. High Point II sets the tone for some of the rather mannered, modernistic, curvaceous clichés prevalent in the 1950's.

Lubetkin's sense of social experimentation found an outlet in The Finsbury Health Centre of 1938 which again indicates some of the architect's deeply embedded neo-Baroque tendencies. The building is symmetrical and has clearly arranged hierarchies of fixed and changeable functions—a formal and functional strategy to be taken over in the post-war years

by Denys Lasdun, the most gifted of the young architects to pass through Lubetkin's office.

In the late 1940's Lubetkin was temporarily involved with the design of Peterlee, a new town, which called for the full range of his social and formal powers. However, his principles and his clients' were not in accord, and, strangely, Lubetkin all but ceased to practice by the early 1950's. Still, Lubetkin's influence in England has been considerable. At its weakest this has been a matter of a diluted vocabulary of strip windows, hump-shaped roofs, colored tiles and flats on stilts; at its strongest (particularly via the original talent of Lasdun), it has been a matter of the extension of basic ideological and formal messages from early modern architecture.

—William J. R. Curtis

LUCAS, Colin (Anderson).

British. Born in London, 29 December 1906. Educated at Cheltenham College, Gloucestershire, 1919–25; Trinity College, Cambridge (Cambridge University Architectural School), 1925–28. Married Dione Wilson in 1931; Pamela Campbell in 1952; sons: Mark and Peter. Director, Lucas Lloyd and Company, builders, Greenwich, London, 1928–33; Partner, with Amyas Connell, *q.v.,* and Basil Ward, Connell, Ward and Lucas, London, 1933–39; Architect, Ministry of Works, Building Research Station, and Ministry of Home Security, 1941–51, and with the Housing Division, London County Council and Greater London Council, 1951–78. Exhibitions: *Contemporary Industrial Design in the Home,* Dorland Hall, London, 1934; Exhibition of Drawings of Blocks of Working Class Flats in Reinforced Concrete, Imperial Institute, London, 1935; *Contemporary Industrial Design,* London, 1935; Museum of Modern Art, New York, 1935; Royal Academy, London, 1938. Fellow, Royal Institute of British Architects, 1939. O.B.E. (Officer, Order of the British Empire), 1972. Address: 2 Queen's Grove Studios, Green's Grove, London N.W.8, England.

Works:

1927 "Silver Birches" (house), Burghclere, Hampshire

1930 "Noah's House" (house and boathouse), Spade Oak Reach, Bourne End, Buckinghamshire

1931 "Sun House", Chelwood Gate, Ashdown Forest, Sussex

1933 "The Hop Field" (house), St. Marys Platt, Wrotham, Kent (with Amyas Connell and Basil Ward)

1934 4 Houses, High and Over Estate, Amersham, Buckinghamshire (with Amyas Connell and Basil Ward)

1935 Kent House Flats, Ferdinand Street, Chalk Farm, London (with Amyas Connell and Basil Ward)

2 pairs of semi-detached houses, Parkwood Estate, Ruislip, Middlesex (with Amyas Connell and Basil Ward)

"The Firs" (house), Brighton Road, Redhill, Surrey (with Amyas Connell and Basil Ward)

Hertford County Buildings (competition project; with Amyas Connell and Basil Ward)

1936 "Dragons" (house), Woodmancote, Sussex (with Amyas Connell and Basil Ward)

"Concrete House" (Ronald Gunn House), The Ridgeway, Westbury-on-Trym, Bristol (with Amyas Connell and Basil Ward)

Civic Buildings, Newport, Monmouthshire (competition project; with Amyas Connell and Basil Ward)

1937 House, Wentworth, Virginia Water, Surrey (with Amyas Connell and Basil Ward)

Geoffrey Walford house, 66 Frognal, Hampstead, London (with Amyas Connell and Basil Ward)

House, Worcester Park. Surrey (with Amyas Connell and Basil Ward)

Sound City Film Studios, Shepperton, Middlesex (with Amyas Connell and Basil Ward)

1937/
38 H. Tarburn House, 6 Temple Gardens, Moor Park, Hertfordshire (with Amyas Connell and Basil Ward)

1938 "Potcraft" (Dr. Thomas House), Sutton, Surrey (with Amyas Connell and Basil Ward)

1938/
39 Major Proudman house, 26 Bessborough Gardens, Roehampton, London (with Amyas Connell and Basil Ward)

1939 Lords Court (apartment building and shops), 32 St. John's Wood Road, London (partially built with Amyas Connell and Basil Ward)

With Greater London Council Architects Department Housing Division:

1951/
78 Alton Estate West, Roehampton
Ackroydon Estate
Canada Estate
Somerset Estate
Westbury Street Estate
Kidbrooke Estate

Publications:

On LUCAS: articles—"Heroes of the Modern Movement" by Amyas Connell and Walter Menzies in *Building Design* (London), 27 February 1976; "Building Revisited: Alton Estate, Roehampton" by Michael Fleetwood in *The Architects' Journal* (London), 30 March 1977.

My work as an architect was originally—and is still —inspired by a feeling for the material one is using, and particularly its structural possibilities. This, coupled with the three-dimensional disposition of space dictated by the client's requirements, combines to give the opportunity for the expression of certain proportions in the structure as a whole. Thus materials, space, and proportion are the three main design elements. Whether the finished building is doomed to be reminiscent of this or that period or style is irrelevant. Ideally, it should have no style other than its own.

—Colin Lucas

The international style architecture of Continental Europe was usually constructed of concrete blocks plastered and painted to give the illusion of a building completely constructed of reinforced concrete. That did not worry Le Corbusier, but it did worry the moralizing, puritanical English who felt that if it looked as if it was all made of reinforced concrete, then it should indeed all be made of reinforced concrete. It was Colin Lucas who showed them how to do it.

Colin Lucas felt that the new architecture in England was continually frustrated by the conservatism of builders, so he formed his own building company, Lucas Lloyd and Co., to build unconventional buildings. He evolved a system of building in reinforced concrete, using 100mm walls and 125mm floor and roof slabs, and built the first reinforced concrete houses in England. His Noah's House and Boathouse at Spade Oak Reach, Bourne End, Bucking-

Colin Lucas: "The Hop Field," St. Marys Platt, Wrotham, Kent, 1933

hamshire, exploits the potential of reinforced concrete construction; some of the details, such as the curved stair balustrades, seem curiously dated, but the way that the construction allows one whole wall of the living room to be of thin concrete mullions and glass is as fresh today as when it was built. Lucas followed up the success of Noah's House with "The Hopfield," St Mary's Platt, Wrotham, Kent, a truly beautiful little building, with a very solid outside staircase tying the house down to the ground.

In 1933 Colin Lucas joined Amyas Connell and Basil Ward to form Connell, Ward and Lucas and was able to bring to the firm his unparalleled knowledge of reinforced concrete house-building. For six years they produced a series of houses that no other contemporary firm could match. They were world class architects.

Connell, Ward and Lucas acted as a team, and Lucas's experience in concrete construction is evident in all the houses built by the firm. However, the individual authorship of the firm's houses is known, and Lucas is seen at his best in the final flowering of the firm just before the war. Lucas's 66 Frognal in London, the firm's most famous house, is inventive, beautifully built and very habitable; his Roehampton house explores emphasized horizontals and is a response to some of the detailing failures of the earlier houses. Lucas's "Potcraft" at Sutton is an intriguing tailpiece; built of timber boarding on a timber frame, and with a sloping roof, it shows that the architect has gained sufficient confidence to re-introduce traditional forms and materials.

After the war Colin Lucas worked in the Architects Department of the London County Council. His role there was largely administrative, but it was the kind of administration that enabled architecture to happen. It was the young architects under Colin Lucas that built the great Roehampton scheme, only a few hundred yards from Connell, Ward and Lucas's last house.

—John Winter

LUCKHARDT, Hans.

German. Born in Berlin, 16 June 1890. Educated at the Technische Hochschule, Karlsruhe. Served in the German Army. In partnership with his brother Wassili Luckhardt, q.v., Berlin, 1921 until his death, 1954. Recipient: First Prize, with Wassili Luckhardt, Alexanderplatz Competition, Berlin, 1929. *Died* (in Bad Wiessee, Germany) *in 1954.*

See LUCKHARDT, Wassili

LUCKHARDT, Wassili.

German. Born in Berlin, 22 July 1889. Educated at the Technische Hochschule, Charlottenburg, Berlin. Served in the German Army. In partnership with his brother Hans Luckhardt, q.v., Berlin, 1921–54; in private practice, Berlin, 1954 until his death, 1972. Recipient: First Prize, with Hans Luckhardt, Alexanderplatz Competition, Berlin, 1929; Kunstpreis, Berlin, 1958. D.Eng.: Technische Hochschule, Berlin, 1962. Member, Akademie der Künste, Berlin, 1956. *Died* (in Berlin) *2 December 1972.*

Works:

1919 Glass Banqueting Hall (project)
      Cinema (project)
1920 Private House (project)
1921 Theatre (project)

      Museum of Hygiene (project; with Hans Luckhardt)
1922 Skyscraper, Friedrichstrasse, Berlin (competition project; with Hans Luckhardt)
1923 Private house, Westend, Berlin (with Hans Luckhardt)
      Norma Tool Factory, Berlin (competition project; with Hans Luckhardt)
      Office building conversion, Tauentzienstrasse, Berlin (with Hans Luckhardt)
1924 Housing estate, Dahlem, Berlin (with Hans Luckhardt)
1927 Experimental housing development, Schorlemer Allee, Berlin (with Hans Luckhardt)
      Exhibition Room, Thannhauser Art Gallery, Bellevuestrasse, Berlin (with Hans Luckhardt)
      Office building, Kurfürstendamm, Berlin (with Hans Luckhardt)
1928 3 houses, Rupenhorn, Berlin (with Hans Luckhardt and Alfons Anker)
      Pavilion, *Heim und Technik* exhibition, Munich (with Hans Luckhardt)
1929 Telschow-Haus Department Store, Potsdamer Platz, Berlin (with Hans Luckhardt and Alfons Anker)
      Alexanderplatz redevelopment, Berlin (competition project; with Hans Luckhardt)
      Housing development, Gohlis, Leipzig (project; with Hans Luckhardt)
1930 Berlin House, Potsdamer Platz, Berlin (project; with Hans Luckhardt)
1931 Central Law Courts, Berlin (project; with Hans Luckhardt)
1932 Private house, Velten, near Berlin (with Hans Luckhardt)
      Private house, Lankwitz, Berlin (with Hans Luckhardt)
1933 Pavilion, *Building Exhibition,* Berlin (with Hans Luckhardt)
1946 Building for the University of Jena (competition project; with Hans Luckhardt)
1948 Bridge, Stockholm (project; with Hans Luckhardt)
1951 Berlin Pavilion, and Terrace House, *Constructa Exhibition,* Hanover (with Hans Luckhardt)
1952 American Memorial Library, Berlin (competition project; with Hans Luckhardt)
      Institute of Plant Physiology, Free University of Berlin (competition project; with Hans Luckhardt)
      Treasury Building, Steglitz, Berlin (project; with Hans Luckhardt)
1954 German Student Residence, Cité Universitaire, Paris (with Hans Luckhardt)
1956 Apartment building, Kottbusser Tor, Berlin
1957 Social Welfare Administration Centre for Bavaria, Munich (initial design with Hans Luckhardt)
      Berlin Pavilion, *International Building Exhibition,* Berlin (project)
      Town Hall, Bremen (competition project)
      Luckhardt House, Dahlem, Berlin
      Apartment building, Hansa District, Berlin (with Hubert Hoffmann)
      City Hall, Toronto (competition project)
1962/
69 Deputies Assembly Hall, Bremen
1962/
70 Institute for Plant Physiology, Free University of Berlin
1963/
68 Institute for Veterinary Medicine, Free University of Berlin

Publications:

By LUCKHARDT: books—*Zur neuen Wohnform,* with Hans Luckhardt, Berlin 1930; *Lichtarchitektur,* with Walter Kohler, Berlin 1956; letters in *Die Glaserne Kette,* exhibition catalogue, Berlin 1963.

On LUCKHARDT: books—*Wassili und Hans Luckhardt: Bauten und Entwürfe* by Udo Kultermann, Tubingen 1958; *Wassili Luckhardt,* edited by Helga Kliemann, Tubingen 1973; articles—"Die Wohnung unserer Zeit" by Ludwig Hilberseimer in *Die Form* (Berlin), 15 July 1931; "A House Near Berlin by the Brothers Luckhardt" in *Architectural Journal* (London), July 1936; "Wohnhochhausgruppe am Kottbusser Tor in Berlin" in *Bauen und Wohnen* (Zurich), June 1956; "Das Landesversorgungsamt Bayern in Munich" in *Bauen und Wohnen* (Zurich), July 1958; "Das Werk von Wassili und Hans Luckhardt" in *Bauen und Wohnen* (Zurich), February 1959; "Wassili Luckhardt" in *Der Aufbau* (Vienna), June 1959; "Provincial Offices, Munich" in *Architectural Review* (London), September 1960; "Das Haus der Bürgerschaft in Bremen" in *Bauwelt* (Berlin), 13 February 1967; "Pflanzenphysiologisches Institut der Freien Universität Berlin" in *Bauwelt* (Berlin), 10 August 1970.

Wassili Luckhardt worked mainly in collaboration with his younger brother Hans until the latter's death in 1954. Like most of the significant German architects who were active in the 1920's they went through an expressionist phase at a time when, because of a shortage of clients with money, there was little opportunity to construct actual buildings. Those visionary and utopian expressionist architects who were genuinely striving to find new forms for new functions, to provide architecture with a new basis, exchanged ideas and discussed aesthetic questions in their contributions to Bruno Taut's magazine *Frühlicht,* which enabled them to publish designs of projects that were never actually realized. These projects include some highly imaginative designs by Wassili Luckhardt for theatres and cinemas, which would have been as strange in psychological atmosphere as the highly stylized sets of the German silent films of the time—yet these designs have had some influence on younger architects since the Second World War.

In the early 1920's the clients for German housing were largely the building societies; consequently, many housing estates and garden suburbs were built at the time. The Luckhardt brothers designed one of the first modern housing estates in Dahlem, Berlin, in 1924. They showed a marked inclination towards geometrical architecture, rectangular and blocky, with a strong emphasis on such motifs as horizontal bands of windows. Despite this concern with the purity of rectangular shapes, they also explored the possibilities of free curved facades, as in the shop frontage of the Telschow-Haus Department Store, or of dynamically-curved blocks divided up by continuous horizontal bands of windows, as in their winning entry for the Berlin Alexanderplatz.

During the same period they built three modern residences on the western outskirts of Berlin at Ruperhorn: the houses take full advantage of the splendid view and other special features of a site where Erich Mendelsohn also chose to build his own house in the same year. The first of these houses to be built is particularly interesting in design, on three floors with a roof garden, full use being made of the steel-frame structure in obtaining the utmost flexibility in the planning of each floor. The first floor living room has six large bays all along its front with large glass panels, alternately fixed and sliding horizontally on rollers, opening out onto a terrace irregularly shaped like half of a tennis-racket, providing maximum opportunity for enjoying the sun and the view throughout the day.

A typical example of the Luckhardt brothers' work after the interruption of the Hitler period and the destruction of the Second World War was the Berlin Pavilion at the *Constructa Exhibition* of 1951 in Hanover. The Pavilion was intended to demonstrate, by a display of drawings and models, Berlin's progress in building since 1945; the construction consisted of a steel frame carrying both roofs and walls, the walls being taken to only half the height of the building, with the intervening spaces entirely

Wassili and Hans Luckhardt: Museum of Hygiene, 1921 (project)

glazed with plate glass, producing a partially transparent building: the impression of lightness and floating was heightened by the view of the trees seen through it.

In 1954, before Hans' death, they had produced the final design for the Munich offices of the Social Welfare Administration, which was built in 1957. The special design problem faced here was that since the offices would be regularly visited by many war disabled and other invalids, it was essential that these visitors should not have to climb stairs—nor did the use of lifts seem practical. The Luckhardts' solution was to situate all the offices to which the public would have access in ground-floor, single-storey, pontoon-shaped buildings, while the offices to which the public would not have access are on three floors of a long building that appears to float on pilotis at right angles to the pontoons.

Wassili Luckhardt's apartment building on the Kottbusser Tor, Berlin, shares the propensity to balconies of other German architects of the time, the balconies being built into the structure, shielded by the walls, to produce a flat though indented facade. Even while Hans was alive the brothers had often collaborated with other architects (for example, Alfons Anker), and in 1957 Wassili worked with Hubert Hoffmann in designing a block of flats in the Hansa Quarter, Berlin, consisting of a range of five terrace structures divided longitudinally by staircase towers, with different sizes and plans of flats permitting a wide variety of dwelling types.

In 1958 Wassili Luckhardt was awarded the Kunstpreis of the City of Berlin, where most of his work was built.

—Konstantin Bazarov

LUMSDEN, Anthony.

American. Born (of Australian nationality) in Bournemouth, Hampshire, England, 16 May 1928; emigrated to the United States, 1954. Educated at the University of Sydney School of Architecture, 1947–51, B.Arch. 1951. Married Anne Fowler in 1964; children: John, Thomas and Fiona. Project Designer, Eero Saarinen and Associates, Bloomfield Hills, Michigan, 1954–60; Senior Designer, Kevin Roche/John Dinkeloo, Hamden, Connecticut, 1962–64. Since 1964, Vice-President and Principal in charge of Design, Daniel, Mann, Johnson and Mendenhall, Los Angeles. Exhibitions: *Three Worlds of Los Angeles,* Brussels, 1974, Paris, 1975; *Los Angeles 12,* Pacific Design Center, Los Angeles, and tour, 1975–76; *California Architects,* Museum of Modern Art, San Francisco, and tour, 1977. Recipient: First Design Award, 1966, and Annual Design Award, 1972, *Progressive Architecture;* Merit Award, United States Department of Housing and Urban Development, 1967; Excellence in Human Factors Design Award, Institute of Human Engineering Sciences, 1967; Architectural Award of Excellence, American Institute of Steel Construction, 1968, 1972; Special Award for Architectural and Engineering Excellence in Design, 1969, and Award of Engineering Excellence, 1973, Portland Cement Association; Award of Honor, 1969, 1975 (twice), 1976, and Award of Merit, 1969, 1973, 1976, American Institute of Architects, Southern California Chapter; Award of Merit, AIA/National Center for Low and Moderate Income Housing/National Urban Coalition/Urban Design and Development Corporation, 1970; Honor Award, AIA/*House and Home,* 1970; Design Award, 1970, and Honor Award, 1973, AIA, Hawaii Chapter; Award of Merit, National Society of Professional Engineers, 1972; Eminent Conceptor Award, 1972, and Award of Excellence, 1973, Consulting Engineers Association of California. Fellow, American Institute of Architects. Address: DMJM, 3250 Wilshire Boulevard, Los Angeles, California 90010, U.S.A.

Works:

1966	Beverly Hills Jewelry Store, Los Angeles (with Cesar Pelli)
	Sunset Mountain Park, Santa Monica, California (project; with Cesar Pelli)
1967	Los Angeles Rapid Transit
1967/ 68	Third Street Tunnel, Los Angeles (with Cesar Pelli)
1967/ 69	Worldway Post Office, Los Angeles (with Cesar Pelli)
1967/ 70	Kukui Gardens, Honolulu
1967/ 73	Federal Aviation Administration Agency, Lawndale, California
1968	Teledyne Systems Research and Manufacturing Facility, Northridge, California (with Cesar Pelli)
1969	Beneficial Life Building, Los Angeles
	Century City Medical Plaza, Los Angeles (with Cesar Pelli)
	Pacific Ocean Park, Los Angeles
	Lockheed Offices, Sunnyvale, California
1970	Hillrise Apartments, Honolulu (project)
1970/ 72	One Park Plaza, Los Angeles
1971/ 72	Century Bank, Los Angeles
1972	Naval Air Reworks Facility, San Diego, California
	Immobiliaire Apartments, Los Angeles (project)
	Convention Center, Lugano, Switzerland (project)
	Sepulveda Water Reclamation Plant, Los Angeles (project)
1972/ 75	Marina City, Los Angeles
1972/ 76	Bank Bumi Daya, Jakarta, Indonesia (project)

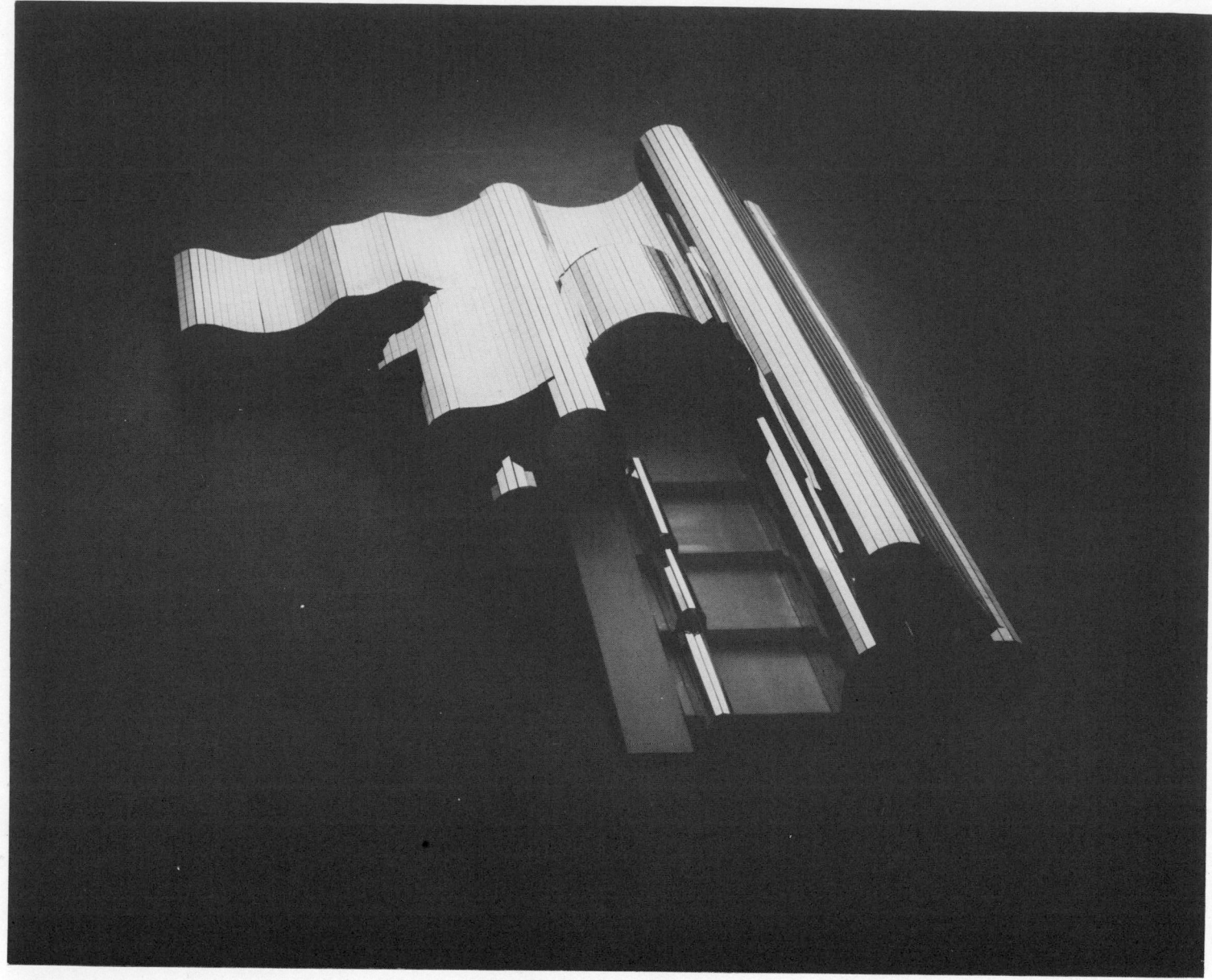

Anthony Lumsden: Convention Center, Lugano, Switzerland, 1972 (project)

1973 A La Wai Plaza Skyrise Building, Honolulu
City Hall, Las Vegas, Nevada
Sears Warehouse, Los Angeles
Beverly Hills Hotel, California (project)
Sepulveda Bridge, Los Angeles
1974 Holyoke Community College Gymnasium
and Natatorium Building, and Student
Center, Holyoke, Massachusetts
El Monte Bus Station, Los Angeles
Banyan Tree Apartments, Honolulu
Portland Plaza, Oregon
Roxbury Plaza, Beverly Hills, California
Santa Clara Office Building, California
Van Nuys Housing, Los Angeles
Kodak Office Building, Whittier, California
(project)
Trident Naval Warehouse, Seattle
1974/
76 Jacksonville Community College, Jackson-
ville, Florida (with Reynolds, Smith, and
Hills)
Van Camp Food Processing Factory, San
Diego, California
1975 Baltimore Community College
Ford Office Building, Bethesda, Maryland
Tempe Mall, Arizona
University Station, Los Angeles
Library, Santa Monica Community College,
California
East Los Angeles Medical Clinic

Plan for the Moda Medical Center, Al Kharj,
Saudi Arabia
1976 Northlake Community College, Irving, Texas
(with Envirodynamics Inc.)
Lawrence Laser Laboratories, Livermore,
California
Saudi Youth Evaluation Center, Riyadh,
Saudi Arabia
Detention facility at Peoria, Illinois
Engine test facility at Tullahoma, Tennessee
Riyadh New Town, Saudi Arabia
1976/
77 Pedestrian bridges, Los Angeles
1977 Gajah Mada Commercial Complex, Jakarta,
Indonesia
Music Building, Santa Monica Community
College, California
Harapan Plaza, Jakarta, Indonesia
Longview Community College, Kansas City,
Missouri
Maplewood Community College, Kansas
City, Missouri
Capitol Building, St. Paul, Minnesota (com-
petition project)
Ambassador College Office Building,
Pasadena, California
Office building, Anchorage, Alaska
1978 Peoplemover, Los Angeles
Los Angeles Valley College, Van Nuys, Cali-
fornia

Publications:

On LUMSDEN: articles—"Anthony Lumsden,
DMJM" in *Architecture + Urbanism* (Tokyo),
March 1975; "The Development of an Esthetic System at DMJM" by Michael Franklin Ross in *Architectural Record* (New York), May 1975; "Post-
Mies: Architecture di Anthony Lumsden" by Esther
McCoy in *Domus* (Milan), November 1975; "Images
from a Silver Screen" in *Progressive Architecture*
(New York), October 1976; "Architecture-Promo-
tion, Architecte-Promoteur" in *L'Architecture d'Aujourd'hui* (Paris), October 1977.

Anthony Lumsden is an architect of polemics, of
keen visual awareness, and of bold imagery. His architectural skill is displayed in a large body of work
that often breaks from modern precepts to forge new
directions and explore previously uncharted waters.
The strength of his convictions can be seen in the
powerful images of the Lugano Convention Center,
the Beverly Hills Hotel and the Bank Bumi Daya.
Lumsden's somewhat unconventional approach to
design sometimes leaves the uninitiated and less sophisticated wondering as to the full intent of his
work. Careful analysis and patient review of the
work reveal a clear, consistent attitude toward the
design process, which often manifests itself in diverse

and unsuspected exterior forms.

Lumsden is fond of examining the relationship of form and function in nature and applying it to architecture. Any school of fish in the sea or swarm of butterflies clearly indicates a visual diversity that has far more to do with the exterior environment than it has to do with the internal workings of the particular species. Similarly, Lumsden maintains that an architect can solve the internal functions and quite independently develop an exterior that is appropriate to a given environment. The Beverly Hills Hotel, for example, has a dramatic silhouette that steps up along the diagonal in a series of extruded cylinders that enclose a variable-height galleria of terraced shops. By employing a membrane skin enclosure that is not dependent on the structure for its esthetic, Lumsden can allow the rolling surface to respond to variations in site configuration and programmatic requirements. The combination of the sophisticated high-tech membrane enclosure and the extruded, vernacular esthetic was a bold departure for Lumsden that heralded new explorations in the 1970's. The FAA Building, the Sepulveda Water Reclamation Plant, and the Beverly Hills Hotel, signaled a departure from current architectural preoccupations of the period.

Lumsden's design approach has been applied to both high-rise office towers and horizontal stepping universities and college campuses. The rolling surfaces of Roxbury Plaza, the angled, folded planes of Century Bank Plaza and the extended curved corners of One Park Plaza, headquarters of DMJM, of which Lumsden is Vice President and Principal for Design, form an interesting evolution of the variable surface membrane enclosure as it is applied to commercial office structures.

Perhaps the most successful application of the extrusion esthetic yet to be realized by Lumsden is the Northlake Community College in Irving, Texas. Set on a rolling 276-acre wooded hillside, the new campus is composed of a series of stepping volumes that repeat a similar profile. By employing the extrusion esthetic, Lumsden makes the building step up the hillside in what he describes as, "a series of little buildings like you get in a Japanese village . . . like vernacular architecture." The use of horizontal planters at grade and cantilevering off the roof is the continuation of an esthetic system that Lumsden first worked on as project architect under Kevin Roche for the Oakland Museum.

The separation of membrane enclosure from structure departs from the trabeated esthetic of Mies van der Rohe and of his Chicago disciples at Skidmore, Owings and Merrill, but it is not really all that radical. Le Corbusier's Domino House concept and his villas at Vaucresson and at Garches clearly led the way for these more recent explorations. In his *Age of Modern Masters,* Reyner Banham uses Lumsden's Century Bank Plaza and Corbu's Parliament Building at Chandigarh to illustrate his point that,

> In a world where art-movements like Pop and Op have evaporated like the morning dew, the style that runs—visually—from Gropius's Fagus factory of 1911 to Le Corbusier's Capitol buildings at Chandigarh and on to the prismatic mirror-glass skyscrapers being built in the US in the early Seventies, is a style to be reckoned with, durable beyond the expectations of our time.

There is no question that these visual explorations by Lumsden and others will continue. It is interesting to note, looking back over the body of work designed by Tony Lumsden in the last two decades, that his most compelling and original projects have not been built. One can only speculate on the impact a Sepulveda Water Reclamation Plant, a Beverly Hills Hotel or a Bank Bumi Daya might have had on the profession had they been constructed, and whether future projects will again develop this high level of originality and vision.

—Michael Franklin Ross

LUND, Kjell.

Norwegian. Born in Lillehammer, 18 June 1927. Educated at the Norges Tekniske Høyskole, Trondheim, Dip.Arch. 1950. Married Tove Berg in 1954; children: Martine, Johanne, and Bendik. In private practice, Oslo, 1950–58. In partnership with Nils Slaatto, *q.v.,* Oslo, since 1958. Assistant Editor, *Byggekunst,* Oslo, 1959–70. Exhibition: *Works of Lund and Slaatto,* Det Kongelige Danske Kunstakademie, Copenhagen, and Det Finske Arkitekturmuseum, Helsinki, 1975, toured universities and architecture schools in Europe and the United Kingdom, 1975–78. Recipient: First Prize, Akerhaus County Agricultural School Competition, Årnes, Norway, 1958; The Concrete Award, Federation of Norwegian Architects/Norwegian Concrete Association, 1964, 1977; The Wood Prize, Norwegian Concrete Association/Council for Tree Information, 1966; Sundt's Award, 1972, and Houen's Award, 1976, Federation of Norwegian Architects; First Prize, Norwegian Civil Engineers Main Office Building Competition, Oslo, 1970; First Prize, Eidsvåg Church Competition, Bergen, 1970; First Prize, National Gallery Extension Competition, Oslo, 1972; First Prize, National Theatre Extension Competition, Oslo, 1973; First Prize, Bank of Norway Competition, Oslo, 1973. Address: Kjell Lund og Nils Slaatto Arkitekter, Bygdøy Allé 13, Oslo 2, Norway.

Works (with Nils Slaatto):

1958　Sawdust silo, Romedal Almenning, Norway
1958/
　60　Primary school, Vik, Ringerike, Norway
1958/
　63　Town Hall, Asker, Norway
1958/
　66　St. Hallvard Church and Monastery, Oslo
1958/
　68　Akerhaus County Agricultural School, Årnes, Norway
1959/
　61　House, Rostad, Oslo
1961　Bookshop, Gol, Hallingdal, Norway
1961/
　66　Farm, Trones, Verdal, Norway
1961/
　68　Nic Waals Child Psychiatry Institute, Oslo
1961/
　70　Chateau Neuf: Norwegian Student Association Center, Oslo
1962/
　63　Farm, Rua, Hønefoss, Norway
1963　House, Andersen, Lysaker, Norway
1963/
　64　House, Lund, Oslo
　　　House, Lystrup, Asker, Norway
1964　Henie-Onstad Art Center, Høvikodden, Norway (competition project)
　　　Radio station, Vardø, Norway
　　　Employers' Association Study Center, Jevnaker, Norway (competition project)
1966　Pyramiden Mountain Cabin (project)
1967　House, Haraldseid, Gol, Norway
1968　House, Botheim, Oslo
1968/
　69　Farmhouse, Rustad, As, Norway
1968/
　70　House, Kionig, Fredrikstad, Norway
　　　European Youth Center (Council of Europe), Strasbourg
1969　Bekkefaret Church, Stavanger, Norway (project)
1970　Center for Environmental Studies, Interlaken, Switzerland (competition project)
1972　Eidsvåg Church, Bergen (competition project)
　　　National Gallery extension, Oslo (competition project)
1972/
　74　Høvik Stål Factory and Office Building, Hønefoss, Norway

1972/
　76　Det Norske Veritas Administration/Research Center, Høvik, Norway
1973　National Theatre extension, Oslo (competition project)
　　　The Bank of Norway, Oslo (competition project)
1974　Plan for the center of Oslo
1974/
　75　Plan for the central park area, Oslo (partially executed, 1975–79)
1976　Farmhouse, Biri, Norway
1976/
　78　Bank building, Bagn, Valdres, Norway
　　　Andersen Factory, Larvik, Norway
1976/
　79　Police School, Oslo
　　　Nestlé-Findus Administration Center, Asker, Norway
　　　Norwegian Civil Engineers Main Office Building, Oslo
1977/
　78　Henrikke Outdoor Restaurant, Oslo
1979/
　80　Paviljongen Outdoor Restaurant, Oslo

Publications:

On LUND/SLAATTO: books—*World Architecture 2* and *4* by John Donat, London 1965, 1967; articles—"St. Hallvard" by Nils Ole Lund and Martin Drouzy in *Dansk Arkitektur* (Copenhagen), June 1966; "Works of Lund and Slaatto" by Poul Erik Shriver in *Dansk Arkitektur* (Copenhagen), January 1972; "Modern Scandinavian Architecture," special issue of *Process: Architecture* (Tokyo/Pittsburgh), January 1977; "Veritus Center" by Karen Zahle in *Dansk Arkitektur* (Copenhagen), April 1977.

Educated in the philosophy of the modern movement, but at the same time steeped in the traditions of timber buildings, Kjell Lund and Nils Slaatto are producing a concrete, tile and glass architecture which, although unashamedly modern, is tempered by a knowledge and understanding of timber construction and by the unavoidable influence of Norway's powerful natural surroundings. The Norwegian people respect nature. Nature is never far away; it is both the scenario and the backdrop for daily life, forcing the Norwegian into an intimate relationship that is essential to the national character. This relationship at once involves submission to and confrontation with the natural processes, and this duality is apparent in the traditional timber buildings. For although the farmsteads and hamlets were clearly man-made and man-arranged, expressing a determination to protect and order existence, yet they were in harmony with the land. And to construct these places, the Norwegians took the materials that nature offered. They devised a simple but highly practicable method of building—placing individual timber components side by side or one above the other. They built by assembly, and while the joints between components were shaped with precision, the surfaces were invariably left untouched. Only the junctions, the corners, consistently provoked more conscious articulation.

The work of Lund and Slaatto clearly expresses this connection with their country's past. Their buildings are assembled piece by piece, and the simple framework produced is brought to life by the detailing of the junctions, of the materials and surfaces and volumes.

Their relationship to the present is also clear, but less conscious and somehow less satisfying. There is a systematic logic in these buildings which, while producing a pleasing coherency, denies incident, spontaneity and fun. This is an architecture with no hierarchy, no hierarchy of forms, spaces or materials. There is no mystery, for order, logic and and equalization defy the existence of the unexpected. These buildings are serious—the occasional flash of

Kjell Lund and Nils Slaatto: House, Lund, Oslo, 1964

a sun blind produces the only light relief. But this is a fair reflection of Norwegian society today, one that is fiercely democratic. Life is ordered, forming a pattern to which everyone is forced to conform, a routine whose only changes are those determined by the passing of the seasons.

The achievement, then, of Lund and Slaatto is to have shown that it is possible today to create an architecture that embodies the aspirations of a contemporary society while maintaining a necessary continuity with the past and a sensitivity to the qualities of place.

—Linda Martin

LUNDY, Victor A(lfred).

American. Born in New York City, 1 February 1923. Educated at Harvard University, Cambridge, Massachusetts, 1939–43, 1947–48 (Charles Hayden Scholar, 1939–43; Edward H. Kendall Scholar, 1947–48), B. Arch. 1947, M. Arch. 1948; awarded Rotch Travelling Scholarship in Architecture, 1948–49. Served in the United States Army, 26th Infantry Division, 1943–46. Married to Anstis Burwell; children: Nicholas, Jennifer, and Mark. In private practice, New York, since 1951. Visiting Lecturer, Harvard University, 1957, University of California, Berkeley, 1958, University of Florida, Gainesville, 1958, Columbia University, New York, 1963, and Yale University, New Haven, Connecticut, 1964. Recipient: Award of Merit, 1960, 1966, and First

Honor Award, 1965, American Institute of Architects. Address (office): 1345 Third Avenue, New York, New York, U.S.A.

Works:

1956 Venice-Nokomis Presbyterian Church, Venice, Florida
1957 Bee Ridge Presbyterian School, Sarasota, Florida
1958 Warm Mineral Springs Inn, Venice, Florida
      Samuel H. Herron House, Sarasota, Florida
1960 St. Paul's Lutheran Church, Sarasota, Florida
      Elvgren House, Siesta Key, Sarasota, Florida
1961 I. Miller Shoe Salon, 730 Fifth Avenue, New York
      First Unitarian Church, Westport, Connecticut
      Hillspoint Elementary School, Westport, Connecticut
      Ski Center, Lincoln National Forest, Ruidoso, New Mexico
1964 Church of the Resurrection, East Harlem, New York
      IBM Garden State Office Building, Cranford, New Jersey
      United States Embassy, Colombo, Ceylon
1965 Singer Showroom, Rockefeller Center, New York
1970 St. Bernard's School, Gladstone, New Jersey
1972 Intermediate School 53, Nameoke Street, Far Rockaway, Queens, New York
1973 St. Paul's Lutheran Church, Sarasota, Florida

1976 United States Tax Court, Washington, D.C. (with Lyles Bissett Carlisle and Wolff)

Publications:

On LUNDY: articles—"Florida's Parasol Motel" in *Architectural Forum* (New York), May 1958; "Eglise Luthérienne à Sarasota" in *L'Architecture d'Aujourd'hui* (Paris), April/May 1960; "Young Architects in the U.S." by Esther McCoy in *Zodiac* (Milan), no. 8, 1961; "New Ideas of Victor A. Lundy" in *Architectural Record* (New York), February 1962; "Victor Lundy: Réalisations et Projects Récents" in *L'Architecture d'Aujourd'hui* (Paris), February/March 1962; "Victor Lundy et l'Evolution de la Tradition Architecturale Américaine" by H. F. Lenning and P. Simond in *Architecture: Formes et Fonctions* (Lausanne), 1964–65; "Magic Architecture for the Singer Sewing Center" in *Interiors* (New York), August 1965; "Justice on a Pedestal" in *Architectural Forum* (New York), September 1967; "Church under a Great Tent" in *Architectural Forum* (New York), July/August 1970; "Sculpture in Space" in *Architectural Forum* (New York), April 1971; "Sanctuary for St. Paul's Lutheran Church, Sarasota, Florida" in *Architecture + Urbanism* (Tokyo), June 1973; "The Public School as Architecture" in *Architecture Plus* (New York), August 1973; "Monumental Suspense" by Stanley Abercrombie in *Progressive Architecture* (New York), July 1976.

Although Victor Lundy's architecture is serene, quiet, delicately balanced and carefully resolved, it is not synthesized from purely intellectual concerns. It is the result of a passionate process that is spontaneous and intuitive. "I strive to make a perfect thing . . . I seek equilibrium," Lundy claims. Still, he admits, "I am usually in turmoil, agitated and mercurial." Lundy is an intellectual, and his work no doubt reflects the keenness of his mind, but he claims his ultimate strength is drawn not from thinking or discussion, but from what "my own eye sees and tells me, and my own hand does. . . . I do things intuitively, by sheer work, by the act of doing, testing, trying over and over until I get the ultimate irreducible expression of what it is I am after."

Lundy's work reveals an acute concern with pure form. His shapes have been worked out laboriously and joined with great exactitude, and materials and textures are mixed with equal precision. At the same time, though, evidence of his visceral approach is always apparent. His buildings are dramatic, with touches of whimsical artistic action that are not indulgent, but nevertheless clearly express distance from a purely rational approach.

Lundy's new building for the United States Tax Court, recently constructed in Washington D.C., is a case in point. Clear, careful application of pure geometry and monolithic forms characterize the design, but this sedate approach is broken by a dynamic structural system that allows a 200 foot long slab to cantilever more than 50' over the entrance to the building. This feat is accomplished by steel cables mounted to a central structural core. They have been hidden, however, so that the cantilever appears to be floating miraculously.

Steel cables also create an unusual roof silhouette at St. Paul's Lutheran Church in Sarasota, Florida. Still, the building was erected within a very restricted budget. Inside, the plan is straightforward, and the congregation faces a barren, concrete wall. The pulpit and chancel are finished cleanly, with severely minimal furnishing and accoutrements. Dramatic contrast between bright light at the ends of the church and relative darkness in the central portion adds more drama to the building, however, contrasting sharply with the starkness of the detailing.

Indeed, many of Lundy's buildings have successfully met the challenges imposed by very small budgets, while still providing architectural interest, even excitement. It seems that the difficulty of making an artistic statement with little means has been the catalyst of some of Lundy's finest expressions and attest to the vibrancy of his personality and artistic intent. Lundy also draws, sculpts and paints well; he is one of the few remaining architects still adhering to the Beaux Arts system, which emphasizes the importance of sketching and formal comprehensibility achieved through symmetry.

While never losing sight of the importance of precision and sensibility in plan, Lundy has been able to let other forces emerge more freely. His buildings are not pretentious, but rich in genuine architectural delight.

—Ching-Yu Chang

LURCAT, André.

French. Born in Bruyeres, Vosges, 27 August 1894. Educated at the Ecole Municipale des Beaux-Arts, Nancy, 1911–13; Ecole Nationale Supérieur des Beaux-Arts, Paris, 1913–14, 1918–23. Served in the Infantry, French Army, 1914–18: military medal and 5 citations of honor; organized the Architects' National Resistance Front, Paris, 1942; imprisoned, Prison de la Santé, Paris, 1943–45. Married to Renée Michel. In private practice, Paris, 1923–34: Director, Lurcat Atelier, rue Daguerre, Paris, 1932–34; emigrated to Russia: Professor of Town Planning, Institute of Architecture, Moscow, 1934–35; Architect-in-Chief, Commissariat of Public Health of the U.S.S.R., Moscow, 1935–36; returned to France: in private practice, Paris, 1937 until his death, 1970. City Planner and Architect-in-Chief, Saint-Denis, Paris, 1945; Chief City Planner for the Reconstruction of Maubeuge, France, 1945; Consultant Architect, Ministry of Reconstruction and City Planning, Paris, 1945; Member, Commission for the Monnet Modernization Plan, Paris, 1945; Consultant City Planner for the reconstruction of Warsaw, 1946. Appointed Director, Academy of Architecture, Ankara, Turkey, 1939 (declined); Lecturer in Architecture, Ecole des Arts Décoratifs, Paris, 1939–43. Founder Member, CIAM (Congrès Internationaux d'Architecture Moderne), 1928. Exhibitions: *Salon d'Automne,* Paris, 1923, 1924; *Exposition des Arts Décoratifs,* Paris, 1925; *Arts Plastiques en France,* Vienna, 1926; *Architecture Internationale,* Nancy, 1926; *Exposition Coloniale,* Vincennes, France, 1931; *Triennale,* Milan, 1933 (one-man); Atelier Lurcat, Paris, 1934 (one-man); Museum of Western Art, Moscow, 1935 (one-man); Town Planning and Housing Exhibition, Saint-Denis, 1947; *André Lurcat, Architecte,* Centre National des Arts et Metiers, Paris, 1967–68; toured Nancy and Vienna. Collection: Conservatoire Nationale des Arts et Metiers, Paris. *Died* (in Sceaux, Hauts-de-Seine), *10 July 1970.*

Works:

1917 Villa, Cote d'Azur, France (project)
1923 Villa by the Sea, *Salon d'Automne,* Paris (exhibition project)
Semi-detached house, *Salon d'Automne,* Paris (exhibition project)
1924 Rousset Villa, Eaubonne, Seine-et-Oise, France (demolished)
1924/
25 Jean Lurcat House, 4 Villa Seurat, Paris
Quille House, 8 Villa Seurat, Paris
1925 Bertrand Houses, 5 and 9 Villa Seurat, Paris
Gromaire House, 3 Villa Seurat, Paris
Townshend House, 1 Villa Seurat, Paris
Galerie Bignou interiors, Paris (destroyed)
Galerie Barbazanges interiors, Paris (destroyed)
Galerie Pierre interiors, Paris (destroyed)
Galerie Leonce Rosenberg interiors, Paris (destroyed)
Galerie Bernheim interiors, Paris (destroyed)
Galerie Georges Petit interiors, Paris (destroyed)
1926 Huggler House, Villa Seurat, Paris
Bomsel House, Versailles
Michel House, rue Georges-Ville, Versailles
Workers' Housing Complex (project)
Housing Complex for Professional People (project)
Workers' Housing, Villeneuve-Saint-Georges, France (competition project)
Myrbor Fashion House, Paris
Group of villas, Parma, Italy (project)
1927 Guggenbuhl House, 14 rue Nansouty, Paris (since altered)
Housing Complex (project)
Mediterranean Tourist Hotel (project)
Apartment building, Bagneux, Seine, France
Michel House, Bagneux, Seine, France
Froriep de Salis House, Boulogne, Paris
Galerie Barbazanges shop-front and interiors, Paris
1928 Workers' Housing, Versailles (2 competition projects)
Luxury hotel, La Baule, France (project)
Residential quarter development, Paris (project)
Small apartments complex, Choisy-le-Roi, Paris (project)
Living room for M. P. David Weill, 1 rue Silvestre de Sacy, Paris
1929 Sanatorium, Durdol, Puy-de-Dome, France (project)
1930 Hotel Nord-Sud, Calvi, Corsica
1931 Tourist Airport on the Seine, Paris (project)
1932 4 Werkbund Exhibition Houses, Lainz, near Vienna
Hefferlin House, rue de Garches, Ville d'Avray, Seine-et-Oise, France
Housing development, Villejuif, Seine, France (project)
1933 Karl-Marx School Complex, Villejuif, Seine, France
1934 Metro Engineers' Residential Building, Moscow (project)
1935 Children's Hospital for Contagious Diseases, Moscow (project)
Institutue of Physics and Chemistry, Moscow (project)
Faculty of Medicine, Moscow (project)
1945/
50 Reconstruction plan for Maubeuge, France
1946 Karl-Marx School additons, Villejuif, Seine, France
1948 Cité Paul Langevin, Saint-Denis, Paris
Cité Fabien, Saint-Denis, Paris
Housing, Avenue de la Gare, Maubeuge, France
1949 Boys' and Girls' School, Nevers, France
André Lurcat House, Sceaux, France
1950 Holiday Village, Meriel, Seine-et-Oise, France
1951 Leduc House, Sceaux, France
1953 Cité Paul Eluard, Saint-Denis, Paris
Housing development, Blanc-Mesnil, France
Michaut House, Sceaux, France
Hospital Centre additions and alterations, Saint-Paris, Paris
School complex, Blanc-Mesnil, France
Fabien Infants School, Saint-Denis, Paris
Holiday house, Franceuil, Indre-et-Loire, France
1954 Cité Paul Semard, Saint-Denis, Paris
Cité Auguste Delaune, Saint-Denis, Paris
J. Currie School Complex, Saint-Denis, Paris
Paul Semard School Complex, Saint-Denis, Paris
Cité Daniele Casanova, Blanc-Mesnil, Paris
1957 Henri Barbusse Nursery School, Saint-Denis, Paris
1958 Paul Vaillant-Couturier School Complex, Villejuif, Seine, France
Church of Saint-Pierre et Saint-Paul, Maubeuge, France
Town Hall, Maubeuge, France
1960 Cité Gabriele Peri, Saint-Denis, Paris
Square Saint-Livier, Nancy-Saint-Max, France
1962 Palace of Sports, Saint-Denis, Paris
Paul Langevin School Complex, Ivry-sur-Seine, France
Cité Roger Semat, Saint-Denis, Paris
Cité Emmaus, Blanc-Mesnil, France
1963 Haut Rivage Development, Nancy-Saint-Max, France
André Lurcat Country House, Sancerre, France
1964 Town Hall, Blanc-Mesnil, France
1965 Cité M. Cachin, Saint-Denis, Paris
1966 Cité Paul Vaillant-Courturier, Villejuif, Seine, France
1968 Cité Guyemer, Saint-Denis, Paris

Publications:

By LURCAT: books—*Architecture,* Paris 1929; *André Lurcat: Projets et Réalisations,* Paris 1929; *Terrasses et Jardins,* Paris 1929; *Urbanisme et Architecture,* Paris 1942; *Forms, Composition et Lois d'Harmonie,* 5 volumes, Paris 1953–57; *André Lurcat: Oeuvres Récentes,* Paris 1961; *Scritti sull'esperienza Sovietica,* with E. May and H. Schmidt, edited by M. de Michelis and B. Cassetti, Padua 1972; articles—in *Architecture Internationale,* exhibition catalogue, Nancy 1926; "La Formation de l'Architecte" in *L'Architecture d'Aujourd'hui* (Paris), October/November 1933; "L'Architecture Contemporaine en Occident" in *Arhitektura SSSR* (Moscow), March 1934; "Retour d'Union Sovietique" in *L'Art Vivant* (Paris), March 1934; "Néoclassicisme ou Constructivisme" in *Arhitektura SSSR* (Moscow), July 1934; "L'Architecture dans la Crise" in *L'Architecture d'Aujourd'hui* (Paris), June 1935; "Evolution d'Architecture" in *L'Architecture d'Aujourd'hui* (Paris), September 1935; "L'Homme, La Technique, L'Architecture" in *Izvestija* (Moscow), 12 June 1937; "L'Architecture en U.R.S.S." in *Bulletin de l'Union des Architectes* (Paris), February 1938; "Récherche et Creation" in *André Lurcat, Architecte,* exhibition catalogue, Paris 1967.

On LURCAT: book—*André Lurcat, Architecte,* exhibition catalogue, Paris 1967; articles—"Arbeithauser von André Lurcat" in *Moderne Bauformen* (Stuttgart), vol. 27, 1928; "André Lurcat's Architecture" by P. Morton Shand in *The Architects' Journal* (London), 29 April 1931; "André Lurcat" by Edoardo Persico in *Casabella* (Milan), January 1935; "La Reconstruction de Maubeuge" in *Techniques et Architecture* (Paris), vol. 6, no. 7/8, 1946; "Reconstruction and Housing in France" in *Techniques et Architecture* (Paris), vol. 12, no. 11/12, 1953; "Un'ideologia per la ricostruzione: Le Opere Recenti di André Lurcat" by S. Tintori in *Casabella* (Milan), March 1962; "Omaggio a André Lurcat, ma senza equivoci" by Bruno Zevi in *L'Architettura* (Rome), March 1968; "André Lurcat: 48 Ans d'Architecture" by J. B. Ache in *La Construction Moderne* (Paris), September/October 1970; "Il Municipio di Blanc-Mesnil di André Lurcat" in *L'Architettura* (Rome), October 1970; "André Lurcat in U.R.S.S." by B. Cassetti in *Socialismo, Città, Architettura U.R.S.S. 1917–1937,* Rome 1971; "Lurcat" by J. L. Cohen and others, in *Architecture Mouvement Continuité* (Paris), September 1976.

The drama of André Lurcat is one of a conflict of loyalties—loyalty to his convictions as an architect, loyalty to his political convictions.

At first the two struggles could run in parallel; they complemented each other. The young member of the revolutionary pacifist student organization was able to follow his path as a modern architect, which, after the house of his brother Jean, built in 1925, led him to that courageous masterpiece, the Karl-Marx School at Villejuif, designed five years later.

Unfortunately, Lurcat's active sympathies led him to Moscow, to the Institute of Architecture and the Health Commissariat, where, from 1934 to 1937, he did his best to defend the architectural "line" of the Bauhaus and CIAM and to justify the system that rejected it. Returning to France, he courageously joined the Resistance, supported the Communist Party despite his disappointments, spent time in prison, and took part in the reconstruction of liberated France. But the purity and impetus of his architectural vision had been destroyed, more by the exhausting ideological struggle from 1934–37 than by any physical ordeals.

Lurcat thereafter was a man who had to accept compromise and the surrender of principles, who built groups of dwellings, schools, a town hall and other works (none of great importance), and in numerous writings criticized the "capitalist system," incapable of producing a genuine urbanism, and the "cosmopolitan" propositions of Le Corbusier. He praised the middle way in architecture and in urbanism. His experiences nevertheless led the honest man that he had always been to condemn severely in France policies that continued to be rife in the U.S.S.R. and the countries she inspires—the policy of "models," the systematic application of heavy prefabrication, etc.

How André Lurcat, who always dreamed about the "freedom of creation," must have suffered.

—Pierre Vago

LUTYENS, Sir Edwin (Landseer).

British. Born in London, 29 March 1869. Educated privately and at the South Kensington School of Art, now the Royal College of Art, London, 1885–87. Married Emily Lytton in 1897; children: Robert, and four daughters. Worked in the office of Ernest George and Peto, London, 1887–88; in private practice, London, 1890 until his death, 1944. Adviser to the Indian Government on the new government buildings at Delhi, from 1912; Principal Architect, Imperial War Graves Commission, London, 1916–44; Consultant, with Sir Charles Bressey, London Road Survey, later Royal Academy Plan for London, 1934. Member, Royal Fine Art Commission, 1924–44; President, Royal Academy, London, 1938–44. Recipient: Gold Medal, Royal Institute of British Architects, 1921; Gold Medal, American Institute of Architects, 1924. Associate, Royal College of Art, 1913; LL.D.: University of Liverpool, 1928; D.C.L.: Oxford University, 1934. Royal Academician; Fellow, Society of Antiquaries. Honorary Member, Royal Scottish Academy; Honorary Fellow, Institute of Landscape Architects. Knighted, 1918; K.C.I.E. (Knight Commander, Order of the Indian Empire, 1930; O.M. (Order of Merit), 1942. *Died* (in London) *1 January 1944.*

Works:

1888 Edmund Gray Cottage alterations, Thursley, Surrey
1889 H. A. Mangles Cottage, Littleworth, Surrey
      Lodge, Park Hatch, Hascombe, Surrey
      Lodge, Hoe Farm, Hascombe, Surrey
1890 Stables for Cowley Lambert, Little Tangley, Surrey
      A. W. Chapman House additions I, and Gardener's Cottage, Crooksbury, Surrey
      "The Corner" (C. D. Heatley House) additions, Thursley, Surrey
1892 Shop, cottage and lych gate for Sir Reginald Bray, Shere, Surrey
1893 "Woodside" (Duchess of Bedford House) garden, Chenies, Buckinghamshire
1894 "Clinthurst" (Miss Guthrie House), near Guildford, Surrey
      "Ruckmans" (Miss Lyell House), Oakwood Park, Surrey
      "Lascombe" (Colonel Spencer House) alterations, Puttenham, Sussex
1896 Cottages and shop for the Earl of Northbrook, Micheldever, Hampshire
      "Munstead Wood" (Gertrude Jekyll House), Godalming, Surrey
      "Sullingstead" (C. A. Cook House), Hascombe, Surrey
1897 "Binfield Lodge" (Captain Ernest Rhodes House), Newbury, Berkshire
      Streatfield House, Fulbrook, Surrey
      "Woodend" (Lady Stewart House) alterations, Witley, Surrey
      The Liberal Club, Farnham, Surrey
1898 A. W. Chapman House additions II, Crooksbury, Surrey
      "Orchards" (Sir William Chance House), Godalming, Surrey
      "Berrydown" (Archibald Grove House), Hampshire
      Longman Cottage and Wheelwright's Shop, Hemel Hempstead, Hertfordshire
      Church alterations, Busbridge, Surrey
      "Witwood" (house), Camberley, Surrey
      "Les Bois des Moutiers" (Guillaume Mallet House), Varengeville, France
      Nonconformist Chapel, Overstrand, Norfolk
      Roseneath House alterations, Dumbartonshire
      Inn alterations, Roseneath, Dumbartonshire
      "Rowfant" (Locker Lampson House), Sussex
1899 Overstrand Hall, Norfolk
      "The Pleasaunce" (Lord Battersea House) alterations, Overstrand, Norfolk
      Post Office, Abinger, Surrey

Mrs. Cavan Irving House alterations, 94 Eaton Place, London S.W.1
"Tigbourne Court" (Edgar Horne House), Witley, Surrey
Reverend A. Wickham House, Mayfield, Sussex
Stoke College alterations, Suffolk
"Littlecroft" (Mrs. Bowes Watson House), Guildford, Surrey
Rev. W. H. Evans House, Charterhouse, Surrey
"Goddards" (Sir Frederick Mirrielees House), Abinger Common, Surrey
1900 British Pavilion, *World's Fair,* Paris
      Rake Manor additions, Milford, Hampshire
      Thursley Institute, Surrey
      "Fisher's Hill" (Gerald Balfour House), Woking, Surrey
      Cottages for the Earl of Lytton, Knebworth, Hertfordshire
      Golf Clubhouse, Knebworth, Hertfordshire
      Lych gate for Lord Hylton, Kilmersdon, Somerset
      "Grey Walls" (Alfred Lyttelton House), Gullane, Scotland
      "The Den" (H. Avery House) garden, Pershore, Worcestershire
1901 Deanery Garden, for Edward Hudson, Sonning, Berkshire
      St. Peter's Home, Ipswich, Suffolk
      "Abbotswood" (Mark Fenwick House) alterations and garden, Stow-on-the-Wold, Gloucestershire
      Cottage for Walter Hoare, Basing, Surrey
      "Marshcourt" (Herbert Johnson House), Stockbridge, Hampshire
      Knebworth House alterations, Hertfordshire
      "Homewood" (Earl of Lytton House), Knebworth, Hertfordshire
      Folly Farm additions I, Sulhampstead, Berkshire
      F. Debenham House alterations, 1 Fitzjohns Avenue, London N.W.3
      "Holmwood" (Wildman Catley House) alterations, Dorking, Surrey
      Cottages for Robert Webb, Thursley, Surrey
      Cottage for the Countess of Warwick, Easton Park, Essex
1902 Summer Farm, Clandon, Surrey
      "The Great Holt" (Major Boyce Combe House) additions, Frensham, Surrey
      "The Hoo" (Alexander Wedderburn House) alterations and garden, Willingdon, Sussex
      Blackburn House, Little Thakeham, Sussex
      "Monkton House" (William James House), Singleton, Sussex
      Stainton House alterations, 11 Stanhope Place, London W.2
      Berkeley Hotel alterations, Piccadilly, London W.1
      Earl of Lytton House alterations, 10 Buckingham Street, London W.C.2
      Scenery designs for the play *Quality Street,* Vaudeville Theatre, London
      Dalham Hall Lodge and Entrance, Newmarket, Suffolk
      "Rossall" (T. B. Lumb House), near Blackpool
      A. W. Chapman House stables and garden, Crooksbury, Surrey
      "Ruckmans" (Miss Lyell House) music room addition, Oakwood Park, Surrey
      "Ammerdown" (Lord Hylton House) garden, Somerset
      Devonshire Club alterations, London (project)
      Bridge, over the River Thames, Sonning, Berkshire (project)
1903 "Buckhurst" (R. H. Benson House) alterations, Withyham, Kent
      Papillon Hall, Leicestershire
      Church room, Dorking, Surrey
      Munstead House additions, Godalming, Surrey

Sir Edwin Lutyens: Viceroy's House, New Delhi, 1930

"Lindisfarne" (Edward Hudson House), Holy Island, Northumbria (partially built)

The Mount School, Hindhead, Surrey

"Daneshill" (Walter Hoare House), Old Basing, Hampshire

Adam Black House alterations, 7 Petersham Terrace, London S.W.7

"Sullingstead" (C. A. Cook House) additions, Hascombe, Surrey

Chichely Hall alterations, Buckinghamshire (project)

Archibald Grove House, Chalfont, Buckinghamshire

1904 Ivor Guest House alterations I, Ashby St. Ledger's, near Rugby, Warwickshire

"Millmead" (Gertrude Jekyll House), Bramley, Surrey

"La Mascot" (F. W. Pethick-Lawrence House) alterations, Surrey

Country Life Offices, Covent Garden, London

Decoration of the *Queen of Scots* yacht, for W. A. Coats

"Hestercombe" (E. W. Portman House) gardens, Somerset

The Manor House alterations, Wells, Somerset

1905 "Marshcourt" (Herbert Johnson House) stables, Stockbridge, Hampshire

Forest House alterations, Forest Row, Sussex

St. John's Institute, Westminster, London

Lambay Castle, Dublin

"Nashdom" (Princess Alexis Dolgoronki House), Taplow, Buckinghamshire

Hobson House gardens, Esholt, Sheffield, Yorkshire

Lady Helen Vincent House sunken garden, Esher Place, Surrey

Queen's House alterations, Chelsea, London

"Bodrog Olaszi" (Count Elemer Lonyay House) alterations, Zemplen, Hungary

1906 Dormy House, Walton Heath Golf Club, Surrey

Viscount Haldane House alterations, 28 Queen Anne's Gate, London S.W.1

Sir Basil Montgomery House alterations, 51 Berkeley Square, London W.1

Sir William Bird House alterations, Eartham, near Chichester, Sussex

Sir G. Munro Miller House, Barton St. Mary, East Grinstead, Sussex

"Heathcote" (Hemingway House), Ilkley, Yorkshire

Copse Hill House alterations, Upper Slaughter, Gloucestershire

Miss F. Mirrielees House gardens, Pasture Wood, Dorking, Surrey

Hurlingham Club interiors, London

Edward Hudson House alterations, 15 Queen Anne's Gate, London S.W.1

Stonehouse Court alterations, Gloucestershire

Office building, Kingsway, London W.C.2

"Heywood" (E. Hucheson Poe House) gardens, Ireland

Folly Farm additions II, Sulhampstead, Berkshire

"New Place" (A. S. Franklyn House), Shedfield, Hampshire

1907 House at Repton School, Yorkshire

Memorial tablets, Glasgow Crematorium

"Fisher's Hill" (Gerald Balfour House) cottage, Woking, Surrey

Wittersham House alterations, Kent

"Angerton" (F. Straker House) gardens, Morpeth, Northumberland

Lady Allendale House alterations, 32 Queen Anne's Gate, London S.W.1

1908 Whalton Manor, Northumberland

County Hall, London (competition project)

Layout for Hampstead Garden City, London (project)

Institute Building additions, Hampstead Garden City, London

Fenwick House alterations, Temple Dinsley, Hertfordshire

Small house and cottages for Lord St. Ledgers, Ashby St. Ledger's, near Rugby, Warwickshire

Lady Battersea House alterations, 10 Connaught Place, London W.2

Knebworth House alterations II, Hertfordshire

Brick Pavilion, *Building Trades Exhibition*, London

"Chussex" (W. H. Fowler House), Walton Heath, Surrey

"Middlefield" (Henry Bond House), Great Shelford, Cambridgeshire

1909 "Great Maytham" (H. J. Tennant House), Rolvenden, Kent

Sir John Horner House alterations, 16 Lower Berkeley Street, London W.1

Ivor Guest House alterations II, Ashby St. Ledger's, near Rugby, Warwickshire

"Les Communes" (Guillaume Mallet House), Varengeville-sur-Mer, France

Renishaw Hall alterations, Chesterfield, Derbyshire

"Warren Lodge" (R. W. Webb House) alterations, Thursley, Surrey

Lambay Castle gardens, Dublin

Cottages for the Duke of Bedford, Tavistock Estate, Devon

1910 Exhibition Building, *International Exposition*, Rome

Howth Castle restoration, Dublin

"Great Dixter" (Nathaniel Lloyd House) reconstruction, Northiam, Kent

Hanover Lodge alterations, Regent's Park, London

Houses, North Square, Hampstead Garden City, London

St. Jude's Church, with Vicarage and Manse, Hampstead Garden City, London

Lowesby Hall alterations, Leicestershire

Sir Hugh Lane House garden, 100 Cheyne Walk, London S.W.3

1910/
30 Castle Drogo, Devon

1911 Rand Regiments Memorial, South Africa

Gaspard and Farrer House, 7 St. James's Square, London S.W.1

"The Salutation" (Henry Farrer House), Sandwich, Kent

H. G. Fenwick House additions II, Temple Dinsley, Hertfordshire

"Hill End" (Fenwick House), Hitchin, Hertfordshire

Reginald McKenna House, 36 Smith Square, London S.W.1

Cecil Baring House alterations, 26a Bryanston Square, London W.1

Parliament Chamber interiors, Inner Temple, London E.C.4

Theosophical Society Headquarters, Gloucester Place, London W.1

Design of the *Shakespeare's England* Exhibition, London

Design of the decorations for the Coronation Ball, Albert Hall, London S.W.7

1912 British School, Rome

Barham Court additions, Kent

McLaran House, Westminster, London

Johannesburg Art Gallery, South Africa

Mark Fenwick House alterations, 22 Bruton Street, London W.1

The Lodge, Knowlton Court, Camberley, Surrey

Roehampton House additions, London

Folly Farm additions III, Sulhampstead, Berkshire

Alfred Lyttelton House, 18 Little College Street, London S.W.1

"Ranguin" (Guillaume Mallet House) alterations, Grasse, France

Bridge Design (project)

Ednaston Manor, Derbyshire

Master plan for New Delhi, India

Jaipur Column, New Delhi, India

Indian Garden, New Delhi, India

1912/
30 Viceroy's House, Staff Residences and Stables, New Delhi, India

1913 Mrs. Edgar House gardener's cottage, Chalfont, Buckinghamshire

Grill Room decoration, Berkeley Hotel, London W.1

Alfred Mildmay House alterations, 28 Portman Square, London W.1

Imperial Tobacco Company office alterations, Nottingham

Abbey House, Barrow-in-Furness, Lancashire

"Frog's Island" (Countess of Londesborough House), Walton Heath, Surrey

Mrs. Sofer Whitburn House garden, Addington Park, Surrey

Moreton Frewen House alterations, Brede Place, Sussex

1914 Renishaw Golf Clubhouse additions, Chesterfield, Derbyshire

St. Martin's Church, Knebworth, Hertfordshire

Philipson Family Mausoleum, Golder's Green, London

F. E. Briggs House additions, Crooksbury, Surrey

New billiard room, Shenley Hill House, Hertfordshire

H. Philipson House alterations, 74 Portland Place, London W.1

1915 Grange Court alterations, Chigwell, Essex

El Guadalperal Castle alterations, Spain (project)

1916 Lambay Castle chapel and gardens, Dublin

Nizam of Hyderabad House, New Delhi, India (as consultant)

1917 Sir James Barrie House alterations, Adelphi Terrace, London W.C.2

1918 Town plan for Alwar, India (as consultant)

Lady Sackville House alterations, 40 Sussex Square, Brighton, Sussex

Lady Cooper House alterations, 96 Cheyne Walk, London S.W.3

Lady Sackville House alterations, 182 Ebury Street, London S.W.1

"Bell House" (Lady Lucas House) alterations, Dulwich, London

Colonel Morrison House layout and alterations, Basildon Park, Essex

H. Pennoyer House alterations, 20 New Cavendish Street, London W.1

Wimborne House alterations, Arlington Street, London S.W.1

Breccles Hall alterations, Norfolk

Lady Sackville House reconstruction, 34 Hill Street, London W.1

1919 Tomb, Muncaster, Ravenglass, Cumberland

The Cenotaph, Whitehall, London S.W.1

Memorials to Captain Geoffrey Congreve, V.C., at Corbie, France, and Chartley, England

War memorials at Southampton, and Shere, Surrey

Noel Willis House additions, Miserden Park, Gloucestershire

Maharajah of Kashmir House, New Delhi, India (project)

University of Cape Town, South Africa (project)

Clifford Manor restoration, Stratford upon Avon

Ivor Guest House alterations III, Ashby St. Ledger's, near Rugby, Warwickshire

"The Grange" (George Lewis House) alterations, Rottingdean, Sussex

1920 War memorials in Etaples, France; Richmond, South Africa; and Gerrards Cross, Ravenglass, Luton, Leeds, Ely, Busbridge, Stockbridge, King's Somborne, Hartburn Village, Southend, Wargrave, and Wells, England

Imperial Tobacco Company War Memorial, Bristol

Chapel of St. John, St. Jude's Church, Hampstead, London

Penheale Manor restoration, Egloskerry, Cornwall

Britannic House, Finsbury Circus, London E.C.2

1921 War memorials at Rolvenden, Stow-on-the-Wold, Hove, Rochdale, Abinger, Hampstead (London), Ashwell, Derby, and Reading, England; and Colombo, Ceylon

P. Vaughan Morgan House alterations, 43 Green Street, London W.1

Gaekwar of Baroda House, New Delhi, India

Master plan for the University of Lucknow, India (project)

City redevelopment plan for Madras, India (as consultant)

1922 Oliver Lyttelton House alterations, 104 Eaton Square, London S.W.1

House alterations, 11 Carlton House Terrace, London S.W.1

Midland Bank, Piccadilly, London W.1

War memorials in Sandhurst, and York, England; Hong Kong; and Bermuda

1923 Motecomb House additions, Yealmpton, Devon

"White Lodge-on-the-Cliff" (Lady Sackville House), Roedean, Sussex

"Mesnil Warren" (George Lambton House) alterations, Newmarket, Suffolk

The Times Stand, *British Empire Exhibition,* Wembley, London

Filtration plant, Newport, Monmouthshire (project)

Ivor Guest alterations IV, Ashby St. Ledger's, near Rugby, Warwickshire

Gledstone Hall, Yorkshire

General B. Freyburg House alterations, 7 Clarendon Place, London W.2

Sir Alfred Mond House alterations, 35 Lowndes Square, London S.W.1

British Medical Association Offices (extension to Theosophical Society Headquarters), Gloucester Place, London W.1

Mells Park House, Somerset

Mrs. H. Fordham House reconstruction, Ashwell Bury, Hertfordshire

War memorials in Cowley, Leicester, and Manchester, England

1924 "Beechwood" (Cecil Baring House) alterations, Slough, Buckinghamshire

F. A. Konig House, Tyringham Park, Newport Pagnell, Buckinghamshire

Midland Bank, Poultry, London E.C.2

Warwick House alterations, Norfolk Street, London W.2

All India War Memorial Arch, New Delhi, India

War memorials in Northampton, London, and York, England; and Thiepval, France

"Marshcourt" (Herbert Johnson House) great hall addition, Stockbridge, Surrey

Grosvenor House elevations, Park Lane, London W.1

New stone bridge for St. James's Park, London S.W.1 (project)

Sir George Lewis House alterations, 43 Bryanston Square, London W.1

1925 "Foxbury" (Sir John Lloyd House) alterations, Sevenoaks, Kent

Lady Apsley House alterations, 18 Buckingham Gate, London S.W.1

Mrs. Harris Lebus House alterations, 29 Belgrave Square, London S.W.1

1927 British Embassy, Washington, D.C.

Terminal House elevations, Westminister, London (as consultant)

Euston Station interiors, London N.W.1

Edward Hudson House lakes and gardens, Plumpton Place, Sussex

Mill House restoration, Plumpton, Sussex

War memorials, Faubourg d'Amiens, France, and Norwich, England

Gold and crystal communion plate, St. Paul's Cathedral, London

Monument to James K. Hackett, New York

Hereford House elevations, Oxford Street, London W.1 (as consultant)

1928 Grosvenor Housing Development, Millbank, London S.W.1

Y.M.C.A. Central Club and Hostel, Tottenham Court Road, London W.1

Edward Hudson House cottages, entrance gate and bridge, Plumpton Place, Sussex

Sir Roderick Jones House alterations, 29 Hyde Park Gate, London S.W.7

Bridge at Hampton Court, Middlesex

Building elevations, 68 Pall Mall, London S.W.1

Midland Bank, Leadenhall Street, London E.C.3

British Pavilion, *International Exposition,* Antwerp

The Benson Wing, Magdalen College, Cambridge

"Marvells" (George Plank House), Five Ashes, Sussex

1929 Oliver Lyttelton House alterations, 4 Connaught Place, London W.2

Crane Bennett Ltd. Offices, 120 Pall Mall, London S.W.1 (now Holland Building)

New Charing Cross Bridge, London S.W.1 (project)

Midland Bank, King Street, Manchester

Johannesburg Art Gallery extensions, South Africa

Earl of Kenmare House alterations, 117

Eaton Square, London S.W.1
War memorial, London, Ontario, Canada

1929/
41 Metropolitan Cathedral, Liverpool (project)
1930 Aldford House elevations, Park Lane, London W.1 (as consultant)
River Ember and railway bridges, near Hampton Court, Middlesex
Fleet House alterations, Weymouth, Dorset
Farrer and Company office front restoration, 66 Lincoln's Inn Fields, London W.C.2
Memorial lodges and piers for Lord Fairhaven, Runnymede, Berkshire
Mrs. Guy Liddell House, 42 Cheyne Walk, London S.W.3
King George V Memorial/Fountains, New Delhi, India
Sir Jonathan North Memorial Lodges and Entrance Gates, Victoria Park, Leicester
War memorials, Dublin, Ireland, and Auckland, New Zealand
1931 Pilgrim's Way Bridge, Guildford, Surrey
T. J. Ley House alterations, 11 Connaught Place, London W.2
1932 Brook House elevations, Park Lane, London W.1 (as consultant)
Lord Revelstoke Guest-House, Lambay Island, Dublin
1933 Saunton Court, Barnstaple, Devon
Lamp standards, West Front, St. Paul's Cathedral, London
Legh Manor alterations, Cuckfield, Sussex
North House, Princes Way, London S.W.19
"Brent Eleigh" (H. Pennoyer House) alterations, Lavenham, Suffolk
Lady Cynthia Mosley Tomb, Denham, Buckinghamshire
Dame Nellie Melba Memorial, Melbourne
Mrs. Clark Tomb, Windlesham, Surrey
1934 The Cedar House, Chobham, Surrey
Memorial bridge, Eton
Campion Hall, Oxford
The Drum Inn, Cockington, Sussex
Louis Lebus House alterations, 5 Balfour Place, London W.1
"Middleton Park" (Earl of Jersey House), Bicester, Oxfordshire
1935 Baroness Porcelli Mews House conversion, 36 Hill Street, London W.1
Reuters/Press Association Building, Fleet Street, London E.C.4
West Wing, St. Jude's Church, Hampstead, London
Ivor Guest House bridge and garden alterations, Ashby St. Ledger's, near Rugby, Warwickshire
Midland Bank extension I, Poultry, London E.C.2
Highway Development Survey (with Sir Charles Bressey)
General Miller Memorial Stone, Wheatley, Nottinghamshire
1936 New Wing, Johannesburg Art Gallery, South Africa
"Halnaker" (Reginald McKenna House), Chichester, Sussex
"The Cogers" Public House, Salisbury Court, London E.C.4
Elliptical Room, Greenwich Maritime Museum, London S.E.10
King George V Memorial, Windsor Castle, Berkshire
Australian National War Memorial, Villers Bretonneux, France
1937 Midland Bank extension II, Poultry, London E.C.3
Leslie Hore-Belisha House alterations, 16 Stafford Place, London S.W.1
Cricket pavilion and cottages, Reigate, Surrey
Passenham Manor alterations, Stony Stratford, Buckinghamshire
Viscount Ridley House garden alterations, Blagdon, Northumberland

Design of the decorations for the Coronation Ball, Albert Hall, London S.W.7
National Theatre, South Kensington, London (project)
King George V Tomb, Windsor Castle, Berkshire (as consultant)
Myer Memorial, Melbourne
1938 Ivor Guest House final alterations, Ashby St. Ledger's, near Rugby, Warwickshire
Clock Tower, Filgrave, Buckinghamshire
Plan for Tower Hill, London E.C.3 (project)
Bronze barriers, Cenotaph, Whitehall, London S.W.1
Earl Beatty Tomb, St. Paul's Cathedral, London
1939 Processional arch, Jaipur, India
Liria Palace reconstruction, Madrid (project)
Fountains, Trafalgar Square, London W.C.2
1940 Tomb for the Earl and Countess of Strathmore and Kinghorne, Glamis, Scotland
1942 National Theatre, South Bank, London S.E.1 (project)
1943 Plans for post-war reconstruction (with Sir Patrick Abercrombie)
Mackintosh Book Production Works, Brockham Green, Surrey (project)
Six Sacton Noble Memorial, Batheaston, Somerset

Publications:

On LUTYENS: books—*The Architecture of Sir Edwin Lutyens* by A. S. G. Butler and Christopher Hussey, London 1950; *The Life of Sir Edwin Lutyens* by Christopher Hussey, London 1953; articles—"Building with Wit" by Nikolaus Pevsner in *Architectural Review* (London), April 1951; "In the Character of the Country" by J. F. Lewis in *Ideal Home* (London), March 1975; "Collective Design" by Peter Smithson in *Architectural Design* (London), May 1975; "A Lutyens Legacy" by J. Brown in *Landscape Design* (London), May 1977; "Lutyens at Varengeville-sur-Mer" by D. Mangin in *Architecture Mouvement Continuité* (Paris), November 1977; "Lutyens Enjoys Belated Recognition of His Genius" by D. Pearce in *Building Design* (London), 29 September 1978.

Edwin Lutyens influenced his own generation of like-minded architects by raising English domestic architecture from the vernacular to the palatial. His country houses (it is through them that he is best known) went back for their detailing to the craftsmanship and knowledge of materials and their use of the country builder. The builder was never an architect as we know the architect of today, but he was ever a craftsman and learned his craft from his predecessors, for the working of timber and stone and the use of brick had changed little over the centuries. Lutyens said of old Tickner, the Milford builder, that he taught him most of all.

An important architectural influence on Lutyens was to be found in the work of Philip Webb, greater even than that of Shaw and Nesfield who were the more sophisticated members of that hierarchy. Webb's designs all exhibit a sureness of touch and a calm confidence, the use and appearance of all his materials seeming to be utterly inevitable. This comes out in the early Lutyens work, which was influenced by Tudor manors and farmhouses, and is particularly so in the Deanery Garden at Sonning in which his mastery of visible proportion and material fitness is finely displayed.

Robert Lutyens in a biographical sketch of his father quite understandably joins the voices of the eulogisers, writing that his father's work "has profoundly influenced every living practitioner of the art of architecture." This is a remark that cannot possibly hold up, for Lutyens was not a forerunner so much as a designer who reinterpreted in traditional terms the visual atmosphere of a past. In fact, his son writes a little later in the same book that to Lutyens only manual skill and craftsmanship were enduring, advances in mechanical technique were ephemeral—his great achievement lying in the re-orientation of

domestic building "backwards, as it were." Surely this gifted man represented, although in the highest imaginative degree, but a recapitulation of the things that were passing away, for the influence I had on his few devoted successors did almost nothing to increase his following.

Entirely admirable, however, is this use of the imagination in an utterly concentrated dedication to his materials, by which it seemed he was able to put out of mind his great learning of the traditional European styles of the Renaissance and to use that deep knowledge only to reinforce his most original interpretation of it.

In the great houses the Renaissance itself showed through, particularly in the noble entrance halls and staircases and the frequent quite useless features, such as balconettes, which nevertheless contributed to an overall richness. His clients were often maddened by his extravagance and planned inconveniences. Even A. S. G. Butler in the volumes on Lutyen's buildings allows himself the gentle understatement that Lutyens's internal arrangements were "sometimes not wholly convenient." The architect himself, however, did not let this bother him; he was too sure of what he wanted and what he considered the client should want. Writing of his professional colleagues he expressed the view that "they should give no heed as to what the critics may or may not say, but should face their problems with the same sincerity as the sap within a tree." This may or may not be an apposite metaphor, but I would doubt its validity.

When he arrived at the stage of building for commerce—in such imposing works as the Midland Bank in Poultry in the City of London, or Reuters, off Fleet Street—Lutyens had to have recourse to steel construction for his frame, the "ephemeral" technique he thought must be eschewed; it was no doubt a matter of cost that made him use it, for, as with Bentley in Westminster Cathedral, he would have preferred stone upon stone and brick upon brick, with short spans of timber to support the intermediate floors and possibly a large-span timber open roof or a series of Byzantine brick domes, for he was nothing if not an eclectic.

He paraphrased Wren, but in this paraphrase came the supremely imaginative interpretation, bridging the centuries in a new presentation of a traditional development. This is certainly what the continuation of an architectural period should present, but all architectural periods, by certain social, economic or political considerations, come to an end. Lutyens ignored this fact, and in his grandiose designs nailed his flag to the mast of Wren's English baroque.

New Delhi was undoubtedly his greatest work, his apogee, not even excepting the unfulfilled design for the Catholic cathedral of Liverpool, which always seemed to me to be a forced competitor with St. Peter's, Rome: the dome, although exceeding the dimensions of St. Peter's, in spite of its hugeness and great height could only have *contrasted* with St. Peter's and could never have rivalled the beauty of Wren's St. Paul's. At New Delhi, however, Lutyens achieved the truly magnificent, again at fantastic expense but with a perfect artistic economy. Its greatest appreciator was perhaps Robert Byron who, in his *Country Life* articles, wrote: "The beauty of this building transcends the merely panoramic.... Never was so large, so arrogant, yet so lovely a palace. The climax, the shout of Imperial suggestion, is the dome, reared blind and sudden from the middle of the house—an offence against democracy, a slap in the face of the modern average man—" and so on; and all this imperial symbolism was finished within some fifteen years of the disintegration of the Indian Empire!

What of the man? He was as arrogant as his New Delhi, as perfectly sure of his mission as any dictator, "not gifted," as his son writes, "with wide sympathy, with charity, and his heart has ever been unmoved by deep emotion." Away from his studio, and sometimes in it, he was even naive, perpetrating the most fearful and irreverent puns. Lunching with his son at the Garrick, he referred to the fish course as "the piece of cod which passeth all understanding." On occasion, and perhaps perforce, he could be humorously gracious and ingratiating, ending a humble apology to Lady Harding, the vice-reign of India, after ignoring her instructions, by writing that he would sue for forgiveness by washing her feet with his tears and drying them with his hair. "It is true," he ended, "that I have very little hair. But then you have such very little feet."

Here was a man who once he was engaged in the act of concentrating on architectural creation could not consider any other pre-occupation. His light shone out of an otherwise somewhat immature schoolboyish character that, overlaid by immense gifts, nevertheless left behind some outstanding works in the art of architecture.

—H. A. N. Brockman

LUZ, Hans.

German. Born in Stuttgart, 10 June 1926. Educated at the Dillmann Real-Gymnasium, Stuttgart, 1936–44, graduated 1944; apprenticed to the landscape architect Adolf Haag, Stuttgart, 1948–50. Served in the Germany Army, and prisoner of war, 1944–47. Married Gretel Reinhardt in 1952; children: Christof, Frieder, Heiner, and Henrike. Landscape-Gardener and Site Manager for Adolf Haag, Stuttgart, 1950–52; Landscape Gardener with Otto Valentien, Stuttgart, 1953–55, and Dr. J. Schweizer, Basel, 1955–56. Free-lance landscape gardener since 1956: opened planning office with small nursery, Birkach, Stuttgart, 1958; Principal, Hans Luz und Partner, Birkach, since 1961. Lecturer, 1973, and since 1975 Honorary Professor, Technical University of Stuttgart. Exhibitions: *Bundesgartenschau*, Stuttgart, 1961, Karlsruhe, 1967, Mannheim, 1975, and Stuttgart, 1977. Recipient: Paul Bonatz Prize, in collaboration, 1959, 1967; First Prize, Leonberg Cemetery Competition, 1966; First Prize, Höher Odenwald Recreation Center Competition, 1968; First Prize, Leinfelden Cemetery Competition, 1969; Hugo Häring Prize, in collaboration, 1969, 1970; First Prize, Oberboihingen Cemetery Competition, 1972; First Prize, Reichenbach Recreation Center Competition, 1974; First Prize, *Bundesgartenschau* Competition, Stuttgart, 1974; First Prize, with Dieter Bohnet, Federal Chancellor's Office Competition, Bonn, 1974; Federation of Landscape Architects (BDLA) Prize, 1977. Member, Akademie der Künste, Berlin, 1975. Address: Hans Luz und Partner, Dinkelstrasse 40, Postfach 72 02 04, 7000 Stuttgart 70 (Birkach), West Germany.

Works (landscape architecture):

1958 Luz House, Birkach, Stuttgart
1960 University of Karlsruhe
1961 *Bundesgartenschau,* Stuttgart
State Parliament House, Stuttgart
1961– University of Stuttgart
1963/
65 ICI Factory, Östingen, Germany
1964/
67 Teachers Training College, Ludwigsburg, Germany
University of Tubingen at Morgenstelle
1964/
68 Hospital, Leonberg, Germany
1965 Agricultural University of Hohenheim, Stuttgart (with Walter Rossow)
1967 Marwitz House, Sindelfingen, Germany
Bundesgartenschau (25 m² gardens), Karlsruhe
1967/
71 Cemetery, Leonberg, Germany
1967/
73 Asemwald Residential Complex, Stuttgart
1967/
77 Health Resort Park, Wildbad, Germany (with Walter Rossow)
Oberbettringen Residential Complex, Schwäbisch Gmünd
1968 Beer House, Pflaumloch bei Nördlingen, Germany
1968/
73 Höher Odenwald Recreation Center, Germany
1969/
73 Cemetery, Leinfelden, Germany
1969/
78 Tannenplatz Residential Complex, Ulm
1970 German Pavilion, *Expo '70*, Osaka, Japan
1970/
72 Central University Sports Complex, Olympia, Munich (with Wolfgang Miller)
1972/
74 Cemetery, Oberboihingen, Germany

Hans Luz: Garden, Luz House, Birkach, Stuttgart, 1958

Geno House, Stuttgart
1974/
76 Reichenbach Recreation Center, Germany
1975/
76 Federal Chancellor's Office, Bonn (with Dieter Bohnet)
1975/
77 Königstrasse, Stuttgart (competition project)
1977 *Bundesgartenschau*, Stuttgart (with Planungsgruppe 1)
1979 City Center, Leonberg, Germany

Publications:

By LUZ: articles—"Planzung ohne Erdanschluss" in *Gartenamt* (Hanover), June 1973; "Friedhof Leinfelden" in *Garten und Landschaft* (Munich), November 1974; "Beton" in *Garten und Landschaftsbau*, Stuttgart 1977.

On LUZ: articles—"Platz für Garten ist Überall" by Irene Mutz in *Mein schöner Garten* (Offenburg, Germany), April 1977; "In der Luftröhre ein Park" by Manfred Sack in *Garten und Landschaft* (Munich), November 1977; article by K. H. Rucker in *Gartenpraxis* (Stuttgart), March 1979.

As a practicing landscape-architect, I see my task as follows: 1) to make sure that as little harm is done to our landscape as possible (this is unfortunately inevitable at the present time, because of the strain put on the landscape by continual building and other engineering projects); 2) to try to repair the damage caused by these processes; but, above all, 3) to plan and design the new open spaces that should be created with the "genius loci" and the tradition of our predecessors in mind, so that they really become spaces in which we can live.

As a result of my gardening background, vegetation plays an important role in my work.

I feel that landscape architects should not forget their creative, imaginative role.

—Hans Luz

Hans Luz has become one of the most prominent garden architects in Southern Germany: he employs a wealth of innovations and new ideas, and he has achieved wide public recognition. He has extended the disciplines of small-scale gardening through domestic projects to the more complex open space systems of community housing and the university campus. He has a reputation for care in detailing—particularly when relating constructional features to planting—which suffuses the whole of his work.

The work of Hans Luz is characterized by a number of clearly definable attributes. He is particularly at ease in dealing with complex level changes. The complicated steps and retainers, often intricately interwoven, that he uses are always subservient to the texture and pattern of the whole design. His enclosures are usually simple (see, for example, his treatment of the ICI Factory at Östingen). He uses natural material when possible, but, when juxtaposed with concrete, both the concrete and the plants echo the form of the construction. The use of natural material, in particular, is always dependent upon a high standard of craftsmanship. As regards concrete, he has developed a number of system blocks that can produce dramatic sculptural effects, e.g. the chevron walling at Dr. Zabel's garden. There is often a strong formality to his designs and a tendency toward pattern making.

There is repeatedly a strong feeling of anti-suggestion—as with, say, cube blocks within school playgrounds. Traditional garden features are frequently translated into a modern vernacular—for example, concrete stools and plant containers. There is always a strong division of elements in his designs, but with little or no duality of purpose. He is masterful at joining different surfaces, often employs Oriental techniques of planting, and is as sparing in his use of water as he is of plant material, a technique that lends great individuality of expression to the species employed.

Among Luz's best-known works may be included a wide of variety of private gardens, notably his own at Stuttgart-Birkach, Garten Marwitz, and Garten Beer, the University of Karlsruhe and the University of Stuttgart-Hohenheim, and various school and municipal projects. His international reputation derives from the *Bundesgartenschau* at Stuttgart in 1961 and Karlsruhe in 1967 and, most notably, from the German Pavilion at *Expo '70* in Osaka.

—Gordon Patterson

LYNDON, Donlyn.

American. Born in California, 1936; son of the architect Maynard Lyndon. Educated at Princeton University, New Jersey, B.Arch. 1959. Partner, MLTW: Moore, Lyndon, Turnbull and Whitaker, Berkeley, California, 1960–65. Principal, Lyndon Associates, Cambridge, Massachusetts, since 1965. Professor at Massachusetts Institute of Technology, Cambridge. Address: Lyndon Associates, 948 Parker Street, Cambridge, Massachusetts 02138, U.S.A.

Works:

1960 Jobson House, Big Sur, California
1961 Bonham House, Boulder Creek, California
1962 Jenkins House, Rutherford, California
Otus House, Berkeley, California
Seaside Professional Building, Seaside, California
West Plaza Condominiums, Coronado, California (project)
1963 Jewell House, Orinda, California
Monte Vista Apartments, Monterey, California
Monte Vista Village, Monterey, California (project)
1964 Hoover-Slater House, Stinson Beach, California
Lone Hill Winery Housing, San Jose, California
Morris-LaForge House, Boulder Creek, California (project)
Speculation II Prototype House, Sea Ranch, California
1965 Condominium I, Sea Ranch, California
Sea Ranch Athletic Club I, Sea Ranch, California (with Lawrence Halprin)
Talbert House, Oakland, California
1968/
75 Pembroke Dormitory, Brown University, Providence, Rhode Island

Publications:

By LYNDON: book—*The Place of Houses*, with Charles Moore and Gerald Allen, New York 1974; articles—"Filologia dell'architettura americana" in *Casabella* (Milan), November 1963; "Sea Ranch: The Process of Design" in *World Architecture 2*, London 1965; "Seattle: Metamorphosis from Fair into Center" in *Progressive Architecture* (New York), July 1965; "In Canada: The Continent's First Single-Structure Campus" in *Architectural Forum* (New York), December 1965; "Big Happening in Berkeley" in *Architectural Forum* (New York), January/February 1966; "Student Dorms: A University Tries Variety" in *Architectural Forum* (New York), March 1966; "Concrete Cascade in Portland" in *Architectural Forum* (New York), July/August 1966; "The Environment and the Market" in *World Architecture 4*, London 1967; "Sea Ranch: A Second Look," with Charles Moore and Gerald Allen, in *Architectural Record* (New York), November 1974; "Five Ways to People Places" in *Architectural Record* (New York), November 1975; "Commentary" in *Progressive Architecture* (New York), February 1976; "Architectural Education Here" in *Journal of Architectural Education* (Washington, D.C.), February 1978.

On LYNDON: article—"Charles W. Moore and His Partners" by Misawa, Ehira and Sugawara in *The Japan Architect* (Tokyo), September 1965.

Donlyn Lyndon is the "L" in MLTW—Moore, Lyndon, Turnbull, and Whitaker—an extraordinary and resilient fraternity, more often apart than together, who first came to prominence as a team with their design of Sea Ranch in 1964. Donlyn Lyndon's father is a distinguished architect in the California modern manner, and growing up in such an environment was a formative influence. However, it is Princeton and the Class of '59 that established the basis for his architecture: the teaching of Jean Labatut, an anachronism then anticipating the collapse of faith in Modernism because he had never had any, and the stimulus of a shared belief in new possibilities for architecture among fellow students and young faculty, including William Turnbull and Charles Moore. The nature of each individual's contribution to MLTW may be impossible to define. Even for those involved, a shared creative process doesn't have simple boundaries. In judging their independent work, it seems that the genius of the group differs markedly in many ways from the sum of its parts: Turnbull has matured and expanded the innovations of Sea Ranch; Moore has flourished brilliantly; Lyndon has spent most of his time teaching.

Yet, with Lyndon, there has been a limited but significant production. With Moore, he wrote *The Place of Houses:* with great skill and sensitivity they share the lessons and insights from their lives of making houses and experiencing places. The principles underlying the book are wise and robust and have a quiet universality. Essentially the concern is for poetic contextualism. After the book had been published, Lyndon reviewed its major themes in an article. They were: use elements that suggest the presence of people; emphasize forms that relate to the human body and reveal its functions; create pride of place by continuing care; be open to conflicting claims of use; incorporate what others have built and re-invest their care; give a measured and varied structure to space; make spaces that are contestable and encourage improvised use; make places that nurture celebration and encourage people to pay attention to each other.

These principles were put to the test in Lyndon's major work since Sea Ranch—the Pembroke Dormitory at Brown University in Providence, Rhode Island. Coping with a limited budget, Lyndon has produced a building that is simply and directly made, yet filled with rich and complex invention. With simple means, he creates continuing variation both in the private and public spaces. The individual is left to complete his own celebration of the space given, while the architecture strives to provide a stage for joyous communion. This stage management is most self-conscious in the decorated arches and gateways and in the use of color, particularly on the public street side. The decoration of the arches demands too much and interjects a discordant personality into the internal setting, but the space is strong enough to survive the intrusion. The use of color to modulate the wall surfaces creates a highly effective transformation of mood, which could have been extended.

Lyndon's work is tougher intellectually and less sensual than that of his contemporaries to whom he might be compared. As does his writing, his work, particularly Pembroke, has a didactic quality from which it is possible to learn without merely emulating style.

—Alan Balfour

LYONS, Eric (Alfred).
British. Born in London, 2 October 1912. Trained as an articled pupil and part-time student at the Regent Street Polytechnic, London. Married Catherine Joyce Townsend in 1944; children: Richard, Jane, Antony, and Naomi. Worked in the office of Walter Gropius and Maxwell Fry, London, 1936–37; in partnership with G. Paulson Townsend, London, 1945–50; in private practice, London, 1950–63. Since 1963, Partner, with Ivor Cunningham, Eric Lyons Cunningham Partnership, London (Richard Lyons joined partnership, 1972). Member of the Council, 1960–63, Vice-President, 1967–68, Senior Vice-President, 1974, and President, 1975–77, Royal Institute of British Architects; Chairman, Association of Consultant Architects, 1973. Recipient: Civic Trust Award, 1961 (twice), 1962, 1964, 1965, 1967; Ministry of Housing and Local Government Medal, 1961 (3 times), 1963, 1964 (3 times), 1965, 1966, 1967, 1968; Distinction in Town Planning, 1961, and Eastern Region Architecture Award, 1966, Royal Institute of British Architects. Fellow, Royal Institute of British Architects, and Society of Industrial Artists and Designers. Honorary Fellow, American Institute of Architects; Member, Académie d'Architecture, France. C.B.E. (Commander, Order of the British Empire), 1979. Address: Eric Lyons Cunningham Partnership, Mill House Studio, Bridge Road, East Molesey, Surrey KT8 9HF, England.

Works:

1951 Box Corner (flats), Twickenham, Middlesex
1952 Onslow Court (flats), Richmond, Surrey
1954 Cavendish Court (flats), Richmond, Surrey
1955 The Priory (flats), Blackheath, London
1955/
57 Parkleys (flats), Ham Common, Richmond, Surrey
1956 The Hall (flats), Blackheath, London
1957 Flats for the Soviet Trade Delegation, West Hill, Highgate, London
1958 The Cedars (housing), Teddington, Middlesex
1959 Applecourt (flats), Cambridge
Corner Green (housing), Blackheath, London
Hallgate (flats), Blackheath, London
Howard House (old people's housing), Bognor Regis, Sussex
1960 Fieldend (housing), Twickenham, Middlesex
Hall 2 (housing), Blackheath, London
Highsett (flats), Cambridge
Parkgate (flats), Hove, Sussex
1962 Lansdowne Hill (flats, public housing), Southampton
Married soldiers quarters, Pirbright, Surrey
Pitcairn House (public housing), Hackney, London
The Hamlet (old people's housing), Bognor Regis, Sussex
1963 Spangate (flats), Blackheath, London
Southrow (flats), Blackheath, London
The Lane (housing), Blackheath, London
The Paddox (housing), Oxford
1963/
64 Blackheath Park (private housing), Blackheath, London
1964 Albion Primary School, Bermondsey, London
Friar's Primary School, Southwark, London
Highsett II (housing), Cambridge
Rayners Road (housing), Putney, London
Templemere (housing), Weybridge, Surrey
1964/
78 World's End Redevelopment (high-density public housing complex), Chelsea, London
1965 Brackley (housing), Weybridge, Surrey
Castle Green (housing), Weybridge, Surrey
Castle House (public housing), Southampton
Hall 4 (housing), Blackheath, London
Highsett III (housing), Cambridge
1965/
70 New Ash Green (new village), Kent

1966 Cedar Chase (housing), Taplow, Buckinghamshire
Offices, Holly Road, Hampton Hill, Middlesex
Public housing, Harlow New Town, Essex
Weymede (housing), Byfleet, Surrey
1967 Dryden House (flats), Cambridge
Grasmere (housing), Byfleet, Surrey
Parkend (housing), Blackheath, London
1969 Westfield (housing), Ashtead, Surrey
1971 Married soldiers quarters, Pirbright, Surrey
Mayford (public housing), Camden, London
New Ash Green County Primary School, Kent
1972 Walsingham Lodge (old people's housing), Barnes, London
1973 Plan for the central area, and housing and shops, Vilamoura, Algarve, Portugal
1974 Plan for centre redevelopment, and public housing and old people's home, Chertsey, Surrey
Wates House (staff common rooms, etc.), University of Surrey, Guildford
1977 Master plan for the new village of Aqueduct Green, Telford, Shropshire
Caledonian Estate (public housing), Islington, London
Westbourne Neighbourhood (public housing, medical centre, community centre, and old people's home), Islington, London
1978 Holm Walk (housing), Blackheath, London
1979 Delhi/Outram Streets (public housing), Islington, London
Fieldend (housing), Telford New Town, Shropshire
Mallard Place (housing), Twickenham, Middlesex

Publications:

By LYONS: articles—"Domestic Building and Speculative Development" in *RIBA Journal* (London), May 1958; "Few New Ideas for Homes" in *The Times* (London), 3 July 1961; "Rebuilding Britain," with others, special issue of *Twentieth Century* (London), Summer 1962; "Criticism of Work Submitted for RIBA Prizes and Studentships 1963" in *RIBA Journal* (London), June 1963; "Managing Without Design?" in *RIBA Journal* (London), October 1966; "Pushing Hard—But in What Direction?" in *RIBA Journal* (London), March 1967; "Why We Want More Competitions" in *RIBA Journal* (London), January 1968; "Too Often We Justify Our Ineptitudes by Moral Postures" in *RIBA Journal* (London), May 1968; "Back to Blackheath" in *The Architect* (London), July 1971; "I Am Sure It Will Go Away" in *The Architects' Journal* (London), 12 July 1972; "A New Lease for Lyons" in *Building* (London), 18 October 1974; "Pruning Can Be Fruitful" in *RIBA Journal* (London), April 1975; "What Happened to Housing?" in *The Spectator* (London), 17 May 1975; "Eric's Whistle-Stop Tours" in *RIBA Journal* (London), February 1976; "The President's Column" in *RIBA Journal* (London), March 1976; "Eric Lyons Ponders on the Nature of Modern Architecture" in *RIBA Journal* (London), April 1976; "Membership Involvement" in *RIBA Journal* (London), June 1976; "Aesthetic Control" and "User Involvement in Housing" in *RIBA Journal* (London), July 1976; "Habitat Architectural Competition" in *RIBA Journal* (London), August 1976; "Architects' Pattern Books" in *RIBA Journal* (London), September 1976; "The Need for an RIBA" and "Architecture and Place" in *RIBA Journal* (London), October 1976; "Housing Experiments" in *RIBA Journal* (London), December 1976; "Building Failures" and "Small Is Beautiful" in *RIBA Journal* (London), January 1977; "Growth Points for the Profession" in *RIBA Journal* (London), March 1977; "Not Waving, but Drowning" and "Death of the Cowboy" in *RIBA Journal* (London), April 1977; "Private Housing" in *RIBA Journal* (London), May 1977;

"What Is the RIBA Doing for Its Members?" in *RIBA Journal* (London), June 1977.

On LYONS: articles—"The Team in the Office" in *Architecture and Building* (London), June 1956; "SPAN" by Robert Furneaux Jordan in *Architectural Review* (London), February 1959; "The Man about the Houses" by Richard Findlater in *Punch* (London), 17 January 1962; "The Spanman Cometh" in the *Sunday Times* (London), 10 November 1968; "What We Need Are *Friendly* Homes," interview with Rex Grizell, in *Evening News* (London), 26 November 1969; "Out of the Strong . . ." in *The Architect* (London), February/-March 1975; interview with Judy Hillman in *The Times* (London), 28 June 1975; "Rus in Urbe" in *The Architects' Journal* (London), 9 July 1975; "Building Gardens with Houses in Them" by Caroline Moorehead in *The Times* (London), 21 July 1975; "Eric Lyons: Architect President" in *The Architects' Journal* (London), 30 July 1975; "Eric Lyons and RIBA 1976" in *Building Design* (London), 9 June 1976; "Mid-Span," interview with John Donat, in *Building* (London), 16 July 1976.

From the moment an architect begins his professional education, he is conditioned to geometry and the T-square. That conditioning is almost inevitable; mathematics and proportion form his basic aesthetic. But the more he becomes absorbed in his art, the further he may lose touch with biological form. In many schools of architecture, for instance, the tree is reduced to the mathematical symbol of a circle, harsh treatment for one of the most expressive forms in nature. But there are exceptions, and Eric Lyons is one who has consistently held the balance between architecture and nature without which the average human subconsciously feels disoriented.

Although Lyons' practice covers a wide field, he will be remembered mainly for his contribution to domestic housing, conceived more as landscape architecture than as architecture itself. The elegant Span housing he built for a private company at Petersham, Blackheath and Weybridge, mainly for the professional classes within commuting distance of London, have been a success speculatively as well as aesthetically. "Good landscape is good business" was proved right. Together with his assistant, Ivor Cunningham (now a partner), Lyons evolved a form of terrace houses enclosing common gardens in a single total landscape concept—in contrast to the usual configuration of buildings encircling a space into which gardens have later been inserted. This unity is partly achieved by ground modelling, so that, in contrast to the standard London square, vertical and horizontal have an agreeable plastic relationship. There are small private patio gardens, but the collective gardens are so beautifully and intricately planted that they have maintained some of the mystique of nature without being disordered.

In this age of concrete jungles and the mass production of architecture, the preservation of human values is vital. This quality in Eric Lyons was recognized by the profession in Britain when it elected him its president. He does, in fact, stand astride the two professions of architecture and landscape design, and if his endeavours to repeat the success of Span at New Ash Green in Kent did not succeed, the fault lay in the market for which his work had to be designed. A Lyons house is only for the sensitive and the appreciative, where the sight, touch and smell of a plant has as much meaning as a work of art.

—Geoffrey Jellicoe

Eric Lyons: Templemere, Weybridge, Surrey, 1964

LYONS, ISRAEL, ELLIS AND GRAY.

Partnership; established, London, 1947, as Lyons, Israel and Ellis, by E. D. Lyons (born 1905), Lawrence Israel (born 1909), and Tom Ellis (born 1911); additional partner, David Gray (born 1928), since 1975. Exhibition: *Transformations in Modern Architecture*, Museum of Modern Art, New York, 1979. Recipient: First Prize, Falmouth Secondary Modern School Competition, 1952; First Prize, Finchley Town Hall Competition, London, 1954; Bronze Medal, Ministry of Housing, 1958; Architectural Design Award, 1966, 1967; Civic Design Award, 1968. Address: 43 Portland Place, London W1N 3AG, England.

Works:

1952 Millbrook Junior School, Southampton
Orpington Infants and Junior School, Kent
1953 Chislehurst Boys' Secondary School, Kent
Middleton Mixed Secondary School, Lancashire
1954 Herne Bay Mixed Secondary School, Kent
1957 Millbrook Infants' School, Southampton
Falmouth Mixed Secondary School, Cornwall
Hoe Secondary School, Kent
1958 Barnsley Mixed Secondary School, Yorkshire
Peckham Comprehensive School, London
Orrell Mixed Secondary School, phase I, Lancashire
Bridgnorth Boys' Secondary School, Shropshire
Hoglands Housing Scheme, Southampton
Vyse Lane Housing Scheme, Southampton
1959 Jordanthorpe Girls' Secondary School, Sheffield
Workshop Annex, Old Vic Theatre, London
1960 Weston Park Boys' Secondary School, Southampton
Northfleet Girls' Secondary School, Kent
Bridgnorth Girls' Secondary School, Shropshire
1961 Wolfson Institute, Royal Postgraduate Medical School, Ducane Road, Hammersmith, London
Workshop Block, Hammersmith Hospital, London
Avenham Estate, Preston, Lancashire
1962 Upholland Mixed Secondary School, Lancashire
Chorley Mixed Grammar School, Lancashire
Harrow Weald Grammar School extension, London
Bridgnorth Boys' Secondary School extension, Shropshire
1963 Urmston Boys' Grammar School, Lancashire
1964 Barnsley College of Technology, Yorkshire
Parkhouse Mixed Secondary School, Sheffield
1965 Windsor Girls' Grammar School, Berkshire
Wokingham Mixed Secondary School, Berkshire
David Lister High School, Kingston-upon-Hull, Yorkshire
1966 Royal Postgraduate Medical School, Ducane Road, Hammersmith, London
Animal Quarters and Animal Kitchen, Department of Experimental Medicine, 5 Shaftesbury Road, Cambridge
Wentworth Teachers' Training College, phase I, Barnsley, Yorkshire
Middleton Mixed Secondary School extension, phase I, Yorkshire
National Sea Training School, Gravesend, Kent
Wickersley Mixed Secondary School, phase I, West Riding, Yorkshire
Bentley Mixed Secondary School, West Riding, Yorkshire
Home for the Aged, Dorinda Street, Islington, London
Town Hall, phase I, Middleton, Lancashire

1967 Dunn Nutritional Laboratories, Milton Road, Cambridge
Orpington Junior School, Kent
Hoe Secondary School extension, Kent
1968 Housing, Polthorne Street, Woolwich, London
1969 Housing, Southampton Central Redevelopment Area
1970 College of Engineering and Science, Polytechnic of Central London, New Cavendish Street, London W1
Hollybrook Infants' and Junior School, Southampton
Shipping Federation Offices, Tilbury, Essex
1971 Beckenham Girls' Comprehensive School extensions, Bromley, Kent
1972 Queen Elizabeth Hospital for Children, Hackney Road, London E2
1973 Southampton Retail Trades College, phase I
1974 College of Communication, Polytechnic of Central London, Riding House Street, London W1
1975/
76 Medical Research Laboratories, Mill Hill, Middlesex

Publications:

On LYONS/ISRAEL: articles—"Southampton Technical College Food Trades Department and Communal Building" in *The Architects' Journal* (London), 2 August 1972; "Endowment in Concrete" by A. Best in *Design* (London), March 1973.

*   *   *

The vigorous expansion of the schools building programme in England in the immediate post-war years gave the young firm of Lyons, Israel and Ellis the opportunity to put into effect some of the aspirations of the Modern Movement. The movement had had a minimal effect on school design in the established pre-war architectural practices—despite a number of outstanding entries in the *News Chronicle* Schools Competition of 1937. The ideas generated in this competition had to wait for the impetus of the 1944 Education Act, and the consequent enlightened administration of the Ministry of Education, before they could be exploited. Lyons, Israel and Ellis built up their practice through their active participation in this programme, for which they built thirty primary, secondary, grammar, technical, and comprehensive schools.

The shortage of building materials and stringent building restrictions stimulated them to a series of imaginative and ingenious solutions. The "handwriting" of their work became evident in the sensitive use of materials, the skillful exploitation of technical solutions as an integral part of the design, and the fastidious attention to detailing. The early schools were all responses to very restrictive briefs from the client as well as some exceptionally difficult sites; they varied in plan from the cross-wall design of the Upholland School, Lancashire, with the corridor "spine" punched through the classroom block; the volute plan of Jordanthorpe School, Sheffield; the prize winning linear answer to the shelving site at Falmouth, Cornwall; to the inward-turned "walled town" at the David Lister School, Kingston-upon-Hull.

In the 1960's and 1970's the firm went on to design technical colleges, laboratories for research units, polytechnics, and hospital and university buildings. Two buildings in particular illustrate their architectural aims:

The Wolfson Institute is a complex of three lecture theatres, common rooms, restaurant and social facilities, built for the Royal Post-Graduate Medical School of London University on the site of the Hammersmith Hospital. The two smaller lecture theatres are slung beneath the counterbalancing large theatre, and this dramatic structure is echoed visually in the stark, clear-cut white concrete volumes. Around the dominant central fortress of the theatres, the wide corridors, stairs and social areas flow in a single continuum of space. A remarkable feature of the lecture theatres is their perfect two-way acoustics. Not only can the lecturer be heard in the back row of the 500-seat auditorium without any mechanical aids, but any member of the audience can audibly join in the discussion. The aims, derived from Le Corbusier, were to design a building that would be

the symbol of an idea, using a coherent system, a sustained discipline to produce a recognized order in content, route and structure. The most important parts of a building internally to be recognizable externally, the form expressing the inherent use and structure of the various parts. The plan to have a clearly defined route (way in and way out), with the major destinations clearly identifiable.

The College of Engineering of the Polytechnic of Central London is a further attempt to synthesize all these aims. The result is a sophisticated complex, comprising a cranked 8-storey laboratory block, a 5-storey tutorial block, and a focal node containing entrance area, two lecture theatres, common rooms and library. In the basement there are extensive engineering workshops and garaging. The planning constraints of the cramped triangular site have been vigorously exploited and turned to advantage, and a feeling of spaciousness has been achieved, particularly in the triple height entrance hall and the communal areas. Here students and staff are brought together throughout the day from all the faculties, with no hierarchical segregation.

The floor to ceiling glazing on the tutorial block, which is the street facade, provides visual interest and involvement in the life of the Polytechnic for the passerby. It is a building that, very deliberately, does not cut itself off from its immediate environment. It has been designed in white concrete and bronze, and the bronze is used as a unifying element throughout, not only in the windows and spandrel panels but also, inside, on balustrades and door fittings. The bronze may seem costly, but because of its greater structural strength, the architects were able to use much thinner sections ($3'' \times 1/10''$ extruded) where $6''$ thick aluminum sections would otherwise have been necessary to withstand the windloading. Standardization of parts throughout the building also kept the costs down, for, as in all the firm's previous work, a prime consideration was to achieve a building with low operational and maintenance costs. Again, the consistent and sustained use of the 2 ft. bronze module throughout clarifies and makes comprehensible the complex geometry of the building.

Interest in the aims of the partnership over the years have attracted many younger architects to work for the firm. Among them have been James Stirling, James Gowan, Alan Colquhoun and John Miller, Ronald Simpson, Neave Brown, and David Gray, who became a partner in 1975.

—Mary Hayes

Lyons, Israel, Ellis and Gray: College of Engineering and Science, Polytechnic of Central London, 1970

MACKAY, David (John).

British. Born in Eastbourne, Sussex, 25 March 1933; moved to Spain, 1958. Educated at the Northern Polytechnic, London, 1951–58, Dip.Arch. 1958; Escuela Técnica Superior de Arquitectura, Barcelona, 1967–68, Dip.Arch. 1968. Married Roser Jarque in 1957; children: John, Anna, Martha, Sonia, Monica, and Mark. In partnership with Josep Martorell, *q.v.,* and Oriol Bohigas, *q.v.,* Barcelona, since 1962. Recipient: Essay Prize, Royal Institute of British Architects, 1949–50; Andrew N. Prentice Prize, RIBA, 1960; Puig i Cadafalch Prize, Colegio de Arquitectos de Cataluña y Baleares, 1968. Associate, Royal Institute of British Architects, 1959. Address: Martorell, Bohigas, Mackay, Camp 61, Barcelona 6, Spain.

Publications:

By MACKAY: books—*World Architecture,* with others, 4 volumes, London 1967; *Contradictions in Living Environment,* London 1971, as *Contradicciones en el Entorno Habitado,* Barcelona 1972; *The Anti-Rationalists,* with others, edited by Nikolaus Pevsner and J. M. Richards, London 1973; *Wohnungsbau im Wandel,* Stuttgart 1977, as *Multiple Family Housing,* London, New York and Toronto 1977, as *Viviendas Plurifamiliares,* Barcelona 1979

See MARTORELL, BOHIGAS, MACKAY

MACKINTOSH, Charles Rennie.

British. Born in Glasgow, Scotland, 7 June 1868. Educated at Reid's Public School, Glasgow, 1875–77; Alan Glen's High School, Glasgow, 1877–83; School of Art, Glasgow, evenings 1884–89. Married Margaret Macdonald in 1900. Apprentice, office of John Hutchison, Glasgow, 1884–89; Draughtsman, 1889–94, Architect, 1894–1904, and Partner, 1904–13, Honeyman and Keppie, Glasgow; temporarily retired from architecture to take up watercolour painting, Suffolk, England, 1913–14; in private architectural practice, Chelsea, London, 1916–20; concentrated entirely on painting, Port Vendres, France, 1923–27, and London, 1927–28. Founder Member, with Herbert McNair, Frances Macdonald, and Margaret Macdonald, The Four group, Glasgow, 1895. Exhibitions: Maison de l'Art Nouveau, Paris, 1895; *The Four,* Arts and Crafts Society, London, 1896; *Wiener Sezession Exhibition,* Vienna, 1900; *International Exposition of Decorative Art,* Turin, 1902; *Furniture Exhibition,* Moscow, 1903, 1913; *Kunstschau,* Vienna, 1909; *International Exhibition,* Chicago, 1925; one-man shows—McLellan Galleries, Glasgow, 1933; *Charles Rennie Mackintosh 1868–1928,* Edinburgh Festival, 1953; *Charles Rennie Mackintosh and the Glasgow School of Art,* Glasgow School of Art, 1961; *Charles Rennie Mackintosh: Furniture* and *Ironwork and Metalwork,* Glasgow School of Art, 1964; *Charles Rennie Mack-* *intosh 1868–1928: Architecture, Design and Painting,* Edinburgh Festival, 1968; *Charles Rennie Mackintosh,* Museum des 20.Jahrhunderts, Vienna, 1969; *Mackintosh Watercolours,* Glasgow Art Gallery, 1978, toured Edinburgh and London. Collections: Hunterian Art Gallery, University of Glasgow; Glasgow School of Art; Glasgow Museum and Art Gallery; Charles Rennie Mackintosh Society, Queen's Cross Church, 870 Garscube Street, Glasgow (founded 1973). Recipient: Institute of Architects Prize, Glasgow, 1887, 1888; Bronze Medal, 1888, Queen's Prize, 1889, Silver Medal, 1891, and Gold Medal, 1892, South Kensington National Competition, London; Diploma of Honour, *International Exposition of Decorative Art,* Turin, 1902. Fellow, Royal Institute of British Architects, 1906, and Royal Corporation of Architects in Scotland, 1908; Member, Glasgow Institute of Architects, 1908. Honorary Member, Wiener Sezession, 1900. *Died* (in London) *10 December 1928.*

Works:

1888 Mountain Chapel (competition project)
1889 Presbyterian Church (competition project)
1890 Public Hall (competition project)
     Science and Art Museum (competition project)
     Redclyffe (pair of semi-detached houses), 140 Balgrayhill Road, Springburn, Glasgow
1891 Tenement Buildings (competition project)
1892 Chapter House (competition project)
1893 Railway Terminus (competition project)
1894 Royal Insurance Building, Glasgow (competition project)
     Queen Margaret's Medical College, Hamilton Drive, Glasgow (now altered)
1894/
95 Gladsmuir (William Davidson House) interiors, Kilmacolm, Renfrewshire (destroyed)
1895 *Glasgow Herald* Building extensions, Mitchell Street, Glasgow
     Lennox Castle Inn alterations, Lennoxtown, Stirlingshire (destroyed)
1895/
96 Cranston Tea Rooms interiors, 91–93 Buchanan Street, Glasgow (with G. Walton; now altered)
1896 Martyr's Public School, Parson Street, Glasgow
1897/
98 Cranston Tea Rooms interiors, Argyle Street, Glasgow (with G. Walton; now altered)
1897/
99 Glasgow School of Art, 167 Renfrew Street
1898 St. Matthew's Church, 866 Garscube Road, Glasgow (subsequently Queen's Cross Church; now the Charles Rennie Mackintosh Society)
     National Bank of Scotland, Glasgow (competition project)
     Ruchill Street Church Hall, 24 Ruchill Street, Maryhill, Glasgow
1899 Dunglass Castle interiors, Bowling, Dunbartonshire

1899/
1901 Windyhill (William Davidson House), Kilmacolm, Renfrewshire
1900 Rowat House interiors, 34 Kingsborough Gardens, Glasgow
     Westdel (J. Maclehose House) interiors, Queen's Place, Glasgow
     St. Serf's Church interiors, Dysart, Fife
1900/
01 Cranston Tea Rooms interiors, 205–209 Ingram Street, Glasgow (now altered)
     Artist's Country Cottage (project)
     Artist's Town House and Studio (project)
1900/
06 Mackintosh Studio/Apartment interiors, 120 Mains Street, now Blythswood Street, Glasgow
1901 Auchenbothie Gate Lodge, Kilmacolm, Renfrewshire
     Daily Record Building, Renfield Lane, Glasgow (now altered)
     Concert Hall and Industrial Hall, *International Exhibition,* Glasgow (competition project)
     "Innendekoration" House for an Art-Lover, Darmstadt (competition project)
1902 Scottish Section, *International Exposition of Decorative Art,* Turin
1902/
03 Hill House (W. W. Blackie House), Helensburgh, Dunbartonshire
1902/
07 Warndorfer Music Room interiors, Vienna (destroyed)
1903 Anglican Cathedral, Liverpool (competition project)
1903/
04 Willow Tea Rooms interiors, Sauchiehall Street, Glasgow (now altered)
1903/
05 Cochrane House alterations, Nitshill, Glasgow (destroyed by fire, 1935)
1903/
06 Scotland Street School, Glasgow
1904 Holy Trinity Church interiors, Bridge of Allan, Stirlingshire
1904/
06 Auchenibert (F. J. Shand House), near Killearn, Stirlingshire
1906 Mosside (H. B. Collins House), near Kilmacolm, Renfrewshire
     Mackintosh House alterations and interiors, 6 Florentine Terrace, now 78 Southpark Avenue, Glasgow (destroyed)
     Abbey Close Church furniture, Paisley, Renfrewshire (destroyed)
1907/
09 Glasgow School of Art additions, 167 Renfrew Street, Glasgow
1908 Lady Artists' Club entrance and hall interiors, Blythswood Square, Glasgow
1911 White Cockade Restaurant interiors, *International Exhibition,* Glasgow
1912 Ritchie Hairdressing Salon alterations, Union Street, Glasgow (destroyed)

Charles Rennie Mackintosh: Hill House, Helensburgh, Dunbartonshire, 1903

Mosside (H. B. Collins House) alterations, near Kilmacolm, Renfrewshire
1915/
17   W. J. Bassett-Lowke House conversion, 78 Derngate, Northampton
1917   F. M. Jones House interiors, The Drive, Northampton
1917/
19   The Dugout (Willow Tea Rooms basement) extension, Sauchiehall Street, Glasgow (now altered)
1919   E. O. Hoppe Studio House extensions and conversion, Little Hedgecourt, East Grinstead, Sussex
1920   Harold Squire Studio House, Glebe Place, Chelsea, London S.W.3
         Brooks Cottage alterations, Burgess Hill, Sussex
         F. Derwent-Wood/A. Blunt Studio House, Chelsea, London (project)
         Arts League of Service Studio Apartments, Chelsea, London (project)
         Theatre for Margaret Morris, Chelsea, London (project)

Publications:

On MACKINTOSH: books—*Charles Rennie Mackintosh* by Hermann Muthesius, Darmstadt 1902; *Haus eines Kunstfreundes* by Hermann Muthesius, Darmstadt 1902; *Charles Rennie Mackintosh* by Nikolaus Pevsner, Milan 1950; *Charles Rennie Mackintosh and the Modern Movement* by Thomas Howarth, London 1952, 1977; *Charles Rennie Mackintosh 1868–1928*, exhibition catalogue, by Thomas Howarth, Edinburgh 1953; *Charles Rennie Mackintosh and the Glasgow School of Art*, exhibition catalogue, by D. P. Bliss, Glasgow 1961; *Charles Rennie Mackintosh: Furniture* and *Ironwork and Metalwork*, exhibition catalogues, by H. Jefferson Barnes, Glasgow 1964; *Architectural Jottings by Charles Rennie Mackintosh*, edited by Archibald M.

Doak and Andrew McLaren Young, Glasgow 1968; *Charles Rennie Mackintosh* by Robert Macleod, London 1968; *Charles Rennie Mackintosh 1868–1928: Architecture, Design and Painting*, exhibition catalogue, by Andrew McLaren Young, Edinburgh 1968; *Charles Rennie Mackintosh*, exhibition catalogue, by Andrew McLaren Young and Eduard Sekler, Vienna 1969; *Charles Rennie Mackintosh as a Designer of Chairs* by Filippo Alison, Milan 1973, London 1974; *Mackintosh Watercolours*, exhibition catalogue, by Roger Billcliffe, London 1978; *Mackintosh and Architecture*, edited by J. Cooper, London 1978; *Charles Rennie Mackintosh: Complete Furniture, Furniture Drawings and Interior Designs* by Roger Billcliffe, Guildford, Surrey 1979.

It is becoming increasingly obvious that it is necessary to see the work of Charles Rennie Mackintosh as belonging firmly to the 20th century and not the 19th, as has been the tendency in the recent past. Though his international reputation rests primarily on the design for the Glasgow School of Art, which he began in 1897, it is worth remembering that the Library Wing of the building dates from 1907–1909, and it is the work on this second phase that shows him to be essentially of the Modern Movement.

The School of Art played an important part in his early years. He first enrolled there in 1884, at the age of 16, as an Evening Class student; he intended to study painting and drawing though he did in fact also attend classes in architecture. At the time he was apprenticed as a junior draughtsman, but the decision to enrol was his own. Under its progressive principal, Francis Newbery, the School had a well founded reputation for forward thinking, and the policy of creative individuality, based on a sound study of natural forms, was to Mackintosh's liking.

He had remarkable talents as a descriptive draughtsman, and this ability soon developed along more knowing lines when he became aware of the work of others through the newly established art and

design magazine *The Studio*, which first appeared in 1893. The influence of the decadent and somewhat sinister drawings of Aubrey Beardsley is clear, and so is that of the Dutchman Jan Toorop, but perhaps the most important influence, architecturally at least, was C.F.A. Voysey, who figured prominently in the earlier editions.

With his friend Herbert MacNair and the Macdonald sisters—he was later to marry Margaret Macdonald—Mackintosh evolved a poetic "spooky" curvilinear style that it is often convenient to link with the organic swirlings of European Art Nouveau. Known as "The Four," their most important group contribution was to the 1902 *International Exposition of Decorative Art* in Turin. Mackintosh is truly European and was far more widely known on the Continent, through reproductions of his work in various journals, than he was in England. His first real success was in Vienna where he was to exhibit his designs for a Tea Room at the 1900 *Wiener Sezession Exhibition.*

His social attitudes were influenced by the writings of John Ruskin, and like the critic he clearly saw the value of keeping a sketchbook in which he made notes of anything he might well incorporate into future designs. There is a growing interest in the note-books, and they are proving a reliable chronological source for his "thinking aloud" working method.

Mackintosh's first independent commission, a rather orthodox terraced house, dates from 1890; by the end of 1916 his professional architectural career was over. The emphasis on the Glasgow School of Art is justified, and it has become one of the most written about buildings in the whole story of architecture, but it is a mistake not to take full notice of the other work. The large private houses and certainly the tea rooms designed for Catherine Cranston have an individual vigour and charm that is very much the artist's trademark. The tea rooms in particular are important in their influence on subsequent interior design, for Mackintosh very deliberately relates the furniture and fittings to the overall larger scheme in a way that is definitely Modern. The cage-like furniture of the Willow Tea Rooms of 1903/04 is a good example of this total concept of integrated design. Again the ideas expressed were widely appreciated in Europe, and again the impact on the Viennese was considerable.

Late in his life, when he moved away from Scotland and dropped out of professional life, Mackintosh turned to the study of nature; his truly beautiful tinted flower drawings have a certain tartness not unlike that of the now popular Gustave Klimt and Egon Schiele.

To the end there is an appealing decadent quality about his work, and the subtle difference between it and the more obvious extrovert line of Art Nouveau is where the turn of the century problem lies. His concept of total environmental design belongs to the 20th Century, as the Glasgow School of Art makes clear. Its whole meaning is set firmly within the ethos of the Modern Movement.

—John Furse

MADIGAN, Col(in Frederick).

Australian. Born in Glen Innes, New South Wales, 22 July 1921. Educated at Inverell High School, New South Wales, 1932–37; Sydney Technical High School, 1938–39; Sydney Technical College, 1940, Dip.Arch. 1950. Served as a Sub-Lieutenant in the Royal Australian Navy, 1941–46. Married Ruby Miriam Court-Rice in 1950; son: Guy. Worked with his father, the architect F. J. Madigan, Inverell,

1950–54. In practice with Jack Torzillo and Maurice C. Edwards, in Sydney, since 1948: in partnership as Edwards Madigan and Torzillo, 1954–66, and, with David Briggs, as Edwards Madigan Torzillo and Briggs, 1966–77; Director, Edwards Madigan Torzillo Briggs International, since 1977; office established in Canberra, 1973. Recipient: First Prize, Sydney Rocks Area Competition, 1963; Sulman Medal, 1967, 1971, and Blackett Award, 1968, Royal Australian Institute of Architects; First Prize, Australian National Gallery Competition, Canberra, 1968; First Prize, Town Centre Competition, Mount Druitt, New South Wales, 1970; First Prize, High Court of Australia Competition, Canberra, 1973. Address: Edwards Madigan Torzillo Briggs International Pty. Ltd., 201 Pacific Highway, North Sydney, New South Wales 2060, Australia.

Works:

1967 Warringah Shire Library, New South Wales
1968 Library, Warren, New South Wales
1970 Plan for the town centre of Mount Druitt, New South Wales (competition project)
1971 Australian Government Office Centre, Woolloomooloo, New South Wales
Student Dormitories, Mitchell College of Advanced Education, Bathurst, New South Wales
1980 High Court of Australia, Canberra
1981 Australian National Gallery, Canberra

Publications:

On MADIGAN: books—*Ladenbauten* by Karl Kaspar, Stuttgart 1967; *Toward an Australian Architecture* by Harry Sowden, Sydney 1968; *Living and*

Partly Living: Housing in Australia by Ian McKay and others, Melbourne 1971; articles—"Domestic Architecture in Australia" in *Art and Australia* (Sydney), June 1971; "High Court of Australia" in *Law News* (Canberra), May 1978.

*

It is apparent that new purpose and new functions demand new forms which may even become recognized to be beautiful. By comparison functionless form denotes atrophy, purposelessness, inertia, a replica of provisional existence, a wasted potential—as we may now consider the effect of much of our built environment.

I tend to think of our architecture—the work I'm involved in—as being "inclusive" because it reveals its function and purpose readily, allowing each observer to participate in its workings.

The design process is from the inside out to achieve this proper "fit," and the physical expression reveals this desired intention.

"Exclusive" architecture, so called, can be the opposite to this.

In some instances, it develops from a pre-conceived idea (object or product oriented) unrelated to the free expression of the function, where the preconception dominates the form and the programmed requirements are forced into it. The necessary evolution, which at times demands additions or variations to this embalmed architecture, is difficult to formulate.

Participating architecture makes functional space (how it works) its best asset and gives priority to this event over and above what may be considered the conservative "luxury of fine finishes." Instead of the spurious solution by covering up structure that we see so much of in present day building, the nobility of primary materials, such as reinforced concrete,

Col Madigan: Australian National Gallery, Canberra, 1981

which makes the architecture, must be judged in relation to the spatial forms that it produces, unfolding the sense of a "luxury of space" and a release from the conservative containment of the box.

The proper and obvious development of theme is "how" the aesthetic is made relevant and valid. The art of architecture is measured by the exposure of a logical development of theme—and, depending on the degree of exposure, and its degree of consistency, so too can we judge the integrity of that expression.

One can enter a building and see its structure, services and function expressed. It immediately "includes" the visitor in the way it works.
—Col Madigan

Col Madigan is one of those blunt "Australian" Australians that people from other lands sometimes find difficult to understand. He is a pragmatist, but at the same time he is a social philosopher who holds deep convictions as to ideal relationships of man to man and man to buildings. Madigan states that his work is based on his belief in the potential of architecture to extend the freedom of man and to relate man to his context in time and place. He defines his position "as a Romantic one, governed by ideals." Fundamental to the aims of his architecture is the need for a clear communication between the building and those who use it. Consequently Madigan's buildings are articulate (though not always understood), involving, and explicit in their delineation of purpose.

The firm of Edwards, Madigan and Torzillo (and, since 1966, Briggs) was founded in 1954. By Australian standards it is a large firm, employing up to seventy staff members. The work is diversified, but its reputation is based primarily on civic buildings in and around Sydney and on the winning of the two major national competitions held in this country since the war: the Australian National Gallery (1968), and the High Court of Australia (1973), both for Canberra. While in the work of joint partnerships it is often difficult to discern the role of one man, the trademarks of Madigan's hand show clearly on projects with which he was closely involved.

The civic buildings, which include several libraries, are characterized internally by an expansive sense of space arising from the arrangement of particular use areas around a large central zone and from the connections established from room to room and level to level. Spaces are regulated in size and height to fit use, and the functional organization of the buildings shows clearly in the planning (which often indicates a potential for expansion).

Madigan employs contemporary technologies in an innovative manner to achieve the sought-after consonance of form and purpose, and does not hesitate to combine varied structural systems in one building. Structures and services are commonly left exposed. The confidence shown with structure is also evident in his handling of materials and in the obvious attention to detail and quality throughout the buildings. Organization, structure and services are further clarified visually by the extensive use of natural light from both high and low sources.

The external forms of the buildings clearly reflect the major design focus on the generation of specific internal spaces. This gives rise to boldly expressive exteriors with complex profiles of skylights, window shades, door canopies and roof overhangs. The High Court of Australia and the Australian National Gallery stand as focal buildings on adjacent sites on the edge of the lake in the Parliamentary Triangle in Canberra. The High Court is an obvious extension of concepts previously explored but here translated into the monumental language of the angular concrete forms of this imposing structure. With the design for the National Art Gallery Madigan adhered to his accustomed organization of internal space, but the freedom accorded previous buildings is disciplined by the imposed order throughout of a three-dimensional geometry based on the equilateral triangle: "the equilateral triangle is the nucleus of the structural code, dictating the dimensions and character of the building." In-situ concrete has allowed for a vig-

orous, but here a more restrained, modelling of the exterior.

Col Madigan is a concerned and creative architect who has accepted the challenges posed by his own philosophy. His sometimes controversial architecture has arisen out of his refusal to accept the mediocre and his determination to continually raise consumer expectations of building performance in all respects. Perhaps the highest compliment comes from John Andrews (who worked for the firm in his early years): "Col Madigan taught me what integrity in architecture is all about."

—Jennifer Taylor

MAILLART, Robert.

Swiss. Born in Berne, 6 February 1872. Educated at ETH: Eidgenössische Technische Hochschule, Zurich, 1890–94, Dip.Eng. 1894. Married; had two sons, one daughter. Worked for Pümpin and Herzog, Zurich, 1894–97, Städtisches Tiefbauamt, Zurich, 1897–99, and Froté and Westermann, Zurich, 1899–1902. In private practice as Maillart and Company, Zurich, 1902–12; practised in Russia, 1912–14; Principal, Maillart Engineering Office, Geneva, 1919 until his death, 1940; opened branches in Berne and Zurich, 1924. Lecturer, ETH, Zurich, 1911. Honorary Member, Royal Institute of British Architects, 1936; Honorary Member, Special Department for Bridge Builders, Schweizerischer Ingenieur und Architekten-Verein, 1940. *Died* (in Geneva) *5 April 1940.*

Works:

1901   Inn Bridge, Zuoz, Switzerland
1904   Thur Bridge, Billwil-Oberbüren, St. Gallen, Switzerland
1905   Rhine Bridge, Tavanasa, Graubünden, Switzerland (destroyed, 1927)
1908   Mushroom Structure, Zurich (project)
1910   Warehouse, Giesshübel, Zurich
1912   Grain Depot, Altdorf, Switzerland
       Aare Bridge, Aarburg, Switzerland
       Warehouse, Petrograd, Russia
1913   Muota Bridge, Vorder Ibach, Switzerland
       Shelter, Chiasso, Ticino, Switzerland
1914   Box Factory, Lancey, France
       Cable Factory, Villanueva y Geltrù, Spain
1920   Textile Hall, Sallent, Spain
       Benet Factory, Barcelona
       Arve Bridge, Marignier, France
1924   Rempen Aqueduct, Schwyz, Switzerland
       Schrahbach Bridge, Innerthal, Switzerland
       Flienglibach Bridge, Innerthal, Switzerland
       Ziggenbach Bridge, Waggital, Switzerland
1925   Magazzini Generali S.A., Chiasso, Ticino, Switzerland
       Chatelard Aqueduct, Wallis, Switzerland
       Val-Tschiel Bridge, Donath, Switzerland
1926   Sihl Post Office, Zurich
1930   Salginatobel Bridge, Schiers, Switzerland
       Landquart Bridge, Klosters, Switzerland
1931   Spital Bridge, Frutigen-Adelboden, Berne
       Ladholz Bridge, Frutigen, Berne
       Hombach Bridge, Schangnau, Berne
       Luterstalden Bridge, Schangnau, Berne
       Aqueduct, Gadmen, Berne
1932   Traubach Bridge, Habkern-Bohl, Berne
       Bohlbach Bridge, Habkern, Berne
       Rossgraben Bridge, near Schwarzenburg, Berne
       Tessin Bridge, Giubiasco-Sementina, Ticino, Switzerland
       Gorge-du-Trent Bridge, Wallis, Switzerland
       Quai Perdonnet, Vevey, Switzerland

1933   Screw factory, Gerlafingen, Switzerland
       Schwandbach Bridge, Berne
       Thur Bridge, Felsegg, St. Gallen, Switzerland
1934   Viaduct, Sarajevo, Yugoslavia
       Sitter Bridge, Haggen-Stein, St. Gallen, Switzerland
       Aare Bridge, Innertkirchen, Berne
       Toss Footbridge, Wülflingen-Winterthur, Zurich
1935   Rhine Bridge, Schaffhausen, Switzerland
       Rhine Bridge, near Schaffhausen, Switzerland
       Birs Bridge, Liesberg, Berne
       Aare Bridge, Berne
       Footbridge, Huttwill, Berne
1936   Twannbach Bridge, Twann-Ligerz, Berne
       Aarne Bridge, Vessey, Geneva
       Ticino Footpath, Someo, Ticino, Switzerland
       Quai Turrettini, Geneva
1937   Tara Bridge, Yugoslavia
       Gründlischwand Bridge, Berne
1938   Footbridge, Weissensteinstrasse, Berne
1939   Zementhalle, *Swiss Provinces Exhibition,* Zurich (with Hans Leuzinger)
       Footbridge, Altendorf, Switzerland
       Rhone Bridge, Aire-la-Ville-Peney, Geneva
1940   Simme Bridge, near Laubegg, Berne
       Simme Bridge, Garstatt, Berne
       Footbridge, Lachen, Altendorf, Switzerland
1947   Marchgraben Bridge, Saanenmöser, Berne (completed by others)
1954   Aire Bridge, Lancy, Geneva (completed by others)

Publications:

On MAILLART: books—*Circle* by Herbert Read and Morton Shand, London 1937, 1971; *Maillart Ingenieurbureau: Zurich und Berne,* Zurich and Berne 1938; *Robert Maillart* by M. Ros, Zurich 1940; *Space, Time and Architecture* by Sigfried Giedion, Cambridge, Massachusetts 1941; *Robert Maillart* by Max Bill, Zurich, 1948, 1969; *The World's Great Bridges* by H. Shirley-Smith, London 1964; *Bridges* by Derrick Beckett, London 1969; articles—"Robert Maillart: The Architecture of a Great Swiss Engineer" by Morton Shand in *RIBA Journal* (London), September 1938; "Early and Late Works of Robert Maillart" by Sigfried Giedion in *The Architect and Building News* (London), January 1948; "Brücken von Robert Maillart" by Walther Schmidt in *Bauen und Wohnen* (Zurich), vol. 4, no. 5, 1949; "En Memorie de Robert Maillart" by Pierre Tremblet in *Journal de Geneve,* April 1965; "Robert Maillart: Pioneer Extraordinary" by Martin Hunt in *Concrete* (London), October 1972; "Robert Maillart," special edition of *Bulletin Technique de Suisse Romande* (Lausanne), September 1973; "An Example of Structural Art: The Salginatobel Bridge of Robert Maillart" by David P. Billington in *Journal of the Society of Architectural Historians* (Philadelphia), March 1974; "Structural Art and Robert Maillart" by David P. Billington in *Architectural Science Review* (Melbourne), June 1977.

Robert Maillart was the Swiss engineer who, in a long career spanning the first forty years of this century, brought reinforced concrete design from its crude beginnings to its position as a major engineering material of great aesthetic and structural possibilities. When Maillart was young, reinforced concrete was in the hands of its inventors, men like Hennebique who made the breakthrough to the new material but could not see its potential except as a substitute for stone. When Maillart died, he was able to hand on the skill of designing beautifully in reinforced concrete to the talented men of the next generation, Nervi, Morandi, Candela, and others.

The discipline of structural engineering can easily lead to codified solutions, with columns calculated separately from beams and framing members seen as the structure that carries non-load-bearing members.

Robert Maillart: Salginatobel Bridge, Schiers, Switzerland, 1930

60mm thick cantilevering off the sides of the arches. Beautifully lit at night, the shell was a memorable advertisement for concrete.

Either by natural sympathy or pure chance, Maillart found that his approach to design coincided with that of many of the architects and artists of the modern movement. After the First World War, Maillart no longer used decoration on his bridges, and ten years later he abandoned the traditional massive stone faced approaches, for, he said, engineers had to choose "between mass or quality." The clear forms of his bridges, their understated elegance and their reinforced concrete construction endeared Maillart to the historians of the Modern Movement both in Europe and the United States, who placed Maillart firmly amongst the great designers of the first half of the 20th century.

—John Winter

MAKI, Fumihiko.
Japanese. Born in Tokyo, 16 September 1928. Educated at the University of Tokyo, 1948–52, B.Arch. 1952; Cranbrook Academy of Art, Bloomfield Hills, Michigan, 1952–53, M.Arch. 1953; Harvard Graduate School of Design, Cambridge, Massachusetts, 1953–54, M.Arch. 1954. Married Misao Matsumoto in 1960; children: Midori and Naomi. Designer, Skidmore, Owings and Merrill, New York, and Sert Jackson and Associates, Cambridge, 1954–56; Assistant Professor, Washington University, St. Louis, 1956–58; Fellow of the Graham Foundation, Chicago, 1958–60; Associate Professor, Washington University School of Architecture, 1960–62, and Harvard Graduate School of Design, 1962–65. Since 1965, Principal, Maki and Associates, Tokyo. Lecturer, Department of Urban Design, University of Tokyo, since 1965. Visiting Professor, Harvard Graduate School of Design, 1967–68, and University of California, Berkeley, 1970–71. Founder Member, Metabolism Group. Recipient: Japan Institute of Architects Award, 1963; Joint First Prize, United Nations Low-Cost Housing Competition, Lima, Peru, 1969; Mainichi Art Prize, Tokyo, 1969; 24th Art Prize, Minister of Education, Japan, 1973. Member, Japan Institute of Architects. Address: Maki and Associates, 3-6-2 Nihonbashi, Chuo-ku, Tokyo, Japan.

Works:

1960 Toyoda Memorial Hall, Nagoya University, Nagoya, Japan
Steinberg Arts Center, Washington University, St. Louis
1962 Memorial Hall, Chiba University, Chiba, Japan
1966 Sakai Sports Park Outdoor Sports Facilities, Sakai, Osaka
1967 Osaka Rinkai Center Building, Sakai, Osaka
Rissho University, stage I, Kumagaya, Japan
1968 Rissho University, stage II, Kumagaya, Japan
Hagoromo Station Area and Takaishi City Plan, Osaka
Korakuen Sports, Recreational and Entertainment Complex redevelopment, Tokyo
1969 Civic Center Building, Senri New Town, Osaka
Community Center, Mogusa Housing Estate, Tokyo
Hillside Terrace Apartment Complex, stage I, Tokyo
Master plan for the Marine Recreational Youth Complex, Tannowa, Osaka
1970 Sirogane Park House, Tokyo
Archaeological Museum, Senboku New Town, Osaka
Sumitomo Trading Company Office Feasibil-

To the tentative design ideas of the earliest reinforced concrete engineers, Maillart brought the power of lateral thinking and the ability to see the problem as a whole. For his multi-storey structures he invented the mushroom column, so that beams are not required and columns and slabs act together to resist the stresses upon them. In his bridges, he showed that an arch need not support a road deck: the entire structure can act as a whole.

The most memorable images of Maillart's work are his bridges, and in a series of some forty reinforced concrete bridges, plus many abandoned projects, he innovated and refined for forty years. The first mature design is the bridge at Zuoz, built in the first year of this century, in which the box girder is used for the first time, thus changing the structural role of the deck from that of passive thing to that of part of the structural whole. Looking at this bridge three-quarters of a century later, one is convinced of its early date only by the incontrovertible documentary evidence, for its image is twenty or thirty years ahead of its time. In the Tavanasa bridge, redundant spandrels to the box girder are omitted, creating triangular openings in the side that separate the arch from the deck—a development that reaches a logical conclusion in Aarburg bridge: the hollow spandrel has framing members across it, to ensure that deck and arch act together in a bridge that is very open

for its size. This schema reaches perfection in the 90m span Salginatobel Bridge, set in a beautiful natural landscape. Whereas the earlier bridges had solid, stone faced abutments, in the Salginatobel Bridge the row of vertical framing members under the roadway is continued under the approach spans, so that the entire construction is light: gone are the heavy abutments reminiscent of masonry arch bridges. Four years later, in the Schwandbach Bridge, the entire plan is curved to suit the U-turn on the road, and at this time Maillart built a series of bridges that twist, turn and slope to suit the road engineer's wishes: because the entire bridge structure was in each case working as a single structural element, Maillart was able to warp and bend it freely. In the Felsegg bridge, he obtained greater structural efficiency by pointing the arch, and in a small bridge over the Simme at Garstatt he abandoned the curved form and made the underside of each half of the bridge a straight line from springing to apex, a solution most enticing in its simplicity.

Although it was bridges that brought him fame, Robert Maillart busied himself with retaining walls, aqueducts, warehouses, and other engineering structures all his working life. His most famous building, the Zementhalle, built for the *Swiss Provinces Exhibition* in Zurich in 1939, is a pioneer shell structure with arches spanning some 15 metres and shells only

ity Study, Singapore
Master plan for Sea Park, Yokohama
1970/
75   Low-cost experimental housing, Lima, Peru
1971   Kanazawa Ward Office and Community Center, Yokohama
New town development, Kanazawa, Yokohama
Development plan for Kotesashi Housing Estate, Saitama, Japan
1972   St. Mary's International School, Tokyo
Kato Gakuen Elementary School, Numazu, Shizuoka Prefecture, Japan
Windsor House, Tokyo
Hiroo Homes, Towers, Apartments and Condominium, Tokyo
Osaka Prefectural Sports Center, Sakai, Osaka
Design of the *Japanese Painters Annual Exhibition,* Tokyo
N.I.R.A. Research Institute (project)
Development plan for the Yatsugatake Resort Community, Nagano, Japan
1972/
73   Sennan Residential and Recreation Community Development, Osaka
1972/
75   Kanazawa Housing Estate Development Plan, Yokohama
1973   Hillside Terrace Apartment Complex, stage II, Tokyo

Embassy of Japan, Chancellery and Ambassador's Residence, stage I, Brasilia
1974   Center for the School of Art and Physical Education, Tsukuba University, Ibaragi Prefecture, Japan
Noba Kindergarten, Noba Housing Estate, Yokohama
Toyota Memorial Museum and Guest Pavilion, Kuragaike, Toyota, Japan
Irish Embassy Chancellery, Tokyo
National Institute of Research Advancement Headquarters, Tokyo
Private research institute main office, Tokyo
1975   Embassy of Japan, Chancellery and Ambassador's Residence, stage II, Brasilia
Marine Life Park, *Expo '75,* Motobu, Okinawa
Chiba City Development Plan
Master plan for the Kota Kinabalu Sports Complex and Park, Malaysia
Development plan for the Shima Peninsula Resort Complex, Mie Prefecture, Japan
1976   Tsukuba University Center, Ibaragi Prefecture, Japan
School of Art Building, Tsukuba University, Ibaragi Prefecture, Japan
Austrian Embassy, Chancellery and Ambassador's Residence, Tokyo
1978   Hillside Terrace Apartment Complex, stage III, Tokyo
National Museum of Modern Art, Kyoto

Publications:

By MAKI: books—*Metabolism 1960,* with others, Tokyo 1960; *Investigations in Collective Form,* St. Louis 1964; *Movement Systems in the City,* Cambridge, Massachusetts 1965; translation of *Communitas* by Paul and Percival Goodman, Tokyo 1967; *What Is Urban Space?,* with Kawazoe Noboru, Tokyo 1970; article—"Some Thoughts on Collective Form" in *Structure in Art and Science,* edited by Gyorgy Kepes, New York 1965; "Dialogue: On Architecture," with Richard Meier, in *Space Design* (Tokyo), January 1978

On MAKI: articles—"Fumihiko Maki," special feature of *Architectural Record* (New York), August 1976.

Fumihiko Maki is a student of two cultures, and the value of his work stems from his successful fusion of both influences. After receiving an undergraduate degree from Japan's most prestigious architectural school, Tokyo University, Maki studied in America at Cranbrook and Harvard, and he has since taught at several American universities. He never lost touch with his Japanese acquaintances, however, and in 1960 he helped establish the Metabolism Group.

Along with many other young Japanese designers, Maki has maintained an obsessive interest in new technology and rational design. He uses modular systems in the planning phases and standardized

Fumihiko Maki. Kato Gakuen Elementary School, Numazu, Japan, 1972

building components in construction. His aesthetic is firmly placed in the modern age, and his favorite materials are metal, glass, and poured concrete. At the same time, however, Maki has not always resorted to the grandiose, monumental expressions of either his Japanese or American colleagues. With all of his keen interest in theory and technology, Maki is a populist, and his buildings display a warmth and sense of excitement and surprise that is rarely found in contemporary architecture.

At ground level even his most enormous buildings are scaled appropriately, and his several streetfront designs, notably the Austrian Embassy in Tokyo and his award winning Hillside Terrace Apartments, exhibit carefully manipulated shapes and textures that humanize their total effect. Both buildings are sculptural and plastic, with clean horizontal lines reinforcing the street patterns.

In a different setting, Maki's approach may become entirely different, attesting to his constant concern with contextual response. His recent design for Tsukuba University is massive, but it is intended to serve as an architectural pivot for the entire campus, which will soon be built on a large, open site. The huge, metalled walls suggest a modern, machine image, but they are carefully reduced, dimensionally, by the relatively small size of the glass blocks that comprise the curtain wall.

At the Toyota Memorial Museum, Maki's concerns are more traditional, and he incorporates directional changes that arise from the intersections of two conflicting grids to express a traditional Japanese spatial property: incompleteness of view. Not only can you not see far ahead or behind you in this very long progression, but although the museum is at the side of a very beautiful lake, only a very limited number of openings reveal views of the outside.

Fewer still are directed towards the lake, and the result is that those few have become sacred, and are cherished.

While Maki has rightly gained considerable notoriety as a theoretician, he has clearly not allowed his thinking to become clouded with esoteric ideas. He applies his belief in module, standardized parts and adaptability for change in a very utilitarian, pragmatic way. It is apparent that the thrust of his design attention is not the glorification of these concepts, but the successful employment of them to create inclusive, highly contextual architecture that is in strict accord with human, psychological preferences.

Maki has recently been studying traditional Japanese conceptual notions with increasing depth. Incorporating these ideas into his design work has added even more breadth to his architecture. Far ahead of that of many of his Japanese colleagues who continue to be intrigued solely with pure form, Maki's design work is remarkably mature, not merely in choice of concept, but in terms of compositional sophistication as well.

—Ching-Yu Chang

MAKOVECZ, Imre.

Hungarian. Born in Budapest, 20 November 1935. Educated at the Technical University of Budapest, under Dr. Károly Weichinger, György Szrogh, and György Jánossy, 1954–59, Dip.Arch. 1959. Served in the Hungarian Army, 1955, 1956. Married Marianne Szabó in 1961; children: Benjamin, Anna, and

Pál. Architect/Designer in the Bureau of Urban Studies, "Buvati," Budapest, 1959–62, and in SZÖV-TERV, Budapest, 1962–71; Chief of the Architectural Studio, VÁTTI, Budapest, 1971–77. Since 1977, Architect/Designer with the Forestière Organization, Budapest. Member of the Board of the Hungarian Architects Association. Exhibitions: *Biennale,* Venice, 1973; Hajduszoboszló, 1976; Dombóvár, 1978. Recipient: Ybl Prize, 1969. Address: Villányi ut. 8, 1114 Budapest, Hungary.

Works (all Hungary):

1963   Restaurant, Velence
       Restaurant, Balatonszepezd
1965   Hotel, Dombóvár
       Restaurant, Balatonszepezd
1967   Hotel, Sárospatak
       Restaurant, Balatonfured
1968   Restaurant, Tatabánya
       Department store, Letenye
       Department store, Csorna
1971   Department store, Sárospatak
1975   Belvedere, on the River Tisza, Töserdö
       Week-end house, Budapest
       Studio/Apartment, Budapest
1976   Cabana Hoffmann Tourist Hotel and Restaurant, near Budapest
1977   Mortuary Hall, Farkasrét Cemetery, Budapest (with Gábor Mezei)
1978   Collective Housing, Tokaj
       Excursion Centre, Visegrád

Publications:

By MAKOVECZ: books—*Architectural Forms and Movements,* privately printed 1970; *The Regulation*

Imre Makovecz: Mortuary Hall, Farkasrét Cemetery, Budapest, 1977

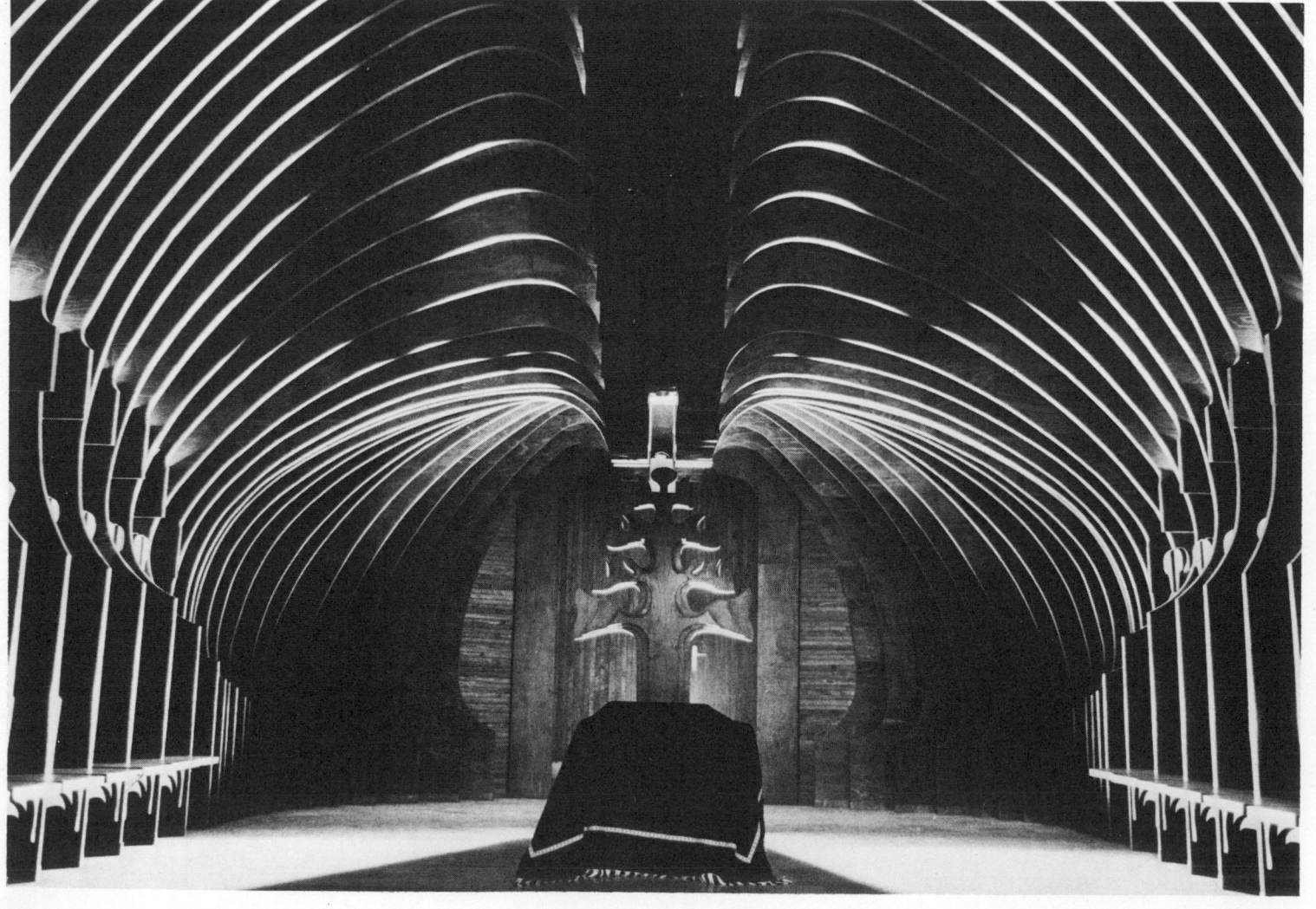

of Private Competitions, Budapest 1972, 1974; *Art Almanach,* Budapest 1977, 1978; articles—in *Magyar Építőmüvészet* (Budapest), April 1966; *Magyar Építőmüvészet* (Budapest), January and February 1968; *Magyar Építőmüvészet* (Budapest), January 1969; *DBZ* (Gutersloh, Germany), May 1971; *Magyar Építőmüvészet* (Budapest), June 1971; *Magyar Építőmüvészet* (Budapest), March 1972; *Müvészet* (Budapest), March and April 1972; *Müvészet* (Budapest), June and December 1973; *Müvészet* (Budapest), August 1975.

On MAKOVECZ: books—*Imre Makovecz* by Attila Komjáthy, Budapest 1977; *Imre Makovecz* by János Frank, Budapest 1979; articles—by Ferenc Merényi in *Magyar Építészet,* 1967; by Ferenc Mendele in *Magyar Építőmüvészet* (Budapest), February 1968; by Mihály Kubinszky in *Magyar Építőmüvészet* (Budapest), February 1970; by Jenö Szendröi in *Magyar Építészet* (Budapest), 1972; by Mihály Kubinszky in *Építészeti lexikon* (Budapest), 1978.

Architecture in a socialist country is subject to demands for a constant raising in the standard of living and to the demands of centralized planning which dictates a whole range of approaches. The work of Imre Makovecz fits only marginally into this framework. Much as he seeks to fulfil general requirements, he searches, equally, for personal solutions to particular circumstances, solutions directly linked to his creed as a designer.

His work is multi-coloured, like a mountain crystal. The facets it shows are as multifarious as the rigorous principals which underlie it. With his passion for the organic architecture of Frank Lloyd Wright and for the anthroposophy of Rudolf Steiner, Makovecz refuses a simple repetition of forms and materials to create, in each of his buildings, a specific work that is at once personal and proper to its site.

Makovecz's architecture resounds with echoes of the Hungarian "pousta," transposing into contemporary terms the traditions of the country (as in the week-end house, Budapest; or the restaurant at Tatabanya). At the same time it remains aesthetically linked to the new physical, economic and political conditions of the country (for example, the Belvedere on the River Tisza).

Makovecz searches for forms that delimit and give character to the interior or exterior space. In this endeavour so much can come into play—from simple building materials to the nature of the direct participation by the users. A good example of this kind of concern is the impressive oak ceiling structure in the Mortuary Hall at the Farkasret Cemetery, Budapest, which creates an exceptional consonance with the vigil of grief.

A designer who is extremely conscientious in his duty to his country and to his people, Markovecz is not afraid to struggle for the sake of his creations, preferring, rather than simply fulfilling quantitative needs, to remain honest with himself and his fundamental principles. His work is a quest for communication between human beings, a communication that can only come about if architecture transcends the realm of the functional and fulfils its psychological and educational obligations.

—Zdravko Natchev

MALLET-STEVENS, Robert.
French. Born in Paris, 24 March 1886. Educated at the Ecole Spéciale d'Architecture, Paris. Served in the French Air Force, 1914–18. In private practice as an architect/interior decorator, Paris, from 1920. Professor, Ecole Spéciale d'Architecture, Paris, from 1924. Founder, with Chareau, Barbe, Herbst, Jourdain and Perriand, Union des Artistes Modernes, Paris, 1929. Exhibitions: *Salon d'Automne,* Paris,

1912, 1922; Ghent, 1913; London, Lyons and Brussels, 1914; San Francisco, 1915; *Exposition des Arts Décoratifs,* Paris, 1925. *Died* (in Paris) *in 1945.*

Works:

1914 Workman's house, Saint Cloud, Paris (project)
1922 Electricity Transformer Station (project)
Aéro-Club de France Pavilion, *Salon d'Automne,* Paris
1923 Bookshop, Paris
Vicomte de Noailles Villa, Hyères, Var, France (with others)
Street facades for the Cafés du Brésil, Paris
1924 Film sets for Marcel l'Herbier's *L'Inhumaine*
Poiret Chateau, Mezy, Seine et Oise, France
Hotel des Roches Noires reconstruction, Trouville, France
1925 Pavilion of Tourism, *Exposition des Arts Décoratifs,* Paris (with Poulenc, Honneger, Léger, and Robert Delaunay)
Alfa Romeo Building, rue Marbeuf, Paris
1926 House, Ville d'Avray, France
Freres Martel House, Paris
House, Boulogne-sur-Seine, Paris
1926/
27 Houses, rue Mallet-Stevens, Paris
1927 Mallet-Stevens House, Paris
1928 Casino, Saint Jean de Luz, France
1929 Apartment building, rue Mechain, Paris
House, Pernambuco, Brazil
Offices for the P. F. Department Stores, Paris
Bally Shoe Shop, Boulevard de la Madeleine, Paris
1930 Municipal Theatre, Grasse, Alpes Maritimes, France
Government Distillery, Istanbul, Turkey
Delza Shop, rue de la Paix, Paris
Shop front, rue d'Assas, Paris
Layouts for the *Exposition des Artistes Modernes,* Paris
1931 C. House, Roubaix, France
T House, Sceaux, France
House/Studio for the master glassmaker Barillet, Paris
1934 Houses, Roubaix, France
1935/
36 Fire station, rue Mesnil, Paris
1937 Palais d'Electricité, *World's Fair,* Paris
Olympic Stadium, Paris (project)

Publications:

By MALLET-STEVENS: books—*A Modern City,* London 1922; *Pour l'Art Moderne, Cadre de la Vie Contemporaine,* Paris 1934; *Grandes Constructions,* Paris 1928; *Vitraux Modernes,* Paris 1937; articles—"Architecture Moderne" in *L'Architecture d'Aujourd'hui* (Paris), November 1932; "Architecture d'Aujourd'hui" in *L'Architecture d'Aujourd'hui* (Paris), no. 6, 1935; "Union des Artistes Modernes" in *L'Architecture d'Aujourd'hui* (Paris), July 1937; "L'Esprit des Expositions" in *L'Architecture d'Aujourd'hui* (Paris), no. 1/2, 1940.

On MALLET-STEVENS: books—*Robert Mallet-Stevens, Architecte* by Alberto Sartoris, Paris 1930; *Robert Mallet-Stevens: Dix Années de Réalisations en Architecture et Décoration* by M. Raynal, Paris 1930; *Mallet-Stevens* by Léon Moussinac, Paris 1931; articles—"Architects and Their Offices: Robert Mallet-Stevens" in *Architectural Record* (New York), October 1928; "House at Roubaix, France, by Robert Mallet-Stevens" in *Architect and Building News* (London), 29 June 1934; "Robert Mallet-Stevens" by A. Bluysen in *L'Architecture d'Aujourd'hui* (Paris), January 1945; "Mallet-Stevens" by Guy Habasque in *L'Oeil* (Paris), no. 60, 1959; "Wohnhauser an der rue Mallet-Stevens" in *Werk* (Zurich), February 1965; "Le Corbusier, Mallet-Stevens and Some Others" by Michel Lugnier in *Architecture Francaise* (Paris), October 1975; "Mallet Stevens: A Cross-Section of His Architecture" by Dominique Deshoulieres, Hubert Jeanneau and others in *Architecture Mouvement Continuité* (Paris), March 1977.

Robert Mallet-Stevens was the most successful of the French rationalist school of architects in the years 1920–30. In fact, one could almost talk of that period in architecture in France as the Era of Mallet-Stevens. During fourteen years of activity he completed a score of apartment buildings, various exhibition halls, half a dozen important public buildings, and shops, cafes and restaurants as well as interior design schemes and furniture. He also designed film sets.

Perhaps his popularity had something to do with the fact that, among his colleagues and among the intellectuals who lived and worked in Paris at that time, he was a "true Frenchman"—or perhaps it had something to do with the fact that he was not a disciple of Le Corbusier! Nevertheless, he received a stimulating training precisely because of the international Parisian milieu. And even if he was not in agreement with Le Corbusier's polemic, he greatly admired his work. His upbringing, too, had brought him into early contact with artistic and aesthetic matters: his father was an art expert; his uncle, Stoclet, was the silent partner in Josef Hoffmann's master work in Brussels. Hoffmann and Mackintosh were two strong early influences, and at about the same time he discovered Japanese architecture. He studied at the Ecole Spéciale d'Architecture in Paris, but his real training was at the *Salons d'Automne* of 1912–14. There he met and came to know the work of young architects and designers like Jourdain, Chareau and Bourgeois. After the war, Mallet-Stevens continued to study and become involved in international artistic events. Well-informed, cultured and tolerant, he typified the European intellectual of the 1920's.

His approach to his work was also characterized by the same breadth of vision: he did not regard an architect as someone withdrawn, hemmed in by absolutes. For each important commission he formed a team. For the Noailles Villa in Hyères, for instance, he called on Jourdain, Chareau, Ruhlmann, Bourgeois, Guevrékian and van Doesburg. As a result of his friendship with van Doesburg he made the important discovery of De Stijl and of Oud: he discovered Dutch culture. He became friends with Dudok, who influenced him strongly, especially in his later work. Contemporary music and painting were also components of his culture and influences on his architecture. Poulenc, Honneger, Léger and Robert Delaunay collaborated with him on the Pavilion of Tourism at the 1925 *Exposition des Arts Décoratifs.*

With his good technical training, Mallet-Stevens was an expert in reinforced concrete and metal frames. His work is impregnated with his awareness of current cultural movements; it shows a mastery of modern techniques, even if it occasionally presents superficial solutions. As he himself said, he "preferred to unify the aspect of the facades," for he believed that "volumes are more important than constructional details." The characteristic "play of volumes" of his architecture resulted from this approach, influenced no doubt by his first experiments in the cinema.

In 1929 Mallet-Stevens was one of the founders of the Union des Artistes Modernes, and throughout the 1930's he struggled sincerely for an international architecture at a time when nationalist and racist ideas were taking hold in almost the whole of Europe.

—Luciana Miotto-Muret

MANGIAROTTI, Angelo.
Italian. Born in Milan, 26 February 1921. Educated at the Milan Polytechnic School of Architecture, 1945–48, Dip.Arch. 1948. In partnership with Bruno Morassutti, Milan, 1955–60. In private practice, Milan, since 1960. Consultant to Le Porte Echappement Universal, La Chaux de Fonds, Switzerland, 1955–68, CGE, Milan, 1959, Alfa Romeo, Milan, 1960, and Electrolux, Stockholm, 1961. Visiting Professor, Institute of Design, Illinois Institute of Technology, Chicago, 1953–54; Lecturer, Istituto Superiore di Disegno Industriale, Venice, 1963–64; Visiting Professor, University of Hawaii, Honolulu, 1970, Ecole Polytechnique Federale, Lausanne, 1975, University of Adelaide, and South Australian Institute of Technology, Adelaide, 1976, and University of Sao Paulo, 1978. Exhibitions: *La Casa Abitata,* Palazzo Strozzi, Florence, 1965; University of Zurich, 1966; Delft, Holland, 1966; *Ten Italian Architects,* Los Angeles County Museum of Art, 1967; *Exposicion Internacional de la Vivienda,* Santiago, Chile, 1972. Recipient: Olimpiadi della Cultura Boys' Club Prize, Milan, 1952; Economic Development Center Prize, Trieste, 1953; *Domus* Prize, 1956; Gold Medal, Villa Comunale dell'Olmo, Como, 1957; Award of Distinction, AITEC (Associazione Italiana Tecnico Economica del Cemento), 1962; IN-ARCH Regional Prize, Lombary, 1963; Prize for Industrial Design, Nazionale del Golfo de la Spezia, 1963; Associazione Italiana Prefabbricati Prize, 1972. Address (office): Via Cappuccio 7, 20123 Milan, Italy.

Works:

1953 Master plan for Cervia, Milano Marittima, Ravenna (competition project)
1953– Multi-use furniture in moulded plywood, bronze, and hammered metals; clocks, sewing machines, bronze vases, and other household items
1954 Professional Studio, Perrysburg, Ohio (project)
1955 Skyscraper, Port of Genoa (project; with Bruno Morassutti)
 Tomb, Udine
1957 Matris Misericordiae Church, Baranzate, Milan (with Bruno Morassutti)
 3 houses, San Martino di Castrozza, Trento, Italy (with Bruno Morassutti)
 INA-CASA Housing Development, Feltre, Milan
 INA-CASA Housing Development, Ferrara, Italy
 Clinic and Nursery, Udine (project; with Bruno Morassutti)
 Club 44 interiors, La Chaux de Fonds, Switzerland (with Bruno Morassutti)
1958 Warehouse, Padua (with Bruno Morassutti and Aldo Favini)
 Apartment building, Via Fezzan, Milan (project; with Bruno Morassutti)
1959 Apartment building, Via Gavirate, Milan (with Bruno Morassutti)
 House restoration, La Chaux de Fonds, Swit-

zerland (with Bruno Morassutti; original building by Le Corbusier, 1914/16)
1960 Apartment building, Via Quadronno, Milan (with Bruno Morassutti)
 Sports Stadium, Geneva (competition project; with Bruno Morassutti and Aldo Favini)
1961 Furniture shop, Corsico, Milan
 Water Tower and Reservoir, near Rome (project; with Aldo Favini)
 Residential complex, Piombino, Livorno
1962 Car Testing Wind Tunnel (project)
 SIAG Industrial Complex, with housing, Marcianise, Caserta, Italy
 Società Poretti Warehouse, Mestre, Venice
 Industrial building, Arese, Italy (project)
1963 Italsider Steel Pavilion, *International Fair of the Sea,* Genoa
 Industrial building, Cesena, Forli, Italy (project)
1964 Società Elmag Building, Monza, Milan
 School and houses in pre-fabricated metal components (project)
1964/
 65 House conversion and interiors, Camogli, Genoa
1965 Policentro Megastructure (project)
 Pre-fabricated houses in sheet zinc (project)
 Overpass, Piazza della Republica, Milan (project)
1966 Industrial building, Rovellasca, Como
1967 CUB 8 Interwall
1968 Pre-fabricated structure in prestressed concrete for a tile factory, Salerno (project)

Angelo Mangiarotti: Office Building, Snaidero Industrial Complex, Mayano del Friuli, Udine. 1978

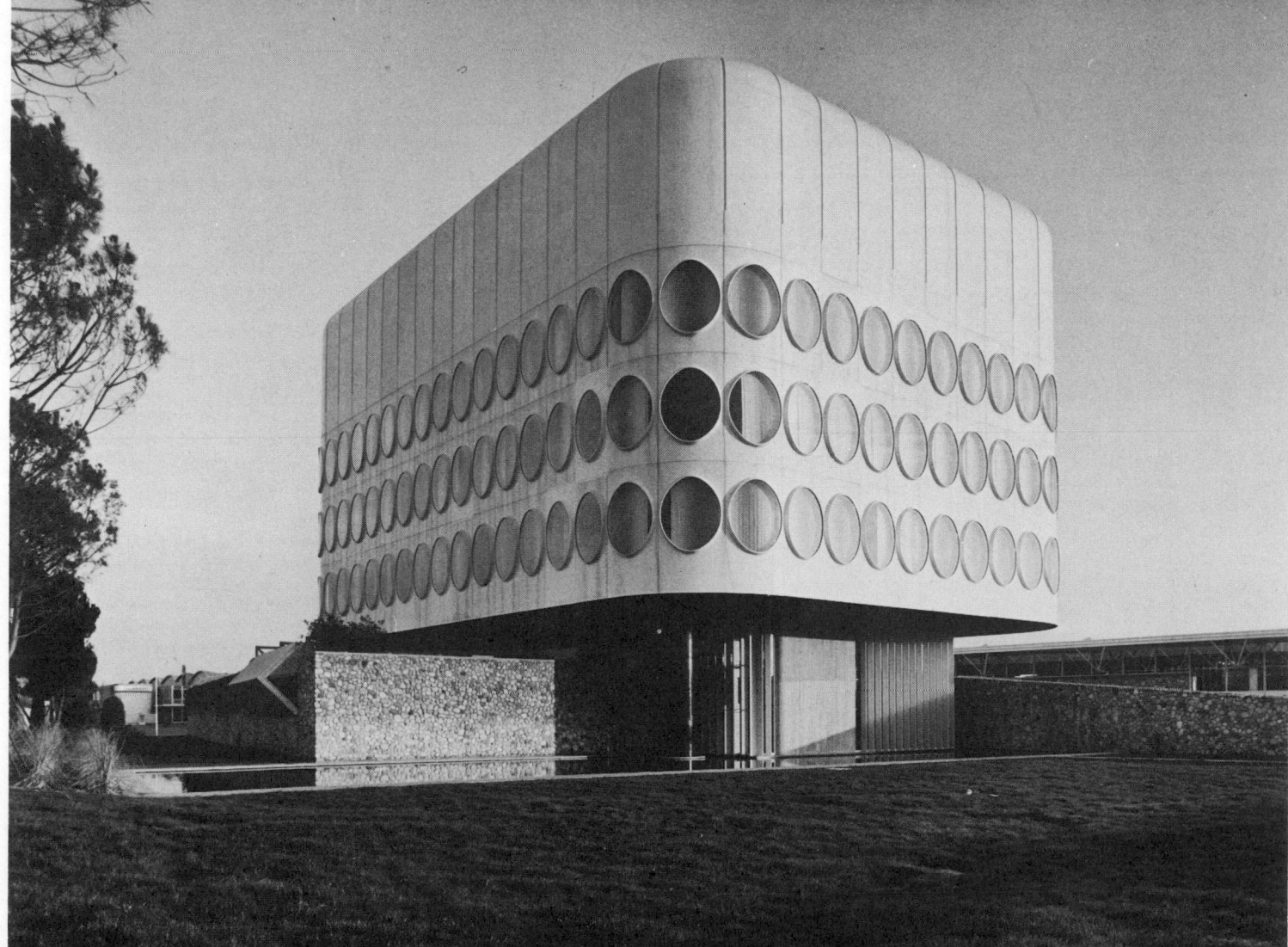

House, Marina di Pietrasanta, Lucca, Italy
House, Piadena, Cremona, Italy
Commissioner of Automobiles Office, Dome-
    gliara, Verona
Design of the *Furniture Exhibition,* Corsico,
    Milan
1969 Industrial building in prestressed concrete,
        Alzata Brianza, Como
1971 Villa, Bardolino, Verona
        Tourist Center, Murlongo, Verona
        Villa, Somma Lombardo, Varese, Italy
        Industrial structure in prestressed concrete
1972 Apartment building, Monza, Milan
1973 Pre-fabricated industrial-use structure in
        reinforced concrete (project)
1975 *Fiera di Padova* Headquarters, Padua (pro-
        ject; with others)
1976 Pre-fabricated industrial-use structure in
        prestressed concrete
1977 Apartment building, Arosio, Como
1978 Snaidero Industrial Complex, Mayano del
        Friuli, Udine

Publications:

By MANGIAROTTI: articles—numerous in
Domus (Milan), 1949–78; *Arts and Architecture* (Los
Angeles), 1953–70; *L'Architecture d'Aujourd'hui*
(Paris), 1953–73; *Casabella* (Milan), 1955–78;
L'Oeil (Paris), 1956–72; *Architectural Forum* (New
York), 1959–63; *Bauen und Wohnen* (Zurich),
1959–77; *Moebel Interior Design* (Stuttgart), 1960–
75; *L'Industria Italiana del Cemento* (Rome), 1963–
77; *Ottagono* (Milan), 1966–78; *Interni* (Milan),
1967–77; *Casa Vogue* (Milan), 1968–77; etc.

On MANGIAROTTI: books—*Italian Contemporary Architecture,* London 1952; *New Furniture,* edited by Gerd Hatje, Stuttgart 1952, 1956; *Architettura Moderna in Milano,* Milan 1964; *Angelo
Mangiarotti,* Tokyo 1965; *World Architecture,* volume 2, edited by John Donat, London 1965; *Architettura Italiana Contemporanea* by Alberto
Galardi, Milan 1967; *Pannelli di Copertura Prefabbricati* by Alberto dal Lago, Milan 1972; *Progettare
un Edificio* by Ludovico Quaroni, Milan 1977; *Angelo Mangiarotti: Il Processo del Costruire* by Enrico
D. Bona, Milan 1979; articles—"Architettura recen-
tissime di Angelo Mangiarotti" by Giulia Veronesi
in *Zodiac* (Milan), no. 11, 1963; "The Work of Angelo Mangiarotti and Bruno Morassutti" in *Architectural Design* (London), March 1964; "The 'Avan-
guardia' di Mangiarotti" by Pier Carlo Santini in
Ottagono (Milan), March 1971; "Angelo Mangiarotti" in *Architecture + Urbanism* (Tokyo), September 1974.

After a period spent in a progressive search for simplification of the language of the modern architectural tradition—mainly that of rationalism and particularly that of Mies van der Rohe—Angelo
Mangiarotti has concentrated on working out a fluid
formal language of his own. He has, at the same
time, defined articulate modular principles for pre-
fabricated industrial buildings, so constructed that
they can be arranged in complex, plastically significant forms.

His research concerns the working out of a construction methodology that is a reflection of his own
philosophical program for private and social life, one
founded on a search for a new and properly motivated relationship between man and his environment, and this research has constantly moulded the
actual design of his architecture: he has tried to form
a single, coherent whole in accordance with his basic
principles.

Mangiarotti modulates space and surfaces in
fluent, almost musical movements—as in the sensitive handling of interior space in his houses, for example the old house at Camogli, in which horizontal
and vertical lines create spatial relations of a restful
and agreeable clarity.

In his other buildings, too, Mangiarotti makes use
of a delicate spatial modulation and employs components from the local countryside, making his architecture almost a scaled-down part of its surroundings. The Steel Pavilion at the entrance to Genoa
Harbor, built for the *International Fair of the Sea,*
has an open framework, a platform with a hollow-
moulded roof of great plastic delicacy supported
above it on steel columns. Beneath the exhibition
platform, half underground, there is a hall for film
shows, conferences and meetings. The Società Elmag
Building is an example of Mangiarotti's total use of
pre-fabrication: the three elements (pillar, rafter,
roof-tile) are fitted into one another without expansion joints in a structural assembly that is light and
organic. The SIAG Industrial Complex, which includes residential buildings, uses as its basic building
material the panels produced by SIAG themselves,
by a secret process, from a residue (canapulo) of the
hemp that is grown locally. The proportions of the
buildings depend on the measurements of the panel,
in a coherent design that makes use both of the
environmental features and of the most advanced
experimental research: the solution is simple and
extremely flexible and at the same time formally acceptable.

The same methods of working and the same flexibility and delicacy are revealed in his residential
buildings, as are the means for almost indefinite
practical expansion. Mangiarotti's industrial design
shows the same characteristics—simplicity, refinement, flexibility—whether he is designing furniture,
interiors, or such useful objects as the clock in the
Secticon series.

—Lara-Vinca Masini

MANSFELD, Al(fred).

Israeli. Born in St. Petersburg, now Leningrad,
Russia, 2 March 1912; emigrated to Israel, 1935.
Educated at the Technische Hochschule, Berlin,
1931–33, and at the Ecole Spéciale d'Architecture,
Paris, under Auguste Perret, 1933–35. Served as a
Second Lieutenant in the Israeli Army, 1948–49.
Married Bella Reinin in 1946; children: Michael and
Yoel. In private practice, Haifa, since 1938: in part-
nership with Munio Weinraub, 1951–59. Head,
Northern Area Department, Ministry of Building,
Tel Aviv, 1949–50. Senior Lecturer, 1949–70, and
since 1970 Professor of Architecture, Technion: Is-
rael Institute of Technology, Haifa. President, Israel
Institute of Architects, 1968–70. Exhibitions: *Forms
from Israel,* American Federation of Arts, New
York, 1958; Museum of Modern Art, Haifa (one-
man), 1963; *Architecture in Israel,* Israel Museum,
Jerusalem, 1966, and Tel Aviv Museum, 1967; *Architecture of Museums,* Museum of Modern Art,
New York, 1968; *Bauhaus,* Musée National d'Art
Moderne, Paris, 1969. Recipient: First Prize, Israel
Museum Competition, 1959; First Prize, Lod Airport Competition, Tel Aviv, 1962; Israel Prize for
Architecture, 1964; First and Second Prizes, Jerusalem Town Hall Competition, 1964; Gold Plaquette
for Foreign Architects, Bund Deutscher Architekten, 1966. Member, Akademie der Künste, Berlin,
1970. Address: Al Mansfeld, Architect, 5 Keller
Street, Haifa, Israel.

Works:

1951 Cultural Centre, Kiryat Haim, near Haifa
        (with Munio Weinrabu)
        Commemorative monument, Kiryat Haim,
        near Haifa (with Munio Weinraub)
1953 Housing development, Mount Carmel, Haifa
        (with Munio Weinraub)
1956 Institute for Hebrew Studies, Hebrew Univer-
        sity of Jerusalem (with Munio Weinraub)

Centre for the Re-education of the Blind,
        Haifa (with Munio Weinraub)
        Kiryat Eliahu Housing Development, Haifa
        (with Munio Weinraub)
1957 Hydrotechnical Institute, Technion, Haifa
        (with Munio Weinraub)
        Mansfeld Residence, Mount Carmel, Haifa
        Ramat Hadar Residential Quarter, Haifa
        (with Munio Weinraub)
        S. S. Israel and S. S. Theodor Herzl interiors
        (with Dora Gad)
1960 University of Nigeria, Nsukka (project, partly
        executed; with Dani Havkin)
        Library, Trinity College, Dublin (competition
        project; with Dani Havkin and J. Polatsek)
1962 Lod Airport, Tel Aviv (competition project;
        with Dani Havkin)
        Mausoleum, Rangoon, Burma (project)
1963 Centre for Nuclear Studies, Technion, Haifa
        Israel Pavilion, *World's Fair,* New York
        (competition project)
1964 *S. S. Shalom* interior (with Dora Gad)
1965 Israel Museum, Jerusalem (with Dora Gad)
1972 Mount Carmel Auditorium, Haifa (with Dani
        Havkin)
1978 Shaar Ha'aliya Housing (250 units), Haifa
        (with Dani Havkin)
        Kindergarten, Shaar Ha'aliya, Haifa
        Town Hall and Civic Precinct, Jerusalem
        (with Dani Havkin)

Publications:

By MANSFELD: book—*Designing for Growth and
Change,* Haifa 1976; articles—"Meinungen zu Mies
van der Rohe, Al. Mansfeld" in *Baumeister* (Munich), March 1966; "Architecture in Israel—Past
and Present" in *Technion Magazine* (Haifa), February 1970; "Building a New Land" in *Tarbut* (New
York), Summer 1970; essay in *Design: Umwelt wird
in Frage gestellt,* Berlin 1970; "Kann der Designer
die Welt retten?" in *Architektur und Wohnen* (Hamburg), no. 2, 1973; "Building a New Land: Architecture in Israel" in *International Technion Diary 1977,*
Haifa 1977.

On MANSFELD: books—*Strukturformen der Modernen Architektur* by Curt Siegel, Munich 1960; *Industriebau* by Walter Henn, Munich 1962; *Balkone*
by F. Schuster, Stuttgart 1962; *Neues Bauen in der
Welt* by Udo Kultermann, Tubingen 1965; *House
Plans* by the editors of the *Daily Mail,* London 1965;
The Aesthetics of Contemporary Architecture by
Michel Ragon, Neuchatel 1967; *Betonkonstruk-
tionen in Hochbau* by P. G. Wieschemann and K.
Gatz, Munich 1968; *Mehrzweck-Gebaüde für Gesell-
schaftliche Funktionen* by Friedeman Wild, Munich
1970; *A History of Building Types* by Nikolaus
Pevsner, London 1975; articles—"Centre de Culture
à Kiryat Haim" in *Techniques et Architecture*
(Paris), January 1951; "S. S. Israel and S. S. Theodor
Herzl" in *Architectural Review* (London), September
1957; "Israel's First Passenger Ship" in *Interiors*
(New York), September 1958; "Israeli Culture" in
Architectural Forum (New York), February 1961;
"Dublin University Library Competition" in *Archi-
tect and Building News* (London), June 1961; "A
Visit to Israel" in *Concrete Quarterly* (London),
July/September 1963; "L'Art en Israel" in *Les Let-
tres Francaises* (Paris), August 1963; *L'Architecture
d'Aujourd'hui* (Paris), March 1965; "Profilo dell'ar-
chitetto Alfred Mansfeld" in *L'Architettura* (Rome),
May 1965; "Israel" by Dore Ashton in *Arts and
Architecture* (Los Angeles), October 1965; "The Art
That History Shaped—A Report from Israel" by
Katharine Kuh in *Saturday Review* (New York),
January 1966; "The Planning and Architecture of
the Israel Museum" by Willem Sandberg in *Museum*
(Unesco: Paris), January 1966; special issue of *Koku-
sai-Kentiku* (Tokyo), May 1967; "Architectuur in
Israel" in *Cement* (Amsterdam), March 1969; "Var-
ious Buildings by Al Mansfeld" in *Kindai-Kenchiku*

Al Mansfeld: Israel Museum, Jerusalem, 1965

(Tokyo), April 1970; "Alfred Mansfeld: Tre Opere Communitarie" in *L'Architettura* (Rome), March 1971; "Leisure Centre and Multi-Purpose Auditorium, Mount Carmel" in *Architecture + Urbanism* (Tokyo), May 1976; "Shaar Ha'aliya, Haifa" in *AC: International Asbestos and Cement Review* (Zurich), April 1977.

CREDO

I believe in the architect's responsibility towards society, his "ultimate customer" (although the immediate client does not always represent the real needs of society).

I believe that this responsibility results in the conception that design is indivisible, and therefore:

that there is no inherent difference in the act of designing a city, a building, a chair or a spoon, and that the "complete" architect should aspire to universality in this sense;

that in our age of narrow specialization an architect should use his creative forces in order to re-establish the disrupted balance between matter and spirit, and to integrate, humanize and harmonize man's heterogeneous surroundings;

that dreams are the basis of reality and that expediency is not equivalent with practicality;

that true practicality is at the root of any technological development, and that therefore architecture will be decisively influenced by the process of industrialization;

that this development, far from restricting architecture, will produce new systems and values and provide the artist with new tools to create new forms and dimensions;

that an architect should use these tools not only to provide the logical and efficient physical framework for the man of today, but also to create joy and delight in man's visual environment and harmonious space-patterns around him;

that this spatial and plastic order can best be achieved through the use of three-dimensional mathematical elements and systems, and through a combination of a scientist's sobriety and an artist's intuition and vision.

that permanence and transience in architecture are reconcilable twin-phenomena and that our built environment should be structured in such a way that the resulting space-order, in spite of being "complete in itself" should remain open for growth and change;

that such open design-systems are a more appropriate expression of our epoch than architectural "frozen music" compositions.

that the architect's calling is to join, to fit, to create order and to relate, not to separate, to disrupt, to set apart or to cause gaps.

I believe in true team-work, where every member of the team contributes his special knowledge and talent towards a harmonized whole; but I also believe in an undivided responsibility vested in the architect as the leader of the team

I do not believe that the creative tasks and responsibility of the architect can be delegated to committees or "technical offices." I do believe that much good can come out of a close collaboration between the architect and imaginative and enlightened public bodies qualified to formulate the true needs of society.

—Al Mansfeld

Al Mansfeld has practised architecture for the past four decades in Haifa, but he received his formal architectural training in Berlin and Paris, and a touch of European elegance and sophistication has always been evident in his work. This was perhaps to be expected when, in the 1950's, he was in partnership with the late Munio Weinraub, himself a product of the Bauhaus in its Mies van der Rohe phase; but these characteristics carry over into his later association with Israeli-born Dani Havkin, and even to his present-day "Team Mansfeld," a group of young and talented designers—a category he has always attracted to his office, where they found rich opportunities for creative interaction. Mansfeld believes in "true team-work, where every member of the team contributes his special knowledge and talent towards the harmonized whole;" but this is obviously no egalitarian, unstructured team, for he also believes in the undivided responsibility and leadership of the architect.

While there has been variety and a natural evolution in the character of Mansfeld's output, it has always been marked by distinctiveness, which sets it apart from the general run of contemporary Israeli work. It has, moreover, been characterized in recent years by a certain consistency of architectural approach, which derives not only from Mansfeld's design personality, but also from the discipline of a guiding philosophy. Mansfeld's "Credo" casts the architect in a universalistic role, the "humanizer and harmonizer" of man's surroundings, responding to the needs of society as the "ultimate customer." Lately he has attempted to translate the somewhat lyrical images of this credo into the more hardedged, precise terms of an architectural theory: this he calls his structuralist approach, utilising open, cumulative design systems as a way of designing for growth, change and uncertainty.

This hierarchical and open-ended approach to design replaced the finiteness of his earlier work: the massive Ramat Hadar flats, with their Corbusian overtones, and the striking Kiryat Eliahu high-rise tower, an exercise in structural formalism. The new approach is first evident in his Israel-prize winning design (with Dora Gad) for the Israel Museum in Jerusalem with its articulated and elegant pavilions; it may also be seen in his multi-purpose auditorium for Haifa, the later development of the Jerusalem town hall project (as yet unbuilt), and the Shaar Ha'aliya housing scheme for Haifa. The theory, as it is here demonstrated, is not a strait-jacket but a framework within which ingenious solutions to diverse problems may be postulated, resulting in characterful but essentially modest architectural complexes which seek to enhance rather than to dominate their urban context.

Generally, even the largest projects break down into small-scale units, whose picturesque grouping is disciplined by the overall structural grid and the insistent morphology. Because of the decomposition of the larger masses, the pictorial quality of surfaces, and the refinement and elegance of detail, the work of the Mansfeld office is anti-monumental, but when the need arises, the monumental form is handled convincingly and with great power: the high-rise version of the Jerusalem town hall project, for instance, is a tower of soaring beauty that somehow captures those elusive qualities of grandeur, gravity and grace that one usually associates with an I.M. Pei masterpiece.

—Gilbert Herbert

MANTEOLA, SÁNCHEZ GÓMEZ, SANTOS, SOLSONA, VIÑOLY, ARCHITECTS.
Partnership; established as Manteola, Petchersky, Sánchez Gómez, Santos, Solsona, Viñoly, in Buenos Aires, 1964, by Flora Manteola (born 1936), Ignacio Petchersky (now deceased), Javier Sánchez Gómez (born 1936), Josefa Santos (born 1931), Justos Jorge Solsona (born 1931), and Rafael Viñoly (born 1944). Address: Florida 890, 3rd Floor, Buenos Aires 1005, Argentina.

Works:

1960	Church, Venado Tuerto, Argentina (project)
1963	National Library, Buenos Aires (project)
1964	House, La Lucila, Buenos Aires
	Tire (Tyre) sales and warehouse buildings in Buenos Aires, Neuquen, and Santa Fe, Argentina
	Argentine Pavilion, *World's Fair,* New York
1965	Museum and Park, La Plata, Argentina
	Municipal development schemes for Buenos Aires (2 projects)
1966	Hall of Deputies extension, Buenos Aires
	Dental Association Building, Buenos Aires
	Devoto Co-operative Villa, Buenos Aires (with Aftalion, Bischof and Vidal)
	Energy Company Headquarters, Cordoba, Argentina (project)
	Mar del Plata Auditorium, Buenos Aires (competition project)
1967	Housing, Santa Teresita, Buenos Aires
	Tower Restaurant, Buenos Aires
	Teaching Hospital, Cordoba, Argentina (project; with Ernesto Katzenstein)
	City Hall, Amsterdam (competition project)
1968	Bank of the City of Buenos Aires Branch at Casa Matriz, Buenos Aires
	Argentine Industrial Union Building, Buenos Aires
	Hotel, Taormina, Italy
1969	Housing complex, Acoyte, Buenos Aires
	Housing complex, Rioja, Buenos Aires
	Ventas Bank Main Building, Buenos Aires
	Bank of the City of Buenos Aires Branches at Patricios, Barracas, and Liniers, Buenos Aires
	Mental Health Centre, Tucuman, Argentina
	Mental Health Centre, Santiago del Estero, Argentina
	Bialik School, Buenos Aires
	Oks House, Buenos Aires
1970	Hotel Internacional, Buenos Aires
	Bank building, Tucuman, Argentina
	Naval Hospital, Buenos Aires
	Bank building, Chaco, Argentina
	IBM Building, Buenos Aires
	Housing, La Matanza, Buenos Aires
	Bank of the City of Buenos Aires Branches at Villa Urquiza, Flores, Condor, and Retiro, Buenos Aires
	Housing complex, Entre Rios, Argentina
	Argentine Embassy, Brasilia (project)
1971	Durand Hospital, Buenos Aires
	Costanera Avenue Development, Misiones, Argentina
	National Pediatric Hospital, Buenos Aires (project)
	Hospital, Misiones, Argentina (project)
	Hospital, La Rioja, Argentina (project)
	Almirante Brown Hospital, Buenos Aires
1972	Plaza and car park, Buenos Aires
	CGE Office Building, Buenos Aires
	Housing complex, Buenos Aires
	Redevelopment plan for the central area of Santiago, Chile (project; with Bielus, Goldemberg and Wainstein)
	Boatin Club House, Buenos Aires
	Auditorium, Buenos Aires (project)
	Goethe School, Buenos Aires
1973	Housing complex, San Isidro, Buenos Aires
	Paper factory, Buenos Aires
	Housing complex, Buenos Aires
1974	Department of Social Work Headquarters, Buenos Aires (with Sabbatiello and Terzoni)
	Ranelagh Housing Complex, Buenos Aires
	Housing complex, Chubut, Argentina
	Piedrabuena Housing Complex, Buenos Aires
	Housing complex, Chaco, Argentina
1975	Urban housing developments (2), Buenos Aires (with Irajtenber, Cano, Lluma and Grennon)

	Sports Centre Complex, Corrientes, Argentina
	Energy Authority Headquarters, Buenos Aires (project)
1976	Aerolineas Argentinas Headquarters, Buenos Aires (project)
	Football stadium, Mendoza, Argentina
	Football stadium, Rosario, Santa Fe, Argentina (with Pujals and Hope)
	Television Production Center, Buenos Aires (with Sadkowska, Trajtenberg, Lluma, Cano and Grannon)
1977	Prourban Office Building, Buenos Aires
	Summer holiday housing complex, Punta del Este, Uruguay
	Country club house, Buenos Aires
1978	Bank headquarters, Buenos Aires

Publications:

On MANTEOLA/SANCHEZ GOMEZ: book—*Manteola, Sánchez Gómez, Santos, Solsona, Viñoly,* Buenos Aires 1978; articles—"Acerca de la Practica" in *Summa* (Buenos Aires), no. 57, 1972; "Buenos Aires" in *Casabella* (Milan), February 1973.

In order to write this statement, we have had to try to put into words those motives that underlie all our work, motives that normally remain unspoken. This task would pose problems for anyone, but it does so in our case for a particular reason: we are not in the habit of verbalizing, in any organized sense, those thought processes that form part of our daily routine.

It is now about 15 years since we began working together, and despite the natural changes in each of us during that time and the irreparable loss of Ignacio Petchersky, we have still managed to retain our original character as a team. The reason for the continuity of this identity, which goes beyond the given eclecticism of our work, seems to us to lie in an almost fanatical attitude towards what we do and in the very real way in which we relate to our projects. Our works have always been, and continue to be, very close to our hearts. Simply as a means of repeating the pleasure we take in seeing the way that the ideas of our sketches become reality, we have always managed to overcome the various obstacles that make it so difficult to set up and maintain an independent practice in a profession as closed as architecture.

Working in architecture in Argentina—as, probably, in many other environments and countries in the world—presents a challenge that resolves itself somewhere between logic and effrontery. To consolidate a coherent style and method, then to attempt a minimum of continuity, and at the same time to remain intellectually faithful to those principles that are generally associated with youthfulness and inexperience—these goals are almost impossible to achieve. Yet we try; even today, each theme provides an exercise that tests the very limits of our capacity for reinterpretation. By adhering to this principle, we believe that we can give the finished objects a certain critical quality; as well, we can fill our daily activity with cultural significance and contribute something to the language of architecture.

The evolution of our activities has gradually caused us to question our beliefs about the "function of form"—ideologies that we all inherited; we have come to the conclusion, gained as a result of concrete experience, that the essence of architecture is not the reconciling of opposing ends within a forced equilibrium that is always bound to end in instability. Because this idea, enforced with such strictness and authority, has come to seem to us unsatisfactory, it has recently brought us to a serious exercise in self-criticism. This questioning is now the basis of our approach to design, and it seems to us the most legitimate way of dealing with our natural desire to improve or revise our preconceptions.

—Manteola, Sánchez Gómez, Santos, Solsona, Viñoly

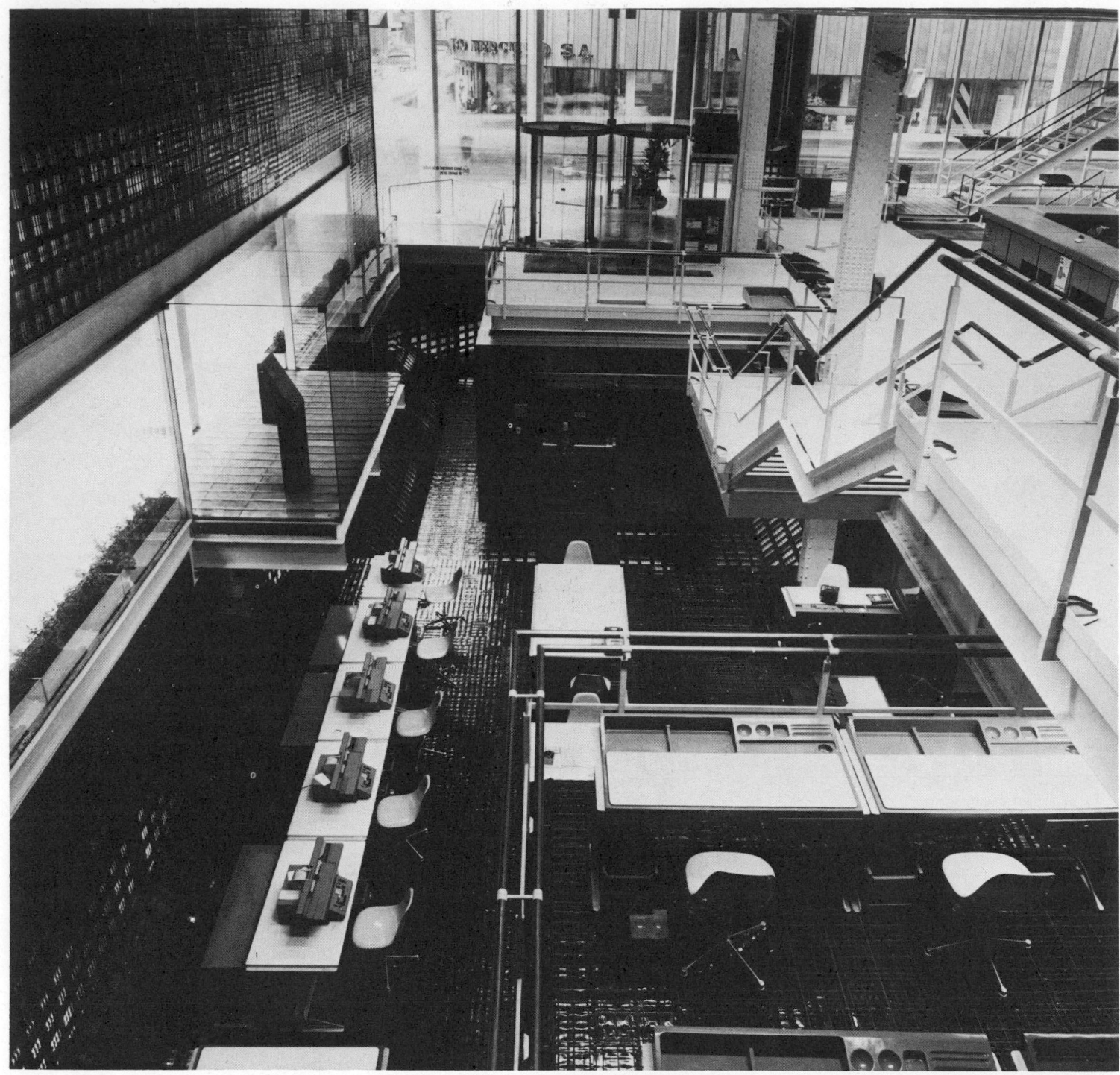

Manteola, Sánchez Gómez, Santos, Solsona, Viñoly: Bank of the City of Buenos Aires branch at Casa Matriz, 1968

The team of Manteola, Sánchez Gómez, Santos, Solsona, and Viñoly are undeniably one of the most original and vital contributors to the "making of architecture" in Argentina in recent years. They are the creators of the Television Production Center, one of the best buildings in Buenos Aires in the last decade.

The team approaches each project by a process of analysis and discussion in which each one participates: in this way they interpret the subject, formulate the basic ideas, and define the fundamental generators of the project. The advantage of the method is that it allows the team a "fresh start" with each project; it has also contributed to the enrichment of their repertory of ideas on architecture.

With this method, and given the fact that each member of the team is an individual architect, working and changing with one another for nearly 15 years, their work ought to reveal an almost casebook eclecticism. And to a certain extent it does. To the extent, that is, that architecture is revealed in forms,

and that forms are or are not expressive, and that the ideas that inform a project are valid only for a particular case, having been conceived as abstract simplifications that solve the problems of manipulation of a complex language—to that extent, their work is eclectic. And, because of their technique and philosophy of working, it *is* difficult to attempt a survey of the studio's style (with the possible exception of the series of banks in Buenos Aires from the period 1967–72, which brought them international fame) for the simple reason that it is difficult to point to formal similarities among their buildings or any givens in their use of architectural elements. Yet a "constant" does run throughout the output of the studio, an insistence on "visuality" and a concern for the relation of the constructed object to the environment. What is obvious, too, is their manifest capacity for creating striking architectural images.

Their management of space in creating and confirming the image of the city is outstanding. High-rise apartments, they have said, "are like

bridges, avenues, public squares: they reinforce the urban geography of the neighborhood and transcend the mere fact of containing apartments; they constitute in themselves a modern social and technical phenomenon, that of being able to accommodate 100 dwellings in space at a height of 80 metres. Hence the domestic aspect disappears both in the realization of aesthetics and in the election of materials." This idea, that works of a certain magnitude can both transcend the image of predecessor forms yet simultaneously partake of the established image of their environment, could describe much of their work.

The team's interest in the environment also reveals itself in their propensity to design for flexibility, especially in those works—office buildings, public buildings, hospitals—in which spaces may need to adapt to future changes. The degree of non-determination is obviously variable, but, mainly, the team attempt to leave "free" the space that is otherwise limited or defined by the outside enveloping line. That may sound like a diffusive kind of architecture, but in their ordering of volumes, in their treatment of structural elements, and in their use of color and light, the team establishes a precise form in each building.

The team's manner of approaching architectural problems is not scientific, and design is not subordinated to technological resources—rather the reverse: such resources are put at the service of space and function (if, at some point, they become manifest, they are being used as communication signs). This attitude allows the team complete freedom with each project, a freedom in which to exercise their critical attitudes, to come up with new solutions. A good example is their headquarters for a bank in Buenos Aires. In place of the usual atmosphere of solemnity the team have created a colorful spectacle in which employees and public both participate, as do (perhaps without even wanting to) the pedestrians on the pavement outside. Thanks to the treatment of space and the technological resources adopted, the passerby is both observer and observed.

Perhaps the most accurate impression one can gain from the work of the team is that they have never stood still. They have stuck to certain principles (a fresh approach to each project; a concern for the visual image and the management of space; a concern for the environment, involving a flexibility in design; a refusal to allow technological means to dominate the expressive goal)—yet, in the course of their practice, they have passed through periods in which they subscribed to various of the architectural concepts of our time—modular coordination, technological purity, anti-stylism, synthesis on ground plan, subdivision of the program into generic categories, softness in formal definition (the cult of additive aesthetics), open forms, growth systems, geometricalization of composition, urban connection, general systems theory, etc.

That Manteola, Sánchez Gómez, Santos, Solsona, and Viñoly have seemed to operate as from one of these concepts, then from another, and another, is evidence of nothing more than the sincerity of their critical search. Many of these concepts—and the discipline they impose—have helped the team to create some of their most important work, and, in designing from particular concepts, in changing one for another in a process of continual "testing," the team has really demonstrated the breadth of their vision —that each architectural problem is complex and the instruments of control notoriously precarious.

—Jorge Glusberg

MARDALL, C(yril) S(jostrom).
British. Born in Helsinki, Finland, 21 September 1909; emigrated to England, 1927: naturalized, 1928. Educated at the Northern Polytechnic, London; Architectural Association School, London, 1931–32. Served in the Royal Naval Volunteer Reserve, 1940–44: Lieutenant. Married the architect (Hilary) June Park in 1948; children: Georgia and Charles. Year Master, Architectural Association School, 1936–39; Chief of the Shelter Section, UNRRA (United Nations Relief and Rehabilitation Agency), 1944–45; Partner, with F. R. S. Yorke, *q.v.* (died, 1962), and Eugene Rosenberg, *q.v.*, Yorke, Rosenberg and Mardall, 1944 until he retired, 1975. In private practice, with June Park, since 1975. Member of the Council of the Architectural Association, 1950–52. Recipient: Council of Industrial Design Award, 1959; Civic Trust Award, 1961, 1964, 1965, 1966, 1967, 1969; Bronze Medal, Royal Institute of British Architects, 1961, 1966, 1967, 1972; *Financial Times* Award, 1966, 1969. Fellow, Royal Institute of British Architects. Commander, Order of the Lion of Finland, 1966. Address: 5 Boyne Terrace Mews, London W11 3LR, England.

Works:

1947 Cowley Peachey Housing, Middlesex
1948 Linden Doors Factory, Stowmarket, Suffolk (project)
1949 Temporary Outpatients Department, St. Thomas' Hospital, London
     Shebbear College Boarding School alterations, Devon
     Factories, Dagenham Docks, London (project)
1951 Housing, King's Langley, Hertfordshire
     Susan Lawrence Primary School, London
     Elizabeth Lansbury Nursery School, London
     Housing, Brynmawr, Brecknock, Wales
     Hainault Forest Secondary School, Essex
1952 College of Further Education, Merthyr Tydfil, Glamorgan, Wales
1953 Warren Wood Secondary School, Rochester, Kent
     Upholland Grammar School, Wigan, Lancashire
     West Park Secondary School, Leeds
     Sheerwater Primary School, Woking, Surrey
     Causeway Green Primary School, Oldbury, Worcestershire
1954 Queensmead Secondary School, Ruislip, Middlesex
1955 Quarles Secondary Modern School, Romford, Essex
     Master plan and stage I of the Leeds Polytechnic
     Mark Hall Local Authority Housing, Harlow, Essex
     Kingswood School, Essex
1956 Boxgrove Housing prototypes
     Jack Straw's Lane House, Oxford
     East Anglian Girls School, Bury St Edmunds, Suffolk
     Bradfield Secondary School, Yorkshire
     Kingswood School extensions, Essex
1957 Southlands College Lecture Block and Dining Room extensions, Wimbledon, London
     Temple Moor Grammar School, Leeds
     Stanley Outwood Secondary School, Yorkshire
     Oak Park Secondary School, Havant, Hampshire
     Dawley Secondary School, Shropshire
     Master plan for the Bromsgrove Education Centre, Worcestershire
     Timberlog Secondary School, Basildon, Essex
     St. Paul's Secondary School, Addlestone, Surrey
1958 Unilever House, Hamburg (competition project)
     Finnish Seamen's Mission, London
     Chaucer Secondary School, Sheffield
     Leeds Polytechnic, stage II
1959 Elephant and Castle Development, London (project)
     World Health Organization Offices, Geneva (competition project)
     St. Paul's School Hall alterations, Chertsey, Surrey
     Brays Grove Secondary School, Harlow, Essex
     Upholland Grammar School extensions, Wigan, Lancashire
1960 Rothwell Secondary School, stage II, Yorkshire
     Warslow School, Staffordshire
     United States Embassy, Grosvenor Square, London (with Eero Saarinen Associates)
     Passmores Comprehensive School, Harlow, Essex
     Brierly Hill Secondary School, Staffordshire
     Rolls Royce Offices, Derby (project)
1961 Royal Masonic School, Ascot, Berkshire (project)
     YRM Offices, Greystoke Place, London
     Kew Bridge Development for British Rail, London (project)

Kingswood School extensions, stage II, Essex
1962 Elliott Brothers Welfare Building, Rochester, Kent (project)
     Rotameter Factory, Croydon, Surrey (project)
     Library, Cambridge University (project)
     Southlands College: Queensmere Hostels, Lecture Block and Gymnasium, Wimbledon, London
     Barstable Comprehensive School, Basildon, Essex
     College of Further Education extensions, stage II, Merthyr Tydfil, Glamorgan, Wales
     Oak Park Secondary School extensions, Havant, Hampshire
     Timberlog Secondary School extensions, Basildon, Essex
1963 Rolleston Secondary School, Staffordshire
     Rochdale College, Lancashire
     Redevelopment scheme for the Dawley schools, Shropshire
     A. Johnson and Company Factory and Offices, Wokingham, Berkshire
     Harlow Training Centre, Essex
     Bradford Secondary School extensions, Yorkshire
1964 Southlands College Staff Accommodation, Wimbledon, London
     Development plan for the central area of Blackpool, Lancashire
     Blythe Bridge Secondary School, Staffordshire
     Mildmay Secondary School, Aveley, Essex
     Dawley Secondary School extensions, Shropshire
     Chaucer Secondary School extensions, Sheffield
1965 Bakewell Secondary School, Derbyshire
     Simestow Comprehensive School, Tettenhall, Staffordshire
     Romford Technical College, Essex
     Chalvedon Comprehensive School, Basildon, Essex
     German Sailors' Home, London
     Gibbons Road Secondary School, West Willesden, London
     Rochdale College extensions, Lancashire
1966 Local authority housing, Cadell Street, Tower Hamlets, London
     Elliott Brothers Factory extensions, Borehamwood, Hertfordshire
     Westwood Hall and St. Edward's School, Leek, Staffordshire
     Elliott Brothers Factory, Rochester, Kent
     St. Paul's Secondary School extensions, Addlestone, Surrey
     Clements Store extensions, Watford, Hertfordshire
1967 Bacton Street Housing, Tower Hamlets, London
     Ilford Training Centre, Essex
     Sceptre Road Housing, Tower Hamlets, London
     Queensmead Secondary School extensions, Ruislip, Middlesex
     Brays Grove Secondary School extensions, Harlow, Essex
1968 Uxbridge Technical College, London
     Willesden Secondary School, London
     Old Street Concourse, London
     Timberlog Secondary School extensions, stage II, Basildon, Essex
     St. Paul's Secondary School extensions, stage II, Addlestone, Surrey
1969 Kingshold Estate, King Edward's Road, Hackney, London
     Osprey Estate Housing, Bermondsey, London
     Chalvedon Comprehensive School extensions, Basildon, Essex
1970 Rochdale College extensions, stage II, Lancashire

Sceptre Road Housing extensions, Tower Hamlets, London

1972 Tomo Estates Factory, Cowley Peachey, Middlesex

Hindrey Place Housing, Hackney, London

High Park School extensions, Stourbridge, Worcestershire

1973/

75 Camden Health Centre, London

Community Centre, King Edward's Road, Hackney, London

Los Llanos Recreational Centre, Costa del Sol, Spain (project)

Library and Community Building, Albion Street, Southwark, London

Brixton Road Development, London

Territorial Army Centre, Camden, London (project)

Tomo Estates Offices, Cowley Peachey, Middlesex

Queensmead School extension, Ruislip, Middlesex

Hillingdon Sports Hall, Ruislip, Middlesex

Residence Hacienda la Mota, Costa del Sol, Spain

1976/

78 Hotel, West Cork, Ireland (with June Park)

Housing and restoration of ruins, St. Maarten, Netherlands West Indies (with June Park)

Cultural Centre and Sunday School for Finnish Nationals, Albion Street, London (with June Park)

Publications:

On MARDALL: book—*The Architecture of Yorke Rosenberg Mardall,* introduction by Reyner Banham, London and New York 1972.

C. S. Mardall was born in Finland in 1909 and was educated at Northern Polytechnic and at the Architectural Association. His name is most familiar from the partnership with Eugene Rosenberg and F.R.S. Yorke (who died in 1962), which he formed in 1944. All three were associated with the early years of the MARS group and the foundation of modern architecture in Britain.

YRM, as the partnership is known, has become identified with an uncompromising form of the postwar International Style almost always produced for public sector clients. It was formed in conscious imitation of larger groups like TAC: The Architects Collaborative and has recently established firmer ties still with its trans-Atlantic equivalent, Skidmore, Owings and Merrill. The output of the partnership has been predominately flats, stores, industrial buildings and hospitals. Best known of all, Mardall and his partners have, since 1955, been the architects of Gatwick Airport, an exercise that began in an Anglicised version of Mies' idiom and developed into the partnership's characteristic white-tile-and-Helvetica idiom of the mid-1960's.

YRM has a corporate obsession with detail and claims, popularly, never to have cut a facing tile, so perfect are the drawings and so well supervised is the execution of each building. The partnership, which is prosperous and successful, is run on hierarchical lines and in a "statement of principles," issued as late as 1966, declared that "a dynamic and developing architectural mainstream, originating from the modern international movement as established in the 20's and 30's, is still the correct course to follow." This doctrine compounds the partnership's vaguely leftish sentiments with a sense of social commitment that owes its origins to a belief in "total solutions," an inheritance of the architectural avant-garde from between the wars.

The partnership, the better to advance its austere

aesthetic policies, has a "rationalisation section" and prepares its own design manuals for its staff of two hundred.

—Stephen Bayley

MARKELIUS, Sven (Gottfrid).

Swedish. Born in Stockholm, 25 October 1889. Educated at the Institute of Technology, Stockholm, graduated 1913; Academy of Fine Arts, Stockholm, graduated 1915. Worked in the offices of the architects Östberg, Tengbom, Lallerstadt and Grut, Stockholm, 1915; in private practice, Stockholm, from 1915; concentrated on urban planning and building standardization for the Stockholm City Council, 1915–31; Director of the Planning Department, Stockholm Building Institute, 1938–44; Director of the Planning Regulation Office, Stockholm, 1944–54. Assistant, 1919–21, and Professor, 1937–39, Department of Construction Sciences, Stockholm Polytechnic. Visiting Professor, Yale University, New Haven, Connecticut, 1949; Visiting Professor, Massachusetts Institute of Technology, Cambridge, and University of California, Berkeley, 1962. Member, State Committee for Building Technology and Production, Stockholm, 1938–43; Member, Consultants Group for the United Nations Building, New York, 1947; Member, Supervising Committee for the Unesco Buildings, Paris, 1952–58; President, Federation of Swedish Architects, 1953–56; Member, Unesco Arts Committee, 1954. Exhibitions: *Bygge och Bo,* Lidingo, Sweden, 1925; *Stockholm Exhibition,* 1930; *Standard 1934,* Gallery Liljewalchs, Stockholm, 1934; *House with Collective Services,* Stockholm, 1936; *World's Fair,* New York, 1939. Recipient: First Prize—Bergsatra Building So-

C. S. Mardall: Hindrey Place Housing, Hackney, London, 1972

Sven Markelius: Stockholm suburb of Vallingby, 1967

ciety Competition, Lidingo, Sweden, 1917; Railway Bridge Competition, Hammarbyleden, Sweden, 1920; Bygge och Bo Town Development Competition, Lidingo, Sweden, 1925; Hälsingborg Concert Hall Competition, 1925; Kristineberg District Urban Redevelopment Plan Competition, Stockholm, 1927; St. Lars Hospital Pavilion Competition, Lund, Sweden, 1934; and Association of Constructors Building Competition, Stockholm, 1935; Howaldn Memorial Prize, Yale University, 1949; St. Erik's Medal, Stockholm, 1959; Federation of Swedish Architects Award, 1961; Prince Eugene Medal, 1961; Patrick Abercrombie Prize, International Union of Architects, 1961; Gold Medal, Royal Institute of British Architects, 1962; Statlig Konstnarsbeloning, Stockholm, 1967. Honorary doctorate: Polytechnic of Rheinland/Westphalia, Aachen, 1966. *Died 27 February 1972.*

Works:

1916   Cemetery, Malmo (competition project; with O. Lundgren)
1917   Urban plan for a residential district, Lidingo, Sweden (competition project)
       Urban plan for the Graakalbanen Society, near Trondheim, Norway (competition project)
       Urban plan for Palsjo Hälsingborg, Sweden (competition project; with O. Lundgren)
1918   Plan for the Central Station, Stockholm (project)
1919   Hotel complex, Saltsjobaden, Sweden (competition project)
1920   Railway bridge, Hammarbyleden, Sweden

(competition project; with O. Lundgren)
1923   Redevelopment plan for the Old City, Stockholm (competition project; with E. Sundhal)
1925   Pavilion, and Urban Complex, *Bygge och Bo* exhibition, Lidingo, Sweden
1926   School, Sundsvall, Sweden (competition project)
       Ewald Engineering Building, Hälsingborg, Sweden
1927   Urban plan for the Kristineberg District, Stockholm (competition project)
1929   Students Club Building, Stockholm Polytechnic (with U. Ahren)
       Apartment building, Berget, Stockholm
       Ohman Villa, Salstjo-Duvnas, Sweden
1930   Pavilion, *Stockholm Exhibition*
       Hangar, Lindaragnen, Sweden (with Professor Forsel)
       Villa, Nockeby, Sweden
       Apartment and office block, Sjokatten, Stockholm (project)
1931   Low-cost housing, Graset, Sweden
1932   Engkvist Villa, Eldtomta, Sweden
       Liden Villa, Vasteras, Sweden
1933   *Morgonbris* newspaper Editorial Offices, Skolan, Stockholm
       Syndicate Headquarters Building, Göteborg, Sweden (project)
       Syndicate Headquarters Building, Ilgodset, Stockholm (project)
1934   Concert Hall, Hälsingborg, Sweden
       Air Terminal, Bromma, Sweden (project)
       House with Collective Services, *Standard 1934* exhibition, Stockholm

Theatre, Malmo (competition project; with V. Goransson)
1935   Office and Cinema Building, Apotekaren 4, Lund, Sweden (project)
       Villa, Asen, Lidingo, Sweden (project)
       Engkvist Villa expansion and alterations, Eldtomta, Sweden
       Blomberg Building, Stocksund, Sweden
       Kollektivhus (House with Collective Services; apartment building), Fagelbarstradet, Stockholm
       Provincial Records Office, Harnosand, Sweden
1936   EPA Building, Sundsvall, Sweden
       Obstetrics clinic, Sandiviken, Sweden (project)
       Commercial building, Trasket, Stockholm (project)
       Industrial building, Morgardshammars, Sweden (project)
       ASEA Company Building (project)
1937   Association of Constructors Building, Stockholm
       St. Lars Hospital Pavilion, Lund, Sweden
       Housing for families with children, at Roda Rummet, Hemsoborna, Kristineberg, Boras, Hasseleholm, Nörrköping, Skara, Karlshamm, and Sala, Sweden
       Myrdal Villa, Stockholm
       Office building, Sirius, Stockholm (project)
1938   Svenska Flatfabriken Turbine Factory, Humlegarden, Stockholm (project)
1939   Swedish Pavilion, *World's Fair,* New York
       EPA Commercial and Office Buildings, Sweden (projects)

Syndicate Buildings and Urban Renewal Plans, Stockholm (project)

Nynas Petroleum Service Station, Lindköping and Karlstad, Sweden (projects)

1944/
54 Various plans for the city and region of Stockholm

1945 Markelius Villa, Kevinge, Sweden

1947/
52 United Nations Building, New York (with international team of architects, including Le Corbusier and Oscar Niemeyer—Wallace K. Harrison, Chairman)

1952 Syndicate Headquarters, Linköping, Sweden

1958 Munkbrobadet, Stockholm (project)
Hotel, Alvadalen, Sweden (project)

1959 Sailor's House, Lappskon, Stockholm (project)

1960 Syndicate Headquarters and Municipal Theatre Building, Stockholm
Office building, Alvadalen, Sweden
Swedish Forest Industry Offices, Stockholm
Apartment building, Granen, Stockholm

1963 Commercial and office building, Beridarenbanan, Stockholm
Sverigehuset, Stockholm

1965 Apartment building, Reven, Stockholm
New Municipal Theatre, Overkikaren, Stockholm (project)

1966 Burgerhaus Cultural and Congress Centre, Giessen, Essen, Germany

1968 Hotel, Lonnen, Stockholm

Publications:

By MARKELIUS: books—*Acceptera,* with Asplund, Gahn, Paulsson and Sundahl, Stockholm 1930; *Kollektivhuset som bostadsform,* Stockholm 1935; *Det framtida Stockholm,* with Ahlberg, Hofsten and Sidenbladh, Stockholm 1946; *Report on the United Nations Headquarters,* with others, Stockholm 1947; articles—"Sverige i New York" in *Byggmastaren* (Stockholm), no. 33, 1939; "Villa i Kevinge" in *Byggmastaren* (Stockholm), "Manniskan i centrum?" in *Plan* (Zurich), no. 1/2, 1950; "Nuovi sviluppi urbanistici a Stoccolma" in *Urbanistica* (Turin), no. 10/11, 1952; "Urban Land Policies in Sweden" in *United Nations Housing and Town and Country Planning Bulletin* (New York), no. 7, 1953; "Om—och Tillbyggnad av tekniska Hogskolans Karhus, Stockholm" in *Byggmastaren,* no. 7, 1953; "Hoghus ger Stockholm dess nya stadsbild 2050" in *Byggnadsindustrin* (Stockholm), no. 8, 1955; "Stockholms struktur. Synpunkter pa ett storstadsproblem" in *Byggmastaren* (Stockholm), no. 3, 1956; "Projekt till enfamiljshus" in *Arkitektur* (Stockholm), no. 3, 1959; "Villa pa Lidingo" in *Arkitektur* (Stockholm), no. 8, 1960; "Stockholms Folkets Hus" in *Arkitektur* (Stockholm), no. 11, 1961; "Il Nuovo centro di Stoccolma" in *Casabella* (Milan), no. 275, 1963.

On MARKELIUS: books—*Architecture in Sweden* by A. Hahn, Stockholm 1938; *New Swedish Architecture,* edited by G. Paulsson, Stockholm 1940; *Nordische Baukunst* by S. E. Rasmussen, Berlin 1940; *Ny Arkitektur* by T. Paulsson, Stockholm 1948; *Ten Lessons on Swedish Architecture,* edited by T. P. Jacobson and E. Silow, Stockholm 1949; *Ny Svensk Byggnadskonst* by E. Cornell, Stockholm 1950; *Svensk stad* by G. Paulsson, 3 volumes, Stockholm 1950–53; *Scandinavian Architecture* by T. Paulsson, London 1958; *Ny stad* by T. Paulsson, Stockholm 1958; *International History of City Development, II: The Alpine and Scandinavian Countries* by E. A. Gutkind, New York 1965; *Il Contributo Svedese all'Architettura Contemporanea e l'Opera di Sven Markelius* by Stefano Ray, Rome 1969; articles—"Vicende dell'urbanistica svedese" by F. Malusardi in *Quaderni della Societa Generale Immobiliare* (Rome), no. 13, 1960; "Building a City and a Metropolis: The Planned Development of Stockholm" by Y. Larsson in *Journal of the American Institute of Planners* (Washington, D.C.), no. 28, 1962; "Il nuovo centro di Stoccolma" by S. Bracco in *La Cittaterritorio,* Bari, Italy 1964; "Stockholm: A Planned City" by G. Sidenbladh in *Scientific American* (New York), September 1965.

One of the outstanding Swedish architects and urban planners of the century, Sven Markelius shows in his work an awareness of most of the modern developments in architectural design and building technology both in Europe and America. He availed himself of these methods whenever they answered requirements, but at the same time he made his own contribution to new and ingenious solutions of problems presented by changing social economic and cultural needs. It could be claimed that his contributions to domestic architecture, concert hall design and urban planning made him to some extent an innovator.

An outstanding early work of domestic architecture is the 1935 Kollektivhus in Stockholm, which was designed to answer the needs of working parents. The flats are mostly one, two and three roomed; they are grouped on each floor with short corridor access, and architecturally attractive and well secluded balconies are provided for the larger flats. There are food lifts, a restaurant, and provision for the collective care of children.

Of the many well designed family houses by Markelius, that which he built for himself at Kevinge (1945) is notable. It is one story in an L-shaped plan; the rooms are in functional sequence, and careful attention has been paid to the best orientation for the various rooms. It is well integrated with its large garden, for full enjoyment of the long summer days.

The building by which Markelius first became famous is the Concert Hall at Hälsingborg of 1934. The design is a new and original departure from traditional halls. It is rectangular with a flat ceiling; the floor rises gently from the orchestra in the front and then steeply in the rear, and was designed to be removed in sections so that the hall could also be used for banquets and dances. Above the orchestra there is a canopied, well-integrated reflector. Large plain masses, with little ornament, characterize the design, and the interior is reflected in the exterior dispositions of forms which combine with the setting of trees into a pleasing ensemble. A similar original and progressive spirit is seen in Markelius' later Syndicate Headquarters Building, Stockholm, which includes a municipal theatre. The large congress hall is shaped like a Greek theatre, with concentric seating round the orchestra, a foreshadowing of many later theatre and hall designs.

Markelius is best known internationally as planning director in Stockholm, responsible for the planning of the modern city and its surroundings. Markelius' conception was that of a city developed in the centre with a degree of pedestrianization, with several large neighbourhoods or satellite towns planned in the surrounding areas to accommodate the increasing population. Several of these satellites have been built and are distinguished for their imaginative planning. The most famous, Vallingby, has many ingenious features and architectural excellencies, especially in the residential areas on undulating sites. The pedestrian centre built over the railway station has also proved to be very successful. It is significant that Vallingby and also Farsta, another Stockholm satellite in the plan, received the Reynolds Memorial Award for Community Architecture in 1967, the other two so honoured being Cumbernauld and Tapiola.

In all his work Markelius showed the impulses of an artist sensitive to architectural character and proportion, and this artistry distinguishes all his original and ingenious utilizations of modern developments in architectural design and building technology.

—Arnold Whittick

MARKSON, Jerome.

Canadian. Born in Toronto, Ontario, 21 March 1929. Educated at the University of Toronto, 1948–53, B.Arch. 1953; Cranbrook Academy of Art, Bloomfield Hills, Michigan, 1952. Married Mayta Ruth in 1953; children: Nancy and Anna. Principal, Jerome Markson Architects, Toronto, since 1955. Vice-Chairman, Toronto Chapter of the Ontario Association of Architects, 1969–70; Member of the Board, 1976, and Vice-President, 1978, Toronto Chapter of the Architectural Conservancy of Ontario. Recipient: Canadian Housing Design Council Award, 1960, 1967, 1969, 1971, 1977; Massey Medal for Architecture, 1964; Ontario Association of Architects Award, 1964, 1970, 1977; Canadian Wood Design Award, 1965; Ontario Masons Relations Council Award, 1966, 1973, 1977; *Canadian Architect* Award, 1968, 1970; Design Award, Steel Company of Canada, 1978. Address: Jerome Markson Architects, 161 Davenport Road, Toronto, Ontario M5R 1J1, Canada.

Works:

1954 Dawes Road Cemetery Chapel, 3169 St. Clair Avenue East, East York, Ontario

1955 House, 167 Valley Road, North York, Ontario
House, 45 Amelia Street, Hamilton, Ontario

1956 House, 16 Monsheen Drive, Woodbridge, Ontario
Dr. Miklos Office Building, Newcastle, Ontario

1957 Woodview Development Houses, Seneca Heights, Woodbridge, Ontario
Stanrock Mines Multiple Housing, Elliott Lake, Ontario
House, 67 Old Park Road, Forest Hill, Ontario
Shops and offices, Elliot Lake, Ontario
House, 79 Amelia Street, Hamilton, Ontario
Whitburn Apartments, Whitburn Avenue, North York, Ontario (with Klein and Sears)

1958 Art Studio and Theatre, Camp Manitou-Wabing, near Parry Sound, Ontario
House I, Winston Avenue, Hamilton, Ontario

1959 House, Mayfair Place, Hamilton, Ontario
House, 125 Amelia Street, Hamilton, Ontario
House, Dixie Road, Mississauga, Ontario
House II, 90 Winston Avenue, Hamilton, Ontario
Ritualarium, Kline Avenue South, Hamilton, Ontario

1960 House, 23 Park Lane Circle, North York, Ontario
Munk House alterations, 63 Woodlawn Avenue, Toronto
House, 32 Saintfield Avenue, North York, Ontario
House alterations, 44 Elm Avenue, Toronto
Architect's house alterations, 15 Poplar Plains Crescent, Toronto

1961 International Woodworkers of America Office Building, 2088 Weston Road, Weston, Ontario
Jewish Home for the Aged, 3560 Bathurst Street, North York, Ontario (with Marani, Routhwaite and Dick)
Cottage at Big Cedar Point, Lake Simcoe, Ontario
Corvette School addition, 30 Corvette Avenue, Scarborough, Ontario

1962 Health Centre, for United Steelworkers of America, 240 McNabb Street, Sault Ste. Marie, Ontario
House, 53 Montressor Drive, North York, Ontario

1963 Chatelaine Houses, Montreal and Brampton, Ontario

1964 House, 63 The Bridle Path Road, North York, Ontario

Clubhouse, Cedarvale Park, East York, Ontario
Dr. Ascah House, Huntsville, Ontario
1965 Alexandra Park Public Housing, Dundas at Spadina, Toronto (with Klein and Sears, Webb, Zerafa, Menkes)
Place Ste. Helene, *Expo '67*, Montreal
Cottage at Kempenfeld Bay, Lake Simcoe, Ontario
1966 Dr. Baida House, Etobicoke, Ontario
Currie House, Claremont, Ontario
1967 Sherman Mine Staff Lodge, Pirates Cove, Lake Timagami, Ontario
Group Health Centre, United Automobile Workers of America, 14 Queen Street, St. Catharines, Ontario
House, 538 Scenic Drive, Hamilton, Ontario
Dylex Diversified Offices and Showroom, Toronto
True Davidson Home for the Aged, 200 Dawes Road, East York, Ontario
1968 Sabre Saw Chain Offices, Hamilton, Ontario
North York Medical Arts Building, 1333 Sheppard Avenue East, North York, Ontario
Country Home, Bolton, Ontario
Housing, Martingrove Road, Etobicoke, Ontario
6-storey stacked housing, Bramalea, Ontario
1969 Glazier Medical Centre, 136 Simcoe Street North, Oshawa, Ontario

Architect's weekend house, Brock Township, Ontario
105 Maitland Street renovations, Toronto
House, 25 Forest Wood, Toronto
C. A. Pitts Head Office, 30 Commercial Road, Toronto
1970 Nurses' residence, Sioux Lookout, Ontario
1971 Office building, 562 Eglinton Avenue East, Toronto
Y.M.-Y.W.H.A. (including Lean Posluns Theatre and Koffler Centre for the Arts), 4588 Bathurst Street, Willowdale, Ontario
1972 Johnson House, Claremont, Ontario
Community and day care centre, 1386 Victoria Park Avenue, East York, Ontario
Neighbourhood shopping centre, Don Mills and Cliffwood Corners, Don Mills, Ontario
Apartment building, 336 Lakeshore Drive, North Bay, Ontario
Architect's offices, 161 Davenport Road, Toronto
1973 Sherwood Park Manor Nursing Home, Highway 2, Brockville, Ontario
Civic Garden Centre (Edwards Gardens), 777 Lawrence Avenue East, Toronto
Weekend house, near Rosemont, Ontario
Eddie Bauer Shop, 22 Bloor Street West, Toronto
Urban Transportation Development Corporation Offices, 20 Eglinton Avenue West,

Toronto
1974 House, 320 Courtleigh Boulevard, Toronto
Neighbourhood shopping centre, Malvern, Scarborough, Ontario
Parkette for Sefton Memorial, Bay and Hagerman Streets, Toronto
Sherbourne-Pembroke Housing, Toronto
1976 Grace MacInnis Co-op Housing, Church/-Gloucester Streets, Toronto
David B. Archer Co-Op Housing, St. Lawrence Project, Toronto
Brantwood Park Housing, Brantford, Ontario
1977 McDonald's Restaurant, Bayview and Eglinton, Toronto
Barn, Manvers Township, Ontario
House, Parkers Point, Lake Muskoka, Ontario
Cambridge Clothes Offices, 56 York Boulevard, Hamilton, Ontario

Publications:

By MARKSON: book—*Exploring Toronto: Its Buildings, People and Places,* Toronto 1972.

On MARKSON: books—*New Buildings in the Commonwealth* by J. M. Richards, London 1961; *Canadian Architecture* by Carol Moore Ede, Toronto 1971.

Jerome Markson: Civic Garden Centre (Edwards Gardens), Toronto, 1973

Since completing my schooling twenty-five years ago I have been struggling to forget the rigid rules gently—and not so gently—imposed. There really aren't any rules other than those of nature—gravity pulling down, water trying to get in and freezing, and so on.

One of the struggles is to break from the ascetic and rigid confines of these teachings and dogmas; the box form and boxed space, the sacred techniques of joining forms and parts together, lightness, separation of the man-made from the natural. Rather, we try to tie a building more easily to its site, to respect a good milieu when it exists, to enhance space and form, to explore better ways of putting things together. Surely it must mean something to the people we serve for architects to respect and, where necessary, to improve upon the past. We attempt to attain a sense of appropriateness and scale in the city or countryside—for our clients, for the users, and for the greater urban context.

To be a sponge, to absorb what we admire in the past and present and adapt it when suitable, to further explore the tendencies we feel developing in our work, to have, however, a sense of realism and to get things built if worthwhile, to free ourselves from the bonds of rigid teachings—these preoccupations and influences are numerous, changing and, at best, tacit. They are manifested through our buildings which, in turn, are tempered by their physical and social context.

Urban problems in Canada remain our first concern, particularly those of affordable housing. This concern for the form and role of housing in a changing urban setting influences our intentions in architecture. Much of our work lies in this area, and the remainder consists of the special "one-off" problem buildings which seem to revitalize and energize our efforts.

For us, the design and building process seems to be a constant struggle. Like architects everywhere, we are constantly ambushed by innumerable constraints on every project, so that a successful building is something of a wonder.

All we can do is plug away, sometimes succeeding, sometimes not, trying all the while to keep our broader objectives from being overly compromised by bureaucratic requirements and the exigencies of practice, as well as the limitations of our own abilities.

—Jerome Markson

In very general terms the contemporary practice of architecture in Toronto may be viewed as comprising three generations. The first of these—the pre-1950 generation—was led by a group of architects who had mostly grown up and been trained in Toronto and belonged to or were associated with the old established Anglo-Saxon families of the city. The second generation, that of the 1950's themselves, also consists largely of architects who grew up and were educated in Toronto, but this generation began for the first time to represent the social and ethnic diversity which has increasingly characterized the life of the city. Jerome Markson is one of a group of young Jewish architects who entered practice at that time, a group which also includes Irving Grossman, Jack Klein and Henry Sears.

Yet, if he entered practice with that peer group, in the perspective of the past 25 years, Markson's career seems increasingly distinct from theirs. Where their work has grown increasingly large in scale, his has remained relatively small; where theirs has grown increasingly commercial, his has continued to consist primarily of custom-designed "one-off" works. Where they have turned increasingly to planning and research, he has continued to place built projects at the centre of his area of interest.

If Markson cannot now be plausibly seen together with the local peer group of his own circle and generation, neither can he be seen to be one with the varied group of architects who have immigrated to this city since the late 50's, which forms what may be thought of as a third generation. This group includes such well-known figures as Ron Thom, John Andrews,

Macy Dubois, A. J. Diamond and Barton Myers. All of these figures, having been educated elsewhere, brought to Toronto much more clearly articulated design philosophies than it would have been possible for anyone to have gleaned from a Toronto architectural education in the early 1950's. Unlike the members of his own peer group, in his preoccupation with the particularity of individual building tasks, Markson is also uneasy in this circle of notable immigrants to Toronto because of his aversion to their various modes of precocious public theorizing. Instead, Markson has, over the past quarter century of his career, pursued a quite individual course within the territory of Canadian architecture, evidently untheoretical, highly particular and unarticulated.

Given all this, it is predictable that Markson's practice has never grown to a large size; that he has never been awarded a major public commission; that his work lacks a high public profile in this country. From time to time, when his work has come up for more explicit critical consideration, it has often been dismissed as a marginal eclecticism, irrelevant to the main course of Canadian architectural history. Yet notwithstanding a certain apparent plausibility, this simple dismissal fails in the end to take adequate account of the strengths of his work.

One can say that it fails to recognize the implicit psychological qualities that characterize the spatial organization of his projects. It fails to acknowledge the strong consistency—at another level than parti—of the detail and finish of his buildings. Beyond, and I think deeper than both of these, there is also, I think—at least in the best of his works—a characteristic almost unique in contemporary Canadian architecture: a subconscious tactile iconography of the materiality of building, a materiality that is, for me, reminiscent of some aspects of the work of Aalto and Le Corbusier. Albeit an elusive characteristic of any contemporary architecture, this is particularly important in the Canadian context on account of its extreme rarity here. Not only is it usually entirely absent from the work of the large commercial practices; it is often less forceful than one might expect even in the work of such better known architects as Dubois and Thom.

Where this tactile iconography of materials *can* readily be found, of course, is in the vernacular architectures of many parts of the world, and Markson's strong devotion to these other architectures is well-known in his circle of admirers. In the most successful of his projects—I would cite as examples, the Camp Manitou-Wabing Art Studio and Theatre (1958); the renovation to the Munk Residence in Toronto (1960); and the True Davidson Home for the Aged, in Toronto, (1967)—these qualities of intense materiality rank Markson's underrated work with the best that has been accomplished in Canada in the past two decades.

—George Baird

MARTIENSSEN, Rex (Distin).
South African. Born in Queenstown, Cape Province, 26 February 1905. Educated at King Edward School, Johannesburg, under Desmond Davis, 1916–22; University of the Witwatersrand, Johannesburg, under G. E. Pearse and A. S. Furner, 1923–29, Dip.Arch. 1929; student-apprentice in the office Cowin, Powers and Ellis, Gordon Leith, and Kallenbach, Kennedy and Furner, Johannesburg, 1924–29. Served in the Air Force Sub Unit, Rand University Training Corps, Johannesburg, 1942: 2nd Lieutenant. Married Heather Bush in 1937. In private practice, Johannesburg, 1930–34; Partner, with John Fassler and Bernard Cooke, Martienssen/Fassler/Cooke, Johannesburg, 1934–35; in virtual retirement from architectural practice, 1935–42. Temporary Head of the Architectural School, 1932, and Lecturer, 1932–42, University of the Witwatersrand, Honorary Editor, *South African Architectural Record,* Johannesburg, 1932–42. Founder Member, Alpha Club architectural group, Johannesburg, 1931, and, with Norman Hanson and Gordon McIntosh, Zerohour, Johannesburg, 1932. President, Transvaal Institute of Architects, 1939; Member of the Central Council, South African Institute of Architects, 1939. *Died* (in military hospital, Voortrekkerhoogte, South Africa) *23 August 1942.*

Works:

1926   Archives Building, Johannesburg (student project)
       Martienssen Family House, Wychwood Road, Johannesburg
1928   Repertory Theatre, Johannesburg (student project)
1931   Holmes-a-Court House, Greenside, Johannesburg (project)
       Sharp House, Valley Road, Johannesburg
       Waterside House (project)
1932   Krahmann House, Westcliff, Johannesburg (project; with Gordon McIntosh)
1933   Flats, Berea, Johannesburg (project; with Norman Hanson)
1934   Peterhouse Building, Johannesburg (with John Fassler and Bernard Cooke)
       McLea House, Dunkeld, Johannesburg (project; with John Fassler and Bernard Cooke)
       Apartment building, near Joubert Park, Johannesburg (project; with John Fassler and Bernard Cooke)
       Cook House, Johannesburg (project; with John Fassler and Bernard Cooke)
       Hersov House (project; with John Fassler and Bernard Cooke)
       Magistrates Court, Johannesburg (competition project; with John Fassler and Bernard Cooke)
1934/
  35   Crown Motors Garage, Johannesburg (with John Fassler and Bernard Cooke)
       Stern House, Houghton, Johannesburg (with John Fassler and Bernard Cooke)
1935   Gaydon House, Melrose, Johannesburg (with John Fassler and Bernard Cooke)
1937   Argu Ideal House (competition project; with John Fassler and Bernard Cooke)
1938   Double-storey house, Bryanston, Johannesburg (project)
       Single-storey house, Bryanston, Johannesburg (project)
1939   Hayne and Gibson Printing Works, Johannesburg (project)
1940   Rex Martienssen House, Greenside, Johannesburg

Publications:

By MARTIENSSEN: books—*Zerohour* (monograph), editor with Norman Hanson and Gordon McIntosh, Johannesburg 1933; *The Idea of Space in Greek Architecture: with Special Reference to the Doric Temple and Its Setting,* Johannesburg 1956, 1964; articles—"Wine Cellars and Minor Farm Buildings of the Cape" in *Architectural Review* (London), October 1928; numerous articles in *South African Architectural Record* (Johannesburg), 1931–33.

On MARTIENSSEN: book—*Martienssen and the International Style* by Gilbert Herbert, Cape Town and Rotterdam 1975; articles—"In Memoriam: Rex Martienssen," special issue of *South African Architectural Record* (Johannesburg), November 1942; "The Anatomy of a Revolution" by Gilbert Herbert in *South African Architectural Record* (Johannesburg), February 1967; "The Legacy of Martienssen" by Ronald Lewcock in *Architectural Association Quarterly* (London), no. 2/3, 1977.

Rex Martienssen was appointed a lecturer in the School of Architecture at the University of the Witwatersrand, and an Editor of the *South African Architectural Record,* at the beginning of 1932. During the decade that followed, until his untimely death in 1942, the architectural scene in South Africa underwent a dramatic metamorphosis. Through the powerful intervention of a few highly-motivated and gifted architects, it was swept from the backwaters of architectural provincialism into the main stream of the International Style. This small band of idealists—the "Transvaal Group", as Le Corbusier called them—were nurtured in the School of Architecture, and their principal forum of expression was the *Record.* Martienssen was a nodal point in the constellation of the Transvaal Group, at once its prophet, spokesman, standard-bearer and measuring rod.

Those of his generation who let themselves come into his field of force were transmuted by it, and were lifted to new planes of achievement. From each of his colleagues and his students he drew out every ounce of latent ability, and informed it and directed it. He was, in this, a true educator, and every facet of his work had a didactic message. He shaped the architectural revolution that brought modern architecture to South Africa, using the full range of his formidable talents as a speaker, a writer, a designer, by the power of his words, the strength of his example, and the clarity, integrity and single-mindedness of his purpose.

Martienssen designed very few buildings, but they were among the pioneer examples of modern architecture, and their quality was outstanding. His short-lived but highly creative partnership with John Fassler and Bernard Cooke produced but a few private houses, the climax of achievement perhaps being Stern House, a lyrical exercise in the Corbusian manner; one small centre-city building, Peterhouse, a block of flats set above a funeral parlour—and Martienssen's handling of the problem of this incongruous juxtaposition of the quick and the dead is as sure in its psychological insights as it is effective in its formal articulation; and several unrealized but influential projects, notably the bravura Hersov House and the exciting Joubert Park block of duplex flats. These works represent an ongoing search for form, based on the language of the International Style, rich in quotations from Le Corbusier, Mies van der Rohe, and Gropius, and yet relevant to the South African scene. In his own house at Greenside, his last building, this universality is modified, if not compromised, by a more personal—almost idiosyncratic—architecture, simpler in form, more highly intellectualized, and almost classical in its response.

Martienssen was hardly a compulsive builder, but a highly selective architect interested in undertaking a project only if it could be used to underwrite his general theme. In the evolution of modern architecture in South Africa each new work by Martienssen was a cause celebre, each new building an instant monument, each new project a thesis for discussion and debate. The remnants of his work have been sadly abused by man and time, but they evoke images of a heroic and, somehow, an innocent age seeking for clarity and excellence.

If a new architecture, universal in character, but valid for our time, was Martienssen's message, then his chosen medium was the *South African Architectural Record.* Not only the built form, but all other forms of communication—lectures, symposia, exhibitions—were ultimately encapsulated in its pages. As an editor Martienssen selected with rigour only that material supportive of his thesis; as a writer he used his fluent pen to entertain, to inform, and to inspire, as he wove a skilful fabric of past and present, art and architecture, concept and form, a heady blend of philosophy, poetry and propaganda.

Within the wider framework of the International Style, it was principally upon Martienssen and the Transvaal Group that attention was focussed: upon the pioneer architecture they produced, the progressive educational policy of the School of Architecture, and upon the avant-garde nature of the *Record.* The

modern movement derived strength from its international affiliations, which saved it from parochial isolation: and it was Rex Martienssen who constituted the essential bridge between the Transvaal and Europe, who—through his on-going association with Le Corbusier, first as disciple, then as respected colleague, and through the esteem in which he was held by Léger—opened a direct channel of communication to the very fountainhead of the modern movement in art and architecture in Europe.

—Gilbert Herbert

MARTIN, Sir (John) Leslie.

British. Born in Manchester, 17 August 1908. Educated at the University of Manchester School of Architecture, 1927–30 (Royal Institute of British Architects Silver Medallist, 1929; Soane Medallist, 1930), M.A. 1930, Ph.D. 1934. Married the architect Sadie Speight in 1934; children: Susan and Christopher. Assistant Lecturer, University of Manchester School of Architecture, 1930–34; Head of the School of Architecture, University of Hull, Yorkshire, and in private practice in Hull, 1934–39; Principal Assistant Architect, LMS Railway, London, 1939–48; Deputy Architect, 1949–53, and Architect, 1953–56, London County Council. In private practice, Cambridge, since 1956. Consultant to the Universities of Leicester, Hull, and London, 1956–78; Consultant to the Gulbenkian Foundation, Lisbon, 1956–69. Professor of Architecture, 1956–72, and since 1973 Emeritus Professor, Cambridge University; also, Fellow, 1956–73, Honorary Fellow, 1973, and since 1976 Emeritus Fellow, Jesus College, Cambridge. Slade Professor of Fine Art, Oxford University, 1965–66; Gropius Lecturer, Harvard University, Cambridge, Massachusetts, 1966; Ferens Professor of Fine Art, University of Hull, 1967–68; William Henry Bishop Visiting Professor of Architecture, Yale University, New Haven, Connecticut, 1973–74. Member of the Council, 1952–58, and Vice-President, 1955–57, Royal Institute of British Architects; Member, Royal Fine Art Commission, 1958–72. Recipient: Bronze Medal, 1954, Distinction in Town Planning, 1956, and the Royal Gold Medal, 1973, Royal Institute of British Architects; Civic Trust Award, 1967; Concrete Society Award, 1972. M.A.: Cambridge University, 1956; Oxford University, 1965; LL.D.: University of Leicester, 1963; University of Hull, 1967; University of Manchester, 1972; D.Univ.: University of Essex, Colchester, 1976. Fellow, Royal Institute of British Architects, 1937. Honorary Member, Association of Finnish Architects; Accademico Corrispondente, National Academy of San Lucca, Italy; Commander, Order of Santiago da Espada, Portugal. Knighted, 1957. Address (office): The Kings Mill, Great Shelford, Cambridge CB2 5EN, England.

Works:

1934/
39   Houses at Ferriby, Yorkshire, and Brampton and Dockray, Cumbria
      Nursery school, Northwich, Cheshire
      Unit furniture (early models)
1939/
48   Emergency wartime buildings
1951 Royal Festival Hall, London (with Sir Robert Matthew, Peter Moro and Edwin Williams)
1956 Sports Centre, Crystal Palace, London (project; with others)
1956/
59   College Hall, Knighton, Leicester (with Trevor Dannatt)
1956/
58   Martin House, The Mill, Great Shelford, Cambridge
      General layout for the University of Leicester, University of Hull, and Royal Holloway College of the University of London (with Colin St. John Wilson)
      General layout of the University of London (with Trevor Dannatt)
1957/
58   King's Hostel, Cambridge (with Colin St. John Wilson)
1957/
62   Harvey Court Residential Building, Gonville and Caius College, Cambridge (with Colin St. John Wilson)
1958 Low-rise housing project, St. Pancras, London (with Colin St. John Wilson)
1959/
64   Group of library buildings, Manor Road, Oxford (with Colin St. John Wilson)
1960/
64   William Stone Residential Building, Peterhouse, Cambridge (with Colin St. John Wilson)

Sir Leslie Martin: Zoology/Psychology Building, Oxford University, 1970

Arts Building and Middleton Hall, University of Hull

1962/
64 British Museum Library, London (first project; with Colin St. John Wilson)

1964/
67 Graduate Building, Balliol and St. Anne's Colleges, Oxford

1964/
70 Zoology/Psychology Building, Oxford University

1968/
70 Kettle's Yard Gallery, Cambridge (with David Owers)
General layout of Wellington Square, Oxford (with David Owers)

1970/
78 Government Centre, Taif, Saudi Arabia (with David Owers)

1972/
76 Pembroke College Library and St. Ebbe's Building, Oxford (with Colen Lumley)

1972/
78 Glasgow Cultural Centre (project; with Colen Lumley)

1978 New Music School, Cambridge University (with Colen Lumley and Ivor Richards)

Publications:

By MARTIN: books—*Circle,* editor with Ben Nicholson and Naum Gabo, London 1937; *The Flat Book,* editor with Sadie Speight, London 1939; *Whitehall: A Plan for a National and Government Centre,* London 1965; *Urban Space and Structures,* volume I, editor with Lionel March, London 1972; articles—"Architecture and the Painter" in *Focus* (London), no. 3, 1939; "A Note on Science and Art" in *The Architects Yearbook* (London), 1947; "Design of the Royal Festival Hall" in *RIBA Journal* (London), April 1952; "The Collegiate Plan" in *Architectural Review* (London), July 1959; "Notes on the Study of a Building Type" in *Architectural Design* (London), 1964; "Land Use and Built Forms," with Lionel March, in *Cambridge Research,* April 1966; "An Architect's Approach to Architecture" in *RIBA Journal* (London), May 1967; "Education Without Walls" in *RIBA Journal* (London), August 1968; "Education Around Architecture" in *RIBA Journal* (London), September 1970; "Bridges Between Cultures" in *RIBA Journal* (London), June 1973; "Notes on a Developing Architecture" in *Architectural Review* (London), July 1978.

On MARTIN: articles—"Housing Development, St. Pancras" in *Architectural Design* (London), July 1959; "College Hall, Leicester" in *Architectural Review* (London), June 1961; "Harvey Court" in *Architectural Design* (London), November 1962; "Selected Works" in *Architectural Design* (London), September 1965; "The Third Force in English Architecture" by Thomas Stevens in *Architectural Design* (London), September 1965; "Libraries, University of Oxford" in *Architectural Design* (London), September 1965; "Middleton Hall, University of Hull" in *Architectural Review* (London), October 1967, and in *Baumeister* (Munich), February 1969; "Gold Medal Commendation" in *RIBA Journal* (London), February 1973; "Pure Gold" in *Building Design* (London), 2 February 1973; "Architecture's Gold Medallist" in *Financial Times* (London), 3 February 1978; "Appreciation" by Trevor Dannatt in *RIBA Journal* (London), August 1973; "Faculty of Music" in *Architectural Review* (London), July 1978.

In architecture it seems important to distinguish between external impressions and developing ideas. Superficial form and the imitation of form is fashion. Ideas generate forms, and by consistently developing and elaborating these we build up a language. That language must be effective at the small scale and

anonymous level of the vernacular which creates an environment: at the other end of the scale it communicates through works which by their nature should be powerfully significant. The development of a language of that range is the basis of a tradition.

—Sir Leslie Martin

Sir Leslie Martin's architectural work has always had a firm intellectual basis in an organizing principle. It is achieved through the consistent use of a limited range of materials (notably brick, timber or concrete) to explore the potentialities of space and light. Taken as a whole, the work displays an order and control in which all elements are contained within the completeness of a unifying form—a form that marks, as he himself has said, "the end of a process."

This "process" begins with his concept of architecture as not just an isolated activity but as part of a culture. He has consistently spoken for an architecture in which the design activity is built up around contemporary needs and the belief that, as Trevor Dannatt puts it, architects should be concerned "with a whole range of elements in art and science that have to be brought into harmony, and that this constitutes the theme of architecture in our time."

Such ideas, however, are not static, but developing, as can be seen in the range of projects that Sir Leslie and his associates have produced over many years. His work at all scales shows a developing continuity (he calls it a "developing language") which can be seen in the family of forms produced in various schemes for student housing, or in the modulation within the range of auditoria, or in such university proposals as those to house the departments of Zoology and Psychology at Oxford, where the basic structure plan allows a range of possibilities with each stage of development.

There is a clear link between such an approach and the opportunities, and demands, of education. The stimulus provided by Sir Leslie's attitude to architecture was an essential part of his role as head of the School of Architecture at Cambridge University. Here, principally through the Centre for Land Use and Built Form Studies (now the Martin Centre), he was able to foster the fresh theoretical examination of fundamental architectural issues. The research which he inspired was both challenging and rigorous, as, for instance, in the clear demonstration that tall buildings do not make the most effective use of land and that other forms of layout can place the same floor space on the same land area in one third of the height.

As the citation that accompanied the award of the Royal Gold Medal in 1973 said, "During a most active career, spanning more than 35 years, Sir Leslie Martin has made a truly outstanding contribution to architecture and planning, both through his work in private and public practice and most notably as a leading figure in architectural teaching and research."

—Peter Willis

MARTORELL Codina, Josep (Maria).

Spanish. Born in Barcelona, 21 May 1925. Educated at the Escuela Tecnica Superior de Arquitectura, Barcelona, 1943–51, Dip.Arch. 1951, Dr.Arch. 1963; studied town planning at the Instituto de Estudios de la Administracion Local, Barcelona, 1961. Served in Spanish Army, Campamento de la Granja, Segovia, 1946–47. Married Roser Solanic in 1954. In partnership with Oriol Bohigas, *q.v.,* Barcelona, since 1951, with Bohigas and David Mackay, *q.v.,* Barcelona, since 1962. Worked with Office of the Provincial Commission for Town Planning, Barcelona, 1951–56; President, Cultural Commission of the College of Architecture of Catalunya, Barcelona,

1968–70; Representative, Town Planning and Community Services Commission, Barcelona, 1970–74. Founder-Member, Grupo R, Barcelona, 1951. Recipient: Fundacio Güell Prize, Institut d'Estudis Catalans, Barcelona, 1978. Address: Martorell-Bohigas-Mackay, Camp 61, Barcelona 6, Spain.

Publications:

By MARTORELL: books—*La Inmigracion a Catalunya,* with others, Barcelona 1968; *Guia d'Arquitectura de Menorca,* Barcelona 1978.

See MARTORELL-BOHIGAS-MACKAY

MARTORELL-BOHIGAS-MACKAY.

Partnership; established, Barcelona, 1962, by Josep Martorell, *q.v.,* Oriol Bohigas, *q.v.,* and David Mackay, *q.v.* (predecessor firm, Martorell and Bohigas, 1951–62). Exhibitions: *Grupo R,* Barcelona, 1952–58; *Bienal,* Sao Paulo, 1957; *Biennale,* Venice, 1976; Centro de Arquitectos, Rosario, Argentina, 1977; *Barcelona 1950–77,* Centre Georges Pompidou, Paris, 1978; *Setmanes Catalanes,* Berlin, 1978. Recipient: First Prize, Ministry of Education Centres of Professional Education Competition, 1954; First Prize, University of Barcelona Colleges Competition, 1956; First Prize, Colegio de Arquitectos de Catalunya Headquarters Competition, 1957, 1958; First Prize, Palacio Municipal Extension Competition, Barcelona, 1958; First Prize, Asociacion Ing. Indus. de Barcelona Housing Competition, 1959; FAD Prize, 1959, 1962, 1966; Delta de Plata Prize, ADI/FAD, 1966; Garriga Nogues Prize, 1975; Delta de Oro Prize, ADI/FAD, 1976; 2 First Prizes, Prototype Schools Competition, Ministry of Education, Madrid, 1979. Address: Camp 61, Barcelona 6, Spain.

Works:

Martorell and Bohigas:

1952/
62 Escorial Housing, Calle Escorial 50, Barcelona (with F. Mitjans, M. Ribas, and J. Alemany)

1954/
55 Guardiola House, Argentona, Maresme, Spain

1954/
58 Roger de Flor Housing, Calle Roger de Flor 215, Barcelona

1955/
58 Trade School, Sabinanigo, Huesca, Spain

1955/
59 Mutua Metalurgica de Seguros Clinic, Diagonal 394, Barcelona

1956/
61 Baro de Viver School, Barcelona

1957 Timbaler del Bruc School, Riera d'Horta/-Calle Arnaldo de Oms, Barcelona

1957/
68 Church of the Redeemer, Avenida Mare de Deu de Montserrat 34–40, Barcelona

1958 Provisional Church of St. Sebastian, Via Favencia, Verdum, Barcelona

1958/
59 Housing, Calle Pallars 299–317, Barcelona

1959 Piher Factory, Riera Canado, Badalona, Barcelona

1959/
62 Max Cahner House, Barcelona

Martorell-Bohigas-Mackay: Housing for Teaching Staff, Pińeda, Maresme, Spain, 1969

Martorell, Bohigas, Mackay:

1957/
64 Via Augusta-Muntaner Housing, Via Augusta 168, Barcelona
1959/
62 Lujan House, Palau de Plegamans, Valles Occidental, Barcelona
1959/
65 Meridiana Housing, Avenue Meridiana 312, Barcelona
1960/
63 Navas de Tolosa Housing, Calle Navas de Tolosa 296, Barcelona
1960/
65 Secretari Coloma Housing, Calle Secretari Coloma 79–89/Providencia 133–35, Barcelona
1960/
68 Sant Sebastian Parish Centre, Calle Viladrosa, Verdum, Barcelona
1961/
62 Orpi House, El Figaro, Valles Oriental, Barcelona
Permit Office, Colegio de Arquitectos de Catalunya, Plaza Nova 5, Barcelona
1961/
64 Casa del Pati Housing, Ronda Guinardo 44, Barcelona
1961/
65 Mas Silvestre Children's Holiday Colony, Canyamars, Maresme, Spain
1962/
64 Milans del Bosch Housing, Calle Sant Adria 196, Barcelona
1962/
65 Can Bordoi House, Llinars del Valles, Valles Oriental, Barcelona
La Vanguardia Newspaper Building, Calle Tallers 52–54, Barcelona
1962/
73 Garbi School, Esplugues de Llobregat, Barcelona
1963/
64 Europalma Housing Development, Costa de la Calma, Majorca
1963/
65 Espar Housing, Calle Milanesado 20–22, Barcelona
Pere IV Industrial Complex, Calle Pere IV 162, Barcelona
1963/
66 Sant Marti Housing, Calle Fluvia 200, Barcelona
1964/
67 Doctor Carulla Housing, Calle Dr. Carulla 53, Barcelona
1964/
70 Xaudiera Housing, Calle Entenca 99–101/Arago 20–22, Barcelona
1965/
67 Destino Publisher's Offices and Warehouse, Riera Canada, Badalona, Spain
1965/
69 Church of the Sagrada Familia, Igualada, Anoia, Spain
1966/
67 Santa Agueda Housing Development, Benicassim, Castello, Spain
1966/
69 Montana House, L'Ametlla del Valles, Valles Oriental, Barcelona
Housing, Calle Casp 114, Barcelona
1967/
68 Heredero House, Tredos, Vall d'Aran, Spain
1967/
69 Sant Jordi School, Calle Mn. Cinto Verdaguer, Pineda, Maresme, Spain
Housing, Calle Buscarons 16, Barcelona
1967/
71 Housing Development, Avenida Dr. Moragas, Santa Maria de Barbera, Valles Occidental, Barcelona

1967/
72 Housing Development, Avenida Angel Sallent Terrassa, Valles Occidental, Barcelona
1968/
69 Housing for Teaching Staff, Calle Mn. Cinto Verdaguer, Pineda, Maresme, Spain
1968/
72 Piher Factory, Avenida San Julian, Granollers, Valles Oriental, Barcelona
M. Serras Shop, Calle Anselm Clave 28, Granollers, Valles Oriental, Barcelona
1968/
75 Augusta Clinic, Calle Madrazo 8–10, Barcelona
1969/
71 Piher Factory II, Riera Canado, Badalona, Barcelona
1969/
72 Giro Hnos Textile Factory, Avenida Navarra, Badalona, Barcelona
Haissa Knitwear Factory, Avenida Marti Pujol 273, Badalona, Barcelona
1969/
73 Crescent de Viladecans Housing Development, Calle del Sol. Viladecans, Baix Llobregat, Spain
Manzana la Salut Housing Development, Calle Ruperto Llado/Riera de la Salud, Sant Feliu de Llobregat, Baix Llogregat, Spain
1970 Sant Cugat Golf Club, Sant Cugat del Valles, Valles Occidental, Barcelona (project)
1970/
73 Bonanova Housing, Plaza de la Bonanova 92, Barcelona
Gubern Footwear Shop, Calle del Mar 54–56, Badalona, Barcelona
1971/
73 Pals Golf Houses, Plays de Pals, Baix Emporda, Spain
1971/
74 Illuro Department Store, Calle Sant Antoni 82–88, Mataro, El Maresme, Spain
1971/
75 Casa de la Torre Housing Development, Avenida Mossen Cinto Verdaguer, Santa Perpetua de la Moguda, Valles Occidental, Barcelona
1972/
74 Marti House, Sant Jordi d'Alfama, Baix Ebre, Spain
Cases Bessones Building, Calle Rectoria 36–38, Barcelona
Thau School, Carretera de Esplugues 49–53, Barcelona
1973/
74 Almaina Park Housing Development, Muchamiel, Alacant, Spain (project)
1973/
75 Misser House, Llinars del Valles, Valles Oriental, Barcelona
1974/
75 El Hacho de Manilva Tourist Development, Manilva, Malaga, Spain (project; with Vittorio Gregotti)
1974/
77 Housing, Calle La Costa 59–63, Barcelona
1975 Riudellots Housing Development, Riudellots de la Selva, Girones, Spain (project; with Enric Steegman)
1975/
77 Almirall House, La Garriga, Valles Oriental, Barcelona
Otero House, La Garriga, Valles Oriental, Barcelona
Housing, Calle Ossio 45–53, Barcelona
1975/
78 Amil House, Sant Vicenc de Montalt, Maresme, Spain
1976 Colegio de Arquitectos Headquarters, Plaza Cristo de Burgos, Seville (project; with Enric Steegman)

Colegio de Arquitectos de Catalunya Headquarters extension, Plaza Nova, Barcelona (project; with Enric Steegman)
1979 Vall-Roig Housing Development, Manzana/-Calle Espana-Roma-Sevilla/Diagonal, Cerdanyola, Barcelona

Publications:

On MBM: books—*Antologia Espanola de Arte Contemporaneo* by Cesareo Rodriguez-Aguilera, Barcelona 1955; *El Arte en las Artes* by Juan Perucho, Barcelona 1964; *Panorama del Nuevo Arte Espanol* by Vincente Aguilera Cerni, Madrid 1966; *La Otra Cara de Catalunya* by Jose Carlos Clemente, Barcelona and Mexico City 1968; *Los Encuentros* by Baltasar Porcel, Barcelona 1969; *Temas de Arquitectura Escolar, 1972: Martorell, Bohigas, Mackay* by José Corredor Matheos, Barcelona 1973; *Martorell, Bohigas, Mackay: Arquitectura 1951–1972* by Juan Daniel Fullaondo, Barcelona and Madrid 1974; *Arquitecturas Catalanas* by Helio Pinon, Barcelona 1978 *Martorell-Bohigas-Mackay: Arquitectura 1953–1978* by Helio Pinon and Charles Jencks, Madrid 1979; articles—"Interview mit Josep Maria Martorell, Oriol Bohigas und David Mackay" by Joaquin Gili in *Moebel Interior Design* (Leinfelden, Germany), January 1967; "Testimonianze di Martorell, Bohigas e Mackay" by José Corredor Matheos in *L'Architettura* (Rome), August 1968; "Aportaciones de la Culture Arquitectonica Catalana: Equipo Martorell, Bohigas, Mackay" by Antonio Fernandez Alba in *Nueva Forma* (Madrid), March 1973; "Martorell, Bohigas, Mackay et l'Architecture du Logement a Barcelone" by Ignasi Sola Morales in *L'Architecture d'Aujourd'hui* (Paris), January/February 1975; "MBM and the Barcelona School" by Charles Jencks in *Architectural Review* (London), March 1977.

Between—or beyond—an architecture meant to be drawn and an architecture meant to be built, there is built architecture that can be drawn (to be built, it had to be drawn beforehand). Between Piranesi and the practical manuals on house constructions are the essayists who, like Palladio, establish compositive bases upon either built examples or working drawings. So the drawing—the essential tool to control the composition and to check the design intentions—is, at the same time, a self-sufficient expression of an artistic proposal. It is this artistic proposal, understood as an intention to compose the building —"compose it" and "pose it" in its physical, psychological, or cultural setting—that is underlined in the various works we have carried out during 25 years of professional practice. Instead of attempting a systematic explanation, we can say that each building refers to elements and systems in a visual order composed and "posed." This approach to architecture can be classified in four distinct ways, though in reality they more often than not merge.

1) The conceptual thread leads through the relationship between the architectural project and the architectural and urban elements that have a constant tradition in the built environment. One aspect of this relationship is the minimalization of stylistic elements in an area where these elements are well defined. The relationship concerns not only the total form of the building itself but also the surface texture of the facade, which defines the "skin" of the environment. The persistent constructive play of artificial stone in and around the centre of Barcelona is an example.

2) Another aspect of this relationship is in the use of ordinary, anonymous elements that, even if they do not strictly correspond to the context, allow the architecture to be easily understood, because they are rooted in a solid but living tradition. Timber bay-windows, small scale traditional construction imposed upon a new urban building, and back galleries shifted round to the front facade are a few examples. These elements are often chosen for their delib-

erately fragile nature, which allows the new building to be absorbed into the neighbourhood as something provisional, not yet converted into a monumental object but, rather, a soft addition to a quietly changing neighbourhood whose character is maintained by a succession of these adaptable newcomers. Timber-slats, asbestos-cement, canvas blinds, and wooden shutters all suggest this reserved intention not to intrude with a rude, autocratic imposition: they are consistent with the user's desire for self-expression, within a composition of apparent disorder that supports this structure.

3) The relationship between architecture and the city can also be inverted, with part of the building reflecting the urban structure and texture as though it had allowed the city to carry on inside. This reference is visual rather than functional. The mistake of trying to impose on the left-over spaces the vitality of a city, by copying the social reality of the urban street, is avoided by restricting the image to a sequence of urban references within the architecture, even if the result is rhetorical or theatrical.

4) A more intensive architectural intervention is appropriate when the building or group of buildings act as an instrument of urban revival. When a street or neighbourhood has lost its initial vitality and decay has begun to set in, there is a need to create new centres of interest, rearrange a decadent disorder, reinterpret use, correct street perspectives, and relate urban incidents to the meaning of the places. The limits of this sort of intervention are always within the modest dimensional characteristics of architecture and its capacity to be read and understood in an easy code that is recognized by the man in the street; it must be close to that reality that is rooted in the historical process of the community and guarantees its coherent continuity.

These four "ways" are each an attempt to try to recover the proper role of architecture within the historical centres, its capacity to intervene in form and content without rejecting the familiar references of the social groups that both use and create within a process of continuing dialogue. The architect can work only like a beauty specialist or a cosmetic surgeon, whose task is always partial in that it cannot essentially change the human body or introduce a new interpretative code. Adjusting the contours of a nose or breast involves an agreement that, because of the mistakes of nature or the effects of wear and tear, there is a need for improvement; the make-up artist works according to the same kind of agreement. The make-up man and the cosmetic surgeon achieve, slowly, within the limits of the skills their professions have attained, a partial change in the human figure. The architect in relation to the city is in the same position: it is no exaggeration to say that in some respects the anatomy and biology of reality is the result of an archaeological superimposition of various make-ups and various partial adjustments, and it is that reality with which the architect must work.

To build in Europe almost always means to build in the historical city, especially if we understand by "historical" all that is both old and recent, the result of a dialectical process. Accordingly, the work of the architect in our cities should always be like that of the make-up artist or cosmetic surgeon. But the rapid growth of our cities, combined with the lack of limitation on private speculation, has destroyed the historical dialogue. The "new towns," "residential estates" and "slum clearances" involve attitudes and methods very different from those of the make-up artist and cosmetic surgeon. There is no previous structure upon which to work, so there can be no reflection of the old cities: the reality of their historical process cannot be imitated without the architect's committing the error of the ridiculous, be it the picturesque, monumental, folk, or revival. The challenge of virgin territory should be met with new constructions that are parallel to the large public works that have been refined and adjusted during the last 200 years and are now available to us charged with historical process, however unorthodox. The country is not the city, and to achieve an urban

context rapidly new structures must be used—the ones we have already, the ones with a long visual history, the port, the railroad, the motorway, the dam, the quarry, and the airstrip.

—Martorell-Bohigas-Mackay

The partners in Martorell-Bohigas-Mackay are polemicists, and they have nicely portrayed some of the traps that recent Spanish architecture has fallen into—from the casualties of the revolution, those buildings that avoid reality in a make-believe world, to the particular pseudo-vernacularizing that amounts to a sick architecture, courting reality with formal irony and a certain amount of despair, to the faceless buildings that have come to be symbols of the hollow grey elite of the meritocracy. The architect rushing to stay in one place is the only constant in an inconstant milieu. The MBM answer, however, is not some sort of National Romanticism, with its dead-end in People's Democratic Architecture, nor a Technological Romanticism with its dead-end in a neutral, stillborn architecture, nor some utopian fantasy that never quite emerges from its pseudo-scientific test-tubes. MBM's credo is "poetic realism"—charging a building with imagination and suggesting the purpose of culture, the sort of architecture that always endeavours to be one step ahead of the printed word.

MBM condemns many of the vanities and anomalies of modern Spanish architecture. Neither the adolescent longing for a computer-based architecture with a comic-strip coding nor the overstressed axonometric cut-away mathematical vocabulary entirely escape their critical venom; neither is an "architecture-of-autobiography" nor a "blood-and-earth-architecture" safe. But, perhaps owing to their hypersensitivity to the limitations of most of the styles manifested by Spanish architecture today, they themselves seem unwilling to commit themselves to any style at all, and their "poetic realism" seems to mean no more than adopting a different genre for each design programme, hoping to find a better fit between the immediate conditions of the environment and the functional parameters than a more consistent "style" might allow. This method permits them to invent a succinct style from scratch, then bring it to realization and destruction within the span of a single building.

The rhythmic intermittence of the Meridiana Housing in Barcelona, an urban wall with occasional apertures, is a pertinent solution to the problems of a house-in-the-city, but it was abandoned as soon as it had been devised. MBM moved on to a kind of vernacular-run-amok at Santa Agueda, Benicassim: this labour-intensive-picturesque style, with its broken massing and throw-away feel, was indeed thrown away for the next major project, the housing for teaching staff at Pineda, which is much more compact and exacting. The Piher Factory at Granollers is an unashamed industrial shed. The apartments in Gerona are a Venturian elegy, the Thau School in Barcelona a gasketted dream of modernism. If this is "poetic realism," what is the difference between it and stripped classicism, or tourist architecture, or official monumentalism?

Still, a period of destruction, followed by one of what seems to the observer to be almost wilfully chaotic experimentation, is the classic progress of revolution—and revolutions are sometimes successful. Martorell-Bohigas-Mackay share an acute awareness of the problems and structure of urban life. It may be that the best is yet to come.

—Chris Fawcett

MASUDA, Tomoya.
Japanese. Born on Awaji Island, Hyogo Prefecture, 16 December 1914. Educated at the University of Kyoto, 1935–39, B.Arch. 1939. Lecturer, 1950–58, Assistant Professor, 1958–62, Professor, 1962–78, and since 1978 Emeritus Professor, University of Kyoto (has maintained atelier at the university). D.Arch., University of Kyoto, 1954. Address: Department of Architecture, Faculty of Engineering, Kyoto University, Sakyo-ku, Kyoto 606, Japan.

Works:

1957 Nantan-cho Town Hall, Hyogo Prefecture, Japan
     Institute for Radioactive Macromolecular Research, Neyagawa, Osaka Prefecture, Japan
     City Hall, Nagasaki (competition project)
1958 Rest House, Miyazu, Kyoto Prefecture, Japan
     Keage Purification Plant, Kyoto
     Onomichi City Hall, Hiroshima Prefecture, Japan
1959 Girls' High School, Suma, Kobe, Japan
     Toba Sewage Disposal Plant, Kyoto
     Engineering Faculty Buildings, Kyoto University
1961 Onomichi Assembly Hall, Hiroshima Prefecture, Japan
     Sumoto City Hall, Hyogo Prefecture, Japan
1962 Naruto City Hall, Tokushima Prefecture, Japan
     Kyoto University Atomic Pile Laboratory, Kumatori, Osaka Prefecture, Japan
     Kobayashi House, Kinugasayama, Kyoto
1963 Yamanouchi Purification Plant, Kyoto
     Suzuki Automotive Industries Main Building, Hamana-gun, Shizuoka Prefecture, Japan
     Higashiyama Hall, Kyoto
1964 Chishakuin Hall, Kyoto
     Memorial Assembly Hall, Kyoto University (project)
1965 Dormitory for the Tsuruya-Yoshinobu Company, Kyoto
     Master plan for *Expo '70*, Osaka (project)
1966 Shimizu Central Public Hall, Shizuoka Prefecture, Japan
1967 Heart Institute Laboratories, Tokyo
1968 Japan Furniture Centre, Harumi, Tokyo
1970 Toyooka Civic Centre, Hyogo Prefecture, Japan
     Monument to Typhoon Victims During A-Bomb Investigation, Hiroshima
1971 Engineering Faculty Main Office Building, Kyoto University
     Memorial Gymnasium, Kyoto University
     Okamoto House, Nantan-cho, Hyogo Prefecture, Japan
1972 Kitanada-Higashi Primary School and Kindergarten, Naruto, Tokushima Prefecture, Japan
1973 Hokke Club House, Kyoto
     Naruto Cultural Center, Tokushima Prefecture, Japan (project)
1975 Kuwajima Kindergarten, Naruto, Tokushima Prefecture, Japan
1976 Naruto Welfare Center for the Aged, Tokushima Prefecture, Japan

Publications:

By MASUDA: book—*Architecture Universelle Japon*, Geneva 1969; article—"Struktur und Freiheit" in *Werk* (Zurich), October 1962.

On MASUDA: articles—"Town Hall, Minami-tan machi, Hyogo" in *The Japan Architect* (Tokyo), February 1958; "Onomichi City Hall" in *The Japan Architect* (Tokyo), September 1960; "Hohere Madschenschule in Suma, Kobe, Japan" in *Werk* (Zurich), no. 4, 1962; "A House in Kinugasayama" in

Tomoya Masuda: Higashiyama Hall, Kyoto, 1963

The Japan Architect (Tokyo), August 1964; "Bauchronik: Eigenheim von Prof. Kobayashi, Kinugasayama, Kyoto" in *Werk* (Zurich), no. 5, 1964; "Siedlung mit Terrassenhausern bei Kobe, Japan" in *Werk* (Zurich), no. 10, 1964; "The Japan Furniture Center" in *The Japan Architect* (Tokyo), January/February 1968; "Laboratories for the Heart Institute" in *The Japan Architect* (Tokyo), December 1968; "The Chishaukuin Hall" in *The Japan Architect* (Tokyo), June 1969.

"Nature" is apprehended in two ways in our traditional way of thought. One is: we do not act upon it, we leave it intact; that is, nature is just "the given." The other is: we act freely upon "the given," naively following our own essential nature. These two visions are simultaneous and ambiguous. Just as "the given" is not merely naked physical nature, so is any artificial action not merely arbitrary or illogical. Both "nature" itself, that which the word "nature" signifies, and the attitude toward "nature," I assume to be "a-logical" or "non-logical." If the word "non-logical" does not mean illogical (*id est,* "not logical"), and if it conceivably implies the logical "non" —in other words, a logic of none—then it would be clear what and how the East, following its own nature, has constructed in "nature." It would then become evident how foresighted were the tea-house, flower arranging, gardening and its architecture, and, above all, the sense of time and space.

—Tomoya Masuda

Is Japanese architecture "form above all," as Peter Smithson has suggested—is it reducible to a "rectangular plane and a certain sort of curve"?

The large output of Tomoya Masuda's atelier at Kyoto University has been consistently concerned with assessing the nature and formative roots of the Japanese architectural tradition vis-a-vis Western architectural biography. The fundamental distinction that Masuda draws between the two spatial enterprises rests on the "visible basis" of Western architecture and the "non-visible basis" of the Japanese. He cites the material aspects of classical and gothic forms as forming a visible basis in the European environment, in contrast to the way that columns alone signify Japanese space. Mannerism is the moment in Western history when "visibility" took over and wrapped itself independently around architectural superstructures: it would have continued to appear to us to be the only solution if modernism had not come along and cleared the air. Looking to the traditional Japanese house as an exemplar, the heroic architects chucked out visibility in favour of an architecture not determined by visual rules, proportions and geometries alone. But now visibility is beginning to creep in again through the back door—in the guise of post-modernism, post-metabolism, post-rationalism. The architecture of pure outlines of purpose just passed us by: there was nothing to remember it by, no mnemonic or associational network to make it adhere: it just drifted past as if it had never arrived in the first place. And that brings us back to square one. Visible rules hold sway again. "Difference" has again become a value, when only fifty years ago "difference" had been replaced with "similarity."

Masuda, in such works as the Kyoto University Gymnasium or the Higashiyama Hall, is intent on establishing a middle path, a neutral line between these polarities—not a clear-cut centre parting but an ambiguous zone of double meaning best described by the term *ryogi*. Not so objective and finite as

"balance," it is more a matter of accommodating as many of the extremes on both sides as one can.

Another key consideration for Masuda is that we should see "others" as ourselves: we should design for ourselves, that is, for ourselves-as-others. What is the difference between designing for oneself and for oneself-as-others? An actor on the stage—he plays the part of a killer but must remain himself as well: the architect must become an actor.

—Chris Fawcett

MAY, Ernst.
German. Born in Frankfurt, 27 July 1886. Educated at University College, London, 1907–08; Technische Hochschule, Darmstadt, 1908–10; worked in the town planning office of Raymond Unwin, London, 1910–12; studied at the Technische Hochschule, Munich, under Friedrich von Thiersch and Theodor Fischer, 1912–13. Served in the German Imperial Army on the eastern and western fronts during World War I. Established private practice, Frankfurt, 1913; Technical Director, Regional Planning Authority, Breslau, 1919–21; Director, Public Housing Authority, Breslau, 1921–23; Director, Central Office for Refugee Welfare/Distressed People's Housing, Breslau, 1923–25; City Architect, Frankfurt, 1925–30; Director of the European Town Planning Team in the U.S.S.R., 1930–34; farmed in Tanganyika, 1934–37; in private practice, as architect and town planner, Nairobi, Kenya, 1937–54 (interned as an "enemy alien," 1942–45); Head of the Planning Department, subsequently Adviser on City Planning and Housing Techniques, Neue Heimat Housing Development Organization, Hamburg, 1954–60; in private practice, Hamburg, 1960 until his death, 1970. Founder Editor, *Das Schlesische Heim,* Breslau, 1919–25, *Das Neue Frankfurt,* 1925–30, and *Neue Heimat,* Hamburg, 1954–60. Recipient: German Cross of Merit. Honorary D.Eng.: Technische Hochschule, Hanover; D.Phil.: University of Freiburg; Honorary Professor, Technische Hochschule, Darmstadt. Member, Akademie der Künste, Berlin. Honorary President, German Association of Housing, Town and Country Planning. Honorary Corresponding Member, British Town Planning Institute, and Royal Institute of British Architects. *Died* (in Hamburg) *12 September 1970.*

Works:

1919   Cottages, Goldschmieden-Neukirche, Germany
1922   Plan for a housing development at Ohlau, Lower Silesia
1926   May House, Frankfurt
1926/
27   Bruchfeldstrasse Housing Development, Frankfurt
Ginnheim Housing Development, Frankfurt
Praunheim Housing Development, Frankfurt
1928   Reform School, Bornheimer Hang, Frankfurt (with A. Locher)
Niederrad Housing Development, Frankfurt (with H. Boehm)
Westhausen Housing Development, Frankfurt
Römerstadt Housing Development, Frankfurt
Hohenblick Housing Development, Frankfurt
Bornheimer Hang Housing Development, Frankfurt
Riedhof-East Housing Development, Frankfurt
Gartenstadt Goldstein Development, Frankfurt
Tornow-Gelande Housing Development, Frankfurt

Manundshainerstrasse Housing Development, Frankfurt

Engelsruhe Development, Höchst, Frankfurt

Miquelstrasse Housing Development, Frankfurt

Plans for housing developments at Raimundstrasse, Riederwald, Rutschlehen, and Riedhof-West, Frankfurt

1928/
30 Redevelopment plan for Frankfurt
1930/
34 Town plans for Stseglovsk, Kusnetszk, Tirgan, Magnitogorsk, Stalinsk, Nishni-Tagil, and Leninakan, U.S.S.R.

Regional plan for Moscow

1945/
47 May House, Nairobi

Delamate Avenue Housing Development, Nairobi

1947 City plan for Kampala

Community development plan for Naguru, Uganda

Central Recreation Park, Kampala

Oceanic Hotel, Mombasa, Kenya

Farmer's house, Limuru, Kenya

Farmer's house, Molo, Kenya

Aga Khan House, Oyster Bay, Dar-es-Salaam

1950/
51 Aga Khan School, Kisumu, Kenya

Aga Khan Maternity Hospital, Kisumu, Kenya

Cultural Center, with Shops, Offices and Hotel, Moshi, Tanganyika

1954/
56 Hegholt Housing Development, Hamburg (with Sprotte and Neve)

Grunhofe Housing Development, Weissenstein, Bremerhaven

St. Lorenz Housing Development, Lubeck

Alte Vahr Housing Development, Bremen

Housing development, Aachen-West

Redevelopment plan for Neu-Altona, Germany

Apartment building, Lübeckerstrasse, Hamburg

1956/
70 May House, Hamburg

Rheinhausen Housing Development (competition project)

Fennptuhl Housing Development, Lichtenberg, East Berlin (competition project)

Limes Housing Development, Frankfurt (competition project)

Garath Housing Development, Dusseldorf (project)

Workers' Housing, Wulfen, Germany (competition project)

Neuen Vahr Housing Development, Bremen

Parkfeld Housing Development, Wiesbaden (competition project)

Klarenthal Housing Development, Wiesbaden

Dotzheim Housing Development, Wiesbaden

Rahlstedt Housing Development, Hamburg

Housing development, Stuttgart

Eselsweg Housing Development, Mainz

Plan for the redevelopment of the centre of Bremerhaven

Publications:

By MAY: articles—numerous contributions to *Das Schlesische Heim* (Breslau), *Das Neue Frankfurt,* and *Neue Heimat* (Hamburg).

On MAY: book—*Ernst May: Bauten und Planungen* by J. Buekschmitt, Stuttgart 1963; articles—"House in Kenya by Ernst May" in *The Architects' Journal* (London), 20 July 1939; "Kampala Town Planning" in *The Architects' Yearbook,* London 1947; "Eigenheim des Architekten in Nairobi" in *Werk* (Zurich), June 1949; "House at Dar-es-Salaam" in *Architectural Review* (London), May 1953; "The One-Family House Versus Rebuilding the City" in *American Institute of Planners Journal* (Washington, D.C.), Fall 1956; "Ernst May" in *Der Aufbau* (Vienna), May 1957; "Ernst May: La Sua Abitazione ad Amburgo" in *Abitare* (Milan), May 1964; "Un Architetto e Una Città: Ernst May a Francoforte" by Giorgio Grassi in *Controspazio* (Bari, Italy), April/May 1970.

From the time of his early studies in Munich and in England, Ernst May was much influenced by the ideas of Ebenezer Howard and the architecture of Raymond Unwin. He was an admirer of English domestic architecture championed by Muthesius and a devotee of the Garden City movement. Yet his work for the new *Wohnkultur* was free from social and stylistic constrictions in a way that was not possible in England, for May's professional career coincided with a period of great social and political change in Germany.

As architect of Frankfurt in the 1920's, he designed the celebrated Römerstadt Housing Estate, which embodied some of the best English and Continental ideas of the time. Basically municipal low-income housing, Römerstadt was planned with small gardens and with something of the ideals of the Garden City movement, yet the architecture is avant-garde, owing much to the models of the Bauhaus circle. The peculiar economic difficulties within the Weimar Republic encouraged the use of experimental building techniques for cheapness, and standardized components and units were developed. May must therefore be seen as a major architect working within the tradition of providing low-cost housing that was developed from the 19th century.

He was invited to the Soviet Union to advise on town planning, and he led the teams responsible for the design of Tirgan and for the drafting of the Moscow Regional Plan. After only three years, however, he left Russia for East Africa, where he worked as a planning adviser.

His experience in the design of low-cost housing led to his appointment as consultant to the Heimat housing combine after the Second World War. He specialized in the renewal of the shattered German towns and cities using techniques he had learned at Römerstadt. In his later years he became concerned with the deteriorating quality of the environment and with the dehumanization of planning. Just as Soviet Russia did not live up to his expectations in the 1930's, so the post-war reconstruction in a new era also disappointed him. He became aware that the modern planner had the power to make an environment totally lacking in human qualities, and he saw that the total rejection of the past for a chimerical technological paradise had brought new terrors to modern life.

May was primarily a creative architect who never lost sight of his early aims to create a decent environment for healthy humans. At Römerstadt he made an extraordinary marriage of ultra-modern simplicity in architectural design with the principles of the Garden City movement, and thus broke away from the theories of Camillo Sitte and Muthesius that had influenced him in his early years. His 1919 designs for cottages at Goldschmieden-Neukirche reflect the influence of Unwin, his lifelong friend and mentor. These are still picturesque and traditional, in the enlightened eclecticism advocated by Muthesius, but Römerstadt, with its crisply cubic buildings and bald, even stark, outlines, owes even more to Professor Tessenow's housing schemes at Dresden or Bruno Taut's designs at Berlin-Falkenberg.

May has been represented as a left-wing idealist, an idea that has been fostered after his stay in the Soviet Union. In fact, he was nearest the Fabian Socialist position and remained sympathetic to this very British brand of idealism all his life, partly through his friendship with Unwin and partly through his adherence to the views of the Town and Country Planning Association. Despite internment in Kenya during the war as an "enemy alien," he remained an enthusiastic admirer of liberal ideas from Britain until his death.

—James Stevens Curl

MAYBECK, Bernard (Ralph).

American. Born in New York City, 7 February 1862. Educated at the L'Ecole Nationale dex Beaux-Arts, Paris, 1881–86 (Silver Medal, 1885). Married Annie White in 1890; children: Wallen and Kerna. Worked for Carrere and Hastings, New York, 1886–88; Partner, Russell and Maybeck, Kansas City, 1888; worked for Ernest Coxhead, San Francisco, 1889–90, and for A. Page Brown, San Francisco, 1891–94; in private practice, Berkeley, California, from 1894;

Ernst May: Romerstadt Housing Development, Frankfurt, 1928

Bernard Maybeck: First Church of Christ Scientist, Berkeley, California, 1910

Instructor in Drawing, University of California, Berkeley, 1894–97, and Director of Architectural Studies, Mark Hopkins Institute of Art, San Francisco, 1895–97; Manager of the Phoebe A. Hearst Competition for the architectural design of the University of California campus, 1896–1900 (travelled abroad extensively on competition business); Instructor in Architecture, University of California, Berkeley, 1898–03 (devised first complete curriculum in architecture); opened San Francisco office in 1902; retired from active practice, 1938. Supervising Architect, United States Shipping Board, 1917; Associate Architect, *Golden Gate International Exposition,* 1939. Member, Berkeley City Planning Commission; President, San Francisco Art Association. Exhibitions: *Domestic Architecture of the San Francisco Bay Region,* San Francisco Museum of Art, 1949; *Roots of Contemporary Architecture,* Los Angeles, 1956. Recipient: Gold Medal, American Institute of Architects, 1951. M.A.: Mills College, Oakland, California, 1923; LL.D.: University of California, 1930. *Died* (in Berkeley) *3 October 1957.*

Works:

1886   Ponce de Leon Hotel, St. Petersburg, Florida (with Thomas Hastings)
1891   Crocker Building, San Francisco (as draftsman to A. Page Brown)
1892/
1902   Bernard Maybeck House, Grove and Berryman Streets, Berkeley, California
1894   Swedenborgian Church, San Francisco (as draftsman to A. Page Brown)
1895   Keeler House, Highland Place, Berkeley, California
1896   Emma Kellogg House I, Palo Alto, California (destroyed, 1899)
        Hall House, Highland Place, Berkeley, California (destroyed, 1956)

Lawson House, Waring Street, Berkeley, California (destroyed)
1897   Davis House, Ridge Road, Berkeley, California (destroyed, 1957)
1899   Town and Gown Club, Dwight Way, Berkeley, California (with later additions by other architects)
        Emma Kellogg House II ("Sunbonnet House"), Bryant Street, Palo Alto, California
        Reception Building, for Phoebe A. Hearst, Channing Way, Berkeley, California (moved to the University of California campus and converted to a gymnasium, Hearst Hall, 1901; destroyed, 1922)
        Rieger House, Highland Place, Berkeley, California (destroyed, 1958)
1900   Bridgeman House, La Loma Street, Berkeley, California
        McCrea House, Derby Street, Berkeley, California
1901   Flagg House, Shattuck Avenue, Berkeley, California
1902   Barn, University of California, Berkeley (project)
        Faculty Club, University of California, Berkeley (with later additions by others)
        Whitney House, Hawthorne Terrace, Berkeley, California (destroyed by fire, 1923)
        Hiram Kellogg House, Regent Street, Berkeley California (relocated to Lyndon Street, Berkeley)
        Stockton House, LeRoy Avenue, Berkeley, California (destroyed by fire, 1923)
        Bunnell House addition, San Francisco
        Barnett House, San Francisco (project)
        Boke House, Panoramic Way, Berkeley, California
        Dresslar House, La Conte Avenue, Berkeley, California (destroyed by fire, 1923)

Keeler Studio, Highland Place, Berkeley, California
1902/
   03   Wyntoon (Phoebe Hearst country estate), McCloud River, Siskiyou County, California (destroyed)
1903   Cooley House, Haste Street, Berkeley, California (project)
        Clubhouse, Bohemian Club of San Francisco, Bohemian Grove, Russian River, California (2 projects)
        Newall Brothers Store Building, San Jose, California (remodelled)
        Jones House, Berkeley, California (project)
        Thomas House additions, Berkeley, California (destroyed by fire, 1923)
        University of California Hospital, San Francisco (project)
1904   Gates House, South 13th Street, San Jose, California
        California Wine Association Exhibit, *St. Louis Exposition*
        Newall House remodelling, Pacific Street, San Francisco (with additional remodelling, 1906)
        Bettys House, Berkeley, California (project)
        Bunnell House movement to new site and remodelling, Broadway near Pierce Street, San Francisco
        Newall House remodelling, El Camino Real near Oakgrove, Burlingame, California (destroyed)
        Underhill House I, LeRoy Avenue, Berkeley, California (destroyed by fire, 1923)
        Outdoor Art Club Building, Blithedale Avenue, Mill Valley, California
        Ranson Beach House, Sunnyside Avenue, Oakland, California
1905   Farrington House, Arch Street, Berkeley, California (destroyed by fire, 1923)

Diggles House, Lomita Park, San Mateo, California

Tufts House I, Entrata Avenue, San Anselmo, California

1906 Hamilton Church, Belvedere and Waller, San Francisco (project)

School, Morgan Hill, California

Hillside Club Building, Cedar Street, Berkeley, California (with additions, 1922; destroyed by fire, 1923)

Sanderson House, Lookout Place, Berkeley, California (destroyed by fire, 1923)

Gregory House, Hilgard Street, Berkeley, California (project)

Elston House, Aberdeen, Washington

Unitarian Church, Cowper and Channing Streets, Palo Alto, California (destroyed)

Flagg Studio, Shattuck Avenue, Berkeley, California

Miall House, Burlingame, California (project)

Robinson House, El Camino Real, Burlingame, California (destroyed)

Frey House, Berkeley, California (project)

Stiles House, Piedmont, California (project)

Tait House, East Oakland, California (project)

Hopps House, Winding Way, Ross, California (with additions, 1925)

Paul Elder Bookstore, Van Ness and Pine, San Francisco (destroyed)

de Lemascheffsky House, Le Conte Avenue, Berkeley, California (project)

George Hansen Houses, Berkeley, California (projects)

Evans House, Arch Street, Berkeley, California (project)

Telegraph Hill Neighborhood House, Stockton Street, San Francisco

Welch House, Larkin Street, San Francisco (project)

Read House, Stockton, California (project)

Rees House, La Loma and Virginia, Berkeley, California

1907 French House, Summer Street, Berkeley, California

Senger House, Bay View Place, Berkeley, California

Kern House, Dormidera Street, Piedmont, California

Stebbins House remodelling, Berkeley, California

Oscar Maurer Photographic Studio, LeRoy Avenue, Berkeley, California

Gregory House, Greenwood Terrace, Berkeley, California

Robinson House, Burlingame, California (project)

Schneider House, Arch Street, Berkeley, California

Lawson House, La Loma Avenue, Berkeley, California

Saeltzer House, West Street, Redding, California

Underhill House II, Tamalpais Road, Berkeley, California (destroyed by fire, 1923)

Bath House for Hearst Hall, University of California, Berkeley (destroyed, 1922)

1908 Tufts House II, Culloden Street, San Rafael, California

Roman House, Laurel Place, San Rafael, California

Atkinson House, Durant Avenue, Berkeley, California

Havens House, Wildwood Gardens, Piedmont, California (later remodelled)

Library, for Briggs House, Los Gatos, California

Social Hall, Unity Church, Bancroft and Dana Streets, Berkeley, California (destroyed)

1909 Goodman House, Berkeley, California (project)

Flagg Summer House, Orr's Creek, Ukiah, California (destroyed, 1921)

Roos House, 3500 Jackson Street, San Francisco (with additions: living room, 1913; garage, 1916; dressing room, 1919; study, 1926)

Randolph School, 2700 Belrose Avenue, Berkeley, California (now a residence)

Goslinsky House, 3233 Pacific Avenue, San Francisco

Rowell House, Mildreda and Forthcamp Street, Fresno, California (destroyed)

Fry House, 32nd Avenue, San Francisco

Thomas House, Eldridge Avenue, Mill Valley, California

Bernard Maybeck House II, Buena Vista Way, Berkeley, California (destroyed by fire, 1923)

Randolph School, Shattuck and Berryman, Berkeley, California (project)

1910 Thomas Studio, Greenwood Terrace, Berkeley, California (destroyed by fire, 1923)

Dyer House, Los Gatos, California

Decker House, Buena Vista Way, Berkeley, California (project)

Apartment house, Lombard and Leavenworth Street, San Francisco (project)

Power House, 1526 Masonic Avenue, San Francisco

Shuman House, Sycamore Avenue, San Mateo, California

San Francisco Settlement Association Club Building, 2520 Folsom Street, San Francisco (destroyed)

First Church of Christ Scientist, Dwight Way and Bowditch Street, Berkeley, California

1911 Young House, Green Street, San Francisco (project)

Boynton House, Buena Vista Way, Berkeley, California (temporary house; permanent house completed by A. R. Monro; destroyed by fire, 1923; subsequently rebuilt)

Jockers House, La Loma Avenue, Berkeley, California

Strawberry Canyon Bath House, University of California, Berkeley (project)

Towart House, Buena Vista Way and La Loma Avenue, Berkeley, California (destroyed by fire, 1923)

Design for Canberra, Australia (competition project)

Courthouse, Dayton, Nevada (competition project)

Schwartz House, Oakland, California (project)

1911/
13 Field houses for the de Fermery Playground, Mosswood Park Playground, and Bella Vista Playground, Oakland, California

1912 Flagg House II, Shattuck Avenue, Berkeley, California

Runyon House, Los Molinas, California (project)

Irving House, Sonora, California

Pacific Unitarian Church and School, Dana and Allston Way, Berkeley, California (project)

Steps and walk, for Underhill House, Rose Path and Euclid Avenue, Berkeley, California

San Francisco City Hall (competition project)

1913 Alameda County Infirmary, California (competition project)

Scott House, Vine and Scenic Avenue, Berkeley, California (destroyed by fire, 1923)

Young House, 51 Sotelo Avenue, Forest Hills, San Francisco

Parsons Memorial Lodge, Sierra Club, Tuolumne Meadows, California

1913/
15 Town plan and hotel for Brookings Lumber Company, Brookings, Oregon (as projects: cottages, YMCA Club, and school)

1914 McFarlan House, Hawthorne Terrace, Berkeley, California (destroyed by fire, 1923)

Chick House, Chabot Road, Berkeley, California

Kennedy Studio, Euclid Avenue, Berkeley, California (destroyed by fire, 1923; rebuilt and annex added, 1923)

1915 Palace of Fine Arts, Livestock Pavilion, and "House of Hoo-Hoo" for the Pacific Lumbermen's Association, *International Exposition,* San Francisco

Hunt House, Spruce Street, Berkeley, California (relocated to Domingo Avenue, Berkeley)

Mathewson House, La Loma and Buena Vista Way, Berkeley, California

Whitney House, Keith Avenue, Berkeley, California

1916 Greene House, Chabot Road, Berkeley, California (destroyed)

Erlanger House, 270 Castenada, Forest Hills, San Francisco

Jackson House remodelling, Orchard Lane, Berkeley, California

Bingham House, San Ysidro Road, Montecito, California

Owens House, Ashmount Avenue, Oakland, California (with additions, 1920)

1917 Loeb House, 275 Pacheco Street, San Francisco (with additions, 1922)

Gay House, 196 Clarendon Avenue, San Francisco

1918 Hanna Houses, Crockett, California (project)

Temporary Red Cross Building, Civic Center Plaza, San Francisco

General plan for Mills College, Oakland, California

1918/
19 Town plan for Clyde, California

1919 Garage and service rooms for Rancho Lomo, Live Oak, Sutter County, California

Forest Hills Association Club Building, 381 Magellan Avenue, San Francisco (with E. C. Young)

Freeman Memorial Seat, Tucson, Arizona (with the sculptor Beniamino Bufano)

1920 Greeley House additions, 19th Avenue, Bakersfield, California

Stevensen House, Hollywood, California (project)

Oakland Memorial, California (project)

O'Keefe House, San Jose, California (project)

Morse Community House, Del Monte Properties, Pebble Beach, California (project; with Mark Daniels)

Fagan House, Portola Drive, Woodside, California

National Conservatory of Music, California Branch (project)

1921 Wright House, Etna Street, Berkeley, California

San Carlos de Borromeo Mission reconstruction, Carmel, California (project)

Floete House, Pebble Beach, California (project; with Mark Daniels)

Landsberger House, Carmel, California (project)

Resort buildings, Glen Alpine Springs, El Dorado County, California

Outdoor Theatre for the Pilgrimage Play, Hollywood, California

Peers House, Old Truckee Road, Colfax, California

Calkins House, Rosemont Street, Oakland, California

Clark House, Hawthorne Terrace, Berkeley, California

1922 Ford House, Pebble Beach, California

Thomas House additions and remodelling, Pebble Beach, California

School, Pebble Beach, California (project)

Camp Curry kitchen additions, Yosemite Valley, California

School building on site of the 1915 fair, San Francisco (project)

Manning House, Pebble Beach, California (project)

Beckett House, Berkeley, California (project)

1923 Phoebe Hearst Memorial Building, University of California, Berkeley (project)

Joralemon House and Studio, Southampton Avenue, Berkeley, California

Loy House, Ellsworth Street, Berkeley, California

Sturm House, East Orange Grove Avenue, Glendale, California (project)

Kennedy House, Redding, California (project)

McMurray House, LeConte Avenue, Berkeley, California (destroyed by fire)

1923/
30 General plan for Principia College, East St. Louis, Illinois

1924 Giesler House, Buena Vista Way, Berkeley, California

Burnett House, Hilgard Avenue, Berkeley, California

"Sack House" (Bernard Maybeck House III), Buena Vista Way, Berkeley, California

1924/
29 Auditorium-Gymnasium-Museum, University of California, Berkeley (project)

1925 Hearst Memorial Gymnasium, University of California, Berkeley (with Julia Morgan)

Peers Office Building, Colfax, California (project)

Duncan House, Santa Rosa Avenue, Sausalito, California (project)

de Angulo House, 2815 Buena Vista Way, Berkeley, California

Legge House, Panoramic Way, Berkeley, California (project)

Library and Recreation Hall, Chevy Chase School, Maryland (project)

Anthony House I, 3405 Waverly Place, Los Angeles

Staniford House, Ocean View Drive, Oakland, California

Smith House, San Francisco (project)

1926 Packard Automobile Showrooms, Van Ness Avenue, San Francisco (with Powers and Ahnden)

Hemet Hotel, Hemet, California (project; with M. E. Manning)

Hollis House, La Loma Avenue, Berkeley, California (project)

1927 Anthony House II, 3347 Waverly Drive, Los Angeles

Associated Charities Building, Gough and Eddy Street, San Francisco

Woolsey House, Sunset Drive, Kensington, California

1928 Harrison Memorial Library, Carmel, California

Packard Automobile Showroom, Los Angeles (with John Parkinson and Donald B. Parkinson)

Sunday School for First Church of Christ Scientist, Dwight Way, Berkeley, California (with Henry Gutterson)

Pillsbury House, Alvarado Road, Berkeley, California

Packard Automobile Showroom, Harrison Street, Oakland, California (with Powers and Ahnden; destroyed, 1974)

Anthony House III, with studio and gardens, 3435 Waverly Place, Los Angeles (with Mark Daniels)

1930/
38 Revised general plan for Principia College, Elsah, Illinois (with Julia Morgan)

1931 Chapel, Principia College, Elsah, Illinois (with Julia Morgan)

Maybeck Cabin, Twain Harte, California

Tufts House III, Buena Vista Way, Berkeley, California

1932 Paul Elder Book Store, Geary Street, San Francisco

1933 Wallen Maybeck House I, Buena Vista Way, Berkeley, California

Annie Maybeck House, Buena Vista Way, Berkeley, California

1935 House, 2786 Buena Vista Way, Berkeley, California

1935/
37 Ninth Church of Christ Scientist, San Francisco (project)

1936 Wells Cabin, Fuller Road, Twain Harte, California

Cole Chemical Company, St. Louis (project)

1937 Staniford House, Fresno, California (project)

Women of Berkeley Building, University Avenue, Berkeley, California

Wallen Maybeck House II, Purdue Avenue, Kensington, California

1938 Bernard Maybeck Studio, Maybeck Twin Drive, Berkeley, California

1939 Morris House, Edgecroft Road, Berkeley, California (with Mark White)

1940 Cemetery, South San Francisco (project; with Julia Morgan)

Aikin House, Buena Vista Way, Berkeley, California

Publications:

By MAYBECK: books—*Hillside Building* (booklet), Berkeley, California 1907; *Palace of Fine Arts and Lagoon,* San Francisco 1915; *The Principia College Plans,* St. Louis 1927; articles—"The Planning of a University" in *Blue and Gold* (University of California Yearbook, Berkeley), 1900; "A Dream That Might Be Realized" in *Merchants Association Review* (San Francisco), November 1903; "House of Mrs. Phoebe A. Hearst in Siskiyou County, California" in *Architectural Review* (Boston), January 1904; "Palace of Fine Arts" in *Transactions of the Commonwealth Club of California* (San Francisco), August 1915; "Fine Arts Palace Will Outlast Present Generation" in *Architect and Engineer* (New York), November 1915; "Reflections on the Grauman Metropolitan Theatre, Los Angeles" in *Architect and Engineer* (New York), June 1923.

On MAYBECK: books—*Five California Architects* by Esther McCoy, New York 1960; *Bernard Maybeck: Artisan, Architect, Artist* by Kenneth H. Cardwell, Santa Barbara, California 1977; articles—"San Francisco Bay Portfolio" by William W. Wurster in *Magazine of Art* (New York), December 1944; "Bernard Ralph Maybeck, Architect, Comes Into His Own" by Jean Murray Bangs in *Architectural Record* (New York), January 1948; "Bernard R. Maybeck" by Jean Harris in *AIA Journal* (Washington, D.C.), May 1951; "A Visit with Bernard Maybeck" by F. D. Nichols in *Journal of the Society of Architectural Historians* (Philadelphia), October 1952; "Churches" in *Architectural Record* (New York), December 1956; "Maybeck: The Work of a Grass-Roots Visionary" in *Interiors* (New York), January 1960; "Bernard Maybeck, San Francisco Genius" in *AIA Bulletin* (San Francisco), April 1960; "How to Embalm a Building" in *Architectural Forum* (New York), November 1967; "The Dream Made Permanent" in *Progressive Architecture* (New York), February 1968; "Bernard Ralph Maybeck and the Principia: Architecture as Philosophical Expression" by Robert M. Craig in *Journal of the Society of Architectural Historians* (Philadelphia), October 1972.

*

Bernard Maybeck is one of the pivotal figures in the regionalist architecture of the San Francisco Bay area. He was also an architect in the tradition of the artist—versatile, colorful, inventive, eclectic, full of the whimsy that makes art joyous and loved.

Maybeck was born in 1862 in New York, the son of a German immigrant wood carver in whose shop he apprenticed. He trained as an architect in Paris at the Beaux-Arts, learning that architecture had to be rationally thought out, that it had to utilize not only modern structural techniques but also traditional forms and values. He returned to New York, to work for his classmates Carrere and Hastings, then went to Kansas City and then San Francisco, which was still struggling to be "eastern" in its culture. The work of Maybeck and others pointed to a different, more relaxed, mode of life.

His many skills, ranging from disciplined but broad-handed designer to disciplined craftsman, and his wide eclectic tastes, afforded him an extremely wide palette. He was at home with almost any style, from Richardson to neo-classic, to Byzantine, to rural farm, to medieval, to romanesque—or whatever else he chose. Moreover, he could combine them, and often did.

Maybeck's work is characterized by an emphasis on vertical space dramatized by mixtures of scale in component structured assemblages. He saw architecture as a way of surrounding people with beauty. He used contemporary materials and techniques, direct structural expressions, innovative planning, and he was a master at handling the elements of architecture. He combined decorative crafts with historic images. Often he combined vernacular forms with "low art"—commonplace building materials and pieces, such as a factory-made window sash. His work also had a great deal of wit. He favored the humorous juxtaposition of materials whose scales were mixed and therefore surprising.

His best known building is the Palace of Fine Arts for the *International Exposition* of 1915 in San Francisco. It has, over the years, become so much of a landmark that, when it was faced with demolition, a successful effort was made to restore it. More innovative and expressive of the "Bay Area culture" is the First Church of Christ Scientist in Berkeley, dating from 1910. Its massive wood structure is reminiscent of Japanese wood architecture, but the building is strictly "Bay area." The Oakland Packard Showroom, in Moorish style, is a grand space with rich applied decoration, unlike the First Church where the structure is its own visual embellishment.

Many of Maybeck's 150 buildings are houses. After the great fire in Berkeley he designed a number of houses for quick construction, utilizing a system of dipping burlap bags in wet plaster. Nailed in place, in several layers, they hardened into a strong and permanent wall.

Maybeck's work remains a favorite of the public and of the profession—to a large extent because it is not polemic but, rather, a rich feast for the senses, masterfully composed.

—Paul Spreiregen

MAYEKAWA, Kunio.

Japanese. Born in Niigata City, 14 May 1905. Educated at the University of Tokyo, Department of Architecture, graduated 1928; trained in Le Corbusier's office, Paris, 1928–30, and Antonin Raymond's office, Tokyo, 1930–35. Married Miyo Miura in 1945. In private practice, Tokyo, since 1935. President, Japan Architects Association, 1959–62; Vice-President, International Union of Architects, 1965–69. Recipient: Riddare av Kungl. Vasaorden, Sweden, 1959; Award, 1962, and Grand Prix, 1968, Architectural Institute of Japan; Asahi Newspaper Prize for Contemporary Architecture, 1962; Auguste Perret Prize, International Union of Architects, 1963; Suomen Leijonan Ritarikunnan Luokan Komentajamerkin, Finland, 1967; Japan Art Academy Award, 1974. Member of the Architectural Institute of Japan. Honorary Member, Mexican Institute of Architects, and Peruvian Institute of Architects; Corresponding Member, Royal Institute

Kunio Mayekawa: Metropolitan Festival Hall, Tokyo, 1961

of British Architects; Honorary Fellow, American Institute of Architects. Address: Kunio Mayekawa and Associates, 8 Honshio-cho, Shinjuku-ku, Tokyo, Japan.

Works:

1935	Morinaga Candy Store, Ginza, Tokyo, and 15 other locations
1939	Employees' quarters for Kako Commercial Bank, Shingai, China
	Arimine and Wadagawa Electric Power Station, Toyama, Japan
1940	Kishi Memorial Hall, Tokyo
	Social Welfare Hall, Tokyo
1948	Keio University Hospital, Tokyo
1950/ 62	24 Branch Offices, Nihon sogo Bank, Japan
1952	Head Office, Nihon sogo Bank, Tokyo
1953	National Museum of Modern Art, Tokyo
	Apartment building, Hiroshima
1954	Kanagawa Concert Hall and Library, Yokohama
	Nishihara Engineering Office, Tokyo
1955	International House of Japan, Tokyo (with Junzo Sakakura and Junzo Yoshimura)
1956	Educational Centre, Fukishima, Japan
1957	Prefectural Office, Okayama, Japan
	Hanezawa Apartment Building, Tokyo
	Shuzo Kaikan (Brewers' Club Cooperative Building), Kochi, Japan

	Nippon Petrochemical Industry Office, Kawasaki, Japan
	San-ei shoji Head Office, Nagoya, Japan
1958	Multi-story apartment building, Harumi, Tokyo
	Japanese Pavilion, *World's Fair*, Brussels
	City Hall, Hirosaki, Japan
1959	Setagaya Community Centre, Tokyo
1960	Kyoto Hall
	Setagaya Ward Office, Tokyo
	Gakushuin University, Tokyo
1961	Metropolitan Festival Hall, Tokyo
	National Diet Library, Tokyo (with Makato Tanaka and Mido Associates)
1962	Kanagawa Prefectural Youth Centre, Yokohama
	Cultural Centre, Okayama, Japan
1963	Library, Gakushuin University, Tokyo
	Hotel Yaesu Ryumeikan, Tokyo
	Okayama Museum, Okayama, Japan
1964	Kinokuniya Book Store Building, Tokyo
	Community Centre, Hirosaki, Japan
	Setagaya Museum, Tokyo
	Japanese Pavilion, *World's Fair*, New York
1965	Janome Sewing Machine Company Head Office, Tokyo
1966	Community Centre, Saitama, Japan
1967	Building for the Monopoly Corporation of Japan, Tokyo
1969	Kinokuniya Book Store interior, San Francisco

	Setagaya Ward Secondary Office, Tokyo
1970	Steel Automobile Pavilion, *Expo '70*, Osaka
	Fuji Visitors' Centre, Yamanashi, Japan
1971	Speed Skating Stadium for the Winter Olympic Games, Sapporo, Japan
	City Hospital, Hirosaki, Japan
	Saitama Prefectural Museum, Omiya, Japan
1973	Resort Club House for the Kinokuniya Book Store in Awaji-shima, Hyogo, Japan
.1974	Tokio Kaijo Building (Tokyo Marine and Fire Insurance Company), Tokyo
	City Educational Centre, Yokohama
1975	Metropolitan Art Museum, Tokyo
1976	City Museum, Hirosaki, Japan
1977	Prefectural Museum, Kumamoto, Japan
	Museum of East Asian Art, Cologne
1978	Prefectural Museum, Yamanashi, Japan
1979	City Museum, Fukuoka, Japan

Publications:

By MAYEKAWA: articles—"Thoughts on Civilization and Architecture" in *Bauen und Wohnen* (Zurich), 1965; "Formes et Fonctions" in *Architecture: Formes et Fonctions* (Lausanne), no. 13, 1967; "L'Humanisme et l'Architecture" in *Architecture: Formes et Fonctions* (Lausanne), no. 14, 1968; "La Décadence Psychologique des Architectes" in *Architecture: Formes et Fonctions* (Lausanne), no. 15, 1969; "Hommage à Sakakura" in *L'Architecture d'Aujourd'hui* (Paris), October/November 1969;

"Vom Tod der Architektur" in *Kolner Stadt-Anzeiger* (Cologne), 5 December 1977.

On MAYEKAWA: articles—"Kulturzentrum in Tokio" in *Baukunst und Werkform* (Nuremberg), March 1962; "The Tokyo Metropolitan Festival Hall" in *Progressive Architecture* (New York), April 1965; "Art Museum in Japan" in *Arts and Architecture* (Los Angeles), September 1965; "The Saitama Prefectural Cultural Hall" in *The Japan Architect* (Tokyo), September 1966; "Saitama Prefectural Museum" in *L'Architecture d'Aujourd'hui* (Paris), September 1973; "Tokyo Marine and Fire Insurance Company" in *The Japan Architect* (Tokyo), September 1974.

A half century has passed since I went to Paris for the first time in my life, to learn about "modern architecture." I arrived at the Gare du Nord in Paris ten years after the armistice. France seemed to be enjoying her post-war prosperity but with some anxiety about the destiny of Western civilization. Oswald Spengler had published *Der Untergang des Abendlandes,* and I was shocked by the pessimistic opinions of Paul Valéry at the Société des Nations round table conference in Geneva in 1925.

In the 18th century, during the time of the Industrial Revolution in England, the Occidental countries began to have great confidence in the rationalist way of thinking, which has since been the basis of all science and technology; and it is quite obvious that all the brilliant fruits of modern civilization have encouraged Western people to believe in a rosy future for humanity.

But the optimism of the early 20th century has been destroyed completely by two world wars, and people have been struck dumb with confusion—just like the Babylonians whose ambitious Tower of Babel was torn down by the hands of God as punishment for their arrogance in wanting to equal God by building a tower. Today, it must be the task of the architect to assemble the broken pieces of brick and rebuild the human environment from no other motivation than real human need.

—Kunio Mayekawa

Kunio Mayekawa is undeniably the father of modern Japanese architecture. He has the unique distinction of having worked directly with Le Corbusier from 1928 to 1930 and with Frank Lloyd Wright's disciple Antonin Raymond from 1930 to 1935. During this period Mayekawa developed a keen understanding of the International Style. While in Le Corbusier's atelier, he worked on the Villa Savoye and the Pavillon Suisse, two of Corbu's most sophisticated and acclaimed projects. The experience left an indelible mark on his own work.

The Harumi Apartment Complex of 1958 is clearly indebted to the concepts developed for the Unité d'habitation at Marseilles by Le Corbusier. At Harumi, Mayekawa introduced to Japan the skip-floor apartment concept, while pioneering the use of reinforced concrete. Mayekawa first began using exposed concrete before the Second World War, and he continued to refine its use after the war in such outstanding projects as the Tokyo Metropolitan Festival Hall and the Gakushuin University buildings. In each case the articulation of architectural mass and the precision of detail reinforced the strength and clarity of the design.

Today, looking back over fifty years of architectural practice since his graduation from Tokyo University in 1928, Mayekawa draws a distinction between "pre-industrial architecture and post-industrial architecture," emphasizing the gradual shift from natural materials like stone and wood to man-made materials like steel, concrete and plastic. A pioneer of exposed concrete, Mayekawa has said of his own work, "I think the most outstanding example is the Tokyo Metropolitan Festival Hall."

A landmark building that integrated a cluster of theaters, performance and exhibition spaces into a unified architectural statement, the Tokyo Festival Hall, completed nearly two decades ago, remains one of the most influential and well conceived works of modern Japanese architecture. The heavy lintel which wraps around the interlocking theatrical spaces is reminiscent of Le Corbusier's bold entrance canopy to the Palace of the Assembly building in Chandigarh (also designed in the late 1950's). An unfortunate footnote to Japan's industrial growth is the destruction of the concrete at the Festival Hall due to the air pollution. Mayekawa laments, "We had to abandon this type of finish because of the air in Tokyo."

In the final analysis Kunio Mayekawa remains a creative artist and a master of his craft who has influenced nearly three generations of modern architects beginning with Kenzo Tange, who worked for Mayekawa from 1938 to 1942. Today Mayekawa continues to strive for architectural excellence: "I wish to create my architecture as the expression of my identity. I do not want to throw myself away as a merchandise in the market of the capitalist society!"

—Michael Franklin Ross

McCUE, Gerald (Mallon).

American. Born in Woodland, California, 5 December 1928. Educated at the University of California, Berkeley, 1947–52, A.B. 1951, M.A. 1952. Married Barbara Walrond in 1951; children: Scott, Mark, and Kent. Partner, with Joseph P. Milano, in Milano and McCue, Berkeley, 1953–59; Principal, McCue and Associates, Berkeley, 1963–70; Principal, with David C. Boone and Frank Tomsick, McCue, Boone and Tomsick, San Francisco, 1970–76. Since 1976, Consulting Principal, MBT Associates, San Francisco. Member of the faculty, University of California, Berkeley, 1954–76: Professor of Architecture and Urban Design, 1966–76, and Chairman of the Department, 1966–71. Since 1976, Professor of Architecture and Urban Design, Chairman of the Department, and Associate Dean of the Graduate School of Design, Harvard University, Cambridge, Massachusetts. Exhibitions: *The Art of San Francisco,* San Francisco Museum of Art, 1962; *The Work of Gerald McCue and Associates,* University of California, Berkeley, 1966; *Architectural Work of McCue Boone Tomsick,* Redwood Association Gallery, San Francisco, 1972; *San Francisco Group Show,* California State Polytechnic University, Pomona, 1978, toured California. Recipient: Masonry Institute Award, 1963, 1964; National Design Merit Award, United States Department of Health, Education and Welfare, 1966; Governor's Honor Award, California, 1966; Prestressed Concrete Institute Award, 1968; National Council of Architectural Registration Boards Award, 1969; American Institute of Planners Award, Northern California Chapter, 1970; American Institute of Steel Construction Award, 1971; Edward C. Kemper Award, American Institute of Architects, 1971; United States General Services Administration Award, 1973; *Architectural Record* Award, 1973; Beautification Award, San Francisco Chamber of Commerce, 1976, 1977; *Print Magazine* Award, 1978. M.A.: Harvard University, 1977. Member, Lambda Alpha Honorary Land Economics Society, 1968. Fellow, American Institute of Architects, 1969. Address: Department of Architecture and Urban Design, Gund Hall, Harvard University, Cambridge, Massachusetts 02138, U.S.A.

Works:

1960 88-Inch Cyclotron, for the Lawrence Radiation Laboratory, University of California, Berkeley
1961 Stauffer Chemical Company Research Building, Richmond, California
1963 Dow Chemical Company Research Center, Walnut Creek, California
1966 Fire House II, Berkeley, California
       Marina Master Plan and Harbormaster's Building, Berkeley Marina, California
1967 Chevron Research Laboratory, Richmond, California
1968 Gerald McCue House, Berkeley, California
       Milligan House, Galleon Ranch Road, Sea Ranch, California
       Ames Research Center, Moffett Field, California
1969 Life Sciences Building, Mills College, Oakland, California
1970 Djerassi House, Santa Cruz Mountains, California
       Alza Headquarters, Palo Alto, California
       12th and 19th Street/Broadway Subway Stations, Oakland, California, for the Bay Area Rapid Transit District
1972 Syntex Corporation Laboratories, Palo Alto, California
1975 Epstein House, Orinda, California
1976 IBM Santa Teresa Computer Programming Center, San Jose, California
1978 Oakes College, University of California at Santa Cruz

Publications:

By McCUE: book—*Creating the Human Environment,* with others, Urbana, Illinois 1970; articles—"Implications for ACSA of New Approach to Architectural Education" in *Journal of Architectural Education* (Washington, D.C.), August/December 1966; "The Role of the College of Environmental Design at Berkeley as a Training Ground for Architects" in *Architectural and Engineering News* (Philadelphia), June 1968; "Mendelsohn as a Teacher" in *Eric Mendelsohn,* Berkeley, California 1969; "Report of the AIA Committee on the Future of the Profession" in *Journal of Architectural Education* (Washington, D.C.), April 1970; "The Social Environment for Planning and Design" in *The Future Role of Professionals in the Built Environment,* Cambridge, Massachusetts 1974; "The Arch: An Appreciation" in *AIA Journal* (Washington, D.C.), November 1978.

On McCUE: articles—"The Talent for the Sixties" and "Cyclotron in California" in *Architectural Forum* (New York), August 1961; "Roof of Red Cedar" in *Architectural Design* (London), March 1968; "McCue Boone Tomsick" in *Architectural Forum* (New York), April 1973; "Work by McCue Boone Tomsick" in *Architecture + Urbanism* (Tokyo), July 1977; "IBM's Santa Teresa Laboratory" in *Architectural Record* (New York), August 1977; "Oakes College, Santa Cruz" in *Baumeister* (Munich), November 1978; "U.C. Santa Cruz" in *AIA Journal* (Washington, D.C.), August 1979.

Gerald McCue has combined an active career in architectural practice with theoretical and practical work as a professor and researcher; he has, as well, maintained a high degree of involvement with professional organizations. His design theory and architectural practice are closely related. His primary aim is, and has been, to further the aims and the continued development of the modern movement in architecture. In McCue's theory and practice, this has involved a striving for a number of objectives. The prime objective is to utilize the most advanced technologies and methods of construction available. Ancillary objectives are the creation of forms that show user or observer the nature of the structure, the materials of construction, and the methods of assembly. These objectives are accomplished by the creation of prototypic designs that establish patterns of honest and direct expression.

McCue's career has progressed from following the classic prototypes of the modern movement to the production of new prototypes. In his view, new prototypes are necessary when neither Miesian exposed steel frames nor Corbusian concrete frames provide the best synthesis between activity enclosing space form and the materials and means of construction supporting it. His rocket testing station at Ames Research Center, Moffett Field, California, is an example of a contemporary and original expression of the Corbusian prototype. It follows what McCue calls a "homogeneous model," where structure and finish—whether wall, floor, columns, etc.—are as homogeneous as possible. This achieves, from the viewpoint of the modern movement, the fusion between modern building technology and honesty.

The IBM Santa Teresa Computer Programming Center near San Jose, California, serves as an example of a new prototype. It follows what McCue calls a "heterogeneous model" in that there is no consistency in structure and finish—whether walls, floor, columns, etc.—between the inside and the outside of the structure. Here honesty does not mean a mapping of inside unto outside, or vice versa; thus, the "honesty" of the modern movement undergoes some redefinition. To be honest now means that outside and inside both are contemporary and readable but that one is not readable from the other. To a certain extent, this is a return to the concept of a façade that is separable from the interiorscape of a building complex.

The "heterogenous model" as new prototype reveals a number of converging forces on contemporary versions of the modern movement in architecture. Many people find the modern construction methods and materials displeasing and alienating, and for that if for no other reason desire a certain amount of artifice in the constructed environment. The distance between façade and interior may provide that degree of artifice. The current concern for security and defensibility of private space makes forms that demand high consistency between interior and exterior seem both psychologically and physically insecure. This often cited contemporary "narcissism" bespeaks a division between person and persona: interior and exterior. The realities of truly contemporary construction methods also make the "homogeneous model" a luxury few clients can afford. Interior finishes can be made much more cheaply from materials that are not suitable for exposure to the weather.

An architecture that is truly modern will forcefully symbolize a reading of the modern condition. McCue's recent work reflects an alienated, narcissistic, security conscious and fragile post-industrial society of corporate and governmental gigantism. I wonder if different clients or a fundamentally nonmodern design philosophy might have given rise to a different reflection.

—Joseph B. Juhasz

McGRATH, Raymond.

British. Born in Sydney, New South Wales, Australia, 7 March 1903; emigrated to England, 1926, and to Ireland, 1940. Educated at Fort Street School, Sydney; University of Sydney (University Medal for English Verse, 1926), B.Arch. (first-class honours) 1926; awarded Wentworth Travel Fellowship, 1926; Research Student, Clare College, Cambridge, England, 1927–29. Served as an Official War Artist, England, 1939–40. Married Mary Catherine Crozier in 1930; children: Norman and Jennifer. In private practice, London, 1930–39; worked in the Office of Public Works, Dublin, 1940–68: Principal Architect, 1948–68; returned to private practice, Dublin, 1968 until his death, 1977. Consultant Architect, British Broadcasting Corporation, London, 1932. Professor, Royal Hibernian Academy, Dublin, 1968–77. Member of the 20th Century Group, and of the MARS (Modern Architecture Research) Group, London, in the 1930's. President, Royal Hibernian Academy, 1977. Fellow, Royal Institute of British Architects, Royal Institute of Architects of Ireland, and Society of Industrial Artists. *Died* (in Dublin) *2 December 1977.*

Works:

1928   Finella House remodelling and interiors, Queen's Road, Cambridge
1930   General Electric Company Stand, *Building Exhibition,* Olympia, London
1932   Fischer's Restaurant, New Bond Street, London W.1
          Studio, Broadcasting House, London W.1

Gerald McCue: Epstein House, Orinda, California, 1975

Raymond McGrath: Fischer's Restaurant, London, 1932

Rudderbar House (project)
1937 St. Anne's Hill (house), Chertsey, Surrey
Kingstone Store, Belgrave Gate, Leicester
1938 James Clark and Sons Stand, *Building Exhibition,* Olympia, London
1939 Chemical Factory, Buckinghamshire
House, Hampstead, London
Airport Hotel (project)
Keene House, Carrygate, Leicestershire
1950 Cenotaph, Leinster Lawn, Dublin
Irish Embassy conversion, 17 Grosvenor Place, London S.W.1
President of Ireland's House restoration, Dublin
1964 Kennedy Memorial Concert Hall, Dublin (project)
Dublin Castle restoration
1970 Matthew Gallagher Art Gallery, Royal Hibernian Academy, Dublin
1974 St. Anne's (house), Carrickmines, County Dublin
1979 New Headquarters for the Royal Hibernian Academy, Dublin

Publications:

By McGRATH: books—*Twentieth Century Houses,* London 1934; *Glass in Architecture and Decoration,* with Al Frost, London 1937, 1961; articles—"El Hospital de la Santa Cruz" in *Architectural Review* (London), May 1929; "Light Opera" in *Architectural Review* (London), January 1930; "Looking into Glass" in *Architectural Review* (London), January 1932; "Glass: An Integrally Decorative Material for the Architect and for the Industrial Designer" in *Country Life* (London), September 1941; "Aus-

tralian Early Colonial" in *Architectural Review* (London), July 1948; numerous articles in *The Bell* (Dublin), 1940–54.

On McGRATH: articles—"Finella: A House for Mansfield D. Forbes" by A. C. Frost in *Architectural Review* (London), December 1929; "Architects of Europe Today: Raymond McGrath, England" in *Pencil Points* (New York), June 1936; "A House in Surrey" in *RIBA Journal* (London), January 1938; "Chemical Factory, Buckinghamshire, England" in *Architectural Record* (New York), February 1940; "Keene House, Carrygate, Leicestershire" by Christopher Hussey in *Country Life* (London), August 1942; "Irish Embassy" in *Architectural Review* (London), May 1953; "Ireland's Modern Buildings" in *The Architects' Journal* (London), September 1966; article in *Irish Builder and Engineer* (Dublin), 19 February 1972; "House at Carrickmines" in *Build Ireland* (Dublin), July 1975; "Rhapsody in Black Glass," interview, by Brian Hanson, in *Architectural Review* (London), July 1977.

*

Raymond McGrath remains one of the great enigmas of architecture, in particular Irish architecture. Arriving in Ireland in 1940, at the age of 37, to take up a public appointment, he experienced not an architectural consciousness, as had been his good fortune in England, but a newly emerging literary consciousness born out of Ireland's declared policy of neutrality during World War II. John Betjeman, now Poet Laureate, was in Dublin then. So was Maurice Craig, the historian, who was later to become McGrath's great friend. The ambience of Dublin suited him admirably, for he was a splendid

writer as well as architect. He had published in England. His essay "The History of Architecture, the History of the Window," for his book *Glass in Architecture and Decoration,* written with Al Frost in 1937, remains one of the finest expositions of architecture from 1800 to that year.

Raymond McGrath's writing talents were soon in evidence in Dublin. In the leading literary journal of the time, *The Bell,* published by Sean O Faolain and Peadar O'Donnell, he wrote as well as illustrated many articles on architecture and the arts. He became intimately associated with the Royal Hibernian Academy, first as a Full Member, then as Professor of Architecture, and finally as President—the first Architect/President since its founder, Francis Johnston.

McGrath had arrived, no less auspiciously, in England in 1926, and while undertaking post-graduate studies in Cambridge met his first client, Mansfield Forbes. The conversion of the Victorian house "Finella" for Forbes in 1928 has become legendary. Although a general awareness of the International Style was just being felt in England, it was clearly in evidence in Amyas Connell's "High and Over" of 1929. Connell, from New Zealand, was later joined by his fellow countryman Basil Ward, and later still by Colin Lucas, to form a practice that is generally credited with the introduction of the International Style in England. "Finella," however, was still an architecture of surfaces. But it did bring McGrath into contact with many other innovators including the artists Henry Moore, Jacob Epstein, and Paul Nash, and the architects Wells Coates and Serge Chermayeff.

The International Style, then well established in Germany, Holland and France, became widely known in England through the 1932 essays of the *Architectural Review*. McGrath, fresh from "Finella," was now working on Fischer's Restaurant, London, and, in conjunction with Coates and Chermayeff, on interiors for the BBC. These projects, together with a house, were illustrated in *Architectural Review*. His work began to have a significant effect on furniture and interior design, particularly his work in tubular steel and plywood. But it was his capacity to handle his projects as a series of planes using curved forms, neon lighting and glass, the elements of Art Deco, that set McGrath apart at this time. And his collaboration with two conventional photographers, Dell and Wainwright, to illustrate his interiors, was a significant contribution to the development of architectural photography.

In 1934, after many years of preparation, he published *Twentieth Century Houses*. His best known work, St. Anne's Hill, Chertsey, Surrey, a reinforced concrete house with landscaping by Christopher Tunnard, was completed in 1937. McGrath was now practicing in the company of many emigrés who were involved in firmly establishing the International Style in England. They included the Tecton and Mars groups, Gropius, Breuer, Moholy-Nagy and Mendelsohn, as well as F.R.S. Yorke, Maxwell Fry, and Denys Lasdun. But, in 1940, rather than continue as a war artist, like many of his contemporaries, McGrath chose instead to accept an official appointment in Dublin as an architect with the Office of Public Works. Apart from the resulting cultural isolation, this appointment, by its nature, precluded private practice. He became Principal Architect in 1948, a post he held until 1968.

His works in Ireland include the unrealized projects for the Kennedy Memorial Concert Hall and a new headquarters for the Royal Hibernian Academy. His one piece of domestic architecture in Ireland, St. Anne's, Carrickmines, County Dublin, is very reminiscent of the earlier work, St. Anne's Hill, Chertsey.

McGrath's life was one of architectural and intellectual fulfillment, which, for its second half at least, seemed undiminished by the apparent indifference with which he was treated.

—Kevin Spencer

McHARG, Ian (Lennox).

American. Born in Clydebank, Scotland, 20 November 1920; emigrated to the United States, 1954: naturalized, 1960. Educated at Harvard University, Cambridge, Massachusetts, 1946–50, B.Landscape Arch. 1949, M.Landscape Arch. 1950, M.City Planning 1951. Served as a Major in the British Army, commanding parachute troops, 1939–46. Married Pauline Crena de Iongh in 1947 (died, 1974); children: Alistair and Malcolm; married Carol Ann Smyser in 1977. Planner, Department of Health for Scotland, 1950–54. Since 1954, Professor of City Planning and Chairman of the Department of Landscape Architecture and Regional Planning, University of Pennsylvania, Philadelphia. Since 1963, Partner, with David A. Wallace, *q.v.*, William H. Roberts, and Thomas A. Todd, Wallace McHarg Roberts and Todd, Philadelphia; offices subsequently established in Los Angeles and Miami. Distinguished Science Lecturer, Brookhaven National Laboratory, Long Island, New York, 1968; Horace Albright Memorial Lecturer, University of California, Berkeley, 1969; Danz Lecturer, University of Washington, Seattle, 1971; Brown and Haley Lecturer, University of Puget Sound, Tacoma, Washington, 1972; Green Visiting Professor, University of British Columbia, Vancouver, 1974. Member, Committee on the Profession, American Society of Landscape Architects; Member of the Committee, White House Conference on Children and Youth; Member, United States Committee on Public Works. Recipient: Bradford Williams Medal, American Society of Landscape Architects, 1968, 1976; Morrison Medal, North American Wildlife Management Association, 1971; Creative Arts Award, Brandeis University, Waltham, Massachusetts, 1972; Allied Professions Medal, American Institute of Architects, 1972. D.H.L.: Amherst College, Massachusetts, 1970; D.H.: Lewis and Clarke College, Portland, Oregon, 1970; Bates College, Lewiston, Maine, 1978. Fellow, American Society of Landscape Architects, and Institute of Landscape Architects. Honorary Member, American Institute of Architects. Honorary Fellow, Royal Institute of British Architects. Address: Wallace, McHarg, Roberts and Todd, 1737 Chestnut Street, Philadelphia, Pennsylvania 19103, U.S.A.

Works:

1964 Plan for the valleys of Baltimore County
        Inner Harbor and Municipal Center, Baltimore
1966 Plan for Lower Manhattan (with others)
1967 Landscape plan for Washington, D.C.
1968 Richmond Parkway, Staten Island, New York (project)
1969 Ecological study for Minneapolis-St. Paul
1970 Metro Center, Baltimore (project)
        Skippack Ecological Study, Montgomery County, Pennsylvania
1972 Plan for the center of Los Angeles
1973 Plan for Northwest Baltimore (with I. M. Pei and Partners)
        Regional transportation plan for Denver
1974 Development plan for Amelia Island, Florida
1975 Pardisan Environmental Park, Tehran (project)
        I-95 Route Selection Study, Princeton, New Jersey
1976 Capitol Building, Washington, D.C. (project)

Publications:

By McHARG: book—*Design with Nature*, New York 1969; articles—"The Functions of Open Space Housing" in *The Architects Yearbook*, London 1955; "Can We Afford Open Space" in *The Architects' Journal* (London), 8–15 March 1956; "The Court house Concept" in *Architectural Record* (New York), September 1957; "Ecology of the City" in *AIA Journal* (Washington, D.C.), December 1962; "Man and Environment" in *The Urban Condition,* edited by Leonard Duhl, New York 1963; "Ecological Determinism" in *The Future Environments of North America,* edited by Fraser Darling and John P. Milton, New York 1966; "Blight or a Noble City" in *Audubon Magazine* (New York), February/-March 1966; "An Ecological Method for Landscape Architecture" in *Landscape Architecture* (Louisville, Kentucky), January 1967; "The Place of Nature in the City of Man" in *Challenge for Survival,* edited by Pierre Bansereau and V. A. Weadock, New York 1970; "Towards Comprehensive Ecological Planning" in *Plan* (Johannesburg), no. 10, 1973.

On McHARG: articles—in *Life* (New York), 15 August 1969; in *Time* (New York), 10 October 1969; in *Fortune* (New York), February 1970; "A Sensible Plan for Future Development" in *Reader's Digest* (New York), August 1970; "Ian McHarg" by Dennis Fahrney in the *Wall Street Journal* (New York), 30 August 1971; article in the *Atlantic Monthly* (Boston), January 1974; "Planning for the Brave New World" by Roger Yee in *Progressive Architecture* (New York), June 1974; "Ian McHarg: Champion for Design with Nature" by Constance Holden in *Landscape Architecture* (Louisville, Kentucky), March 1977.

With his book *Design with Nature*, Ian McHarg established himself as America's foremost landscape architect to stress the relationship of ecology to human land use. He believes that, prior to any development, the study of an area's ecological balances is imperative, if the impact of humanity on nature is to be better ascertained and minimized. In exhorting land use planners and developers to confront the totality of the landscape (and the implications of destruction of even a portion of that landscape), McHarg delights conservationists and greatly expands of province of traditional landscape architecture.

Viewing human actions as those of "a blind, witless, low-brow, anthropocentric clod who inflicts lesions upon the earth," he asserts that people must act in harmony with nature rather than ignore it. Too much of our civilization has been constructed in spite of nature and has led to both human and natural catastrophe. Using such stunning examples as the flooding of the New Jersey shore, McHarg reveals the senseless waste that results from humanity's blindness to the needs of nature. He persuasively argues for an intensely ecological approach to development, one that would reconcile environmental and human needs.

McHarg has had the opportunity to implement his ideas on various projects. He employs a strict methodology that identifies flood plains, erosion prone areas, frigid sites, soil drainage capacity, water table polluting areas, unstable bedrock, animal trails, flora patterns, outstanding scenery, historic structures, etc. on a series of overlapping maps. Through a process of elimination—as colored overlay is piled atop colored overlay—the area best suited for development emerges as the white portion of the map. From these pin-pointed areas McHarg is able to make his final recommendations with regard to the proposed project.

Because it is such a pure, apparently deterministic approach, McHarg has been criticized for expounding mechanical solutions to difficult problems. Critics note his inability to deal with local political and business situations and point to the frequency with which political interests have compromised McHarg's theoretical solutions. His plan for northwest Baltimore certainly suffered this fate. A sprawling open valley, which McHarg had recommended remain intact while development occurred on adjoining hills and plateaus, is now the victim of urban sprawl, the result of far too many "practical" decisions. That travesties of this sort occur comments more upon American political practice than upon McHarg's design procedures. To suggest that McHarg should encompass political considerations within his project plans is to completely misunderstand the man. He is a man with a purpose, a message to preach, and a plan to unfold. He expresses the need, and reveals a means, for people to develop in harmony with nature; the implementation of his schemes demands communal sanity. He is a teacher, who looks toward the long term results of education rather than the short term accomplishments of compromise.

—Don J. Hibbard

McINTYRE, (Robert) Peter.

Australian. Born in Melbourne, Victoria, 24 August 1927. Educated at Trinity Grammar School, Melbourne, matriculated 1944; University of Melbourne, 1944–50, B.Arch. 1950; Royal Melbourne Technical College, Dip.Arch. 1953; University of Melbourne, Dip.Town and Regional Planning 1955. Married the architect Dione Beatrice Cohen in 1954; children: Robert, Jane, Susan and Anne. Employed in the office of his father, the architect Robert H. McIntyre, Melbourne, 1947, and for Stephenson and Turner, and Buchan Laird and Buchan, Melbourne, 1948; in private practice, Melbourne, 1950–53; Partner, with John and Phyllis Murphy and Kevin Borland, in Borland, Murphy and McIntyre, Melbourne, 1953–56; Partner, Peter and Dione McIntyre, Melbourne, 1956–61. Since 1961, Principal of McIntyre McIntyre and Partners Pty. Ltd., Melbourne (firm formed by consolidation of practices of Peter and Robert H. McIntyre). Director, International Planning Collaborative, Melbourne, since 1972 (partners: George Connor and Donald Wolbrink). Tutor, School of Architecture, University of Melbourne, 1951–53; Lecturer, Royal Melbourne Institute of Technology, 1957–60; Member of the Faculty of Architecture and Building, University of Melbourne, 1968–72. Founder and Director, *The Architects' Revue,* University of Melbourne, 1948–54; Editor, with Robin Boyd, *Cross-Section,* Melbourne, 1951–53. Councillor, Royal Victorian Institute of Architects, 1963; President, Victorian Chapter, Royal Australian Institute of Architects, 1969–71; President, Royal Australian Institute of Architects, 1973–75. Exhibitions: *Olympic Pool Competition,* 1950; Academy of Science, Canberra, 1956; *High Court of Australia* travelling exhibition, 1972. Recipient: First Prize, Olympic Swimming Stadium Competition, Melbourne, 1953; Housing Service Award, 1954, Robin Boyd Environmental Award, 1975, Architectural Projects Award, 1975, and Bronze Medal, 1977, 1978, Royal Australian Institute of Architects; Sir James Barrett Memorial Medal, Town and Country Planning Institute, Melbourne, 1974; Special Recognition Award, American Society of Landscape Architects, Hawaii, 1968. Life Fellow, Royal Australian Institute of Architects, Royal Melbourne Institute of Technology, and Royal Australian Planning Institute. Associate, Royal Institute of British Architects. Address: McIntyre McIntyre and Partners Pty. Ltd., 570 Bourke Street, Melbourne, Victoria 3000, Australia.

Works:

1953   Beulah Hospital, Victoria
1954   Brunt House, The Belvedere, Kew, Victoria
        Snelleman House, 40 Kean Street, East Ivanhoe, Victoria
1954/
56   Olympic Swimming Stadium, Melbourne (with Kevin Borland and John and Phyllis Murphy)
1955   Stephenson House, 42 Kean Street, East Ivanhoe, Victoria
        McIntyre House, 2 Hodgson Street, Kew, Victoria
1958   Shaw House, Eglington Street, Kew, Victoria
1959   Seymour Swimming Pool (project)
1961   McIntyre Ski Lodge, Mt. Buller, Victoria
        Peter Office Building, La Trobe Street, Melbourne
1962   Auski Ski Hire, Mt. Buller, Victoria
1963   Butt House, 16 View Road, Vermont, Victoria
        Molony's Ski Hire, Falls Creek, Victoria

1964   Ski Club of Victoria Apartments, Mt. Buller, Victoria
        Fairchild Factory, Croydon, Victoria
1965   Collingwood Football Club Grandstand, Victoria
        Loveridge Country Hardware Store, Berwick, Victoria
1966   Baldwin Country House, Birmingham Road, Mooroolbark, Victoria
1967   Ski Flats, Falls Creek, Victoria
1968   Morgan House, 9 Wheriside Avenue, Toorak, Victoria
1969   George Bass Motel, Lakes Entrance, Victoria
        Offices, 150 Lonsdale Street, Melbourne
        Motel, West Wyalong, New South Wales
1970   Offices, 180 William Street, Melbourne
1971   Ashley House, St. Kilda Road, Melbourne
        Offices, 450 St. Kilda Road, Melbourne
        Offices, 444 St. Kilda Road, Melbourne
1972   Bayside Shopping Centre, Frankston, Victoria
1973   A.M.P. Society Offices, Shepparton, Victoria
1973/
74   Melbourne Strategy Plan
1974   Cadbury-Schweppes House, St. Kilda Junction, Melbourne
        Mt. Buller Planning Scheme, Victoria
        Hardies Offices, Braybrook, Victoria
1976   Apartments, Dryburgh Street, North Melbourne
1977   Knox City Shopping Centre, Stud Road, Knoxfield, Victoria

Peter McIntyre: Knox City Shopping Centre, Melbourne, 1977

Park Circle Shopping Centre, South Melbourne

1978 Australia Pacific House, 136 Exhibition Street, Melbourne

Rob's Restaurant, Bulleen, Victoria

The objective of my work has been to find innovative solutions to architectural problems and at the same time to seek an appropriate emotional response from the user of the building and the community.

—Peter McIntyre

If Peter McIntyre were asked to summarize his design philosophy in one word, it would be "innovation." His practice has grown rapidly since he joined the family firm in the mid-1950's. The firm's output has been erratic in quality, reflecting a clientele with a wide range of attitudes to architecture.

When McIntyre was designing his first houses, Harry Seidler's book on architecture in Australia had just been published, and was having a profound influence on the thinking of young graduates. The same forces that influenced Seidler are, to some extent, reflected in McIntyre's own early work. There is the same interest in expressing structure and the same preoccupation with simple forms and direct geometry. The crowning achievement of this early period is the competition winning swimming complex for the Olympic Games held in Melbourne in 1956. The concept is remarkably simple. The major compression members are raked to accommodate seating on each side of the pool. They are tied together by roof trusses, the depth of which is reduced by the counterbalancing tension forces, and the whole is braced by delicate tension rods which are exposed on the exterior.

McIntyre had used the principle of tension structures before, in the Bush Nursing hospital at Beulah and in his own house at Kew. A number of his other houses of the same period are also noteworthy: like the works of many contemporary Australian architects (notably Robin Boyd and Roy Grounds, also from Melbourne) each house is an exercise emphasizing one aspect of architecture, such as shape, structure, volume, space, finish, or geometry.

During the 1960's the office of McIntyre and McIntyre turned its attention to commercial work, particularly low-cost, low-rental office buildings, pubs, and the development of winter sports facilities in the snow country just a few hours drive north of Melbourne. During the past decade the firm has been engaged with Donald Wolbrink in the preparation of the City of Melbourne Strategy Plan—the first of its kind in Australia. The main feature of the plan is that it lays down the key strategies and goals for future growth without dictating the physical form it will take. The constraints of form are laid down in Action Plans that are developed for specific areas as and when required. It is unfortunate that rather than acting to prevent unrestrained development in the central business area, the strategy plan has merely stretched the ingenuity of commercial property developers who have brought every political, legal, and financial pressure on the city council to delay its adoption.

Most recently, Peter McIntyre has won acclaim for two buildings. Park Circle Shopping Centre is a small collection of single-storey shops built around a tiny public open space. The whole is tied together by a canopy of glass supported by a steel trussed folded plate. The construction is simple and finishes are cheap, indicating that this is a temporary use for a valuable development site. A delightful place to be in fine weather.

Knox City is a regional shopping centre and bus terminal located on the edge of metropolitan Melbourne. In external appearance and finish this building stands like a stronghold warding off the surrounding sea of cars and offering protection to the shopper. This image of a crusader castle is strengthened by the hollow concrete barbican guarding the covered way to the main entry. The interior is an enclosed pedestrian street two storeys high lined with small shops. At each end there is a department store. Attached to one side of the street is a tower containing rentable professional offices, a restaurant, and two small cinemas. Inside the protective walls the scale of the building is reduced to people-size as the street meanders and branches. At the junction, the floor is transformed into a small amphitheatre and the roof is pierced by pyramidal skylights. Here McIntyre has ignored the opportunity for exciting structural expression that was the hallmark of his earlier work. Instead of being directed upwards, the eye is invited to look at the shoppers below. This is an architecture in which people are the important ingredient.

—David Watson

McKINNELL, Noel Michael.

British. Born in Salford, Lancashire, 25 December 1935; moved to the United States, 1960. Educated at the University of Manchester School of Architecture, 1953–58 (University of Manchester Traveling Scholarship, 1956), B.A. (honours) 1958; Columbia University School of Architecture, New York, 1959–60 (Fulbright Scholar, 1960), M.S.Arch. 1960; awarded Royal Manchester Institute Silver Medal, 1960. Married Jane D'Esopo in 1961; children: Caitlin and Phoebe. Associate Professor, Columbia University, 1960–62; Assistant Professor, 1963–66, Associate Professor, 1966–71, and since 1971 Professor of Architecture, Harvard Graduate School of Design, Cambridge, Massachusetts. Since 1962, Partner, with Gerhard M. Kallmann, q.v., and Henry Wood, Kallmann, McKinnell and Wood, Architects, Inc., Boston. Professor of Architecture, University of Manchester (on leave from Harvard), 1972–74; Visiting Professor, Yale University, New Haven, Connecticut, 1976; Adjunct Professor, Columbia University, 1976–77. Exhibitions: Museum of Fine Arts, Boston, 1962; National Institute of Arts and Letters, New York, 1969; Metropolitan Museum of Art, New York, 1970; De Cordova Museum, Lincoln, Massachusetts, 1974. Recipient: Brunner Prize, National Institute of Arts and Letters, 1969; Honor Award, American Institute of Architects, 1969; Precast Concrete Institute Award, 1969; Bartlett Award, 1969; Harleston Parker Medal, 1970, 1975; Award of Merit, Concrete Industry Board, 1974; Bard Award, City Club of New York, 1977. Address: Kallmann, McKinnell and Wood, Architects, Inc., 127 Tremont Street, Boston, Massachusetts 02108, U.S.A.

Publications:

By McKINNELL: books—World Architecture, contributing editor, London 1964–65; articles—interview in Architects on Architecture, edited by Paul Heyer, New York 1966, London 1967; "Movement Systems as Generators of Built Form," with Gerhard M. Kallmann, in Architectural Record (New York), November 1975.

See KALLMANN, Gerhard M.

MEIER, Richard (Alan).

American. Born in Newark, New Jersey, 12 October 1934. Educated at Cornell University, Ithaca, New York, 1953–57, B.Arch. 1957. Worked with Frank Grad and Sons, New Jersey, 1957, Davis, Brody and Wisniewski, New York, 1958–59, Skidmore, Owings and Merrill, New York, 1959–60, and Marcel Breuer and Associates, New York, 1960–63. Since 1963, Principal, Richard Meier and Associates, Architects, New York. Adjunct Instructor, 1963–66, Assistant Professor, 1966–69, and Adjunct Professor of Architecture, 1969–73, Cooper Union, New York; Visiting Lecturer/Critic, Princeton University, New Jersey, 1963, Syracuse University, Syracuse, New York, 1964, Pratt Institute, New York, 1965, and Yale University, New Haven, Connecticut, 1967; Resident Architect, American Academy in Rome, 1973; William Henry Bishop Professor of Architecture, Yale University, 1975, 1977; Visiting Professor of Architecture, Harvard University, Cambridge, Massachusetts, 1977. Chairman of the Awards Jury, American Institute of Architects, Philadelphia Chapter, 1972, American Academy in Rome, 1974, national AIA, 1975, and Pennsylvania Society of Architects, 1975. Exhibitions: AIA National Convention Exhibition, Washington, D.C., 1965, Portland, 1968, Boston, 1970, Detroit, 1971, and Washington, D.C., 1974; 40 under 40, American Federation of the Arts, New York, 1966; Benjamin Franklin Parkway Fountain Competition, Architectural League, New York, 1966; Vacation Houses, AIA, New York, 1968; Architecture U.S.A., United States Pavilion, World's Fair, Osaka, 1970; Another Chance for Cities, Whitney Museum, New York, 1970; National Housing Conference Exhibition, Washington, D.C., 1971; Younger New York Architects, Columbia University, New York, 1971; National Institute of Arts and Letters Exhibition, New York, 1971; Low Rise High Density Housing, Museum of Modern Art, New York, 1973; Triennale, Milan, 1973; Due Architetti Americani, United States Information Service, Milan, 1974; Columbia University, New York, 1974; Residential Design Exhibit, AIA, New York, 1974; University of California at Los Angeles, 1974; Five Architects, Princeton University School of Architecture, 1974; Cornell University, Ithaca, New York, 1974; Architectural Studies and Projects, Museum of Modern Art, New York, 1975; University of Houston School of Architecture, Texas, 1975; The New York Five, Art Net, London, 1975; La Città di Michelucci, Basilica Alessandro, Fiesole, Italy, 1976; Five Architects, New York, at the Mostra di Architettura, Naples, and toured Genoa, Zurich, Lausanne, Paris, Brussels and Helsinki, 1976; Suburban Alternative, at the Biennale, Venice, 1976; Cooper Union, New York, 1976; Man Transforms, Cooper-Hewitt Museum, New York, 1976; University of California at Los Angeles, 1976; Idea as Model, Institute for Architecture and Urban Studies, New York, 1976; Graham Foundation, Chicago, 1977; 200 Years of American Architectural Drawing, Cooper-Hewitt Museum, New York, 1977; New York: The State of Art, Cultural Education Center, Albany, New York, 1977; Design in Michigan, Cranbrook Academy of Art Museum, Bloomfield Hills, Michigan, 1977; Architecture, Leo Castelli Gallery, New York, 1977; Architecture: Seven Architects, Institute of Contemporary Art, University of Pennsylvania, Philadelphia, 1977 The Atheneum, Historic New Harmony, Indiana, School of Architecture, Princeton University, New Jersey, 1978; Architecture: Service/Craft/Art, Rosa Esman Gallery, New York, and New Jersey State Museum, Trenton, 1978. Recipient: Excellence for House Design Award, 1964, 1968, 1969, and Award of Excellence for Design, 1977, Architectural Record; Homes for Better Living: Award of Merit, 1965, 1973, 1975, Homes for Better Living: First Honor Award, 1968, 1969, 1971, 1977, National Honor Award, 1969, 1971, 1974, 1976, 1977, Award of Merit, 1970, Low and Moderate Income Housing National Award, 1970, and Bartlett Award, 1977, American Institute of Architects; House Competition Prize, 1965, and Award for Outstanding Residential Design, 1968, AIA, New York Chapter; Honor Award, AIA, New England Regional Council, 1968; Honor Award, United States Department of Housing and Urban Development, 1970; Brunner Prize, National Institute of Arts and Letters, 1972; Bard Award, City Club of New York, 1973, 1977; Award of Honor, New York Society of Architects, 1973; R. S. Reynolds Memorial Award, 1977; Design Award, New York State Association of Architects/AIA, 1978; Architectural Award of Excellence, American Institute of Steel Construction, 1978; Annual Award, *Progressive Architecture,* 1978. Fellow, American Institute of Architects, 1976. Address: Richard Meier and Associates, 136 East 57th Street, New York, New York 10022, U.S.A.

Works:

1962   Lambert Beach House, Fire Island, New York
1963   Design of *Recent American Synagogue Architecture* exhibition, Jewish Museum, New York
1964   Monumental Fountain, Benjamin Franklin Parkway, Philadelphia (competition project; with Frank Stella)
1965   Mr. and Mrs. Jerome Meier House, Essex Fells, New Jersey
        Frank Stella Studio and Apartment, New York (project)
1966   Dotson House, Ithaca, New York
        Renfield House, Chester, New Jersey
1967   Sona Shop, New York
        Smith House, Darien, Connecticut
        Mental Health Facilities, West Orange, New Jersey (project)
        Hoffman House, East Hampton, Long Island, New York
        Rubin Loft renovation, New York (project)
1969   Saltzmann House, East Hampton, Long Island, New York
        Bronx Redevelopment Planning Study, New York
        House, Pound Ridge, New York
1970   Westbeth Artists' Housing, New York
        Health and Physical Education Building, State University College of New York at Fredonia (project)
        Charles Evans Industrial Buildings, at Fairfield and Piscataway, New Jersey (project)
1971   House, Old Westbury, New York
        Olivetti Branch Office Prototype, and Branch Office Prototype Modification
        Olivetti Training Center Dormitory, Tarrytown, New York (project)
        Olivetti Headquarters, Fairfax, Virginia (project)
1972   Twin Parks Northeast Housing, Bronx, New York
        Robert R. Young Housing, New York (project)
1972/
74   East Side Housing, New York (project)
1973   Douglas House, Harbor Springs, Michigan
        Paddington Station Housing, New York (project)
1974   Monroe Development Center, Rochester, New York (with Todd and Giroux)
        Shamberg House, Chappaqua, New York
        Museum of Modern Art, Villa Strozzi, Florence, Italy (project)
        Condominium House, Yonkers, New York (project)
        Undergraduate housing, Cornell University, Ithaca, New York (project)
1975   The Theatrum, New Harmony, Indiana
        Commercial building and hotel, Springfield, Massachusetts (project)
        Wingfield Racquet Club, Greenwich, Connecticut (project)
1976   Bronx Developmental Center, New York
        Maidman House, Sands Point, Long Island, New York
        de Lone-Plukas House, Concord, Massachusetts (project)
        Weber-Frankel Gallery, New York (project)
1978   Bronx Psychiatric Center Warehouse rehabilitation, New York

The Atheneum, and The Pottery Shed, New Harmony, Indiana
Aye Simon Reading Room, Guggenheim Museum, New York

Publications:

By MEIER: books—*Recent American Synagogue Architecture,* exhibition catalogue, New York 1963; *Richard Meier, Architect: Buildings and Projects 1966-1976,* New York 1976; *Richard Meier: Drawings of Four Objects, A Post Card Book 1976,* New York 1977; articles—"Planning for Jerusalem" in *Architectural Forum* (New York), April 1971; introduction to *Le Corbusier: Villa Savoye,* edited by Yukio Futagawa, Tokyo 1973; "Strategies: Eight Projects" in *Casabella* (Milan), May 1974; "Tre Recenti Progetti" in *Controspazio* (Bari, Italy), September 1975; "My Statement" in *Architecture + Urbanism* (Tokyo), April 1976; "Dialogue," with Arata Isozaki, in *Architecture + Urbanism* (Tokyo), August 1976; "General Remarks" in *The Japan Architect* (Tokyo), December 1976; "Olivetti Prototypes" in *L'Architecture d'Aujourd'hui* (Paris), December 1976; "A Word from Richard Meier" and "Dialogue: On Architecture," with Fumihiko Maki, in "White Existence—Richard Meier 1961-77," a special feature in *Space Design* (Tokyo), January 1978.

On MEIER: books—*The New York Times Book of Interior Design and Decoration,* New York 1966; *Art Today* by Ray Faulkner and Edwin Ziegfeld, New York 1969; *Young Designs in Living* by Barbara Plumb, New York 1969; *Architectural Record Book of Vacation Houses,* New York 1970; *History of Notable American Houses* by Marshall Davidson, New York 1971; *Decorative Art in Modern Interiors* by Ella Moody, London 1971; *Architecture in a Revolutionary Era* by Julian Kulski, Nashville, Tennessee 1971; *Observations on American Architecture* by Ivan Chermayeff, New York 1972; *Five Architects: Eisenman/Graves/Gwathmey/Hejduk/Meier* by Kenneth Frampton and Colin Rowe, New York 1972; *Young Designs in Color* by Barbara Plumb, New York 1972; *Richard Meier: Smith House and House in Old Westbury* by Yukio Futagawa, Tokyo 1973; *Urban Design as Public Housing* by Jonathan Barnett, New York 1974; *Houses in the U.S.A.,* edited by Yukio Futagawa, Tokyo 1974; *Richard Meier: Douglas House, Michigan,* edited by Yukio Futagawa, Tokyo 1975; *Great Houses* by Walter Wagner, New York 1976; *Five Architects, New York* by Manfredo Tafuri, Rome 1976; *Wohnungsbau im Wandel von der Addition zur Integration* by David Mackay, Stuttgart 1977; *200 Years of American Architectural Drawing* by David Gebhard and Deborah Nevins, New York 1977; articles—"The Very Personal Work of Richard Meier and Associates" by Joseph Rykwert in *Architectural Forum* (New York), March 1972; "Five on Five" in *Architectural Forum* (New York), May 1973; "Richard Meier: Public Space and Private Space" by Charles Hoyt in *Architectural Record* (New York), July 1973; "Architecture's Big Five Elevate Form" by Paul Goldberger in *The New York Times,* 26 November 1973; "Process Versus Style" by Wolf Von Eckardt in *The Washington Post,* 27 April 1974; "4 Projects by Richard Meier: Change and Consistency" by Charles Hoyt in *Architectural Record* (New York), March 1975; "Spatial Structure: Richard Meier," special issue of *Architecture + Urbanism* (Tokyo), April 1976; "The Gospel According to Giedion and Gropius Is Under Attack" by Ada Louise Huxtable in *The New York Times,* 27 June 1976; "Richard Meier: Architect" by Paul Goldberger in *The New York Times Book Review* (New York), 5 December 1976; "The Individual: Richard Meier" by Suzanne Stephens in *Progressive Architecture* (New York), May 1977; "Architectural Drawings as Art" by Ada Louise Huxtable in *The New York Times,* 12 June 1977; "Bronx Developmental Center," special issue of *Architecture + Ur-*

banism (Tokyo), November 1977; "White Existence—Richard Meier 1961-77," special feature in *Space Design* (Tokyo), January 1978; "Architecture: Richard Meier" by Paul Goldberger in *Architectural Digest* (Los Angeles), September 1978; "Five Frontiersmen" in *Newsweek* (New York), 6 November 1978.

The paradox of the great cities is that in spite of the apparent denial of individual existence, there are human needs and hungers that the city answers. Large institutions are the city in microcosm. Their order is analagous to the articulation of public and private zones within a city. And within them exists wider possibilities of human intercourse within the continuity of urban existence.

Mine is an attempt to clarify and redefine a sense of order within society, to understand then a relationship between what has been and what can be.

But to gain any sense of my involvement, it is necessary to consult my work. Beyond theory, beyond historical reference, my meditations are on space, shape, light and how to make them. My goal is presence, not illusion, and I pursue it with an unrelenting vigor.

—Richard Meier

To Richard Meier the process of building is an inorganic activity from the start; it is an intellectual pursuit to be thoughtfully considered from all angles. It is not surprising, then, that all aspects of his buildings are conceived in relation to their natural setting, even though to Meier the destruction of nature is implicit in man's creation of something new.

Perhaps this is why Meier articulates the material of his buildings with white paint: this brings out the surface and expresses the planar quality in relation to the more amorphous forms found in nature. He chooses white because it can creatively reflect the interchange between vertical space and natural light. The whiteness of his buildings is in purposeful contrast to natural surroundings.

In all of Richard Meier's houses, too, there is wood flooring which usually extends through the glass wall to an outside deck. He does not cover the floor in white tile because he wishes to express the difference between the horizontal floor plane and the vertical walls. (If the flooring were white, the spatial experience would be volumetric rather than planar.) The decking does not break with Meier's expression of contrast with nature, since, according to his philosophy, any material that has been shaped and reformed by man is already unnatural.

This is the era of the International Style, with the mass media making architectural information available throughout the world. Anyone's architectural style today is certainly influenced by this massive flow of information, and Richard Meier is no exception. The simplicity of Meier's work reflects some visual images of Le Corbusier and Alvar Aalto as well as some traits of the Japanese architectural style.

Comparing two of Meier's houses, the Smith House and the Douglas House, one can see that the latter is an improvement on the former; nevertheless, the intentions of the architect are clearly revealed in both cases. Both contain a clear separation of public and private spaces, with the circulation areas that connect these either articulated or not articulated. The interplay of the various spaces is well organized and designed according to his own, personal sense of aesthetics. From the exterior, one can always see a clear distinction between solid spaces and penetration of space derived from the building's relationship to the sun as well as from internal spatial arrangements.

The most distinctive aspect of Meier's design philosophy calls for the wrapping of spaces and their extension vertically, rather than horizontally—in contrast to, say, the Japanese house, which uses horizontal space to open the house toward the outside. Another important aspect of Meier's design is his

Richard Meier: Bronx Developmental Center, New York, 1976

University of Munich, under Theodor Fischer, 1911–12. Served in the German Army, on the Russian and Western fronts, 1917–18. Married Luise Maas in 1915: daughter: Esther. Worked as a theatre designer and interior decorator, in Munich, 1912–14; associated with the expressionist artists of the Blaue Reiter Group, Munich, 1914–15; practiced in Berlin, 1919–33; left Germany to escape persecution of the Jews, and lived alternately in London and Palestine, 1933–41; in partnership with Serge Chermayeff, *q.v.,* in London, 1933–39; settled in New York, 1941; practiced in San Francisco, 1945 until his death, 1953. Exhibitions: *Architecture in Concrete and Steel,* Galerie Paul Cassirer, Berlin, 1919; sculptural effect. He creates this by adding and subtracting masses inside and outside the building, with the whiteness also contributing to the effect by unifying the surface and making volumetric deformations more pronounced.

It is wrong to assume, however, that Meier is devoted only to house design, for he has had such varied commissions as a modern museum in Florence, Italy and a hospital for the mentally retarded in the Bronx, New York. Both are superb designs and further evidence of his skillful articulation of circulation and precise composition of architectural elements.

—Ching-Yu Chang

MENDELSOHN, Eric.
American. Born Erich Mendelsohn in Allenstein, East Prussia, Germany, now Olsztyn, Poland, 21 March 1887; emigrated to England, 1933: naturalized, 1938; emigrated to the United States, 1941: naturalized, 1946. Studied economics at the University of Munich, 1907, and architecture at the Technische Hochschule of Berlin, 1908–10, and at the

Gallery Contempora, New York, 1929; Architectural Association, London, 1931; *Triennale,* Milan, 1932; Museum of Modern Art, San Francisco, 1942; Art Institute of Chicago, 1942; City Art Museum, St. Louis, Missouri, 1944; Jewish Museum, New York, 1952; Royal Institute of British Architects, London, 1962; *Eric Mendelsohn,* Akademie der Künste, Berlin, 1968; *L'Opera di Eric Mendelsohn,* Istituto Nazionale di Architettura, Rome, 1972. Recipient: First Prize, Cathedral Square Competition, Magdeburg, Germany, 1930; First Prize, Berlin Passenger Transport Co. Administration Building, 1931. *Died* (in San Francisco) *15 September 1953.*

Works:

1911 Chapel, Hebrew Cemetery, Allenstein, Germany, now Olsztyn, Poland
1915 Becker House, Chemnitz, now Karlmarxstadt, Germany (project)
1920 Hausleben, Dorotheenstrasse, Berlin (destroyed)
1920/
  24 Einstein Tower, Potsdam, Germany
1921 Office building, Kemperplatz, Berlin (project)
1921/
  23 Herman and Company Hat Factory, Luckenwalde, Germany
      Berliner Tageblatt Building, Jerusalemerstrasse, Berlin
1922 Two-family villa, Karolingerplatz, Charlottenburg, Berlin
1923 Weichmann Silk Store and Offices, Gleiwitz, Germany, now Gliwice, Poland
      Meyer-Kaufmann Textile Factory Power Station Building, Wuestegiersdorf, Germany
      Sternfeld House, Heerstrasse, Berlin
      Ruthenberg Central Electrical Works, Haifa, Palestine, now Israel (project)
      Commercial Center, Haifa, Palestine, now Israel (competition project)
1924 Herpich Furriers Building, Leipzigerstrasse, Berlin

1925/
  26 Temple of the Three Patriarchs, Tilsit, now Sovetsk, U.S.S.R.
1925/
  27 Textile factory and industrial complex, Leningrad
1926 Schocken Department Store, Nuremberg
      Cohen-Epstein Department Store extensions, Duisburg, Germany
1926/
  28 Schocken Department Store, Stuttgart (destroyed)
1926/
  29 Universum Cinema, Berlin
1927 Petersdorff Department Store, Breslau, Germany, now Poland
      Deukon Dressmaking Building, Berlin
      Power Station, Berliner Tageblatt Building, Jerusalemerstrasse, Berlin
      Dr. Bejach House, New Babelsberg, Germany
      Zoo Exhibition Hall, Berlin (project)
      Yacht Club, Wannsee, Berlin (project)
      Hebrew Cemetery, Königsberg, Germany (destroyed by Nazis)
      Herpich Shop, Berlin
      Trade Union Administration Building, Germany (project)
1927/
  28 Woga Building Complex, Kurfürstendamm, Berlin
1928 Rudolf Mosse Pavilion, *Press Exhibition,* Cologne
      Galerie Lafayette, Potsdamerplatz, Berlin
1928/ (project)
  29 Schocken Department Store, Chemnitz, now Karlmarxstadt, Germany
      Metal Workers Union Building and Lindenstrasse redevelopment, Berlin (project)
1929 Chemical Syndicate Administrative Building, Berlin (project)
      Palace of the Soviets, Moscow (competition project)

Mendelsohn House, Rupenhorn, Berlin
1930 Cathedral Square, Magdeburg, Germany (competition project)
Hebrew Youth Center, Essen
1930/
33 Bachner Department Store, Moravska-Ostrava, Czechoslovakia
1931 Columbus House, Potsdamerplatz, Berlin (destroyed)
Alexanderplatz redevelopment, Berlin (project)
Administration Building, Berlin Passenger Transport Co., Friedrichstrasse, Berlin (competition project)
Villa for the Duke of Alba, Madrid (project)
1932 Zinc Works, Magdeburg, Germany
1934/
36 Weizmann House, Rehovot, Palestine, now Israel
1935 Hotel, Southsea, Hampshire (project; with Serge Chermayeff)
de la Warr Pavilion, Bexhill-on-Sea, Sussex (with Serge Chermayeff)
Nimmo House, Chalfont St. Giles, Buckinghamshire (with Serge Chermayeff)
1935/
36 Master plan for Hebrew University, Mount Scopus, Jerusalem (project)
1936 Salman Schocken House, Jerusalem
Schocken Library, Jerusalem
House, Frinton Park, Essex (with Serge Chermayeff)
White City Housing Development, London (project; with Serge Chermayeff)
House, 64 Old Church Street, Chelsea, London (with Serge Chermayeff)
1937 Hotel, Garages and Shops Complex, Blackpool, Lancashire (project)
Commercial School, Jagur, Palestine, now Israel
1937/
38 Government Hospital, Haifa, Palestine, now Israel
1937/
39 Anglo-Palestine Bank, now National Bank of Israel, Jerusalem
Hadassah University Medical Centre, Mount Scopus, Jerusalem (renovated by Rechter-Zarhy-Rechter, 1976)
1939 Agricultural Institute, Rehovot, Palestine, now Israel
Daniel Wolf Research Laboratories, Rehovot, Palestine, now Israel
1942 Kaplan House renovation, Long Island, New York
1946/
50 Maimonides Health Center for the Chronic Sick, San Francisco (remodelled by others, 1953)
B'nai Amoona Temple and Community Center, St. Louis
Temple and Community Center, Cleveland
1947 Apartment building, Chestnut Street, San Francisco (project)
Walter Heller House, San Francisco (project)
Walter Haas House, San Francisco (project)
1948 Temple and Community Center, Washington, D.C. (project)
Beth El Temple and Community Center, Baltimore (project)
1948/
52 Emanu-El Temple and Community Center, Grand Rapids, Michigan
1950/
51 Russell House, Pacific Heights, San Francisco
1950/
53 Varian Associates Electronic Research and Development Plant, Palo Alto, California
1950/
54 Mount Zion Temple and Community Center, St. Paul, Minnesota
1951 Emanu-El Temple and Community Center, Dallas (project)

Monument to the Jewish War Dead, New York (project)
1951/
53 Atomic Energy Commission Laboratories, Berkeley, California

Publications:

By MENDELSOHN: books—*Erich Mendelsohn: Structures and Sketches,* translated by H. G. Scheffauer, London 1924; *Amerika: Bilderbuch eines Architekten,* Berlin 1926; *Russland, Europa, Amerika: Ein Architektonische Querschnitt,* Berlin 1929; *Erich Mendelsohn: Das Gesamtschaffen des Architekten: Skizzen, Entwürfe, Bauten,* Berlin 1930; *Neues Haus—Neue Welt,* Berlin 1931; *Der Schöpferische Sinn der Krise,* Berlin 1932; *Three Lectures on Architecture,* Berkeley, California 1944; *Erich Mendelsohn: Letters of an Architect,* edited by Oskar Beyer, Munich 1961, New York and London 1967; articles—"Das Problem einer neuen Baukunst" in *Arbeitsrat für Kunst* (Berlin), 1919; "Architecture of Our Own Times" in *Architectural Association Journal* (London), June 1930; "Background to Design" in *Architectural Forum* (New York), April 1953; "The 3-Dimensions of Architecture: Their Symbolic Significance" in *Symbols and Values,* New York 1954.

On MENDELSOHN: books—*Wright, Dudok, Mendelsohn* by Hermann Soergel, Munich 1926; *Moderner Zweckbau* by Adolf Behne, Munich 1926; *Eric Mendelsohn* by Arnold Whittick, London 1940, 3rd ed. 1965; *Il contributo di Mendelsohn alla evoluzione dell'architettura moderna,* Milan 1952; *Eric Mendelsohn* by Wolf Von Eckardt, New York and London 1960; *Theory and Design in the First Machine Age* by Reyner Banham, London 1960; *Modern Architecture: Expressionism* by Dennis Sharp, London 1966; *Eric Mendelsohn,* exhibition catalogue, Berlin 1968; *Eric Mendelsohn: Opera Completa* by Bruno Zevi, with Louise Mendelsohn, Milan 1970; *Eric Mendelsohn,* exhibition catalogue, by Bruno Zevi, Rome 1972; articles—"Erich Mendelsohn" by H. G. Scheffauer in *Architectural Review* (London), May 1923; "Puritanism in Art" by Aldous Huxley in *The Studio* (London), March 1930; "Erich Mendelsohn," special issue of *L'Architecture Vivante*

(Paris), Autumn/Winter 1932; "Mendelsohn" by Julius Posener in *L'Architecture d'Aujourd'hui* (Paris), May 1932; "Undici Opera di Mendelsohn" by Edoardo Persico in *Casabella* (Milan), April 1934; "Current Architecture: Hospitals" in *Architectural Review* (London), February 1939; "Eric Mendelsohn" in *Architectural Forum* (New York), May 1947; "Eric Mendelsohn" in *Architectural Forum* (New York), April 1953; "Eric Mendelsohn" by Bruno Zevi in *Metron* (Rome), no. 49/50, 1954; "Mendelsohn" by Reyner Banham in *Architectural Review* (London), August 1954; "The Last Work of a Great Architect" by H. Schiller in *Architectural Forum* (New York), February 1955; "Eric Mendelsohn" by Irving D. Shapiro in *AIA Journal* (Washington, D.C.), June 1958; special issue of *L'Architettura* (Rome), September 1963.

Many influences served to form Eric Mendelsohn's architecture, which he absorbed and combined into a strongly individual style. These influences could be enumerated as the spectacular and efficient engineering structures of the 19th century—he had a tremendous admiration for the Crystal Palace—the evolution of the modern machine, and modern art movements, especially art nouveau and expressionism. As well, he had a strong feeling for the structural potentialities of steel and reinforced concrete. All this is strongly reflected in the large number of sketch projects that he exhibited in 1919 at the outset of his career.

Among them were sketch projects for observatories which secured for him his first important commission: the observatory at Potsdam built for further researches into Einstein's theory of relativity. This, now famous, building is one of the best examples of Expressionist architecture. The exterior conforms to the interior structure of a square shaft with a square stairway, but the tower and base is a design of rhythms and curved shapes with deep massive recesses derived partly from optical instruments. With the help of the light and shadow created by the design, it succeeds in giving an impression of mystery and symbolizes its purpose of scientific investigation into the nature of the universe. Mendelsohn's principal conscious aim in the design, however, was to achieve organic unity, a guiding principle in all his work. Einstein himself thought of it as organic. A

Eric Mendelsohn: Schocken Department Store, Stuttgart, 1928

notable circumstance is that the finished building conforms in essential shapes to the original sketch. Mendelsohn always began an architectural project with a perspective sketch—a three dimensional concept—and the final in the series of such sketches was often like the finished building, as for example in the Schocken Store at Stuttgart. Mendelsohn used to say, "Look at the sketch, it's all there."

Most of Mendelsohn's subsequent buildings did not give quite the same scope for symbolic expression as the Einstein Tower. They are often distinguished by the careful relation of curved and rectangular forms, seen in his German work mainly in a series of departmental stores of which the most impressive are those at Stuttgart (now destroyed) and Chemnitz. In the former the long horizontal lines of the main front are arrested by the spiral staircase glass tower, like a passage of music arrested by a vibrating chord. Mendelsohn used this motif frequently in a wide variety of buildings, in the de la Warr Pavilion, at Bexhill, in several buildings in Palestine, and perhaps most beautifully of all in the series of balcony-fronts in the Maimonides Health Center in San Francisco, where the straight horizontals are punctuated by a series of semi-circular projections. The relation of large curved form to straight is used with good effect in the Chemnitz store with the long convex horizontal bands of golden travertine and glass in eight storeys arrested at both ends by staircase and lift grills. A similar dramatic treatment of curved forms is seen in the interior of the Universum Cinema, where the grand unbroken sweep of the balcony front and seats is continued in the horizontal straight forms of the walls and echoed in the ceiling pattern.

One early influence on Mendelsohn is that of Greek art, which became apparent in a few designs such as the immense Columbus haus in Berlin, in his own house in Berlin, in two houses in England, in the Hadassah University Medical Centre, Mount Scopus, Jerusalem, and in the Schocken House in Jerusalem. In these buildings, curved forms are used with great restraint; the main forms are of large plain pale masses broken only by windows and a carefully calculated relation of verticals and horizontals to convey feelings of serenity and repose. This is seen particularly in his own house, which is very largely a design of square shapes, and it is significant that a partly enclosed exterior space against the house is designed for the performance of Greek plays.

To appreciate fully the de la Warr Pavilion, which Mendelsohn designed in collaboration with Serge Chermayeff, one must see a model of the whole design, for the building as it is now is only a part, and it has suffered from subsequent maltreatment. In the original complete scheme the building extends seawards with a circular swimming pool opposite the glass enclosure of the spiral staircase, with a lawn between, and a pier projecting from the swimming bath enclosure. The whole design is a fine combination of curved and rectangular forms.

Mendelsohn emigrated to the United States in 1941 and his principal works there were a series of temples and community centres for Jewish communities. They exhibit considerable variety of design. One of the most beautiful and characteristic is that at Cleveland, with its 100 ft. dome. The site is slightly hilly and, in designing both the temple and the community centre, Mendelsohn carefully related the curved forms to the contours of the site. This is one of the best examples of his sense of organic unity, where a building is an integral part of its setting. In this guiding principle of Mendelsohn designs, each part shows by its character its relation to the whole. In addition his work is characterised by decorative emphasis of purpose, which at times is symbolic.

The ideas like dignity, aspiration, power, repose, solemnity and gaiety suggested by the purpose and character of buildings imply symbolic shapes to which Mendelsohn gives dramatic emphasis, while taking these shapes as subjects for aesthetic effect.

—Arnold Whittick

Paulo Mendes da Rocha: Covered Gymnasium for the Paulistano Athletic Club, Sao Paulo, 1958

MENDES da ROCHA, Paulo (Archias).

Brazilian. Born in Vitoria, Espirito Santo, 25 October 1928. Educated at Mackenzie University, Faculty of Architecture and Town Planning, Sao Paulo, Dip.Arch. 1955. Served in the Brazilian Officers Reserve Corps (CPOR), Sao Paulo, 1949–51. Married Virginia Ferraz Navarro in 1955; children: Renata, Guilherme, Paulo, Pedro, and Joana. In private practice, Sao Paulo, since 1955. Professor, 1961–69, Director of Projects and University Councillor, 1965–67, and Co-ordinator of the Projects Department, 1969, University of Sao Paulo Faculty of Architecture and Town Planning. Member of the Council, 1958–61, Director of the Habitat Commission, 1971, and President, 1972–78, Brazilian Institute of Architects (IAB), Sao Paulo. Exhibitions: *Bienal,* Sao Paulo, 1961; *Beaubourg Competition Exhibition,* International Union of Architects, Paris, 1971; Museum of Contemporary Art, Sao Paulo, 1975. Recipient: First Prize, Legislative Palace Competition, Santa Catarina, Brazil, 1957; First Prize, Athletic Club Competition, Sao Paulo, 1958; President's Prize, *Bienal,* Sao Paulo, 1961; First Prize, Jockey Club Competition, Goias, Brazil, 1963. Address (office): Rua Bento Freitas 306, 5th Floor, Suite 51, 01220 Sao Paulo, Brazil.

Works:

1957 Legislative Palace, Florianopolis, Santa Catarina, Brazil (with Pedro Paulo de Melo Saraivo and Alfredo S. Paesani)

1958 Covered Gymnasium for the Paulistano Athletic Club, Rua Honduras, Sao Paulo

1960 Center for Child Care and Social Assistance, Cedral, Sao Paulo State

1962 Vila Maria School Complex, Sao Jose dos Campos, Sao Paulo State
Taboao School Complex, Sao Bernardo do Campo, Sao Paulo State
Forum Building, Avare, Sao Paulo State
National Industrial Federation Headquarters, Brasilia
Silveira Mello House, Piracicalia Garden City, Sao Paulo State (with Joao E. de Gennaro)
Gaetano Miani House, Granja Julieta, Sao Paulo (with Joao E. de Gennaro)

1963 Jockey Club, Goiania, Goias, Brazil
Malta Cardoso House, Jardim Guedala, Sao Paulo (with Joao E. de Gennaro)

1964 Cruz Secco House, Butanta, Sao Paulo (with Joao E. de Gennaro)

Camargo Correia Building Company Office
Building, Sao Paulo (competition project;
with Joao E. de Gennaro)
Apartment building, Haddock Lobo Street,
Sao Paulo (with Joao E. de Gennaro)
House, Mooca, Sao Paulo (with Joao E. de
Gennaro)
Paulo Mendes da Rocha House, Sao Paulo
1967 Vila Baeta School Complex, Sao Bernardo do
Campo, Sao Paulo State
COHAB Prefabricated Housing, Sao Paulo
(project; with Joao E. de Gennaro)
Cumbica Housing Estate, Sao Paulo (with J.
B. Vilanova Artigas and Fabio Penteado)
1968 President Roosevelt State College, Sao Paulo
Housing complex, Guarulhos, Sao Paulo
State
SENAI Technical School, Sao Paulo
SENAC Technical School, Campinas, Sao
Paulo State
1970 Brazilian Pavilion, *Expo '70,* Osaka, Japan
(with Flavio Motta, Julio Katinsky, and
Ruy Ohtake)
Fernando Millan House, Sao Paulo
Mario Masetti House, Sao Paulo
1972 James Francis King House, Sao Paulo
Children's Educational Centre, Jardim
Calux, Sao Bernardo do Campo, Sao
Paulo State
1973 Serra Dourada Municipal Stadium, Giania,
Goias, Brazil
1974 Grota da Bela Vista Development, Sao Paulo
(project)
1975 Municipal Insurance Headquarters, in the
New Administrative Center, Sao Paulo
Museum of Contemporary Art, University of
Sao Paulo (with Jorge Wilhelm)
Park Housing Development, Itatibam, Sao
Paulo State (with Alfredo Paesani)
1976 Cultural and Convention Center, Campos do
Jordao, Sao Paulo State
National Agricultural Engineering Center,
Fazenda Ipanema 7, Sorocaba, Sao Paulo
State
Antonio Junqueira de Azevedo House, Sao
Paulo
1977 Monorail Station, Cuiaba, Mato Grosso, Bra-
zil
Comgas Company Administration and Tech-
nical Buildings, Sao Paulo
University Center, Rondonopolis, Mato
Grosso, Brazil
1978 Governor's Residence, Cuiaba, Mato Grosso,
Brazil

Publications:

On MENDES da ROCHA: books—*Neue Möbel,*
Stuttgart 1961; *Concours International pour la Réali-
sation du Centre Beaubourg,* Paris 1971; *Grota da
Bela Vista* (planning authority report), Sao Paulo
1974; articles—"Ginasio Coberto Clube Atletico
Paulistano" in *Acropole* (Sao Paulo), November
1961; "Obra do Arquiteto Paulo A. Mendes da
Rocha," edited by Flavio Motta, special issue of
Acropole (Sao Paulo), August/September 1967;
"Pavilhao Oficial do Brasil, Expo '70" in *Acropole*
(Sao Paulo), March 1969; "Brazil's Pavilion" in
Kokusai Kentiku (Tokyo), vol. 34, 1970; "Wohn-
haus Paulo A. Mendes da Rocha" in *Architektur und
Wohnen* (Hamburg), Summer 1973; "Dos Resi-
dencias en Brasil: Casa Millan e Casa Masetti" in
Summa (Buenos Aires), February 1976; "Museu de
Arte Contemporanea da Universidade de Sao Paulo"
and "Grota da Bela Vista" in *Modulo* (Rio de
Janeiro), no. 42, 1977; "Centro Nacional de Engen-
haria Agricola" in *Modulo* (Rio de Janeiro), no. 46,
1977.

We try to achieve, in our own environment, a constant interaction between theoretical research and
practical experiment, geared to the needs of a rapidly
developing society.

Our designs demonstrate not only our preference
for an economy of language, but also the desire to use
only those technical resources suitable for the revitalization of living and work areas, so as to improve
the quality of life in the urban social environment.
—Paulo Mendes da Rocha

The modern architectural movement is not simply a
movement to "modernize" architecture, to make it
correspond to today's needs. It has as well, at times,
been an attempt to regain an integrity for architecture, to create works that are significant in historical,
artistic and human terms. Paulo Mendes da Rocha
belongs to the generation whose connection with the
modern movement is well established, and he may be
characterized as an architect whose place in that
movement has involved more than simply a response
to the economic needs of people at a particular time
and in a particular place.

To define Mendes da Rocha in terms of influences
and antecedents, however, is to end up with a vast
"family-tree" that, without extensive analysis and
qualification, is more chaotic than illuminating. Although this is an over-simplification, it is more helpful to say that he is an architect of Brazil and that,
in that context, he has been more interested in the
confrontation between architecture and nature than
in the confrontation between architecture and society. The architect to whom he can be most closely
compared is Oscar Niemeyer.

Their works have much in common. Those who
are tackling the problems of "crippling underdevelopment" may well be put off by such works—
by the niceties of light, airy spaces, easy access, efficient circulation, and room for natural growth. For
this world of elegance and charm is far removed
from the world to which the great majority of Brazilians belong. It is almost as if the architecture of
Mendes da Rocha (and Niemeyer) were intended for
a different species. It is an architecture that—like a
sleek, aristocratic heron—lands gently in front of the
inhabitant of central Brazil—a deformed, transformed man, nearer to geography than to history, a
man more familiar with the trees of the Brazilian
bush than the cultural references of a Niemeyer palace. From a certain perspective, it is easy to dismiss
such work as stunning, even beautiful, but superfluous.

Yet such an analysis would miss the "accomplishment." The work of Mendes da Rocha creates a
natural environment, reminding man of the earth's
generosity, never condemning, in itself or by implication, what has gone before. It provides the setting in
which we can examine the relationship of nature and
architecture without recourse to knowledge of "technical," pseudo-scientific disciplines and their aggressive moralities. If this architecture seems remote
from the man who looks at it, then it must be remembered that he looks at it with justified pleasure: because it is beautiful and because it suggests different
perspectives, different kinds of reality. The architect
has not thwarted his basic desire to communicate.

It is also well to remember that we have lived in
a period in which there has been and continues to be
a great deal of talk from architects and planners
about man's "solidarity with nature." What this has
usually meant in practice is a voracious and irreversible appropriation of the landscape to create works
that dehumanize. The simplicity of approach, in
both Mendes da Rocha and Niemeyer, also has to do
with "solidarity," but it neither invades nor disturbs
nature. Their architecture could be called fragile—
not because they lacked the necessary financial resources and certainly not because they intended to
demonstrate some dubious motive. It is a fragility
that pays its respects to nature and rests on a firm
belief in the solidarity of human beings and in the
inevitability of change. It does not seek to impose a
vision of society. Its true accomplishment is to keep
nature intact, to remind man of his potential, and to
allow for the advance of a new and more varied
society.
—Flavio Motta

MERRILL, John (Ogden).
American. Born in St. Paul, Minnesota, 10 August
1896. Educated at the University of Wisconsin,
Madison, 1914–16; Massachusetts Institute of Technology, Cambridge, 1919–21, B.Arch. 1921. Served
as a Captain in the Coast Artillery Corps, United
States Army, 1917–19. Married Ross MacKenzie in
1918; children: Elizabeth Ross, John Jr. and Jean;
married Viola Berg in 1946. Worked for Granger
and Bollenbacher, Chicago; Chief Architect for the
Mid-West States, United States Housing Administration, 1939. Joined Louis Skidmore, *q.v.,* and Nathaniel Owings, *q.v.,* already practicing as Skidmore
and Owings, Chicago (1936–39), to form Skidmore,
Owings and Merrill, Chicago, New York, San Francisco, Portland, Oregon, Washington, D.C., etc.,
from 1939: retired from the firm in 1958. Director,
Chicago Building Code Revision Commission,
1947–49. President, Chicago Chapter, American Institute of Architects. Exhibition: *Skidmore, Owings
and Merrill,* Museum of Modern Art, New York,
1950. Recipient: Honor Award, American Institute
of Architects, 1968. Fellow, American Institute of
Architects. *Died 13 June 1975.*

See SKIDMORE, OWINGS AND MERRILL

MEYER, Hannes.
Swiss. Born in Basle, 18 November 1889. Educated
at the Gewerbeschule, Basle, 1905–09; took evening
courses in aesthetics at the Kunstgewerbeschule,
Berlin, and in economics and land reform at the
Landwirtschafts-Akademie, Berlin, under Professor
Goecke, 1909–12; made study tour of England,
1912–13. Served in the Swiss Army, 1914–16. Married to Lena Bergner. Worked as a site superinten-
dent, Stamm Brothers Building and Architectural
Company, Basle, 1905–09; Assistant Architect, studio of Adolf Frohlich, Charlottenburg, Berlin, 1911–
12; Assistant to Emil Schaudt, Berlin, 1912, and
Georg Metzendorf, Munich, 1916–17; Architect,
under Baurat Schmohl, Housing Welfare Section,
Krupp Building Administration, Essen, 1917–18; in
private practice, Basle, 1919–25; in partnership with
Hans Wittwer, Basle, 1926–27; Master of Architecture, 1927–28, and Director (succeeded Gropius),
1928–30, Bauhaus School, Dessau, Germany: published *Bauhaus,* 1928–29; Chief Architect of the Gi-
provtus Institutes of Technology and Higher Education, Consultant and Chief Architect to the
Giprogor Town Planning Institute, and Chief Architect of the Standardgorproyect Town Planning
Trust, all Moscow, 1930–31; Professor, VASI University of Architecture, Moscow, 1930–33; Professor, and Head of the Housing Advisory Council,
Academy of Architecture, Moscow, 1934–35; in private practice, Geneva, 1936–39; Director, Institute
of Urbanism and Planning, Mexico City, 1939–41; in
private practice, Mexico City, 1941–49: Technical
Director, Department of Workers' Housing, Ministry of Labor, Mexico City, 1942, and of La Estampa
Mexicana Publishing House, Mexico City, 1947–49;
returned to Switzerland, concentrating on theoretical studies for architectural publications, 1949 until
his death, 1954. Member, German Land Reform
Movement; Swiss Free Land Movement; Swiss Co-
operative Movement; ABC Group, Switzerland;
CIRPAC (Directing Committee of CIAM: Congrès
Internationaux d'Architecture Moderne); Der Ring
Architects Association, Berlin; VOPRA Architects'
Association, Moscow; Managing Committee, Moscow Section, Association of Soviet Architects. Recipient: First Prize, German Trade Unions Federation School Competition, 1928. *Died* (in Crocifisso
di Savosa, Switzerland) *19 July 1954.*

Hannes Meyer: German Trades Unions Federation School, Bernau, 1930

Works:

1916/
18   Kiel-gaarden Housing Development, near Essen (project; with Georg Metzendorf)
     Margarethenhöhe Housing Development, near Essen (project; with Georg Metzendorf)

1918/
19   Pic-Pic Housing Development, Geneva (competition project)

1919/
21   Freidorf Co-operative Housing Estate, near Basle
     Urbanization plan for Balsthal, Jura, Switzerland

1923   Central Cemetery, Basle (project)

1924   Co-op Show Window Display, *International Co-operative Exhibition,* Ghent

1926   St. Peter's Primary School for Girls, Basle (competition project; with Hans Wittwer)

1926/
27   Palace of the League of Nations, Geneva (competition project; with Hans Wittwer)

1928/
30   Törten Housing Estate redevelopment, Dessau, Germany (with Bauhaus students; partially built)
     German Trade Unions Federation School, Bernau, near Berlin

1929   Workers' Bank Building, Berlin (competition project)

1931/
32   Development and reconstruction plan for Greater Moscow (project; with Geimanson and Bücking)

1931/
36   Lenin School, Moscow (project; with Bauhaus students)
     Housing development, Ishevsk, U.S.S.R. (project)

1932   Plan for the satellite town of Nishniy-Kurinsk, near Perm, U.S.S.R. (with the Standardgorproyect team; partially built)

Plan for the satellite town of Sozgorod Gorki, near Molotov, U.S.S.R. (with the Standardgorproyect team; partially built)

1933/
34   Plan for the capital city of Birobidjan, U.S.S.R. (with the Giprogor team, Gandurin and Salvin; partially built)
     Redevelopment plan for Tschita, U.S.S.R. (project)
     Redevelopment plan for Krassnojarsk, U.S.S.R. (project)

1934   Plan for the Perm Basin Industrial Zone, U.S.S.R. (project; with the Giprogor team, and Patapov)
     Plan for the reconstruction of the town of Rybinsk, U.S.S.R. (project)

1938/
39   Jäggi Foundation Children's Home, Mümliswil, Solothurn, Switzerland

1941   Sports and Cultural Centre, Mexico City (competition project)

1942   Lomas de Becerra Housing Estate, Tacubaya, near Mexico City (project)

1946/
47   Agua Hedionda Spa Centre, Cuautla, Morelos, Mexico (project)

1947   Banco Nacional/Banco Internacional Headquarters, Mexico City (project)

Publications:

By MEYER: books—*The Freidorf Co-operative Housing Estate,* with J. F. Schar and H. Faucherre, Basle 1921; *Hannes Meyer: Architettura o Rivoluzione: Scritti 1921–1942,* edited by Francesco Dal Co, Padua 1969; articles—numerous in specialist periodicals, including *Bauhaus* (Dessau, Germany), 1927–29.

On MEYER: book—*Hannes Meyer: Buildings, Projects and Writings* by Claude Schnaidt, Teufen, Switzerland and London 1965 (includes bibliography); articles—special issue of *Arquitectura y Decoracion* (Mexico City), October 1938; "Hannes Meyer" by

Paul Artaria in *Werk* (Zurich), October 1954; "Hannes Meyer" by Victor Bourgeois in *Ruimte* (Antwerp), May 1955; "The Work and Activities of the Architect and Town Planner Hannes Meyer 1009–1954" by Walter Münz in *Deutsche Bauzeitung* (Stuttgart), March 1961; "Hannes Meyer e la Scuola di Architettura" by Massimo Scolari in special Bauhaus issue of *Controspazio* (Bari, Italy), April/May 1970; "Hans Schmidt and Hannes Meyer in Moscow" by Christian Borngräber in *Archithese* (Niedertaufen), November/December 1978.

There are three good reasons for remembering and honouring Hannes Meyer. In the late 1920's he was the designer of a few highly progressive competition schemes. He was the second Director of the Bauhaus, after Gropius and before Mies van der Rohe, a post from which he was expelled on political grounds in 1930. And he believed that architecture was not art.

Traditionally his belief is explained as a manifestation of his Marxism, but, as with William Morris, the reverse might as easily be true. Meyer's design philosophy (though he was never plain in formulating his aesthetic principles) patently had the force of personal feeling commanding political philosophy. It probably began that way round—then it grew extreme. If Meyer believed only that design ideals should be subordinate to practical applications, it would have been an unexceptional, and unmemorable, position.

Meyer's pedagogically-forged extremism is durable precisely because it was so radical. His dialectical struggle with Moholy-Nagy (the Bauhaus's prime exponent of visual culture) forced Meyer in to exaggerated statements of the anti-visual. His advocacy of architecture as pure social science and sheer function became implacable. He held no brief for the accommodating pragmatism of formalist training, at least as far as his teaching theories were concerned: he opposed studio discussions about mere form. Ultimately, therefore, an aesthetic of anti-art was Meyer's contribution to architectural thought.

An anti-art aesthetic? What at the time was a seemingly blatant self-contradiction no longer holds after the lesson of an intervening fifty years of modernism and, more particularly, after the rise of semiology and its influence on modern aesthetic theory: Morris, Saussure and others have persuasively shown that nothing is without signification or aesthetic meaning. So Meyer with his contradictions has become a crucial figure to reassess. His conception of non-art architecture, or even anti-art architecture (if such a thing were possible, as it may be in the post-Saussure consciousness), would doubtless come across as a galvanic "statement" and hence a significant manifestation in the semiological books. His pure aesthetic neutrality, once achieved, would be loaded with values. Its very denials—unless invisible—would become emblematic.

Meyer's ironic failure to achieve these realizations of non-art in his own time, for example through the limited appreciation of such conceptual masterpieces as his competition drawings for the St. Peter's School, Basel (1926), has nevertheless not harmed his position with like-minded later fans, e.g. contemporary English neo-rationalists such as Cedric Price and Richard Rogers. In the end Hannes Meyer emerges both as a small historic figure, very much of his time—one especially sympathizes with his sad rootlessness, wandering from Russia to Mexico—and a far larger figure for the future.

—Nathan Silver

MEYER, Wilhelm O(laf).

South African. Born in Pretoria, 14 May 1935. Educated at the University of the Witwatersrand, Johannesburg, 1953–59 (Transvaal Institute of Architects First Prize, 1956, 1959; Gordon Leith Prize, 1959; A. S. Furner Prize, 1959), B.Arch. 1959; University of Pennsylvania, Philadelphia, under Louis I. Kahn, 1960–61 (Postgraduate Study Scholarship; Frank Miles Day Prize), M.Arch. 1961. Married Angela Winsome Murray in 1961; children: Arne and Alessandra. Partner, Watson, Peiser, Grobbelaar and Meyer, Pretoria, later also Johannesburg, 1961–66. Since 1966, Principal of Wilhelm O. Meyer and Partners, Johannesburg (partners since 1971: Francois Pienaar; A. Holley; D. Hoffrichter; G.H.H. Hattingh). Guest Lecturer, University of Capetown, University of Natal, University of Pretoria, University of Potchefstroom, and University of the Witwatersrand, all South Africa, 1963–73. Founder-Member, Urban Action Group, Johannesburg, 1971, and Member of the Urban Action Teaching Group at the University of the Witwatersrand, 1973. Vice-President, 1976, and President, 1977, Transvaal Provincial Institute of Architects. Member of the Council of Architects, South Africa, since 1975; Chairman, South African Institute of Architects Housing Committee, since 1977. Exhibitions: Transvaal Academy Exhibition, Johannesburg, 1968; Pahlavi Library (Tehran) Exhibition, in Tehran, Mexico City, Cape Town and Johannesburg, 1978. Recipient: First Prize, International Johannesburg Civic Centre Competition, 1962; Merit Award, South African Institute of Architects, 1964, 1966, 1972, 1975, 1977; First Prize, Germiston Civic Centre Competition, 1973; Outstanding Young South African Award, 1973. Member, South African Institute of Architects, 1959; Associate, Royal Institute of British Architects, 1959. Address: Wilhelm O. Meyer and Partners Inc., P.O. Box 52317, Saxonwold 2132, Johannesburg, South Africa.

Works:

1961/
62   Kenmauval Apartments, Pretoria (with the Watson Partnership)

1962/
63   Grupels Court Apartments, Pretoria (with the Watson Partnership)
     Botha Mansions Apartments, Pretoria (with the Watson Partnership)
1963   Civic Centre, Johannesburg (with the Watson Partnership and Bryer and Partners)
1963/
64   Robinson House, Johannesburg (with Glen Gallagher)
1966/
67   Meyer House, Plettenberg Bay, South Africa
1968   Development plan for Rand Afrikaans University, Johannesburg (with Jan van Wijk and Partners)
1969   Development plan for Potchefstroom University, South Africa
     Architect's studio, Johannesburg
1969/
76   Student housing, Potchefstroom University, South Africa
1970/
75   Rand Afrikaans University, Johannesburg: Central Academic Facilities; Lecture Theatres; Laboratories and Library; Student Centre, Theatre and Sports Complex; Student Housing; Service Building and Central Plant (with Jan van Wijk and Partners)
1971/
75   Braamridge Head Office and Urban Centre, Johannesburg (with other firms)
1973   Civic Centre, Germiston, South Africa (competition project)
1973/
78   Potchefstroom University Biological Laboratories, stage I, and Education and Psychology Building, South Africa
1973/
79   Potchefstroom University Student Centre, Theatre and Sports Complex, South Africa (with Bannie Britz)
1975   Development plan for the University of Zululand, South Africa
     Urban plan for the Port Zimbali Resort Village, Natal North Coast, South Africa (with Revel Fox and Partners)
     Japan Architect Housing Competition, Tokyo (project)
1975/
76   McAdam House, Plettenberg Bay, South Africa
     Kruger House, Plettenberg Bay, South Africa
     Fihrer House, Plettenberg Bay, South Africa
     Sawmill and Factory, Plettenberg Bay, South Africa
     Sanctuary Vacation Village, Plettenberg Bay, South Africa (project)
1975/
77   Vaal Triangle College of Advanced Technology academic extension, Vanderbijlpark, South Africa
1976   University of Zululand Lecture Theatre Complex, South Africa
     Development plan for the University of the North, Transvaal, South Africa
     Development plan for Mabopane College of Advanced Technology, South Africa
     Rosebank Offices, Johannesburg
     Woodmead Town Houses, Johannesburg (project)
     Montgomery Park Town Houses, Johannesburg (project)
     Workers' Housing Village, Mabopane East, South Africa
1977   Development plan for the New Satellite Campus of Potchefstroom University, Vanderbijlpark, South Africa
     Development plan for University of Fort Hare, Cape Province, South Africa
     Student Housing, University of Fort Hare, Cape Province, South Africa
     Parliament Complex, High Courts, Presidential Suite and Ministries, Mmabatho, Bophuthatswana, Africa
1977/
78   Van der Wat House, Natures Valley, South Africa
     Perdikies House, Sandton, South Africa
     Pahlavi National Library, Tehran, Iran (competition project)
     New campus for Mabopane College of Advanced Technology, South Africa

Publications:

By MEYER: articles—"The World of the House" in *South African Architectural Record* (Johannesburg), April 1965; "Values and the Making of Buildings" in *South African Architectural Record* (Johannesburg), November 1966; "Roofscapes" in *Habitat* (Johannesburg), no. 22, 1976; "The Architect's Responsibility for Better Building" in *Planning and Building* (Braamfontein), January 1976; "Beyond the Pigeonholes" and "Search and Exploration" in *South African Institute of Architects Golden Jubilee Congress Report*, Johannesburg 1977; "Homes Away from It All" in *Planning and Building* (Johannesburg), September 1977; "Pedro the Bull and Assorted Daisy Cows" in *Transvaal Provincial Institute of Architects Papers* (Johannesburg), October 1977.

On MEYER: book—*Meyer and Partners: Projects and Buildings 1967–1978*, Johannesburg 1978; articles—"Come Sara L'Architettura Africa" by J. Beinart in *Edilizia Moderna* (Milan), no. 89/90, 1963; "A Development Plan for Rand Afrikaans University" in *Architect and Builder* (Cape Town), May 1969; "Rand Afrikaans University" in *Bauen und Wohnen* (Zurich), November 1969; "Universities" by Julian Elliott in *Architectural Review* (London), April 1970; "Letter from Cape Town" by J. Morgan in *Architecture Plus* (New York), March 1974; "Johannesburg Revisited" by Theo Crosby in *RIBA Journal* (London), February 1976; "Pahlavi National Library" in *Domus* (Milan), August 1978.

Any place succeeds even if it gives man only a glimpse of his highest aspirations. The great, the monumental, the awe-inspiring, the intimate, the socially responsible, the unassuming, the commonplace can all do this. Man's spirit can be touched by the unique and heroic as well as by the ordinary and humble in the complexity of human requirements and desires. Although these values can be circumstantially varied in their application, they cannot be invalidated or polarised into right or wrong. In man's history they are cyclical elements and not absolute. Order may thus include that which seems to be its opposite in the physical life condition of dualities and polarity. Even in doing so Ultimate Order is never escaped.

The golden thread of endeavour is perceived through anticipation and retrospection; prophecy and memory. Without considering two directions—backward and forward—the thread can have no continuity. Without considering both, in unison, there can be no thread. If something is loved deeply, it cannot be copied, but it can inspire a not dissimilar response. Reverence for the integrity of the original will only allow its essence to inform a later fragment of man's visual history.

In one's work the ramifications of various theories and images of the time are obviously present in suffused fashion behind what one does. But expression as such remains personal and belongs to the individual maker. This is part of his private world and fantasies for which he is not answerable to anyone. The art of the possible is no art without compelling visions in the impossible. But no matter the momentary and transitory foibles of expression one inadvertently journeys through from innovation through boring cliché back to the same innovation in a new guise, the real interest one has in one's own

Wilhelm O. Meyer: Rand Afrikaans University, Johannesburg, 1975

work lies in how far it approaches the personal quest of interpretation of the timeless qualities and values in ever changing conditions and renewing circumstances.

For the architect the work he does should always remain his way of expressing how he feels about and for his fellow man. It is as direct as that with no shorter cut and, constantly kept in mind, will act as the most reliable measure in all his concerns and sensibilities nurtured by deep inner awareness, whether these be social, aesthetic, practical or technical. Architecture means the thoughtful housing of the human spirit in the physical world. The architect becomes the enabling instrument only when he reaches in beyond himself. Ultimately, however, there is no shame or pity in architecture losing if life wins.

—Wilhelm O. Meyer

When Wilhelm O. Meyer studied at the University of the Witwatersrand during the late 1950's, the bloom had already gone off the influence there of the modern movement: that influence had been strongest in the 1930's and early 40's. There was a general searching about for a philosophical framework, for the architecture of the late 1950's was to a great extent dull and derivative, with few memorable works. Meyer was one of a group of young South Africans, which included Roelof Uytenbogaardt, Francois Pienaar, Danie Theron and Glen Gallagher, who studied during the late 1950's and early 60's at the University of Pennsylvania under the then prevailing influence of Louis Kahn. On his return to South Africa, Meyer produced works that showed the influences of Kahn's formal approach: such apartment buildings as Grupels Court and Botha Mansions show a vigorous articulation of form, as does Robertson House (with Glen Gallagher).

Meyer participated with others in the winning scheme for the new Johannesburg Civic Centre, but both in detail and in overall form this scheme seems related to work in Johannesburg of the late 1950's:

at that time the move away from the modern movement was characterized by detailed design, by some classical precedents, and, to an extent, by the influence of Fassler and the later work of Norman Hanson. The formal language of the Johannesburg Civic Centre was significantly different from the forms that Meyer chose for himself in his own work, particularly the design for the Rand Afrikaans University—his major work of the period: with its vigorous forms and its powerfully expressed enclosing shape, it was one of the most powerful images of a university of the 1960's. The style he achieved here expressed also the powerful drives within the Afrikaner community in South Africa. The form and the articulated shape, monumental scale, and, as Theo Crosby put it, "the Piranesian grandeur of the interiors" were entirely appropriate for the period.

There is in Meyer's work the development of two main themes: the search for a strong geometric form on a fairly monumental scale and the attempt to capture the "genius loci." He has been commissioned for several buildings of a similar kind—government, parliament and other institutional buildings—which he has done with considerable panache, and all have by their nature encouraged the formal and the monumental. The geometry of Germiston Civic Centre is somewhat freer than the others and shows a confident approach to the handling of relationships in a tighter urban context.

What distinguishes the latest work, such as the Pahlavi National Library competition entry and the parliament building projects, is the use of a simpler form for the building, with less articulation of the parts. This work is characterized by clarity of detailing and a great consistency of the parts to the whole. What one misses in these large-scale schemes is the gentler geometry and softer forms that only now and again have found their place in his work. Meyer's house for his parents in Plettenberg Bay, with its gentle shaping of the not too greatly articulated elements in plan, shows an appropriateness to site and relative smallness of scale that are welcome. Now that the period of heavy articulated forms in South African architecture has passed, Meyer moves into a period where possibly the commissions will be of a different nature and where this lighter touch and smaller scale may form part of his further development.

Meyer's work and that of his nearest collaborators and associates—Glen Gallagher, Bannie Britz and Francois Pienaar (a partner of long standing)—has been an important influence in South Africa, and there is for the period 1965–75 a discernible "school" in the Witwatersrand area that, though obviously revealing the influence of Louis Kahn, has steadily gained its own characteristic features. Influences have clearly been imported, but it is no longer a question of "alms from abroad," for there is in this work an exportable vision of its own.

—Hans Hallen

MICHELUCCI, Giovanni.

Italian. Born in Pistoia, 2 January 1891. Educated at the School of Architecture, Pistoia, 1908–11, Dip. Arch. 1911; Academy of Fine Arts, Florence, 1911–14. Served in the Italian Army, 1915–16. Married Aloisia Pacini in 1928. In private practice, Fiesole, since 1916. Teacher at the Institute of Art, Pisa, 1916–20, and Rome, 1920–28; Professor of Interior Design, School of Architecture, Florence, 1928–36; Assistant Professor of Interior Design, 1936–39, Professor, 1939–44, Chair in Urban Planning, 1944–45, Chair in Architectural design, 1944–45, and Dean of the School of Architecture, 1944–45, 1947–48, University of Florence; Chair in Architectural Composition, Faculty of Engineering, 1948–66, and since 1966 Emeritus Professor, University of Bologna. Director, *La Nuova Città,* 1945–56; Founder, *Esperienza Artigiana,* 1949; Director, *Panorami della Nuova Città,* 1950–52. Exhibitions: *Esposizione di Architettura Razionale,* Galleria di Palazzo Ferroni, Florence, 1932; *Ten Italian Architects,* Los Angeles, 1967; *La Città di Michelucci,* Palazzo del Comune, Pistoia, Italy, 1976; *Giovanni Michelucci,* Heinz Gallery, Royal Institute of British Architects, London, 1978. Recipient: First Prize, *Italian Gardens Exhibition,* Florence, 1931; First Prize, with others, S. Maria Novella Station Competition, Florence, 1933; First Prize, with others, Master Plan of Pistoia Competition, 1936; First Prize, with others, Grazie Bridge Competition, Florence, 1954; Feltrinelli Prize, 1958; San Luca International Prize for Architecture, 1958. Address (office): Il Roseto, 50014 Fiesole, Florence, Italy.

Works:

1916 Chapel, Caporetto, Italy
1920 House, Via Bellini, Pistoia, Italy
1921 War Memorial, Ancona, Italy (competition project)

Giovanni Michelucci: Church of St. John the Baptist, Autostrada del Sole, Florence, 1964

1924 House, Via Rosselli, Montecatini, Italy
      Valdissena House, Pescia, Italy
1929 Balilla Headquarters, Piazza S. Francesco, Pistoia, Italy (with Raffaello Fagnoni)
1930 Valiani House, Via Mangili, Rome
      Dining Room Pavilion, *Triennale,* Monza, Italy
1931 Valiani Villa, Via Prenestina, Rome
      Alfredo Casella Villa, Rome (project)
1932 Exhibition Halls, *Fiera Nazionale dell'Artigianato,* Florence (with Pier Niccolo Bernardi, Gherardo Bosio, and Sarre Guarnieri)
1933 Master plan for University City, Rome (with others)
1935 S. Maria Novella Station, Florence (with others)
      Institute of General Physiology, Psychology and Anthropology, University City, Rome
      Institute of Mineralogy, Geology, and Paleontology, University City, Rome
      Covered Market, Piazza de Guidici, Florence (project)

1936 Master plan of Pistoia, Italy (competition project; with A. Susini and L. Fuselli)
      Facade for *VI Mostra Mercato dell'Artigianato,* Florence
1938 Government Building, Savona, Italy (competition project)
1939 Government Building, Arezzo, Italy
      Open-Air Theatre, E.42 District, Rome (project)
      Palace of Light and Water, E.42 District, Rome (project)
      Government Building, Savona, Italy (2nd project)
      Villa Contini-Bonacossi extensions, Viale Morin, Forte dei Marmi, Italy
      Tower conversion to house and gallery, Via Guicciardini, Florence (destroyed during World War II)
1946 Reconstruction of the area around the Ponte Vecchio, Florence
1947 Tower conversion, Vicolo dei Ramaglianti, Florence

1948 Funeral Chapel, S. Miniato al Monte, Italy
      House, Lido d'Albaro, Genoa
      Cassa di Risparmio Building, Viareggio, Italy
      Cassa di Risparmio Building, Volterra, Italy
      Cassa di Risparmio Building renovation, Florence

1950 Stock Exchange, Pistoia, Italy
      Bathing Resort, Sori, Genoa (project)
      House, Via Montebello, Florence
      Baldassare House, Fancavilla al Mare, Chieti, Italy (project)
      Skyscraper, Marsaglia Park, San Remo, Italy

1953 Caffe Donnini, Piazza della Republica, Florence

1954 Master plan for Ferrara, Italy (as consultant)
      Collina di Pentolungo Church, Pistoia, Italy
      Grazie Bridge, Florence (competition project; with E. Detti and D. Santi)
      Carrais Bridge, Florence (competition project; with E. Detti and D. Santi)
      Vespucci Bridge, Florence (competition project; with L. Cestelli-Guidi)

1956 Church of the Virgin, Via Bassa della Vergine, Pistoia, Italy

1957 Residential Zone and Church, Sasso Pisano, Italy
      Larderello Workers Village, Pisa
      Ventura House, Via Guicciardini 24, Florence
      INA Apartment Building, Via Guicciardini, Florence
      House, Via Monte Pania 1, Lido di Camaiore, Lucca, Italy
      Cassa di Risparmio Building, Via Bufalini, Florence
      Skyscraper, Livorno (project)
      Cabin, Torre S. Lorenzo, Italy (with L. Lugli)
      Società Larderello Building, Pisa
      Uffizi Gallery re-organization, Florence

1958 Master plan for the Sorgane Quarter of Florence (as co-ordinator)
      Citadel Gardens, Pisa
      Galileo Center, Pisa (project)

1959 Institute of Geology, University of Bologna
      Faculty of Letters and Philosophy, University of Bologna
      Larderello Church, Pisa
      Cemetery Church, Pistoia, Italy
      Institute of Mathematics, University of Bologna

1961 Belvedere Church, Pistoia, Italy
      Apartment building/shops, Lungarno del Tempio, Florence

1962 Giunti House, Viareggio, Italy

1963 Osteria del Gambero Rosso, Collodi, Pistoia, Italy
      Memorial to the Victims of Kindu, Pisa Airport
      Apartment/office building, Piazza Brunelleschi, Florence

1964 Church of St. John the Baptist, Autostrade del Sole at Campi Bisenzio, Florence
      Concert Hall, Montecatini Terme, Italy (project)
      Concert Hall and Art School, Ravenna (project)
      Quadrio House, Milan (project)
      Tomb of Dante (project)

1965 Rosetti House, Ravenna (project)
      Monument to the Carabiniere, Fiesole, Florence
      School and Village Garden, Arzignano, Vicenza, Italy
      Institute of Chemistry, University of Florence (project)

1966 Skyscraper, Livorno
      Borgo Maggiore Church, San Marino

1967 Arzignano Church, Vicenza, Italy
      SIP Headquarters, Via Masaccio, Florence
      Stock Exchange extension, Pistoia, Italy
      Cassa di Risparmio Headquarters, Pistoia, Italy
      Post office, Via Verdi, Florence

1969 Sampiva House, Arzignano, Vicenza, Italy
      Bracco Chapel, Trespiano, Florence

1971 Master plan for Camaiore, Lucca, Italy

1972 Cangioli House, Pistoia, Italy
      Scaglietti Chapel, Collodi Cemetery, Pistoia, Italy (project)

1973 Orangery reconstruction, Villa Strozzi, Florence (project)

1974 Lozzelli House, Pistoia, Italy
      Plan for the center of Sesto Fiorentino, Italy

1975 Bastione Thyrion Secondary School, Pistoia, Italy
      Post office, Viareggio, Lucca, Italy (with A. Pasquinucci)
      Marble Experimental Center, Foce di Pianza, Carrara, Italy (with B. Sacchi)
      Monte dei Paschi di Siena Headquarters, Volle Val d'Elsa, Siena (project; with B. Sacchi)
      Contrada del Palio Valdimontone Headquarters, Siena (project; with B. Sacchi)
      Bini House, Pescia, Pistoia, Italy (with B. Sacchi)
      Plan for the center of Arzignano, Vicenza, Italy (project; with B. Sacchi)

1976 Telecommunications Center, Pisa (with M. Innocenti)
      Cassa di Risparmio Headquarters, Via Montalbano, Pistoia, Italy (with B. Sacchi)
      Church, Livorno (project; with B. Sacchi)
      Lacini House, Montemarcello, La Spezia, Italy (project; with B. Sacchi)
      Friendship Monument, Church of St. John the Baptist, Autostrade del Sole at Campi Bisenzio, Florence

1978 San Bartolomeo Hospital, Sarzana, Italy (with M. Innocenti)
      Novello Church, Cutigliano, Pistoia, Italy (with B. Sacchi)
      Oratorio di San Leonardo conversion, Siena (project; with B. Sacchi)

Publications:

By MICHELUCCI: books—*Filippo Brunelleschi,* Florence 1936; *Il Quartiere di Santa Croce nel Futuro di Firenze,* with A. Ardigo and F. Borsi, Rome 1968; *Brunelleschi Mago,* Florence 1972; *La Nuova Città,* edited by R. Risaliti, Pistoia, Italy 1975; *Non sono un Maestro,* Sarzana, Italy 1976; articles—numerous in *Lo Stile* (Milan), 1942–43, *La Nuova Città* (Florence), 1946–56; "Ambienti Storici e Urbanistica Moderna" in *Domus* (Milan), no. 223 225, 1947; "La Ricostruzione in Toscana nell'Umbria e nelle Marche" in *Edilizia Moderna* (Milan), no. 40/42, 1948; "Felicita dell'Architetto" in *Domus* (Milan), no. 234, 1949; numerous in *Panorami della Nuova Città* (Florence), 1950–52, and *Urbanistica* (Turin), 1951–53; "Lettera per la Casa di Wright sul Canal Grande" in *Metron* (Rome), no. 51, 1954; "Come ho Progettato la Chiesa della Vergine" in *L'Architettura* (Rome), no. 16, 1957; "Sorgane: Quartiere Autosufficiente" in *Edilizia Popolare* (Rome), no. 16, 1957; "Punti Interrogativi" in *Quaderni della Nuova Città,* Florence 1957; "Rispondere ad una Esigenza Popolare con una Forma Culturalmente Efficace" in *L'Architettura* (Rome), no. 31, 1958; "Una Casa che non e un Villino, a Firenze" in *L'Architettura* (Rome), no. 35, 1958; "Chiesa di Larderello" in *L'Architettura* (Rome), no. 46, 1959; "La Scuola e La Città" in *Prospettive Storiche e Problemi Attuali dell'Educazione: Studi in Onore di E. Codignola,* Florence 1960; "La Concezione Architettonica della Chiesa" in *Civiltà delle Macchine* (Rome), no. 5, 1961; "Pensieri di Michelucci" in *L'Architettura* (Rome), no. 76, 1962; "De nombreuses chose d'abord obscures se sont éclairices et m'ont paru nouvelles" in *L'Architecture d'Aujourd'hui* (Paris), no. 113–114, 1964; "Sintonia" in *Domus* (Milan), no. 413, 1964; "Giustificazione di una Forma Architettonica" in *Autostrade* (Rome), no. 3, 1964; "L'Eglise de San Marino" in *L'Architecture d'Aujourd'hui* (Paris), no. 119, 1965; "Urbanistica: Problema Umano" in *Vita Sociale* (Pistoia, Italy), no. 2, 1966; "La Città del Dialogo" in *Testimonianze* (Florence), no. 85, 1966; "Il Cantiere" in *Vita Sociale* (Pistoia, Italy), no. 5/6, 1966; "La Genesi dell'Opera" in *Casabella* (Milan), no. 311, 1966; "Architettura e Società Civile" in *Vita Sociale* (Pistoia, Italy), no. 3, 1967; "Lo Spazio e il Lugo dove l'Uomo construisce la sua Storia" in *Problemi della Città,* Padua 1967; "Considerazione di Urbanistica" in *A Proposito di una Polemica sul P. R. di Fiesole,* Pistoia, Italy 1969; "La Chiesa di Longarone" in *Civiltà delle Macchine* (Rome), no. 1, 1970; "La Città Antica nella Moderna" in *Firenze: Notizario del Commune* (Florence), no. 1, 1971; "Misura e Caratteri Umani della Città" in *Vita Sociale* (Pistoia, Italy), no. 146, 1971; "Giovanni Michelucci sulla Linguistica Architettonica" in *L'Architettura* (Rome), no. 227, 1974; "La Città e La Salute" in *La Riforma Sanitaria,* Pistoia, Italy 1974; "Una Chiesa che serva alla Città" in *Testimonianze* (Florence), April.May 1974; "Per un'altro Città" in *Parametro* (Bologna), May 1975; etc.

On MICHELUCCI: books—*Cassa di Risparmio di Firenze* by E. Berti and M. Gobbo, Florence 1958; *La Chiesa dell'Autostrada del Sole,* Rome 1964; *Giovanni Michelucci,* edited by Franco Borsi, Florence 1966; *Giovanni Michelucci: Il Pensiero e le Opera* by F. Clemente and L. Lugli, Bologna 1966; *Michelucci* by M. Cerasi, Rome 1968; *Firenze Chiesa dell'Autostrada* by A. Ottani Cavina, Bologna 1968; *La Città di Michelucci,* exhibition catalogue, by Franco Borsi and others, Pistoia, Italy 1976; *Giovanni Michelucci* by Fabio Naldi, Florence 1978.

From the detachment and impartiality of his S. Maria Novella Station in Florence, won in competition in 1933, to the saturnalia of the 1964 Church of St. John the Baptist near Florence, dedicated to the memory of the workers who lost their lives during the construction of the Autostrade del Sole, Giovanni Michelucci has never been afraid of practising abstinence one day, epicurism the next. One day he is a model of functionalist virtue, a paragon of philanthropic innocence, stainless and incorruptible, mobilizing architecture for a good and righteous cause—and his buildings are principled and moral havens, harbours of ethical integrity and the cardinal virtues. Another day will find him egocentric, impatient to explore the voluptuousness in a detail here, the carnality in a material there, the earthiness of that section over there—on such a day, many diverse currents are ingeniously assimilated, resulting in intermittent architectonics irradiated with human involvement.

Obdurate members of both camps, the rationalists and the organicists, are usually outraged by Michelucci's blithe disregard for their carefully established and long maintained categories—but both camps might have something to learn from his contribution. Le Corbusier was constantly running into the same problem: architecture will always be bigger than the terms we invent to describe it.

—Chris Fawcett

MIES van der ROHE, Ludwig.
American. Born Ludwig Mies in Aachen, Germany, 27 March 1886 (later adopted mother's name van der Rohe); emigrated to the United States, 1938: naturalized, 1944. Educated at the Domschule, Aachen, 1897–1900; Aachen Trade School, 1900–02. Served in the German Army, in the Engineer Corps, 1914–18. Worked in his father's stonemason business, Aachen, 1900–02; draftsman in a stucco decorating business, Aachen, 1903–04; moved to Berlin

545

and worked briefly in the office of an architect specializing in wood structures, 1905; apprenticed to the
architect and furniture designer Bruno Paul, Berlin,
1905–07; in private architectural practice, Berlin,
1907–08; Assistant, with Walter Gropius and Le
Corbusier, in the office of Peter Behrens, Berlin,
1908–11; in private practice, Berlin, 1911–14, 1919–
37; in private architectural practice, Chicago, 1938
until his death, 1969 (firm continues as FCL Associates). Director of the Bauhaus at Dessau, 1930–32,
and in Berlin, 1932 until it closed, 1933; Director of
Architecture, Illinois Institute of Technology (formerly Armour Institute), Chicago, 1938–59. Co-
Founder, *G* (Gestaltung) magazine, Berlin, 1921;
Director of Architectural Exhibits, Novembergruppe, Berlin, 1921–25; Founder, Zehner Ring,
Berlin, 1925; First Vice-President, Deutscher Werkbund, Berlin, 1926–32, and Director of the Werkbund exhibition *Weissenhofsiedlung,* Stuttgart,
1927, and of the Werkbund section, "The Dwelling,"
at the Berlin Building Exhibition, 1931; President,
CIAM (Congrès International d'Architecture Mo-
derne). Exhibitions (one-man): Museum of Modern
Art, New York, 1947; Art Institute of Chicago,
1968, toured the United States, Canada and Europe;
A New City Square and Office Tower, Royal Ex-
change, London, 1968; *Ludwig Mies van Rohe: Furniture and Furniture Drawings,* Museum of Modern
Art, New York, 1977. Recipient: Royal Gold Medal,
Royal Institute of British Architects, 1959; Gold
Medal, American Institute of Architects, 1960; Gold
Medal of Honor, with Philip Johnson, Architectural
League of New York, 1960; Fine Arts Prize, City of
Berlin, 1961; United States Presidential Medal of
Freedom, 1963; Gold Medal, Bund Deutscher Ar-
chitekten, Germany, 1966. D.F.A.: Carnegie Insti-
tute of Technology, Pittsburgh, 1960; Northwestern
University, Evanston, Illinois, 1963; University of
Illinois, Urbana, 1964; D.Eng.: Institute of Technol-
ogy, Karlsruhe, 1950; Institute of Technology,
Braunschweig, Germany, 1955; LL.D.: University of
North Carolina, Chapel Hill, 1956; D.H.: Wayne
State University, Detroit, 1961. Member, National
Institute of Arts and Letters, 1963. Member, Prus-
sian Academy of Arts and Sciences, 1931; Comman-
der (with cross), German Order of Merit, 1959. *Died*
(in Chicago) *17 August 1969.*

Works:

1907 Riehl House, Neubabelsberg, Berlin
1911 Perls House (later Fuchs House), Zehlendorf,
     Berlin
1912 Kröller House, The Hague (project)
     Bismarck Memorial, Bingen am Rhein, Ger-
     many (competition project)
1913 House, Heerstrasse, Berlin
1914 Urbig House, Neubabelsberg, Berlin
     Mies van der Rohe House, Werder, Germany
1919 Glass Skyscraper, Friedrichstrasse, Berlin
     (competition project)
1920 Kempner House, Berlin (destroyed)
1921 Glass Skyscraper II, Berlin (project)
     Petermann House, Neubabelsberg, Berlin
     (project)
1922 Reinforced Concrete and Glass Office Build-
     ing, Berlin (project)
1923 Brick Country House (project)
     Lessing House, Neubabelsberg, Berlin (pro-
     ject)
     Eliat House, Nedlitz bei Potsdam, near Berlin
     (project)
1924 Reinforced Concrete Villa (project)
     Traffic Tower, Berlin (project)
     Mosler House, Neubabelsberg, Berlin
1925 Municipal housing development, Afrikanis-
     chestrasse, Berlin
1926 Wolf House, Guben, Germany
     Monument to Karl Liebknecht and Rosa

Ludwig Mies van der Rohe: IBM Building,
Chicago, 1967

Luxemburg, Berlin (demolished by the Nazis)

1927 Apartment Building (with furniture—e.g., the MR Chair—and interiors in collaboration with Lilly Reich) and General Plan for the Werkbund exhibition *Weissenhofsiedlung,* Stuttgart

Silk Exhibit, *Exposition de la Mode,* Berlin (with Lilly Reich)

1928 Fuchs House (originally Perls House) additions, Zehlendorf, Berlin

Remodelling of the Alexanderplatz, Berlin (competition project)

Adam Building, Leipzigerstrasse, Berlin (competition project)

Bank Building, Stuttgart (competition project)

Hermann Lange House, Krefeld, Germany (badly damaged in the war)

Esters House, Krefeld, Germany (badly damaged in the war)

1929 Office Building, Friedrichstrasse, Berlin (competition project)

German Pavilion (including furniture, e.g., the Barcelona Chair), *International Exposition,* Barcelona (demolished)

Electricity Pavilion, *International Exposition,* Barcelona (demolished)

Industrial Exhibits, *International Exposition,* Barcelona (with Lilly Reich)

1930 Tugendhat House (with furniture and interiors), Brno, Czechoslovakia (badly damaged in the war; later converted to a gymnasium)

Country Club Building, Krefeld, Germany (competition project)

War Memorial, Berlin (competition project)

Gericke House, Wannsee, Berlin (competition project)

Philip Johnson Apartment interiors, New York

1931 House, and Apartment for a Bachelor, *Building Exhibition,* Berlin (demolished)

Court Houses (project)

1932 Lemcke House, Berlin

1933 Reichsbank, Berlin (competition project)

Factory Building and Power House for the Silk Industry, Vereinigte Seidenwebereien AG., Krefeld, Germany

1934 Mining Exhibit, *German People—German Work* exhibition, Berlin

Mies van der Rohe House, Tyrol, Austria (project)

German Pavilion, *International Exposition,* Brussels (competition project)

Filling Station (competition project)

1935 Lange House, Krefeld, Germany (2 projects)

Hubbe House, Magdeburg, Germany (project)

1937 Silk Industry Administration Building, Krefeld, Germany (project)

1938 Resor House, Jackson Hole, Wyoming (project)

1939 Preliminary master plan for the Illinois Institute of Technology, Chicago

1941 Revised master plan for the Illinois Institute of Technology, Chicago

1942 Museum for a Small City (project)
Concert Hall (project)

1943 Minerals and Metals Research Building, Illinois Institute of Technology, Chicago (with Holabird and Root)

1944 Library/Administration Building, Illinois Institute of Technology, Chicago (project)

1945 Alumni Memorial Hall, Illinois Institute of Technology, Chicago (with Holabird and Root)

Metallurgy and Chemical Engineering Building, Illinois Institute of Technology, Chicago (with Holabird and Root)

Chemistry Building, Illinois Institute of Technology, Chicago (with Friedman, Alschuler and Sincere)

Joe Cantor Drive-In Restaurant, Indianapolis (project)

1947 Cantor House, Indianapolis (project)

1948 Student Union Building, Illinois Institute of Technology, Chicago (project)

1949 Promontory Apartments, 5530 South Shore Drive, Chicago (with Pace Associates, and Holsman, Holsman, Klekamp and Taylor)

1950 Farnsworth House, Plano, Fox River, Illinois

Institute of Gas Technology, Illinois Institute of Technology, Chicago (with Friedman, Alschuler and Sincere)

Boiler Plant, Illinois Institute of Technology, Chicago (with Sargent and and Lundy, and Frank Konnaker)

Central Research Laboratory, for the Association of American Railroads, Illinois Institute of Technology, Chicago (with Friedman, Alschuler and Sincere)

Cantor Commercial Center, Indianapolis (project)

Caine House, Winnetka, Illinois (project)

1951 McCormick House, Elmhurst, Illinois

Mechanical Research Building, for the Armour Research Foundation, Illinois Institute of Technology, Chicago (with Friedman, Alschuler and Sincere)

Steel-Frame Pre-fabricated Row House (project)

Pi Lambda Phi Fraternity House, University of Indiana, Bloomington (project)

Fifty by Fifty Foot-Square House (project)

860 and 880 Lake Shore Drive Apartments, Chicago (with Pace Associates, and Holsman, Holsman, Klekamp and Taylor)

Algonquin Apartments, Chicago (project; with Pace Associates)

1952 Chapel, Illinois Institute of Technology, Chicago

1953 Carman Hall: Faculty and Student Apartment Building, Illinois Institute of Technology, Chicago (with Pace Associates)

Mechanical Laboratory, for the Association of American Railroads, Illinois Institute of Technology, Chicago (with Friedman, Alschuler and Sincere)

Student Commons Building, Illinois Institute of Technology, Chicago (with Friedman, Alschuler and Sincere)

National Theatre, Mannheim, Germany (project)

1954 Convention Hall, Chicago (project)

Master plan for the Houston Museum of Fine Arts

1955 Bailey Hall, Illinois Institute of Technology, Chicago (with Pace Associates)

Cunningham Hall, Illinois Institute of Technology, Chicago (with Pace Associates)

1956 Physics-Electronics Research Building, Illinois Institute of Technology, Chicago (with C. F. Murphy Associates)

Crown Hall: School of Architecture and Design, Illinois Institute of Technology, Chicago (with C. F. Murphy and Associates)

Master plan for Lafayette Park, Detroit

Commonwealth Promenade Apartments, Chicago (with Friedman, Alschuler and Sincere)

900 Esplanade Apartments, Chicago (with Friedman, Alschuler and Sincere)

1957 Laboratory Building, for the Association of American Railroads, Illinois Institute of Technology, Chicago (with Friedman, Alschuler and Sincere)

Siegel Hall, Illinois Institute of Technology, Chicago (with Pace Associates)

United States Consulate, Sao Paulo, Brazil (project)

Quadrangle Apartments, Brooklyn, New York (project)

Bacardi Office Building, Santiago, Cuba (project)

1958 Metals Research Building, Illinois Institute of

Technology, Chicago (with Holabird and Root)

Seagram Building, 375 Park Avenue, New York (with Philip Johnson and Kahn and Jacobs)

Pavilion Apartments, Lafayette Park, Detroit

Joliet, La Salle and Nicolet Street Town Houses, Lafayette Park, Detroit

Battery Park Apartment Development, New York (project)

1959 Cullinan Hall, Houston Museum of Fine Arts (with Staub, Rather and Howze)

Master plan for the Federal Center, Chicago

1960 Pavilion and Colonnade Apartments, Colonnade Park, Newark, New Jersey

1961 Bacardi Office Building, Mexico City (with Saenz, Cancio, Martin, Guttierez)

1962 Georg-Schafer-Museum, Schweinfurt, Germany (project)

Home Federal Savings and Loan Association Building, Des Moines, Iowa (with Smith, Voorhees, Jensen)

1963 Lafayette Towers, Lafayette Park, Detroit

One Charles Center Office Building, Baltimore

2400 Lakeview Apartments, Chicago (with Greenberg and Finfer)

Krupp Administration Building, Essen, Germany (project)

1964 Meredith Memorial Hall, Drake University, Des Moines, Iowa

Mountain Place, Montreal (project)

Highfield House (apartment building), Baltimore

1965 School of Social Service Administration, University of Chicago

1966 Church Street South School, New Haven, Connecticut (project)

Development plan for New Haven, Connecticut

Foster City Apartment Buildings, San Mateo, California (project)

1967 City Square and Office Tower, London (project; with William Holford and Partners)

IBM Building, Chicago (with C. F. Murphy Associates)

1968 Science Center, Duquesne University, Pittsburgh (with Paul Schweikher)

Neue Nationalgalerie, Berlin

Westmount Square, Montreal (with Greenspoon, Freedlander, Plachta and Kyrton)

Esso Service Station, Nun's Island, Montreal (with Paul LaPointe)

Commerzbank Office and Bank Building, Frankfurt (project)

1969 Toronto-Dominion Centre (as consultant; with John B. Parkin Associates and Bregman and Hamann)

Houston Museum additions

Blue Cross Building, Chicago (project)

High Rise Apartment Block I, Nun's Island, Montreal (with Philip Bobrow)

King Broadcasting Studios, Seattle (project)

High Rise Apartment Blocks II and III, Nun's Island, Montreal (with Edgar Tornay)

High Rise Apartment Block IV, Nun's Island, Montreal (completed by others)

Northwest Plaza, Chicago (project)

Dominion Square, Montreal (project)

American Life and Accident Insurance Company Building, Louisville, Kentucky (completed by others)

General plan for the Illinois Central Air Rights Development, Chicago

Two Illinois Center Building, Chicago (completed by others)

Loop College, Chicago (completed by others)

1970 111 East Wacker Drive Building, Chicago (completed by others)

Indiana Bell Telephone Company District Office, Columbus, Indiana (completed by others)

ederal Center, Chicago (with A. E. Epstein
and Sons, C. F. Murphy Associates, and
Schmidt, Garden and Erikson: completed
by associates)

Publications:

By MIES: books—*Bürohaus,* Berlin 1923, revised
edition as *Der Moderne Zweckbau,* Munich 1926;
Industrielles Bauen, Berlin 1924; articles—"Hoch-
haus-projekt für Bahnhof Friedrichstrasse in Berlin"
in *Frühlicht* (Berlin), January 1922; "Baukunst und
Zeitwille" in *Der Querschnitt* (Berlin), April 1924;
"Briefe an die Form" in *Die Form* (Berlin), January
1926; "Runschau: Zum Neuen Jahrgang" in *Die
Form* (Berlin), February 1927; "Preface" and "Zu
Meinen Block" in *Weissenhofsiedlung,* Deutscher
Werkbund exhibition catalog, Stuttgart 1927;
"Werkbundaustellung: Die Wohnung Stuttgart" in
Die Form (Berlin), September 1927; "Zum Thema:
Austellung" in *Die Form* (Berlin), April 1928; "Uber
Kunstkritik" in *Die Kunstblatt* (Berlin), June 1930;
"Frank Lloyd Wright: An Appreciation" in *College
Art Journal* (New Haven, Connecticut), Autumn
1946; "Das Schöne is der Glanz des Wahren" in *Die
Neue Zeitung,* Berlin 1950; "Arbeitsthesen," "Uber
die Form in der Architektur," "Die neue Zeit," and
"Technik und Architektur" in *Programme und
Manifeste zur Architektur des 20. Jahrhunderts,* Ber-
lin 1964.

On MIES: books—*Mies van der Rohe* by Philip
Johnson, New York 1947, 3rd edition 1978; *Ludwig
Mies van der Rohe* by Max Bill, Milan 1955; *Mies
van der Rohe* by Ludwig Hilberseimer, Chicago
1956; *Architecture U.S.A.* by Ian McCallum, New
York and London 1959; *The Master Builders* by
[ ]er Blake, New York 1960; *Ludwig Mies van der
[ ]e* by Arthur Drexler, New York and London
[ ]0; *Contemporary Architecture: Its Roots and
[ ]nds* by Ludwig Hilberseimer, Chicago 1964; *Mies
van der Rohe: The Art of Structure* by Werner Blaser,
New York, Stuttgart and London 1965; *Mies van der
Rohe,* exhibition catalog, by James Speyer and Frederick Koeper, Chicago 1968; *Mies van der Rohe* by
Martin Pawley, Tokyo 1968, London 1970; *Ludwig
Mies van der Rohe: Drawings in the Collection of the
Museum of Modern Art* by Ludwig Glaeser, New
York 1969; *Mies van der Rohe at Work* by Peter
Carter, London and New York 1974; *Ludwig Mies
van der Rohe* by Lorenzo Papi, Florence 1975; *Mies
van der Rohe: Barcelona 1929* by J. P. Bonta, Bar-
celona 1975; *After Mies: Mies van der Rohe: Teach-
ing and Principles* by Werner Blaser, New York,
Basle and Stuttgart 1977; articles—"Farnsworth
House" in *Architectural Forum* (New York), Octo-
ber 1951; "Seagram Building" by Arthur Drexler in
Architectural Record (New York), July 1958; "Sky-
line: The Lesson of the Master" by Lewis Mumford
in *The New Yorker,* 13 September 1958; "Seagram
Assessed" by William Jordy in *Architectural Review*
(London), December 1958; "Ludwig Mies van der
Rohe," edited by H. T. Cadbury Brown, special issue
of *Architectural Association Journal* (London),
July/August 1959; "Mies van der Rohe," edited by
Peter Carter, special issue of *Architectural Design*
(London), March 1961; "New Work of Mies van der
Rohe" in *Architectural Forum* (New York), Septem-
ber 1963; "Mies van der Rohe" by Katherine Kuh
in *Saturday Review* (New York), 23 January 1965;
"Soaring Towers Gave Form to an Age" by Ada
Louise Huxtable in the *New York Times,* 19 August
1969; "Mies and the Closing of the Bauhaus" by
Richard A. M. Stern in *The Nation* (New York), 22
September 1969; "Ludwig Mies van der Rohe" in
Inland Architect (Chicago), May 1977.

Bibliography: *Ludwig Mies van der Rohe: An Annotated Bibliography and Chronology* by David A.
Spaeth, New York 1979.

As the world is a very large place, no sane person
would hope to remake it; at most, an architect of

Europe remained unbuilt, and he entered his most
fruitful period after World War II in the United
States. Meticulously proportioned buildings of glass
supported by slender steel members were to become
his hallmark: the twin towers of flats at 860 North
Lake Shore Drive in Chicago, the country house for
Dr. Farnsworth near Plano, Illinois, and Crown
Hall, the architecture building at IIT—the last being
one of a type in which he suspended the roof from
trusses to leave the interior space all open and flexible. Among his other major buildings were the Seagram Building in New York and the Federal Center
in Chicago.

Today, the discipline and Platonic purity of Mies'
buildings cannot be challenged, but their high abstraction often looks grim and void. Relentless grid
patterns and "universal" spaces too nearly express
the anonymous and the bureaucratic, rather than
any noble aspirations for individual or communal
express "the scientific and technological driving and
sustaining forces of our time" was his moral duty.
("I work so hard," he said in 1963, "to find out what
I have to do, not what I like to do.")

As a boy Mies helped his father in the family
stonecutting shop. He had no formal education in
architecture; at fourteen he went to work as a designer of traditional stucco ornaments. He moved on
to Berlin in 1905 and soon apprenticed to Bruno
Paul, an architect best known as a cartoonist and
furniture designer. Mies very quickly immersed himself in the progressive movement. At twenty-one he
saw his first independent commission, the Riehl
house, built near Berlin; it was not an innovative
design, but a solidly crafted one, already suffused
with his characteristic gravity. Mies' three years in
the office of Peter Behrens, ending in 1911,
confirmed this natural bent and also impressed him
with the model of K.F. Schinkel's work, notably the
Altes Museum (1823–1828) in Berlin, still in his
mind when he designed the New National Gallery,
built in Berlin at the end of his life. Mies went to
Holland in 1912 to work on a project for the Kröller
country house, and there admired the "honesty" of
H.P. Berlage's use of brick. From studying Berlage's
Stock Exchange (1897–1903) in Amsterdam he decided that the goal of architecture should be "a clear
construction."

After the years of his military service in 1914–
1918, Mies' career suddenly matured. Three office-
building projects of 1919–1921 revealed his intent of
"driving to the essence of things." Two were towers
of glass on steel framing; the last had walls with alternating bands of concrete and glass. Interior spaces
were hardly indicated. Cantilever construction was
to lighten the mass while reducing each scheme to
little more than repeated floors and supports. From
his models Mies discerned that "the play of reflections" on the glass would replace the traditional architectural values of sunlight raking across reveals to
create shadows. Such prototypes forecast not only
much of Mies' work during the 1950's and 1960's in
North America but also an entire era of glass curtain-wall skyscrapers.

Having gone far toward an architecture he described as "almost nothing," Mies in a 1923 project
for a brick country house revealed an aesthetic vocabulary drawn from *de Stijl,* the Dutch movement
based on a Calvinist austerity very like his own. He
had met Theo van Doesburg, its chief propagandist,
in 1920. The walls of the brick house were planned
as a dance of asymmetrically balanced meetings and
crossings. *De Stijl* also helped him generate the plans
for the minimal yet elegant Barcelona Pavilion of
1929 (he spoke of his "shock" while designing it
when he realized the aesthetic possibilities of the
"free-standing wall"); for his courtyard house projects of the 1930s; and for the campus of the Illinois
Institute of Technology, in Chicago, where he
headed the department of architecture from 1938 to
1959.

Mies served as first vice-president of the
Deutscher Werkbund, directed the great model
housing exposition at Stuttgart in 1927, and directed

the Bauhaus from 1930 to 1933. Most of his work in
great ambition might offer prototypes. That is what
Ludwig Mies van der Rohe did. He liked to build not
for the single client or site or brief but to solve, as he
said, general "problems of building." He became celebrated as one of the several great masters of the
modernist movement, because as his work grew ever
more basic it attained exceptional sureness and clarity.

Mies—"van der Rohe" was his mother's surname
—was a reformer deeply inspired by the past. Born
in Aachen, Germany, he was taken as a child to
worship each day in the chapel of Charlemagne. In
later years he recalled his admiration for the old and
"clear" masonry buildings strong enough to have
survived the centuries. His temperament was also
formed by the 19th century: his sympathy for neo-
classicism, his belief in the historical notion of the
zeitgeist or spirit of the time, and his idea that to
life. The prototypes appear too similar and unwilling
to recognize the vast variety in human life and its
daily functions. Their testament to science and technology is not so welcome, and their lack of color,
texture, warmth, and joy is noticeable. A new environmental awareness cannot accept their relation to
nature or their emphasis on thermally disastrous
walls of glass along with sealed interiors. In reaching
a naked clarity of structure Mies renounced too
many human associations. Perfect in their own
terms, his buildings hold forth little invitation to
explore, to make one's self at home, or to deepen
one's sense of place through time and intimacy.

—Donald Hoffmann

MINDLIN, Henrique (Ephim).
Brazilian. Born in Sao Paulo, 1 February 1911. Educated at the Mackenzie School of Engineering, University of Sao Paulo, 1929–32, Dip.Arch.Ing. 1932.
Married Helena Muniz de Souza; Vera Maria Bocaiuva Cunha; children: Katia and Tatiana. In private
practice, Sao Paulo, 1933–41; in private practice, Rio
de Janeiro, 1945–63, and also in partnership with
Giancarlo Palanti, Sao Paulo, 1955–63; Partner (in
the successor firm to the two partnerships), Henrique E. Mindlin, Giancarlo Palanti e Arquitetos
Associados S.C. Ltda., Rio de Janeiro, from 1964
(name changed, on withdrawal of Palanti, to Henrique E. Mindlin e Arquitetos Associados S.C. Ltda.,
1966, simplified to Henrique Mindlin Associados
Ltda., 1969). Special Assistant to the Coordinator
for Economic Mobilization, Construction Sector,
Rio de Janeiro, 1942–44 (Representative in the
United States, 1943–44); Member, Subcommission
for Housing, Council for Foreign Trade, Rio de
Janeiro, 1944–45. Lethaby Professor of Architecture, Royal College of Art, London, 1961; Yonge
Lecturer, Auburn University, Alabama, 1961; Professor, Federal University of Brazil, Rio de Janeiro,
1968–71. Member, Editorial Staff, *Acropole,* Sao
Paulo, 1933–41; Editorial Consultant, *Arquitetura,*
Rio de Janeiro, 1961. President, Instituto de Ar-
quitetos do Brasil, 1970. Recipient: First Prize, Min-
istry of Foreign Affairs Annex Competition, Rio de
Janeiro, 1942; Housing Prize, *Bienal,* Sao Paulo,
1951; First Prize, Israeli Paulista Congregation
Headquarters and Synagogue Competition, Sao
Paulo, 1954; Honor Award, *Construcao Ingenieria
Internacional,* 1958; First Prize, Bank of London
and South America Competition, Sao Paulo, 1959;
First Prize, Bank of London and South America
Competition, Brasilia, 1960. Honorary Fellow,
American Institute of Architects, 1960; Honorary
Member, Society of Planning, Architecture and Vi-
sual Arts of Mexico, 1960, and National Society of
Interior Designers, New York, 1960; Honorary Cor-
responding Member, Royal Institute of British Ar-

MIES van der ROHE

1973 Federal Center, Chicago (with A. E. Epstein and Sons, C. F. Murphy Associates, and Schmidt, Garden and Erikson: completed by associates)

Publications:

By MIES: books—*Bürohaus*, Berlin 1923, revised edition as *Der Moderne Zweckbau*, Munich 1926; *Industrielles Bauen*, Berlin 1924; articles—"Hochhaus-projekt für Bahnhof Friedrichstrasse in Berlin" in *Frühlicht* (Berlin), January 1922; "Baukunst und Zeitwille" in *Der Querschnitt* (Berlin), April 1924; "Briefe an die Form" in *Die Form* (Berlin), January 1926; "Runschau: Zum Neuen Jahrgang" in *Die Form* (Berlin), February 1927; "Preface" and "Zu Meinen Block" in *Weissenhofsiedlung*, Deutscher Werkbund exhibition catalog, Stuttgart 1927; "Werkbundaustellung: Die Wohnung Stuttgart" in *Die Form* (Berlin), September 1927; "Zum Thema: Austellung" in *Die Form* (Berlin), April 1928; "Uber Kunstkritik" in *Die Kunstblatt* (Berlin), June 1930; "Frank Lloyd Wright: An Appreciation" in *College Art Journal* (New Haven, Connecticut), Autumn 1946; "Das Schöne is der Glanz des Wahren" in *Die Neue Zeitung*, Berlin 1950; "Arbeitsthesen," "Uber die Form in der Architektur," "Die neue Zeit," and "Technik und Architektur" in *Programme und Manifeste zur Architektur des 20. Jahrhunderts*, Berlin 1964.

On MIES: books—*Mies van der Rohe* by Philip Johnson, New York 1947, 3rd edition 1978; *Ludwig Mies van der Rohe* by Max Bill, Milan 1955; *Mies van der Rohe* by Ludwig Hilberseimer, Chicago 1956; *Architecture U.S.A.* by Ian McCallum, New York and London 1959; *The Master Builders* by Peter Blake, New York 1960; *Ludwig Mies van der Rohe* by Arthur Drexler, New York and London 1960; *Contemporary Architecture: Its Roots and Trends* by Ludwig Hilberseimer, Chicago 1964; *Mies van der Rohe: The Art of Structure* by Werner Blaser, New York, Stuttgart and London 1965; *Mies van der Rohe,* exhibition catalog, by James Speyer and Frederick Koeper, Chicago 1968; *Mies van der Rohe* by Martin Pawley, Tokyo 1968, London 1970; *Ludwig Mies van der Rohe: Drawings in the Collection of the Museum of Modern Art* by Ludwig Glaeser, New York 1969; *Mies van der Rohe at Work* by Peter Carter, London and New York 1974; *Ludwig Mies van der Rohe* by Lorenzo Papi, Florence 1975; *Mies van der Rohe: Barcelona 1929* by J. P. Bonta, Barcelona 1975; *After Mies: Mies van der Rohe: Teaching and Principles* by Werner Blaser, New York, Basle and Stuttgart 1977; articles—"Farnsworth House" in *Architectural Forum* (New York), October 1951; "Seagram Building" by Arthur Drexler in *Architectural Record* (New York), July 1958; "Skyline: The Lesson of the Master" by Lewis Mumford in *The New Yorker,* 13 September 1958; "Seagram Assessed" by William Jordy in *Architectural Review* (London), December 1958; "Ludwig Mies van der Rohe," edited by H. T. Cadbury Brown, special issue of *Architectural Association Journal* (London), July/August 1959; "Mies van der Rohe," edited by Peter Carter, special issue of *Architectural Design* (London), March 1961; "New Work of Mies van der Rohe" in *Architectural Forum* (New York), September 1963; "Mies van der Rohe" by Katherine Kuh in *Saturday Review* (New York), 23 January 1965; "Soaring Towers Gave Form to an Age" by Ada Louise Huxtable in the *New York Times,* 19 August 1969; "Mies and the Closing of the Bauhaus" by Richard A. M. Stern in *The Nation* (New York), 22 September 1969; "Ludwig Mies van der Rohe" in *Inland Architect* (Chicago), May 1977.

Bibliography: *Ludwig Mies van der Rohe: An Annotated Bibliography and Chronology* by David A. Spaeth, New York 1979.

As the world is a very large place, no sane person would hope to remake it; at most, an architect of great ambition might offer prototypes. That is what Ludwig Mies van der Rohe did. He liked to build not for the single client or site or brief but to solve, as he said, general "problems of building." He became celebrated as one of the several great masters of the modernist movement, because as his work grew ever more basic it attained exceptional sureness and clarity.

Mies—"van der Rohe" was his mother's surname —was a reformer deeply inspired by the past. Born in Aachen, Germany, he was taken as a child to worship each day in the chapel of Charlemagne. In later years he recalled his admiration for the old and "clear" masonry buildings strong enough to have survived the centuries. His temperament was also formed by the 19th century: his sympathy for neoclassicism, his belief in the historical notion of *zeitgeist* or spirit of the time, and his idea that to express "the scientific and technological driving and sustaining forces of our time" was his moral duty. ("I work so hard," he said in 1963, "to find out what I have to do, not what I like to do.")

As a boy Mies helped his father in the family stonecutting shop. He had no formal education in architecture; at fourteen he went to work as a designer of traditional stucco ornaments. He moved on to Berlin in 1905 and soon apprenticed to Bruno Paul, an architect best known as a cartoonist and furniture designer. Mies very quickly immersed himself in the progressive movement. At twenty-one he saw his first independent commission, the Riehl house, built near Berlin; it was not an innovative design, but a solidly crafted one, already suffused with his characteristic gravity. Mies' three years in the office of Peter Behrens, ending in 1911, confirmed this natural bent and also impressed him with the model of K.F. Schinkel's work, notably the Altes Museum (1823–1828) in Berlin, still in his mind when he designed the New National Gallery, built in Berlin at the end of his life. Mies went to Holland in 1912 to work on a project for the Kröller country house, and there admired the "honesty" of H.P. Berlage's use of brick. From studying Berlage's Stock Exchange (1897–1903) in Amsterdam he decided that the goal of architecture should be "a clear construction."

After the years of his military service in 1914–1918, Mies' career suddenly matured. Three office-building projects of 1919–1921 revealed his intent of "driving to the essence of things." Two were towers of glass on steel framing; the last had walls of alternating bands of concrete and glass. Interior spaces were hardly indicated. Cantilever construction was to lighten the mass while reducing each scheme to little more than repeated floors and supports. From his models Mies discerned that "the play of reflections" on the glass would replace the traditional architectural values of sunlight raking across reveals to create shadows. Such prototypes forecast not only much of Mies' work during the 1950's and 1960's in North America but also an entire era of glass curtain-wall skyscrapers.

Having gone far toward an architecture he described as "almost nothing," Mies in a 1923 project for a brick country house revealed an aesthetic vocabulary drawn from *de Stijl,* the Dutch movement based on a Calvinist austerity very like his own. He had met Theo van Doesburg, its chief propagandist, in 1920. The walls of the brick house were planned as a dance of asymmetrically balanced meetings and crossings. *De Stijl* also helped him generate the plans for the minimal yet elegant Barcelona Pavilion of 1929 (he spoke of his "shock" while designing it when he realized the aesthetic possibilities of the "free-standing wall"); for his courtyard house projects of the 1930s; and for the campus of the Illinois Institute of Technology, in Chicago, where he headed the department of architecture from 1938 to 1959.

Mies served as first vice-president of the Deutscher Werkbund, directed the great model housing exposition at Stuttgart in 1927, and directed the Bauhaus from 1930 to 1933. Most of his work in Europe remained unbuilt, and he entered his most fruitful period after World War II in the United States. Meticulously proportioned buildings of glass supported by slender steel members were to become his hallmark: the twin towers of flats at 860 North Lake Shore Drive in Chicago, the country house for Dr. Farnsworth near Plano, Illinois, and Crown Hall, the architecture building at IIT—the last being one of a type in which he suspended the roof from trusses to leave the interior space all open and flexible. Among his other major buildings were the Seagram Building in New York and the Federal Center in Chicago.

Today, the discipline and Platonic purity of Mies' buildings cannot be challenged, but their high abstraction often looks grim and void. Relentless grid patterns and "universal" spaces too nearly express the anonymous and the bureaucratic, rather than any noble aspirations for individual or communal life. The prototypes appear too similar and unwilling to recognize the vast variety in human life and its daily functions. Their testament to science and technology is not so welcome, and their lack of color, texture, warmth, and joy is noticeable. A new environmental awareness cannot accept their relation to nature or their emphasis on thermally disastrous walls of glass along with sealed interiors. In reaching a naked clarity of structure Mies renounced too many human associations. Perfect in their own terms, his buildings hold forth little invitation to explore, to make one's self at home, or to deepen one's sense of place through time and intimacy.

—Donald Hoffmann

MINDLIN, Henrique (Ephim).
Brazilian. Born in Sao Paulo, 1 February 1911. Educated at the Mackenzie School of Engineering, University of Sao Paulo, 1929–32, Dip.Arch.Ing. 1932. Married Helena Muniz de Souza; Vera Maria Bocaiuva Cunha; children: Katia and Tatiana. In private practice, Sao Paulo, 1933–41; in private practice, Rio de Janeiro, 1945–63, and also in partnership with Giancarlo Palanti, Sao Paulo, 1955–63; Partner (in the successor firm to the two partnerships), Henrique E. Mindlin, Giancarlo Palanti e Arquitetos Associados S.C. Ltda., Rio de Janeiro, from 1964 (name changed, on withdrawal of Palanti, to Henrique E. Mindlin e Arquitetos Associados S.C. Ltda., 1966, simplified to Henrique Mindlin Associados Ltda., 1969). Special Assistant to the Coordinator for Economic Mobilization, Construction Sector, Rio de Janeiro, 1942–44 (Representative in the United States, 1943–44); Member, Subcommission for Housing, Council for Foreign Trade, Rio de Janeiro, 1944–45. Lethaby Professor of Architecture, Royal College of Art, London, 1961; Yonge Lecturer, Auburn University, Alabama, 1961; Professor, Federal University of Brazil, Rio de Janeiro, 1968–71. Member, Editorial Staff, *Acropole,* Sao Paulo, 1933–41; Editorial Consultant, *Arquitetura,* Rio de Janeiro, 1961. President, Instituto de Arquitetos do Brasil, 1970. Recipient: First Prize, Ministry of Foreign Affairs Annex Competition, Rio de Janeiro, 1942; Housing Prize, *Bienal,* Sao Paulo, 1951; First Prize, Israeli Paulista Congregation Headquarters and Synagogue Competition, Sao Paulo, 1954; Honor Award, *Construcao Ingenieria Internacional,* 1958; First Prize, Bank of London and South America Competition, Sao Paulo, 1959; First Prize, Bank of London and South America Competition, Brasilia, 1960. Honorary Fellow, American Institute of Architects, 1960; Honorary Member, Society of Planning, Architecture and Visual Arts of Mexico, 1960, and National Society of Interior Designers, New York, 1960; Honorary Corresponding Member, Royal Institute of British Ar-

chitects, 1963. Honorary Member, Brazilian Academy of Arts, 1968. *Died* (in Guanabara, Brazil) *6 July 1971.*

Works:

1938 Haberkamp House, Sao Paulo (project)
Gross House, Sumare, Sao Paulo (project)

1939 Sousa Lima House, Sao Paulo (project)
Carlos de Barros House, Sao Paulo (project)
House, Rua Santa Adelaide, Sao Paulo (project)

1940 Santarem Building, Rua Barao de Campinas, Sao Paulo
House, Placa Lucayas 146, Sao Paulo (project)

1942 Ministry of Foreign Affairs Annex, Rio de Janeiro (competition project)
Hungria Machado House, Rio de Janeiro

1944 Palacio Itamarati alterations, Rio de Janeiro (project)
Railway Employees Building modifications, Rio de Janeiro (project)
Clinical Centre, Rua Conde de Lage, Rio de Janeiro
Pan American Hotel, Rio de Janeiro (project)
Hotel Rio Clara, Sao Paulo (project)
Pan American Hotel, Belo Horizonte, Brazil (project)
2 houses, Sao Paulo (project)
Edgard de Almeida House interiors, Rio de Janeiro

1945 José Mindlin House, Sao Paulo (project)
Condominium, Avenida Ipiranga, Sao Paulo
Jacques Bloch House, Sao Paulo (project)
Manoel Casoy House alterations, Sao Paulo (project)
Tres Leoes Building, Sao Paulo (project)
David Bank House interiors, Rio de Janeiro (project)
Arthur Hehl Neiva House interiors, Rio de Janeiro (project)
Samuel Klabin House interiors, Sao Paulo
Palacio Tiradentes Conference Hall conversion, Rio de Janeiro (project)
Sangirardi House, Niteroi, Rio de Janeiro
Apartment building, Al. Barao do Rio Branco, Sao Paulo
Pan American Hotel, Praia Vermelha, Rio de Janeiro (project)

1946 Office building, Rua Mario Ribeiro, Guaruja, Sao Paulo
Apartment building, Rua Barata Ribeiro 432, Rio de Janeiro
Apartment building, Guaruja, Sao Paulo
Apartment building, Rua Belfort Roxo, Rio de Janeiro
Apartment building, Rua Santo Amaro, Guaruja, Sao Paulo
Hotel, Rua Couto Magalhaes 353, Sao Paulo
Apartment building, Rua Araujo Gondim 46, Rio de Janeiro
Jorge Zarur House, Rio de Janeiro
Sao Geraldo Sanatorium, Rio de Janeiro
Office building, Rua Ouvidor, Sao Paulo
Ministry of the Exterior, Rio de Janeiro

1947 Domicini Shop, Rua Xavier de Toledo, Sao Paulo
Claudio Medeiros Lima House, Estrada da Gavea 199, Rio de Janeiro

1948 José Carvalho House, Fazenda Nogueira, Bom Clima, Petropolis, Rio de Janeiro
A Exposicao Copacabana Shop, Avenida N. Senhora Copacabana 791, Rio de Janeiro
Antenor Rezende House alterations, Rio de Janeiro
A Exposicao Copacabana office interiors, Avenida 13 de Maio 23, Rio de Janeiro
Hotel Ambassador modifications, Rua Senador Dantas 25–27, Rio de Janeiro
José V. Carvalho House alterations, Rua Marques de Sao Vicente 205, Rio de Janeiro
Inovacao Shop interiors and alterations, Rua Ouvidor, Rio de Janeiro

1949 Ducal Shop alterations, Sao Paulo
Exposicao Tiradentes Shop interiors and alterations, Rio de Janeiro
Hotel Comodoro interiors, Rua Duque de Caxias, Sao Paulo

1950 Dr. A. Bahia House interiors, Avenida Atlantica, Rio de Janeiro
Capital Bank alterations and interiors, Avenida 13 de Maio, Rio de Janeiro
Shop interiors, Avenida N. Senhora Copacabana 664, Rio de Janeiro
Ceramus Building alterations, Avenida Atlantica 140, Rio de Janeiro
Joao Alberto Dutra Leite Barbosa Inn, Avenida Presidente Dutra, Rio de Janeiro
Ducal Shop interiors, Rua da Quitanda, Rio de Janeiro
Augusto Lohnstein House, Rio de Janeiro
Cogema Office interiors, Rua Mexico 31, Rio de Janeiro
Housing development, Sao Paulo
Ducal Shop interiors, Meier, Rio de Janeiro
Palvino Montenegro Rocha Apartment interiors, Rio de Janeiro
Office building, Rua Formosa 75–89, Sao Paulo
Paulo Lynch House, Rio de Janeiro
Office building, Rua Sao Bento, San Paulo
A Exposicao Modas Building Complex, Exposicao Carioca, Rio de Janeiro
Office building, Rua Barata Ribeiro 432, Rio de Janeiro
Ducal Madureira Shop interiors, Rio de Janeiro
Department store interiors, Copacabana, Rio de Janeiro
Cogema Pavilion, Exposicao Rodoviaria, Rio de Janeiro

1951 Apartment building, Rua Bulhoes de Carvalho 181, Rio de Janeiro
Mark Burke House, Rua Timoteo da Costa, Rio de Janeiro
Apartment building, Rua Aristides Espinola, Rio de Janeiro
Apartment building, Rua Taylor, Rio de Janeiro
Banco do Brasil Headquarters, Rio de Janeiro (competition project)
Banco de Credito Real Headquarters, Rua Sao Bento, Sao Paulo
Harry Wentworth Hollmeyer House, Rua Timoteo da Costa, Rio de Janeiro
José Carlos Moreira Salles House, Avenida Almirante Cochrane, Santos, Sao Paulo
BOAC Office alterations, Avenida Rio Branco 251, Rio de Janeiro
Library interiors, Rua Barao de Itapetininga, Sao Paulo

1952 Bus station, Placa 15 de Novembro, Rio de Janeiro
Office building, Largo de Carioca, Rio de Janeiro
Apartment building, Rua Raul Pompeia, Rio de Janeiro
Natan Doiban House, Ilha do Governador, Rio de Janeiro
Apartment building, Avenida Vieira Souto 336, Rio de Janeiro
Hotel, Avenida Getulio Vargas, Rio de Janeiro
Apartment building, Rua Padre Antonio Vieira, Rio de Janeiro
Hotel, Avenida Ipiranga, Sao Paulo
Apartment building, Rua Consolacao, Sao Paulo
Apartment building, Rua Timoteo da Costa, Rio de Janeiro
Israeli Embassy alterations and new Consulate Building, Rua das Laranjeiras 361, Rio de Janeiro
Urban and rural plan for Praia de Pernambuco, Sao Paulo

Lauro de Carvalho Apartment alterations, Rio de Janeiro

1953 Vemag Shop interiors, Rua Piratini 1128, Rio de Janeiro
Synagogue, Rua Capelao Alvares Silva 15, Copacabana, Rio de Janeiro
Siderurgica Mannesmann, Belo Horizonte, Brazil (as consultant)
Lauro de Souza Carvalho House, Petropolis, Rio de Janeiro
A Exposicao Avenida reconstruction, Rio de Janeiro
Israeli Cultural Headquarters, Rua Jose Higino 240, Rio de Janeiro
Office building alterations and extensions, Rua Sorocaba 696, Botafogo, Rio de Janeiro
Diana Danneman House, Rio de Janeiro
Exposicao Madureira Shop, Rio de Janeiro
Mannesmann City Housing Complex, Belo Horizonte, Brazil (project)

1954 Israeli Religious Association Headquarters, Community Centre and Temple, Rua General Severiano 166–177, Rio de Janeiro (project)
George Hime House, Petropolis, Rio de Janeiro
Israeli Paulista Congregation Headquarters and Synagogue, Rua Antonio Carlos, San Paulo (competition project)
Horst Sekkel House, Rua Iposeira, Rio de Janeiro (project)
Hebraica Headquarters, Rua das Laranjeira 346, Rio de Janeiro (project)
Factory, Avenida Independencia, Sao Paulo (project)
Federal Senate Headquarters, Avenida Rio Branco, Rio de Janeiro (competition project)

1955 Swissair Offices alterations, Rio de Janeiro (project)
Auto Pecas Motorit Factory, Avenida Independencia, Sao Paulo
Apartment building alterations, Ilha do Governador, Rio de Janeiro (project)
KLM Airlines Offices alterations and interiors, Rio de Janeiro (project)

1956 Alzira Perestrello Apartment interiors, Rio de Janeiro (project)
Copacabana Super Shopping Center, Rio de Janeiro (project)
Avenida Central Building, Avenida Rio Branco 152–162, Rio de Janeiro
Conjunto Vieira Souto Building, Rio de Janeiro (project)

1957 Apartment building, Rua Belizario Tavora, Rio de Janeiro (project)
Pilot plan for Brasilia (competition project)
Apartment building alterations, Rua Julio Otoni, Rio de Janeiro (project)

1958 Ultima Hora Building, Niteoi, Rio de Janeiro (project)
Apartment building, Rua Visconde de Piraja 174–176, Rio de Janeiro
Rudolf Mooshake House, Teresopolis, Rio de Janeiro (project)
Feigenson/Telespark Office interiors, Rio de Janeiro (project; with Giancarlo Palanti)
Olivetti Office/Shop interiors, Rio de Janeiro (project; with Giancarlo Palanti)
Luiz Fernando Bocaiuva Cunha House alterations and extensions, Santa Tereza, Rio de Janeiro (project)

1959 Hotel Imperial, Petropolis, Rio de Janeiro (project)
Apartment building, Avenida Rui Barbosa, Rio de Janeiro (project)
Bank of London and South America, Rua 15 de Novembro, Sao Paulo (with Giancarlo Palanti)
Brazilian Pavilion, *Biennale,* Venice (project; with Giancarlo Palanti and Amerigo Nino Marchesin)

1960 Bank of London and South America, Setor Bancario Sul, Brasilia (competition project)
Hotel Rio Hilton, Rio de Janeiro (project)
Intercontinental Hotel, Brasilia (project)
Residential and commercial complex, Rua Jardim Botanico, Rio de Janeiro (project)
First National City Bank of New York, Setor Bancario Sul, Brasilia (project)
Hilton Hotel, Brasilia (project)
First National City Bank of New York, Avenida Rio Branca, Rio de Janeiro (project)
Metro Cinema alterations, Sao Paulo (with Giancarlo Palanti)
Hilton Hotel, Botafogo, Rio de Janeiro (project)

1961 First National City Bank Branch Office, Brasilia (project)
Globo Radio and Television Building, Rua von Martrius, Rio de Janeiro (project)
Vera Simoes Boaiuva Cunha House, Rua Joao Felipe 685, Santa Tereza, Rio de Janeiro
Apartment building, Rua Anibal de Mendonca 22, Rio de Janeiro

1962 José Smith Braz House, Brasilia (project)
First National City Bank of New York, Recife, Brazil
Australian Embassy, Brasilia (project)
State school, Rio Comprido, Rio de Janeiro (project)
State school, Meier, Rio de Janeiro (project)
British School extensions, Botafogo, Rio de Janeiro (project)

1963 Industrial complex, Sao Paulo (project; with Giancarlo Palanti)
Guanabara State Bank Headquarters, Avenida Nilo Pecanha, Rio de Janeiro
Instituto de Resseguros do Brasil Headquarters, Humaita, Rio de Janeiro (competition project)
Especifarma Laboratory, Sao Paulo (project; with Giancarlo Palanti)
Apartment building, Rua Marques de Sao Vicente, Rio de Janeiro (project)
José Mindlin House alterations, Sao Paulo (project; with Giancarlo Palanti)
Madureira de Pinho Building, Rio de Janeiro (project)
Bank of London and South America Headquarters alterations and extensions, Rio de Janeiro
Antonio Carlos de Almeida Braga House alterations, Rua Icatu 93, Gavea, Rio de Janeiro
Apartment building, Jardim Botanico, Rio de Janeiro (project)
Laranjeiras Residential/Commercial Complex, Rio de Janeiro (project)
Madureira National Shopping Center Commercial Complex, Estrada do Portelo 81–91, Madureira, Rio de Janeiro

1964 Bank of London and South America interior alterations, Recife, Brazil (project)
Netherlands Embassy, Brasilia
Town plan for the Troia Peninsula, Portugal
1965 Plan for the City Square, Guanabara, Brazil
1966 Lauro Simoes House alterations, Urca, Rio de Janeiro (project)
1967 *Jornal do Brasil* Headquarters and Industrial Plant, Avenida Brasil, Rio de Janeiro
Merchant Marine Center, Avenida Alfredo Agache, Rio de Janeiro (project)
Feasibility study for a hotel, Avenida Paulista, Sao Paulo
Ladeira do Leme Residential Complex, Rio de Janeiro (project)
1968 Electromar Factory extensions, Rio de Janeiro (project)
Banco da Lavoura Headquarters, Sao Paulo (competition project)
Sheraton Hotel, Avenida Niemeyer 121,

Praia do Vidigal, Rio de Janeiro
Texaco do Brasil Building, Rio de Janeiro (project)
Office building, Rua Mayrink Veiga, Rio de Janeiro (project)
First National City Bank of New York, Belo Horizonte, Brazil (project)
Andarai Residential Complex, Guanabara, Brazil (project)
Divantex Factory, Sao Paulo (project)
IBM Building alterations, Avenida Presidente Vargas 1988, Rio de Janeiro
Banco da Lavoura Branch Office, Praca da Republica, Sao Paulo
Banco da Lavoura offices and computer rooms conversion, Rua Santo Andre 66, Sao Paulo
1969 First National City Bank of New York Branch Office, Avenida Nossa Senhora Copacabana 313, Rio de Janeiro
Elnorsa Factory, Pernambuco, Brazil (project)
IBM Factory and Offices, Sumare, Sao Paulo
First National City Bank of New York Headquarters alterations, Avenida Ipiranga, Sao Paulo
Banco da Lavoura Drive-in Branch Office, Sao Paulo (project)
Sheraton Hotel, Praia de Boa Viagem, Recife, Brazil (project)
Thomas de la Rue Works extensions, Rio de Janeiro (project)
First National City Bank of New York Headquarters alterations, Avenida Rio Branco 85, Rio de Janeiro
Banco Real de Investimentos Meeting Hall alterations, Sao Paulo (project)
Henrique de Botton House, Rua Aprazivel 85, Santa Tereza, Rio de Janeiro
1970 Intercontinental Hotel, Praia de Gavea, Guanabara, Rio de Janeiro
IBM Office Building interiors, Avenida Presidente Vargas, Rio de Janeiro (project)
First National City Bank of New York Branch Office alterations, Sao Paulo (project)
First National City Bank of New York Headquarters, Salvador, Brazil (project)
Credit-Card City Bank, Avenida Ipiranga 104, Sao Paulo
Madureira do Pinho Office alterations, Rua 7 de Setembro 32, Rio de Janeiro

Publications:

By MINDLIN: books—*Modern Architecture in Brazil*, Rio de Janeiro 1956; *O Grande Hotel: Notas Sobre a Evolucao de un Programa* (professorial thesis), Rio de Janeiro 1962; *Prumadas de Circulacao em Edificios Altos* (professorial thesis), Rio de Janeiro 1962; articles—numerous in *Acropole* (Sao Paulo), 1933–41; "Walter Gropius" in *Jornal do Brasil* (Rio de Janeiro), July 1969.

On MINDLIN: book—*Henrique Ephim Mindlin: O Homen e o Arquiteto* by Celia Ballario Yoshida and others, Sao Paulo 1975; articles—"Apartment House, Guaruja, Santos" in *Pencil Points* (New York), April 1947; "Apartment Building, Sao Paulo," "Living in Brazil" and "Luxury Beach Hotel, Praia Vermelha" in *Architectural Forum* (New York), November 1947; "Brésil" in *L'Architecture d'Aujourd'hui* (Paris), January 1948; "Domestic Architecture in Brazil" in *L'Architecture d'Aujourd'hui* (Paris), August 1952; "Hotel Copan, Sao Paulo" in *Architectural Forum* (New York), October 1953; "Brazil: A New Oceanside Community" in *Architectural Record* (New York), June 1954; "Synagogue et Centre Culturel de la Comauté Israelite de Sao Paulo" in *L'Architecture d'Aujourd'hui* (Paris), June/July 1960; "Henrique E. Mindlin" in *Jornal do Brasil* (Rio de Janeiro), 18 February 1961; "Docencia Livre de Mindlin" by Jayme Mauricio in *Correio da Manha* (Rio de Janeiro), 31 August 1962;

"Mindlin: Arquitetura" in *Correio da Manha* (Rio de Janeiro), 3 September 1970.

Henrique Mindlin started his career in Sao Paulo, in the years 1933–41, by erecting a few modernistic houses (following in the footsteps of Warchavchik) and the Santarem Building, a sober construction quite close in spirit to the work that Rino Levi was turning out at that time and to the modern Italian architecture of the years just prior to World War II.

In 1942 Mindlin moved to Rio de Janeiro, then still the capital of Brazil, and there came into contact with those architects who were engaged in the creation of a national architecture based on the theories of Le Corbusier. This influence had a profound effect on his subsequent work, and, with Lúcio Costa, Niemeyer, Reidy, Moreira and the Roberto Brothers, he began to actively contribute to the formation of the architectural idiom that was to give such a recognizable identity to the Brazilian version of the International Style. Some of Mindlin's major unbuilt projects belong to this period—the Foreign Affairs Ministry Annex, the Pan American Hotel at Praia Vermelha, and the Federal Senate Headquarters, all in Rio. But it is in his domestic architecture of the time that Mindlin most revealed his architectural creativity. The elements—butterfly roofs, chamferred walls in raw materials, glazed bays, sunscreens and wooden shutters—that characterize the houses for Lauro de Souza Carvalho and George Hime in Petropolis in 1953–54 are handled in a very personal manner, each plane visually detached from the adjoining one, disrupting the contention of the volumes and stressing a certain tension that exists in the composition of the mass.

In 1956 Mindlin started a new phase with the Avenida Central Building in Rio de Janeiro, the first steel-frame skyscraper erected in Brazil. His next works—for instance, the Bank of London in Sao Paulo and the First National City Bank of New York in Recife (a small, well-proportioned building pleasantly inserted into the existing urban scale)—are attempts to translate American curtain-wall office building principles into the local environment.

The Guanabara State Bank in Rio of 1963 marks another change in style, this time brought about by the use of exposed concrete and a brutalist vocabulary. Ribbon windows and concrete parapets alternate on the facade of the building, creating a strong horizontal pattern tied together by two powerful pylons. This "manner" would continue to be developed by Mindlin until the end of his life—either worked in a sobre vein, as in the project for the Merchant Marine Centre and in the *Jornal do Brasil* Building, both in Rio, or pushed towards more complicated articulations, as in the project for the First National City Bank of New York in Salvador.

The IBM Factory in Sao Paulo (1969) deserves special mention for its pioneering use of the space-frame structure and for the exceptional attention paid to the technical problems inherent in an industrial building.

Henrique Mindlin's contribution to Brazilian architecture is not, however, restricted to his architectural production. As important as his technically innovative work—perhaps even more so—was the influence he exerted on his contemporaries both with the organization of his office and with his book *Modern Architecture in Brazil*, still virtually the only comprehensive source of information on the Brazilian movement.

His architectural firm, organized on a team-work system when the usual mode was still the individual practice, pointed the way to a work method that was suitable for coping with the ever-increasing complexities of projecting and designing architecture in a developing country. The firm is still in operation under the direction of Mindlin's partners, turning out such high quality works as the Souza Cruz Plant in Uberlandia (1975), and the *O Globo* Newspaper Industrial Building and a project for the head offices of C.V.R.D., both in Rio de Janeiro.

—Jorge Czajkowski

MITCHELL, Ehrman B(urkman, Jr.).

American. Born in Harrisburg, Pennsylvania, 25 January 1924. Educated at the Hill School, Pottstown, Pennsylvania, graduated 1941; University of Pennsylvania, Philadelphia, 1941–44, 1946–48 (Emerson Architectural Prize, 1948; Faculty Medal in Architecture, 1948), A.B. 1947, B.Arch. (summa cum laude) 1948. Served in the United States Navy, 1943–46. Married Hermine Strickler in 1948; children: Eric and Marianne. Associate Architect, Bellante and Clauss, London, 1951–58. Since 1958, Partner, with Romaldo Giurgola, *q.v.,* Mitchell/Giurgola Architects, Philadelphia; office established in New York, 1966. Director, Harmony Savings and Loan Association, Philadelphia. Vice-President, 1977, First Vice-President, 1978, and President, 1979, American Institute of Architects. Exhibitions: University of Pennsylvania Museum, Philadelphia, 1965; Pennsylvania Academy of Fine Arts, Philadelphia, 1975; Columbia University, New York, 1977; *200 Years of American Architectural Drawing,* American Federation of Arts travelling exhibition, 1977–78; *Drawings Toward a More Modern Architecture,* The Drawing Center, New York, 1977, and Otis Art Institute Gallery, Los Angeles, 1978; *Roma Interrotta,* Rome, 1978. Recipient: First Award, 1961, Gold Medal, 1964, Honor Award, 1974, 1975, 1977, Architectural Firm Award, 1976, and Award of Merit, 1978, American Institute of Architects; Gold Medal, AIA, Philadelphia Chapter, 1961, 1964, 1972, 1974, 1977; Silver Medal, 1965, 1974, 1975, 1977, Distinguished Building Award, 1971, 1975, 1977, and First Honor Award, 1977, Pennsylvania Society of Architects; Gold Medal, Artists Guild of Philadelphia, 1966; First Prize, Wainwright State Office Complex Competition, St. Louis, 1974; Medal of Honor, AIA, New York City Chapter, 1975; Bard Award, City Club of New York, 1978; Design Award, *Urban Design,* 1978. Fellow, American Institute of Architects, 1969. Address: Mitchell/Giurgola Architects, 12 South 12th Street, Philadelphia, Pennsylvania 19107, U.S.A.

See GIURGOLA, Romaldo

MONEO, José Rafael.

Spanish. Born in Tudela, Navarra, 9 May 1937. Educated at the Escuela de Arquitectura, Madrid, under Leopoldo Torres Balbás and Francisco Javier Saénz de Oíza, 1956–61. Served in the Spanish Army in Segovia, 1958, 1959, and Pamplona, 1962. Married Belén Feduchi in 1963; children: Belén, Teresa, and Clara. Worked in the office of Jørn Utzon, Hellebaek, Denmark, 1961–62; Assistant, Academia de España, Rome, 1963–65. In private practice, Madrid, since 1965. Assistant Professor, Escuela de Arquitectura, Madrid, 1966–70. Since 1971, Professor of Architecture, Escuela de Arquitectura, Barcelona. Co-Founder/Editor, *Arquitecturas-Bis,* Barcelona, since 1974. Visiting Fellow, Institute for Architectural and Urban Studies, New York, 1976–77; Visiting Professor, Cooper Union School of Architecture, New York, 1976–77. Recipient: Premio de Roma, 1962; First Prize, Lacuna District Plan Competition, Victoria, 1977. Address: José Rafael Moneo, Arquitecto, Oria 17, Madrid-2, Spain.

Works:

1964 Madrid Opera House (competition project)
1965 Diestre Factory, Madrid Highway, Zaragoza, Spain
1966 Plaza de Toros extension, Pamplona, Spain
1967 Gómez-Acebo House, La Moraleja, Madrid
     City Hall, Amsterdam (competition project)
1970 Uremea Residential Building, San Sebastian, Spain (with Marquet, Zulaica and Unzurrunzaga)

Primary school, Tudela, Spain
1972 Eibar City Center, Spain (competition project)
1973 Stock Exchange, Madrid (competition project)
1975 Bankinter (bank office building), Paseo de la Castellana, Madrid (with Ramón Bescós)
     Fénix Mutuo Insurance Company Office Building, Ramirez de Arellano 4, Madrid
1976 Town Hall, Huesca, Spain (competition project)
1976/
78 Town Hall, Logroño, Spain
1977 Plan for the Lacuna District, Vitoria, Spain (competition project)

Publications:

By MONEO: articles—"Notas sobre la Arquitectura Griega" in *Hogar y Arquitectura* (Madrid), July 1965; "Madrid: Los Ultimos Veinticinco Años" in *Informacion Comercial Española* (Madrid), no. 402, 1967; "La Escuela de Barcelona" in *Arquitectura* (Madrid), January 1969; "El Desarrollo Urbano de Madrid en los 60" in *Cuadernos para el Dialogo* (Madrid), April 1970; "Vitruvio y el Buen Salvaje" in *Arquitecturas-Bis* (Barcelona), no. 2, 1974; "Gregotti and Rossi" in *Arquitecturas-Bis* (Barcelona), no. 4, 1974; "Arquitecturas en las Margenes" in *Arquitecturas-Bis* (Barcelona), no. 12, 1976; "Aldo Rossi: The Idea of Architecture" in *Oppositions* (New York), no. 5, 1978, and in *Space Design* (Tokyo), March 1978; plus numerous educational papers published by Escuela Tecnica Superior de Arquitectura, Barcelona, since 1971, and other articles in *Arquitecturas-Bis,* Barcelona, since 1974.

On MONEO: books—*Arquitectura Española Contemporanea* by Lluis Domènech, Barcelona 1967; *Contradictions in Living Environment* by David Mckay, London 1971; articles—"José Rafael Moneo: Early Work," special issue of *Hogar y Arquitectura* (Madrid), "Amsterdam City Hall Competition," special issue of *Arquitectura* (Madrid), April 1969; "José Rafael Moneo," special issue of *Nueva Forma* (Madrid), January 1975.

Bankinter, my latest work and one which is my idea of true architecture, rises upon on a site in the Castellana, one of the streets with most character in Madrid, next to a small 18th century palace of delicate workmanship. Its restricted size shows the respect involved in its planning as an unobtrusive background against which the palace would assume greater importance and is indicative of a knowledge of the locality—of the implicit lines and of the limits imposed by law.

However, an interpretation of the frontage, which such planning appears to demand, becomes confused when one approaches the ordinary entrance, since the character of the independent features, which every building possesses, makes a great impression. Such independence is strongly emphasized by the horizontal line of the pavement. It must, then, be clear that the hazards and limitations—or, in short, the influence of the setting to which the work of architecture is subject—do not prevent the appear-

José Rafael Moneo: Bankinter, Madrid, 1975

ance of those disciplinary principles on which ultimately depend the formal structure of the object.

In Bankinter some of these principles are well known and may even be called tradition. Such as: the emphasis placed on proportion, the interest shown in the definition of the various elements, the consideration for the construction, and the desire to give due value to the different materials.

But adherence to such principles has not involved disregarding the value of the whole as a basis on which to found the planning operations; in Bankinter I have not, I hope, fallen into the temptation of concentrating on separate parts.

The desire for perfection, the eagerness to achieve correct proportions—an attribute of so-called classic architecture—has always been present throughout the execution of the work and this explains, perhaps, why both the work of the sculptor, Francisco López Hernández, the creator of the reliefs on the facade, and that of the painter, Pablo Palazuelo, to whom we are indebted for the plaster work in the entrance hall, has been incorporated without any need for special integration.

—José Rafael Moneo

José Rafael Moneo graduated in 1961 from the Escuela de Arquitectura of Madrid where he had been a student of Leopoldo Torres Balbás, the famous historian and curator of the Alhambra, and of Francisco Javier Saénz de Oíza, the most brilliant architectural talent in Spain in the last 25 years. In his work Moneo seems to have brought both of these influences together. He conceives of his professional life as teaching and criticism on one hand and as the practice of architecture on the other. His work—his own personality—is the result of that fortunate synthesis.

Moneo collaborated with Saénz de Oíza in the Torres Blancas projects of 1960–62. Then he went to Denmark to work with Utzon on the Sydney Opera House project. But after he had won the Premio de Roma in 1962 and a place in the Spanish Academy for two years, he began to show in his work that the final flowering of European utilitarian and expressionistic trends—evident in both Torres Blancas and the Sydney Opera House—would not determine his own future.

More careful than his teachers, Moneo produced a softened version of Nordic and Dutch traditions (current architecture in Madrid was sensitive to both): this trend is obvious in his competition projects for the Madrid Opera House and the Amsterdam Town Hall. To this conception he added, as it were, an evaluation of his own historic traditions and the possibility of rejecting what was thought of as modern—the International Style. This range of influences and aims is clear in his works of the 1960's—the splendid Urumea Building in San Sebastian, the Gómez-Acebo House in Madrid, the Primary School in Tudela, or the development in Pamplona.

In these early years, in the 1960's, Moneo was one of the centers of interest and excitement in Madrid architecture. Now, in his maturity, he seems to have overcome the crises implicit in the 1960's with ease and with clarity. As an architect and as a teacher Moneo has become one of the most important and dynamic figures in Spanish architecture.

Against crisis Moneo defends the competence of architecture. From his commanding position as both professor and critic, he points out that discipline is the characteristic common to several architectures. Architecture, then, is a vast history in which the architect conscientiously looks for models and resources to convert or transform. (The courses Moneo taught at the Escuela de Madrid from 1966–70 were "Projects" and "Analysis of Architectural Shapes.") This attitude is evident in the Bankinter in Madrid—even if its main interest has been in having achieved an apt urban solution for the Paseo de la Castellana, the main axis of the capital. In his competition projects for the Stock Exchange in Madrid and the Town Hall in Huesca, and in his Town Hall in Logroño, Moneo presents his reflec-

tions and answers to the way in which architecture can both merge into and build a city.

—Anton Capitel

MONTA, Mozuna (Kikoo).

Japanese. Born in Kushiro City, 14 November 1941. Educated at Kobe University, Department of Architecture, 1961–65. Lecturer at Kobe University, 1965–77; Principal, Monta Mozuna Mobile Molgue, Kobe, 1969–74. Since 1977, Principal of Monta Kikoo Mozuna Architects, Tokyo. Exhibitions: *The Contemporary Art Space,* Yokohama City Museum, 1976; *Post-Metabolism,* Architectural Association, London, 1978; *New Wave of Japanese Architecture,* toured the United States, 1978. Address: Monta Kikoo Mozuna Architects, Sangubashi Silk Haitsu 302, 5-52-6 Yoyogi, Shibuya-ku, Tokyo, Japan.

Works:

1972   Anti-Dwelling Box (M House), Kushiro City, Japan
1973   Labyrinth in the Labyrinth (project)
1975   Uchū-an (Cosmic Hermitage) I, II, III (project)
1976   Heaven Phase (T House), Wakayama, Japan
        Earth Phase, Koyasan, Japan
        Human Phase (T House), Kyoto
1977   Museum in Hokkaido, Kushiro, Japan
        Yin and Yang (S House), Kushiro, Japan
1978   Temple Eishoji, Tokyo

Publications:

By MONTA: articles—"Anti-Construction" in *Kentiku* (Tokyo), September 1972; "Theory of Extension of Architecture" in *Kentiku* (Tokyo), March 1973; "Twin Architecture" in *Gendai Shisoh* (Tokyo), June 1973; "Esashioiwake" in *Kentiku* (Tokyo), April 1974; "Theory of Mobile Molgue" in *Space Design* (Tokyo), September 1974; "Manner of Mirrored Imagine House" in *Toshi-Jutaku* (Tokyo), October 1975; "Temple and Shrine," series, in *Shitsunai* (Tokyo), January 1977 to December 1978; "Manner of the Architecture of Earth, Water, Fire and Wind" in *Dento-To-Gendai* (Tokyo), vol. 50, 1978.

On MONTA: articles—"An Anarchist's Guide to Modern Architecture" by Chris Fawcett in *Architectural Association Quarterly* (London), no. 3, 1975; "Monta Mozuna" by Makoto Ueda in *Japan Interior* (Tokyo), March 1978.

I, Mozuna Monta, the megalomaniac architect, following the examples of Vitruvius and Alberti, have compared architecture to the universe and developed an "architectural cosmos."

As the "cosmos" was created by a man, its endurance is very short and its scale is small. Its firmament can be easily touched by a hand, and its ground can be vibrated or sometimes even treaded through by a foot.

When it is overtaken by a storm, its firmament leaks and its ground is flooded. At a time like this, the "god" who takes charge of the cosmos must mend in a flurry the leaks in its firmament.

The architectural cosmos has the following three aspects: Celestial aspect, Terrestrial aspect and Human aspect. It is a trinitarian world derived from the universe that is symbolized by Zero. It is also a cosmological architecture that, as a universe model, represents the "planeto-terrestrial globe."

The architectural cosmos contains, as its spatial mythos, a reflected image of the beginning of the world or a dually reflected image of the cosmogony (Zohar, Kojiki, etc.).

chitectural prototype of the Human aspect. The Sayadō is a sort of covering "sheath structure" that has been used in a few Japanese religious buildings (e.g. Konjikido of Chusonji). It protects the shrine inside. The shape of the Human aspect is derived from the core of Le Corbusier's Garches. Its grilles are projected on the distorted covering structure.

The art of cosmological architecture is derived from those of the following building structures: Kanshinji, Kōyasan with its lotus flower arrangement, Boro-Budar, Piazza del Campidoglio, etc.

The spatial system and composition of cosmological architecture are derived from the study of the following superbooks: *Kongōkai mandara* (Vajradhātu-mahā-mandala), *Taizōkai mandara* (Mahākarunā-garbhōdbhava-mandala), *Emerald Tablet, Zohar, Yi-King, Yuiitsu-Shinto-Myōbō-yōshū, Abidharmakosa-sastra,* etc.

—Mozuna Monta

Michitaro Tada, in his book *Shigusa no Nihon Bunka (The Japanese Culture of Gesture),* presents a striking analysis of *monomare* (mimicry) as the definitive trait whereby Japanese culture is made known to the world at large and transmitted internally: "Briefly, we feel at the bottom of our hearts it's not a bad thing to copy. In fact, we don't consider it a negative phenomenon but rather something nostalgic we have known a long time." An essential element from which Japanese society is compounded is the rite of invitation into a group by means of identification—the stranger is immediately said to look like someone a member of the group knows—"As for our society, there is a kind of tacit premise among people who are alike that brings them together and into contact."

Where Mozuna Monta scores over Tada's analysis is in his understanding that "mimicry," "identity," "reflection," etc. are axiomatic in any culture, that identical twins are regarded with universal caution, that one's reflection in a mirror provokes speculation in every society, that symmetry is a global perception: his long elaborated "architecture-of-twins" has ruthlessly followed up these hunches. Uchū-an House features two identical forms at different scales.

Its system is based on the principles of Yin and Yang (Yi-King) and the binary system of Sephirot (Cabala). Its sacred structural principle is based on the ins and outs of the mechanism of the universe.

The architectural cosmos, in addition, contains another context. The context consists of constructional theories, architectural idioms and structural techniques of modern architecture and the architectural idioms and techniques of historical architecture. In other words, one can regard it as an architecture that combines modern techniques with symbolism.

The Celestial aspect is the "cast shadow" of a celestial figure (the Great Bear) that is projected on the earth's surface. The constellation projected on the earth has seven columns. The Celestial aspect was planned to eliminate the cartesian co-ordinates. It has, like a constellation, various imaginary lines (e.g. solid lines, broken lines, dotted lines, chain lines, etc.) that constitute implicitly a covering structure. It contains Yin-volumes and Yang-volumes.

The Terrestrial aspect has a "womb of Chimoshin," that is, a symbolizing deity of Mother Earth. It is a "stratigraphic-space-raising architecture." The Terrestrial aspect that has an inclination of 45 degrees is a plan and an elevation at the same time. When it is projected vertically on the ground, it becomes a plan. When it is projected horizontally on human eyes, it becomes an elevation. It has two faces: positive and negative.

The Human aspect is a space that reflects the physical and spiritual structures of microcosm man. It uses a "Sayadō" that can be regarded as an ar-

Mozuna Monta: Anti-Dwelling Box, Kushiro City, Japan, 1972

facing each other; Human Phase (T House) has two identical forms of the same size linked by a bridge; Anti-Dwelling Box (M House) comprises a cube within a cube within a cube—this positing of a world within a world is one of the primal architectural episodes we are condemned to repeat ad nauseam.

More recently, Monta has begun to compliment his ironic mirrorings and knowing repetitions with a cosmological overlay—one house has its columns laid out according to a heavenly constellation, its stairs following a star-shaped course. This paranormal architecture-of-things-that-go-bump-in-the-night points to the supernatural forces conspiring to shape the laws of mimicry and reflection. He projects architecture as an astral body in which "the universe of mind intersects the physical universe at right angles and stretches into a different dimension." He wants to establish a building that corresponds to the centre of gravity of the soul—it involves the discovering and laying out of the working principles of the universe and the gathering of them together into one bag. Design must respect that each of us is not one person but a whole "ladder of selves" whose rungs can take each of us to separate levels of perception of the world's mysterious elements.

—Chris Fawcett

MOORE, Arthur Cotton.

American. Born in Washington, D.C., 12 April 1935. Educated at St. Albans School, Washington, 1950–54, graduated 1954; Princeton University, New Jersey, 1954–60, A.B. (cum laude) 1958, M.F.A. 1960. Served as a Lieutenant in the United States Army, 1961. Married Patricia Stephan in 1966; son: Gregory. Worked in the office of Skidmore, Owings and Merrill, New York, summers 1956–58, Ketchum and Sharp, New York, summer 1959, Satterlee and Smith, Washington, D.C., 1960–61, and Cloethiel Woodward Smith and Associates, Washington, D.C., 1961–65. Since 1965, Principal, Arthur Cotton Moore Associates, Washington, D.C. Contributing Editor on Urban Affairs, *The Washingtonian*, 1965–78. Professional Adviser, Committee Against the National Airport, 1966; Chairman, Committee on International Visitors, American Institute of Architects, Washington Chapter, 1969; Treasurer and Member of the Executive Committee, Georgetown Planning Council, Washington, D.C., 1970; Chairman of the Jury on the Presidential Reviewing Stand, 1972; Chairman, Subcommittee on Airports, Committee of 100 on the Federal City, 1973; United States Representative, State Department Trade Mission to Switzerland, The Netherlands, and Belgium, 1973; Member, Washington City Council Special Citizens Committee on Urban Renewal, 1973; Member of the Bicentennial Assembly of the District of Columbia, 1973; Member of the Board, Metropolitan Washington Planning and Housing Association, 1974; Member, Design Advisory Panel, City of Baltimore, 1975. Recipient: Excellence in Architecture Award, Metropolitan Washington Board of Trade, 1970; Honor Award, American Institute of Architects, Potomac Valley Chapter, 1970; Citizens Association of Georgetown Award, 1971; Honor Award, AIA, Middle Atlantic Region, 1971; *Architectural Record* Award, 1972, 1977; *Progressive Architecture* Award, 1973; First Award, 1973, and Merit Award, 1976 (twice), Historic Preservation and Architectural Design, AIA, Washington, D.C. Chapter; American Association of School Administrators Award, 1976; *Design and Environment* Award, 1976; Owens-Corning Energy Award, 1976, 1977; First Honor Award, 1977 (twice), and Special Energy Citation, 1977, AIA, Northern Virginia Chapter; National Honor Award, AIA, 1977; Grand Award, National Association of Home Builders/*Better Homes and Gardens*, 1978

(twice). Address: Arthur Cotton Moore Associates, 1214 28th Street N.W., Washington, D.C. 20007, U.S.A.

Works:

1967 Rosslyn Air Terminal, Arlington, Virginia (project)
1969 Canal Square, Georgetown, Washington, D.C.
House, 1600 Avon Place, Washington, D.C.
1970 Woodlawn Shopping Center, Woodlawn, Virginia
Air rights proposal for downtown Washington, D.C.
New Republic Office Building, Washington, D.C. (project)
1971 B and D Inland (mixed-use development), Washington, D.C. (project)
Charleston Development, Charleston, South Carolina (project)
1972 Harris House, Arlington, Virginia
1973 Arthur Cotton Moore Associates Office Building, Washington, D.C.
1974 Remely Point Housing Development, South Carolina (project)
Ohlandt Condominium, Charleston, South Carolina (project)
Barney's Mixed-Use Development, Schenectady, New York (project)
1975 Chessie Georgetown Development, Washington, D.C. (project)
1976 The Foundry, Georgetown, Washington, D.C.
The Cairo Apartments, Washington, D.C.
Solar Energy Science Building, Madeira School, Greenway, Virginia
Seven Old Buildings, Vanderbilt University, Nashville, Tennessee (project)
Torpedo Plant (concept plan), Alexandria, Virginia
Frederick Development (Black Horse Tavern and Kline Houses), Frederick, Maryland (project)
1977 Parking Facility, Vanderbilt University, Nashville, Tennessee
Urban design for Columbia Pike, Arlington, Virginia (project)
Times Square Adult Entertainment Center, New York (project)
Shirlington Master Plan, Arlington, Virginia (project)
Baltimore Fish Market (project)

Redevelopment plan for Market Street, Baltimore (project)
Plan for re-use of Lansburgh's Department Store, Washington, D.C. (project)
Fairfax Cultural Center, Fairfax, Virginia (project)
1978 Lafayette Elementary School, Washington, D.C.
Van Ness Apartments, Washington, D.C.
Cooperative Finance Corporation Apartments, Washington, D.C.
Cooperative Finance Corporation Office Complex, Washington, D.C.
Bedford-Stuyvesant Commercial Complex (Restoration Plaza), Brooklyn, New York
Convention Center, Washington, D.C. (project)
Tooks Way Housing Development, Columbia, Maryland
Le Steak (restaurant), Washington, D.C.
Cherry Hill (apartments), phase I and II, Washington, D.C.
Bernstein House, Washington, D.C.
Master plan for development for the Hechinger Company, Washington, D.C.
Mixed-use development, 1312 30th Street, Washington, D.C.
Guardian Federal Office Building, Washington, D.C.
Greenberg Condominium, New Hampshire Avenue, Washington, D.C.
Office building, 3030 M Street, Washington, D.C. (project)
Redevelopment plan for Joseph Square Shopping Center, Columbia, Maryland
1979 Commercial Complex, Schenectady, New York
1980 The Old Post Office Development, Washington, D.C.
Rockefeller Housing Development, Washington, D.C.
Capitol Hill Car Barn, Washington, D.C. (project)
Dupont Circle Shopping Center, Washington, D.C. (project)
Master plan for the Potomac School of Law, Washington, D.C.
1981 3600 M Street Building, Washington, D.C. (project)
Hechinger Plaza Development, Washington, D.C. (project)
Ellington School for the Performing Arts, Washington, D.C. (project)

Arthur Cotton Moore: Canal Square, Georgetown, Washington, D.C., 1969

ACT/Proctor's Theatre, Schenectady, New York (project)

5A Office Building, Baltimore

City Master Plans: Colmar Manor, Maryland, 1974; Downtown Nassau (and Bahamas Master Plan), 1975; York, Pennsylvania, 1976; Petersburg, Virginia, 1976; Columbus, Georgia, 1977; Norfolk, Virginia (waterfront), 1977; Nashville, Tennessee, 1977; Fort Wayne, Indiana, 1977; Baltimore, Maryland, 1978–; Schenectady, New York, 1979; Dearborn, Michigan, 1979; Rockville, Maryland, 1979.

Publications:

By MOORE: books—*New Town Legislation,* Department of Housing and Urban Development, Washington, D.C. 1969; foreword to *Historic Buildings of Washington,* Washington, D.C. 1973; articles —"Politics, Architecture and World Fairs" in *AIA Journal* (Washington, D.C.), April 1965; "The Pennsylvania Avenue Plan" in *St. Albans Bulletin* (Washington, D.C.), May 1965; numerous articles in *The Washingtonian,* 1965–78.

On MOORE: articles—"An Architecture of Issues" in *Progressive Architecture* (New York), July 1973; "A Study in Solar Energy Architecture" by Wolf Von Eckardt in the *Washington Post,* 16 February 1974; "Arthur Cotton Moore Associates of Washington: Practice Profile" by Mary E. Osman in *AIA Journal* (Washington, D.C.), May 1974; "Sunny Side Up" by Jim Murphy in *Progressive Architecture* (New York), February 1976; "Restoration of Confidence" by John Morris Dixon in *Progressive Architecture* (New York), November 1977; "Washington Architect Arthur Cotton Moore" by William Marlin in *Architectural Record* (New York), December 1977; "Arthur Cotton Moore" by Wolf Von Eckardt in *New Republic* (Washington, D.C.), 25 February 1978.

*

ACM is concerned about the increasingly intermural and academic nature of even today's best architectural work. In order to counter architecture's growing separation from the mainstream of society, the firm acts not only as architects and planners but also at times as developers. By understanding and becoming involved in the political and economic basics of society, ACM has gained the freedom to influence the direction of many American cities and the real freedom to do and control the firm's design interests.

In planning, ACM has stressed an alternative-additive-incremental approach which entrepreneurs existing features and buildings with new construction into linkages to strategically reverse urban decline. In architecture, ACM has used adaptive reuse, incorporating of old fragments and historical allusions to build bridges or rapport with the general public. The preserved or evoked old images permit contrasting, free experimentation with new elements increasingly involving complete and curvilinear forms.

—Arthur Cotton Moore

*

Arthur Cotton Moore was an early critic of classic urban renewal and has continually sought means to influence the direction of his city, the nation's capital, and other cities, within and without traditional architectural practice. For more than 10 years, Moore was architectural and urban critic for *The Washingtonian,* a glossy magazine in which he called attention to neglected problems and various proposed planning schemes with which he disagreed. Along with written criticisms of the status quo, he also published drawings and discussions of his suggestions for what should be done, involving himself in economic as well as architectural questions. He also frequently writes this sort of article for Washington's leading newspaper, *The Washington Post,* and serves on many official and ad hoc committees on urban planning. His conviction is that the gap

between the profession and the public must be narrowed—partly by politicizing the population about architectural issues and partly by developing a rapport between people and the buildings themselves.

The project that first made Moore's name is Canal Square, in Washington's Georgetown neighborhood, one of the first major recycling projects in the country. A 19th century warehouse was joined to more than 75,000 square feet of new construction, sheathed in a similar dark brown brick. The complex contains offices, shops and a large restaurant laid out around a series of courtyards. Moore was one of the developers of Canal Square as well as the architect, and he frequently performs that role in other projects and even consults with interested community groups about how to develop such a project, including what retail mix pays and what political coalitions might be required to put the package together. He obviously does not agree that the architect is someone "who designs the building after all the decisions have been made."

Moore is not a preservationist as such but an urbanist with a taste for the variety and density that recycling can provide. His new construction often plays off the materials and details of the old, although until recently it was with a straightforward "clean-it-up-and-magnify-its-scale" modernist approach. The experience of incorporating different buildings into one complex has led him to a design position which values juxtaposition of dissimilar elements. His vocabulary has been quite fluid over the years—from the ribbon window bands and acute angles of his designs from five to ten years ago to the Buck Rogers moderne and neo-Palladian motifs of his current work. What has been consistent is a regard for the street and a propensity toward courtyard arrangements and traditional materials. Moore's practice is also distinguished by an interest in solar energy design, specifically the Madeira School Science Building, one of the first privately-financed, non-residential solar heated buildings in the country.

—Nory Miller

MOORE, Charles W(illard).
American. Born in Benton Harbor, Michigan, 31 October 1925. Educated at the University of Michigan, Ann Arbor, under Roger Bailey, 1942–47, B.Arch. 1947: awarded University of Michigan George Booth Travelling Fellowship, 1949; Princeton University, New Jersey, under Jean Labatut, Enrico Peressutti and Louis I. Kahn, 1954–57 (Council of Humanities Fellowship, 1957), M.F.A., Ph.D. 1957. Served in the United States Army Corps of Engineers, in the United States and Korea, 1952–54: Captain. Partner, Moore-Lyndon-Turnbull-Whitaker, Berkeley, California, 1962–64, and MLTW/Moore Turnbull, Berkeley, 1964–70; Principal, Charles W. Moore Associates, 1970–75. Since 1975, Partner, Moore Grover Harper, Los Angeles. Assistant Professor, University of Utah, Salt Lake City, 1950–52, and Princeton University, New Jersey, 1957–59; Associate Professor, 1959–65, and Chairman of the Department of Architecture, 1962–65, University of California, Berkeley; Chairman of the Department of Architecture, 1965–69, Dean of the School of Architecture, 1969–71, and Professor of Architecture, 1969–75, Yale University, New Haven, Connecticut. Professor of Architecture since 1975, and Program Head in the School of Architecture since 1978, University of California at Los Angeles. Exhibitions: *40 under 40,* Architectural League of New York, 1965; University of Maryland, College Park, 1971; *Biennale,* Venice, 1976; University of Houston, 1976; Bologna, Italy, 1978; University of Michigan, 1978; Williams College, Williamstown, Massachusetts, 1978. Recipient: Award,

Progressive Architecture, 1962, 1963, 1964, 1965, 1966, 1967; Award, American Institute of Architects, 1965, 1966. Address: Moore Grover Harper, 1725A Selby, Los Angeles, California 90024, U.S.A.

Works:

1957 House, 325 Via del Rey Road, Monterey, California
1959 House, 10 Chualar Place, Monterey, California
1961 Studio, 2508 Leavenworth Street, San Francisco
Jobson House, Palo Colorado Canyon, California
1962 Jenkins House I, St. Helena, California (project)
Bonham House I, Boulder Creek, California
Moore House, Orinda, California
West Plaza Condominium, Coronado, California (project)
Seaside Professional Building, Seaside, California
Master plan for the South Coast, Monterey, California (with Skidmore, Owings and Merrill)
Master plan for Lone Hill Housing, San Jose, California
1963 Cortese House, Orinda, California (project)
Legge House additions, Portola Valley, California
Trueblood House additions, Palo Alto, California
Turner House, Pebble Beach, California (project)
Monte Vista Apartments, Monterey, California
1964 Athletic Club I, Sea Ranch, California
Cudabach House renovation, Oakland, California (project)
Gordon House renovation, Berkeley, California
Jackson House, Santa Fe, New Mexico (project)
Jenkins House II, St. Helena, California
Jewell House, Orinda, California
Morris-LaForge House, Boulder Creek, California (project)
Slater House, Stinson Beach, California
Condominium I, Sea Ranch, California
Goldsmith House renovation, Berkeley, California
1965 Bache House additions, Piedmont, California (project)
Cornuelle House, Hillsborough, California (project)
Halprin House I, Sea Ranch, California (project)
Halprin House II, Sea Ranch, California (project)
Johnson House, Sea Ranch, California
Karas House, Monterey, California
Kermeen House renovation, Orinda, California
Krakauer House, Los Altos, California (project)
Lawrence House additions, Palo Alto, California
Martin House, Lake Tahoe, California
Polk House renovation, Berkeley, California
Talbert House, Oakland, California
Condominium Hillside, Sea Ranch, California (project)
Carmel Knolls Housing, Carmel Valley, California (project)
Civic Center, Fremont, California (competition project)
Plan for a Commercial Square, Novato, California
Portland South Park, Lovejoy Plaza, Portland, Oregon (with Lawrence Halprin)
1966 Budge House, Healdsburg, California

Charles W. Moore: Kresge College, University of California at Santa Cruz, 1973

Halprin House III, Sea Ranch, California (project)
Halprin House IV, Sea Ranch, California
Harrison House, Santa Barbara, California (project)
Johnson/Martin House, Lake Tahoe, California
Knutsen House, Sonoma, California
Lawrence House, Sea Ranch, California
McClelland House, Sea Ranch, California (project)
McNiven House renovation, Berkeley, California
Otus House, Berkeley, California
Saltzman House, Carmel, California
Thomasian House, Orinda, California
Truesdale House, Sea Ranch, California
Turnbull Sr. House I, Carbondale, Colorado
Vickery House, Sea Ranch, California (project)
Arts Center, University of California, Berkeley (competition project)
Urban renewal housing, Akron, Ohio (project)
Cascade Project, Akron, Ohio (project)
1967 Boas House, Stinson Beach, California
Moore House renovation, New Haven, Connecticut
Morris House I, Sea Ranch, California (project)
Pirofski House, Palo Alto, California (project)
Spec I House, Sea Ranch, California (project)
Stauffacher House, Mill Valley, California (project)
Beckonridge Housing, Tacoma, Washington (project)
College 6, University of California at Santa Cruz (project)
1968 Dahlen House, Santa Barbara, California (project)
Hines House, Sea Ranch, California

McElrath House, Santa Cruz, California
Morris House II, Sea Ranch, California
Ray House, Sea Ranch, California (project)
Rigler House, Estes Park, Colorado
Spec II House, Sea Ranch, California (prototype)
Spec III House, Sea Ranch, California (prototype)
Weyerhauser Prototype House, Kansas City, Missouri
Bechtel Prototype Housing, Santa Catalina, California (project)
Conifer 4 Housing for the Elderly, Tacoma, Washington
Conifer 5 Housing, Tacoma, Washington
Church Street South Housing, New Haven, Connecticut
Gas Station Plaza Housing for the Elderly, New Haven, Connecticut
Los Angeles Psychiatric Building, Beverly Hills, California
Faculty Club, University of California at Santa Barbara
Housing, Hamden, Connecticut (project)
Athletic Club II, Sea Ranch, California
1968/
72 Peterson House I, Tacoma, Washington (project)
1969 Caygill House, Sea Ranch, California
Cornuelle House, New Hampshire (project)
Goodman House, Montauk, Long Island, New York (project)
Klotz House, Westerly, Rhode Island
La Boyteaux House, Orinda, California (project)
McComber House, Sea Ranch, California
Naff House, Pajaro Dunes, California
Reid House, Sea Ranch, California
Schub House, Long Island, New York (project)
Baker House, Sea Ranch, California
Bartell House, Sea Ranch, California

Binker House, Sea Ranch, California
Eastwood House, Sea Ranch, California
Edgerton House, Sea Ranch, California
Kohlmeister House, Sea Ranch, California
Kreps/Levine House, Sea Ranch, California
Larsen House, Sea Ranch, California
Matthews House, Sea Ranch, California
Whiteside House, Sea Ranch, California
Wickstead House, Sea Ranch, California
Wilson/Moore/King House, Sea Ranch, California
Tempchin House, Bethesda, Maryland (with Rurik Ekstrom)
Turnbull Sr. House II, Carbondale, Colorado
Low-income housing, Whitesburg, Kentucky (project)
Master plan for Russian Harbor, Jenner, California
Kansas City Mall
1970 Baer House addition, Monterey County, California (project)
Bransten House, Muir Beach, California (project)
Bransten House renovation, San Francisco (project)
Gahagan House, Tamales Bay, California (project)
Koizim House, Westport, Connecticut
Moss House, Sea Ranch, California
Mentzer House, Sea Ranch, California
Rush House, Sea Ranch, California
Goodhart House, Sea Ranch, California
Deep River Housing, Essex, Connecticut (project)
Villa del Monte Housing for the Elderly, Seaside, California
Oak Street Turnkey Housing, Haight-Ashbury, San Francisco (project)
Huntington Station Urban Renewal Housing, Huntington, Long Island, New York
Tract A Townhouses, Vail, Colorado (project)
Boas Pontiac Building remodelling, San Francisco
Golden West Savings and Loan Association Office interiors, Capitola, California
Golden West Savings and Loan Association Office remodelling, Castro Valley, California
Golden West Savings and Loan Association Office interiors, Corte Madera, California
Golden West Savings and Loan Association Office interiors, Eastridge, California (project)
Land use analysis: Nuclear Power Station, Davenport, California
1971 Church Street South Housing, New Haven, Connecticut
Robert T. Wolfe Apartments, New Haven, Connecticut
Triangle Pacific Development, Vermon, Connecticut
Housing for the elderly, Seaside, California
1972 Maplewood Terrace Housing, Middletown, Connecticut
Xanadune, St. Simon's Island, Georgia
Talmar Wood, Orono, Maine
Rudolph House, Captive Island, Florida
Goodman House, Long Island, New York (project)
1973 Essex Point Condominiums, Deep River, Connecticut
Anderson Housing Development, Springfield, Massachusetts
Moore House, Essex, Connecticut
Halprin House, Sea Ranch, California
Kresge College, University of California at Santa Cruz
Murray House, Cambridge, Massachusetts
1974 Burns House, Santa Monica Canyon, California
Cold Spring Harbor Laboratories, Huntington, New York

Whitman Village Housing, Huntington, New York

Kingsmill on the James, Williamsburg, Virginia

1974/
75 Owen Brown Village, Columbia, Maryland
1975 Swan House, Southold, New York
Barber House, Guilford, Connecticut
Piazza d'Italia Fountain, New Orleans (project)
House, Madras, India
Moore House, Los Angeles
1976 House, near New York

Publications:

By MOORE: books—*The Place of Houses,* with G. Allen and D. Lyndon, New York 1974; *The Yale Mathematics Building Competition: Architecture for a Time of Questioning,* with N. Pyle, New Haven, Connecticut 1974; *Dimensions,* with G. Allen, New York 1976; *Body Memory and Architecture,* with K.C. Bloomer, New Haven, Connecticut 1977; articles—"New-Old Newport" in *Architectural Record* (New York), February 1959; "Hadrian's Villa" in *Perspecta* (New Haven), no. 6, 1960; "Sagamore" in *Journal of Architectural Education* (Washington, D.C.), Summer 1961; "You Have to Pay for the Public Life" in *Perspecta* (New Haven, Connecticut), no. 9/10, 1965; "Creating of Place" in *Image,* no. 4, 1966; "The Establishment Invites You to Join the Hushed and Sumptuous Appreciation of the Several Arts, Lincoln Center, Most Evenings; Arrival Optional but Difficult" in *Architectural Forum* (New York), September 1966; "Plug It In, Rameses, and See If It Lights Up, Because We Aren't Going to Keep It Unless It Works" in *Perspecta* (New Haven, Connecticut), no. 11, 1967; "Church Street South Housing in New Haven," with G. Allen, in *Architect's Yearbook* (London), 1971; "Eleven Agonies and One Euphoria" in *Michigan Society of Architects Monthly Bulletin,* February 1971; "Charles W. Moore," interview, in *Kenchiku Benka* (Tokyo), April 1971; "How Much Is a Monument Worth?" in *Journal of the Society of Architectural Historians* (Philadelphia), October 1972; "Schindler: Vulnerable and Powerful" in *Progressive Architecture* (New York), January 1973; "In Similar States of Undress" in *Architectural Forum* (New York), May 1973; "After a New Architecture: The Best Shape for a Chimera" in *Oppositions* (New York), May 1974; "Sea Ranch: A Second Look," with G. Allen and D. Lyndon, in *Architectural Record* (New York), November 1974; "Southerness" in *Perspecta* (New Haven), no. 15, 1975; ". . . Where Are We Now, Vincent Scully?" in *Progressive Architecture* (New York), April 1975; "Yale University Mathematics Building-Conclusion" in *Oppositions* (New York), no. 6, 1976; "Self-Portrait" in *L'Architecture d'Aujourd'hui* (Paris), March 1976; "Berlin: alt und neu," with others, in *Lotus International* (Venice), December 1976; "Magic, Nostalgia and a Hint of Greatness in the Workaday World of the Building Types Study," with R. Oliver, in *Architectural Record* (New York), April 1977; address in *North Carolina Architect* (Raleigh), November/December 1978.

On MOORE: books—*40 under 40,* exhibition catalog, by Robert Stern, New York 1965; *The Puzzle of Architecture* by Robin Boyd, Melbourne, London and New York 1965; *Selected Houses from Progressive Architecture,* New York 1966; *American Architecture and Urbanism* by Vincent Scully, New York 1969; *New Directions in American Architecture* by Robert Stern, New York 1969; *Nuove Ville* by Roberto Aloi, Milan 1970; *Global Architecture No. 3: MLTW/Moore Lyndon Turnbull Whitaker: The Sea Ranch* by Yukio Futagawa, Tokyo 1970; *Global Interiors No. 1: Houses in the U.S.A.* by Yukio Futagawa, Tokyo 1971; *Architecture 2000: Predictions and Methods* by Charles Jencks, New York 1971; *Observations in American Architecture* by Ivan Chermayeff, New York 1972; *Adhocism: The Case for Improvisation* by Charles Jencks and Nathan Silver, New York 1972; *A Visual History of Twentieth-Century Architecture* by Dennis Sharp, London and New York 1972; *Conversations with Architects* by J. W. Cook and H. Klotz, New York 1973; *A Guide to Architecture in San Francisco and Northern California* by David Gebhard and others, revised edition, Santa Barbara, California and Salt Lake City, Utah 1973; *Modern Movements in Architecture* by Charles Jencks, New York 1973; *Global Interiors No. 6: Houses in the U.S.A.* by Yukio Futagawa, Tokyo 1974; *Modern Architecture: The Architecture of Democracy* by Vincent Scully, New York 1974; *The Shingle Style Today* by Vincent Scully, New York 1974; *MLTW: Houses, 1959–75* by Yukio Futagawa, Tokyo 1975; articles—"Trends in Architecture: U.S.A.: Work by Charles W. Moore" in *Bauwelt* (Berlin), June 1963; "U.S.A.: Charles Moore, California" in *Architectural Design* (London), September 1963; "Charles Moore: Architecture and the New Vernacular" by David Gebhard in *Artforum* (New York), May 1965; "World Architects 2: Charles W. Moore and His Partners" in *The Japan Architect* (Tokyo), May and September 1965; "Charles W. Moore" in *Kenchiku Bunka* (Tokyo), April 1971; "Should Anyone Care About the 'New York Five'?" by P. Goldberger in *Architectural Record* (New York), February 1974; "White and Grey: Eleven Modern American Architects" in *Architecture + Urbanism* (Tokyo), April 1975; "Interior Architecture: Charles Moore—One Point of View" in *Progressive Architecture* (New York), April 1975; "Moore Is More: Cinq Portraits pour 'Chuck'" in *L'Architecture d'Aujourd'hui* (Paris), March/April 1976; "America Now: Drawing Towards a More Modern Architecture" by R. Stern in *Architectural Design* (London), no. 6, 1977; "Charles W. Moore" by Yukio Futagawa in *Architecture + Urbanism* (Tokyo), 1978; "Art: Architectural Drawings: The Grace of Fine Delineation" in *Architectural Digest* (Los Angeles), March 1978; "Barrier-free Design" in *Progressive Architecture* (New York), April 1978.

*

Charles Moore is a recognized and accomplished spokesman of a group who, together, constitute a dissident movement in American architecture. Born in 1925, he is a graduate of the University of Michigan and Princeton, from which he earned a PhD. His dissertation was on the role of water in architecture.

A characteristic of the "dissident" movement is that its practitioners possess a considerable background of scholarship, including an extensive and insightful knowledge of architectural history. They are also articulate and, since many of them hold teaching positions, they have a wide audience. Moore himself has been a teacher during much of his career, at the University of California at Berkeley, at Yale, and at the University of California at Los Angeles. As a practitioner much of his work has been authored under the firm identification "MLTW"—Moore, Lyndon, Turnbull, Whitaker.

Moore's dissidence is with a somewhat moralistic and socially directed position that modern architecture assumed. One can argue if that has been even partly fulfilled, or if indeed it is not business and institutional exigency that motivates and directs American architecture. Whatever it is, Moore takes exception to it.

As a counter offering, he poses a new set of objectives and possible accomplishments for architecture, and draws on an entirely different set of premises. Essentially his aim is that architecture be personalized, derived out of a condition of personal (client) predilection, out of metaphoric reference to site-setting and its historic and cultural connotation. Architecture should engage fancy, whim, historicism, myth, fantasy. It is less a medium for moralizing an ideal; more an environment of symbols and connotations in the realm of sensed revelation, stimulated by psyche-arousing artifacts in space.

This direction came to wide professional attention with MLTW's design for the Sea Ranch, a coastal recreational community about 100 miles north of San Francisco. The buildings are of the most pragmatic, even ordinary construction. Their forms derive from their inner functions, site form, climate, and from recollections of summer-cottage architecture. It is a brilliant work, simple and elegant. It had great influence.

In the Faculty Club for the University of California at Santa Barbara, Moore has drawn on the personality of the place as a source of his design concept. That personality is one of theatrics, confounded but controlled. It is a reflection of "the California spirit" somewhat thwarted—as indeed that spirit is. The building has elements of "heraldry", befitting the traditional mood and even pretense of historic academic association.

In the design of the Kresge College at the University of California at Santa Cruz he has created a de Chirico-like stage set for the drama of student interchange. Again, it is composed of the most commonplace architectural elements, drawing even on the toy blocks of childhood.

Moore's faith is in the living out of each individual's personal destiny, not a social consciousness moralistically imposing itself through architecture, and certainly not some transposed stylistic architectural identification. His own consciousness is not easily dismissed.

—Paul Spreiregen

MORANDI, Riccardo.
Italian. Born in Rome, 1 September 1902. Educated at the School of Applied Engineering, Rome, Dip.-Ing. 1927. In private practice, Rome, since 1931. Adjunct Professor of Constructional Technique, 1958, and Professor of Bridge Structure/Form, 1959, Faculty of Architecture, University of Florence. Professor of Bridge Construction, University of Rome. Member, Superior Council of the Italian Ministry of Works; Member, Italian National Research Council. Recipient: Italian Association of Cement Manufacturers Prize, 1962; Columbus Prize, International Institute of Communications, 1967; Freyssinet Prize, Federation Internationale de Precontrainte, 1970. Member, Academy of San Luca, Rome. Honorary Member, Royal Society of Arts, London. Address (office): Viale G. Rossini 18, Rome, Italy.

Works:

1931 House, Viale Vaticano, Rome
1933 Piccini Car Park, Via Vittorio Emanuele, Rome
1934 Augustus Cinema, Rome
1935 Parish Church, Colleferro, near Rome
Giulio Cesare Cinema, Via Giulio Cesare, Rome
1939 House, S. Felice Circeo, Latina, Italy
1941 House, via Terme Deciane, Rome
1946 Astoria Cinema, Via Stoppani, Rome
1947 Alcyone Cinema, Via Lago di Lesina, Rome (with G. Gandolfi)
S. Nicolo Bridge, over the River Arno, Florence
1948 Bologna Cinema, Rome
Bridge over the River Fortore, near Serracapriola, Fiuggi, Italy
SRE Thermo-Electric Centre, S. Paolo, Rome
Valentino Bridge enlargement and restoration, River Calore (project)
1949 Calci e Cementi di Segni Cement Factory, Scafa S. Vantino, near Pescara, Italy
Grillo Bridge, over the River Tevere, near Rome

1950 House, Via Martelli, Rome
Espero Cinema, Via Nomentana, Rome
Bridge over the River Elsa, Tuscany, Italy
Match Factory, Zaule, Trieste
Auditorium, Academy of S. Cecilia, Rome
Floating Bridge, Paola Lake, near Sabaudia, Italy (project)

1951 Di Tommaso Barracks, Rome
SST Thermo-Electric Centre, Civitavecchia, Italy
Bridge over the River Arrestra, Genoa/-Savona Motorway, Italy
Bridge over the River Tuy, Venezuela

1952 Eden Cinema, Rome
BPD Study Centre, Collefero, near Rome
Bridge over the Lupara Stream, Genoa/-Savona Motorway, at Arenzano, Italy
Aircraft Hangars, La Guaira, near Caracas, Venezuela (project)

1953 New Republic Bridge, Paguita, Caracas, Venezuela
Bridge over the River Storms, between Port Elizabeth and Cape Town, South Africa
Compere Bridge, over the River Liri, Sori, near Frosinone, Italy
Bridge over the River Adda, Lecco, Italy (project)
Verona Arena reinforcement
Bridges over the Agro and Fiumedinisi streams, Sicily

1954 Gornalunga Bridge, Enna, Sicily
Cerami Bridge, Galliano Castelferrato, Enna, Sicily
Lazzi Car Park, Florence
BPD Metallurgic Centre, Colleferro, Italy
Mooring Towers for electric cables across the Straits of Messina, Sicily
BPD Fibre Plant, Castellaccio, Anagni, Frosinone, Italy

1955 Bridge over the Tambura stream, Vagli di Sotto, near Lucca, Italy
Footbridge over the Lussia stream, Vagli di Sotto, near Lucca, Italy

Hydraulic Reservoir Aqueduct, Livorno (project)
Underground Reservoir, Caracas, Venezuela
SRE Thermo-Electric Centre, Fiumicino, Rome

1956 Maestoso Cinema, Via Appia, Rome
Genoa/Po Valley Motorway alterations, Bolzaneto, Genoa
Oreto Bridge, Palermo, Sicily (project)
Santa Barbara Thermo-Electric Centre, S. Giovanni Valdarno, near Florence
Amerigo Vespucci Bridge, over the River Arno, Florence

1957 Metronio Covered Market and Car Park, Via Magna Grecia, Rome
Calci e Cementi Sengi Cement Factory, Savignano, Italy
Bridge over the Sambro stream, Autostrada del Sole, near Bologna
Bridge over Lake Maracaibo, Venezuela
Fiumicino International Airport Terminal, Rome (competition project; with A. Zavileeri, V. Monacco, and A. Luccichenti)
SENN Nuclear Establishment, Garigliano, near Latina, Italy

1958 Bridge over the Tevere River, Magliana, Rome

1959 ABCD Factory, Ragusa, Sicily
Underground Pavilion, Valentino Park, Turin
Palazzo del Lavoro, *Italia '61*, Turin (project)
Bridge over the River Tevere, Tor di Quinto, Rome (project)

1960 Viaduct, Via Olimpica, Rome
Plan for raising of the Abu Simbel Temples, Aswan, Egypt (project; with G. Colonetti and P. Gazzola)
Bridge over the River Tartaro, Canada, Udine, Italy (project)
SELT Thermo-Electric Centre, Valdarno, Livorno

Bridge over the Columbia River, Canada
Overpass, CISA Motorway, Italy

1961 Olympic Stadium, Tehran (project)
Peugeot Building, Buenos Aires
Viaduct, Fiumarella Valley, near Catanzaro, Italy
Bridge over the River Tevere, Autostrade del Sole, near Attigliano, Viterbo, Italy
Monorail, *Italia '61*, Turin

1962 Aircraft Hangars, Alitalia Building, Fiumicino International Airport, Rome
Bridge over the Port of Göteborg, Sweden (project)
Bridge over the Vella stream, Sulmona, Italy
Piezometric Reservoir, EUR Zone, Rome (project)
Bridge over the River Schelda, Antwerp (project)

1963 Bridge over Lake Paola, Sabaudia, Latina, Italy

1964 Sports Stadium, Munich (project)
Thermo-Electric Centre, Bastardo, Foligno, Italy
Zeppieri Garage, Frosinone, Italy

1965 Bridge and Viaduct over the Polcevera Valley, Genoa/Savona Motorway, Italy
Solferino Bridge, over the River Arno, Pisa (project)
Bridge over the River Parana, Corrientes, Argentina (project)
S. Nicola Bridge, Benevento, Italy
Bridge over the River Riachuelo, Buenos Aires
Entella Viaduct, Genoa/Savona Motorway, S. Luigi, Italy
Viaduct, Modica Valley, Ragusa, Italy (project)
Calci e Cementi di Segni Cement Factory additions, Colleferro, Italy
Bridge over the River Paranda, Zarate, Argentina
Bridge over the Salerno/Reggio Calabria Motorway, Sicily

Riccardo Morandi: Aircraft Hangar, Fiumicino International Airport, Rome, 1962

Hotel/Restaurant, S. Felice Circeo, Latina, Italy
1966 Viaduct, Latte Valley, near the Franco-Italian border (project)
Wadi-Kuf Bridge, Libya
Overpass, Via Cristoforo Colombo, Casal Palocco, Rome
Viaduct over the Favazzina stream, Salerno/-Reggio Calabria Motorway, Sicily
Bridge over the Rome/Fiumicino Airport Motorway, Magliana, Rome
House, Salto di Fondi, Latina, Italy
1967 Bridge over the River Adige, Trento, Italy
Viaduct over the River Ontrano, Salerno/-Reggio Calabria Motorway, Sicily
1968 Bridge over the River Salso, Licata, Agrigento, Sicily
1969 Bridge over the River Guyas, Guayaquil, Ecuador
Sports Centre, Milan (with Ortensi, Mosco, Musmesi and Stegher)
1970 Viaduct over the Tangential, Naples
Alitalia Maintenance Centre for Boeing 747 Aircraft, Fiumicino International Airport, Rome
Catania Airport, Sicily
Viadict over the Valley of Temples, Agrigento, Sicily
Bridge over the River Magdalena, Barranquilla, Colombia
1971 ENEL Thermo-Electric Centre, Piombino, Italy
Underground Car Park, Turin
ENEL Thermo-Electric Centre, Milazzo, Italy
Underground Car Park, Brescia, Italy
Lecco Motorway, Italy
Bridge, Stmigliano, near Rome (project)
1972 Bridge, Barranquilla, Colombia
Naples Port and Motorway alterations
Bridge, Rande, Spain
1973 Focaro, Ruzzi and Arsella Viaducts, near Chieti, Italy
Arvivo Viaduct, Italy
1974 Servia Bridge, Macedonia, Greece
Mededil Car Parks, Naples
Thermo-Electric Centre, Termini Imerese, Italy
Bausan Wharf, Naples
1975 Pyramid Building, Abidjan, Ivory Coast
Carpinteto Viaduct, Potenza, Italy
Aircraft Hangars, at Fertilia, Alghero, Olbia, and Elmas Cagliari, Sicily
Air Force Barracks, Olbia, Sardinia
1976 Ergife Hotel, Via Aurelia, Rome
1977 Irminio Viaduct, Sicily
Apartment/office buildings, Jeddah, Saudi Arabia
FATA Building, Turin (with Oscar Niemeyer)
Bridge, Jeddah, Saudi Arabia (project)
1978 Bridge, Abidjan, Ivory Coast
Bridge over the River Creek, Saudi Arabia (project)

Pre-stressing system employed in hundreds of structures (7 patents)

Publications:

By MORANDI: books—*Strutture di Calcestruzzo armato e di Calcestruzzo Precompresso,* Rome 1954; *Forma e Struttura dei Ponti,* Florence 1959.

On MORANDI: books—*Riccardo Morandi* by Giorgio Boaga and Benito Boni, Milan 1962; *L'Architettura negli Impianti di Produzione e di Distribuzione di Energia Elettrica* by Mario Magistrelli, Rome 1963; *Scienza delle Construzioni e Menzione Architettonica in Architettura Problemi,* Florence 1965; *Guida dell'Architettura Contemporanea in Roma,* Rome 1965; articles—"The Story of a Visit to Northern Italy in October 1956" by R. Pedio in *Concrete Quarterly* (London), January/March 1957; "The Italian 'Morandi' System of Prestressing" by A. Carbone in *Indian Concrete Journal* (Bombay), vol. 31, no. 7, 1957; "An Underground Hall in Prestressed Concrete" in *Concrete Quarterly* (London), no. 47, 1960; "The Use of Prestressed Concrete in Architecture" by Henry J. Cowan in *Architectural Science Review* (Melbourne), March 1960; "Prestressed Concrete Crosses Lake Maracaibo" in *Engineering News Record* (New York), October 1961; "Riccardo Morandi" by Giorgio Boaga and Benito Boni in *Architect and Building News* (London), 27 November 1963; "L'Oeuvre de Riccardo Morandi" by H. Hofacker in *Architecture: Formes et Fonctions* (Lausanne), no. 11, 1964/65; "The Concrete Architecture of Riccardo Morandi" by Giorgio Boaga and Benito Boni in *Forum* (Hilversum, Netherlands), January/February 1966; "Roma senza Cuore" by Paolo Portoghesi in *Controspazio* (Bari, Italy), December 1969; "Les Ingenieurs et l'Architecture" by Serge Ketoff in *L'Architecture d'Aujourd'hui* (Paris), no. 113/114, 1970; "Morandi's Bridges" in *Architectural Forum* (New York), October 1971; "L'Opera di Riccardo Morandi" by Lara-Vinca Masini in *Bolletino degli Ingegneri* (Florence), no. 6, 1972; "Our Lady of the Plateau" in *Architecture Plus* (New York), September/October 1974; "Tre Opere di Riccardo Morandi" in *Industria delle Costruzioni* (Rome), March 1976; "Nuova Sede della Fata" by Massimo Gennari in *Domus* (Milan), May 1977.

*

All of Riccardo Morandi's work since the 1940's has aimed to redefine technological architecture in method and form, based on rationalist experimentation. He has restated and transformed the objects of the engineering tradition of the 19th century to conform to contemporary cultural and social needs. His bridges, viaducts and buildings are intended to be functional, and their relationship with the landscape is, as with all man-made objects, one of seeking to qualify and redefine—but not in accordance with town-planning conceptions of "human scale," the tradition of romantic idealism. Morandi's vision is quite different: he seeks a complete change of dimensional scale in which the architectural work becomes, as it were, a macro-support for a macro-functional operation. The relationship between architecture and space (and between architecture and nature) is identified in a sort of interchange, or interaction, aiming at a new environmental conception. By broadening his scale, he modifies and adapts the outlines of the landscape (as in the Valle del Latte Viaduct, the Wadi-Kuf Bridge, the Valley of the Temples Viaduct in Sicily, or the Columbia River Bridge in Canada), or tends to strain it to the breaking point (as in the Polcevera Viaduct over the "exploded" outskirts of Genoa, passing with a scornful disregard over the poor little buildings of run-down suburbs).

Despite their huge scale, Morandi's constructions are formally and plastically expressive. They relate to contemporary artistic movements, from "minimal art" to "land art." Often they achieve all the delicacy of an intricate gear system—as in the subtle frame of the Magliana Bridge or the Boeing 747 Aircraft Hangar at Fiumicino Airport in Rome. The outstanding feature of the hangar is the great sail roof, raised up and still seeming to rise, suspended like a halo, stretched from three large exterior pillars, transforming the hangar into a sort of shell whose outside form reflects the shape of the huge aircraft. It is this image that gives the work a symbolic character, so that it becomes a piece of token-architecture, one that functions as an ideal "key" for the coordination of site planning—a focus for the laying out of the site, step by step, in ideal proportions, at the culmination of which the channel of communications is transformed from the horizontal or suspended (as in bridges and viaducts) to the aerial, in a gigantic infrastructural supporting network.

Morandi's symbolism is just as apparent in his large industrial structures. For example, the Gari-gliano Nuclear Establishment involves a contemporary image, a "key" image, of a basilica. The image is not gratuitous. Morandi has both precisely read and commented upon a current transformation in architectural symbolism, in which the technological image for the illustration of productive power is being converted to one of a secular/sacral character. His image is encroaching, overwhelming, and apt.

Yet just as Morandi becomes comprehensible, in the sense that one tries to anticipate his visions, he seems to change. "Seems" because, again, it is only the observer who is slow to perceive. In the beautiful spiral steps of the Zeppieri Garage he transforms and interprets the spiral of Frank Lloyd Wright's Guggenheim Museum in a quite deliberate personal manner—directly linking industrial and technological architecture with works of "culture" in contemporary architectural tradition.

—Lara-Vinca Masini

MOREIRA, Jorge Machado.
Brazilian. Born in Paris, of Brazilian parents, 23 February 1904. Educated at the National School of Fine Arts, University of Brazil, now the Federal University of Rio de Janeiro, 1927–32, Dip.Arch.-Ing. 1932. Served as a Reservist in the Brazilian Army, Rio Grande do Sul, 1921. Married the architect Giuseppina Pirro in 1957. Director of Architecture, Baerlein Construction Company, Rio de Janeiro, 1933–37. In private practice, Rio de Janeiro, since 1936. Works Coordinator, 1936–37, Member of the Commission, 1939–41, and Chief Architect, 1949–62, University City of the Federal University of Rio de Janeiro. Vice-President, 1953–55, 1959–61, 1961–63, 1963–65, and Member of the Superior Council, 1957–59, 1974–75, 1976–77, 1978–79, Institute of Brazilian Architects; Vice-President, 4th Congress of Brazilian Architects, Sao Paulo, 1954; President of the Jury, 2nd International Competition for Schools of Architecture, *Bienal,* Sao Paulo, 1955; Vice-President, National Congress of Engineers, Architects, and Agricultural Engineers, Rio de Janeiro, 1959; Member of the Federal Council of Engineering, Architecture and Agronomy, Rio de Janeiro, 1967–68; Member, Superior Council of Urban Planning, Rio de Janeiro, 1972–75; President, 1st Symposium on Development and Environment, Rio de Janeiro, 1973. President, Commission for Landscape Protection of Rio de Janeiro, since 1970. Exhibitions: 6th Pan American Congress of Architects Exhibition, Lima, Peru, 1947; *14th Beaux-Arts National Salon,* Rio de Janeiro, 1949; *Bienal,* Sao Paulo, 1953, 1957, 1961; *World's Fair,* Brussels, 1958. Recipient: First Prize, with Affonso Eduardo Reidy, Rio Grande do Sul Railway Headquarters Competition, 1944; Honorary Prize, 6th Pan American Congress of Architects, Lima, 1947; Gold Medal, *14th Beaux-Arts National Salon,* Rio de Janeiro, 1949; First Prize, *Bienal,* Sao Paulo, 1953, 1957, 1961; Gold Medal, *World's Fair,* Brussels, 1958; Gold Medal, 1967, and Personality of the Year Award, 1978, Institute of Brazilian Architects; Brazilian Government Diploma for Public Service, 1972; State of Guanabara Medal, 1975. Address: Avenida Bartolomeu Mitre 380, CEP 22431, Rio de Janeiro, Brazil.

Works:

1933 2 Apartment buildings, Rua Prudente de Morais 982, Rio de Janeiro (later altered by others)
1934 George White House, Ladeira do Russell 37, Rio de Janeiro
Apartment building, Rua Republica do Peru 305, Rio de Janeiro (later altered by others)

Gaetano Vanutelli House, Rua Senador Correa 50, Rio de Janeiro (demolished)

Apartment building, Rua Senador Vergueiro 23, Rio de Janeiro

1936 Apartment building, Rio de Janeiro (project)

1937 Izabel Silva House, Rua General Rabelo 52, Rio de Janeiro

1937/
43 Ministry of Education and Health, Rio de Janeiro (with Le Corbusier, Oscar Niemeyer, Affonso Eduardo Reidy, Lúcio Costa; now the Palace of Culture)

1940 Administration Building, Rio Grande do Sul Railway System Pension Fund, Porto Alegre, Brazil (project)

1941 Capel Apartments, Rua Senador Vergueiro 66, Rio de Janeiro

S. Vicente de Paulo Home for the Elderly, Sao Borja, Brazil (later altered by others)

Administration Building, Public Service Pension Fund, Porto Alegre, Brazil (project)

1942 Medical Center, Federal University of Rio Grande do Sul, Porto Alegre, Brazil (project)

1943 Civic Center, Porto Alegre, Brazil (project)

1944 Headquarters for the Railway System of Rio Grande do Sul, Porto Alegre, Brazil (competition project; with Affonso Eduardo Reidy)

1945/
46 IPASE Tuberculosis Sanatoria, Correas and Rio de Janeiro (projects)

1946 Itatiaia Apartments, Rio de Janeiro (project; with Carlos Leão)

1947 Administration Building, Ferroviarios and Public Service Pension Fund, Porto Alegre, Brazil (project)

1947/
48 SNT Tuberculosis Sanatoria, Manaus, Salvador, and Belo Horizonte, Brazil (later altered by others)

1948 Antonio Ceppas Apartments, Rua Benjamin Batista 180, Rio de Janeiro

1949/
62 University City, of the Federal University of Rio de Janeiro: general plan; Institute of Child Care; Architecture and Urbanism School; Engineering School; Medical Center; and Printing Works; also, projects for Pharmacy School; Nuclear Physics Institute; Microbiology Institute; Bio-physics Institute; Institute of Tuberculosis; University Stadium; and residential blocks

1950 IAPB Tuberculosis Sanatorium, Salvador, Brazil (project)

1952 Getulio Vargas Foundation Building, Rio de Janeiro (project)

Sergio Correa da Costa House, Rua Campo Belo 88, Rio de Janeiro

Antonio Ceppas House, Praca Atahualpa 86, Rio de Janeiro

Nike Apartments, Rio de Janeiro (project)

1953 IAPB Apartment Building, Rua Voluntarios da Patria 471, Rio de Janeiro (later altered by others)

1954 Floriano Farias House, Rua Eng. Alfredo Duarte 456, Rio de Janeiro

1955 Sergio Marques de Souza House, Rua

Igarapava 14, Rio de Janeiro

1961/
65 Flamengo Park, Rio de Janeiro (with others)

1965 Restaurant for Flamengo Park, Rio de Janeiro (project)

IAPFESP Administration Building, Porto Alegre, Brazil (project)

1970 Alfredo Ornellas House, Nova Friburgo, Brazil (with Giuseppina Pirro de Moreira; later altered by others)

Benfica Park Estate (houses, apartments, and leisure area), Teresopolis, Brazil (project; with Giuseppina Pirro de Moreira)

Publications:

On MOREIRA: books—*Brazil Builds* by Philip Goodwin, New York 1943; *Dix Ans d'Architecture Contemporaine* by Sigfried Giedion, Zurich 1951; *Latin American Architecture since 1945* by Henry-Russell Hitchcock, New York 1955; *Modern Architecture in Brazil* by Henrique Mindlin, Rio de Janeiro 1956; *Brazil* by Elizabeth Bishop, in *Life World Library* series, New York 1962; *Arquitectura Actual de America,* Madrid 1966; *Quem é Quem nas Artes e nas Letras do Brasil,* Rio de Janeiro 1966.

I started my professional life in 1932, identified with the movement that strove to establish a new Architecture. In Brazil as well as in many other countries, this movement was an outcome of the world-wide campaign, from 1928, by CIAM (Congrès Internationaux d'Architecture Moderne). I had begun tak-

Jorge Machado Moreira: Architecture School, Federal University, Rio de Janeiro, 1957

ing an active part in this struggle while still a student at the National School of Fine Arts in Rio de Janeiro. Lúcio Costa had been appointed Director of that School in 1931; he proceeded to change our education by "establishing a new manner of conceiving, projecting and building." Gregori Warchavchik —the pioneer of contemporary architecture in Brazil —was invited to teach us, and he made a very strong impression, arousing our enthusiasm for and understanding of Costa's initiative, and creating our consequent support of it. That same year, Frank Lloyd Wright's visit to Rio de Janeiro, and his activities here, were most important for the consolidation of the Modern Movement.

Having concluded my studies, I went to work for a construction company. All at once I felt how difficult it would be to practice architecture as I had come to feel it. I decided to make it a condition of my stay with the company that they allow me my freedom in designing. This condition having been accepted, I had no further problems during the period that I remained with them.

This basic requirement I still maintain. It is not that I want to impose my point of view; I always try to arrive, through a dialogue, at the most appropriate solutions to the client's needs, without, however, making any concessions that are contrary to the principles that I, as an architect, must fight for. This criterion has never made me walk out on a job. My opinions find justification in solid argumentation, and the client understands that I am trying to defend his own interests. I opened my private office in 1936.

I have enjoyed the privilege of knowing personally Frank Lloyd Wright, Richard Neutra, Walter Gropius, Alvar Aalto, Mies van der Rohe, Kenzo Tange, and Philip Johnson. Of greater significance, however, was the contact I had with Le Corbusier in 1937, when he came to Rio at the invitation of the Minister of Education and Health. The close relationship that we—the architects entrusted with the design of the new Ministry building—had with Le Corbusier during about three weeks, had a decisive influence on my professional development.

In the years that have elapsed since that time, Brazilian architecture has suffered the consequences of political, social, and economic changes, which have also affected the way we practice in our metier. And yet, my way of feeling architecture and its importance has remained unchanged. For me, to make architecture is still to conceive a work that endeavors to solve plastically the proposed problem, in accordance with the times, the materials, the technical and economic possibilities—by analyzing and considering any external factors that might influence the work; by giving heed to the impositions and habits of the milieu; by detailing and articulating all the architectural elements; and, finally, by always seeking the truth of purpose and function, in form as well as in materials. I always try to give my full assistance to the contractors on the building, so that the work is executed as it was conceived, fulfilling the needs of the client, and thus completing my task. I am also concerned with the environment of a proposed work, and of the work's significance within the environment. Once built, it becomes an element of the urban landscape, the harmony of which must always be preserved. For this reason, every architect must be urbanistically oriented.

In accordance with this principle, I have endeavored to collaborate rather actively in the establishing of urban regulations and norms that have in view the structuring of the city and the guidance of its future development, without loss to the natural landscape and to the material evidence of its history, the remains of which it is our duty to preserve.

I have had a constant interest in the institutional aspect of my profession, collaborating with and supporting our various associations—particularly the Institute of Brazilian Architects. This seems to me to be the only way to fulfill completely one's professional obligations.

I hope that the struggles and deceptions that are a part of our professional life will never discourage

me or make me abandon the ideals that I have always held, ideals that are always being updated so that I may better serve architecture, whatever the occasion or the circumstances.

—Jorge Machado Moreira

The work of Jorge Machado Moreira is notable for its strict coherence and for its restrained use of form, which lend a classical simplicity to his buildings, making them the most representative examples of the rationalist tendency in Brazil.

Jorge Machado Moreira was a member of the team that created the design for the Ministry of Education and Health in Rio de Janeiro—with Le Corbusier, Lúcio Costa, Oscar Niemeyer, Affonso Eduardo Reidy, and others. His own first large-scale project was the Medical Center at Porto Alegre in 1942. It sets out architectural ideas that were to be developed in greater depth in the university buildings in Rio de Janeiro. In 1944 he collaborated with Affonso Eduardo Reidy in the national competition to design the new headquarters of the Rio Grande do Sul Railway, and their entry won first prize. The site for the new building was later changed and the project developed mainly by Reidy. In its exuberant use of shapes, the building has obvious links with the architectural movement of the 1940's and 1950's.

From 1949 until 1962 Jorge Machado Moreira directed the design office responsible for the new university at Rio de Janeiro. This enormous task included the urbanization of an area of approximately six square kilometres and the construction of buildings for a total of 40,000 people.

The project was only partially completed and is now being drastically altered. Of the twelve projects undertaken before 1962 (when the architect was indisposed as a result of a serious accident), only four major works were actually built: the Institute of Child Care; the Engineering School; the School of Architecture and Urbanism (which currently also houses the National School of Fine Arts and the University Administrative Center); and the Medical Center (now almost complete). Two of these buildings—the Institute of Child Care of 1953 and the School of Architecture and Urbanism of 1957—were awarded first prize in the 2nd and 4th Sao Paulo *Bienal;* the group of projects won a Gold Medal at the Brussels *World's Fair* in 1958.

The Institute of Child Care is a low building consisting of three parallel blocks (casualty, hospital and crèche) linked by a transverse block and opening onto large gardens. The building is chiefly notable for its uncluttered detail and for its extensive internal and external surfaces, on which finishing materials are combined and juxtaposed with rare skill and taste.

The three larger buildings stand out like topological landmarks against the flat landscape of Fundão Island. A common identity is immediately established by the use of the same external material; by the clarity of line and the simplicity of the skyline; by the regularity of the windows, emphasized by their jutting sills and by the partitions that frame each gap; by the uniformity of design (two-storey buildings separated by landscaped patios and long narrow "blades" with blind lateral walls); and by the uniformity of scale and mood—that of monumental sobriety and simplicity. Yet the individuality of each building becomes apparent at closer range; then it is obvious that there are design features peculiar to each building, a response to specific functional needs. They demonstrate the wealth of possibilities that a limited vocabulary can offer when handled with dexterity.

This balance between individuality and identity— uniformity without monotony—is a rare and important contribution to contemporary town planning— all the more so in that it serves to point out the shortcomings of the more recent university buildings and of the great majority of projects of the same nature, where each building shrieks a strident individualism detrimental to the principles of harmony and restraint.

Two of Moreira's residential works are also outstanding. Despite the limitations imposed by the dimensions of the site and by zoning restrictions, the Ceppas Apartment Building is one of the best works of its kind in Rio de Janeiro. The Ceppas House, also in Rio, and subject to similar limitations, is an exceptional work—a large urban dwelling, extraordinarily spacious inside yet constructed on a site merely 430 metres square. The architect's proverbial perfectionism is obvious again in the fastidious attention to detail.

In his career Jorge Machado Moreira has also been constantly concerned with protecting architectural interests and with conservation. His active role in the profession—whether as a lecturer, competition judge, or member of special committees, particularly those having to do with revision of the laws relating to architecture—have won him innumerable important tributes, notably the Gold Medal and the Personality of the Year Award of the Institute of Brazilian Architects.

—Jorge Czajkowski

MORGAN, William.

American. Born in Jacksonville, Florida, 14 December 1930. Educated at the Harvard University Graduate School of Design, Cambridge, Massachusetts, under Josep Lluis Sert and Sigfried Giedion, 1955–58 (Holloway Scholarship; Lehman Fellow; Appleton Prize Fellow), M.Arch. 1958; Fulbright Grantee in Italy, 1958–59. Served as an officer in the United States Navy, in Korea and the Far East, 1952–55. Married Bernice E. Leimback in 1954; children: Newton and Dylan. Draftsman, for Paul Rudolph, Cambridge, part-time 1955–58, Smith, Hinchman and Grills, Detroit, summer 1957, and Reynolds, Smith and Hills, Jacksonville, Florida, 1959–60. Since 1961, Principal, William Morgan Architects, Jacksonville. Exhibition: *A Decade of Architecture*, Jacksonville University Department of Fine Arts, 1971; *Transformations in Modern Architecture* Museum of Modern Art, New York, 1979. Recipient: Wheelwright Fellowship, Harvard University, 1964; Design Award, American Institute of Architects, Florida Association, 1964, 1965, 1967, 1968, 1970, 1971, 1972, 1973, 1975, 1976, 1978; Graham Foundation grant, 1973; Honor Award, American Institute of Architects, 1974; Design Award, *Progressive Architecture*, 1975; Design Award, United States General Services Administration, 1978; Mid-Career Fellowship, National Endowment for the Arts, 1979. Fellow, American Institute of Architects, 1975. Address: William Morgan Architects, 220 East Forsyth Street, Jacksonville, Florida 32202, U.S.A.

Works:

1961 William Morgan Apartments and Architectural Studio, Atlantic Beach, Florida
1962 James House, Atlantic Beach, Florida
Williams House, Jacksonville Beach, Florida
1964 Gillespie Medical Clinic, Jacksonville Beach, Florida
Rawls House, Jacksonville, Florida
Williamson House, Ponte Vedra Beach, Florida
1966 Hatcher House, Jacksonville, Florida
Place by the Sea Apartments, Atlantic Beach, Florida
Ballentine House, Atlantic Beach, Florida
1968 Jacksonville Children's Museum, Florida
1969 Air Launched Weapons Training Facility, Mayport, Florida
Stanley House, Gainesville, Florida
1970 Goodloe House, Ponte Vedra Beach, Florida
Trainable Mentally Retarded School, Jacksonville, Florida

Norfolk Sheraton Hotel, Virginia
1971 Savannah Elderly Housing, Georgia
Florida State Museum, Gainesville
Sheraton Inn, Hampton, Virginia
Plaza Executive Centers, Miami
1972 Seascape at Hilton Head Apartments, Hilton Head Island, South Carolina
Plummers Cove Apartments, Mandarin, Florida
1973 M. K. Dickinson House, Atlantic Beach, Florida
220 East Forsyth Office Building (William Morgan offices), Jacksonville, Florida
William Morgan House, Atlantic Beach, Florida
1974 Hilltop House, Central Florida
1975 Dunehouse Apartments, Atlantic Beach, Florida
Oceanfront Condominium, Ocean City, Maryland
1976 Riverfront Esplanade, Norfolk, Virginia
McCondichie House, Ponte Vedra Beach, Florida
1977 Police Memorial Building, Jacksonville, Florida
1978 United States Post Office, Murray Hill, Jacksonville, Florida
Regional Service Center for Duval County, Jacksonville, Florida
Federal Building/United States Courthouse, Fort Lauderdale, Florida
Community for Elderly Persons, Asheville, North Carolina
J. C. Dickinson House, Gainesville, Florida

Publications:

By MORGAN: book—*Prehistoric American Architecture*, Cambridge, Massachusetts 1980; article—"Florida's Earth Architecture" in *The Florida Architect* (Miami), May/June 1975.

On MORGAN: articles—"Teatro all Aperto" by Bruno Zevi in *L'Architettura* (Rome), January 1960; "Four Level House" by David Travers in *Arts and Architecture* (Los Angeles), June 1964; "Appartements-Jardins Atlantic Beach" by Renée Diamant-Berger in *L'Architecture d'Aujourd'hui* (Paris), April/May 1965; "William Morgan, Architect" by David Travers in *Arts and Architecture* (Los Angeles), May 1965; "Bright Young Men with Design on the Future" by Walter McQuade in *Fortune* (New York), July 1966; "The Earth" by C. Ray Smith in *Progressive Architecture* (New York), April 1967; "Interpod" by David Travers in *Arts and Architecture* (Los Angeles), April 1967; "From Flying Boxes to Stacked U's" by C. Ray Smith in *Progressive Architecture* (New York), June 1968; "Names: William Morgan" by Peggy Johnson in *Architectural and Engineering News* (Philadelphia), December 1969; "Museum Play In" by C. Ray Smith in *Progressive Architecture* (New York), November 1970; "Museum Architecture" by Michael Webb in *Museum News* (Washington, D.C.), March 1971; "Designing in, under, around and with the Earth" by Wolf Von Eckardt in the *Washington Post,* 8 April 1972; "Molding Our Man Made World" by Bess Balchen in *AIA Journal* (Washington, D.C.), February 1974; "Florida State Museum" by Gaitano Bologna in *Industria della Costruzioni* (Rome), November/December 1974; "Stepped Terrace as Breakwater" by C. Ray Smith in *Interiors* (New York), February 1975; "Earth Form House by William Morgan Echoes Florida's Pre-Colonial Past" by Barclay Gordon in *Architectural Record* (New York), May 1976; "Haus auf Vier Ebenen" by Jürgen Joedicke in *Bauen und Wohnen* (Zurich), September 1976; "Shaping Space" by Ed Fitzell in *Interior Design* (New York), January 1977; "McCondichie Residence, Hilltop Residence, Oceanfront Condominium" by Nakamura in *Architecture + Urbanism* (Tokyo), September 1977; "Breaking Down the Battlements" by Charles Hoyt in *Architectural Record* (New York), January 1978; "Underground Architecture" by Andrea O. Dean in *AIA Journal* (Washington, D.C.), April 1978; "Designs for Living" by Douglas Davis in *Newsweek* (New York), 6 November 1978.

During the last two decades my work has become concerned with the environment as a whole rather than individual building as an isolated entity. Similarly Michelangelo conceived the design of the Compidoglio in relation to Baroque Rome and the Farnesina in relation to the Palazzo Farnese via a proposed new bridge across the Tiber. History has become much more important to me than novelty: I have recently completed 12 years of research on man's experience in shaping his environment in the Eastern United States between 2200 B.C. and A.D. 1500, and have found many of our earlier experiences to be more meaningful than our present ones.

Through this search for design origins in our past I am beginning to find meaningful possibilities for our future of which the Florida State Museum, the Jacksonville Police Memorial Building and State Office Building, and the Federal Courts Building in Fort Lauderdale are examples. The regard for earth as a building material has become increasingly important in my work, again a direct result of my examining man's past with a search of his evolution toward a meaningful future. As a consequence, my

William Morgan: Florida State Museum, Gainesville, 1971

work has taken on a specific character not found widely elsewhere in the latter 20th century.

I sense that we as architects today find ourselves exploring many alternatives toward a meaningful tomorrow. This is not the first time that this fundamental re-examination has occurred in history, nor presumably will it be the last. Where our explorations will lead us we do not know, but the search itself is as refreshing as it is challenging.

—William Morgan

Since embarking upon an independent practice in the early 1960's William Morgan has, in his architectural career, undergone a major metamorphosis. From spinning rather Miesian, functional cocoons of glass and other materials, he emerged from a ten year study as one of the prime proponents of architecture as landscape. What at first appears to be an incredible transition in Morgan's approach reveals itself, upon closer inspection, to be a consistent maturation of ideas.

His early work adhered to strictly traditional, modern movement, neoclassical, functionalist forms, as exemplified by the Rawls and Williamson residences. These box-like dwellings present an austere facade to the public while employing extensive glass panels in the rear. Bold masonry "service towers," which house plumbing, utilities and baths, are a conspicuous design element, and a cantilevered roof provides structural support via hanger rods. A large, open, central living space, often two stories in height, dominates the interior. Snugly integrated within this "noble" space is an intimate fireplace area, and balconies overlook the space to afford myriad views. Morgan further explored the ramifications of this spatial disposition in an apartment complex, the Place by the Sea, and found it provided a "controlled variety within an agreeable order."

With later projects, such as the multi-level Ballentine and Hatcher residences, Morgan proved himself to be a masterful manipulator of interior spaces. These dwellings have as a focal point a central core that provides vertical circulation. Situated off either side of the core, at various levels, are living areas of different heights. The use of intimate fireplaces and balconies are reminiscent of his earlier designs, but the employment of a more complex spatial arrangement allows for a more varied and dynamic experience. The exteriors also display a more sophisticated handling, particularly in the Hatcher house. Numerous balconies penetrate its facade of naturally finished materials to create a dramatic pattern of light and shadow, which transcends the earlier unadorned curtain walls. While retaining a sense of functional utility and formal lines, these houses edge out into the twilight zone and explore the more humanistic aspects of classicism. However, a restrained formalism still dominates these designs, which is readily perceived in the buildings' relationship to their surroundings. The houses are built on and above the landscape and serve as platforms from which to observe nature. The environment is placed at a distance and regarded primarily as a source of scenic interest, to be considered architecturally only in the handling of the fenestration.

Morgan maintains this pronounced sense of classical control and order even in his more recently conceived "architecture as landscape" projects. His major public commissions of the past decade, the Florida State Museum in Gainesville and the Jacksonville Police Memorial Building, both belie the architect's strong commitment to rational order. Such elements as earth berm construction, a human scale, and expansive terraces, courtyards and promenades blend into an exceedingly formal, rigidly controlled pattern of interrelated spaces. These "earth form" designs do not so much disclose their proclaimed end, "buildings as landscape," as they do landscape as buildings. In these projects Morgan blurs the distinctions between building and landscape by employing natural elements as materials to be handled in a functional manner. A number of "earth form" residences, including the Hilltop

House, well demonstrate this point. Featuring earth berm sides, the Hilltop House is a pyramid of monumental proportions that rises above the countryside. Although perpetuating the verdant sweep of the landscape, the residence is distinct from the surrounding terrain and functions in a manner similar to the Hatcher house, as an observatory.

A more successful attempt by Morgan to create a building as landscape is a duplex in Atlantic Beach, which is set into an existing sand dune. Situated on the ocean and following the rolling contours of the dune, the duplex intrudes as minimally as possible upon its natural setting. Only a curvilinear entry and a pair of oval porthole-like patios betray the presence of the dwelling in the earth. As such, this duplex points towards a feasible blending of landscape as architecture; however, the number of natural features that can be molded in such a manner appear to be rather limited.

The different stages of William Morgan's career all disclose him to be an extremely robust and innovative practitioner of functional formalism. He has consistently explored a wide range of possibilities which derive from the synthesis of the classical tradition and modern technology, and has developed various design solutions in an attempt to reconcile a functional approach with humanist needs.

—Don J. Hibbard

MORIYAMA, Raymond.

Canadian. Born in Vancouver, British Columbia, 11 October 1929. Educated at public and private schools in Vancouver, Hamilton, Ontario, and Tokyo; University of Toronto, 1949–54, B.Arch. 1954; McGill University, Montreal, 1954–57, M.Arch. 1957. Married Sachiko Miyauchi in 1954; children: Mark, Murina, Selena, Jason, and Ajon. In private practice, Toronto, since 1958: in partnership with Ted Teshima since 1969. Chairman of the Board, Ecological Research Ltd., Toronto, since 1969; President, Group One Ltd. (museum consultants), Toronto, since 1970. Chairman, Mid-Canada Conference Task Force on Environmental and Ecological Factors, 1969–70. Member, Expert Committee on Societal Aspects of Great Lakes Water Quality, International Joint Commission's Great Lakes Research Advisory Board, since 1975. Exhibitions: National Gallery of Canada, Ottawa, 1977; Art Gallery of Ontario, Toronto, 1978. Recipient: Massey Medal for Architecture, 1961; Award, *Canadian Architects Yearbook*, 1968; Pre-stressed Concrete Institute Award, 1969; Citizen's Award, 1974; Massey Medal for Planning, 1976; Civic Award of Merit, Scarborough, Ontario, 1977; Japan Foundation Award, 1977. LL.D.: Brock University, St. Catherines, Ontario, 1973; York University, Toronto, 1973. Fellow, Royal Architectural Institute of Canada, 1970; Member, Royal Canadian Academy of the Arts, 1973. Fellow, Royal Society of Arts, London, 1970. Address: Raymond Moriyama, Architects and Planners, 32 Davenport Road, Toronto, Ontario M5R 1H3, Canada.

Works:

1958 Private golf course, Toronto
1959 Gatehouse and Equipment Centre, for Crothers Caterpillar Ltd., Toronto
1960 Brady House, Scarborough, Ontario
       Comfort stations, Metropolitan Toronto Parks
1961 Civic Garden Centre, North York, Ontario
1962 Japanese-Canadian Cultural Centre, North York, Ontario
1964 Ernest Thompson Seton Park, North York, Ontario

Master plan for the Ontario Science Centre, North York
1965 Raymond Moriyama, Architects and Planners Offices (renovation of service station), 32 Davenport Road, Toronto
1966 Convention Centre, Nassau, Bahamas (project)
       Master plan and site selection, Metropolitan Toronto Zoological Park, Scarborough, Ontario
       Minota Hagey Residence, University of Waterloo, Ontario
1967 John McCrae Senior Public School, Scarborough, Ontario
       Master plan of the Erindale Campus of the University of Toronto, Mississauga, Ontario
       Centennial Baptist Church, Markham, Ontario (project)
1968 Jack Minor Public School, Scarborough, Ontario
       Human Kinetics Building, University of Guelph, Ontario
1969 Ontario Science Centre, North York
       Bell Telephone Hotel and Training Centre, Belleville, Ontario
1970 Academic Staging Building, Brock University, St. Catharines, Ontario
       Fine Arts Building, phase II, York University, North York, Ontario
1971 Radio Station CKEY, Toronto
       Feasibility study of the Ministry of Urban Affairs, Ottawa, Ontario
1972 Centennial Arboretum Centre, University of Guelph, Ontario
       L'Amoreaux Collegiate, Scarborough, Ontario
       Studios and Headquarters, Global Television Network, North York, Ontario
       Gazebo, King Township, Ontario
1973 Winnipeg Railway Study
       Scarborough Civic Centre, Ontario
1974 Minesing Swamp Study, Simcoe County, Ontario
       Northern Resources Exhibition Centre, Timmins, Ontario (project)
1975 Steam Attraction Centre, Muskoka, Ontario (project)
1976 Burnhamthorpe District Library, Mississauga, Ontario
       Malton Community Centre, Mississauga, Ontario
       Urban design of South Beach, Miami Beach, Florida
1977 The Goh Ohn Bell Shelter, Toronto
       Metropolitan Toronto Library
1979– Regional Art Gallery, London, Ontario
       Black Creek Visitors Centre, North York, Ontario
       Community Art Centre, Guelph, Ontario
       Stage One Experimental Theatre, Stratford, Ontario
       Civic Centre, Calgary, Alberta
       Performing Arts Centre, York University, North York, Ontario
       Church of the Good Shepherd, Markham, Ontario
       Multicultural Media Centre, Toronto
       Government of Canada Building, Scarborough, Ontario
       Civic Centre, Barrie, Ontario

Publications:

By MORIYAMA: articles—"Urban Renewal: Planning the Neighborhood" in *Royal Architectural Institute of Canada Journal* (Toronto), January 1958; "Trends in Motel Design" in *Royal Architectural Institute of Canada Journal* (Toronto), September 1960; "Thought Process and Intent: The Centennial Centre of Science and Technology, Toronto" in *Canadian Architect* (Toronto), September 1969; "Design Process: Scarborough Civic Centre" in *Canadian Architect* (Toronto), November 1973.

On MORIYAMA: articles—"Three Projects by Moriyama and Watts, Toronto" in *Royal Architectural Institute of Canada Journal* (Toronto), June 1960; "Three-Hole Golf Course" in *Progressive Architecture* (New York), July 1962; "Workspace" in *Canadian Architect* (Toronto), February 1967; "Zoological Park, Metropolitan Toronto" in *Canadian Architect* (Toronto), November 1968; "Ontario's Participatory Museum" in *Architectural Record* (New York), August 1970; "A Civic Center for Scarborough, Ontario" in *Architectural Record* (New York), July 1974; "A Richness of Form, Space and Books" by Barry Downs in *Canadian Architect* (Toronto), January 1978; "Architecture, Meaning and Values: Raymond Moriyama and the New Metropolitan Toronto Library" by Joan M. Vastokas in *Artscanada* (Toronto), February/March 1978.

The consistency in the work of Raymond Moriyama is that of architectural personality applied to various building problems. In his designs, the richness of the psyche has remained free from the constraints of dogma. Each commission has brought interaction between the concerns of architect, client and user in the pursuit of an appropriate response. The range of possibilities he chooses to develop is unusual in the practice of modern architecture. Materials vary between buildings of similar use and form. There is a mix of angular and curved geometry. Motifs are sometimes invented or taken over from a generalized style or the work of other architects. The sophisticated viewer may object to the apparent lack of motivating rules or development of a personal style. In actuality, as one of Moriyama's buildings approaches a rule (e.g. a regulating geometry) or a specific style (e.g. a recognizable set of motifs), it unduly stresses that aspect of the design to the detriment of the whole.

There are various kinds of unity. Modern architecture favoured conceptual and formal unity; it rejected emotional and, by extension, spiritual unity if that can be considered descriptive of man's total existence. The architectural vocabulary employed by Moriyama fits within modern architectural practice. While ranging in source in contemporary time and place, it has the same simple, plain, undecorated look. As others do, he uses plants to soften the impact of the built environment. This architectural vocabulary is not one to which the general public is normally responsive, and its only imagistic allusions are to other architectural sources whose use might trouble connoisseurs. To most viewers, however, this issue is irrelevant in that all the forms are newly perceived and therefore equal within the context of the experience. Given the richness and diversity of contemporary existence, no specific form language will necessarily fit all occasions. As functional arrangement, or structural system, or even energy consumption may generate different form solutions, so may less tangible but equal or more important concerns: uniqueness, personality. Or the form language itself might be subservient to other components of the total experience. The very nature of the intended building can establish its own significance which pre-exists the design. The form then becomes supportive of the situation rather than presuming to create it.

Moriyama's success has been to match form with name and place to produce buildings that can be endowed with meanings associated with their purpose. The method of achieving this has been to establish psychological events within the overall fabric. Architects accustomed to conceptualizing the totality of a building design into a symbolic whole of metaphysical import may not see a relationship between the parts. The ordinary user will experience entry, shape, light, movement, colour, space as a series of events which cluster around the concept "library," or "civic centre," or "science centre." Such a set of sequential happenings allows some elements to have no other purpose than to enclose space

or, at least, not to produce negative effects, while other forms create the desired experiences. Possibly because of the complexity of three-dimensional design, architects have learned to respond to simple orthogonal structures. By freeing the total building form from its symbolic function, Moriyama has been able to expend his creativity where it is most effective.

Current architectural dogma demands so many constraints as to severely limit design possibilities. By rejecting such stereotyped systems, Moriyama has freed himself to create effects where and how they are required, and at a scale and character that are appropriate. His buildings thereby include segments of creative brilliance where the non-rational amalgam of architectural elements comes together in a memorable experience. That it is the internal meaning of architectural experience evoked that is remembered, not the external medium of architecture employed, permits this diversity of means. The unifying theme is the inner sense of place where the architect's intent overrides and subjects his building vocabulary to the creation of a shaped event.

That Moriyama's buildings cannot be approached in the traditional formal terms of architectural theory sets them outside the mainstream of the architecture of the recent past. However, their popularity among the general public and the current broadening of architectural interests suggest that their consistent quality of result will lead to a critical reassessment of their value.

—Anthony Jackson

Raymond Moriyama: Metropolitan Toronto Library, 1977

MORO, Peter.

British. Born in Heidelberg, Germany, 27 May 1911; emigrated to England, 1936: naturalized, 1947. Educated at the Technische Hochschule, Stuttgart, 1929–30, Berlin, 1930–34, and Zurich, 1934–36, Dip.Arch. 1936. Married Anne Vanneck in 1940; has three daughters Practised with the Tecton Group, London, 1937–39; Lecturer, Regent Street Polytechnic, London, 1941–47; Associated Architect, Festival Hall, London County Council, 1948–51. Since 1952, Partner, with Michael Mellish and Michael Heard, Peter Moro and Partners, London. Member of the Executive Committee, MARS (Modern Architectural Research) Group, London, 1938; founder-Member, 1961, and Vice President, 1978, Association of British Theatre Technicians; Member of the Council, Royal Institute of British Architects, 1967–73. Recipient: Bronze Medal, Royal Institute of British Architects, 1964. Fellow, Royal Institute of British Architects, 1948, and Society of Industrial Artists and Designers, 1957. C.B.E. (Commander, Order of the British Empire), 1977. Address: Peter Moro and Partners, 13 Rathbone Street, London W1P 1AF, England.

Works:

1939 House, Birdham, Sussex (with Richard Llewelyn Davies)
1948/
   51 Royal Festival Hall interiors, South Bank, London S.E.1
1954 House, Waldringfield, Suffolk
   Independent Television House and Studios, Kingsway, London
1957 Fairlawn Primary School, Lewisham, London
   Peter Moro House, Blackheath Park, London
1962 Hille of London Ltd. Offices and Showroom, Albemarle Street, London W.1
1963 Flats, for Audley Properties Ltd., Mayfair, London
1964 Playhouse Theatre, Nottingham
   Royal Opera House alterations, Convent Garden, London

1965 Secondary School and Youth Club, Cator Street, Peckham, London
Primary School, Birstall, Leicestershire
Hall of Residence, University of Leicester
1968 The Hansen House, Hertfordshire
1969 Gulbenkian Centre, Theatre and Television Studio, University of Hull, Yorkshire
1970 Associated Rediffusion Showrooms and Offices, London
Greater London Council Housing, Comber Grove, Camberwell, London
1971 Theatre Royal alterations/remodelling, Bristol
1972/
74 Greater London Council Housing, Barnado Gardens, Tower Hamlets, London
1973 Borough of Southwark Housing, Old Kent Road, London
1974 Borough of Southwark Housing, Montpelier Road, London
Downside and Worth Boys Club with Swimming Pool, Southwark, London
Greater London Council Housing, Fayland Estate, Wandsworth, London
Greater London Council Housing, Clairview Road, Wandsworth, London
1975 Borough of Southwark Housing, Coxson Place, London
Borough of Southwark Housing, East Street, London
Riverside Theatre, New University of Ulster, Coleraine
1976 Borough of Southwark Housing, Earl Road, London

1977 Greater London Council Housing, Lebanon Gardens, Wandsworth, London
Borough of Southwark Housing, Hamilton Square, London
1978 Borough of Southwark Housing, Queens Road/Pomeroy Street, London
Greater London Council Housing, Hildenborough Gardens, Lewisham, London
Piccadilly Theatre alterations, London
1979 Borough of Southwark Housing, Brimmington Central, London
Borough of Southwark Housing, Pasley Road, London
1980 Plymouth Civic Theatre, Devon

Publications:

By MORO: articles—"Queen Elizabeth Hall Appraisal" in *RIBA Journal* (London), June 1968; "Salle de Spectacles," special issue of *Architecture Francaise* (Paris), January/February 1969; "Theatres: A Design Guide" in *Architectural Design* (London), no. 3, 1973; "Fifteen Years of Theatre Design by Peter Moro," with S. Williams, in *RIBA Journal* (London), February 1979.

On MORO: books—*Architetture per lo Spectacolo* by Roberto Aloi, Milan 1958; *Modern Architecture in Britain* by Trevor Dannatt, London 1959; *Exhibition Design* by Misha Black, London 1959; *New Housing in Britain* by Brickman and Lewis, London 1960; *Ville nel Mondo* by Roberto Aloi, Milan 1961; *Schulbau* by Karl Otto, Stuttgart 1961; *Neue Einfamilienhauser* by Hoffman, Stuttgart 1962; *Archi-* *tecture in Britain Today* by Michael Webb, London 1969; *The Politics of Architecture* by Anthony Jackson, London 1970; *The Modern Theatre* by Hannelore Schubert, London 1971; *Theatre Planning* by Roderick Ham, London 1972; article—"Urban Housing Variations" by J. M. McKean in *Building Design* (London), 28 July 1978.

I regard architecture as a service, not a vehicle for ego trips.

That is to say that a building must, as a matter of course, fulfill all functional requirements, both physical and emotional.

A building that works well but is aesthetically unsatisfactory is as bad as a beautiful building that fails to function properly on the physical plane.

The challenge, therefore, as I see it, is to combine in one's work aesthetic quality with practicability, not one at the expense of the other.

—Peter Moro

Peter Moro is an exemplar of Modern Movement architecture in England. His career began with Tecton before the Second World War, and he was on the executive of the MARS Group, but unlike that of many of his contemporaries his architectural practice into the 1980's retains its integrity; his buildings maintain a clarity and stylishness. There was no commercial sell-out in the '60's, nor loss of design nerve in the '70's; his latest major project, the important Plymouth Civic Theatre, which will be completed in the early 1980's, may be his finest building yet.

Typically, Moro would immediately qualify that

Peter Moro: Gulbenkian Centre, University of Hull, Yorkshire, 1969

word "his," also crediting Michael Mellish and Michael Heard, his partners for nearly 30 years. The practice has remained small and their output modest in quantity, but this is rather the result of the vagaries of patronage than of any ideological limit on size. Best known for a series of theatres, the partnership has designed a wide variety of buildings, and, in recent years, they have been offered a staple diet of local authority housing.

And their reputation need not rest on the larger buildings, for Moro has produced charming and sparkling little gems over a long period, works that clearly demonstrate his skill and intentions. His own house, for example, a cool white box floating over Blackheath greenery, is nevertheless undogmatic and friendly; in the Fairlawn Primary School in Lewisham, the precision of detail, materials and colour echoes the geometric Pasmore abstract which hangs in the hall, yet the school is humane and cheerful; the Hille Showroom and Offices in London's West End, a carefully scaled, modest, curtain-walled corner, hits the ground with a touch of virtuoso wit: the precisely board-marked concrete, instead of being exposed to dirt, lichen and weather-staining, stands half a metre inside its crisp metal and glass cage. The counterpoint of textures, colours, planes and materials in these works is always deft, and the spaces therefore are pleasing both at a distance and in close contact.

Providing visual richness at all scales, but without a traditional decorative vocabulary, had engrossed Moro earlier when, at perhaps the most crucial point in his career, he found himself invited to join the design team for the Royal Festival Hall. It was Britain's first major non-utilitarian building for a decade, and, within Sir Leslie Martin's overall concept, Moro designed and detailed the interior of what is now recognized as one of the very few great buildings in modern Britain. It does not possess the "timelessness" that was the aim of the Modern Movement: not just the detail (the bent plywood, the flying boxes, the patterned carpet) but also the spaces and forms are clearly dated. The RFH is no longer admired as "new" but as "architecture," with its magnificent spaces, its quietly competent functioning, and, particularly, its consistency. Moro explored the decorative potential of the required lighting and the air handling and acoustic devices, well aware that the function of such a hall included an atmosphere of drama, of festivity and of anticipation.

These themes have been developed in the theatre projects that followed, from the very successful Nottingham Playhouse to, hopefully, the Plymouth Civic Theatre. Nottingham excites users and the public alike: its forms are clear and logical, inventively useful; its glittering detail is held within a simple geometry.

Moro is scathing about "false aesthetics," and never tries, for example, to hide a fly tower; rather, he would use it to compositional advantage. His antipathy to the Sydney Opera House is, he says, based on its being unable to perform its intended functions. As clearly, if unspoken, he feels an antipathy to forms that are generated from abstract imposed ideas rather than from the artistic exploitation of utilitarian necessities. This conviction is becoming rare in an era of little faith, but Peter Moro and Partners have shown that, with such convictions, they can produce architecture of consistently fine quality.

—J. M. McKean

MORTLOCK, Bryce.
Australian. Born in Lithgow, New South Wales, 14 October 1921. Educated at the University of Sydney School of Architecture, under Leslie Wilkinson, and George Molnar, 1946–50 (George McCrae Prize for Construction, 1949), B.Arch. (honours and University Medal) 1950; worked in the office of Sydney Ancher, Sydney, 1948–50; awarded Byera Hadley Travelling Scholarship, 1951; travelled in England and Europe, 1950–52. Served as Flying Officer and Instructor in the Royal Australian Air Force, in Australia and Canada, 1942–45. Married Peggy Evelyn Worley in 1948; children: Peter, Richard, and Philip. Worked in the Architect's Department of the London County Council, 1950–52; Partner, with Sydney Ancher, q.v., and Stuart Murray, q.v., Ancher, Mortlock and Murray, Sydney, 1953–64, and, with Ancher, Murray, and Ken Woolley, q.v., Ancher, Mortlock, Murray and Woolley, Sydney, 1964–69; Director, Ancher, Mortlock, Murray and Woolley Pty. Ltd., Sydney, 1969–75. Since 1975, Director, Ancher, Mortlock and Woolley Pty. Ltd., Sydney. Master Planner, University of Melbourne, since 1968; Director, Australian Building Industry Specifications Pty. Ltd., Sydney, since 1975. Member of the Council since 1960, Honorary Treasurer, 1964–66, Vice-President, 1966–70, and President, 1970–72, Royal Australian Institute of Architects, New South Wales Chapter; Member, New South Wales Board of Architects, 1968–72; Member of the Advisory Committee to the New South Wales Minister for Housing, 1968–75; Chairman of the Finance Committee, 1973, Member of the Council, 1973, Vice-President, 1973–75, and President, 1975–76, federal RAIA. Exhibitions: Student Design Exhibition, London, 1951; *Ancher, Mortlock, Murray and Woolley, Sydney Architects, 1946–76,* Art Gallery of New South Wales, 1976, and Australian tour, 1977. Recipient: Alfred Bossom Medal, London, 1951; Sulman Prize, 1960, and Merit Award, 1972, Royal Australian Institute of Architects, New South Wales Chapter; Queen's Jubilee Medal, 1977. Fellow, 1963, and Life Fellow, 1970, Royal Australian Institute of Architects. Address: Ancher, Mortlock and Woolley Pty. Ltd., 10 Ridge Street, North Sydney, New South Wales 2060, Australia.

Works:

1954 House, Rayner Road, Whale Beach, New South Wales
1955 House, Ulm Street, Lane Cove, New South Wales
      House, Flaumont Avenue, Lane Cove, New South Wales
1956 House, Stonehaven Avenue, West Dubbo, New South Wales
1958 House, Herbert Avenue, Newport, New South Wales
1959 Badham House, Dolans Road, Cronulla, New South Wales
      House, Hendy Avenue, Collaroy, New South Wales
      House, Hull Road, Beecroft, New South Wales
1960 Materials and Structures Laboratory, University of Sydney
1961 House, Milray Avenue, Wollstonecraft, New South Wales
      Ski Lodge, Thredbo, New South Wales
      Civil Engineering Building, University of Sydney
1962 House, Cowdroy Avenue, Cammeray, New South Wales
1963 Chemical Engineering Building, University of Sydney
      House, Boronia Parade, Lugarno, New South Wales
      House, Karoo Avenue, East Lindfield, New South Wales
1964 Dental surgery, 40 Haldon Street, Lakemba, New South Wales
      House, Coppins Close, St. Ives, New South Wales
1965 Electrical Engineering Building, University of Sydney
      House, Mount Panorama, Bathurst, New South Wales

House, Boronia Parade, Lugarno, New South Wales
      House, Castle Hill, Townsville, Queensland
1967 Peter Nicol Russell Engineering Faculty Building, University of Sydney
1968 Control Plan for Housing Development, Lyons, A.C.T.
1969 Town houses, 18 Shirley Road, Wollstonecraft, New South Wales
      Royal Australian Institute of Architects Headquarters, 2a Mugga Way, Red Hill, A.C.T.
      Student Union Building, Macquarie University, North Ryde, New South Wales (with Ken Woolley)
1970 Army Holiday Centre, Terrigal, New South Wales
      Master plan for the University of Melbourne
1971 Redevelopment area control plan for Turramurra, New South Wales
1972 City Office Building, 3 Spring Street, Sydney (with McConnel, Smith and Johnson)
      Town houses, 20 Almora Street, Mosman, New South Wales
      House, Fennell Bay, New South Wales
1974 Sports and Recreation Complex Control Plan, Mitchell College of Advanced Education, Bathurst, New South Wales
1975 Initial development work for the National Building Specification
      Durham Street Sports Centre Control Plan, Bathurst, New South Wales
      Markets Campus Plan, New South Wales Institute of Technology, Sydney
1977 University Square Precinct Plan, University of Melbourne

Publications:

By MORTLOCK: books—*University of Melbourne Master Plan Report,* Melbourne 1970; *University of Melbourne Landscape Elements Report,* Melbourne 1974; *BIAC Report No. 5: The Use of the Master Specification,* Sydney 1974; *BIAC Report No. 16: A Building Classification System,* Sydney 1975; articles —"Model of the Design Process and the Problem of Values" in *Architecture in Australia* (Sydney), December 1965; "Towards a Reform of SfB" in *The Architects' Journal* (London), April, May, June 1966; "The Architect in the Community" in *Royal Australian Institute of Architects Journal* (Sydney), 1967; book review in *Australian Quarterly* (Sydney), vol. 40, no. 2, 1968; "Design of Union Buildings" in *University of Adelaide Union Newsletter,* August 1969; "President's Message" (editorials) in *Royal Australian Institute of Architects Bulletin* (Sydney), 1970–72; "Observations on McEwen's *Crisis in Architecture*" in *Architecture in Australia* (Sydney), June 1975; "Commonsense Conservation" in *Architecture in Australia* (Sydney), April/May 1977; "University of Melbourne—University Square Precinct Report" in *Architecture in Australia* (Sydney), July 1977.

On MORTLOCK: book—*Ancher, Mortlock, Murray and Woolley, Sydney Architects, 1946–76,* catalogue by David Saunders and Catherine Bourke, Sydney 1976.

During the 1950's and 60's progressive architects believed that modern architecture's mission was to change the world. The pre-war prophecies of the European moderns—Corbusier, Gropius, Mies and others—were about to be fulfilled. New pure building forms would be based on Cezanne's cube, cone and cylinder. Modern technology would give us new, more efficient building methods and materials. Corb's Radiant City—immense slab blocks on pilotis separated by vast public open spaces—would make existing cities obsolete, to be swept away by comprehensive redevelopment and "sun, space, verdure." People's lives would be transformed. Henceforth

Bryce Mortlock: Royal Australian Institute of Architects Headquarters, Red Hill, A.C.T., 1969

they would be healthier, happier, richer, and eternally grateful for the benefits of modern art and architecture.

Well, of course, today it is only too obvious that it didn't work out like that. For one thing, environmental determinism—the effect of the environment on behaviour—had been grossly overestimated. The ethologists—Lorenz, Tinbergen, Morris, Ardrey, and many others have shown that environments change species only through the mechanism of heredity over many generations and only when survival is involved. Man is no exception. The changes which modern architecture could make to man's environment had little effect on his survival as a species.

But they had a big effect on his capacity for being outraged, and it was the opposite of what modern architects intended. On the whole, people didn't like the new architecture. They acquired spokesmen like Malcolm MacEwen in *Crisis in Architecture* and Conrad Jamieson on BBC-TV. The mutterings swelled to a chorus and spread to the Sunday papers.

Baiting the professions is a popular sport, and the outrage has no doubt been exaggerated; after all, modern architecture has had its popular triumphs too. However, I think one point at least can be made, that insofar as architecture claimed to change the world, the world has given it the thumbs down. Comprehensive development is now a dirty word; it has destroyed potential conservation areas and scattered close-knit communities. The wind whistles through the undercrofts of the post-Corb skyscraper slums; at Pruitt-Igo in the U.S. they even resorted to blowing up the buildings. The spaces between skyscrapers became no man's land owned and loved by nobody. As to land-use efficiency, the residential densities were no higher than in the Georgian squares of London.

Utopia through architecture proved elusive, but unfortunately we didn't stop there. We laid claim to be guardians of the whole environment. I think it was Einstein who first said "the environment is everything that isn't me," and of course everybody is entitled to take an intelligent interest in what so closely concerns him. But we went further than that, and in so doing set outselves up.

The environment became popular, and the heavies began to get into the act. Activist groups were formed to usurp the functions of government. Unions backed them. Builder's labourers took over planning. Everybody began minding everyone else's business.

In the middle of all this were the architects, with negligible political leverage, but in a most vulnerable position as potential scapegoats. Why? Because our work comes at the end of the decision-making chain. All the important decisions affecting the built environment—use, density, built form—are already made by politicians, aldermen, and planners by the time we come on the scene. The gross effects of bad planning decisions will not be mitigated by architectural treatment, no matter how sensitive. But the activist public ignores these decisions until they are embodied in our designs. Then it is we who are the villains, and we who are expected to bring the whole juggernaut to a halt by our sacrifice.

I think the time has come for us to give a lead in a new direction, towards minding one's own business. Voltaire's Candide, at the end of all his adventures, concluded that "il faut cultiver notre jardin." Our architectural garden has always been designing buildings and getting them built. Let us get on with cultivating it, to the best of our ability. If everybody did that, we'd make a better world.

—Bryce Mortlock

Bryce Mortlock first became well known when his Badham House received the Sulman Prize for the best building of the year. The style comprised a true, detailed modular layout, simple materials sensitively but often unconventionally chosen, with an absence of applied finishes. The rational arrangement of economical materials and direct details anticipated what Robin Boyd later called the "Sydney School." It is in line with the Australian tradition of controlling sunlight to limit heat gain in summer while making the best use of it in winter, and of using natural materials such as timber and brick.

In the 1960's many architects in Sydney had the opportunity for large-scale work, and Bryce Mortlock's logical pragmatic approach produced a series of functional and economic buildings, particularly for universities. He was involved not merely in the design of individual buildings but also in university precinct design and eventually in the planning of entire campuses, applying his principles to the logical use of land and the creation of spaces rather than building sites.

Bryce Mortlock was elected to the Council of the New South Wales Chapter of the Royal Australian Institute of Architects in 1960, became Chapter President in 1970, and Federal President in 1975. He was a highly articulate president. He was also active in devising a better method for specifications, which led to the development of a standard specification by a commercial computer specification service, whose copyright he donated to the Royal Australian Institute of Architects.

—Henry Cowan

MOSER, Werner M(ax).

Swiss. Born in Karlsruhe, Germany, 16 July 1896. Educated at E.T.H.: Eidgenössische Technische Hochschule, Zurich, under his father Karl Moser, 1915–19, Dip.Arch. 1919. Married Silva Schindler in 1923; children: Lorenz, Ruth, and Claudia. Worked in Rotterdam, 1921–22, with Frank Lloyd Wright, in Taliesin, Wisconsin, 1923–26, and in his father's architectural studio, Zurich, 1926. In private practice, Zurich, from 1928: in partnership with Max Haefeli and Rudolf Steiger from 1938. Visiting Lecturer, Harvard University, Cambridge, Massachusetts, 1955; Professor, E.T.H., Zurich, 1958–63. Exhibitions: *Der Neue Schulbau*, Kunstgewerbemuseum, Zurich, 1932; *Switzerland Planning and Building Exhibition*, Royal Institute of British Architects, London, 1946; *Frank Lloyd Wright*, Zurich, 1950. Dr.Ing.: Technical University, Stuttgart, 1958. Member, Bund Schweizer Architekten, and Schweizerischer Werkbund. Honorary Fellow, Royal Institute of British Architects. Member, Akademie der Künste, Berlin. *Died* (in Zurich) *19 August 1970.*

Works:

1923 Office building, Chicago (project)
1926 Terraced houses, Zürichbergstrasse, Zurich (project)
1929 Hagmann Boathouse, Erlenbach, Zurich (with Emil Roth)
1930 Semi-detached house, Hegibachstrasse, Zurich
    Budgeheim Old People's Home, Frankfurt (with Mart Stam)
    Eglisee Housing Development, Basle (with Emil Roth)
1931 Moser/Guggenbühl House, Eierbrechtstrasse, Zurich
1932 Neubühl Housing Development, Zurich (with Artaria and Schmidt, Max Haefeli, Rudolf Steiger and Emil Roth)
    Collegiate Building, Basle (competition project)
1933 Höngg School Complex, Zurich (competition project)
1934 Chiodera House, Küsnacht, Zurich
    Affoltern Church Hall, Zurich (competition project)
1935 Sury House, Riehen, Basle
1937 Studio Gubler, Unterengstringen, Switzerland
    Von Schulthess House, Zollikon, Zurich
1939 Congress Building and Concert Hall, Zurich (with Max Haefeli and Rudolf Steiger)
    Allenmoos Swimming Pool, Zurich (with Max Haefeli)
1941 Alstetten Reform Church, Zurich
1945 Prilly Housing Development, Lausanne (project)
1950 New Apostle Church, Geneva
    Church, Witikon, Switzerland (project)
1952 Cantonal Hospital, Zurich (with AKZ)
1953 Kienberger House, God Laret, St. Moritz, Switzerland
    Housing development, Hohenbühlstrasse, Zurich (with Max Haefeli)
1954 Fretz House, Zumikon, Zurich
    Eternit AG Office Building, Niederurnen Glarus, Switzerland (with Max Haefeli)
1957 Farbhof Housing Development, Alstetten, Zurich (with Max Haefeli and Rudolf Steiger)
1959 Jona School, Rapperswil, Switzerland (competition project)
1961 Dental Institute, University of Zurich
    E. F. Schmidt House, Rüschlikon, Switzerland
1962 Kornfeld Church, Riehen, Basle
1964 Palme Building, Zurich (with Max Haefeli, Rudolf Steiger, and André Studer)
1965 Aula University, Zurich (project)
1966 Neubühl Old People's Housing Development, Zurich (with Max Haefeli and Rudolf Steiger)
1967 ASM Administration Building, Zurich (with Max Haefeli and Rudolf Steiger)
1968 Bally Capitol, Bahnhofstrasse, Zurich
1973 Bungertwies School, Zurich (with Max Haefeli)

Publications:

By MOSER: books—*Das Kind und sein Schulhaus,* with Gonzenbach and Schohaus, Zurich 1933; *Frank Lloyd Wright: Sechzig Jahre Lebendige Architektur,* Winterthur, Switzerland 1952; *Wandlungen im Reformierten Kirchenbau in den Letzten Hundert Jahren,* Riehen, Switzerland 1965; *Gedanken über die Schweizer Architektur von 1916–1958,* Zurich 1969; articles—"Das Verhalten des Laien zur Heutigen Baukunst" in *Schweizerische Technische Zeitschrift* (Waben, Switzerland), no. 46, 1956; "Frank Lloyd Wright" in *Bouwkundig Weekblaad* (Antwerp), November 1959; "Die Bedeutung Frank Lloyd Wright für die Entwicklung der Gegenwartsarchitektur" in *Werk* (Zurich), December 1959; "Beiträge zur Schulbaureform" in *Schweizerische Bauzeitung* (Zurich), April 1965.

On MOSER: articles—"Double House near Zurich, Switzerland" in *Architectural Record* (New York), May 1934; "Tonhalle und Kongresshaus, Zurich" in *Werk* (Zurich), December 1939; "Bemerkungen zum Modernen Wohnhausbau" by Friedrich T. Gubler in *Werk* (Zurich), February 1941; "The Congress Building in Zurich" in *Architect and Building News* (London), March 1941; "House at Zollikon" in *Architectural Review* (London), March 1945; "Eglise à Zurich" in *L'Architecture d'Aujourd'hui* (Paris), December 1946; "Kerk te Zurich-Altstetten" in *Bouwkundig Weekblaad* (Antwerp), August 1948; "Werner Moser zum Siebzigsten Geburtstag" in *Werk* (Zurich), July 1966; "Swimming Baths and Sports Hall in School Complex, Zurich-Hottingen" in *Schweizerische Bauzeitung* (Zurich), November 1973; "Railway Architecture in Switzerland: Past Work and Three Contemporary Examples" by Bruno Oldermatt in *Schweizerische Bauzeitung* (Zurich), July 1974.

Werner M. Moser belongs to the generation that established modern architecture in Switzerland. Like Max Haefeli, Rudolf Steiger, Hans Schmidt and Hans Wittwer, he studied at the E.T.H., Zurich, under his father Karl Moser. Yet, during the years 1915–19, when Karl Moser was totally committed to neo-clasicism, Werner Moser's early designs were marked by the influence of expressionism. There were other influences too. During his studies he spent some time with Paul Bonatz in Stuttgart; after graduation, like many other young architects of the time, he worked in Holland; and in 1923 he went to the United States where he worked with Frank Lloyd Wright. Wright's influence is evident in Moser's design for a multi-story Chicago office building—at the same time the project reveals Moser's unequivocal adoption of "modernism."

After he returned to Switzerland, Moser's work revealed his adherence to the tenets of European New Building. Its peculiarly Swiss characteristics were a regard for topography, a breaking away from severe stereometry, and a preoccupation with design. During this period Moser was primarily concerned with school building. He took part in the school building exhibition in Zurich in 1932, published a book on the subject, *Das Kind und sein Schulhaus,* in 1933, and his designs and projects influenced school building in Switzerland for the next decade. Another important interest of his early work was the housing development: with collaborators, he built two Woba Union estates, the Eglisee Housing Development in Basle and the Neubühl Housing Development in Zurich. In these estates—in common with much of modern Swiss architecture—there is strong attention to detail, fine technical execution, and a particular attention to individual rooms. The components—standards of "classical modernism"—are slim, light-weight, and of high quality; there is a variety of materials, and the lighting effects are subtle.

Moser's joint practice with Haefeli and Steiger sprang from their friendship and similar interests. They received a number of major public commissions including the Congress Building and Concert Hall, the Allenmoos Swimming Pool, and the Cantonal Hospital—all in Zurich. These designs have in common their structure, emphasis of tactile qualities, open wall and ceiling elements, continuity of space sequence, transparent (planted) room dividers, and indirect lighting. They are also attempts to create a new festive and ceremonial monumentality in public buildings. They try, too, to relate well to their environments. The swimming pool, for instance, "fits" the totality of its park landscape: green areas are threaded in; the pavilions have a "provisional" quality.

Werner M. Moser: Congress Building, Zurich, 1939

Moser is now most remembered for his handling of space in his post-war plans for housing developments. He took into account the scale of the surroundings. High, medium and low-rise buildings were combined, and he treated the multi-storey building as a town planning element with diverse uses.

Moser was also interested in church building. He wrote on the subject, and he experimented in his own churches—putting the new in an old context (Altstetten Reform Church, Zurich), giving in to the influence of Wright (New Apostle Church, Geneva), or trying out the ideas of Aalto (Kornfeld Church, Riehen).

His openness and his versatility—characteristics that made him a memorable architect—also marked his relationship with his students at the E.T.H.

—Ulrike Jehle-Schulte Strathaus

MOYA, (John) Hidalgo.

British. Born in Los Gatos, California, 5 May 1920. Educated at Oundle School; Royal West of England School of Art, Bristol, 1937–38; Architectural Association School, London, 1938–43, Dip.A.A. 1943. Married Jannifer Mary Innes Hall in 1947; children: Susan, Timothy, and Joanna. Partner, with Philip Powell, q.v., Powell and Moya, and Powell, Moya and Partners, London, since 1946 (Michael Powell, Powell, and Moya, 1946–50; Powell and Moya, 1950–61; Powell, Moya, Robert Henley and Peter Skinner, 1961–73; Powell, Moya, and Skinner, 1973–76; Powell, Moya, Skinner, John Cantwell, and Bernard Throp, since 1976). Exhibitions: Royal Institute of British Architects, London, 1974; Royal Academy, London, yearly since 1974. Recipient: First Prize, Pimlico Housing Competition, London, 1946; Bronze Medal, 1950, 1958, 1961, Architectural Award, 1967, and Royal Gold Medal, 1974, Royal Institute of British Architects; Festival of Britain Award, 1951; Civic Trust Award, 1961; Project Award, Architectural Design, 1965. Associate of the Royal Institute of British Architects, 1956. C.B.E. (Commander, Order of the British Empire), 1966. Address: Powell, Moya and Partners, 21 Upper Cheyne Row, London SW3 5JW, England.

See POWELL, Sir Philip

MUCHOW, William C(harles).

American. Born in Denver, Colorado, 28 July 1922. Educated at the University of Notre Dame, Indiana; University of Illinois, Urbana, B.Arch. 1947; Cranbrook Academy of Art, Bloomfield Hills, Michigan, under Eliel Saarinen, M.Arch. and Urban Planning 1948; awarded Rome Prize, 1948. Served in the United States Navy, 1942–46: Lieutenant junior grade; Captain of the U.S.S. Lovelace DE 198. Married Priscilla Williams in 1948; children: Mark, Marcelyn, Brian, Daryl and Kim. Since 1950, Principal of William C. Muchow Associates, Architects, Denver. Director, Key Savings and Loan Association, since 1972. Member, Colorado State Board of Architectural Examiners, 1967–77; President, National Council of Architectural Registration Boards, 1975–76; Member, Jury of Fellows, 1977–79, and Chairman of the National Awards Committee, 1978, American Institute of Architects. Director, Downtown Denver Inc., since 1969, and the American Automobile Association, since 1970; Member, International Advisory Board, United States General Services Administration, since 1972. Exhibitions: Hardwood Industry Exhibition, Museum of Science and Industry, Chicago, 1955 (furniture), 1959 (building); Muchow Associates, Colorado State University, Fort Collins, 1976; American Association of School Administrators Exhibition, Las Vegas, Nevada, 1977, and Atlanta, Georgia, 1978. Recipient: Award of Merit, 1954, and Honor Award, 1975, American Institute of Architects; Award of Merit, AIA/Sunset Magazine, 1957; Award of Excellence, Architectural Record, 1957; Award of Merit, 1957, 1958, 1967, 1969, 1974, 1976, Design Award, 1960, First Honor Award, 1964, and Honor Award, 1964, 1969 (twice), 1972, AIA, Western Mountain Region; First Honor Award, 1961, 1965, and Design Award, 1977, AIA, Colorado Chapter; Award of Excellence, American Institute of Steel Construction, 1961; Award of Honor, AIA/Structural Clay Products Institute, 1963; Design Award, 1963, and First Design Award, 1971, Progressive Architecture; First Place, Denver Convention Center Competition, 1965; First Honor Award, AIA/United States Office of Education, 1966; Honor Award, AIA, Colorado Chapter/Structural Clay Products Institute, 1969; Placque Award, Downtown Denver Inc., 1974; Barlett Award, President's Committee on Employment of the Handicapped, 1975; Special Service Award Citation, Society of American Registered Architects, 1975; Special Citation, AIA/American Association of School Administrators, 1976; Honor Award, Construction Specifications Institute, 1977. Fellow, American Institute of Architects, 1968. Address: Muchow Associates, 3707 Cherry Creek North Drive, Denver, Colorado 80209, U.S.A.

Works:

1951	Texas Company Office Building, Denver
1952	Merino High School, Merino, Colorado
1953	Two parking garages, Denver (with Fisher and Fisher)
1954	Muchow House, 618 South Monroe Way, Denver
	First Federal Savings and Loan Building, Denver
1956	Brentwood Methodist Church additions, Denver
1958	Mullen High School, Fort Logan, Colorado
	Merino Elementary School, Merino, Colorado
	West Lakewood Elementary School, Lakewood, Colorado
	Washington Park Congregational Church, Denver
	Loveland Ski Lodge, Loveland Basin, Colorado
1960	First Federal Savings and Loan Building additions, Denver
1961	Public Service Building, Denver (with Berne, Baume and Polvnick)
	888 Logan Apartments, Denver (with Nat Sachter)
	Cherry Creek Medical Building, Denver
	Rockland Community Church, Lookout Mountain, Colorado
	Women's Club Building, Denver
	Silver State Savings and Loan Building, Aurora, Colorado
1962	Prince of Peace Church remodelling, Denver
	First Federal Savings and Loan Building, Englewood, Colorado
	Capitol Federal Savings and Loan Building, Arvada, Colorado
1964	Methodist Church, Littleton, Colorado
	First National Bank, Loveland, Colorado
	Lincoln Towers Office Building, Denver (with Robert Hiester)
	Silver State Savings and Loan Main Office Building, Denver
1965	Engineering Sciences Center, University of Colorado, Boulder (with Architectural Associates)
1966	First United Presbyterian Church, Denver
	Anchor Savings Association Building, Lawrence, Kansas
	Congdon House, 4150 East Quincy, Englewood, Colorado
1968	First Methodist Church, Laramie, Wyoming
	Federal Reserve Bank, Denver (with Ken R. White)
	Methodist Church, Cheyenne, Wyoming
	Dormitories, Hiram Scott College, Scottsbluff, Nebraska
	Bonfils-Stanton Regional Library, Lakewood, Colorado
1969	Logan Office Building, Denver
	Currigan Exhibition Hall, Denver (with Ream and Larson)
1970	Financial Programs Office Building, Denver
	Marina Center, Yellowstone National Park, Wyoming
	West Entrance Station, Yellowstone National Park, Wyoming
	Savings and Loan Building, Loveland, Colorado
	Bergen Elementary School, Bergen Park, Colorado
	Denver Center Office Building, Denver
	Lions Head Gondola Terminals, Vail, Colorado
	Farmers Union Office Building, Denver
1971	Albert L. Place Junior High School, Denver
	Denver Technical Center Building II, Englewood, Colorado
	Diners Club Office Building, Englewood, Colorado
1972	Jewish Community Center, Denver
	Lincoln Center Office Building, Denver
	Administration Building, Winter Park, Colorado (with Haller and Larson)
1973	Hellenic Orthodox Church, Denver (with Haller and Larson)
	Park Central Office Building, Denver
	Hamilton Life Insurance Building, Englewood, Colorado
1974	Fleming Law Building, University of Colorado, Boulder
	Del Pueblo Elementary School, Denver
	Greeley National Bank, Greeley, Colorado (with CNC/NHPQ)
	Blue Cross/Blue Shield Office Building, Denver (with Ken R. White)
	KKBNA Office Building, Lakewood, Colorado
	Laredo Middle School, Englewood, Colorado (with Haller and Larson)
	Office building, 18th and Central, Denver
1975	Henry Junior High School, Denver
	Fine Arts Center, Colorado State University, Fort Collins
	Cherry Creek Performing Arts Center, Englewood, Colorado
	First Presbyterian Church additions, Boulder, Colorado
	First National Bank, Westminster, Colorado
	Auraria Higher Education Center Master Plan, Colorado (with A-5 Denver Inc.)
	Auraria Higher Education Center Administration and Shops Buildings, Colorado (with A-5 Denver Inc.)
	Smoky Hill High School, Englewood, Colorado (with Haller and Larson)
	Metrobank Building, Denver
1976	Margaret Walters School for the Retarded, Arvada, Colorado
	Robert Weiland School for the Retarded, Lakewood, Colorado
	Heritage Elementary School, Englewood, Colorado (with Haller and Larson)
1978	Parking Garage, Denver Center for the Performing Arts
	Governmental complex, Littleton, Colorado
	Water Board Administration Building, Denver
	Water Board Shops Building, Denver
	Cherry Creek High School III, Englewood, Colorado (with Haller and Larson)
1979	Events and Conference Center, University of Colorado, Boulder (with Haller and Larson)

William C. Muchow: Engineering Sciences Center, University of Colorado, Boulder, 1965

Publications:

On MUCHOW: books—*Banken und Sparkassen,* Munich 1961; *Mid-Century Architecture in America,* Baltimore 1961; *Contemporary Houses Evaluated by Their Owners* by Thomas H. Creighton and Katherine M. Ford, New York 1961; *City Halls and Emergency Operating Centers,* Office of Civil Defense Brochure TR 32, Washington, D.C. 1966; *Existing Schools: Their Future,* Office of Civil Defense Brochure TR 53, Washington, D.C. 1968; *Housing: Adventures in Design,* New York 1973; *Architecture in America: Pictorial History,* vols. 1 and 2, by G. E. Kidder Smith, New York 1976.

William Muchow is a very successful practicing architect in Denver, Colorado, where nearly all of his architectural work is to be found. He has been able to combine a financially rewarding architectural career with a very high degree of design quality. His work has kept the Denver area abreast of leading international trends in architecture, although it has perhaps not been directly innovative of those trends. The look of the buildings is cosmopolitan; there is no particular striving to create a "Rocky Mountain Look."

Muchow's design philosophy stresses conscious awareness of technical and spatial problems, the solutions to which produce the envelope or facade of the building. Strictly speaking, there is no facade, as the technical/spatial approach produces "honest" buildings, the insides of which directly map unto the outside surface. The buildings have in effect been designed from the inside out. The "form making" then becomes an unconscious selection producing many alternatives which are successively eliminated, again for largely technical reasons. The language or expressive quality of a Muchow-designed building, then, tends to be an excellent representative of designed objects which communicate primarily the implicit value systems of a culture through explicit technological and technical excellence.

A case in point is the celebrated Blue Cross/Blue Shield building in Denver, which has become a kind of local urban landmark. Building-height and zoning limitations produced an air-space or envelope which even when fully filled was hardly financially promising, given local land costs. The solution was to totally fill the air space and send cars to below the building so that no precious land would be wasted on auto access or parking. The resulting building is a conventional skyscraper lying on its side, in the air, with autos sitting under it. The internal circulation plan is signalled on the outside by an outrageous red stripe going down the middle of the sleeping giant. The building, then, through strict attention to technical and spatial problems, is not only extremely interesting and visually striking, but also even a witty if restrained comment on contemporary high-rise architecture. It celebrates this culture's preoccupation with efficiency and tool-like neatness, but in carrying that preoccupation to an extreme becomes an artistic expression of it—perhaps pushing people into a new and deepened awareness of themselves and their values.

The same approach to the Engineering Center at the University of Colorado, Boulder, produced right-side-up, high-rise classroom buildings that tower over the local low-rise, "hill-town" look and psychologically challenge the Rocky Mountain foothills to a face-off. The rigorous and unbending attention to space needs again turned the local scene topsy-turvy, gently mocking Boulder's rural pretensions.

What is missing in all this is an attention to people not as consumers or clients but as users of the insides of the buildings. One is tempted to paraphrase Amos Rapoport and say that, although strictly socio-cultural solutions in architecture often produce technical excellence, sheer attention to technical excellence rarely is satisfactory from a socio-cultural standpoint. Indeed, one could hardly produce a more succinct statement of the unconscious values of our culture than that it values technology more than human beings.

—Joseph B. Juhasz

MULLER, Peter.

Australian. Born in Adelaide, South Australia, 3 July 1927. Educated at St. Peter's School, Adelaide, 1944; University of Adelaide, 1944–48, B.E. 1948; South Australian School of Mines and Industries, Adelaide, 1945–48, F.S.A.S.M.I. 1948; University of Pennsylvania, Philadelphia, 1950–51 (South Australian Travelling Scholarship; Fulbright Scholarship; University Tuition Fellowship), M.Arch. 1951. Married Rosemary Winn Patrick in 1953 (divorced, 1964); married Carole Margaret Mason in 1964; children: Peter, Suzy, and James (died). Since 1953, Principal, The Office of Peter Muller, Sydney; since 1978, Principal, Regional Design and Research, Consultants, Marulan, New South Wales (associates: interior design—Alan Gilbert; research—Adrian Snodgrass; contracts—Christopher Carlisle). Visiting Tutor, University of New South Wales, Sydney, 1962; Director, National Capital Development Commission, Canberra, 1975–77. Address: The Office of Peter Muller, Marulan, New South Wales 2580, Australia.

Works:

1952   Audette House, Edinburgh Road, Castlecrag, Sydney
1954   Winns Department Store, Ware Street, Fairfield, Sydney
       Peter Muller House, 42 Bynya Road, Whale Beach, Sydney
1955   Walcott House, 40 Bynya Road, Whale Beach, Sydney
1956   Richardson House, 949 Barrenjoey Road, Palm Beach, Sydney
1957   McGrath House, 4 Dunara Gardens, Point Piper, Sydney

Nicholson House, Angophora Crescent, Forestville, Sydney
1958   Walker House, 21 Arterial Road, St. Ives, Sydney
       Kindergarten, Barrenjoey Road, Palm Beach, Sydney
       Victa Administration Building, 318 Horsley Road, Milperra, Sydney
       Ward House, Foote Street, Templestowe, Melbourne
1959   Sculfer House, Livistonia Lane, Palm Beach, Sydney
       Richardson Ski Lodge, Thredbo Village, New South Wales
       Fogarty House: Dunalister Stud, Elmore, Victoria
1960   Southside Plaza Shopping Centre, Rockdale, Sydney
       McGrath Ski Lodge, Thredbo Village, New South Wales
       Gunning House, 369 Edinburgh Road, Castlecrag, Sydney
1960/
78   Craftbuilt Prototype Houses (8), various locations around Sydney
1961   Patrick House, The Scarp, Castlecrag, Sydney
       Park House, Prince Alfred Parade, Newport, Sydney
1962   Creaser House, 1 Womerah Street, Turramurra, Sydney
       Hamilton House, 1 Pindari Place, Bayview, Sydney
       Purcell House, 14 Fisher Street, Balgowlah, Sydney
       Lance House, 1 Lindsay Avenue, Darling Point, Sydney

Barling House, 4 Paradise Avenue, Clareville Beach, Sydney
1963   Barton House, Morella Place, Castlecove, Sydney
       Green House, 7 Wolseley Road, Point Piper, Sydney
       Walder House, Cabarita Road, Stokes Point, Sydney
1964   Lance House, Coolong Road, Vaucluse, Sydney
       Mitchell House, 20 Robe Terrace, Adelaide
       I.P.E.C. Headquarters, 259 Glen Osmond Road, Frewville, Adelaide
       Greenwood House, Mulgowrie Avenue, Balgowlah, Sydney
1965   Walder House, 61a Kambala Road, Bellevue Hill, Sydney
       I.P.E.C. Airfreight Terminal, Launceston, Tasmania
       Carroll House, Rockbath Road, Palm Beach, Sydney
       McArthur House, Tor Walk, Castlecrag, Sydney
1966   Dickson Hotel, Dickson, Canberra
       Hoyts Drive-in Theatre, Tamworth, New South Wales
1967   Hoyts Drive-in Theatre, Casula, Sydney
       Hoyts Cinema Centre, Bourke Street, Melbourne
1968   McGrath House, 8 Castra Place, Double Bay, Sydney
       Hoyts Drive-in Theatre, Bulleen Road, Bulleen, Melbourne
       Hoyts Drive-in Theatre, Mountain Highway, Wantirna, Melbourne
       Regent/Paris Theatres and Arcade, Rundle Street, Adelaide

Peter Muller: Peter Muller House, Whale Beach, Sydney, 1954

1969 Town houses, Trelawney Street, Woollahra, Sydney

Turner House, 8 Sylvan Avenue, East Lindfield, Sydney

1970 Dulhunty Homestead: Nant Lodge, Glen Innes, New South Wales (with Albert Read)

Steidler House, 9 Wentworth Street, Point Piper, Sydney (with Albert Read)

1971 Snider House, 12 Wolseley Crescent, Point Piper, Sydney (with Albert Read)

Woolf House, 7 Gulliver Avenue, Vaucluse, Sydney (with Albert Read)

Burrell Homestead: Rockdale, Armidale, New South Wales

1972 Peter Muller House II, Ubud, Bali, Indonesia

1973 Kayu Aya Hotel, Seminyak Kuta Beach, Bali, Indonesia

1978 Lian Cove Hotel, Batangus Luzon, Philippines

Publications:

By MULLER: monographs—*The Esoteric Nature of Griffin's Design for Canberra,* Canberra 1976; *The New and Permanent Parliament House,* with others, Canberra 1977.

On MULLER: book—*An Australian Identity* by Jennifer Taylor, Sydney 1972; articles—"Molinari House" in *Architecture and Arts* (Melbourne), July 1954; "Audette House" in *Architecture in Australia* (Sydney), July/September 1955; special issue of *Architecture and Arts* (Melbourne), December 1955; "Peter Muller House" in *Architecture in Australia* (Sydney), January/March 1956; "Richardon House" in *Architecture and Arts* (Melbourne), August 1956; "House by Peter Muller" in *L'Architettura* (Rome), August 1958; "Craftbuilt Houses" in *Architecture in Australia* (Sydney), September 1961; article by David Saunders in *Art and Architecture* (Sydney), June 1971.

The extent of our understanding and the intensity of our search for meaning and significance is more truthfully reflected and intuitively embodied in the work itself, rather than in anything said.

The power of the Gothic cathedral is locked within the building fabric and the enclosed spaces. The Knights Templar must have believed that any explanation of the inner mysteries of the building would reduce one's intuitive apprehension to a merely intellectual appreciation, thereby imposing upon it all of the attendant limitations, variations and quantifications peculiar to each and every individual.

In an inverse way, the proselytising zeal of today, which aims to explain all, leaves nothing to the imagination. The works may be very professional, technically refined and socially experimental, but they are, however, strangely devoid of inner life and certainly of humour.

—Peter Muller

Peter Muller was the earliest and most original of a circle of Sydney architects in the 1950's who were influenced by Frank Lloyd Wright. By nature an independent individual, he preferred to work alone, seeking new and innovative solutions to problems that arose from his particular response to a site or a client. His determination to use natural materials, to avoid synthetic finishes, and his feeling for the Australian landscape, infected many of his Sydney contemporaries. But it was his creative attitude that set him apart, for much Australian architecture was derivative—and still is—borrowing, whenever necessary, stylistic terms from Europe and America. Muller avoided subservience to overseas styles by allowing himself to be influenced by cultures rather than by styles. He identified with the spiritual principles within a culture and so attained a deeper understanding of that culture's architecture. This attitude

tion of industrialism in his architecture: if anything, his buildings have been a retort to the new International Style. In his Bali hotel he was ideally placed to immerse himself in Balinese culture and to tap the rich decorative possibilities of Balinese crafts. Burley Griffin's buildings.

Wright had a direct influence on Muller, but there can be no doubt that Muller developed in an independent way, that his vision of architecture was sufficiently strong to be sufficiently his own, and that his distance from Wright enabled him to work in a freer manner than Wright's own students. This "distance" is crucial, because it enabled Muller to develop according to his own lights, and while there are similarities in their work Muller has to be seen as an independent architect pursuing an organic ideal within the Australian context, rather than as a slavish neo-Wrightian.

Muller's architecture is characterized by a strong sense of geometry and axial composition; the repetition of simple geometrical elements imparts a pervasive unity to the forms, while the axial disposition of the parts responds to the romantic ideal of a building that is whole and simultaneously in a mystical union with nature. Muller has employed four different kinds of geometry—rectangular shapes organized about several opposed axes, usually three, of which one is dominant (Audette House; Muller House, Whale Beach); a related kind consisting of overlapping or connected squares along a diagonal growth axis (Nicholson House; Walcott House); a hexagonal geometry similar to Wright's; and circles (Richardson House).

Muller's private practice began almost as soon as he returned from overseas in 1952, when he was asked to design Audette House. It is, to some extent, an immature work; it featured exposed timber trusses in much the same fashion as Taliesin West. The form of the building was defined by three axes; there was a longitudinal spine intersected by two transverse axes, one at ground level beside the entrance, the other on an upper level on the other side. Muller employed unprotected, exposed hardwood, and because he was unable to afford rustic masonry of the kind Wright had used in Falling Water, he imitated the appearance of masonry by inventing what came to be called "snotted brickwork."

His own house at Whale Beach, built some three years later, is a much more impressive work. It is based on a main spine intersected by a transverse axis of open galleries, with a third axis through the bedroom, and in his house Muller explored several themes. He carried the main living space out over and free of the precipitous sandstone outcrop on hardwood trusses that he supported on grey cement brick piers, to match the grey bark of the surrounding gum trees. He created maximum openness and identification with the landscape by using floor to ceiling plate glass and a long panel of glass in the roof over the entertainment area. He flooded the flat roofs so as to reflect the gums—a very beautiful, largely aesthetic notion of mirroring the landscape and so rendering the building invisible.

In the late 1950's Muller built a number of modest low-cost houses, such as Nicholson House, the Craftbuilt houses, and the Gunning House at Castlecrag. The Gunning House is a culmination of Muller's ideas on domestic architecture, and subsequent projects (Creaser House; Barton House) are elaborations on a larger scale of the earlier ideas. By the early 1960's Muller was designing substantial commercial buildings for such companies as IPEC and Hoyts Theatres: of these the Hoyts Cinema Centre, Melbourne, with its adaptation of the traditional Japanese system of bracket supports for supporting the edges of the floor slabs, is probably the most interesting.

It wasn't until the 1970's that new possibilities began to emerge in Muller's work, with the Kayu Aya Hotel on Kuta Beach, Bali. For some time Muller had been interested in Asian culture, architecture, and crafts, but it was in Bali, for the first time, that he had an opportunity to further this inter-

est. From the outset Muller has avoided any idealization is peculiarly Australian: Muller conforms to a rural, essentially conservative architectural tradition, issuing from the 19th century English arts and crafts movement and supported by the example of Walter Muller's regionalist approach has considerably validity in Third World countries where it has been found that the whole imposition of International Style forms and techniques is not only expensive but also results in buildings that look alike all around the world. Muller employed Balinese craftsmen, using as much as possible their skills as both carvers and designers, mostly for the decoration of his buildings. But his concept went further: he used local materials and traditional methods of construction, even to the extent of following the ritual of cutting bamboo. The new hotel is a minor masterpiece of its kind.

Peter Muller occupies an important place in postwar Australian architecture as the leading romantic architect of his time, one who has developed, as an alternative to the modern movement, an organic conception of architecture.

—Philip Drew

MURANO, Tohgo.

Japanese. Born in Karatsu, Saga Prefecture, 15 May 1891. Educated at the Waseda University School of Architecture, graduated 1918. Worked in Setsu Watanabe's architectural office, Osaka, 1918–29. Since 1929, Principal of Tohgo Murano Architects, Osaka (in partnership with Tiuchi Mori, as Murano and Mori Architectural Office, from 1949). Has served as Chairman, Japan Architects' Organization; Member of the Central Council of Chartered Architects, Japan. Recipient: Red Cross Honorary Prize, Germany, 1935; Japan Art Academy Prize, 1953; Arts Council Prize, Osaka Prefecture, 1953; Annual Prize, 1954, 1956, 1965, and Special Prize, 1972, Japan Architectural Society; Annual *Architects Yearbook* Prize, Tokyo, 1963; Prime Minister's Prize, Japan, 1974; Imperial Silver Goblet Award, 1974, and Imperial Silver Bowl, 1976. Honorary doctorate: Waseda University. Member, Japan Architects' Organization, and the Japan Art Academy; Honorary Member, Japan Architectural Society. Corresponding Member, Royal Institute of British Architects; Honorary Fellow, American Institute of Architects. Member, Order of the Blue Ribbon, Japan, 1958, and Order of Cultural Merit, Japan, 1967. Knight of St. Gregory, Vatican, 1970. Address (office): 2-3-8 Abeno-suji, Abeno-ku, Osaka, Japan.

Works:

1931 "Osaka Pension" Apartment Hotel, Osaka
Minami Osaka Church, Osaka
Inspector's House, Kobe, Japan
Morigo Company Building, Takara-cho, Tokyo

1935 German Cultural Research Institute, University of Kyoto.

1936 Sogo Department Store, Osaka

1937 Daimaru Department Store, Kobe, Japan
Public Hall, Ube, Japan
Hieizan Hotel, Mount Hiei, near Kyoto

1937/
38 Argentina *Maru* and Brazil *Maru* ships' interiors

1941 Nakabayashi House, Japan
Ishihara Maritime Company Building, Japan

1942 Tohgo Murano House, Ashiya, Osaka

1950 Nagoya Maruei Hotel, Nagoya, Japan

1951 Shima Kanko Hotel, Shima Peninsula, Japan
Tokyo Bank Club House, Takarazuka, Japan
Kansai University, Suita, Osaka

1952 Takashimaya Department Store, Tokyo

Tohgo Murano: New Kubuki Theatre, Osaka, 1958

Nakagawa House, Japan
Daishin Trading Company Office Building, Nagoya, Japan
1953 Chapel for World Peace, Hiroshima
Fujikawa Galleries, Osaka
Sennichimae Grand Theatre, Japan
1954 Kintetsu Hall, Osaka
Kinei Hall, Japan
1955 Dohton Restaurant, Osaka
Maru-ei Department Store, Nagoya, Japan
1956 Printemps Coffee Shop, Shinsaibashi, Osaka
Newspaper Hall, Kobe, Japan
1957 Rokko School Gymnasium and Lecture Hall, Mount Rokko, Kobe, Japan
Kintetsu Department Store, Tennoji, Osaka
Yomiuri Hall and Sogo Department Store, Tokyo
Tonda-ya Restaurant, Osaka
Marubutsu Department Store and Ikeburu Station Building, Japan
1958 City Hall, Yonago, Japan
Yahata Central Community Center, Hobashira Park, Kitakyushu City, Japan
New Kabuki Theatre, Osaka
Fugetsu-do Restaurant, Tokyo
1959 City Hall, Yokohama
Senshu Bank Head Office, near Osaka
Kasuien Annex, Miyako Hotel, Kyoto
Kitagawa House, Tokyo
Myoshin-ji Hanazono Hall, Kyoto
Takarazuka Golf Club House, Takarazuka City, Japan
Kokura Central Community Hall, Central Park, Kokura City, Japan
1960 Miyako Hotel, Mount Higashi, Kyoto
Textile Export Center, Japan
Yoshimoto Building, Osaka
1962 New Literature Department Building, Waseda University, Tokyo
City Hall, Amagasaki, Japan
Morita Building, Japan
Idemitsu Kosan Branch Office, Kyushu, Japan
1963 Miyako Hotel, Nagoya, Japan
Rest House, Meishin Expressway, Nagoya-to-Kobe, Japan
Shin-Osaka Building, Osaka
Nihon-Seimi Insurance Co. Building, and Nissei Theatre, Hibiya, Tokyo
1964 Konan Woman's University, Kobe, Japan

1965 Chiyoda-Seimi Life Insurance Co. Main Building, Tokyo
Shigetsu-Tei House, Tokyo
Takashimaya Department Store, Tokyo
1967 Takarazuka Catholic Church, Takarazuka City, Japan
1969 Nishinomoya Trappist Monastery, Hyogo Prefecture, Japan
1971 Hakone Botanical Gardens and Rest House, Hakone, Japan
1974 Reception Centre and Guest House, Akasaka Palace, Japan
Industrial Bank of Japan, Tokyo
1976 Hitachinomiya Family House, Japan
Keizo Koyama Art Museum, Japan
1977 Nadama Teahouse, New Otani Hotel, Tokyo
Abe Memorial Library, Konan University, Kobe, Japan
1978 Prince Hotel, Hakone, Japan

Publications:

By MURANO: article—"Humanity and Architecture," with Teijiro Muramatsu, in *The Japan Architect* (Tokyo), March 1974.

On MURANO: books—*The Architecture of Tohgo Murano 1931–1963,* Tokyo 1963; *Tohgo Murano,* Tokyo 1965; articles—"Tea Ceremony Rooms in a Department Store" in *The Japan Architect* (Tokyo), October 1973; "Akasaka Palace Guest House" in *The Japan Architect* (Tokyo), September 1974; "Industrial Bank of Japan, Tokyo" in *The Japan Architect* (Tokyo), January 1975; "Keizo Koyama Art Museum" in *The Japan Architect* (Tokyo), July 1976; "Abe Memorial Library, Konan University" in *Kenchiku Bunka* (Tokyo), January 1977; "Nadama Teahouse" in *The Japan Architect* (Tokyo), April 1977; "Abe Memorial Library" in *The Japan Architect* (Tokyo), May 1977.

*   *   *

It is a privilege to write about the work of one of the major figures of modern Japanese architecture. The work of Tohgo Murano of the past fifty years provides a wealth of buildings that range in expression from direct functionalism, to a rich sensuousness, to the restrained elegance of the sukiya style. Unlike several of his contemporaries, Murano did not study in Europe, yet perhaps more than any other architect

in Japan, his buildings show a subtle blending of past and present western architecture with the artistic heritage of Japan.

After graduation from Waseda University in 1918, Murano joined the Setsu Watanabe office in Osaka. In 1929 he established his own firm in that city, and completed its first modern building, the Sogo Department Store, in 1936. The success of this building led to further commissions in commercial architecture, on which his early practice primarily was based.

Murano was among the pioneers who steered Japanese architecture through the reactionary years of the early post-war period. His buildings of that time show the spectrum of his diverse abilities that determined the characteristics of future work. Further commercial projects included the Takashimaya Department Store, Tokyo, 1952, which remains one of the most practical and pleasant of its kind anywhere in the world. At Hiroshima the Chapel for World Peace, 1953, displays his fascinating translation of western design. This strangely austere building appears to combine the concrete framing of Perret, with Parisian Art Deco, and a dash of Byzantine design. The massive volumetric composition of the Yonago City Hall of 1958 shows Murano in a rare structurally expressive mood. Closely akin to this building is the Industrial Bank of Japan, Tokyo, of 1974. But for the Industrial Bank, the rough concrete, brick, and tile textures of Yonago have been replaced by the sleek precision of gleaming granite.

The most amazing of his works of the early 1960's is his building in Hibiya, Tokyo, which, behind its ordered and balanced Renaissance-inspired façade, houses Murano's most exuberant spaces—the foyers and auditorium of the Nissei Theatre. The rich materials and sinuous lines of the foyers are but preliminaries to the Gaudi-like colours and undulating curves of the continuous walls and ceiling of the auditorium, which gleam with glass mosaics and pearl oyster shells. Lighting from concealed sources adds to the mysterious quality of this truly fantastic space. A few years earlier Murano had designed the new Kabuki Theatre in Osaka in a pseudo-traditional style.

Murano's imaginative expressionism shows most clearly in the Takarazuka Catholic Church of 1967. The organically curved white walls of the structure are capped by a continuous copper roof that sweeps up from the spine with a fluidity that would be envied by Mendelsohn. Several of Murano's later buildings, including the Keizo Koyama Museum of 1976, show a related earthy sensuality in their curved forms and white stuccoed walls that appear to grow organically out of the soil of their sites.

All that is best in Murano's architecture is evident in the Chiyoda Life Insurance Building in Tokyo (1965). The orderly structure that cleverly reduces the scale, the subtle blend of a delicate landscape with a large building accommodating 1,400 office workers, the gentle transition from site to building, the restrained yet mystical richness of the entry foyer, and the sensitivity of the Aikei teahouse in the sukiya style, make this one of the most accomplished buildings of its era.

Murano is a master of the modern sukiya style. The Kasuien Annex of the Miyako Hotel, Kyoto, 1959, the Shigetsu-Tei residence, Tokyo, 1965, and the recently completed Nadama Teahouse of the New Otani Hotel, Tokyo, amongst others, are harmonious and innovative compositions in this tradition.

Today, at the age of eighty-seven, Tohgo Murano remains a respected leader of the profession in Japan. In retrospect his work now appears more relevant than perhaps it was even at the time of its construction. Murano's greatest attribute is that, despite the borrowing of compositional principles of the West, he has always remained a traditional Japanese architect, introducing a fresh sensitivity into the discipline of modern technology. He has provided a humanistic architecture rich with visual and tactile delights.

—Jennifer Taylor

MURCUTT, Glenn (Marcus).

Australian. Born in London, England, of Australian parents, 25 July 1936; lived in New Guinea, 1936–41. Educated at the University of New South Wales, Sydney, under Noel Bazeley, 1956–61; while a student, worked with Neville Gruzman and Bill Lucas, Sydney, 1956, and with John Allen and Russel Jack, Sydney, 1957–61; lived in Europe, 1962–64. Served in the Australian Air Force, 1956. Married Helen Kay in 1962 (divorced, 1979); children: Nicholas and Daniel. Worked in the offices of Ancher, Mortlock, Murray and Woolley, Sydney, 1964–69. In private practice, Mosman, Sydney, since 1969. Design Tutor, University of Sydney, 1970–78. Recipient: Architectural Award of Merit, 1972, 1975 (twice), 1976, 1977, 1978, Wilkinson Award, 1976, and Blacket Award, 1977, Royal Australian Institute of Architects. Address: Glenn Murcutt, Architect, 176a Raglan Street, Mosman, New South Wales 2088, Australia.

Works:

1961 House, Beacon Hill, Sydney
1968 Staff House, University of Newcastle, New South Wales
1970 House, Killara, Sydney
1972 House, Belrose, Sydney
    Murcutt House renovation, Mosman, Sydney
1973 House, Terrey Hills, Sydney
    House, Balmain, Sydney
1974 House renovation, Mosman, Sydney
1975 House, Kempsey, New South Wales
    House, Canberra, A.C.T.
1976 House restoration, Longueville, Sydney
1977 House, Kempsey, New South Wales
1978 House, Cromer, Sydney
    Berowra Waters Inn, Berowra Waters, Sydney
    House, Woollahra, Sydney
    House, Balmain, Sydney
    House, Clontarf, Sydney
    Houses (2), Mount Irvine, New South Wales

Since I am interested in people as individuals rather than as anonymous consumers of architecture, much of my architecture is domestic in character, with the bulk of the work consisting of renovations. I have avoided major buildings by preference because in designing them one is isolated from the users. Such large projects deprive one of both the stimulus and personal satisfaction of developing a building design from a close personal understanding of the client and his requirements.

The significant influences on my architecture have been the work of the Sydney architect S. E. Ancher; Mies van der Rohe's Farnsworth House; Pierre Chareau's Maison d'Alsace in Paris; the simple use of materials and forms, the movement of traffic, the modulation of daylight and the spatial coherence of the folk architecture of the Greek islands; and, now, the Australian landscape.

I find myself strongly directed by climate when designing, allowing the penetration of the winter sunlight and excluding the sun in summer, thus modifying and affecting the micro-environment of my buildings. The use of gardens, pergolas, and simple sunlight and wind filters establishes a temperate gradient between the interior of my buildings and the surrounding environment. It should also be possible to be able to establish what the day is like outside whilst within one of my buildings. I am particularly interested in the language of a site, the question of appropriateness of building to landform, whether one designs merely a house on a farm or a farmhouse, for example.

The strong Australian sunlight, like that of Greece, requires for me simple forms, often white both outside and inside, allowing the structure of the native flora to be clearly silhouetted, and that the interest and variety develops from the play of light over the interior surfaces—a kind of natural decoration. We live in an era of organic decoration, though there'll always be a place for applied decoration. The ultimate decoration for me is a white cube. In this sense, then, decoration should be inseparable from an outcome of materials, the light, and the site. Thus decoration which consists entirely of applied textures and patterns has a life of perhaps one or two years before it has to be changed. But decoration that is the integration of objects, and the clarification of space and materials, has an enduring appeal.

I like simple ordinary forms. The plans of many of my buildings are composed of pavilions on rectangular platforms which, while they are simple enough, represent a resolution of a complex series of demands. I see simplicity not so much as a disregard of complexity but as the clarification of the significant. In this regard I am very much in sympathy with Mies van der Rohe's philosophy of design.

My interest in the ordinary expresses itself in my renovation work of typical Sydney suburban bungalows—of giving the ordinary something special—and in the use of galvanised corrugated iron not only for roofing but also for the walls of some of my houses. The proper recognition of galvanised corrugated iron as a handsome, versatile industrial building material was hampered by the prejudice derived from the wholesale misuse of this material in the 19th century, when it was inadequately insulated, and by the "tamed romantic Brutalism" which, until recently, has typified the Sydney School of architecture. I reject the affected rusticity, pretentious merging of building with the natural landscape, and feverish search for an "Australian style" of the Sydney School of architecture in favour of a more honest, straight-forward kind of architecture.

I see the house as a comfortable refuge from the tensions and conflicts of the public world. Nevertheless, the house, particularly where it is located in an established street, should conform to the existing street patterns. In the future, architects will spend more time in renovating the existing building stock. This change is healthy in my view because it means that the architect will need to think much more carefully about how his decisions affect both people and the existing architectural environment. I enjoy working with old buildings, or simply giving them a new life, in order to improve the well being of the occupants—no matter how small the project.

—Glenn Murcutt

Glenn Murcutt's architecture is characterized by a Miesian clarity in the planning, architectonic form and conception, allied with predominantly Finnish or Aalto interiors and treatment of materials. But, in addition, Murcutt has resurrected the ubiquitous corrugated iron shed and given it a fresh domestic interpretation as a tent-like open pavilion not unrelated to Mies' pavilions.

Glenn Murcutt's appropriation of the corrugated iron shed for his houses after 1973 should not be interpreted as indicating that his work is merely an extension of the romantic values of the Sydney School. Such an assessment ignores the strong Miesian and Finnish inspiration in his own house in Mosman and the houses at Belrose and Terry Hills, Sydney, all of which reveal Murcutt's debt to Mies, particularly Mies' Farnsworth House. Murcutt's houses represent a serious interpretation of the Miesian vocabulary. Thus while he has learned from the simple rectangular and clearly articulated, even classical, plans of Mies' buildings, there are important differences. Murcutt's space is cellular, not fluid, and he shows a much greater regard for sun control than does Mies in his buildings. Moreover, his later corrugated iron houses at Balmain and Kempsey possess a hard-light quality in marked contrast to the warm tweedy textures of the Sydney School.

Another factor that should not be overlooked is the close relationship between Glenn Murcutt and Sydney Ancher. To some extent Murcutt's houses provide a bridge to the largely discredited Functionalist mainstream of modern architecture. The choice of the "tin shed" as a prototype has two advantages besides its cheapness and ease of construction: it serves to maintain a connection with the Functionalist ethic of modern architecture while at the same time providing a link with Australian tradition.

—Philip Drew

Glenn Murcutt: House, Terrey Hills, Sydney, 1973

MURRAY, Stuart.

Australian. Born in Sydney, New South Wales, 27 October 1926. Educated at Fort Street Boys High School, Sydney, 1938–42; worked as a draughtsman with Wunderlich Ltd., Sydney, 1943–44; studied at the Sydney Technical College School of Architecture, under Henry Pynor, Sydney Ancher and Morton Herman, 1944–49, Dip.Arch. (civic design distinction) 1949; awarded New South Wales Board of Architects Research Bursary, 1950. Married Elizabeth Grime in 1952 (divorced, 1966); children: Anna, Andrew, Ruth and Daniel. Architectural Assistant with W. B. Griffin and Nicholls, Sydney, 1945–47, and with Sydney Ancher, Sydney, 1948–49; Architect with Denis Clarke Hall, London, 1949–51; Senior Architect, Intercon Ltd., London, 1952–53; Partner, with Sydney Ancher, *q.v.*, and Bryce Mortlock, *q.v.*, Ancher, Mortlock and Murray, Sydney, 1953–64; Partner/Director, with Ancher, Mortlock, and Ken Woolley, *q.v.*, Ancher, Mortlock, Murray and Woolley, Sydney, 1964–75; Founder-Director, North Sydney Planning Consultants, 1970–73. Since 1976, Principal, Stuart Murray Architect, North Sydney. Design Tutor, University of New South Wales Faculty of Architecture, Sydney, 1962, 1974–78; Member of the faculty, University of Sydney, 1965–75. Member of the Housing Committee, 1966–67, and Councillor and Chairman of the Environment Board, 1972–76, Royal Australian Institute of Architects, New South Wales Chapter. Exhibition: *Ancher, Mortlock, Murray and Woolley, Sydney Architects, 1946–76,* Art Gallery of New South Wales, 1976, and Australian tour, 1977. Recipient: First Prize, Waverley, New South Wales Town Hall Competition, 1957; First Prize, University of Newcastle Great Hall Competition, 1968. Fellow, Royal Australian Institute of Architects, 1966. Address: Stuart Murray Architect, 119 High Street, North Sydney, New South Wales 2060, Australia.

Works:

1949 House, Scotland Island, Sydney
1952 House, Amaroo Avenue, Turramurra, Sydney
 Hotel, Kingsford, Sydney
1959 House, Montah Avenue, Killara, Sydney
 House, Karoo Avenue, Lindfield, Sydney
1963 Housing, Northbourne Avenue, Canberra (with Sydney Ancher)
1964 Chemical Engineering School, University of Sydney
 Public Library, Gordon, Sydney
1965 Offices, Milperra, Sydney
 Architects' Studio, North Sydney
 House, Careening Cove, Sydney
1966 House, Bilgola Heights, Sydney
 Baby Health Centre, West Pymble, Sydney
 Public Library, Turramurra, Sydney
1967 Carpark, Gordon, Sydney
 Drive-In Restaurant, Bass Hill, Sydney
 Town houses, Cremorne, Sydney
1968 Flats, Church Street, Woollongong, New South Wales
 Flats, Liverpool, Sydney
1970 Apartments, Elizabeth Bay, Sydney
 Faculty Building, University of Sydney
1971 Nursing Hospital, Parramatta, Sydney
1972 Ski Lodge, North Perisher, Mount Kosciusko, New South Wales
 Great Hall, University of Newcastle, New South Wales
1973 Offices, Ashfield, Sydney
1974 Aeronautics School, University of Sydney
 Gymnasium and Library, Fort Street High School, Petersham, Sydney
1976 Holiday Lodge, Robertson, New South Wales
 Factory/Studio, North Sydney

Publications:

By MURRAY: papers—*Elements of Urban Environment,* Sydney 1972; *Contemporary Architecture and Environment,* Canberra 1976.

On MURRAY: books—*Australian Housing of the*

Stuart Murray: Apartments, Elizabeth Bay, Sydney, 1970

70's by Howard Tanner, Sydney 1976; *Ancher, Mortlock, Murray and Woolley, Sydney Architects, 1946–76,* exhibition catalogue, by David Saunders and Catherine Bourke, Sydney 1976; articles—"Community Housing, Canberra" in *Cross Section* (Melbourne), May 1963; "Apartments, Elizabeth Bay, Sydney" in *Cross Section* (Melbourne), July 1967; "Great Hall, University, Newcastle" in *L'Architecture d'Aujourd'hui* (Paris), no. 142, 1969; article by Diane Kell in *Constructional Review* (Sydney), May 1972; "Offices, Ashfield, Sydney" in *New South Wales Builder* (Sydney), June 1974; "Aeronautics School, University of Sydney" by Diane Kell in *Constructional Review* (Sydney), December 1974.

*

The early work attempted urbane, concise architecture, sparse and rectilinear; housing groups expressed privacy, and early sensitivity to environmental spaces (1959). Unity was sought in expression of quietly vivid Australian character under the influence of Sydney Ancher.

By the mid-1960's the use of more highly individual forms expressed the different influences of the programmes, producing sophisticated urban building (Apartments, Elizabeth Bay) of strongly sculpted construction, a blend of technical discipline with bold shaping (strong European influence).

Later a more complex organic technology produced handsomely rugged structures, strong and characterful. The Great Hall is scaled to total form rather than its component parts; it has large intention and a vivid series memorable in distant view, approach, entry and circulation (some Aalto influence).

In the early 70's a frankly industrial approach was adopted—the severing of building functions, building-block assemblies, overlapping profiles, glass canopy roofs (Aeronautics School, University of Sydney)—all the true components of the neo-functionalism of Stirling's work in the United Kingdom.

The buildings are lively in planning devices, internal spaces, external forms and siting, the latter two being used to integrate building and environment.

Inventiveness is used not merely to produce personal display, but as an imaginative and sensible response to the building programme, producing an intelligent solution to problems with a rich variety of architectural images.

—Stuart Murray

*

On the edge of a promontory overlooking Sydney Harbour stands a small jewel-like block of luxury apartments. Beaten copper gates open onto a travertine paved courtyard edged with regimented bay trees. But beyond this court one dare not go. Electronic sentinels guard this place as securely as did the eunuchs of Shahryar watch over his hareem. Inside the tower Shahrazad combs her hair and watches the boats sail past.

Stuart Murray looks upon his wayward and untypical building with some affection. He cheerfully acknowledges that his inspiration for the tight detailing and the opulent materials came from Italy via *Domus.* The baroque curves of the tower are reminiscent of Mendelsohn and Rudolph, whilst the urbane treatment of the ground floor entry shows the influence of Mangiarotti. The product of these diverse influences is one of the most sophisticated and elegant small buildings in Sydney.

Murray maintains that, in architecture as in the other arts, it is necessary to recognize influences and acknowledge sources. Two later buildings are typical of this approach and illustrate the way in which he is able to transform his inspirational sources into a personal style.

The Aeronautics School at the University of Sydney was completed while Murray was still a director of the firm Ancher, Mortlock, Murray and Woolley, and is one of a number of buildings in this precinct undertaken by them. This is a memorable building that can only be understood by spending some time in it. At first glance it is simply a long slab that spans a service road. The slab contains offices, service rooms, and access spaces. Tacked along the side of the slab, and articulated by a glazed slit at the junction, are the main workshop, laboratory and teaching spaces. This is an indeterminate plan: bits can be added or taken away from the central spine without destroying the basic form. But the simple plan is developed into a complicated and maze-like long section with branches and dead-ends in which it is easy to become lost. The interior of the spine is dominated by a glazed space which extends from ground level to the topmost storey. Finely detailed industrial glazing is supported by a three dimensional steel truss that hangs above stair and light wells. Finishes in this building are uncompromisingly industrial—concrete off-form without any special surface treat-

ment, fairfaced brickwork infill panels inside and out, and heavy duty flooring. There is a certain maritime air about the place, and this quality is reinforced by the direct and simple details. Influences of Le Corbusier and James Stirling are recognizable but do not dominate the design. They do, however, endow this building with references that illuminate the way in which it is experienced.

The second building is a small office block located on a typical urban strip for a firm of building contractors. It is a simple, economic slab in bush-hammered concrete. Varying space requirements on each floor result in a stepped profile on the street facade. The lowest storey is set below ground level. The offices at this level look out onto a garden light-court and are protected from street noise by a landscaped embankment. Pedestrian access is via a bridge across the courtyard to a reception area on a gallery overlooking a public waiting space below. The introduction of the double-height space and the conservatory style glazing on the external wall are reminiscent of the Aeronautics School. They transform an ordinary building into a delightful, urbane workplace.

The common thread that runs through Murray's work is a masterful understanding of scale. His buildings fit unfussily into the urban fabric, carefully maintaining the visual character of the street without in any way attempting to echo the architectural details of their neighbours. Those who come into contact with them find the experience essentially humanizing.

—David Watson

Barton Myers: Housing Union Building, University of Alberta, Edmonton, 1969

MYERS, Barton.
American. Born in Norfolk, Virginia, 6 November 1934; moved to Canada, 1968. Educated at the Norfolk Academy, Virginia, graduated 1932; United States Naval Academy, Annapolis, Maryland, 1952–56, B.S. 1956; University of Pennsylvania, Philadelphia, 1961–64, M.Arch. 1964; awarded University of Pennsylvania Chandler Travel Scholarship, 1965. Served as a Pilot in the United States Air Force, in the United States and England, 1956–61: Lieutenant. Married Victoria George in 1959; daughter: Suzanne. Worked with Louis Kahn, Philadelphia, 1964–66; Assistant Architect, Bower and Fradley, Philadelphia, 1966–68; Partner, with A. J. Diamond, *q.v.,* Diamond and Myers, Toronto, 1968–75. Since 1975, Principal, Barton Myers Associates, architects and planners, Toronto (associates: Donald Clinton; Robert Hill; Bruce Kuwabara; Kristine Martin; David W. Oleson). Assistant Professor, University of Toronto Department of Architecture, 1968–70; Lecturer, Ontario College of Art, Toronto, 1970–71, and Division of Environmental Studies, University of Waterloo School of Architecture, Ontario, 1971–73. Assistant Editor, Royal Architectural Institute of Canada journal *Architecture Canada,* Toronto, 1968–69; Member, Advisory Committee for Design, National Capital Commission, Ottawa, 1968–74; Executive, Toronto Chapter, Ontario Association of Architects, 1972; Vice-Chairman, Toronto Chapter of Architects, 1973; Member, North Midtown Planning Group, Toronto, 1974–75. Exhibitions: *Harbour Front,* Toronto, 1975; *Urban Infill,* Science Centre, Toronto, 1975; Architectural Awareness Week Exhibition, Queens Park, Toronto, 1977. Recipient: Society of Graphic Designers of Canada Award, 1968 (twice); Annual Design Award, Ontario Association of Architects, Toronto Chapter, 1969, 1971 (twice), 1976 (twice); Residential Design Award, Canadian Housing Design Council, 1971, 1975; Masonry Award, Canadian Design Council, 1972; Canada Council Grant, 1972; Design in Steel Award, 1973; Award of Merit, Toronto Historical Board, 1974; Landscape Ontario Award, 1977; House Award, *Architectural Record,* 1977; Design Award, City of Edmonton, 1978; Stelco Design Award, 1978; Habitation Space International Award, Switzerland, 1978; Design Award, *Progressive Architecture,* 1978; Award, *Urban Design,* 1978. Member, Royal Architectural Institute of Canada, Society of Architectural Historians, Tau Sigma Delta, Heritage Canada, and the Royal Canadian Academy of Art. Address: Barton Myers Associates, 322 King Street West, Toronto, Ontario M5V 1J4, Canada.

Works:

1969 York Square (restaurant/shops complex), Yorkville, Toronto (with A. J. Diamond)

Housing Union Building, University of Alberta, Edmonton (with R. L. Wilkin)

Alcan Executive Headquarters interiors, Toronto (with A. J. Diamond)

Long range development plan for the University of Alberta, Edmonton (with A. J. Diamond)

Vidal Sassoon Salon interiors, Toronto (with A. J. Diamond)

1970 Ontario Medical Association Headquarters, Toronto

Blade House, Virginia Beach, Virginia

Schwartz House, Virginia Beach, Virginia

Barton Myers House, Berryman Street, Toronto

Steel Equipment Building interiors, Toronto

1971 Canadian Television Housing Study, Toronto (with A. J. Diamond)

1972 Kew Beach Infill Housing and renovation, Toronto

Long range development plan for the University of Alberta, stage II, Edmonton

1973 Apogee Infill Housing, Toronto

Union Facilities, University of Maryland, Baltimore

Town plan for Bronte, Ontario
1974 Wolf House, Roxborough Drive, Toronto
       Rideau Street Mall, Ottawa
1975 Pickle Lake New Town and Housing, Ontario
       Citadel Theatre, Edmonton, Alberta (with R. L. Wilkin)
       Barton Myers Associates Office interiors, Toronto
       Dundas/Sherbourne Housing, Toronto
1976 Lincoln Park Development Plan, Calgary, Alberta (with James McKellar)
       York Row Infill Housing, Yorkville, Toronto (project)
       Canadian National Railway Yards and Mainline Development Plan, Regina, Saskatchewan (project; with Stephen McLaughlin)
       Canadian Pacific Railway Express Building, Toronto (project)
       Canadian Pacific Railway Yards and Mainline Development Plan, Regina, Saskatchewan (competition project)
       Canadian National Railway Station for Parkdale, Toronto (relocation)
       Jones Avenue Branch Library renovations, Toronto
       Spadina Commuter Parking Facility, Toronto (project)
       Cinema Park Housing, Calgary, Alberta (project)
1977 Smith/Hamilton House, Newcastle, Ontario (project)
       Townhouses, Ghent Square, Norfolk, Virginia
       Urban Outdoors Inc. interiors, Toronto
       Munn's United Church renovations, Oakville, Ontario
       Monticello Arcade renovation, Norfolk, Virginia
       Downtown plan review, Norfolk, Virginia
1978 Freemason Harbor Development Plan, Norfolk, Virginia
       Alternatives to high-rise study, Edmonton, Alberta
       Urban design study for the Urban Transportation Development Corporation
       Downtown revitalization plan for Cambridge, Ontario
       Yorkville Public Library alterations and additions, Toronto
       Omnitown Housing Project, Toronto
       Alcan interiors, Toronto
       Downtown Athletic Club and Housing Project, Norfolk, Virginia

Publications:

By MYERS: articles—"The Architecture of Accommodation" in *Habitat* (Ottawa), no. 3/4, 1977; "Weighting the Elements" in *Canadian Architect* (Toronto), November 1977; "Vacant Lottery" in *Design Quarterly* (Minneapolis), no. 108, 1978.

On MYERS: articles—"York Square" in *Canadian Architect* (Toronto), June 1969; "York Square" in *Progressive Architecture* (New York), September 1969; "York Square" in *Byggekunst* (Oslo), September 1969; "York Square" in *Abitare* (Milan), October 1970; "Alcan Interiors" in *Canadian Architect* (Toronto), March 1971; "Ontario Medical Association" in *Canadian Architect* (Toronto), June 1971; "York Square" in *Architecture + Urbanism* (Tokyo), November 1971; "Work of Diamond and Myers" in *Architecture + Urbanism* (Tokyo), May 1972; "The Campus as a Lesson in Urban Form—Students' Union Housing" in *Progressive Architecture* (New York), September 1972; "York Square in Toronto" in *Baumeister* (Munich), October 1972; "The Low Rise Alternative Urban Recycling" in *Time* (New York), 16 April 1973; "To Save a Fabric" in *Progressive Architecture* (New York), May 1973; "Student Street" in *Progressive Architecture* (New York), February 1974; "Students' Union Housing, University of Alberta" in *Architecture + Urbanism* (Tokyo), December 1974; "Diamond and Myers: Form and Reform" in *City Magazine* (Toronto), August/September 1975; "The Cutlery of Progress" by John Morris Dixon in *Progressive Architecture* (New York), February 1977; "Barton Myers" by C. Ray Smith in *Urban Design* (New York), Summer 1977; "A View of Contemporary World Architecture" in *The Japan Architect* (Tokyo), December 1977.

Barton Myers Associates believes that architects and planners are most creative when confronting problems with difficult constraints, whether they be social, economic or physical. The ability to exploit circumstance and constraints is crucial to help bring about the accommodating aspects which make the work responsive to complex situations.

Members of the firm share personal interests in how things work and how things are made, and believe that the user as well as the builder appreciates these interests. The goal is to design buildings and details which are expressive of how they are put together. Buildings designed by the office of Barton Myers demonstrate how common off-the-shelf component parts, standard industrial systems, and composite structures can be selected, controlled, and modified to meet very particular building situations in the North American builders' market.

Each construction system and element is rigorously considered with respect to its functional, symbolic and cost appropriateness within the overall scheme. The assemblage and detail of the construction and the exposure of elemental system components create a sense of texture that is lacking in most contemporary buildings. Many of the projects make use of contemporary warehouse steel frame, metal decking and open-web steel joists, and the overlay of building sub-systems, when exposed and finely finished, contributes significantly to a quality of lightness and spaciousness.

The ultimate stress is on design excellence, and the resulting architecture is clear, composite, simply ordered in plan, while more complex spatially, and endowed with scale and ornamentation by means of elegant details, fittings and finishes. Stylistically, the work combines multiple references drawn from historical, vernacular and contemporary sources to increase the possible meanings. The projects of the office attempt to achieve a closely knit social and physical matrix where form and program are mutually supportive and the important issues of contemporary cities are addressed.

Barton Myers Associates has argued publicly for a strategy of consolidation of the inefficient physical fabric and building forms that continue to be developed in and around the typical uni-centred North American city with its high-density, high-rise downtown core and low-density suburban sprawl. The concept of urban consolidation demands a multi-centred city with a more balanced pattern of development densities and population distribution, with emphasis particularly on the middle-density range for low- and mid-rise residential design alternatives. Clearly, the major goals of a consolidation program are better utilization of land and municipal servicing, effective public transit networks, mixed land use development policies, and a wider range of housing choices with higher dwelling amenity.

The contextual aspects of our work are based on a respect for existing rights, urban fabric, and old/new combinations. An appreciation of tradition, historical models, popular culture, climate and building technology further influences the form and meaning of the architecture.

—Barton Myers

Barton Myers is a graduate of the University of Pennsylvania, influenced by Louis Kahn and the Philadelphia School. Since immigrating to Canada, Myers has been an active critic of the inefficiencies of the uni-centred North American city. He advocates an alternative strategy of *urban consolidation*, arguing for a multi-centred city of connected neighbourhoods, a more balanced distribution of development densities employing low-rise street-related forms, and efficient use of land, services and public transportation. Myers' architecture of consolidation must be understood within this polemic of urban reform, which reflects a pragmatic idealism working within the market place. His conception of the city is influenced by Jane Jacobs and Edmund Bacon.

Nearly all of the projects are either "infill" building types, which respect existing urban fabric, or connected, additive buildings as opposed to buildings as separate, isolated objects. Many of the projects retain existing buildings integrating "old" and "new" to maintain cultural continuity. Each project generally proposes a new social space in the form of the courtyard, the square and the galleria street.

Myers' work represents deliberate departures from the ideas and work of Louis Kahn. Designing for the Canadian climate, Myers has moved toward making simple, large building envelopes with unarticulated flat exterior surfaces and with articulated building elements within. Where Kahn believed that the "room" is the essential element of architectural composition, creating plans that represent a "society of rooms," Myers establishes the total building envelope as a single large "room" within which enclosures become "rooms within the room." Myers' idealization of the industrial warehouse as a generalized volume for living in is particularly evident in his steel construction essays which create 20th century residential lofts. The incompleteness of the enclosures within the envelopes, the minimization of wall returns, dark corners and spaces, and the substitution of sliding walls for conventional doors disclose a heroic/claustrophobic spatial sensibility. Where Kahn generally maintained a rigorous distinction between "served" and "servant" spaces in his work, Myers integrates environmental support systems within habitable spaces. Service areas are rationally ordered in zones in plan.

The dominant configurative geometries are linear, orthogonal and planar, while the use of the circle, cylinder and curves is reserved to enclose and symbolize places of meeting or indicate special openings. Circumstantial inflections occur sparingly, with consistent use of the 45° angle to resolve corners, directional conditions and to indicate service elements.

The buildings are composite, made up of overlaid orders of exposed structural, mechanical and electrical systems. Connections between the discrete elements, fixtures and fittings are made visible, intentionally didactic.

In a design mode reminiscent of the work of Charles Eames, Myers selects and arranges common "off-the-shelf," "high-tech" and customized building components in out-of-context settings, juxtaposed with traditional, modern, and pop artefacts. The Myers schema, however, places greater weight on the construction elements than on vernacular and folk objects, to achieve a density of texture.

The facades of Myers' buildings fall into two groups. The first group could be called "infill frames," related primarily to the steel constructions in which the principal facades are rendered as minimal compositions of solid and large glazed panels set inside steel frames. The second group are the "faces," related to various concrete and frame structures, where brick is employed as a veneer deliberately expressed through its detailing to wrap the buildings in more complex and often gestural ways. Brick is consistently used as a reference to local vernacular traditions through type and colour selection. Openings are composed as simple geometric cut-outs in the frontal planes, emphasized by the concealment of window jambs and the use of large sheets of glass.

Myers brings together a number of diverse attitudes and tendencies rather than projecting a single "pure" style. The architecture is rational, clear and composite, reflecting the interaction of both a heroic morale and a reformative view of the urban implications of Modern Architecture.

—Bruce Kuwabara

N

NEFF, (Edwin) Wallace.

American. Born in La Mirada, California, 28 January 1895. Studied art in Munich, 1911–13, and in Geneva, 1913–14; attended the School of Architecture, Massachusetts Institute of Technology, under Ralph Adams Cram, 1915–17. Married Louise Up de Graff in 1925; children: Phyllis, Wallace and Arthur. Loft-Molder, American Shipbuilding Company, San Pedro, California, 1917–18; Delineator-Draftsman, office of the architect George Washington Smith, Santa Barbara, California, 1919; Partner, Neff and Edwards, Architects, Santa Barbara, 1919; Principal, Wallace Neff, Architect, Pasadena, California, 1922–33, and Hollywood, California, 1933 until he retired, 1975. Exhibitions: American Institute of Architects Exhibitions, Southern California Chapter, Los Angeles, 1924, 1930, 1938, 1950, 1958; *L.A. in the Thirties,* Art Galleries of the University of California at Santa Barbara, 1975. Collections: University of Southern California, Los Angeles; Huntington Library, San Marino, California. Recipient: Honor Award, American Institute of Architects, 1924 (twice), 1929, 1939, 1950, 1958; Egyptian Government Award for Housing, 1951. Fellow, 1956, and Fellow Emeritus, 1972, American Institute of Architects. Address: 228 Forest Avenue, Laguna Beach, California, U.S.A.

Works:

1919 Edwin Neff House, Santa Barbara, California (with William Edwards)
1923 Walker House, San Pasqual Street, Pasadena, California
      E. D. Libbey Stables, Ojai, California
      Frances Marion Estate, Beverly Hills, California
1924 Ojai Valley Country Club, Ojai, California
      Johnson House, Burleigh Dr., Pasadena, California
      Delano House, Allen Avenue, Pasadena, California

1925 Wallace Neff House, Mendocino Street, Altadena, California
      St. Elizabeth's Roman Catholic Church, Altadena, California
      Hall House, Woodstock Road, San Marino, California
      Motor Sales Building, Altadena, California
      Bourne House, Lombardy Road, San Marino, California
      Dumbolton House, Allen Avenue, Pasadena, California
      Toms House, Lombardy Road, San Marino, California
      Doane House, Shenandoah Road, San Marino, California
1926 Post House, Orlando Road, San Marino, California
      Fairbanks House, Orlando Road, San Marino, California
      Noble House, Burleigh Drive, Pasadena, California
      Johnson House, Burleigh Drive, Pasadena, California
      Bryant Ranch, Santa Ana Canyon, California
      Visscher House, Prospect Lane, Pasadena, California
      Lecky House, Armada Drive, Pasadena, California
      Burr House, Carolwood Drive, Holmby Hills, California
1927 Barlow Estate, Sierra Madre, California
      California Security Loan Building, Pasadena
      Van Deinse Estate, Pasadena, California
      Pickfair Estate additions, Beverly Hills, California
      Forthman House, La Fayette Park Place, Los Angeles
1928 Gillette Ranch, Calabasas, California
      Bush House, Lake Wells, Florida
      Busch House, Hillcrest Avenue, Pasadena, California
      Norman Chandler House, Nottingham Road,

Los Angeles
      Harry Culver Estate, Cheviot Hills, California
      Collins House, Pasadena, California
      Gartz House, Via Almar, Palos Verdes, California
      King Vidor Estate, Tower Road, Beverly Hills, California
1929 Anderson House, Sunset Boulevard, Beverly Hills, California
      Doheny Ranch, Santa Paula Canyon, California
      Wallace Neff Office Building, Pasadena, California
      Neff House, Orlando Road, San Marino, California
      Edwin Neff House, South Orange Grove Boulevard, Pasadena, California
      Turner House, Orlando Road, San Marino, California
      Baer House, La Vereda Road, Santa Barbara, California
      Thorne House, Los Altos Drive, Pasadena, California
1930 Richter House, Virginia Road, San Marino, California
      Niblo Estate, Beverly Hills, California
      Brigham Estate, Bel-Air, Los Angeles
      Wurtzel Estate, Bel-Air, Los Angeles
1931 Millikan House, Normandy Drive, Pasadena, California
1932 William Goetz House (Louis B. Mayer House), St. Pierre Road, Bel-Air, Los Angeles
1933 Factory-built "Mobile Home," Los Angeles
1934 Doheny House alterations, Chester Place, Los Angeles
1936 Fredric March Estate, Beverly Hills, California
      Garner House, Holliday Road, San Marino, California
1937 Miller Estate, Bel-Air, Los Angeles

Wallace Neff: Gillette Ranch, Calabasas, California, 1928

1938 Joan Bennett House, Mapleton Drive, Holmby Hills, California

King Vidor Estate II, Beverly Hills, California

1939 Doheny Memorial Library, Camarillo, California

1940 William Goetz House, Santa Monica, California

1941 "Air-form" concrete structures, Falls Church, Virginia

Doheny Memorial House of Studies, Washington, D.C.

1942 Thomas Ince Memorial Hospital, 29 Palms, California

1946 A. Neff "Air-form" House, Los Robles Avenue, Pasadena, California

1948 Bourne Estate, Palm Springs, California

1949 Hornstein Estate, Hidden Valley, California

1950 Duff Estate, Hollywood, California

1952 Browne Estate, Bel-Air, Los Angeles

1953 Groucho Marx Estate, Beverly Hills, California

Factor House, Beverly Hills, California

1955 Harpo Marx House, Palm Springs, California

1956 Gummo Marx House, Beverly Hills, California

George B. Miller House, Smoke Tree Ranch, Palm Springs, California

1957 Manressa Jesuit Retreat House Chapel, Azusa, California

Gymnasium, Pomona College, Claremont, California

1958 Edgar Richards Estate, Palm Springs, California

1960 Ralph Chandler House, Rossmore Street, Los Angeles

1963 Roy Eaton Estate, Hope Ranch, Santa Barbara, California

1964 Elizabeth Hay Bechtel Estate, Santa Barbara, California

1965 Singleton Estate, Holmby Hills, California

1969 Robert K. Straus House, Hope Ranch, Santa Barbara, California

1975 Browne Estate II, Big Canyon, Newport Beach, California

Publications:

By NEFF: book—*Thin Shell Concrete Construction,* privately printed 1965.

On NEFF: book—*Architecture of Southern California: A Selection of Photographs, Plans and Scale Details from the Work of Wallace Neff,* Chicago 1964; articles—"An Artist in Adobe" by Harris Allen in *Pacific Coast Architect* (Los Angeles), August 1924; "Adventures in Architecture" by Harris Allen in *Pacific Coast Architect* (Los Angeles), September 1927; "Ranch House for E. L. Doheny, Santa Paula Canyon, California" in *Architectural Record* (New York), November 1930; "Residence of Joan Bennett, Holmby Hills, California" in *California Arts and Architecture* (Los Angeles), September 1938; "Wallace Neff, Architect: Some of His Recent Work" by Mark Daniels in *Architect and Engineer* (Los Angeles), January 1941; "Ballyhooed Balloon" in *Architectural Forum* (New York), December 1941; "Bubble House" in *Architectural Record* (New York), December 1941; "Bubble House for Defense" in *Architect and Engineer* (Los Angeles), January 1942; "Grain Bins in Southwest Arizona" in *Architect and Building News* (London), 23 April 1943; "Airform House for a Desert Colony" in *Architectural Record* (New York), July 1944; "U.S.A." by André Bruyere in *L'Architecture d'Aujourd'hui* (Paris), July/August 1945; "Air-formed Concrete Domes" in *Progressive Architecture* (New York), June 1954.

My practice has been almost entirely confined to California, where problems of climate and site have to be contended with on every job. During the first years I applied the lessons I learned in five years study of the traditional architecture of Europe (1910–1914), when "modernism" was virtually unheard of.

I always admired the simpler architecture on the Continent. Clients in California were enthusiastic about having houses (my practice was domestic), which were reminiscent of the simpler architecture of Italy and France, and I was enthusiastic about giving them the "right" solution for their needs, using European precedents. However, I never had any illusion that my work was anything other than "Californian" in style, never "authentic" copies of something alien. I was always interested in structure (I learned the importance of structure from Ralph Adams Cram at MIT).

When the Depression of the 1930's wiped out my practice, I became interested in the problems of mass housing. The factory-built home I designed in 1934 sold for $800, but no one could afford even that.

My interest in "modern" was not stylistic. A thin shell concrete structure erected without forms seemed a rational answer to the problem of low-cost shelter at a time when low-cost shelter was needed. The "Airform" method of construction which I developed and patented proved more applicable in the underdeveloped countries than it did in the United States, where building was hemmed in by codes and special interests.

I was in practice for such a long time that my early work began to be admired in a nostalgic sort of way, and I got a lot of clients who were in love with the recent past. Once again, however, I was not under any illusion that my late work was "authentically" "1920's" or "1930's." It was done for people who lived in a different era, and I feel solves the problems of contemporary living.

—Wallace Neff

In 1921 Wallace Neff started a practice as an architect of large country and suburban houses. His involvement in the design and production of a factory-built "Mobile Home" in 1933, followed by his invention of the "Airform" concrete structure in 1941, seem a startling reversal of direction in mid-career. A close examination of his design approach reveals less inconsistency than might at first appear.

At the time that Neff started his practice California was still receptive to almost any architectural influence. Frank Lloyd Wright and others had built "Mayan" buildings, and Schindler and Neutra were able to flourish as "moderns." Neff, who had spent years in Europe and received a "Beaux-Arts" education at M.I.T., turned out work which was closer in spirit to that of Bernard Maybeck. Each house was in a "style" appropriate to the client and the site, but the style was freely interpreted. The estate that Neff built in 1923 for Frances Marion, a hugely paid script writer, and her husband, a cowboy actor, was the architect's interpretation of "Hollywood." It included a Spanish bullring where the cowboy might perform, a Baroque gatehouse, an approach through Moorish arches, and a huge voissoired portal flanked by engaged columns which emerged above the roof as turrets topped by Oriental finials. The next year he built a very irregularly planned "Normandy" mansion in a scale so small that the eaves almost touched the ground in many places. The reason for the adoption of this scale was to save as many as possible of the old oaks that covered the site.

Neff's work proved very popular in Southern California. As early as 1927 critics pointed out that it was widely imitated. Perhaps no single architect was more responsible than Neff for creating the eclectic "style" we associate with Southern California in the 1920's and 1930's.

In his country houses, where he did not have to contend with building codes, Neff pursued his interest in structure. The Bryant Ranch (1926) and the Gillette Ranch (1928) employed a combination of adobe (mud) bricks, manufactured on the site, and reinforced concrete.

The Neff-designed "Mobile Home," christened the "Honeymoon Cottage" by its promoters, was assembled in the factory and trucked to the site.

In "Airform" construction a rubber-coated balloon is inflated and sprayed with concrete or plastic. The balloon is deflated and re-used as soon as the concrete or plastic is self-supporting. As far as is known, the twenty-one shells erected at Falls Church, Virginia, in 1941, were the first pneumatically formed structures where the entire structure was thin shell concrete. Neff went on to patent the process in 1942, and by the 1950's worthwhile social and general housing projects, including entire villages, had been built in South Africa, French West Africa, Pakistan and Brazil.

Wallace Neff's services were constantly in demand because he approached each job in an uninhibited manner. His life left little time for polemics or introspection. Each client, whether a Hollywood millionaire or a native of an underdeveloped country, had a problem to be solved. This interest in problem solving gives philosophical consistency to Wallace Neff's prodigious career as an architect.

—Alson Clark

NELSON, George.

American. Born in Hartford, Connecticut, 29 May 1908. Educated at Yale University, New Haven, Connecticut, B.A. 1929, M.A. 1931; Catholic University of America, Washington, D.C., 1932; American Academy, Rome, 1932–34 (Rome Scholarship). In partnership with William Hamby, New York, 1936–41; Design Director, Herman Miller Furniture Company, Zeeland, Michigan, 1946. Since 1947, Principal, George Nelson and Company, industrial designers, New York; since 1953, Partner, Nelson and Chadwick, architects, New York. Design Instructor, Yale University, 1931–32; Teacher of Design, Columbia University, New York, 1942–45; Visiting Critic in Architecture, Graduate School of Design, Harvard University, Cambridge, Massachusetts, 1972–73. Associate Editor, 1935–43, Co-Managing Editor, 1943–44, and Consultant, 1944–49, *Architectural Forum,* New York; Head, *Fortune/Forum* Experimental Department, Time Inc., New York, 1944–45; Editor, *Interiors,* New York, 1948–75. Member, New York State Council on Architecture, 1968–75. Program Chairman of the 15th Conference, 1965, and since 1965 Member of the Board of Directors, International Design Conference, Aspen, Colorado; Member, Board of Directors, Industrial Designers Society of America, 1967–69, and since 1972. Exhibition: *Nelson/ Eames/Girard/Propst: The Design Center at Herman Miller,* Walker Art Center, Minneapolis, 1975–76. Recipient: Industrial Arts Medal, American Institute of Architects, 1964; Contribution to Design Award, Industrial Designers Society of America, 1974; Elsie de Wolfe Award, American Society of Interior Designers, 1975. Address: George Nelson and Company Inc., 251 Park Avenue South, New York, New York 10010, U.S.A.

Works:

1940/
41 Fairchild House, 17 East 56th Street, New York (with William Hamby)

1944 Storagewall (with Henry Wright)

1946 Basic Storage Components

Gateleg Table

Slat Bench

1948 Herman Miller Showroom, Chicago

Executive Office Group

1950 Holiday house, Quoque, Long Island, New York (with Gordon Chadwick)

1952 Bubble Lamp, for the Howard Miller Clock Company

Rosewood Cases

1953 Herman Miller Showroom, New York
1954 Pedestal End Tables
Steelframe Group
1956 Information Center, Colonial Williamsburg, Virginia
Coconut Chair
Modular Seating
Omni System, for Structural Products Inc.
Thin Edge Cases
1957 Design of the *Education for Theatrical Design* exhibition, for the United States Information Agency, at the Sao Paulo *Bienal*
Day Bed
1958 Fire Alarm, for Acme Fire Alarm Company
Comprehensive Storage System
1958/
60 Design of the *Design Today in America and Europe* exhibition, for the Government of India; toured India
Design of the *Peaceful Uses of Atomic Energy* exhibition, for the Atomic Energy Commission, Cairo
Design of the *American National Exhibition,* for the United States Information Agency, in Moscow
1959 Loeb Student Center interiors, New York University, 566–576 La Guardia Place, New York
Catenary Group
1960 Tower Suite, Time-Life Building, 1271 Sixth Avenue, New York
1961 Design of the *Transportation USA* exhibition, for the United States Information Agency; toured Russia
1962 Design of the Abbott Medical Exhibit, *World's Fair,* Seattle
Herman Miller Factory, Zeeland, Michigan
1963 Design of the *U.S.-Us Show,* for Herman Miller Company, toured the United States
Sling Sofa
1964 Herman Miller Showroom, Washington, D.C.
Action Office 1
Design of the Chrysler Exhibition, *World's Fair,* New York
Design of the United States Department of State exhibition, Hall of Presidents, *World's Fair,* New York
Design of the Irish Pavilion, *World's Fair,* New York
1966 Herman Miller Factory additions, Zeeland, Michigan
Herman Miller Showroom, New York
1967 Design of the *Industrial Design USA* exhibition, for the United States Information Agency; toured Russia
1968 Rosenthal Studio, New York
1970 Design of the *U.S. Treasury* exhibition, United States Department of the Treasury, Washington, D.C.
1970/
72 Design of the *Research and Development in

the U.S.* exhibition, for the United States Information Agency; toured Eastern Europe
1971 Executive Office Group
1972 La Potagerie, 554 Fifth Avenue, New York
The Children's Place, West Hartford, Connecticut
The Children's Place, Willowbrook, New Jersey
The Children's Place, Echelon, New Jersey
1973 Aid Association for Lutherans Hospital, Appleton, Wisconsin
1974/
76 Design of the *USA '76: The First Two Hundred Years* exhibition, for the American Revolution Bicentennial Administration; toured 10 American cities
1976 Design of the *Latin American Exhibition,* Inter-American Cultural and Trade Center, Miami

Publications:

By NELSON: books—*Industrial Architecture of Albert Kahn Inc.,* New York 1939; *Tomorrow's House,* with Henry Wright, New York 1945; foreword to *Miller Furniture Company,* catalogue, Zeeland, Michigan 1952; *Living Spaces,* editor, New York 1952; *Chairs,* editor, New York 1953; *Display,* editor, New York 1953; *Storage,* editor, New York 1954; *Problems of Design,* New York 1957; *How to See: Visual Adventures in a World God Never Made,* Boston 1977; articles—"Architects of Europe Today" in *Pencil* Points (New York), January/March, May, July, September and November 1936, and January, March, June, August and October 1937; "Wright's Houses" in *Fortune* (New York), August 1946; "There's a New Pattern in Furniture Behavior" in *House Beautiful* (New York), July 1947; "Styling Organization/Design" in *Arts and Architecture* (Los Angeles), August 1947; "Problems of Design: Ends and Means" in *Interiors* (New York), May 1948; "Blessed Are the Poor" in *Interiors* (New York), July 1948; "Problems of Design: The Dead-End Room" in *Interiors* (New York), November 1948; "Beware of Trends" in *Interiors* (New York), December 1948; "Mr Roark Goes to Hollywood: A Comment on Warner Brothers' Attempt to Intrepret Frank Lloyd Wright to the Masses" in *Interiors* (New York), April 1949; "Modern Furniture" in *Interiors* (New York), July 1949; "Business and the Industrial Designer" in *Fortune* (New York), July 1949; "Problems of Design: Modern Decoration [Notes on the Subscape, The Enlargement of Vision]" in *Interiors* (New York), November 1949, November 1950, and November 1951; "After the Modern House" in *Interiors* (New York), July 1952; "Good Design: What Is It For" in *Interiors* (New York), July 1954; "Handbook of European Architecture" in *Holiday* (New York), January 1960; "A Question for George Nelson and Paul Rudolph," with Paul Rudolph, in *Zodiac* (Milan), no.

8, 1961; "People-to-Product Relationship" in *Industrial Design* (New York), May 1962; "The French Like Glass" in *Architectural Forum* (New York), November 1962; "Switzerland" in *Architectural Forum* (New York), June 1963; "Prima dell'apertura, una visita alla Fiera di New York" in *Domus* (Milan), May 1964; "Design in America: The Last 25 Years: A Series of Interviews" in *Interiors* (New York), November 1965; "Obsolescence" in *Perspecta* (New Haven, Connecticut), no. 11, 1967; "Architecture for the New Itinerants" in *Saturday Review* (New York), 22 April 1967; "Design, Technology, and the Pursuit of Ugliness" in *Saturday Review* (New York), 2 October 1971; "The End of Architecture: Are Buildings About to Be Driven Underground or to Disappear" in *Architecture Plus* (New York), April 1973; "The Humane Designer" in *Industrial Design* (New York), June 1973; "The Designer as Social Catalyst" in *Canadian Architect* (Toronto), June 1973; "From Monuments to Bell Jars: George Nelson Predicts the End of Architecture" in *RIBA Journal* (London), October 1973; "The Hidden City: Making Our Cities Less Boring by Making Them Less Visible" in *Architecture Plus* (New York), November/December 1974; "Design: The Business of Survival" in *Industrial Design* (New York), March 1975; "Do Small Companies Need Design?" in *Industrial Design* (New York), May/June 1975; "Interiors: The Emerging Dominant Reality" in *Interiors* (New York), November 1975.

On NELSON: articles—"The Storagewall" in *Architectural Forum* (New York), November 1944; "What Is Happening to Modern Architecture" in *Museum of Modern Art Bulletin* (New York), Spring 1948; "George Nelson Joins Interiors" in *Interiors* (New York), October 1948; "About the Job of Designing a Furniture Showroom" in *Interiors* (New York), May 1949; "The Projection of Industrial Design into Advertising" by Mildred Constantine in *Graphis* (Zurich), November 1953; "Examples of Work by George Nelson" and "The George Nelson Office: A Comprehensive Design Organization" in *Architectural Record* (New York), December 1957; "Designing the Moscow Exhibit" in *Architectural Record* (New York), November 1959; "The World of George Nelson" by Enzo Fratelli in *Zodiac* (Milan), no. 8, 1961; "Nelson's Way" in *Interiors* (New York), November 1963; "The Herman Miller Action Office" in *Interiors* (New York), December 1964; "Seven Significant Designers: An In-Depth Report" in *House Beautiful* (New York), October 1966; "Portfolio: Architecture" in *Perspecta* (New Haven, Connecticut), no. 11, 1967; "Conversation with George Nelson" in *Industrial Design* (New York), April 1969; "Designers in America: George Nelson and Company" in *Industrial Design* (New York), October 1973; "The Design Process at Herman Miller" in *Design Quarterly* (Minneapolis), no. 98/99, 1975.

George Nelson: Comprehensive Storagé System, 1958

Although he was trained as an architect, George Nelson's accomplishments extend to all phases of environmental design, and today he is known as one of the most talented industrial, graphic, and urban designers of the 20th century. He has received international acclaim for his interiors, his unique designs for exhibition displays, his home and office furnishing inventions, and recently for proposing new concepts of urban growth.

After completing his undergraduate education at Yale University, Nelson began his career as a writer for several American architectural journals, and he was associate editor of *Architectural Forum* for almost a decade. During that time, he independently developed several new prefabricated architectural components. The most notable of these was a combination storage unit and room divider, known commercially as Storagewall (released in 1945). At roughly the same time, he invented, but did not develop, a complete, pre-formed one wall kitchen unit.

Storagewall brought Nelson to the attention of Herman Miller Inc., then still a small furniture manufacturer in Wisconsin. Even though Nelson had no experience in interior or industrial design besides his few, semi-architectural inventions, the president of that company still managed to eventually persuade him to join their staff. There, he continued to apply his keen mind towards creating radically new products for interior use, and soon Nelson was a catalytic force in Herman Miller's growth.

He brought the now famous Charles Eames, a designer with similar multi-disciplinary inclinations, to the company, and Herman Miller soon became a mecca for the most talented industrial designers in the country. The company has always valued its design team as its chief commodity, and allowed them complete economic and temporal freedom to fully develop their new ideas. Herman Miller has remained dedicated to innovational design and high quality production, and has gained a reputation for European styling and craftsmanship. Today, largely as a result of Nelson's perseverance, it is America's most respected manufacturer of home and office furnishings.

Nelson's extraordinary ability to conceptualize environments in their totality, and erase distinguishing lines that have traditionally existed between interior, industrial, architectural and urban design, has been his chief asset throughout his career. With Herman Miller, and in independent practice, Nelson has developed countless schemes that are combinations of these disciplines, and are particularly effective because of this. Many of his designs for Herman Miller were complete living environments that were both furniture and architecture at once.

In the late 1950's, he applied this skill to a logical cause, the design of exhibitions. Soon he was clearly the leading American exhibition designer, and in 1959 he designed his acclaimed structure for the American national exhibition in Moscow. It used translucent fiberglass, molded into umbrella shapes, to create the roof and the display areas, while the columns regulated circulatory movement. Nelson has also designed many display cases, panel systems for vertical exhibitions, and numerous accompanying catalogues, including the brochure that accompanied the first exhibit of the Cooper Hewitt Museum, the Smithsonian Institution's National Museum of Design.

Throughout his professional career Nelson has remained a prolific writer, and his books and articles have had as much impact on contemporary design as have the ingenuity of his own creations. His 1977 release entitled *How to See* is his most personal. It is an extraordinary pictorial essay that displays design throughout our environment. There is some commentary, but the strongest statement is expressed by the careful selection of visual material.

Nelson is a quick thinker who has remained in the forefront of the design world for a third of a century, and continues to offer meaningful suggestions for future growth. Lately he has been concentrating more directly on issues of urban design, and he published numerous articles in the mid-seventies proclaiming the importance of revolutionizing our attitude towards architecture and the city as a whole. But whether the subject is architectural, industrial, or even completely hypothetical, Nelson has shown himself to be one of the sharpest problem solvers around, still happily kicking for design to bring more order and more beauty to our man-made environment.

—Mitchell B. Rouda

NELSON, Paul (Daniel).

French. Born in Chicago, Illinois, 8 November 1895; emigrated to France, 1920: naturalized, 1973. Educated at Princeton University, New Jersey, 1913–17 (President, Princeton Triangle Club, 1916–17), Litt.B. 1917; Ecole des Beaux-Arts, Paris, 1920–27 (Prix Guadet, 1927), D.P.L.G. 1927; influenced by the work of the Ecole de Paris: Braque, Léger, Miró, Giacometti, Arp, Derain, Hélion, Laurens, Calder, Bissière, Picasso, etc. Volunteered to join the Lafayette Escadrille, 1917, then served in the United States Air Force, in Italy and France, 1917–19: Lieutenant; Member, 1941, and President of the Washington, D.C. Chapter, 1942–43, American National Committee of "France Forever." Married Francine Lecoeur in 1920 (died, 1951); married the painter Maddalena Giannattasio in 1952; children: Ugo and Rory. In private practice, Paris, 1928–40; Architectural Consultant, 1941–42, and Job Captain, 1942–43, United States Housing Authority, Washington, D.C.; Consultant, Board of Economic Warfare and National Housing Agency, Washington, 1943–44; Chief of the Division of Urbanism and Building Industries, Supply Mission for France, Washington, 1944–45; returned to Paris and re-opened office there, 1945–67; Technical Assistant, French Ministry of Reconstruction, Paris, 1945–46; Professor and Director of the Franco-American Atelier of Architecture, Ecole Nationale Supérieure des Beaux-Arts, Paris, 1965–67; moved practice to Marseilles, and served as Professor and Director of the Franco-American International Atelier of Architecture, Ecole d'Art et d'Architecture de Marseille-Luminy, 1967–78. Special Consultant to the United States Public Health Service, 1959, and to the Technical Department of the French Ministry of Public Health, 1961–62. Visiting Professor, School of Architecture, Pratt Institute, New York, 1957–58; Visiting Critic in charge of the Hopper Fellowship Competition, Yale University School of Architecture, New Haven, Connecticut, 1958–59; Visiting Professor, School of Architecture, Harvard University, Cambridge, Massachusetts, and School of Architecture, Massachusetts Institute of Technology, Cambridge, 1959–60, and Fellow of the Joint MIT/-Harvard Center for Urban Studies, Cambridge, 1960. Exhibitions: Museum of Modern Art, New York, 1936; Palais de la Découverte, Paris, 1937. Collection: Museum of Modern Art, New York. Recipient: Graham Foundation Fellowship, 1957; Gold Medal, Société d'Encouragement à l'Art et à l'Industrie, 1968; Grand Medal of Honor, Académie d'Architecture, Paris, 1978. Honorary Member, Sociedad de Arquitectos Mexicanos, 1943; Member, American Institute of Architects, 1958. Chevalier, 1946, and Officer, 1956, Légion d'Honneur; Commandeur des Arts et Lettres, 1964. Address: Chemin Rousset, Quartier Pommé, 13530 Trets, France.

Works:

1928 Brooks House, 80 Boulevard Arago, Paris
1929 Art direction and sets for the United Artists' film *What a Widow!*, Hollywood, California
1930 Audio-visual theatre for the Joseph Kennedy House, Bronxville, New York (project)

1930/
32 Petite Maison de Santé, near Paris (project)
1932/
33 Health City of Lille, France (project)
1934 Surgical Pavilion of Ismailia, Egypt (project)
1936 National Center for the Columbia Broadcasting System, New York (project)
1936/
38 Suspended House, France (project)
1937/
38 Museum of Scientific Discovery, Paris (project; with Oscar Nitzchke and Frantz Jourdain)
1938 W.G.N. Broadcasting Theatre, Chicago (competition project; with Fernand Léger)
1941/
46 Research in urban planning for the United States Government
1946/
56 France-U.S.A. Memorial Hospital, Saint-Lô, France (with Roger Gilbert, Charles Sébillotte and Marcel Mersier)
1951/
52 Nurses' Home, Doctors' Home, and renovation of nursing units in the existing hospital, American Hospital of Neuilly, Paris
1954/
55 Badin Experimental House, rue Paul Couderc, Sceaux, France
1955/
56 Museum for Fernand Léger, Biot, France (project)
1957/
60 Research in America on hospital architecture
1961/
62 J. Walter Thompson Administrative Center, Paris (project)
1963/
68 Hospital, Dinan, France (with P. Devinoy and R. Lamourec)
1965/
74 Master plan and 500-bed hospital for the Arles Community Health Center, France (with P. Devinoy and Remondet)
1971 Plan for health care facilities in Tunisia (with P. Devinoy)
1975/
76 Paul Nelson House, Trets, France

Publications:

By NELSON: books—*La Cité Hospitalière de Lille,* Paris 1932; *Deux Etudes Hospitalières par Paul Nelson,* Paris 1936; *La Maison Suspendue,* Paris 1937; *Transformation de l'Architecture aux Etats-Unis,* Paris 1946; articles—"La Maison de la rue Saint-Guillaume" in *L'Architecture d'Aujourd'hui* (Paris), November/December 1933; "L'Organisation Internationale des Cité Hospitalières" and "L'air conditionné" in *La Revue des Hôpitaux* (Lyons), 1934; "Le Pavillon Chirurgical de Suez" in *Cahiers d'Art* (Paris), December 1935; "A Method of Architectural Procedure" in *Architectural Record* (New York), June 1937; "La Peinture Spatiale de Léger" in *Cahiers d'Art* (Paris), June 1937; "Le Palais de la Découverte" in *Cahiers d'Art* (Paris), no. 3/4, 1940; "American Architecture 1891–1941" in *Architectural Record* (New York), February 1941; "Researching for a New Standard of Living" in *Revere Copper and Brass Company Magazine* (New York), no. 2, 1942; "War Dormitories" in *Public Housing* (F.P.H.A.: Washington, D.C.), May 1942; "Design for Tomorrow" in *Perspecta* (New Haven, Connecticut), 1959; "An Integrated Approach to Design" in *Journal of the American Hospital Association* (Chicago), June 1959; "Mon ami Braque" in *Les Lettres Françaises* (Paris), 6 and 12 September 1962; "Le Théâtre et les Loisirs" in "Le Lieu Théâtral dans la Société Moderne" in *Revue du Centre National de la Recherche Scientifique* (Paris), 1963; "Collaboration Artistes-Architectes" in *Melpomène* (Paris), 16 December 1964; "Corbu: C'était un géant" in *Paris-Normandie* (Paris), 30 August 1965; "Un Brûleur d'Etapes" in *Les Lettres Francaises* (Paris), 2 and 7 September 1965; "Plomberie et Sanitaires Industrialisés" in *Les Tables Rondes du Second Oeuvre* (Paris), October 1965; "L'homme, l'architecte, l'industrie du bâtiment" in *Techniques et Architecture* (Paris), 1966; "Vers le Centre de Santé" in *La Table Ronde* (Paris), March 1968; "Mutation ou Cessation" in *Le Carré Bleu* (Helsinki), no. 3/4, 1969.

On NELSON: books—*Hospitals: Integrated Design* by Isadore Rosenfield, 2nd edition, New York 1956; *Nouvelle Architecture Francaise* by Maurice Besset, Teufen, Switzerland 1967; *The New Architecture of Europe* by G. E. Kidder Smith, New York 1967; articles—"La Cité Hospitalière de Lille" by Christian Zervos in *Cahiers d'Art* (Paris), no. 8/10, 1932; preface by Christian Zervos to *La Cité Hospitalière de Lille* by Paul Nelson, Paris 1932; "The Surgical Pavilion of Suez" in *Architectural Record* (New York), June 1934; preface by Jean Hélion, "Termes de vie, Termes d'espace," to "Le Pavillon Chirurgical de Suez" by Paul Nelson in *Cahiers d'Art* (Paris), December 1935; "Health City of Lille" in *Architectural Record* (New York), June 1938; "The Suspended House" in *Architectural Record* (New York), December 1938; "The Palace of Scientific Discovery" by John Burchard in *MIT Review* (Cambridge, Massachusetts), January/February 1939; "The Palace of Scientific Discovery" in *Architectural Record* (New York), February 1939; "Hôpital Hospice de Saint-Lô" in *L'Architecture d'Aujourd'hui* (Paris), November 1947; "Hôpital Hospice de Saint-Lô" in *L'Architecture d'Aujourd'hui* (Paris), January 1948; "Sun for Surgery at Saint-Lô" in *Life* (New York), July 1948; "L'Hôpital de Saint-Lô" in *L'Architecture d'Aujourd'hui* (Paris), no. 27, 1949; "Hospital at Saint-Lo, France" in *Architectural Review* (London), March 1949; "The Saint-Lo Hospital" in *Architectural Forum* (New York), September 1949; "Hôpital Memorial France-Etat-Unis, Saint-Lô, France" by Bridgeman in *L'Architecture d'Aujourd'hui* (Paris), no. 70, 1956; "Une Maison aux couleurs de Fernand Léger" in *Maison et Jardin* (Paris), July 1956; "Vers un Nouvel Humanisme," interview, by D. Valeix in *L'Architecture d'Aujourd'hui* (Paris), 1957; "Memorial Hospital" in *Progressive Architecture* (New York), October 1957; "Paul Nelson: La Maison Suspendue" by Aulis Blomstedt in *Le Carré Bleu* (Helsinki), no. 2, 1958; "For the Jersey Meadows: A Serpentine Band of Housing" in *Architectural Forum* (New York), April 1958; "Pratt Studies Jersey Meadows" in *Progressive Architecture* (New York), 1958; "La Forme Architecturale" by Aulis Blomstedt in *Le Carré Bleu* (Helsinki), no. 1, 1961; "Paul Nelson: Un Architecte Humaniste" by Michel-Louis Lacoste in *Informations et Documents* (U.S. Embassy, Paris), 1 November 1963; "Présentation Préliminaire de l'Hôpital de Dinan" in *L'Architecture d'Aujourd'hui* (Paris), no. 115, 1964; "Projet de l'Hôpital de Dinan" in *Techniques et Architecture* (Paris), no. 2, 1965; "Un Américain à Paris" by Ch. Galperine in *Notre République* (Paris), 3 February 1967; "Vers un Centre de Santé pour la Communauté: Arles" in *La Vie Collective* (Paris), October 1971; "Paul Nelson: An Interview" by Judith Applegate in *Perspecta* (New Haven, Connecticut) no. 13/14, 1971; "Plaidoyer pour le changement" by Anne Kandelman in *Le Carré Bleu* (Helsinki), no. 1, 1978.

*

Ever since I began my studies of architecture in Paris I intended to be a creator, not a businessman (therefore I never maintained a big agency but chose the best associates, designers and engineers, as I went along, according to need). I was always interested in development. My interest in new methods and materials was combined with a constant interest in the development of "man"—this I learned from the artists of the Ecole de Paris, particularly from Braque. And I attempted to realize a synthesis between American technology and French humanism.

As my architecture was devoted to the development of man, I needed to learn how "man-in-progress" develops himself. And I discovered that he develops in two ways at the same time—as an individual and as a collective or social being. Parallel ways, but complementary: man goes from one to the other, and it is this alternation that enriches him—indirectly, while enriching his collectivity. From the moment that this process is admitted, then the conception of the house changes, because it becomes a closed form where it is possible for man and family to isolate themselves momentarily for their development needs (the Suspended House project). Conversely, collective architecture must be a free-standing form, opened on all sides. The "enriching" must result necessarily from the contrast between the activities pertaining to these two forms (the goal is not form but man). In my opinion, therefore, the objective of architecture and of urban planning consists finally in responding to the needs of development of total man, from birth to death.

In my research in urban planning I discovered the fact that the most economical community units were also the most efficient—a discovery that was both economically staggering and qualitatively desirable. I came to believe that it is not a question of creating services—education, health, communications, etc.— for a given population, but rather one of discovering the standards that determine the size of population necessary for the optimum efficiency of each service. And this led me to my theory about the organic structuration of the town as it should be.

To realize such a profound study of man's needs, and to reach an answer to these questions of needs by taking into account the future (with the hope of creating the least number of barriers to development), I was helped by a method of architectural procedure that I created in 1933–35 which I have used systematically ever since. This methodology is composed of three stages: the "non-architectural analysis," where the over-all aims are established by all concerned (specialists, engineers, artists and users); the "architectural analysis," devoted to the planning of ideal systems or forms of inter-relationships; and the "architectural synthesis," when design first crystallizes. This approach is dialectical in essence because it is based on continuous interchange (opposition and resolution) of the forces involved in the different fields. And, finally, it relies for beauty on the contrapuntal form of harmony that these melodies constitute as they enter into unison at certain points in the planning for over-all aims and principles.

These principles led me as an architect to develop a method of planning to facilitate to the maximum the provision of desirable development for man. Therefore, I have always started with "what should be done," which would permit me to lower my aim to "what can be done." This method eliminates immediately and continually any possibility of giving in to "what is usually done."

—Paul Nelson

*

"It has always been a principle of my architecture," Paul Nelson remarked in an interview, "to never limit the user to one way of doing things," and throughout his career he has been dedicated to the idea of "flexibility" as an architectural imperative.

Nelson was born in Chicago in 1895 and educated at Princeton University. A bomber pilot in France during World War I, he returned to Paris after the war to attend the Ecole des Beaux-Arts. In 1923, at the suggestion of his friend Le Corbusier, Nelson and several other young architects established an atelier under Auguste Perret, France's leading exponent in the use of reinforced concrete. By 1928 Nelson had his own office, and in 1930 he received a commission to design a small private clinic near Paris. In this project Nelson was to define several major themes that he would pursue for the remainder of his career. The psychological comfort of both patient and visitor, the architectural ramifications of modern medical technology, and the need for flexibility to accommodate changing environmental conditions were issues confronted in the clinic. They were greatly elaborated upon just two years later with a project for a teaching hospital and medical and nursing school complex in Lille. For this project Nelson invented and patented a "flexible curtain-wall" to allow for greater interior partition arrangements, though the wall was not put into use until construction of the France-U.S.A. Hospital at St Lô.

Throughout the 1930's Nelson was involved in highly imaginative, often speculative architectural work, and in the invention of building or constructional systems. Specializing in hospital design, Nelson developed an egg-shaped operating room that allowed increased control over asepsis and lighting. It was also at this time that Nelson designed perhaps his best known project, the Suspended House (Maison Suspendue). Greatly influenced by Pierre Chareau's Maison de Verre, the Maison Suspendue consisted of prefabricated units for different functions suspended within a fixed steel cage. Touted as an "all-steel house," the Maison Suspendue was, for a short time, under consideration as the main theme construction for the 1939 New York *World's Fair*. Despite its wide publication, however, the house was never built, and the Trylon and Sphere were constructed at the Fair instead.

During World War II Nelson left France, though he was able to collaborate with Frantz Jourdain and Oskar Nitzchke on a research project for a Museum of Scientific Discovery (Palais de la Découverte). Drawings made for this unrealized building show a huge domed structure, strung with cables, and owing much to both Le Corbusier's design for the Palace of the Soviets and several of Melnikov's large exhibition projects.

Returning to France after the war, Nelson was named chief-architect for the France-U.S.A. Memorial hospital of St. Lô; it was completed in 1956 and is Nelson's finest medical building, incorporating many of his technological innovations. The architect's old friend Ferdinand Léger contributed a large mural to the entry of the hospital and, shortly before his death, collaborated with Nelson on a small residence near Paris (the Badin house at Sceaux), which boasted painted wall panels. After Léger's death, Nelson was asked to design a memorial museum for the painter. Situated over a hair-pin turn in the little winding town of Biot, the Léger museum, regrettably never built, is Nelson's most ingenious piece of site-planning, with the roof-terrace of the building creating a public plaza.

In 1957 Nelson received a Graham Foundation fellowship and returned to the United States, and his renewed contacts thereafter brought him back with increasing frequency. In 1959–1960 he taught at both Harvard and M.I.T., directing studies on a Progressive Patient Care Hospital in Cambridge.

Between 1960 and 1967 Nelson designed several large hospital complexes, including the 450 bed facility for the city of Dinan and a technologically sophisticated hospital and community mental health center in Arles. While working on the Arles center, Nelson moved to Marseilles where he helped set up the Franco-American Atelier of Architecture in the new School of Art and Architecture.

—Richard Lavenstein

NERVI, Pier Luigi.

Italian. Born in Sondrio, 21 June 1891. Educated at the University of Bologna, Dip.Ing. 1913. Officer in the Engineering Corps of the Italian Army, 1915–18. Married Irene Calosin in 1924; children: Antonio, Vittorio, and Mario. Engineer with the Societa per Costruzioni Cementizie, Bologna, 1913–15, 1918–23. In private practice, Rome, from 1923: Partner, Nervi and Nebbiosi, 1923–32; President, Ingg. Nervi and Bartolia, from 1932; Partner, with sons Antonio, Mario and Vittorio, Studio Nervi, 1960 until his death, 1979. Consultant Engineer, Unesco, Paris, 1952. Professor of the Technology and Technique of Construction, Faculty of Architecture, University of Rome, 1947–61. Exhibition: *Pier Luigi Nervi,* Centre d'Information du Bâtiment, Paris, 1962. Recipient: Certificate of Commendation, Institute of Structural Engineers, London, 1955; Brown Medal, Franklin Institute, Philadelphia, 1957; Exner Medal, Osterreiche Gewerbevereines, Vienna, 1957; Gold Medal, American Institute of Architects, Philadelphia Chapter, 1958; Gold Medal, Confederazione Generale Italiana Professionisti-Artisti, Rome, 1958; Gold Medal, Royal Institute of British Architects, London, 1960; Alfred Lindau Award, American Concrete Institute, 1963; Award, Concrete Industry Board, New York, 1963; Emil Morsch Award, Deutsche Beton Verein, 1963; Gold Medal, American Institute of Architects, 1964; Gold Medal, Institute of Structural Engineers, London, 1968; Feltrinelli Award, Rome, 1968; Gold Medal, Académie d'Architecture, Paris, 1971. Honorary doctorates: University of Buenos Aires, 1950; University of Edinburgh, 1960; Technische Hochschule, Munich, 1960; University of Warsaw, 1961; Harvard University, Cambridge, Massachusetts, 1962; Dartmouth College, Hanover, New Hampshire, 1963; Prague Polytechnic, 1966; University of London, 1969. Member, Accademia di San Luca, Rome, 1960. Honorary Member, American Institute of Architects, 1956; Honorary Member, National Institute of Arts and Letters, U.S.A., 1957; Foreign Member, Royal Academy of Fine Arts, Stockholm, 1957; Corresponding Member, Academia Nacional de Ciencias Exactas Fisicas y Naturales, Buenos Aires, 1959; Honorary Member, American Academy of Arts and Sciences, 1960; Corresponding Member, Bayerischen Akademie der Schönen Künste, Munich, 1960; Member, Royal Institute of Dutch Engineers, 1964; Member, Akademie der Künste, Berlin, 1964; Member, Institut des Beaux Arts, Paris, 1973; Foreign Member, Institut de France, Paris, 1973. *Died* (in Rome) *9 January 1979.*

Works (as structural engineer):

1927 August Cinema, Naples
1932 Municipal Stadium, Florence
 Circular Hangars in re-inforced concrete and steel (projects)
 Monumento della Bandiera, Monte Mario, Rome (project; with Rubens Magnani)
1934 Revolving House (project)
1935 Stadium, Rome (project; with Cesare Valle)
1936 Aircraft Hangars, for the Italian Air Force, Orvieto, Italy
 Biedano Valley Bridge, Viterbo, Italy (project)
1938 Silos for the Societa Solvay, Rosignano, Italy (project)
1939 Viaduct (project)
1940 Pavilion of Italian Civilization, for the *Esposizione Universale* of 1942 (project; with P. M. Bardi)
 Palace of Water and Light, for the *Esposizione Universale* of 1942 (project)
1941 Aircraft Hangars, for the Italian Air Force, at Orbetello, Torre del Lago, Italy (destroyed in 1944)
1942 Underground Gasoline Storage Tanks, Italy
1943 984 foot span (project)
 660 foot span for railway station (project)
1945 Ferro-Cemento Warehouse, Rome Factory (project)
1946 Central Station, Palermo, Sicily (project)
 Pre-fabricated circular house (project)
1947 Swimming Baths, Naval Academy, Livorno
 Conte Trossi Wharf, San Michele di Pagano, Genoa (with Luigi Carlo Daneri)
1949 Air-insulated shed roof (project)
 Aircraft Hangar, Buenos Aires (project)
1950 Restaurant Roof, Kursaal Beach Casino, Ostia, Italy (with Attilio La Padula)
 Exhibition Halls, Salone B and Salone C, Turin
1951 Salt Warehouse, Tortona, Italy
 Bridge over the River Reno, Sasso Marconi, Italy (project; with Carlo Castelli-Guidi)
1952 Tobacco Factory, Bologna
 Roof of Hall, Chianciano Terme, Italy (with Mario Loreti and Mario Marchi)
1953 Gatti Wool Factory, Rome
 "System Nervi" pressure pipeline
 Lancia Factory, Turin (project)
 Sports Palace, Vienna (project; with Antonio Nervi)
1954 Main Railway Station, Naples (project; with Giusseppe Vaccaro and Mario Campanella)
 Italian Cultural Institute, Stockholm (with Gio Ponti and Ture Wenerholm)

Pier Luigi Nervi: Palazzo dello Sport, Rome, 1959

Storehouses for Tobacco Factory, Bologna
Tobacco Factory and Storehouses, Turin
Tramcar Depot, Turin
1955 Fiat Factory, Turin
Bridge over the River Tenza, Italy (project)
Centre National des Industries, Paris (project; with Camelot, de Mailly and Bernard Zehrfuss)
1956 Exhibition Hall, Caracas, Venezuela (project)
1957 Unesco Headquarters, Paris (with Marcel Breuer and Bernard Zehrfuss)
Palazzetto dello Sport, Rome (with Annibale Vitellozzi)
1958 Pirelli Building, Milan (with Gio Ponti, Alberto Rosselli, Antonio Fornaroli, Giuseppe Valtolina, Egidio dell'Orto, and Arturo Danusso)
1959 Palazzo dello Sport, Rome (with Marcello Piacentini)
Flaminio Stadium, Rome (with Antonio Nervi)
Via Olimpica Overpass, Rome
New Norcia Cathedral and Abbey, near Perth, Western Australia (project; with Antonio Nervi and Carlo Vannoni)
Railway Station, Savona, Italy (competition project)
1961 Palazzo del Lavoro, *Italia '61* exhibition, Turin
George Washington Bridge Bus Station, New York
Nathaniel Leverone Field House, Dartmouth College, Hanover, New Hampshire
1962 Burgo Paper Mill, Mantua, Italy
1963 Overpass, Genoa
1964 Covered Swimming Pool (project)
Palazzetto dello Sport, Vicenza, Italy (project; with P. Maltauro)
1966 Portsmouth Cathedral extension, Hampshire, England (project; with Seeley and Paget)
Cromodora Factory, Venoria Realie, Turin
Stock Exchange Tower, Montreal (with Luigi Moretti)
Office Building, Verona (project)
Risorgimento Bridge, Verona
1967 MOTTA Autogrill, Padua (with M. Bega)
Cultural Center, Tripoli, Libya (project)
1971 Church, San Remo, Italy (project; to be constructed)
Papal Audience Hall, Vatican City
St. Mary's Cathedral, San Francisco (with Pietro Belluschi, and McSweeney, Ryan and Lee)
Cassa di Risparmio Headquarters, Venice (with A. Scattolin)
Cultural and Convention Center, Norfolk, Virginia (with Williams and Tazewell)
1975 Ebute-Metta Station, Lagos, Nigeria (project)
Stadium, Novara, Italy
Ice Hockey Rink, Dartmouth College, Hanover, New Hampshire
Um-Al-Khanezeer Island Development, Baghdad, Iraq (project)
1978 International Labour Organization Office, Geneva (with Eugène Beaudouin)
Pitt Rivers Museum, Oxford (project; with Powell and Moya)
1978– African Development Bank Headquarters, Abidjan, Ivory Coast (with E. Olympio)
Italian Embassy, Brasilia
Apartment/Office Building, Riyadh, Saudi Arabia (with ICE, Orsi and Koerne, Giudici and Stoppa, and Italprogetti)
Australian Embassy, Paris (as structural consultant; with Harry Seidler and Marcel Breuer)
Railway Station, Cosenza, Italy (with Sara Rossi)
Civic Library, Verona
Church of S. Gaspare del Bufalo, Rome
Good Hope Centre (exhibition hall), Cape Town

Publications:

By NERVI: books—*El Lenguaje Arquitectonico,* Buenos Aires 1950; *Arte o Scienza del Construire?,* Rome 1954; *Concrete and Structural Form,* London 1955; *Costruire Correttamente,* Milan 1955, as *Structures,* New York 1956; *Nuove Strutture,* Milan 1963, as *New Structures,* London and Stuttgart 1963; *Aesthetics and Technology in Building,* Cambridge, Massachusetts and London 1966; articles—"Arte e Technica del Costruire" in *Quadrante* (Milan), June 1931; "Pensieri sull/Ingegneria" in *Quadrante* (Milan), October 1932; "Monumento alla Bandiera" in *Quadrante* (Milan), December 1933; "Problemi della Realizzazione Architettonica" in *Casabella* (Milan), February 1934; "Una Aviorimessa in Cemento Armato" in *Casabella* (Milan), April 1938; "Un Arco Monumentale in Conglomerato non Armato" in *Casabella* (Milan), August 1942; "Ancora sul senso dell Architettura" in *Domus* (Milan), March 1950; "Economica Edilizia" in *La Casa* (Rome), April 1950; "Le Proporzioni nella Tecnica" in *Domus* (Milan), December 1951; "Possibilitá Costruttive ed Architettonica della Pre-Fabbricazione Strutturale" in *L'Architettura* (Rome), January 1952; "Precast Concrete Offers New Possibilities for Design of Shell Structures" in *American Concrete Institute Journal* (Detroit), February 1953; "L'Architecture du Beton Arme et le Problème des Coffrages" in *L'Architecture d'Aujourd'hui* (Paris), July 1953; "Concrete and Structural Form" in *The Structural Engineer* (London), May 1956; "The Place of Structure in Architecture" in *Architectural Record* (New York), July 1956; "Reinforced Concrete Construction" in *Progressive Architecture* (New York), September 1957; "Critica delle Strutture" in *Casabella* (Milan), January, February, March and April 1959; "Le Strutture dell'Unesco" in *Casabella* (Milan), April 1959; etc.

On NERVI: books—*Gli Elementi dell'Architettura Funzionale* by Alberto Sartoris, Milan 1935; *Nuova Architettura Italiana* by Agnoldomenico Pica, Milan 1939; *Architettura Moderna in Italia* by Agnoldomenico Pica, Milan 1941; *Italy Builds* by G. E. Kidder Smith, London and Milan 1955; *Pier Luigi Nervi* by G. C. Argan, Milan 1955; *The Works of Pier Luigi Nervi* by Jürgen Joedicke and Ernesto Rogers, Stuttgart and London 1957; *Pier Luigi Nervi* by Ada Louise Huxtable, New York 1960; *Structure in Architecture* by Mario Salvadori, Englewood Cliffs, New Jersey 1963; *Architettura Moderna in Milano* by Agnoldomenico Pica, Milan 1964; *Architectural Engineering: New Structures* by Agnoldomenico Pica, New York 1964; *Pier Luigi Nervi* by Mate Major, Budapest 1966, Berlin 1970; *Nervi* by Jan Tomes, Prague 1967; *Pier Luigi Nervi* by Agnoldomenico Pica, Rome 1969.

*

As an architect in reinforced concrete, Pier Luigi Nervi was one of the most notable of this century. He evolved his own system of structural design, independently of others. It was mainly for large buildings of the hall type—exhibition pavilions, covered sports arenas, railway stations, aircraft hangars, warehouses and sports stadia—and into the system he introduced variations in answer to needs and economy. The structures proved not only very efficient but also visually attractive. In many buildings he was both the structural engineer and the architect. In others he collaborated with architects, but his special contribution to the design of the structure is usually strongly apparent. In the early years of his practice he realized the limitations of in-situ concrete, especially if speed and economy were to be secured, and he went on to design numerous pre-cast units that he used in conjunction with poured concrete in situ. One of these he termed "ferro-cemento." It consists of layers of fine steel mesh sprayed with cement mortar, and it can be used either for shell construction or for heavier units, with reinforcing rods inserted between the layers of mortar and mesh. With this basic system he was able to introduce many variations as solutions to the different problems presented by each project.

Among his early spectacular works is the large Municipal Stadium at Florence for 35,000 people. (During the construction of the stadium he realized the difficulties in creating such a structure of in-situ concrete.) The stadium has several impressive features, among them the series of unusual spiral staircases projecting from the outer circumference of the building by means of curved cantilevered members: they have the appearance of modern abstract sculpture. Impressive too is the shell canopy of the grandstand supported by a series of curved cantilevered beams.

The series of about a dozen large aircraft hangars for the Italian Air Force reveal Nervi's constant experimentation and evolution towards more efficient methods. For the earliest of these hangars he employed in-situ concrete for the roof beams, and the method involved complicated shuttering. In the later hangars he designed much lighter lattice pre-cast ribs for the roof, which were made in sections, assembled, jointed and held together at intervals by poured concrete ribs with forked ground supports. The arch is a low pointed Gothic, and the lattice beams make a diamond pattern, visually very attractive.

Among Nervi's finest achievements as an architect in reinforced concrete are the two immense exhibition halls in Turin, Salone B and Salone C, both very large structures erected in the incredibly short time of seven and six months. Salone B has a segmental roof span of 310 feet of corrugated section in which Nervi used his own method of pre-cast units of ferrocemento. These units have windows for roof lights, and are jointed and linked by ribs poured in situ, supported by four ribbed fans converging to the massive main supporting inclined concrete stanchions. At the end of the hall is an apse for which he employed a different method. Here the precast units, also made of ferro-cemento, form channels into which concrete is poured. In contrast to the perforated corrugated main roof, the half dome of the apse has a diamond pattern. The pattern of both roofs, although structurally determined, is highly decorative. In Salone C the diamond pattern is used, and light is admitted through a band between the triangular supports and the upper part of the roof.

Both of these methods were used in two well known later structures, the Palazzetto and the Palazzo dello Sport in Rome. Although he collaborated with two noted Italian architects—Vitellozzi in the Palazzetto and Piacentini in the Palazzo—it is clear that the essential design of the structures is Nervi's work. In the Palazzetto dello Sport Nervi used the diamond pattern roof as in the Turin Salone C (with a similar, almost vertical band of fenestration at the lower edge of the roof), which, in this saucer dome, creates a very beautiful effect. It has been likened in effect to the fan valuting of late Gothic. The external sloping piers with triangular forked heads, which take the thrust of the roof ribs, provide a dramatic external effect. Here the sense of powerful structure and dramatic decorative effect are one.

In the Palazzo dello Sport, which is much larger, the corrugated form of roofing, as in the Turin Salone B, is adapted to the saucer dome with impressive effect, especially at the apex where the ribs converge to the cylindrical lantern. The thrust of the roof is taken by the mass of terraced seating, which in turn is supported by sloping piers. This construction is not, however, apparent in the general exterior view but is enclosed in a colonnade of slender members, which provides a covered passageway all around the building. Because of the colonnade the exterior effect is not so impressive and structurally decorative as in the Palazzetto. Possibly, it was introduced by the collaborating architect.

The Unesco Headquarters in Paris is also a collaborative effort. Though different from his other work, it clearly shows Nervi's contribution in the structural design. The Y-shaped 8-storey office block is supported on heavy inclined concrete piers; adjoining it is the fan-shaped concrete conference hall of folded concrete slab construction. In this complex Nervi permitted himself two very attractive decorative features: the generous sweep of a cantilevered shell canopy for the entrance and the external spiral stairway the whole height of the building, like a series of fans in concrete. Both have been mistaken, at first sight, for works of decorative abstract sculpture—which, of course, they are, while at the same time fulfilling a practical purpose.

Pier Luigi Nervi belongs to that small group of structural engineers who have introduced methods that have created structures that are both spectacular and efficient. He was an engineer who was also an artist.

—Arnold Whittick

Walter A. Netsch: East Wing, Art Institute of Chicago, 1976

NETSCH, Walter A(ndrew Jr.).

American. Born in Chicago, Illinois, 23 February 1920. Educated at the Massachusetts Institute of Technology, Cambridge, 1939–43, B.Arch. 1943. Served in the United States Army Corps of Engineers, 1943–46. Married Dawn Clark in 1963. Designer, for L. Morgan Yost, Kenilworth, Illinois, 1946–47. Joined Skidmore, Owings and Merrill, 1947: Designer, Chicago, 1947, Oak Ridge, Illinois, 1947–49, San Francisco, 1949–53, Tokyo, 1954, and Chicago, 1955; Partner, for Design, Chicago, 1955–72, Baltimore, 1972, and Chicago, since 1972. Has served as Member, Board of Directors, Metropolitan Housing and Planning Council of Chicago; Trustee, Museum of Contemporary Art, Chicago; Chairman, Planning Committee, American Institute of Architects, Chicago Chapter; Member, United States General Services Administration National Public Advisory Panel on Architectural Services; Chairman, Jury on Institute Honors, American Institute of Architects; and Member, Advisory Council, Film Center, Art Institute of Chicago. Exhibitions: United States Air Force Academy, Colorado Springs, 1954; Miami University Art Museum, Oxford, Ohio, 1979; *Transformations in American Architecture,* Museum of Modern Art, New York, 1979. Recipient: R. S. Reynolds Award, 1964; Honor Award, and Bartlett Award, American Institute of Architects, 1978; Library Building Award, American Institute of Architects/American Library Association, 1978. D.F.A.: Lawrence University, Appleton, Wisconsin, 1968; Miami University, Oxford, Ohio, 1979. Fellow, American Institute of Architects, 1967. Address: Skidmore, Owings and Merrill, 30 West Monroe Street, Chicago, Illinois 60603, U.S.A.

Works:

1954 United States Naval Postgraduate School, Monterey, California
1962 Expansion plan for Northwestern University, Evanston, Illinois
1964 Chapel, United States Air Force Academy, Colorado Springs, Colorado
1965 Student Center, Grinnell College, Iowa
1965/
71 University of Illinois at Chicago Circle
1966 Lindheimer Astronomical Research Center, Northwestern University, Evanston, Illinois
1969 Louis Jefferson Long Library, Wells College, Aurora, New York
1970 Joseph Regenstein Library, University of Chicago
1971 Library, Northwestern University, Evanston, Illinois

Hogan Biological Sciences Research Building, Northwestern University, Evanston, Illinois
1972 Engineering Library remodelling, Massachusetts Institute of Technology, Cambridge
St. Matthew's Methodist Church, Chicago
1976 East Wing, Art Institute of Chicago
Walter Netsch House, 1700 North Hudson, Chicago
1978 Selby Public Library, Sarasota, Florida
1979 Pavilion, University of Illinois at Chicago Circle
Central Library, Sophia University, Tokyo
School of Music remodelling, University of Chicago
Library, Texas Christian University, Fort Worth

Publications:

By NETSCH: article—"Comprehensive Building Systems: Threat or Promise?" in *Building Research* (Washington, D.C.), September/October 1966.

On NETSCH: articles—"Northwestern University Expansion Plan" in *Progressive Architecture* (New York), August 1962; "Air Force Academy Chapel" in *Architectural Record* (New York), December 1962; "University of Illinois Campus Plan" in *Architectural Forum* (New York), May 1966; "University of Illinois" in *Architectural Forum* (New York), December 1968; "Field Theory: Forms as Process" in *Progressive Architecture* (New York), March 1969; "The Field Theory of Walter A. Netsch" in *Space Design* (Tokyo), June 1969; "The 'Visual Library' of Walter Netsch" in *Inland Architect* (Chicago), December 1970; "Field Theory" in *Bauen und Wohnen* (Zurich), October 1974; "Art Institute of Chicago" in *Architectural Review* (London), October 1977; "Netsch House" in *L'Architettura* (Rome), December 1977.

With an M.I.T. background and a history of design experience, not only in the midwest but also in California and in Japan, Walter A. Netsch has made his name within the framework of Skidmore, Owings and Merrill, with whom he has been associated for more than thirty years.

Netsch is responsible for such works as the libraries of Northwestern University and the University of Chicago and the East Wing of the Art Institute of Chicago—dramatic, functional, beautiful by any standards. But perhaps the greatest interest has been in Netsch as the prime mover in "field theory." He has worked on the development of this theory since the 1960's, and in his own townhouse in Chicago he has created a kind of prototype, spaces with a variety of uses, main and subsidiary, from one basic unit. There are no corridors, and the open space dimension is carried out on the vertical as well as on the horizontal planes. The various levels spiral round a service core, engendering a diagonal more than a horizontal direction. Netsch is aware that the mode of living created by such surroundings will not suit the tastes and way of life of many people. It is not a style in which to grow old; superb agility is required to move around the different level accesses.

Netsch's aim has always been to apply the theory to larger constructions, to get away from the boredom of the square box. His first building to break away from the single rectangle was the United States Air Force Academy Chapel, and the first to actually employ the elements of field theory was the Community Social Center at Grinnell College, Iowa. But Netsch really drew attention to the theory with Chicago Circle.

Chicago Circle Campus of the University of Illinois took five years to plan and three years to build, and in 1965, with the completion of the first phase of building, the campus opened to 9,000 students. There are no residential buildings; Chicago Circle is essentially planned as an active commuter area, with a central open-air amphitheatre, relevantly an exposed gathering place, an allegory of the service core from which the life of a building generates. The Architecture and Arts Building shows strict adherence to field theory. Ground plans show the lattice work formed from the basic octagon, itself created from one rotating square placed upon another. These shapes lie beside each other, overlap, or extend, creating pinked edges instead of sharped angled corners.

Of the same period, Louis Jefferson Long Library at Wells College, Aurora, New York, is also constructed according to the principles of field theory. Space was required for a quarter million books, on open shelves, and seating for 328. Netsch's design comprises nine interlocking octagon "buds," forming an irregularly shaped perimeter, and there are magnificent wooded views from huge windows in all directions and at all angles. The odd-angled tent-like roof is supported by a series of eight interwoven beams sprouting from brick pillar bases, juxtaposing the trees, creating a link between nature and man. The two upper levels protrude at angles like giant theatre boxes, making the roof visible from all levels.

There has been considerable controversy on the advisability of the theory. The great point in its favour is, naturally, its flexibility; from the central core, "walls," in the form of library shelves, laboratory cabinets, or whatever corresponds to the function of the proposed building, create mobile boundaries. Allowances can be made for change and growth without great expense. On the other hand, perimeter walls are immense and costly.

Yet Netsch is not hardened in his principles. In the second phase at Chicago Circle he made every effort to solve the problems noted by students and faculty about the first phase. Netsch claims only that the "field theory is an ordering device, a way of looking at things." He most certainly compels us to look, and to think.

—Muriel Emanuel

NEUTRA, Richard J(osef).

American. Born in Vienna, Austria, 8 April 1892; emigrated to the United States, 1923: naturalized, 1929. Educated at the Technische Hochschule, Vienna, graduated (with honors) 1917: influenced by Otto Wagner and Adolf Loos. Served as an Artillery Officer in the Imperial Austrian Army, in the Balkans, 1914–17. Married Dione Niedermann in 1922; children: Frank, Dion and Raymond. Conducted seminar, with Karl Moser, at the Eidgenössische Technische Hochschule, Zurich, 1919; worked with the landscape architect Gustav Amann, Zurich, 1919–20, and with Erich Mendelsohn, Berlin, 1921–22; worked in various architects' offices, New York, 1923, and in the office of Holabird and Roche, Chicago, 1924 (met Louis Sullivan, Chicago, 1924); lived for three months at Frank Lloyd Wright's Taliesin, Wisconsin, 1924; lived in the house of Rudolf Schindler, Los Angeles, collaborating with him on various projects, including the League of Nations competition and the Group of Industry and Commerce projects, 1925–30; in private practice, Los Angeles, from 1925: in partnership with Robert E. Alexander, Los Angeles, 1949–58, and with his son Dion in Richard and Dion Neutra and Associates, Los Angeles, 1965 until his death, 1970. Tutor, Academy of Modern Art, Los Angeles, 1928–29 (students: Harwell Harris and Gregory Ain). American Representative, CIAM Conference, Brussels, 1929; Member, 1939–41, and Chairman, 1941–44, California State Planning Board; Member, California Board of Examiners, 1942–46; Member, Architectural Review and Advisory Panel, United States Navy, 1965; Consultant to the Austrian Government on the Building Research Organization, Vienna, 1969. Exhibitions (one-man): Museo de Arte, Sao Paulo, Brazil, 1950; University of California at Los Angeles, 1958; Kunstgewerbemuseum, Zurich, 1959. Recipient: Honor Award, American Institute of Architects, Southern California Chapter, 1939, 1947, 1949, 1963; Membership in Hall of Fame, *World's Fair,* New York, 1939; Bicentennial Silver Medallion, Columbia University, New York, 1954; *Wisdom Magazine* Award, 1957; Citation, United States Department of Commerce, 1957; Honor Prize for Architecture, City of Vienna, 1958; Gold Medal, Cuban Association of Architects, 1958; Order of Merit, Federal Republic of Germany, 1959; Wilhelm Exner Medal, Austrian Association of Crafts, 1959; Citation, United States Housing and Home Finance Agency, 1959; Arcadia Honor Award, 1959; Klimt Honor (Vereiningung Bildender Kunstler), Vienna Secession, 1961; Gold Medal, Ethiopia, 1967; Cross of the Republic of Germany, 1967; Gold Ring, City of Vienna, 1968; Gold

Medal, American Institute of Architects (posthumous), 1977. Honorary doctorate: University of Graz, Austria, 1948; Technical University of Berlin, 1954; Adelphi University, Garden City, New York, 1963; University of Rome, 1965; and University of California at Los Angeles, 1969; Honorary Professor of Architecture, University of Madrid, 1969. Richard Neutra Room established at the Library of the University of California at Los Angeles, 1953. Fellow, American Institute of Architects, 1947; Member, National Institute of Arts and Letters, 1964; Member, National Academy of Design, 1964. Honorary Member, American Institute of Landscape Architects, 1970. Corresponding Member, League of Philippine Architects, 1941; Honorary Member, La Sociedad de Arquitectos, Mexico, 1944; Honorary Member, Academy of Fine Arts, Brussels, 1952; Honorary Member, Royal Institute of British Architects, 1954; Fellow, Royal Society for the Encouragement of Arts, Manufactures and Commerce, 1957; Honorary Member, Alberta Association of Architects, 1957; Corresponding Member, Accademia di San Luca, Rome, 1957; Honorary Member, Colombia Association of Architects, 1957; Honorary Member, Belgian Institute of Architects, 1958; Honorary Member, College of Academicians, Accademia di Belle Arti, Venice, 1958; Honorary Member, East African Institute of Architects, 1958; Corresponding Member, Académie d'Architecture, Paris, 1959; Honorary President, Tekhne: Office de Coopération et d'Assistance, Brussels, 1960; Honorary Member, Union of Hungarian Architects, 1963; Benjamin Franklin Fellow, Royal Society of Arts, London, 1965; Honorary Fellow, Sociedad Central de Arquitectos, Argentina, 1965; Honorary Member, Colegio de Arquitectos, Peru, 1965; Honorary President, Bund Deutscher Architekten, Germany, 1969; Honorary Member, Leonardo da Vinca Society, Italy, 1969. *Died* (in Wuppertal, Germany), *16 April 1970.*

Works:

1926/
30   Rush City Reformed, Los Angeles (project)
1927   Jardinette Apartments, Los Angeles
      League of Nations Secretariat Plan (competition project; with Rudolph Schindler)
1929   Lovell House (Health House), Los Angeles
1933   Van Der Leeuw Research House (Neutra House), Silverlake, Los Angeles (destroyed by fire, 1963; rebuilt by Neutra, with his son Dion, 1964)
1935   Beard House, Altadena, California
      Corona Avenue School, Bell, Los Angeles
1936   Plywood Model House, Los Angeles
      Von Sternberg House (Ayn Rand House), San Fernando Valley, Los Angeles (demolished)
      California Military Academy, Los Angeles
1937   Beckstrand House, Palos Verdes, California
1938   Strathmore Apartments, Westwood, Los Angeles
      Emerson Junior High School, Westwood, Los Angeles
1939   National Youth Administration Centers, Sacramento and San Luis Obispo, California
      Amity Village, Compton, California
1940   Kahn House, San Francisco
1941   Avion Village, Texas
1942   Nesbitt House, Brentwood, Los Angeles
      Channel Heights, San Pedro, California
      Kelton Apartments, Westwood, Los Angeles
1944   Rural school buildings, Puerto Rico
      Health centers, Puerto Rico (projects)
1946   Kaufmann House (Desert House), Palm Springs, California
1948   Tremaine House, Santa Barbara, California
      Aloe Medical Supply Building, Los Angeles
      Holiday House, Malibu, California
1950   Urban redevelopment plan for Sacramento, California (project; with Robert E. Alexander)

1950/
53   Redevelopment plan for Elysian Heights, Los Angeles (project; with Robert E. Alexander)
      Eagle Rock Playground Club House, Los Angeles
1951   Hinds House, Los Angeles
      Northwestern Mutual Fire Insurance Building, Los Angeles
1952   Moore House, Ojai, California
1953   Kester Avenue Elementary School, Los Angeles
1954   Child guidance clinic, Los Angeles (with Robert E. Alexander)
      Business Education Building, Orange Coast College, Costa Mesa, California (with Robert E. Alexander)
1955   Medical Center, San Bernardino, California
      Science Building and Auditorium, St. John's College, Annapolis, Maryland (with Robert E. Alexander)
1956   Gemological Institute of America Building, Brentwood, Los Angeles
1957   Science Building, Arts and Music Auditorium, and Sports Facilities, Orange Coast College, Costa Mesa, California (with Robert E. Alexander)
      Miramar Chapel, La Jolla, California (with Robert E. Alexander)
      Alamitos Intermediate School, Garden Grove, California (with Robert E. Alexander)
1958   Riviera Methodist Church, Redondo Beach, California (with Robert E. Alexander)
      Elementary Training School, University of California at Los Angeles (with Robert E. Alexander)
1959   Theatre, Dusseldorf (competition project)
      Museum of Natural History and Planetarium, Dayton, Ohio (with Robert E. Alexander)
1960   Singleton House, Los Angeles
1962   Community Church, Garden Grove, California
1963   Swirlbul Library, Adelphi University, Garden City, Long Island, New York (with Robert E. Alexander)
      United States Embassy, Karachi, Pakistan (with Robert E. Alexander)
      Mariners' Medical Arts Center, Newport Beach, California
      Lincoln Memorial Museum, Gettysburg, Pennsylvania (with Robert E. Alexander)
1964   Hall of Records, Los Angeles (with Robert E. Alexander)
      Richard J. Neutra Elementary School, Lemoore, California (with Robert E. Alexander)
1965   Friedland House, Philadelphia
1966   Bucerius House, Navegna, Switzerland
      Bewobau Housing Colony, Quickborn, near Hamburg, Germany
      Bewobau Housing Colony, Waldorf, near Frankfurt, Germany
      Grelling House, Ascona, Switzerland
1967   Tower of Hope, Garden Grove Church, California (with Dion Neutra)
      Rang House, Koenigstein, Germany
      Kemper House, Wuppertal, Germany
      Reutsch House, Wengen, Switzerland
1968   Pescher House, Wuppertal, Germany
1969   Orange County Courthouse, Santa Ana, California (with Ramberg and Lowrie)

Publications:

By NEUTRA: books—*Wie Baut Amerika,* Stuttgart 1926, in English edition, edited by Thomas Hines, Los Angeles 1979; *Amerika* (Neues Bauen in der Welt series), Vienna 1930, in English edition, edited by Thomas Hines, Los Angeles 1979; *National Planning Methods of Mass Housing,* with the editors of the International Congress for New Building, Lon-

Richard J. Neutra: Van Der Leeuw Research House, Silverlake, Los Angeles, 1933, rebuilt 1964

don 1930; *House and Home,* with others, New York 1935; *Circle: Routes of Housing Advance,* with others, London 1938; *Preface to a Master Plan,* with others, Los Angeles 1942; *New Architecture and City Planning,* with Paul Zucker, New York 1945; *Architecture of Social Concern in Regions of Mild Climate,* Sao Paulo 1948; *Mysteries and Realities of the Site,* Scarsdale, New York 1951; *Survival Through Design,* New York and London 1954, Hamburg, Milan and Mexico City 1955; *Life and Human Habitat,* Stuttgart 1956; *Realismo Biologico Renacimiento Humanistico en Arquitectura,* Buenos Aires 1958, 1974; *Life and Shape* (autobiography), New York and Hamburg 1962, Buenos Aires 1973; *World and Dwelling,* Stuttgart 1962, Barcelona 1963; *Building with Nature,* Stuttgart and Barcelona 1970, New York 1971; *Bauen und die Sinneswelt,* Dresden 1977; articles—"Terminals-Transfers" in *Architectural Record* (New York), August 1930; "Gegenwärtige Bauarbeit in Japan" in *Die Form* (Berlin), January 1931; "Japanische Wohnung, Ableitung, Schwierigkeiten" in *Die Form* (Berlin), March 1931; "Umbildung chinesischer Städte" in *Die Form* (Berlin), January 1932; "Die industriell hergestellte Wohnung in USA Typungsschwierigkeiten" in *Die Form* (Berlin), March 1932; "New Elementary Schools for America" in *Architectural Forum* (New York), January 1935; "School in the Making" in *Nation's Schools* (Chicago), November 1937; "Regionalism in Architecture" in *Architectural Forum* (New York), February 1939; "Research on Design of Dwelling-Units with Regard to Regional Differentiation" in *South African Architectural Record* (Johannesburg), February 1940; "Governmental Architecture in California" in *Arts and Architecture* (Los Angeles), August 1941; "Index of Liveability" in *Sunset* (Menlo Park, California), November 1943; "Classrooms and Livingrooms" in *New Architecture and City Planning* by Paul Zucker, New York 1944; "Sea-land-transfer" in *Architectural Record* (New York), September 1946; "Human Setting in an Industrial Civilization" in *Zodiac* (Milan), no. 2, 1957;

"Experience of the Theatre: Its Physiology" in *Arts and Architecture* (Los Angeles), May 1960; etc.

On NEUTRA: books—*Richard Neutra,* exhibition catalogue, Sao Paulo, Brazil 1950; *Richard Neutra: Buildings and Projects,* edited by Willy Boesiger, vol. I, 1923–50, Zurich 1951, London 1965, vol. II, 1950–60, Zurich 1959, and London 1965, vol. III, 1961–66, Zurich, London and New York 1966; *Richard Neutra* by Bruno Zevi, Milan 1954; *Richard Neutra: Is Planning Possible?* by Frederick Wright, Los Angeles 1958; *Richard Neutra* by Esther McCoy, New York 1960, London 1961; *Richard Neutra* (Contemporary Architects series), Tokyo 1969; *Richard Neutra* by Maté Pal, Budapest 1970; *Richard Neutra* by Rupert Spade, New York and London 1971; *Richard and Dion Neutra: Pflanzen, Wasser, Steine, Licht,* edited by H. Exner, D. Neutra, and H. Hammerbacher, Berlin and Hamburg 1974; *Richard Neutra and the Search for Modern Architecture* by Thomas Hines, New York 1980; articles—special issue of *L'Architecture d'Aujourd'hui* (Paris), June 1948; cover story in *Time* (New York), 15 August 1949; special issue of *Baukunst und Werkform* (Darmstadt), June 1955; special issue of *Espacio* (Havana), July 1955; special issue of *The Canadian Architect* (Toronto), November/December 1957; special issue of *Vitrum* (Milan), May/June 1962; "Neutra est Arrivé" in *Réalitiés* (Paris), March 1965; special issue of *Arquitectura* (Madrid), September 1965; special issue of *DLW-Nachrichten* (Bietigheim/Wuertt, Germany), no. 75, 1967; special issue of *Kindai Kenchiku* (Tokyo), February 1968; special issue of *Home Magazine* (Los Angeles), February 1968; special obituary issue of *L'Architettura* (Rome), November 1970; film—*The Ideas of Richard Neutra,* Vienna 1968.

Richard J. Neutra is one of the seminal figures in 20th century American architecture. His roots are wide and his influences strong. His work bears the unmistakable identity of its author, yet each project is uniquely appropriate.

He was born in the Vienna of the Hapsburgs in 1892, and the plan and imperious architecture of that city left a sense of richness and elegance that was to emerge in his mature work, but in entirely new forms. It is a richness not normally found in the architecture of the first half of this century. That richness and complexity, never contrived, extended to his manipulation of space, internal and external.

The Vienna of his childhood and student days was a city rich in artistic and intellectual cross-currents. Among those architects whose work impressed him were Otto Wagner and Adolph Loos, whose dictum against ornament directed Neutra away from traditional forms. He graduated from the Vienna Technische Hochschule after serving in the Austrian Army in World War I. He left Austria in 1919 to work in Switzerland and then moved to Germany. In 1921 he joined Erich Mendelsohn, to work on the Berliner Tageblatt Building remodelling and the landmark Zehlendorf Housing Group. Believing that the future of modern architecture lay in America, he emigrated in 1923, worked in the east, and then in Chicago for the firm of Holabird and Roche. There he met Louis Sullivan in that master's final days. At Sullivan's funeral in 1924 he met Frank Lloyd Wright. He spent some time with Wright at Taliesen East. Most of Wright's work at that time was in Los Angeles, and Neutra decided to go there. Rudolph Schindler, a friend of student days, was also working in Los Angeles, and Neutra was to collaborate with Schindler on several projects.

In southern California Neutra developed an especially appropriate regional architecture, adding a new dimension and direction to the several regional design systems in that area. His motifs, based on simple post and beam construction, were decidedly modern. He avoided a certain dependence on Mexican references that his predecessors utilized. In residential architecture, with its range of design demands, his design philosophy came into its full range of effects and expressions. A particular hallmark of his work was the relationship between interior and exterior spaces. He utilized large areas of glass and inter-penetrations of interior and exterior space to achieve that relationship. He also employed rich landscaping to affirm his buildings' relationship to their climates and sites and to enrich his designs texturally.

Neutra was a great draftsman. His skill is seen in his renderings, plans, and in his travel sketches, done in telling and rapid pastels. The originality of his creative mind is epitomized in this episode. He was once given a psychological test. Asked where he would add an additional right arm to a perfectly formed human body, his reply started his interrogators. "The human body is the result of millions of years of evolution. I would not do anything to change it. I reject the question!"

Neutra was a man of great physical stature. He was commanding in appearance and in word, and not a little arrogant. That may have accounted for the lack of major commissions that might otherwise have come to a man of such talent.

But his work was popular—due, in part, to skilful architectural photography, namely that of Julius Shulman. That is not to demean the work but to recognize a then growing method of communicating architectural concepts and achievements.

Neutra's influence spawned a branch of southern California architecture—open, straight-forward, assertive, unafraid of adjustment to site shape, and often possessing elements of formalistic flair, even bordering on playfulness. Among his more distinguished disciples are Robert E. Alexander, Gregory Ain, and Harwell Hamilton Harris, and the work of the large California firm, Welton Beckett, bears a considerable Neutra influence.

—Paul Spreiregen

NIEMEYER, Oscar.

Brazilian. Born in Rio de Janeiro, 15 December 1907. Educated at the Escola Nacional de Belas Artes, Rio de Janeiro, 1930–34, Dip. Arch. 1934. Married Annita Baldo in 1929; daughter: Anna Maria. Worked in the architectural studio of Lúcio Costa and Carlos Leão, Rio de Janeiro, 1935, and the studio of Le Corbusier, Paris, 1936; Architect, Departamento de Patrimonio Historico e Artistico Nacional, Rio de Janeiro, 1936–37; in private practice, Rio de Janeiro, 1937–56; Chief Architect, NOVA-CAP (Government Building Authority), Brasilia, 1956–61 (architectural adviser since 1961); returned to private practice, Rio de Janeiro, 1961. Lecturer, School of Architecture, Federal University of Rio de Janeiro, since 1968. Founder Editor, *Modulo,* Rio de Janeiro, 1955. Exhibitions: *Oscar Niemeyer,* Musée des Arts Décoratifs, Paris, 1965; *Oscar Niemeyer,* Centre Georges Pompidou, Paris, 1979. Recipient: Honorary Citizen Award, New York, 1939; First Prize, National Athletic Center Competition, Rio de Janeiro, 1941; First Prize, Aeronautical Training Center Competition, Sao Jose dos Campos, Sao Paulo, 1947; Prix Joliot-Curie, Paris, 1956; Work Medal, Brazil, 1959; Lenin Award of the U.S.S.R., 1963; Benito Juarez Award, *Mexican Revolution Centennial,* Mexico City, 1964; Medal of the Polish Architectural Association, 1967; *L'Architecture d'Aujourd'hui* Award, 1968. Honorary Member, American Academy of Arts and Sciences, 1949. Address (office): Avenida Atlantica 3940, Cobertura, Copacabana, Rio de Janeiro, Brazil.

Works:

1936   Henrique Xavier House, Rio de Janeiro (project)
1937   Obra do Berco Nursery and Maternity Clinic, Rio de Janeiro

1937/
43   Ministry of Education and Health, Rio de Janeiro (with Le Corbusier, Lúcio Costa, Jorge Machado Moreira, and Affonso Eduardo Reidy; now the Palace of Culture)
1938   Oswald de Andrade House, Sao Paulo
        Grande Hotel, Ouro Preto, Minas Gerais, Brazil
1939   Brazilian Pavilion, *World's Fair,* New York (with Le Corbusier)
1940   Design of the *Brazilian Industrial Exhibition,* Buenos Aires
1941   National Stadium, Rio de Janeiro
        Water Tower, Rio de Janeiro
1942   Pampulha Development, with the Church of St. Francis of Assisi, Yacht Club, and Restaurant, Minas Gerais, Brazil
        Oscar Niemeyer House, Gavea, Rio de Janeiro
1943   Kubitschek House, Pampulha, Minas Gerais, Brazil
        Ofair House, Rio de Janeiro
1944   Prudente de Morais Neto House, Rio de Janeiro
        Recreation Center, Rodrigos de Freitas Lagoon, Rio de Janeiro
1945   Yacht Club, Rio de Janeiro
1946   Boavista Bank, Rio de Janeiro
1947   Burton Tremaine House, Santa Barbara, California
1947/
52   United Nations Building, New York (with international team of architects, including Le Corbusier and Sven Markelius—Wallace K. Harrison, Chairman)
1948   Auditorium, Rio de Janeiro
1949   Mendes Country House, Rio de Janeiro
        Gavea Hotel, Rio de Janeiro
        House, Carvalho de Azevedo Street, Rio de Janeiro
        O Cruzeiro Headquarters, Rio de Janeiro (project)
1950   Duchen Biscuit Factory, Sao Paulo
        Libanais Club, Belo Horizonte, Brazil
        Montreal Office Building, Sao Paulo
        Quitandinha Hotel, Petropolis, Rio de Janeiro
        House, Gavea, Rio de Janeiro
        COPAN Office Building, Sao Paulo
        Carlos de Britto Food Factory, Sao Paulo (project)
        Julia Kubitschek Elementary School, Diamantina, Brazil
1951   Kubitschek Building Complex, Belo Horizonte, Brazil
        Diamantina Hotel, Minas Gerais, Brazil
        Ibirapuera, *IV Centennial Exhibition,* Sao Paulo (with Helio Uchoa, Zenon Lotufo, Eduardo Kneese de Mello, Gauss Estelita, and Carlos Lemos)
1952   Sul American Hospital, Rio de Janeiro
        Miranda House, Gavea, Rio de Janeiro
1953   Aeronautical Training Center, Sao Jose dos Campos, Sao Paulo
        Mineiro da Praducao Bank Headquarters, Belo Horizonte, Brazil
        Oscar Niemeyer House, Canoas, Rio de Janeiro
1954   Apartment building, Belo Horizonte, Brazil
        Cavanelas House, Pedro do Rio, Rio de Janeiro
1955   Museum of Modern Art, Caracas
        Secondary school, Belo Horizonte, Brazil
        Apartment building, Berlin
        Public Library, Belo Horizonte, Brazil (project)
        Getulio Vargas Foundation Headquarters, Rio de Janeiro
1957   Alvorada Palace (President's Residence), Brasilia
        Brasilia Palace Hotel
1958   Supreme Court, Brasilia

        Presidential Chapel, Brasilia
        Planalto Palace (Presidential Offices), Brasilia
        Three Powers Square, Brasilia
        Congress Buildings, Brasilia
        Brazilian Foundation Museum, Brasilia
        Chapel of Our Lady of Fatima, Brasilia
        National Theatre, Brasilia
1960   Main Square, University of Brasilia
        Sciences Faculty, University of Brasilia
        CEPLAN, University of Brasilia
        National Steel Company Building, Brasilia
        Dominican Theological Institute, Brasilia
1961   Stadium, Brasilia
1962   Arches Palace (Foreign Office), Brasilia
        New Yacht Club, Pampulha, Minas Gerais, Brazil
        Design of the *International Fair,* Tripoli
1963   Ministry of Justice, Brasilia
1964   Nordia Building Complex, Haifa, Israel (project)
        Panorama Building Complex, Haifa, Israel (project)
        University of Haifa, Israel
        City in the Negev Desert, Israel (project)
1965   Rothschild House, Israel (project)
        Redevelopment plan for the Algarve, Portugal
        Brasilia Airport
        Brazzaville Palace, Congo (project)
1966   Hotel, Madeira
        French Community Party Headquarters, Paris (with Jean de Roche and Chemetof)
        Bloch Building, Rio de Janeiro
        Redevelopment plan for Grasse, France (with Marc Emery)
1967   Dominican Convent, Saint Baume, France
1968   Mosque, Algiers
        Redevelopment plan for Algiers
        Civic Center, Algiers
        Vertical Palace, Belo Horizonte, Brazil
        Satetyles (Telecommunications Complex), Rio de Janeiro
        Mondadori Building, Milan (with Luciano Pozzo)
        Cuiaba University, Mato Grosso, Brazil
        Ministry of Defense, Brasilia
1969   Constantine University, Algeria
        Renault Office Building, Paris
1970   Hotel Nacional Rio, Rio de Janeiro
        Brazilian Architects Institute, Brasilia
        Stadium, Brasilia (project)
        Cathedral, Brasilia
1971   Sciences and Technology Faculty, University of Algeria, Algiers
        Human Sciences Faculty, University of Algeria, Algiers
1972   Moura Lacerda University, Ribeirao Preto, Sao Paulo
        Denasa and Oscar Niemeyer Office Building, Brasilia
        Frederico Gomes House, Rio de Janeiro
        Bobigny Office Building, Paris
        Cultural Center, Le Havre, France
        Redevelopment plan for Dieppe, France (with Marc Emery)
        Trade Center, Miami, Florida (project)
1973   Tour de la Défense (office building), Paris
        Residence Hall, Oxford (project)
        Music Center, Rio de Janeiro
        Central Railway Station, Brasilia
1974   Foreign Office, Algiers
        Safra Bank, Sao Paulo
        Vice-President's Residence, Brasilia
        Rio Towers, Rio de Janeiro
        Telebras Office Building, Brasilia (with Carlos Magalhaes)
        Josephine Jordan House, Rio de Janeiro
1975   Foreign Office Building II, Brasilia
1976   National Party Headquarters, Algiers
        Mirza House, Rio de Janeiro
1977   Barra da Tijuca Redevelopment, Rio de Janeiro (with Marc Emery)

Oscar Niemeyer: Ministry of Defense, Brasilia, 1968

FATA Building, Turin (with Riccardo Morandi)
Bus Terminal, Londrina, Parana, Brazil
1978 Convention Center, Foz do Iguacu, Brazil
Theatre, Vicenza, Italy (with Frederico Motterle)
Anthropological Museum, Belo Horizonte, Brazil
Deputies Office Building, Brasilia
1979 Zoological Gardens, Algiers
Embratur Office Building, Brasilia
CESP Office Building, Sao Paulo
Business Quarter, Algiers
City Center Redevelopment, Barra, Rio de Janeiro

Publications:

By NIEMEYER: books—*Mina Experiencia em Brasilia,* Rio de Janeiro 1961, Paris and Moscow 1963; *Textes et Dessins pour Brasilia,* Paris 1965; *Viagens: Quase Memorias,* Rio de Janeiro 1966; *Oscar Niemeyer,* Milan 1977; *A Forma na Arquitetura,* Rio de Janeiro and Milan 1978, Paris 1979; articles—"Ce qui manque à notre Architecture" in *Le Corbusier: Oeuvres Completes,* edited by W. Boesiger, Zurich 1938; "Témoignages" in *L'Architecture d'Aujourd'hui* (Paris), October/November 1958; numerous articles in *Modulo* (Rio de Janeiro).

On NIEMEYER: books—*The Work of Oscar Niemeyer* by Stamo Papadaki, New York and Tokyo 1950; *Modern Architecture in Brazil* by Henrique Mindlin, New York 1956; *Oscar Niemeyer: Works in Progress* by Stamo Papadaki, New York 1956; *Oscar Niemeyer* by Stamo Papadaki, New York and Ravensburg, Germany 1960; *Oscar Niemeyer* by Rupert Spade, London 1971; *Oscar Niemeyer* by Nelson Werncek Sodre, Rio de Janeiro 1978; articles—special issue of *Architectural Review* (London), March 1944; special issue of *Progressive Architecture* (New York), April 1947; special issue of *L'Architecture d'Aujourd'hui* (Paris), September 1947; special issue of *Architectural Forum* (New York), November 1947; special issue of *Architectural Review* (London), October 1950; "The Works of Oscar Niemeyer" in *L'Architecture d'Aujourd'hui* (Paris), August 1952; special issue of *L'Architecture d'Aujourd'hui* (Paris), October 1952; special issue of *Architectural Review* (London), October 1954; special issue of *L'Architecture d'Aujourd'hui* (Paris), October/November 1958; "Brasilia," special issue of *Acropole* (Sao Paulo), July/August 1970; special issue of *L'Architecture d'Aujourd'hui* (Paris), January/February 1974; "The Paradoxes of Oscar Niemeyer" by Bernard Huet in *L'Architecture d'Aujourd'hui* (Paris), March/April 1976; "Niemeyer in Turin" by Massimo Gennari in *Domus* (Milan), May 1977; "Niemeyer's One-Man Paris Show" by Odile Fillion in *Building Design* (London), 2 March 1979.

*

When a form creates beauty it becomes functional and therefore fundamental in architecture.

The straight line, hard, inflexible, created by man, does not attract me. What does draw me is the free and sensual curve. The curve that I find in the mountains of my country, in the sinuousness of her rivers, in the clouds of the sky and the waves of the sea. The whole universe is made of the curve, the curved universe of Einstein.

—Oscar Niemeyer

*

Walter Gropius, discussing the work of Oscar Niemeyer with a group of his students at Harvard in the 1940's, referred to him as the *Paradiesvogel* (bird of paradise) of the architectural world. His work has always provoked very divergent responses—sometimes admiration, sometimes disparagement. Even today, it continues to be controversial.

The modern architecture of Europe, born in the depressed economy of the years following World War I, had necessarily a minimal standard morality or ethic as its basis. Exuberant, flamboyant images were never part of the modernist credo, and it took many years and divers influences before any visual richness began to be considered, much less explored. Even then, the suggestion was of forbidden fruit, an interest that needed constant justification. Although the influence of Le Corbusier has always been stressed in describing Niemeyer (and the description is apt, especially of the early work), the comparison is unnecessary for most of his buildings. Niemeyer's creative genius is born of, and is a uniquely integral part of, the spirit and imagery of Brazil. One need only consider the almost unreal drama of those giant sugar loaf granite mountains right in the middle of Rio de Janeiro to recognize some of the profiles of Niemeyer's seemingly equally unreal building ideas.

Niemeyer has always accompanied the presentation of his designs with the most telling of thumbnail sketches. They contain the very essence of his design methodology. In a disarming way, they proceed along a logical path, outlining a process of elimination. First they suggest, then they are crossed out because of rational unsuitability, then they take a more logical direction—then take a leap and present an utterly disarming, simple, direct and yet visually poetic solution. To many architects who proceed in design with all kinds of hangups, who shackle their creative senses, these sketches often appear too simple, too easy—almost child-like and impossible—and they would be if it were not for the fact that on the next pages there invariably appears, quite miraculously and impeccably, the end result, an elegantly finished building, not deviating in the slightest from the essence contained in the seminal early sketches.

During some months in 1948 I briefly worked with Niemeyer and observed him at his work. In contrast to my experience of European/American procedure, he worked as I would imagine a painter or sculptor works. Sketches—intuitive gestures—ideas presented in a way to make the rationalist-oriented designer cringe. But my suspicions soon melted away when I subsequently realized how fundamentally unassailable were the inherent logic, the clarity, the structural and constructional plausibility of his work. This is not simply a personal perception; the results bear out the generalizations. Consider how many of his stunning concepts—Brasilia, huge universities in different parts of the world, museums, vast housing and office complexes—have in fact become reality. In our world, distrustful of artistic gestures, none of these projects would have been executed if they were not, however flamboyant the concepts, essentially of rationalist substance.

Niemeyer is an unassuming and humble man. While I worked for him he tried to discourage me from a long journey to Belo Horizonte just to see his buildings placed around a lake at Pampulha. "They are badly maintained, they are going to change the casino into a radio station . . . don't go." But I did—and seeing those structures under the brilliant tropical sky remains one of the memorable impressions of my career! They were certainly powerful enough to visually overcome disarranged interiors and dirty windows—more than one can say about most other modern architecture.

The deep humility and social consciousness of Niemeyer at first seem as unbelievable as his architectural visions. He accepted no fees for his first job, a nursery in Rio, and when the *brise-soleils* would not work, he paid for new ones out of his own pocket. For the design of his master work, Brasilia, he refused any fees other than his humble civil servant's salary. The evidence bears him out when he says, "I should be ashamed to be rich." When accepting the Lenin Prize at Brasilia, he spoke only of the need for government action to ease the miserable conditions of the workers who had built the city. He did not bask in the praise for his own work, but pointed out the social discrimination threatened by an imminent change to Lúcio Costa's plan for the city.

With all its looming social problems, there must indeed be hope for the future of Brazil—when the country has poets of the visual world with the humility of an Oscar Niemeyer.

—Harry Seidler

NOWICKI, Matthew.

Polish. Born Maciej Nowicki in Chita, Russia, of Polish parents, 26 June 1910; travelled extensively as a child and lived for some years in Chicago. Educated at the Art Institute of Chicago, 1921; School of Design, Gerson, Warsaw, 1925; Warsaw Polytechnic, 1929–36, M.Arch. 1936. Served as a Lieutenant in the Polish Army Artillery, 1939; participated in the Warsaw Insurrection, Home Army, 1944. Married Stanislawa Sandecka in 1935; had one son. In private practice, Warsaw, 1936–39; Assistant to Professor Swierczynski, Institute of Public Buildings, Warsaw, 1937–39; taught underground classes in architecture and town planning during the Nazi occupation, Warsaw, 1939–45; Leader, Architectural Discussion Studio and Workshop, Warsaw, 1945; Design Chief, Capital Rebuilding Bureau (BOS), Warsaw, 1945–46; Cultural Attaché, Polish Consulate, Chicago, 1946; Polish Representative, United Nations Site and Building Committee, New York, 1946–47; Visiting Critic, Pratt Institute, Brooklyn, New York, 1947–48; Senior Professor of Architecture and Acting Head of the School of Design, North Carolina State College, Raleigh, 1948–51; employed by the architectural firm of Mayer and Whittlessey, New York, to begin firm's study for Chandigarh, the new capital city of the Punjab, India, 1949 until his death, 1951. Exhibition: Museum of Modern Art, New York, 1950. *Died* (in an airplane crash, in the Nile delta) *31 August 1951.*

Works:

1936/
37 National Bank Building, Warsaw (project)
    Ministry of Communications Building, Warsaw (project)
    Ministry of Work and Social Security Building, Warsaw (project)
    City redevelopment plan for Warsaw
1938 Local Government Building, Lodz
    Health Center, Druskienniki, Poland
    Tourist hotel, Augsutow, Poland
    Sports and recreation center, ul. Podskarbinska, Warsaw
1939 Polish Pavilion, *World's Fair,* New York
1939/
45 Post-war city development plan for Warsaw
1943 Fregata Cafe interiors, Warsaw (with S. Sandecka)
    Latona Cafe interiors, Warsaw (with S. Sandecka)
1944/
45 Development plan for the city center of Warsaw
1944/
48 Chapel and Residence Hall, Center for the Blind, Laski, near Warsaw
1948/
53 Dorton Arena, *North Carolina State Fair,* Raleigh (project; with William Henry Dietrick)
1949 Buildings for Brandeis University, Waltham, Massachusetts (project; with Eero Saarinen)
1949/
51 State Library and Museum, Raleigh, North Carolina (project; with William Henry Dietrick)
    Preliminary studies for Chandigarh New Capital City, Punjab, India (for Mayer and Whittlessey)
1950 Circular Shopping Center, Columbus Circle, New York (project; with Clarence Stein)

Publications:

By NOWICKI: book—*The Writings and Sketches of Matthew Nowicki,* compiled by Bruce Harold Schafer, Charlottesville, Virginia 1973.

On NOWICKI: books—*Geschichte der Modernen Architektur* by Jürgen Joedicke, Stuttgart 1958; *Roots of Contemporary American Architecture,* edited by Lewis Mumford, New York 1959; *Polish Avant-Garde Architecture* 1918–1939 by Izabella Wislocka, Warsaw 1970; articles—"Matthew Nowicki" in *Architectural Forum* (New York), October 1950; "Matthew Nowicki," special issue of the *North Carolina State College School of Design Student Publication* (Raleigh), Winter 1951; "The Life, Teaching and the Architecture of Matthew Nowicki" by Lewis Mumford in *Architectural Record* (New York),

June/August 1954; "Matthew Nowicki 1910–1951" by J. Hryniewiecki in *Projekt* (Warsaw), no. 1, 1957; "Matthew Nowicki" in *L'Architecture d'Aujourd'hui* (Paris), September 1957; "The Writings and Sketches of Matthew Nowicki" by Bruce H. Schafer in *AIA Journal* (Washington, D.C.), July 1974.

Matthew Nowicki was one of the most creative architects of his generation. But for his untimely death in 1951, he could well have found his place among the top few architects of the 20th century. At the time of his death he was on the verge of realizing some of his most important projects, including a new city of Chandigarh in India, the planning of which was later completed by Le Corbusier. Although Le Corbusier's Chandigarh plans are well documented, there is little record of Nowicki's concept of super blocks and sketches for a whole range of civic and residential buildings. These admirably show how Nowicki sympathetically and sensitively married the European design approach to local Indian materials, arts and building crafts. They show his love of drawing, which enabled him to express his ideas in three dimension rather than through plans and elevations.

Nowicki's early Polish training in engineering found a new scope in the United States where he was able to extend his mastery of somewhat repetitive post and beam construction to more daring and innovative structures. His sketches and projects, such as the Dorton Arena for the *North Carolina State Fair* and the State Library and Museum in Raleigh, are eloquent testimony to his creative abilities. His Arena is enclosed in two parabolic concrete arches that intersect each other close to the ground and support the roof and frame the grandstands. His other designs include a circular shopping centre in Columbus Circle, New York, set above traffic at a busy intersection.

A less happy phase of Nowicki's work was his one time concern with the application of module to building, which he considered as a panacea for all architectural problems. This invariably produced monotony and occasionally forced solutions that were inappropriate to specific programmes.

As a teacher Nowicki is well remembered for his brief stint as a senior Professor of Architecture at North Carolina State College in Raleigh, where he was able to introduce important changes in a new curriculum. It united architecture, landscape architecture and city planning into a "single frame for the changing picture of the life of man," as he put it. His programme had four streams: design, structure, descriptive drawing and humanities. In many ways it was the forerunner of courses that schools of architecture later adopted during the 1960's and 70's. However, owing to the difficulties of implementation inherent in the bureaucratic environment of American tertiary institutions, many of his ideas were diluted.

Matthew Nowicki was far ahead of his time. He will be remembered for being one of the few architects who was able to get away from the then well accepted functional and somewhat stark approach of the modern movement and strive towards understanding and expression of a more humane architecture, softened by the local environment, tradition and culture, as his work in India so clearly indicates.

—B. S. Saini

NOYES, Eliot (Fette).

American. Born in Boston, Massachusetts, 12 August 1910. Educated at Phillips Academy, Andover, Massachusetts, graduated 1928; Harvard College, Cambridge, Massachusetts, 1928–32, B.A. 1932; Harvard Graduate School of Architecture, Cambridge, 1932–35, 1937–38 (Eugene Dodd Medal,

1935; Alpha Rho Chi Medal, 1938; American Institute of Architects Medal, 1938), M.Arch. 1938; awarded Wheelwright Travelling Fellowship, 1939. Served in the United States Air Force, 1942–45: Major. Married Mary Duncan Weed in 1938; children: Mary, Eliot Jr., Frederick and Margaret. Worked as an architect on the Iranian Archaeological Expedition of the Oriental Institute of the University of Chicago, 1935–37; Draftsman in the office of Coolidge, Shepley, Bulfinch and Abbot, Boston, 1938, and in the office of Walter Gropius and Marcel Breuer, Cambridge, 1939–40; Director of the Department of Industrial Design, Museum of Modern Art, New York, 1940–42, 1945–46; Design Director for Normal Bel Geddes and Company, New York, 1946–47; in private practice, as Eliot Noyes and Associates, New Canaan, Connecticut, 1947 until his death, 1977. Curator of Exhibitions, 1948–50, and Associate Professor and Critic of Architecture, 1948–53, Yale University, New Haven, Connecticut. Consultant Director of Design, IBM Corporation, 1956–77, and Mobil Oil Corporation, 1964–77; Design Consultant to Westinghouse Electric Corporation, 1960–76, and to Pan American World Airways, 1969–72; Consultant on Design to the President of the Massachusetts Institute of Technology, Cambridge, 1972–77. President, International Design Conference in Aspen, Colorado, 1965–70. Recipient: Design Award, *Progressive Architecture,* 1954; Award of Excellence for House Design, *Architectural Record,* 1956, 1957, 1959, 1971, 1974; First Honor Award, and Centennial Medal, 1957, and Industrial Arts Medal, 1965, American Institute of Architects; Award of Merit, *House and Home,* 1957; Merit Award, United States Department of Housing and Urban Development, 1968; Merit Award, American Society of Landscape Architects, 1970; Design Medal, Society of Industrial Artists and Designers, London, 1971; Honor Award, Connecticut Society of Architects/AIA, 1975 (twice); Design Excellence Award, *Industrial Design,* 1975. D.F.A.: Carnegie-Mellon University, Pittsburgh, Pennsylvania, 1969. Fellow, American Institute of Architects, and Industrial Designers Society of America; Associate, National Academy of Design. Fellow, Royal Society of Arts, London. *Died* (in New Canaan, Connecticut) *18 July 1977.*

Works:

1941 Jackson House, Dover, Massachusetts
1950 Tallman House, New Canaan, Connecticut
    Bremer House, New Canaan, Connecticut
1951 Ault House, New Canaan, Connecticut
    Stackpole House, New Canaan, Connecticut
    Hersey House, Southport, Connecticut
1952 Weeks House, New Canaan, Connecticut
1953 Briggs House, Redding, Connecticut
    Bubble Houses, Hobe Sound, Florida
1954 Bareiss House, Greenwich, Connecticut
    General Electric Corporation Wonder Home (exhibition project)
1955 Noyes House, New Canaan, Connecticut
1956 Bernhard House, Port Chester, New York
1958 IBM Corporation Office additions, Harrison, New York
1959 Simonsen Vacation House, Martha's Vineyard, Massachusetts
1960 Ohly Vacation House, Sherburne, Vermont
    First Federal Savings and Loan Association Building, Hagerstown, Maryland
1961 Noyes Ski House, Sherburne, Vermont
    IBM Branch Office Building, Arlington, Virginia
    IBM Branch Office Building, Los Angeles
1963 Rantoul Vacation House, Martha's Vineyard, Massachusetts
1964 IBM Aerospace Building Parking Garage, Los Angeles
    Timothy Dwight School, New Haven, Connecticut
    Time Capsule Pavilion, for Westinghouse Electric, *World's Fair,* New York

1965 IBM Aerospace Building, Los Angeles
Mobil Service Station Prototypes (55 built throughout the United States)
Xerox Corporation Showroom interior, New York
Westinghouse executive suite interior, Pittsburgh

1966 McKay Vacation House, Stratton, Vermont
Westinghouse Telecomputer Center and Office Building, Pittsburgh
IBM Branch Office Building, Garden City, Long Island, New York
General Fireproofing Company Showroom interior, New York

1967 General Fireproofing Company Sales Office and Showroom, Toronto
Oliver Wolcott Library, Litchfield, Connecticut
Salisbury Elementary School, Connecticut
General Fireproofing Company Showroom interior, Toronto
United Nations Pavilion, *Expo '67,* Montreal

1968 IBM Office Building additions, Harrison, New York
Mobil Oil Company boardroom interior, New York
IBM Pavilion, *Hemisfair,* San Antonio, Texas

1969 Preston House, Martha's Vineyard, Massachusetts
Cummins Engine Company Sales and Service Buildings Prototypes
IBM Computer Room Annex, Poughkeepsie, New York
Meadow Street Fire Station, Norwalk, Connecticut
Fire Drill Tower, Norwalk, Connecticut
Study of elevated subway train stations, New York (project)

1970 Graham House, Greenwich, Connecticut
Hodgson Vacation House, Snowmass at Aspen, Colorado
Mobil Oil Refinery Administration Building, Joliet, Illinois
IBM Branch Office Building, Hamden, Connecticut
Southside Junior High School, Columbus, Indiana
Mobil Site Feasibility Study, Farmers Branch, Texas

1971 Mobil Stonybrook Center Engineering Building, Hopewell Township, New Jersey
Mobil Stonybrook Center Customer Service Laboratory, Hopewell Township, New Jersey
Mobil Oil Portuguese Headquarters Building, Lisbon
Master plan for Mobil Stonybrook Center, Hopewell Township, New Jersey
Pan American World Airways Passenger Terminal interiors, Kennedy Airport, New York

1972 Horton House, Stamford, Connecticut
Feasibility study: Wilton Library, Connecticut
Survey: Intercontinental Hotel, Cotonou, Dahomey
New Passenger Ship Terminal interiors, New York
IBM Headquarters lobby design, Armonk, New York
Mobil Oil Corporation Interior Design Standards (manual)
IBM Branch Office interiors, Baltimore

1975 Johnson House, Mystic, Connecticut
Wilton Library, Connecticut

1980 IBM Management Development Center, Armonk, New York

Publications:

By NOYES: book—*Organic Design and Home Furnishing,* New York 1941; articles—regular column in *Consumer Reports* (Mount Vernon, New York), 1947–54; "Moods Are Not Accidents" in *Life* (New York), 15 February 1963.

On NOYES: books—*Masters of Modern Architecture* by John Peter, New York 1958; *Architecture USA* by Ian McCallum, New York 1959; *Architecture Today and Tomorrow* by Cranston Jones, New York 1961; *Vacation Houses* by William J. Hennessey, New York 1962; *Modern Houses of the World* by Sherban Cantacuzino, New York 1964; *Design and Planning,* Waterloo, Ontario 1965; *Design Coordination and Corporate Image* by F. H. K. Henrion and Alan Parkin, London and New York 1967; *Design in America* by Ralph Caplan, New York 1969; *The Corporate Search for Visual Identity* by Ben Rosen, New York 1970; *The Architectural Record Book of Vacation Houses,* New York 1970; *International Vacation Houses,* Stuttgart 1967; *International Shop Design,* Stuttgart 1967; *Great Houses,* edited by Walter F. Wagner, Jr., New York 1976; *Ferro-cement* by Stanley Abercrombie, New York 1977; articles—"Concrete Bubble House" in *Architectural Record* (New York), May 1954; "IBM's New Corporate Face" in *Architectural Forum* (New York), February 1957; "Art at Home by Eliot Noyes" in *Art in America* (New York), Summer 1958; "A House for All Seasons" in *Life* (New York), 15 February 1963; "The Work of Eliot Noyes and Associates" in *Industrial Design* (New York), June 1966; "Eliot Noyes" in *Crée* (Paris), January/February 1971; "Design for the Corporation" in *Progressive Architecture* (New York), October 1975.

Eliot Noyes is as well known for his industrial design as he is for his architecture. He studied at Harvard Graduate School of Design in the early thirties when the Beaux-Arts tradition was still the accepted curriculum. But, during his years at Harvard, he enlightened himself with the works of Le Corbusier who was drawing away from traditionalism towards a revolutionary style of functional modernism. He interrupted his education at Harvard to participate as the delineator/recorder member of an archaeological expedition to Iran, as if to take a new perspective look at the Beaux-Arts curriculum with which he, too, was discontented.

He returned to Harvard to find that Gropius and Breuer had joined the faculty and were injecting into the curriculum this new spirit of modernism. His study of the Bauhaus, expounded by the new faculty, inspired his career-long reverence for the interrelationship of industrial design, architecture, painting, and sculpture. For Noyes, the complete architect was, like Le Corbusier, a painter, a sculptor, a furniture designer as well as a designer of building structure. Engineering, function, and art are the combined generators of design.

Noyes was, for a time, the Director of the Department of Industrial Design at the Museum of Modern Art, and there organized the furniture design competition out of which came the famous Eames chair. A wartime friendship with Thomas Watson, the future executive of IBM, developed into a designer-client association that changed the look of many IBM products. Noyes gave typewriters a sleek smooth modern design that showed that intricate, complicated machines can have an aesthetic beauty not inconsistant with their underlying expression of function. Noyes put aesthetics into Mobil gas stations, pumps and accessories, giving that company a new corporate image through uniformity of design of its standardized parts with simple bold graphics. The function of the products was not compromised, just given an extra dimension with pleasing looks.

Noyes's houses convey his attempts to simplify the complicated. Usually they are comprised of simple rectilinear spaces, sometimes separated not by a material closure, but by the suggestion of closure through the use of furniture placement or wall screens. Almost a trademark of his, is the common division of living space from dining space by a free-standing fireplace. There are definite separate activity areas in his houses, but often one borrows extra expanse from an adjacent space.

Noyes predominantly used natural materials in simple configurations where each material often expresses more than itself. A stone fireplace in a house, for example, may extend to become a major structural element—a stone wall running the full length of the house perhaps terminating as a garden wall on the exterior. His own houses have a sparse, open geometric plan and a straightforward, simply expressed structure that creates an uncluttered background where his many art treasures and artifacts from extensive travels easily find places for display. He exhibits the Miesian celebration of the unadorned and straightforward use of materials to generate the bare structural essential space, refined or clad with a clean tight skin.

—Stephen P. Hamilton

Eliot Noyes: Graham House, Greenwich, Connecticut, 1970

OBATA, Gyo.

American. Born in San Francisco, California, 28 February 1923. Educated at the University of California, Berkeley, 1941–42; Washington University, St. Louis, 1942–45, B.Arch. 1945; Cranbrook Academy of Art, Bloomfield Hills, Michigan, 1945–46, M.Arch. 1946. Married Majel Beth Chance in 1948 (divorced, 1971): children: Kiku, Nori, and Gen; married Nancy J. McGeehon in 1971. Sr. Designer, Skidmore, Owings and Merrill, Chicago, 1947–50; Associate in charge of Design, Hellmuth, Yamasaki and Leinweber, St. Louis, 1951–55. Since 1955, Principal, with George Hellmuth, *q.v.*, and George Kassabaum, *q.v.*, Hellmuth, Obata and Kassabaum, St. Louis. Affiliate Professor of Architecture, Washington University, St. Louis, since 1971. Recipient: Outstanding Alumni Citation, Washington University, 1964. Fellow, American Institute of Architects. Address: Hellmuth, Obata and Kassabaum Inc., Architects, 100 North Broadway, St. Louis, Missouri 63102, U.S.A.

Publications:

By OBATA: article—"Some Suggestions for Urban Housing" in *Architectural Record* (New York), March 1961.

See HELLMUTH, OBATA AND KASSABAUM

OESTERLEN, Dieter.

German. Born in Heidenheim, Württemberg, 5 April 1911. Educated at the Goethe Gymnasium, Hanover, graduated 1930; Technische Hochschule, Stuttgart, under Professor Schmitthenner, 1930–32; Technische Hochschule, Berlin, under Heinrich Tessenow and Hans Polzeig, 1932–36, Diploma 1936, M.Arch. 1939. Married Eva Freise in 1939; children: Friedrich, Mathis and Bettina; married Eva Maria Stroedel in 1957. In private practice, Hanover, since 1945. Professor at the Technical University, Braunschweig, 1952–76. Exhibitions: Art Circle, Hameln, 1961; Kunstverein, Oldenburg, 1971; Stadtisches Museum, Braunschweig, 1972. Recipient: Schinkelplakette, Berlin, 1938; First Prize, Hanover Cinema Competition, 1950; 3 Laves Prize, City of Hanover, 1954; Krahe Prize, City of Braunschweig, 1960; Award of Distinction, City of Bochum, 1965; Bund Deutscher Architekten Prize, Bremen, 1974; Recognition Prize, International Cembureau, Paris, 1975; 3 Prizes of the Bund Deutscher Architekten, Niedersachsen, 1976; German Architecture Concrete Prize, 1977. Member, Akademie der Künste, Berlin, since 1966. Address (office): Baumstrasse 11, 3000 Hanover 1, Germany.

Works:

1946/
60 Market Church restoration, Hanover

1951/
53 Filmstudio Cinema, Hanover
1956/
58 Wilhelm-Busch School, Hanover
1957/
59 Christ Church, Bochum, Germany
1957/
62 Parliament Building for the Council of Niedersachsen, Hanover
1959/
65 Church of Our Lady restoration, Bremen
1960/
62 Andreanum School, Hildesheim, Germany
1961/
67 German Soldiers Cemetery, Futa Pass, Florence
1962/
63 Church of Jesus Christ, Sennestadt, near Bielefeld, Germany
1962/
66 Conference and Concert Hall, Saarbrucken
1963/
66 History Museum, Am Hohen Ufer, Hanover
1964/
67 Church of the Twelve Apostles, Hildesheim, Germany
1967/
69 Administration Building, Volkswagen Works Foundation, Hanover
Administration Building, Chamber of Commerce and Industry, Bielefeld, Germany
IBM Administration Building, Hanover
1970/
71 Lamberti Church restoration, Oldenburg, Germany
1971/
72 Institute for the Study of Materials and Soldering Techniques, Technical University, Braunschweig, Germany
1971/
73 Town Hall, Greven, Germany
1972/
74 Administration Building, Concordia Insurance Company, Hanover
1974/
75 Bischof Stahlin Geriatric Center, Oldenburg, Germany
City Art Gallery, Herford, Germany
1976/
77 Theatre restoration and alterations, Mainz
1978 Church of St. Tomas Community Center, Laatzen, near Hanover
Post Office Headquarters Administration Building, Bremen (project)
Playhouse for the State Theatre, Braunschweig, Germany (project)
German Embassy, Buenos Aires (project)
Guesthouse for the University of Göttingen (project)

Publications:

On OESTERLEN: book—*Dieter Oesterlen: Buildings and Projects 1946–63* by Alexander Koch, Stuttgart 1964.

I have been building for only a little more than twenty years, having began at about 45 years of age. After I received my diploma in Berlin in 1936 I was occupied with town planning in the pre-war Nazi era, then there was the war until 1945, and then until 1955 there was a need to make up for the time lost as an architect in Germany cut off from architectural development.

I believe that a building arrangement grows from the actual town planning situation and that its characteristic plastic expression of shape (form-content) develops from the actual building problem. Since Mies van der Rohe and Scharoun I regard the interlinking of exterior and interior spaces as an important specific of the new architecture. Everything—space as well as large and small forms—should be seized by this dynamic. Accordingly, I try to achieve a liveliness in my buildings with a tension in their spatial deployment and with pervasive, appropriate atmosphere, both goals to be achieved within controlled homogeneity of the interior and exterior appearance.

I have always considered the restoration of historic buildings (and the process of supplementing them with new buildings) as self-instructive, self-introspective and self-measuring. A "feeling for" restoration seems essential to me.

Nostalgia, which can be advantageous in momentary recollection, and its consequences—decorativeness, eclecticism—can only happen if the aims for the productive development of a new architecture are unclear or are intentionally abandoned.

—Dieter Oesterlen

I consider one of Dieter Oesterlen's buildings as particularly typical of his feeling for form, already apparent at the beginning of the still-disdained 1950's. It is his cinema in Hanover, with 600 seats in an underground area. There are two neon-lit words on the street facade: Film and Studio. The three straight lines of the "F" are continued down the outside wall, bend to the ceiling of the box office foyer, twist as a triple spiral around the central support of the main stairway, and glide freely with an asymmetric verve into the underground foyer. There the projection room rises in a gentle arch in the ellipse of the auditorium. The side walls and ceiling are indirectly lit with strip lighting behind wood panels that become visible through the back lighting. For Oesterlen (as he says) a film lives from light. And so, architecturally, this cinema involves a play of light.

Oesterlen does without a curtain in front of the screen. Nothing in this Filmstudio is to remind us of the opera or the theatre, where the curtain still has a meaning: it covers the scenery, allows players surprise entries. In this cinema, and for the first time, Oesterlen designed a screen with two wings: they open at the beginning of the presentation like a book and close again at the end. Both wings have irregu-

Dieter Oesterlen: Christ Church, Bochum, Germany, 1959

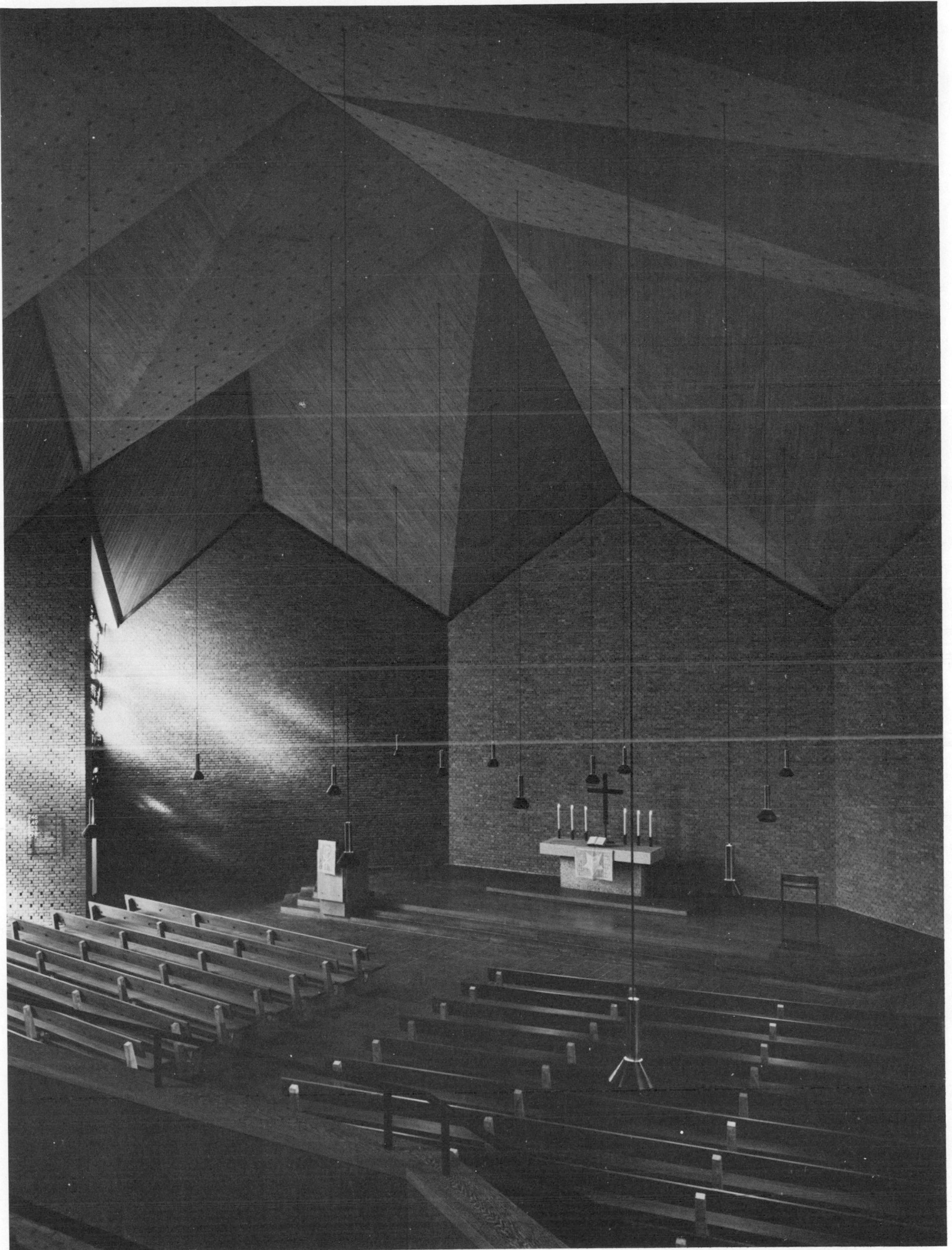

larly curved metal inserts which recall the highlights of an imaginary landscape.

The Hanover cinema is not typical of the whole of Oesterlen's work, of the crystalline body of his Christ Church in Bochum or of the cubist blocks of his housing and administration buildings. Yet this cinema is one of the best German examples of an architecture which, in its feeling for freedom of form, avoids the right angle and seeks a connection with organic growth.

—Christian Borngräber

O'GORMAN, Juan.

Mexican. Born in Coyoacán, Mexico City, 6 July 1905. Educated at Jesuit schools in Mexico City; National University of Mexico, School of Architecture, Mexico City, 1922–26, Dip.Arch. 1926; apprenticed to Carlos Obregón Santacilia, 1927; studied painting with Antonio Ruiz, Ramon Alba Guedarrama, and Diego Rivera. Married Helen Fowler in 1941; daughter: Maria Elena. Worked in the architectural offices of José Villagrán García, Carlos Tarditi, and Carlos Contreros, Mexico City, 1927–29; Chief Draftsman, office of Carlos Obregón Santacilia, 1929–32; Head, Mexico City Department of Building Construction, 1932–34. In private practice, Mexico City, from 1934. Co-Founder, School of Architecture, 1932, and Professor of Architecture and Architectural Composition, 1932–48, National Polytechnic Institute, Mexico City. Founder, Workers' Housing Study Group, Mexico City, 1936. Exhibitions: *Anniversary of the Revolution,* Palace of Fine Arts, Mexico City, 1934; Museum of Modern Art, Palace of Fine Arts, Mexico City, 1948; Galerias del Bosque de Chapultepec, Mexico City, 1949; *Realismo y Fantasia en la Obra de Juan O'Gorman,* Palace of Fine Arts, Mexico City, 1950, and Morelia, Mexico, 1951; Institute of Mexican Art, Mexico City, 1961; *Salon de la Plastica Mexicana,* Mexico City, 1964; San Fernando Valley State College, California, 1964; *Art of Latin America since Independence,* Yale University, New Haven, Connecticut, 1966, and toured the United States; *Proyectos de Murales de Juan O'Gorman,* Palace of Fine Arts, Mexico City, 1968. Recipient: First Prize, La Tolteca Painting Competition, Mexico City, 1930; First Prize for Mexico City, Excelsior Painting Competition, 1948; Diploma, City of Morelia, 1952; Diploma and Medal of Honor, School of Engineering and Architecture, National Polytechnic Institute, Mexico City, 1959; Diploma, National Institute of Mexican Youth, 1969; Diploma, Mexican College of Architects, 1970; Mexican National Art Prize, 1972. Member, National College of Architects of Mexico, 1956. Member, Bolivarian Society of Architects, Caracas, 1967. Member, Academy of Arts, Mexico City, 1971. Address: Calle Jardin 88, San Angel Inn, Mexico 20, D.F., Mexico.

Works:

1924/
25 Frescoes for the Salon Bach (bar), Mexico City
Numerous murals in Mexico City
1925/
28 Bank of Mexico reconstruction, Mexico City (with Carlos Obregón Santacilia)
SSA (Secretaria de Salubridad y Asistencia Publica) Building, Mexico City (with Carlos Obregón Santacilia)
1927/
28 Lomas House, Chapultepec, Mexico City
Mural, Pascual Ortiz Rubio House, Tizapán, Mexico
1929/
30 Diego Rivera House and Studio, San Angel Inn, Mexico City

Juan O'Gorman House I, San Angel Inn, Mexico City
1931 Thomas O'Gorman House, Palmas, San Angel Inn, Mexico City
Murals, Public Library, Azcapotzalco, Mexico (with Julio Castellaños)
1932/
34 28 primary schools throughout Mexico, for the Ministry of Education, including schools at Tampico, Colonia Portales, Ilahuac Village, Xochimilco Village, Peravillo, and Coyoacán
Technical School, Tresguerras Street, Mexico City
1934 Julio Castellaños House, Mexico City
Manuel Toussaint House, Mexico City (project)
Mexican Confederation of Labor Offices and Auditorium, Mexico City (project)
Frances Toor House, Mexico City
1936 Sindicato de Electricistas Building, Calle Orozco and Berra, Mexico City
1936/
37 3 murals, Mexico City Airport (2 now in the History Museum, Chapultepec Castle, Mexico City)
1939 Mural, Xochimilco Primary School, Mexico City
1940 12 murals, Cultural Association of Jewish Youth, Pittsburgh (project)
1941 Mural, Gertrude Bocanegra Public Library, San Agustin Church, Patzcuaro, Michoacán, Mexico
1941/
42 Mural, private house, San Angel Inn, Mexico City
1942/
43 Mural, Fred Davis House, San Jeronimo Lidice, Mexico (destroyed)
1944/
45 Museo Anahuacalli, Mexico (as consultant; with Diego Rivera)
1948 Mosaic murals, Conlon Nancarrow House, Las Aguilas, Mexico
1952/
53 National Library, State University of Mexico, University City, Mexico City (with Gustavo Saavedra and Juan Martinez de Velasco)
Mosaic mural, Ministry of Communication and Public Works, Mexico City
1953/
56 Juan O'Gorman House II, Avenida San Jeronimo, San Angel Inn, Mexico City (destroyed, 1970)
1954/
56 Mosaic mural, Posada de la Mision Hotel, Taxco, Mexico
1960/
61 Mural, History Museum, Chapultepec Castle, Mexico City
1962/
65 Mural, Entrance Hall, Centro Interamericano del Seguro Social de la Unidad Independencia, San Jeronimo Lidice, Mexico (with Roberto Berdecio)
Mural, Banco Internacional del Paseo de la Reforma, Mexico City
Mosaic mural, San Cristobal Park, Santiago, Chile (as consultant/supervisor)
1966/
67 Mosaic mural, Convention Center Theatre, San Antonio, Texas
1968/
79 Murals, Room of the Revolution, History Museum, Chapultepec Castle, Mexico City

Publications:

On O'GORMAN: book—*Builders in the Sun: Five Mexican Architects* by Clive Bamford Smith, New

York 1967; articles—"Federal Schools of Mexico" in *Architectural Record* (New York), May 1934; "Contenido Politico de la Arquitectura" in *Edificacion* (Mexico City), September/October 1937; "Jardines del Pedregal da San Angel" in *Arts and Architecture* (Los Angeles), August 1951; "Biblioteca y Hemeroteca Nacional" in *Arquitectura* (Mexico City), September 1952; "Mexico City University: Its New Campus and Buildings" in *Northwest Architect* (Minneapolis), September/October 1952; "Mosaic Details from a House" in *Arts and Architecture* (Los Angeles), March 1955; "Mosaics" in *Art and Architecture* (Los Angeles), February 1959; "Juan O'Gorman" by Mathias Goeritz in *Arquitectura* (Mexico City), December 1960; "Habitation à Mexico" in *L'Architecture d'Aujourd'hui* (Paris), June/July 1962; "O'Gorman Cave House Disappears" in *Progressive Architecture* (New York), March 1970; "O'Gorman House" in *Architectural Design* (London), September 1970.

Juan O'Gorman is the oldest son of an Irish father and a Mexican mother, a genetic combination bound to produce of preponderance of imagination and fantasy over rational impulse, a condition favorable to creative work of fascinating iridescence as well as complex contradictions in theoretical pronouncements.

O'Gorman belonged to that generation of architects educated in the years when Le Corbusier's *Vers une Architecture* appeared and the architectural avant-garde hotly defended the favorite line, "La maison est une machine à demeurer," while conveniently forgetting such sentences as "L'architecture, c'est l'art par excellence" or ". . . est au delà des choses utilitaires" or "L'architecture est le jeu savant, correct et magnifique des volumes assemblées sous la lumière." After graduating from the Architecture School of the National University of Mexico and working for some years in the offices of various architects, O'Gorman built, between 1929 and 1932, a series of houses that are generally considered the first in Mexico to be designed according to the doctrines of Functionalism. Among these houses there was one for himself and two (a house and a studio) for Diego Rivera. At the time he was criticized for copying Le Corbusier's early houses in Paris. There is some truth in the charge—especially in the Diego studio, with its spiral stairs and sawtooth roof. But O'Gorman was only 24 years old at the time, and if he copied, he made the right choice.

During the following years O'Gorman designed and supervised the construction of 28 schools for the Ministry of Education, strictly observing the rule of "maximum of utility for minimum of expense." And, while teaching design at the National Polytechnic Institute, O'Gorman instilled in his students the spirit of Functionalism: "Copying the monuments of antiquity, be they Aztec, Mayan, colonial or more recent works, means, as a pedagogical discipline, to engrave and to impress upon the mind of youth forms that were the product of other necessities and other construction methods and are therefore the farther away from our way of life the more mankind makes material progress."

Twenty years later, in a paper read at the Palace of Fine Arts, O'Gorman made this statement about his early architectural work (it sounds somehow like the confession of a penitent defector, accusing himself of having given in to bourgeois temptations): "What I want to have clearly established in writing is the fact that, for my own work, I took the architecture of Le Corbusier as a model and that makes me partly responsible for the implanting of Functionalism in our country; it is, at the same time, valid proof of my own lack of talent. This happened between 1926 and 1936, years during which I worked at actively applying the principles of Functionalism in Mexico. This mistake was especially grave, considering that within my reach was the knowledge of Frank Lloyd Wright's work, which was, at that time as it still is today, the contemporary expression of

Juan O'Gorman: O'Gorman House II, San Angel Inn, Mexico City, 1956

our own tradition. When I finally realized this error, I renounced architecture to dedicate myself to painting. . . . The Swiss puritanism of Le Corbusier's architecture is exactly the antithesis to the plastic arts of Mexico, from the antique Anáhuac down to the popular expressions of today."

If Frank Lloyd Wright's organic architecture was the supreme expression of the artistic tradition of Meso-America, Mexican architecture, too, should be, against all evidence, organic. On the other hand, Wright's Taliesin West is, according to O'Gorman, "the most magnificent modern house . . . and one of the most important works of art of all time. Its Mexican character is evident."

Today, all of these intertwined theories may seem both confusing and irrelevant, but the fortunate fact is that, about ten years after his flight from Functionalism (time that he spent painting a series of great al fresco murals and numerous excellent easel paintings in tempera), the architect O'Gorman suddenly emerged from his self-imposed exile, with the sword of Anti-Functionalism, the shield of Organic Architecture, and the battle cry Integration, ready to design, construct and complete in five years two buildings in Mexico City that made him famous through the world: the National Library at University City and his own house in the Avenida San Jeronimo.

Many murals had been painted in Mexico since the revolution, all of them on existing walls and mostly without any satisfactory relation to the architecture until, at mid-century, the idea of integrating sculpture and painting more closely into the building process became more widely discussed. As with the great architectural monuments of the past from very

different cultures—the Parthenon, Angkor Vat, Uxmal, or Chartres—the three arts should not be elaborated separately and later "put together," but should be worked out on the job, by the same people, in an act of simultaneous creation.

Conditions at the National Library were ideal for integration: O'Gorman was one of the three architects responsible for the project at the same time that he was the creator of the magnificent stone mosaics that surround the book stacks. The library was widely admired and more photographed than any other modern building in the world, but it did not satisfy O'Gorman's desire for total integration: the murals that covered the rectangular box could not possibly hide it.

O'Gorman's own house, begun while he was finishing the library, is a work of ecologically integrated, pure organic architecture; it is the most significant creation of his life. He had bought a rather large plot at the edge of the vast lava bed south of Mexico City. Here he found a grotto hidden in the vegetation and used it to form two sides of the wonderful living room; part of the existing rock formation became the ceiling, and the remaining surfaces, mostly curved, he covered with coloured stone mosaics inside and outside. All kinds of minor technical difficulties beset him, but at last he realized his dream castle. He wrote in 1976: "This experiment in organic architecture was realized . . . for the principal purpose of being an outcry of protest in favor of humanism, perishing in the technological desert of our marvellous civilization."

After living in it for fifteen years, O'Gorman had to sell the house, and the subsequent owner de-

stroyed it by pulling down a great part of the walls and covering the rest totally with a thick layer of cement—a crime that deprived the Mexican people of a singular monument that should have been protected by law. The loss almost broke O'Gorman's heart. He renounced architecture and now dedicates himself to painting apocalyptic images haunting the deserts of technology.

—Max Cetto

OKADA, Shin'ichi.
Japanese. Born in Tokyo, 9 January 1928. Educated at the University of Tokyo School of Architecture and Graduate School of Architecture, B.Arch. 1955, M.A. 1957; Yale University Graduate School of Art and Architecture, 1962–63, M.A. 1963. Married Hiroko Sakata in 1956; children: Makiko and Namihei. Architect for the Kajima Corporation, Tokyo, 1956–62; Designer, Skidmore, Owings and Merrill, New York, 1964–65; Chief Architect, Kajima Corporation, Tokyo, 1965–69. Since 1969, President, Shin'ichi Okada, Architect, and Associates, Tokyo. Lecturer, Chiba University, 1966–69, and the University of Tokyo, 1971–73. Lecturer, Tokyo Metropolitan University, since 1974. Recipient: Kanagawa Prefecture Award, 1967; First Prize, Japanese Supreme Court Competition, 1969; Building Contractors Society Award, 1970, 1974; Architectural Insti-

tute Award, 1975. Address: Shin'ichi Okada Architect and Associates, No. 2—Kawa Building, 1-11-39 Akasaka, Minato-ku, Tokyo 107, Japan.

Works:

1966 Omura Children's Home, Nagasaki
1967 Idemitsu Kosan Clubhouse, Kanagawa, Japan
1968 Gymnasium, Nippon Dental College, Tokyo
1969 Osaka Business Terminal Urban Renewal (project)
    Hitachi Industries General Hospital, Hitachi, Japan
1970 Kajima Sendai Branch Office Building, Sendai, Japan
    Kajima Kyushu Branch Office Building, Fukuoka, Japan
    Kajima Head Office, Tokyo
1971 Gumma Cultural Center, Maebashi, Japan
    Yanase Motors Branch Office, Fukuoka, Japan
1972 Hotel Ricci Sapporo, Sapporo, Japan
    Idemitsu Kosan Research Center, Chiba, Japan
    Niigata Campus, Nippon Dental College, Niigata, Japan
    Toa Real Housing Estate, Tokyo
    Grant Heights Housing, Japan Housing Corporation, Tokyo (project)
1973 City General Hospital, Kurashiki, Japan
    Fukuoka Welfare Facility for the Elderly, Fukuoka, Japan
    Okayama Young People's Lodge-in-Nature, Okayama, Japan
1974 The Japanese Supreme Court, Tokyo
    Hotel Ricci Fukuoka, Fukuoka, Japan
    Bridgestone Tire Training Center, Saitama, Japan (project)
    Nissei Sangyo Hayama Clubhouse, Hayama, Japan
    Research Laboratory, Japan Petroleum Exploration Company, Hamura, Japan
    Japan Red Cross Blood Supply Center, Niigata, Japan
1975 SVAX Shinjuku Office Building, Tokyo
    Okayama General Welfare Center, Okayama, Japan
    Kurashiki Young People's Lodge-in-Nature, Kurashiki, Japan
1976 Tsukuba University, Tsukuba, Japan
1977 Anzen Motors Office Building, Tokyo
1978 Gumma Prefectural Library, Maebashi, Japan
    Nissei Sangyo Yamanaka-Lake Clubhouse, Yamanashi, Japan
    Niigata City Music Center, Niigata, Japan
    Singapore Embassy, Tokyo
    SVAX Nishishimmbashi Office Building, Tokyo
1978- Home for the Elderly, Yokohama, Japan
    Public Library, Tokorozawa, Japan
    Main Library, Tsukuba University, Tsukuba, Japan
    Cultural Center, Tomakomai, Japan
    Cultural Center of Kamojima, Tokushima, Japan
    Metropolitan Police Headquarters, Tokyo
    The Orient Museum, Okayama, Japan
    Idemitsu Museum in Mitaka, Tokyo
    Tobihino Rest Home, Nara, Japan
    Urban renewal of Mihara, Japan
    Gyosei International High School, Chiba, Japan
    Community Center for Handicapped Persons, Nerima, Japan
    Community Village for Handicapped Persons, Hokkaido, Japan

Shin'ichi Okada: The Japanese Supreme Court, Tokyo, 1974

Publications:

By OKADA: books—*Overseas Architecture,* nos. 1–6 (Kajima, Tokyo), 1972–75; articles—"The Meaning of System in Design" in *Space Design* (Tokyo), May 1969; "Organization and Design: From Concept to Decision in Design" in *Kenchiku-Bunka* (Tokyo), March 1970; "The Process Toward the Physicalization of Architecture" in *Space Design* (Tokyo), January 1972; "The Meaning of System in Design" in *The Japan Architect* (Tokyo), January 1973; "The Inter-Relation Between Architecture and Human Life" in *Space Design* (Tokyo), December 1973; "Space and Symbol: The Development of the Architectural Concept in the Design of the Japanese Supreme Court" in *Space Design* (Tokyo), special issue 1974.

On OKADA: book—*Beyond Metabolism: The New Japanese Architecture* by Michael Franklin Ross, New York 1978; article—"Okada and Associates" in *Kenchiku-Gaho* (Tokyo), December 1973.

*

Several fundamental thoughts have occurred to me in the process of design:

The Wall: I find the wall a fundamental component that serves to create and determine space. By manipulating it by imposition, we succeed in generating and moving space as well as enclosing it. In the process it brings humankind into its fold. Furthermore, the wall becomes a step in the direction of developing the town.

The Heart Space: Of the spaces thus formed by the manipulation of the wall, we find generated the heart space. It is space that is able to adapt itself to the human situation—the place for a group to form, the place of communication, of human amelioration. A space fit to be called human, motherly space. The heart space might correspond to what Louis Kahn calls the "Room."

Catalytic Region: It is the region in which an object and another object lie contiguous to each other, confronting each other. Now the two objects exert force upon each other. It is a boundary region formed of two regions in touch with each other—such as the site and the road, the building and the earth, etc. These I find important and I believe that they deserve full attention when carrying out design. For we shall, in so developing the catalytic region, lead it into the realm of the urban.

Trunk Space: For complex architecture, and even for simple, independent structures, but more so for urban-size projects, the generation of the trunk space is indispensable. In my design it becomes a key vocabulary. The street, the plaza and the mall are examples. But it is the region becoming more internalized, as is the spine, which deserves to be called the trunk space. The external/internal space of the main hall of the Japanese Supreme Court Building is one example that is very close to what I mean by trunk space.

Architectural Language: There is meaning in every architectural element. They form what we call the physical vocabulary. But against these there must be the vocabularization of each architectural concept, and the meaning of expression of each part of its content, that is, the conceptual vocabulary. By means of these two vocabularies (condensed into the architectural vocabulary), the complex structure may be brought into being, thereby evolving the architectural language. What is now the structuring architectural language device becomes the basis of a building structuring process. This we term the system of design.

—Shin'ichi Okada

*

Shin'ichi Okada is one of a select few Japanese architects who have had the technical skill, courage, and extraordinary design ability to leave the fold of one of Japan's Big Five design-build conglomerates. Okada succeeded in developing his own practice after being the chief designer for Kajima Corpora-

tion by winning the Japanese Supreme Court Building competition in 1969. His work for Kajima and his own work subsequently reveal the strong influence of his mentors at Yale University, Paul Rudolph and Louis I. Kahn.

Okada's buildings inevitably reflect the simple geometry and bold massing most often associated with Kahn. The head office of Kajima Corporation is composed of two massive towers shifted in plan to create a slot of space between them as an entrance, not unlike the shafts of brick at Richards Medical Building by Kahn. These large volumes shifted in plan appear again in Okada's "space walls" at the Supreme Court Building and, later, in a more refined statement at the Niigata Campus of the Nippon Dental College.

The overall impact of the Supreme Court Building itself is one of monumentality. It is massive, bold and imposing. Okada intended this impression, and in fact he believes in the need for monumentality in the overall urban design framework of our cities. He defines monumentality as possessing "scale that permits transmission into the future, continuity, long life, and the dream of durability in the face of change."

It is interesting to realize that "durability in the face of change" need not always be achieved through the heavy-handed use of bulky, capacious forms. It is true that the Egyptians employed a combination of massive size with simplicity of form to achieve longevity, but the delicate and serene Katsura Detached Palace has stood the test of time, albeit a shorter span, through the creative use of vernacular, natural materials and forms. This lesson was somehow never incorporated into Okada's design vocabulary.

A more sophisticated integration of forms and spaces with their environment was achieved by Okada at the Niigata Campus of the Nippon Dental College. Clusters of connected square blocks, with their projecting stair and service towers sheathed in clay tile, are arranged around a major campus outdoor quadrangle. The general esthetic is indebted to Kahn's Richards Medical Building, but the design attempts to develop Kahn's concept further and adapt it to this particular site. In this respect Okada is quite successful. The long, gray cold winters of this region produce powdery, white salt deposits from the ocean, which tend to collect on vertical panes of glass and erode exposed metal. Okada developed a system of clay-tiled vertical walls and steeply sloping glass skylights that protect the inhabitants from the bleak winters and shed the unsightly salt deposits, while allowing the warm sun to brighten the interior spaces.

All of Shin'ichi Okada's buildings tend to incorporate exterior space into the overall design concept, often with pleasing results. His structures, however, remain massive and geometrically purist. The success of the Niigata Campus and such other projects as the Gunma Cultural Center, the Omura Children's Home at Nagasaki, and the Kurashiki Young People's Lodge, indicates that we can expect a continuation of significant strong statements from the office of Shin'ichi Okada.

—Michael Franklin Ross

OTAKA, Masato.
Japanese. Born in Fukushima Prefecture in 1923. Educated at Tokyo University, Architecture Department, Dip.Arch. 1947, and Tokyo University Graduate School. Worked in the office of Kunio Mayekawa and Associates, Tokyo, 1949–61. In private practice, Tokyo, since 1961. Lecturer, Waseda University, Tokyo, and Tokyo University. Director, Japan Architects Association: Member of the Council, Architectural Institute of Japan: President, Agricultural Co-operation Architectural Study Society,

Tokyo; Member, Board of Directors, Environmental Development Center, Tokyo. Founder Member, with Noboru Kawazoe, Kiyonori Kikutake, Fumihiko Maki, Noriaki Kurokawa, Kiyoshi Awazu, and Shinya Izumi, The Metabolist Group, Tokyo, 1960. Address: Masato Otaka and Associates, Yoyogi Building, 5-18-21 Sendagaya, Shibuya-ku, Tokyo 151, Japan.

Works:

1954 Kanagawa Concert Hall and Library, Yokohama
1956 Education Center, Fukishima, Japan (with Kunio Mayekawa and Associates)
1958 Multi-story apartment building, Harumi, Tokyo (with Kunio Mayekawa and Associates)
1961 Metropolitan Festival Hall, Tokyo (with Kunio Mayekawa and Associates)
1961/
69 Kataoka Agricultural Union Co-operative Building, Japan
Yamanouchi Agricultural Union Co-operative Building, Japan
Hanaizumi Agricultural Union Co-operative Building, Japan
City over Tokyo Bay (project)
Urban Platform Development, Otemachi, Japan (project)
Urban Platform Development, Sakaide City, Japan (project)
Katayama Agricultural Union Co-operative Union Hall, Japan
Tochiji Prefectural Health Insurance Hall, Japan
Japan Marine Workers' Union Hall, Tokyo
Silk Center, Yokohama (competition project)
Ueno Commemorative Hall, Japan
1967 Prefectural Center, Chiba, Japan
1969 Mango-cho Agricultural Co-operative Union Building, Japan
Makinohara Service Area and Rest House, Tokyo-Nagoya Expressway
1970 Central Library, Chiba, Japan
Niihama Agricultural Co-operative Union Hall, Japan
1971 Shizuoka Agricultural Co-operative Association Center, Japan
1972 Federation of Japan Automobile Workers' Union Education Center, Gotemba, Japan
Housing development, Chojuen, Japan
Housing development, Motomachi, Japan
1973 Apartment building development, Hiroshima
1974 Library, College of Industrial Technology, Nihon University, Japan
1977 Memorial Visitors' Center, Tsukuba, Japan
Prefectural Art Museum, Chiba, Japan

Publications:

On OTAKA: articles—"Masato Otaka" in *Zodiac* (Milan), no. 3, 1958; "The Architects" in special issue on Japan of *Architectural Review* (London), September 1962; "New Architecture Assessed: Masato Otaka's Chiba Cultural Hall" in *Kokusai Kentiku* (Tokyo), May 1967; "Two Agricultural Co-operatives" in *The Japan Architect* (Tokyo), July 1967; "Experiments from Japan" in *Casabella* (Milan), March 1969; "New Developments in Japanese Architecture" in *Architectural Record* (New York), September 1970; "Education Center at Gotemba" in *The Japan Architect* (Tokyo), December 1972; "Apartments in Hiroshima" by Masaya Fujimoto in *The Japan Architect* (Tokyo), August 1973; "Mass Production in Housing" in *Bauen und Wohnen* (Zurich), March 1975; "Library, College of Industrial Technology, Nihon University" by Isao Takada in *The Japan Architect* (Tokyo), June 1974; and "Chiba Prefectural Art Museum" by Noboru Kijima in *The Japan Architect* (Tokyo), February 1977.

Having worked in Mayekawa's office for twelve years, during which time he was largely responsible for various works, including the Harumi Apartment Block on Tokyo Bay, Masato Otaka went on to become the oldest founder member of the Metabolist Group. Working particularly with Maki, he insisted on "Group Form" as the only valid urban instrument. To the dimensions of time and the three spatial dimensions, he added a fifth, the "dimension of the group." He hoped to generate fertile circumstances for the prismatic realization of city, and, in a series of projected urban accommodations and floating arcadia, he illustrated how "Group Form" could contribute to that ideal.

But those projects, when actually built, came to have a bitter realism about them. Otaka had learned (along with architects of Tange's generation) that despite the Metabolist plea for an untrammelled architecture, the result, when actually built, was inevitably a concrete and determinate object in the field of environmental relations. The resultant architecture has been a positing of lines and barriers in an ongoing filtering process whereby positive is separated from negative, yin from yang, wabi from sabi. The built element in Otaka's projects has come to assume a very deliberate and directing role: it does not try to be an entrepreneurial mechanism whereby urban transactions are effected; it manifests itself as the actual stuff (quiditas) of these exchanges.

Take his Chiba Prefectural Center of 1967: here the "thingness" is very evident: it is a place where civic justice is quite patently to be administered, a place where power is obviously manifest, a single object-crystal of self-evident truth to which all else must bow. There is no room to wonder whether this kind of justice is, in fact, as true as the whole enterprise is making out. Of course, answering such a question was not part of the architect's brief, and in a way he was right to gloss it over—yet one regrets that there isn't even the slightest crack or blemish in the building's logic of authority.

There is an interesting similarly between this project and the main sanctuaries of some of the more prosperous of the new Japanese religions such as Soka Gakkai. The languages of civic and religious power overlap to an extent that might embarrass the Western observer, but to the Japanese they are reconcilable. I asked the architect responsible for the design of a temple in Kyoto for the new Buddhist sect, Konko-Kyo, why he had treated it in much the same vein as the coffee house he had designed elsewhere in Kyoto. With the headquarters of the sect carried out in Shinto style, the main sanctuary in Buddhist style, and the temple in Kyoto in a contemporary guise—under such conditions, he could make no sense of my question. The Japanese perceives and divides up his universe in a way quite distinct from ours, and we shouldn't be surprised by such apparent stylistic anomalies, any more than we should be surprised to find that in a recent poll of the religious practices of the Japanese, a great percentage of those polled professed to be believers in both Buddhism and Shinto.

—Chris Fawcett

OTANI, Sachio.
Japanese. Born in Tokyo, 20 February 1924. Educated at the University of Tokyo, Dip.Arch. 1946, D.Arch. 1951. Married Akiko Ochiai in 1952; daughter: Michiko. Worked as an architectural designer, office of Kenzo Tange, Tokyo, 1946-60. In private practice, Tokyo, since 1960. Lecturer, Department of Architecture, 1955-64, Assistant Professor of City Planning, 1964-71, and since 1971 Professor of City Planning, University of Tokyo. Exhibitions: *Contemporary Japanese Architecture*, toured Italy, 1968; *Sachio Otani: Pan-Pacific Prize
Exhibition*, Honolulu, 1969. Recipient: First Prize, International Conference Hall Competition, Kyoto, 1963; Pan-Pacific Prize, American Institute of Architects, Hawaii Chapter, 1969. Member, Architectural Institute of Japan, and the City Planning Institute of Japan. Address: 3-22-15 Shoan, Suginami-ku, Tokyo 167, Japan.

Works:

1960/
61 Kojimachi District Redevelopment, Tokyo (project)
1960/
64 Tensho Kotai Jingu Religious Sect Headquarters, Yamaguchi Prefecture, Japan
1961/
63 Tokyo Children's Cultural Center
1963/
66 Kyoto International Conference Hall
1964/
69 The Wholesalers' Market Center, Toyama, Japan
1965/
66 Pavilion for Children, Children's Land, Kanagawa Prefecture, Japan (with sculptor Isamu Noguchi)
Japan Social Insurance Agency Office Building, Tokyo
1967/
68 Sagamihara Campus of Kitazato University, Kanagawa Prefecture, Japan
1967/
69 Kanazawa Institute of Technology, Ishikawa Prefecture, Japan
1967/
70 Sumitomo Fairytale Pavilion, *Expo '70*, Osaka
Tensho Kotai Jingu Religious Sect Headquarters extension, Yamaguchi Prefecture, Japan
1969/
70 Ohtsuka House, Tokyo
Kawaramachi High-rise Housing Estate, Kawasaki, Kanagawa Prefecture, Japan (project)
1969/
73 Kyoto International Conference Hall extension
1970/
71 Master plan for the west part of the Kawasaki Station Redevelopment, Kawasaki, Kanagawa Prefecture, Japan
1973/
75 Tensho Kotai Jingu Religious Sect Complex, Honolulu
1973/
77 Tensho Kotai Jingu Religious Sect Complex, Tokyo
1973/
80 National Institute of Environmental Study, Tsukuba Kenkyu Gakuen Toshi, Ibaragi Prefecture, Japan
1975/
76 Kanazawa Institute of Technology extensions, Ishikawa Prefecture, Japan
1978 Singapore Convention Center (project)
Ohtsuka Company Office Building, Tokyo

Publications:

By OTANI: books—*History of Urban Space Composition*, Tokyo 1972; *Regional Planning and Environment*, Tokyo 1972; *Life and the City*, Tokyo 1974; articles—"Urban Design and Architecture" in *Journal of Architecture and Building Science* (Tokyo), October 1965; "Urban Space and Community" in *Chiiki Kaihatsu* (Tokyo), May 1971; "Logic in Space Composition" in *Toshi Jutaku* (Tokyo), December 1971; "Matters Relating to Urban Renewal" in *Man and City*, Tokyo 1973; "Composition of Urban Space" in *Contemporary Policies in City Planning*, Tokyo 1973; "Historical Landscape Design and City

Sachio Otanı: Kyoto International Conference Hall, 1966

Planning" in *Journal of Architecture and Building Science* (Tokyo), December 1973; "City Planning and Cultural Properties" in *Gekkan Bunkazai* (Tokyo), June 1975; "Contemporary Architecture and the Quality of Urban Space" in *Toshi Jutaku* (Tokyo), October 1975; "Low-rise Collective Housing" in *Toshi Jutaku* (Tokyo), May 1977; "The Role of City Planning in the Conservation of Historical Towns" in *Kankyo Bunka* (Tokyo), February 1978.

On OTANI: book—*The Complete Works of Contemporary Japanese Architects,* volume 18, edited by Isamu Kurita, Tokyo 1970; articles—"The Tokyo Children's Culture Center" in *The Japan Architect* (Tokyo), September 1964; "The Headquarters of the Tensho Kotai Jingu Sect" in *The Japan Architect* (Tokyo), March 1966; "Kyoto International Conference Hall" in *Kokusai Kentiku* (Tokyo), July 1966; "Trapezoids Shape International Conference Center in Kyoto, Japan" in *Progressive Architecture* (New York), August 1966; "Palais des Conférences Internationales à Kyoto" and "Centre Religieux de la secte Tensho Kotai Jingu à Tabuse, District de Yamaguchi" in *L'Architecture d'Aujourd'hui* (Paris), September 1966; "The Architecture of Japan" in *Canadian Architect* (Toronto), January 1967; "Japanische Architektur," special issue of *Baumeister* (Munich), August 1967; "Children's Land Juvenile Hall" in *The Japan Architect* (Tokyo), November 1967; "The Kitasate University, Sagamihara Campus" in *The Japan Architect* (Tokyo), October 1968; "Expo '70 Projects," special issue of *The Japan Architect* (Tokyo), April 1969; "Kanazawa Institute of Technology: Its Center and Its Civil Engineering Building" in *Kenchiku Bunka* (Tokyo), October 1969; "New Developments in Jap-

anese Architecture" in *Architectural Record* (New York), September 1970; "New Trends in the Design of Public Operated Apartment Houses" in *Kenchiku Bunka* (Tokyo), December 1972; "Additions to the Kyoto International Conference Hall" in *The Japan Architect* (Tokyo), August 1973; "Kanazawa Institute of Technology" in *The Japan Architect* (Tokyo), April 1977.

Sachio Otani was one of Kenzo Tange's close collaborators, working on some of the latter's earliest and best works such as the Hiroshima Peace Center. With the Tokyo Children's Cultural Center, he began his independent career, and since then his buildings, though few, have been marked by a distinct style.

The Children's Center revealed his design approach, which has basically remained unchanged: an aggressive expression of the structure, a bold, sculptural handling of masses, and an intense articulation of functions. It also raised questions, which have persisted throughout his career, about his monumental sense of scale, here especially troubling in a building intended for children. More in keeping with its use is the Tensho Kotai Jingu Sect Headquarters, where the exposed concrete masses form an even more heroic ensemble.

The Kyoto International Conference Hall, which Otani designed on the basis of his winning entry in an open competition, is his representative building and shows both his strengths and weaknesses. One must applaud his effort to make a novel structural system of slanting columns and precast wall panels work. The system creates trapezoidal sections of different sizes and recalls a traditional method of wood construction in Japan called *gassho zukuri;* thus the

Hall may be considered Otani's contribution to the "Tradition Debate" that took place in the 1950's and 1960's. Otani has explored the architectural possibilities of this framework and has produced exciting visual effects, particularly on the outside, where (for example) interpreters' booths jut out of the conference hall. Yet the effort is all too visible inside, and the merit of having chosen this unorthodox system becomes debatable as the novelty wears off—when you have seen one room with a trapezoidal section, you have seen them all.

Otani is known as a theoretician and educator, and his Kojimachi Redevelopment Project is his essay in experimental urban design and housing. The dwelling units are self-contained and raised off the ground on stilts. The possibility of their fitting various ground contours is investigated, yet little else is shown to indicate that the project was meant for a specific site, much less one in central Tokyo.

The same slightly academic air prevails in Otani's more recent public housing project in Kawasaki, which was actually built. One can see his characteristic desire to explore new spatial organizations. In a typical building, the bottom half of the slab splays outward, creating inside what was intended to be a sheltered semi-public space. Unfortunately, nothing has been done with this space and it is dark and cavernous; one expects manacled prisoners to file past, not children and adults engaged in those spontaneous encounters the architect undoubtedly sought to promote.

In the end, it is not for his earnest investigations into new spatial organizations but for the indisputably dramatic sculptural expression of his forms that Otani's work will be remembered.

—Hiroshi Watanabe

OTTO, Frei.

German. Born in Siegmar, Saxony, 31 May 1925. Educated at the Schadow School, Zehlendorf, Berlin, as a trainee stone-mason, 1931–43; Technische Hochschule, Charlottenburg, Berlin, 1932; Technical University of Berlin, under Freese, Bickenbach and Jobst, 1948–50 (on study trip to the United States, 1950–51), Dip.Ing. 1952, Dr.Ing. 1954. Did compulsory labour service, then served as a Fighter Pilot in the German Air Force, 1943–45; prisoner of war in France, 1945–47: Prison Camp Architect, Depot 501, Chartres, France, 1946–47. Married Ingrid Smolla in 1952; children: Angela, Bettina, Christine, Dietmar, and Erdmute. In private practice, Zehlendorf, 1952–58; established architecture studio in Zehlendorf, with Lohs, Bubner, Frank, Wehrhan, Medlin, etc., 1958–68. Since 1968, associated with Studio Warmbronn, with Bubner, Krier, Thorsteinn, Wright, Goedert, Goldsmith, Fritz, Doster, etc., Warmbronn, Germany: since 1972 has worked only in collaboration with other architects, engineers, and surveyors. Adviser to the Large Tent Construction Division, L. Stromeyer and Company, Constance, 1953–74; Adviser to Höchst AG on the use of technical fibers, 1973–75. Founder, Development Center for Lightweight Construction, Berlin, 1957. Since 1964 Professor and Director of the Institute for Lightweight Structures, and since 1976 Professor-in-Ordinary, University of Stuttgart. Visiting Professor of Design, Washington University, St. Louis, 1958, Design Academy, Ulm, 1969, Yale University, New Haven, Connecticut, 1960, University of California, Berkeley, 1962, Massachusetts Institute of Technology/Harvard University, Cambridge, Massachusetts, 1962, University of Zulia, Maracaibo, 1962, National Institute of Design, Ahmedabad, India, 1966, and the International Summer Academy, Salzburg, 1971. Exhibitions: *The Work of Frei Otto*, Museum of Modern Art, New York, 1971; *Leichtarchitektur: Frei Otto and His Teams 1955–1976*, travelling exhibition, North America, Europe, South Africa and the Middle East, 1975–78. Recipient: Paul Bonatz Prize, Stuttgart, 1971; City Architecture Prize, Cologne, 1971; Honorary Award for Use of Plastics, Club of Plastics Use, Munich, 1972; Thomas Jefferson Memorial Medal, University of Virginia, Charlottesville, 1974; Berlin Arts Prize, 1976; Auguste Perret Prize, with Rolf Gutbrod, International Union of Architects, 1976; Plaque, Bund Deutscher Architekten, 1978. Dr.Art/Arch.: Washington University, St. Louis, 1973; Honorary Professor, Technische Hochschule, Stuttgart, 1965, and University Federico Villareal, Lima, Peru, 1977. Honorary Fellow, American Institute of Architects, 1968. Member, Akademie der Künste, Berlin, 1970. Address: Institute for Lightweight Structures, Passenwaldring 14, 7000 Stuttgart 80, West Germany.

Works:

1953/
  56 Social housing, Alexandrastiftung, Templehof, Berlin
1955 Tent Pavilions, *Bundesgartenschau*, Kassel
1956 Tents, and Aircraft Hangars, *Gartenschau*, Saarbrucken
     Observation Pavilion, *Oktoberfest*, Munich
1957 Dance Floor Tent, Entrance Canopy, and Tent Shelters, *Bundesgartenschau*, Cologne
     City of Tomorrow Pavilion, *Interbau*, Berlin
     Small Exhibition Halls, *Interbau*, Berlin (with Gunschel and Carl Otto)
     Cafe at Schloss Bellevue, Gropius Building, *Interbau*, Berlin (with Bubner and Lohs)
1958 Inselcafe Tent, *Saffa Exhibition*, Zurich
     Tent Pavilion, *Gartenschau*, Saarbrucken
1959 Frei Otto Studio, Türksteinweg 5, Berlin 37
1960 Tent for evangelist Billy Graham, Berlin
1961 Design of Evangelical Church Day celebrations, Olympic Stadium, Berlin
1962 Experimental structures, Deubau, Germany

1963 Undulating Tent, Membrane Structure Hall, and Star Halls/Pavilions, *Bundesgartenschau*, Hamburg
1964 Snow and Rocks Restaurant Pavilion, *Swiss National Exhibition*, Lausanne
1965 Retractable roof, Cannes (for Roger Taillibert)
     Mobile theatre, for the Dutch Opera Foundation (project; with van den Broek and Bakema)
1967 German Pavilion, *Expo '67*, Montreal (with Rolf Gutbrod)
1968 Retractable roof for the Open-Air Theatre, Bad Hersfeld, Germany (with Romberg and Bubner)
     Institute of Light Surface Structures, Vaihingen, Germany
1969 Arctic City (project; with Sir Ove Arup and Kenzo Tange)
1970 Luisenburg Roof (project; with Rombert)
1971 Mobile large umbrella roof for the Music Pavilion, *Bundesgartenschau*, Cologne
1972 Roofs for the Olympic Stadium and Arenas, Munich (for Günter Behnisch; with Bubner, Aver, Büxel, and Fritz Leonhardt)
1973 Cultural Center, Abidjah, Ivory Coast (project; with Sir Ove Arup and Rolf Gutbrod)
1974 Hotel and Conference Center, Mecca, Saudi Arabia (with Sir Ove Arup and Rolf Gutbrod)
     Mannheim Multi-Hall
     Spa and Recreation Center, Baden-Baden (competition project; with Rolf Gutbrod)
1976 Ministry of Industry and Electricity, Riyadh, Saudi Arabia (project; with Sir Ove Arup and Rolf Gutbrod)
1978 Airfish High Performance Airship (project)
1978- Council of Ministers Building, Riyadh, Saudi Arabia (with Sir Ove Arup and Rolf Gutbrod)

Publications:

By OTTO: books—*The Suspended Roof*, Berlin 1954; *Tensile Structures*, volume 1, with R. Trostel, Berlin 1962, and volume 2, with F.-K. Schleyer, Berlin 1966; editor of *IL Publications*, 17 volumes, Stuttgart, 1969–78; articles—"Vom Nest zur modernen Wohnstadt" in *Der Architekt* (Stuttgart), vol. 3, no. 12, 1954; "Vom ungeheizt schön warmen Haus und neuen Fenstern" in *Deutsche Bauzeitschrift* (Gutersloh), no. 3, 1955; "Bauten für morgen?" in *Bauen und Wohnen* (Zurich), vol. 10, no. 3, 1955; "Die Stadt von morgen und das Einfamilienhaus" in *Baukunst und Werkform* (Nuremberg), vol. 9, no. 12, 1956; "Formes, Techniques et constructions humaines" in *L'Architecture d'Aujourd'hui* (Paris), vol. 29, no. 78, 1958; "Imagination et Architecture" in *L'Architecture d'Aujourd'hui* (Paris), vol. 33, no. 102, 1962; "Die Erdoberfläche" in *Bauen und Wohnen* (Zurich), vol. 18, no. 1, 1964; "Villes futures" in *L'Architecture d'Aujourd'hui* (Paris), vol. 35, no. 115, 1964; "Ein Interbau und ein Spinnerzentrum" in *Deutsche Bauzeitung* (Stuttgart), September 1970; "Die neue Zeit der vielen Architekturen" in *Deutsche Bauzeitung* (Stuttgart), December 1972; "Die Europastadt" in *Deutsche Bauzeitung* (Stuttgart), December 1973; "Creation, Creativity and Architecture" in *Architectural Design* (London), vol. 45, no. 7, 1975; "Mit Leichtigkeit gegen Brutalitat" in *Deutsche Bauzeitung* (Stuttgart), January 1976; "Les formules qui ménent l'architecture" in *L'Architecture* (Paris), no. 396, 1976; "Widernatürliche Architektur" in *Universitatsnachrichten* (Stuttgart), no. 50, 1977; "Wie weiter?" in *Schweizerische Bauzeitung* (Zurich), vol. 95, no. 16, 1977; etc.

On OTTO: books—*The Work of Frei Otto*, exhibition catalogue, by Ludwig Glaeser, New York 1971, revised as *Leichtarchitektur: Frei Otto and His Teams 1955–1976*, 1975, 1977; *Frei Otto: Form und Konstruktion* by Philip Drew, Stuttgart 1976; article

—"Frei Otto at Work" in *Architectural Design* (London), March 1971.

Frei Otto is wholly responsible for the revival of the tent as a leading species of modern tensile architecture. The grid shell, of which the 1974 Mannheim Multi-Hall is the most recent example, may appear at first glance to be unrelated to pre-industrial tents, but in reality it is a modern version of the traditional trellis tent of Central Asia. The tent and monumental architecture are not isolated phenomena: at various times in history each has had an influence on the other. Frei Otto's modest early textile structures and his later regular mesh steel cablenet structures are open pavilions of the kind that has been such an important archetype of modern architecture and achieved its purest expression in the hands of Mies van der Rohe.

Modern tensile building was inspired, in the main, by the industrial suspension bridge; consequently, Frei Otto's promotion of modest prestressed textile pavilions as an alternative prototype involved such a radically different conception of tensile form that he challenged current ideas on the nature and application of these structures. The much freer small scale development of prestressed textile and cablenet pavilions in the 1960's is due, to a considerable extent, to Otto's pioneering efforts.

If, as Sigfried Giedion has asserted, construction is the subconscious of modern architecture, then Frei Otto's role has been to enlarge and enrich its resources by the addition of an entirely new vocabulary of structural forms. His contribution is comparable to that of the other great 20th century shell builders and structural innovators, notably Candela, Torroja, Nervi and Fuller.

Otto's architecture is a curious combination of Rationalism and Romanticism; it is, in the finest sense, an organic architecture that seeks to realize minimal-energy structures with shapes that correspond to the fundamental spatial laws of the universe. He belongs to the Rationalist strand of modern architecture in which architectural expression is achieved through the unhindered revelation of structure. Frei Otto's emphasis on structural clarity, pure compression or tension stressed shapes, minimal surface and material constructions all suggest a strong Rationalist bias and an extreme commitment to structural determinism of architectural form.

Frei Otto's obvious Rationalism is allied to a thoroughly German kind of Romanticism, as shown in his reliance on such automatic processes as hanging chains, minimal soap films, and stretched fabrics and membranes to establish structural form, and in his consuming interest in biological structures. His emphasis on structural process as a primary design tool is innately Romantic because it represents a rejection of culturally determined styles in architecture and a return to Nature.

The highly curved shapes of Otto's pavilions are in striking harmony with landscape and biological forms: the artificial terrain of the large cablenet roofs counterpoint adjacent natural earth contours, and the Institute of Light Surface Structures at Vaihingen and the grid shell at Mannheim display disconcerting reptilian characteristics.

Frei Otto's innovations have been of outstanding importance for the advancement of tensile architecture because he has combined research into the best forms for prestressed surface structures with the creation of the technical means to construct them. Traditional urban tents had pre-determined simple shapes, and 20th century engineers tended to follow this practice by adopting mathematically defined shapes for their structures. At a time when the analysis of cable structures was relatively undeveloped, Frei Otto was able to explore a host of complex indeterminate shapes and establish optimal geometries for his structures by using a range of model testing techniques. From the outset Frei Otto sought to discover the full range of anti-classically curved surfaces, the effect of various methods of supporting them, and the influence of various edge arrangements on the final shape.

Frei Otto: Institute of Light Surface Structures, Vaihingen, Germany, 1968

The Snow and Rocks Restaurant pavilions at the *Swiss National Exhibition* at Lausanne in 1964 were Otto's first cablenets. Previously, all his roofs were made of cotton canvas with modest spans of from 20 to 30m. The Lausanne pavilions were transitional membrane-cablenet structures. The German Pavilion at *Expo '67* was Otto's first truly large scale cablenet roof. With the completion of this pavilion, prestressed cablenet structures came of age, and, for the first time, the constructional means used matched the structural demands of large scale prestressed structures having a freely sculptured surface topography. A new identity of form, structure and construction was now feasible. The roofs of the main stadium and arenas of the 1972 Olympic Games at Munich added little to the Montreal achievement beyond the development of purely mathematical computer-based procedures for determining cablenet patterns.

The small early *Bundesgartenschau* textile pavilions are amongst Frei Otto's most lyrical and successful works—the riverside shelter and dance pavilions at Cologne, 1957, and the small undulating star pavilions at Hamburg, 1963, were outstanding for their integration of aesthetics and construction. The close association of Frei Otto and Peter Stromeyer, a leading tent manufacturer from Konstanz, undoubtedly contributed to the excellence of these early pavilions. The pre-1963 textile pavilions usually consisted of standard membrane elements arranged symmetrically in additive compositions. It was not until the mid-1960's, and his collaboration with the Stuttgart architect Rolf Gutbrod, that Otto began to explore picturesque asymmetrical surfaces divided unevenly with interior low or high points. The Montreal Pavilion is the outstanding example of such a freely formed roofscape with its evocation of earthforms. The simply suspended auditoria roofs of the Hotel and Conference Centre at Mecca, 1974, are later fruits of Otto's collaboration with Gutbrod.

Frei Otto exploited the inherent flexibility of textile structures by devising the convertible roof; its variable geometry allows the roof membrane to be retracted when not required. A great many such roofs have been constructed in Germany, France and elsewhere, but none is so captivating as the roof for the Open-Air Theatre at Bad Hersfeld, 1968.

Since 1970 Frei Otto has concentrated his attention on the analysis of biological material. Most of his genuine innovations were made prior to 1964, and his work subsequently has involved an elaboration and detailed development of these early proposals. Frei Otto's researches in the area of structure are remarkable for their diversity and inclusiveness. Today, he is no longer so active as a designer, and his influential role in German architecture is increasingly one of stimulating and guiding advanced architectural theory.

—Philip Drew

OUD, J(acobus) J(ohannes) P(ieter).

Dutch. Born in Purmerend, 9 February 1890. Educated at the Quellinus Arts and Crafts School, Amsterdam; Rijksnormal School, Amsterdam; Technical University, Delft. Worked in the offices of Cuypers and Stuyt, Amsterdam, and of Theodor Fischer, Munich. In private practice, Purmerend, 1913–14; worked with W. M. Dudok in his studio, Leiden, 1915–16; in private practice, Leiden, 1916–18; City Architect, Rotterdam, 1918–33; in private practice, Rotterdam, 1933–54, and in Wassenaar, near The Hague, 1954 until his death, 1963. Founder Member, with Theo van Doesburg and others, De Stijl group, Leiden, 1916–20; Founder, with Jan Wils and van Doesburg, De Sphinx Art Club, Leiden, 1917, and, with van Doesburg, *De Stijl* magazine, Leiden, 1917. Exhibitions: *Modern Architects,* Museum of Modern Art, New York, 1932; *J. J. P. Oud,* Rotterdam, 1951; *J. J. P. Oud: Bauten 1906–63,* Die Neue Sammlung, Munich, 1965, and Akademie der Künste, Berlin, 1966. Honorary doctorate: Technical University, Delft, 1945. *Died* (in Wassenaar) *5 April 1963.*

Works:

1906 House, Purmerend, Netherlands
1911 Housing, for the Vooruit Company, Purmerend, Netherlands
1912 Cinema, Purmerend, Netherlands
     Country house, Aalsmeer, Netherlands
1915 Country house, Blaricum, Netherlands
     Public Baths, Purmerend, Netherlands (project)
     Military Convalescent Home, Den Helder, Netherlands (project)
1916 Leidendorp Housing Estate, Leiden (with W. M. Dudok)
     House, Broek, Waterland, Netherlands
     Housing, Velp, Netherlands (project)
1917 De Vonk Boarding School, Nordwijkerhout, Netherlands
     Allegonda House, Katwijk, Netherlands

(with M. Kamerlingh Onnes; enlarged, 1927)
     School of Art and Trade, Den Helder, Netherlands (project)
     Terraced beach houses, Scheveningen, Netherlands (project)
1918 Terraced Housing (project)
     Reinforced Concrete Semi-Detached Housing (project)
1919 Spangen Housing Estate, Rotterdam (destroyed in World War II)
     Distillery/Shop, Purmerend, Netherlands (project)
     Factory/Offices, Purmerend, Netherlands (project)
1920 Tusschendijken Housing Estate, Rotterdam (damaged, 1943; reconstructed, 1950)
1922 Oud Mathenesse (semi-permanent) Housing Estate, Rotterdam
     House, Grunewald, Berlin (project)
1923 Temporary Administration Building, Oud Mathenesse Quarter, Rotterdam
1924 Workers' housing blocks (2), Hook of Holland
1925 De Unie Cafe, Rotterdam (destroyed, 1940)
     Kiefhoek Workers' Village, Rotterdam
1926 Stianssi Hotel, Brno, Czechoslovakia (project)
     New Stock Exchange Building, Rotterdam (project)
1927 Basic Terraced Housing, Weissenhofsiedlung, Stuttgart
     Allegonda House extensions and remodelling, Katwijk, Netherlands
     People's University, Rotterdam (project)
1928 Church, Kiefhoek Workers' Village, Rotterdam
     3-family house, Brno, Czechoslovakia (project)
1931 Blijdorp Workers' Housing Quarter, Rotterdam (project)
1934 Apartment Types (preliminary projects)
     Dinaux House, Rotterdam (project)
1935 House/Studio, Hillegersberg, Netherlands (project)
1936 Pfeffer Country House, Blaricum, Netherlands (project)
1938/
  42 Shell Company Corporate Headquarters, The Hague
1942/
  43 Plan for the centre of Rotterdam (project)
1943 Central Savings Bank, Rotterdam
1947 Workers' Terraced Housing Types (project)
1948 Dutch Steelworks Headquarters, Ijmuiden, Netherlands (project)
     Dutch Soldiers' Monument, Grebbeberg Cemetery, Rhenen, Netherlands
1949 War Memorial, Dam Square, Amsterdam (with the sculptors John and Han Radecker)
1950 Esveha Company Offices, Rotterdam
     Semi-detached house, Bloemendaal, Netherlands (project)
     Plan for the San Lorenzo Complex, Rotterdam (project)
1951 Religious Centre, The Hague (project)
     Workers' terraced housing, Arnhem, Netherlands (with N.P.A.M. van Hassel)
     Water/Bell Tower, Emmeloord, Netherlands (project)
1952 South Holland Local Government Headquarters, The Hague
1952/
  60 Bio Children's Convalescent Home, near Arnhem, Netherlands
     School, The Hague
1954/
  56 Utrecht Life Insurance Company Building, Rotterdam
1956/
  63 Congress Hall Complex, The Hague
1958 De Hoge Veluwe Park-Keeper's House (project)

1960 House, Voorburg, Netherlands (project)
1962 Town Hall, Almelo, Netherlands (project)

Publications:

By OUD: books—*Het Hofplein-plan van Dr. Berlage,* Rotterdam 1922; *Hollandische Architektur,* Munich 1926; *Nieuwe Bouwkunst in Holland en Europa,* 's Graveland, Netherlands 1935; *Il Palazzo B.I.M. Shell,* The Hague 1951; *Zijn er nog architecten?,* The Hague 1959; *Mondriaan,* with L. J. F. Wijsenbeek, Zeist, Netherlands 1962; *Architecturalia voor bouwheren en architecten,* 's Gravenhage, Netherlands 1963; *Mein Weg in De Stijl,* Rotterdam 1962; articles—numerous in *De Stijl* (Leiden), *De 8 en Opbouw* (Amsterdam), *i 10* (Amsterdam), and *De Groene Amsterdammer;* "Landhauser von Hermann Muthesius" in *Bouwkundig Weekblad* (The Hague), November 1913; "Over Cubisme, Futurisme, Moderne Bouwkunst" in *Bouwkundig Weekblad* (The Hague), September 1916; "Glas in lood van Theo van Doesburg" in *Bouwkundig Weekblad* (The Hague), August 1918; "Wohin fuhrt das neue Bauen: Kunst und Standard" in *Neue Zürcher Zeitung* (Zurich), September 1927; "Das flache Dachin Holland" in *Das Neue Frankfurt,* October/December 1927; "Architecture and the Future" in *The Studio* (London), December 1928; "The European Movement Towards a New Architecture" in *The Studio* (London), April 1933; "Mr. Oud Replies" in *Architectural Record* (New York), March 1947; "United Nations Headquarters" in *RIBA Journal* (London), October 1948; "Clarity in Town Planning" in *Housing and Town and Country Planning* (London), April 1949; etc.

On OUD: books—*J. J. P. Oud* by Henry-Russell Hitchcock, Paris 1931; *Modern Architects,* exhibition catalogue, by Alfred Barr, Henry-Russell Hitchcock, and Lewis Mumford, New York 1932; *J. J. P. Oud,* exhibition catalogue, by W. Jos. de Gruyter, Rotterdam 1951; *J. J. P. Oud* by Giuliana Veronesi, Milan 1953; *J. J. P. Oud* by K. Wiekart, Amsterdam 1965; *J. J. P. Oud: Bauten 1906–63,* exhibition catalogue, by Wend Fischer, Munich 1965; articles—special issue of *Sikentiku* (Tokyo), 1924; "Entretiens sur l'Architecture Vivante: l'Urbanisme en Hollande" by Jean Badovici in *Architecture Vivante* (Paris), Summer 1925; "L'Evolution de l'Architecture Moderne en Hollande" by Theo van Doesburg in *Architecture Vivante* (Paris), Autumn 1925; "The Architectural Work of J. J. P. Oud" by Henry-Russell Hitchcock in *The Arts* (New York), February 1928; "J. J. P. Oud" by H. P. L. Wiessing in *Building* (London), July 1938; "Mr. Oud Embroiders a Theme" in *Architectural Record* (New York), December 1946; "Building at The Hague" in *Architectural Review* (London), April 1948; special issue of *Forum* (Amsterdam), no. 5/6, 1951; "Oud at 70" in *Bouwkundig Weekblad* (The Hague), no. 23, 1960; "J. J. P. Oud" by Giuliana Veronesi in *Zodiac* (Milan), no. 12, 1963; "Notes on Oud" by Sergio Polano in *Lotus* (Venice), September 1977.

*

Of all the leaders of the Modern Movement it is the Dutchman J.J.P.Oud with his early method based on the mass-production and standardization of inexpensive working-class housing that has meant most to many of today's leading architects. A founder member of the De Stijl group, Oud developed a style that is firmly that of the interrelationship of horizontal and vertical planes first understood by the Cubist painters and culminating in the severely geometric designs of the Neoplastic art of fellow De Stijl artist Piet Mondrian. The model for the proposed Purmerend factory, made in 1919, is a deliberate attempt to reproduce this severity with an obvious reliance on the simple relationships involving a series of interlocking forms and the inevitable cubic spaces left in between.

The influence of Frank Lloyd Wright is also crucial, arising partly from the exhibition of 1910 and partly from the fact that the spread of architectural magazines had resulted in Wright's ideas being both more widely known and certainly more accepted in Europe than in his native America.

This sympathetic amalgam of Wright and analytical Cubism led Oud to an essentially abstract concept of architecture and an intense distrust of the previous concern with hand-craft detailing and fussy ornamentation. This he saw as mere sentiment and even worse—"expressionistic;" he believed that materials, construction systems, and methods of production must be of the present and well geared to the new machine age—fitted in fact to a life dependent on the machine. The standardization of the method of mass-production not only produced cheaper materials with which to build but also resulted in a uniformity that would inevitably lead to a social uniformity if used intelligently. Straight lines and clearcut forms were what was needed.

In 1917 Oud designed a row of seaside houses intended for an esplanade above the beach at Scheveningen, which are little more than a series of simple cubic masses, and it can be argued that in this unexecuted project of models and drawings he is more concerned with the surface facade than with controlled volume and that the link with Mondrian is clear.

The first built Rotterdam housing-estates at Spangen (1918–19) and Tusschendijken (1920), both of which were destroyed in the Second World War, were among the earliest schemes for low-cost working-class housing and austerely built of brick. The later estates at Hook of Holland and Kiefhoek, also in Rotterdam, had a streamlined smoothness and sophisticated line that reflected an interest in something new. Oud's aim was to produce inexpensive building of a quality that would hint at real architecture.

The smallest cheapest house could be mass-produced with enough variety in its design to provide a good varied way of living for the workers who lived there. The style would be neutral and suggest a common anonymity, and nowhere is this ideal better illustrated than in Oud's contribution to the Weissenhofsiedlung at Stuttgart in 1927. Here he is seen at his inventive best amongst architects from five different countries who offered their solutions to the growing housing problem and whose work had a remarkable consistency which led inevitably to what we now see as the International Style. Oud's terraced row was constructed of poured concrete—on-the-spot pre-fabrication—with typically vigorous projections and recessions and with the now almost obligatory flat roof. A well thought out arrangement of screens separated the houses that were stepped to conform to the slope of the ground. The interiors catered for accepted aspects of working-class life—"those without servants can well eat in the kitchen"—and the back-yards offered ample opportunity for the necessary social contact. Modest in scale and in cost, they seemed the ideal solution.

In the early 1930's, however, Oud began to have doubts. He feared the danger of monotony and a sense of possible boredom and felt that his method limited him to little more than basic utilitarian problems. What he now envisaged was a happier balance between a strict objectivity of shape and an underlying gaiety which he hoped might bring an added richness through an increased variety of forms. He argued that the early fight for Modernism was over and that the battle had been won. A new evaluation was needed.

Oud's doubts have become our doubts and an admiration for the early work which is undoubtedly superior to anything he achieved later leaves us thinking the same way. A new evaluation is needed and perhaps the revived interest in J.J.P.Oud, especially by the new re-thinking Post-Modernists, will help to provide the answer.

—John Furse

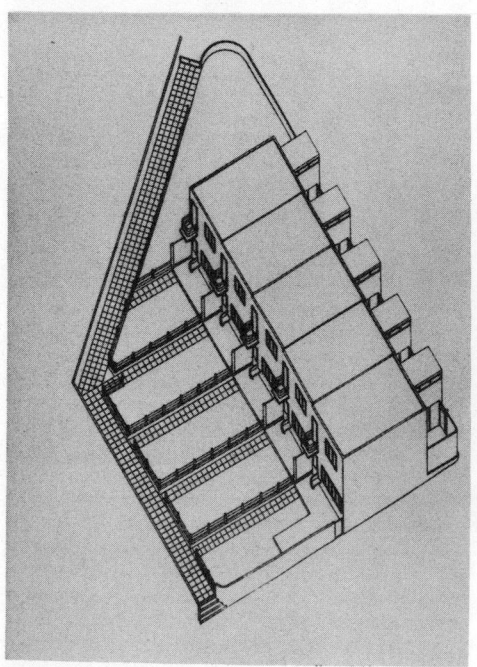

J. J. P. Oud: Basic Terraced Housing, Weissenhofsiedlung, Stuttgart, 1927

OWINGS, Nathaniel (Alexander).

American. Born in Indianapolis, Indiana, 5 February 1903. Educated at the University of Illinois, Urbana, 1921–22; Cornell University, Ithaca, New York, 1927. Married Emily Otis in 1931 (divorced, 1953); children: Emily, Jennifer, Natalie, and Nathaniel Jr.; married Margaret Wentworth in 1954. Co-Founding Partner, with Louis Skidmore, *q.v.,* Skidmore and Owings, Chicago, 1936–39, and, with John Merrill, *q.v.,* Skidmore, Owings and Merrill, Chicago, New York, San Francisco, Portland, Oregon, Washington, D.C., etc., from 1939: now retired. Chairman, Chicago Plan Commission, 1948–51; Vice-Chairman, California Highway Scenic Roads Commission, 1964–67; Chairman, Temporary Commission on the Design of Pennsylvania Avenue, Washington, D.C., 1964–73, and since 1973 Member of the Permanent Commission; Member, 1966–70, and Chairman, 1970–72, United States Secretary of the Interior's Advisory Board on the National Parks, Historic Sites, Building and Monuments, Washington, D.C.; Chairman, Urban Design Concept Team for the United States Interstate Highway System, 1967–70. Trustee, American Academy in Rome. Exhibition: *Skidmore, Owings and Merrill,* Museum of Modern Art, New York, 1950. Recipient: Conservation Service Award, United States Department of the Interior, 1968. LL.D.: Ball State University, Muncie, Indiana, 1970; L.H.D.: Indiana University, Bloomington, 1973; Butler University, Indianapolis, 1976. Fellow, American Institute of Architects. Address: Big Sur, California 93920, U.S.A.

Publications:

By OWINGS: books—*The American Aesthetic,* New York 1969; *The Spaces in Between: An Architect's Journey,* Boston 1973; articles—"New Materials and Building Methods for the Chicago Exposition" in *Architectural Record* (New York), April 1932; "Economics of Department Store Planning" in *Architectural Record* (New York), February 1947; "What's New in Planning an Office Building?" in *Building* (London), December 1947; "Do We or Do We Not Orient the Bedroom?" in *Royal Architectural Institute of Canada Journal* (Toronto), September 1948; "Two Looks at Preservation" in *AIA Journal* (Washington, D.C.), February 1962.

See SKIDMORE, OWINGS AND MERRILL

P

PANI, Mario

Mexican. Born in Mexico City, 29 March 1911. Educated at elementary schools in Belgium and Italy; Lycée Janson de Sailly-Bachellor, Paris; Ecole Nationale Supérieure des Beaux-Arts, Paris, 1928–34, Dip.Arch. 1934; also awarded degree by the University of Mexico, Mexico City, 1934. Married Margarita Linaae in 1933; children: Margara, Mario Jr., Ana, Eugenia, Enrique, Federico, and Arturo. In private architectural practice, Mexico City, since 1934. Chairman of the Board, Deplan S.A., international consultants, Mexico City, 1974–78. Professor of Architecture, University of Mexico, 1940–48. Founder and President, *Arquitectura Mexico* magazine, Mexico City, 1938–78. President of the Executive Board, Federal Public School Construction Program, Mexico City, 1944–48; Founder and Member of the Board, Colegio de Arquitectos de Mexico, 1946; Member of the Board, Committee for the Construction of Mexico City University, 1948–52; President, Regional Planning Commission of Acapulco, Mexico, 1951–53; Patron, San Carlos Museum of Art, 1954–78; Director, National Institute of Housing, Mexico City, 1955–64. Recipient: First Prize, Ciudad Victoria Stadium Competition, 1938; Bronze Medal, Marti Monument Competition, 1938; First Prize, House of Spain Competition, 1940; Gold Medal, VI Pan-American Congress, Lima, Peru, 1947; Gold Medal, VII Pan-American Congress, Havana, Cuba, 1950. Honorary Fellow, Peruvian Institute of Urbanism, 1942, and American Institute of Architects, 1964. Address: (office) Paseo de la Reforma 369-1 Mezzanine, Mexico 5, D.F., Mexico.

Works:

1936   Reforma Hotel, Mexico City
1938   Tomas Bay Residence, Mexico City
1940   Hamburgo 293, 295, and 297, Mexico City
1941   Explanada, Mexico City
1942   Perote Tuberculosis Hospital, Veracruz
        Medical Center Master Plan, Mexico City (with José Villagrán García)
        Alpes 1105, Mexico City
1943   Balsas 36, Mexico City
        Rincon del Bosque, Mexico City
        General Hospital, Saltillo, Mexico
        Regional Hospital, Tulancingo, Mexico
1944   Alameda Hotel, Morelia, Mexico
        Avenida Juarez 88, Mexico City
1945   Plaza Hotel, Mexico City
        National School of Teachers, Mexico City
        Reforma 334, Mexico City
1946   National Conservatory of Music, Mexico City
1947   5 elementary schools, Mexico City
        Reforma-La Fragua, Mexico City (with Jesus García Collantes)
1948   V. Carranza 70, Mexico City (with H. Galguera)
1949   Aleman 1080 Apartments, Mexico City (with Salvador Ortega)
1950   Secretariat of Water Resources Building, Paseo de la Reforma, Mexico City (with Enrique del Moral)

Costera 505, Acapulco (with Enrique del Moral)
1951   Regional plan for Yucatan, Mexico (with José Luis Cuevas and D. Garcia)
        Regional plan for Merida, Mexico (with José Luis Cuevas and D. Garcia)
        Dumas 130, Mexico City (with Enrique del Moral)
1952   Central Administration Building, University City, Mexico City (with Enrique del Moral and Salvador Ortega)
        Juarez 950 Apartments, Mexico City (with Salvador Ortega)
        Regional plan for Acapulco (with José Luis Cuevas)
        Master plan for Guaymas, Sinaloa, Mexico (with José Luis Cuevas and D. Garcia)
        Master plan for Culiacan, Sinaloa, Mexico (with José Luis Cuevas and D. Garcia)
        Master plan for Mazatlan, Sinaloa, Mexico (with José Luis Cuevas and D. Garcia)
        Mazaryk 170, Mexico City (with Enrique del Moral)
        Lima House, Cuernavaca, Mexico
        Master plan for University City, Mexico City (with Enrique del Moral)
1953   L. R. Montes House, Acapulco (with Enrique del Moral)
        Pozo del Rey, Acapulco (with Enrique del Moral)
1954   Satellite City, Mexico City (with José Luis Cuevas and D. Garcia)
1955   Ixtlan, Mexico City
        Ixtlan-Lomas Altas, Mexico City
        Acapulco Airport (with Enrique del Moral)
1956   Reforma 369 Condominium, Mexico City (with Salvador Ortega)
        Santa Fe (2500 houses and apartments), Mexico City (with Luis Ramos)
1957   Los Cocos Condominium, Acapulco (with Salvador Ortega)
1958   Master plan for Matamoros, Mexico (with José Luis Cuevas and D. Garcia)
        Tlanepantla 2000 Houses and Apartments, Mexico City (with Luis Ramos)
        Reforma 368 Condominium, Mexico City (with Salvador Ortega)
        Stadium, Ciudad Victoria, Mexico
1959   Banco Popular, Monterrey (with Salvador Ortega)
1960   Commercial Center, Satellite City, Mexico City (with Jesus García Collantes)
1963   Immigration and Customs Building, Matamoros, Mexico (with H. Galguera)
        Commercial Center, Cuernavaca, Mexico (with H. Gualguera)
        Master plan for Juarez, Mexico
        Master plan for Piedras Negras, Tamaulipas, Mexico
1964   Immigration and Customs Building, Nogales, Mexico (with H. Gualguera)
        Nonoalco Tower, Mexico City (with Luis Ramos)
        Commercial Center, Juarez, Mexico (with E. Molinar)

Exposition Center, Juarez, Mexico (with E. Molinar)
        Commercial Center, Matamoros, Mexico (with H. Gualguera)
        Tlatelolco City (12000 apartments), Mexico City (with Luis Ramos)
        John F. Kennedy 5070 Apartments, Mexico City (with Luis Ramos)
        General studies for Mexican border cities, Baja California
        Master plan for Nogales, Mexico
1965   5 tourism developments, Baja California
        Vallejo 5600 Apartments, Mexico City (with H. Galguera)
        Platcros 5510 Apartments, Mexico City (with Luis Ramos)
1970   Condesa del Mar Hotel, Acapulco
1974   Master plan for the reconstruction of Managua City, Nicaragua

Publications:

By PANI: books—*Eupalinos o el Arquitecto,* translation of the work by Paul Valéry, Mexico City 1938; *Los Multifamiliares de Pensiones,* Mexico City 1953; articles—"Presentation of the First Issue of Arquitectura" in *Arquitectura Mexico* (Mexico City), no. 1, 1938; "El Arquitecto Mario Pani escribe" in *Manana* (Mexico City), 3 December 1948; "The Housing Problem in Mexico City" in *Arquitectura Mexico* (Mexico City), no. 27, 1949; "Mario Pani lanza un reto a la critica" in *Mexico de Hoy* (Mexico City), 7 May 1949; "The Master Plan of the University City" in *Arquitectura Mexico* (Mexico City), no. 39, 1952; "Fundamental Ideas in the Planification of Acapulco" in *Arquitectura Mexico* (Mexico City), no. 46, 1954; "First Housing Project for the Seguro Social Institute" in *Arquitectura Mexico* (Mexico City), no. 53, 1956; "Mexico: One Problem, One Solution" in *Arquitectura Mexico* (Mexico City), no. 60, 1957; "La Ciudad Satellite" in *Nivel* (Mexico City), May 1959; "Las Ciudades y sus planos reguladores" in *Novedades* (Mexico City), 23 August 1959; "Construction Control to Limit the Population Density in a Master Plan" in *Arquitectura Mexico* (Mexico City), no. 71, 1960; "Urban Renewal of Mexico City" in *Arquitectura Mexico* (Mexico City), no. 72, 1960; "La Ciudad Universitaria obra de equipo" in *Revista de America* (Mexico City), 20 January 1960; "Urban Renewal" in *Arquitectura Mexico* (Mexico City), no. 81, 1963; "25 Years Anniversary" in *Arquitectura Mexico* (Mexico City), no. 83, 1963; "Comentarios" in *Arquitectura Mexico* (Mexico City), no. 84, 1969; "Tlatelolco" and "The Economic Structure and Density of Tlatelolco City" in *Arquitectura Mexico* (Mexico City), no. 94/95, 1966; "Presentation" in *Arquitectura Mexico* (Mexico City), no. 96/97, 1967; "La Construccion de Tlatelolco" in *Siempre* (Mexico City), no. 877, 1970; "Eupalinos, the Architect" in *Arquitectura Mexico* (Mexico City), no. 106, 1972; "Urban Problems: The Street" in *Arquitectura Mexico* (Mexico City), no. 107, 1972; "Urban Problems" in *Arquitectura Mexico* (Mexico City), no. 109, 1974; "Richard J. Neutra" in *Arquitectura Mexico* (Mexico City), no. 110,

Mario Pani: National School of Teachers, Mexico City, 1945

1974; "6th Centennial of Filippo Brunelleschi" in *Arquitectura Mexico* (Mexico City), no. 115, 1977.

On PANI: books—*Mexico's Modern Architecture* by I. E. Myers, New York 1952; *Builders in the Sun: Five Mexican Architects* by Clive Bamford Smith, New York 1967; articles—"Mario Pani" in *Life* (New York), 17 March 1947; "Modern Mexico" by Ann Binkley Horn in *Architectural Record* (New York), July 1947; "Arte Moderne Mexicano" in *Arquitectura* (Havana), August/September 1948; "La Arquitectura Mexicana" in *Revista Nacional de Arquitectura* (Madrid), July 1949; "Arquitectura Actual" in *Arquitectura* (Lisbon), May 1950; "Urban Progress in Latin America" by Anatole A. Solow in *The American City* (New York), November 1950; "The Overall Plan of Ciudad Universitaria" in *Arts and Architecture* (Los Angeles), August 1952; "Arquitectura Abstracta o Realista" in *Manana* (Mexico City), July 1953; "El Arquitecto Mario Pani" in *Arquitectura* (Havana), September 1953; "La Nueva Arquitectura Mexicana" in *Estudios Americanos* (Seville), November 1953; "Mexiko Heute" in *Bauwelt* (Berlin), December 1953; "La Propieta orizontale arriva in Messico" in *L'Architettura* (Rome), January 1957; "Acapulco Airport, Mexico" in *Architectural Design* (London), February 1957; "Satellite City" in *Dimension* (Ann Arbor, Michigan), no. 1, 1958; "Presidente Juarez Center" in *Architect and Building News* (London), January 1958; "The Towers of Satellite City" in *Arts and Architecture* (Los Angeles), May 1958; "Superblock in Mexico" in *Ar-*

chitectural Forum (New York), May 1959; "Mario Pani" in *Construccion Moderna* (Mexico City), September 1959; "Tlatelolco" in *L'Architecture d'Aujourd'hui* (Paris), September 1960; "El Club de Yates de Acapulco y Mario Pani" in *Mundo Hispanico* (Madrid), July 1968; etc.

Educated in France, I obtained a degree in architecture at the Ecole des Beaux-Arts in Paris in 1934, and returned to my country with the intention to adapt my European learning to the social and cultural profiles of Mexico.

It has been my continuous task to apply in Mexico the international principles of urbanism and architecture; for this reason I have consistently promoted projects in which those principles could be applied without affecting the Mexican character and idiosyncracies.

The following projects are the ones in which I achieved this goal, introducing in Mexico new concepts in urbanism and architecture:

1936: The first hotel to meet international standards
1947: Buildings high enough to allow a population density appropriate to Mexico City's subsoil characteristics
1948: The first multi-habitational building with 1000 apartments
1950: The first super block (University City)
1956: The first co-ownership building

1964: The first co-ownership city (Tlatelolco housing complex in Mexico City for 80,000 inhabitants)

The visual expression in vogue at the beginning of my studies in architecture was Art Deco of which there are excellent examples in Mexico; however, there is no trace of it in my work. My "architectural language" is that of the Bauhaus adapted to local climates and materials.

In Mexico, after Art Deco the Muralistic Movement came into being with formal expression in colonial as well as in contemporary buildings.

My participation in that movement known in Mexico as "plastic integration" was with Jose Clemente Orozco, one of the greatest painters of all times. Together we experimented with what should rather be called "Interaction" than "Integration" between architecture and the visual arts: The National School of Teachers.

—Mario Pani

Mario Pani's Tlatelolco housing development, in the heart of Mexico City, typifies his concern with an affinity between the old and the new. This gigantic urban renewal project, covering 198 acres, was created to replace a squalid ghetto of 70,000 inhabitants. While excavating for this city within a city, the builders discovered many treasures from antiquity—among them a colonial chapel, Aztec pyramids, and a 16th century cross—all of which were preserved in the Plaza of the Three Cultures.

Tlatelolco's 12,000 apartments are contained in 101 buildings ranging in height from four to twenty-two stories. Dominating the skyline is the tower of the administration and office building topped by a campanile. The project has three medical and dental clinics, twelve creches, sports and social clubs, a cinema, multiple shopping areas, parking lots, and a total of thirteen schools. The green spaces, which make up fifty percent of the total area, alleviate the harshness of the surrounding skyscrapers of concrete and steel.

Educated in Europe, Pani, on the return to his native Mexico, was appalled by the living conditions of the masses; subsequently, he became not only an architect but also a city planner. Because of his dedication and expertise, the Mexican Government has retained him to develop master plans for almost every city and region in Mexico—Acapulco, Mexico City, Yucatan, Guaymas, and even Baja California. He designed Mexico's first planned community—a satellite city for the capital. The color, forms, and scale of this city produce visual impact of impressive magnitude.

In 1947, Pani and Enrique del Moral were chosen to prepare the master plan for Mexico's University City. While directing this majestic project, they also found time to design the campus, the gardens, the sports stadium, and the Central Administration Building. This building, at the entrance to the University, exemplifies the beauty in Pani's work: the contrast of rough planes against smooth, the constant interplay of light and shadow, and the unique juxtaposition of muted serenity and blazing color. A three dimensional mural by David Alfaro Siqueiros adorns one wall, while adjacent to it, around the corner, is a wall of golden translucent onyx. The administrative offices are located in a twelve-story tower connected to a three-story structure containing offices for student affairs. The tower, which rests on columns, is also adorned with a mural, and has a facade of glazed tiles, glass bricks, concrete, and carrera glass.

Pani's first commission, in 1936, was the design of Mexico City's first hotel—the Reforma. The success of this luxury hotel led to other hotel commissions: the Plaza and the Alameda in Mexico City, and the Condesa del Mar in Acapulco. Also, in Acapulco, he designed the International Airport with Enrique del Moral, the Yacht Club, and the Los Cocos Condominium.

In the late 1930's, he furthered his practice by entering every competition in which architects were invited to submit plans. His original, contemporary designs not only won awards but also attracted much attention. As a result, he was chosen to design Mexico City's first condominium of thirteen stories with a penthouse and, one of the first modern skyscrapers, the twenty-two story Secretariat of Hydraulic Resources Building, both on the Paseo de la Reforma.

In 1956, with Architect Luis Ramos, he designed The Social Services and Housing Unit of Santa Fe in Mexico City. This complete community for 14,000 inhabitants includes schools, creches, sports fields, social clubs, a medical clinic, a theatre, a shopping center, and public gardens.

"Mankind must build, in the next thirty-five years, more homes than it has built in the past five thousand years," says Pani, "to keep up with the growing population." Pani is one of the architects who, in combining beauty with efficiency, has shown the way.

—Peggy Cochrane

PARKIN, John B(urnett).

Canadian. Born in Toronto, Ontario in 1911. Educated at the University of Toronto, Dip.Arch. 1935. Married; son: John Burnett Jr. Worked for National Coal Board, London, and in office of architects Howard and Souster, London, 1935–37; in private practice, as John Burnett Parkin, Toronto, 1937–47; Partner, with his brother Edmund T. Parkin and with John C. Parkin (no relation), *q.v.*, John B. Parkin Associates, 1947–68, subsequently Parkin Architects Engineers and Planners, 1968–70; Partner, with Roy Marshall, Parkin Architects Engineers and Planners, Los Angeles, 1970 until his death, 1975. *Died* (in Los Angeles) *in August 1975.*

Works:

1946 Sunnylea School, Glenroy Avenue, Etobicoke, Ontario
1948 Christadelphian Church, Church Street, Toronto
1950 Central Collegiate Institute, Simcoe Street South, Oshawa, Ontario
   Hamden Memorial Hospital, Church Street, Weston, Ontario
1952 George Harvey Vocational School, Keele Street, York Township, Ontario
   Northwestern General Hospital, Keele Street, York Township, Ontario
1953 Yardley of London Plant and Offices, Curity Avenue, East York, Ontario
   Unity Church of Truth, Eglinton Avenue West, Toronto
1954 Robert Simpson Company Service Building, Lawrence Avenue West, North York, Ontario
   Ontario Association of Architects Headquarters, Park Road, Toronto
1955 Kenmore Industrial Development Plant, Warehouse and Power Plant, Etobicoke, Ontario
   Imperial Oil Office and Research Building, Sarnia, Ontario
   Ortho Pharmaceutical Office Building and Plant, North York, Ontario
1955/
57 Don Mills Shopping Centre, North York, Ontario
1956 Salvation Army National Headquarters and Temple Corps Building, Albert Street, Toronto
1958 Barber-Greene Plant and Offices, Barber-Greene Road, North York, Ontario
   Greater Niagara General Hospital, Niagara Falls, Ontario
   W. H. Collins Memorial Centre, Elliot Lake, Jamestown, Ontario
1959 Don Mills Collegiate Institute and Junior High School, The Donway East, North York, Ontario
   George Kennedy Public School, Weber Drive, Georgetown, Ontario
1960 Adams Brands Plant and Offices, Bertrand Avenue, Scarborough, Ontario
   Northern Electric Company Plant and Offices, London, Ontario
   Sun-Life Building, University Avenue, Toronto
   Hilldale Manor Home for the Aged, Oshawa, Ontario
   Primrose Club Building, Saint Clair Avenue West, Toronto
   Holy Blossom Temple additions, Bathurst Street, Toronto
   Imperial Oil Offices, North York, Ontario
1961 Elgin Centre Car Showrooms and Offices, Bay Street, Toronto
   Sidney Smith Building, University of Toronto
   St. Michael's College School additions and staff residences, Bathurst Street, Toronto
   Bawating Collegiate and Vocational School, Second Line East, Sault Sainte Marie, Ontario

   Knox Fellowship Centre and Chapel, Spadina Avenue, Toronto
   Dorothy Cameron Art Gallery, Yonge Street, Toronto
   Holy Rosary Parish Hall, Saint Clair Avenue West, Toronto
1963 Thomas J. Lipton Offices and Food Processing Plant, Bramalea, Ontario
   Sifto Salt Mill and Warehouse, Oxford Street, Goderich, Ontario
   Bell Telephone Company Equipment Building (No. 5 Crossbar Building), Markham, Ontario
   St. Mark's Presbyterian Church, Greenland Road, North York, Ontario
1963/
66 Toronto International Airport: Master Plan, Aeroquay, Control Tower, Administration Building, and Central Utilities Building
1964 Parking Garage, Germain Street, St. John, New Brunswick
   H. J. Heinz Company Factory extension, Leamington, Ontario
   Barber-Ellis Warehouse and Offices, Overlea Boulevard, Leaside, Ontario
   Simpson's Shop, Yorkdale Shopping Centre, North York, Ontario
   Huntington University Residence, Larch Street, Sudbury, Ontario
   Canadian Dental Association Office Building additions, St. George Street, Toronto
1965 McKinnon Industries Ltd. Building, St. Catharines, Ontario
   Bata International Shoe Company Head Office, North York, Ontario
   City Hall, Toronto (with Viljo Revell)
   Oshawa Catholic High School, Stevenson Road North, Oshawa, Ontario
1965/
80 York University, Keele Street, North York, Ontario
1966 International Nickel Research Laboratory and Offices, Sheridan Park, Ontario
   Warner-Lambert Research Institute, Sheridan Park, Ontario
   Residential complex, University of Waterloo, Ontario
   Thorvaldson Building, University of Saskatchewan, Saskatoon
   Clarke Institute of Psychiatry, College Street, Toronto
   Riverside Golf and Country Club, East Riverside, New Brunswick
1966/
75 Brock University, St. Catharines, Ontario
1967 I.B.M. Canada Head Office, North York, Ontario
   Foundation Scottish Properties Office Building, Place du Canada, Montreal
   Theatre, MacKay Pier, *Expo '67,* Montreal
   Canadian National Pavilion, Ile Notre Dame, *Expo '67,* Montreal
1968 Simpson Tower Office Building, Toronto
1969 Union Railway Station, Ottawa
   Toronto-Dominion Centre (consultant: Mies van der Rohe)

Publications:

By PARKIN: articles—"Post-War Planning of Schools" in *Royal Architectural Institute of Canada Journal* (Toronto), September 1942; "Tomorrow's Schools" in *Royal Architectural Institute of Canada Journal* (Toronto), July 1943.

On PARKIN: books—*Toronto International Airport,* Ottawa 1962; *John B. Parkin Associates,* Toronto 1966; articles—"Two Buildings by John B. Parkin Associates" in *Architectural Review* (London), November 1958; "Complete Professional Service for Diverse Industries" in *Architectural Record*

(New York), December 1959; "John B. Parkin: Recent Work" in *Arquitectura* (Madrid), September 1966; "1500 Don Mills Road" by John C. Parkin in *Canadian Architect* (Toronto), May 1978; "Parkin" by John C. Parkin and Thomas Howarth in *Canadian Interiors* (Toronto), May 1978.

Together with his younger partner, John Cresswell Parkin (not related, despite the surname), John B. Parkin was a major figure in the establishment of modern architecture in Canada in the years following World War II. He helped to define architectural practice as a comprehensive corporate service. At the same time, he gained an international reputation for his firm, John B. Parkin Associates, as purveyors of a Canadian version of the austere and disciplined design associated in the U.S.A. with Skidmore, Owings and Merrill and in the U.K. with Yorke, Rosenberg and Mardall. John B. Parkin was himself a highly disciplined person of strong religious (Christadelphian) convictions who applied that rigor to his support of modern architecture in the late 1960's when Canadian architecture wavered uneasily between the familiar and comfortable historical eclecticism of the well established architects, and the evangelical claims of younger protagonists of "modern."

Educated in the late Beaux Arts approach still taught at the University of Toronto in the 1930's, Parkin travelled in Europe after graduation and worked in England for the National Coal Board and Howard and Souster. He returned to Toronto to establish a small practice in 1937. Though his early work shows his personal interest and ability in design, his firm's design eminence became most closely associated with his younger partner, John Cresswell Parkin, who, in the firm's dominant years, carried responsibility for design. Nonetheless, John B. Parkin's interest and strongly expressed convictions about design provided a firm foundation for the work of his partner, as it did for the many talented architects who worked under their direction.

John B. Parkin's first houses, from the one-man practice he established on his return from Europe, were examples of that attenuated historicism that is almost styleless but carries implicit references to either the mediaeval or classical tradition. There is certainly in Parkin's early work an emphasis on clarity, simplicity and consistency that later emerged as the leading characteristic of the firm's design.

John B. Parkin's later role was that of administrative leader rather than designer. He was known as a man of great integrity, direct and plainspoken, but also of great charm, who had the complete respect and trust of both colleagues and clients. He was able to reach important clients and attract and retain associates of outstanding ability to carry out their commissions. He shaped the firm to offer a service that was the corporate, industrial, equivalent of the arts and crafts model exemplified by Philip Webb and pioneered in the 20th century by U.S. practices such as Skidmore, Owings and Merrill. Total design by the unified group was the objective. To this end the firm incorporated specialists in the design of structures, mechanical and electrical systems, interiors and furnishings, landscaping and graphics. Furthermore, particular partners and associates developed specialized interests ranging from hospitals to airports. This objective was further expressed through a decided preference for prestigious and institutional clients who were prepared to allow the architect this complete control over programming, design and construction.

The results are exemplified in the well-known buildings from the 1950's and 60's, the Ontario Association of Architects Headquarters, Ortho Pharmaceutical, Toronto International Airport: Terminal One (the Aeroquay), Ottawa Union Station, Bata Shoes Head Office and the IBM Head Office, all in or near Toronto. Terminal One is an outstanding example. Within John B. Parkin Associates the key figure in its design was Lloyd Laity (later with John Carl Warnecke in San Francisco). The building

united clarity of form and structure—central cubic parking garage in concrete elevated over arrival and departure levels, a ring structure in steel frame leading to departure gates—a masterly resolution of the interweaving movement of cars, buses, planes, passengers, friends and spectators—with somewhat cold and formal interiors that displayed a remarkable wealth of specially commissioned Canadian art. The unanticipated advent of the jumbo-jet necessitated subsequent alteration and adaptation, but as originally conceived and executed within the Parkin airport plan, the building was a triumphant expression of the firm's virtues, themselves the result of John B. Parkin's vision.

—Michael McMordie

PARKIN, John C(resswell).
Canadian. Born in Sheffield, England, of Canadian parents, 22 March 1922. Educated at the University of Manitoba, Winnipeg, 1940–44 (received University of Manitoba Travelling Fellowship; Thesis Prize, 1944), B.Arch. (honours) 1944; Harvard University, Cambridge, Massachusetts, under Walter Gropius, 1944–47, M.Arch. (honours) 1947. Married Margaret Jeanne Warmith in 1948; children: John Jr., Geoffrey and Jennifer. Co-Founding Partner, with John B. Parkin, *q.v.*, and Edmund T. Parkin, and Partner in charge of Design, John B. Parkin Associates, Toronto, 1947–68; Senior and Managing Partner, Parkin Architects Engineers Planners, Toronto, 1968–70. Since 1971, Senior Partner, Parkin Architects Planners, Toronto (restyled as Parkin Partnership Architects Planners, 1976); current partners: Jack B. Mar, Peter H. Warren and Donald L. Wilson. President, Parkin Engineers Ltd., and Parkin-Arpac Ltd.; Director, Transo Corporation Ltd., Eastern Utilities Ltd., and Trans-Canada Freezers Ltd. Lecturer, University of Toronto, 1947–48; Visiting Professor, McGill University, Montreal, 1966–67. President, 1955–58, and Chairman of the Committee of Past Presidents, 1958–60, Canadian Conference of the Arts; Chairman, National Industrial Design Council, 1959–61; Chairman, National Design Council, 1961–70; Governor, National Film Board of Canada, 1964–67; Chairman, Architectural Advisory Board, *Expo '67*, Montreal, 1965–67; Vice-Chairman, 1973, and Chairman, 1978, Board of Governors, Ryerson Polytechnical Institute, Toronto. Consultant, National Capital Commission, Ottawa, since 1962; Member of the International Council, Museum of Modern Art, New York, since 1966; President, Royal Canadian Academy of Arts, since 1970. Recipient: Massey Medal in Architecture, 1950, 1955, 1958, 1964; Premier Canadian Architecture Award, Olympic Art Exhibition, Helsinki, 1952; Oscar Cahen Memorial Award, Art Directors of Toronto, 1960; Centennial Medal, Canada, 1967; Citation, Board of Directors, Canadian Corporation for the 1967 World Exhibition, 1968; Alumni Jubilee Award, University of Manitoba, 1968; Citation, Prime Minister of Canada, 1970; First Prize, National Gallery of Canada Competition, 1976; Queen's Silver Jubilee Medal, 1977. D.Eng.: Nova Scotia Technical College, Halifax, 1977. Fellow, Royal Architectural Institute of Canada, 1960. Fellow, Royal Institute of British Architects, 1954, Royal Society of Arts, London, 1962, and Society of Industrial Artists and Designers, London, 1967. Honorary Member, Japanese Canadian Cultural Centre, Toronto, 1966, Chambre de Commerce Francaise au Canada, 1967, and Association of Canadian Industrial Designers, 1972. C.C. (Companion, Order of Canada), 1972. Address: Parkin Partnership, 147 Front Street West, Toronto, Ontario M5J 1E9, Canada.

Works:

1953 John C. Parkin House, North York, Ontario
1954 Ontario Association of Architects Headquarters, Toronto
1955 Ortho Pharmaceutical Office Building and Plant, North York, Ontario
1960 Imperial Oil Offices, North York, Ontario
1963 Thomas J. Lipton Offices and Food Processing Plant, Bramalea, Ontario
1963/
66 Toronto International Airport: Master Plan, Aeroquay, Control Tower, Administration Building, and Central Utilities Building
1965 Bata International Shoe Company Head Office, North York, Ontario
McKinnon Industries Ltd. Building, St. Catharines, Ontario
1966 International Nickel Research Laboratory and Offices, Sheridan Park, Ontario
Etobicoke General Hospital, Ontario
1967 IBM Canada Head Office, North York, Ontario
1968 Simpson Tower Office Building, Toronto
1969 Union Railway Station, Ottawa
1971 Health Sciences Complex, Memorial University of Newfoundland, St. John's
1972 Safeco Insurance Company of America Offices, Mississauga, Ontario
1973 Eaton's of Canada Executive Offices interiors, Toronto
1976 New National Gallery of Canada, Ottawa
1977 Computer Centre, Bank of Montreal, Scarborough, Ontario

Publications:

By PARKIN: articles—"Relationships: Art and Architecture" in *The Structurist* (Saskatoon), October 1961; "Toronto 1980" in *The Globe and Mail* (Toronto), 4 November 1961; "Canadian Architecture since 1945" in the *Royal Architectural Institute of Canada Journal* (Toronto), January 1962; "Responsibility of the Architect to the Public and the Profession" in *AIA Journal* (Washington, D.C.), January 1964; "Architectural Disorder in Our Cities" in *AIA Journal* (Washington, D.C.), June 1965; two articles in the special issue on Canada of *Progressive Architecture* (New York), September 1972; "1500 Don Mills Road" in *Canadian Architect* (Toronto), May 1978; "Parkin," with Thomas Howarth, in *Canadian Interiors* (Toronto), May 1978.

On PARKIN: book—*John B. Parkin Associates*, Toronto 1966; article—"Canadian Cubes" in *The Architects' Journal* (London), December 1977.

There are certain principles which I believe I have held fast for 30 years. My firms were never highly mobile ones in the sense that a one-man practice could be. We have never apologized for this, for we have always viewed this as a positive virtue necessitating, as it does, our avoidance of the ephemeral. We have never used the arbitrary, what is unreasonable, illogical or irrational. We have sought clarity of plan, clarity of structure, clarity in the use of materials and clarity of form.

The creation of beautiful plans and the creative pleasure attendant to the process has always been fundamental to architectural art. We have sought to place each and everything in its appropriate place.

The expression of our structures has usually been clearly evident in both elevation and plan; the bizarre structural forms which have been fashionable from time to time have never been of our concern.

In the use of materials we have probably been doctrinaire in avoiding any arbitrary change of materials in the same wall plane, for example. We have always attempted to make materials do what is in their true nature. Our forms have been, I trust, a direct expression of plan and structure.

John B. Parkin. Ortho Pharmaceutical Office Building and Plant, North York, Ontario, 1955

Our better buildings, the Ottawa Union Station and the Aeroquay (Terminal 1: Toronto Airport) for example, have always tended to accept the realities of convenience. In both these buildings the automobile was invited inside—surely a sensible notion in our climate. Both these buildings also demonstrate an idea which has always intrigued me, that is, the interaction of the two most important materials of our age—steel and concrete in juxtaposition. The circular ring building of the Aeroquay is steel, and its exterior clad in metal: the central rectangular solid is of concrete and of composite design directly expressed as such. The Union Station follows in the great railway tradition of a conspicuous metal roof poised against symmetric one-storey pavilions, wholly concrete in design. I was once told that the success of Union Station in Ottawa rested on the fact that it "looked like a station."

Architecture should enliven, ennoble and inspire, and not gratify or glorify the banal. The doctrine of innovation for its own sake, founded on creative obsolescence, is a practice we have always resisted. Our budgets and programs are sufficiently spartan and austere, although our forms need never reflect an austerity.

In attempting to set an even course in design policy over these more than 30 years, I have counselled my clients to avoid the momentary and the merely fashionable. No hyperbolic-paraboloids, and thin shells only where necessary: no fortresses in concrete and, I trust, only a rare judgmental error in the overwhelmingly pervasive use of concrete in the 1960's.

If I have a major regret it would be related to a lack of opportunity to work to a greater extent in wood. This was owed, in the main, to the fact that most of our commissions have been of an institutional or commercial nature and in urban settings with inhibiting codes. Otherwise, my partners and I have been privileged to undertake work in almost every building type—the regrettable exception being the high-rise residential apartment building.

We have always tended to agree with the idea that every problem must be solved in an entirely radical way and believe, as others do, that the practice of architecture involves an accumulating sum of experience, the "softwear" of design method as well as the "hardware" of building technique.

—John C. Parkin

John C. Parkin has been completely identified first with the design work of John B. Parkin Associates and subsequently with the work of the firm he established following the end of the original firm in 1970, Parkin Architects Planners (now Parkin Partnership), winners of the 1976 competition for the new National Gallery of Canada.

With a large firm the work of the senior design administrator is inextricably bound up with the work of the colleagues whose work he supervises. One of the great achievements of John C. Parkin has been his ability to attract and collaborate with a succession of outstanding partners and associates, such men as Douglas Rowland, now a partner in the successor firm to John B. Parkin Associates, Neish Owen Rowland and Roy, Toronto. Many others

have passed through a period of apprenticeship with John C. Parkin and his colleagues to later eminence elsewhere.

Parkin is, nonetheless, directly identified with the design of the building that marked the first clear recognition of John B. Parkin Associates by Canadian colleagues, the Ontario Association of Architects Headquarters. The competition scheme had the same clear rectilinear frame and buff brick infill of the final structure, but in the course of development the design progressed from in situ reinforced concrete to the exposed steel frame that became a preferred feature of the Parkin style.

Other early projects of the firm show some variant tendencies that were to be resolved by the mid-1950's. An early butterfly-roofed rural school is one, the Toronto Salvation Army National Headquarters of 1956 is another. The latter, clad in buff brick, supported by round concrete columns, has sun shades extended over (south facing) windows, and perches a smaller flat as a separate block atop the main office building, which rises in turn from the ground level Auditorium block. The result seems close to Gropius's work of the same period, with perhaps a distant acknowledgement of Le Corbusier. The later work, of the 1950's and early 60's, is more comparable to the work carried out under Gordon Bunshaft by Skidmore Owings and Merrill and to that of Mies van der Rohe. Certainly the work of the firm's peak years was more in tune with contemporary American than European architecture. One exception was the Toronto City Hall of 1965, but even there execution of Revell's competition scheme through collaboration between the Finnish team and the Parkin staff led to a more closed, solid looking, earthbound building than the original drawings suggested.

John C. Parkin's influence within and without his practices has been pervasive both as a propagandist for good design and as a design critic. With John B. Parkin he became identified with the comprehensive "total" design best exemplified by buildings like Ortho Pharmaceutical, Terminal One (The Aeroquay at Toronto International Airport), the Bata Shoe Company and IBM Head Offices. These are buildings designed to stand apart as objects complete in themselves, set in landscapes varying from informal (Ortho Pharmaceutical) to the more formal (the Bata building on its platform). The buildings recall the 18th century play of Palladian formality against the "designed" landscape, none more so than John C. Parkin's own house.

The structures themselves were executed in black and white as far as possible with accent colours reserved for interiors and furnishings. For a while all lettering was (sans serif) Standard Medium, and Mies's Barcelona chairs were a popular adornment. The black painted recess at junctions (the "negative detail") was a ubiquitous device.

The result was a considerable achievement in terms of consistency, clarity, quality of execution and, above all, in establishing a recognizable and memorable image for modern architecture.

In the mid-1960's, as the influence of Paul Rudolph and others became strong, the Simpson Tower and other buildings, in bush-hammered concrete and more plastic, irregular forms, reflected a slackening of the earlier discipline, as well as receptivity to the ideas of younger designers. This greater freedom continues to be apparent in the more recent work of the Parkin Partnership, though the great strength of

the competition winning scheme for Canada's National Gallery was its use of a massively scaled three-dimensional grid to unify and discipline an unwieldy program.

—Michael McMordie

PASANELLA, Giovanni.

American. Born in New York City, 13 January 1931. Educated at the Cooper Union, New York, 1949–53; Yale University, New Haven, Connecticut, 1954–58, M.Arch. 1958; awarded Yale Traveling Fellowship, 1958–59. Married Ann Kenigson in 1958; children: Marco and Nicolas. Designer with Edward Larrabee Barnes, New York, 1959–64; in private practice, as Giovanni Pasanella, Architect, New York, 1964–76. Since 1976, Partner, with Arvid Klein, Pasanella and Klein, Architects, New York. Architectural Consultant to the Chairman of the New York City Planning Commission, 1967, and to the Little Italy Restoration Association, New York, 1974–75. Critic in Architecture, Yale University, New Haven, Connecticut, 1963, and University of Kentucky, Lexington, 1964; Associate Professor of Architecture, 1965–68, and Project Director at the Institute of Urban Environment, 1965–66, Columbia University, New York; Critic in Architecture, and Visiting Fellow, Institute for Architectural and Urban Studies, New York, 1974. Exhibitions: Yale University Art Gallery, 1964; Columbia University School of Architecture, 1965; *40 under 40,* The Architectural League of New York, 1966; *The New City: Architectural and Urban Renewal,* Museum of Modern Art, New York, 1967;

Urban Design in New York, New York City Planning Commission, 1969; *Architecture for the State University of New York College at Potsdam,* Katonah Gallery, Katonah, New York 1970; *Can Our Cities Survive?,* Whitney Museum, New York, 1970; *Architecture for the Arts,* Museum of Modern Art, New York, 1971; *Younger New York Architects,* Columbia University School of Architecture, 1972; *Architecture Lecture Series Exhibition,* Yale University School of Architecture, 1973; *Twin Parks,* Columbia University School of Architecture, 1973. Recipient: *Architectural Record* Award, 1968, 1970, 1974; Residential Award, American Institute of Architects, New York Chapter, 1970. Address: Pasanella and Klein, 154 West 57th Street, New York, New York 10019, U.S.A.

Works:

1965 Intensive Therapy Center for Infants, Staten Island, New York
      Richard Lemon House, Bedford, New York
      Godfrey Rockefeller House, Greenwich, Connecticut
      New campus master plan for Wykeham Rise School, Washington, Connecticut
1966 Giovanni Pasanella House, New York
1967 Science Building II, State University of New York College at Potsdam
      Twin Parks Urban Renewal Plan, Bronx, New York (with Jonathan Barnett, J. T. Robertson, Richard Weinstein, and M. Weintraub)
      Harlem Housing Study, New York (exhibition project)
      Alan Gray House, Wellfleet, Massachusetts
      Alex Rapaport House, Scarsdale, New York

Giovanni Pasanella: Twin Parks West, Bronx, New York, 1973

1968 Negril Development Plan, Jamaica, West Indies (with Jonathan Barnett, Adelates Technical Services, J. T. Robertson, and Richard Weinstein)
Chester Weinberg House, New York
Charles Dunbar House, Winhall, Vermont
1969 Classrooms, Offices and Computer Center, State University of New York College at Potsdam
Firehouse and Chief's Headquarters, New York
Harry J. Brown House, Ringoes, New Jersey
Robert L. B. Tobin House, New York
1969/
73 Twin Parks West, Bronx, New York
1970 Residential Complex B, State University of New York College at Purchase (project)
Administration Building, State University of New York College at Potsdam
Twin Parks Community Development, Bronx, New York (as consultant)
1970/
74 Twin Parks East, Bronx, New York
1971 Entrance Gates, Roads and Parking Area, State University of New York College at Potsdam
William Clark House, Hilton Head Island, North Carolina (project)
Albert Bernstein House, Roslyn Heights, New York
1972 Elementary School P205, New York
Planning study for the Manhattan Landing Hotel Complex, New York
Planning study for Hartz Mountain Industries, Hackensack Meadowlands, New Jersey
Melrose Renewal Area Housing, New York (project)
Three Towns Program Housing, Albany, New York (project)
40-storey luxury apartment block, New York (project)
Ralph Peters House, Minerva, New York
Howard Bissell House, Ponte Vedra, Florida
William Josephson House, New York
Jane Campbell House, Ghent, New York
Cavendish Corporation office interiors, New York
Discount Corporation trading room and office interiors, New York
1973 Joseph E. Seagram and Sons office interiors, 375 Park Avenue and 800 Third Avenue, New York
Harry Winston Inc. office interiors, New York
1976 Joseph E. Seagram and Sons Office Building, Des Plaines, Illinois
1978 Columbia Grammar and Preparatory School, New York
Pueblo Nuevo (housing), New York
Little Italy (housing), New York

Publications:

On PASANELLA: books—*Architectural Record Houses of 1969* and *1970*, New York 1969, 1970; *The Shingle Style Today* by Vincent Scully, New York 1974; *Urban Design as Public Policy* by Jonathan Barnett, New York 1974, Tokyo 1978; articles —"Lemon House" in *Art in America* (New York), May/June 1966; "The Work of Giovanni Pasanella" in *House Beautiful* (New York), July 1966; "Lemon House" in *L'Architecture d'Aujourd'hui* (Paris), May 1967; "Lemon House" in the *New York Times*, 17 March 1968; "Residential Complex II" in *Architectural Forum* (New York), November 1970; "Twin Parks West" in the *New York Times*, 8 August 1971; "Twin Parks West" in *Building Design and Construction* (Chicago), April 1972; "Administration Building, Science II" in *Architectural Record* (New York), August 1972; "Grey House" *L'Architecture d'Aujourd'hui* (Paris), September 1972; "Twin Parks West" in *Architectural Forum* (New York), June 1973; "Twin Parks West" in *Architectural Record* (New York), June 1973; "Twin Parks West" in *Apartment Construction News* (New York), August 1973; "Twin Parks West" in *Real Estate Forum* (New York), August 1973; "Joseph E. Seagram and Sons Inc." in *Progressive Architecture* (New York), September 1973; "Twin Parks West" in *Professional Builder* (Chicago), September 1973; "Bissell House" in *Architectural Forum* (New York), October 1973; "Twin Parks West" in the *New York Times*, December 1973; "Joseph E. Seagram and Sons Inc." in *Contract* (New York), March 1974; "Joseph E. Seagram and Sons Inc." in *Lighting Design and Application* (New York), July 1974; "Twin Parks West" in *Architecture + Urbanism* (Tokyo), July 1974; "The Work of Giovanni Pasanella" in *Architecture + Urbanism* (Tokyo), April 1975; "The Work of Giovanni Pasanella" in *L'Espresso* (Rome), 13 July 1975; "Joseph E. Seagram and Sons Inc." in *Interiors* (New York), September 1975; "Twin Parks West" in *Controspazio* (Bari, Italy), September 1975; "Twin Parks East" in *Architectural Record* (New York), August 1976; "Seagram Des Plaines" in *L'Architecture d'Aujourd'hui* (Paris), August 1976; "Seagram Des Plaines" in *Architectural Record* (New York), June 1977; "Twin Parks East" in *Controspazio* (Bari, Italy), June/July 1977; "Twin Parks East" in *Tosh Jutaku* (Tokyo), March 1978.

Giovanni Pasanella established his own practice in 1964 after working as a designer with Edward Larrabee Barnes, and since January 1976 he has been in partnership with Arvid Klein. He first attained prominence in 1967 as one of a group of young architects serving as consultants to the then chairman of the New York City Planning Commission. These advisers helped establish an urban design group within the Planning Commission which still functions today.

His firm does school and college buildings, medical and correctional facilities, urban planning and community development, commercial buildings and banks, multiple dwellings, houses and interior design. But, to date, Pasanella is best known for his low- and middle-income housing projects constructed by the New York State Urban Development Corporation, the New York City Housing Authority, or various other public agencies, on so-called "vest pocket" sites. Such sites are irregular in shape and varied in topography, unlike the vast sites formerly cleared and leveled for urban renewal. These sites demanded a new kind of housing and massing design.

Three projects in the Bronx—Twin Parks Southwest, Twin Parks West and Twin Parks East—were a new departure when they were built in the late 1960's and early 1970's. The first two projects have floor-through split-level apartments in which living and sleeping areas are separated by a half-level change in elevation. For what was believed to be the first time in any New York City high-rise structure, public corridors and elevator stops do not serve every building level. Rather, one corridor and elevator stop serves 2½ floors, saving 60 per cent of the public corridor space for redistribution into the apartments.

Twin Parks East is notable for the way in which it integrates 599 apartments at a density of 135 units per acre, an elementary school, parking facilities, community spaces and a center for the aged.

Pasanella's multiple dwellings prove that high-rise, high-density housing doesn't have to be bad. His work thus has served a major public purpose.

—Mildred F. Schmertz

PAYSSÉ-REYES, Mario.

Uruguayan. Born in Montevideo, 5 March 1913. Educated at the University of Montevideo Faculty of Architecture, under J. Vilamajo, 1932–37, Dip. Arch. 1937. Married Emma Alvarez in 1940; children: Emma, Mario, Marcos, Monica, and Marcelo. Worked in the studio of J. Vilamajo, Montevideo, 1939–43. In private practice, Montevideo, since 1943. Professor of Architectural Projects, 1943–56, and since 1975 Director of the Faculty of Architecture, University of Montevideo. Secretary, First Assembly of the Institute of Architecture, Montevideo, 1945. Exhibitions (one-man shows): Faculty of Architecture, University of Montevideo, 1944, 1946, 1951, 1956, 1961, 1976; Center of Arts and Letters, Montevideo, 1963. Recipient: Medal of the Society of Uruguayan Architects, 1952, 1957, 1959, 1961, 1974. Member, College of Jurors, Society of Uruguayan Architects. Honorary Life Member, Central Society of Architects, Buenos Aires, 1969. Officer of the Academy of France, 1955; Academician, National Academy of Fine Arts, Buenos Aires, 1977. Address (office): General Santander 1725, Montevideo, Uruguay.

Works:

1936 House, Malvin, Uruguay
1937 Faculty of Architecture, University of Montevideo (competition project; with Julio Duhalde and G. Garcia Selgas)
1942 Low-cost housing, Uruguay (competition project)
1944 House, Carrasco, Uruguay (with Walter Chappe and Architectural Project School)
1945 Apartment building, Boulevard Artigas, Montevideo (with Julio Duhalde and G. Garcia Selgas)
1945/
48 Zoological Gardens, Santiago Vasquez, Montevideo
1948 Apartment building, Pocitos, Montevideo
Hotel Waldorf Astoria, Punta del Este, Uruguay (competition project; with G. Garcia Selgas)
1950 House, Parque de los Aliados, Montevideo (project)
1951 House, Punta del Este, Uruguay
1955 Low-cost housing, Salinas, Uruguay
Payssé-Reyes House, Carrasco, Uruguay
Archdiocese of Montevideo Seminary (with Enrique Monestier and Walter Chappe)
1956 Transformable Building (project)
1957 Social Security Building, Calle Mercedes, Montevideo (competition project; with Walter Chappe, Fedor Tisch, and Mario Harispe)
1959 National Party Mutual Association Building, Montevideo (project; with N. Bascou, E. Faget, E. Ross, and C. Peluffo)
1961 Banco de La República Branch Office, Punta del Este, Uruguay (with Adolfo Poszi-Guelfi)
1964 Mount Olympus Building, Montevideo (competition project; with Perla Estable)
1965 Euro-Kursaal Building, Montevideo (competition project; with others)
1967 City Hall, Amsterdam (competition project; with Luis Patrone and Perla Estable)
1970 La Brava Housing Complex, Punta del Este, Uruguay (with Villegas-Berro, Mario Harispe, Gomez-Platero, Lopez-Rey, Perla Estable, and G. Lussich-Payssé)
La Pastora Housing Complex, Punta del Este, Uruguay (with Villegas-Berro, Mario Harispe, Gomez-Platero, Lopez-Ray, Perla Estable, and G. Lussich-Payssé)
1971 Belgrano University, Buenos Aires (with Villegas-Berro, Mario Harispe, Perla Estable, and G. Lussich-Payssé)
1972 Montecarlo Center, Montevideo (with Villegas-Berro, Mario Harispe, Perla Estable, and G. Guerra)

Mario Payssé-Reyes: Payssé-Reyes House, Carrasco, Uruguay, 1955

1973   Central Bus Station, Buenos Aires (with Villegas-Berro, U. Herran, Gomez-Platero, Perla Estable, Mario Harispe, A. Meijide, and G. Lussich-Payssé)

1974   Paraguayan Embassy, Brasilia (competition project; with Perla Estable, Nayla and Carlos Peluffo, G. Hughes, and M. Payssé-Alvarez)

Publications:

By PAYSSÉ-REYES: book—*Where Are We in Architecture?*, Montevideo 1967; articles—numerous, particularly in *Arquitectura* (Montevideo).

On PAYSSÉ-REYES: books—*Art in Latin American Architecture* by Paul F. Damaz, New York 1963; *New Directions in Latin American Architecture* by Francisco Bullrich, New York 1969; article—"Mario Payssé-Reyes," special issue of *Arquitectura* (Montevideo), December 1959.

The dwelling pictured was built in 1954–55 at the seaside resort of Carrasco, 17 kilometres from the city of Montevideo, and involved putting into practice theories that I had long been developing. It takes into account the climate, construction, economics, materials used, and the determinants of country and place.

Generally, my theories comprise these goals: that the architecture ought to be realized in such a way that the dwelling contributes to the happiness of the family; that it should allow for development, the possibility of change; and that the principles employed in a particular house should be the same in any house, no matter what the budget of the family, or the cost of the house, might be.

I am also concerned with these principles:

A house ought to have spaces that are both sheltered and open to the garden or exterior spaces. These intermediate spaces ought to be realized in such a way that they can be part of the exterior when the outside temperature allows and part of the inside when there is rain, wind, damp or too much sun and it is not pleasant or possible to be outdoors.

Good geometry is the guide to good architecture. Free spaces should be used only when there are determinants for those spaces: without autonomy of space there cannot be autonomy of shape or expression.

The proportion of openings to the outside should be adequate for light, temperature and comfort—for human sensibility. In Uruguay, the correct total area of outside openings is more or less 20%.

Materials should be used in their natural aspect and colour, to create an appearance of reality.

The plastic arts ought to be used in accordance with the principle laid down by Piet Mondrian 30 years ago: "By means of the unification of architecture, sculpture and painting, a new plastic reality will be created. Painting and sculpture should not be manifest apart from architecture, nor as mural art that destroys real architecture, nor as applied art. They should be part of the construction, to create an ambience not merely useful or rational but also pure and complete in its beauty."

The house at Carrasco conforms to Axel Munthe's description in his *Book of San Michele:* "The house was small, with few rooms, but it had courtyards and terraces from which to admire nature: the soul needs more space than the body."

—Mario Payssé-Reyes

One of the most outstanding figures in Uruguayan architecture in this century is Mario Payssé-Reyes. His importance derives from his work not only as an architect but also as a teacher: he is responsible for having dynamically revised the curriculum at the School of Architecture at the University of Uruguay, and he has been the unchallenged master of generations of Uruguayan architects. His solid theoretical grounding is obvious in his writings, yet he doesn't speak of architecture as only a play of forms but essentially sees it as being at the service of man. To him, architecture consists in working in accordance with determinants—the climate or the materials available for construction; in accordance with directives—function, building systems, economic imperatives, etc.; and, lastly, in accordance with norms—plastic, aesthetic, or social. Architecture today is something more than simply the art of building; it is the art of transforming the entire habitat of man.

Some of Payssé-Reyes' works are already part of modern architectural tradition—for example, the Banco de La República in Punta del Este or his own private house in Carrasco: the latter has won praise from such internationally renowned figures as Richard Neutra and Bruno Zevi. For Payssé-Reyes, architectural emotion is achieved with the exaltation of the proposed program or subject, and his general principles may be summarized as: a simple and clear functional criterion; unification of interior spaces; relation of interior to exterior space, and full use made of the exterior; lighter, quicker, and cheaper building systems, such as steel or concrete; the employment of new materials and a greater use of transparent ones; a simplification of ornamentation; and a new integration of plastic arts. What architecture must be, according to Payssé-Reyes, is utilitarian in its objectives, and structurally rigorous, aesthetically demanding, and economically limited. The principal virtue of his architecture is simplicity, and functional and spatial values are his prime concerns. In this, he reveals the influence of the masters of the rationalist period, Le Corbusier, Gropius, and van der Rohe, although the work of Frank Lloyd Wright has also left its mark.

Payssé-Reyes has always been concerned to improve the conditions of architecture in Uruguay. He carried out a series of studies of the climate of country, evaluating light, temperature, humidity, rains, winds, etc., from which he concluded that it was necessary to complement the enclosed and covered areas of buildings, particularly dwellings, with open and covered spaces; he also determined the proportion that must exist between built and empty spaces, taking into account, too, questions of economy, maintenance, security, and the sensibility of the local inhabitants. Payssé-Reyes also tends to make use of materials in the most expressive and simple way; he respects their constructive possibilities and tries to preserve their unique textures and colors. And his rigorous geometry confers on his work an unmistakable language, which is in turn reinforced by the manifest integration between architecture, sculpture and painting, in the plastic tradition of Joaquín Torres García.

—Jorge Glusberg

PEI, I(eoh) M(ing).
American. Born in Canton, China, 26 April 1917; emigrated to the United States, 1935: naturalized, 1948. Educated at St. John's Middle School, Shanghai; Massachusetts Institute of Technology, Cambridge, B.Arch. 1940; Harvard Graduate School of Design, Cambridge, Massachusetts, M.Arch. 1946. Served on the National Defense Research Committee, 1943–45. Married Eileen Loo in 1942; children: T'ing, Chien, Li, and Liane. Instructor, then Assistant Professor, Harvard Graduate School of Design, 1945–48; Director of Architecture, Webb and Knapp Inc., New York, 1948–55. Since 1955, Partner, I. M. Pei and Partners, New York. Member, Urban Design Council of the City of New York; Member, National Urban Policy Task Force, American Institute of Architects; Member, National Council on the Humanities, Washington, D.C.; Member, Corporation of the Massachusetts Institute of Technology. Recipient: Arnold Brunner Award, National Institute of Arts and Letters, 1961; Medal of Honor, American Institute of Architects, New York Chapter, 1963; Golden Door Award, International Institute of Boston, 1970; "For New York" Award, City Club of New York, 1973; Thomas Jefferson Memorial Medal, University of Virginia, Charlottesville, 1976; Elsie de Wolfe Award, American Society of Interior Designers, New York Chapter, 1978; Gold Medal, American Institute of Architects, 1979.

D.F.A.: University of Pennsylvania, Philadelphia, 1970; Rensselaer Polytechnic Institute, Troy, New York, 1978; LL.D.: Chinese University of Hong Kong, 1970; Pace University, New York, 1972; President's Fellow, Rhode Island School of Design, Providence, 1979. Fellow, American Institute of Architects; Honorary Fellow, American Society of Interior Designers; Member, American Academy and Institute of Arts and Letters, American Academy of Arts and Sciences, and the National Academy of Design. Honorary Fellow, Royal Institute of British Architects. Address: I. M. Pei and Partners, 600 Madison Avenue, New York, New York 10022, U.S.A.

Works:

1954/
59 Hyde Park Redevelopment, Chicago (with Harry Weese)
1955 Mile High Center, Denver
1956/
65 Place Ville Marie, Montreal (with Ray Affleck)
1958 Plan for Society Hill, Philadelphia (with Edmund N. Bacon)
1961 Plan for the Government Center, Boston
1962 Kips Bay Plaza, New York
Slayton House, 3411 Ordway Street N.W., Washington, D.C.
Town Center Plaza, stage I, 3rd/6th Streets N.W., Washington, D.C.
1963 Henry R. Luce Foundation Chapel, Taiwan
1964 Washington Square East/Society Hill, Philadelphia
Green Center for the Earth Sciences, Massachusetts Institute of Technology, Cambridge
Plan for the central business district of Oklahoma City
School of Journalism: Newhouse Communications Center, Syracuse University, Syracuse, New York
1965 L'Enfant Plaza, stage I, Washington, D.C.

1966/
67 Area Renewal plan for Bedford-Stuyvesant, Brooklyn, New York (with David A. Crane)
1967 University Plaza, New York University, New York
Hoffman Hall, University of Southern California, Los Angeles
National Center for Atmospheric Research, Boulder, Colorado
1967/
70 Air Traffic Control Tower, for the Federal Aviation Agency, at various airports in the United States
1968 Everson Museum of Art, Syracuse, New York
Des Moines Art Center addition, Iowa
Polaroid Corporation, Waltham, Massachusetts
1969 Bedford-Stuyvesant Superblock, Brooklyn, New York
1970 Master plan for Columbia University, New York
The Wilmington Tower, Delaware
Dreyfus Chemistry Building, Massachusetts Institute of Technology, Cambridge
National Airlines Terminal, Kennedy Airport, New York
1971 Cleo Rogers Memorial Library, Columbus, Indiana
1972 Mellon Art Center, The Choate School, Wallingford, Connecticut
Third Church of Christ Scientist and the *Christian Science Monitor* Building, 16th and Eye Streets, Washington, D.C.
Canadian Imperial Bank of Commerce Complex, Toronto
1973 John Hancock Tower, Boston
Harbor Towers, Boston
Christian Science Church Center, Boston (with Arnaldo Cossutta)
88 Pine Street (office building), New York
Herbert F. Johnson Museum of Art, Cornell University, Ithaca, New York

I. M. Pei: East Building, National Gallery of Art, Washington, D.C., 1978

1975 Chemical Engineering Facility: Ralph Landau Building, Massachusetts Institute of Technology, Cambridge
1976 Wilson Commons Building, University of Rochester, New York
Chinese Banking Corporation Headquarters, Singapore
1977 Dallas Municipal Center
1978 East Building, National Gallery of Art, Washington, D.C.
1979 John Fitzgerald Kennedy Library Complex, Boston
Hotel, Peking (project)
Art Museum, University of Indiana, Bloomington
Convention and Exhibition Center, New York (project)
Industrial Credit Bank, Tehran
1980 West Wing, Museum of Fine Arts, Boston
Akzona Inc. Corporate Headquarters, Asheville, North Carolina
1981 El Paso Tower: Texas Commerce Plaza, Houston
Nestle Corporate Headquarters, Purchase, New York

Publications:

By PEI: article—"The Nature of Urban Space" in *The People's Architects,* edited by Harry S. Ransom, Chicago 1964.

On PEI: book—*Global Architecture 41: National Center for Atmospheric Research, Boulder, Colorado/Christian Science Church Center, Boston, Massachusetts,* edited by Yukio Futagawa, Tokyo 1976; articles—"Pei in the Sky" by Astragal in *The Architects' Journal* (London), 28 August 1952; "How They Go About the Problem in Pei's Office" in *Architectural Record* (New York), September 1956; "The Builder's Architect" in *Architectural Forum* (New York), January 1959; "Paeans for Pei" in *Progressive Architecture* (New York), October 1963; "Good Luck, Mr. Pei!" in *Progressive Architecture* (New York), January 1965; "I. M. Pei and Partners" in *Architecture Plus* (New York), February 1973; "Humble Pei" in *Architectural Design* (London), July 1976; "Winning Ways of I. M. Pei" by Paul Goldberger in the *New York Times Magazine,* 20 May 1979.

Ambiguity is everywhere in architecture, and most architects do a great deal of talking about it. I.M. Pei doesn't talk much, and his buildings don't represent manifestos of one architectural theory or another. Instead, he stands apart from the dispute and just builds the best way he knows how. There is still a cohesive philosophy evident in his work, but it is rational, not theoretical, and it is seldom stated verbally.

Pei has certainly been prolific: his firm has designed more than fifty major buildings, including several of the largest civic and corporate constructions of the decade. His work is strong, aggressively modern and highly successful. Nevertheless, Pei has hardly been an architectural hero. He doesn't spew the necessary epigramatic pronouncements. Stripped of the hype that surrounds the work of many more "conceptual" architects, though, the work of I.M. Pei emerges clear, consistent, yet still innovative.

Design is very important to I.M. Pei, yet in many areas he has accepted the fact that a certain amount of standardization is necessary within the current uses of technology. He uses standardized parts frequently, but with restraint, for he is an exacting designer who refines details carefully, even at the occasional expense of maximum structural efficiency. His skilled use of technology both in terms of parts and modern structure is bold and expressive; nevertheless, he focuses on the interest of the client more than personal formal expressions.

Pei understands the importance of a philosophical approach, but he also knows the practical limitations that inevitably occur within design. He perfects the building functionally and emphasizes total, comprehensive planning, rather than the philosophical statement related to it. In the end, he embodies classical form with modern technology.

Pei's 12 year association with developer William Zeckendorf taught him a great deal: he understands architecture in a broad context, both environmentally and economically. His sense of reason and balance reflect this understanding, and the combination of rational restraint with a keen aesthetic sense and the unabashed use of structure and technical innovation is responsible for the vibrancy of his design.

Pei will not deny that he often compromises, but to him architecture is a profession of compromises relying on adept problem solving relative to constraints. The process of design is a perfecting one, a pragmatic effort at successfully synthesizing a product from a total view of diverse and occasionally contradictory design issues. Pei remains aware and responsive to different contemporary architectural movements, but he continues to demonstrate a more acute concern for rational and structural architectural approaches.

—Ching-Yu Chang

PEICHL, Gustav.

Austrian. Born in Vienna, 18 March 1928. Educated at the Staatsgewerbeschule, Mödling, Vienna, 1943–44; Bundesgewerbeschule, Linz, 1946–48; Academy of Fine Arts, Vienna, under Clemens Holzmeister, 1949–53, Dip.Arch. 1953. Married Elfriede Weinmayr in 1957; children: Markus, Katharina, and Sebastian. In private practice, Vienna, since 1953. Professor at the Academy of Fine Arts, Vienna, since 1973. Political Cartoonist, as "Ironimus," in the *Süddeutsche Zeitung,* Munich, and *Die Presse,* Vienna, since 1955. Recipient: City of Vienna Award for Architecture, 1969; Austrian State Award for Architecture, 1971; Reynolds Memorial Award, U.S.A., 1975. Address (office): Opernring 4, A-1010 Vienna, Austria.

Works:

1958 Urban plan for Gartenstadt Süd, Vienna (with Wilhelm Hubatsch and Franz Kiener)
1960 Public housing, Vienna
1960/
62 Residential home, Grinzing, Vienna
1961 Elementary school, Krim, Vienna
Interior design of the Caravelle Aircraft of Austrian Airlines
1962/
64 Austrian Pavilion, *World's Fair,* New York
1963 Austrian Airlines Branch Office, Sofia
1963/
65 Konvent der Dominikanerinnen: High School, Dormitories, Gymnasium and Cafeteria, Hacking, Vienna
1964 Austrian Pavilion, *Expo '67,* Montreal (project)
1965/
67 RZ-Meidling Rehabilitation Center, Vienna
1967 Junior College with audio-visual display systems, Mistelbach, Austria (project)
Contower Urban Housing (project)
1968 Austrian Pavilion, *Helsinki Trade Fair*
1969 ORF (Austrian Broadcasting Company) Branch Studio, Eisenstadt, Austria
1969/
77 City of Vienna Public School, Diesterweggasse, Vienna
1970/
72 ORF (Austrian Broadcasting Company) Stations at Linz, Salzburg, Innsbruck, and Dornbirn, Austria
1974 "Die Freyung zu Wien" Redevelopment Project, Vienna

1976 "Molino Stucky" Redevelopment Project, *Biennale,* Venice
1976/
79 Earth Station for EFA (satellite communication company), Aflenz, Austria
1977 ORF (Austrian Broadcasting Company) Station, Graz, Austria
Vaduz Art Gallery, Liechtenstein (project)

Publications:

By PEICHL: article—"Architektur ist Sinnlich" in *Deutsche Bauzeitung* (Stuttgart), no. 5, 1978.

On PEICHL: articles—"ORF Studios" in *L'Architecture d'Aujourd'hui* (Paris), December/January 1972/73; "ORF Radio Stations" in *Architectural Design* (London), January 1973; "Radio Four" by A. Best in *Design* (London), June 1973.

In the contemporary climate of specialization in the arts and sciences, there are a few strongholds where universality is preserved. Architecture is one of them.

Architecture exerts its influence over several generations. It is a prospect, an outlook, a vision of a new environment: that is the basis of its universality. It is equally clear that the claim to universality in no way implies a claim to totality. However, the interlinking of science, politics, research and architecture is in full swing, and in recent years the radical increase in man's conscious awareness of research activity is equal to the development in science itself.

But what makes planning and architecture so important are not only the economic and ethical but also the political and social consequences. In the typical State, politics makes use of architecture as a symbol. The better the architecture, the better the State.

We architects are the favorite scapegoats and whipping-boys in our society, but it is the client who is more guilty than the architect: architecture is, after all, conceivable without architects, but not without clients. Clients create the spirit of the age that architects have to portray.

The contemporary public client does not build, he consumes—building materials, money, the environment. For him, building is a meeting of requirements, an exhaustion of budget funds; building for the public client rarely has an aspect of "bringing up" or "bringing about." The large and powerful clients are the municipality, the town or city council, the company entrepreneur, and industry. The anonymity of the client leads to a loss of quality. Today's client is rarely one individual.

I should like architecture's aim to be understood as the process and structure of alterations in the spatial environment in which human society develops and changes. If we consider the invasion of the town and country by the same bleak curtain facades, then we realize the importance of the character of a locality and of individual personality to a lively picture of this world. It is worth recognizing the importance of the genius loci as a defence mechanism against the devastation of architecture.

Architectural criticism is also a question of aesthetics. I do not mean classical aesthetics, but a new aesthetic that is abstract or mathematical. It is not dependent, as is the classical aesthetic, on a philosophic concept, but—far removed—on a methodological one. It is not oriented towards subjective but largely towards objective measures. This aesthetic uses mathematical and empirical methods of procedure and makes use of abstract concepts. I love the classical aesthetic, but I am a willing slave to the technical aesthetic. There are technically perfect works that are aesthetically expressionless and unsatisfactory, but there is no architecture that is outstanding from an aesthetic viewpoint which is not also superb technically.

If the environment is not to become a routine copy, we must shape it not exclusively according to

Gustav Peichl: ORF (Austrian Broadcasting Company) Station, Salzburg, 1972

reason and purpose but also according to the senses. Architecture makes you feel serious or cheerful—according to its scale, volume or color. Architecture makes you sensuous!

—Gustav Peichl

From the same diploma year of 1953 at the Vienna Academy of Fine Arts as Gsteu and Holzbauer, and like them influenced by Clemens Holzmeister, Gustav Peichl is perhaps the leading representative of the new generation of post-war Austrian architects.

His first works, of the early 1960's—for example, the Krim Elementary School and the Dominican Convent, both in Vienna—embody a feeling for pure form expressed in plain concrete and rendered surfaces. The explicit references to the International Style of the 1930's are emphasized by the strong horizontals that pervade the designs, and the buildings are superb examples of a finely perfected philosophy of internal planning.

Peichl's work developed in the later 1960's, becoming richer as the buildings shed their stylistically pure shells. The Meidling Rehabilitation Center in Vienna, though rational in planning terms, has a brutalist aesthetic of overhanging concrete terraces overlaid with symbolic gestures—three giant shiny metal spheres housing services on the roof—images that prefigure the mechanistic overtones of Peichl's

series of near-identical radio stations for the ORF network throughout Austria.

Each radio station complex—organically planned with varying sized studios, control rooms and offices ranged around a central entrance hall—is given expression by a forest of gleaming aluminum ductwork that punches through a glazed roof—similar in feeling to the images of Bruno Taut. These ducts occasionally sprout out over the immaculately cast board-marked concrete exterior. The overall result is one of an unusually fine blend of whimsy and rationality, and the effect of architectural collage is heightened by the lattice-grids of walkways and antennae that seem to float above the ensemble. In these buildings Peichl never allows structure and services to impose their own rationale, regardless of the architectonic implications: elements are assembled for their picturesque effect, not their literal face value.

In his recent work there is a growing concern for contextual design, in which buildings are considered relative to the surrounding built fabric. "Die Freyung zu Wien" is no run-of-the-mill rehabilitation scheme, but Peichl's earnest attempt at a symbiosis of nature and architecture—something also hinted at in his submission for the Venice *Biennale* of 1976. In the Vaduz Arts Center project the building is no longer treated as a free-standing sculptural

object at all. Indeed, it is hard to discern a single "building" as such, so well integrated is the complex into the existing town morphology.

With these most recent works, Peichl's talents seem to have matured, so much so that he has become one of the leading modern movement architects who still finds he has a role in these post-modern times. In abandoning the monument, he has not forsaken architecture.

Yet, despite his eminence in the profession, Peichl's fame among the Austrian public at large comes from his alternative career as a political and social caricaturist. He remains best known as "Ironimus."

—Gerald Adler

PELLI, Cesar.
American. Born in Tucuman, Argentina, 12 October 1926; emigrated to the United States, 1952: naturalized, 1964. Educated at the University of Tucuman, 1944–49, Dip.Arch. 1949; University of Illinois, Urbana, 1952–54, M.S.Arch. 1954; influenced by the teaching of J. Vivanco, E. Sacriste, E. Rogers and A. Richardson and by the work of Eero Saarinen. Married Diana Balmori in 1950; children: Denis and Rafael. Director of Design, OFEMPE (government organization), Tucuman, 1950–52; Associate Architect, Eero Saarinen and Associates, Bloomfield Hills, Michigan and Hamden, Connecticut, 1954–64; Director of Design, DMJM (Daniel, Mann, Johnson and Mendenhall), Los Angeles, 1964–68; Partner in charge of Design, Gruen Associates, Los Angeles, 1968–77. Since 1977, Principal of Cesar Pelli and Associates, New Haven, Connecticut, and Dean of the School of Architecture of Yale University, New Haven. Visiting Professor, University of Tucuman, 1960; Visiting Professor of Architectural Design, University of Cordoba, Argentina, 1960; Charlotte Shepard Davenport Visiting Professor, 1972, and William Henry Bishop Visiting Professor of Architecture, 1974, Yale University School of Architecture; Visiting Professor, University of California at Los Angeles, 1975, 1976. Exhibitions: *Los Angeles 12*, Pacific Design Center, Los Angeles, 1976; *Biennale*, Venice, 1976; *A View of California Architecture: 1960–1976*, Museum of Modern Art, San Francisco, 1976–77. Recipient: Design Award, *Progressive Architecture*, 1966; Honor Award, American Institute of Architects, Southern California Chapter, 1968, 1969, 1975 (twice), 1976; First Prize, United Nations City Competition, Vienna, 1969; Arnold W. Brunner Prize, National Institute of Arts and Letters, 1978. Address: Cesar Pelli and Associates, 1056 Chapel Street, New Haven, Connecticut 06510, U.S.A.

Works:

1965 Sunset Mountain Park Urban Nucleus, Santa Monica, California (competition project)
1966 Century City Medical Plaza, Los Angeles
     Teledyne Systems Laboratories, Northridge, California
     Worldway Postal Center, Los Angeles
     Federal Aviation Authority Office Building, Lawndale, California
1967 COMSAT Laboratories, Clarksburg, Maryland
     Kukui Gardens Housing, Honolulu, Hawaii
     Bunker Hill Third Street Tunnel extension, Los Angeles
1968 Pacific Center (offices and commercial complex), Vancouver, British Columbia
1969 Western Electric Office Building, Newark, New Jersey
     United Nations City, Vienna (competition project)

Cesar Pelli: United States Embassy Office Building, Tokyo, 1972

City Hall, San Bernardino, California
1970 Commons and Courthouse Center, Columbus, Indiana
Security Pacific National Bank Building, San Bernardino, California
Ohrbach's Del Amo Department Store, Torrance, California
1971 Ohrbach's Cerritos Department Store, Cerritos, California
Pacific Design Center, Los Angeles
1972 Wells Fargo Office Building, Oakland, California
United States Embassy, Tokyo, Japan
1973 Clorox Office Building, Oakland, California
1974 Yale Music Center, New Haven, Connecticut (project)
Fox Hills Mall, Culver City, California
1975 Rainbow Center Mall and Winter Gardens, Niagara Falls, New York
1976 Daehan Kyoyuk Life Insurance Building, Seoul, Korea
1977 Museum of Modern Art gallery expansion and residential tower, New York (project)

Publications:

By PELLI: articles—"Open Line City" in *Progressive Architecture* (New York), June 1970; "Third Generation Architects" in *Architecture + Urbanism* (Tokyo), March 1971; "Nisson Motors Building" in *Architecture + Urbanism (Tokyo), December 1972;* *"Four Days in May"* in *Architecture + Urbanism* (Tokyo), September 1974; "Transparency: Physical and Perceptual" in *Architecture + Urbanism* (Tokyo), November 1976.

On PELLI: articles—"Cesar Pelli: Public Architect" by Sibyl Moholy-Nagy in *Architectural Forum* (New York), March 1970; "Cesar Pelli," special issue of *Architecture + Urbanism* (Tokyo), March 1971; "Cesar Pelli," special feature in *Architecture + Urbanism* (Tokyo), November 1976.

*

Architecture can claim to be the Mother of the Arts because of its deep roots in reality. A reality that nurtures it and establishes its limits. I need to work close to these roots. They are the primary source and feedback of my ideas. The circumstances in the reality of each project are for me, when properly understood, the source of opportunities in design. Design grows and expands from these firm roots. Within them is the potential for the project. How far it will be carried and in which direction depend on the quality of my judgement and my artistic skill. Seeking opportunities within a well-understood problem is the obverse of functionalism that sees in the same circumstances only a problem to be solved: a deterministic view that reduces options and allows no room for life. And much different from the formalist attitudes that will impose the same pre-conceived intentions on any circumstances. My commitment is to an architecture that celebrates life. For too long architecture has been absorbed with its death-defying qualities. An architecture that defies death has to accent the qualities of the non-living. It seeks above all massiveness and durability and it avoids the temporary or fragile. An architecture that enhances life accents perception, lightness and change. The difference between a flower and a stone. Architecture is not in the empty building but in the vital interchange between building and participant.

—Cesar Pelli

*

Cesar Pelli's buildings executed while he was head of design at DMJM and then Gruen Associates in Los Angeles from 1964 through 1977 are evidence of his impatience with permanent, monumental architecture. His name is associated with elegant glass towers which, by the suppression of the mullions, the nondirectional flow of the glass skin, and the absence of a masonry base, create wide glass screens for the reflection of the cityscape. The impermanent aspect of the buildings is heightened by the extruded form, a form which allows the building to be cut off at many points (United States Embassy in Tokyo; Pacific Design Center; glass tower for the Museum of Modern Art expansion). His interest in the glass box was brief, but his preoccupation with transparency remains. He explored sculptural forms in glass, using recesses and projections, and often bands of glass set at an angle to distort the images (San Bernardino City Hall); and in the Pacific Design Center he turned the box on its side and introduced color—the glass is blue.

Another of his concerns, the changing use of buildings, is demonstrated in the design for two laboratories of the 1960's, both linear in plan with a circulation spine along a high glazed wall through which additions can project (Teledyne Laboratories; COMSAT Laboratories). The circulation spine usually replaced stairwells, lobby and lounges; and always a view across existing fields or groves replaced the typical over-designed gardens. The most dramatic use of the circulation spine along the perimeter was in his award-winning design for United Nations Headquarters in Vienna, a multi-layered space stretching the entire length of the seven attached towers.

His intellectual approach to design had been sharpened by his ten years in the office of Eero Saarinen where there were ample time to study fully schemes for a variety of building types, and this was a factor in his quick adjustment in Los Angeles to reduced time for design as well as smaller budgets. Although he limited himself to standard catalogue materials, standard methods of construction, and sacrificed fine detailing, the quality of his buildings established his reputation as one of the important young designers. Working in his favor was the greater latitude in Los Angeles to experiment, greater than he would have enjoyed in more traditional cities. By 1977 when he left Los Angeles to become Dean of the School of Architecture at Yale University, and subsequently to open his own office, he had developed a unique style that was bold and prognostic, often poetic, as in the Winter Garden and Mall, Niagara Falls. More than anyone else in his generation, Pelli is an architect's architect.

—Esther McCoy

PEÑA Ganghegui, Luis.

Spanish. Born in Oñate, Guipúzcoa, 29 March 1926. Educated at the National School, Oñate; College of Santa Maria, Vitoria, 1938–40; College of Santa Maria, San Sebastian, 1940–46; studied architecture and painting at the Mayor Nebrija College, Escuela Técnica Superior de Arquitectura, Madrid, 1946–58, Dr.Arch. 1958. Served in the University Militia, La Granja, Segovia. Married to Rosario Azpilicueta Aguilar; children: Maria, Rocio, Domingo, and Miguel. City Architect, San Sebastian, 1963–64. In private practice, San Sebastian, since 1964. Professor (in San Sebastian Department), Escuela Técnica Superior de Arquitectura, Barcelona. Recipient: First Prize, Ulia National Competition, San Sebastian, 1962; Aizpurua Prize, 1964. Member, Conjunto Monumental de San Esteban, Murcia, Spain, 1977. Address (office): Reyes Católicos 14, 7th Floor, San Sebastian, Spain.

Works:

1959 Vista Alegre Tower, Zaraux, Guipúzcoa, Spain (with Juan M. Encio)
1963 Plaza de la Trinidad redevelopment, San Sebastian
1964 Housing, Plaza Alcibar, Motrico, Guipúzcoa, Spain
1965 Entzus Housing, Motrico, Guipúzcoa, Spain
 Imanolena House, Paseo de San Nicolás, Motrico, Guipúzcoa, Spain
1966 Rosa Housing, Motrico, Guipúzcoa, Spain
1967 Maria y Jose College, Zumaya, Guipúzcoa, Spain
1968 Church of St. Francis, Vitoria, Spain
1969 Housing, Oyarzun, Guipúzcoa, Spain
 Elu Housing, Motrico, Guipúzcoa, Spain
 50 houses, Ataun, Guipúzcoa, Spain

1970 Housing, El Puerto, Motrico, Guipúzcoa, Spain
 Juan XXIII Co-operative Housing, San Sebastian
1972 Escoriaza Social Workshops Building, Irún, Guipúzcoa, Spain
1973 Pharmaceutical Union Building, Eibar, Guipúzcoa, Spain
 20 houses, Ataun, Guipúzcoa, Spain
1974 Pharmaceutical Union Building, San Sebastian
 Housing, Lequeitio, Vizacaya, Spain
 Development plan for Silvestre Pérez, Motrico, Guipúzcoa, Spain
 Secondary school, Oyarzun, Guipúzcoa, Spain
 Iparraguirre Housing Complex, Motrico, Guipúzcoa, Spain
1978 Plaza a la Mar, Paseo del Tenis, San Sebastian (with sculptures by Eduardo Chillida)
 Euzkadi Monument to the Dead, Oyarzun Cemetery, Guipúzcoa, Spain
1979 Plaza Monumento a los Fueros, Vitoria, Spain (with sculptures by Eduardo Chillida)

Publications:

On PENA: articles—"Live Tradition in the Work of Luis Peña" by Miguel Angel Baldellou in *Hogar y Arquitectura* (Madrid), July/October 1974; "Six Guipúzcoan Architects" in *Arquitectura* (Madrid), no. 206/207, 1977.

Since my time in Madrid came to an end, I have worked as an architect mainly in Motrico, a small village of some 5,000 inhabitants in Guipúzcoa, in the Basque Country. Because I work in a small Spanish village, the work I do is very far from using any kind of advanced technology.

In 1963 I was given the opportunity to take over the job of Municipal Architect of the beautiful city of San Sebastian, and I planned and directed the construction of the Plaza de la Trinidad in the Old Quarter, a square devoted to the Basque popular games. I gave up my post because I had strong feelings of incompatibility with the way in which the town was progressing and because I disagreed with the urban development plan that had been adopted.

I now carry on my profession in small communities of Guipúzcoa, such as Oyarzun (4,000 inhabitants) and Ataun (1,500 inhabitants) as well as in

Luis Peña: Plaza de la Trinidad, San Sebastian, 1963

Motrico. Nevertheless, I do have continual contact with architects in Barcelona and Madrid through the "sesiones de critica" which take place each year in different cities of Spain.

Recently I have been involved in the planning of important urban spaces, such as the Plaza a la Mar in the Paseo del Tenis in San Sebastian, with sculptures by Eduardo Chillida, and the Plaza Monumento a los Fueros in Vitoria, also in collaboration with the same sculptor.

An interesting experience has been the construction of the Monumento a los Muertos for Euzkadi in the Cemetary of Oyarzun, built with a single mason, at the cost of 500,000 pesetas.

From the time that the Catalan architect, Oriol Bohigas, joined the Escuela de Barcelona, I have been attached to the school as a professor, working in its department in San Sebastian.

—Luis Peña

Over the past 20 years Luis Peña has produced work dedicated to a response to its surroundings. Without falling into the trap of local colour, he has contributed to the international movement in architecture with works suffused with local and national sentiment. As a result of this continuous search for the right ingredients, his work lacks the rigor of the avant-garde, but it has an uncanny feeling for place. His response to what the "feeling of place" means to people is so strong that his buildings seem to be a natural background to the everyday life of the Basques. His buildings, once built, seem always to have been there.

Mackintosh combined a national culture with an international movement; Luis Peña also looks for means to integration, but within the Basque Country. As far as architecture is concerned, the most significant feature of Basque culture is the closely-knit relationship of the community as expressed through the love of sport—that of the players and that of the spectators, who gamble on the outcome. Every corner, porch, street and square becomes a pitch for a favorite ball game; the characteristics and obstacles of each "pitch" influence the rules of each particular game, and the rules are agreed upon before play begins. This kind of full participation by neighbours in the use and management of their public spaces is inbred in all of Peña's architecture—so much so that he now seems to have deserted the architecture of buildings for the architecture of squares. His best are in San Sebastian—El Trinidad by the church and El Tenis by the sea.

His housing developments consist of either large

barn-like structures or an erratic string of street facades covered with a spider-like web of thin metal balconies. Both forms are characteristic of the Basque vernacular, translated by Peña into the language of modern architecture. His best housing is in Oyarzun and Motrico.

Peña's exploration of the relationship of the modern movement to place does not, however, merely consist of translating vernacular features; it also involves introducing a formal investigation of the movement itself into the local context. This intention is clear in the Mies-like precision of his Pharmaceutical Union Building in San Sebastian and his secondary school in Oyarzun. In the Pharmaceutical Union Building curved walls of glass brick and aluminium, mixed with concrete and rendered wall surfaces, do not, at first, look at all Basque. But it is a warehouse on a factory estate: it does not demand more, and Peña does not force the issue. The school, however, has been designed literally as a bridge between two neighbourhoods, and forms the background and wings of an open-air stage and playground—a building acting an urban role.

Perhaps the most moving of Peña's designs is his small monument in Oyarzun Cemetery to those who died defending Basque liberties against Franco. It is like the old tombstones that lie up against the cemetery wall. Peña has rebuilt part of the rose-coloured wall with an open window that looks out onto the green farmlands beyond, marked with a black metal band like that that marks out the area on the wall and floor of a Basque ballgame. The window is "out of bounds"—symbolic of the injustice suffered by the martyrs. A flagpole is placed horizontally across the centre so that the Basque national flag can be hung either outside the cemetery or inside over the tomb. The flagpole leads the eye from the tomb to the fields, from the dead to the life they died for. Such symbolism would seem to suggest that Peña is a romantic, but, though he has a romantic streak, he is too much of an intellectual to fit any such easy generalization.

Luis Peña is still a practising architect, but now he devotes much of his time to teaching the younger generation in the small Basque school of architecture that he is creating.

—David Mackay

PENTEADO, Fabio (Moura).

Brazilian. Born in Campinas, Sao Paulo State, 3 June 1929. Educated at the Ophelia Fonseca School, Sao Paulo, 1935–39; Instituto Mackenzie, Sao Paulo, 1940–48; Mackenzie University, Faculty of Architecture and Urbanism, Sao Paulo, under Eliziario Bahiana, 1948–53, Dip.Arch. 1953. Served in the Brazilian Air Force, 1948–49. Married Claude de Barros in 1958; children: Gabriel and Adriana. In private practice, Sao Paulo, since 1953. Member, Underground Transport Commission, Sao Paulo, 1959; Counsellor for Urbanism, National Planning Advisory Board, Brasilia, 1966. Instructor, School of Architecture and Urbanism, Mackenzie University, Sao Paulo, 1962–64. Architectural Editor, *Revista Visão,* Sao Paulo, 1956–62; Organizer and Editor, *Brazilian Building Data Catalogue,* Sao Paulo, 1958; Director, *Arquitetos na TV,* Excelsior Television Network, Brazil, 1961–62. Director, *Arquiteto,* Sao Paulo, since 1974. Vice-President, Institute of Brazilian Architects, Sao Paulo Chapter, 1960–61; President, Executive Council, Brazilian Institute of Architects, 1966–68; Member, Executive Committee, International Union of Architects, Paris, 1969. Exhibitions: *Playa Girón Monument Competition Exhibition,* Havana, 1962; *International Theatre Exhibition,* Prague, 1967; *Bienal,* Sao Paulo, 1969; *Latin American Biennale,* Lima, 1970; *International Architecture Bienal,* Sao Paulo, 1973; *International Theatre Exhibition,* Prague, 1975. Recipient: First Prize, State Bank and Campineiro Club Competition, Campinas, Brazil, 1954; First Prize, Harmonia Club Competition, Sao Paulo, 1958; First Prize, and Gold Medal, *International Theatre Exhibition,* Prague, 1967; Gold Chain, Brazilian Institute of Architects, 1969; First Prize, Jockey Club Social Building Competition, Sao Paulo, 1974. Life Member of the Executive Committee, Brazilian Institute of Architects, 1968. Honorary Member, Colegio de Arquitectos de Mexico, 1969, Colegio de Arquitectos del Peru, 1969, and the American Institute of Architects, 1972. Address (office): Rua Bento Freitas 306, Sl. 801, 01220 Sao Paulo, Brazil.

Works:

1950 Domingos Solha House, Souzas, Sao Paulo
1954 Arnaldo Barbosa Apartment Building, Sao Paulo
     Sao Bernardo, Sao Caetano, and Santo Andre Water Treatment Stations, Sao Paulo State (with Ringo Kubota)

State Bank and Campineiro Club, Campinas, Sao Paulo (competition project)
1956 Carlos Wathely Apartment Building, Sao Paulo
     Water Treatment Plant, Campinas, Sao Paulo (with Alfredo Paesani)
1958 Cabo Frio Hotel, Rio de Janeiro (project; with Ringo Kubota)
1960 Forum Building, Araras, Sao Paulo
     School, Campinas, Sao Paulo
     Sanitary Building, Barretos, Sao Paulo (project)
     Conselheiro Antonio Prado Technical School, Campinas, Sao Paulo
     Coffee Museum, Campinas, Sao Paulo (project)
     Carlos Monteiro Silva House, Sao Paulo
     Piracicaba Municipal Theatre, Sao Paulo (project; with José Ribeiro)
1961 School, Sao Caetano do Sul, Sao Paulo
     Electrotechnical Institute, Sao Paulo (project)
     Secondary school, Sao Bernardo do Campo, Sao Paulo (project)
1962 Apartment building, Dona Viridiana Street, Sao Paulo
     Noroeste Bank Branch Office, Guarulhos, Sao Paulo
     Bairro do Limão Housing Development, Sao Paulo (project)
     Playa Girón Monument, Museum, and Square, Cuba (competition project; with Ubirajara Gigliolli, José Ribeiro, Tito Livio Fraschino, and Vasco de Mello)
1963 Dock Workers' Housing Development, Santos, Sao Paulo (project)
1964 Harmonia Tennis Club Building, Sao Paulo (with Alfredo Paesani and Teru Tamaki)
     Founders' Monument, Goiania, Goias State, Brazil (project; with José Ribeiro)
1965 Water Treatment Plant, Pirassununga, Sao Paulo (project; with Alfredo Paesani and Teru Tamaki)
     Tourist Centre, San Sebastian, Spain (competition project; with Alfredo Paesani and Teru Tamaki)
1966 Water Treatment Plant II, Campinas, Sao Paulo (with Alfredo Paesani and Teru Tamaki)
     Opera House, Campinas, Sao Paulo (project; with Alfredo Paesani and Teru Tamaki)

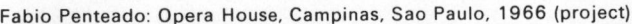

Fabio Penteado: Opera House, Campinas, Sao Paulo, 1966 (project)

Sondeiker House, Jardim Marajoara, Sao Paulo (with Alfred Paesani and Teru Tamaki)

1967 Cumbica Housing Estate, Sao Paulo (with J. B. Vilanova Artigas and Paulo Mendes da Rocha)

1968 Cultural Centre, Campinas, Sao Paulo (with Alfredo Paesani and Teru Tamaki)

Old People's Home, Campinas, Sao Paulo (project; with Teru Tamaki)

Praca dos Azulejos Hotel, Campinas, Sao Paulo (project; with Alfred Paesani and Teru Tamaki)

Julio de Mesquita Filho Hospital and School, Sao Paulo (with Teru Tamaki, Eduardo Almeida, and Giselda Visconti)

1969 Technical School, Vila Alpina, Sao Paulo (with J. P. Vilanova Artigas)

Santa Casa da Misericordia Experimental Health Centre, Sao Paulo (with Teru Tamaki)

1970 Federal Technical School, Santos, Sao Paulo (project; with J. B. Vilanova Artigas and Paulo Mendes da Rocha)

Alto Pinheiros Club Building, Sao Paulo (with Teru Tamaki)

Fritz Strauss House, Campinas, Sao Paulo (with Teru Tamaki)

Aziz Maluf House, Vinhedo, Sao Paulo (with Teru Tamaki)

1971 Tennis Club Building, Campinas, Sao Paulo (with Teru Tamaki)

Twin Office Towers, Sao Paulo (project; with Teru Tamaki and Tito Livio Fraschino)

Franklin Guidler House, Campinas, Sao Paulo (with Teru Tamaki)

1972 Office building, Alameda Santos, Sao Paulo (project; with Teru Tamaki)

Pasargada Park Housing Estate, Sao Paulo (with Teru Tamaki; since altered)

Ralton Purina Company Office Building, Volta Redonda, Rio de Janeiro (with Teru Tamaki)

José Roberto Penteado House, Campinas, Sao Paulo (with Teru Tamaki)

1973 Cyrel Imobiliaria Housing Estate, Sao Paulo (project; with Teru Tamaki and Vasco de Mello)

Chacara do Piqueri Housing Complex, with office tower and shops, Sao Paulo (project; with Decio Tozzi, João Walter Toscano, and Telesforo Christofani)

State Administration Centre, Sao Paulo (project; with Teru Tamaki, Tito Livio Fraschino, and Hercules Merigo)

Renewal plan for the historic town centre of Campinas, Sao Paulo (project; with Teru Tamaki and Tito Livio Fraschino)

Ibiuna Land Development, Sao Paulo (with Teru Tamaki and Tito Livio Fraschino)

Master plan for Fazenda Nossa Senhora do Carmo, Itaquera, Sao Paulo (with Teru Tamaki)

Salto Housing Development, Sao Paulo (with Teru Tamaki)

Ronald Levinsohn House, Rio de Janeiro (with Teru Tamaki and Tito Livio Fraschino)

1974 Jockey Club Social Building, Sao Paulo (competition project; with Teru Tamaki and Tito Livio Fraschino)

Hermitage Hotel, Campinas, Sao Paulo (with Teru Tamaki)

F.E.A.C. Urban Development, Campinas, Sao Paulo (project; with Teru Tamaki)

Granja Sao Martinho Land Development, Campinas, Sao Paulo (project; with Teru Tamaki and Tito Livio Fraschino)

San Carlos Housing Development, Sao Paulo (project; with Teru Tamaki)

1975 Heleno Fragoso House, Rio de Janeiro (with Teru Tamaki)

1975/
77 10 school buildings, Sao Paulo State (with Teru Tamaki and Hercules Merigo)

8 branch offices for the Sao Paulo Savings Bank, Sao Paulo State (with Teru Tamaki, Hercules Merigo, and Nadia Cahen)

1977 Sao Paulo Light and Power Company Technical Installation Buildings, Sorocaba, Sao José dos Campos, Sao Paulo (with Teru Tamaki, Hercules Merigo, and Nadia Cahen)

Luiz Antonio Pires House, Campinas, Sao Paulo (with Teru Tamaki and Hercules Merigo)

1978 Cultural Centre: Theatre, Library and Art Gallery, Sao Bernardo do Campo, Sao Paulo (project; with Teru Tamaki)

Urban development plan for Sao Carlos do Pinnal, Sao Paulo (project; with Teru Tamaki and José Borelli)

Marcelino P. Barbosa House, Campinas, Sao Paulo (with Teru Tamaki and José Borelli)

José Steinberg House, Campinas, Sao Paulo (with Teru Tamaki, Hercules Merigo, and José Borelli)

Publications:

By PENTEADO: articles—monthly column on architecture in *Visão* (Sao Paulo), 1956–62.

On PENTEADO: articles—"Architectural Works Around Sao Paulo After Brasilia" in *Kokusai Kentiku* (Tokyo), June 1967; "Open Air Theatre Designed by Fabio Penteado" in *Binario* (Lisbon), January/February 1974.

*

For a long time Sao Paulo, in spite of its reputation as "the largest industrial centre in Latin America," remained a city whose cultural outlook was extremely conservative. Indeed, at Mackenzie University, where I studied architecture, any expression of modernism was generally considered bad taste, and architects such as Le Corbusier and even Oscar Niemeyer were sometimes quoted as being the dangerous proponents of Communist architecture.

After I received my diploma in 1953, combining my own efforts with those of a few of my more persistent colleagues, I began to use my first professional assignments as a means of teaching myself the necessary knowledge that I had not yet acquired. This self-teaching process was complemented by the experience that I gained as the architectural editor (1956–62) of an important Brazilian weekly, *Revista Visão*. As I was writing and learning, one of the aspects with which I was most concerned was the gap between the notions of human solidarity described in "Preliminary Thoughts" and what was actually achieved in the completed projects. Even when these projects incorporated the best design and the latest technology, they hardly ever seemed to me to fulfil the basic requirements of the original objectives.

After twenty-five years and several completed projects which, if nothing else, have kept my business alive, I believe that there have been a few occasions when I have been able to put into practice some of the ideas with which I was most concerned. These ideas can be seen in a few of the projects which try to live up to the ideal of total collective participation, although I do not know if the projects represent any real contribution: they were not specifically comissioned with this ideal in mind, nor was their value sufficiently appreciated. I like to regard them, however, as the preliminary plans for a party to which, when it takes place, I would very much like to be invited.

—Fabio Penteado

*

No study of Fabio Penteado's work should be restricted to questions of form, function and technique, although these aspects are sufficient evidence in themselves of the unquestionable quality of his buildings. The prime consideration is really one of response to purpose. Though function is partly determined by fixed parameters, a building is also influenced to a great extent by the architect's notions of the social role of architecture. The people/function relationship is carefully considered by Penteado in his projects, and the implicit possibilities are rethought and dealt with in a very dynamic way.

In practical terms: there is, in his work, a delicate balance between functional nuclei, the elements of which are precisely defined, and spatial complexes that are open to a variety of uses, that are designed to allow the user a wide range of interpretation. Further, his architectural aims are defined conceptually. A building may have a specific use, but it must never compartmentalize or exclude the changing world. A building should live *with* the world, inviting active participation from the user, assuming an almost didactic character by accepting and provoking a constant rediscovery of *rôle* and the consequent change in its social function.

Fabio Penteado's clients are the great Brazilian public: crushed, intimidated, discriminated against, and disoriented by the astonishing population explosion. His basic concern is with restoring dignity to their daily use of the man-made environment—a concern that is fundamental to his buildings. And, hence, his wider role, that of putting forward creative ideas and blueprints for mass architecture.

This task is of utmost importance: it is now forecast that the population of Brazil will double within the next 25 years. The capacity to implement such ideas as Penteado's will fall pitifully short of the expansion that is required. The deadlines for completion hardly allow time for prototypes to be tested or for monitoring the mistakes that multiply at an alarming rate in undertakings of this scale. There would be no point in proposing standardized models: they would be impracticable, not least because of the variety of cultural and geographical conditions. More relevant is any dialogue of ideas that can serve as a departure point in the formation of conceptual models. Penteado's work is concerned with just such ideas.

The Campinas Cultural Centre is one of a series of theatre projects that are the result of his research into architectural responses to leisure and culture. (His projects for the Piracicaba Municipal Theatre, the award winning Campinas Opera House, and the Sao Bernardo do Campo Cultural Centre are other examples.) The Campinas Cultural Centre is situated in the middle of a traditional Campinas square, but instead of "invading" the square, it replaces it: pedestrians pass over or through it in their search for the shortest way from A to B, and the building puts its various functions at the disposal of even the most casual user. Its four blocks are surmounted by an area that is entirely given over to the public, with tiered seating forming a large open-air theatre available for spontaneous events and public gatherings. Usable space is doubled. The volumes, laid out in the form of a mandala, are wonderfully dynamic: they vary in composition as the observer moves, standing out against each other with archaic monumentality, opening or closing the vistas. The tip of the large, leaning obelisk-tower does not emphasize its own base but marks the centre of the square and of the avenue that leads to it.

The Julio de Mesquita Filho Hospital and School, part of the Santa Casa de Misericordia Health Centre in Sao Paulo, is dedicated to the complex problem of providing medical care for a population of two million people in a state of abject poverty. This technical, dimensional and psychological impasse is resolved by a simple horizontal layout that can be grasped by the humblest of people. The hospital becomes a small town: the wards are the "suburbs" and the corridors are the "streets" where patients, doctors and visitors come and go, as do cleaning trolleys, food trolleys, and stretchers—as much as possible as if they were ordinary streets. In the centre of the building there is a large park with playing fields and places designed for the leisure needs of people of varying ages. It is all an attempt to incorporate the notion of healthiness within the community and to remove the tabu and disturbing connotations of sickness.

The "Santa Casa" is recognizable by its pediment of bare concrete, broken on each of the four sides by three arches 71 metres wide. This simple design suggests both the scale of the undertaking and the magnitude of its public function.

Penteado is also concerned to blend architecture with its surroundings—either through contrast or integration, depending on the individual circumstances. In the theatre projects, the space is developed architecturally to allow an expansion of activities centred around the buildings. This is also the case in the Aziz Maluf House in Vinhedo, the Fritz Strauss House in Campinas and, inversely—by landscaping the interior—in the Harmonia Tennis Club Building in Sao Paulo. Conversely, the "Santa Casa" and the Water Treatment Plant II in Campinas stand out in sharp definition against the surrounding landscape by virtue of the purity of their volumes.

Penteado has also expressed his ideas (and his idealism) in large urban plans. Of these, the Cumbica Housing Estate, already partially complete, has served for experiments in the establishment of work and planning systems hitherto not attempted on this scale; it has provided basic data for a study of the quality/quantity relationship and its economic implications in such a large-scale complex.

Penteado's profound involvement in activities specifically related to architecture is also characterized by a breadth of understanding born of his humanist viewpoint. As President of the Brazilian Institute of Architects during one of the most trying times in the political life of the country, he took great pains to grant his colleagues in need the support and solidarity of the Institute.

—Jorge Czajkowski

PENTTILÄ, Timo.

Finnish. Born in Tampere, 16 March 1931. Educated at the Institute of Technology, Helsinki, 1950–56, Dip.Arch. 1956. Served as an Ensign in the Finnish Infantry, 1956–57. Worked as a designer for Hytönen and Luukonen, Helsinki, 1953–54, Ström and Tuomisto, Helsinki, 1954–55, and for Aarne Ervi, Helsinki, 1957–59. In private practice, Helsinki, since 1959; in partnership with Heikki Saarela, since 1970. Visiting Lecturer, University of California, Berkeley, 1968–69. Vice-Chairman of the Finnish Architects Association, 1968, and of the Museum of Finnish Architecture, Helsinki, 1976–78. Exhibition: *Bienal,* Sao Paulo, 1969. Recipient: First Prize, City Theatre Competition, Helsinki, 1961; Architecture Award, State of Finland, 1976. Address: Arkkitehtuuritoimisto Timo Penttilä & Heikki Saarela Oy, Kuusiniementie 5, 00340 Helsinki 34, Finland.

Works:

1958 Town Hall, Seinäjoki, Finland (competition project; with Kari Virta)
1960 Sports Hall, Turku, Finland (competition project; with Kari Virta)
1961 City Hall, Helsinki (competition project)
1962 Civic School and Workers' Institute, Tampere, Finland (with Kari Virta)
     Parish Hall, Karkku, Finland
1963 City centre plan for Oulu, Finland (competition project)
1964 Cultural Centre, Kemi, Finland (competition project)
1965 Commercial Institute, Tampere, Finland (with Kari Virta)
     Edvard Grieg Concert Hall, Bergen, Norway (competition project)
     Master plan for Amager, Denmark (competition project)
1966 Pellonperäntie Rowhouses, Helsinki
1967 Ratina Stadium, Tampere, Finland
     Reima-Pukine Textile Factory, Kankaanpää, Finland
     City Theatre, Helsinki
1969 Sauna and Health Club, Humallahti, Helsinki (competition project)
1971 Yyteri Resort Hotel, Pori, Finland (competition project)
1974 Master plan for the extension of Tapiola Garden City Centre, Espoo, Finland
1975 Training and Education Centre, Espoo, Finland
     Kop Bank Headquarters, Helsinki (competition project)
1976 National Cultural Centre, Manama, Bahrain (competition project)
1977 Hanasaari Power Plant, Helsinki
     Art Museum, Vaduz, Liechtenstein (competition project)

Publications:

On PENTTILÄ: articles—"Helsingfors Stadsteater" in *Arkitektur* (Stockholm), vol. 68, no. 2, 1968; "Helsinki Stadsteater" in *Arkitektur* (Copenhagen), vol. 13, no. 4, 1969; "Kraftwerk in Hanasaari" in *Bauen und Wohnen* (Zurich), vol. 29, no. 11, 1975.

Architecture is a vitally important means of intellectually and emotionally unlimited expression to man, and as such is part of his cultural heritage. This is true even though architecture, also by its very nature, is intertwined with all the necessities of everyday life.

Timo Penttilä: City Theatre, Helsinki, 1967

Architecture comes into existence only through the materialization of the ideas in unique situations, which is due to its heterogenous nature and the relative importance of many influencing factors.

In an inexplicable way architecture also transcends the mere self-evident sum of these factors.

Therefore I try to avoid pre-conceived ideas and the fallacies of dogmatism. My inspiration usually comes from the inside of the situation and differs case by case.

The architecture of the Helsinki City Theatre (see the photo), for example, reflects the unison of the natural topography of the site and the flow of people in the public spaces.

Modern technology and methodology are indispensable assets in the service of man, but they should not be the ultimate issues of architectural morality. The emphasis of my work has been and shall be on the satisfaction of human needs—practical as well as emotional.

—Timo Penttilä

Finland nowadays has only a few internationally-known architects. Timo Penttilä is, without doubt, one of them. The number of his works is relatively small, but their quality is the better for that. It is significant that almost every one of his works has been published.

Penttilä's most important work is the City Theatre of Helsinki, which was built in 1964–67. Penttilä won the competition in 1961 when he was 29 years old with an entry that showed a sensitive adaptation to the site in a park district. This sensitivity remained constant throughout the entire building, right down to the smallest detail. The generous and finely harmonized succession of areas, beginning with the entrance up to the interior of the auditorium, is overwhelming. The materials are also finely harmonized, with bronze and ceramic tiles prevailing.

Certainly the Helsinki Theatre does not belong to the avant-garde—if that means untreated concrete and visible installations. But it would also be wrong to call the building "conservative;" its conception is quite too advanced for that. What, then, is it? And what sort of architect is Penttilä? In what "category" should he be placed?

Considering his previous buildings, one does find similarities to the designs of Alvar Aalto. His functional solutions and his generous conceptions of space suggest Aalto too. Nevertheless, he cannot really be called a student of Aalto, and he never worked with him. Contemplating again the equalized detail work of the Helsinki Theatre, one thinks of only one direct model—Aarne Ervi. The humanity of Ervi's architecture and his fine feeling for detail must surely have influenced Penttilä during the two years that he worked for him.

But, finally, Penttilä can't be classified. It would perhaps be more interesting to discover why his buildings are generally well accepted by their users and thought "beautiful" by other people. It is worth pointing out, because it becomes more and more obvious, how little recent experimental architecture has contributed to the beauty of our environment. This facts seems to be increasingly realized by the general public. This is not the place to discuss the so-called "lack of understanding" by the public and by builders of much modern architecture; I wish simply to pose the question, Should not good architecture be something that is accepted by its users even when it involves innovations? Penttilä's architecture becomes something that is accepted by its users even when it involves innovations? Penttilä's architecture becomes more understandable in this context.

Penttilä does not follow vogue trends, and he does not build for architectural critics. He is not a teacher who tries to educate his public; he refers to symbols and traditions that are accepted by his public, that is, by the users of his buildings. He is not seduced by the now dominant Bauhaus building purism; on the contrary, he is looking for values that functionalism is supposed to have thrown overboard. His interest is in the variety and continuity of forms and materials that belong to the tradition of our building cul-

ture, that are of significance and value. A comparison obtrudes with Eliel Saarinen, who, in spite of his generous conceptions, found the means to relate the forms and materials as well as the building tradition of Finland to the international movement (this is best seen in his former national romantic works, especially in the Helsinki Railway Station). Is Penttilä the successor of Eliel Saarinen?

—Antero Markelin

PEREIRA, William L(eonard).

American. Born in Chicago, Illinois, 25 April 1909. Educated at the University of Illinois School of Architecture, Urbana, 1926–30, B.Arch. 1931. Served as an Assistant Regional Director, for California, United States Office of Civilian Defense, 1942–44. Married Margaret McConnell in 1934; children: William Jr. and Monica. Associated with Holabird and Root, Chicago, 1930–31; in private practice as William L. Pereira, Architect, Los Angeles, 1931–50; Partner, with Charles Luckman, Pereira and Luckman, Los Angeles, 1950–58. Since 1958, Principal and Chairman of William L. Pereira Associates, Los Angeles (other principals: G. L. Garvey; Jack Kassel; Neil W. Birnbrauer; Otto H. Kilian). Professor of Architecture, Design and Planning, University of Southern California, Los Angeles, 1949–59. Chairman, California Governor's Task Force on Transportation, 1967–68; Member, National Council of the Arts, 1967–68; Member, California Governor's Commission on Ocean Resources, 1967; Adviser, Aeronautics and Space Engineering Board, National Academy of Engineering, 1969–70; Member of the Science and Technology Council of the California Assembly, 1970; Architect-in-Residence, American Academy in Rome, 1971. Member of the Advisory Committee, Crocker National Bank, California, since 1963; Director, Urban America Inc., since 1965; Director, American Film Institute, Washington, D.C., since 1965. Recipient: Honor Award, American Institute of Architects, Southern California Chapter, 1963 (twice); Award of Merit, American Library Association, 1963; Alumni Achievement Award, University of Illinois, 1973. Honorary doctorate: Otis Art Institute, Los Angeles, 1964; D.F.A.: Art Center College of Design, Los Angeles, 1971; D.L.: Pepperdine University, Malibu, California, 1974. Fellow, American Institute of Architects, 1958. Fellow, Academy of Motion Picture Arts and Sciences. Commander, Order of the Ivory Coast, West Africa. Address: William L. Pereira Associates, 5657 Wilshire Boulevard, Los Angeles, California 90036, U.S.A.

Works:

1939   Lake County Tuberculosis Sanitorium, Waukegan, Illinois
1950   Robinson's Department Store, 777 East Colorado, Pasadena, California
1952   CBS Television City, Beverly and Fairfax, Los Angeles
1953/
58   University of California at Santa Barbara (as supervising architect)
1954   Marineland of the Pacific, Palos Verdes, California
1959/
62   Master plan, new terminals and restaurant, Los Angeles International Airport
1960   Development plan for Irvine, California
1963   Public Library, Santa Fe Springs, California
Olin Hall of Engineering, University of Southern California, Los Angeles
West Fullerton Library, Fullerton, California
1964   Los Angeles County Museum of Art

Avco Savings and Loan Association Building, 250 South Mills, Ventura, California
Ahmanson Center, University of Southern California, Los Angeles
1965   Library, Crawford Hall, Steinhaus Hall, and Humanities-Social Sciences Building, University of California at Irvine (with Jones and Emmons, and Blurock and Ellerbrock)
Dickenson Art Center, University of California at Los Angeles
Booth Memorial Hall, University of Southern California, Los Angeles
1966   Norris Residence Hall, Occidental College, Eagle Rock, California
1969   Public Library, Buena Park, California
Master plan for the Houston Center, Texas
Seaver Science Center, University of Southern California, Los Angeles
1970   Central Library, University of California at San Diego
Braille Institute Library, Los Angeles
Fine Arts Building, University of California at Irvine
1970/
73   *Los Angeles Times* Building addition, Spring and 1st Streets, Los Angeles
1971   Cityview, Queens, New York
1971/
73   Pepperdine University, Malibu, California
1972   Transamerica Corporation Building, San Francisco
St. Francis Hotel tower addition, San Francisco
Irvine Towers, Newport Center, Newport Beach, California
1973   Pacific Mutual Building, Newport Center, Newport Beach, California
Great Western Savings Center, Beverly Hills, California
Security Pacific Building, Flower and 6th Streets, Los Angeles
Charles Lee Powell Hall, University of Southern California, Los Angeles
1974   Wells Fargo Bank Building, Newport Center, Newport Beach, California
1976   Library/Multimedia Center, Golden West College, Huntington Beach, California

Publications:

By PEREIRA: articles—"The Architect and the Entrepreneur" in *AIA Journal* (Washington, D.C.), July 1962; "Campus Planning, University of California" in *Architectural Record* (New York), November 1964.

On PEREIRA: articles—"Two Current Works by William Pereira" in *Architectural Design* (London) September 1972; "Houston Center" by Charles Delfante in *Urbanisme* (Paris), no. 137, 1973; "Great Western Savings Center" in *Domus* (Milan), September 1973; "Cityview Renewal Project, Borough of Queens, New York City" in *L'Architecture d'Aujourd'hui* (Paris), September/October 1973; "Pyramid from San Francisco" by F. E. Rontgen in *Polytechnische Tijdschrift* (The Hague), 21 December 1973; "Library of the University of California at San Diego" by L. Kahan in *Technique des Travaux* (Liege), January/February 1974; "Houston Center" by Edward K. Carpenter in *Urban Design* (New York), Autumn 1977.

Chicago-born William L. Pereira is a product of the Midwest. He studied at the University of Illinois, one of the great American schools of architecture, and worked in Chicago before settling in Los Angeles. But his work is a manifestation of an architectural and cultural energy that is clearly Californian.

Pereira's architectural work covers a broad range, including large-scale planning. His clients have been large corporations and public companies as well as

governmental agencies. His buildings are characterized not so much by a style as by stylistic wholeness and expression, for his goal seems always to have been to establish a fluent and immediately recognizable formal entity—a complete and spirited object as architecture.

Identifiability and symbol are always a principal emphasis of his work. In this respect his design reflects an urge identified with the Beaux-Arts approach to architecture, while the particular forms he employs are derived from those familiar in 20th century Western art and sculpture. At the same time his designs are always extremely functional. One discerns in his finished work a disciplined search for functional appropriateness, a fluidity in the movement of people and processes. The combination of form and function is a clear headed and optimistic California blend. If it is not profound, it is workable and affirmative, celebrating a moment and a time rather than attempting to probe depths. The work, like the man, is most congenial.

Among his accomplishments is the Marineland of the Pacific—a high achievement in the viewing of aquatic life and in handling large groups of people. Los Angeles International Airport, a far larger and more complex work, is a well-handled portal for the city. His Transamerica Corporation Building in San Francisco is a tall pyramidal tower standing with its own distinct identity amidst other tall buildings. Pereira also designed the striking tree-like library of the University of California at San Diego.

—Paul Spreiregen

PERESSUTTI, Enrico.

Italian. Born in Pinzano al Tagliamento (Udine), 28 August 1908. Educated at the Milan Polytechnic School of Architecture, 1927–32, Dip.Arch. 1932. Served in the Italian Army, 1941–43. Married Emma Pasquinelli in 1944; daughter: Marina. Founder Partner, with Gianluigi Banfi, q.v., Ludovico Belgiojoso, q.v., and Ernesto Nathan Rogers, q.v., BBPR Architectural Studio, q.v., Milan, 1932 until his death, 1973. Vice-Commissioner, CLNAI (Comitato di Liberazione Nazionale per l'Alta Italia), 1943; Member, Municipal Committee for the Master Plan for the City of Milan, 1946–47; Consultant Architect and Planner, CECA (Communauté Européenne Charbon Acier), Luxembourg, from 1953; Consultant, Metropolitana Veneta, Venice, 1967–73. Member, CIAM (Congrès Internationaux d'Architecture Moderne), from 1935; Vice-President, ICSIL (International Council of Societies of Industrial Design), 1957–59. Member, Commissione per le Manifestazioni d'Arte Moderna dell'Associazione tra i Cultori d'Architettura, 1935, and Maison des Artistes, Lausanne, 1939; Founder Member, Société Européenne de Culture, 1950. Died (in Milan) in 1973.

Publications:

By PERESSUTTI: articles—"Sulla Funzione dei Materiali" in Quadrante (Milan), January 1934; "Urbanistica Corporativa: Piani Regolatori" in Quadrante (Milan), December 1934; "Architettura Mediterranea" in Quadrante (Milan), January 1935; "Incontri in Russia" in Almanacco Letterario Bompiani, Milan 1942; "Il Passaggio Ideale per la Casa" in Domus (Milan), August 1942; "Un Arredamento e una Dichiarazione" in Domus (Milan), October 1944; "Sul Convegno della Ricostruzione" in Metron (Rome), November/December 1945; "L'Uomo e gli

Oggetti: Bere" in Domus (Milan), January 1946; "Sul Piano Regolatore: Funzioni e Caratteri della Città" in La Voce di Milano, February 1946; "L'Uomo e gli Oggetti: Dormire" in Domus (Milan), February 1946; "L'Uomo e gli Oggetti: Giocare" in Domus (Milan), March 1946; "L'Uomo e gli Oggetti: Mangiare" in Domus (Milan), April 1946; "La Lupa di Stagno non piace agli Architetti" in Cronache di Bologna, May 1947; "Sistemazione del Piazzale della Stazione di Bergamo" in Metron (Rome), May/June 1948; "Parliamo di Gropius" in Epoca (Milan), September 1951; "Risolvere il Problema del Traffico" in Milano-Sera, 7 January 1954; "Moral Training for the Architect" in Architecture and the University, Princeton, New Jersey 1954; "La Sedia Thonet" in Domus (Milan), no. 290, 1954; "Case della CECA per gli Operai Siderurgici" in Edilizia Popolare (Rome), November 1955; "Un Convegno per la Protezione di Erice" in Casabella (Milan), no. 215, 1957; "Il Convegno dell'ASID a Beaford Springs" in Stile Industria (Milan), March 1959.

See BBPR ARCHITECTURAL STUDIO

PERKINS, Lawrence B(radford).

American. Born in Evanston, Illinois, 12 February 1907. Educated at the University of Wisconsin, Madison, 1924–25; Cornell University College of Architecture, Ithaca, New York, 1926–30, B.Arch. 1930. Married Margery Isabella Blair in 1932; children: Dwight, Blair, L. Bradford, and Julia. Founding Partner, with Philip Will Jr., q.v., and E. Todd Wheeler, Perkins, Wheeler and Will, Chicago, 1935–46, subsequently Perkins and Will, 1946–64, and the Perkins and Will Partnership, 1964–70; Chairman of the Board, 1970–73, and since 1973 Director, Perkins and Will Architects Inc., Chicago; offices established in New York, 1951, and Washington, D.C., 1962. Since 1974, Adjunct Professor of Architectural Design, University of Illinois at Chicago Circle. Member, 1945–65, and Chairman, 1948–54, 1963–65, Evanston Planning Commission; Chairman, Advisory Board, Cook County (Chicago) Building Codes Commission, 1963–66; Director, Adlai Stevenson Institute of International Affairs, Chicago, 1965–75. Member of the Advisory Committee of the Cook County Forest Preserves, since 1963. Recipient: Chicagoan of the Year Award, 1960; 25 Year Award, American Institute of Architects, 1971; Distinguished Service Award, American Association of School Administrators, 1975. Fellow, American Institute of Architects, 1953. Address: Perkins and Will Architects Inc., 309 West Jackson Boulevard, Chicago, Illinois 60606, U.S.A.

Works:

1940 Crow Island Elementary School, Winnetka, Illinois (with Eliel and Eero Saarinen)
1942 Rugen Elementary School, Glenview, Illinois
Clyde Lyon Elementary School, Glenview, Illinois
1948 Greenbriar School, Northbrook, Illinois
Blythe Park Elementary School, Riverside, Illinois
1949 Westwood Elementary School, Woodstock, Illinois
1952 Heathcote Elementary School, Scarsdale, New York
Greenwood Elementary School, Woodstock, Illinois
Glenbrook North High School, Glenview/Northbrook, Illinois
Hoover Elementary School, Neenah, Wisconsin
1953 Washington School, Evanston, Illinois
Ralph Smith Elementary School, Hyde Park, Chicago

1954 Kellogg High School, Idaho (with Culler, Gale, Martell and Norie)
1955 Byron Junior High School, Shaker Heights, Ohio (with Michael Kane)
1956 Linton High School, Schenectady, New York
Paige Elementary School, Schenectady, New York
1958 Richard E. Byrd School, Chicago
1960 Rockford College, Illinois
1963 United States Gypsum Building, Chicago
1964 Evanston Township High School, Illinois
Charles Gates Dawes School, Evanston, Illinois
1965 Chute School, Evanston, Illinois
Dalton Elementary School, Illinois
Winnetka Public Library, Illinois
First National Bank Building, Chicago (with C. F. Murphy Associates)
1976 Chapel, Ithaca College, Ithaca, New York (with A. Egner)

Publications:

By PERKINS: books—Schools, with Walter Cocking, New York 1949; Workplace for Learning, New York 1957; article—"Must We Live in Unlovely Cities" in The School Administrator (Arlington, Virginia), Summer 1971.

On PERKINS: article—"The Perkins and Will Partnership" in Building Construction (Chicago), April 1969.

Our architectural concern through the years has been service rather than architectural formulas. We have attempted to derive our architecture from the activities appropriate for the users, rather than impose some patent rectangle.

—Lawrence B. Perkins

Lawrence B. Perkins built the firm of Perkins and Will on two basic concepts. The first related to the nature of architecture, the second to the men and women who produce it. Perkins has always believed that a successful building project is the result of the combined contributions of many capable individuals. Furthermore, once the right team has been gathered, he believes that it should be allowed to operate freely so that the most creative ideas about design and technology can rise to the surface and be applied to the job at hand. Perkins and Will, founded in 1935, is now one of the largest firms in the United States, yet the team approach within a permissive atmosphere continues to prevail. And consequently, their architecture remains varied in style and use of materials.

Rather than reflecting any preconceived stylistic or structural dogma, each project evolves from the compound circumstances of a particular building program, locale, client, and job team. Although projects may differ outwardly from one to another, there is nevertheless a common denominator that runs throughout the firm's work: buildings are appropriate to their situation and requirements.

The company's first major commission was the Crow Island School in Winnetka, Illinois, done in conjunction with Eliel and Eero Saarinen. Crow Island embodied a progressive design that turned away from traditional educational philosophy and form. Instead of a single anonymous rectangle, the school extends wings from a central block in order to distinguish age groups and activities through architectural massing. Each classroom opens onto a landscaped courtyard and has its own lavatory, sink and drinking fountain. Every aspect of the building is scaled to the children, right down to the furniture. Crow Island School had a tremendous influence on American academic design. It was a landmark in every sense, and it established the firm as a sensitive expert in educational architecture, a reputation that it still deservedly enjoys.

Although Perkins and Will has long specialized in

Lawrence B. Perkins: Heathcote Elementary School, Scarsdale, New York, 1952

institutional buildings, schools and hospitals particularly, the office has also expanded its interest and skill in commercial projects. Of all the commissions undertaken for the private sector, Perkins is perhaps most proud of and the firm most recognized for the soaring, plastic design of the 60-story First National Bank of Chicago.

Throughout his career, Perkins has assumed responsibility for some design and a great deal of management and client contact, and his leadership is indelibly stamped on every aspect of the firm's practice. He has always taken great interest in young people, and this is evidenced in both his commitment to teaching and in his willingness to create opportunities for the younger members of his organization.

—Linda Legner

PERRET, Auguste.

French. Born in Brussels, Belgium, of French parents, 12 February 1874. Educated at the Ecole des Beaux-Arts, Paris, under Julien Guadet, 1891–95 (Réconnaissance des Architectes Americains Prize, 1895). Married in 1899. Worked in his father's building construction firm, Paris, 1897–1905, and Partner, with brothers Gustave and Claude, in the successor company, Perret Frères, from 1905. Inspector-General of Public Works and National Palaces, France; Member, French National Committee for the Reconstruction; Chief Architect, Reconstruction of Le Havre; Member, Conseil Artistique des Musées Nationaux, Paris. President, Conseil Superieur de l'Ordre des Architectes, Cercle d'Etudes Architecturales, and Salon des Tuileries, all Paris. Recipient: Royal Gold Medal, Royal Institute of British Architects, 1948; Medal of Honor, Académie des Beaux-Arts, Denmark, 1949. Honorary doctorate: Helsinki Polytechnic, 1949. Officier, Légion d'Honneur, 1926. Officer, Order of the White Lion, Czechoslovakia, 1925, and of La Couronne du Chêne, Luxembourg, 1925. *Died* (in Paris) *25 February 1954.*

Works:

1889 Temple Tower, *Exposition Universale,* Paris
1890 House, Berneval, France
1894/
  96 4 six-storey houses, rue Sorbier, Paris

1898 Office building, 10 Faubourg Poissonière, Paris
1899 Municipal Casino, Saint Malo, France
1902 Apartment building, 119 Avenue de Wagram, Paris
1903 Cathedral, Oran, Algeria (project)
  Apartment building, 22 bis rue Franklin, Paris
1904 School, rue de la Tour, Paris
  Office building, Avenue Niel, Paris
1905 Garage, 51 rue de Ponthieu, Paris
  Villa, Montereau, France
1906 Office building, 48 rue Raynouard, Paris
1907 La Saulot Hunting Lodge, Salbris, France
1908 Docks at Saïda, Tiaret and Sidi-Bel-Abbès, Algeria (projects)
1911 French Legation, Istanbul
  House extensions, Bièvre, France
1913 Théâtre des Champs Elysées, Paris (original project by van de Velde)
1914 Société Royale d'Harmonie Building, Antwerp (project)
1915 House, rue Claude-Lorrain, Paris
1916 Société Industrielle Docks [I], Casablanca
  Chapel, Maurice Denis House, Saint Germain, Paris
1919 Société Industrielle Docks [II], Casablanca
  Esders Clothing Workshops, 78 Avenue Philippe-Auguste, Paris
1921 Madame Paul Jamot Monument, Montparnasse Cemetery, Paris

Marinoni Workshops, Wallut Foundry Buildings, and Grange Foundry Buildings, Montataire, Oise, France
Rozanes Jewellery Shop, rue de la Paix, Paris
FER Factory, Aulnois, France
Aircraft hangar, Villacomblay, France (project)
Terraced housing, Paris (project)

1922 Société Marseillaise de Crédit Building, 4 rue Auber, Paris
High-rise building (project)
Housing, Tours, France (project)

1923 Notre Dame Church, Le Raincy, near Paris
Durand Décors Workshops, rue Olivier-Metra, Paris
Grand-Quevilly House, near Rouen
Gaut House, rue Nansouty, Paris
Pont d'Argent (temporary aluminum structure), Théâtre des Champs Elysées, Paris

1924 Church Bell Tower, Saint Vaury, Creuse, France
Palais de Bois (temporary exhibition building), Porte Maillot, Paris

1925 Theatre, and Albert Levy Pavilion, *Exposition des Arts Décoratifs,* Paris
Crédit Hôtelier Building, rue de la Ville-l'Evêque, Paris
Church of Saint Thérèse, Montmagny, Seine et Oise, France
Observation Tower, *Grenoble Exhibition*
House, Tours, France (project)

1926 Cassandre House, Versailles
Veret House, Noyon, France
Chana Orloff House, rue de la Tombe-Issoire, Paris
Aghia House, Alexandria, Egypt
Joan of Arc Basilica, Paris (project)

1927 Braque House, rue du Douanier, Paris
School, Parc Montsouris, Paris
Palace of the League of Nations, Geneva (competition project)
Dominican Convent, Cairo (project)
School for Young Girls, Constantine, Algeria (project)

1928 Bresy House, Villa Said, Algeria
Chapel, Arceuil, Seine, France

1929 Mela Muter House, Villa Seurat, Algeria
Church extensions, Juvisy-sur-Orge, France
Eiffel Monument, Paris
Chapel, Chalons, France
Colpach Monument, Luxembourg
Huré House, Boulogne-sur-Seine, Paris
Gordine House, Boulogne-sur-Seine, Paris
Galerie Katia Granoff Gallery extensions, Quai Conti, Paris
Ecole Normale de Musique, rue Cardinet, Paris
Oblates Convent, Saint Benoit, France

1930 Lange House, Avenue Ingrès, Paris
Musée Moderne (project)
Facade for the Galeries Lafayette, Paris (project)

1931 Capucine Monastery alterations, Saint Symphorien, France
Magnin Museum alterations, Dijon, France
Nubar Bey House, Garches, France
Society of Naval Works and Construction Building, Paris
Chapel, Vanves, France
Porte Maillot Redevelopment, Paris (project)
Palace of the Soviets, Moscow (competition project)

1932 Apartment building, 51–55 rue Raynouard, Paris
Marine National Building, Paris
State Printing Buildings, Paris (project)
Awad Bey House, Cairo
Chapel, Strasbourg (project)
Arsenal Building, Toulon (project)
Military Headquarters Complex, Algiers (project)

1933 Aghun House, Alexandria, Egypt
Government Buildings, Algiers (project)

Auguste Perret: Mobilier National Building, Paris, 1934

Palace of Agriculture, Algiers (project)
Redevelopment plan for the Port of Metz, France (project)

1934 Master plan, and Trocadéro, for the *World's Fair* of 1937, Paris (project)
Paul Lefèvre House, Sceaux, France
Mobilier National (National Guard) Building, Paris

1935 Pont de l'Arc, Paris

1936 Pershing Monument, Route de Versailles (project)

1937 Museum of Public Works, Paris
Palais de Chaillot, Paris (project)

1939 Iron and Aluminum Foundry, Issoire, France
Clock and Watch Factory, Besançon, France
Barbier Hugo Hospital, Algiers
Church, Carmaux, France (project)
Attaturk Monument, Turkey (project)

1940 Comedy Theatre, Istanbul (project)
Thermal Baths, Paris (project)
Champs Elysées and Invalides Developments, Paris (projects)
Plaine de l'Arc Airport, Marseilles (project)

1945 Master plan for the reconstruction of Le Havre

1947 Place de la Gare reconstruction, Amiens

1948 Perret Tower, Amiens
Midy Laboratories, Neuilly, Paris
Olympic Stadium, Montessou, France (project)

1948/
53 Atomic Energy Commission Establishment, Saclay, France

1949 Airport, Marignane, France
Airport, Berre, France (project)

1950 New Town of Gif, France

1952 Church of St. Joseph, Le Havre

Town Hall, Le Havre
Aircraft hangars, Marignane, France

1953/
55 David Weill Building, Boulevard Berthier, Paris

Publications:

By PERRET: book—*Contribution à une Théorie de l'Architecture,* Paris 1952; articles—"Le Musée Moderne" in *Mouseion* (Paris), December 1929; "Architecture, Science et Poésie" in *La Construction Moderne* (Paris), October 1932; "Construire un Musée" in *Encyclopedie Francaise,* Paris 1938.

On PERRET: books—*A. et G. Perret et l'Architecture du Beton Armée* by P. Jamot, Paris and Brussels 1927; *Auguste Perret* by Ernesto N. Rogers, Milan 1955; *Auguste Perret* by Bernard Champigneulle, Paris 1959; *D'Une Doctrine d'Architecture: Auguste Perret* by Marcel Zahar, Paris 1959; *Concrete: The Vision of a New Architecture* by Peter Collins, London 1959; articles—"A. et G. Perret" by Jean Badovici in *Architecture Vivante* (Paris), Summer 1925; "Auguste Perret and Brothers" in *The Architects' Journal* (London), December 1926; "Auguste Perret" by M. E. Cahen in *L'Architecture d'Aujourd'hui* (Paris), January 1930; special issue of *L'Architecture d'Aujourd'hui* (Paris), October 1932; "The Doctrine of Auguste Perret" by Peter Collins in *Architectural Review* (London), August 1953; "The Work of Auguste Perret" by Ernö Goldfinger in *Architectural Association Journal* (London), January 1955; "Classicism and Rationalism in Perret" by Jean Prouvé and Vittorio Gregotti in *Domus* (Milan), May 1974; "The Last of the Master Builders" by Ernö Goldfinger in *Building Design* (London), 7 March 1975; "Auguste Perret" by Francoise Very in *Architecture Mouvement Continuité* (Paris), November 1975; "A. et G. Perret" by J.-B. Ache in *Construction Moderne* (Paris), May 1976.

Auguste Perret can justifiably be regarded as the creator of reinforced-concrete architecture, i.e. of an architecture in which all the elements of the reinforced-concrete structure remain visible externally and—as far as is practical—internally. Two fortuitous circumstances oriented him toward this research: the earliest systematic experiments in reinforced-concrete frame construction (patented in France by Hennebique in 1892) coincided with his own architectural training at the Ecole des Beaux-Arts; and his father, Claude Perret, was a building contractor who taught him to see architecture as literally "the art of building"—a methodical, carefully supervised process of assembling tectonic components.

Auguste Perret was also greatly influenced by Julien Guadet, who was not only his teacher at the Ecole des Beaux-Arts but also a personal friend. Guadet's theory of architecture was eventually published in book form, when it became the standard text on this topic for the next fifty years. Phrases such as "Truth is indispensable to architecture, and every architectural lie corrupts," and "Any project is bad if it is more difficult or more complicated to construct than necessary" indicate the doctrine he taught concerning the relationship between form and structure.

Auguste Perret's first opportunity to experiment systematically with the Hennebique system came in 1903 (i.e. when he was nearly thirty). His father wanted to construct an apartment building on a vacant lot in the fashionable residential district behind the Palais de Chaillot, but the area was too small for a profitable multi-story building in masonry. He initially opposed his son's proposal to build in reinforced-concrete (since Hennebique's patent precluded him from being the main contractor), but Auguste Perret eventually obtained his consent, and designed the building (22b rue Franklin) to take ingenious advantages of the topographical and legal constraints, and every advantage of the new structural system. The facade was covered with faience tiles, since concrete surfaces could not, at that time, be relied upon to resist the penetration of moisture. But the tiles were arranged in such as way as to express as clearly as possible the forms of the structural system employed.

After Claude Perret's death in 1905, Auguste and his brother Gustave changed the name of the firm to Perret Frères, and began specializing in reinforced-concrete construction. Initially they built only for other architects in accordance with the plans provided, but while so doing they experimented with the fundamental architectural problems that the new structural system presented. Of these, the most important (in Auguste Perret's opinion) was the problem of building reinforced-concrete *visibly*, as distinct from the then current assumption that the new material was only practicable as a concealed structural support.

Perret's first opportunity to demonstrate his solution to these problems occurred in 1922, when he was commissioned to design and build a large war-memorial church at Le Raincy, near Paris. Internally and externally, it was entirely of bare concrete. The roof was a thin shell; the slender vertical supports were carefully profiled monoliths; and the walls were a continuous grille of precast elements filled with stained glass. The beauty of the overall appearance effectively established the feasibility of using the new material to create a new architecture. As Henry-Russell Hitchcock asserts, it was at Notre Dame du Raincy that reinforced-concrete "came of age as a building material."

From then onward Auguste Perret's reputation as the pioneer of reinforced-concrete architecture was unchallengeable. But whereas the avant-garde theorists of the 1920's were mainly concerned with mass-produced housing and industrialization, Perret's research was directed towards technical refinements, whereby the system used at Le Raincy could be extended to every kind of monumental or multi-story building.

His main concern was to find methods of displaying the richness of the aggregate, to develop means of precasting all non-loadbearing elements, and to improve timber formwork in ways that would produce the most elegant profiles. The extent of his achievement can best be assessed by studying the apartment building that he designed and constructed at 51–55 rue Raynouard in 1932, and the Mobilier National (also in Paris) designed and built in 1934.

After World War II Auguste Perret was charged with the reconstruction of Le Havre, a large seaport completely flattened by aerial bombardment. His scheme was subject to some criticism at the time because it did not conform to the precepts of the CIAM "Athens Charter," but it effectively demonstrated his concept of architecture as a harmonious environment in sympathy with existing urban traditions.

—Peter Collins

PERSICO, Edoardo.

Italian. Born in Naples in 1900. Educated at the University of Naples, as a law student, 1920–24; Atelier Lionello Venturi, Turin, 1927–29. Worked as an art critic, Turin, 1925–28, and as a laborer, Fiat Automobile Company, Turin, 1927–28; on the editorial staff of *Motor Italia*, Turin, 1927; Founder Member, Group of Six, Turin, 1928; Founder Director, with Pietro Maria Bardi, Bardi Art Gallery (later renamed Galleria Bardi, then Galleria del Milione), and Editor of the gallery's journal *Belvedere*, Milan, 1929–36; Editor, 1930–33, and Co-Director, with Giuseppe Pagano, 1933–36, *Casabella*, Milan; concentrated on architecture, associating with the architects Giuseppe Pagano, Levi-Montalcini, Alberto Sartoris, and Ettore Sottsass, Milan, 1931–36. *Died* (in Milan) *10 January 1936.*

Works:

1927   Edoardo Persico House interiors, Naples
1933   Design of the *Triennale*, Milan
1934   Advertising Display Structure, Galleria, Milan (with Marcello Nizzoli)
      Hall of Gold Medals, *Italian Aeronautical Exhibition*, Milan
      Art Gallery, Milan (with Marcello Nizzoli)
      Gianni Mazzocchi Studio interiors, Milan
      Antonio Cazzaniga Studio interiors, Milan
1934/
  35   Parker Shop, Largo Santa Margherita, Milan (with Marcello Nizzoli)
      Parker Shop, Corso Vittorio Emanuele, Milan (with Marcello Nizzoli)
1935   Domus Stand, *Trade Fair*, Bari, Italy
1936   Salon of Honor, *Triennale*, Milan (with G. Palanti and Marcello Nizzoli)

Publications:

By PERSICO: books—*Arte Romana*, Milan 1935; *Dopo Sant'Elia*, editor, Milan 1935; *Profezia dell'Architettura*, Milan 1947; *Edoardo Persico: Tutte le Opere*, edited by Giulia Veronesi, Milan 1964; *Edoardo Persico: Oltre l'Architettura, Scritti Scelti e Lettere*, edited by R. Mariani, Milan 1977.

On PERSICO: books—*Edoardo Persico*, Milan 1936; *Edoardo Persico: Introduzione agli scritti critici e polemici* by Alfonso Gatto, Milan 1947; *Storia dell' Architettura Moderna* by Bruno Zevi, Turin 1950; *Difficolta Politiche dell'Architettura in Italia* by Giulia Veronesi, Milan 1953; *Diario in Pubblico* by E. Vittorini, Milan 1957; *L'Idea di Architettura: Storia della Critica da Viollet-le-Duc a Persico* by R. de Fusco, Milan 1964; articles—"Edoardo Persico e Morto" by Alfonso Gatto in *Casabella* (Milan), January 1936; "Negozi a Milano" by R. Giolli in *Casabella* (Milan), January 1937; "Edoardo Persico e la Crisi dell'Architettura" by L. Sinisgalli in *Furor Mathematicus*, Milan 1950; "Edoardo Persico" by Nikolaus Pevsner in *Architectural Review* (London), February 1966; "The Designs of Persico" by Maria Luisa Madonna in *Ottagono* (Milan), June 1978.

As a law student in Naples, Edoardo Persico submitted a thesis on the right to strike: perhaps not unexpectedly, it was not accepted. Soon afterwards, however, he found his milieu. While studying at the school of Lionello Venturi in Turin, he made contact with the circle of Gobetti and Gramsci and began to contribute to Gobetti's review, and it was from this group that the first germ of a left-wing culture in Italy emerged. From that time Persico showed great intellectual and moral firmness, together with an unyielding, courageous anti-Fascism. He became the leading spirit in the Group of Six, the first group of Italian artists who, supported by Venturi and Casorati, tried to fight their way out of a narrow provincial culture.

His life in Turin was hard. He was actually an unskilled worker at Fiat, at the time that Matté Trucco's Fiat Nugget, a lovely example of a new architecture, was being built. It may have been the start of his passion for architecture. While still in Turin he studied the avant-garde architects—Pagano, Levi-Montalcini, Sartoris, Perona, Sottsass. But, whatever the source, he came to believe that the future liberty of man would spring from freedom of the arts.

Toward the end of his time in Turin he was imprisoned on a political charge and suffered severe beatings, and when he was released his health was in ruins. In 1929 he moved to Milan. With Pietro Maria Bardi, he founded the Bardi Art Gallery (which in the 1930's mounted the first exhibition of Italian abstract artists), and became the editor of the gallery's arts review, *Belvedere*. His association with Giuseppe Pagano on the architectural review *La Casa Bella* (later *Casabella*) was even more fruitful. Pagano was less dogmatic than Persico in his attitude to the cultural fashions of the time, but his spontaneous enthusiasm combined with Persico's lucidity and intransigence made *Casabella* a valuable instrument in the defense of freedom of expression.

Persico's opposition to the cultural tenets of Fascism found expression in the fierce political criticism contained in his polemics on architecture: he contrasted international culture with the shut-in situation in Italy; he resisted the regime and the culture it tried to impose. He was an outspoken supporter of rational architecture, and found its roots not in Cubism ("or it would have died in infancy") but "in the wake of Impressionism: Wright may be looked on as the Cezanne of the new architecture."

Besides giving *Casabella* a graphic quality in harmony with the lines of rationalist culture, Persico was also responsible, with Marcello Nizzoli, for exhibits, interior design, and shops. His most important works include the Hall of Gold Medals at the *Italian Aeronautical Exhibition* in Milan in 1934 and the Salon of Honor at the sixth Milan *Triennale*, in which the lucid, severe vision of limpid linear scansion rises up into a highly calibrated spaciousness lit by soft, diffused light.

Edoardo Persico died before he could know what would happen to the brave new world he imagined. Manfredo Tafuri speaks of the "meta-historic abstraction of architecture that tends to enclose itself in the incommunicable abstraction of its own aura," and he singles out this period as one in which research and theory could be disinterested, compelled as the researchers and theorists were to shut themselves away in a hermeticism that, psychologically at least, could give them the hope of their own convictions. But Persico was probably more of a realist

Edoardo Persico: Hall of Gold Medals, *Italian Aeronautical Exhibition*, Milan, 1934

than that description suggests. As Giulia Veronesi has pointed out, Persico, in his attempt to link all varieties of culture together, "identified the problem of literature with that of painting and that of architecture: all of them involved the problems of life itself, the hard life of every man."

—Lara-Vinca Masini

PIACENTINI, Marcello.

Italian. Born in Rome, 8 December 1881; son of the architect Pio Piacentini. Educated at the Accademia di San Luca, Rome, 1901–04, Dip.Arch. 1904. Served in the Italian Army during World War I. In private practice, Rome, from 1906. Served as the Government Architect (principal architect to Mussolini). Professor, Scuola Superiore di Architettura. Rome. Editor, *L'Architettura*, Rome, 1922–43. President, National Committee on City Planning, and National Council of Architects. Recipient: First Prize, Civic Centre Competition, Bergamo, Italy, 1903; First Prize, Quirinal Traffic Tunnel Competition, Rome, 1908; First Prize, University of Bergamo Competition, 1910; Grand Prize for Architecture, *World's Fair*, Brussels, 1910; Grand Prize and Gold Medal, *Esposizione di Roma*, 1911; Special Grand Prize, *Pan Pacific Exposition*, San Francisco, 1915; First Prize, Memorial Arch Competition, Genoa, 1923; Gold Medal, City of Turin, 1935. Honorary doctorates: Accademia di Genoa, Urbino, Perugia, and Bologna. *Died* (in Rome) *in 1960.*

Works:

1903   Civic Centre, Bergamo, Italy (competition project)
1908   Quirinal Traffic Tunnel, Rome (competition project)
1910   Italian Pavilion, *World's Fair*, Brussels
       Master plan for the University of Bergamo, Italy

1911   Plan for the *Esposizione di Roma* (with A. Giustini and C. Bazzani)
       Palazzo delle Feste, Rome
       Pavilion, Piazza Colonna, Rome
       Villa Berlingier, Rome (with Pio Piacentini)
1915   Quirino Theatre restoration, Rome
       Villa Rusconi, Rome
       Villa Cavaglieri, Rome
       Villa Allegri, Rome
       Villa Page, Rome
       Villa Nobili, Rome
       Villa Gaspari, Rome
       Italian Pavilion, *Pan Pacific Exposition*, San Francisco
1917   Cinema, Rome (competition project)
       Villa, Via Settembrini, Rome
       2 villas, Viale della Regina, Rome
       Villa, Viale Liegi, Rome
       Terraced houses, Piazza del Viminale, Rome
       Restaurant, Rinascente Department Store, Rome
1918   Banca d'Italia Building, Piazza del Paramento, Rome
1919   Marmorata Bridge, Rome
1922   Cinema-Theatre Savoia, Florence
1925   Quirinetta Theatre, Rome
       Palazzo Pateras, Rome
       Villa Giovve, Rome
       Villa della Bitta, Rome
       Villa Peragallo, Rome
       Villa Testasecca, Rome
1926   Ambassador's Hotel, Rome
1927   Villa Glori Racecourse, Rome
       Master plan for the centre of Bergamo, Italy
       Argentina Theatre restoration, Rome
       Palace of the League of Nations, Geneva (competition project)
1927/
   32 Piazza della Vittoria, Brescia, Italy: Central Post Office, National Assurance Institute, and National Treasury of Social Assurance
1928   Casa Madre dei Mutilati, Rome
       War Memorial, Bolzano, Italy
       Law Courts, Messina
1930   Cinema-Theatre Barberini, Rome
       Piazza Missori, Milan
       Cassa Nazionale delle Assicurazioni Sociali Building, Milan
1932   Memorial Arch, Genoa
       Via Regina Elena, Rome
       City Corporation Building, Rome (with G. Vaccaro)
       International Temple of Peace, Rome
       City Centre and Via della Conciliazione, Rome (with Attilio Spacciarelli)
       Luigi Cadorna Mausoleum, Pallanza, now Verbania, Italy
       Palazzo degli Studi, Foggia, Italy
       Wedekind Mausoleum, Acqui Ottolenghi, Italy
1933   University City, Rome (as chief architect; with Arnaldo Poschini, Pietro Aschieri, Giuseppe Capponi, Giuseppe Pagano, Giovanni Michelucci, Gaetano Rapisardi, and Gio Ponti)
1934   Church of Christ the King, Rome
1936   Banca Nazionale del Lavoro Headquarters, Rome
       Rectorate, University City, Rome
       General Insurance Building, Jerusalem
1937   Italian Pavilion, *Exposition Internationale*, Paris
1937/
   40 *Esposizone Universale*, Rome (as supervising architect)
1938   Via Roma, Turin
1940   Law Courts, Milan
1941   Magna Grecia Museum, Reggio Calabria, Italy
1942   Master plan for the E.42 district, Rome (with others)
       Piazza della Vittoria, Genoa

Marcello Piacentini: University City, Rome, 1933

Master plan for University City, Rio de Janeiro (with V. Morpurgo)
1959 Palazzo dello Sport, Rome (with Pier Luigi Nervi)

Publications:

By PIACENTINI: books—*Architettura d'Oggi,* Rome 1930; *Volto di Roma,* Rome 1945.

On PIACENTINI: books—*Architettura Moderna in Italia* by A. Pica, Milan 1941; *L'Eclettismo a Roma 1870–1922* by Paulo Portoghesi, Rome 1969; *European Architecture of the Twentieth Century* by Arnold Whittick, London 1974; articles—"Marcello Piacentini mori nel 1925" by Bruno Zevi in *L'Architettura* (Rome), 1958; article by P. Marconi in *L'Architetto* (Rome), August 1960.

To appreciate the work of Marcello Piacentini it is essential to know its political and social background. Piacentini was Mussolini's principal architect throughout the major period of the Fascist regime. Mussolini dreamed of restoring the ancient glories of Imperial Rome and instigated numerous large reconstruction schemes for the centres of some of the principal cities. Piacentini carried out and made projects for several of these, principally at Brescia, Turin and Rome. His best work, in which his qualities as a planner and architect are most conspicuous, is the University City in Rome. Piacentini aimed in his design to combine the severe simple character of modern concrete building with classical monumentality—to combine in short the grandeur of Rome with the modern spirit, a goal inspired by his principal client.

His earliest large scale urban scheme, the Piazza della Vittoria at Brescia and the surrounding buildings, gives a clear indication of the character of his work. The buildings are constructed of reinforced concrete frames with brick infillings faced with mar-

ble, occasionally patterned, in the traditional Italian mediaeval and Renaissance manner. There is some mixture of traditional influences, Greek, Roman and Romanesque, but each is much simplified to flatness and bare outlines. The immense Post Office building is a massive square Greek portico; the National Assurance Institute and Social Assurance Buildings have flat simplified treatment with marble encrustation and Romanesque arcading.

A notable achievement in urban renewal is Piacentini's replanning and reconstruction of a central area of Rome to improve transport facilities as well as the setting of the fine buildings of ancient Rome and the Renaissance. The work was done in collaboration with Attilio Spacciarelli and involved the demolition of mean buildings and the introduction of a handsome avenue—the via della Conciliazione—from the Tiber to the Piazza S. Pietro. It is a vast improvement in this central area, and it is difficult to resist the belief that the adverse criticism that has been made is partly the result of its association with the Fascist regime.

Perhaps Piacentini's most conspicuous success is the University City in Rome, which invites comparison with the new building complex of London University. Both are classically inspired. In the former there is a happier disposition of buildings, for the City is really a large garden in which monumental buildings are grouped and for the most part looking inward. Piacentini was the controlling architect, and he assembled a team of the best known Italian architects to assist him. The general impression of the buildings is that one mind controlled for the most part the essential character of the whole. The aims are explained by Piacentini himself. He is speaking of the Roman piazzi, which he says "are born of a symmetrical order, but the single buildings each take forms characteristic of their service. So it is with this University City. Born of an idea of a basilical and transept plan, it draws all its impressiveness from order and fundamental symmetry," and he speaks of the differences in the buildings. The undoubted unity

of the whole could be criticized as possessing sameness, for the buildings follow in character Piacentini's own immense and dominating Rectorate building which also houses the Great Hall and Library. This sets the keynote of the whole. The lofty square columns of the central portico, the patterning of windows on the plain flanking blocks, the lettered frieze, and the large sculptured reliefs give large scale decorative notes to the walls, and the good proportion and monumental scale are impressive.

This semblance of modernity given to the architecture of a classic Mediterranean clime is also a monumental expression of a political era.

—Arnold Whittick

PIANO, Renzo.

Italian. Born in Genoa, 14 September 1937. Educated at the Polytechnic, Milan, 1959–64, Dip.Arch. 1964. Married Magda Arduino in 1962; children: Carlo, Matteo and Lia. Lecturer, Polytechnic of Milan, 1965–68. Since 1970, Partner, with Richard Rogers, *q.v.,* Piano and Rogers Architects, London, Paris and Genoa; since 1977, Partner, with Peter Rice, Piano and Rice, engineers and architects, Genoa, Paris and London. Visiting Lecturer, Columbia University, New York, 1967, University of Pennsylvania, Philadelphia, 1967, University of Bucharest, 1968, and Polytechnic of Delft, 1969; Professor of Architecture, Architectural Association School, London, and Polytechnic of Central London, 1971; Visiting Lecturer, Unesco, Paris, 1973, and Oslo School of Architecture, 1976. Exhibitions: *Triennale,* Milan, 1967; Architectural Association, London, 1970; Musée des Arts Décoratifs, Paris, 1973. Recipient: First Prize, Place Beaubourg Competition, Paris, 1971; Auguste Perret Prize, International Union of Architects, 1978. Address: Studio Piano and Rice, Viale G. Modugno 22, 16156 Genoa, Italy.

Works:

1968 Olivetti Factory Roof Components, Ivrea, Italy (with M. Zanuso)
1969 Residential district, Genoa
Olivetti-Underwood Factory Roof Components, Harrisburg, Virginia
1970 Shell/Esso Prefabricated Service Station System
Italian Industry Pavilion, *Expo '70*, Osaka, Japan
1970 Fitzroy Street Commercial Centre, Cambridge (with Richard Rogers and Fitzroy Robinson)
ARAM Inc. Medical Centre, Washington, D.C. (with Richard Rogers)
1971 B & B Italia Offices, Como, Italy (with Richard Rogers)
Clasp Italiana Ltd. Brockhouse Steel Structures (building system), Birmingham, England (with Richard Rogers)
1972 Universal Oil Products United Kingdom Head Office, and UOP Fragrances Ltd. Laboratory, Tadworth, Surrey (with Richard Rogers)
1973 Aston Martin Lagonda Ltd. Offices, Showroom, Restaurant, Squash Court and Housing, London (with Richard Rogers)
1975 PA Management Consultants (PATScentre) Research Laboratories, Workshops and Ancillary Administration Building, Cambridge, England (with Richard Rogers)
Housing and recreation areas, for Globe Construction Ltd., at Basildon, Essex, England (with Richard Rogers)
1977 Institut de Récherche et de Coordination Acoustique, for Pierre Boulez, Paris (with Richard Rogers)
Centre Beaubourg, Paris (with Richard Rogers and Ove Arup and Partners)

Publications:

By PIANO: book—*The Building of Beaubourg,* with Richard Rogers and others, London 1978; article—"Architecture and Technology" in *Architectural Association Quarterly* (London), July 1970.

On PIANO: articles—"Structural Plastics in Europe" in *Arts and Architecture* (Los Angeles), August 1966; "Uno Studio Laboratorio" in *Domus* (Milan), October 1968; "Nuove Techniche & Nuove Strutture per L'Edilizia" in *Domus* (Milan) November 1968; "Industrial Roofing" in *Architectural Forum* (New York), March 1970; "Espo '70, Osaka" in *Accaio* (Milan), November 1970; "Industrialized Construction" in *Deutsche Bauzeitung* (Stuttgart), April 1971; "Concours Beaubourg" in *Architecture Mouvement Continuité* (Paris), November 1971; "Centre Beaubourg, Paris" in *Techniques et Architecture* (Paris), February 1972; "L'Evoluzione del Progetto per il Centro Beaubourg" in *Domus* (Milan), June 1972; "Centre Beaubourg" in *Arkitekten* (Copenhagen), September 1972; "Piano † Rogers, Paris" in *L'Architecture d'Aujourd'hui* (Paris), November/December 1973; "B and B Italia Building" in *Architectural Design* (London), April 1974; "Centre Beaubourg" in *Acier-Stahl-Steel* (Brussels), September 1975; "Eiffel vs. Beaubourg" in *Werk-Archithese* (Niedertaufen), September 1977; "Centro Beaubourg" in *Informes de la Construccion* (Madrid), April 1978.

My attitudes about architecture spring from a critical attitude towards static design process definitions. Architectural planning that has been statically conceived and schematically organized in an initial analysis of problems, with a subsequent isolation of

Renzo Piano: Construction of glass reinforced plastic roof, Genoa, 1966

remedies (mostly slow ones), plus the whole university teaching set-up based on analysis and subsequent design synthesis, all combine to show a profound inconsistency with the fluid and changing reality of things. This type of approach inevitably overlooks the complex question of time, which transcends the objective limits of the project.

A different kind of attitude must be pursued. I would define this as a dynamic, open attitude, which interprets analysis as constant critical action and makes the time dimension act within the process. It has to be dynamic in order to counter the attitude hitherto defined as static, inasmuch as it must refuse to freeze reality into a relatively immobile view and, hence, to freeze the intentions and end-purposes of the project itself. This approach is accomplished by means of the completion of operative design tools such as design methods and, within the project itself, structural and technological research.

The use of these reconsidered tools makes it possible to recover a number of control phases within the design process, which have the capacity to introduce levels of complexity that were lost in the initial definition stages.

The result of this design experience is the establishment of a wider range of possible answers to the problem, and the extraction of a conclusive object within this range, which ensures a better adherence to its complex character.

—Renzo Piano

Architecture can be analyzed according to how fully its maker expresses the building as an object, as a construct, or as a container. By "an object" one means primarily an artifact to be appreciated; "construct" refers to the actual building methods and means; and "container" conveys how well the building's intended uses were fulfilled. Of course any successful architectural design has to take account of all three, but a polemical architect may preoccupy him-

self with one or perhaps two. Renzo Piano has been a constructor. While his buildings certainly encompass successfully all three objectives, structural developments are decidedly his conceptual points of departure.

Though national architecture means little today, there was something essentially Italian in his early pursuit of concrete factory frames and in his refining and perfecting of them. As with Nervi and other Italian masters, Piano's opportunities arose through the flexibility of the designer's professional role in Italy (engineers and architects can also be builders or developers, without ethical difficulty), together with the good luck of having industrialists in his own family who were able to commission some of his earlier work.

None of this would have come to international attention had Piano not met Richard Rogers in London and won the Centre Pompidou ("Beaubourg") competition with him and Ove Arup and Partners. Piano's contribution was equal to that of Rogers, but Piano was especially concerned with structure and overall design logic expressed in construction patterns. He functioned as an effective leader but even more as a smooth coordinator. Like Rogers, his social skills in the evolutionary process of that design have been underestimated, but they may be his most solid achievement to date, and even his greatest example to others.

Since 1977 Piano has been in partnership with Peter Rice, the leading structural engineer on Beaubourg's superstructure.

—Nathan Silver

PIETILÄ, Reima.

Finnish. Born in Turku, 25 August 1923. Educated at the Institute of Technology, Helsinki, 1945–53, Dip. Arch. 1953. Served in the Finnish Army, 1942–44: Corporal. Married the architect Raili Paatelainen in 1961; daughter: Annukka. In private practice with Raili Pietilä, Helsinki, since 1960. Professor of Architecture since 1973, and Dean of the Department of Architecture since 1978, University of Oulu, Finland. Exhibitions: *Morphology Urbanism,* Helsinki (one-man), 1960; *Zone,* Helsinki (one-man), 1967; *Space Garden,* Helsinki (one-man), 1972. Recipient: First Prize, Finnish Pavilion for the Brussels *World's Fair* Competition, 1956; First Prize, Finnish Embassy at New Delhi Competition, 1963; First Prize, New Tampere Library Competition, 1979. Honorary Professor of Arts, Finland, 1971–72. Honorary Member, Swedish Royal Academy of Arts, 1969; Honorary Fellow, American Institute of Architects, 1975; Honorary Member, SAFA (Finnish Architects Association). Address: Raili and Reima Pietilä Architects, Laivurinrinne 1A, 17 Helsinki 12, Finland.

Works:

1953 Porin Sato Housing (competition project; with Viljo Revell and M. Jaatinen)
1958 Finnish Pavilion, *World's Fair,* Brussels

With Raili Pietilä:

1963 Finnish Embassy, New Delhi, India (competition project)
1966 Kaleva Church, Tampere, Finland
      Dipoli International Conference Centre, Institute of Technology, Otaniemi, Finland
1966/
  69 Suvikumpu Housing Development, Tapiola New Town, Espoo, Finland
1967 Malmi Church, Helsinki (project)
1970 Central Government Offices Plan, Sief Palace Area, Kuwait City (project)
1972 Hvitträsk Sauna Bath Building, Eliel Saarinen Museum Centre, Kirkkonummi, Finland
      Reidar Särestoniemi Swimming Pool, Sauna and Art Gallery, Kittilä, Lapland, Finland
1974 Dubai Corniche (project)
1975 Cultural Services Master Plan, Hervanta New Town, Tampere, Finland
1979 Congregational Centre, Leisure Centre, and Shopping Hall, Hervanta New Town, Tampere, Finland
      City Library, Tampere, Finland (competition project)
1981 His Highness The Emir's Office reception area extension, Sief Palace, Kuwait City
      Council of Ministers Building, and Ministry of Foreign Affairs Building, Sief Palace Area, Kuwait City

Publications:

By PIETILÄ: books—*Centres and Noncentres,* Helsinki 1969; *Concept of Visual Entity in Environmental Design,* Wageningen, Holland 1971; *Architectures "Totales" et "Partielles" dans le Contexte d'une Image Morphologique de l'Environnement,* Arc-et-Senans, France 1973; *Notion, Image, Idea: Notes on Architectural Teaching,* Otaniemi, Finland 1974; *Leisure Time Architecture,* Helsinki 1977; articles—"La Morphologie de l'Expression Plastique" and "La Théorie de la Composition" in *Le Carré Bleu* (Paris), no. 1, 1958.

On PIETILÄ: books—*Arquitectura Finlandesa* by Maria Borras, Barcelona 1967; *Novaij Architektura*

Finlandii by A. Ikonnikov, Moscow 1972; *Meaning in Western Architecture* by Christian Norberg-Schulz, New York 1975; articles—in *Perspecta* (New Haven, Connecticut), no. 8, 1963; *Comunità* (Milan), no. 131, 1965; *Archetype* (Melbourne), no. 6, 1971; *Architecture + Urbanism* (Tokyo), no. 9, 1974.

*

My wife and I are figuratively married to architecture as we live and work together as a married couple. Architecture is present also in our domestic life. Sitting over breakfast from 6 until 8 in the mornings we talk of new ideas and solve practical detail problems: thus the most creative and genuine experience of architecture comes to us undisturbed by the later busy work in the studio. Our weekends are completely dedicated to creative activity: thus architecture is our leisure, our hobby.

There are several working teams of married architects like ourselves still active in Finland, and we believe they will have an important role to play in improving the quality of architecture in the future.

We also believe that architecture, in its contemporary and inimitable form, is our basic cultural commodity and as such is original as art. And only as such can architecture help man to experience his environment profoundly and conceive the quality of his own culture. A genuine architecture helps man to be positively more acceptable and perceptive to himself. Design should not stop at the stage of a mere performance—form has also to convey emotion.

Architecture must be "local," expressing an appearance of the local nature. Finnish architecture should be organically one with its own evergreen Arctic forest, united with the "form-language" of the forest. Also, the rhythms of architectural structure and form should be national and characteristic, expressing the shape of space. Colours are to be closely related to nature, providing a strong tie to our cultural heritage.

This architecture is freed from the international types of superficial generality and without fashionable names.

We strive for an architecture that by nature makes minds more sensitive to the built-up environment. We aim for this with all possible means, independent of any modern direction and moving freely amongst all the cultural periods of man. We try to do this without repeating ourselves.

We try to renew our basic grasp and vision in each new task. Thus we hope to bring forth a development and show that there are still areas in contemporary architecture open to exploration.

—Reima Pietilä

*

Reima Pietilä was born in Turku two years after Alvar Aalto received his architectural diploma in Helsinki at the age of 23. This places him in the generation of Finnish architects we might refer to as "post-Aalto," although Pietilä did not graduate until he was 30 and his first commission was not undertaken until 1957, when he was already 34. Thus, hardly precocious, he was a late developer who has balanced relatively short spells of building with longer periods of thinking and working out his architectural philosophy. He is widely read in psychology, philosophy and cultural history; and, one of the most articulate of modern practitioners, he expresses himself wittily in English.

He first attracted international attention with the design for the Finnish Pavilion at the Brussels *World Fair,* won in competition in 1956 and executed in 1958. References to Aalto are clearly detectable in this pavilion, particularly to the sports hall at Otaniemi (1949–54). No further buildings came from Pietilä's studio until the mid-1960's. In the meantime, he married a fellow architect, Raili Paatelainen, in 1961, which has resulted in a charming continuity and harmony between home and office that is firmly within the Finnish tradition. The first products of this partnership were the "Dipoli" International Conference Centre for Otaniemi, and the Kaleva Church in Tampere, both completed in 1966.

The Kaleva Church is indisputably one of the most successful religious interiors of this century, although the original concrete exterior was modified and clad in brick tiles at the request of the parish council, divorcing it entirely from the interior quality and expression it was intended to reflect.

With the successes of "Dipoli", the Kaleva Church and the unrealised Finnish Embassy at New Delhi, Pietilä established himself as the master of an original architectural expression, a mastery he has retained in his recent successful competition entry for the new Tampere City Library. Also, by the time he undertook the design of the Suvikumpu housing area for Tapiola, Pietilä had emerged as the intellectual leader of his generation of Finnish architects, a situation deriving very much from his years of enforced contemplation, his model experiments and his contributions to *Le Carré Bleu.*

In recognition of this stature, he was awarded the national Professorship of Arts in 1971–72 and appointed to the Chair of Design in Oulu University in 1973. Since then he has divided his time between Oulu and an increasingly busy office in Helsinki. In 1972 he completed a sauna at Hvitträsk Culture Centre (formerly the studio home of Saarinen, Gesellius and Lindgren) and a sauna and art gallery for the artist Särestoniemi at Kittilä in Lapland. But his major works of the 70's have centered on Tampere and Kuwait City. Just outside Tampere in the New Town of Hervanta there is a parish centre, leisure centre, and a shopping hall, due to be completed in 1979; while 1979 also gave him first prize in the competition for the new Tampere Library and with it a chance to leave another mark on the city proper. In Kuwait City the Pietiläs have designed the Ministry of Foreign Affairs, the Council of Ministers Building and an extension to the Emir's reception hall in the Sief Palace, the interiors especially reflecting the strength of their collaboration.

—Malcolm Quantrill

PIKIONIS, Dimitris A.

Greek. Born in Piraeus in June 1887. Studied civil engineering at the Athens Polytechnic, 1904–08; painting and sculpture in Munich, 1908; architecture in Paris, 1909–12; drawing and ornamentation at the School of Fine Arts, Athens, 1923, Diploma 1923. Served in the Greek Army, 1912–21. Married Alexandra Anastasion in 1927; had two daughters and three sons. In private practice, Athens, 1923 until his death, 1968. Head, Architectural Team, Ministry of Rebuilding, Athens, 1946–47. Lecturer, 1921–23, Associate Professor, 1925–30, and Professor, 1930–57, National Technical University, Athens. Member, Greek Popular Art Association, 1937–40. Exhibitions: Academy of Fine Arts, Munich, 1961; *Dimitris Pikionis,* National Gallery, Athens, 1978. Member, Academy of Athens, 1966. Member, Academy of Fine Arts, Munich, 1966. *Died* (in Athens) *27 August 1968.*

Works:

1921/
  23 Moraitis House, Tzitzifies, Neo Faliro, Greece
1925 Karamanos House, Patissia, Irakliou Road, Athens
1926 School and Residence, Island of Egina, Greece (project; with E. Kriezis)
1927 Church of Agion Anargyron, Nea Ionia, Athens (project; with E. Kriezis)
      Papaloukas House, Chalepa Square, Athens
1928 Carayannis House, Mitsaki Road, Athens
1930 Papaioannou House, Markora Road, Patissia, Athens
1932 Summer Theatre, Marika-Kotopouli, Hayden Road, Athens

Reima Pietilä: Kaleva Church, Tampere, Finland, 1966

1933 School of Lycabetus, Athens
1933/
35 Garis House, Psychico, Athens
Gionis House, Ellinico, Athens
Caloyannis House, Ellinico, Athens
Porfyras Tomb, Anastaseas Cemetery, Piraeus
Paoli Family Tomb, Anastaseas Cemetery, Piraeus
Gounaraki Family Tomb, First Cemetery, Athens
Experimental School, University of Salonika
1936 Small building, Hayden Road, Athens (with N. Mitsakis)
1938 Craftsman's Pavilion, Neo Faliro, Greece (project)
1942 Mitsakis Gravestone design
1949 Efthymiadi-Menegaki Studio/House, Grypari Road, Patissia, Athens
1950/
57 Aixoni Housing Development, Glyfada, Greece (with others)
Master plan for the surroundings of the Acropolis and the Hill of Philopappou, Athens
Building complex, St. Dimitrios-Lombardiaris, Athens
1953 University of Salonika Forest Village, Pertouli-Trikalon, Greece
Hotel Xenia, Delphi, Greece (with A. Papageorgiou)
Garis House, Parnassos Road, Psychico, Athens
Potamianos House, Ano Philothei, Athens
1960/
68 Children's playground, Philothei, Athens (with P. Pikionis and A. Coutsoyannis)
Town Hall, Volos, Greece (project)
Fortetzas Tourist Development, Rethymnon, Crete (project)
Stamatopoulos House, Kypriadou, Athens
Development surrounding the Velissarios Monument, Kymymi, Greece
St. Paul's Church, Ethniki Estia, Greece

Publications:

By PIKIONIS: books—*Dodecanissos* (The Problem of Form), Athens 1950; *Antonis Sochos,* Athens 1961; *Fortetzas Tourist Development,* Athens 1966; *Autobiographical Notes,* Athens 1968; articles—"Our Popular Art and Us" in *Filiki Eteria* (Athens), April 1925; "The Painter Steris" in *Proia* (Athens), 23 April 1931; numerous articles in *Technica Chronica* (Athens), 1933–58, *To Trito Mati* (Athens), 1935–37, *Aixoni* (Athens), 1950–54, and *Zygos* (Athens), 1956–66; "About Greek Tradition" in *Epoches* (Athens), January 1964.

On PIKIONIS: books—*Greek Art and Architecture 1945–1967* by Dimitris A. Fatouros, volume 8 of *Balkan Studies,* Salonika 1967; *The Architect Dimitris Pikionis* by Z. Lorentzatos, Athens 1969; *The Life and Work of Pikionis* by Ch. Tsilalis, Salonika 1969; *Dimitris Pikionis,* exhibition catalogue, Athens 1978; articles—"Entyposis ke Crisis" by Fotis Politis in *Politia* (Athens), 26, 28 and 29 June and 4 July 1923; "House of Filotlei" in *Architectoniki* (Athens), no. 1, 1957; special issue of *Zygos* (Athens), January/February 1958; "A Quiet Creator Who Deeply Influenced Greek Architecture" by M. Kalligas in *To Vima* (Athens), 20 May 1962; "Virtue and Form" by David Holden in *The Guardian* (London), 22 August 1963; "Architecture of the Road" by N. Kurokawa in *Ekistics* (Athens), November 1963; "The New Academician: Dimitris Pikionis" by A. Provelegios in *Nea Estia* (Athens), 1 June 1966; "An Unknown Work of Pikionis" by N. Moutsopoulos in *Icones* (Athens), 26 August 1966; "L'Architecture en Grèce" by Fr. Loyer in *SADG* (Paris), 2 July 1967; "Kinderspielplatze: Garten in Filothei bei Athen" by A. Papageorgiou in *Bauwelt* (Berlin), 1 July 1968; "Dimitris Pikionis: A Great Maître" by

K. Doxiades and "Pikionis: An Indelible Presence in the Neo-Hellenic World" by P. Psomopoulos in *To Vima* (Athens), 1 September 1968; "The Life and Work of Pikionis" in *Architektoniki* (Athens), September/October 1970; "Dimitris Pikionis: His Work Lies Underfoot on Athen's Hills" by Anthony C. Antoniades in *Landscape Architecture* (Louisville, Kentucky), March 1977; "Pikionis: Architecture as a Way of Life" by Dimitris A. Fatouros in *To Vima* (Athens), 14 February 1979.

*

Dimitris A. Pikionis played a singularly leading role in the formation of contemporary Greek architecture, and, even now, more than a decade after his death, he continues to influence Greek architectural thinking. Pikionis also contributed to the development of Greek art, working with such artists as Kondoglou, Diamandopoulos, Gkika and Tsarouhis. He tried to coordinate architecture with artistic creation and to define their functions within the particular conditions of the Greek environment.

Pikionis used two basic organizing systems: one is the spatial relationship—geometric organization; the other is, as it were, life, the behavior that is evoked or even demanded by each space, the socio-cultural relationship.

The first system is one of relations between the under, over and in between limits (the "three limits" space definition); the continuous and non-continuous; light and dark; the small and large in any spatio-situation; the interior and exterior of a building. He is concerned with neighborhood—the narrow pavement, moving between high walls, with a sudden opening where one lingers. That concern reveals itself in the volumes, small in size, in different variations, probably organized in "accumulative" order, with enclosures of large perpendicular planes—windows, doors, etc.

The second system involves human activities and behavior in each of these spaces—in the small atrium, enclosed all around by a high wall, next to, but removed from, the road; in the semi-covered space with the deep sensual shadow; inside a cavity on a bright road; in the spaces of the many different occasions of private life, man alone, in small groups, or in public.

Relying on these two systems, Pikionis organized his space according to the demands (and possibilities) of his country and in the service of its people—so far as his time allowed and always with admirable virtuosity..

The works of Pikionis anticipate by twenty years the tendencies of today's architecture to avoid large monolithic constructions, the high-rise and the oversize, and create small units structured in communications networks, closely related to the natural environment and to the psychological and physical scale of man.

All of his ideals are clearly revealed in his large and singularly significant reorganization of the area around the Acropolis with its carefully designed access routes, roads for cars and pedestrians, and its pavilions and small squares. His abiding socio-cultural philosophy is also expressed in the low-rise housing at Aixoni, near Athens, and in the playground at Philothei, where the spaces for games reflect elements of mythology.

The inspiration of Pikionis's architecture is not, obviously, a superficial reading of what is called, conventionally, "popular architecture." His buildings are his own interpretation of a Greek and Mediterranean reality—an interpretation with a worldwide utility and a revolutionary strength.

—Dimitris A. Fatouros

POELZIG, Hans.

German. Born in Berlin, 30 April 1869. Educated at the Viktoria-Gymnasium, Potsdam, Berlin, 1879; Technische Hochschule, Charlottenburg, Berlin, 1888–95; worked in Hugo Häring's Building Büro, Berlin, 1893–94; studied for the architect's license, 1896–98; licensed architect, 1899. Served in the German Army Infantry, 1894–95. Settled in Breslau, and practised there, 1899–1916; City Architect of Dresden, 1916–20; practised in Berlin, 1920 until his death, 1936. Director, Breslau Kunst Akademie, 1903–16; Head of the Department of Architecture, Kunst Akademie, Berlin, 1920–24; Professor, Technische Hochschule, Charlottenburg, 1924–33; Director of the Combined Schools of Art, Berlin, 1933 (resigned). Exhibition: *Poelzig, Endell, Moll und die Breslauer Kunst Akademie 1911–32,* Berlin, 1965. D.Eng.: Technische Hochschule, Stuttgart, 1929. Associate of the Akademie de Bildenkunst, 1933. *Died* (in Berlin) *in 1936.*

Works:

1901 Church tower, Breslau
Church organ loft, Trebnitz, Germany
1902 Organ for the University, Breslau (project)
1903 Castle and Parish Church renovation, Oels, Germany
1904 Single-family house, for the *Breslau Art Fair*
1905 Evangelical Church, Wultschkau, Germany
1906 Town Hall renovation, Lowenberg, Germany
Poelzig House, Leerbeutel, Breslau
Watermill, Breslau (project)
Evangelical Church, Maltsch, Germany
High Altar, Catholic Parish Church, Ziegenhals, Germany
1909 Castle Bridge, Königsberg, Germany (project)
1910 Water Tower, Hamburg (project)
Zwirner Youth House, Lowenberg, Germany
Castle, Brustawe, Germany (project)
1911 Water Tower, Posen, Germany, now Poznan, Poland
Bridge and Bridgehead, Cologne (project)
Bismarck Monument, Bingerbruck, Germany (project)
1912 Office building, Junkernstrasse, Breslau
Housing development, Breslau
Chemical factory and workers' housing, Luban, Germany, now Poland
Opera House, Berlin (project)
1913 Building Centenary Exhibition Building, Breslau
Chapel for a castle, Carolath, Germany
1914 Youth Hostel and Assembly Hall, Emmagrube (Oberschlesien), Germany (project)
Single-family house for the Community Garden City Society of Brockau, Breslau
1915 Franciscan Monastery, Glatz, Germany (project)
1916 Gasworks in Reick, Dresden
House of Friendship, Constantinople (project)
Fire Station, Dresden (project)
2 schools, Dresden (projects)
1917 Gasometer, Dresden (project)
Town house, Dresden (project)
Museum Complex, Dresden (project)
City plan for Dresden
1918 Bridge over the Elb, Dresden (project)
Concert Hall, Dresden (project)
1919 Grosses Schauspielhaus, Berlin
1920 Exhibition Pavilion, Dresden
Majolica Church, Dresden (project)
Film sets for *Der Golem*
1921 Hotel, Dresden (project)
Bank Building, Dresden (project)
Wooden housing, Hellerau, Germany (project)
1922 Festspielhaus, Salzburg (project)
Railway Headquarters Building, Friedrichstrasse, Berlin (project)
Majolica Fountain, Dresden

Hans Poelzig: Grosses Schauspielhaus, Berlin, 1919

1924 Meyer Company Administration Building,
       Vinnhorst, Hanover
     Meyer Company Storage Depot, Hanover
     City Theatre, Rheydt, Germany (project)
     Hotel Atlantic, Chemnitz, Germany (project)
     Shop renovations at the Zoo, Berlin
1925 Capitol Cinema Building, with shops, Berlin
     Concert Hall restoration, Breslau
     Exhibition Hall, Hamburg (project)
     Bridgehead, Cologne (project)
1926 Mosaic Fountain, Dresden
     Deli Cinema, Breslau
     House for the Free Secession, Berlin (project)
     Sportsground and Student Housing, Berlin
       (project)
1927 Sigmund Goeritz Factory, Chemnitz, Ger-
       many, now Karlmarxstadt, East Germany
     Sports Hall, Berlin (project)
     Professional Schools, Charlottenburg, Berlin
       (project)
     Concert Hall renovation, Beuthen, Germany
     Weekend house, Berlin
     Single-family house, Weissenhof Estate,
       Stuttgart
     Redevelopment plan for Republic Squares,
       Berlin (project)
     Palace of the League of Nations, Geneva
       (competition project)
1928 Redevelopment plan for the Scheunenviertels
       District, Berlin
     City centre plan for Hindenburg, Germany
     Housing block, Scheunenviertel District, Ber-
       lin
     Adam Building, Berlin (project)
     Single-family housing in the Gafgah District,
       Zehlendorf, Berlin

     Bridge over the Rhine at Speyer, Germany
       (project; with Gollnow und Sohn)
     Bridge over the Rhine at Maxau, Germany
       (project; with Gollnow und Sohn)
     Friedrich-Ebert Bridge, Mannheim (project)
     Tietz Company Warehouse, Breslau (project)
1929 Power station, Schulau, Germany (with
       Werner Issel)
     Babylon Cinema, Berlin
     Cassirer and Company Ltd. Cableworks,
       Spandau, Berlin
     Professional school in Urban, Berlin
     Community Centre, Kammin, Germany
     Reichstag Building extension, Berlin (project)
     Student House, Charlottenburg, Berlin (pro-
       ject)
     Stickstoffs Syndicate Administration Build-
       ing, Berlin (project)
     Single-family house, Kliedbruch, Krefeld,
       Germany
     Zoo extensions, Breslau (project)
     Bridge over the Rhine at Ludwigshafen, Ger-
       many (project; with Gollnow und Sohn)
1930 I. G. Farben Administration Building,
       Frankfurt
     Trade Fair, Berlin (with Martin Wagner)
     Broadcasting House, Berlin
     Theatre, Charkov, Russia (project)
1931 Palace of the Soviets, Moscow (project)
     Savings Bank, Wolgast, Germany
     Docks, Niederfinow, Germany (project)
1932 Single-family house, Berlin (exhibition pro-
       ject)
     Schauburg Theatre, Thuringer Wald, Ger-
       many (project)
     Film Studios, Gatow, Berlin (project)

     Development plan for the Dahlem District,
       Berlin
     Development plan for the Eichkamp District,
       Berlin
     Development plan for Am Waldfriedhof, Ber-
       lin
1933 Model Housing
     Development plan for the Augustaplatz,
       Leipzig
     Reichsbank extensions, Berlin (project)
     City Hall, Rostock, Germany (project)
1934 I. G. Farben Transport Building, Höchst,
       Germany (project)
1935 Opera House and Conservatoire, Istanbul
       (project)
     Friedrich Theatre, Dessau, Germany (pro-
       ject)
     Diplomat's house, Ankara (project)
     Barracks, Ankara (project)

Publications:

By POELZIG: book—*Der Architekt,* Stuttgart 1931;
article—"Werkbund" in *Wendingen* (Amsterdam),
November 1919.

On POELZIG: books—*Die Baukunst der Neuesten
Zeit* by G. A. Platz, Berlin 1930; *Hans Poelzig: Le-
bensbild eines Baumeister* by Theodor Heuss, Tubingen 1939, 1955; *Hans Poelzig: Bauten und Entwürfe*
by Theodor Heuss, Berlin 1939; *Poelzig, Endell,
Moll und die Breslauer Kunst Akademie 1911–32,*
exhibition catalogue, Berlin 1965; *Modern Architecture and Expressionism* by Dennis Sharp, London
1966; *Architecture and Politics in Germany 1918–
1945* by B. Miller Lane, Cambridge, Massachusetts

1968; *Hans Poelzig* by Julius Posener, Berlin 1970; articles—"Hans Poelzig" by H. G. Scheffauer in *Architectural Review* (London), October 1923; "Modern Tendencies in Architecture: The Work of Hans Poelzig" by A. Dresdner in *The Studio* (London), May 1931; "Poelzig" by Julius Posener in *Architectural Review* (London), June 1963; "Hans Poelzig" by F. Borsi in *Casabella* (Milan), October 1967.

Hans Poelzig could be described as an adventurous romantic. In the early part of his career he was restless, striving for an expressive architecture, impatient of imitating the styles of the past. In this striving for an originality that should be expressive, he was inevitably attracted to the new materials for large scale construction—steel and concrete, especially the plastic possibilities of concrete. If not a technical innovator, Poelzig was well abreast of modern movements and utilized technological developments to the full.

In his early buildings fulfilment of function is often enlivened with fanciful motifs, as in the introduction of segmental windows in a project for a watermill, combined with a modern steel and glass facade treatment in another part of the building. The segmental window was also introduced into the chemical factory that he built a little later at Luban, which schematically links with circular headed arcading. In his office building at Breslau (1912) Poelzig designed one of the earliest modern buildings with long horizontal emphasis—alternating horizontal bands of fenestration and wall—that was to become a familiar theme in departmental store and office buildings.

Varied experimentation is also characteristic of other works of his middle period. The water tower at Posen of 1911, which externally is a rather dull engineering structure of steel and glass with filed walling, yet has many ingenious fanciful internal features such as the serpentlike stairways. The exhibition building at Breslau is a modern essay in classicism, with domed halls and a heavy Dovic-like colonnade.

In his search for motifs to incorporate into architectural designs Poelzig turned to natural forms: we find them in some of his details for interior decoration where plant forms are sometimes rendered almost naturalistically. On a larger scale, mountain and rock forms often provided ideas, as in his project for the Festspielhaus, Salzburg. His crowning achievement of this kind is the Grosse Schauspielhaus, Berlin (1918–19), a reconstruction of a Schumann Circus building designed as a setting for Max Reinhardt's spectacular productions. This immense domed structure was clearly inspired by the cave with a profusion of stalactites, for these provide the interior decorative character. This building is often cited as an example of architectural expressionism, a movement of which Poelzig is sometimes regarded in architectural histories as one of the prime forces. The character of the Grosse Schauspielhaus results primarily, I think, from Poelzig's romantic feelings and from ideas derived from natural forms and his exploitation of the plasticity of concrete. Its conversion from a circus building facilitated the design with the Greek orchestra and open stage, while the stalactites have some acoustical justification.

Poelzig's fanciful and romantic impulses were again to combine successfully with functional design in cinemas built in the late 1920's in Berlin and Breslau, although these are much more restrained. His romantic impulses were never again to find so complete an expression in an actual building as in the unique Grosse Schauspielhaus.

—Arnold Whittick

POLLINI, Gino.

Italian. Born in Rovereto, 13 January 1903. Educated at the Milan Polytechnic, 1922–27, Dip.Arch. 1927. Served in the Italian Army, 1943. Married Renata Melotti in 1931; son: the pianist Maurizio Pollini. Founder Member, with Luigi Figini, *q.v.*, Guido Frette, Sebastiano Larco, Adalberto Libera, Carlo Enrico Rava and Giuseppe Terragni, *q.v.*, Gruppo 7, Milan, 1927–29. Since 1929, in partnership with Luigi Figini, Milan. Member, Municipal Committee for the Master Plan for the City of Milan, 1946. Professor-in-Charge, Faculty of Architecture, Milan Polytechnic, 1963–68; Professor and Director of the School of Architecture, University of Palermo, 1969–78. President, Lombardy Section, INU (Istituto Nazionale di Urbanistica), 1955–56. Member, CIAM (Congrés Internationaux d'Architecture Moderne), from 1929; Member, MIAR (Movimento Italiano per l'Architettura Razionale), 1930–32, and Quadrante, Milan, 1933–35. Exhibitions: Rationalist Architecture Exhibition, *Biennale*, Monza, Italy, 1927; *Triennale*, Monza, 1930; *Modern Architecture Exhibition*, Museum of Modern Art, New York, 1931; Union des Artistes Modernes, Paris, 1932; IV CIAM, Athens, 1933; CIAM Pavilion, *Triennale*, Milan, 1933; *Italian Aeronautical Exhibition*, Milan, 1934; *Triennale*, Milan, 1936; VII CIAM, Bergamo, 1949; *Italian Architecture*, London, and toured the United Kingdom, 1952; *The Modern Movement in Italy: Architecture and Design*, Museum of Modern Art, New York, and toured the United States, 1953; *Triennale*, Milan, 1954; *Mostra Documentaria dell' Architettura Sacra Italiana del Dopoguerra*, Bologna, 1955; *Triennale*, Milan, 1960; *Milano 70-70*, Museo Poldi Pezzoli, Milan, 1971; *Domus: 45 Anni de Architettura*, Louvre, Paris, 1973; *Il Razionalismo e l'Architettura Italiana durante il fascismo*, Venice, 1976. Member, Accademia di San Luca, 1963 Address: Architetti Figini/Pollini, Via Manin 3, 20121 Milan, Italy.

Works:

1927   Garage (project; with Gruppo 7)
        Casa del Dopolavoro (project; with Gruppo 7)
1930   Electric House, *Triennale*, Monza, Italy (with Gruppo 7)
1931   De Angeli-Frua Offices, Milan (with Luigi Figini and Luciano Baldessari)
        Bar Craja, Milan (with Luigi Figini and Luciano Baldessari)
1933   Artist's House and Studio, *Triennale*, Milan (with Luigi Figini)
1934   Sala dei Precursori, *Italian Aeronautical Exhibition*, Milan (with Luigi Figini)
        Palazzo del Littorio, *Mostra della Rivoluzione Fascista*, Rome (competition project; with Luigi Figini, BBPR, and Luigi Danusso)
1934/
57   Olivetti Factory, Nursery School, Workers' Housing and Social Services Centre, Ivrea, Italy (with Luigi Figini)
1935   Plan for the New Town of Ivrea, Italy (with Luigi Figini)
1936   Living Room and Roof Garden, *Triennale*, Milan (with Luigi Figini)
        Brera Academy, Milan (with Luigi Figini, Pietro Lingeri, and Giuseppe Terragni)
        Master plan for the Valle d'Aosta (with Luigi Figini, BBPR, Piero Bottoni and others)
1939   Sala del Volo, Milan (exhibition project; with Luigi Figini)
1942   Villa Manusardi, Cartabbia, Italy (with Luigi Figini)
1946   Master plan for the centre of Milan (with Luigi Figini, BBPR, Piero Bottoni, Franco Albini, and others)
1948   Apartment and Office Building, Via Broletto, Milan (with Luigi Figini)
1951   INA-CASA Housing Estate, Via Harar, Milan (with Luigi Figini and Gio Ponti)
1952   Plan for the Borgo Porto Conte, Sardinia (with Luigi Figini)
1954   Church of the Madonna of the Poor, Milan (with Luigi Figini)
1957   Apartment building, Via Circo, Milan (with Luigi Figini)
        Hoepli Building, Milan (with Luigi Figini)
1963   Pozzi Ceramic Factory Industrial Complex, Sparanise, near Caserta, Italy (with Luigi Figini)
        Church for the CEP Housing Scheme, near Bergamo (project; with Luigi Figini)
        Hotel Largo Augusta, Milan (with Luigi Figini and C. Blasi)
1968   Apartments, Milan
1972   Department of Science Building, University of Palermo (with V. Gregotti and G. Caronia)
1974   Student Study Centre, Conservatorio della SS. Nunziata, Palermo (with P. Culotta, G. Laudicina, T. Marra and F. Purini)
        Villa Guida, Guanzate, Italy (with Luigi Figini)
1976   IACP Housing Development, S. Giuliano Milanese, Italy (with Luigi Figini and G. Marini)
1977   Church of Mater Ecclesiae, Rome (project; with Luigi Figini and G. Marini)

Publications:

By POLLINI: books—*Il Piano Regolatore della Valle d'Aosta*, with Luigi Figini, BBPR, Piero Bottoni and others, Ivrea, Italy 1943; *Elementi di Architettura*, Milan 1966; *La Residenza: Esperienze di Progettazione*, Palermo 1973; articles—"Architettura," with Gruppo 7, in *Rassegna Italiana* (Milan), December 1926; "Gli Stranieri," with Gruppo 7, in *Rassegna Italiana* (Milan), February 1927; "Impreparazione, Incomprensione, Pregiudizi," with Gruppo 7, in *Rassegna Italiana* (Milan), March 1927; "Una Nuova Epoca Arcaica," with Gruppo 7, in *Rassegna Italiana* (Milan), May 1927; "Un Programma di Architettura," with Luigi Figini and others, in *Quadrante* (Milan), May 1933; "Relazione al Progetto del Palazzo del Littorio," with Luigi Figini, BBPR, and Luigi Danusso, in *Quadrante* (Milan), August/September 1934; "Origines de l'Architecture Moderne en Italie," with Luigi Figini, in *L'Architecture d'Aujourd'hui* (Paris), June 1952; "Architettura e Tecnica dall'Inghilterra" in *Parametro* (Bologna), February 1975; "CIAM da Bruxelles ad Atene: La Citta Funzionale" in *Parametro* (Bologna), December 1976.

On POLLINI: books—*Figini e Pollini* by Eugenio Gentili, Milan 1959; *Figini e Pollini* by Cesare Blasi, Milan 1963 (includes bibliography).

See FIGINI, Luigi

POLSHEK, James Stewart.

American. Born in Akron, Ohio, 11 February 1930. Educated at Case Western Reserve University, Cleveland, Ohio, 1947–51, B.S. 1951; Yale University School of Architecture, New Haven, Connecticut, 1951–55, M.Arch. 1955; Royal Academy of Fine Arts, Copenhagen (Fulbright Fellow), 1956–57. Served as a meteorologist in the United States Air Corps Reserve, 1953–60. Married Ellyn May Margolis in 1952; children: Peter and Jennifer. Worked with I. M. Pei and Associates, New York, 1955–56, with Ulrich Franzen and Associates, New York, 1957–60, and with Westermann and Miller and Associates, New York, 1960–61. In private practice, as James Stewart Polshek and Associates, New York, since 1962. Dean of the Faculty of the Graduate School of Architecture and Planning, Columbia University, New York, and Special Adviser to the President of Columbia for Planning and Development, since 1973. First Vice-President, American Institute of Architects, New York Chapter, 1970–71. Vice-President, Municipal Art Society, New York, since 1974. Exhibitions: *40 under 40,* American Federation of Arts, New York, 1966; *Expo '70,* Osaka, Japan, 1970; *Another Chance for Cities,* Whitney Museum, New York, 1970; *Rise of an American Architecture,* Metropolitan Museum of Art, New York, 1970. Recipient: Building Contractors Society Prize, Japan, 1965; Osaka Prefecture Architecture Prize, Japan, 1965; Gold Medal, Architectural League of New York, 1965; Project Award, *Progressive Architecture,* 1969; Hudson River Valley Commission Certificate, New York, 1969; Award of Excellence, American Institute of Steel Construction, 1971; Honor Award, American Institute of Architects, 1972; First Honor Award, Connecticut Building Congress, 1974; Bard Award, City Club of New York, 1978. Fellow, American Institute of Architects, 1972. Address: James Stewart Polshek and Associates, 295 Madison Avenue, New York, New York 10017, U.S.A.

Works:

1959 Oster House, Stony Point, New York
1962 Oster Townhouse, New York
1964 Teijin Central Research Institute, Tokyo
1965 Teijin Textile Processing Research Institute, Osaka, Japan
1966 Big Brothers Inc. Residence, New York
1967 Stable Quadrangle rehabilitation, State University College of New York at Old Westbury (project)
  Bedford-Stuyvesant Community Center, Brooklyn, New York (project)
  Expo '70 Competition (project)
1968 Donovan House, Port Washington, Long Island, New York
  Williams House, New York
  Atlantic Terminal Urban Renewal Area Concept Plan, Brooklyn, New York
1969 Student Center, Wesleyan University, Middletown, Connecticut (project)
  Recreation Structure, for Mr. and Mrs. Edgar Bronfman, Purchase, New York
1970 Clinton Youth and Family Center, YMCA of New York
  Centennial Exhibit, Metropolitan Museum of Art, New York
  George Jensen Store, Madison Avenue, New York (modified by others, 1974)
  Planning study for undergraduate dormitories at Wesleyan University, Middletown, Connecticut
1971 Dormitory and Academic Buildings, Rosemary Hall, Wallingford, Connecticut
  New York State Bar Center, Albany
  Service Group, State University of New York at Old Westbury
  Atura Site 4B Housing (300 units), Atlanta Terminal Urban Renewal Area, Brooklyn, New York
  Planning study for the Paterson, New Jersey Redevelopment Agency
  Clinton Youth Center, West 54th Street, New York
  Gellert House, Chappaqua, New York
  Student Center, Wesleyan University, Middletown, Connecticut (project)
  Central Plant, Wesleyan University, Middletown, Connecticut
1972 Materials Research Center, Allied Chemical Corporation, Morristown, New Jersey
  Twin Parks East (housing), Bronx, New York
  New student housing, Vassar College, Poughkeepsie, New York (project)
  Comprehensive Consulting Center, Columbus, Indiana
  Recycle Fuels Plant, Westinghouse Electric Corporation, Columbia, South Carolina
1973 Intermediate School 1972, New York

  Glen Ellen Ski and Recreation Center, Fayston, Vermont (project)
1974 Prototype manufacturing facility for the Westinghouse Company, Pittsburgh
1975 Helen Owen Carey Playhouse, Brooklyn Academy of Music, New York
1975- Health and Physical Education Building, State University of New York at Old Westbury
1976 Brotherhood Synagogue restoration, New York
  Health and Physical Education Building, Kingsborough Community College, Brooklyn, New York
  Empire State Plaza (Albany Mall) Planning Study, Albany, New York
  Allied Chemical Process Development, phase II (project)
  Planning study for the Church of the Heavenly Rest and Day School
1977 Public Works Building, Englewood, New Jersey
  Simon and Schuster Corporate Offices, New York
  Student Residence, Skidmore College, Saratoga, New York (project)

1978 Trancas Associates Medical Center, Napa, California (with Peter Gluck)
  Urban Issues Center, Villard House Restoration, New York (project)

Publications:

On POLSHEK: articles—"Functional Grid in Japan" in *Architectural Forum* (New York), August 1964; "An American Castle in Japan" in *Fortune* (New York), May 1965; "Laboratory 3: Research Placed on a Podium" in *Architectural Forum* (New York), May 1965; "A New York Studio di Architettura al Quaratasettesimo Piano" in *Domus* (Milan), February 1966; "The Young Innovators 1966" in *House Beautiful* (New York), July 1966; "Fluid Space" in *Interiors* (New York), September 1966; "Design Awards Program" in *Progressive Architecture* (New York), January 1969; "Teahouse by the Pool" in *Architectural Forum* (New York), May 1970; "Design for Merchandising" in *Architectural Record* (New York), February 1971; "Jugend und Familien-Treffpunkt in New York" in *Baumeister* (Munich), June 1971; "Clinton Youth and Family Center" in *Architectural Record* (New York), June 1971; "Work in Progress/James Polshek" in *Intellectual Digest* (New York), February 1972; "Tale of

James Stewart Polshek: Teijin Central Research Institute, Tokyo, 1964

the Twin Park" in *Architectural Forum* (New York), June 1973; "Rosemary and Time" in *Architectural Forum* (New York), September 1973; "Allied Chemical's New Research Center" in *Architectural Record* (New York), August 1974; "James Polshek and Associates" in *Architecture + Urbanism* (Tokyo), April 1976; special issue of *Space Design* (Tokyo), June 1978.

For 16 years my work has been characterized by a pattern of dependence on classical 2- and 3-dimensional systems of geometric organization modified by an intellectual scepticism about the implications of those systems. Most of my major works have depended on bi-axial symmetries that have used the human body as a model. These attitudes have manifested themselves in my work since my student days at Yale where I often rejected current architectural fashions, preferring instead to depend on a combination of visual intuition and natural morphologies. One result of this was that my design solutions often bore vague resemblances to indigenous or vernacular architecture. This combination of "primitive" and neo-platonic forms has characterized my work ever since. As a student I spoke frequently of my antipathy to an architecture that would eschew historical consistency for programmatic appropriateness. Ironically, it is exactly the opposite that has signified most of my work. My interest in commissions that emphasized contextualism and historic preservation represent two specific examples. In commission after commission I have sought out form determinants that have de-emphasized the massive ego involvement that is required in virgin design challenges. Therefore I have been little interested in the single house design as an outlet for my art and have been more interested in (and therefore more successful in securing) commissions that have depended on socially justifiable or scientifically (technologically) determined programs such as schools and community centers or laboratories and industrial buildings.

Current debates about the validity of modernism or the meaningfulness of "post-modern" architecture have little interest for me. My mid-western pragmatism and my belief in the value of criticism have led me to believe in the *act* of building as being more important than the *theory* of building and therefore have little interest in or sympathy with recent obscurantist theorizing. Alex Tzonis (an architect and critic currently at Harvard) characterizes these new theoretical architects as "narcissistic"—embracing elitism and hedonism while rejecting any interest in social responsibility and technological advancement. I agree with him. And although my own work clearly depends on highly-ordered geometrics, the interpretation and expressions of the specific programs and the client dreams that have generated them are what I have striven to perfect.

There are aspects of my work that are so recurrent as to cause me to believe in the Freudian-defined role of the unconscious in physical design. Specifically I refer to the earlier described bi-axial symmetry and also to my dependence on a tripartite system of organization. With regard to this latter manifestation, one need only refer to my designs for the Teijin Central Research Institute (3 service tower cores); my Service Group at the State University in Old Westbury (designed as 3 "L"-shaped buildings); the Bar Center in Albany, New York (tri-partite building organization); the Pool Pavillion in 1967 (3 interlocking squares); the Wesleyan Student Center (3 part scale breakdown of the High Street facade); Intermediate School 1972 (the 3 school tower organization); and the private residence in Chappaqua, New York (3 wing organization).

I have sought also to develop prototypical solutions to a *variety* of problems. The result of this desire for diversity is that for 15 years our office has had commissions in many aspects of practice that are less romantic (or prestigious) than the "one-off" building—the monument or singular "masterpiece." Since 1968 historic preservation has been an impor-

tant part of the practice. Although long before 1968 I had designed at least six townhouses where the constraints of a partywall system and the necessity to make on-site changes and extrapolations set many patterns for later practice. Not all of these patterns have been positive. For instance, construction phase changes made without reliance on drawings created a somewhat less than rigorous attitude about the development of working drawings. The joy (and power) of "inventing" details on the job proved to be extremely gratifying.

I referred earlier to my lack of interest in individual house clients. Part of this lack of interest certainly stemmed from my not needing those clients to help me establish a "market." My "Cinderella" commissions in Japan largely solved that problem. In addition to the market aspect, however, I had (and still have) other reasons for preferring less personal commissions. Clients who come to one for "ART" rather than problem-solving have always proved to be less interesting, and the complex intellectual chemistry of architect-client communications which is necessary before a truly significant design solution can be achieved is missing. My most interesting house clients have been problem-solvers themselves —specifically scientists and journalists.

It is this same dichotomy of ad-hocism and belief in rationality that finally caused me to become interested in architectural education. And while this has been an almost totally consuming passion and responsibility for the past six years, it has also been of great value to me intellectually and therefore ultimately will be of great significance to my future work.

—James Stewart Polshek

James Stewart Polshek calls them his Cinderella commissions, but it must be one of the most extraordinary strokes of good fortune to befall any young architect. A Japanese visitor was so taken with Polshek's first independent commission, the Oster House, Stony Point, New York, that he invited Polshek to be the architect for a new central research institute for his company, Teijin Ltd., to be located outside Tokyo, a 32 million dollar project. Polshek moved his family to Japan, established an office, and designed and supervised construction of a range of buildings, complex both organizationally and technically. The results show a calm strength and remarkable maturity. Much that is formative in Polshek's subsequent work seems to result from this experience.

As a whole his architecture has some unusual characteristics. There is distinct lack of stylistic continuity. Although the character of the work is strong, the strength comes not by idiosyncratic invention but from a programmatic and technical response to specific problems and specific contexts. He has undertaken a diverse range of projects: education buildings, institutional buildings, industrial buildings, labs, interiors work, exhibitions. Diverse, yet united in that they mostly pose unusual and demanding problems. The work has no dominate theme. It is in every case an intelligent response to the unique aspects of the program.

His architecture is at its best when there are strong constraints and a demand for ingenuity. In the accommodations for the New York State Bar Center, for example, the need to relate to a terrace of 19th century town houses enriched a work of sensitive contextualism. The new buildings are not simply respectful of the old, but in their mass and urban presence (apart from the curved stair), they seem almost vital new growth out of the old context. His work is least successful when neither context not problem offers any guidance. This is particularly true of the moderate income housing project for the South Bronx, Twin Parks East. Here the result is the antithesis of the previous example—raw, brutal, confused.

This lack of any kind of stylistic continuity is a puzzle. The work is engaging yet somewhat devoid of personality. Perhaps the early success in Japan

provided so much personal fulfillment that there has been no need for self-indulgence in subsequent work. But mainly, I believe, its character results from his preoccupation with the stuff of building, the legacy of the teaching of Eugen Nalles at Yale. In many ways the nature of his architecture fits into that period after Gropius and before Kahn. Formal freedom is excused through contextualism; formal invention is excused through aspects of building technique or performance. He doesn't fit easily with his contemporaries: compared with that of his New York colleagues, his work is conservative and makes few concessions to poetry. Yet, in his role as undemonstrative orchestrator of a building's parts, Polshek produces work of strength and honesty, and his inventiveness with technique and context raises it above the ordinary.

—Alan Balfour

PONTI, Gio(vanni).

Italian. Born in Milan, 18 November 1891. Educated at the Milan Polytechnic School of Architecture, 1918–21, Dip.Arch. 1921. Served in the Italian Army, 1916–18: awarded War Cross and Military Performance Medal. Married Giulia Vimercati in 1921; has four children. Worked in the architectural studio of Mino Fiocchi and Emilio Lancia, Milan, 1921; Designer and Production Renovator, Richard Ginori Ceramics Factory, Milan and Florence, 1923–30; Partner, with Emilio Lancia, Studio Ponti e Lancia, Milan, 1927–33; Partner, with Antonio Fornaroli and Eugenio Soncini, Studio Ponti-Fornaroli-Soncini, Milan, 1933–45; Partner, with Fornaroli and Alberto Rosselli, Studio Ponti-Fornaroli-Rosselli, Milan, 1952 until he retired, 1976. Professor, Faculty of Architecture, Milan Polytechnic, 1936–61. Director, *Stile,* Milan, 1941–47. Founder Editor, *Domus,* Milan, 1928–41, 1948–79. Director, Executive Board of the *Biennale,* Monza, subsequently the *Triennale,* Milan, 1933–79; General Supervisor, *Italia 61* exhibition, Turin, 1961, and the *Eurodomus* exhibition, Genoa and other Italian cities, 1966–69. President, Collegio Regionale Lombardo degli Architetti, Milan, 1957–60, and International Museum of Modern Architecture, Milan, 1961. Exhibitions: Florence, 1937; Galleria Gianferrari, Milan, 1939, 1951; Galleria dell' Obelisco, Rome, 1950; Institute of Contemporary Art, Boston, 1954, and toured the United States; Galleria La Bussola, Turin, 1955; AB Ferdinand Lundquist, Göteborg, Sweden, 1956; Galleria del Sole, Milan, 1956; Christofle, Paris, 1957; Liberty's, London, 1957; Galleria del Designo, Milan, 1959; *The Expression of Gio Ponti,* University of California at Los Angeles, 1966, and toured the United States; Galleria de Nieubourg, Milan, 1967; Galleria Toselli, Milan, 1978. Recipient: First Prize for Art, Accademia d'Italia, 1945; First Prize, University of Padua Faculty of English Competition, 1934; Compasso d'Oro for Industrial Design, 1956; Gold Medal, Académie d'Architecture, Paris, 1968. Honorary doctorate: Royal College of Art, London, 1968. Corresponding Member, Royal Institute of British Architects; Honorary Associate, American Institute of Architects. Member, Accademia di San Luca, Rome. *Died in September 1979.*

Works:

1921 Church, *Biennale,* Rome (exhibition project)
1925 House, via Randaccio, Milan (with Emilio Lancia)

Gio Ponti: Pirelli Tower, Milan, 1956

Richard Ginori Ceramics Factories conversions, Florence and Milan
1926 Bouilhet House, Paris
1927 Rinascente Department Store vestibule, Milan (with Emilio Lancia)
Pavilion, *Fiera Campionaria,* Milan (with Emilio Lancia)
1928 Semanza House interiors, Levanto, Italy
Memorial Monument, Milan (with G. Muzio, O. Cabiati, A. Alpago Novello and T. Buzzi)
1929 Hairdresser's salon, Malagoti, Milan
1930 Pavilion, *Biennale,* Monza, Italy (with Emilio Lancia)
Design of a flag for the Ospedale Maggiore, Milan
1931 Union Bank, Milan (with Emilio Lancia)
House, via Domenichino, Milan (with Emilio Lancia)
Borletti Tomb, Monumental Cemetery, Milan
1932 Borletti House, via S. Vittore, Milan (with Emilio Lancia)
House, Bastioni di Porta Venezia, Milan (with Emilio Lancia)
1933 Littoria Tower (in steel), Parco di Milano, Milan (with Cesare Chiodi)
University City, Rome (with Giovanni Michelucci, Arnaldo Foschini, Pietro Aschieri, Giuseppe Capponi, Giuseppe Pagano, and Gaetano Rapisardi; Marcello Piacentini, chief architect)
House, corso Venezia, Milan
1934 Faculty of Mathematics Building, University City, Rome
House, via de Togni, Milan (with Emilio Lancia)
Palazzo de Littorio, Rome (competition project)
Faculty of English, University of Padua (competition project)
House, viale C. Zugna, Milan
1935 CIMA Building, Milan (with Luciano Baldissari)
Laporte House, Milan
Hotel, via Martello, Alto Adige, Italy (with Antonio Fornaroli and Eugenio Soncini)
House, via Ceradini, Milan
House, via Hajech, Milan
House, via Gustavo Modena, Milan
House, viale Regina Margherita, Milan (with Antonio Fornaroli and Eugenio Soncini)
House, corso Italia, Milan (with Antonio Fornaroli and Eugenio Soncini)
De Bartolemeis a Bratto Villas, Brescia, Italy
Entrance Hall, Ministero delle Corporazione, Rome
1936 Montecatini Building I, Milan (with Antonio Fornaroli and Eugenio Soncini)
Design of the *Catholic Press International Exhibition,* Vatican City
Italian Institute, Fürstenberg Palace, Vienna
Villa Marzotto, Valdagno, Italy (project; with Antonio Fornaroli, Eugenio Soncini, and Francesco Bonfanti)
Urban plan for Addis Abiba (with Giuseppe Vaccaro and Enrico del Dobbio)
1937 Liviano Building, School of Archeology, University of Padua (with the painter Massimo Campigli)
Domus Alba, via Goldoni, Milan (with Antonio Fornaroli and Eugenio Soncini)
Italian Pavilion (furnishings and ceramics), *World's Fair,* Paris
1938 Design of the *Vittoria Exhibition,* Padua
San Michele Hotel, Capri (project; with Bernardo Rudofsky)
Bungalows, Hotel Eden Roc, Cap d'Antibes, France (project)
RAI (Radio Associazione Italiana) Building, Milan (with Antonio Fornaroli, Eugenio Soncini and Nino Bertolata)
1939 Villa Donegani, Bordighera, Italy

Ferrania Office Building, corso Matteotti, Milan (with Antonio Fornaroli and Eugenio Soncini)
Building, San Babita, Milan (with Antonio Fornaroli and Eugenio Soncini)
Urban plan for Scalo Sempione, Milan (with de Finetti)
Costumes and scenery for *Il Pulcinella,* at the Teatro della Triennale, Milan
Great Hall and Basilica, Palazzo del Bo, University of Padua
Foreign Office, Rome (competition project; with Guglielmo Ulrich, R. Angeli, C. de Carli, and Eugenio Soncini)
Palazzo Marzotto, Milan (project; with Antonio Fornaroli, Eugenio Soncini, and Francesco Bonfanti)
1940 Villa Tataru, Cluj, Rumania (with Elsie Lazar)
Villa Marchesano, Bordighera, Italy
Staircase frescoes, University of Padua
Columbus Clinic for the Missionary Sisters of the Sacred Heart, Milan (with Antonio Fornaroli and Eugenio Soncini)
Ledoga Building, Milan (with Antonio Fornaroli and Eugenio Soncini)
Palazzina Salvatelli, Piazza Duse, Rome (with Antonio Fornaroli and Eugenio Soncini)
House, via Appiani, Milan (with Antonio Fornaroli and Eugenio Soncini)
INA-CASA Development, via Manin, Milan (project; with Antonio Fornaroli and Eugenio Soncini)
Giustiniani Apartment, Milan (project)
Fiat Building, Milan (with Antonio Fornaroli and Eugenio Soncini)
1943 Mondadori Building, Milan (project; with Antonio Fornaroli and Eugenio Soncini)
1944 Casa Barzanti, via Spiga, Milan
1945 North Railway Hotel and Office Building, Milan (project; with Antonio Fornaroli)
Ponti House I, Civate, Como, Italy
1946 Brustio Apartment, Milan
1948 Monument to the Victims of Ebensee Concentration Camp, Austria
House, via Lamarmora, Milan (with Antonio Fornaroli)
1949 Costumes and scenery for *Orfeo,* at La Scala, Milan
Villa Piodari, Rapallo, Italy (with Antonio Fornaroli)
Swimming Pool, Hotel Royal, San Remo, Italy
Self-illuminating furniture for the Casa Cremaschi, Milan
Mazzocchi Studio furnishings, via Monte di Pieta, Milan
Caffe espresso machinery, for La Pavoni, Milan
Sewing machines for La Visa, Voghera, Italy
1950 First Class Lobby, *Conte Grande* Liner (with Nino Zoncada)
Casino interiors, San Remo, Italy (with Antonio Fornaroli)
Villa Marchesano, San Remo, Italy
RAS Building, corseo Vittorio Emanuele, Milan (with Antonio Fornaroli)
Ceccato furnishings, Milan
Dulciora Shop, Milan
Vembi-Burroughs Offices, Genoa and Turin (with Antonio Fornaroli)
Villa Cremaschi interiors, Carate Urio, Como, Italy
1951 INA-CASA Housing Estate, via Harrar, Milan (with Luigi Figini and Gino Pollini)
Montecatini Building II, Milan
First Class interiors, on the liners *Giulio Cesare, Andrea Doria* and *Conte Biancamano* (with Nino Zoncada)
School complex, Chiavenna, Sondrio, Italy (with Antonio Fornaroli)
Model Hotel Room, *Triennale,* Milan

Steel cutlery for Argenteria Krupp, Milan, and Fraser, New York
Silver articles for Argenteria Krupp, Milan
Lamps for Greco, Milan
Leggera Chair, for Cassina, Milan
1952 Edison Electrical Centers, at Santa Giustina, Chiavenna, Cimego, Liri, Vinadio, Plantano d'Avio, and Stura Demonte, Italy (with Antonio Fornaroli and Alberto Rosselli)
Edison Building, Milan (with Antonio Fornaroli)
Villa Arata, Naples (with Antonio Fornaroli)
Oceania and *Africa* ships interiors
Technical School, Gonzaga Institute, Crescenzago, Milan (with Antonio Fornaroli)
Tables for the Singer Company, New York
1953 Faculty of Nuclear Physics, University of Sao Paulo (project)
Italian-Brazilian Center, Sao Paulo (project; with Luiz Contrucci)
Taglianotti House, Sao Paulo (project)
Swimming Pool, Hotel Royal, Naples
Distex Armchair, for Cassina, Milan
Furniture and Partition Walls, for Altamira, New York
Tap Fittings, for Gallieni, Vigano, and Marazza, Milan
Sanitary Fittings, for Ideal Standard, Milan
Lancia Building, Turin (with Antonio Fornaroli, Alberto Rosselli, and Nino Rosani)
Furniture, for Nordiska Kompaniet, Stockholm
Design of car bodywork, for Carrozzeria Touring, Milan
1954 Villa Planchart, Caracas
Italian Cultural Institute, Stockholm (with Pier Luigi Nervi and Ture Wenerholm)
Aldo Garzanti Center, Forli, Italy (with Antonio Fornaroli and Giulio Bosisio)
Industrialized House, *Triennale,* Milan (exhibition project)
1955 Arreaza House, Caracas
San Lucca Church, Milan (with Antonio Fornaroli and Alberto Rosselli)
Villa Marmont, Zoagli, Genoa (with Antonio Fornaroli and Alberto Rosselli)
Ponti House II, Civate, Como, Italy
Superleggera Chair, for Cassina, Milan
Town Hall, Cesanatico, Pesaro, Italy (with Antonio Fornaroli and Alberto Rosselli)
Summer house, Arenzano, Genoa
Lamps, for La Luma, Milan
Alitalia Offices, New York
Cutlery, for Christofle, Paris
Supermarket, viale Zara, Milan (with Antonio Fornaroli and Alberto Rosselli)
Metal Desk, for Rima, Padua
Desk, for Chiesa, Milan
Cowhide carpet, for Colombi, Milan
1956 Pirelli Tower, Milan (with Pier Luigi Nervi, Arturo Danusso, Antonio Fornaroli, Alberto Rosselli, Giuseppe Valtolina, and Egidio dell'Orto)
Handles, for Olivar, Borgomanero, Italy
Faculty of Architecture, Milan Polytechnic (with Giordano Forti)
Silver articles, for Christofle, Paris
Steel cutlery, for Argenteria Krupp, Milan
RAS House, via Nievo, Milan (with Antonio Fornaroli and Alberto Rosselli)
1957 House, via Dezza, Milan (with Antonio Fornaroli and Alberto Rosselli)
Melandri House, Milan (with Antonio Fornaroli and Alberto Rosselli)
FEAL Pre-Fabricated House, *Triennale,* Milan
Gorrondona House, Caracas (project)
Lamps, for Arredoiuce, Milan
1958 Carmelite Convent, San Remo, Italy (with Antonio Fornaroli and Alberto Rosselli)
Government Office Building, Baghdad (with

Antonio Fornaroli, Alberto Rosselli, Giuseppe Valtolina, and Egidio dell'Orto)

Assolombarda Building, Milan (with Antonio Fornaroli and Alberto Rosselli)

Villa Guzman-Bianco, Caracas (project)

Gallini Center, Voghera, Italy (with Antonio Fornaroli and Alberto Rosselli)

Cutlery, for Christofle, Paris

Eighth Floor Auditorium, Time and Life Building, New York

1960 Villa Nemazee, Tehran

Philips Building, Rome (with Antonio Fornaroli and Alberto Rosselli)

Alitalia Air Terminal interiors, Central Station, Milan

Hotel Parco dei Principi, Sorrento

1961 Montreal Tower (project)

Design of the *Italia '61* exhibition, Turin (with Pier Luigi Nervi)

1962 RAS Building, Milan (with Antonio Fornaroli, Alberto Rosselli, and Piero Portaluppi)

Montecatini Pavilion, *Milan Fair*

2 villas, Capo Stella, Elba (with Cesare Casati)

Hotel Storione, Padua (with Antonio Fornaroli and Alberto Rosselli)

Banca Antoniana, Padua (with Antonio Fornaroli and Alberto Rosselli)

Cassa di Risparmio di Padova e Rovigo, Padua (with Antonio Fornaroli and Alberto Rosselli)

House for the Mother Superior of Notre Dame de Sion, Rome (with Antonio Fornaroli and Alberto Rosselli)

Pakistan House Hotel, Islamabad (with Antonio Fornaroli and Alberto Rosselli)

1963 Shui Hing Stores, Hong Kong

Daniel Koo House, Hong Kong

Church of San Francesco, Milan

Bruckner Cultural Center, Linz, Austria (competition project; with Costanino Corsini and Giorgio Wiskeman)

Employees Residence, Varese Shoe Factory, Italy (with Antonio Fornaroli and Alberto Roselli)

Cassa di Risparmio, Modena, Italy (with Antonio Fornaroli and Alberto Rosselli)

1964 Ministry Buildings, Islamabad, West Pakistan (with Antonio Fornaroli and Alberto Rosselli)

Anguissola House, Lido di Camaiore, Italy (project)

Hotel Parco dei Principi, Rome (with Antonio Fornaroli and Alberto Rosselli)

Chair, for Knoll, Milan

Banca dei Monte di Pieta Office and Apartment Building, Milan (with Antonio Fornaroli and Alberto Rosselli)

House Under Foil (project)

1965 Church, San Carlo Borromeo Hospital, Milan

Apartment/Office Building, Beirut (project; with Antonio Fornaroli and Alberto Rosselli)

1966 Law Courts, Verona (project; with Antonio Fornaroli and Alberto Rosselli)

1967 Bijenkorf Shopping Center, Eindhoven, Netherlands (with Theo Boosten, and the sculptors Mario Negri and Frans Gast)

Office building, via San Paulo, Milan (with Antonio Fornaroli and Alberto Rosselli)

1968 Plastic lamps, for Guzzini, Macerata, Italy

Furniture, for La Tecno, Milan

Piltello Housing Estate, Milan (with Antonio Fornaroli, Alberto Rosselli, A. Ferrari Angilella, and Giulio Ponti)

1969 Daniel Koo House, Marin County, California (project)

1970 Savoia Assicurazioni e Riassicurazioni Building, Milan (with Antonio Fornaroli and Alberto Rosselli)

Plan for the center of Monaco di Baviera,

Italy (competition project; with Antonio Fornaroli and Alberto Rosselli)

1971 Taranto Cathedral, Italy

FEAL Building (project)

Centre Beaubourg, Paris (competition project; with Alberto Ferrari)

Coordinating designs, for Zucchi, Milan

1972 Salzburg University (as consultant to Otto Prosinger and Martin Windisch)

Museum of Modern Art, Denver (with James Sudler and Joal Cronenwett)

1973 Decor, for D'Agostino Pottery, Salerno, Italy

1976 Tiled flooring in Agostino ceramics, for Salzburger Nachrichten, Austria

1978 Painting on perspex, for the Shui Hing Stores, Singapore

Publications:

By PONTI: books—*La Casa all'Italiana,* Milan 1933; *Italiani,* with Leonardo Sinisgalli, Milan 1937; *Il Coro,* Milan 1944; *Cifre Parlanti,* Milan 1944; *Politica dell'Architettura,* Milan 1944; *Ideario,* Milan 1945; *L'Architettura e un Cristallo,* Milan 1945; *Verso la Casa Esatta,* Milan 1945; *Ringrazio Iddio che le Cose non vanno a Mode Mio,* Milan 1946; *Paradiso Perduto,* Milan 1956; *Amate l'Architettura,* Genoa 1957, as *In Praise of Architecture,* New York 1960, Tokyo 1963; *Milano Oggi,* Milan 1957; *Nuvole sono Immagini,* Milan 1968; articles—numerous in *Domus* and *Stile,* Milan, and in other architectural and design periodicals throughout the world.

On PONTI: books—*Architettura d'Oggi* by Marcello Piacentini, Rome 1930; *Mobili Tipici Moderni* by G. C. Palanti, Milan 1933; *Tecnica dell'Abitazione* by G. Pagano, Milan 1936; *Architettura Moderna in Italia* by A. Pica, Milan 1941; *Difficolta Politiche dell'Architettura in Italia 1920–40* by Giulia Veronesi, Milan 1953; *Espressione di Giovanni Ponti* by James S. Plaut, Milan 1954; *Ponti: Summing Up* by Mario Labo, Milan 1958; *Modern Architecture* by Vincent Scully, New York 1965; *The Expression of Gio Ponti,* edited by Nathan H. Shapira, Minneapolis 1967; articles—"Giovanni Ponti: dell' Architettura al Disegno per l'Industria" by P. E. Gennarini in *Pirelli* (Milan), November/December 1951; "Pirelli Building, Milan" by Reyner Banham in *Architectural Review* (London), March 1961; "Scraping the Skies of Italy" by Edgar Kaufmann in *Art News* (New York), February 1966.

Modern man is born in a clinic and dies in a clinic. Is it therefore not surprising that he should spent the intermediate period between these two paramount events of his life in utterly soulless clinical environments? Architects, in moulding man's surroundings, have today unfortunately lost their magic touch. In the past, members of the profession were priests, astronomers or philosophers; in more ancient times they were conversant in the secret knowledge of celestial bodies and proficient in the understanding of essential terrestrial forms. This knowledge helped them to produce rarified works of art. Today, architecture is rarely able to transcend purely materialistic requirements. Architecture has become subservient solely to business interests and speculation. What started as a path to enlightenment is now just a job!

Not so for Gio Ponti. From the beginning of his career, Ponti's quest was for a unique, individual creative ideology. Although a contemporary of members of the Italian Futurist movement, he was never in any way associated with their philosophy. Even in those early days he moved in a path isolated from surrounding thoughts and fashions. Gradually he developed an individualistic, sensitive approach in a multivalent and pluralistic expression of total design. His main influences came from close intimate friendships with Edoardo Persico, Bernard Rudofsky and the painter Massimo Campigli: a reflection of his wide scope of vision. Following an initial academic and classical period of activity, he produced such significant pre-war projects as the Mathematics Building at Rome University (1934), the first Montecatini Building in Milan (1936) and the RAI offices in Milan (1938). The Montecatini design involved a remarkable evolution of standardization and architectural simplicity, in comparison to other works in Italy of that period. Contemporary to these works and also worthy of notice is his evocative hotel project for the Island of Capri, unfortunately never built, which manifested a deep ethnic understanding of the Mediterranean tradition. The particular relationship to site revealed in this project was to develop into a sensitive proficiency in grafting his work on to essential roots and in creating a progressive process of continuity, evolution and harmony in adapting his buildings to their particular environment.

Ponti's major contributions were, however, to come in later years in a remarkable integration of multi-disciplinary activities ranging from ceramics, painting, furniture and industrial design, theatre-sets and graphics, to architecture itself and town planning. In all of these activities (as well as in his long editorship of *Domus*), Ponti transcended purely materialistic requirements into a rare contemporary embodiment of truly poetic design concepts. The dogmatic imperatives of the early Modern movement, accompanied by declamatory revolutionary dialogue, resulted in a loss of spiritual values. In the mechanized soulless era of mass production that was to follow, Ponti's belief, plea and commitment was essentially for the individual, the particular and the unique. His total approach to architecture remained incontestably humanistic and essentially personal, respecting and glorifying both the onlookers and users of his buildings. In the best of Italian tradition (and what tradition it is!), Ponti's work evokes in its spectators a magical sense of ecstasy and fantasy. This is an expression of love and joy that transcends purely intellectual and technological values into the realm of the spiritual.

In all of his work there is constant evidence of his deep concern and inclination towards producing effects of lightness as opposed to heaviness and finite closed forms as opposite to infinite open ones; most of all, there is evidence of a deep understanding of what he referred to as the "poetry of precisions." This highly personalized approach produced a series of architectural masterpieces that, despite their floating fantasy, are logically anchored to economic and rational criteria.

The Pirelli Tower in Milan (despite the changes from model to realization) must be considered as the jewel of modern skyscrapers: a diamond well cut and beautifully faceted. His Bijenkorf Shopping Center in Eindhoven brings a welcome Southern air to the overcast sombre Northern skies of Holland: a space conceived for the glorification of the city. The Museum of Modern Art in Denver is as over-indulgent and Italianate as Caruso singing Neopolitan melodies, but equally infectious: a Baroque, mannerist expression as welcome and necessary as a golden touch of Mediterranean sun and as vital and rewarding as the best of Italian wines. The Cathedral in Taranto is perhaps his most successful religious building. A man of devout faith, Ponti manages to evolve the pure architectural spatial concept to a higher religious-spiritual one. "Religious architecture is not a matter of architecture but a matter of religion," Ponti tells us . . . and so it is here. Its sun-scorched perforated lace-like facade evokes sculptured sounds against the timelessness of eternity. The rising fastigium recalls the elegant music of Tomaso Albinoni or Benedetto Marcello: crystallized sounds of romantic elegance. Ponti's concept of removing the stained glass evolves beyond that of the medieval cathedral and rings in clarion tones of conceptual clarity. Taranto's saffron-screen offers us a contact between spectator and infinity, between man and his Creator. The joy, belief and involvement of its maker is convincingly conveyed to the observer.

In the wide variety of his activities there is constant evidence that life, art and architecture were inseparable to Ponti. His versatility was part of the grand tradition of the ancient masters of his land. In today's world, overwhelmed by the stolid faceless-ness of modern rationalism, we ask whether it is still possible for a contemporary building to be trans-formed into a poem. In perhaps the most difficult period of modern architecture Gio Ponti gave us a hopeful glimpse of a personal, positive, exuberant answer. For that accomplishment, his place in his-tory is secure.

—Richard England

PORTMAN, John (Calvin, Jr.).
American. Born in Walhalla, South Carolina, 4 De-cember 1924. Educated at the United States Naval Academy, Annapolis, Maryland, 1944; Georgia In-stitute of Technology, Atlanta, B.Arch. 1950. Served in the United States Naval Reserve, 1942–44. Mar-ried Joan Newton in 1944; children: Michael, John III, Jae, Jeffrey, Jana, and Jarel. Worked for Ketchum, Gina and Sharp, H. M. Heatley Associ-ates, New York and Atlanta, 1945–49, and Stevens and Wilkinson, Atlanta, 1950–53; in private prac-tice, Atlanta, 1953–56; Partner, Edwards and Port-man, Atlanta, 1956–68. Since 1968, President of John Portman and Associates, Atlanta. President,

Central Atlanta Progress, 1970–72. President, At-lanta Development Corporation, Atlanta Trade Shows Corporation, Peachtree-Harris Corporation, Atlanta, and Jamestown Shopping Center, College Park, Georgia; Principal, Portman Properties; Chairman, Atlanta Merchandise Mart; Co-Owner, Atlanta Decorative Arts Center, and of Peachtree Center Development Company; Partner, Crown and Portman (development firm), Atlanta; Vice-Presi-dent, Regency Hotel, Atlanta; Honorary Consul of Denmark in Atlanta. Recipient: National Citation, *Progressive Architecture,* 1956; Outstanding Young Man of the Year Award, Georgia Junior Chamber of Commerce, 1959; Distinguished Service Award, De-Kalb County Junior Chamber of Commerce, Georgia, 1960; Ivan Allen Award, American Insti-tute of Architects, Northern Georgia Chapter, 1964; Outstanding Public Relations Award, Public Rela-tions Society of America, Atlanta Chapter, 1967; Salesman of the Year Award, Sales and Marketing Executives of Atlanta Association, 1968; Golden Plate Award, American Academy of Achievement, 1968; Tau Sigma Delta Honorary Society Award, Georgia Institute of Technology, Atlanta, 1972; At-lanta Civic Design Commission Award, 1973; Ar-chitectural Excellence Award, American Institute of Steel Construction, 1973; Outstanding Humanitar-ian Award, National Jewish Hospital, 1973; Omi-cron Delta Kappa Award, Georgia State University, 1974; Design in Steel Award, American Iron and Steel Institute, 1975; Elsie de Wolfe Award, Ameri-

can Society of Interior Design, 1976; Georgian of the Year Award, Georgia Association of Broadcasters, 1976; City Association Award, Los Angeles, 1976; Brewer Award, Atlanta Convention Bureau, 1976; Merit Award, National Council for Community Ser-vices to International Visitors, 1976; Distinguished Service Medal, Georgia Business and Industry Asso-ciation, 1977; Civic Leadership Award, Building Owners and Managers Association of Atlanta, 1977; Medal for Innovation in Hotel Design, American Institute of Architects, 1978. LL.D.: Emory Univer-sity, Atlanta, 1974. Fellow, American Institute of Architects. Member, Royal Order of the Knights of Dannenborg, Denmark, 1975; Officer, Royal Belgian Order of the Crown, 1975. Address: John Portman and Associates, 225 Peachtree Center, Atlanta, Georgia 30303, U.S.A.

Works:

1953 Fraternal Order of Eagles Building, Atlanta
1954 Henderson Office Building, Atlanta
1955 Lemer House, Atlanta
      Toubman House, Atlanta
1956 Midway Elementary School, DeKalb County, Georgia
1957 Southern Bell Executive Suite, Hurt Building, Atlanta
      Coggins Clinic and Drugstore, Atlanta
      Oglethorpe Demonstration School, Atlanta

John Portman: Renaissance Center, Detroit, 1977

1958 Jeff Davis Elementary School addition, Hazelhurst, Georgia
1959 YMCA Building, Southwest Side, Atlanta
YMCA Building, West Side, Atlanta
YMCA Building, Decatur, Georgia
1960 Carey Reynolds Elementary School, Doraville, Georgia (addition, 1966)
1961 Infirmary, Georgia Institute of Technology, Atlanta
YMCA Building, Rome, Georgia
Decorative Arts Center, Atlanta (addition, 1970)
1961- Peachtree Center, Atlanta
1962 Jamestown Shopping Center, College Park, Georgia
Hawthorne Elementary School, Atlanta (additions, 1963, 1965)
Fairburn High School addition, Fulton County, Georgia
1963 Pollack Paper Company Atlanta Plant addition
Perry Homes addition, Atlanta
Sequoyah High School, Doraville, Georgia (additions, 1964, 1965)
1964 John Portman House, Atlanta
Trailways Bus Company Garage and Parking Deck, Atlanta
Pollack Paper Company Plant addition, Birmingham, Alabama
1965 Greenbriar Shopping Center, Atlanta
Service Center School, Atlanta
Peachtree Center Building, Atlanta
Antoine Graves House, Atlanta
Dana Fine Arts Center, Agnes Scott College, Decatur, Georgia
Herndon Elementary School, Atlanta
Greenbriar Tire Center, Atlanta
Greenbriar First National Bank, Atlanta
Rich's Department Store, Greenbriar Shopping Center, Atlanta
Greenbriar Theatre, Atlanta
Trailways Bus Company Temporary Terminal, Atlanta
1966 Spalding Elementary School, Atlanta (addition, 1967)
One Peachtree Street Building alterations and addition, Atlanta
Midway Elementary School, Decatur, Georgia (addition, 1969)
Pollack Paper Company Atlantic Plant addition
1967 Hyatt Regency Hotel, Peachtree Center, Atlanta (addition, 1971)
C. W. Hill School, Atlanta
Henderson High School, Chamblee, Georgia (additions, 1968, 1969)
1968 Merchandise Mart addition, Peachtree Center, Atlanta
1970 South Building, Peachtree Center, Atlanta
1971 J. F. Kennedy School and Community Center, Atlanta
Hyatt Regency O'Hare Hotel, Chicago
Blue Cross Office Building, Chattanooga, Tennessee
Alfred Blalock Elementary School, Atlanta
John Portman and Associates office interiors, Peachtree Center, Atlanta
Park Central Company Office Buildings (2), Dallas
Security Pacific National Bank, San Francisco
1974 Peachtree Cain Building, Peachtree Center, Atlanta
Hyatt Regency Hotel, Embarcadero Center, San Francisco
Levi Strauss Building, Embarcadero Center, San Francisco
Fort Worth National Bank, Texas
1975 Peachtree Cain Company Shopping Gallery, Atlanta
World Trade Mart, Brussels
1976 Embarcadero Center, San Francisco
Peachtree Plaza Hotel, Peachtree Center, Atlanta

Peachtree Harris Tower, Peachtree Center, Atlanta
1977 Bonaventure Hotel, Los Angeles
Renaissance Center, Detroit
1979 Apparel Mart, Peachtree Center, Atlanta

Publications:

By PORTMAN: book—*The Architect as Developer,* with Jonathan Barnett, New York 1976; articles—"Atlanta Decorative Arts Center" in *Interiors* (New York), January 1961; "An Architecture for People and Not for Things" in *Architectural Record* (New York), January 1977.

On PORTMAN: articles—"John Portman: Atlanta's One-Man Urban Renewal Program" in *Architectural Record* (New York), January 1966; "Atlanta" in *Architectural Forum* (New York), April 1969; "The Architects Want a Voice in Redesigning America" by Gurney Breckenfield in *Fortune* (New York), November 1971; "John Portman: Architecture Is Not a Building" by Bernhard Leitner in *Arts in America* (New York), March/April 1973; "John Portman, Architect Plus" by Cathy Stanton in *AIA Journal* (Washington, D.C.), April 1975; "What to Do for an Encore" in *Architectural Record* (New York), June 1976; "John Portman, Architect-Developer" by Yukio Futagawa in *Approach* (Osaka), Autumn 1976; "Evaluation: San Francisco's Hyatt Regency Hotel as a Spatial Landmark" by John Pastier in *AIA Journal* (Washington, D.C.), October 1977; "Architect/Developer John Portman" in *RIBA Journal* (London), December 1977; "Hotels" and "In Progress: Portman Projects" in *Progressive Architecture* (New York), February 1978.

John Portman is Georgia-born and Georgia-educated, as an architect and as a businessman. His work is the epitome of a successful blend of high finance and high-style architecture. That combination is as old in architecture as capitalism, but Portman has given it a new and fresh expression and dimension in American practice. At the same time as his work is financially successful, it is also enormously popular. People who would seldom go to see architecture visit Portman buildings and show them off to their visitors.

It is a tendency of American hotel architecture to be led in a particular direction at a particular time, usually by a particular architect. That architect is, currently, John Portman. His design motif is the urban hotel, self-contained in all its services and functions, and featuring an extremely large central atrium. His atriums are latter day urban forums. They are outfitted with shops, restaurants and lounges to assure a continuous vitality and animation, and they are spectacular in their vertical dimensions.

Portman's office provides all the design services required for executing one of his projects. He has also a commanding knowledge of the fiscal process of building development. Thus, his design skill is amply fortified by the normally controlling focus of financing. The two, combined, are powerful and unswerving. He commands resources of information that can withstand the severest forces of compromise.

As to the quality of his design, he is stylish without being superficial, and his lines, colors, materials and spaces are of great elegance. His buildings furnish a "sense of place" in many American cities that are otherwise lacking in such attributes of sociability.

Portman has practiced solely under his own name since 1968. Although most of his work is to be found in Georgia (particularly in Atlanta, and most notably in the Peachtree Center), his commissions include the Ambarcadero Center in San Francisco, the Hyatt Regency O'Hare Hotel in Chicago, the World Trade Mart in Brussels, and—one of his most ambitious projects—the Renaissance Center in Detroit.

—Paul Spreiregen

PORTOGHESI, Paolo.

Italian. Born in Rome, 2 November 1931. Educated at the University of Rome, Dip.Arch. 1957. In private practice, Rome, since 1958: in partnership with Vittorio Gigliotti, since 1964. Assistant Professor, 1958–61, and Professor, Faculty of Architecture and School for Monument Restoration, 1961–68, University of Rome. Since 1967, Professor of the History of Architecture, Milan Polytechnic (Dean of the Faculty of Architecture, 1968–75). Art Director, Officinia Edizioni, Rome, since 1964; Director/Editor, *Controspazio,* Bari, Italy, since 1969; Editor, *ITACA,* Rome, since 1977. Exhibitions: *Actual Alternatives,* L'Aquila, Italy, 1962; Galleria Il Bilico, Rome, 1966; Bauzentrum, Vienna, 1967; *Festival of Two Worlds,* Spoleto, Italy, 1967; *I Mostra Triennale Itinerante della Architettura Moderna Italiana,* toured Italy, 1968; Hochschule für Bildende Künste und Bauzentrum, Hamburg, 1969; Hochschule für Bildende Künste, Berlin, 1970; Kunst Haus, Göttingen, 1970; Galleria Farnese, Rome, 1970; *Expo '70,* Osaka, Japan, 1970; Architects Association, Oslo, 1971; *Il Mostra Triennale Iterinerante dell'Architettura Moderna Italiani,* toured Italy, 1973; Galleria Il Milione, Milan, 1977; Galleria Pan, Rome, 1978; *Roma Interrotta,* Rome, 1978; Galleria Numerosette, Naples, 1978. Recipient: National Award, Italian Institute of Architecture, 1963; Gold Medal, Ministry of Public Works, Rome, 1971. Member, Accademia di San Luca, Rome, 1966. Address (office): via XXIV Maggio 43, 00187 Rome, Italy.

Works:

1958 ENPAS Building, Pistoia, Italy
1959 Workers' housing, Castrovillari and Villa San Giovanni, Italy
Children's Hospital, Bari, Italy (project)
Baldi House, Rome
1960 Workers' housing, Modena, Italy
1961 Housing development (for 6,000 people), Reggio Calabria, Italy
INA-CASA Housing, in Cariati, San Marco Argentano, Carolei, and Mangone, Italy
1962 Housing development, Bagnara Calabra, Italy
1963 Old People's Home, Montecatini, Italy (project)
Office building, Rome
ENPAS Health Resort, Cesenatico, Italy
1964 Design of the *Michelangelo Exhibition,* Rome
1964/
67 Andreis House, Scandriglia, Italy
1965 600 houses, Naples (competition project)
Opera House, Cagliari, Italy
Canadian Pacific Tower, Montreal (project)
1966 SPECI Residential Development (for 1,000 people), Santa Marinella, Italy
1966/
71 Bevilacqua House, Gaeta, Naples
1967 Papanice Building, Rome
Master plan for the town of Colleferro, Italy
Italian Chamber of Deputies Office Building, Rome (competition project)
1968 Primary and secondary schools, Naples and Palermo
Church of the Holy Family, Salerno, Italy
Palace Hotel, Chianciano, Italy
Master plan for the town of Salerno, Italy (competition project)
1969 5,000 pre-fabricated houses, Kuwait
Social Services Center and Library, Avezzano, Vasto, Sulmona, Italy
Apartment building, Colle d'Arcaccio, Rome
Pre-fabricated schools, Asti and Rome
1969/
78 Technical college, L'Aquila, Italy
1970 Tersigni House, Ariccia, Italy
1972 Restoration of the old town of Salerno, Italy (as consultant)
Aparthotel Andalucia Mar, Marbella, Spain
Royal Jordanian Airlines and Royal Jordanian Army Housing (project)
Tourism development plan for Jordan

Paolo Portoghesi: Mosque and Islamic Center, Rome, 1976 (model)

1973   International Airport, Khartoum
          Master plan for Khartoum
1973/
   74 Officers' Club, Khartoum
1973/
   78 The Royal Court, Amman
1976   The Mosque and Islamic Center, Rome

Publications:

By PORTOGHESI: books—*Guarino Guarini,* Milan 1956; *Borromini nella Cultura Europea,* Rome 1964; *Michelangelo, Architetto,* with others, Turin 1964; *Il Tempio Malatestiano,* Florence 1965; *Infanzia dell'Macchine,* Rome 1965; *Bernardo Vittone,* Rome 1966; *Roma Barocca,* Rome 1966; *Borromini: Architettura come Linguaggio,* Rome 1967; *Dizionario di Architettura e Urbanistica,* editor, Rome 1968; *Roma: un'altra Città,* Rome 1968; *L'Eclettismo a Roma 1870–1922,* Rome 1969; *Victor Horta,* Rome 1969, Tokyo 1976; *Roma del Rinascimento,* Rome 1970, London 1972; *Le Inibizioni dell'Architettura,* Rome 1974; *La Seggiola di Vienna,* Rome 1975; *Album del Liberta,* Rome 1975; *Album degli Anni Venti,* Rome 1976; *Album degli Anni Cinquanta,* Rome 1977; articles—"Fear at Montecitorio: The New Building for the Chamber of Deputies: A Renunciation of Architecture" in *Controspazio* (Bari, Italy), September 1973; "Bottoni: 40 Years Fighting for Architecture," with others, in *Controspazio* (Bari, Italy), October 1973; "The Roman Palazzina" in *Casabella* (Milan), November 1975; "Le Inibizione dell'Architettura Moderna" in

Casabella (Milan), December 1975; "The Research Continues" in *Controspazio* (Bari, Italy), December 1975; "Paolo Portoghesi and Vittorio Gigliotti," interview with Tatsuji Arono, in *Architecture + Urbanism* (Tokyo), May 1977; "Ideology and Original Sin" in *Controspazio* (Bari, Italy), June 1977; "National Competition for the New Administrative Centre of Florence" in *Controspazio* (Bari, Italy), December 1977; "The Architecture of Doubt" in *Controspazio* (Bari, Italy), January/February 1978.

On PORTOGHESI: book—*Alla Ricerca dell'Architettura Perduta: Le Opere di Paolo Portoghesi e Vittorio Gigliotti* by Christian Norberg-Schulz, Rome 1975; articles—"Fortress-Like House on the Clifftop at Fontania, near Gaeta" in *Architecture Francaise* (Paris), October 1975; "Locus: Works by Paolo Portoghesi and Vittorio Gigliotti, 1971–1975" by Christian Norberg-Schulz in *Controspazio* (Bari, Italy), December 1975; "Project for the New State Palace in Amman" by Alfredo Passeri in *Industria delle Costruzioni* (Rome), November 1977.

*   *   *

The works of Paolo Portoghesi, with Vittorio Gigliotti, overcome the concern with rigid limits in the tradition of functional modern architecture and explore more imaginative possibilities of form and meaning. Portoghesi has re-discovered the "gestalt" qualities of Oriental architecture and Gothic, Baroque and Art Nouveau buildings. His concern with tradition does not, however, involve some passive or limited interpretation of the forms and typologies of

the past. He uses tradition in a new and creative way by absorbing the values of the past into the forms of contemporary architecture. Portoghesi is also concerned with the environmental qualities of the site; he works to create harmony between a building and its users.

In the spirit of the revival of Baroque architecture (to which Portoghesi, one of our outstanding architectural historians, contributed immensely), his buildings rediscover space and movement as structural elements. In houses and large complexes he uses a geometric vocabulary in a disciplined manner, relating the uniqueness of the topographical conditions to the specific aims of the client: examples are the Baldi, Andreis, Bevilacqua and Tersigni houses, built between 1959 and 1971.

The rectangular geometry of the earlier phase of modern architecture is amplified and enriched by Portoghesi in these works with combinations of concave and convex spatial elements. In the later works carried out in the Middle East, he has successfully integrated European and Islamic traditions into the formal vocabulary in a new synthesis.

As a teacher and writer, as an architect and planner, Portoghesi has made an important contribution to international architecture.

—Udo Kultermann

POWELL, Sir (Arnold Joseph) Philip.

British. Born in Bedford, 15 March 1921. Educated at Epsom College, Surrey, 1934–39; Architectural Association School, London, 1939–43 (SADG Medallist, 1943), Dip.A.A. (honours) 1943. Married Philippa June Eccles in 1953; children: Dido and Ben. Architectural Assistant to Frederick Gibberd, London, 1943–45. Partner, with Hidalgo Moya, *q.v.*, Powell and Moya, and Powell, Moya and Partners, London, since 1946 (Michael Powell, Powell, and Moya, 1946–50; Powell and Moya, 1950–61; Powell, Moya, Robert Henley, and Peter Skinner, 1961–73; Powell, Moya, and Skinner, 1973–76; Powell, Moya, Skinner, John Cantwell, and Bernard Throp, since 1976). Member of the Royal Fine Art Commission since 1969. Exhibitions: Royal Institute of British Architects, London, 1974; Royal Academy, London, yearly since 1974. Recipient: First Prize, Pimlico Housing Competition, London, 1946; Bronze Medal, 1950, and Royal Gold Medal, 1974, Royal Institute of British Architects; Ministry of Housing and Local Government Award, 1953. Associate, 1944, and Fellow, 1956, Royal Institute of British Architects. Associate of the Royal Academy of Arts, 1972, and Royal Academician, 1977. O.B.E. (Officer, Order of the British Empire), 1957; Knighted, 1975. Address: Powell, Moya and Partners, 21 Upper Cheyne Row, London SW3 5JW, England.

Works (with Hidalgo Moya):

1946/
62 Churchill Gardens, Grosvenor Road, London S.W.1
1949 Houses, Mount Lane, Chichester, Sussex
1951 Skylon, *Festival of Britain,* South Bank, London
1953 Houses and flats, Gospel Oak, London N.W.5
       Local authority housing, Inhurst, Baughurst, near Kingsclere, Hampshire (with Eric Chick)
1954 House, Toy's Hill, near Westerham, Kent
1955 Houses, Stokesheath Road, Oxshott, Surrey
1956 House, Leamington Spa, Warwickshire
       Mayfield School, West Hill, Putney, London S.W.15
1957 Admission Unit, Fairmile Hospital, near Wallingford, Berkshire
1961 Festival Theatre, Chichester, Sussex
1961/
72 Princess Margaret Hospital, Swindon, Wiltshire
1962 New building for Brasenose College, Oxford
1964 Admission Unit, Borocourt Hospital, near Henley, Oxfordshire
1966 Wexham Park Hospital, Slough, Buckinghamshire
1966/
75 Wycombe General Hospital, High Wycombe, Buckinghamshire
1967 Cripps Building, St. John's College, Cambridge
1967/
71 Wythenshawe Hospital, near Manchester
1968 Blue Boar Quad, Christ Church, Oxford
       Swimming baths and assembly hall, Upper Richmond Road, Putney, London S.W.15
       Christ Church Picture Gallery, Oxford
1969 Magpie Lane Annex, Corpus Christi College, Oxford
1970 Dining Rooms, Bath Academy of Art, Beechfield House, Corsham, Wiltshire
       British Pavilion, *Expo '70,* Osaka, Japan (with Takaki and Dodd)
1973 Plumstead Manor School, Plumstead Common, Woolwich, London S.E.18
1974 Wolfson College, Oxford
       Dining Rooms, Eton College, Buckinghamshire
1976 Museum of London, London Wall, London E.C.1
1976/
78 New buildings, Queens' College, Cambridge
1977/
78 Woolwich Military Hospital, London S.E.18
1978 London and Manchester Assurance Company Headquarters, Winslade Park, Clyst St. Mary, Devon

Sir Philip Powell and Hidalgo Moya: Wexham Park Hospital, Slough, Buckinghamshire, 1966

Publications:

On POWELL/MOYA: books—*The New Architecture in Great Britain* by Edward D. Mills, London 1953; *World's Contemporary Architecture,* volume 8, by Ino and Koike, Tokyo 1953; *Come si costruische oggi nel mondo* by Carpanelli, Milan 1955; *Encyclopédie de l'Architecture-Immeubles collectifs,* Paris 1956; *Die neue Schule* by Alfred Roth, Zurich 1957; *Encyclopédie de l'Architecture nouvelle,* volume 2, by Alberto Sartoris, Milan 1957; *New Housing in Great Britain* by H. Bruckmann and D. L. Lewis, Stuttgart and London 1960; *Ebenerdig wohnen* by Meyer-Bohe, Stuttgart 1963; *Encyclopaedia of Modern Architecture* by Gert Hatje, London 1963; *Modern Buildings in London* by Ian Nairn, London 1964; *The New Museum* by Brawne, London 1965; *Architecture in Britain Today* by Webb, London 1969; *Versammlungssttatten* by Ruhnau, Gutersloh 1969; *Cambridge New Architecture* by Booth and Taylor, London 1970; *Student Housing* by Munnings and Allen, London 1971; *Neue englische Architektur* by Robert Maxwell, Stuttgart 1972; *Ospedali* by Aloi and Bassi, Milan 1972.

*

To define, even to myself, my approach to architecture, I find difficult. If I can detect principles, they are too often negative or humdrum—perhaps some are not principles at all: a mistrust of conscious struggling after originality (if originality grows out of the originalities of the problem, well and good); a mistrust, typically English perhaps, of the monumental approach, of making things big when they need not be; a mistrust of the attitude which treats any job as a "prestige job." A belief that each job—large or small, repetitive and standardized or nigglingly tailor-made—has an identity of its own and should not, in order to save its designer time and trouble, be allowed to become an arbitrary re-hash of one of its predecessors.

—Sir Philip Powell

Philip Powell and Hildago Moya both trained at the Architectural Association School of Architecture during the war years when Frederick Gibberd was the principal, and Gibberd's individual approach to modern architecture is reflected in the work of Powell and Moya. They established their architectural practice in 1946 after winning the Pimlico Housing Architectural Competion. This development on the north bank of the River Thames was built in phases between 1946 and 1962 to replace some 33 acres of war damaged property. Churchill Gardens, as it is now called, houses some 6,500 people in flats and maisonettes in a high density layout devised to make the best use of this important riverside site. Every flat has a view of the river, and the general flat planning and site layout is strongly reminiscent of the early 1930's housing work of Walter Gropius in Berlin. Churchill Gardens, built with concrete frame and brick panels, is undoubtedly one of the most outstanding examples of post war housing in Britain, and today, nearly 20 years after completion, it is still well cared for and clearly appreciated by the residents. The human scale of this large complex and the excellent detail planning and design made Churchill Gardens a model that, unfortunately, too few have followed in recent years.

This attention to detail and understanding of human scale has become a Powell and Moya trademark, and although they have designed very little housing since Churchill Gardens, the standard of their work has been consistently high. Mayfield School, Putney, 1956, has been rightly described as "subtle, elegant and humane." That description could be equally applied to all their subsequent work, which has included hospitals, swimming baths and many college buildings at Oxford and Cambridge.

The Festival Theatre in Chichester in 1961, a low-budget hexagonal building, was one of the earliest examples of an arena stage in Britain. The design proved that good modern architecture is not necessarily dependent on expensive materials or a huge budget. In such works as the Cripps Building, St John's College, Cambridge, 1967, Powell and Moya, with inherent sensitivity and understanding of materials applied to each new design problem, have produced architecture that is not original for the sake of originality but of a consistent high standard. They have earned many awards and the appreciation of those who use the buildings.

Powell and Moya received the Royal Gold Medal of the Royal Institute of British Architects in 1974: this was the first and only occasion in more than 130 years that the award was made to an architectural practice rather than an individual architect. One of the most recent buildings by this distinguished practice is the new London Museum, located on a difficult central city site: once again the resultant building is not only eminently practical; it also sets a high architectural standard, in striking contrast to much of the frankly commercial building that surrounds it.

—Edward D. Mills

PRATT, James (Reece).

American. Born in Stamford, Texas, 25 March 1927. Educated at the University of Texas, Austin, 1944–50, B.Arch. 1950; Harvard University Graduate School of Design, Cambridge, Massachusetts, 1952–53, M.Arch. 1953. Served in the United States Navy, in the Pacific Theatre, 1945–46. Married Joanne Henderson in 1955; children: Sabrina, Alexandra, and Ilya. Field Administrator, Broad and Nelson, Dallas, 1951; Design Architect, A. L. Aydelott, Memphis, Tennessee, 1952, I. M. Pei, New York, 1953, Haefeli Moser Steiger, Zurich, 1954, and Broad and Nelson, Dallas, 1955–57; Partner, with Harold Box, Pratt and Box, Dallas, 1958–61. Since 1961, Partner, with Box and Philip Henderson, Pratt Box and Henderson, Dallas. Trustee, Dallas Museum of Fine Arts, 1964–68; Member, Professional Advisory Committee to the Dallas County Mental Health/Mental Retardation Board, 1967–71; Member, Board of Directors, The Greenhill School, Addison, Texas, 1967–73; Member, Task Force on Higher Education, Goals for Dallas, 1968–70; Member, Community Council of Greater Dallas Health Panel, 1971–75. Trustee, Dallas Health and Science Museum, since 1962; Trustee and Member of the Executive Committee, North Texas Educational Television Foundation, since 1969. Co-Designer of the exhibitions, *A Study of Downtown Dallas,* 1957, and *The Better/Best Dallas,* 1958. Recipient: First Prize, Matico National Homes for Better Living Competition, 1959. Fellow, American Institute of Architects, 1973. Address: Pratt Box Henderson and Partners, 3526 Cedar Springs, Post Office Box 19647, Dallas, Texas 75219, U.S.A.

Works:

1960 Children's Development Center (school for mentally handicapped children), Dallas
1961 Wilson House, 9035 Broken Arrow, Dallas
1962 St. Stephen Church, Mesquite, Texas
1963 The Great Hall, Apparel Mart, Dallas
1964 Hochstim House, 3725 Maplewood, Dallas
1965 College Inn, Eugene, Oregon
1966 Quadrangle Shopping Center, Dallas
1967 Master plan for the *State Fair of Texas,* Dallas
1968 Master plan for Griffin Square, Dallas
1969 Recognition Equipment Manufacturing Plant, Irving, Texas
1970 Waste Water Research Laboratory, Dallas
1971 Montgomery House, 3712 Beverly Drive, Highland Park, Texas
1972 Apparel Mart, phase III, Dallas
1973 Master plan for the Surrey Docks, London
1974 Greenhill Middle School and Laboratory Theatre, Addison, Texas
1975 Master plan for Brookhaven College, Farmers Branch, Texas
1976 Sloman House, 6009 St. Andrews Drive, University Park, Texas
1977 Patterson House addition, Crooked Lane at Strait Lane, Dallas
1978 Brookhaven College, phase I, Farmers Branch, Texas
1979 County Court House restoration, Dallas

Publications:

By PRATT: books—*The Prairie's Yield: Forces Shaping Dallas Architecture from 1840–1962,* co-author, New York 1962; *COPE Guide to Environmental Education,* editor, Washington, D.C. 1970; *Urban Design in Dallas, Part I: Objectives,* Dallas 1970; *Environmental Encounter: Experiences in Decision Making for the Built and the Natural Environment,* co-author, Dallas 1979; articles—"A Matter of Choice" in *AIA Journal* (Washington, D.C.), May 1970; "How to Make Fair Park a Fair Park" in *D Magazine* (Dallas), March 1975; "An Architect in Search of Dallas" in *Texas Architect* (Austin), November/December 1976.

On PRATT: books—*Architectural Design Preview U.S.A.* by John Dixon, New York 1962; *Dallasights* by Lu, Weiming and others, Dallas 1978; articles—in *Architectural Forum* (New York), November 1959; in *Interiors* (New York), June 1974; "Dallas" by Donald Canty in *AIA Journal* (Washington, D.C.), March 1978.

*

I was trained just at the end of the era when Texas buildings still relied on a particular natural ventilation and were planned for the sun control needed in a hot, as well as a cold, locale. There was always a conflict between the logical form required by this sine qua non of comfort and the then-fashionable imported style. High styles had been derived in far more northern climes, and their forms only came to be possible in Texas when total climate control was available in the 1950's. We thought we could ignore nature. This was a critical point of architecture in the United States. From this time we would always have some form of climate control.

To an architect who grew up when one *had* to dine in the garden in the evening because it was the comfortable place, had to study in the shaded breezeway, and who slept on a deck in preference to a stifling bedroom, climate control was a great panacea for environmental ills, but it was not enough. The smells, the sounds, and the textures were missing. Before climate control we were trained to make buildings thin in one dimension to encourage the breeze. The fortunate side benefit was ever-changing daylight from at least two directions. There was bred in us an unconscious demand for a variety of sensory stimuli which the never-varying fluorescent bulb and the fixed windows of big square boxes ignores.

From a goal of satisfying immediate sensory demands in a single building one can expand to the wider purpose of answering more psychological needs in the design of environments. Clarifying and expressing those psychological purposes of art in architecture are what I want to be about as an architect. For their solutions are what make for excellence in building any environment.

The interrelation of forms in environment is one aspect of this attitude that is most often overlooked in building. The response of one creation to its existing neighbor helps make extra spaces for the one just added and gives more meaning to both. New possibilities for human contacts are revealed by these spaces between buildings when they are positively designed. In the city, buildings are spread into small pedestrian islands by the motor car. I want to consciously knit them back together into a viable pedestrian fabric. It is the indoor or outdoor spaces which

James Pratt: Brookhaven College, Farmers Branch, Texas, 1978

may facilitate community contact for the individual that interest me; I have gone about the world studying the components of such spaces for the past 30 years to better prepare myself to design them. They nearly always are multi-purposed in nature, and even though they have a formal working purpose, they as well have a recreational use. Creating the design solution to these complex functions is what challenges my ingenuity and imagination.

Another aspect of psychological purpose in architecture which interests me as a design problem is the creation of a more unique sense of place—but as part of its surrounding whole city. What are the constituent elements of a particular place? Physical and social? How can I employ them as architectural devices which both relate that place to its history and contribute to fresh buildings for today?

High art in the past came out of the vernacular of a particular locale—from down deep in its roots. Local materials, local cultural patterns, and local nature each contributed. Understanding and drawing from that vernacular are acts I want to better employ to help give substance to what I create. How can industrial artifacts and processes make as strong, as pungent, as special environments as those pre-industrial ones we admire? In what ways can a design be heightened with the particular light—both the quantity of light and its quality, its sharp direct hardness, or its soft diffuseness; its shadow and its color? What will enhance the particular topography, distill local nature to express the essence of that

place? What should man's relation to the plant and animal world become in that locale?

I want to contribute pieces to a whole, be able to create a quiet background as well as a strong focal one. A work of architecture needs to be in harmony both with other buildings and with nature. I see a need to help man perceive better his relationship with his surroundings—both far and near—as he sits, stands, and moves at all kinds of speeds. How can I help men achieve grace in environments?

—James Pratt

James Pratt and his principal partners, Harold Box and Philip Henderson, make up a Dallas office young in age but capable of wise decisions. In a diverse portfolio of work there is a strength of confident design. Like certain firms in the past (that of Eero Saarinen, for instance), Pratt and his partners make sure that each project is unique, as individual as the program requires—but totally designed.

No two projects have resembled one another; the linking thread is innovation and a progressive outlook. The European design of the Quadrangle Shopping Center, the witty and precise masonry construction of Brookhaven College, and the handling of scale within the Great Hall of the Apparel Mart, all in Dallas, are results of closely coordinated concepts, details, and materials.

In works for heavy public use, maintaining interest is a paramount consideration. Pratt has designed the Great Hall with separate sub-spaces functioning

within the massive exhibition space, providing for multiple usage and comfortable scale. At Brookhaven College the structural intrigue of floating brick beams add to the minute detailing. And Pratt is not afraid to test the new. His readiness to tamper with social habits is best seen in the Quadrangle, a little jewel of a shopping center not from the PBH offices. Off the beaten track but in a very swank area of Dallas, the Quadrangle is neither a mommoth, mindless shopping mall nor a endless American commercial strip à la Venturi. It invites the shopper to a quiet walk through many luxurious shops. Asking an American to abandon his automobile is a risky if not dangerous business, but the Quadrangle overcomes any withdrawal symptoms with intimate courtyards and spaces that invite exploration.

Pratt believes in "projects that can influence the form of the city." The volume of his firm is low but of high quality. Though an expansion to large scale projects is his goal, that goal is being achieved slowly, by careful choice. Pratt, Box, Henderson is a close-knit firm that believes in good design—often total design down to the doorknobs. Each of the partners doubles on duties, permitting closer contact to projects. It is a firm of involvement, stressing teamwork and a flow of ideas throughout the staff.

Look to James Pratt and his partners to influence all areas of architecture. Their designs are confident and clear in vision. They are also interested in their community and the development of their profession: they helped in establishing a school of architecture at the University of Texas in Arlington. Their own lives involve the arts and urban affairs. Their varied capabilities and innovative approach puts them a cut above local and Texas-typical architecture, and will light the way to national and international fame.

—Logan Cravens

PRICE, Cedric.

British. Born in Stone, Staffordshire, 11 September 1934. Educated at the Cambridge University School of Architecture, 1952–55, M.A. 1955; Architectural Association School, London, 1955–57, Dip.A.A. 1957. Principal, Cedric Price Architects, London, since 1960. Co-Founder, with Frank Newby, Lightweight Enclosures Unit, London, since 1969; Founder, Polyark: Architectural Schools Network, London, since 1971. Part-time Teacher, Architectural Association School, London, 1958–64. Chairman, Quality of Life Committee, Science Policy Foundation Ltd., London, 1970–71. Exhibition: *Cedric Price: The Evolving Image*, Heinz Gallery, Royal Institute of British Architects, London, 1975. Associate, Royal Institute of British Architects, 1959. Address: Cedric Price Architects, 38 Alfred Place, London WC1E 7DP, England.

Works:

1961 Aviary, London Zoo, Regent's Park, London (with Lord Snowdon and Frank Newby)
Fun Palace, for Joan Littlewood, Stratford East, London (project)
1964 Potteries Thinkbelt, Staffordshire (project)
1966 Oxford Corner House (public information hive), Central London (project)

1968 Development plan for the North Side of London Airport, Heathrow
Plan for adult education network and components, Greater Detroit and Oakland County, Michigan
1969 Computer Centre, British Transport Docks Board, London
Research on air structures, for the Ministry of Public Buildings and Works, London
1969- Design of short life adaptive housing
1970 Temporary theatre, Amsterdam
Birmingham and Midland Institute Headquarters, Birmingham
1971 Catering Complex, for J. Lyons and Company, Blackpool Zoological Gardens, Lancashire
1972 Community Centre, for Inter-Action Trust, Kentish Town, London
Inflatable Roof Pedestrian Precinct, Southend, Essex
Olympia Information Complex, Olympic Village, Munich
Development plan for the central area of Stuttgart (competition project; with Heinie Wischer and Partners)
Two Tree Island Development, Southend, Essex (with Yorke, Rosenberg and Mardall)
1973 Variable, truckable conference facilities and specialized motor bus design (project)
Floating Breakwater and Marina, Abu Dhabi (project)
Draft building code for single skin air structures, Department of the Environment, London
1974 Students Residential/Social Centre, Trondheim, Norway (competition project; with Archigram Architects)
1978 Generator, North Florida
1979 Westpen experimental cattle and sheep handling plant, Hampshire
Greenbird adjustable experimental aviary, Hampshire

Publications:

By PRICE: books—*Learning: Developing Patterns of Urbanisation*, London 1970; *Air Structures*, London 1971; *Air Structures Bibliography*, 2 volumes, London 1972, 1973; *Predicament of Man*, London 1972; articles—guest editor of "What About Learning?," special issue of *Architectural Design* (London), May 1968; "Non-Plan: An Experiment in Freedom" in *New Society* (London), 21 March 1969; "Expediency" in *Architectural Design* (London), September 1969; "Safety Pins and Other Magnificent Designs" in *Pegasus* (New York), Spring 1972; "Public Spaces" in *London Architecture Club Magazine*, no. 2, 1978.

On PRICE: book—*Planning for Diversity and Choice* by Stanford Anderson, Cambridge, Massachusetts 1968; *New Directions in British Architecture* by Royston Landau, London 1968; articles—"Life Conditioning" in *Architectural Design* (London), October 1966; "The Future Starts Now" in *Interior Design* (London), March 1968; "Rhetoric and Architecture" by Charles Jencks in *Architectural Association Quarterly* (London), Summer 1972; "Approaching an Architecture of Approximation" in *Architectural Design* (London), October 1972; "Price's Process" in *RIBA Journal* (London), January 1976; "Cedric Price—or Still Keeps Going When Everything Else Has Stopped" in *Architectural Design* (London), May 1976.

Architecture and planning must through its content increase the range of imagination, invention and ingenuity of its users.

The reason for architecture is to encourage rather than satisfy people's appetite to behave, mentally and physically, in ways which they had previously thought impossible.

Architecture can best be judged by the untruths it establishes in other disciplines.

—Cedric Price

Cedric Price: Community Centre for Inter-Action Trust, Kentish Town, London, 1972

The ideological debate in British architecture during the last two decades has gained considerable strength and definition from Cedric Price, who represents one extreme point of view most articulately. Although his built work is by its very nature unlikely to appeal aesthetically to many of his fellow architects, he is nonetheless widely respected for his ideas and for his ability to defend them against considerable odds.

Price draws our attention to the negative and repressive side of architecture: to the way in which our actions are all too often restricted and conditioned by buildings originally constructed for other purposes and made incapable of change. He calls for flexibility and adaptability in architecture, believes in unpretentious and expedient buildings that can be used in a variety of foreseen and unforeseen ways, and believes, too, that buildings should have a predetermined life-span—in the case of most of his own built works, less than twenty years. In the interests of flexibility and easy demolition, he constructs most of his buildings of lightweight dismantable materials. He is keen to exploit contemporary technology and disapproves of the widespread use of heavy permanent construction, particularly in high buildings. He has pointed out how seldom architects seem to think, as they build, about how their work could be safely demolished.

Underlying Price's attitudes is a strong political commitment. He has long been a member of the Labour Party, and he dislikes architectural elitism and the production of monuments. Most of the profession, he says, is obsolete and incapable of responding to the needs of our time. Architecture should not be concerned with making statements or sending messages: that is surely the task of newsprint or television. Price's work can be consciously anti-aesthetic in its pursuit of expediency. In his Inter-Action Centre, for example, he used temporary huts called Portakabins for part of the accommodation, generating the kind of ad hoc untidiness that most architects strive to avoid!

Price is also a pioneer of the non-building. An ingenious project for a university in Staffordshire, for example, involved the re-use of an abandoned railway with specially adapted carriages for lecture halls, which could move from town to town. Whereas most architects are only too keen to immortalize their thoughts in bricks and mortar, Price seems to strive to avoid doing so: if possible, he finds a solution to the problem that does not actually involve building, and he takes a perverse pride in seeing his works destroyed as they reach the ends of their allotted life-spans.

Price argues vigorously against the production of permanent specific spaces for particular functions, always stressing the need for flexibility and the unpredictability of future use. He does not take very seriously the need for character and identity in buildings or the danger of disorientation in surroundings that change too frequently—issues that many other architects would put above flexibility and efficiency in use. It seems strangely inconsistent of Price that he acknowledges so fiercely the negative effects of architecture, yet remains so silent about the positive ones.

—Peter Blundell Jones

PROUVÉ, Jean.
French. Born in Paris, 8 April 1901; son of the painter Victor Prouvé. Self-taught; trained as a blacksmith and ironmonger, Paris, 1917–22. Served in the French Army; worked with the Resistance during World War II. Married Madeleine Schott in 1924; children: Françoise, Claude, Simone, Helene and Catherine. Established and managed a furniture factory, Nancy, France, 1922–54. Since 1954, in private practice as a building counsellor, Paris. Exhibi-

tions: Pavillon de Marsan, Musée des Arts Decoratifs, Paris, 1964, 1966; Berne, 1965; Munich, 1965; Copenhagen, 1966; Zurich, 1973; Karlsruhe, 1976; Geneva, 1977; Vienna, 1977. Recipient: Diploma of Honour, *Exposition de Paris,* 1925. Honorary doctorates: L'Ecole Polytechnique, Lausanne, 1969; University of Stuttgart, 1976. Chevalier of the Order of Arts and Letters, Paris, 1965; Member, L'Académie d'Architecture, Paris, 1972. Chevalier, 1950, and Officier, 1975, of the Légion d'Honneur; Chevalier of the L'Etoile d'Anjouan, 1952, and of the Order of Leopold, Belgium, 1958. Address. 37 rue de Blancs Manteaux, 75004 Paris; and 4-6 rue Augustine Hacquard, 54000 Nancy, France.

Works:

1918/
24   Numerous iron and metalwork pieces, Monumental Gates to the War Dead, Verdun, France
1924/
40   Furniture and metal partitions, Paris, Nancy, etc.
     Grilles and architectural ironmongery, Nancy and Paris (with Le Corbusier and Robert Mallet-Stevens)
1937 Roland Garros Aero-Club, Buc, France (with Marcel Lods and Eugène Beaudouin; dismantled by the Germans during the Occupation, 1940–44)
     Wall and screen units, Nancy, France
1939 Maison du Peuple, Clichy, Paris (with Marcel Lods, Eugène Beaudouin and Vladimir Bodiansky)
     French Embassy, Ottawa, Canada
     Weekend House prototype, Nancy, France
1940 Refugee School (project; with Le Corbusier)
1944 Houses for the Sinistres de Lorraine
1947/
49   School of Glassmaking, Croismare, France
1949 Tropical House, Niamey, West Africa
1950 Palace for the *International Fair,* Lille
1951 Firemen's Barracks, Bordeaux
1952 Apartment building, Paris
1953 City Administration Building, Bayonne, France
     Social Security Building, Marseilles
1954 Pavilion, *Centenaire de l'Aluminium,* Paris
     Residential blocks in St. Etienne and St. Jean de Maurienne, France
     Institute of Astronomical Research, St. Germaine en Laye, France
     Jean Prouvé House, Nancy, France
1955 Holiday resort, Arbonne, France
1956 Source Cachat Pump-Room, Evian, France
1956 Pre-fabricated houses, Lagny, France (project; with Le Corbusier)
1957 Low-cost housing, Panama (project; with Georges Candilis)
1958 French Pavilion, *World's Fair,* Brussels (as consultant)
     Luxembourg Pavilion, *World's Fair,* Brussels
1961 Workshops for the French Atomic Energy Commission, Pierrelatte, France
1965 Ski Resort, Vallée de Belleville, France (with Georges Candilis and Shadrach Woods)
1966 Exhibition Village, St. Michel-sur-Orge, France
     Holiday Village, for Air France, Fontainebleau, France
1967 Palais de la Foire, Grenoble
     Maison des Jeunes, Pantin, France
     School complex, St. Michel-sur-Orge, France

Publications:

By PROUVÉ: articles—"L'Habitation de notre époque," edited by Colin Davidson, in *Architectural Association Journal* (London), December 1965; "Auguste Perret," with Vittorio Gregotti, in *Domus* (Milan), May 1974.

On PROUVÉ: book—*Jean Prouvé: Prefabrication—Structures and Elements* by Benedikt Huber and Jean Claude Steinegger, Zurich and London 1971; articles—"Jean Prouvé," special number of *Architecture* (Brussels), December 1954; "Jean Prouvé" in *Esthetique Industrielle* (Paris), January/February 1957; "Jean Prouvé" by Francoise Choay in *L'Oeil* (Paris), no. 46, 1958; "Jean Prouvé" by G. Gassiot-Talabot in *Cimaise* (Paris), no. 54, 1961; article in *Architectural Review* (London), August 1966; article in *Architectural Design* (London), February 1967: "The Future of Structures: Robert Le Ricolais, Jean Prouvé and René Sanger interviewed by Marie-Therese Mathieu" in *Récherches et Architecture* (Paris), no. 10, 1973.

Where have we got to with the industrialization of building (a subject on which we never stop talking). Should we not, having stumbled about for nearly 30 years, take a new leap and finally find ourselves in front, this time, with the obstacles behind us? Really, the buildings of our time, small and large, industrial or commercial, are not on the whole as yet "of age." As for myself, I find only rarely that they harmonize with the other industrial productions of our time. They are too diffuse.

In fact, I do not know of any factory that is building, in large quantities, "conditioned" building elements which, benefiting from the industrial economic miracle of our time, could be used by all the specialists, architects, entrepreneurs, and eventually by the users.

I will try to explain what I mean. I think we must take stock of the position—ask ourselves the question, Where have we got to? Certainly there is an architecture being built that we can call "modern;" let's say that it is contemporary. Most of us are agreed that it does not, on the whole, provoke the same architectural experience as that felt by people in front of the great ensembles of the past; that is undeniable. Would the reason not be a lack of courage in our use of the new materials that mechanization has put at our disposal? Is there not, too, a deficiency of architectural inspiration in relation to these means?

It is important—and honest—to note that, amongst the mass productions of contemporary architecture, there are exceptions, exceptional, striking works—but, one must recognize, they are perhaps too particular. But these works are deceptive in the extent to which they involve a spirit of industrialization, for they come from an execution that is only "semi-industrial;" they involve the fabrication of a limited number of pieces. They are nothing more—for these unique works want to be personalized and signed.

Some think that this kind of peculiarity and diversity is desirable, but personally I think that it leads to disorder.

We note that the old and admired architectural entities were often very uniform. That's a troubling thought. Industrialists are confused because, for the "personalities" of architecture, they are obliged to study and adapt continuously. The Master Builders, who are tempted to evolve, often make industrialists suffer by their personal demands, demands that are often inappropriate to the materials chosen. Such tasks are superhuman and cruel both to men and tools. Prices, too, are very high. And it happens that certain clever artisans, capable of improvisation, compete with the industrialists.

In fact, one has to be very competent to know, for example, what it is possible to obtain simply from a tipper press. It is only when one uses the press as a starting point that constructive inspiration can happen. To know how to take advantage of simplicity is, of course, not easy. But, in my opinion, everything stems from that. Any torment or any exploitation imposed on a basic material and in consequence on machines is economically indefensible.

Yet we must industrialize; we really have no choice. And, in my opinion, as an old practitioner, we must:

Jean Prouvé: School complex, St. Michel-sur-Orge, France, 1967

but no one else was going all the way and making the whole building an industrially designed and produced object. Destruction in the war probably prevented the Buc building from becoming a seminal 20th century building. A few years later, again with Beaudouin and Lods and this time also with Bodiansky, Prouvé built the "Maison du Peuple" in the Paris suburb of Clichy. It was a sizeable building with large moving parts—the 2,000 seat auditorium had floor, walls and roof that moved at the press of a button to change the space or to open it to the sky—and all was wrapped in an ingenious curtain wall of stressed skin panels held apart by coil springs. Forty years of weathering have not dealt kindly with the Maison du Peuple, for the weathering problems were not all solved and the building has not had the sympathetic maintenance that it needed.

The second peak in Prouvé's career occurs in the 1960's with a series of single-storey pressed metal buildings. Workshops for the French atomic energy scientists at Pierrelatte, a holiday village for Air France at Fontainebleau, an exhibition village at St Michel-sur-Orge and many other structures stand as evidence of a well thought out way of building in light pressed metal. It is the way that these buildings are worked out with finesse in every detail that impresses.

It may well be that the prime importance of Jean Prouvé is that he has nagged at the consciences of architects everywhere. No one can say of industrialized building that it cannot be done, for Prouvé has done it. He has not adapted building to machine processes; he has worked it all out from scratch as if no one had ever built a building before. He has shown us all that there is a real alternative to the building construction that we have inherited from the middle ages. Through Prouvé we can see that there is the alternative tradition of industrial design and industrial production. His single-minded life-long dedication has produced some tangible results, but the road is too hard for there to be many following the the way that he is treading.

—John Winter

1) Bring architects closer to manufacturing. That will probably lead them to specialize, perhaps to integrate—but why not? Action at the heart of an innovative industry can be very exciting;

2) Imagine buildings as composed of elements, because the present way of manufacture is useless: it involves new materials being put to use in a traditional manner;

3) Use the elements as a starting point, from which all sorts of possible variations will come to mind—and those variations will in turn become new elements.

This process will lead to a worthwhile industrialization.

The construction of motor cars—is that not the best example of what I mean? We owe the rationalization and the simplicity of the motor car to the recognition by the constructor of that which is technically possible. The same is now true for works of art, even for household items. Shall we remain incapable of that kind of perception in regard to that which is the framework of our lives—our accommodation?

Is it not depressing that, in regard to that subject, a return to the past is now being advocated? What a failure that would be!

—Jean Prouvé

For sixty years Jean Prouvé has been the major figure in using industrial techniques in building. His especial love is for thin sheets of metal, formed and crimped to give them strength. Prouvé has usually worked closely and constructively with architects, but he is not an architect himself and is, in fact, critical of the profession of architecture, believing that the separation of designer and producer is one of the reasons for the low standard, both of design and construction, which is prevalent today.

During his long and diligent working life, Prouvé has been an opportunist, taking the jobs that come, innovating and evolving where he can, often compromising and doing the ordinary where necessary for the continuity of his business. Two moments of this working life seem to be peaks when Prouvé was in the forefront of thought and development in architecture and building technology.

The first high spot in Prouvé's career was in the late 1930's when he built a series of buildings with the architects Beaudouin and Lods. Their Roland Garros Club for flying enthusiasts is a fair claimant to being the first totally industrialized building—walls, roof, floors, ramp, etc. were all pressed metal in this amazing building. The architects of the modern movement at that time were anxious to give their buildings a machine-made look, and machine-made elements, such as windows, were becoming normal,

PRUS, Victor.
Canadian. Born in Poland, 24 April 1917; emigrated to England, 1940; emigrated to Canada, 1952: naturalized, 1957. Educated at the Technical University, Warsaw, 1935–39, Diploma 1939; University of Liverpool School of Architecture, 1945–47, Dip.Ing. Arch. 1947. Served as a Flying Officer in the Royal Air Force, in the Middle East and Great Britain, 1940–45: Polish Cross of Valour (twice). Married the architect Maria Fisz in 1948. Assistant professor, Polish University College, London, 1947–50; Senior Executive Officer, *Festival of Britain,* London, 1949–51; Partner, with George Scolly, Prus and Scolly, Architects, London, 1950–52; Associate, V. Rother and Associates, Montreal, 1952–54; Assistant to Buckminster Fuller, Princeton University, New Jersey, 1953. Principal, Victor Prus, Architect, Montreal, 1954–70, and Victor Prus and Associates, Montreal, since 1970 (associates: Maria Prus; Jean Gareau). Visiting Professor, McGill University, Montreal, 1953, 1966, 1972; Professor, Ecole d'Architecture, Quebec, 1959; Visiting Professor, Graduate School of Architecture, Washington University, St. Louis, Missouri, 1978. Member, Canadian Housing Design Council, 1973–1974. Exhibitions: Victoria and Albert Museum, London, 1950; Montreal Museum of Fine Arts, 1958, 1960, 1963; Musée du Québec, 1964; Canadian Education Showplace, Toronto, 1968; Royal Canadian Academy, 1972; National Gallery of Canada, Ottawa, 1977; Place Desjardins, Montreal, 1978. Recipient: Massey Medal for Architecture, 1963; First Prize, Quebec Centennial Centre Competition, 1964; First Prize, Royal Canadian Air Force Memorial Competition,

Victor Prus: Metro Bonaventure Terminus Complex, Montreal, 1966

1969; First Prize, Montreal Congrès Centre Competition, 1978. Fellow, Royal Architectural Institute of Canada, 1968; Academician, Royal Canadian Academy, 1972; Member, Order of Architects of Quebec; Member, Town Planning Institute of Canada; Member, Corporation of Urbanists of Quebec. Honorary Fellow, American Institute of Architects, 1977. Address: Victor Prus and Associates, 1420 Sherbrooke Street West, Montreal, Quebec H3G 1K5 Canada.

Works:

1950 Public House, London (competition project; with Ernst Pollak)
1951 Display design, Physical World Exhibition, H.M.S. Campania, and Shipbuilding Section, Sea and Ships Pavilion, *Festival of Britain,* London
1952 Office building, Jidda, Saudi Arabia (with G. Scolly)
1954 Webster House, Maitland, Ontario
1955 Public school, Lyn, Ontario
1956 Public school, Montague, Ontario
      Recreation centre, Kaplan, Louisiana (with N. Nehrbass)
1957 Experimental farm, Baton Rouge, Louisiana (with N. Nehrbass)
      Bowen House, Cornwall, Ontario

Country club, Massena, New York (with Norval White)
1958 Lighter House, Westmount, Montreal
1959 McLeod House, Brockville, Ontario
      Strub House, Beaurepaire, Quebec
1960 Rockland Shopping Centre, Mount Royal, Montreal (with I. Martin)
      Yacht club, Senneville, Quebec
1961 Normandie Shopping Centre, Montreal (with I. Martin)
1962 Savoie Apartment Building, Westmount, Montreal
      Master plan for Nuns' Island, Montreal (with Norbert Schoenauer)
      Polar Bear Zoo Enclosure, Granby, Quebec (with Buckminster Fuller)
1963 Hodgson House, Mount Tremblant, Quebec
1964 Centre Simard, Lac à l'Eau Claire, Quebec (project)
1966 Mount Royal Metro Station, Montreal
      Metro Bonaventure Terminus Complex, Montreal
1967 *Expo '67* Stadium, Montreal
      Place Longueuil Civic and Shopping Centre, Longueuil, Quebec
1968 St. Augustin's Church, St. Bruno, Quebec
      James Lyng Polyvalent School, Montreal
1969 Royal Canadian Air Force Memorial Com-

plex, Trenton, Ontario (competition project)
1970 Brudenell River Resort, Prince Edward Island
1971 Langelier Metro Station, Montreal
      Grand Théâtre de Québec, Quebec City
1972 Conservatory of Music, Quebec City
1973 Molson House, Mount Tremblant, Quebec
1975 Centaur Theatres One and Two, Montreal
1977 Canada/France Astronomical Observatory, Mauna Kea, Hawaii
      National Gallery of Canada, Ottawa (competition project)
1978 Astronomical Observatory, Mount Megantic, Quebec
1979 Grantley Adams International Airport, Barbados, West Indies
      Congrès Centre, Montreal

Publications:

By PRUS: papers—*Architecture et Terre des Hommes,* Montreal 1964; *Architecture and Human Ecology,* Montreal 1966; *The Role of the Arts in Contemporary Society,* Montreal 1967; *Two Theatres,* Urbana, Illinois 1970; *Architecture of Little Presence,* St. Louis 1975; *Theatre in North America,* Adelaide, South Australia 1975; *Architecture at* the *Service of the Community Theatre*, Adelaide, South Australia 1975; *Architecture of Condition: Heuristic Approach to Design*, St. Louis 1978; articles —"The Place of Shopping Centres in the City Today" in *Canadian Architect* (Toronto), February 1960; "On Subterranean Architecture" in *Canadian Architect* (Toronto), April 1963; "Metro Architecture" in *Architectural Design* (London), July 1967; "Expo Stadium in Retrospect" in *Architecture Canada* (Ottawa), April 1970; "Un Immeuble à la Mesure du Québec" in *Culture Vivante* (Quebec), May 1970; "Competitions for Canada" in *Review* (Toronto), Spring 1977.

On PRUS: books—*Three Centuries of Architecture in Canada* by John Bland, Ottawa 1971; *Canadian Architecture 1960–1970* by Carol Moore Ede, Toronto 1971; *Pedestrian Revolution: Streets Without Cars* by Simon Breines, New York 1974; *Barbados Airport* by Mary Hall, Montreal 1978; articles —"Public House Design" in *The Times* (London) 5 April 1950; "Pub Competition" in *Architectural Review* (London) April 1950; "Rockland Shopping Centre" in *Canadian Architect* (Toronto), February 1960; "Stadium for Expo '67" in *Architectural Design* (London), April 1967; "Two Subways" by Donald Canty in *Urban America* (Washington, D.C.), November 1967; "James Lyng School" in *Canadian Architect* (Toronto), January 1968; "Prus Wins RCAF Competition" in *Architecture Canada* (Ottawa), September 1969; "Le Grand Théâtre" by Jacob Siskind in *The Gazette* (Montreal), 16 January 1971; "What's Up in Quebec's New Theatre" by Eric McLean in *The Montreal Star,* 23 January 1971; "Le Grand Théâtre de Québec" by André Blouin in *Vie des Arts* (Montreal), Summer 1971; "Brudenell Park" by J. A. Murray and others in *Canadian Architect* (Toronto), December 1971; "The House of the Five Pavilions" by Dan MacMasters in the *Los Angeles Times,* 28 April 1974; "Architects Praise Towns" by Patricia Lowe in the *Montreal Star,* 24 October 1974; "National Gallery Competition" in *Canadian Architect* (Toronto), April 1977; "Un Palais des Congrès sortant de l'ordinaire pour Montréal" by Marc Castro in *Bâtiment* (Montreal), October 1978; television—*Dossier*, CBC, Quebec, 1972.

*

The reality of architecture lies not in the walls, the roof nor even in the spaces they enclose but rather in the ambience that results from the entire complex process. Such ambience is subjectively perceived by the user and it must be our ultimate objective—as surely as making a home is the object of building a house. The form is merely a medium: it proceeds from a particular desire for a particular ambience.

Ambience is the abstract quality of condition, and I believe in architecture of condition rather than in architecture as a rhetorical statement or as an object of synthesis. Perhaps one can talk of the language of form, but it is preposterous to talk of the language of architecture. Our affectivity is pre-discursive: ambience affects us totally and at once. It is in such experience of architecture that its meaning resides.

But apprehension of meaning is often difficult in this post-modern frantic scramble for attention. The over-use of extravagant form places an impossible strain on the already over-taxed human sensibility. In this context the architecture of condition must be the architecture of moderate presence: neither stunning to the senses nor boggling to the mind but acceptive, inclusive and accountable.

—Victor Prus

*

Orthodox modern architecture grew out of the teachings and practice of the Bauhaus in the 1920's. It was a revolutionary ideology based on a doctrine of moral integrity, rationalism, social relevance and puritanism. The movement came to flower during the post-war years, and like most pioneering movements, it overlooked, in its zeal, many of the important issues of architecture.

Victor Prus entered the architectural mainstream

during the early 1950's, and except for a brief period of work in England, his professional life has centered in Ontario and Quebec.

Ideologically, his work often diverges from the accepted canons of modern architecture, insofar as he shifts the emphasis from traditional concerns of programme and construction techniques to expressional and humanitarian considerations. This does not mean that Prus's architecture is not contemporary. Quite the contrary, it attempts to fill a void by introducing extrinsic questions. Prus sees architecture as an intermediary process. He refers to his architecture as an "Architecture of Condition," one that finds its meaning in experience rather than expedience. Condition is the provision, or the prerequisite, for the occurrence and the actualization of an *ambiance;* and *ambiance* is the abstract quality of condition which, for Prus, is the ultimate reality of architecture.

It is this pre-occupation that has created different attitudes and design expectations in his architecture. By rejecting the ultimate authority of programme, Prus accepts architecture as an act both subjective and objective, an interplay between intuition and reason. His architecture is one of accommodation, one that is willing to address itself to conflicting requirements without diffidence.

In the Grand Theatre de Quebec, two opposing objectives merge; the relationship of internal spacial considerations and contextual issues. Thus, the design strives to create an *ambiance* of illusion in which the spectator reacts to a continuum of experiences during the time-lapse of a journey through the theatre. At the same time, the design lets itself be governed by a powerful, if somewhat traditional, urbanistic consideration, namely, that the building becomes a visual focal point for the neighborhood. The result is a rich interior environment, dressed in a formal and very polite vestment. It is, what Venturi refers to, an "Architecture of Complexity and Contradiction."

In a similar manner, contradiction and opposition are acknowledged and used successfully in the design of the Montreal Congrès Centre. The building, an oblong, straddles a sunken, exposed expressway in a longitudinal manner. The roadway separates two natural and very different zones of the city. Relating to each zone on its own terms, Prus produced a building with two totally different elevations, making his architectural integration a sympathetic graft in the urban tissue.

In the Royal Canadian Air Force Memorial Complex, Prus explores the possibility of superimposing varying *ambiances,* related to different spacial or movement conditions of the observer. The design recognizes three totally different, but equally important, levels of perception: from the air, from a motoring passer-by, and from a visitor on foot. Prus meets his objectives by making the building a landscape-form in which scale and form are perceived differently, depending upon the space-time relationship of the observer.

Whereas the French tradition of the Beaux Arts regarded the *plan* as the indispensable basis of architectural composition, Prus employs the *section* as his principal compositional tool. The Grand Theatre de Quebec, James Lyng Polyvalent School in Montreal, the Bonaventure Subway Station in Montreal, and the Grantley Adams International Airport in Barbados, all tell their story most clearly in their cross-sections, which disclose not only the formal substance of the design, but the hierarchical organization of space, the principal nodal points, the circulation lines and the structure.

It is difficult to sum up the work of Victor Prus. Unlike Rudolph or Mies, there is no neat chain of sequential events in which each part is developed or derived from the preceding one; there is no obvious chronology; there are no conspicuous common denominators. There is, however, a common concern and a consistency in attitude.

Prus's buildings are generally microcosmic statements of urbanism, in that they deal with inter-rela-

tionships of scales, conflicts and functions. They are structured around hierarchical principles of order and priorities. Prus is not a formalist. He is not a designer of beautiful objects, per se, nor is he a confirmed rationalist. He does not follow the credo that form is absolutely decided by its fulfilling function. Although he is a contemporary architect, he is not an avid camp-follower of the modern movement.

The architecture of Victor Prus is one of refinement, classical order, and is controlled by a sense of formal appropriateness. His architecture is a premeditative act striving for complete physical and psychological meaning.

—Adrian Sheppard

PUIG i CADAFALCH, Josep.

Spanish. Born in Mataro, 15 October 1867. Educated at the Colegio de Padres Escolapios, Mataro; studied physics and mathematics at the University of Barcelona, 1883–88, and the University of Madrid, 1888, D.Sc. 1888; studied architecture at the Escuela Provincial de Arquitectura, Barcelona, 1883–91, Dip.Arch. 1891. Worked as an architect with the Municipal Works Department, Mataro, 1891–97; in private practice as an architect, Barcelona, from 1897; also worked as an archaeologist and writer, 1889 until his death, 1956. Professor, Escuela de Arquitectura, Barcelona. Guest Lecturer, Sorbonne, Paris, 1918, 1930, Harvard University, Cambridge, Massachusetts, 1918, Cornell University, Ithaca, New York, 1918, and the Metropolitan Museum of Art, New York, 1918. Councillor, City of Barcelona, 1902–05; Deputy, 1907–10, and Provincial Deputy, 1913–23, Las Cortes (Parliament), Barcelona; President, Mancomunidad of Catalonia, Barcelona, 1917–23. President, Institute of Catalan Studies, Barcelona. Recipient: First Prize, Concurso Martorell, Barcelona, 1907. Honorary doctorate: Universities of Paris, Freiburg, Barcelona, and Toulouse. Honorary Member, Académie des Belles Lettres, Paris, 1927. *Died* (in Barcelona) *24 December 1956.*

Works:

1896   Casa Marti, Calle Montesió 3, Barcelona
       Mystery of the Rosary Statuary Group, Camino de la Cueva, Montserrat, Spain (commission from Antoni Gaudí; with J. Llimona)
       Pantheon, New Municipal Cemetery, Barcelona
1897/
1900   Puig i Cadafalch House, Argentona, Spain
1900   Casa Coll y Pagés, Mataro, Spain
       Casa Gari (El Cros), Argentona, Spain
       Casa Amatller, Paseo de Gracia 41, Barcelona
       Casa Macaya, Paseo General Mola 8, Barcelona
1901   Casa Bofill, Viladrau, Spain
       Cross for the Monumental Rosary, Montserrat, Spain
       House, Calle Trinquete 2, Barcelona
1903   Casa Muntadas, Avenida Dr. Andreu 48, Barcelona
       Hotel Terminus, Calle de Aragon 282, Barcelona
1903/
07   Casa Serra, Rambla de Catalunya 126, Barcelona (now a religious school)
       House, La Garriga, Spain

Josep Puig i Cadafalch: Casa Terrades, Barcelona, 1905

1904 Champaña Codorníu Vaults, San Sadurní de
      Noya, Spain
      Casa Trinxet, Calle Corcega 268, Barcelona
      (demolished)
      Casa Llorach, Calle Muntaner 263, Bar-
      celona (demolished)
1905 Casa Terrades (Casa de los Punxes), Diagonal
      416–420, Barcelona
      Dr. Sastre i Marques Pharmacy, Calle del
      Hospital 109, Barcelona
      Casa Muley-Afid, Paseo de la Bonanova 55,
      Barcelona
1906 Palacio Quadras, Diagonal 373, Barcelona
1909 Church of the Immaculate Heart, Buenos
      Aires (project; with J. Goday)
      Casa Sobrieva, Las Guilleries, Spain
      Design of the Plaza de Catalunya, Barcelona
      (project)
      House, Calle Montesion 5, Barcelona
1911 Casarramona Factory, Calle Mexico, Mont-
      juich, Barcelona (now police barracks)
      Casa Pastor, Tibidabo, Barcelona
      Casa Company, Calle Casanova 203, Bar-
      celona
1914 Institute of Catalan Studies Library conver-
      sion, Barcelona
1917 Master plan for the *Esposicion de Industrias
      Electricas,* Montjuich, Barcelona (project)

Publications:

By PUIG: books—*Notes Arquitectoniques sobre les Esglésies de Sant Pere de Terrassa,* Barcelona 1889; *Estudi d'Arqueologia sobre el Sepulcre Roma de Favara,* Barcelona 1892; *Arquitectura,* 2 volumes in the *Historia General del Arte,* Barcelona 1901; *L'Arquitectura Romànica a Cataluñya,* 3 volumes, with J. Goday y Canals and A. de Falguera, Barcelona 1909–18, as *La Geografia i els Origens del Primer Art Romànic,* Barcelona 1930; *L'Architecture Religieuse dans le Domaine Byzantin en Espagne,* Paris and Liege 1924; *La Transmissió de la Cupula Oriental en la Basilica Romanica del Segle XI,* Barcelona 1926; *Decorative Forms of the First Romanesque Style: Their Diffusion by Moslem Art,* Cambridge, Massachusetts 1928; *Le Premier Art Roman: L'Architecture en Catalogne et dans l'Occident Mediterranéen au Xe et XIe Siècle,* Paris 1928; *La Catalogne à L'Epoque Romane,* with Folch i Torres, P. Lauer, and N. d'Oliver, Paris 1932; *La Place de la Catalogne dans la Géographie Generale et la Chronologie du Premier Art Roman,* Paris 1932; *Noves Descobertes a la Catedral d'Egars,* Barcelona 1948; *L'Art Visigothique et ses Survivances: Récherches sur les Origines et le Développement de l'Art en France et en Espagne du IV au XIIe Siècle,* Paris 1961; articles —numerous in *Anuari del Institut d'Estudis Catalans* (Barcelona).

On PUIG: books—*Puig i Cadafalch 1896–1904,* Barcelona 1904; *Arquitectura Modernista* by Oriol Bohigas, Barcelona 1968, Turin 1969; articles— "Puig i Cadafalch" by J. F. Rafols in *Cuadernos de Arquitectura* (Barcelona), no. 28, 1956; "La Arquitectura de Puig i Cadafalch" by A. Cirici Pellicer in *Cuadernos de Arquitectura* (Barcelona), no. 63, 1963; "Puig y Cadafalch, arquitecto, hisoriador de arte y arqueologo" in *Cuadernos de Arquitectura* (Barcelona), no. 68/69, 1967.

Josep Puig i Cadafalch figured prominently in Catalonia's Modernisme Movement. Overshadowed by the movement's leading exponents, Gaudí and Domènech i Montaner, Puig was no less distinguished and extraordinary as an architect, archaeologist, politician, writer and architectural journalist.

After obtaining a doctorate in physics and mathematics, he turned to architecture and graduated from the Escuela Provincial de Arquitectura, Barcelona, where he was exposed to the ideas of Ruskin and Viollet-le-Duc. He began his career by working in the Municipal Works Department in Mataro,

where he built the Casa Coll y Pagés, a pleasing neo-Gothic house. After being appointed to the faculty of the Escuela de Arquitectura, Barcelona, he published many erudite works, including *Arquitectura* (2 volumes) in the *Historia General del Arte* for Montaner y Simon, and *La Geographia i els Origens del Primer Art Romànic,* which established his reputation as a scholar and authority on Romanesque. Apart from his historical treatises, he wrote enthusiastically on contemporary architecture in Germany, England and France, disseminating new ideas into Spain. As early as 1902 he had made thorough analyses of the work of Scott, Olbrich, van de Velde, Wagner and Hoffmann. Through extensive travelling and reading, Puig developed a profound knowledge and understanding of modern architecture in Central Europe. Like Domènech i Montaner, he was also a fervent politician; he served as a deputy in the Cortes (Parliament) and eventually as President of the Mancomunidad de Cataluna.

His first important work as an architect was the charming Casa Marti in the Calle Montesió, Barcelona, in 1896. Here an artistic group that included Utrillo Casas and Rusinol founded the cabaret "Els Quatre Gats," which became a famous rendezvous for those interested in the advancement of the Modernisme Movement. The year 1900 was particularly productive for Puig. He finished the Casa Gari in Argentona and the Casas Amatller and Macaya in Barcelona. These houses, together with the Palacio Quadras in Barcelona's Diagonal, are among his most mature works. Distinctly neo-Gothic in appearance, they are all picturesque and feature highly-ornamented portals, windows, balconies, and rich surface ornament, so reminiscent of plateresque. Tastefully executed and composed, they radiate comfort, warmth and intimacy. Intensely human, they are free of the monotony and monumentality that characterized neo-classical works.

Similar skill is evident in Puig's house in Argentona, where several old houses were converted into single use. Here the continuity of space and planning is impressive. Two further domestic works command attention, the Casa Trinxet (chalet) in Barcelona, which shows influence of Olbrich's Darmstadt Colony, and the Casa Terradas (or Casa de los Punxes) in Barcelona's Diagonal, a large complex, picturesque in composition, with a rich and varied silhouette. At Montjuich, Puig's Casarramona Factory (1911) is imaginatively conceived and displays an attractive silhouette—ideal, comments Oriol Bohigas, for a museum of Modernisme. His project for the *Exposicion de Industrias Electricas* of 1917 demonstrates his versatility and ability to plan a large and extensive complex with conviction.

In assessing Puig's contribution to Modernisme it would be easy to classify his work according to neo-Gothic and archaeological sources, but doing so would be grossly unfair to his spatial skills and general inventiveness. Despite his Gothic preferences, Puig had ability as an architect that is never in question. His work is always lively in composition and visually stimulating. Space and structure are always supported by a love of refined if lavish decoration in tile, iron and stone. His work closely relates to the ideals of the Art and Crafts Movement, but responds intensely to the creative influence of Wagner and Olbrich's Darmstadt Colony. In fact, through his buildings, scholarship, erudition and insight into European developments generally, Puig added new and exciting dimensions to the Catalan Modernisme Movement.

—Harold Booton

Q

QUARONI, Ludovico.

Italian. Born in Rome, 28 March 1911. Educated at the University of Rome School of Architecture, 1928–34, Dip. Arch. 1934, and School of Town Planning, 1934–35. Served as a Lieutenant in the Italian Army, 1938–46: prisoner-of-war in India, 1941–46. Married Marcella Coromaldi in 1946; daughter: Sofia; married Gabriella Esposito in 1973; son: Massimiliano. In private practice, Rome, since 1935. Professor of Town Planning, University of Rome and University of Naples, 1949–54; Professor of Planning, University of Florence, 1955–65. Professor of Architectural Composition, University of Rome School of Architecture, since 1964. Member, Advisory Board for Public Works, Rome; Member, Advisory Board, Academy of Fine Art, Rome; Vice Chairman, Instituto Nazionale di Urbanistica; Recipient: Olivetti Prize for Planning, 1956; First Prize, with others, Turin Master Plan Competition, 1962; First Prize, with others, Government Office Building Competition, Rome, 1965. Member, Accademia del Disegno, Florence, 1958; Member, Accademia Nazionale di San Luca, Rome, 1972. Address: Studio Quaroni, Via I. Nievo 61, 00153 Rome, Italy.

Works:

1948/
58 Church of S. Franco, Francavilla a Mare, Italy
1950 Housing development, Tiburtino Quarter, Rome (with Carlo Aymonino)
1951 La Martella Housing Development, Matera, Italy (with M. Agati, F. Gorio, P. M. Lugli, and M. Valori)
       House, Via Innocenzo X, Rome (with Carlo Aymonino)
1952 La Martella Church, Matera, Italy
       Master plan for Ivrea, Italy (with A. Fiocchi, E. Ranieri, and N. Renacco)
1955 Master plan for the Canton Vesco, Ivrea, Italy
       School, Canton Vesco, Ivrea, Italy (with A. De Carlo)
1956 Master plan for Ravenna (with A. De Carlo, G. Salmoni, and P. L. Giordani)
       Church of the Holy Family, Genoa (with A. De Carlo, A. Mor, and A. Sibilla)
       "Pineta di Donoratico," Castagneto Carducci, Italy (project; with F. Gorio and A. De Carlo)
       Church of S. Gottardo, Genoa (project; with A. De Carlo, A. Mor, and A. Sibilla)
1957 INA–CASA Housing Development, S. Giusto, Prato, Italy (with M. Boschetti, A. De Carlo, and M. Giovannini)
       2-level bridge, Dora River, Ivrea, Italy (project; with A. De Carlo, S. Musmeci, and B. Zevi)

Ludovico Quaroni: Barene di S. Giuliano, Mestre, Venice, 1959 (model)

1958 Master plan for Cortona, Italy (with A. De Carlo and M. Uccelli)

Italian Pavilion, *World's Fair,* Brussels (with others)

1959 Plan for Barene di S. Giuliano, Mestre, Venice (with M. Boschetti, A. De Carlo, G. Esposito, L. Giovannini, L. Menozzi, A. Polizzi, and T. Musho)

Master plans for the towns of Palmyra, Hasseke, Raqua, Kameshlie, and Sahra, Syria (with A. De Carlo, M. Boschetti, A. Livadiotti, and L. Giovannini)

1960

Master plan for the center of Tunis (with A. De Carlo, M. Amodei, and R. Consiglio)

1962 Punta Ala and Il Gualdo Developments, Castiglione della Pescaia, Italy (with R. Maestro, G. Esposito, S. Paoli, and A. Ponis)

Master plan for the center of Turin (competition project; with others)

1963 Lido di Classe Tourist Development, Ravenna (with N. D'Olivo, A. Manzone, and A. Quistelli)

1965 Government Office Building, Rome (competition project; with G. Esposito, M. Mibelli, and A. Quistelli)

Cassa di Risparmio Building, Ravenna (with E. Calanca, A. De Carlo, and C. Salmoni)

Marcellus Theatre restoration and additions, Orsini Palace, Rome (with L. Giovannini and G. Esposito)

Casilino Housing Development, Rome (with G. Esposito, R. Maestro, and L. Rubino)

1967 Master plan for Bari, Italy (with A. Quistelli, A. Renzulli, and R. Ferrari)

1969 Master plan for Reggio Calabria, Italy (with A. Quistelli and F. D'Orsi Villani)

Housing development, Lungomare Quarter, Bari, Italy (with A. Quistelli, A. Renzilli, and R. C. Ferrari)

Government Center, Kaskah, Tunis (project; with A. Amodei, R. Berardi, A. De Carlo, and B. Hagler)

1970 Lagoon Development, Tunis (with A. De Carlo)

Straits of Messina Bridge (competition project; with others)

New Gibellina Parish Church, Italy (with L. Anversa and G. D'Ardia)

Multi-purpose building, Grosseto, Italy (with E. Calanca)

1971 Banco di Roma, Filiale Romana, Rome (with E. Calanca)

1973 University of Calabria, Cosenza, Italy (competition project; with others)

University of Somalia Campus, Mogadishu (with S. Dierna)

Po River Industrial Area, Chioggia, Italy (project; with BBPR and others)

1975 University of Lecce, Italy (with R. C. Ferrari, S. Dierna, and A. Renzulli)

Plan for the "Asse Attrezzato," Rome (with M. Fiorentino, L. Passarelli, and B. Zevi)

1976 FIAT Housing Developments at several towns near Termoli and Cassino, Italy (with F. Karrer and L. Passarelli)

1977 Development plan for the S. Paolo and Collegno areas of Turin (with L. Passarelli and Livo Quaroni)

Publications:

By QUARONI: books—*La Torre de Babele,* Padua 1967; *Immagine di Roma,* Bari, Italy 1969; introduction to *Die Stadtkrone* by Bruno Taut, Milan 1973; *Progettare un Edificio,* Milan 1977; articles— "La Communità Indiana" in *Metron* (Rome), 1947; "La Situazione dell'Architettura Moderna in Italia" in *Metron* (Rome), 1948; "Urbanistica e Architettura" in *Urbanistica* (Milan), 1949; "L'Urbanistica per l'Unita della Cultura" in *Comunità* (Milan), 1952; "Indagine Edilizia su Granasco," with L. Anversa and others, in *Inchiesta Parlamentare sulla Miseria,* Rome 1954; "La Città" in *Comunità* (Milan), 1954; "L'Architetto e L'Urbanistica" in *L'Architettura d'Oggi,* Florence 1954; "Volto della Città" in *Comunità* (Milan), 1954; "Pianificazione senza Urbanisti" in *Casabella* (Milan), 1954; "La Chiesa, lo Spazio Interno" in *Casabella* (Milan), 1955; "Pianificazione Urbanistica come Mezzo di Difesa dell'Ambiente" in *L'Architettura* (Rome), 1956; "La Difesa ed Il Rinnovamento del Paesaggio Urbano e Rurale" in *L'Architettura* (Rome), 1957; "Politica del Quartiere" in *Urbanistica* (Turin), 1957; "Una Città Eterna: Quattro Lezioni da Ventisette Secoli" in *Urbanistica* (Turin), 1959; "Qualcosa si Muove" in *Casabella* (Milan), May 1964; "School, Academy, Architecture" in *Controspazio* (Bari, Italy), November 1975; "Material for the Modern Movement" in *Parametro* (Bologna), March/April 1978.

On QUARONI: book—*Ludovico Quaroni e lo Sviluppo dell'Architettura Moderna in Italia* by Manfredo Tafuri, Milan 1964; articles—"Profilo di Ludovico Quaroni" by Riccardo Musatti in *Comunità* (Milan), no. 6, 1950; "Architetti Italiani: Ludovico Quaroni" by Raffaella Crespi in *Comunità* (Milan), no. 54, 1957; "Progetti dello Studio Quaroni" by Antonio Quistelli in *Controspazio* (Bari, Italy), no. 2, 1973; "The Variety of Invariants" in *L'Architettura* (Rome), October 1977; "Multipurpose Development in Grossetto" by Giuseppe Nannerini in *Industria delle Costruzioni* (Rome), February 1979.

*

I am both architect and planner. I can not conceive the division between the two. I am interested in the life within the buildings in the city, the people in the town, and the life of the town in its natural environment. Before 1960 I worked in support of town planning against architecture; since 1960 I have worked in support of architecture against planning. I have always been fond of town design and of an architecture integrated into the city. I believe that, even today, with new methods of analysis and design, architecture is a synthesis of function, technology and form—but form has to arise from a correct use of the integration of functional and technological planning and design.

—Ludovico Quaroni

*

Among the generation of Italians who graduated in the early and mid-1930's, Ludovico Quaroni holds an important place not only as an architect but also as a planner and teacher.

It is perhaps his influence as a didact and as a collaborator with younger architects in the post-war period for which he is best known in Italy. Outside Italy, however, his best known works are his churches, notably the Church of S. Franco at Francavilla al Mare, the church in his La Martella Housing Development at Matera, and the Church of the Holy Family in Genoa. None of these buildings is large, but they are startling. Not flamboyant, they have a great richness of conception and of detail. Their charm lies in clever and self-conscious manipulation of form, materials and space, to tease the eye and propose visual paradox.

Quaroni's career has been interesting. Always a neo-classicist at heart, even in college, he slipped easily into the Fascist idiom in the late 1930's and produced elegant compositions of great skill, the drawings for which are still admired. He served in the Italian Army during the war, was captured by the British in North Africa, and spent five years in a POW camp in India, where he worked on a few projects and taught architecture to his fellow prisoners. After the war his work became softer. He became greatly involved with low-cost housing—at Tiburtino (an early conscious attempt to recreate a Roman urban vernacular), at La Martella and at Prato. These schemes are characterized by modern planning ideas—buildings set back from streets, free geometry, and functional zoning—married to gracefully eclectic housing forms, and the result is surprisingly successful.

But since 1958, when he was one of the huge team responsible for the Italian Pavilion at the Brussels *World's Fair,* Quaroni has built comparatively little. He has, instead, concentrated on urban planning and on the teaching of that subject. It is a matter of regret that Quaroni's planning work reflects none of the charm and consideration of his buildings. His plans tend to be grandiose, to involve steadfastly illogical pattern-making—a far cry from the village of La Martella, which was admired throughout the world. Yet his reputation is assured: Quaroni can justly be accounted one of the great post-war Italian architects, if only for his housing projects and for his churches.

—Andrew Rabeneck

R

RAINER, Roland.

Austrian. Born in Klagenfurt, 1 May 1910. Educated at the Technische Hochschule, Vienna. In private practice, Vienna. Chief Planning Officer of Vienna, 1958–63. Professor of Housing and Town and Country Planning, Technische Hochschule, Hanover, Germany, 1953–54; Professor of Building and Design, Technische Hochschule, Graz, Austria, 1955. Since 1956, Leader of the Architecture Master Class at the Akademie der Bildenden Künste, Vienna. Recipient: City of Vienna Architecture Prize, 1954; Austrian Cross of Honour in the Arts and Sciences, 1962; National Prize for Architecture, 1962. Honorary Fellow, American Institute of Architects, 1973. Address: Akademie der Bildenden Künste, Schillerplatz 3, A–1010 Vienna, Austria.

Works:

1954 Pre-fabricated housing estate, Vienna (with Carl Auböck)
        Apprentices' Hall of Residence, Vienna
1956 Terraced housing, Ternitz, Lower Austria
1957 Artist's House, Kitzbühel, Austria
        "Town of the Future," *Interbau Exhibition,* Berlin
1958 Municipal Hall, Vienna
        Böhler Brothers Office Building, Elizabeth-strasse 12, Vienna
1960 Steinbruch House, Burgenland, Austria
1961 New town for 100,000 people, near Bilbao, Spain (competition project; with others)
        Municipal Hall, Swimming Pool, and Housing Development, Ternitz, Lower Austria
1962 Mountain Holiday House (project)
1963 Lido, Ternitz, Lower Austria
        Housing development, Mauerberggasse, Vienna
        Evangelical church, Simmering, Vienna
1964 Housing development, Linz, Austria (project)
        Municipal Hall, Bremen (with Säume and Hafemann)
1965 Stadium, Munich (competition project)
        Municipal Hall, Ludwigshafen, Germany
1966 Austrian Pavilion, Plovdiv, Bulgaria
1967 Austrian Pavilion, *Expo '67,* Montreal (competition project)
1969 Puchenau Garden City, phase I, Linz, Austria
1973 High School, Kagraner Anger, Vienna
        Television Centre, Kuniglberg, Vienna
        Covered swimming pool, adjacent to City Hall, Vienna
1976 Roman Catholic Pastoral Centre, Puchenau, Linz, Austria
1978 Puchenau Garden City, phase II, Linz, Austria

Publications:

By RAINER: books—*Die Behausungsfrage,* Zurich 1947; *Städtebauliche Prosa,* Tübingen 1948; *Die Gegliederte und Aufgelockerte Stadt,* with Hubert Hoffmann and Johannes Göderitz, Tübingen 1957; *Anonymes Bauen Nordburgenland,* Salzburg 1961; *Planungskonzept Wien,* Vienna 1963; *Lebensgerechte Aussenräume,* Zurich 1972; *Für Eine Lebensgerechtere Stadt,* Vienna 1974; *Die Welt als Garten: China,* Graz, Austria 1976; *Anonymes Bauen im Iran,* Graz, Austria 1977; *Kriterien der Wohnlichen Stadt,* Graz, Austria 1978; *Lebensgerechtes Bauen,* Graz, Austria 1978.

On RAINER: book—*Roland Rainer: Bauten, Schriften und Projekte* by Peter Kamm, Tübingen 1973.

After the disillusionment and disappointment over the results of post-war architecture and planning, our euphoria has changed to a world-wide scepticism about the triumph of production and the passion for technology and efficiency. We are now concerned

Roland Rainer: Municipal Hall, Ludwigshafen, Germany, 1965

with regaining personal, independent living areas—with space and volume in town planning—aims with which I have been concerned for 30 years in my speeches, my writings, and in my work for dwellings, housing estates and garden cities.

We must still and continually defend this trend towards a more humane and more natural environment, a respect for ecology, against the latest inclinations of many architects to monumentality and "Architecture."

—Roland Rainer

Roland Rainer was Chief Planning Officer for the city of Vienna from 1958 to 1963—though it was only after a long struggle that he was able to carry out his general plan for rebuilding in the city. He first really made his mark there with the 1954 experimental estate of pre-fabricated detached houses that he designed with Carl Auböck in deliberate contrast to the fortress-like blocks of flats built for workers in Vienna during the 1920's. His ideas on low buildings in cities were put forward in his book *Die Gegliederte und Aufgelockerte Stadt.* These ideas, both theoretically and practically, have had a great influence on younger Austrian architects, and post-war reconstruction in Austria has been largely inspired by Rainer and his school, with its emphasis on strict economy and rationality.

Rainer's own urban planning schemes outside Vienna include a municipal hall, swimming pool and housing estate in Ternitz and Puchenau Garden City near Linz. He has been particularly in demand for his municipal halls with steel and reinforced concrete shells and suspension roofs: the first, Vienna Municipal Hall, for 16,000 people, was followed by municipal halls in the German cities of Bremen and Ludwigshafen. They are great multi-purpose buildings, the hall in Bremen being designed to cater for such varied events as cycle racing, ice shows and

political meetings, with grandstands placed along the two sides of a central arena that can be adapted as a track or an ice rink. The basic idea of the design consists in fusing the girders of the grandstands with the tensile members of the suspended roof into a single structure—in contrast to the Vienna hall, where the reinforced concrete grandstands support a steel trusswork.

After a visit to China in 1973, Rainer wrote the book *Die Welt als Garten: China,* which begins by asking the question, "Was könnte uns China sagen?" (What can China tell us?). Rainer's conclusion is that, above all, it can point the way to an improvement in urban living. Summing up some of the problems of modern cities, he argues: "At such a moment we must find interesting a world that for three or four thousand years has enabled many hundreds of millions of people in a relatively small area to live a cultivated existence—a world constructed not as a mechanism but grown like a garden."

—Konstantin Bazarov

RAMIREZ VAZQUEZ, Pedro.

Mexican. Born in Mexico City, 16 April 1919. Studied with the architects José Luis Cuevas and Domingo Garcia Ramos, Mexico City. Married Olga Campuzano in 1947; children: Pedro, Olga Maria, Javier and Gabriella. In private practice, Mexico City, since 1944. Zone Chief for the State of Tabasco, Federal School Construction Program, Mexico, 1944–47; Head of the Department of Building Preservation, Mexican Ministry of Public Education, 1947–58; General Manager of the Administra-

tive Committee, Federal School Construction Program, Mexico, 1958–64; Founder and Technical Director, Regional Center for School Construction, Mexico City, 1964–66. Secretary of Human Settlements and Public Works of the Mexican Government, since 1976. Professor of Architectural Design and Town Planning, National School of Architecture, Mexico City, 1942–58. Member of the Executive Committee, International Union of Architects, 1953–57; President, Society of Mexican Architects, and National Federation of Architects of Mexico, 1953–59; Founder and Director, Chapultepec Park Artistic and Cultural Unit, Mexico City, 1953–65; Member, ICOMOS (International Council of Monuments and Sites), 1965–76; President, XIX Olympic Games Organization Committee, Mexico City, 1966–70, and President of the Mexican Olympic Committee, 1972–74; Technical Adviser to the Institute of Political, Economic and Social Studies, 1969–70, and Secretary of Press and Propaganda, 1975, Institutional Revolutionary Party of Mexico; President, Industrial Design Seminar, Mexico City, 1970; Member of the International Council, Museum of Modern Art, New York, 1970; President, Metropolitan Autonomous University, Mexico City, 1974–75. Member of the International Olympic Committee, since 1972; Founder and Chairman of the Board of Directors of the Association of Friends of the National Museum of Anthropology, Mexico City, since 1974. Exhibitions: *World's Fair,* Brussels, 1958; *World's Fair,* New York, 1964. Recipient: Golden Star, Belgium, 1958; Grand Prize, *Triennale,* Milan, 1960; Grand Prize and Gold Medal, *Bienal,* Sao Paulo, 1965; Gold Medal, Mexico City, 1969; Jean Tschumi Prize, International Union of Architects, 1969; Special Award, Industrial Designers Society of America, 1969; National Arts Prize, Mexico, 1973; Gold Medal, Académie d'Architecture, Paris, 1978. Member, Society of Mexican Architects, 1953, and

Pedro Ramirez Vazquez: National Museum of Anthropology, Mexico City, 1964

National Federation of Architects of Mexico, 1953; Acting Member, National Academy of History and Geography, Mexico, 1965; Founding Member, Academy of Arts of Mexico, 1968. Honorary Member, American Institute of Architects, 1953; Honorary Member, Industrial Designers Society of America, 1970; Member, Royal Society of Arts, London, 1972. Knight of the Order of the Crown of King Leopold II, Belgium, 1958; Great Officer, Vasa Royal Order of Sweden, 1968; Great Chief, Ghana, 1968; Entrant, Golden Book of Israel, 1969; Great Officer, Order of the White Rose of Finland, 1969; Commander, Order of the Crown of Belgium, 1970. Address (office): Avenida de las Fuentes 170, Mexico 20, D.F., Mexico.

Works:

1944/
64 35,000 schools throughout Mexico (while working for the Mexican Ministry of Education)
1953 National School of Medicine, Mexico City (with Alvarez Espinosa, Hector Velazquez and Ramon Torres)
1954 Ministry of Labor and Social Welfare, Mexico City
1955/
57 15 markets in Mexico City
1958 Mexican Pavilion, *World's Fair,* Brussels
1960 National Institute for the Protection of Infancy, Mexico City
        Gallery of History, Chapultepec Park, Mexico City
1962 National Labor Conciliation Board, Mexico City
        Mexican Pavilion, *World's Fair,* Seattle
        Borderline Museum, Juarez, Mexico
1963/
64 Museum of the City of Mexico
        Museum of Modern Art, Chapultepec Park, Mexico City
        National Museum of Anthropology, Mexico City
        Mexican Pavilion, *World's Fair,* New York
1965 Ministry of Foreign Relations, Plaza of Three Cultures, Mexico City
        Aztec Soccer Stadium, Mexico City
1968 National Confederation of Chambers of Commerce, Mexico City
        Cauhtemoc Soccer Stadium, Puebla, Mexico
1970 The Home for Girls and the Children's Hospital, Mexican Institution of Assistance to Children, Mexico City
1971 Market municipal plan for San Salvador, El Salvador (as technical adviser)
1972 Museum of African Art, Dakar, Senegal (project)
1974/
75 Pilsen High School, Chicago
1975 *Siempre* Magazine Building, Mexico City (project)
        Urban plan for a new capital city, Dodoma, Tanzania
1975/
76 Japanese Embassy, Mexico City (with Manuel Rosen and Kenzo Tange)
        Shrine of Guadalupe, Villa Gustavo A. Madero, Mexico City
1976 Master plan for Paseo Residencial, Monterrey, Mexico
        Fertilizantes de Centro America Building, San Jose, Costa Rica
        Mexican-Japanese School, Mexico City (with Manuel Rosen)
        Clinic and Social and Sports Centre, Monterrey, Mexico
        Lomas Cemetery, Mexico City (project)
        Museum of Anthropology, Lima, Peru (project; as adviser)

Publications:

By RAMIREZ VAZQUEZ: books—*4,000 Years of Mexican Architecture,* Mexico City 1956; introduction to *Mayan Architecture* by Henri Stierlin, Geneva 1964; *The National Museum of Anthropology,* Geneva 1968.

On RAMIREZ VAZQUEZ: book—*Mexico's Modern Architecture* by I. E. Myers, New York 1952; articles—"National School of Medicine" in *L'Architecture d'Aujourd'hui* (Paris), April 1955; articles on prefabricated rural schools in *Der Architekt* (Stuttgart), August 1960, *Comunità* (Milan), September 1960, *L'Architecture d'Aujourd'hui* (Paris), September 1960, *L'Oeil* (Paris), September 1960, *Industrial Design* (New York), September 1960, *L'Architettura* (Rome), November 1960, *Architectural Review* (London), November 1960, and in *Domus* (Milan), December 1960; "National Museum of Anthropology" in *Architectural Record* (New York), June 1969; "Paseo Tollocan" in *Landscape Architecture* (Louisville, Kentucky), November 1976.

In my opinion the mission of architecture is to give form to the spaces where man lives; it should be governed by the system of life and the technique of a given time, respecting at the same time the permanent and traditional esthetic values. In my work I have always endeavored to preserve these values, using contemporary solutions. Without imitating forms or repeating solutions I have tried, in the formal aspects, to preserve in the open spaces—in the patios, for instance—proportion and respect for the environment and the landscape, a generosity of dimensions, color, and the natural texture of materials, emphasizing the clarity and the sobriety of their use and harmony with their objective.

I also believe that architecture is a discipline meant to serve man; its mission consists not only in contributing forms and in planning works, but basically in representing an instrument of social politics. It is necessary to produce, simply and clearly, the architecture needed by our country, based on a deep knowledge of the peculiarities of our needs, both individual and collective, applying the technological progress of our time to the level of our economic possibilities in order to lead a better life at home, in the country and in the city. I tried to reflect that concept in the rural school, in the house that grows, in the museums, in all sorts of buildings. Architecture is the material expression of its time, its objective being to serve man, not to achieve a form. Therefore, I have always been concerned with the importance of the work, giving it a human scale, not from a material point of view but bearing in mind the dignity of man and the social group he belongs to.

Hence the scope of the museums I have built. These were conceived with the same idea: a museum, an objective and permanent educational building, must be easily understood by people of all cultural levels, must be a place where visitors will behold the objects it contains, will learn and be proud of their past and help them to be useful in the future.

The above ideas, which have inspired and guided my architectural work, reflect a desire to be useful to society and to act with intellectual honesty.

—Pedro Ramirez Vazquez

*   *   *

The architectural design of Pedro Ramirez Vazquez is stunningly original.

Although he has designed many museums, in Mexico, Africa, and Peru, his most famous is the National Museum of Anthropology in Mexico City. Housing one of the world's richest collection of archaeological treasures, this imposing edifice features an immense forecourt with bowers of trees shading benches of hand-hewn stone. The impressive entrance of smooth concrete and glass planes is flanked on either side with massive walls of rough, natural stone. Covering an eleven acre site, the complex contains an inner 600 foot long patio with an umbrella-like fountain fashioned from a sculptured bronze column topped with an aluminum overhang. The water, which cascades onto black cantara paving, is re-circulated through small holes in the floor. Cut and fitted by hand, the cantara stone is evidence of Mexico's "mano de obra"—hand labor—reflecting pride of craftsmanship. Immense glass walls open the surrounding gardens and forests of the park into the interior of the museum, creating a blending of the indoors and outdoors, in conjunction with the past and the present, surpassing space and time.

His other work includes the School of Medicine for Mexico's University City: the buildings comprise three distinct units—the lecture halls, the laboratories, and a fan-shaped auditorium with 1,050 seats. From 1944 to 1964, 35,000 prefabricated schools were built from his plans in rural areas throughout Mexico. The Mexican Government also commissioned him to design the Mexican pavilions for three World's Fairs—New York, Seattle, and Brussels. Ramirez Vazquez's pavilion in Brussels was a small jewel set among the large pavilions of other countries. Comprising only 950 square yards, the structure was designed to represent Mexico as a progressive country rooted in an ancient culture.

Clean swept volumes and planes mark his Ministry of Labor and Social Security Building in Mexico City. Supported on round columns, the facade makes use of concrete, glass and light sandstone contrasting with dark lava. Ramirez Vazquez also designed many markets with thin-shell concrete roofs shaped like inverted umbrellas. These forms, derived from the awnings that cover the rural open markets, allow for natural light and cross-ventilation.

His work is both distinguished and varied.

—Peggy Cochrane

RAPSON, Ralph.

American. Born in Alma, Michigan, 13 September 1914. Educated at Alma College, 1933–35; University of Michigan, Ann Arbor, 1935–38 (Phi Beta Kappa), B.Arch. 1938; graduate studies in urban and regional planning at Cranbrook Academy of Art, Bloomfield Hills, Michigan, 1938–40 (Cranbrook Scholarship). Married Mary Dolan in 1949; children: Richard and Thomas. In private practice, Chicago, 1942–46, and Cambridge, Massachusetts, 1946–54. Since 1954, in private practice, as Ralph Rapson and Associates Inc., Minneapolis. Head, Department of Architecture, Institute of Design, Chicago, 1942–46; Associate Professor, School of Architecture, Massachusetts Institute of Technology, Cambridge, 1946–54. Since 1954, Professor and Head, School of Architecture, University of Minnesota, Minneapolis. Thomas Jefferson Visiting Professor, University of Virginia, Charlottesville, 1967. Member of the Editorial Board, *Northwest Architect,* 1955–65; Commissioner, Minneapolis City Planning Commission, 1957–60; Member, Board of Directors, Walker Art Center, Minneapolis, 1959–63; Member, Architectural Advisory Board, United States General Services Administration, 1965–69; President, Minneapolis Chapter of the American Institute of Architects, 1967–68; Member, Board of Directors, Minnesota Society of Architects, 1967–70; Member, Low Income Housing Advisory Board, United States Metropolitan Planning Commission, 1969–72; Member, Transportation Task Force, Capitol Long Range Improvement Committee, Minneapolis, 1969–71. Architecture and Planning Consultant, University of Manitoba, Winnipeg, since 1957; Member, Minneapolis Committee on Urban Environment, since 1968 (past Vice-Chairman); Member, Architectural Advisory Board, University of Kansas, Lawrence, since 1970; Member, Community Development Task Force, Minneapolis, since 1971; Member, Architectural Advisory Board, United States Federal Reserve System, since 1977. Recipient: Parker Medal, State of Massachusetts, 1951; First Honor Award, 1954, 1975, Merit Award, 1955 (four times), and Bartlett Award, 1975, American Institute of Architects; Danish Government Medal, 1955; First Honor Award, 1958, 1959 (twice), 1963, 1964, 1972, 1973, Merit Award, 1960, 1961 (three times), 1965 (twice), 1972, 1974 (twice), and Honor Award, 1976, 1977, Minnesota Society of Architects; First Honor Award, Minneapolis Downtown Council, 1964; Award of Merit, Community Facilities Administration, 1964; First Design Award, *Progressive Architecture,* 1968, 1972; Honor Award, Pacific Region White Cement Architectural Awards Program, 1972; Honor Award, Minneapolis Committee on Urban Environment, 1972; Honor Award, United States Department of Housing and Urban Design, 1974 (twice); Barbara Flanagan Award, Minneapolis Committee for Urban Design, 1977; Honor Award, American Institute of Architects, Minnesota Chapter, 1977, 1978. Fellow, American Institute of Architects. Address: Ralph Rapson and Associates Inc., 1503 Washington Avenue South, Minneapolis, Minnesota 55454, U.S.A.

Works:

1942 Willow Run Schools (3), Michigan (with Eero Saarinen)
1946 Gidwitz House, Chicago
1948 Gladstone Clinic and Apartments, McHenry, Illinois

1950 Eastgate Apartments, Cambridge, Massachusetts
1951/
53 United States Embassy Staff Apartments, Neuilly, Paris (with J. Vander Meuler)
1953 United States Embassy Office Building, Stockholm (with J. Vander Meuler)
United States Embassy Office Building, Copenhagen (with J. Vander Meuler)
United States Consulate and Apartments, Le Havre, France (with J. Vander Meuler)
United States Embassy, Athens (project; with J. Vander Meuler)
United States Embassy, The Hague (project; with J. Vander Meuler)
United States Embassy, Oslo (project; with J. Vander Meuler)
1954 United States Embassy Staff Apartments, Boulogne, Paris (with J. Vander Meuler)
1955 Gidwitz House II, Ravinia, Illinois
Hillside School and Dormitories, Northboro, Massachusetts
St. Peter's Lutheran Church, Edina, Minnesota
1958 Prince of Peace Lutheran Church for the Deaf, St. Paul, Minnesota
1959 Fargo City Hall and Memorial Auditorium, North Dakota
1960 St. Luke's Presbyterian Church, Minnetonka, Minnesota
1961 Mrs. Edward Brooks House, Long Lake, Minnesota

1963 Tyrone Guthrie Theatre, Minneapolis
State Capitol Credit Union Branch Office, Minneapolis
Wilder Residences for the Elderly, St. Paul, Minnesota
Pillsbury House, Wayzata, Minnesota
1964 Chateau Co-op Dining Club, Minneapolis
1969 St. Thomas Aquinas Church, St. Paul Park, Minnesota
1970 Hope Lutheran Church, Minneapolis
Butwin House, Mendota Heights, Minnesota
Cedar Riverside (housing and community complex), stage I, Minneapolis
1971 International Studies Building, University of Chicago (with Burnham and Hammond)
Performing Arts Center, University of California at Santa Cruz (with Henrick Bull)
1972 Rarig Building: Performing Arts Center, University of Minnesota, Minneapolis
1973 Humanities/Fine Arts Center, University of Minnesota at Morris
1974 Cedar Riverside (housing and community complex), stage II, Minneapolis
Cedar Square West (housing and community complex), stage I, Minneapolis
1975 Weyer House, Excelsior, Minnesota
1976 Recreation Facilities Building, Southern Illinois University, Carbondale
Classroom/Laboratory Building, St. Mary's Junior College, Minneapolis
The Glass Cube (Rapson House), Amery, Wisconsin

Ralph Rapson: Humanities/Fine Arts Center, University of Minnesota at Morris, 1973

1977 First Federal Savings and Loan, Estherville, Iowa
1978 Tew House, Wayzata, Minnesota
       Liu House, North Oaks, Minnesota
1978– Flesch/Davis House, Afton, Minnesota
       Okoboji Condominiums, Estherville, Iowa

Publications:

By RAPSON: book—*Architects on Architecture,* edited by Paul Heyer, New York 1965; article—"The Ten Commandments of Architectural Design" in *Architecture Minnesota* (Minneapolis), November/-December 1977.

On RAPSON: books—*Architecture U.S.A.* by Ian McCallum, New York 1959; *The Tyrone Guthrie Theatre,* Minneapolis 1963; *A New Theatre* by Tyrone Guthrie, New York 1964; *Contemporary Theatre Architecture* by Maxwell Silverman, New York 1965; *Theatre Design* by George Izenour, New York 1965; *Structure Systems* by Heinrich Engel, Stuttgart 1967; *A Concise History of Western Architecture* by R. Furneaux Jordan, New York 1969; *New Town in America: The Design and Development Process,* edited by James Bailey, New York 1973; *Drawings by American Architects,* edited by Alfred M. Kemper, New York 1973; *Towards a Quality of Life,* edited by Lelah Bakhtiar, Tehran 1974; *Theatres and Auditoriums* by Harold Burris-Meyer and Edward Cole, Huntington, New York 1975; *The Architecture Book* by Norval White, New York 1976; *The New Downtowns* by Louis G. Redstone, New York 1976; *Architectural Presentation Techniques* by William Wilson Atkins, New York 1976; *Architecture in the United States* by Ralph Hammett, New York 1976; articles—"Architecture for the Stage" in *Walker Design Quarterly* (Minneapolis), no. 58, 1963; "Tyrone Guthrie Theatre" in *Progressive Architecture* (New York), December 1963; "Theatres U.S.A.: Recent Designs by Ralph Rapson and John Johansen" in *Architectural Review* (London), April 1964; "Ralph Rapson: Artistic Virtuoso" by Mike Wilkinson in *Architecture Minnesota* (Minneapolis), May 1975.

*   *   *

Architecture is not only a highly precise social and physical science but also a fine art—the processing of organizing and ordering space and relating it to society for our use, comfort, pleasure and spiritual satisfaction. In other words, it is the total act of converting and controlling, shaping and ordering the entire physical environment into an effective, expressive and harmonious setting for human life. Quality and totality must be stressed; there is a dichotomy here. It is a conflict imposed by the effort to simultaneously satisfy both practical human needs and human aspirations. In a sense this dilemma is the conflict of technology versus cultural value.

In our search for significant environment the art of architecture must always control the science and technology of architecture, and the total must control the parts. The creative act must govern. Frank Lloyd Wright has given a clue in a beautifully stated passage:

> In the arts, every problem carries within itself its own solution, and the only way yet discovered to reach it is a very painstaking way: to look sympathetically within the thing itself, to proceed to analyze and sift it, to extract its own consistent and essential beauty, which means its common sense truthfully idealized. There lies the heart of the poetry that lives in architecture.

Clearly this is the design process; however, the physical synthesis is quite another thing. Creativity is neither consistent nor predictable. The magic which the individual architect brings to each situation will vary, but it is nonetheless his grave responsibility to society.

An ancient Chinese Taoist philosopher—perhaps it was Confucius—wrote: "Lay more stress on the process through which perfection is sought than upon perfection itself." While I'm not certain that I agree completely with this—for no matter how excellent the process, the resultant design may still be poor—still, the process, the orderly systematic search, is vital and essential to a quality solution. Natural scientists have long perceived that form and process are indivisible aspects in organic growth.

As an educator, as well as a practicing architect and planner, I subscribe to the importance of the design process. This is particularly true in the education of designers, where it is far more important to establish rational and creative thought process than simply a final design product.

Over the years I have organized ten check-points in my design search. These "ten commandments" are not listed here in any particular order; quite obviously one or another of these points will take precedence in any one specific situation. While laying little claim to their originality, I do try to work with integrity and vigor within this general framework: 1) the need for economic/managerial responsibility; 2) need for historical continuity; 3) concern for the regional context and site conditions; 4) functional integrity in planning; 5) structural integrity; 6) integrity of technological advantage; 7) creative space; 8) the need for architectural expression; 9) the understanding and utilizing the potential of the period; and 10) totality of concept and totality of the creative act.

Igor Stravinsky has written: "The uninitiated imagine that one must await inspiration in order to create. That is a mistake." How true! Creative design is an agonizing and often lonely process. But it's an exhilarating, joyous and rewarding effort. And creativity is hard, loving work; while little is understood of creativity, near the heart of the creative process is the ability to maintain broad intuitive and emotional activity freely within the framework of endless hours of search and a vast amount of acquired knowledge along with endless experience.

Concerned and motivated as it is with the problems of humanity, there is seldom a black and white solution to any given environmental problem; rather, there is the great richness of the entire palette, limited only by the architect's inherent and developed qualities. Quite obviously, there is running through all of this the violent conflict of our highest hopes and aspirations with the daily press of reality—the dilemma of the dichotomy of the intellectual versus the emotional aspects of life. Technical means have always been and will continue to be the necessary means of achieving an enriched environment, but our great advantages will be of little value unless inspired by truly cultural values—values based on a genuine desire for harmonious and orderly environment, all stemming from an understanding and appreciation of the dignity of man and his aspirations. Fundamental to human survival is man's need to bring order to his environment. Unless he brings life's situations to an integrated whole, he cannot continue to grow and develop.

What I have been saying can perhaps best be summed up in this one short prescription found in Buddhism: "Develop an infallible technique, and then place yourself at the mercy of inspiration."

—Ralph Rapson

*   *   *

The architecture of Ralph Rapson emphasizes the straight line and its accompanying geometric shapes. Although his work displays many mechanistic and functionalist tendencies, this Minnesota architect has attempted to move beyond mere structural and material dictates to create spatially intriguing sculptural buildings. Grounded in a strong Miesian tradition, Rapson respects the need for structural integrity and functional planning; however, he does not limit himself by these approaches. He expands upon their theoretical foundations to create a more ornate, humanistic cube. For Rapson an architectural form is more than just a machine; it is a machine which may be enhanced via playful manipulation of space through the extension/accentuation of structural elements in a strictly decorative manner.

Control and order are the primary concerns of Rapson's architecture, and many restrained, formal designs have come out of his office. Such straightforward, unadorned structures as the United States embassies in Sweden and Denmark, St. Thomas Acquinas Catholic Church, the Prince of Peace Lutheran Church, and the State Capitol Credit Union indicate the main thrust of his work. However, a more dynamic plan, the Pillsbury House in Wayzata, Minnesota, more aptly reveals Rapson's ideals at their best.

One of the most ambitious domestic designs of the past fifteen years, the Pillsbury House consists of five separate, cube-shaped, brick pavilions which are linked by glass enclosed bridges. Skylights of various heights project above the flat roof and ostensibly serve as natural illumination sources. These functional elements provide a sculptural dimension and further enhance the aloftness of the building which a cantilevered patio and raised concrete block foundation already establish. The fenestration, much of which is inset, further contributes to the sculptural nature of the dwelling through the creation of an undulating surface. The use of separate pavilions produces various courtyards whose spaces are determined by concrete block walls of varying heights. The sculptural approach applied to the exterior is vigorously perpetuated on the interior with a cubistic ceiling treatment resulting in multiple ceiling heights within each room. These interior and exterior elements combine to achieve a subtle, yet complex, spatial experience.

The Pillsbury House is an example of Rapson at his best. His handling of space mediates the formalistic geometric lines to create a provocative design. Such a playful use of space and forms fulfills Rapson's definition of architecture, the organization and ordering of an environment which relates to people's physical and spiritual use, comfort and pleasure. How well his more formal designs attain such an end depends upon how austere a definition is applied to the human condition and its needs.

—Don J. Hibbard

RAUCH, John.

American. Born in Philadelphia, Pennsylvania, 23 October 1930. Educated at Wesleyan University, Middletown, Connecticut, 1951; University of Pennsylvania, Philadelphia, 1953–57, B.Arch. 1957. Served in the United States Army, 1951–53, and in the reserves, 1953–55: Lieutenant. Partner, with Robert Venturi, *q.v.,* since 1964, and with Venturi and Denise Scott Brown, *q.v.,* since 1967, Venturi and Rauch, Philadelphia (associates: Steven Izenour; David Vaughan). Lecturer, University of Pennsylvania, 1967–69. Chairman of the Awards Committee, 1968, and Chairman of the Official Practice Committee, 1969–70, American Institute of Architects. Exhibitions: *Gold Medal Awards,* Architectural League of New York, 1965; *The Work of Venturi and Rauch,* toured the United States, 1965; *40 under 40,* Architectural League of New York, 1965; *The Work of Venturi and Rauch,* Whitney Museum, New York, 1971; *The Invisible Artist,* Philadelphia Museum of Art, 1974; *The Work of Venturi and Rauch,* Pennsylvania Academy of Fine Arts, Philadelphia, 1975; *Suburban Alternatives: 11 American Projects,* Biennale, Venice, 1976; *200 Years of American Architectural Drawing,* Cooper-Hewitt Museum, New York, 1977; *Drawings for a More Modern Architecture,* Drawing Center, New York, and Cooper-Hewitt Museum, New York, 1977; *Architecture 1: An Exhibition,* Leo Castelli Gallery, New York, and Institute of Contemporary Art, Philadelphia, 1977; *Roma Interotta,* Incontri

Internazionali d'Arte, Rome, 1977–78; *Palaces for People,* Cooper-Hewitt Museum, New York, 1977; *Presence and Absence,* Galleria d'Arte Moderna, Bologna, Italy, 1977. Recipient: Graham Foundation Grant, 1963; Design Award, *Progressive Architecture,* 1967; First Prize, Yale University Mathematics Building Competition, 1970; Gold Medal, 1972, and Adaptive Re-use Award, 1976, American Institute of Architects, Philadelphia Chapter; Award of Merit, *House and Home/AIA,* 1973; Arnold Brunner Prize, National Institute of Arts and Letters, 1973; Creative Arts Award, Brandeis University, Waltham, Massachusetts, 1976; Casebook Award, *Print Magazine,* 1976 (three times); Honor Award, 1977, and Medal, 1978, AIA; Case Studies Award, *Urban Design,* 1977; Medal of Achievement, Philadelphia Art Alliance, 1978. Address: Venturi and Rauch, 333 South 16th Street, Philadelphia, Pennsylvania 19102, U.S.A.

See VENTURI, Robert

RAYMOND, Antonin.

American. Born Antonin Rajman in Kladno, Bohemia, now Czechoslovakia, 10 May 1888; emigrated to the United States, 1910: naturalized, 1914. Educated at the Realko, Kladno; Czech Higher Technical Institute, University of Prague, 1906–10; influenced by the work of Otto Wagner. Served in the United States Army Intelligence Corps, in France and Switzerland, 1917–19: 2nd Lieutenant. Married Noémi Pernessin in 1914; son: Claude. Worked in the office of Cass Gilbert, New York, 1910–12, and Frank Lloyd Wright, Chicago and Taliesin, 1912–17, and for Wright in Tokyo, assisting on Wright's Imperial Hotel, 1919–20; established American Architect-Engineers, Tokyo, 1920–23; in private practice, Tokyo, 1923–37; returned to the United States via India, 1937: opened an office in New York, 1938, and a design studio in New Hope, Pennsylvania, 1939; in partnership with L. L. Rado, from 1946; returned to Japan and re-established practice there, 1947. Exhibitions: Rockefeller Center, New York, 1938; Takashimaya Department Store, Tokyo, 1952. Recipient: Medal of Honor, 1956, and Award of Merit and First Honor Award, 1957, American Institute of Architects. Fellow, American Institute of Architects, 1952. Honorary Life Member, Japanese Institute of Architects. Chevalier of the Légion d'Honneur, France; Officer of the Order of the White Lion, Czechoslovakia; Member, Order of the Corona d'Italia, Italy, and the Order of the Rising Sun, Japan. *Died* (in Langhorne, Pennsylvania) *21 November 1976.*

Works:

1917 de Vieux Columbier Theatre, New York
1920 Hoshi School, Tokyo
     Tanaka House, Tokyo
     Tokyo Lawn Tennis Club, Tokyo
1921 Women's Christian College, Tokyo
1922 Andrews Warehouse, Osaka
     Fukui House, Tokyo
1923 Goto House, Tokyo
     Raymond House, Reinanzaka, Tokyo (later re-erected at Morito Beach, Hayama, Japan)
1923/
33 St. Luke's International Hospital, Tokyo
1924 Convent and School of the Sisters of Notre Dame, Tokyo
     Dr. Read House, Reinanzaka, Tokyo
     Teten House, Tokyo
1925 Hagiwara House, Tokyo
     Siber-Hegner Warehouse, Yokohama
     Seaside Hotel, Kamakura, Japan (project)

1926 Convent and School for the Sisters of Notre Dame, Kobe, Japan
     Rising Sun Petroleum Company Offices, Yokohama
1927 Viscountess Hamao Summer House, Tokyo
     Socony Office Building, Yokohama
1928 Convent and School of the Sisters of the Sacred Heart, Okayama, Japan
     French Embassy alterations, Tokyo
     Italian Embassy Villa, Nikko, Japan
     Nagoaka House, Tokyo
     Oko House, Tokyo
1929 Manager's House, and Staff Housing, Rising Sun Petroleum Company, Yokohama
     Soviet Embassy, Tokyo (not supervised)
1930 Dunlop Rubber Company Factory, Kobe, Japan
     Rising Sun Petroleum Company Service Stations in Tokyo, Yokohama, etc.
     Tokyo Golf Club, Saitama
1931 Akaboshi Summer Cottage, Fujisawa, Japan
     Troedsson Summer House, Nikko, Japan
     Tokyo Steel Products Company Office Building, Kawasaki, Japan
1932 Akaboshi House, Tokyo
     Otis Company Factory, Tokyo
     Viscount S. House, Tokyo (project)
1933 Hatoyama House, Tokyo
     Raymond Summer House, Karuizawa, Japan
1934 Brazil Coffee Shop, Tokyo
     Chapel and Auditorium, Women's Christian College, Tokyo
     Kawasaki House, Tokyo
     James House, Shanghai, China
     Ford Motor Company Assembly Plant and Office Building, Tsurumi, Japan (project)
     Gymnasium, Sisters of Notre Dame School, Kobe, Japan
     St. Paul's Church, Tokyo
     Fukui Summer House, Atami, Japan
     Kodera Summer House, Karuizawa, Japan
     Oda Summer House, Karuizawa
1935 Blake House, Tokyo
     Keller House, Tokyo
     Walker House, Karuizawa, Japan
1936 National Cash Register Company Offices, Tokyo (project)
1938 Dormitories, Sri Aurobindo Ashram, Pondicherry, India
     Piano designs for the Wurlitzer Company
1939 Pitt Petri Shop, Buffalo, New York
     Raymond Farm, New Hope, Pennsylvania
1940 Defence Housing, Bethlehem, Pennsylvania
1941 Cambridge Glass Co. Wholesale Showroom, New York
     Camp Upton (facilities for 3 Coast Artillery Regiments), Camp Upton, Long Island, New York
     Docks for Panama (preliminary reports)
1942 Camp Kilmer Staging Area, Shelton, New Jersey
     Camp Shanks Staging Area, Orangeburg, New York

Japanese Model Housing (for test purposes), Utah Proving Grounds
     Prefabrication system for housing for Drycembly, Baltimore
1943 Airport, housing and hospital facilities, Fort Dix, New Jersey
1944 New York City Department of Sanitation Garage, Brooklyn
     U.S. Plywood Company Showroom, Boston
1945 Analysis and design proposals for Idlewild Airport, now Kennedy Airport, New York
     Edward Keith Store, Kansas City, Missouri
     Leister Housing, Bristol, Pennsylvania (project)
     Long Island Railroad Station, Great River, New York
     Prefabricated farm structures for the Stran Steel Company, Detroit
     Regional Airport, Lexington, Kentucky (project)
     Stores for Brown Fence and Wire Company, New Jersey
1946 Commercial Pacific Cable Company Offices, Guam (project; with L. L. Rado)
     General Bronze Corporation Showroom, New York
     Roadway Express Company Freight Terminal, Hoboken, New Jersey
1947 Master plan for the George School, Newton, Pennsylvania
     Myrtle Beach Development, South Carolina (with L. L. Rado)
1948 Community Center, Summit, New Jersey (with the Allen Organization)
     Community Center, Hickory, North Carolina (with the Allen Organization)
     Electrolux Corporation Field House, Bronx, New York
     Indian Government Office, New York
     Master plan for the Levi Center Park, Omaha, Nebraska
     Midtown Art Galleries, New York
     St. Joseph's Catholic Church, Negros, Philippines
     State Farm Insurance Co. Recreation Center, Bloomington, Illinois
     War Memorial Community Buildings, Housatonic, Massachusetts
     Research and survey of glass use in farm buildings for the Libby Owens Ford Company
1949 Electrolux Corporation Recreation Center, Old Greenwich, Connecticut
     Reader's Digest Building, Tokyo
     Electrolux Corporation Industrial Building, Old Greenwich, Connecticut
1950 Standard Vacuum Oil Company Houses (2), Yokohama
1951 Master plan for Anderson Air Base, Guam
     Anderson Air Base Theatre, Guam
     Neighborhood Recreation Center, Summit, New Jersey

Antonin Raymond: Dormitories, Sri Aurobindo Ashram, Pondicherry, India, 1938

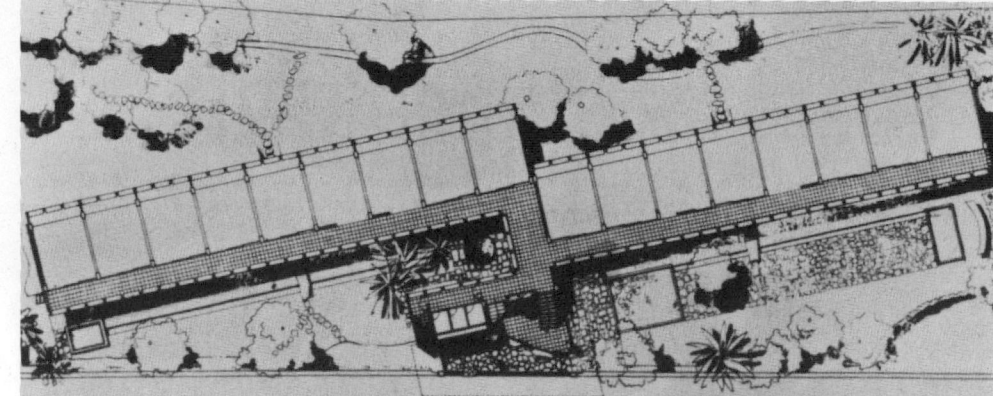

Nippon Gakki Building and Yamaha Concert Hall, Tokyo

United States Army Engineers Base Maintenance Shop, Schenectady, New York

Harris House: United States Embassy Apartments, Tokyo

Perry House: United States Embassy Apartments, Tokyo

Jai Alai Arena, Tokyo (project)

Pan American World Airways Hotel, Tokyo (project)

1952 First National City Bank, Nagoya, Japan
Mikimoto Pearl Shop, Tokyo
Tokyo Film Building and Film Vault, Tokyo
United States Army Camp Drake and Camp Zama, Asaka, Japan

1953 Kitao Book Store (project)
Nippon Ita Garasu Office Building, Osaka (project)
Raymond Office and House, Azabu, Japan
Cunningham House, Tokyo

1954 St. Anselm's Church, Tokyo
Yasukawa Electric Company Office Building and Factory, Yawata, Japan
Yawata Steelworkers Union Memorial Hall, Yawata, Japan

1955 St. Alban's Church, Tokyo
St. Patrick's Church, Tokyo
Master plan for development of the shoreline, Long Beach, California
Yasukawa Gymnasium, Yawata, Japan

1957 Fuji Golf Club, Gotenba, Japan
Lutheran Church, Nobeoka, Miyazaki, Japan
Ito House, Matsuzakaya, Tokyo

1958/
60 Library, International Christian University, Mitaka, Tokyo

1958/
61 Gunma Music Center, Takasaki, Tokyo

1959 Golf Club, Moji, Japan
Rikkyo High School, Saitama, Japan

1959/
60 Iran Embassy, Azabu, Tokyo

1960/
66 Nanzan University, Nagoya, Japan

1961 Holy Cross Church, Tokyo
Chapel, Holy Ghost Hospital, Nagoya, Japan
Rikkyo High School, Shiki, Tokyo
St. Paul's Chapel, Rikkyo High School, Shiki, Tokyo

1961/
64 Matsuzakaya Department Store, Ginza, Tokyo

1963 Society Verbi Divini Monastery, Tokyo
Society Verbi Divini Seminary and Chapel, Nagoya, Japan

1965 San Carlos University, Cebu, Philippines

1966 Catholic Church, Shibata, Japan
International School, Nagoya, Japan
Society Verbi Divini Hostel, Maynooth, Ireland
Anglican Episcopal Church, Tokyo

1966/
69 Pan Pacific Forum, University of Hawaii, Honolulu

1968 Israeli Pavilion, *Expo '70*, Osaka (project)

Publications:

By RAYMOND: books—*Architectural Details,* with Noémi Raymond, Tokyo 1938, New York 1947; *Antonin Raymond: An Autobiography,* Rutland, Vermont 1973; articles—"On Japanese Residences," with Noémi Raymond, in *Antonin Raymond: His Work in Japan 1920-1935,* edited by K. Nakamura, Tokyo 1935; "Concrete for New Designs" in *Architectural Record* (New York), January 1936; "Raymond Will Take Apprentices" in *Pencil Points* (New York), December 1939; "Working with USHA under the Lanham Act" in *Pencil Points* (New York), December 1941; "Toward True Modernism" in *Pencil Points* (New York), August 1942; "Buildings of 94X" in *Architectural Forum* (New York), May 1943; "A Hillside Built This House" in *Better Living* (New York), no. 18, 1943; "Housing: A Post-War Responsibility and Opportunity" in *AIA Journal* (Washington, D.C.), December 1945; "The Spirit of Japanese Architecture" in *AIA Journal* (Washington, D.C.), December 1953; "The Doctrine of Auguste Perret" in *Architectural Record* (New York), January 1954; "Some Ideas Regarding an Organized Effort to Provide Public Housing in Japan" in *Hisaakira Kano* (Tokyo), 12 August 1955.

On RAYMOND: books—*Raymond's House,* Tokyo 1931; *Collection of Antonin Raymond's Work,* Tokyo 1931; *Antonin Raymond: His Work in Japan 1920-1935,* edited by K. Nakamura, Tokyo 1935; *Modern Furnishings,* series 10, Tokyo 1937; articles—"Architect Comes Home from Japan" in *Architectural Forum* (New York), February 1939; "A Portfolio of Recent Works by Antonin Raymond" in *Architectural Forum* (New York), November 1941; "U.S. Architecture Abroad" in *Architectural Forum* (New York), March 1953; "U.S.A. Abroad" in *Architectural Forum* (New York), December 1957; "Antonin Raymond, Architect," edited by J. Killick, special edition of *Architectural Association Journal* (London), August 1962; "Urban School Design" in *Progressive Architecture* (London), March 1967; "A Conversation with Ladislav Rado" by William Marlin in *Architectural Record* (New York), May 1978.

It is difficult to summarize the architectural achievements of Antonin Raymond. His working life lasted for over half a century, and his buildings are dotted all over the globe. However, during that long career he sometimes changed direction, and his widely scattered buildings are usually located far from the centres of architectural thought and development.

Like Richard Neutra and Rudolph Schindler, Raymond left Central Europe for the U.S.A. and gravitated to Frank Lloyd Wright. It was chance that made Frank Lloyd Wright send him to Japan to help with the hotel that he was building in Tokyo, but it was a chance that changed Raymond's life. Japan amazed the young Raymond and his designer wife Noémi. They felt that the architecture and the culture of Japan placed man more at ease with nature than was possible in the frenetic life of the cities of the west. The Raymonds' life was rootless, but Japan gave them a home for much of their working lives.

At a time when the Japanese were full of admiration for all things Western, Antonin Raymond found great scope for his talents in Tokyo as numerous sizeable commissions came to him while he was still young. His earliest independent works were designed very much in the manner of Frank Lloyd Wright, and Raymond admitted that he found it difficult to throw off the style of his erstwhile employer. His own house, at Reinanzaka, Tokyo, completed in 1923, is the first break with the Frank Lloyd Wright manner and is Raymond's first mature design; it uses plain surfaces and cubic forms and must rate as a very early example of the international style, as if Raymond was looking to Europe to free himself from Wright.

The decade following the completion of the Reinanzaka house saw the construction of a series of buildings of ever increasing quality. These buildings, in the cool international style of the time, were often comparable with the German work of the same period. The 1928 alterations to the French Embassy in Tokyo were followed a couple of years later by the Tokyo Golf Club; this sequence of designs reached its apotheosis in two very beautiful houses, the Akaboshi House of 1932 and the Kawasaki house of 1934. Noémi designed the interiors for the houses.

Like Le Corbusier, Raymond became dissatisfied with the limitations of the international style and by the early 1930's he was looking for richer forms and more tactile materials. His own summer house of 1933 at Karuizawa used sloping roofs and timber. It was based on the parti of the house Le Corbusier designed for a site in Chile, and Raymond suffered some cutting remarks from Le Corbusier for this shameless piece of cribbing, but the storm passed and Le Corbusier became an admirer of Raymond's work.

In 1937 the political climate made it difficult for an American to obtain work in Japan, and Raymond was asked to design some dormitories for an ashram in Pondicherry, India. Eighteen years previously Raymond had imbibed the traditional spirit of Japan, now he did the same in India, living and working as a member of the ashram. The resulting buildings are perhaps Raymond's most distinguished design. Calm, elegant, climatically suitable with their vaulted roofs and louvred facades, they were his last buildings in Asia for a decade.

The approach of war brought Raymond back to the United States. At New Hope, Pennsylvania, he established his version of Wright's Taliesin. Here the family, assistants and disciples would farm, build and draw. The war-time years were spent as part of a large practice involved in wartime housing. After the war, in partnership with Ladislav Rado, he embarked on a second creative period. The post-war American work of Raymond and Rado as typified by the buildings for Electrolux at Old Greenwich, Connecticut, are pleasant, modest structures, but do not have the elan of his Japanese houses of the 1930's.

The commission by *Reader's Digest* magazine to build their new building in Tokyo brought Raymond back once again to his beloved Japan. The Reader's Digest Building, completed in 1949, was designed in Raymond and Rado's New York office; it was the first major post-war building in Japan and immediately revived Raymond's Japanese practice. The Readers Digest Building took the light exposed regular structure of the traditional Japanese building and added the louvres that he had learned to use at Pondicherry. A Japanese garden designed by Isamu Noguchi completed the scene of a revivified Japanese design.

In 1933 with his Karuizawa House, Raymond had turned away from the international style to more folky, friendly forms. In 1953, making a similar turn, he built a house and office for himself at Azabu, with shoji screens and other features of traditional Japanese houses and framed the building in round logs.

Reinanzaka, Karuizawa, New Hope, Azabu—it is in the peaceful atmosphere of the houses that Raymond built for himself that we see him at his best. Raymond's buildings for others were sometimes good, often indifferent, but in his own home is an atmosphere of calm for the relaxation and restoration of the human spirit.

—John Winter

RECHTER, Yacov.

Israeli. Born in Tel Aviv, 14 June 1924; son of the architect Ze'ev Rechter. Educated at the Technion: Hebrew Technical Institute, Haifa, 1943–47, Dip. Arch. 1947. Served as a Lieutenant in the Israeli Army, 1947–49. Married Sarah Segal in 1947; Hannah Marron in 1957; children: Yonatan, Michael, Amnon, Ofra and Daphna. Assistant Architect to Ze'ev Rechter, Tel Aviv, 1946–50; Partner, with Ze'ev Rechter and Moshe Zarhy, in Rechter-Zarhy-Rechter, Tel Aviv, 1950–60, and, with Zarhy and Michael Peri, in Rechter, Zarhy—Architects, Peri Engineer, Tel Aviv, 1960–75. Since 1975, in private practice as Yacov Rechter, Architect, Tel Aviv. Recipient: Israel Prize for Architecture, 1973. Address (office): 150 Arlozorov Street, Tel Aviv, Israel.

Works:

1957 Mann Auditorium, Tel Aviv (associate architect)

1960 Sprinzak Resort Hotel, Nazareth
1963 Lynn Polyclinic, Haifa
1965 Hilton Hotel, Tel Aviv
1968 Mivtakhim Resort Hotel, Zikhron-Ya'acov, Israel
1970 Conservatoire, Be'er-Sheva, Israel
      Polyclinic, Ramat Gan, Israel
1974 Memorial and Cultural Building, Herzlia, Israel
1975 Hilton Hotel, Jerusalem
1976 Carmel Hospital, Mount Carmel, Haifa
      Hadassah Hospital, Mount Scopus, Jerusalem
      Namir Square and Clal Building, Tel Aviv
      Migdal-Binyan Insurance Company Building, Tel Aviv

Publications:

On RECHTER: articles—article in *Baumeister* (Munich), September 1975; "Three Buildings in Israel" in *L'Architettura* (Rome), November 1975; article in *Baumeister* (Munich), September 1976; "High on Giv'at Ram: The Jerusalem Hilton" by Betty Raymond in *Interiors* (New York), September 1976; "Recent Works of the Israeli architects Rechter Zarhy Peri" in *L'Architettura* (Rome), December 1976; article in *Baumeister* (Munich), May 1977; article in *Architectural Record* (New York), October 1977.

*

Immediately upon graduating from the Haifa Technion's faculty of architecture, Yacov Rechter joined with his father, the notable architect Ze'ev Rechter, to form (in 1950) the firm Rechter-Zarhy-Rechter, which during the 1950's produced such major buildings as the Convention Halls (Binyanei Ha'oomah) in Jerusalem and the Mann Auditorium and Cultural Centre in Tel Aviv. After his father's death in 1960 the imprint of Yacov Rechter's design personality was felt even more strongly in the firm, and in the succeeding decades he has been largely responsible for several significant projects of high quality, for one of which—the Mivtakhim Resort Hotel in Zikhron-Ya'acov—he was awarded the prestigious Israel Prize in 1973.

At first glance his work is stylistically diverse, but analysis reveals some persistent architectural themes. Of these perhaps the most important leitmotif is the device of the cellular façade, that is, the repetitive use of a basic element to create the overall form and pattern of the building. We see two significant variations of this theme: in many buildings—the Hilton Hotels in Tel Aviv and Jerusalem come to mind here—the individual elements are either highly-modelled or sharply facetted, uniting to create a rather simple overall form of great surface brilliance and intricacy of texture; in the Mivtakhim Resort Hotel, on the other hand, the individual cell is a rectilinear unit of pristine simplicity, but the manner of assembly is such as to generate an undulating façade form of great complexity. Thus the tension between simplicity and complexity, standardization and diversity, is always present in Rechter's work.

Rechter has an eye for a dramatic site, and the skylines of Jerusalem, Haifa and Zikhron Ya'acov are dominated by his designs. The Hilton tower is an elegant marker of one's approach to Jerusalem, if not an unquestionably appropriate symbol. The sinuous façade of the Zikhron-Ya'acov hotel, hugging the escarpment of the Carmel range, not only respects the landform but enhances it, in what must be one of Israel's most successful symbioses of landscape and the man-made object. The siting of Rechter's Carmel Hospital, recently completed in Haifa, is more controversial. Again, there is a sympathetic resonance between the spur of the mountain on which the building is located, and the magnificent,

Yacov Rechter: Migdal-Binyan Insurance Company Building, Tel Aviv, 1976

slope-wall, sculptured form of the hospital: but one may question whether the dominance of hill and flanking coastal plain by this massive, fortress-like structure is the appropriate expression of a hospital in the urban hierarchy.

Another hospital recently completed by Rechter, of a less virtuoso kind, shows this talented architect at his very best. It is his reconstruction and radical expansion of Erich Mendelsohn's historic Hadassah Hospital on Mount Scopus, whose war-torn hulk was recovered through the reunification of Jerusalem in 1967. Here Rechter, with great skill and understanding, combines the rigorous and complicated functional demands of a modern hospital with a loving care for the integrity of Mendelsohn's sadly-abused masterpiece. This respect for another's work shows restraint and sensitivity, qualities which, together with a precision in planning, a nicety of detail, and a response to context, combine to make Yacov Rechter one of the foremost of his generation in Israel's architecture.

—Gilbert Herbert

REIDY, Affonso Eduardo.

Brazilian. Born in Paris, France, 27 October 1909. Educated at the Escola Nacional de Belas Artes, Rio de Janeiro, 1927–30, Dip.Arch. 1930. Married Carmen Portinho in 1934. Worked in the Municipal Service Department, Rio de Janeiro, from 1934; Chief of the Division of Architecture, Municipal Works Department, Rio de Janeiro, 1934–47; Chief of the Planning Service, Housing Department, Rio de Janeiro, 1947; Director, Department of Urbanism, Municipal Works Department, Rio de Janeiro, 1948 and 1950–54. Assistant to Professor Warchavchik, 1930–31, Professor of Small Architectural Compositions, 1931, and Professor of City Planning, 1954, Faculty of Architecture and Urbanism, Federal University of Rio de Janeiro. Vice-President, 1944–45, and Life Member of the Advisory Board, Brazilian Institute of Architects. Exhibitions: *Bienal*, Sao Paulo, 1963; Lima, Peru, 1964; Tokyo, 1965. Recipient: Gold Medal, Escola Nacional de Belas Artes, Rio de Janeiro, 1930; First Prize, with Gerson Pompeu Pinheiro, House of Good Will Competition, Rio de Janeiro, 1931; First Prize, *Bienal*, Sao Paulo, 1951. Livre Docente, Federal University of Rio de Janeiro, 1954. Honorary Fellow, American Institute of Architects, 1964. *Died* (in Rio de Janeiro) *10 August 1964*.

Works:

1931/
32 Home of Good Will (Hostel for Homeless Persons), Rio de Janeiro (with Gerson Pompeu Pinheiro)
1937/
43 Ministry of Education and Health, Rio de Janeiro (with Le Corbusier, Lucio Costa, Jorge Machado Moreira, and Oscar Niemeyer; now the Palace of Culture)
1938 Government Administration Building for the City Area, Rio de Janeiro (project)
1939 City Transport Service Offices and Workshops, Rio de Janeiro (project)
1944 Rio Grande do Sul Railway Administration Building, Porto Alegre, Brazil (project)
1947 Aviation Training Center, Sao Jose do Campos, Sao Paulo (project)
1947/
52 Pedregulho Housing Estate, Rio de Janeiro
1948 Redevelopment plan for the center of Rio de Janeiro (project)
      Plan for Santo Antonio Hill Development, Rio de Janeiro

Pharmaceutical Factory, Rio de Janeiro (project)
1949 Pumping Station, Rio de Janeiro (project)
1951 Marechal Hermes Community Theatre, Rio de Janeiro
1952 Carmen Portinho House, Rio de Janeiro
      Museum of Visual Arts, Sao Paulo (project)
      Gavea Housing Development, Rio de Janeiro
1954 Museum of Modern Art, Rio de Janeiro (destroyed by fire, 1978; now being reconstructed by Henrique Mindlin Associados)
      Experimental school, Asuncion, Paraguay
1955 Dr. Couto e Silva House, Rio de Janeiro
      Museum of Modern Art gardens, Rio de Janeiro (with Roberto Burle Marx)
      Student Theatre, Rio de Janeiro (project)
1956 Master plan for Flamengo Park, Rio de Janeiro (with Roberto Burle Marx)
1957 City Employees Insurance Fund Headquarters, Rio de Janeiro
1959 World Health Organization Headquarters, Geneva (competition project)
1960 National Museum, Kuwait (competition project)
      Bank of London and South America, Brasilia (competition project)
      Paulo Bittencourt Footbridge, Rio de Janeiro
1960/
64 Open-Air Theatre, and Bandstand, Flamengo Park, Rio de Janeiro (projects)
    Pavilions, Flamengo Park, Rio de Janeiro
    Pavilion, Morro da Viuva Recreation Park, Rio de Janeiro (project)
1962 Country house, Petropolis, Brazil
      Forum, Pinacicaba, Sao Paulo (project)

Publications:

On REIDY: book—*The Works of Affonso Eduardo Reidy* by K. Franck, New York and London 1960; articles—"Some New Architecture in Brazil" by S. Loweth in *The Architects' Journal* (London) 31 January 1946; "Pedregulho: ein wohnquartier in Rio de Janeiro" in *Werk* (Zurich), August 1953; "Brazil: Museum of Modern Art in Rio de Janeiro" in *L'Architecture d'Aujourd'hui* (Paris), January/February 1954; "Rio de Janeiro Museum of Modern Art" in *Architectural Review* (London), May 1954; "Conjunto Residencial Pedregulho" in *Informes de la Construccion* (Madrid), December 1956; "Versicherungsgebaude in Rio de Janeiro" in *Bauen und Wohnen* (Zurich), March 1960; "Affonso Eduardo Reidy" in *Zodiac* (Milan), no. 6, 1960; "Affonso Eduardo Reidy" in *Baukunst und Werkform* (Nuremberg) January 1962; "Affonso Eduardo Reidy" by Oscar Niemeyer in *L'Architecture d'Aujourd'hui* (Paris), September/November 1964.

*

Affonso Eduardo Reidy was, from the start of his career, involved with the introduction of functional modernism into Brazil. After absorbing various formative influences, he went on to build upon firmly based principles of form and design and rapidly made his own distinctive contribution to the modern movement. When Lúcio Costa, the acknowledged father of modern architecture in Brazil, became director of the Escola Nacional de Belas Artes in 1931, he gathered round him a team of young architects, including Oscar Niemeyer and Reidy, and he appointed as head of his School of Architecture the Russian-born Gregori Warchavchik, who had been responsible for the very first modern-style architecture in Brazil. Reidy was made Warchavchik's assistant and thereafter combined practice with teaching. Another notable influence was Le Corbusier, who was invited to Rio in 1936 to design the now famous Ministry of Education and Health with a team which included Costa, Niemeyer and Reidy. Le Corbusier's forceful personality and powerful ideas naturally had a considerable effect, which can be seen in several characteristic features of Reidy's work as in Brazilian architecture in general, though they were modified and adapted to suit the particular climatic conditions of Brazil.

Reidy developed a subtly personal style that reached its full fruition in his Pedregulho Housing Estate, a loosely organized residential quarter for low-income public employees at subsidized rents; the estate included all the basic amenities such as a primary school, a health service clinic, a laundry, a market, a gymnasium, a swimming pool and recreation areas. Traffic is not allowed in the area, and there are many interesting geometrical contrasts and decorative features such as the murals of characteristic Latin *azulejos,* glazed tiles, of the school. The most striking feature is the great serpentine multistorey block of flats, 260 metres long, dominating the south side in great sweeping curves that follow the winding contours of the sloping hillside. The whole layout of the estate is indeed closely linked to the contours of the site, with the tall serpentine block of flats entered at middle-level from the hill slope, an idea suggested by earlier Le Corbusier projects in North Africa.

Many of Reidy's other projects are major urban planning schemes, such as his Gavea Housing Development in Rio, which extends the principles applied in the Pedregulho Estate. His superb plan for developing a new civic centre for Rio de Janeiro on Santo Antonio Hill was drawn up in 1948 and carried into execution in the following decades, though not without bureaucratic antagonism that prevented its full realization. The plan incorporates the ancient convent of Santo Antonio on the highest ground and other historic features such as the aqueduct, which becomes an enduring landmark of the city's tradi-

tional past, while a very considerable part of the land is given over to open spaces.

The Carmen Portinho house is on a steep hillside, with the garage and servants' quarters built directly on the ground, joined by the two sides of a sunken patio following the slope of the land to a main block which is raised on the characteristic pillars known as *pilotis,* with a huge glass wall to the living room offering a view of the rich forest vegetation and a vast distant panorama.

With Carmen Portinho as construction engineer, the Museum of Modern Art in Rio de Janeiro is a further example of Reidy's designs in which two groups of buildings of different volumes are characterized by freely flowing wide spaces as well as by the novel ways in which natural daylight is combined with artificial lighting. The Museum clearly demonstrates the essentially spatial qualities of his architecture, with its geometrical contrasts almost sculptural in their impact, and his liking for an ingenious play of light and shade created by a combination of natural and artificial lighting. This is also true of his Museum of Visual Arts in Sao Paulo, again on a highly irregular site, but here given an expressive base structure with the Museum rising as a clear-cut triangular prism from it. His two theatres in Rio both have ingenious roofs. The earlier, the Marechal Hermes Community Theatre, in an industrial suburb of Rio, has a small auditorium seating only 300, and is also used for amateur performances as well as popular productions by professionals. The inverted double slope roof helps to integrate the external aspect with the internal layout, with the interpenetration of the two roof slopes, which corresponds to the

auditorium section, serving a dual purpose: to the rear of the building it allows sufficient height for the stage with its scenery and cyclorama, while to the front it allows the lobby to be lit by a clerestory. Like all Reidy's projects, it shows him as a highly inventive architect who always arrived at technical and architectural solutions that are both personal and yet characteristically Brazilian.

—Konstantin Bazarov

REINIUS, Leif.

Swedish. Born in Stockholm, 24 May 1907. Educated at the Högre Realläroverket, Stockholm, graduated 1925; Royal Technical University, Stockholm, 1925–29, Dip.Arch. 1929. Married Ingrid Bergsten in 1936; children: Kristofer, Silja (died), Mikael, and Cornelia. In partnership with Sven Backström, *q.v.,* Stockholm, since 1936. Editor, *Byggmästaren,* Stockholm, 1944–50. Recipient: Kasper Salin Award, Svenska Arkitekters Riksförbund, 1967; Prince Eugen Medal, 1970; Olle Engkvist Medal, 1973. Member, Royal Academy for Free Arts, 1962. Knight Commander, Royal Order of Vasa, 1973. Address: Backström and Reinius, Storgatan 11, S-114 44 Stockholm.

See BACKSTRÖM, Sven

Affonso Eduardo Reidy: Pedregulho Housing Estate, Rio de Janeiro, 1952

Andrew Renton: Saint Katharine Dock House (now World Trade Centre), London E.1, 1965

RENTON, Andrew.

British. Born in Dunfermline, Scotland, 22 May 1917. Educated at Dunfermline High School, 1929–34; Edinburgh College of Art School of Architecture, 1934–37, 1938–40 (Andrew Grant Travel Scholarship to the Cotswolds and Somerset, 1935, 1936; Royal Institute of British Architects Bronze Medallist, 1937; RIBA Scholarship to Italy, 1939), Dip.Arch. 1940. Served in the Royal Air Force in England, South Africa, India, and Burma, 1940–46. Married Jessie Baillie Leith in 1940; Marjorie Julia Esdaile in 1977; sons: John and Andrew. Worked during college vacations for architect James Shearer, Dunfermline, 1932, 1933; worked in the office of Sir John Burnet Tait and Lorne, Edinburgh and London, 1937–38, in the office of Sir Robert Lorimer and Matthew, Edinburgh, 1946–48, and in the office of Basil Spence and Partners, London, 1948–49; Partner, Basil Spence and Partners, 1949–61; Principal, Andrew Renton and Associates, London, 1961–66; Partner, with Peter Howard and Humphrey Wood, Renton, Howard, Wood Associates, London, 1966–73, and Renton, Howard, Wood Partnership, London, 1973–74; Partner, Renton, Howard, Wood, Levin Partnership (with Gerald Levin), London, since 1974. Principal, Andrew Renton (Edinburgh), 1973–77. Member, Royal Institute of British Architects Publications Committee, 1961–65, Public Relations Committee, 1961–65, Council, 1968–74, London Regional Council, 1970–72, and London Environment Group, 1970–75; Member of the Council, Architects' Benevolent Society, 1962–64,

1967–69; Member of the Council, Society of Industrial Artists and Designers, 1966–70, and Joint Honorary Treasurer, 1968–70; President, Cities of London and Westminster Society of Architects, 1970–72, and Founder and Chairman of the society's Conservation Group, 1970–74. Member of the Design Council Scottish Committee, since 1974, and of the Design Index Selection Committee, since 1975. Recipient: RIBA Architecture Award for London Region, 1967, and for Yorkshire Region, 1972; Civic Trust Award, 1967, 1972; Concours Cembureau Award, 1975. Associate of the Royal Institute of British Architects, 1940, and Fellow of RIBA, 1960. O.B.E. (Officer, Order of the British Empire), 1972. Address: 31 Harmont House, 20 Harley Street, London W1A 1AA, England.

Works:

1959   Thorn House Office Building, Upper St. Martin's Lane, London W.C.2

1965   Saint Katharine Dock House (now the World Trade Centre), London E.1

1970   Edinburgh College of Domestic Science (now Queen Margaret College)

1971   Crucible Theatre, Sheffield

1972   Pure and Applied Sciences Buildings, University of Nottingham

         Department of Psychology, University of Sheffield

1974   River Clyde Study, Scotland (competition project)

1977   Apartment restoration and conversion, Kensington Palace, London

1978–   Saint Katharine by the Tower redevelopment, London E.1

Publications:

By RENTON: articles—"Saint Katharine Dock House" in *East London Papers* (London), Summer 1969; "The Waterfront," with Charles McKean, in *Save the City: A Conservation Study of the City of London,* London 1977.

*

My teaching always led me to believe that the building (in the three-dimensional sense) made the university, the church, the house, or whatever the project happened to be. Experience has however taught me that it is only people who can bring buildings alive. Nowadays it is only when the clients have a completely clear idea of what they wish to achieve and the politicians are in support of the project that the architect can get on with his job.

Architects now must get down to hard physical, social and economic facts and cannot as in the past create their own monuments with little regard for the users and their needs, buildings being treated as *objets d'art.* In my opinion, this present day challenge is all to the good.

—Andrew Renton

What is it that characterizes the varied output of Andrew Renton?—is it possible to find a common thread running through his various projects? The approach is clearly an inclusivist one, bent on establishing good urban manners and coming up with an appropriateness for each site in turn—for example, the way that even the sinuous rhythm of the distant Park Hill Housing Estate is embodied in the roof form of his Crucible Theatre, Sheffield. What is it that links this work with, say, the grand civic statement at St. Katharine Dock, London.

As far as one can see, it seems impossible to trace much of a connection between these projects (and our "auteur" theory might fail us), but in fact there is one idea enshrined and explored in most of Renton's work. The idea repeatedly tested and so far not discarded is, in fact, affirmation of interior at the expense of exterior: the latter is deliberately sacrified on behalf of the former.

This modus operandi is best demonstrated at the Crucible Theatre. The interior lobby is an eloquent conclave of ramps, directions and stops, highlighted in dramatic colour coding: the experience is synaesthetic, whereby all of one's senses are fused together into one human receptor. But, outside, one is hard pushed to find even the slightest external corroboration of the internal event. The external super-structure enjoys a complicity of its parts one with another—there is clearly a vague, soft effort by each part to individualize itself, falling back and emptied of any correspondence with the logic of the interior. While the inside gives itself all at once, the exterior sits more like a delayed-action fuse, releasing itself by degrees. . . . Whereas the interior is a fine denouement, the exterior can be only provisional.

To design from in to out is to restore the private at the cost of the public. Everything goes on "behind the door," and one needs a key to enter.

—Chris Fawcett

REVELL, Viljo (Gabriel).
Finnish. Born in Vaasa, 25 January 1910. Educated at the Technical University, Helsinki, 1928–36. Married Maire Hellin Myntti in 1941; children: Tuula, Sonja and Kati. Partner, Kokko-Revell-Riihimäki, Helsinki, 1934–36; in private practice, Helsinki, 1936–64. Head of the Bureau of Reconstruction, Association of Finnish Architects, Helsinki, 1942–45. *Died (in Helsinki) 8 November 1964.*

Works:

1935 "Glass Palace" Office Building, Helsinki (with N. Kokko and H. Riihimäki)
1937 Kesko Office Building, Vaasa, Finland
Kuntsi House, Vaasa, Finland
1938 Halli Oy Office and Apartment Building, Vaasa, Finland
1945 Pihlajatie Apartment House, Helsinki
Vänr. Stoolinkatu Apartment House, Helsinki
Ollonqvist House, Espoo, Finland
1948 War Consumptives Rehabilitation Centre, Liperi, Finland
Salo Villa, Karjalohja, Finland
Henriksson Villa, Espoo, Finland
Havula Villa, Tuusula, Finland
Sato Oy Apartment Houses, Vaasa, Finland
National Pensions Institute, Helsinki (competition project; with Keijo Petäjä and Torben Valeur)
1949 Helenius Villa, Vaasa, Finland
1950 Kelopuu Summer House, Sipoo, Finland
1951 Laajasalo Terrace House, Helsinki
1952 Teollisuuskeskus Industrial Centre, Office Building and Hotel, Helsinki (with Keijo Petäjä)

Viljo Revell: Teollisuuskeskus Office Building, Helsinki, 1952

Rantakatu Apartment House, Vaasa, Finland
Maunula Apartment Houses, Helsinki (with Keijo Petäjä)
Hakasalmi Oy Office Building, Helsinki (competition project)
1953 Meilahti Primary School, Helsinki (with Osmo Sipari)
Children's Home, Tapiola, Finland
Terrace house, Tapiola, Finland
Tampereen Tasa Housing, Tampere, Finland (competition project; with E. Eerikainen)
Housing Reform Plan (competition project; with E. Eerikäinen)
Porin Sato Housing (competition project; with M. Jaatinen and Reima Pietilä)
1954 Sufika and Mäntyviita Housing, Tapiola, Finland
Elementary school, Joensuu, Finland
1955 Hyvon-Kudeneule Knitwear Factory, Hanko, Finland
Tallberg Villa, Helsinki
1956 Vaasanpuistikko Apartment Houses, Vaasa, Finland

Malmönkatu Apartment House, Vaasa, Finland
1957 Didrichsen Villa, Helsinki
Slev Factory, Kirkkonummi, Finland
1958 Tricol Factory, Inkoo, Finland
Pyykönen House, Helsinki
City Hall, Toronto, Canada (competition project; with Heikki Castren, Bengt Lundsten and Seppo Valjus)
1959 Hietalahdenkatu Apartment House, Vaasa, Finland
Kaskenkaatajantie Apartment Houses, Tapiola, Finland
Kaksoistornit Apartment House, Pori, Finland
1960 Tornitaso Apartment Houses, Tapiola, Finland
World Health Organization Office Building, Geneva, Switzerland (competition project; with Robert Ellenrieder, Bengt Lundsten and Seppo Valjus)
1961 Garrison Annex, Helsinki (with Heikki Castrén)

Didrichsen Art Gallery, Helsinki
Vatiala Funeral Chapel, Tampere, Finland
1962 Elementary school, Kauriala, Hämeenlinna,
Finland
Commercial Centre, Vaasa, Finland
Nallentorni Apartment House, Tapiola, Finland
Peugeot Office Building, Buenos Aires, Argentina (competition project; with Heikki Castrén, Taivo Caspi and Kimmo Söderholm)
1963 KOP Bank Building, Turku, Finland
Munkkiniemenranta Apartment House, Helsinki
Koulukatu Apartment House, Vaasa, Finland
Kaunisto House, Helsinki
Kaskenhovi Terrace House, Tapiola, Finland
1964 City Hall, Toronto, Canada (with John B. Parkin Associates)
Oulunkylä Church, Helsinki (competition project; with Heikki Castrén)

Publications:

On REVELL: book—*Viljo Revell: Buildings and Projects,* edited by Kyösti Ålander, Helsinki 1966; articles—"Projet pour l'hôtel de ville de Toronto" in *L'Architecture d'Aujourd'hui* (Paris), vol. 33, no. 100, 1962; "Neues Rathaus in Toronto" in *Bauen und Wohnen* (Zurich), vol. 20, no. 8, 1968.

The young Viljo Revell's breakthrough in Finland came with the Lasipalatsi (Glass Palace) in 1935, which he designed in cooperation with Kokko and Riihimäki. This early functionalist building, originally intended to be only temporary, reflects influences of the 1930 Stockholm exhibition. From the beginning of his career, Revell acknowledged that he worked to promote international trends. As Alvar Aalto's assistant, together with Aarne Ervi, he worked, for instance, on the design of the Finnish Pavilion at the Paris *World's Fair* in 1937. After World War II, Revell's own work showed that his approach diverged from the highly individual Aalto line, which was based on harmony and a conscious restraint with materials. Revell's works reflect the changes that were going on in post-war architecture internationally: he used the full potential of new materials, new concrete techniques and pre-fabricated elements to produce a non-ornamental mechanized urbanism that was completely new, particularly in Finland.

In 1948 Revell won a competition for a commercial building sponsored by various Finnish industrial organizations; it was to be the first large Finnish business building in the post-war period. Its strip windows and colonnade point to the International Style, and it also symbolized the emergence of the Finnish economy into a new era after the problems of the war and the post-war period of scarcity. The same new industrial modernism can be found in Revell's unit-built houses in the first phase of Tapiola (1954). He later turned to a more traditional technique in his designs for Tapiola, aiming at strong horizontal line. A large-scale town planning competition entry in 1953, for a suburb to the north of the city, never got beyond the competition stage. It featured two three-story lamellas of housing almost a kilometre long, following the ups and downs of the terrain, with an internal service corridor. Revell and Osmo Sipari had experimented with this kind of twisting volume on a smaller scale in the Meilahti Primary School of 1953. In 1955 the Kudeneule Knitwear Factory was completed in Hanko, one of the Revell office's main projects before the design for Toronto City Hall. The factory integrated the rational qualities called for by industry into a basically rectangular, almost artificially modern, milieu.

The team involved in the Toronto City Hall competition of 1958—Heikki Castren, Bengt Lundsten and Seppo Valjus as well as Revell himself—created a powerful, symbolic-looking construction in which two concave towers shield a circular City Council Chamber. The final version (completed in 1964) made several compromises over the original plan in order to meet local demands. In a form that dominates the city centre, Toronto City Hall is a building that bears the hallmark of Revell's architecture, embodying the belief in technology of the '50s combined with the International Style's aspirations for the monumental. Here, as in several projects for city blocks (Helsinki, Vaasa), Revell reveals his powerful instinct towards the large entity, sometimes at the expense of detail. Yet, his small houses, such as the Villa Didrichsen in Helsinki, are also worked out down to the last detail, and the formalism that is sometimes perceptible in the larger works is not present.

The style of Revell's architecture has points of contact with Scandinavian functionalism, with the works of Le Corbusier, and with International Style and post-war industrial formalism. He was an architect of great character who made a major contribution to orienting Finnish architecture internationally and opening up its potential at home.

—Pekka Suhonen

RICCI, Leonardo.

Italian. Born in Florence, 8 June 1918. Educated at the University of Florence, under Giovanni Michelucci, 1938–41, Dip.Arch. 1941. In partnership with Leonardo Savioli, *q.v.,* and G. Gori, Florence, 1944–49. In private practice, Florence, since 1949. Member of the Architecture Faculty, University of Florence, since 1945: Assistant Professor of Architecture, 1945–54; Professor of Architectural Composition and Design, 1954; Professor of Interior Design, 1954–55; Professor of Art and Architecture, 1954–60; Professor in charge of the Industrial Design Course, 1955–60; Professor in charge of the Second-Year Drafting Course, 1960–65; Professor of the Elements of Architectural Composition and Design, 1964–65; Director, Town Planning Institute, since 1965; Professor of Town Planning, 1966–70; Head of the Faculty of Architecture, since 1971. Visiting Professor, Massachusetts Institute of Technology, Cambridge, 1960. Director, Town Planning Research Program, Italian National Committee for Research, 1964–66, 1966–67. Exhibitions: *La Casa Abitata,* Palazzo Strozzi, Florence, 1965; *Italian Architecture,* toured Italy 1965, 1973. Recipient: Architecture Prize, *Bienal,* Sao Paulo, 1953; Naples Architecture Prize, 1955; Gold Medal, *Triennale,* Milan, 1958; Gold Florin Award, Florence, 1964; INARCH Prize, Florence, 1966. Member, Fine Arts Academy, Rome, 1962, San Luca Academy, Rome, 1963, and Teatina Academy for Sciences, Rome, 1964. Address (office): Via Bolognese Nuova, Monterinaldi, Florence, Italy.

Works:

1944/
45   Victory Bridge, Florence (competition project; with R. Gizdulich, G. Gori, G. Neumann, and Leonardo Savioli)
1945/
46   Plan for the reconstruction and redevelopment of Vicchio and Dicomano, Italy (with Leonardo Savioli)
Carraia Bridge, Florence (competition project; with G. Gori, G. Neumann, and Leonardo Savioli)
1946   Plan for the reconstruction and redevelopment of Empoli, Italy (competition project; with G. Gori and Leonardo Savioli)
Tourist and urban development plan for the Lido, Venice (competition project; with G. Gori and Leonardo Savioli)

Piazza d'Armi, Perugia, Italy (competition project; with G. Gori and Leonardo Savioli)
Grazie Bridge, Florence (competition project; with G. Gori and Leonardo Savioli)
1946/
47   Reconstruction plan for the Pontevecchio War-Damaged District, Florence (competition project; with G. Gori, E. Brizzi, and Leonardo Savioli)
Bridge over the Sieve River, Rufina, Italy (with G. Gori, G. Neumann, and Leonardo Savioli)
Bridge over the Arno River, Terranuova Braciolini, Italy (with G. Gori, E. Brizzi, and Leonardo Savioli)
Bridge over the Arno River, Figline Valdarno, Italy (with G. Gori, E. Brizzi, and Leonardo Savioli)
Group of 4 villas, for the directors of the Vetroflex Company, Florence (with G. Gori and Leonardo Savioli)
1947   San Romando District Redevelopment, Ferrara, Italy (competition project; with E. Gori, G. Gori, and Leonardo Savioli)
Bridge over the Arno River, Signa, Italy (competition project; with G. Gori, E. Brizzi, and Leonardo Savioli)
San Niccolo Bridge, Florence (competition project; with G. Gori, E. Brizzi, and Leonardo Savioli)
Bridge over the Serchio River, Calavorno, Italy (competition project; with G. Gori, E. Brizzi, and Leonardo Savioli)
Bridge over the Cecina River, Ponteginori, Italy (competition project; with G. Gori and Leonardo Savioli)
Mezzo Bridge, Pisa (competition project; with G. Gori and Leonardo Savioli)
Bridge over the Bisenzio River, Signa, Italy (with G. Gori and Leonardo Savioli)
Municipal Cemetery, Settignano, Italy (project; with E. Detti, R. Gizdulich, G. Gori, and Leonardo Savioli)
Saint-Gobain Workers' Garden City, Pisa (project; with G. Gori and Leonardo Savioli)
Design of the *Artisans' Trade Fair,* Florence (with E. Gori, G. Gori, and Leonardo Savioli)
1948   Bridge over the Sterza River, Bottaccina, Volterra, Italy (competition project; with G. Gori and Leonardo Savioli)
Design of the *Artisans' Trade Fair,* Florence (with E. Gori, G. Gori, and Leonardo Savioli)
Bridge over the Sterza River, Salitone, Volterra, Italy (with G. Gori and Leonardo Savioli)
Urban development building code for Lido di Camaiore, Italy (competition project; with G. Gori, E. Isotta, and Leonardo Savioli)
1948/
51   Flower and Fruit Market, Pescia, Italy (with E. Gori, G. Gori, E. Brizzi, and Leonardo Savioli)
1949   Design of the *Artisans' Trade Fair,* Florence (with E. Gori, G. Gori, and Leonardo Savioli)
1951/
63   Village of 16 villas, Monterinaldi, Florence
1952   House, Beverly Hills, California
1953   Sets and costumes for the Boboli Garden Ballet, Florence
1953/
54   Village for 2,000 in the Sesto Hills, Florence (competition project; with G. Petrelli, Danilo Santi, and Leonardo Savioli)
1954   Quercianella Tourist Village, Livorno (project)
1954/
55   Plan for the San Frediano District, Florence (competition project; with G. Petrelli, Danilo Santi, and Leonardo Savioli)

1955 Leonardo Ricci Villa, Monterinaldi, Florence
Stage sets and scenery for Monteverdi's *Orfeo*, International Festival, Aix-les-Bains, France
Plan for Albisola Marina and for Albisola Superiore, Italy

1957 Borghese-Mann House, Forte dei Marmi, Italy
Housing Development Study for the CEP Workers' Housing Institution, Sorgane, Florence (project; with others)

1958 Balmain House, Island of Elba
Flower Market, San Remo, Italy (project)

1959 Goti Spinning Factory, Campi Bisenzio, Florence

1962 Plan for the Novoli Quarter, Florence (project; with others)

1962/
74 Montepiano Residential Village, Florence

1963 Cardon House, Castiglioncello, Livorno
Rossell House, Le Focette, Lucca, Italy
Experimental village, Riesi, Sicily
Workers Housing Development, Granaiolo, Genoa (project)
Residential Village, for GESCAL National Institute for Workers' Housing, Sorgane, Florence

1964 Giannini House, Rome
Design of the *Expressionism* exhibition, Palazzo Strozzi, Florence

1964/
68 Monte degli Uliva Village, Riesi, Caltanissetta, Italy

1965 Megalopolis (project; with Pennsylvania State University students)
Town plan for Pachino, Sicily

1967 Permanent Exhibition Centre, for the *Artisans' Trade Fair*, Florence (competition project)
Municipal Cemetery Redevelopment, Montecatini, Lucca, Italy (project)
Layouts for the Italian Pavilion, *Expo '67*, Montreal

1972/
73 Master plan for the University of Florence (competition project; with others)

1977/
78 Administrative Centre, Florence (competition project; with others)

Publications:

By RICCI: books—*Anonymous, XX Century*, New York 1962, as *Anonimo del XX Secolo*, Milan 1965; *Leonardo Savioli*, with others, edited by Giovanni Fanelli, Florence 1966; articles—"Problemi per una nuova Maggioranza" in *Casabella* (Milan), May 1964; "The Architect: For Which Society?" in *Casabella* (Milan), December 1973; "Modern Art Gallery in Bologna" in *L'Architettura* (Rome), April 1976.

On RICCI: book—*Italian Architecture 1965–70*, exhibition catalogue, by Giuseppe Tucci, Florence 1973; articles—"A Monterinaldi, presso Firenze" in *Domus* (Milan), December 1957; "New Look on the Hills Near Florence" by Giulia Veronesi in *Zodiac* (Milan), no. 4, 1959; "The Involved Man: Leonardo Ricci" in *Progressive Architecture* (New York), August 1960; "La Nascita di un Villaggio per una Nuova Comunità, in Sicilia" in *Domus* (Milan), December 1963; "Birth of a Village in an Underdeveloped Area" in *Arts and Architecture* (Los Angeles), October 1966; "Città della Terra: Récherches d'Urbanisme, Faculté de Florence" in *L'Architecture d'Aujourd'hui* (Paris), October/November 1966; "Exploratory Research in Urban Form and the Future of Florence" in *Arts and Architecture* (Los Angeles), February 1967; "Abitazione à Firenze" in *Architecture: Formes et Fonctions* (Lausanne), no. 15, 1969; "Architettura a Scala Urbana" in *L'Architettura* (Rome), May 1971.

After his studies under Giovanni Michelucci at the University of Florence, Leonardo Ricci soon purged his style of anything that suggested self-satisfaction or any notions of "subject before form." He thereafter devoted himself to international architectural questions—without reference to historic culture, conscious of the profound significance of contemporary conditions.

Ricci was one of the first Italian architects to change the treatment of materials in architecture, and he employs free, organic, natural forms full of powerful expressive content, putting forward the possibility of a new way of life related to today's needs in today's consumer society.

Ricci has anticipated some of the liberating alternative proposals of much of the current generation's radical architecture. In his research he has combined the lessons of Frank Lloyd Wright with neo-expressionist demands, and this synthesis has led, in his work, to an individual version of International Brutalism.

More recently, Ricci has extended his architectural ideas to town planning. In his lectures he has been offering theories on macrostructures and fluid communication facilities, proposing a whole series of investigations into great, organic "district cities" in which the natural components of the district are seen as parts of incessant, vital patterns of circulation.

—Lara-Vinca Masini

RICHARD SHEPPARD, ROBSON AND PARTNERS.

Partnership; established, London, 1958. Partners: Richard Sheppard, Geoffrey Robson, William Mullins, Gordon Taylor, John Heywood, A. C. F. Morris, Anthony Furlong, and Richard Young. Associated firm: Richard Sheppard, Robson and Partners (Overseas), Jersey, Channel Islands, established 1976. Recipient: Regional Award, Royal Institute of British Architects, 1953, 1961, 1962, 1967, 1968 (twice), 1969 (twice), 1974; First Prize, Churchill College Competition, Cambridge, 1959; Civic Trust Award, 1966, 1968, 1969, 1975. Address: 77 Parkway, Camden Town, London NW1 7PU, England.

Works:

1952 Harrowfield Secondary Boys School, Harold Hill, Essex

1953 Offices for Swan Hunter and Wigham Richardson, Wallsend on Tyne

1954/
66 Royston School, Hertfordshire

1954/
67 Churchfields School, West Bromwich, Staffordshire

1954/
70 Burton-on-Trent Technical College, Staffordshire

1955 Oswestry Secondary Modern School, Shropshire

1956 Tollington School, Creighton Avenue, London N.10
Hurlingham Girls School, Peterborough Road, Fulham, London

1956/
61 Riley Comprehensive School, Bloxwich, Walsall, Staffordshire

1959/
66 School of Navigation, Newtown Road, Warsash, Southampton

1959/
68 Chatham Walderslade Secondary School, Kent

1960/
71 Worcester Technical College

1960/
76 William Edwards School, Stifford Clays Road, Grays, Essex

1961/
66 Loughborough University, Leicestershire

1961/
73 Redditch College of Further Education, Worcestershire

1963 Digby Hall, University of Leicester

1964/
68 Imperial College of Science and Technology, South Kensington, London

1964/
72 West Midlands College of Education, Gorway, Walsall, Staffordshire

1964/
73 Merz Court, Science/Arts Buildings, and Hatton Gallery, University of Newcastle upon Tyne

1965/
73 Brunel University, Uxbridge, Middlesex
Churchill College, Cambridge

1967 Wallasey Grammar School, Cheshire

1968 St. Albans School, Hertfordshire

1968/
77 South Bromsgrove School, Charford Road, Bromsgrove, Worcestershire

1969 Administration Building, University of Southampton

1969/
75 Central redevelopment of Waltham Cross, Hertfordshire

1969/
76 The City University, St. John Street, London

1974 Collingwood College, University of Durham
Social Amenity Centre and Library, Campus West, Welwyn Garden City, Hertfordshire
Welwyn/Hatfield Sports Centre, Welwyn Garden City, Hertfordshire
Richard Sheppard, Robson and Partners Offices, Parkway, London N.W.1

1974/
75 Offices and shops at 12/13 and 34/36 Lime Street, London

1976 Conference Centre and Library for King Edward's Hospital Fund for London, Albert Street, London N.W.1
Offices at 150/152 Fenchurch Street, London

1976/
80 Wood Green Shopping City, London N.22

1977/
78 Manchester Polytechnic

1978 Offices at 105/109 Cannon Street, London

Publications:

On SHEPPARD/ROBSON: articles—"The Work of Richard Sheppard, Robson and Partners" in *Architectural Design* (London), July 1957; "Churchill College, Cambridge: An Essay in Form and Quality" by H. N. Brockman in *The Financial Times* (London), 5 June 1964; "The Oxbridge Double" by Michael Manser in *The Observer* (London), 26 July 1964; "Brunel University" by Diana Rowntree in *The Guardian* (London), 25 February 1965; "Massive Simplicity Beside the Cam" by Michael Webb in *Country Life* (London), 25 November 1965; article in *Kentiku* (Tokyo), March 1968; "The City University" by H. N. Brockman in *The Financial Times* (London), 8 October 1970; "Sheppard's Path" in *The Architects' Journal* (London), 14 March 1973; "Friendly Face of Culture" by Stephen Gardiner in *The Observer* (London), 21 April 1974; "Architects Have the Best Office" by Roy Levine in *The Financial Times* (London), 20 October 1975; articles in *Art and Architecture* (Tehran), December 1975, March 1976; "Higher Education at Lower Cost" by Tony Aldous in *Country Life* (London), 12 February 1976; "Finding the Perfect Partnership" by Stephen Gardiner in *The Observer* (London), 24 September 1978.

Richard Sheppard, Robson and Partners: The City University, St. John Street, London, 1976

intention but are distant in the result. We believe that the purpose, form and organisation of a building should be immediately comprehensible externally and internally by the disposition of volumes and their expression. Scale and mass must also be manipulated in relation to site and intention. It is important that buildings should create a sense of relation and responsibility with the user. The vandal insults authority but if we can produce something which people are proud of and pleased to occupy, then environmental conditions are enriched and dignified.

—Richard Sheppard, Robson and Partners

Richard Sheppard, Robson and Partners originated at the Architectural Association School of Architecture during its wartime evacuation to Hadley Wood, near Barnet. As a member of the teaching staff, Dick Sheppard recognized the qualities in one of the leading students, Geoffrey Robson, and after office experience a partnership was formed that has both personally and professionally been an outstanding success. Both partners are designers first and businessmen afterwards, and so consistent is the firm's work, which is always of a high standard, that it is difficult to tell who was individually responsible. No building is more revealing than their own offices in Camden Town, London—an imaginative re-use of poor space at the rear of shops.

Sheppard and Robson's chief claim to fame, however, will undoubtedly rest with Churchill College, Cambridge, resulting from a competition which they won in 1959. Although visually the architectural idiom is modern, the plan shows Sheppard's particular sensitivity to history and appreciation of the values of the form of the traditional Oxford and Cambridge colleges. These were based on the square quadrangle, a shape both practical and contemplative that grew from the medieval cloister. At Churchill College the squares are planned to follow one another in informal sequence, re-composed from history to be free and liberal in their grouping (not unlike academics in converse). The elevation of this unusual plan reflects the advanced way of thought at the time and, like all the firm's detailing, is strong, sometimes to the point of abruptness. Truth to material suggested that the concrete which forms the building material should express its timber shuttering, and sometimes (as with the Greek conversion of timber form into stone) timber form has been transposed into concrete.

It was in a similar vein of boldness, imagination and appreciation of arts other than architecture that this distinguished firm organized the removal of a famous modern fresco that was deteriorating in a barn in Cumbria to a new position in their university buildings at Newcastle.

—Geoffrey Jellicoe

"Modern" architecture seeks to derive its formal content from the exploration of a problem rather than its adaptation to a pre-conceived form.

As a practice we believe that "modern" architecture is vigorous and vital and that its full growth and development is to come. We do not think that it has become an historical digression and that a return to past forms is likely or desirable—although certainly possible. We think there is a place for the vernacular in in-filling but that generally only a design discipline based upon the scale and technological resources of our society can meet present conditions.

Our approach is thus pragmatic and we hope that every one of our buildings creates its own identity. There is no identity kit, and if there is a resemblance between one and another we are glad but this is not our aim. We do not theorise about forms, techniques and user needs but endeavour to find an answer which most nearly fits our information about these requirements and think that the design should meet them in an economic, practical and significant way. We do not seek, indeed have never produced, personal, individual, quirky expressions, nor distorted the problem in any respect in order to do so. We believe that form, proportion, rhythm, texture and consequently style are functions which vary in terms of the problem and are never constant. We are extremely conscious of the dichotomy inherent in the architect's role. We are engaged as the owner's agent to design for a (usually) unknown and anonymous tenant. Society has created a chasm between the user, a tenant, and the owner and his architect. The interests of the two seldom coincide and we all, in our various ways, try to bridge the gap. But in this relationship lies the impersonality of modern building and the modern state. Both may be benevolent by

RICKARD, Bruce (Arthur Lancelot).
Australian. Born in Sydney, New South Wales, 1 December 1929. Educated at Barker College, Sydney, 1937–46; studied architecture at Sydney Technical College, 1947–53, Dip.Arch. 1953; studied landscape architecture at University College London, 1954, and the University of Pennsylvania, Philadelphia, 1956–57 (fellowship), M.Landscape Arch. 1957, studied town planning at the University of Sydney, 1958–59. Married Norma Mary Nivison Charley in 1954; children: Peter (deceased), Jane; married Robin May Cooke in 1960; children: Samuel, James and Nicholas. Worked as a Junior in the offices of H. Ruskin Rowe, Sydney, 1947–49, Sydney Ancher, Sydney, 1949–53, and Fowell, Mansfield and McLurcan, Sydney, 1952; Assistant, Wallis Gilbert and Partners, London, 1954–55, Garner and White, Philadelphia, 1956, George Patton, Philadel-

Bruce Rickard: Rickard House, Wahroonga, New South Wales, 1961

phia, 1956, and Harberson, Hough, Livingston and Larson, Philadelphia, 1957. Since 1959, Principal, Bruce Rickard and Associates, Sydney. Temporary Lecturer, University of Sydney, 1958–59; Part-time Tutor, University of New South Wales, Sydney, 1962–72, 1974–76. Exhibitions: *Modern Sydney Domestic Architecture,* Museum of Modern Art, Melbourne, 1961; Farmer's Blaxland Gallery, Sydney, 1961; Royal Agricultural Society Easter Show, Sydney, 1964; Royal Australian Institute of Architects Awards Exhibition, 1977, and toured Australia. Recipient: Merit Award, Royal Australian Institute of Architects Award, New South Wales Chapter, 1972, 1977. Address: Bruce Rickard and Associates, 7 Ridge Street, North Sydney, New South Wales 2060, Australia.

Works:

1953 Dickinson House, 26 Finlay Road, Turramurra, New South Wales

1954 Treloar House, The Avenue, Newport, New South Wales

1957 Clifton House, Prince Edward Parade, Hunters Hill, New South Wales

1958 Cohen House, 19 Rembrandt Drive, Middle Cove, New South Wales

1959 Malone House, Parni Place, Forestville, New South Wales

    Rickard House I, 51 Finlay Road, Warrawee, New South Wales

    Dibbs House, 39a Bardo Road, Newport, New South Wales

    Coventry House, Albert Parade, North Avalon, New South Wales

    Nairn House, Cronulla, New South Wales

1960 Reid House, 372 Old Northern Road, Castle Hill, New South Wales

    Marks House, 4 Deakin Place, Killara, New South Wales

1961 Midgley House, Whale Beach Road, Whale Beach, New South Wales

    Smith House, Walker Place, McCarrs Creek, New South Wales

    Rickard House II, 10 Kokoda Avenue, Wahroonga, New South Wales

    Courthouse, Narommine, New South Wales (with Ian McKay)

1962 Rolf House, 25a Finlay Road, Turramurra, New South Wales

    Armstrong House, 10 Cutler Road, Clontarf, New South Wales

    Armit House, 22 Currugul Road, North Turramurra, New South Wales

    Cobb and Co. Drive-in Restaurant, Tempe, New South Wales

1963 Tennisen House, Burra Close, Mount Colah, New South Wales

    Fienberg House I, 27 Valerie Avenue, Chatswood, New South Wales

    Riddle House, 378 Deepwater Road, Castle Cove, New South Wales

    Shereline Homes Farmstead House, Showground, Sydney

1964 Lewis House, 37 Lynbrae Avenue, Beecroft, New South Wales

    Spring House, "Cloverdale," via Walcha, New South Wales

    Shereline Homes Executive House, Pennant Hills Road, Carlingford, New South Wales

1965 Marshall House, 61 Gordon Street, Clontarf, New South Wales

    Resanceff House, 14 Morella Place, Castle Cove, New South Wales

    Zador House, Boulevarde Street, Strathfield, New South Wales

    Mitchell House, 23 Rembrandt Drive, Middle Cove, New South Wales

    Sooster House, White Road, New Berrima, New South Wales

1966 Madden House, 27 Glenhaven Road, Glenhaven, New South Wales

    Davison House, The Esplanade, Kangaroo Point, New South Wales

    Hickey House, 2073 Pittwater Road, Bayview, New South Wales

1967 Armstrong House, 233 Cooyong Road, Terrey Hills, New South Wales

    Curry House, 13 Sunnyridge Place, Bayview, New South Wales

    Dell House, 169 Campbell Drive, Wahroonga, New South Wales

    Heritage Homes Houses I, II and III, Monterey Street, St. Ives, New South Wales

1968 Dolphin House, 3 Glenhaven Road, Glenhaven, New South Wales

1969 Connolly House, Colbran Road, Cheltenham, New South Wales

    Mortuary chapel, Lady Davidson Hospital, St. Ives, New South Wales

1970 Allum House, 7 Berrillee Lane, Turramurra, New South Wales

Freeman House, 9 Kennedy Place, Church Point, New South Wales

McCreadie House, 72 Wandeen Road, Clareville, New South Wales

1971 Chapel, Lady Davidson Hospital, St. Ives, New South Wales

Car wash facilities, Mosman, Crows Nest, and Parramatta, New South Wales

1972 Car wash facilities, Canberra

1973 Whale Carwash, Gordon, New South Wales

1974 Car wash facilities, Bondi Junction, New South Wales

Fienberg House II, 19 Ocean Road, Palm Beach, New South Wales

Taylor House, Duke Street, Mittagong, New South Wales

1975 Townhouses, Ocean Shores, New South Wales (project)

Howard House, 3 Barclay Close, Pymble, New South Wales

Gee House, 2b North Parade, Hunters Hill, New South Wales

Lesslie House, Whitehall Road, Kenthurst, New South Wales

1977 Medium-density houses, Thurgoona, Albury-Wodonga, New South Wales (project)

1978 Medium-density houses, Bathurst, New South Wales (project)

Publications:

By RICKARD: article—"The Development of Canberra Landscaping" in *Architecture Australia* (Sydney), December 1959.

On RICKARD: books—*Australian Housing in the Seventies* by Howard Tanner, Sydney 1967; *Living and Partly Living: Housing in Australia* by Ian McKay, Robin Boyd, Hugh Stretton and John Mant, Melbourne 1971; *An Australian Identity: Houses for Sydney 1953–1963* by Jennifer Taylor, Sydney 1972; articles—"The Growth of an Australian Architecture" by Milo Dunphy in *Hemisphere* (Canberra), August 1962; "Whale Carwash, Pacific Highway, Gordon, N.S.W." in *Architecture in Australia* (Sydney), August 1973; "House, Palm Beach" in *Architecture Australia* (Melbourne), January 1978.

The bulk of my architectural work that has been built has been individual houses, the remainder being commercial work. Although I am very interested in housing on a larger scale and have designed some medium density housing groups for government and developer/clients, none have, so far, been built.

I am not concerned merely with designing adequate buildings which shelter human activities from unpleasant sensations (like wet, cold, heat) but buildings that allow and encourage people in their everyday life to enjoy and partake of the pleasant sensations emanating from climate and the natural and built environment such as the well being felt from sun in winter and shade in summer; the delight of seeing trees, plants, the sky, and the aesthetic pleasure of contemplating the play of space in a well put together built environment. The houses which I have built express this preoccupation, for example my houses always, if possible, face north (similar to the south of the northern hemisphere) to catch the winter sun all day and have northern terraces where it is as convenient for living activities to take place as it is indoors and often more pleasant. The outdoor areas also expand the usable living area of the house allowing the family members greater choices for community or private activities. This aspect is of great importance to small units of medium and high density housing where often families are condemned to living indoors only in crowded conditions with little privacy and sometimes in units oriented in such a way as to never receive winter sun.

I care about the relationship of building to the site environment. My approach is to integrate the building with the site, for the building to reflect and em-

phasise in form, materials and colour the dominant character of the site environment whether it be on an undistrubed natural site with trees and rocks or a site in a man-made urban environment.

Even though I consider the design of exterior appearance of my buildings and the spatial relationships that my buildings make with others, of greater moment to me is the interior spatial relationship and the play of major and minor spaces flowing together and sliding in sequence both horizontally and vertically as one moves about. While I try to obtain and be disciplined by a neat structural system, I try not to let the system dominate my design at the expense of spatial quality but rather I try to exploit the unifying rhythmic elements of the structural system. In small buildings I prefer to build with warm materials that require no further coating or decorating like brick, stone, timber and glass. In buildings requiring large spans I take up the challenge of building with steel and concrete and try to turn to account their innate qualities.

—Bruce Rickard

By the time Bruce Rickard returned to Australia in 1958, after four years overseas studying landscape design at the University of London and the University of Pennsylvania, the tide had turned and was beginning to run against the modern movement in Australia. Something of the conservatism of rural Australia had survived well into the 1950's in Sydney, and this factor, coupled with an undercurrent of romantic nationalism from the 1890's, led to a wholesale rejection of the internationalism and machine aesthetics of modern architecture. Bruce Rickard arrived back in Australia at the crucial moment when the call for regionalism, climatic appropriateness, and an Australian identity in architecture was being voiced.

Wright's Usonian houses were a revelation to Rickard who recalls that on seeing Taliesin he was "impressed for the first time by a man-made environment." Bruce Rickard's free interpretation of Wright's 1930's language provided a focus for this somewhat romantic rejection of modern architecture, a movement which coalesced in a Wrightian school of domestic architecture in Sydney. Besides Bruce Rickard, the Sydney Wrightian School included Peter Muller, Neville Gruzman, Ian McKay and several others, and had a considerable impact on later post-war domestic architecture.

Bruce Rickard's style—he has built some sixty houses—unlike the romantic individualism of Peter Muller, is a rationalized version of Wrightian motifs from the late 30's which have been stripped of their more idiosyncratic details. It would be trite to dismiss Rickard's Wrightian houses as mere copies and no more, for although Rickard has selected the best from Wright and adapted it to Australian circumstances, there are important, and fundamental, differences. For one thing, Wright's conception of the house as a protective cave-like refuge contrasts with the basic optimism of Rickard's houses which open onto the landscape and welcome light from the outside. Rickard avoids the cruciform plan and interpenetrating volumes intersecting at a central core of Wright's houses, and prefers instead an elongated plan comprising a series of horizontally layered roof planes all facing north and, where the site permits, stepping back up the slope to admit daylight to the interior. The sun is a controlling factor in Rickard's houses. He strictly orients each house to the north and carefully calculates the roof overhangs to admit sunlight in winter and exclude it in summer. And instead of Wright's double pitched roofs, Rickard often uses a simple skillion roof superimposed above a lower horizontal one, to admit light deep within his houses. Rickard's houses are an intelligent interpretation of Wright, thus there are similarities of style in the spatial form, horizontal expression, use of materials and comfortable human scale. Rickard uses continuous strip windows, stained natural timber, rough sandstone walls, and progressive spatial sequences resulting in masterly Wrightian spatial

compositions. The precise details throughout Rickard's houses demand a high standard of craft.

The Cohen house at Middle Cove, 1958, is a long low brick building with strong horizontal roof planes stepping backwards from the central living room. Bruce Rickard's house I at Warrawee, 1959, and house II at Wahroonga, 1961, particularly the latter, are consumate expressions of Rickard's artistry.

Bruce Rickard's reputation as an outstanding interpreter of the Wrightian domestic style is unfortunate in that it tends to obscure other quite different achievements. In the 1960's Rickard designed a number of excellent carwash and service centres in Sydney with a precise engineering expression. Rickard's concern for extending quality design into the mass-housing market led to his involvement in a series of project houses for Shereline Homes and Heritage Homes; of these, the Executive Project House for Shereline is the most interesting. In his planning of individual house and town house types for the Ocean Shores Resort New Town, Brunswick Heads, Rickard was enabled to pursue his interest in the Usonian ideal.

Bruce Rickard's training as an architect and landscape designer allows him to see architecture as being of lesser importance than the design of the whole environment. In this respect, Rickard continues the tradition established in Australia by Walter Burley Griffin of land planning and environmental design.

—Philip Drew

RIETVELD, Gerrit (Thomas).

Dutch. Born in Utrecht, 24 June 1888. Studied drawing at the Municipal Evening School, Utrecht, 1906–08; architectural drawing with the architect P. Houtzagers, Utrecht, 1908–11; architecture with P. J. Klaarhamer, Utrecht, 1911–15. Worked in his father's cabinet making business, Utrecht, 1899–1906; Draughtsman, C. J. Begeer's Jewellery Studio, Utrecht, 1906–11; in private practice as a cabinetmaker, Utrecht, 1911–19, and as an architect, Utrecht, 1919–60: collaborated on architectural and interior projects with Mrs. Truus Schroder-Schrader, Utrecht, 1921–64; Partner, with J. van Dillen and J. van Tricht, Rietveld, van Dillen and van Tricht, Utrecht, 1960 until his death, 1964. Instructor in Industrial and Architectural Design, Academie voor Beeldende Kunsten, Rotterdam and The Hague, Academie van Beeldende Kunst en Kunstnijverheids, Arnhem, and Academie voor Baukunst, Amsterdam, 1942–58. Member, with Van Doesburg, Huszar, Oud and Wils, De Stijl Group, Leiden and Utrecht, 1919–31; Founder-Member, CIAM (Congrès Internationaux d'Architecture Moderne), 1928; Dutch Delegate, CIAM, Frankfurt, 1929. Exhibitions: Modern Architecture Exhibition, Moscow, 1927; *Werkbund,* Vienna, 1932; *Biennale,* Venice, 1953; *Gerrit Rietveld,* Centraal Museum, Utrecht, 1958; *Rietveld Rietveld, Architect,* Stedelijk Museum, Amsterdam, and Hayward Gallery, London, 1971–72; *Rietveld Schroder Huis 1925–1975,* Utrecht, 1975. Honorary doctorate: Technical College, Delft, 1964. Honorary Member, Bond van Nederlandse Architecten, 1963. *Died* (in Utrecht) *25 June 1964.*

Works:

1920 Cornelis Begeer Shop, Utrecht

Dr. Hartog House interiors, Maarssen, Netherlands

1920/
22 Jeweller's shop, Amsterdam (destroyed)

1923/
24 Wessels Shop, Utrecht

1924 Van Huffel Chemist's Shop interiors, The Hague

Schroder House, Prins Hendriklaan, Utrecht (with Mrs. T. Schroder-Schrader)

Gerrit Rietveld: Schroder House, Utrecht, 1924

1925 P. Ketting Study interiors, Utrecht
Dr. Muller Nursery, Utrecht
1926 Dr. Harrenstein Living Room, Amsterdam
(with Mrs. T. Schroder-Schrader)
Weteringschans Bedroom, Amsterdam (with
Mrs. T. Schroder-Schrader)
1927 Lommen House, Wassenaer, Netherlands (altered by others)
Birza Family House interiors, Utrecht (with
Mrs. T. Schroder-Schrader; destroyed)
Normaal Housing (project; with Mrs. T.
Schroeder-Schrader)
1928 Garage with Chauffeur's Living Quarters,
Waldeck Pyrmontkade 10, Utrecht
1929/
58 Core Houses (projects)
1930/
31 Row houses, Erasmuslaan, Utrecht (interiors
with Mrs. T. Schroder-Schrader)
1930/
32 Row-houses, for the Wiener Werkbund,
Vienna
1931 Klep House, Montenspark 8, Breda, Netherlands
1931/
34 Studio houses, Blaricum and Laren, Netherlands (projects)
1932 Row houses, Robert Schumannstraat,
Utrecht
House and Music School, Henriette van Lyn-
denlaan 6, Zeist, Netherlands
1933 Small Practical Houses (project)
Metz and Company Shop, Hoogstraat, The
Hague (with W. Penaat)
1934 Row houses, Erasmuslaan, Utrecht (with
Mrs. T. Schroder-Schrader)
Szekely House, Joh. Verhulstweg 70, Santpoort, Netherlands
1935 Hondius-Crone House interiors, Bloemen-
daal, Netherlands
Hillebrand House, Bloemlandscheweg 3,
Blaricum, Netherlands
1936 Vreeburg Cinema, Utrecht (with Mrs. T.
Schroder-Schrader)
Smedes House, van Weerden Poelmanlaan 1,
Den Dolder, Netherlands
Mees House, Van Ouwenlaan 42, The Hague
1939 Hypothecair Crediet Bank, The Hague
Brandt-Corstius Summer House, Petten,
Netherlands
1941 Verrijn Stuart Summer House, Breukeler-
veen, Netherlands

1942 Rietveld House (project)
1949 Smit House, Puntweg 8, Kinderdijk, Nether-
lands (project)
Van Ommeren House, Rijksstraatweg 158,
Elst, Netherlands
1951 Stoop House, Beekhuizenseweg 48a, Velp,
Netherlands
Home for Spastic Children, Willemstad,
Curacao
1952 Klaasen House, Taveernelaan 9, Den Dolder,
Netherlands
1953 Bicycle Shed, Utrecht (destroyed)
1954 Van Ravensteijn-Hintzen House, Hoeflo 14,
Laren, Netherlands
Driessen House, Hulkesteinscheweg 21, Arn-
hem, Netherlands
Dutch Pavilion, *Biennale,* Venice
Sculpture Pavilion, Sonsbeek Park, Arnheim,
Netherlands (rebuild at the Kroller-
Museum, Otterlo, Netherlands, 1965)
1954/
57 Housing, Hoograven, Utrecht (with van
Grunsven and H. Schroder)
1955/
57 Housing, Utrecht (project; with J. Rietveld)
1956 Juliana Hall, and Entrance, *Trade Fair,*
Utrecht (with others)
Visser House, Bergerdreed 6, Bergeyk, Neth-
erlands (with H. Schroder)
De Ploeg Textile Works, Bergeyk, Netherlands (with G. Beltman, Engineers)
Institute for Applied Art, Wibautstraat, Amsterdam (project)
1956/
58 Scholten House, Kleiweg 32b, Baambrugge,
Netherlands
1956/
68 Institute for Applied Art (Gerrit Rietveld
Academy), Prinses Irenestraat 96, Amsterdam (completed by van Dillen and van
Tricht)
1957 Blaha House, Villaparklaan 5, Best, Netherlands
Van Daalen House, Fasantlaan 14, Bergeyk,
Netherlands
Press Room, Unesco, Paris
1957/
58 Schrale Beton Offices, Willemsvaart 21,
Zwolle, Netherlands
1957/
59 Housing, Erasmusweg, Reeuwijk, Netherlands

1957/
63 Academy for Arts and Crafts, Onderlangs 9,
Arnhem, Netherlands (completed by van
Dillen)
1958 Parkhurst House, Oberlin, Ohio
1958/
59 De Zonnehof Exhibition Hall, Amersfoort,
Netherlands
Van den Doel House, Monnikendammerzij-
weg 31, Ilpendam, Netherlands
1958/
61 Housing, Kanaleneiland, Utrecht
1958/
64 Primary school, Badhoevedorp, Netherlands
1958/
66 Auditorium, Hoofddorp Cemetery, Netherlands (completed by van Dillen)
1959 Ket Shop, Leeuwarden, Netherlands
Gemeentelijk Lyceum School, Doetinchem,
Netherlands (with van Tricht)
1959/
60 Hamburger House, Korswater 9, Noordwijk,
Netherlands
van Dantzig House, Harddraverslaan 60,
Santpoort, Netherlands
Theissing House, Breitnerlaan 1, Utrecht
1960 Koot House, van Soutelandelaan, The Hague
1960/
65 Protestant Church, Zijdeveld, Uithoorn,
Netherlands (with van Tricht)
1961/
62 Showroom, Design Centre, Amsterdam
(partly destroyed, 1971)
1961/
63 Mado Shop, Oudegracht 119, Utrecht
1961/
64 Van Slobbe House, Zandweg 122, Heerlen,
Netherlands
1961/
72 Centraal Museum extensions, Utrecht (with
van Dillen)
1962 Poster Column, Eindhoven, Netherlands
1962/
63 Town Hall, Leerdam, Netherlands (project)
1962/
65 Savings Bank, Dedemsvaart, Netherlands
1963/
67 Steltman Jewellery Shop interiors, The Hague
Bosschaert House, Langewijnen 9, Laren,
Netherlands (completed by T. Bakker)
1963/
72 Vincent van Gogh Museum, Amsterdam
(with van Dillen and van Tricht)
1964 Miners' Barracks interiors, Eygelshoven,
Limburg, Netherlands
Twente Technical High School Science Centre, Enschede, Netherlands (project)
1964/
67 Engelhard House, Straat van Mozambique 3,
Amstelveen, Netherlands

Designs: Red-Blue Chair, 1918; Hanging Lamp,
1920; Berlin Chair, 1923; One-Piece Moulded Chair,
1927; Zig-Zag Chair, 1934; One-Piece Stamped
Chair, 1942; etc.

Publications:

By RIETVELD: books—*Over Kennis en Kunst, lez-
ing-cyclus over stedebouw,* Amsterdam 1946;
Schroder Huis, Amsterdam 1963; articles—numerous in *De 8 en Opbouw* (Amsterdam), 1932–1941,
and "Aanteekening bij Kinderstoel" in *De Stijl*
(Leiden), no. 9, 1919; "Niet een landhuis maar een
gewoon huis" in *Bouwkundig Weekblad* (The
Hague), no. 44, 1926; "Interieur" in *International
leergang voor nieuwe architectuur,* Delft 1930;
"Nieuwe zakelijkheid in de Nederlandsche architectuur" in *De Vrije Bladen,* Amsterdam 1932; "De
nieuwe zkelijkheid in de architectuur" in *Leeu-
warder Courant* (Leeuwarden, Netherlands), February 1933; "Vakverrotting" in *Bouwkundig Weekblad*
(The Hague), no. 47, 1935; "Aangifte" in *Bond van*

Nederlandsche Architecten, Amsterdam 1940; "De verhouding tusschen beeldhouwer en architect" in *Nieuwe Utrechtsch Dagblad* (Utrecht), February 1947; "Het interieur" in *Bouwkundig Weekblad* (The Hague), no. 25, 1948; "Aspecten van het nieuwe bouwen" in *Forum* (Amsterdam), no. 2/3, 1949; "De bedoeling van de tentoonstelling" in *Schoonheid in huis en hof,* Amersfoort, Netherlands 1950; "Die Nachkriegsarchitektur in Holland" in *Werk* (Zurich), no. 11, 1951; "De Consequenties van het structuurplan van Utrecht voor de binnenstad" in *Bouwkundig Weekblad* (The Hague), no. 23/24, 1954; "Mondrian en het nieuwe bouwen" in *Bouwkundig Weekblad* (The Hague), no. 11, 1955; "Moord op Utrechts binnenstad: of levensvoorwaarde voor een stad" in *Elseviers Weekblad* (Amsterdam), October 1955; "De Jaarbeursgebouwen in 40 jaren" in *Forum* (Amsterdam), no. 3, 1956; "Ontwerper en materiaal" in *Visie* (Leiderdorp, Netherlands), no. 5, 1957.

On RIETVELD: books—*The Work of Gerrit Rietveld, Architect* by Theodore M. Brown, Cambridge and Utrecht 1958; *Gerrit Rietveld: Bouwmeester van ein nieuwe tijd* by H. Schaafsma, Utrecht 1959; *Gerrit Thomas Rietveld* by A. Buffinga, Amsterdam 1971; *Gerrit Rietveld, Architect,* exhibition catalogue, by I. L. Szenassy, Amsterdam 1971, London 1972; *Rietveld Schroder Huis 1925-1975,* exhibition catalog, Utrecht 1975; *Gerrit Thomas Rietveld: Furniture* by Daniele Baroni, Milan 1977, London 1978; articles—"Proeve van kleurencompositie in interieur" by Theo van Doesburg in *De Stijl* (Leiden), no. 12, 1920; "Sculpture Pavilion, Arnhem, Holland" in *Architectural Design* (London), no. 25, 1955; "Nieuw werk van G. Rietveld" in *De Groene Amsterdammer,* March 1956; special issue of *Forum* (Amsterdam), no. 3, 1958; "L'Oeuvre de Gerrit Rietveld" in *Architecture: Formes et Fonctions* (Lausanne), no. 6, 1959; "Gerrit Rietveld" in *Domus* (Milan), September 1965; "The Examples of Rational Buildings" by K. Drugowitsch in *Bauforum* (Vienna), January/February 1974; "Rietveld and His Museum Buildings" by E. Berg and H. Bak in *Arkitekten* (Copenhagen), 12 March 1974; "A Touch of De Stijl" by R. Yee in *Progressive Architecture* (New York), March 1975; "The Schroder House, 1924" by S. Nagao and Y. Tominaga in *Space Design* (Tokyo), March 1976.

Gerrit Rietveld is an extraordinary architect. Almost all his work is provincial, even boring, yet there were brief moments when he was the most important architect and furniture designer in the world.

In 1918 Holland was an oasis of peace in a Europe at war, and it was in this Holland that Gerrit Rietveld produced his "red-blue" chair—a piece of furniture that was not too comfortable to sit on but was a delight to look at. It can be seen, in retrospect, as a demonstration of many of the concepts of the modern architecture that were to be invented during the course of the next decade. Rietveld was a cabinet maker by training and made the chair himself; simple enough in construction, it was in its aesthetic that it was truly prophetic. Rietveld was a member of the de Stijl group and shared their love of bright colours and of rectangular planes sliding past one another. The red-blue chair was a de Stijl construction with bright colours and flat planes, but it also carried, in embryo, concepts such as the clear separation of supported planes and supporting framework and such as the reduction of designs to simple unadorned rectangles that later architects were to develop in the design of buildings.

The chair was important, but the house that Rietveld designed for and with his friend Mrs. T. Schroder-Schrader was even more so. The house is small and stands on a tiny lot on Utrecht's Prins Hendriklaan, but it is clearly a manifesto building and the passing of more than half a century has not dimmed its impact. In 1924, when it was completed, Le Corbusier and Mies Van der Rohe were still fumbling

through their early house designs, but Rietveld was not fumbling. The Schroder House is a mature work, a clear statement unequalled in Northern Europe this century.

De Stijl claimed to be liberators of space, and the Schroder House does not disappoint in that respect. In all the years since the Renaissance, space had been seen as confined, enclosed, ordered. Frank Lloyd Wright broke away from this limiting tradition and used space in a much freer way, and, due to the influence of Robert van't Hoff, Wright was admired and understood in Holland. But the Schroder House frees space far beyond that which Wright would sanction. The first floor is a flexible space—screens can be operated to make enclosed rooms or an open space. Big windows open the room to the outside: by placing side hung casement windows opening away from the corner with no corner mullion, Rietveld removed the solidity and space-enclosing nature of the walls. For years corners had been made solid; in the Schroder house the corner can be made nonexistent, and a new sensation of space, of limitless openness, has been gained.

The new sense of space achieved in the Schroder House would have been less meaningful were it not for the steel frame, used in a showy, wilful, but utterly consistent way. The architecture of open, flowing space is appropriate for steel framed buildings, and here steel columns are enjoyed for their own sake and carried past the structure they support to emphasize the mood of continuity, of space extending beyond the confines of the house.

Ten years after the completion of the Schroder House, Rietveld built the everyday version, a row of houses, on an adjoining site in Utrecht's Erasmuslaan. Thoughtful, beautifully put together and obviously very habitable, they are amongst the finest houses built in Europe at that time, but they lack the magic and the space games of the Schroder House, for by 1934 Rietveld had left the de Stijl movement, and he never again found a clear direction for his work. If the Erasmuslaan terrace is a come-down after the Schroder House, the later work of Rietveld can be said to continue the decline, for never again in thirty more years of practice did he design a building of world-scale influence and importance. He became a respectable but very local architect.

It was not only in Nazi Germany that modern architecture was frowned upon: for twenty years Rietveld had little work and was considered demodé by the critics. Either because he had some sympathy with the reaction of the time or because he had to compromise to build at all, Rietveld's work in this period is often traditional, dull and insipid. The nadir is reached in 1941 with the Verrijn Stuart Summer House at Breukelerveen, all thatch and waney-edge boarding, as if Hansel and Gretel had built a home by the lake.

The Schroder House made all the history books on Modern Architecture, while its architect seemed lost in a world of vernacular revival. In 1954 he staged a minor come-back. The Sculpture Pavilion in Arnheim's Sonsbeek Park stood for only a short while, but a decade later it was built again at Otterlo. This building has none of the smooth surfaces of the early buildings, but it does play de Stijl space-games, with walls extending outwards like the Barcelona pavilion. Then, in 1956, Rietveld turned to the curtain wall, which he handled very beautifully in the Institute for Applied Art, Amsterdam, with a totally high-tech image. The 1964 Van Slobbe House at Heerlen is probably the finest work from Rietveld's post-war period. A regular, almost Miesian frame is married with de Stijl planes—an irreconcilable combination that somehow comes off in this calm, masterly house. The Slobbe House is, however, the exception, and the general standard of the late work is not high. More typical is the brick de Stijl of the Dedemsvaart Savings Bank; structurally illogical, the design seems dated and dull.

—John Winter

ROBERTO ARCHITECTS.

Partnership; established, Rio de Janeiro, 1933, as M. M. Roberto, by Marcello Roberto (died, 1965) and Milton Roberto (died, 1955); known as M. M. M. Roberto Architects, with Mauricio Roberto, 1942–65, and, under the direction of Mauricio Roberto, as M. Roberto Architects, since 1966. Exhibitions: Museum of Modern Art, Sao Paulo, 1958; *Brazilian Architecture,* Jedda, Saudi Arabia, and Lagos, Nigeria, 1976. Recipient: First Prize, Brazilian Press Association Headquarters Competition, Rio de Janeiro, 1936; Grand Golden Collar Award, Brazilian Institute of Architects, 1970; First Prize—Mint Building Competition, Rio de Janeiro, 1971; Alagados Urban Planning Competition, Salvador, Brazil, 1973; Taubate Administration Centre Competition, Sao Paulo, 1974; Usiminas Housing Competition, Ipatinga, Minas Gerais, Brazil, 1975; Convention Centre Competition, Salvador, Brazil, 1976; Tres Rios Urban Expansion Competition, 1976; Caji City Plan Competition, Salvador, Brazil, 1977; Buraquinho Tourist City Plan Competition, Salvador, Brazil, 1978. Address: M. Roberto Arquitetos, Rua Siqueira Campos 43, Grupo 1006, Copacabana, Rio de Janeiro 22.031, Brazil.

Works:

1936 Brazilian Press Association Headquarters (ABI), Rio de Janeiro
1937 Airport Terminal Building and Hangars, Santos Dumont Airport, Rio de Janeiro
1941 Brazilian Insurance Institute Headquarters (IRB), Rio de Janeiro
1943 Industrial Institute Headquarters, Rio de Janeiro
　　 Brazilian Insurance Institute Employees' Recreational Centre, Rio de Janeiro
1944 Pianco Apartment Building, Rio de Janeiro
　　 Mamamguape Apartment Building, Rio de Janeiro
1944/
46 Sotreq Caterpillar Industrial Plant, Rio de Janeiro
1945 Roberto Building, Rio de Janeiro
1946 Mechanics' School, Rio de Janeiro
　　 Faria Goes Summer Residence, Lake Araruama, Rio de Janeiro
1947 Institute of Pensions (IPASE) Employees' Apartment Building, Rio de Janeiro
1948 Faria Goes House, Rio de Janeiro
　　 Naval Carpentry School, Niterói, Rio de Janeiro
1949 Carpentry and Weaving School, Vassouras, Rio de Janeiro
　　 Brazilian Insurance Institute Office Building, Rio de Janeiro
1950 Weaving School, Petrópolis, Rio de Janeiro
　　 Herbert Moses House, Gavea, Rio de Janeiro
1951 Ricardo de Albuquerque Workers' City, Rio de Janeiro
1952 Marques do Herval Offices and Shops, Rio de Janeiro
　　 Arthur Monteiro Coimbra House, Jacarepagua, Rio de Janeiro
　　 Apartment building, Cataguases, Brazil
1953 Samambaiba Apartment Building, Rio de Janeiro
1954 Shop and office, Samambaia, Rio de Janeiro
　　 School of Motor Engineering, Rio de Janeiro
　　 Fátima e Finusia Apartment Building, Rio de Janeiro
　　 Angel Ramirez Apartment Building, Rio de Janeiro
　　 Guarabira Apartment Building, Rio de Janeiro
　　 Tacito Prado House, Petrópolis, Rio de Janeiro
1955 Campello Apartment Building, Rio de Janeiro
　　 Grumari Seaside Tourist Resort Development Plan, Rio de Janeiro
　　 Tourist plan for the Cabo Frio Region of Rio de Janeiro

1956 School of Civil Construction, Rio de Janeiro
Polynuclear Metropolis: Urban Unit Cities Study (competition project)
Master plan of Imbituba City, Santa Catarina, Brazil
1957 Expansion plan for Tunis
1958 Souza Cruz Cigarette Company Headquarters, Rio de Janeiro
Banco da Amazonia, Brasilia
Guarapes Apartment Building, Rio de Janeiro
Bela Vista Apartment Building, Rio de Janeiro
Dalton Apartment Building, Rio de Janeiro
Barao de Sao Clemente Apartment Building, Rio de Janeiro
1960 Regina Yolanda Werneck House, Isle of Paqueta, Rio de Janeiro
Self-service garage, Rio de Janeiro
1961 Cesar Thedim House, Cabo Frio, Rio de Janeiro
Apartment building, Laranjeiras, Rio de Janeiro
1962 Residential and hotel complex, Arenzano, Riviera del Poente, Italy
Getulio Vargas Hospital Annex and Ancillary Buildings, Rio de Janeiro
Ambulance, tuberculosis and public health buildings, Tijuco District, Rio de Janeiro
Moncorvo Filho Hospital, Rio de Janeiro
Club Building, Guinle Park, Rio de Janeiro
Apartment building I, Botafogo, Rio de Janeiro
1966 Apartment building II, Botafogo, Rio de Janeiro
1967 Development plan for Tres Rios, Rio de Janeiro
Building code for Araruama, Rio de Janeiro
Government Building, Sao Luiz, Brazil
1968 Bus Station, Tres Rios, Rio de Janeiro
Plan for Ribeirao Preto, Sao Paulo
Development plan for Betim, Minas Gerais, Brazil
1969 Apartment building, Ipanema, Rio de Janeiro
1969/
77 Bank of Brazil Administration and Data Processing Centre, Porto Alegre, Brazil
1969/
78 Bank of Brazil Administration and Data Processing Centre, Rio de Janeiro
1970 Development plan for Duque de Caxias, Rio de Janeiro
Development plan for Vitória, Espirito Santo, Brazil
Bank of Brazil Regional Headquarters, Sao Luiz, Brazil
1970/
77 Bank of Brazil Administration and Data Processing Centre, Sao Paulo
1971 Morro Nova Cintra Housing Development, Rio de Janeiro
1972 Priorities plan for Cabo Frio, Rio de Janeiro
Plan for the Niterói/Rio das Ostras Highway, Brazil
Urban master plan for Alagados, Salvador, Brazil (competition project)
BANESPA Banking Corporation Administration Centre, Sao Paulo
Nossa Senhora de Copacabana Parish Centre, Rio de Janeiro
Vera Simões Summer Residence, Cabo Frio, Rio de Janeiro
1972/
77 Brazilian Academy of Letters, Rio de Janeiro
1973 Regional Bank of Brazil additions, Brasilia
Bank of Brazil Central Treasury, Rio de Janeiro

Roberto Architects: Bank of Brazil Administration and Data Processing Centre, Sao Paulo, 1977

1974 Taubate Administration Centre, Sao Paulo
Marine Ministry interiors, Rio de Janeiro
Urban plan for Vila Oficinas, Curitiba, Brazil
Urban plans for Itapevi, Santo Andre, and Cotia, Sao Paulo
Santo Antonio do Catagua Urban Development, Taubate, Sao Paulo
1975 6th Naval District Headquarters, Sao Paulo
Youth Centre, Belo Horizonte, Minas Gerais, Brazil
Geovia Company Industrial Plant, Vitória, Espirito Santo, Brazil
Tourist development plan for Praia de Cacandoca, Ubatuba, Sao Paulo
1976 Santa Maria da Serra Tourist Centre, Barra Bonita, Sao Paulo
Bahia Convention Centre, Salvador, Brazil
Usiminas Housing, Ipatinga, Minas Gerais, Brazil
Bairro Ouro Verde Urban Development, Belo Horizonte, Minas Gerais, Brazil
Cidade Verde Urban Development, Betim, Minas Gerais, Brazil
Tourist plan for Barra Bonita, Sao Paulo
Plan for Caji, Salvador, Brazil
1977 International Insurance Company Headquarters, Rio de Janeiro
Urban expansion plan for Tres Rios, Rio de Janeiro
Acu da Torre Urban Development, Sao Joao da Mata, Bahia, Brazil
Urban development plan for Itapevi, Sao Paulo
1978 ERCO Company Factory, Santa Cruz, Rio de Janeiro
Urban development plan for Nova Lima, Minas Gerais, Brazil
Urban development plan for Santa Cruz, Rio de Janeiro
Tourism development plan for Buraquinho, Salvador, Brazil (competition project)
Tourism development plan for Morro de Guaratiba, Rio de Janeiro
1979 Data Processing Centre, Curitiba, Parana, Brazil
Data Processing Centre, Recife, Pernambuco, Brazil

Publications:

On ROBERTO ARCHITECTS: articles—"Building for Business: New and Remodelled Office Buildings" in *Architectural Record* (New York), December 1940; "Brazilian Press Building" in *The Architects' Journal* (London), March 1941; "Cantilever Hangar, Santos Dumont Airport, Rio de Janeiro" in *Architectural Record* (New York), December 1942; "Cantilever Hangar" in *Architect and Building News* (London), March 1943; "Rio de Janeiro Airport" in *Architectural Review* (London), March 1947; "Flats in Rio de Janeiro" in *Architectural Review* (London), August 1947; "Building ABI, Rio de Janeiro" in *L'Architecture d'Aujourd-'hui* (Paris), September 1947; "Education and Welfare in Brazil," "Living in Brazil," and "Office Buildings" in *Architectural Forum* (New York), November 1947; "Brésil" in *L'Architecture d'Aujourd-'hui* (Paris), January 1948; "IRB Building at Rio de Janeiro" in *Architectural Review* (London), January 1948; "Archéd Industrial Building Integrates Displat Repair and Office Space" in *Architectural Forum* (New York), November 1950; "Factory at Rio de Janeiro" in *Architectural Review* (London), January 1951; "The Work of Roberto, Roberto and Roberto, Architects" in *L'Architecture d'Aujourd-'hui* (Paris), August 1952; "Buildings for Education" in *Progressive Architecture* (New York), February 1957; "Marcelo e Mauricio Roberto: Scioltezza e Liberta" by Giulia Veronesi in *Zodiac* (Milan), no. 6, 1960; "Data Processing Centre for the Sao Paulo Region Banco do Brasil" in *Modulo* (Rio de Janeiro), December/January 1977–78.

It is a fact that in almost all under-developed or developing countries one of the greatest worries is to find some way to create a just and correct distribution of income. Brazil, for example, seems to have reached a stage where it is of the utmost necessity to correct such unjust distortions. That money is concentrated in the hands of very few people is patently obvious to everyone. In consequence, many houses are sub-standard, and often there is no housing in our cities for people of the lower economic level. This state of affairs is reaching a point of such flagrant injustice that the government is seriously worried and searching for a solution.

In my opinion, in order to attain it, we architects should be perfectly aware of the vastness of the problem and be utterly modest. To insist on importing the models of developed countries, applying them without any further adaptation, is of no use to Brazil. On the contrary, the notion is almost ridiculous. Such models, which are not consistent with the reality of Brazil, can be harmful. We need to be modest in order to be able to plan our cities in a way consistent with our socio-economic reality, with our scale.

A large part of the population earns very little and suffers from a natural, universal, and irreversible problem—urbanization. These people have been affected by technological change: the need for manual workers in the countryside is gradually decreasing, and the promise of a more secure employment in the city is a constant lure. It is within such a reality—taking into account the economic/cultural development of a population that has changed its habitat—that the problem has to be solved.

We must understand that a house is not a number one priority for these people. It would represent a stage in urban development that they have not yet reached. Not because they are lesser human beings but because, in the country, they have always been badly sheltered, in very poor, utterly rustic huts, in places where malaria, tuberculosis, Chagas disease, and ignorance are endemic. For such people an urban shack—the "barracos"—appropriate to their urban development, yet safe and free of disease, means almost complete satisfaction. Health, education and a job are far more important to them than a house. This is the basic difference between the inhabitants of "sub-dwellings" in a developed country and in a country like Brazil. In a developed country the poor end in a slum as an end of a process. They are, therefore, a desperate people, and when the government offers them a house, it represents a stage in the cultural process that they had already attained; they are, in fact, winning back "status." In the developing countries, on the other hand, squatter communities such as the "favela," the "mocambo," the "barriada" and the "villa miseria" are the *beginning*, the hope and future in the lives of the poor. Hence the music they compose, the "escolas de samba" they create, the big football rallies they organize.

As an architect and urbanist my challenge lies not in the avenues of Brasilia, Rio de Janeiro or Sao Paulo, but in Caxias, in Alagados, in all the cities or urban settlements where the sub-dwellings predominate. My challenge is to put an end to such barbarities as the "Low-Cost Housing Complex": they are still being planned and built. The government should no longer build houses; they should instead invest in large-scale infrastructures, in adequate solutions to shelter all of these people. If we could provide for their survival, they would be able to integrate the labour force of our country, and then, with the growth that would inevitably follow, with the increase of the gross national product, we would actually have contributed to a more humane and equitable distribution of income and to human satisfaction.

—Mauricio Roberto

One of the teams most closely involved with the birth and development of modern architecture in Brazil was that of the Roberto brothers. The partnership was initially formed by the two elder brothers, Marcello and Milton, and was later expanded to include

Mauricio, who eventually took the office over on his own after the premature death of his brothers (in 1964 and 1955 respectively). Up until the mid-1950's the Roberto brothers produced one of the most exuberant and personal strains of the Brazilian version of the "International Style," and contributed considerably to the freshness of its vocabulary.

The team's most notable building, the Brazilian Press Association Headquarters (ABI) in Rio in 1936, was one of the first modern designs to win an open architectural competition. This building is as important—historically and chronologically—as the famous Ministry of Education and Health Building built during the same period and in the same part of the city. The ABI Building brought together all the elements that were to become features of the Roberto brothers' subsequent work during this first phase of their practice: functionalist treatment of volume and facades, transparency of construction method, fluidity and ambiguity of interior/exterior limits, and spatial dynamism.

The ABI Building is also a pioneer in the use of *brises-soleil*—originally proposed by Le Corbusier, first used on this building, and subsequently almost the trademark of the Roberto brothers. These "sunbreaks" are made of fixed vertical "blades" that protect the office balconies from excessive sunlight: they seem to be carved out of the surface of the building and turned inwards, which gives the facade a somewhat compact and monolithic appearance. These superimposed sun-breaks were to appear in other projects in a more clearly stated form—for example, the concrete *grille* becomes a striking architectural feature in the case of the Santos Dumont Terminal, the Roberto Building, and the Fátima-Finusia Apartments. In other buildings—the Brazilian Insurance Institute Office Building or the Marques do Herval Building—the Roberto brothers employ another ingenious system—a light-weight structure with pivoted or swivelling aluminium parts.

The design of the headquarters of the Brazilian Insurance Institute (1941) is a more sophisticated and explicit expression of the principles of the ABI Building. The functional treatment of facades and volumes correspond more closely to the requirements of the interior. The symbolic functions—the director's office, for example—are expressed in an exceptionally free way. The colour scheme picks out the various elements of construction, emphasizing the rational construction approach while remaining discreet. This polychrome experiment was later to be developed and would become another hallmark of the Roberto brothers' work. It is evident in all its splendour in the facades of Santos Dumont Airport.

Also notable in this first phase of the Roberto brothers' work is their treatment of the relationship between interior and exterior. In the case of the ABI Building and the Brazilian Insurance Institute, the entrance halls merge with the urban space: there is no separation of interior and pavement. The broad, open concourse of Santos Dumont Airport has a monumentality prescribed by its numerous columns —a technological requirement of its day. From the pavement outside, one can look through the concourse and enjoy an uninterrupted view of the airplanes. The concourse itself becomes an enormous symbolic portico: with its adjacent gallery, it puts passengers in the mood for the excitement of air travel. In the Brazilian Insurance Institute Recreation Centre—a building of exceptional lightness and simplicity—the areas designated for living, leisure and games are interlinked and flow freely into one another.

In the Sotreq Caterpillar Industrial Plant, the Naval Carpentry School, and the School of Motor Engineering, the spatial dynamics are handled in a much more complex and unusual way. Several features—such as the stairways, mezzanines, walls or even secondary volumes—break with tradition and contribute to a closer link between interior and exterior. In the Sotreq building, three domes with different radii seem to shoot out at random, finally merging with the central body. In the schools, especially

the latter, the architectural features are organized in an almost abstract way reminiscent of the constructivists. A similar treatment can be seen in certain of Rino Levi's projects and in Henrique Mindlin's houses, which attempt to dynamize the volume by separating it onto several planes. But with the Roberto brothers it is not the *volume* that is made dynamic but the *space* itself. This is perhaps their greatest contribution to Brazilian architecture. Sometimes the volume is maintained, but the surrounding space is opened up and its very "bareness" exploited. In other cases, shapes that create space are added or juxtaposed—the mouldings on the Fátima-Finusia and Marques do Herval buildings, for example. The treatment of these facades may at first sight appear gratuitous, but the rationale is precisely that of spatial dynamics.

It is strange that there is no expression of this language in the Roberto brothers' domestic architecture, which tends to be somewhat stilted or pretentious. Two rare exceptions are the Tacito Prado House in Petrópolis and the Sales Pavilion at Samambaia (now completely transformed)

The designs of the first phase of the Roberto brothers' work, ending about the mid-1950's, involved an inventiveness and an intuitive, revolutionary treatment of architectural features that has only recently been studied and applied consistently. By contrast, their more recent buildings are chiefly concerned with mass and volume, to the detriment of spatial and symbolico-functional techniques.

The architectural output of this second phase can be divided into three different "styles." The most conventional of these styles comprises work such as the Banco da Amazonia in Brasilia and the Brazilian Academy of Letters in Rio, variations of the theme of a monolithic volume supported by chamfered pillars. In the second "style" there is greater emphasis on the composition of the mass, as in the Nossa Senhora de Copacabana Parish Centre in Rio and the Bank of Brazil Administration and Data Processing Centres in Rio and in Sao Paulo. Of three cylindrical volumes of different heights and radii, the Saolo Paulo Centre is perhaps their most expressive design in this style. The third "style" is characterized by structures of tall pillars set out in proportion, supporting isolated volumes containing the functional components of the design. Theoretically it would be possible to place extra "boxes" in the spaces between the existing volumes without interfering with the normal running of the building. The visual effect of numerous columns crossing the remaining area is one of both chaos and fragility. Of the projects that were conceived along these lines, only one was built: the Bank of Brazil Administration and Data Processing Centre in Porto Alegre.

Town planning is now the most important part of Mauricio Roberto's work. The Robertos' first venture into this field was in 1955, with their design for a resort at Grumari Beach near Rio. This was soon followed by another plan of a similar nature for the Cabo Frio region. In 1956 Marcelo and Mauricio Roberto took part in the competition for a pilot plan for Brasilia. They were awarded third prize for their "Polynuclear Metropolis," which was to have consisted of seven urban units, each for 72,000 people. The units would have been urbanized and constructed in accordance with the requirements of the city's growth.

Of the more recent projects, the following are noteworthy: the plans for the integrated development of the towns of Duque de Caxias and Vitória and the designs for the area surrounding the Niterói/Rio das Ostras Highway and for the Barra Bonita Tourist Centre. The last two were designed to preserve and improve areas important to the ecologist and tourist alike. But of all the projects, the most interesting is a plan for the Alagados region of Salvador, which aims to regenerate a slum area of houses built on stilts without destroying the spontaneous urban structure and the community spirit that exists among the area's 90,000 inhabitants.

—Jorge Czajkowski

ROBERTSON, Sir Howard (Morley).
British. Born in Salt Lake City, Utah, U.S.A., of British parents, 18 August 1888. Educated at Eastfield House, Ditchling, Sussex; Malvern College, Worcestershire; Architectural Association School, London; Ecole des Beaux-Arts, Paris, Diploma 1913. Served in the British Army, in France, 1915–19: Military Cross, 1919. Married Doris Adeney Lewis in 1927. In partnership with the architect J. Murray Easton, London, 1919–31, and with Easton and E. Stanley Hall, London, 1932–40; Partner, Easton and Robertson, London, 1940–59, and Easton, Robertson, Cusdin, Preston and Smith, London, 1959 until his death, 1963. Technical Adviser, League of Nations Building, Geneva, 1927–29; Consultant Architect, National Services Hostels Corporation, London, 1939–45; Member of the Advisory Committee, United Nations Building, New York, 1947–48; Consultant, Unesco Building, Paris, 1951. Principal, and Director of Education, Architectural Association School, London, 1920–35. President, Royal Institute of British Architects, 1952–54. Recipient: Bronze Medal, 1928, 1936, Godwin Bursary, 1933, and Royal Gold Medal, 1949, Royal Institute of British Architects; Medal of the Essex, Cambridgeshire and Hertfordshire Allied Society of Architects, 1937. Fellow, Royal Institute of British Architects, 1925. Knighted, 1954. *Died* (in London) *5 May 1963.*

Works:

1925 British Pavilion, *International Exposition,* Paris (destroyed)
      Royal Horticultural Hall, London (with J. Murray Easton)
1928 Private cinema, Imperial Institute, London
1929/
  32 Liberty's Department Store, Regent Street, London W.1 (with J. Murray Easton)
1930 Office building, 52 Cornhill, London E.C.3
      House, South Kensington, London
      Oxford University Press Warehouse, Neasden, London N.W.10
1930/
  39 Savoy Hotel modernization, London
1931/
  39 Berkeley Hotel modernization, London
1932 Royal Bank of Canada Building, 6 Lothbury, London E.C.2
1932/
  33 Nurses' Home, Children's Hospital, 37–46 Guilford Street, London W.C.1
1933 Private cinema for Fox Films, London House, Lake Zug, Switzerland
1935 British Pavilion, *International Exposition,* Brussels (destroyed)
1935/
  39 Claridge's Hotel modernization, London
1936 British Pavilion, *World's Fair,* Johannesburg (destroyed)
      Norbury House Hotel, Droitwich, Worcestershire
1937 *The Practitioner* Office Building, 5 Bentinck Street, London W.1
      Private cinema for Publicity Films, London
      Apartment block, Avenue Close, Regent's Park, London
      Apartment block, St. Edmund's Terrace, Regent's Park, London
1938 Metropolitan Water Board Laboratories, New River Head, Rosebery Avenue, London E.C.1 (with J. Murray Easton)
1939 Electricity Company Showrooms, London E.C. (destroyed)
      British Pavilion, *World's Fair,* New York
      Sadler's Wells Theatre alterations and additions, London E.C.1
1946 Sanatorium, Uppingham School, Rutland
1947/
  52 Savoy Hotel modernization II, London
      Berkeley Hotel modernization II, London
1949 Institute of Brewing Laboratories, Nutfield, Surrey

S. S. *Rangitoto* interiors, New Zealand Shipping Company (destroyed)

S. S. *Rangitane* interiors, New Zealand Shipping Company (now floating hotel, at Sullom Voe, Zetland)

1950   Cargo ship's interiors and living quarters, for Messrs. Watts, Watts and Company (destroyed)

Apartment block, Church Street, London W.1

Apartment block, St. John's Wood Road, London N.W.8

1951   Hatfield Technical College, Hertfordshire (now altered)

Hatfield Secondary Technical School, Hertfordshire (now altered)

S. S. *Ruahine* interiors, New Zealand Shipping Company (destroyed)

1952/
63   Master plan for the University of Reading, Berkshire (now altered)

1956   Bank of England Printing Works, Loughton, Essex

Faculty of Letters, University of Reading, Berkshire

1958   Bank of England Returned Note Building, Loughton, Essex

1961   Shell Centre Building, York Road, London S.E.1

1961/
67   Lloyds Bank Regional Head Offices, Birmingham

1963   Bank of England Branch Offices, Bristol (now altered)

Publications:

By ROBERTSON: books—*The Principles of Architectural Composition,* London 1924; *Architecture Explained,* London and New York 1926; *Examples of Modern French Architecture,* with F. R. Yerbury, New York and Berlin 1928; *The Four Inns of Court,* New York 1930; *Modern Architectural Design,* London 1932, 1952; *The Post-War Home,* with others, London 1942; *Architecture Arising,* London 1944; *Reconstruction and the Home,* London and New York 1947; articles—"Modern Dutch Architecture" in *Architectural Review* (London), August 1922; "Modern Sweden" in *Architectural Review* (London), July 1924; "The Architecture of Finland" in *Architectural Review* (London), December 1924 and January 1925; "Architecture 1927—at the RIBA Galleries" in *Architectural Review* (London), June 1927; "Architecture 1928" in *Architectural Review* (London), June 1928; "A Pictorial Review of Modern Architecture in Europe," with F. R. Yerbury, in *Architecture* (London), November 1928/December 1930; "La Formation de l'Architecte en Angleterre" in *L'Architecture d'Aujourd'hui* (Paris), October/November 1933; "Architecture in Ankara" in *The Architect and Building News* (London), 8 April 1938; "The Domestic Scene: Contemporary Trends" in *Royal Architectural Institute of Canada Journal* (Toronto), November 1938; "The British Pavilion, New York World's Fair" in *The Builder* (London), 2 June 1939; "The New York World's Fair" in *Architectural Association Journal* (London), July 1939; "Architecture 1919–1939" in *The Builder* (London), 2 February 1940; "B.I.N.C.: An Assessment" in *The*

Architect and Building News (London), 28 November 1941; "Defence Housing in the U.S.A." in *The Architect and Building News* (London), 27 February 1942; "Como se evita el desordenado crecimiento de las ciudades" in *Ingenieria y Arquitectura* (Bogota), November/December 1945; "Design of Interiors" in *Architectural Association Journal* (London), February/March 1947; "Quality in Architecture" in *The Architects' Journal* (London), 6 November 1947; "The American Scene" in *The Architect and Building News* (London), 19 March 1948; "The Seven Vamps of Architecture" in *The Builder* (London), 25 March 1949; "Inaugural Address" in *RIBA Journal* (London), November 1952; "The Architect's Dilemma" in *AIA Journal* (Washington, D.C.), February 1954.

On ROBERTSON: articles—"The Brussels Exhibition, 1935" in *Architectural Association Journal* (London), October 1934; "RIBA's New President, Mr. Howard Robertson" in *The Builder* (London), 20 June 1952; "Work by RIBA's New President" in *The Architects' Journal* (London), 26 June 1952; "Men of the Year—Howard Robertson" in *The Architects' Journal* (London), 15 January 1953; "Howard Robertson" by Reyner Banham in *Architectural Review* (London), September 1953; "A Traditional Architect" (obituary) in *The Times* (London), 6 May 1963; "Obituary" in *RIBA Journal* (London), June 1963.

Much of Sir Howard Robertson's work is in the late Renaissance manner, simplified by the deletion of

Sir Howard Robertson: Royal Horticultural Hall, London, 1925

classical ornament and the influence of the underlying steel and concrete construction, yet in a few buildings, such as those of the hall type, he was, with his partner, J. Murray Easton, in the forefront of modern developments. This emanated in part from his admiration, often expressed in his writings, of some of the best modern continental architecture.

A notable development in Europe in the first quarter of the century for large buildings of the hall type was the parabolic rib construction, generally of reinforced concrete. An example of this in Robertson's work is the Royal Horticultural Hall, London, which he designed in collaboration with Easton. By a series of arches, approximately parabolic, a step structure is supported on either side, the vertical sections of which make four tiers of windows, while additional lighting is provided by an elliptical window in each bay. Ceiling heating, an early example, is provided by water-pipes embedded in the concrete soffit. This, for its time, very modern construction resulted in one of the most beautiful modern exhibition halls in Europe.

Robertson also designed many industrial buildings, offices and blocks of flats. Among the most typical of his designs, in the traditional simplified Renaissance manner, is the Nurses' Home of the Children's Hospital in Guilford Street, London, a steel-framed, brick-faced building with stone dressing on the two lower floors. It is a design of rectangular masses, well related, and there is an effective Greek reminiscence in the fluted columns of the two south portico entrances.

Robertson admired Mendelsohn's treatment of long horizontal facades arrested by circular vertical features, and it was possibly this influence that prompted his design (in collaboration with Easton) of the Metropolitan Water Board Laboratories, London, in which a long curved two storey facade abuts a circular projecting entrance hall with vertical windows—but it lacks the cohesion of Mendelsohn's designs.

A spectacular later building, which must rank with the Horticultural Hall as among Robertson's finest, is the Bank of England Printing Works, with its vast production hall, 800 feet long, with a clear span of 125 feet. (The structural engineer was Ove Arup.) The roof consists of a series of asymmetrical arches which hold, on the north side, a stepped structure with windows forming the verticals. This is clearly an echo of the roof of the Horticultural Hall. Abutting it, on the south side, is the administration building, with a tall, six-storey vertically-emphasized entrance block and two long wings, one with continuous glazing forming a horizontal motif relating well with the verticals of the central blocks. Here are two contrasting structures determined by function, without stylistic integration—but the production hall is impressive.

Some of Robertson's latest work in the simplified Renaissance manner, such as the immense and too obtrusive Shell Building on the South Bank, is apt to be rather dull, and it lacks the occasional originality of his best work. The demands of clients, however, can be inhibiting.

Sir Howard Robertson's work is of varied excellence: it includes some of the best modern buildings, but some is rather stereotyped. He was not immune to the influence of the wave of neo-classicism that spread over Europe during the 1930's.

—Arnold Whittick

ROBERTSON, Jaquelin (Taylor).
American. Born in Richmond, Virginia, 20 March 1933. Educated at St. Mark's School, Southboro, Massachusetts, graduated 1951; Yale University, New Haven, Connecticut, 1951–55, B.A. 1955; Magdalen College, Oxford (Rhodes Scholar), M.A. 1957; Yale University (Koppers Student Architectural Design Scholarship), M.Arch. 1961; awarded Yale Travelling Fellowship, 1961. Married Marianna Neze in 1962. Worked as an architectural designer in the office of Sir Leslie Martin, Cambridge, England, 1962–63, and Edward Larrabee Barnes, New York, 1963–66; Principal Urban Designer, Urban Design Group, City Planning Commission, New York, 1968–69; Director, Office of Midtown Planning and Development, New York, 1969–72; City Planning Commissioner, New York, 1973; Vice-President, Arlen Realty and Development Corporation, New York, 1974–75; Director, Llewelyn-Davies and Partners, Tehran, 1975–77; Chairman, Llewelyn-Davies Associates, New York, 1977–78. Since 1978, Partner, J. T. Robertson Associates, New York. Lecturer, Yale School of Architecture, 1964–65, and Columbia University School of Architecture, New York, 1965–67; Visiting Lecturer, Salzburg Seminar, Austria, 1973, and The New School, New York, 1973. Member, Board of Visitors, University of California at Los Angeles, 1971–72; Director, Parks Council, New York, 1971–75, International Design Conference at Aspen, Colorado, 1972–75, Architectural League of New York, 1972–75, Circle in the Square Theatre, New York, 1972–75, and Municipal Arts Society, New York, 1972–76. Exhibitions: *Forty under Forty,* Architectural League of New York, 1966; *The New City,* Museum of Modern Art, New York, 1967; *Urban Design,* New York, 1969; Institute of Architecture and Urban Studies, New York, 1977. Recipient: Albert S. Bard Award, City Club of New York, 1970; Parks Council Award, New York, 1971; Annual Design Award, *Progressive Architecture,* 1977. Address: 211 East 70th Street, New York, New York 10021, U.S.A.

Works:

1962 Louis Camu House, Alöst, Belgium (with Herman Lemaire)
1967 Isador Seltzer House, Sagaponick, New York Madden House (project)
Master plan for Negril, Jamaica (with Sam Chang Associates)
1968 Twin Parks Urban Renewal Plan, Bronx, New York (with Jonathan Barnett, Giovanni Pasanella, and Richard Weinstein)
Lincoln Square Special Zoning District Plan, New York (with the Urban Design Group)
1969 Coney Island Urban Renewal Plan, Brooklyn, New York (with the Urban Design Group)
Plan for the Special Theatre District, New York (with the Urban Design Group)
Air Rights Transfer Legislation for New York City Landmarks (for Grand Central Terminal)
1969/
70 West Midtown Master Plan, New York (as Director, Office of Midtown Planning and Development)
1970 Jaquelin Robertson House renovation, 11 Punemere Lane, Easthampton, New York
Agronomics Office Building, Tehran (with Sam Chang Associates)
Clinton Urban Renewal Plan, New York (as Director, Office of Midtown Planning and Development)
1970/
72 Midtown Circulation Study and Plan, New York (as Director, Office of Midtown Planning and Development)
1971 Residential Multi-Use Zoning District Plan, New York (as Director, Office of Midtown Planning and Development)
1972 Fifth Avenue Special District Plan, New York (as Director, Office of Midtown Planning and Development)
Air Rights Transfer Legislation for Open Space, New York (as Director, Office of Midtown Planning and Development)
Times Square Special District Plan, New York (as Director, Office of Midtown Planning and Development)
1973 Queensboro Bridge Development Plan, New York (as Director, Office of Midtown Planning and Development)
Kaikaakko Development Plan, Honolulu (with Chester Rapkin)
1974 Hartford Square, Connecticut (with the Arlen Design Group)
Griffin Square, Dallas (with the Arlen Design Group)
1975/
78 Shahestan Pahlavi, Tehran (with Llewelyn-Davies and Partners, Tehran)
1977 Buford Scott House, 7612 Hill Drive, Richmond, Virginia (with Fred Cox)
1978 Lawrence Flinn House, Spaeth Lane, Easthampton, New York
Arco Chemical Corporation Research and Development Center, New Town Square, Philadelphia (with Davis Brody Associates)
1978- Museum of Modern Art Tower, New York (with Cesar Pelli)

Publications:

By ROBERTSON: articles—contributor, with Richard Weinstein, to *Urban Design as Public Policy* by Jonathan Barnett, New York 1973; "Machines in the Garden" in *Architectural Forum* (New York), April 1973; "Five on Five," with others, in *Architectural Forum* (New York), May 1973; "The Rediscovery of the Street" in *Architectural Forum* (New York), November 1973; "Shahestan Pahlavi" in *RIBA Journal* (London), February 1977.

On ROBERTSON: articles—"Jaquelin Robertson: Ex New York City Planner Turned Developer's Architect" by Jane Holtz Kay in *Building Design* (London), 26 April 1974; "The Gamesman: Jaquelin Robertson" by Suzanne Stephens in *Progressive Architecture* (New York), May 1977; "A New City Center in Tehran" in *Progressive Architecture* (New York), January 1978.

Architecture is a COMMUNAL art, both dependent upon and reactive to its surroundings. Unlike painting or sculpture, use and active social engagement is necessary to its appreciation. It is, very simply, man's most lasting and revealing artifact, as well as his most crucial and difficult aesthetic endeavor.

Architecture is not meant for museums—nor should it be judged by museum standards. It requires and serves LIVING—not VIEWING.

As an architect, I have been continually interested in the dialogue connecting seemingly opposite poles: ART and COMMERCE; OLD and NEW; LARGE and SMALL-SCALE DESIGN: PUBLIC and PRIVATE PRACTICE; OBJECT and CONTEXT; PLANNING and DESIGN; FLEXIBILITY and DETERMINACY; CITY and SUBURB; CAR and PEDESTRIAN. It is the comparison, juxtaposition, reconciliation, or delineation of these kinds of DIFFERENCES which leads to the creation of RELEVANT, LIVABLE and SATISFYING ORDERS, which it is the architect's task to uncover.

My architectural concerns have largely focused on: a) *Historical Continuity:* Architecture is conservative and architectural changes are healthily INCREMENTAL not REVOLUTIONARY. Dictim: Mistrust POLEMICS; eschew UTOPIAS. b) *The Primacy of Context:* Buildings should observe the MANNERS OF THE PLACE. History, social/-political and economic patterns, local conventions, the natural surroundings, taste and established language. These provide the architectural SETTING. Dictum: Ignore them at great risk. c) *Originality:* Not as important as it's cracked up to be. Dictum: Better to be good than original. d) *The Design of Cities:* Architects were intended to design cities. The order of the whole is more important than the order of the parts. Dictum: Designing cities is NOT like designing chairs. e) *Architecture/Planning/Development:* The three are inextricably interconnected. No architect who is ignorant of the *requirements* of the other two will be very useful as an urban designer, or even an aesthetically concerned citizen. Dictum: The architect should know how the world around him works. f) *Politics and Public Life:* All decisions, especially political ones, have design implications. If one wants to *positively* affect the quality of the built environment, one has to participate in government; they write the rules. Dictum: Pluralistic democracies depend on Citizen Bureaucrats: you get what you deserve. g) *Money:* It's important. Architects need it and need to understand how it works. Dictum: Only fools ignore money and power. h) *Variety:* Greatly over-rated. Most of the world's best architecture has been the *elaboration* of a few simple ideas, schemes, partis, details, etc. Dictum: There is greatness in consistency; variety is most often a lack of focus— a handmaiden of triviality.

As a consequence of these concerns, my professional life has shifted between architectural design, urban design, planning and development activity as well as between private practice and public sector involvement. I have worked for myself, for government, for a real estate firm and for traditional architectural firms. I have taught and at the same time tried to understand and to participate in the market place. I have planned transit/pedestrian malls for large cities with the same enthusiasm as I have written zoning legislation, and have designed cities in foreign cultures with the same attention to context as I have given small country houses in established regional settings. I have lived with compromise and accommodation. While I remain a "closet aesthete" and humanist whose motivating energies and tastes are essentially artistic, I am continually and fundamentally tainted by an undying addiction to the pulp world of politics and commerce, to art serving life.
—Jaquelin Robertson

Jaquelin Robertson, the architect, is an anomaly. An able designer whose reputation until recently has rested on three small house designs (one unbuilt), Robertson has for most of his career forsaken architecture for planning. He is an activist whose politics have led him away from building in the hope of serving architecture more broadly. His career provides interesting evidence of the degree to which participation in politics and development can allow a gifted architect to influence strongly the quality of the built environment.

Robertson's public career began when he joined with a group of friends to work with New York's mayor, John Lindsay, on problems of planning and development for the city. Robertson became Director of the Office of Midtown Planning and Development. His group had two modes of behavior. As architectural polemicists, they produced a number of elegantly detailed conceptual studies of areas in Midtown Manhattan in the cause of influencing subsequent development. These studies have had little tangible effect. As urban strategists, they devised incentive zoning plans in an attempt to advance certain qualities they considered valuable in the city. Developers were given concessions that could result in greater revenue from the development, in return for participating in improving the street level experience. Here there has been some success.

In 1974 Robertson moved from public to private participation in the process he had created. He became Vice-President of Planning and Design for Arlen Realty, who were engaged at that time with the Olympic Tower development. The building, designed by SOM, discreetly incorporates an arcade, the product of Robertson's incentive zoning. When compared with Rockefeller Center across the street, however, the benefits to the pedestrian are hard to find.

His work with Llewelyn-Davies on Shahestan Pahlavi, a new town center for Tehran, as with the products of the Midtown Planning Office, has a markedly architectural character. In the careful drawings and sensitive diagrams, and in the superb model, there is marvellous invention, a curious hybrid of New York formalism and Iranian contextualism.

Until recently, Robertson's independent work as an architect comprised three little houses—one in Belgium, one in New York, and one never built. The two American designs—Seltzer House (built) and Madden House (projected)—are both remarkable and yet quite dissimilar. The Seltzer House is raw and bony: it shows all the inventive concerns of the early 1960's, but with a maturity, poise and restraint that are remarkable for work so early in a career. The Madden House (from limited evidence) is an exceptional invention. Again, there are influences: a curious blend of Kahn and Rudolph, the composition has a dramatic and theatrical originality. It plays with illusional transparency in a way that belies its date. Perhaps, in all of Robinson's urban work, it has been the architect in him that has dominated. For example, one sees echoes of the Madden House in the buildings flanking the Nation Square of Shahestan Pahlavi.

Robertson's opportunism appears to involve a constant search for a setting that will allow the application of all his creative skills. The political game can encompass a vast range of intentions. In Robertson's work, they seem above all to be a desire for architectural place-making, irrespective of the social or political context.

—Alan Balfour

ROCHE, (Eamonn) Kevin.

American. Born in Dublin, Ireland, 14 June 1922; emigrated to the United States, 1948; naturalized, 1964. Educated at the National University of Ireland, Dublin, 1940–45, B.Arch. 1945; did postgraduate work at the Illinois Institute of Technology, Chicago, 1948–49. Married Jane Tuohy in 1963; children: Eamon, Paud, Mary, Ann, and Alice. Designer, Michael Scott and Partners, Dublin, 1945–46, 1947–48; Architect with Maxwell Fry and Jane Drew, London, 1946, and with the United Nations Planning Office, New York, 1949; Associate, Eero Saarinen and Associates, Bloomfield Hills and Birmingham, Michigan, and Hamden, Connecticut, 1950–66 (Principal Associate in Design to Saarinen, 1954–61). Since 1966, Founder Partner, with John Dinkeloo, *q.v.*, Kevin Roche John Dinkeloo and Associates, Hamden, Connecticut. Member, Board of Trustees, American Academy in Rome, 1968–71, and Woodrow Wilson International Center for Scholars, Smithsonian Institution, Washington, D.C., 1969–71. Member of the Commission of Fine Arts, Washington, D.C., since 1969. Exhibitions: Museum of Modern Art, New York, 1968, 1971. Recipient: Arnold Brunner Award, American Institute of Arts and Letters, 1965; Creative Arts Award in Architecture, Brandeis University, Waltham, Massachusetts, 1967; Medal of Honor, American Institute of Architects, New York Chapter, 1968; Bard Award, City Club of New York, 1968, 1977; California Governor's Award for Excellence in Design, 1968; New York State Award, 1968; Bard Citation, Citizens' Union of New York, 1968; Total Design Award, American Society of Industrial Design, 1976. D.Sc.: National University of Ireland, 1977. Academician, National Academy of Design; Member, National Institute of Arts and Letters. Address: Kevin Roche John Dinkeloo and Associates, 20 Davis Street, Hamden, Connecticut 06517, U.S.A.

Works (with John Dinkeloo):

1961/
68 Oakland Museum, California

1962/
64 IBM Pavilion, *World's Fair,* New York

1962/
67 Richard C. Lee High School, New Haven, Connecticut

1962/
69 Administration, Student Union, and Physical Education Buildings, Rochester Institute of Technology, New York

1963 Air Force Museum, Wright-Patterson Air Force Base, Ohio (project)
Women's Resident Colleges, University of Pennsylvania, Philadelphia (project)

1963/
65 Cummins Engine Company Components Plant, Darlington, England

1963/
68 Ford Foundation Headquarters, New York

1964 National Center for Higher Education, Washington, D.C. (project)

1964/
74 Fine Arts Center, University of Massachusetts, Amherst

1965/
69 Knights of Columbus Headquarters, New Haven, Connecticut
United States Post Office, Columbus, Indiana

1965/
71 Power Center for the Performing Arts, University of Michigan, Ann Arbor

1965/
72 Veterans Memorial Coliseum, New Haven, Connecticut

1965/
73 Creative Arts Center, Wesleyan University, Middletown, Connecticut

1966 Institute for the Study of Human Reproduction, Columbia University, New York (project)
National Fisheries Center and Aquarium, Washington, D.C. (project)

1966/
72 Irwin Union Bank and Trust Company, Columbus, Indiana
Aetna Life and Casualty Computer Building, Hartford, Connecticut

1967/
71 College Life Insurance Company of America Headquarters, Indianapolis

1967/
78 Master plan for additions to the Metropolitan Museum of Art, New York (Temple of Dendur Pavilion; American Wing; Robert Lehman Pavilion; Michael C. Rockefeller Primitive Art Wing; European Art Wing; Sculpture Court)

1968 Small Orangerie, Columbus, Indiana (project)

1969 IBM Computer Technology Museum, Armonk, New York (project)

1969/
75 Hotel and Office Building, stage I of the United Nations Development, New York

1969/
77 Federal Reserve Bank of New York

1970/
73 Cummins Engine Company Sub-Assembly Plant, Columbus, Indiana

1970/
74 Richardson-Merrell Inc. Headquarters, Wilton, Connecticut
Worcester County National Bank, Worcester, Massachusetts

1971 Design of the *Bicentennial* celebrations, Philadelphia (project)
Office complex, Toronto (project)

1972 Indiana and Michigan Power Company Complex/Headquarters, Fort Wayne, Indiana
Cummins Engine Company Corporate Headquarters, Columbus, Indiana

1973/
76 Fiat World Headquarters, Turin
Kentucky Power Company Headquarters, Ashland

Kevin Roche and John Dinkeloo: Ford Foundation Headquarters, New York, 1963

1974 Center for the Performing Arts, Denver (project)
1975/
  79 West Office Building, John Deere and Company Headquarters, Moline, Illinois
1976 Visual and Communication Arts Building, Texas Christian University, Fort Worth
      Thomas J. Watson Research Center addition, IBM Corporation, Yorktown Heights, New York
      Union Carbide Corporation World Headquarters, Danbury, Connecticut
1977 Exxon Chemical Company Headquarters, Fairfield, Connecticut

Publications:

On ROCHE/DINKELOO: books—*Modern Architecture* by Vincent Scully, New York 1961, 1974; *New Architecture in New Haven* by Don Metz, Cambridge, Massachusetts 1966; *Architects on Architecture,* edited by Paul Heyer, London 1967; *American Architecture and Urbanism* by Vincent Scully, New York 1969; *New Directions in American Architecture* by Robert A. M. Stern, New York 1969, 1977; *Will They Ever Finish Bruckner Boulevard* by Ada Louise Huxtable, New York 1970; *Observations on American Architecture* by Ivan Chermayeff, New York 1972; *Third Generation: The Changing Meaning of Architecture* by Philip Drew, London 1972; *Kevin Roche John Dinkeloo and Associates 1962–1975* by Yukio Futagawa, Tokyo and Fribourg 1975; articles —"Horizon" by Wolf Von Eckardt in *American Heritage* (New York), Summer 1971; "Kevin Roche and John Dinkeloo 1964–1974," a special number of *Architectural Forum* (New York), March 1974.

Kevin Roche-John Dinkeloo and Associates is the most aesthetically daring and innovative American firm of architects now working in the realm of governmental, educational, and corporate clients. As successors to the firm of Eero Saarinen and Associates, they appear to be also the successors, or at least strong contenders, to Skidmore Owings and Merrill in the area of large corporate facilities. The reasons are not difficult to see.

Their work in the past 18 years—some 35 major projects built and not built—demonstrates a kind of problem solving for each specific situation that has produced, as it did for Eero Saarinen, works of distinct individuality and stylistic variety from project to project. We need only compare the Union Carbide headquarters in Connecticut, with the Fiat headquarters in Turin and the College Life Insurance headquarters in Indianapolis, to see the range of invention and variation applied to the design of suburban office complexes.

Their work has also continuously shown perceptive planning in relation to the environment—both urban and suburban. They were early innovators of urban public spaces—with the interior courts at the Ford Foundation Headquarters, the National Fisheries Center project, the National Center for Higher Education project, and the United Nations Development; with the park-covered Oakland Museum, which is the major monument of underground architecture; and with portico-arcades such as the one at the Columbus, Indiana Post Office. In terms of interior planning also they have been consistently innovative and refined in detailing inside and out, from the days when Warren Platner was the head of their interior design department to the more recent office landscape scheme for Fiat headquarters. Their urban planning has been influential on other contemporary architects, especially the first schemes for the Worcester County National Bank and the Federal Reserve Bank of New York.

Their technological achievement, which is the province of John Dinkeloo, has made noteworthy advances in the use of slip-form concrete construction with inset steel members (Knights of Columbus Headquarters), of vast steel trusses (New Haven Coliseum) as well as in the use of materials such as raw poured concrete (Richard C. Lee High School; University of Massachusetts Fine Arts Center); weathering steel (Cummins Engine Plant, Darlington, England; Ford Foundation Headquarters); silo tiles (Knights of Columbus); and steel-and-glass curtain walls that are elegantly refined.

In their formal invention developed for individual planning requirements, there is always an element of surprise. Generally their solutions are so geometrically primal that they seem like the first project sketches or like first models blown up and built. Sometimes that surprise comes from an insight that appears unfailingly on target, reminding us of Dr. Johnson's definition of wit as that which makes us ask why we did not think of the idea ourselves. The work of Roche-Dinkeloo so often seems just right, obvious once revealed, almost inevitable—the idea of an urban interior park as at the Ford Foundation, the idea of elevating an urban tower high enough to let sunlight onto virtually all of a site, as at the Federal Reserve Bank of New York. Sometimes, on the other hand, their work appears to come from a flair for the arbitrary and the wilful, a kind of latter-day Boullée minimalism that makes us ask how the architects themselves ever got such an idea, as in the College Life Insurance complex.

At all times, however, the work of Roche-Dinkeloo is beautifully executed, daring and innovative, refined, and economically detailed. It is an architecture of contemporary size, of today's grandeur and richness. Yet it raises questions about our psychological responses. For all its currentness, the work of Roche-Dinkeloo is almost entirely abstract—in the mainstream of the Modern movement—and therefore virtually without reference to any recognizable traditional cultural symbolism. In this regard the architects come under censure from post-modern proponents of "representational" architecture, which attempts, through associations with vernacular building or through analogies to classical or other forms and colors, to tell us about itself. The abstract geometries of Roche-Dinkeloo, their glassy, slick, smooth, impersonal surfaces, are, to a degree, alienated from mankind, almost other-worldly.

The principal cause of this alienation is the scale of their work. The Ford Foundation is only 12 stories high but houses a garden that is 1/3 of an acre; the Air Force Museum project is designed to cover 3½ city blocks, the United Nations Development project is planned to cover 2 city blocks, and the National Fisheries Center project to have a greenhouse 600 feet long. But size alone is not the issue. Roche-Dinkeloo's projects are vast in appearance even when not in fact. The Knights of Columbus building, though only 23 stories tall, presents an astonishing image when one is driving into New Haven. It looks as if the city built an electric plant as a gateway. "Please say 'Power Plant,'" Kevin Roche urged when I first made that observation. (Was it inevitable that he should design Power Center?)

Roche has long been enamored of the bigness and power of American industrial architecture—its factories and roadways—and the forms of that architecture are often reinterpreted, however abstractly, in his designs. The broad concrete bands (Richard C. Lee High School; Oakland Museum; Wesleyan University Arts Center) derive as much from highway bridges as from Frank Lloyd Wright's Falling Water; the weathering steel structures for factories (Cummins Engine Company projects) are idealized industrial architecture of the most direct analogy and progression.

In the design of delicate and continuous steel-and-glass structures, however, the firm makes some of its highest marks. Those greenhouses are taut and uniform, pristine and elegant; they are at the same time abstract and generalized, even when they mirror and reflect the natural landscape, as at Power Center. With their awning-like structures (U.N. Plaza Hotel; Union Carbide Headquarters), they are only slightly more human. In their phantom awning development of steel without glass (Irwin Union Bank and Trust) they are dehumanized to an unearthly, dazzling degree.

These glistening greenhouse factories feed the aspirations of corporate magnates. The work of Roche-Dinkeloo realizes, it seems, the utopian dream of the industrial revolution, when, as now, corporations have progressed from manu-factories to management headquarters. The dream seems, in their work, realized, expanded to a superscale, ordered to a glittering tidiness, and suggesting the overbearing authority and the de-humanity of corporate existence. Roche-Dinkeloo designs appropriately and consummately for the princes of our day.

—C. Ray Smith

ROGERS, Archibald C(oleman).
American. Born in Annapolis, Maryland, 29 September 1917. Educated at Lawrenceville School, New Jersey, 1932–35; Princeton University, New Jersey, 1935–39, B.A. 1939, M.F.A. 1942; United States Naval Postgraduate School, Annapolis, 1942–43, Dip.Naval Arch. 1943. Served in the United States Navy, 1942–46: Lieutenant. Married Lucia Bernadine Evans in 1947; children: Lucia and Coleman. Draftsman in the office of Cross and Cross, New York, 1939–40. Founder Partner, with Francis Taliaferro, George Kostritsky, and Charles Lamb, Rogers-Taliaferro-Kostritsky-Lamb, Baltimore, 1946–69, and Chairman of the Board of the successor firm, RTKL Associates, Baltimore, since 1969. Zoning Commissioner, 1946–52, and Chairman of the Sanitary Commission, 1965, Anne Arundel County, Maryland. Lecturer, Virginia Theological Seminary, Alexandria, 1967–72. Member, Maryland Architectural Registration Board, 1958–67; Member, Architectural Review Board of Washington, D.C., 1963–66; Member, Maryland Arts Council, 1967–68; Chairman, Soviet-American Symposium on Urban Design, 1968, Israeli-American Symposium, 1969, and Indian Symposium, 1970; Trustee, Princeton University, 1972–76; President, American Institute of Architects, 1974. Address: RTKL Associates, Village Square, Village of Cross Keys, Baltimore, Maryland 21210, U.S.A.

Works:

1962 Charles Center, Baltimore
Urban redevelopment plan for Hartford, Connecticut

1966 Plan for downtown Cincinnati
Plan for downtown Eugene, Oregon
1968 Fountain Square, Cincinnati
1972 Plan for downtown Jacksonville, Florida

Publications:

By ROGERS: novel—*The Monticello Fault*, Durham, North Carolina 1979; articles—"Towards a National Design Policy" in *Architectural Record* (New York), June 1967, "Russian Reconnaissance: Stresses of Change" in *Progressive Architecture* (New York), August 1969; "The Ideas" in *Architecture: Formes et Fonctions* (Lausanne), 1971.

On ROGERS: articles—"Successful Cincinnati" by Ann Ferebee in *Design and Environment* (New York), Winter 1972; "Profile of the President of the AIA: Archibald C. Rogers" by Carol Rose in *AIA Journal* (Washington, D.C.), December 1973; "When an Architect Becomes a Novelist" by Andrea O. Dean in *AIA Journal* (Washington, D.C.), February 1979.

The following is an extract from my novel *The Monticello Fault* in which the hero and heroine argue about the nature of architecture. Joel, the architect, has become bogged down in the nuts-and-bolts of his design for a new museum building: the driving force

of his original concept now eludes him. Lila, a painter, attempts to clarify, and perhaps help solve, his problem:

"Architecture no doubt lives by economics and stands by technology, but the architect is called to be an artist. It is an artist who stands at the heart of you, Joel Pellegrini, even if he is camouflaged in a business suit and is licensed to practice a profession. When you deny admittance to your intuition, you deny your calling. When you deny your calling, you risk atrophy. Intuition may be cruel, Joel, as cruel as living can be. But both are preferable to a walking death."

Joel could be stubborn, nearly as stubborn as Lila. He fought back.

"That's great! 'What is an architect?' The answer to this enigma appears below, inverted. So I stand on my head. 'An architect is an artist wrapped in a professional inside a businessman.' It sounds positively Churchillian, Lila."

Lila glared at him, her lips compressed, her eyes flashing a warning which Joel chose to ignore.

"I'll grant you this, Lila. Architecture *is* an art, but it's not architecture until it's built. To be built it has to be practical, its concept has to be realistic. Architecture isn't free like other arts, like music or poetry or painting. The architect is trammeled by reality. His art must be rational or it won't be built and won't be art. Where is there room for inspiration? Your paintings are inspired, Lila. I know that

Archibald C. Rogers: Fountain Square, Cincinnati, 1968

679

just as I know that a Mozart sonata or a Shakespearean sonnet is inspired. But what would happen if I admitted inspiration to my mind? How could a flash of insight, a pure and simple idea, survive translation into an economically sound and structurally safe building?"

Lila let him have it.

"*Never* say that to me. Never say that mine is the easier calling, that my art is freer than yours, that it is less rational, less real. *Never* again put me down, Joel Pellegrini."

She stormed at him, stamping her small, sandaled foot in fury. Joel was shaken. He sat down upon the drafting stool, regarding the new Lila.

Here was a Lila few had seen—imperious, passionate, flashing fire. Joel decided that he enjoyed this Lila, enjoyed too the contest that was building up between them. He started to interrupt. She ignored him and swept on, one question crowding upon the next.

"Is my palette more tractable than your economics or your stresses-and-strains? Is my canvas less limiting than your site? Are not my visions compromised by my medium? My painting disciplined by my tools. Is my work unreal, irrational because it looks beyond time?" She again stamped her foot. "Is there no reality but this, this moment when one's foot treads the earth?"

Lila paused. Joel broke in. He meant to soothe her. He instead annoyed her.

Joel waffled.

"You are right, Lila. Of course you are right and I agree with you. Still, there is something different, more difficult, about architecture, about the art of architecture."

Lila was scornful.

"There *isn't* any real difference, Joel. Architecture is an art like any other art, like music or poetry, and no more difficult. One art differs from another only in its raw material and in its medium for translating this material. Mozart's music flowed from his mind through his fingers to the keyboard. It flowed back to his mind through his ears. Was what came back identical with what flowed forth? How could it be? The poet wrestles with words to express his images, and words may well be the most intractable of all the media. My raw material is what I see about me and in my mind, translated imperfectly by my painting. Yours is the problem of sheltering society. Its solutions are translated, also imperfectly, by your buildings."

Lila smiled softly and to herself.

"We, you and I, Joel, are put here to be artists. We didn't ask for this assignment, but we cannot evade it. And what is our assignment?" Lila paused as if awaiting an answer. But she was no longer looking at Joel.

She answered.

"It is this. To listen. To accept within our emptiness the fertile radiance from eternity. To nurture the offspring it conceives within us. To let this then escape to life in the flesh with which we, and we alone, can clothe it so that it, my painting or your building, can then fulfill *its* assignment."

"But what is *its* assignment, Lila? My building shelters a fragment of society. Your painting delights the eye and, from what I have seen, teases the mind. What more is there?"

"Those are the assignments of time, Joel. But art has another assignment from its parent beyond time. It is this. To speak its universal and wordless language to those it touches, to those who see my paintings and who indwell your buildings. To knit back together time and eternity during the brief moment of its speaking."

—Archibald C. Rogers

Archibald C. Rogers is the Founder and Chairman of the Board of RTKL Associates (established in 1946 as Rogers, Taliaferro, Kostritsky, Lamb), one of the leading practitioners of urban design in the United States and also a significant architectural firm.

Rogers and his firm had an important role in the Charles Center redevelopment in downtown Baltimore, his home city, including the design of the public spaces. However, the firm's most important work is probably the plan for downtown Cincinnati, completed in 1966. This plan has become an exemplar of the way to include decision-makers necessary to the implementation of the plan in the process of creating the plan itself. Rogers set up a four-stage process: 1) reaching a consensus on the nature of the problems; 2) systematically reviewing available alternatives; 3) selecting the most desirable alternative; and 4) choosing the most effective way of attaining the selected objectives. Within each stage Rogers was able to structure a series of decisions which were voted upon by a working committee of community leaders and then ratified by the Planning Commission and City Council. The plan, when completed, had also to be enacted in this way. Rogers had devised a planning process with its political support built in.

As a consequence of this process, the Cincinnati plan has been implemented much more successfully than most other planning documents. One of its most important features is Fountain Square, also designed by RTKL. This Square has given downtown Cincinnati a new and important public space, which confers focus and identity on the new developments around it.

While RTKL has subsequently prepared downtown plans for many other cities, including Eugene, Oregon and Jacksonville, Florida, Rogers himself became interested in creating a national planning context. As president-elect and then president of the American Institute of Architects during 1973 and 1974, Rogers worked to create a National Growth Policy. It was adopted by the AIA. He then spent an additional year trying to create a coalition of other organizations that would support such a policy. The key to the National Growth Policy was the Growth Unit, which would produce a balanced plan and design for new development whether it took place as a new community or within an existing urban area. So far Rogers' national planning efforts have met with little direct success, but they play an important part in creating the climate of opinion that may eventually lead to the adoption of such policies.

Rogers was more successful in influencing urban highway design. Through his efforts, an Urban Design Concept Team was established as part of the process of redesigning a controversial expressway project in Baltimore. Although the plans for this expressway have not gone forward, the concept of integrating land-use decisions and urban design with urban highway planning has been adopted in Federal highway legislation, and projects such as Westway in New York City would not have been possible without the work of Rogers and the Baltimore experience.

—Jonathan Barnett

ROGERS, Ernesto Nathan.
Italian. Born in Trieste, of an Italian mother and English father, 16 March 1909; acquired Italian citizenship, 1930. Educated at elementary school in Zurich, 1915–18; Gymnasium Tasso, Milan, 1918–21; Liceo Parini, Milan, 1921–27; Milan Polytechnic, 1927–32, Dip.Arch. 1932. Served in the Italian Army, 1933–35; during World War II interned in Vevey, Switzerland, 1943–45. Founder Partner, with Gianluigi Banfi, *q.v.,* Ludovico Belgiojoso, *q.v.,* and Enrico Peressutti, *q.v.,* BBPR Architectural Studio, *q.v.,* Milan, 1932 until his death, 1969. Lecturer, School of Architecture, 1962–65, Lecturer, Faculty of Art History, 1964–65, and Professor and Director of the Institute of Humanities, 1964–69, Milan Polytechnic. Editor, *Le Arti Plastiche,* Milan, 1931–33;

Architectural Critic, *La Fiera Letteraria,* Milan, 1932–33; Editorial Adviser, *Rassegne d'Architettura,* Milan, 1932–34; Co-Editor, *Quadrante,* Milan, 1933–36; Editor, *Atti del Sindicato Inter-provinciale Fascista degli Architetti,* 1936; Joint Editor/Manager, *Bulletin du Centre d'Etudes pour le Bâtiment,* Lausanne, 1944–45; Editor/Publisher, *Domus,* Milan, 1946–47; Director, Architetti del Movimento Moderne, and Editor of their periodical *Il Balcone,* Milan, 1947; Editor, *Casabella-Continuità,* Milan, 1953–64. Member of CIAM (Congrès Internationaux d'Architecture Moderne), from 1935; Member of the Secretariat, Commissione per le Manifestazione d'Arte Moderna dell'Associazione tra i Cultori d'Architettura, 1935, and Maison des Artistes, Lausanne, 1939; Member of the Committee, CNR (Consiglio Nazionale delle Ricerche), 1945; Founder Member, MSA (Movimento Studi Architettura), 1945, INU (Istituto Nazionale di Urbanistica), 1949, and Société Européenne de Culture, 1950; Member, Cercle d'Etudes Architecturales, Paris, 1950, Institut d'Esthetique Industrielle, Paris, 1951, Centro Studi Estetici, Milan, 1953, Zentralvereinignung der Architekten, Vienna, 1957, Association Internationale Critique d'Art, 1958, and Lega d'Igiene e di Profilassi Mentale, Rome, 1961. Honorary Member, American Institute of Architects, 1956, and Royal Institute of British Architects, 1963. *Died* (in Gardone, Italy) *7 November 1969.*

Publications:

By ROGERS: books—*Auguste Perret,* Milan 1955; *The Works of Pier Luigi Nervi,* with Jürgen Joedicke, Stuttgart and London 1957; *Esperienze dell'Architettura* (collected essays), Turin 1958; *Editoriali di Architettura* (collected essays), Turin 1968.

Besides his activity as an architect, Ernesto Nathan Rogers was also a very prolific writer, the most influential writer among the Italians to reach a European public.

The son of a British insurance agent in Trieste and an Italian mother, Rogers was brought up in a literary household; his father was one of James Joyce's Trieste friends. Much of his secondary education was in Switzerland, and he was naturally cosmopolitan and polygot. An early flirtation with Futurism prompted his entry into the Fascist Party and into renouncing his British nationality. In 1927 he entered Milan Polytechnic with Banfi and Belgiojoso, whom he had met towards the end of his secondary schooling, and as a student he became editor of the general arts periodical *Le Arti Plastiche* to which he was already a contributor. With his associates he edited *Quadrante,* from 1933–36, which carried some of the most important polemics of the interwar years. In 1935 all four associates joined CIAM. Rogers, as site architect of the Italian Merchant Navy Pavilion, on a barge moored in the Seine, travelled to Paris during the *Exposition Internationale* in 1937, but in 1938, when Italy adopted the German racial laws, he retired into anonymity, though he remained in Milan until forced to flee to Switzerland in 1943.

Rogers' disillusion with fascism was gradual, but by the beginning of the war it had passed into violent opposition. The internment camp at Vevey was regarded by such inmates as Rogers as a kind of college and contributed to the formation of the Partito d'Azione, which was to play an important part in immediate post-war Italian politics. Rogers was its agent at Vevey. He returned to practice with his surviving partners in 1945, and took over the editorship of *Domus* (to which, as well as *Casabella,* he had contributed before the war) from its politically compromised editors, making it the most exciting architectural magazine of the time; unfortunately, its high international reputation also led to its being abandoned by its usual lay home public, and Rogers was edged out. This, and other activities, lead to his becoming a permanent member of the Council of

CIAM, with which he remained connected until its demise in 1959/60.

Rogers' most important influence was exercised through his editorship of *Casabella-Continuità* (1953–64) around which he gathered a group of young and and important contributors (Giancarlo De Carlo, Vittorio Gregotti, Gae Aulenti, Marco Zanusso, Aldo Rossi, etc.) and which he regarded as an open seminar. *Casabella* became the most accurate recorder of the changes in Italian taste, which were taken up immediately by younger architects in Europe and the United States. Rogers consolidated this influence by his many lectures in Europe, America, Latin America, and China. His professorship in Milan was not to come until later, in 1964.

Although he never published a major book, Rogers' publications were frequent and prolific: some are collected in two volumes, *Espierienza dell'Architettura* in 1958 and *Editoriali di Architettura* in 1968. There is also a moving monograph on Auguste Perret. While, since the war, the Roman group of architects, with Bruno Zevi as their spokesman, wanted a concentration on local problems under the banner, oddly, of Frank Lloyd Wright, Rogers made Milan the centre of a cosmopolitan architectural activity by making the outside world familiar with Italian developments through the maximum exposure of the younger Italians to European and American cross-currents. His own philosophical developments are reflected more accurately in his writings than in the later work of BBPR, of which he continued to be an active partner. His particular concern with recent history as a foreshadow of current trends and his fascination with the Viennese brand of liberal rationalism and the architecture which it produced (Loos, Hoffmann, Behrens) has influenced the architecture of the 1970's more than it did that of his own lifetime, and it will probably continue to do so, through the group which he formed round *Casabella*.

—Joseph Rykwert

See BBPR ARCHITECTURAL STUDIO

ROGERS, Richard.

British. Born in Florence, Italy, of British parents, 23 July 1933. Educated at the Architectural Association School, London, 1953–59 (First Year Prize), Dip.A.A. 1959; Yale University School of Architecture, New Haven, Connecticut, 1961–62 (Fulbright, Edward D. Stone and Yale Scholar), M.Arch. 1962. Served in the British Army, 1951–53. Married the architect Su Brumwell in 1960; Ruth Elias in 1973; children: Ben, Ab, Zad and Roo. Partner, with Norman and Wendy Foster and Su Rogers, Team 4, London, 1963–68, and Richard and Su Rogers, London, 1968–70. Since 1970, Partner, with Renzo Piano, *q.v.,* Piano + Rogers Architects, London, Paris and Genoa. Exhibitions: *Biennale de Paris,* 1963, 1967. Recipient: *Architectural Design* Awards, 1964, 1964, 1965, 1968; Industrial Architecture

Richard Rogers: Lloyd's of London Headquarters, 1979

Award, *Financial Times*, 1967, 1976; House for
Today Award, *Ideal Home*, 1968; Work of Out-
standing Quality Award, 1969, and Research
Award, 1970, Royal Institute of British Architects;
First Prize, Basildon Housing Competition, 1971;
First Prize, Place Beaubourg Competition, Paris,
1971; Design Award, British Steel Corporation,
1975. Royal Academician, 1979. Address: Piano +
Rogers Architects, 3 Avon Estate, Avonmore Road,
London W14 8TS, England.

Works:

1967 Reliance Controls Ltd. Electrical Factory,
 Swindon, Wiltshire
1970 Italian Industry Pavilion, *Expo '70*, Osaka
 (with Renzo Piano)
1970- Fitzroy Street Commercial Centre, Cam-
 bridge (with Renzo Piano and Fitzroy
 Robinson)
 ARAM Inc. Medical Centre, Washington,
 D.C. (with Renzo Piano)
1971 B and B Italia Offices, Como, Italy (with
 Renzo Piano)
 Clasp Italia Ltd. Brockhouse Steel Structures
 (building system), Birmingham (with
 Renzo Piano)
 International Distillers and Vintners Ware-
 house/Office conversion, London
1972 Universal Oil Products United Kingdom
 Head Office, and UOP Fragrances Ltd.
 Laboratory, Tadworth, Surrey (with
 Renzo Piano)
1973 Aston Martin Lagonda Ltd. Offices, Show-
 room, Restaurant, Squash Court and
 Housing, London (with Renzo Piano)
1975 PA Management Consultants (PATScentre)
 Research Laboratories, Workshops and
 Ancillary Administration Building, Cam-
 bridge (with Renzo Piano)
 Housing and recreation areas, for Globe Con-
 struction Ltd., Basildon, Essex (with
 Renzo Piano)
1977 Institut de Récherche et de Coordination
 Acoustique, for Pierre Boulez, Paris (with
 Renzo Piano)
 Centre Beaubourg, Paris (with Renzo Piano
 and Sir Ove Arup and Partners)
1979- Lloyd's of London Headquarters

Publications:

By ROGERS: book—*The Building of Beaubourg*,
with Renzo Piano and others, London 1979.

On ROGERS: articles—"Piano and Rogers—Beaubourg" in *Domus* (Milan), October 1971; "Centre du
Plateau Beaubourg: Concours d'Idées," special issue
of *Techniques et Architecture* (Paris), February 1972;
"Piano and Rogers" in *The Architects' Journal* (London), 21 April 1972; "Piano and Rogers: Centre
Beaubourg" in *Architectural Design* (London), July
1972; "Piano and Rogers" in *Architectural Design*
(London), no. 5, 1975; "Piano and Rogers: Architectural Method" in *Architecture + Urbanism*
(Tokyo), June 1976; "RIBA Discourse" in *RIBA
Journal* (London), January 1977; "Centre Pom-
pidou" in *Architectural Design* (London), no. 2,
1977; "Richard Rogers: Interview with Dennis
Sharp" in *Building* (London), 6 April 1979.

Ideology cannot be divided from architecture.
Change will clearly come from radical changes in
social and political structures. In the face of such
immediate crises as starvation, rising population,
homelessness, pollution, mis-use of non-renewable
resources and industrial and agricultural production, we simply anaesthetise our consciences. With
problems so numerous and so profound, with no
control except by starvation, disease and war, we
respond with detachment. Today, at best, we can
hope to diminish the coming catastrophe by the rec-

ognition of the existing human conditions and by
rational research and practice.
 The importance of technology is in the application
of method to technique, whether one is talking of
sophisticated or primitive technology. The aim of
technology is to satisfy the needs of all levels of
society. Technology cannot be an end in itself but
must aim at solving long-term social and ecological
problems. This is impossible in a world where short-
term profit for the "haves" is seen as a goal, at the
expense of developing more efficient technology for
the "have nots." All forms of technology—from low
energy intensive to high energy intensive—must aim
at conserving natural resources while minimising ecological, visual and social damage to the environment, so that by using as little material as possible
as functionally as possible to answer new briefs, we
reach a self-sustaining situation where input = output.
 A new distribution of ends and means is needed,
not based purely on a limited financial evolution of
human needs. In this context, it is as difficult to
create a truly socially oriented brief as it is to adapt
and translate it by the use of the correct technological means.

—Richard Rogers

Richard Rogers is one of the few *emblematic* contemporary architects. He stands for something in
particular: namely, Hi-Tech. Rogers's concern with
advanced technology in architecture would put him
deeply at risk of failure, or at least at risk of design
eccentricity, if he wasn't also a skilled manager. This
he has proved to be without a doubt. Though many
architects have aspired to produce highly technological works, Rogers has the ability to carry them out
with repeated success. The formula seems to be that
his clear design intentions are coupled with persua-
siveness to clients, charisma to staff, and exhaustive
research within a deceptively relaxed approach.
These administrative and technical skills make his
difficult design objectives attainable. If "design process" (to use that familiar if inert phrase) is a subject
worth study, Rogers is a key person with whom to
study it. High technology involves little risk of failure if ruthless practicality governs—and that seems
to be Rogers's way.
 Winning the Beaubourg competition was a great
achievement for Piano and Rogers, but not nearly so
great as building it. Rogers was the most dynamic of
the leaders. His team members later perceived their
contributions as individually strong but also heightened by Rogers—a significant hint of how "effectiveness" was managed. A few slight (and diminishing)
Archigram-style design resemblances therefore have
little to do with Rogers's central qualities, the best of
which prove a vital case for cultural progress and
optimism (the weakest show an artiness that unfortunately gets well appreciated too).
 Characteristic Rogers work are the PATScentre,
the Centre Pompidou (Beaubourg), and the recent
project for Lloyd's of London. His works are deve-
lopmentally consistent, so singling out a few is not
to suggest the special but the more or less typical.
His most admirable work to date is the Institut de
Récherche et de Coordination Acoustique, Paris, in
collaboration with Renzo Piano.

—Nathan Silver

ROSE, Peter.
Canadian. Born in Montreal, Quebec, 1 August
1943. Educated at Lower Canada College, Montreal,
1955–61; Yale University, New Haven, Connecticut,
1961–70, B.A. 1966, M.Arch. 1970. Partner, with F.
Andrus Burr and J. V. Righter, Rose/Burr/Righter
Associates, Montreal, 1970–74; Designer, Arcop Associates, Montreal, 1972. Since 1970, President of

Endless Construction Company, Montreal; since
1974, in private practice, as Peter Rose, Architect,
Montreal. Visiting Critic in Architecture, Yale University, 1974–78, Columbia University, New York,
1977, Carleton University, Ottawa, 1978, and Nova
Scotia Technical College, Halifax, 1978. Recipient:
Design Award, *Progressive Architecture*, 1978; Design Award, Ordre des Architectes du Québec, 1978;
Post Prize, McGill University School of Architecture, Montreal, 1978. Member, Ordre des Architectes du Québec. Address (office): 1407 rue de la
Montagne, Montreal, Quebec H3G 1Z4, Canada.

Works:

1970 Peter Rose House, Magog, Quebec
1971 Graham House, Maisonville, Quebec (with F.
 Andrus Burr)
 Restaurant, Montreal (with F. Andrus Burr)
1972 2 prototype houses for native people, Bala,
 Ontario (with F. Andrus Burr)
 Vacation condominiums (300 units), St. Fé-
 reol, Quebec (project; with F. Andrus
 Burr)
 Prototype housing system for under-
 developed countries (project; with F. Andrus Burr)
1973 Plan for the ski area at St. Sauveur, Quebec
 (with F. Andrus Burr)
 Sinclair House, Jay Peak, Vermont (with F.
 Andrus Burr)
 Cummings House alterations, Knowlton,
 Quebec (with F. Andrus Burr)
 Cluster housing for doctors, Trudeau Institute, Saranac, New York (project; with F.
 Andrus Burr)
1974 Fortier House alterations, Magog, Quebec
 (with F. Andrus Burr)
 Winser House, Magog, Quebec (with F. Andrus Burr)
1975 4-block recycling scheme for Old Montreal
 (project; with F. Andrus Burr)
1976 Finlayson House, North Hatley, Quebec
 (with Mill Design and Research Center)
 Office Tower, Pointe Claire, Quebec (project;
 with Mill Design and Research Center)
 Elmwood School for Girls additions and alterations, Ottawa (project; with Mill Design and Research Center)
 Marosi House, North Hatley, Quebec
 Fortier House alterations, Magog, Quebec
1977 Bradley House, North Hatley, Quebec
 Johnson House, Ste. Agathe, Quebec
 Richer House, Ste. Agathe, Quebec
 C.I.C. Screen Printers Offices and Ware-
 house, Laval, Quebec
 Pavillon 70 (ski pavilion), St. Sauveur, Que-
 bec (with Peter Lanken and J. V. Righter)
1978 Survey/evaluation of all Cree schools in Que-
 bec
 Pavillon 70 alterations, and swimming pool,
 tennis courts and landscaping at St. Sau-
 veur, Quebec
1978- Housing for Crees (Nemeska Band), Cham-
 pion Lake, Quebec
 Cousineau House, Ayers Cliff, Quebec
 Clubhouse, for Redbird Ski Club, Mont
 Tremblant, Quebec
 Pinsonnault House alterations, Knowlton,
 Quebec
 Shaughnessy House alterations, Montreal
 Clubhouse, for the Montreal Skeet Club

Publications:

On ROSE: books—*Supermannerism* by C. Ray
Smith, New York 1977; *The Language of Post Modern Architecture* by Charles Jencks, New York 1978.

The influence of Charles Moore and Robert Venturi
has, since the early 1960's, spread rapidly throughout the world, and most of the architecture designed

Peter Rose: Bradley House, North Hatley, Quebec, 1977

under this influence is, at best, mediocre. This is largely due to the filtering down of architectural ideas and images—the second-hand, third-hand, and fourth-hand exposure (through books, journals, lectures, etc.) of most architects to the work of the Moore/Venturi High Architectural World. The level of understanding is shallow, and the resulting work is usually shallower. Accomplished people like Moore and Venturi must shudder at much of what gets built under their international wings.

But there are important exceptions to this general condition, such as the work of Peter Rose in Quebec. A native of Montreal, Rose completed his undergraduate and graduate degrees at Yale University. Robert Venturi and James Stirling were influential at Yale then; but of more significance is the fact that Rose was in the first class taught by Charles Moore in the Yale School of Architecture in 1966. The ideas and images came to Rose first-hand. And these ideas and images—particularly Moore's late 60's rediscovery of vernacular architecture—were reinforced by Rose's travels between Montreal and New Haven through New England villages and farm country.

In addition to his use of false fronts and scale juxtapositions from Venturi and places of memories and big-time dreams from Moore, Rose's architecture has an additional layer of intelligently handled Quebec responses and references which save the works from being uncomfortable American transplants. In three buildings since 1975—two houses and a ski-lodge in Quebec—the huge chimneys are reminiscent of the chimney on the house Venturi designed for his mother in Chestnut Hill, Pennsylvania in 1962, and they recall Moore's 1969 Koizim House chimney in Westport, Connecticut; but Rose's chimneys are also like the prominent chimneys of 17th and 18th century Quebecois houses. His use of big sweeping roofs recalls Venturi's 1962 Meis House Project for Princeton, New Jersey and Moore's California Sea Ranch roofs of 1966; but

they are also functional snow shedding devices and relatives of the great Canadian railway hotel roofs. There is an overriding Northerness in Rose's compact plans (environmentally sensible), extensive use of wood, and most noticeably, Northerness in the proper, polite, serious composition of architectural elements.

Although there are teasers in his work (the very dramatic "sundeck as ski stage" in the *Pavillion Soixante-Dix* or the kitsch ceramic tile/fieldstone juxtaposition in the Marosi House fireplace), the work does not carry the sophisticated ironies and the complex readings available in Moore and Venturi's very American designs. Rose's work is not very ordinary, not very erotic, not very political, and not very controversial, all of which are possibilities taught by Moore and Venturi. But through learning from Quebec vernacular, Peter Rose produces spirited architecture which has a friendly familiarity and a sense of belonging in the North.

—Larry Richards

ROSENBERG, Eugene.
British. Born in Topolčany, Czechoslovakia, 24 February 1907; emigrated to England, 1939; naturalized, 1947. Educated at primary and secondary schools in Nagy Tapolcsány, Hungary, 1912–18; secondary school in Topolčany, Czechoslovakia, 1918–20; State Industrial School for Building, Bratislava, Czechoslovakia, 1920–24; Technical University, Brno, Czechoslovakia, 1924–26; Technical University, Prague, 1926–28; Academy of Fine Arts School of Architecture, Prague, 1928, 1930–32, Dip.Arch. and Town Planning 1932; Atelier Le Corbusier,

Paris, 1929; awarded Royal Institute of British Architects Diploma, London, 1946. Served in the Home Guard, 1943–45. Married Penelope Dorothy Wilkinson in 1946. Assistant to Havlíček and Honzík, Prague, 1932–33, Jan Gillar, Prague, 1933–34, and Josef Stepánek, Prague, 1934; in private practice, Prague, 1934–38; worked in the Department of Civic Design, University of Liverpool, under William Holford, 1939–40; in internment camp in Australia, 1940–42; Assistant to Rodney Thomas, London, 1942–43, and to F. R. S. Yorke, *q.v.*, London, 1943–44; Partner, F. R. S. Yorke and Eugene Rosenberg, London, 1944; Partner, with Yorke and Cyril Mardall, *q.v.*, Yorke, Rosenberg and Mardall, London, 1944–75. Recipient: Council of Industrial Design Award, 1959; Civic Trust Award, 1961, 1964, 1965, 1966, 1967, 1969; Bronze Medal, Royal Institute of British Architects, 1961, 1966, 1967, 1972; *Financial Times* Award, 1966, 1969. Fellow, Royal Institute of British Architects, 1948. C.B.E. (Commander, Order of the British Empire), 1971. Address: 9 Chelwood House, Gloucester Square, London W2 2SY, England.

Works:

1929 Housing, Holešovice, Prague (project)
1931 Town plan for Trencin, Czechoslovakia (competition project; with J. Kucera)
     Airport, Ruzyne, Prague (competition project; with J. and K. Fiser, and J. Kincl)
1931/
33 Red Cross Tuberculosis and Maternity Clinics, Topolčany, Czechoslovakia
1932 Workers Faculty Building, Prague (project)
1933 Town plan for Mukačevo, U.S.S.R. (competition project)
1934/
35 Apartment block, Letrohradská, Prague 7
   Dr. Mokr House and Surgery, Topolčany, Czechoslovakia

1934/
36 Apartment block, u. Průhonu, Prague 8
2 apartment blocks, u. Elektrárny, Prague 7

1935/
37 Shops, offices and flats complex, Belkrediho Ul., Prague 7
Low-cost apartment block, Schnirchova ul., Prague 7

1936 "Humanita" Workers' Co-operative Housing, Prague (project)

1936/
38 Shopping arcades, offices and apartment blocks, Stepánská-Smečeky, Prague 2

1937 Grammar school, Topolčany, Czechoslovakia (project)
Grammar school, Bratislava, Czechoslovakia (project)
Primary school, Ludanice, Czechoslovakia (project)
Stores, Nitra, Czechoslovakia (project)
Stores, offices and flats complex, Prague 19 (project)

1938 Department store, offices and flats complex, Prague 2 (project)

With Yorke, Rosenberg and Mardall

1947 Luccombe House, Isle of Wight
Cowley Peachey Housing, Middlesex
Exhibition stands, Council of Industrial Design and Board of Trade, London

1948 Sigmund Pumps Factory, Gateshead, Durham
Fort Corbletts House conversion, Alderney, Channel Islands
Linden Doors Factory, Stowmarket, Suffolk (project)

1949 Temporary Outpatients Department, St. Thomas' Hospital, London
Shebbear College Boarding School alterations, Devon
Factories, Dagenham Docks, London (project)

1950 Barclay Secondary School, Stevenage, Hertfordshire

1951 John Lewis Department Store, Southsea, Hampshire (project)
Dr. Cole House, Londonderry, Northern Ireland (with Corr and McCormick)
Housing, King's Langley, Hertfordshire
Susan Lawrence Primary School, London
Elizabeth Lansbury Nursery School, London
Housing, Brynmawr, Brecknock, Wales
Hainault Forest Secondary School, Essex

1952 Sir William Nottidge School, Whitstable, Kent
Sish Lane Housing, Stevenage, Hertfordshire
College of Further Education, Merthyr Tydfil, Glamorgan, Wales

1953 Williams and Williams Exhibition Stand, *Building Trades Exhibition*, London
The Mill House conversion, Wootton, Oxfordshire
Warren Wood Secondeary School, Rochester, Kent
Upholland Grammar School, Wigan, Lancashire
West Park Secondary School, Leeds
Southlands Teachers' Training College Assembly Hall, Wimbledon, London
Sheerwater Primary School, Woking, Surrey
Causeway Green Primary School, Oldbury, Worcestershire
North Mimms Boy's and Infants' School, Hertfordshire

1954 Steddall's Warehouse alterations, London
Birchen Coppice Primary School, Kidderminster, Worcestershire
Queensmead Secondary School, Ruislip, Middlesex
London Transport Bus Garage and Depot, Loughton, Essex
Hammerson Group Offices, Great New Street, London (project)

1955 Tudor House Home for the Infirm, Grayshott, Hertfordshire (project)
Kerris Artists Studio conversion, Mousehole, Cornwall
Williams and Williams Offices, London (project)
Quarles Secondary Modern School, Romford, Essex
Master plan and stage I of the Leeds Polytechnic
Mark Hall Local Authority Housing, Harlow, Essex
Haileybury Boys Club, London
Bewdley Secondary School, Worcestershire
Kirkwall Place Housing, Bethnal Green, London
Kingswood School, Essex

1956 Boxgrove Housing prototypes
Wootton Rectory, Oxfordshire
Jack Straw's Lane House, Oxford
Tyrell and Green Store, Southampton
Dick Sheppard School, Tulse Hill, London
East Anglian Girls School, Bury St. Edmunds, Suffolk
Bradfield Secondary School, Yorkshire
Sigmund Pumps Factory extension, Gateshead, Durham (project)
North Mimms Boys' and Infants' School additions, Hertfordshire
College of Further Education extensions, Merthyr Tydfil, Glamorgan, Wales
Kingswood School extensions, Essex

1957 Southlands College Lecture Block and Dining Room extensions, Wimbledon, London
Temple Moor Grammar School, Leeds
Stanley Outwood Secondary School, Yorkshire
Jewish Theological College, Montagu Square, London

Eugene Rosenberg: St. Thomas' Hospital, London, 1975

Oak Park Secondary School, Havant, Hampshire

Philip Harben House, 115 Great George Street, London

Dawley Secondary School, Shropshire

Interbau Housing, Berlin (project; with Werner Düttmann)

Master plan for the Bromsgrove Education Centre, Worcestershire

Timberlog Secondary School, Basildon, Essex

St. Paul's Secondary School, Addlestone, Surrey

Gatwick Airport, stage I, Sussex

Sir William Nottidge School extensions, Whitstable, Kent

1958 Unilever House, Hamburg (competition project)

Wokingham Infants School, Berkshire (competition project)

Jewish Board of Guardians Offices, London

Finnish Seamen's Mission, London

Chaucer Secondary School, Sheffield

Carmel College extensions, Wallingford, Berkshire

Brixton Synagogue Hall remodelling, London

Leeds Polytechnic, stage II

Tyrell and Green Store extensions, Southampton

East Anglian Girls School alterations and additions, Bury St. Edmunds, Suffolk

1959 J. Spedan Lewis House, Longstock, Hampshire

Morsons Chemical Works, Enfield, Middlesex

Elephant and Castle Development, London (project)

World Health Organization Offices, Geneva (competition project)

Timber Development Association Office Furniture, London (competition project)

Formation Furniture prototypes, for Bath Cabinet Makers Ltd.

Roman Road Housing, Bethnal Green, London

High Park School, Stourbridge, Worcestershire

St. Paul's School Hall alterations, Chertsey, Surrey

Brays Grove Secondary School, Harlow, Essex

College of Further Education, Bromsgrove, Worcestershire

Tennant Brothers Exhibition Stand, *Club Trades Fair,* London

Churchill College, Cambridge (competition project)

Upholland Grammar School extensions, Wigan, Lancashire

East Anglian Girls School alterations and additions, stage II, Bury St. Edmunds, Suffolk

1960 Watford Shopping Centre, Hertfordshire (project)

Rothwell Secondary School, stage II, Yorkshire

Warslow School, Staffordshire

United States Embassy, Grosvenor Square, London (with Eero Saarinen Associates)

Supasave Store, Southend, Essex

Staincliffe Hospital Geriatric Unit, Leeds

Altnagelvin Hospital, Londonderry, Northern Ireland

Passmores Comprehensive School, Harlow, Essex

D. Allford House, Persham, Surrey (project)

Brierly Hill Secondary School, Staffordshire

Rolls Royce Offices, Derby (project)

Telecommunications Engineering Building, Gatwick Airport, Sussex

Leeds Polytechnic, stage III

1961 N. J. Payne House, Shamley Green, Norfolk

Royal Masonic School, Ascot, Berkshire (project)

Bromsgrove High School, Worcestershire

Hob Green Primary School, Worcestershire

YRM and Norwich Union Insurance Societies Offices, Greystoke Place, London

Maternity and Outpatients Departments, Crawley Hospital, Sussex

Kew Bridge Development for British Rail, London (project)

Report on Creekside Refuse Disposal Depot, Deptford, London

Timber Development Association Wooden Furniture, London (competition project)

Kingswood School extensions, stage II, Essex

1962 Master plan for Kuwait Airport (with Sir Frederick Snow and Partners)

Elliott Brothers Welfare Building, Rochester, Kent (project)

Rotameter Factory, Croydon, Surrey (project)

Library, Cambridge University (project)

Southlands College: Queensmere Hostels, Lecture Block and Gymnasium, Wimbledon, London

Ark House, Rochford, Essex

Staff Residence, Crawley Hospital, Sussex

Barstable Comprehensive School, Basildon, Essex

College of Further Education extensions, stage II, Merthyr Tydfil, Glamorgan, Wales

North Mimms Boys' and Infants' School additions, stage II, Hertfordshire

Haileybury Boys Club, stage II, London

Oak Park Secondary School extensions, Havant, Hampshire

Timberlog Secondary School extensions, Basildon, Essex

1963 Stamford House Swimming Pool, London

Rolleston Secondary School, Staffordshire

Rochdale College, Lancashire

Redevelopment scheme for the Dawley schools, Shropshire

John Lewis Warehouse, Stevenage, Hertfordshire (with Felix Candela)

Brewery redevelopment, Luton, Bedfordshire (project)

T. R. Evans House, Lacey Green, Buckinghamshire

A. Johnson and Company Factory and Offices, Wokingham, Berkshire

Harlow Training Centre, Essex

Cole Brothers Store, Sheffield

Shebbear College additions, Devon

East Anglian Girls School additions and alterations, stage III, Bury St. Edmunds, Suffolk

Bradford Secondary School extensions, Yorkshire

1964 Southlands College Staff Accommodation, Wimbledon, London

Development plan for the central area of Blackpool

Staff Residences, Altnagelvin Hospital, Londonderry, Northern Ireland

Kidd's Store, Leeds

Keddies Store, Southend, Essex

Temporary buildings for Crawley Hospital, Sussex

Development report on Luton Airport, Bedfordshire

Clements Store, Watford, Hertfordshire

Blythe Bridge Secondary School, Staffordshire

Belfast Synagogue

Mildmay Secondary School, Aveley, Essex

Adler Street Unit Workshops, London

Taylorian Institute Modern Languages Faculty, Oxford (project)

Dawley Secondary School extensions, Shropshire

Chaucer Secondary School extensions, Sheffield

College of Further Education extensions, Bromsgrove, Worcestershire

1965 Bakewell Secondary School, Derbyshire (project)

Gatwick Airport, stage II, Sussex

Simestow Comprehensive School, Tittenhall, Staffordshire

Romford Technical College, Essex

Chalvedon Comprehensive School, Basildon, Essex

Department of Electrical Engineering and Electronics, University of Liverpool

German Sailors' Home, London

Nurses Home and School, Crawley Hospital, Sussex

Gibbons Road Secondary School, West Willesden, London (project)

Control Building, Kuwait Airport

Rochdale College extensions, Lancashire

John Lewis Warehouse extensions, Stevenage, Hertfordshire

1966 Residential Buildings, Hamble College of Air Training, Hampshire (project)

Ada Street Unit Workshops, London

Local authority housing, Cadell Street, Tower Hamlets, London

Elliott Brothers Factory extensions, Borehamwood, Hertfordshire

Westwood Hall and St. Edward's School, Leek, Staffordshire

Intermediate Terminal, Luton Airport, Bedfordshire

St. Thomas' Hospital, stage I, London (with W. Fowler Howitt)

Revision of the development plan, Library, Molecular and Engineering Sciences Building, stage I, and First Hall of Residence and Boilerhouse, University of Warwick

B. Henderson Guest Pavilion, Great Bedwin, Wiltshire

Elliott Brothers Factory, Rochester, Kent

College of Further Education extensions, stage III, Merthyr Tydfil, Glamorgan, Wales

Leeds Polytechnic, stage IV

St. Paul's Secondary School extensions, Addlestone, Surrey

Clements Store extensions, Watford, Hertfordshire

1967 Milkhouse Water House, Pewsey, Wiltshire

Operating theatres, Lambeth Hospital, London

Ancillary buildings, Redhill Hospital, Surrey

Avalon Furniture Offices and Showrooms, Yatton, Somerset

Bacton Street Housing, Tower Hamlets, London

Bath Cabinet Makers Furniture Factory

Royal Infirmary and Ancillary Buildings, Hull, Yorkshire

Ilford Training Centre, Essex

Sceptre Road Housing, Tower Hamlets, London

Stamford House Remand Home, Hammersmith, London

Terminal, Newcastle Airport

First Hall of Residence, stage II, University of Warwick

General Aviation Terminal, Gatwick Airport, Sussex

Queensmead Secondary School extensions, Ruislip, Middlesex

Leeds Polytechnic, stage V

Brays Grove Secondary School extensions, Harlow, Essex

1968 Boots Pure Drug Company Head Office, Nottingham (with Skidmore, Owings and Merrill)

Cottam Power Station, Nottinghamshire

Office Block, Gatwick Airport, Sussex

Cargo Area Canteen, Heathrow Airport, London

Cargo Area Airside Operations Building, Heathrow Airport, London

Second Hall of Residence, stage I, Physics Building, stage I, and Sports Pavilion and Playing Fields, University of Warwick
Fire Station, Luton Airport, Bedfordshire
Uxbridge Technical College, London
Willesden Secondary School, London
B. Henderson House conversion, Regent's Park, London
Old Street Concourse, London
Development plan for the University of Zambia, Lusaka
Timberlog Secondary School extensions, stage II, Basildon, Essex
St. Paul's Secondary School extensions, stage II, Addlestone, Surrey
Chaucer Secondary School extensions, stage II, Sheffield
John Lewis Warehouse extensions, stage II, Stevenage, Hertfordshire

1969 Computer Laboratory, University of Liverpool
Ealing Children's Home, London
Cargo Agents' Building, Heathrow Airport, London
Willis-Faber-Dumas Ltd. Computer Office interiors, Southend, Essex
Terminal, Stansted Airport, Essex
Kingshold Estate, King Edward's Road, Hackney, London
Second Hall of Residence, stage II, University of Warwick
Arts Centre and Chapel, University of Warwick (project)
Osprey Estate Housing, Bermondsey, London
Nash House Club Rooms interiors, The Mall, London
Associated Portland Cement Manufacturers Offices, Northfleet, Kent
Leeds Polytechnic, stage VI
Chalvedon Comprehensive School extensions, Basildon, Essex

1970 Crawley Hospital, stage II, Sussex
Furness Withy and Company Apartment interior conversions, London
Sir William Gathwaite House interiors, London
Herman Miller Furniture Factory and Showrooms, Bath
Hangar, Luton Airport, Bedfordshire
Renal Dialysis Unit, St. Thomas's Hospital, London
Computer Centre, Lambeth Hospital, London
College of Further Education extensions, stage II, Bromsgrove, Worcestershire
Rochdale College extensions, stage II, Lancashire
Sceptre Road Housing extensions, Tower Hamlets, London

1970/
72 Royal Infirmary and Ancillary Building extensions, Leeds

1971 Armstrong Cork Company Office interiors, Uxbridge, Middlesex
Magistrates Court, Manchester
Keddies Store extensions, stage II, Southend, Essex
Arts Building, Computer Centre and Sports Centre, University of Warwick
Parsons Brown Office Building, Amoco Jetty, Milford Haven, Wales (project)
BEA (British European Airways) Office Building, Ruislip, Middlesex
BEA (British European Airways) Operational Offices, Heathrow Airport, London (project)
Chemistry Building, University of Zambia, Lusaka
Sizewell "B" Power Station, Suffolk (project)
Bromsgrove High School extensions, Worcestershire
Keddies Store extensions, Southend, Essex

1972 Tomo Estates Factory, Cowley Peachey, Middlesex
Furness House Office interiors, London
C and A Modes Computer Suite interiors, London
Battle Hospital, Reading, Berkshire
John Radcliffe Hospital, stage I, Oxford
Fieldhead Hospital, Wakefield, Yorkshire
Alcan Aluminium Smelter and Power Station, Lynemouth
Staff Residences, Churchill Hospital, Oxford
Schools of Education and Engineering, University of Zambia, Lusaka
South Western Hospital Departments, Lambeth, London
St. Thomas' Hospital Offices, Leadenhall Street, London
Keddie Commercial Centre, Southend, Essex (project)
Two Tree Island Marina, Essex (project; with Cedric Price)
New Arts Building, University of Liverpool
Feasibility study: Theodore Herzl Memorial Hospital, Israel
Northern Extension Terminal Building, Gatwick Airport, Sussex
Hindrey Place Housing, Hackney, London
John Radcliffe Hospital, stage II, Oxford
St. Thomas' Hospital, phase II, London
Wellington Hospital, St. John's Wood, London
W. D. and H. O. Wills Head and Western Division Offices and Factory, Bristol (with Skidmore, Owings and Merrill)
Central Electricity Generating Board Divisional Offices, Gloucester
Dashwood House Offices, Old Broad Street, London
St. Thomas' Hospital Office Development, Lambeth, London
Birchen Coppice Primary School extensions, Kidderminster, Worcestershire
High Park School extensions, Stourbridge, Worcestershire
Fire Station extensions, Luton Airport, Bedfordshire

1973/
75 Amersham General Hospital, Buckinghamshire
C and A Head Offices remodelling, London
Offices, Eastcheap, London
Camden Health Centre, London
Development plan for Churchill/Warneford Hospitals, Oxford
Southern Extension and East Land Development, Gatwick Airport, Sussex
Slade Industrial Site, Oxford
National Westminster Bank Office Building, Southend, Essex
New Terminal, Luton Airport, Bedfordshire
John Radcliffe Hospital, stage III, Oxford
Feasibility study: Bio-Medical Centre, Lambeth, London (with Cusdin, Burden and Howitt)
Renslade Investments Ltd. Offices, The Hague, Netherlands
St. Thomas' Hospital, phase B, London
Guardian Properties Offices, The Hague
Ashmolean Art Gallery, Oxford
Organizational and building evaluation study: Commonwealth Development Finance Corporation Offices, London
Los Llanos Recreational Centre, Costa del Sol, Spain (project)
Library and Community Building, Albion Street, Southwark, London
Brixton Road Development, London
Territorial Army Centre, Camden, London
Tomo Estates Offices, Cowley Peachey, Middlesex
Royal Infirmary additions, Hull, Yorkshire
Keddies Store and Offices, stage III, Southend, Essex (project)

Psychiatric Day Unit, Battle Hospital, Reading, Berkshire
Crawley Hospital, stage IIa, Sussex
Yorke, Rosenberg, Mardall Offices, Turnmill Street, London

Publications:

By ROSENBERG: article—"Rebuilding and the Human Environment" in *Nove Ceskoslovensko* (London), November 1943.

On ROSENBERG: books—*The Modern Flat* by F. R. S. Yorke and Frederick Gibberd, London 1948; *The Architecture of Yorke Rosenberg Mardall,* introduction by Reyner Banham, London and New York 1972; articles—"Projekt zu einem Wohnblock in Holešovice" in *Stein Holz Eisen* (Stuttgart), no. 13, 1931; "Town Planning Competition: Horní-Sihot, Trencin" in *Stavitel* (Prague), no. 1, 1932; "Competition: Airport Prague-Ruzyne" in *Stavitel* (Prague), no. 4/5, 1932; "Workers Faculty" in *Stavitel* (Prague), no. 13, 1932; "Zwei Neuzeitliche Wohnbauten" by R. Hoffman in *Prager Tagblatt* (Prague), 28 January 1937; "Arcades in Stepánská, Prague" by Frantisek Zelenka in *Lidove Noviny* (Prague), 25 November 1938; "Immeubles de Rapport à Prague" in *L'Architecture d'Aujourd'hui* (Paris), October 1938; "Block of Flats, Prague" in *The Architects' Journal* (London), 18 April 1940; "Arcades, Offices and Flats, Prague" in *The Architects' Journal* (London), 11 July 1940; "Modern Architecture in Czechoslovakia" by F. R. S. Yorke in *Review* (London), no. 3, 1943; "The English Approach" by Hugh Casson in *Kvart* (Prague), no. 5, 1946; "Conversations with an Overseas Architect" by M. Kadlečíková in *Domov* (Prague), no. 3, 1964; "YRM's Shining Pot" in *The Architects' Journal* (London), 8 May 1974; "Trouble at Two Tree Island" in *Building. Design* (London), 19 July 1974; "Sickness and Wealth" in *Design* (London), September 1974; "Alcan Smelting Works in Lynemouth, Great Britain" in *Deutsche Bauzeitschrift* (Gutersloh), October 1974; "Wills Factory and Headquarters, Hartcliff, Bristol" in *The Architects' Journal* (London), 24 September 1975; "A Healthy New Building" by Vincent Smith in *Architecture Australia* (Melbourne), August/September 1976; "British Art Gallery" in *L'Architecture d'Aujourd'hui* (Paris), January/February 1977; "New Offices for Yorke Rosenberg Mardall in Britton Street" by Stevan Brown in *RIBA Journal* (London), March 1978; "A Place for Art" by Annette LeCuyer in *Building Design* (London), 1 December 1978; "Taking Off at Gatwick" by Jack Christopher in *Building Design* (London), 2 March 1979.

Eugene Rosenberg was born in Slovakia and graduated in 1932 from the Academy of Fine Arts in Prague. Before qualifying he had spent a year working intermittently in Paris for Le Corbusier, and when he left the Academy he worked for Havlíček and Honzík on the famous Pensions Institute in Prague, perhaps one of the first great monoliths in reinforced concrete and finished in white tiles. In 1939, two days before Hitler marched into Prague, Rosenberg arrived in London never to return permanently to Czechoslovakia. His reputation then rested on a series of modern buildings he had designed in Prague and elsewhere and his future upon an acquaintance in England with F. R. S. Yorke, Max Fry and Frederick Gibberd.

To understand and appreciate Rosenberg's work and its origins, one should keep in mind this background, as by 1934, when he was practising on his own account, Prague and Brno had become two acknowledged centres of the "international" modern movement and stood perhaps in the same relation to East Europe as Rotterdam to the West. The international movement—already being suppressed in Germany by Hitler—flourished in Prague and in Brno where Mies van der Rohe had built his celebrated Tudendhat House and where Bohuslav Fuchs also worked. It was a mainstream movement there, uncompromising and committed, with a strict geometrical discipline and much influenced by Le Corbusier and with close links with the Bauhaus. This was the architectural environment in which Rosenberg was brought up and in which he emerged to practice. His early work already outlined the course his architecture was to take in his maturity in England.

Most of these early buildings in Prague were blocks of flats and offices, and they already display a mastery of plan and section which was later to distinguish the work of the partnership Yorke, Rosenberg and Mardall, founded in London in 1944, with which Rosenberg was to spend most of his working life. These early buildings—offices and flats in the Stepánská-Smeceky and the Schnirchova ul.—also exhibit another characteristic, a clearly-stated structural geometry with a very sophisticated feeling for the plasticity of concrete. Rosenberg began his education as an engineer and subsequently switched to architecture, and throughout his career his planning has always related to a logical and consistent sense of structure.

The immediate impact of Rosenberg's work is one of ruthless logic, succeeded by a realization of the beauty that emerges from an intellectual discipline clearly expressed in the built form. It is Cartesian. It emerges in Prague and reaches through to the work in London years later. The major works of the partnership are, in the highest sense of the word, professional. There is nothing adventitious or casual but a classical, even Roman, simplicity of mass, a rigorous elimination of the irrelevant. Their buildings always make a clear, and often a grand, statement of intention and structure in the idiom of the international movement and demonstrate its increasing range and versatility—just as did Rosenberg's individual work in Prague.

In the early works, too, there is an elegance of detail, originating from simple elements. The structural discipline is echoed in the details such as shop fronts, balustrades and railings formed from standard sections. Indeed, there seems to be a coherence in design, in structure, and in the use of materials between these buildings in Prague and some of those being built in England during the period—like Highpoint I. It was indeed an international movement, and Rosenberg has played no small part in it.

—Richard Sheppard

ROSSI, Aldo.

Italian. Born in Milan, 3 May 1931. Educated at the Polytechnic, Milan, under Ernesto N. Rogers and Giuseppe Salmona, Dip.Arch. 1959. In private practice, Milan. Editor, *Casabella,* Milan. Professor of Architectural Composition, Polytechnic, Milan, 1970–71. Director, International Seminar of Architecture, Santiago de Compostela, Spain, 1976. Exhibitions: *Triennale,* Milan, 1960; Centro Arte Viva, Trieste, 1967 (one-man show); *Aldo Rossi: Bauten, Projekte,* Eidgenössische Technische Hochschule, Zurich, 1973; *Aldo Rossi/Louis Kahn/John Hejduk,* University of Stuttgart, 1974; *Aldo Rossi: Architektur des Rationalismus,* IDZ, Berlin, 1974; *Aldo Rossi + 21 Arquitectos Espanoles,* Palau de la Virrenia, Barcelona, 1975, toured Spain; *Aldo Rossi,* Institute for Architecture and Urban Studies, New York, 1976; *Aldo Rossi, Architetto,* Galleria Solferino, Milan, 1976. Recipient: First Prize, with G. Braghieri, Municipal Cemetery Competition, Modena, 1971. Address (office): Via Rugabella 8, 20122 Milan, Italy.

Works:

1960 Redevelopment plan for the Via Farina, Milan (project; with G. U. Polesello and F. Tentori)

Ronchini Villa, Versilia, Italy (with L. Ferrari)

1961 Peugeot Building, Buenos Aires (competition project; with V. Magistretti and G. U. Polesello)

1962 Monument to the Resistance, Cuneo, Italy (competition project; with Luca Meda and G. U. Polesello)

Monumental Fountain, City Hall, Milan (competition project; with Luca Meda)

Country Club Building, Fagagna, Italy (project; with G. U. Polesello)

School, Villa Reale Park, Monza, Italy (competition project; with V. Gavazzeni and G. Grassi)

Museum of Contemporary History interiors, Milan (with M. Baffa, Luca Meda, and U. Rivolta)

City Hall, Turin (competition project; with G. U. Polesello and Luca Meda)

1964 General plan and Steel Bridge, for the *Triennale,* Milan (with Luca Meda)

Abbiategrasso Sports and Leisure Facilities, Ticino, Italy (project)

Paganini Theatre and Piazza della Pilotta, Parma, Italy (competition project)

1965 Residential redevelopment, Naples (competition project; with G. Grassi)

Town Hall Square and Monumental Fountain, Segrate, Milan (partially realized)

General building code and plan for Broni, Italy (project)

1966 Regional plan for Veneto, Italy (project; with G. Salmona)

Building code and plan for Certosa di Pavia, Italy (project)

San Rocco Residential Complex, Monza, Italy (competition project; with G. Grassi)

1967 Building code and plan for the town centre of Sannazzaro de' Burgondi, Italy (competition project)

1968 City Hall, Scandicci, Italy (competition project; with M. Fortis and M. Scolari)

1969 School, Trieste (project; with R. Agosto, G. Grassi, and F. Tentori)

1970 Gallaratese 2 Apartment Complex, Milan

De Amicis School restoration and additions, Broni, Italy

1971 General building code and plan for Abbiategrasso, Italy (project; with A. Balzani)

Municipal Cemetery, Modena, Italy (competition project; with G. Braghieri)

1972 Town Hall, Muggio, Italy (competition project; with G. Braghieri)

1973 Municipal Cemetery, Modena, Italy (2nd competition project; with G. Braghieri)

Single-family housing, Borni, Italy (with G. Braghieri)

Layout of the International Architecture Section, *Triennale,* Milan

Villa, Borgo Ticino, Italy (project; with G. Braghieri)

General building code and plan for Fagnano Olona, Italy (project)

1974 Castle restoration and Bridge, Bellinzona, Italy (with G. Braghieri, B. Reichlin, and F. Reinhart)

Single-family housing, Robbiate, Italy (with G. Braghieri)

Local Government Office Building, Trieste (competition project; with G. Braghieri and M. Bosshard)

Student Building, University of Trieste (competition project; with G. Braghieri, M. Bosshard, and A. Cantafora)

1976 Student Building, University of Chieti, Italy (competition project; with G. Braghieri and A. Cantafora)

Municipal Cemetery, Modena, Italy (3rd project; with G. Braghieri)

1978 Plan for the city center of Florence (competition project; with Carlo Aymonino and others)

Elementary school, Fagnano Olona, Italy

Publications:

By ROSSI: books—*Concorso per la Ricostruzione del Teatro Paganini di Parma,* with Carlo Aymonino, Venice 1966; *L'Architettura della Città,* Padua 1966; *Scritti scelti sull'architettura e la città,* edited by Rosaldo Bonicalzi, Milan 1975; articles—"Un Monumento ai Partigiani" in *Casabella* (Milan), no. 208, 1955; "L'Architetto e l'Urbanistica" in *L'Urbanisme au Service de l'Homme,* edited by A. Gutton, Paris 1962; "Conversacion con Aldo Rossi" in *Construccion del la Ciudad 2C* (Barcelona), 1972; "L'Habitation et la Ville" in *L'Architecture d'Aujourd'hui* (Paris), no. 174, 1974; "Architecture and Rationalism" in *Construccion de la Ciudad 2C* (Barcelona), March 1977; "H. Schmidt and the Problem of Monotony" in *Werk/Archithese* (Niedertaufen, Switzerland), May/June 1978.

On ROSSI: books—*Aldo Rossi: Bauten, Projekte,* exhibition catalogue, Zurich 1973; *Aldo Rossi: Architektur des Rationalismus,* exhibition catalogue, Berlin 1974; *Aldo Rossi,* exhibition catalogue, New York 1976; *Aldo Rossi, Architetto,* exhibition catalogue, Milan 1976; *L'Architettura di Aldo Rossi* by Vittorio Savi, Milan 1977; articles—"Elementi e Costruzione: Note sull'Architettura di Aldo Rossi" by E. Bonfanti in *Controspazio* (Bari, Italy), no. 10, 1970; "Zu einer Ausstellung der Projekte von Aldo Rossi an der ETH—Zurich" by B. Reichlin in *Werk* (Zurich), no. 4, 1972; "La Idea de Arquitectura en Rossi y el Cementiero de Modena" by Jose Rafael Moneo in *Elementi di Composizione,* Barcelona 1973; "Aldo Rossi," special issue of *Construccion de la Ciudad 2C* (Barcelona), no. 2, 1975; "Rational Architecture" by Alan Colquhoun in *Architectural Design* (London), no. 6, 1975; "Aldo Rossi," special issue of *Architecture + Urbanism* (Tokyo), no. 65, 1976; "Aldo Rossi," special issue of *Construccion de la Ciudad 2C* (Barcelona), no. 5, 1976; "Aldo Rossi: Una Alternativa Progresista para la Arquitectura" by S. Frago and Malo de Molina in *Triunfo* (Madrid), no. 719, 1976; "Aldo Rossi: The Idea of Architecture" by José Rafael Moneo in *Oppositions* (New York), no. 5, 1978; "The Architecture of Dissent: Aldo Rossi and Ettore Sottsass" by Pier Carlo Santini in *Ottagono* (Milan), June 1978; "Elementary School at Fagnano Olona" in *Architecture + Urbanism* (Tokyo), June 1978.

The work and theory of Aldo Rossi together make up one of the most important statements in international contemporary architecture. Building practice needs reflection, theory needs practical experience, and Rossi's work benefits from his complex activities as teacher, editor of the magazine *Casabella,* and architectural historian. His studies in the typology and morphology of cities resulted in the book *L'Architettura della Città,* a fundamental text in contemporary urbanism.

Building and the city are united in Rossi's work, and he deals with the urban fabric as an architect, not as a planner or designer. According to Rossi, the city is an agglomeration of objects of meaning and identity ("urban facts") relevant to the specific life of people in time and place. Cities are built over a long period of time; they include history; they are manifestations of political and social ideologies that shape the urban form. For Rossi the architect, history is not so much a sequence of events in time as objects recalled by memory and used as elements in the design process. The "urban fact" emerges from this process, the form that for Rossi is the basis of the architect's work, that which reveals the identity of each given place. A strong emphasis on regional and local aspects of building and cities is also necessarily part of his work.

Rossi refers to his working method as "rational", but he means more than a logical deduction from abstract facts. He means analogical thought—more

complex than logical considerations. Rationalism deals with environment and people, meaning and history. In Rossi's own words: "the reducible specificity of architecture . . . resides in the capacity to produce typical forms, which requires a particular knowledge of the past." Design thus becomes a process of selecting the appropriate type of "plan" in a given context rather than a subjective statement.

Rationalism in architecture in Rossi's sense is a continuation of the thinking patterns of the Enlightenment of the 18th century, as manifested in Boullée and Ledoux, and their transformation into contemporary reality. Rossi's goal is the reconstitution of the architectural profession by these criteria, the creation of an autonomous architecture.

—Udo Kultermann

ROTH, Alfred.

Swiss. Born in Wangen, near Berne, 21 May 1903. Educated at primary and secondary schools in Wangen; Intermediate School, Solothurn, baccalaureate 1922; Federal Institute of Technology, Zurich, 1922–26. Worked with Le Corbusier and Pierre Jeanneret in Paris, 1927–28; in private practice, Göteborg, Sweden, Sweden, 1928–30. In private practice, Zurich, since 1931. Design Critic, Washington University, St. Louis, Missouri, 1949–52, and Harvard University, Cambridge, Massachusetts, 1953; Professor of Architecture, Federal Institute of Technology, Zurich, 1957–71. Editor, *Werk*, Winterthur, Switzerland, 1943–56. Exhibitions: *Switzerland Planning and Building Exhibition*, Royal Institute of British Architects, London, 1946; *Triennale*, Milan, 1957; *National Exhibition of Switzerland*, Lausanne, 1964. Honorary doctorate: Technical University, Munich, 1977. Honorary Member: Royal Institute of British Architects, 1948; Royal Flemish Academy of Arts, Letters and Sciences, Brussels, 1948; Union of Modern Artists, Paris, 1949; Austrian Federation of Architects, 1955; Swedish Association of Arts and Crafts, 1956; Honorary Fellow, American Institute of Architects, 1966. Address: Bergstrasse 71, 8032 Zurich, Switzerland.

Works:

1928/
65 Industrial buildings in Wangen, Switzerland
1929/
30 200 low-cost apartments, Göteborg, Sweden
1930 Private house, near Göteborg, Sweden
1935/
36 Doldertal Apartment Blocks, Zurich (with Emil Roth and Marcel Breuer)
1936/
61 Houses in Zurich and Wangen, Switzerland
1937 Weekend House, Mammern, Lake Constance, Switzerland
1938/
46 Military buildings, Wangen, Switzerland
1939 Pavilion of Commerce, *National Exhibition of Switzerland,* Zurich (with Emil Roth)
1948 Kindergarten, Wangen, Switzerland
Mechanical Laboratory extension, Federal Institute of Technology, Zurich
1948/
49 Swiss Tourist Office, Trafalgar Square, London
1950/
52 Primary school, Berkeley (St. Louis), Missouri

Alfred Roth: Commercial Centre Sabbaz, Beirut, Lebanon, 1970

1953/
55 *Contemporary Swiss Architecture* exhibition layouts, United States and Canada
1956 Secondary school, Wangen, Switzerland
1957 Swiss Pavilion, *Triennale,* Milan
1960 Roth House, Zurich
1961/
63 Primary school, Zurich
1962 Metal factory, Oerlikon/Zurich
1962/
72 Main Building and Natural Science Institute extensions, Federal Institute of Technology, Zurich
1965/
66 Shopping centre, Lucerne
1965/
69 Secondary school, Skopje, Yugoslavia
1966/
69 Schools, Kuwait, Persian Gulf
1968/
70 Commercial Centre Sabbaz, Beirut, Lebanon
1972 Commercial building, Zurich
1977 Urban housing with shops and offices, Ajman, Persian Gulf (project)
Bahrain National Oil Co., Bahrain, Persian Gulf (project)
1978/
79 Prefabricated schools, Kuwait, Persian Gulf
1978/
80 Abu Nuseir New Town, near Amman, Jordan (with Schindler and Schindler, Zurich, and Al Muhandis-Al Arabi, Amman)

Publications:

By ROTH: books—*Zwei Wohnhäuser von Le Corbusier und Pierre Jeanneret,* Stuttgart 1927; *The New Architecture,* Zurich 1939, 6th edition 1976; *The New Schoolhouse,* Zurich 1950; *Begegnung mit Pionieren,* Zurich and Basle 1973, Tokyo 1975; articles—in *Werk* (Winterthur), 1943–56.

On ROTH: books—*Gli Elementi dell'Architettura Funzionale* by Alberto Sartoris, Milan 1931; *The Modern House* by F. R. S. Yorke, London 1934; *Switzerland Builds* by G. E. Kidder Smith, New York and Stockholm 1950; *A Decade of New Architecture* by Sigfried Giedion, Zurich 1951; *Contemporary Architecture: Switzerland* by Yuichi Ino, Tokyo 1953; *Geschichte Meines Lebens* by Henry van de Velde, Munich 1962; *Nationalisme et Internationalisme dans l'Architecture de la Suisse* by Jacques Gubler, Lausanne 1975.

All my architectural endeavours and all my thinking are firmly based on the principles of the so-called functional architecture. But, for me, the complexity of the manifold functions does not permit me to reduce them to purely practical, technical and economic ones—as is unfortunately true for the majority of present-day designs and buildings. The most important functions originate in man's psychological and human behavior and in the demand for beauty, harmony, nobility and inventiveness in general. This has been true for the architecture of all great historic periods. The differences between the essence and form of their art of building and ours can be found in the very different nature and multitude of functions to be considered today and in our very different creative possibilities to express them technically and artistically.

—Alfred Roth

The architectural ideas and creations of Alfred Roth are a logical continuation of the work of the pioneers of New Building in an honestly objective and constructive form of architecture. Roth believes in the undiminished validity of an architecture that answers its purpose. Functional appropriateness is a prime requirement of the user of this architecture and must be satisfied. From a conviction that our modern age is, at heart, creative and not imitative, as was the 19th century for example, Roth subordi-

nates all conceivable questions of form to practical exigencies and holds the view that in this manner the psychological, spiritual and aesthetic requirements in a building can be satisfied.

In particular Alfred Roth has projected and built schools both at home and abroad which are a portrait of the logical consequence of an architectural creativity which finds its overwhelming expression in urbanistic, climatic and logical functionality. Roth sees his works as timeless and resistant to the constant changes in architectural notions and views. He says: "Unfortunately today we see a progressive degeneration in established functional creative form. The most obvious causes are a spreading commercialization of architectural works and a frenzied striving for permanent novelty, chiefly for new forms which have no inner reason."

It is an interesting opinion of Roth's that a serious scientific criticism of architecture is lacking and that the extremely large range of possibilities in architectural form, broadcast through excessive commercial publication in architectural journals, has had a bad influence on the work of architects who, uncritically, pick up impulses from all sides and incorporate them in their own work without adequate reflection. In this respect one has to support him. It really is incomprehensible that we do not have an adequate critical examination of the suitability of today's architecture to its time, of an architecture which is in fact a portrait of a disunited, spiritually and ethically divided pluralistic society. I fully support Roth's view that we must prevent the architecture that shapes the face of our cities from becoming a plaything used for fashionable trends and cheap effects which nevertheless sell very well. We need a new draught of architectural ideas, feelings and treatment, a revaluation of the ethical principles of our profession which, even if not scientific, must nevertheless be an honestly based expression of creative work. How compatible the striving of Alfred Roth for a timelessness in architecture would be is another question. Architecture is always the portrait of a society and thus the expression of its culture. Even a society cannot escape its own shadow. Creative developments in the last decades have been particularly short winded and short lived. We see the frenzy of a modern age which less and less reflects upon itself in all spheres of life and must consequently stand the test of history.

—Justus Dahinden

ROUX-SPITZ, Michel.

French. Born in Lyons, France, 13 June 1888. Educated at the Lycée Ampere, Lyons, 1904–07; Ecole des Beaux-Arts, Lyons, under Tony Garnier, 1908–12; student/apprentice, studio of Redon, Paris, 1912–13, 1919–20, and studio of Duquesne Recoura, Paris, 1913–14; Prix de Rome Scholar, 1920–23. Served in the French Army during World War I. Married Suzanne Marcel in 1923; children: Jean and Francine. In private practice, Paris, 1924 until his death, 1957. Professor of Architectural Theory, Ecole des Beaux-Arts, Paris, 1943–44. Editor, *L'Architecture,* Paris, 1925–32; Contributing Editor, *Architecture Francaise,* Paris, 1943–50. *Died* (in Dinard, France) *15 July 1957.*

Works:

1924/
29 Dental School and Dispensary, Lyons
Municipal Hall, La Croix Rousse, Lyons
1925 Monument to the Heroes of Dixmunde, Pierrefeu, France
Apartment building, Rue Guynemer, Paris

Publications:

By ROUX-SPITZ: book—*Bâtiments et Jardins à l'Exposition des Arts Décoratifs,* Paris 1925.

Michel Roux-Spitz: Apartment building, rue Guynemer, Paris, 1925

On ROUX-SPITZ: books—*Michel Roux-Spitz: Réalisations,* 3 volumes, *1924–1932,* Paris 1936, *1932–1932,* Paris 1950, and *1943–1957,* Paris 1959; articles—"Tendencies of the School of Modern French Architecture" in *Architectural Record* (New York), April 1929; "New Post Office, Lyons" in *The Architect and Building News* (London), 12 May 1939; "Cité des Hauts-Paves à Nantes" and "Quartier du Grand-Clos à Nantes" in *Architecture Francaise* (Paris), vol. 8, no. 73/74, 1947; "Le Centre Technique Forestier Tropical à Nogent-sur-Marne" in *Construction Moderne* (Paris), June 1954; "Postes et Telecommunications" in *Architecture Francaise* (Paris), November/December 1966; "Michel Roux-Spitz" by M. Raymond, P. Saddy and P. Celeste in *Architecture Mouvement Continuité* (Paris), no. 39, 1976.

*   *   *

Born in Lyons in 1888, Michel Roux-Spitz was a member of the generation that turned towards new underlying principles for architecture. He sought primarily the beauty of forms—and their logic, the kind of logic that Auguste Perret asserted in the economic, aesthetic and rational use of concrete.

Roux-Spitz reacted against the solemn mediocrities and rejected the decorative pastries that litter our towns. He drew up simple, logical and unadorned architectural plans that achieve the quality of expression appropriate to pure forms and appropri-

ate, too, to the laws of architecture and construction. As well, he sought new solutions that would yet allow the user to "adapt;" at the same time he looked for new methods of building. He used techniques that allowed him to advance towards tomorrow's architecture.

In 1925 Roux-Spitz achieved a simple and significant kind of building. He erected in Paris, opposite the Luxembourg Gardens, a rental building of a hitherto unknown purity. He built in concrete clad with polished stones. The windows were treated in horizontal bands, one of the series being brought forward to break the monotony of the facade. This kind of housing provided agreeable and practical arrangements for the occupiers. Roux-Spitz conceived a number of this kind of building, always of impeccable quality, for he knew how to combine convenience with elegance.

Rouz-Spitz was aware of all the currents in international architecture and with progress in technology, but his knowledge and his much-envied organizational methods were always at the service of a sure sense of taste. He had a certain liking for pomp as well as for order, which reveals itself in his sumptuous villa in Dinard where stylish furniture seems to be at one with the architecture and where the garden is a succession of constructive elements. He believed in the permanence of certain laws of harmony.

When he was entrusted with the redevelopment

and renovation of the National Library, he had to face very complicated, important and delicate problems. He solved them with a kind of lucid authority. On the one hand, he treated the Mansart gallery masterpiece and neighboring rooms with sober refinement. On the other hand, he dealt very surely with the depository at Versailles, giving it an aspect of totally serviceable functional modernism.

—Bernard Champigneulle

RUDOLPH, Paul (Marvin).

American. Born in Elkton, Kentucky, 28 October 1918. Educated at the Alabama Polytechnic Institute, Auburn, 1935–40, B.Arch. 1940; Harvard Graduate School of Design, Cambridge, Massachusetts, under Walter Gropius, 1940–43, 1946–47, M.Arch. 1947; Wheelwright Scholar, in Europe, 1948. Served as a Lieutenant in the United States Navy, 1943–46. In partnership with Ralph Twitchell, Sarasota, Florida, 1948–52; in private practice, Sarasota, and New Haven, Connecticut, 1952–58; Chairman, School of Architecture, Yale University, New Haven, 1958–65. In private practice, New York, since 1965. Exhibition: *Building Arts Exhibition,* Jewett Arts Center, Wellesley College, Massachusetts, 1960. Recipient: First Prize, Rorimer Competition, American Institute of Decorators, 1940; Award of Merit, 1949, 1959, 1962, 1964, and First Honor Award, 1964, American Institute of Architects; Outstanding Young Architect Award, *Bienal,* Sao Paulo, 1954; First Design Award, *Progressive Architecture,* 1955; Arnold Brunner Prize, National Institute of Arts and Letters, 1958; National Gold Medal, *Building Arts Exhibition,* Wellesley College, Massachusetts, 1960; Architectural Award, Boston Arts Festival, 1961; Award of Excellence for House Design, *Architectural Record,* 1963; Honor Award, AIA, New York Chapter, 1969. D.Arts: Colgate University, Hamilton, New York, 1966; D.F.A.: Florida State University, Tallahassee, 1970; Southeastern Massachusetts Technological Institute, North Dartmouth, 1970; H.H.D.: Auburn University, Montgomery, Alabama, 1972. Fellow, American Institute of Architects, 1970. Address (office): 54 West 57th Street, New York, New York 10019, U.S.A.

Works:

1946 Denman House, Siesta Key, Sarasota, Florida (with Ralph Twitchell)

1947 Finney Guest House, Siesta Key, Sarasota, Florida (project)

Miller House, Casey Key, Sarasota, Florida (with Ralph Twitchell)

1948 Revere Quality House, Siesta Key, Sarasota, Florida (with Ralph Twitchell)

Healy Guest House ("Cocoon House"), Siesta Key, Sarasota, Florida (with Ralph Twitchell)

Russell House, Sarasota, Florida (with Ralph Twitchell)

1949 Cheatham House, Lakeland, Florida (with Ralph Twitchell)

Deeds House, Siesta Key, Sarasota, Florida (with Ralph Twitchell)

1951 Leavengood House, St. Petersburg, Florida (with Ralph Twitchell)

Coward House, Siesta Key, Sarasota, Florida (with Ralph Twitchell)

Burnette House, Sarasota, Florida (with Ralph Twitchell)

Wheelan Cottage, Siesta Key, Sarasota, Florida (with Ralph Twitchell)

Hook Cottage, Siesta Key, Sarasota, Florida

Knott House, Yankeetown, Florida

1952 Design and layout of the *Good Design Exhibition,* Merchandise Mart, Chicago, and Museum of Modern Art, New York

Walker Guest House, Sanibel Island, Florida

Cohen House, Siesta Key, Sarasota, Florida

Sanderling Beach Club, Siesta Key, Sarasota, Florida

1953 Siegrist House, Venice, Florida (with Ralph Twitchell)

Biggs House, Delray Beach, Florida

Hiss House ("Umbrella House"), Lido Shores, Florida

1954 United States Embassy, Amman, Jordan (project)

Bostwick House, Palm Beach, Florida (project)

Wilson House, Sarasota, Florida

Taylor House, Venice, Florida

1955 Jewett Arts Center, Wellesley College, Massachusetts (with Anderson, Beckwith and Haible)

Sarasota-Bradenton Airport, Florida (project)

Burgess House, Burgess Island, Florida (project)

Plywood Association Experimental School (project)

1956 4 model houses for *Woman's Home Companion*

Model house for the Homestyle Center, Grand Rapids, Michigan

Applebee House, Auburn, Alabama

Bramlett Equipment Company Office Building, Miami (project)

Davidson House, Bradenton, Florida

Inter-American Center, Miami (project: as architectural design consultant)

Yanofsky House, Newton, Massachusetts

1957 Riverview High School, Sarasota, Florida

Harkavy House, Lido Shores, Florida

Blue Cross/Blue Shield Headquarters, Boston (with Anderson, Beckwith and Haible)

Greeley Memorial Laboratory, Yale University Forestry School, New Haven, Connecticut

Burkhardt House, Casey Key, Florida

1958 High school, Sarasota, Florida

Art and Architecture Building, Yale University, New Haven, Connecticut

Redevelopment plan for Church Street, New Haven, Connecticut (as consultant)

McCandlish House, Cambridge, Massachusetts

Master plan for Tuskegee Institute, Alabama (project; with John S. Chase)

Deering House, Casey Key, Florida

1959 Parking garage, Temple Street, New Haven, Connecticut

May Memorial Unitarian Church, Syracuse, New York

Lake Region Yacht and Country Club, Winter Haven, Florida

Liggett House, Tampa, Florida

1960 Married Student Housing, Yale University, New Haven, Connecticut

Friedberg House, Baltimore

Interdenominational Chapel, Tuskegee Institute, Alabama (with Fry and Welch)

Vacation house, Greenwich, Connecticut, for *Woman's Day*

Milam House, Jacksonville, Florida

Daisley House, Inlet Cay, Florida

Portland Cement Company Theme Center, *World's Fair,* New York (project)

Cultural Center, Tuskegee Institute, Alabama (project; with Fry and Welch)

RCA Advanced Designing and Styling Center (project)

Pi Kappa Phi Fraternity House, University of Florida, Gainesville

1961 Ciba Pharmaceutical Company additions and cafeteria, Summit, New Jersey (project)

Kappa Sigma Fraternity House, Auburn University, Alabama

Manager's Office, Parking Authority, New Haven, Connecticut

O'Brien Motor Inn, Waverly, New York (project)

Silvas House, Greenwich, Connecticut

Wallace House, Athens, Alabama

Juvenile Detention Home additions, Bridgeport, Connecticut

1962 IBM Complex, East Fishkill, New York (with Walter Kidde)

Ford Foundation Theatre (project)

Free Library, Guilford, Connecticut

Paul Rudolph: Government Service Center, Boston, 1963

Endo Laboratories Complex, Garden City, Long Island, New York (with Walter Kidde)

Crawford Manor Housing for the Elderly, New Haven, Connecticut

Master plan, dormitories, auditorium, and classroom building, Hotchkiss School, Lakeville, Connecticut

Mental Health Building, Government Center, Boston (with Desmond and Lord, H. A. Dyer, and Pedersen and Tilney)

Health, Welfare and Education Building, Government Center, Boston (with Desmond and Lord, H. A. Dyer, and Pedersen and Tilney)

Christian Science Organization Building, University of Illinois, Urbana (with Smith, Seaton and Olach)

1963 Government Service Center, Boston (as co-ordinating architect)

Orange County Government Center Office and Court House Building, Goshen, New York (with Peter Barbone)

Southeastern Massachusetts Technological Institute, North Dartmouth (with Desmond and Lord)

Creative Arts Center, Colgate University, Hamilton, New York

Beneficent Church High-Rise Apartment Building, Weybosset Hill Housing Complex, Providence, Rhode Island

1964 City Hall, Syracuse, New York (project; with Ketcham-Miller-Arnold)

John W. Chorley Elementary School, Middletown, New York (with Peter Barbone)

Paul Rudolph Offices, West 57th Street, New York

1965 International Bazaar, Interama Project, Miami (project)

Callahan House ("Southern House"), Birmingham, Alabama (project)

1966 Manoa Campus Visual Arts Center, University of Hawaii, Honolulu (project)

Master plan for the East Pakistan Agricultural University, Mymensingh (with William Grindereng)

Master plan for Stafford Harbor Resort Community, Virginia

Physical Sciences Building, Texas Christian University, Fort Worth (with Preston M. Geren)

Kinney House, Hamilton, New York (project)

Monteith College Center, Wayne State University, Detroit (project)

Hirsch House, New York

Brookhollow Corporation Office Building, Dallas (with Harwood K. Smith and Partners)

John Jay Park, New York (project)

Master plan for Northwest No. 1 Urban Renewal Area, Washington, D.C.

Caspi Penthouse, New York (project)

Beth El Synagogue additions, New London, Connecticut

1967 Graphic Arts Center and Apartments, New York (project)

Lower Manhattan Expressway Study, New York

Parcells House, Grosse Pointe, Michigan

Brown House, New York

Shore Dental Offices, New York

3 parks and playgrounds, New York (project)

Kaiser Apartment, New York

Endo Laboratories Office Building additions, Garden City, New York

2 apartment buildings, Bronx, New York

Master plan for Fox Hill, Staten Island, New York (with Jerrald L. Karlan)

Tracey Towers (apartment buildings and plaza), Bronx, New York (with Jerrald L. Karlan)

1968 Wilmot Road/Brookside Avenue Housing

(mobile homes), New Haven, Connecticut

Married Student Housing (mobile homes), University of Virginia, Charlottesville (project)

Student Union, Southeastern Massachusetts Technological Institute, North Dartmouth

Stadium, Dammam, Saudi Arabia (project)

Magnolia Homes (mobile homes), Vicksburg, Mississippi (project)

Government Center (city hall, library, plaza, and police station), New Haven, Connecticut

Fort Lincoln Housing (mobile homes), Washington, D.C. (project)

Green House, Cherry Ridge, Pennsylvania

Additional buildings for First Church in Boston

1969 Raich House, Quoque, Long Island, New York (project)

Lewis House, Boston (project)

Burroughs Wellcome and Company Corporate Headquarters, Research Triangle Park, Durham, North Carolina

Central City Library, Niagara Falls, New York

Waterfront Development (housing, school, commercial and community facilities), Buffalo, New York

Pistell House, Lyford Cay, Nassau, Bahamas (project)

Natural Science Building, State University of New York at Purchase

Gardner Cowles Apartment, New York

1970 Deare House, Great Neck, Long Island, New York

106th Street Housing and Neighborhood Development, New York (project)

10 apartment towers, Kew Gardens, New York (project)

Rockford Center, Illinois

Industrial Park (office, industrial and commercial buildings), Hauppage, New York

House, Fort Worth, Texas

Shuey House, Bloomfield Hills, Michigan

Edersheim Apartment, New York

1971 Urban complex (apartments, commercial, recreational, and administration buildings), Beirut

Dweck House, Deal, New Jersey

Daiei Company Office Building, Nagoya, Japan

Davidson House additions, Bloomfield Hills, Michigan

1972 Community College, Staten Island, New York (project)

Entrecanales y Tavora Office Building, Madrid

1973 Apartment Complex, Miami (project)

Paul Rudolph Apartment, New York

Modular Housing (project)

East Northport Jewish Center Synagogue additions, East Northport, New York (project)

Dormitory, Davidson College, North Carolina (project)

1974 Pan-Lon Apartment Hotel, Jerusalem (project)

Os House, Atlanta

Pitts Theology Library addition, Emory University, Atlanta

Publications:

By RUDOLPH: books—*Architectural Education in the United States,* Washington, D.C. 1962; *Global Architecture 2: Frank Lloyd Wright—Fallingwater,* with Yukio Futagawa, Tokyo 1970; *Drawings,* edited by Yukio Futagawa, Tokyo 1972, Fribourg, Switzerland 1974; *The Evolving City,* with Ulrich Franzen and Peter Wolf, New York 1974, 1976; articles—"The Spread of an Idea," editor, special issue

of *L'Architecture d'Aujourd'hui* (Paris), 1950; "New Directions" in *Perspecta* (New Haven, Connecticut), Summer 1952; "Criticism of the United Nations Building" in *Architectural Forum* (New York), October 1952; "The Orientation of Modern Architecture" in *Sarasota Review* (Sarasota, Florida), 1953; "Notes on Row Housing" in *Pennsylvania Triangle* (Philadelphia), January 1953; "Regionalism and the South" in *AIA Journal* (Washington, D.C.), April 1953; "Evaluation of North Carolina Livestock Judging Pavilion" in *Architectural Forum* (New York), April 1954; "The Changing Philosophy of Architecture" in *Architectural Forum* (New York), July 1954; "On the New School Design Research Team" in *Architectural Forum* (New York), September 1956; "The Six Determinants of Architectural Form" in *Architectural Record* (New York), October 1956; "Regionalism in Architecture" in *Perspecta* (New Haven, Connecticut), vol. 4, 1957; "A Personal Contribution to American Architecture" in *Architectural Review* (London), June 1957; "The Changing Face of New York" in *AIA Journal* (Washington, D.C.), April 1959; "On Arts and Architecture" in *Arts and Architecture* (Los Angeles), August 1959; "The Creative Use of Architectural Material" in *Progressive Architecture* (New York), September 1959; "Architectural Education in the United States" and "A Question for George Nelson and Paul Rudolph," with George Nelson, in *Zodiac* (Milan), no. 8, 1961; "Paul Rudolph Cites Old Principles as a Basis for Analysis of Today's Work" in *Architectural Record* (New York), January 1962; "In Search of a Comprehensive Style" in *New Homes Guides,* New York 1963; "A View of Washington as a Capitol; or, What Is Civic Design" in *Architectural Forum* (New York), January 1963; "Architecture: The Patron and the Public" in *Response* (Princeton, New Jersey), April 1963; "Rudolph Calls Students to Task of Urban Design" in *Architectural Record* (New York), May 1964; "The Essence of Architecture Is Space" in *House and Garden* (New York), November 1969; "Sibyl Moholy-Nagy" in *Architectural Forum* (New York), June 1971; "Alumni Day Speech: Yale School of Architecture, February 1958" in *Oppositions* (New York), October 1974.

On RUDOLPH: books—*Architecture USA* by Ian McCallum, London 1959; *Theory and Design in the First Machine Age* by Reyner Banham, London 1960; *Architects on Architecture,* edited by Paul Heyer, New York and London 1967; *Paul Rudolph* by Yukio Futagawa, Tokyo 1968, English translation, by Rupert Spade, London 1971; *American Architecture and Urbanism* by Vincent Scully, New York and London 1969; *New Directions in American Architecture* by Robert A. M. Stern, New York and London 1969; *The Architecture of Paul Rudolph* by Sibyl Moholy-Nagy, New York and London 1970; *Global Architecture 20: Paul Rudolph—Interdenominational Chapel, Tuskegee Institute and Boston Government Service Center* by Yukio Futagawa and Carl Black Jr., Tokyo 1973; articles—"Yale's Paul Rudolph" by Russell Bourne in *Architectural Forum* (New York), April 1958; "Paul Rudolph: Away from Genealogy of the Celebrated Architects" by Hiroyasu Yamada in *Kokusai Kentiku* (Tokyo), June 1960; "Rudolph at the Cross-Roads" by Henry A. Millon in *Architectural Design* (London), December 1960; "Paul Rudolph" by Giulia Veronesi in *Zodiac* (Milan), no. 8, 1961; "Whither Paul Rudolph" by Peter Collins in *Progressive Architecture* (New York), August 1961; "Paul Rudolph: A Series of Articles," special issue of *Kokusai Kentiku* (Tokyo), April 1965; special issue of *The Japan Architect* (Tokyo), July 1970; special issue of *Architecture + Urbanism* (Tokyo), January 1975, July 1977; "Paul Rudolph's Manhattan Apartment" in *Architectural Record* (New York), January 1978.

Paul Rudolph's volume of accomplishment is immense. He was fortunate that his talent and energy were ted by the American building boom of the 1950's and 60's. From the start of his own office in 1952 (after a four year partnership with Ralph Twitchell in Florida) to the present, Rudolph has worked upon approximately 160 commissions, built and unbuilt, 58 of which were houses, apartment interiors or additions and remodelings.

The remaining commissions comprise almost every conceivable building type or urban design problem of today: an embassy in Jordan, 19 educational buildings, 7 campus plans, master plans including buildings for 26 major housing or civic projects, an airport, a parking garage, a motor inn, a theatre, a stadium for the kingdom of Saudi Arabia, a yacht and country club, 12 office buildings, 5 religious buildings including the superb Tuskegee Chapel, 4 libraries, 8 government or civic buildings, 2 important exhibitions, various plans for parks and other recreational facilities, and uncounted miscellaneous projects. Some of this work was done during his seven year stint as Chairman of the Department of Architecture at Yale University. All of it was done, and is being done, without a partner. Rudolph once said: "Let's face it, architects were never meant to design together. . . . Architecture is a personal effort, and the fewer people coming between you and your work the better. . . . If an architect cares enough and practices architecture as an art, then he must initiate design—he must create rather than make judgements."

Rudolph's initiations and creations have prefigured much of the design that has followed in the United States, Europe and Japan. He continues to bring new concepts to the world of architecture which find their way into the work of nearly everyone else, becoming part of generalized building practice. His design is a synthesis of the ideas of Le Corbusier, Wright and Kahn. It is heroic, humanistic and sculpturally alive. His buildings are powerful interventions, creating new scale relationships in their surroundings. They are gateways, bridges, rallying points, creating great swirling outdoor environments and dynamic, intricately juxtaposed interior spaces. According to Ulrich Franzen: "He started the first real dialogue about architecture in the context of the city . . . this was a new approach to analyze problems of form and scale, space and function, as urban problems, rather than in the context of individual buildings." His two most spectacular exercises in urban form are the Boston Government Service Center and the Southeastern Massachusetts Technological Institute.

Rudolph continues to be interested in the concept of the industralized, plug-in city and has devised several unbuilt schemes in which housing units similar to mobile homes and indeed manufactured by that industry would be hoisted into a steel or concrete framework and connected to the mechanical and electrical services. His unbuilt Graphic Arts Center project for New York City proposed, in his words, that "mobile homes be used as 20th century bricks" hung from cantilevered trusses.

In spite of his interest in industrialized processes, Rudolph long ago began to question the precepts of the Modern Movement. The generation of architects following him (led by Philip Johnson, who preceded him) do the same thing—declaring themselves to be Post-Modernists. Rudolph is one of the unacknowledged fathers of this new way of thinking. He was prescient as far back as the early 1960's when he said: "Action has outstripped theory. The last decade has thrown a glaring light on the omissions, thinness, paucity of ideas, naiveté with regard to symbols, lack of creativeness, and expressiveness of architectural philosophy as it developed during the 20's. . . . Many of our difficulties stem from the concept of functionalism as the only determinant of form. We cannot pretend to solve problems of space without precedent in form." Rudolph differs from the Post-Modernists, however, to the degree that his work is highly personal, competitive and aggressive. The Post-Modernists claim to have more modest aims, but this may also reflect the fact that they have matured in

a more modest economy. Like that of the Post-Modernists, Rudolph's work has, from the beginning, been tied to history, yet transformed in ways that are uncompromisingly his own.

—Mildred F. Schmertz

RUSSELL, David.

British. Born in London, 5 April 1935. Educated at the School of Architecture, Regent Street Polytechnic, London, under John Reed, James Stirling, William Howell and David Jenkins, 1952–54, 1956–59, Dip.Arch. 1959. Served in the Royal Artillery, 1954–56. Married the architect Srisurang Sriuttamayothin in 1971; children: Ratanasuda and Parichart. Assistant Architect, Pinckney and Gott, London, 1959–60; Architect, with Ronald Cuddon, London, 1960, Denys Lasdun and Partners, London, 1962–65, and Intaren, Bangkok, 1965–69; Partner, Russell and Montochio, Bangkok, 1969–71. Since 1971, Partner, Russell and Dreyer, Hong Kong and Bangkok; since 1977, Partner, Russell/Poon Group Partnership, Hong Kong. Part-time Lecturer at the Department of Architecture, Hong Kong, since 1976. Member of the Council, Hong Kong Institute of Architects, 1976–79. Founder Member and Chairman, Hong Kong Heritage Society, since 1978. Recipient: Silver Medal Award, Hong Kong Institute of Architects, 1977. Address: Russell and Dreyer, 13B Bonaventure House, 85–91 Leighton Road, Hong Kong.

Works:

1967 Zeullig Company Office Building, Bangkok (with Intaren)
1968 Esso Office Building, Bangkok (with Intaren)
1969 Multi-storey Car Park and Sports Centre, for the Royal Bangkok Sports Club
1974 Dairy Farm Shopping Centre, Hong Kong
 Dairy Farm Office Building, Hong Kong
 "Pendragon" (housing project), Hong Kong
1975 Dairy Farm Shopping Centre, Repulse Bay, Hong Kong
1977 Aircraft Catering Building, Hong Kong

Publications:

By RUSSELL: articles—in *Asian Architect* (Hong Kong), since 1966.

David Russell: Aircraft Catering Building, Hong Kong, 1977

A product of the Regent Street Polytechnic, David Russell has travelled extensively in the Middle East and India and has lived in Southeast Asia since 1965. If I were to describe his work I should say that it is not unlike that of some of the intelligent but unrecognized expatriate architects of the British Empire who left buildings of great charm and sensitivity in India, Malaysia and Hong Kong, work that shows qualities of "commodity, firmness and delight" and, with them, an understanding and sensitivity to a place and its people.

Russell is still very much an Englishman, with his strong sense of the picturesque and his awareness of history. He is an extremely modest, unassuming man, but he holds strong views on the state of our environment in Hong Kong: he acts as a rebuking conscience to those who are destroying our architectural heritage.

His own work is urbane in quality, with a relaxed, intellectual English atmosphere about it that often gives it a presence—not obvious yet still pervasive. His architecture is always an ensemble of ideas, spiced with inexpensive innovations producing that "ordinariness" of form that Smithson speaks about. Russell's architecture can probably be described as a well-worn Harris Tweed jacket, looking comfortably warm and firm, with the added dash of a fresh rose on its lapel.

—K. C. Lye

RUUSUVUORI, Aarno.

Finnish. Born in Kuopio, 14 January 1925. Educated at Tehtaanpuisto High School, Helsinki, graduated 1943; studied architecture at the Technical University, Helsinki, 1946–50, Dip. Arch. 1951; influenced by Aulis Blomstedt in whose office he worked while a student. Served as a Corporal in the Finnish Army, 1943–45. Married Anna Maria E. Jäämeri in 1970; children: Eva and Anu. In private practice, Helsinki, since 1952. Editor, 1952–55, and Editor-in-Chief, 1956–57, *Arkkitehtilehti* magazine,

Helsinki; Assistant, 1952–59, Acting Professor of Architecture, 1959–63, and Professor of Architecture, 1963–66, Technical University, Helsinki; Director, Museum of Finnish Architecture, Helsinki, 1975–78. Chairman, Finnish National Committee of ICOMOS (International Council of Monuments and Sites), 1967–70, and of the Finnish Friends of Architecture, 1967–76. Exhibitions: Jyväskylä, Finland (one-man), 1969; Brno and Bratislava, Czechoslovakia (one-man), 1969–70; *Contemporary Architecture in Finland,* toured the United States, 1955; *World's Fair,* Brussels, 1958; *Bienal,* Sao Paulo, 1961, 1969; Royal Institute of British Architects, London, 1961; *Church Exhibition,* Milan, 1962. Recipient: Vainö Vähäkallio Scholarship, Helsinki, 1955; Lindahl-Thomé Scholarship, Helsinki, 1955; Kordelin Scholarship, Helsinki, 1957; Artist Scholarship, Helsinki, 1970, 1973–75. Professor of Art, Finland, 1978–83. Member of SAFA (Finnish Architects Association), 1952; Honorary Member, Architectguild, Helsinki, 1966. Address: Architectural Office Aarno Ruusuvuori, Annankatu 15 B 10, 00120 Helsinki 12, Finland.

Works:

1961 Hyvinkää Church and Parish Center, Hyvinkää, Finland
       Pietinen Studio, Helsinki
1962 Apartment building, Merimienenk. 32, Helsinki
       City Real-Estate Office renovation, Helsinki
1964 Huutoniemi Church and Parish Center, Vaasa, Finland
1965 Church and Parish Center, Tapiola, Espoo, Finland
1966 Weilin and Göös Printing Works, Tapiola, Espoo, Finland
       Orijärvi Mansion renovation, Orijärvi, Finland
       Prefabricated System House, Bökars, Finland
1967 Elementary school, Roihuvuori, Helsinki
       Marimekko Printing Works, Helsinki
1968 Police Headquarters, Mikkeli, Finland
       Kluuvi Office renovation, Helsinki
1969 Hellekis Mansion renovation, Hällekis, Sweden

1970 Helsinki City Hall renovation, stage I
1972 Rauhannummi Chapel and Cemetery, Hyvinkää, Finland
       Stunkel House, Grenolier, Switzerland
1973 Aberra House, Addis Ababa, Ethiopia
       Lilibeth House, Addis Ababa, Ethiopia
       Helsinki City Office Building renovation
       Paragon Office Building, Helsinki
1976 Real Estate Development Center, Addis Ababa, Ethiopia
       Klingspor Villa, Rossö, Sweden
1977 Halonen House, Kuusisaari, Helsinki
1979 Parate Printing Works, Helsinki

Publications:

By RUUSUVUORI: article—"Rauhannummi Funeral Chapel and Cemetery" in *Arkkitehti* (Helsinki), vol. 70, no. 7, 1973.

On RUUSUVUORI: books—*The New Churches of Europe* by G. E. Kidder Smith, London 1964; *World Architecture 2,* London 1965; *Asumme Lähellä Luontoa* by Anna-Liisa Ahmavaara, Helsinki 1966; *Uutta suomalaista arkkitehtuuria* by Pekka Suhonen, Helsinki 1967; *Neue Finnische Architektur* by Egon Tempel, Stuttgart 1968; *Architettura Finlandese,* Turin 1973; *Finnish Architecture,* The Hague 1975; *Suočasná finská architektura* by by Vladislav Dlesek, Prague 1975; *Mai finn építészet* by Elemér Nagy, Budapest 1976; article—general survey of works in *Kokusai Kentiku* (Tokyo), April 1967.

To me architecture is a problem of space and light. The solution to this problem is backed by a rational structure.

In my work I look for an appropriate frame for various human activities, a point of departure reduced to simple basic elements, rounded out and supplemented by developing activity.

—Aarno Ruusuvuori

Aarno Ruusuvuori graduated as an architect in 1951, a memorable year in the history of modern Finnish architecture. For various reasons the Second World War had interrupted the purity and simplicity of functionalism, which had made its breakthrough in the 1930's. During and after the war, in the 1940's, architects returned to traditional building forms, and their romanticism was reflected not only in the overall structure but in the details as well. In 1951, however, some of the older generation of architects— Aulis Blomstedt, Yrjö Lindegren, Viljo Revell—rejected this romanticism in their work in favour of a return to international modernism.

Not enough attention has been paid to this period in architecture, but Ruusuvuori's thesis work—a project for the Finnish Embassy in Rome—is evidence that there was great admiration for the traditions of functionalism among students. Rationalism became Ruusuvuori's symbol. He prefers using cast fairface concrete, which he combines with other ascetic building materials. Nevertheless, it is the cool aestheticism and elegant detail that offer proof of his professional skill and give him his individuality.

Almost without exception, Ruusuvuori's buildings impress themselves on the mind; they have a certain pregnant form. One of the most expressive is the pyramid-shaped church in Hyvinkää, but generally speaking his individuality has been achieved with simpler overall forms.

In addition to the design of new buildings Ruusuvuori has done a considerable amount of restoration—churches, town halls, business premises and manor houses. In some cases, such as the renovation of the neo-classical Helsinki City Hall (from 1833), his methods have been extremely radical: only the outer walls and the most valuable rooms have been restored; everything else has become new modern architecture. In work like this, Ruusuvuori's reveals his characteristic striving for simplicity and strong forms.

—Asko Salokorpi

Aarno Ruusuvuori: Helsinki City Hall renovation, 1970

S

SAARINEN, Eero.

American. Born in Kirkkonummi, Finland, 20 August 1910; son of the architect Eliel Saarinen, *q.v.*, and the sculptor Louise (Loja) Gesellius Saarinen; emigrated with his family to the United States, 1923: naturalized, 1940. Educated at primary and secondary schools in Michigan; studied sculpture at the Académie de la Grand Chaumière, Paris, 1929–30; studied architecture at Yale University, New Haven, Connecticut, B.F.A. 1934; awarded Charles O. Matcham Fellowship, for travel in Europe, 1934–36. Worked in the Office of Strategic Studies, Washington, D.C., 1942–45. Married Lily Swann in 1939 (divorced, 1953); children: Eric and Susan; married Aline Bernstein Louchheim in 1954; son: Eames. Joined his father's architectural practice, Ann Arbor, Michigan, 1936: practised with his father, 1937–41; Partner, with his father and J. Robert Swanson, Saarinen-Swanson-Saarinen, Ann Arbor, 1941–47, then, with his father, Saarinen, Saarinen and Associates, Ann Arbor, 1947 until his father's death, 1950; Principal of the successor firm, Eero Saarinen and Associates, Birmingham, Michigan, 1950 until his own death, 1961. Recipient: 2 First Prizes, with Charles Eames, Furniture Design Competition, Museum of Modern Art, New York, 1940; First Prize, Jefferson National Expansion Memorial Competition, St. Louis, 1948; Grand Architectural Award, Boston Arts Festival, 1953; First Honor Award, American Institute of Architects, 1955, 1956; First Prize, American Embassy Competition, London, 1965; Gold Medal, American Institute of Architects, 1962. M.A.: Yale University, 1949; LL.D.: Wayne State University, Detroit, 1961. Fellow, American Institute of Architects, and American Academy of Arts and Sciences. *Died* (in Ann Arbor) *1 September 1961.*

Works:

1937/
38 Community House, Fenton, Michigan (with Eliel Saarinen)
1938 Area plan for Goucher College, Baltimore (competition project; with Eliel Saarinen)
Berkshire Music Center, Tanglewood, Massachusetts (with Eliel Saarinen)
1938/
40 Kleinhans Music Hall, Buffalo, New York (with Eliel Saarinen)
1939 Smithsonian Institution Art Gallery, Washington, D.C. (project; with Eliel Saarinen and J. Robert Swanson)
1939/
40 Crow Island School, Winnetka, Illinois (with Eliel Saarinen, and Perkins, Wheeler and Will)
1940 Molded Plywood Chair (competition project; with Charles Eames)
1940/
42 Tabernacle Church of Christ, Columbus, Indiana (with Eliel Saarinen)
1941 Oberlin College, Ohio (project; with Eliel Saarinen and Richard Kimball)
Houses, school and community hall, Center

Line, Michigan (with Eliel Saarinen and J. Robert Swanson)
1941/
42 A. C. Wermuth House, Fort Wayne, Indiana (with Eliel Saarinen)
Willow Run Housing Units, Michigan (with Eliel Saarinen and J. Robert Swanson)
1942 Schools, Willow Run, Michigan (with Eliel Saarinen and J. Robert Swanson)
Group plan and architectural scheme for Wayne State University, Detroit (competition project; with Eliel Saarinen and J. Robert Swanson)
Summer Opera House and Chamber Music Hall, Berkshire Music Center, Tanglewood, Massachusetts (with Eliel Saarinen)
1943 Lincoln Heights Housing Area, Washington, D.C. (with Eliel Saarinen and J. Robert Swanson)
1943/
44 Parliament Building, Quito, Ecuador (competition project; with Eliel Saarinen and J. Robert Swanson)
1944 Town plan for New Castle, Indiana (with Eliel Saarinen and J. Robert Swanson)
1944/
48 Edmundson Memorial Museum, Des Moines Art Center, Iowa (with Eliel Saarinen and J. Robert Swanson)
1945 Plan for Washtenaw County, Michigan (with Eliel Saarinen and J. Robert Swanson)
Development plan for Antioch College, Yellow Springs, Ohio (with Eliel Saarinen and J. Robert Swanson)
1945/
49 Women's Dormitory, Antioch College, Yellow Springs, Ohio (with Eliel Saarinen and J. Robert Swanson)
1946 H. H. Houston Community Development Plan, Outer Roxborough, Philadelphia (with Eliel Saarinen)
1946/
47 Campus development plan for Drake University, Des Moines, Iowa (with Eliel Saarinen and J. Robert Swanson)
Women's Dormitory, Drake University, Des Moines, Iowa (with Eliel Saarinen)
1946/
48 Christ Church, Cincinnati, Ohio (with Eliel Saarinen)
1946/
49 Science and Pharmacy Building, Drake University, Des Moines, Iowa (with Eliel Saarinen, J. Robert Swanson, and Brooks and Borg)
1947 Civic Center, Detroit (with Eliel Saarinen)
Campus development plan for Stephens College, Columbia, Missouri (with Eliel Saarinen)
Chapel, Stephens College, Columbia, Missouri (with Eliel Saarinen)
Peoples Bank and Trust Company Building, Fort Wayne, Indiana (with Eliel Saarinen)
1948/
56 General Motors Technical Center, including

interiors and furniture, Warren, Michigan (with Smith, Hinchman and Grylls)
1949 Buildings for Brandeis University, Waltham, Massachusetts (project; with Eliel Saarinen)
1951/
55 Dormitories/Dining Hall, Drake University, Des Moines, Iowa
1952/
55 Irwin Union Bank and Trust Company, Columbus, Indiana
1953/
55 Kresge Auditorium and Chapel, Massachusetts Institute of Technology, Cambridge
1953/
57 Milwaukee County War Memorial, Wisconsin
Miller House, Columbus, Indiana
1954 Master plan for the University of Michigan, Ann Arbor
1954/
58 Concordia College, Fort Wayne, Indiana
Dormitory, Vassar College, Poughkeepsie, New York
1955/
58 Women's Dormitory/Dining Hall, University of Chicago
1955/
59 United States Chancellery, Oslo
1955/
60 United States Embassy, Grosvenor Square, London (with Yorke, Rosenberg, Mardall)
1956/
59 IBM Building, Rochester, Minnesota
1956/
60 Law School, University of Chicago
1956/
62 Trans World Airlines Terminal, Idlewild Airport, now Kennedy Airport, New York
1957/
60 Law School, and Women's Dormitories, University of Pennsylvania, Philadelphia
1957/
61 Thomas J. Watson Research Center, IBM, Yorktown, New York
1957/
62 Bell Telephone Corporation Research Laboratories, Holmdel, New Jersey
1957/
63 John Deere and Company Administration Center, Moline, Illinois
1958 David S. Ingalls Hockey Rink, Yale University, New Haven, Connecticut
1958/
62 Ezra Stiles College, and Morse College, Yale University, New Haven, Connecticut
1958/
63 Terminal Building, Dulles International Airport, Washington, D.C. (Chantilly, Virginia)
1958/
64 Repertory Theatre and Theatre Library/Museum, Lincoln Center, New York (with Skidmore, Owings and Merrill)

Eero Saarinen: Trans World Airlines Terminal, Kennedy Airport, New York, 1962

Publications:

By SAARINEN: book—*Eero Saarinen on His Work,* edited by Aline B. Saarinen, New Haven, Connecticut 1968; articles—"The Architecture of Defense Housing," edited by Edmond H. Hoben, in *National Association of Housing Officials Journal* (Chicago), no. 165, 1942; "Trends in Modern Architecture" in *Michigan Society of Architects Bulletin* (Detroit), May 1951; "Our Epoch of Architecture" in *AIA Journal* (Washington, D.C.), December 1952; "Six Broad Currents of Modern Architecture" in *Architectural Forum* (New York), July 1953; "The Changing Philosophy of Architecture" in *Architectural Record* (New York), August 1954; "Function, Structure and Beauty" in *AIA Journal* (Washington, D.C.), July/August 1957; "Campus Planning: The Unique World of the University" in *Architectural Record* (New York), November 1960.

On SAARINEN: books—*Eero Saarinen* by Allan Temko, New York and London 1962; *Great Modern Architecture* by Sherban G. Cantacuzino, New York and London 1966; *Eero Saarinen* by E. J. Iglesia, Buenos Aires 1966; *Eero Saarinen* by Rupert Spade, New York and London 1971; *The Fourth Dimension in Architecture* by Edward and Mildred Hall, Santa Fe, New Mexico 1975; articles—"Now Saarinen the Son" by Aline B. Louchheim in the *New York Times Magazine,* 26 April 1953; special issue of the *Michigan Society of Architects Bulletin* (Detroit), July 1953; "Recent Works of Eero Saarinen" in *Zodiac* (Milan), no. 4, 1959; "The Diversity of Eero Saarinen" by Lawrence Lessing in *Architectural Forum* (New York), July 1960; "Eero Saarinen: Something Between Earth and Sky" by Allan Temko in *Horizon* (New York), July 1960; "Recent Work by Eero Saarinen" in *RIBA Journal* (London), November 1960; "Eero Saarinen 1910–1961" by Douglas Haskell in *Architectural Forum* (New York), October 1961; "Eero Saarinen 1910–1961" by Peter Carter in *Architectural Design* (London), December 1961; "Eero Saarinen: A Complete Architect" by Walter McQuade in *Architectural Forum* (New York), October 1962; "On Eero Saarinen" by Raymond Lifchez in *Zodiac* (Milan), no. 17, 1967; "Pluralismo e pop-Architettura" by Bruno Zevi in *L'Architettura* (Rome), September 1967; "A View of Contemporary World Architecture," special issue of *The Japan Architect* (Tokyo), July 1970; "The Genesis of a Great Building and an Unusual Friendship" by William Hewitt in *AIA Journal* (Washington, D.C.), August 1977.

Bibliography: *Eero Saarinen: His Life and Work* by Robert A. Kuhner, Monticello, Illinois 1975.

To be born the child of a talented parent may be a blessing or a curse. Being the child of two such parents can only compound the situation. And for a child to follow in the profession of a talented parent may bring with it an even greater boon or risk.

For Eero Saarinen, being the son of the talented and famous architect, Eliel Saarinen, and the talented artist and artisan, Loja Gesellius Saarinen, was definitely a blessing. He lived in a home filled with creative activity and with creative people, visitors as well as his mother, father and sister. His early formal training was sporadic, at best, but he had ample opportunity for his own creative endeavours.

Having moved with his family to Bloomfield Hills, Michigan, when he was 13 years old, Eero Saarinen decided that, of all the arts, sculpture was his favorite and that he would become a sculptor. After a year in art school, he decided to become an architect rather than a sculptor, in spite of the fact that while a teenager his designs were mostly for sculpture and sculptural furniture. In later years, his love of sculpture was never lost. And eventually, when he became famous, as great an architect as his father had been —some think even greater—he also became the most sculptural architect of his era.

Eliel Saarinen was a notable architect before winning the second prize in the competition for the Chicago Tribune Tower in 1922. The elder Saarinen's design, considered by many to be superior to the winner by Raymond Hood and John Mead Howells, brought with it world-wide publicity and recognition. Like his father before him, Eero Saarinen became a notable architect who later received worldwide recognition for winning a competition, in 1948, that for the design of the Jefferson National Expansion Memorial in St. Louis, later known as the Gateway Arch. He had achieved considerable stature before the competition in partnership with his father, and together they had designed a number of important buildings, including the Kleinhans Music Hall, Buffalo, New York, Crow Island School, Winnetka, Illinois, in association with Perkins, Wheeler and Will, and Tabernacle Church, Columbus, Indiana. He had won competitions before, the first for a design with matchsticks when he was 12 years of age and two first prizes, in 1940, for furniture designs made with Charles Eames for the Museum of Modern Art of New York City.

But the Gateway Arch established him firmly as

one of the world's most important architects and established him as an individual architect, independently of his father. After his father's death in 1950, Eero Saarinen started his own practice, which grew quite rapidly. His buildings received wide publicity and won awards.

The buildings designed by the two Saarinens together gave little hint of the future development of Eero Saarinen as a designer. Most were excellent but unspectacular; they were relatively small and utilized natural materials. An exception was the large and complex General Motors Technical Center, in Warren, Michigan, designed in association with Smith, Hinchman and Grylls, a multi-million dollar project completed in the 1950's after the elder Saarinen had died. The Technical Center style was what might be called classic modern of its time, with straight, clean lines, rectangular forms, in an almost Miesian manner. It, too, gave no indication of the future design directions of Eero Saarinen.

What followed was a tremendous outpouring of original work, each building different from the last and seemingly derived from some inner drive of Saarinen's toward inventive and sculptural forms. The Kresge Auditorium and Chapel, completed in 1955, at Massachusetts Institute of Technology, Cambridge, were, perhaps, the first buildings to indicate the future directions of Saarinen's work. Both are daring in concept and sculptural in form. To follow were such notable buildings as those at Concordia College, Fort Wayne, Indiana, two buildings for IBM, the John Deere and Company Administration Center in Moline, Illinois, the Ingalls Hockey Rink at Yale, and the Trans World Airlines Terminal Building at John F. Kennedy Airport, New York City. In each succeeding design, Saarinen appeared to be trying to outdo the predecessors. And each brought him added fame and recognition. Along the way, he designed other buildings, some of which, such as the United States Embassy in London, were admired but not considered among his best.

During all the years of the 1950's, Saarinen continued to surprise and delight his admirers and to confound his critics. To both groups, he always seemed to be searching for the one design scheme that would be absolutely appropriate for each new building, searching for new horizons and seldom, if ever, looking back. While other noted architects seemed to be attempting to develop personal styles, in which each succeeding building derived from those that they had designed before, Saarinen seemed to be developing an almost styleless philosophy in which each design sprang full blown from his talent and toil almost as if he had never previously designed another building.

Needless to say, Saarinen's designs were, for the most part, fresh, intriguing, even mysterious. Saarinen himself came to be something of an enigma to the public and to his fellow architects. Some accused him of being primarily a showman, but others thought of him as possibly the most creative architect of his time. In the end, most had concluded that he really was a very creative architect, who was also a consummate showman.

In the late 1950's, Saarinen designed some of his greatest buildings. In 1961, successful, famous and almost inevitably destined for even greater achievements, Eero Saarinen died while undergoing brain surgery. He was only 51 years of age with what many thought would be the best of his architectural years ahead of him. A year later, he was awarded, posthumously, the highest honor of his fellow architects, the gold medal of the American Institute of Architects, an award his father had also won 15 years before. In 1963, what many people consider his masterpiece, Dulles Airport, was completed.

Although he had not developed a style that others could follow and, perhaps, develop further, Eero Saarinen had left a creative legacy of originality in design that has influenced later architecture profoundly.

—William Dudley Hunt, Jr.

SAARINEN, (Gottlieb) Eliel.
American. Born in Rantasalmi, Finland, 20 August 1873; emigrated to the United States, 1923; naturalized, 1945. Educated at Klassillinenlyseo secondary school, Viborg, Finalnd, 1883–89; Realyceum secondary school, Tammerfors, Finland, 1889–93; simultaneously studied painting at the University of Helsinki and architecture at the Polytekniska Institutet, Helsinki, 1893–97, Dip.Arch. 1897. Married the sculptor Louise (Loja) Gesellius in 1904; children: Eva-Lisa (Pipsan) and the architect Eero Saarinen, *q.v.* Partner, with Herman Gesellius and Armas Lindgren, Gesellius-Lindgren-Saarinen, Helsinki, 1896–1905, and Gesellius-Saarinen, Helsinki, 1905–07; in private practice as Eliel Saarinen, architect, Helsinki, 1907–23, Evanston, Illinois, 1923–24, and Ann Arbor, Michigan, 1924–37; practised with son Eero in Ann Arbor, 1937–41; Partner, with Eero and J. Robert Swanson, Saarinen-Swanson-Saarinen, Ann Arbor, 1941–47; Partner, Saarinen, Saarinen and Associates, Ann Arbor, Michigan, 1947–50. Visiting Professor of Architecture, University of Michigan, Ann Arbor, 1924; Director, 1925–32, President, 1932–50, and Director of the Graduate Department of Architecture and City Planning, 1948–50, Cranbrook Academy of Art, Bloomfield Hills, Michigan. Chairman, City and Regional Planning Committee, American Institute of Architects, 1935. Exhibitions: *Salon d'Automne,* Paris, 1907; *Die Grosse Kunstausstellung,* Berlin, 1909; *Internationale Baufach Ausstellung,* Leipzig, 1913; *Deutsche Werkbund Ausstellung,* Cologne, 1914; Munksnas-Haga exhibition, *Riddarhuset,* Helsinki, 1915; *Thumb Tack Club Annual Exhibition,* Detroit Institute of Arts, 1924; *Ausstellung Neuer Amerikanischer Baukunst,* Berlin, 1926; *International Architectural and Arts Exposition,* New York, 1930; *Loja and Eliel Saarinen,* Architectural League of New York, 1931; *Nordiska Byggnadsdag,* Helsinki, 1932; *Saarinen Family Exhibition,* Detroit Institute of Arts, 1932; *Saarinen Family Exhibition,* Cranbrook Pavilion, Bloomfield Hills, Michigan, 1935; *World's Fair,* Paris, 1937; *Loja and Eliel Saarinen,* Norfolk Museum of Art and Science, Virginia, 1937; *America Builds,* Museum of Modern Art, New York, 1942, toured the United States and Europe; *Eliel and Loja Saarinen,* Berea College, Kentucky, 1943; *New Architecture of the United States,* Cairo, Egypt, 1944. Recipient: Bronze, Silver and Gold medals, State of Finland, 1900; Gold Medal, Leipzig Exhibition, 1913; Gold Medal, Architectural League of New York, 1934; Academic Architects Society Medal, Copenhagen, 1939; Gold Medal, American Institute of Architects, 1947. Honorary Doctorates:

Eliel Saarinen: Museum and Library, Cranbrook Academy of Art, Bloomfield Hills, Michigan, 1943

Technische Hochschule, Karlsruhe, Germany, 1925; University of Helsinki, 1932; University of Michigan, 1933; Bethany College, Lindsburg, Kansas, 1936; Harvard University, Cambridge, Massachusetts, 1940; Drake University, Des Moines, Iowa, 1948. Honorary Professor, Finland, 1918. Fellow, American Institute of Architects, 1944; Academician, National Academy of Design, U.S.A., 1946. Honorary Member: Imperial Academy of Art, St. Petersburg, 1906; Deutsche Werkbund, 1913; Die Zentrale Vereinigung der Architekten Osterreichs, Vienna, 1913; Finnish Academy of Art, 1920; Society of Arts and Crafts, Budapest, 1921; Freie Deutsche Academie des Stadtebaues, 1922; Royal Institute of British Architects, 1924; Michigan Chapter of the American Institute of Architects, 1925; Swedish Engineers Society, Detroit, 1926; Society of Finnish Architects, 1930; Architects Society of Uruguay, 1931; Central Institute of Architects of Brazil, 1931; Council of Confidence, Art Academy of Finland, 1932; Michigan Society of Architects, 1936; Detroit Chapter of the American Institute of Architects, 1936. Commander First Class, Finnish Order of the White Rose, 1925; Grand Cross, Finnish Order of the Lion, 1946. *Died* (in Cranbrook Hills, Michigan) *1 July 1950.*

Works:

1897 Tallberg Apartment Building, Helsinki (with Herman Gesellius and Armas Lindgren)
Market Hall, Tampere, Finland (competition project; with Herman Gesellius and Armas Lindgren)

1898 Verdandi Insurance Company Building, Turku, Finland (competition project; with Herman Gesellius and Armas Lindgren)
Henry van Gilse van der Pals Country House, Paloniemi, Lohja, Finland (with Herman Gesellius and Armas Lindgren)
Municipal Library, Turku, Finland (competition project; with Herman Gesellius and Armas Lindgren)

1899 Apartment block, Siltasaarentaku 12, Helsinki (with Herman Gesellius and Armas Lindgren)
Vuorio Villa, Helsinki (with Herman Gesellius and Armas Lindgren)
Pellervo Insurance Company Building, Helsinki (project; with Herman Gesellius and Armas Lindgren)

1899/
1900 Finnish Pavilion, *World's Fair,* Paris (with Herman Gesellius and Armas Lindgren)

1899/
1901 Pohjola Insurance Company Building, Helsinki (with Herman Gesellius and Armas Lindgren)

1900 Törngren Villa, Espoo, Finland (with Herman Gesellius and Armas Lindgren)

1900/
01 Pulkanranta Villa, Mäntyharju, Finland (with Herman Gesellius and Armas Lindgren)
Apartment block, Fabianinkatu 17, Helsinki (with Herman Gesellius and Armas Lindgren)

1900/
03 Savings Bank, Tampere, Finland (with Herman Gesellius and Armas Lindgren)

1901 Sievers Villa, Helsinki (with Herman Gesellius and Armas Lindgren)
Church, Janakkala, Finland (project; with Herman Gesellius and Armas Lindgren)
EOL Apartment Block, Helsinki (with Herman Gesellius and Armas Lindgren)

1901/
03 Olofsborg Apartment Block, Helsinki (with Herman Gesellius and Armas Lindgren)

1902 Hvitträsk (architects' houses and studio), Kirkkonummi, Finland (with Herman Gesellius and Armas Lindgren)
Westerlund Country House, Hvittorp, Kirk-

konummi, Finland (with Herman Gesellius and Armas Lindgren)
Selin Villa, Miniato, Sökö, Espoo, Finland (with Herman Gesellius and Armas Lindgren)
Suur-Merijoki Country House, Viipuri, Finland (with Herman Gesellius and Armas Lindgren)
Paper mill, Voikkaa, Finland (with Herman Gesellius and Armas Lindgren)
Vicarage, Jokioinen, Finland (with Herman Gesellius and Armas Lindgren)
Municipal Library, Oulu, Finland (competition project: with Herman Gesellius and Armas Lindgren)

1902/
06 Edelfelt EKA Villa, Kilo, Espoo, Finland (with Herman Gesellius and Armas Lindgren)

1903 Church, Nilsiä, Finland (project; with Herman Gesellius and Armas Lindgren)
Bobrinsky Villa, Moscow (project; with Herman Gesellius and Armas Lindgren)
Castrén Villa, Espoo, Finland (with Herman Gesellius and Armas Lindgren)

1904 Pirtti Artists' Club, Helsinki (with Herman Gesellius and Armas Lindgren)
Luther Factory Club, Tallinn, Estonia (with Herman Gesellius and Armas Lindgren)
Count Schouvaloff Memorial, Kursk, Russia (with Herman Gesellius and Armas Lindgren)
Bank building, Sortavala, Finland (with Herman Gesellius and Armas Lindgren)
Methodist church, Helsinki (with Herman Gesellius and Armas Lindgren)
Nordic Bank Building, Helsinki (with Herman Gesellius and Armas Lindgren)
Private house, Essen, Germany (competition project; with Herman Gesellius and Armas Lindgren)
Päivälehti Newspaper Building, Helsinki (with Herman Gesellius and Armas Lindgren)

1904/
10 Finnish National Museum, Helsinki (with Herman Gesellius and Armas Lindgren)

1905 Emmanuel Church, Helsinki (with Herman Gesellius)
Palace of Peace, The Hague (competition project; with Herman Gesellius)
Labour Union Building, Kotka, Finland (with Herman Gesellius)

1905/
07 Molchow House, Remer Country Estate, Mark Brandenburg, Germany (with Herman Gesellius)

1905/
14 Helsinki Railway Station

1906 Helsingin Sanomat Newspaper Building, Helsinki (with Herman Gesellius)
Oma Apartment Block, Helsinki (with Herman Gesellius)
Town Hall, Lappeenranta, Finland (project; with Herman Gesellius)

1907 School building, Helsinki (project)
Keirkner Apartment interiors, Helsinki

1908 Parliament Building, Helsinki (competition project)
School building, Turku, Finland (project)
Salamandra Insurance Company Building, St. Petersburg, Russia (project)

1908/
13 Viipuri Railway Station, Finland (with Herman Gesellius)

1909 Winter Villa, Sortavala, Finland
Cederberg Mausoleum, Joensuu, Finland (project)

1910 Tallberg Office Building II, Helsinki
Municipal Theatre, Tampere, Finland (competition project)
Industrial Exhibition Design, Helsinki (competition project)

Huber Office Building, Helsinki (competition project)

1910/
15 Town plan for Munkkiniemi-Haaga, Finland

1911 Rigaer Gesellschaft Gegenseitigen Credits Office and Apartment Building, Riga, Latvia (competition project)
Esto-Bank Building, Tallinn, Estonia (competition project)

1911/
12 Town Hall, Lahti, Finland
Esto-Bank Building, Tallinn, Estonia

1911/
13 Town plan for Tallinn, Estonia (competition project)

1912 Town plan for Budapest, Hungary
Suomi Insurance Company Building, Helsinki (competition project)
Trade Union Building, Riga, Latvia (competition project)
School for Girls, Lahti, Finland
Town Hall, Tallinn, Estonia (project)
Town plan for Canberra, Australia (competition project)

1912/
13 Town Hall, Joensuu, Finland

1913 Paulus Church, Tarto (Dorpat), Estonia

1914 Finnish Pavilion, *San Francisco Fair* (competition project)
Finnish Lutheran Congregational Hall, St. Petersburg, Russia (project)

1915 Keirkner Villa, Helsinki

1916 Town plan for Munkkiniemi-Haaga, Finland
Keskuskatu Street layout, Helsinki
Swedish Theatre Annex and restoration, Helsinki (project)

1916/
18 Pensionat Hotel, Munkkiniemi, Finland

1917 Tirkkonen Office Building, Helsinki (project)
Tirkkonen House, Helsinki (project)

1917/
18 City plan for Greater Helsinki

1919 Hospital, Cairo, Egypt (project)
Kalevala House, Munkkiniemi, Finland (project)

1922 Tribune Tower, Chicago (competition project)

1923 Plan for the lake front, Chicago (project)

1925 Christian Science Church, Minneapolis (project)

1926/
30 Cranbrook School for Boys, Bloomfield Hills, Michigan

1926/
41 Cranbrook Academy of Art, Bloomfield Hills, Michigan

1927 Palace of the League of Nations, Geneva, Switzerland (competition project)

1928/
29 Saarinen House, Bloomfield Hills, Michigan

1929/
30 Kingswood School for Girls, Cranbrook, Bloomfield Hills, Michigan
Hudnut House, New York (with Ely Jacques Kahn)

1931 Stevens Institute of Technology, Hoboken, New Jersey

1931/
33 Institute of Science, Cranbrook, Bloomfield Hills, Michigan

1933 Alexander Hamilton Memorial, Chicago (project)

1935 Alko Factory and Office Building, Helsinki (competition project)

1937/
38 Community House, Fenton, Michigan (with Eero Saarinen)

1938 Area plan for Goucher College, Baltimore, Maryland (competition project; with Eero Saarinen)
Berkshire Music Center, Tanglewood, Massachusetts (with Eero Saarinen)

1938/
40   Kleinhans Music Hall, Buffalo, New York (with Eero Saarinen)

1939   Smithsonian Institution Art Gallery, Washington, D.C. (project; with Eero Saarinen and J. Robert Swanson)

1939/
40   Crow Island School, Winnetka, Illinois (with Eero Saarinen, and Perkins, Wheeler and Will)

1940/
42   Tabernacle Church of Christ, Columbus, Indiana (with Eero Saarinen)

1940/
43   Museum and Library, Cranbrook Academy of Art, Bloomfield Hills, Michigan

1941   Oberlin College, Ohio (project; with Eero Saarinen and Richard Kimball)
  Houses, school and community hall, Center Line, Michigan (with Eero Saarinen and J. Robert Swanson)

1941/
42   A. C. Wermuth House, Fort Wayne, Indiana (with Eero Saarinen)
  Willow Run Housing Units, Michigan (with Eero Saarinen and J. Robert Swanson)

1942   Schools, Willow Run, Michigan (with Eero Saarinen and J. Robert Swanson)
  Group plan and architectural scheme for Wayne State University, Detroit (competition project; with Eero Saarinen and J. Robert Swanson)
  Summer Opera House and Chamber Music Hall, Berkshire Music Center, Tanglewood, Massachusetts (with Eero Saarinen)

1943   Lincoln Heights Housing Area, Washington, D.C. (with Eero Saarinen and J. Robert Swanson)

1943/
44   Parliament Building, Quito, Ecuador (competition project; with Eero Saarinen and J. Robert Swanson)

1944   Town plan for New Castle, Indiana (with Eero Saarinen and J. Robert Swanson)

1944/
48   Edmundson Memorial Museum, Des Moines Art Center, Iowa (with Eero Saarinen and J. Robert Swanson)

1945   Plan for Washtenaw County, Michigan (with Eero Saarinen and J. Robert Swanson)
  Development plan for Antioch College, Yellow Springs, Ohio (with Eero Saarinen and J. Robert Swanson)

1945/
49   Women's Dormitory, Antioch College, Yellow Springs, Ohio (with Eero Saarinen and J. Robert Swanson)

1946   H. H. Houston Community Development Plan, Outer Roxborough, Philadelphia (with Eero Saarinen)

1946/
47   Campus development plan for Drake University, Des Moines, Iowa (with Eero Saarinen and J. Robert Swanson)
  Women's Dormitory, Drake University, Des Moines, Iowa (with Eero Saarinen)

1946/
48   Christ Church, Cincinnati, Ohio (with Eero Saarinen)

1946/
49   Science and Pharmacy Building, Drake University, Des Moines, Iowa (with Eero Saarinen, J. Robert Swanson, and Brooks and Borg)

1947   Civic Center, Detroit (with Eero Saarinen)
  Campus development plan for Stephens College, Columbia, Missouri (with Eero Saarinen)
  Chapel, Stephens College, Columbia, Missouri (with Eero Saarinen)
  Peoples Bank and Trust Company Building, Fort Wayne, Indiana (with Eero Saarinen)

Publications:

By SAARINEN: books—*Munksnas-Haga*, with Gustaf Strengell, Helsinki 1915; The *Cranbrook Development*, Bloomfield Hills, Michigan 1931; *The City: Its Growth, Its Decay, Its Future*, New York 1943; *Search for Form*, New York 1948; articles—"Stadtplanung für Reval" in *Der Stadtbau* (Cologne), vol. XVIII, no. 5/6, 1921; "Lausunto Eraista Helsingin Kaupungin Asemakaavakysmyksista" in *Helsingin Kaupungin Keskiosien Yleisasemakaavaehdotus*, Helsinki 1932; "Architecture in the Post-War World" in *Art Digest* (New York), August 1943; "Eliel Saarinen Receives the Gold Medal: The Citation and Mr. Saarinen's Response" in *AIA Journal* (Washington, D.C.), June 1947.

On SAARINEN: books—*L'Architecture à l'Exposition Universelle de 1900*, Paris 1900; *Konhistoria* by Carl G. Laurin, Stockholm 1901; *Kun Suuret Olivat Pienia* by Helmi Setala, Helsinki 1911; *Suomen Taiteen Historia* by Johannes Ohquist, Helsinki 1912; *Pro Helsingfors* by Bertel Jung, Helsinki 1918; *Ausstellung neuer amerikanischer Baukunst*, publication of the Akademie der Künste, Berlin 1926; *The Story of Architecture in America* by Thomas E. Tallmadge, New York 1927; *Byggnaden som Konstverk* by Gustaf Strengell, Helsinki 1928; *Modern Architecture* by Henry-Russell Hitchcock Jr., New York 1929; *History of the Skyscraper* by Francisco Mujica, Paris 1929; *Living Architecture* by Arthur Woltersdorf, Chicago 1930; *Byggnadskonst i Finland*, Helsinki 1932; *The New Architecture and the Bauhaus* by Walter Gropius, London 1935; *Modern Building* by Walter Curt Behrendt, New York 1937; *Architecture Through the Ages* by Talbot Hamlin, New York 1940; *Space, Time and Architecture* by Sigfried Giedion, Cambridge, Massachusetts 1941; *The Architectonic City in the Americas* by Hugo Leipziger, Austin, Texas 1944; *Tolv kapitel om Munksnas* by Per Nystrom, Helsinki 1945; *Asemakaavaoppi* by Otto Meurman, Helsinki 1947; *Eliel Saarinen* by Albert Christ-Janer, Chicago, London and Toronto 1948; articles—"Eliel Saarinen" by J. Robert Swanson in *Michigan Technic* (Ann Arbor,), May 1924; "Eliel Saarinen" by Donnell Tilghman in *Architectural Record* (New York), May 1928; "L'Architecte Eliel Saarinen" by Gustaf Strengell in *L'Art Vivant* (Paris), 15 October 1928; "Eliel Saarinen" by Bertel Jung in *Arkitekten* (Copenhagen), vol. XXIX, no. 3, 1932; "Eliel Saarinen, Master of Design" by Kenneth Reid in *Pencil Points* (New York), September 1936; "Eliel Saarinen" by Aulis Blomstedt in *Arkkitehti* (Helsinki), no. 11/12, 1943; "Eliel Saarinen: An Appreciation" by Kent Barker in *Journal of the Royal Architectural Institute of Canada* (Toronto), December 1944; "Gesellius-Lindgren-Saarinen" by Marika Hausen in *Arkkitehti* (Helsinki), no 9, 1967; "The Helsinki Railway Station in Eliel Saarinen's First Versions, 1904" by Marika Hausen in *Studies in Art History 3*, Helsinki 1977.

*

Eliel Saarinen is one of the few architects of modern times who has received less credit than he deserves. Many of his ideas are rooted in the pre-International Style days. During the height of the International Style vogue they were virtually lost. However, they were ideas of such power that they have survived its demise, and only now are they beginning to establish their place in the forefront.

In his drawing for the Chicago Tribune Tower competition, Saarinen, without resorting to stylistic eclecticism, established the concept of a tall building woven in all of its parts into a harmonious whole, a continuous flow from ground to sky. This is a stark contrast to the usual "high rise" of today in which the typical floor is repeated mindlessly to the top, where the building is brutally cut off as a pair of scissors might cut a mechanically printed ribbon. Only now is the whole building beginning to return as the design unit.

Yet Saarinen's greatest message is that the object

of architecture is not the building at all but rather the harmonious relationship of building and open space, and that this harmony does not stop at any arbitrary boundary or lot line but extends ever outward into the depths of the city. This led him to a major preoccupation with city planning.

In 1912 Saarinen entered the competition for the design of the new Capital for Australia, Canberra. Here, as in Chicago, his design was given second place, so his ideas remained on paper.

Saarinen's opportunity actually to build the environment he had dreamed about came some ten years after his arrival in the United States from Finland, when George and Ellen Scripps Booth founded the Cranbrook Academy of Art in Bloomfield Hills outside of Detroit, and asked Saarinen to design it and the nearby boys' and girls' schools. Through his collaboration with Swedish sculptor Carl Milles, and his work with his wife, the great weaver Loja, and others, he integrated art and crafts into architecture in a way that still is unmatched, and he created here one of the very few totally harmonious environments in the United States.

Saarinen did everything he could to turn the central flow of architectural energy away from preoccupation with the individual structure into concern for the larger organism of the city. The fact that his voice was ignored has exacted a tragic toll because of the inability of the design profession to deal with the creative possibilities offered by the government program of Urban Renewal. Because so few had heeded his admonition the profession as a whole was unprepared for the avalanche of responsibility that Urban Renewal placed on it, and made a terrible botch of a wonderful opportunity. In city after city in the United States the basic urban fabric was torn apart for architectural non-entities, or, even worse, for vacant open wounds which still remain.

Saarinen saw clearly that his ideas would have their fullest expression in the distant future, and set about to bridge the gap created by the misunderstanding and rejection which surrounded him. At Cranbrook he established an Academy which, more than any other, resembled the Academy of classical times. Here, through personal contact, he was able to influence young minds with the vision he possessed in a way far more effective than he ever was able to achieve through his books. The students who worked with him there, including Charles Eames, Carl Feiss, Harry Weese, Harry Bertoia, Florence Knoll and myself, are trying to bring these ideas alive today.

Eliel Saarinen laid out for the architectural profession a design for its future course which it may well decide to follow.

—Edmund N. Bacon

SAÉNZ DE OÍZA, Francisco (Javier).

Spanish. Born in Madrid, 12 October 1918. Educated at the Escuela Tecnica Superior Arquitectura, Madrid; Colegio de Çataluna y Baleares, Barcelona, Dip.Arch. 1946. In private practice, Madrid, since 1947. Professor, Escuela Tecnica Superior Arquitectura, Madrid. Recipient: First Prize, with Laorga, Basilica of Aránzazu Competition, 1949; First Prize, with Laorga, Basilica of La Merced Competition, 1949; Spanish National Architecture Prize, with Romaní y Oteiza, 1954; First Prize, Universidad Autonoma de Madrid Competition, 1970; First Prize, Montecarlo Competition, 1970; First Prize, University of Cordoba Competition, 1978. Address (office): Avenida de Portugal 55, Madrid, Spain.

Works:

1949   Basilica, Aránzazu, Spain (competition project; with Laorga)

Basilica, La Merced, Spain (competition project; with Laorga)
1951 Entrevías Public Housing Development, Madrid
1954 Camino de Santiago Chapel, Spain (with Romaní y Oteiza)
     Fuencarral Public Housing Development, Madrid
     Barrios de Puerta del Angel Public Housing Development, Madrid
1955 Batán Public Housing Development, Madrid
1960 House, Talavera de la Reina, Spain
1961 Ciudad Blanca Terraced Housing Development, Alcudia, Majorca
     Exhibition Hall, Huarte, Spain
1962 Torres Blancas Apartment Complex, Madrid
     Loyola Housing Development, Carabanchel, Spain (with J. L. Romany Aranda, E. Mangada Samain, and C. Ferran Alfaro)
1965 Horizonte Satellite Town, near Madrid (project; with J. L. Romany Aranda, E. Mangada Samain, and C. Ferran Alfaro)
1969/
70 Universidad Autónoma de Madrid y Bilbao, Madrid
1970 Montecarlo Development (competition project)
1971 Casa Huarte, Majorca
1971/
78 Bank of Bilbao, Madrid
1978 University of Cordoba, Spain (competition project)

Publications:

By SAENZ DE OIZA: article—"El Vidrio y la Arquitectura" in *Revista Nacional de Arquitectura* (Madrid), September/October 1952.

On SAENZ DE OIZA: articles—"Urbanizacion 'Ciudad Blanca,' Alcudia (Mallorca)" in *Cuadernos de Arquitectura* (Barcelona), no. 58, 1964; "Grupo de Vivendas Loyola" in *Hogar y Arquitectura* (Madrid), August 1965; "Einfamilienhauser" in *Baumeister* (Munich), December 1966; "Espagne—Madrid, Barcelone" in *L'Architecture d'Aujourd'hui* (Paris), April/May 1970; "Competition in Cordoba" by Jeronimo Junquera in *Arquitectura* (Madrid), January/February 1978; "Seven Masters of Madrid and 7 + 7 Young Architects" by Alberto Campo Baeza in *Architecture + Urbanism* (Tokyo), March 1978.

Francisco Saénz de Oíza is possibly the most complex and attractive personality in Spanish architecture of the last 25 years. His work is an exacting history of the progress of modern trends in this country.

His early career belongs to that period of historical reaction of the first years of Franco's regime, and his works of that time are a modernized version and revision of previously accepted conceptions. It was only during the 1950's that he began to break with these traditions. His original tendencies are still evident in the projects for basilicas in Aránzazu and La Merced, designed in collaboration with Laorga, both of which won their respective competitions to become accepted as "standards." But as the 1950's progressed, Saénz de Oíza's work began to show the growing influence of modernist ideals. In trying to make up for lost time, Saénz de Oíza (and other Spanish architects) moved quickly, with an almost pre-ordained determination, towards the goal of "modernism," a goal that had been abandoned and lost among the tragedies and upheavals of the 1930's and 40's.

Saénz de Oíza became one of the staunchest critics of official modern culture. He identified his ideal as that of the most orthodox modernism—a faith in architecture as a social response, encompassing what is functional and constructive. This ideal helps to explain his total dedication in the early 1950's to state sponsored housing developments in Madrid—Barrios de Puerta del Angel, Fuencarral, Batán, and Entrevías. All of these developments reveal his careful realism, his professionalism: they became the basis of his influence.

In 1954 Saénz de Oíza and Romaní y Oteiza shared the National Architecture Prize for the Chapel on the Camino de Santiago. The influence of Mies is evident in the use of technology as an expressive tool. The Chapel testifies to the poetic force of such language; it seems to demonstrate that, no matter how diverse the subjects of works may be, technology is always of paramount importance.

In the late 1950's Saénz de Oíza seemed to change again, to be reacting to positions like that of Bruno Zevi, who criticized the early ideas of the modern movement. The Ciudad Blanca in Alcudia expresses itself in terms of crude realism, and the House in Talavera de la Reina, or the Exhibition Hall in Huarte, reveal a Nordic influence—like much of the architecture of Madrid in the 1960's. Thereafter his career, and his notions, progressed rapidly. In 1962, with the Torres Blancas Apartment Complex, his work transcended strictly national boundaries and, like the Sydney Opera House by Utzon, became the center of an international controversy. The explosion, to a great extent, was the destruction of early modernist ideals.

Yet if this was a revolutionary moment in Spanish architecture, it was not pure revolution. The irony is that destruction of some of the primitive ideals of modernism co-exist in Torres Blancas with a near perfect realization of other of those ideals. It may be that in Spain the very eagerness to import modern trends (trends that had developed more slowly in other countries) caused this kind of error; what is certain is that the work of Saénz de Oíza, and that of many other architects of the time, is guilty of the error. Saénz de Oíza can be justly accused of searching for new ideals while in practice skilfully rescuing a concept of architecture that insists on rigorous functionalism and technological means.

Yet, in the late 1960's and the 1970's there has been notable progress. Saénz de Oíza *has* gone on to produce works that more closely approximate his own ideals—the Universidad Autónoma de Madrid y Bilbao, the Montecarlo Development project, and the Casa Huarte in Majorca all show an increasing mastery. The Banco de Bilbao in Madrid confirms the trend; it is certainly one of the most sophisticated tower buildings in Europe. And recently, in the project for the University of Cordoba, Saénz de Oíza has created a strong work far removed from the mirage of modernism. His motto, "Utilitas, Firmitas, Venestas," suggests that he will persevere in his belief that the knowledge of architectural means is the way to make the old adage come true.

—Anton Capitel

SAFDIE, Moshe.
Canadian/Israeli. Born in Haifa, Israel, 14 July 1938; moved to Canada, 1955; acquired Canadian nationality (also retaining Israeli nationality), 1959. Educated at McGill University, Montreal, 1955–61, B.Arch. (honours) 1961. Reserve Soldier (Private) in the Israeli Army Corps of Education. Married Nina Nusynowicz in 1959; children: Taal and Oren. Architect with van Ginkel and Associates, Montreal, 1961–62, and with Louis I. Kahn, Philadelphia, 1962–63; Section Head, Canadian Corporation for the 1967 World Exhibition, Montreal, 1963–64. In private practice, Montreal, since 1964, and Jerusalem, since 1971. Visiting Professor, McGill University, 1970; Davenport Professor of Architecture, Yale University, New Haven, Connecticut, 1971. Since 1975, Professor of Architecture and Director of the Desert Architecture and Environment Department, Desert Research Institute, Ben Gurion University, Beersheva, Negev, Israel; since 1978, Professor of Architecture and Urban Design, Graduate School of Design, Harvard University, Cambridge, Massachusetts. Exhibitions: Baltimore Museum of Art, subsequently toured San Francisco, New York, Chicago, Ottawa, and Des Moines, Iowa, 1973. Recipient: Canadian Lieutenant-Governor's Gold Medal, 1961; Massey Medal for Architecture, Canada, 1968; Gold Star Award, Philadelphia College of Art, 1970; Architect of the Year Award, American Institute of Registered Architects, 1971; Award of Excellence, *Canadian Architect*, 1972, 1973. Address: Moshe Safdie Architect, 1315 Boulevard de Maisonneuve West, Montreal, Quebec H3G 1M4, Canada.

Works:

1967 Habitat '67, Montreal
1968 Habitat New York (project)
     Student Union, San Francisco State College (project)
     Fort Lincoln Urban Renewal Plan, Washington, D.C. (project)
1968/
72 Habitat Puerto Rico, San Juan
1970 Habitat for Tropaco, U.S. Virgin Islands (project)
     Habitat, Indian Carry, Saranac Lake, New York (project)
1971 Plan for Coldspring New Town, Baltimore
1971/
79 Yeshivat Porat Joseph Rabbinical College, Jerusalem
1972 Master plan for Mamilah Central Business District, Jerusalem
1974 Desert Research Institute and Ben Gurion Archives, Sde Boqer, Negev, Israel
     Master plan for the Western Wall Precinct, Jerusalem
1976 Paley Youth Wing, Jerusalem
     Master plan for Keur Farah Pahlavi New Town, Senegal, West Africa
1977 Habitat Elahieh, Tehran
     Blood Transfusion Centres, Ivory Coast, West Africa

Publications:

By SAFDIE: books—*Beyond Habitat*, Cambridge, Massachusetts 1970; *For Everyone a Garden*, Cambridge, Massachusetts 1974; *Habitat Bill of Rights* (pamphlet), with Sert, Ardalan, Doshi, and Candilis, Tehran 1976; articles—"On from Habitat" in *Design* (London), October 1967; "Post Mortem on Habitat: Anatomy of a System" in *RIBA Journal* (London), November 1967; "The Changing Environment: Hell or Utopia?" in *Midway* (Chicago), Summer 1968; "Industrialized Buildings: Variety Within Repetition" in *Architecture Canada* (Toronto), November 1968; "Habitat '67" in *Beyond Left and Right*, edited by Richard Kostelanetz, New York 1968; "Presentation of Habitat, Puerto Rico and New York, Fort Lincoln and San Francisco" in *Architectural Design* (London), January 1969; "New Environmental Requirements for Urban Building" in *Zodiac* (Milan), no. 19, 1969; "A View of Cities in 2024 A.D." in *Saturday Review World* (New York), August 1974; "Collective Consciousness in Making Environment" in *The Frontiers of Knowledge*, New York 1975.

On SAFDIE: book—*Habitat '67*, Ottawa 1967; articles—"Habitat '67" in *Engineering News Record* (New York), April 1965; "Habitat '67" in *Building Management* (Toronto), October 1965; "Correspondence Exchanged on Urban Problems" in *Business Quarterly* (London, Ontario), Summer 1966; "Habitat '67" in *Progressive Architecture* (New York), October 1966; "Habitat '67" by David Jacobs in *Horizon* (New York), Winter 1967; "Habitat '67" by

Moshe Safdie: Habitat '67, Montreal, 1967

Alexander Pyke in *Architectural Design* (London), March 1967; "Post Mortem on Habitat '67" by A. E. Komendant in *Progressive Architecture* (New York), March 1968; "Fort Lincoln Urban Renewal Project" in *Bauen und Wohnen* (Zurich), May 1969; "Moshe Safdie" by Israel Shenker in *Horizon* (New York), Winter 1973; "An Interview with Safdie" in *Ariel* (Jerusalem), 1973; "Building Systems and Growth: A Look into the Future in *The Designer* (New York), February 1974; "Seven Years after Habitat" in *Time* (Montreal), 15 July 1974; "Entre-vue avec l'architecte Moshe Safdie" in *Regards sur Israel* (Montreal), March/April 1975; "Five Architects" in *Art and Architecture* (Tehran), April 1975; "Habitat Lives" in *Newsweek* (New York), 9 February 1976; "Safdie's Design for the Western Wall Precinct, Jerusalem" in *Baumeister* (Munich), August 1976; "New Mamilah Will Rise Outside Jerusalem's Walls" in *Architectural Record* (New York), October 1977; "A New Setting for the Western Wall" by Mildred F. Schmertz in *Architectural Record* (New York), April 1978; "Rebuilding Jerusalem: The Work of Moshe Safdie's Practice" by Alan and Sylvia Blanc in *Building Design* (London), 10 November 1978; "Building a New Jerusalem" by Peter Davey in *The Architects' Journal* (London), 29 November 1978; "Safdie Goes Back to Basics" by Annette LeCuyer in *Building Design* (London), 11 May 1979.

Rather than attempting to make a statement here on my work, I would prefer that readers refer to my writings listed above to learn of my theories and work as an architect.

—Moshe Safdie

Although nearly fifteen years have passed since the revolutionary housing project "Habitat" was erected in Montreal in 1967, Israeli born Moshe Safdie is still best known for this, the first major project of his career. Safdie studied at McGill University in Montreal, and then worked for two years in the office of Louis Kahn. He opened private practice in 1964, and he designed "Habitat" shortly thereafter. Nevertheless, his offices in Montreal and Jerusalem have been far from quiet since then, and much of his more recent work has demonstrated a continuing commitment to progressive experimentation, but with a more ripened sense of design and architectural finesse.

"Habitat" was a controversial project, criticized both because it looked unlike any piece of architecture that had ever been produced before that time, and because, like any prototype, it suffered from various miscalculations and mistakes that made the building terribly costly, partially inefficient, and occasionally unworkable. Still, as the first major prefabricated housing complex in the world, "Habitat" was indeed a breakthrough. Safdie's unabashed design made no aesthetic compromises towards more conventional construction, which it wasn't, and the use of the units as building blocks celebrated the independence and integrity of each component. An even more exciting gesture was Safdie's careful consideration of amenities such as private gardens, unobstructed views, and individual access which proved that mass produced housing need not be aimed only for the poor.

Far too few units (only 158) were built at "Habitat" to make the project and the prefabricating operation cost efficient, but Safdie repeated the project in Puerto Rico for a fraction of the cost. There, the bottom line per unit was low enough to qualify for government assisted programs designated for low to middle income housing.

In the late 1960's and early 1970's Safdie's work became more diffuse, and his work included both small building projects, such as the San Francisco State College Student Union, and massive urban design schemes, including a much documented plan for a new town near Baltimore, Maryland, called Cold-spring.

Transferring his attention to issues unlike those confronted in school and during his early career, when he focused his efforts almost exclusively on prefabricated housing, gave Safdie a chance to explore the potentials of prefabrication and his own personal expression in completely different contexts. The experience proved to be a strengthening one, and when he began work on several projects in Jerusalem in the mid-1970's, he appeared more confident and capable than his earlier work had demonstrated. He designed a huge plaza for the large area now cleared in front of the Western Wall, the last remaining remnant of the retaining wall of the Second Temple and the holiest relic on Earth for the Jewish people. It expertly uses level changes and geometrical ordering devices to create a space that allows ten people to pray in comfort, but could also accommodate a celebration of three thousand people, or a demonstration of fifty thousand. He also designed a twenty acre business district for Mamilah, the former demilitarized zone that separated the old and new cities when the older portion was controlled by Jordan.

The most impressive of the Jerusalem projects, though, and the most significant in terms of Safdie's own personal expression, is his Yeshivat Porat Joseph Rabbinical College, recently completed in the heart of the Jewish Quarter of the old city, and overlooking the Western Wall Plaza. The school is an interesting mixture of bold structure, modern highlights (including repetitive, transparent glass domes that diffract colored light on their inner surfaces), and environmental sensitivity and response. Despite the frankness of the contemporary structure, the Yeshivat blends into the ancient city perfectly, and mimics traditional patterns of color, texture, shape, and proportion.

All of the Jerusalem projects display the frenzied, but handsome sense of movement that has been a trademark of Safdie's work, but they also demonstrate an improved ability to deform that expression to remain sensitive to surroundings. Still, in plan, all of the projects continue to be organized largely based on geometrical maneuvers, not unlike those used at "Habitat" and the San Francisco Student Union. While the geometries that Safdie has favored throughout his career have certainly increased the rationality of his arrangements, they have also frequently been the biggest cause of economic difficulty, by jacking expense needlessly to retain theoretical design purity.

Regardless of the effectiveness of Safdie's geometry, his resolution of problems of high density construction with completely three dimensional solutions has been a great architectural contribution. Safdie is a theorist who should be admired for the boldness of his experimentation. If occasionally his work lacks the refinement of a more conservative practitioner, it is only because Safdie realizes that unless one dares to skirt failure, no advance can be made.

—Mitchell B. Rouda

SAKAKURA, Junzo.

Japanese. Born in Hashima City, Gifu Prefecture, 29 May 1901. Educated at the Tokyo University School of Art, 1923–27; studied architecture in Paris, 1929–30; apprentice/assistant in the office of Le Corbusier, Paris, 1931–36. Married Yuri Sakakura in 1939; children: Haruna, Miho, and Takenosuke. Worked as a community planner in Manchuria, 1939; in private practice, Tokyo, 1939–46; Principal, Junzo Sakakura and Associates, Tokyo, 1947 until his death, 1969 (associates: Fumitaka Nishizawa, now President; Taisaku Cho; Seizo Sakata; Akira Yamaki; Shinichiro Takemura; Takanobu Ohta; and Toshitsugu Nunokawa); branch office established in Osaka, 1948. President, Japan Architects Association, 1964–68. Recipient: Grand Prize, *World's Fair*, Paris, 1937. *Died 1 September 1969.*

Works:

1937 Japanese Pavilion, *World's Fair*, Paris
1941 Iihashi House, Todoroki, Setagaya-ku, Tokyo
1941/
50 Pre-fabricated wooden houses, Tokyo
1944 Tatsumura House, Takarazuka, Hyogo Prefecture, Japan
1948 Low-cost bamboo furniture
1950 Osaka Baseball Stadium
Takashimaya Department Store remodelling, Namba, Osaka
1951 Department of Higher Education, Franco-Japanese Institute, Tokyo
Kamakura Museum of Modern Art, Kamakura, Kanagawa Prefecture, Japan
Club Kanto, Chiyoda-ku, Tokyo
1952 Club Kansai, Osaka

1954 Taro Okamoto House, Minato-ku, Tokyo
Muroga House, Nikawa, Nishinomiya, Hyogo Prefecture, Japan
Suzuki House, Ashiya City, Hyogo Prefecture, Japan
Maruyama Hydro-Electric Power Plant, Gifu Prefecture, Japan
Tohkyu Kaikan Building, Shibuya, Tokyo
1955 International House of Japan, Minato-ku, Tokyo (with Kunio Mayekawa and Junzo Yoshimura)
Shiono House, Shukugawa, Nishinomiya, Hyogo Prefecture, Japan
1956 Tohkyu Bunka Kaikan Building, Shibuya, Tokyo
Diesel Memorial Garden, Augsburg, West Germany
1957 Exhibition design at the *Triennale*, Milan
1958 Shirokiya Department Store remodelling, Tokyo
1959 Hajima City Hall, Gifu Prefecture, Japan
National Museum of Western Art, Taito-ku, Tokyo (with Le Corbusier, Kunio Mayekawa, and Takamasa Yosizaka)
Silk Center, Yokohama
Hakuba Tokyu Hotel, Nagano Prefecture, Japan
Iga-Ueno City Public Hall, Mie Prefecture, Japan
Yamaha Company Employees' Seaside Recreation Center, Bentenjima, Hamamatsu, Shizuoka, Japan
1960 Exhibition design at the *Triennale*, Milan
Air France Office, in the Hibiya Mitsui Building, Tokyo (with Charlotte Perriand)

Junzo Sakakura: Kamakura Museum of Modern Art, Kamakura, Kanagawa Prefecture, Japan, 1951

Hannan High School, Osaka
1961 Shionogi Pharmaceutical Company Central Laboratory, Osaka
1962 Kure City Hall and Cultural Center, Hiroshima Prefecture, Japan
Shionogi Pharmaceutical Company Warehouse and Office, Kuise, Hyogo Prefecture, Japan
Toray Company Basic Research Laboratory, Kanagawa Prefecture, Japan
1963 Saga Prefectural Gymnasium, Saga City, Japan
Highway Toll-Gate (prototype)
1964 Hiraoka City Hall, Osaka
Hotel Sanai (Park Hotel), Sapporo, Hokkaido, Japan
Iwate Broadcasting Company Building, Morioka City, Iwate Prefecture, Japan
Shipping Center, Takashimaya Department Store, Osaka
1965 Annex, Kamakura Museum of Modern Art, Kanagawa Prefecture, Japan
Iga-Ueno City Hall, Mie Prefecture, Japan
Shin Akasaka Building, Minato-ku, Tokyo
Gymnasium, Ueno Municipal Nishi Primary School, Ueno City, Mie Prefecture, Japan
1966 Nagoya Terminal Station Building, Aichi Prefecture, Japan
Westside Concourse, Shinjiku Station, and Underground Parking Garage, Shinjuku, Tokyo
Osaka Youth Outdoor Activities Center
1967 Gifu City Municipal Culture Center, Japan
Yamaguchi Prefectural Museum, Yamaguchi City, Japan
Kohshiro Matsumoto House, Minato-ku, Tokyo
Odakyu Department Store and Shinjuku Terminal, Shinjuku, Tokyo
1968 Takashimaya Kohsakusho Furniture Factory, Minoh City, Osaka
Hajima City Municipal Cultural Center, Gifu Prefecture, Japan
Shionogi Pharmaceutical Company Factory, Settsu City, Osaka
1969 Hotel Blue Sky, Shirahama, Wakayama Prefecture, Japan
Kashikojima Country Club House, Mic Prefecture, Japan
Electric Power Pavilion, *Expo '70*, Osaka
25 vocational schools, Thailand
Westside Annex Building, Shibuya Station, Tokyo

Publications:

By SAKAKURA: article—"Témoinages pour Le Corbusier," with Nicholas Colley, in *L'Architecture d'Aujourd'hui* (Paris), February/March 1966.

On SAKAKURA: articles—"Three New Buildings in Osaka by Junzo Sakakura and Associates" in *Kokusai Kentiku* (Tokyo), May 1956; "Air France, Tokyo" in *The Japan Architect* (Tokyo), December 1960; "The Architects," in special issue on Japan of *Architectural Review* (London), September 1962; "Gusto di Junzo Sakakura" in *L'Architettura* (Rome), September 1965; "A Profile of Junzo Sakakura" by Ryuichi Hamaguchi in *The Japan Architect* (Tokyo), November 1966; "Hommage à Sakakura" by Mayekawa, Sato, Perriand, Prouvé and Takemura in *L'Architecture d'Aujourd'hui* (Paris), October/November 1969.

Architecture is presented to us by Junzo Sakakura as a compact entity that patiently awaits our coming in order to exist, then overflows our conception; it is there, in our midst, dense and impenetrable, like a stone or a tree; it endures; finally, it is what it is. These characteristics are perhaps a consequence of Sakakura's six-year meditation in the office of Le Corbusier.

At best, as in the courtyard houses in Osaka, Sakakura's work has a cave-like quality, featuring an interiority well directed and orchestrated by the thick concrete threshold he sometimes mounted around the site to present the architectural entity. At worst, the raw concrete imprisons, the entity interrupts the flow of human occurrences, making of the architecture a ludicrously heavy mass. Sometimes the whole is relieved by a delicacy of curve, an organic incident, such as the pitched roofs on the Osaka Youth Outdoor Activities Centre, or an improbable angle or an unprecedented detail, such as the giant ventilation snorkels undermining the overzealous devotion to the developer's dream in the Shinjuku Station project.

Massive concrete work doesn't necessarily insist on absolute and nihilistic enclosure; there are ways of relieving it through modelling and perforation. Too often, however, Sakakura thought only of keeping out the forces of the Japanese city—for him, unknown terrors lurked in every corner, and his only thought was to keep them out of the private domain of his own project. But, of course, by so doing, he unwittingly added to the terrors of the public domain.

Some Japanese architects tend to design as if they were sitting an exam: each one works on his own, jealous of his own performance, selfish, ready to come up with a tenuous, barely consolidated result rather than own up that he might welcome a bit of help from his neighbour. In architecture, this attitude can produce an environment of urgent morphologies and sensational architectural monsters or one of notorious vanity and ostentatious consumption. Although much of Sakakura's work was strong and possibly enduring, it as often seemed to be guilty of one or the other of these flaws.

—Chris Fawcett

SALMONA, Rogelio.

Colombian. Born in Paris, France, 28 April 1929. Educated at the Universidad Nacional de Colombia, Bogota, 1947–48, 1957–62, Dip.Arch. 1962; student-/apprentice, studio of Le Corbusier, Paris, 1949–58; Ecole des Hautes Etudes Sociales, Sorbonne, Paris, under Pierre Francastel, 1948–57; Ecole d'Arts et Metiers, Paris, 1952–56. Married Michelle Clement in 1959; children: Pablo and Juan. In private practice, Bogota, since 1958. Exhibition: Universidad Autonoma de Mexico City, 1977 (one-man show). Recipient: First Prize, Colombian Architects Association Headquarters Competition, Bogota, 1971; National Prize, Colombian Architects Association, 1977. Address: Residencias El Parque, Carrera 5, No. 26–39, Bogota, Colombia.

Works:

1959 El Polo (apartment building), Bogota (with Guillermo Bermudez)
High School, Bogota
1961 House, Santa Ana Sector, Bogota
1961/
63 Residencias los Cerros (low-income apartments), Bogota
1962 High School, Bogota
1963 Residencias San Cristobal (low-income apartments), Bogota
1965 Timiza (housing and urban development), Bogota (project)
House, Cabrera Sector, Bogota
House, Santa Margerita Sector, Bogota
1965/
70 Residencias El Parque (apartments), Bogota
1966 House, Los Rosales Sector, Bogota
1968 House, El Refugio Sector, Bogota
1969 Usatama (urban development), Bogota (project)

Low-rise, multi-family housing development, Pereira, Colombia (project)
1970 Calle 72 (apartment building), Bogota
El Museo (apartment building), Bogota
City Hall, Bogota
Independence Park renovation, Bogota
Alba House, El Chico Sector, Bogota
1971 El Rodadero (apartment building), Santa Marta, Colombia
El Retiro (apartment building), Bogota
Colombian Architects Association Headquarters, Bogota
Automobile and Touring Club Headquarters, Bogota (with Luis Esguerra)
House, Bosque el Retiro Sector, Bogota
1974 Rafael Nunez (housing and urban development), Bogota
1975 San Diego (office and housing complex), Bogota
Museum of Modern Art, Bogota
House, Suba Sector, Bogota
1976 El Pinar (apartment building), Bogota
House, Bosque el Retiro Sector, Bogota
1977 Arango House, Bogota
1978 Alto de Los Pinos (apartment building), Bogota
Country house, Tabio, Colombia
1978/
79 Housing and Urban Development, Cali, Colombia (project)
1979 Gaitan Popular Museum, Bogota

Publications:

On SALMONA: books—*New Directions in Latin-American Architecture* by Francisco Bullrich, New York and London 1969; *Multi-Storey Housing* by Karl W. Smith, Stuttgart 1970; articles—"In South America: After Corbu, What's Happening?" in *Progressive Architecture* (New York), September 1966; "Immeuble d'Habitation à Bogota" and "Habitat" in *Architecture d'Aujourd'hui* (Paris), February/-March 1967; "Logements Economiques à Bogota" in *A.C. 49* (Zurich), 1968; "L'Architettura di Rogelio Salmona" in *Controspazio* (Bari, Italy), no. 8, 1972; "The Architecture of Rogelio Salmona" by J. A. Acebillo in *Arquitecturas Bis* (Barcelona), September 1975; "Amaral House, Bogota" in *Architecture d'Aujourd'hui* (Paris), no. 192, 1977.

The works of Le Corbusier exerted a notable influence throughout the world, particularly in Latin America, where his ideas were adopted by a generation of architects who carried out the modernization of local architecture. Le Corbusier had also proposed urbanization plans for the South American cities of Buenos Aires and Rio de Janeiro, and in 1949 the Colombian government commissioned him to draw up a pilot plan for the capital, Bogota, a plan that was later developed by Josep Lluis Sert and Paul Lester Wiener. The plan is based on the principle of urban sectors; the land is divided into rectangular areas; there is an efficient rapid transit system. As in other Latin American countries, the influence of the International Style was already great in Colombia, and with the creation of the Bogota plan, Colombian architecture took a markedly rationalist road. It is within this context that the work of Rogelio Salmona should be analyzed.

Salmona worked for a number of years in Le Corbusier's studio in Paris, but on returning to Colombia he became, paradoxically, one of his former teacher's most outspoken critics. One of the reasons may well have been that the great man's precepts had begun to look more and more inappropriate in Colombia. During the 1950's a series of profound social changes had taken place: there was a displacement of masses of people to the cities, with an attendant deterioration of the environment; simultaneously, of course, there was wholesale real estate speculation, from which it followed that "rentability" became a prime criterion even for the architect. It is precisely in response to this new situation that Salmona developed his own ideas on architecture and urbanization —and these ideas have informed his work ever since.

His ideas are easily summarized. Architecture and city planning in Colombia are in a state of crisis created by the country's rapid urbanization and its attendant economic structure. This crisis is manifested in works that deny the most significant values of Colombian architectural culture, works that offer impoverished images and serve to decrease (rather than enhance) the variety of the urban morphology. Although there are excellent examples of modern architecture in Colombia, most modern works unfortunately support the generalization. By sacrificing the most important social, cultural and topological values, architecture has given in to commercialism and conformity. The ideals of rationalist architecture do not provide the answer, for rationalist models are, almost by intention, foreign to the social and cultural values of their surroundings.

Salmona practices what he preaches. His vision is of an architecture that identifies with a particular and historical place and site, one that adds to by participating in its environment, and this vision is manifest in all his works, particularly the outstanding Residencias El Parque.

Salmona does not accept that the city must look like a chessboard—an image that has become almost an immutable fact of contemporary architecture. Because, with each project, he tries, as it were, to visualize the city afresh, his works are often greeted with controversy and an initial rejection that gradually

dissipates as the virtues of his proposals become apparent. Further, he makes himself unpopular with a certain segment of his society by rejecting the goals of land speculation: in his work, he maintains occupation densities that are appropriate to people. And he often surprises by using his works to incorporate urban space into the environment—evidence of his belief that architecture is made for the whole man, that architecture is as much the property of the community as the sky.

Although this adroit handling of spatial volume is its most notable characteristic, his work is also interesting in other ways. For example, he is concerned with creating original, well-designed low-cost housing for low-income groups. So are architects in many other parts of the world, but in Colombia there is a general attitude that fashionable architects create for fashionable clients: architecture involves a series of signs that denote prestige. As well, Salmona often uses brick, a material that is traditional to Colombia. The choice is not gratuitous. By using brick, he can relate his work to the existing urban landscape.

Yet perhaps, after all, Salmona's greatest accomplishment is that he has made his countrymen look at their cities. His main criticism of rationalist architecture, and its seeming triumph, is that now all cities, particularly Colombian ones, despite their historical, cultural and regional differences, increasingly resemble one another: there is no sense of place; the constructions have no cultural or social meaning. He blames architects themselves for this decline— makes them responsible for contributing to urban

chaos, for responding to extravagant rather than real needs, for giving in to economic power. He makes his countrymen regard the seemingly ubiquitous cement wall that destroys or blocks the Colombian landscape, and reminds them that buildings occupy an urban space that belongs to the entire community.

Salmona has created an alternative. The Residencias El Parque are a good example. The building code allowed for 100% land occupancy. Salmona used 20% of it for buildings, and used the rest for open promenades and gardens for the use of the public. He proposed a series of volumes that would balance the needs of the program, economic rentability, and the characteristics of the site—and created buildings that present an outline appropriate to Bogota, encompass the green background of the city's mountains, and make use of the natural materials of the area.

The never less than superb execution of his vision makes Rogelio Salmona the most important figure in contemporary Colombian architecture.

—Jorge Glusberg

Rogelio Salmona: Residencias El Parque, Bogota, 1970

O. R. Salvisberg: Roche Products Factory, Welwyn Garden City, England, 1939

SALVISBERG, O(tto) R(udolf).

Swiss. Born in Koniz bei Berne, 19 October 1882. Studied painting and architecture at the Technikum, Biel, Switzerland. Assistant in the office of the architects Thiersch and Hocheder, Munich, and subsequently in the office of Curjel and Moser, Karlsruhe, 1906–08; in private practice, Berlin, 1908–29, and in Zurich, 1929 until his death, 1940. Professor, and Head of the Department of Architecture, E.T.H.: Eidgenössische Technischen Hochschule, Zurich, 1929–40. Exhibition: *O. R. Salvisberg*, E.T.H., Zurich, 1941. Recipient: First Prize, Swiss Volksbank Competition, Solothurn, 1926. Honorary Member, Royal Institute of British Architects. *Died* (in Arosa, Switzerland) *23 December 1940*.

Works:

1914 Housing development, Pieseritz bei Wittenberg, Germany
1919 Housing development, Nauen, Germany
1921 Housing development, Dortsfeld bei Dortmund, Germany
1923/
28 Housing development, Kopenick, Germany
1926 Housing development, Ganching i Obbay, Germany
Geyer Film Works, Adlershof, Berlin
Housing, Lichtenberg, Berlin
Housing development, Zehlendorf, Berlin (with Bruno Taut and Hugo Häring)
1927 Church, Stieglitz, Berlin
Town Hall, Pieseritz bei Wittenberg, Germany
Housing development, Schwaz in Bohmen, Germany

1927/
28 Schweizerische Volksbank, Solothurn, Switzerland
1927/
29 Lory Hospital, Berne
1928 Geyer Film Works, Neukolln, Germany
1929/
30 Sauglings- und Murterheim Building, Berne
1930 Community Centre, Stieglitz, Berlin
Health Insurance Building, Schöneberg, Berlin
Workers' apartment buildings, Reinickendorf, Berlin
Salvisberg House, Restelbergstrasse, Zurich
1930/
31 Administration Building and Laboratories, University of Berne
Suva House, Berne
Pavilions for Wander, Suglingsheim and Hyspa companies, Berne
Technological Laboratories, E.T.H.: Eidgenössische Technische Hochschule, Zurich
1931 Forest Housing Development, stage I, near Onkel Toms Hutte, Zehlendorf, Berlin (with Hugo Häring and Bruno Taut)
1932 Insurance Company Building, Berne
1936 Apartment building, Alfred-Escherstrasse, Zurich
1936/
37 Hoffman-La Roche Company Factory and Office Buildings, Basle
1937 Apartment building, Manesstrasse, Zurich
1939 Roche Products Factory, Welwyn Garden City, England (with C. Stanley Brown)
1939/
40 Bleicherhof Office Building, Zurich
1940 Apartment building, Stockerstrasse, Dreikönigsh, Zurich

Publications:

On SALVISBERG: books—*Thieme-Becker Künstler-Lexikon,* edited by Hans Vollmer, Leipzig 1935; *Schwiezer Architektur* by Hans Volkart, Ravensburg 1951; *Otto Rudolf Salvisberg: Zum Andenken,* Zurich 1972; articles—*L'Architecture d'Aujourd'hui* (Paris), December 1933; *Werk* (Zurich), November 1941; *Architetti* (Florence), no. 17, 1953.

*

The main impression of the architecture of O.R. Salvisberg is of an expressive use of modern structural methods and materials, employed, as in the work of most progressive architects, better to satisfy functional requirements, which Salvisberg combined with classical dignity and restraint occasionally enlivened with more dynamic features.

He was the architect of a varied range of buildings —houses, offices, industrial and university buildings. He was a protagonist of reinforced concrete construction in the late 1920's and 1930's, realizing its structural and aesthetic potentialities. His designs in this medium are often ingenious, and his own house in Zurich is a good example. It is L-shaped on plan, with the inner corner towards the south. The reinforced concrete frame structure employed permitted very wide window openings. One in the south-west wing is a complete wall-opening to a terrace and pool. In the south east wing there is a verandah under the first floor, which is supported on very slender columns, expressive of the structural capability of the material, and relating well to the large plain white walls—a motif introduced often in later buildings.

In the Bleicherhof Office Building in Zurich the arcading of light column supports under a massive five-storey building is a notable feature. The structural elements, however, are set back, which permits a band of uninterrupted fenestration on the first floor and a light rectangular concrete grill on the upper floors.

Salvisberg adopted Maillart's mushroom construction in several buildings. In the Hoffman-La Roche Building at Basle, he set the mushrooms well back from the main facades, which made possible a structural lightness, with long continuous horizontal bands of fenestration.

The essential characteristics of Salvisberg's architecture are eloquently displayed in the famous factory for Roche Products at Welwyn Garden City, which he built with the assistance of an English architect, C. Stanley Brown. It was not uncommon at this time in England for the office of an industrial building to have a dignified or pretentious palatial character, while behind it the factories or workshops were little more than a series of sheds. The Roche building, on the contrary, is a unified architectural whole, with the white concrete blocks transversely arranged on the northern side of the extensive site and lawns spreading to the south. A two-storey office block abuts a four-storey factory and warehouse, with lower blocks adjoining. The endwise entrance facade of the office block is distinctive. The first floor, which holds the Conference Room at this end, projects well forward of the ground floor, forming a porch, and is supported on even more slender columns than Salvisberg had previously used. The relation of these columns to the plain walls, well proportioned and spaced windows, and overhanging flat roof result in a felicitous architectural composition.

Salvisberg did, in fact, occasionally introduce motifs that contrasted with the quiescent character of his designs. In the Bleicherhof Office Building there are two rather dramatically introduced elliptical spiral staircases a little reminiscent of those of the late Renaissance; while in the La Roche building a spiral staircase right of the entrance hall gives access to the Conference Room. This provides a dynamic note in the interior, but is rather a discordant than a harmonizing effect in the fine exterior.

—Arnold Whittick

SAMONÀ, Giuseppe.

Italian. Born in Palermo, Sicily, 8 April 1898. Educated at the University of Palermo, Dip.Civ.Ing. 1922. Married Teresa Favara in 1923; children: Adele, Carmelo and Alberto. In private practice, Messina, 1922–58. Established office in Venice, 1936; Principal, with Giuseppina Marcialis Samonà and Alberto Samonà, Studio Samonà, Rome, since 1958. Assistant Design Instructor, Faculty of Engineering, University of Messina, 1927–30; Instructor, Faculty of Architecture, University of Naples, 1931–36; Instructor, 1936–45, and Professor of Architectural Composition, and Director, 1945–71, Institute of Architecture, Venice. Member, National Planning Legislation Committee, 1963–65; Senator of the Republic of Italy, 1972. Exhibition: *Giuseppe Samonà*, Palazzo Grassi, Venice, 1975. Recipient: First Prize, Palazzata Resort Complex Competition, Messina, 1930; First Prize, Emergency Hospital Competition, Rome, 1947; Olivetti National Prize, 1958; First Prize, Regional Development Plan Competition, Messina, 1960; First Prize, City Centre Competition, Turin, 1962; Special Prize, New Sacca del Tronchetto Competition, Venice, 1964; IN-ARCH National Prize for Architecture, 1964. Address (office): via Isonzo 42, 00198 Rome, Italy.

Works:

1922 Monument to the War Dead, Milan.(project)
1923 Monument to the War Dead, Milan (2nd project)

1925 New Pulpit, Cathedral of Trento, Italy (competition project)
1928 Parish churches, Calabria, Italy (projects)
      Postal and Telecommunications Building, Naples (competition project)
      Municipal Hall, Merano, Italy (competition project)
1929 Cathedral, La Spezia, Italy (competition project)
      Palace of Justice, Campobasso, Italy (competition project)
1930 School of Science and Technical Institute, Syracuse, Italy (project; with Camillo Autore)
      Villa Bellini restoration and alterations, Catania, Italy (with Camillo Autore)
      New Seaside Resort Centre, Messina (competition project; with Camillo Autore)
      Development plan for Bolzano, Italy (competition project; with Enrico Calandra and Camillo Autore)
1931 Wool and Grain Market Building, Foggia, Italy (competition project)
1932 Giuffrida Funeral Chapel, Montevago, Agrigento, Italy
      Giuffrida Country Villa, Montevago, Agrigento, Italy (project)
      Church in Paradiso, Messina (competition project)
      Church of Mary, Milazzo, Messina (competition project)
      Church of San Filippo Neri, Messina (competition project)
      Civil Service Office Building, Bari, Italy (competition project)
1933 Castellaneta Villa, San Severo, Foggia, Italy (project)
      Passenger Terminal Building, Santa Maria Novena Station, Florence (competition project)

P.T.T. Services Building, Nomentano Quarter, Rome (competition project)
1933/
36 P.T.T. Services Building, Appio Quarter, Rome
1934 Exhibition Hall, *Exposition of the Fascist Revolution,* Rome (competition project)
1934/
35 Savings Bank Headquarters, Modena, Italy (competition project)
      Apartment Building Development, Palermo (project)
      Cinema lobby alterations, Ostia, Italy (project)
      Auditorium, Rome (competition project)
1936 Police Magistrates Office Complex, Rome (competition project; with Mario de Renzi)
      P.T.T. Employees' Apartment Building, via Taranto, Rome (project)
1936/
40 Government Officials House, Messina
1937 Casa Littoria, Rome (competition project)
1938/
40 Villa, Baia, Italy (project)
      GIL Building, Messina (project)
      INFAIL Headquarters, Messina (project)
      San Paolo Bridge, Rome (project)
      Apartment building, via Dalmazia, Rome (partially built)
      Palace of Italian Civilization, E 42 Development, Rome (competition project; with Viola)
      Palace of Agriculture and Land Reclamation, E 42 Development, Rome (project; with Marconi and Viola)
1939 INFPS Headquarters, Rome (competition project; with Viola)
      Central Residential Development, Gaeta, Italy (project)

Giuseppe Samonà: Banco d'Italia Headquarters, Padua, 1968

Development study of the Via Latina and Via Appia, Rome
1945 Crystal Palace Development, London (competition project)
Urban development plan for the Lavinaio Quarter, Naples
1946 Entrance Building, *Mediterranean Fair,* Palermo (project)
1947 INAIL Hospital, Rome (competition project)
1948 Apartment Building, Livorno (project)
Apartment Building, Turin (project)
1949 Office/Apartment Building, Sampierdarena, Genoa (project)
INA Office/Apartment Building, Treviso, Italy
1950 Scimeni Villa, Mondello, Palermo
Apartment building, Rome
INAIL Revenue Building, Venice
1951 INA-CASA Housing Development, San Giuliano Mestre, Venice (with L. Piccinato and others)
INAIL Office Building, Livorno (project)
INAIL Hospital, Palermo (project)
1952 INAIL Office/Apartment Building, San Simeone, Venice (1st project; with E. Trincanato)
INA-CASA Housing Development, Palma Montechiaro, Italy (project)
INA-CASA Housing Development, Sciacca, Italy
1953 INCIS Housing Development, Padua
INAIL Orthopaedic Hospital, Bari, Italy
Messina Seaside Resort Centre
SGES Headquarters, Palermo (1st project)
1954 INAIL Apartment Building, Livorno (project)
1955 Palazzo Camarata interior renovations, Palermo (project)
SGES Headquarters, Palermo (2nd project)
1956 Borgo Ulivia Experimental Housing Estate, Palermo (with Bonafede, Calandra, and Caracciolo)
INPS Headquarters, Messina Seaside Resort Centre
TIFEO Electrical Centre, Augusta, Italy
INAIL Office/Apartment Building, San Simeone, Venice
1957 Apartment Block, Block XI, Messina Seaside Resort Centre
Urban development plan for Brescia, Italy
1959 CEP Housing Development, Barene di San Giuliano Mestre, Venice (competition project; with Piccinato, Astengo, Calabi, and Majoli)
National Library, Rome (competition project; with Pizzetti and Quilici)
1960 Regional development plan for Messina (competition project)
Thermo Electric Stations (prototypes)
Apartment building, Syracuse, Italy
Villa in the Parco Flora, Albaro, Genoa (project)
Apartment/office building, Palermo
1961 ENEL Office Building, Milazzo, Italy (project)
SGES-ENEL Office Building, Palermo
TIFEO Thermo-Electric Station, Termini Imerese, Italy
ENEL Office Building, Syracuse, Italy
1962 Regional development plan for Milazzo, Italy (competition project)
Provincial development plan for Messina
Machinery/Servicing Buildings, Hydro-Electric Centre, Sardinia (project)
Directional Centre for Turin (competition project; with Dardi, Mattioni, Pastor, Semerani, Tamaro, Trincanato, and Vianello Vos)
ENEL Thermo-Electric Centre, Trapani, Italy (project)
Provincial town plan for Trento, Italy
Regional development plan for Cavarzere, Venice (with Dardi, Trincanato and Bellemo)

Macchi House, Zitelle, Venice (project)
1963 National Providence and Credit Institute Headquarters, Palermo (competition project)
Morroy-Persico Inn, via delle Regione, Palermo (project)
SCEIS commercial and development plan for Palermo
1964 Regional development plan for Villa San Giovanni, Italy
Office building conversion, Mestre, Venice (project)
Territorial plan for the industrial belt of Milazzo, Messina (project; with Calandra and Bonafede)
New development plan for the Sacca del Tronchetto, Venice (competition project; with Dardi, Mattioni, Pastor, Polesello, Tamaro, Semarani, and Trincanato)
Regional development plan for Scilla, Italy
Comprehensive urban plan for Vajont, Italy
Group of villas, Falconarossa Baida, Palermo
1965 Regional development plan for Castiglione dello Stiviere, Garda, Italy (project; with Giovanazzi and Marconi)
Regional development plan for Cefalu, Sicily (project; with Doglio, Calandra, and Bonafede)
Regional development for Meda, Milan (project; with Cagna)
ANAS Divisional Headquarters, Palermo (project; with Cappellani and Di Cristina)
Mutual Insurance Company Building renovations, Largo Chigi, Rome (with Pizzetti)
1966 Mountain colony, near Ravenna
School complex, near Ravenna (project; as consultant architect)
Corso Clatafimi Residential Complex, Palermo (project)
Palazzo Francavilla restoration, Palermo (project; with Ziino)
Regional development plan for Palmi, Italy (with Doglio and Morabito)
1967 Chamber of Deputies Building, Rome (competition project)
Plan for the Veneta region, Italy (project; with others)
1968 Banco d'Italia Headquarters, Padua (with Pizzetti)
1969 Civic and Cultural Centre, Secondigliano, Naples (project; with Giannattasio)
Vulcanello Tourist Village, Vulcano, Italy (project)
Permanent Road-Link Between Sicily and the Italian Mainland (competition project; with others)
1970 Civic, Cultural and Commercial Centre, Gibellina, Italy (project; with Gregotti and Pirrone)
1971 Portonovo Beach Development, Ancona, Italy (project)
Bank of Sicily Headquarters and Piazza Croci Redevelopment, Palermo (project)
New University of Cagliari, Italy (competition project; with others)
Territorial plan for the thermal zone of Sciacca, Sicily
1973 University of Calabria, Italy (competition project)
1974/
79 Theatre, Sciacca, Sicily
1975 Master plan for the centre of Florence (competition project; with others)
1976/
79 Plan for the old town centre of Montepulciano, Italy
1978 Apartment and office building, Fano, Italy
1979 Plan for the old town centre of Palermo (with others)

Publications:

By SAMONÀ: books—*Elementi Medioevali nell'ar-chitettura del secolo XVI in Provincia di Messina,* Naples 1935; *Monumenti Medioevali nel Retroterra di Cefalu,* Naples 1935; *Schemi Compositivi di Palazzi Napoletani del '500,* Naples 1935; *La Casa Popolare,* Naples 1935; *Il Duomo di Cefalu,* Rome 1940; *L'Urbanisticà e l'Avvenire della Città,* Bari, Italy 1959; *Venezia, Caduta e Salvezza,* Florence 1970; *L'Unità Architettura Urbanistica,* Milan 1975; *L'Urbanistica e l'Avvenire della Città negli Stati Europei,* Rome 1975; articles—numerous in Italian periodicals since 1928, including *L'Architettura, Metron, Casabella, Urbanistica,* and *Zodiac.*

On SAMONÀ: books—*Giuseppe Samonà: La Casa Popolare degli Anni '30,* introduction by Mario Manieri-Elia, Padua 1973; *Giuseppe Samonà: L'Unità Architettura Urbanistica: Scritti e Progetti 1929–73* by Pasquale Lovero, Milan 1975; *Giuseppe Samonà: Cinquant'Anni di Architettura,* exhibition catalogue, by Carlo Aymonino, Giorgio Cucci, Francesco dal Co, and Manfredo Tafuri, Rome 1975; articles—"Risveglio Architettonico in Sicilia" in *L'Architettura* (Rome), no. 11, 1932; "Recensione a Giuseppe Samonà: La Casa Popolare" by Enrico Calandra in *L'Architettura* (Rome), no. 14, 1935; "Il Centro Traumatologico di Bari e Il Nucelo Residenziale in Padova dell'Architetto Giuseppe Samonà" by Giancarlo De Carlo in *Casabella* (Milan), no. 206, 1955; "Giuseppe Samonà" in *Cronache di Architettura* (Bari, Italy), no. 273, 1971; "Progetti dello Studio Giuseppe e Alberto Samonà 1968–72" by Pasquale Lovero in *Controspazio* (Bari, Italy), no. 2, 1973; "Samonà and Urban Architectural Unity" by Pasquale Lovero in *Parametro* (Bologna), September/October 1975.

Giuseppe Samonà summarizes his own career as one devoted to architectural design, urban planning and political involvement. To this must be added a long and illustrious history as an educator.

In his architecture Samonà admits to leaning toward eclecticism and expressionism, the result of an interest in the differences rather than the commonalities in architectural-urban problems. General rules fail too often, he says, because they do not fit specific cases. Thus his eclecticism—which has allowed him to range over a wide variety of forms and approaches in his architectural compositions, even allowing him the audacity to design a single building with quite dissimilar facades (the Banca d'Italia in Padua) in an attempt to harmonize with the particular character of each of the urban ambiences toward which the facades happened to face. Thus also his interest in expressionism in architecture, which avoids standardization and emphasizes the uniqueness of each problem.

The unifying themes behind his work have been: the vision of nature with its complex interrelationships as an exemplar of cities and buildings; and a strong political bias toward socialism and a related emphasis on an architecture that can simultaneously respond to and fulfil political, social and economic goals together with those that are aesthetic and functional.

Several of his most dramatic architectural projects have been unrealized. These include the competition project for the Chamber of Deputies Building in Rome in 1967, which displays a vigorously thrusting composition of cantilevered volumes and planes partially supported by an irregular arrangement of exaggeratedly slender "pilotis;" the Directional Centre for the city of Turin, 1962, similarly composed of floating planes, but within an attenuated complex stretching for nearly a kilometer from end to end; and the project for a villa in Baia, near Naples, of 1938–40, which, like the later works cited, seems to synthesize ideas derived from Wright, Le Corbusier and constructivism, but displays a compositional sophistication seldom realized by other architects until several decades later.

As much renowned as an educator as a practicing

architect, Samonà, immediately after World War II, gathered together in the School of Architecture in Venice a variety of architects and artists who had been excluded from full participation in their professions by the Fascist regime, and in a manner reminiscent of Walter Gropius and the Bauhaus, forged a community spirit of progressivism which, for at least two decades, kept the Venice School in the forefront of modern architectural thought.

—Abraham Rogatnick

SANDROCK, Brian.

South African. Born in Bloemfontein, South Africa, 10 November 1925. Educated at the Boys High School, Kimberley; University of Pretoria, M.Arch. Served as a Pilot in the South African Air Force, seconded to the Royal Air Force, Italy, 1942–45. Married Thelma Athene Wilson in 1951; son: Peter. In private practice, Pretoria, since 1953. Lecturer in Design and the History of Architecture, University of Pretoria, 1954–59. Address: Halcyon Place, 426 King's Highway, Lynnwood, Pretoria 0081, South Africa.

Works:

1956– Various buildings for the University of Pretoria

1960– National Nuclear Research Centre, Pelindaba, near Pretoria

1962– New campus for the University of South Africa, Pretoria

1975 Sandrock Studio and Penthouse, Lynnwood, Pretoria

Brian Sandrock is probably the most distinguished and least publicized of the new generation of South African architects who emerged after the end of World War II. His architectural training began during the post-war years of building austerity when the hoped-for architectural developments had not yet arrived and the profession was mainly occupied in overcoming the backlog of housing and in utilitarian building. The new wave of industry generated during the war was growing however; a shift in political power, large scale immigration from other parts of the world and a loosening of ties with the United Kingdom brought new attitudes and values. One of the effects of these events on South African architecture was that the former English and American beaux-arts oriented influence on architectural practice and education (which had, in the 1930's, been breached by the influence of German and French thinking) faded.

Sandrock's teaching career at the new department of architecture at the University of Pretoria occurred during a period of radical change in architectural education: courses were no longer confined to design with particular emphasis on its artistic aspects but towards an integrated and total concept of architecture; design was combined with the practical and technical subjects of technical construction and the

different faces of building sciences and services. In time, administration and economics came to be given more weight than before, and courses were broadened to include the humanities and the work of other design specialists.

The beginning of practice for Sandrock, and the accomplished associates he gathered round him after 1950, was in a climate of economic and population growth and expanding technological and scientific developments in the field of electric power, the production of steel and other materials and building components—with architecture, subject to such imperatives, becoming less a personal art or the personal interpretation of individual needs. Sandrock's recognition of and use of science and technology in architecture has always gone hand in hand with his respect and concern for the needs of the human spirit, an approach which led him to the creation of fine architecture. In the main this approach has been revealed within his exploration of the notably complex aspects of comprehensive planning for the long term development of universities and nuclear research installations.

The rationality of his planning, the enormous scale of projects, enriched by exotic and indigenous plants, creepers, shrubs and trees, and, on occasion, their spectacular nature, reveals a talent that provides not only vigour but also wit and elegance in buildings of an independent kind. He has also the ability, which is evident at Pelindaba, to make the Transvaal vernacular of brick and concrete merge into its setting or, with a splendid sense of structure and theatre, to command it: the delta-shaped administration block on the campus of the University of Pretoria, with its tall, swept back walls composed

Brian Sandrock: New campus, University of South Africa, Pretoria, 1962

Hideo Sasaki: Greenacre Park, New York, 1972

Arch. 1948. Married Kisa Noguchi in 1951; children: Rin and Ann. Principal, Sasaki Associates, Watertown, Massachusetts, 1951–52; Partner, Sasaki, Walker, Roberts Associates, San Francisco, 1952–60; Partner, Sasaki, Strong and Associates, of complex, curving surfaces to shield the building against the western sun and traffic noise, provides a flat suburban setting with a point of focus. At the University of South Africa the long, tiered administrative building, partly supported and cantilevered from a single, giant square column, dominates the capital city contained in the valley below.

—Doreen Greig

SASAKI, Hideo.

American. Born in Reedley, California, 25 November 1919. Educated at Reedley Junior College, California, 1939; University of California, Berkeley, 1939–41; Central YMCA College, Chicago, 1943–44; University of Illinois, Urbana, 1944–46, B.F.A. in Landscape Arch. 1946; Harvard University, Cambridge, Massachusetts, 1946–48, M.Landscape

Toronto, 1960–66; Partner, Sasaki, Dawson, DeMay Associates, Watertown, Massachusetts, 1966–78. Since 1978, Principal, Sasaki Associates Inc., Watertown. Instructor, University of Illinois, Urbana, 1948–50, 1952–53; Instructor, 1950–52, 1953–70, and Chairman of the Department of Landscape Architecture, 1958–68, Harvard University. Member, United States Commission on the Fine Arts, 1962–71. Member of the Advisory Committee on Arts and Architecture, Kennedy Memorial Library, Boston, since 1970. Recipient: Design Award, *Progressive Architecture,* 1958, 1960, 1965; Award, 1960, 1962, 1963, 1964, 1972, Certificate of Merit, 1972, and Allied Professions Medal, 1973, American Institute of Architects; Collaborative Medal of Honor, with Eero Saarinen, Architectural League of New York, 1962; Landscape Architecture Prize, Boston Arts Festival, 1962; First Honor Award, United States Federal Housing Authority, 1963; Gold Medal, Massachusetts Horticulture Society, 1964; 5 United States Housing and Home Finance Agency Awards, 1964; First Honor Award, United States Bureau of Higher Education/AIA, 1966; First Prize, Copley Square Competition, Boston, 1966; Award, Ontario Association of Architects, 1967; First Prize, St. Louis Gateway Mall Competition, 1967; Landscape Award, American Association of Nurserymen, 1968, 1972; First Prize, Providence College Library

Competition, 1970; Award of Merit, United States Army Corps of Engineers, 1970; Award, 1970, 1971, and Medal, 1971, American Society of Landscape Architects; Design Award, United States Department of Housing and Urban Renewal, 1970; American Institute of Steel Construction Award, 1971; New York Society of Architects Award, 1973; Grand Award, Associated Landscape Contractors of America, 1975. Fellow, American Society of Landscape Architects, 1969. Address: Sasaki Associates Inc., 64 Pleasant Street, Watertown, Massachusetts 02172, U.S.A.

Works (landscape architecture):

1952 Jaycee Headquarters, Tulsa, Oklahoma
1959 Golden Gateway Development, San Francisco
1961 Stauffer Chemical Company Office Building, Richmond, California
1962 Foothill College, Los Altos Hills, California
1963 Pomeroy Green Industrial Center, Santa Clara Valley, California
1964 Alcoa Building, 1 Maritime Plaza, San Francisco

Dormitories, University of Rhode Island, Kingston

Engineering Complex, University of Colorado, Boulder

1965   Pomeroy West Industrial Center, Santa Clara Valley, California
        Cabot, Cabot and Forbes Industrial Park, San Francisco
1966   Sasaki, Dawson, DeMay Associates Offices, Watertown, Massachusetts
        Master plan for the University of Massachusetts at Amherst
        Master plan for the University of Colorado, Boulder
        Master plan for Kent State University, Ohio
1967   Gateway Mall, St. Louis (competition project)
        Bell Telephone Laboratories, Holmdel, New Jersey
        Civic Center, Los Gatos, California
        Place Bonaventure Hotel, Montreal
1969   Alexandra Park, Toronto
        Library Building, School of Architecture, University of Virginia, Charlottesville
1970   Copley Square Development, Boston
        Library, Providence College, Rhode Island
1971   Norfolk Airport, Virginia
        State University of New York at Buffalo/Amherst
        Wightman Tennis Center, Weston, Massachusetts
1972   MGIC Investment Corporation Headquarters, Milwaukee
        Greenacre Park, New York
        Weyerhaeuser Company Headquarters, Tacoma, Washington
1973   Constitution Plaza, Hartford, Connecticut
        Plan for the Old Savannah historical district, Savannah, Georgia
1974   Master plan for the Columbia Point campus of the University of Massachusetts
        Cedar Square West, Minneapolis
        Promontory Point Housing, Newport Bay, California
        Tobin Elementary School, Cambridge, Massachusetts

Publications:

On SASAKI: articles—"Design of Exterior Space" by Jan C. Rowan in *Progressive Architecture* (New York), July 1960; "New England Portfolio" in *Landscape Architecture* (Louisville, Kentucky), April 1965; "Focusing University Development" in *Progressive Architecture* (New York), October 1966; "Castle in the Sky: Hotel Bonaventure" in *Interiors* (New York), October 1967; "Place Bonaventure" in *Architectural Design* (London), January 1968; "Most Popular Campus" in *Progressive Architecture* (New York), June 1973; "Place Bonaventure" in *Landscape Design* (London), February 1977; "Planting with Evergreens" in *Concrete Quarterly* (London), April/June 1977.

Hideo Sasaki is one of the great professional success stories of our time. He was born and raised in California's hot south Central Valley and educated at Berkeley. With the onset of World War II and his family were caught in the hysteria that resulted in the relocation of all west coast Japanese in various concentration camps. From there, as a result of a government policy that apparently considered Japanese in the east less dangerous than they would be in the west, he was able to go east to study and work in his field of landscape architecture. He taught at Illinois and Harvard (he had studied at both universities), and in 1958 became the Chairman of the Department of Landscape Architecture at Harvard. Here his extraordinary talents for communication, organization, and leadership began to blossom. Educational programs and his professional practice grew together, each reinforcing and supporting the other. Students gained practical as well as theoretical knowledge, and Sasaki's office had a constant supply of eager workers. At no other school has there been

such a consistent, thorough, and successful integration of teaching and practice.

So happily balanced a process could not maintain equilibrium forever. Eventually the office practice grew so demanding that Sasaki had to make a choice. He decided to give up teaching: the school was now well established, with a good faculty ready to take over. Thereafter the Sasaki office, in Watertown, Massachusetts, grew rapidly into a multi-disciplinary firm that eventually employed 300 people, involved in architecture, engineering, and planning as well as landscape architecture.

That is the success story. What has been the qualitative level of the work turned out by this astonishing firm? Remarkably high. Sasaki went to Harvard in the wake of the modern design revolution that had occurred there in the late 1930's. He absorbed it, along with previous historical experience, and created a design/planning vocabulary that had both the freedom and the strength of that combination. Perhaps a little conservative from the free-swinging western point of view, his work, rich, strong and solid, struck the right notes at the right times and places, and earned him an enviable clientele; and graduates from his classes and office have built what may well be called a Sasaki tradition throughout North America. Designer, planner, teacher, organizer, communicator, and salesman par excellence for the profession, Sasaki occupies a secure leading position in 20th century landscape architecture.

—Garrett Eckbo

SAUER, Louis.
American. Born in Park Forest, Illinois, 15 June 1928. Studied medicine at DePauw University, Greencastle, Indiana, 1946–49, and architecture at Illinois Institute of Technology, Chicago, 1949–53, B.Arch. 1953; International School of City Planning, Venice, 1956; University of Pennsylvania, Philadelphia, 1957–59, M.Arch. 1959. Served in the United States Army, 1953–55. Married Elizabeth Mason in 1956; children: Christopher and Kathryn. Worked in the office of Jules Gregory, Lambertville, New Jersey, 1955–57, Milton Schwarz, Philadelphia, 1957–61, and Esbach, Pullinger, Stevens and Bruder, Philadelphia, 1959–61; Partner, with William Winchell, in Winchell and Sauer, Philadelphia, 1961–62; in private practice as Louis Sauer, Architect, Philadelphia, 1962–67; Partner, with Anthony Devito, Sauer and Devito, Philadelphia, 1967–69. Since 1969, Principal, Louis Sauer Associates, Philadelphia. Instructor, Drexel Institute of Technology, Philadelphia, 1960–65; Associate Professor, 1965–67, 1974–77, and Adjunct Professor of Architecture, 1977–79, University of Pennsylvania, Philadelphia. Professor, and Head of Department of Architecture, Carnegie-Mellon University, Pittsburgh, since 1979. Member, Housing Research Committee, and Design Committee, American Institute of Architects Commission on Environment and Design, 1973–74; Member, Design Advisory Panel, Department of Housing and Community Development, Baltimore, 1973–74; Member, Research Advisory Panel, American Institute of Architects, 1974–75; Member, Advisory Committee on Behavior Science Research and Architectural Practice, AIA Research Corporation and National Endowment for the Arts, 1975–77. Member of the Editorial Board, 1974–77, and since 1977 Contributing Editor, *Journal of Architectural Research,* Philadelphia; Member, Community Development Committee, AIA, since 1978; Research Adviser, National Science Foundation, since 1979. Exhibitions: United States Pavilion, *World's Fair,* New York, 1964; Art Alliance of Philadelphia, 1975; University of Texas at Austin, 1974. Recipient: Honor Award, 1963, 1964, 1965, 1967, 1970, 1971,

1972, 1978, and Silver Medal, 1967, 1973, Pennsylvania Society of Architects; AIA Award, 1963, 1965, 1968, 1969, 1970, 1971, 1972, 1974; Annual Award, Montgomery County Planning Commission, Pennsylvania, 1967; *Architectural Record* Award, 1967; National Plywood Design Award, 1972; Biennial Award, United States Department of Housing and Urban Development, 1972, 1976; Honor Award, Connecticut Society of Architects, 1974; Design Award, Greater Wilmington Development Council and Newcastle County Planning Board, Delaware, 1975; *Design and Environment* Award, 1975; Fellowship in Design, National Endowment for the Arts, 1978. Fellow, American Institute of Architects, 1973. Address: Louis Sauer Associates, 1185 Fort Washington Avenue, Fort Washington, Pennsylvania 19034, U.S.A.

Works:

1961   Sachse Factory, Philadelphia (project)
        Winchell House conversion, Philadelphia
1962   Urban renewal plan for the Morton area, Philadelphia
        Louis Sauer House conversion, Lambertville, New Jersey
        Cripps House, Lambertville, New Jersey
        Hamilton House conversion, New Hope, Pennsylvania
        Buten Duplex Townhouse conversion, Philadelphia
1963   Watson House conversion, Philadelphia
        Waverly Court Housing, group I, Philadelphia (project)
1964   North Crossing Rental Housing, Willow Grove, Pennsylvania
        Pastorius Mews Housing Development, Philadelphia (project)
        Cooper House, Margate, New Jersey (project)
        Drake Mill House conversion, Chester County, Pennsylvania (project)
        Addison Court Housing Development, Philadelphia (project)
        Housing development, 7th and Lombard Streets, Philadelphia (project)
1965   Atrium Court Housing Development, Philadelphia (project)
        Hornung House conversion, Philadelphia
        Housing development, Willinboro, New Jersey (project)
        Golf Course Island Housing Development, Reston, Virginia
        McClennan House, Philadelphia
        Park Purchase Condominium, Baltimore (project)
        St. Simeon's-by-the-Sea, Wildwood, New Jersey
1966   Waverly Court Housing, group II, Philadelphia.
        Housing conversions, 10th and Lombard Streets, Philadelphia
        Rental apartments conversion, 11th Street, Philadelphia
        Viewmont Village (rental housing development), Scranton, Pennsylvania
        Spring Pond (rental apartments and houses), Corning, New York
        Housing development, 5th and Spruce Streets, Philadelphia (project)
1967   Lakeside Housing Development, Reston, Virginia (project)
        Offutt Houses, Reston, Virginia
        Penn's View Housing, Philadelphia (project)
        Devito House conversion, Philadelphia
        Harmony House Co-operative Housing Development, New Haven, Connecticut
        Canterbury Gardens Co-operative Housing Development, New Haven, Connecticut
        Grant and Morrison Houses, Philadelphia
        Urban renewal plan for the Newhallville area, New Haven, Connecticut

Louis Sauer: Spring Pond, Corning, New York, 1966

Head House East Shops and Housing Development, Philadelphia (project)

Reed House, Great Barrington, Massachusetts

Leonard Frankel House, Margate, New Jersey

William Frankel House, Margate, New Jersey

Penn's Landing Square One Housing Development, Philadelphia (project)

Oakland Mills Village Centre, Columbia, Maryland

1968 Housing development, Locust Street, Philadelphia

Grundy Tower Housing Development, Bristol, Pennsylvania

Development plan for Fox Chase, Pennsylvania (project)

1969 Regency Square Housing Development, Cincinnati

Second Street Housing Development, Philadelphia

Penn's Landing Square Two Housing Development, Society Hill, Philadelphia

Genesee Crossroads Housing Development, Rochester, New York (project)

Governor's Grove Housing Development, Middletown, Connecticut

North Crossing Rental Housing II, Philadelphia

Central Island Village, Islip, New York (project)

Sauer House conversion, Chestnut Hill, Philadelphia

1970 Condominium, Lombard Street, Philadelphia

High-rise low-cost rental apartment building, Warburton and Lamartine Streets, Yonkers, New York

Low-cost rental row-housing development, Warburton and Ashburton Streets, Yonkers, New York

1971 Oak Hill Terrace Housing Development, Penn Valley, Pennsylvania

Motel Complex, Penn's Landing Square, Philadelphia (project)

Strathallan Rental Housing for the Elderly, Rochester, New York (project)

Riverton Patio Housing Development, Rochester, New York (project)

Housing post-occupancy evaluation for the United States Department of Health, Education and Welfare

1972 Wilton Condominium, Wilmington, Delaware

Wilton Clubhouse, Wilmington, Delaware

Seascape Condominium, Avalon, New Jersey

1973 Plan for development of riverfront land, Cincinnati

Headmaster's House, Westtown School, Pennsylvania

Graver's Lane Rental Housing conversions, Philadelphia

1974 Development plan for Fell's Point, Baltimore

Land development plan for Boca Lago, Florida

Gypsy Hill Road Housing, Lehighton, Pennsylvania (project)

Crystal Gardens Housing Development, Corning, New York (project)

Western Savings Bank at New Market, Society Hill, Philadelphia

Parcel 76 Housing Development, Washington, D.C.

Orchard Mews Low-cost Housing Development, Baltimore

Crystal Gardens Housing Feasibility Study, Corning, New York (project)

Newmarket Commercial Complex, Philadelphia

1975 Hord House, Philadelphia

Broadway Market Rehabilitation, Fells Point, Baltimore

1976 Inner Harbor West Housing Development Plan, Baltimore

Marren House renovation, Harvey Cedars, New Jersey

1977 York Re-use Housing, York, Pennsylvania

Penn Housing, Philadelphia

Pine Street Houses, Philadelphia

Cincinnati Riverfront Plaza

1978 One West Conway Rental Housing for the Elderly, Baltimore

Harbor Walk Sales Housing, Baltimore

Lower Town Development Strategy, St. Paul, Minnesota

1979 House rehabilitation, 1185 Fort Washington Avenue, Fort Washington, Pennsylvania

Washington Square West Low-Cost Housing rehabilitation, Philadelphia

Roberts House, Society Hill, Philadelphia

Publications:

By SAUER: articles—"The Architect and User Needs" in *Behavior, Design and Policy Aspects of Human Habitats,* Madison, Wisconsin 1972; "How Six Families Use Space in Their Homes" in *Proceedings of the Third EDRA Conference,* Los Angeles 1973; "Some Thoughts on Design and Process in Housing" in *Modulus 10* (Charlottesville, Virginia), June 1974; "Differing Fates for Two Nearly Identical Housing Developments" in *AIA Journal* (Washington, D.C.), February 1977; "Man-Environment Knowledge and Design Criteria" and "A Framework for Considering Housing Costs" in *Proceedings of the Lebanon Housing Seminar,* Washington, D.C. 1977.

On SAUER: articles—"Louis Sauer's Works" in *Aujourd'hui* (Paris), January 1967; "Works and Methods of Louis Sauer" in *Toshi-Jutaku* (Tokyo), January 1969; "How to Work with Developers and Actually Enjoy It" in *Architectural Record* (New York), April 1973; "Penn's Landing Square" in *Progressive Architecture* (New York), March 1976; "Working Toward an Approach That Will Yield Lessons for Future Design" in *AIA Journal* (Washington, D.C.), August 1976; "Spring Pond Apartments" in *Wohnungsbau im Wandel* by David Mackay, Stuttgart 1977; "Building Types Study 523: Low-Rise Housing" in *Architectural Record* (New York), October 1978.

I understand architecture to be a technological process and a product of society for heightening people's self-identity through solving specific man-environment problems. As a process, it is intrinsically a cultural action for resource allocation involving complex issues and varied participants, to achieve political purposes. The major aspects concerning architecture are human needs, policies and programs allocating resources, community and neighborhood development, physical design, construction, distribution and occupancy, property maintenance and management. I have found that, to the extent the interactions, separate goals and disciplines of the individual participants in these aspects are understood, one can be effective in predicting and modifying the outcomes of the designed environment. Thus, architects, or others, may choose to intervene for greater influence upon the quality of the built environment.

—Louis Sauer

Louis Sauer is a no-nonsense, user oriented architect from Philadelphia, Pennsylvania. His firm has been quite prolific, and they have completed many fine buildings that have been conservative, but not conventional, and completely up-to-date, without being trendy. Sauer himself is a pragmatist, greatly aware of the importance of communication with the client, and sensitive to issues far broader than merely architectural design. Still, his buildings are neatly handsome and often slick. He has frequently proposed unique and surprisingly successful solutions to many difficult problems facing contemporary architects. He has readily accepted the challenges of some of the toughest building programs in America, and his portfolio includes an impressive number of successful public housing projects and in-fill urban designs.

In the Society Hill area of Philadelphia, Sauer has completed many six to ten unit attached house complexes that have blended easily with the existing street patterns without compromising modernity or design freshness. By maintaining certain volumetric dimensions but distorting others, Sauer's houses are unusual and exciting in and of themselves, without damaging or significantly altering the local environmental character.

In the same neighborhood, but adjacent to the Delaware River, Sauer designed a new shopping center that clearly demonstrated his facile capability to produce a boldly imaginative solution reflecting the individual issues of a particular program. Residents had been long opposed to the development of a commercial center in the heart of this historic district, but Sauer finally developed a plan that did nothing to destroy the neighborhood's appearance. What is most surprising is that the new building he designed is a high-tech glass and stainless steel affair with exposed columns, beams, ducts and pipes, all painted in bright, primary colors. This was accomplished by completely hiding the new center on all sides except the waterfront. Newmarket, as the complex is called, is masked on the other three sides by older residential units that were maintained and refurbished. The stores are located in the area that was once the yards for the surrounding homes, and it remains invisible until the pedestrian leaves the street zone, and enters a passage to penetrate within. An outdoor activity area designed for pedestrians surrounds the buildings of Newmarket, and extends to the backs of the houses. Towards the water, the complex is allowed to reveal itself, where there is no concern with maintaining the quiet rhythms of the colonial streets.

Newmarket is also unusual because it explores a new method of merchandise display. There are no store windows, per se. Instead, the entire glass facade of the market reveals store interiors intended to serve as the displays themselves. The outdoor areas are certainly more exciting because of the interior motion visible through the glass walls.

Sauer has also completed a variety of public housing projects that are worthy of commendation. Two developments near New Haven, Connecticut, and

several near Philadelphia, have proven Sauer to be capable of handling the hardest assignments. In all, he made snappy structures with easily identifiable individual units, and surprising variation for low income developments. In Connecticut, he conducted interviews with future occupants to discover changes they would like to implement, and he revised the floor plan accordingly, without changing the size or overall cost of the housing.

Sauer is a strong, energetic, and forceful designer who is impressed by action, not words. He has made a strong commitment to keep architecture in close touch with the people it serves, and he has stayed a bit removed from the polemical debates of architecture, in order to be in the thick of its production.

—Mitchell B. Rouda

SAUVAGE, (Frederic) Henri.

French. Born in Rouen, 10 May 1873. Educated at the Ecole Gerson, Paris, 1888–90; Ecole des Beaux-Arts, Paris, under Pascal, 1890–95. Served as a Sub-Lieutenant in the French Army, 1914–18. Married Marie-Louise Charpentier in 1898; son: Jean. Proprietor of a wallpaper shop, rue de Rohan, Paris, 1896–1904; in partnership as an architect with Charles Sarazin, Paris, 1898–1912; in private practice, Paris, 1919 until his death, 1932. Professor of Architecture, Ecole des Arts Décoratifs, Paris, 1928, and Ecole des Beaux-Arts, Paris, 1929–31. Exhibitions: *Salon de la Société Nationale des Beaux-Arts,* Paris, 1898, 1899, 1901, 1902, 1903, 1904, 1909; *Salon des Artistes Décorateurs,* Paris, 1904; *Salon d'Automne,* Paris, 1904, 1907, 1908, 1913; *Henri Sauvage: Travaux d'Architecture 1907–1930,* Strasbourg 1932; *Henri Sauvage 1873–1932,* Société des Architectes, Paris, 1976, and Ecole Nationale Supérieure d'Architecture, Brussels, 1977; *Henri Sauvage,* Architectural Association, London, 1978. *Died* (in Paris) *in 1932.*

Works:

1896 Furniture (projects)
1897 Cover design for *Art et Décoration* magazine (competition project)
1898 Villa Majorelle, 1 rue Louis Majorelle, Nancy
1899 Café de Paris interiors, 41 Avenue de l'Opera, Paris 8 (destroyed, 1955)
1900 Loïe Fuller Pavilion, Giugnol Parisien Pavilion, Sauvage and Jolly Fils Printed Materials Exhibit, Maison Majorelle Pavilion, and decorative flagmasts, *Exposition Universelle,* Paris
 Bathing Cabins (project)
 Madame Majorelle Country House (project)
 Jansen Shops interiors, 9 rue Royale, Paris 8 (destroyed)
1901/
02 Public Baths by the Sea, Algiers (project)
 Bathroom (project)
 Seaside Villa (project)
 Building Facade (project)
1902 Small Country House (project)
 House, 17 rue Damrémont, Paris 18
 Coudyser Fabrics shop front and alterations, Paris
 Low-cost housing, 7 rue de Trétaigne, Paris 18
 Low-cost housing, 1 rue Ferdinand Flocon, Paris 18
 de Lestapis Villa (Villa Oceana), Biarritz
 Cité l'Argentine, 111 Avenue Victor Hugo, Paris 16
1904 Villa in Brittany, for *Art et Décoration* magazine (project)

 Apartment building, 22 rue Laugier, Paris 17
 Apartment for an Actress, *Salon des Artistes Décorateurs,* Paris
1905 Low-cost housing, 10 rue Danville, Paris 14
 Low-cost housing, 20 rue Severo, Paris 14
1906 City Fortifications Plan, for the Association of Cités-Jardins, *Exposition of Milan*
1907 Leubas House, 110 rue d'Espagne, Biarritz
 Hotel, Biarritz (project)
1908 Majorelle House, Avenue Thiers, Compiègne, France
 Low-cost housing, 165 Boulevard de l'Hôpital, Paris 13
1909 Low-cost housing, 1 rue de Chine, Paris 18
 Les Terrasses Hotel, Tréport, France (destroyed)
1911 Apartment building, 29 rue de la Boétie, Paris 8
1912 Apartment building, 26 rue Vavin, Paris 6
1913 Majorelle Offices/Shops Complex, 126 rue de Provence, Paris 9
1919 S.E.C.B. Director's House, Mimizan, France
1920 Gambetta Cinema, 4 rue Belgrand, Paris 20
 Terraced Housing (project)
1921 Theatre, Boulevard Raspail, Paris 6 (project)
1922 Sèvres Cinema, 68 rue de Sèvres, Paris 7 (destroyed, 1976)
 Low-cost housing, 13 rue des Amiraux, Paris 18
 Cottage-type Terraced Houses (project)
 Villa-type Terraced Houses (project)
1923 Hotel, America House, and other buildings for the 1925 Exposition, Porte de Villiers, Paris (project; with Guimard, Brachet, Richard, Sezille, and Roemrich)
1924 Apartment building, 50 Avenue Duquesne, Paris 7
 Apartment building, 14–16 Boulevard Raspail, Paris 7
 Apartment building, 19 Boulevard Raspail, Paris 7
 Apartment building, 137 Boulevard Raspail, Paris 6
1925 Apartment building, 42 rue de la Pompe, Paris 16
 Apartment building, 6 rue de Sully Prud-homme, Paris 7
 Galerie Constantine, Primavera Pavilion, and Electric Transformer Station, *Exposition des Arts Décoratifs,* Paris (with Zette Sauvage)
 Hallari House, Combs-la-Ville, France (project)
1926 La Samaritaine (department store) extension, Paris (with Frantz Jourdain)
 Studio Building, 65 rue La Fontaine, Paris 16
 Sauvage House, Saint-Martin-la-Garenne, France
 Garage, rue Campagne-Première, Paris 14
 Prefabricated building components, *Salon des Appareils Ménagers,* Paris, and erected at Auteil, France
1927 Steel Housing (project)
 Grand Hotel (project)
 Varilla House, Orsay, Seine et Oise, near Paris
 Institut du Syntol, Neuilly, Paris (destroyed)
 Le Sphinx Club, Boulevard Edgar Quinet, Paris 14
1928 Terraced Building and Garage by the Seine, Paris (project)
 Apartment building, 27 rue Légendre, Paris 17
 Apartment building, 8 bis Boulevard Maillot, Paris 16
 Pyramid-Shaped Tower, Montparnasse Cemetery, Paris
1929 Office building, 10 rue Saint-Marc, Paris 7
 Monteils Type B Industrialized Housing (project)
 Hotel, Neuilly, Paris
1930 Monument to the First Victory of the Marne (competition project; with Zette Sauvage)

Galeries Lafayette Facade, Paris (competition project)
Process T Housing (project)
Type B and C Villas (project)
1931 Decre Shops, Nantes, France (destroyed, 1943)
Triumphal Parade for the Etoile, La Défense, Paris (competition project)
Redevelopment Plan for a Large City (project; with André Ventre)
1932 Apartment building, 42 Quai des Orfevres, Paris 1 (now the Auberge du Vert-Galant)

Publications:

By SAUVAGE: books—*La Boutique à Treize*, Paris 1923; *Méthodes Economiques de Construction des Habitations et Standardisation des Matériaux*, Rennes 1931; articles—"Les Tendances de l'Architecture Moderne" in *L'Amour de l'Art* (Paris), October 1922; "Interview d'Henri Sauvage" in *La Journée Industrielle* (Paris), (Paris), January 1923; "Notes sur une Simplification Possible de Certains Articles du Décret du 13 Aout 1902" in *L'Architecture* (Paris), 10 January 1923; "Les Immeubles Collectifs" in *L'Illustration Economique et Foncière* (Paris), 22 November 1924; "Maison de Rapport" in *L'Illustration* (Paris), 30 March 1929; "Les Maisons à Elements Tubulaires" in *Revue de l'Habitation* (Paris), September 1930; "De la Fantaisie en Architecture" in *L'Architecture d'Aujourd'hui* (Paris), June/July 1931; "Considerations en Faveur de l'Usinage de la Maison" in *La Construction Moderne* (Paris), January 1932.

On SAUVAGE: books—*Henri Sauvage* by Gabriel Mourey, Paris 1928; *L'Art en 1900* by Maurice Rheims, Paris 1965; *Henri Sauvage* by Dominique Dumerle, and Elizabeth and René Hasson, Paris 1974; *Henri Sauvage 1873-1932*, exhibition catalogue, by R. L. Delevoy, F. Loyer, B. Brace Taylor, Luciana Miotto-Muret, and others, Paris and Brussels 1976; articles—"Sauvage and Hygienic Housing; or, The Cleanliness Revolution in Paris" by B. Brace Taylor in *Archithese* (Niedertaufen), no. 12, 1974; "Henri Sauvage" by Dominique Dumerle, and Elizabeth and René Hasson in *Architecture Mouvement Continuité* (Paris), no. 37, 1975; "Henri Sauvage (1873-1932)" by Luciana Miotto-Muret in *Architecture* (Paris), February 1976.

Henri Sauvage once remarked, "Perhaps I shall have served as a hyphen between tradition and the avant-garde," and it is certainly true that elements of both are constantly mingled throughout his work. Indeed, in his complex personality, there is an ambiguity that is both embarrassing and fascinating.

The fundamental influences of his training—the Art Nouveau movement and the rationalist teaching of Viollet-le-Duc—are apparent in his earliest achievements. He was one of the first French architects to recognize and promote a renewal of the arts through architecture—as in the Villa Majorelle of 1898. But in the series of low-cost housing developments from that in the rue Trétaigne to that in the boulevard de l'Hôpital in 1908, he went further: he abandoned a certain decorative formalism and attempted a genuine social renewal of architecture.

Influenced by his initial training, and by the Parisian milieu which he frequented with Frantz Jourdain and Alexandre Charpentier, he maintained throughout his life a certain kind of involvement in his profession and at the same time a certain readiness to compromise. This ambiguity is very apparent in various works of his middle period—the Leubas House in Biarritz of 1908 and the Majorelle House in Compiègne of 1908, in which he used (with ease) regional architectural elements mingled with purely academic elements. His earlier rationalist language is completely denied.

A similar attitude obtains in the works of his maturity from 1912 to 1932. Side by side with a series of innovative projects for tiered housing and prefabricated houses of standardized elements, Sauvage executed buildings for the rich clients of the 8th and 16th districts of Paris in which the design conforms to the most reactionary models of the years 1920–30: the work is academic, and it shows little evidence of the new technologies. The connecting principle of these rather ill-assorted works would seem to be Sauvage's relationship with his client. When designing for the rich, he behaves like a routine professional who wants to give his clients what they want, without too much effort. Yet, when he had to solve a problem of collective or mass housing, he was transformed into a genuine innovator in both ideas and techniques. It is undeniable, for example, that he conceived "tiered" housing: his first projects for such structures date from 1909 (Sant'Elia, another innovator in the field, did not design his versions until 1914).

In his Utopian projects, Sauvage used the unit system of tiered dwellings as a model for works on an urban and suburban scale, producing not only new solutions for public housing but also innovations in collective structures. The swimming pool inside the building in the rue des Amiraux in Paris is unfortunately the only one of his projects of this kind that was actually realized.

Another anomaly is that, despite the evidence of some of his works, Henri Sauvage was also a great investigator and experimenter in modern building technology, a worthy member of the great technological tradition of the French architect/engineers such as Perret, Hennebique, de Baudot, and Tony Garnier.

—Luciana Miotto-Muret

SAVIOLI, Leonardo.
Italian. Born in Florence, 30 March 1917. Educated at the Humanities Gymnasium, Florence, graduated 1935; University of Florence, under Giovanni Michelucci, 1935–40, Dip.Arch. 1941. Married Flora Wiechmann in 1950. In partnership with G. Gori and Leonardo Ricci, Florence, 1944–49. In partnership with Danilo Santi, Florence, since 1950. Member of the Faculty of Architecture, University of Florence, since 1940: Professor of Town Planning and Landscape Architecture, since 1951. Exhibitions: *Mostra della Ricostruzione*, Rome, 1950; *Bienal*, Sao Paulo, 1953, 1957; *Disegni di Leonardo Savioli*, Galleria XXII Marzo, Venice, 1960; *Aspetti dell'Arte Contemporanea*, L'Aquila, 1963; *Disegni di Leonardo Savioli*, Galleria La Strozzina, Florence, 1963; *La Casa Abitata*, Florence, 1965; *Quadriennale*, Rome, 1966; *Mostra del Marmo*, Carrara, Italy, 1966; *Italia 1965*, Tokyo, 1966. Recipient: Prize, *Bienal*, Sao Paulo, 1953; INARCH-DOMOSIC Prize, 1960; IN-ARCH Prize, 1963; Il Siglio d'Oro, 1965; Donatello Prize, 1965; First Prize, Flower Market Building Competition, Pescia, Italy, 1970; First Prize, Resort Development Competition, Cannes, 1973; INARCH-ANIACAP Prize, 1973. Member, Italian Art Academy, 1960. Address (office): Via delle Romite 12a, 50124 Florence, Italy.

Works:

1942 District development plan for Livorno
1944/
45 Victory Bridge, Florence (competition project; with R. Gizdulich, G. Gori, Leonardo Ricci, and G. Neumann)
1945/
46 Plan for the reconstruction and redevelopment of Vicchio and Dicomano, Italy (with Leonardo Ricci)
Carraia Bridge, Florence (competition project; with G. Gori, Leonardo Ricci, and G. Neumann)
1946 Plan for the reconstruction and redevelopment of Empoli, Italy (competition project; with G. Gori and Leonardo Ricci)
Tourist and urban development plan for the Lido, Venice (competition project; with G. Gori and Leonardo Ricci)
Piazza d'Armi, Perugia, Italy (competition project; with G. Gori and Leonardo Ricci)
Grazie Bridge, Florence (competition project; with G. Gori and Leonardo Ricci)
1946/
47 Reconstruction plan for the Pontevecchio War-Damaged District, Florence (competition project; with G. Gori, Leonardo Ricci, and E. Brizzi)
Bridge over the River Sieve, Rufina, Italy (with G. Gori, Leonardo Ricci, and G. Neumann)
Bridge over the Arno River, Terranuova Braciolini, Italy (with G. Gori, Leonardo Ricci, and E. Brizzi)
Bridge over the Arno River, Figline Valdarno, Italy (with G. Gori, Leonardo Ricci, and E. Brizzi)
Group of 4 villas, for the Directors of the Vetroflex Company, Florence (with G. Gori and Leonardo Ricci)
1947 San Romando District Redevelopment, Ferrara, Italy (competition project; with E. Gori, G. Gori, and Leonardo Ricci)
Bridge over the Arno River, Signa, Italy (competition project; with G. Gori, Leonardo Ricci, and E. Brizzi)
San Niccolo Bridge, Florence (competition project; with G. Gori, Leonardo Ricci, and E. Brizzi)
Bridge over the Serchio River, Calavorno, Italy (competition project; with G. Gori, Leonardo Ricci, and E. Brizzi)
Bridge over the Cecina River, Ponteginori, Italy (competition project; with G. Gori and Leonardo Ricci)
Mezzo Bridge, Pisa (competition project; with G. Gori and Leonardo Ricci)
Bridge over the Bisenzio River, Signa, Italy (with G. Gori and Leonardo Ricci)
Municipal Cemetery, Settignano, Italy (project; with E. Detti, R. Gizdulich, G. Gori, and Leonardo Ricci)
Saint-Gobain Workers' Garden City, Pisa (project; with G. Gori and Leonardo Ricci)
Design of the *Artisans' Trade Fair*, Florence (with E. Gori, G. Gori, and Leonardo Ricci)
1948 Bridge over the Sterza River, Bottaccina, Volterra, Italy (competition project; with G. Gori and Leonardo Ricci)
Design of the *Artisans' Trade Fair*, Florence (with E. Gori, G. Gori, and Leonardo Ricci)
Bridge over the Sterza River, Salitone, Volterra, Italy (with G. Gori and Leonardo Ricci)
Urban development building code for Lido di Camaiore, Italy (competition project; with G. Gori, E. Isotta, and Leonardo Ricci)
1948/
49 2 pre-fabricated semi-detached villas (project; with E. Detti and Danilo Santi)
Villa, via del Larione, Ricoboli, Florence (with E. Detti and Danilo Santi)
Villa, San Domenico, Regresso, Florence (with E. Detti and Danilo Santi)
1948/
51 Flower and Fruit Market, Pescia, Italy (with E. Gori, G. Gori, Leonardo Ricci and E. Brizzi)
1949 Design of the *Artisans' Trade Fair*, Florence (with E. Gori, G. Gori, and Leonardo Ricci)

Leonardo Savioli: Office Building, Florence, 1976 (project)

Residential Zone, Savona, Italy (competition project; with E. Detti and Danilo Santi)

Pension, Forte dei Marmi, Italy (with E. Detti and Danilo Santi)

Design of the *Music Exhibition,* Palazzo Davanzati, Florence (with E. Detti and Danilo Santi)

1949/
51 Urban development building code for Florence (with L. Bartoli, E. Detti, S. Pastorini, G. Sagrestani, and the Florence City Technical Office)

1950/
51 Leonardo Savioli House, Certosa del Galluzzo, Florence

1951/
52 Piazzale Leonardo da Vinci, Mount Morello, Italy (project; with Danilo Santi)

1951/
58 2 semi-detached villas, San Francesco Village, Florence

Single-family house, San Francesco Village, Florence (with Danilo Santi)

1952/
53 Development plan for San Francesco Village, Florence (with Danilo Santi)

8 semi-detached apartments, 6 apartments with shop, and complex of 16 apartments, San Francesco Village, Florence (project; with Danilo Santi)

1953 Pinocchio Monument, Collodi, Pescia, Italy (competition project; with Danilo Santi and G. Gambone)

Fabrics shop, Prato, Italy (with Danilo Santi)

1953/
54 Village for 2,000 in the Sesto Hills, Florence (competition project; with Leonardo Ricci, Danilo Santi, and G. Petrelli)

Granary Barn conversion to Macchioro House, via delle Campora, Florence (with Danilo Santi)

1953/
64 Apartment building, San Francesco Village, Florence (with Danilo Santi)

1954/
55 Plan for the San Frediano District, Florence (competition project; with Leonardo Ricci, Danilo Santi, and G. Petrelli)

2 semi-detached villas, Poggio Gherardo, Florence (with Danilo Santi)

Torelli Villa, via Pana, Bellosguardo, Florence (with Danilo Santi)

1956/
57 Plan for Pomarance, Pisa

1956/
58 General plan for Prato, Italy (with T. Gatti and E. Rafanelli)

General plan for Montemurio, Italy (with Danilo Santi)

1957/
59 Building complex, Belvedere Quarter, Pistoia, Italy (with Danilo Santi and P. Melucci)

1958 Cinema, La Briglia, Florence (with Danilo Santi)

Villa Ventura, Regello, Italy (with Danilo Santi)

1958/
59 Urban development on the left bank of the Arno River, near Piazza G. Guerra, Empoli, Italy (competition project; with Danilo Santi)

1959 Church, Caprese Michelangelo, Italy (with Danilo Santi)

1959/
60 General plan for Volterra, Italy (competition project; with Danilo Santi)

1959/
61 Co-operative Housing Block, Pomarance, Italy (project; with Danilo Santi)

1960 Gebendinger Villa, Marignolle, Florence (with Danilo Santi)

Sacchelli Pension, Tonfano, Viareggio, Italy (with Danilo Santi)

Apartment building, via del Ponte alle Mosse, Florence (with Danilo Santi)

1960/
61 Covered market, Pomarance, Italy (with Danilo Santi)

Fischer Villa, Castello, Florence (with Danilo Santi)

1960/
65 Plan for Vaiano, Florence

1961 Melloni House, San Gaggio, Florence

1961/
62 Plan for the San Jacopino District, Florence (with Danilo Santi)

1961/
65 Building code and various buildings, via Torcicoda, Isolotto, Florence (project; with Danilo Santi)

1962 Low-cost holiday house, Tonfano, Italy (with Danilo Santi)

Building on a Platform (projects; with M. Dezzi Bardeschi, V. Giorgini, F. Gori, and Danilo Santi)

Pension, Tonfano, Italy (project; with Danilo Santi)

Design of L'Oggetto Moderno in Italia exhibition, Palazzo Strozzi, Florence (with Danilo Santi and R. Vernuccio)

1962/
63 Plan for the Novoli District of Florence

1962/
64 Sandroni Villa, Arezzo, Italy (with Danilo Santi)

1963 Design of Le Corbusier exhibition, Palazzo Strozzi, Florence (with Danilo Santi and R. Vernuccio)

Design of the Jewellery Exhibition, La Strozzina Gallery, Florence

Inn with 80 Rooms, Tropea, Italy (project; with Danilo Santi and S. Fabbri)

Wine Connoisseurs' Restaurant, San Casciano, Florence (project; with Danilo Santi)

Giandalia Villa, via Chiantigiana, Florence (with Danilo Santi)

1963/
64 Development plan for the Green Belt, Castello, Florence (with Danilo Santi and S. Fabbri)

1964 Torrini Building Plan, near via delle Campora, Florence (with Danilo Santi)

Urban plan for Caprese Michelangelo, Italy

Jewellery Shop, Ponte Vecchio, Florence (project; with Danilo Santi and S. Fabbri)

Glassware Shop, Venice (project)

1964/
65 Municipal Building Plan, Castiglio Fiorentino, Arezzo, Italy (with G. Fanelli and F. Trivisonno)

Taddei Villa, San Domenico, Florence (with Danilo Santi)

1964/
67 Apartment building, via Piagentina Florence (with Danilo Santi)

1965 Civic Center Plaza, San Francisco, California (competition project; with G. Fanelli, Danilo Santi, and F. Trivisonno)

Urban plan for the enactment of Statute 167, Castiglioni Fiorentino, Arezzo, Italy (with G. Fanelli, Danilo Santi, and F. Trivisonno)

1965/
73 Bayon Villa, San Gaggio, Florence

1966 Design of the Florence at the Time of Dante exhibition, Certosa del Galluzzo, Florence (with Danilo Santi)

Pre-fabricated room units, La Casa Abitata exhibition, Palazzo Strozzi, Florence

1966/
68 Montecatini Cemetery extension (with E. Brizzi and Danilo Santi)

1967/
71 Verrazzano Bridge, Florence (with C. Damerini and V. Scalese)

1971 City Planning Structure (project; with Danilo Santi, G. Corradetti, and R. Buti)

1971/
72 Viaduct Bridge, over the River Indiano, Florence (competition project)

Workers' Village, Volterrano, Italy (project; with Danilo Santi, G. Corradetti, and S. Giubbi)

1972 Catanzaro Airport, Italy (competition project)

1973 Genoa Airport (competition project)

Resort Development, Cannes (competition project)

1976 Office Building, Florence (project)

1976/
78 Administrative Centre, Florence (competition project)

Publications:

By SAVIOLI: books—Il Piano di Ricostruzione di Dicomano, Florence 1950; I Potessi di Spazio, Florence 1969; Problemi di Architettura Contemporanea, Florence 1973; articles—"Concorso per il Lido di Camaiore" in Urbanistica (Turin), no. 2, 1949; "Per un significato piu vero della pianificazione" and "La sistemazione urbanistica della piazza d'Armi a Perugia" in Architetti (Florence), no. 2, 1950; "Compiti attuali dell'Urbanistica e dell'Architettura" in Architetti (Florence), no. 6, 1951; "Gli sviluppi di Firenze dal 1900 fino ad oggi" and "Il Piano Regolatore di Firenze del 1951" in Urbanistica (Turin), no. 12, 1953; "Le case minime a Firenze" in Urbanistica (Turin), no. 14, 1954; "Il Piano Intercommunale del Territorio Fiorentino" in Firenze, Florence 1954; "I Problemi del Piano di Ricostruzione di Firenze" in La Planificazione Intercomunale, Turin 1957; "Urbanistica e Architettura Moderna nei Centri Storici Monumentali" in Quaderni della Nuova Città, Florence 1958; "Note su una Villa a Populonia" in Aujourd'hui (Paris), no. 41, 1963; "Note su un Negozio di Calzature ad Arezzo" in L'Architettura (Rome), no. 120, 1965.

On SAVIOLI: books—Disegni di Leonardo Savioli, exhibition catalogue, by Giuseppe Marchiori, Venice 1960; Disegni di Leonardo Savioli, exhibition catalogue, by Umbro Apollonio, Florence 1963; Leonardo Savioli, edited by Giovanni Fanelli, Florence 1966; Leonardo Savioli, edited by Massimo Becattini, Florence 1974; articles—"La Mostra dell'Oggetto Moderne Italiano" by Lara-Vinca Masini in Abitare (Milan), no. 14, 1963; "La Casa Abitata" by Lara-Vinca Masini and A. Pica in Domus (Milan), no. 426, 1965; "Leonardo Savioli" by M. Bottero in World Architecture 3, London 1966; "Art for the People: The Work of Leonardo Savioli" by Giuliano Chelazzi in Deutsche Bauzeitung (Stuttgart), January 1977; "The Cemetery of Montecatini" by Giovanni Klaus Koenig in L'Architettura (Rome), July 1978.

*

Leonardo Savioli has always combined architectural research with a constant graphic and pictorial activity, in which he relies on the rhythmic repetition of a symbol to generate form; in turn, rhythm and symbol have become essential elements of his architecture. It is always by way of a symbol that Savioli relives and recreates the artistic experience of the past while proposing concepts for the future of the city—such as the stratification and concretization of plastic elements of different periods that, assembled in "technological" strata, project the present and future configuration of the city.

Starting from a spare, clear architectural language, worked out in parallel slabs arranged in depth perspective (as in his own house at Certosa), Savioli has moved on to the elaboration of rhythmically arranged volumetric units, which became the foundation of his conception of self-contained composition, the creation of a landscape of forms not planned in advance but obtained from a series of additions. He moved from the plastic-technological object—detached, finite and complete in itself (like the Via Piagentina block in Florence)—to a rejection of architecture that is self-contained and inward-looking for one that is global, directly connected with the

course of life. This rejection followed a period of academic experiment and the university dispute of 1968. He calls his new work the "architecture of behavior."

After a series of lectures—before and during the university dispute—like that of 1967 on "Poor Equipment for a Collective Structure" (during which some of the first proposals for "radical architecture" also emerged), Savioli shifted his theoretical research toward the elaboration of proposals for polyfunctional systems for contemporary art.

His most recent architecture reflects his theoretical position. He plans a modular structure in advance; it has a distinct technological-industrial reference, is roofed in and extensible, and provides a base containing all the technical necessities on which the user is able to erect a series of pre-fabricated concrete elements for his particular use. The structure is efficient, easy to build and easy to manage, and creates residential units each different from the other—as in the two-apartment Bayon Villa at San Gaggio and in the project for a Workers' Village in the Volterrano.

—Lara-Vinca Masini

SCARPA, Carlo.

Italian. Born in Venice, 2 June 1906. Educated at the Accademia di Belle Arti, Venice, Dip.Arch. 1926; student assistant to Professor Guido Girilli, Institute of Architecture, University of Venice, 1926–27. Married. In private practice, Venice, 1927 until his death, 1978. Artistic Counsellor to the Murano Cappellin and Company Glassworks, Venice, 1927–30, to the Venice Biennale from 1941, and to the Venice Institute of Work, for the 8th Triennale, Milan, 1947. Drawing Instructor, Art and Industry Institute, Venice, 1945–47; Professor of Architectural Composition, 1972–74, and Director, 1972–78, Institute of Architecture, University of Venice. Exhibitions: Nine Architects, Venice, 1960; Architecture of the Museum, Museum of Modern Art, New York, 1966; Pursuit of New Structures, at the Biennale, Venice, 1968; Great Drawings from the Collection, Royal Institute of British Architects, London, 1972; Carlo Scarpa—Architetto Poeta, Royal Institute of British Architects, London, 1974; Carlo Scarpa, Accademia Olimpico, Vicenza, Italy, 1974; 28/78 Architettura, Palazzo delle Stelline, Milan, 1979. Recipient: National Olivetti Award, 1956; IN-ARCH National Award, 1962; Regional Architecture Prize, Verona, 1964; Accademia dei Lincei Prize, 1971. D.Arch.: University of Venice, 1955. Died (in Tokyo) 28 November 1978.

Works:

1928 Glassware Shop interiors, Lungarno Guicciardini, Florence (demolished)

1931 Pastry Shop interiors, Frezzeria, Venice (demolished)

Ferruccio Asta House interiors and furnishings, Venice

1932 Academy Bridge, Venice (competition project)

1934 Plan for Mestre, Venice (competition project; with Mario de Luigi)

Lido Airport, Venice (project)

1935 Bassani Apartment, Cortina, near Belluno, Italy (project)

1936/
37 Ca Foscari (Faculty of Economics and Commerce) restoration, University of Venice

1937 Design of the Venetian Jewels exhibition, Venice

1940 Small apartments, San Gregorio, Venice (project)

1941 Design of the Biennale, Venice

Rizzo Tomb, Cemetery of San Michele, Venice

1942 Galleria Il Cavallino interiors, Riva degli Schiavoni, Venice
1946 Cinema, Valdobbiadene, Treviso, Italy (project)
1947 Giacomuzzi House, Udine, Italy (project)
Rental apartments and shops, Spalato Square, Padua (project)
Trans-Adriatic Society Offices, Venice (project)
1947/
49 Catholic Bank Headquarters, Tarvisio, Udine (project)
1948 Design of the *Paul Klee* exhibition, *Biennale*, Venice
Catholic Bank, Cervignano, Udine (competition project)
Bus Station, Piazza Mazzini, Padua (project)
Parish Church, Torre di Mosto, Venice (project)
1948/
49 Cinema, San Dona di Piave, Venice (project)
1949 Bauer Hotel, San Moise, Venice (project)
Design of the *Giovanni Bellini* exhibition, Palazzo Ducale, Venice
Il Cavallino Gallery office interiors, Frezzeria, Venice
Apartment Building, Padua (project)
Guarnieri House, Lido, Venice (project)
4-storey rental apartment building, Feltre, Belluno, Italy (project)
Danieli Hotel lobby, Venice (project)
1949/
50 Storeroom, and design of the *Publications Exhibition*, at the *Venice Film Festival*
1950 Ala Piavola de Franza Shop alterations, Venice (demolished)
Ferdinando Ongania Shop interiors, San Marco, Venice (demolished)
Telephone Company office alterations, San Marco, Venice (demolished)
Galleria Il Cavallino Art Publications Pavilion, *Biennale*, Venice
Bortolatto House, Cervignano, Udine (project)
1952 Design of the Italian Pavilion, and of the *Tiepolo* exhibition, *Biennale*, Venice
Design of the *Graphic Works by Toulouse-Lautrec* exhibition, Palazzo Napoleonico, Venice
Historical Archives of Contemporary Art alterations, Ca'Giustinian, Venice (project)
Academy Gallery interiors and furnishings, Venice
1953 Design of *The 15th Century* exhibition, Town Hall, Messina
Correr Museum first floor gallery alterations, Venice
Villa Zoppas, Conegliano, Treviso, Italy (project)
National Gallery of Sicily restoration, Palazzo Abbatellis, Palermo
1954 Design of the *Art of Ancient China* exhibition, Palazzo Ducale, Venice
1954/
56 Academy Gallery interiors II, Venice
1955 Manlio Capitolo (public court) alterations, Rialto, Venice
Scatturin Lawyers' Office alterations, Venice
Museum, Library and Cultural Centre, La Spezia, Italy (competition project; with G. d'Agaro, E. Detti, and V. Pastor)
1955/
57 Pedestal, for the Monument to a Partisan, Venice (demolished)
1955/
61 Veritti House, Udine
1956 Design of the *Piet Mondrian* exhibition, Gallery of Modern Art, Rome
Olivetti Mountain Colony, Brusson, Ivrea, Italy (competition project; with G. d'Agaro, E. Detti, and V. Pastor)
Main Auditorium alterations, Ca'Foscari, Venice

Venezuelan Pavilion, *Biennale*, Venice
Six exhibition rooms remodelling. Uffizi Gallery, Florence (with Ignazio Gardella and Giovanni Michelucci)
1956/
57 Canova Museum alterations, Possagno, Treviso, Italy
1957 Taddei House, Dorsoduro, Venice (project)
1957/
58 Olivetti Showroom, San Marco, Venice
1958 Design of the *From Altichiero to Pisanello* exhibition, Castelvecchio Museum, Verona
Italian Pavilion interiors, *Biennale*, Venice
Design of the *Murano Glassware* exhibition, Salviati and Company, San Gregorio, Venice
1959 Design of the *Vitality in Art* exhibition, Palazzo Grassi, Venice
Design of *A Century of Art in Murano Glass* exhibition, Verona
1960 Correr Museum second floor galleries alterations, Venice
Design of the *Frank Lloyd Wright Memorial Exhibition*, Venice
Design of the *Erich Mendelsohn* exhibition, *Biennale*, Venice
1961 Design of the *Sense of Colour and the Mastery of Water* exhibition, *Italia '61*, Turin
Gavina Shop, Bologna (now the Simon Shop)
1961/
63 Querini Stampalia Library ground floor restoration and courtyard, Venice
1962 Design of the *Cima da Conegliano* exhibition, Treviso, Italy
1962/
63 Italian Pavilion alterations, *Biennale*, Venice (project)
1963 Cassina House, Ronco di Carimate, Italy (project)
Revoltella Museum alterations, Trieste (with Franco Vattolo)
Carlo Felice Theatre reconstruction, Genoa (project)
1964 Castelvecchio Museum restoration and alterations, Verona
Design of the *Giacomo Manzu* exhibition, Palazzo Napoleonico, Venice
1964/
65 Apartment Building, Grand Canal, Venice (project)
1964/
68 Zentner House alterations, Zurich
1965/
72 Benedetti House, Rome (project)
1966 Piazza del Duomo Development, Modena, Italy (project)
New Gallery reconstruction, Munich (competition project)
Design of the *Giorgio Morandi* exhibition, Italian Pavilion, *Biennale*, Venice
Entrance, Institute of Architecture, University of Venice (project)
1967 Design of *The Poem* exhibition, Italian Pavilion, *Expo '67*, Montreal
Design of the *Arturo Martini* exhibition, Treviso, Italy
1968 Design of the *Pursuit of New Structures* exhibition, *Biennale*, Venice
Design of *The Drawings of Erich Mendelsohn* exhibition, University of California, Berkeley
Design of the *Frescoes from Florence* exhibition, Hayward Gallery, London
Santini House, near Lucca, Italy (project)
Municipal Theatre, Vicenza, Italy (competition project)
1970 Design of the *Morandi* exhibition, Royal Academy, London
Masieri Memorial: Students Library and Housing, Grand Canal, Venice
1970/
72 Brion-Vega Tomb and Cemetery, San Vito, Treviso, Italy

1971/
72 Roth House, Asolo, Treviso, Italy (project)
1972 Lupi House, near Vicenza, Italy (project)
1972/
78 Carlo Felice Theatre, Genoa
1973 Fini Restaurant, Modena, Italy (project)
Library and Guest Rooms Annex, Querini Stampalia Library, Venice (project)
Museum remodelling (final stage), Villa Strozzi, Florence (project)
1973/
75 People's Mutual Bank, Verona
1974 Design of the *Gino Rossi* exhibition, Treviso, Italy
Design of the *Venezia-Byzantium* exhibition, Palazzo Ducale, Venice
1974/
75 Villa Palazzetto exterior alterations, Monselice, Padua
Santa Caterina Convent conversion to museum, Treviso, Italy (project)
Annex, Villa Matteazzi-Chiesa, Venice
1974/
78 National Museum, Messina
1975 Monument to the Victims of the '72 Terrorist Outrage, Brescio, near Milan
1975/
76 Convent of San Sebastiano reconstruction and extensions, Faculty of Literature and Philosophy, University of Venice
1975/
77 Preservation plan for the ancient Roman housing of Feltre, Italy
1976 Picasso Museum, Paris (project)
1977 Antoniana Bank Branch Office, Monselice, near Padua (project)
1977/
78 Week-end house for 3 families, Belluno, Italy (with Hiroyuki Toyota)

Designs: glassware for Murano Cappelin and Company, Venice, 1927–30, and for the Venini Company, Murano, Venice, 1933–47; furniture, particularly for the Gavina (now the Simon) Shop, Bologna; and silverware.

Publications:

By SCARPA: article—"Interview with Carlo Scarpa," with Barbara Radice, in *Modo* (Milan), January/February 1979.

On SCARPA: books—*Carlo Scarpa—Architetto Poeta* by Sergio Los, Venice 1967; *Carlo Scarpa—Architetto Poeta*, exhibition catalogue, by Sherban Cantacuzino, London 1974; *Carlo Scarpa*, exhibition catalogue, by Neri Pozza, Vicenza, Italy 1974; *28/78 Architettura: Fifty Years of Italian Architecture, 1928 to 1978*, exhibition catalogue, Milan 1979; articles—"Opere dell'Architetto Carlo Scarpa" by G. Mazzariol in *L'Architettura* (Rome), no. 3, 1955; "I Premi Nazionali di Architettura e Urbanistica a Carlo Scarpa e Ludovico Quaroni" by Bruno Zevi in *L'Architettura* (Rome), no. 15, 1957; "Progetti di Carlo Scarpa" by F. Tentori in *Casabella* (Milan), no. 222, 1958; "Object on View" by Michael Brawne in *Architectural Review* (London), no. 753, 1959; "L'Architettura di Carlo Scarpa" by S. Bettini in *Zodiac* (Milan), no. 6, 1960; " 'Italia '61' Visual Poetry" by P. Gray in *The Observer* (London), 14 May 1961; "Un'Opera Distrutta di Carlo Scarpa" by Pier Carlo Santini in *Zodiac* (Milan), no. 9, 1962; "Carlo Scarpa il Veneziano" by M. Bottero, in *World Architecture 2*, London 1965; "Carlo Scarpa—Architetto Veneziano" by M. Brusatin in *Controspazio* (Bari, Italy), no. 3/4, 1972; "Scarpa: L'Ornement est un Crime" by Pierre Joly in *L'Oeil* (Lausanne), no. 223, 1973; "Carlo Scarpa" in *Architectural Review* (London), December 1973; "La 'Magie' de Carlo Scarpa" by Manfredo Tafuri and "Locus Solus—Carlo Scarpa et le Cimetière de San Vito d'Altivole" by P. Duboy in *L'Architecture d'Aujourd'hui* (Paris), no. 181, 1975; "Carlo Scarpa" by Tadashi Yokoyama and Hiroyuki Toyota, special issue of *Space Design* (Tokyo), June 1977; "Carlo Scarpa: The Greatest Designer of Contemporary Italian Architecture" in *L'Architettura* (Rome), January 1979; "Obituary: Carlo Scarpa" in *Architectural Review* (London), February 1979.

Post-war Italian architecture made a number of quite specific and recognizable contributions; prominent among them was the design of museum interiors. Carlo Scarpa belonged to a small group of architects who renovated a number of the great Italian museums and who were occasionally also able to demonstrate that their design skills did not depend entirely on the juxtaposition of new elements within an old context. To thousands of visitors to the Palazzo Abbatellis in Palermo, the Castelvecchio in Verona, or the Correr Museum in Venice, it must have come as perhaps both a surprise and a revelation that a contemporary architect could treat the art of the past—whether a painting or a building—with such sympathy yet freshness. It was not what they immediately associated with modern architecture.

Scarpa's success may have been aided by two strong interests that are closely related to each other: decoration and the craft of building. What makes an immediate impression in a building such as the Venezuelan Pavilion in the grounds of the Venice *Biennale* is not only the relation between the major and minor volumes or the dissolution of the corner in the way in which the glass in the roof joins the glass in the wall, but also the detail of the screen hinge. A simple device becomes a celebration that explains an action, focuses the eye on an element of decoration, and speaks of the care and skill with which the building has been designed and put together.

These skills have also been put at the service of showing objects of art in ways that have radically altered our way of seeing and understanding them. No setting can ever be non-existent or even neutral; at its best it should be sympathetic. Scarpa has been able to devise such settings through an understanding of the unique attributes of the object. At the Palazzo Abbatellis, for instance, Francesco Laurana's bust of Eleanor of Aragon, seen at the end of a vista through two doorways, is raised slightly above its metal support so that none of its form will be visually interrupted; behind it the background of green painted panels emphasizes the outline of the white marble and at the same time provides within a tall room an environment in scale with the size of the sculpture and the delicacy of its carving.

Scarpa's work is deeply rooted in the Venetian tradition; at the same time he has been enormously influenced by Frank Lloyd Wright. Not only do his drawings resemble those of Wright, but he has taken up Wright's preoccupation with architecture as a plastic, intensely three-dimensional art. From Wright and Charles Rennie Mackintosh he has also inherited a belief in a kind of visual density that derives from both form and materials and the way in which they are detailed—what Kahn writing about Scarpa described as "the sense of the wholeness of inseparable elements."

Scarpa's work began to make an impact in the middle 1950's, long before notions of conservation, respect for the past, or the recognition of the possibilities of decoration were seriously mooted. The contribution that he and a number of his Italian contemporaries made was thus to awaken among architects both an alternative view of the past and a new way of relating it to the present—of perhaps understanding the value of a continuity in tradition.

—Michael Brawne

SCHAROUN, Hans.

German. Born in Bremen, 20 September 1893. Educated at the Technische Hochschule, Charlottenburg, Berlin, 1912–15. Worked in the office of Paul Kruchen, Berlin, 1913–15, and served as site architect to Kruchen on the East Prussia Rebuilding Programme, 1915–18; in private practice, Insterburg, Germany, 1919–25; in partnership with Adolf Rading, Berlin, 1926–28; in private practice, Berlin, 1932 until his death, 1972. City Planning Officer, Berlin, 1945–47; Founder, Planungskollektiv, Berlin, 1946. Professor of Architecture, Academy of Arts, Breslau, 1925–32; Senior Professor of Town Planning, Technical University, Berlin, 1946–58; Head, Institute of Building Studies, Berlin, 1947–51. Member, Glaserne Kette (Glass Chain), Berlin, 1919; Member, Works Council for the Arts, Berlin, 1919; Member of Der Ring, Berlin, 1926. Exhibitions: *Weissenhofsiedlung,* Stuttgart, 1927; *German Garden and Industry Exhibition,* Leignitz, 1927–28; *Deutscher Werkbund Exhibition,* Breslau, 1929; *Building Exhibition,* Berlin, 1931; *Hans Scharoun,* Akademie der Künste, Berlin, 1967, 1969; *Hans Scharoun,* Institute of Contemporary Arts, London, 1974. Recipient: First Prize, Cathedral Square Competition, Prenzlau, 1919; First Prize, Market Place Competition, Insterburg, 1921; First Prize, Leiderhalle Competition, Stuttgart, 1949; First Prize, Theatre Competition, Kassel, 1952; First Prize, Old People's Home Competition, Berlin, 1952; Fritz Schumacher Prize, Hamburg, 1954; Berliner Kunst Prize, 1954; First Prize, Town Planning Competition, Bremen, 1956; First Prize, Berlin Philharmonie Competition, 1956; Federal Grand Cross of Merit, 1959; Medallion, Free Arts Academy, Hamburg, 1959; First Prize, Mehringplatz Development Competition, Berlin, 1963; Bund Deutscher Architekten Prize, 1964; First Prize, Library of Prussian Culture Competition, Berlin, 1964; Auguste Perret Prize, International Union of Architects, 1965; First Prize, Wolfsburg Theatre Competition, 1965; Honorary Citizenship, Berlin, 1969. Honorary doctorates: Technische Hochschule, Stuttgart, 1954; University of Rome, 1965. Senator of the Technical University of Berlin, 1962. *Died* (in Berlin) *25 November 1972.*

Works:

1911 Church, Bremerhaven, Germany (competition project)
1913 Plan for the Kaiser-Wilhelm-Platz, Geestemunde, Germany (competition project)
 Kruchen House, Buch, near Berlin (with Paul Kruchen)
 Freymuth Sanatorium, Babelsberg, near Berlin (with Paul Kruchen)
 Grunewald Sanatorium, near Berlin (project; with Paul Kruchen)
1914 Hospital, Mariendorf, near Berlin (with Paul Kruchen)
 Community Hall, Angerburg, Germany (competition project)
1915 Town plan for Gumbinnen, East Prussia (project)
1916 Riding School/Temporary Church conversion, Walterkehmen, East Prussia
 Inn, Goldaper Lake, East Prussia (project)
1917 Community Hall, Kattenau, East Prussia
1917/
 18 Farmhouse, Thierfeld, near Gumbinnen, East Prussia
1918 Semi-detached houses, with stables, near Insterburg, East Prussia
1919 State Housing Development, Insterburg, East Prussia (project)
 Tivoli Theatre conversion, Insterburg, East Prussia (project)
 Cemetery, Dortmund, Germany (competition project)
 Cathedral Square, Prenzlau, Germany (competition project)
 Town Hall, Emmerich, Germany (competition project)

 Swimming Baths, Prenzlau, Germany (competition project)
1920 2 houses, Pregelstrasse, Insterburg, East Prussia
 Gutzheit House conversion, near Gumbinnen, East Prussia
 Kamswyken Housing Development, near Insterburg, East Prussia
 Cultural Centre, Gelsenkirchen, Germany (competition project)
 Matheus Muller Works extensions, Eltville, Rheinhessen, Germany (competition project)
 Town Hall and Church Square, Lyck, East Prussia (competition project)
 Museum of Medicine, Dresden (competition project)
1920/
 21 Town planning scheme for Insterburg, East Prussia (competition project)
1921 Railway Station Post Office, Bremen (competition project)
 Market Place, Insterburg, East Prussia (competition project)
1921/
 22 Farmhouse conversion, Sahtilten, East Prussia
1922 Farmyard with forge and riding stables, Kuinen, East Prussia
 Stock Exchange Building, Königsberg, East Prussia (competition project)
 Chicago Tribune Building (competition project)
 Multi-Storey Office Building, Friedrichstrasse, Berlin (competition project)
 Granary Building, Wertheim, East Prussia
 Town Hall, Wesel, Germany (competition project)
 Single-family houses, Insterburg, East Prussia
 Gobert House, Sodehnen, East Prussia
 Kant Monument, Königsberg, East Prussia (competition project)
1923 Office and apartment building conversion, Insterburg, East Prussia
1923/
 24 Apartment blocks, Parkring, Insterburg, East Prussia
1924 Prince Albrecht Gardens Buildings, Berlin (competition project)
1924/
 25 Munsterplatz, Ulm, Germany (competition project)
 Public Buildings, Bad Mergentheim Spa, Württemberg, Germany
 Business Premises, Frankfurt (competition project)
1925 Professor Siegel House, Insterburg, East Prussia (project)
 Tannenberg Monument, Germany (competition project)
 Town Hall, Bochum, Germany (competition project)
 Konitzer Shop, Marienburg, East Prussia (project)
 Water Tower (3 competition projects)
 Bridgehead Building, Cologne (competition project)
1926 Station Square, Duisburg, Germany (competition project)
 Variable Apartment Block Dwellings (project)
 Popelwitz Housing Development, Breslau (competition project)
1927 Exhibition Site and Fairground, Berlin (competition project)
 Town Hall, Insterburg, East Prussia (competition project)
 Exhibition Hall, Breslau (2 projects)
 Transportable Wooden House, *German Garden and Industry Exhibition,* Liegnitz
 Single-family house, *Weissenhofsiedlung,* Stuttgart

Hans Scharoun: State Library, Berlin, 1978

Redevelopment plan for Ministry Gardens, Berlin (project; with Peter Behrens, Adolf Rading, Heinrich Tessenow and Martin Wagner)

Offices and fire station, Breslau (competition project)

Reichstag Building extensions, Berlin (2 competition projects)

Swimming Baths, near the Zoo, Berlin (project)

Apartment block, Dahlem, Berlin (project)

1928 Evangelical Church, Zimpel, Breslau (competition project)

School, Zimpel, Breslau (competition project)

Civic Hall and Exhibition Hall, Bremen (competition project)

School buildings, Schlichtallee, Lichtenberg, Berlin (competition project)

Single-Family House (competition project)

Hotel, Wesermunde, Germany (project)

Richard Wagner Monument, Leipzig (competition project)

1928/
29 Apartment block, Kaiserdamm, Charlottenburg, Berlin

1929 Single People's Apartment Block, *Deutscher Werkbund Exhibition,* Breslau

Housing, Kaiserstrasse, Bremerhaven, Germany

Apartment block, Heidelberger Platz, Wilmersdorf, Berlin (project)

Apartment block, Paulsbornerstrasse, Wilmersdorf, Berlin (project)

German Iron and Steel Company Exhibition Pavilion, Desta, Germany (project)

1929/
30 Apartment block, Hohenzollerndamm 35–36, Wilmersdorf, Berlin

1930 Law Courts, Invalidenstrasse, Tiergarten, Berlin (competition project)

Housing development, Siemenstadt, Berlin

Apartment block, Lindner, Berlin (project)

Schlachtensee-type Terraced Housing (project)

Halensee-type Terraced Housing (project)

Apartment block, Flinsberger Platz, Wilmersdorf, Berlin (destroyed, 1944; rebuild by others, 1963)

Civic Hall, Rostock, Germany (competition project)

1931 Leiser Company Shop Sign, Berlin (project)

War Memorial, Thuringer Wald, Germany (competition project)

Steinhausen House conversion, Falkenhain, near Berlin (project)

Bauwelt Contemporary House, Berlin (competition project)

Housing, Kottbusser Tor, Kreuzberg, Berlin (project)

Housing, Treseburger Ufer, Neukolln, Berlin (project)

Housing, Hauptstrasse, Schöneberg, Berlin (project)

Housing, Kaiserdamm, Charlottenburg, Berlin (project)

"Worolet" Housing Types (project)

3 Moller Single-Family Houses, Potsdam, near Berlin (project)

Apartment Block with Access Galleries, Berlin (project)

Lobau-type Single-Family House (project)

2 semi-detached houses (project)

Suburban Housing Scheme, Berlin (project; with Edwin Gutkind)

Housing and Cinema, Spandauer Damm, Charlottenburg, Berlin (project)

2-storey apartment blocks, Berlin (project)

4-storey apartment blocks, Berlin (project)

Housing, Wannsee, Berlin (project)

Apartment block, Reichstrasse, Charlottenburg, Berlin (project)

Plan for Central Corridor Block Apartments, Berlin (project)

Apartment block, Hindenburgplatz, Bremerhaven, Germany (project)

1932 Single-Family House (3 projects)

Square Building Apartment, Berlin (project)

"The Growing House," Berlin (exhibition project)

Apartment block, Landsberger Allee, Lichtenberg, Berlin (project)

Cinema, Bremerhaven, Germany (project)

Panke Park, near Berlin (project)

Transportable House (project)

Apartment block, Hohenzollernring, Spandau, Berlin

Wenzeck House, Frohnau, Berlin

Schuldenfrey House, Garystrasse 26, Dahlem, Berlin

Apartment block with variable flats (project)

Apartment block, Berlin (project)

Single-family house with arcade (project)

1933 Apartment block, Zweibruckerstrasse 38–46, Spandau, Berlin

Variable Dwelling (project)

Schminke House, Löbau, Saxony, Germany

Strauss House, Huninger Strasse, Dahlem, Berlin

Town plan for Stockholm (competition project)

Apartment block, Alexanderplatz, Berlin (project)

Mattern House, Bornim, Potsdam, near Berlin

Housing development, Kladow-Hottengrund, Berlin
1934 Loeser and Richter Works conversion and extensions, Lobau, Saxony, Germany
Single-family housing group, Burgerpark, Wesermunde, Germany (project)
Hotel holiday houses, Vietznau, Switzerland (project)
Muller-Oerlinhausen Mosaic Works Shop, Charlottenburg, Berlin
Professor Gocht House, Berlin (project)
1935 Baensch House, Hohenweg 9, Spandau, Berlin
Hoffmeyer House, Friesenstrasse 6, Bremerhaven, Germany
Pflaum House, Falkensee, near Berlin
1936 Housing, Kaiserstrasse 224, Bremerhaven, Germany
House, Heiligensee, Berlin
Moll House, Grunewald, Berlin (destroyed, 1944)
1937 Housing, Elbestrasse, Bremerhaven, Germany
Moller House, Zermutzelsee, near Altruppin, Brandenburg, Germany
1937/
38 Noack House, Potsdam, near Berlin
1938 Biskupski House, Zermutzelsee, near Altruppin, Brandenburg, Germany
Housing, Blessmannstrasse, Bremerhaven, Germany
Kruger House conversion, Rehwiese 4, Nikolasse, Berlin
Bonk House, Bornim, Potsdam, near Berlin
Housing, Humboldtstrasse, Reinickendorf, Berlin (project)
Just House, Schlachtensee, Berlin (project)
Apartment Block conversion, Yorkstrasse, Bremerhaven, Germany (project)
1939 Weidhaas House, Leipzig (2 projects)
Silbermann Family Garden Bath-House, Havel, Brandenburg, Germany
Scharf House, Miquelstrasse 39a/b, Schmargendorf, Berlin
Mohrmann House, Falkensteinstrasse 10, Lichtenrade, Berlin
1940 Housing, Kaiserstrasse 240–54, Bremerhaven, Germany
Endell House, Kleinen Wannsee 30b, Wannsee, Berlin
Studio conversion, Kantstrasse 12, Charlottenburg, Berlin
1941/
43 Central Laundry, Berlin (project)
1942 Weigand House, Borgsdorf, near Berlin
1943 Muller-Oerlinghausen House conversion, Kressbroon/Bodensee, Germany
Moller House extension, Zermutzelsee, near Altruppin, Brandenburg, Germany
1946 Berlin City Plan (project; with Planungskollektiv Group)
Deutschland Plastic House (project; with Karl Bottcher)
Exhibition Gallery, Friedrichstrasse Station, Berlin (project)
1948 Wilhelm House, Kladow, Berlin (project)
America House conversion, Bremerhaven, Germany
Gerd Rosen Exhibition Gallery (project)
1949 Opera House, Leipzig (competition project)
Cellulose Factory, Rothensee, Magdeburg, Germany (project)
Neighborhood Unit Housing, Friedrichshain, Berlin (project)
Leiderhalle, Stuttgart (competition project)
Institute of Building conversion, German Academy of Sciences, Berlin
1950 Schminke House extensions, Löbau, Saxony, Germany (project)
Shops and apartments, Kurfurstendamm 182, Charlottenburg, Berlin (project)
1951 Primary school, Darmstadt (project)
American Memorial Library, Blucherplatz,

Kreuzberg, Berlin (competition project)
1952 Heinrich-Mendelsohn Building, Kaiserdamm, Charlottenburg, Berlin (competition project)
Siemenstadt Centre, Jungfernheideweg, Berlin (project)
City Theatre, Kassel, Germany (competition project)
Old People's Home, Tiergarten, Berlin (competition project)
Plan for the development of Heligoland, Germany (competition project)
1953 National Theatre, Mannheim (competition project)
1954 Theatre, Gelsenkirchen, Germany (competition project)
1954/
59 "Romeo and Juliet" Flats, Zuffenhausen, Stuttgart
1955 Private school, Bergneustadt, Germany (competition project)
Office building, Hanover (competition project)
New Market, Hamburg (competition project)
City Plan for Marl, Westphalia, Germany (as project consultant)
Restaurant, Hansaviertel, Berlin (project)
Wella Company Administration Buildings, Darmstadt (2 competition projects)
Stroeher House, Darmstadt
Apartment block extensions, Goebelstrasse 1–9, Siemenstadt, Berlin (original building by Bartning)
1956 Town plan for Bremen (competition project)
Orphanage, Botnang, Stuttgart (project)
Krupp Convent, Essen (competition project)
Development plan for the Hansaviertel, Tiergarten, Berlin (project)
Single-family houses, Hansaviertel, Tiergarten, Berlin (project)
1956/
61 Housing, North Charlottenburg, Berlin
1956/
62 Geschwister Secondary School, Lunen, Westphalia, Germany
1957 School, Holterhofchen, Hilden, Westphalia, Germany (competition project)
Civic Hall, Bremen (competition project)
Shopping centre, Goebelplatz, North Charlottenburg, Berlin (project)
1958 Concert Hall, Saarbrucken (competition project)
Plan for Spandau Old Town, Berlin (project)
Rothenburg House conversion, Dahlem, Berlin (project)
State Savings Bank, Stuttgart (project)
Town Hall, Marl, Westphalia, Germany (competition project)
1959 Berlin as Capital City (competition project)
Plan for Reeperbahn-Millerntor, Hamburg (project)
1960 Studio flat, Berlin (project)
1961 School for Social Studies, Linz, Austria (competition project)
1961/
63 "Salute" High-Rise Block, Stuttgart
1961/
68 School, Marl, Westphalia, Germany
1962 Foreign Students Hostel (project)
Leere Vasen Housing Development, Boblingen, near Stuttgart
Dumont Schauberg Publishers Offices, Cologne (project)
1963 Dom-Romerberg-Bereich, Frankfurt (competition project)
Berlin Philharmonie, Kemperplatz, Tiergarten, Berlin
Redevelopment plan for Mehringplatz, Kreuzberg, Berlin (competition project)
1963/
71 German Embassy, Brasilia
1964 Neven-DuMont House, Cologne (project)
Concert Hall, Pforzheim, Germany (competi-

tion project)
Theatre, Zurich (competition project)
BP Offices, Hamburg (competition project)
Library of Prussian Culture, Tiergarten, Berlin (competition project)
1965 Housing, Rauhe Kapf, Boblingen, near Stuttgart
1966 Tormann House, Bad Homburg van der Hohe, Germany
Faculty of Architecture Building, Technical University of Berlin
Chapel of St. John, Glockengarten, Bochum, Germany
Church of the Transfiguration of Christ, Viktoria-Luise-Platz, Schöneberg, Berlin (project)
Art Centre and Hostel, Matthaikirchplatz, Tiergarten, Berlin (project)
1967/
78 State Library, Berlin
1968 "Red Garage," Zuffenhausen, Stuttgart
Kopke House, Im Dol 10, Dahlem, Berlin
1969 Housing, Hasenbergsteige, Stuttgart (project)
1970 Church and Parish Centre, Rabenberg, Wolfsburg, Germany
Kindergarten, Detmerode, Wolfsburg, Germany
High-rise apartment block, Zabel-Kruger-Damm, Reinickendorf, Berlin
AOK Headquarters Building, Mehringplatz, Kreuzberg, Berlin
German Maritime Museum, Bremerhaven, Germany
1971 "Orplid" High-Rise Apartment Block, Boblingen, near Stuttgart
1973 City Theatre, Wolfsburg, Germany
1978 Philharmonie Chamber Music Hall, Tiergarten, Berlin (completed by others)
State Institute for Musical Research and Museum of Musical Instruments, Tiergarten, Berlin (completed by others)

Publications:

By SCHAROUN: articles—"Struktur in Raum und Zeit" in *Handbuch Moderner Architektur,* Berlin 1957; "Raum und Milieu der Schule" in *Bauen und Wohnen* (Zurich), April 1961; preface to *Baroque: Italie et Europe Centrale* by Pierre Charpentrat, Fribourg 1964.

On SCHAROUN: books—*Hans Scharoun,* exhibition catalogues, by Heinrich Lauterbach, Berlin 1967, 1969; *Global Architecture: The Berlin Philharmonic Concert Hall* by Yukio Futagawa and Hiroshi Sasaki, Tokyo 1973; *Expressionist Architecture* by Wolfgang Pehnt, London 1973; *Fantastic Architecture* by Ulrich Conrads and Hans G. Sperlich, London 1973; *Hans Scharoun: Bauten, Entwürfe, Texte,* edited by Peter Pfankuch, Berlin 1974; *Hans Scharoun* by Peter Blundell Jones, London 1978; articles—"Hans Scharoun: Oeuvres Récentes" in *L'Architecture d'Aujourd'hui* (Paris), September/November 1960; "Hans Scharoun: Ein Beitrag zum organischen Bauen" by Margit Staber in *Zodiac* (Milan), no. 10, 1962; "L'Opera di Hans Scharoun e la sua influenza a Lunen" in *L'Architettura* (Rome), October 1963; "Hans Scharoun," special issue of *Bouwkundig Weekblad* (Amsterdam), October 1963; "The Work of Hans Scharoun" by Udo Kultermann in *Binario* (Lisbon), January/February 1974; "Hans Scharoun: An Exhibition of His Work" by Peter Blundell Jones in *Building Design* (London), 8 November 1974; "Hans Scharoun: A Short Discussion of His Work" in *The Architect* (London), December 1974; "Late Work of Scharoun" by Peter Blundell Jones in *Architectural Review* (London), March 1975; "Hans Scharoun: An Introduction" by Peter Blundell Jones in *Architectural Design* (London), July 1978; "Hans Scharoun" by Peter Blundell Jones in *RIBA Journal* (London), November 1978.

Hans Scharoun's early work was a mixture of international modernism and expressionism. His flats at the *Deutscher Werkbund Exhibition* in 1929, though strictly functional in conception, have some expressionist features and are full of curves and pierced splayed walls. He was responsible for the general layout of the housing at Siemenstadt, Berlin, in 1930, and his own contribution to the scheme also shows traces of expressionism.

Although Scharoun's work falls into two distinct parts, before and after the Second World War, the buildings he designed during the war are of considerable interest. Scharoun was not a popular architect before the war, but he built a number of remarkable houses, among which the Schminke House, Löbau, is outstanding. Arranged at first floor level, it has a free open plan divided only by light-weight moveable partitions. The house has generous balconies which curve and sweep around it.

His houses were always very skilfully sited, making the maximum use of ground and cross-country views. He did not hesitate to plan a living room facing north if the best outlook was in that direction, but he always compensated for the lack of sunlight by providing smaller windows in the same room looking southward. His greatest skill was in the creation of interior space incorporating outlook, comfort, and surprise, the last often obtained by the use of converging and then widening walls in the form of a venturi. The direction of the best views was always marked on his sketch plans; houses were clearly seen to be created round these axes. Apart from this determination to make the best use of the site, there is nothing geometrical about his plans: they flow freely and logically and without constraint. He never seems to have been much concerned with external appearances, usually leaving them to take care of themselves, sometimes with not very happy results.

During the Second World War his designs were officially unpopular, but he still continued to design private houses, clothing his expressionist plans in skilfully designed traditional exteriors which either deceived or satisfied the authorities.

It was not until after the war that Scharoun came into his own as the Expressionist of the age. Outstanding among his post-war designs was the City Theatre for Kassel, which was never built because the client doubted whether the design could be constructed. It was the design for the Romeo and Juliet Flats in Stuttgart-Zuffenhausen, in 1954–59, that firmly established him. Here the plan, almost devoid of right angles, points in nine different directions, while odd-shaped curved and pointed balconies add to the startling and dramatic silhouette. In spite of their curious and even frightening appearance, the flats are extremely popular and are snapped up the moment they come onto the market.

Scharoun's best-known work, The Berlin Philharmonie, is one of the world's great concert hall interiors clad in a drab and collapsed-looking exterior. The hall, reached from a dramatic polygonal foyer where staircases shoot off Piranesi-like at all angles, is built up of parcels of seating round the orchestra. Each parcel contains about the same number of seats as there are players in the orchestra, and the effect is to reduce the overall scale of the interior without lessening the total sense of space. For once the siting of the building is far from ideal. It deserves an enclosed site; instead, it looks over-exposed, like jelly on a flat dish.

Scharoun's German Embassy in Brasilia shows his use of floor space at its most prodigal, with frequent changes of level and many oddly-shaped rooms. Externally, boldly expressionist use is made of sun screens.

Scharoun also built several schools notable for their immense spread and their logical planning within what at first appears to be an incomprehensible jumble. Elevations—or, more properly, exteriors—were allowed to develop themselves, and detailing is heavy but simple and modest.

The Maritime Museum in Bremen contrasts with most of Scharoun's other buildings in that it is comparatively simple in conception. But the plan and general conception of the City Theatre in Wolfsburg astounds by the extravagance of its spread, above all in its foyer and cloakrooms. It has much in common with the Berlin Philharmonie. The Berlin City Library, sited opposite Mies van der Rohe's National Gallery, is Scharoun's last and largest building. At first sight its plan seems very wasteful, although the various functions are skilfully integrated. No doubt, as in all Scharoun's buildings, it will be found to have some fine interiors.

—Gontran Goulden

SCHINDLER, Rudolph.

American. Born in Vienna, 5 September 1887; emigrated to the United States, 1914. Educated at the Imperial Technical Institute of Vienna, 1906–11; Vienna Academy of Arts, under Otto Wagner, 1909–14. Married Sophie Pauline Gibling in 1919 (separated in the 1930's). Worked as a Draftsman for Mayr and Mayer, Vienna, 1911, and for Ottenheimer, Stern and Reichert, Chicago, 1914; joined the office of Frank Lloyd Wright, Chicago, as an unsalaried employee, 1916: became a paid employee, 1918; sent by Wright to oversee work on the Barnsdall Houses, Los Angeles, 1920–21; in private practice, Los Angeles, 1921 until his death, 1953. Lecturer, Chicago School of Applied Art, 1917. Exhibitions: Scripps College, Claremont, California, 1950; University of California at Santa Barbara, 1967; Stedelijk Museum, Amsterdam, 1969; Royal Institute of British Architects, London, 1969. *Died (in Los Angeles) 22 August 1953.*

Works:

1912 Hotel Rong, Vienna (project)
Hunting Lodge, Vienna (project)
Actors' Clubhouse, 6 Dorotheergasse, Vienna (for Mayr and Mayer)
1912/
13 Crematorium and Chapel, Vienna (project)
1914 Summer House, near Vienna (project)
Neighborhood Center, Chicago (competition project)
1915 Hotel, Chicago (project)
Bar, Chicago (project)
Martin House, Taos, New Mexico (project)
1915/
16 Homer Emunim Temple and School, Chicago (project)
1916 Store Front, Chicago (project)
Central Administration Building, Chicago (project)
Women's Club, Chicago (project)
Lee House remodelling, Maywood, Illinois
Hampden Club, Chicago
1916/
17 Log House (project)
1917 House, Oak Park, Illinois (project)
1917/
18 Buena Shore Club, Chicago
1918 Children's Corner, Art Institute of Chicago (project)
1919 One-room Apartment, Chicago (project)
Memorial Community Center, Wenatchee, Washington
Staley House, Waukegan, Illinois
Shampay House, Chicago
Workmen's Colony ("Monolith Homes"), Chicago (project)
1920 Temporary House for J. B. Irving, Wilmette, Illinois (project)
Theatre, shops and apartments, Olive Hill, Los Angeles (project; with Frank Lloyd Wright)
Barnsdall Houses A and B, Olive Hill, Los Angeles (with Frank Lloyd Wright)
Bergen Free Public Library, Jersey City, New Jersey (competition project)
Industrial Housing, Los Angeles (project)
House, 7 Greenwood Common, Berkeley, California
1921 Walt Whitman School, Los Angeles (project)
Korsen Bungalow Court, Los Angeles (project)
The Playmart Skyscraper, Los Angeles (project)
1921/
22 Schindler/Clyde Chase Double House, 833 North Kings Road, Hollywood, California
1922 Helena Rubinstein Beauty Salon, Los Angeles
Binder and Gross Apartment Buildings, Soto Street, Los Angeles
Burrell Duplex, Hollywood, California
Henderson Double House, Los Angeles
Caplan Apartment Building remodelling, Los Angeles
Lacey Duplex, 830–832 Laguna Avenue, Los Angeles
Kent House, Los Angeles (project)
Mix House, Los Angeles (project)
Campbell House, Los Angeles (project)
Duncan House, Los Angeles (project)
Lindquist House, Hollywood, California (project)
Baker Photographic Studio, Los Angeles
Temple Apartment Building, Hollywood, California (project)
Popinoff Cabin, Coachella, California
Burrell House, Los Angeles (project)
1922/
24 Davies House, Los Angeles (project)
1922/
25 Floren Duplexes and Apartments, Harper and Romaine and La Jolla and Romaine, Hollywood, California
1923 Friedman/Kopley Apartment Building, 115 North Soto Street, Los Angeles
Paine Duplex, 1024 Havenhurst Avenue, Los Angeles
Lovell House, Hollywood, California (project)
Lowe House, Eagle Rock, California (with Frank Lloyd Wright)
Hotel Wind and Sea alterations, La Jolla, California (project)
Warne House, Hollywood, California (project)
Art Room, Hollywood Public Library, California (project; with Douglas Donaldson)
Physical Education Club Lodge, Topanga Ranch, Topanga Canyon, Los Angeles County (project)
Neville Store and Hotel, Hollywood, California (project)
Helena Rubinstein House alterations and remodelling, Greenwich, Connecticut
Leswin/Leepa Beach Studio and Store, Castel La Mar, California
Pueblo Ribera Community, 230 Gravilla Street, La Jolla, California
Baker House, Hollywood, California (project)
Kruetzer Apartment Building, 1620–1626 North Gower Street, Los Angeles
Four-flat building, 4327 Harold Way, Los Angeles
1924 Popinoff Desert House, Coachella, California (project)
Lovell Vacation House, Wrightwood, California
Braun Apartment Building remodelling, 6092 Selma Avenue, Los Angeles
Packard House, 931 North Gainsborough Drive, South Pasadena, California
The Peoples Bank, Los Angeles (project)
Plotkin House, Los Angeles (project)
Barnsdall Houses garden wall and landscaping, Olive Hill, Los Angeles
Gibling House, Los Angeles

Rudolph Schindler: Lovell Beach House, Newport Beach, California, 1926

Nurembega Heights Hotel, Burbank, California (project)

1924/
33 Levin House, 2376 Dundee Place, Los Angeles
1925 Barnsdall Houses remodelling, Olive Hill, Los Angeles
Popinoff Hotel and Bungalow Community, Coachella, California (project)
Howe House, 2422 Silver Ridge Avenue, Los Angeles
Hotel Elsinore, Elsinore, California (project; with A. R. Brandner and Richard Neutra)
Wading Pool and Pergola, for Barnsdall Houses, Olive Hill, Los Angeles
Photographic Studio, Ambassador Hotel, Los Angeles (project)
Lovell Ranch House, Fallbrook, California
Furniture for Lovell House children's workshop, Los Angeles
Sullivan/Kent Tea Room, Los Angeles
Brudin House, El Monte, California (project)

Breacher Apartment Building, Los Angeles
Park Ranch House, Fallbrook, California
1925/
26 Lovell Beach House, 1242 Ocean Avenue, Newport Beach, California
1926 Weiner House remodelling, 1120 Court Street, Los Angeles
Briggs House, Newport Beach, California (project)
Sorg House, 600 South Putney Avenue, San Gabriel, California
Exhibition Room, Berkeley, California (project)
Morgenthau Studio, Palm Springs, California (project)
Leah-Ruth Shop, Long Beach, California
Haines Health Food Store, Los Angeles
League of Nations Building (competition project; with Richard Neutra)
Brown Apartments, Hollywood, California (project)
Hain House, Los Angeles

Hennessey Brothers Apartment Building, Los Angeles (project)
Levy Apartment Building, Los Angeles (project)
1926/
28 Martec House, Los Angeles (project)
Price House, Los Angeles (project)
1926/
40 Manola Court Apartment Building, 1811–1813 Edgecliff Drive, Los Angeles
1927 Freeman House furniture, 1965 Glencoe Way, Hollywood, California
Hotel Elsinore, Elsinore, California (2nd project; with A. R. Brandner)
Miller Apartment Building, Los Angeles (project)
Four-flat building, Pasadena, California
Aesop's Store, Los Angeles
Temporary outdoor exhibition pavilion, Barnsdall Houses, Olive Hill, Los Angeles
Garden Apartments, Los Angeles (project)
Miller Apartment Building, Los Angeles (project)
Napolitano Oil Mill, 676 Clover Street, Los Angeles
Richardson House remodelling, 8272 Marmont Way, Los Angeles
Zaczek House, Los Angeles (project)
Translucent House (Barnsdall House), Palos Verdes, California (project)
Amusement Center, Los Angeles (project)
1927/
28 Falcon Flyers Country Club, near Wasco, Kern County, California (project)
1928 Twin Harbor Community, Catalina Island, California (project)
Slemons House, Los Angeles (project)
Art Gallery, Lake Merritt, Oakland, California (project)
Braxton House, Venice, California (project)
Barnsdall House remodelling, Olive Hill, Los Angeles
The Golden Pyramid, Los Angeles (project)
Wolfe Summer House, Avalon, Catalina Island, California
Sets for *Soul of Raphael*, Trinity Auditorium, Los Angeles
Braxton Gallery, Hollywood, California
Grokowsky House, 816 Bonita Drive, South Pasadena, California
1929 Hotel, Hollywood, California (project)
Diffen House remodelling, Avalon, Catalina Island, California (project)
Coffee Shop for Tucson Holding Company, Arizona (project)
Wolfe School of Costume Designing, Los Angeles
Satyr Bookshop, Los Angeles
Lavana Studio Building, Los Angeles (project)
Automobile Show Room, Lincoln Garage Building, Beverly Hills, California (with H. Sachs)
Lingerbrink Cabin, Calabasas, California
J. J. Newberry Storefront, Los Angeles (project; with H. Sachs)
Paradise Resort, Ontario, California (project)
Cabin No. 1, Park Moderne, Blackbird Way, Woodland Hills, California
Effie Dean Cafe, Los Angeles (project)
Frankel Apartment Building, Los Angeles (project)
Vorkapic House remodelling, 2100 Benedict Canyon, Beverly Hills, California
Easter Puppet Show, Los Angeles
1930 Shore House, Venice, California (project)
Cohan Market, Los Angeles (project)
Exposition Buildings and Park, Los Angeles (project)
Bennati House remodelling, Los Angeles (partially executed)
Elliot House, 4237 Newdale Drive, Los Angeles

Wing Hotel and Subdivision, Banning, California (project)
Nobby Knit Store, Los Angeles (project)
Kopenlanoff Desert House, Palm Springs, California (project)
Kopenlanoff Subdivision, Palm Springs, California (project)
Auditorium and Civic Center, Richmond, California (competition project)

1930/
31 George/Freedman Store, Los Angeles (project)

1931 Cherry Apartment House, 3910 South Walton Street, Los Angeles
Marx House remodelling, 1557 North Courtney Avenue, Los Angeles
Stojano House garage, 8501 Dahlia Street, Los Angeles
Highway Bungalow Hotel (project)
Von Koerber House, 408 Monte d'Oro, Hollywood Riviera, Torrance, California
The Embassy Restaurant and Arcade, Los Angeles

1932 House, Park Moderne, Blackbird Way, Woodland Hills, California
Hanna House, Los Angeles (project)
Lierd/Todd House, Los Angeles (project)
Standard Oil Service Station (prototype)
Donnell's Desert Hotel, Twenty-nine Palms, California (project)
Brown, Smith and Moore Automobile Store, Los Angeles (project)
Max Company Show Windows, Los Angeles (project; with A. R. Brandner and B. P. Paradise)

1932/
33 Bread Pit Stores, Los Angeles

1932/
34 Sardi's Restaurant, Hollywood, California
Lindy's Restaurant, Hollywood, California

1932/
36 Veissi House, Hollywood, California

1933 Schindler Shelters (prototypes)
Farr Dance Hall, Denver (project)
Oliver House, 2236 Micheltorena Street, Los Angeles
Union Oil Service Station (prototype)
Lock House, Los Angeles (2 projects)
Perstein House remodelling and furniture, 111 Tamalpais Road, Berkeley, California
The Oven (retail bakery), Los Angeles
Grauman Restaurant, Los Angeles (project)
Panel Post Constructions (prototypes)

1934 Buck House, 8th and Genessee Streets, Los Angeles
Dondo House remodelling, 583 Tamalpais Road, Berkeley, California (project)
King House remodelling and furniture, 10354 La Grange, Westwood, California
Kipp House remodelling, 1773 Griffith Park Boulevard, Los Angeles
Pavaroff House remodelling and furniture, 1641 North Crescent Heights Boulevard, Los Angeles
Ransom House, Palm Springs, California (project)
Rheingold House remodelling, 8730 Sunset Boulevard, Los Angeles
House, Leimert Park, Los Angeles (project)
Nerenbaum Service Station (project)

1934/
35 Van Patten House, 2324 Moreno Drive, Los Angeles
Haines House, 5112 Alishia Drive, Dana Point, California

1934/
37 Bennati Mountain Cabin, Lake Arrowhead, California

1935 Stander House remodelling, 2006 La Brea Terrace, Hollywood, California
Stander Apartments, Los Angeles (project)
O'Reilly Mountain Cabins (project)
Heraty House, Los Angeles (project)

Delahoyde House, Los Angeles (project)
First Baptist Church of Hollywood, California (project)
DeKeyser Double House, 1911 Highland Avenue, Hollywood, California
Shep House, Los Angeles (2 projects)
Stander House remodelling, Los Angeles

1935/
36 Geggie House, Pasadena, California (2 projects)
Walker House, 2100 Kenilworth Avenue, Los Angeles

1936 Fitzpatrick House, 8078 Woodrow Wilson Drive, Hollywood Hills, California
Sunset Medical Building, 6642 Sunset Boulevard, Hollywood, California
Jacobs House, Beverly Glen, California (2 projects)
Mack House, Hollywood, California (project)
Kaun Beach House, 112 Western Drive, Richmond, California
Schuettner House, Los Angeles (project)
Seligson House remodelling, 1671 Orange Grove Drive, Los Angeles
Seff House remodelling and furniture, Los Angeles
Miller House, Los Angeles (project)
Warshaw House, Los Angeles
Kipp Craft Workshop, Los Angeles
Pavaroff House, Beverly Hills, California (project)
Mack House, Los Angeles (project)
McAlmon Houses (2), 2721 Waverly Drive, Los Angeles
Panel Post Constructions (2nd prototypes)

1936/
37 Berkoff House, Los Angeles (project)

1936/
38 Zaczek Beach House, 114 Ellen Avenue, Playa Del Rey, California
Modern Creators Store, Holloway Drive and Palm Avenue, Hollywood, California

1937 Lingenbrink Store, 8750 Holloway Drive, Hollywood, California
Lowe House II, Eagle Rock, California
Rodakiewicz House, 9121 Alto Cedro Drive, Los Angeles
Rose Beach Colony (project)
Warren House remodelling and furniture, 1115 North Beverly Drive, Hollywood Hills, California
Ryan Beach House (project)
Renisoff House, Los Angeles (project)
Kipp House remodelling, 1773 Griffith Park Boulevard, Los Angeles

1938 Yates House remodelling, 1735 Micheltorena Street, Los Angeles
Bubeshko Apartment Building, 2036 Griffith Park Boulevard, Los Angeles
Rosenthal Apartment Building, Los Angeles (project)
Sharpless Studio House, Los Angeles (project)
Southall Studio House, 1855 Park Avenue, Los Angeles
Timme House, Los Angeles (project)
Westby House, 1805 Maltman Avenue, Los Angeles
Wilson House, 2090 Redcliff Street, Los Angeles
Wolff House, 4008 Sunnyslope Avenue, Studio City, California
Francis House, Hollywood Hills, California (project)
Hanna House, Los Angeles (project)
Morgan Photographic Shop, Hollywood, California (project)
Shep House, Los Angeles (project)
Burke House/Apartment, Newport Beach, California (project)
Djey/Aldrich House, Los Angeles (project)
Lockheed 27 Airplane interiors (2 projects; with H. Sachs)

Panel Post Constructions (3rd prototypes)

1939 Falk Apartment Building, 3631 Carnation Avenue, Los Angeles
Goodman House remodelling, 2149 Casitas Avenue, Altadena, California
Lingenbrink Store, 12560 Ventura Boulevard, Studio City, California
Bissiri House, Los Angeles (project)
Balkany House, North Hollywood, California (project)
Hub Office Building, Los Angeles (project)
Mackey Apartment Building, 1137 South Cochran Avenue, Los Angeles
Wong House remodelling, Santa Monica, California
Kaun Beach House, Richmond, California

1940 Lingenbrink Store, Studio City, California
Droste House, 2035 Kenilworth Avenue, Los Angeles
Goodwin House, 3807 Reklaw Drive, Studio City, California
Hodel House remodelling and furniture, 1800 Huntington Drive, San Marino, California
Rodriguez House, Glendale, California (project)
Lapotka Apartments, Los Angeles (project)
Houses, 423, 429 and 433 Ellis Avenue, Inglewood, California (with E. Richard Lind)
Van Dekker House, 5230 Penfield Avenue, Canoga Park, California
Sax House, Los Angeles (project)
Strader House, North Hollywood, California (project)
Taylor House, South Pasadena, California (project)

1941 Rodriguez House, 1845 Niodrara Drive, Glendale, California
Carre House, Los Angeles (project)
Hartigan House, Hollywood Park, California (project)
Hiler Studio House, Hollywood, California
Bubeshko Apartment Building addition, 2036 Griffith Park Boulevard, Los Angeles
Byers House, Van Nuys, California (project)
Gibling House, Los Angeles (project)
Druckman House, 2764 Outpost Drive, Los Angeles
Periere House, Los Angeles (project)
Karz Apartments, Los Angeles (project)

1942 Albers House remodelling, 2781 Outpost Drive, Los Angeles
Harris House, Los Angeles
Pennington House remodelling, Thousand Oaks, Camarillo, California
Falk Apartment Building, Los Angeles (3 projects)
Officers' Club, Palm Springs, California (project)

1943 Howenstein House remodelling, South Pasadena, California
Fisher House, Los Angeles (project)
Langley House remodelling, 841 Stone Canyon, Brentwood, California
Marker House remodelling, Los Angeles (project)

1944 Bethlehem Baptist Church, 4900 South Compton Avenue, Los Angeles
Litt House remodelling, 3050 Menlo, Glendake, California
Nickerson House remodelling, 681 Norton Street, Los Angeles
Hollywood Women's Club remodelling, Los Angeles (project)
Rosco Duplex remodelling, 6000–6002 La Prada Park, Los Angeles
Thomasset Apartment remodelling, Los Angeles (project)
Starkey House remodelling, 2330 Merrywood, Los Angeles
Sabsay House studio addition, Los Angeles

1945 Roth House, 3624 Buena Park Drive, North Hollywood, California
Schick House, North Hollywood, California

(project)
Braden House, North Hollywood, California (project)
Compinsky House, Burbank, California (project)
Gold House, 3758 Reklaw Drive, Los Angeles
Medical Arts Building, 12307 Ventura Boulevard, Studio City, California
Presburger House, 4255 Agnes Avenue, Studio City, California
1946 Daugherty House, 4635 Louise Avenue, Encino, California
Kermin Medical Building, Los Angeles (project)
Toole Desert House, Palm Village, California
Kallis House, 3580 Multiview Drive, Studio City, California
Harvey House remodelling, Los Angeles
Howatt House, Laguna Beach, California (project)
Lord Leigh Showroom and Offices, 847 South Santee, Los Angeles
Redesdale Avenue Apartments, Los Angeles (project)
Spangler House, Los Angeles (project)
Lingenbrink Store additions, 8750 Holloway Drive, Hollywood, California
West Pottery Works, Los Angeles
Gallagher Apartments, Los Angeles (project)
1946/
49 Tietz Medical Offices, Los Angeles
Armon House, 470 West Avenue 43, Los Angeles
1947 Mangaldas House, Los Angeles (project)
Courcio House remodelling, Los Angeles (project)
Schick and Associates Rest Home, Los Angeles (project)
Virginia Duplex, Los Angeles (project)
Trumbo House, Los Angeles (project)
Borisof House, Los Angeles (project)
1948 Lechner House, 11606 Amanda Drive, Studio City, California
Schick and Associates Motel, Los Angeles (project)
Gibling House, Los Angeles (project)
Ott Apartment Building, Beverly Hills, California (project)
Laurelwood Apartments, 11833 Laurelwood Drive, Studio City, California
Sax House, Los Angeles (project)
Drive-In Theatre, Los Angeles
1949 Washington Palace Motel, Los Angeles (project)
Janson House, 8704 Skyline Drive, Hollywood Hills, California
Penthouse, Beverly Hills, California (project)
Blembel House, Hollywood, California (project)
Meyers House remodelling, 2040 Oakstone Way, Hollywood, California
1949/
50 Tischler House, 175 Greenfield Avenue, Bel Air, Los Angeles
Inaya House, Beverly Hills, California (project)
1950 Tucker House, 8010 Fareholm Drive, Hollywood, California
Gordon House remodelling, 6853 Pacific View Drive, Hollywood Hills, California
Kaynor Manufacturing Company, 811 East 17th Street, Los Angeles
Zaczek Beach House additions, Playa Del Rey, California
1950/
51 Ries House, 1404 Miller Drive, Los Angeles
Erlik House, 1757 Curson Avenue, Hollywood, California
1950/
52 Skolnik House, 2567 Glendower Avenue, Los Angeles
1952 Apartment, Los Angeles (project)

Elmer House, Hollywood, California (project)
Esther McCoy House into Duplex conversion, 2434 Beverly Boulevard, Santa Monica, California (not completed)
Schlesinger House, 1901 Myra Avenue, Los Angeles
1953 Marks House remodelling, 1052 Manzanita Street, Los Angeles

Publications:

By SCHLINDER: book—*Collected Papers,* Los Angeles 1948.

On SCHINDLER: books—*International Neue Baukunst* by Ludwig Hilberseimer, Stuttgart 1928; *New World Architecture* by Sheldon Cheney, New York 1930; *The Book of Modern Houses* by Patrick Abercrombie, London 1936; *Southern California Country* by Carey McWilliams, New York 1946; *Architecture, Ambition and Americans* by Wayne Andrews, New York 1955; *Five California Architects* by Esther McCoy, New York 1960; *R. M. Schindler,* exhibition catalogue, Santa Barbara, California 1967; *The Architecture of the Well-Tempered Environment* by Reyner Banham, London 1969; *Schindler* by David Gebhard, New York 1972; articles—"An Eastern Critic Looks at Western Architecture" by Henry-Russell Hitchcock in *California Arts and Architecture* (Los Angeles), December 1940; "West Coast Architecture: A Romantic Movement Ends" by Esther McCoy in *Pacific Spectator* (Stanford, California), Winter 1953; "Four Schindler Houses of the 1920's" by Esther McCoy in *Arts and Architecture* (Los Angeles), September 1953; "Roots of Contemporary Architecture" by Esther McCoy in *Arts and Architecture* (Los Angeles), October 1956; "Rudolph Schindler" by Hans Hollein in *Der Aufbau* (Vienna), no. 3, 1961; "Letters of Louis H. Sullivan to R. M. Schindler" by Esther McCoy in *Journal of the Society of Architectural Historians* (Philadelphia), December 1961; "Rudolph Schindler" by Hans Hollein in *Bau* (Vienna), no. 4, 1966; "Dedicato a Schindler" by Herman Hertzberger in *Domus* (Milan), September 1967; "The Renewed Interest in Popularity of Schindler's Architecture" by Esther McCoy in the *Los Angeles Times,* 23 October 1967; "Rudolph Schindler: A Pioneer Without Tears" by Reyner Banham in *Architectural Design* (London), December 1967; "Ambiguity in the Work of R. M. Schindler" by David Gebhard in *Lotus* (Milan), no. 5, 1968; "R. M. Schindler" by Esther McCoy in *Lotus* (Milan), no. 5, 1968; "The Least Appreciated: Rudolph Schindler" by Walter Segal in *The Architects' Journal* (London), 19 February 1969; "The High and Low Art of Rudolph Schindler" by Dan O'Neill in *Architectural Review* (London), April 1973.

The importance of Rudolph Schindler as a highly original architect of the modern movement is a recently accepted fact, and much of this reassessment depends on the tardy recognition that his Beach House, designed in 1922 and built during 1925–26 for the naturist author Dr. Phillip Lovell, compares most favourably with what Le Corbusier, particularly in his innovative "Maison Citrohan," was doing at the same time. Schindler, it is now realized, is not merely an "interesting outsider"—outside the limits of the International Style, that is—but a builder of immense subtlety of meaning, well able to handle the most diverse structural and symbolic problems.

Trained in Vienna by Otto Wagner and influenced by the designs of Charles Rennie Mackintosh and the thinking of Adolf Loos—his essay on "Ornament and Crime" had a lasting effect—Schindler is very much the artist-architect and indeed his tentatively erotic figure drawings are close in manner to those of Gustave Klimt and Egon Schiele. In a Manifesto published in 1912 he stated, "The cave was the origi-

nal dwelling. A hollow adobe pile was the first permanent house. To build meant to gather and mass material, allowing it to form empty cells for human shelter." And this sculptural method is the basis of much of what he built. The Manifesto is an important document, for everything that Schindler achieved is in some way related directly to its youthful ideals.

In America, first in Chicago and then in Los Angeles, he proved a most prolific designer, both when working alone and later with Frank Lloyd Wright, a man he much admired. Eventually he found Wright a little too overpowering, and began to work in collaboration with his close friend, the engineer Clyde Chase. In 1921, with Chase, he built their two-family house on Kings Road to the west of Hollywood, at a time when the newly emerging motion-picture industry was all the rage. From this time on Schindler and Los Angeles are pretty well inseparable.

The house is of prime importance to a full understanding of his basic architectural philosophy. It is one of the most original concepts of the 1920's, being conceived solely in terms of living needs and not as an essay in spatial form or formal virtuosity! The mood is very much one of modestry and restraint. For the first time the garden is seen as an integral part of the house, and the accepted traditional distinction between the outside and inside is taken to be false. This is, of course, an important legacy of his association with Wright. The house is designed as a series of private rooms and co-operative areas—"zones"—and conceived primarily as a single enclosed environment intended to "combine the solidity of the cave with the light-weight characteristics of a tent." Here again there are hints of Wright and the thinking of the Manifesto. Schindler was obviously happy with the house and lived and worked in it until his death in 1953.

The Lovell Beach House is one of the most important early modern houses. It is almost Constructivist in feeling. The open, box-like inner area consists of two tray-like planes supported on the outside by a concrete frame which enables the two planes to connect easily with each other. The outside-inside counter-balance is well controlled and typically restrained.

Schindler kept in touch with developments in Europe, and a detailed file of cuttings from the leading architectural magazines was ever at hand. He was very aware of the Dutch De Stijl group—especially the work of the architect-designer Gerrit Rietveld—and there is certainly something of Rietveld in the Beach House. Its form is a knowing amalgam of the positive expression of structure as advocated by the Constructivists and the sculptural interplay of the planes and volumes of De Stijl.

Dr. Lovell was an ideal client, and the two men worked in complete harmony to achieve a synthesis of health and modernity based on privacy and informal communal living in the open air.

In recent years interest in the philosophy behind the building of the Beach House has served to point out the fact that at a time when Le Corbusier was making his no doubt well deserved reputation as the leading architect of the new style and publishing *Towards a New Architecture,* Schindler had, in two houses, built a logical extension to the thinking of his own equally pertinent Manifesto—yet was virtually unknown. It is now clear that his partial distaste for the International Style—the style for the 20th century—is the reason for Schindler's past neglect, but now that a new evaluation of the concept of internationalism is called for, there can be little doubt that Schindler will rightly be seen to have been one of the most original architects of the Modern Movement.
—John Furse

Frank Schlesinger: 1301 Pennsylvania Avenue Office Building, Washington, D.C., 1976

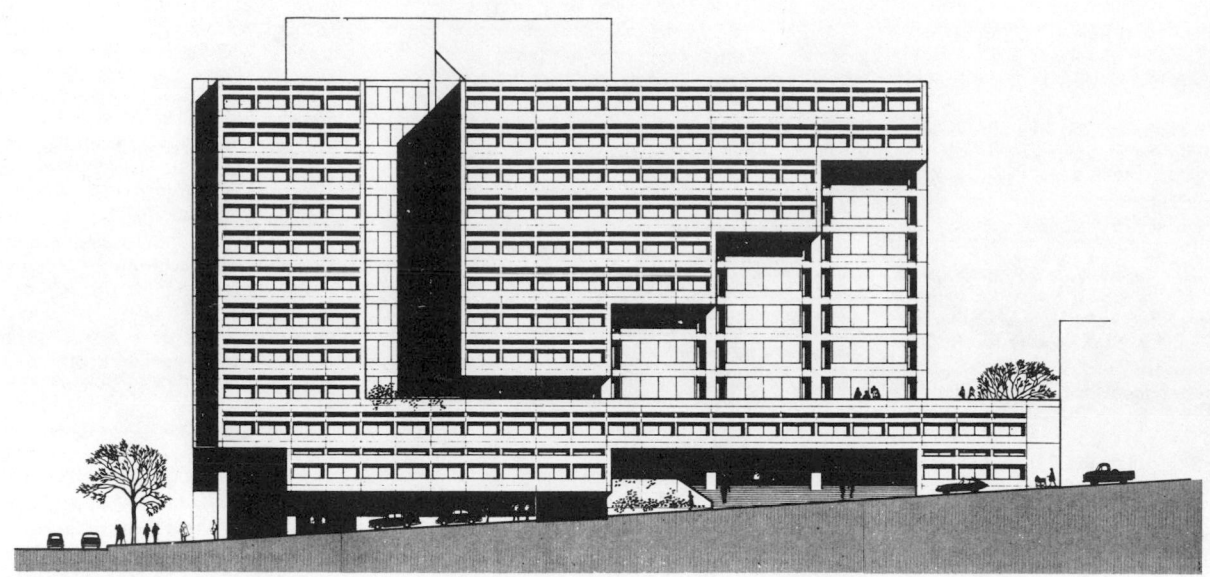

SCHLESINGER, Frank.

American. Born in New York City, 17 September 1925. Educated at Middlebury College, Vermont, 1946–48; University of Illinois, Urbana, 1948–50, B.S. 1950; Harvard University Graduate School of Design, Cambridge, Massachusetts, 1950–54, M.Arch. 1954. Served in the United States Navy, 1943–46. Married Draga Ann Christy in 1971; children: Christy, Katherine, Danny, Nike, Jeff, and (stepson) Francis. Designer, for Hugh Stubbins, Cambridge, Massachusetts, 1953–55, for Marcel Breuer, New York, 1955–56, and (part-time) for Louis I. Kahn, Philadelphia, 1957–58. Principal, Frank Schlesinger, Architect, Philadelphia since 1956 and Washington, D.C. since 1972. Instructor, University of Pennsylvania, Philadelphia, 1957–58; Visiting Critic, Columbia University, New York, 1962–63, and University of Pennsylvania, 1965. Since 1971, Professor of Architecture, University of Maryland, College Park. President, Harvard Graduate School of Design Alumni Association, 1971–73. Exhibitions: *National Gold Medal Exhibit,* Architectural League of New York, 1965; *40 under 40,* Architectural League of New York, 1965; *Frank Schlesinger, Architect,* Philadelphia Art Alliance, 1968. Recipient: Honor Award, American Institute of Architects, Philadelphia Chapter, 1960–65, 1968, 1969; Honor Award, 1960, 1961, 1963–65, Bronze Medal, 1965, 1969, and Silver Medal, 1973, Pennsylvania Society of Architects; Design Award, *Architectural Record,* 1960, 1974; Arthur Wheelright Fellowship in Architecture, Harvard University, 1963; Design Award, *Progressive Architecture,* 1966, 1967, 1969, 1972, 1974. Fellow, American Institute of Architects, 1970. Address (office): 732 17th Street N.W., Washington, D.C. 20006, U.S.A.

Works:

1953 Schlesinger House, Lexington, Massachusetts
1958 Bernstein House, Princeton, New Jersey
1960 Schlesinger House, Doylestown, Pennsylvania
1960/
 70 Girl Scout Camp Structures, Quakertown, Pennsylvania
1962 Oberman House, Princeton, New Jersey (project)
 Katz House, Norristown, Pennsylvania (project)
 Rittenhouse Swim Club, Philadelphia (with T. R. Vreeland)

Research Laboratory, University of Pennsylvania, Philadelphia (with T. R. Vreeland)
1963 Beachcomber Swim Club, Philadelphia (with T. R. Vreeland)
1964 Blumenthal House, Princeton, New Jersey
 Zisman House, New York (project)
 Lemmon House, Gladwyne, Pennsylvania
1965 Medical Offices/Apartments, Bristol, Pennsylvania (project)
 Plan for the urban renewal of the Mercer-Jackson area, Trenton, New Jersey
1965/
 66 Plan for the urban renewal of the Genesee Crossroads area, Rochester, New York
1967 Service station, Buffalo, New York
 Oritsky House, Reading, Pennsylvania
 Fisher House, Doylestown, Pennsylvania (project)
1967/
 69 Plan for the urban renewal of the Waterfront area, Buffalo, New York
1968 Fairmount Park Nature Center, Philadelphia
 Malkiel House, Princeton, New Jersey (project)
1969 Office Building, South Coventry, Connecticut (project)
1970 Genesee Crossroads Plaza, Rochester, New York
 St. Mary's at the Cathedral, Philadelphia
 Girl Scout Dining Hall, Quakertown, Pennsylvania
 Dining Hall, Cheyney, Pennsylvania (project)
1971 Dino's Restaurant, Columbia, Maryland
1972 Housing for the Elderly, Bristol, Pennsylvania
1973 Wisconsin Avenue Condominiums, Washington, D.C. (project)
 Low and Middle-Income Housing, Rochester, New York (with Gindel and Johnson)
 Christy Village Ski Condominiums, Beech Mountain, North Carolina
 Marina and Village Center, Syracuse, New York
1974 Waterfront Condominiums, Annapolis, Maryland
1975 Senate Auto Service Center/Garage, Washington, D.C.
 Westover Apartments, Washington, D.C. (with Kerr-Reno)
 Boathouse, Syracuse, New York (project)
1976 1301 Pennsylvania Avenue Office Building, Washington, D.C.
1978 National Plaza Hotel/Office Building, Washington, D.C. (with Mitchell/Giurgola)

Publications:

On SCHLESINGER: articles—"Megastructures" in *Progressive Architecture* (New York), July 1968; "Genesee Crossroads Plaza" in *L'Architecture d'Aujourd'hui* (Paris), September 1968; "Fairmount Park Nature Center" in *Progressive Architecture* (New York), January 1969; "Oritsky Residence" in *Progressive Architecture* (New York), April 1970; "Girl Scout Dining Hall" in *Architectural Forum* (New York), October 1971; "Tubular Steel Residence" in *Progressive Architecture* (New York), January 1972; "Genesee Crossroads Plaza" in *Progressive Architecture* (New York), March 1972; "St. Mary's at the Cathedral" in *Progressive Architecture* (New York), January 1974; "Christie Village Condominiums" in *Architectural Record* (New York), May 1974.

The name of Frank Schlesinger is far from being a household word in Washington, D.C., where he has maintained an office since 1972. But that status could change drastically in the not too distant future for Schlesinger, whose architectural roots are in Philadelphia—both in the city and in the so-called Philadelphia School.

When Schlesinger became Professor of Architecture at the University of Maryland at College Park, near Washington, he decided to open an office in the nation's capital. He admits that having retained a recent client—a developer—has indeed been a breakthrough for his relatively small firm, which now is associated with a $110 million commission. The developer happens to be involved in the revitalization of Pennsylvania Avenue, and the project is the first major one to be constructed as part of that grand plan. This kind of affiliation with a developer might seem somewhat paradoxical for an architect who probably has exercised his greatest influence in the field of education, even though his firm has won more than 30 design awards at national, state and local levels. Yet, upon closer observation, it becomes obvious that Schlesinger is not to be associated with the ivy-covered halls of learning. "I have no starry-eyed sense of purpose," he emphatically states, referring not only to the classroom but also to his own practice.

It is interesting to note that in his office brochure under "Education," Schlesinger lists the offices of Hugh Stubbins, Marcel Breuer, and Louis Kahn. These men have moulded his philosophy as much as, if not more than, the institutions he attended. He questions out loud, however, whether this kind of "devotion" is a healthy thing, whether it might inhibit the development of one's own style. He expresses the hope that his work does not respond to a fad or to a particular time. One thing is for certain: he has brought a high level of design to a number of projects with which aesthetics are seldom associated, such as an underground garage and pedestrian bridge project and a prototype service station, to mention just two.

Schlesinger is deeply concerned about today's architectural students and about the world they observe and will soon join as practitioners. Modern architecture, as he sees it, is not dead; instead, it allows for a range of styles from Wright to Mies to a variety of present-day innovators. Students somehow tend to look at all of this in terms of "fashion," he explains. "What it amounts to is a misreading of architectural history. Buildings are seen as having no continuity with the past, but this is not necessarily true."

Schlesinger knows that, for the small architectural firm to survive, principals like himself must provide extensive experience in the coordination and direction of interdisciplinary teams of planners, landscape architects, engineers, as well as traffic, market and graphic consultants. When the scale or nature of the project requires special expertise, specialists (who work with the firm on a continuing basis) must be brought in.

Modern architecture can take its rightful place in the fabric of society today, and architects such as Frank Schlesinger are attempting to make it happen —both in the classroom and in the nitty-gritty business of practice.

—Robert E. Koehler

SCHWARZ, Rudolf.

German. Born in Strasbourg, 15 May 1897. Educated at the Technical University of Berlin, 1915–19; State Academy of Arts, Berlin, under Hans Poelzig, 1919–23. Worked as a government architect in Cologne, 1923–25; taught at the Bau- und Kunstgewerbeschule, Offenbach, 1925–27; Director, Kunstgewerbeschule, Aachen, 1927–34; in private practice, Aachen, 1934–40; Chief of Reconstruction and Planning, Lothringen, 1941–44; prisoner-of-war, 1944–46; Chief City Planner, Cologne, 1946–52; Professor of Town Planning, Staatliche Kunstakademie, Dusseldorf, 1953 until his death, 1961. Member of the Deutscher Werkbund. Recipient: German Service Cross, 1951; Fritz Schumacher Prize, Hamburg, 1952; Art Prize, Nordrhein-Westfalen, 1958. Member, Akademie der Künste, Berlin. *Died* (in Cologne) *3 April 1961.*

Works:

1928 Castle, Festival Hall and Chapel reconstruction, Rothenfels-am-Main, Germany
1929 Youth Hall, Aachen (with Hans Schwippert and Johannes Krahn)
　　　Waldfriedhof Cemetery, Aachen (with Johannes Krahn)
1930 Corpus Christi Church, Aachen (with Hans Schwippert and Johannes Krahn)
1931 College of Sociology, Aachen (with Hans Schwippert and Johannes Krahn)
1932 Liebfrauen Church interiors, Leipzig
　　　Parish Church, Ilsenburg/Harz, Germany (project)
　　　Parish Church, Milwaukee, Wisconsin (project)
1933 St. Abert Chapel, Leversbach, near Düren, Germany

Semi-detached house, Lovenich, near Cologne
Schrage House, Bruck, Cologne
Parish Church, Grosssteinheim-am-Main, Germany (project)
2 houses, Landhaus, Essen
Doctor's house, Duisburg, Germany
1936 Parish Church with Hall, Lichterfelde, Berlin (project; with Emil Steffan)
　　　Parish Church, Aschaffenburg-Damm, Germany (project)
　　　Dr. Fruhauf Surgery, Offenbach/Main, Germany
1937 Church, Gross Zschocher, Leipzig (project)
　　　Church and Parish Hall, Windorf, Leipzig (project)
　　　Gothic Parish Church extensions, Burgstadt-/Main, Germany
　　　Baroque Parish Church interiors, Wasserlos-in-Unterfranken, Germany
　　　Parish Church interiors, Ketzin, Brandenburg, Germany
　　　Fluhe House, Duisburg, Germany
1938 Gymnasium/Church of Christ the King conversion, Fulda, Germany
　　　Schwarz House, Frankfurt
　　　Church and Parish Hall, Gropelingen, Bremen (project)
1940 Pilgrimage Church interiors, Mariental, Westerwald, Germany
1941 Cathedral interiors, Trier, Germany (as consultant architect)
1941/
44   Regional and reconstruction plans for Lothringen, Germany
1942 Parish Church, Hanau, Germany (project)
　　　New Gothic Church interiors, Bockenheim, Frankfurt

Rudolf Schwarz: St. Joseph's Church, Braunsfeld, Cologne, 1954

1943 Church of Mary Queen of Peace, Oberroding-hausen, Germany (with Johannes Krahn)
1944 St. Catherine's Church extensions, Krick-enau, Germany
1946/
52 Reconstruction plans for the city of Cologne
1947 Saint Heribert Church reconstruction, Deutz, Cologne (with Josef Bernard)
Church, Durwiss, near Aachen (project)
Temporary church, Gey, near Düren, Germany (project)
Church, Bilderstockenhen, Cologne (project; with Emil Steffan)
Church, Kirchen/Sieg, Germany (project)
1948 St. Paul's Church/Political Discussion Hall conversion, Frankfurt (with Eugen Blank, Johannes Krahn, and Gottlob Schaupp)
Liebfrauen Church choir fittings, Frankfurt
Marien Hospital Chapel interiors, Frankfurt
1949 Borromeo Chapel reconstruction, Munster (competition project)
1950 Pilgrimage Church reconstruction, Kalk, Cologne
St. Catherine's Church reconstruction, Niehl, Cologne (with Hermann Pfeiffer)
1952 Roman Church reconstruction, Johannis-berg, Rheingau, Germany (with Rudolf Steinbach)
Maria Himmelfahrt Church, Wesel, Germany
Girls' Upper School, Darmstadt (project)
All Saints' Anglican Church, Marienburg, Cologne (with Josef Bernard)
Cathedral interiors, Munster (competition project)
1953 Liebfrauen Church interiors, Trier, Germany
St. Anna's Church, Parish Hall and Kindergarten, Duisburg, Germany
State Theatre, Mannheim (project; with Josef Bernard and Wilhelm Kiphahn)
Industrial development plans for Kopasack, Germany (with Josef Bernard)
1954 St. Albert's Church, Andernach, Germany
St. Michael's Church and Oratory, Frankfurt
St. Joseph's Church, Braunsfeld, Cologne (with Josef Bernard)
1955 Plan for the Rhein Braun Colliery, Germany
Mechtern Church reconstruction, Ehrenfeld, Cologne
Liebfrauen Church reconstruction, Mulheim, Cologne
1956 St. Anna's Church, Düren, Germany
Parish Church with Rectory and Meeting Hall, Graveneck/Lahn, Germany
Altar, for the Assembly of German Catholics, Cologne
Schwarz House, Mungersdorf, Cologne
Festival Hall reconstruction, with Chapel, Gurzenich, near Cologne (with Karl Band)
Pedagogical Academy, Munster (competition project; with Josef Bernard)
1957 Cathedral Precinct, Cologne (competition project; with Karl Band)
Wallraf-Richartz Museum reconstruction, Cologne (with Josef Bernard)
St. Mary's Church interiors, Oberhausen, Germany (with Josef Bernard)
Church of the Holy Cross, Bottrop, Germany (with Josef Bernard)
St. Francis Church, Bedingrade, Essen
Parish Hall and Youth Centre, Niehl, Cologne
St. Andrew's Parish Church, Ruttenscheid, Essen
St. Joseph's Church, Merzig, Saarland, Germany (competition project)
1958 Parish Church of the Holy Family, Oberhausen, Germany (with Josef Bernard)
Collegiate Church Spire, Bocholt, Germany (with Josef Bernard)
St. Mauritius Church, Wiesbaden (competition project)

Town Hall, Marl, Germany (competition project)
Memorial Church to the Victims of National Socialism, Plotzensee, Berlin (as consultant architect)
1959 Vetus-Latina Institute, Archbishopric of Kloster Beuron, Germany
St. Antonius' Church, Frohnhausen, Essen
Church of Mary the Queen, Saarbrucken
St. Boniface's Church, Forst, Aachen
St. Pius' Church with Rectory and Parish Hall, Barmen, Wuppertal, Germany
1960 St. Christophorus Church and Social Centre, Niehl, Cologne
St. Gertrude's Church and Social Centre, Schweinheim, Aschaffenburg, Germany
Primary school, Nippes, Cologne
St. Boniface's Church and Social Centre, Wetzlar, Germany
St. Raphael's Church, Gatow, Berlin
St. Vitalis Church interiors, Mungersdorf, Cologne
St. Ludger's Church, Vohwinkel, Wuppertal, Germany
St. Florian's Church and Social Centre, Vienna
St. Teresa's Church and Social Centre, Donau, Linz, Austria
Church with Rectory and Kindergarten, Hausen, near Offenbach, Germany
Theatre, Dusseldorf (competition project)
Catholic Church, Soest, Westphalia, Germany (competition project)
Reichstag, Berlin (competition project)
Town Hall, Cologne (competition project)
Chamber of Commerce, Bremen (competition project)
Plan for a Town Square, Wolfsburg, Germany (competition project; with S. Szekessy)

Publications:

By SCHWARZ: books—*Vom Bau der Kirche,* Aachen 1938, as *The Church Incarnate,* Chicago and London 1958; *Kirchenbau,* Heidelberg 1960; articles—"Dominikus Böhm und sein Werk" in *Moderne Bauformen* (Stuttgart), vol. 26, 1927; "Das Zukunftige Köln" in *Bauen und Wohnen* (Zurich), vol. 4, 1949; "Der Neue Kirchenbau" in *Werk* (Zurich), April 1949; "Dominikus Böhm" in *Baukunst und Werkform* (Nuremberg), February 1955; "Einige Bemerkungen zu St. Michael in Frankfurt" in *Das Münster* (Munich), July/August 1955; "Architektur als heiliges Bild" in *Baukunst und Werkform* (Nuremberg), vol. 10, no. 3, 1957; "Die Kirche zum Heiligen Kreuz in Bottrop" in *Das Münster* (Munich), May/June 1958.

On SCHWARZ: articles—"The Architecture of Rudolf Schwarz" in H. A. Reinhold in *Architectural Forum* (New York), January 1939; "Neuen Kirchenbauten von Rudolf Schwarz" in *Bauen und Wohnen* (Zurich), no. 12, 1949; "Europe's Great New Churches" in *Architectural Forum* (New York), December 1957; "Das Erste Museum der Nachkriegszeit" in *Baukunst und Werkform* (Nuremberg), no. 1, 1958; "The 'Seven Archetypes' of Rudolf Schwarz" in *Architectural Record* (New York), June 1958; "New Church Architecture in Germany" by G. E. Kidder Smith in *Architectural Record* (New York), June 1962; "Das Erbe von Rudolf Schwarz" in *Das Münster* (Munich), January/February 1967; "In Memoriam Rudolf Schwarz" by Rudolf Bernard in *Das Münster* (Munich), January/February 1972.

Rudolf Schwarz is best known for his Catholic churches, though he was not so exclusively a church architect as his older contemporary Dominikus Böhm—he designed such important secular buildings as the College of Sociology in Aachen and the Wallraf-Richartz Museum in Cologne, and he worked in city planning and post-war reconstruction. But he has been described (by G.E. Kidder Smith) as "probably the most profound church architect of our time," because for him religious architecture was not limited to mere building, but reflected the basic philosophical thinking that is strongly evident in his book *Vom Bau der Kirche.* Schwarz's work has been called an "*architecture parlante*" because the buildings are meant to suggest and embody metaphysical ideas, to be "high inhabitable pictures like life-size parables."

This does not mean that Schwarz was not a modern functionalist architect, for it was in accordance with that basic doctrine "form follows function" that he became a pioneer of the one-room open-plan type of church interior. His work was part of the Liturgical Revival, a movement to return to the most ancient concept of Christianity in which priest and laity were intimately one within the mystical body of the Church, and the prototypes of his early church buildings were the great basilicas of pagan Rome, which were open halls of justice. A highly significant example, which prompted much controversy when it was first built in 1930, is the Corpus Christi Church at Aachen, a very plain simple rectangular hall without aisles, a severe enclosed space, with the altar mounted on a platform so that it is clearly visible from any point, the outside with its belfry tower having an equally stark simplicity, the whole full of a concentrated austere religious purpose.

Schwarz felt that a religious building should be a "mighty refuge," and in many of his post-war designs he sought to provide a spiritual "fortress" of enduring solidity and strength against the outside world. The solid towering walls of St. Michael's Church in Frankfurt rise unbroken by windows, for this church is lit only by a continuous window band just below the roof. The plan is an ellipse with trefoil chapels, so that the main body is a great oval room surrounded by a gently curving wall which gives much less feeling of confinement than would a similar rectangular space, producing a serenely calm interior lit only from high above. The idea came on a journey through the Aare Gorge, when Schwarz found himself "hemmed in by staring rocks lit only high up through a small gap to the open sky. I saw this gorge as a common human experience: a menacing world towering all around with but a glimpse of the open sky whose silver light shimmers down from the highest region. This experience found its architectural expression in St. Michael's."

Another highly original shape, which is equally a thoughtful interpretation of the new liturgical concepts, is St. Anna's Church in Düren (a town almost totally destroyed by bombing), built with stone retrieved from rubble to make a large massive L-shaped church with sheer exterior walls. The highly unusual plan of the Church of the Holy Cross, Bottrop, a brick parabola with the open end sheathed only in glass, is a direct realization of an idea put forward in the form of a parable years earlier in Schwarz's book. Similarly, the Church of Mary the Queen in Saarbrucken expresses the idea of Mary as Queen directly in its plan of four horizontal conjoined parabolas which give the appearance of a crown, lit by glazed half parabolas at the meeting point, so that light is focused as a dazzling architectural spotlight at the crossing.

These highly original constructions are never mere gimmicks, but always attempts to make the buildings more directly functional and open in accordance with the requirements of the modern liturgical movement. And they have made Schwarz generally acknowledged, along with Dominikus Böhm, as one of the great innovators of modern church design.

—Konstantin Bazarov

SCHWEIKHER, Paul.

American. Born in Denver, Colorado, 28 July 1903. Educated at the University of Colorado, Boulder, 1921–22; Art Institute of Chicago, 1922–23; Illinois Institute of Technology, Chicago, also the Chicago Atelier, nights 1924–26; Yale University School of Architecture, New Haven, Connecticut, under Otto Faelton and Sheppard Stevens, 1927–29, B.F.A. 1929; travelled and studied in Europe (Matcham Fellowship), 1929–30. Served in the United States Naval Reserve, in Virginia, Illinois and California, 1942–45: Lieutenant junior grade to Lieutenant Commander. Married Dorothy Miller in 1923; son: Paul. Worked as a draftsman with Granger and Bollenbacher, Chicago, 1923–25, and with David Adler, Chicago, 1925–27; assistant designer with Russell Wolcott, Chicago, 1927, 1928; free-lance architect, 1930–31; Chief Designer with Philip B. Maher, Chicago, 1931–33; Designer and Site Planner, General Houses Inc., Chicago, 1933–34; Principal and Senior Partner, with Theodore Warren Lamb and Winston Elting, Schweikher, Lamb and Elting, Architects, Chicago, 1934–42, and Schweikher and Elting, Chicago, 1946–52; Professor of Architecture and Chairman of the School of Architecture, Yale University, also in private practice as Paul Schweikher Associates, New Haven, Connecticut, 1953–57; Professor of Architecture and Head of the Department of Architecture, Carnegie-Mellon University, Pittsburgh, also in private practice as Paul Schweikher Associates, Pittsburgh, 1957–69. In private practice, Sedona, Arizona, since 1970. Director, American Institute of Architects Chicago Chapter School, 1939–40; Member, Board of Directors, Arts Club of Chicago, 1939–56; Member, Civic Design Committee of Chicago, 1941–42; Member, City Planning Commission of Pittsburgh, 1961–63; Member of the Advisory Council, Princeton University School of Architecture, New Jersey, 1961–69. Visiting Critic/-Lecturer: School of Fine Arts, Art Institute of Chicago, 1939; University of Illinois, Urbana, 1947, 1952; Yale University, 1947, 1950, 1951; Washington University, St. Louis, 1949; Arizona State University, Tempe, 1949, 1975; Tulane University, New Orleans, 1950; University of Kansas, Lawrence, 1950; University of Minnesota, Minneapolis, 1952; Western Reserve University, Cleveland, 1957; Syracuse University, New York, 1959; Princeton University, 1960. Exhibitions: one-man—Art Institute of Chicago, 1941; Yale University, 1947, 1969; Akron Art Institute, Ohio, 1948; University of Chicago, 1949; University of Illinois, 1949–50; Tulane University, 1949–50; University of Texas at Austin, 1951; University of Kansas, 1951; University of Minnesota, 1951; Carnegie Institute of Technology, Pittsburgh, 1957; Princeton University, 1960, 1963; Catholic University, Washington, D.C., 1960; Carnegie Institute Museum, Pittsburgh, 1962, 1965; Arts and Crafts Center, Pittsburgh, 1967; Harvard University, Cambridge, Massachusetts, 1968; Arizona State University, Tempe, 1974; group—Museum of Modern Art, New York, 1933, 1951; Sokolniki Park, Moscow, 1959; Architectural League of New York, 1960; American Institute of Architects Center, Washington, D.C., 1960; American Federation of Arts, toured U.S.A. and South America, 1962–64; *Chicago Architects,* toured U.S.A. 1976–77. Recipient: Grand Prize, General Electric Homes Competition, 1935; First Award, Church Architectural Guild of America, 1955; Design Award, *Progressive Architecture,* 1956, 1957, 1960; Distinguished Citizen Award, Denver, 1958; Honor Award, 1959, and Merit Citation, 1962, American Institute of Architects, Chicago Chapter; Ford Foundation Research Grant, 1962; Architect of the Year Award, Junior Chamber of Commerce, Pittsburgh, 1966; Artist of the Year Award, Arts and Crafts Center, Pittsburgh, 1967. Honorary M.A.: Yale University, 1953. Address: R.R. No. 3. High Tor, Sedona, Arizona 86336, U.S.A.

Works:

1936   Berg House I, Glen Ellyn, Illinois
      Third Unitarian Church, Chicago
      Dushkin House, Winnetka, Illinois
      Johnson House, Chicago
      Lowenstein House, Highland Park, Illinois
1937/
  41   Upton House I, Scottsdale, Arizona
      Berg House II, Glen Ellyn, Illinois
1938   Rinaldo House, Downers Grove, Illinois
      Schweikher House, Roselle, Illinois
1939   Emerson Settlement House, Chicago
      Housing project, Rockford, Illinois
      Barry House, Glenview, Illinois
      Cooperative Community, Glenview, Illinois
      Foster House, Hinsdale, Illinois
      Guenther House, LaPorte, Indiana
      L. D. Kern House, Roselle, Illinois
      M. A. Kern House, Roselle, Illinois
      Williams House, Glen Ellyn, Illinois
      Voevodsky House, Libertyville, Illinois
1940   Flatley House, Western Springs, Illinois
      Stone House, Topeka, Kansas

Paul Schweikher: Student Union Building, Duquesne University, Pittsburgh, 1967

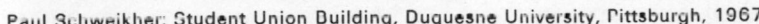

1941 McVey House, Glen Ellyn, Illinois
1942 Officers Quarters, United States Naval Training Station, Great Lakes, Illinois
William Fleming House, Highland Park, Illinois (project)
1946 Goebel House, Barrington, Illinois
House for *Life* magazine, New York
Usonia Cooperative II, White Plains, New York
Wooster House, Skokie, Illinois
1947 Burda House, Mount Prospect, Illinois
Kessel House, Glenview, Illinois
Landis House, Flora, Indiana
Stary House, Lisle, Illinois
1948 Lew House, White Plains, New York
Upton House addition, St. Joseph, Michigan
Upton House II, Scottsdale, Arizona
Tom Darlington House, Paradise Valley, Arizona (project)
1949 Fine Arts Center, Maryville College, Tennessee
Beatty House, Lake Forest, Illinois
1950 Burhans House, Peoria, Illinois
Finch House, Paradise Valley, Arizona
Horton House, Valparaiso, Indiana
Rockwell House, Flossmoor, Illinois
Eli Brown Office Building, Louisville, Kentucky (project)
Porter Office Building, Chicago (project)
1951 First Methodist Church, Plainfield, Iowa
Faith United Protestant Church School, Park Forest, Illinois
Carpenter House, Libertyville, Illinois
Elting House, Libertyville, Illinois
Harring House, Highland Park, Illinois
Keller House, South Bend, Indiana
Otis House, Libertyville, Illinois
Orphan asylum, Chicago (project)
Decker House, Peoria, Illinois (project)
1952 Cazenovia Elementary School, New York
Residence for the Mentally Ill, Chicago Medical Center
Beaugureau House, Barrington, Illinois
Bennett House, Tryon, North Carolina
Harvey Studio, Libertyville, Illinois
Shiller House, Glen Ellyn, Illinois
Yacht club, St. Joseph, Michigan (project)
1953 Elementary school, Roselle, Illinois
Samuel Tyndale Wilson Chapel/Theatre, Maryville College, Tennessee
Elementary school, Schaumburg, Illinois
Faith United Protestant Church, Park Forest, Illinois
Gray House, St. Joseph, Michigan
Lloyd-Smith House, Huron Mountain, Michigan
Parker House, Palatine, Illinois
Ross House, St. Joseph, Michigan
1954 Frazel House, Wayne, Illinois
Law School, University of Chicago (project)
Grace Lutheran School and Church, Teaneck, New Jersey (project)
1955 First Universalist Church, Chicago
Josiah Willard Gibbs Research Laboratory, Yale University, New Haven, Connecticut (with Douglas Orr)
Long-range plan for Yale University, New Haven, Connecticut (project)
1956 Reactor Building, University of Buffalo, New York (project)
Seymour Knox Wing, Museum of Fine Arts, Buffalo, New York (project)
Hotel Machu Picchu, Lima, Peru (project)
1957 Fine Arts Center and Music Unit, University of Buffalo, New York
Women's Dormitory, New Haven State Teachers College, Connecticut (with Earl Carlin)
1958 Unitarian Church, Evanston, Illinois
Studio Theatre, Carnegie Institute of Technology, Pittsburgh
Carnegie Institute Museum alterations, Pittsburgh

Public library, Watertown, Connecticut
Campus Activities Building, Carnegie Institute of Technology, Pittsburgh
1959 Women's Dormitory, Maryville College, Tennessee
Chicago Hall Language Center, Vassar College, Poughkeepsie, New York
1960 Trinity United Presbyterian Church, East Liverpool, Ohio (with James Porter)
Somerville Hospital, Massachusetts (project; with William Metcalf)
1961 Exhibition cases for the Carnegie Institute Museum, Pittsburgh
1962 The Ideal Theatre, Pittsburgh (project; with George Izenour)
1965 Knoxville Branch, Carnegie Library, Pittsburgh
1966 Cooperative apartments, Kittanning, Pennsylvania (project)
1967 Student Union Building, Duquesne University, Pittsburgh
Medical Office Building, Steubenville, Ohio (with James Porter)
Wright House, Fox Chapel, Pennsylvania
Municipal Fine Arts Center, Concert House and Theatre, Erie, Pennsylvania (project; with George Izenour)
1968 Thompson House, Seal Harbor, Maine
Apartment building for the elderly, Pittsburgh (project)
Scattered hillside housing, Pittsburgh (project)
Keller House, St. Joseph, Michigan (project)
1969 Science Center, Duquesne University, Pittsburgh (with Mies van der Rohe as supervising associate)
1970 WQED-WQEX Educational Television Station, Pittsburgh
YMCA Building, Pittsburgh (project)
1974 Schweikher House II, Sedona, Arizona
1978– Schweikher studio, workshop and house complex, Sedona, Arizona

Publications:

By SCHWEIKHER: articles—"Chicago Must Plan to Save Its Life" in *Real Estate Magazine* (Chicago), July 1939; "Decay and Revival of American Cities" in *Illinois Society of Architects Bulletin* (Chicago), September 1939; "Architectural Bandwagon" in *The New Humanist* (Chicago), March 1955; "The Architectural Virtues" in *Pittsburgh Post-Gazette,* July 1961; "The Architecture of Usefulness" in *Yale Literary Review* (New Haven, Connecticut), September 1966.

On SCHWEIKHER: books—*Neuzeitlicher Verkehrsbau* by K. Wittman, Potsdam 1931; *Tomorrow's Houses* by Nelson and Wright, New York 1945; *Built in USA: Postwar Architecture,* edited by Henry-Russell Hitchcock and Arthur Drexler, New York 1952; *Churches and Temples* by Paul Thiry, Richard M. Bennett and Henry L. Kamphoefner, New York 1954; *Architecture USA* by Ian McCallum, New York 1959; *The Architecture of America* by Burchard and Bush-Brown, Boston 1961; *Chicago's Famous Buildings,* edited by Arthur Siegel, Chicago 1966; *Chicago Architects* by Stuart E. Cohen, Chicago 1976; articles—buildings and projects published in articles in *Architectural Forum* (New York), November 1939, October 1940, August 1942, January 1946, May 1947, October 1947, December 1952, April 1956, May 1959, December 1961, January 1962, March 1966, and July/August 1967; *Architectural Record* (New York), November 1941, March 1943, December 1946, July 1947, November 1947, December 1951, April 1955, June 1955, June 1956, August 1957, April 1959, September 1959, and February 1966; *Architecture + Urbanism* (Tokyo), July 1971; *House and Garden* (New York), December 1950; *House and Home* (New York), October 1957; *Architecture d'Aujourd-*

'hui (Paris), April/May 1957; *Life* (New York), April 1947; *Nuestra Arquitectura* (Buenos Aires), April 1947, August 1952, October 1952, November/December 1956; *Pencil Points* (New York), February 1940, December 1946; *Progressive Architecture* (New York), November 1950, January 1957, November 1957, January 1960, December 1961, February 1962, December 1965, and September 1967; *Vogue* (New York), July 1957; "Austerity in Concrete" in *Architectural Forum* (New York), December 1961; "Four Theaters for the Ford Foundation" in *Progressive Architecture* (New York), February 1962; "Homage to Paul Schweikher" in *Charette* (Philadelphia), January 1963; "Power for Culture" in *Progressive Architecture* (New York), December 1965; "Pittsburgh Library—Class Amid the Clutter" in *Architectural Forum* (New York), March 1966; "Architecture on Campus" in *Architectural Forum* (New York), July/August 1967; "Three Houses, Three Generations" in *Progressive Architecture* (New York), November 1967.

The April 1939 issue of *Architectural Forum* presented some of the work done up to that time by my associate Theodore Warren Lamb and me. The editor had asked that we write a short introduction. We wrote in part the following:

A working philosophy of made up of growing and changing ideas and we hesitate to crystallize it into irrevocable statements.

If we solve the vital problem of satisfying the requirements, creating simple, workable structure, orienting the structure to sunlight, to prevailing winds and to the physical character of the site . . . we find little need for serious discussion of the building's style.

Ted Lamb was killed in an airplane accident in 1943 while on his way to London. I have had a number of partners and associates since, but the above tenet serves still as a direction-finder.

Otto Faelton and Sheppard Stevens influenced me as a student at Yale. Longer lasting influences were those of: David Adler—my employer for two years; from him I learned to see scale, proportion, and detail. Mies van der Rohe—a close friend; we had many long talks about architecture, other architects, and his collection of Schwitters. Buckminster Fuller—I was one of a small group that worked (nights) with Fuller on the first "Dymaxion" house in 1933; we are still in touch from time to time. George Howe—my predecessor (as Chairman of the School of Architecture) at Yale, a dear friend, a cherished companion: he was a sharp critic. Louis Kahn—it was my privilege to teach with him (and to be taught by him) at Yale; he was an occasional guest at Carnegie-Mellon in the '60s.

—Paul Schweikher

Paul Schweikher's forte is sensitive selection and honest expression of materials. He uses materials with enduring qualities and indigenous textures: brick, stone, tile, wood, copper, lead, steel and concrete. Rarely does he resort to traditional finish materials; when he does, it is usually for functional reasons. As he has said:

It is better as a whole to be satisfied with a closer acquaintance with a few basic materials and to concentrate on those with the same sincerity and honesty given to present day plan—that an integration of plan and material and ultimately building may become a truly representative architecture.

Schweikher makes little distinction between exterior and interior materials, as at the Knoxville Branch Library in Pittsburgh: concrete block walls, exposed concrete structural frame, and granite paving carry the material theme throughout the building, unifying the design. He conceives of walls as complete three-dimensional units without front and back, finished or unfinished side. The interior face of an exterior wall, by definition, is of the same material.

The design of Trinity United Presbyterian Church, East Liverpool, Ohio, demonstrates Schweikher's thorough knowledge of precast concrete. At the intersection of columns and beams, exposed lead beam caps and lead plugs skillfully express the inner function of post-tensioning strands. Slit windows separate the concrete block exterior walls from the columns, clearly defining structural and non-structural elements. Concrete blocks, carefully proportioned and left exposed reveal the indigenous aggregates.

At the Unitarian Church in Evanston, Illinois, Schweikher turned to reinforced concrete and glass to make a brutal statement in material. The exterior has two end walls entirely of glass, captured between massive concrete sidewalls and roof structure. Huge fins project out from the sidewalls and merge with the main concrete roof beams to form a rigid frame. Very narrow glass slits punctuate the otherwise unrelenting severity of the smoothly-finished, inward-sloping sidewalls.

Schweikher's quest for explicit honesty in exposing natural finishes and structural elements required careful integration of architectural, mechanical and electrical systems. A narrow mechanical bay bisecting the Knoxville Branch Library supplies air through the sidewalls of the high-ceilinged, sky-lit reading rooms. Strip fluorescent down lights, mounted on the shelving units, provide lighting in the stack areas and keep the exposed concrete, double-tee ceiling uncluttered. At the Fine Arts Center at Maryville College, Tennessee, Schweikher made no attempt to conceal the mechanical and electrical systems; he deliberately exposed pipes, conduits, light fixtures and heating units in front of finished materials. At the Stone House in Topeka, Kansas, a symbiotic relationship exists between material expression and mechanical function. Here, an underfloor radiant heating system freed the living space of mechanical equipment and necessitated the use of brick pavers as a floor material and heat sink.

With the proliferation of today's dropped-ceiling, extruded-aluminum, gypsum board buildings, Paul Schweikher's work stands pointing in another direction, honest expression of basic materials resulting in a more representative architecture.

—Geoffrey Lee Farnsworth

SCOTT, Michael.

Irish. Born in Drogheda, 24 June 1905. Educated at Belvedere College, Dublin, 1917–23; School of Art, Dublin, and School of Acting, Abbey Theatre, Dublin, 1923–26; articled to Jones and Kelly, architects, Dublin, 1923–26. Married Patricia Nixon in 1932; children: Anthony, Michael, Brian, Niall, and Ciarin. Architectural Assistant, Charles J. Dunlop, Architect, Dublin, 1926, and Office of Public Works, Dublin, 1927; acted with the Abbey Players, Dublin, on tour of the United States, winter 1927–28. In private practice, Dublin, since 1928, as Principal, Michael Scott, Architect, 1928–59, and Michael Scott and Associates, 1959–66, and Director, Michael Scott and Partners, 1966–74, and Scott Tallon Walker/Architects, 1974 until he retired, 1977; now Consultant to Scott Tallon Walker (senior partners: Robin Walker; Ronald Tallon; Niall Scott); office established in London, 1973. Co-Founder and Chairman, Building Centre of Ireland, 1958–77. Co-Founder and Chairman of the Executive Committee of ROSC (international art exhibitions), Dublin,

since 1967; Chairman of the Council, Dublin Theatre Festival, since 1968. Exhibitions: Dawson Gallery, Dublin (landscape drawings), 1967, 1975; Royal Institute of the Architects of Ireland, Dublin (architecture), 1975. Recipient: Silver Medal, City of New York, 1939; Triennial Gold Medal, Royal Institute of the Architects of Ireland, 1953–55; Royal Gold Medal, Royal Institute of British Architects, 1975; Distinguished Service Cross, Federal Republic of Germany, 1977. Hon.Dip.Arch.: College of Technology, Bolton Street, Dublin, 1967; Hon.Dr.: Royal College of Art, London, 1969; Litt.D.: Dublin University, 1970; D.Sc.: Queen's University of Belfast, 1977. Fellow, Royal Institute of the Architects of Ireland, 1948. Honorary Member, Royal Society of Ulster Architects, 1967; Honorary Fellow, American Institute of Architects, 1972; Honorary Fellow, Institute of Structural Engineers, London, 1976. Member, Icelandic Order of the Falcon, 1974. Address (office): 19 Merrion Square, Dublin 2, Ireland.

Works:

1929   North Wing, St. Ultan's Children's Hospital, Dublin 2
1930   Gate Theatre conversion, Dublin 1
1936   Laois County Hospital, Portlaoise, Ireland
1937   Offaly County Hospital, Tullamore, Ireland
1938   "Geragh" (Scott House), Sandycove Point, Dun Laoghaire, County Dublin
1939   Pavilion of Ireland, World's Fair, New York
1949   Irish Transport Board Bus Chassis Factory, Dublin 8 (now Central Engineering Workshops of the Office of Public Works)
1951   Irish Transport Board Bus Garage, Donnybrook, Dublin 4
1953   Irish Transport Board Bus Station/Department of Social Welfare Office Building, Store Street, Dublin 1
1954   McCairns Motors Ltd. Car Assembly and Service Garage, Santry, Dublin 9
1956   Stewarts and Lloyds of Ireland Ltd. Warehouse and Office Building, Port of Dublin Ballroom, Shelbourne Hotel, Dublin 2
1959   Brown and Polson Ltd. Factory, Inchicore, Dublin 12
1966   Abbey Theatre, Dublin (with Ronald Tallon)

Publications:

By SCOTT: articles—"Inaugural Address" in Green Book: Journal of the Architectural Association of Ireland (Dublin), 1937–38; "The Abbey as I Remember It" in The New Abbey Theatre, supplement to The Irish Times (Dublin), 18 July 1966; "An Aspect of Man and His Environment" in Green Book: Journal of the Architectural Association in Ireland (Dublin), 1968; "Art and Architecture" in Art about Ireland, Dublin 1979.

On SCOTT: articles—"Comhaimsirigh Michael Scott" in Indui (Dublin), 10 August 1951; "Men of the Year" in The Architects' Journal (London), 20 January 1955; "Michael Scott" in The Irish Times (Dublin), 17 September 1955; "Michael Scott" in Irish Architect and Contractor (Dublin), October 1956; "Michael Scott and Partners" by Alan Colquhoun in Architectural Design (London), February 1968; editorial comment by Martin Reynolds in Irish Builder and Engineer (Dublin), 7 September 1968; "Michael Scott: Father Figure of Irish Architecture" in Building and Contract Journal (Dublin), 12 June 1969; "The Royal Scott" by Lancé Wright in The Architects' Journal (London), 22 January 1975; "Irish Gold" by Neil Steedman in Building Design (London), 24 January 1975; "Michael Scott, Man and Architect" in Build (Dublin), February 1975; "Scott/Tallon/Walker" by Neil Steedman in Yearbook of the Royal Institute of the Architects of Ireland (Dublin), 1975–76; "Michael Scott on Dublin," interview with Consuelo O'Connor, in An Taisce: Ireland's Conservation Journal (Dublin), September/October 1978.

As a pupil of Jones and Kelly I recall playing my part in the detailing of Ireland's last classical civic building, Cork City Hall. I was, of course, also expected to "switch to Gothic" when it was thought that the occasion demanded this. On first encountering modern architecture, initially in its Swedish (and Dutch) forms, through the eyes of Frank Yerbury, those of us who were weaned to it from this training background tended to see the modern movement as something which we were "for," in opposition to others who were "against," without analyzing too clearly the various strands which made it up, or our own positions in it. Those who were "against" were forced into some species of eclecticism (full dress classical or gothic had by that time priced itself out of all but the ecclesiastical market) or Art Deco, a style in which I also served by brief time (but distinctions among different segments of the opposition were considered irrelevant once a commitment to modern architecture had been declared).

I would consider my glass-walled Irish Pavilion in the 1939 New York World's Fair, along with my own house at Sandycove Point, to be my first recognizably modern movement buildings, although my county hospitals at Portlaoise and Tullamore were both significant steps—albeit in somewhat different directions—along my chosen path: Portlaoise a very frank expression of both the hospital brief and its crude, or at least low-tech, mass concrete structure, painted in the stunning white of the period, and Tullamore with its juxtaposition of stone arches and Dudok-type stair towers.

My Irish Pavilion was to be, however, my last exercise in its genre. Although Ireland was neutral in the 1939–45 war, shortages of supply put building on any scale out of the question, and my practice was hard put to survive on small alteration works, offering little scope for creativity of any kind. As with a great many architects of my generation, who took their first faltering steps in modern architecture within the shadow of war clouds ahead, a magic moment had passed beyond recall by the time the major commissions from Coras Iompair Eireann (nationalized transport) reached me in the immediate post-war years. Although the bus terminal and offices at Store Street, Dublin, must be reckoned the principal work of my architectural career, and is therefore chosen as the subject of the accompanying photograph, this building bears many signs of the loss of architectural foothold, perhaps loss of innocence, which those who reached their maturity just as war broke out suffered from the interruption of their creative flow.

The Store Street building was completed in 1953. From then on to the end of the decade was a lean time in Ireland, during which emigration reached its peak. Although bitterly disappointed that the immediate post-war boom had proved yet another false start to my chances of creating a real corpus of good modern buildings in Ireland, I did at least have the opportunity, with this enforced freedom from major commissions, to look at the several directions in which modern architecture was seen to be dividing. The still well from which I first drew inspiration had become a whirlpool in which I was now trying to define my position.

What I began to see as the true gospel of modern architecture was clarified for me most eloquently, many years later, by Peter Carter, at one time a member of Mies van der Rohe's staff and author of Mies van der Rohe at Work, in a lecture delivered in University College, Dublin, in December 1975. As this lecture was delivered in my honour—as one of a series of events organized by my colleagues in Ireland to celebrate my Royal Gold Medal year—I take leave to quote from it, in lieu of any profession of my own faith:

> . . . because today's technology provides architects with a wide range of choice, the freedoms it brings may only too easily be interpreted as license for irrational individualism of a most egregious kind.

Michael Scott: Irish Transport Board Bus Station, Store Street, Dublin, 1953

By concentrating upon a STRUCTUR-ALLY oriented architecture, our work as a whole would acquire REASON as its basis, and GENERALITY in its application. For, in a MORPHOLOGICAL interpretation of STRUCTURE may be found a sound GENERAL PRINCIPLE upon which the architecture of *our time* might develop, as it indeed did in the past.

While this PRINCIPLE OF STRUCTURE remains secure, the MAINSTREAM of architectural development will not be easily side-tracked.

And, furthermore, we shall be properly prepared for the time when our present *needs* and *means* give way to others and so initiate a new cycle in the development of architecture.

The *philosophy of architecture* could be interpreted as having both CONSERVATIVE and RADICAL strains, without implying contradictory aims.

CONSERVATIVE: Because in its basic ingredients are to be found the *traditional* principles of structural order, spatial relation and proportion.

RADICAL: Because it accepts as prime determinants the significant driving and sustaining forces of our time—those of science, technology, industrialism and economy.

Furthermore, in its realization as *architecture,* this philosophy often becomes *sociologically* radical, in that we may sense in the very HUMILITY of the spaces many of its buildings offer, the acquisition of civilizing freedoms from wilful architectural manipulation and anachronistic custom.

At the beginning of this lecture I noted that the one characteristic shared by all the

great architectural epochs of the past was that their BUILDERS restricted themselves to very clear PRINCIPLES, yet this did not inhibit the range or the variety of their work. And, upon due reflection, I think that many will agree that *that* is, perhaps, the only way we too may make an architecture of *some* SIGNIFICANCE.

When, in 1959, at the onset of a new period of great expansion in Ireland, I decided to make my chief assistants at that time, Robin Walker and Ronald Tallon, associates in a reconstituted practice, to become partners later, I was happy to feel that this doctrine of architecture would be safe in their hands and, subsequently, in the hands of my son Niall. The third member of my 1959 crew, Patrick Scott, also joined in the creation of this new firm but left shortly afterwards to devote his full time to painting and free-lance designing. He continues his association with the firm—as I do, since my own retirement—in a consultant capacity.

—Michael Scott

Michael Scott has never, at least publicly, acknowledged any architectural influences—but then neither did Frank Lloyd Wright.

There were three important aspects of his formative years. He chose an articled training, a decision precipitated no doubt by the rather erratic nature of academic facilities at that time in Ireland. He went into private practice very early in his life, which, somehow, gave him the opportunity to travel and to pursue and ultimately dismiss other careers in acting, in ballet no less, even as a painter. Then there was the relative isolation of Ireland. Little effective dialogue with European mainland influences was possible. It is doubtful that Corbusier's *Towards a New Architecture* of 1927 would have reached Ireland, or Pevsner's *Pioneers of Modern Design* of 1936, not to mention the *Architectural Review* and,

in particular, its famous essays of 1932 by Morton Shand and Wells Coates. Certainly there were murmurings like the Christ the King Church, Cork, of 1936, by Barry Byrne, a Chicago architect; there was, too, the whole literary revival in Ireland, then in full ferment; finally, there was the Irish Stained Glass movement, which had reached its zenith in the work of artists like Michael Healy, Harry Clarke and Evie Hone. All this in a country struggling to find its nationalistic feet, putting together only in 1937 a constitutional basis for its future.

Nevertheless, Scott was learning the language of contemporary expression in architecture. An early office block by Jones and Kelly, his employers, provided him with an introduction. On establishing his own practice in 1928 there were many projects such as his own house, hospitals, and theatre conversions to allow him to extend his syntax. But it was the Irish Pavilion for the New York *World's Fair* in 1939 that demonstrated his command. In this stylish curvilinear work, with its glazed curtain wall cladding, flat roof slab, and two-storey volume may be seen an excellent manifestation of Scott's fluency. There are echoes of the Mies' Barcelona Pavilion of 1929. There is the same comprehension of space, one rectilinear, one curvilinear, but three dimensional for all that: the canvas of architecture had, for Scott, been laid out. Sculpture and paintings were included too, not as idle artifacts but as integral elements of his design.

Back in Dublin coincidentally this very architecture was finding another expression in a new terminal for the airport (1939) by Professor Desmond Fitzgerald—a Bauhaus-inspired design. With these two buildings, then, though separated by several thousand miles, Ireland had, at last, shaken off the pseudo-classicism of the revival period.

In the mid 1940's there came the commission for the Bus Station in Dublin and, with it, official recognition at home as well as abroad. Opened in 1953, after many vicissitudes, including a change of client, it still retains its original qualities—the planning of the awkward island site; the use again of architectural volumes, particularly the great curving concourse enhanced and unified by its column disposition and diagonal floor finish; the complex planning so evident at each floor level; the superb detailing throughout.

Of course there have been criticisms; it has been condemned as eclectic. But then, as Peter Collins says in his book *Changing Ideals in Modern Architecture,* this is no bad thing. In the Dublin Bus Station Scott eschews all formalism in detail planning in favour of a freer interpretation of the design brief. His capacity to do this is demonstrated in the way that spaces are put together, the way each reflects its function, the way that their complex hierarchy is evolved. Their disparate environmental needs are provided for; the rationale of structure in architecture is well articulated. Scott has—albeit with notable assistance from Ove Arup and Jorgan Varming—become fully literate.

Naturally it is tempting to look for overseas influences. Le Corbusier's Cité de Refuge, a Salvation Army hostel opened in Paris in 1933, has an obvious elevational similarity but it would be impertinent to labour it.

The introduction of associates into his practice in 1959 and partners some years later brought to an end the accredited architectural work of Michael Scott. Yet for Scott an evangelical role, with a very special concern for the visual arts, continued: he has participated, and continues to participate, in virtually every national institution having to do with the arts. Most citations concerning Michael Scott highlight his pioneering role in architecture, indeed in all the arts in Ireland, and his inclusion in this publication is further endorsement of his achievements.

—Kevin Spencer

SCOTT BROWN, Denise.

American. Born Denise Lakofski in 'Nkana, Zambia, 3 October 1931; emigrated to the United States, 1958: naturalized, 1967. Educated at Kingsmead College, Johannesburg, South Africa, 1938–47; University of the Witwatersrand, Johannesburg, 1948–51; Architectural Association School, London, under Arthur Korn, 1952–55, A.A. Diploma and Certificate in Tropical Architecture 1956; University of Pennsylvania, Philadelphia, under H. Gans, Louis I. Kahn, D. A. Crane, R. B. Mitchell, W. L. C. Wheaton, W. Isard, C. Rapkin, P. Davidoff and B. Harris, 1958–60, M.City Planning 1960, M.Arch. 1965. Married the architect Robert Scott Brown in 1955 (died, 1959); married the architect Robert Venturi, *q.v.,* in 1967; son: James. Worked as a student architect with various firms in Johannesburg and London, 1946–52; Architectural Assistant to Ernö Goldfinger and Dennis Clarke Hall, London, 1955–56, to Giuseppe Vaccaro, Rome, 1956–57, and to Cowin, DeBruyn and Cook, Johannesburg, 1957–58; Assistant Professor, School of Fine Arts, University of Pennsylvania, Philadelphia, 1960–65; Visiting Professor, School of Environmental Design, University of California, Berkeley, 1965; Associate Professor, School of Architecture and Urban Planning, University of California at Los Angeles, 1965–68 (initiated Urban Design Program). Since 1967, Architect and Planner, and later Partner, with Robert Venturi and John Rauch, *q.v.* (associates: Steven Izenour; David Vaughan), Venturi and Rauch, Philadelphia: Partner-in-Charge of Urban Planning. Visiting Professor in Urban Design, Yale University School of Architecture, New Haven, Connecticut, 1967–70 (Fellow of Morse College since 1970); Visiting Critic, Rice University, Houston, Texas, 1969; Regents Lecturer, University of California at Santa

Barbara, 1972; Chairwoman, Evaluation Committee for the Industrial Design Program, Philadelphia College of Art, 1972; Member of the Visiting Committee, School of Architecture and Urban Planning, Massachusetts Institute of Technology, Cambridge, 1973–79; Baldwin Lecturer, Oberlin College, Ohio, 1975. Exhibitions: *The Work of Venturi and Rauch,* Whitney Museum, New York 1971; *The Invisible Artist,* Philadelphia Museum of Art, 1974; *The Work of Venturi and Rauch,* Pennsylvania Academy of Fine Arts, Philadelphia, 1975; *Suburban Alternatives: 11 American Projects,* Venice, 1976; *Women in American Architecture,* Brooklyn Museum, New York, 1977. Recipient: First Prize, Yale University Mathematics Building Competition, 1970; Gold Medal, 1972, and Adaptive Re-use Award, 1976, American Institute of Architects, Philadelphia Chapter; Casebook Award, *Print Magazine,* 1976 (twice); *Urban Design* Case Studies Award, 1977. D.F.A.: Oberlin College, Ohio, 1977. Member, Association of Women in Architecture, and the Architects Registration Council of the United Kingdom; Associate of the Royal Institute of British Architects. Address: Venturi and Rauch, 333 South 16th Street, Philadelphia, Pennsylvania 19102, U.S.A.

Works:

1963 Study of the Neighborhood Garden Association of Philadelphia
     Plan for the new tri-state New York Metropolitan Region, for the Office of Regional Development of the State of New York (with Marc Emery)
1967/
 70 "Mass Communication on the People Freeway" (project: subway stop design; with Robert Venturi and B. Adams)
     "Learning from Las Vegas" (research project on symbolism in commercial architecture; with Robert Venturi and Steven Izenour)
     "Remedial Housing for Architects; or, Learning from Levittown" (research project on residential symbolism and popular taste; with Robert Venturi and P. Schmitt)

With Venturi and Rauch:

1968 Walker and Dunlop Office Building, Transportation Square, Washington, D.C. (project; with Caudill Rowlett Scott)
1968/
 70 Rehabilitation plan for South Street, Philadelphia
1970 Mathematics Building, Yale University, New Haven, Connecticut
     Survey and analysis of subway station facilities, Philadelphia
     Humanities Classroom Building, State University of New York at Purchase
     Master plan and urban design of California City, California
1971 Lawton Plaza redevelopment plan, New Rochelle, New York
     Great Western Cities Inc. Office Building, California City, California (project)
1972 Master plan for the Bicentennial International Exposition Site at Eastwick, Philadelphia (with other firms)
1973 Windsor Hotel conversion plan, Cape May, New Jersey
     Preliminary design for prototypical neighborhood and community shopping centers for Saga Harbor, new community south of Miami, Florida
     Housing, Washington Square West Urban Renewal Area, Philadelphia (project)
     Renewal plan for the Seneca-Susquehanna area, Harrisburg, Pennsylvania
     Design of the Bicentennial celebration on and around Benjamin Franklin Parkway, Philadelphia

     South Central Philadelphia Neighborhood Development Program
1973/
 75 Fairmount Manor and the Poplar Community (planning study for lawsuit, Shannon v. H.U.D.)
1974 Natural Science Museum, Roanoke, Virginia (project)
     City Edges: design study for the improvement of road and water entrances to Philadelphia (with Murphy Levy Wurman)
     Feasibility study for a residential community near Phoenix, Arizona
1975 Revitalization study of The Strand, Galveston, Texas
1976 Franklin Court, Independence National Historical Park, Philadelphia
     Allen Memorial Art Museum renovation and additions, Oberlin College, Ohio
     Faculty Club, Pennsylvania State University, University Park
     Signs of Life: Symbols in the American City exhibition plan, Smithsonian Institution, Washington, D.C.
1977 Proposal for the rejuvenation of Main Street and The Hollow, Boonton, New Jersey
     Urban design study for Heritage Plaza West, Salem, Massachusetts
     Planning study for St. Christopher's Hospital for Children, Philadelphia
     Expert testimony on environmental impact for Harvey Cedars, New Jersey
     Planning study for Old City, Philadelphia
1978 Planning study for Washington Avenue, Miami Beach
     Planning study for Jim Thorpe, Pennsylvania
     Urban design for Western Plaza, Pennsylvania Avenue, Washington, D.C.

Publications:

By SCOTT BROWN: books—*The Highway,* exhibition catalog, with Robert Venturi, Philadelphia 1970; *Aprendiendo de Todas Las Cosas,* with Robert Venturi, Barcelona 1971; *Learning from Las Vegas,* with Robert Venturi and Steven Izenour, Cambridge, Massachusetts 1972, 1977; *Signs of Life: Symbols in the American City,* exhibition catalog, with Steven Izenour, New York 1976; articles—"Natal Plans" in *Journal of the American Institute of Planners* (Washington, D.C.), May 1964; "The Meaningful City" in *Journal of the American Institute of Planners* (Washington, D.C.), January 1965; "Development Proposal for Dodge House Park" in *Arts and Architecture* (Los Angeles), April 1966; "Will Salvation Spoil the Dodge House?" in *Architectural Forum* (New York), October 1966; "Team 10, Perspecta 10, and the Present State of Architectural Theory" in *Journal of the American Institute of Planners* (Washington, D.C.), January 1967; "The Function of a Table" in *Architectural Design* (London), April 1967; "Planning the Powder Room" in *AIA Journal* (Washington, D.C.), April 1967; "Housing 1863" in *Journal of the American Institute of Planners* (Washington, D.C.), May 1967; "Teaching Architectural History" in *Arts and Architecture* (Los Angeles), May 1967; "Planning the Expo" in *Journal of the American Institute of Planners* (Washington, D.C.), July 1967; "The Bicentennial's Fantasy Stage" in *Philadelphia Evening Bulletin,* 8 March 1968; "A Significance for A & P Parking Lots; or, Learning from Las Vegas," with Robert Venturi, in *Architectural Forum* (New York), March 1968; "Mapping the City: Symbols and Systems" in *Landscape* (Santa Fe, New Mexico), Spring 1968; "Little Magazines in Architecture and Urbanism" in *Journal of the American Institute of Planners* (Washington, D.C.), July 1968; "Urbino" in *Journal of the American Institute of Planners* (Washington, D.C.), September 1968; "On Ducks and Decoration," with Robert Venturi, in *Architecture Canada* (Toronto), October 1968; "Venturi versus Gowan," with Robert Venturi, in

A PROPOSAL FOR
PLANNING AND DESIGN SERVICES
FOR WASHINGTON AVENUE

MIAMI BEACH

VENTURI AND RAUCH · ARCHITECTS AND PLANNERS
Philadelphia, Pennsylvania

DAVID JAY FEINBERG · ARCHITECT
Miami, Florida

JANUARY 1978

Denise Scott Brown: Planning study for Washington Avenue, Miami Beach, 1978

Architectural Design (London), January 1969; "On Pop Art, Permissiveness and Planning" in *Journal of the American Institute of Planners* (Washington, D.C.), May 1969; "Learning from Lutyens," with Robert Venturi, in *RIBA Journal* (London), August 1969; "The Bicentennial Commemoration 1976," with Robert Venturi, in *Architectural Forum* (New York), October 1969; "Mass Communication on the People Freeway; or, Piranesi Is Too Easy," with Robert Venturi, in *Perspecta* (New Haven, Connecticut), no. 12, 1969; "Co-op City: Learning to Like It," with Robert Venturi, in *Progressive Architecture* (New York), February 1970; "Reply to Pawley— 'Leading from the Rear'," with Robert Venturi, in *Architectural Design* (London), July 1970; "Education in the 1970's—Teaching for an Altered Reality" in *Architectural Record* (New York), October 1970; "Learning from Pop" and "Reply to Frampton" in *Casabella* (Milan), May/June 1971; "Some Houses of Ill-Repute: A Discourse with Apologia on Recent Houses of Venturi and Rauch," with Robert Venturi, in *Perspecta* (New Haven, Connecticut), no. 13/14, 1971; "Ugly and Ordinary Architecture; or, The Decorated Shed," with Robert Venturi, in *Architectural Forum* (New York), part I, November

1971, and part II, December 1971; "Bicentenaire de l'Independence Americaine," with Robert Venturi, in *L'Architecture d'Aujourd'hui* (Paris), November 1973; "Evaluation of the Humanities Building at Purchase," with Elizabeth and Steven Izenour, in *Architectural Record* (New York), October 1974; "Functionalism Yes, But . . . ," with Robert Venturi, in *Architecture + Urbanism* (Tokyo), November 1974; "House Language," with others, in *American Home* (New York), August 1976; "On Architectural Formalism and Social Concern: A Discourse for Social Planners and Radical Chic Architects" in *Oppositions 5* (New York), Summer 1976; "Suburban Space, Scale and Symbol," with others, in *Via* (Philadelphia), 1976; "Zeichen des Lebens, Signes de Vie" in *Archithese* (Zurich), no. 19, 1976; "Elusive Outcome" in *Progressive Architecture* (New York), May 1977.

On SCOTT BROWN: books—*American Architecture and Urbanism* by Vincent Scully, New York 1969; *New Directions in American Architecture* by Robert A.M. Stern, New York 1969; *Will They Ever Finish Bruckner Boulevard?* by Ada Louise Huxtable, New York 1970; *After the Planners* by Robert

Goodman, New York 1971; *Wasteland: Building the American Dream* by Stephen A. Kurtz, New York 1973; *Conversations with Architects* by John W. Cook and Heinrich Klotz, New York and London 1973; *Architettura Radicale* by Paolo Navone and Bruno Orlando, Milan 1974; *Supermannerism: New Attitudes in Post Modern Architecture* by C. Ray Smith, New York 1977; *Women in American Architecture: A Historic and Contemporary Perspective,* by Susana Torre, New York 1977; articles—"Are the Venturis Putting Us On" by Ursula Cliff in *Design and Environment* (New York), Summer 1971; special issue of *Architecture + Urbanism* (Tokyo), October 1971; "Ms. Scott Brown Keeps Her Own Taste to Herself" by Patsy McLaughlin in *Pennsylvania Gazette* (Philadelphia), December 1971; "Interview: Denise Scott Brown" by Linda Groat in *Networks* (Los Angeles), no. 1, 1972; "Venturi and Venturi, Architectural Anti-Heroes" by Barbara Flanagan in *34th Street Magazine* (New York), 13 April 1972; "The Venturis—American Selection" by Deborah Waroff in *Building Design* (London), 4 August 1972; "Women in Professions: Architecture" by Vivien Raynor in *Viva* (London), May 1974; "Venturi and Rauch 1970–74," special issue of *Architecture + Urbanism* (Tokyo), November 1974; "Thirty-Six Women with Real Power Who Can Help You" by Donnal Israel and David C. Berliner in *Cosmopolitan* (New York), April 1975; "Architect for Pop Culture" by Maralyn Lois Polak in *Philadelphia Inquirer,* 8 June 1975; special issue of *Progressive Architecture* (New York), October 1977; "The Social Thought of Denise Scott Brown and Robert Venturi" and "Venturi and Rauch as Planners" by Jean-Louis Sarbib in *L'Architecture d'Aujourd'hui* (Paris), June 1978.

From radical chic architects to social planners, and including most architects and planners in between, we are all against the melting pot and in favor of cultural pluralism and the richness it affords this nation. But when it comes to the aesthetic and formal implications of cultural pluralism we all of us run scared. Social planners of my acquaintance seem to be scared of art and aesthetics in general, perhaps because they see them as intuitive, spontaneous behavior beyond rational control. In fact, social planners tend to see the totality of urban design and architectural behavior as intuitively based and not subject to rational discourse. And, although aesthetic preference patently affects in some way the urban decision making behavior of a majority of the population, rich and poor, social planners define aesthetic concern as "elitist," which, for them, means it should be disdained and ignored.

Architects are afraid that if they are forced to pay attention to the aesthetic preferences of people and groups different from themselves they will lose aesthetic control. For the architect, the sensation induced by the loss of aesthetic control is one akin to drowning.

Given such, not altogether misplaced, fears on both sides, we have had unsurprisingly little rational discourse on the subject.

—Denise Scott Brown

As a principal in the firm of Venturi and Rauch, Denise Scott Brown has pursued a career in both the practice and teaching of architecture, planning and urban design. Educated at the University of Witwatersrand, Johannesburg, the Architectural Association School, London, and at the University of Pennsylvania, Scott Brown has made a significant theoretical contribution to the firm's production, notably in the development of large planning projects and exhibitions. She has written extensively, particularly on issues of social conditions and their relation to architecture and planning.

Since the publication of Robert Venturi's *Complexity and Contradiction in Architecture* in 1966, the firm has publicly established a polemical attitude that utilizes history as a model for architectural problem solving. In numerous articles and a later book, *Learning from Las Vegas*, Denise Scott Brown has, as co-author, put considerable emphasis on the inherent value of the commercial vernacular of America's recent past and continuing present. She has consistently theorized that the current cultural environment is not one that calls for heroic communication through pure architecture. She advocates, instead, a richness in architectural meaning through the use and adaptation of conventional forms.

Consistently, the firm's projects seem to be designed around a parti that is unassertive and familiar. The development of the partis, however, most often yields details that can best be thought of as discordant fragments. The complexity and confusion introduced by these transfigured elements is intended to provoke a re-evaluation of conceptual content of the work. This architecture may be ordinary or "familiar" in two basic modes: in how it is constructed and in how it is seen. Artistically, the use of conventional elements in Venturi's work involves careful adaptations of symbolic imagery. This approach, while remaining functionally conventional, promotes an architecture of meaning rather than expression.

Denise Scott Brown's interests, however, extend beyond the realm of architecture's traditional limits. Her particular education and consequent exposure to the social planning theories of writers such as Paul Davidoff and Herbert Gans have instilled a deeply-rooted concern for the philosophical gap between architects and sociologists. Her research, in both theory and practice, has focused on ways in which architects can better utilize social insight and express social concern. Approaching this investigation as both an architect and a planner, Scott Brown more readily distinguishes formal components as being defined by both perceptual and symbolic qualities. She is concerned not only with what we see in form, but also with what we understand from what we see. Her aim has been to show that the architect's concern with form and its aesthetics can be reconciled with social concern and social idealism.

In defense of the firm's investigative work with Las Vegas and Levittown, Scott Brown repeatedly differentiates between the concepts of "learning" and "enjoying." She promotes the separation of one variable, such as the formal vernacular of Levittown or Las Vegas, as part of a process of analysis and design. This investigation of form is intended as a means of producing innovations in architectural theory and form-making that are more receptive to the needs and life-styles of different types of people. The appeal is to architects not to be overly self-righteous—to allow the lower middle class its own version of the suburban environment. In defense against the charges of social irresponsibility, Scott Brown responds that the origin of these charges lies not in the avowed realms of capitalist social evils or in isolated formal doctrine, but in the fact that the lower middle class symbolism of the forms of Las Vegas and Levittown is offensive to the upper middle class tastes of many architects.

Although this view might be construed as being non-dialectical in nature, it does raise the issues of social concern in architecture to a highly consequential level. We have here an almost polemical stance that calls for a comprehensive understanding of the social concerns and immediate problems confronting architecture today. This is not a philosophy that replaces idealism with realism but rather one that concentrates visionary and idealistic energies on immediate concerns within the confines of existing means.

—S. Fiske Crowell, Jr.

SEGAL, Walter.

British. Born in Ascona, Switzerland, 15 May 1907; emigrated to England, 1936: naturalized, 1939. Educated at the Technische Hoogeschule, Delft, 1927; Technische Hochschule, Berlin, 1929; E.T.H.: Eidgenössische Technische Hochschule, Zurich, 1931–32, Dip.Arch. 1932. Married Eva Bradt in 1938 (died, 1950); married Mary Moran Scott in 1962; has six children. In private practice, Ascona, near Locarno, Switzerland, 1932–33, Porza sopra Lugano, Switzerland, 1933–34, and Palma, Majorca, 1934–35; Excavation Architect, Cairo Museum, 1935. In private practice, London, since 1936. Studio Master, Architectural Association School, London, 1944–48; Bannister Fletcher Professor, Bartlett School, University College London, 1973; Assistant Lecturer, Thames Polytechnic, London, 1976; Visiting Professor, University of Pennsylvania, Philadelphia, 1978. Address (office): 8 North Hill, Highgate, London N.6, England.

Works:

1931 Small House, Berlin (competition project)
1932 Casa Piccolo, Ascona, Switzerland
1933 House, Terreno, Palma, Majorca
House, Calle Dos de Mayo, Palma, Majorca
Restaurant, Ciudad Marina, Ibiza
1937 School, for the *News Chronicle*, London (competition project)
Factory, Holly Street, London E.8
1938 Furniture designs
1940 U.K. Ministry of Supply Hostels in Blackpole, Gloucestershire; Steeton, Gloucestershire; and Kirby, Liverpool (2).
1945 Block of flats, Leigham Court Road, Streatham, London
1950 Housing estate, St. Anne's Close, Highgate, London N.6
Housing estate, West Heath Gardens, Hampstead, London N.W.3
1951/
61 House, Crooked Usage, Finchley, London
House, Neeld Crescent, Hendon, London
House, Dennis Lane, Stanmore, Middlesex
House, Brent, London
House, The Boltons, Kensington, London
House, Church Road, Bushill Park, London N.19
1961 House, Rugby Road, Twickenham, Middlesex
1963 House, West Heath Road, Hampstead, London N.W.3
House, Fideris, Grisons, Switzerland
Tretol Office Building, Edgware Road, Colindale, London
Block of flats, Chesham Street, Chelsea, London S.W.3
Factory and office building, Ramsgate Street, Dalston, London E.8
1964 Block of flats, Rutland Gate, London
Block of flats, Ovington Square, London
1965 Maisonettes, Compayne Gardens, Hampstead, London N.W.3
Terraced housing, Tasker Road, Hampstead, London N.W.3
Temporary "rationalized timber" house, Highgate, London N.6
1966 Block of flats, Cat Hill, East Barnet, London
Block of flats, Salmon Way, Wembley, Middlesex
1967 Block of flats, Bedford Road, Feltham, Middlesex
Walter Segal House, Highgate, London N.6
1968 Timber House, Ballygarrett, Ireland
1969 Timber house, Chapel Street, Halstead, Essex
1970 Timber house, Main Street, Yelling, Huntingdonshire
Timber house, North Chailey, Lewes, Sussex
House addition, 40 Old Church Lane, Wembley, London N.W.9
1971 House, Ballycummisk, County Cork, Ireland
House, North Common, Chailey, Sussex
House, Woodbridge, Suffolk
1974 House extension, Woodbridge, Suffolk
1976 Social Centre, University of Sussex, Brighton (project)
1977 Two-storey house, Mill Hill, London
1977/
80 Lewisham Self-Build Housing Association, London
1978 Housing schemes for the Solon Housing Association, London (project)

Publications:

By SEGAL: books—*Planning and Transport*, London 1945; *Home and Environment*, London 1948, 1953; *Housing: A Survey of the Post-War Housing Work of the London County Council 1945–49*, London 1949; *Housing for People*, London 1979; articles—"Building a House in Majorca" in *Architect and Building News* (London), June 1942; "Patio House: Variations on a Theme" in *Architect and Building News* (London), February 1943; "The Small House in Urban Areas" in *Architect and Building News* (London), June 1943; "Site Layout and Technique" in *Journal of the Royal Architectural Institute of Canada* (Toronto), January 1945; "Small Houses in America" in *Architect and Building News* (London), July 1948; "Changing Trends in Site Layout" in *Arena* (London), March 1966; "A Man on His Own" in *Architect and Building News* (London), October 1968; "Architecture: The Assertive and the Unobtrusive" in *Architect and Building News* (London), September 1969; "Readier for Compromise" in *The Architects' Journal* (London), April 1970; "Mart Stam" in *The Architects' Journal* (London), June 1970; "Ernst May 1886–1970" in *The Architects' Journal* (London), September 1970; "Art in Revolution" in *The Architects' Journal* (London), February 1971; "Aalto Up-to-Date" in *The Architects' Journal* (London), January 1972; "The Neo-Purist School of Architecture" in *Architectural Design* (London), June 1972; "Scharoun" in *Architectural Review* (London), February 1973; "Home—Sweet Home?" in *RIBA Journal* (London), October 1973; "Into the Twenties" in *Architectural Review* (London), January 1974; "Meeting Gropius Again" in *The Architects' Journal* (London), 13 February 1974; "Wood in Architecture" in *The International Book of Timber*, London 1975; "An Architect's Approach to Architecture" in *RIBA Journal* (London), July 1977.

On SEGAL: book—*Walter Segal* by John Maule McKean, Stuttgart and Zurich 1980; articles—"Hostel for Factory Workers" in *Architect and Building News* (London), May 1942; "Proposed House at Mill Hill" in *Architect and Building News* (London), November 1947; "The ABSE House" in *Architect and Building News* (London), April 1949; "Factory and Warehouse" in *The Architects' Journal* (London), October 1958; "House at Highgate" in *The Architects' Journal* (London), March 1966; "A Certain Satisfaction in Building a Shelter for Oneself" by John Maule McKean in *The Architects' Journal* (London), 3 September 1975; "Das Segal Konzept: Hauser aus der Baustoffhandlung" in *Baumeister* (Munich), November 1975; "Walter Segal: Pioneer" by John Maule McKean in *Building Design* (London), 20 and 27 February 1976; "Liberation Through Technology" in *Building Design* (London), 27 February 1976; "The Segal System" by John Maule McKean in *Architectural Design* (London), no. 5, 1976.

It is extremely interesting to see the way that Walter Segal's reputation has grown on the basis of a relatively small number of buildings. In particular, he has attracted the attention of a generation of younger architects who have grown dissatisfied with the increasingly detached and managerial role of the architect. There is no doubt that Professionalism has had some of the effects that its original critics like Lethaby feared: architects have become detached from the building process to such an extent that many problems like building faults, high costs, uninventive construction, failure to realize the potential of either traditional crafts or new techniques, can be attributed to it.

Walter Segal, perhaps without really intending it, began to point a way back to a better synthesis with building, when he had to design himself a temporary and extremely low cost house in his garden in the mid 1960's. Using standard and uniform timber members, board sizes, rationalized framing and a radically different attitude to foundations, he produced a prototype that became a model for a series of other designs in which he has gone on refining and developing his method. It was an approach which lent itself as well to owner-builders as to clients who wanted low cost buildings put up by builders. He developed a system of drawings that greatly simplified communication with the few tradesmen that were needed to construct his designs, and he personally supervised and took on many of the tasks of a general contractor for his clients, thus being able to control costs, details and quality in a way few architects who operate in conventional practice are able to do.

In the course of this development, Segal has naturally encountered those authorities who administer regulations and control development, and Segal's reputation among many architects has been enhanced by his having become quite militant in the fight against petty bureaucrats who cannot tolerate the refreshing iconoclasm of his general approach to design.

—Cedric Green

SEIDLER, Harry.

Australian. Born in Vienna, Austria, 25 June 1923; emigrated to Australia in 1948: acquired Australian nationality, 1958. Educated at the Wasagymnasium, Vienna, 1932–38; University of Manitoba, Winnipeg, 1941–44, B.Arch. 1944; Harvard University, Cambridge, Massachusetts, under Walter Gropius and Marcel Breuer, 1945–46, M.Arch. 1946. Married Penelope A. M. Evatt in 1958; children: Timothy and Pauline. Chief Assistant to Marcel Breuer, New York, 1946–48; worked with Oscar Niemeyer, Rio de Janeiro, 1948. Since 1948, Principal of Harry Seidler and Associates, Sydney. Visiting Professor, Harvard University Graduate School of Design, Autumn 1976–77, and University of British Columbia, Vancouver, Winter 1977–78; Thomas Jefferson Professor of Architecture, University of Virginia, Charlottesville, Autumn 1978. Trustee, Art Gallery of New South Wales, Sydney; Counsellor, University of New South Wales, Sydney. Collections: Museum of Modern Art, New York; Harvard University. Recipient: Sir John Sulman Medal, Royal Australian Institute of Architects, 1951, 1967; Wilkinson Award, RAIA, 1965, 1966, 1967; Pan Pacific Citation, American Institute of Architects, 1968; Gold Medal, RAIA, 1976. Fellow, Royal Australian Institute of Architects. Honorary Fellow of the American Institute of Architects. O.B.E. (Officer, Order of the British Empire), 1972. Address: Harry Seidler and Associates, 2 Glen Street, Milsons Point, New South Wales 2061, Australia.

Works:

1949/
54 Houses, Sydney

1957 Master Plan for McMahons Point high density housing, Sydney

1960 Apartment block, Ithaca Gardens, Elizabeth Bay, Sydney

Ciba Chemical Company Administration and Warehouse Building, Orion Road, Lane Cove, Sydney

1960/
67 Australia Square redevelopment, Sydney (with Pier Luigi Nervi)

1961 Blues Point Tower apartment block, McMahons Point, Sydney

Office and Warehouse Building, Harris Street, Ultimo, Sydney

Lend Lease House office building, Macquarie Street, Sydney

1962 The Rocks redevelopment project, Sydney Cove

Apartment block, 40 Victoria Street, Potts Point, Sydney

1963 Apartment block, Stephen Street, Paddington, Sydney

Apartment block, Kimberley Street, Diamond Bay, Sydney

1963/
65 Apartment block, 58 Roslyn Gardens, Rushcutters Bay, Sydney

1964 Town houses and apartment housing, Canberra

1965 Apartment block, 85 Elizabeth Bay Road, Elizabeth Bay, Sydney

1965/
66 Apartment block, 29 Ocean Avenue, Double Bay, Sydney

1965/
68 Space Frame Building, Bourke Road, Alexandria, Sydney

Harry Seidler: Commonwealth Government Trade Group Offices, Barton, Canberra, 1975

1966/
67 Apartment blocks, Edgecliff Road, Edgecliff, Sydney
Seidler House, Killara, Sydney
1967 Apartment blocks, Maloney Street, Rosebery, Sydney
1967/
68 Housing project for fellows and research scholars, Australian National University, Canberra
1968 Urban redevelopment scheme, Sydney
Apartment block, 100 Elizabeth Bay Road, Elizabeth Bay, Sydney
1970 Condominium apartments, Acapulco, Mexico
Memorial to Martyrs, Rookwood, Sydney
1970/
75 Commonwealth Government Trade Group Offices, Kings Avenue, Barton, Canberra
1971 Mid-City Centre, George and Pitt Streets, Sydney
1971/
72 Office building, 21 McLaren Street, North Sydney
1971/
73 Seidler and Associates Office and Administration Building, Milsons Point, Sydney
1971/
77 M.L.C. Centre Office Tower and Theatre Royal, Martin Place, Sydney
1972 Conzinc Riotinto of Australia Headquarters, office tower and commercial redevelopment, Collins Street, Melbourne
1973 Apartment housing project, Bushey Park, Singapore
Commonwealth Government Offices, Tuggeranong, Canberra
1973/
77 Australian Embassy, Quai Branly, Paris
1974/
76 Fairfield Central Library, Cabramatta, Sydney
Torin Factory, Penrith, Sydney (with Marcel Breuer and Associates)
1976 La Trobe University Library, Victoria

Publications:

By SEIDLER: articles—in *Arts and Architecture* (Los Angeles), January 1948, January, February, and June 1949, January, May, and September 1950, November 1951, November 1953, May 1954, May, November, and December 1955, August and December 1956, January and September 1957, February, April and July 1958, January, October and December 1959, January, March, July and November 1960, January, May, June, August and December 1961, May, June, August and November 1962, February and October 1963, June and July 1964, October and November 1965; *Architectural Review* (London), September, October and November 1951, November 1952, May 1954, August 1956, October 1959, May 1961, July and August 1963, November 1964, July 1966, November 1967, June 1968, March 1969, October 1970, and April, May and September 1972; *Bauen und Wohnen* (Zurich), October 1952, April 1955, March and July 1956, September 1957, March 1958, December 1959, March 1960, July 1961, October 1962, November 1963, June 1964, January, May and June 1966, January and February 1969; *M.D.* (Stuttgart), April 1958, July 1961, June 1962, August and October 1963, May, June, October and December 1964, March, April and November 1965, April 1968, July 1969, June 1971, May 1972, February 1973; *L'Architecture d'Aujourd'hui* (Paris), no. 20, 1952, September 1954, no. 73, 1957, no. 86, 1959, no. 103, 1962, nos. 113–114, 1964, no. 120, 1965, no. 130, 1967, no. 150, 1970; *Domus* (Milan), February 1952, September 1953, July 1963, April 1964, August 1968, May 1972; *Architectural Design* (London), April 1959, April 1960, December 1961, November 1962, May 1963, September, October and November 1963, October and November

1964, September 1965, October 1966, June 1967, March 1972; *Architectural Forum* (New York), September 1960, January 1962, August 1963, March 1968, April 1969, November 1970; *Deutsche Bauzeitschrift* (Gutersloh), June 1961, May and October 1962, October 1963, July 1964, February 1965, September and November 1966, May, August and September 1967, January, February, July and August 1969, April 1970, July 1972; *Architecture Plus* (New York), February 1973; *Architecture in Australia* (Sydney), October 1949, December 1951, April and July 1954, January 1955, December 1958, May and June 1961, May 1962, June 1965, July 1966, February, June, August and December 1967, April, August and November 1968, June 1969, February and August 1970, April 1971, April and June 1972.

On SEIDLER: books—*Living Spaces* by G. Nelson, New York 1952; *Houses, Interiors and Projects 1949–54*, Sydney 1954, 1959; *The Modern Factory* by Edward D. Mills, London 1959; *The Australian Ugliness* by Robin Boyd, Melbourne 1960; *Best Australian Houses* by N. Clerehan, Melbourne 1961; *New Buildings in the Commonwealth* by J. M. Richards, London 1962; *Encyclopaedia of Modern Architecture* by G. Hatje, London 1963; *Harry Seidler 1955–63*, Sydney, Paris and Stuttgart, 1963; *High Density Living* by R. Jensen, London 1966; *Apartments* by S. Paul, New York 1967; *Architecture in Australia: A History* by J. M. Freeland, Melbourne 1968; *Australia Square*, Sydney 1969; *Australian Style* by B. Hayes, London 1970; *Office Buildings* by R. Hohl, London 1968; *Living and Partly Living* by McKay, Boyd, Stretton and Mant, Melbourne 1972; *Architecture for the New World: The Work of Harry Seidler* by Peter Blake, Sydney, New York and Stuttgart, 1973.

*

The underlying credo of morality in modern architecture has largely been lost, forgotten or undergone such mutation as to become unrecognizable.

The demand that there be a consequential three-way simultaneous design process at the basis of architectural design decisions, which brings into a happy marriage considerations of social use, aesthetics and technology, is ignored in the wilful capriciousness which characterizes so much of the new man-made world that has come into existence.

To regain some direction which could restore a discernible cultural aim to take the place of the prevalent "free for all"—and the commercially motivated "something new every Monday morning"—desperate efforts of the unskilled—it may be well to recall the high principles and clear consequentiality expressed by some of the pioneers; their demand was for basic integrity and an intrinsic honesty of approach. Let us think simply and realistically of the tasks. It is the cardinal brief for the designer to find solutions which in addition to all "architectural" considerations will be objects that can be produced naturally and appropriately in a given socio-economic climate. To extract from an existing environment the essential character that is its very own and develop an inevitably complimentary solution, is as important as finding answers simultaneously to technological questions. One can not exist at the exclusion of the other.

Practically such solutions will:

Strive toward the exquisite understatement inherent in consequential systems to take the place of today's fashionable devotion to ostentatious complexity.

Contrive systematic solutions and their components such as will "invite" variation. The more parts of a system are assembled, the more interesting and visually enticing the totality will become, rather than duller and more soul-destroying, as is the present-day norm.

Devise and maximize systems of mechanization appropriate and "in tune" with the particular task. These must not

only stop at considerations of structure and cladding (as is so often the limit of prevalent thought), but will also encompass simultaneously integral solutions to the problems posed by all services (without the usual nightmarish after-thought complications of most "modern" buildings).

Pursue with purity and directness the problems of connections and detail which will re-occur wherever identical situations generate them (in contrast to ad-hoc traditional detailing which contributes so much to high cost of building).

In the shaping of elements, give free reign to the expression of the laws of nature —not what is "imagined" to be so by many structurally naive architects—but the unassailable physical truth of statics. Great richness of expression can result from such a search which will have that irreplaceable quality of longevity—of remaining valid— being born of the immutable and irrevocable truth of nature.

Aesthetically such solutions will:

Exploit a visual vocabulary which stems from the conviction that architecture is and always was above all an ART form, and that an interrelation and interdependence exists between all the visual arts.

Be aware that consistent visual phenomena have emerged in our time which have given rise to recognizable basic design criteria forming a common denominator to most visual endeavours; amongst these are:

The subtle orchestration of the intricacies of space. 20th century man's eyes and senses crave space in a new way as only our technology can muster (as against the great spatial work of, for instance, the Baroque). The sense of the infinite and yet simultaneously intimate—the sense of the beyond.

The channelling of space and surfaces in opposition or tension; the "pulling apart" of confining areas and their disposition in contradiction (the curve against counter-curve—the juxtaposition and sequencing of compressive low to the surprise of high).

Visual tension, the balance of unequals, generated in surfaces as in the juxtaposition of material (synthetic smooth against natural rough—warm colour against cold).

The use of counterpoint; once a strong visual element is chosen, it must find its re-use or echo throughout the work (as against the arbitrary assembly of unrelated forms).

A single strong idea of form coupled with a solution to planning which must be disarmingly simple—a "Gordian Knot" kind of solution, with the character of the inevitable and that of a reproducible prototype.

—Harry Seidler

Harry Seidler's early houses from 1949 to 1954 established an authentic version of modern architecture in conformity with Bauhaus principles in Australia. The consistency and unfailing high quality design and execution of Seidler's subsequent work set a standard for modern architecture in Australia. Seidler's design orientation presents a number of contrasts with the mainstream of post-war architecture in Australia; his buildings are uncompromisingly international in a country where conservative regionalism is the rule. And whereas the creative wave of Australian architecture has tended towards a kind of romanticism inspired by Wright and Scandinavian ideas, Harry Seidler's architecture is an example of academic rationalism in so far as it emphasizes standardization and concentration, the perfection of a limited number of established themes, the clear articulation of architectonic form and the expression of architecture as structural form. Seidler frequently bases his architectural forms on motifs taken from contemporary painting or sculpture which he uses to generate a range of compositions from which he selects the most suitable form.

The Australia Square Office Tower marks the beginning of a change in Seidler's architecture away from tensional composition derived from Albers and a De Stijl type of elementarist composition, towards a more static classical type of composition inspired by Norman Carlberg's sculpture and the paintings of Frank Stella. The use of circular and quadrant geometries in Seidler's architecture in the 1970's betrays a significant shift away from functionalism and towards classicism. The Trade Group Offices, Canberra, are the clearest expression of the new classicism in Seidler's work. Seidler's rationalism is manifested in the meticulous consideration of details and their standardisation and in a preoccupation with the mastery of technology. In his recent public buildings Seidler has transformed structure and services into decorative sculpture. Seidler was assisted in the sculptural expression of his structures (notably the variable profile concrete "T" beams) by Peter Miller, a Sydney structural engineer, and Pier Luigi Nervi.

The main influences on Seidler were Josef Albers and Marcel Breuer: from Albers, Seidler learned to think in visual terms, while Breuer showed him how to assemble and articulate his building elements. Breuer's influence can also be detected in Seidler's choice of materials, especially Breuer's juxtaposition of smooth artificial materials and natural rough materials and the fluid treatment of space.

Of the early houses, it was the Rose Seidler (1949–50) and the Rose houses built at Turramurra that made the greatest impact on Seidler's Australian contemporaries. While working in Breuer's New York office from September 1946 to March 1948 Seidler was involved in the Robinson House, Williamstown (1946–47), and the Breuer House I in New Canaan, Connecticut (1947). Some features, mainly relating to the planning, were carried over from these American houses and reapplied in Seidler's new Australian houses. The R. Seidler House, for example, had a bi-nuclear plan (developed by Breuer in 1943) similar to the Robinson House, and the Rose House was closely related in its plan to the Breuer House. These early Seidler houses should not be thought of as mere copies, since they reveal an independence of thought, professional competence and care for the quality of construction that compares more than favourably with Breuer's own houses.

Seidler was busy throughout the 1950's designing houses for private clients, then in the early 60's he received commissions for apartment and office buildings. In nearly all his apartment buildings, from the earliest ones close to the centre of Sydney at Camperdown, Elizabeth Bay, Rushcutter's Bay, and Edgecliff, to the apartments for Australian embassy staff in Paris, Seidler consistently applied a split level arrangement with access on alternate floors. The Blues Point Tower Apartments, North Sydney, with its staccato rhythm of staggered glass enlivening the exposed facades, is probably the most interesting of Seidler's apartment buildings. In 1961 Seidler designed Lend Lease House Offices, Sydney, which, with its prominent use of adjustable aluminium louvres for sun control, was the first of a series of important projects, of which the M.L.C. Centre, Sydney, is the most recent. The most famous, and deservedly so, is the Australia Square project, Sydney, which was a major town planning triumph in overcoming the problems of piecemeal development in the central business district, and a formidable statement of Seidler's uncompromising rationalism. Pier Luigi Nervi made an important contribution in the design of the floor system for the first two floors of the tower.

In 1964–68 Seidler was also involved in group housing schemes in Canberra which were remarkably successful. Seidler's own house at Killara

(1966–67), located in a bush setting reminiscent of Wright's Falling Water, is an essential statement of the architect's values. Seidler is still very much a European, never having lost the Viennese sense of decorum from which his buildings take their formal quality and dignity. The major themes of structural clarity, material economy in the construction, spatial interplay of related levels and disciplined selection of materials are all there.

The early 1970's were an expansive period for Seidler; he built offices for his firm at Milson's Point, Sydney, and completed three major projects: the Trade Group Offices, Canberra, the Australian Embassy in Paris, and the M.L.C. Centre, Sydney. The offices at Milson's Point and the Embassy are major works typifying the shift in Seidler's style towards classicism.

Seidler has played an important role in the establishment of modern architecture in Australia. His stature as an architect can be assessed in two ways: firstly in relation to his Australian contemporaries, and secondly as a student of Gropius, Albers and Breuer who happened to work in Australia. His architecture is therefore an extension rather than a reflection, as most Australian architecture is, of the international modern movement. Seidler's architecture is unquestionably important both in a local sense and internationally, although recognition has tended to come more readily from outside Australia.

—Philip Drew

SEIFERT, Ivan.

French. Born in Zagreb, Yugoslavia, 23 December 1926; emigrated to France, 1955: naturalized, 1969. Educated at the University of Zagreb, Department of Architecture, under Vladimir Turina, 1945–51 (Student Prize, 1950), Dip.Arch.Ing. 1951. Married Miryana Vujicic in 1955; children: Sanda, Marc, Patrick and Anne. Town Planner, Town Planning Institute, Zagreb, 1951; Architect, Office Haberle, Zagreb, 1952–55, office of Pierre Vago, Paris, 1955–57, Stafford, Moor and Farington, Sydney, Australia, 1957–58, and Atelier L.W.D., Paris, 1958–61. Since 1961, Partner, A.T.E.A. (Atelier d'Etudes Architecturales), Neuilly, Meudon, France (partners: Guy Lagneau; Michel Weill; Jean Dimitrijevic; Paul Cordoliani; Henri Coulomb; Renzo Moro). Technical Adviser, S.E.T.A.P. (Société pour l'Etude Technique d'Aménagements Planifies), Neuilly, Meudon, since 1961. Address: A.T.E.A., 3 rue Marcel Allegot, 92190 Meudon, France.

Works:

1952 Cinema, restaurant and bowling club complex, Bregana, Yugoslavia
Electrical Centre, Institute for Shipbuilding Research, Zagreb
1954 Hydroelectric Power Station, Jablanica, Yugoslavia
1956 Apartment building, rue Erlanger, Paris
1957 McMahons Point Residential Development, Sydney (project; with others)
Laboratories, University of Sydney
Office building, Sydney
Villas, University of Sydney
Factory, Sydney
1958 Qantas Airlines Airport Hangar, Sydney
Slaughterhouse, University of Veterinary Studies, Sydney
Central Bank for the West African States, Lome, Togo
1959 Citroen Exhibition Hall, Abidjan, Ivory Coast
1960 Hotel Transatlantique, Ouargla, Sahara
Chargeurs Reunis Apartment Buildings, Libreville and Port Gentile, Gabon

1961 Low-cost housing, Ouargla, Sahara
1962 Apartment buildings, Gif-sur-Yvette, France
Apartment buildings, Brest, France
1963 High School and College of Education, Bamako, Mali (with Tekhne)
1964 Faculty of Literature Building, University of Nice
Library, University of Nice
1966 National Bank of Madagascar, Tananarive
1967 Bank of France, Cannes
Apartment building, Landivisiau, France
1968 Apartment buildings and houses, Cergy-Pontoise, France
1969 E.S.S.E.C.: Institute for Advanced Studies in Economics and Commerce, Cergy-Pontoise, France
1970 Highway Bridge Restaurant, Lancon, France
1971 Airport, Bamako, Mali (with Tekhne)
Highway Hotel, Macon, France
1972 Apartment building, Cergy-Pontoise, France
1973 Bank of France, Clermont-Ferrand, France
1974 Bank of France, Creteil, France
1975 Popular Bank Group Training Centre, Cergy-Pontoise, France
1976 Teaching and Research Centre for Advanced Studies in Commerce and Management, Sophia-Antipolis, France

Publications:

On SEIFERT: articles—"Sport Parc Rijeka-Susak" in *L'Architecture d'Aujourd'hui* (Paris), December 1949; "Institute for Shipbuilding Research" in *Arhitektura* (Zagreb), no. 1, 1954; "Skyscraper or Eight-Story Building?" in *Vjesnik* (Zagreb), 21 December 1954; "A Redevelopment Project for McMahons Point" in *Arts and Architecture* (Los Angeles), February 1958; "Central Bank for West African States" in *Progressive Architecture* (New York), December 1962; "University of Nice—Faculty of Literature" in *Technique et Architecture* (Paris), December 1964; "Creators of the Institute" in *Le Courier* (Tananarive), 9 March 1968; "High School and College of Education, Bamako, Mali" in *L'Architecture d'Aujourd'hui* (Paris), November 1968; "University of Nice Faculty of Literature and University Library" in *Technique et Architecture* (Paris), October 1969; "Hopes and Possibilities—Ivan Seifert, Architect" in *Telegram* (Zagreb), 21 December 1971; "E.S.S.E.C.: Institute for Advanced Studies in Economics and Commerce" in *Architecture Intérieure* (Paris), November 1973; "E.S.S.E.C." in *Reflets* (Paris), January 1974; "E.S.S.E.C.: Institute for Advanced Studies in Economics and Commerce" in *Planen und Bauen* (Zurich), June 1974; "Training Centre for the Popular Bank Group, Cergy-Pontoise" in *Le Bâtiment-Bâtir* (Paris), May 1977.

Architecture and architects have not been spared by the crisis which has shaken our economy for some years; I think, however, that the problems of our profession arose much earlier. The profession of architect, once regarded as one of the most eminent, has lost its prestige and its respectability.

We are told daily that we have not learnt to adapt ourselves to new situations, to new techniques, to a society in continuous evolution. Perhaps some architects have known how to adapt to new situations only too well, and perhaps this is precisely the reason for a certain deterioration in the profession. The sudden increase in demand for dwellings and installations after the war provoked a tidal wave in construction. The demand was such that speed was often more important than quality: to have a roof over one's head was of greater consequence than the proportions of a facade! Suddenly architects faced a promising future, and a large number of young people were attracted to the profession; unfortunately, vocation and talent were not always deciding factors in their choice. With high stakes and few references, the problem was how to make one's name, how to

Ivan Seifert: E.S.S.E.C.: Institute for Advanced Studies in Economics and Commerce, Cergy-Pontoise, France, 1969

sell one's architecture. Instead of becoming a creator, the architect became a "salesman."

For the less gifted, to be effective was enough. They claimed that they could solve any problem by using curtain walls to replace facades and by using system building which allowed everyone to produce everything (except good projects). By eliminating practically all research and by always repeating ready-made solutions from other projects, they became ubiquitous "specialists" in dwellings, educational establishments, etc., monopolizing entire building sectors. They became essential assistants, because legislation required that an architect be called in for certain kinds of buildings.

We have this kind of architect to thank for a large number of housing estates, for school buildings that recall barracks, and for the contempt of the public at large for "contemporary architecture."

More gifted architects had to take the opposite path. In order to sell their architecture, they had to be different. They had to invent a new architecture every day: architecture became a consumer item, following fashion, changing with ever-increasing rhythm.

It is not surprising that the public, disgusted with the mediocrity of some architects and confused by the search for ever more unusual forms of other architects (forms often accentuated by aggressive colour), sought refuge in the so-called "inspired" values of the past (witness the current infatuation for the individual house "in the French manner" and certain very formal projects for the center of Paris). One wonders whether architecture will arrive at the year 2000 in reverse gear.

To get out of this absurd situation, we must rethink the art of building. Before you can find a remedy you must establish a diagnosis.

In the old towns every building was different. Nevertheless, the whole gave an impression of unity and harmony by the use of identical or similar materials, by the same building techniques, by the human scale; and form clearly expressed function. Architecture in the past was easily understood by the public: it provided a sense of security. Our towns today are no longer reassuring. We flee from them at every opportunity. The best proof: the congestion on

the motorways every weekend. The perfection of completely rationalized plans that do not take into account the human being's deepest desires has produced neither towns nor habitat but groups of zones of specific activity and machines for living, working or shopping. In our towns disorder and a lack of unity are the consequences of the desire of many architects to do their work without bothering to adapt their project to what already exists.

The global result is generally disappointing despite the sometimes undeniable quality of the components. It is not surprising that, with such results, the public doubts the competence of our profession. It is up to us to give proof to the contrary.

—Ivan Seifert

From Yugoslavia, where he was born, trained as an architect, and worked for a time, Ivan Seifert came to France to broaden his experience, then settled permanently.

He first worked with me, collaborating notably on the Interbau Hansaviertel Apartment Building and in the competition for the Library of the University of Bonn. After working in Australia, Seifert returned to France, and for many years now has been a member of the A.T.E.A. architectural team within which he has conceived and executed numerous works, in Africa as well as France, that are always interesting and often of great quality—for example, E.S.S.E.C.: Institute for Advanced Studies in Economics and Commerce in the new town of Cergy-Pontoise, near Paris.

Seifert's work is characterized by a thorough research into form and volume—not by arbitrary plastic compositions but by a dynamic expression of functions and a studied use of materials.

—Pierre Vago

SEIFERT, Robin (Richard Seifert).
British. Born of Swiss parents, 25 November 1910. Educated at the Central Foundation School, London, 1920–28; University College, University of London, 1928–33, Dip.Arch. 1934. Served in the Corps of Royal Engineers, 1940–44, and in the Indian Army, 1944–46: Certificate for Meritorious Services, Home Forces, 1943; Honorary Lieutenant Colonel, 1946. Married Josephine Jeanette Harding in 1939; children: Brian, John, and Anne. Since 1934, Principal of R. Seifert and Partners, London (current partners: H. G. Marsh; A. G. Henderson; J. M. Seifert; R. F. Morris; R. J. Jenkins; S. Alexander; H. E. Morgan; and J. Clowes); office established in Glasgow, 1970. Member of the Road Safety Council, 1970–73; Member, British Waterways Board, 1971–74; Member of the Council, Royal Institute of British Architects, 1971–74. Recipient: Civic Design Award, 1970; E.E.C. Constructional Steelwork Award, 1978. Fellow, University College London, 1971. Fellow, Royal Institute of British Architects, 1945, and Royal Society of Arts, 1976. Address: R. Seifert and Partners, 164 Shaftesbury Avenue, London WC2H 8HZ, England.

Works:

1955 Woolworth House, Marylebone Road, London N.W.1
1960 Kellogg House, Baker Street, London W.1
1962 Dunlop House, King Street, St. James's, London S.W.1
1965 Nat. West House, Stratford Place, Piccadilly, London W.1
1966 Centre Point (office building), St. Giles Circus, London W.C.2
     Royal Garden Hotel, Kensington, London W.8
     I.C.T. Headquarters Building, Putney, London
1967 Drapers Gardens (bank headquarters), London E.C.4
     Gateway House, Piccadilly, Manchester
1968 Tolworth Towers (local council offices), Surbiton, Surrey

Guinness Mahon Bank, Gracechurch Street, London

1969 Britannia Hotel, Grosvenor Square, London W.1

1970 I.C.I. Research Laboratories, Blackley, Manchester

1971 A.T.V. Centre, Birmingham
Lloyds Bank, City of London

1971/
72 Shopping Centre and Council Housing, Erith, Kent

1972 Whittington House, Alfred Place, London W.1
Anderston Cross (shopping mall, offices, residential buildings, and bus station), Glasgow

1973 Park Tower Hotel, Knightsbridge, London S.W.1
Sobell Sports Centre, Islington, London N.1
International Press Centre, Shoe Lane, London
Holiday Inn, George Street, London W.1
Surrey Lane Housing, Wandsworth, London
London Metropole Hotel, Edgware Road, London N.W.2

1974 *Times* Newspaper Building, Printing House Square, London E.C.4
London Penta Hotel, Cromwell Road, London
St. John's Ambulance Headquarters, Windsor, Berkshire

1975 National Exhibition Centre and Metropole Hotel, Birmingham
British Steel Corporation Research Laboratories, Middlesbrough, Yorkshire
IPC Offices, Kings Reach, Southwark, London
Melia Hotel and Residential Complex, South Bank, London

1976 London Heathrow Airport Hotel
Maples Furniture Store, Tottenham Court Road, London W.1

1977 Wembley Conference Centre, London
Tower Warehouse, London Docks
Princess Grace Hospital, Nottingham Place, London W.1
Houses and offices, King Street, Hammersmith, London

1978 Minet Insurance Company Headquarters, Leman Street, London E.11
Metropolitan Police Headquarters, Putney, London
B.A.T. Building, Victoria Street, London S.W.1
New Blackfriar's Station and Guinness Peat's Headquarters, London

1979 Shopping mall, King Street, Hammersmith, London
Gamages redevelopment, Holborn, London
National Westminster Bank Tower, Bishopsgate, London
Euston Square (new station and office development), Euston, London N.W.1

Publications:

By SEIFERT: article—"London's Buildings: Technical Advances Point to an Exciting Future" in *Chartered Surveyor* (London), September 1972.

On SEIFERT: articles—"The Man Who Did All This and Became an Architect by Accident" by Judy Hillman in the *Evening Standard* (London), 22 June 1965; "Architects and Their Offices: R. Seifert and Partners" by Mary Haddock in *Building* (London), 10 February 1967; "Centre Point: Symbol of the Sixties" in *Building* (London), 24 May 1968; "Drap-

Robin Seifert: Centre Point, London, 1966

ers Gardens" in *Building* (London), 6 August 1968; "Seifert-on-the-Hill" in *The Architects' Journal* (London), 7 October 1969; "Tomorrow's Hotels" in *Architect and Building News* (London), 5 November 1970; "Seifert on Our Skyline" in the *Sunday Times Magazine* (London), 13 February 1972; "The Post House Hotel, London Airport" in *Architectural Review* (London), September 1972; "R. Seifert" in *Building Design* (London), October 1972; "Two Sides of a Street" in *The Architects' Journal* (London), 22 August 1973; "Hospital Remedy: Princess Grace Hospital, London" by Martin Spring in *Building* (London), 21 July 1978; "The Highest Building in Europe: The National Westminster Bank Tower" in *Building* (London), 4 August 1978; "Seifert's Wrenaissance" by David Atwell in *The Architects' Journal* (London), 21 February 1979.

Post-war architecture has long been the subject of debate, clouded by strong criticism against all that has been done. There is no defence against bad architecture, but I would prefer to treat all the mistakes and successes as part of an experimental era leading to the unique in design and technology. All architecture communicates—many try to evade this fact whilst under the spell of modernistic dogma.

It is right that everyone is now taking an interest in the design of our buildings. If there had been the same kind of interest in the early 1950's, the building boom might have started off on the right foot. Most people live and work in buildings that are far removed from their architectural ideal. Many of us have a preference for Nash terraces and there has been much talk about a "human scale" in building, but one must try to balance the preservation of historic and architectural places with the vital need of a community to rebuild. Whilst Nash terraces have their remarkable attraction (and it must be remembered that they were "speculative" housing developments), it would be monotonous and uninteresting if urban cities were full of Nash terraces without a variation of style. Comprehensive developments that respect their neighbours, the skyline, conservation areas and views from the parks and bridges, should not be architecturally frustrated, unless we wish to see our great cities submerged into a skyline that can only be viewed from the street and not from panoramic points of vantage.

The architect has always been a creator, but today, among other things, he has to be a technologist, a lawyer, a cost controller, conservationist, sociologist and administrator. When he has been all these things to his client and to society—only then perhaps can he dwell on the hope for the future. He must grapple with the problems of energy saving, pollution, economics, road sprawl—the combination of these problems must, in the future, necessarily tax the mind of every architect, who, with the encouragement of governments and the people, must look to an architectural era when technology, together with the elements of nature, will create a new architectural definition to our way of working and living.

I hope that we are now moving into a new postmodern period. We have learnt a great deal about spatial organization, clarity and refinement of details, which have characterized most of the world's greatest epochs of architecture. They stand for the rational, the abstract and the universal in their internal competition with the subjective, the evocative and the particular.

—Robin Seifert

Robin (also known as Richard) Seifert formed his architectural practice when he qualified in 1934. His first works were on private housing estates. After the Second World War his office won a number of commissions for industrial estates, including large complexes at Woolwich and at Brighton. His interest in new techniques in building, and his desire to reject the traditional methods of cladding and construction, led him to develop an expertise in concrete as a structural and expressed material at a time when brick and stone were difficult to obtain in Britain. He embraced technologies and models developed in America and in Europe, involving the maximum use of concrete in sculptured forms for the buildings themselves, and exploiting the homogeneous possibilities of concrete as the skin and bones of architecture.

His architecture is, in his own estimation, greatly influenced by Gropius, and Seifert sees Gropius as the seminal force on modern architecture, mid-way between the philosophies of Lloyd Wright on the one hand and those of Le Corbusier on the other. Seifert has certainly created buildings that startle. The complicated castings needed for Centre Point, for example, are indicative of his commitment to concrete as a cladding and structural material, and have made possible a tall building with a distinctively modelled character. The Royal Garden Hotel in Kensington is a more conventional slab with antecedents firmly in both the Gropius and Corbusier camps, while the London Penta Hotel combines both sculptured shapes and the simpler rectangular slabs. Yet the apparent clarity of the main forms of these buildings is perhaps dimmed by the handling of their bases. The slender tower of Centre Point, for example, becomes confused with the lower building at its foot, while the simple slab-like form of the Royal Garden Hotel has several structures at the *pilotti*-like base that detract from the simple geometry of the building as a whole.

Although Seifert moved away from concrete as a cladding material after 1971, and now favours a return to traditional claddings such as brick and granite for their appearance and durability, his latest great tower-block for the National Westminster Bank in the City of London is perhaps the apotheosis of his belief in advanced building technology. It certainly promises to be among the most elegant of all the towers in the City, and it will be technically the most sophisticated. The concrete core is surrounded by light, curtain-walled offices and will support the tallest office-block in the United Kingdom.

Robin Seifert has succeeded in building up one of the largest and most successful practices in the United Kingdom. His firm has carried out a great number of large schemes that are startling, dynamic, and spectacular, but the true sophisticated of Seifert's work lies in his exploitation of technology to achieve his effects, of which perhaps the National Westminster Tower is the greatest expression.

—James Stevens Curl

SELIGMANN, Werner.
American. Born in Osnäbruck, Germany, 30 March 1930; emigrated to the United States, 1949: naturalized, 1955. Educated at Cornell University, Ithaca, New York, under Romaldo Giurgola, Thomas Canfield, Abraham Geller, and Buckminster Fuller, 1950–54, B.Arch. 1954; Technische Hochschule, Braunschweig, Germany, under F. W. Kraemer, 1958–59. Married Jean Lois Liberman in 1954; children: Raphael and Sabina. Principal, Werner Seligmann and Associates, Cortland, New York, since 1961. Instructor, University of Texas at Austin, 1956–58; Research Assistant, Technische Hochschule, Braunschweig, 1958–59; Instructor, E.T.H.: Eidgenössische Technische Hochschule, Zurich, 1959–61; Assistant Professor, 1961–65, and Associate Professor, 1965–74, Cornell University; Professor, Harvard University, Cambridge, Massachusetts, 1974–76. Since 1976, Dean of the School of Architecture, Syracuse University, New York. Exhibitions: *American Synagogue Architecture,* Jewish Museum of New York, 1963; *40 under 40,* Architectural League of New York, 1965; *American Architecture,* Musée d'Art Moderne, Paris, 1966; *Another Chance for Cities,* Whitney Museum, New York 1971; *Works of Werner Seligmann and Associates,* Andrew Dickson White Museum, Cornell University, 1971; *Another Chance for Housing,* Museum of Modern Art, New York, 1973; *White and Gray,* University of California at Los Angeles, and Museum of Modern Art, Pasadena, California, 1974; *Istituto Nazionale di Architettura,* Rome, 1974; *Two Hundred Years of American Synagogue Architecture,* Rose Art Museum, Brandeis University, Waltham, Massachusetts, 1976. Address: Werner Seligmann and Associates, 9 Homer Avenue, Cortland, New York 13045, U.S.A.

Works:

1963 Beth David Synagogue, Binghamton, New York

1966 Plan for Urban Renewal Area, I, Binghamton, New York

1967 Science Building II, State University of New York at Cortland

1967/
   69 Heritage Park, Elmira, New York (project)

1968/
   to Community renewal plan for Utica, New York
       Plan for the Model Cities Area, Binghamton, New York
       Plan for the Woodburn Court Area, Binghamton, New York

1971 Administration Building, Willard State Hospital, Willard, New York

1972 Rehabilitation Center, Willard State Hospital, Willard, New York (with F. P. Wiedersum)
       Dormitory, Huntington Camp, Raquette Lake, New York

1973 New York State Urban Development Corporation Low- and Middle-Income Housing, Elm Street, Ithaca, New York
       New York State Urban Development Corporation Low- and Middle-Income Housing, Maple Avenue, Ithaca, New York
       Rehabilitation study of the Court Street Area, Binghamton, New York

1974 New York State Urban Development Corporation Low- and Middle-Income Housing, Menands, New York

1975 New York State Urban Development Corporation Housing for the Elderly, Olean, New York
       Impact study for the Capri Theatre, Binghamton, New York

1979 Central Fire Station, Olean, New York

Publications:

By SELIGMANN: articles—"Assessing Broadway East" in *Progressive Architecture* (New York), October 1974; "Runcorn: Historical Precedent and the Rational Design Process" in *Oppositions 7* (New York), Winter 1976–77.

On SELIGMANN: book—*Low-rise Housing* by John Macsai, New York 1976; articles—"Rehabilitation Center, Willard State Hospital" in *Architectural Forum* (New York), December 1970; feature article in *Progressive Architecture* (New York), May 1973; "U.D.C. Housing, Ithaca, New York" by Charles Moore in *Oppositions 3* (New York), May 1974; "Willard Administration Building" by Michael Dennis in *Progressive Architecture* (New York), May 1976; special issue of *Architecture + Urbanism* (Tokyo), December 1976.

In an age of widespread architectural fads, rapidly changing stylistic trends and an often arcane language of explanation, Werner Seligmann's work remains rooted in the mode of classical modernism. Born in Germany, but educated in the United States (at Cornell University,) Seligmann has developed an architectural vocabulary whose sources can be

Werner Seligmann: Administration Building, Willard State Hospital, Willard, New York, 1971

traced to Frank Lloyd Wright and, principally, Le Corbusier.

Seligmann's early work, particularly his Beth David Synagogue in Binghamton, New York, is ambitious, even in its obvious enthusiasm and debt to Frank Lloyd Wright. In its overall appearance and general massing (and in the revealing symmetrical cross-section), Beth David Synagogue shares significant resemblances to Wright's Unity Temple. The plan is an amalgam, however, exhibiting a Wrightian symmetry but inflected with modern mannerist tendencies, as in the skewed geometry of the stairs that run from the lower level to the sanctuary. The special, sculptural spaces (the small chapel, for instance,) recall a more distinctly Corbusian aesthetic. Constructed of concrete block, the building is both oddly rugged and elegant, a sensitive composition in the delineation and contrast between exposed block bearing walls and non-bearing plastered screen walls.

Seligmann's subsequent work shows the influence of Wright supplanted by the ghostly presence of Le Corbusier. The Willard State Hospital Administration Building, Willard, New York, is, in boldest terms, a Corbusian white box set in the landscape. A study in clarity, the double loaded corridor plan is rigorously simple, as is the overall organization of the building. Architectural interest and complexity comes through a series of contrasting polar opposites: the thin-ness of the structure and cladding system (a simple steel frame and metal enclosure) versus the spatial depth of the plan. A centralized service wall runs the length of the corridor; functional interruptions along the wall punctuate the space, providing pocket entries for offices and special rooms. The lobby exhibits its own particular dispositions of a free plan, where oversized stairs and landing float within a space which is, in turn, enclosed by a free glass facade.

Built during a time of considerably revived interest in the architecture of Le Corbusier, Seligmann's Willard Administration Building is an interpretive excursus into an historical approach to building, not unlike those historistic, distinctly Corbusian referential buildings by Richard Meier (and in some cases, Michael Graves) which date from the same period.

Seligmann's best known project to date is his

Urban Development Corporation housing, which comprises 235 units of publically assisted low-cost housing in the college town of Ithaca, New York. Here it is the spirit rather than the actual example of Le Corbusier that pervades the complex, while the real inspiration for the design comes from the brilliant Halen Housing Estate by Switzerland's Atelier 5 in 1961.

Like the Halen scheme, Seligmann's UDC housing is situated on a sloped site and comprises a variety of individual unit types. Instead of including the landscaped roof terraces that distinguish Halen, which Seligmann could not use due to UDC budget restrictions, most units enclose an atrium. Within a rigorous, tightly-controlled framework Seligmann manages to develop both the intensely repetitive basis of the scheme and a sense of each unit's individuality, aided by a series of internal pedestrian streets. An earlier site plan, more lavishly landscaped with a green fissure running through it, is more attractive, though, like other amenities, unhappily cut for lack of funds.

Currently dean of the Architecture School at Syracuse University, Werner Seligmann formerly taught architecture at Harvard, Texas, Cornell and the ETH in Zurich. Committed to the principles and, seemingly, the aesthetic of the modern movement, Seligmann has managed to stamp his architecture with a spirit of rational clarity, tempered with sensitivity and elegance.

—Richard Lavenstein

SERT, Josep Lluis.

American. Born in Barcelona, Spain, 1 July 1902; emigrated to the United States, 1939: naturalized, 1951. Educated at the Escuela Superior de Arquitectura, Barcelona, M.Arch. 1929. Married Ramona Longás in 1938; daughter: Maria. Assistant to Le Corbusier and Pierre Jeanneret, Paris, 1929–31; in private practice, Barcelona, 1929–37 (organized GATCPAC group of architects affiliated with CIAM: International Congress of Modern Architec-

ture); lived in Paris, 1937–39; Co-Founder and Partner, with Paul Lester Wiener and Paul Schulz, Town Planning Associates, New York, 1939–57; in private practice, Cambridge, Massachusetts, 1957–58. Partner, with Huson Jackson and Ronald Gourley, Sert, Jackson and Gourley, Cambridge, 1958–63, and Sert, Jackson and Associates, Cambridge, since 1963. Professor of City Planning, Yale University, New Haven, Connecticut, 1944–45; Professor of Architecture and Dean of the Graduate School of Design, Harvard University, Cambridge, 1953–69, also Consultant to the Harvard Planning Office, 1956–69 (now Emeritus Professor); Thomas Jefferson Memorial Foundation Professor of Architecture, University of Virginia, Charlottesville, 1970–71. Member, Board of Directors and Planning Committee, Citizens Housing Council of New York, 1945; President, CIAM, 1947–56; Chairman, Planning Board of Cambridge, Massachusetts, 1957; Chairman, American Institute of Architects Committee on the National Capital, 1964; Member of the Advisory Council, Princeton University School of Architecture and Urban Planning, 1972–74. Exhibition: *J.L. Sert,* Spanish Museum of Contemporary Art, Madrid, 1978. Recipient: Thomas Jefferson Medal, University of Virginia, 1970; FAD (Fomento de las Artes Decorativas) Award, Barcelona, 1974; Gold Medal, Académie d'Architecture, Paris, 1975; Architectural Firm Award, American Institute of Architects, 1977. Honorary M.A.: Harvard University, 1953; Lit.D.: Boston University, 1963; Art.D.: Boston University, 1968. Fellow, American Institute of Architects; Member, National Institute of Arts and Letters, and American Academy of Arts and Sciences. Honorary Member: Royal Architectural Institute, Canada; Royal Society of Arts, London; Royal Institute of British Architects; Academie Royale, Belgium; Akademie der Künste, Berlin; Society of Architects, Mexico; Institute of Urbanism, Peru; Académie d'Architecture, France; Sociedad de Arquitectos, Colombia. Address (office): 44 Brattle Street, Cambridge, Massachusetts 02138, U.S.A.

Works:

1929 New resort community for the Costa Brava, Spain (exhibition project)

1931 Apartment house, Calle Muntaner 342–348, Barcelona

1933/
35 Master plan for the City of Barcelona (with GATCPAC, Le Corbusier and Pierre Jeanneret)

1934 Leisure City, Castelldefels, near Barcelona (project; with GATCPAC)

1934/
36 Casa Bloc (low-rent apartments), Paseo Torras y Bages 105, Barcelona (with GATCPAC)

1935 Week-end houses, Garraf, Spain
Central Anti-Tubercular Dispensary, Calle Torres Amat, Barcelona (with J. Torres and J. Subirana)

1937 Spanish Pavilion, *World's Fair,* Paris (with Luis Lacasa)

1945 Motor City, Brazil (project)

1948 New City of Chimbote, Peru (project)

1949 Sert House, Locust Valley, Long Island, New York

1949/
51 Master plan for Medellin, Colombia

1950/
52 Master plan for Tumaco, Colombia
Master plan for Cali, Colombia

1951 Church, Puerto Ordaz, Venezuela (project)

1951/
53 Master plan for Bogota, Colombia (with Le Corbusier)

1954/
55 Pilot plan for the resort of Varadero, Cuba

1955/
56 Studio for Joan Miró, Palma, Majorca

1955/
57 Presidential Palace, Havana (project)

Josep Lluis Sert: Miró Center for the Study of Contemporary Art, Barcelona, 1975

1955/
58 Master plan for Havana
1955/
60 United States Embassy, Baghdad
1958 Sert House, Cambridge, Massachusetts
1958/
59 Center for the Study of World Religions, Harvard University, Cambridge, Massachusetts
1958/
60 New England Gas and Electric Association Headquarters, Boston
1958/
65 Holyoke Center, Harvard University, Cambridge, Massachusetts
1959/
64 Museum of Contemporary Art, for the

Maeght Foundation, Saint-Paul-de-Vence, France (with Bellini, Lizero and Gozzi)

1960 House for Georges Braque, Saint-Paul-de-Vence, France (project)
East Hills Housing (Action Housing), Pittsburgh (demonstration Planned Unit Development project; with Walter Gropius, Carl Koch, John Ormsbee Simonds, and B. Kenneth Johnstone)
1960/
67 Charles River Campus of Boston University (with Hoyle, Doran and Berry and Edward T. Steffian and Associates)
1961 House, Ibiza, Spain
1963 Carpenter Center for the Visual Arts, Har-

vard University, Cambridge, Massachusetts (with Le Corbusier; as supervisory architect)
1963/
65 Peabody Terrace Married Students Housing, Harvard University, Cambridge, Massachusetts
1964/
66 Dormitory, Library, Dining and Activity Center, Guelph University, Ontario (with Project Planning Associates)
1965/
70 6 houses, Punta Martinet, Ibiza, Spain
1966/
72 Martin Luther King Elementary School, Cambridge, Massachusetts

1967/
68 Urban renewal plan for the central business district of Worcester, Massachusetts
1969 Carmelite Convent, Carmel de la Paix, Mazille (Cluny), France
Master plan for a resort community on the Frioul Islands, Marseilles, France
1970/
73 Undergraduate Science Center, Harvard University, Cambridge, Massachusetts
1971/
75 Eastwood Housing, Roosevelt Island, New York
Riverview Housing, Yonkers, New York
1972/
75 Fundación Joan Miró Center for the Study of Contemporary Art, Montjuich Park, Barcelona (with Anglada, Gelabert and Ribas)
1974 Les Escales Park Housing, Barcelona (with Anglada, Gelabert and Ribas)
1977 Caixa d'Estalvis de Catalunya (offices and cultural center), Barcelona
1978- Autopistas (road service buildings, hotel, shops and restaurants), La Junquera, Spain

Publications:

By SERT: books—*Can Our Cities Survive?*, Cambridge, Massachusetts and London 1942; *The Heart of the City*, edited with E. N. Rogers and J. Tyrwhitt, New York and London 1952; *Antoni Gaudí*, with James Johnson Sweeney, Stuttgart, London and New York 1960; *The Shape of Our Cities*, with J. Tyrwhitt, Tokyo 1961; *Ibiza: Fuerte y Luminosa*, Barcelona 1967; *Cripta de la Colonia Güell de Antoni Gaudí*, Barcelona 1969; articles—"The Human Scale in City Planning" in *New Architecture and City Planning*, edited by Paul Zucker, New York 1944; "Urbanism en Amerique du Sud," with Paul Lester Wiener, in *L'Architecture d'Aujourd'hui* (Paris), December 1950/January 1951; "The Changing Philosophy of Architecture" in *Architectural Record* (New York), August 1954; "Architecture and the Visual Arts" in *Harvard Foundation for Advanced Study and Research Newsletter* (Cambridge, Massachusetts), 31 December 1954; "The Architect and the City" in *The City in Mid-Century*, edited by H. Warren Dunham, Detroit 1957; "What Became of CIAM?," with Walter Gropius, Le Corbusier, and Sigfried Giedion, in *Architectural Review* (London), March 1961; "Remembering Le Corbusier" in *AIA Journal* (Washington, D.C.), November 1965.

On SERT: books—*José Luis Sert* by Knud Bastlund, Zurich and London 1967; *Sert: Mediterranean Architecture*, edited by Maria Lluisa Borrás, Barcelona and Paris 1974, Boston 1975; *Sert's Architecture in the Miró Foundation* by Bruno Zevi, Barcelona 1976; *J. L. Sert* by Jaume Freixa, Barcelona 1978; *J. L. Sert*, exhibition catalog, Madrid 1978; articles—"Sert's Concept of Living" by S. Anderson in *Architectural Design* (London), August 1965; "Sert: Works and Projects 1929–1973," special edition of *Cuardenos de Arquitectura* (Barcelona), November/December 1972; "Ten Years Past at Peabody Terrace" by Jonathan Hale in *Progressive Architecture* (New York), October 1974; "A Portfolio of Design for Display" by Gerald Allen in *Architectural Record* (New York), October 1974; "The Last Works of J. L. Sert in Barcelona" by David Ferrer in *Arquitectura* (Madrid), March 1975; "A Certain Feeling: Interview with J. L. Sert" by Peter Murray in *Building Design* (London), 23 May 1975; "Miró and Sert in Barcelona" by Pierre Joly in *L'Oeil* (Paris), September 1975; "Towards a Housing Manifesto" by Marie Dulac in *Architecte* (Paris), June 1976; "A Study Center for Contemporary Art" by Roland Penrose and "Sert for Miro" by David Mackay in *Architectural Review* (London), July 1976; "Homage to Catalonia—Fundación Joan Miró" by Mildred F. Schmertz in *Architectural Record* (New York), March 1977; "The Urbane and Varied Buildings of Sert, Jackson and Associates" by Andrea O. Dean in *AIA Journal* (Washington, D.C.), May 1977.

*

Josep Lluis Sert, as a disciple of Le Corbusier, and former President of CIAM, played an important role in the development of the early planning theories of the Modern Movement and through his design projects and writings contributed significantly to their acceptance. For example, he helped prepare the Modern Movement's seminal planning manifesto, the Athens Charter of 1933, which formalized and codified the new concepts.

With the exception of Le Corbusier, Sert has had more influence upon the built world of housing and planning than any other CIAM member and as much as any architect of his generation. In his long career he has collaborated in the preparation of approximately twelve master plans at the scale of the city or town, at least three within the scope of a neighborhood or district, six for large scale housing developments and two for entire campuses.

Sert's high-rise, high-density housing projects disprove the currently fashionable criticism that such housing is inhumane, the cause of feelings of isolation and helplessness and contributory to delinquency, vandalism and the collapse of the family. Sert's housing—most notably the Peabody Terrace Married Student's Housing at Harvard University, Eastwood on Roosevelt Island in New York City and Riverview in Yonkers—is very humane indeed. Sert is a leading spokesman for, and designer of, balanced, compact housing designed with an equal emphasis upon community and privacy within a range of densities. In his housing Sert manages to achieve a workable balance between the number of dwelling units and the supporting services provided, such as schools, day-care centers, recreational facilities, shopping and other amenities. He strives to obtain a proper balance between people and automobiles, buildings and open space, people and trees, as well as passive and active recreation.

His housing offers a variety of dwelling sizes and plan layouts to provide a range of choices to families and individuals of different needs and life styles. In his schemes most units have cross ventilation, good views in two directions, natural light and sunlight. In massing and fenestration Sert follows the Modulor dimensioning of Le Corbusier, paying great attention to scale, color and texture.

Sert's campus work at Harvard and for the Charles River Campus of Boston University also exhibits his interest in high density urban design. He has written, "An urban campus is a cultural center within a city, and should set an example of good planning and good design for the city. It is, in a way, a micro-city, and its urbanity is the expression of a better, more civilized way of life."

Sert has also done distinguished work at the scale of the single building. He has, for example, shown great skill in the design of museums. The Foundation Maeght in St. Paul de Vence and his most recent museum in Barcelona are both composed of carefully proportioned spaces, shaped in a variety of ways, with many different ceiling heights, sources of light and degrees of openness. For museums and other buildings which need to make maximum use of natural light, Sert has developed prominent semi-circular light scoops, which he has used so often they have become a trademark.

The Barcelona museum houses the paintings and sculpture of Sert's friend, Joan Miró. The work of the latter—spontaneous, joyful, rooted in the subconscious—is at the opposite end of the spectrum from Sert's eminently rational, scientific, conscious design.

—Mildred F. Schmertz

SHARON, Arieh.

Israeli. Born in Yaroslaw, Poland, 28 May 1902; emigrated to Palestine in 1920, and worked and lived on the Kubbutz Gan Shmuel, 1920–26; acquired Israeli nationality, 1948. Educated at the Staatliche Bauhaus, Dessau, Germany, under Walter Gropius, Hannes Meyer, Josef Albers, Paul Klee, and Wassily Kandinsky, 1926–29, graduated 1929. Married Gunta Stoelzl in 1928; Haya Sankowsky in 1932; children: Yael, Eldar, and Uri. In charge of the architectural office of Hannes Meyer in Berlin, and supervised building of the Educational Centre of the Trade Unions in Bernau, Berlin, 1929–31; in private architectural practice, Tel Aviv, 1932–39; townplanner and civic designer, Tel Aviv, 1940–48; Director and Chief Architect of the National Planning Agency of Israel, 1948–53; Partner, in an architectural practice, with Benjamin Idelson, Tel Aviv, 1954–64, and with his son Eldar Sharon, Tel Aviv, since 1964. Member of the Executive Committee, International Union of Architects, Paris, 1963–67; Chairman, National Council for National Parks and Nature Reserves, Israel, 1964; Chairman, Standards Institution of Israel, 1965–69; President, Association of Engineers and Architects in Israel, 1965–71. Exhibitions: *Kibbutz und Bauhaus*, Bauhaus Archive, Berlin, and tour of Germany, Switzerland, Mexico and U.S.A., 1977–79. Recipient: Israel Prize for Architecture, 1962; Gold Medal, Mexican Institute of Architecture, 1964; Rokach Award, Tel Aviv, 1963, 1971. Honorary Member, Royal Institute of British Architects, 1962, Akademie der Künste, Berlin, 1965, and the Bund Deutscher Architekten, 1967; Honorary Fellow of the American Institute of Architects, 1970. Address: Arieh Sharon/Eldar Sharon, Architects and Townplanners Ltd., Hayarkon Street 70, Tel Aviv, Israel.

Works:

1924/
26 Buildings for the Kibbutz Gan Shmuel, Palestine
1929 Vocational school in Zlin, Czechoslovakia (competition project; with Anton Urban)
1932 Histadrut Pavilions, *Levant Fair*, Tel Aviv
1933/
34 Cooperative housing, Tel Aviv
1934/
35 Brenner House, Histadrut Centre, Tel Aviv
1935/
37 Beilinson Hospital, Petah Tikva, Palestine
1936 Institute for Physical Culture, Haifa
Agricultural Cooperative Centre, Tel Aviv
1937/
38 Hamashbir Cooperative Centre, Jaffa
1937/
39 Apartment houses, Tel Aviv
Apartment houses, Ramat Gan, Palestine
Apartment houses, Haifa
1938 Kibbutz layout, Ein Hashofet, Palestine
1938/
40 Cooperative housing, Tel Aviv
1939 Kibbutz Dining Hall, Gan Shmuel, Palestine
Kibbutz Dining Hall, Sarid, Palestine
Kibbutz layout, Dalia, Palestine
1940 Kibbutz layout, Kfar Glikson, Palestine
1940/
42 Ohel Theatre Building, Tel Aviv
1941 Kibbutz layout, Mishmar Hayam, Palestine
1942 Kibbutz layout, Alumot, Palestine
1944 Vocational school, Tel Mond, Palestine
1945 Kibbutz Kindergarten, Gan Shmuel, Palestine
Kibbutz school community, Beit Alpha, Palestine
1945/
48 Chen Movie Theatre and Offices, Tel Aviv
1946 Kibbutz school community, Ma'abarot, Palestine
Histadrut Trade Union School, Tel Aviv
1947 Wingate Institute for Physical Education, Nethanya, Palestine
1948 Lessin House of Culture, Tel Aviv

Arieh Sharon: Convalescent home, Tiberias, Israel, 1971

1948/
52 Solel Boneh Headquarters, Tel Aviv (with Dov Karmi)
1949 School building, Kiryat Yam, Israel
1949/
53 Urban and new town plans for Israel (with National Planning Agency)
1950/
70 Beilinson General Hospital, Peta Tikvah, Israel (with Ora Fradis and Benjamin Idelson)
1954 Forum, Technion, Haifa (with Benjamin Idelson)
1954/
60 Municipal Hospital, Ichilov, Tel Aviv (with Ora Fradis, M. Rafaeli, and Benjamin Idelson)
1955/
57 Neighbourhood housing, Nazareth (with Benjamin Idelson)
1955/
62 Regional Hospital, Beersheba, Israel (with Benjamin Idelson)
1956/
58 Churchill Auditorium, Technion, Haifa (with Y. Bregman, A. Kinsbrunner, and Benjamin Idelson)
1958 Israel Pavilion, *World's Fair*, Brussels (with Arieh Elhanani and Benjamin Idelson)
1958/
60 Library and Senate Building, Technion, Haifa (with Moshe Kletter and Benjamin Idelson)
1959/
60 Workers Bank Headquarters, Tel Aviv (with

Neomi Paz and Benjamin Idelson)
1959/
61 Yakhin Pectin Factory, Petah Tikva, Israel (with Ziona Leshem and Benjamin Idelson)
1959/
64 Yad Vashem Memorial, Jerusalem (with Arieh Elhanani and Benjamin Idelson)
1960 Dormitories, Hebrew University, Jerusalem (with Benjamin Idelson)
1960/
65 Housing, Kiryat Yam, Israel (with Y. Rosenberg and Benjamin Idelson)
1961 Faculty of Chemistry, Hebrew University, Jerusalem (with Benjamin Idelson)
Ezrat Nashim Mental Hospital, Jerusalem (with Benjamin Idelson)
1961/
63 Gratz Elementary School, Tel Aviv (with Benjamin Idelson)
1961/
65 Jewish Agency Headquarters, Tel Aviv (with Benjamin Idelson)
1962 Beit Yakhin Office Building, Tel Aviv (with Shmuel Schwartz and Benjamin Idelson)
1963 Master plan for Ife University, Nigeria (with Benjamin Idelson)
1963/
65 Labour Sick Fund Headquarters, Tel Aviv (with Ziona Leshem and Benjamin Idelson)
Regional Clinic, Rehovot, Israel (with Micha Amitai and Benjamin Idelson)
Humanities Building, Ife University, Nigeria

(with AMY Limited and Benjamin Idelson)
1964 Halls of Residence, Ife University, Nigeria (with AMY Limited and Benjamin Idelson)
Hasneh Building, Beersheba, Israel (with Benjamin Idelson)
Radio and Television Building, Jerusalem (with Elling Bureau, Eldar Sharon, and Moshe Kletter)
1964/
66 Electric power station, Ashdod, Israel (with Moshe Kletter and Benjamin Idelson)
1964/
68 Regional Hospital, Eilat, Israel (with A. Yaski, A. Alexandroni, and Benjamin Idelson)
1964/
70 Hamaschbir Office Building, Tel Aviv (with Shmuel Schwartz and Benjamin Idelson)
1965/
68 Agricultural Cooperative Headquarters, Tel Aviv (with A. Kaplan, E. Mashiah, and Eldar Sharon)
1965/
71 Convalescent home, Tiberias, Israel (with Harold Rubin and Eldar Sharon)
1965/
72 Rambam Government Hospital, Haifa, (with E. Kanner, Ora Fradis, and Eldar Sharon)
1965/
76 Tel Giborim General Hospital, Tel Aviv (with Moshe Kletter, Zalman Shohat, and Eldar Sharon)

1966 Medical Centre, Tel Aviv (with Moshe Kletter, Ora Fradis, Yuval Geni, and Eldar Sharon)

Regional Hospital, Ashdod, Israel (project; with Y. Rosenberg, Ziona Leshem, and Eldar Sharon)

1966/
68 Kibbutz Memorial Museum, Yad Mordechai, Israel (with Yoram Diamant, M. Dubravsky, and Eldar Sharon)

1966/
70 Geha Mental Hospital, Petah Tikva, Israel (with Yoram Diamant and Eldar Sharon)

1966/
74 Tel Giborim Nurses School, Tel Aviv (with Moshe Kletter, Zalman Shohat, and Eldar Sharon)

1967 Pavilion Hospital for Developing Countries (project; with others)

Israel Pavilion, Expo '67, Montreal (with David Resnik and Eldar Sharon)

Beeri Apartment Houses, Tel Aviv (with Dov Karmi, E. Mashiah, and Eldar Sharon)

1967/
68 Housing, Beersheba, Israel (with Shmuel Schwartz and Eldar Sharon)

1967/
69 Housing estate, Nazareth (with Avi Kaplan and Eldar Sharon)

1967/
70 Library, Ife University, Nigeria (with AMY Limited, Harold Rubin, and Eldar Sharon)

1967/
72 University Medical School, Tel Aviv (with Eldar Sharon)

1968 Health Sciences Centre, Bangkok (with Benjamin Idelson, G. Zippor, AMY Limited, and Eldar Sharon)

Vice-Chancellor's Residence, Ife University, Nigeria (with AMY Limited, Harold Rubin, and Eldar Sharon)

1968/
69 Town Hall, Kiryat Yam, Israel (with E. Kanner and Eldar Sharon)

1968/
70 Master plan for the Old City and environs, Jerusalem (with David A. Brutzkus and Eldar Sharon)

1968/
72 Institute of Education, and Secretariat, Ife University, Nigeria (with AMY Limited, Harold Rubin, and Eldar Sharon)

1969 Tiergarten Museum, Berlin (competition project; with Eldar Sharon)

Civic Centre, Sdeh Boker, Israel (with Eldar Sharon)

1969/
74 Bank of Israel Headquarters, Jerusalem (with Y. Rosenberg and Eldar Sharon)

1970 Military hospital, San Salvador (with AMY Limited and Eldar Sharon)

Adam Hacohen Apartment Houses, Tel Aviv (with Shmuel Schwartz and Eldar Sharon)

1970/
73 Israel America House, Tel Aviv (with M. Tintner, George Perel, and Eldar Sharon)

1971 City Hall, Amsterdam (competition project; with Eldar Sharon)

1972 Oncology Pavilion, Rambam Hospital, Haifa (with D. Rubinstein and Eldar Sharon)

Neighbourhood housing, Eilat, Israel (with Eldar Sharon)

UNIDO and IAEA Conference Centre, Vienna (competition project; with Eldar Sharon)

Pre-fabricated bungalows, Ghana (with Eldar Sharon)

1972/
73 Fast Hotel, Jerusalem (with George Perel and Eldar Sharon)

1972/
75 Radar Memorial, near Jerusalem (with George Perel and Eldar Sharon)

1972/
76 Hotel, Sharem-el-Sheikh, Israel (with Yoram Diamant and Eldar Sharon)

Municipal Centre, Rehovot, Israel (with George Perel and Eldar Sharon)

Assembly Hall, Ife University, Nigeria (with AMY Limited, Harold Rubin, and Eldar Sharon)

Soroka Health Centre, Beersheba, Israel (with Micha Amitai, Ora Fradis, and Eldar Sharon)

1972/
82 Medical Centre, Tel Aviv (with Moshe Kletter, Yuval Geni, and Eldar Sharon)

1973 Container housing for OHW, New York (project; with Harold Rubin and Eldar Sharon)

Misawa Home Housing Scheme, Japan (project; with Harold Rubin and Eldar Sharon)

1973/
75 Field School, Kfar Etzion, Israel (with Charles Dorell and Eldar Sharon)

1973/
76 Gilo Neighbourhood, Jerusalem (with Y. Rosenberg and Eldar Sharon)

Maccabi Sports Centre, Tel Aviv (with George Perel and Eldar Sharon)

1974 Negev Museum, Sdeh Boker, Israel (with Eldar Sharon)

1974/
78 Asaf Harofe Hospital, Zerifin, Israel (with Eldar Sharon)

1977 Apical Hospital and College for Health Sciences, Ife, Nigeria (with Eldar Sharon, Egboramy Company, and Yeheskel Rosenberg)

1978 Isaka Island Vacation Village, Nigeria (project; with Eldar Sharon, Egboramy Company and Yuval Geni)

Publications:

By SHARON: books—*Physical Planning in Israel,* Tel Aviv 1955; *Hospitals in Developing Countries,* Tel Aviv 1967; *Hospitals in Israel and Developing Countries,* Tel Aviv 1968; *Planning Jerusalem: The Old City and Its Environs,* Jerusalem 1973; *Kibbutz + Bauhaus,* Stuttgart and Massada 1976; articles— "Planning and Israel" in *Israel and Middle East* (Tel Aviv), March 1952, and in *Town Planning Review* (Liverpool), April 1952; "Collective Settlements in Israel" in *Town Planning Review* (Liverpool) January 1955; "Hospitals in Israel" in *World Hospitals* (London), vol. 1, 1964; "Medical Centres and Hospitals in Developing Countries" in *Dialogue in Development* (Proceedings of the 2nd World Congress of Engineers and Architects in Israel), Tel Aviv 1970; "Planning Jerusalem" in *Ekistics* (Athens), November 1974.

On SHARON: books—*Ospedali* by Roberto Aloi and Carlo Bassi, Milan 1973; *Wohnen im Eigenen Haus* by Gerhard Schwab, Stuttgart 1976; article— "Cast in History, Not in Concrete" by Wolf Von Eckardt in the *Washington Post* (Washington, D.C.), 26 August 1972.

*   *   *

The long and productive career of Arieh Sharon, extending over half a century, embraces many phases: the farmer and practical builder on the kibbutz; the pioneer modern architect; the public servant, directing the urban and regional planning programmes of the new state of Israel; and the successful architect in private practice, not only helping to shape Israel's architecture, but also significantly contributing to the development of the Third World. Threaded through this long saga of achievement there are three continuous strands, three components of his attitude to architecture and to life. It is only when these strands are woven together that the pattern is complete; and it is when the components are brought into congruence that Sharon's architecture is at its most powerful.

The first component is idealism, the capacity to be moved by an idea, the capacity for devotion and service to a cause, be it the Zionist-socialism of his youth or the ideal of the new architecture that he imbibed at the Bauhaus—both, in their ways, dreams of building a shining new world. It was this idealism that led Sharon to devote many creative years to the design of kibbutzim; which almost tempted him to follow Hannes Meyer to a career in the Soviet Union; and which, after the founding of the State of Israel in 1948, induced him to accept the new government's invitation to create and direct a National Planning Agency, through which he advocated that policy of decentralization which underlay Israel's new towns programme, which initiated the proper planning of the major urban concentrations, and which sought—through propaganda and exhibition—to make the general public planning-conscious.

After idealism—or perhaps linked to it—is Sharon's eternal avant-gardism, his pioneering spirit, his eagerness to be in the vanguard of new development, in the forefront of new movements—not only in responding to new challenges, but also in creating new symbols. The spirit of the "chalutz," or pioneer, brought Sharon to Eretz Israel in 1920; during the 1930's he played a central role in the making of a modern architecture in Israel, a natural revolutionary stance for an architect who had sought out the Bauhaus for his education; and even today, in the past decade, as advanced architectural posture moves into its post-modern phase, he has joined forces with his son Eldar and other young Israeli architects of that generation that he delights to call "the sabra avant-garde," seeking once again to put a new face on Israel's architecture and perhaps to attempt to give it new meaning.

It must be said that the drive to be in the avant-garde is both a strength and a weakness: at best the pioneering spirit is a creative force, discarding the shackles of the past, generating new and valid solutions to present and future problems; but there is always an inherent danger, when new architectural forms are sought, that it is not for their relevancy, but for mere novelty's sake. The control mechanism that prevents this trivialization of the creative spirit is found in the third component of Arieh Sharon's architectural attitude: his essential pragmatism, his concern with reality as well as dream, practice as well as theory, action as well as idea. It is Sharon the pragmatist who first learned architecture through direct building experience, in his kibbutz days; who was more strongly attracted by the Bauhaus's credo of learning by doing than by its polemical debates on abstract issues; and who found his architectural inspiration in the guidance of Hannes Meyer, the apostle of the functionalist approach and the *neue sachlichkeit.* Pragmatism is the very essence of Sharon's early architectural work: the honest and direct use of materials, the austere simplicity of architectural form, the functional efficiency of his planning, the growing awareness of climatic constraints. It is in evidence not only in his more modest projects, such as his many apartment blocks or in his kibbutz and housing area developments (where economic factors are a powerful lever for pragmatism), but also in the larger, more complex, and functionally more demanding institutional buildings—especially the university complexes and hospitals—that he has designed. This pragmatism is particularly evident in the fecund period when he worked in association with Benjamin Idelson, when, in my view, his creative talent was at its peak—mature, disciplined, yet powerfully inventive.

The motivating power of Sharon's work is his idealism, expressed both in architectural and social terms; the freshness and excitement lies in his natural thrust towards the vanguard, the new and the untried. It is when these traits are coupled with the iron discipline of the pragmatist, who harnesses his dream to the real world, and derives his vision from the constraints of reality, that good architecture can be made. It is to Arieh Sharon's credit, and greatly to architecture's benefit, that he has so often succeeded in achieving this elusive synthesis of the real and the ideal.

—Gilbert Herbert

SHEPPARD, ROBSON AND PARTNERS. *See* RICHARD SHEPPARD, ROBSON AND PARTNERS.

SHINOHARA, Kazuo.
Japanese. Born in Shizuoka, 2 April 1925. Educated at the Institute of Technology, Tokyo, B.Eng. 1953, D.Eng. 1967. Served in the Japanese Army, in Japan and Korea, 1945. Married Kumiko Sasaki in 1951; children: Miwako, Rieko and Hikaru. Instructor, 1953–61, Associate Professor, 1962–69, and since 1970 Professor of Architecture, Tokyo Institute of Technology. Began architectural practice privately, 1954; studio established at Tokyo Institute of Technology, 1962. Exhibition: *Two Houses in a Department Store,* Odakyu Department Store, Shinjuku, Tokyo, 1964. Recipient: Architectural Institute of Japan Prize, 1972. Address: Tokyo Institute of Technology, O-Okayama 2–12–1, Meguro-ku, Tokyo, Japan.

Works:

1954	House in Kugayama, Tokyo
1958	House in Kugayama II, Tokyo
	Tanikawa Residence, Tokyo
1960	House in Komae, Tokyo
1961	House in Chigasaki, Japan
1962	Umbrella House, Tokyo
1963	House with a Big Roof, Tokyo
	House with an Earthen Floor, Karuizawa, Japan
1965	North House in Hanayama, Kobe, Japan
1966	Asakura Residence, Tokyo
	House in White, Tokyo
	House of Earth, Tokyo
1968	South House in Hanayama, Kobe, Japan
	Yamashiro Residence, Yokohama
	Suzusho Residence, Hayama, Japan
1970	Shino Residence, Tokyo
	The Uncompleted House, Tokyo
1971	Cubic Forest (private house), Kawasaki, Japan
	Repeating Crevice (private house), Tokyo
	Sea Stairway (private house), Tokyo
	Sky Rectangle (private house), Tokyo
	Prism House, Yamanaka-ko, Japan
1972	House in Kugahara, Tokyo
1973	House in Higashi-Tamagawa, Tokyo
	House in Seijo, Tokyo
1974	Tanikawa Residence, Karuizawa, Japan
1975	Cylindrical Quadrants (private house and art gallery), Karuizawa, Japan
1976	House in Uehara, Tokyo
1978	House in Ashitaka, Numazu, Japan
	Third House in Hanayama, Kobe, Japan
	House in Uehara II, Tokyo

Publications:

By SHINOHARA: books—*Residential Architecture,* Tokyo 1964; *Theories on Residences,* Tokyo 1970; *Kazuo Shinohara: 16 Houses and Architectural Theory,* Tokyo 1971; *Theories on Residences II,* Tokyo 1975; *Kazuo Shinohara II: 11 Houses and Architectural Theory,* Tokyo 1976; articles—

Kazuo Shinohara: Tanikawa Residence, Karuizawa, Japan, 1974

"Houses Are Art" in *Shinkenchiku* (Tokyo), May 1962; "The Three Primary Spaces" in *The Japan Architect* (Tokyo), August 1964; "A Theory of Residential Architecture" in *The Japan Architect* (Tokyo), October 1967; "Beyond Symbol Spaces" in *The Japan Architect* (Tokyo), April 1971; "Abstractions from the East" in *The Japan Architect* (Tokyo), May 1974; "Irrational City and Space Machine" in *Shinkenchiku* (Tokyo), March 1975; "When Naked Space Is Traversed" in *The Japan Architect* (Tokyo), February 1976; "The Third Style" in *Shinkenchiku* (Tokyo), January 1977.

On SHINOHARA: book—*New Directions in Japanese Architecture* by Robin Boyd, New York and London 1968; articles—"Kazuo Shinohara's Architectural Theory" by Hiroki Onobayashi in *The Japan Architect* (Tokyo), February 1967; "Heretical Spaces" by Koji Taki in *Shinkenchiku* (Tokyo), July 1968; "Kazuo Shinohara und die japanische Wohnarchitektur" by Irmtraud Schaarschmidt in *Die Kunst* (Munich), March 1971; "Significant Spaces" by Koji Taki in *The Japan Architect* (Tokyo), April 1971; "Kazuo Shinohara and Residences" by Akira Ohashi in *To the Age of Interior,* Tokyo 1971; "With a Sensation of Freedom: Houses Designed by Kazuo Shinohara" by Irmtraud Schaarschmidt in *Bauwelt* (Berlin), February 1976; "Kazuo Shinohara" by

Toyoo Itow in *History of Residences in Showa Era,* Tokyo 1976; "Jap Savagery" in *Architectural Review* (London), August 1977; "Kazuo Shinohara: Una Filosofia de la Vivienda," special issue of *Summarios* (Buenos Aires), October 1977; "Absence of Architecture" by Yasumitsu Matsunaga in *Kenchiku Bunka* (Tokyo), October 1978.

I try to think of houses in terms of symbolic words, such as "things with naked forms," "machine," and "savagery." I believe that this is part of the process of creating a new theory of residential architecture, but there are times when I wonder whether I am not doing the opposite, which is to say dismantling the theory. Whenever I add a new concept, the prospect becomes more cloudy. The categories to which the concepts belong are different, and there is no sign of a structure that will bring them together. When I design a house, it is difficult to find a sure point of reference such as I gained from my dialogue with Japanese tradition. When I selected elementary geometrical shapes as an inorganic framework for expression, it was because of the certainty they afforded. This is a necessary step in the process of creation, but I cannot help feeling uncertain and ill at ease. The one single word that comes to me now is "concreteness." I do not see it as merely an addition to the vocabulary, or even as the structural concept that will tie everything together, but simply as the one word which can strike through all the various orders and categories of words before me.

I had never once foreseen that I would confront concreteness, because it is the diametric opposite of abstraction, which I have always considered the foundational concept linking my houses and my themes. If I am now unconsciously trying to shift to concreteness, which is the concept that seems nearest at the moment, my architecture will have to be dismembered in the strictest sense of the word. Yet I cannot escape the feeling that somehow I can link this dangerous word "concreteness" with the various concepts that lie before me and with the houses built in an effort to cope with them.

I jumped into the tradition of Japanese architecture because I responded instinctively to its beauty, without the benefit of logic or theory. After finishing my first house, I strongly felt the need to re-examine tradition from a logical viewpoint, and at this point abstraction, or the process of abstracting, became a central feature of my theories. This does not mean, however, that each individual space was preceded by an abstract theory. In the case of the "Umbrella House," for example, I was quite conscious of linking the geometrical forms of the structure and the divisional forms of the floor plan with an abstract theory, but the original image of the space came from the dark dirt-floored kitchen of an old farmhouse, in which I had discovered a powerful symbolism. It was, without doubt, a concrete thing that existed within me. Someone said that "House in White" gave him the feeling that he was a child playing in a field of grass. Whether the space actually inspires such feelings or not, I do not hesitate to say that it came from something concrete that was inside me.

To shift directly from abstract to concrete is beyond my ability. A space in which a high level of abstraction co-exists with forceful concreteness seems to me to be the living space that I am seeking now, as well as the structure that forms it. When I began to think of concreteness as a phase of this sort, I felt that the uncertain, structureless point of reference within me had begun slowly to move, and not in the direction of dismemberment.

—Kazuo Shinohara

A cursory glance at Kazuo Shinohara's houses from the outside suggests nothing more than a slightly smug, suburban formula. Then the questions occur. Why is it that his name is on every Japanese architecture student's lips? Why is it that Shinohara vies with only Shirai for the title of "architect's architect" in Japan—Isozaki is, to the practising Japanese architect, an upstart in comparison. It is necessary to penetrate deep into the paradoxical folds of his houses to find the answers.

When we are told that in his House with an Earthen Floor there is a room with a beaten earth floor, we immediately assume that it is in the basement: this makes the surprise so much greater when we enter to find that the earthen floor is the ground floor. It is through the manipulation of such devices that Shinohara has achieved the apotheosis of "house," and it is this quality that has made his work so much discussed in Japan. His programme is uninterrupted homage to, long extended offering to, and devout confirmation of "house:" he is in no rush to get to "housing." He has, over the years, in concentrating on the single-house, projected himself with such commitment to "dwelling" that we are obliged to recognize his depth of sensitivity in spite of the modest size of the field of enquiry. His attention to detail is microscopic, and his intuition of texture, space and material all point towards "dwelling" of the purist kind.

Beginning in a traditional syntax, he was suffocated by the cramped results that such a vernacular necessitated in a modern economy. The irrealisability of the archaic space of traditional dreams made itself felt, and some new equation was needed; he turned to blank concrete walls, earthen floors and characterless space definers in order to amplify the delicate schema of the old historical lines. The vignette was a re-enacting, within the house, of what was going on in Japanese culture as a whole. His work turned more towards an existential minimum, and it became an increasingly internal affair: witness the Cubic Forest House or the Tanikawa Residence. He took the external characteristics of modern architecture, complete with its aloof blanks, and turned them inside-out, parodying them with his bleached, featureless, numbed interiors: Shino Residence, with its ambiguous interior void, is a case in point: it could be said that here the courtyard as an exterior space has been completely transformed into an interior space.

Shinohara demonstrated the course that has brought architecture to its knees in the contemporary metropolis and has charted the way it has been perverted into a degraded approximation of need. We "make do," "get by," but only just. The future lies in one of two directions: we become architecture or architecture becomes man. Which course does Shinohara recommend? It is basically one of creating "operationally abstract space with a view to producing a new quality of the extraordinary." He plans to "express the eternal, one of the most radical expectations of man;" in doing so, Shinohara has advanced from "substantial symbols to insubstantial, fictitious ones," culminating in "uninhibited pleas for a characterless, disinterested space."

—Chris Fawcett

SHIRAI, Seiichi.

Japanese. Born in Kyoto, 5 February 1905. Studied philosophy and architectural history at the Karl Reprecht University, Heidelberg, and the Friedrich Humboldt University, Berlin, under Karl Jaspers and Max Desoir, 1928–31. Married Teruko Kawamura in 1938; children: Hyōsuke and Ikuma. Director, Shirai Architectural Institute, Tokyo, since 1935. Recipient: Kōtarō Takamura Award, 1960; Architectural Annual Prize, 1969; Architectural Institute of Japan Award, 1969; Mainichi Art Award, 1970. Address: 2-31-10 Ebara-cho, Nakano-ku, Tokyo, Japan.

Works:

1936 Kawamura House, Tokyo
1937 Kanki-sō (house), Shizueka Prefecture, Japan
1942 Shimanaka Mountain Lodge, Nagano Prefecture, Japan
1950/
51 Akinomiya Village Office, Akita Prefecture, Japan
1954/
55 Atomic Bomb Memorial Building (project)
1955 Hansobo Buddhist Temple (project)
1955/
56 Matsuida Town Office, Gunma Prefecture, Japan
1956 Ogachi Town Office, Akita Prefecture, Japan
1958 Hondō of the Zenshoji (main part of a Buddhist temple), Tokyo
1962/
63 Ohato Branch of the Shinwa Bank, Nagasaki Prefecture, Japan
1963 Tokyo Branch of the Shinwa Bank
1963/
65 Shicho-sha (private house), Kureha, Toyama, Japan
1966/
75 Shinwa Bank Head Office, Sasebo, Nagasaki Prefecture, Japan
1967/
70 Kohaku-an (Shirai House), Ebara-cho, Nakano-ku, Tokyo
1968/
71 Sakusetsu-ken (private house), Negishi-cho, Yokote, Akita Prefecture, Japan
1971/
72 Shiribetsusan-ryo (villa residence for a pharmaceutical company), Hokkaido, Japan
St. Sebastian House (class room), Ibaraki Christian Junior College, Ibaraki Prefecture, Japan
1972/
74 NOA Building, Tokyo
1974 Santa Chiara Chapel, Ibaraki Christian Junior College, Ibaraki Prefecture, Japan

Publications:

By SHIRAI: book—Buddhism and Architecture, volume 12 of the Complete Works of World Architecture, Tokyo 1960; Koshikyo-shocho (The World of My Calligraphy), 3 volumes, Tokyo 1970, 1976, 1978; articles—"Tendan" in Shinkenchiku (Tokyo), September 1955; "Stone Buddhist Images of China" in Shinkenchiku (Tokyo), October 1955; "Something Jomon-like" in Shinkenchiku (Tokyo), August 1956; "Tofu" in Living Design (Tokyo), October 1956; "Meshi" in Living Design (Tokyo), November 1956; "Taian no nijo" in Shinkenchiku (Tokyo), August 1957.

On SHIRAI: books—Seiichi Shirai, volume 9 of The Complete Works of Contemporary Japanese Architects by Isamu Kurita, Tokyo 1970; The Architecture of Seiichi Shirai by Takashi Hasegawa and others, Tokyo 1974; Seiichi Shirai, edited by Aiko Hasegawa, Tokyo 1976; The Architecture of Seiichi Shirai and His World, edited by Noboru Kawazoe, Tokyo 1978; Study of the Works of Seiichi Shirai, Tokyo 1978.

As the noted writer Junichiro Tanizaki observed, Japanese architecture begins with the spreading of a roof over the land to create a domain of shadows which is then partitioned as necessary. One might say, on the other hand, that Western architecture begins with the creation of the wall in vertical contradistinction to the land. Despite the century of modernization and the apparent adaptation to Western building methods, the Japanese, lacking a tradition of masonry construction, have yet to fully exploit the architectonic qualities of walls.

Educated in Europe (where he studied German philosophy) but sensitive to traditional Japanese culture, Seiichi Shirai is very conscious of this. Perhaps no other Japanese architect is so aware of what one might call the existential meaning of the wall and of the expressive potential of wall surfaces.

The Kaisho-kan and the NOA Building are two exercises in the startling juxtaposition (in the former, lateral; in the latter, vertical) of roughly dressed stone and slick metal panels. The facade of his famous Shinwa Bank Head Office in Sasebo consists of two seemingly unconnected masses: one a dark bronze mass on a white stone base and the other a white travertine mass cantilevered from a dark core. Unlike, say, Louis Kahn, his concern for walls is not structuralist. Through the interplay of different tactile and visual values, Shirai compels us to confront the wall as surface.

His buildings repel the casual visitor. In the Kaisho-kan, the oddly shaped windows, deliberately unaligned, seem to encode some recondite wisdom or the enigmatic language of a secret fraternal society. In the Shinwa Bank, the building's base literally curls away from the sidewalk like a fastidious man who finds himself in low company.

Entry (i.e., the penetration of the wall), as one might expect, is never a simple matter in a Shirai building. This is true even in his earliest work. In the residence called Kanki-so, built in the 1930's, an exterior stairway takes one to the second floor terrace from which entrance is effected. Inside, one finds oneself on a theatrically raised stage with

Seiichi Shirai: Hondō of the Zenshoji, Tokyo, 1958

carved balustrade from which one steps down into a whitewashed room with dark exposed timber members and a fireplace at the other end. There is the same (sometimes exaggerated) sense of drama in his other works. In the Kaisho-kan, which is, of all things, a computer center, the prevailing image is distinctly sexual: one enters via a thin slit in the sandstone-faced front of the building. The same overtly womb-like image is used for the entrance to the NOA Building. It is, however, his unbuilt project for the Atomic Bomb Building, designed to house drawings of the catastrophe, which most graphically expresses the theme of re-birth or resurrection. The actual exhibition area is a white volume cantilevered from a dark core, standing aloof and protected by a moat of water. One enters from a separate building, via a tunnel from which one rises by a stairway inside the core, which is lit from above.

His interiors are often sealed, artificially lit spaces. Shirai has remarked that philosophy is born only where there is enclosure and that the only truly enclosed space in traditional Japanese architecture is the tea-ceremony room. In the sense that his spaces turn the visitor back onto himself and are essentially contemplative, Shirai's work is in great contrast to much of postwar Japanese architecture, which was long preoccupied with technological utopia and the rapidly growing economy.

His Japanese-style buildings, too, are striking, but it is his so-called Western buildings that are the most remarkable for their somewhat eccentric individuality and for the commentary that they make on modern society by the aloofness of their external forms and the reflective quality of their inner spaces.

—Hiroshi Watanabe

SIMONDS, John Ormsbee.

American. Born in Jamestown, North Dakota, 11 March 1913. Educated at Michigan State University, East Lansing, 1930–35 (Arnold Scheele Award), B.S. in Landscape Architecture 1935; Graduate School of Design, Harvard University, Cambridge, Massachusetts, under Joseph Hudnut, Bremer Pond, Walter Chambers, Marcel Breuer and Walter Gropius, 1936–39 (Topiarian Cup, 1938; Samuel Hershey Prize, 1938; Eugene Dodd Medal, 1939), M. Landscape Arch. 1939. Served as a site planner for war housing and military construction during World War II. Married Marjorie C. Todd in 1943; children: Taye, Todd, Polly and Leslie. Park Planner and Construction Supervisor, Michigan State Department of Parks, in the Upper Peninsula, 1935–36; Partner, Simonds and Simonds, landscape architects, Pittsburgh, 1939–70, and Collins, Simonds and Simonds, landscape architects-planners, Washington, D.C. and Pittsburgh, 1952–70. Since 1970, Partner, EPD: The Environmental Planning and Design Partnership, Pittsburgh and Miami Lakes, Florida (partners: Philip Douglas Simonds; Paul Dorr Wolfe; C. Richard Hays; Geoffrey L. Rausch; Jack R. Scholl). Instructor in Site, Community, Urban and Regional Planning, Department of Architecture, Carnegie Institute of Technology, Pittsburgh, 1955–67. Chairman of the Committee on Education, 1952–53, Vice-President, 1959–63, Member of the Executive Committee, 1959–67, President, 1963–65, and Chairman of the Committee on the Profession, 1961–63, American Society of Landscape Architects, and President of the ASLA Foundation, 1965–67; United States Consultant on Community Planning, Inter-American Center for Housing and Planning, Bogota, Colombia, 1960, 1961; Member of the Executive Council, Harvard Graduate School of Design Alumni Association, 1960–63; Founding Member, Interprofessional Commission on Environmental Design, 1963; Member, Joint Committee on the National Capitol, 1964–65; Chairman, Urban Parks and Open Spaces Panel, White House Conference, 1965; Member of the Board of Urban Advisers, Federal Highway Administration, 1966–68; Chairman, Design Awards Jury, Landscape Architecture and Conservation, United States Army Corps of Engineers, 1968; Member, President's Task Force on Resources and the Environment, 1968–70; Chairman, Panel on Environmental Impact Statements, Interprofessional Commission on Environmental Design, Airlie Conference, 1972. Exhibitions: American Society of Landscape Architects exhibitions, 1945–75. Recipient: Honor Awards in the categories of community planning, housing, civic design, parks and recreation, school and campus planning, transportation, and environmental design, from the American Society of Landscape Architects; Honorary Citation, ASLA, Pennsylvania Chapter, 1968; ASLA Medal, 1973; Top Men of the Year Citation, *Engineering News-Record,* 1973. D.Sc.: Michigan State University, 1968. Fellow, American Society of Landscape Architects, 1965; Associate, National Academy of Design, 1969; Honorary Associate, American Institute of Architects, Pennsylvania Chapter. Fellow, Royal Academy of Design, London, 1970; Honorary Corresponding Member, Royal Town Planning Institute, London, 1973. Address: EPD: The Environmental Planning and Design Partnership, 100 Ross Street, Pittsburgh, Pennsylvania 15219, U.S.A.

Works (landscape architecture/planning):

1936   Marquette State Park, Michigan
1939/
  55   Site and landscape planning for more than 200 private residences and estates in Pennsylvania, Ohio, Indiana and Michigan
1947/
  49   10 prototype parklets, The City of Pittsburgh

1952 North Allegheny High School and Campus, Allegheny County, Pennsylvania (with Mitchell and Ritchey)

Aviary/Conservatory, Pittsburgh (with Button and McLean)

Broadhead Manor (public housing community), Pittsburgh (with Mitchell and Ritchey)

Beechwood Park and Swimming Pool, Pittsburgh (with B. Kenneth Johnstone and Associates)

Greater Pittsburgh Airport (with Joseph Hoover)

John Kane Hospital, Allegheny County, Pennsylvania (with Mitchell and Ritchey)

General Medical Hospital, Pittsburgh (with Mitchell and Ritchey)

North View Heights (public housing community), Summer Hill, Pittsburgh (with Mitchell and Ritchey)

1953 Mellon Square, Pittsburgh (with Mitchell and Ritchey)

St. Clair Hospital, Allegheny County, Pennsylvania (with Kuhn, Newcomer and Valentour)

Lower Hill Redevelopment, Pittsburgh (with Mitchell and Ritchey)

1954 North Allegheny Elementary School, Allegheny County, Pennsylvania (with Mitchell and Ritchey)

Fraternities, Carnegie Tech, Pittsburgh (with Lawrence and Anthony Wolfe)

Civic Auditorium, Pittsburgh (with Mitchell and Ritchey)

Sewickley Academy, Pennsylvania (with B. Kenneth Johnstone)

1955 Cannon-McMillan High School, Cannonsburg, Pennsylvania (with Kuhn, Newcomer and Valentour)

Improvement program for the Pittsburgh City Reservoirs

Seton Hill College Campus, Pennsylvania (with Celli-Flynn)

United States Army Nike Housing (5 sites), Allegheny County, Pennsylvania

1956 Redevelopment plan for Rankin, Pennsylvania

North Triangle Redevelopment, Philadelphia (with Lester A. Collins)

Clara Barton School, Allegheny County, Pennsylvania (with Button and McLean)

Improvements to Fort Meade, Maryland (with Lester A. Collins)

1957 Grandview Park, Pittsburgh

Equitable Plaza, Pittsburgh (with Schell and Deeter)

Mt. Lebanon High School Campus and Fields, Mt. Lebanon, Pennsylvania (with Kuhn, Newcomber and Valentour)

Lockhaven Hospital, Lockhaven, Pennsylvania (with B. Kenneth Johnstone)

Physically Handicapped Children's School,

Allegheny County, Pennsylvania (with B. Kenneth Johnstone)

1958 Sewickley Heights Estates, Pennsylvania

Development plan for Allegheny College Campus, Meadville, Pennsylvania

Allegheny Center Redevelopment, Pittsburgh (with Mitchell and Ritchey)

Santee Fill, Annapolis Campus, Maryland (with Lester A. Collins)

Children's Hospital, Pittsburgh (with B. Kenneth Johnstone)

1959 Chautauqua Institution Campus, Chautauqua, New York (with Lester A. Collins)

Allegheny County Regional Park System, Pennsylvania (with Griswold, Winters and Swain, and Ezra Stiles)

1960 Physical Education Complex, University of Pittsburgh (with Mitchell and Ritchey)

Underground Zoo, Pittsburgh (with Lawrence and Anthony Wolfe)

East Hills Housing (Action Housing), Pittsburgh (demonstration Planned Unit Development project; with Walter Gropius, Josep Lluis Sert, Carl Koch, and B. Kenneth Johnstone)

St. Thomas of the Fields, Allegheny County, Pennsylvania (with John Pekruhn)

1960– Miami Lakes New Town, Miami Lakes, Florida (with Lester A. Collins)

1961 Recreation study for the Kinzua Reservoir, Warren County, Pennsylvania

John Ormsbee Simonds: Allegheny Center Redevelopment, Pittsburgh, 1958

Comprehensive plan for Clairton, Pennsylvania

Pittsburgh Stadium and Riverfront Park (with Deeter, Ritchey and Sippel)

Westinghouse Research Center, Pittsburgh (with Deeter, Ritchey and Sippel)

1962 Conceptual plans for Wacker Drive, Chicago (with Barton-Aschman)

Mount Union Public Housing Community, Pennsylvania (with Curry, Martin and Taylor)

1963 Recreation plan for Twelve Mile Island, Allegheny County, Pennsylvania (project)

1964 Shopping Mall, East Liberty, Pennsylvania

1965 Allegheny Commons (revised master development plan), Pittsburgh

Virginia Outdoor Recreation Study

1966 Comprehensive parks and recreation plan for Baltimore

Downtown urban renewal plan for Parkersburg, West Virginia

Founder's Square, Louisville, Kentucky (with Lawrence Melillo)

1967 Redevelopment plan for the central area of McLean, Virginia

Master plan for the proposed community of Tatoosh, Washington (project)

Washington Road Shopping Mall, Mt. Lebanon Township, Pennsylvania

1968 Environmental action plan for Chattanooga and Hamilton County, Tennessee

1968– Landscape architecture for the Metropolitan Area Transit Authority, Washington, D.C.

Jacaranda (planned community of 9 square miles), Broward County, Florida

1969 Center City Redevelopment, Cumberland, Maryland

Multiple use opportunities plan, East-West Freeway, Milwaukee

1970 Downtown urban renewal plan for Huntington, West Virginia

Riverfront, Louisville, Kentucky (with Lawrence Melillo, and Doxiades and Associates)

Transit Expressway Revenue Line, Allegheny County, Pennsylvania (project; as planning consultant)

1971 Master plan for Ohiopyle State Park, Pennsylvania

Development plans for the new community of Saga Bay, Dade County, Florida

Highway illumination concept plan, Virginia Department of Highways (with Hayes, Seay, Mattern and Mattern)

The Springs (new community), Orlando, Florida (with Nils Sweitzer)

1972 Master plan for Fisher Island, Dade County, Florida (project)

Opportunity Park and Redevelopment, Akron, Ohio

Cary Arboretum, Duchess County, New York

Revised master plan for the Missouri Botanic Garden, St. Louis

Corridor location, design and multiple use opportunities plan, Interstate Highway 110, Pensacola, Florida (with Beiswenger, Hock and Associates)

Location alternatives, Leesburg, Virginia Bypass

1973 Space utilization study, Interstate Highways 64 and 77, Charleston, West Virginia

Development plan for the waterfront, Toledo, Ohio

Multimodal transportation study for Pennsylvania state park and recreation areas (project)

Shoreline protection and development program, Lake Ontario, Finger Lakes Region, New York

Environmental improvement study of Highway VA I-66, Fairfax and Arlington

Counties, Virginia

1974 Community development plans for Indian Trace, Broward County, Florida

Riverbend Plaza, South Bend, Indiana (with Clyde E. Williams and Associates)

1975 Transportation alternatives study, I-66 Corridor, Fairfax and Arlington Counties, Virginia (with Howard, Needles, Tammen and Bergendoff)

1976 Revised master plan and site development, Holden Arboretum, Mentor, Ohio

Comprehensive plan for St. George Island, Franklin County, Florida

Development plan for West Palm Beach, Florida

Master plan for the new community of Pelican Bay, Florida

Replanning of Palm Coast, Flagler County, Florida

Plan for Key Island, Naples, Florida

1977 Campus planning, Pennsylvania State University, University Park

Pennsylvania National Cemetery, Indiantown Gap (with Burt, Hill and Associates)

Neville Island Regional Park, Allegheny County, Pennsylvania

Beachfront, Hollywood, Florida (project)

Corridor study, Grant Street, Pittsburgh (project)

1978 Toledo International Park, Ohio (project)

Dade County Marina, Florida (project)

Plan for the Carnegie Mellon University Campus, Pittsburgh (project)

Publications:

By SIMONDS: books—*Landscape Architecture: The Shaping of Man's Natural Environment,* New York 1961; *A Report on the Profession of Landscape Architecture,* editor, Washington, D.C. 1963; *Virginia's Commonwealth,* editor, Richmond 1965; introduction to *Landscape Gardening* by Andrew Jackson Downing, New York 1967; *The Freeway in the City,* editor, Washington, D.C. 1968; *Outdoor Recreation Facilities Manual,* U.S. Army Corps of Engineers, Washington, D.C. 1973; contributions to *Encyclopaedia of Urban Planning,* edited by Arnold Whittick, New York 1974; *Earthscape: A Manual of Environmental Planning,* New York 1978; articles—"Miami Lakes New Town" in *Parks and Recreation* (Washington, D.C.), October 1970; "The Mobile Society: A Look to the Future" in *Consulting Engineer* (New York), March/April 1974; "Self-Destruction of an Island Paradise" in *Landscape Architecture* (Louisville, Kentucky), January 1976; "From Scrabble and Ooze" in *Landscape Architecture* (Louisville, Kentucky), March 1978.

On SIMONDS: articles—"Figures in a Landscape" in *Landscape Architecture* (Louisville, Kentucky), January 1964; article in *The Engineering News Record* (New York), 9 March 1972; article in *AIA Journal* (Washington, D.C.), October 1978.

*

The work of the landscape architect, or "architect of the landscape," is the design of functional and expressive out of door spaces and places. These are created within the context of the natural and man-built environment, and range in scope and complexity from a child's playlot to a recreational park, university campus, or the conceptual planning of a community or new town.

On larger commissions the landscape architect often serves as a member of a closely coordinated professional team, which includes architects, engineers, planners, and scientist-advisers. A generalist, the landscape architect brings to the planning-design process specialized training in the physical sciences —such as physiography, geology, hydrology, biology, and ecology—and a feeling for the land, human relationships and design.

The past several decades have witnessed a remarkable evolution in the practice of landscape architecture. Within this brief span of time the emphasis has shifted from the design of large estates and sumptuous resorts for the wealthy to subdivisions, public works projects, public housing, urban renewal, military installations, freeway improvements, national, state and urban parks—and more recently to river basin studies and comprehensive resource planning. It has been the privilege of the members of our firm to have had an active role in this dynamic transformation.

—John Ormsbee Simonds

John Ormsbee Simonds is a founding partner of Environmental Planning and Design, a firm that consists of more than thirty professionals who are experienced in all phases of landscape architecture and planning. It has engaged in more than 500 projects since the founding of the original partnership in 1939. The firm is national in scope, and its work includes programs in regional development, urban renewal and municipal comprehensive planning and zoning. The office engages in the design of waterfront and water related projects, pedestrian malls, downtown urban plazas and botanical gardens. It plans industrial sites, highway and transit facilities, and park and recreational space, and serves a large variety of institutions including hospitals, schools and churches.

Since such work demands highly complex forms of collaboration, it is difficult to assess Simonds as an individual designer. Because of the immense success of his firm in both its volume and quality of work, Simonds must be considered first as an immensely skillful specialist, a man who knows how to respond to the expressed needs of many segments of society, how to formulate problems and agree upon alternatives. His books, most notably *Landscape Architecture: The Shaping of Man's Natural Environment,* reveal a philosophy of planning rooted in a knowledge of historical forms enriched by extensive travel as a young man in Japan, Korea, China, Burma, Bali, India and Tibet. By his own account his travels taught him that "one plans not places or spaces or things—one plans experiences. . . . Form must take its shape from the planned experience, rather than the experience from the preconceived form. . . . The living, pulsing, vital experience, if conceived as a diagram of harmonious relationships, will develop its own expressive forms. And the forms evolved will be as organic as the shell of the nautilus; and perhaps, if the plan is successful, they may be as beautiful."

—Mildred F. Schmertz

SIREN, Heikki.

Finnish. Born in Helsinki, 5 October 1918. Educated at Suomalainen Yhteiskoulu, Helsinki, matriculated 1939; Technical University, Helsinki, under J. S. Sirén, Dip.Arch. 1946. Served in the Finnish Army, 1939–45: Lieutenant. Married the architect Kaija Tuominen (i.e., Kaija Siren, *q.v.*) in 1944; children: Kirsi, Sara, Jukka and Hannu. Worked in the office of Professor J. S. Sirén, Helsinki, 1944–48. Since 1948, Partner, with Kaija Siren, Arkkitehtitoimisto Kaija ja Heikki Siren, Helsinki; branch office established in Linz, Austria, 1962–74, and Kotka, Finland, 1969–75. Guest Lecturer, University of Technology, Trondheim, Norway, 1960; Director, Architectural Seminar, University of Technology, Vienna, 1966. Exhibitions: *Bienal,* Sao Paulo, 1957, 1961; *Exposition d'Art Contemporain* (own stand), Paris, 1963. Recipient: Väino Vähäkallio Fellowship, 1948; Gold Medal, *Bienal,* Sao Paulo, 1957, 1961. Honorary Professor, Helsinki, 1970; Member, Finnish Academy of Technical Sciences, 1971. Address: Arkkitehtitoimisto Kaija ja Heikki Siren, Lounaisväylä 8A, 00200 Helsinki 20, Finland.

Heikki and Kaija Siren: Chapel, Otaniemi, Finland, 1957

Works (with Kaija Siren):
1948 Scenery for the play *Miriam,* Kansanteatteri, Helsinki
1949 Tomb of the Fallen, Tarvasjoki, Finland
1950 Apartment building, Kalevankatu 46, Helsinki
    Apartment building, Savonkulma, Kuopio, Finland
1950/
73 Tech Town, Otaniemi, Finland
1951 Kankainen Manor House restoration, Kalvola, Finland
    Tech Town Sauna, Otaniemi, Finland
1951/
60 Siren House, Lauttasaari, Helsinki
1952 Servin Mökki Restaurant, Otaniemi, Finland
    Apartment building, Hatsalanpuisto, Kuopio, Finland
1953 Tuura Vacation House, Suomusjärvi, Finland
    Soiniemi Villa, Vihtr, Finland
    Tikkakoski Home for Children, Tikkakoski, Finland
    Apartment building, Otakallio 1, Otaniemi, Finland
1954 Small Stage, Finnish National Theatre, Helsinki
    Kimmeltie Rowhouse Development, Tapiola, Finland
    Scenery for the play *Wanderer,* Finnish National Theatre, Helsinki
    Concert Hall, Lahti, Finland
    Kontiontie Rowhouse Development, Tapiola, Finland
1955 Ylitalo Vacation House, Sjökulla, Finland
    Leppäniemi Manor restoration, Loppi, Finland
    Apartment building, Kivalterintie 18–20, Helsinki
    Otsolahden Lämpö Garage, Tapiola, Finland

1956 Suomen Koneliike Office Building, Helsinki
    Helkama Villa, Vihti, Finland
    Otalaakso Apartment Building, Otaniemi, Finland
    Apartment building, Kivalterintie 17–19, Helsinki
    Apartment buildings, Ritokalliontie 1 and 3, Helsinki
    Bockholm Sauna, Barösund, Finland
1956/
72 Shell Service Stations, Finland
1957 Otaharju Apartment House, Otaniemi, Finland
    Aarnivalkea School, Tapiola, Finland
    Aarnivalkea School Teachers' Apartments, Tapiola, Finland
    Rowhouses, Näätätie 19, Helsinki
    Chapel, Otaniemi, Finland
1958 Eskola Vacation House, Sjökulla, Finland
    School, Kauklahti, Espoo, Finland
    Housekeeper Institute, Kauniainen, Finland
1959 Otanotko Apartment Building, Otaniemi, Finland
    Otsonpesä Linked Houses, Tapiola, Finland
    House interior, Välskärinkatu 7, Helsinki
    Finlayson Industrial Building elevation, Tampere, Finland
1960 Maria Sauna, Iniö, Finland
    Olkahinen Elementary School, Aitolahti, Finland
    Rowhouses, Kanneltie, Helsinki
    Kehrääjä Apartment Building, Tapiola, Finland
    OSA I Apartment Building, Otaniemi, Finland
    Peurasaari School, Kemi, Finland
1961 Interior for the yacht *Kuohhuneiti,* Helsinki
    Water Tower, Loviisa, Finland
    Church, Orivesi, Finland

    J. S. Sirén Tombstone, Helsinki
    Alppilan Tehdastalo Building for small industries, Helsinki
    Finnish Workers' Savings Bank, Kotka, Finland
    Tapiolan Lämpö Central Garage, Tapiola, Finland
    Kauklahti Children's Complex, Espoo, Finland
1962 Interior for Valtimo KOP, Porvoo, Finland
    Karhuranta Apartment Building, Tapiola, Finland
    Sauna at Kankainen Manor, Kalvola, Finland
    Otsonlinna Apartment Building, Tapiola, Finland
    OAS II Apartment Building, Otaniemi, Finland
    Otakallio II Apartment Building, Otaniemi, Finland
    Iltarusko Rowhouses, Tapiola, Finland
    Finnish National Theatre restoration, Helsinki
    Pappilansalmi School, Hamina, Finland
    Complex for the Aged, Kauklahti, Espoo, Finland
    Apartment building, Kauklahti, Espoo, Finland
1963 New chapel and cemetery, Espoo, Finland
    Ympyräkeskus Office Building, Hamina, Finland
    Rowhouse development, Hagen, West Germany
    Helsinki Cathedral restoration, Helsinki (plan by J. S. Sirén)
    Oulu Oy Office Building, Oulu, Finland
    Pihlajamäki Shopping Centre, Helsinki
    Apartment building, Oravankatu 3–5, Karhula, Finland

Apartment building development, North Tapiola, Finland

Apartment building, Kauklahti, Espoo, Finland

Siren stand, *Exposition d'Art Contemporain,* Paris

1964 Apartment building, Lounaisväylä 8, Helsinki

Pusenius House, Kotka, Finland

Rauma-Repola Kitchen Furniture (project)

Apartment building, Pikalähetintie 14–18, Helsinki

Nurmes Administration Building, Nurmes, Finland (plan by J. S. Sirén)

Konela Automobile Repair Shop, Helsinki

1964/
65 Bird House and Ostrich Hall, Korkeasaari Zoo, Helsinki

1965 Kallio Municipal Offices, Helsinki

Finnish Workers' Savings Bank, Tampere, Finland

Bank of Finland restoration, Vaasa, Finland

Log cabins, Rantasalmi Oy, Finland

Björkbodan Tehdas Oy Fittings, Finland

Tapionsolu Linked Houses, Tapiola, Finland

1966 Shopping centre, North Tapiola, Finland

Atrium House Development, Louhentie 1, Tapiola, Finland

5 private houses, Tapiola, Finland

Apartment building development, Kalliola, Kotka, Finland

Residential development, Krefeld, West Germany

Pieksämäki Savings Bank, Finland

1966/
69 Lingonso Vacation Island, Barösund, Finland

1966/
70 Polar houses and row houses, Finland

1967 Sisko Aho Tombstone, Helsinki

Spiral staircase, Högfors, Finland

Town Hall, Kankaanpää, Finland

Tornionlaakso Savings Bank, Tornio, Finland

Punjo Villa, Espoo, Finland

Apartment building, Kääpäkatu 8, Karhula, Finland

1967/
74 Vacation village, Lacanau, France

1968 Scenery for the play *Rosencrantz and Guildenstern Are Dead,* Finnish National Theatre, Helsinki

Linked houses development, Polar Village, Vantaa, Finland

KOP Circular Building, Helsinki

Tapion Auto Office Building, Tapiola, Finland

Tampereen Keskus Office Building, Tampere, Finland

Oy Lohja Ab Directors' Residence, Lohja, Finland

Asko Kitchen Furniture (project)

1968/
71 Apartment house development, Ristinkallio, Karhula, Finland

1968/
74 Pirkkola Sports Park, Helsinki

1968/
76 Apartment building development, Karhuvuori, Kotka, Finland

1969 Kontula Parish Hall, Helsinki

Myllypuro Parish Hall, Helsinki

Espoonlahti Apartment Building, Espoo, Finland

House interior, Hollantilaisentie 1, Helsinki

Espoo Mixed Secondary School, Kauklahti, Espoo, Finland

Roinela Sauna, Järvenpää, Finland

1970 Apartment building, Jukolantie 11, Kouvola, Finland

"La Pierrefitte" attached houses development, Paris

Lauttasaari Co-Educational School, Helsinki

Apartment building, Kauklahti, Espoo, Finland

Parish Centre, Kankaanpää, Finland

1971 Oiva Soini Tombstone, Helsinki

Apartment building, Kääpäkatu 12, Karhula, Finland

Jussi Vacation House, Barösund, Finland

Co-operative Bank, Kotka, Finland

1971/
75 Sports Center, Kankaanpää, Finland

1972 Apartment building, Kymenlaaksonkatu 14, Kotka, Finland

Finnish Co-Educational School of Helsinki

"Johanna" Trawler

Björkholm Vacation House, Snappertuna, Finland

1973 Kaikka Vacation House, Barösund, Finland

Hakkarainen Vacation House, Bromarv, Finland

Muurahainen Vacation House, Kangasala, Finland

Suulisniemi Apartment Building Development, Karhula, Finland

1974 Brucknerhaus Concert Hall, Linz, Austria

Apartment buildings, Kalliola, Kotka, Finland

Viitamaki Apartment Building, Kouvola, Finland

Town plan for Lentävänniemi, Tampere, Finland

Rank Xerox Head Office, Espoo, Finland

Utsjoki Golf Club and Restaurant, Karuizawa, Japan

Sapokan Vuokratalot Apartment Buildings, Kotka, Finland

1974/
75 Kolmio Apartment House Development, Kotka, Finland

1975 Viitapuisto Apartment Building, Kouvola, Finland

Log Buildings, Huvila Seppälä, Finland (project)

Raatimikko Business Building, Mikkeli, Finland

1976 Alatornio Parish Hall, Tornio, Finland

Golf Club, Onuma, Hokkaido, Japan

Vacation Centre, Hakone, Japan

1977 Juvatalo Office Building, Tapiola, Finland

Reichsbrücke, Vienna

1978 Opetustalo School of Economy, Helsinki

Conference Palace, Baghdad

Publications:

On the SIRENS: book—*Kaija and Heikki Siren, Architects,* edited by Erik Bruun and Sara Popovits, Helsinki 1977, Dusseldorf 1978.

*

The Finnish log-built village, old grey buildings with their fences, gates and courtyards; white plastered houses on the Mediterranean; restrained and disciplined wooden architecture that blends into the Japanese landscape—indigenous architecture has still some amazing power; it can move one with its simplicity and genuineness.

It is obvious that the lasting significance of these buildings stems from the strength of creation behind them. They do not only meet the given need, but also often rise beyond it to the non-rational quality of architecture. Instinct, intuition and imagination are integral to creative work of permanent value.

An architect's working methods arise from his own characteristic quality, his experience and his training. The stress laid on different aspects of planning varies, depending on the requirements and conditions of age. The special character of each project is the primary premise for planning, which may have a visionary, technological, aesthetic or purely morphological basis.

Still, a clear plan is absolutely vital, as it is a synthesis based on all aspects of the problem.

Max Reinhardt, an "architect" of the stage, said

that even in his most fantastic productions he was operating in a sphere "only a hand's breadth" above reality.

Architecture creates the "stage" for human life, which has in itself all the elements for illusion. The unrestrained imagination of the designer can easily break the delicate balance that should exist between nature and the built environment.

The architect has to define the desired atmosphere, the relationship between the building and its surroundings, and then to find the appropriate means to create this intangible quality of the work.

—Kaija and Heikki Siren

*

The work of Kaija and Heikki Siren began in the 1950's and reached its first peak towards the end of the decade, when the University of Technology area in Otaniemi was built.

At that juncture Brutalism was beginning to spread throughout the world; a few years later Metabolism appeared in public for the first time, with utopic proposals for bearing constructions of great span and interchangeable secondary units, which later materialized in a simplified form. Then, under the influence of the demand for variability and flexibility, came what is called container architecture, the architecture of neutral cells in which it was often only possible to find one's bearings by means of various information systems—when it appeared both unnecessary and unavoidable to introduce industrialized building. The youth revolt in the U.S.A. led the way to dome and shelter architecture and the houseboats in Sausalito. On the other hand, the single family house facing a garden appeared to be a hopeless anachronism, while densely populated areas and high-rise buildings were thought to be a necessity.

Those who consciously experienced these tendencies and currents finally have had to accept with resignation that many of the waves have disappeared, leaving no trace in the sand. When the waters calmed there were a few rocks left on the beach, recently covered but now once more a visible witness to their own abiding quality. If I am not mistaken, some of Kaija and Heikki Siren's buildings can be counted among these survivors.

Here we confront an architectural problem of long standing and one that will persist into the future. It concerns the relationship between form and space, the creation of a frame that does not limit human activity but facilitates it, the relationship between redundancy and information, the relationship between the known and the new. Undoubtedly it is sound architecture, not that of exaggeration and the grandiose gesture, which finds expression in the work of these architects—an architecture characterized by clarity and restraint.

The chapel in Otaniemi was one of the buildings which at that time made an abiding impression and exercised an influence on us younger architects on the Continent: two walls which enclose the forecourt and church area, a sloping roof, light coming in from the rear and a view over the altar area out into a natural setting—a simple house of brick and wood. Seldom has more been created by such simple means! This building, apparently so simple, contains, however, a set of problems which are worth thinking over. Much in modern architecture appears simple, but is in fact not simple, merely monotonous. True simplicity lies in that which has, so to speak, regained simplicity; it does not constitute the first step but the last step in a lengthy and laborious process. Simplicity is so rare today because we lack the patience and time to allow the form to mature. Thus some buildings strive to make an impression at any price, because some people—and rightly—revolt against monotony, but on the other hand do not have sufficient time or patience to make their way from the stage of great and unbridled gestures back to simplicity. For those actually participating in an epoch it is often difficult to realize when this stage of simplicity has been reached. One often has to be content with assumptions. Presumably the only criteria are stability in time and durability over a longer, if also limited, period of time.

Reflections on architecture are linked, beyond the rational, with values that are not based on reason. Heikki Siren once expressed this more simply. According to him, anything that cannot be grasped comes from the heart.

Anonymous indigenous architecture is one of the sources of inspiration for both these architects. What they find fascinating in it is not just its simplicity and originality, but the creative power, the unerring instinct.

Heikki Siren, who has himself designed stage-settings, labels architecture a stage for human life. If this formula is taken in earnest, we find that behind it lies hidden the idea that playfulness is a legitimate and necessary means in architecture. This element of playfulness is indeed found in their work. It does not force itself upon one; it appears instead with restraint; it is no guiding principle, merely a hint—for example, the white fencing outside the row houses on Kontiontie in Tapiola.

In any discussion of Finnish architecture the landscape typical of the country is often mentioned. In the Western world God and nature are typically conceived to be at different poles. For the Japanese, on the other hand, the divine reveals itself in nature, and nature is itself divine. Something of this latter concept is perceptible in the work of the Sirens, for otherwise it is difficult to understand why, for example, the natural setting seen through the glass altar wall in the Otaniemi chapel is permitted to be a part of the church area and why the cross does not stand inside the church, but in front of it, in the forest.

I have attempted here a few notes that may contribute to an understanding of the Sirens. Of course I hardly dare hope that I have succeeded in explaining very much, but I might add that, with Kaija and Heikki Siren, life and architecture complement one another: the simplicity, originality and sincerity of their own lives is reflected in their architecture.

—Jürgen Joedicke

Alvaro Siza: Caxinas Housing Estate, Vila do Conde, Portugal, 1972

SIREN, Kaija.
Finnish. Born Katri Anna-Maija Helena Tuominen in Kotka, 23 October 1920. Educated at Kotkan Tyttölyseo, Kotka, matriculated 1939; Technical University, Helsinki, under J. S. Sirén, Dip.Arch. 1948. Married the architect Heikki Siren, *q.v.,* in 1944; children: Kirsi, Sara, Jukka and Hannu. Since 1948, Partner, with Heikki Siren, Arkkitehtitoimi: Kaija ja Heikki Siren, Helsinki; branch office established in Linz, Austria, 1962–74, and Kotka, Finland, 1969–75. Exhibitions: *Bienal,* Sao Paulo, 1957, 1961; *Exposition d'Art Contemporain* (own stand), Paris, 1963. Recipient: Gold Medal, *Bienal,* Sao Paulo, 1957, 1961. Address: Arkkitehtitoimisto Kaija ja Heikki Siren, Lounaisväylä 8A, 00200 Helsinki 20, Finland.

See SIREN, Heikki

SIZA, Alvaro.
Portuguese. Born in Matosinhos, 25 June 1933. Educated at the University of Oporto School of Architecture, under Fernando Tavora, 1949–55, Dip. Arch. 1955. Married Maria Antonia Marinho Leite in 1962 (died, 1973); children: Alvaro and Joana. In private practice, Porto, since 1954: worked with Fernando Tavora, 1955–58. Professor of Architecture, University of Oporto, since 1965. Exhibitions: *Siza Arkitekt i Porto,* Copenhagen, 1975, and Aarhus,

Denmark, 1976; *Alvaro Siza, Arquitecto,* Barcelona, 1976; *Europa/America,* at the *Biennale,* Venice, 1978; *Alvaro Siza, Architetto 1954–79,* Milan, 1979. Correspondent, L'Académie d'Architecture, Paris, 1971. Address (office): Rua da Alegria 399, Porto 4000, Portugal.

Works:

1954/
57 4 houses, Afonso Henriques Avenue 394, Matosinhos, Portugal

1956/
59 Parish Center, Matosinhos, Portugal (partially built)

1957/
59 Carneiro de Melo House, Boavista Avenue, Porto

1958/
63 Boanova Restaurant, Avenue Marginal, Leca da Palmeira, Matosinhos, Portugal (with Alberto Neves, Antonio Meneres, Botelho Dias, and Joaquim Sampaio)

1958/
65 Quinta da Conceicad Swimming Pool, Matosinhos, Portugal

1959 Caulkers Monument, Porto (project; with Alcino Soutinho, Augusto Amaral, and the sculptor Lagoa)

1960 Factory canteen, Matosinhos, Portugal (demolished)

1960/
62 Rocha Ribeiro House, Duarte Pacheco 502, Maia, Portugal

1960/
63 Lordelo Cooperative Building, Prof. Augusto Nobre 193, Porto

1961/
66 Leca Swimming Pool, Avenue Marginal, Leca da Palmeira, Matosinhos, Portugal (partially built)

1962/
65 Ferreiro da Costa House, Azenha Decima Street 258, Matosinhos, Portugal

1964/
68 Alves Costa House, Praia de Moledo, Moledo do Minho, Portugal

1965/
69 Alves Santos House, Padre Afonso Soares Street, Povoa do Varzim, Portugal

1966 Cotton warehouse, Sousa Aroso Street, Matosinhos, Portugal

1967 Motel, Coimbra (project)
1967/
70 Manuel Magalhaes House, Combatentes Avenue 1954, Porto
1968 Office Building, Porto (project)
1969 Borges Bank, Vila do Conde, Portugal (project)
1970 Domus Co-operative Supermarket, Boavista Avenue 3324, Porto
1970/
72 Caxinas Housing Estate, Praia de Caxinas, Vila do Conde, Portugal (partially built)
1971 Alcino Cardoso House, Lugar da Gateira, Moledo do Minho, Portugal
1971/
74 Sottomayor Bank, Dr. Antonio José de Almeida, Oliveira de Azemeis, Portugal
1972 Mobil Housing Estate, Matosinhos, Portugal (project)
Marques Pinto House, Porto (project)
Domus Co-operative Supermarket, Alvaro Gomes 112, Porto
Housing estate, Ovar, Portugal (project)
1972/
73 Sottomayor Bank, Visconde Guedes Teixeira Avenue, Lamego, Portugal
1973 Housing estate, Ovar, Portugal (2nd project)
Gallery, Campo Alegre 1192, Porto (partially built)
Azeitad House, Azeitad, Portugal (project)
1973/
76 Beires House, Alberto Pimentel Street, Povoa do Varzim, Portugal
1973/
77 Bonca Residents Association Housing, Boavista Avenue, Porto
1974/
77 S. Victor Residents Association Housing, Senhora das Dores, Porto
1975 Restaurant Pico do Areeiro, Madeira (project)
1976 Barredo Renewal, Fontetaurina 191–192, Porto
Largo da Lada Barredo Renewal, Porto (project)
1976/
77 Antonio Carlos House, S. Joao de Deus Street, Santo Tirso, Portugal
1977 Francelos House, V. Nova de Gaia, Portugal (project)
1977/
79 Co-operative housing, Bairro da Malagueira, Evora, Portugal
1979 Görlitzer Bad Swimming Pool, Berlin (competition project)

Publications:

By SIZA: articles—in *Lotus 13* (Milan), December 1976; in *Proceedings of the Seminario Internacional de Arquitectura,* Santiago de Compostela, Spain 1977; in *Europa/America,* exhibition catalogue of the *Biennale,* Venice 1978; in *Arquitectura* (Lisbon), March 1979.

On SIZA: articles—"Tres Obras de Alvaro Siza" by Nuno Portas in *Arquitectura* (Lisbon), July 1960; "Un Analisis de la Obra de Alvaro Siza" by Pedro Vieira de Almeida in *Hogar y Arquitectura* (Madrid), January 1967; "Architettura Recenti di Alvaro Siza" by Vittorio Gregotti and "Note sul Significato dell'Architettura di Alvaro Siza nell' Ambiente Portoghese" by Nuno Portas in *Controspazio* (Bari, Italy), September 1972; "Arquitecturas en Las Margenes" by José Rafael Moneo and "Alvaro Siza" by Oriol Bohigas in *Arquitecturas Bis* (Barcelona), March 1976; "Alvaro Siza, Architetto" by Bernard Huet and "Il Metodo di Siza" by Pierluigi Nicolin in *Alvaro Siza, Architetto 1954–79,* exhibition catalogue, Milan 1979.

Most of my works were never fulfilled; some of the things I did were carried out only in part, others were profoundly changed or destroyed.

That's only to be expected.

An architectonic proposition, whose aim it is to go deep into the existing transforming trends, into the clashes and strains that make up reality, a proposition that intends to be more than a passive materialization, refusing to reduce that same reality, analysing each of its aspects, one by one—that proposition can't find support on a fixed image, can't follow a linear evolution.

Nevertheless, and for the same reason, that proposition can't be ambiguous, neither can it restrain itself to a disciplinary discourse, however sure it seems to be.

Each design is bound to catch, with the utmost rigour, a precise moment of a flittering image in all its shades. The better you can recognize that flittering quality of reality, the clearer must your design arise. It is the more vulnerable as it is true.

That may be the reason why only marginal works (a quiet dwelling, a holiday-house miles away) have been kept as they were originally designed.

This is the outcome of participation in a process of cultural transformation, of construction/destruction. But something remains. Pieces are kept here and there, inside ourselves, perhaps gathered by someone, leaving marks on space and on people, melting in a process of total transformation.

We are now putting them together, to make the spaces between them become images and give them a meaning and to make each of them have a meaning when faced with the others "sous la lumière."

In that space there can be found the last little stone and the last little conflict.

We change space as we change ourselves—by pieces, confronted with "the other" collectively and individually.

Nature, the abode of man, and man, the creator of Nature, both absorb everything, embodying or rejecting it in a transitory way, as everything leaves its mark on them.

Departing from isolated pieces we search the space that bears the pieces.

—Alvaro Siza

Possibly the most important characteristic of Alvaro Siza's work—that to which the new Portuguese architecture owes so much—is his ability to break down the stylistic elements of "Racionalismo" and recompose them so that they come to be part of "Manierismo." The Modernist tradition of Form expresses itself with originality in Siza's work in three different ways: in the autonomy of space; in relation to surroundings; and in method of positioning.

Siza's works are always based on unity of space and volume, and it is this that makes them stand out as autonomous objects. They are all comprehensible as artefacts in which, thanks to the handling of components, there is an absolute coherence of function and form, varied though they may all be in content and arrangement. Thus, in the case of the Magalhaes House the walls, screens and pillars all play their part in implying the dialectic of continuous fluidity within finite and limited space; in contrast, the Sottomayor Bank in Oliveira de Azemis uses these same elements to give the impression of spatial fluidity, broken up, as it were, into an unlimited succession of independent sectors. The fundamental reasoning behind the finished work lies in the way in which space can be held under tension, always achieved through the use of familiar means in an ambiguous setting within the actual composition.

Architecture is fundamentally intended, then, as an independent unity of concept and form; but despite this independence, it always manages, without sacrificing its radicality, to accommodate well to its surroundings. All Siza's work can also be understood, therefore, as a response to the rural or urban context to which it belongs, despite the fact that this accommodation is never achieved through imitation, and certainly not in terms of those "environmental pre-existences" of which the Italians were so fond in the 1950's and 1960's. Siza is able to respond to the environment without detracting from the functional and stylistic identity of his architecture, and, moreover, he establishes an effective dialectical tension within it. In his plans for the Via Alfonso Henriques, Porto, he manages to make the new buildings stand out even though they are adapting to the existing curve of the street; they are integrated into the existing architecture in a now almost legendary manner. The way in which the surroundings are reflected in the mirror surface of the facade is characteristic of the way in which he visually re-integrates the urban landscape, without, however, affecting the independent value of his own contribution. Another example is the way in which the swimming pool at Leça hides between the structure of the roadway and the first rocks of the beach, but nevertheless yields nothing of its own identity to its surroundings and does not disappear as though camouflaged. In the case of the residential complex in the Bonça district of Porto, Siza even seems to introduce a fundamental change of form and typology in the surroundings themselves, suggesting that architecture has within it the means of transformation—the view of the Modernists in their most optimistic moments; but he also makes a sufficient response to the basic topographical, as well as sociological and symbolic, elements of the residential area of which it forms a part.

The differences between (on the one hand) the Bonça development and (on the other) the incomplete Caxinas Housing Estate indicate that, when faced with the same conflicting objectives of autonomy versus appropriateness, Siza evolves very different solutions, depending on the individual situation, the physical, economic, productive and environmental needs. In this sense one might say that his designs are always based on situation—or that they are more appropriately defined according to the "contextual whole" than to any dogma or a priori assumptions—more of a conditioned response than an abstract ideology. Siza would without doubt have the approval of John Dewey, who defined research as "the controlled transformation of an indeterminate situation into one so determined in its constituent relations that it converts the separate elements of the original situation into a unified whole." In Siza's work the disruption and recomposition of Rationalist language has shown itself to be a fitting instrument for adaptation to the expressive force of situation.

—Oriol Bohigas

SKIDMORE, Louis.
American. Born in Lawrenceburg, Indiana, 8 April 1897. Educated at the Bradley Polytechnic Institute, now Bradley University, Peoria, Illinois, graduated 1917; Massachusetts Institute of Technology, Cambridge, 1921–24 (Rotch Special Student Prize, 1924), B.Arch. 1924; awarded Rotch Travelling Fellowship, 1926–29: Visiting Scholar, American Academy in Rome, 1927. Served in the United States Army, in England, 1918–19. Married Eloise Owings in 1930; children: Louis Jr. and Phillip. Worked for Maginnius and Walsh, 1924–26; Chief of Design, and Assistant to the General Manager, *Century of Progress Exposition,* Chicago, 1929–35. Co-Founding Partner, with Nathaniel Owings, *q.v.,* Skidmore and Owings, Chicago, 1936–39 (established New York branch, 1937), and, with John Merrill, *q.v.,* Skidmore, Owings and Merrill, Chicago, New York, San Francisco, Portland, Oregon, Washington, D.C., etc., from 1939: retired from the firm in 1955. Served as President, New York Building Congress; Chairman, Advisory Council of the School of Architecture, Princeton University, New Jersey; Consultant Architect to the United Nations, New York, and to

the University of Michigan, Ann Arbor. Exhibition: *Skidmore, Owings and Merrill*, Museum of Modern Art, New York, 1950. Recipient: Medal of Honor, 1948, and Gold Medal, 1957, American Institute of Architects; Distinguished Alumni Award, Bradley University, 1952. LL.D.: Bradley University, 1952. Fellow, American Institute of Architects. *Died* (in Winter Haven, Florida) *27 September 1962*.

Publications:

By SKIDMORE: book—illustrations for *Tudor in Architecture* by Richard Chamberlain, New York 1929; article—"New York Proposes a World Capital for the United Nations" in *Architectural Forum* (New York), November 1946.

See SKIDMORE, OWINGS AND MERRILL

SKIDMORE, OWINGS AND MERRILL.
Partnership; established, Chicago, by Louis Skidmore, *q.v.*, and Nathaniel Owings, *q.v.*, as Skidmore and Owings, 1936, and, with John Merrill, *q.v.*, as Skidmore, Owings and Merrill, 1939; branch offices established in New York, 1937, subsequently in San Francisco, Portland, Oregon, and Washington, D.C. Current partners include: Charles Bassett; Gordon Bunshaft, *q.v.*, Myron Goldsmith, *q.v.*, Bruce J. Graham, *q.v.*, Fazlur Khan, *q.v.*, and Walter Netsch, *q.v.* Exhibition: *Skidmore, Owings and Merrill*, Museum of Modern Art, New York, 1950. Addresses: 30 West Monroe Street, Chicago, Illinois 60603; 400 Park Avenue, New York, New York 10022; 1 Maritime Plaza, San Francisco, California 94111, U.S.A.

Principal Works:

1942/
46   Atom City, Oak Ridge, Tennessee
       Recreation and Welfare Buildings, Great Lakes Training Center, Illinois
1949/
50   Lake Meadows (housing development), Chicago
       Terrace Plaza Hotel, Cincinnati
       Brooklyn Hospital, New York
1952   Lever House, Park Avenue, New York
       H. J. Heinz Company Vinegar Plant, Pittsburgh
1954   Manufacturers Hanover Trust, Fifth Avenue Branch, New York
       United States Consulate, Dusseldorf
1955   Hilton Hotel, Istanbul
1957   Connecticut General Life Insurance Company, Bloomfield, Connecticut
       United States Navy Service School, Great Lakes, Illinois
       Karl Taylor Compton Laboratories, Massachusetts Institute of Technology, Cambridge
1958   Reynolds Metals Company Building, Richmond, Virginia
       Inland Steel Company Headquarters, Dearborn and Monroe Streets, Chicago
1959   John Hancock Mutual Life Insurance Company Building, San Francisco
       Crown Zellerbach Corporate Headquarters, San Francisco
1960   PepsiCo Inc. World Headquarters, Park Avenue, New York

Skidmore, Owings and Merrill:
Lever House, New York, 1952

United Airlines Hangars and Flight Kitchen Complex, San Francisco
       Union Carbide Building, Park Avenue, New York
       Parke Davis and Company Offices and Research Laboratories, Kalamazoo, Michigan
1961   Chase Manhattan Bank, New York
       Upjohn Pharmaceuticals Company, Kalamazoo, Michigan
       First National City Bank, Houston
1962   United States Air Force Academy, Colorado Springs
       United Airlines Headquarters, Chicago
       Solar Telescope, Kitt Peak, Arizona
1963   Emhart Manufacturing Company Offices, Bloomfield, Connecticut
       Beinecke Rare Book and Manuscript Library, Yale University, New Haven, Connecticut
1964   Tennessee Gas Corporation Headquarters, Houston
1965   American Republic Insurance Company Building, Des Moines, Iowa
       Civic Center, Chicago
       Brunswick Building, Chicago
       Library/Museum and Vivian Beaumont Theatre, Lincoln Center, New York
       Mauna Kea Beach Hotel, Hawaii
       University of Illinois at Chicago Circle
       Banque Lambert Office and Bank Building, Brussels
       H. J. Heinz Company Ltd. Headquarters, Hayes Park, Middlesex, England
1966   Life Sciences Building, Illinois Institute of Technology, Chicago
1967   Marine Midland Building, 140 Broadway, New York
       Hartford Fire Insurance Company Building, San Francisco
1968   Oakland-Alameda County Coliseum, Oakland, California
       Alcoa Building, Golden Gate Center, San Francisco
       Bank of America Headquarters, San Francisco
       Boots Pure Drug Company Ltd. Headquarters, Nottingham, England
1970   John Hancock Center, Chicago
       International Bank for Reconstruction and Development, Washington, D.C.
1971   One Shell Plaza Office Building, Houston
       Lyndon Baines Johnson Library and Sid W. Richardson Hall, University of Texas at Austin
       Trans World Airlines Office Building, Kansas City
1973   W. R. Grace Building, 1114 Avenue of the Americas, New York
1974   First Wisconsin Center (bank/office building), Milwaukee
       Royal Gazette Newspaper Plant, Hamilton, Bermuda
       Sears Tower, Chicago (world's tallest building)
       Hirshhorn Museum and Sculpture Garden, Washington, D.C.
       W. D. and H. O. Wills Headquarters and Tobacco Processing Facility, Bristol, England
       Philip Morris Cigarette Manufacturing Plant, Richmond, Virginia
1975   Harris Trust and Savings Bank, Chicago
1975/
89   Jeddah International Airport, Saudi Arabia
1977   Apparel Mart and Holiday Inn, Wolf Point, Chicago
       Khaneh Center (multi-use complex), Tehran
1978   New World Center (multi-use complex), Hong Kong
       Hyatt International Hotel, Surabaya, Indonesia
       Europoint IV Office Building, Amsterdam
1979   National City Bank Building, Cleveland

1980   Arab International Bank (multi-use complex), Cairo
       International Museum of Photography, George Eastman House, Rochester, New York
1981   Hyatt International Hotel and Cultural Center, Kuwait City

Publications:

On SKIDMORE/OWINGS/MERRILL: books—*Skidmore, Owings and Merrill* by Mario José Buschiazzo, Buenos Aires 1958; *Skidmore, Owings and Merrill: Architects*, New York 1960; *The Architecture of Skidmore, Owings and Merrill 1950–1962* by Henry-Russell Hitchcock and Ernst Danz, New York and Stuttgart 1962, London 1963; *Skidmore, Owings and Merrill* by Christopher Woodward and Yukio Futagawa, Tokyo 1968, New York and London 1970; *The Architecture of Skidmore, Owings and Merrill 1963–73* by Arthur Drexler and A. Menges, Stuttgart and New York 1974.

When Louis Skidmore and Nathaniel Owings worked together on the Chicago *Century of Progress Exposition* in 1933, it became clear that they were a good team. They formed their partnership in Chicago in 1936, and Skidmore opened their New York office a year later. As they were aiming at large-scale commissions to be tackled by a group approach, it was inevitable that the office would become multidisciplinary, so, within a few years, John Merrill, an engineer, was made a partner. Whilst all the partners performed primarily organizational and client contact roles, Louis Skidmore was the most sensitive designer, John Merrill the practical engineer, and Nat Owings the organizer.

During its first decade the practice was more renowned for competent large scale work than for individual architectural achievement. In such an environment it is not easy to sort out where the individual talents lay, but the fact remains that the first design breakthrough for Skidmore, Owings and Merrill came from the New York office whilst it was in Louis Skidmore's care.

The founding partners of S.O.M. did not claim to be great architects, but they did claim to be able to "produce the people who produce the architecture." After the Second World War the New York office produced Gordon Bunshaft, and his Lever House of 1952 and his Manufacturers Hanover Trust Company of 1954 put S.O.M. at the forefront of the world architectural scene. Gordon Bunshaft is rightly credited with the design of these spare shiny buildings. Louis Skidmore retired just at the moment when his office was producing architecture of fame and quality. Gordon Bunshaft became famous, but it was Louis Skidmore who made it all possible.

John Merrill was involved with the laying of the foundations for the mighty architectural practice that S.O.M. was to become. His retirement in the 1950's meant that did not stay long to share the period of world-wide fame that the firm enjoyed in the decades following the completion of Lever House. Yet the legacy of the engineer amongst the founding partners is clear to see, for S.O.M. now numbers amongst its partners engineers of the stature of Fazlur Khan and Myron Goldsmith, and much of the firm's work concerns the relationship between architecture and structure.

Because he was younger than his two partners and because they retired early, Nathaniel Owings was the only one of the three founding partners to have been involved with the firm in its two halcyon decades following the completion of Lever House. Owings makes no claim to be a first-rate designer; he is the organizer, the impresario who recognizes and supports talent, who can get others to give of their best. The system at S.O.M. was for each project to have a partner in charge to deal with the client, a project manager to deal with the business side, and a designer to be cossetted and supported and encouraged to design the best possible building with the minimum of interference. Owings had observed how other firms had designers at a fairly low level in the hierarchy, and how these designers got frustrated as their seniors chopped and changed their work, so he saw to it that at S.O.M. talented designers were backed up and supported by others in the firm.

It was its organizational ability, not its design ability, that first brought fame to Skidmore, Owings and Merrill, and it is precisely in getting a large team of architects to work well together that Nathaniel Owings excelled. During the Second World War, when most American practices were severely reduced in size, S.O.M. was commissioned to design and build Oak Ridge, Tennessee, the city for the workers on the first A-bomb. S.O.M. required an office some 450 strong for this project, and this gave Owings the chance to exercise his talents and the firm the experience to tackle the big jobs, the organization clients, and the bureaucracy of the post-war decades.

Chicago played a big part in the origins of S.O.M., and Chicago had, at the turn of the century, a considerable skill at urban organization. S.O.M. revived this tradition and put its own organizational talents into action with vast urban redevelopment schemes such as Lake Meadows on Chicago's South Side, which started construction in 1950. Such developments, where the land is cleared and a series of towers erected, have since gone out of favour, but Lake Meadows remains one of the best in that genre.

Gordon Bunshaft put the firm on the architectural, as opposed to the organizational, map with Lever House in 1952. The shiny glamorous skin and the open space around this tower made it an instant success, and businessmen the world over wanted similar buildings to give them the image of sophistication and efficiency. The powerful combination of organizational and design skills put S.O.M. in a class of its own, and a long series of corporate headquarters of magnificence gave the firm a well-deserved place as world pace setter of this building type. As time went by, other talented designers within S.O.M. took its designs in different directions, and Bunshaft himself shifted his ground, so that by the mid-1960's, S.O.M. buildings ceased to be clearly recognizable from the products of other offices. But the concern for quality, for detail, and for intelligent building remained.

—John Winter

SLAATTO, Nils.

Norwegian. Born in Lillehammer, 22 June 1923. Educated at the Norges Tekniske Høyskole, Trondheim, Dip.Arch. 1947. Married Margit Bleken in 1949; children: Helge, Egill Eindride, Martin, and Brynhild. Division Architect, Vadsø-Tana, during the rebuilding of Finmark, 1948–50; worked in the Farmers Building Office, Oslo, 1950–58. In partnership with Kjell Lund, q.v., Oslo, since 1958. Vice-President, Federation of Norwegian Architects, 1969–71. Exhibitions: *Works of Lund and Slaatto*, Det Kongelige Danske Kunstakademie, Copenhagen, and Det Finske Arkitekturmuseum, Helsinki, 1975, toured universities and architecture schools in Europe and England, 1975–78. Recipient: First Prize, Akerhaus County Agricultural School Competition, Årnes, Norway, 1958; The Concrete Award, Federation of Norwegian Architects/-Norwegian Concrete Association, 1964, 1977; The Wood Prize, Norwegian Concrete Association/-Council for Tree Information, 1966; Sundt's Award, 1972, and Houen's Award, 1976, Federation of Norwegian Architects; First Prize, Norwegian Civil Engineers Main Office Building Competition, Oslo, 1970; First Prize, Eidsvåg Church Competition, Bergen, 1970; First Prize, National Gallery Extension Competition, Oslo, 1972; First Prize, National Theatre Extension Competition, Oslo, 1973; First

Prize, Bank of Norway Competition, Oslo, 1973. Address: Kjell Lund og Nils Slaatto, Arkitekter, Bygdøy Allé 13, Oslo 2, Norway.

See LUND, Kjell

SMITH, Ivor (Stanley).

British. Born in Leigh-on-Sea, Essex, 27 January 1926. Educated at the School of Art, Southend-on-Sea, Essex, 1941–42; Bartlett School of Architecture, University College, University of London, 1943–45; Cambridge University School of Architecture, 1948–50, M.A. 1950; Architectural Association School, London, 1950–52, Dip.A.A. 1952. Married Audrey Laurence in 1947; has 4 children. Senior Architect, City Architect's Department, Sheffield, Yorkshire, 1952–61. Partner, Lupton and Smith, Oxford, 1962–66, subsequently Ivor Smith and Cailey Hutton, Oxford and Bristol, since 1966. Visiting Teacher, Cambridge University School of Architecture, 1963–69; Professor of Architecture, and Director, University College School of Architecture, Dublin, 1969–73. Since 1975, Professor of Architecture, and Head, University of Bristol School of Architecture. Recipient: Bronze Medal, Royal Institute of British Architects, 1961; Civic Trust Award, 1967, 1969; Ministry of Housing and Local Government Medal, 1969; Department of the Environment Award, 1970, and Design Medal, 1975. LL.D.: National University of Ireland, Dublin, 1974. Associate, Royal Institute of British Architects. Address: Ivor Smith and Cailey Hutton Architects, 19 Charlotte Street, Bristol 1, England.

Works:

1961 Park Hill Neighbourhood Development, Sheffield
1966 Housing, Heston Grange, Middlesex
1967 2 houses and studio, Ewelme, Oxford
1969 Old people's and family housing, Dibleys, Blewbury, Berkshire
1970 Suburban housing, Rushey Mead, Leicester
1971 King Street redevelopment, stage I, Cambridge
1974 Magdalen College School master plan, stage I, Oxford
 Magdalen College feasibility studies for student residences, Oxford
1977 King Street redevelopment, stage II, Cambridge
 Greenleys Activity Centre, Milton Keynes, Buckinghamshire
 SSM Priory, Willen, Buckinghamshire
 Somerville College alterations and additions, Oxford
1979 Old people's housing, St. Peter's Vicarage, Poole, Dorset
1981 Housing (500 dwellings), Exwick Farm, Exeter, Devon

Publications:

By SMITH: articles—"Louisiana, Museum of Modern Art" in *RIBA Journal* (London), April 1965; "Architect's Approach to Architecture" in *RIBA Journal* (London), July 1967; "Architecture—A Celebration" in *New Universities Quarterly* (Bristol), Autumn 1976.

On SMITH: articles—"Sectional Interests" in *Building* (London), February 1974; article in *The Architects' Journal* (London), December 1974; "Dialogue Indoors" in *Architectural Review* (London), November 1975; article by Robert Langton in *The Architects' Journal* (London), October 1976; article in *Baumeister* (Munich), December 1977.

The practice of Ivor Smith and Cailey Hutton has always had a particular interest in the way cities, towns and villages develop. This has had an influence on the sort of work taken on, which has tended to be especially concerned with the way buildings relate to and modify their context. The office has tried to develop a better understanding of housing, community building and urban design as well as the implications of making buildings in certain ways.

To many people, both laymen and professionals, the present situation in architecture appears confused. Yet there is a growing amount of work being done which has as its basis a rational approach, an endeavour to see whole issues, and an understanding of the way things relate. At the same time, this recognizes the need for acknowledging in a very human way the complexities of living. It includes an awakened interest into what gives architecture meaning—the way everything is affected by and yet modifies its context, whether at the scale of a building within the urban fabric or at the scale of detail within a building.

Some aspects of our work can be easily defined and measured, but many aspects are indeterminate. Even though these involve value judgements, they can nevertheless be studied in as rigorous a way as the more easily measurable issues. From this can be built up a body of understanding which can be called "theory," substantial enough to support decisions and quite apart from matters of taste.

—Ivor Smith

Underlying Ivor Smith's work is a reasoned approach to architecture, seen as a complex series of inter-relationships between people and their surroundings. He regards as too simple the tendency to concentrate on particular aspects as conveyed by such puritanical slogans as "Form follows Function" or "Honesty of Structure" or the notion that architecture is an expression of the architect's personality. For Ivor Smith the architect's role is to provide a background to human activity. Human living is what matters, and the architect's job is to provide a background full of meaning and significance in relation to its context.

Ivor Smith's developing architectural theory has emerged as a synthesis of his accumulated experience. The underlying assumption is that there are a number of universal principles or standards related to problems generated by our times that can be identified and understood. They exist as a complex series of inter-relationships that always occur, at every scale, whatever technology is used. They are generating factors in design work, supplying reason and motivation to support the decisions and choices made; everything else is of less importance. When all these relationships and interactions are considered in a rational way, the number of options left that must be determined by personal opinion, preference or taste is drastically reduced and no longer a cause of conflict; instead, they can serve to give the necessary richness and diversity or character to places.

Among the basic generators of design, Ivor Smith distinguishes the following relationships: the work to *context* (landscape, urban fabric, land use); to *routes* (external, internal); to *environment* (climate, heat, light, sound); to *groupings* (individuals, groups, crowds); and to *interface* (outside/inside, public/-private). These relationships are brought together in a complex "fit."

By concentrating on these primary relationships, the designer is more likely to get the large elements right. The finer details relating to the functional activity are then more likely to be right and to occupy their proper role. Smith refers often to historical analogy or precedent, which for him provides a way of transferring ideas from similar situations, relates to common experience that can be shared, communicated and discussed, evokes broader issues, and opens up opportunities. This concern is "not with the images of the past but with the underlying order; not with appearances but with the innate structure and the relationships from which it has sprung."

Ivor Smith: King Street redevelopment, stage I, Cambridge, 1971

One aspect of *context* that he sees as important is a respect for the "grain" of the map—the pattern and intensity of black on white. The "grain" is caused by a variety of factors—routes, uses, life styles—that have established themselves in balance over the years. If architects ignore the grain, they are likely to upset this balance and damage the city system and cause it to lose its coherence.

The relationship of build form to *routes* is a generative factor determining the pattern of settlements as well as buildings. Routes provide a "coding" system, a comprehensive large-scale frame within which small scale diversity can occur without chaos. "They can provide the public order that allows for private freedom, informal social contacts or public celebrations." Relationship to *environment* means the way in which buildings are used to moderate climate, light, heat and sound. They should be planned to

require the minimum correction to their internal environment and minimum artificial heating, lighting and ventilation—and to consume the minimum amount of energy.

By *groupings,* the vast numbers of people involved in almost any activity, Smith conveys his concern with ways of breaking down these numbers "in order to make the world a more humane and hospitable place." However, he criticizes the concept of dividing settlements into neighbourhood units, clustered around a primary school and other communal facilities, arguing that that kind of imposition does not allow people the necessary freedom to choose contacts and patterns of living. But he also criticizes the concept of open plan offices, without corridors and with maximum contact between great numbers of workers, for imposing too much freedom, which may have a paralysing effect. "The problem of large

numbers applies elsewhere. It is not just that 'small is beautiful'—which has the ring of putting the clocks back—but that small when it is identifiable in relation to the large is meaningful."

Such architectural factors as the need to mark the entrance, or the different treatment of outside and inside, are referred to by Smith as *interface* relationships. Interface is about edges, where the internal demands of the street are simultaneously ordered. This implies reconciliation, and it is in this reconciliation that the architect exploits his skill.

The inter-relationship between all these factors is very complex: they do not always fit. But Ivor Smith does not look for an exact fit, for something that is neat and tidy. He argues that the people for whom he designs do not operate precisely, they change their minds and do unpredictable things; he is, therefore, looking for something looser, not too specific,

Whitney R. Smith: Neighborhood Church, Pasadena, California, 1972

even ambiguous, that will allow for a range of opportunities and choices, so that people can live in the way they want.

—Teresa Czaplinska-Archer

SMITH, Whitney R(owland).

American. Born in Pasadena, California, 16 January 1911. Educated at the University of Southern California, Los Angeles, 1929–34, B.Arch. 1934. Married Virginia Hill in 1936; children: Annabel and Gregory. Worked in various architects' offices, and in private practice, Pasadena, 1941–46; Partner, with Wayne R. Williams, Smith and Williams, Pasadena, 1946–73. In private practice, Pasadena, since 1973. Instructor in Advanced Planning and Architecture, University of Southern California, Los Angeles, 1941; Instructor in Architecture and Planning, Scripps College, Pomona, California, 1945–52. Member, Planning Commission of South Pasadena, 1953, and Community Redevelopment Agency of South Pasadena, 1954–62. Recipient: Honor Award, 1946 (twice), 1951 (three times), 1954, 1957 (twice), and Merit Award, 1957 (twice), American Institute of Architects, Southern California Chapter; Honor Award, 1950, 1957, Merit Award, 1957, 1959, and Award of Excellence, 1959, AIA, Pasadena Chapter; Merit Award, national AIA, 1952, 1954 (twice),

1958; First Award, Community Arts Association, Santa Barbara, California, 1954; Merit Award, *House and Home/Sunset Magazine/*AIA, 1956 (twice); Merit Award, *House and Home,* 1956; Merit Award, National Association of Home Builders, 1957; First Award, *American Home,* 1957; Merit Award, 1957, 1961, and Honor Award, 1961, *Sunset Magazine/*AIA; Los Angeles Beautiful Award, 1958; Merit Award, Church Architectural Guild, 1959; Merit Award, AIA: Homes for Better Living, 1962. Fellow, American Institute of Architects, 1957. Address (office): 1517 Fair Oaks Avenue, South Pasadena, California 91030, U.S.A.

Works:

1937 Milton R. Jones House and Office, Claremont, California
1938 George L. Coates House, 232 N. Oliveras, Altadena, California
1942 Bradley House, Pasadena, California
    MacLean House, Pasadena, California
1943 Linda Vista Shopping Center, San Diego
1947/
 50 Mutual Housing Association Community Development, Hanley Avenue at Rochedale, Los Angeles (with A. Quincy Jones and Edgardo Contini)
1948 Williams House, 4211 Glenwood, Mount Washington, Los Angeles
    Johnson Motors Showroom and Shops, Pasadena, California

1949 Whitney R. Smith House, Pasadena, California
    Griffith Park Girls' Camp, Griffith Park Boulevard, East Hollywood, Los Angeles
    Sale House, 1455 Oriole Drive, Beverly Hills, California
1950 Clarke House, 1557 Oriole Lane, Beverly Hills, California
1951 Dean's Residence, Occidental College, Los Angeles
    Nursery School, All Saints Episcopal Church, Pasadena, California
1952 Blaisdell Medical Building, 547 East Union, Pasadena, California
    Crowell House, 949 South San Rafael, Pasadena, California
1953 Fisher-Hauch Clinic, Pomona, California
1954 Blue Ribbon Tract Housing, Northridge, California
    Manning Medical Building, Pasadena, California
    Children's Chapel, Neighborhood Church, Pasadena, California
1956 Thorpe Insulation Plant, Los Angeles
    Grandview Construction Company Office Building, Gardena, California
    Millikan Religious Education Building, Neighborhood Church, Pasadena, California
1957 Smith and Williams Architectural Office, Pasadena, California
    Mobil Service Station, Anaheim, California

Mobil Service Station, La Mirada, California
Royce Children's Clinic, Pasadena, California
College Car Wash, Pasadena, California
1958 Van Vechten Laundry, Pasadena, California
Office building, 1414 Fair Oaks, South Pasadena, California
1959 Swimming Facilities, Scripps College, Pomona, California
International Chemical Workers Local 146, Lompoc, California
Seabyrd Restaurant, Newport Beach, California
Oscar's Restaurant Chain, Southern California and Arizona
Civic Center, Buena Park, California
Westcott Building, Los Angeles
Port Holiday Recreation Community, Lake Meade, Nevada
1960 Community development, California City
1961 Mission Bay Water Recreation Development, San Diego (as consultant)
McCarthy Office Building, Pasadena, California
St. Paul's Lutheran Church, Monrovia, California
1964 Recreation Center, University of California at Los Angeles
1965 W. H. Friend Offices and Warehouse, 100 West Green at DeLacey, Pasadena, California
1967 Residence Halls, California Polytechnic State University, Pomona
Central Power Plant, California Institute of Technology, Pasadena
1972 Neighborhood Church, 1 Westmoreland Place, Pasadena, California
Ikebana House Flower Arranging Studio, San Marino, California
1973 Vedanta Society Convent, Hollywood, California
1977 Science and Art Buildings, Westridge School for Girls, Pasadena, California
1979 Gymnasium, Westridge School for Girls, Pasadena, California
Henry E. Huntington Memorial Library addition, San Marino, California (project)

Publications:

By SMITH: books—*The Architect Looks at Housing the Aging,* editor, Los Angeles 1958; *Planning of Homes for the Aged,* with others, Chicago 1959.

On SMITH: book—*Standards for Regional Recreation* by Wayne R. Williams and others, Washington, D.C. 1958; articles—"Planning for Specialists" in *Los Angeles County Medical Bulletin,* October 1956; "Buildings by Smith and Williams" in *Architectural Review* (London), May 1957.

Southern California from 1941 to the present has been a good place for an architect to work. First, there have been interesting clients in a wide variety of fields, and, second, there have been many vital and qualified consultants and collaborators with whom to work.

I have had the good fortune to practice as an architectural partner with Wayne R. Williams over a period of 27 years. Together we designed nearly every classification of architectural work from a garden tea house to a complete city. We expanded our architectural team as required: corporate members included Robert P. Meyerhof, Philip C. Patterson, R. Stuart Denker and others. A permanent collaboration was formed with Simon Eisner (city planner) and Garrett Eckbo (the landscape architect), and was called Community Facilities Planners (C.F.P.). C.F.P. developed plans for more than 40 major projects.

Other ad hoc team members have included Victor Gruen and Associates; Kariotis and Kesler; Selje,

Bond and Stewart; Edgardo Contini; A. Quincy Jones; Joseph Amestoy; and many others.

I have acted as developer for four office buildings. I believe that all architects can improve their understanding and experience by developing some projects for themselves.

I have taught "architectural appreciation" courses, and I strongly believe that any major improvement in architectural design will come from emphasizing the education of the general public rather than the practicing architect.

For the past six years I have been in private practice as an individual. I contract for all supporting design and engineering services and retain on an ad hoc basis some 40 consultants for this purpose. These consultants are highly qualified persons, many of whom I have worked with for many years, and they make possible what I consider to be a highly efficient and creative team.

—Whitney R. Smith

Whitney R. Smith worked for a short time in the office of Harwell Hamilton Harris, and he considers Harris to have been a great influence on his work; he also acknowledges his debt to Kem Weber and Charles and Henry Greene.

During World War II Smith designed the Linda Vista Shopping Center at San Diego, notable because it was one of the first such projects to be built around a central green ("Grass Grows on Main Street"), with parking on the perimeter behind the buildings. After the war, during a short partnership with Quincy Jones and Edgardo Contini, he was instrumental in designing two important projects in the Los Angeles area—the "goodsie-woodsie" Mutual Housing Association Community in upper Brentwood and the Griffith Park Girls' Camp, a wood, post-and-beam structure which is more of an open shelter than a building.

During his long partnership with Wayne R. Williams, he had many commissions for commercial buildings, schools, churches, etc., but his greatest contribution was in domestic architecture, much of it in Pasadena. His partner liked verticals. Smith—reflecting perhaps his debt to the Greene Brothers—worked with horizontals. He customarily used panel-post construction with 4′ × 8′ infills, usually of plywood and glass. Smith coped with Pasadena's hot summer climate by using materials such as adobe brick and by opening interior spaces to the prevailing breezes through sliding glass doors. Often the entrance to his houses was through a lath greenhouse with planting by Garrett Eckbo visible from all parts of the living space. This lath house treatment was also a characteristic of some of his larger designs, such as the office building at 1414 Fair Oaks in South Pasadena.

Since most of his houses were built on sub-divisions of old estates, they were from the first usually surrounded by large trees which formed a theatrical setting for the precise modular buildings.

In the 1970's Smith has usually designed in what might be called a neo-Shingle style, the new buildings at Westridge School in Pasadena being cases in point. His project in 1979 for a major addition to the Henry E. Huntington Memorial Library in San Marino is appropriately Beaux Arts in inspiration.

—Robert Winter

SMITHSON, Alison.

British. Born Alison Margaret Gill in Sheffield, 22 June 1928. Educated at Sunderland Church High School, County Durham; George Watson's Ladies College, Edinburgh; South Shields High School for Girls, County Durham; School of Architecture, University of Durham; influenced by the work of Le Corbusier. Married Peter Smithson, *q.v.,* in 1949;

children: Simon, Samantha, and Soraya. Temporary Technical Assistant, London County Council Architects Department, London 1949–50. In partnership with Peter Smithson, London, since 1950. Associated with the Independent Group and with Team 10. Exhibitions: *Parallel of Life and Art,* Institute of Contemporary Arts, London, 1953; *Architecture and Technology,* London, 1961; *Triennale,* Milan, 1968; *Line of Trees . . . A Steel Frame,* Art Net, London, 1975, and Arts Council Fruit Market Gallery, Edinburgh, 1976; *Sticks and Stones,* at the *Biennale,* Venice, 1976. Collections: Victoria and Albert Museum, London; Royal Institute of British Architects Drawings Collection, London. Address: Alison and Peter Smithson, Architects, Cato Lodge, 24 Gilston Road, London SW10 9SR, England.

Works (with Peter Smithson):

1954 Hunstanton Secondary Modern School, Norfolk
1956 Sanders Garage, Bark Place, London
The House of the Future, *Ideal Home Exhibition,* Olympia, London
Patio and Pavilion, *This Is Tomorrow* exhibition, Whitechapel Gallery, London
1957 Watford House, Devereux Drive, Watford, Hertfordshire
1960 Caro House, Frognal, Hampstead, London
Wayland Young Pavilion, 100 Bayswater Road, London
1961 Iraqi House, Piccadilly, London
1962 Fonthill Folly, Upper Lawn, West Tisbury, Wiltshire
1963 Occupational Health Unit, Park Royal Hospital, London
1964 The Economist Building, St. James's Street, London
1970 Road, etc., in Street, Somerset
Garden Building, St. Hilda's College, Oxford
1972 Robin Hood Gardens (housing), Robin Hood Lane, London E.14
Ansty Plum Studio, Garage and Store, Wiltshire

Publications:

By Alison SMITHSON: books—*Uppercase,* with Peter Smithson, London 1960, revised edition as *Urban Structuring,* London and New York 1967; *Team 10 Primer,* editor, London 1965, Cambridge, Massachusetts 1968; *Portrait of the Female Mind as a Young Girl,* novel, London 1966; *The Euston Arch,* with Peter Smithson, 1968; contribution to *The Evacuees,* edited by B. S. Johnson, London 1968; *Ordinariness and Light: Urban Theories '52–'60 and Their Application in a Building Project '63–'70,* with Peter Smithson, London 1970; *Without Rhetoric: An Architectural Aesthetic 1955–1972,* with Peter Smithson, London and Cambridge, Massachusetts 1973; articles—numerous articles since 1952, including, most recently: "Florence: Arno Approach," with Peter Smithson, in *Architectural Design* (London), September 1972; "Ruminations on Founders Court" in *Architectural Design* (London), August 1973; "Collage of Photographs" in *Architectural Design* (London), November 1973; "Travel Notes" in *Feedback* (London), December 1973; "Collective Design: The Violent Consumer; or, Waiting for the Goodies" in *Architectural Design* (London), May 1974; "Collective Design: Reappraisal of Concepts in Urbanism" in *Architectural Design* (London), July 1974; "How to Read and Recognize Mat-Building" in *Architectural Design* (London), September 1974; "Collective Design: Collective Quality" in *Architectural Design* (London), November 1974; "Collective Design: The Good-Tempered Gas Man" in *Architectural Design* (London), March 1975; "Team 10 at Royaumont, 1962" in *Architectural Design* (London), November 1975; "The Tram Rats: A Story for Adults and Children" in *Art Net* (London), July 1976; statement on The Tram Rats, with Peter Smithson, in *Net 3* (London), July 1976; "Alvar

Aalto," with Peter Smithson, in *Ark: Arkkitehti* (Helsinki), August 1976; "In Pursuit of Lyrical Appropriateness" in *Spazio e Società* (Florence), Autumn 1976; "Kreutzburg Study: Berlin 1975" in *Lotus* (Venice), December 1976; "Four Visits: Arme de Salut: 1948, '54, '59, '76," with Peter Smithson, in *Bauwelt* (Berlin), January 1977; "Adamsez Sanitary Fittings" in *Design Magazine* (London), June 1977.

On the SMITHSONS: articles—"Beyond Garden Lane" by Anthony Pangaro in *Architecture Plus* (New York), June 1973; "Robin Hood Gardens" in *Architecture + Urbanism* (Tokyo), February 1974; "Alison and Peter Smithson: Gentle Cultural Accommodation" in *L'Architecture d'Aujourd'hui* (Paris), January/February 1975; "The Smithsons: A Profile" by John Maule McKean in *Building Design* (London), May 1977.

Bibliography: *Bibliography of the Works of Alison and Peter Smithson* by the Smithsons, London 1975.

My current concern is with the quality of place. Related to the built environment, quality is not only visual; it concerns a satisfactory life in various kinds of place . . . supportive places that give out energy . . . the revitalization of existing groups of buildings by new buildings . . . the pleasure of use of the environment transmitted through the other four senses: touch, smell, feel, sound. The term Quality of Place can be further rounded out to include such aspects of experience as the sense of reassurance which certain densities convey . . . the time-ordering of a city by the ebb and flow of under or over use of such a place as the market . . . the quality of placement of new buildings so that they renew each town's own identity . . . that reconnective quality that dovetails each building into place . . . the rightness of choice of site for the patterns of movement a development will attract . . . the voice in terms of the bulk of a new building and whether this speaks truly of the contribution the activity in the building will make to the quality of life in the town . . . whether the rightness of placement reflects a sense of social order. In this rounded-out definition, quality of place seems to have two natures: the tangible, or built-form; and the intangible, or social-form. The tangible qualities are man-made; ordered, articulate, classifiable, physical, often very obvious forms. The intangible qualities are those of human connection; attitude, and accepted, therefore difficult to observe, patterns of use. The tangible quality of place has to do with the acts of form-giving. Intangible quality of place has to do with those acts by which the community clothes the built fabric with further levels of meaning . . . the stuff and decoration of the urban scene . . . the feeling of knowing how to use spaces responsibly.

My act of form giving has to invite the occupiers to add their intangible quality of use.

—Alison Smithson

Alison Smithson's contribution to the highly-successful partnership with her husband Peter is less noticeable than one might expect as The Smithsons admit to no division of labour and consequently speak with one voice. This has been the accepted pattern since their marriage in 1949 when they began work on the Hunstanton School. Credit and comment are equally shared, and the solidarity against criticism is total. When asked to contribute personally to the "Women in Architecture" edition of *Architectural Design* in August 1975, Alison Smithson began her statement with the usual "We."

Like her husband she finds the constant need to express herself in words, and it is perhaps here, in the many contributions to the influential architectural press, that we see her at her most personal. A short piece in *The Evacuees* tells of the early years, and in her novel *Portrait of the Female Mind as a Young Girl* there are clear insights into the sources of much

of her architectural philosophy. Her commitment to Team 10 is well illustrated by the care and consideration she took in editing the *Team 10 Primer*—a vital document for those concerned with the evolution of the Modern Movement.

In the early days of the meetings of the Independent Group her concern with the difficulties of everyday living and intuitive understanding of the social implications of working-class street "culture" played an important part in the thinking around the 1952 Golden Lane Project and consequently in the ideas behind the recent scheme for Robin Hood Gardens.

The affection she retains for the days at the Institute of Contemporary Arts and the real influence they had on English "Pop" Art is genuine, and her many broadsides fired at Banham offer some of the more stimulating comments on what she sees as the inadequacies of the architectural establishment. Often aggressive in her tone of voice, she is ever concerned with the idea of identity and meaning of the most mundane day-to-day existence, and her contribution to the most important husband and wife team of recent times cannot be doubted.

—John Furse

SMITHSON, Peter (Denham).

British. Born in Stockton-on-Tees, County Durham, 18 September 1923. Educated at Stockton-on-Tees Grammar School; School of Architecture, University of Durham; Royal Academy Schools, London; influenced by the work of Le Corbusier and Mies van der Rohe. Served as a Lieutenant in the British Army, Queen Victoria's Own Madras Sappers and Miners, in India and Burma, 1942–45. Married Alison Margaret Gill (i.e., Alison Smithson, *q.v.*) in 1949; children: Simon, Samantha, and Soraya. Temporary Technical Assistant, London County Council Architects Department, 1949–50. In partnership with Alison Smithson, London, since 1950. Associated with the Independent Group and with Team 10. Exhibitions: *Parallel of Life and Art,* Institute of Contemporary Arts, London, 1953; *Architecture and Technology,* London, 1961; *Triennale,* Milan, 1968; *Line of Trees . . . A Steel Frame,* Art Net, London, 1975, and Arts Council Fruit Market Gallery, Edinburgh, 1976; *Sticks and Stones, Biennale,* Venice 1976. Collections: Victoria and Albert Museum, London; Royal Institute of British Architects Drawings Collection, London. Address: Alison and Peter Smithson, Architects, Cato Lodge, 24 Gilston Road, London SW10 9SR, England.

Publications:

By Peter SMITHSON: books—*Uppercase,* with Alison Smithson, London 1960, revised edition as *Urban Structuring,* London and New York 1967; *The Euston Arch,* with Alison Smithson, London 1968; *Ordinariness and Light: Urban Theories '52–'60 and Their Application in a Building Project '63–'70,* with Alison Smithson, London 1970; *Bath: Walks Within the Walls,* London 1971; *Without Rhetoric: An Architectural Aesthetic 1955–1972,* with Alison Smithson, London and Cambridge, Massachusetts 1973; articles—numerous articles since 1952, including, most recently: "Simple Thoughts on Repetition" in *Architectural Design* (London), August 1971; "Toulouse-le-Mirail: Reactions" in *Architectural Design* (London), October 1971; "Signs of Occupancy" in *Architectural Design* (London), February 1972; "Vehicles, Mechanisms, Services: Another Ordering" in *Architectural Design* (London), June 1972; "Florence: Arno Approach," with Alison Smithson, in *Architectural Design* (London), September 1972; "Collective Design: Initiators and Successors" in *Architectural Design* (London), October 1973; "Shadrach Woods" in *Architectural*

Design (London), November 1973; "Interactions and Transformations: Urban Structure and Urban Form" in *Architectural Design* (London), January 1974; "To Embrace the Machine" in *Architectural Design* (London), April 1974; "The Free University and the Language of Modern Architecture" in *Domus* (Milan), May 1974; "Collective Design: Lightness of Touch" in *Architectural Design* (London), June 1974; "Thorpe Thewles Viaduct" in *Architectural Design* (London), July 1974; "Collective Design: Making the Connections" in *Architectural Design* (London), May 1975; "Affirmation: Church at The Hague, Aldo van Eyck architect" in *Architectural Design* (London), June 1975; "Thinking of Louis Kahn" in *Architecture + Urbanism* (Tokyo), September 1975; "The Space Between" in *Oppositions* (New York), October 1975; "Louis Kahn's Centre for British Art, Yale" in *RIBA Journal* (London), April 1976; "Ronald Jenkins: Oration" in *Arup Journal* (London), April 1976; "Oxford and Cambridge Walks" in *Architectural Design* (London), June 1976; statement on The Tram Rats, with Alison Smithson, in *Net 3* (London), July 1976; "Alvar Aalto," with Alison Smithson, in *Ark: Arkkitehti* (Helsinki), August 1976; "Four Visits: Arme de Salut: 1948, '54, '59, '76," with Alison Smithson, in *Bauwelt* (Berlin), January 1977; "Apropos Terni + Words on Centre Pompidou" in *L'Architecture d'Aujourd'hui* (Paris), February 1977; "Making Another Connection" in *Arkitekten* (Copenhagen), June 1977.

As I find I can only read the theoretical writings of those architects whose work I have already fallen in love with, this has led my life into the channel cut in this century by Le Corbusier, Mies van der Rohe, and Walter Gropius. Action first, writing later. With a strong sense of obligation to the continuity of architecture itself. Of English theoretical writing only Uvedale Price remains in my mind, ill-rememberedly important. And Ruskin, in snatches. But always the thing itself catches me first . . . the English landscape garden, Florence, and Venice. It was Palladio who took me to Wittkower.

It is architecture on the ground, buildings being built, that I enjoy; like Maigret I feel suffocated by theory without the intention of action and not arising from it. My own work and theoretical writing is somehow always the same . . . deeper into the same things. But it is for others to talk about that.

—Peter Smithson

In equal partnership with his wife Alison, Peter Smithson is responsible for three of the most important buildings built in England since the Second World War. The legendary secondary school at Hunstanton, Norfolk, designed in 1949, started in 1952 and finished in 1954, is the true foundation of The Smithsons' youthful international reputation. The Economist Building in St. James's Street, London, completed in 1964, is one of the most sophisticated complexes in 20th century architecture, and the most recent major work, the housing at Robin Hood Gardens, also in London and completed in 1972, is a concrete attempt at solving the ever-present problem of mass-housing.

Labelled "New Brutalist" by Banham, the influences are clear. "Mies is great but Corb communicates" is the familiar admission, and this subtle combination of formal articulate styling tempered by an essentially human understanding of the day-to-day working pattern of ordinary people is the basis of the method.

The Hunstanton School is essentially Miesian in concept: wherever you stand you see exactly how the building is made and with what materials. There is no ambiguity.

The Economist Building is conceived as an articulate series of functional movements involving not only those who work there and those who play in the select confines of the adjacent Boodles, but also the man in the street, the pedestrian who cuts through the piazza to avoid the traffic chaos in nearby Piccadilly.

Robin Hood Gardens, in London's East End, is an attempt to put into built fact the ideas on mass-housing—working-class housing, that is—first suggested in the Golden Lane Project of 1952 with its Le Corbusier-inspired "street-decks" and the thinking based on the fascination for "street culture" that so obsessed those connected with the *This Is Tomorrow* exhibition held at the Whitechapel Gallery in 1956. Much of Peter Smithson's early ideas can be seen in relation to the Independent Group meetings held at the Institute of Contemporary Arts, London, in the mid 1950's and his reaction to the sudden influx of imagery from across the Atlantic. His later visits to America and to Japan are of prime importance.

Unquestionably the most articulate of recent architectural polemicists, he has made an important contribution to the academic side of the profession; words have been as important to him as the buildings. The Smithsons have, in fact, written much and built comparatively little. The continually provocative writing—especially in the early days of *Architectural Design*—has had a telling effect on those to whom The Smithsons embody the continuation of the progressive ideas of the Modern Movement. This reputation has been enhanced by their regular involvement with other leading young architects in the highly influential and truly international Team 10. The importance of this "loose association of friends"

to the Modern Movement, since its formation at Dubrovnik in 1956, is well illustrated in the *Team 10 Primer*—edited by Alison Smithson.

Recently, in a short piece written for the Jubilee Edition of the *Architectural Review*, Peter Smithson has drawn attention to the change that has taken place in the neighbourhoods that he has come to know well over the last twenty-five years and states that a new "form" is needed to ensure that the reality of these neighbourhoods is retained. It is true to say that, twenty-five years after Hunstanton, those concerned with what must be done are waiting to hear what "form" he has in mind.

—John Furse

See SMITHSON, Alison

SOLERI, Paolo.

American. Born in Turin, Italy, 21 June 1919; emigrated to the United States, 1955. Educated at the Turin Polytechnic, 1941–46, D.Arch. (honors) 1946; Fellow, Frank Lloyd Wright Foundation, Taliesin West, Scottsdale, Arizona, 1947–48. Married Carolyn Woods in 1949; children: Kristine and Daniela. In private practice, Turin, and Southern Italy, 1950–55. Since 1956, President, the Cosanti Foundation, Scottsdale. Distinguished Visiting Lecturer, Arizona State University, Tempe. Exhibitions: *Visionary Ar-*

chitecture, Museum of Modern Art, New York, 1961; *Two Urbanists: The Architecture of Buckminster Fuller and Paolo Soleri*, Brandeis University, Waltham, Massachusetts, 1964; *The Architectural Vision of Paolo Soleri*, Corcoran Gallery, Washington, D.C., 1970, toured New York, Chicago, Ottawa, Berkeley, California, and Phoenix, Arizona; *2 Suns Arcology: The City Energized by the Sun*, Xerox Center, Rochester, New York, 1976. Collection: Soleri Archives, Howe Architecture Library, Arizona State University, Tempe. Recipient: Graham Foundation Fellowship, 1962; Guggenheim grant, 1964, 1967. Honorary doctorates: Dickinson College, Carlisle, Pennsylvania; Moore College of Art, Philadelphia; Arizona State University. Address: The Cosanti Foundation, 6433 Doubletree Road, Scottsdale, Arizona 85253, U.S.A.

Works:

1948 Bridge (project)
1949 The Dome House, Cave Creek, Arizona (with Mark Mills)
1953 Artistica Ceramica Solimene Ceramics Factory, Vietri-sul-Mare, near Palermo
1956 Earth House, Scottsdale, Arizona
1956/
  76 The Cosanti Foundation, Scottsdale, Arizona
1958/
  61 Mesa City (project)
1966 Outdoor Theatre, Institute of American Indian Arts, Santa Fe, New Mexico

Paolo Soleri: Arcosanti, near Cordes Junction, Arizona, 1970

1970– Arcosanti (community for 5,000 people), near Cordes Junction, Arizona

Publications:

By SOLERI: books—*Arcology: The City in the Image of Man,* Cambridge, Massachusetts 1970; *The Sketchbooks of Paolo Soleri,* Cambridge, Massachusetts 1971; *The Bridge Between Matter and Spirit Is Matter Becoming Spirit,* New York 1973; article—"Two Suns Arcology" in *Architecture Association Quarterly* (London), vol. 7, no. 2, 1976.

On SOLERI: book—*The Architecture of Bridges,* New York 1948; articles—"Paolo Soleri" by Jeffrey Cook in *Architectural Association Quarterly* (London), April 1969; "Quella che Soleri Chiama Arcologia" in *Domus* (Milan), May 1969; "Prophet in the Desert" by Ada Louise Huxtable in the *New York Times,* 15 March 1970; "Arcology of Paolo Soleri" by Sybil Maholy-Nagy in *Architectural Forum* (New York), May 1970; "Paolo Soleri Thinks Very Big" by Sherwood Davidson Kohn in the *New York Times Magazine,* 28 July 1970; "The Architectural Vision of Paolo Soleri" in *L'Architecture d'Aujourd'hui* (Paris), October 1970; "Paolo Soleri: The Philosophy of Urban Life" by Henryk Skolimowski in *Architectural Association Quarterly* (London), Winter 1971; "Soleri: 'Plumber with a Mind of St. Augustine'" by E. Higbee in *AIA Journal* (Washington, D.C.), February 1971; "Soleri's Arcology: A New Design for the City" by S. Kostof in *Art in America* (New York), March 1971; "The Individual as Institution" by W. I. Thompson in *Harper's* (New York), September 1972; "Job Site for Utopia" by J. M. Dixon in *Progressive Architecture* (New York), April 1973; "Arcosanti: Pueblo and Acropolis" by Chuck Simmons in *Mountain Gazette* (Denver), October 1973; "Paolo Soleri: A Flight from Flatness" by John Elkington in *Architectural Association Quarterly* (London), vol. 6, no. 1, 1974; "Arcosanti: Dream City" by Douglas Davis in *Newsweek* (New York), 16 August 1976.

The Cosanti Foundation is a not-for-profit organization pursuing the research and development of an alternative urban environment. Given that the ecological, logistic, economic, cultural and energy problems of present cities are closely interwoven, it is the Foundation's understanding that long-term solutions must be sought within a comprehensive perspective. For the past 15 years the Cosanti Foundation has been experimenting with an urban reorganization of highly integrated 3-dimensional complexes called ARCOLOGIES (from architecture-ecology), urban concepts reinforcing the interdependence between population, resources and diverse urban functions. Arcology is seen also as a societal framework that can give a higher quality to humankind's physical, psychological and aesthetic well-being.

Present related research investigates the use of solar energy within arcologies. The focus is on the use of peripheral, extensive greenhouses employed for both food production and as solar collectors from which heat energy is directed to the town complex to meet heating and cooling needs on a community scale.

The gathering and structuring of cities into 3-dimensional space maximizes the urban benefits of interaction and accessibility while minimizing the costs of energy, raw materials, and land. Logistically, the self-contained design of the arcology would result in: conservation of energy and resources; preservation of land for agriculture and recreation; elimination of the diffused sprawl of commercial services and community facilities; elimination of the need within the urban landscape for the automobile, a prime cause of pollution and waste; and highly integrated and economically efficient heating, cooling, lighting, delivery systems and waste disposal mech-

anisms. In addition, arcology can be an instrument for cultural intensification and social integration while meeting the private needs of the individual. Every resident would have immediate and unlimited access to the lively urban center as well as to a vast natural landscape. Arcology is an environment that offers a satisfying synthesis of city and country dwelling.

The construction of Arcosanti began in 1970 in the mesa country of central Arizona, 70 miles north of Phoenix. When completed the town of 4,500–5,000 people will rise 25 stories, cover 13 acres of an 860 acre land preserve, and will serve as a study center for the social, economic, and ecological implications of its architectural framework. To date, more than 2,500 students and professionals of all ages, races and backgrounds have participated in experiental workshops and seminars, teaching and learning from one another through the building of Arcosanti.

—Paolo Soleri

Paolo Soleri received his training at Turin Polytechnic, graduating with a doctorate in architecture in 1946. Awarded a scholarship, he went to the United States where he took up an apprenticeship with Frank Lloyd Wright in Arizona from January 1947–September 1948. Somewhat disillusioned with Taliesin West and accompanied by his equally disenchanted friend Mark Mills, Soleri set up—hermit-like—in the desert. In 1949, having just married his best client's daughter, Soleri together with Mills built a remarkable masonry and dome house for his mother-in-law at Cave Creek, Arizona. The next year Soleri returned to Turin with his wife; they designed craft objects and built a *Leoncino* (a camper converted from a lorry large enough to house three people), which incorporated a solar device. In it they moved to Southern Italy in 1951 and began specializing in ceramics. At Vietri-sul-mare, near Palermo, Soleri designed his first major building, a ceramics studio and workshop large enough for a one-family business. The Ceramica Artistica Solimene, completed in 1953, faces the Mediterranean and consists of an expansive top-lit workshop built from reinforced concrete and faced externally with glazed pots. It was an early experiment in the strict use of locally available materials, handcraft and engineering, all of which were to become important features of Soleri's later work in Arizona.

Soleri and his wife returned to the American desert in 1955 and settled into the, then, relative peace of Scottsdale in Paradise Valley, Arizona, close to Phoenix and Taliesin and near to mother-in-law. On a flat arid five-acre site Soleri began to build his Cosanti Foundation and sketch out his blueprints for alternative urban environments. Cosanti was the original workshop base out of which came the ideas for *Arcologies* (a name given to the alternative urban habitats compounded of *arc*hitecture and ec*ology*) and eventually "Arcosanti," the prototype settlement now under construction at Cordes Junction eighty miles further north from Scottsdale. At Cosanti the first experiments in new building techniques and forms commenced, firstly with the so-called "earth house" (concrete forms cut from the ground) and most recently with the newly opened (1978) concrete exhibition gallery. Here Paolo Soleri started making ceramic wind bells and eventually established a foundry and workshop on site for casting metal bells. This activity, still the main income-making source for Cosanti, now also operates at Arcosanti.

A recurring design theme in Soleri's work has been on bridges and "bridge-cities." He first achieved recognition in this engineering field through the publication of some of his designs in the book *The Architecture of Bridges* issued by the Museum of Modern Art, New York in 1948. Soleri's work came to the wider attention of the American public through a large scale exhibition of his arcology and bridge projects held at the Corcoran Gallery, Washington, in 1970. There he presented his

ideas in model form, establishing his priorities for an alternative urban future based on a concentration or "a miniaturization" (after Teilhard de Chardin) of city elements into single large urban structures. His concept was in direct opposition to the ideas of planners such as Doxiades and their notion of spread-out cities (Ecumenopolis) which, in Soleri's view, lacked both ecological balance and architectural significance.

The same year Soleri set out to build one of these arcologies, the one for an "Arcosanti," on the 860-acre site at Cordes Junction, a point on the Arizona map that gives access to the main highways. Situated on a mesa which has similar characteristics to a hypothetical scheme he drew up some years before, Arcosanti will eventually provide accommodation for 4500–5000 people. It will rise 25 stories, will be pedestrian oriented and will cover only 13 acres of the incredibly beautiful site. It is unique and, according to Soleri, will serve as a prototype for further schemes. The design aspects of the project are interesting and innovative. What was learnt at Cosanti about concrete casting has been developed to a high degree at Arcosanti, and experiments have been carried out in the decoration of surfaces and moulding. Two large vaults have been constructed as well as "solar" apses and a more conventional workshop block. The whole scheme is being built largely by volunteers, summer student apprentices and workpeople who share Soleri's personal vision. It has gone through numerous modifications but is at last emerging as a viable alternative proposition for the future.

Soleri has developed his original design to take into account the new urgent needs for energy conservation in building; in conjunction with experts from the University of Arizona, he has designed more advanced solar systems. He explains this development at some length in his article "Two Suns Arcology" (*AA Quarterly,* vol. 7, no. 2, 1976).

His involvement with the project has been time consuming, and the need to raise the necessary capital to complete the project (possibly 15–20 years from now) has taken Soleri from Los Angeles to Delhi as well as most of the European capitals over the past decade on lectures, broadcasts and promotional tours. Most recently the Arcosanti yearly Arts and Music Festivals have been arranged to bring large numbers to the site (10,000 people in one day in 1978), not simply to share in the delights of Arizona's special musical event but also to experience at first hand the new environmental concept. The next stage of the project will include theatre and workshop centres to house such events.

Through all this activity Paolo Soleri himself remains a calm, introspective, frugally minded individual possessed by the desire to continue and complete the vision of a new order for "urban man." His own writings and pronouncements on the wider implications of his philosophy (enshrined in his completely unfathomable book *The Bridge Between Matter and Spirit*) are now displaying a much more intense interest in metaphysics, theology and what he calls "eschatology." He defines man's (and by that he means also woman's) present situation as untenable and the modern city—with its inherent destructive characteristics—as unacceptable. Thus he seeks to find restitution in the "new man" who has a vision strong enough to take him forward into new areas of spirituality and find new hope in a close knit urban way of life.

—Dennis Sharp

SORIANO, Raphael (Simon).
American. Born in Rhodes, Greece, 1 August 1907; emigrated to the United States, 1924: naturalized, 1930. Educated at Rhodes College, St. Jean, 1919–22; University of Southern California, Los Angeles,

Julius Shulman House and Studio, 7875 Woodrow Wilson, Los Angeles
Touriel Medical Building, 2608 West Santa Barbara, Los Angeles
1951 Schrage-Hallauer House, 2648 Commonwealth, Los Angeles
1959 Houses, 20 and 24 Longfellow Road, Mill Valley, California
1969 World Peace Center, Alcatraz Island, San Francisco Bay (project)

Publications:

On SORIANO: articles—"Dos Casas en California: Raphael S. Soriano, Arquitecto" in *Arquitectura* (Mexico City), July 1941; "House by Raphael Soriano" in *Arts and Architecture* (Los Angeles), October 1945; "Un Architetto in una Società Industrializzata" by Geoffrey Holroyd in *Edilizia Moderna* (Milan), April 1955; "Steel Frame House by Raphael S. Soriano" in *Arts and Architecture* (Los Angeles), January 1956; "Genetrix: Personal Contributions to American Architecture" in *Architectural Review* (London), May 1957; "A Hillside House by Raphael S. Soriano" in *Arts and Architecture* (Los Angeles), August 1960; "Raphael S. Soriano, FAIA" in *Architectural and Engineering News* (Philadelphia), February 1963; "Recent Domestic Architecture" in *Bauen und Wohnen* (Zurich), June 1967; "Scholars Back Soriano Proposal" in *San Francisco Examiner*, 13 October 1969.

The modern movement in California, at a certain moment in time, owed much to European emigrés—Richard Neutra, Rudolph Schindler and Raphael Soriano. Soriano emerged out of Neutra's office and his architecture owed much to Neutra, but his work was more ordered, more regular, more classic. An amalgam, one is tempted to think, of the California of his adoption and his native Aegean.

There is a fundamental difference in his pre-war and his post-war work. Before the war he was a mainstream, modern architect, designing white cubes in the Bauhaus tradition, but after the Case Study House of the late 1940's, he changed to structures of steel and to a less formal way of building.

It was his houses of the late 1930's that first brought him fame. Influenced by Neutra's designs for the Kahn house and the Brown house, they marry the rectangular white aesthetic of the European modern movement with the ubiquitous American balloon frame and try to express the balloon frame by exposing the studs as vertical elements through the long strips of glazing. Without going all the way with Neutra and his "Biorealism," Soriano nevertheless shared Neutra's underlying care for climate and environment, and the sharp forms of the early houses are softened in the later structures by broad overhangs to protect the windows from the powerful Los Angeles sun.

In the late 1940's, the West Coast magazine *Arts and Architecture* commissioned a series of "Case Study Houses" by Los Angeles architects, and these houses tended to be steel framed, with a hard-edged structure enclosing relaxed indoor/outdoor living spaces so appropriate to the local climate and life style. These houses launched Charles Eames, Pierre Koenig and others on their architectural careers, but Soriano was already a mature house designer. His case study house, with a steel frame of round columns, and a heavy fascia combined with lush semitropical planting and light infill panels, made the steel frame seem at home in Southern California and led to a series of commissions for steel houses which must be regarded as his most beautiful works. Of particular delight is the house for the architectural photographer Julius Shulman, where the steel frame extends out over the terrace to enclose it with planting. A particular Soriano skill was the filtering of the strong California sun through diffuse membranes to make habitable outdoor spaces; the filter could be plants as at the Shulman house, corrugated plastic

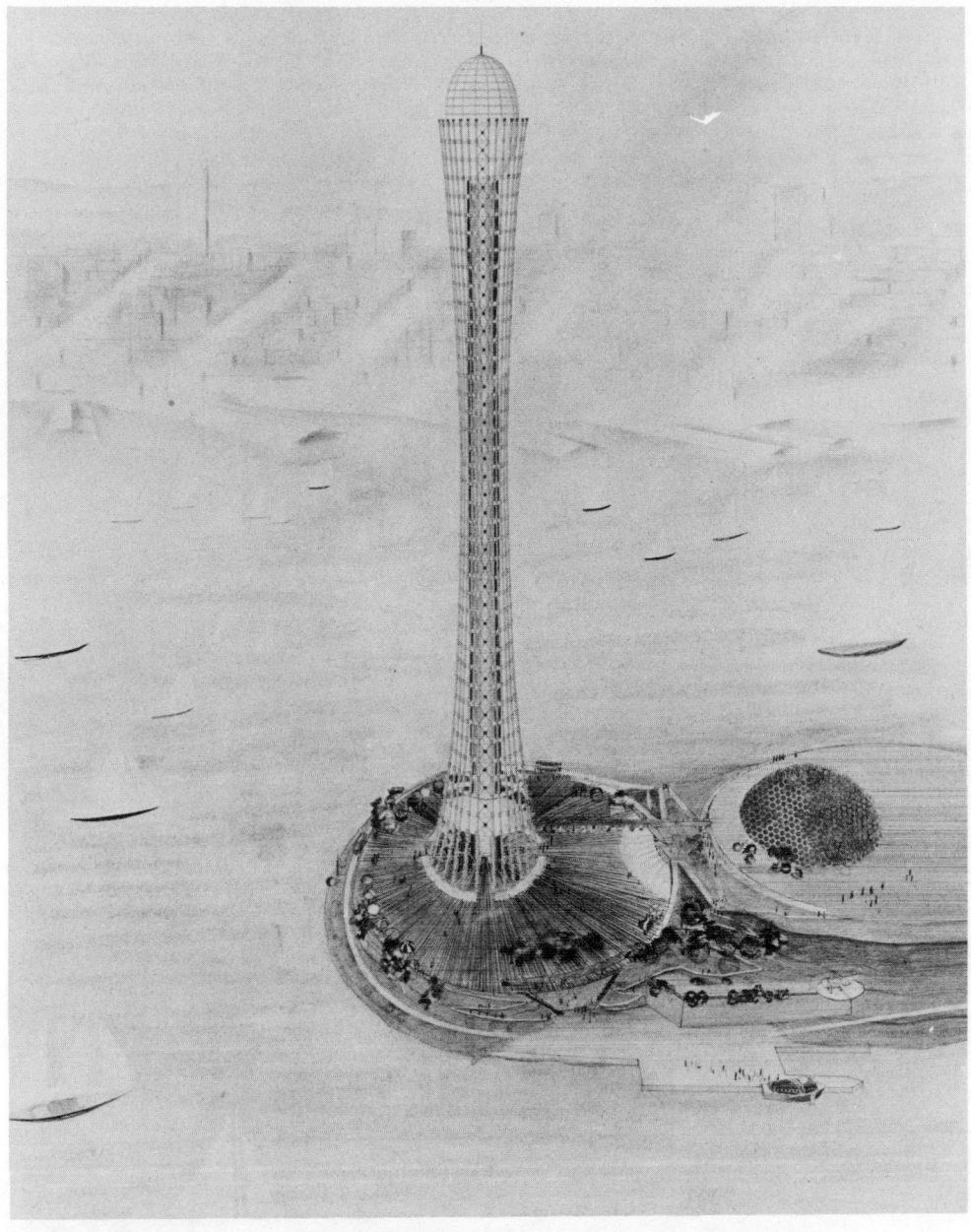

Raphael Soriano: World Peace Center, Alcatraz Island, San Francisco Bay, 1969 (project)

B.Arch. 1934. Worked with Richard Neutra, Los Angeles, 1932–35, and with the Los Angeles City Planning Commission, 1935–36. In private practice, Los Angeles, 1936–53, and Tiburon, California, since 1953. Visiting Professor, Tulane University, New Orleans, 1956, University of Arizona, Tucson, 1959, McGill University, Montreal, 1959, Yale University, New Haven, Connecticut, 1959–60, Cornell University, Ithaca, New York, 1961–62, and Washington University, St. Louis, 1962–63. Exhibitions: *World's Fair*, Paris, 1937; Pan-American Congress, Havana, 1951, and Mexico City, 1952; Museum of Modern Art, New York, 1952; Fine Arts Museum, Houston, 1952; *Bienal*, Sao Paulo, 1953; *International Industrial Exhibition*, Moscow, 1958; Yale University, New Haven, Connecticut, 1960; City Art Museum, St. Louis, 1962; *The Twentieth Century House*, Museum of Modern Art, New York, 1962; *Historical Housing 1930–1940*, University of California at Santa Barbara, 1975. Recipient: *Progressive Architecture* Award, 1947; American Institute of Architects Award, 1949, 1951, 1956, 1957, 1958, 1959, 1960, 1962; Pan American Congress Award, 1951, 1954; *Architectural Record* Award, 1956; *House and Home* Award, 1960. Fellow, American Institute of Architects. Honorary Member, Society of Mexican Architects. Address (office): 21 Main Street, Belvedere, Tiburon, California 94920, U.S.A.

Works:

1935 Lipetz House, 1843 Dillon, Los Angeles
1936 Kimpson-Nixon House, 380 Orlena, Los Angeles
1937 Los Angeles Jewish Community Center, 2317 East Michigan, Los Angeles
1938 Ross House, 2123 Valentine, Los Angeles
1939 Polito House, 1650 Queens Road, Hollywood, Los Angeles
     Gogol House, 2190 Talmadge, Los Angeles
1940 Lukens House, 3425 West 27th Street, Los Angeles
     Koosis House, 1941 Glencoe, Los Angeles
     Strauss-Lewis House, 3131 Queensbury, Los Angeles
1941 House, Avenue 37, Mt. Washington, Los Angeles
1948 Horticultural Center, for the Hallawell Seed Company, San Francisco (demolished, 1965)
     Ciro of Bond Street Shop, San Francisco (with Serge Chermayeff)
     Case Study House, for *Arts and Architecture*, Pacific Palisades, California
1950 Colby Apartments, 1312 Beverly Green Drive, Los Angeles
     Noyes House, 111 Stone Canyon, Los Angeles

sheet in the Griffiths Park Apartments, wood slats for a nursery garden in San Francisco.

The 1953 move from Los Angeles to a waterside office in Marin County gave him a delightful place in which to work, but little local success. The woodsy Bay Region Style was too strong in the San Francisco area for Soriano to be appreciated and understood, and he remained an outsider.

—John Winter

SOSTRES Maluquer, Josep Maria.
Spanish. Born in La Seu d'Urgell, Lerida, 15 May 1915. Educated at the Escuela Superior de Arquitectura, Barcelona, Dip.Arch. 1946. In private practice, Barcelona, since 1947. Adjunct Professor of Art and Architectural History, 1957, Head of the First Year Course, 1958–59, Antoni Gaudí Professor of Architecture, 1960–61, and since 1962 Professor of Architectural History, Escuela Tecnica Superior Arquitectura, Barcelona. Founder Member, Group R, Barcelona, 1952; Member of the Founding Committee, Amigos de Gaudí Foundation, Barcelona, 1953.

Exhibitions: Galerias Layetanas, Barcelona, 1952, 1958; *Bienal,* Sao Paulo, 1957. Recipient: First Prize, Low-Cost Housing Competition, Barcelona, 1949. Corresponding Member, Union Professionelle des Architectes, Saint Luc, Brussels. Address (office): Aragon 250, Barcelona, Spain.

Works:

1948   Elias Family House alterations and extension, Bellver de Cerdanya. Lerida, Spain

Josep Maria Sostres: *El Noticiero Universal* Building, Barcelona, 1965

1948/
50 6 houses, Tallo District, Bellver de Cerdanya, Lerida, Spain
    Hotel, Montseny, Spain (project; completed by Fogars de Montclus)
1949 Low-Cost Housing, Barcelona (competition project; with others)
1951 Elias Family Vault, Tallo Cemetery, Bellver de Cerdanya, Lerida, Spain
1952 Cusi House, La Seu d'Urgell, Lerida, Spain
      Tibau House, Bellver de Cerdanya, Lerida, Spain
1953 Brau House, Muntaner and Reus Streets, Barcelona (project)
1953/
55 Farras House, Andorra
    Agustí House, Sitges, Spain ·
1955 Design of the *Third Exhibition of Group R,* Barcelona (with F. Basso)
      Hostel Valira, Andorra (project)
      Alonso House, Ciudad Diagonal, Barcelona (completed by others)
      4 apartments, Torredembarra, Tarragona, Spain
1955/
58 M.M.I. House, Ciudad Diagonal, Barcelona
1956 Design of the *Gaudí Exhibition,* Salon del Tinell, Barcelona
1956/
57 Hotel Maria Victoria, Puigcerdà, Gerona, Spain
1957 Iranzo House, Ciudad Diagonal, Barcelona
1960/
61 Cloister Garden landscaping, Cathedral of La Seu d'Urgell, Lerida, Spain
1963/
65 *El Noticiero Universal* (newspaper) Building, Barcelona
1968 Hernandez Pijuan Studio interiors, Barcelona
1971/
73 Xampeny House, Ventola, Gerona, Spain
    Campana House, Ventola, Gerona, Spain

Publications:

By SOSTRES: articles—"Sentiment and Symbolism of Space" in *Projects and Materials* (New York), September/October 1949; "El Funcionalismo y la Nueva Plastica" in *Boletin de Informacion de la Direccion General de Arquitectura* (Madrid), July 1950; "La Arquitectura Monumental" in *Revista Nacional de Arquitectura* (Madrid), May 1951; "Nikolaus Pevsner: Primer Historiador de la Arquitectura Moderna" in *Destino* (Barcelona), May 1952; "Situacion de la obra de Gaudí en relacion con su epoca y trascendencia actual en Arquitectura" in *Revista Nacional de Arquitectura* (Madrid), July 1953; "Luis Domènech y Montaner: Arquitecto del Orfeo Catala" in *La Vanguardia* (Barcelona), 13 February 1958; "Henry van de Velde" in *Cuadernos de Arquitectura* (Barcelona), no. 13, 1958; "Frank Lloyd Wright" in *Cuadernos de Arquitectura* (Barcelona), no. 37, 1959; "Un Esquema de la Arquitectura actual en Finlandia" in *Cuadernos de Arquitectura* (Barcelona), no. 39, 1960; "Paisaje y diseno" in *Cuadernos de Arquitectura* (Barcelona), no. 64, 1966.

On SOSTRES: books—*La Arquitectura Moderna* by Gillo Dorfles, Oriol Bohigas, and José Martorell, Barcelona 1956; *Arquitectura Espanola Contemporanea* by Luis Domènech, Barcelona 1968; *Polèmica d'Arquitectura Catalana* by Oriol Bohigas, Barcelona 1970; articles—"Bellver de Cerdaña (Lerida)" in *Revista Nacional de Arquitectura* (Madrid), June 1953; "Josep Maria Sostres" by Luis Domènech in *Arquitecturas Bis* (Barcelona), May 1974; "Dos Obras Recientes de Josep Maria Sostres" in *2C Construccion de la Ciudad* (Barcelona), June 1975; "Josep Maria Sostres," special issue of *2C Construccion de la Ciudad* (Barcelona), August 1975.

Because of the Civil War, and because he had been ill as a child, Josep Maria Sostres did not quality as an architect until he was 30 years old. It was during these long formative years that he acquired a wider culture than is usual in the study of architecture. He not only read about architecture, he also read poetry; in addition, painting became more than just a pastime to him. He could count among his friends both artists and poets. After qualifying in 1946 he visited Italy and was impressed by Terragni's buildings. This background led him into direct opposition to the general cultureless atmosphere that gripped Spain, in particular the universities. Under Franco's dictatorship the Modern Movement was associated with the Republican Government and was actively discouraged. Within this context a small group of architects gathered together in Barcelona under the open-ended name of "Grupo R" in 1952: the main objective of the group was to establish connections back to the rationalist architects of the 1930's, to recover a lost culture and to bring it back into Spanish society. Sostres, who had already published four fundamental articles on the subject, became the natural theoretical leader of the group. At the same time his keen interest in Antoni Gaudí led him to become one of the founder-members of the "Amigos de Gaudí," and it was as a result of his hard work that Gaudí was finally recognized internationally.

Yet Sostres is more than just an influential theoretician and polemicist. Although he has constructed only about a dozen architectural works, four of these works constitute corner-stones of modern architecture in Catalonia: Hotel Maria Victoria in Puigcerdà; Casa Agustí in Sitges; M.M.I. House in Ciudad Diagonal; and the *El Noticiero Univeral* Building in Barcelona.

Hotel Maria Victoria, in the Pyrenees border town of Puigcerdà, is within the mainstream of functional architecture with its clearly expressed structure and use, but at the same time it incorporates an Aalto-like organic appreciation of place, each of its three facades responding to the little square and narrow side street, with commanding views over the cliffs of this hillside town. The facades have been designed to fit into the urban context rather than to serve as a functional expression of internal use.

The Casa Agustí, on the Mediterranean, responds to the climate by breaking down the essentially simple cubic concept to create a series of sheltered outside rooms. A double facade protects the bedrooms from the heat, and the cube is excavated away under the staircase to allow light and breezes across the ground floor living area. The single-storey library and study are separated from the main house by a pergola, and the walls of the house extend, Mies-like, into the garden, to create an enclosure.

The M.M.I. House reveals an extraordinary synthesis of early modern architecture, including nearly all of the classical Mondrian-like compositional elements—flat roof terrace, alternative walls of glass and solid rendered surfaces—and a plan that revolves around a glass-walled patio. In this very carefully detailed building, Sostres made the rich vocabulary of the 1930's available for the 1950's.

Sostres is a firm believer in the Modern Movement. He is capable of absorbing the lessons of history and place without rejecting the Movement's early rational tradition. His *El Noticiero Universal* Building, with its severe regular window pattern, glazed on the same plane as the stone facing, is a superb example of civic manners in providing a background architecture to complement Cerda's Barcelona street plan and to fit in beside its neighbours.

In 1962 Sostres was awarded the chair of history at the Barcelona School of Architecture. Since then, however, he has led a somewhat retired life both academically and professionally.

—David Mackay

SOTTSASS, Ettore, Jr.

Italian. Born in Innsbruck, Austria, of Italian parents, 14 September 1917. Educated at the Polytechnic, Turin, 1935–39, Dip.Arch. 1939. Served in the Italian Army, in Montenegro and Sargiaccato, 1942–45. Married in 1948. Associated with the designer Luigi Spazzapan, Turin, 1937–40. In private practice, as architect and designer, Milan, since 1946. Designer Consultant to the Olivetti Company since 1958: established additional design office for Olivetti, at Ivrea, near Turin, 1960. Exhibitions: *Triennale,* Milan, 1954, 1957, 1960; *Miljö för en ny planet,* National Museum, Stockholm, 1969; *Italy: The New Domestic Landscape,* Museum of Modern Art, New York, 1972; *Ettore Sottsass Jr.,* International Design Centre, Berlin, 1976, toured Europe, Israel and Australia; Cooper-Hewitt Museum, New York, 1976. Recipient: Premio Compasso d'Oro, Milan, 1959. Honorary doctorate: Royal College of Art, London. Address (office): Via Manzoni 14, 20121 Milan, Italy.

Works:

1934 Apartment Building, Turin (project)
1947 Church, QT8 Quarter, Milan (competition project)
      Design of the Oggetti per la Casa exhibition, *Triennale,* Milan
      Chair design in "legno panforte"
      Salon Réalités Nouvelles, Paris
1948 Grassotti Display Stand, *Food Fair,* Turin
      Cogne Display Stand, *Automobile Show,* Turin
1949 Villas (projects)
1950 INA-CASA Housing Development, Savona, Italy (competition project)
1951 INA-CASA Housing Development, Novara, Italy (competition project)
1952 School, Siliqua, Sardinia (project; with Ettore Sottsass Sr.)
      Golf Club, Lerici, Italy
      4 two-storey houses, Romentino, Novara, Italy (project)
      INA-CASA Apartment Building, Arborea, Sardinia (project)
1952/
54 INA-CASA Housing Development, Carmagnola, near Turin
    INA-CASA Housing Development, Meina, Lake Maggiore, Italy
1956 Galleria del Naviglio, Milan
      Galleria del Cavallino, Venice
1957 Cineaste's Apartment interiors, Milan
      Design of the Italian Glass Exhibition, *Triennale,* Milan
1958 Dentist's House interiors, Genoa
1960 Atrium Entrance Hall, *Triennale,* Milan
1961 Design of the Prime Materials Exhibition, *Italia '61,* Turin
      Design of the *Italian Painting Exhibition,* Bolles Gallery, San Francisco
      Villa by the Sea (project)
1963 Design of *I Biennale d'Arte,* Bari, Italy
1964 Galleria Il Quadrante, Florence
1965 Galleria Sperone, Turin
      Fetrinelli Photographic Library, Turin
      Living Room, *La Casa Abitata,* Florence
1968 Olivetti Display Stand, *La Macchina della Informazione,* Turin
      Pomodoro Apartment interiors, via Vigevano 3, Milan
1969– "Sistema 45" Office Equipment and Furnishings, for the Olivetti Company

Publications:

By SOTTSASS: books—*Europa e America,* exhibition catalogue, Turin 1946; *Arte Astratta e Concreta,* exhibition catalogue, Rome 1948; *Ceramiche dell Tenebre,* exhibition catalogue, Milan 1963; *Miljö för en ny Planet,* exhibition catalogue, Stockholm 1969; articles—"Coerenza di Neutra" in *Domus* (Milan),

November 1946; "Le Case Camminano" and "E inutile che cerchiate sezioni auree nelle case di Wright" in *Avanti* (Milan), April 1947; "Case false e vere" and "Standard" in *Avanti* (Milan), May 1947; "La Triennale" in *Avanti* (Milan), June 1947; "L'Architettura no fu Nuova" in *Avanti* (Milan), August 1947; "La Carta degli Architetti e degli Operai" in *Avanti* (Milan), December 1947; "Significato dello Standard" in *Comunità* (Rome), March/April 1949; "Architettura Popolare in Sardegna" in *Comunità* (Rome), June 1951; "Antoine Pevsner" in *Domus* (Milan), April 1953; "Alberghi e Tende" in *Domus* (Milan), October 1953; "Gusto per il Rustico" in *Domus* (Milan), January 1954; "Le Corbusier e il Mediterraneo: Due Mostre di Le Corbusier" in *Domus* (Milan), February 1954; "Liberty: La Bibbia di Mezzo Secolo" in *Domus* (Milan), March 1954; "Struttura e Colore" in *Domus* (Milan), October 1954; "Katsura: Villa Imperiale a Sud-Ouest di Kyoto" in *Domus* (Milan), November 1954; "Lussuoso e finito" in *Domus* (Milan), December 1954; "Piccola Storia del Cartellone Pubblicitario" in *Stile Industria* (Milan), January 1955; "Graffica Popolare" in *Stile Industria* (Milan), April 1955; "Disegno Magico" in *Stile Industria* (Milan), October 1956; "Disegno e Produzione del Mobile" in *Atti del Collegio Regionale Lombardo degli Architetti,* Milan 1957; "Chiariti i Misteri della Pittura Astratta" in *Avanti* (Milan), February 1958; "Adriano Olivetti" in *Stile Industria* (Milan), May 1960; "Design" in *Domus* (Milan), January 1962; "Automatizzazione e Design" in *Stile Industria* (Milan), April 1962; "Viaggio a Oriente: Birmania" in *Domus* (Milan), June 1962; "Viaggio a Oriento: Japur e il Palazzo" in *Domus* (Milan), August 1962; "Viaggio a Oriente: Templi in India" in *Domus* (Milan), November 1962; "Dada, New Dada, New Realists" in *Domus* (Milan), February 1963; "Civiltà del Danubio nelle Riviste" in *Domus* (Milan), May 1963; "Man Ray: Il Dada è morto: Viva Il Dada" and "Viagga a Oriente: Agra e le Pitture Sulle Case" in *Domus* (Milan), January 1964; "Pop e non Pop (a proposito di Michelangelo Pistoletto)" in *Domus* (Milan), May 1964; "Offerta a Siva" in *Domus* (Milan), January 1965; "Viaggio a Occidente: Che cosa fanno il dentro?" and "Viaggio a Oriente: Nepal" in *Domus* (Milan), March 1966; "Breve Sondaggio in Germania" in *Domus* (Milan), April 1966; "Mémoires di Panna Montata" in *Domus* (Milan), December 1966, January 1967, December 1967, March 1969, and March 1970; "Gli Archizoom" in *Domus* (Milan), October 1967; "Un Posto in Città" in *Domus* (Milan), July 1968; "A Philosophy of Light" in *Space Design* (Tokyo), February 1970; "Una Lettera in Ritardo" in *Domus* (Milan), February 1971; "Graffi d'Amore sulla pelle del Pianeta" in *L'Uomo Vogue* (Milan), April 1971; "Environment per il Lavoro d'Ufficio" in *Rassegna Modi di Abitare Oggi* (Milan), November/December 1971; "Objects as Memories" in *Casabella* (Milan), February 1974; "Ettore Sottsass 1955–1975" in *Binario* (Lisbon), August/September 1976; "A Day in the Life of a Designer" in *Crée* (Paris), September 1977.

On SOTTSASS: book—*Sottsass's Scrap Book: Drawings and Notes by Ettore Sottsass Jr.,* edited by Federica Di Castro, Milan 1976; articles—"Introduzione ad Ettore Sottsass Jr." by Pier Carlo Santini in *Zodiac* (Milan), no. 11, 1963; "Ettore Sottsass Jr.: Mobili 1965" in *Domus* (Milan), December 1965; "Cahier di Ettore Sottsass Jr., 1966" in *Lotus* (Venice), no. 3, 1966–67; "Six Design Offices in Europe: Ettore Sottsass Jr." by Gilles de Bure and Gerard Negreanu in *Crée* (Paris), May 1974; "Ettore Sottsass" by Solange Thierry, Monelle Hayot, and Odette-Helene Gasnier in *L'Oeil* (Lausanne), January/February 1977; "Architecture of Dissent: Aldo Rossi and Ettore Sottsass" by Pier Carlo Santini in *Ottagono* (Milan), June 1978.

*   *   *

What Ettore Sottsass Jr. exhibited at *Italy: The New Domestic Landscape* at the Museum of Modern Art

in 1972 were super-sensual postulates for a ritualized interior, counter-design, building as commentary.

His works "represent a series of ideas, and not a series of objects to be put on the market this evening or tomorrow morning. . . . The aim is not to achieve a product but to . . . provide ideas." Sottsass is not in the least concerned with making furniture, or in creating an elegant, "cute," sweet or amusing environment, and still less is he concerned with designing "silent" objects that will allow the spectator to remain calm and happy within his psychic and cultural status quo. His aim is to break "the interminable chain of psycho-erotic self-indulgences about 'possession' . . . of objects." And one can only reflect that that kind of goal will certainly impose a responsibility on whomever ventures to use the objects. "Eliminating the protective layer of alibis we build around ourselves always necessitates great commitment."

Sottsass wants design to come to terms with that catalogue of needs that our industrial-productive society has drawn up, and he insists that this can happen only if the designed objects have a detached, disinterested, uninvolved quality—so that they gradually fade away, disappearing into the general texture of domestic life, acting as a frame for the rites of cooking, sleeping, entertaining. He envisages "house" not as a barricaded fortress, containing the tombs of the occupants' memories, but rather as a sort of living plasma of demountable elements that can at any moment provide the most suitable setting —sinuous or rigid, transparent or closed—for the drama that is about to take place. "The pieces of furniture move like beasts of the sea; they diminish or increase, they go to right or left, up or down; they coalesce into colonies, dissolve into dust, solidify into rocks or soften to plankton." By being so amorphous and chameleon-like, and by means of its neutrality and mobility and its ability to clothe any ceremony without becoming involved it it, "house" may promote a greater consciousness of environment and of the creative role that we can play. Surely, if we can accept "house" in the way that Sottsass describes, then this would be an auspicious beginning to the demystification of that solemn morbidness with which the environment is normally regarded.

Sottsass's prototypical wardrobes and cupboards suggest totems of domesticity: around them flow the rites of the bed, the oven, the hearth, the front door, the stairs. His house is a shrine-like chamber in which the acts of greeting, discussion, eating, cleaning, breathing, get separated from their human vessels and lay on the floor like debris. This is no orgy of consumption, no diversion, no camp operetta, but a perspective onto an expanded inventory of urban qualities.

—Chris Fawcett

SPEER, Albert.

German. Born in Mannheim, 19 March 1905. Educated at the Oberrealsschule, Heidelberg, 1913–23; Technische Hochschule, Munich, 1923–25; Technische Hochschule, Berlin, under Heinrich Tessenow, 1925–27, Dip.Ing. 1927. Married Margarete Weber in 1928; children: Albert, Hilde, Fritz, Margret, Arnold, and Ernst. Assistant Professor to Professor Tessenow at the Technische Hochschule, Berlin, 1928–31; Architect to Adolf Hitler, 1933–42; Inspector-General of Buildings, for the Renovation of the Federal Capital, Berlin, 1937–45; German Minister of Armaments, 1942–45; incarcerated by the Allies in Nuremberg and in Spandau Prison, Berlin, 1945–66. Exhibition: *World's Fair,* Paris, 1937. Recipient: Grand Prix, and Gold Medal, *World's Fair,* Paris, 1937. Address: Schloss-Wolfsbrunnenweg 50, 6900 Heidelberg 1, Germany.

Works:

1930   Private family house, Heidelberg
1931   Humboldtstiftung (home for foreign students) conversion, Charlottenburg, Berlin
        Professor Romberg House extension and pleasure grounds, Nikolasee, Berlin
1932   Nazi Party Headquarters renovation, Berlin
1933   Ministry of Propaganda interiors, Berlin
        Annex to a hall of the official residence of Dr. Goebbels, Berlin
        Design for Party rallies
1934   Stands at Zeppelinfield, and at Luitpold Arena, Luitpold hall, Nuremberg
1935   Speer House, Nikolasee, Berlin
1936   Thorak Sculpture Studio, Baldham, Munich
        Speer Studio, Berchtesgaden, Obersalzberg, Germany
        Stadium of the Four Hundred Thousand, Nuremberg (project)
        Märzfeld (Marching Field), Nuremberg (project)
1937   German Pavilion, *World's Fair,* Paris
1938   Reichsmarschallamt (office of Hermann Göring), Berlin (project)
        Grosse Halle (Great Hall), Berlin (project)
1938/
   39   Reichschancellery, Berlin
1939   Oberkommando der Wehrmacht, Berlin (project)
        Führerpalais, Berlin (project)
        Central Station, Berlin (project)
        Urban development plan for Berlin

Publications:

By SPEER: books—*Inside the Third Reich,* Berlin 1969, London and New York 1970; *Spandau: The Secret Diaries,* Berlin 1975, London and New York 1976.

On SPEER: book—*Albert Speer: Architektur,* Berlin 1978.

*   *   *

It cannot be denied that in the socio-political domain, powerful consequences operating in the future can often be kindled through the architect's work. I think, for example, about the consequences which monotonous rental housing will have on the minds of several generations of children. Many architects are necessarily aware of having to contribute to the depersonalization of our future environment because of financial and technical constraints. Because buildings stand for decades. Goethe wrote in *Wilhelm Meisters Wanderjahren* that an insurmountable truth is inherent in illusion as long as illusion lasts. I wonder whether in the coming decades we will recognize as the illusion of our time the belief, elevated to the mystical, in the miracle of technology?

I take the point of view that it *should* have been my duty to refuse to be Hitler's architect—in spite of all temptations which these commissions, with their unlimited financial and material resources, provided—because I was aware that my buildings would promote his goals. But basically, an architect's office work is apolitical, because he has no control over the socio-economic conditions which determine what his buildings can become. The problem sources are based within the society, not the buildings. Not only forests, lakes, maintaining pure air and water but also our buildings are an essential part of our environment. Perhaps they are the most important part because they influence daily life in every way.

—Albert Speer

*   *   *

It is perhaps significant that the young Albert Speer, as a student of architecture, wanted Poelzig as his tutor. Instead, however, he came under the influence of Professor Heinrich Tessenow whose insistence on simplicity and purity of form was a catalyst to a number of students of the period in Berlin.

Speer joined the N.S.D.A.P., and in 1932 was asked to refurbish the Party Headquarters in Berlin. The finished job impressed Hitler, and, after the elec-

Albert Speer: Reichschancellery, Berlin, 1939

tions of March 1933, Speer was commissioned to redesign the interiors of Schinkel's building in the Wilhelmsplatz for Goebbels' Ministry of Propaganda. Soon afterwards Speer created his first stage-sets for Party rallies at the Tempelhof Field, using vast banners, searchlights, and raised podia which were to become features of the later Nuremberg Rallies. Tessenow was not amused by his former pupil's work, and dismissed it as "showy." Hitler, however, was impressed with Speer's designs for the Zeppelin Field as well as being struck by the architect's remarkable organizing ability in getting Goebbels' house reorganized in record time. The result was that Speer was asked to work with Paul Ludwig Troost on the rehabilitation and refurnishing of the Chancellor's Residence in Berlin, and this success brought him close to Hitler at the age of only twenty-eight.

The restrained neo-classicism of Troost derived from a respectable 19th century tradition fostered by Schinkel, von Klenze, and others. Speer became greatly influenced by Troost's approach to a stripped-down classicism, and on Troost's death in 1934 he became the most important architect in the Reich. He designed the funeral of Paul von Hindenburg, and shortly afterwards his enormous scheme for a permanent podium and colonnade for the Zeppelin Field was approved by Hitler. The work of Speer now assumed a totally neo-classical manner, and his Zeppelin Field stands derive almost entirely from the altar at Pergamon. The details are stripped and coarsened, but the greatest difference is one of scale. Speer's designs began to take on something of the architectural megalomania pioneered by Boullée and other architects of the late 18th century in France, and indeed he recognized the similarities of his work for the Nuremberg Rallies to the designs for the Champs de Mars in Paris during the French Revolution. Greek rather than Roman neo-classicism became part of Speer's palette, although the scale of his work became positively Roman, mixed with a strong dose of French neo-classicism derived from the period of Boullée and Ledoux.

Speer's vast projects for the Nuremberg Stadium won the Grand Prix at the Paris Exhibition of 1937, while his Pavilion, a massive vertical pier topped by an eagle, won a gold medal. His success in getting designs out quickly, and his ability to organise the erection and completion of his projects in remarkably quick time, persuaded Hitler to entrust him with the planning of a new, monumental Berlin. This huge plan, with processional ways, triumphal avenues and arches, monumental buildings, and a megalomaniac scale, was to outdo anything Boullée had envisaged. Speer's designs for the palaces of Göring and Hitler were grandiose essays in 20th century neo-classicism characterized by their huge scale but with curious echoes of the refined work of Schinkel and others.

The accidental death of Todt caused Speer to be promoted to the post of Armaments Minister in 1942, a position he held until the end of the Second World War. Speer's efficiency, intelligence, and organizational genius helped him to run his Ministry with great success, despite a steadily worsening situation. His trial and twenty years in Spandau showed

that he, and perhaps he alone among all the Nazi hierarchy, had the courage to admit his appalling moral failure. His memoirs are a fascinating record of his rise as an architect in the Nazi ranks, as well as offering an insight into the neo-classical architecture of the Third Reich.

—James Stevens Curl

SPENCE, Sir Basil (Urwin).

British. Born in Bombay, India, of British parents, 13 August 1907. Educated at George Watson's College, Edinburgh; Heriot-Watt University Architectural School, Edinburgh; Bartlett School of Architecture, University College London. Served in the British Army, 1939–45: Major. Married Mary Joan Ferris in 1934; children: Milton and Gillian. Worked as an assistant in the office of Sir Edwin Lutyens, London, and in the office of Rowland Anderson, London; subsequently, Partner, Kinninmonth and Spence, Edinburgh, Spence, Glover and Ferguson, Edinburgh, and Spence, Bonnington and Collins, London and St. Albans; then Principal, Sir Basil Spencer and Partners, London. Adviser to the Board of Trade for the *British Industries Fair*, London, 1947, 1948, 1949; served as Planning Consultant to universities of Edinburgh, Southampton, and Nottingham, and to Basildon New Town. First Hoffman Wood Professor of Architecture, University of Leeds, 1955–56; Professor of Architecture, Royal Academy, London, 1961–68. Member of the Council, 1952, Vice-President, 1954–55, Honorary Secretary, 1956, and President, 1958–60, Royal Institute of British Architects; Member, Fine Arts Commission, London, 1956–70; Treasurer, Royal Academy, London, 1962–64. Recipient: *Festival of Britain* Award, 1951; First Prize, Coventry Cathedral Competition, 1951; Saltire Society Award, 1952; Bronze Medal, Royal Institute of British Architects, 1962; Award of Merit, City of Coventry, 1970; Grand Medaille d'Or, Académie d'Architecture, Paris, 1974. Honorary Fellow, Royal College of Art, London, 1962; D.Litt.: University of Leicester, 1963, University of Southampton, 1965; LL.D.: University of Manitoba, 1963. Fellow, Royal Institute of British Architects, 1947; Associate of the Royal Scottish Academy, 1952; Associate of the Royal Academy, 1953, and Royal Academician, 1960; Royal Designer for Industry, 1960. Honorary Fellow, American Institute of Architects, 1963; Honorary Member, Accademia di San Luca, Rome, 1973. Knighted, 1960; O.M. (Order of Merit), 1962. *Died* (in Eye, Suffolk), *19 November 1976.*

Works:

1935 House for Miss Reid, Murryfield, Edinburgh
1938 House for Mrs. Spence (his mother), Edinburgh
1946 *Britain Can Make It* exhibition, London (as Chief Architect)
1947 *Enterprise Scotland* exhibition, Edinburgh (as Chief Architect)
1949 *Scottish Industries Exhibition,* Glasgow (as Chief Architect)
1950 Housing, Dunbar, East Lothian, Scotland
     Housing, Selkirk, Scotland
1951 *Heavy Industries Exhibition,* at the *Festival of Britain,* London (as Chief Architect)
     Sea and Ships Pavilion, *Festival of Britain,* London
     Housing, Shepperton, Middlesex
1952 Saltire Award Flats, Newhaven, Sussex
     Duncanrigg Secondary School, East Kilbride, Scotland
1954 Ecclesfield Secondary Modern School, Yorkshire

School, Sydenham, London
     St. Ninian and St. Martin's Church, Whilthorn, Scotland
1955 Parsons Cross Secondary School, Sheffield
     Church, Clermiston, Scotland
1956 Trinity College Chapel, Glenmorgan, Scotland
1957 St. Martin's School, Shropshire
     St. Chad's Church, Bell Green, Coventry
     St. Oswald's Church, Tile Hill, Coventry
     Church of St. John the Divine, Willenhall, Coventry
1958 St. Paul's Church, Ecclesfield, Yorkshire
     Housing, Basildon New Town, Essex
     House, Oxlease Estate, Hatfield, Hertfordshire
     Wray House, Wimbledon, London
1959 St. Catherine's Church, Sheffield
     St. Aidan's Church, Leicester
     Thorn House (office building), St. Martin's Lane, London
     Research and Teaching Building, University of Liverpool
1960 Undergraduate Residence, Queen's College, Cambridge
     Physics Building, University of Liverpool
     Aeronautics and Mechanical Engineering Building, University of Southampton
     Glen Eyre Residences, and Economics Building, University of Southampton
1961 St. Francis' Church, Newall Green, Wythershawe, Lancashire
     Spence House, Beaulieu, Hampshire
1962 Cathedral of St. Michael, Coventry
     Scottish Widows Life Assurance Building, Edinburgh
     Power Station, Trawafynydd, Wales (original design and as consultant)
     Housing II, Basildon New Town, Essex
     High-rise housing, Gorbals, Glasgow
     Senior Common Room, University of Southampton
     Falmer House, University of Sussex, Brighton
1963 Music Rooms, Trinity College, Glenmorgan, Scotland
     Arts Building, and Chemistry Building, University of Southampton
1964 Hampstead Civic Centre, Library and Swimming Baths, London
     2 houses, Banalbufar, Majorca
     Research Building, University of Edinburgh
     Nuffield Theatre, and Civil and Electrical Engineering Building, University of Southampton
     Library, phase I, University of Sussex, Brighton
1965 Princes Street Housing, Edinburgh
     Animal Research Building, University of Edinburgh
     Chemistry Building, University of Exeter
     Chemistry Building, University of Sussex, Brighton
     St. Aidan's College, University of Durham
1966 Crematorium, Mortonhall, Edinburgh
     Terminal, Glasgow Airport
     Meeting House, University of Sussex, Brighton
     Students Union Building, Physics Building, and Animal House, University of Southampton
     Lecture Theatre, University of Exeter
1967 Library, Staff Club and Canteen, University of Edinburgh
     Physics Building, University of Exeter
     Geology/Botany Building, University of Southampton
     Physics Building, University of Sussex, Brighton
     St. Matthew's Church, Reading, Berkshire
1969 Municipal Library, Newcastle upon Tyne
     Tizard Building extension, University of Southampton

Sir Basil Spence: Meeting House, University of Sussex, Brighton, 1966

Recreation Building, and Biology Building, University of Sussex, Brighton
1970 Household Cavalry Barracks, Knightsbridge, London
Town Hall and Civic Centre, Sunderland
House, Fawwara, Malta
Boathouse, Carmel College, Wallingford, Berkshire
Institute of Development Studies, University of Sussex, Brighton
1971 Chancery, British Embassy, Rome
Rivierstaete Building, Amsterdam (original design and as consultant)
Library, phase II, University of Sussex, Brighton
1972 Administration Building, University of Sussex, Brighton
1973 Zoology Building, University of Southampton
1974 Parliament Building extension, Wellington, New Zealand (original design and as consultant)
Palais des Nations extension, Geneva (as consultant)
1975 Bank of Piraeus, Athens
Northampton Lodge, Canonbury, London
Arts Building, University of Sussex, Brighton
Geology and Mining Building, University of Newcastle
1976 Queen Anne's Mansions Office Development, London (original design and as consultant)

1977 Kensington and Chelsea Civic Centre, London
Mariposa Luxury Apartments, Cannes
Ionian Popular Bank, Piraeus

Publications:

By SPENCE: books—*Exhibition Design,* with others, edited by Misha Black, London 1950; *The Cathedral of St. Michael, Coventry,* London 1962; *Phoenix at Coventry: The Building of a Cathedral,* London 1962, 1964; *Out of the Ashes: A Progress Through Coventry Cathedral,* with Henk Snoek, London 1963; *The Idea of a New University: An Experiment in Sussex,* with others, edited by David Daiches, London 1964; *New Buildings in Old Cities,* Southampton 1973; article—"The Modern Church" in *RIBA Journal* (London), July 1956.

On SPENCE: articles—"Basil Spence" in *The Observer* (London), 14 June 1959; "The Very Model of a Monumental O.M." by Peter Lewis in *Queen* (London), 4 December 1962; "Pillar of Architecture" by David Pryce-Jones in *Telegraph Magazine* (London), 28 September 1973; "Obituary" by Richard Sheppard in *RIBA Journal* (London), January 1977; "Obituary" by Sir Frederick Gibberd in *Architectural Review* (London), April 1977; "Sir Basil Spence: An Architect's Appreciation" by Colin Campbell in *Scottish Review* (Edinburgh), Spring 1977.

Sir Basil Spence was raised and received part of his

architectural training in Edinburgh. He came to London to work in the office of Sir Edwin Lutyens on the designs of the government buildings for New Delhi in India. His association with Lutyens influenced the whole of his architectural career, for Basil Spence's work carried the Lutyens stamp of monumentality complete with a deep appreciation of building form and composition. In a truly individual way Spence developed a form of modern architecture that carried on the Lutyens tradition in contemporary terms, using both modern and traditional forms and materials.

His work immediately following World War II was largely concerned with exhibitions and he designed part of the 1951 *Festival of Britain* South Bank Exhibition, the Sea and Ships Pavilion. In 1950 he entered and subsequently won the architectural competition for the rebuilding of Coventry Anglican Cathedral: this event was to have a profound effect on his life's work. The assessors report described the design as "one which shows the author has qualities of spirit and imagination of the highest order." The design, for which Spence prepared all the drawings personally, retained the ruins of the war-damaged Cathedral Church as a memorial shrine and entrance to the new Cathedral, which was planned at right angles to the ruined shell.

The New Coventry Cathedral, which can seat 2,000 people, was consecrated on 25th May 1962; it has been hailed by many critics as one of the outstanding religious buildings of our time. Some, less enthusiastic, pointed out that the elongated plan is not in keeping with recent liturgical thinking, which favours a plan form that encourages the congregation to gather round the altar, rather than view it from a distance. This criticism takes no account of the difficulties of the site, and ignores the fact that it was Spence's wish to bring the altar forward, in front of the choir, to reduce the apparent distance between the focal point of the Cathedral and the congregation. This revision to the design was not approved by the Reconstruction Committee, and the original plan was therefore retained. Time alone will decide the place of Coventry Cathedral in the history of British architecture, but there is no doubt that the ordinary visitor finds much that is satisfying and inspiring. Each year thousands of people visit the Cathedral: it is estimated that more than one million visitors have passed through its doors since the day of consecration.

Spence's intention was that the Cathedral should represent all that is best in our day and age, to the glory of God, and the work of many artists has been included: the tapestry by Graham Sutherland, stained glass by John Piper and Lawrence Lee, sculpture by Jacob Epstein and many others, all designed to compliment rather than compete with the building. Of all the buildings Basil Spence designed, Coventry Cathedral stands out as his personal work, for he involved himself in arduous lecture and money raising tours on behalf of the Reconstruction Committee and concerned himself with every detail of the design and execution of the work.

To many laymen Coventry Cathedral represents the best of contemporary architecture, and apart from Wren, Basil Spence is the only architect that they can name. This one building will rightly ensure that Spence's name is never forgotten.

The controversy that developed over the design of Coventry Cathedral was often repeated with other buildings designed by Basil Spence, for although, initially, the Cathedral dominated his life and work, his services were in constant demand and he received many other commissions. Among the more important were Thorn House, the University of Sussex, the British Embassy in Rome, the Knightsbridge Barracks, and the Hampstead and Kensington Civic Centres. Each of these works has received its share of praise and condemnation. In particular, the Knightsbridge Barracks was considered by some critics as too massive a structure for a site on the edge of Hyde Park, but when the smaller, mediocre towers that fringe the Royal Parks are considered in relation to Spence's tower, they become insignificant, petty intrusions, whereas the Knightsbridge tower has a monumental character, boldly modelled and challenging. Basil Spence was a rare architectural genius, able to develop a genuine monumentality through the medium of contemporary design.

This particular skill is clearly shown in his Rome Embassy design. In a city of great monuments, Spence fitted in naturally and produced a building of great personal character that nevertheless acknowledged the scale and character of its neighbours.

Towards the end of his career Basil Spence seemed to feel, not without justification, that the professional critics were often unfair in their comments about his buildings. For example, the building that replaced Queen Anne's Mansions by St James's Park, for which he was consultant, was severely castigated by the architectural press when the designs were first published. This very large office building faced with Portland stone occupies a very important site in London. Now that it is complete, it is clear that once again the critics have misjudged Spence's skill, for the new building is exactly right in its setting—primarily because of the scale, sculptural form, and massing developed by its architect.

Basil Spence received many honours at home and overseas, including a knighthood and the Order of Merit. He was always able to pass his enthusiasm on to others—students, friends, or audience; he was totally committed to architecture, and his boundless enthusiasm and total sincerity won clients and even

critics over to his side in the end. History will without doubt regard Basil Spence as perhaps the last great architectural figure of the 20th century, who perhaps would have been more at home in earlier times, but who nevertheless left a permanent record of personal achievement, in times when anonymity seems to be regarded as a desirable characteristic.

—Edward D. Mills

STAM, Mart(inus Adrianus).

Dutch. Born in Purmerend, 5 August 1899. Studied drawing at the Rijksnormaalschool voor Tekenonderwijs, Amsterdam, 1917–19. Married the architect Lotte Beese in 1934. Student/Draughtsman, office of J. M. van der Mey, Amsterdam, 1917–19; Draughtsman, office of Granpré Molière, Verhagen and Kok, Rotterdam, 1919–22; worked in the offices of Hans Poelzig and Max Taut, Berlin, 1922, Werner Moser, Zurich, 1923–24, A. Itten, Thun, Switzerland, 1924–25, and J. A. Brinkman and L. C. van der Vlugt, Rotterdam, 1925–28; Guest Lecturer in City Planning, Bauhaus School, Dessau, Germany, 1928–29; worked with Ernst May on city planning in the U.S.S.R., 1930–34; in private practice, with Lotte Beese and W. van Tijen, Amsterdam, 1935–39; Director, Institute for Industrial Arts Education, Amsterdam, 1937–48, Academy of Fine Arts, Dresden, 1948–50, and of the Kunsthochschule für Bildende und Angewandte Künste, East Berlin, 1950–52; worked in collaboration with B. Merkelbach and P. Elling, Amsterdam, 1953–56; established own practice, Amsterdam, 1956: closed studio in 1966 and moved to Switzerland. Editor, with Hans Schmidt, Hannes Meyer, El Lissitzky, and Emil Roth, *ABC*, Zurich, 1924–28; President, Opbouw Group, Rotterdam, 1926–28; Founder Member, CIAM (Congrès Internationaux d'Architecture Moderne), 1928; Co-Founder, GKF (Association of Practitioners of Applied Arts), Amsterdam, 1945; Editor, with Brusse, Jaffé, Kloos, Rietveld and Sandberg, *Open Oog*, Amsterdam, 1946; Co-Organizer, with Mesquita, Sandberg, and van den Broek, Goed Wonen (Good Living) Foundation, Amsterdam, 1947. Exhibition. *Building 20–40*, van Abbemuseum, Eindhoven, Netherlands, 1971.

Works:

1920 City plan for The Hague (competition project)

1920/
30 Budge Foundation Old People's Home, Frankfurt (with Werner Moser)

1922 German Bookprinters Association Building, Dudenstrasse, Berlin (with Max Taut)
Am Knie Office Building (project)
Reinforced Concrete and Glass Office Building, Königsberg, Germany (competition project; with W. von Walthausen)

1924 Wolkenbügel Office Building, Moscow (project; with El Lissitzky)
City plan for Trautenau, Czechoslovakia (competition project)
St. Wendel School, Germany (project)

1925 School, Thun, Switzerland (project)
Shopping Centre with Cafe-Restaurant, Laan van Meerdervoort, The Hague (competition project)
Railway Station, Cornavin, Geneva (project)

1926 Plan for Rokin Square, Amsterdam (competition project)

1926/
27 Housing Block with Three Apartment Types, Amsterdam (project)

1926/
30 van Nelle Factory, Rotterdam (with Brinkman and van der Vlugt)

1927 Bus Station (project)
Terraced housing, Weissenhof Estate, Stuttgart
Water Tower, Amsterdam (project)

1927/
28 Plan for the Hofplein, Rotterdam (project; with the Opbouw Group)

1928 N. V. Van Berkel's Patent Office, Keileweg, Rotterdam (project)
Baba House, Prague (project; built in 1933 to revised plans)

1929/
31 Hellerhof Housing Development, Frankfurt

1930/
31 City plan for Magnitogorsk, U.S.S.R.

1931 Open-Air Theatre, Urals, U.S.S.R. (project)

1932/
33 City redevelopment and reconstruction plan for Makejevka, U.S.S.R.

1933/
34 City Plan for Orsk, U.S.S.R.

1936 Apartment building, Anthonie van Dijckstraat, Amsterdam (with W. van Tijen and Lotte Beese)

1937 Town Hall, Amsterdam (competition project; with W. van Tijen, Lotte Beese and H. A. Maaskant)

1938 Plan for the Bos and Lommer District, Amsterdam

1938/
39 Layout for *De Trein* (Dutch Railways Centenary Exhibition), Amsterdam

1939 Fokker Factory Exhibition Stand (project)
Dutch Pavilion, *World's Fair*, New York

1940 Dutch Pavilion, *Trade Fair*, Cologne (project)

1942 Crematorium with Columbarium, The Hague (competition project)
City expansion plan for Rotterdam (with the De 8 Group)

1949 Reconstruction plan for the Old City, Dresden

1954 City plan for Nagele, Nordoostpolder, Netherlands

1956/
59 Housing Complex, for the Het Osten Catholic Building Commission, Dr. H. Colijnstraat, Amsterdam (with Merkelbach and Elling)

1957 Plan for the Hansaviertel District, Berlin

1957/
59 N. V. De Geillustreerde Pers Office Building, Stadhouderskade, Amsterdam (with Merkelbach and Elling)

1958 Beatrix Apartment Building, Dopperkade/Beethovenstraat, Amsterdam

1959/
61 Princesse Apartment Building/Office/Garage Complex, Beethovenstraat, Amsterdam

1962 Apartment building with self-service shop, Linnaeusstraat/Polderweg, Amsterdam

1963 Mahuko High-Rise Office Building, De Tijd-Maasbode, Amsterdam

1964 Sports Center, De Boelelaan, Amsterdam

1965 Country house, Hierden, near Harderwijk, Netherlands

Publications:

By STAM: articles—"Kollektive Gestaltung" in *ABC* 1 (Zurich), no. 1, 1924–25; "Die Reklame," with El Lissitzky, and "Modernes Bauen 1" in *ABC 1* (Zurich), no. 2, 1924–25; "Modernes Bauen 2" and "Modernes Bauen 3" in *ABC 1* (Zurich), no. 3/4, 1924–25; "Der Raum die Fläche, das Volumen, der Volumenkomplex," with H. Schmidt, in *ABC 1* (Zurich), no. 5, 1924–25; "Der Zusammenbruch der Monumentalität in Rotterdam 1922, 1926, 1928" in *ABC 2* (Zurich), no. 4, 1927–28; "Das Mass—Das richtige Mass—Das Minimum-Mass" in *Das Neue Frankfurt*, no. 3, 1929; numerous articles in *De 8 en Opbouw* (Amsterdam), 1935–42; "Die Architektur-Konzeption El Lissitzkys" in *El Lissitzky*, exhibition catalogue, Basle and Hanover 1965, 1966; "Armoede of Welstand" in *Open Oog* (Amsterdam), no. 1, 1946; "Behoudzucht" in *Open Oog* (Amsterdam), no. 2, 1946.

On STAM: books—*Holländische Architektur* by J. J. P. Oud, Munich 1926, 1927; *Grossstadt Architektur* by Ludwig Hilberseimer, Stuttgart 1927; *Modern Dutch Builders* by F. R. Yerbury, London 1931; *De Stijl 1917–1931: The Dutch Contribution to Modern Art* by H. L. C. Jaffé, Amsterdam 1956; *Theory and Design in the First Machine Age* by Reyner Banham, London 1960; *Die Weissenhofsiedlung* by Jürgen Joedicke and Christian Plath, Stuttgart 1968; *Mart Stam* by G. Oorthuys, London 1970; *Building 20–40*, exhibition catalogue, Eindhoven, Netherlands 1971; articles—special issue of *Bouwkundig Weekblad* (The Hague), 23 December 1969; "Mart Stam" by Walter Segal in *The Architects' Journal* (London), 3 June 1970; "Weissenhof, 50 Years Later" by Norbert W. Daldrop in *Moebel Interior Design* (Leinfelden), February 1977; "The Development of the Weissenhof Estate in Stuttgart" by Babo Rasch in *Deutsche Bauzeitung* (Stuttgart), November 1977.

Mart Stam belongs to that group of functionalist architects who, in the late 1920's, had an appreciable influence on the development of international architecture and, in particular, its ideology. Among the members of this group were the collaborators on the social critical review *ABC* (1924–28): Stam, Hans Schmidt, Hannes Meyer and El Lissitzky. Their influence was such that in 1928 Meyer became Director of the Bauhaus in Dessau and Mart Stam Guest Lecturer. And it was Stam, Meyer and Schmidt who, in 1928, created the famous concluding declaration at the first CIAM (Congrès Internationaux d'Architecture Moderne), thereby thwarting Le Corbusier's intention of putting forward his own conceptions. Even during the preparations for the Weissenhof Estate in Stuttgart in 1927, Mart Stam, with his socialist ideas, was an opponent of Le Corbusier, the independent artist. In Holland, from 1926–28, after Oud's resignation, Stam took over as the active President of the architects' association Opbouw.

This group of architects, which was known as the radical left wing of the avant garde, had strong social commitments. Van Loghem, a colleague of Stam's, has expressed their attitude as follows: "The whole of our creative thinking was directed to ideas of so

cial revolution." Because the West did not offer these architects an opportunity to realize the goal of a renewal of society, they hoped to achieve it in Communist Russia within the framework of the Five Year Plan. From 1930 onwards, Stam, Schmidt and Meyer, together with Ernst May, André Lurcat and others, went to Russia as specialists, involved mainly in the building of the new Russian industrial towns. Between 1932 and 1934, however, a change occurred in Communist dogma: the "Ideology of Labor" was transformed into the "Ideology of Socialist Man." The foreign specialists were reproached with building inhuman towns, and, as a result, they had to leave Russia. There was something ironically comic in their situation: in Russia they were dismissed as decadent bourgeois architects; in the West they were received as cultural bolshevists.

And, yet, the group was completely serious. Influenced by Marxist theory, the *ABC* architects wanted to fulfil the essential spiritual and material needs of all mankind. In order to achieve this goal, they took the path of pure science and technique; they consistently turned away from the traditional formal demands of architecture. They believed in the technical neutrality of architecture: they saw architecture as a problem of organization. Hannes Meyer said: "The devaluation of all works of art is indisputable, and without doubt their replacement by an exact science is only a question of time. Art is on the These basic ideas permeate the 1928 CIAM Declaration: "Town planning is the organization of all the functions of collective life in the town and in the country. Town planning can never be determined by aesthetic considerations but exclusively by functional deductions. The most important factor in town planning is the systematic arrangement of functions—a) housing; b) work; and c) recreation (sport, pleasure). Means to the fulfilment of these functions are a) land division; b) traffic regulation; and c) legislation." The Athens Charter of 1933— with its well-known four functions division and its scientific, analytic method of Functionalism—also owes much to the work of the *ABC* architects group.

The understanding of architecture as science (analysis) as opposed to architecture as art (intuition) brought about tensions in the CIAM. In 1938 Giedion described the two opposing tendencies as productive of architectural discussion, but after the Second World War a shift took place within the CIAM and more emphasis was thereafter placed on architecture as art (Team 10).

Mart Stam's work can be divided into two periods, 1920–34 and 1934–65: the transition coincides roughly with his return from Russia in 1934. It is the first period that is of most importance.

Stam is a representative of the Dutch "Whites" of the 1920's, along with Rietveld, Oud, Duiker and van der Vlugt. During this period he played a very special role, which can be perhaps be compared with that of Theo van Doesburg: they were spokesmen for new tendencies, and both made a creative contribution to conceptions of architecture. While van Doesburg propagated the De Stijl aesthetic with his cubes and squares composition, Mart Stam took a new road. Influenced by Russian Constructivism and Futurism, he became one of the leading spokesmen of Functionalism.

Architectonically, Stam's Constructivist contribution is of particular importance. With brilliantly drawn constructivist perspective-projects, he created a sensation in international specialist offices—with the Königsberg Office Building, the Wolkenbügel variations, the Geneva-Cornavin Railway Station, the Rokin in Amsterdam, etc. It was in a similar spirit that these well-known Constructivist-inspired buildings were exected in Holland at the end of the 20's—Duiker's Sanatorium in Hilversum and the Open-Air School in Amsterdam, and van der Vlugt's Rotterdam Stadium and, to a certain extent, the van Nelle Factory. (Compare, too, the Constructivist project by Le Corbusier for the Soviet Palace in 1931.)

Of Mart Stam's dozen or so executed buildings, his contribution to the Weissenhof Estate is architecturally the most valuable. He created this work, terraced housing, during the period when he collaborated, between 1925–28, in the architectural practice of Brinkman and van der Vlugt (when he also took part in various works for which van der Vlugt was responsible, for example, the van Nelle Factory). Stimulated by Marcel Breuer's chair experiments, Stam also designed for the Weissenhof Estate a 2-legged sprung tubular steel chair—as did Mies van der Rohe: it was presumably in preliminary discussions about the exhibition that Mies adopted Stam's basic idea. Further, Stam's functionalist town planning schemes for Russia (1930–34) are remarkable, as is his project for an open-air theatre in the Urals.

Thanks to the currently available monographs on the Dutch "Whites" of the 1920's, and because of the research that was necessary to produce these studies, this group can now be assigned their appropriate

Mart Stam: Baba House, Prague, 1928 (project)

place in architectural history. Besides his contribution to Stuttgart, Mart Stam is important principally for his Constructivist and town planning projects and for his inspirational role as spokesman for Functionalism. In a critical examination of his completed works, one should be guided not only by his own ideologies but also by this directive from his adversary Le Corbusier who, at the beginning of the 1920's, said: "The development of form is the architect's touchstone."

—Arnulf Lüchinger

STEPHEN, Douglas (Cruden).

British. Born in Fraserburgh, Scotland, 4 May 1923. Educated at the American School, Shanghai, China, 1929–33; China Inland Mission School for Boys, Chefoo, now Yentai, Shantung, China, 1934–37; Royal High School, Edinburgh, 1938–39; St. Asaph County Grammar School, North Wales, 1940–42; University of Liverpool School of Architecture, 1942–43; Architectural Association School, London, under Arthur Korn and H. T. Cadbury-Brown, 1945–48, 1952–53. Married the architect Margaret Olivia Dent in 1947 (divorced, 1965); children: John and Jan. Assistant Designer with John Lansdell, London, 1948–49; Architectural Assistant to Ernö Goldfinger, London, 1949–50; Part-time Architectural Assistant to H. T. Cadbury Brown, London, 1950. Since 1954, Founder Partner, with Margaret Dent, Douglas Stephen and Partners, London (current partners: Stephen; Dent; Barnaby Milburn; Robert Maxwell). Exhibitions: Royal Academy, London, 1974; Museum of Modern Art, New York, 1978. Recipient: Ministry of Housing and Local Government Award, 1964; South West Region Award, Royal Institute of British Architects, 1977; Constrato-Steel Award, 1978. Address: Douglas Stephen and Partners, 42–44 Beak Street, London W1R 4DS, England.

Works:

1949/
54 Manor house modernization, North Houghton, Hampshire (with Margaret Dent)
House conversions, London (with Margaret Dent)
Exhibitions and shops, London and Glasgow (with Margaret Dent)
House, East Horsley, Surrey
1951 Civil Engineering and Irrigation sections, *Festival of Britain,* Kelvin Hall, Glasgow (with Margaret Dent)
1954 Pottery showroom and offices, Baker Street, London (now demolished)
1955 Showroom and maisonettes, Crawford Street, London W.1 (project)
1956 Haslerigge Road Primary School extension, South London
Apartment block, Lansdowne Road, London W.11 (project)
Apartment block, 103–105 Harley Street, London W.1
Apartment block, 62–64 Wimpole Street, London W.1
1959/
63 Office building, Deansgate and St. Mary's Gate, Manchester
1959/
64 Centre Heights (shops, offices and flats development), Swiss Cottage, London (with Panos Koulermos)
1961/
64 The Mount (apartment block), Bedford Gardens, London W.1
Pre- and post-natal clinic, Acton, London (with Alan Forrest)

1962/
65 Crossover maisonettes, Craven Hill Gardens, Paddington, London (with Kenneth Frampton)
1963/
67 Hereward Centre (shopping centre), Peterborough (with Elia Zenghelis and David Bradley)
1964 Evelyn's Secondary School, Yewsley, Middlesex (project; with Alan Forrest)
Southwood Park Apartments, Highgate, London (with Robert Maxwell)
UAM House (office building), Watford, Hertfordshire (with David Wild and Ed Jones)
1965 Evelyn's Secondary School, Yewsley, Middlesex (with Alan Forrest and Claire Watson)
1965/
66 Housing, Dover, Kent (with Margaret Dent)
Old people's housing, Cosser Street, London (project; with David Bradley)
Low-rise high-density housing, Cramer Street, London (project; with David Bradley)
1965/
69 Rodwell Tower, Piccadilly, Manchester
1966 Housing, Joel Street, Middlesex (project)
Royal College of Art conversion, London (with Elia Zenghelis)
Office building, Waltham Cross, Hertfordshire (project; with Robin Spence)
Brunel Centre, stage I and master plan, Swindon, Wiltshire (with Robert Maxwell)
Shops, offices and flats development, Swiss Cottage, London (project)
Housing, Breakspear Road, Hillingdon, London (project)
Kitchen range for Boulton and Paul (project; with Robin Spence and David Bradley)
Greater London Council low-rise high-density housing, Drummond Street, Camden, London (with Robert Maxwell)
French Embassy high-security penthouse extension, London (with Robert Maxwell and Barnaby Milburn)
1967 Greater London Council Housing, Middleton Street, Bethnal Green, London (with Robin Spence and David Bradley)
Branch Library, South Ruislip, Middlesex (with Robin Spence)
1968 Brunel Centre, stage II, Swindon, Wiltshire (with Adrian Gale, Gerard Gilgallon and Barnaby Milburn)
1969 St. Paul de l'Etoile Satellite Town, La Gude, Var, France (project; with Martin Richardson and Margaret Dent)
Mechanical garage, Boston (project; with Anton Furst)
1971 Office building, Manchester (project; with Barnaby Milburn)
Hotel, Earl's Court, London (project)
Low-income housing, Nassau (with David Bradley)
Hotel, Bahamas (project; with Kenneth Frampton)
Historic building rehabilitation, London (project; with Margaret Dent)
Housing rehabilitation, Southwark, London (project; with Margaret Dent)
1972 2 social services buildings, Luton, Bedfordshire (project; with Robert Maxwell)
Housing Advice Centre, Hillingdon, London (with Charles Sands)
1973 Brunel Centre, stage III, Swindon, Wiltshire (with Barnaby Milburn and BDP)
Hotel complex, M4 Motorway, Wiltshire (project; with Barnaby Milburn)
2 libraries and 3 social services buildings, Hillingdon, London (with Charles Sands)
Apartment block, Fitzjohn's Avenue, London N.W.3 (project)
Office building, London Road, East Grinstead, Sussex (project; with Barnaby Milburn and Stephen Gage)

Flats, Hove, Sussex (project; with Charles Sands)
Housing, Ascot Road, Haringay, London (with Robert Maxwell, Andrew Preece, David Lyall and Margaret Dent)
Health Centre, Bounds Green, London (with Stephen Gage)
Neo-classical house, Hampstead, London
1974 Gallagher Tobacco Showroom, Bond Street, London W.1 (project; with Achille Castiglione)
1975 St. James's Churchyard Shopping Centre conversion, Piccadilly, London W.1 (project)
1976 Historic house rehabilitation, Chelsea, London (project)
1977 National Magazine Company Headquarters, London (project)
3 permanent exhibition buildings for 'Concorde' prototypes (project I: with Robert Maxwell; project II: with Barnaby Milburn, Stephen Gage and Stephen Buck; project III: with Carl Laubin and Robert Hughes)
4 hotels for shrine sites for pilgrims, Iraq (project; with Barnaby Milburn, Robert Hughes, Stephen Buck and Carl Laubin)
1977/
78 Urban renewal plan for Kendall Square, Cambridge, Massachusetts (project; with Barnaby Milburn, Stephen Buck, Robert Hughes, Robert Maxwell and Carl Laubin)
1978 Brunel Centre, stage IV, Swindon, Wiltshire (with Barnaby Milburn, Robert Hughes, Stephen Buck and Carl Laubin)
Victorian office building rehabilitation, Poland Street, Soho, London (with Stephen Gage)
Victorian warehouse rehabilitation, Folgate Street, London E.1 (project)
1979 Above Bar Church, Southampton (project; with Stephen Buck)

Publications:

By STEPHEN: book—*British Buildings 1960–64,* with Kenneth Frampton and Michael Carapetian, London 1965; articles—"Institute of Technology at Otaniemi, Finland" in *Architectural Design* (London), February 1968; "25 Years of British Architecture 1952–1977: Commercial Buildings" in *RIBA Journal* (London), May 1977.

On STEPHEN: article—"Douglas Stephen and Partners" by Robert Maxwell in *Architectural Design* (London), September/October 1977.

*

Having entered architectural practice at the beginning of the fifties, I belong to an immediate post-war generation which felt very closely in touch with the sources of the modern movement on the Continent, and indeed saw modern architecture as a cause to fight for in Britain.

The enjoyment of functional empiricism in the post-war period was partly an appreciation of its flexibility in relation to the varying demands of different jobs, but also a desire to exploit its own potential for structuring this diversity with a visual order. There were crucial differences in the modern style as practised in Le Corbusier and Terragni, say, or in Gropius or Breuer, and I belonged to a circle whose discrimination between such stylistic nuances had been sharpened by the teaching of Colin Rowe. It was this unequivocal influence also which enabled one to see modern architecture as being as much due to stylistic invention as to empirical necessity.

The willingness to accept an arbitrary or pre-conceived mental element in works of architecture enables them to be treated as vehicles of expression for ideas. This approach is probably the main explanation for the marked classicism and narrow eclecti-

cism which has characterized my own work of our practice today.

I have never ceased to regard architecture as a practical art, which uses technology of necessity but never becomes subservient to it. Between demands of the programme, the resources of technology, I always look to a means of making the buildings communicate. In that way I hope to be equal to the task of responding to the social implications in a programme, and enlarging the depths of meaning that mere buildings may have for most people.

—Douglas Stephen

As a student Douglas Stephen was remarkable amongst his contemporaries for his enthusiasm and drive. While still a student he undertook many small commissions for exhibition stands, and this led to his being responsible for an extensive area of the exhibition mounted in Glasgow in 1951 as part of the *Festival of Britain* celebrations, under the aegis of the late Sir Basil Spence. This experience of actually getting things built was an important factor in his early success as a practitioner.

The buildings of this early period are in one sense works of immaturity, but they also display a thorough professionalism and certainly reflect the confidence which during the post-war period most architects placed in the benefits of redevelopment. However, two aspects of the work of this early period were remarkable: the apartments at Harley Street and Wimpole Street stand out, not for their functionalist aesthetic, but for their classicism; while the flats at Bedford Gardens are ultra-modern in a distinctly European, not an English, way. The difference of approach suggests the opening up of a polemic within Stephen's understanding of architecture, and betrays an interest in style and the theory of style which is quite other than the single-mindedness of a practitioner who wants only to get things built.

Stephen's awareness of these stylistic choices indicates an inner intellectuality at variance with his surface qualities of empiricism and entrepreneurial initiative. The potential was present from the beginning for the discovery of an approach to architecture which could reconcile the demands of the programme with a conscious refusal of a purely programmatic inspiration. This also perhaps explains how his practice developed into a gentle patronage in which others could join in this quest. The recital of those who worked there as associates and later distinguished themselves in their own right as radical designers or theorists is testimony to the generous spirit in which he worked: Panos Koulermis, Kenneth Frampton, Elia Zenghelis, Robin Spence, Adrian Gale, Edward Jones and Peter Jamieson all contributed to the work of the office and helped to produce a varied output which never took the facile imprint of a "house style."

In the early 1970's this period of eclectic search was succeeded by a more concentrated period of consolidation. The practice was enlarged by the addition of Robert Maxwell and Barnaby Milburn, and gave itself the task of attempting to reconcile the diversity of approaches in a more consistent theoretical method. From this middle period have come the various buildings constructed at Swindon for the Borough of Thamesdown. These buildings make positive spaces between each other and with the adjoining parts of the town. Each building is distinctive, so that a single character is not imposed on a large slice of the town, but rather between them they sketch out a way of dealing with the comprehensive redevelopment without the usual penalties of uniformity and visual impoverishment. Technological possibilities are explored in the interests of making an up-to-date facility, but they do not take over as the predominant content of the architecture, imposing a uniformity of appearance. The various glazed

Douglas Stephen: Brunel Center, Swindon, Wiltshire, 1978

canopies are made out of modern materials with modern technology, yet they are also reminiscent of 19th century arcades and railway architecture, appropriate to a railway town. These buildings represent the maturing of Stephen's original perception that style and function have to be attended to separately, and reconciled, along with a more general reconciliation between classical and modern, between the claims of development and those of environment and history.

—Robert Maxwell

STERN, Robert A. M.

American. Born in New York City, 23 May 1939. Educated at Columbia University, New York, B.A. 1960; Yale University, New Haven, Connecticut, M.Arch. 1965. Married Lynn Solinger in 1966 (divorced, 1978); son: Nicholas. Worked for the Perkins and Will Partnership, Washington, D.C., summer 1964; Program Director, The Architectural League of New York, 1965–66; Designer, Office of Richard Meier, New York, 1966; Consultant to Philip Johnson for *Eye on New York* television documentary, CBS-TV, and Member, Mayor Lindsay's Task Force on Urban Design, 1966–67; Consultant, Small Parks Program, New York, 1966–70; Urban Designer and Assistant for Design Policy to Assistant Administrator Samuel Ratensky, Housing and Development Administration, New York, 1967–70; Partner, Robert A. M. Stern and John S. Hagmann, architects, New York, 1969–77. Since 1977, Principal, Robert A. M. Stern Architects, New York. Lecturer, 1970–72, Assistant Professor, 1973–77, and since 1977 Associate Professor, Columbia University (Chairman, Committee on Lectures and Exhibits, since 1971, and College Departmental Representative, since 1973). William Henry Bishop Visiting Professor, Yale University, 1978. Member, Board of Directors, Yale Arts Association, 1968–72; Vice-President, Cunningham Dance Foundation, 1969–73; Member, Architecture Committee, Whitney Museum, New York, 1970–76; President, Architectural League of New York, 1973–77; Director, New York Chapter, American Institute of Architects, 1976–78. Trustee, American Federation of the Arts, since 1967; Member, Mayor's Panel of Architects, New York, since 1975. Exhibitions: group shows—*The Roosevelt Island Competition*, Architectural League of New York, 1975; *Biennale*, Venice, 1976; *Palaces for the People*, Cooper-Hewitt Museum, New York, 1977; *Drawing Toward a More Modern Architecture*, Drawing Center and Cooper-Hewitt Museum, New York, 1977; *Art and Contemporary Architecture*, David Findlay Galleries, New York, Fall 1977; *Celebration of Water*, Cooper-Hewitt Museum, New York, 1978; *Transformations in Modern Architecture*, Museum of Modern Art, New York, 1979; one-man shows—North Carolina School of Design, Raleigh, 1976; Art Net, London, 1977; Architectural Club, Miami, 1978. Organized: continuing series of exhibits for the Architectural League of New York, 1965–66; *40 under 40*, American Federation of the Arts travelling exhibition, 1966; *Another Chance for Cities*, Whitney Museum, New York, and tour, 1970–71; *Some Younger New York Architects*, Columbia University and Boston Architectural Center, 1971–72; *Ornament in the 20th Century*, Cooper-Hewitt Museum, New York, Fall 1978; *Trends in Contemporary Architecture*, New Gallery of Contemporary Art, Cleveland, 1978. Collection: Tehran Museum of Contemporary Art. Recipient: Award of Honor, New York Society of Architects, 1974; First Prize, Roosevelt Island Housing Competition, New York, 1975; Certificate of Honor, New York State Association of Architects, 1975; Certificate of Merit, New York State Association of Architects/American Institute of Architects, 1976;

Award of Merit, *House and Home*/AIA, 1977; Residential Design Award, AIA, New York Chapter, 1977; First Honor Award, Homes for Better Living, *Housing*, 1978; Lumen Award, New York Section, Illuminating Engineering Society/International Association of Lighting Designers, 1978. Address: Robert A. M. Stern Architects, 200 West 72nd Street, New York, New York 10023, U.S.A.

Works:

1968 Wiseman House, Montauk, Long Island, New York

1969 Tiffeau-Busch Ltd. Showroom and Offices, New York

1970 Showrooms for Helen Harper Inc., New York

1971 William White Jr. Apartment, New York
      Poolhouse and related facilities, Danziger House, Purchase, New York

1972 Beebe House and outbuildings, Montauk, Long Island, New York
      Kretchmer Apartment, New York
      Danziger Apartment, New York

1973 Eisner Apartment, New York
      Source Securities Corporation office alterations, New York (additional alterations, 1975, 1976)

1974 Poolhouse, for Bourke House, Greenwich, Connecticut
      Ferris Booth Hall additions and alterations, Columbia University, New York (project)
      Lang House, Washington, Connecticut
      Library, Museum, and Civic Plaza, Biloxi, Mississippi (project)
      University Hotel, John Jay Hall, Columbia University, New York (project)

1975 Dooney and Bourke Factory, Norwalk, Connecticut (project)
      Tennis Club, for King/Hitzig Productions, New York (project)
      Squash Courts and Club Facility, for Bourke Enterprises, Newton, Massachusetts (project)
      Development plan for the city of Regina, Saskatchewan (competition project)
      Cullman House additions and alterations, Stamford, Connecticut
      Ehrman House and outbuildings, Armonk, New York
      Leonard Stern Townhouse, New York
      Hope Solinger Apartment, New York
      Solinger and Gordon Law Offices, New York
      Roosevelt Island Housing, New York (competition project)

1976 Danziger House additions and alterations, Purchase, New York
      Ferrin House, East Hampton, Long Island, New York
      Ski Lodge, Killington, Vermont (competition project)
      Development plan for Singer Island, City of Riviera Beach, Florida (competition project)
      St. Joseph's Village for Senior Citizens (competition project)
      Student Television Studio, Ferris Booth Hall, Columbia University, New York (project)
      State Capitol Annex Building, St. Paul, Minnesota (competition project)
      Subway Suburb, *Biennale*, Venice

1977 Jerome Greene Building, School of Law, Columbia University, New York
      Bourke House, Seal Harbor, Maine

1978 Rodman Rockefeller Apartment, New York
      Millstein Townhouse, New York

1979 Erbun Fabrics Inc. Showroom, New York
      First Avenue Squash Club, New York
      Catlin House, Dublin, New Hampshire
      Maynard House, East Hampton, Long Island, New York
      Cohen Apartment, New York
      Silvera House, Deal, New Jersey

STERN

Hitzig Apartment, New York
International House renovation, New York
Smetana Medical Suite, New York
Prototypical facade for Best Inc.
1980 Cohn House, Llewellyn Park, New Jersey
Cohn House, Chilmark, Martha's Vineyard, Massachusetts
Lawson House, East Quoque, Long Island, New York

Publications:

By STERN: books—*40 Under 40: Young Talent in Architecture,* exhibition catalogue, New York 1966; *New Directions in American Architecture,* New York 1969, 1977; *George Howe: Toward a Modern American Architecture,* New Haven, Connecticut 1975; introduction to *The PSFS Building* (booklet), Philadelphia 1976; foreword, with Wilder Green, to *200 Years of American Architectural Drawings* by David Gebhard and Deborah Nevins, New York 1977; *Europa/America: Architetture Urbane Alternative Suburbane,* with others, *Biennale* exhibition catalogue, Venice 1978; commentary to *Philip Johnson: Collected Writings,* New York 1979; *American Architectural Drawings,* with Deborah Nevins, New York 1979; articles—"PSFS: Beaux Arts Theory and Rational Expressionism" in *Journal of the Society of Architectural Historians* (Philadelphia), May 1962; "Relevance of the Decade 1929–1939" in *Journal of the Society of Architectural Historians* (Phila-

delphia), March 1965; "Paul Rudolph: The First Twenty-Five Years" in *Kokusai Kenchiku* (Tokyo), May 1965; editor of *Perspecta* (New Haven, Connecticut), no. 9/10, 1965; "Constitution Plaza One Year After" in *Progressive Architecture* (New York), December 1965; "A Static Gallery" in *Progressive Architecture* (New York), April 1966; "Random Shots at USA '65" in *Progressive Architecture* (New York), May 1966; "Stompin' at the Savoye" in *Architectural Forum* (New York), May 1973; "Tape Recorder Chats" in *Architectural Record* (New York), May 1973; "Raymond Hood" in *Progressive Architecture* (New York), July 1974; "Yale 1950–1965" in *Oppositions* (New York), October 1974; "Toward an Architecture of Symbolic Assemblage" in *Progressive Architecture* (New York), April 1975; editor of "White and Gray," special issue of *Architecture + Urbanism* (Tokyo), April 1975; "A Serious Discussion of an Apparently Whimsical House" in *Architectural Record* (New York), July 1975; "Park Avenue Is Almost All Right (Maybe)" in *Architectural Record* (New York), February 1976; "Letter to the Editor" in *Oppositions* (New York), Winter 1976; "Robert Stern on Jim Stirling" in *Design Quarterly 100* (Minneapolis), Spring 1976; "Gray Architecture: Quelques Variations Post-Modernistes Autour de l'Orthodoxie" in *L'Architecture d'Aujourd'hui* (Paris), August/September 1976; guest editor of "40 Under 40 + 10," special issue of *Architecture + Urbanism* (Tokyo), January 1977; "At the Edge of Modernism" in *Architectural Design*

(London), April 1977; "Forum: The Beaux-Arts Exhibition" in *Oppositions* (New York), Spring 1977; "Letter to the Editor" in *Contract Interiors* (New York), July 1977; "Further Thoughts on Millbank," with George Baird and Charles Jencks, in *Architectural Design* (London), July/August 1977; "Report: New York Notebook" in *Architecture + Urbanism* (Tokyo), August 1977; "The Evolution of Philip Johnson's Glass House, 1947–48" in *Oppositions* (New York), Fall 1977; "Something Borrowed, Something New" in *Horizon* (New York), December 1977; "After the Modern Movement" in *The Japan Architect* (Tokyo), December 1977; "Venturi and Rauch: Learning to Love Them" in *Architectural Monographs* (London), vol. 1, 1978; "New Directions in Modern American Architecture: Postscript" in *Architectural Association Quarterly* (London), nos. 2/3, 1978; "The Suburban Alternative: Coping with the Middle City" in *Architectural Record* (New York), August 1978; "How to Redesign New York" in *Art News* (New York), November 1978; "Models for Reality: Some Observations" in *Great Models* (Student Publication: North Carolina State University School of Design, Raleigh), no. 27, 1978; "Drawing from Models," with Frances Halsband, R. M. Kliment, and Richard B. Oliver, in *Journal of Architectural Education* (Washington, D.C.), September 1978; "Doubles of Post-Modern" in *Harvard Architecture Review* (Cambridge, Massachusetts), vol. 1, 1979; "With Rhetoric, The New York Apartment House" in *Via* (Philadelphia), no. 4, 1979;

Robert A. M. Stern: Lang House, Washington, Connecticut, 1974

774

"Not Spaces but . . . Rooms" in *Global House* (Tokyo), December 1978.

On STERN: books—*The Roosevelt Island Competition,* exhibition catalogue, edited by Barbara Goldstein, New York 1975; *Wohnen im Eigenen Haus* by Gerhard Schwab, Stuttgart 1976; *The Form of Housing,* edited by Sam Davis, New York 1977; *The Language of Post-Modern Architecture* by Charles Jencks, London 1977; *Decorative Art and Modern Interiors 1978,* volume 67, edited by Maria Schofield, New York 1978; articles—"Lang Residence: Where Are We Now, Vincent Scully?" by Charles Moore in *Progressive Architecture* (New York), April 1975; "Residence for an Academical Couple, Washington, Connecticut, 1973–74" in *Architecture + Urbanism* (Tokyo), April 1975; "The Work of Robert A. M. Stern and John S. Hagmann," special feature in *Architecture + Urbanism* (Tokyo), October 1975; "Stern Dimensions" in *Progressive Architecture* (New York), June 1976; "Les Cendres de Jefferson" by Manfredo Tafuri and "Robert Stern-/John Hagmann" in *L'Architecture d'Aujourd'hui* (Paris), August/September 1976; "Architecture: Letting Go with Color" in *House and Garden* (New York), September 1976; "Stern Star Estrella: La Obra de Robert A. M. Stern" in *Arquitecturas Bis* (Barcelona), September 1976; "40-under 40: Robert A. M. Stern" in *Architecture + Urbanism* (Tokyo), January 1977; "Grand Allusions" by Suzanne Stephens in *Progressive Architecture* (New York), February 1977; "The Stern View" by Jane Holtz Kay in *Building Design* (London), 11 February 1977; "Robert Stern," interview, by Bob Maltz in *Building Design* (London), 10 June 1977; "Robert A. M. Stern's Two Houses" by Paul Goldberger in *Architecture + Urbanism* (Tokyo), September 1977; "The Re-emergence of Color as a Design Tool" by Nory Miller in *AIA Journal* (Washington, D.C.), October 1978; "Designs for Living" by Douglas Davis in *Newsweek* (New York), 6 November 1978; "U.S. Architects: Doing Their Own Thing" by Robert Hughes in *Time* (New York), 8 January 1979.

*   *   *

Many of the cherished orthodoxies of the Modern Movement are now being supplanted by new concerns and beliefs. While these may not yet define a theory of architecture, a few beliefs that now guide my work may have wider implications for understanding the architectural climate of our time: 1) applied ornament is no crime; 2) buildings that refer to other buildings in the history of architecture are more meaningful than those which do not (this used to be called "eclecticism"); 3) buildings that refer and defer to the buildings around them gain strength over those that do not (this might be called "contextual integration"); 4) buildings that associate with ideas about specific events which caused them to be made are more meaningful than those which do not; the pursuit of specific images to convey ideas about buildings is relevant to design; 5) architecture is a story-telling or communicative art. Facades are not diaphanous veils; nor are they the affirmation of deep structural secrets. They are mediators between buildings as "real" constructs and those illusions, allusions and perceptions necessary to put buildings in closer contact with their social, cultural, historical and physical milieu.

Language and Meaning: In issues of form, as opposed to issues of technology or functional accommodation, orthodox modern architecture has been unwilling to accept known paradigms; over and over, the leading architects of the past generation have struggled to invent new forms that would replace those from the past which had become widely accepted as symbols. Rather than searching for ways of saying new things in traditional languages, our most inventive Modern architects have attempted with very modest success to invent a new, exclusive, absolute, universal architectural language. Nonetheless, at this point in time, the new language of modernism cannot be ignored no matter how limited it may appear to be in relationship to the great architectural languages of the past. In certain situations the modernist language is very potent: as in the designs of factories and other industrial buildings and especially in the components of buildings including the furniture which was the specialty of the Bauhaus. But, for most situations, especially those affecting the private realm of habitation and the public realm of institutional and urban design, the language of modernism—especially its dialect known as the International Style—has often proven incapable of subtle expression. The modernist styles are abstract rather than associative, conceptual rather than perceptual, technologically rather than culturally based. Modernism has become a narcissistic exercise about the making of buildings. As such, it has cut itself off not only from its role as a cultural act but also from its own formal traditions.

I believe that architectural form is related to symbolic intention and not technological expression; that architectural design is based on a known integration of lessons learned from those buildings that one admires and clients value—whether the client be individuals or the public and its institutions; and that forms from the past must be manipulated in relationship to particular and environmental situations. I believe that such a process of integration and manipulation—which used to be called eclecticism—can enrich our work and thereby make it more familiar and, possibly, more meaningful not only to the people who use buildings directly but also to those who merely see them in passing. The idea of eclecticism in architecture ought not to be embarrassing; after all, virtually every architect chose his or her art and profession out of admiration for buildings which were already in existence.

In the same way that many architects talk about functional programs which cause work to emerge in a particular way, and about the constraints of site, budget, and so on, which also serve to shape it, architects should be willing to talk about the forms of earlier architecture which have spoken directly to them. And it seems perfectly logical to me that details and sometimes whole images from admired work of the past find their way into current work just as portions of the literature of the past find their way into much of the poetry and prose of our time and just as our spoken language has within it certain phrases adopted whole from foreign languages.

Ornamentalism is the handmaiden of eclecticism. It is a paradox that when the Modern Movement threw out applied ornament it took over the characteristics of ornamentation—natural imagery, plasticity and continuity—even, on occasion, representationalism—and used them to establish not only a new language but also a new grammar of building form. This had the effect of turning whole buildings into utilitarian ornaments. Contrast Howell and Hood's *Chicago Tribune* building with Adolf Loos's project: one an image of a gothic tower, the other literally a doric column. At present, it seems that the use of familiar ornamental devices from the past is one way of making architecture more accessible. The articulation of new and old elements is deliberately blurred in my work: my feet are firmly placed on both sides of the line of historical imperative. I am both Modern and contemporary, anxious to reinforce tradition without losing sight of the fact that though I can choose to speak an old language, I will need to coin new phrases and, of course, to say new things.

I believe that design is, in part, a process of cultural assimilation. Though design includes problem-solving, the functional and technological paradigms called for in the vast majority of situations with which we deal have been established over the past 200 years: hence we can discuss building typology. Our task is to question the formal prejudices—or are they paradigms?—which dog us at what I regard as the end of modernism. And such questioning cannot come only from within the well-spring of an individual architect's "talent"; it must also emerge from a knowledge of history, a concern for the state of the architectural art at a given moment, and a serious respect for the aspirations of clients. It must be continuously reaffirmed that individual buildings, no matter how remotely situated from other works of architecture, form part of a cultural and physical context. As a culture, as architects, we know so very much. What must be done is to face this knowledge squarely—and in so doing face the world around us, taking it for what it is, incrementally adapting the objects and ideas in it to our needs, while we in turn adapt to its demands. My attitude toward form, based on *a love for and knowledge of history,* is not concerned with accurate replication. It is eclectic and uses collage and juxtaposition as techniques to give new meaning to familiar forms and, in so doing, to cover different though not necessarily new ground. Mine is a confidence in the power of memory (history) combined with the action of people (function) to infuse design with richness and meaning. If architecture is to succeed in its efforts to participate creatively in the present, it must go beyond the iconoclasm of the Modern Movement of the last 50 years as well as the personal and often self-indulgent formalism of so much recent work and, strengthened by the fullest possible reading of its own past, recapture for itself a basis in culture.

—Robert A. M. Stern

*   *   *

An architect whose didactic gifts need to be assessed in his historical essays, lectures, and critical writing, as well as in his buildings, Robert A. M. Stern was a notable author and teacher of design before he began his own practice. This particular position as critic-*cum*-architect may look a bit like that of Robert Venturi, and it does somewhat derive from him, but Stern is more than somewhat stylistically at variance with Venturi. Taking off from Venturi's preoccupations with American vernacular design and the sense of history (Venturi always seems more concerned with the sensation than the history), Stern has developed a stronger historicism, its sensations dogmatically controlled into sensibilities.

In Stern's own presentation of his work, he has seen himself as an "inclusivist," for his mix of references and themes, as opposed to the "exclusivists," the modern movement masters and, latterly (according to Stern) their partly neo-Corbusian acolytes like Graves, Meier, and Hejduk. For observers outside the salons and schools of New York, New Haven, and Philadelphia, with their esoteric architectural preoccupations, the inclusivists and exclusivists might look the same, since Venturi, Stern, Graves and the rest use like vocabularies of stucco, contrasting solids and voids, flat planes, thin surfaces, deliberately skimpy details, tepid shapes, and (in Stern and several, but not all, practitioners) seductive curves, decorator-y colours, and no interest in expressing structure. Occasional infighting between such as the "New York Five" and their critics, the "Five on Five" (the latter including Stern), seems remote and precious in places like England, where Piano and Rogers and Norman Foster show their remorseless technological bent, or in Japan, France and Belgium, where really hairy ad-hocists offer a more relaxed, more vulgar, less contrived manifestation of what could be read as the linguistic analogy in aesthetics.

But Stern was only 40 in 1979. His admirers can find him at his present best in and near New York, notably in the Lang House in Washington, Connecticut.

—Nathan Silver

STILLMAN AND EASTWICK-FIELD.

Partnership; established, London, 1949, by John Stillman (born 1920), Elizabeth Eastwick-Field (born 1919), and John Eastwick-Field (born 1919). Current associates: Humphrey Lukyn Williams; John Howe; David Stephens. Exhibition: *150th Anniversary Retrospective Exhibition,* University College London, 1978. Recipient: Bronze Medal, Ministry of Housing and Local Government, 1962; First Prize, Special Categories Competition, Royal Institute of British Architects, 1977; Bronze Medal, Department of the Environment, 1977. Address: 18 Highbury Place, London N5 1QT, England.

Works:

1946 Cecil Sharp House/English Folk Dance and Song Headquarters rebuilding, London (pre-partnership: J. and E. Eastwick-Field with Hugh Pite)
1953 Crocker Farm Buildings, Minety, Wiltshire
1955 Blackwell School Hall and Gymnasia, Harrow, Middlesex
1956 Krabbe House, Calcot, Reading, Berkshire
Camden School for Girls redevelopment, London
Goldup House, Whitchurch, Berkshire
1958 New Wing for the Children's Hospital, Marlborough, Wiltshire
1959 Concrete Ltd. Exhibition Stand, *Building Exhibition,* London
1960 Post Office, Putney, London
Fulbourne Housing Estate, Bethnal Green, London
Halls of Residence and Staff Housing, College of Aeronautics, Cranfield, Bedfordshire
Rayners School for the Deaf, Penn, Buckinghamshire
1961 Municipal Depot, Welwyn Garden City, Hertfordshire
1962 Hide Tower Housing Scheme, Westminster, London
Housing, Oxlease, Hatfield, Hertfordshire
1963 Students Union Building, University of Keele, Staffordshire
1964 Mackintosh Hall Cultural Centre and Girls School, Gibraltar
1965 Hampstead School, London
1966 Housing, community centre and shopping development, West Ham, London
Residential school for the partially sighted, Exeter, Devon
Residential and commercial development, Dufours Place/Marshall Street, Soho, London
Advanced Science Wing, Camden School for Girls, London
New Assembly Hall, Market Harborough Grammar School, Leicestershire

Primary school, Market Harborough, Leicestershire
Engineering Complex, Brunel University, Uxbridge, Middlesex
Training centre for the handicapped, Hackney, London
1968 Sports Hall, Totnes School, Devon
Trevelyan College for Women, University of Durham
1970 Allington Park Primary School, Allington, Kent
Grove Lane Housing Scheme, Camberwell, London
Brixham Primary School, Devon
Plympton Grammar School Development, Devon
Ilfracombe Comprehensive School, Devon
1971 Physics, Polymer Science and Nuclear Science Buildings, Brunel University, Uxbridge, Middlesex
Edward VI School, Totnes, Devon
Clissold Park Comprehensive School, Stoke Newington, London
Housing, Brecknock Road, Holloway, London
1972 Princess Marina Psychiatric Hospital, Northamptonshire
1973 Sir James Knott Hall, Trevelyan College, University of Durham
1975 New VIth Form House, Roedean School, Brighton
Weedon Bec Primary School, Northamptonshire
Blackheath Bluecoat School Development, London
Malpas County High School Development, Cheshire
Frodsham County Secondary School, Cheshire
Drama Workshop and Science Extensions, Hampstead School, London
1976 Housing and day nursery, Gresham Road, Brixton, London
Housing, Wheelwright Street, Islington, London
Welldon Park First School, Harrow, Middlesex
University College development plan and stage I, Buckingham
Chace Wing, Enfield District Hospital, Middlesex
Nantwich School Development, Cheshire
Newton Abbot Schools Development, Devon
Housing, nursery and community buildings, Walterton Road, Paddington, London
School sports hall, Axminster, Devon
1977 Corby Community Hospital and Health Centre development, phase I, Northamptonshire

Housing, Nelson Gardens, Bethnal Green, London
School for Delicate Children, Kennington, London
Sheltered housing for old people, Myatts Fields, Brixton, London
Housing, phase II, Wheelwright Street, Islington, London
Palmers Estate housing rehabilitation, Tufnell Park, London
Working girls hostel and adult training centre, Highbury, London
Irthlingborough School Development, Northamptonshire
1978 Old people's housing, Prentis Road, Streatham, London
Old people's housing, Stockwell Road, Clapham, London
Flats rehabilitation, Nevern Place, Earls Court, London
Gymnasium, Camden School for Girls, London
New comprehensive school, Gibraltar
Housing, Palmers Estate, Tufnell Park, London
Mayflower Family Centre, London E.1

Publications:

On STILLMAN AND EASTWICK-FIELD: books —*Scheibe, Punkt und Hugel* by Gustav Hassenpflug and Paulhans Peters, Munich 1966; *Planning for Play,* edited by Lady Allen of Hurtwood, London 1968; *New British Architecture* by Robert Maxwell, London 1972; *A Guide to Modern Buildings in London,* edited by Charles McKean and Tom Jestico, London 1976; articles—"Hexagon College for Durham" in *Times Educational Supplement* (London), 15 March 1958; "Young Architects" by James Stirling in *Architectural Design* (London) June 1958; "The Brains Behind the Builders" in *The Times* (London), September 1958; "Hide Tower, London" in *Bauen und Wohnen* (Zurich), September 1962; "Building Brunel" by Diana Rowntree in *The Guardian* (London), 25 February 1965; "The Visionary Village" by Diana Rowntree in *The Guardian* (London), 22 March 1966; "Architects Top Ten" by George Mansell in the *Sunday Telegraph* (London), 1 July 1966.

*

We do not bring to projects preconceived ideas of planning, design or construction. We believe that a closer study of clients' needs and of the site and its surroundings is the key to successful design. Each project will make its own demands for the type of construction and materials—as witness the many beautiful and unselfconscious indigenous buildings throughout the world.

Stillman and Eastwick-Field: Trevelyan College for Women, University of Durham, 1968

We believe that building must ultimately become far more sophisticated, but until economic and other circumstances permit a more rapid development to technology, we realize there are risks in setting aside tradition and using substitute methods and materials.

We believe that architects have an obligation both to build soundly and to use their trained sensibilities to stretch visual imagination.

—John Stillman
John Eastwick-Field
Elizabeth Eastwick-Field

Years ago the critic Ian Nairn wrote that Stillman and Eastwick-Field "have always been honest and sometimes dull also. Not the dullness of someone with nothing to say, but the honesty which if presented with an unexciting programme refuses to dramatise it artificially." There are no great set-pieces in the portfolio of Stillman and Eastwick-Field. Rather theirs is a record of sound and honest architecture, architecture that desires first and foremost to satisfy the people who use it while remaining true to the materials and methods of construction it has employed.

The practice started life in 1949, full of the zeal of building a better Britain out of the wreckage of the war. By that time John Eastwick-Field had put in a period working for the Building Research Station, and when he joined John Stillman in partnership his interest in the technological aspect of building was married with what has proved to be a lifelong interest of Stillman's in standards and specifications. In addition to architecture, Elizabeth Eastwick-Field brought to the practice a background in designing film sets and the sociological aspects of town planning. The three combined an admiration for the work of Mies, Aalto and Le Corbusier with a healthy scepticism for the strict mores of the Modern Movement. While their buildings have never been far from the forefront of the current fashion, they have been preoccupied with combining style with technical excellence. An example is the 226 foot high Hide Tower, Westminster, which was an early and successful example of prefabrication in a tall residential building (incidentally, for elderly people) in Britain.

Since the early 1960's, however, a new strain has appeared in their work: a concern to make their buildings smaller in scale and readily comprehensible to their users. This has been particularly true of their schools which have often been designed for the handicapped or for very young children. The West of England School for Partially Sighted Children, in Exeter, completed in 1966, was conceived in traditional manner as an intimate group of brick-clad buildings designed to encourage the children to venture out of doors. Again, in 1971, at their Edward VI School at Totnes, traditional materials were skillfully handled to produce a sensitive alternative to the conventional post-war school. More recent work in housing also displays a preoccupation with domesticity and privacy: at the Lydford Estate for the Greater London Council and Gresham Road, Lambeth.

—Stephanie Williams

STIRLING, James (Frazer).
British. Born in Glasgow, Scotland, 22 April 1926. Educated at the Quarry Bank High School, Liverpool, until 1941; Liverpool School of Art, 1942; University of Liverpool School of Architecture, 1945–50 (exchange student in New York, 1949), Dip.Arch. 1950; School of Town Planning and Regional Research, London, 1950–52. Served as a Lieutenant in the Paratroops, 1942–45: in D-Day Landing with 6th Airborne Division, 1944. Married Mary Shand in 1966; children: Benjamin, Kate and Sophie.

Worked as Senior Assistant, Lyons, Israel and Ellis, London, 1953–56; in partnership with James Gowan, London, 1956–63; in private practice, London, 1964–70. Since 1971, Partner, with Michael Wilford, James Stirling and Partner, London. Visiting Teacher, Architectural Association, London, 1955, Regent Street Polytechnic, London, 1956–57, and Cambridge University School of Architecture, 1958; Royal Institute of British Architects Lecturer, 1965. Davenport Professor, Yale University, New Haven, Connecticut, since 1967; Visiting Professor, Akademie der Künste, Dusseldorf, since 1977. Exhibitions: *James Stirling: Three Buildings,* Museum of Modern Art, New York, 1969; Heinz Gallery, RIBA, London, 1974; *Biennale,* Venice, 1976; Walker Art Center, Minneapolis, Minnesota, 1977; Leo Castelli Gallery, New York, 1977. Recipient: Brunner Award, National Institute of Arts and Letters, U.S.A., 1976; Alvar Aalto Medal, Finland, 1978. Associate of the Royal Institute of British Architects, 1950. Address: James Stirling and Partner, 75 Gloucester Place, London W1H 3PF, England.

Works:

1956 House, Isle of Wight
1957 Expandable House (project)
 Low-rise flats, Ham Common, Richmond, London
 Private house conversion, London
 Churchill College, Cambridge (project)
1957/
59 Low-rise houses and flats, Preston, Lancashire
1958/
61 Dining Hall, Brunswick Park Primary School, London
1959 Selwyn College, Cambridge (project)
1959/
63 Engineering Department, University of Leicester
1960/
64 Old people's home, Blackheath, London
 Children's home, Frogmore, Wandsworth, London
1964/
67 History Building, Cambridge University
1964/
68 Flats, Camden Town, London
 Andrew Melville Hall, University of St. Andrews, Scotland
1965 Dorman Long Headquarters Building, Middlesbrough, Yorkshire
1966/
71 Florey Building, Queen's College, Oxford
1967/
76 Housing, Runcorn New Town, Cheshire
1968 Redevelopment study, New York (with A. Baker)
1969 Siemens AG Building, Munich (project)
1969/
72 Olivetti Training School, Haslemere, Surrey
1969/
76 Low-cost housing, Lima, Peru
1970 Derby Town Centre (project)
1971 Olivetti Headquarters, Milton Keynes, Buckinghamshire (project)
 Arts Centre, University of St. Andrews, Scotland (project)
1975 Wallraf-Richartz Museum, Cologne (project)
 Museum for Northrhine/Westphalia, Dusseldorf (project)
1976 Government Centre, Doha Qatar, Persian Gulf (project)
 Regional Centre for Tuscany, Florence (with Castore, Malanima, Rizzi)
1977 Revision to the Nolli Plan for Rome (project)
1977- Administration Centre, Wilaya de Skikda, Algeria
 Museum of Science and Technology, Tehran
 Dresdner Bank, Marburg, Germany
 Art Gallery addition, National Museum, Stuttgart

1979 Design and Feasibility Study for Tate Gallery extensions, Millbank, London

Publications:

On STIRLING: books—*The New Brutalism* by Reyner Banham, London 1966; *Architecture in Britain Today* by Michael Webb, London 1969; *The Politics of Architecture* by Anthony Jackson, London 1969; *Dizionario Encyclopaedia d'Architettura e Urbanistica* by Paolo Portoghesi, Rome 1969; *Architecture 2000* by Charles Jencks, London 1971; *The Third Generation* by Philip Drew, Stuttgart 1972; *New British Architecture* by Robert Maxwell, Stuttgart 1972; *Modern Movements in Architecture* by Charles Jencks, London 1973; *Design in Architecture* by G. Broadbent, London 1973; *Saper Vedere L'Architettura Moderne* by Bruno Zevi, Turin 1973; *James Stirling: Buildings and Projects 1950–74,* London, New York, Stuttgart, Milan and Tokyo 1975; articles—"The Work of Stirling and Gowan" by Arthur Korn in *Architecture and Building News* (London), January 1959; "Two Works by James Stirling: A Portrait" by Hiroshi Hara and Yukio Futagawa in *Kohusai Kentiku* (Tokyo), January 1965; "The Anti-Pioneers" by Nikolaus Pevsner in *The Listener* (London), 5 January 1967; "L'Opera di James Stirling" by L. Biscogli in *Casabella* (Milan), June 1967; "Observations on New British Architecture" by T. Stevens in *Bauen und Wohnen* (Zurich), December 1967; "Pop non Pop" by Charles Jencks in *Architectural Association Journal* (London), Winter 1968; "James Stirling: Buildings and Projects 1950–1967" in *Kentiku Architecture* (Tokyo), January 1968; "Lucky Jim" in *Building Design* (London), 25 May 1973; "James Stirling: Five Projects" in *Genghia Architecture* (Taiwan), June 1973; "An Extra Dimension" by N. Jones in *RIBA Journal* (London), April 1974; "A Modern Neo-Classicist" by M. Girouard in *Country Life* (London), May 1974; "A Detonation in Glass and Brick" by Charles Jencks in *Times Literary Supplement* (London), 21 June 1974; "Transformations in Style" by Kenneth Frampton in *Architecture + Urbanism* (Tokyo), February 1975; "Jim the Great" by G. K. Koenig in *Casabella* (Milan), March 1975; "James Stirling at the IUA Congress, Spain" in *Building Design* (London), May 1975; "The Language of Architecture" by Charles Jencks in *Sunday Times Magazine* (London), 10 August 1975, "Anglo-Scottish Architect with Anglo-International Reputation" in *House and Garden* (London), October 1975; "Inside James Stirling" in *Design Quarterly* (Minneapolis), April 1976; film—*James Stirling's Architecture,* BBC/Arts Council, London 1973.

I ceased to believe in Frank Lloyd Wright's philosophy of "truth to materials" when I saw for the first time a building by Palladio—where the peeling columns showed that the columns were in fact made of bricks—and not of marble or stone which I had naively assumed from the books.

I believe that the shapes of a building should indicate—perhaps display—the usage and way of life of its occupants, and it is therefore likely to be rich and varied in appearance, and its expression is unlikely to be simple. The collection (in a building) of forms and shapes which the everyday public can *associate* with and be *familiar* with—and *identify* with—seems to me essential. These forms may derive from staircases, windows, corridors, rooms, entrances, etc., and the total building could be thought of as an assemblage of everyday elements recognizable to a normal man and not only an architect. For instance, in a building we did at Oxford University some years ago, it was intended that you could recognize the historic elements of courtyard, entrance gate towers, cloisters; also a central object replacing the traditional fountain or statue of the college founder. In this way we hoped that students and public would not be *disassociated* from their cultural past. The particular way in which functional-symbolic ele-

James Stirling: Olivetti Training School, Haslemere, Surrey, 1972

ments are put together may be the "art" in the architecture.

I am wary of what seems to me banal and arrogant solutions of tents, space frames, domes and bubbles covering everything—these technocratic solutions may be valid for single usage spectator activities, but if carried into normal everyday building can only *subvert* the richness and variety of life.

If the expression of functional-symbolic forms and familiar elements is foremost, the expression of structure will be secondary, and if structure shows it is not in my opinion the engineering which counts but the way in which the building is put together that is important. It is desirable not to eliminate the traces of the human hand in carpentry or bricklaying and by the same token it is necessary to express the assemblage process of most prefabricated systems; similarly with the use of colour pigmentation in plastics to delineate the separate parts.

We are not much concerned with the imagery of space flight or super-advanced technology, as I think an architect usually has to make do with the technology which is normal and is cost-wise available to him. According to what is appropriate for a particular building problem, the building could, I think, be made of any materials—old or new, traditional or technological—and the whole spectrum of the past, from earth works to plastics, is usable according to the differing economic/climate conditions prevailing in different countries.

—James Stirling

In terms of architectural ingenuity the work of James Stirling can be seen as the most powerful expression of the contemporary international situation. His development over more than two decades has rightly been described as the mirror of architectural development in general: "It has fallen to James Stirling to express the revolutionary intentions of a new generation in the medium of hard building and all this has provided a tradition which makes questioning not only to be expected but du jour, which is in its own way moving architecture forward on an international front" (Alvin Boyarsky in *Architectural Design,* November 1968). In comparison with his fellow architects of the "Third Generation," Stirling, who has always been more articulate, has thus become a prototype for post-war international architectural development.

Stirling's early work reflects his critical dialogue with the late work of Le Corbusier and architectural history and at the same time is a statement of independence. In 1957 he wrote: "Today, Stonehenge is more significant than the architecture of Sir Christopher Wren." His housing in Ham Common and Preston and his old people's home in Blackheath document the concern for communal vitality and neighborliness in terms of a direct articulation of space and circulation which is in direct opposition to prevalent stylistic and aesthetic concerns. Since 1962 Stirling has argued against the obsession with decorating the skin of buildings. He does not accept the traditional functionalist attitude but prefers instead an integration of form and function using imagery as

the connecting link. Architecture is, in his own words, "not a question of style of appearance; it is how you organize spaces and movement for a place and activity." Form and space are to be experienced in relation to an inherent meaning given to the building by the architect.

A second phase in Stirling's development is strongly articulated in a sculptural and ambivalent use of materials and a dialectical approach toward meaning. This is documented in his buildings for the engineering faculty of the University of Leicester, the history department at Cambridge, the dormitories for the University of St. Andrews, and in the Runcorn New Town housing—each a powerful articulation of the required solution. Stirling integrates the industrial potential appropriately into the architectural form. Metaphorically he is using the image of the green house, the battle ship, constructivist architecture in Russia, and skycraper design in America as well as engineering structures like the launching ramps at Cape Kennedy and housing of the 18th century in England. The integration of pre-existing imagery into the built form gives complex meaning to his work and creates a greater harmony between environment and tradition.

Since 1970 Stirling has intensified historical imagery and urban concern, the project for the Town Centre at Derby being the most radical example. In other projects, such as the museum in Dusseldorf, he has included parts of the existing urban fabric which surrounds the new building. The project for the Wallraf-Richartz Museum in Cologne goes even further in an attempt to correct the existing urban site. By means of the new museum he unifies the three isolated units—the Cathedral, the railway station, and the Hohenzollern Bridge.

Stirling's concept of contemporary architecture is concerned with the humanization of the environment. Humanistic considerations dominate all technological, economic and aesthetic preconceived ideas and ideologies. Architecture has to re-establish its own criteria for evaluation: for Stirling this obviously means creating in harmony with common sense, tradition, the existing environment, and a concern for people.

—Udo Kultermann

STONE, Edward Durell.

American. Born in Fayetteville, Arkansas, 9 March 1902. Educated at the University of Arkansas, Fayetteville, 1920–23; as apprentice to Henry R. Shepley, Boston, 1923–25; Harvard University, 1925–26; Massachusetts Institute of Technology School of Architecture, 1925–26; Rotch Travelling Scholar, in Europe, 1927–29. Served as a Major in the United States Air Force, 1942–45. Married Orlean Vandiver in 1931 (divorced, 1950); children: Edward Jr. and Robert; married Maria Eleana Torchio in 1954 (divorced); son: Benjamin; married Violet Campbell Moffat in 1972; daughter: Fiona. Worked with the consortium of architects designing Rockefeller Center, New York, 1929–35; in private practice, New York, 1935 until his death, 1978: President, Edward Durell Stone and Associates, New York; offices established in Palo Alto, California, Los Angeles, and Chicago. Instructor in Advanced Design, New York University, 1935–40; Associate Professor of Architecture, Yale University, New Haven, Connecticut, 1946–52; Visiting Critic, Princeton University, New Jersey, 1953, and University of Arkansas, Fayetteville, 1955, 1957–59. Trustee, American Federation of the Arts; Director, American National Theatre and Academy; Director, Whitney Museum, New York. Recipient: Architectural League of New York Medal, 1937, 1950, 1953; Grand Prize, Pittsburgh Glass Competition, 1938; First Prize, *House and Garden,* 1939; Gold Medal, 1955, and Honor Award, 1958, 1967, American Institute of Architects; Architectural Achievement Award, Copper and Brass Reserve Association, 1963; Architectural Excellence Award, Metropolitan Washington Board of Trade, 1965; John F. Kennedy Award, Institute of North American Studies, Barcelona, 1966; Building Award, *Business Magazine,* 1966; First Prize, American Society of Landscape Architects Competition, 1973. D.F.A.: University of Arkansas, Fayetteville, 1951; Colby College, Waterville, Maine, 1959; Hamilton College, Clinton, New York, 1962; M.F.A.: Otis Art Institute, Los Angeles, 1961; L.H.D.: University of South Carolina, Columbia, 1964. Fellow, American Institute of Architects; Member, National Academy of Design. Member, National Institute of Arts and Letters, and Fellow, American Academy of Arts and Sciences, 1960. Fellow, Royal Society of Arts, London, 1960. *Died* (in New York) *6 August 1978.*

Works:

1933 Mandel House, Mt. Kisco, New York
1937 House, 4 Buckingham Street, Cambridge, Massachusetts (with Carl Koch)
1939 Goodyear House, Old Westbury, Long Island, New York
     Museum of Modern Art, West 53rd Street, New York (with Philip Goodwin)
1946 El Panama Hotel, Panama City

1951 Fine Arts Center, University of Arkansas, Fayetteville
1954 United States Embassy, New Delhi
1957 Government Hospital, Lima, Peru
     Stanford University Medical School and Hospital, Palo Alto, California
     Graf House, Dallas
1958 United States Pavilion, *World's Fair,* Brussels
     Stuart Pharmaceutical Company, Pasadena, California
1959 Edward Durell Stone House (conversion of brownstone), 130 East 64th Street, New York
     Gulf Service Station, Kennedy International Airport, New York
     Central Library, 1213 Newell Avenue, Palo Alto, California
     Mitchell Park Branch Library, 3700 Middlefield Road, Palo Alto, California
1960 American Federation of the Arts Building interior conversion, 41 East 65th Street, New York
1961 Harvey Mudd College, Claremont, California
     Institute of Nuclear Science and Technology, Islamabad, Pakistan
1962 Perpetual Savings Bank, Wilshire Boulevard and Malcolm, Los Angeles
     Perpetual Savings Bank, Wilshire Boulevard and McCarty, Los Angeles
     Foster and Wells Fargo Buildings, 1015 East Hillside Boulevard, Foster City, California
     Commodore Apartments, Foster City Boulevard, Foster City, California
1963 State University of New York at Albany
     Beckman Auditorium, California Institute of Technology, Pasadena
     General Community Hospital of the Monterey Peninsula, Carmel Highway, Monterey, California
     Theatre, Loyola University, 7101 West 80th Street, Los Angeles
     Center for Continuing Education, University of Chicago
     Public School 199, 270 West 70th Street, New York
1964 National Geographic Society, 17th and M Streets N.W., Washington, D.C.
1965 Huntington Hartford Gallery of Modern Art, Columbus Circle, New York (now the New York City Department of Cultural Affairs)
     City Hall, Paducah, Kentucky
1966 Museum of Art, Ponce, Puerto Rico
     Bush Memorial Stadium, St. Louis
1968 General Motors Building and Plaza, 58th/59th Streets at Fifth Avenue, New York (with Emery Roth and Sons)
     Phillips Hall of Education, University of Southern California, Los Angeles
     Social Science Building, University of Southern California, Los Angeles
1969 *Buffalo Evening News* Building, Buffalo, New York
     Fine Arts Center, Amarillo, Texas
     Master plan for the Florida State Capitol Complex, Tallahassee (with Smith and Hills)
     Civic Center, Seaside, California
1970 Ahmanson Center, 3731 Wilshire Boulevard, Los Angeles
     NASA Building, Cambridge, Massachusetts (now the Federal Department of Transportation)
     School of Law, University of Alabama, University
     Eisenhower Hospital, Palm Desert, California
     City Hall, Palo Alto, California
1971 John F. Kennedy Center for the Performing Arts, Washington, D.C.
1972 Gerontology Center, University of Southern California, Los Angeles
     Law Center, Georgetown University, Wash-

ington, D.C.
1973 PepsiCo World Headquarters, Purchase, New York
1974 Standard Oil Building and Plaza, East Randolph Street, Chicago (with Perkins and Will)
1975 Bankamericard Center, Green and Arroyo Parkway, Pasadena, California
     Davidson Conference Center, University of Southern California, Los Angeles

Publications:

By STONE: books—*The Evolution of an Architect,* New York 1962; *Recent and Future Architecture,* New York 1967; article—"Kitchens: Efficiency Is Not Enough" in *Architectural Record* (New York), May 1962.

On STONE: articles—"Recent Work by Edward Durell Stone" in *Architectural Forum* (New York), July 1941; "Meet Edward Stone" in *House Beautiful* (New York), September 1945; "Genetrix: Personal Contributions to American Architecture" in *Architectural Review* (London), May 1957; "Educational Work of Edward D. Stone" in *Architectural Record* (New York), February 1958; "The Work of Edward D. Stone" in *Architectural Record* (New York), March 1959; "Minoru Yamasaki and Edward Durell Stone" in *Zodiac* (Milan), no. 8, 1961; "New York Is the Office of Ed Stone" in *Architectural Forum* (New York), October 1961; "New Work, Serene and Classic, by Edward Durell Stone" in *Architectural Record* (New York), October 1962; "Recent Work of Edward Durell Stone" in *Architectural Record* (New York), October 1964; "Theatres" in *Progressive Architecture* (New York), October 1965; "Public Buildings" in *Architectural Forum* (New York), November 1971; "Two California Hospitals by Edward Durell Stone" in *Architectural Record* (New York) September 1972; "Sculpture in a Broad Landscape" by Lanning Roper in *Country Life* (London), 21 April 1977.

At the least, Edward Durell Stone was representative of the essentially fragmentary nature of the history of modern architecture. In the course of a career which emerged from the infancy of the International Style and ended in the unsettled eclecticism of the late 1970's, Stone's work was periodically, and often temporarily, emblematic of that congruence of forces that generate "newness" in architecture. The significance of the work is as discontinuous and erratic as the vagaries of popular taste. Stone himself disparaged mass culture: "It is impossible for me to associate these mass-assembled, catch-penny structures with permanent architecture. They bear more resemblance to the latest automobile, dependent upon shining, metallic finish and doomed to obsolescence." Yet much of his own legacy is similarly fleeting, dependent upon surface manipulations and the repeated application of "stock parts."

In his later, most productive years (the Monumental Period), the deterioration of intended permanence into transience became increasingly pronounced as Stone settled into a more restricted vocabulary, rooted in the classicism of the New Delhi Embassy and reapplied endlessly from Paducah to the Potomac. Supported by the popular press and a certain cultural appropriateness (to both India and the United States), New Delhi quickly became a symbol of a "new architecture," its lacy grillwork and sensuous courtyard juxtaposed with a classic symmetry and proportion, the elephantine Great Seal above the entry. As a result, the building was accepted and praised by both the giver and receiver, and, indeed, some twenty years later, John Kenneth Galbraith (then the Ambassador) was to pronounce it "perhaps the most beautiful building ever accomplished by the government of the United States." Frank Lloyd Wright, according to Stone, called it "one of the finest buildings of the past hundred

Edward Durell Stone: Standard Oil Building, Chicago, 1974

Stone's contribution must be judged in terms of the considerable popular impact of his later work. However, the episodic nature of his career contains strata—each somewhat separate from the other—that contain some elements of lasting worth. For example, his early flirtation with the International Style followed an important contribution to the design of the interior of Radio City Music Hall, and resulted in the elegant Panama Hotel and residences that helped introduce the modern style to the Northeastern United States. The signal building of this period—and, perhaps, of Stone's career—was the Museum of Modern Art in New York City (with Philip Goodwin). Even with later additions, the exterior of the museum building has sustained virtues of high modernism that are absent in his later, more monumental work. At the same time, the careful manipulation of the interior space of the rectangle is vastly superior to Stone's other cultural palaces—the Kennedy Center or the Huntington Hartford Gallery of Modern Art in New York.

Stone urged that each architect should "try to find his own handwriting . . . his own expression" yet, save for the early work, there is little that is personal and private in his work.

—Robert Segrest

STONOROV, Oscar.

American. Born in Frankfurt, Germany, 2 December 1905; emigrated to the United States, 1929: naturalized, 1937. Apprenticed to a stonecutter in Florence, and studied anatomy and mathematics at the University of Florence, 1924–25; studied at E.T.H.: Swiss Federal Institute of Technology, Zurich, 1925–28; worked for the architectural firm of André Lurcat, and studied sculpture with Aristide Maillol, Paris, 1928–29. Married Elizabeth Foster in 1938; children: Katrina, Andrea, Barbara, and Derek. In private practice, Philadelphia, 1932 until his death, 1970: in partnership with Alfred Kastner, 1932–36, George Howe, *q.v.*, 1942–43 and Louis I. Kahn, *q.v.*, 1942–48. Organized the exhibition *Sixty Years of Living Architecture: The Work of Frank Lloyd Wright*, Palazzo Strozzi, Florence, 1951, European tour, 1951–53, and North American tour, 1953–54. Served as Director of the Philadelphia Housing Association, and of the Philadelphia Citizens Council on City Planning. Exhibition: *Better Philadelphia Exhibition,* Philadelphia, 1947. Recipient: Fairmont Art Association Award, Philadelphia, 1965. Fellow, American Institute of Architects. *Died* (in a plane crash, with union leader Walter Reuther) *9 May 1970.*

Works:

1928/
29   Karlsruhe Municipal Hospital, Germany (project; with Edwin Blos)
1929   2 houses, Zurich (with Willy Boesiger)
      Private clinic, Karlsruhe (project)
1930   State Theatre of the Ukraine, U.S.S.R. (competition project; with Willy Boesiger)
      Rural Hospital for the Southern States, for the Julius Rosenwald Foundation (project)
      Forrest House, Java Farm, Edgewater, Maryland (project)
1931   Weyman Biological Laboratory, North Carolina
      Clark Foreman Apartment interiors, New York
      Palace of the Soviets, Moscow (competition project; with Alfred Kastner)
1932   Carl Mackley Houses (housing development), for the Federation of Full-Fashioned Hosiery Workers, Philadelphia (with W. P. Barney)

years." In the context of Stone's work, the Embassy was a rare example of a building that synthesized both potent cause and dramatic effect.

The subsequent output of building designs—both built and unbuilt—eroded the pedestal which supported the Embassy's reputation by displaying in endless redundancy not only the formalism of the composition, but its elements as well. The fragile determinism of New Delhi disappeared in a search for "universality."

The distillation of the vocabulary was accompanied by the increasingly messianical perception of the architect's role (no doubt infused by the aura of Frank Lloyd Wright). The result is disastrous. Where there can be tolerance for such romantic banality in lesser structures—gas stations and resort hotels—the magnitude of intention in such buildings as the Kennedy Center in Washington, D.C., the General Motors Building in New York and the

Florida State Capitol turns the object to portentous kitsch. Like other artifacts of mass-culture—the automobile, the mobile home—they attempt to signify status by the manipulation of styles. At best, they are objects for unconsidered or uneducated enjoyment; at worst, they are pompous and dull. They are merely buildings of effect.

Just as Stone's later buildings pander to man's instincts for beauty in a way that annihilates meaning, his ventures into complex and large scale design reveal a similar vacuousness. The consummation of the Stone-Rockefeller Connection—the campus of the State University of New York at Albany—is the academic companion of Wallace Harrison's South Mall and reflects Stone's "quest for order" and formal simplicity. The result is exemplary of the academic fascism of the 1960's. The architect, overly consumed with occupying the podium of good taste, became the conveyor of banality.

1933 Mrs. Frank Foster House interiors, Haverford, Pennsylvania
Mrs. John Wintersteen House interiors, Chestnut Hill, Pennsylvania
M. B. Montgomery Studio, Philadelphia
Howard City (housing development), Washington, D.C. (project; with Hilyard Robinson)

1934 Public housing development, Meadville, Pennsylvania (project)
Pre-fabricated houses, for the Republic Steel Corporation, various locations including Huntington Terrace, Bethesda, Maryland
Recreation Center, Bangor, Pennsylvania
Minard Hamilton Penthouse interiors, New York
Federation of Hosiery Workers Union Hall, Philadelphia

1935 Public housing (Public Works Administration No. 6002), Camden, New Jersey
Academy of Music interiors, Philadelphia
Freedman Store, Philadelphia
Housing renovation, Waverly Street, Philadelphia

1936 Westfield Acres (public housing development), Camden, New Jersey (with Joseph Hettel)
Collier House, Arlington, Virginia (project)
Frank B. Foster House remodelling and additions, Phoenixville, Pennsylvania
Mouth Hygiene Clinic, Philadelphia
Patchell Estate Housing Development, Philadelphia (project)
Rosenfeld Apartments, Camden, New Jersey
Spooner House, Philadelphia (project)
Public housing development, Paterson, New Jersey (project)

1938 School, Charlestown Playhouse, Pennsylvania
Oscar Stonorov House, Avon Lea, Phoenixville, Pennsylvania
Louis Dublin Week-end House, Westport, Connecticut (project)
Cavanaugh House, Falls Church, Virginia (project)
Davis House alterations, Chestnut Hill, Pennsylvania
Clement T. Branch Village (public housing development), Camden, New Jersey (with Hettel Associates)
Public housing development, New Britain, Connecticut (project; with Ludorf and Bishop)

1939 Youth Center, East Springfield, Pennsylvania (project)
Children's World Exhibition, *New York World's Fair* (with George Howe, Herbert Spiegel and Cornelius Bogert)
Public housing development, Aliquippa, Pennsylvania
Public housing development, Ambridge, Pennsylvania
Public housing development, Beaver Falls, Pennsylvania (2 projects)

1940 Resident workshop, National Youth Administration, Philadelphia
Public housing development, Audubon Village, New Jersey (with Hettel Associates)
Tonnies House, Bryn Mawr, Pennsylvania

1941 Sidney Biddle House, Philadelphia
Walter Phillips House, Torresdale, Pennsylvania (with Edmund N. Bacon)
Design of the *Organic Design* Exhibition, Museum of Modern Art, New York
Design of a furniture exhibition at Bloomingdale's Department Store, New York
Design of a furniture/defense house exhibition at Gimbel's Department Store, Philadelphia
Eunice Richardson Apartment interiors, New York
Public housing development, Middletown, Pennsylvania

1941/
43 Carver Court Housing, Coatesville, Pennsylvania (with George Howe and Louis I. Kahn)

1942 Pennypack Housing, Philadelphia (project; with George Howe and Louis I. Kahn)
Phoenixville Hospital alterations and additions, Pennsylvania (project)
Broudo House, Philadelphia
Display house for the *Ladies Home Journal*
Frey House remodelling, Radnor, Pennsylvania

1943 Lincoln Road Housing, Coatesville, Pennsylvania (project; with George Howe and Louis I. Kahn)
Lily Ponds Housing, Washington, D.C. (project; with George Howe and Louis I. Kahn)
Willow Run Housing, Detroit (project; with Louis I. Kahn)
Thermostore, Gimbel's, Phoenixville, Pennsylvania
194X Hotel, Philadelphia (competition project; with Louis I. Kahn)
International Ladies Garment Workers Union Offices interior alterations, Philadelphia
International Upholsterers Union Offices interior alterations, Philadelphia
International Union of Master Ship Workers Offices, Camden, New Jersey

1944 Motion Picture Operators Union Building, Philadelphia
Pennypack Buildings, Philadelphia (with Louis I. Kahn)
Borough Hall alterations and additions, Phoenixville, Pennsylvania
Lucius Crowell House additions, Charlestown, Pennsylvania
Cosmetics Department and Shoe Salon, Gimbel's Department Store, Philadelphia

1945 Health Clinic extension and alterations, 22nd and Locust Streets, Philadelphia (with Louis I. Kahn)
Paul Darrow House alterations and additions, Philadelphia
Pre-fabricated steel house, for the Harman Corporation
Moskalik House, 2018 Spruce Street, Philadelphia
Plan for the North Triangle, Philadelphia
Philadelphia Psychiatric Hospital extension (project)
Radbill House, Merion, Pennsylvania
Coward Shoe Company alterations, Philadelphia

1946 Charlestown Playhouse additions, Pennsylvania
Unity House (International Ladies Garment Workers Union Building), Pike County, Pennsylvania (project)
Thom McCann Shoe Store alterations and additions, 69th Street, Philadelphia
Solar House (project)
House, 2036 Rittenhouse Square, Philadelphia
Memorial Playground, Philadelphia
Evans House, Philadelphia (project)
Psychiatric Hospital, Monument Avenue, Philadelphia (project; with Louis I. Kahn)

1947 Offices and Cafeteria, Container Corporation of America, Philadelphia (project; with Louis I. Kahn)
DuPont Theatre (project)
Plan for the expansion of the Drexel Institute, Philadelphia
Franklin Institute additions, Philadelphia
Plan for the redevelopment of the "Triangle," University of Pennsylvania, Philadelphia
Design of the *Better Philadelphia Exhibition*, Philadelphia (with Edmund N. Bacon)
Garage, Filbert Street, Philadelphia (project)

1948 Captain Beczewski House, Philadelphia
Lucius Crowell House alterations and additions, Charlestown, Pennsylvania
Design of the *Yardville Exhibition* for *McCall's Magazine* and Gimbel's Department Store, Philadelphia
Plan for the redevelopment of North 8th Street, Philadelphia

1949 Coward Glass Front Shoe Store, Philadelphia (with Louis I. Kahn)
Brégy House alterations and additions, Philadelphia
Redevelopment plans for the Harman Corporation
Cherokee Village (housing development), Philadelphia
Kelly's Oyster House (restaurant), Philadelphia
Housing development, Valley Forge, Pennsylvania (project)
Leonni's Restaurant, Philadelphia
Plan for the Southwest Temple Redevelopment Area, Philadelphia
Plan for the 32nd and Walnut Streets Area, Philadelphia
Plan for the 22nd and College Avenue Area, Philadelphia
Solidarity House (United Auto Workers Office Building), Detroit
Design of the *Washington Sesquicentennial Exhibition*, Corcoran Gallery, Washington, D.C.
Penn Drexel Corporation Building, Philadelphia
Holmes House alterations and additions, Charlestown, Pennsylvania

1950 Flower Service Corporation Offices, Philadelphia
Exhibition house for *Life* magazine
Exhibition house for Peasewood Woodwork Company, Cincinnati
Fleer Corporation Offices, Philadelphia

1951 Clark House, Philadelphia
Louis Martin House, Cheltenham, Pennsylvania
Y.M.C.A. Building remodelling, Philadelphia

1952 Alexander Frey House, Pocano Hills, Pennsylvania

1953 Display House, *Philadelphia Home Show*
Louis Forman House, Wyncotte, Pennsylvania
East Falls Elementary School, Pennsylvania

1954 Playground, 8th and Brown Streets, Philadelphia
Hetzell Playground, Philadelphia
Penrose Playground, Philadelphia

1955 Solidarity House additions, Detroit
Plan for the redevelopment of the Gratiot-Lafayette Area, Detroit
Hasselquist House, Charlestown, Pennsylvania

1956 Northeast Municipal Building, Bustleton Avenue, Philadelphia
Cow/Sheep Barn, Pennsylvania State University, University Park

1958 Plan for the redevelopment of the Washington Square East Area, Philadelphia

1959 Plan for the redevelopment of Newark Plaza, New Jersey

1961 Hillman Brass and Copper Company Offices and Warehouse, Willow Grove, Pennsylvania
Plan for Hartford, Connecticut
Plan for the central business district of Sharon, Pennsylvania

1962 Unitarian Fellowship Hall, Cherry Hill, New Jersey
Hopkinson House (apartments), Philadelphia
Oakland Park Apartments, Philadelphia (project)
Schuykill Falls (public housing development), Philadelphia

1963 Forestry Center, Pennsylvania State University, University Park
Schenk Memorial Building (Lutheran Church), Philadelphia
Plan for the central business district of Lansdale, Pennsylvania

1964 Georgia Pacific Corporation Offices and Warehouse, King of Prussia, Pennsylvania
Hotel, Bombay (project)
Government of India Pavilion, *World's Fair*, New York
Lincoln National Bank alterations, Philadelphia
Charlestown Elementary School, Pennsylvania
Housing development, for the Andean Development Corporation, Bogota, Colombia (project)
Lutheran Memorial Church, Blackwood, New Jersey

1965 *India Caravan Exhibition* (project)
Stonorov Architectural Offices, Chestnut Street, Philadelphia
Northeast Medical Center, Philadelphia
Computer Facilities Center, Pennsylvania State University, University Park
Plaza Apartments, Philadelphia
Valley Forge Medical Center and Hospital alterations, Pennsylvania

1966 Rural Teaching Hospital Prototype, for Dr. Lalla Iverson, India
Best of Life Park Housing for the Elderly, Atlantic City, New Jersey
Casa Fermi Housing for the Elderly, Philadelphia
Pump Valve Company additions, Philadelphia
Plan for the central business district of Burlington, New Jersey
Plan for Merchantville, Pennsylvania

1967 Public housing development, South Coatesville, Pennsylvania
Stephen Smith Towers Housing for the Elderly, Philadelphia
Master plan for the Smith, Kline and French Corporation, Applebrock Farm, Pennsylvania

1968 James Sutton House additions, Bryn Mawr, Pennsylvania
John F. Hartranft School and Community Services Center, Philadelphia
St. Paul's Church School, Annapolis, Maryland
Animal Health Research Complex, East Goshen Township, Pennsylvania
Welsh Road Branch Library, Philadelphia
Community plan for East Park, Philadelphia

1969 318–320 South 4th Street additions and alterations, Philadelphia
Community Health Care Center, Temple University, Philadelphia
Lutheran Home for the Elderly, Germantown, Philadelphia
Teaching Hospital, Temple University, Philadelphia

1970 Henry Most House alterations, Charlestown, Pennsylvania
United Auto Workers Family Education Center, Onoway, Michigan (renamed Walter and Mary Reuther Memorial Family Education Center)
Urban renewal plan for the Downtown East Area, Reading, Pennsylvania
Study of mental retardation facilities, for the Pennsylvania State Office of Mental Retardation
Veterans Stadium, Philadelphia
St. Christopher's Hospital for Children, Philadelphia
Library, Cheney State College, Chester County, Pennsylvania
Plan for the township of East Windsor, New Jersey

Master plan for the *Michigan State Fair*
Youth Study Center, Philadelphia
Smith, Kline and French Laboratories, Chester County, Pennsylvania
Casa Vivarelli, Pistoia, Italy

Publications:

By STONOROV: books—*Le Corbusier: His Work 1909–1929*, with Willy Boesiger, Zurich 1929; *Why City Planning Is Your Responsibility*, with Louis I. Kahn, New York 1942; *You and Your Neighborhood*, with Louis I. Kahn, New York 1944; article—"Theatres" in *New Architecture and City Planning*, edited by Paul Zucker, New York 1944.

On STONOROV: articles—"Philadelphia Exhibition" in *Architectural Forum* (New York), December 1947; "Yardville" in *McCall's* (New York), February 1949; "Three Shoe Stores" in *Architectural Forum* (New York), December 1949; "Good Land Use + Good Architecture + Long Earning Life" in *House and Home* (New York), February 1956; "Die Stadt in Automobilizertalter" in *Bauen und Wohnen* (Zurich), September 1957; "The Importance of Being Oscar" in *Greater Philadelphia*, November 1962; "Philadelphia Landmark: Hopkinson House" in *Architectural Forum* (New York), April 1963; "Housing—Still Man's Primary Building Need" by Arthur Ziegler Jr. in *Charette* (Philadelphia), July/August 1967; "Profile" in *The New Yorker*, 5 August 1967; "L'idea di Oscar Stonorov" by Bruno Zevi in *L'Architettura* (Rome), July 1970; "Oscar Stonorov: Public Housing Pioneer" by Ursula Cliff in *Design and Environment* (New York), Fall 1971; special issue of *L'Architettura* (Rome), June 1972; "An Architecture for Labor in Post-Industrial America" in *AIA Journal* (Washington, D.C.), October 1972.

Although Oscar Stonorov was a strongly individual figure, his work is almost a diagram of the development of the social concerns of architecture over the forty years in which he practiced.

One of his first prize-winning designs, in 1931, was the Moscow Palace of the Soviets (with Alfred Kastner), a monument to what seemed to be the new era in art and architecture. As the world-wide depression deepened, and as monumental opportunities for architects diminished, he turned his attention increasingly to the problem of providing decent, pleasant housing for the urban working class. Stonorov always had an unusual facility for seeing where the intellectual action was, and during the 1930's he joined an extraordinary group of young architects and planners in Philadelphia who made that city the pioneer in contemporary American city planning.

Stonorov's first important Philadelphia work, Carl Mackley Houses, housing for the hosiery workers' union, reflects his conviction that "housing . . . is no longer so much a question of naked shelter only. It is the demand for the reorganization of rotten communities into stable, sane, and healthy societies." In addition to the bright, airy apartments, Stonorov's design incorporates the ideals of mutual aid that were then part of the intellectual climate: a cooperative nursery school (which flourished for years) and a cooperative grocery. Stonorov was not only co-designer of the project, but, as an adroit political manipulator, was also largely responsible for having funding for it and other low-cost housing included in the National Industrial Recovery Act of 1933.

After the war, when he and Edmund N. Bacon designed the enormously influential *Better Philadelphia Exhibition*, his planning had become more ambitious, and the wide boulevards, rehabilitated neighborhoods, and multi-level shopping malls set a pattern that Philadelphia is still following. In neighborhood rehabilitation, Stonorov used methods thirty years ago that contemporary planners keep rediscovering. He went into the neighborhoods himself and talked to residents on street corners and candy stores, finding out from them what they wanted in their future environment. He devised a system in which the future owners themselves worked out their down-payments by participating in the construction.

Stonorov had begun his career as a sculptor, studying under Maillol in Paris, and he remained a practicing sculptor all his life, in later years maintaining a studio outside Florence. His last major work, the United Auto Workers Family Education Center, represents a fusion at last of his architecture and sculpture: from the austerity of his earliest housing for the hosiery workers he had moved to buildings where the richness of sculptural form is as important as the structural elements.

—Ursula Cliff

STUBBINS, Hugh A(sher), Jr.

American. Born in Birmingham, Alabama, 11 January 1912. Educated at the Georgia Institute of Technology, Atlanta, 1929–33, B.S. in Architecture 1933; Harvard University Graduate School of Design, Cambridge, Massachusetts, 1933–35 (Appleton Scholarship, 1933–34; Boston Society of Architects Prize, 1934; Warren Prize, 1934, 1935), M.Arch. 1935. Served in the United States Naval Reserve, 1933–39. Married Diana Hamilton Moore in 1938 (divorced, 1960); children: Michael and Hugh Asher III; married Colette Fadeuihle in 1961. Worked as a designer draftsman with R. B. Wills, Boston, 1935–37; Principal, with Marc Peter, in Peter and Stubbins, Boston, 1937–39; Chief Designer, Miller, Martin and Lewis, Birmingham, Alabama, 1939–40; in private practice, Boston, 1940–41; Vice-President, The Stereographic Company, Cambridge, 1941–42; Draftsman, Radio Research Laboratory, Cambridge, 1942–43; Assistant to the President, Polaroid Corporation, Cambridge, 1943–45. Since 1949, President of Hugh Stubbins and Associates, Cambridge; since 1969, Principal, Hugh Stubbins/Rex Allen Partnership, Cambridge and San Francisco. Instructor and Assistant to Walter Gropius, Graduate School of Design, 1940, Assistant Professor, 1945, Associate Professor, 1946–52, Chairman of the Department of Architecture, 1953, Member of the Visiting Committee, Graduate School of Design, 1958–72, and since 1978 Member of the Alumni Council of the Graduate School of Design, Harvard University; Visiting Critic-in-Residence, Yale University, New Haven, Connecticut, 1948–49, and University of Oregon, Eugene, 1950. Member, Arts and Architecture Committee, Kennedy Memorial Library, 1964; Vice-President, American Institute of Architects, 1964–65; Director, Benjamin Franklin Foundation, Berlin, 1964–69; Chairman, Design Advisory Committee, Boston Redevelopment Authority, 1964–76; Chairman, Selection Committee, Thomas Jefferson Memorial Chair, University of Virginia, Charlottesville, 1965–70; Vice-President, 1968–69, and President, 1969–70, Boston Society of Architects; Chairman, South Atlantic Regional Conference Awards Committee, 1974; Member, Jury of Fellows, American Institute of Architects, 1974–75. Member, Design Review Panel, Worcester, Massachusetts, Redevelopment Authority, since 1966; Secretary, Rotch Traveling Scholarship Committee, since 1971; Member, Mayor's Panel of Architects, New York City, since 1972; Member, AIA Housing Committee, since 1978; Member, National Advisory Board, Georgia Institute of Technology, since 1978; Member of the Foreign Business Council of Massachusetts, since 1978. Exhibitions: Museum

Hugh A. Stubbins, Jr.: Citicorp Center, New York, 1978

of Modern Art, New York, 1946; *Triennale,* Milan, 1947. Recipient: First Prize, American Gas Association National Competition, 1938; First Prize, *Progressive Architecture* National Competition, 1946; Award of Merit, American Institute of Architects, 1950, 1961, 1966, 1970; First Design Award, *Progressive Architecture,* 1954; Harleston Parker Gold Medal, 1955; Top Award, *The School Executive,* 1956; Silver Medal, Architectural League of New York, 1958; Award of Excellence, *Architectural Record,* 1959, 1967; Boston Arts Festival Award, 1961, 1963; Design Award, *Progressive Architecture,* 1961; Award of Merit, American Library Association, 1966; Design Award, AIA, New England Regional Council, 1966; Award of Merit, United States Office of Education, 1966; Award of Excellence, American Institute of Steel Construction, 1966, 1970; Architectural Firm Award, AIA, 1967; Award of Excellence for Design, *Architectural Record,* 1971; Award of the Year, Prestressed Concrete Institute, 1971; Collaborative Achievement in Architecture Medal, AIA, 1972; Award of Merit, Institute of Southern Affairs and the Southern Academy of Letters, Arts and Sciences, 1973; Gold Medal for Excellence in Design, Tau Sigma Delta, 1975; Award for Excellence, *Design and Environment,* 1975; Award of Merit, AIA/American Library Association, 1976; Merit Award for Excellence in Design, Guild for Religious Architecture, 1976; Special Energy Award, AIA/American Association of School Administrators, 1978; Bard Award, City Club of New York, 1978; AIA New York Chapter Award, 1978; Boston Society of Architects Award, 1978; Boston Exports Honor Award, 1978; Award of Excellence, Building Owners and Managers Association of New York, 1978; Award of Excellence, *Urban Design,* 1978. Fellow of the American Academy of Arts and Sciences, 1957, and of the American Institute of Architects, 1960; Academician, National Academy of Design, 1974. Honorary Fellow, Mexican Society of Architects, 1974. Address: Hugh Stubbins and Associates Inc., 1033 Massachusetts Avenue, Cambridge, Massachusetts 02138, U.S.A.

Works:

1950 Adams Residence, Concord, Massachusetts
1954 Veterans housing, Wellesley, Massachusetts
        Back Bay Center, Boston (project)
        The Country School, Weston, Massachusetts
1955 United States Legation, Tangier, Morocco
        Better Homes and Gardens House, Chicago
        Dracut Junior/Senior High School, Dracut, Massachusetts
        Piney Point Beach Club, Marion, Massachusetts
1956 Animal Rescue League, Boston
        Sharpe House, Poujac, Rhode Island
        330 Beacon Street Apartment House, Boston
        Shaughnessy Elementary School, Lowell, Massachusetts
1957 Congress Hall, Berlin
1959 Woodland Elementary School, Weston, Massachusetts
        Continental Terrace Apartment House, Cambridge, Massachusetts
        Scientific Engineering Institute, Waltham, Massachusetts
1960 Loeb Drama Center, Harvard University, Cambridge, Massachusetts
        Unitarian Church, Concord, New Hampshire
        Gulf Coast Community College, Panama City, Florida
        Charlesbank Apartment House, Boston
1961 Brookline Farm, Massachusetts (project)
1962 Beverly School for the Deaf, Massachusetts
        Graduate student housing, Massachusetts Institute of Technology, Cambridge
1962/
69   Various buildings, including hi-rise dormitories, dining commons, etc., University of Massachusetts, Amherst
1962/
75   Various buildings, including dormitories,

theatre complex, etc., Mount Holyoke College, South Hadley, Massachusetts
1965 Physics Building and Dormitory, Princeton University, New Jersey
        Maimonides School, Brookline, Massachusetts
        Falmouth Intermediate School, Falmouth, Massachusetts
        Countway Library of Medicine, Harvard University Medical School, Boston
        Gymnasium, Bowdoin College, Brunswick, Maine
1966 North East Primate Center, Harvard University, Southboro, Massachusetts
        Senior Center, Bowdoin College, Brunswick, Maine
1967 Dana Hall School, Wellesley, Massachusetts
        Fine Arts Building, Rochester Institute of Technology, New York
        Administration Center, Brandeis University, Waltham, Massachusetts
1968 Union Mutual Life Insurance Company Office Building, Portland, Maine
        Gymnasium, Oberlin College, Ohio
        National Technical Institute for the Deaf, Rochester Institute of Technology, Rochester, New York
        Decorative Arts Wing, Boston Museum of Fine Arts
        Student Union, Brandeis University, Waltham, Massachusetts
1969 1033 Massachusetts Avenue Office Building, Cambridge, Massachusetts
1971 Veterans Stadium, Philadelphia
1972 Academic complex and hockey rink, Tabor Academy, Marion, Massachusetts
        Technical School, Shiraz Technical Institute, Iran
        Master Plan, Hampshire College, Amherst, Massachusetts
1973 Library, Alfred University, Alfred, New York
1974 The Bank, Manchester, New Hampshire
        Southeastern Massachusetts University, North Dartmouth
1976 Master Plan, Law School, and Graduate School of Business Administration, University of Virginia, Charlottesville
        Public Library, Newburg, New York
        Pusey Library, Harvard University, Cambridge, Massachusetts
1977 Hewlett-Packard Company, Waltham, Massachusetts
        Y.M.C.A., Worcester, Massachusetts
1978 Citicorp Center, New York (with Emery Roth and Sons)
        St. Peter's Church, New York
        Federal Reserve Bank of Boston

Publications:

By STUBBINS: book—*The Design Experience,* New York and London 1976; articles—"College Dormitories: What Do Colleges Really Want?" in *Architectural Record* (New York), April 1946; "Und die Antwort des Architekten" in *Baukunst und Werkform* (Nuremberg), no. 1, 1958.

On STUBBINS: book—*Architects on Architecture,* edited by Paul Heyer, New York 1966, London 1967; articles—in *Architectural Forum* (New York), April 1945; *Architecture d'Aujourd'hui* (Paris), July 1947; *Architectural Forum* (New York), September 1949; *Progressive Architecture* (New York), November 1953; "U.S. Center Slated for Berlin" by Thomas H. Creighton in *Progressive Architecture* (New York), September 1955; "Machine Made America" by Ian McCallum in *Architectural Review* (London), May 1957; "Berlin Congress Hall" in *Architectural Record* (New York), December 1957; *Progressive Architecture* (New York), January 1958; *Architectural Forum* (New York), June 1959; *Architectural Re-*

cord (New York), March 1963; *Architectural Record* (New York) August 1975; *Baumeister* (Munich), June 1976; "Seventh Heaven: Citicorp" in *Building Design* (London), September 1977.

*   *   *

Buildings are built, after all, to fulfill specific needs and to adapt to specific environments. Their ability to do this should form a part of any critical study we make or any buildings we design. "Today we live in a civilization, which in contemporary terms may be measured by the state of its architecture. The primary art of any civilization is that which most immediately dominates and motivates the life styles of people of that civilization. Everywhere, consciously or subconsciously, we are motivated—and often dominated—by the shapes we see and their proportions in relation to us. Contemporary society is reflected to an enormous extent in its shapes and proportions, and indeed it can be said that architecture in the modern world is essentially the cultural bridge between Art and Science, since the modern architect is both an artist and a scientist. While it remains an inspiring pleasure to read the genius of a poet, or to listen to the genius of a musician, or to see the genius of a painter or a photographer, it is for the contemporary mind often a greater inspiration to be able to *feel* the beauty of a structure, which one can touch and exist within. . . ."

I have a deep respect for *function.* The planning problems *must* be solved. The building must not only work for the user, but also be flexible for the future. Structure is of great importance. It should be forthright, logical and honest. It should have integrity, which does not mean it necessarily has to be expressed. A building in some way should express its purpose as well as have a unity in itself. It must be a whole thing, rather than a lot of elements strung together. Integration within its environment is important, for if we are to avoid physical chaos—with which we are now surrounded—we must respect the existing fabric, be it natural or manmade. In the long view, to be new or exciting may not be as important as to be courteous and restrained. I hasten to say that I do not mean that, within these parameters, we should not exploit fully all the ideas and philosophy plus the technology, methods and materials at our command.

Perhaps most of all it is important to realize that at any time we are just a link between the past and the future—and we must see ourselves as evolving from one and leading to the other, despite the ever-present temptation to deny our forebears. Since, in the last analysis, architecture reflects society's priorities and purposes, our architectural heritage is a unique expression of history and the progress of *man.*

What monuments we leave behind us in the form of buildings reveal more clearly than *anything* else, the value we place on the *quality* of life.

Architecture finally speaks of the nobility of man's existence and the desire to make life happier while we live on this earth.

—Hugh A. Stubbins, Jr.

*   *   *

If many young architects had their first choice, or older ones a second, the kind of architect that Hugh Stubbins is might well be the kind they would want to become.

Stubbins is a designer, a very good one, but his concept of design, unlike that of some of his contemporaries, is concerned not only with aspects of space, form and esthetics, but also with rigorous solving of the problems of building sites, circulation, materials, environmental systems and structures, as well as the needs and purposes of clients. And Stubbins is deeply concerned with the needs, problems and aspirations of the people who will occupy and use his buildings. Undoubtedly Stubbins would agree that good design is the essential, central ingredient of all good architecture, but it certainly is not the only one. Enlightened programming and excellence in planning, function and technology are also integral ingredients.

Attention to all of these elements has shaped the kind of architect Hugh Stubbins has become, very close to the ideal of the complete architect, adept at obtaining commissions for his firm, a good business man, a successful designer, a good manager. As a result, he has developed a successful firm that consistently produces buildings that many believe to be beautiful. At the same time, his buildings work, and they are completed on schedule and within their budgets. And, for the most part, his clients are delighted with the results.

Perhaps even more delighted are the people who occupy and use these buildings. This state of affairs has existed for a long time, through the long series of smaller and medium-sized buildings, schools, houses, college buildings and the like that Stubbins has designed over the years. However, it is not uncommon for good architects to produce humane, livable, interesting and comfortable environments in such buildings. Recently, Stubbins has produced such amenities in some very large buildings, a rare occurrence indeed.

In a large office building, Citicorp Center, completed in 1978 in New York City, Stubbins has produced an environment composed of great plazas, shops, restaurants, a church and other elements that capture the imagination, and usually the fancy, of all who experience it. In this building Stubbins gave new life to an urban area that formerly was occupied during the day only by those who were there on business and was completely deserted at night. Perhaps the most telling fact is that the great public spaces of this building are constantly filled with people in action or in repose, all enjoying themselves and experiencing fine architecture, from early morning until late every night, every day including weekends. In the Federal Reserve Plaza, completed in Boston later in 1978, Stubbins has created another such environment. Buildings like these not only provide humane environments for people, but also go a long way toward revitalizing the decaying centers of the cities in which they are built.

Hugh Stubbins admits to having been influenced by Walter Gropius, Marcel Breuer and Alvar Aalto. Their influences have deeply affected his philosophy, his intellect and his ideals, but have affected his style very little. In fact, it might be said that each of his buildings has its own style, derived from its own program, needs and problems. In each, the attempt has been made to discover the exact solution for the individual problems. Accordingly, Hugh Stubbins has not produced any radical, new overall style and no high-sounding theories. All he produces is consistently excellent architecture that people admire and enjoy.

—William Dudley Hunt, Jr.

STUDIO PER.

Partnership; established, Barcelona, 1965. Partners: Pep Bonet, *q.v.;* Cristian Cirici, *q.v.;* Lluis Clotet, *q.v.;* and Oscar Tusquets, *q.v.* Address: Caspe 151, Barcelona 13, Spain.

SULLIVAN, Louis (Henry).

American. Born in Boston, Massachusetts, 3 September 1856. Educated at Boston District Grammar School, 1860–63; Patrick Sullivan Academy, Newburyport, Massachusetts, 1863, and Halifax, Nova Scotia, 1863–64; Brimmer School, Boston, 1864–65; Rice School, Boston, 1865–70; English High School, Boston, 1870–72; studied architecture at the Massachusetts Institute of Technology, Cambridge, under William Ware and Eugene Letang, 1872–73; Ecole des Beaux-Arts, Paris, under Emil Vaudremer, 1874–76. Married Margaret Hattabough in 1899 (separated, 1906; divorced, 1917). Draftsman in the office of Frank Furness and George Hewitt, Philadelphia, 1873; Assistant in the office of William LeBaron Jenney, Chicago, 1874, 1876–79, and in the office of Dankmar Adler, Chicago, 1879–81; Partner, Adler and Sullivan, Chicago, 1881–95 (business declined after confrontation with architect Daniel Burnham at *World's Columbian Exposition,* Chicago, 1893; Adler died, 1900); travelled extensively throughout the United States from 1895 but continued to maintain office in Chicago; in financial difficulties, auctioned library and household effects and gave up office, 1909; died in poverty. Exhibition: *Louis Sullivan and the Architecture of Free Enterprise,* Art Institute of Chicago, 1956. Collection: Avery Architectural Library, Columbia University, New York. Recipient: Gold Medal, American Institute of Architects, 1946. *Died* (in Chicago) *14 April 1924.*

Works:

1879 Central Music Hall, Randolph and State Streets, Chicago (demolished, 1900)
1880 Borden Block, Randolph and Dearborn Streets, Chicago (demolished, 1910)
   Grand Opera House remodelling, North Clark Street, Chicago (demolished, 1927)
   John Borden House, Lake Park Avenue, Chicago
1881 Rothschild Store, West Monroe Street, Chicago
   Levi Rosenfeld Building, Washington and Halsted Streets, Chicago
   Brunswick and Balke Factory, Orleans, Huron, Sedgwick and Superior Streets, Chicago
   Rosenfeld Building extension, Chicago
1882 Brunswick and Balke Warehouse, Chicago
   Martin A. Ryerson Jeweller's Building, Wabash Avenue, Chicago
   Frankenthal Building, South Wells Street, Chicago
   Hammond Library, North Ashland Avenue, Chicago
   Max Rothschild Apartment Building, Prairie Avenue, Chicago
   Leopold House, Indiana Avenue, Chicago (demolished)
   Hyman House, Wabash Avenue, Chicago (demolished)
1883 Brunswick and Balke Lumber Drying Plant, Chicago
   Revell Building, Wabash and Adams Streets, Chicago (remodelled by others, 1929)
   Kniseley Store, Lake Street, Chicago
   3 houses for Max Rothschild, Indiana Avenue, Chicago
   E. L. Brand Store, Jackson Street, Chicago (demolished)
   Wright and Lowther Oil and Lead Manufacturing Company, Chicago
   C. P. Kimball House, East Ontario Street, Chicago
   Sol Bloomenfeld House, West Chicago Avenue, Chicago
   Selz House, South Michigan Avenue, Chicago
   Schwab House, South Michigan Avenue, Chicago (later remodeled)
   Halsted House, Lincoln Avenue, Chicago
   Rubee Store, South Clark Street, Chicago
   Kauffmann Store, Lincoln Avenue, Chicago
   Schoolhouse, Marengo, Illinois
   E. L. Brand Building, East Jackson Street, Chicago (demolished)
1884 F. A. Kennedy and Company Bakery, South Desplaines Street, Chicago
   3 houses for Max Rothschild, 32nd Street and Indiana Avenue, Chicago
   Barbe House, Prairie Avenue, Chicago
   3 houses for Mrs. N. Halsted, North Park Avenue, Chicago
   Ryerson Building, East Randolph Street, Chicago
   Troescher Building, South Market Street, Chicago
   Kniseley Building, West Monroe Street, Chicago
1885 Zion Temple, Washington and Ogden Streets, Chicago (demolished)
   Strauss House, Wabash Avenue, Chicago
   J. W. Scoville Building, West Washington Street, Chicago
   Hooley's Theatre remodelling, Randolph and LaSalle Streets, Chicago (demolished, 1927)
   Chicago Opera Festival Auditorium, *Interstate Exposition,* Grant Park, Chicago (demolished, 1892)
   McVicker's Theatre remodelling, Madison Street, Chicago (destroyed by fire, 1890)
   M. C. Stearns House, Douglas Avenue, Chicago (demolished)
   Lindauer House, Wabash Avenue, Chicago
   House, Prairie Avenue and Gano Street, Chicago
   Henry Stern House, Prairie Avenue, Chicago
   Samuel Stern House, Prairie Avenue, Chicago
   Kuh House, South Michigan Avenue, Chicago (demolished)
1886 Kohn House, Ellis Avenue, Chicago
   Dankmar Adler House, Ellis Avenue, Chicago
   Felsenthal House, Ellis Avenue, Chicago
   Goodman House, Wabash Avenue, Chicago
   Holzheimer House, Ellis Avenue, Chicago
   Eliel House, Ellis Avenue, Chicago
   Peck Building, LaSalle and Water Streets, Chicago (demolished)
   West Chicago Club, Throop Street, Chicago
   Illinois Central Railroad Stations at 39th Street and 43rd Street, Chicago
   Martin Ryerson Charities Trust Building, West Adams Street, Chicago (demolished)
1887 Selz, Schwab and Company Factory, Superior and Roberts Streets, Chicago
   Wirt Dexter Building, South Wabash Avenue, Chicago
   Diemal House, Calumet Avenue, Chicago
   Springer Building remodelling, State and Randolph Streets, Chicago (demolished)
   John Kranz Building remodelling, State Street, Chicago
   Lively House, Oak Street, Chicago
1888 Standard Club, Michigan Avenue and 24th Street, Chicago (demolished, 1931)
1889 Auditorium Building, Michigan Avenue at Congress Street, Chicago
   Walker Warehouse, South Market Street, Chicago
   Felsenthal Building, North Canal Street, Chicago (demolished, 1908)
   Health House, Prairie Avenue, Chicago
   Dexter House addition, Irving Avenue, Chicago
   Ryerson Tomb, Graceland Cemetery, Chicago
1890 Jewish Training School, West 12th Place, Chicago
   Crane Company Factory, Judd Street, Chicago (demolished)
   Getty Tomb, Graceland Cemetery, Chicago
   Louis Sullivan Cottages, Ocean Springs, Mississippi
   3 houses for Victor Falkenau, Wabash Avenue, Chicago
   Opera House Block, Pueblo, Colorado (destroyed by fire, 1922)
   Opera House Block, Seattle (project)
   Hotel Ontario, Salt Lake City, Utah (project)

Das Deutsche Haus remodelling, Milwaukee
1891 Dooly Block, West 2nd South Street, Salt Lake City, Utah
McVicker's Theatre rebuilding, Madison Street, Chicago (demolished, 1925)
Wainwright Building, 7th and Chestnut Streets, St. Louis (with Charles K. Ramsey Associates)
Kehilath Anshe Ma'ariv Synagogue, 33rd Street and Indiana Avenue, Chicago (now Pilgrim Baptist Church)
Chicago Cold Storage Exchange Warehouse, West Water Street (demolished, 1902)
Hotel, Chicago (project)
Apartment hotel, South Michigan Avenue, Chicago (project)
Mercantile Club, St. Louis (project)
Fraternity Temple, Chicago (project)
1892 Schiller Building, West Randolph Street, Chicago (subsequently Garrick Theatre Building; remodelled, 1935)
J. W. Oakley Building, West Austin Street, Chicago (remodelled)
Charnley House, 1365 Astor Street, Chicago
Albert Sullivan House, Lake Park Avenue, Chicago
Wainwright Tomb, Bellefontaine Cemetery, St. Louis
Sinai Temple remodelling, Indiana Avenue and 21st Street, Chicago (demolished)
Illinois Central Railroad Passenger Station, New Orleans
1893 Union Trust Building, 7th and Olive Streets, St. Louis (with Charles K. Ramsey Associates; now the Central National Bank Building)
St. Nicholas Hotel, 8th and Locust Streets, St. Louis (with Charles K. Ramsey Associates; remodelled)
Victoria Hotel, Chicago Heights (remodelled)
Meyer Building, West Van Buren Street, Chicago (remodelled)
Transportation Building, *World's Columbian Exposition*, Chicago (demolished)
1894 Stock Exchange Building, North LaSalle Street, Chicago (demolished; Main Trading Room reconstructed at the Art Institute of Chicago)
1895 Guaranty Building, Church and Pearl Streets, Buffalo, New York
1898 Bayard Building, Bleecker Street, New York (with Lyndon P. Smith Associates)
1899 Gage Building, South Michigan Avenue, Chicago (with Holabird and Roche; remodelled)
Schlesinger and Mayer Department Store, phase I, State and Madison, Chicago (now Carson Pirie Scott)
1900 Euston and Company Linseed Oil Plant, Blackhawk Street, Chicago
Euston and Company Linoleum Plant, Chicago
Crane and Company Foundry and Machine Shop, Canal and 12th Streets, Chicago (remodelled)
1904 Schlesinger and Mayer Department Store, phase II, State and Madison, Chicago (with additions by Burnham and Company, 1906; now Carson Pirie Scott)
Crane Company Office Building, Canal Street and West 12th Place, Chicago (demolished)
1905 Eli Felsenthal Store, East 47th Street, Chicago
1907 Bason House, Riverside Drive, Riverside, Illinois
1908 National Farmers' Bank, Broadway and Cedar Streets, Owatonna, Minnesota

Louis Sullivan: Auditorium Building, Chicago, 1889

1909 Bradley House, North Prospect Street, Madison, Wisconsin (now Sigma Phi Fraternity House, University of Wisconsin)
1911 People's Savings Bank, 3rd Avenue S.W. and 1st Street S.W., Cedar Rapids, Iowa
1913 Henry C. Adams Building, Moore and State Streets, Algona, Iowa
1914 St. Paul's Methodist Episcopal Church, 3rd Avenue S.E. and 14th Street S.E., Cedar Rapids, Iowa
Merchants' National Bank, 4th Avenue and Broad Street, Grinnell, Iowa
Home Building Association Bank, West Main and North 3rd Streets, Newark, Ohio (now Union Trust Company)
Purdue State Bank, State and Vine Streets, West Lafayette, Indiana
1915 John D. Van Allen and Son Dry Goods Store, 5th Avenue and South 2nd Street, Clinton, Iowa
1918 Peoples Saving and Loan Association Bank, Court Street and Ohio Avenue, Sidney, Ohio
1919 Farmers' and Merchants' Union Bank, James Street and Broadway, Columbus, Wisconsin
1922 Krause Music Store and House, Lincoln Avenue, Chicago (with William C. Presto Associates)

Publications:

By SULLIVAN: books—*Kindergarten Chats,* New York 1918, revised edition, edited by Claude Bragdon, Lawrence, Kansas 1934, revised edition, as *Kindergarten Chats and Other Writings,* edited by Isabella Athey, New York 1947; *The Autobiography of an Idea,* New York 1924, London 1956; *A System of Architectural Ornament, According with a Philosophy of Man's Powers,* New York 1924; *Democracy: A Man's Search,* edited by Elaine Hedges, Detroit 1961; *The Testament of Stone: Themes of Idealism and Indignation from the Writings of Louis Sullivan,* edited by Maurice English, Chicago 1963; *Architectural Essays from the Prairie School: Thomas Tallmadge, Louis H. Sullivan, Jens Jensen and Frank Lloyd Wright,* edited by W. R. Hasbrouck, Chicago 1967; numerous articles for the most part included in the above books.

On SULLIVAN: books—*Louis Sullivan: Prophet of Modern Architecture* by Hugh Morrison, New York 1935, revised edition 1952; *The Idea of Louis Sullivan* by J. Szarkowski, Minneapolis 1956; *Louis Sullivan and the Architecture of Free Enterprise,* exhibition catalog, by Edgar Kaufmann Jr., Chicago 1956; *Louis Sullivan as He Lived* by Willard Connely, New York 1960; *Louis Sullivan* by Albert Bush Brown, London and New York 1960; *Louis Sullivan: An Architect in American Thought* by Sherman Paul, Englewood Cliffs, New Jersey 1962; *Culture and Democracy: The Struggle for Form in Society and Architecture in Chicago and the Middle West During the Life and Times of Louis H. Sullivan* by Hugh Dalziel Duncan, Totowa, New Jersey 1965; *American Architecture Comes of Age: European Reaction to H. H. Richardson and Louis Sullivan* by Leonard K. Eaton, Cambridge, Massachusetts 1972; articles— "The Work of Louis H. Sullivan" by Howard Robertson in *The Architects' Journal* (London), 18 June 1924; "Louis Sullivan—His Work" in *Architectural Record* (New York), July 1924; "Sullivan: Decorazione e funzione" in *Domus* (Milan), May 1951; "Sullivan and the Skyscraper" by Henry-Russell Hitchcock in *RIBA Journal* (London), July 1953; "Sullivan and Wright: An Uneasy Union of Celts" in *Architectural Review* (London), November 1955; "Louis Sullivan Today" by Hugh Morrison in *AIA Journal* (Washington, D.C.), September 1956; "Sullivan Salvaged" in *Architectural Review* (London), February 1965; "Moments of Commerce: Louis Sullivan in Chicago" by Marcus Binney in *Country Life*

(London), January 1973 "The European Sources of Louis Sullivan's Ornamental Style" by Paul E. Sprague in *Journal of the Society of Architectural Historians* (Philadelphia), May 1974.

Louis Sullivan was one of the chief form givers of early modern architecture and a germinal figure in the development of the esthetics of the skyscraper. His earliest encounters with the building art were all of brief duration: a year's study at the Massachusetts Institute of Technology from 1872 to 1873; a few months' employment with the Philadelphia firm of Furness and Hewitt in 1873; and a visit to Chicago in the same year which led to a comparably short term of service in the office of William LeBaron Jenney. Sullivan then went to Paris, where he spent just two years, from 1874 to 1876, as a student in the Ecole des Beaux-Arts. The Ecole seems to have confirmed in him the distaste for the orthodox study of style for style's sake which he had begun to develop at M.I.T.

When he returned to Jenney's office in 1876, he met Dankmar Adler, with whom he later formed a partnership. Adler was a skilled engineer whose gifts complemented Sullivan's own abilities as a designer. The body of work the two men produced over a fourteen-year partnership contributed signally to the evolution of the modern tall building.

Adler and Sullivan's most important early work in Chicago was the massive Auditorium Building of 1889, a masonry wall bearing structure whose vigorous facade revealed a debt to the bold arcaded massings and neo-Romanesque character of H. H. Richardson's 1887 Marshall Field Warehouse in Chicago, much admired by Sullivan. The Auditorium took its name from the great operatic theater within, which Adler vaulted with a series of powerful elliptical arches and Sullivan endowed with a monumental rising sweep of space. Sullivan also added a rich program of decoration that made the theater into one of the most opulent interiors of its time.

Sullivan exploited rather than invented the technical advances that had made the metal frame skyscraper possible during the 1880's. In his Wainwright Building in St. Louis in 1891 he abandoned all reference to the stylistic past, including the Richardsonian Romanesque to which he had alluded in the Auditorium. He produced instead a simple and unified volume that pointedly articulated the upward thrust of a multi-story office building without yielding to the monotony of rhythms that such a building type might have forced him into. From a two-story base a strong seven-story shaft rose to a raking cornice, echoing the three-part division associated with Renaissance concepts of the block—not to mention the classical column—but altogether original as Sullivan now conceived it. He introduced a non-bearing column between each pair of supporting piers and added his lavish organic ornament to the spandrels and the top floor facade. The Wainwright was clearly no mere exercise in functional design, but rather a freely poetic expression of the skyscraper form. Sullivan's approach to the Guaranty Building in Buffalo was similar, marked by the same A-B-A vertical rhythms of the Wainwright and the same enhancing use of decoration.

During the 1890's other architects of the energetic Chicago School, notably the firms of Burnham and Root and Holabird and Roche, had themselves carried out ever more straightforwardly the articulation of the metal frame in tall buildings. Yet it remained for Sullivan to create the climactic work of that movement and the culmination of that direction: the Schlesinger and Mayer department store of 1899–1904 (now Carson Pirie Scott), in which the frame was acknowledged with uncompromising candor and stated with stunning compositional force. Structure became virtually identical with expressive form. Again, the bottom floor of the building provided Sullivan with a field in which to design the restless ornament that was the clearest expression of his fundamentally romantic temperament. Akin to Art

Nouveau in the serpentine density of its floral pattern, it was nonetheless a highly personal decorative style and one which provided both richness and grace to the taut vigor of his structural forms.

The Schlesinger and Mayer store was designed after the 1895 breakup of Sullivan's partnership with Adler, and it was the last major building commission he received in Chicago. The final two decades of his life in fact found him frequently in straits, obliged to accept far more modest commissions and to fill idle periods with writing. Yet the last endeavors, both architectural and literary, show a remarkably sustained creative energy. The banks that he built in the small midwestern towns of Owatonna, Minnesota and Grinnell, Iowa, are architectural jewels, in which strength of form is wedded to effulgence of ornament. And the literature Sullivan left, e.g., *Kindergarten Chats* and *The Autobiography of an Idea,* often reflective of the robust American romanticism of Walt Whitman, expounded his belief in an "architecture for democracy," his theories on architecture and his convictions about the destiny of modern building.

He died alone in a Chicago hotel room in 1924.

—Franz Schulze

SYRKUS, Helena.

Polish. Born Helena Niemirowska in Warsaw, 14 May 1900. Studied architecture at the Institute of Technology, Warsaw, 1918–23; humanities and philosophy at the University of Warsaw, 1923–25. Married Szymon Syrkus, *q.v.,* in 1926. Practised with Szymon Syrkus, Warsaw, 1926 until his death, 1964; in private practice, since 1964. Vice-Chairman, 1939–42, and Chairman, 1942–45, PAU (Underground Architecture and Town Planning Studio), of WSM (Warsaw Housing Co-operative); Secretary, Economic and Social Planning Unit, KRN (Underground Polish Government), 1943–45; Chairman, Propaganda Department, and Vice-Chairman of the Spatial Planning Committee, BOS (Capital Rebuilding Bureau), Warsaw, 1945–46; Secretary-General, NROW (Supreme Council for the Reconstruction of Warsaw), 1946. Lecturer, Institute of Architecture and Town Planning, Warsaw, 1949–51. Adjunct, 1949–52, Assistant Professor, 1952–55, Adjunct Professor, 1955–66, Professor, 1966–70, and since 1970 Emeritus Professor, Technical University, Warsaw. Member of the Executive Committee, Union International des Architectes, 1948–58. Member, Committee of Architecture and Town Planning, Polish Academy of Sciences, since 1960. Secretary, Praesens group, Warsaw, 1926–39, Editor of the *Praesens* journal, 1926, 1930, and Member of the Praesens Design Team, 1930–39; Member, 1929–57, and Secretary, 1933–39, Polish Branch of CIAM (Congrès Internationaux d'Architecture Moderne): Vice-President, International Council of CIAM, 1947. Exhibitions: *Warsaw of the Future,* Warsaw, 1936; *Warsaw Lives Again,* toured the United States and the United Kingdom, 1946; Tenth Anniversary Exhibition, Warsaw, 1955; International Union of Architects Exhibition, The Hague, 1955; Warsaw National Institute of Technology for National Economy, 1960; *Constructivism in Poland 1923–1936: Blok/Praesens,* Lodz, Poland, Essen, and Otterlo, Netherlands, 1973; *Tendenzen der Zwanziger Jahre,* Berlin, 1977, London, 1978. Collections: Museum of Modern Art, Lodz, Poland; Museum of Architecture, Wroclaw, Poland. Recipient: First Prize, with Szymon Syrkus, Old People's Home Competition, Kutno, Poland, 1928; First Prize, with Szymon Syrkus, Teachers Sanatorium Competition, Srodborow, Poland, 1932; Polish Medal of Freedom, 1945; Golden Cross of Warsaw Reconstruction, 1947; Polish Anniversary Medal, 1955; Merit Prize, Polish Ministry of Education, 1954, 1966; Honorary Award, International Congress of Intellectuals for Peace, Wroclaw, Poland, 1958; World Peace Committee Award, 1959; Golden Cross of Merit, Warsaw, 1960; Honorary Golden Badge, Central Committee of Housing Co-operatives, Warsaw, 1964; First Prize, Czuby Housing Development Competition, Lublin, 1973; Polish Thirtieth Anniversary Medal, 1974; Polityka Book Prize, Warsaw, 1977; Honorary Award, Polish Historians Association, 1977; Honorary Award, Warsaw City Council Culture Department, 1977; Celebration Medal, Warsaw Institute of Technology, 1977. Commander, Order of Polonia Restituta, 1956. Address: ul. Skolimowska 6 m 12, 00-795 Warsaw, Poland.

Works:

With Szymon Syrkus:

1927 Simultaneous Theatre, Warsaw (with A. Pronaszko and Z. Leski)
1929 Old People's Home, Kutno, Poland
1930 Housing Units with Steel Structures (project; with St. Hempel)
1931 Polish Teachers Association Building, Warsaw
     House, King's Hill, Skolimow, Poland (with St. Hempel)
1932 Teachers' Sanatorium, Srodborow, Poland (competition project; with St. Hempel)
1934 Experimental Theatre, for Irena Solska, Zoliborz, Warsaw
1935 Association of Workers Housing Co-operative, Grudziadz, Poland
1936 Rakowiec Housing Development, stage I, Warsaw (with the Praesens Team)
     House, Warsaw (with St. Hempel)
1937 House, Saska Kepa, Warsaw (with St. Hempel)
     Houses in Grzybowska, Zlota, and Jaworzynska Streets, Warsaw (with St. Hempel)
1939 Rakowiec Housing Development, stages II and III, Warsaw
     Sanatorium, Konstancin, Poland (with St. Hempel)
     Dairy (competition project; with St. Hempel)
1945 Housing developments for Rakowiec and Kolo, Warsaw (projects; with PAU)
     General plan for a "Socialist Warsaw" (project; with PAU)
1949 Meeting Hall, Rakowiec Housing Development, Warsaw (with WSM)
     Kolo Housing Development, stage I, Warsaw
     City Gasworks reconstruction, Kredytowa Street, Warsaw
     Belgian Consulate reconstruction, Warsaw
     Yugoslav Embassy reconstruction, Piekna Street, Warsaw
     Atheneum Theatre conversion, Warsaw
1951 School, Filtrowa Street, Warsaw
     Narodowy Bank Polski, Warsaw (competition project)
     School, Krolikarnia, Warsaw
     OK Saska Plan, Warsaw
     Theatre, Lodz, Poland (competition project)
1954 Praga Housing Development, phase I, Warsaw
1960 Pre-fabricated Slab Systems for Housing Units (project)
     Tatary Housing Development, Lublin, Poland
     Pre-fabricated Reinforced Units (project; with others)
     Praga Housing Development, phase II, Warsaw (project; with others)
     Kolo Housing Development, phase IV, Warsaw (with others)

Helena Syrkus only:

1973 Czuby Housing Development, Lublin, Poland (competition project)
1974 Tarchomin Housing Development, Warsaw (competition project)
1978 Housing Development, Warsaw (competition project)

Publications:

By H. SYRKUS: books—*Nowoczesne Osiedle Robotnicze* (Modern Workers Housing), with Szymon Syrkus, Katowice, Poland 1931; *Le Mur Extérieur,* with Szymon Syrkus (CIAM Paper), Athens 1933; *La Génealogie de l'Architecture Functionnelle,* with Szymon Syrkus (CIAM Paper), Zurich 1938; *Obsluga Spoleczna Jako Czynnik Ksztaltujacy Osiedle* (Communal Services: An Aid to Create a Sense of Community in Housing Estates), with Szymon Syrkus (PAU Paper), Warsaw 1940; *Osiedle Spoleczne na tle Dzielnicy, Miasta, Regionu* (The Social Housing Unit in Relation to District, Town and Region), Warsaw 1941; *Organizacja Wykonawstwa Odbudowy Warszawy* (How to Reconstruct Demolished Warsaw), with Roman Piotrowski, Cracow 1944; *Tezy Urbanistyczne Odbudowy Warszawy* (Town Planning Aspects of Rebuilding Warsaw), with Roman Piotrowski, Warsaw 1945; *Udzial Spoldzielczosci Mieszkaniowej w Realizacji Pierwszego Trzyletniego Planu Godpodarczego dla Warsazwy* (Part Played by Housing Co-operatives in the Realization of the First Three Year Economic Plan for Warsaw), with Szymon Syrkus, Warsaw 1946; *Les Cités ouvrieres à Varsovie,* Zurich 1949; *Hommage à Cor van Eesteren,* with others, Amsterdam 1967; *Hommage à Giedion,* with others, Basle 1971; *Hommage à Walter Gropius,* Berlin 1974; *Ku Idei Osiedla Spolecznego* (Towards the Idea of a Social Housing Estate), Warsaw 1976; *Kazimierz Malewicz* (in French), Warsaw 1978; articles—numerous in Polish architectural journals, and "Production des Logements en Masse," with Szymon Syrkus, in *L'Architecture d'Aujourd'hui* (Paris), no. 1, 1932; "De l'Architecture et de la Production des Logements," with Szymon Syrkus, in *L'Equerre* (Liege), nos. 7/8, 1935; "Industrialisation du Bâtiment en Pologne," with Szymon Syrkus, in *Les Chantiers dans Le Monde* (Paris), no. 3/4, 1948, reprinted in *L'Architecture devant ses Tâches Nouvelles,* Lausanne 1948; "Planning and Housing in Warsaw," with Szymon Syrkus, in *The Architects Yearbook,* London 1949; "La Rationalisation des Projets et de la Construction des Habitation" in *Livre du IVme Congrès UIA,* Rotterdam 1955; "La Recontre d'Architectes et d'Elus Municipaux à Varsovie" in *Revue UIA* (Paris), no. 5, 1954; "Sozialer Wohnungsbau und Baurationalisierung in Warschau: Wohnquartier Kolo," with Szymon Syrkus, in *Das Werk* (Zurich), January 1959.

On H. and S. SYRKUS: books—*Gli Elementi dell'Architettura Funzionale* by Alberto Sartoris, Milan 1932: *Circle: International Survey of Constructive Art,* edited by J. L. Martin, Ben Nicholson and Naum Gabo, London 1937; *The Culture of Cities* by Lewis Mumford, New York and London 1938; *Introduzione all'Architettura Moderna* by Alberto Sartoris, Milan 1944; *Constructivism in Poland 1923–1936: Blok/Praesens,* exhibition catalogue, Lodz 1973; articles—"Kolo Housing Development" in *Revue UIA* (Paris), nos. 4 and 5, 1954; "Habitation 1945–55" in *Livre du IVme Congrès UIA,* Rotterdam 1955; "Simultaneous Theatre and Irena Solska Theatre Projects," summary of a thesis by Bozena Frankowska in *Pamietnik Teatralny* (Warsaw), no. 2, 1962; "Szymon Syrkus und die Gruppe Praesens" in *Bauwelt* (Berlin), January 1965.

The life and work of Helena and Szymon Syrkus are inseparably linked with the history not only of Polish but also of international avant-garde architectural thought. The fundamental principle of their long partnership is that social co-operation is more rewarding than competition and rivalry.

In 1926, through the initiative of Szymon Syrkus, the avant-garde group of Modernists, *Praesens,* was formed, and their journal published their theories of a new architecture. Working within the framework of CIAM, with such internationally eminent architects as Le Corbusier, Gropius, Giedion and Moser, Helena and Szymon Syrkus were co-authors of the Athens Charter, and the Polish Branch, which they represented through the thirty years of its existence, was one of the most radical wings of the organization. They were given moral support in Poland by Toeplitz and Tolwinski, leading organizers of social housing projects. These men entrusted the architects of *Praesens* with the design of the Rakowiec Housing Development for the Warsaw Housing Cooperative, and the *Praesens* architectural/town planning studio was set up to realize this commission.

The Rakowiec project, which was presented to the Third Congress of CIAM in Brussels in 1930, was an illustration of Le Corbusier's dictum, "Il n'y a pas d'Architecture sans Urbanisme." By considering the indelible natural characteristics, such as the geographical location of the city within central Europe, the climate, morphology, and main lines of communication of the country itself, the Syrkus's were able to define the major factors influencing the function of the city and to formulate a rational framework for its development. As a result of this work, they were able to create a theory of social housing for the district, town or region. This theory, first formulated in the Underground Architecture and Town Planning Studio (PAU) during the Nazi occupation of Poland, was later documented by Helena Syrkus in her book *Ku Idei Osiedla Spolecznego.*

The characteristic traits of most of their subsequent work were an emphasis on uniting architecture with social demands, an integration of theoretical architecture and town planning research with the practical design and realization of the social housing estate, and a constant attempt to apply modern building techniques to the construction of cheap, small, and generally accessible apartments, by using standard pre-fabricated units.

There are four consecutive stages in their work. First, between 1917 and 1926, their study and work involved a search for concepts to unify the widely divergent creative aims of the avant-garde—postulates for a new architecture. It was a period of contact with the avant-garde milieu of the 1920's in Moscow, Cracow, Berlin and Paris, and the futurist group Katarynka and later the Blok Group in Warsaw, experiences that helped to form Szymon Syrkus's ideas and their development in *Praesens.*

The formation of *Praesens* is the beginning of the second phase in their career, which was characterized by a crystallization of their ideas about approach and the character and tasks of the new functionalist architecture. They stated their ideology in the first issue of the *Praesens* journal: "By way of experiment, architecture provides new opportunities, not only plastic as it might seem, but also social. For architecture changes the social pattern, as the social pattern changes architecture." According to Syrkus, the only solution measuring up to 20th century expectations was to combine architecture with industry, to adjust it to the technical possibilities offered by industrial production. He assumed that a proper understanding of progress would prompt a flexible architecture, one that could easily be adapted to the rapid changes occurring in everyday life. He believed that architecture had to adapt with these changes—which it could do: new solutions were being continually introduced in the building industry as a result of human inventiveness, the noblest feature of man. New building—making use of all the technical opportunities offered by modern industry, and fulfilling the needs of people—ought as well to integrate dwellings with their surrounding environment.

Their involvement with CIAM greatly influenced their further work and their third period of creativity, which spans the 1930's and the Second World War. It begins with the opening of the *Praes-*

ens Architectural Studio in 1931 and their work on Rakowiec. In designing Rakowiec, they applied an arrangement of columns in the skeleton support structure which created the most advantage conditions for planning flats. By applying and refining this modular system, they managed to formulate certain principles according to which the whole development could be designed, and these principles were later used in planning new housing developments and even new towns. As early as 1931, by introducing a modular system that would allow for mass pre-fabrication, the Syrkus's tried to solve the problem of building houses on a huge developments.

The design of Rakowiec and its partial realization in the pre-war period, combined with their theoretical work with CIAM and CIRPAC, culminated in a full realization of their social housing theory and its illustration in projects created underground during the war years for further housing developments and for a general plan for a future Warsaw. This period is characterized by a continual broadening of interest, a movement towards large-scale spatial and regional planning, and a consciousness of the real social, organizational and political factors responsible for the development of the environment.

The liberation of Poland in 1945 brought a political system that allowed the full realization of the ideas that the Syrkus's had struggled for all of their lives—the fourth and conclusive phase in their work. They saw their theories put into practice, and, at Warsaw Technical University, were able to pass on these theories to others. A high point of this period is the realization of the Kolo Housing Development between 1947–49, which so accurately reflects their ideas that in 1978 it was placed under a preservation order and classified as a historical monument.

During the period 1954–60 Helena and Szymon Syrkus carried out research into the standardization of the construction of houses and prepared a prototype project of pre-fabricated elements. They elaborated their research in further projects, and, in their own view, achieved the "clearest" expression of their theories in the Tatary Housing Development in Lublin of 1960.

Szymon's theoretical work, only partially realized in his lifetime, is now carried on by his widow.

—Teresa Czaplinska-Archer

SYRKUS, Szymon.

Polish. Born in Warsaw, 24 April 1893. Educated at the Technische Hochschule, Vienna, 1911–12, Graz, 1912–14, Riga, Moscow, and Warsaw, 1915–22; studied painting and architecture at the Academy of Fine Art, Cracow, 1918–20, and sculpture at the Ecole dex Beaux-Arts and drawing at the Académie Colarossi, Paris, 1923–24. Served as a technical engineer in the Polish Army, 1915–17; interned in Auschwitz Concentration Camp, 1942–45. Married Helena Niemirowska (i.e., Helena Syrkus, *q.v.*) in 1926. Worked in various architectural practices, on building sites and as a designer in film studios, Berlin, 1922–23; assistant in the architectural studios of Leon Chifflot and Gustave Umdenstock of the Académie des Beaux-Arts, Paris, 1923–24, and in the practice of H. Gay, Warsaw, 1925–26; practised with Helena Syrkus, Warsaw, 1926 until his death, 1964. Chairman, PAU (Underground Architecture and Town Planning Studio) of WSM (Warsaw Housing Co-operative), 1939–42; Vice-Chairman and Director, Town Planning Section, BOS (Capital Rebuilding Bureau), Warsaw, 1945. Chairman, Architecture Department, Unit of Sociology in Architecture, Institute of Architecture and Town Planning, Warsaw, 1949–51; Professor of Design, Technical University, Warsaw, 1949–64. Vice-President, SARP (Polish Architects Association), 1934–37, 1944–46; Chairman of the Research Centre, Polish Association of Housing Reform, 1947–49;

Chairman, Section of Technology Progress in the Building Industry, Polish Committee on State Prizes, 1949–64; First Secretary, Institute of Technology Branch, Communist Party of Warsaw, 1950. Member, Katarynka futurist group, Cracow, 1918–20, and Blok group, Warsaw, 1925; Founder Member, Praesens group, Warsaw, 1926–39, Member of the Editorial Board of the *Praesens* journal, 1926–39, and Member of the Praesens Design Team, 1929–39; Member, Executive Committee, CIRPAC (Comité Internationale pour la Résolution des Problèmes de l'Architecture Contemporaine), 1927–57; Member, Polish Branch of CIAM (Congrès Internationaux d'Architecture Moderne), 1929–57. Exhibitions: Modern Architecture Exhibition, Warsaw, 1926; *Machine Age,* New York, 1927; *International Theatre Exhibition,* New York, 1927; *Functional Warsaw,* London, 1934; *Warsaw of the Future,* Warsaw, 1936; *Warsaw Lives Again,* toured the United States and the United Kingdom, 1946; Tenth Anniversary Exhibition, Warsaw, 1955; International Union of Architects Exhibition, The Hague, 1955; Warsaw National Institute of Technology for National Economy, 1960; *Constructivism in Poland 1923–1936: Blok/Praesens,* Lodz, Poland, Essen, and Otterlo, Netherlands, 1973; *Tendenzen der Zwanziger Jahre,* Berlin, 1977, London, 1978. Collections: Museum of Modern Art, Lodz, Poland; Museum of Architecture, Wroclaw, Poland. Recipient: First Prize, Old People's Home Competition, Brzesc, Poland, 1928; First Prize, with Helena Syrkus, Old People's Home Competition, Kutno, Poland, 1928; First Prize, *Home Trade Fair,* Poznan, 1929; First Prize, with Helena Syrkus, Teachers Sanatorium Competition, Srodborow, Poland, 1932; Polish Medal of Freedom, 1945; Golden Cross of Warsaw Reconstruction, 1947; Diploma, Royal Institute of British Architects, 1954; Polish Anniversary Medal, 1955; Merit Prize, Polish Ministry of Education, 1955; First Class Award, Committee of Town Planning and Architecture, Warsaw, 1956; Golden Cross of Merit, Warsaw, 1960. Honorary doctorate: Technische Hochschule, Graz, Austria, 1963. Honorary Member, Royal Institute of British Architects, 1937. Commander, Order of Polonia Restituta, 1956. *Died* (in Warsaw) *in 1964.*

Works:

1926 Housing Development (project; with T. Zarnower and M. Szczuka)
Bialystok Church (competition project; with H. Oderfeld)
1927 Simultaneous Theatre, Warsaw (with A. Pronaszko, Z. Leski, and Helena Syrkus)
Palace of the League of Nations, Geneva (competition project; with H. Oderfeld)
1928 Old People's Home, Warsaw (with H. Oderfeld and E. Seydenbeutel)
Artificial Silk Factory, Tomaszow Mazowiecki, Poland (with H. Oderfeld)
Old People's Home, Brzesc, Poland
1929 Fertilizer Pavilion, *Home Trade Fair,* Poznan

With Helena Syrkus:

1929 Old People's Home, Kutno, Poland
1930 Housing Units with Steel Structures (project; with St. Hempel)
1931 Polish Teachers Association Building, Warsaw
House, King's Hill, Skolimow, Poland (with St. Hempel)
1932 Teachers' Sanatorium, Srodborow, Poland (competition project; with St. Hempel)
1934 Experimental Theatre, for Irena Solska, Zoliborz, Warsaw
1935 Association of Workers Housing Co-operative, Lodz
Association of Workers Housing Co-operative, Grudziadz, Poland
1936 Rakowiec Housing Development, stage I, Warsaw (with the Praesens Team)

House, Warsaw (with St. Hempel)
1937 House, Saska Kepa, Warsaw (with St. Hempel)
House in Grzybowska, Zlota, and Jaworzynska Streets, Warsaw (with St. Hempel)
1939 Rakowiec Housing Development, stages II and III, Warsaw
Sanatorium, Konstancin, Poland (with St. Hempel)
Dairy (competition project; with St. Hempel)
1945 Housing developments for Rakowiec and Kolo, Warsaw (projects; with PAU)
General plan for a "Socialist Warsaw" (project; with PAU)
1949 Meeting Hall, Rakowiec Housing Development, Warsaw (with WSM)
Kolo Housing Development, stage I, Warsaw
City Gasworks reconstruction, Kredytowa Street, Warsaw
Belgian Consulate reconstruction, Warsaw
Yugoslav Embassy reconstruction, Piekna Street, Warsaw
Atheneum Theatre conversion, Warsaw
1951 School, Filtrowa Street, Warsaw
Narodowy Bank Polski, Warsaw (competition project)
School, Krolikarnia, Warsaw
OK Saska Plan, Warsaw
Theatre, Lodz (competition project)
1954 Praga Housing Development, phase I, Warsaw

1960 Pre-fabricated Slab Systems for Housing Units (project)
Tatary Housing Development, Lublin, Poland
Pre-fabricated Reinforced Units (project; with others)
Praga Housing Development, phase II, Warsaw (project; with others)
Kolo Housing Development, phase IV, Warsaw (with others)

Publications:

By S. SYRKUS: books—*Osiedle w Celle i w Kassel* (Housing in Celle and Kassel), Katowice, Poland 1931; *Nowoczesne Osiedle Robotnicze* (Modern Workers' Housing), with Helena Syrkus, Katowice, Poland 1931; *Le Mur Extérieur,* with Helena Syrkus (CIAM Paper), Athens 1933; *Warschau: Funktionele Stadt,* with Jan Chmielewski (CIAM Paper), Zurich 1934; *Warszawa Funkcjonalna* (Functional Warsaw), with Jan Chmielewski, Warsaw 1935; *La Génealogie de l'Architecture Functionnelle,* with Helena Syrkus (CIAM Paper), Zurich 1938; *Obsluga Spoleczna Jako Czynnik Ksztaltujacy Osiedle* (Communal Services: An Aid to Create a Sense of Community in Housing Estates), with Helena Syrkus (PAU Paper), Warsaw 1940; *Udzial Spoldzielczosci Mieszkaniowej w Realizacji Pierwszego Trzyletniego Planu Godpodarczego dla Warszawy* (Part Played by Housing Co-operatives in the Realization of the First

Three Year Economic Plan for Warsaw), with Helena Syrkus, Warsaw 1946; *Referat o Akademii Architectury* (About the Academy of Architecture), Warsaw 1951; articles—numerous in Polish architectural journals, and "Architecture Opens the Volume" in *Machine Age,* exhibition catalogue, New York 1927; "Debate on the Modern Theatre" in *International Theatre Exhibition,* exhibition catalogue, New York, 1927; "Production des Logements en Masse," with Helena Syrkus, in *L'Architecture d'Aujourd'hui* (Paris), no. 1, 1932; "Nuova Teorie di Teatro" in *Quadrante* (Milan), no. 11, 1934; "De l'Architecture et de la Production des Logements," with Helena Syrkus, in *L'Equerre* (Liege), nos. 7/8, 1935; "Logis et Loisirs: Cas d'Application: Villes et Campagnes" in *Le Livre du Vme Congrès CIAM,* Paris 1938; "Industrialisation du Bâtiment en Pologne," with Helena Syrkus, in *Les Chantiers dans le Monde* (Paris), no. 3/4, 1948, reprinted in *L'Architecture devant ses Tâches Nouvelles,* Lausanne 1948; "Planning and Housing in Warsaw," with Helena Syrkus, in *The Architects Yearbook,* London 1949; "A Critical Appraisal of Habitat at Present" in *Le Livre du Xme Congrès CIAM,* Dubrovnik 1956; "Sozialer Wohnungsbau und Baurationalisierung in Warschau: Wohnquartier Kolo," with Helena Syrkus, in *Das Werk* (Zurich), January 1959.

See SYRKUS, Helena

Helena and Szymon Syrkus: Kolo Housing Development, Warsaw, 1960

T

TAILLIBERT, Roger.
French. Born in Châtres s/Cher, 21 January 1926.
Educated at the Ecole National Supérieure des
Beaux-Arts, Paris: Ecole du Louvre, Paris, Dip.
Arch. (honors) 1955; Prix de Rome Scholar, 1957–
59; Laureate of the Institut de France, for research,
1959. Served in the French Army, 1952. Married
Béatrice Pfister in 1965; daughter: Sophie. In private
practice, Paris. Member, Commission on Public
Buildings, France, 1968–71; Member of the Architectural Commission of Lille and Toulouse,
1972–75; Member, Architectural Commission of
Paris, 1974–77. Researcher in Sports Building Structures, for the French Ministry of Sports, since 1966;
Consultant Architect to the City of Montreal, since
1972; Member of the French National Architectural
Commission, since 1976; Chief Architect and Con-
servator, Grand Palais des Champs-Elysées, Paris,
since 1977. Exhibitions: *Architecture and Sports,*
Mexico City, 1968; *CIAM Exhibition,* Montreal,
1976; *2 Prix Européens,* Cembureau, France, 1978.
Recipient: Gold Medal, Académie d'Architecture,
1971; Grand National Prize in Arts and Letters, for
Architecture, 1976. Architect-in-Chief of Civic
Buildings and National Palaces; Member, Académie
d'Architecture, 1972. Chevalier of the Légion
d'Honneur; Officer of the National Order of Merit,
1972. Member, Royal Society of Arts, London, 1975.
Address (office): 163 rue de la Pompe, 75116 Paris,
France.

Works:

1962 D.A.F. Factory, Survilliers, France
1965 Covered swimming pool, Deauville, France
1967 Olympics Training School, Font-Romeu,
      Pyrenees, France
      Carnot Swimming Pool (with movable roof),
      Paris
1968 Research laboratory, Castres, Tarn, France
1970 Pharmaceutical products factory, Castres,
      Tarn, France
      Parc des Princes Stadium, Paris
1970/
   74 Plateau de Bel Air (new town), near St.-Ger-
      main-en-Laye, France
1972 Stadium Nord, Lille
1972/
   74 Sports and Cultural Center, Chamonix,
      France
1974/
   76 Olympic Complex, Montreal: Stadium,
      Sports Center, Swimming Pools Complex,
      and Plazas
1974/
   78 Sports Center and School, Castres, Tarn,
      France
1975 National Ski and Alpine School, Chamonix,
      France
      Baltimore Stadium, Maryland
1976 Hotel Intercontinental, Montfleury, Cannes
      Municipal Library, Castres, Tarn, France
      Lycée Nord, Toulouse
1977 Nuclear power plant, Tournus, France (pro-
      ject)

Prefecture of Tarn and Garonne Building,
      Montauban, France
1978 Faculty of Pharmacy, University of Toulouse
      National Engineering School, Gabes, Tunisia
      Geographic Institute, Amman, Jordan
      Olympic Water Sports Center, Kirchberg,
      Luxembourg
      European Parliament, Luxembourg
      Jolimont School Complex, Toulouse

Publications:

By TAILLIBERT: books—*Construire l'Avenir,*
Paris 1977; *Annales de l'Institut du Bâtiment,* editor,
Paris 1977.

On TAILLIBERT: books—*Histoire Mondiale de
l'Architecture* by Michel Ragon, Paris 1971; *Guide
d'Architecture Contemporaine de France,* Paris 1972;
Montreal Olympique by Marc Emery, Montreal
1976; *Roger Taillibert* by René Huyghe, Paris 1977.

*

For a quarter of a century architecture has been for
me a means to give better expression to man's needs
and to give him a better way of life.

Each building, each work of art, is an essential
element in scientific, technological development, and
often a delight to the new users. Although materials
have varied little, man exploits their performance
with an ever more precise vision. Architecture,
thanks to the spirit of research and application,
becomes a medium that all developed nations would
like to see applied, with the necessary talent, to all
their needs.

In all my works my most sought-after goal is the
"well-being of man," but there is always also the
possibility that one may find an unknown space
within one's own culture. There should be no superfluity, no aggression, and also one tries to stay as far
as possible from the negative aspects of form, forms
without the conviction of stability or of functional
structure: one tries to explore new paths without
obstacles or servility to past notions.

To have recourse to the purest geometric form, to
adapt it, to carve it in space, to make it audacious
and pleasing—that is an achievement that must
everywhere bring to man the balance that he seeks
in the "chasms of contemporary towns."

Matter shapes space; it does not rend or brutalize
it. In the harmony of its volumes describing the outward appearances of places, the architecture of a
growing world shapes a better way of life in an environment that is always in search of better solutions.
Permanently inventive conceptions cause technique
to blossom, and that is a form of success that only
the erosion of time will ennoble or destroy.

—Roger Taillibert

The ideal that Roger Taillibert pursues is to produce
a structure as if it has sprung from the earth, at the
same time making it appropriate to a given program
and revealing very clearly the resources of contemporary construction. He uses the most modern
means at his disposal to achieve the quintessence of
each project, taking his design to the very limit of
defiance. It is not surprising that he has this attitude

Roger Taillibert: Olympic Complex, Montreal, 1976 (model)

of mind. A great sportsman since his early youth, Taillibert seems driven to push back the limits of the possible.

If he considers architecture as involving a harmonization of space, then he does not attempt to achieve that harmonization according to any dominant aesthetic. It is, rather, an organic and rational harmonization, that which can result from a precise use of materials and techniques selected for their potential. For Taillibert, architecture is an exact and logical organization of matter and space.

This is not to imply that he rejects the aesthetic or social implications of construction as such. They exist for him—but they can only be consequences, not aims. Plastic beauty, functionalism, scale, or symbolic implication are the elements that, in the intuitive process of creation, result from the harmonious combination of other elements—the ingenuity and precision of technical calculations, experimentation, the choice and marriage of materials, adaptation to the economic conditions of the program, and the integration of the project to the site.

These ideas inform his most recent works, the Olympic installations at Montreal, the Olympic Water Sports Center at Kirchberg, Luxembourg, and the nuclear power plant in Tournus—works accomplished with means it would not have been possible to use in earlier works, the Parc des Princes Stadium in Paris, the Sports and Cultural Center in Chamonix, the D.A.F. Factory in Survilliers, or the Olympics Training School at Font-Romeu in the Pyrenees.

—Renée Diamant-Berger

TAKEYAMA, Minoru.

Japanese. Born in Sapporo, 15 March 1934. Educated at Waseda University, Tokyo, 1952–58, B.Arch. 1956, M.Arch. 1958; Harvard University, Cambridge, Massachusetts, 1959–60 (Fulbright Scholar), M.Arch. 1960. Worked for TAC, Josep Lluis Sert, and Hideo Sasaki, Cambridge, 1960–61, for Paul Lester Wiener, Isamu Noguchi, and Harrison and Abramovitz, New York, 1961–62, and for Jørn Utzon, Arne Jacobsen, Finn Juhl and Henning Larsen, in Copenhagen, 1962–64. Since 1965, President of Minoru Takeyama and the United Actions, Tokyo; office established in Sapporo, 1975. Lecturer, School of Architecture, Royal Danish Academy of Fine Arts, 1963–64. Assistant Professor, 1965–76, and since 1976 Professor, Musashino Art University, Tokyo. Visiting Critic, Waseda University, 1965, Hokkaido University, 1966, Kyushuh Institute of Technology, 1972, and Nagoya Institute of Technology, 1972; Visiting Professor, University of California, Berkeley, Spring 1976 and 1977. Member of the Board, Japan Architects Association, since 1975. Member, ArchiteXt, with Takefumi Aida, Takamitsu Azuma, Mayumi Miyawaki, and Makoto Suzuki, since 1971. Exhibitions: Bienal, Sao Paulo, 1957; Body Furniture, Tokyo, 1970; Body Lighting, Tokyo, 1974; Terra-1, Poland, 1975; A New Wave of Japanese Architecture, toured 10 American cities, 1978; Graphic Architecture, Tokyo, 1978. Recipient: Grand Prize, Bienal, Sao Paulo, 1957; Shogyo Design Association Award, 1971, 1974; Wheelwright Fellowship, Harvard University, 1971; Fulbright Research Fellowship, 1975; Silver Medal, Japan Display Design Association, 1975. Address: Minoru Takeyama and the United Actions, 5-1-10-501 Minami-Aoyama, Minato-ku, Tokyo, Japan.

Minoru Takeyama: Hotel Beverley Tom, Tomakomai, Hokkaido, Japan, 1973

Works:

1958 House, Tokyo (ROH)
1959 Recreational facilities for the Mastic Tile Company (COM; competition project)
1960 City Hall, Boston (COB-o; competition project)
1961 Urban design for the Mastic Tile Company (COM; competition project)
1963 National Theatre of Japan (COT; competition project)
1965 Savarian Restaurant interiors, Tokyo (IOG)
  Pandora Restaurant interiors, Tokyo (IOP)
  Design for bath units (DON)
  House, Børnholm, Denmark (ROB; project)
1966 House, Sapporo, Japan (ROT-1)
  Housing units (COB; competition project)
  Mammina Fashion Store interiors, Tokyo (IOM-1)
  Transparent House (ROGg; project)
1967 City Center, Espoo, Finland (COE; competition project)
  Yamagiwa Electric Hardware Store interiors, Tokyo (IOY-1)
  Yamagiwa Parlor interiors, Tokyo (IOY-2)
  Municipal Cemetery, Mito, Japan (POM)
1968 Young Men's Lodge, Nagano, Japan (BON)
  Shingle House, Tokyo (ROK)
  City Hall, Amsterdam (COA; competition project)
  "Situationer" (NOS-1; conceptual model)
  United Nations Conference Center, Vienna (COW; competition project)
  Mammina Fashion Store interiors, Kobe, Japan (IOM-2)
  Yamagiwa Showroom interiors, Tokyo (IOY-3)
  Memorial Tower for War Victims, Hokkaido, Japan (MOO)
  "Shu Pub" Shoe Store, Tokyo (IOO-1)
  Utonai Leisure Center, Hokkaido, Japan (BOU)
  Tops Coffee Shop interiors, Tokyo (IOT)
  Kinichikan Department Store, Sapporo, Japan (BOK; project)
1970 Ichi Ban Kahn Omni-Rental Stores, Tokyo (BOS-1)
  Fuji Heavy Industry Labor Union Hall, Saitama, Japan (BOF)
  Ni Ban Kahn Omni-Rental Stores, Tokyo (BOS-2)
  New experimental college, Thy, Denmark (BONec; project)
  "Living Room" (MOS-2; conceptual model)
  Multi-family house, Tokyo (ROI)
  Relocatable Kindergarten Units, Copenhagen (DOK; project)
  "Body Furniture" (XOF)
1971 Compound houses, Tokyo (ROSh/B)
  Iwakura Office Building, Hokkaido, Japan (BOI-1)
  Place Beaubourg, Paris (COP; competition project)
  Shell Gas Station exterior, Tokyo (EOsh)
  House, Sapporo, Japan (ROSg)
  Yamatake exterior, Sapporo, Japan (EOT)
1972 Pepsi Cola Canning Plant, Mikasa, Hokkaido, Japan (BOP-1)
  Kurashiki Factory conversion (POK; project)
  Tack Restaurant, Hokkaido, Japan (BOI-3)
  Tom Store exterior, Hokkaido, Japan (EOI)
  Redevelopment plan for the Ugawara Coast Line, Japan (POU)
  "Yamaha Sound Woods," Shizuoka, Japan (POY; project)
  House, Lahore, Pakistan (ROPk; project)
  Sambi Restaurant, Los Angeles (BOSn; project)
  "Body Lighting" (lighting fixture; XOE)
1973 Hotel Beverley Tom, Tomakomai, Hokkaido, Japan (BOI-4)
  Island of Chirin, Kyushu, Japan (POT; project)

Nichiro Saloon interiors, Tokyo (ION)
  Combined house, Hakone, Japan (ROT/M; project)
  City of Tomakomai Shopping Arcade, Hokkaido, Japan (EOTm; project)
  Design of store facade for National Electric Shops (EON)
  Onuma Lakeshore Development, Hakodate, Japan (POH; project)
1974 House, Asahikawa, Hokkaido, Japan (ROA)
  House, Tomakomai, Hokkaido, Japan (ROW-1)
  High-density, low-rise housing, Tomakomai, Hokkaido, Japan (ROW-2; project)
  Design of the Environment of the Northern Region exhibition, Sapporo, Japan (XOH)
  Misawa Homes Showroom interiors, Tokyo (ION)
  Yamagiwa Record Shop interiors, Tokyo (IOY-5)
  Yamagiwa Parlor interiors, Chiba, Japan (IOY-6)
  House, Sapporo, Japan (ROIw)
  Stage design for the musical Himiko, Tokyo (DOH)
1975 Porto Santos Island Development (COS; competition project)
  "Earthtecture" (XOT; exhibition project)
  House, Tokyo (ROU)
  House, Sapporo, Japan (ROY)
  Rehabilitation Center, Sapporo, Japan (PON)
  "Shu Pub" Shoe Store, Tokyo (IOO-6)
  Shell Garden Super Market, Tokyo (BOSh; project)
  Self-help community, Manila (COM; competition project)
1976 Sapporo Art Park, Hokkaido, Japan (POS; project)
  Bankei Rehabilitation Center, Sapporo, Japan (PON; project)
  Atelier Indigo (own studio), Sapporo, Japan (ROO)
  Summer House, Hokkaido, Japan (RON)
  Summer House, Hokkaido, Japan (ROOg)
  Prefabricated house, Sapporo, Japan (ROIw)
  "Shu Pub" Shoe Store, Tokyo (IOO-7)
  House, Sapporo, Japan (ROKu)
  House, Tokyo (ROSz)
1977 Medical Center, Sapporo, Japan (BOK; project)
  Design of the Agriculture Fair exhibition, Sapporo, Japan (XOF)
1978 Nakamura Brain Surgery Hospital, Sapporo, Japan (BON)
  TMD Department Store, Tokyo (BOT)
  House, Fukushima, Japan (ROH)
  House, Tokyo (RONm)
  House, Sapporo, Japan (ROKm)
  House, Sapporo, Japan (ROG)

Publications:

By TAKEYAMA: books—Jørn Utzon and His Intentions, Tokyo 1966; Music and Architecture, Tokyo 1966; Space Perception, Tokyo 1966; Scandinavian Design, Tokyo 1967; How to Design Shops and Stores, Tokyo 1972; Blue Nirvana-Language vs. Architecture, Tokyo 1973; Autobiography of an Architect, Tokyo 1973; Food and Environment, Tokyo 1974; Meaning of Street, Tokyo 1977; articles—"Notes on Housing Space" in Kindaikenchiku (Tokyo), June 1959; "On Arne Jacobsen" in Space Design (Tokyo), March 1965; "The Common Trends in Northern Culture" in Design (Tokyo), April 1966; "Urban Design and Architecture in Northern Europe" in Shinkenchiku (Tokyo), January and February 1967; "Tivoli as an Urban Textile" in Design (Tokyo), January 1967; "Situationism in Architecture" in Kindaikenchiku (Tokyo), May 1968; "Space Relationships" in Kenchiku (Tokyo), September 1968; "Henning Larsen and His Works" in Kindaikenchiku (Tokyo), November 1968;

"Space Situationing" in *Toshijutaku* (Tokyo), March 1969; "Revolving Interior" in *Kindaikenchiku* (Tokyo), March 1969; "Forbidden Space" in *Japan Interior* (Tokyo), November 1969; "New Experiments in Space Design" in *Japan Interior* (Tokyo), April 1970; "The Surface Reflects Contents" in *Kenchiku* (Tokyo), July 1970; "Reinstatement of Surface Structure" in *The Japan Architect* (Tokyo), August 1970; "On Territory" in *Space Design* (Tokyo), August 1970; "Expo '70" in *Arkitekten* (Copenhagen), no. 6, 1970; "Street-Scaping" in *Japan Interior* (Tokyo), April 1971; "The Living Room" in *The Japan Architect* (Tokyo), July 1971; "Use-ology" in *Japan Interior* (Tokyo), October 1971; "Civil Design" in *Japan Interior* (Tokyo), November 1971; "IEG (Imago-Encephalo-Graph)" in *Space Design* (Tokyo), March 1972; "Phenomena-Analysis of Urbanity" in *Shotenkenchiku* (Tokyo), April 1972; "Fashion and Architecture" in *Kenchikuzasshi* (Tokyo), July 1972; "Urban Interior" in *Japan Interior* (Tokyo), August 1972; "Language in Architecture" in *Space Design* (Tokyo), January 1973; "Unfinished Harmony in Space" in *Kenchiku* (Tokyo), January 1973; "The Greening Environment" in *Kankyobunka* (Tokyo), March 1973; "Revising Architectural Internationalism" in *Architecture + Urbanism* (Tokyo), May 1973; "Counter Architecture I" in *Kenchikubunka* (Tokyo), August 1973; "Interior Landscape" in *Japan Interior* (Tokyo), August 1973; "Pedagogical Architecture" in *Architecture + Urbanism* (Tokyo), October 1973; "Counter Architecture II" in *Kenchikubunka* (Tokyo), January 1974; "IEG of Minoru Takeyama" in *Space Design* (Tokyo), January 1974; "Distorted Form" in *Japan Interior* (Tokyo), April 1974; "Anthrophobia" in *Kenchikubunka* (Tokyo), June 1974; "Human Grouping and House Collecting" in *Kenchikubunka* (Tokyo), August 1974; "Space Dynamics" in *Japan Interior* (Tokyo), October 1974; "New Dimension of Architects' Education" in *Kenchikuzasshi* (Tokyo), October 1974; "Regionalism in Hokkaido: Design and Community" in *Japan Interior* (Tokyo), January 1975; "Community" in *Japan Interior* (Tokyo), January 1975; "Street Semiology" in *Kenchikubunka* (Tokyo), February 1975; "Urban Environment of San Francisco" in *Japan Interior* (Tokyo), November and December 1975; "Japanese Interior Design as Paradox" in *Japan Interior* (Tokyo), December 1975; "On Japanese Heterogeneity" in *Japan Interior* (Tokyo), February 1976; "Image Synthesizing" in *Kindaikenchiku* (Tokyo), May 1976; "Heterology in Architecture" in *The Japan Architect* (Tokyo), June 1976; "Offensive Space/Defensive Space" in *Japan Interior* (Tokyo), September 1976; "Arts and Urban Environment" in *Mainichi News* (Tokyo), 24 and 31 October 1976; "Outside-in and Inside-out" in *Space Design* (Tokyo), November 1976; "Soft Technology in Architecture" in *Kenchikuka* (Tokyo), November 1976; "White Landscape" in *Japan Interior* (Tokyo), March 1977; "Architecture and Non-Architecture" in *Japan Interior* (Tokyo), August 1977; "Form and Image" in *Shinkenchiku* (Tokyo), September 1977; "Counter Architecture III" in *Kenchikubunka* (Tokyo), September 1977; "Extremely Private Space" in *Japan Interior* (Tokyo), September 1977; "Expressive Urbanism" in *Kenchikubunka* (Tokyo), September 1977; "Atelier Indigo" in *The Japan Architect* (Tokyo), January 1978; "Panoramic Views" in *Intellect and Sensitivity* (Tokyo), February 1978.

On TAKEYAMA: books—*Modern Movements in Architecture* by Charles Jencks, London 1973; *The Language of Post Modern Architecture* by Charles Jencks, London 1977, 1978; *Beyond Metabolism: The New Japanese Architecture* by Michael Franklin Ross, New York 1978; articles—"ArchiteXt and the Problem of Symbolism" by Charles Jencks in *The Japan Architect* (Tokyo), June 1976; "ArchiteXt" in *The Japan Architect* (Tokyo), June 1976; "Post Metabolism" in *The Japan Architect* (Tokyo), October/November 1977; "An Anarchist's Guide to Modern Architecture" by Chris Fawcett in *Architectural Association Quarterly* (London), no. 3, 1978.

*

Architecture is the "relator" which governs the inter-relation between expression and content in its signification. For architectural phenomena, Japan can be compared to a huge kaleidoscope of signs which presents extremely heterogeneous visions. This heterogeneity in visual effects shares a homogeneous content which is socio-culturally characterized by its racial, religious and linguistic univalence. In other words, in this cultural climate, the architect's creativity is the "relator" of heterogeneous expression and homogeneous content.

"Homo" or "hetero"—we can define this "likeness" or "unlikeness" relationship as a basic continuity between two entities, which is one of the fundamental gestalt factors from which a man confirms his orientation and existence. Hypothetically, I have been using a scale to measure a sense of continuity by inserting three degrees, *analogy, homology* and *heterology,* between the extremes of "likeness" and "unlikeness." Simply speaking, *analogy* involves associating similar contents in spite of differences of form and structure; e.g., a bird's wing and an insect's wing. *Homology,* on the other hand, lets us find a similarity of form but not content (such as function); e.g., a bird's wing and a dog's leg. In both cases the continuity can be investigated through similarity or "likeness."

Heterology involves establishing a relationship between two entities in terms of metaphysical meaning. The continuity can still be measured in dissimilar or "unlike" elements. For example, try to relate a turtle's head to a mushroom. They have nothing in common biologically. Their forms and contents are different. However, in Japan, these two are both phallic symbols! They are related not in their intrinsic meaning but in their symbolic meaning, which is a product of the deeply-rooted historical sub-culture of particular human minds.

Through *heterology* we can trace continuous relationships between factors linked neither in structure nor in content in terms of their extrinsic meaning within a particular culture. It is a conceptual tool to cope with the increasing multivalence and dissimilarity of our environmental phenomena. *Heterology* can even be seen to be oriented towards the future if we look back at the evolution of urbanism and architecture. For as the built environment has evolved from the rural to the urban through successive stages of agriculture and industry, and as architectural space has evolved in its primary context from the pragmatic to the semantic through various degrees of functionalism, so too have the concepts dealing with the continuity of such stages changed from the stage of *analogy* to that of *heterology* through that of *homology.* As our perception evolved from one stage to the next, the original meaning of architecture has lost its intrinsic motivation in favor of an increasingly arbitrary intent.

As an architect coping with the sub-culture of a kaleidoscope of multiple architectural signs, I find that one of the basic intentions of my work is to confirm the relation between heterogeneous expression and homogeneous content. Evaluating the phenomena of architectural language, I have changed my aim from time to time—such as reacting against the homogeneity of the content at some times or escalating the heterogeneity of the visual experience at other times. No matter which quality predominated, the architectural meaning has, however, remained with the relationship itself between the two sides, content and expression.

The "discontinuous continuity" of my past challenges in architectural creativity could be classified into the following stages (as far as the chronology of rhetoric is concerned):

During the first period of my architectural practice, after my return to Japan after being abroad for a few years, my intuitive views led me to maintain an arbitrary conception of the surrounding urbanism as a *unicellular* organism. Most architects think analogically; my ideas were analogically oriented too; I emphasized the similarity of contents. In unicellular organisms a single cell is encapsulated by a membrane which functions as a sort of communication link between the internal life and the external stimuli. To me the membrane was more meaningful than the core inside. I expected the surface of material things to have a similar mediating function between the hidden dimensions within buildings and the exposed happenings of the external environment. By and by, however, the surface became, for me, self-contained, independent in its own expression, and even gave up its primary function as a mediator. The first stage of my heterological rhetoric was to disconnect the inter-relation between the inside and the outside, as expressed in those works designated BOS-1, BOS-2, BOF, EOT, EOSh, Earth-texture, etc.

The basic content of the heterogeneous environmental structure of Japan, which is based on a homogeneous socio-culture, seemed to me like the structure of "brotherhood" which is different from that of "neighborhood." Originally various neighbors try to depend upon a certain contract to create a uniform neighborhood of homogeneous quality, while brothers, who have common kinship, often behave in different ways from one another. One brother participating in the same brotherhood does not depend on formal agreement to join the native company. I would compare the difference between "brother" and "neighbor" with the difference between "paradigm" and "syntagm" respectively in linguistics. The syntagmatic context, in my interpretation, is based on a chain of *metonymy* (neighbor to neighborhood) and is, therefore, a contrasting relation, while the paradigmatic context is an oppositional relation, collecting unconscious *metaphors* (brothers to brotherhood).

(In fact, metaphor in architectural language is very arbitrary and unstable. It is absent from man's consciousness and topologically brings up man's memories and associations. Metaphors are the offspring of the *meso-* and *paleo-cortex* of the human brain. While searching for a meta-language of architectural signification, I borrowed immaturely from the knowledge of "brain architects.")

As a result, my surrounding environment was no longer a *unicellular* organism but began to dwell in my own brain, and architecture which seemed to be a relator between expression and content functioned as a *neurone,* the basic element of communication. IEG (Imago-encephalo-graph) is a product of this stage of my architectural conceptions, together with BOP, BOI, SIT-1, SIT-2, and Body Furniture.

Neither a brother nor a neighbor can resist mortality: life and death are the common destiny. It is within a sequence of time, and on that score, that man describes the proof of his existence. According to brain physiologists, time perception is one of the basic human privileges (as well as the privilege of perceiving signs). We share the power of perceiving space with other animals; in fact, a nesting animal can do a better job of creating space ecologically than we can. In notating the syntagmatic context, in terms of time sequence, we need a linear score to show contrasting relations. In the paradigmatic context, the score will become more complicated to include various fragments of metaphor. In order to describe the multivalence of Japanese cultural phenomena, I feel that we need a very particular score that can clarify topologically superimposed signs.

My effort is to conceive space as "time teller," to tell "what time space is" at constantly changing sequences. As far as heterology is a methodology to stipulate "discontinuous continuity" in architecture, this is one of the most promising developments at present. With this conviction, I have done such works as IOO, ROW-1, ROW-2, DOX, COP, ROO, and my challenge is still, patiently, to go on.

—Minoru Takeyama

Minoru Takeyama is one of the wonderful enigmas on Japan's contemporary architectural scene. He is often puzzling and contradictory, yet always creative, inventive and witty. As Robert Venturi pointed out in his classic indictment of modern architecture, complexity and contradiction can be very positive attributes. Venturi claimed that he liked elements "which are hybrid rather than 'pure,' compromising rather than 'clean,' distorted rather than 'straightforward,' ambiguous rather than 'articulated.'" These contradictory qualities of inclusion are an apt place to begin to describe the complex work of Minoru Takeyama.

Like abstract paintings Takeyama named his two attention grabbing pleasure palaces of 1970, Ichiban-khan and Ni-ban-khan, which translate simply into Number-one-building and Number-two-building. Ichi-ban-khan is a black metal and glass space ship with a layering of horizontal stripes to ward off low flying aircraft. Ni-ban-khan, the symbol of postmodern architecture, is a collage of op-art and catalogue components combined into a powerful image in the visually rich Shinjuku entertainment section of Tokyo. Recently Takeyama had Ni-ban-khan repainted into a single piece of op-art sculpture, reinforcing the concept that buildings should be adaptable to change and impermanency.

Like Arata Isozaki, Takeyama represents Japan's new Mannerism in which wit and metaphor are part of the architectural package. In his Pepsi-Cola Canning Plant in Mikasa, Hokkaido, and in the Hotel Beverley Tom in Tomakomai, Takeyama employs visual puns and double entendre to satirize the building functions. The truncated cylindrical form of the Pepsi Canning Plant has a sloped roof which allows melted snow to collect and vaporize at the central boiler plant of the building. As the foggy mist rises on the cold Hokkaido landscape it appears that one of America's most popular soft drinks is being manufactured from melting Japanese snow. At the Hotel Beverley Tom, which is located in a bleak industrial section of Tomakomai, Takeyama has wrapped this large-scale phallic symbol in an industrial black metal skin which parodies the huge oil tankers and silos that accent the landscape.

Takeyama is a master at employing catalogue components and modern technology as visual playthings with which to make larger-than-life toys for people. When his parents asked him to update their somewhat time-tested seventy-year old traditional wooden house, Takeyama wrapped the exterior in diagonal metal siding, giving it a most contemporary look and an energy-efficient insulated enclosure simultaneously; however, he left the interior exactly as it had always been. From the outside it is a sleek, chic modern house, but inside it is a simple traditional Japanese house in which his parents feel most comfortable.

To test the concept of impermanence and flexibility in architecture, Takeyama designed his own house as a series of eight cubes which can theoretically be rearranged in 45,656 configurations. I wonder if anyone is keeping score? Thus far it seems that Minoru Takeyama's richly coded symbolism and mannerist heterogeneity have brought us an architecture that gives the viewer both a sense of joy and wonder.

—Michael Franklin Ross

TANGE, Kenzo.

Japanese. Born in Osaka, 4 September 1913. Educated at the University of Tokyo, Department of Architecture, 1935–38, and Graduate School, 1942–45, D.Eng. 1959. Married Toshiko Kato in 1949; Takako Iwata in 1971; children: Michiko and Noritaka. Principal, Kenzo Tange & Urtec, urbanists and architects, Tokyo, since 1961. Professor of Architecture, 1946–74, and since 1974 Professor Emeritus, University of Tokyo. Visiting Professor, Massachusetts Institute of Technology, Cambridge, 1959–60, and Harvard University, Cambridge, Massachusetts, 1972. Recipient: First Prize, Memorial to the Creation of Greater East Asia Competition, 1942; First Prize, Japanese Cultural Center Competition, Bangkok, 1943; First Prize, Hiroshima Peace Center Competition, 1949; First Prize, Tokyo Metropolitan Government Office Competition, 1952; Annual Prize, Architectural Institute of Japan, 1954, 1955, 1958; Pan Pacific Citation, American Institute of Architects, Hawaii Chapter, 1958; International Prize for Art and Architecture, *L'Architecture d'Aujourd'hui*, 1959; Building Contractors of Japan Society Prize, 1960, 1965, 1966, 1969, 1970; Diploma of Merit, International Olympic Committee, 1964; Gold Medal, Royal Institute of British Architects, 1965; Asahi Newspapers Prize, Japan, 1965; Special Prize, Architectural Institute of Japan, 1965, 1970; President's Medal, Architectural League of New York, 1966; Gold Medal, American Institute of Architects, 1966; Gold Medal, Société d'Encouragement au Progrès, France, 1967; Order of the Yugoslav Star, 1968; Medal of Honor, Royal Academy of Arts, Denmark, 1968; Thomas Jefferson Memorial Foundation Medal, U.S.A., 1970; Gold Medal of the President of Italy, 1970; Prime Minister's Award, Japan, 1971; Gold Medal, Académie d'Architecture, France, 1973; SARP Medal, Institute of Polish Architects, 1973. D.F.A.: State University of New York at Buffalo, 1962; D.Eng.: Technische Hochschule, Stuttgart, 1962; D.Arch.: Polytechnic, Milan, 1964; D.Sc.: University of Hong Kong, 1970; D.Litt.: University of Sheffield, England, 1970; D.Art.: Harvard University, 1971. Honorary Fellow, American Institute of Architects; Honorary Member, American Academy of Arts and Letters, and Akademie der Künste, Germany. Member, Order of St. Gregory the Great, Vatican, 1970, and Order of Merit of Science and Arts, West Germany, 1976; Commander, National Order of Merit, France, 1977. Address: Kenzo Tange & Urtec, 7-2-21 Akasaka, Minato-ku, Tokyo, Japan.

Works:

1942 Memorial to the Creation of Greater East Asia Co-Prosperity Shere, at Mt. Fuji, Japan (competition project)

1943 Japanese Cultural Center, Bangkok (competition project)

1946/
47 Master plan for Hiroshima

1949/
55 Hiroshima Peace Center

1952/
57 Tokyo Metropolitan Government Offices

1953 Kenzo Tange House, Tokyo

1955/
58 Prefectural Government Office, Kagawa, Japan

1957/
58 Imabari City Hall, Ehime, Japan

1958/
60 Kurashiki City Hall, Okayama, Japan

1959/
60 Tokyo Restructuring Plan (project)

1959/
64 Ichinomiya Housing Project, Kagawa, Japan

1960/
61 Totsuka Country Club House, Kanagawa, Japan

1960/
62 Nichinan Cultural Center, Miyazaki, Japan

1960/
64 Tsukiji Redevelopment Plan, Tokyo

1961/
64 National Gymnasia for the Tokyo Olympics St. Mary's Cathedral, Tokyo

1961/
67 Press and Broadcasting Center, Yamanashi, Japan

1962/
64 Prefectural Gymnasium, Kagawa, Japan

1965/
66 Resorts Master Plan, Bandai Inawashiro City, Fukushima, Japan (project)
City Center Reconstruction Project, Skopje, Yugoslavia

1965/
67 Dentsu Office Building, Tokyo
University of the Sacred Heart, Taipei, Taiwan

1966/
67 Yukari Nursery School, Tokyo
Shizuoka Press and Broadcasting Center, Tokyo

1966/
68 Takasaki and Maebashi City Regional Plans, Gunma, Japan (project)
International School of the Sacred Heart, Tokyo
City Axis Master Plan, Kyoto (project)

1966/
70 Kuwait Embassy and Chancery, Tokyo
Master plan, trunk facilities, and Festival Plaza, *Expo '70*, Osaka (as head of group of architects)

1967/
68 Master plan for Flushing Meadow Sports Park, New York City (project; with Marcel Breuer and Lawrence Halprin)

1967/
69 Master plan for Yerba Buena Center, San Francisco (project; with McCue, Boone and Tomsick, and Lawrence Halprin and Associates)

1967/
70 Shizuoka and Shimizu City Regional Plans, Shizuoka, Japan (project)
Olivetti Technical Center, Kanagawa, Japan
Master plan for Morioka City, Iwate, Japan
New Northern Development, Bologna, Italy (project)

1968/
70 Press and Broadcasting Center, Shizuoka, Japan

1968/
71 Japan in the 21st Century Plan, Tokyo (project; as head of a physical and socio-economic team)

1969– New Central Station, Skopje, Yugoslavia
International Air Terminal Building, Kuwait

1970/
71 City Regional Plan, Trieste, Italy (project)

1970/
74 Minneapolis Arts Complex (with Parker Klein Associates)

1971 Sports Arena, Yerba Buena Center, San Francisco (project; with McCue, Boone and Tomsick, and Lawrence Halprin and Associates)
University, hospital, and dormitory, Oran, Algeria
Librino New Town, Catania, Italy (project)

1971/
74 Master plan for Fiera District Center, Bologna, Italy (project)

1972 Akasaka Prince Hotel, Tokyo
Inner Harbor Residential Development, Baltimore (with Cochran, Stephenson and Donkervoet, and Parker Klein Associates)
Palace for King Faisal, Jeddah, Saudi Arabia (project)

1972/
74 Bulgarian Embassy and Chancery, Tokyo

1973 Hokusetsu New Town Center, Hyogo, Japan
Andalouses Tourist Complex, Oran, Algeria
Apartment Towers, Tehran (project)
Pilgrims Accommodation Master Plan, Muna, Saudi Arabia (project; with GK Industrial Design Associates)

1973/
77 Turkish Embassy and Chancery, Tokyo
Headquarters Building, University of Tokyo

Kenzo Tange: National Gymnasia for the Tokyo Olympics, 1964

1974 Farah Park Hotel, Tehran (with Mir-Djalali and Detail Consulting Company)

Sacred Garden of the Buddha's Birthplace, Lumbini, Nepal

Abbasabad New City Centre, Tehran (project; with Louis Kahn)

1974/
75 Matsue City Master Plan, Shimane, Japan (project)

1974/
77 Sogetsu Hall and Offices, Tokyo

1975- Imperial Iranian Embassy, Tokyo

New Presidential Palace, Damascus, Syria (with Mohammad Nofal)

Public Garden, Damascus, Syria (with Mohammad Nofal)

Sports City, Damascus, Syria (with Mohammad Nofal)

Fiera District Center Architectural Design, Bologna, Italy (project; with Pierluigi Giordani, Ferdinando Forlay, Ettore Masi, and Gianpaolo Mazzucato)

1975/
76 Japanese Embassy, Mexico City (with Pedro Ramirez Vazquez and Manuel Rosen)

1976- King Faisal Foundation Headquarters Complex, Saudi Arabia

Institute of Architecture and Urbanism, Oran, Algeria

Bab-Ezzouar III University City, Algeria

Yarmouk University, Amman, Jordan (with Jafar Tukan and Partners)

1976/
78 Hanae Mori Building, Tokyo

1977- Government Center Master Plan, Doha, Qatar (project)

New City Hall, Shahstan Pahlevi, Tehran (project)

King's Palace, and the Crown Prince's Palace, Jeddah, Saudi Arabia

Publications:

By TANGE: books—*Katsura: Tradition and Creation in Japanese Architecture,* Tokyo and New Haven, Connecticut, 1960, 1972; *A Plan for Tokyo,* with the Kenzo Tange Team, 1960; *Ise: Origin of Japanese Architecture,* with Noboru Kawazoe, Tokyo 1962, Cambridge, Massachusetts 1965; *Japan in the Future,* Tokyo 1966; *Japan in the 21st Century,* with the Kenzo Tange Team, Tokyo 1971; *Architecture and Urban Design,* Tokyo 1975; articles— "Creation in Present-Day Architecture and the Japanese Architectural Tradition" in *The Japan Architect* (Tokyo), June 1956; "Architecture and Urbanism" in *The Japan Architect* (Tokyo), October 1960.

On TANGE: books—*Kenzo Tange* by Robin Boyd, New York and London 1962; *Kenzo Tange 1946–58:*

Reality and Creation, Tokyo 1966; *Kenzo Tange 1955–1964: Technology and Humanity,* Tokyo 1966; *Three Japanese Architects: Mayekawa, Tange, Sakakura* by Alfred Alther, Teufen 1968; *Kenzo Tange* by Paolo Riani, Florence and London 1969; *Kenzo Tange* by Isamu Kurita, Tokyo 1970; *Philosophy of Contemporary Architects: Kenzo Tange* by M. Naka, Tokyo 1970; *Kenzo Tange 1946–1969: Architecture and Urban Design* by Udo Kultermann, Zurich and London 1970; *Kenzo Tange* by Noboru Kawazoe, Tokyo 1976; *Kenzo Tange* by A. V. Ikonnikov, Moscow 1976; articles—"Kenzo Tange" by Udo Kultermann in *Das Kunstwerk* (Stuttgart), November/December 1960; "Reflection on Kenzo Tange's Tokyo Bay Plan" by Peter Smithson in *Architectural Design* (London), October 1964; "Junzo Sakakura, Kunio Maekawa and Kenzo Tange" by N. Hozumi and J. Dodd in *Architectural Design* (London), May 1965; "New Arts Complex in Minneapolis" in *Domus* (Milan), September 1973; special number of *The Japan Architect* (Tokyo), August/September 1976.

Kenzo Tange's work reflects and crystallizes the changing political and economic climate of Japan in a quarter century, from the nationalism of World War II, through defeat and reconstruction, to the renewed search for national identity and growth in confidence. Despite finer distinctions to be made in his changing concerns, it is possible to divide his career into two parts, whose major interests are the synthesis of Japanese traditions and modern architecture and the realization of a Metabolist vision of the city.

Western architecture arrived in Japan with the Meiji Restoration more than a century ago. Since then Japanese architectural history for the most part has faithfully mirrored the trends and preoccupations of Europe and America. But recurring throughout those years of adaptation was the idea of a return to native values and forms. (Chuta Ito and Sutemi Horiguchi in their respective ways attempted to broaden the architectural vocabulary to include Japanese and Oriental sources, and they both promoted a reappraisal of traditional works.) World War II and the heightened nationalist sentiment provided the context for Tange's debut, a successful entry in the competition for a Memorial to the Creation of Greater East Asia Co-Prosperity Sphere, followed by another first place in the competition for a Japanese Cultural Center in Bangkok. The former was inspired by Shinto shrines, while the latter made references to palaces. The wartime pressure to employ such references was powerful and even the modernist, Mayekawa, succumbed to it; but with Tange the revivalism seems to have come more naturally, as a personal reaction against conventional modern architecture. After the war, the Occupation naturally dampened such enthusiasms, but even when Tange produced buildings in a modern, specifically Corbusian manner, such as the Hiroshima Peace Center, there were indirect Japanese references.

In the 1950's tradition again became an active issue, and Tange was a leading participant in the so called "Tradition Debate." The blending of Japanese and modern forms in his buildings of the time is more skillful than in his wartime designs. His own house, with its pilotis and core, manages to be modern while recalling ancient "raised floor dwellings" of Japan. The Kagawa Prefectural Government Office, with its application of traditional wood details in concrete on the facade, was much admired and copied. The debate slackened by the 1960's, yet the definitive traditionalist building was finished in 1964. Tange capped the first phase of his career with the National Gymnasia for the Tokyo Olympics. This pair of suspension structures with their sweeping curved roofs is reminiscent of Japanese traditional architecture without indulging in direct references. The masterful asymmetric arrangement of the roofs and the dynamic balance in the siting of the pair show how well Tange had assimilated traditional techniques. Here at last Tange accomplished what his predecessors had not, demonstrating that modern architecture need not necessarily be Western. Ironically, however, this proved to be an end and not a beginning, for Tange was by then engaged in a different problem.

The 1960's in Japan saw the increasing activity of the Metabolists, many of whom had been associated with Tange. The second phase of Tange's career must be seen against that background; even though he himself was not a Metabolist, his work was sympathetic to theirs. In fact they owed a great deal to Tange's proposal to structure the chaotic growth of Tokyo—his Tokyo Plan, 1960—a startling suggestion to extend the city over the bay. It called for a linear trunk of motorways, from which branched giant housing units. This early megastructural approach provided a starting point for the Metabolists. Their attempt to analyze the modern city as an organic unit subject to growth, decay and renewal recall traditional Japanese ideas of cycles and change and thus may be said to continue indirectly the 50's preoccupation with cultural identity.

The movement produced a number of buildings by Kurokawa, Kikutake and others, but none was quite as explicit as or on a scale comparable to that of Tange's Yamanashi Press and Broadcasting Center. Service and stair towers double as structural columns and floors span them freely according to different functional requirements. Gaps were left to indicate the possibility of future growth. It is without

question a striking building. But like a great deal of Metabolist work, the polemics far outdistanced the realized architecture. The random quality of the space layout was more apparent than real—once fixed, the layout was no more flexible than in a conventional structure—and the mechanical services which are housed in the ostensibly more permanent infrastructure may be subject to the most rapid obsolescence.

Yamanashi inaugurated the second phase of Tange's career, one which paralleled Metabolist activity. The Corbusian references disappeared, as did the traditionalist. Gone too was the contained, integrated character of his earlier work. Yukari Nursery School, Sacred Heart University, the original project for Dentsu in Tokyo, and the Kuwait Embassy all suggest in their different ways an incompleteness and the possibility of growth and change. Yet the paradox is that this possibility is forfeited at the same time by the artfulness of the carefully asymmetric designs—one feels that any addition or subtraction would be an unwelcomed disturbance. In his first phase, Tange subordinated parts to the whole, so that structure, mass and space became a tightly integrated unity. In office buildings or single-purpose structures, this mattered less, but there was strain when the program was at all complex. What could not be accommodated conveniently in the whole had to be left out; hence the little boxes that clutter the base of St. Mary's Cathedral. In his second phase, an entire building was fragmented and reassembled into a system. The result, at first glance, may seem more complex, yet the buildings remain expressions of spontaneity and are in reality static and closed.

The 1970 Osaka Exposition, for which he provided the master plan and the theme pavilion, a giant space frame, epitomized the Metabolist movement with its celebration of technology. At last a true megastructure had been built. But like the National Gymnasia, this proved to be the climax of a period and not the start. The era of rapid economic growth came to an end, and with it the more ambitious Metabolist dreams.

Since then Tange's work has been increasingly outside Japan, and he has expressed a loss of interest in the old tradition issue. Yet his successful buildings have all been rooted in the Japanese past directly or indirectly, and it is his National Gymnasia, which best resolved the problem of tradition, that remains his best work and the peak of 20th century Japanese architecture.

—Hiroshi Watanabe

TANIGUCHI, Yoshiro.

Japanese. Born in Kanazawa, Ishikawa Prefecture, in 1904. Educated at Tokyo University, in the Architecture Department of the School of Engineering, 1925-28, Dip.Arch. 1928; made a study tour of Europe, 1928-29. In private practice, Tokyo, from 1930: Partner, with Shinsake Takamiya, in Taniguchi, Takamiya and Associates. Assistant Professor, Tokyo University, 1931; Professor, 1943-65, and Emeritus Professor, 1965-79, Tokyo Institute of Technology. Recipient: Arts and Sciences Prize, 1942, and Works Prize, 1949, Japan Institute of Architects; Japan Academy of Arts Award, 1961. Member, Japan Academy of Arts, 1962. *Died* (in Tokyo) *in 1979.*

Works:

1932 Hydraulics Laboratory, Institute of Technology, Tokyo
1937 K House, Tokyo
       Keio-Gidyuku Primary School, Tokyo
1947 Toson Kinendo Memorial Hall, Kamuro, Japan
1951 Banrai-she Building, Keio University, Tokyo

1952 Lecture Hall, Institute of Technology, Tokyo
1955 10 week-end houses, Karuizawa, Japan
1956 Chichibu Cement Factory, Japan
       Club House, Sagamihara Golf Course, Japan
       Swimming pool, Tokyo
1957 Saeki Week-end House, Japan
1958 Oto-Tachibana-Hime Monument, Sagamihara Golf Course, Japan
       Centennial Monument, Keio University, Tokyo
1959 Chidorigafuchi War Memorial, Tokyo
       City Hall, Aomori, Japan
       Palace for Crown Prince Akihito, Akasaka, Tokyo
       City Hall, Takasaki, Japan
1960 Togu Palace, Japan
1963 Fuzi Zen Study Temple, Japan
       Auditorium, Keio Private School Kindergarten, Shibuya, Tokyo
       Enoshima Yacht Club, Kanagawa Prefecture, Japan
       Shiseido Building, Tokyo
1965 Furukawa Library, Nagoya University, Japan
       Josen-ji Temple, Shibuya, Tokyo
       Yamatane Art Museum, Nihombashi, Tokyo
1966 Imperial Theatre, Marunouchi, Tokyo
1968 Eastern Antiquities Gallery, National Museum, Tokyo
1968/
71 Hotel Okura, Amsterdam (with Yozo Shibata, Bernard Bijvoet, and G.H.M. Holt)
1975 Japan Academy, Tokyo
1976 Fukui Sogo Bank Branch Office, Seiwa, Japan
       House, Yukigawa, Japan

Publications:

By TANIGUCHI: articles—"Gallery of Eastern Antiquities" in *The Japan Architect* (Tokyo), December 1968; "Tokyo Kaikan" in *The Japan Architect* (Tokyo), April 1972.

On TANIGUCHI: articles—"The Personality and Works of Taniguchi" by Ryuichi Hamaguchi in *Shinkenchiku* (Tokyo), January 1956; "Memorials by Yoshiro Taniguchi" in *Shinkenchiku* (Tokyo), October 1958; "Architects of the Month" in *The Japan Architect* (Tokyo), January/February 1959; "Palace for the Crown Prince, Akasaka, Tokyo" in *The Japan Architect* (Tokyo), July 1960; "The Architects," in special issue on Japan of *Architectural Review* (London), September 1962; "The Shiseido Building" in *The Japan Architect* (Tokyo), March 1963; "Yoshiro Taniguchi and His Work" in *The Japan Architect* (Tokyo), May 1966; "Vision de Paix" by Frederic D. Debuyt in *Art d'Eglise* (Ottignies, Belgium), no. 139, 1967; "Hotel Okura, Amsterdam" in *The Japan Architect* (Tokyo), March 1972; "Seiwa Branch of the Fukui Sogo Bank" in *The Japan Architect* (Tokyo), November 1976; "Toward a Revitalization of Form" in *Architecture + Urbanism* (Tokyo), February 1977.

We are apt to perceive Yoshiro Taniguchi as an arch-conservative and reactionary because of the Establishment status that he achieved. It is true that in his public buildings (e.g., Togu Palace, Hotel Okura, and the Eastern Antiquities Gallery of the National Museum), he took the path of traditionalism that modernism had rejected and that he developed a decorative style that had great popular appeal. But he also left behind a body of work, particularly in his youth, which is attractive to the modernist, namely the handsome neo-classical schools (Keio University), the stern and poetic literary monuments and memorial halls (Toson Kinendo), and a factory of a classicist beauty unrivalled in modern Japan (Chichibu Cement); he is indeed one of the masters of modern Japanese architecture.

His work was always in conscious contrast to that of modernists such as Mayekawa and Tange, and he continually broadened the possible range of modern architectural vocabulary in Japan. He had a wide following that included the general public, intellectuals and the ruling elite, yet his architecture was by no means "populist;" it was, in fact, very difficult to understand. Why, then, is its appeal wider and deeper perhaps than that of the work of Tange or Mayekawa?

That appeal is due not simply to the traditionalism of his late work, but also to his classicist rigor and "class," his deep involvement in his design, his attitude toward architecture as philosophy and toward architectural expression as poetry, as well as to the the characteristic decorative spaces of traditionalist motifs in his later years. He managed to reconcile the apparently conflicting worlds of classicism and ornament, insofar as he could maintain the ideals of *Zweckmassichkeit* and *Sachlichkeit,* to create a non-eclectic, non-derivative style. This reconciliation is clear in his Hotel Okura, the Imperial Theatre, and the Tokyo Kogyo University Memorial Hall. These works appealed to the general public, although they were disregarded by many modernists. They constituted his unspoken criticism of the structuralist and heroic yet (for lack of ornament) slightly anaemic forms of modern architecture.

Taniguchi was from the start also a man of letters, and in his writings he expressed the deep impression made on him by the neo-classicism of Schinkel and the traditionalism of Tessenow. What is interesting is that from early on he showered criticism on what he saw as inorganic rationalism and arbitrary formal manipulation. He did not go so far as to espouse decoration, yet he did not reject it either. It was therefore quite natural for him to turn toward traditional decorative patterns via a re-evaluation of traditional culture. Whereas Tessenow created a world of stark, absolute order, taking an anti-international, regionalist stance, Taniguchi, while also anti-international, developed finally a world of ornamental beauty.

His is not a light, simple world of patterns, however, but is unexpectedly dark and heavy. There is, beyond his planar, compositional world, a profound incomprehensibility. There is neither formality nor clarity of concept. His world is created from what most modern architects threw away along with ornament: craftsmanship, studied proportions and treatment of details. It is an expression of corporeality, the aftermath of a struggle between self-restraint and a will to express. Proportions are deliberately distorted in a way contrary to traditional Japanese architectural order *(kiwari).* The cumulative effect of such details contrasts with the conceptuality of modern architecture and results in an illegible totality, yet his work, whether we like it or not, is almost awesomely overpowering and replete in evidence of a will. This corporeality, that is, the vestige of the designer's struggle and thought, requires the maximum self-restraint and formal control. Taniguchi clearly possessed both this restraint and the will to express; that is what gives the effect of darkness and weight to his designs. Yet this quality or "aura" is impossible to capture on photographs, and it is a pity that Taniguchi's architecture may be thus misunderstood. Yet amid the current post-modern reconsideration of what architecture really is, his work is valuable for the alternative approach that it suggests.

—Katsuyoshi Arai

TAO HO.
See HO, Tao.

TAUT, Bruno.
German. Born in Königsberg, 4 May 1880. Educated at the Technische Hochschule, Stuttgart, under Theodor Fischer, 1903–05. Practised in Berlin, 1908–21; City Architect, Magdeburg, Germany, 1921–23; in partnership with his brother Max Taut, *q.v.,* and Franz Hoffmann, Berlin, 1923–31; practised in Moscow, 1932–33, Tokyo, 1933–34, and Ankara and Istanbul, Turkey, 1935 until his death, 1938. Chief Architect, GEHAG Housing Program, Berlin, 1924–32. Chairman, Arbeitsrat für Kunst, Berlin, 1918; Editor/Publisher, *Die Gläserne Kette* chain letter, Berlin, 1919–23, and *Frühlicht* magazine, Magdeburg, 1921–22. Exhibitions: *Arbeitsrat Exhibition of Unknown Architects,* Berlin, 1919; *Paris-Berlin,* Centre Pompidou, Paris, 1978. *Died* (in Ankara, Turkey) *24 December 1938.*

Works:

1902 Crematorium (project)
1903 Monument (project)
1904 Fountain (project)
School, Schramberg, Germany (competition project)
Gravestones (projects)
School, Rottweil, Germany (competition project)
Building Facade Types, Bautzen, Germany (project)
1905 Main Railway Station, Karlsruhe (competition project; with Max Taut)
Country Houses, Tilsit, now Sovetsk, Russia (competition project)
Circular Church (project)
Church, Lichtenthal, Germany (competition project)
Orphanage, Strasbourg, Germany (competition project)
Workers' Housing Development (project)
Kursaal additions, Cannstadt, Germany (project)
Kindergartens (projects)
1906 Village Church interiors, Unterriexingen, Germany
Department Store (competition project)
Grammar School, Diedenhofen, Germany (competition project)
1907 Main Railway Station, Leipzig (competition project)
Church interiors (competition project)
Housing Development, Hamburg (competition project)
1908 Main Railway Station, Darmstadt (competition project; with Karl Bonatz and Georg Martin)
Harkotschen Iron Mills Turbine-House, Wetter/Ruhr, Germany
1909 Apartment building facade, Bismarckstrasse 10, Charlottenburg, Berlin (with Heinz Lassen; demolished)
1910 "Ettershaus" (management recreation facilities), for Siemens-Halske Company, Bad Harzburg, Germany
Wertheim Department Store extensions, Leipzigerstrasse, Berlin
High School, Zehlendorf, Berlin (competition project)
Trade Distribution Company Pavilion, *Clay, Cement and Lime Industries Exhibition,* Baumschulenweg, Berlin
1911 Apartment/office buildings, Bismarckstrasse 1 and 20, Charlottenburg, Berlin (demolished)
Apartment/office buildings, Kottbusser Damm 2–3, Neuköln, Berlin (demolished)
Apartment/office building, Kottsbusser Damm 90, Neuköln, Berlin
Reibedanz House, Dahlem, Berlin
Plan for housing at Johannisthal, Berlin
Apartment buildings, Hardenbergstrasse 1 and 2, Charlottenburg, Berlin (demolished)

Village Church interior restoration, Nieden, Kreis Prenzlau, Germany
Office building facade, Linkstrasse 12, Mitte, Berlin (demolished)
1912 Apartment building, Hardenbergstrasse 3a, Charlottenburg, Berlin (demolished)
Apartment building, Tiergartenstrasse 34a, Tiergarten, Berlin (demolished)
Landscaping of the Rudesheimer Platz, Zehlendorf, Berlin (competition project)
Redevelopment plan for Neuköln, Berlin (competition project; with Max Taut)
1913 "Monument to Steel" Pavilion, *International Building Trades Exhibition,* Leipzig (with Franz Hoffmann)
1914 Master plan for Am Falkenberg (garden suburb), Grunau, Berlin (partly built)
Reform (garden suburb), stage I, Magdeburg, Germany
Heinrich Mittag Department Store alterations, Breiter Weg 155, Magdeburg, Germany (demolished)
Reibedanz Steam Laundry, Teilestrasse 23, Tempelhof, Berlin
Third Secession Building facade, Kurfürstendamm 232, Charlottenburg, Berlin (with Max Taut; demolished)
Luxfer Prism Syndicate "Glashaus" Pavilion, *Werkbund Exhibition,* Cologne (with Franz Hoffmann)
Redevelopment plan for Kladow, Berlin (competition project)
1915 Oheim Mineworkers' Housing Development, Katowice, Poland (partly built)
1916 House of Friendship Building, Istanbul (competition project)
1920 Lindenhof (single-people's housing development), Schöneberg, Berlin (demolished)
Hermann Essig Tombstone (project)
Miners' Housing Development, Ruhland, Senffenberg, Germany (project)
Folkwang School, Hagen, Germany (project)
1921 Reform (garden suburb), stage II, Magdeburg, Germany
Master plan for the development of the Elbe riverbank, Magdeburg, Germany (1st project)
Skyscraper Office Building, Kaiser-Wilhelm-Platz, Magdeburg, Germany (project)
4 exhibition halls, *Middle-German Exhibition,* Rotenhornpark, Magdeburg, Germany
Open-Air Cinema and Park-Keeper's House, *Middle-German Exhibition,* Rotenhornpark, Magdeburg, Germany (projects)
Heinrich Mittag Department Store reconstruction, Magdeburg, Germany (project)
1922 Site utilization plan, Magdeburg, Germany (1st project)
War Memorial, Domplatz, Magdeburg, Germany (project)
Hotel, Kemperlatz, Charlottenburg, Berlin (competition project)
Stadt Köln Hotel/Office Building, Magdeburg, Germany (project)
Chicago Tribune Tower (competition project)
Stadt und Land Agricultural Exhibition Hall, Wilhelm-Kobelt-Strasse, Magdeburg, Germany (now Hermann-Gieseler Sports Hall)
Master plan for the development of the Elbe riverbank, Magdeburg, Germany (2nd project)
Cemetery, Magdeburg, Germany (project)
1923 Site utilization plan, Magdeburg, Germany (2nd project)
Eichwalde Housing Development, stage I, Waldstrasse, near Berlin
Completion plan for Am Falkenberg (garden suburb), with Festival Hall, Grunau, Berlin (project)
1925 Schillerpark Housing Development, stage I, Wedding, Berlin

Plan for the *Hein und Scholle* Exhibition, Braunschweig, Germany

Eichwalde Housing Development, stage II, Waldstrasse, near Berlin

Primary school, Senffenberg, Germany (project)

1927 Hufeisensiedlung Housing Estate, stage I, Britz, Berlin

Housing development, Paul-König-Strasse, Hohenschönhausen, Berlin

Bruno Taut House, Wiesenstrasse, Zossen, Dahlewitz, Germany

Single-family housing development, Waldschulstrasse and Lanchenweg, Eichkamp, Berlin

Apartment building, Weigandufer, Neuköln, Berlin

Apartment building, Leinestrasse, Neuköln, Berlin

Apartment buildings, Fuldastrasse 22–23, Neuköln, Berlin

Terraced houses, Weststrasse, Johannisthal, Berlin

Workers' apartments, Weissenhof Estate, Stuttgart (demolished)

Berthold House, Offenbachstrasse 10, Markkleeberg-West, Germany

Dammweg Community School, Neuköln, Berlin (partly built)

1928 Schillerpark Housing Development, stage II, Wedding, Berlin

Housing development, Grellstrasse, Prenzlauerberg, Berlin

Apartment building, Schönlanker Strasse, Prenzlauerberg, Berlin

Apartment building, Olivaer Strasse 1–11, Prenzlauerberg, Berlin

Attilahohe Housing Development, Attilastrasse, Berlin

Apartment building, Ossastrasse 9–16a, Neuköln, Berlin

Apartment building, Normannenstrasse 13–18, Lichtenberg, Berlin

Apartment building, Trierer Strasse 8–18, Weissensee, Berlin

1929 Beach resort facilities for Zossen, Rangsdorf, Germany (project)

Friedrich Ebert School, Luckenwalde, Germany (project)

1930 Apartment building, Gartenstrasse 22–25, Weissensee, Berlin

Housing development, Carmen-Sylvastrasse, now Erich-Weinert-Strasse, Prenzlauerberg, Berlin

Friedrich Ebert Housing Development, Togostrasse, Wedding, Berlin

Pedagogical Academy, Essen (competition project)

Law Courts, Ivalidenstrasse, Berlin (competition project)

Housing development, Buschallee 24–107, Weissensee, Berlin

Paradies Housing Development, Hundsfelderstrasse, Bohnsdorf, Berlin

Ideal Housing Development, Franz-Konrer-Strasse, Britz, Berlin

1931 Forest Housing Development, stage I, near Onkel Toms Hütte, Zehlendorf, Berlin (with Hugo Häring and O. R. Salvisberg)

Housing development extension, Parchimer Allee, Britz, Berlin

1932 Intourist Hotel, Sverdlor Square, Moscow (competition project)

Housing development, near Kursk Station, Moscow (project)

Trade Union Hall, Moscow (project)

New road plan for the area Gorky Street to Red Square, Moscow (project)

Cultural Centre, Moscow (project)

1934 Ikoma Mountain Development Plan, near Osaka, Japan (project)

Turkish Embassy, Tokyo (project)

1936 Okura House, Tokyo (now altered)

Hingo House interiors, Atami, Japan

1937 Technical University, Ankara, Turkey (project)

Chemical Institute, Ankara, Turkey (project)

Theatre, Ankara, Turkey (project)

1938 Languages and History Faculty Buildings, University of Ankara, Turkey

Bruno Taut House, Ortakoy, Turkey

Ataturk Lyceum, Ankara, Turkey (with Asim Komurcuoglu)

Ministry of Culture Exhibition Buildings, *International Exposition,* Izmir, Turkey

Professor Nissen House, Ortakoy, Turkey (project)

Parliament Building, Ankara, Turkey (project)

Bruno Taut: "Glashaus" Pavilion. **Werkbund Exhibition,** Cologne, 1914

Institute for Girls, Izmir, Turkey (partly built)

Boys' Boarding School, Trabzon, Turkey (completed by Franz Hillinger)

Middle School, Cebeci, Turkey (completed by Franz Hillinger)

Kemal Ataturk Catafalque, Ankara, Turkey

Publications:

By TAUT: books—*Monument der Eisens,* Leipzig 1913; *Glashaus: Werkbundausstellung Köln,* Cologne 1914; *Ein Architekturprogramm,* Berlin 1918, reprinted in *Programme und Manifeste zur Architektur des 20. Jahrhunderts,* edited by Ulrich Conrads, Berlin 1964; *Die Stadtkrone,* with Paul Scheerbart and others, Jena, Germany 1919; *Alpine Architektur,* Hagen, Germany 1919; *Der Weltbaumeister,* Hagen, Germany 1920; *Organisation des Bauwesens,* Berlin 1920; *Die Auflösung der Städte, oder die Erde eine gute Wohnung,* Hagen, Germany 1920; *Die Neue Wohnung,* Leipzig 1924, 4th edition 1926; *Bauen: Der neue Wohnbau,* edited by Der Ring group, Leipzig 1927; *Ein Wohnhaus,* Stuttgart 1927; *Modern Architecture,* London 1929; *Die neue Baukunst in Europa und Amerika,* Berlin 1929; *Nippon mit europaischen Augen gesehen,* Tokyo 1934; *Die Architektur des Westens mit ihrer Bedeutung für Japan,* Tokyo 1934; *Grundlinien der Architektur Japans,* Tokyo 1936; *Bildende und angewandte Kunst,* Tokyo 1936; *Homes and People of Japan,* Tokyo 1937; *Architekturlehre: Grundlagen, Theorie und Kritik,* Tokyo 1936, Istanbul, 1938; *Wiederentdeckung der Schönheit Japans,* Tokyo 1939, 1962, 1965; *Frühlicht: Eine Folge für die Verwirklichung des neuen Baugedankens,* Berlin 1963; articles—numerous in architectural journals, 1913–32, including "Für die neue Baukunst' " in *Das Kunstblatt* (Berlin), no. 1, 1919; "The Nature and Aims of Architecture" in *The Studio* (London), March 1929.

On TAUT: books—*Die Gläserne Kette* by Udo Kultermann, Leverkusen, Germany 1963; *Bruno Taut 1880–1938* by Kurt Junghanns, Berlin 1970; articles —"Bruno Taut: A Visionary in Practice" by H. G. Scheffauer in *Architectural Review* (London), December 1922; "Bruno Taut e la rivista 'Frühlicht' " by Ulrich Conrads in *Edilizia Moderna* (Milan), no. 86, 1965; "Prophet of the Future Environment" by H. H. Waechter in *AIA Journal* (Washington, D.C.), September 1973; "The Glass Dream" by Dennis Sharp in *Architecture + Urbanism* (Tokyo), September 1973; "A Taut Facade and Building Control" in *Bauwelt* (Berlin), 12 August 1977; "Development of the Weissenhof Estate in Stuttgart" by Bodo Rasch in *Deutsche Bauzeitung* (Stuttgart), November 1977.

More than an architect, more than a writer, Bruno Taut was a Utopian, a dreamer. His disillusion with the conservatism, elitism and traditionalism of German society at the start of the new century, which turned to despair as he witnessed the outbreak and the course of the First World War, provoked him to direct his own attentions towards the future. Inspired partly by the new collectivism of the U.S.S.R., and partly by the open democracy of Britain and Holland, he envisaged a new society born of cooperation, constructing for itself an almost magical environment of sparkling alpine cities, with pillars, vaults, arcades and bridges of coloured glass, all radiating as much love as they did light. Taut believed that the stronger the conviction of the society and the more harmonious its spirit, the more extraordinary and the more poetic would be its architecture. His sketches, therefore, should not be read as architectural fantasies but as social fantasies.

But while Taut thought of architecture principally as an expression or a symbol of the quality of the society who created it, he also recognized within it the potential for provoking change. He saw that the new architecture, with its new technologies and its

new materials, might anticipate, and thus encourage, a new social order. Taut regarded the phenomenon of industrialization as significant because it generated these new technologies and new materials, but he rejected its image as the basis for any new architectural aesthetic, any new style. Indeed, his own designs diverged considerably from those of the Bauhaus and his fellow pioneers. Angular, geometric, crystalline structures and motifs recur throughout his work, suggesting the influence of Gothic, oriental and Islamic architecture, each of which, significantly, expressed the aspirations and achievements of their society and culture rather than the genius of a single individual.

The building which most clearly illustrated Taut's architectural vision was the Glass Pavilion at the *Werkbund Exhibition* in Cologne in 1914. A glass dome and glass walls enclosed a gallery with a glass inlaid floor, from which a glass staircase led to a subterranean waterfall—a strangely mystical celebration of a new industrial product. Taut dedicated the Pavilion to Paul Scheerbart, the visionary poet whose lyrical exposition of the potential of a glass architecture had largely inspired the design. Taut's period as planner and architectural adviser to the city of Magdeburg produced little of any architectural significance but did fulfill his commitment to building for a new society. His greater contribution to the new architecture, and to the German Expressionist movement in particular, came not from his buildings but from his writings and his correspondence. It was he who coordinated and broadcast the ideas of the group, first in the Utopian chain letter, *Die Gläserne Kette* (The Glass Chain), which included among its correspondents Hans Scharoun, Walter Gropius, Hermann Finsterlin and Hans and Wassili Luckhardt, and subsequently in his magazine *Frühlicht* (Daybreak), a title fully expressive of Taut's anticipation of the dawning of a new age.

—Bob Allies

TAUT, Max.

German. Born in Königsberg, 15 May 1884. Educated at the Königsberg Gymnasium; apprentice in carpentry and building trades, Königsberg; studied at a building trades school, 1903–05. Served in the Germany Army, 1914–18. Married Margarete Wollgast in 1914. Worked in the office of Mies van der Rohe, Berlin, 1905, and in the studio of Hermann Billing, Karlsruhe, 1906–11; in private practice, Berlin, from 1911: in partnership with Franz Hoffmann, 1918–50 (with Hoffmann and his brother Bruno Taut, *q.v.,* 1923–31); barred from any public commissions by the Nazis, 1933–45. Founder Director, Architectural Department, Fine Arts Academy, Berlin, 1945–53. Founder Member, Berlin Arbeitsrat für Kunst, 1918, Novembergruppe, Berlin, 1919, Der Ring architects' union, Berlin, 1920, Deutscher Werkbund, 1946, and the Bund Deutscher Architekten (BDA), 1948. Exhibitions: *German Arts and Crafts Exhibition,* Dresden, 1906; *Werkbund Exhibition,* Cologne, 1914; *The Growing House,* Berlin, 1928; *Max Taut,* Akademie der Künste, Berlin, 1964. Recipient: Gold Medal, *Arts and Crafts Exhibition,* Dresden, 1906; Gold Medal, *Building Exhibition,* Leipzig, 1913; German Cross of Merit, 1957. D.Eng.: Technische Hochschule, Karlsruhe, 1958. Member, Akademie der Künste, Berlin, 1955. *Died* (in Berlin) *26 February 1967.*

Works:

1905 Main Railway Station, Karlsruhe (competition project; with Bruno Taut)
1911/
12 School, Finsterwalde, Germany
1912 Water Tower, Nauen, Germany (competition project)

Redevelopment plan for Neuköln, Berlin (competition project; with Bruno Taut)
1913 Koswig Textile Factory, Finsterwalde, Germany
Werdandi-Bundes Hall, *Building Exhibition,* Leipzig (with F. Seesselberg)
1913/
15 Real gymnasium, Nauen, Germany
1914 Third Secession Building facade, Kurfürstendamm 232, Charlottenburg, Berlin (with Bruno Taut; demolished)
1919 Church (project)
1920 Wissinger Family Vault, Stahnsdorf, Berlin
Heinrichshofen Exhibition Hall, Magdeburg, Germany (with F. Mutzenbecker)
1921 Revolving House (project)
1922 *Chicago Tribune* Tower (competition project)
1922/
23 Federation of German Trade Unions Building, Wallstrasse, Berlin
1922/
25 German Printers Building, Dudenstrasse, Berlin (with Mart Stam)
1923 S.K.F. Norman Factory, Berlin (competition project)
1926 Federation of German Trade Unions Hall, *Gesolei Exhibition,* Dusseldorf
1927 House, Hiddensee, Germany
Apartment building development, Reinickendorf, Berlin
Werkbund Housing, Weissenhof Estate, Stuttgart
1928 Housing estate, Eichkamp, Berlin
1928/
29 Dorotheen-Lyceum School, Kopenick, Berlin
School complex, Lichtenberg, Berlin
1929/
30 State Administration Building, Breitenbachplatz, Dahlem, Berlin
1929/
31 Federation of German Trade Unions Building, Frankfurt
1930/
32 Co-operative Wholesale Bakery, Spandau, Berlin
1931/
32 Co-operative Department Store, Oranienplatz, Berlin
1949 Radio Station, Hanover (project)
1949/
52 Reuter Housing Estate, Bonn
1952/
53 Ludwig-Georg-Gymnasium, Darmstadt
1954/
55 Apartment building, Methfesselstrasse, Berlin
1955/
64 August-Thyssen Housing Development, Vietlinden, Duisburg, Germany
1957 Apartment building development, Bismarckstrasse, Stieglitz, Berlin
1964 Central Children's Home, Berlin

Publications:

By TAUT: book—*Bauten und Plane,* with introduction by Adolf Behne, Berlin 1927; article—"My Siedlungen" in *Lotus* (Venice), September 1977.

On TAUT: book—*Max Taut,* exhibition catalogue, by Julius Posener, Berlin 1964; articles—"Aufgaben für den Siedlungs-architekten zur Eichkamp-siedlung von Max Taut" by Fritz Hellwag in *Das Schöne Heim* (Berlin), April 1930; "Max Tauts Gewerkschaftshaus in Frankfurt" in *Wasmuths Monatshefte für Baukunst* (Berlin), vol. 15, 1931; "Un Grand Edifice de Max Taut" by Christian Zervos in *Cahiers d'Art* (Paris), no. 3, 1928; "Die Lichtenberger Schulen" in *Wasmuths Monatshefte für Baukunst* (Berlin), vol. 16, 1932; "Entwurf für ein Funkhaus in Hanover" and "Neue Siedlung für Bonn am Rhein" in *Architektur und Wohnform* (Stuttgart),

After the war he was once again able to pursue his career to its full extent, and he went on to create variants of his outstanding structures of the 1920's—for example, the Ludwig-Georg-Gymnasium in Darmstadt. The Reuter Estate in Bonn is one of the outstanding achievements of German post-war building.

—Jürgen Joedicke

Max Taut: Wissinger Family Vault, Stahnsdorf, Berlin, 1920 (drawing)

no. 6, 1949; "Max Taut zum Gedenken" by Kurt Junghanns in *Deutsche Architektur* (East Berlin), February 1968.

Max Taut differed from his brother Bruno in his greater awareness of reality.

After an apprenticeship as a carpenter, Taut attended a building trades school and later worked in Hermann Billing's studio. From 1911 he was active as an architect in private practice, and from 1918 he worked in partnership with Franz Hoffmann. Together with Walter Gropius and Bruno Taut he was a founder of the Berlin Arbeitsrat für Kunst and was later a member of "Der Ring," an association to which all the leading avant-garde architects belonged in the middle 1920's.

From the period immediately after the First World War come several interesting projects like the "Revolving House" of 1921 as well as structures like the expressionistic Wissinger Monument in Berlin-Stahnsdorf of 1920. Taut completed the building for the Federation of German Trade Unions in Berlin in 1923, employing the ferro-concrete framework as a visible element; the interior details reveal an expressionist influence. The Federation of German Trade Unions Building in Frankfurt of 1931 demonstrates in classical form the use of a ferro-concrete framework as an architectural tool.

Taut was invited to build two residential buildings for the Weissenhof Estate in Stuttgart in 1927, evidence of the extraordinary regard in which his work was held by his contemporaries. During this same period, as well as doing residential buildings, housing estates (e.g., the Eichkamp Estate, Berlin, 1928), and administrative and office buildings, he also designed a series of school buildings like the Berlin-Lichtenberg School Complex of 1928–29.

As architect for the trade unions, and as a well-known champion of modern architecture, Taut was excluded, after 1933, from any public commissions. He was able to complete only a few residential buildings.

TENGBOM, Ivar (Justus).

Swedish. Born in Vireda, near Jönköping, Sweden, 7 April 1878. Educated at the School of Building, Chalmers Technical College, Gothenburg, Sweden, 1894–98; Royal Academy of Arts School of Architecture, Stockholm, 1898–1901 (Royal Gold Medal, 1901), Dip.Arch. 1901. Married Hjördis Nordin in 1905; children: Anders, Ann Mari, Yvonne and Ulf; married Madeleine Douglas in 1931. Worked in the office of Erik Lallerstedt, Stockholm, 1901–03; in partnership with Ernst Torulf, Gothenburg, 1903–12: in charge of the Stockholm office of the partnership, 1906–12; in private practice, Stockholm, 1912–62. Architect to the Stockholm Royal Palace, 1922–59, and to the Drottningholm Royal Palace, 1922–62; Director-General, National Board of Building and Planning, Stockholm, 1924–36. Instructor at the Free Academy of Architecture, private school founded by ex-students of the Royal Academy of Arts, including Osvald Almqvist and Sigurd Lewerentz, Stockholm, 1910–11; Professor, Royal Academy of Arts School of Architecture, Stockholm, 1916–20. Recipient: First Prize, with Ernst Torulf, Borås Town Hall Competition, Sweden, 1907; First Prize, Högalid Church Competition, Stockholm, 1912; First Prize, Stockholms Enskilda Bank Competition, 1912; First Prize (shared), Stockholm Concert Hall Competition, 1920; First Prize, with Anders Tengbom, Bonnier Publishing House Competition, Stockholm, 1938; Royal Gold Medal, Royal Institute of British Architects, 1938. *Died* (in Stockholm) *6 August 1968.*

Works:

1904/
05 City Hall, Stockholm (competition project; with Ernst Torulf)
1907/
10 Town Hall, Borås, Sweden (with Ernst Torulf)
1911 Church, Arvika, Sweden
1911/
23 Högalid Church, Stockholm
1912/
15 Stockholms Enskilda Bank Building, Stockholm
1913 Scandinavian Bank Building, Stockholm (competition project)
1919/
20 Johnson Office Building reconstruction, Stockholm
1920/
26 Stockholm Concert Hall
1926 University of Commerce, Stockholm
1926/
28 Swedish Match Company Head Office, Stockholm
1928/
34 Esselte Office Building, Stockholm
1931/
32 "City Palace" Office Building, Stockholm
1935 Savings Bank, Örebro, Sweden
1937/
48 Bonnier Publishing House, Stockholm (with Anders Tengbom)
1938/
40 Swedish Institute, Rome

1938/
41 Church restoration, Halmstad, Sweden
1942/
44 Åtvidaberg Office Building, Stockholm
1943/
44 Savings Bank, Enköping, Sweden
1946/
50 Cathedral restoration, Uppsala (competition project)
1947/
49 Cathedral restoration, Skara, Sweden
1948/
51 Foreign Office rebuilding and restoration, Stockholm
1954/
62 Drottningholm Palace Park restoration, Sweden (with Walter Bauer and Nils G. Wollin)
1956/
58 Royal Palace Museum restoration, Stockholm

Publications:

By TENGBOM: article—"How Yesterday Made Possible Today's Swedish Architecture," interview with Eugene Clute, in *American Architect* (New York), August 1931.

On TENGBOM: articles—"Ivar Tengbom" by George Nelson in *Pencil Points* (New York), November 1935; "Royal Gold Medal Presentation to Professor Ivar Tengbom" in *RIBA Journal* (London), 11 April 1938; "L'Istituto Svedese in Roma" by Francesco Fariello in *L'Architettura* (Rome), September 1942; "Bonnierhuset" and "Fagersta Lasarett" in *Byggmästaren* (Stockholm), 7 June 1951; "Un Immeuble Industriel à Stockholm" by Martin Raberg in *La Construction Moderne* (Paris), March 1956; "Obituary: Ivar Tengbom" in *Building* (London), 16 August 1968; "Ivar Tengbom 1878–1968" by Björn Linn in *Arkitektur* (Stockholm), October 1968.

In 1910 a conflict developed at the Academy of Arts in Stockholm between Professor Grundstrom and some of the students of architecture. Six students, including Osvald Almqvist, Gunnar Asplund, Sigurd Lewerentz, and Melchior Wernstedt, left to found a private school of architecture with Carl Bergsten, Ragnar Östberg, Ivar Tengbom, and Carl Westman as tutors. The ideals on which the school was founded were in opposition to the neoclassicism prevalent at the Academy, and can be best described as those of "national realism," in which traditional Swedish vernacular and structural elements were mixed with a straightforward approach to design that attempted to return to first principles.

If Östberg had been an exponent of a picturesque use of eclectic elements, Ivar Tengbom was perhaps nearer the neoclassical thought of his time than were his colleagues. He began to move away from national realism, even though he had been one of the movement's leading theorists. He commenced a search for geometrical preciseness, and for a crisp, light, rational architecture. His work became gradually restrained and simplified, and his development was marked by his insistence that the earlier neoclassical movement was only a step on the journey in search of purity of form, something that had already been discovered by Boullée, Ledoux, Kreis, Tessenow and Soane. However, instead of the immense build-up of massive forms so characteristic of the French neoclassicists of the Academy in Rome, Tengbom moved steadily towards modernism, although his conversion was scarcely spectacular.

The importance of Ivar Tengbom in the context of Scandinavian architecture lies in his influence as a teacher and as a theorist as well as in his example as a leader in the drive towards a new architecture. His *oeuvre* spans neoclassicism, national realism, and early modernism.

—James Stevens Curl

TERRAGNI, Giuseppe.

Italian. Born in Meda, Milan, 18 April 1904. Educated at the Technical School, Como, 1917–21; Milan Polytechnic, School of Architecture, 1921–26, Dip.Arch. 1926. Served in the Italian Army, on the Greek and Russian fronts, 1939: repatriated to Italy; died of after-effects of exhaustion. In private practice, with his brother Attilio, Como, 1927–39. Founder Member, with Frette, Larco, Libera, Figini, Pollini, and Rava, Gruppo 7, and MIAR (Movimento Italiano per l'Architettura Razionale), 1926. Exhibitions: *I Esposizione di Architettura Razionale*, Rome, 1928; *Giuseppe Terragni*, Como, 1949. Recipient: First Prize, Como Master Plan Competition, 1934; First Prize, Busto Arisizio Secondary School Competition, 1934. *Died* (in Como) *19 July 1942.*

Works:

1926 Villa Saibene (project)
Swiss Metropole Hotel restoration, Como
1927 Gas Works, Rome (project)
1928 Novocomum Apartment Building, Como
1929 Hospital, Milan (competition project)
Tennis Chalet (project)
1930 Vitrum Store, Como
Strecchini Tomb, Como
Ladies' hairdressers shop, Como
1932 Sala del '22, *Mostra della Rivoluzione Fascista,* Rome
War Memorial, Erba Incino, Italy
Ortelli Tomb, Cernobbio, Italy
Tailor's shop, Monza, Italy
Aeroclub, Como (project)
Cathedral (project)
Lake or Seaside House (project)
Land Reclamation Monument (project)
1933 Ghiringhelli House, Milan (with Pietro Lingeri)
Toninello House, Milan (with Pietro Lingeri)
Artist's Lakeside House, *Triennale,* Milan (with Gruppo di Como)
Covered Market, Como
War Memorial, Lake Como (with Enrico Pampolini; from a design by Sant'Elia)
School, Malpensata Quarter, Lecco, Italy
1934 Master plan of Como (competition project; with P. Bottoni, Pietro Lingeri, and others)
Busto Arsizio Secondary School (competition project; with L. Mosca)
Palazzo Littorio, Rome (projects A and B; with Carminati, Lingeri, Vietti, Saliva, and the artists Nizzoli and Sironi)
1935 Rustici House, Milan (with Pietro Lingeri)
Lavezzari House, Milan (with Pietro Lingeri)
Post Hotel, Piazza Volta, Como
Scarfatti Monument, Col d'Echele, Italy
Pedraglio House, Como
1935/
36 Brera Academy School, Milan (two projects; with Pietro Lingeri, Luigi Figini, and Gino Pollini)
Casa del Fascio, Como (now the Casa del Popolo)
Pirovano Tomb, Como
1936 Lakeside Villa (project)
1937 Bianca House, Siveso, Italy
Casa del Floricoltore, Rebbio, Italy
Canton Library, Lugano, Switzerland (competition project)
Nuovo Campari Restaurant, Milan (with Pietro Lingeri and Alberto Sartoris)
Palazzo dei Congressi, E 42 District, Rome (competition project; with Pietro Lingeri and C. Cattaneo)
Asilo Sant'Elia (kindergarten), Como
Palazzo Littorio, stage II, Rome (project)
Danteum, Via dell'Impero, Rome (with Pietro Lingeri)
Satellite quarter, Rebbio, Italy (with Alberto Sartoris)
1938 Tool Factory enlargement, Missagia, Como

Fiera Campionaria, Milan (competition project; with Bottoni, Lingeri, Mucchi, and Pucci)
1939 Palazzo dei Congressi, E 42 District, Rome (2nd project)
Casa del Fascio, Lissone, Italy (with A. Carminati)
Giuliani-Frigerio House, Como
Housing development, Via Anzani, Como

Publications:

By TERRAGNI: articles—"Architettura," with Gruppo 7, in *Rassegna Italiana* (Milan), December 1926; "Gli Stranieri," with Gruppo 7, in *Rassegna Italiana* (Milan), February 1927; "Impreparazione, Incomprensione, Pregiudizi," with Gruppo 7, in *Rassegna Italiana* (Milan), March 1927; "Una Nuova Epoca Arcaica," with Gruppo 7, in *Rassegna Italiana* (Milan), May 1927; "Architettura di Stato?" and "Lettera sull'Architettura" in *L'Ambrosiano* (Milan), February 1931; "Discorso ai Comaschi" in *L'Ambrosiano* (Milan), March 1940.

On TERRAGNI: books—*Giuseppe Terragni* by M. Labo, Milan 1947; *Ritratto di Giuseppe Terragni* by M. Radice, Como 1949; *Difficolta Politiche dell'Architettura in Italia 1920–1940* by Giulia Veronesi, Milan 1953; *Eredeta di Terragni e lo Sviluppo dell' Architettura Italiana 1943–68* (Congress papers), Como 1968; *Omaggio a Terragni* by Bruno Zevi, Milan 1968; articles—"The Casa del Fascio at Como, Architect Giuseppe Terragni" in *The Architect and Building News* (London), July 1937; "Giuseppe Terragni" by P. M. Bardi in *Il Vetro* (Milan), July/August 1943; "Giuseppe Terragni" by Pietro Lingeri in *Quaderni della Facolta di Architettura* (Milan), 1945; "Omaggio a Terragni" by A. Podesta in *Emporium* (Bergamo), April 1948; "Terragni, Lingeri and Italian Rationalism" by Panos Koulermos in *Architectural Design* (London), March 1963; special edition of *L'Architettura* (Rome), July 1968; "Terragni" by A. D. P. in *Domus* (Milan), October 1968; "From Object to Relationship II: Giuseppe Terragni" by Peter D. Eisenman in *Perspecta* (New Haven, Connecticut), no. 13/14, 1971; "Levels of Meaning in Terragni: The Danteum Project" by Thomas Schumacher in *Parametro* (Bologna), May 1976; "Giuseppe Terragni" by Claudio Maneri in *Architecture + Urbanism* (Tokyo), September 1976.

Giuseppe Terragni was one of the pioneer architects of the modern movement in Italy, and produced some of its most significant buildings in a brief career that lasted only 13 years between his graduation in Milan in 1926 and his call-up into Mussolini's army in 1939. Not only was his achievement cut short by his death as a result of his experiences fighting on the Russian front, but also he had less work than he otherwise might have done because he was one of the very few architects who, in the bitter debate that raged round architecture in Italy during the fascist period, held out for a completely new approach.

Wrenching architecture away from neo-classical and neo-baroque revivalism and eclecticism was particularly difficult in Italy: no other country was so heavily overshadowed by its artistic past. The Futurists reacted to this by demanding a violent break with the past, but the principal Futurist architect, Antonio Sant'Elia, was unable to realize any of his utopian visions, leaving only sketches of unbuilt projects behind him when he was killed in the First World War. His example and his legend were the inspiration of the Italian movement for rationalist architecture of the 1920's and 1930's. Some of his drawings for other projects were used by Terragni and Prampolini in the design of their War Memorial, a stark symmetrical composition of abstract forms on the shores of Lake Como.

When, in 1926, Terragni and other progressive members of Gruppo 7 issued the manifesto that made them the leaders in the fight against revivalism, they adopted only a moderately avant-garde position, much less aggressive than that of the Futurists,

Guiseppe Terragni: Casa del Popolo, Como, 1936

calling for clarity and honesty in the use of materials but emphasizing that "we do not intend to break with tradition: tradition transforms itself and takes on new aspects beneath which only a few can recognize it. The new architecture, the true architecture, should be the result of a close association between logic and rationality."

The fight for modern architecture was carried on not only in lively polemics in magazines but also, practically, in exhibitions such as the Monza *Biennale* and Milan *Triennale,* which gave the rationalist architects, who otherwise had to rely on private commissions, rare opportunities for experimentation. Terragni exhibited many fascinating models and projects, and in 1932 he designed a hall for the *Mostra della Rivoluzione Fascista* in Rome.

Those of his designs actually executed form a small but remarkably group; nearly all of them are in Como where he practised and which was then the centre of modern Italian architectural experiment. These works form the nucleus of the language of Italian rationalist or modernistic architecture, the first of them being the Novocomum Apartment Building, a block of flats behind the stadium in Como, harsh and deliberately modernistic, clearly derived from earlier German and Russian experiments. Terragni's architecture achieved both maturity and a more distinctively Mediterranean character in the Casa del Fascio (now known as the Casa del Popolo), which has come to be regarded as one of the most brilliant formal exercises of the 1930's: in it, Terragni translated into a distinctively southern language the possibilities latent in designing with a reinforced concrete skeleton. Floors of offices are simply arranged round an internal court, so that the building is a hollow cube, with the front, which is seen across the piazza outside the cathedral, opening

up an exposed structural frame whose wall does not fill the space between piers and beams but is set back. There is no ornament, simply a beautifully proportioned arrangement of solids and voids whose violent contrasts of light and shade create a dramatically punctuated architectural dialogue. The proportions are those of classical architecture, and it was this complete and cunning fusion of modernism and tradition which once made this building so controversial, leading Giuseppe Pagano to denounce it as an example of "17th century affectation applied to Functionalism." This unique blend has been excellently summed up by Reyner Banham: "For those who believe that modern architecture is still subject to the grand old rules, it is proof that the rules are still valid. For those who believe that modern architecture has to do with social progress, it is the machine aesthetic at its most heartlessly elegant."

Terragni next designed a striking kindergarten, the Asilo Sant'Elia, again using courtyards and open frames to produce airy spaces for children to work and play in. Otherwise, Terragni built a number of houses and apartments, mostly simple unadorned structures that make elegant use of such features as balcony frames and sun screens. At his early death he left behind a large number of architectural and town-planning schemes and a collection of controversial writings on architecture. In many ways his career resembled that of Sant'Elia, except that Terragni did actually manage to realize some of his buildings, buildings that have played an important role in the development of modern Italian architecture.

—Konstantin Bazarov

TESSENOW, Heinrich.

German. Born in Rostock, 7 April 1876. Educated at the College of Education, Rostock, 1892–93; apprentice carpenter in his father's workshop, Rostock, 1894–96; College of Building, Neustadt, Mecklenburg, Germany, 1896; College of Building, Leipzig, 1897; (assistant railway designer, Danzig, 1898–1900); Technische Hochschule, Munich, under Karl Hocheder and Friedrich von Thiersch, 1900–01. Married Elly Mathilde Charlotte Schülke in 1903. Worked with the architect Martin Dülfer, Munich, 1901–02; Instructor, Municipal College of Building, Sternberg, Germany, 1902, and Municipal College of Building, Lüchow, Germany, 1903; worked at Paul Schultze-Naumburg's Saalecker Workshops, 1904; Instructor, Arts and Crafts School, Upper Trier, Germany, 1905–09; Assistant to Professor Martin Dülfer, Technische Hochschule, Dresden, 1909–10; in private practice, in Hellerau, Germany, 1910–13, Vienna, 1913–19, Hellerau, 1919–20, Dresden, 1920–26, and and Berlin, 1926 until his death, 1950. Professor, School of Arts and Crafts, Vienna, 1913–19; Professor, Academy of Arts, Dresden, 1920–26; Head of Master Studio, Academy of Fine Arts, Berlin, 1926–34; Professor, 1926–41, Emeritus Professor, 1941–50, and Lecturer, 1945–50, Technische Hochschule, Charlottenburg, Berlin; Teacher, 1934, and Part-time Director of the Master Studio, 1936, United Schools for Liberal and Applied Arts, Berlin. Founder, Deutscher Werkbund, 1910; Founder, Crafts Center/Community, Hellerau, Germany, 1919; Member, Novembergruppe, Berlin, 1921; Founder Member, Der Ring architects group, Berlin, 1926; Chairman, Deutscher Werkbund, Berlin, 1949. Exhibitions: *Heinrich Tessenow,* Berlin, 1961; *Heinrich Tessenow,* Architectural Association, London, 1977. Honorary doctorates: University of Rostock, 1919; Technische Hochschule, Stuttgart, 1929. Honorary Life Member, Bund Deutscher Architekten, 1950. Honorary Corresponding Member, Royal Institute of British Architects, 1937. Member, Prussian Academy of Fine Arts, Berlin, 1920, and Academy of Arts, Berlin, 1950. *Died* (in Berlin) *1 November 1950.*

Works:

1902   Vicarage (project)
      Tessenow Seaside House, Sternberg, Germany (project)
      Vorstadt Two-Family House (project)
      Garden Pavilion (project)

1902/
03   Schön Boarding House, Sternberg, Germany

1903   Semi-Detached Houses (project)
      Four-Family Houses (project)
      7 Terraced One-Family Workers Houses (project)
      Corner Houses with 2 Shops (project)
      Am Buchenwald Villa (project)
      Facade for a Two-Family House (project)
      Small Town House (project)
      Country House by the Sea (project)
      Porter's House (project)
      Single-Family House (project)
      Bismarck Tower (project)
      Country Lodging House (project)
      Funeral Monument (project)
      Parish Church (project)
      Small Town Hall (project)
      Entrance Gate (project)

1904   Country House (project)
      Haus auf der Höhe (single-family house) (project)
      Two-Family House (projects)
      Burial Vault (project)
      Garden Pavilion (project)
      Three-Family House (project)

1905   Single-family houses, Neu-Dölau Housing Estate, near Halle/Saale, Germany
      4 Terraced Single-Family Houses (project)
      Single-family house, near Mülheim/Ruhr, Germany
      Single-Family House (project)
      Einsiedelei Two-Family House (project)
      4 terraced single-family houses, Weiden Housing Estate, near Cologne
      Country House, Saratoff, Russia (project)
      Workers' House (project)
      Six-Family House (competition project)
      Two-Family Country House (project)
      2 Semi-Detached Workers' Houses (project)
      Forest Cemetery (project)

1906   Country House on the Ruhr (project)
      Single-family house, Mintard, near Mülheim/Ruhr, Germany
      12 Semi-Detached Houses (project)
      Single-family terraced houses, Bad Brösen, near Danzig
      Single-Family Terraced Housing (project)
      Single-Family House, Eifel Plateau, Germany (project)
      2 Single-Family Semi-Detached Houses (project)
      Three-Family House (project)
      2 Semi-Detached Two Family Houses (project)
      Fountain for Small Town Market Square (project)
      Corner House, Bad Brösen, near Danzig (project)

1906/
07   State Electricity Company Workers' Housing, Trier, Germany

1907   Vicarage (2 projects)
      Holiday House, Vorpommern, Germany (competition project)
      Single-Family Terraced Housing, Ohrenstrasse, Trier, Germany (project)
      Rural Single-Family House (project)

      Holiday House on the Ruhr (2 projects)
      Village School, with Teachers' Housing (project)

1908   Single-Family Terraced Housing (project)
      2 Semi-Detached Single-Family Houses (project)
      Single-Family House (project)
      Single Family Terraced House (project)
      2-Storey Terraced Housing (project)
      2 semi-detached houses for civil servants, Mettlach an der Saar, Germany
      Public Baths (project)

1909   Single-Family House in the Ruhr Valley (project)

1910   Haus zum Wolf (Schmidt House), Hopfengarten, near Magdeburg, Germany
      8 single-family houses, Am Schänkenberg, Hellerau, Germany
      Metzges House, Remagen/Rhein, Germany
      Israeli Young Farmers' Educational Institute, Steinhorst, near Celle, Germany
      Dalcroze Institute for Physical Education, Hellerau, Germany
      Single-Family Terraced Housing (project)

1910/
11   12 single-family terraced houses, Am Schänkenberg, Hellerau, Germany
      2 single-family houses, Heideweg 24–26, Hellerau, Germany
      Single-family house, Tännichtweg 2, Hellerau, Germany
      Single-family terraced house, Hohensalza, Germany
      Single-family house, Auf dem Sand 12, Hellerau, Germany
      Single-family house, Heideweg 22, Hellerau, Germany
      Gehlig House, Tännichtweg 1, Hellerau, Germany
      2 semi-detached single-family houses, Am Schänkenberg 17–19, Hellerau, Germany
      2 semi-detached single-family houses, Tännichtweg 6–8, Hellerau, Germany
      Single-family house, Karl-Liebknechtstrasse, Hellerau, Germany
      4 five-family houses, Dresdenerstrasse, Hellerau, Germany (project)

1911/
13   8 single-family houses, Am Schänkenberg and Am Pfarrlehn, Hellerau, Germany

1912   Nau-Rosser Single-Family House and Studio, Lostau, near Magdeburg, Germany
      4 semi-detached single-family houses for factory workers and officials, Waldkirchen-/Erzgebirge, Germany

1912/
13   5 single-family terraced houses, Am Pfarrlehn 4–12, Hellerau, Germany

1913   Single-family house, Falkenberg Garden City, Berlin
      Single-family house, Tännichtweg 14, Hellerau, Germany
      Elementary/High School, Hellerau, Germany (project)
      Six-Family Terraced Housing, Groba-Riesa Housing Estate, Hamburg (project)

1914   4 single-family terraced houses, Am Schänkenberg 38–44, Hellerau, Germany
      Viennese Kunstgewerbeschule Rooms, *Werkbund Exhibition,* Cologne

1916   Cemetery monument, Vienna

1916/
17   Böhler House, Oberalpina/St. Moritz, Switzerland

1917   Single-family terraced houses, Rähnitz, Dresden (project)
      Municipal Monument to the Dead of World War I (competition project)

1919   Post-War Housing Development, Rähnitz, Dresden (project)
      Rural Housing Settlement, Rähnitz, Dresden (project)

1919/
20   Graf Doret Mansion, Czomahaya, Hungary

1920   22 single-family houses and 2 multi-family houses, Public Housing Estate, Possneck, Thuringia, Germany
      Schnitterkaserne Terraced Housing (project)
      Free-Standing Single-Family House (project)
      Workers' Housing, Schleswig-Holstein, Germany (project)
      Mansion for State Secretary Busch, Bussow, Mecklenburg, Germany
      Single-Family Terraced House (project)
      Four-Family House for a Small Town (project)

1921   Kleinstes Dauerhaus (single-family house), Rähnitz, Dresden (project)
      Semi-detached single-family state housing, Rannersdorf Estate, Schwechat, Vienna

1922   11 connected single-family houses, Edwin-Hoernle-Strasse 19–39, Hellerau, Germany

1924   Mansion, Bavaria (project)
      Bridge over the River Elbe, Meissen, Germany
      Krauss Family House, Schwarzenberg, Germany (project)

1925   Regional School, Klotzsche, near Dresden
      Oberbayern Restaurant, and Cupola with 2 Side Halls for Main Exhibitions, *Quadrennial Exhibition,* Dresden
      Dresdener Anzeigers Office Building, Dresden (competition project)
      Berliner Sezession Exhibition Building, Berlin (competition project)

1926   Gallery interiors, and Inner Courtyard, *International Art Exhibition,* Dresden
      Am Rosenhof Restaurant, *Garden Exhibition,* Dresden

1927   Single-family house, Mineworkers' Estate, Finkenherd, Frankfurt an der Oder, Germany
      Freudenberg House, Heidelberg (project)
      City Swimming Hall, Gartenstrasse, Berlin
      Rengen Family Tomb, Kamnist, Germany
      Trade School, Charlottenburg, Berlin (competition project)
      Redevelopment plan for the Ministry Gardens, Berlin (project; with Peter Behrens, Adolf Rading, Hans Scharoun, and Martin Wagner)

1927/
30   Heinrich-Schütz School, Kassel

1928   3 four-family houses, Am Fischtal 58–60, Zehlendorf, Berlin
      6 single-family terraced houses, Am Fischtal 62–66, Zehlendorf, Berlin
      2 single-family houses, Am Fischtal 2 and 2A, Zehlendorf, Berlin
      Castle Hotel conversion, Kassel (destroyed)
      Crown Prince's Palace/Museum of Modern Painting conversion, Berlin (destroyed)
      Country House on the Ruhr (project)

1928/
29   Single-family houses conversion, Neutorstrasse 26, Neubrandenburg, Germany

1929   Music High School, Charlottenburg, Berlin (project)
      Aschrott Foundation Old People's Home, Kassel (competition project)
      Church, Karlshafen, Germany (project)

1930   Tessenow House, Sophie-Charlotte-Strasse 7, Zehlendorf, Berlin
      Busch Family Tomb, Büssow/Neumark, Germany

1930/
31   Memorial to the War Dead, Berlin (renovation/conversion of Schinkel's Neue Wache)

1931   Goethe House enlargement, Am Frauenplan, Weimar
      Church, Karlshafen, Germany (project)
      Elisabeth-Heim Institute for Cripples, Rostock (project)
      Students' Lodging House, Berlin (project)

Regimental Hall of Honor, Magdeburg Cathedral, Germany (project)

1932 Cassinone Family Tomb, Vienna

1933 Reichshauptbank Building extensions, Berlin (competition project)

1934 House, Aue/Erzgebirge, Germany (project)

1935 Crafts School, Königsberg, Germany (project)

Hubbe und Fahrenholtz Administration Building, Magdeburg, Germany

1936 Single-Family House and Three-Family House, Rügen, Germany (competition project)

Hindenburg Memorial and Barracks, Magdeburg, Germany

Hall layouts, *Olympic Art Exhibition,* Berlin

Plan for the Trommelplatz, Königsberg, Germany (competition project)

1937 12 single-family houses, Iserhorstweg, Neustrelitz-Kiefernheide, Germany

Monument to the War Dead of the Stargard Region, Neubrandenburg, Germany

1938 Barracks, Helmstedt, Germany (project)

Dohrn Family Cemetery, Gut Hökersdorf, near Stettin, Germany

Bridge over the River Weichsel (project)

1941 Administration Building, Braunschweig, Germany (competition project)

Junker Works Housing Estate, Magdeburg, Germany (project)

1942 Plan for the Diedrichshagen Satellite Town, Warnemünde, near Rostock

Barlach Tomb, Ratzeburg, Germany (project)

1942 Mosigkau Community Housing Development, near Dessau, Germany (project)

Plan for the Drewitz Satellite Town, Potsdam, Berlin

1943 Cottage/Tessenow House conversion, Güstrow, Siemitz, Germany

1946 Town reconstruction plans for the German towns of Pasewalk, Friedland, Woldegk, Neubrandenburg, Rostock, and Demmin

1947 Small Farmhouse, Single-Family House with Workshop, and Rural Single-Family House, for the Mecklenburg Region, Germany (project)

Plan for the reconstruction of the old city of Lübeck

Plan for the reconstruction of the old town of Mecklenburg

1948 Café Niederegger, Lübeck (project)

Publications:

By TESSENOW: books—*Zimmermannsarbeiten,* Freiburg 1907, Munich 1921; *Der Wohnhausbau,* Munich 1909, 3rd edition 1927; *Hausbau und dergleichen,* Berlin 1916, 3rd edition 1928; *Handwerk und Kleinstadt,* Berlin 1919; *Das Land in der Mitte,* Hellerau, Germany 1921; *Die kleine und die grosse Stadt. Aus dem Nachlass,* edited by Hans Hasche, Munich 1961; *Kleine Schriften von Heinrich Tessenow: Enthält die Aufsätze "Handwerkerarbeit und Fabrikarbeit" und "Die Farbe im Stadtbild,"* Hamburg 1967.

On TESSENOW: books—*Heinrich Tessenow,* exhibition catalogue, Berlin 1961; *Heinrich Tessenow 1876–1950* by Gerda Wangerin and Gerhard Weiss, Essen 1976; articles—"Arbeiten von Heinrich Tessenow und seinen Schulern" by Werner Hegemann in *Wasmuths Monatshefte für Baukunst* (Berlin), vol. 9, no. 9, 1925, and vol. 10, no. 2, 1926; "Paul Wolff und Heinrich Tessenow" in *Wasmuths Monatshefte für Baukunst* (Berlin), vol. 11, no. 4, 1927; "Heinrich Tessenow" by Oskar Gehrig in *Mecklenburgische Monatshefte* (Mecklenburg, Germany), no. 11, 1927; "Heinrich Tessenow" by Peter Meyer in *Werk* (Zurich), no. 8, 1934; "Heinrich Tessenow zum 60. Geburtstag" in *Frankfurter Zeitung* (Frankfurt), 5 April 1936; "Heinrich Tessenow" by Bruno Reichlin in *Casabella* (Milan), no. 7, 1970; "Heinrich Tesse-

now" by Steen Eiler Rasmussen in *Bauwelt* (Berlin), April 1976; "Two Masters: Hans Poelzig and Heinrich Tessenow" by Julius Posener in *Lotus* (Venice), September 1977.

*

Heinrich Tessenow, with his strongly puritanical "reductive-classicism," does not fit easily into any 20th century movements. Although his work is unequivocally associated with the time span of New Building, Tessenow was much more interested in the human and social aspects of a new building than in the creation of a new style.

After completing an apprenticeship as a carpenter in his father's business in Rostock, Tessenow studied building and then studied architecture at the Technische Hochschule, Munich, under Karl Hocheder and Friedrich von Thiersch. He then worked with Martin Dülfer, who became a strong influence, and from 1902–03 he taught at the building colleges in Sternberg (Mecklenburg) and in Lüchow (Hanover). Still in search of solid experience, he joined Paul Schultze-Naumburg's Saalecker Workshop in 1904. This educational history is indicative of Tessenow's goals: like Mebes and Ostendorf, he believed that a fundamental renewal of architecture could be guaranteed only by a return to solid traditions. Because of his disagreement with Schultze-Naumburg's theories, he left the workshop in 1905 and went on to teach in the Arts and Crafts School in Upper Trier. Then, from 1909–1910 he worked as an assistant to Martin Dülfer at the Technische Hochschule in Dresden.

From 1910, Tessenow was able to begin translating into reality his vision of an appropriate, objective architecture, depending less on spectacular artistic ideas than on functional craft traditions. He completed his best known works in 1910–13, the Dalcroze Institute for Physical Education in Hellerau and housing for the Hellerau Garden City. Tessenow's strength lay in the re-use of strong, classical elements in a completely different form. His reduction of the architectonic medium of expression went so far that, to many of his contemporaries, even his houses seemed over-purist. Tessenow considered the objectivity of these buildings not as a style but rather as a necessary result of his function-related work methods. And, in fact, it was especially in his houses that Tessenow best conveyed his extraordinary feeling for spatial atmosphere and the human dimension.

During 1913–19 Tessenow taught at the School of Arts and Crafts in Vienna. World War I and the European revolution made a deep impression on him. Unlike Taut, Mendelsohn or Scharoun, who foresaw the coming of a new age of creativity, Tessenow felt very deeply the burden of the war and the chaos it left behind. He rejected the city. He came to believe that he could achieve a new social cohesion for people only in "organic" and "in themselves viable" small towns. Man again became the center of his attention and his work; his ideals became not dissimilar to those of William Morris, and in 1919 he founded a Crafts Center/Community in Hellerau.

During 1920–26 he taught at the Academy of Arts in Dresden, and in 1926 he was appointed Professor at the Technische Hochschule, Charlottenburg; thereafter he worked and practiced in Berlin. His teaching in Berlin was extraordinarily important to him. He used his position as a forum to criticize all formalism and to propound his belief that "A minimum of display is the decisive factor." During this period, until World War II, Tessenow began to follow new paths, particularly in school architecture. He turned away from symmetry as a principle of order, and in these large buildings rediscovered an objective, purist expression of form. By careful staggering of the structure, he included nature within the ground plan and kept building details within the crafts tradition. It was precisely in this reliance and refinement of a particular tradition that Tessenow differed from Gropius or Mies van der Rohe who wanted to break with tradition, even in building details. In these years Tessenow naturally belonged with representatives of

"New Objectivity" without necessarily adhering to all of their philosophy. Buildings like the Heinrich-Schutz School in Kassel (1927–30) or the City Swimming Hall in Berlin (1927) clearly demonstrate this attitude. In 1928 the estate "Am Fischtalgrund" in Zehlendorf was completed: his work there documents Tessenow's continuing preference for economical, lovingly arranged single-family houses even on high-density estates. In 1930/31 Tessenow was commissioned to transform Schinkel's Neue Wache in Berlin into a memorial to the dead of World War I—a task he handled with extraordinary sensitivity and refinement.

Tessenow soon experienced difficulties after the seizure of power by the National Socialists. In 1934 he was forced to give up his teaching post at the Academy of Fine Arts in Berlin. Under pressure from his former pupil, Albert Speer, he did try to make compromises, but his designs were more and more frequently rejected by the Nazis. Like Paul Bonatz, Tessenow was totally helpless against the continual excessive demands on him, and he was, in effect, forced to retire from teaching and his practice in 1941. But in 1945 he was able to resume teaching at Charlottenburg. He principal post-war activity was in planning the reconstruction of the old town centers, which he regarded as an opportunity to realize the small town ideal he had been propagating since 1918. He worked, on and off, on plans for various towns, most notably Mecklenburg and Lübeck, until his death in 1950.

In the last few decades there has been a continual increase in the estimation of Tessenow's work—despite the fact that he always adopted a middle stance and cannot therefore really be said to belong either to the reactionary "Heimatstil" movement or the radical "New Objectivity." More important than any classification of his style has been the recognition that Tessenow, like Hugo Häring, is one of the very few important 20th century architects who have fostered an individual, primarily modest and human architecture. Few architects have dealt as seriously and as profoundly as Heinrich Tessenow with the problems of high-density housing and of housing for those of modest means.

—Frank Werner

TESTA, Clorindo.

Argentinian. Born in Buenos Aires in 1923. In private practice, Buenos Aires. Member, Buenos Aires Regulating Plan Team, 1948. Member, Group of Thirteen, Buenos Aires. Exhibition: *Clorindo Testa: La Peste en Ceppaloni,* Galeria Florida 948, Buenos Aires, 1978. Recipient: First Prize, Civic Center Competition, La Pampa, Argentina, 1956; First Prize, Provincial Government House Competition, La Pampa, Argentina, 1956; First Prize, Bank of London and South America Headquarters Competition, Buenos Aires, 1960; First Prize, National Library Competition, Buenos Aires, 1962; Grand Prize, *Bienal,* Sao Paulo, 1977. Member, Fine Arts Academy, Buenos Aires. Address (office): Sante Fe 1821-6P, 1123 Buenos Aires, Argentina.

Works:

1956/
61 Bus Terminal, Santa Rosa, La Pampa, Argentina (with Francisco Rossi, Augusto Gaido, and Boris Dabinovic)

1956/
63 Provincial Government House, Santa Rosa, La Pampa, Argentina (with Francisco Rossi, Augusto Gaido, and Boris Dabinovic)

1960/
66 Bank of London and South America Headquarters, Buenos Aires (with SEPRA)

1962 National Library, Buenos Aires (project; with Alicia Cazzaniga de Bullrich and Francisco Bullrich)
1962/
64 Bank of London and South America, Harrod's Branch, Buenos Aires (with SEPRA)
1976 Presidente Plaza Hospital, La Rioja, Argentina
1979 Government Hospital, Ivory Coast

Publications:

By TESTA: paper—*Hacia una Arquitectura Topologica,* with Jorge Glusberg, Lima 1977.

On TESTA: books—*Clorindo Testa* by Julio Llimas, Buenos Aires 1962; *New Directions in Latin American Architecture* by Francisco Bullrich, New York 1969; *Clorindo Testa: La Peste en Ceppaloni,* exhibition catalogue, Buenos Aires 1978; articles—"Clorindo Testa" in *Revista de Arquitectura* (Buenos Aires), no. 38, 1953; "Hospital Presidente Plaza, La Rioja" in *Nuestra Arquitectura* (Buenos Aires), no. 498, 1976.

The most significant figure to have appeared on the Argentine architectural scene in the last two decades is undoubtedly Clorindo Testa. He began his work in 1948 as part of the team for the Buenos Aires Regulating Plan. After spending two years in Italy, where he began painting, he returned to Buenos Aires and developed his activities as an architect, frequently associating with divers colleagues for each project. Since then, it has been as difficult to classify him according to a particular style as it is to comprehend his work according to any explicit (or implicit) theoretical posture. Possessing a bold talent, a powerful creative imagination, and an exquisite sensibility,

Testa likes to allow his buildings to speak for themselves. As he himself points out, "What I wanted to say is what is said by the buildings I made."

Some clues, however, do exist. In a paper presented jointly with the author, before the Frederico Villarreal University in Lima in 1977, entitled *Towards a Topological Architecture,* Testa outlines his attitude about the habitat. Criticizing the urbanization proposals of the Athens Charter, he points out that the assumptions about the quality of life that might be obtained through the division of the city into "functional" areas have been undermined in less than forty years: "Functionalism forgot social reality, and I believe that one cannot speak of an urbanistic change if there exists a division between political, social and human factors." The creation of spaces for particular functions is meaningless, if these spaces don't primarily address the problem of the elimination of the solitude of the individual who lives in the midst of the crowd.

This vision, of an architecture of synthesis, is verifiable in his own works.

The Bank of London and South America is considered by many people to be the most important building erected in Buenos Aires in the last half century because of its significant values. It was done in collaboration with the SEPRA team, which has a wealth of experience in Argentina, and has been praised by critics of international renown such as Nikolaus Pevsner; it has, as well, awakened an unusual interest in the average inhabitant of Buenos Aires. The inside is conceived as one great unitary space which encompasses five levels; these levels jut out or appear as hanging trays, generating series of spaces which are subordinated or integrated to a central one; the structural solution is of a "brutalist" image. The rupture of an image of box-wrapping is manifest in the resolution of the inside-outside link, in the creation of a transition area, coinciding with

the entrance, which allows for the perception of the whole at pedestrian level. Testa was equally concerned with the "linkage" with neighboring buildings and respect for the urban environment, and he has rescued the street as a vital experience. The maturity of the design and the profound technical resolution produce an enormous impact.

Yet despite the formal beauty and ingenuity of the building, function has not been sacrificed to form; on the contrary, a deft integration exists between form and function—as it does in the administrative blocks of La Pampa, which were, additionally, subjected to particular weather conditions. But perhaps the best indication of Testa's ability to combine dazzling form with superb functionalism is his hospital in Africa, his most ambitious work.

The design of the hospital reveals Testa responding to, and solving the problems, of a number of particular conditions: 1) institutional conditions (the client, Health Ministry, Government of the Ivory Coast); 2) social conditions (geographical venue; possible population of the hospital; types of services; assistance activities; teaching centers; research centers); 3) technical conditions (350 beds; 28,000 m² with a central volume in the shape of a hollowed-out prism pierced by ramps); 4) natural conditions (strong winds, heavy rainfall, red earth, vegetation made sparse by clearing work; horizontal land; constant temperature of 30°C); 5) geopolitical conditions (highway crossing in the center of the country; nearby city of 35,000 people); 6) institutional and social conditions of consumption (non-existence of hospital centers in neighboring countries; predominant endemic diseases, etc.); 7) aesthetic conditions (production of an architectural event). The space-time succession, that is to say the constitution of a serial system to which the spectator gains access, is nothing more (or less) than the clear and gradual manifestation of the process of the design, leading to

Clorindo Testa: Provincial Government House, Santa Rosa, La Pampa, Argentina, 1963

an understanding of the final architectural discourse.

The designs of Clorindo Testa do not project a reality—they constitute it. The act of projection and the act of building are not independent stages, but one single proposal within a total structure.

—Jorge Glusberg

THE ARCHITECTS COLLABORATIVE (TAC).
Partnership; established, Cambridge, Massachusetts, 1945, by Walter Gropius, *q.v.*, Norman Fletcher, Jean Fletcher, John Harkness, Sarah Pillsbury Harkness, Robert MacMillan, Louis McMillan, and Benjamin Thompson, *q.v.*; TAC International established in 1960; TAC Incorporated, 1964. Current Principals: Norman Fletcher, John Harkness, Sarah Pillsbury Harkness, Louis McMillen, and Alex Cvijanovic, Roland Kluver, John F. Hayes, Peter W. Morton, Leonard Notkin, Richard Brooker, James E. Burlage, Howard F. Elkus, and H. Morse Payne. Recipient: Boston Arts Festival Award, 1954, 1956, 1959, 1960, 1963, 1964; Parker Medal, Boston Society of Architects, 1961, 1973, 1978; American Institute of Architects Award, 1964, 1966, 1967, 1970, 1971, 1972, 1974, 1976, 1977, 1978, 1979; Prestressed Concrete Institute Award, 1966; American Society of Landscape Architects Award, 1967; United States Department of Housing and Urban Development Award, 1968; American Concrete Institute Award, 1972; United States General Services Administration Award, 1973; First Prize, Johns Manville Building Competition, Colorado, 1973; Connecticut Society of Architects Award, 1974; First Prize, Arab Investment Company Building Competition, 1976; First Prize, Abu Dhabi Library Competition, 1976; American Institute of Steel Construction Award, 1979. Address: 46 Brattle Street, Cambridge, Massachusetts 02138, U.S.A.

Works:

1946 Ryan House, Cambridge, Massachusetts
Poppleton House, Dayton, Ohio
Lexington Nursery School, Massachusetts (project)
Skiing hut, Franconia, New Hampshire (project)
Library, Willimantic, Connecticut (project)
Kaplan House, Newton, Massachusetts
Usiskin House, Long Island, New York (project)
1947 Brockelman House, Worcester, Massachusetts
Neil House, Andover, Massachusetts
Wolfers House, Maine
Peter House, Cape Cod, Massachusetts
Catheron House, Foxboro, Massachusetts
Heywood House reconstruction, Maine
Town plan for Michael Reese Hospital, Chicago
1948 Hua Tung University, Shanghai, China (project)
Peter Thacher Junior High School, Attleboro, Massachusetts
Lawrence House, Lexington, Massachusetts
McMahon House, Lexington, Massachusetts
House, Providence, Rhode Island
England House, Pittsfield, Massachusetts
Howlett House, Belmont, Massachusetts
Elementary school, Sherborn, Massachusetts (project)
1949 Pillsbury House, Rumford, Rhode Island
Field House, Cape Code, Massachusetts
Graduate Center, Harvard University, Cambridge, Massachusetts (with Brown, Lawford and Forbes)
1950 Park buildings, Lexington, Massachusetts
Apthorp House, Concord, Massachusetts
Hechinger House, Washington, D.C.

England House, Washington, D.C.
Napoli House, Concord, Massachusetts
Theatre, New Rochelle, New York (project)
Medical center, Mt. Kisco, New York (project)
Barnes House reconstruction, Belmont, Massachusetts (project)
1950/
65 Dormitory (Boylston, Emerson, Fay) alterations, Harvard University, Cambridge, Massachusetts
1951 Business school, Attleboro, Massachusetts
Burncoat Secondary and Senior Schools, Worcester, Massachusetts (with A. Johnson)
Pillsbury House, Milton, Massachusetts
Vischer House furniture, Indiana
Vannah House, Foxboro, Massachusetts
Stichweh House, Hanover, Massachusetts
Elementary and secondary schools, Amesbury, Massachusetts (project)
Donelly Bureau reconstruction, Boston (project)
Bradley House (project)
Housing and Home Finance Agency Headquarters, San Jose, Costa Rica (project)
Wasco Flashing Corporation, Cambridge, Massachusetts (project)
Five Fields Housing Complex, Lexington, Massachusetts
Houses, Lake Barcroft, Falls Church, Virginia
American University Office Building, Washington, D.C. (project)
Mulcahey Elementary School, Taunton, Massachusetts
Pilgrim Park Elementary School, Warwick, Rhode Island
Elementary school, Providence, Rhode Island
Senior school, Concord, New Hampshire
American Association for the Advancement of Science Office Building, Washington, D.C.
Shops, for the Hechinger Company, Falls Church and Alexandria, Virginia
Designs/models for school and college furniture for the Thonet Factory
Cole House, Cambridge, Massachusetts
Baruch House, Newton, Massachusetts
Lang House, Newton, Massachusetts
Elementary school, Cambridge, Massachusetts
Elementary school, North Adams, Massachusetts
Caulfield House reconstruction, Washington, D.C.
1953 McCormick and Company Office Building, Chicago
Wherry District Housing, for the United States Navy, Quonset, Rhode Island
Back Bay Center, Boston (with Pietro Belluschi, Carl Koch, Hugh Stubbins, and Walter Bogner)
National Education Association Building (project)
Burke House, Center Harbour, New York
1954 Flagg Street Elementary School, Worcester, Massachusetts (with A. Roy)
Shopping center, Saugus, Massachusetts (with Ketchum, Gind and Sharp)
Overholt Thoracic Clinic, Boston
1955 Elementary school, Waltham, Massachusetts
Secondary school, Attleboro, Massachusetts
1956 Elementary school, West Bridgewater, Massachusetts
Housing at Otis Air Force Base, Falmouth, Massachusetts
United States Embassy, Athens
1957 Oheb Shalom Temple, Baltimore
Littleton Junior-Senior High School, Massachusetts
Pioneer Valley Regional High School,

Northfield, Massachusetts
1958 William F. Pollard Junior High School, Needham, Massachusetts
Elementary school, Stoughton, Massachusetts
Dormitories, for Phillips Academy, Andover, Massachusetts
Reyim Synagogue, Newton, Massachusetts
Boylston Hall, Harvard University, Cambridge, Massachusetts
Murchison House, Provincetown, Massachusetts
Pan American Building, New York (as consultant architects; with Pietro Belluschi, on plan of Emery Roth and Sons)
Jewish Community Center, Hartford, Connecticut
1959 Elementary school, Acton, Massachusetts
Britz-Buckow-Rudow Settlement, West Berlin (project)
Apartment block, Hansa District, Berlin
Hollis Hall, Harvard University, Cambridge, Massachusetts
Shiffman Humanities Center and Olin-Sang American Civilization Center, Harvard University, Cambridge, Massachusetts
Putterham Branch Library, Brookline, Massachusetts
Academic Quadrangle, Brandeis University, Waltham, Massachusetts
1960 L. G. Hanscom Field Elementary School, Lincoln, Massachusetts
Elementary school additions, Kingston, Massachusetts
Dormitories, Brandeis University, Waltham, Massachusetts
Northeast Elementary School, Waltham, Massachusetts
East Hills, Pittsburgh (with Carl Koch and Sert, Jackson)
Gould Hospital, Presque Isle, Maine
Parkside Elementary School, Columbus, Indiana
Hoffman Laboratory of Experimental Geology, Harvard University, Cambridge, Massachusetts
Chase Manhattan Bank, Great Neck, Long Island, New York
Hemoglobin Laboratory alterations, Children's Hospital Medical Center, Boston
1961 Levi Warren High School additions, Newton, Massachusetts
Peter Bent Brigham Hospital, Boston
School of Law, Economics and Business Administration, University of Tunis
1961/
73 Wayland High School, Massachusetts
1962 Mount Kisco Elementary School, New York
McCann Regional Vocational High School, North Adams, Massachusetts
Thomas M. Evans Science Building, Arts and Communications Center, George Washington Hall alterations, Sylvia Pratt Kemper Memorial Chapel, and Copley addition to the Oliver Wendell Homes Library, Phillips Academy, Andover, Massachusetts
Julia L. McCarthy Elementary School additions, Acton, Massachusetts
New Trier Township High School, Winnetka, Illinois
IBM Federal Systems Division, Gaithersburg, Maryland
1963 Higher Teacher Training College, Bamako, Mali
Mount Kisco Middle School, New York
Development plan for the Moses Brown School, Providence, Rhode Island
Air-Supported Athletics Facilities, Forman School, Litchfield, Connecticut
St. George's School, Newport, Rhode Island
Pound Ridge Elementary School additions, New York

1964   Britz-Buckow-Rudow Center, West Berlin (project)

Schofield Elementary School, Wellesley, Massachusetts

Lexington High School, Massachusetts

Dormitory and Commons Building Quadrangle, Clark University, Worcester, Massachusetts

Bennington Regional High School, Vermont

North Bennington Fire House, Vermont

Master plan for Redwood Shores, Redwood City, California

Development plan for four state parks in West Virginia

1965   Rosenthal China Factory, Selb, Germany

Master plan for a university at Mosul, Iraq

Clinical Research Center alterations, Children's Hospital Medical Center, Boston

Redwood Shores Community Development, Redwood City, California

Development plan and additional buildings, Eaglebrook School, Deerfield, Massachusetts

Plan for Abbott Academy, Andover, Massachusetts

Chelmsford Junior High School, Massachusetts

YMCA Building, Warren Street and Washington Park Boulevard, Boston

1965/
72   Development plan for the Virginia Polytechnic Institute, Blacksburg

1966   Concord Junior High School, Massachusetts

Faculty Tower, University of Baghdad

Higher Teacher Training College, Kano, Nigeria

Greylock Residential Houses, Williams College, Williamstown, Massachusetts

Jewish Community Center, Worcester, Massachusetts

YMCA Building, Roxbury, Massachusetts

Beveridge Hall additions, Mount Hermon School, Massachusetts

Gymnasium and Swimming Pool, Northfield School, Massachusetts (project)

Multi-Purpose Dormitory Building, Rensselaer Polytechnic Institute, Troy, New York

New Trier West High School, Winnetka, Illinois (with Perkins and Will)

Fox Lane Middle School, Bedford, New York

McFarland Elementary School additions, Chelmsford, Massachusetts

Plum Cove Elementary School, Gloucester, Massachusetts

TAC Office Building, Cambridge, Massachusetts

1966/
76   Blue Hills Regional Vocational High School, Canton, Massachusetts

1967   Experimental buildings for a primary and secondary school at Britz-Buckow-Rudow, West Berlin

Huntington Art Gallery addition, San Marino, California

Tower East Office and Commercial Building, Shaker Heights, Ohio

Thomas Glassworks, Hamburg

Town plan for Selb, Germany

East Greenwich High School, Rhode Island

Camp Hill Auditorium alterations, Mount Hermon School, Massachusetts

1968   Kennedy Federal Building, Civic Center, Boston

Development plan for Butler University, Indianapolis

Boys Club of Boston, Warren and Cliff Streets, Roxbury, Massachusetts

Freshmen Dormitory, Rensselaer Polytechnic Institute, Troy, New York

Weston High School, Massachusetts

School and Child Day Care Center, Gropiusstadt, West Berlin

Westborough Senior High School, Massachusetts

Children's Inn, Children's Hospital Medical Center, Boston

1969   Hillside Elementary School, Needham, Massachusetts

TAC Office Building additions, Cambridge, Massachusetts

Maple Road Elementary School, Chelmsford, Massachusetts

Biology, Geology and Education Building, Virginia Polytechnic Institute, Blacksburg

IBM Space Systems Center, Gaithersburg, Maryland

Chott Maria Agricultural School, Sousse, Tunisia

Optics and Space Guidance Laboratories, NASA Electronics Center, Cambridge, Massachusetts

Composite Medical Facility, Otis Air Force Base, Falmouth, Massachusetts (project)

1970   Chelmsford High School, Massachusetts

Marshfield High School additions, Massachusetts

Peabody School, Concord, Massachusetts

Emerson School additions, Edgartown, Massachusetts

James L. Hanley Education Center, Providence, Rhode Island

Vocational School additions, Providence, Rhode Island

Teaneck Educational Complex, New Jersey (project)

Macgregor House (dormitory), Massachusetts Institute of Technology, Cambridge

Faculty and Classroom Buildings, University of Tunis

Research Buildings, National Institute of Child Health, Bethesda, Maryland (project)

Development plan for Dickinson College, Carlisle, Pennsylvania

Graduate School of Dentistry, Boston University Medical Center

Office and Computer Building, Massachusetts Hospital Association Headquarters, Burlington

1970/
74   Teaching and Research Buildings alterations, Harvard Medical School, Boston

1971   Parking Garage, New England Deaconess Hospital, Boston

Nauset Regional High School, Eastham, Massachusetts

Norwalk Senior High School, Connecticut

Expansion plan for Worcester Academy, Massachusetts

Anita Tuvin Schlechter Auditorium and Arts Center, Dickinson College, Carlisle, Pennsylvania

Jewish Community Center, Wilmington, Delaware

Central Veterinary Laboratory, Sotuba, Mali

Roxse Housing Development, Roxbury, Massachusetts

Khamis Mushayt Hospital, Saudi Arabia

Tabuk Hospital, Saudi Arabia

Basic Pediatric Research Laboratory, Children's Hospital Medical Center, Boston

Park Plaza, Boston (project)

Waterfront Parcel A-6 Commercial Development, Boston (project)

1972   Church Park Apartments, Boston

Museum of Comparative Zoology, Harvard University, Cambridge, Massachusetts

Power House Community Elementary School, Somerville, Massachusetts

Tufts/New England Medical Center, Boston

Electrical and Industrial Engineering Building, Virginia Polytechnic Institute, Blacksburg

Second House (dormitory), Massachusetts

Institute of Technology, Cambridge (project)

Development plan for Southern Illinois University, Edwardsville

Research Laboratories and Animal Quarters Building, Harvard Medical School, Boston

Nursing and Allied Health Sciences Building, University of Vermont Medical School, Burlington

1973   Weston Middle School, Connecticut

Women's Dormitory, Virginia Polytechnic Institute, Blacksburg

IBM Components Building, East Fishkill, New York

Development plan for the United States Military Academy, West Point, New York

Plan for development of tourism in Jaz Valley, Budva, Yugoslavia

Walden Square Housing Development, Cambridge, Massachusetts

Fenway Housing for the Elderly, Boston

Amathus Hotel, Limassol, Cyprus

El Tropicana Hotel, Panama City (project)

Proger Health Services Buildings, and Dental Health Sciences Buildings, Tufts/New England Medical Center, Boston

American Institute of Architects Headquarters, 1735 Pennsylvania Avenue N.W., Washington, D.C.

Ely Park Housing, Binghamton, New York

Health Services Complex, University of Minnesota, Minneapolis

Crown Center, Kansas City, Missouri

1974   Norwell High School, Massachusetts

No. 6 Dormitory alterations, Groton School, Massachusetts

South Station conversion to an Arena, Boston (project)

Maine Medical Center, Portland

Maineway Plaza, Portland (project)

Tozzer Library additions, Harvard University, Cambridge, Massachusetts

Temple Israel, Boston

Sterling and Francine Clark Art Institute, Williamstown, Massachusetts (with Pietro Belluschi)

Coram Library, Bates College, Lewiston, Maine

1974/
79   Development plan for the Capitol Center, Tallahassee, Florida

1975   Angelo Patri School (Bronx Intermediate School 137), 2225 Webster Avenue, Bronx, New York

Pre-fabricated school, Kuwait City

Wolcott House conversion, Milton Academy, Massachusetts

Audubon New Community Development, phase I, Amherst, New York

Echelon Office Building, New Jersey

Tourism development study for the Republic of the Philippines

Classroom and Office Buildings, Southern Illinois University, Edwardsville

Health and Physical Education Building, Virginia Polytechnic Institute, Blacksburg

Radiology and Surgery Department extensions, Children's Hospital Medical Center, Boston

Clinical Laboratory, New England Deaconess Hospital, Boston

National Shawmut Bank, 67 Milk Street, Boston

1976   Foster Gallery of Contemporary Art, Boston

Quincy Elementary School, Boston

Lincoln Park Community School, Somerville, Massachusetts

School of Nursing, New England Deaconess Hospital, Boston

Union Hospital, Lynn, Massachusetts

Johns-Manville Company World Headquarters, Jefferson County, Colorado

Charleston Savings Bank, Boston

Maine State Office Building, Augusta

Hotel Bernardin Resort Complex, Piran, Yugoslavia

Radiation Therapy Building, New England Deaconess Hospital, Boston

Nos. 1–4 Dormitory Units alterations, Groton School, Massachusetts

Forbes House conversion to Student Residences, Milton Academy, Massachusetts

1977 Seeley Mudd and Biochemical Research Buildings, Harvard Medical School, Boston

St. Mary's Hospital extensions and alterations, Kansas City, Missouri

Fiduciary Trust Building, Boston

Athletics Facilities extensions, Harvard University, Cambridge, Massachusetts

Visual Arts Instructional Facility, State University College of New York at Purchase

Building and Grounds Center, and Goodwin House, Milton Academy, Massachusetts

1978 Friends Community Center, Easton, Massachusetts

Porto Carras Tourist Resort, Sithonia, Greece

Sheraton Hotel additions, Kuwait City

Holyoke Revitalization Plan (Heritage State Park), Massachusetts (project)

Environmental impact study of Route 44, Plymouth, Massachusetts

Plan for Smith College, Northampton, Massachusetts

Kuwait Fund Office Building, Kuwait City

Arab Investment Company Headquarters, Riyadh, Saudi Arabia (competition project)

Academic Center, Boston University (project)

Tourist development study of Contadora Island, Panama

Pine Cay Resort Development, Turks and Caicos Islands, West Indies

Tennessee Valley Authority Headquarters, Chattanooga (project)

Sheraton Hotel, Baghdad

Jewish/Hillside Medical Center, New Hyde Park, New York

Amoskeag Bank, Manchester, New Hampshire

Institute of Public Administration, Riyadh, Saudi Arabia

Performing Arts Building, Virginia Commonwealth University, Richmond

Scott Gymnasium additions, Smith College, Northampton, Massachusetts

Physical Education Building, Bates College, Lewiston, Maine (project)

Athletics Facilities, United States Military Academy, West Point, New York (project)

Auditorium, University of Baghdad

Primary Care Center, University of Virginia, Charlottesville

1979 Tourist development study for the Republic of Ireland

Hotel Inter-Continental, Sharjah, United Arab Emirates

Petra Historical Site Development, Jordan

Jerash Historical Site Development, Jordan

Intensive Care Unit, Children's Hospital Medical Center, Boston

New York State Veterans Home, Oxford, New York

Corning YMCA Building conversion, New York

Government Ministerial Office Building, Bahrain

1980 IBM Building, Sterling Forest, New York

Meredith Corporation Headquarters, Des Moines, Iowa

Sheraton Hotel, Basra, Iraq

Abu Dhabi National Library and Cultural Center

1981 National Institute of Electricity and Electronics, Tlemcen, Algeria

School of Natural Resources, University of Vermont Medical School, Burlington

Theatre, Hotel, and Parking Development, Copley Plaza, Boston

St. Francis/St. George Hospital, Cincinnati

Western Pennsylvania Hospital, Pittsburgh

Publications:

By TAC: books—*A Design Manual for Parking Gar-*

The Architects Collaborative: Johns-Manville Company World Headquarters, Jefferson County, Colorado, 1976

ages by Sergio Brizzi and TAC Graphics, Cambridge, Massachusetts 1975; *Streets: A Program to Develop Awareness of the Street Environment,* Boston 1976; *Building Without Barriers for the Disabled* by Sarah P. Harkness and James N. Groom Jr., New York 1976.

On TAC: books—*The Architects Collaborative 1945–1965,* edited by Walter Gropius and others, Teufel, Switzerland, 1966; *The Architects Collaborative Inc.: TAC 1945–1972,* Barcelona 1972; articles —"The Architects Collaborative" in *Arts and Architecture* (Los Angeles), August 1946; "The Architects Collaborative" in *Baukunst und Werkform* (Nuremberg), vol. 10, 1957; "Genetrix: Personal Contributions to American Architecture" in *Architectural Review* (London), May 1957; "The Architects Collaborative" in *Architectural Record* (New York), April 1959; "Gropius e TAC: Lavori Recenti" by Clifford H. Morse and Mario Brunati in *Casabella* (Milan), September 1967; "Unity Within Diversity" by Jane Holtz Kay in *Building Design* (London), 18 October 1974; "The Architects Collaborative: Recent Works" in *Architecture + Urbanism* (Tokyo), July 1978; "Bold Discretions: The Work of TAC Interiors" by David Morton in *Progressive Architecture* (New York), September 1978.

*

"By synchronizing all individual efforts, the team can raise its integrated work to higher potentials than is represented by the sum of the work of just so many individuals." Walter Gropius, 1945

With this statement as a guiding principle, the eight founding partners of TAC recognized at the outset in 1945 that the complex problems facing the profession made the collaborative process essential. Not merely an assemblance of a team of specialists, collaboration is an attitude about how people should work together and toward what ends. The process goes on within an organizational structure that evolved and continues to evolve in response to new needs.

Essential to the structure is a weekly meeting of TAC's Board of Directors to decide business policy and to review work in progress. Policy decisions rely heavily upon recommendations from consultive and research committees, and the decisions that emerge from the weekly meetings are complemented through the office of the President.

Equally essential to TAC's approach is the firm's division into teams varying in number and composition—each working on a specific project. The intimate character of these semi-autonomous groups, headed by senior members of the firm, avoids the anonymity of persons and designs often associated with larger scale.

All projects receive review through the weekly meetings of principals and associates. In order to preserve the artistic integrity of the team, criticisms with respect to design are not binding, but the responsible give and take within these sessions clarifies and broadens the vision of the team members. Collaboration extends as well into work with other firms such as engineers and specialists in the fields of education, health, acoustics and transportation.

It was from a sense of urgency to solve problems on a larger scale that TAC grew from a firm of eight partners to an office of over 200. Had the group remained small, it would have been barred from participation in today's major problems of health, education, and urban design whose solutions require the creative resources of many people. Moreover, the system of teams makes it possible to continue giving problems of smaller scale the same degree of personal attention and involvement.

A mutual respect for each other's interests over the years has led to a wide variety of work, both in this country and abroad. This same breadth of interests will characterize TAC's future work as well. Through all changes, it is intended that the spirit that guides this practice be continuous and reflect

itself in a physical environment which advances the quality of human life.

—The Architects Collaborative

The original nucleus of The Architects Collaborative was Walter Gropius, then Chairman of the Department of Architecture at Harvard University, who believed in the beneficial and even mandatory nature of team effort in the architectural profession. The theoretical tone inherent in this advocacy of collaborative effort finds a direct correspondence in the polemics of Gesalt philosophy, which was pervasive in Western Europe during the 1920's and 1930's; it also relates directly to the teaching methods that were established at the Bauhaus, where Gropius was director from 1919 to 1928. Gropius's participation in the initial development of TAC was integral to the creation of its general and continuing aesthetic philosophy, that the totality of a design is greater than the simple sum of its individual parts or creators.

TAC has grown from the original eight partners to a company of more than 200 people. That growth was a response to the complexity, and size, of many modern design commissions. In turn, the company is now able to draw on the resources of what is now, in effect, a large, multi-disciplinary design organization. At the same time, and unlike some other firms, TAC has retained the original small team concept, making it possible for them to continue to give smaller scale works a high degree of responsible design input.

The idealism of this concept must, of course, become slightly modified in practice, for the economic demands in the operation of a large firm necessitate a very careful evaluation of smaller, less profitable ventures. And, as with all viable business structures in a capitalist society, TAC must make an effort to conduct a successful business venture and must often find it difficult to justify innovative theoretical directives at the risk of corporate profitability. The sheer size of the Collaborative, which gives the firm such a strong core of resources, may also tend to modify and compromise the conceptual and idealistic energy that is possible in more individual solutions.

There are, however, many positive gains. Within TAC, collaboration has aspired to be more than just an assemblance of a team of specialists; it involves an attitude about "group work" that is essentially creative, in that it continues to adapt itself, its methods and solutions, in response to new problems within a dynamic society. The team concept, too, involves both practicality and idealism: TAC teams are each different because each team is a response to a particular job, but each team is a reflection of TAC's attempt to preserve the individuality of persons and their work.

The concept of collaboration extends beyond the confines of the office to directly encompass all professions involved in a particular project. Certainly, the inclusion of engineers and construction-related groups is not unique to the architectural design process of this firm alone, but there is at TAC a professional ambition to be responsible to all peripheral and constituent design issues and to enhance the sensitivity, and skill, of designers by provoking constructive criticism from their associates.

The influence of Walter Gropius is obvious in TAC's approach to architecture as a search to appreciate the specific as it relates to the larger context and the individual as part of the collective, in a modern cultural environment the complexities of which necessitate collaboration and common method. Because of this philosophy and the success of their methods, and because they have denied an esoteric approach in their work in order to achieve a more general exposure, TAC has well designed a wide variety of buildings and dealt with a considerable range of problems. In particular, their interest in the social determinants of architecture has attracted many clients for housing, educational and social projects, not only in the Northeastern United States, but also, increasingly, throughout the world.

—S. Fiske Crowell, Jr.

THIRY, Paul.

American. Born in Nome, Alaska, 11 September 1904. Educated at the University of Washington, Seattle, under Carl Gould and Arthur Herrman, 1923–28 (Bobb and Gould Prize, 1926; Gladding McBean Prize, 1926; American Institute of Architects Medal, 1928; B.Arch. 1928; Ecole des Beaux-Arts, Fontainebleau, France, under Jacques Carlu and Victor Laloux, 1927, Dip.Arch. 1927. Married Mary Thomas in 1940; children: Paul Jr. and Pierre. In private architectural practice, Seattle, since 1929: Partner, Thirty and Shay, 1935–39; Partner, Jones, Bouillon, Thiry and Sylliaasen, involved in war work in Seattle, Renton, Port Orchard, Tacoma and Hanford, Washington, and in Alaska, 1940–45; returned to private practice, 1945–71; since 1971, President of Thiry Architects Inc. Member, 1952–61, and Chairman, 1953–54, City of Seattle Planning Commission; Member of the Executive Board, Puget Sound Regional Planning Council, 1954–57; Member, 1956–61, and Vice-Chairman, 1958–61, United States Department of the Interior Historic American Buildings Survey Board; Member, President's Council on Pennsylvania Avenue, Washington, D.C., 1962–64; Member, 1963–75, and Vice-Chairman, 1972–75, National Capital Planning Commission; Member, John F. Kennedy Memorial Library Committee, Cambridge, Massachusetts, 1964; Member, United States Postmaster-General's Council for Research and Engineering, 1968–70; Architect-in-Residence, American Academy in Rome, 1969. Exhibitions: *World's Fair,* Brussels, 1958; *World's Fair,* New York, 1964; *Salon d'Art Sacre,* Musée d'Art Moderne, Paris, 1954; *National Gold Medal Exhibition,* Architectural League of New York, 1956; *Architectura Actual de America,* Madrid, 1965; Annual Exhibition, National Academy of Design, New York, 1968; *New American Architecture,* New Delhi, 1973. Recipient: Paul Bunyon Award, Seattle Chamber of Commerce, 1949; Distinguished Citizen in the Arts Award, Seattle City Council, 1962; Citation for Community Design, American Institute of Architects, 1965; American Iron and Steel Institute Award, 1965; American Institute of Steel Construction Award, 1965; Herbert Adams Medal, 1974, and Henry Hering Medal, 1976, National Sculpture Society; Certificate of Appreciation, United States Army Corps of Engineers, 1977. Honorary Diploma, Colegio de Arquitectos, Santiago, Chile, 1965; D.F.A.: St. Martin's College, Olympia, Washington, 1970. Fellow, American Institute of Architects, 1951, and Chancellor of the College of Fellows, 1962–64; Member, Society of Architectural Historians (Director, 1967–70); Academician, National Academy of Design, 1967. Honorary Member, American Institute of Interior Designers, 1962, National Sculpture Society, 1963, and American Institute of Planners, 1975. Officier d'Académie, France, 1950. Address: Thiry Architects Inc., 800 Columbia Street, Seattle, Washington 98104, U.S.A.

Works:

1938 Catholic Archbishop's Chancery, Seattle
1940 A. S. Kerry House, Beaconfield, Washington
1940/
44 Federal Public Housing Authority Projects, including 6,000 dwellings and appurtenant community facilities, shopping centers, schools, etc., Port Orchard, Washington (with Jones, Bouillon and Sylliaasen)
1940/
48 Our Lady of the Lake Catholic Church and School, Seattle
1943/
44 United States Navy Advance Base Depot, Tacoma, Washington (with Jones, Bouillon and Sylliaasen)
1944 Du Pont de Nemours Town Plan, Hanford, Washington (with Jones, Bouillon and Sylliaasen)
1945 Ceramics Kiln Building, University of Washington, Seattle

Paul Thiry. Seattle Center Coliseum, 1964

1947 I. F. Laucks House, Orcas Island, Washington

1947/
67 Electrical Engineering Building, University of Washington, Seattle

1948 Botany Experimental Greenhouses, University of Washington, Seattle

1948/
50 Christ the King Catholic Church and School, Seattle

1949 Dairy Plant Plan, Washington State University, Pullman

1950 Museum of History and Industry, Seattle

1950/
58 Regents Hill Women's Residence, Washington State University, Pullman

1952 Charles and Emma Frye Museum, Seattle

1953 St. George Catholic Church and Friary, Seattle

1954 North East Branch Public Library, Seattle
Powerhouse and Visitors Center, Chief Joseph Dam, Bridgeport, Washington

1955 Northgate Public Elementary School, Seattle

1956 St. Pius X Convent, Parish Hall and School, Mountlake Terrace, Washington

1957 Washington State Library, Olympia

1957/
62 *Century 21 Exposition,* Seattle (principal architect)

1958 Francis H. Brownell Jr. House, Seattle
Cedar Park Public Elementary School, Seattle

Haggard Hall of Science, West Washington University, Bellingham

1959 State Capitol Campus Plan, Olympia, Washington

1960 Viking Center-Student Union Building, West Washington University, Billingham
First National Bank Pavilion, *Century 21 Exposition,* Seattle
Corregidor/Bataan Plan, Philippines (competition project)

1961 Presbyterian Church and Center, Mercer Island, Washington
State of Washington Theme Building, International Exhibit Building, and Entertainment Center Buildings, *Century 21 Exposition,* Seattle
United States Embassy, Santiago, Chile

1962 Kalman Brauner House, Seattle
Higginson Hall of Residence for Women, West Washington University, Bellingham
Nalley Theater and Exhibition Building, and Ford Motor Company Pavilion, *Century 21 Exposition,* Seattle
Seattle Center
Libby Dam-Lake Koocanusa Project Comprehensive Plan, Libby, Montana
Libby Dam, Powerhouse, Visitors Center and Facilities, Libby, Montana

1963 West Washington University Campus Plan, Bellingham
Seattle Center Comprehensive Plan

1964 Seattle Center Coliseum
Extension of the West Front of the United States Capitol, Washington, D.C. (as consultant)

1965 Vedanta Center Ramakrishna, Seattle
Seattle Center Contemporary Arts Museum
World War II Memorial, Utah Beach, France (as consultant)

1966 St. Demetrios Greek Orthodox Church and Center, Seattle

1966/
68 National Capital Transit Agency, Washington, D.C. (as consultant)

1966/
70 United States Department of Agriculture Building extension, Washington, D.C. (as consultant)

1967 St. Martin's College Campus Plan, Olympia, Washington
Border Patrol Station, Spokane, Washington
Border Patrol Station, Blaine, Washington

1967/
72 Riverfront development, Spokane, Washington (as consultant)

1968 Aubrey Watzek Campus Library, Lewis and Clark College, Portland, Oregon

1968/
74 Lewis and Clark College Campus Plan, Portland, Oregon

1969 Jewish Community Center, Mercer Island, Washington

Agnes Flanagan College Chapel, Lewis and
Clark College, Portland, Oregon
4th Infantry Division Monument, Sainte
Marie du Mont, France
Burton Hall Men's Residence, St. Martin's
College, Olympia, Washington
1970 Christ Episcopal Church, Tacoma, Washington
1971 Hartsfeld Residence Buildings, and Northwestern School of Law, Lewis and Clark
College, Portland, Oregon
Washington Mutual Savings Bank Headquarters, Seattle
1973 Biology-Psychology Center, Lewis and Clark
College, Portland, Oregon
1975 Enlisted Men's Club, Naval Air Station,
Whidbey Island, Washington

Publications:

By THIRY: books—*Churches and Temples,* with R.
Bennett and H. Kamphoefner, New York 1953; *Eskimo Artifacts,* with Mary Thiry, Seattle 1978; articles—"Architecture Today: A Symposium" in *Liturgical Arts* (New York), November 1950; "Call to
Arms" in *AIA Journal* (Washington, D.C.), December 1954; "Contemporary Church Architecture" in
AIA Journal (Washington, D.C.), October, 1955;
"Esthetics and Architecture" in *AIA Journal*
(Washington, D.C.), June 1956; "Progress Dilemma" in *AIA Journal* (Washington, D.C.), October 1956, and in *Pacific Architect and Builder* (Seattle), April 1957; "Total Design" in *AIA Journal*
(Washington, D.C.), December 1959; "On Design"
in *Pacific Architect and Builder* (Seattle), February
1961; "Unmemorial or in Memoriam" in *AIA Journal* (Washington, D.C.), March 1962; "Basic Needs
of Cities" in *Tacoma News Tribune* (Tacoma, Washington), March 1962; "Washington in Transition" in
AIA Journal (Washington, D.C.), January 1963;
"There Are Many Ways to Create a Desert" in *Architectural Record* (New York), May 1965; "Northwest Today" in *Seattle Post Intelligencer,* December 1965; "Our Cities Today: Chaos or Challenge?" in
AIA Journal (Washington, D.C.), January 1966;
"Water and the Environment" and "Architectural
Treatment of Dams" in *Arts and Architecture* (Los
Angeles), July 1967; "Libby Dam: An Engineer
Talks Esthetics" in *AIA Journal* (Washington,
D.C.), November 1968; "Planning of Washington as
a Capital" in *AIA Journal* (Washington, D.C.),
April 1974; "Washington, D.C., The Capital" in the
Washington Post, May 1974.

On THIRY: books—*Tomorrow's House* by Nelson
and Wright, New York 1945; *Contemporary Church
Art* by Anton Heinze, New York 1956; *Modern
Church Architecture* by Christ-Janer and Foley,
New York 1962; *Architecture in America* by G. E.
Kidder Smith, New York 1976; articles—"The
Work of Paul Thiry" in *Nuestra Arquitectura*
(Buenos Aires), July 1949; articles in *Sinkentiku*
(Tokyo), April 1956 and May 1956; "Profile III:
Paul Thiry" by Robert E. Koehler in *Pacific Architect and Builder* (Seattle), February 1961; "Names:
Paul Thiry FAIA" in *Architecture and Engineering
News* (New York), November 1961; article in *Vitrum* (Milan), November 1963; "West Coast Architects IV: Paul Thiry" by Esther McCoy in *Arts
and Architecture* (Los Angeles), January 1965;
"Paul Thiry, Architect" by Robert Wilmsen in *Symposia* (Portland, Oregon), January 1965; "Una
Capanna Sol Fiume" in *Abitare* (Milan), October
1965; "Seattle Center Coliseum" in *Vitrum* (Milan),
October 1967; "Libby Dam Project" by Andrea O.
Dean in *AIA Journal* (Washington, D.C.), April
1977.

*

For the first time in the history of man we appear to
be faced with an overwhelming urge to build everyplace and anywhere. This urge carries us far beyond
the recognition of existing values or the correctness
of what we do. We are overrun by those obsessed
with the doctrine of progress, who find no place or
thing immune from their immature judgement and
unrestrained activities. Therefore, in a more practical and realistic way, it behooves us to study carefully the requirements of our day. We should do this
with reference to the past and with consideration for
the future. We must know one place is not the same
as another. We need to know the difference between
the wilderness, the rural, and the urban.

ARCHITECTURE
If there is to be physical and mental betterment on
earth it most assuredly rests with the world of architecture to give direction and to take steps to lead the
way. The world of architecture is a world of building
and of planning. It is the privilege of the architect to
provide man with environment. It is singularly his
duty to look at situations objectively . . . because
architecture is the direct result of man's occupation
of space. It would seem significant that architecture
is of prime importance to the life of man and that it
is his inseparable companion, for surely without it,
he reverts to the primitive state. We are faced with
a new pace in architecture, one which does not reconcile itself with the past. It follows no historic pattern nor does it find compatibility in form or appearance with structures of our traditional inheritance.
Inter-mixtures must be viewed with concern.

Architecture can no longer be merely plan and
facade. It is necessary to go beyond, into the wide
ranges of cause and effect of action and reaction, and
into the reasons for force . . . more particularly, into
counter-force. Today we need an architecture that is
in itself counter-force, that extends on a vast scale to
a comprehension of environment, both natural and
man-made. As the pace quickens, the environmental
equations change and methods of realization change
with them. This change cannot be regarded as a
salvation for old patterns. Opposed philosophies
must be reconciled. Where the differences involve
structure, a choice must be made.

ARCHITECTURE: A CONTINUING PROCESS
Our greatness will be measured in how we meet the
progress dilemma—the problem of preservation and
exploitation—and how we cope with the apathetic
and irresistible forces of destruction, which,
strangely enough, move through construction. Others may toy with interplanetary travel and satellite
sub-stations in the stratosphere, but for the present
let us make this a world of beauty and of order.
Where we detract from nature let us add back two
fold with human quality. Before us is the world as it
is and before us is the world as it should be. Ours is
the choice. To labor the day or to envision the morrow.

—Paul Thiry

*

The name of Paul Thiry is synonymous with Pacific
Northwest architecture, although his influence in the
field of design is far more than a regional matter.
This "influence," for the most part, has never really
received the recognition it deserves from his peers.

Since he began his practice in Seattle, 50 years ago,
Thiry has matched his contributions to design with
those to his profession, to his community and to his
country. The latter are particularly noteworthy, for
he was a Presidential appointee to the National Capital Planning Commission for a number of years, always doing his homework, flying from coast to coast
for just about every meeting. A scholar and an historian, he has assembled what is probably one of the
best private collections on the history of the nation's
capital.

Often a champion of unpopular—and generally
controversial—causes, Thiry has refused to remain
silent on affairs of state that affected the environment, man-made or otherwise, whether they be on
the home front in Seattle, where he has lived and
practiced all his adult life, or on the West Front of
the U. S. Capitol itself. More than one delegate to the
national convention of the American Institute of Architects in 1966 remembers when he came to loggerheads with the establishment in what was virtually
a one-man show, convincing the members on the
floor to table a motion regarding the restoration of
the West Front wall.

Thiry, to be sure, has mellowed over the years, but
the truth of the matter is that while he often appeared to be a voice crying in the wilderness, he was
found later to be speaking about the most feasible
solution to the issue at hand.

Thiry is as equally adroit as a writer as he is a
speaker—and his interests are legion.

As for his architecture in general, Thiry has always maintained this basic concern: "buildings
should be good neighbors." And so his have been—
and still are. His Library for the Washington State
Capitol in Olympia, while respecting the traditional
forms already there, was expressed in a contemporary medium. It would be an overstatement to say
that Thiry is truly innovative, yet his Christ the King
Church, Seattle, in 1948, was one of the first to place
the congregation around the altar in a semicircle.

As principal architect for the *Century 21 Exposition* in Seattle in 1962, Thiry employed the same
common sense approach that has been the trademark of his design career. What he wrote before the
fair opened in 1962 was indeed to come true: "Century 21 is designed not only for the excitement of the
moment, but many of its structures and facilities are
planned as a permanent adjunct to a projected Seattle Center of lasting significance.... Seattle World's
Fair will be a phoenix among fairs." Anyone who
has visited the site—to attend an opera, a ballet, or
a sporting event in Thiry's own Coliseum, which he
designed as the theme structure—will attest that
once again the architect was a prophet.

An evaluation of Thiry's work would be incomplete without a reference to Libby Dam in Montana,
which one critic called "a powerful, respected work
of architecture." For any Army Corps of Engineers
project to have an architect involved from start to
finish is almost inconceivable, and few but Thiry
would have seen it through. But in visiting dams
through the U.S.A., he found that the construction
of most of them had disfigured natural surroundings
and that many contained visually discordant and
disconcerting architectural elements.

All of this echoes Thiry's philosophy when he
wrote: "A building's form and relationship to its
neighbors not only affects the visual aspects of the
whole, but the ensemble reflects on the quality of the
individual unit. Too often a nonconformance not
only detracts from itself but also disfigures the total
scene."

Never let it be said that Paul Thiry has been a
nonconformist who detracted from or disfigured the
scene upon which he used his disciplined talents.

—Robert E. Koehler

THOM, Ron(ald James).
Canadian. Born in Penticton, British Columbia, 15
May 1923. Educated at the Vancouver School of
Art, 1941–43, 1944–47, Dip.Art 1947. Served as a
navigator in the Canadian Air Force, 1943–44. Married Molly Golby in 1963; children: Emma, Adam,
and, from previous marriage, Robin, Sidney, Aaron
and Bronwen. Joined Thompson, Berwick, Pratt and
Partners, Vancouver, as an apprentice, 1947: Partner, 1958–63. Since 1963, Principal, Thom Partnership, Toronto. Director, Toronto Cultural Advisory
Corporation, since 1974. Exhibitions: Royal Canadian Academy of Arts Travelling Exhibition, 1971;
National Gallery of Canada, Ottawa, 1973; Institute
for Theatre Technology Exhibition, Anaheim, California, 1975; Toronto City Hall, 1976; *Spectrum*

Ron Thom: Champlain College, Trent University, Peterborough, Ontario, 1971

Canada, Royal Canadian Academy of Arts Travelling Exhibition, 1976; University of Toronto School of Architecture, 1979; *Transformations in Modern Architecture,* Museum of Modern Art, New York, 1979. Collection: University of Calgary Archives, Alberta. Recipient: First Prize, Massey College Competition, Toronto, 1963; Massey Medal, 1963; Citations of Excellence (4), International College and University Conference and Exposition, Atlantic City, New Jersey, 1970; Design Award, Canadian Institute of Architects, Toronto Chapter, 1970; Merit Award, Canadian National Design Council, 1971; Canadian Housing Design Council Award, 1971; First Prize, for North America, Aluminum Building Products Design Competition, 1973; Award of Excellence, *Canadian Architect Yearbook,* 1974; Award of Merit, Ontario Masons' Relations Council Architectural Awards Programme, 1975; Award of Merit, Low Energy Building Design Awards, Public Works Office of Canada, 1979. LL.D.: Trent University, Peterborough, Ontario, 1971; D.Eng.: Nova Scotia Technical College, Halifax, 1973. Associate, 1971, and Member, 1973, Royal Canadian Academy of Arts; Fellow, Royal Architectural Institute of Canada, 1973. Address: The Thom Partnership, 47 Colborne Street, Suite 401, Toronto, Ontario M5E 1E3, Canada.

Works:

1963 Massey College, University of Toronto
1963/
  71 Trent University, Peterborough, Ontario (temporary buildings: Catherine Parr College and Rubidge Hall, 1963–64; Master Plan, 1964; Champlain College, Lady Eaton College, Thomas J. Bata Library, Chemistry Building, and Reginald Faryon Bridge, 1964–71)

1967 Sir Sandford Fleming College, master plan and phase I, Peterborough and Lindsay Campuses, Ontario
Polymer Pavilion, *Expo '67,* Montreal
Pottow House, Toronto
Narod House, Vancouver
Sandwell House, Caledon, Ontario
Stewart House, Caledon, Ontario
1968 College Education Centre, North Bay, Ontario
Social Science Building, Queen's University, Kingston, Ontario
Master plan for the Civic Square, Hamilton, Ontario
1970 Shaw Festival Theatre, Niagara-on-the-Lake, Ontario
Sir Sandford Fleming College, phase II, Peterborough, Ontario
Frum House, Oxbow Avenue, Toronto
1971 Fraser House, Toronto
1972 Price Hotel, Don Mills, Ontario
Metropolitan Toronto Zoo, Scarborough, Ontario (with Clifford and Lawrie, and Crang and Boake)
1973 Home for the Aged, Picton, Ontario
The Thom Partnership Offices, 47 Colborne Street, Toronto
Ridpath's Store, Toronto
Goh House, King City, Ontario
Horne House, Caledon, Ontario
1974 Oakville Theatre, Oakville, Ontario
Sir Sandford Fleming College, phase II, Lindsay, Ontario
1976 Marathon Office Campus, Toronto
Mark Erin Homes, Mississauga, Ontario
Bayview-Finch Townhouses, Toronto
Market Square, Toronto
Bonnycastle House, Calgary, Alberta
1977 Confederation Square, Toronto (project)

Lester Pearson College of the Pacific, Pedder Bay, Vancouver (with Barry Downs)
Dodek Cottage, Roberts Creek, British Columbia
Crematorium, Montreal
Silverspring Apartments, Toronto
Summit Golf Club, Aurora, Ontario
Women's Cultural Centre, Toronto
Troumassee Hotel, St. Lucia, West Indies
1978 Transport Canada Training Institute, Cornwall, Ontario
Ryerson Architecture Building, Toronto
Sir Sandford Fleming College, phase III, Peterborough, Ontario
Convention Centre, Kitchener, Ontario
Creditview Housing, Mississauga, Ontario
1979 Chateau Laurier Hotel renovations, Ottawa
Burlington Hotel and Condominiums, Ontario
Deerfoot Business Centre, Calgary

Publications:

By THOM: book—*Exploring Toronto,* with others, Toronto 1972, 1973, 1974; articles—"Art Centre: A Critical Analysis" in *Canadian Architect* (Toronto), July 1963; "Toronto City Hall: A Critique" in *Canadian Architect* (Toronto), October 1965; "The Many-Headed Client" in *Canadian Architect* (Toronto), September 1966; "Voice" in *Canadian Architect* (Toronto), July 1970; "Comment: Freedom at a Price" in *Canadian Architect* (Toronto), August 1973; "Critique: George Brown College of Applied Arts and Technology, Toronto" in *Canadian Architect* (Toronto), March 1974.

On THOM: articles—"Architect Ron Thom Shapes

a Mantle of Privacy for a Vigorous House" in *House Beautiful* (New York), September 1969; "Thomas J. Bata Library, Trent University" in *Canadian Architect* (Toronto), August 1971; "Progress Report: Metro Zoo, Toronto" in *Canadian Architect* (Toronto), October 1974; "New Theatres on the Niagara River" by Tony Coutade in *Theatre Design and Technology* (New York), Fall 1975; "Stahl" in *Baumeister* (Munich), April 1977; article in *Process: Architecture* (Tokyo/Pittsburgh), May 1978; "The Thom Partnership" in *Canadian Interiors* (Toronto), June 1979.

I see architecture as expression inevitably reflecting time, place, cultural mores and attitudes. This implies both conscious and unconscious expression, and it applies to good and bad architecture alike. Consequently it has always been fairly easy to place very accurate dates on buildings and to be reasonably accurate about their roots.

This suggests that architects should consider architecture as a vehicle of expression that should reflect its raison d'etre.

In order to achieve this, the architect must be as aware as possible of any and all needs that the specific building is to serve. He must be prepared to listen. He must not "create" in his own vain vacuum and expect life to respond by adapting, even though life is forever showing itself capable of doing this. In most cases there need not be unresolvable conflicts between the priorities of the architect and those of users.

As cities increase in size and complexity there becomes a much greater overlapping of the various functions of living, and with that develops a growing interdependence of all the parts. Architects therefore must become increasingly aware of this fact of life, and become more willing than they have been in the past to be affected by conditions surrounding and beyond their immediate work.

Less and less does architecture exist in splendid isolation. Architecture must now recognize the need to assist the cohesiveness of the social fabric, and not be a contributor to mass chaos. To achieve this goal, a greater involvement with other disciplines and the willingness to accept their widsoms will be required of architects in the future than has been expected of them in the past. And this of course demands a change of attitude on the part of architectural educators.

There will also have to be changes in the area of public education as society more and more feels the effects of interdependence and as it becomes more and more a participatory society.

The media in all its forms must become much less oblivious to such a basic and all pervasive topic of life. Even though as a society we are largely visually illiterate, we are not immune to the effects of our created environment.

For all this, it must be said that architecture at its best still has the inherent power to celebrate the human functions it accommodates and that there is nothing to suggest that the new constraints that may come should impede the ability of architecture to extend and enrich life in our society.

—Ron Thom

Integrity is what characterises Ron Thom's work, not simply integrity of overall design but integrity to site and to extant buildings. Even such large projects as Trent University reflect a care for siting and topography on the one hand that is manifested on the other by a meticulous care for all the details of design work down to the cutlery and ashtrays. It is conventional to compare his work to that of Frank Lloyd Wright, but his care for detail has more in common with the work of Arne Jacobsen—as in Jacobsen's St. Catherine's in Oxford. Thom is less dogmatic than Wright; he has more respect for local materials and the quality of the life to be lived within his buildings. Massey College is not only (rightly) turned inward from a noisy intersection around a quiet and decep-

tively arranged quadrangle, but it is also broken up into many "houses," both to preserve intimacy and to reduce noise. Not all of the details of its construction are ideal; residents complain about the inflexibility of the fixtures, but fifteen years after its construction it shows the evidence of contented life—in its public rooms especially—that would be the envy of many other academic architects.

The use of brick with broken, pierced or recessed walls at Massey is characteristic of Thom's conviction that the architect is both activist and observer. He must, Thom believes, "be willing to make adjustments in his design until the architecture becomes a full expression of the life of which it is a part." Plainly, academic work, such as Massey, Trent, the two Sir Sandford Fleming Colleges and the new Pearson College, is congenial to these aims. Its success is attested to by a student at Trent: "One is never conscious of its being architecture. The place works and is comfortable."

Thom's continuing affection for brick and cedar in such varied projects as the Fraser House, the Toronto Zoo, and the Shaw Festival Theatre is evidence of his West Coast roots, but it is of a piece with his concern for detail and site. And in the midst of the blank horror of much that is being built in Ontario, it is a welcome alternative. At Trent it is often overlooked that Thom not only incorporated local stone into the faceted walls of his building but also adapted old houses in the town with a genius and respect that is almost unheard of amongst contemporary renovators. And it is the same genius that he has brought to one of his recent projects, the proposed Confederation Square in Toronto, where a Victorian office building is not only to be preserved but also restored and a new building attached to it, picking up its lines and reticulation.

—D.D.C. Chambers

THOMPSON, Benjamin.

American. Born in St. Paul, Minnesota, 3 July 1918. Educated at Yale University, New Haven, Connecticut, 1937–41, B.F.A. 1941. Served as a Lieutenant in the United States Navy, 1942–45. Married Mary Okes in 1942 (divorced, 1967); children: Deborah, Anthony, Marina, Nicholas and Benjamin Jr.; married Jean Fiske McCullough in 1969. Founder-Partner, TAC: The Architects Collaborative, Cambridge, Massachusetts, 1946–65; Founder and Chairman of the Board, Design Research International Inc., Cambridge, 1953–70. Since 1966, President, Benjamin Thompson and Associates, Cambridge. Chairman, Department of Architecture, Harvard University, Cambridge, 1963–68. Recipient: Honor Award, 1966, 1970, 1972, and First Honor Award, 1974, American Institute of Architects, New England; State Arts Award, Maine, 1967; Centennial Award, Wayne State University, Detroit, 1967; Library Buildings Award, AIA/American Library Association, 1968, 1974; Honor Award, national AIA, 1968, 1971, 1978; Harleston Parker Award, 1971, 1973, 1977, Neighborhood Housing Award, 1974, and Honor Award, 1977, Boston Society of Architects; President's Medal of Honor, Kirkland College, Clinton, New York, 1972; Award of Excellence, AIA, Western Massachusetts, 1974; Case Studies Award, *Urban Design*, 1977; Bartlett Award, AIA/President's Committee on Employment of the Handicapped, 1978; International Design Award, American Society of Interior Designers, 1978; Special Award, American Society of Landscape Architects, 1978. Address: Benjamin Thompson and Associates, One Story Street, Cambridge, Massachusetts 02138, U.S.A.

Works:

With TAC—

1953 Burke House, Center Harbour, New York
1958 Boylston Hall, Harvard University, Cambridge, Massachusetts
1959 Hollis Hall, Harvard University, Cambridge, Massachusetts
    Academic Quadrangle, Brandeis University, Waltham, Massachusetts
1959/
62 Sylvia Pratt Kemper Chapel, Science Building, Arts and Communications Center, and Oliver Wendell Holmes Library, Phillips Academy, Andover, Massachusetts
1960 Chase Manhattan Bank, Great Neck, Long Island, New York
    Dormitories, Brandeis University, Waltham, Massachusetts
1964 North Bennington Fire House, Vermont
1965 Abbott Academy, Andover, Massachusetts (planning only)
1966 Greylock Residential Houses, Williams College, Williamstown, Massachusetts

With Benjamin Thompson and Associates—

1966 Nathan Hale Dormitory, Phillips Academy, Andover, Massachusetts
    Master plan for the new campus of Kirkland College, Clinton, New York
    Heller Buildings, Brandeis University, Waltham, Massachusetts
1967 Rabb Graduate Center and Lown Building, Brandeis University, Waltham, Massachusetts
    Dormitories and Fraternity Building, Colby College, Waterville, Maine
    Mount Anthony Union High School, Bennington, Vermont
1968 Bronfman Science Center, Williams College, Williamstown, Massachusetts
    Music Building and Buckley Recital Hall, Amherst College, Massachusetts
1969 Design Research Project, Cambridge, Massachusetts
1970 Faculty Office Building and Classroom/Administration Building, Harvard Law School, Cambridge, Massachusetts
    Coolidge Bank and Trust Building, Watertown, Massachusetts
1971 New Co-Educational Facility (school conversion), St. Paul Academy, Minnesota
    Plumley Village East Housing Community, Worcester, Massachusetts
1972 J. P. Holland School, Dorcester, Massachusetts
    Berkshire Community College, Pittsfield, Massachusetts
    Gutman Library and Research Center, Harvard University, Cambridge, Massachusetts
    Facilities and dormitories, Kirkland College, Clinton, New York
1973 Housing program for the elderly, Cambridge, Massachusetts
1975 Cape Cod Bank and Trust Building, Hyannis, Massachusetts
1976 Soldiers Field Road Housing, Harvard University, Boston
1977 Alaska State Capital Competition Plan, Willow, Alaska (with Jonathan Barnett and M. Paul Friedberg)
1977/
78 St. Anthony Main (restoration of riverfront district), Minneapolis
    Intercontinental Hotel Complex, Abu Dhabi, United Arab Emirates
1978 Faneuil Hall Marketplace, Boston
1979 Intercontinental Hotel Complex, Al Ain, United Arab Emirates
    Intercontinental Hotel Complex, Cairo, Egypt

Benjamin Thompson: Faneuil Hall Marketplace, Boston, 1978

Publications:

By THOMPSON: articles—in *The New Yorker,* 28 December 1963; "The Spirit of Sanity" in *Connection: Visual Arts at Harvard* (Cambridge, Massachusetts), February 1964; in *Interiors* (New York), June 1964; "Proposal for a Case Method System in Architectural Education" in *Indian Builder Annual* (New Delhi), 1965; "Questions Posed in the Harvard Yard" in *AIA Journal* (Washington, D.C.), April 1965; in *Interiors* (New York), July 1965; "An Interview with Benjamin Thompson" in *Interiors* (New York), November 1965; "An Architect Views His Environment" in *Architectural Record* (New York), January 1966; "Modern Not Monotonous—Let's Build a New Boston for the People" in the *Boston Globe,* 8 May 1966; "Design Research Story" in *Mobilia* (Cambridge, Massachusetts), September 1966; "Boston Is a Growing Thing" in the *Boston Globe,* 26 March 1967; "The World Around Us—Towards an Architecture of Joy and Human Sensibility" in *Architectural Record* (New York), September 1967; "Visual Squalor and Social Disorder—A New Vision of the City of Man" in *Architectural Record* (New York), April 1969.

When we come down from the clouds a meaningful architecture will be created in our time. When we come to grips with our present, there is a chance we will influence the future. Isolation is a terrible state, and architecture of the mountain top has no relevance. Buildings communicate when they connect to the meaningful flow of our own age. Architecture should reflect man's hope and faith, interpret life and transmit joy. The very act of building is a symbolic act of confidence.

We have only begun to recognize architecture's real importance and function in modern life. The space between buildings and the space within buildings may be more important than the photographable facades that preoccupy designers and critics alike. While many professionals continue to design for the static vision of the camera, others are beginning to realize that the dynamics of life and people, the nature of the whole human habitat, is our task. After all, we spend our lives in and around buildings, and, more than we know, our lives are shaped by their qualities—for better or worse.

—Benjamin Thompson

In part, it must come from the association with Gropius, but mostly the moral tone conveyed by Benjamin Thompson's architecture is a reflection of the character of the man. A cultural conservative, Thompson has strong faith in the power of architecture. In his writings, he bemoans the collapse of standards and the continual worsening of the American environment. He is a die-hard modernist in principle as well as style.

He was one of the TAC partners in charge of the Harvard Graduate Center built in Cambridge, Massachusetts in 1949, still the most convincing of all the Gropius work in America. What in the 1940's and 50's was the most advanced of post-war Modernism in America later developed in the 60's and 70's with such calm and evolutionary consistency that its remarkable quality became lost in its unremarkable form. Thompson separated from the Collaborative in 1966, but his work remained faithful to its cause. Until the mid 70's only two problems caused him to stretch his architecture principles into creating works of remarkable quality. The first was a literal showcase for a product design and marketing enterprise, "Design Research," founded by Thompson in 1953, reflecting a concern, as Gropius and Behrens had been before him, not only with producing well designed buildings for working in but also with offering well designed products to serve them. (Thompson remained Chairman of the company until 1970.) The second was the brilliant and theatrical redevelopment of the Faneuil Hall Marketplace, Boston, which revealed a too long hidden sensual and indulgent side to Thompson's nature.

Perhaps, because much of it is hidden in the New England woods, Thompson's twenty years of building mainly for the schools and colleges of the Northeast is not well known. All this work has the same broad characteristics—elegant and ambiguous form, robust structural expression. Though as objects rather anonymous, they are given a sense of place through siting and choice of materials. The heightened emotional range in the Faneuil Hall Marketplace may be there because, unlike much of Thompson's work, the problem demanded it, or perhaps we are seeing a late flowering of his architecture. Whatever the reason, it is most welcome.

The strength and stability of Thompson's work, its utility and essential humanism, seems so much more wholesome and trustworthy than much of the idiosyncratic speculation that has followed the proclamation of post-modernism. One's pleasure in the inventiveness of the present has to do with Modernism's having become so dull: it lost it freshness, and Thompson's architecture even into the 1970's was no exception. Perhaps the failure of Modernism in American was not a failure of principle but a failure to explore the bounds of principle—to care so much for the environment and to do so little to extend the richness of experience that it can offer. Jefferson, Thompson's choice of Architect for a New America, would not have been so timid, but, perhaps, the flaw is inherited. If only Aalto had come instead of Gropius.

—Alan Balfour

TIGERMAN, Stanley.
American. Born in Chicago, Illinois, 20 September 1930. Educated at Senn High School, Chicago, 1944–48; Massachusetts Institute of Technology, Cambridge, 1948–49; Institute of Design, Chicago, 1949–50; Yale University School of Architecture, New Haven, Connecticut, 1959–61 (Alpha Rho Chi Medal, 1961), B.Arch. 1960, M.Arch. 1961. Served as a Petty Officer Second Class in the United States Navy, 1950–54. Married Judith Richards in 1956; JoAnn Kinzelberg in 1968; children: Judson and Tracy. Architectural Draftsman with George Fred Keck, Chicago, 1949–50, T. David Fitz-Gibbon, Norfolk, Virginia, 1952–54, A. J. Del Bianco, Chicago, 1954–56, and with Milton M. Schwartz, Chicago, 1956–57; Designer, Skidmore, Owings and Merrill, Chicago, 1957–59; Architectural Draftsman with Paul M. Rudolph, New Haven, Connecticut, 1959–61; Chief of Design, with Harry M. Weese, Chicago, 1961–62; Partner, with Norman Koglin, Tigerman and Koglin, Chicago, 1962–64. Since 1964, Principal of Stanley Tigerman and Associates Ltd., Chicago. Professor of Architecture, University of Illinois at Chicago Circle, 1965–71. Visiting Critic/Lecturer: Washington University, St. Louis, 1962–64; University of Houston, Texas, 1962–64, 1976, 1977; Northwestern University, Evanston, Illinois, 1962–64; Cornell University, Ithaca, New York, 1964, 1977; Cardiff College of Art, Wales, 1965; Cooper Union, New York, 1966–71; University of Notre Dame, Indiana, 1966–71; University of California, Berkeley, 1966, 1977; Institute for Architecture and Urban Studies, New York, 1975; Smithsonian Institution, Washington, D.C., 1975, 1976; Columbia University, New York, 1976; Virginia Polytechnic Institute, Blacksburg, 1976; Harvard University, Cambridge, Massachusetts, 1976; University of Detroit, 1976; Roosevelt University, Chicago, 1976; University of Kansas, Lawrence, 1976; University of Utah, Salt Lake City, 1977; University of Maryland, Baltimore, 1977; Miami University, Oxford, Ohio, 1977; Rhode Island School of Design, Providence, 1977; University of Illinois, Urbana, 1977; University of Arkansas, Fayetteville, 1977; Society of Fine Arts, Quincy, Illinois, 1977. Chairman, American Institute of Architects Institute Honors Jury, 1977. American Correspondent of *L'Architecture d'Aujourd'hui,* Paris, since 1966. Member, Chicago Seven. Exhibitions: Norfolk Art Museum, Virginia, 1954; Art Institute of Chicago, 1954, 1964, 1965, 1973, 1977; Washington University, St. Louis, 1962; B. C. Holland Gallery, Chicago, 1962; Walker Art Center, Minneapolis, 1965; Art Center, Midland, Michigan, 1965; Northwestern University, 1966; Northern Illinois University, DeKalb, 1966; Roosevelt University, 1966; Evanston Art Center, 1969; Kansas City Art Research Center, 1969; Arts Association, Springfield, Illinois, 1970; University of Chicago, 1975; Cooper Union, New York, 1976; *Seven Chicago Architects,* Richard Gray Gallery, Chicago, 1976; Harvard University, 1976; Museum

of Contemporary Art, Chicago, 1976; *Biennale,* Venice, 1976; University of Houston, 1976, 1977; University of California, Berkeley, 1976, 1977; *Bienal,* Sao Paulo, 1976; Drawing Center, New York, 1977; University of California at Los Angeles, 1977. Also a painter and sculptor: exhibitions at various museums and universities. Recipient: Award of Excellence for Design, *Architectural Record,* New York, 1970; Award of Merit, American Institute of Architects, 1970; Distinguished Building Award, AIA, Chicago Chapter, 1971, 1973 (twice); 1975 (twice), 1977 (twice); Gold Medal Award for Excellence in Masonry, Metropolitan Chicago Masonry Council, 1974; Award of Merit, AIA/*House and Home* and *American Home,* 1974; Annual Award, for continued excellence of design, Illinois AIA, 1976; Award of Merit, Chicago Lighting Institute, 1976; Distinguished Award, Illinois State Council AIA, 1977. Address: Stanley Tigerman and Associates Ltd., 233 North Michigan Avenue, Chicago, Illinois 60601, U.S.A.

Works:

1962/
64 Pickwick Village Townhouses, Chicago
Habenicht House, Elgin, Illinois
1963 O'Grady House, Park Ridge, Illinois (project)
1963/
64 Chaplan House, Park Forest, Illinois
1963/
69 Woodlawn Gardens Low-Rise Housing, Chicago
1966 Kaplan House remodelling, Chicago
Barovsky and Ehrlich Offices, Chicago
Loyola Housing Project, Chicago
1966/
68 Bower's House, Wilmette, Illinois
1966/
69 Nun's Island Low-Rise Housing, Montreal
1966/
76 Five polytechnics in Bangladesh
1968 Chicago Dwelling Association Housing
Inner city apartment remodelling, Chicago
1969 Texas prototype gas station (project)
1969/
74 St. Benedict's Abbey Church and Print Shop remodelling, Benet Lake, Wisconsin
1970 Atlantis Resort Complex, Grand Bahamas (project)
Housing for indigents, Chicago (project)
Park Place Apartments, Chicago

1970/
71 Brodley House, Chicago
1970/
73 Vollen Barn, Burlington, Wisconsin
1972 Instant Football (megastructure project)
Board of Education feasibility study, State of Illinois (project)
Art Museum, Northern Illinois University, DeKalb (project)
1972/
73 Kelmer Arlington Industrial Building, Arlington Heights, Illinois
Hot Dog House, Harvard, Illinois
Frog Hollow, Berrien Springs, Michigan
1973 Metal and Glass House, Glencoe, Illinois
1973/
74 Townhouse, Tucson, Arizona (project)
1974 Richard Gray Gallery, Chicago
Bottega Glascia, Chicago
House and Garden prototype kitchen
Loop College, Chicago (project)
Marks House, Hollywood, California (project)
1974/
78 Piper's Alley Commercial Mall, Old Town, Chicago
Prairie Brook Apartments, Palatine, Illinois
Illinois Regional Library for the Blind and Physically Handicapped, Chicago
1975/
77 Arby's Restaurant, Chicago
Daisy House, Porter, Indiana
1976 Stone-Levin Apartment, Chicago
St. John's Catholic Cathedral, Champaign-Urbana, Illinois (project)
Tackbary House, Barrington, Illinois (project)
Zipper Townhouses (project)
1976/
77 Walner Law Office, Chicago
1976/
78 "Animal Crackers" (Blender House), Highland Park, Illinois
Ukrainian Institute of Modern Art, Chicago
1976/
80 National Archives Center of the Baha'i's of the United States, Wilmette, Illinois
Labadie House, Oakbrook, Illinois (project)
1977/
79 "Tigerman Takes a Bite out of Keck": Walner House addition, Highland Park, Illinois
Kastel House, Chicago

Stanley Tigerman: Illinois Regional Library for the Blind and Physically Handicapped, Chicago, 1978

Anti-Cruelty Society Building, Chicago 1977/
80 Sam's Cut-Rate Liquors Building, Chicago
1978 "A Kosher Kitchen (for a Suburban Jewish American Princess)": Desser House addition, Wilmette, Illinois (project)
"Dante's Bathroom" (project)

Publications:

By TIGERMAN: article—introduction to *Chicago Architects* by Stuart Cohen, Chicago 1976.

On TIGERMAN: books—*Chicago on Foot* by Ira J. Bach, Chicago 1969, 3rd edition 1977; *New Directions in American Architecture* by Robert A. M. Stern, New York 1969; *Urban Structures for the Future* by Justus Dahinden, New York 1972; *Chicago 1930–1970* by Carl Condit, Chicago 1974; *Art: Search and Self-Discovery* by James A. Schinneller, Worcester, Massachusetts 1975; *Housing* by John Macsai and others, New York 1976; *Unbuilt America* by Allison Sky and Michelle Stone, New York 1976; *Megastructure* by Reyner Banham, New York 1976; *Seven Chicago Architects,* catalog of the exhibition at the Richard Gray Gallery, Chicago 1976; articles—"The Nation's Largest Low-Rise Project" in *Architectural Forum* (New York), May 1971; "Aéroport," special issue of *L'Architecture d'Aujourd'hui* (Paris), June/July 1971; "Young Architects in the United States" by Esther McCoy in *Zodiac* (Milan), no. 13, 1973; "Stanley Tigerman in Bangladesh" by M. W. Newman in *Inland Architect* (Chicago), February 1973; "Upgrading Barns to Be Inhabited by People" in *Architectural Record* (New York), June 1974; "Grandes Orgues et Petites Industries" in *L'Architecture d'Aujourd'hui* (Paris), July/August 1974; "Chicago Revisited," special issue of *Interior Design* (New York), December 1974; "Interior Architecture: Fashion with Style" in *Progressive Architecture* (New York), December 1974; "Weese versus Mies" in *Architectural Record* (New York), April 1975; "A House That Thinks for Itself" in *House and Garden* (New York), July 1976; "Tigerman Shapes a Fresh New Library for the Blind" by Nory Miller in *Inland Architect* (Chicago), September 1976.

*

There is a prevailing theory in architecture that the closer, in intention, that a finished object is to its originating abstract concept, the more powerful that object will be. Now does that theory only apply to traditional ideas about Formalism/Functionalism, or can it also relate to symbolic content such as the metaphorical possibilities in theories/buildings? In all events, the underlying central intention of the theory is that *abstraction,* in and of itself, is all important.

Generally speaking, prior to the twentieth century architecture was thought to be more or less representational. Now comes the Modern Movement and with it a reductionist attitude about buildings, through forces such as constructivism and Synthetic Cubism. Buildings, and for that matter all manner of process-items such as drawings and models, became successively more abstract. Rendering in drawings and realistic, materialistic representationism in models were abandoned in favor of that which came to be known (indeed eventually celebrated) as "Dematerialization." That cycle now appears to be completed only to be replaced by more complex concerns in architecture suggesting a kind of new pluralism embracing just about everything from syntactic concerns to energy conservation, and with these pluralist possibilities a rich way of re-presenting ideas.

Three projects of mine can be mentioned that ask (but do not necessarily answer) the question posed above; they also suggest the model-as-conduit as well as the concept-as-model.

Daisy House metaphorically presumes to allude at once to a "Spanish-mission" style (The Alamo) as well as a Ledoux-like, mildly scatological commentary about American Society (The Maison de Plaisir).

Animal Crackers, generated from the cookie-box of the same name, also suggests a calliope, continuing the metaphorical concerns of the Daisy House but employing vestigal, rather than actual, "cut-outs."

The Little House in the Clouds (National Archives Center of the Baha'i's of the United States), a study in timelessness and perpetuity, relates to man's perpetual home (the concretized version) opposed by his original home (its mirror image in topiary).

Now in all three cases something is suggested other than architects talking to each other. In each case, to some degree, the success of the original concept relies upon popular, cultural symbols intended to communicate to the people of that culture in areas not normally exploited and, in all events, tangential to the traditional aspirations of man that architects normally deal with. In each case as well, the model's purpose is somewhat different from the formalist-/functionalist model insofar as what is being conveyed is an idea about ideas rather than an idea about Architecture.

—Stanley Tigerman

*

Stanley Tigerman has tackled with style and imagination many of the architectural issues that have evolved during his career. He has approached middle income and public housing with early and commendable interpretations of vernacular modes. He added his own efforts to the 1960's utopian fascination with high-technology megastructures. And he has worked in the very real forum of third world developing countries in Bangladesh. He has built high-rise and below ground; for speculative developers and the Cuisinart set; in brick, concrete, wood and metal.

Throughout he has been a kind of architectural scavenger, years before (or after) that kind of eclecticism gained acceptance. For the first decade, the strongest influences were his former employers, Walter Netsch and Harry Weese, his teacher Paul Rudolph, and latter-day Chicagoan Mies van der Rohe. Later, the list expanded in all directions to include John Hejduk, Charles Moore, Art Moderne, de Stijl and many more.

In recent years, his previously stylistically diverse practice has begun to come together into a progressive development of designs—some built, some not—that are increasingly sensual and theatrical. As early as the Glass commissions (apartment and boutique), Tigerman's deftness with soft curves and three-dimensional staging became apparent. Subsequent designs have continued to expand the vocabulary which increasingly includes biomorphic shapes, bright color, topiary, and imagery which both in detail (e.g., his repeated use of Magritte cloud-filled skies) and as *objet trouvé* makes allusions to other things.

The names of the buildings have become an element of play as well as explanation: to wit, Hot Dog House, Animal Crackers, Zipper Townhouses, Dante's Bathroom, Kosher Kitchen for a Suburban Jewish-American Princess, Tigerman Takes a Bite out of Keck (a rippled effluvia of an addition to a modernist George Fred Keck house).

The metaphors are sometimes related to the project—for instance, the Daisy House, in the shape of male genitalia, is built for a man who owns strip joints—and sometimes, although not ideologically, surreal. Frequently they are intended to amuse—like a two-car garage shaped and painted like the cars themselves—and just as frequently to shock—church confessionals whose plans come from the sections of standard lavatory fixtures.

Almost invariably the work is marked by formal inventiveness, sculptural and compositional finesse and attentiveness to detail. The pop and pornography, historicism and literary reference are like formal building blocks. That architecture should be jaunty, appealing and an "experience" is really the message.

As well as a prolific architect, Tigerman has been a central influence on the architectural community of Chicago in the 1970's through the group Chicago Seven, conferences, exhibits and competitions. The activities have focused not only on creating a community of discussion among Chicago designers and encouraging talented beginners to participate, but also in putting architectural issues before the architectural, art and general public.

—Nory Miller

TOMBAZIS, Alexandros N(icholas).
Greek. Born in Karachi, Pakistan, 10 April 1939. Educated at elementary and secondary schools in London and Athens, 1945–57; Athens Technical University, 1957–62, Dip.Arch.Eng. 1962. Served as an Officer in the Building Department of the Greek Navy, 1962–64. Married Alexandra Cozzika in 1964; children: Despina and Nicholas. Assistant, Athens Technical University School of Architecture, 1962–65; Scientific Assistant, Doxiades Associates, Athens, 1964–65. Founder and Principal, Alexandros N. Tombazis and Associates, Athens, since 1963, Abu Dhabi, 1974–76, and Dubai, since 1974. Recipient: First Prize—National School Buildings Organization Competition, Athens, 1963; Civil Servants Office Building Competition, Athens, 1968; Demokritos Nuclear Research Centre Headquarters Competition, Athens, 1969; Public Electricity Company Headquarters Competition, Athens, 1971; General Cement Company Headquarters Competition, Athens, 1971; National Bank for Industrial Development Headquarters Competition, Athens, 1972; Chronic Disease Hospital Competition, Korydallos, Piraeus, 1972; Athens University Faculty of Law Competition, 1977; Town Hall Competition, Kifissia, 1977. Address: Alexandros N. Tombazis and Associates, 1 Aristodemou Street, Athens 140, Greece.

Works:

1963 Greek National School Buildings Organization Prototypes (competition project)
1964 Greek State Railways Headquarters, Athens (competition project)
1965 Chios Archaeological Museum (competition project)
1966 Greek Pavilion, for *Expo '67,* Montreal (competition project)
Athens Technical University Boarding House (competition project)
University of Athens Hospital (competition project; with Biris and Sartzetaki)
Urban housing for the Shikenshiku-Sha Company, Tokyo (competition project)
1967 Athens Historical War Museum (competition project)
Espoo City Centre, Finland (competition project)
Epiros Poultry Cooperative Plant, Ioannina, Greece (with Th. Sartzetaki)
1968 Civic Servants Pension Fund Office Building, Athens (competition project)
Telephone booth prototype (competition project)
Hellenica Beauty and Toiletry Laboratory, Maroussi, Athens
A. Svolos House, Kinetta, Greece
V. Katsambas House, Kifissia, Athens
Akti Mytina Tourist Village, Lemnos, Greece
1969 Grava School Complex, Athens (competition project)
Athens Central Market and Commercial Centre (competition project)
E. Diakos Apartment Building, P. Psychico, Athens

Psimaras House, Glyfada, Athens
Nea Smyrni Elementary School Complex, Athens
Van der Graaf Accelerator Building, Demokritos Nuclear Research Centre, Aghia Paraskevi, Athens
Gold Exhibits Section, National Archaeological Museum, Athens
Demokritos Nuclear Research Centre Headquarters, Aghia Paraskevi, Athens
Olympos Cement Depot, Volos, Greece
V.E.S.O. Kernal-Oil Plant, Corinth
1970 Piraeus Port Authority Office Building (competition project)
Technikos Cosmos Company Apartment Complex, Kastri, Athens (competition project)
St. Paul Accident Hospital extension, Kifissia, Athens (project)
1971 Perugia City Centre, Italy (competition project)
Public Electricity Company Headquarters, N. Falero, Athens (competition project)
General Cement Company Headquarters, Kifissia, Athens
Demokritos Nuclear Research Centre Radiation Laboratory, Aghia Paraskevi, Athens
1972 National Electricity Organization Training Centre, Drosia, Athens (competition project)
Prodomi High-rise Residential Complex, Kifissia, Athens
High Tension Laboratory, Athens Polytechnic
King Paul National Foundation Boarding House, Molai, Lakonia, Greece
Athens College Bodosakeio Elementary School, Kantza, Attica, Greece (with Perkins and Will)
National Bank for Industrial Development Headquarters, Athens

Yacht Marina for the Greek Tourist Organization, Salonica
1973 School for Tourist Professions, for the Greek Tourist Organization, Anavissos, Attica, Greece
1974 Technical School, Lamia, Greece
Fix Day Care Centre, P. Falero, Athens
Pediatric Clinic and Spastics Unit, Athens Pediatric Centre, Maroussi, Athens
Catholic Church Office Building, Athens
First-class hotel, Abu Dhabi, United Arab Emirates
A. Chandris Company Cable Plant, Volos, Greece
1975 Abu Dhabi Conference City, United Arab Emirates (competition project)
Apartment complex, Al Saman, Sharjah, United Arab Emirates
Kouloura Fund Health Centre, Hydra, Greece
1976 A. Frangoyiannis House, Ekali, Athens
Al Futtaim House, Dubai, United Arab Emirates
1977 Town Hall, Kifissia, Athens (competition project)
Town Hall, Psychico, Greece (competition project)
Technical Chamber Office Building, Larissa, Greece (competition project)
Secondary school complex, Piraeus, Greece (competition project)
Technical schools complex, Chalkida, Greece (competition project)
National Bank of Greece Pensions Home (competition project)
Secondary schools complex, Chania, Crete (competition project)
Acropolis Archaeological Museum, Athens (competition project)
Chronic Disease Hospital, Korydallos, Piraeus, Greece.

1978 A. Mavrakakis House, Ano Voula, Athens
Agricultural University Library, Athens
Faculty of Law Building, University of Athens
National School Organization school complexes (2), Ano Liossia, Athens
Helos I Solar House, Trapeza Aigialeias, Greece

Publications:

By TOMBAZIS: articles—"The Spacestructure System" in *Architecture in Greece* (Athens), vol. 2, 1968; "Greek Vernacular Architecture" in *Architecture in Greece* (Athens), vol. 3, 1969.

On TOMBAZIS: articles—in *Architektoniki* (Athens), 1963, 1968; *Arkkitehtuuri Kimpailuja* (Helsinki), no. 8, 1967; *Architektur Wettbewerbe* (Stuttgart), vol. 52, 1967; *L'Architecture d'Aujourd'hui* (Paris), no. 134, 1967; *The Japan Architect* (Tokyo), no. 127, 1967; *Architecture in Greece* (Athens), vol. 2, 1968, vol. 3, 1969, vol. 4, 1970, vol. 5, 1971, vol. 6, 1972, vol. 8, 1974, vol. 10, 1976, vol. 11, 1977; *Bauen und Wohnen* (Zurich), no. 8, 1971; *E + P* (Frankfurt), 1971, 1972, 1974; *Design in Greece* (Athens), vol. 3, 1972, vol. 4, 1973, vol. 8, 1977; *L'Architettura* (Rome), August 1972; *Architectural Review* (London), no. 908, 1972; *Technodomica* (Athens), no. 2, 1976, no. 19, 1978; *DBZ* (Gutersloh), no. 22, 1977.

A considerable number of the projects that we have had the opportunity to work on have been awarded to us as the result of architectural competitions called for either by the State or by private individuals. There is a law, in fact, in Greece which requires that most public work be awarded in such a manner which, in my opinion, is a very favourable situation from many points of view. The problems, however,

Alexandros N. Tombazis: General Cement Company Headquarters, Kifissia, Athens, 1971

that exist are many—for example: a number of these projects do not get built; the designer does not supervise construction—he has no say in the alterations that are made to his design!; the whole system for awarding public contracts for construction is not based on any consideration of quality but only upon the lowest price offered; and any large project—of which there are quite a number—is a ten year love affair with at least as many ups and downs!

—Alexandros N. Tombazis

The projects of Alexandros N. Tombazis represent exemplary exceptions to the usual off-hand solutions and the low state of building technology in Greece. He has never preoccupied himself with arguments on Regionalism or the "Greekness" of his projects, as has been the case with many other Greek architects. He can be regarded as the Greek architect par excellence who is constantly alert to advancements of building technology and the state of architecture abroad and who introduces these innovations to his native land. He does so after questioning their adaptability to Greece, through exhaustive and in-depth studies, surrounded by the most gifted technologists of the country. His office, small by Western standards, has produced a great number of diverse building types including residential, educational, industrial, administrative, health and tourist facilities.

Tombazis' work has spread itself across a variety of formal influences. Some of his early projects were heavily influenced by Le Corbusier's form-making language. A number of subsequent projects followed the conceptual and stylistic vocabulary of the Metabolists. The house in Kinetta, one of Tombazis' masterpieces, is perhaps the best "Metabolic" residence ever constructed anywhere on earth. Some of his latest projects—an entry for the first Panhellenic Competition for the new Museum of Acropolis and another entry for the town hall in Psychico—arouse memories of the work of James Stirling, especially his History Faculty Building at Cambridge. There have been a few instances when he dealt with traditional expressions. This happened in circumstances when an historic zoning ordinance or the unique nature of the project demanded such expression. In spite of the multiplicity of Tombazis' formal expressions, one thing is certain: he is a brilliant interpreter of the occasional form vocabulary he sets about to exploit. In every case his projects are integrated design packages, with most appealing craftsmanship and appealing elevations.

Tombazis' office is still young by Western professional standards. It has participated in and won a great number of Greek architectural competitions. It has also been distinguished by major awards in international competitions. There is no doubt that this firm also enjoys the trust of its Greek, as well as its Middle East, clientele. If the firm exploits its authority and the trust gained during the first decade of its practice, and if it goes beyond the conventionalities of generally accepted "good architecture," it will most certainly produce "unique" architecture, distinguished by its own personality, unburdened by the formal memories of other nations, expressive of 20th century Greece. The unfortunate early death in the summer of 1977 of Takis Zenetos, pioneer in the search for a technologically correct Greek architecture, puts an additional burden on the shoulders of Tombazis. His firm has the ability, and he is the only one out of the current Greek practitioners who has the background, to produce a viable, all-inclusive, technologically correct Greek architecture.

—Anthony C. Antoniades

TORROJA y MIRET, Eduardo.

Spanish. Born in Madrid, 27 August 1899. Studied constructional engineering, Dip.Eng. 1923; awarded honorary qualification as architect (posthumously), School of Architecture, Madrid, 1967. Practiced in Madrid from 1923: Partner, with Manuel Sanchez Arcas, 1934–35. Founder-Director, Instituto Técnico de la Construcción y del Cemento, Costillares, Madrid (now, Instituto Eduardo Torroja). Visiting Professor, Harvard University, Cambridge, Massachusetts; Princeton University, New Jersey; Raleigh Architectural College, North Carolina; Massachusetts Institute of Technology, Cambridge; University of Buenos Aires. President, International Federation of Pre-stressing; President, Association of Shell Structures. Collection: Instituto Eduardo Torroja, Costillares, Madrid. Recipient: First Prize, Zarazuela Racecourse Competition, 1936. *Died* (in Madrid) *15 June 1961.*

Works:

1925   Tempul Aqueduct, Guadalete River, Jerez de la Frontera, Spain
1926   Sancti-Petri Bridge, Spain
1933   Market Hall, Algeciras, Spain (with Manuel Sánchez Arcas)
         Aire Aqueduct, University City, Madrid
         Quince Ojos Aqueduct, University City, Madrid (with M. L. Otero and A. Aguirre)
         Stadium Tramcar Station, University City, Madrid (not completed)
         Cantarranas Retaining Wall, Madrid
1934   Operating theatre, and Sun balconies, University City Hospital, Madrid
1935   Zarazuela Racecourse, Madrid (with Carlos Arniches and Martin Dominguez)
         Frontón Recoletos (Pelota Game Hall), Madrid (with Secundino Zuazo; destroyed during the Spanish Civil War)
         Church, Villaverde, Spain
1936   Reinforced Concrete Water Tower, Zarazuela Racecourse, Madrid (project)
1938   Factory Building, Seville (project)
1939   Brick Water Tower, Zarazuela Racecourse, Madrid
         Alloz Aqueduct, Alloz, Spain
         Martin Gil Viaduct, Esla River, near Leon, Spain
         Tordera Bridge, near Barcelona
1939/
47   La Muga Bridge, over the Muga River, Spain
1942/
45   Torrejon Aircraft Hangar, Madrid
         Aircraft Hangar, Barajas, Spain
1943   Las Corts Football Stadium, Barcelona (with J. M. Sagnier)
1948/
51   Instituto Técnico de la Construcción y del Cemento, Costillares, Madrid
1949   Aircraft Hangar, Cuatro Vientos, Spain
1950   Railway Station Roof, Orense, Spain (project)
1952   Church, Pont de Sert, Lerida, Spain (with J. R. Mijares)
         Chapel of the Ascension, Xerrallo, Spain (with J. R. Mijares)
1953   Pre-stressed Concrete Shrine/Shelter, Sancti Spirit, Spain
1956   Half-Mile Aqueduct (project)
         Cañelles Dam, near Lerida, Spain
         Water Tank, Fedala, Morocco
         Cylindrical Shell Chapel (project)
         Timber Church (project)
1957   Shell-Roof, for the Táchira Club, Caracas, Venezuela (with F. Vivas)
         Skew Slab Bridge (project)

Publications:

By TORROJA: books—*The Philosophy of Structures,* Berkeley, California 1958; *The Structures of Eduardo Torroja* (autobiography), New York 1958; *Logik der Form,* Munich 1961: articles—"Problems and Possibilities of Concrete Shells" in *The Builder* (London), 18 April 1958; "The Influence of Structural Form in Architecture" in *Architectural Association Journal* (London), February 1961.

On TORROJA: articles—"Eduardo Torroja" by G. Wastlund in *Byggmastaren* (Copenhagen), 1 February 1950; "Torroja's Sculptural Concrete" in *Architectural Forum* (New York), February 1955; "Vocazione Iberica per la Forma" in *Domus* (Milan), April 1956; "Bridges and Aqueducts" in *North Carolina School of Design Journal* (Raleigh), vol. 7, no. 2, 1957; "Un Maestro delle Strutture: Eduardo Torroja" by G. Pizzetti in *Casabella* (Milan), no. 217, 1957; "Les Structures Spatiales d'Eduardo Torroja" by Alberto Sartoris in *Architecture: Formes et Fonctions* (Lausanne), no. 6, 1959; "Eduardo Torroja" by Jürgen Joedicke in *Bauen und Wohnen* (Zurich), no. 11, 1960; "Eduardo Torroja 1899–1961" by M. Dezzi-Bardeschi in *Casabella* (Milan), August 1961; "Eduardo Torroja" by F. Cassinella in *Cuadernos de Arquitectura* (Barcelona), no. 46, 1961.

*   *   *

Eduardo Torroja y Miret was one of the great architect-engineers of this century, rivalled only by the Italian Pier Luigi Nervi. As a result of Torroja's genius and pioneering efforts, Spanish architecture achieved legendary qualities, particularly in the enclosure of space, structural concepts, and the daring use of material, especially concrete, raising it from prosaic to poetic levels.

Three works, striking for their conceptual simplicity and underlying logic, demonstrate Torroja's incredible structural skill. Moreover, they emphasize the importance of teamwork and collaboration between architect and engineer, which the exploitation of traditional and new materials, and changing ideals, demanded.

In the Market Hall at Algeciras, Torroja, with Manuel Sánchez Arcas, created a superb 156' diameter low profile spherical dome of shell concrete pierced with a zenithal skylight at the centre. In Madrid, Torroja collaborated with Secundino Zuazo to realize the Frontón Recoletos. Designed for the game of pelota, the building was imaginatively roofed with two cylindrical vaults, intersecting at right angles and spanning 107' over a length of 180'. It was built in 80 days. Light was admitted to the interior by ingeniously conceived skylights, integral with the structural shells. The Frontón Recoletos was destroyed during the Spanish Civil War, but Torroja was convinced that its continuous construction would have permitted restoration, especially if it had been shored after damage.

Elsewhere in Madrid, Torroja realized his masterpiece, the Zarazuela Racecourse, designed in association with the architects Carlos Arniche and Martin Dominguez. Determined by the strict functional necessities of racegoers for unrestricted views, shade, and freedom of movement, Torroja's revolutionary roof structure has been described as a "veritable ballet of eggshell concrete butterflies." The roof is composed of a series of shell concrete cantilevered hyperbolic sectors 42' long, counterbalanced by a series of similar shells 23' long, stabilized by anchor ties. The miraculously thin shells vary from 2" to 5.5". It withstood severe bombardment during the Civil War, and its graceful appearance was somewhat marred, but it remains structurally sound.

Without Torroja's engineering skill it is doubtful whether these works would have been realized with such panache. Certainly architecture elsewhere at that time suggests that there was an enormous creative gulf between Torroja and his contemporaries.

Later works by Torroja display his growing confidence; they are all expressions of his dazzling genius. Bridges, aqueducts, dams, water towers, factories, stadia, and even a coal bunker, were raised from a strictly utilitarian level to structural and aesthetic sublimity. Examples are the Alloz Aqueduct, 1,340' in length; Las Corts Football Stadium, Barcelona,

Eduardo Torroja y Miret: Zarazuela Racecourse, Madrid, 1935

where the steel roof cantilevers 83' over the spectators; the water tank at Fedala, with a 925,000 gallon capacity; and the Instituto Técnico de la Construcción y del Cemento in Madrid (founded by Torroja), where a 26' high dodecahedron makes a superb coal bunker and where the circular dining hall and pergola over a peripheral pathway are spectacular.

Torroja's inspiration is also evident in such churches as that at Pont de Sert, Lerida, where the structure of the composite shell vaults is spiritual. His project for the Táchira Club in Caracas, Venezuela, with stepped concrete shell, is masterly and moving as it elegantly adjusts its form to various levels.

Such was the quality of Torroja's work that Frank Lloyd Wright was moved to say, "he has expressed the principals of organic construction better than any engineer I know." His works, moreover, can be understood as a reflection of Spain's precarious economic state: Torroja was prevented from using expensive constructional methods and materials, a limitation that he converted to inspiration.

In his autobiography, *The Structures of Eduardo Torroja,* he makes the following statement: "I have tried to understand as completely as possible all the factors involved and apply my ingenuity to achieve a satisfactory solution both structurally and economically. My final aim has always been for the functional, structural and aesthetic aspects of a project to present an integrated whole both in essence and in appearance."

That is undoubtedly what Eduardo Torroja achieved: he raised structural engineering to un-

precedented heights and created some of the world's most beautiful structures.

—Harold Booton

TOY, R(ichard) H(orton) B(eauclerc).

New Zealander. Born in Ignace, Ontario, Canada, 9 May 1911; emigrated to New Zealand, 1923. Educated at Mt. Albert Grammar School, Auckland, 1927–29; Auckland University College, 1930–36, B.Arch. 1936; St. John's College, Auckland, 1932–34; University of New Zealand Travelling Scholar in Architecture, 1937; Trinity College, Dublin, 1949–50, Ph.D. 1950. Served as a Major in the New Zealand Army, 1939–43. Married Cushla Gwyn Hammond in 1938 (divorced, 1969); married Sally Elizabeth Collier in 1969; children: Michael, Alison, and Brian. Architectural Assistant, offices of E. R. Morton, Auckland, 1936, M. K. Draffin, Auckland, 1936, and S. Heaps, London, 1937–38. In private practice, Auckland, since 1939. Lecturer, 1939–50, Senior Lecturer, 1950–57, Professor of Architectural Design, 1957–77, and since 1977 Professor Emeritus, School of Architecture, University of Auckland. Fellow, St. John's College, Auckland, since 1964. Recipient: Bronze Medal, 1949, and Building of the Year in Auckland Award, 1957, New Zealand Institute of Architects. Address (office): 23 Seccombes Road, Epsom, Auckland 3, New Zealand.

Works:

1936 "Berisville" (block of 7 flats), Symonds Street, Auckland (with E. R. Morton)
1945 House, Selwyn Road, Auckland
1954 Memorial Pavilion, Mt. Albert Grammar School, Auckland
1957 All Saints Church, Ponsonby, Auckland
1958 St. Oswald's Church, Auckland
1961 Christ Church, Papakura, Auckland (with Frank Jones)
1963 St. Matthew's Church, Helensville, Auckland (with Frank Jones)
1964 St. John's Church, Te Awamutu, New Zealand (with Frank Jones)
1970 Private swimming pool and loggia, Mojácar, Spain
1978– Cathedral of the Holy Trinity nave, tower and site development, Auckland (with Gillespie, Newman, Pearce)

Publications:

By TOY: articles—"The University" in *New Zealand Herald* (Auckland), 20 December 1948; "The Adventure of Architecture," parts I and II, in *New Zealand Institute of Architects Journal* (Wellington), May and June 1953; "Architecture 30 Years A.F." in *Home and Building* (Auckland), April 1962; "Design and Its Wholeness" in *New Zealand Institute of Architects Journal* (Wellington), May 1964; "Design Decisions in Architectural Practice" in *New Zealand Institute of Architects Journal* (Wellington), August

1967 and February 1968; "Guest Speaker—Prof. Ole Dybbroe" in *Home and Building* (Auckland), May 1971; "Shapes of Urban Growth in *University of Auckland News,* August 1971; "Auckland: Water City of the South Pacific" in *Auckland at Full Stretch,* edited by Graham Bush and Claudia Scott, Auckland 1977.

On TOY: articles—"Toy Interview," with Ed Haysom, in *Auckland Architectural Association Bulletin,* October 1976; "A Man in His Place" by Boyce Richardson in *New Zealand Listener* (Wellington), 18 June 1977.

In the past, building generally has responded in a whole sort of way, purposefully and often imaginatively, to the shapes and structure of its elemental heritage, its earth-sky-water-light context, wherever that may be. Most modern work makes a minimum response—practical, so-called—the overall and individual effects of which are deadening and especially noticeable in a place like New Zealand where the great bulk of the building in its beautiful landscape is of recent origin. My academic and practical interests have centred round ideas of enhancing what should be in any building project this very vital relationship.

Until recently such ideas received little support, but now it seems to me that the climate is becoming favourable to their growth; there is a more "anima" and less "animus"-like way of relating to the environment, a motivation shown in spreading conservation movements. The pursuit of these ideas involves, on the academic side, developing a theory of nature's structure which can display, in terms corresponding to those of architectural theory, the potentialities of the land, practical and cultural, for human dwelling (and, of course, for letting it be). The potentialities we are concerned with here are those for accommodating and asserting the inward and outward manifestations of life and its transitions. Correspondences and contradictions between the potentialities of natural and architectural forms can then be grasped through a common imagery of closure and openness and movement. Design becomes an orchestration of building and natural structures at all or any levels, from town to room to lamp-post.

If the theory is to be practically effective some way must be found of making it available not just occasionally but generally at the inception of building projects. As a model for this purpose we established at the Auckland School of Architecture a design theatre. This gathered together, round a discussion space, examples of natural and architectural structures graphically interpreted in accordance with the theory, and with particular reference, since this is an Auckland school, to the natural structure of the Auckland region as its base. The theatre was intended to be a tool to help reveal to all those involved the environmental implications of their building design decisions. Such a focus for building work, with appropriate reference to local conditions, could clearly be repeated in other regions and at different levels within the region.

My own practice interest tends to zoom in on the bay form with which, in an infinite variety of nature's proportions, inland as well as by the sea, Auckland and indeed most of New Zealand is bountifully blessed. Three dimensional, and transitional by virtue of its qualities both of connectedness and separateness (connecting by water or land, separated by its land rim), the bay has great potential for resolving many of the apparent conflicts of present day community—the demands, for instance, of outer relatedness on the one hand but of identity on the other. The outstanding example of the bay in its (mainly) built form is to be found in the self-renewing and beautifully modulated piazza and piazzetta of San Marco at Venice.

At the level of smaller gatherings and buildings, the bay form as forecourt, porch, and canopied interior is interesting. This is the "open hand" really,

R. H. B. Toy: St. Oswald's Church, Auckland, 1958

open vertically to the sky still, but as well opening in front over the land—because to receive, to give are transcendent acts certainly, but also warm and earthy things to do. All Saints Church, Ponsonby, is of this type.

Again, the bay is the form of the maori marae, a traditional place for gathering and greetings and farewells. So, whether we are of Polynesian or European descent, this is for us an important form in common. Through it we can, if we wish, build the means for that mutual cultural intercourse and understanding which is one of the happier dreams of people in this land.

—R. H. B. Toy

R. H. B. Toy creates an architecture concerned with the marriage of earth and sky. The words are always on his lips; his hand is always drawing them; his architecture is made with them, an architecture resonant with themes of the immanent and transcendental in human experience. Living and working in the heart of Auckland, he demonstrates in his daily life as in his architecture the intimate connection, for young and old, with the earth's loveliness and the freedom of the open sky. In his architecture—earthbound masonry with light, open timber enclosures above—he continues to work with timber when it has been abandoned by others. His buildings are amongst the loveliest in the country.

Toy has devoted his life to helping others as a teacher: he is loved by students in a society in which it is difficult to admit and express this feeling, and he is recognized by everyone as excelling in the understanding of form in the natural landscape and perceiving the relation of that landscape to built architecture. His buildings are small, but their architectural reference is broad.

Toy is guided by his belief in the public art of

architecture, at home in its natural setting, as a celebration of the society he loves. With this conviction he has quietly embellished a city and region with urban and rural parish churches, culminating in a cathedral. This hierarchy of levels of community is a theme in his work, sensitively grafted to a context of other buildings, characterized by a respect for the old, encouraging gradual shaping of space with time, a tempering of 20th century spatial rhetoric and technical confidence with sensitivity to places and people.

He is concerned with the careful opening of traditional forms without destroying them: floating roof canopies; partial dissolution of massive form into spatial ambiguities and linearities; opened forecourts complemented by the welcoming covering of space in the manner of the Polynesian marae.

All of his themes of space, material and form are embodied in his cathedral design—the tremulous canopy, the enclosure of space, the opened forecourt, the upthrust vertical, the place, the society, aware of itself in its setting. Toy shares with Patrick Geddes a belief in this awareness as a means of growth.

He is prompted in his work by a compelling personal experience of three-dimensional space in relation to the human being, an awareness that the space of architecture is integral to the space of nature. Thus his works, often unassuming in purpose, evince a powerful aesthetic and lead through connection to the deepest purposes in life: it is an architecture quietly assertive of the dignity of man, concerned with universal themes, both encompassed by and encompassing land and society.

It is an architecture that will persist.

—John D. Dickson

TURNBULL, William, Jr.

American. Born in New York City, 1 April 1935. Educated at St. Mark's School, Southboro, Massachusetts, 1948–52; Princeton University, New Jersey, under William Shellman and Heath Licklider, 1952–56, B.A. 1956; Ecole des Beaux-Arts, Fontainebleau, 1956; Princeton University, under Jean Labatut, Enrico Perussutti, and Louis I. Kahn, 1956–59, M.F.A. 1959. Served in the United States Army Corps of Engineers, 1959–60. Married Wendy Woods in 1967; children: Ramsay and Connor. Designer, Skidmore, Owings and Merrill, San Francisco, 1960–63; Designer, President Kennedy's Pennsylvania Avenue Commission, Washington, D.C., 1963; Partner, Moore, Lyndon, Turnbull and Whitaker, Berkeley, California, 1963–65, and MLTW/Moore Turnbull, Berkeley, 1965–70. Since 1970, Principal, MLTW/Turnbull Associates, San Francisco. Lecturer, College of Environmental Design, University of California, Berkeley, 1965–69; Visiting Professor, University of Oregon, Eugene, 1966–68; Lecturer in Architecture, Stanford University, Palo Alto, California, 1974–77; Visiting Critic, Massachusetts Institute of Technology, Cambridge, 1975, Yale University, New Haven, Connecticut, 1977, and University of California, Berkeley, 1978. Chairman, National Honor Awards Jury, American Institute of Architects, 1967–77; Member, Citizens' Technical Advisory Committee to the California Legislative Joint Committee on Open Space Lands, 1968–71; Member, Design Review Board, Sausalito, California, 1976–78. Design Consultant, World Savings and Loan, since 1976; Member of the Council on the Arts, Massachusetts Institute of Technology, since 1976; Design Consultant to The Formica Corporation, since 1977. Exhibitions: *40 under 40,* The Architectural League of New York, 1966; *MLTW,* The Architectural League of New York, 1966; *MLTW,* University of Oregon, 1967; *Centennial Exhibition,* University of California at Santa Barbara, 1968; *The California House,* Oakland Museum of Art, California, 1972, 1975; *Surroundings,* Walnut Creek Civic Arts Gallery, California, 1974; *Two Hundred Years of Santa Clara Valley Architecture,* Triton Museum of Art, Santa Clara, California, 1976; *Princeton Beaux Arts and Its New Academicism,* Institute for Architecture and Urban Studies, New York, 1977; A *View of California Architecture 1960–1976,* Museum of Modern Art, San Francisco, 1977; *50 Years of Princeton Architecture from Labatut to Geddes,* Princeton University, 1977; *200 Years of American Architectural Drawing,* Cooper-Hewitt Museum, New York, 1978; *Drawings for a More Modern Architecture,* Drawing Center, New York, and Otis Art Institute, Los Angeles, 1978; Architecture Exhibition, Ball State University, Muncie, Indiana, 1978. Recipient: House of the Year Award, *Architectural Record,* 1962, 1967, 1969, 1970, 1972, 1973; Merit Award, 1962, 1968, 1975 (twice), Special Award, 1964, 1968, and Honor Award, 1964, 1972 (twice), American Institute of Architects/*Sunset Magazine;* Award of Merit, 1963, 1967, 1978, and Honor Award, 1978, AIA, Bay Region; First Honor Award, 1963, 1976, and Merit Award, 1966, 1970, AIA/*House and Home;* California Governor's Award for Planned Communities, 1966; National Honor Award, AIA, 1967, 1968, 1973; Community Design Award, AIA, California, 1970; First Honor Award, 1970, and Honor Award, 1974, *Progressive Architecture;* Award, AIA/United States Department of Housing and Urban Development, 1972; Honor Award, AIA, Connecticut, 1977; Award of Merit, AIA/American Library Association, 1978. Fellow, Kresge College, University of California at Santa Cruz, 1973. Fellow, American Institute of Architects, 1976. Address: MLTW/Turnbull Associates, Pier 1½, The Embarcadero, San Francisco, California 94111, U.S.A.

Works:

1959 Ellis Island Plan, New York (master's thesis project)

1960 Civic Center Fountain, Seattle (competition project)
Governor's Mansion, Sacramento, California (competition project)
Matterson House, Monterey, California
1961 City Hall, Boston (competition project)
1962 Jenkins House I, St. Helena, California (project)
Moore House, Orinda, California
West Plaza Condominium, Coronado, California (project)
Seaside Professional Building, Seaside, California
Master plan for the South Coast, Monterey, California (with Skidmore, Owings and Merrill)
Master plan for Lone Hill Housing, San Jose, California
1963 Cortese House, Orinda, California (project)
Legge House additions, Portola Valley, California
Trueblood House additions, Palo Alto, California
Turner House, Pebble Beach, California (project)
Monte Vista Apartments, Monterey, California
Plan for Pennsylvania Avenue, Washington, D.C. (project; as staff designer)
1964 Athletic Club I, Sea Ranch, California
Cudabach House renovation, Oakland, California (project)
Jewell House, Orinda, California
Morris-LaForge House, Boulder Creek, California (project)
Slater House, Stinson Beach, California
Condominium I, Sea Ranch, California
1965 Cornuelle House, Hillsborough, California (project)
Halprin House I, Sea Ranch, California (project)
Halprin House II, Sea Ranch, California (project)
Johnson House, Sea Ranch, California
Karas House, Monterey, California
Krakauer House, Los Alto, California (project)
Lawrence House additions, Palo Alto, California
Martin House, Lake Tahoe, California
Polk House renovation, Berkeley, California
Talbert House, Oakland, California
Condominium Hillside, Sea Ranch, California (project)
Carmel Knolls Housing, Carmel Valley, California (project)
Civic Center, Fremont, California (competition project)
Plan for a Commercial Square, Novato, California
Portland South Park, Lovejoy Plaza, Portland, Oregon (with Lawrence Halprin)
1966 Budge House, Healdsburg, California
Halprin House III, Sea Ranch, California (project)
Halprin House IV, Sea Ranch, California
Harrison House, Santa Barbara, California (project)
Knutsen House, Sonoma, California
Lawrence House, Sea Ranch, California
McClelland House, Sea Ranch, California (project)
Otus House, Berkeley, California
Saltzman House, Carmel, California
Thomasian House, Orinda, California
Truesdale House, Sea Ranch, California
Turnbull Sr. House I, Carbondale, Colorado
Vickery House, Sea Ranch, California (project)
Arts Center, University of California, Berkeley (competition project)
Urban renewal housing, Akron, Ohio (project)

Cascade Project, Akron, Ohio (project)
1967 Boas House, Stinson Beach, California
Morris House I, Sea Ranch, California (project)
Pirofski House, Palo Alto, California (project)
Spec I House, Sea Ranch, California (project)
Stauffacher House, Mill Valley, California (project)
Beckonridge Housing, Tacoma, Washington (project)
College 6, University of California at Santa Cruz (project)
1968 Dahlen House, Santa Barbara, California (project)
Hines House, Sea Ranch, California
McElrath House, Santa Cruz, California
Morris House II, Sea Ranch, California
Ray House, Sea Ranch, California (project)
Spec II House, Sea Ranch, California (prototype)
Spec III House, Sea Ranch, California (prototype)
Weyerhauser Prototype House, Kansas City, Missouri
Bechtel Prototype Housing, Santa Catalina, California (project)
Conifer 4 Housing for the Elderly, Tacoma, Washington
Conifer 5 Housing, Tacoma, Washington
Faculty Club, University of California at Santa Barbara
Housing, Hamden, Connecticut (project)
Athletic Club II, Sea Ranch, California
1968/
72 Peterson House I, Tacoma, Washington (project)
1969 Caygill House, Sea Ranch, California
Klotz House, Westerly, Rhode Island
La Boyteaux House, Orinda, California (project)
McComber House, Sea Ranch, California
Naff House, Pajaro Dunes, California
Reid House, Sea Ranch, California
Baker House, Sea Ranch, California
Bartell House, Sea Ranch, California
Binker House, Sea Ranch, California
Eastwood House, Sea Ranch, California
Edgerton House, Sea Ranch, California
Kohlmeister House, Sea Ranch, California
Kreps/Levine House, Sea Ranch, California
Larsen House, Sea Ranch, California
Matthews House, Sea Ranch, California
Whiteside House, Sea Ranch, California
Wickstead House, Sea Ranch, California
Wilson/Moore/King House, Sea Ranch, California
Tempchin House, Bethesda, Maryland (with Rurik Ekstrom)
Turnbull Sr. House II, Carbondale, Colorado
Master plan for Russian Harbor, Jenner, California
Kansas City Mall
1970 Baer House addition, Monterey County, California (project)
Bransten House, Muir Beach, California (project)
Bransten House renovation, San Francisco (project)
Gahagan House, Tamales Bay, California (project)
Mentzer House, Sea Ranch, California
Rush House, Sea Ranch, California
Goodhart House, Sea Ranch, California
Villa del Monte Housing for the Elderly, Seaside, California
Oak Street Turnkey Housing, Haight-Ashbury, San Francisco (project)
Tract A Townhouses, Vail, Colorado (project)
Boas Pontiac Building remodelling, San Francisco
Golden West Savings and Loan Association

Office interiors, Capitola, California

Golden West Savings and Loan Association Office remodelling, Castro Valley, California

Golden West Savings and Loan Association Office remodelling, Corte Madera, California

Golden West Savings and Loan Association Office interiors, Eastridge, California (project)

Pembroke Dormitories, Brown University, Providence, Rhode Island

Land use analysis: Nuclear Power Station, Davenport, California

1971 King House renovation, La Selva Beach, California

Schaefer House, Sonoma County, California (project)

Schink House, Woodside, California (project)

Edgerton House additions, Sea Ranch, California

York House, Oakland, California

Bay Ranch Condominium, Point Reyes, California (project)

Arcata National Building remodelling, San Francisco

Gentry Office Building, Dublin, California (project)

Golden West Savings and Loan Association Building, Albany, California (project)

Golden West Savings and Loan Association Building, Santa Cruz, California (project)

Feasibility plan for low-income housing and housing for the elderly, Pittsburg, California

1972 Boise Cascade System Houses, Lake County, California (project)

Haas House renovation, San Francisco

Hayes House, Comptche, California (project)

Hepler House, Palo Alto, California

Pirofski House additions, Palo Alto, California

O'Connor House, Sea Ranch, California

Dunlavey House, Sea Ranch, California (project)

Starbird House, Santa Clara County, California

MLTW/Turnbull Associates Office remodelling, San Francisco

Beta Theta Pi Fraternity Building remodelling, Stanford University, Palo Alto, California (project)

Hill Plan, Nashville, Tennessee (project)

Vail-Boothcreek Plan, Vail, Colorado (project)

1973 Dillingham House renovation, San Francisco

Foster House renovation, San Francisco

Halprin House additions, Sea Ranch, California

Jacobs House, Sausalito, California (project)

Johnson House additions, Sea Ranch, California

Perini House additions, San Rafael, California

Rosenberg House, Sea Ranch, California (project)

Shanley House, Morris County, New Jersey

Christensen House, Sea Ranch, California

Stone House, San Francisco (project)

Sunset Magazine Prototype House, Menlo Park, California (project)

Sylvia House, Santa Rosa, California

Turnbull Jr. House renovation, Sausalito, California

Kresge College, University of California at Santa Cruz

Owen Brown Village Housing, Columbia, Maryland (project)

Oceanic Properties Cluster Housing, Sea Ranch, California (demonstration unit only)

Richardson Highlands Housing, Marin City, California (project)

Franklin Square, Franklin, Tennessee (project)

Design Research Building remodelling, San Francisco

Sherman Clay Building, Portland, Oregon (project)

Sylvia Corporation Yard, Sea Ranch, California

World Savings and Loan Association Office renovation and interiors, San Francisco

Arts Facility, Kresge College, University of California at Santa Cruz

Old Farm Plan, West Haven, New Jersey (project)

Plan for Owen Brown Village, Columbia, Maryland

1973/
75 Turnbull Sr. House III, Far Hills, New Jersey (project)

1974 Bowles House additions, San Francisco

Devendorf House, Sea Ranch, California

Fall River Cabins, Glenburn, California

Newton Townhouse, San Francisco (project)

Coon House, Sea Ranch, California (project)

Kanner House, Sea Ranch, California

Marshall House, Sea Ranch, California

Potter House, Sea Ranch, California

Wong House, Sea Ranch, California (project)

Ziegler Townhouses, Franklin, Tennessee (project)

Sedway-Cooke Planning Offices, San Francisco

Newman Office interiors, San Francisco

Sterling Vineyards Tasting Room additions and remodelling, Calistoga, California

C.L.O.T.H. Building remodelling and interiors, San Francisco

1975 Bertram House renovation, Sea Ranch, California (project)

Hayes House renovation, San Francisco

Peterson House II, Columbia, Maryland

Sloan House, Franklin, Tennessee

Zimmermann House, Fairfax County, Virginia

La Fuente Restaurant remodelling, San Francisco

1976 House, Lafayette, California

Sagan House, Tahoe, California (project)

Kauai Condominium, Lolea, Kauai, Hawaii (project)

Prince Kuhio Building renovation, Kauai, Hawaii (project)

Wine and Cheese Shop remodelling, San Francisco (project)

Minnesota Capitol addition, St. Paul (competition project)

1977 Lilienthal House additions, Napa, California

Moss House, Sea Ranch, California

Trestle Beach Housing, Santa Cruz County, California

World Savings and Loan Association Building, Santa Maria, California

World Savings and Loan Association Building remodelling, La Jolla, California

World Savings and Loan Association Building, Seal Beach, California

Library and Cultural Center, Biloxi, Mississippi

Master plan and landscaping for Garin Park, Fremont, California (project; with Garrett Eckbo)

A. G. Monastery Plan, Carmel Highlands, California (project)

1978 American Wood Council House Beautiful I, Las Vegas, Nevada (project)

American Wood Council House Beautiful II, Las Vegas, Nevada

Allewelt House, Modesto, California

Brown House, Locke, California

Caygill House addition, Sea Ranch, California

DiGiorgio House, Napa, California

Foster House addition, Healdsburg, California

Hart/Pryor House remodelling, Chevy Chase, Maryland

Hines House, Aspen, Colorado (project)

Keenan House, Napa County, California (project)

Leaper House additions, San Francisco

Lee House, San Francisco

Lindzey House, Sea Ranch, California

Markham Winery additions, Napa County, California

McElrath House additions, Santa Cruz, California

Pirofski House additions, Palo Alto, California

Scarlett House, Woodside, California (project)

Sedway House additions, San Rafael, California

Baxter House, Sea Ranch, California

Steltzner House remodelling, St. Helena, California

Trefethen House additions, Napa County, California

Yoerg House remodelling, Atherton, California

Sausalito Point Housing, Marin County, California (project)

Hart/White Property Housing, West Virginia (project)

Jewels by Jacques Building interiors, Richmond, California

World Savings and Loan Association Offices, Stanford Shopping Center, California

Mark Fenwick Offices interiors, San Francisco (project)

Santos and Haircutter interiors, San Francisco (project)

California Harvest Shops interiors, San Francisco (project)

Schoen-Snedeker/Anchorage interiors, San Francisco

Toys in the Tower interiors, San Francisco

Beadazzled interiors, San Francisco

Almaden Shopping Plaza interiors, San Jose, California

Serramonte Shopping Center remodelling, San Francisco (project)

Sterling Vineyards Private Reserve Building, Calistoga, California (project)

Johnson/Turnbull Vineyards remodelling and planning, Napa County, California

Public Library remodelling, Sausalito, California

Nature Conservancy Interpretive Center, Big Creek, California

Nature Conservancy Interpretive Center, Santa Cruz Island, California

State Coastal Conservancy Plans for Casper, Cambria and Whiskey Shoals, California

Hudson Planning, Big Sur, California

Briggs Property Plan, Carmel Highlands, California

Ocean Meadows Plan, Mendocino, California

A. G. Monastery Union Shell Plan, Monterey, California

Publications:

By TURNBULL: books—*Global Architecture: MLTW/The Sea Ranch,* edited by Yukio Futagawa, Tokyo 1971; illustrations for *The Place of Houses* by Moore, Lyndon and Allen, New York 1974; *Global Architecture: Sea Ranch Details,* Tokyo 1976.

On TURNBULL: books—*The Architecture of Monuments* by Thomas Creighton, New York 1962; *World Architecture 2, 3* and *4: U.S.A.* by John Donat, London and New York 1965, 1966, 1967; *American Architecture and Urbanism* by Vincent Scully, New York 1969; *New Directions in American Architecture* by Robert A. M. Stern, New York 1969, 1977; *Nuove Ville* by Roberto Aloi, Milan

William Turnbull, Jr.: Zimmermann House, Fairfax County, Virginia, 1975

1970; *Observations in American Architecture* by Ivan Chermayeff, New York 1972; *Drawings by American Architects,* New York 1973; *Global Interiors: Houses in the U.S.A. 6,* edited by Yukio Futagawa, Tokyo 1974; *Houses by MLTW, 1959–1975* by Yukio Futagawa, Tokyo 1975; *Unbuilt America* by Alison Sky and Michelle Stone, New York 1976; *Bay Area Houses,* edited by Sally Woodbridge, New York 1976; *Drawings for a More Modern Architecture,* exhibition catalog, Los Angeles 1978; articles—*Geijutsi Seikatsu* (Tokyo), November 1968; *Kenchiku Bunka* (Tokyo), April 1971; *Architecture + Urbanism* (Tokyo), November 1972.

The work of MLTW has evolved in many ways over the last ten year period. Primarily we believe in "place making," that architectural quality derived from site and insight that allows the participant to feel a heightened consciousness of being alive and enjoying the awareness of it. We try to identify and celebrate the individual with all his hopes and aspirations in an increasingly complex and mechanized world.

Within the realm of the automobile, "strip" development, and plastic subdivisions, we in California still look back to the land itself for basic insights—sun, topography and microclimate. We feel that our buildings must be well-rooted in their environments, drawing from the landscape's inherent resources while at the same time commenting on owner's idosyncrasies, desires and budgets.

It seems to us that a building, to provide more than mere shelter, must have a conceptual idea, one that speaks to an insight of the client's needs, both tangible and intangible, and thereby to excellence in architecture. To be successful, a building must be compelling for the mind—as well as keeping out the rain.

The Sea Ranch Condominium (1965) provided a solution for multi-family vacation housing by preserving open land and clustering units. It combined simple repetitive pieces under large roofs that followed the ground contours and resembled "big houses" in the grand seashore tradition (albeit in our case Western and rural). Interiors of vacation homes, we felt, need not be stiff and formal, as proper faces put on for neighborhood consumption in the everyday world. Our condominiums had kitchens and baths stacked like furniture (and painted that way), while bedrooms were two-story derivations of an old four-poster bed. Construction as a heavy timber cage pragmatically solved the structural forces of wind and earthquake, while poetically reminding the inhabitant that the northern coast of California is still a rough, wild, frontier environment.

Ten years later the Zimmermann House, outside Washington, D.C., is a maturation of our concerns with "place" and conceptual image. In this project the owners were at odds with one another about what constituted a house. Mr. Zimmermann felt that a house should be a place of light-filled spaces, while Mrs. Zimmermann wished to have one of many porches recalling her childhood in the old summer houses of Maine. The house wanted to be, in essence, a "grand porch" enclosing an inner house whose roofs themselves became useful decks within this grand superannuated gazebo. The porch has a translucent fiberglass roof to let in overall light, a device we first used on the Swimming/Tennis Facility at Sea Ranch. The exterior of the porch is covered in 1×4 lattice work to filter the sunshine, frame views, and establish a boundary between the inside and outside worlds. Simple plywood walls and aluminum windows of the inside house continue our respectful involvement with common builder materials and the simplicity of detail. The structure of the porch cage is made up of groupings of small pieces of wood, from 2×12's to 2×6's, with fewer pieces as the structure grows above the ground. Like the Condominium, these carrying and bracing members are all exposed for the eye and the mind to perceive. The deceptively simple structure sits quietly on a rise of ground overlooking farmland and the Potomac River. A paradox pleasantly resolved.

Architecture without space and light is devoid of interest. In its making, architecture should delight the mind, respect the purse, and consume the intellect.

—William Turnbull, Jr.

William Turnbull Jr. is a narrative architect. His buildings are carefully crafted fables about shelter, program, site, climate, tradition, and movement through space. His Zimmermann house near Washington D.C. makes a virtue of a contradictory program. The husband wanted lots of light and the wife wanted lots of porch, to recall summers on the verandah of a house in Maine. But a conventional porch would have cut off much of the light. So Turnbull made it unconventional. He abstracted a traditional porch relative—the gazebo—and cast it over the entire house. He produced a dramatic compromise: a sunshade which is also a light filter. The net-like pattern of lathwork even recalls the porch screens of McKim, Meade and White's Newport Casino and the general porch look of late 19th Century New England summer houses. The moral here is that history is always new.

Another house, on a ranch near Modesto in the hot San Joaquin Valley of California, required greater protection from the sun as well as privacy for each member of a large family, which nevertheless liked to live out of doors. The house appears to be a large, simple, rectangular, hip roofed pavilion surrounded by verandahs rhythmically marked off in bays. The image combines the sheltering quality of General Mariano Vallejo's verandah-girt Petaluma Adobe—the classic California ranch house—with an almost Palladian manipulation of symmetry and proportion. It looks new but familiar at the same time, in the manner of the best Bay Region work of William Wurster. But the interior reveals a surprise O. Henry ending to this tale of life on the ranch. For the single enclosing roof form hides two quite separate houses—one for the parents and one for the children. The two structures are connected by a courtyard which is protected but not covered by a section of the roof which has been cut away leaving only the supporting timbers. Here, too, the light is filtered, now through a timber screen, and the court becomes a down-home oasis for recuperation after the round-up.

It is fitting that a storytelling architect should design a house for books. Turnbull's new Biloxi Library and Cultural Center in Mississippi provides the backdrop for the imaginary journey which every reader makes. A library is a place for people to sit while their minds wander away. But before they sit down they can be put in the proper reflective mood. The story here is about entrance and departure, about the way a series of thresholds can accentuate the sensation of arrival. The building resembles an abstracted lobster: the two pincers or wings define a central entrance courtyard, past a flagpole and the original tiny wood frame library which has been preserved. The door is framed in a flat gable capped with a rectangular cut-out or empty belfry at the top. The simple abstract image brings to mind the front stoops of small town churches, schools, and meeting houses of once upon a time. A short passage leads to the high, wide main reading room. To the left is the two story circular circulation (!) "temple," a central desk surrounded by interpenetrating framing devices. Beyond and through the circulation desk, which is also a circulation space, lies the exhibition hall. Entrance here consists of a passage dividing a dramatic double stairway leading up to the light. Another major entrance, or exit, leads outside through the corner of the building. The walk from either side of the building to the circulation desk at the center is a theatrically controlled journey. After all, borrowing a book is a very special event and should be commemorated.

Turnbull's architecture is important because it fashions memorable and modern settings out of ordinary and historical elements. He transforms buildings into places and makes them fun to read.

—Daniel Gregory

TUSQUETS Guillen, Oscar.

Spanish. Born in Barcelona, 14 June 1941. Educated at the Deutsche Schule, Barcelona, 1950–54; Escuela de Artes y Oficios Artísticos, Llotja, Barcelona, 1954–58; Escuela Tecnica Superior de Arquitectura, Barcelona, 1958–65: studied with Federico Correa Ruiz. Served in the Spanish Army, in Tarragona and Lérida, 1961, 1962, 1965: 2nd Lieutenant. Married Beatriz de Moura in 1964. Formed the partnership, Studio PER, with Christian Cirici, q.v., Lluis Clotet, q.v., and Pep Bonet, q.v., Barcelona, 1965. Professor in charge of Projects, Escuela Tecnica Superior de Arquitectura, Barcelona, 1975–76. Member of the Cultural Delegation, Colego Arquitectos Cataluña y Baleares, 1966–67, 1976–78. Exhibitions: *Arquitectura del Studio PER*, Lérida, 1971; *Triennale*, Milan, 1973; *Arquitectura y Lágrimas*, Sala Vincon, Barcelona, 1975; *Centenario de la Escuela Tecnica Superior de Arquitectura de Barcelona*, Palacio Nacional, Barcelona, 1977; *Festival of Films about Architecture*, Centre Georges Pompidou, Paris, 1978. Recipient: Premio F.A.D., 1965, 1972. Address: Studio PER, Caspe 151, Barcelona 13, Spain.

Works:

1963 Colegio Mayor San Raimundo de Peñafort, Barcelona (with Lluis Clotet)
1965 Editorial Lumen Offices, Barcelona (with Lluis Clotet)
 Emilio Blay House interiors, Barcelona (with Lluis Clotet)
 Apartment Block I, Cadaqués, Gerona, Spain (with Lluis Clotet and Xavier Carulla)
 Sonor Hi-Fi shop and studio, Barcelona (with Lluis Clotet and Xavier Carulla)
1968 Gremio Vidrieros Building, Barcelona (with Lluis Clotet and Xavier Carulla)
 Maspons-Ubina Studio, Barcelona (with Lluis Clotet and Xavier Carulla)
 Fonda Sala Restaurant, Olost de Llusanes, Barcelona (with Lluis Clotet and Xavier Carulla)
 Ibars Offices, Barcelona (with Lluis Clotet and Xavier Carulla)
 Casa Fullá apartment building, Barcelona (with Lluis Clotet and Santiago Loperena)
 Single-family housing, La Atmella del Vallés, Barcelona (with Lluis Clotet and Xavier Carulla)
 Solitari Apartments, Cadaqués, Gerona,

Spain (with Lluis Clotet and Xavier Carulla)
 El Colomer Apartment Complex, Cadaqués, Gerona, Spain (with Lluis Clotet, Santiago Loperena, and Anna Bohigas)
 Casa Penina (house), Cardedeu, Barcelona (with Lluis Clotet, Santiago Loperena, and Anna Bohigas)
 Ancla Roja Apartments, Salou, Tarragona, Spain (with Lluis Clotet and Anna Bohigas)
 Miró Otro exhibition plan, Barcelona (with Lluis Clotet, Pep Bonet, and Cristian Cirici)
1970 Gil Sala residential additions, Barcelona (with Lluis Clotet, Santiago Loperena, and Anna Bohigas)
1971 Casa Regás (house), Llofriu, Gerona, Spain (with Lluis Clotet, Santiago Loperena, and Anna Bohigas)
 Puig and Cadafalch Housing Block, Mataró, Barcelona (with Lluis Clotet, Santiago Loperena, and Anna Bohigas)
 Unión Lloyd Travel Agency Building, Barcelona (with Lluis Clotet, Santiago Loperena, and Anna Bohigas)
1972 Aerojet Travel Offices, Barcelona (with Lluis Clotet, Santiago Loperena, and Anna Bohigas)
 Belvedere Georgina (house), Llofriu, Gerona, Spain (with Lluis Clotet, Santiago Loperena, and Anna Bohigas)
1973 Mozart-Fortuny Apartments, Sant Cugat del Valles, Barcelona (with Lluis Clotet, Santiago Loperena, and Anna Bohigas)
 Aerojet Travel Offices, Palma, Majorca (with Lluis Clotet and Santiago Loperena)
 Alpes Building, Hospitalet, Barcelona (with Lluis Clotet, Santiago Loperena, and Anna Bohigas)
1974 Tusquets Family Apartment alterations, Barcelona (with Lluis Clotet, Santiago Loperena, and Anna Bohigas)
 Casa Vittoria (house), Pantelleria, Italy (with Lluis Clotet)
 Stephanie Apartment, Barcelona (with Lluis Clotet, Santiago Loperena, and Anna Bohigas)
 Sahutuje Studio, Barcelona (with Lluis Clotet, Santiago Loperena, and Anna Bohigas)
1975 Jacob Levy Apartment, Barcelona (with Lluis Clotet, Santiago Loperena, and Anna Bohigas)
 Feria Textiles Exhibition Stand, Valencia (with Lluis Clotet)
1976 Housing group, Sardanola, Barcelona (with Lluis Clotet, Santiago Loperena, and Anna Bohigas)

Publications:

By TUSQUETS: books—*Arquitectura Modernista,* with Lluis Clotet, Barcelona 1968; *Arquitectura Gótica Catalana,* with Lluis Clotet, Barcelona 1968; *Arquitectura y Lágrimas,* with Lluis Clotet, Barcelona, 1975; *Vivir en la Ciudad,* Barcelona 1976; articles—"Elogio de los espacios tontos" in *Nuevo Ambiente* (Barcelona), no. 16, 1969; "Porque Cruyff si y Alvar Aalto no?" in *Arquitectura Bis* (Barcelona), May 1974; "B.D. Ediciones de Diseño y su local en Madrid" in *Arquitectura* (Madrid), nos. 204–205, 1977; articles, with Lluis Clotet—"Acondicionamento sala estar y comedor" in *Cuadernos Arquitectura* (Barcelona), no. 4, 1965; "Viviendas en Hospitalet de Llobregat" in *Hogar y Arquitectura* (Madrid), October 1968; "Casa Regás" in *Cuadernos Arquitectura* (Barcelona), July/August 1972; "El chalet masia" in *Mobelart* (Barcelona), October 1972; "Belvedere Georgina casita unifamiliar" in *Cuadernos Arquitectura* (Barcelona), September-/October 1973; "Mi Terraza, Studio PER en el In-

dustrial Design de la Triennales de Milan" in *Hogares Modernos* (Barcelona), November 1973; "Biblioscala de un piso en Barcelona" in *Nuevo Ambiente* (Barcelona), March/April 1974; "Manzana Puig i Cadafalch" in *Cuadernos de Arquitectura Anuario* (Barcelona), no. 109, 1975; "Viviendas en Sant Cugat" in *Cuadernos de Arquitectura Anuario* (Barcelona), no. 110, 1975.

On TUSQUETS: books—*Casa Vittoria, Pantelleria* by the Habitat editors, Barcelona 1976; *El Studio PER o los confines de la Arquitectura actual* by J. Muntañola, Barcelona 1976; *Arquitecturas Catalanas* by Helio Piñón, Barcelona 1977; articles—"Los Premios FAD" by Oriol Bohigas in *Serra d'Or* (Barcelona), January 1967; "Canaletas Neighbourhood" by David Mackay in *World Architecture,* London 1968; "Uma lonja em Barcelona" in *Arquitectura* (Lisbon), January 1968; "Chalet en una ciudad jard." in *Nuevo Ambiente* (Barcelona), no. 15, 1969; "Exposición Miró Otro" in *Summa* (Buenos Aires), 20 November 1969; "Vivre dehors: Autour de patios-terrasses" in *Maison Francaise* (Paris), June 1971; "Obras de Clotet-Tusquets," special issue of *Hogar y Arquitectura* (Madrid), July 1971; "Los Premios de interiorismo FAD 1971" in *Hogares Modernos* (Barcelona), January 1972; "Allestimento a Barcelona" in *Domus* (Milan), October 1972; "Nuevas Tendencias de la Arquitectura española" in *Arquitectura* (Madrid), May 1972; "Belvedere Georgina" in *Nuevo Ambiente* (Barcelona), September 1973; "Casa Regas Llofriu" in *Nuevo Ambiente* (Barcelona), November 1973; "Casa Georgina" in *Toshi Yutaku* (Tokyo), November 1973; "Introducir una vivienda functional en un Belvedere Palladiano" in *Domus* (Milan), no. 522, 1973; "Opiniones sobre el Belvedere" by Correa, Sust, and Flores in *Jano Arquitectura* (Barcelona), December 1973; "Agencia Viajes Aerojet" in *Nuevo Ambiente* (Barcelona), March 1974; "Gil Sala Building" in *Toshi Yutaku* (Tokyo), no. 8, 1975; "El plano en el espacio" by X. Sust in *Jano Arquitectura* (Barcelona), December 1975; "Casa Vittoria en la isla de Pantelleria" in *Arquitecturas Bis* (Barcelona), May/June 1976; "Anarchist's Guide" by Chris Fawcett in *Architectural Association Quarterly* (London), vol. 7, no. 3, 1976; "C'e un designer sul trapezio" by Bruno Zevi in *Espresso* (Milan), 23 July 1977; "Studio PER," special issue of *Architecture + Urbanism* (Tokyo), April 1977; "Per, uno per uno, tutti per tutti" by Alessandro Mendini in *Modo Milano* (Milan), November 1977.

There it comes, the Great Circus of the Culture of Architecture with artists from all over the world. The foolhardy Archigrams, the Tendenzas, rigorous lion-tamers, the Radicals, famous contortionists, the Five Architects, reincarnation of the clown in the thirties . . . and a lot more.

The happy strolling band runs untiring around the world, sets up its tent in any Congress or University and develops the show, always new, always repeated. Ideal towns, universal panaceas, paternalist warnings . . . there isn't any relation with what one really builds, but the circus is like that: a healthy evasion.

It is very difficult to be able to perform in this show, yet from time to time some death or the dictation of fashions causes some vacancies. The new artists are recruited in the most sophisticated universities, where one doesn't waste time in practical training, as its pupils are not going to build that much. It isn't easy for Spanish provincials like us to obtain a role in this troupe.

Nevertheless, as every day the possibility to realize a work becomes more remote, a work that would allow us to really intervene in our surroundings—that is, an architectural work—we exercise ourselves in pirouettes and jumps, hoping that one day the great circus will notice us.

—Oscar Tusquets

See CLOTET Ballus, Lluis.

U

UNGERS, O(swald) M(athias).

German. Born in Kaiseresch/Eifel, 7 December 1926. Educated at elementary and high schools in Mayen, Germany, 1932–47; Technische Hochschule, Karlsruhe, under Egon Eiermann, 1947–50, Dip.Arch. 1950. Served in the Germany Army, 1945–46. Married Liselotte Ungers in 1956; has one son and two daughters. In private practice, Cologne, since 1950, Berlin, since 1964, and Ithaca, New York, since 1970. Professor and Ordinarius (Chair in Urban Design), Technical University, Berlin, since 1963 (Dean of the Faculty of Architecture, and Senator, 1965–67; Vice-Dean of the Faculty of Architecture, 1967–68); Visiting Critic, 1965, 1967, Chairman of the Department of Architecture, 1969–75, and since 1975 Professor of Architecture, Cornell University, Ithaca, New York. Visiting Professor, Harvard University, Cambridge, Massachusetts, 1973; Professor of Architecture, University of California at Los Angeles, 1974–75. Exhibitions: *Bienal,* Sao Paulo, Brazil, 1957; *20 German Architects,* Warsaw and Chicago, 1960; *Cologne Architects' Buildings,* Cologne, 1963; *James Stirling and O. M. Ungers,* Zurich, 1965; *German Architecture,* Moscow, 1967; *Rational Architecture,* London, 1975; *Nine International Architects,* Dortmund, 1976; *Biennale,* Venice, 1976; *MantransForms,* Cooper-Hewitt Museum, New York, 1976; *The Sparkling Metropolis,* Guggenheim Museum, New York, 1978. Recipient: First Prize, Frankfurt Kommende Competition, 1960; First Prize, Berlin 4. Ring Competition, 1975; Special Award, University of Bremen, 1976; First Prize, Hotel Berlin Competition, 1977. Address (office): 60 Belvederstrasse, 5000 Cologne 41, Germany.

Works:

1953/
58   Institute for Science Studies, Oberhausen, Germany
1956   Student housing, Lindenthal, Cologne
1957   Housing complex, Nippes, Cologne
        Apartment block, Dellbrück, Cologne
        Two-family house, Cologne
1958   Apartment block, Hansaring, Cologne
1959   Ungers House, Müngersdorf, Cologne
        Apartment block, Wuppertal, Germany
1959/
62   Housing complex, Poll, Cologne
        "Deutsche Order" (renovation, Frankfurt Kommende), Frankfurt
1960   Art Gallery, Dusseldorf (competition project)
        Single-family house, Bensberg, Germany (project)
1960/
61   Single-family house, Odenthal-Erberich, near Cologne (with Max Bill and Olivio Ferrari)

        Bold House, Odenthal-Erberich, near Cologne (with Max Bill and Olivio Ferrari)
1961   Single-family house, Bad Homburg, Germany
        Single-family house, Overath, Germany
        Roman-German Museum, Cologne (competition project)
        Preparatory School, Beuel, Germany (competition project)
1961/
63   Garden City Development, Zollstock, Cologne (competition project)
1962   Single-family house, Henneg/Sieg, Germany
1962/
65   Master plan for a housing complex and apartment block for the elderly, Cologne New City, Seeberg, Cologne (competition project)
1964   Student housing, Enschede, Netherlands (competition project; with J. Sawade and G. Geist)
1964/
66   Märkisches Viertel Housing Estate, West Berlin
1965   Museum Complex, Tiergarten, West Berlin (competition project)
        German Embassy, Rome (competition project; with J. Sawade)
        Preparatory School, Mayen, Germany (competition project; with U. Fleming)

O. M. Ungers: Ungers House, Müngersdorf, Cologne, 1959

1966 Housing Estate, Ruhwald, Berlin (competition project)
1967/
68 Housing II, Ruhwald, Berlin (project; with Josef Paul Kleihues, H. H. Moldenschardt, and others)
1972 Blauer See Development, Rüsselheim, Germany (competition project)
Federal Ministries, Bonn (competition project)
1973 Plan for the district redevelopment of Düren, Germany (competition project; with R. Koolhaas, K. L. Dietzsch and A. Krieger)
Systematization master plan for the Tiergarten, Berlin (competition project; with R. Koolhaas, P. Allison and D. Allison)
1975 4th Ring Reconstruction, Lichterfelde, Berlin (competition project; with R. Koolhaas and K. Dietzsch)
Aller-Möhe New Town, Hamburg (competition project; with B. Haffner and K. Mekeez)
Housing, Roosevelt Island, New York (competition project)
Housing estate, Widdesdorf, Cologne (project)
Wallraf-Richartz Museum, Cologne (competition project)
1976 University Complex, Bremen (competition project)
Castle Park, Braunschweig, Germany (project)
Morsbroich Castle addition, Leverkusen, Germany (project)
Housing, Marburg, Germany (project)
1977 Hotel Berlin, West Berlin (competition project)

Publications:

BY UNGERS: books—*Die gläserne Kette: Visionare Architekturen aus dem Kreis un Bruno Taut 1919–1920*, exhibition catalog, with Udo Kultermann, Leverkusen, Germany 1963; *Rudolf Schwarz*, 1963; *Die Erscheinungs Formen des Expressionismus der Architektur*, Cologne 1964; *Veroffentlichungen zur Architektur*, 27 volumes, general editor, Berlin 1965–69; *Optimale Wohngebietsplanung*, with Horst Albach, Wiesbaden 1969; *Kommunen in der Neuen Welt 1740–1971*, with Liselotte Ungers, Cologne 1972, Barcelona 1978; articles—"Für eine Lebendige Baukunst" in *Bauwelt* (Berlin), August 1961; "Aus einem vortrag vor dem Akademischen Architektenverein in Hannover" in *Baukunst und Werkform* (Nuremberg), August 1961; "Zum 'Weltplanungsprogramm' von Buckminster Fuller" in *Bauwelt* (Berlin), no. 45, 1961; "Insegnamento sviluppo e ricerca" in *Casabella* (Milan), no. 300, 1965; "Planning and Accident" and "Structure-Quality-Dimension" in *Bau* (Zurich), June 1967; "Grossform" in *Aujourd'hui: Arts et Architecture* (Paris), October 1967; "Form in der Grosstadt" in *Werk* (Zurich), November 1967; "Big Forms in Habitation" in *L'Architecture d'Aujourd'hui* (Paris), May 1969; "Utopische Kommune in Amerika" in *Werk* (Zurich), June 1970, July 1970, August 1970, March 1971, and August 1971; "Northwest-Zentrum: Ad-hoc Heart of a City?", with Liselotte Ungers, in *Architectural Forum* (New York), October 1970; "City Problems in a Pluralistic Mass Society" in *Transparent* (Vienna), May 1971; "Towards a New Architecture," with Reinhard Gieselmann in *Programs and Manifestoes in 20th Century Architecture* by Ulrich Conrads, Cambridge, Massachusetts 1972; "Early Communes in the U.S.A.," with Liselotte Ungers, in *Architectural Design* (London), August 1972; "Berlin Free University: Nine Evaluations," with others, in *Architecture Plus* (New York), January/February 1974; "Le Comuni del Nuovo Mondo," with Liselotte Ungers, in *Lotus* (Venice), no. 8, 1974; "Oswald Mathias Ungers: Theories, Ideas and Proposals," with Vittorio Gregotti, in *Lotus* (Venice), no. 11, 1976; "A Vocabulary: Oswald Mathias Ungers' Plans for Rebuilding the Town of Marburg" in *Lotus* (Venice), June 1977; "Suggestions and Proposals for Five Workers' Housing Estates," with Josef Paul Kleihues, in *Bauwelt* (Berlin), April 1978.

On UNGERS: books—*Neue Deutsche Architektur* by Ulrich Conrads and Werner Marschall, Stuttgart 1962, as *Contemporary Architecture in Germany*, New York 1962, as *Modern Architecture in Germany*, London 1962; *Architettura tedesca del secondo dopoguerra* by Giovanni Klaus Koenig, Bologna 1965; *Wohnen in neuen Siedlungen*, Stuttgart 1965; *Neue Wohnhauser* by Olinde and Walter Meyer-Bohe, Stuttgart 1966; *The New Brutalism* by Reyner Banham, New York 1966; *Twentieth Century Architecture: The Middle Years 1940–65* by John Jacobus, New York 1966; *Mehrgeschossiger Wohnungsbau* by Karl Wilhelm Schmitt, Stuttgart 1966, as *Multi-story Housing*, New York 1966; *Neue Stadt Köln-Chorweiler* by Harald Ludmann and Joachim Reidel, Stuttgart 1967; *New Directions in German Architecture* by Gunther Feuerstein, New York and London 1968; *Reisefuhrer zur modernen Architektur—Deutschland* by Grete Hoffman, Stuttgart 1968; *German Architecture 1960–1970* by Wolfgang Pehnt, New York 1970; *Architettura Rationale* by Enzio Bonfanti and others, Milan 1973; *Wohnungsbau—The Dwelling—L'Habitat* by Harald Deilmann and others, Stuttgart 1973; articles—"Bauten und Projekte von O. Mathias Ungers" in *Bauwelt* (Berlin), 22 February 1960; "Focus VI: O. M. Ungers" by Ulrich Conrads in *Zodiac* (Milan), no. 9, 1962; "I protagonisti dell'architettura contemporanea: O. M. Ungers" in *Rassegna dell'Istituto di Architettura e Urbanistica* (Rome), December 1965; "Germania di Oggi: O. M. Ungers" by L. Bisogli in *Casabella* (Milan), May 1966; "Betrachtungen über das Schaffen der Architekten O. M. Ungers" by Jürgen Paul and "Oswald Mathias Ungers: Ein Beitrag zur Architektur" in *Deutsche Bauzeitung* (Stuttgart), July 1966; "O. M. Ungers—Sozialer Wohnungsbau 1953–1966" in *Baumeister* (Munich), May 1967; "The Contribution of Oswald Mathias Ungers to Architecture" by Carlo Aymonino in *Controspazio* (Bari, Italy), November 1975; "O. Mathias Ungers" by Vittorio Gregotti in *Lotus* (Venice), January 1976; "Oswald Mathias Ungers" in *Dortmunder Architekturausstellung*, edited by Josef Paul Kleihues, Dortmund 1976.

Bibliography: *The Architecture of Oswald Mathias Ungers: A Bibliography* by Gerardo Brown-Manrique, Council of Planning Librarians, Monticello, Illinois 1977.

On a fine Spring day in Vienna I met with O. M. Ungers to talk about architecture.

We discovered that there are three trends that lead us both to expect the worst for the development of architecture: first, the trend towards imitative historicism in which the new is merely a banal quotation from the past, and design exhausts itself in copying and signifies nothing; secondly, the trend to romanticism through kitsch, which discerns the lofty pretension of architecture as artistic concern and considers itself original in the sense of "something for everyone;" and thirdly, the trend of the "down-path path," that is, the architect's flight from his own responsibility into the political hide-and-seek of so-called "participation" in which (in a democratic interpretation of architecture) the will of the people decides how a house or a street or a square in the town shall look. Ungers believes that the architect alone must take full responsibility for the shaping of the environment, that this responsibility is also political and above all undivided and entire. Architects must find the courage to represent their understanding of form.

Ungers wants to advance to autonomy of form by means of asceticism and discipline in planning, so that with simple forms, on the one hand, geometric systems will break down complexity, but, on the other hand, chance as a creative dimension will be impossible. An intellectualized aesthetic with a certain monumental pretension will result.

Ungers says, "Architecture means an analytical discussion with the environment which is developed and stamped by time." Form is the outcome of a dialectical process between the complex given facts of a situation and a particular period of time as well as the defined ideal images that result. So that architecture may remain humanistic and not become hostile to the user, Ungers proposes Contextualism, the integration of actual circumstances without imitating those circumstances. Contextualism is not pragmatic or solely utilitarian, nor should it prevent innovation in architecture.

Ungers regards architectural creations as individual solo performances for which the architect is responsible and must assume the associated challenges. He feels that the collective or civil initiative has not yet furnished any convincing evidence that it is a discoverer or producer of cultural performances. In the history of the West these performances have always been produced by individuals. Twenty years ago, in a manifesto, Ungers said: "Freedom lives only in the constant discussion of individuals with reality and in the perception of inner personal responsibility towards place, time and man."

I asked Ungers what he meant, then, by social architecture, and what significance he attached to his archetypal forms.

He said: "Social architecture is a degree of quality (not quantity) in the design of public places—that is, halls, foyers, galleries, streets, squares. The public place, experienced and lived in by the community, is the most important basis of identity for people in the town."

And he regards the archetypes not simply as fixed forms that allow for continual use and which everyone understands, but also as the conceptual in architecture, its maintenance of value, its timeless expression of excellence. By means of analogies which the architect works at and recomposes, architecture as expression, despite its pretensions to "autonomous form," will become abundant and full of fantasy.

—Justus Dahinden

URABE, Shizutaro.

Japanese. Born in Settsu, Japan. In partnership with Mazakazu Morimoto, Osaka. Address: Urabe and Morimoto, Shin-Hankyu Building, 8 Umeda, Kitaku, Osaka, Japan.

Works:

1961 Japan Craft Museum, Osaka
Ohara Art Museum, Kurashiki, Japan
1962 Apartment building, Osaka
1963 Aizen Children's Welfare School, Japan
1964 Kokusai International Hotel, Kurashiki, Japan
Rayon Konodai Apartment Building, Kurashiki, Japan
1966 Suita Rest House, Nagoya-Kobe Expressway
Zokei University of Art and Design, Tokyo
1967 Nara Youth Hostel, Japan
1968 Rayon Research Center, Kurashiki, Japan
1969 Nishitetsu Grand Hotel, Fukuoka, Japan
1970 Hotel Plaza, Oyodo, Osaka
1972 Civic Center, Kurashiki, Japan
Matsushita Memorial Archives Building, Kii Scenic Memorial Hills Park, Japan
1973 Ibusuki Tourist Hotel, Japan
1974 Tamano Civic Hospital, Japan
Ivy Square, Kurashiki, Japan

Shizutaro Urabe: Kokusai International Hotel, Kurashiki, Japan, 1964

Publications:

By URABE: articles—"A Personal View of Frank Lloyd Wright" in *Kohusai Kentiku* (Tokyo), March 1965; "Nature and Humanity" in *The Japan Architect* (Tokyo), October 1972; "Osaragi Jiro Commemorative Hall" in *Kenchiku Bunka* (Tokyo), June 1978.

On URABE: articles—"Japan Craft Museum, Osaka" in *The Japan Architect* (Tokyo), January 1961; "Kurashiki International Hotel" in *The Japan Architect* (Tokyo), May 1964; "Tokyo University of Art and Design" in *Kenchiku Bunka* (Tokyo), June 1966; "The Kurashiki Central Research Center" in *The Japan Architect* (Tokyo), November 1968; "The Nishitetsu Grand Hotel, Fukuoka" in *The Japan Architect* (Tokyo), October 1969; "The Hotel Plaza, Oyodo, Osaka" in *The Japan Architect* (Tokyo), February 1970; "Kurashiki Civic Center" in *The Japan Architect* (Tokyo), October 1972; "Tamano Civic Hospital" in *The Japan Architect* (Tokyo), April 1974; "Kurashiki Ivy Square" by Masakazu Morimoto in *The Japan Architect* (Tokyo), October 1974.

Kurashiki at 6:30 in the morning; a place reveals itself before one's eyes into the gradual build-up of a picture. The light fashions a sense of direction: one is conscious, with every step, of facing this way or that. Kurashiki, where day meets night exactly half way, was a good setting for morning. No one was there. I was free to look at just what I pleased. The river. A bridge spans it in a low arc that recognizes the fundamental properties of matter. The sublime reflection of the thick green water. The place is well made, solid and void in the right mix. Walking through it is a matter of following the walls. There are times when everyone likes to withdraw from the world of immediate pressures: this is a good place for that. One's thought, like one's feet, follows the walls—a series of right and left turns into scenes differentiated in volume and colour. Again and again, one's path crosses where one has been before, but always the approach is from a fresh angle, eye and foot taking it in, surveying it all. It could be a channel made from stone walls some two or three metres high, the path itself a metre broad. From time to time the channel bends, so that although the path is heading straight it leads, in fact, through a series of gentle curves. Imprisoned by the walls, one gets along as best one can, subject to the will of the walls at all times. Nonetheless, I walk.

Shizutaro Urabe. His is a vernacular rescued from the museums and resuscitated. A revivalist fervour is tempered by a sober analysis of actuality. 1001 nights of Japanese architecture. His method—the plastic reorganization of the *kura* (storehouse), which, along with the castle, constitutes the heavy, massive stream of Japanese history. (For Urabe, Japan is a rampart.) The Ohara Museum is a fortified city wall: he ennobles the concrete by craft techniques, suggesting an alternative to concrete brut, leading towards a kind of archivist's architecture.

Though tendentious, what he says is never without substance. Inside the Kokusai Hotel, there is an explicit medievalizing tendency—heavy wood and cast-iron bannisters, copper light fittings, bulky, textured elements—a fortress against modernity. The interior of the Ohara Museum comprises violent juxtapositions of opposing histories in space: one walks through Bannister Fletcher, its pages reorganized randomly, with the Japanese section more or less at the beginning. Even Tange, in his nearby City Hall, takes a temporary break from his exclusivism. Wood details are transposed into concrete, but this tentative move out to Kurashiki is cancelled by the universal interior, where piles of civic documents lay inaccessible and gathering dust in the liquid and undefined space. There's no mark man can make on it. Urabe goes in the opposite direction, making all the marks himself and, consequently, little room for man as well. But that's to exaggerate. It's perhaps best to describe it as a didactic quality, like a basic primer in architectural history, and the graphic quality there is part of it. Problems? One might mistake the inside of the theatre for a play, the interior of the museum for the exhibits—but it's hard to consider them as real problems.

Urabe maintains that man doesn't make history, but history makes man. He swims against the current of architecture. His brief-case is full of books on world history. He speaks of Greece, Rome and Kurashiki in the same breath. (To a packed hall, he writes on the board "shapes are shadows.") He has his arms outstretched and slowly brings them together in front of him, compressing more and more history into a single crystal form, which acts as the paradigm for all of his designs.

—Chris Fawcett

UTZON, Jørn.

Danish. Born in Copenhagen, in 1918. Educated at the Academy of Arts School of Architecture, Copenhagen, under Steen Ejler Rasmussen and Kay Fisker, 1937–42, Dip.Arch. 1942. Worked in the office of Gunnar Asplund, Stockholm, 1942–45, and in the office of Alvar Aalto, Helsinki, 1946; made study tours of Europe and North Africa, 1947–48, and the United States (Taliesin) and Mexico, 1949. In private practice, Copenhagen, since 1950. Recipient: First Prize, Sydney Opera House Competition, 1956. Address (office): 3150 Hellebaek, Copenhagen, Denmark.

Works:

1945 Crystal Palace Development, London (competition project, with Tobias Faber)
Crematorium (project)
1947 Housing Development, Morocco (project)
Central Railway Station, Oslo (project; with Arne Korsmo)
Paper Factory, Morocco (project)
1948 School of Commerce, Gothenberg, Sweden (project; with Arne Korsmo)
Development plan for the Vestre Vika area, Oslo (project; with Arne Korsmo)
1952 Jørn Utzon House, Hellebaek, Copenhagen
Development plan for the Skøyen-Oppsal area, Oslo (project; with Arne Korsmo)
1952/
53 House, Holte, Denmark
House, near Lake Furesö, Denmark
1954/
60 Elineberg Housing Estate, Denmark (with E. and H. Andersson)
1956/
66 Opera House, Sydney (completed by others, 1973)
1957/
60 Kingohusene Housing Estate, near Elsinore, Denmark
1958 Workers' High School, Hojstrup, Denmark
High School, Hellebaek, Copenhagen (project)
1959 Melli Bank, Tehran
Pavilions Complex, *World's Fair,* Copenhagen (competition project)
1960 National Museum, Copenhagen (competition project)
Town development plan for Elviria, Denmark (competition project)
1962/
63 Danish Co-operative Building Company Housing Development, Fredensborg, Denmark
1963 Art Museum, Silkeborg, Denmark (project)
1964 Municipal Theatre, Zurich (competition project)
1968 Utsep Mobler Flexible Furniture (project)
1969 School Centre, with Technical College, Herning, Denmark (project)
Espansiva Byg A/S Timber Component House System (project)
1976 Bagsüaerd Church, Copenhagen

Publications:

On UTZON: articles—"Jørn Utzon: A New Personality" in *Zodiac* (Milan), no. 5, 1959; "The Sydney Opera House" in *Architecture in Australia* (Sydney), September 1960; "Platforms and Plateaux: Ideas of a Danish Architect" in *Zodiac* (Milan), no. 10, 1962; "Terrasserne, Fredensborg" in *Arkitektur* (Copenhagen), August 1964; "The Work of Jørn Utzon" in *Kokusai Kentiku* (Tokyo), November 1965; "The Sydney Opera House" by Peter Keys and Colin Brewer in *Architecture in Australia* (Sydney), December 1965; "Utzon: The End" by Robin Boyd in *Architectural Forum* (New York), June 1966; "The Utzon Story" in *Architectural Review* (London), June 1966; "Jørn Utzon" in *Bauen und Wohnen* (Zurich), September 1966; "The Work of Jørn

Jørn Utzon: Sydney Opera House, 1973

Utzon," special issue of *Arkitektur* (Copenhagen), no. 1, 1970; "Pedagogical Architect" in *Architecture / Urbanism* (Tokyo), October 1973; "Magnum Opus" by Kerry Stephenson in *Building Design* (London), 12 October 1973; "Utzon's Medal for Life-Saving" in *The Architects' Journal* (London), 28 June 1978; "Utzon's Latest: Church in Bagsvaerd" by Philip McLean in *Building Design* (London), 27 October 1978.

Jørn Utzon became well-known with one extraordinary piece of architecture, the Sydney Opera House, which is probably the most outstanding building designed in modern times. Yet all of his work, from an early competition for the Crystal Palace in London to the Bagsvaerd Church in Copenhagen, shows a powerful imagination and a sensitive skill that goes far beyond Danish "impeccability" and makes him one of the most important contemporary architects. In the aftermath of many recent intellectual debates, young architects today frequently look at his work in search of what is "real" in architecture in its most basic sense.

Utzon graduated from the architectural school of the Royal Academy of Fine Arts in 1942, having as his teachers the enormously influential and respected Kay Fisker and Ejler Rasmussen. Initially he worked in the office of Gunnar Asplund and Alvar Aalto; later he spent a period of study at Taliesin East. Eventually the work of the three masters shaped the convictions and the character of Utzon's architecture: he was able to incorporate into his own work the balanced, disciplined juxtaposition of Asplund, the imaginative gestures of Aalto, and the organic structures of Frank Lloyd Wright. Yet his own work matured in an absolutely singular way, with poetical statement strengthened by a professional skill and a spontaneous dedication to those infinite manifestations of human life that make architecture.

Utzon's architecture is founded and developed upon four main principles: the influence of the work of his masters, a laboriously-achieved adherence to a tradition, the understanding that architecture is to be lived in, and an attention to structure and constructive processes. The result is an architecture from which one inevitably learns, since rather than declaring a prior intellectual intent, it contains that intent not only within the strength of a personality but also as the synthesis of the aspirations of all those who will live within its spaces. An early indication of Utzon's preference for an impeccable construction sequence is the two houses built in 1952–53, one for himself in Hellebaek, the other near Lake Fureso, where a distinctive relation between supporting and supported elements is realized.

Utzon experimented extensively with the idea of raised terraces, platforms, and imaginary roofs that make gestures toward the sky like foliage of tall trees tossed by the wind. A number of his terrace sketches are evocative of the ground platforms of Monte Alban in Mexico. In fact, the design that gave him fame, the Sydney Opera House, is conceived as a structure of grand dimensions rising above a system of terraces, so ingeniously proportioned in its parts as to appear much smaller in drawings. The two series of carefully-shaped reinforced concrete shells covering the halls, described as elliptic paraboloids, rise more than two hundred feet above the ground level. They were engineered by Ove Arup, and by virtue of their shape, their mass is placed where it is most advantageous structurally. Thus the design is the result of a successful integration of the work of an architect and an engineer who together produced an unforgettable architectural image. The overall scale achieved in the complex is not only adequate to Sydney Harbor, but it also develops a focus which collects into one vision the otherwise scattered elements built on its periphery. Unfortunately Utzon was forced to abandon the supervision of the work in the midst of construction, and the interior work of the building clearly reflects his departure.

After the Sydney Opera House, Utzon received a number of commissions and prizes not necessarily followed by construction, like the project for the Zurich Theatre in 1964. In 1976 construction was completed of the Bagsvaerd Church, a subtle and beautiful building. It rises like a simple cluster of farm buildings in a suburban area of Copenhagen, its masses of light grey walls complemented by the glittering reflection of glass roofs. The plan consists of a sequence of meeting rooms, courts, and halls which gradually increase in dimension, culminating in the church assembly hall. This changing of vertical dimension is reflected outside, while in plan all rooms are continued within the limit of two skylighted corridors, which eventually become part of the assembly hall itself. To this alternate sequence of dimensions corresponds a particular choice of materials that includes an undulating reinforced concrete ceiling, terminating in a larger wave and capturing the penetration of daylight into the central hall. The free profile of the shell is framed by the rhythmical sequence of the 2.2 meter module of the supporting elements, and is complemented by transparent wood partitions. An harmonious intimacy is achieved within the building in contrast to the subtle ambiguity of the outside, thus reflecting the public and private nature of the architecture. This building expresses an aspiration for spirituality which is complex, intimate and yet common to people; it does so with simple protective signs, leaving the actual making of symbols to the user. The architecture here does not declare a malaise or the inner contradiction of a society, for the architect knows that architecture can be generated only by aspirations for a better world built from life experience: a hopeful aspect of man's endeavors, not the mirror of his confusion.

The work of Jørn Utzon always proceeds from an accurate consideration of site conditions into the articulation of a program within a precise building discipline. Such a discipline comes from the observance of natural laws and from structural integrity, but Utzon's architecture transcends the mere art of building: it evolves its forms into a poetic invention that has a strength and harmony not unlike the forms of Nature herself.

—Romaldo Giurgola

UYTENBOGAARDT, Roelof S(arel)

South African. Born in Cape Town, 23 June 1933. Educated at the Voortrekker High School, Cape Town, 1947–50; University of Cape Town, under L. W. Thornton-White, 1950–56, B.Arch. 1956; British Academy in Rome, 1957–59 (Royal Institute of British Architects Rome Scholarship); University of Pennsylvania, Philadelphia, under Louis I. Kahn and David A. Crane, 1959–61 (University of Pennsylvania Scholarship; Kahn Scholarship; American Institute of Planners Student Award, 1961), M.Arch. and M.C.P. 1961. Married Mariane Meyer in 1957; children: Ritva, Renera, Mariane. Assistant to the architect Koppel Brown, Kitwe, Zambia, 1955–57; City Planning Designer, Boston Redevelopment Authority, 1961–63; Partner, with Peter J.

Pelser, Uytenbogaardt and Pelser, Cape Town, 1963–66; Principal, Roelof S. Uytenbogaardt, Architect, Cape Town, 1966–71; Principal, with Ian Macaskill and Peter Schneider, Uytenbogaardt, Macaskill and Schneider, Cape Town, 1971–77. Since 1977, Principal, Uytenbogaardt and Macaskill. Senior Lecturer in Architecture, 1966–70, since 1971 Professor and Head of the Department of Urban and Regional Planning, and since 1977 Dean of the Faculty of Fine Art and Architecture, University of Cape Town. Visiting Critic, University of Pennsylvania, 1966, and Columbia University, New York, 1967. Member of the Committee, Cape Provincial Institute of Architects, 1966–71. Recipient: Bronze Medal, Cape Provincial Institute of Architects, 1965, 1967. Address: Uytenbogaardt and Macaskill, 204 Werdmuller Centre, Claremont, Cape Town, South Africa.

Works:

1955 McKerrel House, Kitwe, Zambia
DRC Church Manse, Kitwe, Zambia
Small block of flats, Kitwe, Zambia
1956 African Market, Kitwe, Zambia
Hepworth House, Kitwe, Zambia
1963 Van Zyl Shop, Paarl, South Africa
Primary school, Cape Town (project)
Old Age Home, Cape Town (project)
School, for the Cape Provincial Administration, Parow, Cape, South Africa
1964 Dutch Reformed Church, Welkom, Orange Free State, South Africa
Dutch Reformed Seminary, Cape Town (project)
1966 Development plan for Goodwood, Cape Town (with Barac, Hirst and Field)
Small Hotel, Worcester, Cape, South Africa (project)
House, Seaforth, Cape Town (project)
1967 Bonwit Clothing Factory, Cape Town
Mellini House, Cape Town (project)
Suter House garden and pool, Cape Town (projects)
1968 Crown Mines Property Development (for 40,-000 people), Ormonde, Johannesburg (project; with Urban Design Consultants)

1969 Shell International Offices, Bethlehem, Orange Free State, South Africa (project)
Shell International Depot, Ceres, Cape, South Africa (project)
1970 Gunners Circle Shopping Centre, Epping, Cape Town
1972 Plan for the development of the beach front at Jeffreys Bay, South Africa (project)
1973 Werdmuller Centre, Claremont, Cape Town
1974 Dido Valley Group Housing, Simonstown, South Africa (project)
Runciman Drive Housing, Simonstown, South Africa (project)
1975 De Wet House, Caledon, Cape, South Africa
Garden of Remembrance, Simonstown, South Africa
1976 Belhar Housing, Cape Town
Dorman Housing Development, Hout Bay, Cape Town
1977 Sports Centre, University of Cape Town
Mitchell Plain Housing (2,500 units), Cape Town
1978 Belhar Low-Cost Housing (5,500 units), Cape Town
Steinkopf Community Centre, Steinkopf, Cape, South Africa

Publications:

By UYTENBOGAARDT: book—*Housing: A Comparative Analysis of Urbanism in Cape Town,* with others, Cape Town 1977; article—"The New Urban Environment" in *South African Architectural Record* (Johannesburg), 1966.

On UYTENBOGAARDT: books—*World Architecture 2* by John Donat, London 1965; *A Guide to Architecture in South Africa* by Doreen Greig, Cape Town 1971; articles—"The Symbolic City" by David A. Crane in *American Institute of Planners Journal* (Washington, D.C.), November 1960; "N.G. Kerk, Welkom-Wes" by Neville Krige in *Huisgenoot* (Cape Town), February 1967; "Werdmuller Centre" in *Planning and Building Developments* (Braamfontein, South Africa), September-/October 1975; "Werdmuller Centre" in *Architect and Builder* (Cape Town), May 1976; "Belhar

Roelof S. Uytenbogaardt: Sports Centre, University of Cape Town, 1977

Group Housing" in *Planning and Building Developments* (Braamfontein, South Africa), March/April 1977; "UCT Sports Centre" in *Architect and Builder* (Cape Town), January 1978; "Steinkopf" in *Architect and Builder* (Cape Town), June 1978.

The real concerns of architecture belong to the realm of the timeless. Architecture transcends generations and is for all people. Its continued development is sought in the works of individuals responding to the specifics of place. Regional, local and particular context, as the constraints set up by the given reality and purpose of the building program, is of continued assistance to the design process. In architecture is also the beginning of urbanism, and urbanism again acts as a powerful informant to architecture. In this process there is no sense of the frantic, as one is involved in a continuum in which all of architecture plays a part. Originality is not a goal but a wonderful result of the bringing together of all factors of creativity, and at all times it will be steeped in the experience of that which came before, has been assimilated and given new meaning by the understanding of the present.

—Roelof S. Uytenbogaardt

As a result of his brilliant student career at the University of Cape Town School of Architecture, Roelof S. Uytenbogaardt was awarded the Rome Scholarship in 1957 and spent his first post-graduate years at the British School in Rome. This contact with the historical architecture of Rome and Italy was of particular importance in his formative years, which cul-

minated in a period in the United States where, like so many other graduate students at the time, he came under the powerful influences of Kahn, Crane, and the post-Carpenter Center Corbusier.

After two years of study and work in architecture, urban design and planning in Philadelphia and Boston, Uytenbogaardt returned to work in Cape Town: he started with a small church, went on to a shop, some industrial work, a large commercial complex, and an indoor sports centre. At the same time he has been involved in individual and group housing developments.

To some extent this period has been a process of working through an eclectic rag-bag of the dominant influences of the formative period—the Kahnian influence in the Welkom Church of 1964 and the Bonwit Clothing Factory of 1967, the "style Corbu" in parts of the Werdmuller Centre in 1973 and, to a lesser extent, in the University of Cape Town Sports Centre of 1977. An emphasis on influences would, however, create a superficial view about a number of specific and highly-original architectonic assemblages, only the elements of which indicate a genealogy of remembered images and styles. The Werdmuller Centre is a serious attempt to gain new understandings of how to make a naturally conditioned and adaptive shopping complex that is actually habitable. The Sports Centre, again, is a contribution to a clearer understanding of how to put together a complex variety of university space types. His planning work has ranged from a project for a large new sub-urban development for 40,000 persons at Ormonde, Johannesburg, to a review of the Cape

Town Foreshore Scheme, to several other urban design exercises including important research and development in urban low-cost housing of various types.

All the work, whether architecture or urban design, reflects a view that the visible world is shaped by deep structures, underlying causes and human motivations that it is the role of the architect to explore, understand, and make manifest. It also reflects the view of a "true believer" of the 1960's, a believer in absolute values: it is the role of the architect not only to translate these underlying forces into architectonic form but also to interpret human motivations in the name of man in the abstract.

Roelof Uytenbogaardt is one of the major architectural talents on the African sub-continent, and it is sad to reflect that, perhaps because of malign neglect, his work is not better known internationally. His architectonic virtuosity is at least equal to that of the Australian architect John Andrews, but Uytenbogaardt brings to his work additional levels of perception and involvement. It is worth noting that Uytenbogaardt is an experienced light aircraft pilot: perhaps it is this perspective that enables him to X-ray hidden environmental structures and settlement patterns from above. It is also noteworthy that he has recently also become an avid cyclist. We could speculate that his future work may reflect both the lofty contemplation of aerial absolutes and also a stocktaking of the imperfect hopes and aspirations of ordinary people and enterprises.

—Julian Elliott

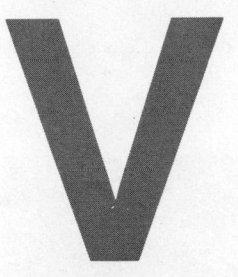

VADÁSZ, György.

Hungarian. Born in Budapest, 18 February 1933. Educated at the Technical University, Budapest, under Károly Weichinger, Pál Csonka, Frigyes Pogany and Máté Major, 1952–57, Dip.Arch. 1957; Master School of the Union of Hungarian Architects, 1958–60, M.Arch. 1960. Served in the Hungarian Army, 1954, 1955. Married Katalin Pusztai in 1954 (divorced, 1964); married Vera Pöhl in 1964; children: György, Katalin, Bence, and Eszter. Architect-Planner with the Office of Urban Studies, Budapest, 1957; Head Planner, Office of Industrial Buildings, Budapest, 1958–64. Since 1964, Head of the Department of Architecture, Office of Urban Studies, Budapest. Lecturer, Faculty of Architecture, Technical University, Budapest, 1963–75. Director, Master School of the Union of Hungarian Architects, since 1978. Exhibitions: *Travelling Theatre*, Royal Festival Hall, London, 1961; Masters School of the Union of Hungarian Architects Exhibition, Budapest, 1961; *International Agricultural Fair*, Budapest, 1962, 1967, 1970; *György Vadász and Tibor Vilt*, Museum of Art, Budapest, 1970; Dwellings Exhibition, Architects Union of the U.S.S.R., Moscow, 1972; *Works of György Vadász*, Sofia, 1973, Varna, 1974, Mongolia, 1975, and Zurich, 1978; Union of Hungarian Architects Exhibition, Budapest, 1977; *Hungarian Architecture 1945–75*, Stuttgart, 1978. Recipient: Ybl Prize, Ministry of Construction, Budapest, 1972; Gold Medal, Ministry of Instruction, Budapest, 1976. Address (office): Herman Otto utca 2/b, 1022 Budapest, Hungary.

Works:

1958   House, Szeged, Hungary (with György Tokar)
1961   ZIM Works, Kecskemét, Hungary
1962   Week-end houses, *International Agricultural Fair*, Budapest (exhibition project)
1963   VTR Office Buildings, Szekesfehérvár, Hungary
        Zugló Knitwear Factory Social Center, Budapest
1967   MHSZ: Hungarian Association of Defence Headquarters, Budapest
        ABC Department Store, Budapest
        Week-end houses, *International Agricultural Fair*, Budapest (exhibition project)
1968/
70   Füred Square Shopping Center, Budapest
1971/
78   Hospital Pavilions, Téténya Street, Budapest (with Péter Katona)
1972   Residence for Diplomats, Budakeszi Street, Budapest (with Anna Perczel)
1976   National Cemetery of Mohács, Hungary (with Gusztáv Szlezák)
1978   City Centre, Zalaegerszeg, Hungary
        MEDOSZ: Agricultural Workers Trade Union Headquarters, Budapest (with András Mészáros)
        Thermal Bath interiors, Gellert Mountain, Budapest (with Márta Fohl)

György Vadász: City Centre, Zalaegerszeg, Hungary, 1978

Publications:

On VADÁSZ: books—*Nagyar épitészettörténet* by Rados Jeno, Budapest 1971; *Hungarian Architecture 1945–75*, exhibition catalogue, Stuttgart 1978; *Modern épitészettörténeti* by Kubinszky, Budapest 1978; articles—"Mohács" in *Baranyai Muvelodes* (Budapest), no. 4, 1976; "Wohnhaus in Budapest" in *Bauwelt* (Berlin), no. 3, 1978.

*

In the new society formed after the Second World War, in which there has been a total upheaval within those professions concerned with faith and the intellect, the architect has had to assume, along with his initial role as a constructor, the increasingly important roles of educator and priest. In Hungary György Vadász has not been afraid to assume this new vocation and responsibility and to leave behind the dead end of ordinary production. He seeks to foresee, to master in advance, the ways in which his architecture will be perceived.

This attitude leads him to work in several directions with different objectives—commercial buildings (large shops, commercial centres), housing (blocks of flats and individual houses), offices and socio-cultural buildings (hospitals, an opera house, a library, etc.); he has even created commemorative furniture and monuments.

In his work Vadász leaves nothing to chance. With the meticulous attention to detail of a goldsmith he has composed such works as the town centre of Zalaegerszeg, where he went beyond the functional and material and made well-orchestrated elements spring into space—the modelling of facades (balcony rails, cornices, copings, the proportions of solids and voids), urban furniture (lighting), urban focal points (fountains), etc. In this spatial sequence much is imparted by the play of materials and the richness of the colours in the prefabricated panels which make up the exterior of the buildings.

Vadász uses a vocabulary of warm materials in coloured plasters, glazed surfaces and metallic tracery, and joins them with an animated placing of volumes to create in space an atmosphere which is both dynamic and static. Vadász fascinates with his ability to say so much with so little.

—Zdravko Natchev

VAGO, Pierre.

French. Born in Budapest, Hungary, 30 August 1910; emigrated to France, 1928; naturalized, 1933. Educated at the Ecole Spéciale d'Architecture, Paris, under Auguste Perret, 1928–32, Diploma (first class) 1932. Served in the Marine Nationale, 1934, 1939–44; Medaille de la Resistance, 1945. Married Monique Lesourd in 1934 (died, 1949); children: Jean-Pierre, Florence, Michel and Catherine; married Nicole Cormier in 1968. In private practice, Paris, since 1934. Director of Architectural Studies, Ecole Supérieure d'Architecture, Tournai, Belgium, 1956–66. Since 1971, Professor of Architecture and Urban Design, Sommerakademie für Bildende Kunst, Salzburg. Chief Editor, 1931–49, and Chairman of the Editorial Board, 1950–75, *L'Architecture d'Aujourd'hui*, Paris. Founder, Réunions Internationals d'Architectes, 1932; Secretary-General, 1948–68, and since 1968 Honorary President, Union Internationale des Architects, Paris; Secretary-General, 1957–59, and President, 1963–65, ICSID (International Council of Societies of Industrial Design), Brussels. Has served on the jury of numerous international competitions including: Berlin Centre; WHO Headquarters, Geneva; Tunis Centre; Tel Aviv Centre; Madrid Opera House; UNIDO Headquarters, Vienna. Recipient: Grand Prix d'Architecture, Paris, 1959. Honorary doctorate: University of Stuttgart, 1972. Honorary Member of the Royal Institute of British Architects, of the American Institute of Architects, and of the Bund Deutscher Architekten. Chevalier of the Légion d'Honneur, 1958. Commander of the Order of Gregoire le Grand, 1959, of the Cross of the South, Brazil, 1961, and of the Order of Alfonso El Savio, Spain, 1975. Member, Akademie der Künste, Berlin. Address: 17 bis Quai Voltaire, 75007 Paris, France.

Works:

1928   Memorial to Joan of Arc (competition project)
1934   Pre-fabricated Steel House, *Exposition de l'Habitation*, Paris
1934/
35   Various houses, apartments and shops, Paris
1936   French Section, *Triennale*, Milan
1937   Architects Club House, *World's Fair*, Paris (with Jean Démaret)
1945/
47   Master plan for the historic cities of Arles, Beaucaire and Tarascon, France
1947/
48   Master plan for Le Mans, France
1948/
54   Reconstruction of the Bouches-du-Rhône area, France (chief architect)
1948/
59   Buildings for the Bank of Algeria in Algiers, Batna, Biskra, etc.
1950   School, Tarascon, France
        Church of St. Pierre, Arles, France
        190 housing units, Martigues, France
1951   School, Arles, France
        Mineral water factory, Arles, France
        Dominican Convent, Monteils, Aveyron, France
        United States Army Depot, Landes-de-Bussac, France
1952   School, Montrouge, Paris
1953   Central Bank of Tunisia, Tunis

Housing units, St. Cloud, Paris
Church, Carry-le-Rouet, France
Dominican Chapel, Etrépagny, France
1954 St. Therese Church, Le Mans, France
Villas, Hydra, Algeria
Housing estates in the South of France
1955 Technical College, Marseilles
1955/
57 Housing (2,000 apartments), Le Mans, France

1956 Le Bon Marché, Algiers
1957 Apartment building, Hansaviertel, West Berlin
Church, St. Cyr, Versailles
1958 Basilica of St. Pius, Lourdes (with Eugene Freyssinet)
St. Michel Clinic, Toulouse
1959 Technical University, Le Mans, France
1960 Residence du Parc, Le Mans, France
1961 Technical School, Beaucaire, France

1962/
76 Sablons Quarter, Le Mans, France
1965 Centre of the new town of Ashdod, Israel (competition project)
1968 Library, University of Bonn (with Fritz Bornemann)
1970 Monastery at Nazareth
Master plan for Luxembourg
1971 Monastery Church, Prouille, France
1973 French Cultural Centre, Jerusalem

Pierre Vago: Basilica of St. Pius, Lourdes, France, 1958

1975 University of Lille
1977 Museum and Hostel, Lourdes
1978 Church for 5,000 worshippers, Lourdes (project)

Publications:

By VAGO: articles—"Architecture in France and the Contemporary Problem of Style" in *The Studio* (London), October 1939; "Architettura e Carattere Urbano" in *Domus* (Milan), December 1955; "France, 1969" in *L'Architecture d'Aujourd'hui* (Paris), July/August 1969; "The Architectural Profession in France" in *Der Architekt* (Stuttgart), June 1974.

On VAGO: articles—"Basilica of St. Pius, Lourdes, France" in *Architectural Design* (London), June 1959; "Bibliothèque de Bonn, Allemagne" in *L'Architecture d'Aujourd'hui* (Paris), February/March 1962; "Siège de Calberson à Paris" in *L'Architecture d'Aujourd'hui* (Paris), December 1963/January 1964.

Pierre Vago was born in Budapest in 1910; his mother was the famous singer Ghita Lenart; his father, Joseph Vago, was a well known architect of the modern movement before 1914, associated with the German Werkbund. When Pierre was eight years old, the family moved to Italy, and Italian became his second language; he also speaks German fluently, and since 1928, when he moved to Paris, French has been his language. His life in different countries prepared him for the international rôle he was to play in architecture.

As a poor student of architecture in Paris, Vago supplemented his meagre allowance by writing. Hard working and astonishingly precocious, he gained his first honours in architecture at the age of eighteen in an international competition for a "memorial to Joan of Arc." He studied under Auguste Perret at the Ecole Spéciale d'Architecture. Perret introduced reinforced concrete into architecture, and the influence on Vago of Perret's doctrine of the paramount importance of construction in architecture has been very strong.

Vago belongs to that generation of young architects who rejected both the traditional architecture still prevalent in France as well as the lack of solid craftsmanship of the avant-garde. From the beginning his aim has been to provide the new architecture with a firm theoretical and practical base, to bring about a concentration of its dispersed efforts and an exchange among proponents of its different tendencies. The periodical *L'Architecture d'Aujourd'hui,* founded in 1930, of which Vago was the editorial secretary and soon the editor, was originally to be named *Construire:* the name implies a programme. *L'Architecture d'Aujourd'hui* was international in outlook. It made known in France the achievements and trends of the new architecture throughout the world. Vago's international background and Perretist outlook enabled him to make the review very quickly the most important publication in architecture in Europe.

In 1932 he founded the Réunions Internationals des Architectes (R.I.A.), which was to develop after the Second World War into the Union Internationale des Architectes (U.I.A., founded in 1948), of which Vago was the Secretary-General, that is to say, the organizer. The organization is less one-sided than the CIAM (of which he was also a member); it is also truly international. From the beginning the socialist countries were represented, and U.I.A. is one of the few associations in which professional people from both parts of the world can engage in a free exchange of opinions. This accomplishment is due to Pierre Vago's wide outlook, his ability to act as a moderator, and his comprehensive and balanced outlook. The first congresses—Moscow, 1932; Milan, 1933; and Prague, 1935—were even then events of outstanding importance. Vago gave a forum and centre to architects in all countries struggling to break away from traditionalism.

It might be said that Vago's organizing activity is the most conspicuous part of his work; however, he has not neglected his professional work as an architect and town planner. In fact, he considers creative work to be the most important part of his life. He has practised architecture since 1934. In that year he showed a prefabricated steel house at the *Exposition de l'Habitation* in Paris; in 1937 he built—with Jean Démaret—the Architects Club House at the *World's Fair in Paris.* Towards the end of the war he supervised the regional planning of the Côte des Maures, the area of the Côte d'Azur between Cannes and Toulon, and in 1947 he was appointed Chief Architect for the reconstruction of the Département Bouches du Rhône. Since 1948 he has realized housing projects at Arles and at Le Mans. He undertook the delicate task of reconstruction and development of the ancient towns of Arles, Avignon, and Beaucaire. As architect for the Bank of Algeria he built a number of office buildings in Algeria and Tunisia. As a result of an international competition, he built, with Fritz Bornemann, the great library at Bonn; and in 1957 he was one of the foreign architects who built blocks of flats in the "Hansaviertel" in Berlin. Pierre Vago's best known building is the underground chapel at Lourdes for 25,000 pilgrims, a great work of architecture—and of construction.

—Julius Posener

VALLE, Gino.
Italian. Born in Udine, 7 December 1923; son of the architect Provino Valle, and brother of the architect Nani Valle. Educated at the Marinelli High School, Udine, 1938–41, graduated 1941; Istituto Universitario di Architettura, Venice, 1942, 1945–48, Dip. Arch. 1948; at Harvard Graduate School of Design, Cambridge, Massachusetts (Fulbright Scholar), 1951–52. Served in the Italian Navy, 1943–45: trained at the Brioni Naval Academy, later prisoner-of-war in Germany. Married Piera Ricci Menichetti in 1961; children: Piero and Carla. Partner, with father Provino, 1948–55, and since 1955 Principal, Studio Architetti Valle, Udine. Associate Professor, 1954–55, 1972–77, and since 1977 Professor of Architecture, Istituto Universitario di Architettura, Venice. Chairman, Industrial Design Course, Venice School of Art, 1962–63; Lecturer, Royal Institute of British Architects, London, 1965; Visiting Professor, University of Natal, Durban, South Africa, winter 1967; Visiting Critic, Harvard Graduate School of Design, 1970–71. Vice-President, ICSID (International Council of Societies of Industrial Design), Brussels, 1967–71. Recipient: Golden Compass Award for Industrial Design, 1956, 1962; First Prize, National Competition for the Monument to the Resistance in Udine, 1959. Member, Accademia di San Luca, Rome, 1975. Address: Studio Architetti Valle, 13 piazza primo Maggio, 33100 Udine, Italy.

Works:

1951 Ghetti House, Codroipo, Italy (with Nani Valle)
1954 Migotto House (now Pozzi House), Pasian di Prato, Italy (with Provino and Nani Valle)
 Quaglia House, Sutrio, Italy (with Provino and Nani Valle)
 Cassa di Risparmio Bank, Udine (with Provino and Nani Valle)
1955 Cassa di Risparmio Bank, Latisana, Italy (with Provino and Nani Valle)
 Bellini House, Udine (with Nani Valle)
 Hospital, Portogruaro, Italy (with Nani Valle)
1957 Flats and offices, Trieste (with Provino and Nani Valle)

1958 Town Hall, Treppo Carnico, Italy (with Nani Valle)
1959 Chiesa Graphic Works, Udine
1960 Apartment building, Udine (with Firmino Toso)
1961 Zanussi Factory Offices, Pordenone, Italy
 Nicoletti House, Udine
1963 Sipre Pre-Fab Factory, Udine
 Zanussi Warehouses, Milan and Rome
1965 Office building, Udine
1966 Twin House (Red House), Udine
1967 Vine Factory, Risano, Italy
1968 Messaggero Veneto Printing Works, Udine
1969 Zanussi Service Spine, Pordenone, Italy
 Monument to the Resistance, Udine (with Federico Marconi and Dino Balsadella)
1971 Apartments and offices, Udine (with P. Ricci Menichetti)
1973 Zanussi DP Centre, Pordenone, Italy
1974 Town Hall, Casarza, Italy (with P. Ricci Menichetti)
 Geatti Warehouse and Showrooms, Terenzano, Italy
 Factory, Portogruaro, Italy
1976 Zoppas Factory Canteen, Susegana, Italy
1978 Fantoni Factory, Offices and Service Buildings, Osoppo, Italy
 Valdadige Pre-Fabricated Schools, Udine and Venice
1979 IACP Public Housing, Udine

Publications:

By VALLE: articles—"La Scuola Internazionale estiva del CIAM 1952 a Venezia" in *La Rivista Pirelli* (Milan), December 1952; "Applicazioni della struttura spaziale continua ad ottaedri" in *Rassegna Tecnica della Regione Friuli Venezia Giulia* (Venice), January 1955; "Friuli Venezia Giulia: Aspetti della regione a statuto speciale e problemi del piano di sviluppo" in *Urbanistica* (Turin), no. 40, 1963; "Discourse: Gino Valle" in *RIBA Journal* (London), May 1965; "La Funzione dell'industrial Designer" in *Congresso Accaio,* Luxembourg 1965; "Otto Riposte sui Problemi del Design: La Educazione dell' Industrial Designer" in *Edilizia Moderna* (Milan), no. 85, 1965; "Intervista Registrata nella Primavera del 1970" in *Zodiac* (Milan), December 1970.

On VALLE: books—*Ville in Italia* by Roberto Aloi, Milan 1960; *Una Svolta nelle Costruzioni* by Konrad Wachsmann, Milan 1960; *10 Profili di Artisti della Regione Friuli Venezia Giulia* by Dino Dardi, Venice 1965; articles—"Architettura di Giovani" by Giuseppe Samonà in *Casabella* (Milan), May 1955; "Tre Banche dello Studio Valle" by Francesco Tentori in *Casabella* (Milan), December 1956; "Una Costruzione a Trieste" by Luciano Semarani in *Casabella* (Milan), April 1958; "The Work of Studio Valle" by Joseph Rykwert in *Architecture and Building* (London), April 1958; "Condominium in Trieste" by Reyner Banham in *Architectural Review* (London), November 1958; "La Distruzione Pianificata" by Francesco Tentori in *Casabella* (Milan), February 1959; "Tre Opere ed un Progetto" by Francesco Tentori in *Casabella* (Milan), April 1959; "Il Monumento alla Resistenza" by Bruno Zevi in *L'Espresso* (Rome), May 1959, and in *L'Architettura* (Rome), August 1959; "10 Anni di Attivita Valle" by Francesco Tentori in *Casabella* (Milan), December 1960; "15 Anni di Architettura Italiana" by Francesco Tentori in *Casabella* (Milan), May 1961; "World Studio Valle" by Reyner Banham in *Architectural Review* (London), June 1961; "World" by Reyner Banham in *Architectural Review* (London), January 1962; "Presente e Futuro della Architettura Industriale in Italia" by Roberto Giuducci in *Zodiac* (Milan), January 1962; "The Look of Industry" in *Architectural Forum* (New York), April 1962; "Gino Valle" by Giuseppe Mazzariol in *Zodiac* (Milan), October 1963; "The Work of Gino Valle" by Joseph Rykwert in *Architectural Design*

Gino Valle: Zanussi Factory Offices, Pordenone, Italy, 1961

(London), March 1964; "Things Seen" by Edward Lucie-Smith in *The Times* (London), 21 April 1964; "Edificio Termale" by Maria Bottero in *Zodiac* (Milan), April 1965; "Architetture di Gino Valle" by Joseph Rykwert in *Domus* (Milan), May 1965; "Alle Porte di Milano" by Joseph Rykwert in *Domus* (Milan), May 1970; "Gino Valle: Edifici Industriali" by Joseph Rykwert in *Domus* (Milan), November 1970; "Italian Suavity," editorial in *Architectural Forum* (New York), April 1971; "Gino Valle" by F. Dal Co and M. Manieri in *L'Architecture d'Aujourd'hui* (Paris), September/October 1975; "La Necessita dell'Architettura" by F. Dal Co in *Lotus International* (Milan), no. 11, 1976; "Incontri con i Protagonisti" by P. Carlo Santini in *Ottagono* (Milan), March 1976.

Italian architecture of the last twenty-five years serves as a dramatic mirror of contradictory tendencies that reflect and epitomize the general condition of Western culture. The ideas and buildings produced have been called the work of an uncertain generation, a generation that has witnessed a progressive alienation from the reality of the process of urban development and construction. With typical generosity, Italian architects have labored under the burden of a great number of attitudes, unfortunately not always bringing them to mature consequences. Any attempt to understand the situation is made even more difficult by the fact that the work of critics and analysts is greatly affected by their political convictions, allegiances that frequently intertwine and react with the political attitudes of the architects themselves. Nevertheless, in spite of a variety of "ruptures" and "alternatives," architectural culture in Italy retains a fundamental continuity. It seems that in Italy transformations are only possible in terms of a deep-rooted philosophy of settlement and its idealization into form. This pressing drive for idealization causes, more than is warranted, a search for the exceptional, at times proposed brilliantly, yet often contrasting sharply with the common sense with which life makes its signs. Gino Valle belongs to that roster of architects who express this common sense in their work; and this may well be the reason for the durable quality of Valle's buildings, both technologically and visually.

The city of Udine, where he works, is a town of respectable and often beautiful buildings, already characterized by the activity of G. D'Aronco, one of the most gifted architects of the Italian "liberty." The tradition of building properly and accurately is deep-seated there, and Valle's office is definitely part of that tradition. It is a family office, a strong qualification in itself, which began with Provino Valle, a designer of several important buildings in the city, and it is now the partnership of his two children, Gino and Nani. Gino Valle was educated both in Italy and at Harvard, where he graduated in 1952. Since that time he has completed a large number of projects, most of them built in the region where he lives. Their design is based on the translation of the tenets of the modern movement into a professional experience pointing toward "significance" in architecture. This significance rests in a methodology of design more than in a vocabulary of forms. Valle focuses upon the realization of a "catalog" of elements, a catalog that includes modules of human activities as well as modules of form. These compositional elements are laboriously investigated, scrutinized, and related to the framework of the urban environment.

The results of this continuous and thoughtful professional activity are buildings the forms of which are generated from the design of a program before the actual "reaching-out" for images. It is appropriate that much of Valle's work deals with industrial buildings. The need for a strict adherence to programmatic demands in such buildings is in keeping with the adoption of a methodology of composition of elements, which ends by having a profound influence on the formal vocabulary. The solutions for the Zanussi Factory Offices of 1961 and the computer center for the same company in 1973 are far apart in time but very close conceptually and in terms of their formal references. It is precisely this sense of continuity, both logical and linguistic, that constitutes the "significance" of Valle's work. The same significance is to be found in the architecture of farmhouses, residences, and other "ordinary" structures in the Friuli region. Few of his works are relatively independent of programmatic limits. One is the somber monument to the Resistance in Udine (1969), while another is the Town Hall of Casarza (1974), where the separate structures of a meeting hall and offices are involved in highly formalistic exercises.

Yet even in these instances Valle's work is in a distinctive position with respect to post-war Italian architecture. Within the process of radical transformation that Italian society is undergoing, Valle's work maintains (and in many ways expands) the responsibilities of professionalism in a free society. His investigations of the process of programming and methods of approach to design consciously place the architect at the center of the process of production. For even if the parameters of the architecture of the present may be different from those of the past, the needs are the same: to relate those humanistic functions to architecture without which it has little reason to exist.

—Romaldo Giurgola

van den BROEK, J(ohannes) H(endrik).
Dutch. Born in Rotterdam, 4 October 1898. Educated at the Rijswerkschool, Nijmegen, Netherlands, 1913–17; Technical University, Delft, 1919–24, Dip. Arch. 1924. In private practice, Rotterdam, 1927–37; in partnership with Johannes Brinkman, *q.v.*, Rotterdam, 1937–48; Principal, with Jacob Bakema, *q.v.*, Architectengemeenschap van den Broek en Bakema, Rotterdam, 1948 until his death, 1978. Professor of Town Planning, Technical University, Delft, 1947–64; Supervisor, Academy of Architecture, Amsterdam, 1966–76. President, Good Living Foundation, Rotterdam, and Efficient Housing Foundation, Rotterdam, 1948–67; Member, Executive and Professional Committees, International Union of Architects, 1948–67; Member of the Council, Bouwcentrum, Rotterdam, 1948–67. Member, CIAM (Congrès Internationaux d'Architecture Moderne), from 1947, and Team 10, from 1963. Exhibitions: *Bouwen voor een open samenleving,* Boymans Museum, Rotterdam, 1963, toured The Netherlands, Germany, Austria and Italy; *Pampus,* Stedelijk Museum, Amsterdam, 1965, toured The Netherlands, Austria and the United States; *Samen Bouwen,* Town Hall, Schoonhoven, Netherlands, 1972, toured Austria and Germany; *Progetti e Opere,* Castello Nuovo, Naples, 1974, toured Italy. Recipient: Dutch Critics Prize, International Association of Art Critics, 1972. Honorary Member, American Institute of Architects, Royal Institute of British Architects, Zentral Vereinigung Architekten Oesterreichs (Austria), and Bund Deutscher Architekten (Germany). Officer, Orange-Nassau Order, Netherlands, 1950; Knight, Order of Nederlandse Neeuw, 1966. Chevalier, Légion d'Honneur, France, 1939; Member, Order of La Couronne, Belgium, 1958. *Died* (in The Hague), *6 September 1978.*

Works:

1927/
29 Housing, with shops and restaurant, Mathenesserplein, Rotterdam
1930/
32 Office and apartment building, Mathenesserlaan-Binnenweg, Rotterdam
1931/
33 High-rise apartment block, Schiekade, Rotterdam
1931/
34 Housing estate, Vroesenlaan, Rotterdam
1934 Low-cost housing, Rotterdam (competition project)
1935/
36 Public housing, Mathenesserdijk, Rotterdam
1936 Doctor's house, Keizersgracht, Amsterdam (competition project)

1936/
37 Public housing, Schepenstraat, Rotterdam
1936/
38 Public housing, Stadhoudersweg, Rotterdam
1937 Dutch Pavilion, *World's Fair,* Paris
Hospital, Terneuzen, Netherlands (project)
Plate Holiday House, Rockanje, Netherlands (project)
1937/
38 Public housing, Statenweg, Rotterdam
Holland-America Lines Departure Hall, Wilhelminakade, Rotterdam
Ten Horst-Vogel House, Vierhouten, Netherlands
Niehuis-van den Berg Office extensions, Pastoriestraat, Rotterdam
1937/
39 Snoek House, C.N.A. Looslaan, Hillergersberg, Rotterdam
1937/
40 Van Ommeren N.V. Office Building, Antwerp
1938 House of Art and Science, Rotterdam (project)
Nygh House, Rotterdam (project)
1938/
39 Public Housing, Vroesenlaan, Rotterdam (with Wilhelmus Theodorus Hyacinthus ten Bosch and Albert Otten)
Gestel House, Bentincklaan, Rotterdam
de Arend Central Club House, Rotterdam
Public housing, Bentincklaan, Rotterdam
1938/
40 Low-cost housing, Tarwebuurt, Rotterdam-South
1939 Mass Exhibition Hall of 1941, Rotterdam (project)
Public housing, Statensingel, Rotterdam (project)
1940/
41 Workers' housing, Rotterdam
Temporary shops, Mathenesserlaan, Rotterdam
1941 Garden Housing Estate, Wilgenplas, Rotterdam (project)
Blaak Development Plan, Rotterdam (competition project)
1941/
43 Tollens and Company Dye and Lacquer Factory, Overschieseweg, Overschie, Netherlands
Public housing, Rotterdam-South
1941/
45 Gispen N.V. Factory and Office Building extensions, Stationsweg, Culemborg, Netherlands
1941/
48 Strijp I Terrace Housing, Strijp, Eindhoven, Netherlands
1942 Development plan for the Hofplein, Rotterdam (competition project)
Engels N.V. Slaughterhouse, Garage and Canteen, Landsmeer, Netherlands (project)
1942/
43 Van Nelle Company Warehouse extensions, van Nelleweg, Rotterdam
1943 Reconstruction plan for Schiedamsesingel-Binnenweg, Rotterdam (project)
Post-war public housing, Rotterdam (project; with the Woning-Architectuur Group)
Maritime Centre, Vasteland, Rotterdam (project)
1944 Slaughterhouse and cattle-market, Rotte, Rotterdam (project)
1945 Wevers Circus, Blijdorp, Rotterdam (project)
Parish Centre, Rotterdam-South (project)
1945/
49 Ardath Tobacco Company extensions, Spuiweg, Dordrecht, Netherlands
1946 Reform Church, Kralingen, Rotterdam (project)

1946/
47 Nederlandse Agrarische Industrie Factory rebuilding, Poeldijk, Netherlands
1946/
48 Aircraft Hangar reconstruction, Ypenburg, Netherlands
1946/
49 Holland-America Lines Warehouse and Office Building, Wilhelminahaven, Rotterdam
Thomsen's Havenbedrif Harbour Building, Lekhaven, Rotterdam
1947 Aula University, Diergaardesingel, Rotterdam (project)
Single-family housing (project)
Terraced housing, Hook of Holland (project)
1947/
50 Strijp II Terrace Housing, Strijp, Eindhoven, Netherlands
Holland America Lines Harbour Building, Rijnhaven, Rotterdam
1947/
51 Lamers and Indemans N.V. Factory, Parallelweg, Hertogenbosch, Netherlands
1948 Church Community Centre, Charlois, Rotterdam (project)
1948/
50 2 semi-detached houses, Hornlaan, Beverwijk, Netherlands
Nederlandse Kroonkurk Mij. N.V. Factory and Office Building, Sluisjesdijk, Rotterdam
1948/
51 Termeulen-Wassen-van Vorst Shopping Bazaar, Binnenweg, Rotterdam
1948/
53 City Transport and Motor Services Building, Schiekanaal, Rotterdam
1949 Pendrecht Housing Estate, Rotterdam (project)
Artists Centre (project)
1949/
50 Layout and buildings for the *Rotterdam Ahoy* exhibition, Stadtpark, Rotterdam
Zuid Shipping Union Medical Services Building, St. Jobsweg, Rotterdam
1949/
51 Van Houten and Zn. Metalworks Shop and Office Building, Bierstraat, Rotterdam
Mill and bakery extensions, Binnenhaven, Wageningen, Netherlands
Anthony Veder N.V. Shipping Bureau extensions, Westplein 11, Rotterdam
1949/
52 Van der Meer House remodelling, Prins Bernhardkade, Rotterdam
1949/
53 Lijnbaan Shopping Centre, Rotterdam
Ypenhof (van den Broek House), Kralingseweg 179, Rotterdam
Secondary school with gymnasium, Coppelstockstraat, Brielle, Netherlands
1950 Cinema, Hengelo, Netherlands (project)
Public housing, Drente, Netherlands (project)
van den Broek/Bakema Office extensions, Westerkade, Rotterdam
Van Leer Company Administration Building, Stadionplein, Amsterdam (competition project)
Auction Building, Marconistraat, Rotterdam (project)
Bataafse Petroleum Company Administration Building, The Hague (competition project)
Uttman House, Bennekom, Netherlands (project)
1950/
51 Aircraft hangar, Ypenburg, Netherlands
Terrace housing, Heeswijkstraat, Voorburg, The Hague
1950/
53 Holland-America Lines Works Building, Wilhelminakade, Rotterdam

1951 Hoving House, Drachten, Netherlands (project)
Pendrecht Housing Estate, Rotterdam (project; with Opbouw Group)
Sanders House, Vught, Netherlands (project)
1951/
52 Hispano Suiza N.V. Factory, Terheydenseweg, Breda, Netherlands
Esso Service Station, Ungerplein, Rotterdam
1951/
53 Zuid Shipping Union Station, Bananenstraat, Rotterdam
Veder N.V. Warehouse and Office Building, Ijsselhaven, Rotterdam
Public housing, Blankenburgersingel, Overschie, Rotterdam
1951/
54 Terrace shops and houses, Lange Nieuwstraat, Velsen, Netherlands
1951/
61 Metallurgy Laboratory, Technical University, Delft
1952 Veder House, Kralingseweg, Rotterdam (project)
1952/
53 Niehuis-van den Bergh Works Building, with Housing, Havenstraat, Rotterdam
1952/
54 de Klerk Furniture Shop, Nieuwe Binnenweg, Rotterdam
Public housing, Molenleystraat, Breda, Netherlands
Huf Shoe Store, Hoogstraat, Rotterdam
Horticultural School, Burgmeester H. van Sleenstraat, Brielle, Netherlands
Public housing, with shops, Burgmeester Baumannlaan, Rotterdam
Ten Cate and Company Administration Building, Spoorstraat, Almelo, Netherlands
1952/
55 Public housing, with shops and restaurant, Pleinweg, Zuidplein, Rotterdam
Boilerhouse and Laboratory of Heating Techniques, Technical University, Delft
1952/
56 Terraced and public housing, Maarten Harpertszoon Trompstraat, Brielle, Netherlands
1953 Alexanderpolder Housing Estate, Rotterdam (project; with Opbouw Group)
Van Giessen and Zn. Wharf, Office and Shops enlargement, Krimpen an der Ijssel, Netherlands
Veder N.V. Office remodelling, Westerkade, Rotterdam (project)
Hotel, Rotterdam (project)
Van Ommeren N.V. Office Building, Westerlaan, Rotterdam (project)
1953/
54 Housing, Breedveldsingel, Rotterdam
Layout and buildings for the *E 55* exhibition, Rotterdam
1953/
55 Nurses' Home, Westersingel, Rotterdam
Housing development, Geuzenveld, Amsterdam
Navy Sports Centre, Schulpweg, Rotterdam
1953/
56 Rotterdamsche Kolen Centrale Office and Warehouse Building, Waalhaven, Rotterdam
1954 Sonneveld House Redevelopment, Schiedamsevest, Rotterdam
1954/
56 Public housing, with shops, Mariniersweg, Rotterdam
1954/
57 Galeries Modernes Department Store, Hoogstraat, Rotterdam
Town Hall remodelling, Marktplein, Brielle, Netherlands (with Philippus Bolt and C. Baert de la Faille)

1954/
58 Reformed Church, Burgemeester Honnerlage Gretelaan, Schiedam, Netherlands

T.N.O. Metallurgy Laboratories, Rotterdamseweg, Delft

1955 Visser House, Papendrecht, Netherlands (project)

Zwolsman N.V. Head Office, Utrecht (project)

Sanders House, Juliaanlaan, Rotterdam

Sports Park, Madestein, The Hague (project)

Congress Hall, The Hague (project)

1955/
57 Shopping Centre, Zuiderwinkels, Nagele, Netherlands

School for the Retarded, Burgmeester H. van Sleenstraat, Brielle, Netherlands

Prefabricated public housing, Rijswijk, Netherlands

1955/
59 Terraced and public housing, Vrederust Oost, The Hague

1955/
60 Montessori School, Schimmelpenninckstraat 20, Rotterdam

1956 Hotel, Zeestraat-Javastraat, The Hague (project)

Alexanderpolder Housing Estate, Rotterdam (project; with Opbouw Group)

Single-family housing, Karpendonk, Eindhoven, Netherlands (project)

Diepen House, Wassenaar, Netherlands (project)

Youth Hostel, Oostvoorne, Netherlands (project)

Theatre, Zwartenweg, The Hague (project)

Nievelt-Goudriaan and Company Office Building, Veerkade, Rotterdam (project)

Frik House extensions, Heerenveen, Netherlands (project)

Centre Building, Emmen, Netherlands (project)

1956/
57 Public housing, Hengelolaan, The Hague

Van Giessen and Zn. Offices remodelling, Krimpen an der Ijssel, Netherlands

Wieringa House, Hobbemastraat 2, Middelharnis, Netherlands

1956/
58 Klein Driene Development, Hengelo, Netherlands

Ierland-van Zanten Shop, Lijnbaan, Rotterdam

1956/
61 World Broadcasting Building, Witte Kruislaan 55, Hilversum, Netherlands

1957 Viewing Tower, Stadtpark, Rotterdam (project)

Shopping Centre, Vlaardingen, Netherlands (project)

Maritime Centre, Scheveningen, The Hague (project)

1957/
58 'T Heechterp District Development, Leeuwarden Ost, Netherlands

1957/
59 Nord-Kennermerland Regional Plan, North Holland

1957/
60 Apartment tower block, Hansaviertel, Berlin

Diaconessenhuis Clinic extensions, Westersingel, Rotterdam

Medical Centre, de Cordesstraat, Hook of Holland

Aero- and Hydro-dynamics Laboratories, Technical University, Delft

Het Parool Newspaper Building, Amsterdam

1958 Netherlands Pavilion, World's Fair, Brussels (with Gerrit Rietveld and Joost Willem Cornelis Boks)

Lummus Nederland N.V. Office Building, Plaspoelpolder, Rijswijk, Netherlands (project)

Landbouwhuis (Agricultural Centre), Paternosterstraat, Alkmaar, Netherlands (project)

Capital Centre, Berlin (competition project)

Ter Meulen House, Oude Zeeweg, Noordwijk, Netherlands (project)

Vlaardingen Nord Building, Vlaardingen, Netherlands (project)

Margarine AG/Unilever Office Building, Valentinskamp, Hamburg (competition project)

Shopping Centre, Culemborg, Netherlands (project)

1958/
59 Van Welzenes N.V. Factory, Spijkenisse, Netherlands

1958/
60 *Floriade* horticultural exhibition layouts, Stadpark, Rotterdam

Reformed Church, Ring, Nagele, Netherlands

van Roosbroeck House, Barendrechtseweg, Barendrecht, Netherlands (demolished)

1958/
61 Dura N.V. Office Building, Raadhuisplein, Rotterdam

Analytical Chemistry Laboratories, Technical University, Delft

1958/
62 Town Hall, Marl, Germany

1958/
63 Central Post Office Building, Prinses Beatrixlaan, The Hague

1959 De Nederlanden 1845 Insurance Building, Adelheidstraat, The Hague (competition project)

Shopping Centre, Laan van Meerdervoort, The Hague (project)

1959/
61 Meerwaldt House, Baarsweg, Hoogvliet, Netherlands

Lamers and Indemans N.V. Factory extensions, Parallelweg, Hertogenbosch, Netherlands

Shopping Centre, with maisonettes, Bergen, Netherlands

Terraced houses with shops, Prins Hendrikstraat, Hook of Holland

1959/
62 Grain Testing Laboratories, Technical University, Delft

Leeuwarden Noord Housing Estate, Leeuwarden, Netherlands

Shopping Centre, with houses, Binnenhof, Amstelveen, Netherlands

1959/
63 Road Construction Laboratories, Technical University, Delft

1959/
64 School of Engineering Lecture Building, and School of Architecture Lecture Building, Technical University, Delft

1960 World Health Organization Building, Geneva (competition project)

Radio and television station, Kuwait (project)

Cultural Centre, Leverkusen, Germany (competition project)

1960/
61 Van Buchem House, Offenbachlaan 5, Hillegersberg, Rotterdam

Van Wijk House, Distelstraat 4, Hook of Holland

De Klerk House, Tsjaikofskilaan 7, Hillegersberg, Rotterdam

1960/
62 Post Office, Binnenhof 64, Amstelveen, Netherlands

Junior School and Kindergarten, Smeetslandsedijk, Rotterdam

Raiffeisenbank Building, Prins Hendrikstraat, Hook of Holland

Van Giessen and Zn. Canteen and Drawing Office, Krimpen an der Ijssel, Netherlands

Office building with shops, Tuftmarkt-Kalvermarkt, The Hague

1960/
63 High-rise apartment block, Mariahoeve, The Hague (project)

Office building, Oostingstraat, Emmen, Netherlands

Elementary School, Emmercompascum, Emmen, Netherlands

1960/
68 Town Hall, Terneuzen, Netherlands

1961 Elementary School, Erica, Emmen, Netherlands (project)

Fortgens House, Straatweg, Rotterdam (project)

Timp House extensions, Grindbank, Laren, Netherlands (project)

Steilshoop Housing Estate, Hamburg (competition project)

Frik House, Heerenveen, Netherlands (project)

Shopping Centre, Heemskerk, Netherlands (project)

High School for the Social Sciences, Linz, Austria (competition project)

Plan for Wulfen New Town, Westphalia, Germany (competition project)

Shopping Centre, Jagershoef, Eindhoven, Netherlands (project)

High-rise apartment block, Rozenburg, Netherlands (project)

1961/
62 Auditorium, Technical University, Delft

Central Post Office, Velperweg, Arnhem, Netherlands

Wierda House, Burgemeester Falkenlaan, Heerenveen, Netherlands

1961/
63 Philips N.V. Works Housing, Strijpsestraat, Eindhoven, Netherlands

Van Wilgen House, Mahlersingel, Rotterdam

1962 Development plan for the Woensel District, Eindhoven, Netherlands

Town Hall, Offenbach am Main, Germany (competition project)

Nordweststadt Centre, Frankfurt (competition project)

Centre Building, Spoorstraat, Nimwegen, Netherlands (project)

Van der Sande Wijbrand House, Straatweg, Rotterdam (project)

Lijnbaan Shopping Centre extension, Lijnbaan, Rotterdam

University of the Ruhr, Bochum, Germany (competition project)

Philips N.V. Works Housing, Geldorp, Netherlands

1962/
63 Expansion plans for Hengelo North, Netherlands

1964 Protestant Student Community Centre, Mainz, Germany (competition project)

Town Hall, Jerusalem (competition project)

Town plan for Skopje, Yugoslavia (competition project)

Sociedad Immobiliaria y del Gran Kurssal Maritimo S.A., San Sebastian, Spain (competition project)

1964/
68 Drachten Elementary School, Netherlands

1964/
69 Hermes Student Club, Rotterdam

1965 Zwijndrecht Secondary School, Netherlands

Leo van Ierland House, Rotterdam

Mobile Theatre, for the Dutch Opera Foundation (project; with Frei Otto)

1965/
70 M.B.O. Covered Shopping Centre, Leeuwarden, Netherlands

1965/
71 Drachten Elementary School for Handicapped Children, Netherlands

J. H. van den Broek and Jacob Bakema: Lijnbaan Shopping Centre, Rotterdam, 1953

1965/
76 Town Hall, Ede, Netherlands
1966/
68 Corpac Office Building, Tilburg, Netherlands
1966/
69 Apartment building, Tilburg, Netherlands
1966/
73 Nurses' Dormitory, Leidschendam, Netherlands
1966/
74 I.C.Z. Hospital, Apeldoorn, Netherlands
1967 Sanders House Reconstruction, Schiedam, Netherlands
1968 Medical School, Accra, Ghana
Urban district development plan for Diemen, Netherlands
Exotarium (tropical garden), The Hague
Town Hall, Amsterdam (competition project)
1968/
73 Cultural and Community Centre, Winschoten, Netherlands
1968/
76 D.S.H.B. Old People's Housing, Delft, Netherlands
1969 Shell Company Administration Building, Hamburg (competition project)
Lommerrijk Sports Centre Residential Buildings, Rotterdam
Town Hall and Apartments, Weert, Netherlands
University of Brussels (competition project)
Mummelmannsberg Comprehensive School, Hamburg (competition project)
Student Dormitories, Delft, Netherlands
1970 Netherlands Pavilion, *World's Fair*, Osaka,

Japan (with Carel Weeber)
1971 University Economics Faculty Building extension, Rotterdam (project)
1971/
73 de Grave Home for the Retarded, Gorinchem, Netherlands
1971/
76 Erasmus College Secondary School, Zoetermeer, Netherlands
1973 Zeckendorf House, The Bahamas
Sunter Town Plan, Djakarta, Indonesia (project)
Kurhaus District redevelopment, Scheveningen, Netherlands (as supervising architect)
Barre Molen Windmill restoration, Zoeterwoude, Netherlands
1974 City centre plan for Eindhoven (project; with Herman Hertzberger)
World Trade Centre, Rotterdam (competition project)
Traffic plan for Kloekamp and Main Railway Station, The Hague
Kaatstraat renovation, Utrecht
1975 Renovation of the Weerdjes District, including apartment buildings, Arnhem, Netherlands

Publications:

By van den BROEK: books—*Habitation*, volumes 1–3, Rotterdam 1945–65; *Creatieve Krachten in de Architectonische Conceptie*, Delft 1948; *Woonmogelijkheden in het nieuwe Rotterdam*, with Willem van Tijen, Johannes Brinkman and Huig A. Maaskant. Rotterdam 1941; *Beginselen van Kerk-*

bouw, The Hague 1954; *Gids voor Nederlandse Architectuur*, with Meischke and Boot, Rotterdam 1955; *Scholen*, Rotterdam 1956; articles—"Wie wil goed wonen?" in *Goed Wonen* (Amsterdam), January 1948; "1898–1948: Viftig jaar Nederlandse Architectuur" in *Bouw* (Rotterdam), September 1948; "Open Brief aan J.J.P. Oud," with Jacob Bakema, in *De Groene Amsterdammer* (Amsterdam), 6 December 1952; "Bedrifsgebouwen" in *Forum* (Amsterdam), April/May 1953; "Bouwkunst in dienst van de kerk" in *Wending 8* (Amsterdam), no. 10/11, 1953/54; "Moderne Architektur in moderner Stadtplanung" in *Aachener Zeitung* (Aachen), 25 January 1955; "Efficiente Woningbouw, Standaardplattegronden," with others, in *Bouw* (Rotterdam), 18 July 1955; "Cultuur, Architectuur, Techniek" in *Bouw* (Rotterdam), 23 July 1955; "Efficiente Woningbouw: Hernieuwde activeit van de Studiegroep," with others, in *Bouw* (Rotterdam), 24 January 1959; "Stadt und Wohnung im heutigen Licht" and "Konstruktion und Gestaltung im industriellen Wohnungsbau" in *Der Architekt* (Stuttgart), April 1959; "Stad en jeugd—jeugd en stad" in *Bouw* (Rotterdam), 16 July 1960; "Uit- en Inleiding" and "Doelmatigheid en creativiteit in de woningbouw" in *Delftse School* (Delft), November 1961; "Velen hebben vaal aan hem te danken: In Memoriam B. Merkelbach" in *Bouw* (Rotterdam), no. 44, 1962; "Bewoners moeten mogelijkheid tot variatie hebben" in *Algemeen Dagblaad* (Rotterdam), 3 November 1962.

On van den BROEK: books—*CIAM 1959 in Otterlo*, Stuttgart 1959; *Architektur und Stadtebau: Das*

Werk van den Broek und Bakema, edited by Jürgen Joedicke, Stuttgart 1963; *Bouwen voor een open samenleving,* exhibition catalogue, Rotterdam 1963; *van den Broek/Bakema,* edited by Camillo Gubitosi and Alberto Izzo, Rome 1976; *Architecture-Urbanism: Architecten-gemeenschap van der Broek en Bakema,* edited by Jürgen Joedicke, Stuttgart 1976; articles—"Het Bureau van den Broek en Bakema" by Willem van Tijen in *Forum* (Amsterdam) June 1957; "Costruzioni degli Architetti Jacob Bakema e Johannes van den Broek" by G. Perugini in *L'Architettura* (Rome), September 1959; "van den Broek und Bakema," special issue of *Bauen und Wohnen* (Zurich), October 1959; "Brinkman, Brinkman, van der Vlugt, van den Broek, Bakema" by B. Housden, special issue of *Architectural Association Journal* (London), December 1960.

*

J. H. van den Broek (he was always known by his initials), was born in 1898 at Rotterdam in the Netherlands, where he also studied architecture. Between 1924 and 1937 he was in practice on his own account; from 1937 to 1948 he was in partnership with Brinkman, and in 1948 he joined Jacob Bakema.

van den Broek was of the same generation as architects like Ernö Goldfinger, born at the right time to witness the remarkable architectural developments in Europe of the 1920's and 30's, but not then experienced or practised enough to influence them. In the work and career of van den Broek, as of Goldfinger, we can see the realization and extension of the Modernist ideals made relevant to a more realistic and politically secure Europe than the one before the war.

Although van den Broek's Dutch Pavilion at the Paris exhibition of 1937 secured his reputation as a practitioner of an elevated version of the International Style, his most familiar contribution to European architecture has been with Team 10, a post-war off-shoot of CIAM. Team 10 encouraged a view of architecture which reflected the utopianism of the 1960's. Of the members of Team 10 (Candilis, Josic, Woods, the Smithsons, Ralph Erskine and Stefan Werweka), van den Broek's contribution is perhaps the most anonymous and one which can be least appropriately applied to the group's credo of "building towards society's realisation of itself."

Stylistically, van den Broek refined the Modernism of the 1930's into a thin, tight and neat glacial mode, well suited to the corporate needs of the 1950's. Precision and lightness are twin dominating characteristics of his style.

—Stephen Bayley

van de VELDE, Henry.

Belgian. Born in Antwerp, 3 April 1863. Educated at the Atheneum, Antwerp, 1878–82; studied painting at the Académie des Beaux-Arts, Antwerp, under Charles Verlat, 1882–84, and with the painter Carolus Duran, in Paris, 1884–85. Married Maria Sethe in 1894 (died, 1943); son: Thyl. Worked as a painter and interior decorator, Antwerp and Brussels, 1885–94; produced first architectural works, Brussels, 1894; in private practice as an architect and designer, Brussels, 1895–98, and as Société van de Velde, architecture, furniture and interiors, Brussels, 1898–1900; in private practice, Berlin, 1900–05, Weimar, 1906–14, Switzerland, 1914–21, Wassenaar, near The Hague, 1921–25, and in Brussels, 1925 until he retired to Oberägeri, Switzerland, 1947. Artistic Adviser to the Grand Duke of Saxony, at Weimar, 1901–08, and Founder/Director, Kunstgewerbeschule, later the Bauhaus School, Weimar, 1908–14; Founder and Principal, Institut Supérieur des Arts Décoratifs, later the Ecole Nationale Supérieure d'Architecture, Brussels, 1925–36; Professor of Architectural History, University of Ghent, 1926–35. Founder Member, Als ik Kan cultural

group, Antwerp, 1886, and L'Art Indépendant group, Antwerp, 1887; Member, Les XX group, Brussels, from 1889; Contributor, *Van Nu en Straks* magazine, Brussels, 1890; Member of the Deutscher Werkbund. Exhibitions: *Henry van de Velde 1863–1957: Personlichkeit und Werk,* Kunstgewerbemuseum, Zurich, 1958; *Henry van de Velde 1863–1957: Das Lebenswerk,* Die Neue Sammlung, Munich, 1959; *Henry van de Velde,* Palais des Beaux-Arts, Brussels, 1963; *Henry van de Velde 1863–1957,* Rijksmuseum Kröller-Müller, Otterlo, Netherlands, 1964; *Henry van de Velde,* Salon l'Ecuyer, Brussels, 1970; *Pionniers du XX Siècle: Guimard, Horta, van de Velde,* Paris, 1971; *Henry van de Velde: Theatre Designs 1904–1914,* Architectural Association, London, 1974. Collections: Association Henry van de Velde, Abbaye de la Cambre 21, Brussels 5; Henry van de Velde Gesellschaft, Hochstrasse 73, Hagen, Germany. *Died* (in Zurich) *25 October 1957.*

Works:

1894	Hotel Otlet interiors, Brussels
1896	Interiors and furnishings for the *Libre Esthétique* exhibition, Brussels
	"Bloemenwerf" (van de Velde House), 80 Avenue Vanderaey, Uccle, Brussels
	L'Art Nouveau shop interiors, for the art dealer S. Bing, Paris
1896/97	Salon de Repos interiors and furnishings, *Exposition des Arts Appliqués,* Dresden
1897	Director's Office interiors, Ixelles, Belgium (now in the Osterreichisches Museum für Angewandte Kunst, Vienna)
1898	Loeffler Office interiors, Berlin (now in the Germanisches Nationalmuseum, Nuremberg)
	Director's Office interiors, Brussels (now in the Nordenfeldske Kunstindustrimuseum, Trondheim, Norway)
	Keller und Reiner Art Gallery interiors, Berlin
	Dining Room, *Salon of Arts and Crafts,* The Hague
	Study/Workroom interiors, *Secession Exhibition,* Munich
1898/99	Maison Moderne interiors, for Julius Meier-Graefe, rue Pergolese, Paris
1899	Habana Company shop interiors, Berlin
1900	Stern House alterations, Berlin
1901	Haby Coiffures interiors, Berlin
1901/02	Folkwang Museum interiors, Hagen, Germany (now the Karl Ernst Osthaus Museum; restored, 1955–56)
1902	Herbert Esche House, Chemnitz, now Karl-marxstadt, Germany
1902/03	Leuring House, Scheveningen, Netherlands
1903	Deutsche Bank Building interiors, Augsburg, Germany
	Count Kessler House alterations, Weimar
1903/04	Museum of Fine Arts, Weimar (project)
1903/05	Louise Dumont Theatre, Weimar (project)
1904	Webicht Restaurant, Weimar (project)
	Institut de Sociologie, Parc Leopold, Brussels (project)
	Hermann Harkort Office, Wettern, Ruhr, Germany
	R. and H. Vorster Studio, Hagen, Germany
	Schede House alterations, Wettern, Ruhr, Germany
1904/06	Kunstgewerbeschule, Weimar
1906	Boardroom, for Hagener Textilindustrie, Hagen, Germany
	Museum Gallery, *Kunstgewerbeausstellung,* Dresden

	"Hohenhof" (Karl Ernst Osthaus Country House), Hagen, Germany (now the Henry van de Velde Gesellschaft)
	van de Velde House, Ehringsdorf, near Weimar
1907	Springmann House, Hagen, Germany
	Esche House, Lauterbach, Germany
	Design for the *German Painters Exhibition,* London
1908	Monument, Jena, Germany
1909	Frose House, Hanover, Germany
1910	Vicarage, Riga (project)
1910/11	Theatre des Champs Elysées, Paris (project; built by Auguste Perret, with revisions, 1911–13)
1912	Durkheim House, Weimar
	Nietzsche Monument, Weimar (project)
1913	Baron Henneberg House, Weimar
	Theo Korner House, Chemnitz, now Karl-marxstadt, Germany
	Springmann House II, Hagen, Germany
	Schulenberg House, Gera, Germany
	Museum of Fine Arts, Erfurt, Germany (project)
1914	Baron de Golubeff House, Paris
	Theatre, *Werkbund Exhibition,* Cologne (destroyed)
1921	van de Velde House, Wassenaar, near The Hague
1925	Fyffes Company Offices, Rotterdam
1926	Plan for the Left Bank of Antwerp
	Schinckel-Blankenese House, near Hamburg
1927	"La Nouvelle Maison" (van de Velde House), Tervueren, Belgium
	Cohen House, Avenue des Nations, Brussels
1929	Old people's housing, Hanover, Germany
1930	Wolfers House, Brussels
	Country house, Wassenaar, near The Hague
1930/54	Kröller-Müller Museum, Otterlo, Netherlands
1931	Colman/Saverys Duplex House, Zoute, Brussels
1932	Marquis de Brion Apartment interiors, Avenue Kléber, Paris
	D. and R. De Bodt Duplex House, Brussels
1937	Belgian Pavilion, *World's Fair,* Paris (with I. Eggeriey)
1939	Belgian Pavilion, *World's Fair,* New York (with Victor Bourgeois)
1939/40	Library, University of Ghent

Publications:

By van de VELDE: books—*Déblaiement d'Art,* Brussels 1894; *Apercu en vue d'une Synthèse d'Art,* Brussels 1895; *Die künstleriche Hebung der Frauentracht,* Krefeld 1900; *Die Renaissance im modernen Künstgewerbe,* Berlin 1901; *Künstgewerbliche Laienpredigten,* Leipzig 1902; *Notizen von einer Reise nach Griechenland,* Weimar 1905; *Der neue Stil,* Weimar 1906, 1907; *Vernunftsgemässe Schönheit,* Weimar 1909; *Amo,* Leipzig 1909, 1912; *Essays,* Leipzig 1910; *Werkbund Diskussion 1914,* Jena, Germany 1914; *Les Formules de la Beauté Architectonique Moderne,* Weimar 1916, as *Formules d'une Esthetique Moderne,* Brussels 1923; *Die drei Sünden wider die Schönheit,* Zurich 1918; *Le Théâtre de l'Exposition du Werkbund à Cologne, 1914, et la Scène Tripartite,* Antwerp 1925; *Der neue Stil in Frankreich,* Berlin 1925; *Le Nouveau,* Brussels 1929; *Deux Rapports,* Brussels 1931; *La Voie Sacrée,* Brussels 1933; *Les fondements du style moderne,* Brussels 1933; *L'Art et l'Etat,* with others, Paris 1934; *Vie et Mort de la Colonne,* Brussels 1942; *Pages de Doctrines,* Brussels 1942; *Leerstelling op zoek naar een bestendige schoonheid,* Antwerp 1944; *Geschichte Meines Lebens,* edited by Hans Curjel, Munich 1962; articles—numerous, in architectural journals in Belgium and Germany.

Henry van de Velde: Theatre, **Werkbund Exhibition,** Cologne, 1914

On van de VELDE: books *Henry van de Velde: Vier Essays* by Karl Scheffler, Leipzig 1913; *Henry van de Velde: Leben und Schaffen des Künstlers* by Karl Ernst Osthaus, Hagen, Germany 1920; *Henry van de Velde et le Théâtre des Champs Elysées* by Jacques Mesnil, Brussels and Paris 1925; *Die Künstlerfamilie van de Velde* by K. Zoege von Manteuffel, Bielefeld and Leipzig 1927; *Henry van de Velde* by Maurice Casteels, Brussels 1932; *Stilwende* by Friedrich Ahlers-Hesterman, Berlin 1941; *Henry van de Welde* by Hans Curjel, Munich 1955; *Die Schriften Henry van de Veldes* by Clement L. Ressegnier, Zurich 1951, New York 1955; *Henry van de Velde 1863–1957: Personlichkeit und Werk,* exhibition catalogue, by Hans Curjel, Zurich 1958; *Les Architectes Celèbres* by A. M. Hammacher, Paris 1959; *Henry van de Velde 1863–1957: Das Lebenswerk,* exhibition catalogue, Munich 1959; *Henry van de Velde* by Herman Teirlinck, Brussels 1959; *Henry van de Velde 1863–1957,* exhibition catalogue, by R. Verwilgen, Brussels 1963; *Henry van de Velde,* exhibition catalogue, Otterlo, Netherlands 1964; *Le Monde de Henry van de Velde* by A. M. Hammacher, Antwerp and Paris 1967; *Henry van de Velde* by K. H. Huter, East Berlin 1967; *Henry van de Velde 1863–1957,* exhibition catalogue, Brussels 1970; *Pionniers du XX Siècle: Guimard, Horta, van de Velde,* exhibition catalogue, Paris 1971; *Henry van de Velde: Theatre Designs 1904–1914,* exhibition catalogue, by Dennis Sharp and Maurice Culot, London 1974; articles—special issue of *L'Art Décoratif* (Paris), October 1898; "Henry van de Velde" by Julius Meier-Graefe in *Dekorative Kunst* (Munich), no. 2, 1899; special issue of *Les Cahiers de Belgique* (Brussels), 1931; special issue of *La Cité* (Brussels), April/May 1933; "van de Velde to Wagner" by P. Morton Shand in *Architectural Review* (London), October 1934; "Henry van de Velde: Extracts from His Memoirs 1891–1901" by P. Morton Shand in *Architectural Review* (London), September 1952; "Henry van de Velde zum 90 Geburtstag" by Alfred Roth in *Werk* (Zurich), April 1953; "Omaggio a Henry van de Velde" by Ernesto N. Rogers in *Casabella* (Milan), no. 217, 1957; special issue of *Casabella* (Milan), March 1960; "Gropius and van de Velde" by Nikolaus Pevsner in *Architectural Review* (London), March 1963; "Van de Velde: Theatres" by Dennis Sharp in *Building Design* (London), 28 June 1974; "Kröller-Müller Art Gallery, Otterlo" by R. Padovan in *Architectural Review* (London), February 1978; "The Hohenhof in Hagen" in *Bauwelt* (Berlin), 5 May 1978; "Reflections on the 'Sacred Way'" by Maurice Culot in *Architecture Mouvement Continuité* (Paris), May 1978.

The early years of Henry van de Velde's career, until he was thirty, were spent first as a painter and then as an interior decorator. As a painter he was much influenced by the neo-impressionists, especially Seurat and Van Gogh. When he turned to interior decoration he designed almost everything for the home from fabrics to tea-cups and furniture. He was associated with the beginnings of Art Nouveau, which was essentially the search for a contemporary non-historical style. It undoubtedly derived partly from the linear rhythms conspicuous in the work of the Pre-Raphaelites and their followers (which van de Velde acknowledged), which in turn was derived from the work of 15th century Florentine painters and sculptors. The linear patterns so conspicuous in Art Nouveau designs were also a distinctive feature of much of van de Velde's furniture, decoration and architecture, but he made an effort to link them with natural forms and with a sense of structure. He often alluded to the inspiration of natural forms, especially moving forms like sea waves, clouds and human figures in action. His association of linear rhythms with structure and lines of force is seen in his stair-case designs and furniture, as in many of his early houses and in the Folkwang Museum at Hagen.

The identification of natural forms with structural design led to the theory that the principles of organic structure should determine architectural design, a creed that not only controlled his own work but also influenced many later architects, among them Erich Mendelsohn. Van de Velde's early practice of painting and interior decoration and furniture design influenced his whole approach to architecture, so that however functional his building succeeded in being, there is always strongly present the decorative character with linear motifs. He designed many houses, several of them fairly large. Among the early ones is that which he built for himself (1896) after he married, which offers a parallel to William Morris' Red House built 35 years earlier. Finding, like Morris, that contemporary interior decoration and furnishing were of a very low quality, he designed everything for his own house.

Most of his houses are heavy massive structures with curved forms introduced in a variety of ways such as the frequent use of elliptical and circular shaped dormer windows, curved roofs, curved porch entrances and bow windows. The plans of these large houses approximated mostly to a symmetrical arrangement of rooms on either side of a main axis, and the hall was often in the centre with rooms all round reached by a corridor from the entrance. He sometimes introduced a first floor gallery round the hall. For fairly large houses this central hall proved to be a functional arrangement.

One of his earliest non-domestic architectural works was the remodelling of the interior of the Folkwang Museum at Hagen, where in the treatment of arches, columns and capitals, balustrading and furniture, his introduction of linear forms is seen to good effect.

Appointed the art director at Weimar in 1901, he

Aldo van Eyck: Children's Home, Amsterdam, 1960

founded and built the famous art school there, a long building with central hall flanked by long corridors with an elliptical staircase at the rear. The top floor has large studio windows, while flanking the centre of the main facade there are bow windows between heavy plasters. It became a famous school of design. Van de Velde remained its head until the First World War and was succeeded, on his own recommendation, by Walter Gropius in 1919, when it was reorganized and became the celebrated Bauhaus.

Van de Velde was a member of the Deutscher Werkbund and took a prominent part together with other notable architects in the Cologne Exhibition of 1914 for which he designed a theatre (now destroyed). This was probably his most famous building. The design makes a satisfactory whole with an efficient integration of its various parts: it is one of the earliest modern theatres where the traditional sharp separation between the stage and auditorium by means of the proscenium wall and arch is elimi-

nated and the whole is conceived as one room. Curved forms like the ogival roof help to give a unifying rhythm to the building.

Van de Velde's last important building is the large Kröller-Müller Museum at Otterlo. This represents a departure from his usual work. Here are few curves and very little linear emphasis; instead, it is a design of large rectangular masses, with plain walls and simple rectangular windows, with a nicely calculated balance of verticals and horizontals, while simple columns of the interior are without embellishment. The whole creates a feeling of classic repose.

Van de Velde was essentially an individualist who believed that architecture should be a matter of individual artistic expression. He was opposed to standardization and team work. When Muthesius advocated at the Deutscher Werkbund Congress of 1911 that perfection of form could be reached by mathematical calculation, and made possible the acceptance of the machine and of standardization, he

met with strong opposition from Van de Velde who contended that an artist was always an individualist who could not be subservient to rules and standards.

—Arnold Whittick

van der VLUGT, L(eendert) C(ornelis).
Dutch. Born in Rotterdam, 13 April 1894. Educated at the Akademie van Beeldende Kunsten, Rotterdam. Worked in the office of Michiel Brinkman, Rotterdam, 1921–25; in partnership with Johannes Brinkman, q.v., 1925 until his death, 1936. Exhibition: *Bouwen voor een open samenleving*, Boymans Museum, Rotterdam, 1963, toured The Netherlands, Germany, Austria and Italy. *Died* (in Rotterdam) *25 April 1936.*

Works:

1921 Public housing, Beukelsdijk, Rotterdam
1922 M.T.S. Technical School, P. Driessenstraat 3, Groningen, Netherlands (with Jan Gerko Wiebenga)
1923 Avondrood House, Ermelo, Netherlands
1924/
25 Vink House, Burgemeester de Vrieslaan, Nordhorn, Netherlands
1925/
26 Theosophical Union Meeting Hall and Administration, Tolstraat, Amsterdam
1925/
27 Van Nelle Tobacco Company Offices, Aalmarkt, Leiden
1926 Theosophical Union Building, Ommen, Netherlands
Van Nelle Company Boilerhouse, van Nelleweg 1, Rotterdam
1926/
27 Public housing, Mathenesserweg, Rotterdam
1926/
29 Van Nelle Tobacco Company Factory, van Nelleweg 1, Rotterdam
1928/
29 Van der Leeuw Villa, Kralingseplaslaan, Rotterdam
1929 Tennis Club, Delftshavensee Schie, Rotterdam
Internationale Crediet en Handelsvereiniging Headquarters extensions, Wolfshoek, Rotterdam
1929/
31 Grain silos, Maashaven, Rotterdam
1930 Mees and Zoonen Bank Building, Beursplein, Rotterdam (project)
Van der Leeuw Holiday House, Rockanje, Netherlands
De Maas Steam Mills extensions, Maashaven, Rotterdam
1930/
31 De Bruyn Villa, Ary Prinslaan, Schiedam, Netherlands
Mees and Zoonen Bank Building, 's-Gravendijkwal, Rotterdam
1930/
32 Van Stolk and Zn. Office Building, Abraham van Stolkweg, Rotterdam
1931 Concert Hall and Cultural Centre, Coolsingel, Rotterdam (project)
1931/
32 Graansilo N.V. Offices and Housing, Maashaven, Rotterdam
Van Ommeren N.V. Travel Bureau rebuilding, rue Auber, Paris
Maas Millworks Office Building, Canteen and Porter's House, Brielselaan, Rotterdam
Prototype telephone booth, Rotterdam
1932 University buildings, Rotterdam (project)
1932/
33 Sonneveld Villa, Jongkindstraat, Rotterdam
1932/
34 Boeve Villa, Mathenesserlaan, Rotterdam
1932/
38 Van der Leeuw Holiday House, Ommen, Netherlands
1933 Van Hoey-Smith Weekend House, Rockanje, Netherlands (project)
Golf Club, Kralingseweg, Rotterdam
1933/
34 Rotterdamse Kunstring rebuilding, Witte de Withstraat, Rotterdam
1933/
35 Steel Skyscraper Block, Bergpolder, Rotterdam (with Willem van Tijen)
Maas Grain and Coal Silos, Brielselaan, Rotterdam
1934 Zoological Gardens, Rotterdam (project)
Diaconessenhuis/Schwesternheim Clinic, Westersingel, Rotterdam (project)
Holland-America Lines Ticket Offices, rue Scribe, Paris

Low-cost housing, Amsterdam (competition project)
1934/
35 Zuid Navigational Union Station, Vierhavenstraat, Rotterdam
1934/
36 Vaes Villa, Kortekade, Rotterdam
1935 University Extension Buildings, Westzeedijk, Rotterdam (project)
van der Vlugt Holiday House, Noordwijk aan Zee, Netherlands
1935/
36 Feijenoord Stadium, Olympiaweg, Rotterdam
Airport Reception Building, Ypenburg, Netherlands
Tennis Club, Rotterdam
1936/
37 Muntz Country House, de Koog, Texel, Netherlands
1936/
38 Diaconessenhuis Clinic extensions, Westersingel, Rotterdam
1937 Hoogendijk Villa, Holyweg, Vlaardingen-Ambacht, Netherlands

Publications:

On van der VLUGT: books—*Nuova Architettura nel Mondo* by A. Pica, Milan 1938; *Geschichte der Moderne Architektur* by Jürgen Joedicke, Stuttgart 1963; *Bouwen Voor een open samenleving,* exhibition catalogue, Rotterdam 1963; *L. C. van der Vlugt* by Jacob Bakema, Amsterdam 1968; articles—"Usines de Tabac, Rotterdam" in *Cahiers d'Art* (Paris), vol. 4, 1929; "La Nuova Architettura Olandese" by Leo Lionni in *Casabella* (Milan), May 1934; "Twee Woonhuizen te Rotterdam van de Architecten Brinkman en van der Vlugt" by B. Merkelbach in *De 8 en Opbouw* (Amsterdam), no. 11/12, 1934; "Casa Populare a Rotterdam" by R. Rothschild in *Casabella* (Milan), December 1934; "Brinkman e van der Vlugt, Architetti" by Edoardo Persico and Leo Lionni in *Casabella* (Milan), March 1935; special issue of *De 8 en Opbouw* (Amsterdam), October 1936; "House van der Leeuw, Rotterdam" in *Architectural Record* (New York), October 1950; "van den Broek und Bakema: A Contribution to the History of Architecture" by Franz Fueg in *Bauen und Wohnen* (Zurich), October 1959; "Brinkman, Brinkman, van der Vlugt, van den Broek, Bakema" by B. Housden, special issue of *Architectural Association Journal* (London), December 1960; "Van Nelle Factory in Rotterdam" in *Architecture* (Paris), April 1975.

See BRINKMAN, Johannes

van EYCK, Aldo.

Dutch. Born in Driebergen, Netherlands, 16 March 1918. Educated at King Alfred School, Hampstead, London, 1924–32; Sidcot School, Winscombe, Somerset, 1932–35; Building School, The Hague, 1938; E.T.H.: Eidgenössische Technische Hochschule, Zurich, 1939–43. Married Hannie van Roojen in 1943; children: Tess and Quinten. Worked as an architect in the Public Works Department, Amsterdam, 1946–50. In private practice, The Hague and Amsterdam, since 1952: in partnership with Theo Bosch since 1971. Editor, *Dutch Forum,* Amsterdam, 1959–67. Lecturer in Art History, Enschede Art School, Netherlands, 1951–55; Visiting Critic/Lecturer, University of Pennsylvania, Philadelphia, Washington University, St. Louis, Harvard University, Cambridge, Massachusetts, Tulane University, New Orleans, and the School of Architecture, Sin-

gapore, 1961–68; Guest Professor, E.T.H., Zurich, 1977–78. Professor, Institute of Technology, Delft, since 1967; Paul Philippe Cret Professor of Architecture, University of Pennsylvania, since 1978. Member, COBRA, Copenhagen, Brussels, and Amsterdam, 1948–51. Member, Team 10, since 1953. Exhibitions: *Greater Number,* at the *Triennale,* Milan, 1968; *Europa-America: 25 Contemporary Architects,* at the *Biennale,* Venice, 1976; *Nine Architects,* toured Germany and Switzerland, 1976–77. Recipient: City of Amsterdam Architecture Prize, 1964; First Prize, Protestant Church Competition, Driebergen, Netherlands, 1965; First Prize, Town Hall Competition, Deventer, Netherlands, 1967; First Prize, with Theo Bosch, Nieuw Markt Master Plan Competition, Amsterdam, 1970; First Prize, with Hannie van Eyck, Historical Museum Competition, Zwolle, Netherlands, 1971. Honorary doctorate: New Jersey Institute of Technology, 1979; Tulane University, 1979. Address (office): Dorpstraat 44, Loenen a.d. Vecht, Netherlands.

Works:

1946 Tower Room conversion, Zurich
1947/
74 Approximately 700 children's playgrounds, Amsterdam (with the Public Works Department)
1948 Heldring en Pierson Bank conversion, The Hague
1949 van Eyck Apartment conversion, Amsterdam
1950 "Ahoy" Entrance Sign, *National Maritime Exhibition,* Rotterdam
1952 Blue-Violet Room, Stedelijk Museum, Amsterdam
1954 64 houses for the elderly, Amsterdam (with Jan Rietveld)
1955 House, Herman Gorterstraat, Amsterdam (with Jan Rietveld)
1955/
56 3 schools, Nagele, N.E. polder, Netherlands (with H. P. D. van Ginkel)
1957/
60 Children's Home, Amsterdam
1965 Protestant Church, Driebergen, Netherlands (competition project)
1966 Sculpture Pavilion, Arnhem, Netherlands
1967 Town Hall, Deventer, Netherlands (competition project)
1968 Design of the Greater Number Pavilion, *Triennale,* Milan
Camping sanitary facilities, Loenen a.d. Vecht, Netherlands
1968/
70 Low-income housing, Lima, Peru (with Sean Wellesley Miller)
Roman Catholic Church, The Hague
1969 Visser House extensions, Bergeik, Netherlands (original house by Gerrit Rietveld)
Schmela Art Building, Dusseldorf
1970 Verberk House, Venlo, Netherlands
Master plan for the Nieuw Markt area, Amsterdam (competition project; with Theo Bosch)
1971 Historical Museum, Zwolle, Netherlands (competition project; with Hannie van Eyck)
1974/
76 G. J. Visser House, Retie, Belgium
1975/
77 Housing, Zwolle, Netherlands (with Theo Bosch)
1975/
79 Hubertus Home (for single parents and their children), Amsterdam (with Hannie van Eyck)

Publications:

By van EYCK: articles—"CIAM 6, Bridgewater: Statement Against Rationalism, 1947" in *A Decade*

of Modern Architecture by Sigfried Giedion, Zurich 1954 and *CIAM Otterlo* by Oscar Newman, Stuttgart and London 1961; numerous articles in *Dutch Forum* (Amsterdam), including "Wij Ontdekken Stijl" (We Discover Style), no. 2/3, 1949; "De Bal Kaatst Terug" (The Ball Bounces Back), no. 3, 1958; "Het Verhaal van een Andere Gedachte" (The Story of Another Idea), no. 7, 1959; "There Is a Garden in Her Face," no. 3, 1960/61; "The Medicine of Reciprocity, Tentatively Illustrated," no. 6/7, 1962; "Steps Toward a Configurative Discipline," "The Pueblos of New Mexico," and "The False Client and the Great Word NO," no. 4, 1962; "Anna Was, Livia Is, Plurabelle's To Be," July 1967; and "Dogon," July 1967, reprinted as "The Interior of Time: A Miracle of Moderation" in *The Meaning of Architecture*, edited by Charles Jencks and George Baird, London 1969, and, with "The Kaleidoscope of the Mind," in *Via* (Philadelphia), no. 1, 1968; "Giancarlo De Carlo and Urbino" in *Zodiac* (Milan), no. 16, 1966; "The Enigma of Multiplicity (Mourn Also for All Butterflies)" in *Harvard Educational Review* (Cambridge, Massachusetts), vol. 39, no. 4, 1969.

On van EYCK: books—*Netherlands Architecture since 1900* by R. Blijstra, Amsterdam 1960; *Modern Movements in Architecture* by Charles Jencks, London 1973; *Onze Arquitectos* by Oriol Bohigas, Barcelona 1976, Cambridge, Massachusetts 1977; articles—"Polder and Playground" by John Voelcker in *The Architects Yearbook*, London 1955; "Children's Home in Amsterdam" by Bruno Zevi in *L'Architettura* (Rome), no. 6, 1961; "The Vicissitudes of Ideology" by Kenneth Frampton in *L'Architecture d'Aujourd'hui* (Paris), no. 177, 1975; "Church at The Hague" by Peter Smithson in *Architectural Design* (London), June 1975; "The Web and the Labyrinth" by Pierluigi Nicolin in *Lotus* (Milan), no. 11, 1976.

Blight has crept over our field in recent years. I shall, therefore, draw on the *Team 10 Primer* and say what I have said before. I wish—still wish—to identify a building with that same building entered—hence, with those it shelters; and define space—each space built—simply as the appreciation of it. This "circular" definition, whilst excluding all academic abracadabra, includes what should never be excluded: those entering that space, appreciating it. Architecture can do no more, nor should it ever do less, than accommodate people well, assist their homecoming. The "rest"—a sign here or a symbol there—will either take care of itself or does not matter.

If making a building has become too difficult, the dilemma is complete. But is it really all that difficult? Does it really require a genius to avoid the meagre or a sage to bypass silliness? It is painfully true of architecture that it is not just good quality that counts, but a sufficient quantity of that quality. A nice school built here is of no use to a child elsewhere. So why not start with this: persuade those narrow border lines—the hard and harsh ones—to loop generously and gracefully into articulated in-between places and, having done so, give each space the right "inner horizon" for the gratifying sense of reference it provides. That buildings could help mitigate stress is no longer a desirable objective! On the contrary: fostering conflict—even provoking it wilfully—has become a trend, like those other flirtations with absurdity, irony, banality, inconsistency and "Rome," of course. Affecting mannerism by misquoting from true mannerism, which, though re-

flecting inner conflict, also resolved it by coaxing troublesome paradoxes into significant form, is particularly selfish. Essential meaning is thus abused and wasted. Eclectics everywhere are producing little more than a single standard mono-mix with the opposite in mind no doubt. But never mind the Minnesota Six and their like! What is needed is better functionalism. For there is no such thing as a solid teapot that also pours tea. Such an object might be a penetrating statement about something, but it simply is not a teapot. Neither is there, nor shall it come to pass that there ever will be, such a thing as a building intentionally contradictory, absurd, banal, trivial or disconcerting that is still a building—or architecture. Marcel Duchamp invented many puzzling things, but they were significantly *not* buildings. Anyway, history—that great gathering body of experience—is there in the mind's interior—to be used and not spilt.

—Aldo van Eyck

Aldo van Eyck's reputation as a leading architect of the post war European avant-garde is based on his simple concern that a building must not only provide real practical space but also offer the opportunity for possible alternative activities for those who come to use it. It must be structurally and formally adaptable; consequently, the language of its construction can have more than one meaning.

Van Eyck is a man of considerable personal charm and modesty, and there is a fundamental humanity about his whole approach to architecture that is clearly reflected in everything he has done. From the early, and much admired, Amsterdam Children's Home to the recent housing at Zwolle, there is a continuity of common sense that underlines his very real concern for the identity of the individual and a realization that the architect must build for each man and all men, as quite obviously they no longer feel the necessity to build for themselves. Worrying about the increasingly formless nature of society, coupled with an avowed distaste for the "boredom of hygiene," van Eyck has increasingly looked outside the accepted Western European tradition for his solutions. The Pueblos and the Dogon and later his work in the shanty-town "Barriados" of Peru have led him away from his original formal mathematical method into an area that always involves some element of surprise. He likes us to come upon his buildings without quite knowing what to expect and without fully understanding the reason for them until we recognize it instinctively. There is a real horror of what he has called the "organized nowhere." His comment that architecture need do no more than "assist man's homecoming" suggests the basis of his obvious attraction for the "ad-hoc" re-thinking Post-Modernists, with their affection for a controlled molecular form that offers an opportunity for individual interpretation of function. But it is a concern for controlled alternatives, not mere irrational ambiguity, that preoccupies van Eyck.

The much quoted act of sympathetic recognition —"Bump!—sorry. What's this? Oh hello!"—is typical of his fondness for what he sees as a poetic approach to architecture; it hints at a lingering admiration for Le Corbusier and also accounts for his commitment to Team 10—the "loose association of friends" whose admitted responsibility for the recent evolution of mainstream Modern Movement thinking has proved so fruitful for the continuation of the European tradition.

Though undeniably part of this tradition, van Eyck refuses to be a part of mere history, and that is his appeal to those concerned with the vital problem of retaining a formal identity, both socially and architecturally, in the face of intense commercial pressure. The concern for the individual is genuine, and the need for a form that offers more than one solution essential. Van Eyck is not concerned with "Utopia" but with the day-to-day existence of the individual in what he sees as a formless society.

—John Furse

van WIJK, Jan.
South African. Born in Roberts Heights, 2 May 1926. Educated at Oranje Meisieskool, Bloemfontein, 1933; Robert Heights Primary School 1934; Beach Primary School, East London, 1935–. Roberts Heights Primary School, 1937; Grey College, Bloemfontein, 1938; Langenhoven Primary School, Pretoria, 1939; General Brink Primary School, Roberts Heights, 1939; Afrikaans Boys High School, Pretoria, 1940–43; University of Pretoria School of Architecture, 1944–49, B.Arch. 1949. Married Erna Marais in 1960. Student Assistant in the offices of Verhoef, Smit and Viljoen, Pretoria, 1946, and office of Norman Eaton, Pretoria, 1948; Assistant Architect, Meiring and Naude, Pretoria, 1949–50, Cape Town, 1951–56; Brian Colquhoun and Partners, London, 1956; Kahn and Jacobs, New York, 1957, and Smit and Viljoen, Pretoria, 1958; Partner, Daan Kesting and Jan van Wijk, Pretoria, 1959–62; in private practice, Pretoria, 1962–67; Senior Partner, Jan van Wijk and Partners, Pretoria and Johannesburg, 1968–75. Since 1975, Chairman of the Jan van Wijk Partnership Inc., Johannesburg, with branches at Pretoria and George, Cape Province; also, Director, Letra Printing Company, Johannesburg, and Condenda Investment Company, Pretoria, since 1975. Exhibitions: Museum Gideon Malherbe, Paarl, South Africa, 1975. Recipient: Institute of South African Architects Award, 1973, 1978. Address: Jan van Wijk Partnership, Prentice Place, 163 D. F. Malan Drive, Northcliff, Johannesburg 2195, South Africa.

Works:

1950/ 56	South African Broadcasting Corporation Studios and Offices, Cape Town (with Meiring and Naude)
1957	Hotel, Jamaica, West Indies (project)
	Motel, Long Island, New York (project)
	American Airlines Terminal, Kennedy Airport, New York (as assistant)
	Seagrams Building, New York (as assistant)
1959	Tennis Clubhouse, Pretoria
	Shops, offices and flats complex, Lydenburg, South Africa
	Church Hall, Parkhurst, Johannesburg
	Church, Moregloed, Pretoria
1960	Church, Universiteitsoord, Pretoria
	Streicher House, Lydenburg, South Africa
	Dr. van der Merwe House, Machadodorp, South Africa
1962	Chemist's shop, offices, and bank complex, Thabazimbi, South Africa
1963	De Leeuw House, Pretoria
	Dr. Aucamp Cave House, Pretoria
	Jan van Wijk House, Pretoria
	Motel, Thabazimbi, South Africa (project)
1964	Rembrandt Tobacco Corporation Art Pavilion, Johannesburg
	Motel, Nelspruit, South Africa (project)
1965	Post Office, Kleinbos, Stormsriver, South Africa
	Luckhoff Beach House, Kleinmond, South Africa
	Bonuskor Offices and Shops, Nelspruit, South Africa
1966	Church, Sasolburg, South Africa
1967	Resort Town, Natal Northcoast, South Africa (project; with D. Theron)
	Bonuskor Company House, Komatipoort, South Africa
	Municipal Electric Company Substation, Offices and Workshops, Paarl, South Africa
	Ster Theatres Cinemas, Shops and Ice Rink Complex, Pretoria
	Fire Brigade Station and Housing, Verwoerdburg, South Africa
	Arconpark Church, Vereeniging, South Africa
	Rand Afrikaans University, Johannesburg (with Wilhelm O. Meyer)

Jan van Wijk: Afrikaans Language Symbol, Paarl, South Africa, 1975

1968 Dr. Wessels Bushveld House, Hoedspruit, South Africa
1969 De Necker Bushveld Camp, Klaserie, South Africa
      Indian Reformed Church, Laudium, Pretoria
      Telephone Exchange Secretariat/Laboratories, Pretoria (with O. Verhoef, W. Mare and F. Viljoen)
1971 De Necker Holiday Bungalow, Knysna, South Africa
1973 Municipal Electricity Company Offices and Workshops, Kempton Park, South Africa
      Rembrandt Tobacco Corporation Cigarette Factory, Heidelberg, Transvaal, South Africa
      Rembrandt Tobacco Corporation Store, Paarl, South Africa
      Fruit Stall, Sabie Park, South Africa
      Housing development, Sabie Park, South Africa
      Rembrandt Tobacco Corporation Workers' Housing Scheme, Paarl, South Africa
      Dr. Wessels Bushveld House, Sabie-Sand Game Reserve, South Africa
      Recreation Centre, Sabie Park, South Africa
      Dr. Rupert Bushveld House, Transvaal Lowveld, South Africa
1974 Church Hall, Aucklandpark, Johannesburg
      Church complex, Brackenhurst, South Africa
      Irish Brigade/Anglo-Boer War Monument, Johannesburg
      Students Housing, phase II, Rand Afrikaans University, Johannesburg
      Wilderness House, Wilderness, South Africa
      Sub-Economic Housing Scheme, Kleinkrantz, South Africa (project)
1975 Afrikaans Language Symbol, Paarl, South Africa
      Condeda Development Company Office Building, Pretoria
      Belvidere Holiday Resort, Knysna, South Africa (project)
      Church complex, College Park, Vereninging, South Africa
      Sub-economic houses and town development, Breidbach, King Williamstown, South Africa
      Gazankulu Government Buildings, Giyani, Transvaal, South Africa
      Kruger House, Johannesburg
      Kloof-en-Dal Church Complex, Johannesburg
1976 Students Housing, phase III, Rand Afrikaans University, Johannesburg
      Experimental holiday houses, Sabie Park, South Africa
      Town Square Development, Paarl, South Africa
1977 Tourist camp, Pacaltsdorp, South Africa
      Oudemeester Workers' Housing, Stellenbosch, South Africa
      Van der Merwe Beach House, Still Bay, South Africa
      Housing scheme, Tembisa, Transvaal, South Africa
      Economic housing, Breidbach, King Williamstown, South Africa
      Jan van Wijk Beach House, Wilderness, South Africa
1978 I. C. Breweries Beer Distribution Depot, Johannesburg
      Gazankulu Ministers' Houses, Giyani, Transvaal, South Africa
      Holiday resort, Oyster Bay, South Africa
      Historic houses restoration, Stellenbosch, South Africa
      Army Mess and Single Men's Headquarters, Middleburg, Transvaal, South Africa

Being of Africa, this continent, especially South Africa where I was born and bred, had a marked influence on my development as an architect. Its wide ranges, its plains and semi deserts, its mountains, rocks, trees, its bush and semi-tropical regions brought me close to nature. Africa's indigenous architecture—reed huts, adobe huts, thatched roofed settlements near the waterhole, the organically-shaped enclaves with meandering walls, encircling baobab trees, the earthy whole encompassing the social structure, the patterns of plains and dry riverbeds, the patchland agriculture, the greys, the yellows, the reds, oranges and browns, and bright blue skies, tremendous thunderstorms and droughts —all these made me believe that architecture is a clayey thing, a moulded sculpture, flowing as part of the soil.

A rock, a tree, a hillock, a dry riverbed, would ask for a building—no, would ask for someone to outline the building that is already there, has been there since long past, to define what it wants to be given shape to in its midst. Difficult requests, set by nature, because what do you do to a commercial building in a city where nature in a sense is excluded? And yet, the building is "seen," defined in the mind's eye, then sketched and modelled, given shape, and then drawn by means of instruments, in order to have it built. At times even the computer questions the validity of the resulting curves. And those materials that come straight, are bent, cut, moulded so that they do not form a box but enclose spaces of various shapes and experience, as if the soil or site itself gave birth. And those that cannot be bent and shaped are so arranged that the whole seems plastic, organic. Granted, only one of the many avenues of architecture but one that constantly asserts itself and wants to be explored. In the city proper, with its constraints and harsh building regulations, the battle is really on, with some success. In the suburban scene, where nature is present, more success. With housing schemes and smaller buildings, churches, clinics, club houses, theatres, etc., having fun becomes possible.

The chosen example of my work is a culmination of the above, being a dynamic symbol in reinforced hammered concrete made and moulded from and rooted in the soil of Africa and depicting the origin and growth potential of a dynamic language, Afrikaans, my mother tongue, which is a modern Western language of Africa. Height: 57m.; two years building time; completed 1975.

But this is only part of the big game of architecture, from Vitruvius to moon landings, art and technology, intuition and reason, feeling and logic. From preconceived visions, to be drawn, to be built, or from the other end, a logical sequence of structured thinking through the vision to the product—all trying to seek the golden thread of man's never-ending quest of enclosing a space.

—Jan van Wijk

*

The symbiotic relationship of architectural education at the University of Pretoria with the work of the city's most prominent architects lead to a most productive architecture in Pretoria during the late 1940's and early 1950's. The leaders of that movement included Norman Eaton, Helmut Stauch, Professor Meiring and Gordon Mackintosh. The influences upon them and upon the young architects ranged from the spluttering end of the modern movement of the 1930's that had revolved around Martienssen in Johannesburg to the strong influence of Le Corbusier, as seen in the Brazilian work of the time and published in *Brazil Builds*. Jan van Wijk worked on the South African Broadcasting Building in Cape Town, by Meiring and Naude, and there the Brazilian influence is most clearly seen.

The influences of this period seem the strongest in van Wijk's houses and other projects of the early 1960's. The organic forms that Eaton at times sought and (possibly because of his strong roots in the classical) could not reach except in the paving and site works of some of his buildings, and which draw upon the free forms of African themes, such as those represented by the Zimbabwe ruins, van Wijk was to develop and take further. His design for the Monument at Paarl is an excellent example of these qualities in his work.

Van Wijk's collaboration with Meyer on the Rand Afrikaans University lead to a design that, with its tightly expressed and articulated shapes, is much more characteristic of Meyer and his colleague Pienaar. This influence clearly had an effect on van Wijk's subsequent work, for that work shows much greater geometric formalism than previously—as in the New Telephone Exchange in Pretoria.

The importance of van Wijk's work lies in its roots in one of the most vigorous architectural periods in South Africa and in its continuation of the themes that grew out of that time: a direct sensitivity to climate, excellence in siting, and an inventive freedom in the choice of an appropriate form. Some of these influences have been suppressed in South Africa in the last decade or so, as articulated forms and geometric rigidity have become the dominant themes, supported as they are by a strong and imported philosophic influence. Van Wijk may well return to the earlier themes in his work.

—Hans Hallen

VECSEI, Eva.

Canadian. Born Eva Hollo in Vienna, Austria, of Hungarian nationality, 21 August 1930; emigrated to Canada, 1957: naturalized, 1962. Educated at the School of Architecture, University of Technical Sciences, Budapest, 1948–52, B.A. 1952. Married the architect Andrew Vecsei in 1952; children: Andrea and Paul. Assistant Professor, School of Architecture, University of Technical Sciences, Budapest, 1952–53; Architect, Architectural Institute of Residential Design (Lakoterv), Budapest, 1953–56; Design Developer, 1958–64, and Associate, 1964–70, Affleck, Desbarais, Dimakopoulos, Lebenswold, Size, architects, Montreal; Associate, Dimitri Dimakopoulos, Architect, Montreal, 1970–73; Principal, Eva H. Vecsei, Architect, Montreal, 1973–76; Partner, Eva Vecsei—Dan Hanganu, Montreal, 1977. Since 1978, Principal, Eva Vecsei, Architect, Montreal. Exhibition: *Les Femmes Architectes Exposent,* Centre Pompidou, Paris, 1978. Address: Eva Vecsei, Architect, La Tour de la Cité, 300 Leo Pariseu, Suite 1801, Montreal, Quebec H2W 2N1, Canada.

Works:

1954 Housing for miners, Tatabanya, Hungary
1955/
56   Lagymanyos School and Housing Project, Budapest
1973/
77   La Cité, Montreal: 3 residential buildings; office building; hotel; recreational club; 3 cinemas; shopping centre; parking, gardens and terraces (with Dobush, Stewart, Longpré, Marchand and Goudreau)
1976 City Centre, Karachi, Pakistan: 5 interconnected office buildings; hotel; conference centre; cinema; residences; retail space and parking (project; with Yasmeen Lari and John Schreiber)
      Restaurant interiors (5), Montreal
1977 Studio 2 renovation, National Film Board, Montreal (with Dan Hanganu)
1978 Conceptual and feasibility study: East Block, 1910 Wing, Parliament Hill, Ottawa

Publications:

By VECSEI: article—La Cité de la métropole" in *Architectural Concept* (Montreal), May/June 1977.

Eva Vecsei: La Cité, Montreal, 1977 (model)

On VECSEI: books—*History of Modern American Architects* by Zoltan Kosa, Budapest 1973; *History of Modern Architecture* by Zoltan Kosa, Budapest 1975; articles—"Human Settlements: World News: L'Architecte de La Cité—Eva Vecsei" by Claude R. Lussier in *Décormag* (Montreal), January 1977; article by Mildred F. Schmertz in *Architectural Record* (New York), January 1978.

My definition of Architecture: building of shelters which satisfy the psycho-sociological needs of our society.

The prehistoric shelter-building or even the creation of present day working space is not architecture per se; it becomes architecture when it goes beyond its mere function, i.e., when it appeals to us at the *intellectual level* and at the *level of sensory perception* as well.

The modern movement is almost blameless on the intellectual level. It taught us to look for harmony between the structural system and the plan, materials and details. We learned the beauty of simplicity and economy of repetitiveness. It taught us to respect function—or, at least, the physical aspect of it. But repetition, simplicity and predictability alone are not yet virtues; they often mean the absence of creativity and inventiveness. Simplicity is often boring, and it is well known that a boring environment often provokes neurotic behavior.

If we acknowledge the necessity of a perceptually more stimulating architecture, especially in urban environments, we should also recognize all the parties to whom it should be addressed. The effect on the so-called "other users" is equally important: those who live nearby or, by seeing our structures every day, are affected by their presence, i.e., those whose environment is altered by our architectural activity.

I feel that present day architectural design should put more accent on the sensory level. Instead of the uniform surface, anonymous massing, parts of the building should be identifiable by and with the user. (Apartments, working spaces, etc. should be recognized from the exterior.) The "episode of decoration" should have a comeback, together with the more adventurous surface treatment, the greater variation of void and solid on the facade.

The dual role of roofscape should be fully exploited again; i.e., as the fifth elevation of the building (this cannot be ignored in urban situations, where it is often within view) and as a new source of semi-public space. The surface of our buildings should have the tactile appeal which makes the architecture of the great epochs so visually exciting.

These are some of the aspects I tried to incorporate in the recent La Cité mixed-use project. The 3 residential buildings—1350 units—are strongly sculptured by the variety of different expressions of some 80 apartment types. These towers are adjacent to pools, recreational terraces, and a plaza—all built over the commercial infrastructure utilizing the landscaped roof slabs as public and semi-public spaces.

To sum up: the aesthetic quality of our urban environment must be improved. Architecture should become a perceptually more stimulating experience than it is presently. It should become, again, *the* source of visual pleasure and civic pride.

—Eva Vecsei

Hungarian-born Eva Vecsei spent her first twelve years as an architect in Montreal working first as a design developer then as an associate of Affleck, Desbarais, Dimakopoulos, Lebensold and Size. While there, she was in charge of the design of several large projects, and, still in her thirties, she became head project designer with partner-in-charge R.T. Affleck for one of the largest buildings in the world—Place Bonaventure in Montreal. Constructed on a six-acre site with one million square feet of retail mart space, 100 thousand square feet of office space, and a 400-room roof top hotel, Place Bonaventure was built just in time for the opening of *Expo '67* and cost $80 million in 1967 dollars.

Her second mammoth project is La Cité, Montreal's first large-scale mixed-use comprehensive downtown development. This project, completed in 1977, is the first job designed by Vecsei as head of her own office, which she opened in 1973. The project, constructed on a seven-acre site, consists of a 26-story office building, a 500-room hotel, three 30-story residential towers, and a two-level, 220 thousand-square-foot retail area that provides all weather connection between all parts of the project. The total cost of La Cité was $120 million in 1976 dollars.

These facts and figures are significant because no woman architect has ever before had such broad responsibility for the design and construction of projects of this magnitude and excellence. Vecsei has had the opportunity to display a nearly full range of design abilities—her own geometric and spatial skills, her knowledge of architectural form and theory, and the power to coordinate, integrate and synthesize the knowledge of others.

It is unlikely that projects of the size of Place Bonaventure and La Cité will be built again in Canada in the near future. Vecsei is now engaged in smaller work that makes a lesser demand upon her organizational talents and a larger one upon her expressive skills. The results will deserve attention.

—Mildred F. Schmertz

VENTURI, Robert.

American. Born in Philadelphia, Pennsylvania, 25 June 1925. Educated at the Episcopal Academy, Philadelphia, graduated 1943; Princeton University, New Jersey, under Donald Drew Egbert and Jean Labatut, 1943–50, B.A. 1947 (Phi Beta Kappa), M.F.A. 1950; American Academy, Rome (Rome Prize Fellowship), 1954–56. Married the architect Denise Scott Brown, *q.v.,* in 1967; son: James. Worked as a designer for the firms of Oscar Stonorov, Philadelphia, Eero Saarinen, Bloomfield Hills, Michigan, and Louis I. Kahn, Philadelphia, 1950–58; Partner, with Paul Cope and H. Mather Lippincott, Venturi, Cope and Lippincott, Philadelphia, 1958–61, and, with William Short, Venturi and Short, Philadelphia, 1961–64. Partner, with John Rauch, *q.v.,* since 1964, and with Rauch and Denise Scott Brown since 1967, Venturi and Rauch, Philadelphia: Partner-in-Charge of Design (associates: Steven Izenour, David Vaughan). Assistant Professor, then Associate Professor of Architecture, University of Pennsylvania, Philadelphia, 1957–65; State Department Lecturer in the U.S.S.R., 1965; Architect-in-Residence, American Academy, Rome, 1966; Charlotte Shepherd Davenport Professor of Architecture, Yale University, New Haven, Connecticut, 1966–70; Visiting Critic, Rice University, Houston, Texas, 1969. Member, Panel of Visitors, School of Architecture and Urban Planning, University of California at Los Angeles, 1966–67; Trustee, American Academy, Rome, 1966–71; Member, Board of Advisers, Department of Art and Archaeology, Princeton University, New Jersey, 1969–72. Member, Board of Advisers, School of Architecture and Urban Design, Princeton University, New Jersey, since 1977, and of the Ossabaw Island Project, Savannah, Georgia, since 1977. Exhibitions: *Gold Medal Awards,* Architectural League of New York, 1965; *The Work of Venturi and Rauch,* toured the United States, 1965; *40 under 40,* Architectural League of New York, 1965; *The Work of Venturi and Rauch,* Whitney Museum, New York, 1971; *The Invisible Artist,* Philadelphia Museum of Art, 1974; *The Work of Venturi and Rauch,* Pennsylvania Academy of Fine Arts, Philadelphia, 1975; *Suburban Alternatives: 11 American Projects,* at the Biennale, Venice, 1976; *200 Years of American Architectural Drawing,* Cooper-Hewitt Museum, New York, 1977; *Drawings for a More Modern Architecture,* Drawing Center, New York, and Cooper-Hewitt Museum, New York, 1977; *Architecture 1: An Exhibition,* Leo Castelli Gallery, New York, and Institute of Contemporary Art, Philadelphia, 1977; *Roma Interotta,* Incontri Internazionali d'Arte, Rome, 1977–78; *Palaces for People,* Cooper-Hewitt Museum, New York, 1977; *Presence and Absence,* Galleria d'Arte Moderna, Bologna, Italy, 1977. Recipient: Graham Foundation Grant, 1963; Design Award, *Progressive Architecture,* 1967; First Prize, Yale University Mathematics Building Competition, 1970; Gold Medal, 1972, and Adaptive Re-use Award, 1976, American Institute of Architects, Philadelphia Chapter; Award of Merit, *House and Home/*AIA, 1973; Arnold W. Brunner Memorial Prize in Architecture, National Institute of Arts and Letters, 1973; Creative Arts Award, Brandeis University, Waltham, Massachusetts, 1976; Casebook Award, *Print Magazine,* 1976 (three times); Honor Award, 1977, and Medal, 1978, AIA; Case Studies Award, *Urban Design,* 1977; Medal of Achievement, Philadelphia Art Alliance, 1978. D.F.A.: Oberlin College, Ohio, 1977. Fellow, American Institute of Architects, 1978. Address: Venturi and Rauch, 333 South 16th Street, Philadelphia, Pennsylvania 19102, U.S.A.

Works:

1960 Dudley L. Miller House, East Hampton, Long Island, New York
1963 Alan Zinzer House, Woodbury, Connecticut
      Vanna Venturi House, Philadelphia
1964 H. Justice Williams House restoration, stage I, Philadelphia
1965 Guild House: Elderly People's Housing, Philadelphia
      Footlighters Theatre, Paoli, Pennsylvania (project)
1965/
69 Philadelphia General Hospital renovation and additions
1965– F. Otto Haas House additions, Ambler, Pennsylvania
1966 Entrance Building, Mausoleum and Memorial Tower, Princeton Memorial Park, New Jersey (project; with Richard Cripps)
1967 Community Center: Y.M.C.A., City Hall and Library addition, Philadelphia (project)
      Renewal plan for Hennepin Avenue, Minneapolis
1968 Renewal feasibility study of Hot Springs, Arkansas
      H. Justice Williams House restoration, stage II, Philadelphia
      Nathaniel Lieb House, Long Beach Island, New Jersey
      Two-Bay Fire Station, Columbus, Indiana
      Walker and Dunlop Office Building, Transportation Square, Washington, D.C. (project; with Caudill Rowlett Scott)
      Drs. George Varga and Frank Brigio Medical Office Building, Bridgeton, New Jersey
1968/
70 Rehabilitation plan for South Street, Philadelphia
1969 St. Francis de Sales Church renovation, Philadelphia
1970 Feasibility study of office, commercial and theatre complex for Times Square, New York
      Survey and analysis of subway station facilities, Philadelphia
      Master plan and urban design of California City
1971 Lawton Plaza redevelopment plan, New Rochelle, New York
      Great Western Cities Inc. Office Building, California City (project)
1972 Bato Paper Company Warehouse, Greenwich, Connecticut
      Convention Center conversion plan, Niagara Falls, Ontario
      Master plan for the Bicentennial International Exposition Site at Eastwick, Philadelphia (with other firms)
1973 West Mount Airy Clustered Housing Plan, Philadelphia
      Preliminary design for prototypical neighborhood and community shopping centers for Saga Harbor, new community south of Miami, Florida
      Horace Bushnell Memorial Hall alterations, Hartford, Connecticut (with George Izenour)
      Humanities Classroom Building, State University of New York at Purchase
      Feasibility study for the re-use of the Philadelphia College of Art
      Neighborhood health center for the Southeast Philadelphia Community Corporation (project; with William Mann Sr.)
      Housing, Washington Square West Urban Renewal Area, Philadelphia (project)
      David Trubek House, Nantucket Island, Massachusetts
      George Wislocki House, Nantucket Island, Massachusetts
      Renewal plan for the Seneca-Susquehanna area, Harrisburg, Pennsylvania
      Prototype designs for lighting, street furniture and signs, University of Pennsylvania (competition project)
      Design of the Bicentennial celebration on and around Benjamin Franklin Parkway, Philadelphia
      South Central Philadelphia Neighborhood

Development Program (as consulting architect and planner)

1974 Four-Bay Fire Station, New Haven, Connecticut

Natural Science Museum, Roanoke, Virginia (project)

Public park and recreational facility, East River, New York (project; with Coffey Levine and Blumberg)

Kevin Cusak House, Sea Isle City, New Jersey

Peter Brant House, Greenwich, Connecticut

Design study for the improvement of road and water entrances to Philadelphia (with Murphy Levy Wurman)

Feasibility study for a residential community, phase I, near Phoenix, Arizona

1975 Revitalization study of The Strand, Galveston, Texas

Carll Tucker II House, Mount Kisco, New York

Community Center Building, Philadelphia Naval Base

1976 Franklin Court, Independence National Historical Park, Philadelphia

Allen Memorial Art Museum renovation and additions, Oberlin College, Ohio

Faculty Club, Pennsylvania State University, University Park

Educational Facility for Morris Arboretum, Philadelphia (project)

Peter Brant House, Vail, Colorado

200 Years of American Sculpture installation design, Whitney Museum, New York

American Painting Bicentennial exhibition design, Pennsylvania Academy of Fine Arts, Philadelphia

Philadelphia: Three Centuries of American Art exhibition design, Philadelphia Museum of Art

1977 Catalog-Showroom for Basco Inc., Concord, Delaware

Marlborough-Blenheim Hotel renovation and additions, Atlantic City, New Jersey (project)

Palley's Jewellers renovation, Atlantic City, New Jersey

INA Capital Management Corporation office interiors, Philadelphia

Peter Brant House, Bermuda

Proposal for the rejuvenation of Main Street and The Hollow, Boonton, New Jersey

Urban design study for Heritage Plaza West, Salem, Massachusetts

Planning study for St. Christopher's Hospital for Children, phase I, Philadelphia

Signs for the central business district of Salem, Massachusetts

Publications:

By VENTURI: books—*Complexity and Contradic-*

tion in Architecture, New York 1966, Tokyo 1969, Paris 1971, Barcelona 1972; *The Highway,* exhibition catalogue, with Denise Scott Brown, Philadelphia 1970; *Aprendiendo de Todas Las Cosas,* with Denise Scott Brown, Barcelona 1971; *Learning from Las Vegas,* with Denise Scott Brown and Steven Izenour, Cambridge, Massachusetts 1972, 1977; articles—"The Campidoglio: A Case Study" in *Architectural Review* (London), May 1953; "Project for a Beach House" in *Architectural Design* (London), November 1960; "Weekend House" in *Progressive Architecture* (New York), April 1961; "A Justification for a Pop Architecture" in *Arts and Architecture* (Los Angeles), April 1965; "Three Projects: Architecture and Landscape, Architecture and Sculpture, Architecture and City Planning" in *Perspecta* (New Haven, Connecticut), no. 11, 1967; "Trois bâtiments pour une ville de l'Ohio" in *L'Architecture d'Aujourd'hui* (Paris), December 1967/January 1968; "A Significance for A & P Parking Lots; or, Learning from Las Vegas," with Denise Scott Brown, in *Architectural Forum* (New York), March 1968; "A Bill-Ding Board Involving Movies, Relics and Space" in *Architectural Forum* (New York), April 1968; "On Architecture" in *L'Architecture d'Aujourd'hui* (Paris), September 1968; "On Ducks and Decoration," with Denise Scott Brown, in *Architecture Canada* (Toronto), October 1968; "Venturi versus Gowan," with Denise Scott Brown, in *Architectural Design* (London), January 1969; "Learning from Lutyens," with Denise Scott Brown, in *RIBA*

Robert Venturi: Franklin Court, Independence National Historical Park, Philadelphia, 1976

Journal (London), August 1969; "The Bicentennial Commemoration 1976," with Denise Scott Brown, in *Architectural Forum* (New York), October 1969; "Mass Communications on the People Freeway; or, Piranesi Is Too Easy," with Denise Scott Brown, in *Perspecta* (New Haven, Connecticut), no. 12, 1969; "Co-op City: Learning to Like It," with Denise Scott Brown, in *Progressive Architecture* (New York), February 1970; "Reply to Pawley—'Leading from the Rear'," with Denise Scott Brown, in *Architectural Design* (London), July 1970; "Some Houses of Ill-Repute: A Discourse with Apologia on Recent Houses of Venturi and Rauch," with Denise Scott Brown, in *Perspecta* (New Haven, Connecticut), no. 13/14, 1971; "Ugly and Ordinary Architecture; or, The Decorated Shed," with Denise Scott Brown, in *Architectural Forum* (New York), part I, November 1971, part II, December 1971; "Bicentenaire de l'Indépendance Américaine," with Denise Scott Brown, in *L'Architecture d'Aujourd'hui* (Paris), November 1973; "Functionalism Yes, But . . . ," with Denise Scott Brown, in *Architecture + Urbanism* (Tokyo), November 1974; "Plain and Fancy Architecture by Cass Gilbert at Oberlin" in *Apollo* (London), February 1976, in an expanded version in *Allen Memorial Art Museum Bulletin* (Oberlin, Ohio), no. 2, 1976-77; "A Reaction to Complexity and Contradiction in the Work of Furness" in *Pennsylvania Academy of the Fine Arts Newsletter* (Philadelphia), Spring 1976; "Learning from Aalto" in *Progressive Architecture* (New York), April 1977.

On VENTURI/RAUCH: books—*American Architecture and Urbanism* by Vincent Scully, New York 1969; *New Directions in American Architecture* by Robert A. M. Stern, New York 1969; *Will They Ever Finish Bruckner Boulevard?* by Ada Louise Huxtable, New York 1970; *Architecture for the Arts: The State University of New York College at Purchase*, New York 1971; *The Work of Venturi and Rauch*, exhibition catalogue, by Vincent Scully, New York 1971; *After the Planners* by Robert Goodman, New York 1971; *Third Generation: The Changing Meaning of Architecture* by Philip Drew, New York 1972; *Wasteland: Building the American Dream* by Stephen A. Kurtz, New York 1973; *Conversations with Architects* by John W. Cook and Heinrich Klotz, New York and London 1973; *Architettura Radicale* by Paolo Navone and Bruno Orlando, Milan 1974; *The Shingle Style Today* by Vincent Scully, New York 1974; *Global Architecture 39: Venturi and Rauch* by Paul Goldberger and Yukio Futagawa, Tokyo 1976; *Supermannerism: New Attitudes in Post Modern Architecture* by C. Ray Smith, New York 1977; articles—"Are the Venturis Putting Us On" by Ursula Cliff in *Design and Environment* (New York), Summer 1971; "Robert Venturi," special issue of *Architecture + Urbanism* (Tokyo), October 1971; "Venturi and Rauch" in *L'Architecture d'Aujourd'hui* (Paris), December 1971/January 1972; "Architecture in '71: Lively Confusion" by Ada Louise Huxtable in the *New York Times*, 4 January 1972; "Venturi and Venturi, Architectural Anti-Heroes" by Barbara Flanagan in *34th Street Magazine* (New York), 13 April 1972; "The Venturis—American Selection" by Deborah Waroff in *Building Design* (London), 4 August 1972; "In Love with Times Square" by Ada Louise Huxtable in the *New York Review of Books*, 18 October 1973; "Venturi and Rauch 1970-74," special issue of *Architecture + Urbanism* (Tokyo), November 1974; "Franklin Court" in *Progressive Architecture* (New York), April 1976; "The Rise and Fall of Main Street" by Ada Louise Huxtable in the *New York Times Magazine*, 30 May 1976; "The Venturi 'Anti-Style' of Architecture" by Ada Louise Huxtable in the *New York Times*, 30 January 1977; special issue of *Progressive Architecture* (New York), October 1977; "The Recent Nine Works of Venturi and Rauch" by Shinichiro Kikuchi in *Architecture + Urbanism* (Tokyo), January 1978; "Venturi and Rauch," special issue of *L'Architecture Aujourd'hui* (Paris), June 1978.

*

We promote an architecture responsive to the complexities and contradictions of modern experience, the particularities of context, the varieties of the users' taste cultures, and the symbolic and decorative dictates of the program.

—Robert Venturi

Robert Venturi is presently one of the most original talents in contemporary architecture in the United States; his projects and writings provide a critical, underlying strength for the alternatives to the American functionalism that developed in the late 1950's. He has also been instrumental in devising an architectural language that has its counterpart in the Pop movement in the figurative arts.

A knowledge of Venturi's preparation as an architect is important for an understanding of his attitudes and his work. He graduated from the Princeton University School of Architecture, which was directed at that time by the revered Professor Labatut, one of the last representatives of the Beaux Arts system in education. Venturi first became associated with the office of Eero Saarinen, where, among other projects, he worked on the design of the Milwaukee County War Memorial Center. The building design retains the characteristics of Saarinen's work; nevertheless, the dynamic contrast between the cantilevered elements and the rigid setting of the plan reveals Venturi's characteristic search for an ambiguous balance within the structure as a whole. After spending a term as a Fellow of the American Academy in Rome, he designed a house in Chestnut Hill, Philadelphia, where an intense concern for the quality of daylight is revealed in his emphasis upon the large roof-top light chambers; it is a concern that, during his time in Italy, Venturi must have seen similarly embodied in the architecture of the late Roman Baroque and the late 18th century in Naples. In 1957 Venturi became a member of the faculty of the University of Pennsylvania School of Architecture, where he taught a course on architectural criticism; this course eventually provided the basis for his book *Complexity and Contradiction in Architecture*. The book made his ideas well-known among architects, students, and critics; for Vincent Scully, for example, it is the most important writing on the making of architecture since Le Corbusier's *Vers une architecture*. The book elaborates the articles of a gentle manifesto in which Venturi makes a clear break with the multitude of "-isms" presented as alternatives to the shallow surface of Functionalism; it re-introduced architecture in the multitude of its spontaneous manifestations, including that of the often-condemned current building industry. It is an imaginative manifesto, inspired in part by the "will to be" of the great Louis Kahn, who nevertheless was unable to comprehend Venturi's appreciation of the circumstantial and the ordinary. During his tenure at the University of Pennsylvania, Venturi stated his case as an architect with the design submitted for the F.D. Roosevelt Memorial in Washington, D.C. It is a work of unquestionable quality, one that exists simultaneously as a large billboard perceptible at great distance, a place for cars to pass by and park, and an area of small gardens for art objects to be perceived at close range.

During the same period Venturi designed a number of small houses, including a house for his mother in Chestnut Hill, built in 1963. At this point the conceptual attitude and the formal vocabulary of Venturi's work are clearly pronounced and decisively developed on two levels: the large-scale element of distant view (billboard, chimney, roof shapes), responding in part to the Kevin Lynch precepts in urban design, and the texture of surfaces in close view, the current products of the American building industry and home developers (aluminum sash, varieties of textured bricks, colored tiles, etc.). The Brutalist tendency in architecture had already conditioned the current American taste for such choices. However, the implication of Venturi's reinforcement of these choices was far-reaching, as it involved a substantial criticism of the modern movement, particularly of Mies van der Rohe's aesthetics ("Less is more"), a criticism that Brutalism never shared. Venturi's reply, "More is more," became programmatic; the "true" honest things for which to search became the objects of everyday use, particularly those that were used as symbols of activities: the products of the advertising and distribution industry, used furniture, light signs, and graphic announcements.

However, Venturi's work still remains firmly bound to the basic tenets of the modern movement. His building plans always observe the requirements of function, program, and activities, and his architecture never becomes lost in the stimulus of historicism. In reacting to post-modernist claims heavily dependent upon historical recollections, Venturi recently declared that for him the "modern movement was almost right." His architecture above all gives importance to the making of a place; the juxtaposition of textures and materials is used to establish a condition quite different from the one obtained when the main preoccupation is the abstract depiction of space. Instead, his architecture is inherently scaled to human use, comfort, entertainment, and memories.

The theoretical preoccupations that often make Venturi a vigorous polemicist also frequently affect his architecture, which at times cannot overcome the limitation of being demonstrative. However, Venturi shows an uncommon artistic sensitivity in projects such as the Transportation Building in Washington D.C. (rejected by the Art Commission), the Humanities Classroom Building for the State University of New York at Purchase, the competition project for the Yale Mathematics Building, a series of houses built on Nantucket Island, which represent a sophisticated view of contextual architecture, and finally in Franklin Court in Philadelphia, where he becomes totally free from polemic positions. The work done in close collaboration with Denise Scott Brown is of great significance in defining conceptual approaches, as well as in developing a consciousness for social conditions. This partnership made possible the extensive exploration into the nature of the suburbs that culminated in the book *Learning from Las Vegas*, in which Venturi's familiar theory of the "ordinary" was further illustrated.

If a single statement could express Robert Venturi's contribution to architecture, it would have to be that, with his work and his writings, Venturi has opened a window on the contradictory and yet extraordinary landscape of built America. In doing so he caused the improvised, the casual, and the contingent to become part of our real environment, not bypassed or ignored; new structures both inspire and become part of such a reality. This view has rightly captivated the imagination of many young architects, and will continue to have a lasting effect on their work.

—Romaldo Giurgola

VILLAGRÁN GARCÍA, José.
Mexican. Born in Mexico City, 22 September 1901. Educated at the Colegio del Sagrado Corazon, Mexico City, 1908-13, 1914-15; Colegio Frances, Mexico City, 1916-17; School of Architecture of the Academia de San Carlos, now the National School of Architecture of the Universidad Nacional Autonoma de Mexico, Mexico City, 1918-22, Dip. Arch. 1923. Married Concepcion de la Mora in 1935; son: Enrique. Worked as an architect for the Department of Public Health, Mexico City, 1924-35. In private practice, Mexico City, since 1935. Consultant Architect, National Committee of the Campaign Against Tuberculosis, 1939-47; Consultant Architect for Hospital Construction, Secretariat of Public Health and Welfare, Mexico City, 1943-

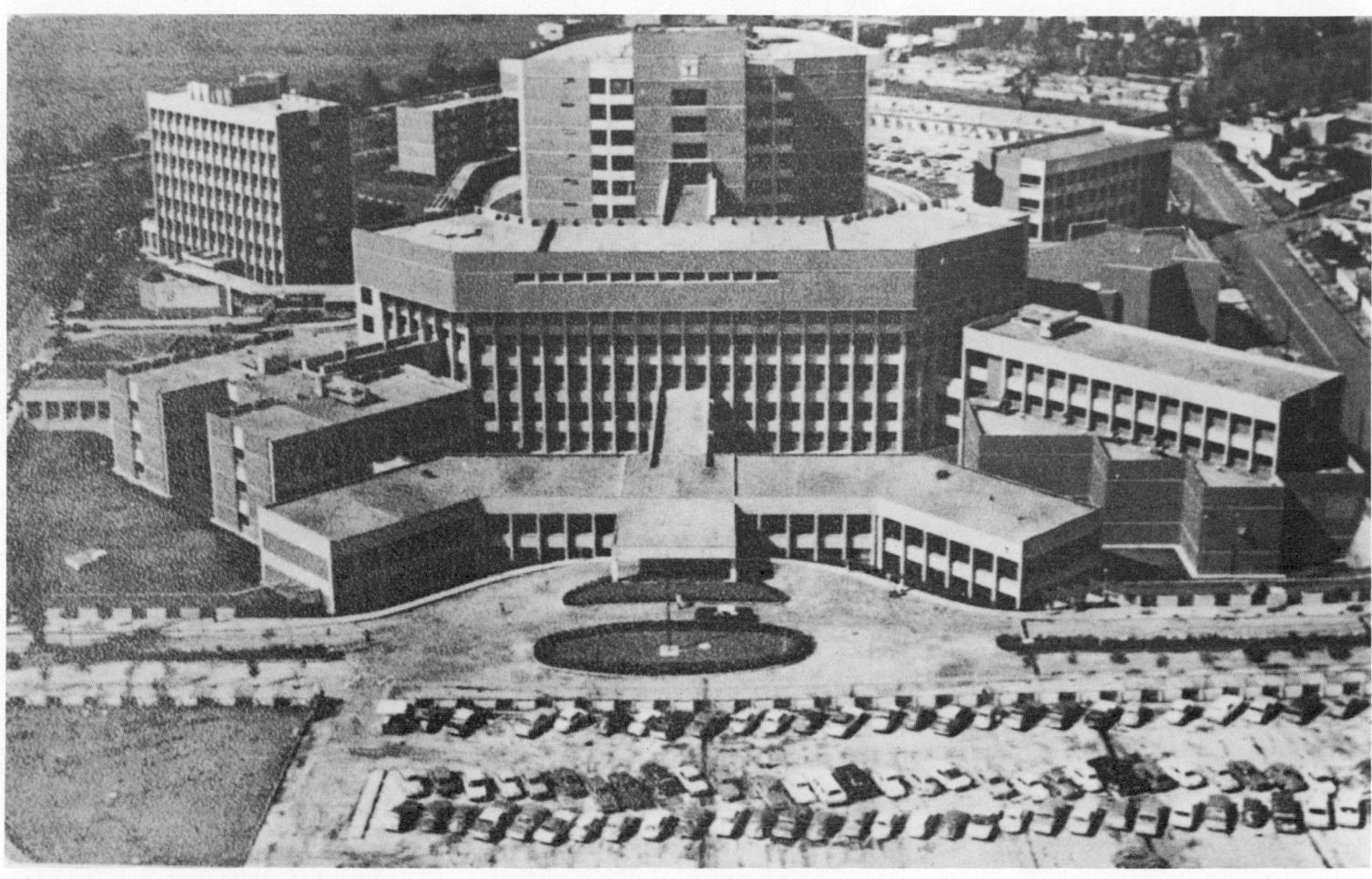

José Villagrán García: National Cardiological Institute, Mexico City, 1976

45; Consultant Architect for Hospitals in the Western Hemisphere, World Health Organization, Washington, D.C., 1951. Professor of Architectural Composition, 1924–35, Professor of Architectural Theory, 1926–35, 1936–57, and Director, 1933–35, National School of Architecture, Mexico City. Member, Board of Governors, Universidad Nacional Autonoma de Mexico, 1953–70. Exhibition: *Bienal,* Sao Paulo, 1955. Recipient: Architecture Prize, *Bienal,* Sao Paulo, 1955; National Art Prize, Mexico, 1968. Member, Colegio Nacional de Arquitectos de Mexico. Address (office): Dublin 7, Mexico 6, D.F., Mexico.

Works:

1922 Hotel, Lake Patzcuaro, Mexico (project)
1925 Institute of Hygiene, Popotla, Mexico City
1929 Tuberculosis Sanatorium, Huipulco, Tlalpam, Mexico City
     Children's Health Dispensary Building, Mexico City
     Milk Production Building, Popotla, Mexico City
1934 Children's Day School No. 5, Mexico City
1935 José Villagrán García House, Dublin 7, Mexico City
     Palma Office Building, Mexico City
1937 National Cardiological Institute, Mexico City
1941 Apartment building, Avenida Insurgentes 444, Mexico City
     Surgical Block, Huipulco Sanatorium, Tlalpam, Mexico City
     Children's Hospital, Mexico City
1942 Chronic Tuberculosis Patients' Block, and Manuel Gea Gonzalez Hospital, Huipulco Sanatorium, Tlalpam, Mexico City
     Medical Center Master Plan, Mexico City (with Mario Pani)
     Tuberculosis Sanatorium, Zoquipan, Jalisco, Mexico

1943 Mundet Sports Park, Mexico City
     Hospital de Jesus Office Building, Mexico City
1943/
  46 Hospitals plan for the Republic of Mexico
1944 Mexico University College, Mexico City
1945/
  46 Regional schools plan for Mexico
     Costa Rica Primary School, Mexico City
1946/
  50 Condesa Office Building, Mexico City
1948 Gante Parking Garage, Mexico City
1951 National School of Architecture Complex, Universidad Nacional de Mexico, Mexico City
1952 Las Americas Cinema and Office Building, Mexico City
1953 Cumbres Primary and Secondary School, Mexico City
     Lafragua Office Building, Mexico City
     National Mission Seminary, Tlalpam, Mexico City
1954 Centro Inmobiliario America Complex, Mexico City
     Rastro y Frigorificos Works/Office Complex, Mexico City
     San Cosme Market Building, Mexico City
     San Lucas Market Building, Mexico City
1963 Hotel Maria Isabel, Mexico City
     Hotel Alameda, Mexico City
     Ford Motor Company Office Building, Mexico City
     Tacubaya, La Viga, and Coyoacan Preparatory Schools, Universidad Nacional de Mexico, Mexico City
1965 Mixcoac and Insurgentes Preparatory Schools, Universidad Nacional de Mexico, Mexico City
1966 National School of Architecture additions, Universidad Nacional de Mexico, Mexico City

1967 University Centre additions, Universidad Nacional de Mexico, Mexico City
1970 ICA Constructora Company Offices, Mexico City
1976 Complex of 20 buildings for the National Cardiological Institute, Mexico City (Hospital, Outpatients Clinic, Scientific Research Block, Nursing School, Cardiologists' School, Residential Block)

Publications:

By VILLAGRÁN GARCÍA: books—*Panorama de 50 Anos de Arquitectura Mexicana Contemporanea,* Mexico City 1950; *Problemas en la Formacion del Arquitecto,* Mexico City 1964; *Arquitectura y Restauracion de Monumentos,* Mexico City 1967; introduction to *Builders in the Sun* by Clive Bamford Smith, New York 1967; *Estructura Teorica del Programa Arquitectonico,* Mexico City 1972; *Esencia de lo Arquitectonico,* Mexico City 1972; *El Mayor Problema de la Arquitectura Actual,* Mexico City 1974; *La Forma en Arquitectura,* Mexico City 1975. articles—"Apuntes para un estudio" in *Arquitectura* (Mexico City), nos. 3–12, 1939–43; "La Iglesia Catolica ante la Arquitectura de la Epoca" in *Arquitectura* (Mexico City), no. 14, 1943; "Poco para Mucho y Mucho para Poco" in *Arquitectura y lo Demas* (Mexico City), vol. 1, no. 4, 1945; "Ideas Regentes en la Arquitectura Actual" in *Arquitectura* (Mexico City), no. 48, 1954; "La Ensenanza de la Arquitectura" in *Revista ENA* (Mexico City), no. 1, 1959; "Notas acerca de la carrera de arquitecto" in *Revista ENA* (Mexico City), no. 3, 1960; "Meditaciones sobre una crisis formal de la arquitectura" in *Cuadernos de Arquitectura* (Mexico City), no. 4, 1962; "6 Temas sobre la Proporcion en Arquitectura" in *Cuadernos de Bellas Artes* (Mexico City), nos. 7, 8 and 10, 1962; "Teoria de la Arquitectura" in *Cuadernos de Arquitectura* (Mexico City), 1964.

On VILLAGRÁN GARCÍA: book—*Parkhauser Tiefgaragen* by Dietrich-Klose, Stuttgart 1965; articles—"School/Home for Small Children" in *Architectural Record* (New York), June 1936; "Arquitectura en Mexico" in *Arquitectura* (Mexico City), April 1939; "Children's Hospital, Mexico City" in *Architectural Record* (New York), October 1944; "Edificios para estacionamento de automoviles" and "Edificios para despachos" in *Arquitectura* (Mexico City), June 1951; "Museo de Arte y Escuelo de Arquitectura" in *Arquitectura* (Mexico City), September 1952; "José Villagrán García," special issue of *Arquitectura* (Mexico City), September 1956; "Hotel Maria Isabel, Mexico, D.F." in *Arquitectura* (Mexico City), June 1962; "Fabrique de Ventilateurs près de Mexico" and "Hotel Alameda a Mexico" in *L'Architecture d'Aujourd'hui* (Paris), September 1963; "Hotel Maria Isabel, Mexico City" in *Architectural Design* (London), September 1963.

*

The work which I have developed during the 56 years of service to my country as an architect can be divided into two categories. The first is of a didactic nature; the second is professional architecture itself.

The Didactic: The idea that is basic to my teaching of the Theory of Architecture is that architecture is *the art of constructing habitable space for the human being;* or, to put it into its four dimensions—the physical, the biological, the psycho-instinctive, and that pertaining to the spirit. Or, as summed up in the classical definition of Seneca: the animal, the rational, and the free.

Professional Architecture: I have tried, for 56 years, to realize and apply in my works the ideas explained in my architectural teaching, invariably pursuing these aims, that works should have axiological and concurrent worth as objects with economic/constructive usefulness; that they should be factological—in other words, that their form should accord with complex totality; that they should be aesthetically positive and expressive in themselves; and, finally, that they should have social value in the service of the community in which they find themselves.

—José Villagrán García

*

After the turn of the century revolution, Mexican artists tried to find a link with pre-Hispanic times through the subjects developed in their murals, the battle of the Indian race against the conquistador—Diego Rivera is an example. And a similar phenomenon, an approach to a past destroyed by violence, happened in architecture during the first decades of this century as the result of a search for authentic expressions. It is in this context that the work of José Villagrán García, known as the father of modern rationalism in Mexico, really achieves its importance.

Villagrán's influence stems not so much from works actually built (although some of them, such as the National School of Architecture in Mexico's University City, are an example in themselves), but from his constant preaching in classrooms and lectures, based on a profound analysis of the European theoreticians. Villagrán was always solidly against the imitation of historic styles, even if Mexican: "What originally was a spontaneous identification with Colonial and pre-Cortez forms has become more and more critically inconsistent and has led our people down pathways to the worst expression of taste in this century."

According to Villagrán, a work of architecture acquires status as such only if utilitarianism, technology, and social, functional and formal factors have been integrated in the design. This makes it easy to understand his opposition to "dressing" architecture with fashionable silks. In 1925 he suggested that "Mexican contemporary architecture is the fruit of the historical development of our art in search of theoretical doctrinal orientation and of expressions which are part of our culture."

Villagrán's ideas were initially influenced by Le Corbusier, particularly *Vers une Architecture* and Le Corbusier's "living machine" concept, and by Gropius, to whom he specifically refers. Discussing criticism of the new Mexican architecture that he proposed, he said: "Those who have referred to the new Mexican architecture as functionalist, meaning by that to imply that it has ignored the aesthetic in order to satisfy utility and society, are unaware of the doctrine put forward by our School of Architecture, and probably also unaware of what has been pointed out in a similar vein, although in a different way, by European functionalists like Gropius."

Villagrán repeatedly urged young Mexican architects to identify with their time and place. He warned against a divorce between doctrine and practice and against expressions of a decorativist, atechtonic and extemporaneous formalism. One of Villagran's principles is truth in architecture, accompanied by logical thought (the object is created through objective reasoning, not subjective emotion). Truth and logic, in a milieu tending towards exalting rediscovered native pre-Columbian values, will ensure that modern architecture's message is heard, with all the risks implicit in a movement that precisely has as an objective the abolishing of all ornamentalism (as in Loos) and all vestiges of "picturesque-ism." This is why Villagrán's architecture, for example, did not involve (as did the work of some of his disciples and followers) the integration of the wall with its surfaces—a mode that, nevertheless, to a considerable extent, identifies some of the best-known works of modern Mexico.

The opposition between a culture that possessed traditional and popular artistic elements, a culture that welcomed any stance that stressed national values, and the principles of a different attitude in architecture, one that appealed to design guidelines unassociated with whatever is not "functionalist," and therefore tending to impress forms not identifiable with specific sectors and places—this opposition was not exclusive to Mexico after the second decade of this century. But it was intense in Mexico, and the effort to popularize the ideas of modern architecture had to overcome difficulties not present in other places. The importance of José Villagrán García and his lessons is that, by sheer effort, he was able to introduce the contemporary world to Mexican architecture.

—Jorge Glusberg

*

VILLANUEVA, Carlos Raúl.

Venezuelan. Born in Croydon, Surrey, England, of Venezuelan parents, 30 May 1900. Educated at the Lycée Condorcet, Paris; Ecole des Beaux-Arts, Paris, under Gabriel Heraud, Dip.Arch. 1928. In private practice, Caracas, Venezuela, 1929 until his death, 1975. Architect to the Ministry of Public Works, Caracas, 1929–39; Consultant Architect, Banco Obrero (Workers' Bank), Caracas, 1940–60. Founding Professor of Architecture, University of Venezuela, Caracas, from 1944. Founder President, Venezuelan Association of Architects; President, Venezuelan National Board for Historic and Artistic Protection and Conservation; Founder Director, National Planning Commission. Exhibition: *Carlos Raúl Villanueva,* Museo de Caracas, 1976. Recipient: Diploma of Merit, Pan American Congress of Architecture, Lima, Peru, 1947; Citation of Merit, *Bienal,* Sao Paulo, 1957; National Architecture Prize, Venezuela, 1963. Dr.Arch.: University of Venezuela, Caracas, 1961. Honorary President, College of Architects of Venezuela; Officer, Orden del Libertador, Venezuela, 1945. Chevalier, Légion d'Honneur, France, 1939; Honorary Corresponding Member, French Society of Urbanism, 1948; Honorary Member, American Institute of Architects, 1952, and Royal Institute of British Architects, 1959. *Died* (in Caracas) *16 August 1975.*

Works:

1929/
30   Church of San Francisco de Yare, Caracas
     Bolivar House restoration, Caracas
1931   Bullring, Maracay, Venezuela
1935   Museo de los Caobos, Caracas
1937   Venezuelan Pavilion, *World's Fair,* Paris
1939   Gran Colombia School, Caracas
1941   Redevelopment of the El Silencio Quarter, Avenida Bolivar, Caracas
1943/
44   General Rafael Urdaneta Housing Development, Maracaibo, Venezuela
1943/
45   Dos de Diciembre Housing Development, Caracas (with José Manuel Mijares, José Hoffman and Carlos Branco)
1944/
47   Master plan for University City, University of Venezuela, Caracas
1945   Medical Center, University City, Caracas
1947   Technical/Industrial School, Caracas
1948   Francisco de Mirando Housing Development, Caracas
1950   Ciudad Tablitas (housing development), Caracas
1950/
52   Olympic Stadium, University City, Caracas
1951   Villanueva House, La Florida, Caracas
1952   Aula Magna (main auditorium), Library, Plaza Cubierta and Walks, and the Botanical Institute, University City, Caracas
1953   Small Concert Hall, University City, Caracas
1954   El Paraiso Housing Development, Caracas (with Carlos Celis and José Manuel Mijares)
     Humanities, Science, and Physics buildings, University City, Caracas
     Cerro Piloto Housing Development, Caracas
1955   School of Dentistry, University City, Caracas
1955/
57   23 de Enero High-Rise Housing Development, Caracas (with C. C. Cepero and José Manuel Mijares)
1956   Institute of Petroleum Engineering, University of Zulia, Maracaibo, Venezuela
1957   School of Architecture and Urbanism, School of Pharmacy, and Olympic Swimming Stadium, University City, Caracas
     Ascension Chapel, 23 de Enero Development, Caracas
1958   Villanueva House, Caraballeda, Venezuela
1961/
64   Fundación La Salle Office Building, Caracas
1967   Venezuelan Pavilion, *Expo '67,* Montreal (with E. Trujillo)
1968   Museo de Bellas Artes, Caracas (project)

Publications:

By VILLANUEVA: books—*Caracas of Yesterday and Today,* Caracas 1943, 1950; *Caracas en tres tiempos,* Caracas 1966; articles—"La Ciudad y su Historia" in *Boletin de Universidad Central* (Caracas), January 1964; "Lettre de Colombia" in *Architecture: Formes et Fonctions* (Lausanne), vol. 12, 1965/66; "Fonction-Formation-Position" in *Architecture: Formes et Fonctions* (Lausanne), vol. 15, 1969.

On VILLANUEVA: books—*Latin American Architecture since 1945* by Henry-Russell Hitchcock, New York 1955; *Masters of Modern Architecture* by John Peter, New York 1958; *Baukunst der Gegenwart* by Udo Kultermann, Tübingen 1958; *Art in Latin American Architecture* by Paul F. Damaz, New York 1961; *Carlos Raúl Villanueva and the Architecture of Venezuela* by Sibyl Moholy-Nagy, Stuttgart and London 1964; articles—"Caracas University City" in *Arts and Architecture* (Los Angeles), November 1954; "La Casa di Villanueva" and "Nuovi

Quartieri a Caracas" in *Domus* (Milan), April 1956; "Housing Projects in Caracas," "La Maison de l'architecte Carlos Raúl Villanueva" and "Unité d'Habitation à Caracas" in *L'Architecture d'Aujourd'hui* (Paris), October 1956; "Three Cubes" in *Architectural Forum* (New York), September 1967; "Obituary" in *AIA Journal* (Washington, D.C.), December 1975; "Homage from Venezuela to Carlos Raúl Villanueva" in *Arquitecturas Bis* (Barcelona), November 1976.

Carlos Raúl Villanueva's real importance lies not merely in his built works, but also in his underlying attitude to architectural design, for much of his work has become a prototype for subsequent works by architects throughout Latin America. An initiator of new methods and new standards, Villanueva was also a creator of the first rank.

At first the bullring at Maracay, his earliest major work, does seem particularly "modern." Bullfighting is a rigidly traditional sport, a fact that Villanueva acknowledges in his design: the structure is a compromise of new materials, the demands of expanded space, and historical continuity. Thus, the massive arena is surmounted all around by the lacelike lightness of its top arcade, and Moorish-style horse-shoe arches span its entrance. But, with this work, Villanueva introduced to South America a skeleton structure actually *expressed* through its concrete stress-members, as Perret had done in Europe some 50 years previously.

In his redevelopment of the El Silencio Quarter in Caracas, Villanueva revealed his concern for the quality of the human environment, and in his development of the University City of the University of Venezuela, Caracas, this feeling is most triumphantly expressed. His accomplishment is particularly evident in his conception of the covered plazas and walks: more than a mile of covered walkway undulates around the hillsides on which the university is situated, its wave-like progression, varying in height, providing a cool shelter as its pre-stressed, pre-poured concrete units on cantilevered supports curve around planted islands. Low shelters give way to lofty halls, which in turn give onto terrazzo-floored plazas that provide shaded gathering places throughout the university complex. At almost every focal point in this vast structure Villanueva collaborated with artists who created sculptural and mural "accents" integrated into the work as a complete architectural entity—a notable success being Alexander Calder's multi-coloured "clouds" hanging from the ceiling of the main auditorium (the Aula Magna), not only acting as sound baffles for musical concerts, but also transforming the massive interior into a light and airy space.

Villanueva's Olympic Stadium at University City illustrates how severely practical his designs could be, while at the same time achieving an aesthetic magnificence. Seating 30,000 people, the stadium is supported on almost invisible concrete columns; the grandstand, with locker-rooms and other facilities ingeniously tucked below, is covered by a breathtaking cantilevered free span of pre-stressed concrete beams. Clean ramps, also in concrete, sweep up to the terraces of seating to complete a totally harmonious blend of stressed forms.

University City is magnificent, the work of a master. Villanueva may, however, have his most lasting influence in housing.

Just prior to commencing work on University City, he was commissioned to design a low-cost housing development for low-income families in Maracaibo. Previously such developments had been sponsored by industrial concerns whose only interest was to locate workers in rows of conveniently drab and monotonous barracks for as little expense as possible. Villanueva rose to the occasion by creating a new standard of housing at an equally low cost, arranging the 1,000 one-family houses and several 3-storey multiple dwellings concentrically around urban centres of community facilities—schools,

shops, churches, and gathering-places. Short but broad streets opened out at the fronts of the houses, and individual yards and pedestrian walkways at the rear were designed to enhance the character of the neighborhood. Villanueva had built up to a standard, rather than down to a cost.

While he was Consultant Architect to the Workers' Bank, Villanueva further developed the lessons of Maracaibo in two residential estates in Caracas—23 de Enero and El Paraiso—perhaps the finest low- to middle-income housing complexes in Venezuela. Instead of spreading single-storey "ranchos" all over what was (and still is, thanks to his scheme) an environmentally beautiful hillside, he built a blend of low-rise and high-rise blocks in a coherent pattern that stresses horizontal movement rather than a vertical stabbing at the sky. The peasants who live in these blocks enjoy cool breezes from the hillside, rather than the expensive ground-level mugginess reserved for the fashionable rich.

It is difficult to believe that these developments were greeted with harsh and bitter criticism when they were first built, for today they have become a synonym—as has all of Villanueva's work—for qualitative rather than quantitative design.

—Colin Naylor

von BRANCA, Alexander (Freiherr).
German. Born in Munich, 11 January 1919. Educated at the Landeschulheim, Neubeuern, Germany, 1931–37; University of Munich, 1946–48; E.T.H.: Eidgenössischen Technischen Hochschule, Zurich, 1948–50. Served in the German Army, 1938–40. Married Theresa Freifau zu Guttenberg in 1952 (died, 1953); married Carolina Bernasconi in 1955; children: Franziskus, Emanuela, Alexandrea, Matthias, and Benedicta. In private practice, Munich. Architect, Heimat Building Department, City of Munich, since 1972. Recipient: Cultural Prize, City of Munich; Honor Award, City of Burghausen, Germany. Member, Bavarian Order of Merit, and Akademie der Künste, Munich. Member, Papal Order of Sylvester, and Accademia dei Virtuosi al Phanteon, Rome. Address (office): Gauss-strasse 1, 8000 Munich 80, West Germany.

Works:

1954	Volksbank, Weiden, Germany
	Church, Herzogspitalstrasse, Munich
1955	Buttermelcher Church, Munich
	Flats for diplomats, Thiemestrasse, Munich
1957	Klenze Grammar School, Munich
1957/	
58	Old people's home, Pullach, Munich
1957/	
60	Monastery for the Styler Missionaries, Munich
1958	Church, Greifenberg, Germany
1959/	
61	Church, Rohrbach, Germany
1960	Haniel House, Haimhausen, Germany
1962	Church, Weissenburg, Germany
1962/	
64	Stanischeff House, Munich
1962/	
65	St. Matthias Church, Fürstenried, Germany
1963/	
66	German Embassy, Madrid
1963/	
67	Savings Bank, Wasserburg, Germany
1963/	
71	Family holiday house, Naumburg, Germany
1964	von Branca House, Oberfohringerstrasse, Munich
	Church, Langwasser, Germany
1964/	
68	Raiffeisen Insurance Building, Munich
1964/	
69	Church, Beuel, Bonn
1965/	
67	Church, Jettingen, Germany
1965/	
68	Catholic Monastery and Church, Schönstatt, Germany
1966/	
69	Castle Church, Hirschberg, Germany
1966/	
71	Treatment Center, Bad Füssing, Germany
1967/	
69	Claas House, Harsewinkel, Germany
1969	Dante Grammar School, Munich
1970/	
71	Underground (Subway) Station, Marienplatz, Munich
1970/	
74	St. Thomas More Church, Neusäss, Augsburg
	Central Library, University of Regensburg
1971	Flats for old people, Heidelberg
1971/	
72	Village school, Neubeuern, Germany
	Press City, Olympic Village, Munich
1971/	
75	Postal Administration Building, Freiburg
	St. Ulrich's Catholic Academy, Augsburg
1972/	
74	Regional Insurance Building (LVA), Perlach, Munich
1972/	
78	Student Union, University of Würzburg
1973–	Neue Pinakothek Art Gallery, Munich
	Library, University of Würzburg
1973/	
75	4 underground (subway) stations, Bonn
1973/	
77	Chapel and School, Catholic Monastery, Schönstatt, Germany
1977–	Guest House, Bad Füssing, Germany
	Church Center, Diesenbach/Regenstauf, Germany
	Hertie Department Store, Würzburg
	Savings Bank Headquarters, Aschaffenburg, Germany
1978–	Raiffeisen-Zentralbank Administration Building, Munich
	Local Government Administration Building, Aschaffenburg, Germany
	Museum, Vaduz, Liechtenstein
	German Embassy, Vatican City
1979–	Raiffeisen-Zentralbank, Augsburg

Publications:

By von BRANCA: articles—"Aufsatz über das Wohnen" in *Süddeutsche Zeitung* (Munich), July 1972; "Augsatz über Architektur und Denkmalsschutz" in *Augsburger Allgemeine*, July 1974; "Denkmal- und Stadtbilpflege in Bamberg" in *Schönere Heimat* (Munich), March 1975; "Das Zeitgemässe—oder der Mut zum Unzeitgemässen" in *Der Architekt* (Stuttgart), 1976; "Die Chance des Regionalismus in der Architektur" in *Der Architekt* (Stuttgart), 1976; "Brücken zwischen moderner Architektur und Denkmalspflege" in *Deutsches Architektenblatt* (Stuttgart), May 1976; "Verfall der Gestaltsaussage" in *Civitas/Rund um den Bau* (Zurich), 1977; "I Feel an Obligation to Form" in *Der Architekt* (Stuttgart), January 1979.

On von BRANCA: articles—"L'Architecte Alexandre von Branca" in *Art d'Eglise* (Ottignies, Belgium), no. 114, 1961; "Klenze-Oberrealschule, München" in *Baumeister* (Munich), March 1964; "Architect-Parents Plan Their Own Highly Modern House in Munich" in *House Beautiful* (New York), January 1966; "Meeting Place for Church and the World: St. Ulrich, Augsburg" in *Architektur und*

Wohnform (Stuttgart), July 1975; "Administration Building in Munich-Perlach for Landesversicherungsanstalt Oberbayern" in *Baumeister* (Munich), October 1975; "Regensburg University" in *Baumeister* (Munich), May 1976; "Oberpostdirektion Freiburg" in *Bauwelt* (Berlin), January 1977.

The abundant work of Alexander von Branca suggests community and a profound basis, that which, over the ages, can be transposed and reflected with strength in architecture. I therefore put to him the question of art in architecture—art as a message from man to man about his place in the world, his seeing and non-seeing, his perception and non-perception.

Von Branca believes that in a work of art both primitive and contemporary human experience are similarly visible; the work of art, therefore, has an irrefutably informatory content. The true value of a creative work is not merely its quality within its particular aesthetic category; the value is also in its message to the next one, to the other, who, as a human being, lives with the same horizon of experience, even when hundreds of years intervene. Von Branca confirms the absolute necessity of continuity through tradition and the symbolic value of architecture as expression over ages and generations. There is a "supertemporal truth" in architecture. In other words, we can not extract modern architecture from its historical context, its associations with history, and regard "modern" as a quality per se.

Or, rather, we should not be able to do so. If the architecture of our century is regarded within a historical context, there is more conformism than courage—uniformity, lovelessness, a technical ingenuity with a failure of design. Von Branca thinks that our work has become spiritually poorer; that is, it has failed to "connect" with the life of man. Most of our works involve a giving in to the ethos of small effort for high return; all want to rule but none will serve. Von Branca, conversely, sees art as involving a high seriousness—listening to, looking at, serving and giving to the purpose of the work, so that man, the observer, can understand and explain why it exists.

Everything that is created lives. Even the apparently dead lives, and in many ways the historic is more alive than the contemporary. There can be no such thing as historicism! Von Branca sees architecture's present task as primarily that of revealing to mankind the life in things. We must be concerned with discovery and with revelation; we must create works that prove themselves by persuading us to look at the environment not only with the outer eye but also with the inner eye. Von Branca believes that architecture must be associative, must inform, must contribute to the world of the imagination without which we, as creative beings, cannot live. Architecture must construct horizons of expectation, and it must have an aura like that of people themselves, who meet each other, who respond, who are attracted or repulsed. Von Branca told me of his first visit to the Pantheon in Rome, when, on entering, he stopped, moved back, because the "inner radiance" of the building was so powerful.

Our materialistic architecture cannot express such radiance. It can no longer seize hold of life. Von Branca deplores the one-sidedness, the functionalism of our works: they are comfortable, well-made, and often they have quality, but they do not live, and their lifelessness makes people sad and drives them to escape into the past, where liveliness is easier to find. Von Branca wants to bring it back to our time, as a "message upwards and downwards," and he defines the message as that of love. For von Branca sees the absence of life as the absence of love, and he fears that lovelessness is the fate of our time.

Alexander von Branca: Chapel, Catholic Monastery, Schönstatt, Germany, 1977

It is a serious and earnest vision, and it pervades all of his work.

Yet there are problems. Von Branca wants to eliminate isolated individualism as the inheritance of a misunderstood notion of "artistic freedom." One could argue that, even if it appears to be a medium of expression for everyone, art is always isolated and individual in its development: the great works of architectural history are always unique, the product of the individual ego. And an architecture that is humble yet resolute in its autonomy is often the one that sets free the creative potential that separates the real work of art from the indifferent average. Also, von Branca thinks that the future development of architecture depends on whether people can escape from the slavery of materialism. But materialism is increasingly the only aim of our lives, and if the possible renaissance of architecture depends not so much on constructed details as on an attitude to life —well, that is a tall order.

I asked von Branca about the relationship of theory to practice, between his philosophy and reality. His answer was unequivocal: theory and practice are one! That is a lofty claim, and with von Branca it is entirely sincere. Yet, I wonder. Even with the greatest care for, and love in, our work, we architects have to accept a good measure of impotence in our achievements, and I think we seek to compensate for this impotency with theory. But this is not to offer a darker vision, or to contradict von Branca. "Theory corrects practice, practice corrects theory," and in the reciprocal fertilization of correction there can be a creative beginning.

—Justus Dahinden

von GERKAN, Meinhard.

German. Born in Riga, Lithuania, 3 January 1935. Studied physics and law at the University of Hamburg; architecture at the Technical University of Berlin, 1958–60, and Technical University of Braunschweig, 1961–64, Dip.Arch.Eng. 1964. Married Gerda Kuhn in 1959; children: Florence and Franziska. Since 1965, Partner, with Volkwin Marg, von Gerkan-Marg + Partner, Hamburg; branch offices in Berlin and Munich (additional partners since 1972: Rolf Niedballa; Karsten Brauer; Andreas Sack; Klaus Staratzke). Professor of Architectural Design, Technical University of Braunschweig, since 1974. Member of the Board, Chamber of Architects, Hamburg, since 1969. Recipient: First Prize, Pahlavi National Library Competition, Tehran, 1978. Member, Bund Deutscher Architekten; Free Academy of Arts, Hamburg. Address: von Gerkan-Marg + Partner, St. Benedictstrasse 8, 2 Hamburg 13, Germany.

Works:

1966 Kohnemann House, Hamburg
1966/
68 Stormarn Public Hall, Oldesloe, Germany (with Schmedje)
1966/
69 Max Planck Institute, Lindau, Germany (with Störmer)
1967/
70 Sports Complex, Diekirch, Luxembourg (with Störmer)
1968/
70 Poppenbuttel Apartment House, Hamburg
1968/
74 Terminal, roads, bridges and other facilities at Tegel Airport, Berlin (with Nickels)
1969/
71 Alsterufer Apartment House, Hamburg
1970/
74 Control Tower, Power Station and Operations Building, Tegel Airport, Berlin (with Nickels)

1972/
74 Shell Company Head Offices, Hamburg (with Wiehe)
Sports Centre, University of Kiel (with Nickels)
1973/
74 Sound-deadening bunkers, Tegel Airport, Berlin
1973/
75 Aral Company Head Office, Bochum, Germany
1974 Munich Airport II
Billwerder-Allermohe New Town, Hamburg (with Erler, Wolske, Nickels and Ohrt)
1974/
75 Tax Office, Oldenburg, Germany (with Patschan)
1974/
77 Psychiatric Institute, Rickling, Germany
1975/
76 Kohlhofen Residential Area, Hamburg
1975/
77 Technical College, Bad Oldesloe, Germany (with Wiehe)
European Patent Office, Munich
1976 Dar El Beida Airport, Algeria
1976/
78 Gross Bleichen modernization, Hamburg
Bergedorf Polytechnic, Hamburg
1977 Hyatt Hotel, Abu Dhabi, Dubai
Moscow Airport (project)
1977/
78 Town houses, Hamburg
MAK Company Head Office Building, Kiel (with Brockstedt and Discher)
Ministry of the Interior, Kiel
Otto Company Head Office, Hamburg
Taima Housing Project, Saudi Arabia
1978 Parish Hall, Stade, Germany
Pahlavi National Library, Tehran
Ministry Offices, Stuttgart

Publications:

By von GERKAN: articles—"Neubau des Flughafen Berlin Tagel" in *Berliner Bauwirtschaft,* no. 598, 1972; "Quo Vadi? Zum Wettbewerbswesen" in *Deutsches Architektenblatt* (Stuttgart), no. 13, 1974; "Vielfalt in der Einheit: Neuplanung für den Flughafen Berlin-Tegel" in *Deutsches Architektenblatt* (Stuttgart), no. 21, 1974; "Architekten sind nicht an allem schuld" in *Die Zeit* (Hamburg), 21 February 1975; "Gedanken zum Berufsbild und zur Berufspraxis des Architekten heute" in *Detail* (Munich), no. 3, 1975; "Schnorkel gegen Raster" in *Die Zeit* (Hamburg), 29 August 1975; "Gestaltung unserer Unwelt" in *Verband Bayerischer Wohnungsunternehmen* (Munich), no. 11, 1975; "Architektur kritisch—Ein Bau widerlegt seine Ideologie: FU-Berlin —'Die Rostlaube' " in *Der Architekt* (Stuttgart), no. 11, 1975; "Elemente der Flughafenplanung: Hamburg-Kaltenkirchen, Flughafen München II, Flughafen Berlin-Tegel" in *Bauen und Wohnen* (Zurich), March 1976; "Verkehrsbauten als zentrale Aufgabe der Umweltgestaltung" in *Der Architekt* (Stuttgart), no. 11, 1976; "Der Computer als Ersatz für den hohlen Bauch" in *Bauwelt* (Berlin), no. 34, 1976.

On von GERKAN: book—*Deutsche Kunst seit 1960,* vol. 4: *Architecture* by Paolo Nestler and Peter M. Bode, Munich 1976; articles—"Ein Burg aus Glas" in *Stern* (Hamburg), no. 30, 1970; article on the Shell Headquarters in *Baumeister* (Munich), no. 5, 1970; "Architektenportrat Meinhard von Gerkan und Volkwin Marg" in *Deutsche Bauzeitung* (Stuttgart), no. 5, 1972; article on the European Patent Office in *Baumeister* (Munich), no. 11, 1972; article on Berlin Airport in *Bauwelt* (Berlin), no. 45, 1974; "Weihe nach Wehen—Flughafen Berlin-Tegel" in *Der Spiegel* (Berlin), 14 October 1974; "Ein Hallelujah für Zwei Architekten" in *Die Zeit* (Hamburg), 25 October 1974; "Die glorreichen Sieben der

Meinhard von Gerkan: Sports Centre, University of Kiel, 1974

deutschen Architektur" in *Welt am Sonntag* (Bonn), 7 November 1976; article on the Sports Centre at the University of Kiel in *Domus* (Milan), December 1977; article on the Pahlavi National Library in *Stern* (Hamburg), 18 May 1978.

Primary in importance in our design efforts is the attempt to render "personality" and "identity" to each building. The diversity of our construction tasks—from the one-family dwelling to the airport—and their respective situations with regard to environment and ecology—extending from Schleswig Holstein to the Persian Gulf—entails a multitude of differences in identity. We have never attempted to conceal such differences by means of standardizing. We much prefer to discover the substance-oriented peculiarity of a project, or its particular reference to environment, to ultimately find for the traits of identity we have thus discovered the best and most suitable means of design.

The means by which we try to establish correspondence of form to the respective content are various —constructional, spatial, plastic three-dimensional, decorative-aesthetical, topographical—but they are in no way merely of a formal nature—in the usual meaning of the term in the architectural vocabulary. We do not use any preconceived formal solution which we can fit to every problem, but we try to find a specific answer to every specific question.

More than by any other factor our design work is determined by the regularity of geometry. When it has not seemed feasible to derive from the specific requirements posed by the building site or from the urban environment components to shape the architectural character, we have drawn the structuring framework of our designs from geometry. With geometry the law of the natural sciences becomes the guide for artistic form-finding and creation. That

may seem to imply a lack of creative power or of formal imagination, but it is the means to discover self-discipline, to seek out valid and timeless forms of architecture. We have almost never freely invented an architectural form: each form is either bound to the requirements imposed by the building site and/or to the specific function, but mostly it is bound to both of these and also to geometric laws.

As variously as we may try to solve each architectural assignment—without any dogmatic prejudices —we do also claim to understand our role as architects in society. We consider ourselves experts in the design and maintenance of order in our environment. That role demands, on the one hand, taking into account the needs of society and, on the other hand, resolutely and purposefully influencing, with the authority of competent experts, permanent changes in the environment. Ideological contempt, or a know-it-all attitude, in these concerns is surely just as inappropriate as is an uncritical striving for fulfillment at any price.

—Meinhard von Gerkan

Although as students they were already successful in architectural competitions (anonymously, in the service of other architects), Meinhard von Gerkan and his partner Volkwin Marg won seven first prizes, some of them in international competitions, in the first year of their joint practice. The exceptional and meteoric rise of two beginners, unknown and without means, to the rank of international stars was made possible by the modern practice, particularly prevalent in Germany, of finding architects through competition for practically all public and most large private building projects.

The principal reasons for von Gerkan and Marg's success are that they conscientiously fulfil the quantitative programme, pragmatically develop their architecture from an analysis of function, local envi-

ronment, and topography, and only rarely seek support from geometric forms. Their designs do not obey a universal repertoire of form or direction but are an "interpretation related to the content and situation of the actual project." Their buildings are not stylistically characterized by an unmistakable personal handwriting; they can, and do, include all the architectural features of our time.

All of Von Gerkan and Marg's buildings are brilliantly conceived and executed. Some are exemplary —for example, the Sports Centre at the University of Kiel. Others, like the airport buildings at Berlin-Tegel, are of international stature.

—Manfred Sack

VOYSEY, C(harles) F(rancis) A(nnesley).
British. Born in Hessle, Yorkshire, 28 May 1857. Educated at Dulwich College, London, 1871–73, and with a private tutor, London, 1873–74; articled to the architect John Pollard Seddon, London, 1879. Married Mary Maria Evans in 1885. Assistant in the office of Saxon Snell, London, 1879, and George Devey, London, 1880–81; in private practice, London, 1881 until his death, 1942; associated with the designer A. H. Mackmurdo, London, 1882–83; designed carpets, textiles and wallpapers for Jeffrey and Company, the Essex Company, Sanderson and Company, and other British companies, from 1883. Member, Art Workers' Guild, London, from 1884. Exhibitions: Art Workers' Guild exhibitions, London, 1884–; *International Exposition,* Antwerp, 1892; *World's Columbian Exposition,* Chicago, 1893; *International Exposition,* Paris, 1900; *Exposi-*

tion of Decorative Arts, Turin, 1902; C.F.A. Voysey, Batsford Gallery, London, 1931; C. F. A. Voysey 1857–1941, University of California at Santa Barbara, 1970; C. F. A. Voysey, Architect and Designer, 1857–1941, Royal Pavilion, Brighton, 1978. Collections: Victoria and Albert Museum, London; Royal Institute of British Architects, London. Recipient: Gold Medal, Royal Institute of British Architects, 1940. Honorary Master, Art Workers' Guild, London, 1924; Fellow, Royal Institute of British Architects, 1929; Royal Designer for Industry, Royal Society of Arts, London, 1936. Died (in Winchester, Hampshire) 12 February 1941.

Works:

1877 Model Housing (project)
1878 Cottages, Kenmore, County Kerry, Ireland (project)
1880 H. W. Vowler Offices, Canning Town, London (project)
1881 Housing, Epping Forest, Essex (project)
      Cottages, Northampton
1882 Shop alterations, Notting Hill, London
      Summer house, Sunbury-on-Thames, Middlesex
1883 Woodhams House alterations, Dulwich, London
      Studio, Oakley Street, Chelsea, London (project)
1884 Sanatorium and baths, South Devon (project)
      Royal Hotel conversion, Teignmouth, Devon (project)
      Victoria Mansions interiors, London
      Crematorium and chapel, Sundrum, Ayr, Scotland (project)
      Carlyle Memorial Tablet, Cheyne Walk, Chelsea, London
1885 Church alterations and interiors, Swallow Street, Piccadilly, London
1887 House alterations, 61 Bedford Gardens, London W.8
1888 Mural paintings for St. Andrew's Church, Cardiff
1889 Studio, 26 Bridge Road West, Battersea, London
      Lakin Cottage, Bishops Itchington, Warwickshire
      Cliff House interiors, Warwick
      Railway Hotel alterations, Camberwell, London
      Heath Brow Cottage interiors, Hampstead, London
      Ward House, Dovercourt (project)
1890 Cliff House addition, Warwick
      Larkin Cottage, Llandrindod, Wales
      Forster House and Studio, 14 South Parade, Bedford Park, London W.4
      Deudraeth Castle alterations, Penrhyndeudraeth, North Wales
      Walnut Tree Farm, Castlemorton, Malvern, Herefordshire/Worcestershire (now Bannut Farm)
1891 Houses, Wentworth Estate, Swan Walk, Chelsea, London
      Britten Studio, 17 St. Dunstan's Road, West Kensington, London
      Plan for Hans Court, London (project)
1892 Studios, Glebe Place, Chelsea, London
      Studio, 7 Hill Road, London N.W.8
      Houses, 14 and 16 Hans Road, London S.W.3 (now offices and flats)
1893 The Mansion alterations, Wood Green, London
      Canwell House additions, Tite Street, Chelsea, London
      Almshouse Chapel decorations, Castle Rising, near Lynn, Norfolk
      House alterations, 12 King Street, Westminster, London
      Studio, Brook Green, London W.6
      Perrycroft House, Lodge and Stables, Jubilee Drive, Colwall, Herefordshire

1894 Verandah for a house at 54 Circus Road, London N.W.8
      House extension, 12 The Parade, Bedford Park, London
      Church House alterations, Trinity College, Camberwell, London
      Lord Lovelace House, Ockham Park, Surrey
      Cottages and outbuildings, Alton, Hampshire
      Lowicks House, Stables and Garden, Sandy Lane, Tilford, Frensham, Surrey
1895 Wentworth Arms Inn, for Lord Lovelace, Elmesthorpe, Hinckley, Leicestershire
      Annesley Lodge, Platt's Lane, Hampstead, London
      Hill Close House, Studland Bay, Swanage, Dorset
1896 Wortley Cottages, Elmesthorpe, Leicestershire
      Shields Studio, Merton, Surrey
      Greyfriars House, Hog's Back, Guildford, Surrey
      Essex Mills frontage, Lavender Hill, London S.W.4
      Sturgis Stables and Lodge, Puttenham, Surrey
1897 Woodcote House additions, Horsley, Surrey
      Free Church Trustees House, Riggindale Road, Streatham, London
      Grane House (Norney Grange), Norney, near Shackleford, Surrey
      Hill House, Thorpe Mandeville, Northamptonshire
      Cottages, houses, and shops, Brackley, Northamptonshire
      Voysey House, Colwall, Herefordshire
      Studios, 32 Queens Road, London S.W.19
      Cattler House, Limpsfield, Surrey
      New Place (Stedman House), Haslemere, Surrey
1898 Broadleys (A. Currer Briggs House), Windermere, Westmorland
      Rickards House, Windermere, Westmorland (project)
      Moorcrag (Buckley House), Windermere, Westmorland (now the Racing Motor Boat Club)
      Barker House, Collington Avenue, Bexhill, Sussex
      Sewell House, Limpsfield, Surrey
      Rowley House, Glassonby, Cumberland
      Lock House, Oxshott, Surrey
      Heyworth House and Stables, Blackburn, Lancashire
      Whalley House additions, 16 Chalcot Gardens, London N.W.3
1899 Wilson Pavilion, Oldbury, Birmingham
      Spade House (H. G. Wells House), Sandgate, Kent (now a hotel)
      Mayers House, Kidderminster, Worcestershire
      Beaworthy Cottage Hospital, Hanwill, Devon (now Winsford Cottage Hospital)
      Fitch House, Putney, London
      Mieville Stables, Kingsbury, Middlesex
      Simmons Studio Buildings, 65 Hamilton Terrace, London N.W.8
      Blyth House, Sandwich, Kent
      Woodcote Lodge additions, Horsley, Surrey
      Bowie House and Garden, Colnbrooke, Buckinghamshire
1900 Oakhurst House, Fernehurst, Sussex
      Chambers House, Priorsgarth, Puttenham, Surrey (now Priorsfield School)
      The Orchard (Voysey House), Chorley Wood, Hertfordshire
      Mieville Coachman's and Men's Residence, and Stables, Kingsbury, Middlesex
      Pinker House, Worcester Park, Surrey
      Lakin Cottage additions, Bishops Itchington, Warwickshire
      Barendt House additions and repairs, 73 Fitzjohns Avenue, London N.W.3
1901 Plyton House, Cuttycroft, Malvern, Here-

fordshire
      Cottages for Earl Beauchamp, Madresfield, Worcestershire
      Lord Lovelace House additions, Ockham Park, Surrey
      Grammar school, Lincoln (project)
      The Pastures (Miss G. Conant House) and Stables, North Luffenham, Rutland
1902 Phillips House, Shooters Hill, Kent
      Sanderson and Sons Factory, Barley Mow Passage, Chiswick, London W.4 (now offices)
      Roughwood Farm additions, Chalfont St. Giles, Buckinghamshire
      Angus House, Vache Estate, Chalfont St. Giles, Buckinghamshire
      Heathdene Stables, Langley Road, Watford, Hertfordshire
      Vodin (F. Walters House), Old Woking Road, Pyrford Common, Woking, Surrey (now Little Court)
1903 Stable, Perrycroft, Colwall, Herefordshire
      Spade House (H. G. Wells House) additional storey, Sandgate, Kent
      2 cottages, Pole Cat Lane, Shotter Mill, Surrey
      Lawrence House, Bracknell Gardens, Hampstead, London (project)
      Ty-Bronner (W. Hastings House), St. Fagan's Road, Fairwater Estate, Cardiff
      Higgs House, Bognor Regis, Sussex
      La Thaugue House, Bedford Park, London (project)
      Toulmin House, Rayrigg Estate, Windermere, Westmorland (project)
      White Cottage (Clarence T. Coggin House), 68 Lyford Road, London S.W.18
      Tilehurst (Miss E. Somers House), 10 Bushey Grange Road, Bushey, Hertfordshire
      Stables, Grane House (Norney Grange), Norney, near Shackleford, Surrey
      Hollybank (Fort House), Shire Lane, Chorley Wood, Hertfordshire (now Sunnybank)
1904 Stable and Garage, and Electricity Generator Building, Vodin (F. Walters House), Pyrford Common, Woking, Surrey
      Stables, Ty-Bronner (Hastings House), St. Fagan's Road, Fairwater Estate, Cardiff
      Stables and Garage, New Place (Stedman House), Haslemere, Surrey
      Lady Henry Somerset House, Lodge and Garage, Higham, Woodford, Essex
      Houses and Workmen's Institute, Whitwood, Normanton, Yorkshire (now The Rising Sun Public House)
      Myholme (Miss E. Somers Nursing Home for Children), Merry Hill Lane, Bushey, Hertfordshire
      Wilson Summer House, Perrycroft, Colwall, Herefordshire
      Carnegie Library, Limerick, Ireland (competition project)
1905 Canon Grave House, Cobham, Surrey
      White Horse Inn, Stetchworth, near Newmarket, Suffolk (now White Horse Stables)
      Mrs. Tytus House, Ashintelly, Tyringham, Massachusetts, U.S.A.
      Woodbrook (Heyworth House) alterations, Alderley Edge, Cheshire
      Leigh Causey House, Aswan, Egypt
      Hollymount (Burke House), Amersham Road, Knotty Green, Beaconsfield, Buckinghamshire
      The Homestead (Turner House), Frinton, Essex
      Fensom House, Chorley Wood, Hertfordshire
1906 Pickards Farm House, St. Nicholas, Guildford, Surrey
      Hatton House, Grays Park, Stoke Poges, near Slough, Buckinghamshire
      3 cottages, Laugham Road, Blackburn, Lancashire (project)

3 shops, Chorley, near Blackburn, Lancashire (project)

1906/
07 Wilverley (Goodhart House) extensions, Stables and Cottages, Holtye Common, Sussex (now Highlands)

1906/
10 Essex and Suffolk Equitable Insurance Company Office reconstruction, 56 and 62 New Broad Street, London E.C.2

1907 Littlehome, Guildford, Surrey
2 houses for Vernon Hart, Finchley Road, Burgess Park, London (destroyed)
Lovelace Sepulchre and Mausoleum, Ockham Park, Surrey
Turner Bungalow, Frinton, Essex (project)
Turner House, Frinton, Essex (project)

1908 3 houses for S. C. Turner, Frinton, Essex
Wilson Coachman's Cottage, Perrycroft, Colwall, Herefordshire
Burke House, Beaconsfield, Buckinghamshire
Lady Lovelace Tomb alterations, Kirby Mallory, Leicestershire

1909 Cotterell Lodge-Style House, Coombe Down, near Bath
Essex and Suffolk Equitable Insurance Company Offices, High Street, Colchester, Essex
Littleholme (Simpson House), 103 Sedbergh Road, Kendal, Westmorland
Voysey House, Slindon, near Barnham Junction, Sussex
Ling House, Hampstead, London (project)
Brooke End (Miss F. Knight House), Stables and Garden, Henley-in-Arden, Warwickshire

1910 2 office/apartment blocks, Tudor Street, London E.C.4 (project)
2 houses for G. E. Marshall, Sea Road, Wallasey, Cheshire
Queen's University extensions, Belfast (competition project)
Convalescent home, Pasture Wood, near Dorking, Surrey

1911 Lowicks (E. J. Horniman House) additions and Summer House, Frensham, Surrey
Myholme (Miss E. Somers Nursing Home for Children) additions, Bushey, Hertfordshire
Hetherington House, Malone Road, Belfast
Playground, Kentish Town, London
Littlehome (gardener's cottage), Guildford, Surrey
Village Hall, Porlock, Somerset
Mirrielees Convalescent Home (barn conversion), Pasture Wood, near Dorking, Surrey
Atkinson and Company Shop, Old Bond Street, London W.1 (demolished)

1912 Lady Lovelace House, Lilycombe, Porlock, Somerset (based on Lovelace design)
Chambers Funeral Monument, Ludham, near Great Yarmouth, Norfolk
Perry and Company Shop, 165 Victoria Street, Westminster, London
Lord Lovelace Memorial, Ashley Combe, Somerset
Burial Grounds for Carl Low, Helenenthal, Moravia, Czechoslovakia (2 projects)
Country Cottages (2 competition projects)

1913 Lodge and Garage, Hill Close House, Studland Bay, Swanage, Dorset
Government Buildings, Ottawa, Canada (competition project)

1914 Voysey House, Wilmslow, Cheshire (project)
Tingey House, Thatcham, Cold Ash, Berkshire (project)
6 cottages rebuilding, Elmesthorpe, Leicestershire
Terrell House, Ashmonsworth, near Newbury, Berkshire (project)
White Cliffe (Barendt House) alterations and

extensions, St. Margaret's-at-Cliffe, Kent (now High Gant)

1915 Garden Studio, Woodbrook, Alderley Edge, Cheshire
2 cottages (project)

1919 Haslington (cottage; coachhouse conversion), Malvern Wells, Worcestershire
2 cottages, Bradfield, Berkshire
Village War Memorial, Malvern Wells, Worcestershire
Cottages, Alderley Edge, Cheshire (project)

1920 Hambledon Hurst (Van Gruisen House) gardens, Hambledon, Surrey
Potters Bar War Memorial, Hertfordshire
Taylor House, Lodge and Garden, Laughton, Market Harborough, Leicestershire
King's Own Yorkshire Light Infantry War Memorial, York Minster
Entrance doors, Sanderson and Sons, 55 Berners Street, London W.1
Manor House War Memorial, Tonbridge School, Kent

1921 Stewart Tomb, Hampstead Cemetery, London

1922 St. Merryn House, Cornwall (project)
Jones House, St. Nicholas-at-Wade, Isle of Thanet, Kent (project)
Low House, Helenenthal, Iglau, Czechoslovakia

1923 Street Telephone Booth (project)

1926 Leigh House, Hillingdon, Middlesex

1930 Memorial Tablet, Ludlow Cottage Hospital, Shropshire
Venesta Ltd. Exhibition Stand, Building Trades Exhibition, Manchester

1932 Lady Diana Gibb Bungalow, South Africa (project)

1933 Manchester Exhibition Hall (competition project)

1936 Robert Donat House, Bishops Avenue, Hampstead, London

Various designs for furniture, textiles, wallpapers, carpets and tiles.

Publications:

By VOYSEY; books—*Reason as the Basis of Art,* London 1906; *Individuality,* London 1915; articles —"An Interview with Mr. Charles F. Annesley Voysey" in *The Studio* (London), no. 1, 1893; "Domestic Furniture in *RIBA Journal* (London), no. 1, 1894; "Art in Decoration and Design" in *The Builder* (London), 23 February 1895; "The Aims and Conditions of the Modern Decorator" in *Journal of Decorative Art* (London), April 1895; "Contribution to Discussion on Style for Liverpool Cathedral" in *Architectural Review* (London), November 1901; "Remarks on Domestic Entrance Halls" in *The Studio* (London), no. 21, 1901; "L'Art Nouveau: What It Is and What Is Thought of It—A Symposium" in *Magazine of Art* (New York), no. 2, 1904; "Ideas in Things" in *Arts Connected with Building,* edited by Raffles Davison, London 1909; "The English Home" in *British Architect* (London), 27 January 1911; "Patriotism in Architecture" in *Architectural Association Journal* (London), June 1912; "The Quality of Fitness in Architecture" in *The Craftsman* (London), November 1912; "Open Letter to the Royal Institute of British Architects" in *British Architect* (London), 29 November 1912; "Modern Symbolism" in *Architect and Contract Report* (London), 15 February 1918; "The Aesthetic Aspects of Concrete Construction" in *The Architect and Engineer* (London), May 1919; "On Town Planning" in *Architectural Review* (London), July 1919; "Self-Expression in Art" in *RIBA Journal* (London), 30 February 1923; "Some Fundamental Ideas in Relation to Art" in *RIBA Journal* (London), 22 March 1924; "The Arts and Crafts Exhibition of 1928" in *RIBA Journal* (London), 8 December 1928; "English Church Art" in *RIBA Journal* (London),

12 July 1930; "1874 and After" in *Architectural Review* (London), October 1931; "Unfamiliar Uses for Stained Glass" in *Apollo* (London), April 1933; "Letter to the Editor" in *The Architects' Journal* (London), 14 March 1935; "Architecture and Archaeology" in *RIBA Journal* (London), 7 November 1936.

On VOYSEY: books—*Modern British Domestic Architecture and Decoration,* edited by Charles Holme, London 1901; *Modern Cottage Architecture* by Maurice B. Adams, London 1904; *The British Home of Today* by W. Shaw Sparrow, London 1904; *Das Englische Haus* by Hermann Muthesius, 3 volumes, Berlin 1904–05; *Ideals in Art* by Walter Crane, London 1905; *Das Moderne Landhaus* by Hermann Muthesius, Munich 1905; *Country Cottages and Weekend Homes* by J. H. Elder-Duncan, London 1906; *The Modern Home* by W. Shaw Sparrow, London 1906; *Landhaus und Garten* by Hermann Muthesius, Munich 1907; *Modern Homes* by T. Raffles Davison, London 1909; *Our Homes and How to Make the Best of Them* by W. Shaw Sparrow, London 1909; *Small Country Houses of Today* by Lawrence Weaver, London 1910; *The House and Its Equipment* by Lawrence Weaver, London 1912; *Gardens for Small Country Houses* by Gertrude Jekyll and Lawrence Weaver, London 1914; *New Place, Haslemere, and Its Gardens,* London 1921; *Floral Forms in Historic Design* by L. P. Butterfield, London 1922; *A History of English Wallpaper 1509–1914* by Alan Sugden and John Edmondson, London 1926; *A History of Everyday Things in England* by Marjorie and C. H. B. Quennell, London 1934; *Pioneers of the Modern Movement* by Nikolaus Pevsner, London 1936, New York 1937; *Sarum Chase* by Frank D. Salisbury, London 1953; *C. F. A. Voysey: A Memoir* by John Brandon-Jones, London and New York 1957; *Architecture: 19th and 20th Centuries* by Henry-Russell Hitchcock, London 1957; *Anfänge des Funktionalismus* by Julius Posener, Berlin 1964; *Sources of Modern Architecture* by Dennis Sharp, London 1967; *Studies in Art, Architecture and Design* by Nikolaus Pevsner, London 1968; *Style and Society: Architectural Ideology in Britain 1836–1914* by Robert Macleod, London 1971; *European Architecture in the Twentieth Century* by Arnold Whittick, London 1974; *Charles F. A. Voysey, Architect* by David Gebhard, Los Angeles 1975; *Catalogue of Drawings by C. F. A. Voysey in the Drawings Collection of the Royal Institute of British Architects,* compiled by Joanna Symonds, Farnborough, Hampshire 1976; *C. F. A. Voysey: Architect and Designer, 1857–1941* by John Brandon-Jones, London 1978.

C. F. A. Voysey began his practice in the early 1880's, at the time of the battle of the styles. He was a strong adherent of the Gothic tradition, as opposed to the Classic and Renaissance, because he felt that it was more suitable to the English climate and environment. Voysey's important work was almost entirely in the field of domestic architecture. The Gothic that he followed was not that of the ornate cathedrals and churches, but the simpler style of domestic buildings which emerged from local conditions and materials. He felt that these mediaeval Gothic buildings were designed from within outwards and not, as in classic architecture, from without inwards, and this accorded with the increasingly held theory of fitness for purpose together with the rejection of much traditional ornament. From such thinking he evolved his own domestic architecture.

The guiding principles, therefore, were fitness for purpose, simplicity, and expressive use of materials. The first is seen mainly in his plans, which were either rectangular or L-shaped. As Philip Webb and Norman Shaw had done, Voysey found it necessary to break with the tradition of formal planning where the convenient relation of rooms was too often sacrificed for symmetry. In the best Voysey plans there is a considerable advance in the functional sequence

C. F. A. Voysey: Broadleys, Windermere, Westmorland, 1898

of rooms: scullery, kitchen (sometimes with pantry), dining-room and drawing-room. But even in this planning, tradition sometimes prevented, to modern eyes, a sufficiently close sequence. There is often a separation by the hall or stairs of kitchen and dining-room. Voysey conceived the house as a unified whole and aimed at the integration of garden—which he often designed—with the house. He also liked to design the interior decoration and furnishing. He was very successful with wallpapers and fabrics, influenced a little by William Morris but introducing more lightness and freshness, which proved very appealing to contemporary taste.

Voysey's liking for simplicity is seen both in his exteriors and interiors, especially in the use of large plain, pale wall surfaces. That is why Voysey liked stucco walls which created large white areas punctuated with bay and flat casement windows. Good examples are Walnut Tree Farm at Castlemorton (1890), Forster House at Bedford Park (1890), Perrycroft, Colwall (1893), Grane House, Shackleford (1897) and his own house at Chorley Wood (1900).

Although Voysey had almost a passion for simplicity and largely rejected ornament, he yet had a great liking for large roofs and prominent chimneys which, as he used them, were really decorative motifs derived from the mediaeval domestic architecture that he so much admired. This introduction of the large, sharply-pitched roof did not always conduce to functional design as it sometimes meant sloping ceilings when flat ones would have been more convenient. The conspicuous pitched roof is seen in Lowicks House at Frensham (1894), where it projects downwards, between the first floor windows, making very wide overhanging eaves, which largely determine the external character.

Voysey, together with Webb and Shaw, had a tremendous influence on domestic architecture in Europe, especially in Germany, through the enthusiastic missionary work of Muthesius, an influence which contributed to the functionalist movement in the first half of the 20th century. It is significant that Behrens' Haus Obenauer of 1905 is very like in character to Voysey's Forster House of 1890.

—Arnold Whittick

WACHSMANN, Konrad.

American. Born in Frankfurt-on-Oder, Germany, in 1901; emigrated to the United States, 1941. Educated at the Arts and Crafts School, Berlin and Dresden, under Heinrich Tessenow and Hans Poelzig. Practiced in Germany, 1925–41; collaborated with Walter Gropius, New York, 1941–49: formed General Panel Corporation, New York, for the manufacture of pre-fabricated housing elements, 1941; Professor of Design, and Director of the Department of Advanced Building Research, Illinois Institute of Technology, Chicago, 1949–64. Professor of Architecture, Director of the Building Research Division, and Chairman of the Graduate Program on Industrialization, 1964–73, and since 1973 Professor Emeritus, University of Southern California, Los Angeles. Exhibitions: *Mobilar Structure,* Museum of Modern Art, New York, 1946; Museum of Science and Industry, Chicago, 1973. Recipient: Rome Prize, German Academy in Rome, 1932. Address: 10347 Calvin Avenue, Los Angeles, California 90025, U.S.A

Works:

1925   Rance River Bridge, France (project)
         Standardized Panel System for Pre-Fabricated Housing
1926   Pre-fabricated hotel, Curacao, West Indies
1927   Pre-fabricated tennis court pavilion, Berlin
1928   Albert Einstein Country House, Caputh, near Potsdam, Germany
1931   Advertising Tower, *International Building Exhibition,* Berlin
1935   Covered market, Rome (project)
1936   Office building and recreational complex, Rome
1940   Leisure Center, Key West, Florida (project; with Walter Gropius)
1942   General Panel Corporation Building System (with Walter Gropius)
         Convalescent home, Key West, Florida (project; with Walter Gropius)
1945/
47   Factory, Burbank, California
1946   Mobilar Structure Building System
         Studio, New York (with Serge Chermayeff)
1948   Marshall House, 6643 Lindenhurst, Los Angeles
1950   General Panel House, 2861 Nichols Canyon, Los Angeles
1954   Convention Center, Chicago (project; with Mies van der Rohe)
1961   Plan for the center and harbor of Genoa
1963   Italsider Headquarters, Genoa
1966   City Hall, California City

Publications:

By WACHSMANN: books—*Holzhausbau: Tecnik und Gestaltung,* Berlin 1931; *Wendepunkt im Bauen,* Wiesbaden 1959, English translation, by Thomas E. Burton, as *The Turning Point in Building: Structure and Design,* New York 1961; *Aspekte* (photographs), New York 1961; articles—"Mobilar Structures" in *Pencil Points* (New York), March 1946; "Ein Konstruktionssystem für Hallenbauten" in *Baukunst und Werkform* (Nuremberg), no. 9, 1954; "Building in Our Time" in *Architectural Association Journal* (London), April 1957; "Das Stadium in Team" in *Bauen und Wohnen* (Zurich), October 1960; "Concetti di Architettura" in *Casabella* (Milan), October 1960; "Research: The Mother of Invention" in *Arts and Architecture* (Los Angeles), April 1967; interview, with Walter Menzies, in *Building Design* (London), 6 August 1976.

On WACHSMANN: articles—"Construction: A Revolutionary Structural System" in *Arts and Architecture* (Los Angeles), April 1946; "General Panel Corporation System" in *Techniques et Architecture* (Paris), nos. 11/12, 1946; "Industrialized House" in *Architectural Forum* (New York), February 1947; "House in Industry: A System for the Manufacture of Industrialized Building Elements" in *Arts and Architecture* (Los Angeles), November 1947; "Profile" in *Der Aufbau* (Vienna), February 1959; "The Work of Konrad Wachsmann" in *Arts and Architecture* (Los Angeles), May 1967; "A View of Contemporary World Architecture" in *The Japan Architect* (Tokyo), July 1970; "Konrad Wachsmann: Toward Industrialization of Building" by Robertson Ward in *AIA Journal* (Washington, D.C.), March 1972; "Whole Earth Men: Fuller and Wachsmann" in *Inland Architect* (Chicago), July 1973.

*

For more than fifty years, Konrad Wachsmann has devoted his life's energy toward the industrialization of building, and his effect on the development of the architectural profession has been staggering. As inventor, architect, and engineer, Wachsmann is a truly monumental figure. Although few of his schemes have ever been executed or mass produced to the extent that he envisioned, his innovative ideas continue to dominate technical advancement in architecture; he remains the giant of his field.

Already prolific in Germany before World War II, Wachsmann matured substantially after emigrating to America in 1941. In 1942, in collaboration with Walter Gropius, Wachsmann developed the building system for General Panel Corporation, which was the first time true flexibility was achieved using standardized building parts. Then, in 1946, his Mobilar Structures offered similar universal variability in a primarily structural component system. His philosophy in both inventions was to standardize basic units, rather than complete walls, windows, columns or beams. Further, his joints were directionless, and the components could be used in horizontal or vertical positions; they were fully interchangable. This enabled infinite combinations to be made with a very limited number of prefabricated elements. The desirable economic advantages of standardization and mass production were finally achieved without compromising the possibility of original architectural expression.

Wachsmann has continued to explore the potentials of industrialized building in the thirty years since then, centering his activities first at the Illinois Institute of Technology, and then at the University of Southern California's Graduate Program on Industrialization, which he founded in 1965. In all that time his message has remained clear. All of his designs allow great freedom in construction and connection, and never impose monotony. For all his interest in mass production, he has never stood apart from the world of architecture and its spirit.

His book *The Turning Point,* released in English in 1961, revealed his love for the precision of modern technology, but ended with a powerful statement insisting that technology and art did not stand apart. The same year he published *Aspekte,* a collection of his own photos. It demonstrated his own sense of precision, but still bore testament to his acute sensitivity to detail and impulse.

Wachsmann has consistently propounded this dual message of precision and sensitivity throughout his life. His devotion to technology has been unfaltering, but it has been tamed by an extraordinary understanding of art and the value of beauty.

—Mitchell B. Rouda

WALKER, Derek.

British. Born in Ribchester, Lancashire, 15 June 1931. Educated at the Leeds School of Architecture and Town Planning, and at the University of Pennsylvania, Philadelphia, 1951–57. Married Jill Messenger in 1958; children: Matthew and Icarus. Principal, Derek Walker and Partners, architects and planners, Leeds, London and Liverpool, 1958–60, and Walker, Wright, Schofield, interiors and graphics, London, 1965–70; Chief Architect and Planner, with overall responsibility for architectural design and planning, Milton Keynes Development Corporation, Buckinghamshire, 1970–76. Since 1976, Principal, Derek Walker Associates, architects, planners and landscape architects, Milton Keynes, London and Rome, and Walker, Wright, Botschi, interiors, graphics, and lightweight structures, London. Representative and Vice-Chairman, Consortium of Consultants to the Società Generale Immobiliare, Italy, since 1978. Exhibitions: *Derek Walker: Furniture and Sculpture,* Woollands, London, 1960; *Milton Keynes,* Salone Internazionale dell'Industrializzazione Edilizia, Bologna, 1976; *Derek Walker: Projects,* University of Southern California, Los Angeles, 1976; *Art into Landscape,* Serpentine Gallery, London, 1977–78; *Derek Walker: Recent Projects,* Architects Gallery, Rome, 1978; *Transformations in Modern Architecture,* Museum of Modern Art, New York, 1979. Recipient: Civic Trust Award, 1965 (twice), 1967, 1968; *Architectural Design* Award, 1966, 1967, 1968, and Grand Project Award, 1966; Industrial Architecture Award, *Financial Times,* 1969; Constrado Steel Award, 1972; Housing Award, Department of the Environment, 1973, 1977; Office of the Year Award, 1974; First Prize,

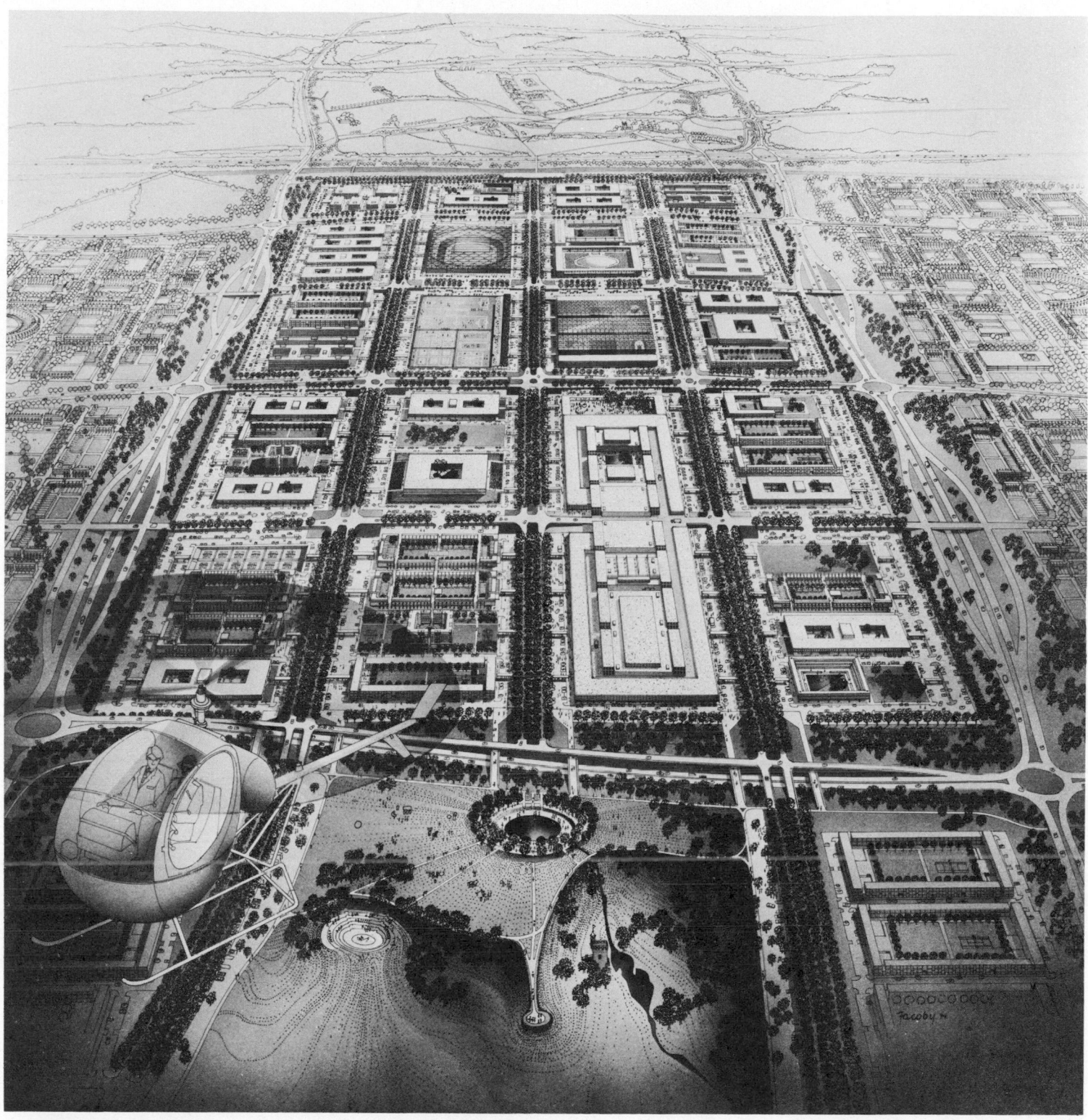

Derek Walker: Central Milton Keynes, Buckinghamshire, AD 1991

Silver Jubilee Architectural Competition, London, 1976. Address: Derek Walker Associates, The Old Rectory, Great Linford, Milton Keynes, Buckinghamshire MK14 5AX, England.

Works:

1964 Johnson House, North Rigton, Yorkshire
1965 Churnin House, Collingham, Yorkshire
 Holiday village, Scarborough, Yorkshire
 Templenewsam Urban Planning Development, Leeds
 Cayton Bay Holiday Village, Yorkshire
1966 Gould House, Leeds
 Village plan for Sherburn in Elmet, Yorkshire
 Housing Association, Park Place, Harrogate, Yorkshire

Housing, Cheadle, Manchester
1967 Hollies Old People's Home, Leeds
 St. Benedict's Church, Garforth, near Leeds
 Serenson House, Liverpool
 Sacred Heart Church, Leeds
 Heckmondwike School, Yorkshire
1968 Ingledew Housing Association, Leeds
 VW Showroom System, United Kingdom
 Shaw Lane Housing, Leeds
 Pontefract Church, Yorkshire
 Doyle Dane Bernbach Advertising Agency, London
1969 Housing, Runcorn New Town, Cheshire
 Mental Villas, Royal Earlswood Hospital, Surrey
 WASS Car Showrooms and Maintenance Depot, Leeds

1970/
76 Milton Keynes, Buckinghamshire (as Chief Architect and Planner)—Central Area development; Central Area housing for 30,000 people; developments in existing towns, Cofferidge Close in Stony Stratford and Brunel Centre in Bletchley; village plans for Great Linford, Woughton, Woolstones, Broughton, Shenley Church End, Shenley Brook End, Loughton, Willen, Milton Keynes Village, Simpson, and Old Bradwell; infrastructure system; housing, Coffee Hall, Neath Hill, Fullers Slade, Bradville, Linford, Fishermead, Springfield, and Tinkers Bridge; industrial developments, Kiln Farm, Stacey Bushes, Bleak Hall, and Manor Farm; City Club, Central

Milton Keynes; SBI System for Industry; Lanhall Private Housing; Canalside Private Housing; Scicon Computer Centre; Parks System; Grid Road Landscape Strategy

1977 City Club Mark III, Sculpture Park, Oldbrook Housing Structure Plan, and El.2 Housing, Milton Keynes, Buckinghamshire

1978 Heelands 9 Housing, Milton Keynes, Buckinghamshire

Housing and schools, Jubail, Saudi Arabia

Plan for MIZDA Village Development, Libya

Building system for Habitat, Milan

VW Distribution Depot, Grimsby, Lincolnshire

Whitney Museum Development, New York (with Foster Associates)

Islamic Cultural Centre, Riyadh, Saudi Arabia

Publications:

By WALKER: book—*Architecture and Planning of Milton Keynes,* London 1979; articles—"System Building for Industry" in *Architectural Design* (London), October 1972; "Milton Keynes" in *Domus* (Milan), April 1973; "The Design Policy of Milton Keynes," special issue of *Architectural Design* (London), June 1973; "Central Area and Central Area Housing, Milton Keynes," special issue of *Architectural Design* (London), August 1974; "The Housing Dilemma" in *Architectural Association Quarterly* (London), no. 3, 1974; "The Social Planning of Milton Keynes" in *Architectural Association Quarterly* (London), no. 4, 1974; "Central Area of Milton Keynes" in *Domus* (Milan), December 1974; "The Emerging City," special issue of *Architectural Design* (London), December 1975; "Landscaping: Clipped and Unclipped" in *Architectural Design* (London), September 1976; "Aluminium in Building" in *RIBA Journal* (London), May 1977; "The Management and Politics of City Building" in *Industrialization Forum* (Montreal), October 1977; "Shopping Building, Milton Keynes" in *RIBA Journal* (London), May 1979.

On WALKER: book—*Architecture in Britain* by Michael Webb, London 1968; articles—"A City of Villages" by David Rock in *The Build Environment* (London), October 1973; "A Celebration of Systems" in *Progressive Architecture* (New York), November 1973; "System Building for Industry" in *Techniques et Architecture* (Paris), February 1974; "Milton Keynes: The Beautiful City" by Robert Maxwell in *Architectural Association Quarterly* (London), vol. 6, 1974; "GRP Housing" in *Bauen und Wohnen* (Zurich), June 1975; "GRP—Those in Favour" by Alastair Best in *Design* (London), June 1975; "The Price of Street Appeal" by Alastair Best in *Design* (London), August 1975; "Milton Keynes: New Town in England" by Rene Elvin in *Architektur der DDR* (Berlin), December 1975; "Milton Keynes Factories" by John Winter in *The Architects' Journal* (London), 22 and 27 December 1976; "Cofferidge Close, Stony Stratford" by Terence Farrell in *The Architects' Journal* (London), 1 November 1978.

An interest in design in all scales, furniture and component design to city design and urban structuring, the inter-relationship of people and places, the manipulation of interior and exterior space.

A fascination with the relative quagmire of large-scale housing after experiment and failures, a new optimism in one's approach, following close studies of the eclectic California tradition and recent experiments in scale breakdown and the extension of a courtyard tradition.

More and more I see architecture as a response to personal initiative and public demand. It is useless to sell outworn stylistic philosophies in the name of historic succession. Large-scale opportunity has freed me from the need to compromise within "house style" formality. My practice will always seek to express itself within a tradition of experiment and widening experience, with a particular emphasis on variety of approach, as each project develops its momentum by analysis of needs, site location, local tradition, client response and personal curiosity.

I hope to remain internationally oriented with the realization that the shared experience in education, film making, graphics, writing and landscape can combine with one's major experience in architecture and planning to offer, particularly in schools of architecture and the confines of a "teaching" office, the kind of background in which the young architect and designer can flourish and develop.

—Derek Walker

Derek Walker is principally known as the chief architect and planner of Milton Keynes, Britain's newest, and possibly last, "New City," where, from 1970 to 1976, he directed the architectural and planning team assembled for the project.

Appointed chief architect at the age of 38, Walker was responsible for knitting the new city of 250,000 people into the existing rural structure of 22,000 acres of North Buckinghamshire. It was a challenge to which Walker responded with characteristic and infectious enthusiasm, assembling around him some of the brightest available people; indeed, for several years, his team became something of a Mecca for the most talented British graduate designers.

The work of the Milton Keynes group also became a prime focus of interest for those involved in architecture in its widest meaning. There was a vast array of projects, including housing for 10,000 newcomers a year, eleven village plans, the largest central area scheme in Europe, a parkland system of 5,000 acres, a new system for industrial building, a blueprint for infrastructure standards, as well as experimental mass produced glass reinforced plastic housing units, lightweight structure enclosures, a pop art City Club with electric-toy play-gardens, and romantic tree-lined walks through a central park with observation cone, water carpet, and water organ to be "played" by the inhabitants of the new-style City. The scheme encapsulated many of the life style aspirations of the 1960's, but they were designed as serious contributions to a richer urban experience.

Walker, however, eventually found himself unable to involve himself fully in projects beyond the design stage, being simultaneously active as administrator, "salesman," and dismantler of bureaucracies. So, in 1976, he resigned from the Milton Keynes Development Board to re-establish his former practice, where he had previously achieved considerable success and a full mantle-shelf of architectural awards, with work ranging from large-scale planning solutions, housing, churches, community and commercial buildings, to major interiors and furniture design, all illustrating his obvious enjoyment of technique and the art of "putting the bits together." He has reformed the practice in the direction of his ideal vision—a design group that might be characterized as an amalgam of the practices of Eero Saarinen and Charles Eames (an "amalgam" because Saarinen never did enough graphics and Eames never did enough architecture): it is their inherent flexibility that Walker so much admires, and he is building a small team of 12–14 designers drawn from many disciplines and able to work together effectively at many different levels.

In late 1978 a consortium was formed to act as consultants to the Italian multi-national group, Società Generale Immobiliare. Besides Walker, the group includes such internationally known figures as James Stirling, Richard Rogers, Frei Otto, Norman Foster, Renzo Piano, and Ove Arup and Partners. Walker's position as Consultant Representative and Vice-Chairman gives some indication of the importance he has achieved internationally and the respect that these associates have for them. Walker recognizes the Utopian optimism in the aspirations of the group, but he argues forcibly that, even if the group is unsupported by major commissions, it will at least achieve a regular dialogue between idea makers that can only be helpful to the individuals and to their work.

Unlike most of his collaborators in the consortium —Foster, Stirling, Rogers, etc.—Walker's personal stylistic enthusiasms are difficult to characterize. He insists that his only criteria is appropriateness and that he therefore refuses to adopt or even search for a "house style." In his commercial and industrial work he can be said to be nearest to his close friend, Norman Foster—with an interest in flexibility, clean detailing, and prototype solutions. But his domestic work achieves a character born out of a fascination, developed from his experiences at Milton Keynes, with the breakdown in scales necessary in the field of large-scale public housing.

Walker is a designer of liberal interests. Cautious of gratuitous architectural gestures in his own work, he refuses to post-intellectualize his buildings after the design process. He feels a pragmatic realism about the architect's responsibility to the user, an overwhelming optimism for the future, and a belief in the designer's ability to work effectively towards it.

—Tom Heneghan

WALLACE, David A.

American. Born in Chicago, Illinois, 30 August 1917. Educated at the University of Pennsylvania, Philadelphia (Chandler Fellow; Paris Prize in Architecture, 1939), B.Arch. 1941, M.Arch. 1950; Harvard University Graduate School of Design, Cambridge, Massachusetts, M.City Planning 1950, Ph.D. in Planning 1953. Served in the United States Army Corps of Engineers, in the United States, England, France, Belgium, and Germany, 1941–46: Major. Married Joan Heatly Dulles in 1954; stepson: Robert. Supervising Planner, Chicago Housing Authority, 1950–51; Partner, Wallace and Schoenbrod, Chicago, 1950–53; Assistant Director, Marshall Field Foundation Study of Housing of Low-Income Groups, Chicago, 1951–53; Director of Planning and Development, Redevelopment Authority of the City of Philadelphia, 1953–57; Director, Planning Council of the Greater Baltimore Committee, 1957–61. Since 1963, Partner, with Ian L. McHarg, *q.v.,* William H. Roberts, and Thomas A. Todd, Wallace McHarg Roberts and Todd, Philadelphia. Assistant Professor of Planning, University of Chicago, 1953. Professor of Planning, 1961–72, and since 1972 Adjunct Professor of Planning, University of Pennsylvania. Member, Board of Governors, American Institute of Planners. Recipient: Design Award, *Progressive Architecture,* 1973. Fellow, American Institute of Architects. Address: Wallace McHarg Roberts and Todd, 1737 Chestnut Street, Philadelphia, Pennsylvania 19103, U.S.A.

Works:

1964 Plan for the valleys of Baltimore County

1964– Inner Harbor and Municipal Center, Baltimore

1966 Plan for Lower Manhattan (with others)

1967 Landscape plan for Washington, D.C.

1968 Richmond Parkway, Staten Island, New York (project)

1969 Ecological study for Minneapolis-St. Paul

1970 Metro Center, Baltimore (project)

Skippack Ecological Study, Montgomery County, Pennsylvania

1972 Plan for the center of Los Angeles

1973 Plan for Northwest Baltimore (with I. M. Pei and Partners)

Regional transportation plan for Denver

David A. Wallace: Baltimore Inner Harbor, 1964

Publications:

By WALLACE: books—*The Future of Metro Center/Baltimore*, Baltimore 1969; *Metropolitan Open Space and Natural Process*, editor and co-author, Philadelphia 1970; articles—"The Relationship of Official and Citizen Planning Programs" in *Planning 1958* (American Society of Planning Officials), Chicago 1958; "Renaissance in Baltimore" in *Traffic Quarterly* (Westport, Connecticut), January 1960; "Renaissancemanship" in *Journal of the American Institute of Planners* (Washington, D.C.), August 1960; "Planning the City's Center," senior editor, in *Journal of the American Institute of Planners* (Washington, D.C.), February 1961; "Conceptualizing Urban Renewal" in *University of Toronto Law Journal*, vol. XVIII, no. 3, 1968; "Diary of a Plan," with William C. McDonnell, in *Journal of the American Institute of Planners* (Washington, D.C.), January 1971.

David A. Wallace is a founder and senior partner of WMRT (Wallace, McHarg, Roberts and Todd), a leading urban design and planning firm located in Philadelphia.

Wallace's most important early experience was as Supervising Planner for the Chicago Housing Authority, Director of Planning for the Philadelphia Redevelopment Authority, and then Staff Director of the Planning Council of the Greater Baltimore Committee, the latter a not-for-profit group that had a quasi-governmental character. These experiences gave him a thorough knowledge of the nature and workings of American city government and became the foundation of his work as a consultant urban designer and planner. In 1961, Wallace became Professor of Planning at the University of Pennsylvania, and he has been closely identified with that university ever since. Ian McHarg, the noted environmen-

talist, who joined him in founding WMRT, was and is a faculty colleague.

The early work of the firm followed naturally from Wallace's Baltimore experience: the Inner Harbor Plan for Baltimore and the Plan for the Valleys of Baltimore County. The Inner Harbor Plan has continued to occupy the firm up to the present time, and many of its proposals have now been realized. An outmoded pier area has been replaced by a public park, surrounded by office towers and housing.

The WMRT has now done plans for cities all over the United States and some work overseas, specializing in downtown redevelopment and environmental analysis. The firm's work is characterized by its application of the planning philosophy identified with the University of Pennsylvania.

That philosophy involves "comprehensive planning," a theory devised to combat the short-sightedness found in many specific plans which focus too closely on an immediate problem. WMRT likes to begin with an environmental analysis and, often, with extensive social and demographic analyses, such as those used in their planning for the Denver Rapid Transit District. "Scientific rigor" is another principle long-pursued at the University of Pennsylvania, and, within the limits of the budgets for planning studies, at WMRT. The difficulty is, of course, that planning requires predictions about human behavior, and predicting human behavior is not an area in which scientific progress has been very marked.

Pursuit of comprehensiveness and science has not diminished the WMRT's commitment to practical answers for immediate problems, and they continue to demonstrate a clear-headed awareness of both the usefulness and the limitations of city planning.

—Jonathan Barnett

WARCHAVCHIK, Gregori.

Brazilian. Born in Odessa, Russia, 2 April 1896; emigrated to Brazil, 1923: naturalized, 1930. Studied architecture at the University of Odessa; Reale Instituto Superiore di Belle Arti, Rome, Dip.Arch. 1920. Married Mina Klabin in 1927; children: Ilia Mauricio and Sonia. Worked in the office of Marcello Piacentini, Rome, 1920–23; in private practice, Sao Paulo, 1923–31, Rio de Janeiro (collaborating with Lúcio Costa), 1931–33, and Sao Paulo from 1934. Professor of Small Architectural Compositions, National School of Fine Arts, Rio de Janeiro, 1931. Member, CIAM (Congrès Internationaux d'Architecture Moderne), 1929–42. Exhibitions: Housing Congress Exhibition, Sao Paulo, 1931; Beaux-Arts Exhibition, Rio de Janeiro, 1931; *Salon of Tropical Architecture,* Rio de Janeiro, 1933; Modern Art Exhibition of the Sociedade Pro-Arte Moderna, Sao Paulo, 1933; *Brazil Builds,* Museum of Modern Art, New York, 1943; *Bienal,* Sao Paulo, 1951, 1953, 1959, 1963; *Brazilian Architecture,* London, Copenhagen and Aarhus, 1957; *Warchavchik e la Introducao da Nova Arquitectura no Brasil,* Museo de Arte, Sao Paulo, 1965–66; *Gregori Warchavchik: Retrospective,* Museo de Arte, Sao Paulo, 1975. Recipient: Architecture Prize, *Correio da Manha,* Rio de Janeiro, 1965. *Died* (in Sao Paulo) *27 July 1972.*

Works:

1927/
28 Gregori Warchavchik House, Santa Cruz Street, Sao Paulo (altered, 1935)
1928/
29 Max Graf House, Mello Alves Street, Sao Paulo (destroyed)
1929 House, Avanhandava Street, Sao Paulo (destroyed)
  Joao Souza Lima House, Sao Paulo

Gregori Warchavchik: Warchavchik House, Sao Paulo, 1928

Candido da Silva House, Sao Paulo
Public housing estate, Barao de Jaguara Street, Sao Paulo
Studio for Two Artists (project)
1930 Middle-class housing estate, Dona Berta and Affonso Celso Streets, Sao Paulo
"Modernistic House," Itapolis Street, Sao Paulo
Luiz da Silva Prado House, Bahia Street, Sao Paulo
Studio for an Artist (project)
1931 Antonio da Silva Prado House, Estados Unidos Street, Sao Paulo (destroyed)
Medical Association Building interiors, Sao Paulo
Nordschild House, Toneleros Street, Rio de Janeiro (destroyed)
Harmonia Tennis Club House, Sao Paulo (project)
Guimaraes da Fonseca House, Sao Paulo (project)
Lincoln Nodari Apartment Building, Rio de Janeiro (project)
Bar and Restaurant, Copacabana, Rio de Janeiro (project)
1932 Manoel Dias Penthouse Apartment interiors, Rio de Janeiro
Rolim Goncalves House, Sao Paulo (project)
Alfredo Schwartz House, Rio de Janeiro (with Lúcio Costa; destroyed)
2 houses for Mrs. Gallo, Rio de Janeiro
1933 Duarte Coelho House, Rio de Janeiro (destroyed)
Workers' housing estate, Gamboa, Rio de Janeiro

1938 Cia. de Melhoramentos Gopouva House, Sao Paulo (destroyed)
1939 Apartment building, Barao de Limeira Street, Sao Paulo
Praca da Republica Redevelopment, Sao Paulo (competition project)
3 rental houses, Avenida Europa, Sao Paulo
1940 Liuba Klabin House, Sao Paulo (since altered)
Town Hall, Sao Paulo (competition project; with Villanova Artigas)
1943 Rau Crespi House, Guaruja, Sao Paulo
1946 Mrs. Jorge Prado Beach Pavilion, Guaruja, Sao Paulo (since altered)
1949 Warchavchik Beach House, Guaruja, Sao Paulo
1950 Raquel Simonsen House, Alemanha Street, Sao Paulo
Crespi Farm House, Sao Paulo State (project)
1952 Renzo Palhari House, Alemanha Street, Sao Paulo
Paulistano Club Building, Sao Paulo
1953 Pinheiros Club Ballroom, Sao Paulo
1954 Cicero Prado Office Building, Avenida Rio Branco, Sao Paulo
Regatas Tiete Club Building, Sao Paulo

Publications:

By WARCHAVCHIK: articles—"Acerca de Arquitectura Moderna" [The 1925 Manifesto] in *Correio da Manha* (Rio de Janeiro), 1 November 1925, reprinted in *Tribuna da Imprensa* (Rio de

Janeiro), 27/28 August 1960; "Architecture: Report on the 3rd CIAM Congress in Brussels 1930" in *Cahiers d'Art* (Paris), no. 2, 1931; "Arquitectura Viva" in *O Jornal* (Rio de Janeiro), 1 December 1931; introduction to *Architecture of Social Concern in Regions of Mild Climate* by Richard Neutra, Sao Paulo 1948; plus numerous other writings in the daily newspapers of Rio de Janeiro and Sao Paulo, 1925–61.

On WARCHAVCHIK: books—*Gli Elementi dell' Architettura Funzionale* by Alberto Sartoris, Milan 1931; *Brazil Builds* by Philip L. Goodwin, New York 1943; *Modern Architecture in Brazil* by Henrique Mindlin, Rio de Janeiro and Amsterdam, 1956; *The New Art in Brazil* by Pietro Maria Bardi, Milan 1956; *Arquitectura Contemporanea* by Udo Kultermann, Barcelona 1958; *Warchavchik e la Introducao da Nova Arquitectura no Brasil* by Gilberto Ferraz, Sao Paulo 1965 (includes complete list of Warchavchik's newspaper articles); *Gregori Warchavchik: Retrospective,* exhibition catalogue, Sao Paulo 1975; articles—"L'Architecture Moderne au Brésil" by Pierre Louis Flouquet in *Chantiers* (Brussels), October 1947; "Habitations Individuelles au Brésil" in *L'Architecture d'Aujourd'hui* (Paris), June 1948; "Les Origines de l'Architecture Nouvelle à l'Amerique Latine" by Alberto Sartoris in *Architecture: Formes et Fonctions* (Lausanne), 1958; "La Nueva Arquitectura Brasilena" by Alberto Sartoris in *Informes de la Construccion* (Madrid), no. 105, 1958.

Gregori Warchavchik was the great pioneer of modern architecture in Brazil. Born in Russia and trained in Italy, he arrived in Brazil in 1923 and settled in Sao Paulo where he became closely associated with a group of avant-garde intellectuals who had taken part in the "Modern Art Week" in 1922. Architecture had had no important representation at that seminal event, and it was only in 1925, with the publication of Warchavchik's manifesto "About Modern Architecture," that the issue of creating a new architecture suitable to the times was raised.

The first modernistic work built in Brazil was Warchavchik's own house in 1927/28. Seen today, it strikes one as a sober building of classicizing tendencies solved in a simplified Art-Deco vocabulary, with matching interiors. At the time, however, it provoked a turmoil, because the prevailing taste militated against so straightforward an architecture. One of the most interesting features of the house is the large covered veranda onto which the main rooms open at the rear. Although ill matched to the rest of the house (it is rather picturesque in appearance), it shows the architect's concern with the local climate.

During the 1930's, one-family houses predominated in Warchavchik's professional practice. The "Modernistic House" of 1930 and the houses for Luiz da Silva Prado of 1930 and Antonio da Silva Prado of 1932 deserve being singled out for the mature handling of their cubistic volumes, enhanced by the use of very few architectural elements.

The "Modernistic House" has a unique place in the history of the development of modern Brazilian architecture. It was exhibited for a whole month, fully furnished and decorated, and during that time was visited by 30,000 people, and this fact, and the polemics the house provoked, helped to bring about a gradual change in public opinion. In Rio de Janeiro the same role was performed by Warchavchik's Nordschild House of 1931 and the Manoel Dias penthouse apartment, displayed in 1932.

The Antonio da Silva Prado house was, however, unquestionably the best project of the period. Outstanding for the daring cantilever of the roof over the front terrace and for the enormous hide-away sliding glass doors which connect the living room directly to the outside, it was much ahead of its time stylistically.

In 1940 Warchavchik took the second prize at a competition for the Sao Paulo Town Hall. It was one of the few large scale projects in his career, and its main interest was in the flexibility of the internal partitioning and in the careful reorganization of the urban space in which it was to be placed.

During the 1940's, Warchavchik's vocabulary, until then decidedly puristic, took a new look, fostered by his use of natural, raw materials. The Crespi House (1943), where the small site inspired the ingenious solution of lifting the bedroom wing on stilts and fitting the other rooms and a veranda underneath, and Mrs. Prado's thatched beach house (1946), both built in the sea-side resort of Guaruja, exemplify quite clearly this new tendency.

But at about this time, Brazilian architecture would take a course that was not foreseen in Warchavchik's work. In Rio de Janeiro a direct contact with Le Curbusier, coupled with a growing awareness of the country's cultural heritage, spurred by the recent creation of the Historical and Artistic Patrimony Protection Service, would result in a highly original indigenous movement, which flourished in the work of Lúcio Costa, Niemeyer, Reidy, Moreira, and the Roberto brothers, a movement that would become internationally renowned in the next 20 years. The main difference between this movement and Warchavchik's work is in the markedly national feeling of the movement and its creativeness, brought about by a freedom in the handling of the orthodox modern vocabulary.

Nevertheless, Warchavchik remains an important figure, as much for the the articles he published to defend his principles as for his architectural work. And his brief stay as a teacher at the Architectural Department of the Beaux Arts School in Rio de Janeiro (1931), together with the work he was then erecting in Rio, had a profound influence on the first generation of modern Brazilian architects.

—Jorge Czajkowski

WARNECKE, John Carl.

American. Born in Oakland, California, 24 February 1919. Educated at Oakland High School, graduated 1937; Stanford University, California, 1937–41, B.Arch. (cum laude) 1941; Graduate School of Design, Harvard University, Cambridge, Massachusetts, under Walter Gropius, 1941–42, M.Arch. 1942. Children: John Carl Jr., Rodger, Margaret, and Frederick. Worked for Miller and Warnecke (father's firm), Oakland, California, 1945; Principal, John Carl Warnecke and Associates, San Francisco, 1946–58, and Warnecke and Warnecke, San Francisco, 1951–58. Since 1958, Chairman and Chief Executive Officer, John Carl Warnecke and Associates, San Francisco, New York, Washington, D.C., and Los Angeles. Member, National Commission on the Fine Arts, Washington, D.C., 1963–67. Recipient: Arnold Brunner Prize, National Institute of Arts and Letters, 1957. Associate, National Academy of Design, 1958; Fellow, American Institute of Architects, 1962. Address: John Carl Warnecke and Associates, 61 New Montgomery Street, San Francisco, California 94105, U.S.A.

Works:

1956   American Embassy, Bangkok, Thailand (project)
1960/
68   Asilomar Hotel and Conference Grounds, Pacific Grove, California
1960/
69   Stanford University, California: University Bookstore and Post Office; J. Henry Meyer Undergraduate Library; Nathan Cummings Art Building; Roscoe Maples Athletic Pavilion; Student Residences
1962   Mabel McDowell Elementary School, Columbus, Indiana
1963   Nob Hill Condominium, San Francisco
1964/
69   Student residences, University of California, Berkeley
1965   Del Monte Regional Shopping Center, Monterey, California
1966   College of the Desert, Palm Desert, California
       John F. Kennedy Memorial, Arlington Cemetery, Virginia
1967   Lafayette Square, Washington, D.C.: New Executive Office Building; United States Court of Claims Building; Townhouse renovation and Park
1969   Master plan for the California State Capitol, Sacramento
       Hawaii State Capitol, Honolulu (with Belt, Lemmon and Lo)
       Renwick Gallery restoration, Washington, D.C.
1970   Moffitt Library, University of California, Berkeley
       Lauinger Library, Georgetown University, Washington, D.C.
       Kaiser Center for Technology, Pleasanton, California
       Residence Halls, University of Massachusetts, Amherst
       Regency at Kahala Hotel, Honolulu
1971   Chinese Cultural Center/Holiday Inn Hotel, San Francisco
       Hilton Hotel Tower, San Francisco
1972   Marco Polo Apartments, Honolulu

Pacific Telephone and Telegraph Equipment Building, stage I and II, Oakland, California
1972/
78   Neiman-Marcus Stores in Beverly Hills, California; Fort Worth, Texas; Newport Beach, California; Northbrook, Illinois; and St. Louis
1974   Bergdorf Goodman Store, White Plains, New York
       New York Telephone Equipment Building, New York
       The Pasadena Center, Pasadena, California
       Rhode Island Hospital Trust National Bank Headquarters, Providence
       United States Naval Academy, Annapolis, Maryland: Master Plan; Mickelson and Chauvenet Halls; Nimitz Library; and Rickover Engineering Building (with George M. Ewing Co.)
1976   Hewlett-Packard Microelectronics Plant, Santa Rosa, California
       Student Residences, Georgetown University, Washington, D.C.
1977   American Telephone and Telegraph Co. Lines Headquarters, Bedminster, New Jersey
       South Terminal, Logan International Airport, Boston
       Breakers Row Apartments, Palm Beach, Florida
       Aid Association for Lutherans Headquarters, Appleton, Wisconsin
       Hennepin County Government Center, Minneapolis
       Sun Oil Co. Headquarters, Radnor, Pennsylvania
       Trident Training Facility, Bangor, Washington (with Tracey-Brunstrom and George M. Ewing Co.)
       Science Center, University of Richmond, Virginia
       Neiman-Marcus Gallerie, Washington, D.C.
       State Compensation Insurance Fund Home Office Building, San Francisco
1978   Ventura County Government Center, Ventura, California (with Daniel L. Dworsky)

Publications:

On WARNECKE: articles—"The Recent Work of John Carl Warnecke" in *Architectural Record* (New York), March 1960; "The Humanist Architecture of John Carl Warnecke" in *Architectural Forum* (New York), December 1960; "Those New Buildings on Lafayette Square" in *Architectural Record* (New York), April 1968; "Hawaii State Capitol: New Forms for the Newest State" in *Architectural Record* (New York), May 1969; "The 1974 AIA Honor Awards: Seven New Buildings, Two Not So New" in *AIA Journal* (Washington, D.C.), May 1974; "John Carl Warnecke, Architect" in *Amerika Magazine* (Moscow), 1975; "Neiman-Marcus: Northbrook" in *Interior Design* (New York), November 1976; "Impressive New Government Center Around a Grand Atrium" in *Architectural Record* (New York), March 1977; "Logan Airport: The New South Terminal" in *Architectural Record* (New York), September 1977; "The Aid Association for Lutherans" in *Architectural Record* (New York) February 1978.

The key to the firm's approach to each problem is its belief that the right solution will grow out of a sensitive, comprehensive understanding of each client. Every project is approached with a searching examination of the client's traditions, needs, and aspirations. The firm believes that each institutional or individual client has a spirit and style uniquely his own, and it is this spirit and style that the firm seeks to discover and express. The precisely right solutions vary greatly in physical form and appearance, depending as they do upon the unique combination of

John Carl Warnecke: United States Court of Claims Building, Lafayette Square, Washington, D.C., 1967

the client, his program, his budget, his site, and its environment.

The site and environment have a powerful influence on the design of each project. Every new project, whatever its size, is a part of a larger community. The project's total physical, social, and historical setting is the subject of a careful study that precedes design.

The firm has been asked to work in some of the world's most beautiful natural environments where nature provides inspiration for design: the hills of San Francisco; California's Redwood Forests; the tropical beauty of Hawaii and Tahiti; the Great Plains of the Midwest; the deserts of Palm Springs and Saudi Arabia; the dramatic Navajo lands; the rich color of Cali, Colombia adjacent to the lush tropical Andes; and the canals and klongs of Bangkok. In these places the approach is to blend the buildings harmoniously into the surroundings—so it might be said that the structures were shaped in such a way that the setting is more beautiful than it was before.

The firm has been asked to design in places—equally beautiful—which were built by man over generations: the environs of the White House; historic Annapolis; the campuses of the University of California and Stanford University; old Monterey; the Royal Palace grounds of Honolulu; fashionable Nob Hill; a site adjacent to the Imperial Palace in Tokyo; and the historic residential area of Neuilly in Paris. In historic places such as these, the needs of the present must show respect for the past. Here,

basic plans, new forms, masses, materials, colors, and textures are designed in sympathy with the place and its history. At the same time each element is planned to solve the problems of the present and to express the continuity that provides a link to the future as well as the past.

In other environments, such as busy commercial districts or the featureless patterns of unplanned suburbs, the setting has less influence on the designs. Here a structure is treated as an entity in itself. In the design of a big city hospital, an airport, an industrial plant, a suburban research center or a downtown office building, new types of buildings and twentieth-century architecture emerge to meet today's needs. Contemporary forms, structural systems and new functions make the strong statements needed to express the purpose, vigor, and significance of each client.

In other places we have created whole new environments—new communities, parks, college campuses, capitol complexes. Here, in projects of broad scope and scale, new ideas and images must be developed. In these places creative solutions to design give new character to the surroundings and evoke new moods, and establish new ways of life.

Another aspect of the firm's approach to design is best expressed by its diversity of experience. By working on all types of projects in the mainstream of contemporary life, the firm maintains the breadth and vitality essential to creative design. This diversity also provides an enlarged knowledge within the firm which can be used to deal with new problems

or channeled into the specialized development and refinement of any particular project or building type. Although each design grows out of its unique program, site, and place in history, strong threads of continuity run through all the firm's work.

Finally, experience has proved that a complete integration of planning, architecture, engineering, landscape architecture, and interior design is necessary for excellence in design. The firm believes that there is basically one unified design profession rising above the separate design disciplines.

—John Carl Warnecke

John Carl Warnecke belongs to that generation of unstructured dissidents who in the late 1950's and '60s searched for ways out of the minimalism to which modern architectural thought seemed to lead. Like others of that period, among them Harry Weese, Edward Durell Stone, Philip Johnson, and Paul Rudolph, Warnecke turned to traditional materials, the forms of exotic as well as classical architecture, and urban design configurations from Mediterranean cultures. Educated under Gropius at Harvard but also schooled in the firm of his Beaux-Arts-trained architect father, Warnecke talks in terms of buildings being good neighbors, both culturally and physically.

His design for the American Embassy in Thailand, the project that made his reputation but was never built, is an attempt to approximate traditional Thai architecture. It was to be raised on stilts over a man-made pool, colonnaded, flanked by a decorative screen balustrade, and topped by a floating pagoda-like roof.

That design led to the Hawaian State Capitol commission, with its volcano-like silhouette, open to the sky in homage to a culture that had once worshipped the forces of weather and edged in emphatic ribbed patterns in recollection of the traditional wood construction.

Within his own culture, Warnecke's taste for non-Western sensibilities sometimes outstripped his good neighborliness. His elementary school in Columbus, Indiana, which he describes as reflecting "the character of South Indiana with its flat terrain accentuated by tall Victorian houses, barns and silos" strikes most visitors as bearing far more noticeable resemblance to a Japanese teahouse than to a midwestern farm.

Warnecke's penchant for decoration as well as place has led to a co-mingling of stylistic motifs on most projects. The famous Lafayette Square design, which found a way to save a row of 19th century houses and a historic park and still provide needed government offices, combines mansard roofs, bay windows, colonial brick (albeit in high-rise form), tracery and Saracen arches. Throughout his career materials (except for the most recent buildings such as the Aid to Lutherans Association Headquarters), inflected massing to minimize scale, and articulation of public space. Like others of his generation, he turned to Italy and Greece for direction. Fountains, arcades, colonnades, atriums, courtyards, paved piazzas and balconies are used in various interpretations in most of the important projects.

Although Warnecke's work can be criticized for less than fastidious proportions and historical details that can be as coy as convincing, his career has thrown the issues of context and non-monumentality into the public eye as effectively as anyone's. And especially during the early 1960's, when his friendship with President John F. Kennedy made him particularly visible, Warnecke gave an impetus to the preservation movement that has never been fully acknowledged.

As Warnecke's reputation grew, so did the firm, now numbering almost 200 people with permanent offices in four major American cities. The design approach has undergone a concomitant expansion but continues to emphasize blending new architecture with old, mitigating the impact of modern size and materials, and providing public gathering spaces.

—Nory Miller

WARREN, (Frederick) Miles.

New Zealander. Born in Christchurch, 10 May 1929. Educated at Christ's College, Christchurch (Soames Scholarship); University of Auckland School of Architecture, 1949–50 (Auckland University College Prize for Excellence in Architecture), Dip.Arch. 1951. Worked for the architects Cecil Wood, Christchurch, 1946–47, R. C. Munro, Christchurch, 1948,

and W. H. Trengrove, Christchurch, 1951–52, and for the London County Council, England, 1953–54. In private practice, Christchurch, since 1955: in partnership with G. T. Lucas, 1956–57, and, with M. E. Mahoney, as Warren and Mahoney, since 1958. Member of the Council, New Zealand Institute of Architects, 1967–68. Chairman, New Zealand Architects Education and Registration Board, since 1976. Exhibition: New Zealand Institute of Architects Exhibition, C.S.A. Gallery, Christchurch, 1973. Recipient: Gold Medal, 1960, 1964, 1969, and Silver Medal, 1969, 1973, 1979, New Zealand Institute of Architects; Pan Pacific Architectural Citation, 1966. Fellow, New Zealand Institute of Architects, 1965. C.B.E. (Commander, Order of the British Empire), 1974. Address: Warren and Mahoney, Post Office Box 1527, Christchurch, New Zealand.

Works:

1958 Flats, Dorset Street, Christchurch
      South Island Dental Nurses Training School, Christchurch
      Karitane Hospital, Christchurch
1959 J. Ballantyne and Company Department Store, Christchurch
      Haywrights Riccarton Department Store, Christchurch
1960 Hall of Residence, Christchurch College
      Laboratories, Christ's College, Christchurch
1961 Wool Exchange, Christchurch
      Christchurch Memorial Garden Crematorium

Miles Warren: Christchurch Town Hall, 1965

1962 Student Union and Ngaio Marsh Theatre, Canterbury University, Christchurch
1963 Student Union, Auckland University
1964 Student Union, Massey University, New Zealand
    British Secondary Boarding School, Port Vila, New Hebrides
    Wool Exchange, Dunedin, New Zealand
    Warren and Mahoney Office and House, Christchurch
1965 Christchurch Town Hall and Civic Centre
    Government House, Honiara, Solomon Islands
    Condominium Government Office, Port Vila, New Hebrides
    British Primary School, Port Vila, New Hebrides
    Lenakel Hospital, Tanna, New Hebrides
    Mendana Hotel, Honiara, Solomon Islands
1966 Burns Philp Ltd. Department Store, New Hebrides
    S.I.M.U. Office Building, Christchurch
    Haywrights Department Store, Ashburton, New Zealand
1967 Canterbury Frozen Meat Company Offices, Christchurch
    International Importing Company Offices, Christchurch
1968 Thorngate (office building), Christchurch
    Northlands Shopping Centre, Christchurch
1969 North Canterbury Catchment Board Offices, Christchurch
    Guardian Royal Exchange Building, Christchurch
    British Service Base Hospital, Vila, New Hebrides
    Maidment Theatre, Auckland
    Medbury Preparatory School, Christchurch
1970 Library, Christ's College, Christchurch
    Travelodge Hotel, Queenstown, New Zealand
    Haywrights Department Store, Christchurch
    Frankton Arms Hotel, Queenstown, New Zealand
    Wendover Maternity Hospital, Christchurch
1972 A.E.Q. Office Building, Christchurch
    Williams City Centre, Wellington
    Maheno Tavern, Oamaru, New Zealand
    Brydone Hotel, Oamaru, New Zealand
    S.I.M.U. Office Building, Timaru, New Zealand
    Avon Broadcasting Company Office Building, Christchurch
    Woolshed Restaurant, Wellington
    Terrace House (office building), Christchurch
1973 City Library, Timaru, New Zealand
    Dominion Mutual Securities Building, Christchurch
    Colonial Mutual Life Insurance Building, Christchurch
    Burma Motor Lodge, Wellington
    Assembly Hall, Medbury Boys School, Christchurch
    Gloucester Street Shopping Arcade, Christchurch
    ICI Office Building, Christchurch
1974 Sports Hall, Christ's College, Christchurch
    Gymnasium and Laboratories, Rangi Ruru Girls School, Christchurch
    St. Peter and Paul Primary School, Lower Hutt, New Zealand
    Atkinson and Forbes Car Park and Shops, Christchurch
    Haywrights Sydenham Supermarket, Christchurch
    S. R. Halliwell Office Building, Christchurch
    Leisure Lodge Motor Inn, Nelson, New Zealand
    Transport House Offices, Christchurch
1974/
  79 Chancery, New Zealand Embassy, Washington, D.C.
1975 S.I.M.U. Office Building, Dunedin, New Zealand

Leisure Lodge Motor Inn, Dunedin, New Zealand
    Roman Catholic Cathedral Restoration, Christchurch
1976 Radio New Zealand Office Building, Christchurch
    Latimer View House (office building), Christchurch
    Feltex House (office building), Auckland
1977 Haywrights Ltd. Shopping Mall, Christchurch
1978 Shopping Arcade, Greenwood Estate, Christchurch
    New Zealand Army Memorial Museum, Waiouru, New Zealand
    New Zealand Refrigeration Nominees Office Building, Christchurch
    Allied Properties Office Building, Auckland
    House Restoration, Governors Bay, New Zealand
1979 National Mutual Life Association Office Building, Christchurch
    Canterbury Library, Christchurch

Publications:

By WARREN: article—"Style in New Zealand Architecture" in *New Zealand Architect* (Wellington), no. 3, 1979.

On WARREN: articles—in *Architectural Review* (London), October 1959; "Three Christchurch Office Buildings by Warren and Mahoney" in *New Zealand Institute of Architects Journal* (Wellington), September 1972; "Ownership Flats for Williams Development Holdings Ltd." in *New Zealand Institute of Architects Journal* (Wellington), April 1975.

*   *   *

Miles Warren, a distinguished, compulsive designer who really enjoys his profession, is New Zealand's most outstanding architect. His buildings, from a highly productive office, are dotted all around his home city of Christchurch and appear up and down New Zealand, even extending as far as the Pacific Islands and Washington, D.C.

His work includes government, university and office buildings; hospitals, theatres and auditoriums; commercial, retail and sports buildings; banks, hotels and restaurants; religious buildings, restorations, flats and "one off" houses for special clients. In all this variety and development, Miles Warren has produced two outstanding works: the Christchurch Town Hall and his own office-town house. Both are designed from a clear rational basis, with spaces sensitively and scientifically organized, and are a vivid indictment of all those who think that modern architecture is dead. Indeed, to attend a concert in the main auditorium of the Christchurch Town Hall is to savour not only the finest modern architectural space in New Zealand, but also one that ranks favourably with any in the world.

Architecture for Miles Warren is the delight and pleasure of making things well. It is the craft of good workmanship—a minor science and technique. At the same time he is hard-headed enough to realize that though architecture occasionally becomes high art, such work has to be subsidized by more standard and repetitive projects.

Historically Miles Warren is the product of the last stages of the arts and crafts free school tradition in New Zealand. Trained by Cecil Wood, Miles Warren experienced early in his career the craft of the architect at work. The great merit of this system was the value it placed upon the all-embracing approach to design: everything was seen to matter. Even draughtmanship was worthy of attention. This love of drawing is still there in Miles Warren, and he has the confidence and skill to draw in front of his clients. In this way he seeks out their needs and inspires their confidence.

Warren supplemented the last stages of his arts and crafts training with full-time study at the Auck-

land School of Architecture when it was under the influence of the "Group" architects. His post-graduate years were spent working on Roehampton and travelling in Europe, where he came under the influence of Le Corbusier's *beton brut* and the Italian formalists. Returning to New Zealand in the mid-1950's, he worked these Brutalist influences out in concrete at Christchurch College, which won him a gold medal.

More recently his work has developed in response to the ever-increasing opportunities available to New Zealand's top architect. Despite added pressure, he still creates work that seems remarkably fresh and invigorating, at a time when the architectural profession throughout the world has been in general losing confidence. Perhaps Miles Warren's secret lies in his ability to gain creative revitalization from constantly building a new house for himself and living in his own architecture. Currently his romanticism is served by restoring a colonial country retreat in the foothills of the Banks Peninsula.

Miles Warren is totally committed to his profession and to the pursuit of excellence. He believes that order is better than chaos, creation better than destruction, gracefulness and forgiveness better than violence and vendetta.

—Russell Walden

WATANABE, Youji.

Japanese. Born in Naoetsu City, 14 June 1923. Educated at the High School of Arts and Crafts, Takada, 1936–41; Assistant to Professor Takamasa Yosizaka at the Architectural Institute of Waseda University, Tokyo, 1955–58; qualified as an architect, 1957; special postgraduate student of city planning at Waseda University, 1969–73. Served in the Japanese Marine Corps, 1944–45: 2nd Lieutenant. Worked for the Nippon Stainless Steel Manufacturing Company, Tokyo and Naoetsu, 1941–47, and in Dr. Kume's Architectural Office, Tokyo, 1947–55. In private practice, Tokyo, since 1958. Lecturer in Architecture, Waseda University, since 1964. Exhibitions: *VIII Salone Internazionale della Industrializzazione Edilizia,* Bologna, 1972; Centre Georges Pompidou, Paris, 1976; *CAYC Travelling Exhibition,* Argentina, 1977; Centro Edile Library, Milan, 1977; Museum of Modern Art, New York, 1978. Address (office): 1–6–13 Hirakawa-cho, Chiyoda-ku, Tokyo, Japan.

Works:

1949 Reinforced concrete apartment houses (competition project)
1950 Fujisawa City Hall, Japan
    Grave of the Unknown Soldier (competition project)
    Restaurant, Yokohama/Kaikan Building, Yokohama (with Dr. Kume's Office)
1952 Hamamatsu City Hall, Japan (with Dr. Kume's Office)
    Tenrikyo Hall, Tokyo (competition project)
1953 Shimbashi Branch of the Daiwa Bank, Tokyo (with Dr. Kume's Office)
    Makino House, Tokyo (with Dr. Kume's Office)
1954 Shibuya Toei Theatre, Tokyo (with Dr. Kume's Office)
    Cultural Center for Aichi Prefecture (competition project)
    Cultural Center for Shizuoka Prefecture (competition project)

Youji Watanabe: Sky Building No. 3, Tokyo, 1970

National Diet Library (competition project)
1955 Asai House, Tokyo (with Dr. Kume's Office)
Town Hall, Takaoka, Japan (with Dr. Kume's Office)
1956 Ryumon Book Warehouse, Nara, Japan
Monument of the 2000th Anniversary of the Birth of Buddha, India (competition project)
City Hall, Nagasaki (competition project)
1958 Osawa Fishing House, Chichibu-Tama National Park, Japan
Niigata Hospital of Labor Office, Naoetsu, Japan
House with store (competition project)
1959 Kagoshima Office and House, Niigata, Japan
Hatonosu Youth Hostel, Chichibu-Tama National Park, Japan
Konishi Building, Tokyo
1960 Otaba Fishing House, Chichibu-Tama National Park, Japan
1961 Miyama Heights (rest house), Chichibu-Tama National Park, Japan
Youji Watanabe Office Building, Tokyo
Zendoji (temple), Itoigawa, Japan
1962 Miyakozushi Restaurant, Tokyo
Yamazaki House ("Tategarami"), Tokyo
1963 Japanese National Theatre (competition project)
International Conference Hall, Kyoto (competition project)
1964 Monden Villa, Fuji, Japan
Minoda House ("Igeta"), Tokyo
Allegheny Public Square, Pittsburgh, Pennsylvania (competition project)
Master plan for Naniwa University of the Arts, Japan (competition project)
Single-family houses (3), Hollywood, California (competition project)
Shijo Ohashi Bridge, Kyoto (competition project)
1965 Plan for the development of tourism in Nippon-Land (competition project)
Exhibition Hall, Japan Architecture Center, Tokyo (competition project)
Fune Teahouse, Tokyo
1966 Takagi House, Isogo, Japan
Miyata House, Tokyo
Shinozaki House, Matsudo, Japan
Yotsuya Station, Japan National Railways (competition project)
The Farmhouse (competition project)
1967 Head Office Building, *Expo '70*, Osaka (competition project)
High-rise Apartment Buildings in Steel (competition project)
Hokkaido Memorial Tower, Japan (competition project)
Sanwa Building, Tokyo
Iwakata House, Naoetsu, Japan
1968 Nishida House, Tokyo
Sky Building No. 2, Tokyo
Ishida House, Tokyo
Dr. Minezaki House ("Dragon Fort"), Ito, Japan
Pavilion, *Expo '70*, Osaka (competition project)
1969 Japanese Supreme Court (competition project)
1970 Sky Building No. 3, Tokyo
Meiwa Building, Tokyo
International Tourism Center, Hakone, Japan (competition project)
1971 Habitat '70 (project)
Sky Building No. 5, Tokyo
W-H Concrete Prefab (project)
Opera House, Belgrade, Yugoslavia (competition project)
Centre Beaubourg, Paris (competition project)
National Headquarters for TANU, Tanzania (competition project)
1972 Community Plaza (competition project)
Kamoshida Building, Tokyo

Yamazaki House ("Site in Air"), Tokyo
1973 Kuramae Tower Building, Tokyo
Daisho Building, Tokyo
Housing, Komyoike-Senboku New Town, Japan (competition project)
1974 Public Housing, Damascus, Syria (competition project)
1975 Tanaka House, Naoetsu, Japan
Polto Santo Island (competition project)
Urban Environment of Developing Countries, centering on Manila (competition project)
1976 U.A.E. Development Bank International Hotel (competition project)
Dr. Minezaki Clinic, Tokyo
1977/
78 Pahlavi National Library, Tehran (competition project)
Center and Shops for Little New Town, Shizuoka, Japan
1978 Nago City Hall, Okinawa (competition project)

Publications:

By WATANABE: book—*Approach to Architecture*, Tokyo 1974; articles—"An Argument on Architectural Offices" in *Kenchiku-bunka* (Tokyo), May 1956; "Religious Architecture and Glass" in *Glass* (Tokyo), August 1962; "The Interior Without Upholstery" in *Kenchiku-chishiki* (Tokyo), November 1964; "Zendoji Temple of Shunanzan" in *Kenchiku-chishiki* (Tokyo), December 1964; "Miscellaneous Thoughts on the Architecture of South America" in *Kenchiku-techo* (Tokyo), March 1969; "The Architectural Competition for the Supreme Court" in *Shinkenchiku* (Tokyo), April 1969; "An Account of a Trip to Iceland" in *Kenchiku-kai* (Tokyo), June 1969; "Opinion to the Supreme Court" in *Kentiku* (Tokyo), June 1969; "History and Race in Architecture: Impressions of Latin America" in *Densetsu Guide* (Tokyo), no. 41, 1970; "Sky Building No. 3/HABITAT '70" in *The Japan Architect* (Tokyo), October 1970; "Industrialization of the Japanese House" in *Technical Japan* (Tokyo), no. 2, 1971; "Residence Tategarami" in *Kentiku* (Tokyo), November 1971; "My Heretical Architecture" in *Shitsunai* (Tokyo), November 1971; "W-H Concrete Prefab" in *Kenchiku-kai* (Tokyo), January 1972; "Campus Layout" in *Waseda University News* (Tokyo), June 1972; "Housing of Tomorrow—More Pilotis" in *Kanna* (Tokyo), no. 56, 1972; "At the Invitation of SAIE '72" in *Journal of Architecture* (Tokyo), January 1973; " 'See,' 'Know,' 'Comprehend:' Architecture of Europe" in *Kenchiku-kai* (Tokyo), January 1973; "My View of Architecture" in *Contemporary Architects of Japan*, volume 23, Tokyo 1974; "My Education in Architecture" in *Journal of Architecture* (Tokyo), April 1976.

On WATANABE: books—*Modern Movements in Architecture* by Charles Jencks, New York 1973, Tokyo 1976; *Contemporary Architects of Japan*, volume 23, Tokyo 1974; articles—"Some Thoughts on the Dragon Fort" by Takamasa Yosizaka in *Shinkenchiku* (Tokyo), April 1969, and in *The Japan Architect* (Tokyo), June 1969; "Architechnics" in *Architecture Plus* (New York), May/June 1974; "Heretical Architecture of Y. Watanabe" in *The Asahi* (Tokyo), 11 September 1974; "It's a Building" in *International Herald Tribune* (Paris), 25 September 1974; "Paradoxical Solid of Isozaki" by Charles Jencks in *Shinkenchiku* (Tokyo), January 1975.

Commentary on my project HABITAT PLAN

1. Argument against the existing conception of "facing south," the "East-West Axis (Latitude)" in architecture. It is a "South-North Axis (Longitude)" project. (Connection with the universe, the earth, plants and human beings is the

starting point of this idea.)
2. Desire to produce and industrialize architecture and experiment with iron architecture.
3. Announcement of the argument against the contemporary world which is mainly occupied by researchers, like civil engineers who do not understand the arts, the city planners.
4. An experiment which is a transcendental condition and "art" without allowing variations to human beings, the city and life by industrialization.

Basis of the HABITAT PLAN

A. 1) Sun. 2) View. 3) Equality for all, and infinity in privacy.
B. 1) Whether or not to include streets and transportation in the city. 2) If the city is altered, the existing method of redeveloping a city will not be used. First of all, streets will be constructed for transportation; after that, buildings around the street will be taken away to create public plazas and schools—it's an opposite view that streets and house lots should be changed to buildings and plazas.

Advantages and defects of my plan, in the event of the alteration of Tokyo

1) In that case, a window or a balcony with a width of 2m, facing south, will be installed per person: the same number of people will be accommodated in only one-half to one-third of existing residential quarters.
2) Surplus residential quarters will be changed to park and public establishments: the area of each establishment will be definite, accordingly the city will be operated smoothly and will be habitable.
3) Transportation will be by pilotis methods; accordingly, there will be no difficulty in commuting and traffic jams will be dissolved.

It is, however, still doubtful whether the conditions mentioned above will be essential or possible, and the HABITAT PLAN may be an experiment in irrationality: the result may be realizations as in Sky Building No. 3.

—Youji Watanabe

Youji Watanabe (not to be confused with Toyokazu Watanabe, that other architectural controversialist in Osaka) has the tendency, once having established the metaphor by which a particular building is to be known, to court that metaphor to the very end. Having got hold of some legitimate analogy by which to approach a project, he follows it right through and out the other side—beginning on one side in the cool lucid dawn of rationalism, he ends up in the steamy dusk of the irrational and the spooky.

In all our thinking we are guided by models and archetypes, metaphors that allow our individual concepts to come together—"The Tree of Life," "The Pyramid of Power," "The Scales of Justice." Through exaggeration and caricature he mocks these deep-seated correspondences. The image of a house-as-a-bus that haunted the prefabrication boffins for a long while he appropriated for his Sky Building No. 3, and the metaphor is somehow left dangling before us while all else has vanished. The image of architecture as lithe and supple, as a bird, as in Saarinen's TWA Terminal in New York—Watanabe pricks its pretensions by making an apartment block in the semblance of a penguin. He took on similar imagery in the Dragon Fort in Ito, a house and clinic for a pediatrician, Dr. Minezaki: initially the house was to resemble the bridge of a battleship, but the plan was

Clifford Wearden: "Ferdene," Kingsbury, London, 1964

later modified to suggest the coiled body of a great dragon. "Children usually dislike doctors, but this house has become a playground for them because of the rising vehicular approach, the rotating turntable in the entrance and the limitless appeal of the spiralling shape."

Architecture need not necessarily be a cage, a lost tract, a suicide machine, a monster of brilliant and erudite torture let loose on man. It need not ride roughshod over man, that abstract and negligible entity. Architecture need not be that thing that architects have recourse to in the same way that alcoholics have recourse to drink. It need not be a cast-off fancy dress, a box of obsolete gadgets, a clockwork toy with the key missing. Watanabe has shown us that in some buildings we can feel our perceptions heightened, as though we had just sprouted antennae. He demonstrates that the "instant of the world" that the architect builds need not necessarily threaten, that it can equally calm and soothe to such an extent that a building can even come out to us, flowing, throbbing, beating up against us both from without and within. The voice we hear in architecture need not necessarily be that of the architect's but can be the unification of all aspirations.

—Chris Fawcett

WEARDEN, Clifford.
British. Born in Preston, Lancashire, 15 August 1920. Educated at Preston Grammar School, 1932–37; University of Liverpool, School of Architecture, 1938–40, 1946–48, B.Arch. (honours) 1948, and Department of Civic Design, 1948–49, Dip. Civic Design 1949. Served as a Pilot in the Fleet Air Arm of the Royal Navy, 1940–46; Lieutenant, Royal Naval Volunteer Reserve. Married Elsie Sherman in 1953; Pauline Noel Tinsley in 1969; children: Amanda, Sarah and Charlotte. Assistant Architect, Lipson and Kaad, Sydney, 1945, York and Sawyer, New York, 1946–47, and George Grenfell Baines Group, Preston, 1947; Architect/Planner, Architekt Wilhelm, Zug, Switzerland, 1948; Project Architect, Sir Basil Spence and Partners, London, 1949–54, and Trehearne and Norman Preston and Partners, London, 1954–55. Since 1955, Principal, Clifford Wearden and Associates, architects/town planning consultants/designers, London. Member of the Council of the Architects Registration Council, since 1966. Exhibitions: *Summer Exhibition*, Royal Academy, London, 1963, 1971; *National Federation of Housing Societies Exhibition*, Royal Institute of British Architects, London 1971; *Jubilee Exhibition*, Architectural Association, London, 1977; *Transformations in Modern Architecture*, Museum of Modern Art, New York, 1979. Member, Society of Industrial Artists and Designers, 1969. Address: Clifford Wearden and Associates, Harewood Row, London NW1 6SE, England.

Works:

1950 Ecclesfield Colley Secondary Modern School, Sheffield (with Sir Basil Spence and Partners)
1952 Coventry Cathedral ruins preservation (with Sir Basil Spence and Partners)
1953 Noonamena House, Onslow Road, Burwood Park, Weybridge, Surrey
1958 Service House, Inchmery, Exbury Estate, Hampshire
1960 Banqueting Hall, Carpenters Hall, London Wall, London E.C.2 (with H. Austen Hall)
1961 Interiors of directors' offices, Watney House, Palace Street, London S.W.1
1963 Pepler House (apartment block), Wornington Road, London W.10 (with Peter Deakins)
1964 Ferndene (cluster housing complex), 123 Slough Lane, Kingsbury, London N.W.9 (with Peter Deakins)
1965 Office interiors, 17 Lansdowne Road, Croydon, Surrey (with Malcolm Wildsmith)
1967 National Westminster Bank, 43 Kingsway, London W.C.2
1968 Lancaster West Urban Village Master Plan, London W.11 (with Malcolm Wildsmith, Peter Simpson and Derek Latham)
1970 Lancaster West Urban Village, stage I, London W.11 (with Ken Price and Nigel Whitbread)
1972 *Readers Digest* Service Department, Plym-

outh, Devon (project; with Ken Price and John Chatwin)

1974 Director's Office, Royal Botanic Gardens, Kew, London (project; with Simon Bensasson)

1977 Public Cleansing and Social Services Departments Sub-Depot, Kensington and Chelsea Borough Council, Barandon Road, London W.11 (with Siu Wing Kwok)

Publications:

On WEARDEN: books—*Architecture in Britain Today* by Michael Webb, London 1969; *Dwelling Houses* by Giampiero Aloi, Milan 1970; *Guide to Modern Buildings in London* by Charles McKean and Tom Jestico, London 1976; articles—"Comprehensive Redevelopment, Kensington" in *Architectural Review* (London), January 1966; "Housing, Kensington, London" in *Architect and Building News* (London), 7 September 1966; "Housing, Kingsbury, London" in *Architectural Review* (London), November 1966; "Housing" in *Architects' Journal* (London), 16 November 1966; "Group d'Immeubles à Kingsbury, Londres" in *L'Architecture d'Aujourd'hui* (Paris), February/March 1967; "Double-Decked Village" in *Architectural Forum* (New York), April 1967; "Hausgruppe in Kingsbury, London" in *Baumeister* (Munich), May 1967; "Hausgruppe in Kingsbury, London" in *Bauwelt* (Berlin), 24 July 1967; "Statt Stadtteil-nurteilsanierung" in *Baumeister* (Munich), December 1970; "Models of Integration 1: Housing Group in Slough Lane, Kingsbury" by Horst Klement and Peter Rumpf in *Bauwelt* (Berlin), 6 May 1974.

For as long as I can remember, I have had a compelling desire to be totally involved with the design and construction of buildings, their interiors and the space between. This force has directed my life's pursuit, but although I have practised architecture and its allied disciplines now for more than thirty years, I am as much at a loss as ever to comprehend why it dominates my life, although I am aware that many others share this compulsion in varying degrees and directions.

I believe it is the existence of this force that makes it difficult for most creative people to explain their aims, and I have found the process of self-analysis involved in preparing this statement a very valuable experience.

During the total creative process I try to involve my clients as much as possible to ensure that their needs and values are fully appreciated and put into effect. The process usually starts with a series of informal discussions, and in this build-up of the brief I encourage thinking in terms of actual needs rather than preconceived images of solutions.

I consider it dangerous to resort to realistic shapes and forms too early in the design process, and I prefer to make only diagrammatic studies until I am satisfied that the brief has been properly formulated, the broad-based research completed, and a hierarchy of values evolved.

Through the years I have employed increasingly more sophisticated methods of working as new techniques—such as network analysis and cost planning —have been devised.

I make use of scale models to assist in the design process and, wherever necessary, full-size mockups of complex structural details and full-size samples to agree such things as texture and colour.

I regard every stage as having a design content, whether it be the formulation of the brief, writing a specification, making a working drawing, or instructing the builder during construction. I believe it is this constant concern for detail in the general pursuit of excellence that leads me to have successive love affairs with my buildings.

This must be the most difficult period to date in which to practise and survive for any sensitive architect. As a profession we have been mercilessly and I

believe unfairly criticised for our recent works, and this has coincided with an economic recession within an age of rapid technological, social and cultural change. In this country there has, at the same time, been a rapid increase in the amount of complicated, restricting and often senseless building and planning legislation published and constantly amended.

It is therefore more than ever vital to remain as flexible as possible within this constantly changing situation and to endeavour to satisfy every need presented by the brief from the most commonplace to delight.

There is, of course, no perfect solution, and the most that one can hope to achieve is the most appropriate balance of the needs presented by the brief within the framework of the existing situation.

—Clifford Wearden

Clifford Wearden's most successful project must be "Ferndene" at Kingsbury, London, a group of 37 dwellings for the Hastoe Housing Society. A plan with a restrained thrust to it in three directions (the fourth being the approach way), the building suddenly assumes in section and elevation a multitude of variegations, facets, and apertures picked out in concrete or brick; the houses break out into a multiplanar mass whose juggling and high-wire antics suggest a clowning all-the-fun-of-the-fair vernacular of the best kind, without having to actually resort to pitched roofs or pantiles to make its case. Out of the slow, well-considered and easy rotation of the plan, the actual architecture of it all pops out as a more mobile and witty affair—where the plan drags its heels, the building as a whole is eager and on the alert, looking for anything that might come its way. The complexity of reference, the sustained orchestration, the little nodes of interest here and there—all such elements point to different readings of the plan-as-text: it is as though, in this instance, the section was not just a resolution of the plan but an urban commentary on it, a caricature no less.

An "island of urbanity in Metroland," it compresses bits of village, town and suburb together in the making of a little sample of city. In the eyes of the Local Authority it makes sense in costguide and Parker Morris terms, yet in more earth-related terms it also makes sense. Of course, its organic constitution could have been played up more, but the complex's suggestions are nonetheless sufficient to lift us out of Metroland into some more substantial place.

—Chris Fawcett

WEEKS, John.

British. Born in London, 5 March 1921. Educated at Dulwich College, London, 1933–38; Architectural Association School, London, 1938–42, 1946–47, A.A. Diploma 1947. Served as a Sergeant in the Education Corps of the British Army, 1942–45. Married Barbara Lilian Munn in 1955; children: Julia and Timothy. Assistant Architect, Research Division, London Midland and Scottish Railways, London, 1947–48; Architect, Hills West Bromich Ltd., West Bromich, Staffordshire, 1949; Assistant Architect, involved in an investigation into function and design of hospitals, London, 1950–56; Deputy Director, Division of Architectural Studies, Nuffield Foundation, London, 1956–60; Studio Master, Architectural Association School, London, 1960. In partnership with Richard Llewelyn-Davies, *q.v.*, London, since 1960: currently, Senior Director of the successor firm, Llewelyn-Davies Weeks Forestier-Walker and Bor, in charge of the firm's hospital and health services planning practices. Part-time Senior Lecturer, Bartlett School of Architecture and Planning, University College, University of London,

1961–72. Member of the Council, Centre on Environment for the Handicapped, 1975–77; Vice-President, 1976–77, and since 1975 Member of the Council, Architectural Association, London. Deputy Chairman of the British Health Care Export Council, since 1976. Exhibitions: *This Is Tomorrow,* Whitechapel Gallery, London, 1956; *Artist Versus the Machine,* Building Centre, London, 1963; *Cybernetic Serendipity,* Institute of Contemporary Arts, London, 1968; *Jubilee Exhibition,* Architectural Association, London, 1977. Recipient: Bronze Medal, Royal Institute of British Architects, 1957; West Suffolk Award to Architects, 1957. Fellow, Royal Institute of British Architects, 1964. Address: Llewelyn-Davies Weeks, 39 Jacksons Lane, London N6 5SR, England.

Works (all with Richard Llewelyn-Davies):

1952 Nuffield House, Musgrave Park Hospital, Belfast

1954 Diagnostic Centre, Corby, Northamptonshire

1955 House, Mayford, Surrey

1957 Mignot Memorial Hospital, Alderney, Channel Islands
Rushbrooke Village Housing, Bury St. Edmunds, Suffolk

1958 *The Times* Newspaper Office Building, London (with Ellis, Clarke and Galleraugh)

1960 Students Residence and Dining Room, Imperial College of Tropical Agriculture, Trinidad, West Indies (with Colin Laird Associates)
Meeting halls and laboratories, Zoological Society, London
Nuffield Institute of Comparative Medicine, London

1961 The Stock Exchange redevelopment, London (with Fitzroy Robinson)
Sun Alliance Insurance Building, London (with Fitzroy Robinson)
Northwick Park Hospital and Clinical Research Centre, Harrow, Middlesex

1963 Tate Gallery extension, London
Town Centre Development, phase I, and Sports Centre, Basingstoke, Hampshire (with Ian Fraser Associates)

1966 Barmston Village Housing Project, Washington New Town, County Durham

1968 Experimental Pathology Research Building, St. Mary's Hospital, Paddington, London
Stantonbury Housing Scheme, Milton Keynes, Buckinghamshire

1970 Youth Treatment Centre, Birmingham
University Children's Hospital, Leuven, Belgium (with Felix Tanghe and Delarue)
Medical Centre, Flinders University, Adelaide, South Australia (with the South Australia Department of Public Works)

1971 York District Hospital
Sciences laboratories, National Hospital for Nervous Diseases, London
Salmaniya Medical Centre, Bahrain

1972 Metal Box Company Headquarters Building, Reading, Berkshire
Singapore General Hospital, Outram Road, Singapore (with INDECO)
General Hospital, Doha, State of Qatar

1973 Normanby College Education Centre, King's College Hospital, London

1974 Health Sciences Centre, University of Khon Kaen, Thailand (with Kingston Reynolds Thom and Allardice)

1975 Cancer Research Foundation, Sutton, Surrey
Rayne Institute Research Laboratories, University College Hospital, London

1976 Voluntary Research Trust Research Laboratory Building, King's College Hospital, London

John Weeks: Northwick Park Hospital, Harrow, Middlesex, 1961

Publications:

By WEEKS: articles—"The Hertfordshire Achievement," with Richard Llewelyn-Davies, in *Architectural Review* (London), June 1952; "Progress in Planning Hospitals" in *RIBA Journal* (London), January 1959; "New Developments in Hospital Design and Construction" in *The Hospital* (London), July 1959; "Sterilizing Practice in Hospital—Architectural Problems" in *The Hospital* (London), October 1959; "Current Trends in Hospital Planning" in *The Hospital* (London), October 1959; "Planning for Growth and Change" in *The Architects' Journal* (London), July 1960; "The Children's House, Amsterdam" in *Architectural Design* (London), July 1960; "Mechanization and Hospital Design" in *Architectural Design* (London), January 1961; "Cost Control—Hospital Building" in *Architectural Design* (London), January 1961; "Review of General Hospitals—Functional Studies of the Main Departments (Bouwcentrum, Rotterdam)" in *The Architects' Journal* (London), April 1962; "Indeterminate Architecture" in *Transactions of the Bartlett Society* (London), May 1964; "Hospitals for the 1970's" in *Hospital Management Planning and Equipment* (London), November 1964, and in *RIBA Journal* (London), December 1964; editor, special issue on hospital architecture of *Architectural Review* (London), June 1965; "Indeterminate Hospital Design on Urban Sites" in *Hospital Management* (London), June 1966; "Indeterminacy in Architecture" in *The Listener* (London), June 1967; "Hospital: Design for Growth and Change" in *World Hospitals* (London), January 1969; "Studies in Hospital Design" in *La Maison* (Brussels), May 1969; "Hospital Design During the Next Twenty-One Years," with Peter Cowan in *Hospital Management Planning and Equipment* (London), May 1969; "Hospital Design (Architecture in Israel)" in *Journal of the Association of Engineers and Architects in Israel* (Haifa), June 1969; "Multi-Strategy Buildings" in *Architectural Design* (London), October 1969; "Designing for Patient Care, Education and Research" in *World Hospitals* (London), November 1969; "Indeterminate Dimensions in Architecture" in *Baumeister* (Munich), November 1969; "Planning the Gasthuisberg Project," with Gavin Maxwell, in *World Hospitals* (London), April 1970; "Northwick Park Hospital" in *L'Architecture d'Aujourd'hui* (Paris), July 1970; "Design Strategy for Flexible Health Sciences Facilities," with Gordon Best, in *Health Services Research* (Chicago), Autumn 1970; "Designing for Indeterminacy" in *Architectural Review* (London), November 1971; "Hospital Design" in *Architectural Design* (London), July 1973; "Alvar Aalto" in *The Listener* (London), Summer 1976; "Distribution of Room Sizes in Hospitals," with Gordon Best, James Cheyne and Ellen Leopold, in *Health Services Research* (London), Autumn 1976; "The Wellington Hospital, St. John's Wood" in *The Architects' Journal* (London), Spring 1977; "Hospital Building" in *RIBA Journal* (London), Jubilee Issue, May 1977.

On WEEKS: books—*Meaning in Architecture* by Charles Jencks, London 1969; *Parameters and Images* by L. Brett, London 1970; article—review in *The Architects' Journal* (London), 2 February 1972.

*

For the greater part of my professional life I have specialized in hospital design. Hospitals as a building type have a number of curious properties (aside from the expected ones of complicated function and, often, great size) which marks them off from typical architect's commissions. All hospitals require to grow and change as they adjust to the changes in their catchment area population and as medical and nursing techniques alter. Since they may take many years to design and construct, it is not unusual for the architect's original brief to be out of date in many places as soon as they are opened.

The architect's brief is only one incident in the life of a hospital which will continue to change during the whole of its existence. Thus the architect is deprived of the traditional basis for his design—a full and accurate description of the functions his building will have to accommodate.

It follows that the architect is not able to determine the final form of the building and that he must design an "indeterminate" hospital, on the assumption that his brief is incomplete and probably wrong.

In successive projects I have been searching for a method of design which takes as its starting point provision for irregular and unforeseeable growth and change—an indeterminate architecture—to replace the conventional ideal of finite formal composition.

—John Weeks

*

In 1960, John Weeks, now a partner in Llewelyn-Davies Weeks Forestier-Walker and Bor, was already advocating an approach to planning that would allow for growth of unforseeable volumes, while still maintaining some kind of comprehensible form—he was reacting against the typical urban growth patterns, best illustrated by hospitals, whereby expedient additions and fillings-in created the characteristic formlessness which the city was assuming. By the principle of space continuity, he managed to establish a way of reliquishing our concept of planning as an exercise in finite geometry in favour of a concept based on an extendible communication system. In other words, to use his analogy, a duffle coat in place of a tailor-made suit. But he added a rider to his manifesto right from the start: the danger exists that flexibility, if uncritically adopted, costs too much and tempts those concerned not to think out their problems in advance—"it is not to be used simply to justify indecisive planning."

By the 1970's, with the completion of his Northwick Park Hospital and of the Medical Centre, Flinders University, Adelaide, his fledgeling "responsiveness" had matured into a full-scale multi-strategy architecture of indeterminacy. This I-Ching architecture of lattice systems and independent subsystems demotes determinism to second place behind that of the life of the building; it entails the letting go of the Platonic side to design and understanding architecture as a kind of time-frame. Japanese Metabolist projects failed, for they only had the appearance of indeterminacy—their real guts were nostalgic and heroic. Cedric Price's Interaction Centre, Weeks feels, is much better resolved, for it carries more vividly evidence of its users' lives.

An indeterminate architecture doesn't get in the way; at a fundamental level it recognizes and appreciates the reality of people's opinions and gives them the right to exercise them. At Northwick Park, Weeks was trying to deal with the problem of sheltering an organization which has a rate of growth and change so great that it makes its buildings obsolete before they decay naturally. Looking at such precedents as the 19th century railway station and exhibition shed, where engineers, uninhibited by the contemporary architectural morality that expects a close fit between form and function, fabricated easily extendible linear spaces which at the same time did not condition the arrangement of internal affairs. His only criticism of these 19th century buildings was that they nonethelesss still looked finite and complete. At Northwick Park he deployed the elements of 19th century flexibility—separate buildings tied together by an independent internal street—but he didn't insist on achieving a unity of constant relationships; instead he came up with a geometric aformalism that wrapped around the close-knit communications clusters. This demonstration of an architecture of kinetic densities and intervals, however, has hardly been matched by some of recent work of the partnership, and one is inclined to wonder if that doesn't make the theory of an architecture-of-chance sound rather hollow today?

—Chris Fawcett

WEESE, Harry (Mohr).

American. Born in Evanston, Illinois, 30 June 1915. Educated at Massachusetts Institute of Technology, Cambridge, 1934–38 (Roche Prize, American Institute of Architects, 1938), B.Arch. 1938; Yale University, New Haven, Connecticut, 1936–37; Cranbrook Academy of Art, Bloomfield Hills, Michigan, 1938–39 (Fellow in City Planning); Research Assistant, Bemis Housing Foundation, M.I.T., 1939–40. Served as an Engineering Officer in the United States Navy, 1942–46. Married Kate Baldwin in 1945; children: Shirley, Kate and Marcia. Designer, Skidmore, Owings and Merrill, Chicago, 1940–41, 1946–47; Partner, with Benjamin Baldwin, Baldwin and Weese, Kenilworth, Illinois, 1941–42. Since 1947, Chairman of the Board of Harry Weese and Associates, Chicago; office established in Washington, D.C., 1966, Miami, Florida, 1977. Chairman, Building Committee, Council for the Restoration of the Adler-Sullivan Auditorium Theatre, Chicago, 1964–67; Member of the Mayor's Committee for the Preservation of Chicago's Historic Architecture, 1972; Member of the Task Force on Federal Architecture, National Endowment for the Arts, 1973; Chairman of the Task Force on Rebuilding the City, 1973, and President of the Chicago Chapter, 1975, American Institute of Architects; Architectural Consultant, United States Department of State Foreign Buildings Program, 1973–76. Chairman of the Urban Form Committee since 1968, and Member of the Lakefront Committee since 1968 and of the Transportation Committee since 1970, Metropolitan Housing and Planning Council of Chicago; Member, American Institute of Architects Capital Architects Advisory Committee, since 1972; Member, National Council on the Arts, since 1974; Member, Architectural Review Panel of the Board of Governors of the United States Federal Reserve System, since 1974. Recipient: Distinguished Building Award, 1959, 1967, 1969, 1970 (twice), 1971, 1974, 1975, 1978, and Honor Award, 1968, 1970, American Institute of Architects, Chicago Chapter; Honor Award, 1960, and Restoration and Rehabilitation Award, 1963, American Institute of Architects/Chicago Association of Commerce and Industry; First Prize, Masonry Institute, 1962; Brunner Prize, National Institute of Arts and Letters, 1964; Merit Award for Design Excellence, United States Department of Housing and Urban Development, 1965 (twice); National Honor Award, 1969, 1970, 1973, 1977, and Firm of the Year Award, 1978, American Institute of Architects; Chicago Beautiful Award, 1969, 1976; Award of Excellence for House Design, *Architectural Record*, 1970; Architectural Award of Excellence, American Institute of Steel Construction, 1970; Award of Excellence, Chicago Tile Institute, 1971; Honor Award, United States General Services Administration, 1972; Honor Award, *House and Home*, 1973; Award of Excellence, Development Council Foundation, Champaign County, Illinois, 1973; City Beautiful Award, Dayton, Ohio, 1973; Prestressed Concrete Institute Award, 1974, 1975; Illinois Association of School Boards Award, 1974; Award for Excellence, *Environmental Design*, 1975; Design Award, Greater Wilmington, Delaware Development Council, 1975. Fellow, American Institute of Architects, 1961; Member, National Academy of Design. Address: Harry Weese and Associates, 10 West Hubbard Street, Chicago, Illinois 60610, U.S.A.

Works:

1951　Master plan for the Cummins Engine Company, Columbus, Indiana

1953　Master plan for Drake University, Des Moines, Iowa

1956　United States Consulate Staff Apartments, Accra, Ghana
　　　　Apartment building, 227 East Walton Street, Chicago
　　　　Residence Hall, University of Chicago

1958 United States Embassy and Staff Apartments, Accra, Ghana
1959 Professor Gale Johnson House, Chicago
Hyde Park Redevelopment, Chicago (with I. M. Pei and Loewenberg and Loewenberg)
1960 KLM Airlines Offices, Chicago
Old Town Apartment Building, 235 West Eugenie Street, Chicago
Master plan for Cornell College, Mount Vernon, Iowa
1962 Arena Stage Theatre I, Washington, D.C.
1963 Illinois Center for the Visually Handicapped, Chicago
Northern Baptist Theological Seminary, Hinsdale, Illinois
1964 Newberry Library renovation, Chicago
Otter Creek Country Club, Columbus, Indiana
1965 Jens Jensen School, Chicago
IBM Office Building, Milwaukee
First Baptist Church, Columbus, Indiana
Kenwood Gardens, Chicago
1966 Cummins Engine Company Manufacturing Plant, Columbus, Indiana
Outdoor Garden, Art Institute of Chicago
Science Complex, University of Colorado, Boulder
Chicago Teachers' Union Apartment Building
1966– Metro Subway System, Washington, D.C.
1967 Adler-Sullivan Auditorium Theatre restoration, Chicago
Orchestra Hall renovation, Chicago
Master plan for the Lincoln Park Zoo, Chicago
Master plan for the Field Museum of Natural History, Chicago
1968 Air India Staff Housing, Bombay
Building 64, Cummins Engine Company, Columbus, Indiana
Library and Auditorium, Rochester Institute of Technology, New York
South Lower Campus Project, University of Wisconsin, Madison
Science Building, Beloit College, Wisconsin
Time & Life Building, East Ohio Street, Chicago
Fort Lincoln Housing for the Elderly, Washington, D.C.
Master plan for Reed College, Portland, Oregon
1969 Seventeenth Church of Christ Scientist, Chicago
Latin School, Chicago
Center for the Performing Arts, Milwaukee
St. Louis Junior College
1970 Bank Street College of Education, New York
Interama: Caribbean Pavilion, Miami, Florida (project)
Atlas Crankshaft Manufacturing Facility, Fostoria, Ohio
District of Columbia Interstate Highway Study
Southwest Washington (D.C.) Urban Renewal
1971 Greenwood Park Apartments, Chicago
Science Building, Cornell College, Mount Vernon, Iowa
Shadowcliff (house), Door County, Wisconsin
Office Building and Art Center, Cincinnati
Education and Communications Building, and Physical Education Building, University of Illinois at Chicago Circle
Master plan for Lake Michigan College, Benton Harbor, Michigan
Master plan for Park Forest South, Illinois
Master plan for St. Louis Junior College
Master plan for the new town of Lake Lure, Waukegan, Illinois
Master plan for the Avery Coonley School, Downers Grove, Illinois
1972 Arena Stage Theatre II, Washington, D.C.

Actors Theatre, Louisville, Kentucky
Given Institute of Pathobiology, Aspen, Colorado
IBM Laboratory and Office Building, Endicott, New York
Master plan for the West Campus of Massachusetts Institute of Technology, Cambridge
Master plan for the Theatre of Western Springs, Illinois
Master plan for Ghent District Housing, Norfolk, Virginia
1973 Crown Center Hotel, Kansas City
Research Building, Chicago Botanical Gardens
Credit Card Center, American Oil Company, Raleigh, North Carolina
IBM Central Utilities Plant, Endicott, New York
Levis Faculty Center, University of Illinois, Urbana
Center for Advanced Study, University of Illinois, Urbana
LaSalle Plaza Office Building, LaSalle and Lake Streets, Chicago
First National Bank, Dayton, Ohio
1974 Lake Village East, Chicago
Credit Card Center, American Oil Company, Des Moines, Iowa
Northwest Medical Arts Building, Arlington Heights, Illinois
Theatre remodelling, Boston University
Fine Arts Building, Carleton College, Northfield, Minnesota
345 West Fullerton Apartment Building, Chicago
Hyde Park Townhouses, Chicago
Village Hall, Oak Park, Illinois
Social Sciences Campus, State University of New York, Buffalo-Amherst Branch
Plan for the restoration and expansion of the State Capitol, Montgomery, Alabama
Master plan for Pershing Square, Kansas City
1975 Federal Correctional Center, Chicago
Fine Arts Building and Student Center, Drake University, Des Moines, Iowa
51st and King Drive Building rehabilitation, Chicago
Grand Central Station redevelopment, New York (project)
Solar House, University of Delaware, Wilmington
Library, University of Massachusetts, Boston
United States Courthouse Annex, Chicago
John Knox Home Apartment Building, Norfolk, Virginia
Grace Street Housing for the Elderly, Chicago
West Willow Townhouses, Chicago
Master plan for the Downtown Core of Baltimore
Master plan for the 3A Interstate Highway System, Baltimore
1976 Mercantile Bank, Kansas City
Library, Williams College, Williamstown, Massachusetts
First National Bank, Albuquerque, New Mexico
Gymnasium, New Trier High School, Winnetka, Illinois
Northwest Industries office interiors, Chicago
Science Building, Cornell College, Mt. Vernon, Iowa
School of Medicine, Southern Illinois University, Carbondale
Plan for the development of the riverbank, Chicago
Trans Union Corporation Office Building, Lincolnshire, Illinois
1977 Wheaton National Bank, Wheaton, Illinois
Civic Center, Middletown, Ohio
Terman Engineering Center, Stanford University, California

Keck, Cushman, Mahin and Cate office interiors, Chicago
1978 Marriott Hotel, North Michigan Avenue, Chicago
Euclid Place, Oak Park, Illinois
Rosenberg Townhouses, Chicago
Study for the National Park Service, Chicago
Floating marina, Navy Pier, Chicago (project)
Plan for the renovation of the Loop Elevated Railway, Chicago
1978– Dade County, Florida Transportation System (as architectural consultant)
Plan for the Northeast Corridor (Boston to Washington, D.C.), for the United States Federal Railroad Administration
Riyadh Airport Community, Saudi Arabia
Field Museum of Natural History renovation, Chicago
Convention/Entertainment Center, Grand Rapids, Michigan
Newberry Library renovation and expansion, Chicago
Multi-Purpose Building, Stateville Prison, Joliet, Illinois
1100 Lake Shore Drive (apartments), Chicago
Harwick Administration Building, Mayo Clinic, Rochester, Minnesota
Theatre, University of Chicago
Pesch House, Lake Forest, Illinois
Plan for the Niagara Frontier Transportation Authority
Minnesota State Prison, Stillwater
Steelcase Showroom, Chicago
200 South Wacker Drive Office Building, Chicago
Plan for Printer's Row (housing), South Dearborn Street, Chicago

Publications:

By WEESE—articles—"Chicago and Urban Design" in *American Institute of Planners Reporter and Review* (Washington, D.C.), December 1958; "Random Thoughts on Architectural Controls and Their Effect on Cities" in *AIA Journal* (Washington, D.C.), March 1961; "Opinion: Tax Reform and Land Reform" in *Inland Architect* (Chicago), July 1972; "The Issue Is Tall Buildings" in *AIA Journal* (Washington, D.C.), January 1973; "Arbor Day Thoughts" in *Morton Arboretum Quarterly* (Lisle, Illinois), Spring 1974; "What's Next for Chicago" in *Commerce Magazine* (Chicago), October 1974; "Tribute to Alvar Aalto" in *Arkkitehti* (Helsinki), August 1976; "Perspective III: Preservation" in *Journal of Architectural Education* (Washington, D.C.), November 1976; "What Next, Chicago?" in the *Chicago Daily News,* 7 May 1977.

On WEESE: book—*Der Offene Kamin-Folge 3* by Fritz Barran, Stuttgart 1976; articles—"Wide-Open Bank" in *Architectural Forum* (New York), August 1952; "Suburban Menace" in *AIA Bulletin* (Chicago), November 1954; "Starting a Tradition" in *Time* (New York), 4 March 1957; "The Office of Harry Weese Associates, Chicago" in *Inland Architect* (Chicago), September 1957; "Eyeful in Africa" in *Architectural Forum* (New York), September 1959; "Arena Stage" in *Architectural Review* (London), June 1960; "Washington Builds a True Theatre-in-the-Round" in *The Times* (London), 27 December 1961; "Il Teatro Arena Stage a Washington" in *Edilizia Moderna* (Milan), March 1963; "Architect Counts City's Blessings" in *Milwaukee Journal,* 10 March 1964; "A Baptist Church by Weese" in *Architectural Record* (New York), December 1965; "First Baptist Church" in *L'Architecture d'Aujourd'hui* (Paris), April/May 1966; "How to Keep Your Landmarks and Have Them, Too" in *Progressive Architecture* (New York), October 1966; "Subways Don't Have to Be Miserable" in *Fortune*

Harry Weese: First Baptist Church, Columbus, Indiana, 1965

(New York), April 1967; "Harry Weese Should Have His Way with Chicago" in *Esquire* (New York), June 1968; "Monumental Weese" in *Architectural Review* (London), December 1968; "Summer House in Muskola Lake District" in *DBZ/Deutsche Bauzeitschrift* (Gutersloh), May 1969; "New Weese Buildings Create a Downtown Complex" in *Progressive Architecture* (New York), June 1969; "Harry Weese, FAIA" in *Interiors* (New York), November 1970; "Vacanze a picco sul lago Michigan" in *Domus* (Milan), October 1971; "Apartments in Chicago" in *Architecture + Urbanism* (Tokyo), October 1971; "Good Weese" in *Architectural Review* (London), February 1972; "Harry Weese" in *Revue Moderne des Arts et de la Vie* (Paris), January 1973; "Harry Weese and Associates of Chicago" in *Space Design* (Tokyo), February 1976; "Metro's Designer" in *Washington Post,* 24 June 1977; "Goodbye Art Deco" in *Progressive Architecture* (New York), August 1977; "Washington Metro" by Colin Amery in *Architectural Review* (London), February 1978.

From the perception of need and the opportunity seized, the resultant work speaks for itself and in many tongues.

—Harry Weese

Harry Weese is a native of Chicago, where he has based his practice, begun in 1947. He received his architectural training at the Massachusetts Institute

of Technology in the 1930's, a time when the curriculum revolved around both the Beaux-Arts and Bauhaus influences. He subsequently studied urban planning at the Cranbrook Academy near Detroit, under Eliel Saarinen. There, Eero Saarinen, though his junior, became a mentor.

Unlike the work of many noted contemporary architects, Weese's work does not bear a recognizable stamp. Weese's work is characterized, rather, by a painstaking attention to the specific design problem at hand. It is from a deep understanding of each problem—its setting, its historical relations, and particularly its unique functional requirements—that his design solutions arise. The nature of his projects and the requirements of American practice compel him to operate a large office, but he has always been in full control of it. Every design project is done under his guidance.

His work includes a wide range of building types —theatres, office buildings, houses, churches, public housing, schools, etc. He has also maintained a position of spokesman for causes and issues in planning and architecture which he feels compelled to address, mainly in Chicago.

Weese was among the first major designer-architects to work in the area of historic restoration. The specific work was the great Chicago Auditorium Theatre, originally designed in the 19th century by Louis Sullivan and Dankmar Adler.

He was also selected to be the design architect for the rail rapid transit system of Washington, D.C.— the stations and public facilities. His approach to this

project indicates his general approach to all problems. He saw that the problem of the station designs was recognizability by passengers—a familiar sequence of arrival or departure experiences. The varying constraints and conditions of each station needed a familiar consistency of theme rather than "variety." Indeed, there would be more than enough forces trying to pull the stations apart, creating confusion. His solution was to design a system of component parts, a "system of systems," for individual designers to utilize in the many stations. It has worked admirably and is among the outstanding works of public architecture in America.

Weese's other projects include the First Baptist Church, Columbus, Indiana; the renovation of the Field Museum of Natural History and Orchestra Hall in Chicago; the Time-Life Building in Chicago; Arena Stage in Washington, D.C.; the Latin School, Chicago; the Federal Correctional Center, Chicago; and the Terman Engineering Center at Stanford University, California.

—Paul Spreiregen

WEINSTEIN, Richard S.

American. Born in New York City, 30 November 1932. Educated at Brown University, Providence, Rhode Island, B.A. 1956; Columbia University, New York, M.A. in clinical psychology; Harvard University, Cambridge, Massachusetts; University of Pennsylvania, Philadelphia, under Louis I. Kahn, Romaldo Giurgola, Robert Venturi, and Robert Le Ricolais (Arthur Spade Brook Gold Medal for Design, 1961), M.Arch. 1961; Prix de Rome Scholar, American Academy in Rome, 1963. Served in the United States Army, 1956–58. Married to Sandra Cohen; children: Alexander and Nicolas. Worked for I. M. Pei, Edward Larrabee Barnes, and Skidmore, Owings and Merrill, New York; Director, Manhattan Planning Office, Department of City Planning, New York, 1966–68, and Mayor's Office of Lower Manhattan Development, New York, 1968–74. Since 1974, in private practice, as Richard S. Weinstein Associates Inc., New York. Project Director, Museum of Modern Art Expansion Projects, 1975–77. Project Director, 42nd Street Redevelopment Projects, New York, since 1978; President, New Sources of Funding Inc., New York, since 1978. Member, Board of Directors, The Theatre Development Fund, New York, New York Landmarks Conservancy, and the Architectural League of New York; Member, Visiting Committee, Harvard Graduate School of Design. Exhibition: Museum of Modern Art, New York, 1966. Address: Richard S. Weinstein Associates Inc., 200 Park Avenue, Suite 3024, New York, New York 10017, U.S.A.

Works:

1966/
67 Twin Parks Urban Renewal Plan, Bronx, New York (with Giovanni Pasanella, Jonathan Barnett, Jaquelin Robertson, and M. Weintraub)
1966/
74 Numerous zoning ordinances, embodying complex urban design criteria, for the Lower Manhattan Waterfront, Lincoln Square, Greenwich Street, Theatre District, etc., for the New York City Government
1969 Negril Development Plan, Jamaica, West Indies (with Giovanni Pasanella, Jonathan Barnett, Adelates Technical Services, and Jaquelin Robertson)
1971 House, Montreal
1974/
75 Master plan/design guidelines for Park Central (mixed commercial development), near Dallas
1975/
77 Apartment Tower, for the Museum of Modern Art, New York (project)
1976/
77 Development plan for Floyd Bennett Field, Gateway National Recreation Area, New York
    Museum of Pueblo and Navajo Art, Santa Fe, New Mexico (project)

Publications:

By WEINSTEIN: article—"Demeter and the Snow Queen" in *Architectural Forum* (New York), October 1973.

On WEINSTEIN: article—"White and Gray: Twelve Modern American Architects" in *Architecture + Urbanism* (Tokyo), April 1975.

Architecture is about institutions. Architects should understand and be able to use to their advantage the legal, financial, and political methodologies of the market place, which underline the institutional structure of contemporary society. This should enable them to find metaphors which express directly the character of our experience of institutional structure, our experience of membership, and our search for a system of values from which to make choices. Mastery of these methodologies also places the architect in a position of advantage with the political and financial establishments which have always controlled the construction of buildings and cities.

—Richard S. Weinstein

Richard S. Weinstein is a leading exponent of the practice of urban design using innovative forms of public-private partnerships and what he calls "venture philanthropy."

One of a group of young architects who joined the administration of New York City Mayor John Lindsay in 1967, Richard Weinstein became the head of the Mayor's Office of Lower Manhattan Development. His most notable achievements were the creation of special zoning districts, in which land-use regulations—previously proscriptive in nature—were used to achieve positive architectural results. These districts, including the Theatre District, the Lincoln Square District, the Greenwich Street District, and the Lower Manhattan Waterfront, became increasingly complex and sophisticated. For the first time they created a means of achieving co-ordinated development of portions of a city incrementally through the medium of land-use regulation. Whether these innovations will prove completely successful still remains to be seen. They are dependent on the vagaries of the private real-estate market, and it will be years before any one district will be developed completely.

After leaving the New York City government in 1974 to start his own practice, Weinstein wrote design guidelines for the 300-acre Park Central project near Dallas. These guidelines amount to a voluntary special zoning district that co-ordinates and gives form to a development proceeding incrementally over a long period of time. It is to be used by the developer in drawing up lease and sale agreements for individual parcels within the project.

Weinstein also has put together a controversial proposal in which the Museum of Modern Art in New York City has sought to develop an apartment house using the "air-rights" (additional floor area permitted by zoning) of the Museum and Garden, transferring these development rights to property adjacent to the Museum. The unused asset of these building rights would thus be put to work and become part of the Museum's endowment. Weinstein is now taking this principle farther by establishing a not-for-profit corporation, New Sources of Funding, which specializes in helping non-profit institutions realize the potential of similar "sleeping assets."

Before entering city government, Richard Weinstein worked for a number of architectural firms, including I. M. Pei and Partners and the Office of Edward Larrabee Barnes, and received the Prix de Rome of the American Academy in 1963. He continues to keep his hand in as an architectural designer. His best-known building is a large private house in Canada, which shows the influence of his teacher, Louis I. Kahn, but also evokes recollections of French Chateaux and the work of H. H. Richardson.

—Jonathan Barnett

WEJCHERT, Hanna.

Polish. Born Hanna Adamczewska in Radom, 29 July 1920. Educated at the Warsaw Technical University, 1939–46, Dip.Arch. 1946, Ph.D. 1959. Interned in Ravensbruck concentration camp, 1944–45. Married Kazimierz Wejchert, *q.v.*, in 1962; daughter: Dorota. In partnership with Kazimierz Wejchert since 1947. Member of the faculty of the Warsaw School of Architecture since 1946: Assistant Lecturer in Town Planning, 1946–59; Lecturer, 1959–62; Assistant Professor, 1962–70; Associate Professor, 1970–75; Professor, since 1975. Vice-Chairman of the Council, TUP (Towarzystwo Urbanistow Polskich), Warsaw, 1968–72; Member of the Town Council of Tychy, Poland, 1969–73; Member, Committee of Architecture and Town Planning, Polish Academy of Science, 1978. Vice-Chairman, SARP (Architectural Association of Poland), since 1974. Exhibitions: *Terra 1,* Wroclaw, Poland, 1975; Exhibition of County Regional Plans, Warsaw, Poland. Recipient: Golden Cross of Merit, 1951; Ministry of Town Planning and Architecture Award, 1955, 1957; Golden Badge of Merit, Katowice, Poland, 1959; Polish State Prize, 1964; Ministry of the Environment Prize, 1974; Ministry of Higher Education Prize, 1977; Badge of Merit, Tychy New Town, 1978. Address (office): ul. Orezna 45, Warsaw, Poland.

Works (all with Kazimierz Wejchert):

1951 Master plan for Tychy New Town, Poland
1952 Master plan for the North District of Tychy, Poland
1958 Recreation Centre, Paprocany, Poland (project; with Z. Lojewski)
      Memorial Monument, Tychy, Poland (project)
1960 North Park, Tychy, Poland (with H. Okolowicz-Krzes)
1962 Master plan for the South District of Tychy, Poland
      Tychy Central Railway Station Area Development, Poland (with N. Niklewicz)
      Town Hall and District Community Party Headquarters, Tychy, Poland (with W. Jaciow and E. Piasecki)
1965 MNO Apartment Buildings, Tychy, Poland (with A. M. Czyzewski)
      Eartecznik Holiday Centre, Wisla Reservoir, Poland (with W. Jaciow and E. Piasecki)
1966 Krzyki District Development, Wroclaw, Poland (competition project; with A. and M. Czyzewscy)
1967 Victoria Palace, Warsaw (competition project; with G. Chodkowski)
      Atrium Housing Development, Tychy, Poland (with M. and A. Czyzewscy)
      Paderewski Housing Development, Katowice, Poland (competition project; with A. and M. Czyzewscy)
      One-family houses, North District, Tychy, Poland (project)
1968 Local Shopping Development, Poland (project; with M. Czyzewska, H. Drzewiecki, and S. Gzell)
      Mokotow Field, Warsaw Technical University
1969 Monument, Tychy, Poland (with J. Jarnuszkiewicz)
1970 Plan for the centre of Sieradz, Poland (competition project; with J. Chmielewski, G. Chodko, and Z. Dembowska)
1971 Town Centre, Jena, East Germany (with G. Chodkowski)
      Recreation Centre, Dzierzno Lake, near Gliwice, Poland (competition project; with A. Gawlikowski and S. Gzell)
1972 Polanczyk Recreation Centre, Solina Reservoir, Poland (with A. Gawlikowski and S. Gzell)
      Sports Stadium, Tychy, Poland (with Z. Kojewski)
      Development plan for the town of Ostroleka, Poland (competition project; with H. Drzewiecki and G. Chodkowski)
      Plan for the centre of Wloclawek, Poland (competition project)
1973 Shopping and Community Centre, Tychy, Poland (competition project; with M. Dziekonski)
1974 Atrium Housing Development, ul. Orezna, Warsaw

Hanna and Kazimierz Wejchert and their plans for Tychy New Town, Poland

1975   Plans for the urban centre and for housing, South District of Tychy, Poland
1976   Master plan for the expansion of Podkowa Lesna, near Warsaw (with K. Domaradzki)
        Plan for the centre of Lomza, Poland (project; with J. Chmielewski, A. Gawlikowski, and E. Gaduch)
1977   Master plan for the satellite town of Jaroszowice, Tychy, Poland
        City Centre, Kiel, Germany (competition project; with M. Dziekonski)
1978   Master plan for the Stella district of Tychy, Poland

Publications:

By H. WEJCHERT: books—*Wplyw Realizacji na Przemiany Miasto* (The Influence of Realization on the Changing Image of a Town), Warsaw 1964; *Przestrzenne Uksztaltowanie Osiedli Mieszkaniowych Wznoszonych Metoda Uprzemyslowiona w Swietle ich Realizacji w Polsce* (monograph), Warsaw 1964; *Mieszkanie, Zespol Mieszkaniowy i Miasto na tle Budowy N. Tychow: Sprawy Mieszkaniowe* (Flats, Housing Estates and Town: The New Town of Tychy), Warsaw 1964; *Z Problemow Urbanistyki Miast Poludniowej Szwecji* (monograph), Warsaw 1967; *Miasto Przyszlosci* (Town of the Future), with Kazimierz Wejchert, Warsaw 1973; *Domy Atrialne* (Atrium Housing), Warsaw 1974; articles—"O Realizacji Planu Zagospodarowania m. Garwolin" in *Dom: Osiedle: Mieszkanie* (Warsaw), January 1947; "Studia Zakladu Urbanistyki w Malych Miastach" in *Biuletyn Historii Kultury* (Warsaw), April 1949; "Szesc Ratuszy," with Kazimierz Wejchert, in *Architektura* (Warsaw), April 1950; "Prace Planist. przy Odbudowie Starego Miasta w Olsztynie" in *Miasto* (Warsaw), May 1951; "Problemy Malego Regionu" in *Architektura* (Warsaw), May 1962; "Problemy Miast Szybko Rozwijajacych sie w Polsce," with Kazimierz Wejchert, in *Miasto* (Warsaw), September 1964; "Uzbrojenie Podziemne Miasta a Przemiany Struktury Przestrzennej Osadnictwa," with Kazimierz Wejchert, in *Miasto* (Warsaw), April 1965; "Hidden Remains of Old Buildings as a Problem of Modern Local Planning" in *The City* (London), no. 3/4, 1970; "Indywidualne Budownictwo Miszkaniowe w Planowaniu Miast i Stref

Zurbanizowanych" in *Sprawy Mieszkaniowe* (Warsaw), February 1971; "Presentation: Tychy New Town," with Kazimierz Wejchert, in *Architektura* (Warsaw), February 1972; "Historia Nadal Optymistyczna" in *Architektura* (Warsaw), February 1972; "Uwagi o Mieszkaniu Przyszlosci," with Kazimierz Wejchert, in *Sprawy Mieszkaniowe* (Warsaw), February 1973; "Nowe Tendecje w Ksztaltowaniu Zespolow Mieszkalnych w Miastach" in *Architektura* (Warsaw), September/October 1974; "Spatial Structure of Small and Middle Size Towns," with Kazimierz Wejchert, in *Geographia Polonica* (Warsaw), no. 32, 1975; "New Towns in Poland," with Kazimierz Wejchert, in *New Towns,* University Park, Pennsylvania 1976.

On H. and K. WEJCHERT: books—*Vom Städtebau der Welt* by F. Jaspert, Berlin 1961; *Les Ville Nouvelle* by Merlin Pierre, Paris 1969; *L'Urbanisme Contemporaine* by W. Ostrowski, Paris 1970; *The Architecture of Poland* by Brian Knox, London 1971; *Städtebau der Socialistischer Lander* by E. Goldzamt, Berlin 1975; articles—"Neue Städte in Polen" by J. Heuer in *Neue Heimat* (Hamburg), no. 8, 1958; "Der Nachbar in Osten" by G. Kuhne in *Bauwelt* (Berlin), no. 19, 1962; "L'Urbanisme Pologne" by H. Skibniewska in *L'Architecture d'Aujourd'hui* (Paris), no. 118, 1964/65; "La Ville Nouvelle: Nowe Tychy" by J. Fourquier in *Planification et Urbanisme en Pologne,* Paris 1970; "We Present Attitudes: The Wejcherts on the City," editorial in *Architektura* (Warsaw), April 1977.

Contemporary architecture should grow from the roots of local conditions and traditions and from national culture.

The architect's task—resulting from the needs of rapid population growth—has changed from the scale of one building to the scale of the building complex. One should, therefore, not speak merely about the architecture of buildings; rather, one has to compose and create the architecture of space. Its form, proportions and tensions generate the framework of people's lives to a much greater extent than do particular buildings.

The large-scale character of the building industry, the size of the areas that are being urbanized, and the industrial production of building elements increase the danger of uniformity and lack of character in urban patterns. The way to counteract this possibility lies in the conscious design of space, backed up by an acquaintance with the theory of appearances, seeing, the analysis of perception, and psychological factors.

On an urban scale the creation of new values has become necessary. It should happen through the introduction of new urban patterns, which would become plan-generating elements and would provide the basis for further rational developments of urban form.

The unplanned development of the great towns creates the danger that conditions of life may deteriorate. This can be prevented if planning authorities attempt to create settlements of medium-sized towns (100,000–150,000 inhabitants): such units encourage conditions that are suited to people and closer to nature.

The space in an urban environment should divide itself—should be so formed that it divides—into intimate housing space, one's everyday surroundings, and into communal space, accessible to everyone.

Housing environments should ensure contact between the dwellings and the local terrain and landscape, a goal that can be obtained by creating buildings "not exceeding the height of trees," i.e. not more than four stories.

In order that each generation need only contribute a small stage to the historical process of building, we should respect the achievements of previous ages and the resources accumulated by the current generation. A skillful reference to existing buildings is the most appropriate cultural continuation.

In the field of education we consider it most im-

portant that the teachers transmit to their students not only knowledge but also creative and social attitudes.

We consider the role of the architect to be that of servant to society. Architectural work is not owned by the designer but by the consumer. In making plans for the future, the designer still has the right and the obligation to rely not only on reason, knowledge and skill, but also, to an equal degree, on intuition. This combination is nearly always decisive in the development of architectural thought.

—Hanna and Kazimierz Wejchert

The most important aspect of the career of Hanna and Kazimierz Wejchert has been their design work, which involves both architecture and town planning. They have also been involved in forming a "team," for most of the tasks in which they have been engaged exceed the capabilities of two people. Equally important has been their theoretical work, which they treat as a synthesis of their accumulated experience. They are regarded as the founders of a "new school of architectural thinking, combining the European cultural heritage with new social ideas to guide future development."

Their basic principles include the acceptance of the social role of the architect/town planner (they regard their profession as providing a social service) and the belief that architectural and town-planning problems are inseparable. The designer should not think to himself, "I built my town" or "My town includes . . .," but should instead regard the town as belonging to the people who live there, for whom he designs only a certain framework that they can assimilate, accept and develop.

Another crucial principle is their treatment of space as architecture: they refer to the spaces between buildings, and to streets, squares and green areas as being capable of creating feelings of belonging and social identification. The Wejcherts have also developed techniques for producing and motivating design decisions—techniques that do not always precisely conform with accepted regulations and conventions. And, finally, this too might be listed as a principle, that the Wejcherts believe in communication—with the public, with their team, with the client/investor, and with the contractor and other specialists in the design process—a communication informed by an understanding of users' needs and the specialists' tasks.

The Wejcherts produced the master plan for the new town of Tychy in 1951, and construction of the town, for 100,000 inhabitants, has been proceeding under their supervision for the past 25 years. It has proved to be for them an experimental testing ground, where the architectural and town-planning concepts propagated and taught by them at the Warsaw School of Architecture have been tried and corrected over a long period.

Their basic assumption in the planning was that, as Tychy would be a new town with no existing roots, it had to have a clear pattern that could be easily comprehended. From a social point of view, it had to be a Socialist city in which there could be no "good" or "bad" districts. As well, they tried to create a certain framework of commonly used space differentiated from the space of the individual—the space within a dwelling and its immediate surroundings.

Their work on the Tychy plan gave rise to a new theory about crystallizing plan elements. In the first stage of the project, the Wejcherts approached the planning, as they themselves admit, in an intuitive way. But as they worked, certain elements—crystallizing elements—suggested themselves, elements that, comprehensible to each user, help in the orientation and readability of urban space. In medieval towns the marketplace usually provided one such element; it explicity defined a particular space, the shape and character of which depended entirely on the wealth of the inhabitants and on local cultural traditions. In the plan for Tychy the basic planning element was provided by two intersecting axes: a railway line running East-West and a green belt running North-South, with an explicitly articulated central point—the station. The main streets, just over ½ mile long, were built on the grid and defined the area of the centre. On each of the corners they planned a complex of squares with district services for the four housing districts, each with 25,000 inhabitants.

The Wejcherts attempted to preserve the hierarchical structure of the city, from the neighbourhood unit through the estate and community, up to the district. They regarded this hierarchy as one that should not be tampered with. "Our task has been to build a town, not a group of housing estates separated from each other and not creating an urban formation. The town is not an agglomeration of housing estates with a shopping centre. The town is an organic creature." The Wejcherts believe that the "natural" development of the town often creates spatially unattractive patterns. In their opinion, the most interesting towns are those of the Middle Ages that had one market, towns that later, in the 17th century, grew into new towns seeded with new elements that crystallized their plans and ordered the areas of development—new clusters of service and trading units, town halls, churches, squares, etc. The Wejcherts believe that many contemporary plans (including those in Poland), the creation of which has involved great difficulties, have suffered just precisely because of the absence of such crystallizing elements.

Another major subject of their research has been in devising a theory of urban composition: man's perception of space, the creation of specific images, the planner's ability to use a variety of elements for spatial composition.

Parallel with their work at Tychy, the Wejcherts are conducting research on the inner spatial structure of small and medium-sized towns. This work will provide the basis in the future for evolving strategic development plans for Tychy. Another practical result will be development plans for a number of small towns conceived of as plans for buildings rather than simply plans for general spatial development—for, as the Wejcherts often stress, "in small towns each building plays a role."

The Wejcherts live in two towns—Warsaw, where they teach, and Tychy, where they build. They are, as they say, fascinated by reality and by the need to realize their projects, a strong characteristic of the War generation, who have a dominating sense of duty to their country.

—Teresa Czaplinska-Archer

WEJCHERT, Kazimierz.

Polish. Born in Smolensk, Russia, 14 May 1912. Educated at the Warsaw Technical University, 1929–35, Dip.Arch. 1935, Ph.D. 1944. Served in the Polish Army, 1935–36, 1939; prisoner-of-war in Bergen-Belsen, 1944–45. Married Janina Pawluc in 1934 (divorced); children: Kazimierz, Ewa, and Dorota; married Hanna Adamczewska (i.e., Hanna Wejchert, q.v.) in 1962. Inspector, Warsaw Surveying Office, 1936–37; in private practice, Warsaw, 1937–39; Member, Polish Country Planning Team, 1946–47. In partnership with Hanna Wejchert since 1947. Chief Designer of Tychy New Town, Poland, since 1951. Member of the faculty of the Warsaw School of Architecture since 1946: Assistant Lecturer on Town Planning, 1946–51; Deputy Professor, 1951–55; Associate Professor, 1955–65; Professor, since 1965, and Director of the Spatial Planning Institute, since 1971. Visiting Professor, Wroclaw University, 1948, Technical University of Berlin, 1962, Technische Hochschule, Hamburg, 1962, and Essen, 1963, Technical University of Helsinki, 1969, Technische Hochschule, Dresden, 1972, and Darmstadt, 1973, Institute of Regional Planning, Bar-

celona, 1974, Technical University of Vilnius, 1974, Institute of Architecture, Moscow, 1975, and Technische Hochschule, Dresden, 1976. Member of the Council, SARP (Architectural Association of Poland), 1949–55, 1960–70, 1974, and Chairman of the SARP Section at Tychy, Poland, 1955–70; Chairman, Society of Polish Town Planners, 1955–57; Chairman, Town Planning Section, Committee of Architecture and Town Planning, Polish Academy of Science, 1960–75. Exhibitions: *Terra 1*, Wroclaw, Poland, 1975; Exhibition of County Regional Plans, Warsaw, 1978. Collection: Architectural Museum, Wroclaw, Poland. Recipient: Polish 10th Anniversary Medal, 1955; Ministry of Town Planning and Architecture Award, 1955, 1957; Polish Golden Cross of Merit, 1956; Polonia Restituta Cross, 1956; Golden Badge of Merit, Katowice, Poland, 1959; Polish State Prize, 1964; Ministry of Higher Education Prize, 1974; Ministry of the Environment Prize, 1974; 30th Anniversary Medal, 1974; Polish Medal of Merit, 1975; Gottfried von Herder Prize, Vienna, 1976. Member, Order of the Banner of Labour, 1970. Address (office): ul. Orezna 45, Warsaw, Poland.

Publications:

By K. WEJCHERT: books—*The Polish Small Town as a Town Planning Problem*, Warsaw 1947; *Tychy New Town*, Warsaw 1960; *Miasto na warsztacie* (Town in the Making), Warsaw 1969, Warsaw and Washington, D.C. 1974; *Sociological Studies as an Element of Town Planning* (monograph), Warsaw 1970; *Miasto Przyszlosci* (Town of the Future), with Hanna Wejchert, Warsaw 1973; *Elementy kompozycji urbanistycznek* (Elements of Town Planning Composition), Warsaw 1974, in German: Warsaw 1978; *Problemy identyfikacji przestrzeni we wspolczesnyck zespolach mieszkaniowych* (Space Identification in Contemporary Mass Housing Development), Warsaw 1975; *Rola elementow krystalizujacych w planach zabudowania* (Role Played by the Crystallizing Elements in Development Plans), Warsaw 1977; articles—"Prace Zakl. Urb. PW. na Ziemiach Odzyskanych" in *Architektura* (Warsaw), September 1948; "Szesc Ratuszy," with Hanna Wejchert, in *Architektura* (Warsaw), April 1950; "Piekne miasta" in *Miasto* (Warsaw), August 1952; "Indywidualnosc miasta a prefabrykacja" in *Miasto* (Warsaw), April 1956; "Tychy New Town" in *Town and Country Planning* (London), April 1956; "Nowe Tychy" in *Architektura* (Warsaw), June 1957; "Städtebau in Polen" in *Städtebau in Ausland*, Berlin 1963; "Problemy Miast Szybko Rozwijajacych sie w Polsce," with Hanna Wejchert, in *Miasto* (Warsaw), September 1964; "Uzbrojenie Podziemne Miasta a Przemiany Struktury Przestrzennej Osadnictwa," with Hanna Wejchert, in *Miasto* (Warsaw), April 1965; "Tereny i urzadzenia sportowe w planowaniu przestrzennym" in *Urzadzenia sportowe*, Warsaw 1966; "Designing and Executing Sports Facilities in Tychy" in *Biuletyn IUA* (Warsaw), no. 30, 1972; "Presentation: Tychy New Town," with Hanna Wejchert, in *Architektura* (Warsaw), February 1972; "Uwagi o Mieszkaniu Przyszlosci," with Hanna Wejchert, in *Sprawy Mieszkaniowe* (Warsaw), February 1973; "Spatial Structure of Small and Middle Size Towns," with Hanna Wejchert, in *Geographia Polonica* (Warsaw), no. 32, 1975; "New Towns in Poland," with Hanna Wejchert, in *New Towns*, University Park, Pennsylvania 1976.

See WEJCHERT, Hanna

WIENS, Clifford (Donald).

Canadian. Born in Glen Kerr, Saskatchewan, 27 April 1926. Educated at Banff School of Fine Arts, Alberta, 1945; University of Saskatchewan, Saskatoon, 1946; Moose Jaw Technical School, Saskatchewan, 1948; Rhode Island School of Design, Providence, 1949–54, B.Arch. 1954. Married Patricia Elizabeth Leigh in 1955; children: Mieka, Robin, Inga, Susan, Nathan, and Lisa. Designer, Stock and Ramsay, architects, Regina, Saskatchewan, 1954–55, and Joseph Pettick, architect, Regina, 1955–57. Since 1957, President, Wiens and Associates, Regina. Visiting Lecturer, University of Saskatchewan Faculty of Sociology and Faculty of Art, 1966–67; Visiting Professor, University of Manitoba, Winnipeg, 1968; Visiting Lecturer, North Dakota State University, Grand Forks, 1970; Visiting Professor, University of Calgary, 1977. President, Saskatchewan Association of Architects, 1970; Member of the Canadian Advisory Committee on Art for Public Buildings, Ottawa, 1974–76. Exhibitions: Canadian Federation of Artists Exhibition, 1964, 1969, 1970; *The Architecture of Clifford Wiens*, Art Gallery of Ontario, Toronto, 1967. Recipient: Merit Award, and Award of Excellence, National Design Council of Canada, 1967; Precast Concrete Institute Award, United States and Canada, 1967; Massey Medal, 1967, 1970; First Award, American Institute of Architects, 1975. Fellow, Royal Architectural Institute of Canada; Associate, Royal Canadian Academy of Arts. Address (office): 2139 Albert Street, Regina, Saskatchewan S4P 2V1, Canada.

Works:

1959   St. Joseph's Church, Whitewood, Saskatchewan
       Pense Elementary School, Pense, Saskatchewan
1960   Pilot Butte School, Pilot Butte, Saskatchewan
       Bell City Motel, Regina
       Kern Motel, Regina
       Kenley Apartments, Regina
       Interprovincial Steel Company Building, Regina
       Balgonie School, Balgonie, Saskatchewan
       Lumsden Eight-Room School, Lumsden, Saskatchewan
1961   St. Mark's Candle Schop, Lumsden, Saskatchewan
       Spivak Apartments, Regina
       Cindercrete Plant, Regina
       4 auditoriums for the Regina Public School Board
1962   Mennonite Brethren Church, Hill Avenue, Regina
       Morse High School, Morse, Saskatchewan
       Kramer House, Mission Lake, Saskatchewan
1963   Lashburn Ten-Room School, Lashburn, Saskatchewan
       Morton House, Regina
       Lough House, Regina
1964   Lebret School, Lebret, Saskatchewan
       Herbert School additions, Herbert, Saskatchewan
1965   McCannell School, Regina
       Darke Hall additions, University of Saskatchewan, Regina
       Weyburn Service Centre, Weyburn, Saskatchewan
       Poultry Science and Horticultural Building, University of Saskatchewan, Saskatoon (project)
1966   North Battleford Service Centre, North Battleford, Saskatchewan
       Lumsden School, Lumsden, Saskatchewan
       Maple Creek Camp and Picnic Grounds Administration Building, Trans-Canada Highway, Maple Creek, Saskatchewan
       Ward Johnston Warehouse, Saskatoon, Saskatchewan
       Lloydminster Creamery Plant, Lloydminster, Saskatchewan

Clifford Wiens: Central Heating and Cooling Plant, University of Saskatchewan, Regina, 1967

1967 Minto Christian Education Centre, Moose
      Jaw, Saskatchewan
      Church of Our Lady, Moose Jaw, Saskatche-
      wan
      Central Heating and Cooling Plant, Univer-
      sity of Saskatchewan, Regina
      Percival Mercury Motor Sales Building,
      Regina
      Melfort Co-op Creamery Plant, Melfort, Sas-
      katchewan
1968 4-H Campsite, Birsay, Saskatchewan
      Hodgeville-Central Butte School additions,
      Saskatchewan
1969 Crestview Chrysler Showroom, Regina
      Silton Chapel, Silton, Saskatchewan
1970 Simpson School additions, Yorkton, Sas-
      katchewan
      Holy Rosary Cathedral interior renovations,
      Regina
      Bertmar Investments Store, Moose Jaw, Sas-
      katchewan
1971 Blakeney House, Regina
1972 St. Joseph School additions, Regina
      Maintenance Building, University of Sas-
      katchewan, Regina
      Unity Separate School additions, Unity, Sas-
      katchewan
      Legislative Building renovations, Regina
      Engineering and Physics Building, University
      of Saskatchewan, Regina (project; with
      others)

1973 Motor Services Shop, Regina
      Traders' Building renovations, Regina
      Mount Royal School, Regina
      Yorkton Creamery Plant, Yorkton, Saskatch-
      ewan
1974 Toronto/Dominion Head Office Building,
      Regina
      Public Library and Art Gallery, Swift Cur-
      rent, Saskatchewan
      Spa Building, Nakusp Hot Springs, British
      Columbia
1975 Native Auto Shredder Plant, Regina
      East Central School, Prince Albert, Saskatch-
      ewan
      Saskatchewan Association of Rural
      Municipalities Office Building, Regina
1976 Dr. Martin LeBoldus High School, Regina
      Joseph Burr Tyrrell High School, Fort Smith,
      North West Territories
      Native Metal Industries Office Building,
      Regina

1977 Elementary School, Regina
      Senior Citizens Recreation Centre, Prince Al-
      bert, Saskatchewan
      Senior Citizens Apartment Complex, Wey-
      burn, Saskatchewan
      Canadian Imperial Bank of Commerce Data
      Service Centre, Regina
      Holy Rosary Cathedral restoration (after
      fire), Regina

1978 Royal Bank of Canada Office Building,
      Regina
      Fire Station No. 6, Regina
      Hillsdale Baptist Church, Regina
      Royal Canadian Mounted Police Swimming
      Pool, Regina (project)
      Canadian Broadcasting Corporation Studio,
      Regina (project)
      Camrose Lutheran College, Camrose, Al-
      berta (project)
      Study of the Moose Jaw River Valley, Sas-
      katchewan
      National Gallery of Canada, Ottawa (compe-
      tition project)

Publications:

By WIENS: book—*Silton Chapel,* Vancouver 1970;
articles—"The Design Canada Structural Steel
Awards Program" in *Design Canada* (Ottawa),
1966; "The Design Canada Concrete Institute
Awards Program" in *Design Canada* (Ottawa),
1967; "Weather Shelter" in *Canadian Architect*
(Toronto), October 1972; "Spiral Tee Pee" in *Wood
World* (Vancouver), Summer 1972.

On WIENS: book—*The Architecture of Clifford
Wiens,* exhibition catalogue, Toronto 1967; articles
—"St. Joseph's, Whitewood, Saskatchewan" in *Ca-
nadian Architect* (Toronto), February 1961; "Inter-

provincial Steel Office Building" and "St. Mark's Shop" in *Canadian Architect* (Toronto), March 1962; "Hill Avenue Mennonite Brethren Church, Regina" in *Royal Architectural Institute of Canada Journal* (Toronto), December 1963; "Architecture of the Prairies" by Hans Elte in *Royal Architectural Institute of Canada Journal* (Toronto), June 1965; "Administration Building" in *Canadian Architect* (Toronto), November 1966; "Significant Architects '67" in the *Canadian Architects Yearbook,* Toronto 1967; "Out on the Plains" in *Progressive Architecture* (New York), September 1970; "That Magnificent Mud-Reinforced Concrete" by Walter McQuade in *Fortune* (New York), December 1970; "National Gallery Competition Results" in *Canadian Architect* (Toronto), April 1977; "Superstars of the Skyscrapers" in *En Route* (Toronto), March 1978.

The process of design for an architectural commission has become extremely complex. It is a complexity that needs to be understood and identified. A kind of equation must be struck that gives weight to the order of priorities that will guide the design process. Central to this equation is the reality of the client. With each commission the fullest respect and attention should be given to the client's needs and resources. To do otherwise is to lose credibility and consequently the opportunity to serve again, for without the client the privilege of shaping space does not exist. That the client may experience a new design awareness in the design process should be anticipated and understood by the architect. Frequently the limits set by the client at the beginning of a project are not the same limits set at the end of the project. The architect must therefore develop the ability to communicate the evolutionary design possibilities to the client at the formative stages.

The focus of architecture exists in the expression of both the essential and the unique. It is my conviction that there is a quality of uniqueness inherent in each design problem. To remove the element of uniqueness from architecture, as is occurring in the somewhat mindless mass production of buildings today, represents a kind of technical cloning for which we can, at best, only congratulate ourselves at having mastered technique. To clearly articulate the essential and unique activities of human use, the essential and unique aspects of the site and the essential and unique characteristics of available materials and construction systems represents, for me, the excitement of the design process.

The design process can begin very slowly towards synthesis or spring full blown, depending on the understanding that is brought to the design problem. Where it must begin slowly, the process is one of developing a working relationship of all elements, however mediocre the articulation of that relationship may be at first. As these relationships develop, I begin to identify what is essential and what is unique and concurrently begin to search for the kind of spatial configurations that will enclose and separate human activity with the greatest clarity. From the understanding of spatial needs, a structural framework begins to suggest itself. It is extremely important, at this point, that the fullest implications of all technical and environmental concerns are fully realized. Each element of the design should fulfill itself in terms of its own discipline while contributing to the whole. The design process, therefore, involves many cycles of critical analysis, each cycle spawning its own mutations. It is often these mutative developments that offer the greatest opportunity for unique and expressive qualities in the design. When a design is most fitting to its use and to the spirit of its own making, it can be considered to be complete, to be fully synthesized, to be unique.

—Clifford Wiens

Clifford Wiens has the ability to distill a building to its essence and to express the distillation in simple floor plans and eye-catching forms. Most of his buildings are modest in size and limited in function,

so his approach to design has yet to pass the test of a complex programme. This does not, however, detract from the effectiveness of what he has already done.

His Administration Building for Maple Creek Camp, the Silton Chapel, the Mennonite Brethren Church in Regina, the Interprovincial Steel Company Building and his Heating Plant for the University of Saskatchewan all have symmetrical plans. The Silton Chapel and the heating plant are perfect squares. His weather shelter design is a helix; the St. Mark's Shop is a circle, with circular port-hole windows. Wiens' preoccupation, then, with rigid and simple geometry is evident.

Although his plans are formal and static, it is in three dimensional form that Wiens lightens his seriousness and achieves some of the memorable effects that have enhanced his reputation. It must be remembered that he is designing for the Canadian prairie, and he seems to want to do two things: to express in built form the horizontality of his sites and also to interrupt this horizontality visually in order to make his building stand out as an "event." One of his standard techniques is to isolate the roof structure from the main base of the building; in effect, this allows a horizontal plan to pass visually through the elevation. The floating roof structure is then free to be exploited as a "flag" and is frequently enhanced by sinking the base of the building into the ground (as in the Silton Chapel and the St. Mark's Shop). By these means he achieves both purposes—expressing the horizontal site yet interrupting it. Lowering the building also gives a sense of shelter (though, ironically, his weather shelter is not lowered). This is one of the few concessions Wiens makes to the harshness of his environment; he is more consistently concerned with a visual response than a physical one. Nevertheless, his buildings are not inappropriate, and visually they make a strong and sensible contribution to the built environment of his region.

—Kent Hurley

WILL, Philip, Jr.
American. Born in Rochester, New York, 15 February 1906. Educated in Rochester public schools, 1912–22; Phillips Academy, Exeter, New Hampshire, 1922–24; Cornell University College of Architecture, Ithaca, New York, 1924–30 (Clifton Beckwith Brown Medal; Charles Goodwin Sands Medal; Thesis Medal, 1930), B.Arch. 1930. Married Caroline Elizabeth Sinclair in 1933; children: Elizabeth and Philip. Worked as an architectural draftsman, Gordon and Kaelber Architects, Rochester, 1928–29, and Shreve, Lamb and Harmon, New York, 1930–33; Associate Architect, General Houses Inc., Chicago, 1933–34, and South Park Gardens, 1934. Founding Partner, with Lawrence Perkins, *q.v.*, and E. Todd Wheeler, Perkins, Wheeler and Will, Chicago, 1935–46, subsequently Perkins and Will, 1946–64, and the Perkins and Will Partnership, 1964–70; Senior Vice-President, 1970–71, and Vice-Chairman, 1970–73, Director since 1973, and Chairman since 1975, Perkins and Will Architects Inc., Chicago; offices established in New York, 1951, and Washington, D.C., 1962. Director, Illinois Council, American Institute of Architects, 1947–49; Director, 1947–51, Second Vice-President, 1951–52, and President, 1952–54, Chicago Chapter of the AIA; Chairman, Citizens of Greater Chicago, 1954; President of the Alumni Council of the College of Architecture, 1954–56, Trustee, 1963–73, and Chairman of the Trustee Committee on Buildings and Grounds, 1966–73, Cornell University; Second Vice-President, 1956–58, First Vice-President, 1958–60, and President, 1960–62, National AIA; Member, 1959–64, and Chairman, 1965, City of Evanston (Illinois) Planning Commission; Chairman, Committee on the

Performance Concept, Building Research Advisory Board, Washington, D.C., 1965. Recipient: Cruceiro Sul do Brasil, 1961; Special Citation of Merit, AIA, 1968; 25 Year Award, AIA, 1971; The Cornell Medal, 1973. Fellow, American Institute of Architects, 1951. Honorary Fellow, Royal Architectural Institute of Canada, and the Philippine Institute of Architects; Honorary Member, Le Sociedad de Arquitectos Mexicanos, and La Sociedad de Arquitectos del Peru. Address: Perkins and Will Architects Inc., 309 West Jackson Boulevard, Chicago, Illinois 60606, U.S.A.

Works:

1933 Logan House, Northfield, Illinois (as associate architect to Howard Fisher)
1934 Steel House, *Century of Progress Exposition,* Chicago (for General Houses Inc.)
1937 Philip Will Jr. Residence, Evanston, Illinois
1939/
40 Crow Island School, Winnetka, Illinois (with Eliel and Eero Saarinen)
1952 Heathcote School, Scarsdale, New York
1954 Rockford Memorial Hospital, Illinois
1957 Willage (Philip Will Jr. Summer Cottage), Higgins Lake, Michigan
1958 Cornell University Engineering Campus, Ithaca, New York
      International Minerals and Chemical Corporation Building, Skokie, Illinois
1960 Pure Oil Company Office Building, Palatine, Illinois
      Stamford Hospital, Connecticut
1963 U.S. Gypsum Building, Chicago
1964 National College of Agriculture, Chapingo, Mexico
1965 Scott Foresman Office Building, Glenview, Illinois
      Lutheran School of Theology, Chicago
1966 First National Bank, Chicago (with C. F. Murphy Associates)
      Salsbury Laboratories, Charles City, Iowa
1967 Orchard Ridge Campus, Oakland Community College, Farmington, Michigan
1969 Abbott Laboratories, Lake County, Illinois

Publications:

By WILL: articles—"The Future of the Architectural Profession" in *Louisiana Architect* (New Orleans), December 1961; "Ahead Lies a New Frontier" in *Florida Architect* (Miami), January 1962; "The Architect Serves His Community" in *AIA Journal* (Washington, D.C.), May 1962.

On WILL: articles—"The Perkins and Will Partnership" in *Building Construction* (Chicago), April 1969; "Return of the Megastructure" by Suzanne Stephens in *Architectural Forum* (New York), September 1973; "First National Bank, Chicago" in *Informes de la Construccion* (Madrid), November 1973; "Medical Facilities" in *Architectural Record* (New York), September 1975.

As humane architecture, a building must relate to people. It must provide an environment that delights beholder and occupant, which inspires respect, productivity, and ultimate sense of rightness.

—Philip Will Jr.

Philip Will Jr. is co-founder (with Lawrence Perkins) of Perkins and Will of Chicago, one of America's largest and most active architectural firms.

After working for Gordon and Kaelber in his home town of Rochester, New York, and Shreve, Lamb and Harmon in New York City, Will moved to Chicago and a position with General Houses Inc., a firm headed by architect Howard Fisher. General Houses did early work in pre-fabricated house designs, mostly in the modernist manner. Will, in fact,

Philip Will, Jr.: Heathcote School, Scarsdale, New York, 1952

was responsible for the pre-fabricated steel house that General Houses showed in the 1934 *Century of Progress Exposition* in Chicago. Three years later he built his own house in Evanston, Illinois, an elegant frame structure whose originality rested in a graceful mixture of the ground-hugging profiles of Frank Lloyd Wright's earlier Prairie Style, with volumetric elements related to the International Style.

The firm of Perkins, Wheeler and Will was established in 1935. Following the lean Depression years, which were marked by only occasional modest residential work, Will and his colleagues undertook their first major commission (with Eliel and Eero Saarinen), the Crow Island School in Winnetka, Illinois. This was a radical design which featured the articulation of individual classrooms and study areas, and Will played a far greater role in the overall planning of Crow Island than he has been given credit for. The project launched Perkins and Will (Wheeler left the firm in 1946) in the design of academic institutions, a field in which they have continued to distinguish themselves.

Perkins and Will's more recent work has been wide-ranging in function and often large in scale. Will himself was chiefly involved in the design of the headquarters for Scott Foresman in Glenview, Illinois and the U. S. Gypsum Building, one of the most discussed works of the post-World War II phase of Chicago commercial building.

—Franz Schulze

WILLERVAL, Jean.

French. Born in Tourcoing, 28 September 1924. Educated at the Ecole Nationale Supérieure des Beaux-Arts, Paris: studied painting, 1943–44, and architecture, 1945–51. Married the architect Anna Mazurkiewicz in 1951; children: Carine, Isabelle and Bruno. In private practice, Paris, since 1959; established office in Lille, 1962 (associates: Pierre Rignols; André Lagarde). Consultant Architect to the French Ministry of Equipment, since 1964; Consultant Architect for the Paris Master Plan, since 1975; Member of the Commission on Architecture and Urbanism of the City of Paris, since 1976. Professor, Department of Architecture, Ecole Nationale Supérieure des Beaux-Arts, Paris, since 1958; Professor and Chairman, l'Ecole Supérieure d'Architecture de San Luc, Tournai, Belgium, since 1964. Recipient: First Prize, Pre-Fabricated Schools Competition, 1960; First Prize, Town Hall Plaza Competition, Lille, 1961; First Prize, Palace of Justice Competition, Lille, 1962; First Prize, National Agronomic Research Center Competition, Theix, 1962; First Prize, Lille-Roubaix-Tourcoing Center Competition, 1970; First Prize, Doubs District Administration Buildings Competition, 1972; Grand Silver Medal, Académie d'Architecture, 1972; First Prize, Lille-Est New Town Commercial Center Competition, 1973; First Prize, National Family House Competition, 1974; Grand National Prize in Architecture, 1975. Member, Académie d'Architecture; Chevalier, Order of Arts and Letters, 1976. Address

(office): 52 rue Pernety, 75014 Paris, France.

Works:

1962/
73   12,000 flats in French new towns
1963/
75   National Institute of Agronomic Research, Theix, France
1968   Hall of Justice, Lille
1973   Fire Brigade Barracks (Caserne Masséna), Boulevard Masséna, Paris
1974   Pernod Factory and Headquarters, Créteil, France
1975   Town Hall, Bordeaux
1976   Banque Populaire du Nord Headquarters, Lille
      Lock Lookout Station, Lille
      "Le Forum" Business and Shopping Center, Lille
1977   Nuclear power plants in Flamanville, Belleville, and St. Alban/St. Maurice, France
      Town Hall, Fort-de-France, Martinique
      "Le Mercure" Business Center, Roubaix, France
      Hypermarket, Lille, France
1978   Polish Consulate, Lille

Publications:

On WILLERVAL: articles—"Fire Station on the Boulevard Masséna" in *Architecture Francaise*

Jean Willerval: Fire Brigade Barracks, Boulevard Masséna, Paris, 1973

(Paris), July/August 1973; "Nuclear Centres" in *Crée* (Paris), February 1976; "Centre Mercure, Roubaix" in *L'Architecture d'Aujourd'hui* (Paris), February 1979.

My ideas on architecture are simple. When I have to construct a building, whatever it is, I always start with the principle that I have to create a master work —in the medieval sense of the word—that is to say, a perfect work, complete in all its details. This work is meant for the men who will live or work there. Of course, it must meet all the functional criteria that our age requires, but I am less and less of a purist in this respect. Contrary to what one might think, dry and precise functionalism is not an exact science and can be adapted to an unusual fantasy born from structural requirements or the nature of the site.

The problem with architecture is mastery of the constructed space: interior and exterior are but one, and one must pass from one to the other without a break. There is no facade street, no facade garden; all facets of the work must be treated nobly. Man inhabits this place, and he has to find himself at ease both inside and out, and there is no detail that can be neglected in the arrangement of the place where he lives and works.

When I am asked to construct large buildings that are to take their place in a city's profile, I still believe that we must construct buildings that, by their quality, their proportions, their beauty, will polarize the diffuse feelings of citizens who like to refer to "places" that attract them and of which they are proud. A town hall is not a magma of cells more or less well put together; it is a public "place." It is built once every 100 or 200 years and is above passion and party. It must be exemplary; it must provoke the pride of citizens by its serene beauty.

I do not construct a building thinking that it may be destroyed in ten years. I have a horror of provisional architecture. I take my profession seriously.

As for the architectural signature that I seek, it is to be found in three complimentary goals: 1) unity within and without—emphasis on the built sector without artifice and without deceit but without depriving oneself of the pleasure of the design of forms, and a search for transparencies, for the path of light through the building, giving it life, as with time passing; 2) creation according to the scale of vision of the passerby who doesn't lift his head, a varied and familiar world that both attracts and distracts him; and 3) appropriateness—the consideration, finally, that a large building takes its place in the city and that its own beauty can be an end in itself. One reaches for another scale of values. This architecture is seen; it belongs to everyone; it should be a source of joy for those who contemplate it every day.

—Jean Willerval

Jean Willerval occupies a not insignificant position among French architects of the post-war generation. He is a conscientious worker who wants to do architecture rather than business and to recognize his responsibilities rather than to escape them in woolly theorizing, absurd non-architecture, scandalous utopias or the fashion for the past. His work is distinguished not by any apparent consistency but by a continual search, more or less successful and always sincere. He does not yet seem to have found the way to express his personality, but it is likely that maturity will help him to develop a more distinctive line.

Worthy of particular mention among his principal executions are the Hall of Justice, Lille, still bearing the traces of his academic training as an architect but already showing his desire to be of his time; the excellent Fire Station on on the Boulevard Masséna in Paris; but especially his building for the apertif firm of Pernod in the new town of Créteil, near Paris, where Willerval gives proof of a great mastery of form and of a controlled freedom in the conception of the whole as well as in the details.

—Pierre Vago

WILLIAMS, Amancio.

Argentinian. Born in Buenos Aires, 19 February 1913. Educated at the University of Buenos Aires, Faculty of Engineering, 1931–34, and Faculty of Architecture, 1938–41, Dip.Arch. 1941. Served as a Reserve Officer in the Argentine Air Force, 1934–38. Married; children: Veronica, Florencia, Teresa, Ines, Gloria, Claudio, and Pablo. In private practice, as architect, designer and city planner, Buenos Aires, since 1941. Exhibitions: International Exhibition of Architecture, Paris, 1947; Harvard University, Cambridge, Massachusetts, 1951, 1955 (one-man); *Architecture of Latin America,* Museum of Modern Art, New York, 1955–56; University of Buenos Aires, 1955 (one-man); *World's Fair,* Brussels, 1958; International Exposition, Moscow, 1958; *Bienal,* Sao Paulo, 1961; *Art of Latin America Since Independence,* Yale University, New Haven, Connecticut, 1966; Museum of Modern Art, New York, 1968; Universidad de la Republica, Montevideo, 1975; *Visionary Drawing of Architecture and Planning,* Drawing Center, New York, 1979. Recipient: Gold Medal, *World's Fair,* Brussels, 1958; Laurel de Plata Award, Ateneo Roariano, Buenos Aires, 1971; Biennial Honor Award, Sociedad Central de Arquitectos, Argentina, 1972. Member, National Academy of Fine Arts, Buenos Aires, 1959. Honorary Fellow, American Institute of Architects, 1962; Honorary Member, Institute of Hispanic Culture, 1965; Honorary Member, College of Architects of Peru, 1965; Honorary Architect, University of Montevideo, 1970; Honorary Professor, Universidad Nacional Federico Villareal, Lima, Peru, 1977. Address (office): Virrey Loreto 1940, Buenos Aires 1426, Argentina.

Works:

1939 High-Rise Building (project)
1942 Dwellings in Space, Buenos Aires (project; with Delfina Galvez de Williams and Jorge Vivanco)
    Jorge Black House, Bariloche, Argentina
1942/
43 Casa Amarilla O.V.R.A. Housing Development, Buenos Aires (project)
    Extendible Partition Wall (project)
1942/
53 Concert Hall (Hall for Plastic Spectacle and Sound), Buenos Aires
1943 Complex of Apartment Blocks, Buenos Aires (project)
    House in the Parque Pereyra Iraola, Mar del Plata, Argentina
    House in Martinez, Albardon, Buenos Aires Province
    House, Buenos Aires (project)
    Triangular Housing Block, Mar del Plata, Argentina (project)
    Regional plan for Patagonia, Argentina
1943/
45 "House on the Stream," Mar del Plata River Valley, Argentina
1944 House, Escobar, Buenos Aires Province
    Transport and communications study, Buenos Aires
1945 Country house, General Pueyrredon District, near Mar del Plata, Argentina (with Jorge Butler)
    International Airport, Buenos Aires (project; with Cesar Janello, Colette Boccara and Jorge Butler)
    Plan for the City of Buenos Aires
1946 Armchair in Leather and Wood
    Office and commercial complex, Buenos Aires (with Cesar Janello, Colette Boccara and Jorge Butler)
1947 National master plan for the Ministry of Public Health, Argentina
1947/
58 Regional plan for the Parana Delta and Buenos Aires Region

1948 Central City Redevelopment, Cordoba, Argentina (project; with Gomes Molina)
    City and regional plan for Corrientes, Argentina
    Missionary-Boat for Disease Prevention in the Parana Delta, Argentina (project)
    Office Building Suspended by Cables, Buenos Aires (project)
1948/
53 Curuzu-Cuatia Hospital, Corrientes, Argentina
    Esquina Hospital, Corrientes, Argentina
    Mburucuya Hospital, Corrientes, Argentina
1949 Design of the *Architecture and Urbanism of Our Times* exhibition, Galeria Kraft, Calle Florida, Buenos Aires
    Doctor's house and surgery, Palermo, Buenos Aires
1949/
50 Various objects in steel and plastic
1951 House for a horticulturist, El Tigre, Argentina
1951/
52 Reinforced Concrete Vaulted Roof (prototype; with Julio Pizetti)
1952 House with ground-floor shop, Munro, Argentina
1953 House in the Forest, Parana Delta, Argentina (project)
1954 Various pre-fabricated structures
1954/
55 Reinforced Concrete Shell Service Station, Avellaneda, Argentina (project)
1955 Health Center, Mar del Plata, Argentina (project)
1955/
57 Apartment building, Buenos Aires (project)
1956/
57 Bedroom and library furniture
    Francisco de Ridder Apartment interiors, Avenida Alvear 1491, Buenos Aires
1957/
58 Regional and city plan for El Tigre, Argentina
1958 Ignacio Pirovano Penthouse conversion, Buenos Aires
1959 Universidad Catolica Argentina alterations and renovations, Buenos Aires
1960 Huinca-Loo Mansion extensions and alterations, Province of Buenos Aires
    Industrial School with Shell Roof, Olvarria, Argentina (project)
    Textiles Supermarket and Showrooms, Bernal, Argentina
    Monument for the Marist International Congress, Buenos Aires
1961 Di Tella Family Summer House and Art Gallery, Punta del Este, Argentina (project)
    Olivetti Company Housing Estate (competition project)
1962 Furniture shop (conversion of existing apartment building), Buenos Aires
    20-storey building, Avenida Libertador, Buenos Aires (project)
    Iggam Company Factory and Office Building, Cordoba, Argentina (project)
    Monument to the Composer Alberto Williams, Buenos Aires
1963 Apartment alterations, Gelly Obes and Guido Streets, Buenos Aires
    Alterations to 2 floors of an apartment building, Hippolito Irigoyen 1782, Buenos Aires
1964 Library, Students Residence, Zavalia 2048, Buenos Aires
    Pastoral Care Center, Berlin (project)
1965 Biochemical Laboratory, Juncal 1720, Buenos Aires (project)
1966 Olivetti Shop and Showrooms alterations, Buenos Aires (project)
    Olivetti Exhibition Pavilions (project)
    Bunge y Born Pavilion, Sociedad Rural Building, Buenos Aires

Amancio Williams: Concert Hall, 1953 (model)

1967/
68 Church of Our Lady of Fatima, Pilar, Argentina

1967/
70 Obra Bonomo Architects' Offices, Buenos Aires

1968 West German Embassy, Plaza Alemania, Buenos Aires (project)

Argentine Industrial Union Building, Buenos Aires (competition project; with Luis Santos, Alejandro Bonomo, and Eduardo Rojkind)

High-Rise Building, Buenos Aires (project)

1968/
69 Tilda Thamar House, Vte. Lopez District, Buenos Aires (project)

1968/
71 Sirio Libanes Country Club, Pergamino, Argentina (with Ricardo Mackinlay and Delfina Galvez de Williams)

1969 San Vicente de Paul Hospital, Oran-Salta, Argentina (competition project; with Luis Santos)

Canumar-Empresa Naviera Office Building, Calle 25 de Mayo, Buenos Aires (project; with Luis Santos)

Juan Carlos Ongania House, Las Lomas de San Isidro, Argentina (project; with Luis Santos)

Raul Desmaras House, Las Lomas de San Isidro, Argentina (project; with Luis Santos)

Bernardo Mandelbaum House, San Isidro Boating Club, Argentina (project; with Eduardo Leston)

1969/
70 Cultural Center, Cume-Co Estate, Pirovano, Buenos Aires Province (project)

1970 L.U.9 Radio Station, Mar del Plata, Argentina

1971/
72 City and neighborhood planning study of Corrientes, Argentina

1972 Monument to the Victims of the 1971 Air Disaster, Buenos Aires (project)

1974/
75 The City That Humanity Needs (urban study project)

1977 Bonomo Office alterations, Buenos Aires

Ignacio Pirovano Apartment alterations, Parera 3, Buenos Aires

S.A.C.A.F.I. Offices, Sargentos 435, Buenos Aires

1978 Office building, Belgrano, Buenos Aires (project)

Publications:

By WILLIAMS: articles—"La Ciudad que Necesita la Humanidad" in *Clarín* (Buenos Aires), 25 November 1977; "Orientar al País para Abordar una Nueva Época" in *La Nación* (Buenos Aires), 12 October 1978; film—*Altar Monumental: Primer Congreso Mariano Interamericano,* with Horacio Coppola, Buenos Aires 1960.

On WILLIAMS: book—*Amancio Williams* by Raul Gonzalez Capdevila, Buenos Aires 1955; article—"La Concepciones del diseño en la trascendente obra de Amancio Williams" in *Conviccion* (Buenos Aires), 26 May 1979; films—*Amancio Williams* by Manuel Antin, Buenos Aires 1967; *Amancio Williams,* produced by Sucesos Argentinos, Buenos Aires 1968; *Departamento de Ignacio Pirovano* by David Lamelas, Buenos Aires 1971.

The realization of my work has been very difficult here in Argentina, but I consider that its importance is in the value of its ideas.

In the last few years I have been very active studying and promoting a theme that is, I think, at this moment, the great need of mankind. It has to do with human habitat. Until now I have used as a title (and also as a slogan) "The City That Humanity Needs." The press in Argentina and Uruguay have given me a great deal of support. All of the newspapers and the best magazines have published articles, and I have lectured on the radio and television, at the National Academy of Fine Arts, and at the University of Uruguay. Considering that the Argentina newspapers have a circulation of something like 500,000 copies, I suppose that until now, in different issues, more than 10 million copies have been circulated on this theme. Now, critics in the States have begun paying attention to this work, and I have been asked to lecture there.

—Amancio Williams

As a foreword to a magazine presentation of the works of Amancio Williams, in 1947, Le Corbusier wrote: "The three Americas, which up to fifty years ago were still the land of colonists and colonization, are still countries which aspire to steep themselves in the latest branches of knowledge. Life races ahead there: these countries beckon life, and life bursts in them. It manifests itself through a form of building which develops beyond all our customs, all our conceptions. Here we have Buenos Aires, which, through succeeding jolts, through contrast and reaction, and through the action of limited but intensely cultivated groups, an avant-garde society, reaches the level of the most captivating reality in architecture. Here we find, for instance, as a first post-war contact, the fresh appearance of creations in the fields of city planning and architecture, filled with the breadth of oceans and of the pampas, a great breadth, liberated from meanness. Here, then, are the works of Amancio Williams and of his team in Buenos Aires."

The quotation is apt, for Amancio Williams, who was then 34 years old, had already carried out the Dwellings in Space project, a project for an airport for Buenos Aires, and, in particular, had designed and overseen the construction of the famous House on the Stream in Mar del Plata, considered "the most audacious and independent creation of that generation of Argentine architects." That decade, the 1940's, saw the greatest output from Williams, who was to have a notable influence on a professional environment that was still strongly tied to more or less orthodox "styles" and (with a few isolated exceptions) hadn't seemed to notice the existence of a new architecture emerging as a consequence of European and American movements at least thirty years earlier.

Unfortunately, Williams's studies and projects are much more numerous than his actual buildings, perhaps because, as he himself observes, the necessary finance to realize such projects is always missing. Nevertheless, those studies have profoundly affected not only Argentine architects but also all those who have seen them at exhibitions throughout the world and in the architectural press. He has been, and remains, a master of contemporary Argentine architecture.

His principles, in his own words, are: "working with every freedom in space; handling the three dimensions freely; searching within technology for true expression; working with a sense of unity; reaching a synthesis; working with a sense of the permanent." And, it is necessary to "employ all of our creative forces, the forces of culture, and to apply science to our development." The two constants in all his work are the application of science and the manipulation of, and attention to, space.

A fundamental concern of his work has been to free the ground of the city, to respect or create green spaces—he admires Le Corbusier's "building in space" concept. This interest in spatiality applies to individual buildings as well as to cities as a whole: besides the works mentioned above, his projects for an office building in downtown Buenos Aires and his Hall for Plastic Spectacle and Sound also demonstrate his consistent and continuous interest in space —as do his more recent studies in the field of planning.

Three works remain seminal.

The House on the Stream, completed in 1945, was an attempt to achieve a three-dimensional structure which would leave the ground level free, that is, an integrated and complex system that would do away with pillar supports. His solution was to achieve support via a curved foil with a parabolic section, which works in conjunction with the concrete floor of the main level of the dwelling and with the beams that surround it, in such a way that the tensions of the whole determined the final shape.

In an urban environment, there is his project for an office building. It was conceived as having an outer structure of four huge concrete columns with beams and upper arcades, also made of concrete, from which were hung the horizontal planes of each floor, through the employment of steel struts acting exclusively through traction—thus eliminating columns from the standard storey. The complex was of four blocks separated from one another and from the ground by airy open spaces which, in the case of the access level tier, reached a height of almost twenty metres.

Presenting his project for Dwellings in Space in 1942—set up on an urban lot measuring 14.50 × 43 m., between party walls—Williams stated that "the plastic solution is obtained on the basis of technology, the only road to avoid falling into capriciousness," and its cost "turned out to be, when the calculation was made, considerably less than that of an ordinary apartment house of the same category and capacity, which was studied at the same time and the

cost of which estimated for comparison purposes." As well, the Dwellings in Space had the notable advantages of open yard ventilation, natural lighting, exposure to sunlight, natural insulation, and views.

This kind of dwelling, expanded on an urban scale, showed itself to be ideal for creating different types of housing for social groups of differing economic levels. Marcel Breuer noted that the ground surface was made use of in three different ways: for shops, general circulation, etc.; for dwellings; and for gardens. And, as Williams himself pointed out after creating the project, the ground plan of the dwellings presented fundamental analogies with the typical native country house, through the relationship between the three basic elements: house, verandah, and green space.

—Jorge Glusberg

WILLIAMS, Sir (Evan) Owen.

British. Born in Tottenham, London, in 1890. Educated at Tottenham Grammar School, London; University of London, B.Sc. 1911; student/apprentice, Electric Tramways Company, London, 1905–11. Married Gladys Tustian in 1915 (died, 1947): children: one son and one daughter; married Doreen Baker in 1947: children: one son and one daughter. Architect/Engineer, Trussed Concrete Company, later Truscon, London, 1912–13; Chief Aeroplane Designer, Wells Aviation Ltd., London, 1913; in private practice as civil engineer and architect, London, 1919–39; in partnership with T. S. Vandy, London, 1939 until his death, 1969. Consulting Civil Engineer, British Empire Exhibition, London, 1922–24; Consulting Engineer for Motorway Construction to the Ministry of Transport, London, 1945–69. Recipient: Silver Medal, City and Guilds Institute, London, 1911; Telford Gold Medal, Institute of Civil Engineers, London, 1927, 1961. Member, Institution of Civil Engineers; Associate Fellow, Royal Aeronautical Society. K.B.E. (Knight Commander, Order of the British Empire), 1924. Died 23 May 1969.

Works:

1912 Shipyard in reinforced concrete, Poole, Dorset (with Reinforced Concrete Engineers)
Gramophone company factory, Hayes, Middlesex (with Truscon; now the E.M.I. Building)
1913 Prototype aeroplanes, for Wells Aviation Ltd.
1914/
18 Concrete ships
1919 Walls Factory, Acton, London
1920 Tannery, Runcorn, Cheshire
1921 Ice-making plant, Hull, Yorkshire
1922/
24 Stadium and layouts for the British Empire Exhibition, Wembley, London (with J. Simpson and M. Ayrton)
1923 Palace of Industry, British Empire Exhibition, Wembley, London
1925 Parc des Attractions, International Exposition, Paris
1925/
30 Wansford Bridge, Huntingdon
Findhorn Bridge, Scotland
River Spey Bridge, Scotland
Montrose Bridge, Scotland
Lea Valley Viaduct, North Circular Road, London
1926 Cotton seed crushing mill, Adana, Turkey
1930 Cumberland Garage, near Marble Arch, London
Dorchester Hotel, Park Lane, London (consulting engineer in early stages; completed by others)

1932 Boots Factory, Beeston, Nottingham
Daily Express Building, London (as consulting engineer; in association with Ellis and Clarke)
Road/Rail Bridge, Charing Cross, London (project)
Waterloo Bridge, London (project)
1933 Cement factory, Thurrock, Essex
Hunt Partners Factory extension, London
1934 Empire Swimming Pool and Sports Arena, Wembley, London
Pioneer Health Centre, St. Mary's Road, Peckham, London
Sainsbury's Warehouse, Rennie Street, Southwark, London
1935 Lilley and Skinner Warehouse, Pentonville Road, London
1936 Housing, Stanmore, Middlesex
1937 Odhams Printing Works, Watford, Hertfordshire
Provincial Newspapers Offices, Salisbury Square, London
Daily Express Building, Glasgow (as consulting engineer)
Boots Factory, Beeston, Nottingham
Removable restaurant, Wembley Stadium, London
Synagogue, Dollis Hill, London
1939 Daily Express Building, Manchester (as consulting engineer; in association with Ellis and Clarke)
1939/
45 Concrete ships
1945 Motorway design for the U.K. Ministry of Transport (as consulting engineer)
1948 Olympic Games installations, Wembley Stadium, London
1950/
54 British Overseas Airways Corporation Maintenance Headquarters and Hangars, London Airport, Heathrow
1959 Daily Mirror Building, London (as consulting engineer; in association with Anderson, Forster and Wilcox)
M1 Motorway, stage I: London to Birmingham
1966 Viaduct, Port Talbot, Wales
1967 M1 Motorway, stage II: Birmingham to Doncaster, Yorkshire
River Usk Bridge, Newport, Monmouthshire
1,000-foot twin tunnel, Crindau Ridge, Newport, Monmouthshire
1968 Midland Link Motorways
1969 Box-Girder Bridge over the Channel, England to France (project)

Publications:

By WILLIAMS: books—The Philosophy of Masonry Arches, London 1927; The Design and Construction of the M1, with O. T. Williams, London 1961.

On WILLIAMS: articles—"Pioneer Health Centre, Peckham, London" in Architectural Record (New York), June 1935; "Neue Bauten von Sir Owen Williams" in Moderne Bauformen (Stuttgart), November 1935; "Warehouse for Messrs. Lilley and Skinner" in Architectural Review (London), September 1936; "Synagogue at Dollis Hill" in The Architect and Building News (London), 25 March 1938; "Sir Owen Williams" by Alfred Roth in Werk (Zurich), April 1947; "BOAC Headquarters at London Airport" in The Builder (London), 4 November 1955; "The New Mirror Building" in The Architect and Building News (London), 8 March 1961; "Sir Owen Williams" by Michael Gold in Zodiac (Milan), no. 18, 1968; "Sir Owen Williams" by Stephen Rosenberg, Warren Chalk and Stephen Mullin in Architectural Design (London), July 1969.

*   *   *

After practice in civil engineering Sir Owen Williams became structural engineer and architect of several

Sir Owen Williams: Boots Factory, Beeston, Nottingham, 1932

notable buildings during the 1930's. These were designed when the "new architecture," that is functional building with synthetic materials—steel, concrete, glass, laminated timber, plastics and numerous others, in which precise mathematical calculations are possible—was gradually spreading mainly from Germany and Central Europe to England. Owen Williams was among the first in England to use the constructional methods that had been developed, and he used them with considerable success. Such methods often made possible a more efficient fulfilment of the building's purpose.

Among the more spectacular of these buildings is the Boots Factory at Beeston, Nottingham. In this structure he used, for the first time in England I think, concrete mushroom columns supporting large concrete floor slabs, a method invented by the Swiss engineer, Maillart, several years earlier. The edges of the concrete floors form string courses of the otherwise unbroken glass screens that form the walls of this large factory. By this method the utmost natural light could be introduced into large areas of the interior, and it was, when erected, one of the most progressive industrial buildings in Europe.

Owen Williams used the mushroom column and floor slab construction in many subsequent buildings, such as the cement factory at Thurrock in Essex and the Peckham Health Centre, London.

In Maillart's first use of this method the mushroom heads were circular; in Williams' use of them in the Boots Factory they were large square reversed pyramids. In the Peckham Health Centre cantilevered crossheads surmount cruciform columns, an elegant variation of the structure. Architecturally this building represents Williams' finest achievement. It

is a rectangular three-storey structure of reinforced concrete with concrete slab floors, and glass screens for external walls similar to the Boots Factory. The various parts of the building are grouped round a central swimming bath. Particularly effective is the centre part of the south-west facade which has a series of six circular bow windows on the two upper storeys above the arcade columns of the children's recessed play space.

The Empire Swimming Pool, at Wembley, is also a notable structural design. It is one of the largest covered spaces in England, 341 feet long with a roof span of 236 feet. Its building was based on a horizontal grid which permitted the use of standardized units contributing to a speedy erection in about six months. The ingenious pitched roof is constructed of a series of three hinged arches in reinforced concrete buttressed by vertical concrete shafts linked to the concrete gallery and to the roof members by concrete fins, a very conspicuous, rather heavy external feature.

Although essentially a structural engineer, specializing in reinforced concrete, Owen Williams was, at the same time, architect of some of the most notable buildings erected in England in the 1930's. Like many structural engineers he was inclined to consider that if the structure is right and fulfilled its purpose well, then good appearance would come of itself—yet some of his designs, especially that of the Peckham Health Centre—show an undoubted sensitivity to aesthetic effect.

—Arnold Whittick

WILLIAMS-ELLIS, Sir (Bertram) Clough.

British. Born in Northampton, 28 May 1883. Educated at Oundle School; Trinity College, Cambridge; Architectural Association School, London. Served as a Major in the Welsh Guards and the Royal Tank Corps, British Army, 1914–18: Military Cross; mentioned in despatches. Married Amabel Strachey in 1915: children: Susan, Charlotte, and Christopher (died). In private practice, London and Merioneth Wales, 1905–14, 1919 until his death, 1978. Served as First Chairman, Stevenage New Town Development Corporation, Hertfordshire; President, Institute of Landscape Architects; President, Design and Industry Association; Vice-President, Council for the Preservation of Rural England; Chairman, Glass Industry Working Party; Member, Grand Council, British Travel Association; etc. LL.D.: University of Wales, 1971. Fellow, Royal Institute of British Architects. C.B.E. (Commander, Order of the British Empire), 1958; Knighted, 1972. *Died* (in Penrhyndeudraeth, North Wales) *8 April 1978.*

Works:

1905/
14 Small institution building, Oxford
    5 houses, Oxford
    House alterations and additions (2), Oxford
    Sports Pavilion, University College, Oxford
    Aberuchaf Cottage, Abersoch, Caernarvonshire
    Farmhouse, Glasfryn Estate, Caernarvonshire
    Steam Laundry reconstruction, Cambridge
    Village Hall, Stone, near Aylesbury, Buckinghamshire

Park cottages, Cricket St. Thomas, near Chard, Somerset

Farmstead buildings, Byfleet, Surrey

House restoration and alterations, Moynes Park, Essex

House alterations, Normandy Park, Surrey

House alterations, additions and new lodge, Burton Court, Hertfordshire

Princess Christian's Farm Colony, Kent

Rectory, near Pentraeth, Anglesey

Rectory and Church, Prentrefelin, Caernarvonshire

Llangoed Castle rebuilding, Breconshire

Church restoration, Crickadarn, Breconshire

Village Square, Cushendun, County Antrim, Ireland

Hunting box and stables, Brechfa, Carmarthenshire

Sham ruins, on islet near Holyhead, Anglesey

Old people's housing, Swavesey, Cambridgeshire

School reconstruction, farmhouse, monument and gates, Wroxall Abbey, Warwickshire

House restoration, Plas Hen, Dolgellau, Merioneth

Cottages, Guys Cliff, Warwickshire

House, near Woking, Surrey

Cottages, Compton, Surrey

Battersea Dog's Home master plan and rebuilding, London

House, Stanmore, Middlesex

Hunting box and stable alterations, near Finmere, Buckinghamshire

Waddington Manor restoration and alterations, Oxfordshire

Llechwyddgarth Hall restoration and altera-tions, Llangynog, Montgomeryshire

Small industrial hamlet, near Leamington, Warwickshire

House alterations, Stoke Bruern Park, Northamptonshire

Dower House alterations, Easton Neston, Northamptonshire

Entrance gates, Gayton House, Northamptonshire

Cleve Court alterations, Kent

Wolverton Court reconstruction and additions, Warwickshire

Country Life House, Gidea Park, Essex (competition project)

Ridgeway House, near Wellington College, Berkshire

House alterations, Strawberry Hill, Kent

Plas Brondanw orangery, gardens and new lodge, Merioneth

Spectator Cottage, Marrow Downs, Surrey (competition project)

1918/39

War Memorial Tower, Garreg, Merioneth

Palace of Industry, pavilions and displays, *British Empire Exhibition* (1925), Wembley, London (as co-ordinating architect)

House alterations, Gilwell Park, Essex

Glenmona House rebuilding, Cushendun, County Antrim, Ireland

Maud Cottages, Cushendun, County Antrim, Ireland

Cushendun Village additions, County Antrim, Ireland

Lord McNaughton Memorial Hall and School, Giant's Causeway, County Antrim, Ireland

Bushmill Central School, County Antrim, Ireland

Youth Hostel, Loggerheads, Flintshire

Government House alterations, Guernsey, Channel Islands

Memorial Hospital alterations, Portmadoc, Caernarvonshire

Ex-servicemen's housing scheme, Ashtead, Surrey

Hospital, Blaenau Ffestiniog, Merionethshire

St. Cross Mill alterations, Winchester, Hampshire

House restoration, near Ticehurst, Sussex

House restoration and additions, Carregfelin, Caernarvonshire

House with studio and garden, Swiss Cottage, London

3 houses, Hampstead, London

Savoy Court restoration and additions, Denham, Buckinghamshire

House/public school conversion and additions, Stowe, Buckinghamshire

House/Bonar Law College conversions and additions, Ashridge Park, Berkshire

New hamlet, Ashridge Park, Berkshire

Cumnor House, Oxfordshire

Gardens and temples, Eaglehurst, Hampshire

Farm buildings, Avon Tyrel, Hampshire

Summit Station, Mount Snowdon, Caernarvonshire

Church of Christ Scientist, Belfast

House, Belfast

School, Belfast

House, near Romsey, Hampshire

Bolesworth Castle reconstruction and gardens, Cheshire

Hotel conversion, and Angel and Neptune Houses, Portmeirion, Merioneth

Sir Clough Williams-Ellis: Maud Cottages, Cushendun, Northern Ireland, 1925

Kilve Court restoration and alterations, Somerset
Country house, near Andover, Hampshire
House, Littlestone, Kent
Deudraeth Castle/Hotel conversion, Merioneth
House, near Ashburton, Devon
House, Stapledown, Surrey
House, near Walton Heath, Surrey
House alterations and additions, Royston, Hertfordshire
Doctor's house and surgery, Penrhyndeudraeth, Merioneth
White Cottage, near Portmeirion, Merioneth
Girls' boarding school, near Guildford, Surrey
Great Hundridge Manor alterations and additions, Buckinghamshire
Milton Court restoration, Surrey
House alterations, near Burnham, Somerset
House/Hotel conversion and extensions, Newland's Corner, Surrey
Country house and cottage, Harrowhill Copse, Surrey
Co-operative Society Store, Pwllheli, Caernarvonshire
House, Pencaenewydd, Caernarvonshire
Cross Hill House alterations, Adderbury, Oxfordshire
House alterations, Attingham Park, Shropshire
Aitcham House alterations, Shropshire
Layton Hall alterations, Shropshire
New Ladies' Carlton Club and Swimming Pool, London
Grosvenor Crescent, London (demolished)
English Speaking Union, Charles Street, Mayfair, London
Oxford and Cambridge Club Ladies' Annex, Pall Mall, London
Bladen Lodge reconstruction, The Boltons, Kensington, London (demolished)
House reconstruction, 8 Hill Street, Mayfair, London
Marcel Boulestin Restaurant, Leicester Square, London
Sloane House alterations, London
Romney House reconstruction, Hampstead, London
Coed Coch House reconstruction and alterations, Denbighshire
Palatial Official/Commercial Residence, Shanghai, China
2 small houses, Tientsin, China
Leigh Coppings Farm alterations and extensions, Kent
Laugharne Castle alterations, Carmarthenshire
Brondanw Tower, Merioneth
Hubbards Hall reconstruction and additions, Essex
2 houses, Chichester harbour, Sussex
Funtington Lodge alterations, Bosham, Hampshire
Little Cassiobury House alterations and additions, Hertfordshire
House and gardens, Caversham Place, near Reading, Berkshire
Laughton House extensions, Lincolnshire
Methodist Chapel, Llanstumddwy, Caernarvonshire
Farmhouse, Pentrefelin, Caernarvonshire
Bridge, Carmarthen Town
Caversham Heights House additions, Berkshire
New Hall and Chapel, Bishop's Stortford College, Essex
House, Plover's Field, Newland's Corner, Surrey
House restoration, Maids-of-Honour Row, Richmond, Surrey
Cornwell Manor reconstruction, Oxfordshire
Hartsbourne Grange reconstruction, Hertfordshire

Restaurant, Laughing Water, Cobham, Kent
Plan for the town, and 3 houses, Llanbedrog, Caernarvonshire
Doctor's house/surgery conversion, Pwllheli, Caernarvonshire
House, near Brickenden, Hertfordshire
House, Rhos-on-Sea, Denbighshire
House, Deganway, Caernarvonshire

1945/
71 Portmeirion and Brandanw Estates renovation, Merioneth
Plan for the town of Bewdley, Worcestershire
Plan for the town of Weston-super-Mare, Somerset
Doctor's house, Somerset (with Lionel Brett)
Plan for the town of Reddith, Worcestershire (with Patrick Abercrombie and Lionel Brett)
House restoration, Gegin Fawr, Aberdaron, Caernarvonshire
House restoration, Plas-yn-Rhiw, Caernarvonshire
House, near Llanfaelrhys, Caernarvonshire
Home Farm House, Aston Tirrold Manor, Berkshire
Beudy Newydd reconstruction, Merioneth
Glanddyfi Castle alterations, Montgomeryshire
New mansion building, Rhiwlas, Merioneth
New mansion and pavilion, Voelas, Denbighshire
National Forest Park Hall, Caernarvonshire
Warden's house, Beddgelert, Caernarvonshire
Beach cafe/restaurant, Criccieth, Caernarvonshire
Restaurant, Conway Falls, Denbighshire
Old Bridge House alterations, Pembroke Town
New Lodge, Ty Newydd Llanstumddwy, Caernarvonshire
House rebuilding, Plas Brondanw, Merioneth
The Drum House, Croesor, Merioneth
Lloyd George Grave, Memorial and Museum, Caernarvonshire
House restoration and additions, Tyn-y-rhos, Brynkir, Caernarvonshire
Nantclwyd Hall reconstruction with farmhouse and inn additions, Denbighshire
House reconstruction and extensions, Nant-y-Glyn, Caernarvonshire
Giant's Causeway renovations, County Antrim, Ireland
Entrance gates and monument, Bodrhyddan Park, Flintshire
Crown house and gardens, Barford St. John, Oxfordshire
Prescote Manor Gardens, Oxfordshire
House, Porth-y-Castell, Merioneth
Park layout and extensions, Dunwood House, Yorkshire (partially realized)
House alterations and extensions, Cwm Bychan Gerddi Blwog, Merioneth
New buildings and Plas Canol extensions, Portmeirion, Merioneth
New buildings, Dalton Hall, Westmorland
Temple in the Park, Hatton Grange, Shropshire
Lloyd George Memorial, Westminster Abbey, London
Caroline Thorpe Monument, near Cobbaton, Devon

Publications:

By WILLIAMS-ELLIS: books—*Cottage Building in Cob, Pisé, Chalk and Clay,* London and New York 1919, revised edition, with John and Elizabeth Eastwick-Field, as *Cottage Building in Cob, Pisé, and Stabilised Earth,* London 1947; *The Pleasures of Architecture,* with Amabel Williams-Ellis, London 1924, 3rd edition 1954; *England and the Octopus,* London 1928, Portmeirion, Wales 1975; foreword to *The DIA Cautionary Guide to St. Albans,* London 1929; *The Architect,* London 1929; *Land of My Fathers,* with others, London 1930; *Lawrence Weaver,* London 1933; *Architecture Here and Now,* with John Summerson, London 1934; *Britain and the Beast,* editor, London 1937; *Snowdonia,* Portmeirion, Wales 1939; *Plan for Living,* London 1941, 1944; *The Adventure of Building,* London 1946; *On Trust for the Nation,* London 1947; *Royal Festival Hall,* London 1951; *Town and Country Planning,* London 1951; *Portmeirion Still Further Explained,* Birmingham 1956; *Portmeirion: The Place and Its Meaning,* London 1963, Portmeirion, Wales 1973; *Roads in the Landscape,* London 1967; *Architect Errant,* London 1971; *Around the World in Ninety Years,* London 1979.

On WILLIAMS-ELLIS: articles—"Plas Brondanw, Merioneth" by Christopher Hussey in *Country Life* (London), 5 and 12 September 1957; "From Portmeirion" in *The Architect and Building News* (London), 3 August 1966; "Clough's Magnificent Folly" by James Morris in the *Observer Colour Magazine* (London), 7 September 1969; "Antrim's Discreet Holiday Resort" by James Stevens Curl in *Country Life* (London), 6 May 1976; "The Fanciful Genius of Portmeirion Who Built to Delight" by Martin Wainwright and Michael Morris in *The Guardian* (London), 10 April 1978; "Sir Clough Williams-Ellis: Sensibility, Skill and Intuition" by Frederick Gibberd in *Building Design* (London), 14 April 1978; "Sir Clough Williams-Ellis 1883–1978" by E. Maxwell Fry in *RIBA Journal* (London), June 1978.

The contribution to architecture and to the quality of the environment of Sir Clough Williams-Ellis has been considerable, although critics excessively sympathetic to modernism have tended to ignore his achievements.

From the beginnings of his career, Williams-Ellis showed a concern for the environment and for picturesque and pleasing compositions that was anathema to fashionable "progressives." His most famous work, the village of Portmeirion in north Wales, embraces his most characteristic strengths: a respect for the natural site and a love of eclectic motifs to achieve agreeable compositions. Elements derived from Italy and Spain combine with more indigenous domestic vernacular forms to create a modern village that delights the eye. On a smaller scale, but full of visual pleasures, is his work for Ronald and Maud McNeill at Cushendun, County Antrim, Northern Ireland, comprising The Square, Glenmona House, and Maud Cottages.

Both Portmeirion and Cushendun demonstrate the genius of Williams-Ellis as a composer of picturesque architectural groupings. Less well-known today are his works for the Wembley Exhibition of 1925, the Bishop's Stortford College Chapel, the conversion of Ashridge Park in Hertfordshire, and the various churches and schools in England, Wales, and Ireland. His designs for memorials and monuments possess a serenity that owes much to the classical language of architecture, notably the Lloyd George mausoleum and the Westminster Abbey memorial, and the recent monument to the first wife of Jeremy Thorpe. He wrote a fine appreciation of the life and work of Sir Laurence Weaver, the historian of monuments and memorials.

As a writer himself, Williams-Ellis was entertaining, witty, and civilized. His *Cottage Building, England and the Octopus, The Pleasures of Architecture,* and *Architect Errant* are eloquent testimonies of his great love of beauty, his hatred of ugliness and of philistinism, and his immense worries about waste, destruction, and stupidity. As editor of *Britain and the Beast* (1937) he argued for coherent, wise, and civilized planning policies to protect the countryside and the national heritage from greed, from pusillanimous attitudes, and from destruction. His choice as first Chairman of the first New Town Development

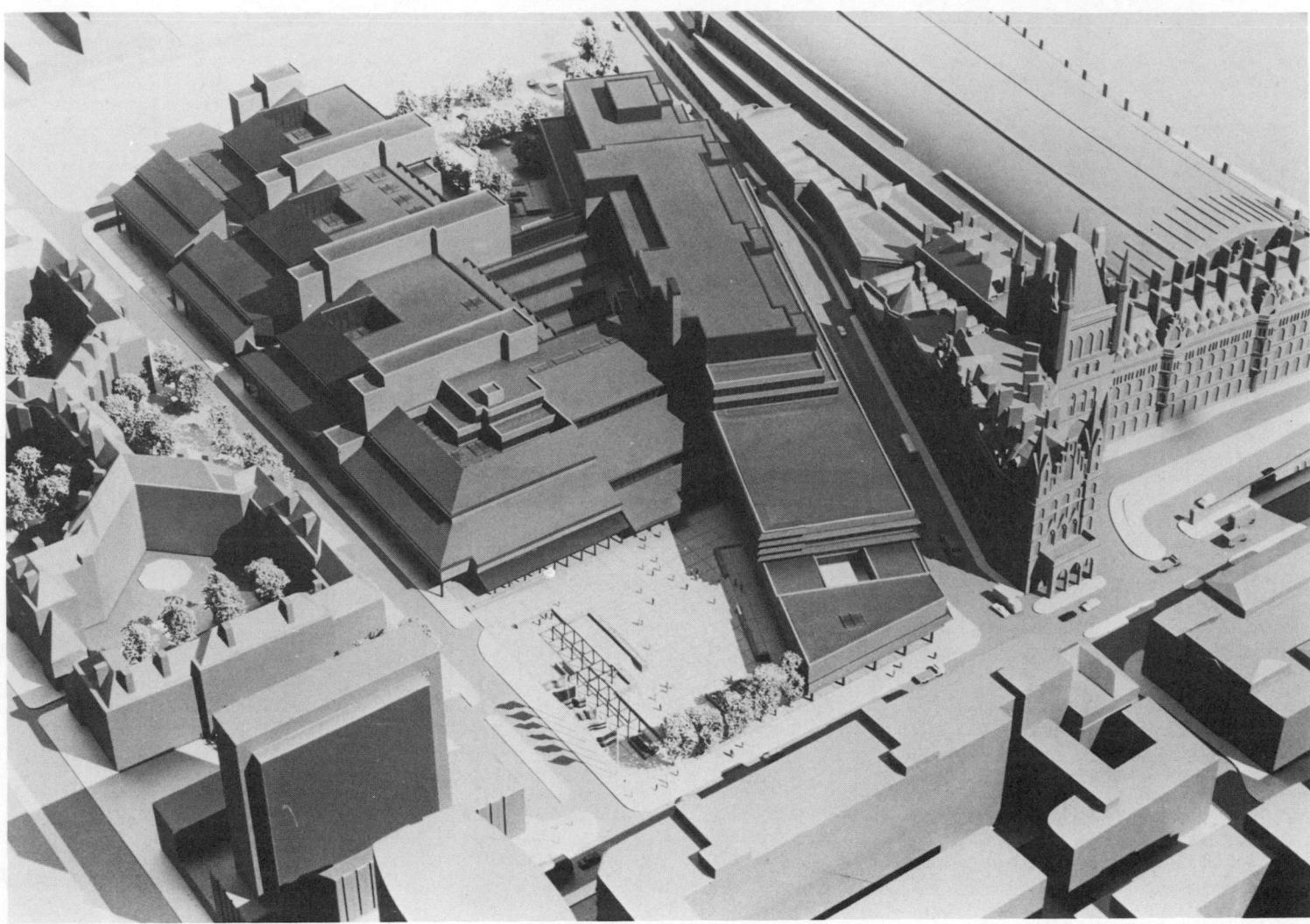

Colin St. John Wilson: British Library Building, Euston Road, London, 1975 (project)

Corporation (Stevenage) might have given us a great new town incorporating the wonderful environmental aspects of Portmeirion and Cushendun on a much larger scale, but unfortunately his brand of cultivated sensibility was out of tune with the realities of post-war Britain as well as with the aims of his colleagues, and so a prosaic utilitarianism with no delight and certainly no "useless" picturesqueness was to prevail.

Williams-Ellis died in 1978. The world, and especially the beleaguered world of traditional architecture and three-dimensional creativity in town planning, is the poorer for his passing.

—James Stevens Curl

WILSON, Colin St. John.

British. Born in Cheltenham, Gloucestershire, 14 March 1922. Educated at Felstead School, Essex, 1935–40; Corpus Christi College, Cambridge, 1940–42, M.A. 1942; Bartlett School of Architecture, University College London, 1946–49, Dip.Arch. 1949. Served as a Lieutenant in the Royal Naval Volunteer Reserve, 1942–46. Married Muriel Lavender in 1955 (divorced); married Mary Jane Long in 1972; children: Sarah and James. Architectural Assistant, Verner O. Rees and Partners, London, 1949–50, and in the Housing Division, London County Council Architects Department, 1950–55; Principal Architect, Property Development Company, London, 1955–56; in private practice, and in association with Professor Sir Leslie Martin, Cambridge and London, 1956–70. Since 1971, Senior Partner, Colin St. John Wilson and Partners, London (partners: John Collier; Douglas Lanham; Peter Carolin; M. J. Long).

Lecturer, Department of Architecture, Cambridge University, 1956–59; Fellow of Churchill College, Cambridge, 1960–72; Visiting Critic, Yale University School of Architecture, New Haven, Connecticut, 1960, 1964; Bemis Visiting Professor of Architecture, Massachusetts Institute of Technology, Cambridge, 1970–71. Professor of Architecture, Cambridge University, since 1975; Fellow of Pembroke College, Cambridge, since 1977. Trustee, Tate Gallery, London, since 1974, and The National Gallery, London, since 1977. Exhibitions: Architectural Association, London, 1951, 1954; *This Is Tomorrow,* Whitechapel Gallery, London, 1956 (designed exhibition); *Contemporary Artists and Architects in the U.K.* (film), at *Expo '67,* Montreal. Address: Colin St. John Wilson and Partners, 9–11 Wilson Street, London EC2M 2TQ, England.

Works:

1951 Coventry Cathedral, Warwickshire (competition project; with Peter Carter)
1952 Narrow-Frontage Maisonette Prototype
Shell Company Service Station (competition project; with Peter Carter)
1954 Housing estate, Bentham Road, Hackney, London
University of Sheffield, Yorkshire (competition project; with Peter Carter)
1955 High-Level Helicopter Station (project; with Peter Carter)
1955/
57 Residential building, Hereford Square, London (with Arthur Baker)
1956 Design of the *This Is Tomorrow* exhibition, Whitechapel Gallery, London
Science Faculty Layout and Physics Build-

ings, University of Leicester (with Sir Leslie Martin)
King's College Hostel, Cambridge (project; with Sir Leslie Martin)
1957/
58 Factory and laboratory, Welwyn Garden City, Hertfordshire (with Sir Leslie Martin and Sir Ove Arup)
1957/
59 Architecture Department extension, Scroope Terrace, Cambridge University (with Alex Hardy)
1957/
62 Harvey Court Residential Building, Gonville and Caius College, West Road, Cambridge (with Sir Leslie Martin)
1958 Housing project, Borough of St. Pancras, London (with Sir Leslie Martin)
1959/
64 3 libraries, Manor Road, Oxford University (with Sir Leslie Martin)
1960 Royal Holloway College Campus Layout, University of London (with Sir Leslie Martin)
1960/
64 William Stone Residential Building, Peterhouse, Trumpington Road, Cambridge (with Sir Leslie Martin)
1961/
64 2 houses, Grantchester Road, Cambridge
1962/
64 British Museum Library, London (project; with Sir Leslie Martin)
1965 Grandstand, Newmarket Racecourse, Suffolk (project)
Residential building, St. John's College, Queens Road, Cambridge (project)

Keiller House, Virginia Water, Surrey (project)
1965/
69 Cornford House, Conduit Head, Madingley
Road, Cambridge
1965/
70 Civic and Social Centre, St. Johns Gardens,
Liverpool (project)
1965/
71 Agricultural Research Council Biochemistry
Laboratory, Babraham, Cambridge (with
Michael Brawne)
1969 British Museum Development Plan, London
(project)
1970 British Library Building, Bloomsbury, London (project)
1970/
79 British Museum West Wing Extension, London
1973 Lucas Industries Corporation Headquarters,
Shirley, Birmingham (competition project)
New County Hall, Northampton (project)
1974/
77 Housing, Borough of Haringey, London
1975 British Library Building, Euston Road, London (project)

Publications:

By WILSON: articles—"Architect and Patron" in
The Observer (London), 4 June 1950; "Towards a
New Cathedral" in *The Observer* (London), 7 Janu-
ary 1951; "The Vertical City" in *The Observer* (Lon-
don), 17 February 1952; "Eduardo Paolozzi and
Nigel Henderson" in *Cambridge Review* (Cam-
bridge), 1957; "The Collegiate Court," with J. L.
Martin, in *Architectural Review* (London), July
1959; "Open and Closed" in *Perspecta* (New Haven,
Connecticut), no. 7, 1961; "Letter to an American
Student" in *Program* (New York), no. 3, 1964; "Ger-
rit Rietveld: 1888–1964" in *Architectural Review*
(London), December 1964; "Modus Operandi" in
Cuadernos de Arquitectura (Barcelona), no. 72,
1969.

On WILSON: articles—"Arbeider 1958–67" by
Christian Norberg-Schulz in *Byggekunst* (Oslo), no.
3, 1967; "Colin St. John Wilson" by Kasumasa
Yamashita in *The Japan Architect* (Tokyo), April
1968; "Colin St. John Wilson o la Seriedad en el
Proceso Arquitectonico" by Marcial Echenique in
Cuadernos de Arquitectura (Barcelona), no. 72,
1969; plus articles on major buildings in *Architectural Design* (London), October 1959, July 1960,
November 1962, November 1965, June 1967, *Architectural Review* (London), September 1965, November 1971, *Domus* (Milan), August 1968, and
RIBA Journal (London), April 1976.

*

I believe that architecture serves a more fundamental
need than we normally suppose. For, harassed by
continual change, we need somehow to be made at
home in the world and to that end we must be served
not only at the level of utility and visual pleasure but
also at a deeper psychological level where both the
reality and the image of wholeness and of structure
in the environment restore us to a measure of balance
amid all our contradictions. If this were not so, then
the present discontent with the state of our cities
would be less impassioned, for I do not believe that
questions of convenience or of aesthetics alone
would lead to such distress.

From this it follows that our first aim is to understand the nature of the real needs for building in our
time, and here the architect's contribution divides
into two. In the first instance he must assist in drawing up a "programme" of those needs which can be
defined in terms of operational order, economic priority and technical feasibility: and it is clear that this
task he cannot perform on his own. I have for nearly

thirty years engaged with this problem in many different ways—working within a local government
office and within private practice, designing buildings for private individuals, for developers, for industry, for universities, for local and for national government agencies; I have built for myself both home
and place of work; and I have been both competitor
and assessor in various competitions. On every occasion it has been a question of starting from scratch!
Furthermore, the "client" in the form of a committee is often a will-of-the-wisp, forever changing personnel, priorities and programme and, in any case,
acting as the sponsor rather than the user of the
proposed building. If we then add to this tenuous
relationship the further strain of continual technological innovation, it becomes clear that we are confronted with a whole pattern of operations which is
cut off from any of the gentle give-and-take by which
traditional procedures have evolved in a balanced
way.

As a teacher (since 1956) I have been able to study
this issue not only in terms of professional practice
but also from a theoretical point of view; and this
view has occasionally been amplified by development
of certain aspects to a level of formal rigour by research students. Out of all this I have built up an
unshakeable conviction that the only course to be
pursued today is in the first instance the patient elaboration of whatever technique is suitable to ensure a
proper dialogue between Architect and user of the
building. This can be laborious in a large building
(for the British Library we had to computerise 8,000
bits of information), but it is the essential foundation.
Secondly, upon that foundation the architect can
then not only invent a design but also submit it to
controlled criticism and revision: and here it is important to realise that, for criticism to be creative, it
must be firmly controlled in this way. Finally, at the
end of the day, the architect must invent a design
which will not only stand up to the test of use but
will also answer to those deep and less rational needs
to which I have alluded above. If it can fulfill them
too, then it will raise the whole issue to that moment
of architectural realization in which a frame for the
actions of men suddenly focuses into a place where
those actions are not merely made possible but are
made manifest, are made, perhaps for the first time,
vivid and recognisable to themselves, and their identity preserved against erosion. When this happens
mere building has become architecture.

That, unlike the drawing up of a statement of
needs, is an act of imagination, and it can be performed only by an architect.
—Colin St. John Wilson

*

A building is a string of events belonging together,
progressing from basement to roof and back again.
This line is derived from the very factual cycle of
living that we can all observe. Colin St. John Wilson,
tired of architects' overblown polemics and sterile
products, has refined his ambitions to following the
chain of existence at its most elementary; he has
elected to elevate the basic living configurations into
a sensitive architecture-of-place. His recent judiciously measured vernacularizing projects also exemplify this caution: he has no truck with the enforced fairy-tale of Post-Modernism.

One ploy he resorts to, in order to avoid the inde-
cent propositions of formalism, is the plan: the plani-
metric interplay of hanging gardens in the Library
Group, Oxford, 1959–64, is an early paean to the
plan, which in this case is made to stand up in a
three-dimensional way. In the pin-wheel massing of
the aborted Liverpool Civic Centre, we can see quite
clearly that the main push is from the plan. Similarly, in the Northampton County Hall project's
Aalto-like sweeping armature, it's the plan that is
leading.

In the splintered, punctured stretched brick and
timber skin of Cornford House, Cambridge, there is
a remarkable break out from the plan, and the perforated, disjointed vernacular wraps around the broken massing in a masterly dwelling spiral. It's only

when Wilson comes to employ this same technique
in the more recent large-scale projects that there is
a sense of mismatching; nonetheless, the vernacular
idiom still allows him a little moderation in the face
of the escalating immoderation that the urban architect feels is expected of him.

Wilson's work is formed by the "twin texts" of
"out-there" (actuality) and "in-here" (in the mind):
he sees the need to re-establish a Cezanne-like *rap-
prochement* between these polarities as the foundation for an architecture that can make sense of whatever may confront it. Only an architecture that can
both embrace and yet distance at the same time has
the possibility of ringing true.

—Chris Fawcett

WINES, James.
American. Born in Oak Park, Illinois, 27 June 1932.
Educated at Syracuse University, New York, 1950–
55, B.A. 1955. Married Gul Seden in 1956 (divorced,
1967); daughter: Suzan. Worked as a sculptor, New
York, exhibiting internationally and completing several large public commissions, 1955–67. Since 1969,
Founder and Principal of SITE Inc., New York: in
partnership with Emilio Sousa, Alison Sky and Michelle Stone, since 1973. Professor of Art, New
School for Social Research, New York, 1960, 1961,
The School of the Visual Arts, New York, 1965,
1971, and New York University, 1965, 1977; Artist-
in-Residence, Cornell University, Ithaca, New York,
1969, and the State University of New York at
Buffalo, 1970; Mellon Professor of Architecture,
Cooper Union, New York, 1977; Architect-in-Residence, Dartmouth College, Hanover, New Hampshire, 1977. Since 1975, Professor of Architecture at
the New Jersey School of Architecture, Newark. Exhibitions: Whitney Museum, New York, 1973; Museum of Modern Art, New York, 1975; *Biennale,*
Venice, 1975; Centre Pompidou, Paris, 1975; Australian Museum Travelling Exhibition, 1976–77. Recipient: Rome Prize, American Academy in Rome,
1956; Guggenheim Fellowship, 1962; Ford Foundation Grant, 1964; National Endowment for the Arts
Grant, 1973; Graham Foundation Grant, 1974. Address: SITE Inc., 60 Greene Street, New York, New
York 10012, U.S.A.

Works:

1969 Education Place, University of Northern
Iowa, Cedar Falls (project; with Cynthia
Eardley and Dana Draper)
Everson Museum Plaza, Syracuse, New York
(project)
1971 Physics/Astronomy Plaza, University of
Wisconsin at Milwaukee (project; with
Dana Draper)
1972 Peeling Facade, Best Products Store, Rich-
mond, Virginia (with Cynthia Eardley)
Crossroads Apartments, Peekskill, New York
(project)

With Emilio Sousa:

1973 Intermediate School 25 Courtyard, New
York (project)
Rainbow Center Plaza, Buffalo, New York
(competition project)
1974 Four Arts Society Plaza, Palm Beach, Florida
(project)
1975 Indeterminate Facade, Best Products Showroom, Houston, Texas
Interstate 80 Roadway, Nebraska (project)
Molino Stucky Grain Mill Plaza, Venice (project)
Parking Lot Building, Best Products Showroom, Southern California (project)
1977 Notch Building, Best Products Showroom,
Sacramento, California

James Wines: Indeterminate Facade, Best Products Showroom, Houston, Texas, 1975

1978 . Ghost Parking Lot, Hamden Plaza, Hamden,
Connecticut
Tilt Showroom, Best Products Showroom,
Towson, Maryland.

Publications:

By WINES: articles—"Public Art, Private Gallery"
in *Art in America* (New York), January 1970; "The
Case for Site Oriented Art" in *Landscape Architecture* (Louisville, Kentucky), July 1971; "Straatkunst," with Nancy Goldring, in *Tijdschrift voor Architectuur en Beeldende Kunsten* (Heerlen), January
1972; "Peekskill Melt," with Nancy Goldring, in
The Art Gallery (Ivorytown, Connecticut), March
1972; "The Case for the Big Duck" in *Architectural
Forum* (New York), April 1972; "La Point de Vue
de l'Automobiliste" in *L'Architecture d'Aujourd'hui*
(Paris), November 1972; "Notes from a Passing
Car" in *Architectural Forum* (New York), September 1973; "Urban Art—Assisting the Assisted
Readymade" in *Casabella* (Milan), May 1974; "De-
architecturization" in *Architecture + Urbanism*
(Tokyo), part I, June 1974, part II, July 1975; "Ent-
Architekturierung" in *Kunstforum International*
(Mainz), October 1974; "The Iconography of Disaster" in *Architectural Design* (London), June 1975;
"De-architecture" in *L'Architettura* (Rome), June
1975; "De-architecturization" in *Arts in Society*
(Madison, Wisconsin), Fall/Winter 1975; "Il Linguaggio Eretico della Disarchitettura" in *Modo*
(Milan), November 1977; "The Architecture of
Risk" in *Architecture Intérieure/Crée* (Paris),
March and May 1978.

On WINES: articles—"Site" in *Art and Artists* (London), October 1971; "New Concepts for Public
Space Combine Art and Architecture" by Janet
Bloom in *Architectural Record* (New York), February 1972; "L'intorno Scolpito" by Bruno Zevi in
L'Architettura (Rome), May 1973; "James Wines"
by Toshio Nakamura in *Architecture + Urbanism*
(Tokyo), Summer 1974; "Indeterminate Facade" by
Toshio Nakamura in *Architecture + Urbanism*
(Tokyo), July 1975; "Pre-disastro nel Texas" by Lisa
Ponti in *Domus* (Milan), October 1975; "SITE-
ations" by Judith Goldman in *Art News* (New York),
October 1975; "Houston Falling" by Douglas Davis
in *Newsweek* (New York), 22 December 1975;
"SITE: Indeterminate Facade" by Franco Raggi in
Casabella (Milan), March 1976; "Surrealism Comes
to Shop Center" by C. Ray Smith in *The Village*

Voice (New York), 15 March 1976; "Crumbling
Facades" by Peter Marsh in *Building Design* (London), 6 August 1976; "Halfway Between Building
Design and Modern Art" by William Marlin in the
Christian Science Monitor (Boston), 11 March 1977;
"Safe as Houses?" by Dennis Sharp in *The Guardian*
(London), 8 June 1977; "Architect's Unstable Designs Relieve Monotony" by Paul Goldberger in the
New York Times, 27 June 1977; "Monumento al
Consumatore" by Bruno Zevi in *L'Espresso* (Rome),
31 July 1977; "Fragmentation in California" by Lisa
Ponti in *Domus* (Milan), August 1977; "The Drums
Go Bang and the Symbols Clang" by Sydney Baggs
in *Architecture Australia* (Sydney), November 1977;
"Business among the Ruins" by Wolf Von Eckardt
in the *Washington Post,* 14 January 1978; "Through
the Looking Glass" by Lance Wright in *Architectural Review* (London), March 1978.

SITE Inc. is a multi-disciplinary architecture and
environmental arts group chartered for the purpose
of exploring new concepts for the urban visual environment. Although originally identified with a kind
of public sculpture, the organization has altered its
direction considerably since formation and is presently involved with subtractive, fragmented, and inversionist aspects of architecture. This work is a category of hybrid endeavor—often suspended between
the definitions of art and architecture—and is usually characterized by social, political, and architectural commentary. These ideas have been variously
referred to as radical architecture, anti-architecture,
arch-art, etc.; however, SITE prefers the term "de-
architecture" to describe its philosophical position.

De-architecture is a general way of defining an
attitude or means for changing standard reactions to
the urban context by using inherent circumstances to
alter and/or invert the original intentions of a particular situation. Whereas, for example, the commonly
sanctioned view of architecture has been exemplified
by a relationship between form and internal motives
of function, the work of SITE deals with a relationship between content and the external influences of
social and cultural context. Or, described another
way, rather than develop architecture as a formalist
endeavor from the inside out, SITE's ideas evolve
from the outside in.

—James Wines

Visions of bricks cascading from a false front, incomplete corners, and peeling walls spring to mind with
the mention of the name of James Wines. Noted for

such deviant design concepts, SITE (originally
Sculpture in the Environment), the firm Wines
heads, injects a whimsical element into the ponderous architectural scene of post-1960's America.
However, more than mere playfulness is at work in
these endeavors; the definition of the role of art and
architecture, architect and artist, is intensely scrutinized and challenged.

Assuming an antagonist role, Wines has proven
himself to be a delightfully literate and refreshingly
engaging critic of the sterile, totalitarian aspects of
function-oriented architecture and the application of
gallery precepts to art in public places. His humorous, almost facetious, essays such as "The Case for
the Big Duck," "Notes from a Passing Car," "De-
Architecturization" and "The Iconography of Disaster" deplore the "Technosplat" sensibility that
pervades so much of modern urban design and reject
the concept of art as applied decoration or exhibitable object. Labeling modern public space art as
"charm bracelet sculpture," and introducing such
sublime ideas as D.D.T. (Duck Design Theory) with
its "form follows fantasy" postulate, Wines raucously re-examines the state of the arts in America.
Finding it totally out of touch with reality, he suggests a rejection of the Bauhaus and avant-garde
traditions and espouses the redefinition of the role of
the artist to a position more responsive to public
needs.

Transcending the written word, Wines attempts to
apply his ideas to the too often impenetrable realm
of implementation. In pre-SITE days, Wines was a
sculptor. He rejected the gallery-museum engendered concept of art as object standing alone, separate from the environment, stressed the need for conceptual site planning, and attempted to eliminate the
focus on public art and architecture as separate entities. The State Street Park in Binghamton, New
York, with its series of massive, undulating, dock-
like structures rolling the length of a full city block,
well reflects his approach. While a monumental
sculpture in its own right, appreciated by both automobilists and pedestrians, it is more than just a
sculpture as it invites and anticipates physical interaction. Functionally reminiscent of Lawrence
Halprin's Lovejoy Fountain in Portland, Oregon, it
serves as a flexible pedestrian, recreation, and leisure
space which adorns the landscape.

More radical and controversial are the SITE
works—for instance, the Best Products showrooms.
By literally decimating the facade of the traditional
functional box, these showrooms breakdown the
conventional expectations of architectural design
and attack the Bauhaus tradition with a vicarious
vengeance. Again sculpture and architecture are integrated to transform a static "art object" into an
event which encourages people to interact with their
surroundings. The juxtaposition of a minimally designed commercial box with a seemingly decomposing facade, provokes at least a second look or a gleeful exclamation of confrontation, if not a questioning
of what it happening. As the antithesis of "Technosplat" design, these structures supplant the intransigent answers of functionalism with a more humanistic situation of action-reaction, question-ponder.

The Best showrooms, while a delight to behold,
present a rather limited solution to the problem of
discovering a new humanistic architecture. Primarily functioning as statements against institutionalized, totalitarian architecture, they are ephemeral
forms that assume the existence of a staid establishment for their impact. Rising from the mire of functionalism, however, these projects may indeed be
valid foundations on which a future of tantalizing
forms will be erected.

—Don J. Hibbard

Peter Womersley: Bernat Klein Studio, Galashiels, Selkirk, Scotland, 1972

WOMERSLEY, Peter.

British. Born in Newark, Nottinghamshire, 24 June 1923. Educated at the Architectural Association School, London, under Arthur Korn, 1947–52, Dip. A.A. (honours) 1952. Served in the British Army, 1942–46. In private practice, Scotland, 1953–78; founded practice in Hong Kong, 1962: in full-time practice in Hong Kong since 1978. Recipient: Grand Project Award, *Architectural Design,* 1964; Civic Trust Award, 1965 (twice), 1968; Edinburgh Architectural Association Medal, 1965, 1973; Bayer International Award, 1974; Scotland Award, Royal Institute of British Architects, 1975. Associate of the Royal Scottish Academy, 1966. Lives in Hong Kong.

Works:

1954 Farnley Hey (house), Huddersfield, Yorkshire

1957 High Sunderland (house), Galashiels, Selkirk, Scotland
      The Rig (architect's house), Gattonside, Melrose, Scotland

1960 Church Square Council Houses, Galashiels, Selkirk, Scotland

1962 House, Camberley, Surrey
      Peninsula Hotel modernization, Hong Kong

1963 Port Murray (house), Maidens, Culzean, Scotland

1964 Fairy Dean Football Stand, Galashiels, Selkirk, Scotland

1965 Psychiatric Admission Unit, Haddington, Lothian, Scotland
      Sports Centre, University of Hull, Yorkshire

1967 Doctors Group Practice Building, Kelso, Scotland
      Roxburgh County Buildings, Newton St. Boswells, Roxburgh, Scotland

1968 House, Bath, Somerset
      Transplantation Surgery Unit, Western General Hospital, Edinburgh

1969 St. George's Office Building, Hong Kong

1970 Midland Bank Headquarters, Huddersfield, Yorkshire

1972 Bernat Klein Studio, Galashiels, Selkirk, Scotland

1978 Boilerhouse, Melrose Hospital, Scotland
      Sports Centre, Coatbridge, Strathclyde, Scotland

Publications:

By WOMERSLEY: article—"Architect's Approach to Architecture" in *RIBA Journal* (London), May 1969.

On WOMERSLEY: articles—"Focus on a Valley View" by S.F. Lewis in *Ideal Home* (London), October 1972; "The Architect's Office, Gattanside" in *Baumeister* (Munich), November 1972; "Bernat Klein Studio" in *Architecture + Urbanism* (Tokyo), July 1974; "Transforming a Drawing-Office into a Living-Room" in *House and Garden* (London), November 1978.

Peter Womersley, although he is English, has spent most of his professional life in Scotland. For much of this time he worked alone, never employing more than three or four assistants, partly because of his belief that he must be personally involved in all his projects. His work consists of small, one-off schemes, in each of which (in his own words) he has striven "to experiment aesthetically, producing at the same time a building which stands up to both gravity and weather, and satisfies the client in use and as an investment." Peter Womersley regards each problem as an individual one, an "affair of the heart," as he puts it, and believes that each architectural solution should be a "fresh re-building of experience gained on other buildings."

That said, one notes that his designs evolve their own constructional and aesthetic systems. Increasingly—due in part to his travels and to his work in Hong Kong—Womersley has become fascinated by the application of basic geometry to architecture. He has always acknowledged his debt to Mies van der Rohe, and expressed it most clearly in his use of a rectangular grid and of simple open volumes broken down into smaller related spaces. However, Womersley recognizes that the Miesian doctrine can easily lead to sterility, and thus we find him turning more to Wright for inspiration in the imaginative expression of materials. In his detailing, as in his planning, he aims to refine "to the apparent simplicity which alone is satisfying."

In the early years of his practice, his preferred material was timber; later, when he turned to reinforced concrete, he used timber as shuttering, and thus suggested a continuing line of development. Such changes were simultaneously an expression of his desire to experiment with more sculptural forms and of his wish to explore the technical potentialities of concrete. With both materials he realizes the importance of structural honesty, but feels that a building should display a "convincing whole" rather than be a "structural demonstration."

The essence of Peter Womersley's architecture is most strikingly demonstrated in the Bernat Klein Studio, near Galashiels, with its beautiful siting and eloquent use of glass, concrete, and blue-black brick. It is arguably the outstanding Scottish building of the 1970's.

—Peter Willis

WONG, Jackson C(hack) S(ang).

Hong Kong Citizen. Born in Hong Kong, 16 June 1930. Educated at St. Joseph's College, Hong Kong, 1945–50; Hong Kong University School of Architecture, under R. Gordon Brown, 1950–55 (Lee Hysan Gold Medal, 1953), B.Arch. (first class honours) 1955. Married Annie Leung Kit Wah in 1962; children: Eugenia, Felix and Raymond. Assistant Architect to Professor R. Gordon Brown, Hong Kong, 1955–57; Founder-Partner, Wong and Ng and Associates, Hong Kong, 1957–64, and Wong, Ng, Ouyang and Associates, Hong Kong, 1964–72. Since 1972, Principal Partner, with Leslie Ouyang, Wong and Ouyang and Associates, Hong Kong (other partners: Thomas W. Y. Kwok; Lam Wo Hei). President, Hong Kong Institute of Architects, 1973–74. Recipient: Wah Yuen Chuen Residential Development Competition, Hong Kong, 1977. Address: Wong and Ouyang and Associates, China Building, 17/F Queen's Road C, Hong Kong.

Works:

1955 House, 8 Purves Road, Hong Kong
House, 12 Cooper Road, Hong Kong
1958 House, Anderson Road, Hong Kong
1959 Jardine's Lookout Residents Association Clubhouse, Hong Kong
Valley Villa, Blue Pool Road, Hong Kong
1960 The Box House, Fei Ngo Shan Road, Hong Kong
1961 House, 21 Cooper Road, Hong Kong
1963 House, Clearwater Bay Road, Hong Kong
Clearwater Bay Apartments, Hong Kong
1964 Kwun Tong District Government Offices, Kowloon, Hong Kong
Kwun Tong Royal Jockey Club Health Centre and Maternity Home, Kowloon, Hong Kong
Hyatt Hotel, Nathan Road, Kowloon, Hong Kong
Skyscraper Apartment Building, Tin Hau Temple Road, Hong Kong
Silver Strand Garden Townhouse, Nam Tau Sha, Hang Hau, Hong Kong
1965 Link's Estate Townhouse, Hong Kong
Kwun Tong Mansion, Yuet Wah Street, Hong Kong
1966 Chinese Y.M.C.A. Building, Waterloo Road, Kowloon, Hong Kong
Villa Monte Roza Apartments, Stubbs Road, Hong Kong
Cape Mansion Apartments, Mount Davis Road, Hong Kong
De La Salle Secondary School, Kam Tsing Village, Fan Ling, New Territories, Hong Kong

Chiap Hua Clocks and Watches Factory, Kwun Tong Road, Hong Kong
Jackson Wong Residence, 80 Chung Hom Kok Road, Hong Kong
1967 Dragon Court Apartments, Waterloo Road, Hong Kong
1968 Man Cheong Office Building, Des Voeux Road West, Hong Kong
Magazine Heights Apartments, 17 Magazine Gap Road, Hong Kong
Tai On Cinema and Apartment Building, Shaukiwan Road, Hong Kong
Harilela House, Cambridge Road, Hong Kong
St. Joseph's Primary School, Morrison Hill, Hong Kong
Belvedere Court Townhouses, Shouson Hill Road, Hong Kong
Concordia Lutheran Anglo-Chinese School, Cloud View Road, Hong Kong
Chan Sui Ki College, Homatin, Hong Kong
1971 Unicorn Gardens Apartments, Shouson Hill Road, Hong Kong
Hong Kong Adventist Hospital, Stubbs Road, Hong Kong
Turtle Cove Villas, Red Hill, Hong Kong
Twin Bay Villa Townhouses, Clearwater Bay Road, Hong Kong
1972 Chong Gene Chong College, Chaiwan, Hong Kong
Pearl City Commercial and Residential Complex, Hong Kong
Dah Chong Hong Motor Services Centre, Cheung Sha Wan, Hong Kong
Din Wai Factory, Hoi Yuen Road, Hong Kong
1973 Residence, 20 D.E.F. Broadwood Road, Kowloon, Hong Kong
1974 Monte Verde Apartments, 41 Repulse Bay Road, Hong Kong
Stephen Mansion Apartments, Belfran Road, Hong Kong
Hutchinson House Office Building, Harcourt Road, Hong Kong
1975 Westlands Gardens Housing, Quarry Bay, North Point, Hong Kong
Oblates Fathers Primary School, Yuk Yat Street, Hong Kong
Holiday Inn, Nathan Road/Mody Road, Kowloon, Hong Kong
1976 Hang Shing Office Building, Hong Kong
Eastern Commercial Centre Office Building, Hong Kong
Causeway Bay Commercial Building, Sugar Street, Hong Kong
Outboard Marine Industrial Building, Tsing Yi Island, Hong Kong
Yan Garden Housing, Waterloo Road, Hong Kong
Hiranand House Office Building, Mody Road, Kowloon, Hong Kong
Holiday Inn, Manila, Philippines
Dah Chong Hong Motors Service Building, Quarry Bay, Hong Kong
1977 CMA Pre-vocational School, Nam Cheong Street, Hong Kong
Car Park and Car Repair Building, Wing Fong Street, Kwai Chung, Hong Kong
Champion Office Building, Nathan Road, Hong Kong
Mrs. Jenny Wong House, Hang Hau, Hong Kong
Yue Hwa Chinese Products Emporium Department Store interiors, Hong Kong
Nan Fung Sun Chuen Housing, Tai Koo Valley, Hong Kong
Hyde Towers Apartments, Kwun Tong, Hong Kong
Honest Motors Car Showroom and Office Building, Leighton Road, Hong Kong
Braemar Hill Mansion Housing, Hong Kong
China Building, Peddar Street/Queen's Road Central, Hong Kong

Publications:

On WONG: articles—"An Architect's House" in *Far East Architect and Builder* (Hong Kong), September 1966; "Holiday Inn: Linking Up" in *Asian Architect and Builder* (Hong Kong), August 1974; "Latest Holiday Inn Has 650 Rooms" in *Asian Building and Construction* (Hong Kong), June 1975; "Cross Design Comes out Tops" in *South China Morning Post* (Hong Kong), 27 July 1977.

Hong Kong as an economic society has been very active, highly efficient, and really realistic, with no exception for the building industry. Land cost in Hong Kong is probably the most expensive among its neighbouring countries, if not the highest in the world. Therefore, to survive in the highly competitive building industry, a developer or his consultants has a unique order of priorities, that is, to achieve: 1) the maximum total floor area in any development; 2) the most economical structure, as most buildings are high-rise; 3) an architectural scheme that requires the least time either for design and/or for construction; and 4) the best form and elevational treatment that does not adversely affect the other priorities, at no significant extra cost to the development.

These priorities are reflected in the works with which I have been involved. As a result they appear simple and straight-forward. I have found that simplicity in form, with explicit structural expression in exterior design, and "clean cut" planning solutions meet less resistance from all concerned.

Coverage of the roof area of a building still plays a crucial part in the development potential of a building site in Hong Kong, which also prevents any architectural articulation or architectural projection or indentation that sacrifices floor area or reduces the commercial viability of a project.

I believe in proportion and consistency. I find that refinement of proportion is one of the few areas with which a client is not concerned; and consistency in architectural detailing enables a building to stand out better in a crowded built environment. Recently my experience has shown that the reflective surface of a building does not necessarily have an adverse visual impact on its surroundings so long as it reflects images.

I believe that the interior of a building should reflect the structural system of the building and, if possible, the architectural form of a building exterior. Occupants in a building—with a few exceptions—should preferably be aware of the exterior surroundings at all times. A building interior to me is a controlled environment, designed for activities within a space. Lighting is an important means of creating an interior atmosphere, even more so than colour. People react to colour differently, and the colour of a surface is subject to changes according to light sources.

The architectural statement of a building should be simple and forceful to maintain its identity harmoniously in busy and over-crowded surroundings.

—Jackson C. S. Wong

Jackson C. S. Wong came from a Swatow background. Among Chinese, the inhabitants of Swatow are known for their defined code of ethics and for their rather Sicilian approach to issues and solutions: Jackson Wong is no exception.

He is a product of the University of Hong Kong under Gordon Brown, the former principal of the Architectural Association. His architecture is direct and controlled. He is committed to the grand scheme of things. He understands thoroughly the spatial determinants used by the private sector to define architecture. He accepts these as his base because they allow him to create the kind of architecture that large development groups and the government can relate to if not understand. He is uncompromising on details, carefully matching these to the scale of his projects.

Jackson C. S. Wong: China Building, Hong Kong, 1977

It is not unreasonable to say that the grand and the formal are still important and essential components necessary to hold urban architecture together. It is unavoidable that such an architecture often suffers from a sense of individual scale but Wong, like Pei and Portman, is committed to the urban collective scale and its purpose. His architecture can be described as sophisticated urban containers for collective activities. Wong's intention in architecture is fundamentally Palladian but his moves and actions leading to this realization must be described as Von Clausewitzian.

—K. C. Lye

WOODS, Shadrach.

American. Born in Yonkers, New York, 30 June 1923. Studied engineering at New York University, and literature at Dublin University, 1945–48. Served in the United States Army during World War II. Married Clarissa Labaugh in 1946. Worked with Georges Candilis, *q.v.*, in the office of Le Corbusier, Paris, 1948–51; associated with Candilis in ATBAT-Afrique, Casablanca, 1951–55; Partner, with Candilis and Alexis Josic, *q.v.*, Candilis-Josic-Woods, Paris, 1955–63; worked with Candilis in Paris, 1963–67; in private practice, New York, 1970–73. Lecturer, Yale University, New Haven, Connecticut, 1967; Professor of Architecture, Harvard Graduate School of Design, Cambridge, Massachusetts, 1968–73; appointed William Henry Bishop Visiting Professor of Architecture, Yale University, 1973 (declined because of ill health). Member, Team 10, from 1962. Recipient: First Prize, Marseilles Housing Competition, 1959; First Prize, Toulouse-le-Mirail New Town Competition, 1960; First Prize, Free University of Berlin Competition, 1963. *Died* (in New York) *in August 1973.*

Works:

1951/
55   Musulman Collective Housing Development, Casablanca (with Vladimir Bodiansky and Georges Candilis)
1952/
54   Master plan for the city of Casablanca (with Vladimir Bodiansky and Georges Candilis)
1954/
55   Opération Million: 3,600 housing units, France, particularly the Paris suburbs (with Georges Candilis and Alexis Josic)
1956/
61   Plan and housing for the new town of Bag-

nols-sur-Cèze, France (with Georges Candilis and Alexis Josic)
1959   Housing (4,000 units), Marseilles (with Georges Candilis and Alexis Josic)
1960   Urban prefabricated houses, Algeria (competition project; with Georges Candilis and Alexis Josic)
      Master plan for the new town of Toulouse-le-Mirail, France (with Georges Candilis and Alexis Josic)
1961   New town of 30,000 inhabitants, Caen, France (competition project; with Georges Candilis and Alexis Josic)
      New town of 10,000 inhabitants, Hamburg (competition project; with Georges Candilis and Alexis Josic)
1962   University for 2,000 students, Bochum, Germany (competition project; with Georges Candilis and Alexis Josic)
1963   Plan for the center of Frankfurt (project; with Georges Candilis and Alexis Josic)
      Master plan for Fort Lamy, Chad, Africa (with Georges Candilis and Alexis Josic)
      Master plan of the Free University of Berlin (with Georges Candilis and Alexis Josic)
1964/
65   Cité Artisanale (Workshop Center for Artisans), Sèvres, France (with Georges Candilis and Alexis Josic)
      Ski Resort, Vallée de Belleville, France (with Georges Candilis and Jean Prouvé)
      Val d'Asua Residential Development, near Bilbao, Spain
1966   Steilshoop Regional Center, Hamburg (with Georges Candilis)
1967   Redevelopment plan for the Bonne Nouvelle, Paris
1969   Redevelopment plan for the SoHo District, New York
1970   Redevelopment plan for Karlsruhe, Germany
      Douglas Circle, Central Park, New York (project)

Publications:

By WOODS: books—*Urbanism Is Everybody's Business,* with J. Pfeufer, Stuttgart 1968, 1970; *What U Can Do,* Houston, Texas 1970; *The Man in the Street: A Polemic on Urbanism,* London 1975; articles—"Why Revisit Le Pavillon Suisse" in *Architectural Forum* (New York), June 1965; "Conversation on Urbanism," with Roger Vailland, in *Perspecta* (New Haven, Connecticut), vol. 11, 1967; "Strive for Uniformity?" in *Architecture Canada* (Toronto), April 1967; "Waiting for Printout" in *Perspecta* (New Haven, Connecticut), vol. 12, 1969.

On WOODS: books—*Candilis, Josic, Woods* by Jürgen Joedicke, Stuttgart 1968; *Toulouse-le-Mirail: Birth of a New Town,* Stuttgart 1975; articles—"Candilis, Josic, Woods" in *Cimaise* (Paris), January/February 1961; "Atelier Candilis, Josic, Woods" in *Architectural Design* (London), January 1965; "Shadrach Woods 1923–1973" by Peter Smithson in *Architectural Design* (London), November 1973; "Shadrach Woods: A Personal Remembrance" by P. C. Papademetriou in *Architecture in Greece* (Athens), vol. 8, 1974; "Team 10 at Royaumont" by Alison Smithson in *Architectural Design* (London), November 1975.

Although Shadrach Woods was trained as an architect and began his career in Le Corbusier's office, his most notable accomplishments were in the field of urban design. As early as the mid 1950's, Woods focused his attention on the increasingly apparent failures of modern urban life, and designed several new town plans, low-income housing projects, and public health facilities for communities throughout the world.

When the radicalism of the 1960's swept the Western world, Woods took a forefront position as champion of the urban inhabitant. During his association with Candilis and Josic in Paris (1955–1967), Woods produced many significant urban schemes as well as several individual buildings. Together, the group developed a policy of "urbanism" that Woods retained after the partnership was dissolved. In the last years of his life, Woods devoted himself even more self-lessly towards the implementation of these ideas.

Urbanism, according to Woods and his associates, is the methodical process by which we organize our cities. It is not a purely physical expression, because it refers not only to the organization of our buildings, but also to the structuring of our service, transportation, and energy networks, as well as to the development of our economic systems. All of these elements determine urban form.

Woods was frustrated by the apparent stagnation of the metabolism of the overall urban form, despite the radical and accelerating changes of the individual systems. For instance, Woods condemned, with others, the singularity of pedestrian and vehicular traffic zones. Such zones had become acutely antiquated, he insisted, because technology had produced new vehicles that now travelled too fast to retain any relationship to human beings on foot.

When he planned, Woods attempted to reform more than just the physical composition of the city, even though he certainly pushed for much physical reformation. "It is clear that no formal composition can provide an answer to these problems," he wrote in 1961, "because the answers of all formal compositions are static, precise, and fixed. Today's buildings are obsolete in five years. Our object is not to make the building flexible, but to make the urban complex flexible enough to foster short life buildings as well as long ones."

Woods felt there was a great urgency to the development of urbanistic solutions, because he sensed that every mistake now being perpetrated would compound itself as we were forced to live in an inadequate environment. In a pamphlet published by Rice University in 1970, Woods pleaded to students to rebel against the status-quo. Despite our limited power as pawns of "the state, the institutions, and the corporations that are the most pernicious forces in society," he told them, we must use whatever skill or power we do wield to alter the current suicidal directions of society. This alteration, he insisted, involved not merely the prevention of negative changes in our cities through the use of organized community resistance, but also the presentation of alternative solutions to real economic problems.

In his final projects in New York, Germany, and France, Woods showed what kind of alternative solutions he meant. His innovative ideas have now become axiomatic: reasonable, anti-opportunistic growth can be accomplished only through sensitive, small scale renewal and renovation, not through the senseless destruction and complete rebuilding of large tracts of still viable communities.

—Mitchell B. Rouda

WOOLLEY, Ken(neth Frank).
Australian. Born in Sydney, New South Wales, 29 May 1933. Educated at Sydney Boys' High School, 1946–49; trainee in the Government Architect's Branch, New South Wales Department of Public Works, Sydney, 1950–54, and studied at the University of Sydney, 1950–54, B.Arch. (honours) 1954 (University Medal; Sulman Medal; Stephenson Turner Medal); awarded Byera Hadley Travelling Scholarship, 1955. Married Cynthia Anne Stuart in 1957; children: Howard, Anna and Simon. Design Architect, Government Architect's Branch, Sydney, 1955–56, 1957–63; Assistant Architect, Chamberlin, Powell and Bon, London, 1956–57; Partner, with Sydney Ancher, *q.v.,* Bruce Mortlock, *q.v.,* and Stuart Murray, *q.v.,* Ancher, Mortlock, Murray and

Woolley, Sydney, 1964–69; Director, Ancher, Mortlock, Murray and Woolley Pty. Ltd., Sydney, 1969–75. Since 1975, Director, Ancher, Mortlock and Woolley Pty. Ltd., Sydney. Visiting Tutor and Critic, University of Sydney, University of New South Wales and New South Wales Institute of Technology, Sydney. Member, New South Wales Board of Architects, 1960–72, New South Wales Board of Architectural Education, 1969–72, and Royal Australian Institute of Architects Aboriginal Housing Panel, 1972–76. Member, New South Wales Building Regulations Advisory Committee, since 1960. Exhibitions: *Sulman Award Exhibition,* Royal Australian Institute of Architects, Sydney, 1963; *RAIA Members Exhibition,* Sydney, 1964; *Australian Exhibition,* at *Expo '67,* Montreal, 1967, and *Expo '70,* Osaka, Japan, 1970; RAIA Awards Exhibitions, Sydney, 1968–77; *Ancher, Mortlock, Murray and Woolley, Sydney Architects, 1946–76,* Art Gallery of New South Wales, Sydney, 1976, and Australian tour, 1977. Recipient: Taubman House Competition Prize (with Michael Dysart), 1958; Sulman Medal, 1962; Bronze Medal, 1962, Wilkinson Award, 1962, 1968, and Blacket Award, 1964, 1969, Royal Australian Institute of Architects; St. Regis-ACI Sisalkraft Travelling Scholarship, 1968; Merit Award, RAIA, New South Wales Chapter, 1972, 1976, 1978. Fellow, 1965, and Life Fellow, 1976, Royal Australian Institute of Architects. Address: Ancher, Mortlock and Woolley Pty. Ltd., 10 Ridge Street, North Sydney, New South Wales 2060, Australia.

Works:

1955/
57   Chapel and Sisters Home, St. Margaret's Hospital, Sydney
      Chemistry School, University of Sydney (with H. Rembert and P. Webber)
1958 Low-Cost Exhibition House, Cherybrooke, Pennant Hills, New South Wales (with Michael Dysart)
1958/
62   Fisher Library, University of Sydney (with T. O'Mahony)
1959 Descon Factory, Brookvale, New South Wales (now demolished)
1960 Mona Vale Hospital, New South Wales (with C. Weatherburn)
1960/
62   Recreation Hall and Chapel, Lidcombe State Hospital, New South Wales
1960/
64   New South Wales State Government Offices, Sydney
1961 Three exhibition houses, Kingsdene, New South Wales (with Michael Dysart)
      Windsor Courthouse restoration, New South Wales
1961/
78   3,000 project houses, Sydney and throughout Australia
1962 Macquarie Field House restoration, Liverpool, New South Wales
      Woolley House, Mosman, New South Wales
1963 Spiral Fountain, State Office Block, Bent Street, Sydney
      Baudish House, Middle Cove, New South Wales
1964 Culhane House, Hunters Hill, New South Wales
      Rothery House, Strathfield, New South Wales
      Theatrette and Premier's Suite interiors, State Office Block, Sydney
      Student Union, University of Newcastle, stage I, New South Wales
1964/
66   St. George Technical College, stage III, New South Wales
      F. C. Pye Field Environment Laboratory, Canberra

1965 Myers House, Mosman, New South Wales
1965/
68   The Penthouses, Darling Point, New South Wales
1965/
69   Student Union Building, Macquarie University, North Ryde, New South Wales (with Bryce Mortlock)
1966 Ullr Ski Lodge, Perisher Valley, New South Wales
      6 townhouses, Milson Road, Cremorne Point, New South Wales
1967 Macquarie Town Housing, Ryde, New South Wales (project)
1967/
68   6 townhouses, Gillies Street, Wollstonecraft, New South Wales
      3-storey apartments, Shirley Road, Wollstonecraft, New South Wales
      Staff House, University of Newcastle, New South Wales
1967/
71   Seventh Day Adventist Church, Canberra
1968 Student Union Building, University of Newcastle, stage II, New South Wales
      Kindergarten, La Perouse, New South Wales
      6-storey apartments, Fairfax Road, Bellevue Hill, New South Wales
      Kinneil Hotel and Apartments (project)
1968/
71   Wentworth Student Union Building, University of Sydney
1969 Steel House for the Future (research project)
      Small office building, Greenmansions Street, St. Leonards, New South Wales
1969/
72   12-storey flats, Reynolds Street, Cremorne, New South Wales
1970/
77   Town Hall House, Sydney Square and Arcade, and Town Hall alterations and restoration, Sydney
1970/
78   Government Detached and Atrium Houses (600), Canberra
      St. Andrew's Cathedral restoration, Sydney
1971 Woden Churches Centre, Canberra
      Woden School for Retarded Children, Canberra
1972 500 apartments, Victoria Point, Sydney (project)
1972/
77   Woden Health Centre and Woden Library, Canberra
1973 108 group houses, Liverpool, New South Wales
      Kippax Health Centre, Canberra
      100 holiday houses, Fiji
1973/
75   Master plan for the Commonwealth Scientific and Industrial Research Organization (C.S.I.R.O.) Black Mountain Campus, Canberra
1973/
78   Australian Embassy, Bangkok, Thailand
1974 High density housing, Rhodes, Sydney (project)
      Wolloomooloo Action Plan Urban Design Study
      Soi Attakarn Prasit Embassy Housing, Bangkok, Thailand (project)
      Woden Child Care Centre, Canberra
1974/
78   Kippax Townhouses, Canberra
      100 townhouses, village centre and new town pilot project, Holsworth, New South Wales
1975 Precast Concrete House (project)
      Master plan and site development for the Academy of Science, Canberra
1975/
78   Infill housing and Victorian period house restoration, Glebe, New South Wales

Ken Woolley: Town Hall House and Sydney Square, 1977

1976   Pettit House, Canberra
1976/
  79   Rare Book Library, University of Sydney
       (project)
       1,000 apartments and urban development,
       Darlinghurst Hill, Sydney
1977/
  79   Radio station, Vila, New Hebrides
1978   West Amenities and Project Control Facility,
       Garden Island Naval Dockyard, Sydney
       Radio station, Honiara, Solomon Islands

Publications:

By WOOLLEY: articles—"Air Conditioning" in *Australian Building Science and Technology* (Sydney) October 1964; "How Australians Should Be Housed" in *Economic Society of Australia Journal* (Sydney), March 1967; statement in *Towards an Australian Architecture* by Harry Sowden, Sydney 1968; "Concrete" in *Building Science Forum* (Sydney), June 1970; "Project Housing" in *Sunday Review* (Sydney), 1971; "Australia's Terrace Houses" in *Architectural Forum* (New York), May 1971; "Australian Domestic Architecture" in *Art and Australia* (Sydney), June 1971; "Tertiary Education Buildings" and "Travel Sketches" in *Architecture in Australia* (Sydney), August/September 1976; "Heritage Legislation in New South Wales" in *Architecture in Australia* (Sydney), May 1978.

On WOOLLEY: books—*Australia's Home* by Robin Boyd, revised edition, Melbourne 1952; *The Puzzle of Architecture* by Robin Boyd, Melbourne 1965; *Towards an Australian Architecture* by Harry Sowden, Sydney 1968; *In the Making* by Craig McGregor, Harry Williamson and David Moore, Melbourne 1969; *Australian Style* by Babette Hayes and April Hersey, Sydney 1970; *Living and Party Living* by McKay, Stretton and Mant, Melbourne 1971; *444 Sydney Buildings* by Richard Apperly and Peter Lind, Sydney 1971; *An Australian Identity* by Jennifer Taylor, Sydney 1972; *Housing in the Seventies* by Howard Tanner, Sydney 1976; *Ancher, Mortlock, Murray and Woolley, Sydney Architects, 1946–76* by David Saunders and Catherine Bourke, Sydney 1976.

*

Early on, it seemed to me that the dogma of the conventional modern movement had not come to terms with humanist values. Its functional and visual shortcomings were apparent in the failure to resolve elements incompatible with an overall concept.

Thus my early work, in the 1950's, tended to pay respect to Aalto for his informal and accidental effects and to Mies for the vigour of his detailing.

There followed a conviction that directness of detail and a reassessment of traditional values were needed and, when applied to domestic and related work, produced a style that Robin Boyd called "a tamed romantic kind of Brutalism" and, with other participants, became known as the Sydney School.

Perhaps because it was expressed in rather warm and traditional materials—brick, tile and timber—there evolved a preconception of the style which often left it unrecognised in other types of buildings, because of its tendency to approach each problem afresh.

I believe, like Venturi, that some buildings are naturally ordinary and demand general, rather traditional responses, whereas others are special and generate particular solutions. I seem to have had many opportunities in both areas, and regard the ordinary buildings, for example the low cost housing, to be just as important as particular special buildings. It is possible to misinterpret the special responses as intentional moves towards a new style or simply as lack of a consistent style.

All of my work, it seems to me now, has been based on finding a framework (not necessarily frame construction) which is capable of acting as a reference for all the functional and aesthetic requirements of the programme. That is, a system or discipline which encompasses the geometry, construction technique and planning arrangements and sets up the potential for variations and complexities which can enhance the design, serving a myriad of minor functional and humanistic subtleties. Ideally, the elements have an inherent capability of permutation by chance and by functional determinants. The achievement of this framework is an effort of synthesis based on analysis and understanding.

The recently completed Town Hall development in Sydney covers a broader range of activities than before. From a basic requirement for ordinary offices on a standard budget, the building becomes the source of a major civic design exercise. The historic Town Hall is restored, its acoustics improved, facilities for audiences extend into the new building, and a new complex of civic spaces forms a Town Square. Direct access is gained to a major underground station, and pedestrian movement on the whole city block is transformed. The restoration work, which also involved St. Andrew's Cathedral for the National Trust, is another interest for which I would like to have more time.

Further new directions are seen in the Australian Embassy in Bangkok, which revives the traditional pavilion standing in water and is clad in golden yellow temple tiles. The most recent project at the Sydney Naval Dockyard is designed with a stressed skin steel plate structure, like the superstructure of the ships it services.

A major central urban high-density housing scheme will start soon and creates new urban streets from a predominantly low-rise solution, utilising them for open space, circulation, visual interest and security. Variation and complexity are developed around a standard low-cost construction technique employing all its geometric possibilities together with added variable components—balconies, doorways, bays and terraces, shop fronts and the like.

Like most architects, I have been plagued in recent years by unbuilt projects, innovative but ill-fated. Many of these are due to the failures of the planning profession, which also deserves criticism for prescribing real building solutions into regulations, stifling creative development.

I am still very involved with drawing, both as a record, like travel sketches, and as a means of communication. Drawing is also the medium in which to work out the development of basic ideas.

As for the future, I hope to see architects concentrating on a truly sensitive language and insisting on the responsibility for the environment's being placed where it belongs, with political planning.

—Ken Woolley

The romantic values of the "Sydney School" are epitomized by Ken Woolley's domestic architecture, which is typified by a selection of warm natural materials, picturesque organization of form and fluid handling of space. Ken Woolley, like many of his contemporaries in the 1960's, is a versatile eclectic. His significance arises from his unerring sense of materials and his ability to relate building forms to materials and their method of assembly, his consistent good taste, and his considerable facility in composing with space. Woolley resembles Eero Saarinen in the way he seeks to respond to the unique and plays down the universal in each problem. Woolley, like Saarinen, often begins design with a consideration of materials, and here his sure sense of materials and selection to suit each context enables him to develop a formal language for each occasion which is invariably appropriate. This flair for materials restrains Woolley's eclecticism and saves his architecture from becoming arbitrary and whimsical.

Ken Woolley and his close contemporaries, Peter Webber, Peter Hall and Michael Dysart, started their careers as trainees in the New South Wales Government Architect's Office. On his return from overseas in 1957, Woolley contributed to the debate on the definition of a regional Australian identity in architecture which was getting under way in Sydney. The question of an international or local expression in Australian architecture was highlighted for Woolley by the dichotomy of Harry Rembert's public and private buildings (Rembert at the time was Senior Design Architect in the Government Architect's Office). Rembert had designed some fine technical colleges in the late 1930's in the manner of Dudok, but his own house in the Blue Mountains was a rustic though not unsophisticated bush house with the outside clad with hardwood fence palings and lined inside with caneite nailed to the stud frame. The only aesthetic concession was the gaily painted window frames. Rembert's bush house started Woolley and

his friends thinking about an Australian idiom, and on his study trip to Europe, after graduation from the University of Sydney, Woolley made a detailed visual analysis of the weathering of materials. The understanding of materials is the departure point for Woolley's architecture.

The change from his position as Government Architect to work in private practice in 1963 is reflected in the type of projects with which he worked. His public phase is identified with such buildings as the Chemistry Block, Sydney University (inspired by Saarinen's G.M. Technical Centre), the Chapel at St. Margaret's Hospital, the Lidcombe State Hospital Recreation Hall and Chapel, the Fisher Library and the New South Wales State Government Offices. The Chapel at St. Margaret's Hospital, the Fisher Library and the State Government Offices are the most important works in Woolley's Government portfolio. The differences of treatment between the Fisher Library and the State Government Offices are revealing. Where a strong horizontal rhythm is achieved in the library by projecting the floor slabs all round, the offices have a vertical expression which is emphasized by recessing the precast concrete floor panels behind the bronze clad columns. The influence of Mies van der Rohe's Seagrams Building is evident in the extensive use of bronze in both buildings.

In 1958 Woolley and Michael Dysart won the Taubman House Competition. The resultant publicity led to an involvement in the design of standard project houses, first with Lend Lease in 1961 and later with Pettit and Sevitt. More than 4,000 houses were built to Woolley designs, and they helped to popularize good design in the highly competitive mass-housing market. The lyrical expression of materials and space in Ken Woolley's own house at Mosman is disciplined by a rationalized carpentry and the use of a 12ft. square bay. This complex, beautiful house is one of Woolley's most personal and important works. The house consists of four staggered platforms on a steep site which are overshot by steeply inclined tiled skillion roofs each subtly freed from the others. Between 1965 and 1968 Woolley helped pioneer the town house type of housing in Australia. "The Penthouses," a terraced group of flats at Darling Point overlooking Rushcutter's Bay, were an important step in gaining acceptance for the town house concept.

The Newcastle University Student Union elaborated the themes of natural materials, tiled skillion roofs and expressive carpentry from his Mosman house and, with the Universities Staff House, represent an outstanding statement of "Sydney School" values. The Wentworth Student Union, Sydney, is similar in style to Denys Lasdun's Royal College of Physicians, London, and is a marked contrast to the Newcastle Union. The new Australian Embassy, Bangkok, resembles Walter Gropius' American Embassy in Athens in its form, which has been given an expressive undercut section and elevated on widely spaced columns over a landscape of ponds and water plants. Of his recent work, the Town Hall House/Sydney Square is the most comprehensive and in terms of civic design the most significant building to date.

Woolley's architecture sums up much that is best in Sydney architecture in the 1960's and 70's. His approach is a mixture of reason and romanticism and of local and international influences. The most important feature of Woolley's architecture is his sensitivity to, and understanding of, the proper expression of materials.

—Philip Drew

WRIGHT, Frank Lloyd.

American. Born in Richland Center, Wisconsin, 8 June 1867; moved with his family to Weymouth, Massachusetts, 1874; settled in Madison, Wisconsin, 1877. Educated at Second Ward School, Madison, 1879–83; University of Wisconsin School of Engineering, Madison, 1885–87. Married Catherine Lee Tobin in 1889 (separated, 1909; subsequently divorced); children: the architect Lloyd Wright, *q.v.*, John, Catherine, Frances, David and Llewellyn; left family to live with Mrs. Mamah Bortwick Cheney, 1909 until her death in the Taliesin fire, 1914; married Miriam Noel in 1915 (separated, 1924; died, 1927); married Olgivanna Lazovich in 1925; children: Iovanna and (by wife's previous marriage) Svetlana. Worked as a Junior Draftsman for Allen D. Conover, Madison, 1885–87, and for Lyman Silsbee, Chicago, 1887; Assistant Architect, 1888–89, and Head of the Planning and Design Department, 1889–93, Adler and Sullivan, Chicago; in partnership with Cecil Corwin, Chicago, 1893–96; in private practice in the Chicago suburb of Oak Park, 1896–97, and in Chicago, 1897–1909; travelled with Mrs. Cheney to Europe, and stayed in Fiesole, near Florence, 1909–11; built first Taliesin house and studio, and resumed practice, Spring Green, Wisconsin, 1911; re-opened Chicago office, 1912; Taliesin partially destroyed by fire and rebuilt as Taliesin II, 1914; established office in Tokyo in conjunction with work on the Imperial Hotel, 1915–20: while in Japan compiled Spaulding Collection of Japanese Prints, now in the Museum of Fine Arts, Boston; worked on first concrete "texture block" houses, California, 1921–24; Taliesin II partially destroyed by fire and rebuilt as Taliesin III, 1925; worked in La Jolla, California, 1928; established southwestern headquarters, Ocatillo, at Chandler, Arizona, 1928–29; established Wright Foundation Fellowship at Taliesin, 1932 (with annual winter transfer of Fellowship activities from Spring Green to Chandler, Arizona, 1933–38, and to Scottsdale, Arizona, from 1938); worked on major theoretical studies for Broadacre City from 1933; built Taliesin West, Paradise Valley, near Scottsdale, Arizona, 1938; continued to practice in Wisconsin and Arizona until his death, 1959; students formed Taliesin Associated Architects on his death to complete various works. Exhibitions: Chicago Architectural Club, 1894, 1898, 1899, 1900, 1901, 1902, 1907; Museum of Modern Art, New York, 1931, toured the United States and Europe; *Broadacre City,* Pittsburgh, 1935; Museum of Modern Art, New York, 1940; *Sixty Years of Living Architecture: The Work of Frank Lloyd Wright,* Palazzo Strozzi, Florence, 1951, European tour, 1951–53, and North American tour, 1953–54; *Mile High Building,* Sherman Hotel, Chicago, 1956; *An Architect and His Client: Frank Lloyd Wright and Francis W. Little,* Metropolitan Museum of Art, New York, 1973; *The Decorative Designs of Frank Lloyd Wright,* Renwick Museum, Smithsonian Institution, Washington, D.C., 1978. Collections: Frank Lloyd Wright Foundation, Taliesin, Spring Green, Wisconsin, and Taliesin West, Paradise Valley, near Scottsdale, Arizona; Frank Lloyd Wright Collection, Avery Library, Columbia University, New York; Northwestern University, Evanston, Illinois. Recipient: Kenchiko Ho Citation, Royal Household of Japan, 1919; Royal Gold Medal, Royal Institute of British Architects, 1941; Gold Medal, American Institute of Architects, 1949; Gold Medal, AIA, Philadelphia Chapter, 1949; Peter Cooper Award, 1949; Centennial Award, *Popular Mechanics,* 1950; Star of Solidarity, City of Venice, 1951; Medici Medal, City of Florence, 1951; Gold Medal, National Institute of Arts and Letters, 1953; Brown Medal, Franklin Institute, Philadelphia, 1954; Freedom of the City, Chicago, 1956. M.A.: Wesleyan University, Middletown, Connecticut, 1939; D.F.A.: Princeton University, New Jersey, 1947; Yale University, New Haven, Connecticut, 1954; University of Wisconsin, Madison, 1955; LL.D.: Florida Southern College, Lakeland, 1950; D.Phil.: University of Wales, Bangor, 1956. Member, National Institute of

Frank Lloyd Wright: Robie House, Chicago, 1909

Arts and Letters, 1949. Honorary Member: Academie Royale des Beaux Arts, Brussels, 1927; Akademie der Künste, Berlin, 1929; National Academy of Brazil, 1932; Royal Institute of British Architects, 1941; National Academy of Architects, Uruguay, 1942; National Academy of Architects, Mexico, 1943; National Academy of Finland, 1946; Royal Academy of Fine Arts, Stockholm, 1953. *Died* (in Phoenix, Arizona), *9 April 1959.*

Works:

1885   University Avenue Power House, Madison, Wisconsin (project)
1887   Hillside Home School Building I, for the Misses Lloyd Jones, Spring Green, Wisconsin (converted to Taliesin Fellowship Complex, 1933)
     Misses Lloyd Jones House, Spring Green, Wisconsin (project)
     Unitarian Chapel, Sioux City, Iowa (project)
1889   Frank Lloyd Wright House, Oak Park, Illinois
1890   Charnley House, Ocean Springs, Mississippi
     MacHarg House, Chicago
     Louis Sullivan House, Ocean Springs, Mississippi
     Cooper House, La Grange, Illinois (project)
1892   Charnley House, 1365 North Astor Street, Chicago
     Blossom House, Chicago
     Clark House, La Grange, Illinois
     Emmond House, La Grange, Illinois
     Mrs. Thomas Gale House, Oak Park, Illinois
     Harlan House, Chicago
     McArthur House, Chicago
     Parker House, Oak Park, Illinois
     Albert Sullivan House, Chicago
     Victoria Hotel remodelling, Chicago Heights
1893   Lake Mendota Boathouse, Madison, Wisconsin
     Walter Gale House, Oak Park, Illinois
     Lamp Cottage, Lake Mendota, Madison, Wisconsin
     Frank Lloyd Wright House playroom addition, Oak Park, Illinois
     Lake Monona Boathouse, Madison, Wisconsin (project)
     Library and Museum, Milwaukee (competition project)
1894   Winslow House, River Forest, Illinois

     Bagley House, Hinsdale, Illinois
     Bassett House remodelling, Oak Park, Illinois
     Peter Goan House, La Grange, Illinois
     Roloson Apartments, Chicago
     Wooley House, Chicago
     Concrete Monolithic Bank (project)
     Orris Goan House, La Grange, Illinois (project)
     McAfee House, Chicago (project)
1895   Francis Apartments, 4304 South Forrestville, Chicago
     Francisco Terrace Apartments, 253 North Francisco, Chicago
     Moore House, Oak Park, Illinois
     Waller Apartments, Chicago
     Williams House, River Forest, Illinois
     Young House alterations, Oak Park, Illinois
     Amusement Park, Wolf Lake, Illinois (project)
     Baldwin House, Oak Park, Illinois (project)
     Lexington Terrace Apartment Building, Chicago (project)
     Luxfer Prism Company Skyscraper, Chicago (project)
1896   Format for *House Beautiful* magazine
     Goodrich House, Oak Park, Illinois
     Roberts House remodelling and Stable, Oak Park, Illinois
     Romeo and Juliet Windmill Tower, Hillside Home School, Spring Green, Wisconsin
     Devin House, Chicago (project)
     Perkins Apartment, Chicago (project)
     Roberts Houses (4), Ridgeland, Illinois (project)
1897   Heller House, 5132 South Woodlawn, Chicago
     Frank Lloyd Wright Studio (addition to house), Oak Park, Illinois
     George Furbeck House, Oak Park, Illinois
     Wallis Boathouse, Lake Delavan, Wisconsin
     All Souls Building, Lincoln Center, Chicago (project)
     Chicago Screw Company Factory Building, Chicago (project)
1898   Rollin Furbeck House, Oak Park, Illinois
     River Forest Golf Club, Illinois
     Smith House, Oak Park, Illinois
     Mozart Gardens Restaurant remodelling, Chicago (project)
     Waller House, River Forest, Illinois
1899   Husser House, Chicago

     Waller House remodelling, River Forest, Illinois
     Cheltenham Beach Resort, near Chicago (project)
     Eckhart House, River Forest, Illinois (project)
     House (project published in *Architectural Review,* London)
1900   Jesse Adams House, Longwood, Illinois
     William Adams House, Chicago
     Bradley House, Kankakee, Illinois
     Dana House, Springfield, Illinois
     Foster House, Chicago
     Goodsmith House, Lake Delavan, Wisconsin
     Hickox House, Kankakee, Illinois
     Pitkin Lodge, Desbarats, Ontario, Canada
     Wallis House, Lake Delavan, Wisconsin
     Abraham Lincoln Center, Chicago (project)
     Home in a Prairie Town (project published in *Ladies Home Journal,* New York)
     Francis W. Little House I, Peoria, Illinois (project)
     Motion Picture Theatre, Los Angeles (project)
     School, Crosbyton, Texas (project)
     A Small House with Lots of Room in It (project published in *Ladies Home Journal,* New York)
1901   Davenport House, River Forest, Illinois
     Universal Portland Cement Company Exhibition Pavilion, Buffalo, New York
     Henderson House, Elmhurst, Illinois
     Hills House remodelling, Oak Park, Illinois
     Jones House, Boathouse and Gate Lodge, Lake Delavan, Wisconsin
     River Forest Golf Club additions, Illinois
     Thomas House, Oak Park, Illinois
     Gatehouse and Gardener's Cottage, for Waller House, River Forest, Illinois
     Gate Lodge remodelling, for Wallis House, Lake Delavan, Wisconsin
     Stables, Wilder House, Elmhurst, Illinois
1902   Willits House, Highland Park, Illinois
     Fricke House, Oak Park, Illinois
     George Gerts Double House, Whitehall, Michigan
     Walter Gerts House, Whitehall, Michigan
     Heurtley House remodelling, Marquette Island, Michigan
     Heurtley House, Oak Park, Illinois
     Hillside Home School Building II, for the Misses Lloyd Jones, Spring Green, Wisconsin (now part of Taliesin)
     Francis Little House II, Peoria, Illinois
     Ross House, Lake Delavan, Wisconsin
     Spencer House, Lake Delavan, Wisconsin
     Lake Delavan Yacht Club, Wisconsin (project)
     Metzger House, Ontario, Canada (project)
     Mosher House (project)
     House, Oak Park, Illinois (project)
     Waller House I, Charlevoix, Michigan (project)
     Yahara Boat Club, Madison, Wisconsin (project)
1903   Barton House, Buffalo, New York
     Freeman House, Hinsdale, Illinois
     Martin House, Oak Park, Illinois
     Scoville Park Fountain, Oak Park, Illinois
     Walser House, Chicago
     Chicago and Northwestern Railway Stations for the Chicago suburbs (project)
     Lamp House I, Madison, Wisconsin (project)
     Roberts Quadruple Block Plan (24 houses), Oak Park, Illinois (project)
     Waller House II, Charlevoix, Michigan (project)
     Frank Lloyd Wright Studio-House, Oak Park, Illinois (project)
1904   Larkin Building, Buffalo, New York
     Cheney House, Oak Park, Illinois
     Lamp House II, Madison, Wisconsin

Martin House and Conservatory, Buffalo, New York

Baldwin House I, Kenilworth, Illinois (project)

Bank Building I, Dwight, Illinois (project)

Clarke House, Peoria, Illinois (project)

House, Highland Park, Illinois (project)

Scudder House, Desbarats, Ontario, Canada (project)

Ullman House, Oak Park, Illinois (project)

Larkin Company Workmens' Rowhouses, Buffalo, New York (project)

1905 Adams House, Highland Park, Illinois

Baldwin House II, Kenilworth, Illinois

Bank Building II, Dwight, Illinois

Brown House, Evanston, Illinois

E-Z Polish Factory, 3005 West Carroll, Chicago

Gilpin House, Oak Park, Illinois

Glasner House, Glencoe, Illinois

Hardy House, Racine, Wisconsin

Heath House, Buffalo, New York

Johnson House, Lake Delavan, Wisconsin

Lawrence Memorial Library interior, Springfield, Illinois

Rookery Building entrance, lobbies and balcony-court remodelling, LaSalle Street, Chicago

Barnes House, McCook, Nebraska (project)

House on a Lake (project)

Varnish Factory (project)

Concrete Apartment Building, Chicago (project)

Pergola and Pavilion, for Moore House, Oak Park, Illinois (project)

1906 Unity Temple, Oak Park, Illinois

Beachy House, Oak Park, Illinois

De Rhodes House, South Bend, Indiana

Fuller House, Glencoe, Illinois

Gridley House, Batavia, Illinois

Hoyt House, Geneva, Illinois

Millard House, Highland Park, Illinois

Nicholas House, Flossmoor, Illinois

Pettit Mortuary Chapel, Belvedere, Illinois

River Forest Tennis Club, Illinois

Shaw House remodelling, Montreal

Bock Studio-House, Maywood, Illinois (project)

Devin House, Eliot, Maine (project)

Fireproof House for $5,000 (project published in *Ladies Home Journal,* New York)

Gerts House, Glencoe, Illinois (project)

Ludington House, Dwight, Illinois (project)

Shaw House, Montreal (project)

Stone House, Glencoe, Illinois (project)

1907 Garage, for Blossom House, Chicago

Cummings Real Estate Office, River Forest, Illinois

Fabyan House remodelling, Geneva, Illinois

Fox River Country Club remodelling, Geneva, Illinois

Hunt House, La Grange, Illinois

Larkin Company Pavilion, *Jamestown Exposition,* Virginia

Fricke House alterations, Oak Park, Illinois

Pebbles and Balch Shop, Oak Park, Illinois

"Tan-y-deri" (Porter House), Spring Green, Wisconsin

Sutton House, McCook, Nebraska

Tomek House, Riverside, Illinois

Westcott House, Springfield, Ohio

McCormick House, Lake Forest, Illinois (project)

Municipal Art Gallery, Chicago (project)

Porter House II, Spring Green, Wisconsin (project)

1908 Coonley House ("Zoned" Prairie House), Riverside, Illinois

Browne's Bookstore, Chicago

Davidson House, Buffalo, New York

Evans House, Chicago

Gilmore House, Madison, Wisconsin

Horner House, Chicago

Francis Little House, Wayzata, Minnesota

May House, Grand Rapids, Michigan

Roberts House, River Forest, Illinois

Stockman House, Mason City, Iowa

Baker House I, Wilmette, Illinois (project)

Stables, for Brigham House (project)

Guthrie House, Sewanee, Tennessee (project)

Horseshoe Inn, Estes Park, Colorado (project)

Melson House, Mason City, Iowa (project)

1909 Robie House, 5757 South Woodlawn, Chicago

Arcade Building, Chicago

Gale House, Oak Park, Illinois

Baker House II, Wilmette, Illinois

City National Bank and Hotel, Mason City, Iowa

Francis Little House additions, Peoria, Illinois

Copeland House alterations, Oak Park, Illinois

Ingalls House, River Forest, Illinois

Steffens House, Chicago

Stewart House, Montecito, California

Thurber Art Gallery, Chicago

Ziegler House, Frankfort, Kentucky

Brown House, Geneva, Illinois (project)

City Dwelling with Glass Front (project)

Larwell House, Muskegon, Michigan (project)

Lexington Terrace, Chicago (2nd project)

Parker Studio remodelling (project)

Roberts House, River Forest, Illinois (project)

Town Hall, Glencoe, Illinois (project)

Town of Bitter Root, Darby, Montana (project)

Bathing Pavilion, for Waller House, Charlevoix, Michigan (project)

Waller Rental Houses (3), River Forest, Illinois (project)

1910 Amberg House, Grand Rapids, Michigan

Blythe and Markley Law Office remodelling, Chicago

Como Orchard Summer Colony, Darby, Montana (partly executed)

Irving House, Decatur, Illinois

Universal Portland Cement Company Exhibit, Madison Square Garden, New York

Frank Lloyd Wright House-Studio, Viale Verdi, Fiesole, Italy (project)

1911 American System Ready-Cut Houses, for Richards Company, Milwaukee (prototypes)

Angster House, Lake Bluff, Illinois

Balch House, Oak Park, Illinois

Pavilion, Banff National Park, Alberta, Canada

Booth House, Glencoe, Illinois

Gardener's Cottage, for Coonley House, Riverside, Illinois

Lake Geneva Inn, Wisconsin

Taliesin, Spring Green, Wisconsin (living quarters destroyed by fire, 1914)

Adams House I, Oak Park, Illinois (project)

Booth Summer Cottage (project)

Christian Catholic Church, Zion, Illinois (project)

Greenhouse, for Coonley House, Riverside, Illinois (project)

Coonley Kindergarten, Riverside, Illinois (project)

Cutten House, Downer's Grove, Illinois (project)

Esbenshade House, Milwaukee (project)

Walter Gerts House alterations, River Forest, Illinois (project)

Garage and Stables, for Heath House, Buffalo, New York (project)

Madison Hotel, Wisconsin (project)

North Shore Electric Train Waiting Stations for the Chicago suburbs (project)

Porter House III, Spring Green, Wisconsin (project)

Schroeder House, Milwaukee (project)

Frank Lloyd Wright House, Chicago (project)

1912 Coonley Playhouse, Riverside, Illinois

Greene House, Aurora, Illinois

Park Ridge Country Club addition and alterations, Illinois

Dress shop, Oak Park, Illinois (project)

Florida House, Palm Beach (project)

Kehl Dance Academy House and Shops, Madison, Wisconsin (project)

San Francisco Call Press Building (project)

Schoolhouse, La Grange, Illinois (project)

Small Townhouse (project)

Taliesin Cottages (2), Spring Green, Wisconsin (project)

1913 Adams House II, Oak Park, Illinois

Francis Little House II, Wayzata, Minnesota

Midway Gardens (including interiors), Chicago (destroyed)

Block of city row houses, Chicago (project)

Carnegie Library, Ottawa, Ontario, Canada (project)

Hilly House, Brookfield, Illinois (project)

Kellogg House, Milwaukee (project)

Mendelsohn House, Albany, New York (project)

1914 Mori Oriental Art Studio, Chicago

Taliesin II, Spring Green, Wisconsin (living quarters; original studios and workshops remained intact; rebuilt living quarters again destroyed by fire, 1925)

Concert Gardens, Chicago (project)

Jackson Houses (3) (project)

State Bank, Spring Green, Wisconsin (project)

United States Embassy, Tokyo (project)

Vogelsang Dinner Gardens, Chicago (project)

1915 Bach House, Chicago

Brigham House, Glencoe, Illinois

German Warehouse, Richland Center, Wisconsin

Ravine Bluffs Housing Development and Bridge, Glencoe, Illinois

Chinese Hospital (project)

Chinese restaurant, Milwaukee (project)

Lake Shore House (project)

Model Quarter-Section Development, Chicago (project)

Wood House, Decatur, Illinois (project)

1916 Bagley House, Grand Beach, Michigan

Hollyhock House (Barnsdall House), Los Angeles

Bock House, Milwaukee

Carr House, Grand Beach, Michigan

Duplex apartments, for Minkwitz Ready-Cut Systems, Milwaukee

Vosburgh House, Grand Beach, Michigan

Behn House, Grand Beach, Michigan (project)

Converse House, Palisades Park, Michigan (project)

William Allen White House remodelling, Emporia, Kansas (project)

1917 Allen House, Wichita, Kansas

Hunt House, Oshkosh, Wisconsin

Hayashi House, Tokyo

Odawara Hotel, Nagoya, Japan (project)

Powell House, Wichita, Kansas (project)

1918 Fukuhara House, Hakone, Japan

Yamamura House, Ashiya, Japan

Count Immu House, Tokyo (project)

Viscount Inouge House, Tokyo (project)

Motion picture theatre, Tokyo (project)

1919 Gallery for Japanese Prints, for the Spaulding Collection, Boston (project)

Monolith Homes, Racine, Wisconsin (project)

1920 Barnsdall Houses A and B, Los Angeles

Cantilevered Skyscraper (project)

Theatre, shops and apartments, Olive Hill, Los Angeles (project)
1921 Mrs. Thomas Gale House, Whitehall, Michigan
Giuy Gakuen School of the Free Spirit, Tokyo
La Miniatura (Millard House), Pasadena, California
Doheny Ranch development, near Los Angeles (project)
Glass and Copper Skyscraper (project)
Baron Goto House, Tokyo (project)
Block House, Los Angeles (project)
1922 Imperial Hotel, Tokyo
Little Dipper (Barnsdall Kindergarten), Los Angeles
Freeman House, Los Angeles
Lowe House, Eagle Rock, California
Storer House, Los Angeles
Johnson Desert Compound and Shrine, Death Valley, California (project)
Merchandising Building, Los Angeles (project)
Desert Springs (house), Mojave Desert, California (project)
Tahoe Summer Colony (cottages and barges), Lake Tahoe, California (project)
1923 Ennis House, Los Angeles
Moore House, Oak Park, Illinois (rebuilding after fire)
Martin House, Buffalo, New York (project)
1924 Indian Figure Sculptures, Madison, Wisconsin (in conjunction with the Nakoma Project)
Gladney House, Fort Worth, Texas (project)
Nakoma Country Club, Madison, Wisconsin (project)
National Life Insurance Company Skyscraper, Chicago (project)
Planetarium, Sugar Loaf Mountain, Maryland (project)
1925 Taliesin III, Spring Green, Wisconsin (living quarters only; original studios and workshops, 1911, remained intact)
Millard Gallery, Pasadena, California (project)
Phi Gamma Delta Fraternity House, University of Wisconsin, Madison (project)
Steel Cathedral, New York (project)
1926 Covers for Liberty magazine
Kinder Symphony Playhouse, Oak Park, Illinois (project)
Skyscraper Regulation, Chicago (project)
Standardized Concrete and Copper Gas Station (project)
1927 Arizona Biltmore Hotel, Phoenix (with Albert McArthur)
Martin House, Derby, New York
1928 Ocatillo (Wright's Southwestern headquarters), Chandler, Arizona
Beach Cottages, Ras-El-Bar Island, Damiette, Egypt (project)
Blue Sky Burial Terraces, Buffalo, New York (project)
Cudney House, Chandler, Arizona (project)
Jones House I, Tulsa, Oklahoma (project)
Low-cost concrete block houses, Chandler, Arizona (project)
San-Marcos-in-the-Desert Resort Hotel, Chandler, Arizona (project)
San Marcos Hotel alterations, Chandler, Arizona (project)
San Marcos Water Gardens, Chandler, Arizona (project)
School for negro children, La Jolla, California (project)
Simple block house, Chandler, Arizona (project)
Young House, Chandler, Arizona (project)
1929 Jones House II, Tulsa, Oklahoma
St. Mark's Tower, New York (project)
1930 Vases and glassware for Leerdam Glass, Netherlands

Automobile with Cantilevered Top (project)
Cabins for desert or woods, Chicago YMCA (project)
Grouped apartment towers, Chicago (project)
Noble Apartment House, Los Angeles (project)
1931 Capital Journal Building, Salem, Oregon (project)
House on the Mesa, Denver (project)
3 schemes for A Century of Progress, 1933 World's Fair, Chicago (project)
1932 Automobile and airplane filling and service stations (project)
Cinema and shops, Michigan City, Indiana (project)
Conventional House (project)
Prefabricated sheet steel farm units (project)
Highway overpass (project)
Life House (project)
New Theatre (project)
Norm of the Prefabricated House (project)
Overhead Filling Station (project)
Prefabricated sheet steel and glass roadside markets (project)
Willey House I, Minneapolis (project)
1933 Taliesin Fellowship Complex, Spring Green, Wisconsin (addition to existing Hillside Home School; partly executed, theatre destroyed by fire, 1952)
1934 Broadacre City model and exhibition plans
Willey House II, Minneapolis
Helicopter (project)
Road Machine (project)
Train (project)
Zoned House No. 1 (project)
1935 Falling Water (Kaufmann House), Bear Run, Pennsylvania
Hoult House (1st Usonian House), Wichita, Kansas (project)
Lusk House, Huron, South Dakota (project)
Marcus House, Dallas (project)
Zoned City House (project)
Zoned Country House (project)
Zoned Suburban House (project)
1936 Hanna House, Palo Alto, California
Jacobs House, Westmoreland, Wisconsin
S. C. Johnson Administration Building, Racine, Wisconsin
Roberts House, Marquette, Michigan
Chandler Hotel remodelling, Chandler, Arizona (project)
Little San Marcos-in-the-Desert Resort Inn, Chandler, Arizona (project)
1937 Wingspread (Johnson House; "The Last Prairie House"), Racine, Wisconsin
Edgar J. Kaufmann Sr. Offices, Pittsburgh
All-steel houses (100), Los Angeles (project)
Borglum Studio, Black Hills, South Dakota (project)
Bramson Dress Shop, Oak Park, Illinois (project)
Memorial to the Soil (chapel), Southern Wisconsin (project)
Notz House, Pittsburgh (project)
Garage, for Parker House, Janesville, Wisconsin (project)
1938 Guest House, for Falling Water (Kaufmann House), Bear Run, Pennsylvania
Midway Farm Buildings, Taliesin, Spring Green, Wisconsin
Rebhohn House, Great Neck, Long Island, New York
Taliesin West (Wright's Winter headquarters), Scottsdale, Arizona
House for a Family of $5,000–$6,000 Income (project for Life, New York)
Jester All-Plywood House, Palos Verdes, California (project)
Johnson Gatehouse and Farm Group, Wind Point, Wisconsin (project)
Jurgensen House, Evanston, Illinois (project)
McCallum House, Northampton, Massachu-

setts (project)
Monona Terrace, Madison Civic Center, Wisconsin (project)
Pinetree House (Smith House), Piedmont Pines, California (project)
1939 Armstrong House, near Gary, Indiana
Goetsch-Winkler House I, Okemos, Michigan
Rosenbaum House, Florence, Alabama
Schwartz House, Two Rivers, Wisconsin
Sturges House, Brentwood Heights, California
Suntop Homes (quadruple house), Ardmore, Pennsylvania
Bell House, Los Angeles (project)
Carlson House, Superior, Wisconsin (project)
Crystal Heights Hotel, Shops and Theatres, Washington, D.C. (project)
Front gates, Taliesin, Spring Green, Wisconsin (project)
Lowenstein House, Mason City, Iowa (project)
Mauer House, Los Angeles (project)
Spivey House, Fort Lauderdale, Florida (project)
Usonian House Development (7 buildings), Okemos, Michigan (project)
1940 Baird House, Amherst, Massachusetts
Bazett House, Hillsborough, California
Christie House, Bernardsville, New Jersey
Community Church, Kansas City, Missouri
Euchtman House, Baltimore
Lewis House, Libertyville, Illinois
Manson House, Wausau, Wisconsin
Pauson House, Phoenix, Arizona
Pew House, Madison, Wisconsin
Pope House, Falls Church, Virginia
Sondern House, Kansas City, Missouri
Auldbrass Plantation, near Yemassee, South Carolina
Model House, Museum of Modern Art, New York (exhibition project)
Nesbitt House, Carmel Bay, California (project)
Eaglefeather (Oboler House), Los Angeles (project)
Pence House, Hilo, Hawaii (project)
Rentz House, Madison, Wisconsin (project)
Watkins Studio, Barnegate City, New Jersey (project)
Methodist church, Spring Green, Wisconsin (project)
1940/
59 Florida Southern College, Lakeland
1941 Affleck House, Bloomfield Hills, Michigan
Griggs House, Tacoma, Washington
Oboler Gatehouse and Retreat, Los Angeles
Richardson House, Glenridge, New Jersey
Snowflake (Wall House), Plymouth, Michigan
Barton House, Pine Bluff, Wisconsin (project)
Dayer Music Studio, Detroit (project)
Ellinwood House, Deerfield, Illinois (project)
Field House, Peru, Illinois (project)
Mountain Lakes (Guenther House), East Caldwell, New Jersey (project)
Petersen House, West Racine, Wisconsin (project)
Schevill House, Tucson, Arizona (project)
Sigma Chi Fraternity House, Hanover, Indiana (project)
Sundt House, Madison, Wisconsin (project)
Waterstreet Studio, near Spring Green, Wisconsin (project)
1942 Solar Hemicycle (Jacobs House), Middleton, Wisconsin
Burlingham House, El Paso, Texas (project)
Circle Pines Center, Cloverdale, Michigan (project)
Cloverleaf Quadruple Housing, Pittsfield, Massachusetts (project)
Cooperative Homesteads (housing for Detroit

Auto Workers; project)

Foreman House, Washington, D.C. (project)

1943 Hein House, Chippewa Falls, Wisconsin (project)

McDonald House, Washington, D.C. (project)

Richardson Restaurant and Service Station, Spring Green, Wisconsin (project)

1944 S. C. Johnson Research Tower, Racine, Wisconsin

Pergola House (Loeb House), Redding, Connecticut (project)

Harlan House, Omaha, Nebraska (project)

Wells House, Minneapolis (project)

1945 Friedman House, Pecos, New Mexico

Grant House, Cedar Rapids, Iowa

Taliesin Dams, Spring Green, Wisconsin

Adelman Laundry, Milwaukee (project)

Berdan House, Ludington, Michigan (project)

Elizabeth Arden Desert Spa, Phoenix, Arizona (project)

Glass House (project for *Ladies Home Journal,* New York)

The Wave (Haldorn House), Carmel, California (project)

Slater House, Rhode Island (project)

Stamm House, Lake Delavan, Wisconsin (project)

1946 Brauner House ("Usonia II"), Okemos, Michigan

Walter House and River Pavilion, Quasqueton, Iowa

President's House, Olivet College, Michigan (project)

Dayer House and Music Pavilion, Bloomfield Hills, Michigan (project)

Garrison House ("Usonia I"), Lansing, Michigan (project)

Hause House, Lansing, Michigan (project)

Housing for the State Teachers College, Lansing, Michigan (project)

Morris House I, San Francisco (project)

Munroe House, Knox County, Ohio (project)

Newman House ("Usonia I"), Lansing, Michigan (project)

Oboler Studio, Los Angeles (project)

Panshin House, State Teachers College, Lansing, Michigan (project)

Pinderton House, Cambridge, Massachusetts (project)

Pinkerton House, Fairfax County, Virginia (project)

Rogers Lacy Hotel, Dallas (project)

Sarabhi Administration Building and Store, Ahmedabad, India (project)

Van Dusen House ("Usonia I"), Lansing, Michigan (project)

1947 Alpauch House, Northport, Michigan

Bullbullian House, Rochester, Minnesota

Master plan for Galesburg Village Dwellings, Kalamazoo, Michigan

Guest House alterations, Falling Water (Kaufmann House), Bear Run, Pennsylvania

Keys House, Rochester, Minnesota

Lamberson House, Oskaloosa, Iowa

First Unitarian Society Meeting House, Madison, Wisconsin

Master plan for Parkwyn Village Dwellings, Kalamazoo, Michigan

Master plan for Usonia Homes, Pleasantville, New York

Wetmore Auto Display Room and Workshop, Detroit (project)

Bell House, East St. Louis, Illinois (project)

Black House, Rochester, Minnesota (project)

Boomer House, Phoenix, Arizona (project)

Butterfly Bridge, over the Wisconsin River, Spring Green, Wisconsin (project)

Cottage Group Resort Hotel, Hollywood, California (project)

San Antonio Transit Company Depot, Texas (project)

Daphne Funeral Chapels, San Francisco (project)

Grieco House, Andover, Massachusetts (project)

Hamilton House, Brookline, Vermont (project)

Hartford House, Hollywood, California (project)

Houston House, Schuyler County, Illinois (project)

Keith House, Oakland County, Michigan (project)

Marting House, Northampton, Ohio (project)

Palmer House, Phoenix, Arizona (project)

Pike House, Los Angeles (project)

Pittsburgh Point Park (project)

Ayn Rand House, near Redding, Connecticut (project)

Sports Club, Hollywood, California (project)

Wheeler House, Hinsdale, Illinois (project)

Wilkie House, Hennepin County, Minnesota (project)

Valley National Bank, Tucson, Arizona (project)

1948 Adelman House, Fox Point, Wisconsin

Alsop House, Oskaloosa, Iowa

Anthony House, Benton Harbor, Michigan

Buehler House, Orinda, California

Eppstein House, Galesburg Village, Kalamazoo, Michigan

Greiner House, Parkwyn Village, Kalamazoo, Michigan

Fountainhead (Hughes House), Jackson, Mississippi

Laurent House, Rockford, Illinois

Levin House, Parkwyn Village, Kalamazoo, Michigan

Mossberg House, South Bend, Indiana

Pratt House, Galesburg Village, Kalamazoo, Michigan

Rosenbaum House addition, Florence, Alabama

Smith House, Bloomfield Hills, Michigan

V. C. Morris Shop, San Francisco

Walker House, Carmel, California

Welziemer House, Oberlin, Ohio

Adelman House, Fox Point, Wisconsin (project)

Barney Cottage, Spring Green, Wisconsin (project)

Bergman House, St. Petersburg, Florida (project)

Bimson Penthouse, Phoenix, Arizona (project)

Crater Resort, Meteor Crater, Arizona (project)

Daphne House, San Francisco (project)

Ellison House, Bridgewater Township, New Jersey (project)

Feenberg House, Fox Point, Wisconsin (project)

Hageman House, Peoria, Illinois (project)

Margolis House, Kalamazoo, Michigan (project)

McCord House, North Arlington, New Jersey (project)

Miller House, Pleasantville, New York (project)

Muehlberger House, East Lansing, Michigan (project)

Pittsburgh Point Park (2nd project)

Prout House, Columbus, Indiana (project)

Scully House, Woodbridge, Connecticut (project)

Smith House, Ann Arbor, Michigan (project)

Valley National Bank and Shopping Center, Sunnyslope, Arizona (project)

1949 Sondern House additions, Kansas City, Missouri

Cabaret-Theatre, Taliesin West, Scottsdale, Arizona

Edwards House, Okemos, Michigan

Friedman House, Usonia Homes, Pleasantville, New York

McCartney House, Parkwyn Village, Kalamazoo, Michigan

Serlin House, Usonia Homes, Pleasantville, New York

Weisblatt House, Galesburg Village, Kalamazoo, Michigan

Bloomfield House, Tucson, Arizona (project)

Dabney House, Chicago (project)

Drummond House, Santa Fe, New Mexico (project)

Goetsch-Winkler House II, Okemos, Michigan (project)

Griswold House, Greenwich, Connecticut (project)

John House, Oconomowoc, Wisconsin (project)

Lea House, Asheville, North Carolina (project)

Publicker House, Haverford, Pennsylvania (project)

Southern Crossing, San Francisco Bay Bridge (project)

Kaufmann Self-Service Garage, Pittsburgh (project)

Theatre, for the New Theatre Corporation, Hartford, Connecticut (project)

Windforhr House, Fort Worth, Texas (project)

YMCA Building, Racine, Wisconsin (project)

1950 Anderton Court Center, Beverly Hills, California

Berger House, San Anselmo, California

Brown House, Parkwyn Village, Kalamazoo, Michigan

Carlson House, Phoenix, Arizona

Carr House, Glenview, Illinois

David House, Marion, Indiana

Gillin House, Dallas

Harper House, St. Joseph, Michigan

Matthews House, Atherton, California

Meyer House, Galesburg Village, Kalamazoo, Michigan

Miller House, Charles City, Iowa

Muirhead House, Plato Center, Illinois

Neils House, Minneapolis

O'Donnell House, East Lansing, Michigan

Palmer House, Ann Arbor, Michigan

Schaberg House, Okemos, Michigan

Shavin House, Chattanooga, Tennessee

Smith House, Jefferson, Wisconsin

Sweeton House, Merchantville, New Jersey

Winn House, Parkwyn Village, Kalamazoo, Michigan

Wright House, Phoenix, Arizona

Zimmerman House, Manchester, New Hampshire

Achuff House, Wauwatosa, Wisconsin (project)

Auerbach House, Pleasantville, New York (project)

Bush House, Arkansas (project)

Carroll House, Wauwatosa, Wisconsin (project)

Chahroudi House I, Lake Mahopac, New York (project)

Conklin House, New Ulm, Minnesota (project)

Grover House, Syracuse, New York (project)

Hargrove House, Berkeley, California (project)

Jackson House, Madison, Wisconsin (project)

Jacobsen House, Montreal (project)

Montooth House, Rushville, Illinois (project)

Sabin House, Battle Creek, Michigan (project)

Leon Small House, West Orange, New Jersey (project)

Southwestern Christian Seminary, Phoenix, Arizona (project)

Stevens House, Park Ridge, Illinois (project)
Strong House, Kalamazoo, Michigan (project)
Wassel House, Philadelphia (project)
1951 "Usonian Automatic" (Adelman House), Phoenix, Arizona
Austin House, Greenville, South Carolina
Chadroudi House II, Lake Mahopac, New York
Elam House, Austin, Minnesota
Fuller House, Pass Christian, Mississippi
Globe House, Lake Forest, Illinois
S. C. Johnson Office alterations, Racine, Wisconsin
Kinney House, Lancaster, Wisconsin
Kraus House, Kirkwood, Missouri
Pearce House, Monrovia, California
Reisley House, Usonia Homes, Pleasantville, New York
Rubin House, Canton, Ohio
Staley House, Madison, Ohio
Clarke Cottage, Carmel, California (project)
Hall House, Ann Arbor, Michigan (project)
Haynes House, Fort Wayne, Indiana (project)
Boulder House (Kaufmann House), Palm Springs, California (project)
Schevill Studio, Tucson, Arizona (project)
1952 Blair House, Cody, Wyoming
Brandes House, Bellevue, Washington
Goddard House, Plymouth, Michigan
Hillside Playhouse redesign and rebuilding, Spring Green, Wisconsin
Hillside Theatre Curtain, Spring Green, Wisconsin
Lewis House, Tallahassee, Florida
Lindholm House, Cloquet, Minnesota
Marden House, McLean, Virginia
Pieper House, Paradise Valley, Arizona
Teater House, Bliss, Idaho
Affleck House II, Bloomfield Hills, Michigan (project)
Bailleres House, Acapulco, Mexico (project)
Clifton House, Oakland, New Jersey (project)
Cooke House, Virginia Beach, Virginia (project)
Leesburg Floating Gardens, Florida (project)
Paradise on Wheels (trailer park), Paradise Valley, Arizona (project)
Sturtevant House, Oakland, California (project)
Swann House, near Detroit (project)
Wainer House, Valdosta, Georgia (project)
Zeta Beta Tau Fraternity House, University of Florida, Gainesville (project)
1953 Boomer Cottage, Phoenix, Arizona
Dobkins House, Canton, Ohio
Penfield House I, Willoughby, Ohio
Riverview Terrace (restaurant), Spring Green, Wisconsin
Sander House, Stamford, Connecticut
Usonian Exhibition House (pavilion), New York
Robert Llewellyn Wright House, Silver Springs, Maryland
Brewer House, East Fishkill, New York (project)
Lee House, Midland, Michigan (project)
Masieri Memorial Building, Grand Canal, Venice (project)
Seacliff (Morris House II), San Francisco (project)
Pieper and Montooth Office Building, Scottsdale, Arizona (project)
Point View Residences (apartment towers), Pittsburgh (project)
FM Radio Station, Jefferson, Wisconsin (project)
Rhododendron Chapel, Bear Run, Pennsylvania (project)
Restaurant, Yosemite National Park, California (project)

1954 Bachman-Wilson House, Millstone, New Jersey
Boulter House, Cincinnati
Christian House, Lafayette, Indiana
Clark-Arnold House, Columbus, Wisconsin
Hollyhock House remodelling, Olive Hill, Los Angeles (exhibition project)
Fawcett House, Los Banos, California
Feiman House, Canton, Ohio
Frederick House, Barrington, Illinois
Greenberg House, Dousman, Wisconsin
Hagan House, Uniontown, Pennsylvania
Keland House, Racine, Wisconsin
Price House, Bartlesville, Oklahoma
Price House, Phoenix, Arizona
Thaxton House, Houston
Barnsdall Park Municipal Gallery, Los Angeles (project)
Christian Science Reading Room, Riverside, Illinois (project)
Tipshus Clinic, Stockton, California (project)
Cornwell House, West Goshen, Pennsylvania (project)
Freund Department Store, San Salvador, El Salvador (project)
Rebhuhn House, Fort Meyers, Florida (project)
Schwenn House, Verona, Wisconsin (project)
1955 Dallas Theatre Centre
Decorative fabrics and wallpapers for Schumacher and Company
Hoffman House III, Manursing Island, Rye, New York
Kalil House, Manchester, New Hampshire
Lovness House, Stillwater, Minnesota
Pappas House, St. Louis County, Mississippi
Rayward House, New Canaan, Connecticut
Sunday House, Marshalltown, Iowa
Tonkens House, Cincinnati
Tracy House, Seattle
Turkel House, Detroit
Adelman House, Whitefish Bay, Wisconsin (project)
Barton House, Downers Grove, Illinois (project)
Blumberg House, Des Moines, Iowa (project)
Boswell House I, Cincinnati (project)
Christian Science Church, Bolinas, California (project)
Coats House, Hillsborough, California (project)
Cooke House (Usonian Block Scheme II), Virginia Beach, Virginia (project)
Dlesk House, Manistee, Michigan (project)
Gillin House, Hollywood, California (project)
Jankowski House I, Oakland County, Michigan (project)
Korrick's Department Store alterations, Phoenix, Arizona (project)
Lenkurt Electric Company Administration/-Manufacturing Building, San Mateo, California (project)
Miller House, Milford, Michigan (project)
Morris Guest House, San Francisco (project)
Neuroseum (hospital and clinic), Madison, Wisconsin (project)
Oboler House II, Los Angeles (project)
"One Room House," Phoenix, Arizona (project)
Pieper House, Phoenix, Arizona (project)
Sussman House, Rye, New York (project)
Wieland Motel, Hagerstown, Maryland (project)
1956 Price Tower (office and apartment building), Bartlesville, Oklahoma
Annunciation Greek Orthodox Church, Milwaukee
Hoffman Auto Showroom, New York
Bott House, Kansas City, Missouri
Kundert Clinic, San Luis Obispo, California
Meyer Clinic, Dayton, Ohio
Friedman House, Deerfield, Illinois

Music Pavilion, Taliesin West, Scottsdale, Arizona
Nooker House (Lloyd Wright Studio) restoration, Oak Park, Illinois
Pre-Fab I, for Marshall Erdman Associates, Madison, Wisconsin
Scott House (Roberts House) alterations, Riverside, Illinois
Smith House, Kane County, Illinois
Spencer House, Brandywine Head, Delaware
Stromquist House, Bountiful, Utah
Walton House, Modesto, California
Boebel House, Boscobel, Wisconsin (project)
Bramlett Hotel, Memphis, Tennessee (project)
Usonian Automatic House Designs (projects; with Taliesin students)
Golden Beacon (skyscraper), Chicago (project)
Gross House, Hackensack, New Jersey (project)
Hunt House, Scottsdale, Arizona (project)
Tonkens Loan Office, Cincinnati (project)
Mile High Skyscraper, Chicago (project)
Mills House I, Princeton, New Jersey (project)
Quietwater (Morris House), Stinson Beach, California (project)
New Sports Pavilion, Belmont, Long Island, New York (project)
O'Keefe House, Santa Barbara, California (project)
Roberts House, Seattle (project)
Schuck House, South Hadley, Massachusetts (project)
Stillman House, Cornwall on Hudson, New York (project)
Vallarino Houses, Panama City (project)
1957 Boswell House II, Cincinnati
Fasbender Clinic, Hastings, Minnesota
Gordon House, Aurora, Oregon
Juvenile Cultural Study Center, Building A, University of Wichita, Kansas
Kinney House, Amarillo, Texas
Pre-Fab II, for Marshall Erdman Associates, Madison, Wisconsin
Schulz House, St. Joseph, Michigan
Lindholm Service Station, Cloquet, Minnesota
Trier House, Des Moines, Iowa
Duey Wright House, Wausau, Wisconsin
Wyoming Valley School, Wisconsin
Adams House, St. Paul, Minnesota (project)
Nezam Ameri Palace, Tehran (project)
Arizona State Capitol, Papago Park, Phoenix (project)
Baghdad Cultural Center, Iraq (project)
University of Baghdad, Iraq (project)
Bimson "Usonian Automatic" House, Phoenix, Arizona (project)
Brooks House, Middleton, Wisconsin (project)
Hartman House, Lansing, Michigan (project)
Hennesy House, Smoke Rise, New Jersey (2 projects)
Herberger House, Maricopa County, Arizona (project)
Highway Motel, Madison, Wisconsin (project)
Fisher Housing Project, Whiteville, North Carolina (project)
Hoyer House, Maricopa County, Arizona (project)
Juvenile Cultural Study Center, Building B, University of Wichita, Kansas (project)
Gate Lodge, Falling Water (Kaufmann House), Bear Run, Pennsylvania (project)
McKinney House, Cloquet, Minnesota (project)
Miller House, near Roxbury, Connecticut (project)
Mills House II, Princeton, New Jersey (project)

U. S. Rubber Company Model Exhibition Houses, New York (exhibition project)

Moreland House, Austin, Texas (project)

Postal Telegraph Building, Baghdad, Iraq (project)

Post Office, Spring Green, Wisconsin (project)

Schanbacher Store, Springfield, Illinois (project)

Shelton House, Long Island, New York (project)

Sottil House, Cuernavaca, Mexico (project)

Stracke House, Appleton, Wisconsin (project)

Wedding Chapel, Claremont Hotel, Berkeley, California (project)

Wilson House, Morgantown, North Carolina (project)

Zieger House, Grosse Island, Michigan (project)

1957/
66 Marin County Government Center, San Rafael, California

1958 Albin House, Bakersfield, California

Lockridge, McIntyre and Whalen Clinic, Whitefish, Montana

Olfelt House, St. Louis Park, Minnesota

Petersen Cottage, Lake Delton, Wisconsin

Pilgrim Congregational Church, Redding, California (partly executed)

Leuchauer Clinic, Fresno, California (project)

Colgrove House, Hamilton, Ohio (project)

Crosby-Lambert House, Colbert County, Alabama (project)

Franklin House, Louisville, Kentucky (project)

Guttierez House, Albuquerque, New Mexico (project)

Hanley Airplane Hangar, Benton Harbor, Michigan (project)

Jones Chapel (Trinity Chapel), University of Oklahoma, Norman (project)

Lagomarsino House, San Jose, California (project)

Libbey House, Grand Rapids, Michigan (project)

Lovness Cottages, Stillwater, Minnesota (project)

Mike Todd Universal Theatre, Los Angeles (project)

Pre-Fab III, for Marshall Erdman Associates, Madison, Wisconsin

Pre-Fab IV, for Marshall Erdman Associates, Madison, Wisconsin

Spring Green Auditorium, Wisconsin (project)

Unity Chapel, Taliesin Valley, Spring Green, Wisconsin (project)

1959 Grady Gammage Memorial Auditorium, Arizona State University, Tempe

Beth Sholom Synagogue, Elkins Park, Pennsylvania

Guggenheim Museum, New York

Art Gallery, Arizona State University, Tempe (project)

Donahoe House, Phoenix, Arizona (project)

Furgatch House, San Diego, California (project)

Mann House, Putnam County, New York (project)

Penfield House II, Willoughby, Ohio (project)

Daniel Wieland House, Hagerstown, Maryland (project)

Gilbert Wieland House, Hagerstown, Maryland (project)

1960 Enclosed Garden, for Mrs. Frank Lloyd Wright, Taliesin, Spring Green, Wisconsin

Publications:

By WRIGHT: books—*Ausgeführte Bauten und Entwürfe von Frank Lloyd Wright* (the Wasmuth Portfolio), Berlin 1910, as *Frank Lloyd Wright: The Early Work,* New York 1968; *The Japanese Print: An Interpretation,* Chicago 1912; *Experimenting with Human Lives,* Los Angeles 1923; *The Life Work of the American Architect Frank Lloyd Wright,* edited by H. Th. Wijdeveld, Sandport, Netherlands 1925, New York 1965; *Modern Architecture,* Princeton, New Jersey 1931; *Two Lectures on Architecture,* Chicago 1931; *An Autobiography,* New York and London 1932, revised edition New York 1943, London 1945; *The Disappearing City,* New York 1932, revised edition as *When Democracy Builds,* Chicago 1945, revised edition as *The Living City,* New York 1958; *Architecture and Modern Life,* with Baker Brownell, New York and London 1937; *An Organic Architecture,* London 1939; *Frank Lloyd Wright on Architecture: Selected Writings 1894-1940,* edited by Frederick Gutheim, New York 1941; *Genius and the Mobocracy,* New York 1949, 1954, London 1972; *The Future of Architecture,* New York 1953, London 1955; *The Natural House,* New York 1954; *An American Architecture,* edited by Edgar Kaufmann, New York 1955; *The Story of the Tower,* New York 1956; *A Testament,* New York 1957; *Drawings for a Living Architecture,* New York 1959; *Frank Lloyd Wright: Writings and Buildings,* edited by Edgar Kaufmann and Ben Raeburn, New York 1960; *The Drawings of Frank* Lloyd Wright, edited by Arthur Drexler, New York 1962; *Architecture: Man in Possession of His Earth,* edited by Iovanna Lloyd Wright and Patricia Coyle Nicholson, New York 1962, London 1963; *Buildings, Plans and Designs,* New York 1963; *Architectural Essays from the Chicago School,* with others, Chicago 1967; *Studies and Executed Buildings,* Chicago 1975; *In the Cause of Architecture: Essays by Frank Lloyd Wright for the Architectural Review 1908-1952,* edited by Frederick Gutheim, New York 1975.

On WRIGHT: books—*Frank Lloyd Wright* by H. de Vries, Berlin 1926; *In the Nature of Materials, 1887-1941: The Buildings of Frank Lloyd Wright* by Henry-Russell Hitchcock, New York 1942; *Frank Lloyd Wright* by Bruno Zevi, Milan 1947; *Taliesin Days: Recent Architecture of Frank Lloyd Wright* by Edgar Kaufmann, New York 1952; *Frank Lloyd Wright* by Enrico Tedeschi, Buenos Aires 1955; *Frank Lloyd Wright to 1910: The First Golden Age* by Grant C. Manson, New York 1958; *Frank Lloyd Wright: Rebel in Concrete* by Alysea Foresee, Philadelphia 1959; *Frank Lloyd Wright* by Vincent Scully Jr., New York and London 1960; *Frank Lloyd Wright* by Peter Blake, New York 1960, London 1963; *Frank Lloyd Wright: A Biography* by Finis Farr, New York 1961; *Frank Lloyd Wright: Living Architecture* by Doris Ransohoff, Chicago 1962; *Frank Lloyd Wright: America's Greatest Architect* by Herbert Jacobs, New York 1965; *Frank Lloyd Wright: A Study in Architectural Content* by Norris Kelly, Englewood Cliffs, New Jersey 1966; *Frank Lloyd Wright: His Life, His Work, His Words,* edited by Olgivanna Lloyd Wright and others, New York 1966; *Frank Lloyd Wright: Public Buildings* by Martin Pawley, Tokyo 1967, London 1970; *Two Great Architects and Their Clients: Frank Lloyd Wright and Howard Van Doren Shaw* by Leonard K. Eaton, Cambridge, Massachusetts 1969; *Frank Lloyd Wright* by Marco Bardeschi, Florence 1970, London and New York 1972; *Frank Lloyd Wright* by Charlotte Willard, New York 1972; *Frank Lloyd Wright: An Interpretive Biography* by Robert Twombly, New York 1973; *The Prairie School: Frank Lloyd Wright and His Midwest Contemporaries* by H. Allen Brooks, Toronto 1972; *Prairie School Town Planning 1900-1915: Wright, Griffin, Drummond* by Courtney Graham Donnell, New York 1974; *The Architecture of Frank Lloyd Wright: A Complete Catalog,* compiled by William Allin Storrer, Cambridge, Massachusetts 1974, 1978; *Houses by Frank Lloyd Wright,* edited by Yukio Futagawa, Tokyo 1975; *Frank Lloyd Wright's Usonian Houses: The Case for Organic Architecture* by John Sergeant, New York 1976; *The Decorative Designs of Frank Lloyd Wright* by David A. Hanks, Washington, D.C. 1977; *Frank Lloyd Wright: His Life and Architecture* by Robert C. Twombly, New York 1979.

Bibliography: *Frank Lloyd Wright in Print 1959-1970* compiled by James Muggenberg, Charlottesville, Virginia 1972; *Frank Lloyd Wright: A Bibliography,* compiled by Kenneth and Jane Starosciak, New Brighton, Minnesota 1973; *Frank Lloyd Wright: An Annotated Bibliography,* compiled by Robert L. Sweeney, Los Angeles 1978.

*

Frank Lloyd Wright is of the American tradition of Emerson, Thoreau, and Whitman; his strength and inspiration were drawn from the soil, the products of natural growth, and the lessons which they taught. His materials were taken from the land—wood (unplaned and stained rather than painted), stone, and clay brick—and though he honoured the machine because of its ability to process, standardize, and simplify, he had passed beyond that stage of feeling obliged, as did his European counterparts, to express symbolically a machine aesthetic in his architecture. A brilliant psychologist, he understood human needs and administered to them through his work. Above all he sought "repose," a restful environment free of tension which catered to the mental health and happiness of the indweller.

To help achieve this, Wright evolved a new concept of interior space: this is his matchless contribution to the future of architecture. Rooms of a house, prior to his time, were box-like although occasionally aligned with large openings in between them. Each room had a single function. Wright changed all that. His "rooms" overlap and interpenetrate—often at the corners. Use areas are defined by screening devices and subtle changes in ceiling heights. A single space serves a variety of functions depending upon (and this is the essential point) the position of the observer. That is to say, spaces are defined rather than enclosed, and use is relative (to the individual) rather than absolute (one room having one use).

Wright also generated a new vocabulary of architectural forms. In the 1920's he began experimenting with shapes other than the right angle. 30, 45, 60, and 120 degree angles began to enter his work, both in plan and in elevation; also the circle, arc, and spiral. Although ridiculed when they first appeared, these forms, in the latter third of our century, have now been generally accepted by the architectural profession.

Wright was born in Richland Center, Wisconsin, in 1867. Two youthful experiences (in addition to his mother's determination that he be an architect) particularly influenced him as a designer. The first was his training with Froebel kindergarten "gifts," which instilled in him a sense of order, proportion, and an appreciation for the relation between basic geometric shapes. Because of this training he based his plans, and later his elevations as well, on a unit (his word) system which governed all elements in the design. The second most significant experience was working summers on his uncle's farm; it was there that he gained his appreciation and respect for the land, nature, and the materials that nature produced.

After a brief, inconclusive stint at the University of Wisconsin where he took some mechanical drawing and basic mathematics courses, Wright departed (1887) for Chicago where he spent some months in J. L. Silsbee's office (an architect devoted to residential designs which for over a decade had an impact on Wright's work) before seeking employment with Adler and Sullivan where he remained until 1893. These were the years of the Auditorium, the Wainwright Building, and the Chicago World's Fair. Once on his own, Wright designed the Winslow house (1894), a strong, monumental work which summed up the ideals of classicism without recourse to Classical forms. This was not, however, what he felt architecture to be, and throughout the decade he sought an expression more suitable to the natural setting and the materials of the region. A variety of experiments characterized these years that concluded in 1900 with what has become known as the prairie house. Long, low, with hovering planes that extend laterally as porches and porte-cocheres, these buildings were L, T, or cruciform in shape with overlapping, interpenetrating spaces. The plans adhered to a basic unit system of design. The materials were either brick or unplaned (stained) wood and plaster.

Until the outbreak of the 1914 war he continually evolved the prairie house toward greater abstraction. Roofs and balconies gradually became flat, hovering slabs, and a geometric interplay between verticals and horizontals replaced an emphasis upon wall. Compare, for example, the Willits house (1902), Robie house (1909), and Coonley playhouse (1912) in this regard. Wright's non-residential work certainly played a role in this development: the Larkin Administration Building (1904) and especially Unity Temple (1906) reiterated the geometric shapes of the Froebel toys and demonstrated the uselessness of a visible roof. When Wright's drawings were published in Europe by Ernst Wasmuth as 100 large lithographs, it is these designs which were included and which irrevocably altered the course of European architecture from that moment onward.

Wright spent more than a year in Europe (he had visited Japan in 1905) preparing the Wasmuth publication, and upon his return began building Taliesin in Wisconsin—on lands he had helped farm in his youth. There, while he was in Chicago finishing the Midway Gardens buildings (the most abstract of his designs to date), a deranged servant murdered seven members of Wright's household and burned Taliesin to the ground. The shock left its impact. In terms of architecture it seemed to direct him toward more solid, protective forms, as if to create a shelter against the outside world. The more formal, massive California houses (Barnsdall, Millard, Ennis, etc) are typical. The 1920's, slighted by Wright's biographers because of his limited number of executed works, were, I believe, incredibly rich in an inventive sense and established the direction of his work for 30 years to come. Domestic tranquility returned to him by the late '20s, and in 1932 he published his *An Autobiography* and founded the Taliesin Fellowship, a group (eventually about 60) of apprentices who built buildings and did domestic chores, as well as working at the drafting boards. He had reached 65, had no commissions, and spent his time giving a few public lectures and designing Broadacre City, which was not really a city at all but rather a car oriented segment of semi-rural America.

In 1936 his luck changed. He designed and built both Fallingwater and the Johnson Administration Building. These thrust Wright into the limelight; the Museum of Modern Art in New York exhibited his work, and the January 17th, 1938 issue of *Time* featured him on its cover—against the backdrop of Fallingwater. Commissions, particularly for lower middle income housing, began to come in. Wright's response was the Usonian (United States-ian) house, a logical development from the earlier prairie house. The Jacobs House was the first of these homes wherein Wright achieved a remarkable degree of variety and openness in buildings of truly restricted size. Built upon a concrete slab into which the radiant heating was incorporated, the house was limited in construction almost entirely to wood, bricks, and glass, these materials having the same natural finish both inside and out.

During this last quarter century of his remarkably long life, Wright produced work the range and variety of which seemingly knew no bounds. Aside from his Usonian and other houses he built the Guggenheim Museum, Price Tower, Beth Sholom Synagogue, Annunciation Greek Orthodox Church, and Marin County Buildings, most of which evolved from his earlier experiments in unorthodox shapes and forms. Near Phoenix, Arizona, he built Taliesin West as a winter retreat and it is there that he died on April 9th, 1959, in his 92nd year, leaving behind a legacy which will nourish architecture for generations to come.

—H. Allen Brooks

WRIGHT, (Frank) Lloyd.

American. Born in Oak Park, Illinois, 31 March 1890; eldest son of the architect Frank Lloyd Wright, *q.v.* Educated at public school in Oak Park, 1895–97; Hillside Home School, near Spring Green, Wisconsin, 1898–1907; University of Wisconsin, Madison, 1907–09. Married Elaine Hyman in 1917 (divorced, 1925); married Helen Taggart in 1926; son: Eric. Assisted his father in the preparation of drawings for the Wasmuth Portfolio, in Florence, and travelled in Europe, 1909; worked at the Harvard Herbarium, Cambridge, Massachusetts, and as a landscape draftsman in the office of Olmsted and Olmsted, Boston, 1910–11; worked in the Olmsted and Olmsted Nursery, and as a landscape architect for the firm of Frederick Law Jr., San Diego, California, 1911; architectural draftsman/delineator, office of Irving J. Gill, San Diego and Los Angeles, 1912–15; in partnership with Paul G. Thiene, as landscape architects, Los Angeles, 1915; established independent office as architect and landscape architect, Los Angeles, and became Head of the Design and Drafting Department of Paramount Studios, Los Angeles, 1916–17; worked for Standard Aircraft Company, Elizabeth, New Jersey, and Curtis Airport Company, Long Island, New York, 1918; Draftsman, Rouse and Goldstone, New York, 1919; worked with his father on the landscaping of Barnsdall Houses and Olive Hill, Los Angeles, 1919–20; worked as a landscape architect for William J. Dodd, Los Angeles, 1920–21; in private practice as a landscape architect, Los Angeles, working closely with his father, 1922–26; in private practice as an architect, Los Angeles, 1927–72. Chairman, Los Angeles Delegation, International Housing Congress, Mexico City, 1939. Exhibitions: *Lloyd Wright,* University of Oklahoma School of Architecture, Norman, 1964; *Four Decades of Living Architecture: Lloyd Wright, Architect,* The Building Center, Los Angeles, 1966; *Lloyd Wright, Architect: 20th Century Architecture in an Organic Exhibition,* University of California at Santa Barbara, 1971. *Died (in Santa Monica, California) 31 May 1978.*

Works:

1910 "A Prairie House," Oak Park, Illinois (project)
1914/
  15 Landscaping of the new industrial city of Torrance, California (with Olmsted and Olmsted)
1915/
  16 Site plan and landscaping for Playa Del Rey, California (project)
      Severence Estate landscaping, Pasadena, California (with Paul G. Thiene)
      Meyer Estate landscaping, Beverly Hills, California (with Paul G. Thiene)
1917/
  18 Various sets for Paramount Studios, Hollywood, California
1919/
  20 Barnsdall Houses/Olive Hill landscaping, Los Angeles
1920 Country Club landscaping, Phoenix, Arizona (project)
      Dodd Estate landscaping, Beverly Hills, California
1921 Preuss Estate landscaping, Hollywood, California
      Weber House, 3923 West 9th Street, Los Angeles
1921/
  22 Santa Monica High School landscaping, California (project)
1922 Henry Bollman House, 1530 Ogden Avenue, Hollywood, California
      Otto Bollman House, 2200 Braidview Terrace, Hollywood, California
      Lyman Commercial Center, Sierra Madre, California (project)
      Taggart House, 5423 Black Oak Drive, Los Angeles

1923 University Club landscaping, Los Angeles
      Stage set for *Julius Caesar* (Gordon Craig production), Hollywood Bowl, Hollywood, California
      Doheny Ranch landscaping, Beverly Hills, California
      Oasis Hotel, 125 Palm Springs Canyon Drive, Palm Springs, California
      Sierra Madre City Park, California (project)
      Storer House landscaping, Hollywood, California (supervised construction for Frank Lloyd Wright)
1924 Ennis House landscaping, Los Angeles (supervised construction for Frank Lloyd Wright)
      Freeman House landscaping, Los Angeles (supervised construction for Frank Lloyd Wright)
      Ellen True Rookery Tent-Houses, Palm Springs, California (one built)
      Mausoleum (project)
1924/
  25 Shell for the Hollywood Bowl, Hollywood, California (project)
1925 Carr House, with landscaping, Lowry and Rowena Streets, Los Angeles
      Gilkerson House landscaping, Chevy Chase, Glendale, California
      Howe House, Beverly Hills, California
      City of the Future, Los Angeles (project)
      Civic Center, Los Angeles (project)
      Stahl House, Beverly Hills, California (project)
      Landscaping plan for Oshkosh, Wisconsin (project)
1925/
  26 House, Palm Springs, California (prototype)
1926 5-Room House, Los Angeles (project)
      Studio House, Los Angeles (project)
      Desert Hacienda, Palm Springs, California (project)
      Concrete Block House, Chevy Chase, Glendale, California (project)
      4-Room House, Chevy Chase, Glendale, California (project)
      Calori House, Chevy Chase Drive, Glendale, California
      Derby House, 2535 Chevy Chase Drive, Glendale, California
      Eliot House, Chevy Chase, Glendale, California (project)
      Fairfax Theatre, Los Angeles (project)
      Farrell House, 3209 Lowry Road, Los Angeles
      Johnson House, Chevy Chase, Glendale, California (project)
      Lewis House, 2947 Graceland Way, Chevy Chase, Glendale, California
      Millard House studio addition, 645 Prospect Crescent Way, Pasadena, California
      Nelson House, Los Angeles (project)
      Oliver House, Chevy Chase, Glendale, California (project)
      Sowden House, 5121 Franklin Avenue, Los Angeles
1926/
  28 Navarro House, 5609 Valley Oak Drive, Hollywood, California
1927 Counselman House, 4905 Lockhaven Street, Eagle Rock, California
      Martin House, Palm Springs, California (project)
      Wilkes Theatre and Shops, Hollywood, California
      Lloyd Wright Studio/House, 858 North Doheny Drive, Los Angeles
      Dune House, near Palm Springs, California (project)
      Connell Hillside House, Los Angeles
1927/
  28 Lake Arrowhead Hotel and Bungalows, California

1928 Behn House, Chevy Chase, Glendale, California (project)
Yucca-Vine Market, for Raymond Griffith, Hollywood, California
McDowell House, Chevy Chase, Glendale, California (project)
Metzler House, Camarillo, California (project)
Upman House garden, Altadena, California
Shell for the Hollywood Bowl, Hollywood, California

1929 Backman Store, Tarzana, California
Bassett House landscaping, Los Angeles
Furniture, for Carrol Jones, Los Angeles
Albert Marple Stores facade remodelling, Los Angeles (project)

1930 Plan for Boeing Airport, Burbank, California (project)
Day House remodelling, Los Angeles
Apollo Baths, Henderson Gymnasium, Los Angeles (project)
Group of Stores, for L. D. Owens, Hollywood, California (project)
Professional Office Building, Hollywood, California (project)
City of Los Angeles Art Department sculpture and garden (project; with Harold Swartz)
Harold Swartz House, Los Angeles (project)
Tibbett House remodelling, Beverly Hills, California
Jake Zeitlin Book Shop, Los Angeles
Plan for Los Angeles Airport (project)
Design of exhibition space for pre-Columbian art, Stendahl Gallery, Los Angeles

1931 Children's Outdoor Theatre, Olive Hill, Los Angeles (project)
Roman Catholic Cathedral, Los Angeles (project)
Kellogg Ranch, Banning, California (project)
Drive-In Open Air Market and Restaurant, Monrovia, California

1932 Furthman House remodelling, Bel Air, Los Angeles
Halfhill Apartments, Los Angeles (project)
Richardson House, Eagle Rock, California (project)
Apartment Building, Hollywood, California (project)

1933 Apollo Baths, Henderson Gymnasium, Los Angeles (2nd project)
Behn House, Westwood, California (project)
Hanna House, Chevy Chase, Glendale, California (project)
Tule Mat Houses, Imperial Valley, California (project)

1933/
34 Howland House, 502 Crescent Drive, Beverly Hills, California
Cascades Club, Palm Springs, California (project)

1934 Connell House remodelling and furniture, Los Angeles
Newman House remodelling, 627 North Canon Drive, Beverly Hills, California
Tony Price/Gladys Barbieri Book Shop and Bindery remodelling, Hollywood, California
Samuel House, 570 North Bundy Drive, Beverly Hills, California

1934/
37 Avery House, 365 Rockingham Avenue, Los Angeles

1935 Claudette Colbert House, 615 North Faring Road, Los Angeles
Kaufman House remodelling, Los Angeles
Niles House, Los Angeles (project)
Sauer House, St. Louis (project)
Smith House, Chevy Chase, Glendale, California (project)
Westlake Medical Building, 676 Westlake Avenue, Los Angeles

1936 Griffith Ranch House, 4965 Rigoletto Street,

Lloyd Wright: Wayfarer's Chapel, Palos Verdes, California, 1951

Canoga Park, California
Theta Chi Fraternity House, University of California at Los Angeles (project)
Jake Zeitlin Book Store, Los Angeles

1936/
41 Day House remodelling, Los Angeles
Evans House, 554 North Bundy Drive, Los Angeles

1937 Butterworth House, Los Angeles (project)
Brower House, Pacific Palisades, California (project)
Edens House remodelling, Los Angeles
Gracy House, Austin, Texas (project)
Haight House, Los Angeles (project)
Jones House, Burbank, California (project)
Lazarus House, Los Angeles (project)
Motel, Los Angeles (project)
Ruby House, Beverly Hills, California (project)

1938 Blalock House, Los Angeles (project)
Christian Science Church, Monrovia, California (project; with William Gray Purcell)

Henricks Press Building, Litchfield, Illinois (project)
Benthuysen House remodelling, Los Angeles
Vidor House, Los Angeles (project)

1939 Four-Square Housing, Los Angeles (project)
Haight House remodelling, Beverly Hills, California
Smith House, Los Angeles (project)
Tibbet Ranch House, near Bakersfield, California (project)

1939/
40 Ramona Gardens Public Housing Project, Los Angeles (with George J. Adams, Ralph C. Flewelling, Eugene Weston Jr., and Lewis Eugene Wilson)

1940 Degener House, Los Angeles
Greer House, 9200 Haskell Avenue, Los Angeles
Lubsen House, 1262 Rubio Avenue, Altadena, California
Othman House, 2200 Broadview Terrace, Los Angeles

Swann House, Hope Ranch, Santa Barbara, California (project)
Tibbet House remodelling, Encino, California (project)

1941 Nelson Eddy Studio, Los Angeles (project)
Kaufman House remodelling, Los Angeles
Kaye House I, Los Angeles (project)
Kellogg Perchino Breeding Farm, Pahrump Valley, Nevada (project)
Lewis House remodelling, Los Angeles
Reuben Mamoullian House, Los Angeles (project)
Robertson House II, Los Angeles (project)
Earl Stendahl Studio-House, Los Angeles

1941/
42 Aliso Village Public Housing Project, First Street and Mission Road, Los Angeles (with George J. Adams, Walter S. Davis, Ralph C. Flewelling, Eugene Weston Jr., and Lewis Eugene Wilson)

1942 Degener House, Los Angeles (project)
1944 Warren Smith House, Los Angeles (project)
Fairmont Hotel remodelling and tower, San Francisco (project)
Schuyler House, Los Angeles (project)
Tourtellotte House, Palos Verdes, California (project)

1945 Benjamin House, Los Angeles
Brewer House, Pacific Palisades, California
Cardenas House, Oracle, Arizona (project)
Crosby House, North Hollywood, California (project)
Greer Dressmaking Plant, Los Angeles
Kaye House II, Westwood, Los Angeles (project)
Mel Smith House, Los Angeles (project)

1946 Loew House, Los Angeles (project)
Antaky Textile Manufacturing Plant, New York (project)
Anne Baxter House remodelling, Los Angeles (project)
Gainsburg House, 1210 Journey's End Drive, La Canada, California
Huntington Hartford Outpost Club, Hollywood, California (project)
Huntington Hartford Reunion Tract, Los Angeles (project)
Kuttler House remodelling, Los Angeles
Caravansary and Administration Buildings, Institute of Mental Physics, Yucca Valley, California
Redlich House, 602 North Arden, Beverly Hills, California
Stendahl Candy Factory, Burbank, California (project)
Frank Wyle Residential Development, Los Angeles

1946/
47 Reitz House, Los Angeles
1946/
48 Jascha Heifetz House remodelling and studio, Beverly Hills, California
1946/
51 Swedenborg Memorial Chapel ("The Wayfarer's Chapel"), Portuguese Bend, Palos Verdes, California

1947 Kenneth Baxter House, San Mateo, California (project)
Beatrice Wood House, Ojai, California
1948 Charles House landscaping, 1210 Benedict Canyon Drive, Beverly Hills, California
Christian Science Reading Room, Fontana, California (project)
Powell House, Los Angeles (project)
1949 Blalock Apartments, Alhambra, California (project)
De Jonghe House, 9020 Crescent Drive, Los Angeles
Dorland House, 1370 Morada, Altadena, California
Healy House, 565 Perugia Way, Los Angeles
Jester House, 32 Narcissa Drive, Portuguese Bend, Palos Verdes, California

Nabel House, 2323 La Mesa Drive, Santa Monica, California
Newman House, 14148 Sunset Boulevard, Pacific Palisades, California
Platt House, Los Angeles (project)
Huntington Hartford Pool Pavilion, Pacific Palisades, California

1949/
50 Hartington Hartford Theatre Square, Hollywood, California (project)

1949/
65 Hill and Dale Nursery and Kindergarten, 16706 Marquez Avenue, Pacific Palisades, California
1950 Alfred Erickson House, 5408 Stauder Circle, Minneapolis
Arthur Erickson House, 5501 Londonderry Road, Edina, Minnesota
Frank Jones House, Covina, California
Shulman House and Carport, Los Angeles
1951 Slater House, La Habra, California (project)
Snow Chapel, Ile Begras, Montreal (project)

1951/
54 Huntington Hartford Vine Street Theatre, Hollywood, California (project)

1951/
59 Jascha Heifetz House additions, 1520 Gilcrest Drive, Beverly Hills, California
1952 Set for the touring production of *John's Brown Body* (Charles Laughton production)
Charles Laughton House pool and dressing room, Los Angeles

1952/
56 Kropp House and Carport, near Grayslake, Illinois
1953 Babcock House, San Diego (project)
Brown House, Los Angeles (project)
Dell House, Los Angeles
Huntington Hartford Fine Arts Galleries, Outdoor Theatre, and Sculpture Gardens, Hollywood, California (project)
Wagner House, Palos Verdes, California (project)

1953/
54 Honeycutt House, 14674 Los Altos Park, Los Angeles
1954 Cafeteria and Cottages, Institute of Mental Physics, Yucca Valley, California
1955 Pent-O-Rama House, Santa Barbara, California (project)
Swedenborg Memorial Chapel, El Cerrito, California (project)
Joshua Tree Land Development, California (project)
1956 Roberts Children's House, Institute of Mental Physics, Yucca Valley, California
Moore House, 504 Paseo del Mar, San Pedro, California
1957 Polster House, Beverly Hills, California
Howard House remodelling and landscaping, Encino, California
Bartfield House, Thousand Oaks, California (project)
Good Shepherd Community Church, Des Plaines, Illinois
1958 Dunham House, Palos Verdes, California
Levand House, Beverly Hills, California
Mace House, 8292 Hollywood Boulevard, Los Angeles
St. Luke's Presbyterian Church, Rolling Hills, California (project)
1959 Lumbleau House, 22158 Pacific Coast Highway, Malibu, California
Stein House and Garage, Granada Hills, California (project)
1960 Charles Laughton House remodelling, furniture, and garden, Los Angeles
Robert Wright House landscaping, Bethesda, Maryland
Pihl House, Edina, Minnesota (project)
Karasik House and Carport, 436 Spaulding Drive, Beverly Hills, California

1961 Pilgrimage Playhouse remodelling, Los Angeles (project)
Mount Olivet Lutheran Church addition, Minneapolis (project)
Piatigorsky/Steiner Chess Club remodelling, Los Angeles

1961/
65 Pico-Robertson Shopping Mall, Los Angeles (project)
1962 Hare House remodelling, Bel Air, Los Angeles
Huntington Hartford Portal Project, Sunset Bay, California (project)
Piatigorsky House entrance gates, Beverly Hills, California
Regional urban plan for Los Angeles County (project)
1963 Bowler House, Palos Verdes, California
Harris House, Orange County, California (project)
Todd Theatre, Los Angeles (project)
Johnson House, 7017 Senalda Road, Hollywood, California
Pfeiffer/Hulet House, Coral Gables, Miami (project)
1964 Terrance Park Apartments, Orange County, California (project)
World Folk Park, Burbank, California (project)
Holiday Bargain Fair and Service Station, Minneapolis (project)
1965 Erickson Family Memorial Garden, Lakewood Memorial Park, Minneapolis (project)
Lombardi House, 804 Los Gatos Road, Palos Verdes, California
Daniel Wright House additions, Phoenix, Arizona
Daniel House landscaping, Los Angeles
Church of the New Jerusalem, Los Angeles (project)
Piatigorsky House guest house remodelling, Los Angeles

1965/
72 First Christian Church, Avenue de los Floras and Kusts Avenue, Thousand Oaks, California
1967 Moorehead House pavilion and loggia additions, Rolling Hills, California
1968 La Rue House, Los Angeles (project)
Alexander House, Thousand Oaks, California (project)

1968/
69 Westfair Shopping Center, Springdale Street and Warner Avenue, Huntington Beach, California (project)
1969 Triangle Park Shopping Center, Long Beach, California (project)
1970 Nabel House landscaping and swimming pool, Santa Monica, California

1970/
71 Urban Recreation Center, Dallas (project)
1971 Bellenson House, Simi Valley, California (project)

Publications:

By WRIGHT: articles—"A New Art" in the *Los Angeles Times,* mid-winter number, 1929; "Woven and Designed by Maria Steinhof" in *California Arts and Architecture* (Los Angeles), November 1940; "Aliso Village Group Housing Project Result of Coordinated Planning" in *Southwest Builders and Contractors* (Los Angeles), May 1943.

On WRIGHT: books—*The Ferro-Concrete Style* by Francis S. Onderdonk, New York 1928; *The New World Architecture* by Sheldon Cheney, New York 1930; *Modern American Design* by R. I. Leonard and C. A. Glassgold, New York 1930; *California Gardens* by Winifred S. Dobyns, New York 1931; *Residential Architecture in Southern California* by

Paul R. Hunter and Walter L. Reichardt, Los Angeles 1939; *Built in U.S.A.* by Henry-Russell Hitchcock and Arthur Drexler, New York 1952; *Lloyd Wright*, exhibition catalogue, Norman, Oklahoma 1964; *Four Decades of Living Architecture: Lloyd Wright, Architect*, exhibition catalogue, Los Angeles 1966; *Lloyd Wright, Architect: 20th Century Architecture in an Organic Exhibition*, exhibition catalogue, by David Gebhard and Harriette von Breton, Santa Barbara, California 1971; articles—"Portrait of Lloyd Wright" by Carter Ludlow in the *Los Angeles Examiner*, 3 November 1961; "So Wright Turns" by Arthur Miller in the *Los Angeles Herald Examiner*, 4 September 1966; "Lloyd Wright" by Esther McCoy in *Arts and Architecture* (Los Angeles), October 1966; "Lloyd Wright on Design" by Judy Cool in the *Los Angeles Herald Examiner*, 21 May 1967; "Lloyd Wright" by Esther McCoy in *Progressive Architecture* (New York), July 1978.

*

Lloyd Wright's talents were scattered over several fields in his formative years, and the unifying thread was his landscape design, which he used to modify or enhance a structure. His early training in landscaping was as a draftsman in the Boston office of Olmsted and Olmsted, a position he took after his return from Europe where he had assisted his father, Frank Lloyd Wright, in preparation of drawings for the Wasmuth Portfolio.

His first job in an architectural office was in San Diego as a draftsman at age 23 for Irving Gill, and his admiration for Gill's unadorned cubic forms of concrete affected his own work. His houses of the twenties and thirties blended his father's decorative style of the teens and twenties with the planar surfaces of Gill; the cubic forms were always clear, and ornament tended to be concentrated in small areas, usually around openings, as in the Churrigueresque style.

Wright's aesthetic was based on the wall, but theatrical features such as overscaled openings, two story fireplaces and complex ornament gave his buildings a closer relationship to German Expressionism than to the work of his father or Gill; but Wright's interest in music and theatre, and his employment for a year in the design department of a film studio (from which industry a number of his clients came), is a more likely source. The houses of the twenties and thirties are often scaleless—or are scaled to the easel rather than the street—which gives them special interest in a post-Miesian age.

Wright had a more temperate side, as seen in designs for less venturesome clients, based on his father's Prairie Style adapted to the California climate. There was also an inventive side—the use of a slip-form technique for the concrete walls of his 1923 Oasis Hotel, Palm Springs; schemes for city plans that proposed elevated roads made of compacted waste from city dumps.

With the completion of his Wayfarers' Chapel at Palos Verdes, Wright's work became more widely known. The glass-walled structure, framed with heavy wood bents and light steel members, is open to a grove of redwoods. The arch form of the bents, and the roof, built up of triangular-shaped solid and transparent materials, give a Gothic character to the open chapel. Wright, as was typical, considered the planting before the design, a sequence that today makes most of his buildings an integral part of the site.

—Esther McCoy

WURSTER, William Wilson.
American. Born in Stockton, California, 20 October 1895. Educated in Stockton elementary schools; Stockton High School, graduated 1913; University of California, Berkeley, 1912–13; worked for a sur-veyor, 1913–14; returned to the University of California, and studied naval architecture and marine engineering, 1914–16; shipped to sea, in the Pacific, as an engineer, 1916–18; returned to the University of California, 1919–20, B.Arch. (honors) 1920. Married Catherine Bauer in 1940; daughter: Sarah. Worked for the architectural firm of John Reid, Jr., San Francisco, 1920; worked in the office of the Filtration Division, City of Sacramento, California, under the architect Charles Dean, 1921–22; travelled in Europe, 1922–23; worked for the firm of Delano and Aldrich, New York, 1923–24; returned to California to design a filtration plant for the East Bay Water Company, 1924–25; in private practice, San Francisco, 1926–43; Partner, with Theodore Bernardi and Donn Emmonds, Wurster, Bernardi and Emmons, San Francisco, 1945 until his death, 1973. Fellow, Graduate School of Design, Harvard University, Cambridge, Massachusetts, 1943–44; Dean of the School of Architecture and Planning, Massachusetts Institute of Technology, Cambridge, 1944–50; Dean, College of Environmental Design, University of California, Berkeley, from 1950. Recipient: First Prize, Golden Gateway Redevelopment Project Competition, San Francisco, 1959; Gold Medal, American Institute of Architects, 1969. Fellow, American Institute of Architects. *Died in 1973.*

Works:

1927 Smith House, Russell Street, Berkeley, California
      Gregory Farmhouse, Canham Road, Scotts Valley, Santa Cruz, California
1931 Yerba Buena Club, *San Francisco Fair*
1932 Henderson House, Bromfield Road, Hillsborough, California
1933 Converse House, Santa Rita Street, Carmel, California
      Eiskamp House, Brewington Avenue, Watsonville, California
1934 Sanderson House, Bristol Avenue, Stockton, California
1936 Pope House, Bromfield Road, Hillsborough, California
      House, 215 Western Drive, Richmond, California
      Jensen House, La Vereda Street, Berkeley, California
1937 Terraced houses, 757–763 Bay Street, San Francisco
      House, 737 Bay Street, San Francisco
      Henning House, Chiltern Road, Hillsborough, California
      Mendenhall House, Emerson Street, Palo Alto, California
1938 Van Deusen House, Hawthorne Terrace, Berkeley, California
1939 House, 2633 Green Street, San Francisco
      House, 30 Cragmont Avenue, San Francisco
      House, 2560 Divisadero Street, San Francisco
      Corbus House, Felton Drive, Menlo Park, California
      Raas House, Cowper Street, Palo Alto, California
      Strauss House, Stonewall Road, Berkeley, California
1940 House, 1641 Green Street, San Francisco
      Dinkelspiel House, Ascot Road, Hillsborough, California
      Farley House, Stonewall Road, Berkeley, California
1941 Carquinez Heights (housing), Vallejo, California
      Parker Houses, Sacramento, California
      Field House, Bristol Avenue, Stockton, California
      Timby House, Knoll Drive, San Carlos, California
1942 Stern Hall, University of California, Berkeley
      Lamberson House, Alvarado Road, Berkeley, California
      House, 3655 Clay Street, San Francisco

Lyman House, Selby Lane, Atherton, California
      Schuckl Canning Company Office Building, Fair Oaks Avenue, Sunnyvale, California (now California Growers and Canners Building)
1943 Valencia Gardens (housing), 15th Street, San Francisco (with Harry Thomsen)
1945 House, 250 Locust Street, San Francisco
1948 House, San Carlos Avenue, Sausalito, California
1949 Shuman House, Mountain Home Road, Portola, California
1951 House, 25 Raycliff Terrace, San Francisco
      House, 2745 Larkin Avenue, San Francisco
1952 House, 2795 Vallejo Street, San Francisco
      House remodelling, Chiltern Road, Hillsborough, California
1954 House, 301 Locust Street, San Francisco
      Center for Advanced Studies in the Behavioral Sciences, Stanford University, Palo Alto, California
1955 2 cottages, Greenwood Terrace, Berkeley, California
1958 House, 850 El Camino del Mar, San Francisco
1958/
65   Capitol Tower Apartments, Sacramento, California (with Edward Larrabee Barnes and DeMars and Reay)
1959 Medical Plaza, Stanford University, Palo Alto, California
      Married Student Housing, Stanford University, Palo Alto, California
      Stern Hall additions, University of California, Berkeley
      Strawberry Canyon Recreation Center, University of California, Berkeley
1960 New building for the Woodside Community Church, Woodside, California
1961 First Unitarian Church, Lawson Road, El Cerrito, California
1961/
63   Golden Gateway Redevelopment Project (master plan, garages, point towers and town houses along Jackson Street), San Francisco (with DeMars and Reay)
1962/
67   Ghirardelli Square renovation and remodelling, San Francisco
1964 Civic Auditorium remodelling, San Francisco (with Skidmore, Owings and Merrill)
1965 Sarah Dix Hamlin School, 2129 Vallejo Street, San Francisco
      Woodlake Residential Community, San Mateo, California
      Cowell College, University of California at Santa Cruz
1967 Northpoint, 2211 Stockton Street, San Francisco
1970 The Ice Houses I and II (conversion of warehouses to interior design showrooms), 1265 Battery and 151 Union Streets, San Francisco
1970/
71   Bank of America World Headquarters, San Francisco (with Skidmore, Owings and Merrill; design consultant Pietro Belluschi)

Publications:

By WURSTER: articles—"From Log Cabin to Modern House" in the *New York Times Magazine*, 20 January 1946; "Building Now: How You Can Meet the 50 Per Cent Rise in Building Costs" in *House and Garden* (New York), May 1946; letter in *Architectural Forum* (New York), March 1947; "When Is a Small House Large" in *House and Garden* (New York), August 1947; "Architectural Education" in *AIA Journal* (Washington, D.C.), January 1948; "Architecture Broadens Its Base" in *AIA Jour-*

William Wilson Wurster: Cowell College, University of California at Santa Cruz, 1965

nal (Washington, D.C.), July 1948; "The Unity of Architecture and Landscape Architecture" in *Landscape Design,* exhibition catalogue, San Francisco 1948; "The Outdoors in Residential Design" in *Architectural Forum* (New York), September 1949; "The Architectural Life" in *Architectural Record* (New York), January 1951; "The Great Arch of the Jefferson National Expansion Memorial in St. Louis, Missouri" in the *St. Louis Post-Dispatch,* September 1956; "Row House Vernacular and High Style Monument" in *Architectural Record* (New York), August 1958; "Indian Vernacular Architecture: Wai and Cochin," with Catherine Bauer, in *Perspecta 5* (New Haven, Connecticut), January 1959; "The University and the Environmental Design Professions" in *College of Environmental Design Exhibition,* exhibition catalogue, Berkeley, California 1959; "College Planning" in *Architectural Record* (New York), September 1959.

On WURSTER: articles—"Building Types: Homes $7,500 and Under" in *Architectural Record* (New York) March 1938; "Case Study House 3" in *Arts and Architecture* (Los Angeles), June 1945; "Meet Wiliam Wurster" in *House Beautiful* (New York), June 1945; "William Wilson Wurster" in *Architectural Forum* (New York), July 1943; "A New Structural Method Builds a New Campus" in *Architectural Forum* (New York), June 1950; "Profilo di un Architetto Americano: William Wilson Wurster" in *Architettura* (Rome), May 1957; "Genetrix: Personal Contributions to American Architecture" in *Architectural Review* (London), May 1957; "L'Architetto William Wilson Wurster" by Richard C. Peters in *Casabella* (Milan), April 1960; "Recent Works of William Wurster" in *Architectural Record* (New York), January 1963; "The Western House" in *AIA Journal* (Washington D.C.), June 1968; "Three Houses Built for Summer" in *House and Garden* (New York), June 1970.

William Wilson Wurster has been called "the great American regionalist—an architect who was both a pioneer and a prophet." Alvar Aalto, the internationally known Finnish architect, said of Wurster, "He is a man who loves people, loves to build for people, and never loses sight of this happiness." As architect, planner and educator, Wurster's achievements were extraordinary. From his famous Gregory Farmhouse, Santa Cruz, in 1927, to the award winning Ghirardelli Square, San Francisco, in 1967, the quality of his work always remained true to his unyielding belief that architecture should be a forthright response to local and regional needs and conditions. His buildings are simple, direct and honest, qualities which, for those who knew him, precisely reflect his philosophy of being—a philosophy of simplicity, directness and honesty of expression. As a person, Wurster was a great humanitarian. As an architect he was internationally known for his leadership in the development of a regional expression. As an educator, Dean Wurster's vision, leadership and determination expanded the scope of professional architectural education to include concern for the total environment.

Wurster's work has a unique place in American architecture. During the late 1920's and in the 1930's he developed an architecture which suited the region, most notably in the Bay Area of Northern California. His understanding of the social and economic conditions, climatic variances, materials, methods of building and the architectural heritage of the area stimulated the expression "Bay Region Style." If style is a conscious language of form, then Wurster's work does not fit this catalog term. His architecture was a rational answer to given conditions rather than the concretization of any predetermined visual image. It was a straightforward expression based on a good deal of knowledge and common sense. Derived from regional sources as a response to local human needs, it transcended the fashionable and exemplified a simple, direct design approach that suited the place, the climate, and the way of life of the people.

Wurster believed architecture, as a complicated social art, had to acknowledge the total environment. This implied that the importance of architecture was not the isolated building itself, but its relation to the people, the community and all other buildings. He knew that human environments created by architects cannot help but influence the ultimate users and thus felt that "the importance of all architectural things must be measured by its meaning for people" and must be concerned with the everyday things that shape their physical and psychological needs and aspirations.

After World War II Wurster joined forces with long-time friends and employees Theodore Bernardi and later Donn Emmons and formed the now famous firm Wurster, Bernardi, and Emmons in 1946.

Because of Wurster's belief that good architecture should be available to people in all walks of life, no work was too big or small for the firm, and they did everything from kitchen remodelings to company headquarters. Even though the scale of the projects dramatically enlarged in later years to include government buildings, college campuses, churches, large housing complexes and bank headquarters, the firm continued in the Wurster tradition, building many wonderful houses. That unfailing sense of simplicity and directness of a decade before is still evident in all the work, and the intentional modesty, informality and lack of strain remained the keynote in their approach.

The significance of Wurster's architecture was perhaps best stated by the noted American landscape architect, Thomas D. Church. When Wurster received the American Institute of Architecture's highest honor, The Gold Medal, in 1969, Church wrote: "Wurster's buildings of 40 years ago sit confidently in the world of today. His buildings of today will seem inevitable 40 years from now."

—Richard C. Peters

Y

YAMASAKI, Minoru.

American. Born in Seattle, Washington, 1 December 1912. Educated at the University of Washington, Seattle, 1930–34, B.Arch. 1934; New York University, 1934–35. Married Teruko Hirashiki in 1941; children: Carol, Taro, and Kim. Designer, Githens and Keally, New York, 1935–37; Designer, Draftsman and Job Captain, Shreve, Lamb and Harmon, New York, 1937–43; Designer, Harrison and Fouilhoux, New York, 1943–44; Designer, Raymond Loewy Associates, New York, 1944–45; Chief Architectural Designer, Smith, Hinchman and Grylls, Detroit, 1945–49. Since 1949, Principal, Minoru Yamasaki and Associates, Troy, Michigan: in partnership, with Joseph Leinweber, Yamasaki, Leinweber and Associates, Detroit, 1949–55; and, with Leinweber and George Hellmuth, *q.v.,* Leinweber, Yamasaki and Hellmuth, St. Louis, 1949–55. Instructor of Water Color, New York University, 1935–36; Instructor of Architectural Design, Columbia University, New York, 1943–45. Exhibitions: *Buildings for Business and Government,* Museum of Modern Art, New York, 1957; *International Building Exposition,* Berlin, 1957; *Living Today,* Corcoran Gallery, Washington, D.C., 1958; *World's Fair,* Brussels, 1958; *American National Exhibition,* Moscow, 1959; University of Chicago, 1959; University of Michigan, Ann Arbor, 1959; Architectural League of New York, 1959 (retrospective); John Herron Art Institute, Indianapolis, 1959 (retrospective); Michigan Society of Architects, Detroit, 1960; Honolulu Academy of Arts, 1960 (retrospective); Michigan State University, East Lansing, 1960; Oberlin College, Ohio, 1960; De Young Museum, San Francisco, 1960 (retrospective); University of Washington, Seattle, 1960; *National Gold Medal Exhibition,* toured the United States 1960–61; *New Directions in Architecture,* American Institute of Architects, Wisconsin Chapter, Milwaukee, 1960; *AIA Convention Exhibition,* Philadelphia, 1961; *Century 21* (World's Fair), Seattle, 1962; *AIA Convention Exhibition,* Miami Beach, 1963; *Arquitectura Actual de America,* Instituto de Cultura Hispanica, Madrid, 1965; *Synagogue Architecture and Sculpture,* Jewish Community Center of Cleveland, 1966; *Minoru Yamasaki: The Architect and His Use of Sculpture as an Integral Part of Design,* Staempfli Gallery, New York, 1967; *Spaces for Sport and Culture,* Olympic Games, Mexico City, 1968; Meadow Brook Art Gallery, Oakland University, Rochester, Michigan, 1974 (retrospective). Recipient: Design Award, *Progressive Architecture,* 1956; Architectural Institute of Japan Award, 1957; Gold Medal, American Institute of Architects, Detroit Chapter, 1959; Alumnus Summa Laude Dignatus Award, University of Washington, Seattle, 1960. D.H.: Wayne State University, Detroit, 1960; D.Arch.: University of Michigan, Ann Arbor, 1961; D.F.A.: Rensselaer Polytechnic Institute, Troy, New York, 1961; Bates College, Lewiston, Maine, 1964; Franklin and Marshall College, Lancaster, Pennsylvania, 1976; D.H.L.: Carleton College, Northfield, Minnesota, 1967; LL.D.: University of Saskatchewan, Regina, 1967; D.Arch. Design: Eastern Michigan University, Ypsilanti, 1979. Fellow, American Institute of Architects, 1960; Fellow, American Academy of Arts and Sciences, 1960. Address: Minoru Yamasaki and Associates, 350 West Big Beaver Road, Troy, Michigan 48084, U.S.A.

Works:

1950   Louis Baker House, Greenwich, Connecticut
Daniel W. Goodenough House, 234 Lothrop, Grosse Pointe Farms, Michigan
1955   S. Brooks Barron House, 19631 Argyle Crescent, Detroit
1956   Terminal Building, Lambert Airport, St. Louis
1957   United States Consulate-General Office Building and Staff Headquarters, Kobe, Japan
1958   McGregor Memorial Community Conference Center, Wayne State University, Detroit
American Concrete Institute, Seven Mile Road, Detroit
1959   Reynolds Metals Regional Sales Office Building, Northland Drive, Southfield, Michigan
United States Pavilion, *Agriculture and Trade Fair,* New Delhi
1961   Civil Air Terminal, Dhahran, Saudi Arabia (architectural design and detailing only)
1962   *Century 21* (World's Fair) Buildings, Seattle (architectural design and detailing only)
1963   Michigan Consolidated Gas Company Office Building, Woodward Avenue, Detroit (architectural design and detailing only)
1964   North Shore Congregation Israel Temple, Sheridan Road, Glencoe, Illinois
Queen Emma Gardens Apartment Buildings, Honolulu
Northwestern National Life Insurance Company Office Building, Minneapolis
IBM Office Building and Garage, Seattle (architectural design and detailing only)
Prentis Building, Wayne State University, Detroit
1965   William James Hall, Harvard University, Cambridge, Massachusetts
Woodrow Wilson School of Public and International Affairs, Princeton University, New Jersey
Classroom and Laboratory Buildings, University of Saskatchewan, Regina
1966   Century Plaza Hotel, Century City, Los Angeles
1967   Manufacturers and Traders Trust Company Office and Bank Building, Buffalo, New York
Library, University of Saskatchewan, Regina
1968   Ala Moana Apartments, Honolulu
Japanese Cultural and Trade Center, San Francisco (with Van Bourg/Nakamura and Associates)
1969   Eastern Air Lines Terminal, Logan International Airport, Boston (architectural design and detailing only)
1972   Styling and Product Planning Building, Chrysler Corporation, Highland Park, Michigan
1973   Horace Mann Educators Office Building, Springfield, Illinois
Basic and Clinical Science Facility, Medical College of Ohio at Toledo
1974   The World Trade Center, New York (with Emery Roth and Sons)
Congregation Beth El Temple, Bloomfield Township, Michigan
Colorado National Bank Office Building, Denver
1975   Montgomery Ward and Company Headquarters Office Building, Chicago
Century Plaza Towers and Garage, Century City, Los Angeles (architectural design and detailing only)
1976   College Center, Franklin and Marshall College, Lancaster, Pennsylvania
Performing Arts Center, Tulsa, Oklahoma
1977   Bank of Oklahoma Office Building, Williams Center, Tulsa, Oklahoma
Rainier Square Bank Tower, Seattle (architectural design and detailing only)
1978   Federal Reserve Bank, Richmond, Virginia
Office Building Complex, for the Arabian Monetary Agency, Riyadh, Saudi Arabia

Publications:

By YAMASAKI: book—*A Life in Architecture,* Tokyo 1979; articles—"Notes in Passing" in *Arts and Architecture* (Los Angeles), July 1959; "The Present State of Architecture" in *Dicta* (St. Louis), January 1963; "Humanist Architecture for America and Its Relation to the Traditional Architecture of Japan" in *RIBA Journal* (London), January 1961; "A Philosophy" in *Design* (Bombay), January 1972; "Architecture East and West" in *Architect and Builder* (Cape Town), February 1976.

On YAMASAKI: articles—"The Morality of Modern Architecture" in *Architectural Forum* (New York), May 1956; "Profilo di un Architetto Americano: Minoru Yamasaki" in *L'Architettura* (Rome), November 1956; "The Architecture of Minoru Yamasaki" in *Architectural Record* (New York), May 1957; "Minoru Yamasaki" in *L'Architecture d'Aujourd'hui* (Paris), April 1958; "American Architect, Yamasaki" by Russell Bourne in *Architectural Forum* (New York), August 1958; "A Conversation with Yamasaki" in *Architectural Forum* (New York), July 1959; "Minoru Yamasaki's Works of Late" in *Kokusai Kentiku* (Tokyo), February 1960; "Minoru Yamasaki: Projets et Réalisations Récents" in *L'Architecture d'Aujourd'hui* (Paris), April/May 1960; "Soaring Ribbed Vaults to Dominate Yamasaki's Design for Seattle Fair" and

Minoru Yamasaki: World Trade Center, New York, 1974

"Yamasaki's New Expression of 'Aspiring Verticality' " in *Architectural Record* (New York), August 1960; "Six New Projects by Yamasaki" in *Architectural Record* (New York), July 1961; "Minoru Yamasaki's Recent Buildings" by Ada Louise Huxtable in *Art in America* (New York), Winter 1962; "Yamasaki's Dhahran Airport" in *Architectural Record* (New York), March 1963; "Yamasaki's First Tower" in *Architectural Forum* (New York), May 1963; "Structure Plays Leading Role in Latest Yamasaki Designs" in *Architectural Record* (New York), December 1963; "Minoru Yamasaki" in *Architectural Record* (New York), September 1964; "Bearing Wall Expressed in a Skyscraper" and "Natural, Appropriate Use of Concrete Shells" in *Architectural Record* (New York), February 1965; "Structure and Design" in *Fortune* (New York), June 1965; "Recent Work of Minoru Yamasaki" in *Casabella* (Milan), January 1966; "The Century Plaza: A Resort in Mid-City" in *Architectural Record* (New York), August 1966; "Minoru Yamasaki Designs His Own Office" in *Architectural Record* (New York), September 1968; "The Greatest Skyscraper of Them All" in *Reader's Digest* (New York), July 1969; "Airports" in *Architectural Record* (New York), August 1970; "Works of Minoru Yamasaki" in *Informes de la Construccion* (Madrid), October 1974; "The Architect Was Told 'World Trade,' So He Planned Big" in *Smithsonian Magazine* (Washington, D.C.), January 1978.

*

For me as an architect, my life has been a constant search for the best possible combination of aesthetics and function in the buildings I design. For several years, as a result of the influences I received during my trips around the world, I tended to overdesign and overdecorate some of our buildings. But about the time of the India Fair, I began to think of the functional needs of people in an urban environment, and this led me to correct these excesses when designing our buildings. For the last fifteen years, I have adhered to the idea of using the least possible amounts of materials to attain the desired strength and stability without compromising either aesthetics or function.

When I read the following Emerson quotation in his essay entitled "Beauty," it only served to strengthen my resolve:

> Beauty rests on necessities: the line of beauty is the result of perfect economy. The cell of the beehive is built at that angle which gives the most strength with the least wax. The bone or the quill of the bird gives the most alar strength with the least weight.
>
> There is not a particle to spare in natural structures. There is a compelling reason in the uses of the plant for every novelty of color or form; and our art saves material by more skillful arrangement; and reaches beauty by taking every superfluous ounce that can be spared from a wall and keeping its strength in the poetry of columns.

I feel very strongly that man is much happier when his environment consists of delicate elements, beautifully proportioned, whether they are of wood or stone, concrete or steel. I thoroughly dislike being in interiors of buildings which are made of cold, rough and massive brick, concrete or stone. I much prefer the softness of wood and plaster and floors of carpet or, in Japan, tatami, because of the comfort they provide and the humane feeling that these materials impart. Obviously, there have been successful spaces built in beautifully polished marbles and other stones but, basically, for the interior, where one must spend most of his time, I prefer the softer materials. I have used polished marbles in both residential and office interiors, relatively sparsely, and in more monumental areas such as public lobbies, where polished or

honed marble seems more appropriate to me. The rougher materials mentioned earlier seem much more suitable in gardens and on exterior walls, not in interior spaces where they are uncomfortable and abrasive when people come into contact with them. I enjoy materials delicately designed and pleasing to the touch as well as to the eye.

Whenever I am in Japan, I try to make time to visit some classic expression of their architectural tradition. Wandering through the structures or sitting in the gardens, I find myself renewed, once again determined to make these the standards by which I will develop my work. Modern man spends too much time thinking of ways to improvise and supposedly improve upon designs, usually to the detriment of true aesthetics. Objects and buildings become too overdone, too trendy, giving them no lasting meaning. It is this we must contemplate on and try to avoid.

A general assessment of what I have learned in my practice is that architecture is to create shelter, usable and livable areas for man so that he may go about living his life productively and happily in all the variety of activities in which he needs and wishes to be involved. We must provide protection from the normal elements of climate—wind, sun, rain, snow, cold and heat—as well as from the more violent aspects of nature, such as fire, earthquakes, hurricanes, etc.

Beyond these basics, the architecture we build should give man an aesthetic emotional fulfillment so that whether he goes from home to work or to other activities in which he may be involved, he can anticipate the pleasure of his destination.

—Minoru Yamasaki

*

Minoru Yamasaki has attempted to provide American architecture with a new tradition of democratic humanism enhanced by his special understanding of the problems of scale and of serenity as derived from Japanese models. This attempt at synthesis of individualistic and democratic Western ideals with Japanese models based on contrary principles takes place in a Miesian concern for purity of understatement. The results have often proven to be contradictory rather than harmonious—an outcome not out of keeping with the ironic and contradictory mode of the times from which the buildings spring.

His Federal Science Pavilion for the *Century 21* World's Fair (Seattle, 1962) was widely heralded as setting such a humanist theme for architecture. With a mood and massing highly reminiscent of St. Mark's Square, this structure constantly combines in its formal aspect the vertical parallels dominant in American high-rise architecture with the arches and spires of Monastic Europe. The scale and serenity derive from the formal arrangement of masses, especially the central sculptural spires.

This theme, especially the formal arrangement of verticality and its resolution in Gothic arches, is, however, stretched to absurdity in the World Trade Center in New York, Yamasaki's most significant and important commission. This design is absurd in much the same way as Theatre of the Absurd or Surrealist Art: in maximization of self-referential incongruity. Extended into the sky, the narrow parallels defining the windows (and the exterior, load-bearing lattice structure) close in on themselves and create sky-spires of negative space. The very towers themselves meet in the infinity of their verticalness, yet forming another Gothic mega-arch infinitely higher than their Seattle predecessors. This theme is set at the base with the "human scale" set of lattices. These lattices actually form physical arches: opposed to the implicit arches of the towers. The final resolution of the human scale, then, as elaborated by this building, occurs in the sky, in the infinity of space: this is an ironic pie-in-the-sky humanism, offering salvation in the not-here and not-now.

From the walkway of the Brooklyn Bridge or the New Jersey Palisades, WTC shimmers. This is architecture as art: Op Art to be exact. The eye cannot discern whether it is looking at a series of crisscross-

ing lines or a series of verticals—here the American-European-Japanese synthesis is clearly unresolvable on the retinal level, and the building is a challenge to the academicism of the New York skyline rather than a solution of its contradictory elements.

In reality, WTC, and for that matter Seattle Science Pavilion, is about as humanistic, democratic, or serene as a 1964 Lincoln Continental. They are physical objects that are humanistic, democratic and serene for those few who can afford them, politically, economically, ecologically. That the WTC uses as much electricity as a Swedish city of 200,000 is neither an accomplishment of socio-technical progress nor a joke. As an office building, WTC provides little in the way of amenity for anyone but the top executives working in it; economically, it is a drain on city and region; politically, it serves a commercial-governmental elite physically and socially isolated from the people whom, by democratic principles, it is supposed to serve.

Rather than creating a humanist tradition or a foretaste of the 21st Century, the architecture of Yamasaki emerges as an ideal realization, an end-of-the-line for a set of technical, social, and aesthetic standards. These standards of accomplishment are expressed by two implicit doctrines brought to final fruition in WTC: 1) architecture is site-free and prototypic—building design is a sub-category of industrial product design; and 2) architecture is the creation of monumental sculpture—purity of form synthesis is a criterion that overrides and is separate and separable from social, political, and environmental responsibility. Judged by these standards, Yamasaki's creations are indeed masterpieces.

—Joseph B. Juhasz

YORKE, F(rancis) R(eginald) S(tevens).

British. Born in Stratford upon Avon, Warwickshire, 3 December 1906. Educated at Chipping Camden School, Gloucestershire; University of Birmingham School of Architecture and Town Planning. Married Thelma Austin Jones in 1930; had two daughters. In private practice, London, 1930–35; in partnership with Marcel Breuer, London, 1935–37; worked under William Holford on government war work, 1939–44; Partner, with Eugene Rosenberg, *q.v.,* and Cyril Mardall, *q.v.,* Yorke, Rosenberg and Mardall, London, 1944 until his death, 1962. Founder Member, MARS Group, London, 1932; Assistant Editor, *The Architects' Journal,* London, 1933; Editor, *Specifications* (annual), London, 1935–62. Recipient: Council of Industrial Design Award, 1959; Civic Trust Award, 1961; Bronze Medal, Royal Institute of British Architects, 1961. Fellow, Royal Institute of British Architects. C.B.E. (Commander, Order of the British Empire), 1962. *Died* (in London) *10 June 1962.*

Works:

1933 Reinforced Concrete Houses (2), Gidea Park, Essex (with William Holford, A. Stephenson and A. Adams)

1935 Reinforced Concrete House, Nast Hyde, Hatfield, Hertfordshire

1936 Civic Centre of the Future (project; with Marcel Breuer)

1937 Sea Lane House, East Preston, Sussex (with Marcel Breuer)

1939 7 cottages, Stratford upon Avon, Warwickshire (with F. W. B. Yorke)

1939/
44 Government depots, camps and factories, England (with William Holford)

1940 Flats, Camberwell, London (with Arthur Korn)

With Yorke, Rosenberg, Mardall:

1947 Luccombe House, Isle of Wight
Cowley Peachey Housing, Middlesex

F. R. S. Yorke: Barclay Secondary School, Stevenage, Hertfordshire, 1950

Exhibition stands, Council of Industrial Design and Board of Trade, London
1948 Sigmund Pumps Factory, Gateshead, Durham
Fort Corbletts House conversion, Alderney, Channel Islands
Linden Doors Factory, Stowmarket, Suffolk (project)
1949 Temporary Outpatients Department, St. Thomas' Hospital, London
Shebbear College Boarding School alterations, Devon
Factories, Dagenham Docks, London (project)
1950 Barclay Secondary School, Stevenage, Hertfordshire
1951 John Lewis Department Store, Southsea, Hampshire (project)
Dr. Cole House, Londonderry, Northern Ireland (with Corr and McCormick)
Housing, King's Langley, Hertfordshire
Susan Lawrence Primary School, London
Elizabeth Lansbury Nursery School, London
Housing, Brynmawr, Brecknock, Wales

Hainault Forest Secondary School, Essex
1952 Sir William Nottidge School, Whitstable, Kent
Sish Lane Housing, Stevenage, Hertfordshire
College of Further Education, Merthyr Tydfil, Glamorgan, Wales
1953 Williams and Williams Exhibition Stand, *Building Trades Exhibition,* London
The Mill House conversion, Wootton, Oxfordshire
Warren Wood Secondary School, Rochester, Kent
Upholland Grammar School, Wigan, Lancashire
West Park Secondary School, Leeds
Southlands Teachers' Training College Assembly Hall, Wimbledon, London
Sheerwater Primary School, Woking, Surrey
Causeway Green Primary School, Oldbury, Worcestershire
North Mimms Boys' and Infants' School, Hertfordshire
1954 Steddall's Warehouse alterations, London
Birchen Coppice Primary School, Kidder-

minster, Worcestershire
Queensmead Secondary School, Ruislip, Middlesex
London Transport Bus Garage and Depot, Loughton, Essex
Hammerson Group Offices, Great New Street, London (project)
1955 Tudor House Home for the Infirm, Grayshott, Hertfordshire (project)
Kerris Artists Studio conversion, Mousehole, Cornwall
Williams and Williams Offices, London (project)
Quarles Secondary Modern School, Romford, Essex
Master plan and stage I of the Leeds Polytechnic
Mark Hall Local Authority Housing, Harlow, Essex
Haileybury Boys Club, London
Bewdley Secondary School, Worcestershire
Kirkwall Place Housing, Bethnal Green, London
Kingswood School, Essex
1956 Boxgrove Housing prototypes
Wootton Rectory, Oxfordshire
Jack Straw's Lane House, Oxford
Tyrell and Green Store, Southampton
Dick Sheppard School, Tulse Hill, London
East Anglian Girls School, Bury St. Edmunds, Suffolk
Bradfield Secondary School, Yorkshire
Sigmund Pumps Factory extension, Gateshead, Durham (project)
North Mimms Boys and Infants School additions, Hertfordshire
College of Further Education extensions, Merthyr Tydfil, Glamorgan, Wales
Kingswood School extensions, Essex
1957 Southlands College Lecture Block and Dining Room extensions, Wimbledon, London
Temple Moor Grammar School, Leeds
Stanley Outwood Secondary School, Yorkshire
Jewish Theological College, Montagu Square, London
Oak Park Secondary School, Havant, Hampshire
Philip Harben House, 115 Great George Street, London
Dawley Secondary School, Shropshire
Interbau Housing, Berlin (project; with Werner Düttmann)
Master plan for the Bromsgrove Education Centre, Worcestershire
Timberlog Secondary School, Basildon, Essex
St. Paul's Secondary School, Addlestone, Surrey
Gatwick Airport, stage I, Sussex
Sir William Nottidge School extensions, Whitstable, Kent
1958 Unilever House, Hamburg (competition project)
Wokingham Infants School, Berkshire (competition project)
Jewish Board of Guardians Offices, London
Finnish Seamen's Mission, London
Chaucer Secondary School, Sheffield
Carmel College extensions, Wallingford, Berkshire
Brixton Synagogue Hall remodelling, London
Leeds Polytechnic, stage II
Tyrell and Green Store extensions, Southampton
East Anglian Girls School alterations and additions, Bury St. Edmunds, Suffolk
1959 J. Spedan Lewis House, Longstock, Hampshire
Morsons Chemical Works, Enfield, Middlesex
Elephant and Castle Development, London (project)

World Health Organization Offices, Geneva (competition project)

Timber Development Association Office Furniture, London (competition project)

Formation Furniture prototypes, for Bath Cabinet Makers Ltd.

Roman Road Housing, Bethnal Green, London

High Park School, Stourbridge, Worcestershire

St. Paul's School Hall alterations, Chertsey, Surrey

Brays Grove Secondary School, Harlow, Essex

College of Further Education, Bromsgrove, Worcestershire

Tennant Brothers Exhibition Stand, *Club Trades Fair,* London

Churchill College, Cambridge (competition project)

Upholland Grammar School extensions, Wigan, Lancashire

East Anglian Girls School alterations and additions, stage II, Bury St. Edmunds, Suffolk

1960 Watford Shopping Centre, Hertfordshire (project)

Rothwell Secondary School, stage II, Yorkshire

Warslow School, Staffordshire

United States Embassy, Grosvenor Square, London (with Eero Saarinen Associates)

Supasave Store, Southend, Essex

Staincliffe Hospital Geriatric Unit, Leeds

Altnagelvin Hospital, Londonderry, Northern Ireland

Passmores Comprehensive School, Harlow, Essex

D. Allford House, Persham, Surrey (project)

Brierly Hill Secondary School, Staffordshire

Rolls Royce Offices, Derby (project)

Telecommunications Engineering Building, Gatwick Airport, Sussex

Leeds Polytechnic, stage III

1961 N. J. Payne House, Shamley Green, Norfolk

Royal Masonic School, Ascot, Berkshire (project)

Bromsgrove High School, Worcestershire

Hob Green Primary School, Worcestershire

YRM and Norwich Union Insurance Societies Offices, Greystoke Place, London

Maternity and Outpatients Departments, Crawley Hospital, Sussex

Kew Bridge Development for British Rail, London (project)

Report on Creekside Refuse Disposal Depot, Deptford, London

Timber Development Association Wooden Furniture, London (competition project)

Kingswood School extensions, stage II, Essex

1962 Master plan for Kuwait Airport (with Sir Frederick Snow and Partners)

Elliott Brothers Welfare Building, Rochester, Kent (project)

Rotameter Factory, Croydon, Surrey (project)

Library, Cambridge University (project)

Southlands College: Queensmere Hostels, Lecture Block and Gymnasium, Wimbledon, London

Ark House, Rochford, Essex

Staff Residence, Crawley Hospital, Sussex

Barstable Comprehensive School, Basildon, Essex

College of Further Education extensions, stage II, Merthyr Tydfil, Glamorgan, Wales

North Mimms Boys' and Infants' School additions, stage II, Hertfordshire

Haileybury Boys Club, stage II, London

Oak Park Secondary School extensions, Havant, Hampshire

Timberlog Secondary School extensions, Basildon, Essex

Publications:

By YORKE: books—*The Modern House,* London 1934; *The Modern House in England,* London 1937; *The Modern Flat,* with Frederick Gibberd, London 1937, 1950; *A Key to Modern Architecture,* with Colin Penn, London 1939; *Flooring Materials,* with C. Roy Fowkes, London 1948; *The New Small House,* with Penelope Whiting, London 1954; article—"Modern Architecture in Czechoslovakia" in *Review* (London), no. 3, 1943.

On YORKE: book—*The Architecture of Yorke Rosenberg Mardall,* introduction by Reyner Banham, London and New York 1972.

F. R. S. Yorke was one of the small group of architects who introduced modern architecture into Britain during the 1930's. While England after the First World War remained true to the tradition of neo-Georgian, the continent had long been seething with 20th century ideas. The most influential revolutionary was Le Corbusier, followed closely by Walter Gropius of the Bauhaus. In the 1920's the ideas percolated into English schools of architecture, but it was not until later that the new concept of internationalism in architecture began to acquire the force of reality. After the Second World War, however, the new style flowered as the expression of a new society, and Yorke was able to practise his art unrestricted by academic tradition.

Although Yorke was undoubtedly inspired by Le Corbusier, he was himself an artist of the highest calibre, not given to imitation. His work at its best was almost classical in its purity of form. Of all his immediate post-war works, perhaps it is for his schools that he will be best remembered. Among these was one specially built for the 1951 *Festival of Britain* exhibition of architecture in the Lansbury neighbourhood in Poplar. The exploitation of glass and reinforced concrete was dramatic. The external space design seemed to flow into the building; from outside, it was possible to see the interior with its rich and colourful ceramics. The so-called International Style was soon to run into difficulties with less experienced and sensitive designers, but during his period Yorke pioneered, illuminated and gave distinction to architecture that will always be part of architectural history.

Yorke was not one to suffer fools gladly, but his personal charm and business acumen enabled him to build up a business with two equally distinguished partners, a firm that has continued after Yorke's death, as Yorke, Rosenberg and Mardall, in his own tradition of the impersonal and international, acknowledging their continuing debt to Le Corbusier and Mies van der Rohe.

—Geoffrey Jellicoe

YOSHIDA, Isoya.

Japanese. Born in Tokyo, 19 December 1894. Educated at the Kaisei Middle School, Tokyo, 1909–13; Department of Architecture, Tokyo Art School, now Tokyo University of Fine Arts, 1915–23, Dip. Arch. 1923; travelled in Europe, 1925. Married Hatsué Yoshida in 1939. In private practice, concentrating on "Sukiya" style (traditional Japanese modular design), Tokyo, 1925 until his death, 1974. Lecturer, 1941–46, Professor of Architecture, 1946–61, and Professor Emeritus, 1962–74, Tokyo University of Fine Arts. Exhibition: *Furniture Designs of Isoya Yoshida,* Takashimaya, Tokyo, 1952; *Expo '70,* Osaka, Japan, 1970. Recipient: Japan Arts Academy Award, 1952; Japan Cultural Medal, 1964. Member, Japan Arts Academy, Japan Architects Association, and Japan Institute of Architects. Honorary Member, Architects Association of Mexico, and American Institute of Architects. *Died* (in Tokyo) *24 March 1974.*

Works:

1931 Sekiya House, Tokyo
1934 Kokei Kobayashi House/Studio, Tokyo
1935 Gimpu-so House, Tokyo
1936 Shuho Yamakawa Studio, Tokyo
 Kineya Villa, Atami, Japan
 Nobuko Yoshiya House, Tokyo
1939 New Park Hotel, Matsushima, Japan
1940 Hoshun Yamaguchi House, Tokyo
 Oshima House, Tokyo
 Iwanami Villa, Atami, Japan
 Aoki House, Tokyo
1940/
 62 Shinkiraku Japanese-style Restaurant, Tokyo
1942 Fugetsu Teahouse, Shizuoka, Japan
1944 Isoya Yoshida House, Kanagawa Prefecture, Japan
1949 Kato House, Kamakura, Japan
1951 Kabukiza Theatre, Tokyo
1951/
 58 Ryuzaburo Umehara House/Studio, Tokyo
1953 Tsurutoku Japanese-style Restaurant, Tokyo
1954 Koyoen Tsuruya Japanese-style Restaurant, Hyogo Prefecture, Japan
 Hoshun Yamaguchi Studio, Kanagawa Prefecture, Japan
1955 Bunrakuza Theatre, Osaka
 Kosaburo Yoshizumi House, Tokyo
1956 Botan Japanese-style Restaurant, Osaka
 Yamagata House, Tokyo
1957 Kanzaburo Nakamura House, Tokyo
 Suzuki House, Tokyo
1958 Meijiza Theatre, Tokyo
 Japan Academy of Arts Center, Tokyo
1959 Tsuruya Japanese-style Restaurant, Osaka
1960 Sasaki House, Tokyo
 Yaeko Mizutani House, Tokyo
 Goto Art Museum, Tokyo
 Yamato Bunka Hall, Nara, Japan
1961 Gyokudo Art Museum, Tokyo
1962 Nobuko Yoshiya House, Kanagawa Prefecture, Japan
 Kitazawa Center, Nagano Prefecture, Japan
 Japan Cultural Center, Rome
1963 Kitamura House, Kyoto
1964 Okazaki Tsuruya Hall, Kyoto
 Shigeru Yoshida House, Kanagawa Prefecture, Japan
1965 Matsuoka House, Kyoto
1965/
 73 Royal Hotel, Osaka
1966 Murakami Kaishin Hall, Tokyo
1967 Inomata House, Tokyo
1968 Narita-san Shinsho-ji Temple, Chiba Prefecture, Japan
 Chugu-ji Temple, Nara, Japan
1969 Sinsuke Kishi House, Shizuoka Prefecture, Japan
 Mangan-ji Temple, Tokyo
1970 Kitagawa Shop, Tokyo
 Matsushita Pavilion, *Expo '70,* Osaka
1971 Mikiya House, Tokyo
 Iikura Hall, Ministry of Foreign Affairs, Tokyo
1972 Prince Chichibu House, Tokyo
 Mitsukoshi Silver House, Tokyo

Publications:

On YOSHIDA: books—*Architect Isoya Yoshida's Work,* edited by Yoshida, Tokyo 1949; *Isoya Yoshida* (Modern Japanese Architects Series), edited by Kurita, Tokyo 1974; *Works of Isoya Yoshida* by Gakuji Yamamoto, Tokyo 1976; articles—"Bunrakuza Theatre" in *Kenchiku Bunka* (Tokyo), April 1956; "Restaurant à Osaka" in *L'Architecture d'Aujourd'hui* (Paris), May 1956; "Classic Modern Hall for the Academy of Arts" in *Shinkenchiku* (Tokyo), July 1958; "Académie d'Art Japonais, Tokio" in *L'Architecture d'Aujourd'hui* (Paris), April/May 1960; "A Profile of Isoya Yoshida" in *The Japan Architect* (Tokyo), January/February 1969; "A

Tribute to the Memory of Isoya Yoshida" by Teijo Ito in *Architecture + Urbanism* (Tokyo), May 1974.

The reconciliation of tradition and modernity was a major theme for modern Japanese architecture. Isoya Yoshida, along with Tange and Kikutake, was one of the few architects to have succeeded in this task, and when one considers that he achieved it in the genre of wood structures, creating the so-called modern *sukiya* style and establishing it as a popular art, his achievement must be ranked at least the equal of Tange's.

Yoshida's work may be divided into that of three periods. The first period saw the pursuit, primarily in private houses and Japanese style restaurants, of a modernization of the *sukiya* and of the establishment of the modern *sukiya* style; the second (postwar) phase saw in public buildings, theaters and art museums the pursuit of a Japanese design in concrete; and the third phase (from the mid-1960's on) saw the formal search for a truly Japanese terminology purged of Chinese influences in religious architecture, a field that had been dominated by very strict stylistic rules.

These phases are distinctions that Yoshida himself once made with regard to his career, but common to these three periods is a search for Japanese spaces and Japanese architecture, and in this search he completely upset the traditional paradigm and its customary order and rules. His approach may be termed *contraventionalism,* and when furthermore one reflects on his love of technical invention, his progressivism and his confident self-advocacy, one may well consider him more akin to Le Corbusier than Le Corbusier's disciple, Mayckawa.

There are many reasons that account for the unique modernity of Yoshida's *sukiya* spaces, but the most striking is his overthrow of the modular system of traditional wood architectural design. Yoshida introduced the *ōkabe* system, a method that hides structural columns inside the wall, into the *sukiya* style, and (disregarding the .9 m. × 1.8 m. module) placed wood pilasters "where [he] wanted to." He also tried such inventive techniques as removing the corner columns from wood structures to create corner windows and reversing the traditional chiaroscuro of Japanese spaces, making the ceiling, wall and floor in that order become darker by the use of artificial lighting. These, together with electrically operated partitions and *shoji* that slide completely into walls, might well have been inspired by the stage mechanisms and lighting effects of the traditional plays that he loved and was familiar with from youth.

In his second phase too he was a traditionalist who constantly rebelled against tradition, often using walls and pilasters and creating a style of flat roof with an extremely thin edge. In his religious architecture, he developed a simple roof-supporting system that did away with the Chinese order *(tokyō).* This spirit of rebellion—the rejection of models and in their stead the espousal of free creation and invention—is indeed true to the original spirit of *sukiya,* which was created in the middle of the 16th century as a style for the emergent bourgeois class, and it is because of this attitude that Yoshida's *sukiya* is truly modern, light and urbane, in contrast to the work of other modern practitioners of traditional wood architecture such as Horiguchi, Murano, Taniguchi and Tange. Yoshida alone spent his entire life removed from the fashion of European modernism or the International Style: his independence can be attributed to his birth and upbringing as a proud, Tokyo bourgeois, his deep confidence in and love of traditional bourgeois culture, and his urbane view of architecture as a background for this culture. This anti-modern modernism that Yoshida embraced lives on and contains within it an unlimited potential for the future.

—Katsuyoshi Arai

Takamasa Yosizaka: Maison Franco-Japonàise, Tokyo, 1959

YOSIZAKA, Takamasa.

Japanese. Born in Tokyo, 13 February 1917. Educated at the Maison des Petits, Geneva, 1921–23; Ecole de l'Etoil du Matin, Tokyo, 1924–29; Ecole Internationale, Geneva, 1929–33; Waseda University, Tokyo, graduated 1941. Served in the Imperial Japanese Army, 1942–45. Married Hukuko Kono in 1945; children: Masakuni, Masamitu and Feliza. In private practice, Tokyo, since 1945; President, Atelier U, Tokyo, since 1965. Worked in the studio of Le Corbusier, Paris, 1950–52; Manager, Equatorial Africa Expedition, 1957–58; Leader, Mount McKinley Expedition, Alaska, 1960. Head of the Department of Architecture, Waseda University, Tokyo, 1964–66, and Sangyo Gizyutu Sensyu Gakko, Tokyo, 1964–69; Dean, School of Science and Engineering, Waseda University, 1969–72. President, Architectural Institute of Japan, 1973–74. Director, Metropolitan Planning Institute, Tokyo, since 1974; President, Japan-China Architectural Technique Friendship Association, since 1974, Institute of Living Studies, Tokyo, since 1975, and Quantity Surveyors Institute, Tokyo, since 1975. Exhibition: *Panoramiru,* Odakyu Hall, Tokyo, 1975. Recipient: First Prize, Ginza Leisure District Project, Tokyo, 1946; First Prize, Sibuya Leisure District Project, Tokyo, 1946; First Prize, *Bienal,* Sao Paulo, 1954, 1955, 1957; Ministry of Education Prize, *Biennale,* Venice, 1957; Leopoldville Cultural Center Prize, Belgian Congo, 1959; Architectural Institute of Japan Award, 1963; Planning Institute of Japan Award, 1974. Member of the Légion d'Honneur, France. Address: Atelier U, 2-17-24 Hyakunintyo, Sinziku-ku, Tokyo 160, Japan.

Works:

1946 Ginza Shopping and Leisure District, Tokyo (project)
      Sibuya Shopping and Leisure District, Tokyo (project)
1947 Waseda Educational/Cultural District, Tokyo (project)
1950 Imamura House, Tokyo
1953 Oikawa House, Tokyo
1955 Yosizaka House, Tokyo

Tiba Nissan Service Station, Iba, Japan
1956 Ura House, Tokyo
Japanese Pavilion, *Biennale,* Venice
1957 Masuda House, Tokyo
Sogo House, Tokyo
Kondo House, Tokyo
Maruyama House, Tokyo
1958 Meisei High School, Osaka
Kaisei High School, Nagasaki
1959 Karasawa Mountain Lodge, Kamikoti, Japan
Maison Franco-Japonaise, Tokyo
National Museum of Western Art, Taito-ku, Tokyo (with Le Corbusier, Kunio Mayekawa and Junzo Sakakura)
1960/
63 Kureha Middle School, Toyama, Japan
1961 Kurosawaike Mountain Lodge, Myoko, Japan
Oosaka Keiza Daigaku Ski Hut, Sirouma, Japan
City Hall, Gozu, Japan
1964 Takeda House, Tokyo
Tateyamaso Mountain Lodge, Midagahara, Japan
1965 Akabosi House, Kugenuma, Japan
Arukokai Ski Hut, Tadesina, Japan
Tenryu River Monument, Hamamatu, Japan
1965/
67 Redevelopment plan for Tokadanobaba, Japan
Daigaku Seminar Housing, Hatiozi, Tokyo
1966 Kurosawaike Mountain Lodge, II, Myoko, Japan
Takayama Rest House, Takayama, Japan
1966/
67 Oosima Pilot Plan, Motomati, Japan
1967 Higuti House, Tokyo
Matudo Minami Primary School, Tiba-ken, Japan
Oosima Daisan Middle School, Oosima, Tokyo
Oosima Daiiti Middle School, Oosima, Tokyo
Oosima Sasikizi Primary School, Oosima, Tokyo
Town Hall and Library, Oosima, Tokyo
Meika Building, Tokyo
1968 Nozawa Spa Lodge, Nozawa, Japan
Husaziiso Mountain Lodge, Tateyama, Japan
Karasawa Mountain Lodge II, Kamikoti, Japan
Space Museum, Ikomayama, Osaka
Development plan for Nagaone, Titibu, Japan
1969 Oono House, Tokyo
Gokurakuzaka Ski Hut, Bizyodaira, Japan
Seikatu Center, Seikatu, Japan
Development plan for Sagamiko, Japan
Redevelopment plan for the shopping quarter, Yamaga and Misumi, Japan
1970 Sin'ei Distribution Center, Tokyo
Printers and Food Manufacturers Collective Estate Development, Kagosima, Japan
1971 Izawa House, Tokyo
Yamada Bokuzyo Mountain Lodge, Nagano-ken, Japan
Kurobedaira Daikanho Mountain Lodge, Toyama-ken, Japan
Working Youth Athletic Center, Asikaka, Japan
Rural housing development, Hirayaga, Japan
Rural housing development, Kamo, Japan
1972 Iizuka House, Takata, Japan
Ootu House, Kasiwa, Japan
Kobayasi House, Matumoto, Japan
Working Women's House, Morioka, Japan
1973 Nisiyama House, Azumi, Japan
Youth Center Covered Pool, Morioka, Japan
Environment renewal plan for Ootamati, Japan
1974 Misawa House, Hayama, Japan
Environment renewal plan for Hiragatyo, Japan

1975 Sakurai High School Gate, Sakurai, Japan
Environment renewal plan for Hatinohe and Sannohe, Japan
1976 Kosizuka House, Tokyo
Horikawa House, Tokyo
Environment renewal plans for Inagawa and for Ninohe, Japan
1977 Metoki Rural Children's Park, Sannohe, Japan
Environment renewal plans for Daitotyo, Kanasago, and Dezima, Japan

Publications:

By YOSIZAKA: books—*Introduction to the Study of Dwellings,* Tokyo 1950; *Le Corbusier,* Tokyo 1953; *Environment and Form,* Tokyo 1955; *A House, A School,* Tokyo 1960; *From Primitive to Civilized,* Tokyo 1961; *Study of Dwelling,* Tokyo 1965; *Directives,* Tokyo 1972; *Century 21 Japan,* with others, Tokyo 1972; *Moi, j'aime pas la mer,* Tokyo 1973; *The Sendai Plan,* with others, Tokyo 1973; *World Architecture,* Tokyo 1976; *Proposition for a Re-Arrangement of Quarters,* with others, Tokyo 1976; *Korean Rural Agglomerations,* with others, Tokyo 1976; translations into Japanese—*Le Modulor* by Le Corbusier, Tokyo 1952; *Le Modulor II* by Le Corbusier, Tokyo 1959; *Silent Cities* by Norman Carver, Tokyo 1966; *Vers Une Architecture* by Le Corbusier, Tokyo 1976; *Le Corbusier: Oeuvres Completes,* 8 volumes, Tokyo 1971–78; *Erreurs Monumentales* by Michel Ragon, Tokyo 1972; *Le Charte d'Athene* by Le Corbusier, Tokyo 1976; *Le Modulor I and II* by Le Corbusier, revised edition, Tokyo 1976.

On YOSIZAKA: book—*Contemporary Japanese Architects: Takamasa Yosizaka,* Tokyo 1971; articles—in *Kentiku* (Tokyo), May 1961, January 1966, January 1971; *Tosi Zyutaku* (Tokyo), August 1975.

What is an architect? It seems that I have been reckoned as an architect, so what I have been doing must be what an architect does. But as for art, a painter or a sculptor will do better; as for enterprise, a business will do better, a politician will do better; as for technique, an engineer will do better; as for workmanship, a craftsman will do better; and as for life, a housewife will do better. Nevertheless, an architect dreams—to build a beautiful house, to build a lively city, a build a prosperous nation, yes, and to build world peace, wielding only the power dictated by the value of his own conscience, believing that it may be the omnipotent key to solve any problem.

People's concern can be classified into five grades: first, the world within and the one immediately in touch with his body; then the world encircling him and useful to him; and the wider world supporting the favorable conditions to realize the above items; further out, there must be a world swarming with disturbing forces which infiltrate everywhere—do we have to conquer this world too? And there is an even bigger world included in the universe which we can only imagine intellectually. Greedily, an architect acts, dealing with this greatest world, wishing to relate it to the first-mentioned world.

Result: the task seems to be beyond his power, but he struggles brandishing a theory named "Discontinuous Unity," and inventing a tool named "Method Through Discovery," trying to bring all the five worlds into a consistent whole and to express them coherently.

"Discontinuous Unity," because the contemporary world drives towards individual respect on one hand and at the same time towards the promotion of group consciousness, the former tending towards diversity and chaos, the latter searching for a discipline of unity yielding to coercion. This contradiction must be solved in plan, section and form. Even floors, walls, ceilings, windows, doors and other elements—as well as building materials and building equipment produced in industry with precision—became independent and need to be gathered together to form one house. It is through finding a

construction method that design can be enhanced to its philosophic and aesthetic value. The clue to the solution can only be reached by "discovering" the fundamental problem through the conditions in each case, on each occasion. Capable of becoming the finding of solutions for other's problems, it is a fascinating play worth risking one's life.

—Takamasa Yosizaka

Takamasa Yosizaka, one of the pioneers of modern architecture in Japan, spent many years in Europe, both as a student and as an employee of Le Corbusier's atelier. Like his compatriots Junzo Sakakura and Kunio Mayekawa, Yosizaka emerged from the experience of working with Le Corbusier deeply colored; his earliest work in Japan greatly recalled the material, formal, and compositional sense of Corbu in the mid-1950's.

Yosizaka's own house (1955), for example, used a visible structural system of concrete posts and slabs, infilled with block much like at Maisons Jaoul. His container and platform system is much like that of the famous Domino House scheme and, physically, the Yosizaka residence resembles Corbusier's early, purist, Citrohan house. The Japan Pavilion at the Venice *Biennale,* designed by Yosizaka in 1956, employs a similar structural frame, but the encasing envelope is less disrupted, and the result is much akin to the Tokyo Museum of Western Art, designed by Corbusier's office with project supervision by Yosizaka, Sakakura, and Mayekawa.

In time, though, Yosizaka's designs moved away from heavy Beton Brut, and other formal explorations that resembled Corbusier. The Gozu City Hall of 1961 must be considered a key work in this regard. Although still constructivist, the building celebrates technology whimsically. A huge office block is thrown into the air, supported by concrete trellises that look like the structural support for a huge bridge, which is, in fact, what the building has become.

The Maison Franco-Francaise, of the same period, demonstrates Yosizaka's growing consciousness of context. It is a very sculptural building finished in a rich, deep red. The front has been masked by a screen studded with Roman letters, however, to confirm the bland massing of many of the simpler buildings in urban Japan.

As his concern for adequate contextual response grew, Yosizaka recieved several planning commissions. In the mid-1960's, in his redevelopment plans for Oosima, Motomati, and Tokadanobaba, he explored three dimensional public spaces and natural, flexible planning within a structured approach. His Daigaku Seminary Housing at Hatiozi, Tokyo, displays the same ideas, but at a more refined level and a smaller scale. The housing units are simple, repeated elements that descend down the slope of the site, but the total plan is dominated by several singular elements. The Headquarters and Main Seminar House tower above the residence blocks like Arabesque minarets or medieval campaniles. They unify the design by offering common, identifiable monuments that have come to characterize the complex.

The combination of many units arranged randomly, with a strong, unifying formal element, reflects Yosizaka's important notion of "Discontinuous Unity." There are many different values of philosophy that must all be expressed in architecture, he claims. While his buildings often suggest this diversity, he also tries to create a "natural understanding that may contribute to peace." He accomplishes this by unification and clarification, by joining complexity with simplicity.

Yosizaka is a highly intelligent designer with a strong background in both Western and Japanese design approach. He has melded these by incorporating in design his understanding of contextual and human concerns, as well as abstract form. His career has been one of transformation, but has been consistently characterized by the inclusion of many different ideas, without compromised integrity.

—Ching-Yu Chang

Z

ZABLOCKI, Wojciech.

Polish. Born in Warsaw, 6 December 1930. Educated at the School of Architecture, Cracow, 1949–54, M.A. 1954; Warsaw School of Architecture, Ph.D. 1968. Married Alina Janowska in 1963; children: Marcin, Michal, and Katarzyna. In private practice, Warsaw, since 1955; has also worked in the State Design Office, Cracow, since 1955. Co-Editor, *Architektura*, Warsaw, 1967–71. Former fencing champion: four times World Fencing Champion, and five times Polish Champion; Member of the Polish Olympic Team in sabre fencing, 1949–65: twice placed second in Olympic Fencing Events. Member, Polish Olympic Committee, 1965–72; Vice-President, Polish Fencing Association, 1968–72. Vice-President, Polich Branch, Sport and Recreation Section, International Union of Architects, since 1970. Exhibition: *Constructions*, Warsaw, 1969. Collection: Museum of Architecture, Wroclaw. Recipient: Polonia Restituta Honorary State Award, 1960; Ministry of Building Award, 1964, 1972, 1975; Ministry of Culture Award, 1968. Address (office): ul. Kaniowska 21B, 01-529 Warsaw, Poland.

Works:

1958 Cement Works, Chelm, Poland
1959 Gypsum Factory, Dolina Nidy, Poland
1962 Olympic Training Centre, Warsaw
1964 Covered Ice Rink, Gdansk, Poland (competition project; with M. Wróbel, W. Szymánski, and Zórawski)
1965 Westerplatte Monument, Gdansk, Poland (competition project; with the sculptor G. Zemla)
    Poznan Museum (competition project)
1966 Monument to the Silesian Uprising, Katowice, Poland (with the sculptor G. Zemla)
1970 Municipal Hall, Lublin (project; with S. Kuś)
    Sports Centre, Nowa Ruda, Poland (project; with W. Humięcki)
1972 Sports Centre, Konin, Poland (with L. Szwedowski)
    Catholic Church, Konin, Poland (project; with S. Kuś)
1973 Sports Hall, Bydgoszcz, Poland (competition project; with W. Humięcki)
    Sports Centre, Glogów, Poland (project; with S. Kuś)
    Covered Ice Rink, Glogów, Poland (project; with S. Kuś)
    Covered Ice Rink, Toruń, Poland (project; with W. Humięcki)
    Cepelia Tower House, Warsaw (project; with W. Humięcki)
1974 Sports Centre, Pulawy, Poland (with S. Kuś)
    Sports Hall, Tarnobrzeg, Poland (project; with J. Bodasiński)
    Sports Centre, Kielce, Poland (competition project; with J. Bodasiński)
    Training Centre, Bydgoszcz, Poland (project; with W. Humięcki)
    Sports Centre, Warsaw (with S. Kuś and R. Wilczynski)
1975 Sports Centre, Tomaszów Maz., Poland (project; with W. Humięcki)
    War Memorial, Tomaszów Maz., Poland (project)
    Twin Atrium House, Warsaw
    Sports Hall, Grudziadz, Poland (with J. Bodasiński)
    Sports Hall, Warsaw (competition project; with J. Bodasiński and S. Kus)
1975– Sports Centre, Zgorzelec, Poland (with S. Kuś)
    Sports and Recreation Park, Tarnobrzeg, Poland
1976 War Memorial, near Kolobrzeg, Poland (project; with the sculptor Pastwa)
    Olympic Sports Centre, Poznan (competition project; with J. Bodasiński)
    Sports Hall, Kielce, Poland (project; with M. Dziurla)
    Elana Sports Hall, Toruń, Poland (project; with T. Spanili)
1976– Sports Park, Kielce, Poland (with J. Bodasiński and M. Dziurla)
1977 Sports Centre, Leszno, Poland (project; with J. Golebiowski)
    Swimming Pool, Ciechanów, Poland (project; with S. Kuś)
    Small Sports Hall (project; with S. Kuś)
1977– Sports Hall, Leszno, Poland (with NOWAK and R. Czyzak)
1978 Slowacki Monument, Warsaw (project; with the sculptor E. Wittig)
    Tennis Centre, Warsaw (project; with R. Czyzak)
1978– Covered Ice Rink, Siedlce, Poland (with W. Humiecki)
    Terrace House, Warsaw (project)
    Tower House 'Polam', Warsaw (project; with A. Derentowicz)

Publications:

By ZABLOCKI: books—*Z Workiem Szermierczym po Świecie* (With Fencing Bag Around the World), Warsaw 1962; *Podroze z Szabla* (Travelling with Sabre), Warsaw 1965; *Czynny Wypoczynek w Zakladzie Pracy* (Recreation in Factories), Warsaw 1966; articles—"Architektura i Konstrukcja Hali Sportowej YoYogi: Kenzo Tange" in *Inzynieria i Budownictwo* (Warsaw), no. 10, 1965; "Architektura Olimpijska" in *Dysk Olimpijski,* Warsaw 1966; "Architektura Obiektów Sportowych" in *Dysk Olimpijski,* Warsaw 1967; "Sport Centrum in Warschau" in *Bauen und Wohnen* (Zurich), no. 7, 1967; "Monument des Insurges Silesiens" in *L'Architecture d'Aujourd'hui* (Paris), no. 9, 1967; "Tworczośćczy Produkcja?" in *Architektura* (Warsaw), no. 133, 1967; "Wladyslaw Hasior: Nowe Relacje" in *Architektura* (Warsaw), no. 410, 1967; "Stalowe Konstrukcje Jerzego Jarnuszkiewicza" in *Architektura* (Warsaw), no. 498, 1967; "Sport we Wspolczesnym Spoleczenstwie" in *Architektura* (Warsaw), no. 213, 1968; "Ogrody Japońskie" in *Architektura* (Warsaw), no. 9, 1969; "Magiczne Kolo Polskiej Architektury" in *Architektura* (Warsaw), no. 2/3, 1969; "Denkmal der Schlesischen Aufstande" in *Deutsche Architektur* (East Berlin), no. 6, 1970; "Sportzentrum Konin" in *Sport und Baderbauten* (Dusseldorf), no. 1, 1972; "Sport Approaches Nature" in *Poland* (Warsaw), no. 3, 1972; "O Architekturze Igrzysk Olimpijskich w Monachium" in *Architektura* (Warsaw), no. 5/6, 1972; "Sala Gier w Warszawie" in *Architektura* (Warsaw), no. 12, 1972; "Salle Sportive Polyvalante à Bydgoszcz" in *L'Architecture d'Aujourd'hui* (Paris), no. 11/12, 1973; "Hallen Sportzentrum in Pulawy" in *Sportstattenbau und Bäderanlagen* (Cologne), no. 4, 1975.

On ZABLOCKI: books—*Ekspresja Sil w Architekturze Wspolczesnej* (Expression of Forces in Contemporary Architecture) by J. Slawinska, Warsaw 1970; *New Polish Architecture* by P. Szafer, Warsaw 1973; *Atlas of Warsaw Architecture* by J. Chroscicki and A. Rottermund, Warsaw 1977; article—"New Sports Architecture of W. Zablocki" by A. Glinski and Bruszewski in *Architektura* (Warsaw), no. 12, 1975.

*

The groups of people to whom I address my work differ greatly. But if we were to make the simple assumption that people are either extrovert or introvert, then my designs would probably be directed to the first group, for I am an extrovert myself. My aim is not to win general applause from a wide range of people: I am happy if my architecture wins the approval of those who find in it the features for which I was looking while designing it.

I am fascinated by the expression of beauty in new structures, the imagined lines of forces—how it stands up, what holds it together. Besides, I like to toy with associations that do not necessarily have geometrical form. One of my designs—the large Sports Hall in Bydgoszcz—suggests the shape of a frog, and while working on this project I studied the movement and structure of the mouths of frogs and fishes. Nevertheless, I did not take this association as "a priori," as I felt that that would be too great a risk.

I do not like to work too long within the framework of one style, for fear of repeating myself, even if that repetition involves a slight improvement. So, from time to time, I try a change in my choice of structure and materials and applied forms, even though the first attempts in a new style may not be so beautiful as those works in styles that are already tried and proved.

I am chiefly involved in sports architecture, because it allows me to experiment in structure and form. However, I also like to design other public buildings such as churches, high-rise buildings, and monuments. I don't have any great ambition to design the perfect building; rather, I try to persist in carrying through some particular intention or idea, closing my eyes to the occasional weakness that may result.

Although I most like those architectonic forms that correspond to my "creative temperament" (such as those of Saarinen and Kenzo Tange), I do,

917

Wojciech Zablocki: Sports Centre, Warsaw, 1974

nevertheless, quite like the obsessive simplicity of Mies and some of the Utopian oddities.

—Wojciech Zablocki

How the architect's mentality and personality are expressed and how his individual mark is made on the designed object are concerns in the work and design approach of Wojciech Zablocki. He belongs to the post-war generation of Polish architects, and for the past twenty years his work has been very specific, individual, and controversial.

Zablocki attempts to integrate the dynamics of structural form with an architecture that aims at the expressive synthesis of new technical possibilities.

He was an active sportsman for many years and an Olympic champion. He is interested in the psychology of sports and recreation, and, indeed, has been responsible for most of the new sports halls and centres in Poland. His personal experience has influenced his views on how space for sports and recreation should be organized. Any sport requires concentration. Also, the technical infrastructure is important, as is easy access to other related sporting activities.

Starting with these assumptions, Zablocki concentrates his interest on the most rational plan for a multi-functional interior. He treats the exterior as a shell requiring large-scale roof profiles; he believes that the exterior must take into account both practical and symbolic functions. A crucial role is played by the form of the architectural-structural solution adopted.

Zablocki is often accused of creating buildings that have "formalistic tendencies" and criticized for not paying sufficient attention to context, the landscape, or neighbouring buildings. He accepts these criticisms, but remarks at the same time that "the search for future and new architectural, structural

and urbanistic solutions is no longer popular today, the reason lying in the crisis of mostly stereotyped and monotonous modern architecture, which has caused people to become interested in the past." He emphasizes that all the visions of romantic utopias, whatever their appeal, were not able to stop the process of civilization, demographic growth, and the development of new technologies.

Zablocki's ideology is close to that of Frei Otto and to the expressionist tendencies of the work of Kenzo Tange and Saarinen. He admits, too, that he often surrenders to an inspiration emerging from a fascination with organic structures.

In 1962, for the Olympic Training Centre in Warsaw, Zablocki conceived of a form of several small pavilions with roof structures hanging on cables, reminiscent of hammocks, sails, or tents stretched between trees. This impression is further intensified by the separation of the suspended form of the roof structure from the horizontal brick podium wall by a band of glazing. After a period of applying suspended roof structures of cable or mixed arch-cable design to many buildings and projects, until repetition of the same structural principle had resulted in its perfection, Zablocki moved away from this concept and explored the possibilities of new forms of expression in frame structures and space-frames. His most recent works are an amalgam of previous experience—hanging structures complemented by frame structures.

A preoccupation with the problems of roof structures for large multi-function sports halls and a search for the expression of logic and beauty in their construction are the dominant traits of Zablocki's work. Accusations that this kind of architecture does not fit many situations and perhaps creates universal but unrelated buildings does not worry him. The descriptions that he uses—hammocks, sails, Con-

corde, bird, butterfly—convey taking off, hovering, flying, and these metaphors suggest perfectly the dynamic character of his architecture. He is unusually consistent in his design approach, does not stand for any compromise solutions, stakes everything on the "natural" beauty of structure and the dynamics of shape, and creates his buildings not for the grey, universal mass but for individuals of a strong and dynamic temperament—very much like his own.

—Teresa Czaplinska-Archer

ZABLUDOVSKY, Abraham.

Mexican. Born in Bialostock, Poland, 14 July 1924; emigrated to Mexico, 1927: naturalized, 1941. Educated at the Universidad Nacional Autonoma, Mexico City, in the National Preparatory School, 1941–42, and the National School of Architecture, 1943–49, Dip.Arch. 1949. Married Alinka Kuper in 1953; children: Gina, Jaime, and Moisés. In private practice, Mexico City, since 1949: in partnership with Teodoro González de León, q.v., since 1968. Director, INURBA S.A., Mexico City, since 1973; Adviser to the Director, CODEUR, Mexico City, since 1978. Teacher of Composition, 1965–67, and currently Lecturer and Adviser, Universidad Nacional Autonoma, Mexico City. Currently, Lecturer and Adviser to the Museum of Modern Art, Mexico City. Exhibitions: *XX Centuries of Mexican Architecture,* El Colegio de México, Mexico City, 1965, and toured Mexico; Colegio Nacional de Arquitectos, Mexico City, 1969; *Arquitectura Contemporánea Mexicana,* Galeria Misrachi, Mexico City, 1969; *The Photography of Architecture and Design,* Los Angeles, 1977; *Mexican Architecture,* Mexico City,

1978; *Transformations in Modern Architecture,* Museum of Modern Art, New York, 1979. Recipient: First Prize, with Teodoro González de León, El Colegio de México Competition, Mexico City, 1974. Address: Zabludovsky/González de León, Avenida Mexico 99, Mexico 11, D.F., Mexico.

Works:

1958 House, Paseo de las Palmas 1210, Mexico City

House, Paseo de las Palmas 1635, Mexico City

1962 Housing development, Satélite, Mexico

1965 Apartment building, Schiller Street, Mexico City

Apartment building, Av. Cumbres de Acultzingo 12 and 20, Mexico City

1966 House, Moraván 180, Mexico City

1967 House, Sierra de la Breña 84, Mexico City

1971 House, Palacio de Versalles 235, Mexico City

With Teodoro González de León:

1963/
77 8 planning surveys for various Mexican cities

1968 José Luis Cuevas House, Galeana 109, Mexico City

1969/
70 Office building, Nuevo León and Campeche, Mexico City

Office building, Campos Eliseos 169, Mexico City

Office building, Presidente Masarik 191, Mexico City

1969/
71 Mixcoac Towers, Mixcoac-Lomas de Plateros, Mexico City

1970/
73 Vallejo-La Patera (1418 apartments), Avenida Vallejo/Torres/de los Cien Metros/Margarita M. de Juárez, Mexico City (with Armando Franco)

1971 Apartment buildings (2), Avenida de las Fuentes and Fuente de la Templanza, Tecamachalco, Mexico City

1972 Apartment buildings (2), Victoria 34, Echegaray, Mexico

Sports and Civic Center (public square; movie theatre; library; club; gymnasium; swimming pool; etc.), Sor Juan Inés de la Cruz 45, Tlalnepantla, Mexico

1972/
73 Cuauhtémoc District Municipal Building, Mexico City (with Luis Antonio Zapiain and Jaime Ortiz Monasterio)

Apartment buildings (2), Fuente de las Pirámides 20 and 22, Tecamachalco, Mexico City (with Rosemberg)

1973 Conasupo Branch Stores, throughout Mexico

INFONAVIT Building (administrative offices for workers' housing development), Mexico City

1973/
75 Mexican Embassy, Brasilia (with J. Francisco Serrano)

1974/
75 El Colegio de México (library; seminar rooms; computer center; offices; auditorium; cafeteria; parking), Mexico City

1975 25-story apartment building, Tecamachalco, Mexico City

Rufino Tamayo Museum, Oaxaca, Mexico (project)

Publications:

By ZABLUDOVSKY: published lectures—*Las ciudades, el hombre, el artista,* Mexico City 1974; *La Arquitectura y las Artes Visuales,* Mexico City 1975; *Arquitectura Contemporánea Israelí,* Mexico City 1976; *Importancia y Significado de la Bauhaus,* Mexico City 1976; *Kibbutz-Bauhaus,* Mexico City 1979.

On ZABLUDOVSKY/GONZÁLEZ DE LEÓN: books—*Arquitectura Contemporánea Mexicana,* exhibition catalogue, Mexico City 1969; *Ocho Conjuntos de Habitacion,* Mexico City 1976; *Ten Mexican Architects* by Alfonso de Neuvillate, Mexico City 1977; *The Photography of Architecture and Design* by Julius Shulman, New York 1977; *Mexican Architecture: The Work of Abraham Zabludovsky and Teodoro González de León* by Paul Heyer, New York 1978; articles—"Immeuble d'habitation à Mexico" in *L'Architecture d'Aujourd'hui* (Paris), September 1963; "Mexico City Office Building" in *American Concrete Institute Journal* (Detroit), May 1976; "Contrapuntal Buildings" by Felix Sanchez in *Arquitectura* (Mexico City), November/December 1976; "An Arresting View to the South" in *Architectural Record* (New York), October 1977; "Mexican Embassy, Brasilia" by G. Cataldi in *Industria delle Costruzioni* (Rome), April 1978; "Colegio de México" by G. Cataldi in *Industria delle Costruzioni* (Rome), May 1978.

Architecture is an activity devoted to confining a space that man uses for some purpose. In fulfilling this function, it is materialized into an object that is, by its nature, plastic volume.

Such a volume is an invention that, like all inven-

Abraham Zabludovsky and Teodoro González de León: El Colegio de México (main entrance), Mexico City, 1975

tions, is based on influences, on existing forms; it springs from its predecessors, from needs.

Sullivan used to say that in the problem lies the solution. The architect's method is the precise conjoining of unknowns to organize space. The first stage in the functional scheme is to delve into the problem, the site, the micro-climate, the psychological and economic context. This is the program. Taking the program as his starting-point, the architect determines the number and size of the spaces, their dimensions and their reciprocal relationships. This, rather than any other point, is where the contemporary architect begins. But the method of creation ends up by being a unitary creative process in which each step arises from the one which precedes it and, at the same time, receives feedback from the one which follows. Everything has its explanation and its own justification. And yet no method automatically leads to a solution. The architect's task is a creative one, and though the form of the object is determined by reference to probable concrete data and to its function, the design process means that different types of influence operate on different individuals.

While it may be true that the solution lies within the problem, it would be simplistic to apply the norm that form follows function. The aim of research into the conditioning factors of a project is not to find the greatest number of relationships between them, but rather the basic ones, the marrow of the problem, and through these to imagine the synthetic spatial relationship. That is, the synthesis of the problem and its basic space must be found first, and into these what is secondary—the vast majority of marginal elements—is easily adapted: the synthesis of the problem lies in the form adopted.

—Abraham Zabludovsky

The work of Abraham Zabludovsky and Teodoro González de León has been one of maturity in linear evolution. Their work is a direct confrontation with the facts of architecture, towards conclusions that are increasingly sophisticated and more sensitized as design responses within the specificity of a building's context, both environmental and cultural. Pedro Ramirez Vazquez, current Minister for Human Settlements and Public Works in the José Lopez Portillo government, identifies González de León and Zabludovsky as Mexico's new generation of architects. He sees their work as truly contemporary because it ignores none of the technical innovations of our time and because it utilizes the available construction systems and materials to the maximum of their potential.

Both men were strongly influenced by Le Corbusier, and González de León spent two years in his atelier. In their work in Mexico, however, performed both singularly and in association, Zabludovsky and González de León have included many more diverse sources, and their response has grown and changed considerably. Their work is plastic, expresses structure coherently and constantly, and has often used color in a boldly imaginative way. Their work is not an isolated effort, and explores many conclusions germane to the seminal ideas of the Modern Movement, but in general theirs is an architecture that is more than the sum of European and United States influences. It is not conditioned by any rationalist or singular idea, but rather it develops from experience. One senses that they see modern architecture as the manifestation of a new and progressive social order rather than of any disciplining ideology.

Zabludovsky and González de León make pragmatic use of simple, available means and their work looks beyond the functionalist premise for a synthesis that includes a form-idea relative to all the functions, the general urban and local conditions, materials and their maintenance, and all pertinent economic factors. They, like many counterparts around the world, find architecture anything but the easy "form follows function" notion; they are more dependent for their inspiration on the main idea that comes from a broader synthesis. This is seen in several of their public projects of recent years, as well as in the consistent development and refinement of their ideas.

Their Colegio de México (1975) is one of their strongest designs, and evokes recollections of convents and monasteries of 16th century Mexico as well as the theme idea of building related to patio. The building is accomplished in an unequivocally 20th century expression. It is not the conscious incorporation or copying of elements and forms from the past but the spirit of the past—the durable values —that the designers seek to respect and capture in a language relevant to their time. The Colegio does not dwell in a wishful land of nostalgia. It deals with reason confirmed by substance and moved by passion.

From the early days of usually solid and well-mannered responses to building problems, Zabludovsky and González de León have emerged to a new, invigorated awareness of the design challenge. "There are no twelve year old geniuses in architecture," remarked Le Corbusier. Architecture is a field for irrepressible optimism and demands a tenacious staying power. Teodoro González de León and Abraham Zabludovsky, as individuals and a collaboration, are filled with both. For them, the Colegio appears as both an end and a beginning, the conclusion of the first half of their careers and the promise of a future that lies ahead. The seeds are sown, and if the fruits are equal to the promise, the architecture of the Americas can only be richer.

—Paul Heyer

ZEHRFUSS, Bernard (Louis).

French. Born in Angers, 20 October 1911. Educated at Stanislas College, Ecole Nationale des Beaux-Arts, Paris, 1928–39 (Premier Grand Prix de Rome, 1939), Dip.Arch. 1939. Volunteer in the Free French Army, 1942; Lieutenant in the Reserves. Married Simone Fanny Samama in 1950; daughter: Dominique. Chief Government Architect and Adjunct Commissioner of City Planning, Housing and Tourism, Tunisia, 1943–48. In private practice, Paris, since 1948. Architect to the Council of Construction, Algeria, 1950–54, and Paris Region, 1955–62. Chief Architect of Civic Buildings and National Monuments, France, since 1955 (Inspector-General of Civic Buildings and National Monuments, 1965–68). Recipient: Gold Medal, Society for the Encouragement of Art and Industry, France, 1960. Honorary Member, American Institute of Architects, and of the Royal Society of Arts, London. Officer of the Légion d'Honneur; Officer of the Order of Merit. Chevalier of the Order of Danebrog, Denmark; Officer of the Republic of Tunisia. Address (office): 9 rue Arsène Houssaye, 75008 Paris, France.

Works:

1943/
48 Public buildings, schools, housing, hospitals and hippodrome, Tunisia
1947 Gammartti National Cemetery, Tunisia
1950 Mame Printing Works, Tours, France
1952 Renault Factory, Flins, France
1955 National Centre for Industry and Technology (CNIT), La Défense, Paris (with Camelot and de Mailly)
1958 Unesco Buildings I, II and III, Paris (with Marcel Breuer and Pier Luigi Nervi)
1958/
78 Housing complexes, Paris Region, Nancy, and St. Etienne, France
1960 University of Tunis
Summer Palace for the Shah of Iran, Tehran (project)
1963 Unesco Building IV, Paris
Cultural Centre, Frankfurt (project)
1965 Faculty of Sciences, University of Tunis
French Embassy, Rabat, Morocco (project)
Hotel du Mont d'Arboir, Megeve, France
1966 Design of the exhibition Hommage à Le Corbusier, Louvre, Paris
1968 Danish Embassy, Paris
1969 Unesco Building V, Paris
1970 French Embassy, Warsaw
1971 Ministry of Finance interiors, Paris
1972 Siemens Company Headquarters, Saint-Denis, Paris (with Burckhardt)
Sandoz Company Headquarters, Paris
1973 Jeumont Schneider Company Headquarters, Paris
1974 Spie Batignolles Headquarters, Paris
1975 Gallo-Roman Underground Museum, Lyons
1976 Design of the exhibition Hommage à André Malraux, Louvre, Paris
1977 Unesco Building VI, Paris

Publications:

By ZEHRFUSS: articles—"Architecture: évolution ou Révolution" in L'Architecture d'Aujourd'hui (Paris), February 1965; "L'homme dans la ville" in La NEF (Paris), July 1965; "Hommage à Le Corbusier" in Lettres Francaises (Paris), August 1965; article on Paris in Figaro (Paris), February 1968; "Fernand Léger and Architecture" in Europe (Paris), 1971; article on Paris in Le Monde (Paris), August 1972; "L'homme et sa ville" in La NEF (Paris), June 1977.

On ZEHRFUSS: books—Tunisie Vivant, Paris 1946; World's Contemporary Architecture, Tokyo 1953; Architecture of the West, Moscow 1972; Les Défis de l'An 2000, Paris 1977; article—"Tunisia" in L'Architecture d'Aujourd'hui (Paris), October 1948. "Fifth Building for Unesco" in Architecture Francaise (Paris), July/August 1973; "Siemens Headquarters in Saint-Denis" in Baumeister (Munich), November 1973; "Archaeological Museum in Lyons" in Architecture Francaise (Paris), April 1975; "Lyon" by Pierre Kjellberg in Connaissance des Arts (Paris), February 1976; "Archaeological Museum in Lyons Which Is Almost Entirely Buried Underground" in Concrete Quarterly (London), April/June 1977; "Archaeology Museum in Lyons" in Casabella (Milan), January 1979.

In all of the works that I have built I have always searched for different solutions and different expressions. Architecture has been, for me, a perpetual beginning again; it is conditioned, in effect, by one's interpretation of the given program and by the function of the chosen site.

The choice of architectural means, the disposition of the plan, the relationship of volumes, the harmony of parts—everything depends on this idea.

Some examples from my works will illustrate this search:

The placement of the Renault Factory in Flins in the countryside on the banks of the Seine or the Mame Printing Works in Tours alongside the Loire.

The grand arch of the Centre National des Industries et des Techniques at Le Défense which stands at the east-west axis of Paris.

The insertion of the building complex of Unesco into an historic environment of Paris; the sunken patios which complete the composition without making it dull.

The swimming pool of the Hotel du Mont d'Arboir in Megeve from which one sees a panorama of the French Alps.

The new University of Tunis modelled on the nearby hills of the town.

The Gallo-Roman Museum in Lyons which, sunken into the slope of a hill, does not change the site of the Roman theatre of Fourvières.

—Bernard Zehrfuss

Bernard Zehrfuss: Gallo-Roman Underground Museum, Lyons, 1975

After the armistice in 1940 Bernard Zehrfuss settled down with a small group of friends in an abandoned village of Provence; ecologists before the fact and in advance of fashion by a quarter of a century, they tried to breathe new life into picturesque Oppède. Then he was called to Tunisia where, with his faithful companions—among them the wise but lazy Paul Herbé, Le Couteur, Auproux, Marmey, Patout, all architects of enthusiasm and merit—he was responsible for the planning and rebuilding of that beautiful country. The "team of twenty" that he inspired did an excellent job, the benefits of which Tunisia keeps to this day.

The successes achieved by Zehrfuss as the head of the Tunisian departments entrusted with development and reconstruction, his human qualities and his organizational capabilities naturally destined him for high responsibilities in liberated France. Important projects were entrusted to him—the Renault complex at Flins, a remarkable industrial achievement; embassies, university buildings, etc. But it was his participation with Breuer and Nervi in the building of Unesco Headquarters in the heart of Paris that brought him to the forefront of current architecture. One recognizes the hand of Nervi in the structure of the great hall and that of Breuer in the conception of the administrative sector—but Zehrfuss, too, was unquestionably important: it was he who was later solely responsible for the numerous enlargements, extensions and new buildings for the world organization, and he has known how to maintain, in spite of very difficult conditions at times, a high quality. Brought into the limelight by this spectacular achievement, Zehrfuss was given commissions for many private sector administrative buildings for important multi-national companies—Sandoz, Siemends, Schneider, etc. Also in collaboration, there is his well-known National Centre for Industry and Technology at La Défense, justifiably criticized for its siting (a criticism acknowledged by Zehrfuss) and whose principal point of interest lies in the great vault by the engineer Esquillan.

Zehrfuss courageously refused to put his name to the alterations required of his project for the development of the Bercy warehouse area in Paris; in his initial prize-winning scheme one finds again all the qualities of this architect. The same is true of a recent but so far little-known work of great quality, the Gallo-Roman Museum in Lyons.

—Pierre Vago

ZEIDLER, Eberhard.

Canadian. Born in Braunsdorf, Germany, 11 January 1926; emigrated to Canada, 1951: naturalized, 1956. Educated at the Bauhaus, Weimar, Germany, 1945–48; Technische Hochschule, Karlsruhe, 1948–49, Dip.Ing. 1949. Married Jane Abbott in 1957; children: Margaret, Robert, Katie and Kristina. Designer, office of Eiermann and Lindner, Karlsruhe and Osnabruck, 1949–51; Associate in charge of Design, Blackwell and Craig, Toronto, 1951. Partner, Blackwell, Craig and Zeidler, Toronto, 1954, and successor firms Craig and Zeidler, 1955–63, Craig, Zeidler and Strong, 1963–75, and Zeidler Partnership/Architects, since 1975. Lecturer in Architectural Design, University of Toronto, 1953–55. Recipient: National Design Award, 1962, 1967, 1972; Design Award, Masonry Council, 1964, 1965, 1966, 1968, 1970, 1971, 1974; Award of Excellence, Canadian Architecture, 1969, 1970, 1971, 1974; Precast Concrete Institute Award, 1970; Eedee Award, 1971; Design Award, Progressive Architecture, 1972; American Iron and Steel Institute Award, 1973; Ordre des Architectes du Québec Award, 1978; Urban Design Award, 1978. Address: Zeidler Partnership/Architects, 98 Queen Street East, Toronto, Ontario M5C 1S7, Canada.

Works:

1953 Grace Church, Peterborough, Ontario
1954 St. Giles Church, Peterborough, Ontario
1955 Memorial Centre, Peterborough, Ontario
Hamilton House, Peterborough, Ontario
1957 West Ellesmere Church, Toronto
1963 Parkwood United Church, Toronto
Beth Israel Synagogue, Peterborough, Ontario
1964 General Hospital, Whitby, Ontario
Ajax and Pickering Hospital, Ajax, Ontario
1965 Forester House, Toronto
Burnview Apartments, Toronto
1966 Grant Sine Public School, Cobourg, Ontario
1967 Health Sciences Centre, McMaster University, Hamilton, Ontario
Physical Sciences Building, University of Guelph, Ontario
Ross Memorial Hospital, Lindsay, Ontario
Centennial Recreation Centre, Scarborough, Ontario
Municipal Building, Ajax, Ontario
Municipal Building, Pickering, Ontario

1968 T. A. Stewart Vocational School, Peterborough, Ontario
1969 Ontario Place, Toronto
Fanshawe School of Applied Arts and Technology, London, Ontario
Korah Collegiate and Vocational School, Sault Sainte Marie, Ontario
1970 Dr. Joseph O. Ruddy Hospital, Whitby, Ontario
Osler School of Nursing, Toronto
1971 Harbour City, Toronto
Regional hospitals, New Brunswick
Willow Park Public School, Scarborough, Ontario
1972 General Hospital, Detroit (with Kessler Associates and Giffels Associates)
Wayne State University Clinic, Detroit (with Kessler Associates and Giffels Associates)
Civic Hospital, Peterborough, Ontario
Sussex Hospital, New Brunswick
Dumont Hospital, New Brunswick
Central Laundry, Hamilton, Ontario
1973 Eaton Centre, Toronto (with Bregman and Hamann)
1975 Health Sciences Centre, Edmonton, Alberta
Mont Sainte Marie Condominiums and Conference Centre, Gatineau, Quebec
Canadian Imperial Bank of Commerce Building, Calgary, Alberta
Regional Hospital, St. Johns, New Brunswick
1976 Century Place, Belleville, Ontario
1977 Chalmers Hospital, Fredericton, New Brunswick
1978 Trinity Square Development, Toronto
Mississauga Hospital, Ontario
Young People's Theatre, Toronto
Kensington Housing Development, Toronto
Glen Cedar Public School, Newmarket, Ontario

Publications:

By ZEIDLER: book—Healing the Hospital, Toronto 1974; articles—"Notes on Church Architecture" in Royal Architectural Institute of Canada Journal (Toronto), December 1956; "Expo '67 in Montreal" in Deutsche Bauzeitung (Stuttgart), August 1967; "Designing for the Unknown Future" in The Business Quarterly (London, Ontario), April 1973; "McMaster and Beyond" in National Hospital and Health Care (Sydney), November 1975; "Planning for Flexibility" in National Hospital and Health Care (Sydney), December 1975; "Montreal Olympics" in Bauen und Wohnen (Zurich), November 1976; "Architects, Developers Have a Moral Duty to Lead the Way to a Better Environment" in Real Estate Development Annual (Toronto), August 1977; "Build Hospitals for Future Change" in Hospital Administration in Canada (Toronto), February 1978; "The Lost Dimension" in Bauen und Wohnen (Zurich), July/August 1978.

On ZEIDLER: articles—"Peterborough Memorial Community Centre" in Canadian Architect (Toronto), November 1957; "Ajax Municipal Building" in Canadian Architect Yearbook (Toronto), 1967; "Madawaska Valley District High School" in Deutsche Bauzeitung (Stuttgart), June 1968; "Thomas A. Stewart and Auburn Vocational Schools" in Domus (Milan), December 1968; "Ajax-Pickering Hospital" in Deutsche Bauzeitung (Stuttgart), September 1969; "McMaster University Health Sciences Centre" in Architectural Review (London), April 1970; "McMaster University" in L'Architecture d'Aujourd'hui (Paris), June 1970; "McMaster University Health Sciences Centre" in The Lancet (London), October 1970; "Harbour City" in Baumeister (Munich), October 1970; "Ontario Place" in Deutsche Bauzeitung (Stuttgart), April 1971; "McMaster University" in Architectural Forum (New York), June 1971; "Dr. Joseph O. Ruddy General Hospital" in Architectural Record (New York), September 1971; "Ontario Place,

Toronto" in *Canadian Architect* (Toronto), October 1971; "Harbour City" in *Progressive Architecture* (New York), January 1972; "University of Guelph-/Fanshawe College" in *Baumeister* (Munich), January 1972; "McMaster University" in *Bauwelt* (Berlin), June 1973; "McMaster University" in *Architectural Design* (London), July 1973; "McMaster University" in *Architecture Francaise* (Paris), November/December 1973; "Ontario Place Children's Village" in *Architectural Review* (London), February 1974; "McMaster University" in *Architektur und Wohwelt* (Stuttgart), October 1974; "Zeidler Residence" in *House Beautiful* (New York), January 1975; "Toronto Eaton Centre" in *Bauen und Wohnen* (Zurich), December 1975; "Toronto Eaton Centre" in *Domus* (Milan), March 1976; "Toronto Eaton Centre" in *Progressive Architecture* (New York), June 1977; "Toronto Eaton Centre" in *Nikkei Architecture* (Tokyo), August 1978.

My architectural training began in one of the sandboxes of a small Silesian town that took most of its architectural heritage from Viennese precedents.

Maybe I should take this into consideration if I want to understand my emotions towards architecture. My architectural amateur status ceased when I started to study in the newly re-opened Bauhaus at Weimar after the War.

In 1951 I came to Canada. I got some small commissions (churches, houses) and taught at the University of Toronto. I was engulfed in a turmoil of frantic activity, the growth period of Canada after the Second World War. I hoped in doing so that I would not only find myself but also build in a better way. I felt that the international style of Bauhaus lacked the emotional quality that I was searching for. Yet the blinds that we all were wearing through the doctrines of Modern Architecture were difficult to discover.

We cannot underestimate the power of architectural theories, especially if they are converted through misuse into dogmas, becoming blinds to the designer, preventing him from seeing the total horizon.

Architecture means something slightly different to all of us; to some it may represent the necessity of building, to others excess of opulence—the Taj Mahal; it may mean the isolated individual building to some, to others the vitality of all man-made environment.

Yet architecture is all of these things. It is necessity and it is folly—if song is folly. It is the detail of the small individual building and it is the totality of our man-made world.

It is only when we equate all of our man-made environment with architecture that we can attempt to understand how it influences our life. Architecture is the shell of our life and therefore our past, our present and our future.

Modern architecture saw beauty in form only as the aftermath of function and construction, but not as an independent emotional force that could equally influence form.

We are looking today with astonishment at Victorian architecture and re-discovering its philosophy, finding many things that are amazingly useable. The irritating thought nags at us, that progress might be a circle rather than a straight line.

Architecture must be seen, walked through, it must be touched and experienced. Architecture must be lived in. Magazines, photographs and theories have become substitutes for the real thing, that obscure the world before us.

And yet here is their power, because theories can either widen or narrow our views of this world. They can help us to understand it better and grasp the meaning of its complexity or they can limit and restrict our creative abilities. We are just awakening from such experience.

Architecture is our life, and like life it is the struggle for survival. It is the job of being alive and is the search for life's meaning.

Architecture will always transcend words and be perceived on a level that cannot be reached by logic. We have realized the dangerous power of a theory to limit our ability to conceive the totality of architecture.

Modern architecture has left us with as rich a heritage as the forgotten masters of Victorian times, now that we have escaped its dogma and are again able to see beyond its borders.

Ultimately, the Pleasure of Form and Space, which is architecture, transcend words and become the poetry of our subconscious.

—Eberhard Zeidler

Tied as it supposedly is to the broad abstracted characteristics of its time—social, economic, political—architecture is usually treated as a very serious art form. Modern architecture particularly has, in the mainstream, taken the mundane forms of ordinary real estate construction as the basis of its style—simple, rectangular, straightforward, with subsequently just a touch of embellishment—forms that derived from warehouses and factories. Collaterally, modern form givers have also been very serious men. The principled Gropius, the enigmatic Mies, the paranoid Corbu were all types well-known in the annals of art where tragedy is felt to be intrinsically superior to comedy.

This situation requires the architectural viewer to ponder the buildings around him soberly. The exception has been the exposition where the general public has expected to be dazzled and architects have allowed themselves (if somewhat self-consciously) to let down their hair and stretch their imaginations. More recently, in our ever more sophisticated consumer society, it has been recognized that while buildings probably do not much affect our behaviour, they can attract or repel; and while certain building types such as schools have captive users, others like fast food outlets need our custom and are their own advertisements. The visual attractions of Main Street have thereby entered the architect's vocabulary. From another direction, the scientific interest in the psycho-sociology of users' needs is recognizing that a joy of living is just as natural as a fascination with suffering and death. Architects representing the spirit of the times can therefore now legitimately include the lighter aspects of human existence: excitement, humour, entertainment, pleasure.

Two large building complexes by Eberhard Zeidler are excellent examples of what might be termed Expo Art. Ontario Place is described as a fun centre and is close in spirit to a permanent exhibition ground. Eaton Centre features a multi-story shopping arcade and offices and is fun architecture made out of a standard building problem. The architectural language employed is generically the same in both and shows that imagination can be extended to buildings that are not functionally designated as amusing. The cable structures, tent forms and dome, over-water walkways and hung stairways at Ontario Place, which sits offshore in Lake Ontario and includes a moored warship, are oddly limited to a more marine aesthetic in Eaton Centre. The connection is not simply that ship-like motifs have been used but that the multi-level space arrangement with its connecting escalators and bridges, and the use of metal and glass with exposed industrial-type components for lighting and air-handling, provide the character of the machine aesthetic with which the early moderns equated such images with a dynamic technologically exciting world. The relationship is furthered by a geometry of angles and curves, and even the street-side advertisements are hung in a manner reminiscent of lifeboats. The quality of design, however, is enlivened and accentuated in subtly amusing details that raise the comparison above a mere copy. The metaphor is elaborated by ad hoc events in layout, shape and connections that enrich the texture of the design and add to the riot of light, movement, sound and colour. Allied to the abundance of planting in the controlled environment under the glass roof, the centre provides a successful contrast to the major street it runs alongside.

The popularity of both Ontario Place and Eaton Centre in a city where a growing number of modern buildings have found favour in the public imagination, indicates the potentialities of the modern style beyond its until recently self-imposed limitations. That this direction needs further broadening is evidenced by another large building designed by Zeidler, the Health Sciences Centre for McMaster University, Hamilton, in which a related form idiom seems less appropriate to the situation. When modern architecture offered a closed style as its response to what was perceived as a definable historical era, it rejected the previous century's concern for the classical principle of propriety. Nonetheless a contemporary architecture has to support the many different qualities of activities that have given rise to various building types. Such a spectrum of needs, each with its own different perceptual requirements, suggests a variety of means to achieve the desired ends. Zeidler's work explores such possibilities.

—Anthony Jackson

Eberhard Zeidler: Ontario Place, Toronto, 1969

NOTES ON ADVISERS AND CONTRIBUTORS

ABERCROMBIE, Stanley. Contributor. Architect in private practice, New York. Former Editor of *Interiors*, and Senior Editor of *Architecture Plus*, New York. Contributor to the *Wall Street Journal*, *Progressive Architecture*, *Artforum*, *Journal of the Society of Architectural Historians*, *Design*, *Architecture + Urbanism*, and other periodicals. **Essays:** Alvar Aalto; Ulrich Franzen.

ACHLEITNER, Friedrich. Contributor. Professor of the History of Building Construction, Akademie der Bildenden Künste, Vienna. Architectural Critic, *Die Presse*, Vienna, 1962–72. Author of *Hosn Rosn Baa* (with H. C. Artmann and Gerhard Rühm), 1959; *Lois Welzenbacher* (with Ottokar Uhl), 1968; *Prosa, Konstellationen, Montagen, Dialektgedichte, Studien*, 1970; *Quadratroman*, 1973; *Die Ware Landschaft* (editor), 1977; *Der Werkbund*, 1978; *Österreich-Architekturführer*, 3 volumes, 1980–83. **Essays:** Hans Hollein; Wilhelm Holzbauer; Clemens Holzmeister.

ACKERMANN, Kurt. Contributor and entrant: see his own entry. **Essay:** Fritz Leonhardt.

ADLER, Gerald. Contributor. Fourth Year Architectural Student, University of Sheffield, Yorkshire. Author of a thesis on William Holden, 1978. **Essay:** Gustav Peichl.

ALINGTON, W. H. Contributor and entrant: see his own entry. **Essay:** Ian Athfield.

ALLIES, Bob. Contributor. Architect in private practice, London. Former Lecturer at the North East London Polytechnic, and at the Open University (U.K.). Contributor to *Building Design* and *The Architects' Journal*. **Essays:** Ahrends Burton and Koralek; Edward Cullinan; Bruno Taut.

ANTONIADES, Anthony C. Contributor. Architect in private practice, Greece and New Mexico. Professor and Director of Architecture, University of Texas at Arlington. Author of *Introduction to Environmental Design*, 1973; *Contemporary Greek Architecture*, 1979; *Architecture and Allied Design*, 1980. **Essays:** Kazuhiro Ishii; Ricardo Legorreta; Alexandros N. Tombazis.

ARAI, Katsuyoshi. Contributor. Lecturer at the Bunka-Gakuin School of Architecture, Tokyo. Author of *A Study of an English New Town: Runcorn*, 1969; *A Study of Modern Architecture: Le Corbusier* (in preparation). Contributor to *Architecture + Urbanism* and *Kenchiku Bunka*. **Essays:** Yoshiro Taniguchi; Isoya Yoshida.

ARNOLD, Christopher. Contributor. President, Building Systems Development Company, San Francisco. Lecturer in the Department of Architecture, University of California, Berkeley, 1975–79. Joint Author of *SLSD: The Project and the Schools*, 1967. **Essays:** Mario J. Ciampi; Ernest J. Kump.

BACON, Edmund N. Contributor and entrant: see his own entry. **Essay:** Eliel Saarinen.

BAIRD, George. Contributor. Associate Professor of Architecture, University of Toronto. Formerly, Tutor, Architectural Association, and Visiting Lecturer, Royal College of Art, London. Author of *Meaning in Architecture* (with Charles Jencks), 1968; *Alvar Aalto*, 1969. **Essays:** Melvin Charney; Jerome Markson.

BALFOUR, Alan. Contributor. Director of Graduate Program in Architecture, Georgia Institute of Technology, Atlanta. Formerly, Research Associate, Massachusetts Institute of Technology, Cambridge. Author of *Portsmouth*, 1970; *Rehab: Strategies and Techniques*, 1973; *Rockefeller Center: Architecture as Theatre*, 1978. **Essays:** John Hejduk; Donlyn Lyndon; James Stewart Polshek; Jaquelin Robertson; Benjamin Thompson.

BARNETT, Jonathan. Contributor and entrant: see his own entry. **Essays:** David A. Crane; David Lewis; Archibald C. Rogers; David A. Wallace;

Richard S. Weinstein.

BATTLE, T. Q. Contributor. Chairman of Towco Gratte Ltd. (U.K.). Author of *The Chimney Book*, 1977. Regular contributor to *The Architects' Journal*. **Essay:** Chamberlin Powell and Bon.

BAYLEY, Stephen. Contributor. Lecturer in Art History and Theory, University of Kent, Canterbury. Formerly, Lecturer in Art History, The Open University (U.K.). Author of *In Good Shape: Design in Industrial Products 1900–1960*, 1979; *The Albert Memorial* (in preparation). **Essays:** Theo Crosby; Howell, Killick, Partridge and Amis; C. S. Mardall; J. H. van den Broek.

BAZAROV, Konstantin. Contributor. Freelance writer and researcher, London. Author of *Landscape Painting*, 1980. **Essays:** Franco Albini; Charles Herbert Aslin; Dominikus Böhm; Rifat Chadirji; Ignazio Gardella; Wassili Luckhardt; Roland Rainer; Affonso Eduardo Reidy; Rudolf Schwarz; Giuseppe Terragni.

BIERMANN, B. E. Contributor. Professor of Architecture, University of Natal, Durban. Author of *Boukuns in Suid-Afrika*, 1954; *Red Wine in South Africa*, 1971. **Essay:** Hans Hallen.

BLUNDELL JONES, Peter. Contributor. Assistant Lecturer in Architecture, Cambridge University. Author of *Hans Scharoun: A Monograph*, 1978. **Essays:** James Gowan; Ron Herron; Cedric Price.

BOHIGAS, Oriol. Contributor and entrant: see his own entry. **Essay:** Alvaro Siza.

BOOTON, Harold. Contributor. Architect and planner in private practice, Leeds, Yorkshire. Principal Lecturer in Architecture, Leeds School of Architecture. Author of *Architecture of Spain*, 1966; *Great Traditions of Western Architecture* (with Bruce Allsopp and Ursula Clark), 1967; *Renaissance Architecture and Ornament in Spain*, 1970. **Essays:** Lluis Domènech; Josep Puig i Cadafalch; Eduardo Torroja y Miret.

BORNGRÄBER, Christian. Contributor. Architectural historian, Berlin, and organizer of exhibitions of German and Russian culture of the 1920's. Author of *Kunst in die Produktion!—Sowjetische Kunst während der Phase der Kollektivierung und Industrialisierung 1927–1933* (with others), 1977; *Stilnovo: Design in den 50'er Jahren—Phantasie und Phantastik*, 1979. **Essays:** Paul Baumgarten; Helmut Hentrich; Dieter Oesterlen.

BRAWNE, Michael. Contributor and entrant: see his own entry. **Essay:** Carlo Scarpa.

BROCKMAN, H. A. N. Contributor. Architectural Correspondent, 1961–79, and now Architectural Consultant, *The Financial Times*, London. Senior Architect, Ministry of Local Government, 1946–61. Author of *The Caliph of Fonthill: An Architectural Biography of William Beckford*, 1956; *The Architect in Industry*, 1965. **Essays:** Trevor Dannatt; Sir Edwin Lutyens.

BROOKS, H. Allen. Contributor. Professor of Fine Art, University of Toronto. Past President, Society of Architectural Historians (U.S.A.). Author of *The Prairie School: Frank Lloyd Wright and His Midwest Contemporaries*, 1972, 1975, and editor of *Prairie School Architecture: Studies from the "Western Architect"*, 1975. **Essay:** Frank Lloyd Wright.

CANDILIS, Georges. Contributor and entrant: see his own entry. **Essay:** Vladimir Bodiansky.

CAPITEL, Anton. Contributor. Architect in private practice, Madrid. Professor of Architectural Design, Escuela Tecnica Superior de Arquitectura, Madrid. Author of *José Antonio Coderch 1945–1976*, 1978. Contributor to *Arquitectura, Arquitecturas Bis, Jano Arquitectura, Controspazio* and *Boden*. **Essays:** Alejandro De La Sota; José Rafael Moneo; Francisco Saénz de Oíza.

CETTO, Max. Adviser, contributor and entrant: see his own entry. **Essay:** Juan O'Gorman.

CHAMBERS, D. D. C. Contributor. Associate Professor of English, University of Toronto. Author of *Lost Cities* (in preparation). **Essays:** A. J. Diamond; Ron Thom.

CHAMPIGNEULLE, Bernard. Contributor. Architectural critic, Paris. Author of *Auguste Perret*, 1959. **Essay:** Michel Roux-Spitz.

CHANG, Ching-Yu. Contributor. Associate Professor and Coordinator of Architectural Design Studies, Nova Scotia Technical College, Halifax. Chief Editor, *Stylos Architecture* (formerly *Process: Architecture*, Tokyo and Pittsburgh). Formerly, Assistant Professor, Carnegie-Mellon University, Pittsburgh. Contributor to *Space Design, Architecture + Urbanism, The Japan Architect*, and *Architecture Plus*. **Essays:** Edward Larrabee Barnes; Jonathan Barnett; Romaldo Giurgola; Victor A. Lundy; Fumihiko Maki; Richard Meier; I.M. Pei; Takamasa Yosizaka.

CHELAZZI, Giuliano. Contributor. Architect in private practice, Marburg, West Germany. Contributor to *Pan Arte, Deutsche Bauzeitung, L'Architettura*. **Essays:** Justus Dahinden; Egon Eiermann; Rolf Gutbrod.

CLARK, Alson. Contributor. Director of the Architecture and Fine Art Libraries, University of Southern California, Los Angeles. President of the Southern California Chapter of the Society of Architectural Historians, 1976–78. **Essays:** Robert E. Alexander; Wallace Neff.

CLIFF, Ursula. Contributor. Associate Editor, *Industrial Design*, New York. **Essay:** Oscar Stonorov.

COCHRANE, Peggy. Contributor. Architect in private practice, California. Past President, Association of Women in Architecture. Member of the Editorial Board, *L. A. Architect*. Author of *Yucatan* (musical), 1977; *I Gave at the Office* (play), 1978; *The Witchdoctor's Cookbook*, 1979; *The Witchdoctor's Manual*, 1979; *How to Reject Rejection*, 1979. **Essays:** Edward A. Killingsworth; Pierre Koenig; Mario Pani; Pedro Ramirez Vazquez.

CODRINGTON FORSYTH, James. Contributor. Technical Officer, Building Standards Institution, Sweden. Formerly, Regional Planner, Järfälla kommun, Sweden; Part-time Instructor in Architecture, Royal Technical College, Stockholm. Joint Editor of *Kök med standard*, 1979. Contributor to *Architectural Review* and *Building Design*. **Essay:** Sven Backström.

COLLINS, Peter. Contributor. Professor of Architecture, McGill University, Montreal. Author of *Concrete: The Vision of a New Architecture*, 1959; *Changing Ideals in Modern Architecture*, 1969; *Architectural Judgement*, 1971. **Essay:** Auguste Perret.

COLLYMORE, Peter. Contributor. Architect in private practice, London. Author of *House Conversion and Renewal*, 1975; *Ralph Erskine* (in preparation). **Essay:** Ralph Erskine.

COLVIN, Brenda. Contributor and entrant: see her own entry. **Essay:** Sir Geoffrey Jellicoe.

COOK, Jeffrey. Contributor. Professor of Architecture, Arizona State University, Tempe. Author of *Architectural Anthology*, 1966, 1969, 1972; *The Architecture of Bruce Goff*, 1978; *Passive Solar '78*, 1979. **Essay:** Bruce Goff.

COWAN, Henry. Contributor. Professor of Architectural Science, University of Sydney (formerly Dean of Architecture). Past President, Building Science Forum of Australia. Author of *The Master Builders; Architectural Structures; Dictionary of Ar-*

chitectural Science; and numerous other books. **Essays:** David Jackson; R. N. Johnson; Bryce Mortlock.

CRAVENS, Logan. Contributor. Freelance designer in Texas. Graduate Research Assistant, University of Texas at Arlington, 1978–79. **Essays:** O'Neil Ford; James Pratt.

CROWELL, S. Fiske, Jr. Contributor. Senior Designer, Perry, Dean, Stahl and Rogers, Boston. Instructor, Boston Architectural Center. **Essays:** Serge Chermayeff; Denise Scott Brown; The Architects Collaborative.

CURL, James Stevens. Contributor. Architect and town planning consultant (U.K.). Author of *European Cities and Society,* 1970; *The Victorian Celebration of Death,* 1972; *City of London Pubs* (with Timothy M. Richards), 1973; *Victorian Architecture: Its Practical Aspects,* 1973; *The Cemeteries and Burial Grounds of Glasgow,* 1975; *The Erosion of Oxford,* 1977; *English Architecture: An Illustrated Glossary,* 1977. **Essays:** Osvald Almqvist; Jacob Bakema; Eugène Beaudouin; Hendrik Petrus Berlage; Victor Bourgeois; Johannes Brinkman; Lúcio Costa; Harald Deilmann; Michel de Klerk; Johannes Duiker; Sigurd Lewerentz; Ernst May; Robin Seifert; Albert Speer; Ivar Tengbom; Sir Clough Williams-Ellis.

CURTIS, William J. R. Contributor. Assistant Professor of Architecture and Urbanism, Carpenter Center for the Visual Arts, Harvard University, Cambridge, Massachusetts. Author of *Le Corbusier-/English Architecture of the 1930's,* 1975; *A Language and a Theme: The Architecture of Denys Lasdun and Partners,* 1977; *Le Corbusier at Work: The Genesis of the Carpenter Center for the Visual Arts* (with Eduard Sekler), 1978. **Essays:** Wells Coates; Sir Denys Lasdun; Bertold Lubetkin.

CZAJKOWSKI, Jorge. Adviser and contributor. Professor of Architecture, Federal University of Rio de Janeiro. Brazilian Correspondent, *Architecture,* Paris, 1975–77. Author of *Since Brasilia: Modern Brazilian Architecture* (in preparation); *Retrato do Brasil* (with others; in preparation). **Essays:** Sergio Bernardes; João Filguéiras; Joaquim Guedes; Rino Levi; Henrique Mindlin; Jorge Machado Moreira; Fabio Penteado; Roberto Architects; Gregori Warchavchik.

CZAPLINSKA-ARCHER, Teresa. Contributor. Assistant Architect with the CMP/John Wheatley Partnership, Cambridge. Supervisor for the Cambridge School of Architecture in History of Modern Architecture. Author of *James Stirling: Theory and Practice* (thesis: Wroclaw Technical University, Poland), 1978. **Essays:** Buszko and Franta; Oskar Hansen; Bohdan Lachert; Ivor Smith; Helena Syrkus; Hanna Wejchert; Wojciech Zablocki.

DAHINDEN, Justus. Contributor and entrant: see his own entry. **Essays:** Günter Behnisch; Alfred Roth; O. M. Ungers; Alexander von Branca.

de MARÉ, Eric. Contributor. Freelance writer and architectural photographer, London. Formerly, Editor of *The Architects' Journal,* London. Author of *The Canals of England,* 1950; *Scandinavia,* 1952; *New Ways of Building* (editor), 1952; *Time on the Thames,* 1952, 1975; *New Ways of Servicing Buildings,* 1954; *The Bridges of Britain,* 1954, 1975; *Gunnar Asplund,* 1955; *London's Riverside,* 1958; *Photography and Architecture,* 1961; *London's River: The Story of a City,* 1964; *Swedish Cross-Cut: The Story of the Göta Canal,* 1965; *London 1851: The Year of the Great Exhibition,* 1972; *The London Doré Saw,* 1973; *Wren's London,* 1975; *The Victorian Wood-Block Illustrators,* 1979; etc. **Essay:** Gunnar Asplund.

DEVINE, Mary Elizabeth. Contributor. Professor of English, Salem State College, Massachusetts. Author of *Restoration and 18th Century Theatre Research: A Bibliography of Criticism 1900–68* (with Carl J. Stratman and David G. Spencer), 1971; *Ap-*

pearances, 1980. **Essay:** Charles William Brubaker.

DIAMANT-BERGER, Renée. Contributor. Writer and architectural historian, Paris. Editor, *L'Architecture d'Aujourd'hui,* Paris, 1948–72. Secretary of the Group Espace, 1950–66. Author of *Group Espace,* 1950; *Arne Jacobsen;* and the monographs *Jean Balladur; Gaston Jaubert; Bernard de la Tour d'Auvergne; Jean Le Couteur;* and *Daniel Badani/-Pierre Roux-Darlut.* **Essays:** Edouard Albert; Daniel Badani; Bernard de la Tour d'Auvergne; Alexis Josic; Roger Taillibert.

DICKSON, John D. Contributor. Senior Lecturer in Architecture, University of Auckland, New Zealand. **Essay:** R. H. B. Toy.

DREW, Philip. Contributor. Senior Lecturer in Architecture, University of Newcastle, New South Wales. Australian Correspondent, *Architecture + Urbanism,* Tokyo. Technical Editor, Architectural Press, London, 1970–71. Author of *Third Generation: The Changing Meaning of Architecture,* 1973; *Frei Otto: Form and Structure,* 1976; *Tensile Architecture,* 1979. **Essays:** John Andrews; Robin Boyd; Peter Corrigan; Walter Burley Griffin; Richard Le Plastrier; Peter Muller; Glenn Murcutt; Frei Otto; Bruce Rickard; Harry Seidler; Ken Woolley.

ECKBO, Garrett. Contributor and entrant: see his own entry. **Essay:** Hideo Sasaki.

EDER, Rita. Contributor. Researcher, Instituto de Investigación Estéticos, National University of Mexico. Author of *Dada Documentos* (with Ida Rodriguez), 1977; *Imagen Historica de la Fotografía en México* (with Nestor García Canelini), 1978; *Alberto Gironella* (in preparation). **Essay:** Mathias Goeritz.

ELLIOTT, Julian. Contributor and entrant: see his own entry. **Essays:** Ron Kirby; Roelof S. Uytenbogaardt.

EMANUEL, Muriel. Editor and contributor. Freelance researcher, editor and writer, London. Editor of *Israel: A Survey and Bibliography,* 1971; *Contemporary Architects,* 1980. **Essays:** Max Abramovitz; Yona Friedman; Walter A. Netsch.

ENGLAND, Richard. Contributor and entrant: see his own entry. **Essay:** Gio Ponti.

FABER, Tobias. Contributor. Professor and Rector, School of Architecture, The Royal Academy of Fine Arts, Copenhagen. Author of *Rum, Form og Funktion,* 1962; *Dansk Arkitektur,* 1963, 1976; *Arne Jacobsen,* 1964; *Alberobello,* 1967; *Neue Dänische Architektur,* 1968. **Essay:** Jørgen Bo.

FARNSWORTH, Geoffrey Lee. Contributor. Architect and Associate with Schmidt, Garden and Erikson, Chicago. **Essay:** Paul Schweikher.

FATOUROS, Dimitris A. Contributor. Professor of Architecture, and Director of the Laboratory of Design and Industrial Aesthetics, University of Thessaloniki, Greece. Member of the Editorial Boards of the annual reviews *Architecture in Greece* and *Design in Greece.* Regular contributor to *To Vima,* Athens. Author of *The Consciousness of Architectural Work,* 1952; *Courses of a Systematic Theory of Architecture,* 2 volumes, 1971–73; *Change and Reality in the University,* 1975; *The Scientist and the Authority,* 1979; *The Syntax of Space and Geometry of the Architectural Work,* 1979; and editor (with others) of *Problems of Production and Organization of Space,* 1979. **Essays:** Dimitris Antonakakis; Aris Konstantinidis; Dimitris A. Pikionis.

FAWCETT, Chris. Contributor. Post-graduate architecture student, University of Essex, Colchester. Formerly, Research Fellow in Architecture, Kyoto University, Japan. Author of *The New Japanese House* (in preparation). Contributor to the *Architectural Association Quarterly, Architectural Design, Tulane Architectural Review, Toshi Jutaku* and *Shinkenchiku.* **Essays:** Takefumi Aida; Yoshinobu

Ashihara; Gae Aulenti; Colquhoun and Miller; Hiromi Fujii; Patrick Gwynne; Hiroshi Hara; John M. Johansen; Martorell-Bohigas-Mackay; Tomoya Masuda; Giovanni Michelucci; Mozuna Monta; Masato Otaka; Andrew Renton; Junzo Sakakura; Kazuo Shinohara; Ettore Sottsass, Jr.; Shizutaro Urabe; Youji Watanabe; Clifford Wearden; John Weeks; Colin St. John Wilson.

FURSE, John. Contributor. Lecturer in Visual Communication, Plymouth Polytechnic, Devon. Formerly, Tutor in Art History, The Open University (U.K.). Author of *Michelangelo,* 1975. **Essays:** Giancarlo De Carlo; Charles Rennie Mackintosh; J. J. P. Oud; Rudolph Schindler; Alison Smithson; Peter Smithson; Aldo van Eyck.

GIURGOLA, Romaldo. Contributor and entrant: see his own entry. **Essays:** Jørn Utzon; Gino Valle; Robert Venturi.

GLUSBERG, Jorge. Contributor. Director, Center of Art and Communication, Buenos Aires. Corresponding Editor for *Leonardo,* Paris; Correspondent, *D'Ars,* Milan, and *Batik,* Barcelona. Vice-President, International Association of Art Critics; Director, International Committee of Architectural Critics. Author of *Towards a Topological Architecture* (with Clorindo Testa), 1977; *Rhetoric of Latin American Art,* 1978; *Socio-Semiotic of Architecture,* 1978; *Myths and Magic of Fire, Gold and Art,* 1978; *From Incan Habitat to the Lima of the Future,* 1979; *Theory and Criticism of Architecture,* 1979. **Essays:** Mario Roberto Alvarez; Antonini Schon Zemborain; Baudizzone-Diaz-Erbin-Lestard-Varas; Eladio Dieste; Manteola, Sánchez Gómez, Santos, Solsona, Viñoly, Architects; Mario Payssé-Reyes; Rogelio Salmona; Clorindo Testa; José Villagrán García; Amancio Williams.

GOULDEN, Gontran. Contributor. Director, The Building Centre, London, 1962–74, and Deputy Chairman, The Building Centre Group, 1974–77. President, The Architectural Association, 1956–57; Treasurer, International Union of Architects, 1965–75. Author of *Bathrooms,* 1966. **Essays:** Otto Bartning; Sir Hugh Casson; Willem Dudok; Kay Fisker; Arne Jacobsen; Hans Scharoun.

GOWAN, James. Contributor and entrant: see his own entry. **Essay:** Peter Cook.

GRAF, Urs. Contributor. Architect, editor and publisher, Berne. Art Critic, *Werk,* Zurich, 1969–75. Author of *Berner Szene* (with Rös Graf), 1973; *Beispiele aus dem Grenzbereich Kunst: Architektur* (exhibition catalogue; with Rös Graf), 1975. **Essay:** Atelier 5.

GREEN, Cedric. Contributor. Senior Lecturer in Architecture, University of Sheffield, Yorkshire. **Essays:** Richard England; Walter Segal.

GREGORY, Daniel. Instructor in Architectural History, Carnegie-Mellon University, Pittsburgh. **Essay:** William Turnbull, Jr.

GREIG, Doreen. Contributor. Architect and writer, Johannesburg. President of the Convocation of the University of the Witwatersrand, Johannesburg. President, Transvaal Institute of Architects, 1959, 1965, South African Institute of Architects, 1972–74, and South African Council for Architects, 1973–75. Author of *Herbert Baker in South Africa,* 1970; *A Guide to Architecture in South Africa,* 1971. **Essays:** Steffen Ahrends; Sir Herbert Baker; Brian Sandrock.

HALLEN, Hans. Contributor and entrant: see his own entry. **Essays:** Julian Elliott; Wilhelm O. Meyer; Jan van Wijk.

HAMILTON, Stephen P. Contributor. Project Architect, Perry, Dean, Stahl and Rogers, Boston. Instructor, Boston Architectural Center. Architectural Book Reviewer for *Library Journal,* New York. **Essays:** Peter Blake; Eduardo Catalano; Dan Kiley;

Carl Koch; Eliot Noyes.

HARROP-ALLIN, Clinton. Contributor. Senior Lecturer, Department of the History of Art, University of South Africa, Pretoria. Author of *Norman Eaton: Architect,* 1975. **Essay:** Norman Eaton.

HAWKINS, Lucinda. Contributor. Deputy Editor, *Studio International,* London. **Essays:** Pietro Belluschi; Charles Warren Callister; Ezra Ehrenkrantz; John Lautner.

HAYES, Mary. Contributor. Freelance writer and lecturer on the visual arts, London. **Essay:** Lyons, Israel, Ellis and Gray.

HEINONEN, Raija-Liisa (died in September 1978). Contributor. Curator of Archives, Museum of Finnish Architecture, Helsinki, 1975–78. Author of *The Breakthrough of Functionalism in Finland,* 1979. **Essay:** Erik Bryggman.

HENEGHAN, Tom. Contributor. Unit Master at the Architectural Association School, London. Freelance writer on architecture for *Building Design,* London. **Essay:** Derek Walker.

HERBERT, Gilbert. Contributor. Mary Hill Swope Professor of Architecture, Technion: Israel Institute of Technology, Haifa. Lecturer in Architecture, University of the Witwatersrand, Johannesburg, 1947–61; Reader in Architecture and Town Planning, University of Adelaide, South Australia, 1961–68. Associate Editor, *South African Architectural Record,* Johannesburg, 1949–60. Author of *The Synthetic Vision of Walter Gropius,* 1959; *Martienssen and the International Style: The Development of Modern Architecture in South Africa,* 1975; *Pioneers of Prefabrication: The British Contribution in the Nineteenth Century,* 1978. **Essays:** Norman Hanson; Dov Karmi; Ram Karmi; Al Mansfeld; Rex Martienssen; Yacov Rechter; Arieh Sharon.

HEYER, Paul. Contributor. Architect in private practice, New York. Professor of Architecture, and Co-Chairman of the Graduate Department of Architecture, Pratt Institute, Brooklyn, New York. Editor of *Architects on Architecture: New Directions in America,* 1966; and author of *Mexican Architecture: The Work of Abraham Zabludovsky and Teodoro González de León,* 1978. **Essay:** Abraham Zabludovsky.

HIBBARD, Don J. Contributor. Architectural Historian, State of Hawaii. Architectural Historian, State of Idaho, 1975–78. Author of *Normal Hill,* 1978; *Weiser: A Look at Idaho Architecture,* 1978. **Essays:** Vernon DeMars; Joseph Esherick; Ian McHarg; William Morgan; Ralph Rapson; James Wines.

HOFFMANN, Donald. Contributor. Art Critic, *The Kansas City Star.* Editor of *The Meaning of Architecture: Buildings and Writings by John Wellborn Root,* 1967; and author of *The Architecture of John Wellborn Root,* 1973; *Frank Lloyd Wright's Fallingwater,* 1978. **Essay:** Ludwig Mies van der Rohe.

HUNT, William Dudley, Jr. Contributor. Architecture Editor, John Wiley and Sons Inc., New York and Chichester. Senior Editor, *Architectural Record,* New York, 1958–63; Publisher, *AIA Journal,* Washington, D.C., 1964–72 (Publishing Director of the AIA, 1970–72). Editor of, and contributor to, *Comprehensive Architectural Services,* 1965; *Creative Control of Building Costs,* 1967; author of *Contemporary Curtain Wall,* 1958; *Total Design,* 1972; *Encyclopedia of American Architecture,* 1979. **Essays:** Welton Becket; Wallace K. Harrison; Raymond Hood; Richard Llewelyn-Davies; Eero Saarinen; Hugh A. Stubbins, Jr.

HURLEY, Kent. Contributor. Assistant Dean, and Director of the Sandwich (Co-op) Program, Faculty of Architecture, Nova Scotia Technical College, Halifax. **Essays:** Gustavo da Roza; Clifford Wiens.

JACKSON, Anthony. Adviser and contributor. Professor of Architecture, Nova Scotia Technical College, Halifax. Author of *The Politics of Architecture,* 1970; *A Place Called Home,* 1976; *The Democratization of Canadian Architecture,* 1978; *The Future of Canadian Architecture,* 1979. **Essays:** Ray Affleck; Barry Downs; Macy DuBois; Raymond Moriyama; Eberhard Zeidler.

JELLICOE, Sir Geoffrey. Contributor and entrant: see his own entry. **Essays:** Holger Blom; Roberto Burle Marx; Brenda Colvin; Dame Sylvia Crowe; Philip Dowson; Eric Lyons; Richard Sheppard, Robson and Partners; F. R. S. Yorke.

JOEDICKE, Jürgen. Contributor. Professor, and Director of the Institut Grundlagen der modernen Architektur und Entwerfen, University of Stuttgart, since 1967; in architectural practice with Walter Mayer, Stuttgart and Nuremberg, since 1973. Editor of the series *Documents of Modern Architecture.* Author of *A History of Modern Architecture,* 1958; *Office Building,* 1959; *Shell Architecture,* 1963; *Hugo Häring: Schriften, Entwürfe, Bauten,* 1965; *Architecture since 1945: Sources and Directions,* 1969; *Angewandte Entwurfsmethodik für Architekten,* 1976; *Architektur im Umbruch: Geschichte, Entwicklung, Ausblick,* 1979. **Essays:** Kurt Ackermann; Richard Döcker; Friedrich Wilhelm Kraemer; Horst Linde; Heikki Siren; Max Taut.

JORDY, William H. Adviser. Henry Ledyard Goddard Professor of Art, Brown University, Providence, Rhode Island. Editor (with Ralph Coe) of *"American Architecture" and Other Writings* by Montgomery Schuyler, 1961; and author of *American Buildings and Their Architects,* 2 volumes, 1976.

JUHASZ, Joseph B. Contributor. Associate Professor of Environmental Design, and Director of the Environmental Design Division, College of Environmental Design, University of Colorado, Boulder. Author of *Environments: Notes and Selections on Objects, Spaces and Behavior* (with Steven Friedman), 1974. **Essays:** Garrett Eckbo; Herb Greene; Victor Horta; Morris Lapidus; Gerald McCue; William C. Muchow; Minoru Yamasaki.

KELL, Diane. Contributor. Editor of the *Constructional Review,* Sydney. **Essay:** Keith E. Cottier.

KINGDON, Jonathan. Contributor. Lecturer in Fine Art, Ruskin School of Drawing, Oxford University. Author of *East African Mammals: An Atlas of Evolution in Africa.* **Essay:** Richard Hughes.

KOEHLER, Robert E. Contributor. Freelance editor and writer, Washington, D.C. Editor, *AIA Journal,* Washington, D.C., 1965–73. Co-editor of *Current Techniques in Architectural Practice,* 1976; editor of *Personnel Practices Handbook,* 1978. **Essays:** Charles Blessing; Frank Schlesinger; Paul Thiry.

KOENIGSBERGER, Otto. Contributor. Emeritus Professor of Development Planning, University College of the University of London. Editor, *Habitat International,* since 1977. Author of *Construction of Ancient Egyptian Doors,* 1936; *Housing in Ghana* (with Charles Abrams and Vladimir Bodiansky), 1956; *Housing in Pakistan* (with Charles Abrams), 1957; *Housing in the Philippine Islands* (with Charles Abrams), 1958; *Metropolitan Lagos* (with others), 1962; *Development and Urban Renewal in Singapore* (with Charles Abrams and Susumu Kobe), 1963; *Roofs in the Warm Humid Tropics* (with Robert Lynn), 1966; *Climate and House Design* (with Carl Mahoney and Martin Evans), 1970; *Manual of Tropical Housing* (with others), 1972; *Planning Legislation,* 1975; *The Implementation of Urban Plans,* 1977; *Planning Education in Poor Countries,* 1977; etc. **Essay:** James Cubitt.

KULTERMANN, Udo. Adviser and contributor. Professor of Architecture, Washington University, St. Louis. Formerly, Director, City Art Museum,

Leverkusen, Germany. Author of *Architecture of Today,* 1958; *Hans und Wassili Luckhardt,* 1958; *Dynamische Architektur,* 1959; *New Japanese Architecture,* 1960; *Junge deutsche Bildhauer,* 1963; *New Architecture in Africa,* 1963; *Der Schluessel zur Architektur von heute,* 1963; *New Architecture in the World,* 1965; *History of Art History,* 1966; *Architektur der Gegenwart,* 1967; *The New Sculpture,* 1967; *Gabriel Grupello,* 1968; *The New Painting,* 1969; *New Directions in African Architecture,* 1969; *Kenzo Tange,* 1970; *Art and Life,* 1970; *New Realism,* 1972; *Die Architektur im 20. Jahrhundert,* 1977; *Ernest Trova,* 1978; *Scultura contemporanea,* 1979; *The Basilica of Maxentius,* 1979; *Architecture of the Seventies,* 1980; *The Renaissance of Contemporary Architecture in the Arab States,* 1980; *Architects of the Third World,* 1980. **Essays:** Arata Isozaki; Uttam C. Jain; Leon Krier; Rob Krier; Paolo Portoghesi; Aldo Rossi; James Stirling.

KUWABARA, Bruce. Associate, Barton Myers Associates, Toronto. Visiting Critic of Architecture, Nova Scotia Technical College, Halifax, and University of Waterloo, Ontario; Tutor, University of Toronto. **Essay:** Barton Myers.

LAURIE, Michael. Contributor. Associate Professor of Landscape Architecture, University of California, Berkeley. Author of *An Introduction to Landscape Architecture,* 1975. **Essay:** Thomas D. Church.

LAVENSTEIN, Richard. Contributor. Architect in private practice, Baltimore. Formerly, Instructor, School of Architecture, Washington University, St. Louis. **Essays:** George Howe; Paul Nelson; Werner Seligmann.

LEGNER, Linda. Contributor. Free-lance writer on architecture, Chicago. **Essays:** Hellmuth, Obata, Kassabaum; Lawrence B. Perkins.

LEWCOCK, Ronald. Contributor. Fellow, Clare Hall, Cambridge; Lecturer, Architectural Association School, London. Formerly, Senior Lecturer, School of Architecture, University of Natal, South Africa. Editor of the architectural entries for the *Encyclopaedia of Southern Africa* and *Everyman's Encyclopaedia.* Author of *Early 19th Century Architecture in South Africa,* 1963. **Essay:** Revel Fox.

LLOYD, Michael. Contributor. Senior Research Fellow, University College London. Formerly: Dean of the Faculty of Architecture, Kumasi, Ghana; Principal, Architectural Association School of Architecture, London; Consultant Head, Hull School of Architecture. Author of *Teknisk Tegning og Skissering,* 1960; *Environmental Impact of Development Activities,* 1975. **Essays:** Ove Bang; Sverre Fehn; Knut Knutsen; Arne Korsmo.

LÜCHINGER, Arnulf. Contributor. Architect and writer, The Hague. Author of *Structuralism,* 1979. Contributor to *Bauen und Wohnen* and *Architecture + Urbanism.* **Essays:** Piet Blom; N. John Habraken; Herman Hertzberger; Mart Stam.

LYE, K. C. Contributor. Professor and Dean of Architecture, University of Hong Kong. Formerly, Professor and Head, Department of Architecture, University of Manitoba. Author of *The Architecture of Self-Help Communities,* 1978. **Essays:** Tao Ho; Sumet Jumsai; David Russell; Jackson C. S. Wong.

MACKAY, David. Adviser, contributor and entrant: see his own entry. **Essays:** Ricardo Bofill; Pep Bonet; Lluis Clotet; José A. Coderch; Antoni Gaudí; Josep María Jujol; Luis Peña; Josep María Sostres.

MAKINSON, Randell L. Contributor. Curator, The Gamble House: Greene and Greene Library, School of Architecture, University of Southern California, Los Angeles. Author of *A Guide to the Work of Greene and Greene,* 1974; *Greene and Greene,* 2 volumes, 1977–78. **Essay:** Greene and Greene.

MARKELIN, Antero. Contributor. Professor of Urban Design, University of Stuttgart. Editor of *Mensch und Stadtgestalt*, 1974; author of *Stadtbild in der Planungspraxis* (with M. Trieb), 1976. **Essay:** Timo Penttilä.

MARTIN, Linda. Contributor. Architect working in the Bristol Housing Association. Formerly in private practice, Oslo. **Essay:** Kjell Lund.

MASINI, Lara-Vinca. Contributor. Art critic and editor, Florence. Author of *Le Tombe dei Re a Saint Denis*, 1966; *La Cattedrale di Wells*, 1967; *Savioli*, 1967; *Gaudí*, 1969; *Riccardo Morandi*, 1973; *Progetto Struttura, Metodologia del Design*, 1975; *Simbolismo*, 1979. Regular contributor to *Domus, Quadrum, NAC, L'Architettura, Art and Artists*, etc. **Essays:** Carlo Aymonino; Angelo Mangiarotti; Riccardo Morandi; Edoardo Persico; Leonardo Ricci; Leonardo Savioli.

MAXWELL, Robert. Contributor. Architect with Douglas Stephen and Partners, London. Professor of Architecture, University College of the University of London. Author of *New British Architecture*, 1972; *Venturi and Rauch*, 1978. **Essay:** Douglas Stephen.

McCOY, Esther. Contributor. Architectural writer and historian, Los Angeles. Contributing Editor, *Arts and Architecture*, Los Angeles, 1951–57. Author of *Five California Architects*, 1960, 1975; *Neutra*, 1960; *Modern California Houses*, 1962, 1978; *Craig Ellwood*, 1968; *Vienna to Los Angeles: Two Journeys*, 1979. **Essays:** Gregory Ain; J. R. Davidson; Harwell Hamilton Harris; A. Quincy Jones; Cesar Pelli; Lloyd Wright.

McKEAN, J. M. Contributor. Freelance architect and critic, London. Tutor, Architectural Association School, London; Director of the First Year Course, North East London Polytechnic School of Architecture. Former Technical, then News Editor of *The Architects' Journal*, London. Author of *Architecture of the Western World* (with others), 1979; *Masterpieces of Architectural Draughtsmanship*, 1980. **Essays:** Michael Brawne; Peter Moro.

McMORDIE, Michael. Contributor. Associate Professor of Architecture, and Programme Director for Architecture, Faculty of Environmental Design, University of Calgary. President, Society for the Study of Architecture in Canada. **Essays:** Arthur Erickson; John B. Parkin; John C. Parkin.

MILLER, Nory. Contributor. Assistant Editor, *AIA Journal*, Washington, D.C. Formerly, Managing Editor, *Inland Architect*, Chicago, and Architecture Critic of the *Chicago Daily News*. **Essays:** Warren J. Cox; Bertrand Goldberg; Hugh Newell Jacobsen; Arthur Cotton Moore; Stanley Tigerman; John Carl Warnecke.

MILLS, Edward D. Contributor. Senior Partner, Edward D. Mills and Partners, Architects, London. Author of *Architecture as a Career*, 1945; *The Modern Factory*, 1951; *The Modern Church*, 1956; *The New Architecture in Great Britain*, 1953; *Factory Building in Great Britain*, 1967; *The Changing Workplace*, 1972; *The National Exhibition Centre*, 1976; *Building Centre Guide to Building Maintenance* (in preparation). **Essays:** Architects Co-Partnership; E. Maxwell Fry; William Graham Holford; Sir Philip Powell; Sir Basil Spence.

MIOTTO-MURET, Luciana. Contributor. Professor of Modern Architectural History, Université de Paris VIII-Vincennes. Author of *Carlo Scarpa*, 1975. Contributor to *L'Architecture d'Aujourd'hui, Revue de l'Art, L'Architecture* and *Spazio e Società*. **Essays:** Pierre Chareau; Tony Garnier; Robert Mallet-Stevens; Henri Sauvage.

MOTTA, Flavio. Contributor. Professor of the History of Art and Architecture, Faculty of Architecture and Urbanism, University of Sao Paulo. Regular contributor to *Acropole*, Sao Paulo. **Essay:** Paulo Mendes da Rocha.

MÜLLER, Michael. Contributor. Professor of Architecture and Environmental Design, University of Bremen, Germany. Author of *Die Villa als Herrschaftsarchitektur* (with R. Beutmann), 1970; *Autonomie der Kunst* (with H. Bredekamp and others), 1972; *Die Verdrängung des Ornaments: zum Verhaltnis von Architektur und Lebenspraxis*, 1977. **Essay:** Adolf Loos.

MURPHY, Elizabeth. Contributor. Final Year Architectural Student, North London Polytechnic. Author of *Eileen Gray* (thesis: North London Polytechnic), 1976; *The Eileen Gray House at Castellar, near Meudon*, 1977. **Essay:** Eileen Gray.

NAIRN, Janet. Contributor. Associate Editor, *Architectural Record*, New York. **Essay:** Frank O. Gehry.

NATCHEV, Zdravko. Contributor. Architect in private practice, Nanterre, France. Contributor to *Neuf, L'Architecture d'Aujourd'hui, Crée*, etc. **Essays:** Imre Makovecz; György Vadász.

NAYLOR, Colin. Associate editor and contributor. Freelance researcher, editor and writer, London. Formerly, Editor, *Art and Artists*, London. Editor of *Contemporary Artists*, 1977. **Essays:** William W. Caudill; Enrique del Moral; Barnett Gruzen; Helmut Jahn; Edward F. Knowles; Lucien Kroll; Carlos Raúl Villanueva.

NEVEL, Robert B. Contributor. Teaching Assistant, School of Architecture, Washington University, St. Louis. **Essay:** Zvi Hecker.

OSBALDESTON, Roger. Contributor. Associate Professor of Landscape Architecture, California Polytechnic State University, San Luis Obispo. **Essay:** Lawrence Halprin.

OSTLER, Timothy. Contributor. Research Fellow, Department of Architecture, University of Sheffield, Yorkshire. Author of *Pancho Guedes: The Collective Unconscious of Architecture* (thesis: University of Sheffield), 1978. **Essay:** Amancio Guedes.

PATTERSON, Gordon. Contributor. Senior Partner, Gordon Patterson and Partners, landscape architects, Stevenage, Hertfordshire. Co-Author of *Gardens of Mughal India*, 1960. **Essay:** Hans Luz.

PEGRUM, Roger. Contributor. Architect in private practice, Sydney. Senior Lecturer in Architecture, University of Sydney. Author of *The Bush Capital* (in preparation); *Fine Detail* (in preparation). **Essay:** Daryl Jackson.

PEHNT, Wolfgang. Adviser. Editor for Arts and Architecture, Deutschlandfunk, Cologne. Editor of *Encyclopedia of Modern Architecture*, 1964; *Die Stadt in der Bundesrepublik*, 1974; and author of *New German Architecture 1960–1970*, 1970; *Expressionist Architecture*, 1973.

PETERS, Richard C. Contributor. Professor and Chairman of the Department of Architecture, College of Environmental Design, University of California, Berkeley. President, Association of Collegiate Schools of Architecture, 1979–82. Author of *William Wilson Wurster: An Architect of Houses*. **Essay:** William Wilson Wurster.

POSENER, Julius. Contributor. Emeritus Professor, Hochschule der Künste, Berlin. Author of *Anfänge des Funktionalismus*, 1964; *Garden Cities of Tomorrow*, 1968; *Hans Poelzig*, 1970; *From Schinkel to the Bauhaus*, 1974; *Berlin on the Road Towards a New Architecture*, 1979; *Collected Writings from Half a Century*, 1979. **Essay:** Pierre Vago.

QUANTRILL, Malcolm. Contributor. Head, Department of Environmental Design, Polytechnic of North London. Founder and Secretary of the Thomas Cubitt Trust. Deputy Editor, *Art International*, Zurich. Director, Architectural Association, London, 1967–69. Author of *Ritual and Response in Architecture*, 1974; *Monuments of Another Age* (with Esther Quantrill), 1975. **Essay:** Reima Pietilä.

RABENECK, Andrew. Contributor. Managing Director, Building Systems Development (U.K.) Ltd., London. Consultant Editor, *Architectural Design*, London, 1970–78. Author of *Planning Office Space* (with others), 1976; *Encyclopaedia of Architecture and Technical Innovation* (with others), 1979. **Essays:** Christopher Alexander; BBPR; Ludovico Quaroni.

RICHARDS, Larry. Contributor. Assistant Professor, Faculty of Architecture, and Campus Design Coordinator, Nova Scotia Technical College, Halifax; Vice-President, Networks Ltd., Halifax. Atlantic Regional Editor, *Decormag*, Montreal. **Essay:** Peter Rose.

RODRIGUEZ, Ida. Contributor. Researcher, Instituto de Investigaciones Estéticos, and Professor, Faculty of Philosophy, National University of Mexico. Author of *La crítica de arte en México*, 1964; *El arte contemporáneo*, 1964; *El surrealismo y el arte fantástico de México*, 1969; *Pedro Friedeberg*, 1972; *Una década de critica de Arte*, 1974; *Herbert Bayer: Un Concepto Total*, 1975; *Dada Documentos* (with Rita Eder), 1977. **Essay:** Max Cetto.

ROGATNICK, Abraham. Contributor. Professor of Architecture, University of British Columbia, Vancouver. Contributor to *Architectural Review, Architectural Design, Artforum, Artscanada* and *The Canadian Architect*. **Essays:** Douglas Cardinal; Giuseppe Samonà.

ROSENBERG, Eugene. Contributor and entrant: see his own entry. **Essays:** Bohuslav Fuchs; Josef Gočár; Josef Havlíček.

ROSS, Michael Franklin. Contributor. Director of Architectural Programs, Daniel, Mann, Johnson and Mendenhall, Los Angeles. Visiting Professor of Architecture, University of California at Los Angeles. West Coast Correspondent, *Progressive Architecture*, New York; Member of the Editorial Board, *L. A. Architect*. Author of *Beyond Metabolism: The New Japanese Architecture*, 1978. **Essays:** Takamitsu Azuma; Kisho Kurokawa; Anthony Lumsden; Kunio Mayekawa; Shin'ichi Okada; Minoru Takeyama.

ROUDA, Mitchell B. Contributor. Freelance architectural writer, New York. Formerly, Assistant Editor, *Stylos Architecture* (formerly *Process: Architecture*, Pittsburgh and Tokyo). Author of *Emerging Architecture in the Emerging World*, 1979. **Essays:** Nader Ardalan; Lewis Davis; Louis I. Kahn; Leandro V. Locsin; George Nelson; Moshe Safdie; Louis Sauer; Konrad Wachsmann; Shadrach Woods.

ROWNTREE, Diana. Contributor. Architect in private practice, Hexham, Northumberland. Architecture Correspondent of *The Guardian*, London, 1955–66. Author of the *Penguin Handbook of Interior Design*, 1964. **Essay:** Sir Ove Arup.

RYKWERT, Joseph. Adviser and contributor. Professor of Art, University of Essex, Colchester, and Slade Professor of Fine Arts, Cambridge University. Author of *The Golden House*, 1947; *Church Building*, 1966; *On Adam's House in Paradise*, 1972; *The Idea of a Town*, 1976; *The First Moderns* (in preparation); and editor of *The Ten Books of Architecture* by Alberti, 1955. **Essays:** Luigi Figini; Vittorio Gregotti; Ernesto Nathan Rogers.

SACK, Manfred. Contributor. Editor of *Die Zeit*, Hamburg. Author of *Architektur in der Zeit*, 1979. **Essays:** Gottfried Böhm; Hermann Fehling; Josef Paul Kleihues; Meinhard von Gerkan.

SAINI, B. S. Contributor. Professor and Head of the Department of Architecture, University of Queensland, Brisbane. Author of *Architecture in Tropical Australia*, 1970; *Building Environment: An Illustrated Analysis of Problems in Hot Dry Lands*,

1973. **Essays:** Charles M. Correa; John Dalton; Robin Gibson; Matthew Nowicki.

SALOKORPI, Asko. Contributor. Chief of the Research Department, Museum of Finnish Architecture, Helsinki. Author of *Modern Finnish Architecture,* 1970; *Guide to Finnish Architecture,* 1979. **Essay:** Aarno Ruusuvuori.

SCHMERTZ, Mildred F. Adviser and contributor. Senior Editor, *Architectural Record,* New York. Visiting Lecturer, Yale University School of Architecture, New Haven, Connecticut. Editor of, and contributor to, *Campus Architecture,* 1972; *Open Space for People,* 1974; *Office Building Design,* 1975. **Essays:** Edmund N. Bacon; Gunnar Birkerts; Cambridge Seven; B. V. Doshi; M. Paul Friedberg; Robert Geddes; Gerhard M. Kallmann; Tasso Katselas; Giovanni Pasanella; Paul Rudolph; Josep Lluis Sert; John Ormsbee Simonds; Eva Vecsei.

SCHNEIDER, Martina. Contributor. Editor with the Abakon Publishing Company, Berlin. Formerly, Editor, *Bauwelt,* Berlin. Editor of *Information über Gestalt,* 1974; *Reihe Suizzenbücher,* 1975; *Reihe Werkstadtbücher,* 1976. **Essay:** Werner Düttmann.

SCHOENAUER, Norbert. Contributor. Professor of Architecture (former Director of the School of Architecture), McGill University, Montreal. Formerly, Senior Adviser for Planning and Design, Canadian Ministry of State for Urban Design. Author of *The Court-Garden House* (with S. Seeman), 1962; *University Housing in Canada* (with J. Bland), 1966; *Architecture Montreal,* 1967; *Introduction to Contemporary Indigenous Housing,* 1973. **Essay:** Irving Grossman.

SCHULZE, Franz. Contributor. Hollender Professor of Art, Lake Forest College, Lake Forest, Illinois. Art Critic of the *Chicago Sun-Times.* Contributing Editor, *Art News,* New York, and *Inland Architect,* Chicago. Author of *Fantastic Images: Chicago Art since 1945,* 1972; *100 Years of Architecture in Chicago* (with Oswald W. Grube and Peter C. Pran), 1976. **Essays:** Thomas Hall Beeby; Irving J. Gill; Bruce J. Graham; Ludwig K. Hilberseimer; George Fred Keck; Fazlur Khan; William Lescaze; Louis Sullivan; Philip Will, Jr.

SEGREST, Robert. Contributor. Associate Professor of Architecture, Georgia Institute of Technology, Atlanta. **Essay:** Edward Durell Stone.

SEIDLER, Harry. Adviser, contributor and entrant: see his own entry. **Essays:** Marcel Breuer; Oscar Niemeyer.

SEKLER, Eduard F. Contributor. Osgood Hooker Professor of Visual Arts and Professor of Architecture, Harvard University, Cambridge, Massachusetts (formerly, Director of the Carpenter Center for the Visual Arts at Harvard). Author of *Wren and His Place in European Architecture,* 1956; *Proportion: A Measure of Order,* 1965; *Le Corbusier at Work: The Genesis of the Carpenter Center for the Visual Arts* (with William J. R. Curtis), 1978; and editor of *Historic Urban Spaces I–IV,* 1962–71; *Master Plan for the Conservation of the Cultural Heritage in the Kathmandu Valley,* 1977. **Essay:** Josef Hoffmann.

SEOW, E. J. Contributor. Professor of Architecture (formerly Head of the School of Architecture), University of Singapore. **Essays:** William S.W. Lim; Lim Chong Keat.

SHARP, Dennis. Architectural consultant, adviser, and contributor. In private practice as an architect, London; Senior Lecturer, Architectural Association School, London, and Founder Editor of the *Architectural Association Quarterly.* Architectural Consultant to *Building,* London. Author of *Area Rejuvenation: Rochdale,* 1965; *Modern Architecture and Expressionism,* 1966; *Sources of Modern Architecture,* 1967; *The Picture Palace and Other Buildings for the Movies,* 1969; *The Bauhaus* (with film strips),

1970; *A Visual History of Twentieth Century Architecture,* 1970; editor of *Planning and Architecture,* 1968; *Glass in Modern Architecture,* 1968; *Glass Architecture by P. Scheerbart,* 1972; *Manchester,* 1969; *Henry van de Velde: Theatres 1904–14,* 1974; *The Rationlists,* 1978; *The English House by H. Muthesius,* 1979. **Essay:** Paolo Soleri.

SHARON, Arieh. Adviser and entrant: see his own entry.

SHEPPARD, Adrian. Contributor. Architect in Montreal. Associate Professor of Architecture, McGill University, Montreal. Former partner in the firm of Desnoyers, Mercure, Gagnon, Sheppard, architects, Montreal. **Essay:** Victor Prus.

SHEPPARD, Richard. Contributor and entrant: see Richard Sheppard, Robson and Partners. **Essay:** Eugene Rosenberg.

SILVER, Nathan. Contributor. Architect in private practice, London. Head of the William Morris School of Architectural Studies, North East London Polytechnic. Formerly, Architecture Critic of the *New Statesman,* London. Author of *Lost New York,* 1967; *Adhocism: The Case for Improvisation* (with Charles Jencks), 1972. **Essays:** Bernard Feilden; Hannes Meyer; Renzo Piano; Richard Rogers; Robert A. M. Stern.

SMITH, C. Ray. Contributor. Writer, editor, design critic, and architecture historian, New York. Formerly, Editor, *Interiors, Residential Interiors,* and *Theatre Crafts,* and Feature Editor, *Progressive Architecture*—New York. Author of *The American Endless Weekend,* 1973; *Supermannerism: New Attitudes in Post-Modern Architecture,* 1977; and editor of *The Shapes of Our Theatre* by Jo Mielziner, 1970; *The Theatre Crafts Book of Costume,* 1973; *The Theatre Crafts Book of Make-Up, Masks, and Wigs,* 1974. **Essays:** Luis Barragán; Peter D. Eisenman; Michael Graves; Charles Gwathmey; Hugh Hardy; Frederick Kiesler; Kevin Roche.

SPENCER, Kevin. Contributor. Architect, Dublin; Research Officer with a state-sponsored organization. **Essays:** Raymond McGrath; Michael Scott.

SPREIREGEN, Paul. Contributor. Architect and planner, Washington, D.C. Broadcaster on National Public Radio (U.S.A.). **Essays:** Gordon Bunshaft; Hassan Fathy; Buckminster Fuller; Bernard Maybeck; Charles W. Moore; Richard J. Neutra; William L. Pereira; John Portman; Harry Weese.

STRATHAUS, Ulrike Jehle-Schulte. Contributor. Member of the staff of the Institute of Architectural History and Theory, Eidgenössische Technische Hochschule, Zurich. Author of *Bauten im 20. Jahrhundert,* 1977; *Kunst der Gegenwart* (with others), 1978. **Essay:** Werner M. Moser.

SUHONEN, Pekka. Contributor. Writer and art critic, Helsinki. Author of *New Finnish Architecture,* 1967; *Finland Creates* (with J. Fields and David Moore), 1976. **Essays:** Aulis Blomstedt; Viljo Revell.

TANNER, Howard. Contributor. Architect in private practice, Sydney. Lecturer in Architectural and Landscape History and Conservation, University of Sydney. Author of *Restoring Old Australian Houses and Buildings,* 1975; *The Great Gardens of Australia,* 1976; *Australian Housing in the Seventies,* 1976; *Architects of Australia,* 1980. **Essay:** Philip Cox.

TAYLOR, Jennifer. Contributor. Senior Lecturer in Architecture, University of Sydney. Author of *An Australian Identity,* 1972; *John Andrews: Architecture and Performing Art* (with John Andrews), 1979. **Essays:** Sydney Ancher; Col Madigan; Tohgo Murano.

UHLIG, Günther. Contributor. Architect in private practice, Aachen. Assistant Professor of Architecture, Technische Hochschule, Aachen. Author of *Kulturelle Modelle der Bau- und Wohnreform-*

bewegungen: Das Zentralküchenhaus im Kontext von Architektur- und Stadtplanungsstrategien bis 1933, 1980. **Essay:** Ludwig Leo.

VAGO, Pierre. Adviser, contributor and entrant: see his own entry. **Essays:** Georges Candilis; Michel Ecochard; Eugène Freyssinet; Jean Ginsberg; Albert Laprade; Marcel Lods; André Lurcat; Ivan Seifert; Jean Willerval; Bernard Zehrfuss.

WALDEN, Russell. Contributor. Reader in Architectural History, Victoria University of Wellington, New Zealand. Senior Lecturer, Birmingham School of Architecture, England, 1972–78. Editor of *The Open Hand: Essays on Le Corbusier,* 1977. **Essays:** W. H. Alington; Le Corbusier; Miles Warren.

WATANABE, Hiroshi. Contributor. Writer and architect, Tokyo. Member of Kenchiku Keikaku Kobo (Architectural Planning Workshop), Tokyo. Author of *The Japanese Conception of Space: Seven Studies of Traditional Cities, Architecture and Gardens* (in preparation). **Essays:** Sutemi Horiguchi; Kiyonori Kikutake; Sachio Otani; Seiichi Shirai; Kenzo Tange.

WATSON, David. Contributor. Senior Lecturer in Architecture, University of Melbourne. **Essays:** Don Hendry Fulton; Peter McIntyre; Stuart Murray.

WERNER, Frank. Contributor. Assistant Professor of Architecture, University of Stuttgart. Architecture Critic, *Stuttgarter Zeitung.* Author of *Old Town with New Life,* 1975; *Paul Bonatz 1877–1956,* 1977. **Essays:** Paul Bonatz; Hugo Häring; Heinrich Tessenow.

WHITTICK, Arnold. Contributor. Architectural historian and writer, London. Formerly, Chief Editor, *Building Materials* and *Encyclopaedia of Urban Planning,* London. Author of *History of Cement Sculpture from Ancient Times to the Norman Conquest,* 1938; *Erich Mendelsohn: A Biography,* 1940, 1955; *War Memorials,* 1946; *The Small House Today and Tomorrow,* 1947; *European Architecture in the Twentieth Century,* 3 volumes, 1950–74; *Symbols and Design,* 1960; *The New Towns: Their Origins, Achievements and Progress* (with Sir Frederic Osborn), 1963; *Ruskin's Venice,* 1976. **Essays:** Peter Behrens; Jane B. Drew; Aarne Ervi; Sir Frederick Gibberd; Walter Gropius; Sir Charles Holden; Sven Markelius; Eric Mendelsohn; Pier Luigi Nervi; Marcello Piacentini; Hans Poelzig; Sir Howard Robertson; O. R. Salvisberg; Henry van de Velde; C. F. A. Voysey; Sir Owen Williams.

WILLIAMS, Sheldon. Contributor. Art critic and journalist, London. Artistic Adviser to Rona Ltd., London. Author of *Situation Humaine,* 1968; *Verlon,* 1969; *A Background to Sfumato,* 1970; *Voodoo and the Art of Haiti,* 1972; *20th Century British Naives and Primitives* (with others), 1978; *The World Encyclopaedia of Naive Painting* (with others), 1979; and editor of *The Rona Guide to the World of Naive Art,* 1979. **Essay:** Max Bill.

WILLIAMS, Stephanie. Contributor. Freelance writer on architecture, London. Formerly, Editor, *Architects News,* and Features Editor, *Building Design,* London. **Essay:** Stillman and Eastwick-Field.

WILLIS, Peter. Contributor. Lecturer in Architecture, University of Newcastle. Editor of *Furor Hortensis: Essays on the History of the English Landscape Garden in Memory of H. F. Clark,* 1975; *The Genius of the Place: The English Landscape Garden 1620–1820,* 1975; and author of *New Architecture in Scotland,* 1977; *Charles Bridgeman and the English Landscape Garden,* 1977. **Essays:** Sir Leslie Martin; Peter Womersley.

WINTER, John. Contributor. Architect in private practice, London. Tutor, University College London and Cambridge University. Author of *Modern Buildings,* 1968; *Industrial Architecture,* 1969. **Essays:** Felix Candela; Amyas Connell; Charles

Eames; Craig Ellwood; Norman Foster; Ernö Goldfinger; Myron Goldsmith; Victor Gruen; Philip Johnson; Arthur Korn; Colin Lucas; Robert Maillart; Jean Prouvé; Antonin Raymond; Gerrit Rietveld; Skidmore, Owings and Merrill; Raphael Soriano.

WINTER, Robert. Contributor. Professor of History, Occidental College, Los Angeles. Chairman, Pasadena, California Cultural Heritage Commission; Vice-President, Los Angeles Cultural Heritage Board. Author (with David Gebhard) of *A Guide to Architecture in San Francisco and Northern California,* 1974, and *A Guide to Architecture in Los Angeles and Southern California,* 1977. **Essay:** Whitney R. Smith.

PHOTO CREDITS

Every attempt has been made to give the appropriate credits. If, however, copyright holders of photographs used in this book find the credits have been omitted, they are invited to contact the publishers. Photographs were supplied by the entrants with the exception of the following: